"No other guide has as much to offer . . . these books are a pleasure to read." Gene Shalit on the *Today Show*

". . . Excellently organized for the casual traveler who is looking for a mix of recreation and cultural insight."
*Washington Post*

★ ★ ★ ★ ★ (5-star rating) "Crisply written and remarkably personable. Cleverly organized so you can pluck out the minutest fact in a moment. Satisfyingly thorough."
*Réalités*

"The information they offer is up-to-date, crisply presented but far from exhaustive, the judgments knowledgeable but not opinionated." *New York Times*

"The individual volumes are compact, the prose succinct, and the coverage up-to-date and knowledgeable . . . The format is portable and the index admirably detailed."
*John Barkham Syndicate*

". . . An abundance of excellent directions, diversions, and facts, including perspectives and getting-ready-to-go advice — succinct, detailed, and well organized in an easy-to-follow style." *Los Angeles Times*

"They contain an amount of information that is truly staggering, besides being surprisingly current."
*Detroit News*

"These guides address themselves to the needs of the modern traveler demanding precise, qualitative information . . . Upbeat, slick, and well put together."
*Dallas Morning News*

". . . Attractive to look at, refreshingly easy to read, and generously packed with information." *Miami Herald*

"These guides are as good as any published, and much better than most." *Louisville* (Kentucky) *Times*

## Stephen Birnbaum Travel Guides

Acapulco
Bahamas, and Turks & Caicos
Barcelona
Bermuda
Boston
Canada
Cancun, Cozumel & Isla Mujeres
Caribbean
Chicago
Disneyland
Eastern Europe
Europe
Europe for Business Travelers
Florence
France
Great Britain
Hawaii
Honolulu
Ireland
Italy
Ixtapa & Zihuatanejo
Las Vegas
London
Los Angeles
Mexico
Miami & Ft. Lauderdale
Montreal & Quebec City
New Orleans
New York
Paris
Portugal
Puerto Vallarta
Rome
San Francisco
South America
Spain
Toronto
United States
USA for Business Travelers
Vancouver
Venice
Walt Disney World
Washington, DC
Western Europe

CONTRIBUTING EDITORS

Ann Arrarte
Agostino Bono
John Branche
Frederick H. Brengelman
Peter Breslow
Tom Bridges
Renee Buencristiano
Rich Campagna
Kevin Causey
Mike Celizic
Paul Century
Fred Clayton
David Constable
Ana Ezcurra
Ernesto Fahrenkrog
Richard Falsone
Maria Luisa de Ferreira
Kathleen Fliegel
Alice Garrard
Dwight V. Gast
Keith Grant

Arnold Greenberg
Harriet Greenberg
Donald Griffis
Steven Gutkin
Earl Hanks
Elizabeth Herrington
Ellen Hoffman
Edward Holland
John Howard
Trish Janeschutz
Delinda Karle
Laurie Kassman
Sharief Khan
Patrick Knight
Kim Knur
Norman Langer
Cathy Langevin
Melinda Liu
Rob MacGregor
Gloria Matute
Alexander Miles

Anne Millman
Tom Murphy
Laurie Nadel
Helen O'Brien
Broewell Peregrine
Christopher Pickard
Dennis Puleston
Monica Ribero
Kathy Rich
Allan Rokach
Tim Ross
Ruth Sanchez
Nina Serefino
Tracy A. Smith
John Treacy
Desi Truideman
Hortensia de Valloton
Bill Verigan
Mary Vogt
Helen Wagg
Laurel Wentz

SYMBOLS  Gloria McKeown

MAPS  B. Andrew Mudryk
Folio Graphics Company, Inc.

A Stephen Birnbaum Travel Guide

# Birnbaum's SOUTH AMERICA 1993

## Alexandra Mayes Birnbaum
EDITOR

## Lois Spritzer
EXECUTIVE EDITOR

Mary A. Dempsey
Anne Kalosh
AREA EDITORS

Laura L. Brengelman
*Managing Editor*

Mary Callahan
Jill Kadetsky
Susan McClung
Beth Schlau
Dana Margaret Schwartz
*Associate Editors*

Gene Gold
*Assistant Editor*

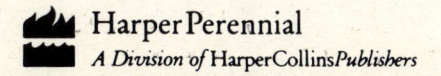

HarperPerennial
*A Division of HarperCollinsPublishers*

*To Stephen, who merely made all this possible.*

BIRNBAUM'S SOUTH AMERICA 1993. Copyright © 1992 by HarperCollins Publishers. All rights reserved. Printed in the United States of America. No part of this book may be used or reproduced in any manner whatsoever without written permission except in the case of brief quotations embodied in critical articles and reviews. For information address HarperCollins*Publishers,* 10 East 53rd Street, New York, NY 10022.

FIRST EDITION

ISSN  0749-2561 (Stephen Birnbaum Travel Guides)
ISSN  0883-2463 (South America)
ISBN  0-06-278052-2 (pbk.)

92 93 94 95 96 CC/WP 10 9 8 7 6 5 4 3 2 1

# Contents

xi **A Word from the Editor**

1 **How to Use This Guide**

## GETTING READY TO GO

All the practical travel data you need to plan your vacation down to the final detail.

### When and How to Go

- 9 What's Where
- 11 When to Go
- 14 Traveling by Plane
- 35 Traveling by Ship
- 44 Traveling by Train
- 48 Traveling by Bus
- 49 Traveling by Car
- 58 Package Tours
- 65 Camping and RVs, Hiking and Biking

### Preparing

- 71 Calculating Costs
- 72 Planning a Trip
- 75 How to Use a Travel Agent
- 77 Entry Requirements and Documents
- 80 Insurance
- 85 How to Pack
- 88 Hints for Handicapped Travelers
- 94 Hints for Single Travelers
- 100 Hints for Older Travelers
- 104 Hints for Traveling with Children

### On the Road

- 109 Credit and Currency
- 116 Accommodations
- 122 Time Zones

## CONTENTS

123 Mail, Telephone, and Electricity
127 Staying Healthy
136 Legal Aid and Consular Services
138 Drinking and Drugs
140 Crime in South America
140 Tipping
142 Duty-Free Shopping
143 Religion on the Road
143 Customs and Returning to the US

### Sources and Resources

148 South American Tourist Offices, Embassies, and Consulates in the US
148 Theater and Special Event Tickets
149 Books, Magazines, Newspapers, and Newsletters
153 Weights and Measures
155 Cameras and Equipment
157 Useful Words and Phrases

## FACTS IN BRIEF

A compilation of pertinent tourist information such as entry requirements and customs, sports, language, currency, clothing requirements, and more for all of the South American countries.

| | | | | | |
|---|---|---|---|---|---|
| 169 | Argentina | 175 | Ecuador | 181 | Peru |
| 170 | Bolivia | 177 | French Guiana | 183 | Suriname |
| 171 | Brazil | 178 | Guyana | 184 | Uruguay |
| 173 | Chile | 179 | Panama | 185 | Venezuela |
| 174 | Colombia | 180 | Paraguay | | |

## PERSPECTIVES

A cultural and historical survey of South America's past and present, its people, politics, and heritage.

189 History
207 Religion
212 Legends and Literature
224 Music and Dance
231 Crafts
239 Food and Drink

## THE CITIES

Thorough, qualitative guides to each of the 13 cities most visited by vacationers and businesspeople. Each section offers a comprehensive report of the city's most compelling attractions and amenities designed to be used on the spot. Directions and recommendations are immediately accessible because each guide is presented in consistent form.

| | | | | | |
|---|---|---|---|---|---|
| 247 | Asunción | 361 | Lima | 476 | Salvador (Bahia) |
| 264 | Bogotá | 387 | Montevideo | | |
| 287 | Buenos Aires | 404 | Panama City | 493 | Santiago |
| 316 | Caracas | 420 | Quito | 514 | São Paulo |
| 339 | La Paz | 440 | Rio de Janeiro | | |

## DIVERSIONS

A selective guide to 18 active and cerebral vacations, including the places to pursue them where the quality of experience is likely to be highest.

539 Introduction

### For the Experience

541 Quintessential South America
546 Luxury Resorts and Special Havens
557 Great Buys: Shopping in South America
564 Fabulous Festivals
569 Casinos Royale
571 Amazonia: Jungle Adventure and Exploration

### For the Body

576 Sinfully Sensuous Beaches
581 Best Depths: Snorkeling and Scuba
584 Sailing
586 Tennis
588 Great Golf
590 Fishing
598 Because It's There: Mountain Climbing
601 The Wild Continent: Trekking, Backpacking, River Rafting, and Camping
611 Parrots, Penguins, Piranhas: Wildlife Expeditions
616 Downhill Skiing
621 Hunting

### For the Mind

624 Lost Worlds: The Archaeological Heritage of South America
630 Memorable Museums

## DIRECTIONS

South America's most spectacular routes and roads, most arresting natural wonders, most magnificent archaeological ruins, all organized into 63 specific driving tours.

637  Introduction

### 639 Argentina

- 641  Buenos Aires to Bahía Blanca
- 648  Bahía Blanca to Bariloche
- 657  Patagonia to Antarctica
- 668  The Falkland Islands/Islas Malvinas
- 672  Mesopotamia
- 678  Mendoza
- 683  Córdoba
- 688  Northwestern Argentina

### 697 Bolivia

- 699  The Highlands
- 710  Cochabamba and Santa Cruz

### 715 Brazil

- 719  The Amazon: Belém to Manaus
- 728  The Northeast
- 743  The Costa Verde: Rio de Janeiro to São Paulo
- 749  Rio de Janeiro to Belo Horizonte
- 757  Belo Horizonte to Brasília
- 763  Brasília to Cuiabá: The Mato Grosso
- 771  São Paulo to the Uruguay Border
- 778  Iguaçu Falls

### 782 Chile

- 784  The North
- 793  Valparaíso and Viña del Mar
- 798  Portillo
- 802  Ovalle to Talca
- 807  Concepción to Laja Falls
- 811  The Lake District
- 819  Chilean Patagonia and the Tierra del Fuego Archipelago
- 825  Easter Island
- 828  The Juan Fernández Archipelago

## 831 **Colombia**

- 833 Cartagena and the Caribbean West Coast
- 842 Riohacha to Villa de Leyva
- 849 Bogotá to Medellín
- 854 Neiva to Cali
- 861 The Amazon

## 864 **Ecuador**

- 866 The North: Tulcán to Machala
- 875 The Oriente
- 880 El Litoral
- 889 The Galápagos Islands

## 897 **French Guiana**

## 903 **Guyana**

## 910 **Panama**

- 912 The Pan-American Highway

## 922 **Paraguay**

- 923 The Golden Triangle
- 928 The Chaco
- 929 The Jesuit Mission Trail/The Central Circuit
- 933 Cattle Country

## 936 **Peru**

- 938 The Outskirts of Lima
- 945 Lima to Cajamarca
- 958 Lima to Nazca
- 964 Arequipa to Puno
- 974 Cuzco and the Inca Ruins
- 985 The Amazon
- 995 Madre de Dios

## 1000 **Suriname**

## 1007 **Uruguay**

- 1008 Montevideo to Salto
- 1013 Montevideo to La Coronilla

## CONTENTS

- 1021 **Venezuela**
- 1024 Caracas to San Francisco de Yare
- 1029 The Andes
- 1037 The Western Coast
- 1040 The Guajira Peninsula
- 1043 The Eastern Venezuelan Coast
- 1048 The Lower Orinoco
- 1052 The Gran Sabana
- 1057 Angel Falls
- 1059 Margarita Island
- 1064 The Upper Orinoco (The Venezuelan Amazon)

- 1069 **Index**

# A Word from the Editor

Despite an early colonial history that closely parallels that of North America, the South American continent has lagged well behind its northern neighbor in recent times and, in terms of sophisticated political and economic progress, is still more notable for its potential than its tangible achievements. What's more, South America remains far less familiar to today's North American travelers than points on the globe that are far more distant and far less similar. So although both continents are part of the Western Hemisphere, their patterns of development over the past several centuries have been markedly different, and modern visitors to South America find a far greater frontier atmosphere than anything that exists in the northern half of the hemisphere.

Though the greedy European "colonists" were no less rapacious south of the equator than north — Pizarro's plundering of the Inca was just about as complete as Cortés's looting of the Aztec — the ensuing years were very different. Whereas industrialization and ever more sophisticated technology came relatively quickly to most areas of North America, they are just now becoming pervasive in South America. But even as this industrial revolution is taking place, economic pressures, political upheavals, and deep divisions among citizens of individual countries have contrived to hamper productive development. In countries including Colombia, Brazil, Argentina, Peru, and Chile, everything from repressive regimes, incendiary rates of inflation, and drug-dominated economies have made reasoned responses to national problems all but impossible to implement. And as the so-called socialist revolution has crumbled in Eastern Europe, Maoist-inspired revolutionaries seem to grow more active in Andean strongholds.

Still, a revolution in tourism is also occurring. Indeed, never before have South America's abundant attractions seemed to tempt so many of the Northern Hemisphere's travelers as at this moment. It's hard to think of a time when North American interest in South American happenings has ever been greater.

It's ironic that many of the same elements that hampered the economic development of South America are the very things that seem to appeal most to current visitors. Extraordinary stretches of deep, untrammeled jungle and vast, lonely llanos (prairies) still survive in many areas of the South American continent, as do the extraordinary, nearly hidden ruins of cultures that may go back to the time of the Egyptians. As recently as 1984, evidence of an entirely new ancient civilization was revealed at the Andean site of Gran Pajaten in Peru, and further discoveries seem to take place with surprising regularity. So it's no surprise that devotees of the ancients, who regularly make pilgrimages to the altars of Greek and Roman civilizations, have come to recognize that stunning reminders of times past also exist in abundance all over South America.

## xii A WORD FROM THE EDITOR

It would be easy to try to treat South America as a single entity with a common continental culture, but that would be misleading. For within this single continent exists an enormous variety of experiences, ranging from the modern high-rise towers of Caracas and Rio de Janeiro to the Stone Age jungle civilizations of the Mato Grosso. And South America is much more than just North America turned upside down, though at least part of South America's allure to tourists from the Northern Hemisphere is the opportunity to ski on fresh powder at a time when northern temperatures are inspiring cases of heat prostration, and, alternately, to sunbathe on one of a bounty of South American beaches while the snow blows north of the equator and the windchill factor falls out of sight.

And there's also much more to visiting South America than just enjoying a happily hedonistic holiday. There are extraordinarily diverse peoples to meet and very complex social and governmental structures to try to comprehend. As with any similarly large landmass, South America has its fair share of genuine heroes and its quota of petty tyrants, with a vast panoply of noteworthy (and notorious) characters in between. To the traveler, this complex human mosaic represents the sort of challenge that enlivens any trip, as the visitor tries to obtain a firsthand grasp of locations and lifestyles that were previously totally unfamiliar.

In creating and revising this book, we've renewed lots of old acquaintances with South America, and many of the new images and impressions have been jarring and surprising. When my husband Stephen Birnbaum was a boy during the 1950s, he spent a significant amount of time visiting and living in South America, and reacquainting himself with once familiar cities (and others not so well-known) had been an odd and often disorienting enterprise. In all candor, Steve's boyhood memories were of a time when the purposeful exploitation of South America's resources by foreigners was at its height, and when relations between outsiders and the native populations were at their nadir. Perhaps a measure of the extent of this insularity is indicated by the fact that when Steve took me to visit the neighborhood in which he had lived in Caracas, he admitted that there had been not a single Venezuelan family within several blocks.

The research for this book and its revisions has dramatically driven home the point that times have indeed changed. The level of nationalistic spirit among South American countries and their pride in their unique heritages has never been higher, and a by-product of this strong sense of national identity is a burst of development almost everywhere on the South American continent. Unfortunately, local politics and ideological anarchy often serve to keep the benefits of this development from the broad mass of citizens. Democratic elections recently seem more the norm than the exception, though tangible improvement in the economic state of the majority of the people doing the electing is less visible.

Despite some less than stable economies, the travel opportunities to South America are almost always extraordinary. Whether lying on the beaches of Bahia, climbing the Andes to ski in Portillo, or exploring Inca ruins near Cuzco, visitors find the experience unforgettable, and there's perhaps more of an opportunity for genuine discovery in South America than anywhere else

## A WORD FROM THE EDITOR

on this planet. It is the basic focus and intent of this guide to make a South American travel experience more accessible to visitors who want to immerse themselves in this unusually rewarding adventure.

What's more, the broadening sophistication of contemporary travelers has made it essential that guidebooks evolve in very fundamental ways in order to keep pace with their readers. That's why Steve and I tried to create a guide to South America that's specifically organized, written, and edited for the more demanding modern traveler headed to this increasingly complex continent. This is a traveler for whom qualitative information is infinitely more desirable than mere quantities of unappraised data. We think that this book, along with the other guides in our series, represents a new generation of travel guides — one that is especially responsive to modern needs and interests.

For years, dating back as far as Herr Baedeker, travel guides have tended to be encyclopedic, seemingly much more concerned with demonstrating expertise in geography and history than with a real analysis of the sorts of things that actually concern a modern tourist. But today, when it is hardly necessary to tell a traveler where Buenos Aires is (in some cases, the traveler has been to a given South American destination as often as the guidebook editors), it becomes the responsibility of those editors to provide new perspectives and to suggest new directions to make a guide genuinely valuable.

That's exactly what we've tried to do in this series. I think you'll notice a different, more contemporary tone to the text, as well as an organization and focus that are distinctive and more functional. And even a random reading of what follows will demonstrate a substantial departure from standard guidebook orientation, for we've not only attempted to provide information of a more compelling sort, but we also have tried to present the data in a format that makes it particularly accessible.

Needless to say, it's difficult to decide just what to include in a guidebook of this size — and what to omit. Early on, we realized that giving up the encyclopedic approach precluded our listing every single route and restaurant, a realization that helped define our overall editorial focus. Similarly, when we discussed the possibility of presenting certain information in other than strict geographic order, we found that the new format enabled us to arrange data in a way that we feel best answers the questions travelers typically ask.

Large numbers of specific questions have provided the real editorial skeleton for this book. The volume of mail we regularly receive emphasizes that modern travelers want very precise information, so we've tried to organize our material in the most responsive way possible. Readers who want to know the best restaurant in Lima or the best beach in Cartagena will have no trouble extracting that data from this guide.

Travel guides are, understandably, reflections of personal taste, and putting one's name on a title page obviously puts one's preferences on the line. But I think I ought to amplify just exactly what "personal" means. Like Steve, I don't believe in the sort of personal guidebook that's a palpable misrepresentation on its face. It is, for example, hardly possible for any single travel writer to visit thousands of restaurants (and nearly as many hotels) in any given year and provide accurate appraisals of each. And even if it were physically possible for one human being to survive such an itinerary, it would of necessity have to be done at a dead sprint, and the perceptions derived therefrom would probably be less valid than those of any other intelligent individual visiting these same establishments. It is, therefore, impossible (especially in a large, annually revised and updated guidebook *series* such as we offer) to have only one person provide all the data on the entire world.

I also happen to think that such individual orientation is of substantially less value to readers. Visiting a single hotel for just one night or eating one hasty meal in a random restaurant hardly equips anyone to provide appraisals that are of more than passing interest. No amount of doggedly alliterative or oppressively onomatopoeic text can camouflage a technique that is essentially specious. We have, therefore, chosen what I like to describe as the "thee and me" approach to restaurant and hotel evaluation and, to a somewhat more limited degree, to the sites and sights we have included in the other sections of our text. What this really reflects is personal sampling tempered by intelligent counsel from informed local sources, and these additional friends-of-the-editors are almost always residents of the city and/or area about which they are consulted.

Despite the presence of several editors, writers, researchers, and local contributors, very precise editing and tailoring keep our text fiercely subjective. So what follows is the gospel according to Birnbaum, and represents as much of our own taste and instincts as we can manage. It is probable, therefore, that if you like your cities sophisticated and your beaches uncrowded, prefer hotels with personality to high-rise anonymities, and can't tolerate good meat or fresh fish that's been relentlessly overcooked, we're likely to have a long and meaningful relationship. Readers with dissimilar tastes may be less enraptured.

I also should point out something about the person to whom this guidebook is directed. Above all, he or she is a "visitor." This means that such elements as restaurants have been specifically picked to provide the visitor with a representative, enlightening, stimulating, and, above all, pleasant experience. Since so many extraneous considerations can affect the reception and service accorded a regular restaurant patron, our choices can in no way be construed as an exhaustive guide to resident dining. We think we've listed all the best places, in various price ranges, but they were chosen with a visitor's enjoyment in mind.

Other evidence of how we've tried to tailor our text to reflect modern travel habits is most apparent in the section we call DIVERSIONS. Where once it was common for travelers to spend a South American visit slothfully nailed to a single spot, the emphasis today is more likely to be directed toward pursuing some favorite activity while visiting foreign turf. So we've organized every activity we could reasonably evaluate and arranged the material in a way that is especially accessible to activists of either athletic or cerebral bent. It is no longer necessary, therefore, to wade through a pound or two of superfluous prose just to find the most challenging golf course or climbable peak within a reasonable distance of your destination.

If there is one single thing that best characterizes the revolution in and evolution of current holiday habits, it is that most travelers now consider

## A WORD FROM THE EDITOR

travel a right rather than a privilege. No longer is a family trip to the far corners of the world necessarily a once-in-a-lifetime thing; nor is the idea of visiting exotic, faraway places in the least worrisome. Travel today translates as the enthusiastic desire to sample all of the world's opportunities, to find that elusive quality of experience that is not only enriching, but comfortable. For that reason, we've tried to make what follows not only helpful and enlightening, but the sort of welcome companion of which every traveler dreams.

Finally, I also should point out that every good travel guide is a living enterprise; that is, no part of this text is carved in stone. In our annual revisions, we refine, expand, and further hone all our material to serve your travel needs better. To this end, no contribution is of greater value to us than your personal reaction to what we have written, as well as information reflecting your own experiences while using our book. We earnestly and enthusiastically solicit your comments about this guide *and* your opinions and perceptions about places you have recently visited. In this way, we will be able to provide the most current information — including the actual experiences of recent travelers — and to make those experiences more readily available to others. Please write to us at 10 E. 53nd St., New York, NY 10022.

We sincerely hope to hear from you.

ALEXANDRA MAYES BIRNBAUM

# HOW TO USE THIS GUIDE 3

## DIRECTIONS

Here are 63 South American driving itineraries, from the Panama Canal to Tierra del Fuego and from Easter Island to the Brazilian jungle. These itineraries include South America's most magnificent ruins and its most spectacular natural wonders. You can travel by car along the Pan-American Highway or use South America's public transportation system: buses (with the exception of their *not* being recommended in Peru, because of terrorism), *colectivos* (taxis shared by several people), and trains. DIRECTIONS is the only section of this book that is organized geographically, and its itineraries cover the touring highlights of the entire continent, in short, independent segments that describe journeys of 1 to 3 days' duration. Itineraries can be "connected" for longer trips or used individually for short explorations.

Each entry includes a guide to sightseeing highlights; a cost-and-quality guide to accommodations along the road (small hostels, country hotels, campgrounds, and off-the-main-road discoveries); and hints and suggestions for activities.

Although each of the book's sections has a distinct format and a special function, they have all been designed to be used together to provide a complete inventory of travel information. To use this book to full advantage, take a few minutes to read the table of contents and random entries in each section to get a firsthand feel for how it all fits together.

Pick and choose needed information. Assume, for example, that you have always been interested in exploring and camping out in South America's pre-Columbian archaeological sites, but never knew exactly how to put such a trip together. Start by reading the short, informative section on camping and hiking in GETTING READY TO GO. This would provide plenty of ideas on how to organize the trip and where to go for more information. But where to go and what to see? Turn to *Lost Worlds: The Archaeological Heritage of South America,* DIVERSIONS, for descriptions of the most fascinating ruins in South America. A look through *History,* PERSPECTIVES, will give you some historical background about the civilizations that once inhabited the cities you will see. Perhaps you choose as one of your destinations Machu Picchu, the dramatic mountain outpost of the Inca Empire and Peru's most famous archaeological zone. Turn next to DIRECTIONS for suggestions on what else to do while in Peru; for example, a flight over the Nazca Desert line drawings or a cruise down the Amazon in a riverboat. You may even decide to take a break from camping in the wilds and visit Peru's capital, Lima, which is fully covered in THE CITIES.

In other words, the sections of this book are building blocks designed to help you put together the best possible trip. Use them selectively as a tool, a source of ideas, a reference work for accurate facts, and a guidebook to the best buys, the most exciting sights, the most pleasant accommodations, and the tastiest food — *the best travel experiences* that you can possibly have.

SOUTH AMERICA
Miles
0 200 400 600 800 1000
0 400 800 1200 1600 km
Cities
Capital cities
Points of interest
Tropical forest
Grassland
CARIBBEAN SEA
San Andrés I. (Colombia)
Ríohacha
Santa Marta
Barranquilla
Cartagena
Colón
David PANAMA
PANAMA
Maracaibo
Coro
Valencia
Barquisimeto
CARACAS
Cumaná
Margarita I.
TRINIDAD
PORT OF SPAIN
VENEZUELA
San Cristóbal
Mérida
Orinoco
Apure
Ciudad Bolívar
Cúcuta
Bucaramanga
Medellín
Cauca
Magdalena
BOGOTÁ
COLOMBIA
Buenaventura
Cali
Neiva
Popayán
Guaviare
Puerto Ayacucho
GUIANA HIGHLANDS
Angel Falls
GEORGETOWN
GUYANA
PARAMARIBO
SURINAME
Devil's Is.
CAYENNE
FR. GUIANA
To Galápagos Islands c. 600 m (see inset map)
Tulcán
Equator
QUITO
ECUADOR
Guayaquil
Riobamba
Cuenca
Machala
Putumayo
Yapurá
Rio Negro
Amazon
Leticia
Iquitos
Manaus
Santarem
Belém
São Luís
Marañón
PERU
Chan-Chan
Trujillo
Pucallpa
Ucayali
Juruá
Purús
Madeira
Tapajóz
Xingú
BRAZIL
Parnaíba
Fortaleza
Natal
João Pessoa
Recife
Maceió
Aracaju
Salvador
Ilhéus
Cerro de Pasco
LIMA
Puerto Maldonado
Machu Picchu
Cuzco
Ica
Nazca
Arequipa
Puno
Lake Titicaca
ALTIPLANOS
Mamoré
MATO GROSSO
Mato Grosso
Araguaya
Tocantins
São Francisco
BOLIVIA
LA PAZ
Cochabamba
Cuiabá
BRASÍLIA
Anápolis
Goiânia
60°
50°
40°
10°
0°
-10°

EASTER ISLAND
(Chile)
Poike Peninsula
Rano Aroi
Pu Katiki
Hanga Roa
Rano Kau
27° 5' S
109° 20' W
GALÁPAGOS ISLANDS
(Ecuador)
San Salvador
Baltra
Santa Cruz
San Cristóbal
Puerto Boquerizo
Fernandina
Isabela
FALKLAND ISLANDS
(Islas Malvinas)
(U.K.)
Port Stanley
Santa Cruz
Calafate
Río Gallegos
Str. of Magellan
Pto Natales
Tierra del Fuego
Punta Arenas
Ushuaia
Cape Horn
Falkland Islands
(Islas Malvinas)
SOUTH PACIFIC OCEAN
SOUTH ATLANTIC OCEAN
Tropic of Capricorn
To Easter Island c. 2,300 miles (see inset map)
Juan Fernández Archipelago
(Robinson Crusoe I.)
Iquique
Chuquicamata
Calama
Antofagasta
Copiapó
La Serena
Ovalle
Viña del Mar
Valparaíso
SANTIAGO
Portillo
Chillán
La Concepción
Valdivia
Osorno
Puerto Montt
Chiloé I.
Potosí
Humahuaca
Jujuy
Salta
Cafayate
Tucumán
La Rioja
Córdoba
San Juan
Mendoza
Santa Fe
Paraná
Rosario
BUENOS AIRES
La Plata
Mar del Plata
Bahía Blanca
Neuquén
Carmen de Patagones
Bariloche
Nahuel Huapi National Park
Puerto Madryn
Comodoro Rivadavia
Puerto Deseado
Santa Cruz
Chubut
Colorado
Salado
Bermejo
Pilcomayo
Paraguay
Paraná
Uruguay
La Plata
Desert of Atacama
Andes Mts.
GRAN CHACO
PAMPAS
PATAGONIA
CHILE
ARGENTINA
PARAGUAY
URUGUAY
Concepción
ASUNCIÓN
Iguaçu Falls
Posadas
Corrientes
Salto
Paysandú
Mercedes
MONTEVIDEO
Punta del Este
Pôrto Alegre
Curitiba
Florianópolis
São Paulo
Rio de Janeiro
Petrópolis
Ouro Prêto
Belo Horizonte
Diamantina
BRAZILIAN HIGHLANDS
20°
30°
40°
50°
60°
70°
80°
90°
0°

# GETTING READY TO GO

# When and How to Go

## What's Where

The South American continent consists of 13 countries. Listing them counterclockwise, they are Colombia, Ecuador, Peru, Bolivia, Chile, Argentina, Uruguay, Paraguay, Brazil, French Guiana, Suriname, Guyana, and Venezuela. A fourteenth nation, Panama, links the South American landmass to Central America, with the Panama Canal joining the Atlantic and Pacific oceans. The main body of the continent roughly resembles a lopsided, upside-down pear with a long, tapering end. South America covers approximately 6,464,037 square miles. Brazil, the largest country on the continent, covers approximately 3,268,470 square miles.

According to the US Department of State geographers, the South American continent's coastline runs approximately 13,415 miles, excluding Panama. The **Caribbean Sea**, the **Atlantic Ocean**, and **Panama** border the continent on the north. The **Pacific Ocean** forms the western border; the **Drake Strait**, the southern border; and the **Atlantic Ocean**, the eastern.

An aerial survey of the terrain reveals a narrow desert band along the Pacific coast from Colombia almost to Tierra del Fuego, bordered on the east by the **Andes Mountains**, a 4,500-mile ridge of giant peaks, the backbone of South America. The eastern slopes of the Andes are *montaña,* gently rolling mountain jungle that levels into *plano* (flatland), or *selva* (flat jungle), for nearly 2,700 miles to Brazil's northeastern coast. The **Amazon** basin takes up more than one-third of Brazil. In the south, the jungle rises to the highlands of the **Mato Grosso**. The **pampas** (grasslands) cover nearly 4,000 square miles of Argentina and Uruguay. South of the Río Colorado, in Argentina and Chile, the **Patagonian** plateau extends to the continent's base, meeting the apex of the triangular tip of the continent at the end of the 1,100-mile-long Tierra del Fuego archipelago. Stretching east-southeast from the isthmus of Panama, the Caribbean and Atlantic coasts are tropical as far south as Patagonia. South America's four great rivers and their plains are the **Orinoco** and its **llanos** (open plains) in Venezuela; the **Amazon** and its *selva* in Peru, Colombia, Ecuador, and Brazil; the **Paraguay** and its **Chaco** in Paraguay; and the **Paraná** and its **pampas** in Argentina and Paraguay.

These are the major topographical and geographical features of the continent:

**Isthmus of Panama** – A narrow neck of land connecting Central America with South America. The isthmus's terrain is mountainous, with agricultural valleys, forests, and thick jungle. The jungle swamps of the Darién region form the main impediment to the successful completion of the Pan-American Highway. International shipping traffic passes through the Panama Canal between the Atlantic and Pacific oceans. Chiriqui Province is the biggest agricultural area. The San Blas Islands archipelago extends offshore along the Atlantic coast to Colombia.

**Caribbean Coast** – Extends for 1,978 nautical miles along the tropical shoreline of Colombia, Venezuela, French Guiana, Guyana, and Suriname. Barranquilla, Colombia; La Guaira, Venezuela; and Georgetown, Guyana, are the major Caribbean ports. Lake Maracaibo produces nearly three-quarters of Venezuela's oil. Maracaibo also is a maritime export center for coffee, from Colombia and the Venezuelan interior, and shrimp.

**Atlantic Coast** – Stretching 6,117 nautical miles from Brazil, along Uruguay and Argentina, with tropical to sub-Arctic climates. The major Atlantic seaports are Recife, Rio de Janeiro, and Santos, Brazil; Montevideo, Uruguay; and Buenos Aires, Argentina. The Atlantic Ocean beach resorts are considered the best in the southern hemisphere and among the finest in the world. The Falkland Islands (called the Islas Malvinas by the Argentines), off the southern Argentine coast, are claimed by both Great Britain and Argentina. As we went to press, Great Britain retained control, but the issue of sovereignty still is very hotly debated.

**Pacific Coast** – Extends from Panama down to Colombia, Ecuador, Peru, and Chile for a total of 5,520 miles. The Colombian and Ecuadoran sections of the coast are tropical. Some areas are hilly. From Peru, south to about 200 miles north of Santiago, the Chilean capital, the coast is a strip of mountainous, arid desert. In southern Peru, the flat Nazca plain has been marked with curious and gigantic drawings left by an ancient Indian culture — believed by some people to have been carved into the sands to demarcate landing areas for extraterrestrial beings.

In northern Chile, the Atacama Desert extends from the coast inland about 50 miles. This is copper mining country. Salt, nitrate, and iodine are mined here, too. The dry, reddish gold coastal sands give way to softer, gray beaches lined with scrub pines about 200 miles north of Santiago. From here to Puerto Montt, the Pacific coast is greener, although rocky cliffs break the shore in places. At Puerto Montt, the land breaks up into fjords, mountains, and glaciers for about 1,100 miles to the tip of Tierra del Fuego.

**The Andes** – Running the length of the continental mainland, some 4,500 miles from the Venezuelan highlands to Tierra del Fuego, the Andes form a spiny, north-south ridge of snow-covered mountains and volcanoes. The tallest, Mt. Aconcagua (also the tallest mountain in the entire Western Hemisphere), towers 23,834 feet near the Chile–Argentina border at Mendoza, Argentina. In Ecuador, 50 volcanoes form the Avenue of the Volcanoes, the most famous of which is Mt. Chimborazo. At 19,882 feet, Mt. Guallatiri is the tallest active volcano in the world. The Andes are separated into two mountain chains by the 600-mile-long altiplano, a grassy plain at an elevation of between 11,500 and 15,000 feet between Cuzco, Peru, and the Bolivian border at Lake Titicaca. At 12,506 feet, Lake Titicaca is the world's highest navigable lake.

The altiplano is home to Indian potato farmers, llamas, and a rare species of flamingo. At 15,000 feet and higher, the *puna*, or high Andes, is even more sparsely settled. There are several ranches where cattle and other livestock are raised. La Paz, Bolivia, at 12,001 feet, one of the world's highest cities, is built in a valley cut into sediments of the altiplano. Around San Carlos de Bariloche in Argentina, the Andes Lake District resorts offer skiing, mountain climbing, and fishing. The eastern slopes of the Andes form the *montaña*, or mountain jungle. Bananas are grown and gold is panned in this terrain, which flattens out about 180 miles from the eastern foothills.

**The Jungle** – Stretching from the eastern slopes of the Andes to the Atlantic coast, the vast South American jungle extends through eastern Colombia, Ecuador, Peru, through most of northern and central Brazil, and as far north as French Guiana, Suriname, Guyana, and Venezuela. The Amazon River forms the world's largest river basin and runs 4,000 miles from Peru to the Atlantic, with a network of thousands of tributaries. The Amazon basin spreads over 2,722,000 square miles. In Venezuela, the Orinoco River flows about 1,600 miles from the Colombia border into the Atlantic. Along one of its tributaries, the Caroní River, near the Guyana Highlands, Angel Falls, the world's highest waterfall, drops 3,281 feet. The Orinoco River plain, or llano, occupies one-third of Venezuela.

The major resource of the jungle is oil. Venezuela, Ecuador, Peru, Colombia, and Brazil now produce petroleum. In Peru and Bolivia, the few remaining natural rubber groves in the world yield high-quality rubber for domestic use. In the rivers of the Peruvian jungle, gold is panned during the dry season. The discovery of new deposits of gold has led to a government-sponsored gold rush, with government engineers helping the miners to develop more efficient techniques. The entire continental jungle also is one of the last strongholds of rare wildlife. Many species are indigenous only to the South American continent. (Travelers to the Brazilian jungles should be aware of the heated controversy between industrialists and other developers — who have been clearing portions of the rain forests for timber and agricultural uses — and conservationist groups worldwide. For more information on this volatile situation, see PERSPECTIVES.)

In southwestern Brazil, the Mato Grosso is a high, flat, savannah swamp. In February, the southern Mato Grosso floods; the northern Mato Grosso floods in June. In September, the entire Mato Grosso dries out and the area becomes a lush pastureland. The jungle is sparsely populated for good reason: Temperatures soar into the 100s, and sudden torrential rains paralyze all transportation. Supplies and medicine are in short supply, and premature death from lack of medical attention is common. Diseases such as malaria are widespread, as are poisonous insects, scorpions, and spiders. For many inhabitants of remote jungle outposts, evening entertainment consists of swatting mosquitoes. The South American jungle is, however, one of the most exotic and spellbinding places on earth.

**The Plains and Pampas** – Extending for about 500 miles east of Buenos Aires, Argentina, and covering the entire country of Uruguay. This is gaucho country, land of the famous South American cowboys. Here, world-renowned Argentine cattle graze on the rich grasses of the pampas. The pampas get fewer than 100 days of rain a year — with most of this precipitation occurring in the eastern portion. The Paraná River flows through the Paraguayan Chaco, or plains, along the border with Brazil and Argentina through the pampas to Buenos Aires, where it joins the Atlantic Ocean. The Paraguay River feeds into the Paraná at Asunción, Paraguay's capital.

**Patagonia** – South of the Río Colorado in Argentina, the terrain becomes a rugged, glacially scarred plateau. Covering a large part of both Chile and Argentina, Patagonia reaches from the Andes to the Atlantic and as far south as Tierra del Fuego. It generally is wilderness with spectacular scenery, not unlike a wilder Scandinavia, and sometimes just as cold.

# When to Go

Think of South America, and the image of people relaxing on a sunlit beach probably is the first thing that comes to mind. But there is much more to South America than sun, sand, and surf. Cosmopolitan cities such as Rio de Janeiro, São Paulo, Caracas, and Buenos Aires have a complete range of sophisticated cultural facilities: museums, parks, the opera, theater, and a plethora of intriguing restaurants. The ski resorts in Chile and Argentina are not only set along some of the most spectacular slopes in the world, but have the advantage of being at their peak between June and September — when ski resorts in the northern hemisphere have gone to pasture — as northern and southern hemisphere seasons are reversed.

The high season varies from country to country and from region to region. During *Carnaval* (held during the days before *Ash Wednesday* in February or March) in Rio de Janeiro, Bahia, and Santos, Brazil, hotel rates are higher than at other times during the year. The beach resort season is at its height — as are prices at the more chic resorts — between November and March throughout South America. High season for ski resorts is between June and September. Although the major capitals do not have

**12 GETTING READY / When to Go**

a tourist season — and seasonal rate variations normally are negligible — the preferable time to visit these cities is in the South American spring (around October) or in the autumn (around March) before winter sets in.

So there really isn't a "best" time to visit South America. It is important to emphasize that more and more vacationers to South America who have a choice are enjoying the substantial advantages of off-season travel; that is, the North American summer (at most of the coastal resorts), winter (inland), and — to some degree — spring and fall (throughout the continent). Getting there and staying there is less expensive during the off-season, as airfares, hotel rooms, and car rental rates go down, less expensive package tours become available, and the independent traveler can go farther on less, too.

The specific dates vary, but South American hotels do observe seasonal delineations and during the off-season hotel prices are routinely 30% to 60% lower than high-season rates. In addition, many resorts offer special off-season promotional packages. The very same activities and amenities — from water sports equipment to greens fees for a round of golf — that can add a not so small fortune in extra charges to your bill during the height of the season often are included in the daily room rates during the rest of the year.

Hotel rates and recreation costs are not the only prices to decrease during the off-season. Airfares also generally are less expensive at these times. What's more, the passing of the high season usually spawns a host of package offerings that can include accommodations, car rentals, and other money-saving extras (see *Package Tours*, in this section).

But financial considerations are only part of the allure of off-season travel. Major tourist attractions, beaches, and other facilities tend to be less crowded during the off-season, and — throughout South America — life proceeds at a more leisurely pace. The destinations themselves actually take on a different, friendlier cast with the passing of the high-season hordes.

An additional bonus to visiting resort areas during the off-season is that even the most basic services are performed more efficiently. In theory, off-season service is identical to that offered during high season, but the fact is that the absence of demanding crowds inevitably begets much more thoughtful and personal attention. The very same staff that barely can manage to get fresh towels onto the racks at beach resorts during January and February has the time to chat pleasantly during June and July.

It is not only hotel service that benefits from the absence of the high-season mobs. Fine restaurants, absolutely unbreachable when the professional high rollers are passing out tips large enough to pay off the maître d's mortgage, pay rapt attention to mere mortals during the off-season. And the food preparation and service also are likely to be best when the chef is required to create only a reasonable number of meals.

It also should be noted that the months immediately before and after the peak months — what the travel industry refers to as shoulder seasons — often are sought out because they offer fair weather and somewhat smaller crowds. But be aware that very near high-season prices can prevail during these periods, most often in the most popular areas — such as Buenos Aires, Rio de Janeiro, and Caracas.

**CLIMATE:** The most common concerns about travel have to do with weather. With its great diversity of latitudes and three major temperature zones created by the western coastal desert, tropics, and mountains, the South American climate fits few generalizations. In countries near the equator with altitudes close to sea level, such as **Suriname**, **French Guiana**, **Guyana**, **Panama**, and a great part of **Brazil**, the weather generally is warm all year; the seasons are marked by the amount of rainfall rather than by temperature variation. On the other hand, the climate of other countries on or near the equator, such as **Ecuador**, **Venezuela**, and **Colombia**, which have vast mountain ranges, are affected by altitude as much as latitude.

Well south of the equator, seasonal changes in South America run the reverse of

## GETTING READY / When to Go

those in North America. When it is summer in the US, it is winter in those countries south of **Peru**. Spring arrives in the southern hemisphere in mid-September and lasts until December, when summer officially begins. Spring temperatures are in the 70s F during the day and cooler at night; in summer, they are in the 80s and 90s F. In tropical regions, temperatures may climb as high as the 100s F in summer. Autumn arrives around March, bringing cooler temperatures in the temperate southern zones and frequently damp fog. In **Argentina** and **Chile**, temperatures drop to the 50s and 40s F in autumn, which falls between March and May. This is the prettiest season in the **Andes**, as the heavy summer rains abate and the mountain slopes turn green. *(Please note that although temperatures usually are recorded on the Celsius scale in South America, for purposes of clarity we use the more familiar Fahrenheit scale throughout this guide.)*

During the height of summer along the coast, the mountains and the jungle have their rainy season. Roads are flooded, more often than not, and flying in and out of isolated regions is a difficult, if not totally impossible, proposition. Even after the rainy season, it can rain every afternoon for a few hours in the jungle — and often in the mountains as well. Winter is the dry season, but the temperature can drop into the 30s F and occasionally even into the 20s F in the **Andes**, southern **Chile**, **Bolivia**, and **Argentina**. The ribbon-like strip of mountainous, coastal desert running south from the **Peru–Ecuador** border to about 200 miles north of **Santiago, Chile**, is hot and dry all year, except for a strip of land around **Lima, Peru**, which is foggy and humid much of the year.

The diversity of climate among South American countries is such that South America really is a year-round destination. Consult the chart below and see FACTS IN BRIEF for more information.

Far and away the best source of accurate, complete information on climate is the *World Climate Chart for South America,* available at no cost from the *International Association for Medical Assistance to Travelers (IAMAT;* 417 Center St., Lewiston, NY 14092; phone: 716-754-4883). This thorough, useful pamphlet contains a month-by-month chart of peak and low temperatures (in Fahrenheit and Celsius); altitude (in meters and feet); humidity; recommendations on the type of clothing to bring for each month; and advice on water, milk, and food. (For information on packing a basic wardrobe, see *How to Pack,* in this section; for information on health precautions regarding fresh food, see *Staying Healthy,* also in this section.)

### A SOUTH AMERICAN CLIMATE CHART (Average Temperature in °F)

| Country | Dec.-Feb. | March-May | June-Aug. | Sept.-Nov. |
|---|---|---|---|---|
| Argentina (Buenos Aires) | 83 | 82 | 57 | 66 |
| Bolivia (La Paz) | 64 | 64 | 62 | 70 |
| Brazil (Rio) | 84 | 80 | 76 | 77 |
| Chile (Santiago) | 85 | 73 | 60 | 72 |
| Colombia (Bogotá) | 67 | 67 | 65 | 66 |
| Ecuador (Quito) | 72 | 70 | 72 | 72 |
| French Guiana | 85 | 86 | 89 | 91 |
| Guyana | 84 | 85 | 86 | 87 |
| Panama | 88 | 87 | 87 | 86 |
| Paraguay (Asunción) | 94 | 84 | 75 | 90 |
| Peru (Lima) | 82 | 78 | 67 | 71 |
| Suriname | 85 | 86 | 88 | 91 |
| Uruguay (Montevideo) | 82 | 71 | 59 | 82 |
| Venezuela (Caracas) | 78 | 80 | 79 | 78 |

**14 GETTING READY / Traveling by Plane**

Travelers can get current readings and extended forecasts through the *Weather Channel Connection,* the worldwide weather report center of the *Weather Channel,* a cable television station. By dialing 900-WEATHER and punching in either the first four letters of the city name or the area code for over 600 cities in the US, and the first four letters of the city name for over 225 international destinations, including 20 cities in South America, an up-to-date recording will provide such information as current temperature, barometric pressure, relative humidity, and wind speed, as well as a general 3-day forecast. (Beach, boating, and highway reports are also provided for some locations in the US.) For instance, to hear the weather report for Buenos Aires, punch in BUEN. To find out which cities (or islands, if applicable) in a given country are covered, enter the first four letters of the *country* name. (Service includes cities in Argentina, Bolivia, Brazil, Chile, Colombia, Ecuador, Panama, Paraguay, Peru, Uruguay, and Venezuela). This 24-hour service can be accessed from any touch-tone phone in the US and costs 95¢ per minute. The charge will show up on your phone bill. For additional information, contact the *Weather Channel Connection,* 2600 Cumberland Pkwy., Atlanta, GA 30339 (phone: 404-434-6800).

# Traveling by Plane

Flying is the best way to get to South America, and it is the quickest, most efficient means of travel once you are there. Touring by car, bus, or train certainly is the most scenic way to travel, but considering the distances between major destinations, is impractical unless you will be covering only one area of a particular country. Cruise ships may dock at one port for several days, but generally they function more as hotels for passengers cruising South America's coastal waters, rather than as especially efficient transportation between individual destinations. Air travel is far faster and more direct — the less time spent in transit, the more time spent at your destination. And that is even truer as nonstop and direct flights to an increasing number of South American destinations become available from US gateways.

Despite recent attempts at price simplification by a number of major US carriers, the airlines offering flights to and between cities in South America continue to sell seats at a variety of prices under a vast spectrum of requirements and restrictions. Since you probably will spend more for your airfare than for any other single item in your travel budget, try to take advantage of the lowest fares offered by either scheduled airlines or charter companies. You should know what kinds of flights are available, the rules under which air travel operates, and all the special package options.

Find out the available flight connections between the points to which you will be traveling — particularly between the interior, main cities, and onward. Since fares and flight schedules are always changing, it is essential to check with a travel agent or the airline when you plan your trip and continue reconfirming all the way. Keep in mind that if you plan to travel around *Christmas, Easter,* or *Carnaval,* or during North Americans' summer vacations, you should make reservations well in advance.

**INTERNATIONAL FLIGHTS AND GATEWAYS:** The major US international airlines serving South America are *American* and *United.* In addition, new discount carriers frequently enter the market for a brief period, then disappear. For most international flights to South America, the major US gateways are Chicago, Dallas, Los Angeles, Miami, and New York — although connecting flights often are offered from other cities.

Below is a list of carriers (identified by country of origin) offering regularly scheduled flights from the listed US gateways to the South American destinations covered in this guide. This list was up-to-date as we went to press, but it is subject to frequent service

## GETTING READY / Traveling by Plane

and scheduling changes by the indvidual carriers. What's more, frequency of service may vary according to the season.

*Aerolíneas Argentinas* (**Argentina**): Los Angeles, Miami, New York
*AeroPerú* (**Peru**): Miami
*Air France* (**France**): Miami
*American* (**US**): Dallas, Miami, New York
*Avensa* (**Venezuela**): Miami, New York
*Avianca* (**Colombia**): Los Angeles, Miami, New York
*British West Indian Airlines* (**Trinidad**): Miami, New York, Toronto
*Copa* (**Panama**): Miami
*Ecuatoriana* (**Ecuador**): Chicago, Los Angeles, Miami, New York
*Faucett* (**Peru**): Miami
*Guyana Airways Corporation* (**Guyana**): Miami, New York
*LAB* (**Bolivia**): Miami
*Ladeco* (**Chile**): Baltimore, Miami, New York
*LanChile* (**Chile**): Miami, Los Angeles, New York
*LAP* (**Paraguay**): Miami
*SAETA* (**Ecuador**): Miami
*Surinam Airways* (**Suriname**): Miami, New York
*Varig* (**Brazil**): Chicago, Los Angeles, Miami, New York, San Francisco
*Viasa* (**Venezuela**): Houston, Miami, New York

**NATIONAL AND INTRACONTINENTAL FLIGHTS:** There are several international South American carriers whose domestic services can be used on unlimited mileage tickets — normally called air passes — for extensive travel within a single country. (Some of these passes also include inexpensive air transportation between different South American countries.) These tickets are well worth considering and must be purchased *prior* to leaving the US, often in conjunction with a round-trip ticket between the US and South America.

International flights from the US to South America also may be less expensive if bought in conjunction with one of these intra-South American tickets. For instance, not only is the Visit Peru fare (for domestic travel within Peru, see below) offered by *Faucett* less expensive if bought along with a ticket from the US on one of these carriers — the fare from Miami also is lower than if bought separately for the same flight.

Some representative examples of special intracontinental air passes are listed below. Call the airlines for current pricing and to double-check restrictions (they fluctuate).

**Argentina:** *Aerolíneas Argentinas* offers a 30-day Visit Argentina I. Passengers are issued coupons, each applicable to any flight offered within Argentina.
**Bolivia:** The 28-day Visit Bolivia air pass offered by *LAB* includes flights to all major cities served by that carrier, provided the passenger holds a round-trip Miami–Bolivia ticket with *LAB*.
**Brazil:** *Varig* has a Brazil Pass, which is valid for flights aboard *Varig* and *Cruzeiro do Sul* (a local carrier; see below), except for shuttle flights between Rio's Santo Dumont Airport and São Paulo. The passenger receives five coupons, which can be used for five flights within a 21-day period; some route restrictions apply. Up to four additional coupons can be purchased for a supplement.
**Chile:** Both *Ladeco* and *LanChile* offer 21-day Visit Chile fares. *LanChile* offers several versions: The Continental I can be bought for flights to destinations within Chile either north *or* south of Santiago; the Continental II includes Chilean flights both north *and* south of Santiago; the Pacific I includes flights between Santiago and Easter Island; the Pacific II covers flights within Chile destinations either north *or* south of Santiago, as well as Easter Island; and the Pacific III includes Chilean flights both north and south of Santiago, as well as

Easter Island. *Ladeco* offers two packages: One includes all intra-Chile flights except Easter Island; the second includes Easter Island.

**Colombia:** *Avianca*'s 30-day, Know Colombia pass offers 10 stopovers anywhere in the country, except the jungle city of Leticia and San Andrés island. A higher-priced pass also includes those destinations. An 8-day pass is good for flights to five cities; another pass includes flights to five cities, plus flights to Leticia and San Andrés.

**Peru:** The Visit Peru ticket offered by *Faucett* offers 30 days of unlimited travel within Peru, if bought with an international ticket on the same carrier. A more expensive version of this pass is availble to passengers arriving in Peru on another carrier. *AeroPerú*'s Tumi Fare includes flights to three destinations within Peru; additional stops may be tacked on at a per-flight cost.

**Venezuela:** *Avensa*'s 10-day pass includes unlimited travel on all of its Venezuelan routes.

And, for travel among a number of South American countries, *AeroPerú* also offers a Visit South America pass which includes six international flights (the round trip from the US to South America is counted as two flights). This pass is good for a maximum of 45 days and includes flights to any of the following cities served by *AeroPerú*: Buenos Aires (Argentina), Caracas (Venezuela), Guayaquil (Ecuador), La Paz (Bolivia), Lima (Peru), Rio de Janeiro and São Paulo (Brazil), and Santiago (Chile). Additional flights within Peru or to other South American countries may be added to the basic package.

In addition, a number of domestic carriers offer regularly scheduled flights within each country and between other South American destinations (**Note:** They do *not* fly between the US and South America). For information on these airlines, see FACTS IN BRIEF.

**Tickets** – When traveling on one of the many regularly scheduled flights, a full-fare ticket provides maximum travel flexibility (although at considerable expense) because there are no advance booking requirements. A prospective passenger can buy a ticket for a flight right up to the minute of takeoff — if a seat is available. If your ticket is for a round trip, you can make the return reservation whenever you wish — months before you leave, or the day before you return. Assuming the foreign immigration requirements are met, you can stay at your destination for as long as you like. (Tickets generally are good for a year and can be renewed if not used.) On some airlines, you may be able to cancel your flight at any time without penalty; on others, cancellation — even of a full-fare ticket — may be subject to a variety of restrictions. It pays to check *before* booking your flight. In addition, while it is true that this category of ticket can be purchased at the last minute, it is advisable to reserve well in advance during popular vacation periods and around holiday times.

**Fares** – Airfares continue to change so rapidly that even the experts find it difficult to keep up with them. This ever-changing situation is due to a number of factors, including airline deregulation, volatile labor relations, increasing fuel costs, and vastly increased competition.

Perhaps the most common misconception about fares on scheduled airlines is that the cost of the ticket determines how much service will be provided on the flight. This is true only to a certain extent. A far more realistic rule of thumb is that the less you pay for your ticket, the more restrictions and qualifications are likely to come into play before you board the plane (as well as after you get off). These qualifying aspects relate to the months (and the days of the week) during which you must travel, how far in advance you must purchase your ticket, the minimum and maximum amount of time you may or must remain away, your willingness to decide on a return date at the time of booking — and your ability to stick to that decision. It is not uncommon for passengers sitting side by side on the same wide-body jet to have paid fares varying by hundreds of dollars, and all too often the traveler paying more would have been equally willing (and able) to accept the terms of the far less expensive ticket.

In general, the great variety of airfares to South America can be reduced to four basic categories, including first class, coach (also called economy or tourist class), and excursion or discount fares. A fourth category, called business class has been added by many airlines in recent years. In addition, Advance Purchase Excursion (APEX) fares offer savings under certain conditions.

A **first class** ticket is your admission to the special section of the aircraft, with larger seats, more legroom, sleeperette seating on some wide-body aircraft, better (or at least more elaborately served) food, free drinks and headsets for movies and music channels, and above all, personal attention. First class fares are about twice those of full-fare economy, although both first class passengers and those paying full-fare economy fares are entitled to reserve seats and are sold tickets on an open reservation system. An additional advantage of a first class ticket is the flexibility to include any number of stops en route to or from your final destination in South America, provided that certain set, but generous, restrictions regarding maximum mileage limits are respected. (Note that it is more likely that you will be able to schedule such stopovers at US rather than other South American destinations en route.)

Not too long ago, there were only two classes of air travel, first class and all the rest, usually called economy or tourist. Then **business class** came into being — one of the most successful recent airline innovations. At first, business class passengers were merely curtained off from the other economy passengers. Now a separate cabin or cabins — usually toward the front of the plane — is the norm. While standards of comfort and service are not as high as in first class, they represent a considerable improvement over conditions in the rear of the plane, with roomier seats, more leg and shoulder space between passengers, and fewer seats abreast. Free liquor and headsets, a choice of meal entrées, and a separate counter for speedier check-in are other inducements. As in first class, a business class passenger may travel on any scheduled flight he or she wishes, may buy a one-way or round-trip ticket, and have the ticket remain valid for a year. There are no minimum or maximum stay requirements, no advance booking requirements, and no cancellation penalties, and the fare allows the same free stopover privileges as first class. Airlines often have their own names for their business class service — such as Connoisseur Class on *United*.

The terms of the **coach** or **economy** fare may vary slightly from airline to airline, and in fact from time to time airlines may be selling more than one type of economy fare. Coach or economy passengers sit more snugly, as many as 10 in a single row on a wide-body jet, behind the first class and business class sections. Normally, alcoholic drinks are not free, nor are the headsets. If there are two economy fares on the books, one (often called "regular economy") still may include a number of free stopovers. The other, less expensive fare (often called "special economy") may limit stopovers to one or two, with a charge (typically $25) for each one. Like first class passengers, travelers paying the full coach fare are subject to none of the restrictions that usually are attached to less expensive excursion and discount fares. There are no advance booking requirements, no minimum stay requirements, and (often) no cancellation penalties — but beware, the rules regarding cancellation vary from carrier to carrier. Tickets are sold on an open reservation system: They can be bought for a flight right up to the minute of takeoff (if seats are available), and if the ticket is round-trip, the return reservation can be made any time you wish. Both first class and coach tickets generally are good for a year, after which they can be renewed if not used, and if you ultimately decide not to fly at all, your money may be refunded (again, policies vary). On some routes between the US and South America, the cost of economy and business class tickets may

## 18 GETTING READY / Traveling by Plane

vary from a basic (low-season) price in effect most of the year to a peak (high-season) price during North American winter months (for coastal resort areas) or summer months (for ski areas).

**Excursion** and other **discount** fares are the airlines' equivalent of a special sale and usually apply to round-trip bookings only. These fares generally differ according to the season and the number of travel days permitted. They are only a bit less flexible than full-fare economy tickets, and are, therefore, often useful for both business and holiday travelers. Most round-trip excursion tickets include strict minimum and maximum stay requirements and reservations can be changed only within the specified time limits. So don't count on extending a ticket beyond the prescribed time of return or staying less time than required. Different airlines may have different regulations concerning the number of stopovers permitted, and sometimes excursion fares are less expensive during midweek. The availability of these reduced-rate seats is most limited at busy times, such as holidays (all of South America seems to take to the air at *Christmas, Easter,* and the end of the US school year). Discount or excursion fare ticket holders sit with the coach passengers and, for all intents and purposes, are indistinguishable from them. They receive all the same basic services, even though they may have paid anywhere between 30% and 55% less for the trip. Obviously, it's wise to make plans early enough to qualify for this less expensive transportation if possible.

These discount or excursion fares may masquerade under a variety of names, they may vary from city to city (from the East Coast to the West Coast, especially), but they invariably have strings attached. A common requirement is that the ticket be purchased a certain number of days — usually between 7 and 21 days — in advance of departure, though it may be booked weeks or months in advance (it has to be "ticketed," or paid for, shortly after booking, however). The return reservation usually has to be made at the time of the original ticketing and often cannot be changed later than a certain number of days (again, usually 7 to 21 days) before the return flight. If events force a change in the return reservation after the date allowed, the passenger may have to pay the difference between the round-trip excursion rate and the round-trip coach rate, although some carriers permit such scheduling changes for a nominal fee. In addition, some airlines may allow passengers to use their discounted fares by standing by for an empty seat, even if they don't otherwise have standby fares. Another common condition is a minimum and maximum stay requirement; for example, 1 to 6 days or 6 to 14 days (but including at least a Saturday night). Last, cancellation penalties of up to 50% of the full price of the ticket have been assessed — if a refund is offered at all — so check the specific penalty in effect when you purchase your discount/excursion ticket.

On some airlines, the ticket bearing the lowest price of all the current discount fares is the ticket where no change at all in departure and/or return flights is permitted, and where the ticket price is totally nonrefundable. If you do buy such a nonrefundable ticket, you should be aware of a new policy followed by some airlines that may make it easier to change your plans if necessary. For a fee — set by each airline and payable at the airport when checking in — you *may* be able to change the time or date of a return flight on a nonrefundable ticket. However, if the nonrefundable ticket price for the replacement flight is higher than that of the original (as often is the case when trading in a weekday for a weekend flight), you will have to pay the difference. Any such change must be made a certain number of days in advance — in some cases as little as 2 days — of either the original or the replacement flight, whichever is earlier; restrictions are set by the individual carrier. (Travelers holding a nonrefundable or other restricted ticket who must change their plans due to a family emergency should know that some carriers may make special allowances in such situations; for further information, see *Staying Healthy,* in this section.)

■ **Note:** Due to recent changes in many US airlines' policies, nonrefundable tickets are now available that carry none of the above restrictions. Although passengers still may *not* be able to obtain a refund for the price paid, the time or date of a

## GETTING READY / Traveling by Plane 19

departing or return flight may be changed at any time (assuming seats are available) for a nominal service charge.

There also is a newer, often less expensive type of excursion fare, the **APEX**, or **Advanced Purchase Excursion**, fare. As with traditional excursion fares, passengers paying an APEX fare sit with and receive the same basic services as any other coach or economy passengers, even though they may have paid up to 50% less for their seats. In return, they are subject to certain restrictions. The ticket usually is good for a minimum of 7 days in South America and a maximum, currently, of anywhere between 1 and 6 months (depending on the airline and the destination); and as its name implies, it must be "ticketed," or paid for in its entirety, a certain period of time before departure — usually 21 days.

The drawback to some APEX fares is that they penalize travelers who change their minds — and travel plans. Usually, the return reservation must be made at the time of the original ticketing, and if for some reason you change your schedule, you will have to pay a penalty of $100 or 10% of the ticket value, whichever is greater, as long as you travel within the validity period of your ticket. More flexible APEX fares recently have been introduced, which allow travelers to make changes in the date or time of their flights for a nominal charge (as low as $25).

With either type of APEX fare, if you change your return to a date less than the minimum stay or more than the maximum stay, the difference between the round-trip APEX fare and the full round-trip coach rate will have to be paid. There also is a penalty of anywhere from $50 to $100 or more for canceling or changing a reservation *before* travel begins — check the specific penalty in effect when you purchase your ticket. No stopovers are allowed on an APEX ticket, but it is possible to create an open-jaw effect by buying an APEX on a split-ticket basis; for example, flying to Rio de Janeiro, Brazil, and returning from Asunción, Paraguay. The total price would be half the price of an APEX to Rio plus half the price of an APEX to Asunción. APEX tickets to South America are sold at basic and peak rates (peak season varies, depending on the destination) and may include surcharges for weekend flights.

**Standby** fares, at one time the rock-bottom price at which a traveler could fly to South America, have become elusive. At the time of this writing, most major scheduled airlines did not regularly offer standby fares on direct flights to South America. Because airline fares and their conditions constantly change, however, bargain hunters should not hesitate to ask if such a fare exists at the time they plan to travel.

While the definition of standby varies somewhat from airline to airline, it generally means that you make yourself available to buy a ticket for a flight (usually no sooner than the day of departure), then literally stand by on the chance that a seat will be empty. Once aboard, however, a standby passenger has the same meal service and frills (or lack of them) enjoyed by others in the economy class compartment.

Something else to check is the possibility of qualifying for a **GIT** (Group Inclusive Travel) fare, which requires that a specific dollar amount of ground arrangements be purchased, in advance, along with the ticket. The requirements vary as to the number of travel days and stopovers permitted, and the minimum number of passengers required for a group. The actual fares also vary, but the cost will be spelled out in brochures distributed by the tour operators handling the ground arrangements. In the past, GIT fares were among the least expensive available from the established carriers, but the prevalence of discount fares has caused group fares to all but disappear from some air routes. Travelers reading brochures on group package tours to South America will find that, in almost all cases, the applicable airfare given as a sample (to be added to the price of the land package to obtain the total tour price) is an APEX fare, the same discount fare available to the independent traveler.

The major airlines serving South America from the US also may offer individual excursion fare rates similar to GIT fares, which are sold in conjunction with ground

## 20 GETTING READY / Traveling by Plane

accommodation packages. Previously called ITX, and sometimes referred to as individual tour-basing fares, these fares generally are offered as part of "air/hotel/car/transfer packages," and can reduce the cost of an economy fare by more than a third. The packages are booked for a specific amount of time, with return dates specified; rescheduling and cancellation restrictions and penalties vary from carrier to carrier. At the time of this writing, these fares were offered to popular destinations throughout South America by *American, Avensa,* and *Avianca.* Check with other carriers at the time you plan to fly. (For further information on package options, see *Package Tours,* in this section.)

Travelers looking for the least expensive possible airfares should, finally, scan the pages of their hometown newspapers (especially the Sunday travel section) for announcements of special promotional fares. Most airlines offer their most attractive special fares to encourage travel during slow seasons, and to inaugurate and publicize new routes. Even if none of these factors applies, prospective passengers can be fairly sure that the number of discount seats per flight at the lowest price is strictly limited, or that the fare offering includes a set expiration date — which means it's absolutely necessary to move fast to enjoy the lowest possible price.

Among other special airline promotional deals for which you should be on the lookout are discount or upgrade coupons sometimes offered by the major carriers and found in mail-order merchandise catalogues. For instance, airlines sometimes issue coupons that typically cost around $25 each and are good for a percentage discount or an upgrade on an international airline ticket — including flights to South America. The only requirement beyond the fee generally is that a coupon purchaser must buy at least one item from the catalogue. There usually are some minimum airfare restrictions before the coupon is redeemable, but in general these are worthwhile offers. Restrictions often include certain blackout days (when the coupon cannot be used at all), usually imposed during peak travel periods. These coupons are particularly valuable to business travelers who tend to buy full-fare tickets, and while the coupons are issued in the buyer's name, they can be used by others who are traveling on the same itinerary.

It's always wise to ask about discount or promotional fares and about any conditions that might restrict booking, payment, cancellation, and changes in plans. Check the prices from neighboring cities. A special rate may be offered in a nearby city but not in yours, and it may be enough of a bargain to warrant your leaving from that city. Ask if there is a difference in price for midweek versus weekend travel, or if there is a further discount for traveling early in the morning or late at night. Also be sure to investigate package deals, which are offered by virtually every airline — although such airline offerings are less common to South America than to other destinations. These may include a car rental, accommodations, and dining and/or sightseeing features, in addition to the basic airfare, and the combined cost of packaged elements usually is considerably less than the cost of the exact same elements when purchased separately.

If in the course of your research you come across a deal that seems too good to be true, keep in mind that logic may not be a component of deeply discounted airfares — there's not always any sane relationship between miles to be flown and the price to get there. More often than not, the level of competition on a given route dictates the degree of discount, and don't be dissuaded from accepting an offer that sounds irresistible just because it also sounds illogical. Better to buy that inexpensive fare while it's being offered and worry about the sense — or absence thereof — while you're flying to your desired destination.

When you're satisfied that you've found the lowest possible price for which you can conveniently qualify (you may have to call the airline more than once, because different airline reservations clerks have been known to quote different prices), make your booking. Then, to protect yourself against fare increases, purchase and pay for your ticket as soon as possible after you've received a confirmed reservation. Airlines generally will honor their tickets, even if the operative price at the time of your flight is higher than the price you paid; if fares go up between the time you *reserve* a flight and the time you *pay* for it, you likely will be out of luck. Finally, with excursion or discount fares, it is important to remember that when a reservations clerk says that you must purchase a ticket by a specific date, this is an absolute deadline. Miss the deadline and the airline may automatically cancel your reservation without telling you.

■ **Note:** Another wrinkle in the airfare scene is that if the fares go *down* after you purchase your ticket, you *may* be entitled to a refund of the difference. However, this is only possible in certain situations — availability and advance purchase restrictions pertaining to the lower rate are set by the airline. If you suspect that you may be able to qualify for such a refund, check with your travel agent or the airline.

**Frequent Flyers** – The leading US carriers serving South America — *American* and *United* — offer a bonus system to frequent travelers. After the first 10,000 miles, for example, a passenger might be eligible for a first class seat for the coach fare; after another 10,000 miles, he or she might receive a discount on his or her next ticket purchase. The value of the bonuses continues to increase as more miles are logged.

Bonus miles also may be earned by patronizing affiliated car rental companies or hotel chains, or by using one of the credit cards that now offer this reward. In deciding whether to accept such a credit card from one of the issuing organizations that tempt you with frequent flyer mileage bonuses on a specific airline, first determine whether the interest rate charged on the unpaid balance is the same as (or less than) possible alternate credit cards, and whether the annual "membership" fee also is equal or lower. If these charges are slightly higher than those of competing cards, weigh the difference against the potential value in airfare savings. Also ask about any bonus miles awarded just for signing up — 1,000 is common, 5,000 generally the maximum.

For the most up-to-date information on frequent flyer bonus options, you may want to send for the monthly newsletter *Frequent*. Issued by Frequent Publications, it provides current information about frequent flyer plans in general, as well as specific data about promotions, awards, and combination deals to help you keep track of the profusion — and confusion — of current and upcoming availabilities. For a year's subscription, send $33 to Frequent Publications, 4715-C Town Center Dr., Colorado Springs, CO 80916 (phone: 800-333-5937).

There also is a monthly magazine called *Frequent Flyer*, but unlike the newsletter mentioned above, its focus is primarily on newsy articles of interest to business travelers and other frequent flyers. Published by Official Airline Guides (PO Box 58543, Boulder, CO 80322-8543; phone: 800-323-3537), *Frequent Flyer* is available for $24 for a 1-year subscription.

**Low-Fare Airlines** – Increasingly, the stimulus for special fares is the appearance of airlines associated with bargain rates. On these airlines, all seats generally sell for the same price, which tends to be somewhat below the lowest discount fare offered by the larger, more established airlines. It is important to note that tickets offered by these smaller companies frequently are not subject to the same restrictions as some of the discounted fares offered by the more established carriers. They may not require advance purchase or minimum and maximum stays, may involve no cancellation penalties, and may be available one way or round trip. A disadvantage to some low-fare airlines, however, is that when something goes wrong, such as delayed baggage or a flight cancellation due to equipment breakdown, their smaller fleets and fewer flights mean that passengers may have to wait longer for a solution than they would on one of the equipment-rich major carriers.

**Taxes and Other Fees** – Travelers who have shopped for the best possible flight at the lowest possible price should be warned that a number of extras will be added to that price and collected by the airline or travel agent who issues the ticket. In addition to the $6 International Air Transportation Tax — a departure tax paid by all passengers flying from the US to a foreign destination — there is a $10 US Federal Inspection Fee levied on all air and cruise passengers who arrive in the US from outside North America (those arriving from Canada, Mexico, the Caribbean, and US territories are exempt). Payable at the time a round-trip or incoming ticket is purchased, it combines a $5 customs inspection fee and a $5 immigration inspection fee, both instituted in 1986 to finance additional inspectors to reduce delays at gateways.

Still another fee is charged by some airlines to cover more stringent security procedures, prompted by recent terrorist incidents. The 10% federal US Transportation Tax applies to travel within the US or US territories. It does not apply to passengers flying between US cities or territories en route to a foreign destination, unless the trip includes a stopover of more than 12 hours at a US point. Someone flying from Seattle to Miami and stopping in Miami for more than 12 hours before boarding a flight to Buenos Aires, Argentina, for instance, would pay the 10% tax on the domestic portion of the trip. Note that these taxes *usually* (but not always) are included in advertised fares and in the prices quoted by airlines reservations clerks.

**Reservations** – For those who don't have the time or patience to investigate personally all possible air departures and connections for a proposed trip, a travel agent can be of inestimable help. A good agent should have all the information on which flights go where and when, and which categories of tickets are available on each. Most have computerized reservation links with the major carriers, so that a seat can be reserved and confirmed in minutes. An increasing number of agents also possess fare-comparison computer programs, so they often are very reliable sources of detailed competitive price data. (For more information, see *How to Use a Travel Agent,* in this section.)

When making plane reservations through a travel agent, ask the agent to give the airline your home phone number, as well as your daytime business phone number. All too often the agent uses the agency number as the official contact for changes in flight plans. Especially during the winter — prime time for an escape to the sunny shores of South America — weather conditions hundreds or even thousands of miles away can wreak havoc with flight schedules. Aircraft are constantly in use, and a plane delayed in the Orient or on the West Coast can miss its scheduled flight from the East Coast the next morning. The airlines are fairly reliable about getting this sort of information to passengers if they can reach them; diligence does little good at 10 PM if the airline has only the agency's or an office number.

Reconfirmation is strongly recommended for all international flights (though it is not generally required on US domestic flights), and, in the case of flights to South America, it is *essential* that you confirm your round-trip reservations — especially the return leg — as well as any point-to-point flights within South America. Some (though increasingly fewer) reservations to and from international destinations are automatically canceled after a required reconfirmation period (typically 72 hours) has passed — even if you have a confirmed, fully paid ticket in hand. It always is wise to call ahead to make sure that the airline did not slip up in entering your original reservation, or in registering any changes you may have made since, and that it has your seat reservation and/or special meal request in the computer. If you look at the printed information on your ticket, you'll see the airline's reconfirmation policy stated explicitly. Don't be lulled into a false sense of security by the "OK" on your ticket next to the number and time of the return flight. This only means that a reservation has been entered; a reconfirmation still may be necessary. If in doubt — call.

Although reconfirmation of a flight *to* South America is easily done by calling the airline, once there, reconfirming a return or ongoing intra-South American flight can be a nuisance. It's almost impossible to reconfirm at the airport or by phone on arrival:

## GETTING READY / Traveling by Plane

instead, this must be done in person at the city ticket office where flight space control is maintained. Reconfirmation is particularly important when traveling within a country from the capital to the provinces. (Airplanes are the primary transport link for most of the continent, and you will find that local flights almost always are fully booked or overbooked — particularly on weekends and holidays.) The city ticket office should, therefore, be the first stop on any city tour (just so you don't forget). An alternative is to arrange in advance for your ground operator (many US tour package operators provide an agent or other local representative to assist you) in each city to handle this for you — in this case, check back with the agent to confirm that this has been done. Some of the better hotels also offer this service to guests.

If you plan not to take a flight on which you hold a confirmed reservation, by all means inform the airline. Because the problem of "no-shows" is a constant expense for airlines, they are allowed to overbook flights, a practice that often contributes to the threat of denied boarding for a certain number of passengers (see "Getting Bumped," below).

**Seating** – For most types of tickets, airline seats usually are assigned on a first-come, first-served basis at check-in, although some airlines make it possible to reserve a seat at the time of ticket purchase. Always check in early for your flight, even with advance seat assignments. A good rule of thumb for international flights is to arrive at the airport *at least* 2 hours before the scheduled departure to give yourself plenty of time in case there are long lines.

Most airlines furnish seating charts, which make choosing a seat much easier, but there are a few basics to consider. You must decide whether you prefer a window, aisle, or middle seat. On flights where smoking is permitted, you also should indicate if you prefer the smoking or nonsmoking section.

The amount of legroom provided (as well as chest room, especially when the seat in front of you is in a reclining position) is determined by something called "pitch," a measure of the distance between the back of the seat in front of you and the front of the back of your seat. The amount of pitch is a matter of airline policy, not the type of plane you fly. First class and business class seats have the greatest pitch, a fact that figures prominently in airline advertising. In economy class or coach, the standard pitch ranges from 33 to as little as 31 inches — downright cramped.

The number of seats abreast, another factor determining comfort, depends on a combination of airline policy and airplane dimensions. First class and business class have the fewest seats per row. Economy generally has 9 seats per row on a DC-10 or an L-1011, making either one slightly more comfortable than a 747, on which there normally are 10 seats per row. Charter flights on DC-10s and L-1011s, however, often have 10 seats per row and can be noticeably more cramped than 747 charters, on which the seating normally remains at 10 per row.

Airline representatives claim that most aircraft are more stable toward the front and midsection, while seats farthest from the engines are quietest. Passengers who have long legs and are traveling on a wide-body aircraft might request a seat directly behind a door or emergency exit, since these seats often have greater than average pitch, or a seat in the first row of a given section, which offers extra legroom — although these seats are increasingly being reserved for passengers who are willing (and able) to perform certain tasks in the event of emergency evacuation. It often is impossible, however, to see the movie from these seats, which are directly behind the plane's exits. Be aware that the first row of the economy section (called a "bulkhead" seat) on a conventional aircraft (not a widebody) does *not* offer extra legroom, since the fixed partition will not permit passengers to slide their feet under it, and that watching a movie from this first-row seat can be difficult and uncomfortable. These bulkhead seats do, however, provide ample room to use a bassinet or safety seat and often are reserved for families traveling with children.

**24 GETTING READY / Traveling by Plane**

A window seat protects you from aisle traffic and clumsy serving carts and also provides a view, while an aisle seat enables you to get up and stretch your legs without disturbing your fellow travelers. Middle seats are the least desirable, and seats in the last row are the worst of all, since they seldom recline fully. If you wish to avoid children on your flight or if you find that you are sitting in an especially noisy section, you usually are free to move to any unoccupied seat — if there is one.

If you are overweight, you may face the prospect of a long flight with special trepidation. Center seats in the alignments of wide-body 747s, L-1011s, and DC-10s are about 1½ inches wider than those on either side, so larger travelers tend to be more comfortable there.

Despite all these rules of thumb, finding out which specific rows are near emergency exits or at the front of a wide-body cabin can be difficult because seating arrangements on two otherwise identical planes vary from airline to airline. There is, however, a quarterly publication called *Airline Seating Guide* that publishes seating charts for most major US airlines and many foreign carriers as well. Your travel agent should have a copy, or you can buy the US edition for $39.95 per year and the international edition for $44.95. Order from Carlson Publishing Co., Box 888, Los Alamitos, CA 90720 (phone: 800-728-4877 or 310-493-4877).

Simply reserving an airline seat in advance, however, actually may guarantee very little. Most airlines require that passengers arrive at the departure gate at least 45 minutes (sometimes more) ahead of time to hold a seat reservation. *American,* for example, may cancel seat assignments and may not honor reservations of passengers who have not checked in some period of time — usually between 30 and 45 minutes, depending on the airport — before the scheduled departure time, and they *ask* travelers to check in at least 1 hour before all domestic flights and 2 hours before international flights. It pays to read the fine print on your ticket carefully and plan ahead.

A far better strategy is to visit an airline ticket office (or one of a select group of travel agents) to secure an actual boarding pass for your specific flight. Once this has been issued, airline computers show you as checked in, and you effectively own the seat you have selected (although some carriers may not honor boarding passes of passengers arriving at the gate less than 10 minutes before departure). This also is good — but not foolproof — insurance against getting bumped from an overbooked flight and is, therefore, an especially valuable tactic at peak travel times.

**Smoking –** One decision regarding choosing a seat has been taken out of the hands of many travelers who smoke. Effective February 25, 1990, the US government imposed a ban that prohibits smoking on all flights scheduled for 6 hours or less within the US and its territories. The new regulation applies to both domestic and international carriers serving these routes.

In the case of flights to South America, these rules do not apply to nonstop flights from the US to destinations in South America or those with a *continuous* flight time of over 6 hours between stops in the US or its territories. Smoking is not permitted on segments of international flights where the time between US landings is under 6 hours — for instance, flights that include a stopover (even with no change of plane), or connecting flights. To further complicate the situation, several individual carriers are banning smoking altogether on certain routes (although as we went to press these bans had not yet extended to South American routes).

On those flights that do permit smoking, the US Department of Transportation has determined that nonsmoking sections must be enlarged to accommodate all passengers who wish to sit in one. The airline does not, however, have to shift seating to accommodate nonsmokers who arrive late for a flight or travelers flying standby, and in general not all airlines can guarantee a seat in the nonsmoking section on international flights. Cigar and pipe smoking are prohibited on all flights, even in the smoking sections.

For a wallet-size guide, which notes in detail the rights of nonsmokers according to these regulations, send a self-addressed, stamped envelope to *ASH (Action on Smoking and Health),* Airline Card, 2013 H St. NW, Washington, DC 20006 (phone: 202-659-4310).

**Meals** – If you have specific dietary requirements, be sure to let the airline know well before departure time. The available meals include vegetarian, seafood, kosher, Muslim, Hindu, high-protein, low-calorie, low-cholesterol, low-fat, low-sodium, diabetic, bland, and children's menus (not all of these may be available on every carrier). There is no extra charge for this option. It usually is necessary to request special meals when you make your reservations — check-in time is too late. It's also wise to reconfirm that your request for a special meal has made its way into the airline's computer — the time to do this is 24 hours before departure. (Note that special meals generally are not available on flights within South America, and definitely not available on the smaller domestic carriers. If this poses a problem, try to eat before you board, or bring a snack with you.)

**Baggage** – Travelers from the US face two different kinds of rules. When you fly on a US airline or on a major international carrier, US baggage regulations will be in effect. Though airline baggage allowances vary slightly, in general, all passengers are allowed to carry on board, without charge, one piece of luggage that will fit easily under a seat of the plane or in an overhead bin and whose combined dimensions (length, width, and depth) do not exceed 45 inches. A reasonable amount of reading material, camera equipment, and a handbag also are allowed. In addition, all passengers are allowed to check two bags in the cargo hold: one usually not to exceed 62 inches when length, width, and depth are combined, the other not to exceed 55 inches in combined dimensions. Generally no single bag may weigh more than 70 pounds.

On domestic South American carriers, baggage allowances may be subject to a different weight determination. The popular flight from Lima to Cuzco on *AeroPerú* is a good example of this situation — the total check-in baggage allowance is 44 pounds. (If you are flying from the US to South America and connecting to a domestic flight, you generally will be allowed the same amount of baggage as on the international flight. If you break your trip and then take a domestic flight, the local carrier's weight restrictions apply.)

Charges for additional, oversize, or overweight bags usually are made at a flat rate; the actual dollar amount varies from carrier to carrier. If you plan to travel with any special equipment or sporting gear, be sure to check with the airline beforehand. Most have specific procedures for handling such baggage, and you may have to pay for transport regardless of how much other baggage you have checked. Golf clubs may be checked through as luggage (most airlines are accustomed to handling them), but tennis rackets should be carried onto the plane. Aqualung tanks, depressurized and appropriately packed with padding, and surfboards (minus the fin and padded) also may go as baggage. Snorkeling gear should be packed in a suitcase, duffel, or tote bag. Some airlines require that bicycles be partially dismantled and packaged (see *Camping and RVs, Hiking and Biking,* in this section).

Airline policies regarding baggage allowances for children vary and usually are based on the percentage of full adult fare paid. Although on many US carriers children who are ticket holders are entitled to the same baggage allowance as a full-fare passenger, some carriers allow only one bag per child, which sometimes must be smaller than an adult's bag (around 39 to 45 inches in combined dimensions). Often there is no luggage allowance for a child traveling on an adult's lap or in a bassinet. Particularly for international carriers, it's always wise to check ahead. (For more information, see *Hints for Traveling with Children,* in this section.)

To reduce the chances of your luggage going astray, remove all airline tags from previous trips, and label each bag inside and out — with your business address rather than your home address on the outside, to prevent thieves from knowing whose house

## 26  GETTING READY / Traveling by Plane

might be unguarded. Lock everything and double-check the tag that the airline attaches to make sure that it is coded correctly for your destination: GRU for São Paulo, or GIG for Rio de Janeiro, for instance.

If your bags are not in the baggage claim area after your flight, or if they're damaged, report the problem to airline personnel immediately. Keep in mind that policies regarding the specific time limit within which you have to make your claim vary from carrier to carrier. Fill out a report form on your lost or damaged luggage and keep a copy of it and your original baggage claim check. If you must surrender the check to claim a damaged bag, get a receipt for it to prove that you did, indeed, check your baggage on the flight. If luggage is missing, be sure to give the airline your destination and/or a telephone number where you can be reached. Also, take the name and number of the person in charge of recovering lost luggage.

Most airlines have emergency funds for passengers stranded away from home without their luggage, but if it turns out that your bags are truly lost and not simply delayed, do not then and there sign any paper indicating you'll accept an offered settlement. Since the airline is responsible for the value of your bags within certain statutory limits ($1,250 per passenger for lost baggage on a US domestic flight; $9.07 per pound or $20 per kilo for checked baggage, and up to $400 per passenger for unchecked baggage, on an international flight), you should take some time to assess the extent of your loss (see *Insurance,* in this section). It's a good idea to keep records indicating the value of the contents of your luggage. A wise alternative is to take a Polaroid picture of the most valuable of your packed items just after putting them in your suitcase.

Considering the increased incidence of damage to baggage, it's now more than ever a good idea to keep the sales slips that confirm how much you paid for your bags. These are invaluable in establishing the value of damaged luggage and eliminate any arguments. A better way to protect your precious gear from the luggage-eating conveyers is to try to carry it on board whenever possible.

Be aware that airport security increasingly is an issue worldwide, and in South America is taken very seriously. Heavily armed police patrol the airports, and unattended luggage of any description may be confiscated and quickly destroyed. Passengers checking in at a foreign airport may undergo at least two separate inspections of their tickets, passports, and luggage by courteous, but nonetheless serious, airline personnel — who ask passengers if their baggage has been out of their possession between packing and the airport, or if they have been given gifts or other items to transport — before checked items are accepted.

**Airline Clubs –** Some US and foreign carriers have clubs for travelers who pay for membership. These clubs are not solely for first class passengers, although a first class ticket *may* entitle a passenger to lounge privileges. Membership entitles the traveler to use of the private lounges at airports along their route, to refreshments served in these lounges, and to check-cashing privileges at most of their counters. Extras include special telephone numbers for individual reservations, embossed luggage tags, and a membership card for identification. Airlines serving South America that offer membership in such clubs include the following:

*American:* The *Admiral's Club.* Single yearly membership $225 for the first year; $125 thereafter; spouse an additional $70 per year.

*United:* The *Red Carpet Club.* Single yearly membership $125 (plus a onetime $100 initiation fee); spouse an additional $50; 3-year and lifetime memberships also available.

Note that such companies do not have club facilities in all airports. Other airlines also offer a variety of special services in many airports.

**Getting Bumped –** A special air travel problem is the possibility that an airline will accept more reservations (and sell more tickets) than there are seats on a given flight.

## GETTING READY / Traveling by Plane

This is entirely legal and is done to make up for "no-shows," passengers who don't show up for a flight for which they have made reservations and bought tickets. If the airline has oversold the flight and everyone does show up, there simply aren't enough seats. When this happens, the airline is subject to stringent rules designed to protect travelers.

In such cases, the airline first seeks ticket holders willing to give up their seats voluntarily in return for a negotiable sum of money or some other inducement, such as an offer of upgraded seating on the next flight or a voucher for a free trip at some other time. If there are not enough volunteers, the airline may bump passengers against their wishes.

Anyone inconvenienced in this way, however, is entitled to an explanation of the criteria used to determine who does and does not get on the flight, as well as compensation if the resulting delay exceeds certain limits. If the airline can put the bumped passengers on an alternate flight that is *scheduled to arrive* at their original destination within 1 hour of their originally scheduled arrival time, no compensation is owed. If the delay is more than 1 hour but less than 2 hours on a domestic US flight, they must be paid denied-boarding compensation equivalent to the one-way fare to their destination (but not more than $200). If the delay is more than 2 hours after the original arrival time on a domestic flight or more than 4 hours on an international flight, the compensation must be doubled (not more than $400). The airline also may offer bumped travelers a voucher for a free flight instead of the denied-boarding compensation. The passenger may be given the choice of either the money or the voucher, the dollar value of which may be no less than the monetary compensation to which the passenger would be entitled. The voucher is not a substitute for the bumped passenger's original ticket; the airline continues to honor that as well.

Keep in mind that the above regulations and policies are only for flights leaving the US, and do *not* apply to charters or to inbound flights originating abroad, even on US carriers. Airlines carrying passengers between foreign destinations are free to determine what compensation they will pay to passengers who are bumped because of overbooking. They generally spell out their policies on airline tickets. Some foreign airline policies are similar to the US policy; however, don't assume all carriers will be as generous.

To protect yourself as best you can against getting bumped, arrive at the airport early, allowing plenty of time to check in and get to the gate. If the flight is oversold, ask immediately for the written statement explaining the airline's policy on denied-boarding compensation and its boarding priorities. If the airline refuses to give you this information, or if you feel it has not handled the situation properly, file a complaint with both the airline and the appropriate government agency (see "Consumer Protection," below).

**Delays and Cancellations** – The above compensation rules also do not apply if the flight is canceled or delayed, or if a smaller aircraft is substituted due to mechanical problems. Each airline has its own policy for assisting passengers whose flights are delayed or canceled or who must wait for another flight because their original one was overbooked. Most airline personnel will make new travel arrangements if necessary. If the delay is longer than 4 hours, the airline may pay for a phone call or telegram, a meal, and, in some cases, a hotel room and transportation to it.

■ **Caution:** If you are bumped or miss a flight, be sure to ask the airline to notify other airlines on which you have reservations or connecting flights. When your name is taken off the passenger list of your initial flight, the computer usually cancels all of your reservations automatically, unless *you* take steps to preserve them.

**CHARTER FLIGHTS:** By booking a block of seats on a specially arranged flight, charter operators offer travelers air transportation for a substantial reduction over the full coach or economy fare. These operators may offer air-only charters (selling transportation alone) or charter packages (the flight plus a combination of land arrangements such as accommodations, meals, tours, or car rentals). Charters are especially attractive to people living in smaller cities or out-of-the-way places, because they frequently leave from nearby airports, saving travelers the inconvenience and expense of getting to a major gateway.

From the consumer's standpoint, charters differ from scheduled airlines in two main respects: You generally need to book and pay in advance, and you can't change the itinerary or the departure and return dates once you've booked the flight. In practice, however, these restrictions don't always apply. Today, most of the charter flights to South America have the more popular resort areas as their prime destinations, and although most still require advance reservations, some permit last-minute bookings (when there are unsold seats available), and some even offer seats on a standby basis.

Though charters almost always are round-trip, and it is unlikely that you would be sold a one-way seat on a round-trip flight, on rare occasions one-way tickets on charters are offered. Although it may be possible to book a one-way charter in the US, giving you more flexibility in scheduling your return, note that US regulations pertaining to charters may be more permissive than the charter laws of other countries. For example, if you want to book a one-way charter back to the US, you may find advance booking rules in force.

Some things to keep in mind about the charter game:

1. It cannot be repeated often enough that if you are forced to cancel your trip, you can lose much (and possibly all) of your money unless you have cancellation insurance, which is a *must* (see *Insurance,* in this section). Frequently, if the cancellation occurs far enough in advance (often 6 weeks or more), you may forfeit only a $25 or $50 penalty. If you cancel only 2 or 3 weeks before the flight, there may be no refund at all unless you or the operator can provide a substitute passenger.
2. Charter flights may be canceled by the operator up to 10 days before departure for any reason, usually underbooking. Your money is returned in this event, but there may be too little time for you to make new arrangements.
3. Most charters have little of the flexibility of regularly scheduled flights regarding refunds and the changing of flight dates; if you book a return flight, you must be on it or lose your money.
4. Charter operators are permitted to assess a surcharge, if fuel or other costs warrant it, of up to 10% of the airfare up to 10 days before departure.
5. Because of the economics of charter flights, your plane almost always will be full, so you will be crowded, though not necessarily uncomfortable. (There is, however, a new movement among charter airlines to provide flight accommodations that are more comfort-oriented, so this situation may change in the near future.)

To avoid problems, *always* choose charter flights with care. When you consider a charter, ask your travel agent who runs it and carefully check the company. The Better Business Bureau in the company's home city can report on how many complaints, if any, have been lodged against it in the past. Protect yourself with trip cancellation and interruption insurance, which can help safeguard your investment if you or a traveling companion is unable to make the trip and must cancel too late to receive a full refund from the company providing your travel services. (This is advisable whether you're buying a charter flight alone or a tour package for which the airfare is provided by charter or scheduled flight.)

**Bookings** – If you do fly on a charter, read the contract's fine print carefully and pay particular attention to the following:

**Instructions concerning the payment of the deposit and its balance and to whom the**

**check is to be made payable.** Ordinarily, checks are made out to an escrow account, which means the charter company can't spend your money until your flight has safely returned. This provides some protection for you. To ensure the safe handling of your money, make out your check to the escrow account, the number of which must appear by law on the brochure, though all too often it is on the back in fine print. Write the details of the charter, including the destination and dates, on the face of the check; on the back, print "For Deposit Only." Your travel agent may prefer that you make out your check to the agency, saying that it will then pay the tour operator the fee minus commission. It is perfectly legal to write the check as we suggest, however, and if your agent objects too vociferously (he or she should trust the tour operator to send the proper commission), consider taking your business elsewhere. If you don't make your check out to the escrow account, you lose the protection of that escrow should the trip be canceled. Furthermore, recent bankruptcies in the travel industry have served to point out that even the protection of escrow may not be enough to safeguard a traveler's investment. More and more, insurance is becoming a necessity. The charter company should be bonded (usually by an insurance company), and if you want to file a claim against it, the claim should be sent to the bonding agent. The contract will set a time limit within which a claim must be filed.

**Specific stipulations and penalties for cancellations.** Most charters allow you to cancel up to 45 days in advance without major penalty, but some cancellation dates are 50 to 60 days before departure.

**Stipulations regarding cancellation and major changes made by the charterer.** US rules say that charter flights may not be canceled within 10 days of departure except when circumstances — such as natural disasters or political upheavals — make it physically impossible to fly. Charterers may make "major changes," however, such as in the date or place of departure or return, but you are entitled to cancel and receive a full refund if you don't wish to accept these changes. A price increase of more than 10% at any time up to 10 days before departure is considered a major change; no price increase at all is allowed during the last 10 days immediately before departure.

For the most current information on charter flight options, the travel newsletter *Jax Fax* regularly features a list of charter companies and packagers offering seats on charter flights and may be a source for charter flights to South America. For a year's subscription send a check or money order for $12 to *Jax Fax*, 397 Post Rd., Darien, CT 06820 (phone: 203-655-8746).

■**Note:** Although charter flights to South America currently are few and far between, at the time of this writing, the following two companies were offering charter flights to the continent: *GWV International* (300 First Ave., Needham, MA 02194; phone: 800-225-5498), a wholesaler (so use a travel agent), and *Suntrips* (2350 Paragon Dr., San Jose, CA 95131; phone: 800-SUN-TRIP in California; 408-432-0700 elsewhere in the US), which retails to the general public.

**DISCOUNTS ON SCHEDULED FLIGHTS:** Promotional fares often are called discount fares because they cost less than what used to be the standard airline fare — full-fare economy. Nevertheless, they cost the traveler the same whether they are bought through a travel agent or directly from the airline. Tickets that cost less if bought from some outlet other than the airline do exist, however. While it is likely that the vast majority of travelers flying to South America in the near future will be doing so on a promotional fare or charter rather than on a "discount" air ticket of this sort, it still is a good idea for cost-conscious consumers to be aware of the latest developments in the budget airfare scene. Note that the following discussion makes clear-cut distinctions among the types of discounts available based on how they reach the consumer; in actual practice, the distinctions are not nearly so precise.

## GETTING READY / Traveling by Plane

**Courier Travel** – There was a time when traveling as a courier was a sort of underground way to save money and visit otherwise unaffordable destinations, but more and more, this once exotic idea of traveling as a courier is becoming a very "establishment" exercise. Being a courier means no more than accompanying freight of one sort or another, and typically that freight replaces what otherwise would be the traveler's checked baggage. Be prepared, therefore, to carry all your own personal travel gear in a carry-on bag. In addition, the so-called courier usually pays only a portion of the total airfare — the freight company pays the remainder — and the courier also may be assessed a small registration fee. Note that many courier flights can be booked in advance (sometimes as much as 3 months) and that flights often are round trip.

There are dozens of courier companies operating actively around the globe, and several publications provide information on courier opportunities:

*A Simple Guide to Courier Travel*, by Jesse L. Riddle, is a particularly good reference guide to courier travel. Published by the Carriage Group (PO Box 2394, Lake Oswego, OR 97035; phone: 800-222-3599), it's available for $15.95, including postage and handling.

*Travel Secrets* (PO Box 2325, New York, NY 10108; phone: 212-245-8703). Provides information useful to those considering traveling as a courier and often lists specific US and Canadian courier companies. Monthly; a year's subscription costs $33.

*Travel Unlimited* (PO Box 1058, Allston, MA 02134-1058; no phone). Lists courier companies and agents worldwide. Monthly; for a year's subscription send $25.

*World Courier News* (PO Box 77471, San Francisco, CA 94107; no phone). Provides information on courier opportunities, as well as useful tips. Each issue highlights a different destination. Monthly; for a year's subscription send $20.

At the time of this writing, two companies were offering courier flights to South America: *Courier Travel Service* (530 Central Ave., Cedarhurst, NY 11516; phone: 800-922-2FLY or 516-374-2299) and *Discount Travel International* (152 W. 72nd St., Suite 223, New York, NY 10023; phone: 212-655-5151). In addition, *Now Voyager* (74 Varick St., Suite 307, New York, NY 10013; phone: 212-431-1616), a referral agency that matches up would-be couriers with courier companies, regularly arranges for courier flights between the US and South America.

**Net Fare Sources** – The newest notion for reducing the costs of travel services comes from travel agents who offer individual travelers "net" fares. Defined simply, a net fare is the bare minimum amount at which an airline or tour operator will carry a prospective traveler. It doesn't include the amount that normally would be paid to the travel agent as a commission. Traditionally, such commissions amount to about 10% on domestic fares and from 10% to 20% on international fares — not counting significant additions to these commission levels that are paid retroactively when agents sell more than a specific volume of tickets or trips for a single supplier. At press time, at least one travel agency in the US was offering travelers the opportunity to purchase tickets and/or tours for a net price. Instead of earning its income from individual commissions, this agency assesses a fixed fee that may or may not provide a bargain for travelers; it requires a little arithmetic to determine whether to use the services of a net travel agent or those of one who accepts conventional commissions. One of the potential drawbacks of buying from agencies selling travel services at net fares is that some airlines refuse to do business with them, thus possibly limiting your flight options.

*Travel Avenue* is a fee-based agency that rebates its ordinary agency commission to the customer. For domestic flights, they will find the lowest retail fare, then rebate 7% to 10% (depending on the airline selected) of that price minus a $10 ticket-writing charge. The rebate percentage for international flights varies from 5% to 16% (again depending on the airline), and the ticket-writing charge is $25. The ticket-writing charge is imposed per ticket; if the ticket includes more than eight separate flights, an additional $10 or $25 fee is charged. Customers using free flight coupons pay the ticket-writing charge, plus an additional $5 coupon-processing fee.

*Travel Avenue* will rebate its commissions on all tickets, including heavily discounted fares and senior citizen passes. Available 7 days a week, reservations should be made far enough in advance to allow the tickets to be sent by first class mail, since extra charges accrue for special handling. It's possible to economize further by making your own airline reservation, then asking *Travel Avenue* only to write/issue your ticket. For travelers outside the Chicago area, business may be transacted by phone and purchases charged to a credit card. For information, contact *Travel Avenue* at 641 W. Lake St., Suite 201, Chicago, IL 60606-1012 (phone: 312-876-1116 in Illinois; 800-333-3335 elsewhere in the US).

**Consolidators and Bucket Shops** – Other vendors of travel services can afford to sell tickets to their customers at an even greater discount because the airline has sold the tickets to them at a substantial discount (usually accomplished by sharply increasing commissions to that vendor), a practice in which many airlines indulge, albeit discreetly, preferring that the general public not know they are undercutting their own "list" prices. Airlines anticipating a slow period on a particular route sometimes sell off a certain portion of their capacity at a very great discount to a wholesaler, or consolidator. The wholesaler sometimes is a charter operator who resells the seats to the public as though they were charter seats, which is why prospective travelers perusing the brochures of charter operators with large programs frequently see a number of flights designated as "scheduled service." As often as not, however, the consolidator, in turn, sells the seats to a travel agency specializing in discounting. Airlines also can sell seats directly to such an agency, which thus acts as its own consolidator. The airline offers the seats either at a net wholesale price, but without the volume-purchase requirement that would be difficult for a modest retail travel agency to fulfill, or at the standard price, but with a commission override large enough (as high as 50%) to allow both a profit and a price reduction to the public.

Travel agencies specializing in discounting sometimes are called "bucket shops," a term once fraught with connotations of unreliability in this country. But in today's highly competitive travel marketplace, more and more conventional travel agencies are selling consolidator-supplied tickets, and the old bucket shops' image is becoming respectable. Agencies that specialize in discounted tickets exist in most large cities, and usually can be found by studying the smaller ads in the travel sections of Sunday newspapers.

Before buying a discounted ticket, whether from a bucket shop or a conventional, full-service travel agency, keep the following considerations in mind: To be in a position to judge how much you'll be saving, first find out the "list" prices of tickets to your destination. Then do some comparison shopping among agencies. Also bear in mind that a ticket that may not differ much in price from one available directly from the airline may, however, allow the circumvention of such things as the advance-purchase requirement. If your plans are less than final, be sure to find out about any other restrictions, such as penalties for canceling a flight or changing a reservation. Most discount tickets are non-endorsable, meaning that they can be used only on the airline that issued them, and they usually are marked "nonrefundable" to prevent their being cashed in for a list price refund.

A great many bucket shops are small businesses operating on a thin margin, so it's a good idea to check the local Better Business Bureau for any complaints registered against the one with which you're dealing — before parting with any money. If you still do not feel reassured, consider buying discounted tickets only through a conventional

**32 GETTING READY / Traveling by Plane**

travel agency, which can be expected to have found its own reliable source of consolidator tickets — some of the largest consolidators, in fact, sell only to travel agencies.

A few bucket shops require payment in cash or by certified check or money order, but if credit cards are accepted, use that option. Note, however, if buying from a charter operator selling both scheduled and charter flights, that the scheduled seats are not protected by the regulations — including the use of escrow accounts — governing the charter seats. Well-established charter operators, nevertheless, may extend the same protections to their scheduled flights, and when this is the case, consumers should be sure that the payment option selected directs their money into the escrow account.

Among the consolidators offering discount fares to South America are the following:

*Bargain Air* (655 Deep Valley Dr., Suite 355, Rolling Hills, CA 90274; phone: 800-347-2345 or 213-377-2919).

*Maharaja/Consumer Wholesale Travel* (34 W. 33rd St., Suite 1014, New York, NY 10001; phone: 212-213-2020 in New York State; 800-223-6862 elsewhere in the US).

*TFI Tours International* (34 W. 32nd St., 12th Floor, New York, NY 10001; phone: 212-736-1140 in New York State; 800-825-3834 elsewhere in the US).

*25 West Tours* (2490 Coral Way, Miami, FL 33145; phone: 305-856-0810; 800-423-6954 in Florida; 800-225-2582 elsewhere in the US).

*Unitravel* (1177 N. Warson Rd., St. Louis, MO 63132; phone: 314-569-2501 in Missouri; 800-325-2222 elsewhere in the US).

Check with your travel agent for other sources of consolidator tickets to South America.

■ **Note:** Although rebating and discounting are becoming increasingly common, there is some legal ambiguity concerning them. Strictly speaking, it is legal to discount domestic tickets but not international tickets. On the other hand, the law that prohibits discounting, the Federal Aviation Act of 1958, is consistently ignored these days, in part because consumers benefit from the practice and in part because many illegal arrangements are indistinguishable from legal ones. Since the line separating the two is so fine that even the authorities can't always tell the difference, it is unlikely that most consumers would be able to do so, and in fact it is not illegal to *buy* a discounted ticket. If the issue of legality bothers you, ask the agency whether any ticket you're about to buy would be permissible under the above-mentioned act.

**OTHER DISCOUNT TRAVEL SOURCES:** An excellent source of information on economical travel opportunities is the *Consumer Reports Travel Letter*, published monthly by Consumers Union. It keeps abreast of the scene on a wide variety of fronts, including package tours, rental cars, insurance, and more, but it is especially helpful for its comprehensive coverage of airfares, offering guidance on all the options from scheduled flights on major or low-fare airlines to charters and discount sources. For a year's subscription, send $37 ($57 for 2 years) to *Consumer Reports Travel Letter* (PO Box 53629, Boulder, CO 80322-3629; phone: 800-234-1970). For information on other travel newsletters, see *Books, Newspapers, Magazines, and Newsletters,* in this section.

**Last-Minute Travel Clubs** – Still another way to take advantage of bargain airfares is open to those who have a flexible schedule. A number of organizations, usually set up as last-minute travel clubs and functioning on a membership basis, routinely keep in touch with travel suppliers to help them dispose of unsold inventory at discounts of between 15% and 60%. A great deal of the inventory consists of complete package tours and cruises, but some clubs offer air-only charter seats and, occasionally, seats on scheduled flights.

Members pay an annual fee and receive a toll-free hotline telephone number to call

## GETTING READY / Traveling by Plane

for information on imminent trips. In some cases, they also receive periodic mailings with information on bargain travel opportunities for which there is more advance notice. Despite the suggestive names of the clubs providing these services, last-minute travel does not necessarily mean that you cannot make plans until literally the last minute. Trips can be announced as little as a few days or as much as 2 months before departure, but the average is from 1 to 4 weeks' notice.

Among the organizations regularly offering such discounted travel opportunities to South America are the following:

*Discount Travel International* (Ives Building, 114 Forrest Ave., Suite 205, Narberth, PA 19072; phone: 800-334-9294 or 215-668-7184). Annual fee: $45 per household.

*Encore/Short Notice* (4501 Forbes Blvd., Lanham, MD 20706; phone: 301-459-8020; 800-638-0930 for customer service). Annual fee: $36 per family for their Short Notice program only; $48 per family to join the Encore program, which provides additional travel services.

*Last Minute Travel* (1249 Boylston St., Boston MA 02215; phone: 800-LAST-MIN or 617-267-9800). No fee.

*Moment's Notice* (425 Madison Ave., New York, NY 10017; phone: 212-486-0500). Annual fee: $45 per family.

*Spur-of-the-Moment Tours and Cruises* (10780 Jefferson Blvd., Culver City, CA 90230; phone: 310-839-2418 in southern California; 800-343-1991 elsewhere in the US). No fee.

*Traveler's Advantage* (3033 S. Parker Rd., Suite 1000, Aurora, CO 80014; phone: 800-548-1116). Annual fee: $49 per family.

*Vacations to Go* (2411 Fountain View, Suite 201, Houston, TX 77057; phone: 800-338-4962). Annual fee: $19.95 per family.

*Worldwide Discount Travel Club* (1674 Meridian Ave., Miami Beach, FL 33139; phone: 305-534-2082). Annual fee: $40 per person; $50 per family.

■ **Note:** A fairly recent development in the world of discount travel is the establishment of a "900" number telephone information service called *Last Minute Travel Connection* (phone: 900-446-8292). For $1 per minute, travelers with touch-tone phones can access recorded advertisements (including numbers to call) of "last-minute" discounted offers on package tours, cruises, airfares, and other travel services. The service is available 24 hours a day, and advertisements are updated as often as once each hour. For more information on this service, contact *La Onda, Ltd.,* 601 Skokie Blvd., Suite 224, Northbrook, IL 60062 (phone: 708-498-9216).

**Generic Air Travel** – Organizations that apply the same flexible-schedule idea to air travel only and arrange for flights at literally the last minute also exist. The service they provide sometimes is known as "generic" air travel, and it operates somewhat like an ordinary airline standby service except that the organizations running it do not guarantee flights to a specific destination, but only to a general region, and offer seats on not one but several scheduled and charter airlines.

One pioneer of generic flights is *Airhitch* (2790 Broadway, Suite 100, New York, NY 10025; phone: 212-864-2000). Prospective travelers stipulate a range of at least five consecutive departure dates and their desired destination, along with alternate choices, and pay the fare in advance. They are then sent a voucher good for travel *on a space-available basis* on flights to their destination *region* (i.e., not necessarily the specific destination requested) during this time period. The week before this range of departure dates begins, travelers must contact *Airhitch* for specific information about flights that will probably be available and instructions on how to proceed for check-in.

(Return flights are arranged in the same manner as the outbound flights — a specified period of travel is decided upon, and a few days before this date range begins, prospective passengers contact *Airhitch* for details about flights that may be available.) If the client does not accept any of the suggested flights or cancels his or her travel plans after selecting a flight, the amount paid may be applied toward a future fare or the flight arrangements can be transferred to another individual (although, in both cases, an additional fee may be charged). No refunds are offered unless the prospective passenger does not ultimately get on any flight in the specified date range; in such a case, the full fare is refunded. (Note that *Airhitch*'s slightly more expensive "Target" program, which provides confirmed reservations on specific dates to specific destinations, offers passengers greater — but not guaranteed — certainty regarding flight arrangements. At the time of this writing, *Airhitch* did not offer flights to South America, but do check at the time you plan to travel.

**Bartered Travel Sources** – Suppose a hotel buys advertising space in a newspaper. As payment, the hotel gives the publishing company the use of a number of hotel rooms in lieu of cash. This is barter, a common means of exchange among hotels, airlines, car rental companies, cruise lines, tour operators, restaurants, and other travel service companies. When a bartering company finds itself with empty airline seats (or excess hotel rooms, or cruise ship cabin space, and so on) and offers them to the public, considerable savings can be enjoyed.

Bartered travel clubs often offer discounts of up to 50% to members who pay an annual fee (approximately $50 at press time) which entitles them to select the flights, cruises, hotel rooms, or other travel services that the club obtained by barter. Members usually present a voucher, club credit card, or scrip (a dollar-denomination voucher negotiable only for the bartered product) to the hotel, which in turn subtracts the dollar amount from the bartering company's account.

Selling bartered travel is a perfectly legitimate means of retailing. One advantage to club members is that they don't have to wait until the last minute to obtain flight or room reservations.

Among the companies specializing in bartered travel, at press time, only *Travel Guild* (18210 Redmond Way, Redmond, WA 98052; phone: 206-861-1900; annual fee: $48 per family) frequently offered members travel services to and within South America. *Travel World Leisure Club* (225 W. 34th St., Suite 2203, New York, NY 10122; phone: 800-444-TWLC or 212-239-4855; annual fee: $50 per family) has in the past offered such services to South America, so call them when planning your trip for information on current offerings.

**CONSUMER PROTECTION:** Consumers who feel that they have not been dealt with fairly by an airline should make their complaints known. Begin with the customer service representative at the airport where the problem occurs. If he or she cannot resolve your complaint to your satisfaction, write to the airline's consumer office. In a businesslike, typed letter, explain what reservations you held, what happened, the names of the employees involved, and what you expect the airline to do to remedy the situation. Send copies (never the originals) of the tickets, receipts, and other documents that back your claims. Ideally, all correspondence should be sent via certified mail, return receipt requested. This provides proof that your complaint was received.

Passengers with consumer complaints — lost baggage, compensation for getting bumped, violations of smoking and nonsmoking rules, deceptive practices by an airline, charter regulations — who are not satisfied with the airline's response should contact the US Department of Transportation (DOT), Consumer Affairs Division (400 Seventh St. SW, Room 10405, Washington, DC 20590; phone: 202-366-2220). DOT personnel stress, however, that consumers initially should direct their complaints to the airline that provoked them.

Travelers with an unresolved complaint involving a foreign carrier also can contact the US Department of Transportation. DOT personnel will do what they can to help resolve all such complaints, although their influence may be limited. Consumers with complaints against specific foreign airlines or other travel-related services should try to contact the tourist authority for the South American country where the problem occurred (see FACTS IN BRIEF for addresses). The agency usually will try to resolve the complaint or, if it is out of their jurisdiction, will refer the matter to the proper authorities.

Remember, too, that the federal Fair Credit Billing Act permits purchasers to refuse to pay for credit card charges for services which have not been delivered, so the onus of dealing with the receiver for a bankrupt airline falls on the credit card company. Do not rely on another airline to honor the ticket you're holding, since the days when virtually all major carriers subscribed to a default protection program that bound them to do so are long gone. Some airlines may voluntarily step forward to accommodate the stranded passengers of a fellow carrier, but this is now an entirely altruistic act.

The deregulation of US airlines has meant that the traveler must find out for himself or herself what he or she is entitled to receive. The US Department of Transportation's informative consumer booklet *Fly Rights* is a good place to start. To receive a copy, send $1 to the Superintendent of Documents (US Government Printing Office, Washington, DC 20402-9325; phone: 202-783-3238). Specify its stock number, 050-000-00513-5, and allow 3 to 4 weeks for delivery.

■ **Note:** Those who tend to experience discomfort due to the change in air pressure while flying may be interested in the free pamphlet *Ears, Altitude, and Airplane Travel;* for a copy send a self-addressed, stamped, business-size envelope to the *American Academy of Otolaryngology* (One Prince St., Alexandria, VA 22314; phone: 703-836-4444). And for when you land, *Overcoming Jet Lag* offers some helpful tips on minimizing post-flight stress; it is available from Berkeley Publishing Group (PO Box 506, Mail Order Dept., East Rutherford, NJ 07073; phone: 800-631-8571) for $6.95, plus shipping and handling.

# Traveling by Ship

There was a time when traveling by ship was extraordinarily expensive, time-consuming, utterly elegant, and was utilized almost exclusively for getting from one point to another. No longer primarily pure transportation, cruising currently is riding a wave of popularity as a leisure activity in its own right, and the host of new ships (and dozens of rebuilt old ones) testifies dramatically to the attraction of vacationing on the high seas. Cruise lines are flocking to South American ports, as repeat passengers seek new, more unusual itineraries, and first-time visitors choose seaborne transportation to experience a taste of this exotic continent.

Among the destinations favored by cruise ship passengers, South America ranks extremely high. Cruise travel today also is the most leisurely way to get to South America. Some of these cruises still sail from New York, but many more sail from such places as Ft. Lauderdale, Miami, Los Angeles, San Francisco, and San Juan, Puerto Rico. From eastern US ports, cruises to South America most often head for Buenos Aires or Rio de Janeiro (also common departure points) and call at a number of popular resort destinations or sail along the coast. Sailings from US West Coast docks often cruise the Pacific coast of the continent, and those that cross through the Panama Canal often include ports of call along South America's Caribbean and Atlantic coasts.

Many modern-day cruise ships seem much more like motels-at-sea than the classic liners of a couple of generations ago, but they are consistently comfortable and passengers often are pampered. Cruise prices can be quite reasonable, and since the single cruise price covers all the major items in a typical vacation — transportation, accommodations, all meals, entertainment, and a full range of social activities, sports, and recreation — a traveler need not fear any unexpected assaults on the family travel budget.

When selecting a cruise, your basic criteria should be where you want to go, the time you have available, how much you want to spend, and the kind of environment that best suits your style and taste (in which case price is an important determinant). Rely on the suggestions of a travel agent — preferably one specializing in cruises (see "A final note on picking a cruise," below) — but be honest with the agent (and with yourself) in describing the type of atmosphere you're seeking. Ask for suggestions from friends who have been on cruises; if you trust their judgment, they should be able to suggest a ship on which you'll feel comfortable.

There are a number of moments in the cruise-planning process when discounts are available from the major cruise lines, so it may be possible to enjoy some diminution of the list price almost anytime you book passage on a cruise ship. For those willing to commit early — say 4 to 6 months before sailing — most of the major cruise lines routinely offer a 10% reduction off posted prices, in addition to the widest selection of cabins. For those who decide to sail rather late in the game — say 4 to 6 weeks before departure — savings often are even greater — an average of 20% — as steamship lines try to fill up their ships. The only negative aspect is that the choice of cabins tends to be limited, although it is possible that a fare upgrade will be offered to make this limited selection more palatable. In addition, there's the option of buying from a discount travel club or a travel agency that specializes in last-minute bargains; these discounters and other discount travel sources are discussed at the end of *Traveling by Plane,* above.

Most of the time, the inclusion of air transportation in the cruise package costs significantly less than if you were to buy the cruise separately and arrange your own air transportation to the port. If you do decide on one of these economical air/sea packages, be forewarned that it is not unusual for the prearranged flight arrangements to be less than convenient. The problems often arrive with the receipt of your cruise ticket, which also includes the airline ticket for the flight to get you to and from the ship dock. This is normally the first time you see the flights on which you have been booked and can appraise the convenience of the departure and arrival times. The cruise ship lines generally are not very forthcoming about altering flight schedules, and your own travel agent also may have difficulty in rearranging flight times or carriers. That means that the only remaining alternative is to ask the line to forget about making your flight arrangements and to pay for them separately by yourself. This may be more costly, but it's more likely to give you an arrival and departure schedule that will best conform to the sailing and docking times of the ship on which you will be cruising.

Generally, people take a cruise ship to South America for the sheer pleasure of being at sea, because it's part of a far broader itinerary, or because of a special interest in a particular area that is best visited by ship. Cruise lines promote sailings to South America as "get away from it all" vacations. But prospective cruise ship passengers will find that the variety of cruises is tremendous, and the quality, while generally high, varies depending on shipboard services, the tone of shipboard life, the cost of the cruise, and operative itineraries.

Although there are less expensive ways to see South America, the romance and enjoyment of a sea voyage remain irresistible for many, so a few points should be considered by such sojourners before they sign on for a seagoing vacation (after all, it's hard to get off in mid-ocean). Herewith, a rundown on what to expect from a cruise, a few suggestions on what to look for and arrange when purchasing passage on one, and some representative sailings to and around South America.

**CABINS:** The most important factor in determining the price of a cruise is the cabin.

## GETTING READY / Traveling by Ship

Cabin prices are set according to size and location. The size can vary considerably on older ships, less so on newer or more recently modernized ones, and may be entirely uniform on the very newest vessels.

Shipboard accommodations utilize the same pricing pattern as hotels. Suites, which consist of a sitting room–bedroom combination and occasionally a small private deck that could be compared to a patio, cost the most. Prices for other cabins (interchangeably called staterooms) usually are more expensive on the upper passenger decks, less expensive on lower decks; if the cabin has a bathtub instead of a shower, the price probably will be higher. The outside cabins with portholes cost more than inside cabins without views and generally are preferred — although many experienced cruise passengers eschew the more expensive accommodations for they know they will spend very few waking hours in their cabins. As in all forms of travel, accommodations are more expensive for single travelers. If you are traveling on your own but want to share a double cabin to reduce the cost, some ship lines will attempt to find someone of the same sex willing to share quarters (also see *Hints for Single Travelers,* in this section).

**FACILITIES AND ACTIVITIES:** You may not use your cabin very much — organized shipboard activities are geared to keep you busy. A standard schedule might consist of swimming, sunbathing, and numerous other outdoor recreations. Evenings are devoted to leisurely dining, lounge shows or movies, bingo and other organized games, gambling, dancing, and a midnight buffet. Your cruise fare normally includes all of these activities — except the cost of drinks.

Most cruise ships have at least one major social lounge, a main dining room, several bars, an entertainment room that may double as a discotheque for late dancing, an exercise room, indoor games facilities, at least one pool, and shopping facilities, which can range from a single boutique to an arcade. Still others have gambling casinos and/or slot machines, card rooms, libraries, children's recreation centers, indoor pools (as well as one or more on open decks), separate movie theaters, and private meeting rooms. Open deck space should be ample, because this is where most passengers spend their days at sea.

Usually there is a social director and staff to organize and coordinate activities. Evening entertainment is provided by professionals. Movies are mostly first-run and drinks are moderate in price (or should be) because a ship is exempt from local taxes when at sea.

■**Note:** To be prepared for possible illnesses at sea, travelers should get a prescription from their doctor for medicine to counteract motion sickness. All ships with more than 12 passengers have a doctor on board, plus facilities for handling sickness or medical emergencies.

**Shore Excursions** – These side trips almost always are optional and available at extra cost. Before you leave, do a little basic research about the South American ports you'll be visiting and decide what sights will interest you. If several of the most compelling of these are some distance from the pier where your ship docks, the chances are that paying for a shore excursion will be worth the money.

Shore excursions usually can be booked through your travel agent at the same time you make your cruise booking, but this is worthwhile only if you can get complete details on the nature of each excursion being offered. If you can't get these details, better opt to purchase your shore arrangements after you're on board. Your enthusiasm for an excursion may be higher once you are on board because you will have met other passengers with whom to share the excitement of "shore leave." And depending on your time in port, you may decide to eschew the guided tour and venture out on your own.

**Meals** – All meals on board almost always are included in the basic price of a cruise, and the food generally is abundant and quite palatable. Evening meals are taken in the

**38 GETTING READY / Traveling by Ship**

main dining room, where tables are assigned according to the passengers' preferences. Tables usually accommodate from 2 to 10; specify your preference when you book your cruise. If there are two sittings, you also can specify which one you want at the time you book or, at the latest, when you first board the ship. Later sittings usually are more leisurely. Breakfast frequently is available in your cabin, as well as in the main dining room. For lunch, many passengers prefer the buffet offered on deck, usually at or near the pool, but again, the main dining room is available.

**DRESS:** Most people pack too much for a cruise on the assumption that their daily attire should be chic and every night is a big event. Comfort is a more realistic criterion. Daytime wear on most ships is decidedly casual. Evening wear for most cruises is dressy-casual. Formal attire probably is not necessary for 1-week cruises, optional for longer ones. (For information on choosing and packing a basic wardrobe, see *How to Pack,* in this section.)

**TIPS:** Tips are a strictly personal expense, and you *are* expected to tip — in particular, your cabin and dining room stewards. The general rule of thumb (or palm) is to expect to pay from 10% to 20% of your total cruise budget for gratuities — the actual amount within this range is based on the length of the cruise and the extent of personalized services provided. Allow $2 to $5 a day for each cabin and dining room steward (more if you wish) and additional sums for very good service. (*Note:* Tips should be paid by and for each individual in a cabin, whether there are one, two, or more.) Others who may merit tips are the deck steward who sets up your chair at the pool or elsewhere, the wine steward in the dining room, porters who handle your luggage (tip them individually at the time they assist you), and any others who provide personal service. On some ships you can charge your bar tab to your cabin; throw in the tip when you pay it at the end of the cruise. Smart travelers tip twice during the trip: about midway through the cruise and at the end; even wiser travelers tip a bit at the start of the trip to ensure better service throughout.

Although some cruise lines do have a no-tipping policy and you are not penalized by the crew for not tipping, naturally, you aren't penalized for tipping, either. If you can restrain yourself, it is better not to tip on those few ships that discourage it. However, never make the mistake of not tipping on the majority of ships, where it is a common, expected practice. (For further information on calculating gratuities, see *Tipping,* in this section.)

**SHIP SANITATION:** The US Public Health Service (PHS) currently inspects all passenger vessels calling at US ports, so very precise information is available on which ships meet its requirements and which do not. The further requirement that ships immediately report any illness that occurs on board adds to the available data.

The problem for a prospective cruise passenger is to determine whether the ship on which he or she plans to sail has met the official sanitary standard. US regulations require the PHS to publish actual grades for the ships inspected (rather than the old pass or fail designation), so it's now easy to determine any cruise ship's status. Nearly 4,000 travel agents, public health organizations, and doctors receive a copy of each monthly ship sanitation summary, but be aware that not all travel agents fully understand what this ship inspection program is all about. The best advice is to deal with a travel agent who specializes in cruise bookings, for he or she is most likely to have the latest information on the sanitary conditions of all cruise ships (see "A final note on picking a cruise," below). To receive a copy of the most recent summary or a particular inspection report, write to Chief, Vessel Sanitation Program, Center for Environmental Health and Injury Control (1015 N. America Way, Room 107, Miami, FL 33132; phone: 305-536-4307). Note that the center requests that all inquiries be made in writing.

**CRUISES TO AND AROUND SOUTH AMERICA:** South American ports of call often are are visited by ships cruising through the Panama Canal. Cruises that include

## GETTING READY / Traveling by Ship

Caribbean destinations commonly visit ports in Venezuela and along the Orinoco River, or travel along coastal Brazil and up the Amazon. Other itineraries include cruises up and down South America's east and west coasts, up and down the Amazon and Orinoco, and special sailings to Antarctica. Note that because of the narcotics trade and associated crime and violence some South American ports of call along the Caribbean Coast have been eliminated from cruise itineraries in recent years due to concerns about the safety of passengers in these ports. Cartagena in Colombia, however, is once again a popular port of call on numerous South American cruises, particularly those visiting the Caribbean Coast.

Below is a list of cruise lines and ships that offer several nights' to several months' sailings to and around South America from US, Caribbean, or South American ports. Some lines position a ship in South American waters — particularly between Rio de Janeiro and Buenos Aires — for several months each year, and these ships alternatively cruise European or Pacific waters.

*Chandris Celebrity Cruises* (5200 Blue Lagoon Dr., Miami, FL 33126; phone: 800-437-3111). The *Meridian* sails from San Juan (Puerto Rico) calling at several Caribbean islands in addition to Caracas (Venezuela).

*Commodore Cruise Line* (800 Douglas Rd., Suite 600, Coral Gables, FL 33134; phone: 800-237-5361). The *Enchanted Isle* makes a 21-day transcanal cruise from San Diego to Caracas (Venezuela), visiting several Mexican ports and Caribbean islands en route. The *Enchanted Seas* makes a 15-day trip between New York and New Orleans that also includes a stop in Caracas.

*Cunard* (555 Fifth Ave., New York, NY 10017; phone: 800-221-4770). The *Sea Goddess* makes a 14-day transcanal sailing from St. Thomas to Acapulco, visiting several Caribbean islands on its way to Cartagena (Colombia). The *QE2* and the *Sagafjord* both stop in Cartagena as part of their New Year's sailings from New York and Ft. Lauderdale, respectively. The *QE2* also includes several stops at South American ports as part of a world tour.

*Epirotiki Lines* (551 Fifth Ave., New York, NY 10176; phone: 800-221-2470 or 212-599-1750). The *World Renaissance* makes a 12-day sailing from Martinique, stopping at several Caribbean islands en route to South America, where it sails up the Amazon River to Manaus (Brazil), visiting Belém, Santarem, and Boca do Valerio as well (all in Brazil).

*Holland America Line* (300 Elliot Ave. W, Seattle, WA 98119; phone: 800-426-0327). The *Rotterdam* makes a 49-day worldwide Grand Circle South America sailing between Norfolk (Virgina) and Los Angeles. Ports of call in South America include Recife, Rio de Janeiro, and Paranagua (Brazil), Devil's Island (French Guiana), Montevideo (Uruguay), Caracas (Venezuela), the Falkland Islands, and Patagonia, as well as several more stops along the western coast.

*Ocean Cruise Lines* (1510 SE 17th St., Ft. Lauderdale, FL 33316; phone: 800-556-8850). The *Ocean Princess* offers a variety of cruises throughout South America ranging in length from 13 to 20 days. Destinations include Argentina, Brazil, Chile, Ecuador, Peru, and Uruguay, as well as Antarctica. Highlights include exploring the Amazon, Patagonia, and the Falkland Islands. City packages that can be added on to the beginning or end of the cruise also are available.

*Princess Cruises* (10100 Santa Monica Blvd., Los Angeles, CA 90067; phone: 800-421-0522). The *Pacific Princess* sails from Manaus (Brazil) and San Juan (Puerto Rico). Yup, this is one of the "Love Boats." Cruises aboard this ship range from 11 to 14 days and ports of call include Recife, Rio de Janeiro, and São Paolo (Brazil), and Montevideo (Uruguay). A 10-day trip aboard the *Regal Princess* includes a stop at Cartagena (Colombia) in addition to other Caribbean ports.

*Regency Cruises* (260 Madison Ave., New York, NY 10016; phone: 800-388-5500 or 212-972-4499). The *Regent Sea* sails from Los Angeles. Cruises last 50 days and ports of call include Buenos Aires (Argentina); Fortaleza, Salvador de Bahia, and Rio de Janeiro (Brazil); Puerto Montt, Tierra del Fuego and Valparaíso (Chile); Devil's Island (off French Guiana); Lima (Peru); and Montevideo (Uruguay); as well as Patagonia (Argentina and Chile). The *Regent Star* also offers a Caribbean sailing that includes a stop at Cartegena (Colombia).

*Renaissance Cruises* (1800 Eller Dr., Suite 300, Ft. Lauderdale, FL 33335-0307; phone: 800-525-2450). The *Renaissance VI*, a particularly luxurious ship, offers 7-day cruises between Rio de Janeiro (Brazil) and Buenos Aires (Argentina), and 10-day sailings from Buenos Aires to Puerto Montt (Chile).

*Royal Cruise Line* (1 Maritime Plaza, Suite 1400, San Francisco, CA 94111 (phone: 800-227-5628, 800-227-0925, or 415-956-7200). The *Crown Odyssey* sails between the island of Barbados and Buenos Aires (Argentina). Cruises last 14 days and ports of call include Belém, Salvador de Bahia, São Paulo and Rio de Janeiro (Brazil), and Montevideo (Uruguay). A post-cruise city package in Buenos Aires also is available.

*Royal Viking Lines:* (95 Merrick Way, Coral Gables, FL 33134; phone: 800-422-8000). The *Royal Viking Sun* offers a 50-day Circle South America cruise from Ft. Lauderdale, which can be broken into 3 segments, each ranging from 15 to 19 days in length. Ports of call include major coastal cities such as Recife and Rio de Janeiro (Brazil), Puerto Montt (Chile), Guayaquil (Ecuador), Lima (Peru), and Montevideo (Uruguay).

*Seabourn Cruise Line* (55 Francisco St., San Francisco, CA 94133 (phone: 800-351-9595). The luxurious *Seabourn Spirit* offers a variety of cruises to South America, ranging from 12 to 28 days and exploring the Amazon, as well as the eastern coastline of the continent. One such cruise is a 14-day trip between Ft. Lauderdale and Manaus (Brazil); ports of call include Rio de Janeiro (Brazil) and Devil's Island (off French Guiana).

*Society Expeditions* (c/o *Abercrombie & Kent International*, 1520 Kensington Rd., Oak Brook, IL 60521; phone: 800-426-7794). This company offers luxury adventure cruises throughout South America and Antarctica, including 9- or 16-day trips between Miami and Manaus (Brazil) which explore the Amazon.

*Special Expeditions* (720 Fifth Ave., Suite 605, New York, NY 10019; phone: 212-765-7740). The MS *Polaris* makes 16-day cruises on the Amazon, starting either from the Caribbean island of Trinidad or from Manaus (far up the Amazon in Brazil).

*Sun Line Cruises* (1 Rockefeller Center, Suite 315, New York, NY 10020; phone: 800-872-6400 or 212-397-6400). The *Stella Solaris* sails from Ft. Lauderdale. Cruises range from 11 to 21 days and ports of call include Buenos Aires (Argentina), Santos (Brazil), and Montevideo (Uruguay). An Amazon River cruise also is offered.

In addition to the standard vacation-on-the-high-seas cruises, specialty packages aboard ships sailing to South America are increasingly popular. For instance, several cruise lines offer special programs or facilities for handicapped, single, or older travelers. See the targeted sections of GETTING READY TO GO for organizations that book special sailings.

Cruise lines also are becoming more sensitive to the special dietary needs and preferences of their passengers. For instance, *Cunard* and other lines feature special low-sugar meals and drinks for people with diabetes. Many cruise lines also will provide — if given sufficient advance notice — pre-packaged frozen kosher meals year-round for passengers requiring such food preparation. (For information, contact the cruise lines listed above.)

**SPECIALTY AND REGIONAL CRUISES:** A number of cruises offered in South

America — aboard some of the large ships mentioned above, as well as smaller vessels — focus on special interests or cover a particular region of coastal or inland waterways. Specialty cruises offer passengers itineraries centered around music, culture, ethnology, and nature study (becoming better known as ecotourism). Other cruises focus on discovering the natural splendors of individual regions or visit popular ports or small towns and villages off the beaten track. And most lines make a point to be in port in Rio de Janeiro during *Carnaval,* offering passengers tickets to major parades and events, while using the ship as a floating hotel.

There also are a large number of motor and sailing yachts which operate chartered and individually booked 3- to 7-night cruises. The yachts carry from 4 to 24 passengers, with accommodations ranging from "tourist basic" to the luxury of private cabins with private baths. (See *Ecuador,* DIRECTIONS, for details.)

Some *Ocean Cruise Line* and *Special Expeditions* itineraries include Ushuaia (Tierra del Fuego, Argentina), the southernmost town in South America. Popular ports on the west coast include Punta Arenas and Valparaíso (Chile), Callao (Peru) — for Lima, Cuzco, and Machu Picchu — and Guayaquil (Ecuador). For the ultimate adventure, *Royal Viking Line* offers at least one circumnavigational cruise around the continent each winter season. *Cunard* also regularly offers around-the-world cruises, including ports of call in South America. For further information on these cruise lines and current offerings, refer to the list above.

Some of the most facinating waterbound trips originate in South America and offer such exotic destinations as the Galápagos Islands off Ecuador, the river system of the Amazon basin, and the glacial fjords of Chile and Antarctica. Two 90-passenger vessels operate 3-, 4-, and 7-night cruises in the Galápagos Islands. Both the *Galapagos Explorer* and the smaller *Santa Cruz* are well-managed ships. Only the former provides an on-board pool, but both ships are air conditioned and carry licensed naturalist guides who lead shore expeditions and lecture on wildlife and conservation. For information on the *Galapagos Explorer,* contact *Galapagos* (7800 Red Rd., Suite 112, Miami, FL 33143; phone: 305-665-0841 in Florida; 800-327-9854 elsewhere in the US). For information on the *Santa Cruz,* contact *Metropolitan Touring* (239 Av. Amazonas, Quito, Ecuador; phone: 2-560550), or its US representative, *Adventure Associates* (13150 Coit Rd., Suite 110, Dallas, TX 75240; phone: 214-907-0414 in Texas; 800-527-2500 elsewhere in the US). Also note that, at press time, a new company called *Galapagos Network* (7200 Corporate Center Dr., Suite 404, Miami, FL 33126; phone: 800-633-7972 or 305-592-2294) had recently begun offering 3-, 4-, and 7-night cruises through the Galápagos Islands aboard their three luxury, 20-passenger ships — the *Eric, Flamingo,* and *Letty.* For information on similar vessels plying these waters, contact the *Galapagos Center* (4203 Ponce de Leon Blvd., Coral Gables, FL 33146; phone: 305-448-8844 in Florida; 800-331-9984 elsewhere in the US).

*Mountain Travel/Sobek* (6420 Fairmont Ave., El Cerrito, CA 94530 (phone: 800-227-2384 throughout the US) sends passengers to Antarctica from Ushuaia (Argentina) with naturalist guides on board, and with zodiac landing craft to take passengers to some of the more remote, inaccessible areas. *Ocean Cruise Line*'s (see listing above) 15-day Antarctic itinerary includes a call at Ushuaia, as well as an exciting 36-hour crossing from Argentina to Chile. This is one of the most dramatic passages in the world, and requires exceptional navigational expertise.

A Chilean company now operates two ships — the M/V *Skorpios I* (carrying 77 passengers) and the M/V *Skorpios II* (a 160-passenger ship) — from Puerto Montt on week-long cruises through the magnificent southern fjords region. With 20 years of experience in these waters, the crew is able, and the officers speak English. The ships attract a well-educated, international clientele, and cruise prices include international and regional menus, Chilean wines and liquors, and drinks of all kinds. In the ship's motorboats, passengers are taken for excursions close into calving glaciers and to small, isolated fishing villages along the way. For information, contact *Tourism Skorpios, Ltd.*

**42 GETTING READY / Traveling by Ship**

(484 MacIver, Office 5, 2nd Floor, Santiago, Chile; phone 33-8715), or contact their US representative, *Ladatco Tours* (2220 Coral Way, Miami, FL 33145; phone: 305-854-8422 in Miami; 800-431-3881 elsewhere in Florida; 800-327-6162 elsewhere in the US).

**Cruising South America's Inland Waterways** – Travel on the Amazon River and its tributaries — particularly from Brazil — is coming into its own. Aside from the numerous luxury cruise ship itineraries on the Brazilian Amazon (some of which are listed above), for the more adventurous there are a number of other passenger boats operating on the Amazon and its major tributaries. (For a thorough discussion of the travel opportunites in the Amazon, see *Amazonia: Jungle Adventure and Exploration*, in DIVERSIONS.)

*Note:* Boat companies, as opposed to cruise ship companies, normally request passengers to pack a separate duffel-type bag for their stay aboard. Storage space is limited, and it is wiser to leave your large suitcase at your hotel in port. Cabins on these boats generally are small, but adequate.

The majority of the Brazilian boats operate out of Manaus, about 1,300 miles upriver from the Atlantic. The *Tuna* is a typical, 2-deck wooden riverboat, refurbished to provide comfortable travel while exploring the nearby rivers, all pretty much off the beaten tourist track. Trips (either for 3 or 6 nights) are intended to provide an in-depth look at ecology, botany, ethnology, and even tropical medicine. The double-hull, 105-passenger catamarans, the *Para* and *Amazonas* (of the Brazilian *ENASA* line), were built in the early 1980s, specifically for Amazon cruising. The ships cruise between Manaus and Belém in 5- and 7-night programs, the longer of which includes a day on Marajo Island, near Belém. Reservations and information on these boats can be obtained either from *Tara Tours* (6595 NW 36th St., Suite 306-A, Miami, FL 33166; phone: 305-871-1246 in Miami; 800-228-5168 elsewhere in Florida; 800-327-0080 elsewhere in the US) or from *Ladatco Tours* (2220 Coral Way, Miami, FL 33145; phone: 800-327-6162 or 305-854-8422).

For those who can rough it a bit more, wooden-hulled cargo boats ply the waters of a number of major rivers in the Amazon basin. Passage is very inexpensive, and they hardly live by a timetable; you also will have to bring your own supplies, hammock, and lots of books. *Brazilian Adventures*, also known as "Brazil Nuts" (1150 Post Rd., Fairfield, CT 06430; phone: 203-259-7900 in Connecticut; 800-553-9959 elsewhere in the US), books its clients on several boats for 3-night programs out of Manaus. They are typical wooden riverboats, some with hammocks and some with cabins, but all with shared facilities.

On the Peruvian Amazon, boat trips typically operate out of Iquitos. There are 3- and 6-night cruises on the M/V *Rio Amazonas* between Iquitos and Leticia (Colombia) and Tabatinga (Brazil) — virtually next to one another on the river. Most major tour operators can book this boat, or contact *Amazon Camp*'s US representative, *South America Reps* (PO Box 39583, Los Angeles, CA 90039; phone: 818-246-4816 in California; 800-423-2791 elsewhere in the US). Another good choice is the M/V *Delfin*, a classic 2-deck Amazon riverboat accommodating 20 passengers on a 3- or 6-night circuit from Iquitos with lots of jungle walks and excursions by small boat. *Tara Tours* (address above) books passage on this ship, as well as the M/V *Rio Amazonas.*

For the ultimate experience, and if you have a month to spare, *Amazon Explorers* (PO Box 815, 499 Ernston Rd., Parlin, NJ 08859; phone: 908-721-2929 in New Jersey; 800-631-5650 elsewhere in the US) takes travelers on an organized, accompanied journey all the way from Pucallpa (Peru) to Belém (Brazil). The program covers extensive areas of virgin jungle and utilizes four different boats of varying levels of luxury.

One of the best "floating" bets on the rivers, perfect for those unsure of just how much roughing it they can take, is the *Flotel Orellana*, a comfortable boat-hotel, offering first class food and facilities, which makes 4- and 5-day cruises on the Aguarico

## GETTING READY / Traveling by Ship 43

River, an Amazon tributary in Ecuador. Accompanied by trained naturalist guides, passengers are taken for jungle walks, visits to native villages, and small-craft rides to interior lakes. More rugged excursions to Pañacocha are available by motor launch. Owned and operated by *Metropolitan Touring,* fly/cruise packages are offered in conjunction with *Ecuatoriana* and *SAETA* airlines. For information on these packages, contact the *Metropolitan Touring* South American office or its US representative *Adventure Associates* (for addresses, see above).

**FREIGHTERS:** An alternative to conventional cruise ships is travel by freighter. These are cargo ships that also take a limited number of passengers (usually about 12) in reasonably comfortable accommodations. The idea of traveling by freighter has long appealed to romantic souls, but there are a number of drawbacks to consider before casting off. Once upon a time, a major advantage of freighter travel was its low cost, but this is no longer the case. Though freighters usually are less expensive than cruise ships, the difference is not as great as it once was. Accommodations and recreational facilities vary, but freighters were not designed to amuse passengers, so it is important to appreciate the idea of freighter travel itself. Schedules are erratic, and travelers must fit their timetable to that of the ship. Passengers have found themselves waiting as long as a month for a promised sailing, and because freighters follow their cargo commitments, it is possible that a scheduled port could be omitted at the last minute or a new one added.

Anyone contemplating taking a freighter from a US port to South America should be aware that at press time, only two freighter lines carried passengers on regular sailings to South American ports. The *Lykes Bros. Steamship Company* (Lykes Center, 300 Poydras St., New Orleans, LA 70130; phone: 800-535-1861 or 504-523-6611) has ships that carry from 4 to 12 passengers and sail from the US through the Panama Canal to Callao (the port for Lima), Matarani, and Salaverry, all in Peru.

*Ivaran Lines* (111 Pavonia Ave., Jersey City, NJ 07310; phone: 800-451-1639 or 201-798-5656) has three freighters, the M/V *Americana* (which can carry 88 passengers), the M/V *Salvador,* and the M/V *Santa Fe,* each of which carries 12 passengers in exceptional comfort. Provides all of the usual cruise ship amenities and a full range of shore excursions available in 18 ports of call. The full cruise aboard all three ships is 45 days of sailing, round trip, from New York to Argentina, although passengers can book shorter segments, including a round trip to Rio de Janeiro (Brazil).

The following specialists deal only (or largely) in freighter travel. They provide information, schedules, and, when you're ready to sail, booking services.

*Freighter World Cruises, Inc.* (180 S. Lake Ave., Suite 335, Pasadena, CA 91101; phone: 818-449-3106). A freighter travel agency that acts as general agent for several freighter lines. Publishes the twice-monthly *Freighter Space Advisory,* listing space available on sailings worldwide. A subscription costs $27 a year, $25 of which can be credited toward the cost of a cruise.

*Pearl's Travel Tips* (9903 Oaks La., Seminole, FL 34642; phone: 813-393-2919). Run by Ilse Hoffman, who finds sailings for her customers and sends them off with all kinds of valuable information and advice.

*TravLtips Cruise and Freighter Travel Association* (PO Box 218, Flushing, NY 11358; phone: 800-872-8584 or 718-939-2400 throughout the US; 800-548-7823 from Canada). A freighter travel agency and club ($15 per year or $25 for 2 years) whose members receive the bimonthly *TravLtips* magazine of cruise and freighter travel.

Those interested in freighter travel also may want to subscribe to *Freighter Travel News,* a publication of the *Freighter Travel Club of America.* A year's subscription to this monthly newsletter costs $18. To subscribe, write to the club at 3524 Harts Lake Rd., Roy, WA 98580.

Another monthly newsletter that may be of interest to those planning to cruise South American waters is *Ocean and Cruise News,* which offers comprehensive coverage of the latest on the cruise ship scene. A year's subscription costs $24. Contact *Ocean and Cruise News,* PO Box 92, Stamford, CT 06904 (phone: 203-329-2787).

> ■ **A final note on picking a cruise:** A "cruise-only" travel agency can best help you choose a cruise ship and itinerary. Cruise-only agents are best equipped to tell you about a particular ship's "personality," the kind of person with whom you'll likely be traveling on a particular ship, what dress is appropriate (it varies from ship to ship), and much more. Travel agencies that specialize in booking cruises usually are members of the *National Association of Cruise Only Agencies (NACOA).* For a listing of the agencies in your area (requests are limited to three states), send a self-addressed, stamped envelope to *NACOA,* PO Box 7209, Freeport, NY 11520, or call 516-378-8006.

# Traveling by Train

Perhaps the most economical, and often the most satisfying, way to see a lot of a foreign country in a relatively short time is by rail. It certainly is the quickest way to travel between two cities up to 300 miles apart (beyond that, a flight normally would be quicker, even counting the time it takes to get to and from the airport). But time isn't always the only consideration. Traveling by train is a way to keep moving and to keep seeing at the same time, and the fares usually are reasonable. You only need to get to a station on time; after that, put your watch in your pocket and relax. You may not get to your destination exactly at the appointed hour, but you'll have a marvelous time looking out the window and enjoying the ride.

**TRAINS:** Whether you enjoy efficient, air conditioned train rides along well-maintained tracks or like the nostalgic wheezing of steam locomotives, you'll find a railway to suit you somewhere in South America. The type and quality of rail service varies considerably from one section of the continent to the other. Generally, trains that run in the southern part of South America are more efficient, comfortable, and modern than those in the northern sections. In the past 10 years, however, train travel in South America has suffered severe setbacks because of financial chaos and political instability — in some cases, terrorism — not to mention cancellations due to natural disasters from flooding and severe storms. Among the routes which can be said to run smoothly and on schedule are those in Argentina, from Buenos Aires north to Asunción (Paraguay) and from Buenos Aires west to Mendoza (Argentina); in Brazil, from Sao Paulo to Rio de Janeiro; and in Chile, from Santiago south to Puerto Montt. Don't be completely disappointed, however. Although many trains are no longer operating, it is still possible to arrange some exciting train tours with one of the private tour companies listed at the end of this section.

In Bolivia, Ecuador, and Peru, trains tend to be considerably more ramshackle on rail lines originally built to connect the coastal cities with the inland mountain settlements close to the mines. Schedules can be erratic, trips tend to take longer than expected, toilets (if they exist) may not always flush, and although porters do their best, English-speaking personnel is limited.

If you can shrug in the face of minor inconveniences and postponements, and sustain an accepting and flexible attitude, you'll find that trains are a wonderful way to get to know the South American people and see the countryside. The scenery in the Andean

## GETTING READY / Traveling by Train

countries, for example, is among the world's most spectacular, and train travel is quite popular in this region — despite the need for indomitable patience, a good sense of humor, and a tolerance for spending long hours jammed in a rickety wooden seat in a passenger car filled with people (and an occasional chicken or goat). It is well worth the discomfort.

Note: In addition to long distances, there are innumerable mechanical delays, flooding during the rainy season, and often rugged terrain to cross, all of which can combine to stretch a distance of some 200 or 300 miles into a 10- to 15-hour trip.

**ACCOMMODATIONS AND FARES:** The quality of train accommodations varies considerably within each country. Argentina's trains have air conditioning, Pullman cars, overnight sleeping compartments, and diners. Some of Brazil's trains, in the state of São Paulo, have air conditioning, Pullman cars, and buffets. On the other end of the scale, the Quito–Riobamba train in Ecuador provides neither heat nor food — although *Metropolitan Touring*'s special train, which runs three times a week on this route, is the exception. For information on this particular train, contact *Metropolitan Touring* (239 Av. Amazonas, PO Box 310, Quito, Ecuador; phone: 2-560550) or its US representative, *Adventure Associates* (13150 Coit Rd., Suite 110, Dallas, TX 75240; phone: 214-907-0404 in Texas; 800-527-2500 elsewhere in the US).

The "tourists' train" from Cuzco to Machu Picchu in Peru has comfortable seats, whereas the "locals' train" along the same route generally is "standing room only." The Bogatá–Nemecón line in Bolivia uses old-fashioned steam engines, as does the railway system in central Paraguay. The overnight train from Santiago to Puerto Montt, Chile, has air conditioning, sleeping cars, and a restaurant. The *Patagonia Express* is an elegant, 1920s steam-engine train that runs between Buenos Aires and Bariloche, Jacobacci, and Esquel.

As in the US, fares are assessed according to the type of accommodation. Some trains have first class and second class cars. First class generally will be less crowded and always is recommended. Train travel anywhere in South America is unbelievably inexpensive compared to that in the US. While it is extremely difficult to generalize about train fares or the quality of South American train services — particularly in Bolivia and Peru — it's wise to pay the extra fare to travel first class. Tickets can be purchased at train stations in each country.

You usually can take as much baggage as you can carry onto a South American train — many people drag their entire worldly possessions along with them. On occasion, however, you may have to pay a small supplement for baggage over a certain amount. Most metropolitan stations have porters who will carry your baggage; a small tip is greatly appreciated. On board, *always* keep track of your belongings, as theft is a common problem throughout South America, as elsewhere.

**RAILWAY OFFICES AND SPECIAL ROUTES:** The major railway offices in South America are as follows:

**Argentina** – *Argentine Railways, Ferrocarriles Argentinos* (*FA;* 735 Florida St., Buenos Aires, Argentina; phone: 1-311-6411 for information; 1-312-3686 for reservations). The Argentine railways have 27,000 miles of track. Formerly a British-owned rail system, it has diesel-drawn engines, new dining cars, and sleepers built by an Argentine subsidiary of Fiat. Two of the most popular routes are the Buenos Aires–San Carlos de Bariloche route in the Lake District, a 35-hour trip, and the Buenos Aires–Mendoza route, which is 13 hours minimum. Also popular are the daily Buenos Aires–Córdoba (12 hours) and Buenos Aires–Tucumán (18 hours) runs.

The new *Argempass* permits unlimited, first class rail travel in Argentina, and is offered for 30-, 60-, and 90-day periods. Discounts are available for groups, families, students, children, men age 60 and up, and women age 55 and up. For information, contact *CIFA* (*Information Center for Argentinian Railroad*), 88 Maipú, 1084 Capital Federal, Argentina (phone: 1-343-7220).

**Bolivia** – *National Railway Company, Empresa Nacional de Ferrocarriles (ENFE;* Estación Central, Av. Manco Capac, 428 Casilla, La Paz, Bolivia; phone: 2-37-306-8169). This 1,400-mile system of railway tracks is divided into an eastern and a western region. A mixed Argentine–Bolivian railroad commission is talking of building a railroad from Santa Cruz, Bolivia, to Río Mamore, Argentina. A second part of this proposed international project would provide a rail link to Peru.

Other Bolivian railway systems include the *Machacamarca–Uncia Railway (Ferrocarril Machacamarca–Uncia)*, Machacamarca; and the *Uyuni–Pulcayo Railway (Empresa Minera Pulcayo)*, Pulcayo. Other important trains operate between Santa Cruz and Puerto Suarez on the Brazilian border, and from La Paz south to the Argentinian border (the *Expresso del Sur).*

**Brazil** – With 23,125 miles of track, Brazil's railways are divided into 22 government-owned divisions that in turn are part of the five regions of the *Rede Ferroviaria Federal, SA (RFFSA).* As in most South American countries, however, trains do not play a central role in the country's transportation system. The *RFFSA* regional offices include:

- **Northeast** (Av. Riocapiparibe, Recife, Brazil; phone: 81-224-2301). Note that there is almost no train service to the northeast part of the country. The only train available from this location provides limited shuttle service within Recife itself.
- **Central** (Ed. D. Pedro II, Praça Cristiano Otoni, 4th Floor, Rio de Janeiro, Brazil; phone: 21-233-3277). The *Rio–São Paulo Cruzeiro do Sul* express, at one point a popular train route, has been canceled. Remaining service consists of local trains making relatively short runs.
- **Central South** (Praça da Luz, Caixa Postal 8061, São Paulo, ZP-01120, Brazil; phone: 11-991-3039). The 3-hour trip between Curitiba and Paranagua in the southern state of Paraná is probably the most scenic rail trip in Brazil. Note that although information and tickets are available from this office, the trains themselves do not depart from this location; connection to the trains is provided via local bus service.
- **South** (Av. Dois Estados, Pôrto Alegre, Brazil; phone: 512-436680).

Other Brazilian railways include: *São Paulo Railways* (Ferrovia Paulista, SA, FEPASA, 39 Rua Libero Badaro, São Paulo, 01009, Brazil; phone: 11-239-0022); and *Victoria a Minas (Cia Vale do Rio Doce;* Caixa Postal 155, Victória, Espirito Santo, Brazil; phone: 27-226-4169).

**Chile** – *Chilean State Railways (Empresa de los Ferrocarriles del Estado;* 3322 Av. Libertador Bernardo O'Higgins, Santiago, Chile; phone: 2-689-1682, 2-689-1825, or 2-689-5199). Tickets also are sold at *Galería Libertador* (853 Alameda, Santiago, Chile; phone: 2-331814 and 2-330746). Most of Chile's train routes run to destinations south of the capital. At the time of this writing, all northern routes except the one to Oruro (Bolivia) from Calama had been discontinued.

The British-owned *Antofagasta and Bolivia Railroad* maintains an office at 225 Bolívar, Antofagasta, Chile (phone: 55-251700). Trains run east from Calama through the northern Atacama Desert and across the Andes into Oruro, Bolivia.

The *Empresa Nacional de Ferrocarriles Bolivianos* (93 21 de Mayo, Arica, Chile; phone: 80-232844) provides rail service across the Atacama Desert to La Paz. The 278-mile trip takes 10 hours.

**Colombia** – *National Railways of Colombia (Ferrocarriles Nacional de Colombia;* 18-24 Calle 13, Bogotá, Colombia; phone: 1-277-5577). As we went to press, the 2,300 miles of Colombian rail track were being served mainly by trains carrying freight. Only one passenger line, the 22-mile Bogotá to Nemocón route, is in operation and travels only on Sundays.

**Ecuador** – *Ecuadorian State Railways* (*Empresa de Nacional Ferrocarriles del Estado;* 433 Carrera Bolívar, Quito, Ecuador; phone: 2-216180). The 253-mile Quito–Guayaquil railway, completed in 1908, was severely damaged by floods in 1984 and, at press time, only the sectors between Quito and Riobamba and Guayaquil and Riobamba were fully operational on a daily basis. The train, however, travels through terrific mountain scenery.

**French Guiana** – No railways.

**Guyana** – No railways.

**Panama** – While rail service is minimal in Panama, the ride from the capital to Colón is particularly interesting. There are five runs daily during the week, three on Saturday, and no service on Sundays, and the route roughly parallels the Canal, with window views of both ship movements and the jungle.

**Paraguay** – *Central Railway of Paraguay President Carlos Antonio López* (*Ferrocarril Central de Paraguay Presidente Carlos Antonio López;* Anteguera y Elígio Ayala, Asunción, Paraguay; phone: 21-43273). One of the oldest railways in South America, the 285-mile Paraguayan system dates from 1861 and has 21 steam locomotives. It is very slow, and bus service between tourist sites is much better. Rail service is also available from Asunción to Posadas, with connecting service to Buenos Aires (Argentina). Every Wednesday, the *San Salvador–Abai* line operates; a restored, antique train, most of its equipment was built before 1914.

**Peru** – *Peruvian National Railroad, Empresa Nacional de Ferrocarriles del Perú* (*ENAFER;* PO Box 1375, 207 Ancash, Lima, Peru; phone: 14-289440). The 1,020-mile Peruvian railway system includes the world's highest standard-gauge railway from Lima to Huancayo, reaching an altitude of 15,688 feet. Unfortunately, at press time, rail service from Lima was temporarily suspended; note that the track between Huancayo and Huancavelica had already been closed for some time to passengers due to the danger of terrorist attacks in the area. When in operation, the Lima to Huancayo portion of the route to Huancavelica normally is recommended — especially to attend Huancayo's Sunday market.

Daily trains for Machu Picchu leave Cuzco early in the morning. There also is a train from Cuzco to Puno, on the shores of Lake Titicaca. A scenic 12-hour journey across the altiplano, it runs daily except Sunday. Most travelers continue into Bolivia, either by bus around the lake or by crossing the lake via the catamaran cruise boat run by the tour company *Transturin* or the hydrofoil operated by *Crillón* (see *Bolivia,* DIRECTIONS). An overnight train operates daily between Puno and Arequipa; the route also is served by day three times a week.

**Suriname** – No railways.

**Uruguay** – Limited to virtually nonexistent passenger service on railways. (Not recommended, in any event, as rail service is unreliable and often unsafe — take a bus instead.)

**Venezuela** – *Venezuela National Railways* (*Ferrocarriles Nacional de Venezuela;* Estación Caño Amarillo, Apdo. 146, Caracas, Venezuela; phone: 2-416141). A poor railway system of 102 miles connects Guanta Naricual and Puerto Cabello with Barquisimeto. Railways are not given high priority as a transportation system in Venezuela; the government favors developing sophisticated highways and airports. As a result, the bus service is extensive.

The *Encanto Historical Railway* (*Empresa del Ferrocarriles Histórico del Encanto;* Caracas y Valencia, Caracas, Venezuela; no phone) takes passengers along an 8-mile track. This is for tourists only.

Finally, although any travel agent can assist you in making arrangements to tour South America by rail, you may want to consult a train travel specialist, such as *Accent on Travel* (1030 Curtis St., Suite 201, Menlo Park, CA 94025; phone: 415-326-7330 in California; 800-347-0645 elsewhere in the US), which books rail tours in a number of

South American countries. *Trains Unlimited Tours* (PO Box 1997, Portola, CA 96122; phone: 916-836-1745) also offers rail adventures in South America, featuring steam locomotives and other interesting trains. Note that itineraries for both of these companies vary significantly from year to year, so call for current information when planning your trip.

# Traveling by Bus

*Because of increased terrorist attacks, the US State Department continued to maintain a travel advisory for tourists regarding travel by public bus in Peru as we went to press. At the time you are planning to travel, check with the State Department or the local US consulate or embassy regarding the safety of this and other areas in South America.*

Going from place to place by bus may not be the fastest way to get from here to there, but that (and, in some cases, a little less comfort) is the primary drawback to bus travel. A persuasive argument in its favor is its cost: Short of walking, it is the least expensive way to cover a long distance. On average, a bus ticket between two cities in South America costs about two-thirds of the corresponding train fare. For this amount, it is *possible* to travel comfortably (the degree of comfort varies widely among routes and buses), if not always speedily, and at the same time enjoy the scenic view.

South American buses are relatively reliable (albeit often dilapidated), and a viable transportation alternative as long as you have time to spare for long delays due to bad roads and poor equipment. The best service is found in Argentina, Brazil, Chile, and Venezuela — but even in these countries it is not necessarily consistent.

The immense distances and the uncertainty of connections make it difficult to be enthusiastic about bus travel to South America from North America, but it is possible. From the US, *Greyhound* serves the Mexico-US border at Laredo, Texas, where you can pick up a Mexican bus for the journey to Mexico City, where you can pick up another bus to points south. (For information on departures from the US, contact the nearest *Greyhound* office or call *Greyhound*'s Laredo office at 512-723-4324). Traveling by bus, however, even to Panama, at the northernmost tip of South America, is a *long* way to go — *if* you can arrange connections through Mexico, Guatemala, Honduras, Nicaragua, and Costa Rica. *Be forewarned: This is a perilous route, through politically unstable areas, and the safety of passengers cannot be guaranteed.*

**FOR COMFORTABLE TRAVEL:** Dress casually in loose-fitting clothes. Be sure you have a sweater or jacket (even in the South American summer) and, for when you disembark, a raincoat or umbrella is recommended in areas of high precipitation and during the rainy season (see "Climate," in *When and How to Go*, in this section). Choose a seat in the front near the driver for the best view or in the middle between the front and rear wheels for the smoothest ride — although, depending on the route and kind of bus, the term "smooth" may be relative.

**SOUTH AMERICAN BUS SERVICES:** A map of South American bus routes is not much different from a road map: If the way is paved, it's likely that a bus — some bus — is assigned to travel it. Buses link nearly all areas of Central and South America, and many South American stations accommodate several private companies. Not only do buses run between major cities, they also travel between out-of-the-way towns and villages, reaching outposts remote from railroad tracks, for those so inclined. (You will find that buses serve almost all the routes outlined in DIRECTIONS.)

Most people in South America depend on buses for transportation, so this is a good place to communicate with them. If you are lucky, you might make the acquaintance of a llama herder, teacher, health worker, farmer, labor union organizer, miner, doctor, missionary, or the lady whose goat may be riding on top of the bus.

**Accommodations and Fares** – Four basic kinds of buses serve South America: those with air conditioning and standard toilets; those with air conditioning and pull-down toilets; those with air conditioning without toilets; and the most common, called regular buses, without air conditioning or toilets, which can be found everywhere. Buses range from luxury Mercedes-Benz vehicles used in Argentina to converted schoolbuses in Bolivia and cramped mini-vans in Ecuador. In rural sections of the continent, buses usually are crowded, cramped, and renowned for infrequent and some desperately needed "pit stops" — they do the donkey work of public conveyance in South America. If you do any extensive traveling by bus, you will undoubtedly ride one at some point.

For obvious reasons, you will be more comfortable on the better grades of "plush," or (usually) air conditioned, first class buses. These buses are clearly marked at the stations throughout South America, and you will pay a bit more for a ticket, though fares normally are inexpensive across the continent (in comparison to fares in the US) so that the difference between a regular and a first class bus will seem quite small to most tourists. Long-distance buses do stop at roadside cafés for food, but most North Americans may be better off providing their own sustenance.

**Booking** – Tickets are purchased at bus stations and tickets are sold on a cash only, first-come, first-served basis. Because many bus companies oversell tickets, it is a good idea to buy your ticket early (the day *before* you travel in Peru) and get to the station in plenty of time to be among the first to board. Particularly during the busiest rush seasons such as *Easter* week or the *Christmas* holidays, purchase your bus tickets as far in advance as possible. Also get to the bus station well before the scheduled departure time to avoid standing in lines for several hours and to make sure you get on the bus. The addresses of the major bus stations are listed in *Getting Around* in some of the individual reports in THE CITIES.

Although South American bus schedules are issued in the country's native language and are rarely available in English, you may be able to decipher them — if not, ask for help. Unless you speak the native language fluently, you also will not get much useful information over the telephone (or at the bus station, for that matter).

One caustic traveler called South American bus schedules "the best Latin American fiction since the Inca legends"; nonetheless, they provide extremely inexpensive long-distance transportation that usually is no more than a few hours off schedule. (In Argentina and Chile, in fact, they *do* run pretty close to on time.) Beyond that very basic service, you will have to fend for yourself.

# Traveling by Car

**DRIVING:** *Given unpredictable road conditions, extremely variable weather and topography, as well as a political climate that often is unstable (and sometimes violent), driving is not currently a recommended mode of transportation to and through much of South America. Although it is possible to drive your own car from the US to South America, following the perilous route through treacherous terrain and unsafe areas in Nicaragua, Honduras, and Panama is not an option that we recommend. However, if you do make the decision to drive in South America, read the following very carefully.*

Driving certainly is the most flexible way to explore out-of-the-way regions of South America. The privacy, comfort, and convenience of touring by car can't be matched by any other form of transport. Trains often whiz much too fast past too many enticing landscapes, tunnel through or pass between hills and mountains rather than climb up and around them for a better view, and frequently deposit passengers in an unappealing part of town. Buses have a greater range, but they still don't permit many spur-of-the-

**50 GETTING READY / Traveling by Car**

moment stops and starts. A car, on the other hand, provides maximum flexibility, allowing visitors to cover large amounts of territory, to visit major cities and sites, or to move from one small town to the next while exploring the countryside. You go where you want when you want, and can stop along the way as often as you like for a meal, a photograph, or a spectacular view.

Your flexibility to drive wherever you please may be somewhat restricted, however, by national borders. Those who plan to rent a car in South America should know that, although policies vary, most car rental companies do not allow rental cars to leave the country in which they are rented. To some extent, this policy is due to governmental restrictions barring rental cars from exiting or entering certain countries; these countries include Argentina, French Guiana, Guyana, Peru, Suriname, and Venezuela. Even in those countries that do allow rental cars to cross the borders, most major rental car companies make it a general policy not to allow inter-country travel. Occasionally, a local or regional rental company *may* allow you to cross borders where it is legal — provided you leave a hefty deposit and return the car to the country of origin. It is, therefore, best to rent a car for driving only within one country at a time (see "Renting a Car," below). If you want to make a short excursion into a bordering country, take advantage of public transportation, guided tours, and package options. South Americans most often fly between countries and rent a car only for local touring.

Those diehards who insist on driving in South America will certainly find the experience an unforgettable adventure. Whether you remember driving in South America with sentimental abandon or with a shudder depends to a great extent on how effectively you prepare for the journey. Surprises are inevitable. Not only is the terrain of astounding variety — tropical jungle and desert, Andean mountains and Patagonian wilds — but driving patterns and road practices are a world apart from standard North American highway courtesy.

When touring by car in South America, it is essential that you know enough Spanish or Portuguese (if you plan to drive in Brazil) to communicate basic needs. You will be spending most of your time on the road in areas uninhabited by English-speaking people. Not only is it inadvisable, it is downright foolhardy to attempt traveling through South America unless you can speak and understand a modicum of the native languages. It is difficult, if not impossible, to find your way unless you can ask directions and understand people's responses. In many parts of South America, roads are not marked. Even in major cities, some streets are not marked.

Be forewarned: Although distances between towns and cities may appear reasonable on a map — this can be misleading due to overall poor road conditions and roundabout routings which circumvent the often mountainous terrain. When planning your driving route be *very* conservative in estimating driving time — *driving or stopping by the roadside after dark can be very dangerous.* Drivers should be aware of latter-day bandits who have been known to stop, assault, and rob tourists (see "Road Safety and Highway Conditions," below). In DIRECTIONS you will find our choices of the most interesting driving itineraries, as well as approximate distances to help in your calculations.

Before setting out, make certain that everything you need is in order. If possible, discuss your intended trip with someone who already has driven the route to find out about road conditions and available services. If you can't speak to someone personally, try to read about others' experiences. Automobile clubs (see below) can be a good source of driving information, although when requesting brochures and maps, be sure to specify the areas you are planning to visit. (Also see "Maps," below.) The local South American tourist boards also may provide useful information on their respective areas; see the individual city reports in THE CITIES for locations.

**License** – To drive in South America, you need an International Driving Permit (IDP), which is a translation of the US license in 9 languages. You can obtain your IDP before you leave from most branches of the *American Automobile Association*

## GETTING READY / Traveling by Car

*(AAA)*. Applicants must be at least 18 years old, and the application must be accompanied by two passport-size photos (some *AAA* branches have a photo machine available), a valid US driver's license, and a fee of $10. The IDP is good for 1 year and must be accompanied by your US license to be valid. Your US license also will be required for renting a car, and in most cases, you will need to present a major credit card and a passport.

**Car Permits and Checkpoints** – With few exceptions, you can only cross international South American borders if driving your own (non-rental) car — which, again, is not recommended. Those few travelers who may do this should know about the *Carnet de Passage en Douanes,* a document with which cars are allowed through various customs points duty-free. Previously issued by the *AAA,* currently you must contact the embassy of each country in which you will be traveling to obtain the documentation required by individual customs services. Allow plenty of time for the exchange of letters and the issuance and receipt of documents — without the correct paperwork, you might be asked to pay a tax for "importing" a vehicle even though you are only in transit. If you will be crossing an international border in a rental car (which is only permitted by some countries and a few rental agencies; see above), be sure to get the proper paperwork from the renting agency — a letter of border authorization and other government papers may be required, depending on the bordering countries.

You will save time at borders if you prepare a sheet of paper with the following information listed clearly in Spanish and/or Portuguese: name, address, nationality, age, place and date of birth, sex, passport number and place of issue, destination, point of departure, profession, driver's license number, *carnet* number (see above), owner of car (when driving a rental car, the renting agency), auto registration number, serial number, license plate number, make, year, and model of car, as well as a checklist including the number of spare tires, radio, tape deck, heater, air conditioning, number and color of seats.

You will encounter many military checkpoints along country roads, as well as at entrances to cities, that will require this information. Generally, major borders between countries will speed you through in about 15 minutes, but there are innumerable smaller road stations where the process is less efficient. In countries with checkpoints, make sure to ask whether your papers must be stamped at each stop. Driving right by a checkpoint may mean that you will have to return to that location if subsequent officials find that you are missing a required stamp — and, in some countries, it can be a long way between checkpoints. It's also not a bad idea to carry an inventory of your possessions written in Spanish and notarized by US customs before you leave home. It can save endless hassles.

**Maps** – Consult road maps. A number of the automobile clubs listed below offer their members (and members of affiliated clubs) free or inexpensive maps. Once in most South American countries, however, good maps may be hard to find; check at local newsstands and tourist information offices.

Instead of waiting until you arrive, contact the *South American Explorers Club* (126 Indian Creek Rd., Ithaca, NY 14850; phone: 800-274-0568 or 607-277-0488), which offers an extensive selection of highway and topographical maps; members receive a discount on all publications. Another good source of maps is *Map Link* (25 E. Mason St., Suite 201, Santa Barbara, CA 93101; phone: 805-965-4402), which carries detailed road maps of most South American countries (the exception is Suriname), as well as hundreds of specialized (topographical, political, and so on) maps of the continent.

A wall map, the *Rand McNally Cosmopolitan Map of South America,* indicates each South American country in a different color. While its size and scale are not practical for touring use, it can be helpful before leaving for South America. All major highways are indicated, and there is no problem figuring out what is near what. This map may be found in bookstores or can be ordered directly for $2.95, plus postage and handling,

**52 GETTING READY / Traveling by Car**

from *Rand McNally,* 150 E. 52nd St., New York, NY 10022 (phone: 212-758-7488).

**Automobile Clubs** – Most South American automobile clubs offer emergency service to any breakdown victim, whether a club member or not; however, only members of these clubs or affiliated clubs may have access to certain information services and receive discounted or free towing and repair services.

Members of the *American Automobile Association (AAA)* often are automatically entitled to a number of services from foreign clubs. With almost 33 million members in chapters throughout the US and Canada, the *AAA* is the largest automobile club in North America. *AAA* affiliates throughout the US provide a variety of travel services to members, including a travel agency, trip planning, fee-free traveler's checks, and roadside assistance. They will help plan an itinerary, send a map with clear routing directions, and will even make hotel reservations. Most of these services apply to traveling in both the US and South America. Note that the *AAA* no longer reimburses members for on-the-road expenses — such as towing and repairs — incurred while in South America. Although *AAA* members receive maps and other brochures for no charge or at a discount (depending on the publication and branch), non-members also can order from an extensive selection of highway and topographical maps. You can join the *AAA* through local chapters (listed in the telephone book under *AAA)* or contact the national office, 1000 AAA Dr., Heathrow, FL 32746-5063 (phone: 407-444-8544).

Automobile clubs in South American countries are listed below. As indicated, some offer fully reciprocal services to *AAA* members from the US; others may require payment for services.

**Argentina:** *Automóvil Club Argentino* (1850 Av. Libertador General San Martín, Buenos Aires, Argentina; phone: 1-802-6061 to 6069). Offers reciprocal services to *AAA* members.

**Bolivia:** *Automóvil Club Boliviano* (2993 Av. 6 de Agosto, San Jorge, La Paz, Bolivia; phone: 2-326132 or 2-342074).

**Brazil:** *Automóvel Club do Brasil* (90 Rua do Passeio, Rio de Janeiro ZC-06, Brazil; phone: 21-240-0440 for emergency service, 21-297-4455 for tourist information); and *Touring Club do Brasil* (4929 Av. Brasil, Bonsucesso, Rio de Janeiro, Brazil; phone: 21-295-7440 for emergency service, 21-210-2180 for tourist information in English — a rare find in South America).

**Chile:** *Automóvil Club de Chile* (main office: 8620 Vitacura, Santiago, Chile; phone: 2-212-5702); branch offices are located throughout Chile (the main office can provide information on other locations). Offers reciprocal services to *AAA* members.

**Colombia:** *Touring y Automóvil Club de Colombia* (46-72 Av. Caracas, Bogotá, Colombia; phone: 1-232-7580). Offers reciprocal services to *AAA* members.

**Ecuador:** *Automóvil Club del Ecuador* (218 Eloy Alfaro y Berlin, Quito, Ecuador; phone: 2-237779 or 2-542130). Offers reciprocal services to *AAA* members.

**Paraguay:** *Touring y Automóvil Club Paraguayo* (25 de Mayo y Brasil, Asunción, Paraguay; phone: 21-24336).

**Peru:** *Touring y Automóvil Club del Perú* (699 Av. Cesar Vallejo, Lince, Lima, Peru; phone: 14-403270). Offers reciprocal services to *AAA* members.

**Uruguay:** *Automóvil Club del Uruguay* (Av. Colonia y Yi, Montevideo, Uruguay; phone: 2-911251, 2-911252, or 2-911253).

**Venezuela:** *Touring y Automóvil Club de Venezuela* (Locales 11-14, Centro Integral, Av. Principal, Santa Rosa de Lima, Caracas, Venezuela; phone: 2-914879). Offers reciprocal services to *AAA* members.

**Breakdowns** – If you break down on the road, immediate emergency procedure is to get the car off the road. Major highways and other two-lane roads tend to have narrower shoulders than you're used to, so make sure you get all the way off, even if you have to hang off the shoulder a bit. To signal for help, raise the hood, and tie a white handkerchief or rag to the door handle or radio antenna. Don't leave the car unattended, and don't try any major repairs on the road.

Unlike Mexico, where the Green Angel emergency service fleet patrols the road, most of South America has no such service. However, people are very helpful, and someone will very likely stop to help you. Truck drivers are usually very good mechanics since they have to be able to repair their own vehicles when they break down in out-of-the-way places.

Automobile clubs also may provide assistance in the event of on-the-road breakdowns. Otherwise, a driver in distress will have to contact the nearest service center by pay phone. And if you don't speak the native language, the local operator should be able to connect you to an English-speaking international operator for assistance. (Better yet, if possible find someone to make the call for you.) Car rental companies also make provisions for breakdowns, emergency service, and assistance; ask for a number to call when you pick up the vehicle.

**Road Safety and Highway Conditions –** The Pan-American Highway is not a well-surfaced superhighway. In many cases, it is only a two-lane gravel road. In Peru and Chile, it is a two- and occasionally a three-lane paved road in good condition. In the Andes, roads are generally gravel. In the rainy season, landslides often make it impossible to pass. Again, if you have to stop on the road, *make sure you get all the way off.*

Be particularly careful about the following:

1. Be aware of recent road incidents involving assaults and robberies of tourists. These are increasingly frequent, and usually befall ill-advised travelers who have underestimated the distances between towns — or the time it takes to cover these distances. Stopping to spend the night in the car or on some deserted stretch of beachfront is the ultimate no-no. Be realistic in calculating the amount of ground you can cover, and make plans on the side of conservatism when you have any doubts. (For a complete description of the major South American driving itineraries, see DIRECTIONS.)
2. Do not drive after dark. Being stranded on a lonely stretch is dangerous at any time — after dark it is downright foolhardy. In addition, there normally are no fences between adjacent fields and jungles, and you never know when a cow, deer, or other animals will decide to see what's on the other side of the road. (Even in the daytime, cows may stand in the middle of the road and stare you down.) Bicycles and other vehicles without lights are other common nighttime road hazards, as are pedestrians.
3. You occasionally will encounter one-lane bridges on two-lane highways. The driver who flashes his or her lights first is supposed to be the one permitted to cross the bridge first. This is standard procedure both day and night. Make sure you slow down as you approach bridges, and go slowly as you cross.
4. Obey speed limits and traffic regulations, especially when driving through towns and cities. As there are very few bypass roads, you will have to slow down as you pass through populated centers. Speeds are always given in kilometers (a kilometer is equal to approximately .62 miles), and most countries use international symbols on highway signs, which are quite easy to understand.
5. If you do get a traffic ticket, follow police instructions and don't argue. You can report any unfair treatment later, but don't expect any quick resolutions of problems that arise far from major cities. (For information on what to do in the event of a serious accident, see *Legal Aid and Consular Services,* in this section.)
6. Make the first days of your trip the shortest, and plan to drive no more than 200 to 300 miles per day (depending on road conditions, about 6 to 7 hours of driving

**54 GETTING READY / Traveling by Car**

time) — if that much. When traveling with children, plan on no more than 150 to 200 miles a day (4 to 5 hours) at the most.

**Gasoline** – In South America, gasoline is sold by the liter, which is slightly more than 1 quart; approximately 3.8 liters equals 1 US gallon. Regular gas is the norm — unleaded gas is often difficult to find on the continent (almost all rental cars take regular leaded gas), although diesel fuel is common.

Gas prices everywhere rise and fall depending upon the world supply of oil, and in South America the price of gasoline varies considerably from country to country. Although North American visitors will generally find gasoline to be more expensive than they are accustomed to paying in the US, in the oil-producing nations of Peru and Venezuela (depending on the current exchange rate) gas may be more reasonably priced.

Be prepared to pay for gas in cash, and when you fill up the gas tank, make sure the attendant first moves the counter back to zero. In many rural areas, gasoline is diluted with water or kerosene. So if the car stops after you have just filled up, it could be due to impure gasoline.

Particularly when traveling in rural areas, fill up whenever you come to a gas station. It may be a long way to the next station, and many areas experience frequent fuel shortages. You *don't* want to get stranded on an isolated stretch — so it is a good idea to bring along an extra few gallons in a steel container. (Plastic containers tend to break when the car is bouncing over rocky roads. This, in turn, creates the danger of fire should the gasoline ignite from a static electricity spark. Plastic containers also may burst at high altitudes.) In some countries, you may carry only a reasonable amount of gasoline in your car for emergencies. Anything more than this "reasonable" amount will require a police permit.

The prudent traveler should plan an itinerary and make as many reservations as possible in advance in order not to waste gas figuring out where to go, stay, or eat. Drive early in the day, when there is less traffic. Then leave your car at the hotel and use local transportation whenever possible after you arrive at your destination.

Make sure that your tires are properly inflated and your engine is tuned correctly to cut gas consumption. Although it may be equally dangerous to drive at a speed much below the posted limit as it is to drive above it — particularly on major highways — at 88 kph (55 mph) a car gets 25% better mileage than at 112 kph (70 mph). The number of miles per liter or gallon also is increased by driving smoothly.

**RENTING A CAR:** Most visitors who want to drive in South America rent a car through a travel agent or international rental firm before leaving home or from a local company once they are in South America. Another possibility, also arranged before departure, is to rent the car as part of a larger travel package.

Renting a car in South America is not inexpensive, but it is possible to economize by determining your own needs and then shopping around among the car rental companies until you find the best deal. As you comparison-shop, keep in mind that rates vary considerably, not only from city to city, but also from location to location within the same city. For instance, it might be less expensive to rent a car from an office in the center of a city rather than at the airport. Ask about special rates or promotional deals, such as weekend or weekly rates, bonus coupons for airline tickets, or 24-hour rates that include gas and unlimited mileage.

Rental car companies operating in South America can be divided into three basic categories: large national or international companies; regional companies; and local companies. *Avis, Budget, Hertz,* and other international firms maintain offices in the major cities, and car rental desks may be found in major hotels. Because of aggressive local competition, the cost of renting a car can be less expensive once a traveler arrives in South America, compared to the prices quoted in advance in the US. Local compa-

## GETTING READY / Traveling by Car

nies usually are less expensive than the international giants (although travelers who do not speak fluent Spanish or Portuguese may have to rule out smaller local companies that rent primarily to natives).

Given this situation, it's tempting to wait until arriving to scout out the lowest priced rental from the company located the farthest from the airport high-rent district and offering no pick-up services. But if your arrival coincides with a holiday or a peak travel period, you may be disappointed to find that even the most expensive car in town was spoken for months ago. Whenever possible, it is best to reserve in advance, anywhere from a few days in slack periods to a month or more during the busier seasons.

If you can read and speak Spanish and/or Portuguese, and decide to wait until after you arrive and let your fingers do the walking through the local phone books, you'll often find a suprising number of small companies listed — particularly in the larger metropolitan areas. Often the best guide to sorting through the options is the local tourist board, which usually can provide recommendations and a list of reputable firms.

Even if you do rent in advance, be aware that many South American car rental experiences bear little resemblance to the normally efficient process found almost everywhere in the US. It is not at all uncommon, for example, to arrive at an airport rental counter — even that of a giant international company — and have your confirmed reservation greeted with a shrug: No cars available. (If you use a car rental firm's toll-free number to reserve a vehicle, it *may* make a difference if you arrive with written confirmation of your reservations in hand — leave enough time for the rental company to mail it to you before you leave home. Also be sure you get a receipt for any deposit.) It is similarly common that the class and make of car you ordered will be notable by its absence. More shrugs. And even when you do get a car, and even when it is precisely the brand and type you want, chances are that its physical appearance and mechanical condition will be substantially inferior to similar rental cars you are used to driving in the US. Caveat renter.

Travel agents can arrange rentals for clients, but it is just as easy to call and rent a car yourself. Listed below are the major international rental companies represented in South America that have information and reservations numbers that can be dialed toll-free from the US (note that these numbers are all for the companies' international divisions, which handle South American rentals):

*Avis* (phone: 800-331-1084). Rents cars throughout South America.

*Auto Europe* (phone 800-223-5555). Rents cars in Argentina, Brazil, Chile, Colombia, French Guiana, Uruguay, and Venezuela.

*Budget Rent-A-Car* (phone: 800-472-3325). Rents cars in all South American countries except Bolivia, French Guiana, Guyana, Paraguay, and Suriname.

*Dollar Rent A Car* (phone: 800-800-4000). Rents cars in Argentina, Brazil, Chile, Colombia, Ecuador, Panama, and Peru.

*Hertz* (phone: 800-654-3001). Rents cars in most South American countries.

*National Car Rental* (phone: 800-CAR-EUROPE). Rents cars in most South American countries.

For information on local car rental companies, as well as sources for other rental and public transportation, see the *Sources and Resources* sections of the individual city chapters in THE CITIES.

**Requirements** – Whether you decide to rent a car in advance from a large international rental company with South American branches or wait to rent from a local company, you should know that renting a car is rarely as simple as signing on the dotted line and roaring off into the night. If you are renting for personal use, you must have a valid driver's license and will have to convince the renting agency that (1) you are personally creditworthy, and (2) you will bring the car back at the stated time. This will be easy if you have a major credit card; most rental companies accept credit cards in lieu of a cash deposit, as well as for payment of your final bill. If you prefer to pay in cash, leave your credit card imprint as a "deposit," then pay your bill in cash when you return the car.

If you are planning to rent a car once in South America, *Avis, Budget, Hertz,* and other US rental companies usually *will* rent to travelers paying in cash and leaving either a credit card imprint or a substantial amount of cash as a deposit. This is not necessarily standard policy, however, as some of the other international chains, and a number of regional and local South American companies will *not* rent to an individual who doesn't have a valid credit card. In this case, you may have to call around to find a company that accepts cash.

Also keep in mind that although the minimum age to drive a car in South America varies from country to country, the minimum age to rent a car is set by the rental company. (Restrictions vary from company to company, as well as at different locations of the same firm.) Many firms have a minimum age requirement of 21 years, some raise that to between 23 and 25 years, and for some models of cars it rises to 30 years. The upper age limit at many companies is between 69 and 75; others have no upper limit or may make drivers above a certain age subject to special conditions.

**Costs** – Finding the most economical car rental will require some telephone shopping on your part. As a *general* rule, expect to hear lower prices quoted by the smaller, strictly local companies than by the well-known international names, with those of the national South American companies falling somewhere between the two.

Comparison shopping always is advisable, however, because the company that has the least expensive rentals in one city — or country — may not have the least expensive cars in another, and even the international giants offer discount plans whose conditions are easy for most travelers to fulfill. For instance, *Budget* and *National* offer discounts of anywhere from 10% to 30% off their usual rates (according to the size of the car and the duration of the rental), provided that the car is reserved a certain number of days before departure (usually 7 to 14 days, but it can be less), is rented for a minimum period (5 days or, more often, a week), is paid for at the time of booking, and in most cases, is returned to the same location that supplied it or to another in the same country. Similar discount plans include *Hertz*'s Leisure Rates and *Avis*'s Supervalue Rates.

If driving short distances for only a day or two, the best deal may be a per-day, per-mile (or per-kilometer) rate: You pay a flat fee for each day you keep the car, plus a per-mile (or per-kilometer) charge. An increasingly common alternative is to be granted a certain number of free miles or kilometers each day and then be charged on a per-mile or per-kilometer basis over that number. Considering the long distances between points in South America, even if you are touring only one area you will be suprised how quickly the miles will add up — the total cost can be astounding.

A better alternative for South American touring is a flat per-day rate with unlimited free mileage; this certainly is the most economical rate if you plan to drive over 100 miles. (Note: When renting a car in South America, the term "mileage" may refer to either miles or kilometers.) Make sure that the low, flat daily rate that catches your eye, however, is indeed a per-day rate: Often the lowest price advertised by a company turns out to be available only with a minimum 3-day rental — fine if you want the car that long, but not the bargain it appears if you really intend to use it no more than 24 hours for in-city driving. Flat weekly rates also are available, and some flat monthly rates that represent a further saving over the daily rate.

Another factor influencing cost is the type of car you rent. Rentals generally are based on a tiered price system, with different sizes of cars — variations of budget, economy, regular, and luxury — often listed as A (the smallest and least expensive) through F, G, or H, and sometimes even higher. Charges may increase by only a few dollars a day through several categories of subcompact and compact cars — where most of the competition is — then increase by great leaps through the remaining classes

## GETTING READY / Traveling by Car

of full-size and luxury cars and passenger vans. The larger the car, the more it costs to rent and the more gas it consumes, but for some people the greater comfort and extra luggage space of a larger car (in which bags and sporting gear can be safely locked out of sight) may make it worth the additional expense. In some countries, models with standard stick-shifts are more common and those with automatic transmissions are, therefore, more expensive.

Electing to pay for collision damage waiver (CDW) protection will add considerably to the cost of renting a car. You may be responsible for the *full value* of the vehicle being rented, but you can dispense with the possible obligation by buying the offered waiver at a cost of around $9 to $15 a day for rentals in South America. Before making any decisions about optional collision damage waivers, check with your own insurance agent and determine whether your personal automobile insurance policy covers rented vehicles; if it does, you probably won't need to pay for the waiver. Be aware, too, that increasing numbers of credit cards automatically provide CDW coverage if the car rental is charged to the appropriate credit card. However, the specific terms of such coverage differ sharply among individual credit card companies, so check with the credit card company for information on the nature and amount of coverage provided. Business travelers also should be aware that, at the time of this writing, *American Express* had withdrawn its automatic CDW coverage from some corporate *Green* card accounts — watch for similar cutbacks by other credit card companies.

When inquiring about CDW coverage and costs, you should be aware that a number of the major international car rental companies now are automatically including the cost of this waiver in their quoted prices. This does not mean that they are absorbing this cost and you are receiving free coverage — total rental prices have increased to include the former CDW charge. The disadvantage of this inclusion is that you probably will not have the option to refuse this coverage, and will end up paying the added charge — even if you already are adequately covered by your own insurance policy or through a credit card company.

Additional costs to be added to the price tag include drop-off charges or one-way service fees. The lowest price quoted by any given company may apply only to a car that is returned to the same location from which it was rented. A slightly higher rate may be charged if the car is to be returned to a different location (even within the same city).

A further consideration: Don't forget that (with some exceptions) the price of gas, on the whole, is higher in South America than in the US. Rental cars usually are delivered with a full tank of gas. (This is not always the case, however, so check the gas gauge when picking up the car, and have the amount of gas noted on your rental agreement if the tank is not full.) Remember to fill the tank before you return the car or you will have to pay to refill it, and gasoline at the car rental company's pump always is much more expensive than at a service station. This policy may vary for smaller, local and regional companies; ask when picking up the vehicle. Before leaving the lot, also check that the rental car has a spare tire and jack in the trunk.

**Fly/Drive Packages** – Airlines, charter companies, car rental companies, and tour operators have been offering fly/drive packages for years, and even though the basic components of the package have changed somewhat — return airfare, a car waiting at the airport, and perhaps a night's lodging all for one inclusive price used to be the rule — the idea remains the same. You rent a car *here* for use *there* by booking it along with other arrangements for the trip. These days, the very minimum arrangement possible is the result of a tie-in between a car rental company and an airline, which entitles customers to a rental car for less than the company's usual rates, provided they show proof of having booked a flight on that airline. For information on available packages, check with the airline or your travel agent.

■ **Note:** When reserving and picking up your rental car, always ask for any available maps and information on the areas in which you will be driving; some companies also may offer brochures outlining scenic driving routes.

# Package Tours

If the mere thought of buying a package for travel to and around South America conjures up visions of a trip spent marching in lock step with a horde of frazzled fellow travelers, remember that packages have come a long way. For one thing, not all packages necessarily are escorted tours, and the one you buy does not have to include any organized touring at all — nor will it necessarily include traveling companions. If it does, however, you'll find that people of all sorts — many just like yourself — are taking advantage of packages today because they are economical and convenient, save you an immense amount of planning time, and exist in such variety that it's virtually impossible not to find one that fits at least the majority of your travel preferences. Given the high cost of travel these days, packages have emerged as a particularly wise buy.

In essence, a package is just an amalgam of travel services that can be purchased in a single transaction. A package (tour or otherwise) to and through South America may include any or all of the following: round-trip transportation from your home to South America, inter-country and local transportation (and/or car rentals), accommodations, some or all meals, sightseeing, entertainment, transfers to and from the hotel at each destination, taxes, tips, escort service, and a variety of incidental features that might be offered as options at additional cost. In other words, a package can be any combination of travel elements, from a fully escorted tour offered at an all-inclusive price to a simple fly/drive booking allowing you to move about totally on your own. Its principal advantage is that it saves money: The cost of the combined arrangements invariably is well below the price of all the same elements if bought separately, and particularly if transportation is provided by charter or discount flight, the whole package could cost less than just a round-trip economy airline ticket on a regularly scheduled flight. A package provides more than economy and convenience: It releases the traveler from having to make individual arrangements for each separate element of a trip.

Tour programs generally can be divided into two categories — "escorted" (or locally hosted) and "independent." An escorted tour means that a guide will accompany the group from the beginning of the tour through to the return flight; a locally hosted tour means that the group will be met upon arrival at each location by a different local host. On independent tours, there generally is a choice of hotels, meal plans, and sightseeing trips, as well as a variety of special excursions. The independent plan is for travelers who do not want a totally set itinerary, but who do prefer confirmed hotel reservations. Whether choosing an escorted or independent tour, always bring along complete contact information for your tour operator in case a problem arises, although US tour operators often have local affiliates who can give additional assistance or make other arrangements on the spot.

To determine whether a package — or, more specifically, *which* package — fits your travel plans, start by evaluating your interests and needs, deciding how much and what you want to spend, see, and do. Gather whatever package tour information is available for your schedule. Be sure that you take the time to read the brochure *carefully* to determine precisely what is included. Keep in mind that travel brochures are written to entice you into signing up for a package tour. Often the language is deceptive and devious. For example, a brochure may quote the lowest prices for a package tour based on facilities that are unavailable during the off-season, undesirable at any season, or just plain nonexistent. Information such as "breakfast included" or "plus tax" (which can add up) should be taken into account. Note, too, that the prices quoted in brochures almost always are based on double occupancy: The rate listed is for each of two people sharing a double room, and if you travel alone, the supplement for single accommodations can raise the price considerably (see *Hints for Single Travelers,* in this section).

In this age of erratic airfares, the brochure most often will *not* include the price of an airline ticket in the price of the package, though sample fares from various gateway cities usually will be listed separately as extras to be added to the price of the ground arrangements. Before figuring your actual cost, check the latest fares with the airlines, because the samples invariably are out of date by the time you read them. If the brochure gives more than one category of sample fares per gateway city — such as an individual tour-basing fare, a group fare, an excursion, APEX, or other discount ticket — your travel agent or airline tour desk will be able to tell you which one applies to the package you choose, depending on when you travel, how far in advance you book, and other factors. (An individual tour-basing fare is a fare computed as part of a package that includes land arrangements, thereby entitling a carrier to reduce the air portion almost to the absolute minimum. Though it always represents a saving over full-fare coach or economy, lately the individual tour-basing fare has not been as inexpensive as the excursion and other discount fares that also are available to individuals. The group fare usually is the least expensive fare, and it is the tour operator, not you, who makes up the group.) When the brochure does include round-trip transportation in the package price, don't forget to add the cost of round-trip transportation from your home to the departure city to come up with the total cost of the package.

Finally, read the general information regarding terms and conditions and the responsibility clause (usually in fine print at the end of the descriptive literature) to determine the precise elements for which the tour operator is — and is not — liable. Here the tour operator frequently expresses the right to change services or schedules as long as equivalent arrangements are offered. This clause also absolves the operator of responsibility for circumstances beyond human control, such as avalanches, earthquakes, or floods, or injury to you or your property. While reading, ask the following questions:

1. Does the tour include airfare or other transportation, sightseeing, meals, transfers, taxes, baggage handling, tips, or any other services? Do you want all these services?
2. If the brochure indicates that "some meals" are included, does this mean a welcoming and farewell dinner, two breakfasts, or every evening meal?
3. What classes of hotels are offered? If you will be traveling alone, what is the single supplement?
4. Does the tour itinerary or price vary according to the season?
5. Are the prices guaranteed; that is, if costs increase between the time you book and the time you depart, can surcharges unilaterally be added?
6. Do you get a full refund if you cancel? If not, be sure to obtain cancellation insurance.
7. Can the operator cancel if too few people join? At what point?

One of the consumer's biggest problems is finding enough information to judge the reliability of a tour packager, since individual travelers seldom have direct contact with the firm putting the package together. Usually, a retail travel agent is interposed between customer and tour operator, and much depends on his or her candor and cooperation. So ask a number of questions about the tour you are considering. For example:

- Has the travel agent ever used a package provided by this tour operator?
- How long has the tour operator been in business? Check the Better Business Bureau in the area where the tour operator is based to see if any complaints have been filed against it.

## 60  GETTING READY / Package Tours

- Is the tour operator a member of the *United States Tour Operators Association (USTOA;* 211 E. 51st St., Suite 12B, New York, NY 10022; phone: 212-944-5727)? The *USTOA* will provide a list of its members on request; it also offers a useful brochure, *How to Select a Package Tour.*
- How many and which companies are involved in the package?
- If air travel is by charter flight, is there an escrow account in which deposits will be held; if so, what is the name of the bank?

This last question is very important. US law requires that tour operators place every charter passenger's deposit and subsequent payment in a proper escrow account. Money paid into such an account cannot legally be used except to pay for the costs of a particular package or as a refund if the trip is canceled. To ensure the safe handling of your money, make your check payable to the escrow account — by law, the name of the depository bank must appear in the operator-participant contract, and usually is found in that mass of minuscule type on the back of the brochure. Write the details of the charter, including the destination and dates, on the face of the check; on the back, print "For Deposit Only." Your travel agent may prefer that you make your check out to the agency, saying that it will then pay the tour operator the fee minus commission. But it is perfectly legal to write your check as we suggest, and if your agent objects too strongly (the agent should have sufficient faith in the tour operator to trust him or her to send the proper commission), consider taking your business elsewhere. If you don't make your check out to the escrow account, you lose the protection of that escrow should the trip be canceled or the tour operator or travel agent fail. Furthermore, recent bankruptcies in the travel industry have served to point out that even the protection of escrow may not be enough to safeguard your investment. Increasingly, insurance is becoming a necessity (see *Insurance,* in this section), and payment by credit card has become popular since it offers some additional safeguards if the tour operator defaults.

■ **A word of advice:** Purchasers of vacation packages who feel they're not getting their money's worth are more likely to get a refund if they complain in writing to the operator — and bail out of the whole package immediately. Alert the tour operator or resort manager to the fact that you are dissatisfied, that you will be leaving for home as soon as transportation can be arranged, and that you expect a refund. They may have forms to fill out detailing your complaint; otherwise, state your case in a letter. Even if difficulty in arranging immediate transportation home detains you, your dated, written complaint should help in procuring a refund from the operator.

**SAMPLE PACKAGES TO SOUTH AMERICA:** As discussed above, a typical package tour in South America might include transportation to and from South America, accommodations for the duration of a stay, a sightseeing tour of the area, and several meals.

Although some packages just cover arrangements at a specific hotel, others offer more extensive arrangements and may be built around activities such as fishing, hunting, or skiing, or special interests such as music, history, native culture, or nature exploration. Simple fly/drive packages including only air transportation and car rental also are offered to South America. (For information on independent car rental options see *Traveling by Car,* in this section, as well as the individual city reports in THE CITIES.)

The following is a list of many of the major US operators who provide escorted or independent tours to South America. Note that most of these tours are either deluxe or first class; however, more and more economy packages are being offered as well. Some offer AP ("American Plan" — including all meals), others MAP ("Modified

## GETTING READY / Package Tours 61

American Plan" — breakfast and one main meal included daily), a few include only breakfast, and others leave you to make your own arrangements for meals. Most tour operators offer several departure dates, depending on the length of the tour and the countries visited. As indicated, some operators are wholesalers only, and will deal only with a travel agent.

*Abercrombie & Kent International* (1420 Kensington Rd., Oak Brook, IL 60521; phone: 800-323-7308 or 708-954-2944). Offers upscale package tours to Argentina, Brazil, Chile, Ecuador, the Galápagos Islands, and Peru; many offer a luxury cruise as an option or part of their itinerary. Independent packages also are available to many destinations in South America.

*Abreu Tours* (317 E. 34th St., New York, NY 10016; phone: 212-661-0555 in New York; 800-223-1580 elsewhere in the US). Specializes in packages to Brazil, which include luxury accommodations.

*Adventure Associates* (13150 Coit Rd., Suite 110, Dallas, TX 75240; phone: 214-907-0414 in Texas; 800-527-2500 elsewhere in the US). The US representative for both *Metropolitan Touring* of Ecuador and Peru's *Lima Tours,* this company offers dozens of independent and escorted tours throughout Bolivia, Ecuador, and Peru.

*Adventure Center* (1311 63rd St., Suite 200, Emeryville, CA 94608; phone: 800-227-8747 or 510-654-1879). This adventure tour specialist offers 13- to 25-day packages to such destinations as the Amazon, the High Andes, the Galápagos Islands, the Inca Trail, Machu Picchu, and Patagonia.

*Adventures on Skiis* (815 North Rd., Westfield, MA 01085; phone: 800-628-9655 or 413-568-2855). Offers skiing packages in Chile.

*Amazon Explorers* (499 Ernston Rd., Parlin, NJ 08859; phone: 908-721-2929 in New Jersey; 800-631-5650 elsewhere in the US). This veteran company offers excursions in Argentina, Bolivia, Brazil, Colombia, and Peru. Many of their trips focus on Amazon locales and expeditions, especially by boat.

*Amazon Tours and Cruises* (8700 W. Flagler, Suite 1A, Miami, FL 33174; phone: 800-423-2791 or 305-227-2266). The US representative for Iquitos-based *Amazon Camp Tourist Service,* their packages include exploration by boat and stays in jungle camps in Brazil, Colombia, and Peru.

*American Express Travel Related Services* (300 Pinnacle Way, Norcross, GA 30071; phone: 800-327-7737 or 404-368-5100). Offers full range of escorted regional and around–South America tours, as well as a variety of programs in single countries for independent travelers. The tour operator is a wholesaler, so use a travel agent.

*Big Five Expeditions* (2151 E. Dublin–Granville Rd., Suite 215, Columbus, OH 43229; phone: 800-541-2790 or 614-898-0036). Offers trips to Ecuador (including the Galápagos Islands) and Peru, with a focus on wildlife and natural history.

*Biological Journeys* (1696 Ocean Dr., McKinleyville, CA 95521; phone: 707-839-0178) This company, which emphasizes ecological awareness, offers whale watching and bird watching tours in the Galápagos Islands and mainland Ecuador.

*Brazilian Adventures* ("*Brazil Nuts*"; 1150 Post Rd., Fairfield, CT 06430; phone: 203-259-7900 in Connecticut; 800-553-9959 elsewhere in the US). These Brazilian specialists offer all the traditional itineraries — such as cruises up the Amazon and city packages in Rio and Recife. Other offerings include wide-ranging adventure programs with an emphasis on wildlife and natural history.

*Breakaway Adventure Travel* (94 Sherman St., Cambridge, MA 02140; phone: 800-955-5635). Specializes in customized tours to South America.

**Brenden Tours** (15137 Califa St., Van Nuys, CA 91411-3021; phone: 818-785-9696 in California; 800-421-8446 elsewhere in the US). Offers 3-day city packages that can be combined with 10- to 22-day escorted tours. The tour operator is a wholesaler, so use a travel agent.

**Equitour** (PO Box 807, Dubois, WY 82513; phone: 800-545-0019 or 307-455-3363). Offers horseback riding packages in Argentina, Chile, and Ecuador — for riders of all ranges of ability.

**Explorama Tours** (*Exploraciones Amazonicas S.A.;* Box 446, Iquitos, Peru; phone: 94-235471). Their tours explore the rain forest of the Amazon basin near Iquitos, Peru.

**Far Horizons** (16 Fern Lane, San Anselmo, CA 94960; phone: 415-457-4575). Special-interest archaeological and cultural trips to Easter Island as well as throughout Chile.

**Fishing International** (4010 Montecito Ave., PO Box 2132, Santa Rosa, CA 95405; phone: 800-950-4242 or 707-542-4242). Specializes in fishing and hunting packages. Offers fishing in Argentina, Chile, Colombia, Panama, and Venezuela, and bird shooting in Colombia. Also books customized packages.

**FITS Equestrian** (2011 Alamo Pintado Rd., Solvang, CA 93463; phone: 800-666-FITS or 805-688-9494). Offers horseback riding packages in Argentina and Chile — not for beginners.

**Forum Travel International** (91 Gregory Lane, Suite 21, Pleasant Hill, CA 94523; phone: 510-671-2900). Offers interesting, off-the-beaten-track itineraries, including destinations such as Brazil's Pantanal and French Guiana.

**Four Winds Travel** (PO Box 693, Old Greenwich, CT 06870; phone: 203-698-0944). Packages regional and around–South America 2- and 3-week escorted, deluxe tours.

**Frontiers International** (PO Box 959, 100 Logan Rd., Wexford, PA 15090; phone: 412-935-1577 in Pennsylvania; 800-245-1950 elsewhere in the US). These experts in top-drawer fishing and hunting trips arrange packages in Argentina, Chile, Colombia, Panama, Uruguay, and Venezuela.

**Geo Expeditions** (PO Box 3656, Sonora, CA 95370; phone: 209-532-0152 in northern California; 800-351-5041 elsewhere in the US). Specializes in natural and cultural in-depth tours to Ecuador, Peru, the Galápagos Islands, and the Amazon.

**Holbrook Travel** (3540 NW 13th St., Gainesville, FL 32609; phone: 904-377-7111 in Florida; 800-451-7111 elsewhere in the US). Offers imaginative, well-run natural history and cultural trips to the Amazon, Chile (including Patagonia), and the Galápagos Islands. Each trip is led by specialists who are knowledgeable about the culture and wildlife of the specific region.

**Ibero Travel** (PO Box 758, Forest Hills, NY 11375; phone: 718-263-0200 or 800-882-6678 in New York State; 800-654-2376 elsewhere). Offers independent city packages to Buenos Aires (Argentina), Caracas (Venezuela), Rio de Janeiro (Brazil), and Santiago (Chile).

**Inca Floats** (1311 63rd St., Emeryville, CA 94608; phone: 510-420-1550). Caters to upscale, well-traveled clients; small expeditions emphasize photo and educational opportunities. Specializes in tours to the Galápagos Islands.

**International Expeditions** (One Environs Park, Helena, AL 35080; phone: 800-633-4734 or 205-428-1700). This company specializes in ecotourism, and offers trips to the Amazon, Argentina, Chile, the Galápagos, and Venezuela. All itineraries focus on the appreciation and preservation of natural and cultural history.

**Ipanema Tours** (9911 W. Pico Blvd., Suite 580, Los Angeles, CA 90035; phone: 800-421-4200 or 213-272-2162). Locally hosted tours or country-by-country packages for independent travelers. The tour operator is a wholesaler, so use a travel agent.

*Ladatco Tours* (2220 Coral Way, Miami, FL 33145 (phone: 800-327-6162 or 305-854-8422). One of the largest tour wholesalers to South America with an extensive catalogue of locally hosted tour segments and complete itineraries; also offers a wide range of cruises. Use a travel agent.

*LATOUR* (15-22 215th St., Bayside, NY 11360; phone: 718-229-6500 in New York City; 800-825-0825 elsewhere in the US). Offers a wide range of packages, including a 19-day Grand Circle tour of South America, which visits Argentina, Brazil, Chile, and Peru. A number of 2- and 3-day city packages also are offered, which can be added onto some of the larger tours.

*Lost World Adventures* (1189 Autumn Ridge Dr., Marietta, GA 30066; phone: 404-971-8586 in Georgia; 800-999-0558 elsewhere in the continental US). While their expertise is based on Venezuela nature expeditions, this company also offers city packages to Caracas, as well as hiking, mountain biking, and horseback riding trips in various parts of the Andes, and several fishing and jungle explorations.

*Marnella Tours* (33 Walt Whitman Rd., Huntington Station, NY 11746; phone: 516-271-6969 in New York State; 800-645-6999 elsewhere in the US). Offers a wide range of independent tour programs all over the continent.

*Maupintour* (PO Box 807, Lawrence, KS 66047; phone: 913-843-1211 in Kansas; 800-255-4266 elsewhere in the US). Offers a 10-day deluxe, escorted tour of Ecuador that includes a cruise to the Galápagos Islands.

*Mountain Travel/Sobek* (6420 Fairmount Ave., El Cerrito, CA 94530; phone: 800-227-2384 or 510-527-8100). This adventure specialist offers tours throughout South America, with a focus on travel into remote areas (on foot whenever possible), mountaineering, and natural history.

*MTA International* (1717 N. Highland Ave., Los Angeles, CA 90028; phone: 213-462-6444 in California; 800-876-6824 elsewhere in the US). Their tour offerings encompass Argentina (including 1-week getaways to Buenos Aires), Brazil, Chile, Ecuador, and Peru. The tour operator is a wholesaler, so use a travel agent.

*Nature Expeditions International* (PO Box 11496, Eugene, OR 97440; phone: 800-869-0639 or 503-484-6529). Their programs in the Brazilian Amazon, Easter Island, Ecuador, the Galápagos Islands, Patagonia, and Peru emphasize wildlife, natural history, and cultural experiences.

*Olson–Travelworld* (100 N. Sepulveda Blvd., Suite 1010, El Segundo, CA 90245; phone: 800-421-5785 or 213-605-0711 in California; 800-421-2255 elsewhere in the US). Specializes in deluxe, all-inclusive, and fully escorted tours throughout South America. The tour operator is a wholesaler, so use a travel agent.

*Overseas Adventure Travel* (349 Broadway, Cambridge, MA 02139; phone: 800-221-0814 or 617-876-0533). This adventure tour operator offers a variety of trekking programs, including special family treks, in Bolivia, the Galápagos Islands, Patagonia, and Peru.

*Path Tours* (12444 Victory Blvd., Suite 407, North Hollywood, CA 91606; phone: 818-980-4442 in California; 800-843-0400 elsewhere in the US). Packages tours to Argentina, Bolivia, Brazil, Chile, Ecuador, and Peru, including skiing in Argentina and Chile. The tour operator is a wholesaler, so use a travel agent.

*Portuguese Tours* (321 Rahway Ave., Elizabeth, NJ 07202; phone: 201-352-6112 in New Jersey; 800-526-4047 elsewhere in the US). Specializes in locally hosted trips throughout Argentina, Brazil, Chile, and Uruguay.

*Questers Tours & Travel* (257 Park Ave. S., New York, NY 10010; phone: 800-468-8668 or 212-673-3120). Offers an extensive line-up of tours to Argentina, Brazil,

Chile, Ecuador, Peru, and Venezuela, with emphasis on natural history, geology, and ecology.

*Raymond & Whitcomb* (400 Madison Ave., New York, NY 10017; phone: 212-759-3960). Offers cruises in conjunction with the *American Geographical Society* to the Amazon and Patagonia. Also offered is a 20-day Art Treasures tour through South America, in conjunction with New York City's *Metropolitan Museum of Art*.

*See & Sea Travel* (50 Francisco St., Suite 205, San Francisco, CA 94133; phone: 415-434-3400 in California; 800-348-9778 elsewhere in the US). These scuba diving specialists with worldwide operations offer 2-week programs in the Galápagos Islands.

*Tara Tours* (Suite 306-A, 6595 NW 36th St., Miami, FL 33166 (phone: 305-871-1246 in Miami; 800-228-5168 elsewhere in Florida; 800-327-0080 elsewhere in the US). Packages a wide range of tours of South and Central America, with a special focus on the Amazon, Bolivia, Brazil, Ecuador, and Peru. The tour operator is a wholesaler, so use a travel agent.

*Tourlite International* (1 E. 42nd St., New York, NY 10017 (phone: 212-599-2727 in New York; 800-272-7600 elsewhere in the US). Offers city packages to Buenos Aires (Argentina) and Rio de Janeiro (Brazil), as well as 12- to 16-day escorted packages to Argentina, Brazil, and Chile.

*Travcoa* (PO Box 2630, Newport Beach, CA 92658; phone: 714-476-2800 or 800-992-2004 in California; 800-992-2003 elsewhere in the US). Their deluxe tours all over South America feature unusual cultural events and activities. The focus is on the Amazon, Easter Island, the Galápagos Islands, Machu Picchu, and Patagonia, as well as Antarctica. The tour operator is a wholesaler, so use a travel agent.

*Travel Plans International* (PO Box 3875, 1200 Harger Rd., Oak Brook, IL 60521; phone: 708-573-1400 in Illinois; 800-323-7600 elsewhere in the US). Specializes in deluxe cultural expeditions to Peru and cruises to the Galápagos.

*Unique Adventures* (9911 W. Pico Blvd., Suite 580, Los Angeles, CA 90035; phone: 800-421-4200 or 213-272-2162 in California; 800-227-3026 elsewhere in the US). This South American specialist can custom design independent packages to any part of South America. The tour operator is a wholesaler, so use a travel agent.

*Venezuela Connection* (958 Higuera St., San Luis Obispo, CA 93401; phone: 800-345-7422). Offers sport fishing packages throughout Venezuela.

*Victor Emanuel Nature Tours* (PO Box 33008, Austin, TX 78764; phone: 512-328-5221 in Austin; 800-328-VENT elsewhere in the US). For bird watching enthusiasts, their tour programs cover the continent.

*Voyagers International* (PO Box 915, Ithaca, NY 14851; phone: 800-633-0299 or 607-257-3091). Offers photographic, natural history, and ecology-oriented packages in the Andes, the Galápagos Islands, and the jungles of the Amazon basin.

*Wilderness Travel* (801 Allston Way, Berkeley, CA 94710; phone: 510-548-0420 in California; 800-247-6700 elsewhere in the US). This adventure specialist offers trekking, river, and general nature-study programs throughout South America.

*Wildland Adventures* (3516 NE 155th St., Seattle, WA 98155; phone: 800-345-4453 or 206-365-0686). Offers a wide variety of itineraries to remote areas in Argentina, Brazil, Chile, Ecuador, the Galápagos Islands, and Venezuela, as well as Antarctica.

*X.O. Travel Consultants* (38 W. 32nd St., Suite 1009, New York, NY 10001; phone: 800-262-9682 or 212-947-5530). This food, wine, and garden tour expert designs a wide variety of special-interest tours. Among their itineraries is a trip up the Amazon that focuses on the lush tropical vegetation of the region.

# Camping and RVs, Hiking and Biking

**CAMPING:** Although there are some countries and areas where camping in South America is not safe and therefore inadvisable — notably Colombia, Peru, and certain areas of other countries — camping still is an exciting way to enjoy the countryside throughout much of the continent. Before planning to pitch your tent, you should know where designated campgrounds are available and where camping is *safe*. With some planning beforehand, you can live well under the stars and enjoy the often spellbinding environment.

If you can speak some Spanish and/or Portuguese, or if you're lucky and the camp director speaks some English, you may discover that he or she is a great source of information about the region, and may even be able to arrange tours or recommend the best restaurants, shops, beaches, or attractions in the immediate area. Campgrounds also provide the atmosphere and opportunity to meet other travelers and exchange useful information.

**Where to Camp** – Camping facilities are located across the South American continent. Some national parks (see *The Wild Continent: Trekking, Backpacking, River Rafting, and Camping* in DIVERSIONS) have areas set aside for camping, but these generally do not have hookups for recreational vehicles — only private facilities do. There often are markets near the entrances to the national parks, but none inside the grounds. (*Note:* For your own safety, *never* camp along the ocean, on an empty beach, or in any other isolated area not specifically designated for camping.)

South American campgrounds are not always well marked, so it's best to have a map and check all available information. Travelers to South America will find it more difficult to collect information on camping facilities than for other destinations. Some of the best practical information is found in the South America backpacking guides done by *Bradt Enterprises*. These guides cover Argentina, Bolivia, Colombia, Ecuador, Peru, and Venezuela. This company also publishes two guides for South America river trips. Found in bookstores, these and other useful publications also are available from the *South American Explorers Club*, 126 Indian Creek Rd., Ithaca, NY 14850 (phone: 800-274-0568 or 607-277-0488).

Other sources of information include North and South American automobile clubs (see *Traveling by Car*) and other special-interest associations (see below). Once in South America, the local tourist offices may be able to provide information on facilities in their respective areas, and it also is advisable to confirm the safety of such options with the US embassy or consulate in the area. (See the individual country listings in FACTS IN BRIEF for addresses.)

Those planning to camp in the vicinity of Brazil's rain forests should be aware of the delicate ecological balance, as well as the heated controversy between those who seek to develop and exploit the jungle and those who wish to preserve it. (For more information on this volatile situation, see PERSPECTIVES.)

**Camping Equipment** – Bring all your own gear. Good camping equipment is very hard to come by in South America. And even when it is available, it is at least two or three times the US price.

■**Note:** Even if you are told that that the campground where you are staying provides purified water, to be safe you should use it only for washing (don't even brush your teeth with it). Use only bottled, purified, or boiled water for drinking. To purify tap water, either use a water purification kit (available at most camping supply stores) or bring the water to a full, *rolling* boil over a campstove. It is inadvisable to use water from streams, rivers, or lakes — even purified. (For further information on health cautions in South America, see *Staying Healthy*, in this section.)

**Organized Camping Trips** – A packaged camping tour in South America is a good way to have your cake and eat it, too. The problems of advance planning and day-to-day organizing are left to someone else, yet you still reap the benefits that shoestring travel affords and can enjoy the insights of experienced guides and the company of other campers. Be aware, however, that these packages usually are geared to the young, with ages 18 to 35 as common limits. Transfer from place to place often is by bus or van (as on other sightseeing tours); overnights are in tents, and meal arrangements vary. Often there is a kitty that covers meals in restaurants or in the camps; sometimes there is a chef, and sometimes the cooking is done by the participants themselves.

When considering a package tour, be sure to find out if equipment is included and what individual participants are required to bring. If you plan to spend a lot of time in the mountains, find out if the group's itinerary includes time to acclimatize. Some of treks offered in the higher regions are much too rigorous, even for people who are in excellent health and physical condition at sea level. (For information on companies and associations offering package tours that include camping, see "Sample Package Tours," below.)

**RECREATIONAL VEHICLES:** The term *recreational vehicles* — RVs — is applied to all manner of camping vehicles, whether towed or self-propelled. RVs will appeal most to the kind of person who prefers the flexibility of accommodations — there are a number of campgrounds in South America that provide RV hookups — and enjoys camping with a little extra comfort.

The level of comfort in an RV is limited only by the amount of money you choose to spend. They range from simple fold-down campers, which provide no more than shelter, to luxurious, fully equipped homes on wheels, requiring electrical hookups at night to run the TV set, air conditioning, and kitchen appliances. An RV undoubtedly saves a traveler a great deal of money on accommodations; in-camp cooking saves money on food as well. However, it is important to remember that renting an RV is a major expense; charges for sewage disposal, propane gas, and electricity (where available) will add to the basic campsite fee. And either driving a motorized model or towing a camper will reduce your gas mileage considerably — a consideration in most parts of South America, as gasoline usually is more expensive than in the US.

It is possible to rent motorized RVs and towable campers in South America, however, they are not as common as in the US and elsewhere — so you may have to do some calling around. As with regular car rentals, they generally will be more expensive than rentals in the US. RV rental rates in South America generally vary depending on the size and complexity of the RV and the number of days rented, and may include customer pick-up and drop-off services at the airport. A common source of vans and towable campers (as well as the larger types of RVs) are the car rental companies listed in *Traveling By Car* in this section. The tourist board offices also may be able to provide recommendations on RV rental sources, as well as where they are permitted.

Useful information on RVs is available from the following sources:

*Living on Wheels* by Richard A. Wolters. Provides useful information on how to choose and operate a recreational vehicle. Though it's currently out of print, check your library.

*Recreational Vehicle Industry Association* (*RVIA;* Dept. RK, PO Box 2999, Reston, VA 22090-0999). Issues a useful complimentary package of information on RVs, as well as a 24-page magazine-size guide, *Set Free in an RV* ($3), and a free catalogue of RV sources and consumer information. Write to the association for these and other publications.

*Recreational Vehicle Rental Association* (*RVRA;* 3251 Old Lee Hwy., Suite 500, Fairfax, VA 22030; phone: 800-336-0355 or 703-591-7130). This RV dealers group publishes an annual rental directory, *Who's Who in RV Rentals* ($7.50).

*TL Enterprises* (29901 Agoura Rd., Agoura, CA 91301; phone: 818-991-4980) publishes two monthly magazines for RV enthusiasts: *Motorhome* ($17.98 for a year's subscription) and *Trailer Life* ($14.98 for a year's subscription). Members of the *TL Enterprises' Good Sam Club* can subscribe to each of these magazines at discounted rates ($12 and $11, respectively), and also receive discounts on a variety of RV services. Membership costs $19 per year.

*Trailblazer* (1000 124th Ave. NE, Bellevue, WA 98005; phone: 206-455-8585). A recreational vehicle and motorhome magazine. A year's subscription costs $24.

**HIKING:** *Never head out for a jaunt in the South American wilderness unless you first check on the safety conditions in the area.* The US Department of State operates a *Citizens' Emergency Center* for up-to-the-minute information on trouble spots, travel advisories, health information, and visa requirements; before leaving, call them at 202-647-5225. Upon arrival, the nearest US consulate or embassy can provide the most up-to-date information on the safety conditions in the area (the addresses are given in *Legal Aid and Consular Services;* also see *Crime in South America* — both are in this section).

If you would rather eliminate all the gear and planning and take to the outdoors unencumbered, park the car and go for a day's hike. It can break up long journeys by car and, more than just giving riders a chance to stretch their legs, is a great way to get to know the country. There are fabulous trails throughout South America. For information on some of the best routes for exploring on foot in South America, see *The Wild Continent: Trekking, Backpacking, River Rafting, and Camping,* in DIVERSIONS.

For those who are hiking on their own, without benefit of a guide or group — not recommended — a map of the trail is a must. Maps of some areas may be available from the local military, but marked trails, both on the maps and in the mountains, are not as complete as those the US American Forest Service issues. Markers range from very poor to nonexistent, so be prepared to get lost more than once, even with a compass.

Many areas of South America are covered by maps in the *International Travel Maps (ITM)* series. These and other maps of use to hikers (and other outdoor adventurers) are available from *Map Link* (25 E. Mason St., Suite 201, Santa Barbara, CA 93101; phone: 805-965-4402), one of the best sources for detailed topographical maps and just about any other type of map (of just about anywhere in the world). Their comprehensive guide *The World Map Directory* ($29.95) includes a wealth of sources for travelers afoot, and if they don't stock a map of the area in which you are interested (or the type of map best suited to your outdoor exploration), they will order it for you. Their stock of topographical maps includes maps of most South American countries. (For information on companies and associations offering package tours that include hiking, see "Sample Package Tours," below.)

**BIKING:** *Before bicycling off on your own into any part of South America, first check on the safety of the area.* See *Crime in South America,* in this section, for specific cautions, and contact the US State Department (see "Hiking," above) and a US embassy or consulate (the addresses may be found in the individual country entries in FACTS IN BRIEF).

For young and/or fit travelers, a bicycle offers a marvelous tool for exploring. Biking does have its drawbacks: Little baggage can be carried, travel is slow, and cyclists are exposed to the elements — in South America, the combined effects of wind and sun can be enervating. And in some areas unless you are in exceptionally good shape and are an avid bike rider at home, you may find steep mountainous terrain and thinner air of the higher altitudes a deterrent to biking. Nevertheless, a lot of people in South America do use bicycles for transportation, and it is not uncommon to join a local cyclist pedaling away, calmly, on desert and mountain highways.

Good maps infinitely improve a biking trip, especially those that provide detailed and clear road references. Good sources of maps, recommendations on popular scenic routes, and other information useful to cyclists are the local tourist authorities (see FACTS IN BRIEF for addresses) and the cycling associations listed below. *Map Link* (see "Hiking," above) also is a good source of maps suitable for cyclists planning South American routes. For general biking information, consult *The Complete Book of Bicycling,* by Eugene A. Sloane (Simon & Schuster; $15.95), and *Anybody's Bike Book,* by Tom Cuthberson (Ten Speed Press; $8.95).

■ **Note:** When biking, wear bright clothes and use lights or wear reflective material to increase your visibility at dusk or at night. Above all, even though many cyclists don't, *always* wear a helmet.

**Renting a Bike** – If you can read the native language, consult local phone directories for bicycle shops; the local tourist authorities also may be able to point you to sources of bicycle rentals. Except in metropolitan areas, you are not likely to find as wide a selection as in the US. The available models *may* include basic (one-gear), 10-speed, and the increasingly popular mountain bikes. As there is no guarantee, however, of the availability or condition of rentals, serious cyclists may prefer to bring their own bikes.

Airlines generally allow bicycles to be checked as baggage; they require that the pedals be removed, handlebars be turned sideways, and the bike be in a shipping carton (which some airlines provide, subject to availability — call ahead to make sure). If buying a shipping carton from a bicycle shop, check the airline's specifications and also ask about storing the carton at the destination airport so that you can use it again for the return flight. Although some airlines charge only a nominal fee, if the traveler already has checked two pieces of baggage, there may be an additional excess baggage charge of $70 to $80 for the bicycle. As regulations vary from carrier to carrier, be sure to call well before departure to find out your airline's specific regulations. If you plan to transport your bike on flights within South America, it is particularly important to check in advance with the local carrier as the smaller planes used may have limited baggage facilities. As with other baggage, make sure that the bike is thoroughly labeled with your name, a business address and phone number, and the correct airport destination code.

**Organized Biking Trips** – A number of organizations offer bike tours in South America. Linking up with a bike tour is more expensive than traveling alone, but with experienced leaders, an organized tour often becomes an educational, as well as a very social, experience. In addition, traveling with a group is *safer.*

One of the attractions of a bike tour is that the shipment of equipment — the bike — is handled by the organizers, and the shipping fee is included in the total tour package. Travelers simply deliver the bike to the airport, already disassembled and boxed; shipping cartons can be obtained from most bicycle shops with little difficulty. Bicylists not with a tour must make their own arrangements with the airline, and there are no standard procedures for this (see above). Although some tour organizers will rent bikes, most prefer that participants bring a bike with which they are already familiar. Another attraction of *some* tours is the existence of a "sag wagon" to carry extra luggage, fatigued cyclists, and their bikes, too, when pedaling another mile is impossible.

Tours vary considerably in style and ambience, so request brochures from several operators in order to make the best decision. When contacting groups, be sure to ask about the maximum number of people on the trip, the maximum number of miles to be traveled each day, and the degree of difficulty of the biking; these details should determine which tour you join and can greatly affect your enjoyment of the experience. Planning ahead is essential because trips often fill up 6 months or more in advance. (For information on companies and associations offering package tours that include biking, see the list below.)

## GETTING READY / Camping and RVs, Hiking and Biking 69

**SAMPLE PACKAGE TOURS:** A number of companies offer tours that feature camping, hiking, and biking, as well as other outdoor activites. While many of them specialize in outdoor adventure packages, others include these activities as part of broader tour programs. Among such companies are the following:

*Above the Clouds Trekking* (PO Box 398, Worchester, MA 01602; phone: 800-233-4499). Offers trekking packages in Argentina, many of which involve camping.

*American Wilderness Experience* (PO Box 1486, Boulder, CO 80306; phone: 800-444-0099). This adventure specialist offers extensive hiking excursions among a variety of adventure packages throughout South America.

*Barron Adventures* (PO Box 3180, Long Beach, CA 90803; phone: 213-438-5664). This adventure, trekking, and expedition specialist, offers 10- and 14-day packages in Peru, and a 21-day Amazon basin expedition. In addition to exploration afoot, horseback riding and rafting also are included.

*Mountain Travel/Sobek* (6420 Fairmont Ave., El Cerrito, CA 94530 (phone: 800-227-2384 or 510-527-8100). This adventure package specialist offers a wide variety of trips in South America, including camping, hiking/trekking, canoeing, and rafting packages in Argentina, Brazil, Chile, Ecuador, Peru, and Venezuela. Hiking expeditions range from easy walks that can be undertaken by anyone in good health to those that require basic or advanced mountaineering experience.

*Nature Expeditions International* (PO Box 11496, Eugene, OR 97440; phone: 800-869-0639 or 503-484-6529). Coordinates cultural and historical study tours throughout South America which involve hiking the sites.

*Overseas Adventure Travel* (349 Broadway, Cambridge, MA 02139; phone: 800-221-0814 or 617-876-0533). Among several South American itineraries is a 21-day camping and hiking expedition through Ecuador, Peru, and the Galápagos Islands. Also occasionally offers biking trips in South America, with an inn-to-inn tour of Ecuador scheduled for this year.

*Wilderness Travel* (811 Allston Way, Berkeley, CA 94710; phone: 510-548-0420 in California; 800-247-6700 elsewhere in the US). Offers 10- to 16-day hiking expedition packages to Argentina, Bolivia, Chile, Ecuador, and Peru.

*Wildland Adventures* (3516 NE 155th St., Seattle, WA 98155; phone: 800-345-4453 or 206-365-0686). Offers a number of leisurely hiking trips in Argentina, Brazil, Ecuador, and Peru, exploring local reefs, ruins, and rain forests.

*Willard's Adventure Club* (Box 10, Barrie, Ontario, L4M 4S9 Canada; phone: 705-737-1881). Features a 16-day hiking and camping expedition in Peru, culminating in a trek to Machu Picchu.

*Yamnuska* (PO Box 1920, 1316 Railway Ave., Canmore, Alberta, T0L 0M0 Canada; phone: 403-678-4164). Offers hiking and trekking expeditions in the Patagonia region of Chile.

In addition to the wilderness specialists listed above, if you are interested in braving the more mountainous regions of South America, you also may want to contact the *American Alpine Institute* (1212 24th St., Bellingham, WA 98225; phone: 206-671-1505), a specialist in mountain climbing expeditions. The institute offers 3- to 4-week organized climbing trips in Argentina, Bolivia, and Ecuador. For further information on climbing the highest peaks, see *Because It's There: Mountain Climbing* in DIVERSIONS.

Another alternative to dealing directly with the above companies is to contact *All Adventure Travel*, a specialist in hiking and biking trips worldwide. This company, which acts as a representative for numerous special tour packagers offering such outdoor adventures, can provide a wealth of detailed information about each packager and programs offered. They also will help you design and arrange all aspects of a

## 70 GETTING READY / Camping and RVs, Hiking and Biking

personalized itinerary. This company operates much like a travel agency, collecting commissions from the packagers. Therefore, there is no additional charge for these services. For information, contact *All Adventure Travel,* PO Box 4307, Boulder, CO 80306 (phone: 800-537-4025 or 303-499-1981).

■ **Note:** The *Specialty Travel Index* (305 San Anselmo Ave., Suite 217, San Anselmo, CA 94960; phone: 415-459-4900 in California; 800-442-4942 elsewhere in the US) is a directory to special-interest travel and an invaluable resource. Listings include tour operators specializing in camping, as well as myriad other interests that combine nicely with a camping trip, such as biking, motorcycling, horseback riding, canoeing, scuba diving, and river rafting. It costs $6 per copy, $10 for a year's subscription of two issues.

**ADDITIONAL RESOURCES:** Other useful sources of information on bicyling in South America include the following:

*American Youth Hostels* (PO Box 37613, Washington, DC 20013-7613; phone: 202-783-6161). This nonprofit organization and its local chapters regularly sponsor a number of foreign hiking and biking tours, including trips to South America. Membership is open to all ages and departures are geared to various age groups and levels of skill and frequently feature accommodations in hostels — along with hotels for adults and campgrounds for younger participants. Contact them for information on current or forthcoming offerings.

*International Bicycle Touring Society* (*IBTS;* PO Box 6979, San Diego, CA 92106-0979; phone: 619-226-TOUR). Regularly sponsors low-cost bicycle tours led by member volunteers. Participants must be over 21. For information, send them $2 plus a self-addressed, stamped envelope.

*League of American Wheelmen* (190 W. Ostend St., Suite 1208, Baltimore, MD 21230; phone: 301-539-3399). This organziation publishes *Tourfinder,* a list of organizations that sponsor bicycle tours of the US and abroad. The list is free with membership ($25 individual, $30 family) and can be obtained by nonmembers who send $5. The *League* also can put you in touch with biking groups in your area.

*Sierra Club* (Outing Dept., 730 Polk St., San Francisco, CA 94109; phone: 415-776-2211). Dedicated to preserving and protecting the natural environment, this nonprofit organization also offers numerous trips each year, including both walking tours and trips which combine hiking and biking. Some are backpacking trips, moving to a new camp each day; others make day hikes from a base camp. Recent offerings included hiking/camping trips in Argentina, Brazil, Ecuador, and Peru.

# **Preparing**

## Calculating Costs

A realistic appraisal of travel expenses is the most crucial bit of planning you will undertake before any trip. It also is, unfortunately, one for which it is most difficult to give precise, practical advice.

Even considering the effects of soaring inflation and the ongoing devaluation of most South American currencies, a vacation to South America normally will cost less than the equivalent time spent in Europe. In capitals and major resort areas, the cost difference between the two continents may be narrowing for hotel accommodations. Meals, services, and local transportation (except car rentals) still cost far less in South America, and the competition for North American visitors often works to inspire some suprisingly affordable travel opportunities.

In South America, estimating travel expenses depends on the mode of transportation you choose, the part or parts of the continent you plan to visit, how long you will stay, and in some cases, what time of year you plan to travel. In addition to the basics of transportation, hotels, meals, and sightseeing, you have to take into account seasonal price changes that apply on certain air routings and in popular resort areas, as well as the vagaries of currency exchange.

In general, it's usually a good idea to organize your trip so that you pay for as much of it as you can in South America, using local currency purchased from South American banks (which, barring interim variations, generally offer a more advantageous rate of exchange than US sources). That means minimizing the amount of advance deposits paid in US greenbacks and deferring as many bills as possible until you arrive on the continent, although the economies possible through prepaid package tours and other special deals may offset the savings in currency exchange. (For further information on managing money abroad, see *Credit and Currency,* in this section.)

**DETERMINING A BUDGET:** When calculating costs, start with the basics, the major expenses being transportation, accommodations, and food. However, don't forget such extras as local transportation, shopping, and such miscellaneous items as laundry and tips. The reasonable cost of these items usually is a positive surprise to your budget. Entries in the individual city reports in THE CITIES give helpful information on local transportation options.

Other expenses, such as the cost of local sightseeing tours and other excursions, will vary from city to city. Tourist information offices are plentiful throughout South America, and most of the better hotels will have someone at the front desk to provide a rundown on the costs of local tours and full-day excursions in and out of the city. Travel agents also can provide this information.

Services, facilities, and meals are either substantially less expensive in South American cities than in major US cities — such as New York — or just plain reasonable, as in Bogotá, Quito, Panama City, Caracas, Lima, La Paz, Asunción, Santiago, Buenos Aires, and Montevideo. Throughout South America, you also will find a great divergence in prices between cities, resort areas, and countryside.

Rural areas offer some of the best travel bargains in the Hemisphere. Haciendas in Colombia and Ecuador, lakeside lodges in Chile, small hotels near pre-Columbian sites in Peru and in colonial centers in Bolivia have comfortable accommodations and fair to fine local cuisine at suprisingly economical prices. In addition to their price-is-right feature, they also are right in or near places you will want to see. The major drawback to planning to stay awhile in the countryside is the limited number of rooms available; this means that trips have to be planned well in advance, especially to well-known areas. Another inconvenience is that, away from the metropolitan areas, travelers will find English even less prevalent, so at least a basic command of Spanish (or in Brazil, Portuguese) often is necessary.

Budget-minded families can take advantage of some of the more economical accommodations options to be found in South America (see our discussion of accommodations in *On the Road*, in this section). Campgrounds are particularly inexpensive and they are located throughout the continent (see *Camping and RVs, Hiking and Biking*, in this section). Picnicking is another excellent way to cut costs, and South America abounds with well-groomed parks, beaches, and idyllic pastoral settings. A stop at a local market can provide a feast of regional delicacies at a surprisingly economical price compared to the cost of a restaurant lunch. (Do, however, read our warnings about fresh produce in *Staying Healthy*, in this section.)

In planning any travel budget, it also is wise to allow a realistic amount for both entertainment and recreation. Are you planning to spend time sightseeing and visiting local tourist attractions? Do you intend to rent a catamaran or take sailing lessons? Is daily golf, tennis, or skiing a part of your plan? Will your children be disappointed if they don't take a guided tour of Inca ruins or go on a jungle wildlife expedition? Finally, don't forget that if haunting discotheques, nightclubs, or other nightspots is an essential part of your vacation, or you feel that one performance of the *Caracas Symphony Orchestra* at the *Teatro Municipal* may not be enough, allow for the extra cost of nightlife.

If at any point in the planning process it appears impossible to estimate expenses, consider this suggestion: The easiest way to put a ceiling on the price of all these elements is to buy a package tour. A totally planned and escorted one, with almost all transportation, rooms, meals, sightseeing, local travel, tips, and a dinner show or two included and prepaid, provides a pretty exact total of what the trip will cost beforehand, and the only surprise will be the one you spring on yourself by succumbing to some irresistible, expensive souvenir. And keep in mind, particularly when calculating the major expenses, that costs vary according to fluctuations in the exchange rate — that is, how much of a given foreign currency a dollar will buy.

■ **Note:** As we went to press, the continuing devaluation of many South American currencies and the resulting volatility of exchange rates, as well as rampant inflation, have created a difficult situation for prospective travelers trying to calculate a travel budget to South America. Between the time you originally make your hotel reservations and arrive, the price in US dollars may vary substantially from the price originally quoted. To avoid paying more than you expected, it's wise to confirm rates by writing directly to hotels or by calling their representative in the US.

# Planning a Trip

Travelers fall into two categories: those who make lists and those who do not. Some people prefer to plot the course of their trip to the finest detail, with contingency plans and alternatives at the ready. For others, the joy of a voyage is its spontaneity; exhaustive planning only lessens the thrill of anticipation and the sense of freedom.

## GETTING READY / Planning a Trip

Neither approach works perfectly in South America. It is an area that requires considerable preparation; internal flights sometimes run only once or twice a week, and an advance booking can mean the difference between continuing to a new city or cooling your heels for several days awaiting another flight. On the other hand, fanatic planners will have to live with a degree of improvisation; arrangements for some of the most exciting tours — into jungles, along rivers, to South America's fantastic natural wonders — are best made from nearby cities after your arrival.

For most travelers, any week-plus trip to South America can be too expensive for an "I'll take my chances" type of attitude . Even perennial gypsies and anarchistic wanderers have to take into account the time-consuming logistics of getting around, and even with minimal baggage, they need to think about packing. Hence, at least some planning is crucial.

This is not to suggest that you work out your itinerary in minute detail before you go; but it's still wise to decide certain basics at the very start: where to go, what to do, and how much to spend. These decisions require a certain amount of consideration. So before rigorously planning specific details, you might want to establish your general travel objectives:

1. How much time will you have for the entire trip, and how much of it are you willing to spend getting where you're going?
2. What interests and/or activities do you want to pursue while on vacation? Do you want to visit one, a few, or several different places?
3. At what time of year do you want to go?
4. What kind of topography or climate would you prefer?
5. Do you want peace and privacy or lots of activity and company?
6. How much money can you afford to spend for the entire vacation?

Sources of information on travel in South America are not as numerous as they are for some destinations, but one excellent resource for planning a trip to the continent is the *South American Explorers Club*. With offices in Ithaca (New York), Lima (Peru), and Quito (Ecuador), their help can be had both before and during a trip. The club is a nonprofit organization and offers none of the standard travel agency services (such as reservations, bookings, and so on) before you leave the US, but it does offer members some of these services once in South America. It also provides a vast amount of first-hand material in the form of reports provided by members who have just returned from their South American sojourns. These reports include prices, where to get the best exchange rates, problems to be wary about, and other useful information, although the club is careful to be unbiased and does not give preferential treatment to any businesses or organizations. Other benefits of membership include a subscription to the club's magazine and discounts on guidebooks; the club's Lima branch even provides storage for equipment and valuables and will sell equipment left by members on previous travels (some of these items are very difficult to find in South America). The tax-deductible membership fee is $25 per person, $35 per couple. Contact the *South American Explorers Club* at 126 Indian Creek Rd., Ithaca, NY 14850 (phone: 800-274-0568 or 607-277-0488). In Lima, they are located at 146 Av. Republica de Portugal, Brena, but mail should be sent to them at 3714 Casilla, Lima 100, Peru. The newest office is in Quito, at 1254 Toledo, La Floresta, Quito, Ecuador (phone: 2-566076); mail should be addressed to Apartado 21-431, Eloy Alfaró, Quito, Ecuador.

Beyond this club, however, you may find it somewhat difficult to collect background and/or current information on travel in South America. You can seek the assistance of travel agents, airlines and cruise ship lines serving South American routes, or use general travel sources such as reliable, yearly updated guidebooks and maps. Motor clubs (see *Traveling by Car)* often can be a good source for brochures and maps, but, in general, there are few good descriptive tourist brochures for South America. (Ecuador's and Chile's are among the best.) Government departments and private clubs

**74 GETTING READY / Planning a Trip**

focusing on outdoor activities and other special interests also may be able to provide information in English.

Of the South American governments, at press time, only Argentina, Brazil, Ecuador, French Guiana, Peru, and Uruguay had tourist offices in the US, and South American consulates and embassies in the US (see FACTS IN BRIEF for individual country listings) are not known for replying punctually (or at all) to written requests for information on tourist facilities or activities. Local tourist offices in South America cannot be counted on to mail materials either; however, they can be very helpful once you arrive in a country — plan on stopping in each city's office on your route. In the US, a visit or phone call to the sales office of an airline with extensive routes on the continent may be more useful. The US Department of State also has a number of free brochures that contain helpful information for travelers in South America. One particularly useful booklet is *Tips for Travelers to Central and South America.* This and other publications can be obtained from the Washington Passport Agency, 1425 K St. NW, Washington, DC 20524 (phone: 202-647-0518).

You now can make almost all of your own travel arrangements if you have time to follow through with hotels, airlines, tour operators, and so on. But you'll probably save considerable time and energy if you have a travel agent make arrangements for you. The agent also should be able to advise you of alternate arrangements of which you may not be aware. Only rarely will a travel agent's services cost a traveler any money, and they may even save you some (see *How to Use a Travel Agent,* below).

Pay particular attention to the dates when off-season rates go into effect. In major resort areas, accommodations may cost less during the off-season (and the weather often is perfectly acceptable at this time). Off-season rates frequently are lower for car rentals and other facilities, too. In general, it is a good idea to be aware of holiday weeks, as rates at hotels generally are higher during these periods and rooms normally are heavily booked.

Make plans early. At the peak of the resort season (December through February), hotel reservations are required months in advance for popular destinations such as beach resorts in Argentina, Brazil, Chile, Panama, and Uruguay. If you plan to attend *Carnaval* in Rio de Janeiro or anywhere else, be prepared to book as much as 10 months to a year in advance at one of the big hotels, and expect to pay considerably more than you would for the same accommodations at any other time. If you are flying at peak times and want to benefit from the savings of discount fares or charter programs, purchase tickets as far ahead as possible. Charter flights (although they are few and far between to the continent) to certain popular destinations — most commonly Buenos Aires — may be completely sold out months in advance. South American hotels may require deposits before they will guarantee reservations, and this most often is the case during peak travel periods. (Be sure to request a receipt for any deposit or use a credit card.) Travel during *Easter Week,* the *Christmas/New Year* period, and local festival and national holiday times also requires reservations well in advance in South America.

Before your departure, find out what the weather is likely to be at your destination. Consult FACTS IN BRIEF for country-specific information on climatic variations and see *When to Go,* in this section, for a chart of average temperatures in South America. See *How to Pack,* also in this section, for some suggestions on how to decide what clothes to take. This information, details regarding special events that may occur during your stay, and essential information on local transportation and other services and resources, also may be found in the individual city reports of THE CITIES.

Make a list of any valuable items you are carrying with you, including credit card numbers and the serial numbers of your traveler's checks. Put copies in your purse or pocket and leave other copies at home. Put a label with your name and home address on the inside of your luggage for identification in case of loss. Put your name and business address — *never your home address* — on a label on the outside of your luggage. (Those who run businesses from home should use the office address of a friend or relative.)

Review your travel documents. If you are traveling by air, check that your ticket has been filled in correctly. The left side of the ticket should have a list of each stop you will make (even if you are only stopping to change planes), beginning with your departure point. Be sure that the list is correct, and count the number of copies to see that you have one for each plane you will take. If you have confirmed reservations, be sure that the column marked "status" says "OK" beside each flight. Have in hand vouchers or proof of payment for any reservation for which you've paid in advance; this includes hotels, transfers to and from the airport, sightseeing tours, car rentals, and tickets to special events.

Although policies vary from carrier to carrier, it's still smart to call to reconfirm your flight 48 to 72 hours before departure, both going and returning. Reconfirmation is recommended for all international flights, however, it is an absolute *must* for point-to-point flights within South America. If you will be driving while in South America, bring your driver's license and any other necessary documentation — such as proof of insurance.

Before traveling to South America, you should consider learning some basic Spanish and/or Portuguese. If you stick to the major resort areas and other popular tourist destinations, you probably can get by without some language facility. However, English is far from the *lingua franca*. Your trip will be much more rewarding and enjoyable (and, in some instances, safer) if you can communicate with the people who live in the countries you will be visiting.

Most adult education programs and community colleges offer courses in Spanish, and a good many teach Portuguese, too. Berlitz, among others, has a series of teach-yourself language courses on audiocassette tapes. To order the Berlitz tapes, send $15.95 (plus postage and handling) to Macmillan Publishing Co., 100 Front St., Riverside, NJ 08075 (phone: 800-257-5755).

South Americans do not frown on or criticize beginners' attempts at speaking their language; rather, they enthusiastically encourage you to continue fumbling your way through prepositional phrases by smiling and profusely assuring you that "*Usted habla bien el castellano*" ("You speak Spanish well") or "*Voce fala bom portugués*" ("You speak good Portuguese"). For information on pronunciation and a list of common travel terms, see *Useful Words and Phrases,* in this section; an introduction to a number of native drinks and dishes that you may encounter can be found in *Food and Drink,* PERSPECTIVES.

Finally, you always should bear in mind that despite the most careful plans, things do not always occur on schedule — especially in South America, where *ahora* ("now") means anytime between today and tomorrow, and *ahorita* ("right now") means anytime within the next few hours. If you maintain a flexible attitude and try to accept minor disruptions as less than cataclysmic, you will enjoy yourself a lot more.

# How to Use a Travel Agent

A reliable travel agent remains the best source of service and information for planning a trip, whether you have a specific itinerary and require an agent only to make reservations or you need extensive help in sorting through the maze of airfares, tour offerings, hotel packages, and the scores of other arrangements that may be involved in a trip to South America.

**Know what you want from a travel agent so that you can evaluate what you are getting.** It is perfectly reasonable to expect your agent to be a thoroughly knowledgeable travel specialist, with information about your destination and, even more crucial, a command of current airfares, ground arrangements, and other wrinkles in the travel scene.

**Most travel agents work through computer reservations systems (CRS).** These are used to assess the availability and cost of flights, hotels, and car rentals, and through them they can book reservations. Despite reports of "computer bias," in which a computer may favor one airline over another, the CRS should provide agents with the entire spectrum of flights available to a given destination and the complete range of fares in considerably less time than it takes to telephone the airlines individually — and at no extra cost to the client.

**Make the most intelligent use of a travel agent's time and expertise; understand the economics of the industry.** As a client, traditionally you pay nothing for the agent's services; with few exceptions, it's all free, from hotel bookings to advice on package tours. Any money the travel agent makes on the time spent arranging your itinerary — booking hotels, resorts, or flights, or suggesting activities — comes from commissions paid by the suppliers of these services — the airlines, hotels, and so on. These commissions generally run from 10% to 15% of the total cost of the service, although suppliers often reward agencies that sell their services in volume with an increased commission, called an override. In most instances, you'll find that travel agents make their time and experience available to you at no charge, and you do not pay more for an airline ticket, package tour, or other product bought from a travel agent than you would for the same one bought directly from the supplier.

**Exceptions to the general rule of free service by a travel agency are the agencies that practice net pricing.** In essence, such agencies return their commissions and overrides to their customers and make their income by charging a flat fee per transaction instead (thus adding a charge after a reduction for the commission has been made). Net fares and fees are a growing practice, though hardly widespread.

**Even a conventional travel agent sometimes may charge a fee for special services.** These chargeable items may include long-distance telephone or cable costs incurred in making a booking, for reserving a room in a place that does not pay a commission (such as a small, out-of-the way hotel), or for a special attention such as planning a highly personalized itinerary. A fee also may be assessed in instances of deeply discounted airfares.

**Choose a travel agent with the same care with which you would choose a doctor or lawyer.** You will be spending a good deal of money on the basis of the agent's judgment, so you have a right to expect that judgment to be mature, informed, and interested. At the moment, unfortunately, there aren't many standards within the travel agent industry to help you gauge competence, and the quality of individual agents varies enormously.

**At present, only nine states have registration, licensing, or other forms of travel agent–related legislation on their books.** Rhode Island licenses travel agents; Florida, Hawaii, Iowa, and Ohio register them; and California, Illinois, Oregon, and Washington have laws governing the sale of transportation or related services. While state licensing of agents cannot absolutely guarantee competence, it can at least ensure that an agent has met some minimum requirements.

Perhaps the best-prepared agents are those who have completed the CTC Travel Management program offered by the *Institute of Certified Travel Agents (ICTA)* and carry the initials CTC (Certified Travel Counselor) after their names. This indicates a relatively high level of expertise. For a free list of CTCs in your area, send a self-addressed, stamped, #10 envelope to *ICTA,* 148 Linden St., Box 82-56, Wellesley, MA 02181 (phone: 617-237-0280 in Massachusetts; 800-542-4282 elsewhere in the US).

An agent's membership in the *American Society of Travel Agents (ASTA)* can be a useful guideline in making a selection. But keep in mind that *ASTA* is an industry organization, requiring only that its members be licensed in those states where required; be accredited to represent the suppliers whose products they sell, including airline and cruise tickets; and adhere to its Principles of Professional Conduct and Ethics code. *ASTA* does not guarantee the competence, ethics, or financial soundness of its members, but it does offer some recourse if you feel you have been dealt with unfairly. Complaints may be registered with *ASTA* (Consumer Affairs Dept., 1101 King St., Alexandria, VA 22314; phone: 703-739-2782). First try to resolve the complaint directly with the supplier. For a list of *ASTA* members in your area, send a self-addressed, stamped, #10 envelope to *ASTA,* Public Relations Dept., at the address above.

There also is the *Association of Retail Travel Agents (ARTA),* a smaller but highly respected trade organization similar to *ASTA.* Its member agencies and agents similarly agree to abide by a code of ethics, and complaints about a member can be made to *ARTA*'s Grievance Committee, 1745 Jeff Davis Hwy., Arlington, VA 22202-3402 (phone: 800-969-6069 or 703-553-7777).

Perhaps the best way to find a travel agent is by word of mouth. If the agent (or agency) has done a good job for your friends over a period of time, it probably indicates a certain level of commitment and competence. Always ask not only for the name of the company, but also for the name of the specific agent with whom your friends dealt, for it is that individual who will serve you, and quality can vary widely within a single agency. There are some superb travel agents in the business, and they can facilitate vacation or business arrangements.

# Entry Requirements and Documents

All of the countries described in this guide require visitors to produce some legal documentation. However you chose to travel to South America, the only universal entry requirement for US citizens is a current passport (for information on obtaining or renewing a passport, see "Passports," below), and that same passport also is needed to re-enter the US. Most countries also require an ongoing or round-trip ticket and some countries also require a tourist card or visa. A few governments also impose a departure tax. For information on the specific entry requirements of the destinations discussed in this guide, see FACTS IN BRIEF. For resident aliens of the US, the requirements are determined by their country of origin, and they should inquire at the nearest consulate or embassy of each country they plan to visit to find out what documents they need to enter South America.

Generally, entering South American countries by air is a routine matter. Customs and immigration officials at airports tend to be fairly easygoing and usually will process anyone who looks reasonable in a few minutes without any hassle. Some countries require that you fill in an embarkation-disembarkation card. At major international airports, such as Rio de Janeiro, São Paulo, Buenos Aires, and Santiago, sophisticated computer technology enables immigration agents to punch in your passport number and quickly obtain clearance.

Yellow fever vaccinations are now required only for entering French Guiana from the US. Other countries in South America require vaccination certificates only if the traveler is arriving from an area of contagion as defined by the World Health Organization and, as the US is considered "free from contagion," an international vaccination certificate is not required for US citizens. Note, however, that some South American countries are *themselves* considered areas of contagion and travelers from the US who visit these countries may have to obtain a vaccination certificate before they can enter one that is considered contagion-free. In addition, there are a number of vaccinations that travelers to South America would be well advised to have before leaving and medicines that should be brought along, particularly if traveling in jungle areas. (See *Staying Healthy,* in this section, for our recommendations and other information on health concerns and precautions.)

Although the applicable period varies from country to country, if planning a stay of 6 months or longer in South America, you should check the individual governments' vaccination and other requirements. Some countries — such as Chile — now also require proof that anyone entering the country for an extended stay is free from AIDS (Acquired Immune Deficiency Syndrome). Check and arrange for any such required tests and health certificates well before your departure date.

**PASSPORTS:** While traveling in South America, carry your passport with you at all times (for an exception to this rule, see our note "When Checking In," below). If you lose your passport while abroad, immediately report the loss to the nearest US embassy or consulate (see FACTS IN BRIEF for information on locations in South America). You can get a 3-month temporary passport directly from the consulate, but you must fill out a "loss of passport" form and follow the same application procedure — and pay the same fees — as you did for the original (see below). It's likely to speed things up if you have a record of your passport number and the place and date of its issue (a photocopy of the first page of your passport is perfect). Keep this information separate from your passport — you might want to give it to a traveling companion to hold or put it in the bottom of your suitcase.

US passports are now valid for 10 years from the date of issue (5 years for those under age 18). The expired passport itself is not renewable, but must be turned in along with your application for a new and valid one (you will get it back, voided, when you receive the new one). Normal passports contain 24 pages, but frequent travelers can request a 48-page passport at no extra cost. Every individual, regardless of age, must have his or her own passport. Family passports no longer are issued.

Passports can be renewed by mail with forms obtained at designated locations only if the expired passport was issued no more than 12 years before the date of application for renewal and if it was not issued before the applicant's 16th birthday. The rules for renewal regarding teens under 16 and younger applicants may vary depending on age and when their previous passport was issued. Those who are eligible to apply by mail must send the completed form with the expired passport, two photos (see description below), and $40 (which includes a $10 execution fee) to the nearest passport agency office. Delivery can take as little as 2 weeks or as long as 6 weeks during the busiest season — from approximately mid-March to mid-September.

Adults applying for the first time and younger applicants who must apply for a passport in person (as well as those who cannot wait for mail application turn around) can do so at one of the following places:

1. The State Department passport agencies in Boston, Chicago, Honolulu, Houston, Long Beach (California), Miami, New Orleans, New York City, Philadelphia, San Francisco, Seattle, Stamford, CT, and Washington, DC.
2. A federal or state courthouse.
3. Any of the 1,000 post offices across the country with designated acceptance facilities.

Application blanks are available at all these offices and must be presented with the following:

1. Proof of US citizenship. This can be a previous passport or one in which you were included. If you are applying for your first passport and were born in the United States, an original or certified birth certificate is the required proof. If you were born abroad, a Certificate of Naturalization, a Certificate of Citizenship, a Report of Birth Abroad of a Citizen of the United States, or a Certification of Birth is necessary.

## GETTING READY / Entry Requirements and Documents 79

2. Two 2-by-2-inch, front-view photographs in color or black and white, with a light, plain background, taken within the previous 6 months. These must be taken by a photographer rather than a machine.
3. A $65 passport fee ($40 for travelers under 16), which includes a $10 execution fee. *Note:* Your best bet is to bring the exact amount in cash (no change is given), or a separate check or money order for each passport (although a family can combine several passport fees on one check or money order).
4. Proof of identity. Again, this can be a previous passport, a Certificate of Naturalization or of Citizenship, a driver's license, or a government ID card with a physical description or a photograph. Failing any of these, you should be accompanied by a blood relative or a friend of at least 5 years' standing who will testify to your identity. Credit cards or social security cards do not suffice as proof of identity — but note that since 1988, US citizens *must* supply their social security numbers.

As getting a passport — or international visa — through the mail can mean waiting as much as 6 weeks or more, a new mini-industry has cropped up in those cities where there is a US passport office. The yellow pages currently list quite a few organizations willing to wait on line to expedite obtaining a visa or passport renewal; there's even one alternative for those who live nowhere near the cities mentioned above. In the nation's capital there's an organization called the *Washington Passport and Visa Service*. It may be the answer for folks in need of special rapid action, since this organization can get a passport application or renewal turned around in a single day. What's more, their proximity to an embassy or consulate of every foreign country represented in the US helps to speed the processing of visa applications as well. The fee for a 5- to 7-day turnaround is $30; for next-day service the charge is $50; for same-day service they charge $90. For information, application forms, and other prices, contact *Washington Passport and Visa Service,* 2318 18th St. NW, Washington, DC 20009 (phone: 800-272-7776). Another company in Washington providing a similar service is *Travisa* (2122 P St. NW, Washington, DC 20037; phone: 800-222-2589). They charge $30 for an 8- to 10-day turnaround on passport applications.

If you need an emergency passport, it also is possible to be issued a passport in a matter of hours by going directly to your nearest passport office (there is no way, however, to avoid waiting in line). Explain the nature of the emergency, usually as serious as a death in the family; a ticket in hand for a flight the following day also will suffice. Should the emergency occur outside of business hours, all is not lost. There's a 24-hour telephone number in Washington, DC (phone: 202-647-4000), that can put you in touch with a State Department duty officer who may be able to expedite your application. Note that if a passport is obtained after regular business hours, a nominal charge will be added to the standard passport fee.

■ **When Checking In:** Occasionally, a foreign hotel may ask you to surrender your passport for 24 hours. While we all get a little nervous when we're parted from our passports, the US State Department's passport division advises that it's a perfectly acceptable procedure. The purpose usually is to check the validity of the passport and ascertain whether the passport holder is a fugitive or has a police record. Many hotels merely will ask that you enter your passport number on your registration card. If a hotel does take your passport, make sure it's returned to you the next day.

**DUTY AND CUSTOMS:** As a general rule, the requirements for bringing the majority of items into South America is that they must be in quantities small enough not to imply commercial import. Most countries in South America impose limitations on the quantities of specific items (such as tobacco products and liquor) which may be imported duty-free. For information on the customs regulations of the area you will be

## 80 GETTING READY / Insurance

visiting, contact the appropriate tourist authority in the US (for addresses, see FACTS IN BRIEF).

If you are bringing along a computer, camera, or other electronic equipment for your own use that you will be taking back to the US, you should register it with the US Customs Service in order to avoid being asked to pay duty both entering and returning from South America. (Also see *Customs and Returning to the US,* in this section.) For information on this procedure, as well as for a variety of informative pamphlets on US Customs regulations, contact the local office of the US Customs Service or the central office, PO Box 7407, Washington, DC 20044 (phone: 202-566-8195).

- **One rule to follow:** When passing through customs, it is illegal not to declare dutiable items; penalties range from stiff fines and seizure of the goods to prison terms. So don't try to sneak anything through — it just isn't worth it.

# Insurance

It is unfortunate that most decisions to buy travel insurance are impulsive and usually are made without any real consideration of the traveler's existing policies. Therefore, the first person with whom you should discuss travel insurance is your own insurance broker, not a travel agent or the clerk behind the airport insurance counter. You may discover that the insurance you already carry — homeowner's policies and/or accident, health, and life insurance — protects you adequately while you travel and that your real needs are in the more mundane areas of excess value insurance for baggage or trip cancellation insurance.

**TYPES OF INSURANCE:** To make insurance decisions intelligently, however, you first should understand the basic categories of travel insurance and what they cover. Then you can decide what you should have in the broader context of your personal insurance needs, and you can choose the most economical way of getting the desired protection: through riders on existing policies; with onetime short-term policies; through a special program put together for the frequent traveler; through coverage that's part of a travel club's benefits; or with a combination policy sold by insurance companies through brokers, automobile clubs, tour operators, and travel agents.

There are seven basic categories of travel insurance:

1. Baggage and personal effects insurance
2. Personal accident and sickness insurance
3. Trip cancellation and interruption insurance
4. Default and/or bankruptcy insurance
5. Flight insurance (to cover injury or death)
6. Automobile insurance (for driving your own or a rented car)
7. Combination policies

**Baggage and Personal Effects Insurance** – Ask your insurance agent if baggage and personal effects are included in your current homeowner's policy, or if you will need a special floater to cover you for the duration of a trip. The object is to protect your bags and their contents in case of damage or theft anytime during your travels, not just while you're in flight and covered by the airline's policy. Furthermore, only limited protection is provided by the airline. Baggage liability varies from carrier to carrier, but generally speaking, on domestic flights, luggage usually is insured to $1,250 — that's per passenger, not per bag. For most international flights, including domestic portions of international flights, the airline's liability limit is approximately $9.07 per pound or $20 per kilo (which comes to about $360 per 40-pound suitcase) for checked baggage and up to $400 per passenger for unchecked baggage. These limits should be specified on your airline ticket, but to be awarded any amount, you'll have to provide an itemized list of lost property, and if you're including new and/or expensive items, be prepared for a request that you back up your claim with sales receipts or other proof of purchase.

If you are carrying goods worth more than the maximum protection offered by the airline, bus, or train company, consider excess value insurance. Additional coverage is available from airlines at an average, currently, of $1 to $2 per $100 worth of coverage, up to a maximum of $5,000. This insurance can be purchased at the airline counter when you check in, though you should arrive early to fill out the necessary forms and to avoid holding up other passengers.

Major credit card companies also provide coverage for lost or delayed baggage — and this coverage often also is over and above what the airline will pay. The basic coverage usually is automatic for all cardholders who use the credit card to purchase tickets, but to qualify for additional coverage, cardholders generally must enroll.

*American Express:* Provides $500 coverage for checked baggage; $1,250 for carry-on baggage; and $250 for valuables, such as cameras and jewelry.

*Carte Blanche and Diners Club:* Provide $1,250 free insurance for checked or carry-on baggage that's lost or damaged.

*Discover Card:* Offers $500 insurance for checked baggage and $1,250 for carry-on baggage — but to qualify for this coverage cardholders first must purchase additional flight insurance (see "Flight Insurance," below).

*MasterCard* and *Visa:* Baggage insurance coverage set by the issuing institution.

Additional baggage and personal effects insurance also is included in certain of the combination travel insurance policies discussed below.

■**A note of warning:** Be sure to read the fine print of any excess value insurance policy; there often are specific exclusions, such as cash, tickets, furs, gold and silver objects, art, and antiques. And remember that insurance companies ordinarily will pay only the depreciated value of the goods rather than their replacement value. The best way to protect the items you're carrying in your luggage is to take photos of your valuables and keep a record of the serial numbers of such items as cameras, typewriters, laptop computers, radios, and so on. This will establish that you do, indeed, own the objects. If your luggage disappears en route or is damaged, deal with the situation immediately. If an airline loses your luggage, you will be asked to fill out a Property Irregularity Report before you leave the airport. If your property disappears at other transportation centers, tell the local company, but also report it to the police (since the insurance company will check with the police when processing the claim). When traveling by train, if you are sending excess luggage as registered baggage, remember that some trains may not have provisions for extra cargo; if your baggage does not arrive when you do, it may not be lost, just on the next train!

**Personal Accident and Sickness Insurance** – This covers you in case of illness during your trip or death in an accident. Most policies insure you for hospital and doctor's expenses, lost income, and so on. In most cases, it is a standard part of existing health insurance policies, though you should check with your insurance broker to be sure that your policy will pay for any medical expenses incurred abroad. If not, take out a separate vacation accident policy or an entire vacation insurance policy that includes health and life coverage.

Two examples of such comprehensive health and life insurance coverage are the travel insurance packages offered by *Wallach & Co:*

*HealthCare Global:* This insurance package, which can be purchased for periods of 10 to 180 days is offered for two age groups: Men and women up to age 75

**82  GETTING READY / Insurance**

receive $25,000 medical insurance and $50,000 death benefit; those from age 76 to 84 are eligible for $12,500 medical insurance and $25,000 death benefit. For either policy, the cost for a l0-day period is $25, with decreasing rates up to 75 days, after which the rate is $1.50 a day.

*HealthCare Abroad:* This program is available to individuals up to age 75. For $3 per day (minimum 10 days, maximum 90 days), policy holders receive $100,000 medical insurance and $25,000 death benefit.

Both of these basic programs also may be bought in combination with trip cancellation and baggage insurance at extra cost. For further information, write to *Wallach & Co.,* 107 West Federal St., Box 480, Middleburg, VA 22117-0480 (phone: 703-687-3166 in Virginia; 800-237-6615 elsewhere in the US).

**Trip Cancellation and Interruption Insurance** – Most charter and package tour passengers pay for their travel well before departure. The disappointment of having to miss a vacation because of illness or any other reason pales before the awful prospect that not all (and sometimes none) of the money paid in advance might be returned. So cancellation insurance for any package tour is a must.

Although cancellation penalties vary (they are listed in the fine print of every tour brochure, and before you purchase a package tour you should know exactly what they are), rarely will a passenger get more than 50% of this money back if forced to cancel within a few weeks of scheduled departure. Therefore, if you book a package tour or charter flight, you should have trip cancellation insurance to guarantee full reimbursement or refund should you, a traveling companion, or a member of your immediate family get sick, forcing you to cancel your trip or *return home early.*

The key here is *not* to buy just enough insurance to guarantee full reimbursement for the cost of the package or charter in case of cancellation. The proper amount of coverage should be sufficient to reimburse you for the cost of having to catch up with a tour after its departure or having to travel home at the full economy airfare if you have to forgo the return flight of your charter. There usually is quite a discrepancy between a charter fare and the amount charged to travel the same distance on a regularly scheduled flight at full economy fare.

Trip cancellation insurance is available from travel agents and tour operators in two forms: as part of a short-term, all-purpose travel insurance package (sold by the travel agent); or as specific cancellation insurance designed by the tour operator for a specific charter tour. Generally, tour operators' policies are less expensive, but also less inclusive. Cancellation insurance also is available directly from insurance companies or their agents as part of a short-term, all-inclusive travel insurance policy.

Before you decide on a policy, read each one carefully. (Either type can be purchased from a travel agent when you book the charter or package tour.) Be certain that your policy includes enough coverage to pay your fare from the farthest destination on your itinerary should you have to miss the charter flight. Also, be sure to check the fine print for stipulations concerning "family members" and "pre-existing medical conditions," as well as allowances for living expenses if you must delay your return due to bodily injury or illness.

**Default and/or Bankruptcy Insurance** – Although trip cancellation insurance usually protects you if *you* are unable to complete — or begin — your trip, a fairly recent innovation is coverage in the event of default and/or bankruptcy on the part of the tour operator, airline, or other travel supplier. In some travel insurance packages, this contingency is included in the trip cancellation portion of the coverage; in others, it is a separate feature. Either way, it is becoming increasingly important. Whereas sophisticated travelers have long known to beware of the possibility of default or bankruptcy when buying a charter flight or tour package, in recent years more than a few respected airlines have unexpectedly revealed their shaky financial condition, sometimes leaving hordes of stranded ticket holders in their wake. Moreover, the value of escrow protection of a charter passenger's funds lately has been unreliable. While default/bankruptcy insurance will not ordinarily result in reimbursement in time to pay for new arrangements, it can ensure that you will get your money back, and even independent travelers buying no more than an airplane ticket may want to consider it.

**Flight Insurance** – Airlines have carefully established limits of liability for injury to or the death of passengers for international flights. For all international flights to, from, or with a stopover in the US, all carriers are liable for up to $75,000 per passenger. For all other international flights, the liability is based on where you purchase the ticket: If booked in advance in the US, the maximum liability is $75,000; if arrangements are made abroad, the liability is $10,000. But remember, these liabilities are not the same thing as insurance policies; every penny that an airline eventually pays in the case of death or injury will likely be subject to a legal battle.

But before you buy last-minute flight insurance from an airport vending machine, consider the purchase in light of your total existing insurance coverage. A careful review of your current policies may reveal that you already are amply covered for accidental death, sometimes up to three times the amount provided for by the flight insurance you're buying at the airport.

Be aware that airport insurance, the kind typically bought at a counter or from a vending machine, is among the most expensive forms of life insurance coverage, and that even within a single airport, rates for approximately the same coverage vary widely. Often policies sold in vending machines are more expensive than those sold over the counter, even when they are with the same national company.

If you buy your plane ticket with a major credit card, you generally receive automatic insurance coverage at no extra cost. Additional coverage usually can be obtained at extremely reasonable prices, but a cardholder must sign up for it in advance. (Note that rates vary slightly for residents of some states.) As we went to press, the travel accident and life insurance policies of the major credit cards were as follows:

*American Express:* Automatically provides $100,000 in insurance to its *Green, Gold,* and *Optima* cardholders, and $500,000 to *Platinum* cardholders. With *American Express,* $4.50 per ticket buys an additional $250,000 worth of flight insurance; $7.50 buys an additional $500,000 worth; and $14 provides an added $1 million worth of coverage.

*Carte Blanche:* Automatically provides $125,000 free flight insurance.

*Diners Club:* Provides $350,000 free flight insurance. An additional $250,000 worth of insurance is available for $4; $500,000 costs $6.50.

*Discover Card:* Provides $500,000 free flight insurance. An additional $250,000 worth of insurance is available for $4.50; $500,000 costs $6.50.

*MasterCard and Visa:* Insurance coverage set by the issuing institution.

**Automobile Insurance** – US insurance policies are *not* recognized in South America, and you must have a special policy for driving in Latin American countries. Due to a number of factors — safety being foremost — we do not recommend driving your own car in South America; therefore, most people who do drive in South America will be driving a rental car. When you rent a car, the rental company is required to offer you collision protection.

In your car rental contract, you'll see that for about $9 to $15 a day, you may buy optional collision damage waiver (CDW) protection. (If partial coverage with a deductible is included in the rental contract, the CDW will cover the deductible in the event of an accident, and can cost as much as $25 per day.)

If you do not accept the CDW coverage, you may be liable for as much as the full retail value of the rental car, and by paying for the CDW you are relieved of all responsibility for any damage to the car. Before agreeing to this coverage, however,

**84 GETTING READY / Insurance**

check with your own broker about your own existing personal automobile insurance policy. It very well may cover your entire liability exposure without any additional cost, or you automatically may be covered by the credit card company to which you are charging the cost of your rental. To find out the amount of rental car insurance provided by major credit cards, contact the issuing institutions.

You also should know that an increasing number of the major international car rental companies automatically are including the cost of the CDW in their basic rates. Car rental prices have increased to include this coverage, although rental company ad campaigns may promote this as a new, improved rental package "benefit." The disadvantage of this inclusion is that you may not have the option to turn down the CDW — even if you already are adequately covered by your own insurance policy or through a credit card company.

If you will be driving your own car, it is necessary to buy special policies for each country of South America through which you will be driving. This can present some difficulties, because few US insurance companies are authorized to issue foreign insurance. Although some South American countries recognize policies issued in the US, others recognize only locally issued policies bought from agencies such as those listed below. Your choices are to go to a US company that can issue a foreign policy (see below), being fully prepared to purchase additional local insurance where it is required, or to go from country to country getting local policies.

The pervasive problem is always the rapidity with which South American insurance laws change, and the difficulty for any agent — even those for South American companies — to stay abreast of the latest developments. If you decide to go the route of single, country-by-country policies, you will discover that often no insurance is available at the border and that you will be forced to drive to the nearest large town before purchasing insurance, leaving you unprotected on the interim journey. When you do buy insurance, it also is best to pay for a policy for a few days beyond the time you expect to need it, just in case you are delayed within the country.

Although we strongly advise that you *not* even consider driving your own car to and through South America, for diehards who refuse to give up their wheels and choose to take on this long and perilous journey, country-specific insurance policies are issued primarily by the New York-based *American International Underwriters* (Automobile Underwriters' Department, 505 Carr St., Wilmington, DE 19809; phone: 302-761-3107; 800-343-5761 for South American information). This office can provide information about the varieties of pan-South American insurance available. As such policies issued in the US may prove inadequate in the eyes of South American local authorities, you may be better off contacting one of the *American International Underwriters* offices (staffed by English-speaking people) in South America; the Wilmington office can provide the locations of these branch locations.

**Combination Policies** – Short-term insurance policies, which may include a combination of any or all of the types of insurance discussed above, are available through retail insurance agencies, automobile clubs, and many travel agents. These combination policies are designed to cover you for the duration of a single trip.

Policies of this type include the following:

*Access America International:* A subsidiary of the Blue Cross/Blue Shield plans of New York and Washington, DC, now available nationwide. Contact *Access America,* PO Box 90310, Richmond, VA 23230 (phone: 800-424-3391 or 804-285-3300).

*Carefree:* Underwritten by The Hartford. Contact *Carefree Travel Insurance,* Arm Coverage, PO Box 310, Mineola, NY 11501 (phone: 800-645-2424 or 516-294-0220).

*NEAR Services:* In addition to a full range of travel services, this organization offers a comprehensive travel insurance package. An added feature is coverage for lost or stolen airline tickets. Contact *NEAR Services,* 450 Prairie Ave., Suite 101, Calumet City, IL 60409 (phone: 708-868-6700 in the Chicago area; 800-654-6700 elsewhere in the US and Canada).

*Tele-Trip:* Underwritten by the Mutual of Omaha Companies. Contact *Tele-Trip Co.,* 3201 Farnam St., Omaha, NE 68131 (phone: 402-345-2400 in Nebraska; 800-228-9792 elsewhere in the US).

*Travel Assistance International:* Provided by Europ Assistance Worldwide Services, and underwritten by Transamerica Occidental Life Insurance. Contact *Travel Assistance International,* 1133 15th St. NW, Suite 400, Washington, DC 20005 (phone: 202-331-1609 in Washington, DC; 800-821-2828 elsewhere in the US).

*Travel Guard International:* Underwritten by the Insurance Company of North America, it is available through authorized travel agents, or contact *Travel Guard International,* 1145 Clark St., Stevens Point, WI 54481 (phone: 715-345-0505 in Wisconsin; 800-826-1300 elsewhere in the US).

*Travel Insurance PAK:* Underwritten by The Travelers. Contact *The Travelers Companies,* Ticket and Travel Plans, One Tower Sq., Hartford, CT 06183-5040 (phone: 203-277-2318 in Connecticut; 800-243-3174 elsewhere in the US).

## How to Pack

No one can provide a completely foolproof list of precisely what to pack, so it's best to let common sense, space, and comfort guide you. Keep one maxim in mind: Less is more. You simply won't need as much clothing as you think, and you are far more likely to need a forgotten accessory — or a needle and thread or scissors — than a particular piece of clothing.

As with almost anything relating to travel, a little planning can go a long way.

1. Where are you going — city, country, or both?
2. How many total days will you be gone?
3. What's the average temperature likely to be during your stay?

The goal is to remain perfectly comfortable, neat, clean, and fashionable, but to pack as little as possible. Learn to travel light by following two firm packing principles:

1. Organize your travel wardrobe around a single color — blue or beige, for example — that allows you to mix, match, and layer clothes. Holding firm to one color scheme will make it easy to eliminate items of clothing that don't harmonize.
2. Never overpack to ensure a supply of fresh clothing — shirts, blouses, underwear — for each day of a long trip. Use hotel laundries to wash and dry clean clothes. There are local laundry services, called *la lavandería* in Spanish and *a lavandaria automatica* in Portuguese, in most towns of any size. (Note that the type of self-service laundromats common in the US generally are not found in South America.)

**CLIMATE AND CLOTHES:** Exactly what you pack for your trip will be a function of where you are going and when, and the kinds of things you intend to do. A few degrees can make all the difference between being comfortably attired and very real suffering, so your initial step should be to find out what the general weather conditions are likely to be in the areas you will visit.

Latin Americans are appearance conscious, and although styles vary from place to place, certain standards apply throughout the major cities. For daytime, informal, comfortable clothes are fine, and although blue jeans are increasingly acceptable, khakis or chinos generally are preferable. (Note that Latin American men rarely wear ties except for business and formal evenings out.)

In beach resorts and Rio de Janeiro, bathing suits are acceptable anywhere near the water. Men often wear shirts over their trunks; women, skimpy sundresses at beach cafés. At night, trousers replace bathing trunks. Women's attire may remain pretty much the same, although less casual dresses are preferable after dark. In cities, beachwear is not acceptable beyond the immediate vicinity of a hotel's swimming pool, and dress generally is more conservative. Even during the South American summer, a sweater or other light wrap is a good idea since the nights can be cool.

Specific information about climate and clothes in South America is given in the individual country listings in FACTS IN BRIEF.

Keeping temperature and climate in mind, consider the problem of luggage. Plan on one suitcase per person (and in a pinch, remember it's always easier to carry two small suitcases than to schlepp one that is roughly the size of downtown Detroit). Standard 26- to 28-inch suitcases can be made to work for 1 week or 1 month, and unless you are going for no more than a weekend, never cram wardrobes for two people into one suitcase. Hanging bags are best for dresses, suits, and jackets.

Before packing, lay out every piece of clothing you think you might want to take. Select clothing on the basis of what can serve several functions (wherever possible, clothes should be chosen that can be used for both daytime and evening wear). Pack clothes that have a lot of pockets for traveler's checks, documents, and tickets. Eliminate items that don't mix, match, or coordinate with your color scheme. If you can't wear it in at least two distinct incarnations, leave it at home. Accessorize everything beforehand so you know exactly what you will be wearing with what.

Layering is a good way to prepare for atypical temperatures or changes in the weather — particularly when traveling in the Andean countries where mornings and evenings can be cold and midday temperatures climb into the high 70s. For unexpectedly cool days or for outings in the mountains (where it may be cooler), recommended basics are a T-shirt and a lightweight wool or heavy cotton turtleneck which can be worn under a shirt and perhaps a third layer, such as a sweater, jacket, or windbreaker. As the weather changes, you can add or remove clothes as needed. (Because of the wide selection of attractive woolen sweaters and ponchos available throughout South America, it usually is easier to keep warm than stay cool — garments made of alpaca wool are a particularly good buy.)

Travelers to the Amazon and jungle regions should include long cotton pants, lightweight long-sleeve shirts, and high socks for protection against insects. In the rainy season, torrential downpours are common, and even in the dryer seasons, rain always is a possibility, so keep an umbrella or waterproof poncho (available from camping supplies stores) with you at all times.

Since you are likely to do more walking than usual in South America — and in small towns and some large cities, streets often are cobbled — it is essential to bring comfortable shoes (often this means an old pair, already broken in). Sneakers or other rubber-soled shoes are good for climbing pyramids and other ancient ruins.

Your carry-on luggage should contain a survival kit with the basic things you will need in case your luggage gets lost or stolen: a toothbrush, toothpaste, all medications, a sweater, nightclothes, and a change of underwear. With these essential items at hand, you will be prepared for any sudden, unexpected occurrence that separates you from your suitcase. If you have many scheduled 1- or 2-night stops, you can live out of your survival case without having to unpack completely at each hotel.

**Sundries** – If you are traveling in the heat of summer and will be spending a lot of time outdoors, be sure to take along a sun hat (to protect hair as well as skin) and sunscreen. Also, remember that in higher altitudes your exposed face and neck are particularly susceptible to a painful sunburn.

Other items you might consider packing are a small bottle in which to carry purified water (if you're driving), a pocket-size flashlight with extra batteries, a small sewing kit, a first-aid kit (see *Staying Healthy,* in this section, for recommended components), binoculars, and a camera or camcorder (see *Cameras and Equipment,* also in this section).

■ **Note:** for those on the go, *Travel Mini Pack* offers numerous products — from toilet articles to wrinkle-remover spray — in handy travel sizes, as well as travel accessories such as money pouches, foreign currency calculators, and even a combination hair dryer/iron. For a catalogue, contact *Travel Mini Pack* (PO Box 571, Stony Point, NY 10980; phone: 914-429-8281). *Pacific Traveler's Supply* (529 State St., Santa Barbara, CA 93101; phone: 805-963-4438) also carries a variety of similar items, as well as an extensive collection of travel guides and maps.

**PACKING:** The basic idea of packing is to get everything into the suitcase and out again with as few wrinkles as possible. Simple, casual clothes — shirts, jeans and slacks, permanent press skirts — can be rolled into neat, tight sausages that keep other packed items in place and leave the clothes themselves amazingly unwrinkled. However, for items that are too bulky or delicate for even careful rolling, a suitcase can be packed with the heaviest items on the bottom, toward the hinges, so that they will not wrinkle more perishable clothes. Candidates for the bottom layer include shoes (stuff them with small items to save space), a toilet kit, handbags (stuff them to help keep their shape), and an alarm clock. Fill out this layer with articles that will not wrinkle or will not matter if they do, such as sweaters, socks, a bathing suit, gloves, and underwear.

If you get this first, heavy layer as smooth as possible with the fill-ins, you will have a shelf for the next layer — the most easily wrinkled items, like slacks, jackets, shirts, dresses, and skirts. These should be buttoned and zipped and laid along the whole length of the suitcase with as little folding as possible. When you do need to make a fold, do it on a crease (as with pants), along a seam in the fabric, or where it will not show (such as shirttails). Alternate each piece of clothing, using one side of the suitcase, then the other, to make the layers as flat as possible. Make the layers even and the total contents of your bag full and firm to keep things from shifting around during transit. On the top layer put the things you will want at once: nightclothes, a bathing suit, an umbrella or raincoat, a sweater.

With men's two-suiter suitcases, follow the same procedure. Then place jackets on hangers, straighten them out, and leave them unbuttoned. If they are too wide for the suitcase, fold them lengthwise down the middle, straighten the shoulders, and fold the sleeves in along the seam.

While packing, it is a good idea to separate each layer of clothes with plastic cleaning bags, which will help preserve pressed clothes while they are in the suitcase. Unpack your bags as soon as you get to your hotel. Nothing so thoroughly destroys freshly cleaned and pressed clothes as sitting for days in a suitcase. Finally, if something is badly wrinkled and can't be professionally pressed before you must wear it, hang it for several hours in a bathroom where the bathtub has been filled with very hot water; keep the bathroom door closed so the room becomes something of a steamroom. It really works miracles.

**SOME FINAL PACKING HINTS:** Apart from the items you pack as carry-on luggage (see above), always keep all necessary medicines, valuable jewelry, and travel or business documents in your purse, briefcase, or carry-on bag — *not in the luggage you will check.* Tuck a bathing suit into your handbag or briefcase, too; in the event of lost baggage, it's frustrating to be without one. And whether in your overnight bag or checked luggage, cosmetics and any liquids should be packed in plastic bottles or at least wrapped in plastic bags and tied.

Golf clubs and skis may be checked through as luggage (most airlines are accustomed to handling them), but tennis rackets should be carried onto the plane. Aqualung tanks (appropriately packed with padding and depressurized) and surfboards (minus the fin and padded) also may go as baggage. Snorkeling gear should be packed in a suitcase, duffel, or tote bag. Some airlines require that bicycles be partially dismantled and packaged (see *Camping and RVs, Hiking and Biking,* in this section). Check with the airline before departure to see if there is a specific regulation concerning any special equipment or sporting gear you plan to take.

# Hints for Handicapped Travelers

From 40 to 50 million people in the US alone have some sort of disability, and over half this number are physically handicapped. Like everyone else today, they — and the uncounted disabled millions around the world — are on the move. More than ever before, they are demanding facilities they can use comfortably, and they are being heard.

Those who have chosen to visit South America are in luck because, in recent years, a series of imaginative, inter-American programs aimed at improving facilities and services for the handicapped in Latin America have been initiated. Chief among these is *Partners of the Americas* with chapters based in 45 states and the District of Columbia, which coordinates joint projects with these states working in various Latin American areas. *Partners of the Americas* also offers information on a variety of programs and volunteer committees for the handicapped throughout Central and South America. For more information, contact the central office of *Partners of the Americas,* 1424 K St. NW, Suite 700, Washington, DC 20005 (phone: 800-322-7844 or 202-628-3300).

Despite this effort to develop special facilities for the disabled, handicapped travelers face pretty much the same problems in South America as in most other parts of the world. Rural areas have no facilities. Cities have some, but there is no consistency, and data on services and facilities are fairly sparse throughout the continent.

**PLANNING:** Collect as much information as you can about your specific disability and facilities for the disabled in South America. Make your travel arrangements well in advance and specify to all services involved the exact nature of your condition or restricted mobility, as your trip will be much more comfortable if you know that there are accommodations and facilities to suit your needs. The best way to find out if your intended destination can accommodate a handicapped traveler is to write or call the local tourist authority or hotel and ask specific questions. If you require a corridor of a certain width to maneuver a wheelchair or if you need handles on the bathroom walls for support, ask the hotel manager. A travel agent or the local chapter or national office of the organization that deals with your particular disability — for example, the *American Foundation for the Blind* or the *American Heart Association* — will supply the most up-to-date information on the subject. The following organizations offer general information on access:

*ACCENT on Living* (PO Box 700, Bloomington, IL 61702; phone: 309-378-2961). This information service for persons with disabilities provides a free list of travel agencies specializing in arranging trips for the disabled; for a copy send a self-addressed, stamped envelope. Also offers a wide range of publications, including a quarterly magazine ($10 per year; $17.50 for 2 years) for persons with disabilities.

*Information Center for Individuals with Disabilities* (Fort Point Pl., 1st Floor, 27-43 Wormwood St., Boston, MA 02210; phone: 800-462-5015 in Massachusetts; 617-727-5540/1 elsewhere in the US; both numbers provide voice and

## GETTING READY / Handicapped Travelers 89

TDD — telecommunications device for the deaf). The center offers information and referral services on disability-related issues, publishes fact sheets on travel agents, tour operators, and other travel resources, and can help you research your trip.

*Mobility International USA* (*MIUSA;* PO Box 3551, Eugene, OR 97403; phone: 503-343-1284; both voice and TDD). This US branch of *Mobility International* (the main office is at 228 Borough High St., London SE1 1JX, England; phone: 44-71-403-5688), a nonprofit British organization with affiliates worldwide, offers members advice and assistance — including information on accommodations and other travel services, and publications applicable to the traveler's disability. *Mobility International* also offers a quarterly newsletter and a comprehensive sourcebook, *A World of Options for the 90s: A Guide to International Education Exchange, Community Service and Travel for Persons with Disabilities* ($14 for members; $16 for non-members). Membership includes the newsletter and is $20 a year; subscription to the newsletter alone is $10 annually.

*National Rehabilitation Information Center* (8455 Colesville Rd., Suite 935, Silver Spring, MD 20910; phone: 301-588-9284). A general information, resource, research, and referral service.

*Paralyzed Veterans of America* (*PVA;* PVA/ATTS Program, 801 18th St. NW, Washington, DC 20006; phone: 202-416-7708 in Washington, DC; 800-424-8200 elsewhere in the US). The members of this national service organization all are veterans who have suffered spinal cord injuries, but it offers advocacy services and information to all persons with a disability. *PVA* also sponsors *Access to the Skies (ATTS),* a program that coordinates the efforts of the national and international air travel industry in providing airport and airplane access for the disabled. Members receive several helpful publications, as well as regular notification of conferences on subjects of interest to the disabled traveler.

*Royal Association for Disability and Rehabilitation* (*RADAR;* 25 Mortimer St., London W1N 8AB, England; phone: 44-71-637-5400). Offers a number of publications for the handicapped, including *Holidays and Travel Abroad 1992/93 — A Guide for Disabled People,* a comprehensive guidebook focusing on international travel. This publication can be ordered by sending payment in British pounds to *RADAR.* As we went to press, this publication cost just over £3; call for current pricing before ordering.

*Society for the Advancement of Travel for the Handicapped* (*SATH;* 347 Fifth Ave., Suite 610, New York, NY 10016; phone: 212-447-7284). To keep abreast of developments in travel for the handicapped as they occur, you may want to join *SATH,* a nonprofit organization whose members include consumers, as well as travel service professionals who have experience (or an interest) in travel for the handicapped. For an annual fee of $45 ($25 for students and travelers who are 65 and older) members receive a quarterly newsletter and have access to extensive information and referral services. *SATH* also offers two useful publications: *Travel Tips for the Handicapped* (a series of informative fact sheets) and *The United States Welcomes Handicapped Visitors* (a 48-page guide covering domestic transportation and accommodations that includes useful hints for travelers with disabilities abroad); to order, send a self-addressed, #10 envelope, and $1 per title for postage.

*Travel Information Service* (Moss Rehabilitation Hospital, 1200 W. Tabor Rd., Philadelphia, PA 19141-3099; phone: 215-456-9600 for voice; 215-456-9602 for TDD). This service assists physically handicapped people in planning trips and supplies detailed information on accessibility for a nominal fee.

Blind travelers should contact the *American Foundation for the Blind* (15 W. 16th St., New York, NY 10011; phone: 800-829-0500 or 212-620-2147) and *The Seeing Eye* (Box 375, Morristown, NJ 07963-0375; phone: 201-539-4425); both provide useful

## GETTING READY / Handicapped Travelers

information on resources for the visually impaired. *Note:* Although requirements vary from country to country, generally, Seeing Eye dogs must be accompanied by a certificate of inoculation against rabies, hepatitis and/or distemper issued within the previous 3 months and certified by the United States Department of Agriculture. These certificates must be authorized by the South American consul of your destination (for a fee of about $20 at press time). *The American Society for the Prevention of Cruelty to Animals (ASPCA,* Education Dept., 441 E. 92 St., New York, NY 10128; phone: 212-876-7700) offers a useful booklet, *Traveling With Your Pet,* which lists inoculation and other requirements by country. It is available for $5 (including postage and handling).

In addition, there are a number of publications — from travel guides to magazines — of interest to handicapped travelers. Among these are the following:

*Access to the World,* by Louise Weiss, offers sound tips for the disabled traveler. Information about South America is included in several sections. Published by Facts on File (460 Park Ave. S., New York, NY 10016; phone: 212-683-2244 in New York State; 800-322-8755 elsewhere in the US; 800-443-8323 in Canada), it costs $16.95. Check with your local bookstore; it also can be ordered by phone with a credit card.

*The Diabetic Traveler* (PO Box 8223 RW, Stamford, CT 06905; phone: 203-327-5832) is a useful quarterly newsletter. Each issue highlights a single destination or type of travel and includes information on general resources and hints for diabetics. A 1-year subscription costs $15. When subscribing, ask for the free fact sheet including an index of special articles; back issues are available for $4 each.

*Guide to Traveling with Arthritis,* a free brochure available by writing to the Upjohn Company (PO Box 307-B, Coventry, CT 06238), provides lots of good, commonsense tips on planning your trip and how to be as comfortable as possible when traveling by car, bus, train, cruise ship, or plane.

*Handicapped Travel Newsletter* is regarded as one of the best sources of information for the disabled traveler. It is edited by wheelchair-bound Vietnam veteran Michael Quigley, who has traveled to 93 countries around the world. Issued every 2 months (plus special issues), a subscription is $10 per year. Write to *Handicapped Travel Newsletter,* PO Box 269, Athens, TX 75751 (phone: 903-677-1260).

*Handi-Travel: A Resource Book for Disabled and Elderly Travellers,* by Cinnie Noble, is a comprehensive travel guide full of practical tips for those with disabilities affecting mobility, hearing, or sight. To order this book, send $12.95, plus shipping and handling, to the *Canadian Rehabilitation Council for the Disabled,* 45 Sheppard Ave. E., Suite 801, Toronto, Ontario M2N 5W9, Canada (phone: 416-250-7490; both voice and TDD).

*The Itinerary* (PO Box 2012, Bayonne, NJ 07002-2012; phone: 201-858-3400). This bimonthly travel newsletter for people with disabilities includes information on accessibility, listings of tours, news of adaptive devices, travel aids, and special services, as well as numerous general travel hints. A subscription costs $10 a year.

*The Physically Disabled Traveler's Guide,* by Rod W. Durgin and Norene Lindsay, rates accessibility of a number of travel services and includes a list of organizations specializing in travel for the disabled. It is available for $9.95, plus $2 for shipping and handling, from *Resource Directories,* 3361 Executive Pkwy., Suite 302, Toledo, OH 43606 (phone: 419-536-5353 in the Toledo area; 800-274-8515 elsewhere in the US).

## GETTING READY / Handicapped Travelers

*Ticket to Safe Travel* offers useful information for travelers with diabetes. A reprint of this article is available free from from local chapters of the *American Diabetes Association*. For the nearest branch, contact the central office at 505 Eighth Ave., 21st Floor, New York, NY 10018 (phone: 212-947-9707 in New York State; 800-232-3472 elsewhere in the US).

*Travel for the Patient with Chronic Obstructive Pulmonary Disease,* a publication of the George Washington University Medical Center, provides some sound practical suggestions for those with emphysema, chronic bronchitis, asthma, or other lung ailments. To order, send $2 to Dr. Harold Silver, 1601 18th St. NW, Washington, DC 20009 (phone: 202-667-0134).

*Traveling Like Everybody Else: A Practical Guide for Disabled Travelers,* by Jacqueline Freedman and Susan Gersten, offers the disabled tips on traveling by car, cruise ship, and plane, as well as lists of accessible accommodations, tour operators specializing in tours for disabled travelers, and other resources. It is available for $11.95, plus postage and handling, from Modan Publishing, PO Box 1202, Bellmore, NY 11710 (phone: 516-679-1380).

*Travel Tips for Hearing-Impaired People,* a free pamphlet for deaf and hearing-impaired travelers, is available from the *American Academy of Otolaryngology* (One Prince St., Alexandria, VA 22314; phone: 703-836-4444). For a copy, send a self-addressed, stamped, business-size envelope to the academy.

*Travel Tips for People with Arthritis,* a 31-page booklet published by the *Arthritis Foundation,* provides helpful information regarding travel by car, bus, train, cruise ship, or plane, planning your trip, medical considerations, and ways to conserve your energy while traveling. It also includes listings of helpful resources, such as associations and travel agencies that operate tours for disabled travelers. For a copy, contact your local *Arthritis Foundation* chapter, or send $1 to the national office, PO Box 19000, Atlanta, GA 30326 (phone: 404-872-7100).

*The Wheelchair Traveler,* by Douglass R. Annand, lists accessible hotels, motels, restaurants, and other sites, including establishments in South America. This valuable resource is available directly from the author. For the price of the most recent edition, contact Douglass R. Annand, 123 Ball Hill Rd., Milford, NH 03055 (phone: 603-673-4539).

A few more basic resources to look for are *Travel for the Disabled,* by Helen Hecker ($19.95), and by the same author, *Directory of Travel Agencies for the Disabled* ($19.95). *Wheelchair Vagabond,* by John G. Nelson, is another useful guide for travelers confined to a wheelchair (hardcover, $14.95; paperback, $9.95). All three titles are published by Twin Peaks Press, PO Box 129, Vancouver, WA 98666 (phone: 800-637-CALM or 206-694-2462). This publisher offers a catalogue of 26 other books on travel for the disabled for $2.

**PLANE:** The US Department of Transportation (DOT) has ruled that US airlines must accept all passengers with disabilities. As a matter of course, US airlines were pretty good about accommodating handicapped passengers even before the ruling, although each airline has somewhat different procedures. South American airlines also are generally good about accommodating disabled travelers, but again, policies vary from carrier to carrier. Most carriers can accommodate passengers in wheelchairs, although advance notice usually is required. Ask for specifics when you book your flight.

Disabled passengers should always make reservations well in advance, and should provide the airline with all relevant details of their condition. These details include information on mobility and equipment that you will need the airline to supply — such as a wheelchair for boarding or portable oxygen for in-flight use. Be sure that the person to whom you speak fully understands the degree of your disability — the more details provided, the more effective help the airline can give you.

On the day before the flight, call back to make sure that all arrangements have been prepared, and arrive early on the day of the flight so that you can board before the rest of the passengers. It's a good idea to bring a medical certificate with you, stating your specific disability or the need to carry particular medicine.

Because most airports have jetways (corridors connecting the terminal with the door of the plane), a disabled passenger usually can be taken as far as the plane, and sometimes right onto it, in a wheelchair. If not, a narrow boarding chair may be used to take you to your seat. Your own wheelchair, which will be folded and put in the baggage compartment, should be tagged as escort luggage to assure that it's available at planeside upon landing rather than in the baggage claim area. Travel is not quite as simple if your wheelchair is battery-operated: Unless it has non-spillable batteries, it might not be accepted on board, and you will have to check with the airline ahead of time to find out how the batteries and the chair should be packaged for the flight. Usually people in wheelchairs are asked to wait until other passengers have disembarked. If you are making a tight connection, be sure to tell the attendant.

Passengers who use oxygen may not use their personal supply in the cabin, though it may be carried on the plane as cargo (the tank must be emptied) when properly packed and labeled. If you will need oxygen during the flight, the airline will supply it to you (there is a charge) provided you have given advance notice — 24 hours to a few days, depending on the carrier.

Among the major carriers serving South America, the following airlines have TDD toll-free lines in the US for the hearing-impaired: *American* (phone: 800-582-1573 in Ohio; 800-543-1586 elsewhere in the US) and *United* (phone: 800-942-8819 in Illinois; 800-323-0170 elsewhere in the US).

The free booklet *Air Transportation of Handicapped Persons* explains the general guidelines that govern air carrier policies. For a copy, write to the US Department of Transportation (Distribution Unit, Publications Section, M-443-2, 400 Seventh St. SW, Washington, DC 20590) and ask for "Free Advisory Circular #AC-120-32." *Access Travel: A Guide to the Accessibility of Airport Terminals,* a free publication of the *Airport Operators Council International,* provides information on more than 500 airports worldwide — including many major South American airports — and offers ratings of 70 features, such as wheelchair-accessible bathrooms, corridor width, and parking spaces. For a copy, contact the Consumer Information Center (Dept. 563W, Pueblo, CO 81009; phone: 719-948-3334). Useful information on every stage of air travel, from planning to arrival, is provided in the booklet *Incapacitated Passengers Air Travel Guide.* To receive a free copy, write to the International Air Transport Association (Publications Sales Department, 2000 Peel St., Montreal, Quebec H3A 2R4, Canada; phone: 514-844-6311).

**SHIP:** Among the ships calling at South American ports, *Princess Cruises' Royal Princess* and *Royal Cruise Line's Crown Odyssey* are considered the best-equipped vessels for the handicapped. Disabled travelers are advised to book reservations at least 90 days in advance to reserve specially equipped cabins.

For those in wheelchairs or with limited mobility, one of the best sources for evaluating a ship's accessibility is the free chart issued by the *Cruise Lines International Association* (500 Fifth Ave., Suite 1407, New York, NY 10110; phone: 212-921-0066). The chart lists accessible ships and indicates whether they accommodate standard-size or only narrow wheelchairs, have ramps, wide doors, low or no doorsills, handrails in the rooms, and so on. (For information on ships cruising South American waters, see *Traveling by Ship,* in this section.)

**GROUND TRANSPORTATION:** Perhaps the simplest solution to getting around is

## GETTING READY / Handicapped Travelers

to travel with an able-bodied companion who can drive. Another alternative in South America is to hire a driver/translator with a car — be sure to get a recommendation from a reputable source. The organizations listed above may be able to help you make arrangements — another source is your hotel concierge.

If you are accustomed to driving your own hand-controlled car and determined to rent one, you may have to do some extensive research, as it is difficult in South America to find rental cars fitted with hand controls. If agencies do provide hand-controlled cars, they are apt to be offered only on a limited basis in major metropolitan areas and usually are in high demand. The best course is to contact the major car rental agencies listed in *Traveling by Car,* in this section, well before your departure, but be forewarned, you still may be out of luck. Other sources for information on vehicles adapted for the handicapped are the organizations discussed above.

The *American Automobile Association (AAA)* publishes a useful book, *The Handicapped Driver's Mobility Guide.* Contact the central office of your local *AAA* club for availability and pricing, which may vary at different branch offices.

In many South American countries, taxis and public transportation also are available, but accessibility for the disabled varies and may be limited in rural areas, as well as in some cities. Check with a travel agent or the country's tourist board for information.

**TRAIN:** There are no special facilities for handicapped travelers on South American trains. However, people usually are quite helpful and will go out of their way to assist disabled people.

**BUS:** Bus travel in South America generally is not recommended for handicapped people, unless you are on a specialized tour.

**TOURS:** Programs designed for the physically impaired are run by specialists who have researched hotels, restaurants, and sites to be sure they present no insurmountable obstacles. The following travel agencies and tour operators specialize in making group and individual arrangements for travelers with physical or other disabilities:

*Access: The Foundation for Accessibility by the Disabled* (PO Box 356, Malverne, NY 11565; phone: 516-887-5798). A travelers' referral service that acts as an intermediary with tour operators and agents worldwide, and provides information on accessibility at various locations.

*Accessible Journeys* (412 S. 45th St., Philadelphia, PA 19104; phone: 215-747-0171). Arranges for traveling companions who are medical professionals — registered or licensed practical nurses, therapists, or doctors (all are experienced travelers). Several prospective companions' profiles and photos are sent to the client for perusal, and if one is acceptable, the "match" is made. The client usually pays all travel expenses for the companion, plus a set fee to compensate for wages the companion would be making at his or her usual job. This company also offers tours and cruises for people with special needs, although you don't have to take one of their tours to hire a companion through them.

*Accessible Tours/Directions Unlimited* (720 N. Bedford Rd., Bedford Hills, NY 10507; phone: 914-241-1700 in New York State; 800-533-5343 elsewhere in the continental US). Arranges group or individual tours for disabled persons traveling in the company of able-bodied friends or family members. Accepts the unaccompanied traveler if completely self-sufficient.

*Dialysis at Sea Cruises* (611 Barry Place, Indian Rocks Beach, FL 34635; phone: 800-544-7604 or 813-596-7604). Offers cruises that include the medical services of a nephrologist (a specialist in kidney disease) and a staff of dialysis nurses. Family, friends, and companions are welcome to travel on these cruises, but the number of dialysis patients usually is limited to roughly ten travelers per trip.

*Evergreen Travel Service* (4114 198th St. SW, Suite 13, Lynnwood, WA 98036-

6742; phone: 800-435-2288 or 206-776-1184). Offers worldwide tours and cruises for the disabled (Wings on Wheels Tours), sight-impaired/blind (White Cane Tours), and hearing-impaired/deaf (Flying Fingers Tours). Most programs are first class or deluxe, and include a trained escort.

*Flying Wheels Travel* (143 W. Bridge St., Box 382, Owatonna, MN 55060; phone: 800-535-6790 or 507-451-5005). Handles both tours and individual arrangements.

*The Guided Tour* (613 W. Cheltenham Ave., Suite 200, Melrose Park, PA 19126; phone: 215-782-1370). Arranges tours for people with developmental and learning disabilities and sponsors separate tours for members of the same population who also are physically disabled or who simply need a slower pace.

*Sprout* (893 Amsterdam Ave., New York, NY 10025; phone: 212-222-9575). Arranges travel programs for mildly and moderately disabled teens and adults.

*USTS Travel Horizons* (11 E. 44th St., New York, NY 10017; phone: 800-487-8787 or 212-687-5121). Travel agent and registered nurse Mary Ann Hamm designs trips for individual travelers requiring all types of kidney dialysis and handles arrangements for the dialysis.

*Whole Person Tours* (PO Box 1084, Bayonne, NJ 07002-1084; phone: 201-858-3400). Handicapped owner Bob Zywicki travels the world with his wheelchair and offers a lineup of escorted tours (many conducted by him) for the disabled. *Whole Person Tours* also publishes *The Itinerary*, a bimonthly newsletter for disabled travelers (see the publication source list above).

Travelers who would benefit from being accompanied by a nurse or physical therapist also can hire a companion through *Traveling Nurses' Network*, a service provided by Twin Peaks Press (PO Box 129, Vancouver, WA 98666; phone: 800-637-CALM or 206-694-2462). For a $10 fee, clients receive the names of three nurses, whom they can then contact directly; for a $125 fee, the agency will make all the hiring arrangements for the client. Travel arrangements also may be made in some cases — the fee for this further service is determined on an individual basis.

A similar service is offered by *MedEscort International* (ABE International Airport, PO Box 8766, Allentown, PA 18105; phone: 800-255-7182 in the continental US; elsewhere call 215-791-3111). Clients can arrange to be accompanied by a nurse, paramedic, respiratory therapist, or physician through *MedEscort*. The fees are based on the disabled traveler's needs. This service also can assist in making travel arrangements.

# Hints for Single Travelers

Just about the last trip in human history on which the participants were neatly paired was the voyage of Noah's Ark. Ever since, passenger lists and tour groups have reflected the same kind of asymmetry that occurs in real life, as countless individuals set forth to see the world unaccompanied (or unencumbered, depending on your outlook) by spouse, lover, friend, or relative. Unfortunately, traveling alone can turn a traveler into a second class citizen.

The truth is that the travel industry is not very fair to people who vacation by themselves. People traveling alone almost invariably end up paying more than individuals traveling in pairs. Most travel bargains, including package tours, accommodations, resort packages, and cruises, are based on *double occupancy* rates. This means that the per-person price is offered on the basis of two people traveling together and sharing a double room (which means they each will spend a good deal more on meals and extras).

The single traveler will have to pay a surcharge, called a single supplement, for exactly the same package. In extreme cases, this can add as much as 35% — and sometimes more — to the basic per-person rate.

Don't despair, however. Throughout South America, there are scores of smaller hotels and other hostelries where, in addition to a cozier atmosphere, prices still are quite reasonable for the single traveler. Some ship lines have begun to offer special cruises for singles, and some resorts cater to the single traveler.

The obvious, most effective alternative is to find a traveling companion. Even special "singles' tours" that promise no supplements are usually based on people sharing double rooms. Perhaps the most recent innovation along these lines is the creation of organizations that "introduce" the single traveler to other single travelers, somewhat like a dating service. Some charge fees, others are free, but the basic service offered is the same: to match an unattached person with a compatible travel mate, often as part of the company's own package tours. Among such organizations are the following:

*Partners-in-Travel* (PO Box 491145, Los Angeles, CA 90049; phone: 213-476-4869). Members receive a list of singles seeking traveling companions; prospective companions make contact through the agency. The membership fee is $40 per year and includes a chatty newsletter (6 issues per year).

*Singleworld* (401 Theodore Fremd Ave., Rye, NY 10580; phone: 914-967-3334 or 800-223-6490 in the continental US). For a yearly fee of $25, this club books members on tours and cruises and arranges shared accommodations, allowing individual travelers to avoid the single supplement charge; members also receive a quarterly newsletter. *Singleworld* also offers its own package tours for singles with departures categorized by age group: 35 or younger and all ages.

*Travel Companion Exchange* (PO Box 833, Amityville, NY 11701 (phone: 516-454-0880). This group publishes a newsletter for singles and a directory of individuals looking for travel companions. On joining, members fill out a lengthy questionnaire and write a small listing (much like an ad in a personal column). Based on these listings, members can request copies of profiles and contact prospective traveling companions. It is wise to join well in advance of your planned vacation so that there's enough time to determine compatibility and plan a joint trip. Membership fees, including the newsletter, are $36 for 6 months or $60 a year for a single-sex listing; $66 and $120, respectively, for a complete listing.

Also note that certain cruise lines offer guaranteed shared rates for single travelers, whereby cabin mates are selected on request. Two cruise lines that provide such rates are *Cunard* (phone: 800-221-4770) and *Royal Cruise Line* (phone: 800-622-0538 or 415-956-7200 in California; 800-227-4534 elsewhere in the US).

In addition, a number of tour packagers cater to single travelers. These companies offer packages designed for individuals interested in vacationing with a group of single travelers or in being matched with a traveling companion. Among the better established of these agencies are the following:

*Gallivanting* (515 E. 79th St., Suite 20F, New York, NY 10021; phone: 800-933-9699 or 212-988-0617). Offers 1- to 2-week tours for singles ages 25 through 55, including cruises and outdoor activities such as hiking, rafting, hot-air ballooning, snorkeling, and sailing. *Gallivanting* also matches singles of the same sex willing to share accommodations in order to avoid paying single supplement charges, and the agency guarantees this arrangement if bookings are paid for at least 75 days in advance.

*Grand Circle Travel* (347 Congress St., Boston, MA 02210 (phone: 800-221-2610 or 617-350-7500). Arranges extended vacations, escorted tours and cruises for the over-50 traveler, including singles. Membership, which is automatic when you book a trip through *Grand Circle,* includes travel discounts and other extras, such as a Pen Pals service for singles seeking traveling companions.

*Marion Smith Singles* (611 Prescott Place, North Woodmere, NY 11581; phone: 516-791-4852, 516-791-4865, or 212-944-2112). Specializes in tours for singles ages 20 to 50, who can choose to share accommodations to avoid paying single supplement charges.

*Saga International Holidays* (120 Boylston St., Boston MA 02116; phone: 800-343-0273 or 617-451-6808). A subsidiary of a British company specializing in older travelers, many of them single, *Saga* offers a broad selection of packages for people age 60 and over or those 50 to 59 traveling with someone 60 or older. Recent offerings included the 32-night South American Odyssey tour, which includes stops in Argentina, Bolivia, Brazil, Chile, Ecuador, Peru, and Uruguay. Although anyone can book a *Saga* trip, a $15 club membership includes a subscription to their newsletter, as well as other publications and travel services — such as a matching service for single travelers.

*Singles in Motion* (545 W. 236th St., Suite 1D, Riverdale, NY 10463; phone: 718-884-4464). Offers a number of packages for single travelers, including tours, cruises, and excursions focusing on outdoor activities such as hiking and biking.

*Solo Flights* (127 S. Compo Rd., Westport, CT 06880; phone: 203-226-9993). Represents a number of packagers and cruise lines and books singles on individual and group tours.

*Travel in Two's* (239 N. Broadway, Suite 3, N. Tarrytown, NY 10591; phone: 914-631-8409). This company books solo travelers on packages offered by a number of companies (at no extra cost to clients), offers its own tours, and matches singles with traveling companions. Many offerings are listed in their quarterly *Singles Vacation Newsletter,* which costs $7.50 per issue or $20 per year.

A good book for single travelers is *Traveling On Your Own,* by Eleanor Berman, which offers tips on traveling solo and includes information on trips for singles, ranging from outdoor adventures to educational programs. Available in bookstores, it also can be ordered by sending $12.95, plus postage and handling, to Random House, Order Dept., 400 Hahn Rd., Westminster, MD 21157 (phone: 800-733-3000).

Single travelers also may want to subscribe to *Going Solo,* a newsletter which offers helpful information on going on your own. Issued eight times a year, a subscription costs $36. Contact Doerfer Communications, PO Box 1035, Cambridge, MA 02238 (phone: 617-876-2764).

An attractive alternative for the single traveler is *Club Med,* which operates scores of resorts in more than 37 countries worldwide and caters to singles, as well as couples and families. Though the clientele is often under 30, there is a considerable age mix; the average age is 37. *Club Med* has two Brazilian resorts — in Rio das Pedras and Itaparica. *Club Med* offers single travelers package-rate vacations including airfare, food, wine, lodging, entertainment, and athletic facilities. The atmosphere is relaxed, the dress informal, and the price reasonable. For information, contact *Club Med* (3 E. 54th St., New York, NY 10022; phone: 800-CLUB-MED). For further information on *Club Med* and other alternatives suitable for singles, see our discussion of accommodations in *On the Road,* in this section.

Not all single travelers are looking for a swinging scene. Some take vacations to rest and relax, and they prefer being by themselves. Generally, people who want this quieter mode of travel have to accept that their accommodations will cost more than if they were part of a couple.

Those interested in a particularly cozy type of accommodation should consider staying in a bed and breakfast establishment or guesthouse. Though a single person will likely pay more than half of the rate quoted for a couple even at these smaller establishments, the prices still are quite reasonable, and the homey atmosphere will make you feel less conspicuously alone.

Another possibility is the *United States Servas Committee* (11 John St., Room 407, New York, NY 10038; phone: 212-267-0252), which maintains a list of hosts around the world who are willing to take visitors into their homes as guests for a 3-night stay. Many private houses and farms throughout the countryside make a pleasant home base and offer a chance to meet local people. *Servas* will send an application form and a list of interviewers at the nearest locations for you to contact. After the interview, if you are accepted as a *Servas* traveler, you'll receive a membership certificate. The membership fee is $45 per year for an individual, with a $15 deposit to receive the host list, refunded upon its return.

And there's always camping. Many areas along the coast in South America, as well as some sites around the countryside, have a place to pitch a tent and enjoy the scenery. However, it is *not* advisable to camp in any isolated area or in a number of South American countries which are politically unstable and could be unsafe. So check — before you pitch your tent. (For more information, see *Camping and RVs, Hiking and Biking,* in this section.)

**WOMEN AND STUDENTS:** Two specific groups of single travelers deserve special mention: women and students. Countless women travel by themselves in South America, and such an adventure need not be feared.

One lingering inhibition many female travelers still harbor is that of eating alone in public places. The trick here is to relax and enjoy your meal and surroundings; while you may run across the occasional unenlightened waiter, dining solo is no longer uncommon.

A woman traveling alone in South America is bound to arouse more than the usual share of attention (by North American standards). This, more than any other single factor, can demoralize a woman on her own. However, exploring South America can be terrifically exciting, and people will go out of their way to be helpful. Once the sense of being foreign wears off, a woman traveler can feel at home in most out-of-the-way places, desert and jungle included. A single woman traveler is such a rarity that in many villages people consider it a privilege to meet one and will invite her to visit their families.

Still, a first-time visitor who speaks no Spanish or Portuguese is advised to join a tour of some kind; and even well-prepared or seasoned women travelers in South America invariably describe the experience with ambivalent feelings. Although there is little danger of physical harm if you apply commonsense guidelines (as you would if you were traveling in the US or Europe), any woman considering a trip to South America on her own must be prepared to encounter psychological discomfort if she minds being whistled at occasionally or if she is self-conscious about traveling alone in a male-dominated, family-oriented society.

Single women traveling in South America also may be taken aback by the "machismo" of South American men in some countries. Women should be forewarned that this male perspective — akin to antediluvian chauvinism in the US — is generally accepted among South Americans. It is unwise to think that an American woman traveler is going to change the national tide single-handedly. Defense is the best offense in this case — don't let it spoil your vacation.

Here are some suggestions for handling difficult situations:

1. Try to take even an abbreviated language course before setting out, and carry a dictionary or phrase book. A little intelligent discourse will go a long way to help you maneuver from place to place with fewer problems.
2. Know where you are going. When you are walking in the street, have some idea

of your destination — whether market, museum, bus station, or hotel. Ignore whistles, jeers, and remarks.
3. Wherever possible, ask women residents of a particular region or city the districts they consider safe.
4. Do not walk alone at night. This applies to the countryside as well as to the city.
5. Bus and railway stations and airports are the areas in which women are approached by offensive individuals most frequently. A single woman waiting for transport can reduce that likelihood by joining a group of women travelers or a family. They usually will be pleased to have you sit with them and may even accept you as part of their group within a short time.
6. In most cases, men who approach women on their own are not dangerous, merely annoying. If ignoring the masher doesn't work, a harsh look and a sharp command (*"Vete,"* in Spanish, or *"Vai embora,"* in Portuguese — "Go away;" *"Un poco de respeto, por favor,"* in Spanish, or *"Un pouco de respeito, por favor,"* in Portuguese — "A little respect, please") tends to discourage unwelcome advances. In the last resort, approach a police officer for help or, if the incident occurs in a public facility, as is often the case, retreat to the ladies' room.
7. Never open a hotel room door to anyone you do not know.

**Studying Abroad** – A large number of single travelers are students. Travel *is* education. Travel broadens a person's knowledge and deepens his or her perception of the world in a way no media or "armchair" experience ever could. In addition, to study a country's language, art, culture, or history in one of its own schools is to enjoy the most productive method of learning.

By "student" we do not necessarily mean a person who wishes to matriculate at a foreign university to earn an academic degree. Nor do we necessarily mean a younger person. A student is anyone who wishes to include some sort of educational program in a trip to South America.

There are many benefits for students abroad, and the way to begin to discover them is to consult the *Council on International Educational Exchange (CIEE)*. This organization, which runs a variety of well-known work, study, and travel programs for students, is the US sponsor of the International Student Identity Card (ISIC). Reductions on airfare, other transportation, and entry fees to most museums and other exhibitions are only some of the advantages of the card. To apply for it, write to *CIEE* at one of the following addresses: 205 E. 42nd St., New York, NY 10017 (phone: 212-661-1414); 2486 Channing Way, Berkeley, CA 94704 (phone: 510-848-8604); 312 Sutter St., Suite 407, San Francisco, CA 94108 (phone: 415-421-3473); or 919 Irving St., Suite 102, San Francisco, CA 94122 (phone: 415-566-6222). Mark the letter "Attn. Student ID." Application requires a $14 fee, a passport-size photograph, and proof that you are a matriculating student (this means either a transcript or a letter or bill from your school registrar with the school's official seal; high school and junior high school students can use their report cards). There is no maximum age limit, but participants must be at least 12 years old. The *ID Discount Guide,* which gives details of the discounts country by country, is free with membership. Another free publication of *CIEE* is the informative, annual, 64-page *Student Travel Catalog,* which covers all aspects of youth travel abroad for vacation trips, jobs, or study programs, and also includes a list of other helpful publications. You can order the catalogue from the Information and Student Services Department at the New York address given above.

Another card of value in South America, and also available through *CIEE*, is the Federation of International Youth Travel Organizations (FIYTO) card, which provides many of the benefits of the ISIC card. In this case, cardholders need not be students, merely under age 26. To apply, send $14 with a passport-size photo and proof of birth date to *CIEE* at one of the addresses above.

Students and singles in general should keep in mind that youth hostels exist in many cities throughout South America. They always are inexpensive, generally clean and well situated, and they are a sure place to meet other people traveling alone. Hostels are run by the hosteling associations of 68 countries that make up the *International Youth Hostel Federation (IYHF);* membership in one of the national associations affords access to the hostels of the rest. To join the American affiliate, *American Youth Hostels (AYH),* contact the national office (PO Box 37613, Washington, DC 20013-7613; phone: 202-783-6161), or the local *AYH* council nearest you. As we went to press, the following membership rates were in effect: $25 for adults (between 18 and 54); $10 for youths (17 and under); $15 for seniors (55 and up); and $35 for family membership. *Hosteling North America,* which lists hostels in the US and Canada, comes with your *AYH* card (non-members can purchase this book for $5, plus postage and handling); the *Guide to Budget Accommodations,* Volume 2, covers hostels in South America (Volume 1 covers Europe and the Mediterranean) and must be purchased ($10.95, plus postage and handling).

Those who go abroad without an *AYH* card may purchase youth hostel International Guest Cards (available in packages of up to six cards, each costs $3 and is good for a night's stay) and obtain information on local youth hostels by contacting some of the youth hostel associations in South America. In addition, local tourist boards in South America also publish information sheets on hostels in their areas (see the individual reports in THE CITIES for locations).

Opportunities for study in South America range from summer or academic-year courses in the language and civilization of a country designed specifically for foreigners (including those whose school days are well behind them) to long-term university attendance by those intending to take a degree.

Those who wish to study in South America have a variety of options. A number of universities in the US sponsor programs at South American universities, and it also is possible to register for courses and programs designed specifically for foreign students under the auspices of a South American institution. Many US universities accept credits from South America, but students are advised to make sure that credits are reciprocal before enrolling. It is advisable to begin researching and planning a study trip to South America about a year before you go and documentation and application forms should be submitted at least 2 months before the semester starts. The academic year varies from country to country — in Venezuela, it runs from September to July; in Argentina and Brazil, from March or April to December, and so on. Most courses are given in Spanish or Portuguese. In addition, there are numerous summer courses and short programs for Americans interested in studying Spanish or Portuguese, South American archaeology, history, or literature, or painting or native crafts, which are offered informally, in English, without credit, and for very reasonable fees.

Complete details on more than 3,000 available courses abroad (including at South American universities) and suggestions on how to apply are contained in two books published by the *Institute of International Education* (IIE Books, Publications Office, 809 UN Plaza, New York, NY 10017; phone 212-984-5412): *Vacation Study Abroad* ($31.95, plus shipping and handling) and *Academic Year Abroad* ($39.95, plus shipping and handling). A third book, *Teaching Abroad,* is out of print; check your local library. IIE Books also offers a free pamphlet called *Basic Facts on Study Abroad.*

The *National Registration Center for Study Abroad (NRCSA,* PO Box 1393, Milwaukee, WI 53201; phone: 414-278-0631) also offers a publication called *The Worldwide Classroom: Study Abroad and Learning Vacations in 40 Countries: 1992-1993,* available for $8.50, plus $3 shipping and handling, which includes information on over 160 schools and cultural centers that offer courses for Americans with the primary focus on foreign language and culture.

Those who are interested in a "learning vacation" also may be interested in *Travel and Learn* by Evelyn Kaye. This guide to educational travel discusses a wide range of opportunities — everything from archaeology to whale watching — and provides information on organizations that offer programs in these areas of interest. The book is available in bookstores for $23.95; or you can send $26 (which includes shipping charges) to Blue Penguin Publications (3031 Fifth St., Boulder, CO 80304; phone: 800-800-8147 or 303-449-8474). *Learning Vacations* by Gerson G. Eisenberg also provides extensive information on seminars, workshops, courses, and so on — in a wide variety of subjects. Available in bookstores, it also can be ordered from Peterson's Guides (PO Box 2123, Princeton, NJ 08543-2123; phone: 800-338-3282 or 609-243-9111) for $11.95, plus shipping and handling.

*Work, Study, Travel Abroad: The Whole World Handbook,* issued by the *Council on International Educational Exchange (CIEE),* is an informative, chatty guide on study programs, work opportunities, and travel hints, with a particularly good section on Latin America. It is available for $10.95, plus shipping and handling, from *CIEE* (address above).

*AFS Intercultural Programs* (313 E. 43rd St., New York, NY 10017; phone: 800-AFS-INFO or 212-949-4242) sets up exchanges between US and foreign high school students on an individual basis for a semester or whole academic year.

If you are interested in a home-stay travel program, in which you learn about another culture by living with a family, contact the *Experiment in International Living,* which sponsors short-term home-stay programs. Designed primarily for high school students, these programs are educational in focus and are offered in over 40 countries, including Bolivia, Brazil, Chile, and Ecuador. For further information, contact *Experiment in International Living,* PO Box 676, Brattleboro, VT 05302-0676 (phone: 802-257-7751 in Vermont; 800-451-4465 elsewhere in the continental US).

**WORKING ABROAD:** For youths age 18 and up who are interested in working abroad as volunteers, the *CIEE* also publishes a helpful book, *Volunteer!,* which includes volunteer programs with nonprofit organizations worldwide, many of which are located in South America. It is available for $6.95, plus shipping and handling, from the *CIEE* at one of the addresses given above. *CIEE* also may be able to provide other information or assistance to those interested in working in South America.

# Hints for Older Travelers

Special discounts and more free time are just two factors that have given Americans over age 65 a chance to see the world at affordable prices. Senior citizens make up an ever-growing segment of the travel population, and the trend among them is to travel more frequently and for longer periods of time. There are some distinct disadvantages to South America as a destination for older travelers, however. Few of the senior citizen discounts so prevalent in North America exist in South American countries.

**PLANNING:** When planning a vacation, prepare your itinerary with one eye on your own physical condition and the other on a topographical map. The greatest obstacles to travel throughout South America are the climate, terrain, and altitudes involved. The average pan–South American tour involves sudden changes from high mountain countries to jungle lowlands. These pose some danger for anyone with heart or breathing problems. In cities like La Paz, Bolivia, everyone has trouble breathing, even the most fit.

Older travelers may find the following publications of interest:

## GETTING READY / Older Travelers

*The Discount Guide for Travelers Over 55,* by Caroline and Walter Weintz, is an excellent book for budget-conscious older travelers. Published by Penguin USA, it is currently out of print; check your local library.

*Going Abroad: 101 Tips for Mature Travelers* offers tips on preparing for your trip, commonsense precautions en route, and some basic travel terminology. This concise, free booklet is available from *Grand Circle Travel,* 347 Congress St., Boston, MA 02210 (phone: 800-221-2610 or 617-350-7500).

*The International Health Guide for Senior Citizen Travelers,* by Dr. W. Robert Lange, covers such topics as trip preparations, food and water precautions, adjusting to weather and climate conditions, finding a doctor, motion sickness, jet lag, and so on. Also includes a list of resource organizations that provide medical assistance for travelers. It is available for $4.95 postpaid from Pilot Books, 103 Cooper St., Babylon, NY 11702 (phone: 516-422-2225).

*The Mature Traveler* is a monthly newsletter that provides information on travel discounts, places of interest, useful tips, and other topics of interest for travelers 49 and up. To subscribe, send $24.50 to GEM Publishing Group, PO Box 50820, Reno, NV 89513 (phone: 702-786-7419).

*Take a Camel to Lunch and Other Adventures for Mature Travelers,* by Nancy O'Connell, offers offbeat and unusual adventures for travelers over 50. Available at bookstores or directly from Bristol Publishing Enterprises for $8.95 (plus shipping and handling), PO Box 1737, San Leandro, CA 94577 (phone: 800-346-4889 or 510-895-4461).

*Travel Tips for Older Americans* is a useful booklet that provides good, basic advice. This US State Department publication (stock number: 044-000-02270-2) can be ordered by sending a check or money order for $1 to the Superintendent of Documents (US Government Printing Office, Washington, DC 20402) or by calling 202-783-3238 and charging the order to a credit card.

*Unbelievably Good Deals & Great Adventures That You Absolutely Can't Get Unless You're Over 50,* by Joan Rattner Heilman, offers travel tips for older travelers, including discounts on accommodations and transportation, as well as a list of organizations for seniors. It is available for $7.95 (plus shipping and handling) from Contemporary Books, 180 N. Michigan Ave., Chicago, IL 60601 (phone: 312-782-9181).

**HEALTH:** Health facilities in major South American cities generally are good; however, an inability to speak the language can pose a serious problem, not in receiving treatment at large hospitals, where many doctors and other staff members will speak English, but in getting help elsewhere or in getting to the place where help is available. A number of organizations exist to help travelers avoid or deal with a medical emergency while traveling. For information on these services, see *Staying Healthy,* in this section.

Medicare is *not* honored in South America. Therefore, before you go, check the applicability of your current insurance coverage while traveling abroad, and if you are not fully covered look into one of the comprehensive insurance packages offered to travelers (see *Insurance,* in this section).

Pre-trip medical and dental checkups are strongly recommended. In addition, be sure to take along any prescription medication you need, enough to last *without a new prescription* for the duration of your trip; pack all medications with a note from your doctor for the benefit of airport authorities. If you have specific medical problems, bring prescriptions and a "medical file" composed of the following:

1. A summary of your medical history and current diagnosis.
2. A list of drugs to which you are allergic.

## 102  GETTING READY / Older Travelers

3. Your most recent electrocardiogram, if you have heart problems.
4. Your doctor's name, address, and telephone number.

**DISCOUNTS AND PACKAGES:** Since guidelines change from place to place, it is a good idea for older travelers to inquire in advance about discounts on transportation, hotels, concerts, movies, museums, and other activities.

Many hotel chains, airlines, cruise lines, bus companies, car rental companies, and other travel suppliers offer discounts to older travelers. Some US airlines offer those age 62 and over (and often one traveling companion per qualifying senior citizen) discounts on flights to South America. For information on current prices and applicable restrictions, contact the individual carriers.

Some discounts, however, are extended only to bona fide members of certain senior citizens organizations. For instance, *Sheraton* offers a 25% discount to any senior citizen and participating *Holiday Inns* offer 10% discounts for *AARP* members — in both cases, these discounts may not apply during certain "blackout" periods. (See listings below for more information on *AARP* benefits.) Because the same organizations frequently offer package tours to both domestic and international destinations, the benefits of membership are twofold: Those who join can take advantage of discounts as individual travelers and also reap the savings that group travel affords. In addition, because the age requirements for some of these organizations are quite low (or nonexistent), the benefits can begin to accrue early.

In order to take advantage of these discounts, you should carry proof of your age (or eligibility). A driver's license, membership card in a recognized senior citizens' organization, or a Medicare card should be adequate. Among the organizations dedicated to helping older travelers see the world are the following:

*American Association of Retired Persons* (*AARP;* 601 E St. NW, Washington, DC 20049; phone: 202-434-2277). The largest and best known of these organizations. Membership is open to anyone 50 or over, whether retired or not; dues are $8 a year, $20 for 3 years, or $45 for 10 years, and include spouse. The *AARP* Travel Experience Worldwide program, available through *American Express Travel Related Services,* offers members tours, cruises, and other travel programs worldwide designed exclusively for older travelers. Members can book these services by calling *American Express* at 800-927-0111 for land and air travel, or 800-745-4567 for cruises.

*Mature Outlook* (Customer Service Center, 6001 N. Clark St., Chicago, IL 60660; phone: 800-336-6330). Through its *TravelAlert,* tours, cruises, and other vacation packages are available to members at special savings. Hotel and car rental discounts and travel accident insurance also are available. Membership is open to anyone 50 years of age or older, costs $9.95 a year, and includes a bimonthly newsletter and magazine, as well as information on package tours.

*National Council of Senior Citizens* (1331 F St. NW, Washington, DC 20004; phone: 202-347-8800). Here, too, the emphasis is on keeping costs low. This nonprofit organization offers members a different roster of package tours each year, as well as individual arrangements through its affiliated travel agency *(Vantage Travel Service).* Although most members are over 50, membership is open to anyone (regardless of age) for an annual fee of $12 per person or couple. Lifetime membership costs $150.

Certain travel agencies and tour operators offer special trips geared to older travelers. Among them are the following:

## GETTING READY / Older Travelers

*Evergreen Travel Service* (4114 198th St. SW, Suite 13, Lynnwood, WA 98036-6742; phone: 800-435-2288 or 206-776-1184). This specialist in trips for persons with disabilities recently introduced Lazybones Tours, a program offering leisurely tours for older travelers. Most programs are first class or deluxe, and include an escort.

*Gadabout Tours* (700 E. Tahquitz, Palm Springs, CA 92262; phone: 619-325-5556 or 800-521-7309 in California; 800-952-5068 elsewhere in the US). Offers escorted tours and cruises to a number of destinations, including South America.

*Grand Circle Travel* (347 Congress St., Boston, MA 02210; phone: 800-221-2610 or 617-350-7500). Caters exclusively to the over-50 traveler and packages a large variety of escorted tours, cruises, and extended vacations, including tours to the Galápagos, Ecuador, and Peru, as well as a program that includes Buenos Aires, Iguassu Falls, and Rio de Janeiro. Amazon cruises also are offered. Membership, which is automatic when you book a trip through *Grand Circle,* includes discount certificates on future trips and other travel services, such as a matching service for single travelers and a helpful free booklet, *Going Abroad: 101 Tips for Mature Travelers* (see the source list above).

*Grandtravel* (6900 Wisconsin Ave., Suite 706, Chevy Chase, MD 20815; phone: 800-247-7651 or 301-986-0790 throughout the US and Canada). This agency specializes in trips for grandparents and their grandchildren (aunts and uncles are welcome, too), bringing the generations together through travel. Several itineraries coincide with school vacations and emphasize historic and natural sites. Transportation, accommodations, and activities are thoughtfully arranged to meet the needs of the young and the young-at-heart. Among their recent offerings was a 2-week cruise to the Galápagos Islands led by a naturalist.

*Saga International Holidays* (120 Boylston St., Boston MA 02116; phone: 800-343-0273 or 617-451-6808). A subsidiary of a British company catering to the older traveler, *Saga* offers a broad selection of packages for people age 60 and over or those 50 to 59 traveling with someone 60 or older. Recent offerings included a 32-night South American Odyssey, with stops in Argentina, Bolivia, Brazil, Chile, Ecuador, Peru, and Uruguay. Although anyone can book a *Saga* trip, a $15 club membership includes a subscription to their newsletter, as well as other publications and travel services.

Many travel agencies, particularly the larger ones, are delighted to make presentations to help a group of senior citizens select destinations. A local chamber of commerce should be able to provide the names of such agencies. Once a time and place are determined, an organization member or travel agent can obtain group quotations for transportation, accommodations, meal plans, and sightseeing. Larger groups usually get the best breaks.

Another choice open to older travelers is a trip that includes an educational element. *Elderhostel,* a nonprofit organization, offers programs at educational institutions worldwide, some of which are in South America (at press time, in Brazil, Ecuador, and Uruguay). The foreign programs generally last about 2 weeks, and include double occupancy accommodations in hotels or student residence halls and all meals. Travel to the programs usually is by designated scheduled flights, and participants can arrange to extend their stay at the end of the program. Elderhostelers must be at least 60 years old (younger if a spouse or companion qualifies), in good health, and not in need of special diets. For a free catalogue describing the program and current offerings, write to *Elderhostel* (75 Federal St., Boston, MA 02110; phone: 617-426-7788). Those interested in the program also can borrow slides at no charge or purchase an informational videotape for $5.

# Hints for Traveling with Children

What better way to encounter the world's variety than in the company of the young, wide-eyed members of your family? Their presence does not have to be a burden or an excessive expense. The current generation of discounts for children and family package deals can make a trip together quite reasonable.

A family trip will be an investment in your children's future, making geography and history come alive to them, and leaving a sure memory that will be among the fondest you will share with them someday. Their insights will be refreshing to you; their impulses may take you to unexpected places with unexpected dividends.

By and large, South Americans are very fond of children and enjoy having them around. No matter where you travel in the southern hemisphere, you will encounter parents with infants and youngsters. Children are treated with affectionate warmth in most hotels and restaurants. They often are fussed over, smiled at, and given extra little treats.

**PLANNING:** Here are several hints for making a trip with children easy and fun.

1. Children, like everyone else, will derive more pleasure from a trip if they know something about their destination before they arrive. Begin their education about a month before you leave. Using maps, travel magazines, and books, give children a clear idea of where you are going and how far away it is.
2. Children should help to plan the itinerary, and where you go and what you do should reflect some of their ideas. If they already know something about the sites they'll visit, they will have the excitement of recognition when they arrive.
3. Children also will enjoy learning some phrases in the languages (generally Spanish or Portuguese) of the countries they will be visiting — a few basics like "hello," "goodbye," and "thank you."
4. Familiarize your children with the foreign currency they will be using. Give them an allowance for the trip and be sure they understand just how far it will or won't go.
5. Give children specific responsibilities: The job of carrying their own flight bags and looking after their personal things, along with some other light chores, will give them a stake in the journey.
6. Give each child a travel diary or scrapbook to take along.

If you are visiting a French- or Spanish-speaking region of South America, you may want to refer to the *Berlitz Jr.* instructional series for children. The series combines an illustrated storybook with a lively 60-minute audiocassette. Each book features a character, Teddy, who goes to school and learns to count and spell and speak Spanish or French phrases. The book/cassette package is available for $19.95, plus shipping and handling, from Macmillan Publishing Company, Front and Brown Sts., Riverside, NJ 08075 (phone: 800-257-5755).

Children's books about South America provide an excellent introduction to various South American countries and cultures and can be found at many general bookstores and in libraries. Bookstores specializing in children's books include the following:

*Books of Wonder* (132 Seventh Ave., New York, NY 10011; phone: 212-989-3270; or 464 Hudson St., New York, NY 10014; phone: 212-645-8006). Carries both new and used books for children.

*Cheshire Cat* (5512 Connecticut Ave. NW, Washington, DC 20015; phone: 202-244-3956). Specializes in books for children of all ages.

*Eeyore's Books for Children* (2212 Broadway, New York, NY 10024; phone:

212-362-0634; or 25 E. 83rd St., New York, NY 10028; phone: 212-988-3404). Carries an extensive selection of children's books; features a special travel section.

*Reading Reptile, Books and Toys for Young Mammals* (4120 Pennsylvania, St., Kansas City, MO 64111; phone: 816-753-0441). Carries books for children and teens to age 15.

*Red Balloon* (891 Grand Ave., St. Paul, MN 55105; phone: 612-224-8320). Carries both new and used children's books.

*White Rabbit Children's Books* (7755 Girard Ave., La Jolla, CA 92037; phone: 619-454-3518). Carries books and music for children (and parents).

Another source of children's books perfect to take on the road is *The Family Travel Guides Catalogue*. This detailed booklet describes a number of informative and fun titles and is available from Carousel Press (PO Box 6061, Albany, CA 94706; phone: 415-527-5849), which also is the mail-order supplier of all titles listed.

And for parents, *Travel With Your Children* (*TWYCH;* 80 Eighth Ave., New York, NY 10011; phone: 212-206-0688) publishes a newsletter, *Family Travel Times,* that focuses on families with young travelers and offers helpful hints. An annual subscription (10 issues) is $35 and includes a copy of the "Airline Guide" issue (updated every other year), which focuses on the subject of flying with children. This special issue is available separately for $10.

Another newsletter devoted to family travel is *Getaways.* This quarterly publication provides reviews of family-oriented literature, activities, and useful travel tips. To subscribe, send $25 to *Getaways,* Attn. Ms. Brooke Kane, PO Box 8282, McLean, VA 22107 (phone: 703-534-8747).

Also of interest to parents traveling with their children is *How to Take Great Trips with Your Kids,* by psychologist Sanford Portnoy and his wife, Joan Flynn Portnoy. The book includes helpful tips from fellow family travelers, a chapter on child development relating to travel, tips on economical accommodations and touring by car, RV, and train, as well as over 50 games to play with your children en route. It is available for $8.95, plus shipping and handling, from Harvard Common Press, 535 Albany St., Boston, MA 02118 (phone: 617-423-5803). Also check out *Great Vacations with Your Kids,* by Dorothy Jordan (Dutton; $12.95).

Another book on family travel, *Travel with Children* by Maureen Wheeler, offers a wide range of practical tips on traveling with children, and includes accounts of the author's family travel experiences. It is available for $10.95, plus shipping and handling, from Lonely Planet Publications, Embarcadero West, 112 Linden St., Oakland, CA 94607 (phone: 510-893-8555).

Finally, parents arranging a trip with their children may want to deal with an agency specializing in family travel such as *Let's Take the Kids* (1268 Devon Ave., Los Angeles, CA 90024; phone: 800-726-4349 or 213-274-7088). In addition to arranging and booking trips for individual families, this group occasionally organizes trips for single-parent families traveling together. They also offer a parent travel network, whereby parents who have been to a particular destination can evaluate it for others.

**GETTING THERE AND GETTING AROUND:** Begin early to investigate all available discount and charter flights, as well as any package deals and special rates offered by the major airlines. Booking is sometimes required up to 2 months in advance. You may well find that charter plans offer no reductions for children, or not enough to offset the risk of last-minute delays or other inconveniences to which charters are subject. Some of the major scheduled airlines, on the other hand, do provide hefty discounts for children. If traveling by ship, note that children under 12 usually travel at a considerably reduced fare on cruise lines. When using local transportation such as a bus or train, ask about lower fares for children or family rates.

## GETTING READY / Traveling with Children

**Plane –** When you make your reservations, tell the airline that you are traveling with a child. Children ages 2 through 12 generally travel at about half to two-thirds of the regular full-fare adult ticket price on most international flights. This children's fare, however, usually is much higher than an excursion fare (which also may be even further reduced for children). On many international flights, children under 2 travel at about 10% of the adult fare if they sit on an adult's lap. A second infant without a second adult would pay the fare applicable to children ages 2 through 11.

Although some airlines will, on request, supply bassinets for infants, most carriers encourage parents to bring their own safety seat on board, which then is strapped into the airline seat with a regular seat belt. This is much safer — and certainly more comfortable — than holding the child in your lap. If you do not purchase a seat for your baby, you have the option of bringing the infant restraint along on the off chance that there might be an empty seat next to yours — in which case some airlines will let you use that seat at no charge for your baby and infant seat. However, if there is no empty seat available, the infant seat no doubt will have to be checked as baggage (and you may have to pay an additional charge), since it generally does not fit under airplane seats or in the overhead racks. The safest bet is to pay for a seat.

Be forewarned: Some safety seats designed primarily for use in cars do not fit into plane seats properly. Although nearly all seats manufactured since 1985 carry labels indicating whether they meet federal standards for use aboard planes, actual seat sizes may vary from carrier to carrier. At the time of this writing, the FAA was in the process of reviewing and revising the federal regulations regarding infant travel and safety devices — it was still to be determined if children should be *required* to sit in safety seats and whether the airlines will have to provide them.

If using one of these infant restraints, you should try to get bulkhead seats, which will provide extra room to care for your child during the flight. You also should request a bulkhead seat when using a bassinet — again, this is not as safe as strapping the child in. On some planes bassinets hook into a bulkhead wall; on others they are placed on the floor in front of you. (Note that bulkhead seats often are reserved for families traveling with children.) As a general rule, babies should be held during takeoff and landing.

Request seats on the aisle if you have a toddler or if you think you will need to use the bathroom frequently. Carry onto the plane all you will need to care for and occupy your children during the flight — formula, diapers, a sweater, books, favorite stuffed animals, and so on. Dress your baby simply, with a minimum of buttons and snaps, because the only place you may have to change a diaper is at your seat or in a small lavatory. The flight attendant can warm a bottle for you.

On most US carriers, you can ask for a hot dog, hamburger, or even a fruit plate, instead of the airline's regular lunch or dinner if you give at least 24 hours' notice. Some, but not all, airlines have baby food aboard. (Note that meals and meal choices are most limited on intra–South American flights, particularly on the smaller domestic carriers.) While you should bring along toys from home, also ask about children's diversions. Some carriers have terrific free packages of games, coloring books, and puzzles.

When the plane takes off and lands, make sure your baby is nursing or has a bottle, pacifier, or thumb in its mouth. This sucking will make the child swallow and help to clear stopped ears. A piece of hard candy will do the same thing for an older child.

Parents traveling by plane with toddlers, children, or young teenagers may want to consult *When Kids Fly,* a free booklet published by Massport (Public Affairs Department, 10 Park Plaza, Boston, MA 02116-3971; phone: 617-973-5600), which includes helpful information on airfares for children, infant seats, what to do in the event of overbooked or cancelled flights, and so on.

■ **Note:** Newborn babies, whose lungs may not be able to adjust to the altitude, should not be taken aboard an airplane. And some airlines may refuse to allow a pregnant woman in her 8th or 9th month to fly. Check with the airline ahead of time, and carry a letter from your doctor stating that you are fit to travel — and indicating the estimated date of birth.

**Ship** – Some shipping lines offer cruises that feature special activities for children, particularly during periods that coincide with major school holidays like *Christmas, Easter,* and the US summer months. On such cruises, children may be charged special cut-rate fares, and there are youth counselors to organize activities. Occasionally, a shipping line even offers free passage during the summer months for children under age 16 occupying a stateroom with two (full-fare) adult passengers. Your travel agent should know which cruise lines offer such programs.

**Car** – Touring by car allows greater flexibility for traveling and packing. (Please, however, read our warnings regarding safety conditions when driving to and in South America in *Traveling by Car,* in this section.) Games and simple toys, such as magnetic checkerboards or drawing pencils and pads, also provide a welcome diversion. And frequent stops so that children can run around make car travel much easier.

**ACCOMMODATIONS AND MEALS:** Often a cot for a child will be placed in a hotel room at little or no extra charge. If you wish to sleep in separate rooms, special rates sometimes are available for families; some places do not charge for children under a certain age. In many of the larger chain hotels, the staffs are more used to children. These hotels also are likely to have swimming pools or gamerooms — both popular with most youngsters. Many large resorts also have recreation centers for children. Cabins, bungalows, condominiums, and other rental options (see our discussions in *On the Road,* in this section) offer families privacy, flexibility, some kitchen facilities, and often lower costs.

A number of hotel chains with properties in South America do not charge for children who occupy the same room as their parents. *Marriott* allows children 18 and under to stay at no charge, and will provide one free extra bed if required; *Sheraton*'s policy allows children under 18 to stay at no charge as long as the hotel does not have to provide extra beds; *Hilton* has a policy similar to *Sheraton*'s with no such age limit (some *Hilton* hotels charge a fee for providing an extra bed).

In addition, a few hotels offer special youth activities programs, particularly during summer months. Detailed information can be obtained from a travel agent.

Several of the *Club Med* resorts also are geared for family vacations, offering a variety of special programs.

Among the least expensive options is a camping facility; many are situated in beautiful, out-of-the-way spots, and generally are good, well equipped, and less expensive than any hotel. Note, however, our warnings on safety; for information on camping facilities, see *Camping, Hiking, and Biking,* in this section.

For the times you will want to be without children — for an evening's entertainment or a particularly rigorous stint of sightseeing, better hotels may be able to arrange for a baby-sitter. Whether the sitter is hired directly or through an agency, ask for and check references and keep in mind that the candidates may not speak much, if any, English.

At mealtime, don't deny yourself or your children the delights of a new style of cooking. Encourage them to try new foods. Children like to know what kind of food to expect, so it will be interesting to look up South American dishes before leaving. And don't forget about picnics.

■ **Be forewarned:** If packing a picnic lunch in a cooler, ice cubes — whether from your hotel kitchen or a local store — should only be used for keeping food chilled in coolers — *never* put them in drinks, as you can't count on the quality of the water from which these were made. If your accommodations include a refrigerator, a good alternative is to make some ice cubes the night before from purified water. (For more information, see *Staying Healthy,* in this section.)

## Things to Remember
1. If you are spending your vacation touring around South America, pace the days with children in mind. Break the trip into half-day segments, with running around or "doing" time built in.
2. Don't forget that a child's attention span is far shorter than an adult's. Children don't have to see every sight or all of any sight to learn something from their trip; watching, playing with, and talking to other children can be equally enlightening.
3. Let your children lead the way sometimes; their perspective is different from yours, and they may lead you to things you would never have noticed on your own.
4. Remember the places that children love to visit: aquariums, zoos, beaches, nature trails, and so on. Among the activities that may pique their interest are bicycling, snorkeling, boat trips, buggy and pony rides, cable car rides, visiting planetariums and children's museums, and viewing rare condors or Amazon creatures at natural habitat exhibits.

Since you are traveling in a foreign country, the number of special programs for children in English is obviously limited, though more and more hotels have cable or satellite TV showing US programs. South American television has all kinds of kiddie shows and cartoons. Children will be fascinated to watch favorite cartoon characters and other old friends dubbed or subtitled in a foreign language.

Try to spend at least 2 nights at each stop on your tour, and find out what festivals, like *Carnaval,* will be taking place during your trip. These *Mardi Gras*-style festivities, complete with samba parades, gargantuan, masked devil dancers, and fireworks, are especially rewarding and colorful experiences for kids. (For information on these and other special events and activities, see the "Special Events" and "Special Places" sections of the individual city reports in THE CITIES.)

# On the Road

## Credit and Currency

It may seem hard to believe, but one of the greatest (and least understood) costs of travel is money itself. If that sounds simplistic, consider the fact that you can lose as much as 30% of your dollar's value simply by changing money at the wrong place or in the wrong form. Your one single objective in relation to the care and retention of your travel funds is to make them stretch as far as possible. When you do spend money, it should be on things that expand and enhance your travel experience, with no buying power lost due to carelessness or lack of knowledge. This requires more than merely ferreting out the best airfare or the most charming budget hotel. It means being canny about the management of money itself. Herewith, a primer on making money go as far as possible while traveling.

**CURRENCY:** Panama actually uses US currency as the official means of exchange. Throughout the rest of South America, however, a local currency is used which fluctuates in value in relation to the US dollar, affected by a wide variety of phenomena. Although US dollars may be accepted in these countries (particularly at points of entry), you certainly will lose a percentage of your dollar's buying power if you do not take the time to convert it into the local legal tender. By paying for goods and services in the local currency, you save money by not negotiating invariably unfavorable exchange rates for every small purchase, and avoid difficulty where US currency is not readily — or happily — accepted. *Throughout this book, unless specifically stated otherwise, prices are given in US dollars.*

Currency is issued in paper bills and coins, often large and heavy, even when denoting small denominations. All South American currencies are based on the decimal system; like the US dollar, each subdivides into 100 smaller units, usually called centavos or cents. Remember that many South American nations use what North Americans recognize as a dollar sign ($) as the symbol of the local currency. More than one uninitiated traveler has been stunned to receive a check of $34 for coffee and rolls before realizing it did not mean 34 US dollars. Another confusing variation is that the use of periods and commas sometimes is reversed — for instance, in Brazil, decimals are used where US currency uses commas. The official currencies for the various countries covered in this guide are listed in FACTS IN BRIEF.

There is no limit to the amount of US currency that can be brought into South America. There also is no restriction on the amount of traveler's checks (in US dollars or foreign currency) that may be brought in, and these usually present no difficulties when you leave, since their US origin is obvious. To avoid problems anywhere along the line, it's advisable to fill out any customs forms provided when leaving the US, on which you can declare all money you are taking with you — cash, traveler's checks, and so on. US law requires that anyone taking more than $10,000 into or out of the US must report this fact on customs form No. 4790, which is available at all international airports or from any office of US Customs. If taking over $10,000 out of the US, you must report this *before* leaving the US; if returning with such an amount, you must include this information on your customs declaration. Although travelers usually are not questioned by customs officials about currency when entering or leaving, the sensible course is to observe all regulations — which vary from country to country — just to be on the safe side.

**FOREIGN EXCHANGE:** Because of the volatility of exchange rates, be sure to check the current value of the local currency in the areas you are planning to visit before finalizing any travel budget. And before you actually depart on your trip, be aware of the most advantageous exchange rate offered by various financial institutions — US banks, currency exchange firms (at home or abroad), or foreign banks.

For the best sense of current trends, follow the rates posted in the financial section of your local newspaper or in such international newspapers as the *International Herald Tribune*. You also can check with your own bank or with *Thomas Cook Foreign Exchange* (for the nearest location, call 800-972-2192 in Illinois; 800-621-0666 elsewhere in the US). In addition, *Harold Reuter and Company*, a currency exchange service in New York City (200 Park Ave., Suite 332 E., New York, NY 10166; phone: 212-661-0826), is particularly helpful in determining current trends in exchange rates. *Ruesch International* offers up-to-date foreign currency information and currency-related services (such as converting foreign currency checks into US dollars). *Ruesch* also offers a pocket-size *Foreign Currency Guide* (good for estimating equivalents while planning) and a helpful brochure, *6 Foreign Exchange Tips for the Traveler*. Contact *Ruesch International* at one of the following addresses: 3 First National Plaza, Suite 2020, Chicago, IL 60602 (phone: 312-332-5900); 1925 Century Park E., Suite 240, Los Angeles, CA 90067 (phone: 213-277-7800); 608 Fifth Ave., "Swiss Center," New York, NY 10020 (phone: 212-977-2700); or 1350 Eye St. NW, 10th Floor and street level, Washington, DC 20005 (phone: 800-424-2923 or 202-408-1200).

As the US dollar continues to be strong in South America, the continent offers many destinations that are travel bargains. As we went to press, however, most South American currencies were in the process of steady devaluation. If this situation has not changed at the time you are traveling, hold onto your US dollars until the last possible minute. By exchanging too early or exchanging too much, you can lose a substantial percentage of your dollar's value. In Brazil, if you are converting dollars at the *technically* unofficial but legal "free market" rate (not the "black market" mentioned under Rule number three, below), convert only what you anticipate spending — do not count on reconverting to dollars on departure from the country. (Note that you cannot convert Brazilian cruzeiros to dollars once you have returned the US.) For information on these "parallel" rates, see FACTS IN BRIEF.

In South America, you will find the official rate of exchange posted in banks, airports, money exchange houses, hotels, and some shops. In some South American countries, the difference between exchange rates offered in banks and in hotels is not as extreme as in other foreign countries — although as a general rule, expect to get more local currency for your US dollar at banks than at any other commercial establishment (with the possible exceptions of Argentina and Brazil). Exchange rates do change from day to day, and most banks offer the same (or very similar) exchange rates. (In a pinch, the convenience of cashing money in your hotel — sometimes on a 24-hour basis — *may* make up for the difference in the exchange rate; anyone who has ever stood in line in a South American bank for 2 hours can attest to this.) Don't try to bargain in banks or hotels — no one will alter the rates for you.

Money exchange houses (*casas de cambio* or *cambios*) are financial institutions that charge a fee for the service of exchanging dollars for local currency. When considering alternatives, be aware that although the rate varies among these establishments, the rates of exchange offered are bound to be slightly less favorable than the terms offered at nearby banks — again, don't be surprised if you get less local currency for your dollar than the rate published in the papers.

You also can change money legally at the main airports, but these facilities are not open 24 hours a day in all countries. If you plan to fly from one South American country to another after regular business hours, you should change enough dollars into the currency of your next destination so that you can take a taxi or bus when you arrive (though, in a pinch, US dollars usually will be accepted). However, when open, airports generally have bank-rate exchanges. Bear in mind, however, that even in airports it is difficult to exchange one foreign currency for another — for instance, when changing Argentine pesos into Peruvian nuevo soles.

That said, however, the following rules of thumb are worth remembering.

**Rule number one: Never (repeat: *never*) exchange more than $10 for foreign currency at hotels, restaurants, or retail shops.** If you do, you are sure to lose a significant amount of your dollar's buying power. If you do come across a storefront exchange counter offering what appears to be an incredible bargain, there's too much counterfeit specie in circulation to take the chance (see Rule number three, below).

**Rule number two: Estimate your needs carefully; if you overbuy, you lose twice — buying and selling back.** Every time you exchange money, someone is making a profit, and rest assured it isn't you. Use up foreign notes before leaving, saving just enough for airport departure taxes (which often must be paid in local currency), other last-minute incidentals, and tips.

**Rule number three: Don't buy money on the black market.** The exchange rate may be better, but it is a common practice to pass off counterfeit bills to unsuspecting foreigners who aren't familiar with the local currency. It's usually a sucker's game, and you almost always are the sucker; it also can land you in jail.

**Rule number four: Learn the local currency quickly and keep abreast of daily fluctuations in the exchange rate.** These are listed in the English-language *International Herald Tribune* daily for the preceding day, as well as in other major international newspapers. Rates change to some degree every day. For rough calculations, it is quick and safe to use round figures, but for purchases and actual currency exchanges, carry a small pocket calculator to help you compute the exact rate. Inexpensive calculators specifically designed to convert currency amounts for travelers are widely available.

When changing money, don't be afraid to ask how much commission you're being charged, and the exact amount of the prevailing exchange rate. In fact, in any exchange of money for goods or services, you should work out the rate before making any payment.

**TIP PACKS:** It's not a bad idea to buy a *small* amount of foreign coins and banknotes before your departure. But note the emphasis on "small," because, for the most part, you are better off carrying the bulk of your travel funds abroad in US dollar traveler's checks (see below). Still the advantages of tip packs are threefold:

1. You become familiar with the currency (really the only way to guard against making mistakes or being cheated during your first few hours in a new country).
2. You are guaranteed some money should you arrive when a bank or exchange counter isn't open or available.
3. You don't have to depend on hotel desks, porters, or taxi drivers to change your money.

A "tip pack" is the only foreign currency you should buy before you leave. If you do run short upon arrival, US dollars often are accepted at points of entry. In other areas, they either *may* be accepted, or someone may accommodate you by changing a small amount — though invariably at a less than advantageous rate.

**TRAVELER'S CHECKS:** It's wise to carry traveler's checks while on the road instead of (or in addition to) cash, since it's possible to replace them if they are stolen or lost; you usually can receive partial or full replacement funds the same day if you have your purchase receipt and proper identification. Issued in various denominations and available in both US dollars and foreign currencies, with adequate proof of identification (credit cards, driver's license, passport), traveler's checks are as good as cash in most hotels, restaurants, stores, and banks.

You will be able to cash traveler's checks fairly easily throughout South America, but don't expect to meander into a small village and be able to get instant cash. Also, even in metropolitan areas, don't assume that restaurants, small shops, and other establishments are going to be able to change checks of large denominations. Worldwide, more and more establishments are beginning to restrict the amount of traveler's checks they will accept or cash, so it is wise to purchase at least some of your checks in small denominations — say, $10 and $20.

At press time, traveler's checks were not available in any South American currencies, so it will be necessary to carry your travel funds abroad in US dollar denomination traveler's checks. If you have not yet changed your US dollar traveler's checks into local currency and want to pay for something with one, ask if change is available in US dollars *before* you countersign your check. You might otherwise end up with a pocketful of foreign coins, and particularly if you will only be in the country for a short time, you are likely to find it cumbersome to change this back into US currency.

Every type of traveler's check is legal tender in banks around the world, and each company guarantees full replacement if checks are lost or stolen. After that the similarity ends. Some charge a fee for purchase, others are free; you can buy traveler's checks at almost any bank, and some are available by mail. Most important, each traveler's check issuer differs slightly in its refund policy — the amount refunded immediately, the accessibility of refund locations, the availability of a 24-hour refund service, and the time it will take for you to receive replacement checks. For instance, *American Express* guarantees replacement of lost or stolen traveler's checks in under 3 hours at any *American Express* office — other companies may not be as prompt. (Note that *American Express*'s 3-hour policy is based on a traveler's being able to provide the serial numbers of the lost checks. Without these numbers, refunds can take much longer.)

We cannot overemphasize the importance of knowing how to replace lost or stolen checks. All of the traveler's check companies have agents around the world, both in their own name and at associated agencies (usually, but not necessarily, banks), where refunds can be obtained during business hours. Most of them also have 24-hour toll-free telephone lines, and some even will provide emergency funds to tide you over on a Sunday.

Be sure to make a photocopy of the refund instructions that will be given to you by the issuing institution at the time of purchase. To avoid complications should you need to redeem lost checks (and to speed up the replacement process), keep the purchase receipt and an accurate list, by serial number, of the checks that have been spent or cashed. You may want to incorporate this information in an "emergency packet," also including your passport number and date of issue, the numbers of the credit cards you are carrying, and any other bits of information you shouldn't be without. Always keep these records separate from the checks and the original records themselves (you may want to give them to a traveling companion to hold).

Although most people understand the desirability of carrying funds in the form of traveler's checks as protection against loss or theft, an equally good reason is that US dollar traveler's checks invariably get a better rate of exchange than cash does — usually by at least 1% (although the discrepancy has been known to be substantially higher). The reasons for this are technical, and less prevalent in some South American countries than elsewhere, but potential savings still exist and it is a fact of travel life that should not be ignored.

That 1% won't do you much good, however, if you already have spent it *buying* your traveler's checks. Several of the major traveler's check companies charge 1% for the

## GETTING READY / Credit and Currency

acquisition of their checks. To receive fee-free traveler's checks you may have to meet certain qualifications — for instance, *Thomas Cook's* checks issued in US currency are free if you make your travel arrangements through its travel agency. *American Express* traveler's checks are available without charge to members of the *American Automobile Association (AAA).* Holders of some credit cards (such as the *American Express Platinum* card) also may be entitled to free traveler's checks. The issuing institution (e.g., the particular bank at which you purchase them) may itself charge a fee. If you purchase traveler's checks at a bank in which you or your company maintains significant accounts (especially commercial accounts of some size), the bank may absorb the 1% fee as a courtesy.

■ **Note:** *American Express* cardholders now can order traveler's checks by phone through a new service called *Cheques On Call.* By dialing 800-55-FOR-TC, *Green* cardholders can order up to $1,000, *Gold* cardholders, $2,500, and *Platinum* cardholders, $10,000 of *American Express* traveler's checks during any 7-day period. The usual 1% acquisition fee is waived for *Gold* and *Platinum* cardholders. There is no postage charge if the checks are sent by first class mail; *Federal Express* delivery is available for a fee.

*American Express, Bank of America, Citicorp, Thomas Cook, MasterCard,* and *Visa* all offer traveler's checks. Here is a list of the major companies issuing traveler's checks and the numbers to call in the event that loss or theft makes replacement necessary:

*American Express:* To report lost or stolen checks in the US, call 800-221-7282. In South America, call the nearest *American Express* office, or 801-964-6665, collect.

*Bank of America:* To report lost or stolen checks in the US, call 800-227-3460. In South America, call 415-624-5400 or 415-622-3800, collect.

*Citicorp:* To report lost or stolen checks in the US, call 800-645-6556. In South America, call 813-623-4100, collect.

*MasterCard:* Note that *Thomas Cook MasterCard* (below) is now handling all *MasterCard* traveler's check inquiries and refunds.

*Thomas Cook MasterCard:* To report lost or stolen checks in the US, call 800-223-7373. In South America, call 212-974-5696 or 609-987-7300, collect, and they will direct you to the nearest branch of *Thomas Cook.*

*Visa:* To report lost or stolen checks in the continental US, call 800-227-6811. In South America, call 415-574-7111, collect.

**CREDIT CARDS:** Some establishments you may encounter during the course of your travels may not honor any credit cards and some may not honor all cards, so there is a practical reason to carry more than one. The following is a list of credit cards that enjoy wide domestic and international acceptance:

*American Express:* Cardholders can cash personal checks for traveler's checks and cash at *American Express* or its representatives' offices in the US up to the following limits (within any 21-day period): $1,000 for *Green* and *Optima* cardholders; $5,000 for *Gold* cardholders; and $10,000 for *Platinum* cardholders. Check cashing also is available to cardholders who are guests at participating hotels (up to $250), and for holders of airline tickets, at participating airlines (up to $50). Free travel accident, baggage, and car rental insurance if ticket or rental is charged to card; additional insurance also is available for additional cost. For further information or to report a lost or stolen *American Express* card, call 800-528-4800 throughout the continental US; elsewhere in the US and in South America, call 212-477-5700, collect.

*Carte Blanche:* Free travel accident, baggage, and car rental insurance if ticket or rental is charged to card; additional insurance also is available at additional cost. For medical, legal, and travel assistance worldwide, call 800-356-3448 throughout the US; in South America, call 214-680-6480, collect. For further information or to report a lost or stolen *Carte Blanche* card, call 800-525-9135 throughout the US; in South America, call 303-790-2433, collect.

*Diners Club:* Emergency personal check cashing for cardholders staying at participating hotels and motels (up to $250 per stay). Free travel, accident, baggage, and car rental insurance if ticket or rental is charged to card; additional insurance also is available for an additional fee. For medical, legal, and travel assistance worldwide, call 800-356-3448 throughout the US; in South America, call 214-680-6480, collect. For further information or to report a lost or stolen *Diners Club* card, call 800-525-9135 throughout the US; in South America, call 303-790-2433, collect.

*Discover Card:* Offered by a subsidiary of Sears, Roebuck & Co., it provides cardholders with cash advances at numerous automatic teller machines and Sears stores throughout the US. For further information and to report a lost or stolen *Discover* card, call 800-DISCOVER throughout the US. Note that at press time, the *Discover* card was not yet accepted in South America; call for current information when planning your trip.

*MasterCard:* Cash advances are available at participating banks worldwide. Check with your issuing bank for information. *MasterCard* also offers a 24-hour emergency lost card service; call 800-826-2181 throughout the US; in South America, call 314-275-6690, collect.

*Visa:* Cash advances are available at participating banks worldwide. Check with your issuing bank for information. *Visa* also offers a 24-hour emergency lost card service; call 800-336-8472 throughout the US. In South America, call 415-574-7700, collect.

One of the thorniest problems relating to the use of credit cards abroad concerns the rate of exchange at which a purchase is charged. Be aware that the exchange rate in effect on the date that you make a foreign purchase or pay for a foreign service has nothing at all to do with the rate of exchange at which your purchase is billed to you when you get the invoice (sometimes months later) in the US. The amount which the credit card company charges is either a function of the exchange rate at which the establishment's bank processed it or the rate in effect on the day your charge is received at the credit card center. (There is a 1-year limit on the time a hotel or other business can take to forward its charge slips.)

The principle at work in this credit card–exchange rate roulette is simple, but very hard to predict. You make a purchase at a particular dollar versus local currency exchange rate. If the dollar gets stronger in the time between purchase and billing, your purchase actually costs you less than you anticipated. (In countries where the local currency is steadily devaluing, the later exchange rate at which your purchase is calculated may work to your substantial advantage.) If the dollar drops in value during the interim, you pay more than you thought you would. There isn't much you can do about these vagaries except to follow one very broad, very clumsy rule of thumb: If the dollar is doing well at the time of purchase, its value increasing against the local currency, use your credit card on the assumption that it still will be doing well when billing takes place. If the dollar is doing badly, assume it will continue to do badly and pay with traveler's checks or cash. If you get too badly stuck, the best recourse is to complain, loudly. Be aware, too, that most credit card companies charge an unannounced, un-itemized 1% fee for converting foreign currency charges to US dollars.

Also, remember that paying with plastic in some South American countries can be an expensive convenience. Since credit card charges are converted to US dollars at the "official" exchange rate — where US dollars often are worth substantially less foreign currency than when calculated at the "alternate" or "free market" rate — you may be

## GETTING READY / Credit and Currency

doubling the cost of South American purchases and travel services. Check carefully on the local scene before deciding whether to settle bills by charging or paying cash.

**SENDING MONEY ABROAD:** If you have used up your traveler's checks, cashed as many emergency personal checks as your credit card allows, drawn on your cash advance line to the fullest extent, and still need money, it is possible to have it sent to you via one of the following services:

*American Express* (phone: 800-543-4080). Offers a service in South America called "Moneygram," completing money transfers in anywhere from 24 hours to 2 days. The sender can go to any *American Express* office in the US and transfer money by presenting cash, a personal check, money order, or credit card — *Discover* (even though not accepted in South America, this card *can* be used to send funds via the "Moneygram" service), *MasterCard, Visa,* or *American Express Optima* card. No other *American Express* or other credit cards are accepted. *American Express Optima* cardholders also can arrange for this transfer over the phone. The minimum transfer charge is $25, which rises with the amount of the transaction. Up to $10,000 can be transferred in each transaction (additional funds can be sent in separate transactions), but credit card users are limited to the amount of their pre-established credit line. To collect at the other end, the receiver must show identification (passport, driver's license, or other picture ID) at an *American Express* office or at a branch of an affiliated bank in South America.

*Western Union Telegraph Company* (phone: 800-325-4176). To send money to South America, a friend or relative can go, cash in hand, to any *Western Union* office in the US, where the funds will be transferred to a branch of *Citibank* in South America (as there are no *Western Union* branches) nearest to the location requested by the sender. The *minimum* charge for sending money is $38 (a $25 charge from *Citibank* is added to the usual $13 *Western Union charge*), which rises with the amount of the transaction. When the money arrives in South America — in the case of most destinations, within 2 business days (although it varies from country to country) — you will not be notified; you must call or go to the *Citibank* branch to inquire. For a higher fee, the US party to this transaction may call *Western Union* with a *MasterCard* or *Visa* number to send up to $2,000, although larger transfers will be sent to a predesignated location.

If you are literally down to your last cent and have no other way to obtain cash, the nearest US consulate (see *Legal Aid and Consular Services,* in this section) will let you call home to set these matters in motion.

**CASH MACHINES:** Automatic teller machines (ATMs) are increasingly common worldwide. If your bank participates in one of the international ATM networks (most do), the bank will issue you a "cash card" along with a personal identification code or number (also called a PIC or PIN). You can use this card at any ATM in the same electronic network to check your account balances, transfer monies between checking and savings accounts, and — most important for a traveler — withdraw cash instantly. Network ATMs generally are located in banks, commercial and transportation centers, and near major tourist attractions.

Some financial institutions offer exclusive automatic teller machines for their own customers only at bank branches. At the time of this writing, ATMs that *are* connected generally belong to one of the following two international networks:

*Cirrus:* Has over 70,000 automatic teller machines worldwide, including over 210 locations in Chile and Venezuela. *MasterCard* and *Visa* cardholders also may use their cards to draw cash against their credit lines. For further information on the *Cirrus* network, call 800-4-CIRRUS.

*Plus System:* Has over 70,000 automatic teller machines worldwide, including over 40 locations in Colombia and Ecuador. *MasterCard* and *Visa* cardholders also may use their cards to draw cash against their credit lines. For further information on the *Plus System* network, call 800-THE-PLUS.

Information about the *Cirrus* and *Plus* systems also is available at member bank branches, where you can obtain free booklets listing the locations of machines worldwide. Note that a recent change in banking regulations permits financial institutions in the US to subscribe to *both* the *Cirrus* and *Plus* systems, allowing users of either network to withdraw funds from ATMs at participating banks. This change does not, however, apply to banks in the South America, and remember, regulations there may vary.

# Accommodations

South American beach resorts, such as Rio de Janeiro, Salvador (Bahia), Guarujá, the Venezuelan/Colombian Caribbean, Contadora Island, Punta del Este, and Viña del Mar, are famous — not always justifiably — for their hotels and settings. The major cities — Caracas, Buenos Aires, Santiago, and São Paulo — have excellent accommodations with every possible amenity and the same conveniences you would find in any European or North American metropolis.

The remarkable increase in the flow of visitors to South America during the 1970s was responsible for the development and construction of dozens of new hotels and resorts. Many of the newer hotels fit into a category now commonly known as "international standard." Rooms are sizable and frequently have two oversize beds, balconies with views, conventional modern facilities, and full room service. They feature a variety of restaurants, poolside bars, and discotheques. A number also have their own casinos (making gambling the primary activity), and some even have a small convention center, or at least meeting facilities. Though rates vary from city to city in South America, they can be as much as 40% lower than those of their sister hotels in Europe.

Many of these establishments are operated by well-known international hotel chains. Following are some examples of international hotel chains represented in South America along with toll-free numbers to call in the US:

*Best Western* (phone: 800-528-1234). Has 1 property in Quito (Ecuador).

*Club Med* (phone: 800-CLUB-MED). Has 2 properties in Brazil.

*Hilton International* (phone: 800-445-8667). Owned by Ladbroke's gambling group of Great Britain, there is no proprietary connection with the US *Hilton* chain. Has 2 properties in Colombia, 3 properties each in Brazil and Venezuela, and 1 each in Argentina, Chile, and Peru.

*Holiday Inn* (phone: 800-465-4329). Has 2 properties in Brazil and 1 in Chile.

*Hyatt* (phone: 800-233-1234). Has 1 property in Argentina.

*Inter-Continental* (phone: 800-332-4246). Has 1 property each in Argentina, Brazil, and Chile.

*Loews* (phone: 800-223-0888). Has 22 properties in Brazil, 2 in Argentina, and 1 each in Bolivia and Ecuador.

*Marriott* (phone: 800-228-9290). Has 1 property in Panama.

*Meliá* (phone: 800-336-3542). Has 3 properties in Venezuela, and 1 each in Brazil and Colombia.

*Meridien* (phone: 800-543-4300). Operates 2 properties in Brazil.

*Novotel* (phone: 800-221-4542). Operates 12 properties in Brazil, and 1 each in French Guiana and Paraguay.

*Sheraton* (phone: 800-325-3535). Has 3 properties in Brazil, and 1 each in Argentina, Chile, Peru, and Venezuela.

## GETTING READY / Accommodations 117

*Utell* (phone: 800-44-UTELL). Has over 100 properties in South America — approximately 25 in Argentina, 20 in Brazil, 10 each in Chile and Peru, 8 each in Ecuador and Venezuela, 6 each in Paraguay and Uruguay, 5 each in Bolivia and Panama, and 1 in Guyana.

*Westin* (phone: 800-228-3000). Has 3 properties in Brazil.

Within the same country, there is little price difference between South American–owned hotels and those owned by international firms. Some properties are not quite as luxurious as the *Hiltons* and *Sheratons;* however, these hotels are aesthetically pleasing, well maintained, and comfortable. The following South American chains are active and should not be overlooked (where available, we have given the numbers of US offices or representatives):

*Cristobal Inn* (phone: 56-55-268259 in Antofagasta, Chile). A Chilean-owned group with 5 properties in Chile.

*Frade* (c/o *D.S.A. International;* phone: 800-882-8908 or 516-271-6565). Has 1 resort property near Rio. (Note that 3 former *Frade* hotels are now members of the new *Porto* group — see below.)

*HORSA* (c/o *Hortur;* phone: 212-371-8885). Has 6 properties in Brazil.

*Luxor* (phone: 21-286-6022, in Rio). Another major Brazilian chain, has 11 hotels.

*Othon* (c/o *Loews Reservations International;* phone: 800-223-0888). The largest South American hotel chain, has 15 hotels in Brazil.

*Porto* (c/o *D.S.A. International;* phone: 800-882-8908 or 516-271-6565). A Brazilian chain with 3 resort properties in Brazil (formerly part of the *Frade* chain).

*Tropical* (phone: 800-468-2744). Owned by *Varig* airlines, this Brazilian chain has 6 properties in Brazil.

Independent, modern establishments in South America often are even more elegant than the chains. Word of mouth among the social set is a mainstay of their reputations, and how good — and well patronized — they are usually is reflected in their prices. *LARC Hotels* (phone: 800-327-3573) is a notable group of distinctive properties of this type located throughout South America; the establishments vary in size and each is individually owned and managed.

Medium-size hotels can be equally modern, or at least modernized, but are more likely to offer local ambience and charm. In general, they're also more reasonably priced. They won't have all the trappings of luxury, the extensive facilities, or the fashionable guests of the super-resorts, however. What you gain in cash you give up in cachet.

In addition to these modern establishments, the growth of tourism has spawned diversified accommodations for economy-minded travelers. Throughout South America, you will find a variety of small *pensiones;* converted haciendas and mansions, thermal spas, gambling centers, ski lodges, jungle lodges, and resorts that offer something special in the way of atmosphere and experience (see *Best in Town* in THE CITIES, *Best en Route* in DIRECTIONS, and *Luxury Resorts and Special Havens* in DIVERSIONS). Many South American countries have some sort of government-run hotel or hostel program, such as Peru's official tourist hotel program, *EnturuPeru* (phone: 14-721928).

In South America, you will not find the types of large budget hotels common in the US, but there are innumerable clean, inexpensive hostelries of all descriptions — modern, colonial, secluded, centrally located, or on the road — that offer basic amenities. Don't expect air conditioning, nightclubs, fancy bars, discos, swimming pools, or TV sets in rustic, out-of-the-way places. Here the charm consists of a genuine welcome, personal hospitality, incredibly gorgeous scenery, and privacy.

**Relais & Châteaux:** Although most members of this association are in France, the group has grown to include dozens of establishments in many other countries, including, currently, two hotels in Brazil, and one each in Argentina, Chile, Colombia, and

**118 GETTING READY / Accommodations**

Uruguay. Members of this group are of particular interest to travelers who wish lodgings reflecting the ambience, style, and frequently the history of the places they are visiting. Accommodations and service from one *relais* or château to another can range from simple but comfortable to elegantly deluxe, but they all maintain very high standards in order to retain their memberships, as they are appraised annually.

An illustrated catalogue of all the *Relais & Châteaux* properties is published annually and is available for $7 from *Relais & Châteaux* (2400 Lazy Hollow, Suite 152D, Houston, TX 77063) or from *Rescorp Reservations Service* (180 Summit Ave., Montvale, NJ 07645; phone: 800-677-3524). The association also can provide information on member properties. Reservations can be made directly with the establishments, through *Rosecorp Reservations Service,* or through a travel agency.

**RENTAL OPTIONS:** An attactive accommodations alternative for the visitor content to stay in one spot for a week or more is to rent one of the numerous properties available throughout South America. These offer a wide range of luxury and convenience, depending on the price you want to pay. One of the charms of staying in an apartment, condominium, cottage, villa, or other rented vacation home is that you will feel much more like a visitor than a tourist.

A vacation in a furnished rental has both the advantages and disadvantages of living "at home" abroad. It can be less expensive than staying in a first class hotel, although very luxurious and expensive rentals are available, too. It has the comforts of home, including a kitchen, which can mean potential savings on food. Furthermore, it gives a sense of the country that a large hotel often cannot. Best of all is the amount of space that no conventional hotel room can equal. On the other hand, a certain amount of housework is involved because if you don't eat out, you have to cook, and though some rentals (especially the luxury ones) include a maid, most don't. (If the rental doesn't include domestic help, arrangements often can be made with a nearby service for far less than in the US.)

For a family, two or more couples, or a group of friends, the per person cost — even for a luxurious rental — can be quite reasonable. Weekly and monthly rates are available to reduce costs still more. As with hotels, the rates for properties in some areas are seasonal, rising during the peak travel season, while for others they remain the same year-round. To have your pick of the properties available, you should begin to make arrangements for a rental at least 6 months in advance.

**Rental Property Agents and Discounts** – There are several ways of finding a suitable rental property. They may be listed along with other accommodations in publications of local tourist boards. Many tour wholesalers regularly include rental packages among their offerings; these generally are available through a travel agent. In addition, a number of companies specialize in rental vacations. Their plans typically include rental of the property (or several properties, but usually for a minimum stay per location), a rental car, and airfare.

The companies listed below rent a variety of properties in South America. They handle the booking and confirmation paperwork and can be expected to provide more information about the properties than that which might ordinarily be gleaned from a short listing in an accommodations guide.

*Rent a Vacation Everywhere* (*RAVE;* 328 Main St. E., Suite 526, Rochester, NY 14604; phone: 716-454-6440). Handles moderate to luxurious apartments in and around Rio de Janeiro, Brazil. Minimum rental usually is 1 week or, occasionally, 2 weeks or 1 month.

*Villas International Ltd.* (605 Market St., San Francisco, CA 94105; phone: 415-281-0910 in California; 800-221-2260 elsewhere in the US). Rents 1- to 4-bedroom apartments in Rio de Janeiro on or close to the beaches. Minimum rental period usually is a week.

In addition, a useful publication, the *Worldwide Home Rental Guide,* lists private villas and cottages throughout South America, as well as the managing agencies. Issued twice annually, single copies may be available at newsstands for $10 an issue. For a year's subscription, send $18 to *Worldwide Home Rental Guide,* PO Box 2842, Santa Fe, NM 87504 (phone: 505-988-5188).

When considering a particular vacation rental property, look for answers to the following questions:

- How do you get from the airport to the condominium?
- If the property is on the shore, how far is the nearest beach? Is it sandy or rocky and is it safe for swimming?
- What size and number of beds are provided?
- How far is the property from whatever else is important to you, such as a golf course or nightlife?
- If there is no grocery store on the premises (which may be comparatively expensive, anyway), how far is the nearest market?
- Are baby-sitters, cribs, bicycles, or anything else you may need for your children available?
- Is maid service provided daily?
- Is air conditioning and/or a phone provided?
- Is a car rental part of the package? Is a car necessary?

Before deciding which rental is for you, make sure you have satisfactory answers to all your questions. Ask your travel agent to find out or call the company involved directly.

**Accommodation Discounts** – Several discount travel organizations provide a substantial savings — up to 50% off list prices — on rental accommodations (and some hotels) throughout South America. Reservations are handled by the central office of the organization or members may deal directly with the rental agencies or individual property owners. To take advantage of the full selection of properties, these organizations often require that reservations be made as much as 6 months in advance — particularly for stays during the holidays or peak travel periods.

*Concierge* (83 S. King St., Suite 106, Seattle, WA 98104; phone: 800-252-0099). Offers up to 50% discounts on week-long apartment rentals in Argentina, Bolivia, and Brazil, as well as 35% discounts on tours, cruises, and car rentals. They also guarantee to obtain the lowest airfare available at the time of booking — and provide a 3% rebate on the fare — to anywhere in the world. Annual membership fee is $69.95 per couple.

*Hotel Express* (3052 El Cajon Blvd., San Diego, CA 92104; phone: 800-634-6526 or 619-280-2582). Offers up to 50% off on rental accommodations throughout South America. One week is the standard minimum stay; shorter rentals may also be available during the off season. Annual membership fee of $49.95 per family provides discounts on other travel services, but membership is not required for bargains on rental accommodations.

*IntlTravel Card* (6001 N. Clark St., Chicago, IL 60660; phone: 800-342-0558 or 312-465-8891). Provides discounts on rental and hotel accommodations in Bolivia, Brazil, Colombia, and Ecuador. The $36 annual membership fee includes spouse.

**BED AND BREAKFAST ESTABLISHMENTS:** Travelers who have become devotees of this homey accommodation alternative will be happy to hear that bed and breakfast establishments (commonly known as B&Bs) are beginning to appear among the alternatives offered to travelers in South America. Although they are not by any means ubiquitous at this time, their worldwide popularity is spreading to the Southern Hemisphere.

Bed and breakfast accommodations provide exactly what their name implies. It is unusual for a bed and breakfast establishment to offer the extra services found in conventional hostelries, so the bed and breakfast route often is the least expensive way to go.

Beyond the obvious fundamentals, nothing else is predictable about bed and breakfast establishments. The bed may be in an extra room in a family home, in an apartment with a separate entrance, or in a freestanding cottage elsewhere on the host's property. A private bath isn't always offered, so check before you reserve. Some homes have only one room to let, whereas others may be large enough to have another party or two in residence at the same time.

Breakfast probably will be a South American version of the continental variety: fruit plus juice, toast, rolls, or homemade bread and preserves, and strong coffee or tea. And as often as not, breakfast will be served along with some helpful tips on what to see and do. If you're in a studio with a kitchenette, you may be furnished with the makings and have to prepare it for yourself. Despite their name, some B&Bs offer an evening meal as well — by prior arrangement and at extra cost.

Some hosts enjoy helping guests with tips on what to see and do and even serve as informal tour guides, while in other places your privacy won't be disturbed. Whichever the case, the beauty of bed and breakfast establishments is that you'll always have a warm reception and the opportunity to meet many more inhabitants of the region than you otherwise would, which means you'll experience their hospitality in a special fashion.

At the time of this writing, unfortunately, there are no US reservations services booking stays at B&Bs in South America. If you are interested in this particularly homey form of hospitality, on arrival check with the local tourist authorities who may be able to point you toward local homeowners offering bed and breakfast accommodations to travelers. A useful source of information on bed and breakfast reservations services and establishments is the *Bed & Breakfast Reservations Services Worldwide* (PO Box 39000, Washington, DC 20016; phone: 800-842-1486), a trade association of B&B reservations services which provides a list of its members for $3.

**HOME EXCHANGES:** Still another alternative for travelers who are content to stay in one place during their South American vacation is a home exchange. The Wright family from St. Louis moves into the home of the Gutierrez family in Argentina, while the Gutierrez's enjoy a stay in the Wright's home. The home exchange is an exceptionally inexpensive way to ensure comfortable, reasonable living quarters with amenities that no hotel could possibly offer; often the trade includes a car. Moreover, it allows you to live in a new community in a way that few tourists ever do: For a little while, at least, you will become something of a resident.

Several companies publish directories of individuals and families willing to trade homes with others for a specific period of time. In some cases, you must be willing to list your own home in the directory; in others, you can subscribe without appearing in it. Most listings are for straight exchanges only, but each directory also has a number of listings placed by people interested in either exchanging or renting (for instance, if they own a second home). Other arrangements include exchanges of hospitality while owners are in residence, or youth exchanges, where your teenager is received as a guest in return for your welcoming their teenager at a later date. A few house-sitting opportunities also are available. In most cases, arrangements for the actual exchange take place directly between you and the foreign host. There is no guarantee that you will find a listing in the area in which you are interested, but each of the organizations noted below includes South American homes among its hundreds or even thousands of foreign and domestic properties:

*Intervac US/International Home Exchange Service* (Box 190070, San Francisco, CA 94119; phone: 415-435-3497). For $45 (plus postage) subscribers receive copies of the three directories published yearly, and are entitled to list their home in one of them; a black-and-white photo may be included with the listing for an additional $10. A $5 discount is given to travelers over age 62.

*Loan-A-Home* (2 Park Lane, Apt. 6E, Mt. Vernon, NY 10552; phone: 914-664-7640). Specializes in long-term (4 months or more — excluding July and August) housing arrangements worldwide for students, professors, businesspeople, and retirees, although its two annual directories (with supplements) carry a small list of short-term rentals and/or exchanges. $35 for a copy of one directory and one supplement; $45 for two directories and two supplements.

*Vacation Exchange Club* (PO Box 820, Haleiwa, HI 96712; phone: 800-638-3841). Offers some 10,000 listings, although, at press time, only a few were in South America. For $50, the subscriber receives quarterly directories, and is listed in one.

*Worldwide Home Exchange Club* (13 Knightsbridge Green, London SW1X 7Q1, England; phone: 44-71-589-6055; or 806 Brantford Ave., Silver Spring, MD 20904; phone: 301-680-8950). Handles over 1,500 listings a year worldwide, including homes in the Caribbean. For $25 a year, you will receive two listings yearly, as well as supplements.

*Better Homes and Travel* (formerly *Home Exchange International*), with offices in New York, and representatives in Los Angeles, London, Paris, and Milan, functions differently in that it publishes no directory and shepherds the exchange process most of the way. Interested parties supply the firm with photographs of themselves and their homes, information on the type of home they want and where, and a registration fee of $50. The company then works with its other offices to propose a few possibilities, and only when a match is made do the parties exchange names, addresses, and phone numbers. For this service, *Better Homes and Travel* charges a closing fee, which ranges from $150 to $500 for switches from 2 weeks to 3 months in duration, and from $300 to $600 for switches longer than 3 months. (Although, at press time, this agency did not arrange exchanges in South America, call when planning your trip for current offerings.) Contact *Better Homes and Travel,* 33 E. 33rd St., New York, NY 10016 (phone: 212-689-6608).

**HOME STAYS:** If the idea of actually staying in a private home as the guest of a foreign family appeals to you, check with the *United States Servas Committee,* which maintains a list of hosts throughout the world willing to throw open their doors to visitors entirely free of charge. At the time of this writing, there were participating hosts in the following South American countries: Argentina, Bolivia, Brazil, Chile, Colombia, Ecuador, French Guiana, Peru, Suriname, Uruguay, and Venezuela.

The aim of this nonprofit cultural program is to promote international understanding and peace, and every effort is made to discourage freeloaders. *Servas* will send you an application form and the name of the nearest of some 200 interviewers around the US for you to contact. After the interview, if you're approved, you'll receive documentation certifying you as a *Servas* traveler. There is a membership fee of $45 for an individual, and there also is a deposit of $15 to receive the host list, refunded on its return. The list gives the name, address, age, occupation, and other particulars of the hosts, including languages spoken. From then on, it is up to you to write to the prospective hosts directly, and *Servas* makes no guarantee that you will be accommodated.

*Servas* stresses that you should choose only people you really want to meet and that during your stay (which normally lasts between 2 nights and 2 weeks) you should be interested mainly in your hosts, not in sightseeing. It also suggests that one way to show your appreciation once you've returned home is to become a host yourself. The minimum age of a *Servas* traveler is 18 (however, children under 18 may accompany their parents), and though quite a few are young people who have just finished college, there are travelers (and hosts) in all age ranges and occupations. Contact *Servas* at 11 John St., Room 407, New York, NY 10038-4009 (phone: 212-267-0252).

You also might be interested in a publication called *International Meet-the-People*

*Directory,* published by the *International Visitor Information Service.* It lists several agencies in a number of foreign countries (about 35 worldwide, including Argentina and Bolivia) that arrange home visits for Americans, either for dinner or overnight stays. To order a copy, send $5.95 to the *International Visitor Information Service* (1623 Belmont St. NW, Washington, DC 20009; phone: 202-939-5566). For other local organizations and services offering home exchanges, contact the appropriate tourist authority.

# Time Zones

Time zones in South America in relation to the US are complicated by the fact that not all South American countries observe daylight saving time. Thus, while Colombia, Ecuador, Panama, and Peru are on eastern standard time — it usually surprises North Americans to discover that South America's west coast is roughly due south of the eastern coast of the US — none of these countries changes its clocks during the year. And, when the eastern US is on daylight saving time, these countries are 1 hour behind. Chile, on the other hand, sets its clocks 2 hours ahead of the eastern US, and it *does* observe daylight saving time (it must be remembered, however, that, as the seasons in North and South America are reversed, Chile is changing its clocks *back* when we are changing ours *forward*). Thus, when the US is observing daylight saving time, the time in Chile is the same as in the eastern US.

Of the remaining South American countries, Argentina, Brazil, and Uruguay are 3 hours ahead of the eastern US when the US is observing standard time, and all of these countries observe daylight saving time — again, at opposite times of the year than the US — so that when it is daylight saving time in the eastern US, these countries are only 1 hour ahead. French Guiana, Guyana, Paraguay, and Suriname are all 2 hours ahead of the eastern US and, as none of these countries changes its clocks, they are 1 hour ahead of the eastern US when it is observing daylight saving time. Bolivia is 1 hour ahead of the eastern US and also does not change its clocks, so that when the eastern US switches to daylight saving time, the time in Bolivia and the eastern US is the same.

South American timetables use a 24-hour clock to denote arrival and departure times, which means that hours are expressed sequentially from 1 AM. By this method, 9 AM is recorded as 0900, noon as 1200, 1 PM as 1300, 6 PM as 1800, midnight as 2400, and so on. For example, the departure of a train at 7 AM will be announced as "0700"; one leaving at 7 PM will be noted as "1900."

Many South Americans have a more flexible concept of time than people in the US. When you set up a social engagement or receive an invitation for a specific time, it often is understood that you are actually expected to meet about an hour later. If you invite friends for dinner at 8 PM, do not expect them until 9 PM. If they have not arrived by 10 PM, you can assume that something came up. This is not intended as a personal insult, nor should you think of yourself as having been stood up. (This is much less likely to happen in a business situation, in which appointments are kept punctually.)

In the jungle, time as we know it does not exist. There is no point in worrying how long it will take to travel from one point to another because there are innumerable unpredictable variables: sudden storms, surprise meetings with the driver's long-lost cousins, mishaps, accidents, contrary river currents, and general procrastination. Jungle guides, aware that gringos like to know how long expeditions are likely to take, are fond of giving estimated times. If a guide tells you a trip will take 3 hours, do not be surprised if it takes at least twice as long.

Most transport systems, such as major airlines, buses, and collective taxis, keep fairly regular schedules, weather permitting. Ask your hotel concierge to call the airport a few hours before your international flight to make sure there are no long delays. People who provide services to tourists, such as tour escorts, generally can be relied upon to be punctual.

If you bear in mind that South Americans say *ahora* (now) when they mean anytime today or tomorrow, *ahorita* (right now) when they mean anytime within the next 3 or 4 hours, and *en seguida* (immediately) when they mean within the hour, you will be spared a lot of anxious waiting. If you adopt a southern attitude toward time during your trip through South America, you will find everything more enjoyable.

# Mail, Telephone, and Electricity

**MAIL:** Although much improved in recent years, mail service in some parts of South America is not all it could be. An airmail letter from the US takes 1 week to 10 days (or longer) to reach one of the capital cities; mail to any of the smaller cities takes anywhere from 2 weeks to forever.

There are several places that will receive and hold mail for travelers in South America. Mail sent to you at a hotel and clearly marked "Guest Mail, Hold for Arrival" is one safe approach. If you do not know what your address will be, have your mail addressed to the nearest post office in care of the local equivalent of General Delivery — for instance, *Lista de Correos* where Spanish is spoken, *Correo Restante* in Portuguese (for Brazil), *Poste Restante* in French (for French Guiana), and *Bezorging Post* in Dutch (for Suriname). Note that you are expected to specify the branch, district, zip code *(codigo postal)* and city — and, under the best conditions, this is very risky. Most foreign post offices have a time limit for holding such mail — 30 days is a common limit. To claim this mail, you must go in person to the post office, ask for the local equivalent of General Delivery, and present identification (driver's license, credit cards, birth certificate, or passport).

When inquiring about mail addressed to you, ask the post office clerk to look for it under the first letter of your first or middle name should there be nothing under the first letter of your last name. Remember, too, that in small towns, separate sets of post office boxes are segregated into *señors* and *señoras*. Your letter may not have landed in the correct sexual category. If you plan to remain in one place for more than a month, consider renting a post office box *(cajón postal, casilla,* or *apartado* in Spanish; *caixa postal* in Portuguese) in the central post office to eliminate the chance of mail getting lost in local delivery.

If you are an *American Express* customer (a cardholder, a carrier of *American Express* traveler's checks, or traveling on an *American Express Travel Related Services* tour), you can have mail sent to an *American Express* branch office in cities on your route (this service is offered in cities throughout South America). Letters are held free of charge — registered mail and packages are not accepted. You must be able to show an *American Express* card, traveler's checks, or a voucher proving you are on one of the company's tours to qualify for mail privileges. Those who aren't clients cannot use the service. There also is a forwarding fee of $5 (at press time). Mail should be addressed to you, care of *American Express,* and should be marked "Client Mail Service." Additional information on its mail service and the addresses of *American Express* offices in South America are listed in the pamphlet *American Express Travelers' Companion,* available from any US branch of *American Express.*

While US embassies and consulates abroad usually will not under ordinary circumstances accept mail for tourists, in some major South American cities, the US embassy will on rare occasions hold mail for US citizens if the papers sent are particularly important. It is best to inform them either by separate letter or cable, or by phone (particularly if you are in the country already), that you will be using their address for this purpose.

When sending mail to South American countries, avoid using middle names. South American surnames, especially those of Spanish origin, are placed in the middle of the full name, followed by the mother's maiden surname. It is only a problem when mail is alphabetized if you have included anything more than a first and last name. Also, *always* include a postal code — the delivery of the letter could depend on it. If you do not have the correct postal code, call the appropriate tourist authority (see FACTS IN BRIEF) — they should be able to look it up for you. Alternatively, you could call the addressee directly — if you have the telephone number — and although this will be costly, it may be worth it to ensure delivery of your correspondence.

In South America, you can send postcards and letters from your hotel with reasonably secure odds of their safe arrival, but it is not a good idea to put anything in a mailbox and expect it to arrive at its destination. Experienced travelers use the central post office — *Correo Central* (*Correio Central* in Brazil) — for the most reliable service. Generally, all mail that leaves any country goes through the central post office, so you can be sure of the most efficient service. Packages should never be sent by surface mail, which is totally unreliable; carry what you can or send it by air freight.

Letters from South America to the US have been known to arrive in as short a time as 5 days, but it is a good idea to allow at least 10 days for delivery in either direction. (If you must contact someone in a hurry, send a cable or telegram through a private — not government-run — telecommunications firm such as *VTR* (*Via Trans Radio*), which has bureaus throughout the southern continent.) In most South American countries, internal surface mail service is highly irregular, and it is worth the few extra centavos to send letters airmail and certified between cities in any country. The best mail service appears to be in Peru (although plagued with strikes in recent years), Ecuador, and Uruguay. Venezuela has one of the worst records.

If your correspondence is important, you may want to send it via one of the special courier services; *Federal Express, DHL,* and other international services are available in most South American capitals and other large cities. The cost is considerably higher than sending something via the postal service — but the assurance of its timely arrival is worth it.

**TELEPHONE:** In many areas of South America, telephone service is so unreliable that it is simply not an effective means of communication, and, even in some major cities, people prefer to drop in on friends unannounced rather than try to phone. Recently, however, telephone service has greatly improved in many big cities, especially for international calls. Where new systems have been introduced, there generally are all new telephone numbers, so if you have a lot of trouble with local calls, ask the hotel operator for assistance. The Brazilian telephone system has been totally overhauled, with city code dialing between state capitals and direct overseas dialing to many countries, including the US. In most countries, however, it is still easier to call South America from the States than vice versa. If at all possible, get someone at your hotel to make calls for you.

Listings elsewhere in this guide include phone numbers, but you may experience some frustration trying to use them, and they change often. And as with anywhere in the world, it's usually easier to get through on an international call either before or after business hours, when the trunk lines are less busy.

Note that the number of digits in phone numbers is not standardized in some South American countries. The phone number for a capital may have more digits than numbers in outlying areas. As making connections in South America for either local or international calls sometimes can be hit-or-miss, those who have to make an important call — to confirm reservations in another city, for instance — should start to do so a few days ahead.

## GETTING READY / Mail, Telephone, and Electricity

Pay telephones in South America are located much as in the US — in restaurants, hotel lobbies, booths on the streets, at post offices, and at most tourist centers. In Argentina, Brazil, Peru, and Suriname, tokens are needed for public telephones (elsewhere you can just use the local coins). You can buy them at hotel desks, post offices, and at some stores. By reaching a US operator, you can charge international calls made on a pay phone to a telephone company credit card number.

The procedure for calling a country in South America from the US is as follows: dial 011 (the international access code) + the country code + the city code + the local number. (If you don't know the country or city code, check the front of a telephone book or ask an international operator.) For example, to place a call from anywhere in the US to Rio de Janeiro, dial 011 + 55 + 21 + the local number.

To call the US from anywhere in South America, dial the international access code + 1 (the US country code) + the US area code + the local number. The procedure is similar for dialing from one South American country to another: dial the international access code + the country code + the city code + the local number. (Although the country codes are based on an international standard and do not change, international access codes will vary, according to the country from which you are calling.) To call from one city to another within the same South American country, simply dial 0 + the city code + the local number (leaving off the country code). And, to dial a number within the same city, simply dial the local number.

Note the following exceptions to the above rules: In French Guiana, Panama, and Suriname, there are no city codes. For instance, to call Panama from the US, dial 011 + 507 (the country code) + the local number. When dialing from other South American countries or within these countries, the above procedures apply, with no need for city codes.

Also note that the procedure for reaching an operator varies throughout South America; you should find out this essential information on arrival in a new area. Usually, you can dial a direct number for a local operator (but don't expect local telephone personnel to be bilingual). For operator-assisted calls between cities or countries in South America, generally you will dial one direct number or the international access code followed by the number for the international operator. If you don't speak Spanish or Portuguese, you also can call an international operator (who will speak English) for information or assistance with local calls or to stay on the line as an interpreter in the event of an emergency. (For information on direct numbers to dial for emergency service, see our country-by-country listing in *Staying Healthy,* in this section.)

**Hotel Surcharges –** Avoiding operator-assisted calls can cut international calling costs considerably and bring rates into a somewhat more reasonable range — except for calls made through hotel switchboards. One of the most unpleasant surprises travelers encounter in many foreign countries is the amount they find tacked on to their hotel bill for telephone calls, because foreign hotels routinely add on astronomical surcharges. (It's not at all uncommon to find 300% to 400% added to the actual telephone charges.)

Until recently, the only recourse against this unconscionable overcharging was to call collect from abroad or to use a telephone credit card — available through a simple procedure from any local US phone company. (Note, however, that even if you use a telephone credit card, some hotels still may charge a fee for line usage.) Now, *American Telephone and Telegraph (AT&T)* offers *USA Direct,* a service that connects users, via a toll-free number, with an *AT&T* operator in the US, who then will put the call through at the standard international rate. An added feature of this service is that travelers abroad can reach US toll-free (800) numbers by calling a *USA Direct* operator, who will connect them. Charges for all calls made through *USA Direct* appear on the caller's regular US phone bill. Note that, as we went to press, this service was offered in Argentina, Brazil, Chile, Colombia, Ecuador, Panama, Peru, and Uruguay. In

Suriname and Venezuela, *USA Direct* can be accessed only by using specially designated phones located in airports and some major hotels. For a brochure and wallet card listing toll-free numbers by country, contact International Information Service, *AT&T Communications,* 635 Grant St., Pittsburgh, PA 15219 (phone: 800-874-4000).

Until such services become universal, it's wise to ask about the surcharge rates *before* calling from a hotel. If the rate is high, it's best to use a telephone credit card; make a collect call; or place the call and ask the party to call right back. Another way to keep down the cost of calling from South America is to leave a copy of your itinerary and telephone numbers with people in the US so that they can call you instead.

A particularly useful service for travelers to non-English-speaking destinations is *AT&T*'s Language Line Service. By calling 800-628-8486 from the US or 408-648-5871 from South America, you will be connected with an interpreter in any one of 143 languages and dialects, who will provide on-line interpretive services for $3.50 a minute. From the US, this service is particularly useful for booking travel services in foreign countries where English is not spoken — or not spoken fluently. Once abroad — this number can be reached by using the *USA Direct* toll-free (800) number connection feature described above — it will enable you to make arrangements at foreign establishments or to reach emergency or other vital services with which you would otherwise have trouble communicating due to the language barrier. For further information, contact *AT&T* at the address above or call 800-752-6096.

**Other Resources** – Particularly useful for planning a trip is *AT&T*'s *Toll-Free 800 Directory,* which lists thousands of companies with 800 numbers, both alphabetically (white pages) and by category (yellow pages), including a wide range of travel services — from travel agents to transportation and accommodations. Issued in a consumer edition for $9.95 and a business edition for $14.95, both are available from *AT&T Phone Centers* or by calling 800-426-8686. Other useful directories for use before you leave and on the road include the *Toll-Free Travel & Vacation Information Directory* ($4.95 postpaid from Pilot Books, 103 Cooper St., Babylon, NY 11702; phone 516-422-2225) and *The Phone Booklet,* which lists the nationwide, toll-free (800) numbers of travel information sources and suppliers — such as major airlines, hotel and motel chains, car rental companies, and tourist information offices (send $2 to *Scott American Corporation,* Box 88, W. Redding, CT 06896).

**ELECTRICITY:** Power failures are not as frequent as they were several years ago, but thunderstorms can produce temporary blackouts, and South American hotels still keep a ready supply of candles. Neither electrical circuits nor plugs and sockets are standardized in South America, and in many countries they differ from those in the US. The American chain hotels may have US-style sockets for electric razors, although beware of plugging larger appliances, such as hair dryers, into these outlets. For the most part, US-made electrical items are useless in South America without some kind of converter and adapter plug.

Travelers can solve the problem by buying a lightweight converter to transform foreign voltage into the US kind (there are several types of converters, depending on the wattage of the appliance) or by buying dual-voltage appliances, which convert from one to the other at the flick of a switch (hair dryers of this sort are common). It also will be necessary to deal with differing socket configurations before plugging in. To be fully prepared, bring along an extension cord (in older or rural establishments the electrical outlet may be farther from the sink than the cord on your razor or hair dryer can reach), and a wall socket adapter with a full set of plugs to ensure that you'll be able to plug in anywhere.

If you are traveling to remote areas, do not be surprised to find the current weak. Your electrical equipment still should work, but not up to maximum capacity. So if you use an electric razor, it is wise to pack a manual safety razor, too, just in case. See FACTS IN BRIEF for individual countries' electrical standards.

One good source for sets of plugs and adapters for use worldwide is the *Franzus Company* (PO Box 142, Beacon Falls, CT 06403; phone: 203-723-6664). *Franzus* also publishes a useful brochure, *Foreign Electricity Is No Deep Dark Secret,* which provides information about converters and adapter plugs for electric appliances to be used abroad but manufactured for use in the US. To obtain a free copy, send a self-addressed, stamped envelope to *Franzus* at the above address; a catalogue of other travel accessories is available on request.

# Staying Healthy

The surest way to return home in good health is to be prepared for medical problems that might occur on vacation. Accidents can happen anytime, but travelers to South America are especially vulnerable to certain illnesses. The change in climate, altitude, and eating habits; the tension of finding yourself in strange places; and the presence of new, unfamiliar bacteria contribute to lowering your resistance to disease. As is always the case with both diseases and accidents, prevention is the best cure. And in South America, this adage applies not only to diarrhea and dysentery, but to more serious diseases like hepatitis and typhoid fever. Below, we've outlined some things you need to think about before your trip.

**BEFORE YOU GO:** Older travelers or anyone suffering from a chronic medical condition, such as diabetes, high blood pressure, cardiopulmonary disease, asthma, or ear, eye, or sinus trouble should consult a physician before leaving home. Those with conditions requiring special consideration when traveling should consider seeing, in addition to their regular physician, a specialist in travel medicine. For a referral in a particular community, contact the nearest medical school or ask a local doctor to recommend such a specialist. Dr. Leonard Marcus, a member of the *American Committee on Clinical Tropical Medicine and Travelers' Health,* provides a directory of more than 100 travel doctors across the country. For a copy, send a 9-by-12-inch, self-addressed, stamped envelope to Dr. Marcus at 148 Highland Ave., Newton, MA 02165 (phone: 617-527-4003).

Also be sure to check with your insurance company ahead of time about the applicability of your hospitalization and major medical policies away from home; many policies do not apply, and others are not accepted in South America. Older travelers should know that Medicare does not make payments outside the US and its territories. If your medical policy does not protect you while you're traveling, there are comprehensive combination policies specifically designed to fill the gap. (For a discussion of medical insurance and a list of inclusive combination policies, see *Insurance,* in this section.)

**Prevention and Immunization** – Specific information on the health status of any area in South America can be secured from its consular services in the US. The Centers for Disease Control publishes a comprehensive booklet, *Health Information for International Travel,* which lists vaccination requirements and other health information for all South American destinations. To order, send a check or money order for $5 to the Superintendent of Documents (US Government Printing Office, Washington, DC 20402), or charge it to your credit card by calling 202-783-3238. For other health-related publications for travelers, see "Helpful Publications," below.

Yellow fever vaccinations now are required only to enter French Guiana, although they are recommended for travelers to Argentina, Bolivia, Brazil, Ecuador, Panama, Paraguay, Peru, and Venezuela. Travelers who will be extending their trip with a visit to Central America should find out about additional required or recommended inoculations. The US Public Health Service advises diphtheria and tetanus shots for people traveling in many of these areas. In addition, children should be inoculated against measles, mumps, rubella, and polio, especially since some of these viruses exist in a more virulent form in South America than at home. Inquire at the consulate or embassy of the country to which you plan to travel about specific immunization requirements. Be sure to ask about any local epidemics (some diseases — like polio — that have been virtually eliminated in the States persist in the South America) so that you can obtain the proper immunization before departure.

A conservative approach to inoculation is especially recommended for multiple-destination travelers, as the entry requirements and areas of infection are changeable. Inquire at the appropriate government tourist offices about the immunization requirements for the areas you will be visiting. Where certificates are required, authorities may demand both the origin and batch number of the serum used.

For further information on vaccination requirements, disease outbreaks, and other health information pertaining to traveling abroad, call the Centers for Disease Control's 24-hour **International Health Requirements and Recommendations Information Hotline: 404-332-4559**.

**First Aid** – Put together a compact, personal medical kit including Band-Aids, first-aid cream, antiseptic, nose drops, insect repellent, aspirin (or non-aspirin tablets), an extra pair of prescription glasses or contact lenses (and a copy of your prescription for glasses or contact lenses), sunglasses, over-the-counter remedies for diarrhea, indigestion, and motion sickness, a thermometer, and a supply of those prescription medicines you take regularly.

In a corner of your kit, keep a list of all the drugs you have brought and their purpose, as well as duplicate copies of your doctor's prescriptions (or a note from your doctor). As brand names may vary in different countries, it's a good idea to ask your doctor for the generic name of any drugs you use so that you can ask for their equivalent should you need a refill. It also is a good idea to ask your doctor to prepare a medical identification card that includes such information as your blood type, your social security number, any allergies or chronic health problems you have, and your medical insurance information. Considering the essential contents of your kit, keep it with you, rather than in your checked luggage.

**MINIMIZING THE RISKS:** Typically, tourists suffer two kinds of health problems in South America, gastrointestinal upset and sunburn. And, as a number of diseases are contracted through bug bites (see below), some precaution against biting insects is strongly advised. Neither these nor any other health problems or illnesses are inevitable, however, and with suitable precautions, your trip to South America can proceed untroubled by ill health.

**Diarrhea and Stomach Upsets** – It is very important to take the first few days easy, especially if you land in a city where the high altitude will be tiring and exacerbate the effect of any alcohol on your system. Because South Americans eat at different times than North Americans (they normally have a light breakfast; a heavy meal in the mid- to late afternoon; and a late dinner, starting any time after 9 PM), your system will have a doubly hard time acclimating to the new regimen — so drink and eat lightly on arrival.

Fortunately, the vast majority of intestinal disorders encountered during travel represent only a temporary inconvenience, which will go away with rest and time. More serious problems may result, however, from the consumption of drinking water contaminated by a particular strain of *E. coli* bacteria. These bacteria inhabit the human intestinal tract and are transmitted through fecal matter, and from there into plumbing and any unpurified water system. The most frequent result is that scourge of travelers known the world over as Cairo crud, Delhi belly, *la turista,* or, in Mexico, Montezuma's Revenge. Its symptoms are dysentery or diarrhea, accompanied by severe intestinal pain and a foul taste in the mouth.

## GETTING READY / Staying Healthy

There is a very simple way to avoid this illness: Don't drink the water. Brush your teeth with bottled purified water (be sure you're not getting a used bottle refilled with tap water). Don't drink iced drinks where the ice has been made from tap water. And take note that those tempting-looking alcoholic concoctions served in coconuts or pineapples, as well as fruit juices — even in the better hotels — may be diluted with tap water, and thus may be unsafe. As a matter of course, it is wise to stick to bottled carbonated water (ask for *agua purificada* or *agua mineral*) or substitute wine or beer at meals. You might also carry standard GI water purification tablets (tetraglycine hydroperiodide). Just drop one of these tablets in a carafe of water and let it stand for half an hour. Or substitute a bottle of tincture of iodine. (Don't worry about what other people think of your precautions — the hours they may spend in transit between bed and bathroom, should they fail to take similar measures, will most likely convince them of the wisdom of your approach.)

Milk sold in supermarkets and groceries is pasteurized, and therefore generally safe to drink, but beware of spoilage due to improper refrigeration during distribution or storage. Stay clear of raw milk and any other unpasteurized or uncooked dairy products. Do not eat unpeeled fruit or any uncooked vegetables. Garnishes of fresh vegetables (even a small amount of shredded lettuce or tomatoes) and salads have often been washed with tap water and can wreak havoc with your gastrointestinal tract the morning after. Stay away from unfamiliar dishes that are hard to identify, as well as creamy or mayonnaise-based dressings that may have been out on serving tables for any period of time. Above all, *do not* buy food from food vendors on streets or beaches.

Be sure to carry along an anti-diarrhea medication and recommended antibiotic in case you do develop symptoms. Before you go, pick up a mild over-the-counter preparation, such as Kaopectate or Pepto Bismol (each is available in tablet as well as liquid form), which, if used according to directions, should have you back on your feet within 12 to 14 hours. An old, favored South American remedy is *manzanilla* (chamomile) tea. You also may want to ask your doctor to recommend one of the stronger medications containing an antibiotic. If you are stricken with diarrhea and have no medication with you, have your hotel call a doctor or visit the nearest pharmacy.

■ **A Warning:** While unpleasant and inconvenient, the type of gastrointestinal disorder discussed above is rarely dangerous; however, a much more serious illness, infectious hepatitis (nicknamed the Big H by gringos), can be contracted from improperly prepared food, contaminated drinking water, and shellfish. It also can be contracted from dirty hypodermic needles, a risk even in hospitals. Its effects may last for weeks or months, and recovery can be slow. Again, care about what and where you eat and — should you need an injection — the use of disposable plastic syringes are the best preventive measures. (If you are a diabetic or require regular injections for any other condition, carry these disposable syringes with you.) An additional measure of protection can also be secured with an immunoglobulin shot from your family doctor before your departure.

**Chagas' Disease** – Travelers who intend to spend time in the jungle areas of South America also should be aware of the threat from the vinchuca. This insect lives in palm trees and is apt to carry a parasite that causes Chagas' disease, which can lead to a number of serious health problems (most usually, chronic heart disease) that may be asymptomatic for years. Although there is no known cure for Chagas' disease, measures can be taken to avoid contact with the insect carrying it: Do not sleep in natives' huts; when camping at night, stay away from palm trees and stone piles, both of which are homes to the vinchuca. Before going to sleep, apply an insecticide that contains DEET (see below).

Should you require medical or surgical treatment involving blood transfusion, go to a university-affiliated hospital in a capital or a major city. Try to avoid foreign private hospitals *(clínicas)* where donors may not have been adequately screened for Chagas' disease.

**Malaria and Yellow Fever** – If you intend to travel into the jungle, where malaria is prevalent, pick up some antimalarial tablets in a pharmacy in a city before you fly into the bush. These very inexpensive tablets are available everywhere. (Malaria is called *paludismo* in Spanish and *malaria* in Portuguese; ask for *medicina contra paludismo* in Spanish-speaking countries, and *remédio contra malaria* in Brazil.) Presently, a yellow fever inoculation and prophylactic medication against malaria are recommended and, in many cases, mandatory for travel in many of the interior tropic and subtropic regions of South America, particularly for visitors making extensive trips in the Amazon basin. As both of these diseases are generally contracted through mosquito bites, precautions against these irritating and potentially harmful bites should be taken (see "Insects and Other Pests," below).

■ **Note:** At the time of this writing, malaria was prevalent in all South American countries except Chile. There also had been cases of jungle yellow fever in forest areas in some countries. In addition, Lima, Peru, was in the midst of a cholera epidemic. Cholera and dysentery have similar symptoms — severe intestinal pain and diarrhea, plus vomiting — and are spread through contaminated water. But while dysentery causes only mild to severe discomfort, cholera is far more *serious* — it has a short incubation period and can become *deadly* through extreme dehydration. If in an area of possible contagion by cholera, take rehydration salt tablets at the first sign of these symptoms and see a doctor immediately.

Before you leave for South America, check with your local county or state health department, or call the US State Department's *Citizens' Emergency Center* at 202-647-5225 for the most up-to-date information on areas of contagion, general health conditions, and other vital information.

**Sunburn** – The burning power of the sun can quickly cause severe sunburn or sunstroke. This is certainly true of South America's coastal areas; however, it also should be noted that at the higher altitudes in which many of the continent's cities and tourist attractions are located, the intensity of the sun's rays is even greater, thus increasing the risks. To protect yourself against these ills, wear sunglasses, take along a broad-brimmed hat and cover-up, and, most importantly, use a sunscreen lotion.

**Altitude Sickness** – One illness for which there is no known preventive is altitude sickness *(soroche)*. Travelers disembarking from planes at El Alto Airport in La Paz, Bolivia (or Cuzco, Peru), more often than not feel the effect of *soroche* during their first steps across the tarmac to the immigration desk. It arrives in the form of a wave of dizziness, frequently accompanied by a minor spasm in the chest. Occasionally, you may feel you are going to faint. (In some ways, *soroche* feels like motion sickness, only the ground below is not moving.) Sit down immediately or, if possible, lie down and take deep breaths. The only cure for *soroche* is acclimatization. If you have the option, travel to higher altitudes gradually. Eat very lightly, mostly or only carbohydrates, and drink lots of liquids (but *no* alcohol) until you feel more comfortable. (Old Andean hands claim it takes a month to get fully acclimated.) Do not exert yourself. If you must walk, walk slowly. Ask someone to carry your luggage. Rest often. It usually takes a few days for the first stages of *soroche* to pass, during which time you also may suffer from headaches and eyestrain. Some hotels and some tourist trains provide *soroche* sufferers with oxygen, which helps to clear the head. You can try coca tea, but the best approach probably would be to check with your doctor or with one of the organizations that provide medical assistance to travelers (see list below) before you take any medications. If you have any kind of medical problem affected by altitude, discuss the problem with your doctor. For most people, *soroche* is a discomfort but not a vital health hazard. For more information, read *Mountain Sickness: Prevention, Recognition, and Treatment,* by Peter Hackett, M.D., available for $6.50 (includes postage and handling) from the *South America Explorers Club,* 126 Indian Creek Rd., Ithaca, NY 14850 (phone: 800-274-0568 or 607-277-0488).

**Insects and Other Pests –** Insects in parts of South America can be not only a nuisance but also a real threat. To avoid contact in areas of infestation, do not sleep on the ground and, if possible, sleep under mosquito netting.

It is a good idea to use some form of topical insect repellent — those containing DEET (N,N-diethyl-m-toluamide) are among the most common and effective. The US Environmental Protection Agency (EPA) stresses that you should not use any pesticide that has not been approved by the EPA (check the label) and that all such preparations should be used in moderation. (Use solutions containing no more than a 15% solution of DEET on children, for example, and apply only to clothing, not directly to the skin.) If picnicking or camping, burn mosquito coils or candles containing allethrin, pyrethrin, or citronella, or use a pyrethrum-containing flying insect spray. For further information about active ingredients in repellents, call the *National Pesticide Telecommunications Network*'s 24-hour hotline: 800-858-7378.

If you do get bitten — by mosquitoes or other bugs — the itching can be relieved with baking soda, topical first-aid creams, or antihistamine tablets. Should a bite become infected, treat it with a disinfectant or antibiotic cream.

Though rarer, bites from scorpions, snakes, or spiders can be serious. If possible, always try to catch the villain for identification purposes. If bitten, the best course of action may be to head directly to the nearest emergency ward or outpatient clinic of a hospital. Cockroaches and termites thrive in warm climates, but pose no serious health threat.

**Water Safety –** Most South American beaches are so beautiful, with sands so caressing and waters so crystalline (although some are less pure than they used to be), that it's hard to remember that the waters of South America also can be treacherous. A few precautions are necessary. Beware of the undertow, that current of water running back down the beach after a wave has washed ashore; it can knock you off your feet and into the surf. Even more dangerous is the riptide, a strong current of water running against the tide, which can pull you out to the sea. If you get caught offshore, don't panic or try to fight the current, because it will only exhaust you; instead, ride it out while waiting for it to subside, which usually happens not too far from shore, or try swimming away parallel to the beach.

Sharks are sometimes sighted, but they usually don't come in close to shore, and they are well fed on fish. Should you meet up with one, just swim away as quietly and smoothly as you can, without shouting or splashing. Although not aggressive, eels can be dangerous when threatened. If snorkeling or diving, beware of crevices where these creatures may be lurking. The tentacled Portuguese man-of-war and other jellyfish may drift in quiet salt waters for food and often wash up onto the beach; the long tentacles of these creatures sting whatever they touch — a paste made of household vinegar and unseasoned meat tenderizer is the recommended treatment.

South America's coral reefs are extensive and razor sharp. Treat all coral cuts with an antiseptic, and then watch carefully since coral is a living organism with bacteria on its surface which may cause an infection. If you step on a sea urchin, you'll find that the spines are very sharp, pierce the skin, and break off easily. Like splinters, the tips left embedded in the skin are difficult to remove, but they will dissolve in a week or two; rinsing with vinegar may help to dissolve them more quickly. To avoid these hazards, keep your feet covered whenever possible. You also should avoid swimming in (or drinking) water from freshwater streams, rivers, or pools, as they may be contaminated with Leptospira, which causes a bacterial disease called leptospirosis (the symptoms resemble influenza).

If complications, allergic reactions (such as breathlessness, fever, or cramps), or signs of serious infection result from any of the above circumstances, *see a doctor.*

Following all these precautions will not guarantee an illness-free trip, but should minimize the risk. For more information regarding preventive health care for travelers, contact the *International Association for Medical Assistance to Travelers* (*IAMAT*; 417 Center St., Lewiston, NY 14092; phone: 716-754-4883). This organization also assists travelers in obtaining emergency medical assistance while abroad (see list of such organizations below).

**MEDICAL ASSISTANCE IN SOUTH AMERICA:** Nothing ruins a vacation or business trip more effectively than sudden injury or illness. Fortunately, should you need medical attention, competent medical professionals perfectly equipped to handle any type of health problem can be found throughout the continent. The type and quality of medical care available, however, vary considerably from place to place. In major metropolitan and large resort areas you will find thorough, well-trained specialists in all fields, both private and public hospitals, clinics (including Anglo-American ones), dentists, optometrists, and pharmacies with pretty much the same drugs as in the US — some available without a prescription and at a lower cost than in the US. In rural and remote areas, however, the quality and availability of health care and the sophistication of medical facilities are far less certain, and for specialized treatment it often is best to arrange for transportation to the nearest metropolitan center.

If you find it necessary to go to a hospital, either for emergency treatment or for admission as a regular patient, try to find one that is affiliated with a university in a capital or major city — this is particularly critical should you need a blood transfusion, as such facilities generally have properly screened blood donors for Chagas' disease, hepatitis, AIDS, and other infectious diseases. (No matter what type of facility you go to, always ask about blood screening.) The next best alternative is to seek treatment at an American or British private hospital. These hospitals, where you can find them, are invariably staffed with English-speaking doctors who were trained in the US or United Kingdom, and are more likely to give you the kind of assurance you need to feel comfortable if you do not speak fluent Spanish or Portuguese. The emergency rooms of most of these hospitals also have staff members who speak English, and your hotel, the nearest US consulate or embassy, tourist office, or the local police can direct you to the nearest facility.

Try to avoid foreign private hospitals — *clinicas* — where blood donors may not have been adequately screened for blood-transmitted diseases. The only exception is if you need highly specialized emergency medical treatment, in which case public hospitals *may* have superior medical equipment. For example, if there is only one kidney dialysis facility, it will be in a public hospital. Remember that if you are hospitalized, you will have to pay, even in an emergency.

**Emergency Treatment** – If a bona fide emergency occurs, the fastest way to get attention may be to go directly to the emergency room of the nearest hospital. An alternative is to dial the local emergency assistance number (see "Emergency Numbers," below) used to summon the police, fire trucks, and ambulances.

Most emergency services send out well-equipped and well-staffed ambulances, although in some areas, ambulances may not be equipped with the advanced EMS technology found in the US and may provide only basic medical attention and be used mainly for transportation. When calling for help, state immediately that you are a foreign tourist and then describe the nature of your problem and your location. Note that the ambulance dispatcher may not be bilingual, and unless you speak the language, he or she will be unable to determine the nature of the emergency, what equipment will

## GETTING READY / Staying Healthy

be needed, or even where to send the ambulance. Travelers with little or no foreign language ability should try to get someone else to make the call. You also can dial for the operator and ask for someone who speaks English. If the situation is desperate, an international operator may be able to make the call to the local emergency service and stay on the line as interpreter.

**Emergency Numbers** – In the event of an accident or other medical emergency, call the applicable number listed below (as you would dial 911 throughout the US).

**Argentina:** Dial 107 for an ambulance or 101 for the police.
**Bolivia:** Dial 110 for emergency assistance throughout Bolivia.
**Brazil:** Dial 190 for the police for emergency assistance.
**Chile:** Dial 133 for emergency assistance.
**Colombia:** Dial 112 for the police for emergency assistance.
**Ecuador:** Dial 101 for the police or 104 for an operator who can connect you to other emergency services.
**French Guiana:** Dial 17 for the police for emergency assistance.
**Guyana:** Dial 911 for emergency assistance.
**Panama:** Dial 102 for emergency assistance.
**Paraguay:** Dial 00 for an operator who will connect you with the police or other emergency services.
**Peru:** Dial 105 for emergency assistance.
**Suriname:** Dial 91111 for an ambulance or 71111 for the police.
**Uruguay:** Dial 999 for emergency assistance.
**Venezuela:** Dial 165 for the police or 169 for an ambulance.

For those countries where you will need to call an operator and ask to be connected to the police or other emergency services, the following phrases should be of help. (Note that although Spanish is spoken throughout the majority of South America, Portuguese is spoken in Brazil, French is spoken in French Guiana, and Dutch is the native language of Suriname.)

**Help! (Assistance!)**
- Spanish: *Socorro!*
- Portuguese: *Socorro!*
- French: *Au secours!*
- Dutch: *Help!*

**Ambulance**
- Spanish: *Ambulancia*
- Portuguese: *Ambulância*
- French and Dutch: *Ambulance*

**Police**
- Spanish: *Policía*
- Portuguese: *Polícia*
- French: *Police*
- Dutch: *Politie*

**Non-Emergency Care** – If a doctor is needed for something less than an emergency, there are several ways to find one. If you are staying in a hotel or at a resort, ask for help in reaching a doctor or other emergency services, or for the house physician, who may visit you in your room or ask you to visit an office. Travelers staying at a hotel of any size probably will find that the doctor on call speaks at least a modicum of English — if not, request one who does. When you register at a hotel, it's not a bad idea to include your home address and telephone number; this will facilitate the process of notifying friends, relatives, or your own doctor in case of an emergency.

Dialing the emergency number, however, may be of help in locating a doctor in a non-emergency situation (again, if you can speak the language). Most likely, you will be given the name of a general practitioner in the area. If you require a specialist, call the appropriate department of a teaching hospital (if one exists nearby) or the nearest US consulate or embassy (see FACTS IN BRIEF for a list of US consuls in South America), which also maintains a list of English-speaking doctors and dentists. If you are already at the hospital, you can see a specialist there or make an appointment to be seen at his or her office.

**Pharmacies and Prescription Drugs** – Pharmacies (*farmacias* in Spanish; *farmácias* in Portuguese) are a slight variation on the theme to which you are accustomed. While they're owned and operated by licensed pharmacists, who fill doctors' prescriptions and provide the same conventional services as druggists in the US, diagnoses and even drug administration are *sometimes* performed by pharmacists or their assistants. This is not as common as it once was, however, as it generally is illegal to sell or administer prescription medications in South America without a doctor's prescription, just as it is in the US. (On the other hand, many medications that are available only with a doctor's prescription in the US are sold over the counter in South America. Be aware, however, that some of these over-the-counter remedies may contain drugs — such as chloramphenicol, an antibiotic sold only by prescription in the US — which may cause allergic reactions or other side effects.) If your complaint is not serious, the local *farmacia* or *farmácia* often will be happy to recommend a (non-prescription) drug, administer it either in bulk or single doses, and recommend a doctor to prescribe a medication or give injections.

In most areas, pharmacies operate on the *Farmacia de Turno* (Rotating Pharmacy) system, where in each neighborhood one pharmacy takes a turn staying open for 24 hours. In small towns, however, where none may be open after normal business hours, you *may* be able to have one open in an emergency situation — such as for a diabetic needing insulin — for a fee. Contact a local hospital or medical clinic for information on the evening's *de Turno* pharmacy or for these on-call pharmacists.

■ **A word of warning:** The threat of AIDS has made medical professionals and patients alike much more cautious about injections, particularly because reusable syringes and needles are often used in South America, and sterilization procedures may be inadequate or inconsistently applied. If you have a condition that may need occasional injections, bring a supply of syringes with you or buy the disposable syringes available without a prescription at most pharmacies in South America.

**ADDITIONAL RESOURCES:** Medical assistance also is available from various organizations and programs designed for travelers who have chronic ailments or whose illness requires them to return home:

*International Association for Medical Assistance to Travelers* (*IAMAT;* 417 Center St., Lewiston, NY 14092; phone: 716-754-4883). Entitles members to the services of participating English-speaking doctors around the world, as well as clinics and hospitals in various locations in South America. Participating physicians agree to adhere to a basic charge of around $40 to see a patient referred by *IAMAT.* To join, simply write to *IAMAT;* in about 3 weeks you will receive a membership card, the booklet of members, and an inoculation chart. A nonprofit organization, *IAMAT* appreciates donations; with a donation of $25 or more, you will receive a set of worldwide climate charts detailing weather and sanitary conditions. (Delivery can take up to 5 weeks, so plan ahead.)

*International Health Care Service* (New York Hospital–Cornell Medical Center, 525 E. 68th St., Box 210, New York, NY 10021; phone: 212-746-1601). This

## GETTING READY / Staying Healthy

service provides a variety of travel-related health services, including information on health conditions and English-speaking physicians in South America and a complete range of immunizations at moderate per-shot rates. A pre-travel counseling and immunization package costs $255 for the first family member and $195 for each additional member; a post-travel consultation is $175 to $275, plus lab work. Consultations are by appointment only, from 4 to 8 PM, Mondays through Thursdays, although 24-hour coverage is available for urgent travel-related problems. In addition, sending $4.50 (with a self-addressed envelope) to the address above will procure the Service's publication, *International Health Care Traveler's Guide*, a compendium of facts and advice on health care and diseases around the world.

*International SOS Assistance* (PO Box 11568, Philadelphia, PA 19116; phone: 800-523-8930 or 215-244-1500). Subscribers are provided with telephone access — 24 hours a day, 365 days a year — to a worldwide, monitored, multilingual network of medical centers. A phone call brings assistance ranging from a telephone consultation to transportation home by ambulance or aircraft, or, in some cases, transportation of a family member to wherever you are hospitalized. Individual rates are $35 for 2 weeks of coverage ($3.50 for each additional day), $70 for 1 month, or $240 for 1 year; couple and family rates also are available.

*Medic Alert Foundation* (2323 N. Colorado, Turlock, CA 95380; phone: 800-ID-ALERT or 209-668-3333). If you have a health condition that may not be readily perceptible to the casual observer — one that might result in a tragic error in an emergency situation — this organization offers identification emblems specifying such conditions. The foundation also maintains a computerized central file from which your complete medical history is available 24 hours a day by phone (the telephone number is clearly inscribed on the emblem). The one-time membership fee, between $25 and $45, is based on the type of metal from which the emblem is made — the choices range from stainless steel to 10K gold-filled.

*TravMed* (PO Box 10623, Baltimore, MD 21204; phone: 800-732-5309 or 301-296-5225). For $3 per day, subscribers receive comprehensive medical assistance while abroad. Major medical expenses are covered up to $100,000, and special transportation home or of a family member to wherever you are hospitalized is provided at no additional cost.

---

■**Note:** Those who are unable to take a reserved flight due to personal illness or who must fly home unexpectedly due to a family emergency should be aware that airlines may offer a discounted airfare (or arrange a partial refund) if the traveler can demonstrate that his or her situation is indeed a legitimate emergency. Your inability to fly or the illness or death of an immediate family member usually must be substantiated by a doctor's note or the name, relationship, and funeral home from which the deceased will be buried. In such cases, airlines often will waive certain advance purchase restrictions or you may receive a refund check or voucher for future travel at a later date. Be aware, however, that this bereavement fare may not necessarily be the least expensive fare available and, if possible, it is best to have a travel agent check all possible flights through a computer reservations system (CRS).

---

**Helpful Publications** – A useful publication, *Health Hints for the Tropics*, offers tips on preventing illnesses and staying healthy in South America, including practical information on immunizations, trip preparation, as well as a list of resources. It is available for $4 postpaid from Dr. Karl A. Western at the *American Society of Tropical Medicine and Hygiene,* 6436 31st St. NW, Washington, DC 20015-2342 (phone: 301-496-6721).

Practically every phase of health care — before, during, and after a trip — is covered in *The New Traveler's Health Guide,* by Drs. Patrick J. Doyle and James E. Banta. It is available for $4.95, plus postage and handling, from Acropolis Books Ltd., 13950 Park Center Rd., Herndon, VA 22071 (phone: 800-451-7771 or 703-709-0006).

The *Traveling Healthy Newsletter,* which is published six times a year, also is brimming with health-related travel tips. For a year's subscription, which costs $24 (sample issues are available for $4), contact Dr. Karl Neumann (108-48 70th Rd., Forest Hills, NY 11375; phone: 718-268-7290). Dr. Neumann also is the editor of the useful free booklet *Traveling Healthy,* which is available by writing to the *Travel Healthy Program* (Clark O'Neill Inc., 1 Broad Ave., Fairview, NJ 07022; phone: 201-945-3400).

# Legal Aid and Consular Services

There is one crucial place to keep in mind when outside the US, namely, the American Services section of the US consulate. If you are injured or become seriously ill, the consulate will direct you to medical assistance and notify your relatives. If, while abroad, you become involved in a dispute that could lead to legal action, the consulate, once again, is the place to turn.

It usually is far more alarming to be arrested abroad than at home. Not only are you alone among strangers, but the punishment can be worse. Granted, the US consulate can advise you of your rights and provide a list of English-speaking lawyers, but it cannot interfere with the local legal process. Except for minor infractions of the local traffic code, there is no reason for any law-abiding traveler to run afoul of immigration, customs, or any other law enforcement authority.

The best advice is to be honest and law-abiding. If you get a traffic ticket, pay it. If you are approached by drug hawkers, ignore them. The penalties for possession of marijuana, cocaine, and other narcotics are even more severe abroad than in the US. (If you are picked up for any drug-related offense, do not expect US foreign service officials to be sympathetic. Chances are, they will notify a lawyer and your family and that's about all. See "Drugs," below.)

Justice in South America is based on the Napoleonic Code, which assumes defendants to be guilty until they prove themselves innocent. This makes any encounter with the police highly uncomfortable. The system of legal rights and requirements which protects citizens in the US is seldom equalled or simply nonexistent in most South American countries. Remember, in many cases you are dealing with a traditionally authoritarian society. By treaty, police are required to inform the US consul if a US citizen is arrested, but the degree of respect that is shown your person will depend to a frightening degree upon the crime of which you are accused and how the police view you.

In the case of minor traffic accidents (such as a fender bender), it often is most expedient to settle the matter before the police get involved. If the police do get involved in minor accidents or violations, try to establish a fine on the spot and pay it quickly. If you speak the language and feel competent, try to bargain the fine, but wisdom decrees that you do what is necessary to get the matter settled on the spot. There are few experiences more distasteful than being hauled off to a South American jail. If it seems that an arrest is imminent, have a friend try to attract the attention of potential witnesses; if you are arrested, have your companion accompany you to the police station.

## GETTING READY / Legal Aid and Consular Services 137

If, however, you are involved in a serious accident, where an injury or fatality results, the first step is to contact the US consulate (see FACTS IN BRIEF for addresses) and ask the consul to locate an attorney to assist you. If you have a traveling companion, ask him or her to call the consulate (unless either of you has a local contact who can help you quickly). Competent English-speaking lawyers practice throughout South America and it is possible to obtain good legal counsel on short notice.

The US Department of State in Washington, DC, insists that any US citizen who is arrested abroad has the right to contact the US embassy or consulate "immediately," but it may be a while before you are given permission to use a phone. Do not labor under the illusion, however, that in a scrape with foreign officialdom, the consulate can act as an arbitrator or ombudsman on a US citizen's behalf. Nothing could be farther from the truth. Consuls have no power, authorized or otherwise, to subvert, alter, or contravene the legal processes, however unfair, of the foreign country in which they serve. Nor can a consul oil the machinery of a foreign bureaucracy or provide legal advice. The consul's responsibilities do encompass "welfare duties," including providing a list of lawyers and information on local sources of legal aid, assigning an interpreter if the police have none, informing relatives in the US, and organizing and administrating any defense monies sent from home. If a case is tried unfairly or the punishment seems unusually severe, the consul can make a formal complaint to the authorities. For questions about US citizens arrested abroad, how to get money to them, and other useful information, call the *Citizens' Emergency Center* of the Office of Special Consular Services in Washington, DC, at 202-647-5225. (For further information about this invaluable hotline, see below.)

Other welfare duties, not involving legal hassles, cover cases of both illness and destitution. If you should get sick, the US consul can provide names of English-speaking doctors and dentists, as well as the names of all local hospitals and clinics; the consul also will contact family members in the US and help arrange special ambulance service for a flight home. In a situation involving "legitimate and proven poverty" of a US citizen stranded abroad without funds, the consul will contact sources of money (such as family or friends in the US), apply for aid to agencies in foreign countries, and in a last resort — which is *rarely* — arrange for repatriation at government expense, although this is a loan that must be repaid. And in case of natural disasters or civil unrest, consulates around the world handle the evacuation of US citizens if it becomes necessary.

The consulate is not occupied solely with emergencies and is certainly not there to aid in trivial situations, such as canceled reservations or lost baggage, no matter how important these matters may seem to the victimized tourist. The main duties of any consulate are administering statutory services, such as the issuance of passports and visas; providing notarial services; distributing VA, social security, and civil service benefits to US citizens; taking depositions; handling extradition cases; and reporting to Washington, DC the births, deaths, and marriages of US citizens living within the consulate's domain.

We hope that none of the information in this section will be necessary during your travels through South America. If you can avoid legal hassles altogether, you will have a much more pleasant trip. And if you run into a confrontation that might lead to legal complications developing with a South American citizen or with local authorities, the best tactic is to apologize and try to leave as gracefully as possible. If you do become involved in an imbroglio, the local authorities may spare you legal complications if you make clear your tourist status. Do not get into fights with residents, no matter how belligerent or provocative they are in a given situation. In a foreign country where machismo is part of the national character, some things are best left unsettled.

For a country-by-country listing of US consulates and embassies in South America, see FACTS IN BRIEF. (If you are not a US citizen, contact the consulate of your own nation.) If you are not in any of the areas mentioned when a problem arises, contact

**138 GETTING READY / Drinking and Drugs**

the nearest office. Note that mailing addresses may be different — so call before sending anything to these offices.

You can obtain a booklet with addresses of most US embassies and consulates around the world by writing to the Superintendent of Documents (US Government Printing Office, Washington, DC 20402; phone: 202-783-3238) and asking for publication #744-006-0000-7-W, *Key Offices of Foreign Service Posts*.

As mentioned above, the US State Department operates a *Citizens' Emergency Center*, which offers a number of services to US citizens traveling abroad and their families at home. In addition to giving callers up-to-date information on trouble spots, the center will contact authorities abroad in an attempt to locate a traveler or deliver an urgent message. In case of illness, death, arrest, destitution, or repatriation of a US citizen on foreign soil, it will relay information to relatives at home if the consulate is unable to do so. Travel advisory information is available 24 hours a day to people with touch-tone phones (phone: 202-647-5225). Callers with rotary phones can get information at this number from 8:15 AM to 10 PM (eastern standard time) on weekdays; 9 AM to 3 PM on Saturdays. In the event of an emergency, this number also may be called during these hours. For emergency calls only, at all other times, call 202-634-3600 and ask for the Duty Officer.

# Drinking and Drugs

**DRINKING:** There are few cultural or legal restrictions on drinking in South America; a person must look extremely young before being denied a drink in a public place. In general, public drunkenness is not a legal offense, and car accidents caused by drunken drivers are depressingly common, as are bar fights. (Although be aware that car accidents that result in any physical injury of pedestrians often result in immediate incarceration of the driver pending trial — therefore, hit-and-run incidents are common.)

That is only a small part of the story, though, and innumerable South American fiestas, at which drinking is an important but not immoderate part, provide wonderful opportunities to get to know and enjoy South Americans. Each country has its own national alcoholic specialty, worth sampling at least once. For information on the native brews of South America, see *Food and Drink*, PERSPECTIVES.

As in the US, national taxes on alcohol affect the prices of liquor in South America, and as a general rule, mixed drinks made from imported liquors (such as whiskey and gin) are more expensive than at home. If you like a drop before dinner, a good way to save money is to buy a bottle of your favorite brand at the airport before leaving the US and enjoy it in your hotel before setting forth. Or stick to locally produced beverages.

Duties on imported liquor vary from country to country; this information is available from the appropriate tourist authorities (for addresses, see the individual country entries in FACTS IN BRIEF). If you are buying any quantity of alcohol (such as a case of Chilean wine) in South America and traveling across national borders (from one South American country to another) en route back to the US, you will have to pass through customs and pay duty at each border crossing, so you might want to arrange to have it shipped home. Whether bringing it with you or shipping, you will have to pay US import duties on any quantity over the allowed 1 liter. And remember that individual US states have the power to impose additional restrictions on the import of liquor above this duty-free amount across their borders, so check with the appropriate state agency before you travel (see *Customs and Returning to the US*, in this section).

**DRUGS:** Another way to avoid legal trouble in South America is to avoid the drug scene — completely. Illegal narcotics are as prevalent in South America as in the US, but the moderate legal penalties and vague social acceptance that marijuana has gained in the US have no equivalents in South American countries. Due to the international war on drugs, enforcement of drug laws is becoming increasingly strict throughout the world. Local South American narcotics officers and customs officials are renowned for their absence of understanding and lack of a sense of humor — especially where North Americans are involved.

Infamous throughout the world (the non-drug world as well as the underworld), Colombian cocaine can be obtained at a costly and dangerous price, the most obvious being imprisonment by the authorities or death at the hands of a drug dealer (especially in such places as Medellín, Colombia). Although marijuana is grown in abundance throughout South America and is widely available in most large South American cities, it is just as illegal in South America as it is in the US, and penalties for selling, growing, and smoking it are just as severe. Opiates and barbiturates, and other increasingly popular drugs — "white powder" substances like heroin and "crack" (the cocaine derivative) — also continue to be of major concern to narcotics officials.

The concerted effort by South American and other foreign authorities to stamp out drug traffic, with the support and encouragement of the United States, has now become a real war on buyers and sellers, a war that has been — and continues to be — deadly. This increased vigilance is particularly avid in South American port areas which are notorious major transshipment areas for the drug underworld — although in the case of Cartagena, Colombia the situation has improved considerably.

Drug dealing itself is a vicious business. One American who has lived in South America for many years reports that cocaine dealers have a nasty habit of supplying gringos with substances ranging from relatively harmless powders to ground glass. Recent news about the violent actions of South American drug dealers — particularly in Colombia — should serve as further incentive to give these criminals a wide berth.

Penalties for possession of even small quantities of marijuana range from deportation with stiff fines to jail terms of at least 2 or 3 years, without bail or appeal. The penalties for other drugs may be more stringent, and smuggling is dealt with even more severely. It is important to bear in mind that the quantity of drugs involved is of very minor importance.

Do not, under any circumstances, take drugs into, out of, or through South America. Persons arrested are subject to the laws of the countries they are visiting, and these laws and their procedures often are very harsh. Most of the Americans repatriated through the prisoner-exchange agreements between the United States and some South American countries were incarcerated for drug offenses. Once you are in jail, the best lawyers in the country won't be able to get you out — and neither will the US government. Eventually, at the whim of the authorities, you will be tried and, upon conviction, given a stiff sentence. The best advice we can offer is this: Don't carry, use, buy, or sell illegal drugs.

Those who carry medicines that contain a controlled drug should be sure to have a current doctor's prescription with them. Ironically, travelers can get into almost as much trouble coming through US Customs with over-the-counter drugs picked up abroad that contain substances that are controlled in the US. Cold medicines, pain relievers, and the like often have codeine or codeine derivatives that are illegal, except by prescription, in the US. Throw them out before leaving for home.

- **■ Be forewarned:** US narcotics agents warn travelers of the increasingly common ploy of drug dealers asking travelers to transport a "gift" or other package back to the US. Don't be fooled into thinking that the protection of US law applies abroad — accused of illegal drug trafficking, you will be considered guilty until you prove your innocence. In other words, do not, under any circumstances, agree to take anything across the border for a stranger.

# Crime in South America

South American countries, like anywhere else in the world, have their share of pickpockets and thieves working the tourist areas. Street crime can happen anywhere, but we recommend particular caution in Cali, Guayaquil, Quito, and Rio de Janeiro. And in countries such as Colombia, Panama, Peru, and Suriname, it pays to exercise *extreme* caution at all times.

At the time of this writing, the US State Department had issued a traveler advisory warning regarding Colombia, Ecuador, Peru, and Suriname — stating that there is no guarantee of safe-conduct in these countries. These warnings and cautions relate to street crime, terrorist attacks, the narcotics trade, and natural disasters. Before you go, you should call the US State Department's *Citizens' Emergency Center* hotline: 202-647-5225. Among the recorded options is specific, up-to-date information on these and other matters concerning the safety of US citizens abroad. The US State Department also recommends contacting the nearest US consulate or embassy upon arrival in South America, and in some countries, such as Suriname, advises US visitors to register with the consular section of the US embassy.

Exercise the normal common-sense precautions you would observe at home — and then some. Be particularly careful in crowded markets, airports, and stations. The US embassy recommends the following precautions:

1. Do not keep your passport, other identification, credit cards, extra traveler's checks, cash, onward tickets, or other valuables in your purse or outside pockets. Carry only what you will need and leave the rest locked in your hotel safe, not in your room (even in a locked suitcase). Do not wear valuable jewelry.
2. If you must carry your passport, it is safer fastened in an inner pocket than in a purse or briefcase. If you do carry a purse or camera, it should be one with a sturdy strap which can be slung across your body and cradled *in front* — with your hand on it at all times.
3. Keep your ID cards separate from your passport because a replacement cannot be issued without some form of identification. Better yet, carry a separate photocopy of your passport (and also photocopy of any visa pages for the countries to be visited). If you lose a passport or visa, make it known at once to the nearest police station. Ask for a copy of the resultant police report; you will need it for a replacement passport, which can be issued by a US consul section only during office hours (see *Entry Requirements and Documents,* in this section).

Frequent travelers to South America swear by money belts as the safest way to carry valuables. In many areas, extreme poverty has bred rampant petty theft (especially in Rio) — visitors often are shocked to discover that young children are common perpetrators. Especially in Colombia, do not accept drinks, candy, or even gum from other passengers on trains and buses; there have been a number of incidents in which travelers have been drugged and robbed.

# Tipping

Although a service charge of between 10% and 20% is levied on most restaurant and hotel bills throughout South America, tipping is still standard practice. Many waiters, waitresses, porters, and bellboys in South America depend upon tips for their livelihood. The salaries they receive, if they do receive salaries, are far below the equivalent paid in the US (even with the lower

South American standards of living taken into consideration). There also are situations in which you wouldn't tip in the US but should in South America.

In restaurants, where a service charge has already been added no tip is expected, although an additional gratuity of 5% to 10% will be greatly appreciated. As a general rule, if service is not included, tip between 10% and 20% of the bill in restaurants, nightclubs, and bars. For average service in an average establishment, a 15% to the waiter or barmaid is reasonable, although one should never hesitate to penalize poor service or reward excellent and efficient attention by leaving less or more.

Although it's not necessary to tip the maître d' of most restaurants — unless he or she has been especially helpful in arranging a special party or providing a table (a few extra bills *may,* however, get you seated sooner or procure a preferred table) — when tipping is desirable or appropriate, the least amount should be the current local equivalent of $5. In the finest restaurants, where a multiplicity of servers are present, plan to tip 5% to the captain. The sommelier (wine waiter) is tipped approximately 10% of the price of the bottle of wine.

In allocating gratuities at a restaurant, pay particular attention to what has become the standard credit card charge form, which now includes separate places for gratuities for waiters and/or captains. If these separate boxes are not on the charge slip, simply ask the waiter or captain how these separate tips should be indicated. Be aware, too, of the increasingly common — and devious — practice of placing the amount of an entire restaurant bill (in which service already has been included) in the top box of a charge slip, leaving the "tip" and "total" boxes ominously empty. Don't be intimidated: Leave the "tip" box blank and just repeat the total amount next to "total" before signing. In some establishments, tips indicated on credit card receipts may not be given to the help, so you may want to leave tips in cash.

If you arrive by air, you probably will find a porter with a cart ready to roll your baggage from customs to the cab stand. He should be paid the current equivalent of about $1 to $2 in local currency, depending on how much luggage you have. If you are traveling by train, porters *expect* a tip of about 25¢ to 35¢ per bag — you might want to go higher. Bellhops, doormen, and porters at hotels generally are tipped at the rate of 50¢ to $1 per piece of luggage, along with a small additional amount if a doorman helps with a cab or car. If you arrive without any foreign coins, tip in US money, preferably in dollars, since quarters and other American coins often are not readily convertible. (When in doubt, it is preferable to tip — in any denomination or currency — than not to tip.)

If a hotel does not automatically add a service charge, it is perfectly proper for guests to ask to have an extra 10% to 15% added to their bill, to be distributed among those who served them. This may be an expecially convenient solution in a large hotel or resort, where it is difficult to determine just who out of a horde of attendants actually performed particular services.

For those who prefer to distribute tips themselves, a chambermaid generally is tipped at the rate of around $1 per day. Tip the concierge or hall porter for specific services only, with the amount of such gratuities dependent on the level of service provided. For any special service you receive in a hotel, a tip is expected — the current equivalent of $1 being the minimum for a small service.

Most South American taxi drivers do not expect tips — except in Uruguay, where 5% of the fare is an acceptable minimum. In Argentina, Brazil, and Chile (and most other countries), rounding the fare up to the next denomination takes the place of tipping. For instance, in Brazil, if the fare is 456 cruzeiros, pay 500.

In South America, tourists often are offered special services by young children in the street. These might include watching your car while you shop and sightsee or cleaning your windshield while you stop at a light. In some instances, these services come more as assaults than offers — you will find someone suddenly propped on the hood of your car wiping your windows with a dirty rag. In such cases, the most expedient thing to do is to give each child a few pesos (or cruzeiros, or francs, and so on) and tell them to go away *(Váyase!)*. Very often children will open the door of your car in an attempt to help you get out. You must tell them *no* immediately. Otherwise they probably will station themselves against your car, allegedly guarding it, until your return. If they insist on "protecting" your car, the wisest recourse is to give them a couple of coins. But first check that everything in the car is as you left it. Arriving and departing from airline terminals also can turn into a battle royal with youngsters over carrying your luggage.

In resort areas, you may come across uniformed adult car watchers who earn their livelihoods this way. If you find one near your car, give him the current local equivalent of $1 when you return — once you've unlocked the car and made sure everything is still there. If you park your car in a garage or lot, the parking attendant who returns it to you will expect a comparable tip. Gas station attendants also expect a small tip, particularly if they wipe your windshield or check the oil.

**Miscellaneous tips:** Ushers in theaters should be given about 50¢ after leading you to a seat and giving you a program. Sightseeing tour guides should be tipped. If you are traveling in a group, decide together what you want to give the guide and present it from the group at the end of the tour ($1 per person is a reasonable tip). If you have been indvidually escorted, the amount paid should depend on the degree of your satisfaction, but it should not be less than 10% of the total tour price. Museum and monument guides also are usually tipped, and it is a nice touch to tip a caretaker who unlocks a small church or turns on the lights in a chapel for you in some out-of-the-way town.

In barbershops and beauty salons, tip as you would at home, keeping in mind that the percentages vary according to the type of establishment — 10% in the most expensive salons; 15% to 20% in less expensive establishments. (As a general rule, the person who washes your hair should get a small additional tip.) Washroom attendants should get a small tip — they usually set out a little plate with a coin already on it indicating the suggested denomination. Coat checks are worth about 50¢ to $1 a coat. For information on tipping aboard ships, see *Traveling by Ship*, in this section.

Customs officials do not expect to be tipped. If you need to secure a police report of a robbery, however, you may have to file your request for such a report on special paper that often must be purchased from street vendors outside the police station or from banks. These papers have to be written in a specialized language. Someone in the police station will write it for you; tip the scribe the equivalent of $1 or $2. In most South American countries, lawyers take care of the complicated transactions involving documents and tips to government officials.

Tipping always is a matter of personal preference. In the situations covered above, as well as in any others that arise where you feel a tip is expected or due, feel free to express your pleasure or displeasure. Again, never hesitate to reward excellent and efficient attention or to penalize poor service. Give an extra gratuity and a word of thanks when someone has gone out of his or her way for you. Either way, the more personal the act of tipping, the more appropriate it seems. And if you didn't like the service — or the attitude — don't tip.

# Duty-Free Shopping

Duty-free shops are located in most major international airports throughout South America. If common sense says that it always is less expensive to buy goods in an airport duty-free shop than to buy them at home or in the streets of a foreign city, travelers should be aware of some basic facts. Duty-free, first of all, does not mean that the goods travelers buy will be free of duty when they return to the US. Rather, it means that the shop has paid no import tax acquiring goods of foreign make because the goods are not to be used in the country where the shop is located. This is why duty-free goods are available only in the restricted, passengers-only area of international airports or are delivered to departing passengers on the plane. In a duty-free store, travelers save money only on goods of foreign make because they are the only items on which an import tax would be charged in any other store.

There is little reason to delay buying locally made merchandise and/or souvenirs until reaching the airport (for information on local specialties, see FACTS IN BRIEF, the individual city chapters in THE CITIES, and *Great Buys: Shopping in South America*, in DIVERSIONS). In fact, because airport duty-free shops usually pay high rents, the locally made goods sold in them may well be more expensive than they would be in downtown stores. The real bargains are foreign goods, but — let the buyer beware — not all foreign goods are automatically less expensive in an airport duty-free shop. You can get a good deal on even small amounts of perfume, costing less than the usually required minimum purchase, tax-free. Other fairly standard bargains include spirits, smoking materials, cameras, clothing, watches, chocolates, and other food and luxury items — but first be sure to know what these items cost elsewhere. Terrific savings do exist (they are the reason for such shops, after all), but so do overpriced items that an unwary shopper might find equally tempting. In addition, if you wait to do your shopping at airport duty-free shops, you will be taking the chance that the desired item is out of stock or unavailable.

## Religion on the Road

South America is a Catholic continent, by and large, and every town, right down to the most isolated village, has its own church. In some more remote southern villages you will find an interesting combination of Catholicism and pre-Christian ritual, as reflected in the common sight of a family leaving Sunday morning mass only to walk across the plaza and set up an idol of some warrior god dating back to Inca times. And in larger, more heavily populated areas, some amount of religious variety is reflected in the numerous Protestant churches, Jewish synagogues, and the occasional mosque or temple.

The surest source of information on English-language religious services in an unfamiliar country is the desk clerk of the hotel or resort in which you are staying; the local tourist information office, a US consul, or a church of another religious affiliation also may be able to provide this information. Services in English are available at various churches and other places of worship in South America, particularly in metropolitan areas and other communities with large English-speaking populations. If you aren't in an area with such services, you might find it interesting to attend a service in a foreign language — even if you don't understand all the words. There are many beautiful churches throughout South America, and whether in a stately cathedral or a small village chapel, visitors are welcome.

## Customs and Returning to the US

Whether you return to the United States by air or sea, you must declare to the US Customs official at the point of entry everything you have bought or acquired while in South America. The customs check can go smoothly, lasting only a few minutes, or can take hours, depending on the officer's instinct. Most customs agents processing return travelers from South America are looking for drugs and fresh fruit and vegetables, although in the Andean countries, they also watch for antiquities, which — if they can be taken out of the country at all — require official export permits. To speed up the process, keep all your receipts handy and try to pack your purchases together in an accessible part of your suitcase. It might save you from unpacking all your belongings.

**DUTY-FREE ARTICLES:** In general, the duty-free allowance for US citizens returning from abroad is $400. This duty-free limit is based on the provision that your purchases accompany you and are for personal use. This limit includes items used or worn while abroad, souvenirs for friends, and gifts received during the trip. A flat 10% duty based on the "fair retail value in country of acquisition" is assessed on the next $1,000 worth of merchandise brought in for personal use or gifts. Amounts over the basic allotment and the 10% dutiable amount are dutiable at a variety of rates. The average rate for typical tourist purchases is about 12%, but you can find out rates on specific items by consulting *Tariff Schedules of the United States* in a library or at any US Customs Service office.

Families traveling together may make a joint declaration to customs, which permits one member to exceed his or her duty-free exemption to the extent that another falls short. Families also may pool purchases dutiable under the flat rate. A family of three, for example, would be eligible for up to a total of $3,000 at the 10% flat duty rate (after each member had used up his or her $400 duty-free exemption) rather than three separate $1,000 allowances. This grouping of purchases is extremely useful when considering the duty on a high-tariff item, such as jewelry or a fur coat.

Personal exemptions can be used once every 30 days; in order to be eligible, an individual must have been out of the country for more than 48 continuous hours. If any portion of the exemption has been used once within any 30-day period or if your trip is less than 48 hours long, the duty-free allowance is cut to $25.

There are certain articles, however, that are duty-free only up to certain limits. The $25 allowance includes the following: 10 cigars (not Cuban), 50 cigarettes, and 4 ounces of perfume. Individuals eligible for the full $400 duty-free limit are allowed 1 carton of cigarettes (200), 100 cigars, and 1 liter of liquor or wine if the traveler is over 21. Under federal law, alcohol above this allowance is liable for both duty and an Internal Revenue Service tax. Note, however, that states are allowed to impose additional restrictions and penalties of their own, including (in Arizona and Utah, for example) confiscation of any quantities of liquor over the statutory limit. Antiques, if they are 100 or more years old and you have proof from the seller of that fact, are duty-free, as are paintings and drawings if done entirely by hand.

To avoid paying duty twice, register the serial numbers of computers, watches, and electronic equipment with the nearest US Customs bureau before departure; receipts of insurance policies also should be carried for other foreign-made items. (Also see the note at the end of *Entry Requirements and Documents,* in this section.)

Gold, gold medals, bullion, and up to $10,000 in currency or negotiable instruments may be brought into the US without being declared. Sums over $10,000 must be declared in writing.

Although we do not recommend that you send any packages through the notoriously unreliable South American postal systems, the allotment for individual "unsolicited" gifts mailed from abroad (no more than one per day per recipient) is $50 retail value per gift. These gifts do not have to be declared and are not included in your duty-free exemption (see below). Although you should include a receipt for purchases with each package, the examiner is empowered to impose a duty based on his or her assessment of the value of the goods. The duty owed is collected by the US Postal Service when the package is delivered (also see below). More information on mailing packages home from abroad is contained in the US Customs Service pamphlet *Buyer Beware, International Mail Imports* (see below for where to write for this and other useful brochures).

**DUTY-FREE CRAFT ITEMS:** In January 1976, the United States passed a Generalized System of Preferences (GSP) to help developing nations improve their economies through exports. The GSP, which recognizes dozens of developing nations — including Argentina, Bolivia, Brazil, Colombia, Ecuador, Guyana, Panama, Peru, Suriname, Uruguay, and Venezuela — allows Americans to bring certain kinds of goods into the US duty-free, and has designated some 3,000 items as eligible for duty-free treatment.

This system entitles you to exceed your $400 duty-free exemption as long as the purchases are eligible for GSP status. The list of eligible goods includes the following categories: baskets and woven bags; cameras and other photographic equipment; candy; china and silverware; cigarette lighters; earthenware; some furniture; games and toys; golf and ski equipment; some jewelry, unset precious or semi-precious stones, and pearls; jewelry and music boxes; musical instruments, radios, tape recorders, records, and tapes; paper goods and printed matter; perfume and toilet preparations; electric shavers; items made of cork, jade, or shell (other than tortoiseshell); wigs; and woodcarvings. Note that, depending on the country of origin, some items may not always be included, and other items not in these categories also may be eligible.

If you have any questions about the GSP status of a particular item, check with the nearest customs office or at the nearest US embassy or consulate (see FACTS IN BRIEF for locations in South America). A useful pamphlet identifying GSP beneficiary nations is *GSP and the Traveler;* to order ask for "US Customs Publication No. 515," from the US Customs Service, Customs Information, 6 World Trade Ctr., Rm. 201, New York, NY 10048 (phone: 212-466-5550).

**CLEARING CUSTOMS:** This is a simple procedure. Forms are distributed by airline or ship personnel before arrival. (Note that a $5-per-person service charge — called a user fee — is collected by airlines and cruise lines to help cover the cost of customs checks, but this is included in the ticket price.) If your purchases total no more than the $400 duty-free limit, you need only fill out the identification part of the form and make an oral declaration to the customs inspector. If entering with more than $400 worth of goods, you must submit a written declaration.

Customs agents are businesslike, efficient, and not unkind. During the peak season, clearance can take time, but this generally is because of the strain imposed by a number of jumbo jets simultaneously discharging their passengers, not because of unwarranted zealousness on the part of the customs people.

Efforts to streamline procedures used to include the so-called Citizens' Bypass Program, which allowed US citizens whose purchases were within their duty-free allowance to go to the "green line," where they simply showed their passports to the customs inspector. Although at the time of this writing this procedure still is being followed at some international airports in the US, most airports have returned to an earlier system. US citizens arriving from abroad now have to go through a passport check by the Immigration & Naturalization Service (INS) prior to recovering their baggage and proceeding to customs. (US citizens will not be on the same line as foreign visitors, but this additional wait does delay clearance on re-entry into the US.) Although all passengers have to go through this obligatory passport inspection, those entering with purchases within the duty-free limit may be spared a thorough customs inspection; however, inspectors still retain the right to search any luggage they choose — so don't do anything foolish.

It is illegal not to declare dutiable items; not to do so, in fact, constitutes smuggling, and the penalty can be anything from stiff fines and seizure of the goods to prison sentences. It simply isn't worth doing. Nor should you go along with the suggestions of foreign merchants who offer to help you secure a bargain by deceiving customs officials in any way. Such transactions frequently are a setup, using the foreign merchant as an agent of US Customs. Another agent of US Customs is TECS, the Treasury Enforcement Communications System, a computer that stores all kinds of pertinent information on returning citizens. There is a basic rule to buying goods abroad, and it should never be broken: *If you can't afford the duty on something, don't buy it.* Your list or verbal declaration should include all items purchased abroad, as well as gifts received abroad, purchases made at the behest of others, the value of repairs, and anything brought in for resale in the US.

Do not include in the list items that do not accompany you, i.e., purchases that you have mailed or had shipped home. As mentioned above, these are dutiable in any case, even if for your own use and even if the items that accompany your return from the same trip do not exhaust your duty-free exemption. It is a good idea, if you have accumulated too much while abroad, to mail home any personal effects (made and bought in the US) that you no longer need rather than your foreign purchases. These personal effects pass through US Customs as "American goods returned" and are not subject to duty. (Again, keep in mind that South American surface mail is notoriously unreliable; for information on suggested alternatives see *Mail, Telephone, and Electricity,* in this section.)

If you cannot avoid shipping home your foreign purchases, however, the US Customs Service suggests that the package be clearly marked "Not for Sale" and that a copy of the bill of sale be included. The US Customs examiner usually will accept this as indicative of the article's fair retail value, but if he or she believes it to be falsified or feels the goods have been seriously undervalued, a higher retail value may be assigned.

**FORBIDDEN IMPORTS:** Narcotics, plants (unless specifically exempt and free of soil), and many types of food are not allowed into the US. Drugs are totally illegal, with the exception of medication prescribed by a physician. It's a good idea not to travel with too large a quantity of any given prescription drug (however, in the event that a pharmacy is not open when you need it, bring along several extra doses) and to have the prescription on hand in case any question arises either abroad or when re-entering the US.

Any authentic archaeological find, colonial art, and other original artifacts cannot be exported from South America unless a special permit is obtained before leaving — although some countries, such as Peru, may ban the export of such items unconditionally. Without such a permit, these items will be confiscated at the border, and the violator runs the risk of being fined or imprisoned. South American countries also restrict the export of gold and silver coins; those interested in such items should check with the country's customs office.

Tourists have long been forbidden to bring into the US foreign-made US trademarked articles purchased abroad (if the trademark is recorded with US Customs) without written permission. It's now permissible to enter with one such item in your possession as long as it's for personal use.

The US Customs Service implements the rigorous Department of Agriculture regulations concerning the importation of vegetable matter, seeds, bulbs, and the like. Living vegetable matter may not be imported without a permit, and everything must be inspected, permit or not. Approved items (which do not require a permit) include dried bamboo and woven items made of straw; beads made of most seeds (but not jequirity beans — the poisonous scarlet and black seed of the rosary pea) and some viable (living) seeds; coconut shells (unhusked and empty); cones of pine and other trees; roasted coffee beans; most flower bulbs; flowers (without roots); dried or canned fruits, jellies, or jams; polished rice, dried beans and teas; herb plants (not witchweed); nuts (but not acorns, chestnuts, or any nuts with outer husks); dried lichens, mushrooms, and seaweed; and most dried spices.

Other processed foods and baked goods usually are okay. Regulations on meat products generally depend on the country of origin and manner of processing. As a rule, commercially canned meat, hermetically sealed and cooked in the can so that it can be stored without refrigeration, is permitted, but not all canned meat fulfills this

## GETTING READY / Customs and Returning to the US

requirement. (The imported brands you see in US stores have been prepared and packaged according to US regulations.) So before stocking up on a newfound favorite, it pays to check in advance — otherwise you might have to leave it behind.

The US Customs Service also enforces federal laws that prohibit the entry of articles made from the furs or hides of animals on the endangered species list. Don't be tempted by sweaters and other garments made from the fine hair of the vicuña (a relative of the domestic llama and alpaca), which is an endangered species. Also beware of shoes, bags, and belts made of crocodile and certain kinds of lizard, and anything made of tortoiseshell; this also applies to preserved crocodiles, lizards, and turtles sometimes sold in gift shops. Most coral — particularly black coral — also is restricted, although small quantities of coral incorporated into jewelry or other crafts items usually are permitted. And if you're shopping for big-ticket items, beware of fur coats made from the skins of spotted cats. They are sold abroad, but they will be confiscated upon your return to the US, and there will be no refund. For information about other animals on the endangered species list, contact the Department of the Interior, US Fish and Wildlife Service, (Publications Unit, 4401 N. Fairfax Dr., Room 130, Arlington, VA 22203; phone: 703-358-1711), and ask for the free publication *Facts About Federal Wildlife Laws.*

Also note that some foreign governments prohibit the export of items made from certain species of wildlife, and the US honors any such restrictions. Before you go shopping in any foreign country, check with the US Department of Agriculture (G110 Federal Bldg., Hyattsville, MD 20782; phone: 301-436-8413) and find out what items are prohibited from the country you will be visiting.

The US Customs Service publishes a series of free pamphlets with customs information. It includes *Know Before You Go,* a basic discussion of customs requirements pertaining to all travelers; *Buyer Beware, International Mail Imports; Travelers' Tips on Bringing Food, Plant, and Animal Products into the United States; Importing a Car; GSP and the Traveler; Pocket Hints; Currency Reporting; Pets, Wildlife, US Customs; Customs Hints for Visitors (Nonresidents);* and *Trademark Information for Travelers.* For the entire series or individual pamphlets, write to the US Customs Service (PO Box 7474, Washington, DC 20044) or contact any of the seven regional offices — in Boston, Chicago, Houston, Long Beach (California), Miami, New Orleans, and New York.

■ **Info Update:** The US Customs Service has a tape-recorded message whereby callers using touch-tone phones can get more information on various travel-related topics; the number is 202-566-8195. These pamphlets provide great briefing material, but if you still have questions when you're in South America contact the nearest US consulate or embassy in the particular country you're visiting.

# Sources and Resources

## South American Tourist Offices, Embassies, and Consulates in the US

South American government tourist offices, consulates, and embassies in the US generally are the best sources of information for their respective countries. As we went to press, however, the only South American governments that had tourist offices in the US were Argentina, Brazil, Ecuador, French Guiana, Peru, and Uruguay.

South American tourist information offices may provide free maps and some travel literature, although in general the selection of brochures is slim compared to that obtainable from airlines and travel agents. Although detailed information on facilities may be somewhat limited, for the best results, request information on specific areas, as well as publications relating to your particular areas of interest: accommodations, restaurants, special events, guided tours, and facilities for specific sports and other activities. There is no need to send a self-addressed, stamped envelope with your request, unless specified. Offices generally are open on weekdays, during normal business hours.

Where required, the embassies or consulates of each country also issue tourist cards and/or special visas for visiting the country and may provide other information useful for travelers. They also are empowered to sign official documents — such as commercial and residence visas — and to notarize copies or translations of American documents, which often is necessary for those papers to be considered legal abroad.

For a complete listing of the best places for tourist information in the US and South America, including South American consulates and embassies in the US, as well as US consulates and embassies in South America, see the individual country entries in FACTS IN BRIEF.

## Theater and Special Event Tickets

In more than one section of this book you will read about events that may spark your interest — everything from theater performances to sporting championships — along with telephone numbers and addresses to which to write for descriptive brochures, reservations, or tickets. The South American tourist offices also may be able to supply information on these and other special events, though they cannot in all cases provide the actual program or detailed information on ticket prices.

Since many of these occasions often are fully booked well in advance, you should think about having your reservation in hand before you go. In some cases, tickets may be reserved over the phone and charged to a credit card, or you can send an international money order or foreign draft. If you write, remember that any request from the

# Books, Newspapers, Magazines, and Newsletters

**BOOKS:** Throughout GETTING READY TO GO, numerous books and brochures have been recommended as good sources of further information on a variety of topics.

The following is a list of books recommended for travelers headed for South America. It includes reading intended to provide background information about South America's past, a foundation for understanding what is found in South American countries today, some ideas about what is happening around you that you may not personally witness, some solid fictional tales set in South America, and a few books that call your attention to things you might otherwise not notice — such as exotic flora, local birdlife, and good buys.

**General Travel** – The following general titles — fiction as well as nonfiction — will provide background and historical information and set the tone for your South American visit.

*Atlas of Ancient America,* by Michael D. Coe, Dean Snow, and Elizabeth Benson (Facts on File; $45).
*Brazilian Phrasebook,* by Mark Balla (Lonely Planet; $3.95).
*The Cloud Forest: A Chronicle of the South American Wilderness,* by Peter Matthiessen (Penguin; $8.95).
*Dusk on the Campo: A Journey in Patagonia,* by Sara Mansfield Taber (Henry Holt and Co.; $19.95).
*Eva Perón,* by Nicholas Fraser and Marysa Navarro (W. W. Norton; $9.95).
*Galápagos Islands: A Traveler's Preview,* by Kit and Art Lane (Pavillion Press; $5.95).
*The Hispanic Way,* by Judith Noble and Jaime Lacasa (National Textbook; $9.95).
*In Patagonia,* by Bruce Chatwin (Penguin; $8.95).
*The Incredible Incas & Their Timeless Land,* by Loren McIntyre (National Geographic Society; $8.95).
*Latin-American Spanish for Travelers,* with a 60-minute audiocassette also available (Berlitz; $15.95).
*Lost City of the Incas,* by Hiram Bingham (Greenwood Press; $59.50).
*Old Patagonia Express,* by Paul Theroux (Simon & Schuster; $6.95).
*The Origin,* (a biography of Charles Darwin) by Irving Stone (New American Library; $5.95).
*The Mythology of South America,* by John Bierhorst (Morrow; $9).
*Peregrenations of a Pariah,* by Flora Tristan (Beacon Press; $9.95).
*Portuguese for Travelers,* with a 90-minute audiocassette also available (Berlitz; $15.95).
*Royal Commentaries of the Incas and General History of Peru,* by Garcilaso de la Vega (University of Texas Press; $15.95).
*The Whispering Land,* by Gerald Durrell (Penguin; $4.95).

**The Outdoors** – These books are guides to outdoor South America. They generally can be found in the travel section in bookstores, or from the *South American Explorers Club* (126 Indian Creek Rd., Ithaca, NY 14850; phone: 800-274-0568 or 607-277-0488), and are useful to sojourners in the great outdoors.

*Adventure Travel in Latin America,* by Scott Graham (Wilderness Press; $12.95).
*Amazon Beaming,* by Petru Popescu (Viking; $25).
*Backpacking in Chile and Argentina,* by Hilary Bradt (Hunter; $17.95).
*Backpacking and Trekking in Peru & Bolivia,* by Hilary Bradt (Hunter; $17.95).
*Climbing & Hiking in Ecuador,* by Rob Rachowiecki (Hunter; $18.95).
*Fool's Guide to Climbing in Ecuador and Peru,* by Michael Kaerner (Michael Kaerner; $3).
*In Kayak Through Peru,* by CanoAndes, the famous Polish whitewater expedition team (Embajada del Viajero, Peru; $14).
*Passage Through El Dorado: Traveling the World's Last Great Wilderness,* by Jonathan Kandell (Avon Books; $9.95).
*Running the Amazon,* by Joe Kane (Vintage Departures; $9.95).
*South America River Trips: Part I,* by George Bradt; *Part II,* by Tanis and Martin Jordan (volume I covers Brazil, Chile, Colombia, and Ecuador; volume II covers Suriname, Venezuela, and Peru; Bradt Enterprises; $6.95 and $12.95, respectively).

**Fiction** – The following fiction titles will make good reading during your trip to and through South America:

*Adventures of a Photographer in La Plata,* by Adolfo Bioy Casares, translated by Suzanne Jill Levine (Penguin; $9.95).
*At Play in the Fields of the Lord,* by Peter Matthiessen (Random House; $10.95).
*Aunt Julia and the Scriptwriter,* by Mario Vargas Llosa (Avon; $9.95).
*Dona Flor and Her Two Husbands,* by Jorge Amado (Avon; $8.95).
*Ficciones,* by Jorge Luis Borges (Grove; $6.95).
*Gabriela, Clove & Cinnamon,* by Jorge Amado (Avon; $9.95).
*The General in His Labyrinth,* by Gabriel Garcia Márquez (Knopf; $19.95).
*Green Mansions,* by W. H. Hudson (Dover Publications; $6.95).
*The House of the Spirits,* by Isabel Allende (Bantam; $5.95).
*In Praise of the Stepmother,* by Mario Vargas Llosa (Farrar, Straus & Giroux; $18.95).
*Kiss of the Spider Woman,* by Manuel Puig (Random House; $10).
*Labyrinths: Selected Short Stories and Other Writings,* by Jorge Luis Borges (Random House; $11.95).
*Memory of Fire I (Genesis), II (Faces & Masks) and III (Century of the Wind),* trilogy by Eduardo Galeano (Pantheon Books; $14 each).
*One Hundred Years of Solitude,* by Gabriel García Márquez (Avon; $5.95).
*The Storyteller,* by Mario Vargas Llosa (Farrar, Straus & Giroux; $17.95).
*The Time of the Hero,* by Mario Vargas Llosa (Farrar, Straus & Giroux; $11.95)
*Tropical Night Falling,* by Manuel Puig, translated by Suzanne Jill Levine (Simon & Schuster; $18.50).

**Music, Art, Photography, and Food** – The following special-interest titles will make good reading in preparation for your trip through South America:

*Amazonia,* with photographs and text by Loren McIntyre (Sierra Club Books; $40).
*Art in Latin America,* by Dawn Ades (Yale University Press; $60).
*The Art of South American Cooking,* by Felipe Rojas-Lombardi (HarperCollins Publishers; $25).
*The Book of Latin American Cooking,* by Elisabeth Ortiz (Knopf; $16.95).
*The Brazilian Sound: Samba, Bossa Nova, and the Popular Music of Brazil,* by Chris McGowan and Ricardo Pessanha (Billboard Books; $18.95).
*Chile from Within,* by Chilean photographers; edited by Susan Meiselas with text by Marco de la Parra and Ariel Dorfman (W. W. Norton; $19.95).
*Cooking the South American Way,* by Helga Parnell (Lerner Publications; $10.95).

*Exploring South America,* with photographs and text by Loren McIntyre (Clarkson N. Potter; $40).
*The Music of Brazil,* by David Applby (University of Texas Press; $10.95).
*The Music of Latin America,* by Nicolas Slonimsky (Da Capo Press; $42.50).
*South American Cooking: Foods and Feasts from the New World,* by Barbara Karoff (Addison-Wesley; 12.95).

**Sources** – The books listed above may be ordered directly from the publishers or found in the travel section of any good general bookstore or sizable public library. If you still can't find something, the following stores and/or mail-order houses also specialize in travel literature. They offer books on South America along with guides to the rest of the world, and in some cases, even an old Baedeker or two.

*Book Passage* (51 Tamal Vista Blvd., Corte Madera, CA 94925; phone: 415-927-0960 in California; 800-321-9785 elsewhere in the US). Travel guides and maps to all areas of the world. A free catalogue is available.

*The Complete Traveller* (199 Madison Ave., New York, NY 10016; phone: 212-685-9007). Travel guides and maps. A catalogue is available for $2.

*Forsyth Travel Library* (PO Box 2975, Shawnee Mission, KS 66201-1375; phone: 800-367-7984 or 913-384-3440). Travel guides and maps, old and new, to all parts of the world, including South America. Ask for the "Worldwide Travel Books and Maps" catalogue.

*Phileas Fogg's Books and Maps* (87 Stanford Shopping Center, Palo Alto, CA 94304; phone: 800-533-FOGG or 415-327-1754). Travel guides, maps, and language aids.

*Powell's Travel Store* (Pioneer Courthouse Sq., 701 SW 6th Ave., Portland, OR 97204; 503-2281108). A panoply of travel-related books and materials (over 15,000 titles, as well as globes, maps, language aids, videos), supplies and accessories (luggage, travel irons, electrical converters, etc.), and service (there is even a travel agency on the premises) — essentially "one-stop shopping" for the traveler.

*The Reader's Catalog* (250 West 57th St., Suite 1330, New York, NY 10107; phone: 800-733-BOOK or 212-262-7198). This general mail-order bookstore will make recommendations on travel — and other — books, and ship them anywhere in the world.

*Tattered Cover* (2955 E. First Ave., Denver, CO 80206; phone: 800-833-9327 or 303-322-7727). The travel department alone of this enormous bookstore carries over 7,000 books, as well as maps and atlases. No catalogue is offered (the list is too extensive), but a newsletter, issued three times a year, is available on request.

*Thomas Brothers Maps & Travel Books* (603 W. Seventh St., Los Angeles, CA 90017; phone: 213-627-4018). Maps (including road atlases, street guides, and wall maps), guidebooks, and travel accessories.

*Traveller's Bookstore* (22 W. 52nd St., New York, NY 10019; phone: 212-664-0995). Travel guides, maps, literature, and accessories. A catalogue is available for $2.

There is at least one good bookstore in every major South American capital, and it is worthwhile to visit it in search of the occasional good locally published guide, which often will be carried in hotel shops as well. Imported books are very expensive, however, and guidebooks in particular will probably be out of date.

In addition, *Culturgrams* is a handy series of pamphlets that provides a good sampling of information on the people, cultures, sights, and bargains to be found in over 90 countries around the world. Each four-page, newsletter-size leaflet covers one country; destinations in South America include Argentina, Bolivia, Brazil, Chile, Ecuador, Panama, Paraguay, Peru, Uruguay, and Venezuela. The topics included range from customs and courtesies to lifestyles and demographics. These fact-filled pamphlets are published by the David M. Kennedy Center for International Studies at Brigham Young University; for an order form contact *Culturgrams,* c/o Publication Services (280 HRCB, Provo, UT 84602; phone: 801-378-6528). When ordering from 1 to 5 *Culturgrams,* the price is $1 each; 6 to 49 pamphlets cost 50¢ each; and for larger quantities, the price per copy goes down proportionately.

Another source of cultural information, is *Do's and Taboos Around the World,* compiled by the Parker Pen Company and edited by Roger E. Axtell. It focuses on protocol, customs, etiquette, hand gestures and body language, gift giving, the dangers of using US jargon, and so on, and can be fun to read even if you're not going anyplace. It's available for $10.95 in bookstores or through John Wiley & Sons (1 Wiley Dr., Somerset, NJ 08875; phone: 908-469-4400).

**NEWSPAPERS AND MAGAZINES:** Among the major US publications that can be bought in South America (generally a day or two after distribution in the US) in many of the larger cities and resort areas, at hotels, airports, and newsstands are the *Miami Herald, The New York Times, USA Today,* and the *Wall Street Journal.* As with other imports, expect these and other US publications to cost considerably more in South America than in the US.

A subscription to the *International Herald Tribune* is a good idea for dedicated travelers. This English-language newspaper is written and edited mostly in Paris, and is *the* newspaper read most regularly and avidly by Americans abroad to keep up with world news, US news, sports, the stock market (US and foreign), fluctuations in exchange rates, and an assortment of help-wanted ads, real estate listings, and personals, global in scope. Published 6 days a week (no Sunday paper), it is available at newsstands throughout the US and in cities worldwide, including major cities in South America. In South America, many large hotels have copies in the lobby for guests — if you don't see a copy, ask the hotel concierge if one is available. A 1-year subscription in the US costs $369 (believe it or not, it's $20 less in New York City: $349). To subscribe, write or call the Subscription Manager, *International Herald Tribune,* 850 Third Ave., 10th Floor, New York, NY 10022 (phone: 800-882-2884 or 212-752-3890).

Sampling the regional fare is likely to be one of the highlights of any visit. You will find reading about local edibles worthwhile before you go or after you return. *Gourmet,* a magazine specializing in food, frequently features mouth-watering articles on the foods of South America, although its scope is much broader. It is available at newsstands throughout the US for $2.50 an issue or for $18 a year from *Gourmet,* PO Box 53780, Boulder, CO 80322-2886 (phone: 800-365-2454).

**NEWSLETTERS:** Throughout GETTING READY TO GO we have mentioned specific newsletters which our readers may be interested in consulting for further information. One of the very best sources of detailed travel information is *Consumer Reports Travel Letter.* Published monthly by Consumers Union (PO Box 53629, Boulder, CO 80322-3629; phone: 800-999-7959), it offers comprehensive coverage of the travel scene on a wide variety of fronts. A year's subscription costs $37; 2 years, $57.

The following travel newsletters also provide useful up-to-date information on travel services and bargains, as well as what's happening and where to go in South America:

> *Center for Latin American and Caribbean Studies Newsletter* (Indiana University, 313 N. Jordan Ave., Bloomington, IN 47405; phone: 812-855-9097). This quarterly publication focuses on cultural, economic, and political issues in South American (and Caribbean) nations. As we went to press this newsletter was available at no cost, however, a subscription fee may be charged in the near future; contact the university for details.
> 
> *Hideaway Report* (Harper Associates, Subscription Office: PO Box 300, Whitefish, MO 59937; phone: 406-862-3480; Editorial Office: PO Box 50, Sun Valley, ID 83353; phone: 208-622-3193). This monthly source highlights retreats — in-

cluding South America island idylls — for sophisticated travelers. A year's subscription costs $90.

***Latin American Monitor*** (370 Old York Rd., London SW1 81SP, UK; phone: 44-81-870-9748). Useful for frequent (particularly business) travelers to South America, this detailed economic and political newsletter is available in three regional series. A year's subscription (10 issues) costs $170 for each series.

***The Latin Travel Review*** (PO Box 897, Coconut Grove, FL 33233; phone: 305-661-1639). Although primarily geared to the travel industry, this quarterly newsletter contains information useful to individual travelers to South America. A year's subscription costs $15.

***Romantic Hideaways*** (217 E. 86th St., Suite 258, New York, NY 10028; phone: 212-969-8682). This monthly newsletter leans toward those special places made for those traveling in twos. A year's subscription costs $65.

***Travel Smart*** (Communications House, 40 Beechdale Rd., Dobbs Ferry, NY 10522; phone: 914-693-8300 in New York State; 800-327-3633 elsewhere in the US). Published monthly, it covers a wide variety of trips and travel discounts. A year's subscription costs $44.

Newsletters focusing on South America are not commonly circulated in North America, however, a number of organizations that specialize in South American travel offer informative newsletters to members only. For instance, membership in the *South American Explorers Club* (126 Indian Creek Rd., Ithaca, NY 14850; phone: 800-274-0568 or 607-277-0488) includes the *South American Explorer* newsletter. The newsletter is issued four times a year; membership costs $25 for an individual or $35 per couple.

■**Computer Services:** Anyone who owns a personal computer and a modem can subscribe to a database service providing everything from airline schedules and fares to restaurant listings. Two such services of particular use to travelers are *CompuServe* (5000 Arlington Center Blvd., Columbus, OH 43220; phone: 800-848-8199 or 614-457-8600; $39.95 to join, plus usage fees of $6 to $12.50 per hour) and *Prodigy Services* (445 Hamilton Ave., White Plains, NY 10601; phone: 800-822-6922 or 914-993-8000; a subscription costs $12.95 a month, plus variable usage fees).

Before using any computer bulletin-board services, be sure to take precautions to prevent downloading of a computer "virus." First install one of the programs designed to screen out such nuisances.

# Weights and Measures

When traveling in South America, you'll find that just about every quantity, whether it is length, weight, or capacity, will be expressed in unfamiliar terms. In fact, this is true for travel almost everywhere in the world, since the US is one of the last countries to make its way to the metric system. Your trip to South America may serve to familiarize you with what one day may be the weights and measures at your grocery store.

There are some specific things to keep in mind during your trip. Fruits and vegetables at a market are recorded in kilos (kilograms), as is your luggage at the airport and your body weight. (This latter is particularly pleasing to people of significant size, who, instead of weighing 220 pounds, hit the scales at a mere 100 kilos.) A kilo equals 2.2 pounds and 1 pound is .45 kilo. Body temperature is measured in degrees centigrade, or Celsius, rather than the Fahrenheit scale, so that a normal body temperature reading is 37C, not 98.6F, and freezing is 0 degrees C rather than 32F.

## GETTING READY / Weights and Measures

Gasoline is sold by the liter (approximately 3.8 liters to 1 US gallon). Tire pressure gauges and other equipment measure in kilograms per square centimeter rather than pounds per square inch. Highway signs are written in kilometers rather than miles (1 mile equals 1.6 km; 1 km equals .62 miles). And speed limits are in kilometers per hour, so think twice before hitting the gas when you see a speed limit of 100. That means 62 miles per hour.

The tables and conversion factors listed below should give you all the information you will need to understand any transaction, road sign, or map you encounter during your travels.

### CONVERSION TABLES: METRIC TO US MEASUREMENTS

| Multiply | by | to convert to |
|---|---|---|
| **LENGTH** | | |
| millimeters | .04 | inches |
| meters | 3.3 | feet |
| meters | 1.1 | yards |
| kilometers | .6 | miles |
| **CAPACITY** | | |
| liters | 2.11 | pints (liquid) |
| liters | 1.06 | quarts (liquid) |
| liters | .26 | gallons (liquid) |
| **WEIGHT** | | |
| grams | .04 | ounces (avoir) |
| kilograms | 2.2 | pounds (avoir) |

### US TO METRIC MEASUREMENTS

| Multiply | by | to convert to |
|---|---|---|
| **LENGTH** | | |
| inches | 25. | millimeters |
| feet | .3 | meters |
| yards | .9 | meters |
| miles | 1.6 | kilometers |
| **CAPACITY** | | |
| pints | .47 | liters |
| quarts | .95 | liters |
| gallons | 3.8 | liters |
| **WEIGHT** | | |
| ounces | 28. | grams |
| pounds | .45 | kilograms |

**TEMPERATURE**

$$°F = (°C \times 9/5) + 32 \qquad °C = (°F - 32) \times 5/9$$

## APPROXIMATE EQUIVALENTS

| Metric Unit | Abbreviation | US Equivalent |
|---|---|---|
| **LENGTH** | | |
| millimeter | mm | .04 inch |
| meter | m | 39.37 inches |
| kilometer | km | .62 mile |
| **AREA** | | |
| square centimeter | sq cm | .155 square inch |
| square meter | sq m | 10.7 square feet |
| hectare | ha | 2.47 acres |
| square kilometer | sq km | .3861 square mile |
| **CAPACITY** | | |
| liter | l | 1.057 quarts |
| **WEIGHT** | | |
| gram | g | .035 ounce |
| kilogram | kg | 2.2 pounds |
| metric ton | MT | 1.1 tons |
| **ENERGY** | | |
| kilowatt | kw | 1.34 horsepower |

# Cameras and Equipment

Vacations are everybody's favorite time for taking pictures and home movies. After all, most of us want to remember the places we visit — and show them off to others. Here are a few suggestions to help you get the best results from your travel photography or videography.

### BEFORE THE TRIP

If you're taking your camera or camcorder out after a long period in mothballs, or have just bought a new one, check it thoroughly before you leave to prevent unexpected breakdowns or disappointing pictures.

1. Still cameras should be cleaned carefully and thoroughly, inside and out. If using a camcorder, run a head cleaner through it. You also may want to have your camcorder professionally serviced (opening the casing yourself will violate the manufacturer's warranty). Always use filters to protect your lens while traveling.
2. Check the batteries for your camera's light meter and flash, and take along extras just in case yours wear out during the trip. For camcorders, bring along extra Nickel-Cadmium (Ni-Cad) batteries; if you use rechargeable batteries, a recharger will cut down on the extras.
3. Using all the settings and features, shoot at least one test roll of film or one videocassette, using the type you plan to take along with you.

## EQUIPMENT TO TAKE ALONG

Keep your gear light and compact. Items that are too heavy or bulky to be carried comfortably on a full-day excursion will likely remain in your hotel room.

1. Invest in a broad camera or camcorder strap if you now have a thin one. It will make carrying the camera much more comfortable.
2. A sturdy canvas, vinyl, or leather camera or camcorder bag, preferably with padded pockets (not an airline bag), will keep your equipment organized and easy to find. If you will be doing much shooting around the water, a waterproof case is best.
3. For cleaning, bring along a camel's hair brush that retracts into a rubber squeeze bulb. Also take plenty of lens tissue, soft cloths, and plastic bags to protect equipment from dust and moisture.

■**Note:** If you will be using your camcorder in South America, note that some countries use electrical currents that differ from the one used in the US, and the battery charger that comes with your camcorder may not be compatible. To ensure that you can plug in anywhere, bring along an electrical converter, as well as a plug adaptor kit. (For further information, see *Mail, Telephone, and Electricity*, in this section.) And if your camcorder system requires a TV set or VCR for playback (most do), you may not be able review your tapes in South America, as some of the countries use a television standard different from that in the US and Canada.

**FILM AND TAPES:** For those travelers concerned about airport security X-rays damaging undeveloped film (X-rays do not affect processed film) or tapes, store them in one of the lead-lined bags sold in camera shops. In the US, and Canada, incidents of X-ray damage to unprocessed film (exposed or unexposed) are few because low-dosage X-ray equipment is used virtually everywhere. While the international trend also is toward equipment that delivers less and less radiation, equipment in South America tends to be less up-to-date than in some other foreign countries, and is, therefore, less predictable.

If you're traveling without a protective bag, you may want to ask to have your photo equipment inspected by hand. One type of film that should never be subjected to X-rays is the very high speed ASA 1000; there are lead-lined bags made especially for it — and, in the event that you are refused a hand inspection, this is the only way to save your film. The walk-through metal detector devices at airports do not affect film, though the film cartridges may set them off.

You should have no problem finding film or tapes throughout South America, particularly in metropolitan and major resort areas. When buying film, tapes, or photo accessories the best rule of thumb is to stick to name brands with which you are familiar. Different countries have their own ways of labeling camcorder tapes, and although variations in recording and playback standards won't affect your ability to use the tape, they will affect how quickly you record and how much time you actually have to record on the tape. The availability of film processing labs and equipment repair shops will vary from country to country.

■**A note about courtesy and caution:** When photographing individuals in South America (and anywhere else in the world), ask first. It's common courtesy. In many of the smaller towns, and even some of the cities, the Indians have superstitions or religious beliefs that photographing them is an insult at best and, at worst, a violation. Furthermore, some governments have security regulations regarding the use of cameras and will not permit the photographing of certain subjects, such as particular government and military installations. For example, in Peru you will not be allowed to photograph airports, railroad stations, military barracks and bases, public water and energy plants, police stations, oil wells, petroleum refineries, or mines. When in doubt, ask.

# Useful Words and Phrases

Unlike the French, who tend to be a bit brusque if you don't speak their language perfectly, South Americans do not expect you to speak Spanish or Portuguese — but are very flattered when you try. In many circumstances, you won't have to, because the staffs of most tourist attractions, museums, and major hotels, as well as a fair number of restaurants, speak serviceable English, which they are usually eager to try — and that means practicing with you. In countries with old ties to England, such as Argentina and Chile, educated people in general know some English. When you get off the beaten path, however, you will find at least a rudimentary knowledge of the local language very helpful. Don't be afraid of misplaced accents or misconjugated verbs. People in all the Latin American countries will appreciate your efforts to speak their language and will do their best to understand you. They will also make an effort to be understood.

As might be expected in such a large area, the languages of South America are not uniform. Although Portuguese is understood almost everywhere in Brazil, as is Spanish in the rest of South America, Quechua, the language of the Inca, is still spoken in Ecuador, Peru, Colombia, Bolivia, and Chile, and other indigenous languages also are widely spoken. There are a number of regional dialects, and it is not uncommon for the same word to have different meanings in different countries. However, a generally accepted educated standard is used in print and on the various national television and radio broadcasts. The list below reflects that standard.

**Spanish** – The spelling of the standard South American Spanish is a very reliable guide to the pronunciation. These rules may be helpful:

The vowel before the last consonant in a word (except *n* or *s*) is accented unless there is an accent mark on another vowel. When the last consonant is *n* or *s,* the vowel before the preceding consonant usually is accented.

* *a* is pronounced as in *father*
* *e* is pronounced as in *red*
* *i* is pronounced as in *machine*
* *o* is pronounced as in *note*
* *u* is pronounced as in *rude*
* *ei/ey* are pronounced as in *vein*
* *oi/oy* are pronounced as in *joy*
* *ai/ay* are pronounced like *y* in *by*
* *au* is pronounced like *ou* in *house*

In general, in other vowel letter sequences (*ae, ie, ue, ia,* etc.) each letter is pronounced.

Spanish consonants are pronounced as in English with these exceptions:

The consonants *b, d,* and *g* are pronounced with the air passage slightly open, producing a softer sound. The consonants *p, t,* and *c/k* are pronounced without the aspiration (the strong puff of breath) which characterizes them in English.

* *b* within words is pronounced like an English *v*
* *d* within words is pronounced like *th* in *other*
* *g* before *e* or *i* is pronounced like a strongly aspirated English *h* or German *ch;* otherwise, as above

*c* is pronounced as in *cell* before *e* or *i;* otherwise it is pronounced like *k*
*h* is silent
*j* is pronounced like a strongly aspirated *h*
*ll* is pronounced like *y* in *youth*
*ñ* is pronounced like *ny* in *canyon*
*qu* is pronounced like *k* before *e* or *i: quilo* — English *kilo*
*r* is pronounced like the casual English *d* in pedal
*rr* is trilled, as in Scottish *farm*
*s* and *z* are pronounced like *z* within words when preceding *b, d, g, m, n, r, l;* otherwise, they are pronounced like *s*

**Portuguese** – The pronunciation of Portuguese does not follow the spelling quite so closely. As in Spanish, the accent (i.e., stress) falls on the vowel preceding the last consonant in the word unless otherwise marked. The vowel letters are pronounced as follows:

*a* is pronounced as in *father*
stressed *e* is pronounced as in *era;* unstressed *e* is pronounced like the *i* in *pin*
stressed *i* is pronounced as in *pique;* an *i* at the beginning of a word is pronounced like *y* in *yet*
stressed *o* is pronounced as in *orb;* unstressed final *o* is pronounced like *u* in *put*
*u* is pronounced as in *boot*
*ei* is pronounced as in *vein*
*ai* is pronounced like *i* in *life*
*oo* is pronounced like the *o* in note
*ou* is pronounced as in *though*
*au* is pronounced like *ow* in *how*

Portuguese vowels are nasalized when marked with a tilde ( ˜ ) or preceding *m, n,* or *nh.* (That is, some air is emitted through the nose while the vowel is pronounced.) Nasalized vowels preceding final vowels are stressed.

Portuguese consonants are pronounced much as in English with these exceptions:

*c* is hard before *a, o, u,* or a consonant, as in *car, core,* and *climb;* it is pronounced *s* before *i* or *e,* or when marked with a cedilla ( ¸ )
*ch* is pronounced like *sh* in *show*
*s* following a stressed vowel is pronounced *z,* as in *rose*
*t* before a final unstressed e is pronounced like English *ch; d* in the same position is pronounced like English *j*
*g* before *e* or *i* is pronounced like *si* in *vision;* otherwise it is hard, as in *go*
*j* is pronounced like *si* in *vision*
*h* is silent
*lh* is pronounced like *lli* in *billiards*
*nh* and *ñ* are pronounced like *ny* in *canyon*
*x* is pronounced like *sh* in *mushy*
*r* is pronounced like the *d* in casual English *pedal*

These are very basic rules, and even though they may seem daunting at first, they shouldn't remain so for long. Nevertheless, if you can't get your mouth to speak Spanish or Portuguese, try your hands at it: With a little observation, you'll pick it up quickly and be surprised at how often your message will get across.

Here are some commonly used words and phrases to speed you on your way. Note that in Spanish and Portuguese all nouns are either masculine or feminine as well as singular and plural, and that the adjectives that modify them must agree in both gender and number. Most nouns ending in *o* are masculine; most nouns ending in *a* are feminine. The articles also show gender. Notice how they are used in the word list below. Plurals are formed by adding *s*. Adjectives almost always follow nouns in Spanish and Portuguese.

## Greetings and Everyday Expressions

|  | *Spanish* | *Portuguese* |
|---|---|---|
| Good morning | *Buenos días* | *Bom dia* |
| Good afternoon, good evening | *Buenas tardes* | *Boa tarde* |
| Good night | *Buenas noches* | *Boa noite* |
| Hello | *Hola!* | *Ola!* |
| How are you? | *Cómo está usted?* | *Como vai?* |
| Pleased to meet you | *Mucho gusto en conocerle.* | *Muito prazer em conhecê-lo (-la).* |
| Good-bye! (formal) | *Adiós!* | *Adeus!* |
| So long! | *Hasta luego!* | *Até logo! Chao!* |
| Yes | *Sí* | *Sim* |
| No | *No* | *Não* |
| Please | *Por favor* | *Por favor* |
| Thank you | *Gracias* | *Obrigado* |
| You're welcome | *De nada* | *De nada* |
| I beg your pardon (Excuse me) | *Perdón* | *Perdão* |
| It doesn't matter | *No importa* | *Não importante* |
| I don't speak Spanish. | *No hablo español.* |  |
| I don't speak Portuguese. |  | *Não falo português.* |
| Do you speak English? | *Habla usted inglés?* | *Fala inglês?* |
| I don't understand. | *No comprendo.* | *Não compreêndo* |
| Do you understand? | *Comprende?/Entiende?* | *Compreênde?* |
| My name is . . . | *Me llamo . . .* | *Me chamo . . .* |
| What is your name? | *Cómo se llama usted?* | *Como se chama?* |
| miss (for an unmarried or young woman) | *señorita* | *menina* |
| madame (for a married or an older woman) | *señora, doña* | *senhora, doña* |
| mister | *señor* | *senhor* |
| open | *abierto/a* | *aberto/a* |
| closed | *cerrado/a* | *fechado/a* |
| entrance | *entrada* | *entrada* |
| exit | *salida* | *saida* |
| push | *empujar* | *empurrar* |
| pull | *tirar* | *puxar* |
| today | *hoy* | *hoje* |
| tomorrow | *mañana* | *amanhã* |
| yesterday | *ayer* | *ontem* – |

## Checking In

| I have a reservation. | *He hecho una reservación.* | *Mandei reservar.* |
|---|---|---|
| I would like . . . | *Quisiera . . .* | *Queria . . .* |
| a single room | *una habitacion sencilla* | *um quarto individual* |

|  | *Spanish* | *Portuguese* |
|---|---|---|
| a double room | una habitación doble | um quarto duplo |
| a quiet room | una habitación tranquila | um quarto tranquilo |
| with bath | con baño | com banho |
| with shower | con ducha | com chuveiro |
| with a sea view | con vista asi el mar | com vista para o mar |
| with air conditioning | con aire acondicionado | com ar condicionado |
| with balcony | con balcón | com varanda |
| overnight only | sólo una noche | só uma noite |
| a few days | unos cuantos días | alguns dias |
| a week (at least) | una semana (por lo menos) | uma semana (pelo menos) |
| with full board | con pensión completa | com pensão completa |
| with half board | con media pensión | com meia-pensão |
| Does that price include | Esta incluído en el precio... | O precio está incluido |
| breakfast? | el desayuno? | café da manhã? |
| taxes? | los impuestos? | as taxas? |
| It doesn't work. | No funciona. | Nõ funciona. |
| Do you accept traveler's checks | Acepta usted cheques de viajero? | Aceita cheques de viagem? |
| Do you accept credit cards? | Acepta tarjetas de credito? | Aceita cartão de crédito? |

## Eating out

|  |  |  |
|---|---|---|
| ashtray | un cenicero | um cinzeiro |
| bottle | una botella | uma garrafa |
| (extra) chair | una silla (adicional) | (mais) uma cadeira |
| cup | una taza | uma xícara |
| fork | un tenedor | um garfo |
| knife | un cuchillo | uma faca |
| napkin | una servilleta | um guardanapo |
| plate | un plato | um prato |
| spoon | una cuchara | uma culher |
| table | una mesa | uma mesa |
| beer | una cerveza | uma cerveja |
| hot cocoa | un chocolate caliente | um chocolate quente |
| black coffee | un café negro | um café |
| coffee with milk | café con leche | café com leite |
| cream | crema | creme |
| milk | leche | leite |
| tea | un té | um chá |
| fruit juice | un jugo de fruta | um suco de fruta |
| lemonade | una limonada | um gaseosa |
| water | agua | água |
| mineral water | agua mineral | água mineral |
| carbonated | con gas | com gás |
| noncarbonated | sin gas | sem gás |
| orangeade | una naranjada | um laranjada |

|  | *Spanish* | *Portuguese* |
|---|---|---|
| soda | *sosa* | *soda* |
| port | *oporto* | *vinho do Porto* |
| sherry | *jerez* | *vinho de Xerez* |
| red wine | *vino tinto* | *vinho tinto* |
| white wine | *vino blanco* | *vinho branco* |
| cold | *frío/a* | *frio/a* |
| hot | *caliente* | *quente* |
| sweet | *dulce* | *doce* |
| (very) dry | *(muy) seco/a* | *(extra) seco/a* |
| bacon | *tocino* | *toicinho* |
| bread | *pan* | *pão* |
| butter | *mantequilla* | *manteiga* |
| eggs | *huevos* | *ovos* |
|   hard-boiled | *un huevo cocido* | *ovos cozidos* |
|   fried | *huevos fritos* | *ovos fritos* |
|   scrambled | *huevos revueltos* | *ovos mexidos* |
|   soft-boiled | *un huevo cocido pasado por agua* | *ovos quentes* |
|   omelette | *torta de huevos* | *omelete* |
| honey | *miel* | *mel* |
| jam, marmalade | *mermelada* | *mermelada* |
| orange juice | *jugo de naranja* | *suco de laranja* |
| pepper | *pimienta* | *pimenta* |
| salt | *sal* | *sal* |
| sugar | *azúcar* | *açúcar* |
| Waiter! | *¡Camarero!/¡Mesero!* | *Criado!* |
| I would like | *Quisiera* | *Queria* |
|   a glass of | *un vaso de* | *um copo de* |
|   a bottle of | *una botella de* | *uma garrafa de* |
|   a half bottle of | *una media botella de* | *uma meia-garrafa de* |
|   a carafe of | *una garrafa de/ una jarra de* | *uma jarra de* |
|   a liter of | *un litro de* | *um litro de* |
| The check, please. | *La cuenta, por favor.* | *A conta, por favor.* |
| Is a service charge included? | *¿Está el servicio incluido?* | *O serviço está incluído?* |
| I think there is a mistake in the bill. | *Creo que hay un error en la cuenta.* | *Acredito que se enganou na conta.* |

## Shopping

|  |  |  |
|---|---|---|
| bakery | *la panadería* | *a padaria* |
| bookstore | *la librería* | *a livraria* |
| butcher shop | *la carnicería* | *o açougue* |
| camera shop | *la tienda de fotografía* | *a loja de artigos fotográficos* |
| delicatessen | *la tienda de comestibles preparados* | *a loja de frios* |
| department store | *el almacén grande* | *as grandes lojas* |
| grocery | *la tienda de comestibles* | *o supermercado* |

|  | *Spanish* | *Portuguese* |
|---|---|---|
| jewelry store | *la joyería* | *a joialharia* |
| newsstand | *el puesto de periódicos* | *a banca de jornal* |
| pastry shop | *la pastelería* | *a pastelaria* |
| perfume (and cosmetics) store | *perfumaría* | *a perfumaria* |
| pharmacy/ drugstore | *la farmacia* | *a farmácia* |
| shoestore | *la zapatería* | *a sapataria* |
| supermarket | *el supermercado* | *o supermercado* |
| tobacconist | *el estanquero* | *a tabacaria* |
| | | |
| inexpensive | *barato/a* | *barato/a* |
| expensive | *caro/a* | *caro/a* |
| large | *grande* | *grande* |
| larger | *más grande* | *maior* |
| too large | *demasiado grande* | *muito grande* |
| small | *pequeño/a* | *pequeno/a* |
| smaller | *más pequeño/a* | *menor* |
| too small | *demasiado pequeño/a* | *muito pequeno/a* |
| long | *largo/a* | *comprido/a* |
| short | *corto/a* | *curto/a* |
| old | *viejo/a* | *velho/a* |
| new | *nuevo/a* | *novo/a* |
| used | *usado/a* | *usado/a* |
| handmade | *hecho/a a mano* | *feito/a á mão* |
| antique | *antiguo* | *antigo* |
| Is it machine washable? | *Es lavable a máquina?* | *Pode se lavar á máquina?* |
| How much does it cost? | *Cuánto cuesta esto?* | *Quanto custa isto?* |
| What is it made of? | *De qué está hecho?* | *Do que qué feito?* |
|   alpaca | *alpaca* | *alpaca* |
|   cotton | *algodón* | *algodão* |
|   corduroy | *pana* | *cotelão* |
|   filigree | *filigrana* | *filigrana* |
|   lace | *encaje* | *renda* |
|   leather | *cuero* | *couro* |
|   linen | *lino* | *linho* |
|   suede | *ante* | *camurça* |
|   silk | *seda* | *seda* |
|   synthetic | *sintético/a* | *sintético/a* |
|   tile | *baldosa* | *telha* |
|   wool | *lana* | *lã* |
|   brass | *latón* | *bronze* |
|   copper | *cobre* | *cobre* |
|   gold | *oro* | *ouro* |
|   gold plated | *dorado* | *com banho de ouro* |
|   silver | *plata* | *prata* |
|   silver plated | *plateado* | *banhado a prata* |
|   stainless steel | *acero inoxidable* | *aço inoxidável* |
|   wood | *madera* | *madeira –* |

## Colors

| | | |
|---|---|---|
| beige | *beige* | *beige* |
| black | *negro/a* | *prêto/a* |
| blue | *azul* | *azul* |

|  | *Spanish* | *Portuguese* |
|---|---|---|
| brown | *moreno/a* | *castanho* |
| green | *verde* | *verde* |
| gray | *gris* | *cinzento/a* |
| orange | *anaranjado/a* | *alaranjado/a* |
| pink | *rosa* | *cor-de-roso* |
| purple | *morado/a* | *roxo/a* |
| red | *rojo/a* | *vermelho/a* |
| white | *blanco/a* | *branco/a* |
| yellow | *amarillo/a* | *amarelo/a* |
| dark | *obscuro/a* | *escuro/a* |
| light | *claro/a* | *claro/a* |

## Getting Around

|  |  |  |
|---|---|---|
| north | *norte* | *norte* |
| south | *sur* | *sul* |
| east | *este* | *este* |
| west | *oeste* | *oeste* |
| right | *derecho/a* | *direita* |
| left | *izquierdo/a* | *esquerda* |
| Go straight ahead | *Siga todo derecho* | *Vá sempre em frente* |
| far | *lejos* | *longe* |
| near | *cerca* | *perto* |
| gas station | *la gasolinería* | *a estação de serviço* |
| train station | *la estación de ferrocarril* | *a estação de trem* |
| bus stop | *la parada de autobuses* | *o ponto de onibus* |
| subway station | *la estación de metro* | *a estação de metró* |
| airport | *el aeropuerto* | *o aeroporto* |
| tourist information | *la información turística* | *informações de turismo* |
| map | *el mapa* | *mapa* |
| one-way ticket | *un billete de ida* | *uma passagem de ida* |
| round-trip ticket | *un billete de ida y vuelta* | *uma passagem de ida e volta* |
| track | *el andén* | *a plataforma* |
| first class | *primera clase* | *primeira classe* |
| second class | *segunda clase* | *segunda classe* |
| no smoking | *no fumar* | *não fumadores* |
| gasoline |  |  |
| regular (leaded) | *gasolina* | *gasolina* |
| unleaded* | *sin plomo* |  |
| diesel | *diesel* | *diesel* |
| tires | *las llantas* | *pneus* |
| oil | *el aceite* | *o óleo* |
| Fill it up, please. | *Llénelo, por favor.* | *Enche o tanque, por favor.* |
| Where is . . . ? | *Dónde está . . . ?* | *Onde éstão . . . ?* |
| Where are . . . ? | *Dónde están . . . ?* | *Onde são . . . ?* |
| How far is it from here to . . . ? | *Qué distancia hay desde aquí hasta . . . ?* | *A que distância estamos de . . . ?* |

*Note that unleaded gasoline is unavailable in Brazil and frequently unavailable in much of the rest of South America. See *Traveling by Car* for more information.

|  | *Spanish* | *Portuguese* |
|---|---|---|
| Does this bus go to . . . ? | *Va este autobús a . . . ?* | *Este onibus pára em . . . ?* |
| What time does it leave? | *A qué hora sale?* | *A que horas sai?* |
| Caution | *Precaución* | *Cuidado* |
| Danger | *Peligro* | *Perigo* |
| Dead End | *Calle Sin Salida* | *Fem Saíoa* |
| Detour | *Desvío* | *Desvío* |
| Do Not Enter | *Paso Prohibido* | *Entrada Proibida* |
| No parking | *Estacionaménto Prohibido* | *Estacionamento Proibido* |
| No Passing | *Prohibido Pasar* | *Proibido Ultrapassar* |
| One Way | *Dirección Unica* | *Sentido Unico* |
| Pay Toll | *Peaje* | *Pedagio* |
| Pedestrian Zone | *Zona Peatonal* | *Pedestres* |
| Reduce Speed | *Despacio* | *Devagar* |
| Steep Incline | *Fuerte Declive* | *Descida Perigosa* |
| Stop | *Alto* | *Alto* |
| Use Headlights | *Encender los faros* | *Acender as Luzes* |
| Yield | *Ceda el Paso* | *Dê Passagem* |

## Personal Items and Services

|  |  |  |
|---|---|---|
| aspirin | *aspirinas* | *aspirinas* |
| Band-Aids | *vendajes* | *Bandaids* |
| barbershop | *la barbería* | *o cabeleireiro* |
| beauty shop | *el salón de belleza* | *o instituto de beleza* |
| condom | *condón* | *a camisinha de Venus* |
| dry cleaner | *la tintorería* | *a tinturaria* |
| hairdresser | *la peluquería* | *o cabeleireiro* |
| laundromat | *establecimiento público de lavadoras automaticas* | *a lavandaria publica automática* |
| laundry | *la lavandería* | *a lavandaria* |
| post office | *el correo* | *o correio* |
| postage stamps | *estampillas* | *selos* |
| sanitary napkins | *unos paños higiénicos* | *Modess* |
| shampoo | *un champú* | *um shampoo* |
| shaving cream | *espuma de afeitar* | *um creme de barba* |
| soap | *el jabón* | *um sabonete* |
| tampons | *unos tampones higiénicos* | *tampōoes higiénicos* |
| tissues | *pañuelo de papel* | *lenços de papel* |
| toilet paper | *papel higiénico* | *papel higiénico* |
| toothpaste | *pasta de dientes* | *pasta de dentes* |
| Where is the bathroom? toilet? | *Dónde está el baño? excusado?* | *Onde está o banheiro?* |
| MEN | *Caballeros* | *Cavalheiros* |
| WOMEN | *Señoras* | *Senhoras* |

## Days of the Week

|  |  |  |
|---|---|---|
| Monday | *Lunes* | *Segunda-feira* |
| Tuesday | *Martes* | *Terça-feira* |

|  | *Spanish* | *Portuguese* |
|---|---|---|
| Wednesday | *Miércoles* | *Quarta-feira* |
| Thursday | *Jueves* | *Quinta-feira* |
| Friday | *Viernes* | *Sexta-feira* |
| Saturday | *Sábado* | *Sábado* |
| Sunday | *Domingo* | *Domingo* – |

## Months

| January | *Enero* | *Janeiro* |
|---|---|---|
| February | *Febrero* | *Fevereiro* |
| March | *Marzo* | *Março* |
| April | *Abril* | *Abril* |
| May | *Mayo* | *Maio* |
| June | *Junio* | *Junho* |
| July | *Julio* | *Julho* |
| August | *Agosto* | *Agosto* |
| September | *Septiembre* | *Setembro* |
| October | *Octubre* | *Outubro* |
| November | *Noviembre* | *Novembro* |
| December | *Diciembre* | *Dezembro* – |

## Numbers

| zero | *cero* | *zero* |
|---|---|---|
| one | *uno* | *um/uma* |
| two | *dos* | *dois/duas* |
| three | *tres* | *três* |
| four | *cuatro* | *quatro* |
| five | *cinco* | *cinco* |
| six | *seis* | *seis* |
| seven | *siete* | *sete* |
| eight | *ocho* | *oito* |
| nine | *nueve* | *nove* |
| ten | *diez* | *dez* |
| eleven | *once* | *onze* |
| twelve | *doce* | *doze* |
| thirteen | *trece* | *treze* |
| fourteen | *catorce* | *catorze* |
| fifteen | *quince* | *quinze* |
| sixteen | *dieciséis* | *dezesseis* |
| seventeen | *diecisiete* | *dezessete* |
| eighteen | *dieciocho* | *dezoito* |
| nineteen | *diecinueve* | *dezenove* |
| twenty | *veinte* | *vinte* |
| thirty | *treinta* | *trinta* |
| forty | *cuarenta* | *quarenta* |
| fifty | *cincuenta* | *cinquênta* |
| sixty | *sesenta* | *sessenta* |
| seventy | *setenta* | *setenta* |
| eighty | *ochenta* | *oitenta* |
| ninety | *noventa* | *noventa* |
| one hundred | *cien* | *cem* |
| one thousand | *mil* | *mil* |

# FACTS IN BRIEF

# Argentina

**TOURIST INFORMATION:** *Argentina National Tourist Offices:* 2655 Le Jeune Rd., Penthouse Suite F, Coral Gables, FL 33134 (phone: 305-442-1366 or 305-442-7029); 12 W. 56th St., New York, NY 10019 (phone: 212-603-0400). *Argentine Embassy:* 1600 New Hampshire Ave. NW, Washington, DC 20009 (phone: 202-939-6400). *Argentine Consulates:* 3550 Wilshire Blvd., Suite 1450, Los Angeles, CA 90010 (phone: 213-739-9977); 12 W. 56th St., New York, NY 10019 (phone: 212-603-0400).

*US Embassy and Consulate in Argentina:* 4300 Av. Columbia, Capital Federal, Buenos Aires 1425 (phone: 1-774-7611).

**ENTRY REQUIREMENTS AND CUSTOMS:** US citizens are required to have a valid passport for visits of up to 90 days. Visits may be extended once you are in Argentina. Travelers may bring in 400 cigarettes, 50 cigars, and 2 liters of alcohol.

**TELEPHONE:** The country code for Argentina is 54.

**GETTING THERE/GETTING AROUND:** The main entrance point is Buenos Aires. The airlines providing direct or nonstop flights from the US to Argentina include *Aerolíneas Argentinas, American, LanChile,* and *United. AeroPerú, Avianca, Ecuatoriana, LAB, LADECO, LAP, Varig,* and *Viasa* offer connecting flights. The domestic airline is *Aerolíneas Argentinas,* which provides the fastest, most efficient way of covering vast distances. Another domestic airline is *Austral;* flights aboard this carrier can be booked when you purchase a ticket for an international flight aboard *Aerolíneas Argentinas.* Argentina has excellent roads linking different sections of the country, as well as Paraguay and Brazil. Buses, which offer comfortable, cross-country service, are a better form of public transportation than trains. Car rentals here, as in most other Latin American countries, are available in major cities for driving where you want within Argentina, but not across borders. Be forewarned that city traffic can be challenging, if not impossible, even for the intrepid.

**CLIMATE:** Dry, temperate climate prevails throughout most of the country. The area around Iguassu Falls has year-round tropical temperatures. The Andes, Patagonia, and Tierra del Fuego are considerably cooler. Seasons are reversed; the Northern Hemisphere's winter (December–March) is Argentina's summer. Buenos Aires temperatures are in the 80s F in summer but drop into the 40s F in winter (June–August), with occasional snow.

**LANGUAGE:** Spanish.

**ELECTRICITY:** 220 volts.

**MONEY:** In January 1992, the peso replaced the austral as the country's unit of currency. Its value is linked to the US dollar — 1 peso equals $1 US. Theoretically this has done away with a need for the black market or free market rates that existed in the past. In practice, this may not always be the case.

**CALCULATING COSTS:** In recent years the inflation rate in Argentina has been one of the world's highest. In Buenos Aires, hotel prices range from $75 up to $250 (double occupancy) in the expensive category; $50–$75, moderate; under $50, inexpensive. Outside the capital, rates average $70–$100, expensive; $45–$70, moderate; under $45, inexpensive. Note: In the Lake District, prices can soar during peak ski season (July–August), often doubling summer rates. Restaurants in Buenos Aires reflect its cosmopolitan taste: Dinner for two costs $80 and more in the very expensive bracket; $60–$80, expensive; $40–$60, moderate; under $30, inexpensive (not including beverages or tips). Other cities and towns are more moderately priced.

**TIPPING:** Tip 10% in restaurants. Cab drivers expect a small tip; porters get the equivalent of 50¢ per piece of luggage, but never less than $1. Washroom attendants should be tipped about 50¢.

**BANKING/BUSINESS HOURS:** Banks are open weekdays from 9 or 10 AM to 3 PM. These hours vary, however, depending on the city and the season. Business hours are 8 or 9 AM to 5 or 6 PM, Mondays through Fridays.

**HOLIDAYS:** *New Year's Day* (January 1), *Holy Thursday* (April 8), *Good Friday* (April 9), *Easter Sunday* (April 11), *Labor Day* (May 1), *Revolution Day* (May 25), *Malvinas Day* (June 10), *National Flag Day* (June 20), *Independence Day* (July 9), *Anniversary of General San Martín's Death* (August 17), *Discovery of America* (October 12), *Immaculate Conception* (December 8), *Christmas* (December 25).

**SPORTS:** Popular participant sports include windsurfing, swimming, tennis, fishing, skiing, horseback riding, and hunting; spectators enjoy soccer, polo, horse racing, auto racing, and *pato,* a gaucho ball game played on horseback.

**SHOPPING:** Leather, suede, well-designed woolen clothes, some furs, and local wine are the best buys.

**AIRPORT DEPARTURE TAX:** Domestic: $3; international: $18.

# Bolivia

**TOURIST INFORMATION:** *Bolivian Embassy:* 3014 Massachusetts Ave. NW, Washington, DC 20008 (phone: 202-483-4410). *Bolivian Consulate:* 211 E. 43rd St., Suite 801, New York, NY 10017 (phone: 212-687-0530).

*US Embassy in Bolivia:* 290 Calle Colón at the corner of Mercado, La Paz (phone: 2-350251). *US Consulate in Bolivia:* Ed Tobia, Calle Potosi, La Paz (phone: 2-320494).

**ENTRY REQUIREMENTS AND CUSTOMS:** US citizens are required to have a valid US passport for visits of up to 30 days. Visits may be extended once you are in Bolivia. Business travelers must obtain a visa (issued in 24 hours) and pay a $50 fee. Diplomats, officials, students, and missionaries are issued a visa at no charge, upon written request to the consulate. Travelers may bring in 1 carton of cigarettes and 2 bottles of liquor.

**TELEPHONE:** The country code for Bolivia is 591.

**GETTING THERE/GETTING AROUND:** The main entrance points are La Paz and Santa Cruz by air, and by land at the Bolivia/Peru checkpoint on Lake Titicaca. The airlines providing direct or nonstop flights from the US to Bolivia include *American* and *LAB,* which both fly to La Paz; *LAB* also connects with Santa Cruz from Miami. *Aerolíneas Argentinas, AeroPerú, LanChile, LAP,* and *Varig* offer connecting flights. The domestic airline, *LAB,* has frequent and fairly reliable service. Although bus and truck routes connect most towns, long distances are best traveled by plane. Railroad buffs will love Bolivia's trains — they're antiques on rails. Routes through the Andes, linking most parts of Bolivia, Peru, and Chile, are especially scenic.

**CLIMATE:** Daytime temperatures in the high Andes generally are in the 40s F in the dry season, between May and November, and in the 50s and 60s F in the rainy season, from mid-November to April. The jungle's climate is tropical all year.

**LANGUAGE:** Spanish is the official language and is spoken by 36% of the total population; Quechua is spoken in almost all of the high plateau and valleys, by 37% of the people (some Spanish is spoken, too); Aymara is spoken in one part of the high plateau, by 25% of Bolivians (about 10% also speak Spanish); and Guaraní is spoken in the south of Bolivia, by 2.5% of the population. Itonama, Yara, Siriono, and other dialects are used by people of the jungle in the eastern part of Bolivia.

**ELECTRICITY:** 110 and 220 volts.

**MONEY:** Boliviano. *Note:* The old Bolivian peso has no value.

**CALCULATING COSTS:** Expect to pay anywhere between $60–$125 per night for a double room at an expensive hotel in La Paz. Costs are much lower in other parts of the country, where a moderately priced double room costs about $25–$40; inexpensive, under $25. Rates in Santa Cruz, a boom-economy town, tend to be higher. A moderately priced double room can cost between $45 and $70. Meals for two in La Paz cost at least $40 (not including drinks) in an expensive restaurant, $20–$40 in one moderately priced, and under $20 at an inexpensive eatery.

**TIPPING:** A 10% service charge is added in restaurants, but tip an additional 5% to 10% above this for particularly good service. Porters get about 50¢ per piece of luggage; taxi drivers are not tipped.

**BANKING/BUSINESS HOURS:** Banks are open weekdays from 8:30 AM to 11:30 AM, and from 2:30 PM to 4:30 PM. Hotels have foreign exchange desks. Business hours are 9 AM to 12:30 PM, and 2:30 to 7 PM, Mondays through Fridays; 9 AM to 12:30 PM, Saturdays.

**HOLIDAYS:** *New Year's Day* (January 1), *Carnaval* (February 20–23), *Good Friday* (April 9), *Easter Monday* (April 12), *Labor Day* (May 1), *Corpus Christi* (June 21), *Independence Day* (August 6), *All Souls' Day* (November 2), and *Christmas* (December 25).

**SPORTS:** Soccer (*fútbol*), mountain climbing, skiing, golf, and tennis.

**SHOPPING:** Ponchos, weavings, fine alpaca knits, colored knit hats (*chullos*) and playful items — miniature reed boats, airplanes, and amulets. Look for *artesanía* beyond the tourist shops and visit local markets.

**AIRPORT DEPARTURE TAX:** There is no domestic airport departure tax; international: $15.

# Brazil

**TOURIST INFORMATION:** *Brazilian Tourism Foundation:* 551 Fifth Ave., Suite 519, New York, NY 10176 (phone: 212-286-9600). *Brazilian Embassy:* 3006 Massachusetts Ave. NW, Washington, DC 20008 (phone: 202-745-2700). *Brazilian Consulates:* 3810 Wilshire Blvd., Suite 1500, Los Angeles, CA 90010 (phone: 213-382-3133); 3009 Whitehaven St. NW, Washington, DC 20008 (phone: 202-745-2828); 630 Fifth Ave., New York, NY 10111 (phone: 212-757-3080).

*US Embassy in Brazil:* Av. das Nações, Lote #3, 70403 Brasília, DF (phone: 61-321-7272). *US Consulates in Brazil:* 147 Av. Presidente Wilson, Rio de Janeiro 20030, RJ (phone: 21-292-7117); 933 Rua Padre João Manoel, São Paulo 01411, SP (phone: 11-881-6511).

**ENTRY REQUIREMENTS AND CUSTOMS:** US citizens are required to have a valid passport and a visa. The visa will be issued free by any Brazilian consulate. Applicants must submit a completed application form (including a passport-size photo) and a copy of their round-trip airline ticket. Travelers under 18 need a copy of their birth certificate. Note that US passports must be valid for 6 months from the date of issue of the visa. Visas are valid for 90 days and may be renewed once. The visa is free if the application is made in person; otherwise, there's a $10 charge. Acquiring a business visa in the US can be a nightmare of red tape, and can take up to a week; as we went to press, a $30 fee for a business visa was pending if the application is made in person, otherwise $40. Even if you're traveling on business, it's suggested that you apply for a tourist visa. Children under 6 must have a certificate of vaccination against polio. Travelers may enter with 1 carton of cigarettes, 2 liters of liquor, and other merchandise totaling not more than $300. Electronic goods and cameras valued at more than $300 must be registered with US Customs at major departure points before traveling to Brazil.

**TELEPHONE:** The country code for Brazil is 55.

**172 FACTS IN BRIEF / Brazil**

**GETTING THERE/GETTING AROUND:** The main entrance points are Rio de Janeiro and São Paulo. The airlines providing direct or nonstop flights from the US to Brazil (to Rio de Janeiro and São Paulo) include *Aerolíneas Argentinas, American, United,* and *Varig. Varig* also has nonstop flights from the US to Belém, Manaus, and Recife. *AeroPerú, Avianca, LAB, LADECO, LanChile, LAP, Surinam Airways,* and *Viasa* offer connecting flights. The domestic line, *Varig,* provides excellent service to major cities, as well as to remote jungle settlements. Amazon cruises and exploratory expeditions along its tributaries are exciting travel experiences. Roads vary from the rugged Trans-Amazon Highway to the sleeker network of highways connecting Rio de Janeiro, São Paulo, Pôrte Alegre, and the Uruguay-Argentina frontiers. Car rentals, however, are not advisable in some areas.

**CLIMATE:** The Northeast, the Amazon, and Rio de Janeiro have a tropical climate (80s F most of the year). During the summer months — December through February — the mercury climbs into the 90s and 100s F. São Paulo is hot and muggy in the summer, in the 50s F in June through August. Seasons are more defined in the southern part of the country, south of the Tropic of Capricorn. Temperatures in winter may drop to near freezing.

**LANGUAGE:** Portuguese.

**ELECTRICITY:** In Rio de Janeiro and São Paulo, the current is almost exclusively 110 volts or 120 volts; in Salvador and Manaus, 127 volts; Recife, Brasília, and a number of other cities have 220 volts. Most hotels provide both 110-volt and 220-volt outlets.

**MONEY:** Cruzeiro. The cruzeiro replaced the cruzado novo in 1990. This is Brazil's fourth currency in almost as many years. *Note:* The cruzado novo was the replacement for the old cruzado, which had replaced the old cruzeiro. You still may come across the old currencies, but they no longer have any value.

Brazil has an unofficial (but officially recognized) and legal "parallel" rate of exchange often called the "free market rate," but more commonly known as the "tourist" rate. This differs from the "black market," where better exchange rates camouflage the practice of passing off counterfeit bills to unsuspecting foreigners who are unfamiliar with the local currency. All *cambios* (exchange houses), hotels, and travel agencies in Brazil use the tourist exchange rate, which offers considerable bonuses in local currency. Most banks handle transactions in both the official rate and the more favorable tourist rate, made available to foreign visitors. Note that this exchange rate usually is better in Rio and other large cities than in small towns. Travel agencies and exchange houses all around Rio offer convenient alternate-exchange-rate access. In Brazil, avoid paying hotel, restaurant, or retail shop bills with credit cards, as purchases paid for with plastic are calculated at the higher *official* exchange rate, which means you will pay much more for goods and services.

**CALCULATING COSTS:** In recent years Brazil's inflation rate has fluctuated dramatically and at press time, hit triple digits. Still, the country remains a relative bargain travel destination because of the strength of the US dollar. The exception is hotel rooms in deluxe properties, especially in Rio and São Paulo, where a double room can cost anywhere between $100–$200. Visitors usually can find a comfortable hotel near the beach in Rio for about $65–$95. Outside major cities, expect to pay $80 and up at an expensive hotel; $40–$80, moderate; under $40, inexpensive. At popular resort destinations, advance reservations are advisable in summer (December–March), and absolutely essential during *Carnaval.* Restaurants generally charge the equivalent of $1–$3 for a *couvert* — bread, chilled vegetables, and other tidbits served as an appetizer — which is optional but appears on the bill if you don't specifically decline it. An expensive meal for two will run $40 and up; moderate, $25–$35; and inexpensive, under $20 (not including beverages and tip).

**TIPPING:** Although a service charge usually is included in the bill at restaurants, it is customary to tip an additional 5%. If no service charge has been added, tip 10% to 15%. When taking a taxi, the usual practice is to round the fare to the next cruzeiro. Tip porters the equivalent of 50¢ per piece of luggage; chambermaids, $1 per room per day. Cloakroom attendants and museum guides also are tipped.

**BANKING/BUSINESS HOURS:** Banks are open weekdays from 10 AM to 4 PM. Business hours are 8 AM to 6 PM, Mondays through Fridays. Some businesses may be open on Saturday mornings.

**HOLIDAYS:** Rio de Janeiro's *Carnaval* (February 20–23) is perhaps the most famous special event in the world. *Carnaval* also takes place in Salvador (Bahia), Santos, Belém, and Guarujá. Other holidays are *New Year's Day* (January 1), *Good Friday* (April 9), *Easter Sunday* (April 11), *Tiradentes' Day* (April 21), *Labor Day* (May 1), *Corpus Christi* (June 21), *Independence Day* (September 7), *Our Lady of Aparecida Day* (October 12), *All Souls' Day* (November 2), *Republic Day* (November 15), and *Christmas* (December 25).

**SPORTS:** Three-time winner of the *World Cup,* Brazil is a country of soccer *(futebol)* fanatics. Swimming, sailing, volleyball, and fishing also draw enthusiasts from all over the world.

**SHOPPING:** Brazilian semi-precious stones — amethyst, aquamarine, topaz, and agate — can be purchased at gem factories around the country. Other good buys are rosewood (jacaranda) carvings, Amazonian dolls, leather goods, and sexy bikinis *(tangas).*

**AIRPORT DEPARTURE TAX:** Both domestic and international departures: about $9 each (depending on the value of the cruzeiro).

# Chile

**TOURIST INFORMATION:** *Chilean Embassy:* 1732 Massachusetts Ave. NW, Washington, DC 20036 (phone: 202-785-1746). *Chilean Consulates:* 510 W. 6th St., Suite 1204, Los Angeles, CA 90014 (phone: 213-624-6357); 870 Market St., Suite 1062, San Francisco, CA 94102 (phone: 415-982-7662); 1110 Brickell Ave., Suite 616, Miami, FL 33131 (phone: 305-373-8623 or 305-373-8624); 866 UN Plaza, Suite 302, New York, NY 10017 (phone: 212-980-3366); 1360 Post Oak Blvd., Suite 2330, Houston, TX 77056 (phone: 713-621-5853).

*US Embassy in Chile:* 1343 Augustina, 5th Floor, Santiago (phone: 2-671-0133). *US Consulate in Chile:* 230 Merced, Santiago (phone: 2-671-0133).

**ENTRY REQUIREMENTS AND CUSTOMS:** No visa is required of US citizens for stays of fewer than 90 days, but a valid passport is required. Travelers may enter with 2 cartons of cigarettes and 3 bottles of liquor.

**TELEPHONE:** The country code for Chile is 56.

**GETTING THERE/GETTING AROUND:** The main entrance point is Santiago. The airlines providing direct or nonstop flights from the US to Chile include *American, LanChile, LADECO,* and *United. Aerolíneas Argentinas, AeroPerú, Avianca, Ecuatoriana, LAB, LAP, Varig,* and *Viasa* offer connecting flights. *LanChile* and *LADECO,* the domestic carriers, also have flights throughout Chile. The Pan-American Highway runs the length of Chile from the Peruvian frontier at Arica to Puerto Montt, where the land breaks into rugged fjords and glaciers. The Pan-American is in good repair. Trains run frequently. A railroad trip through the Andes is unforgettable; so is a boat trip through the southern fjords. For transport between long distances, use domestic airlines and air taxis.

**CLIMATE:** Arid desert in the north; moderate in the central valley, with temperatures in the 90s F in summer (December through March), sometimes dropping into the

20s F in winter (June through September). Southern, mountainous regions are rainy and cool in the summer (temperatures in the 60s F), snowy in winter. The Andes' ski resorts are at their peak between June and September.

**LANGUAGE:** Spanish is the official language; Mopuche and Aymara also are spoken in some rural areas.

**ELECTRICITY:** 220 volts.

**MONEY:** Peso.

**CALCULATING COSTS:** In Santiago, expect to pay top dollar (plus 18% local tax) — $175 and more for a double room in a very expensive hotel; $125–$175 in an international class hotel; $80–$125, moderate; under $80, inexpensive. Throughout the rest of Chile, rates average $75 at an expensive establishment to under $30 for inexpensive accommodations. Prices on Easter Island run about three times higher than those on the mainland, and if you hit ski resorts either in Portillo or the Lake District, prices can skyrocket to well over $100 per night for a double in high season. Advance reservations are advisable in all areas of Chile. Dinner for two in Santiago costs $50 and up in the expensive category; $30–$50, moderate; under $30, inexpensive (not including beverages and tip).

**TIPPING:** Tip 10% in restaurants. Porters get 50¢ per bag, but never less than $1. Taxi drivers expect a small tip.

**BANKING/BUSINESS HOURS:** Banks are open weekdays from 9 AM to 2 PM.. Business hours are 8 or 9 AM to 1 PM, 2 or 3 PM to 6 PM, Mondays through Fridays; some businesses are open on Saturdays from 8 or 9 AM to 1 PM..

**HOLIDAYS:** *New Year's Day* (January 1), *Good Friday* (April 9), *Easter Sunday* (April 11), *Labor Day* (May 1), *Battle of Iquique Day* (May 21), *Assumption Day* (August 16), *Independence Day* (September 18–19), *Columbus Day* (October 18), *All Saints' Day* (November 1), *Immaculate Conception* (December 8), *Christmas* (December 25).

**SPORTS:** Soccer is the most popular spectator sport. Skiing (downhill and cross-country) at world-famous Portillo, Farellones, and Valle Nevado draws skiers from all over the globe. Deep-sea fishing off the Chilean coast and trout and salmon fishing in the Lake District attract anglers.

**SHOPPING:** Weavings, ceramics, lapis lazuli, copper enamel goblets and cutlery, suede, leather, and excellent wine are available at good prices. For crafts, try the *CEMA* cooperatives in Santiago. Seek out small shops in Providencia for unusual ceramics and finely crafted wooden objects.

**AIRPORT DEPARTURE TAX:** There is no domestic airport departure tax; international: $12.50.

# Colombia

**TOURIST INFORMATION:** *Colombian Embassy:* 2118 Leroy Pl. NW, Washington, DC 20008 (phone: 202-387-8338). *Colombian Consulates:* 3580 Wilshire Blvd., Suite 1450, Los Angeles, CA 90010 (phone: 213-382-1136); 10 E. 46th St., New York, NY 10017 (phone: 212-949-9898).

*US Embassy in Colombia:* 8-61 Calle 38, Bogotá (phone: 1-285-1300). *US Consulates in Colombia:* Calle 77 and Carrera 68-15, Centro Comercial Mayorista, Barranquilla (phone: 58-457088).

**ENTRY REQUIREMENTS AND CUSTOMS:** US citizens are required to have a valid passport and a round-trip ticket for visits of up to 90 days. The duty-free allowance fluctuates from time to time; check with the duty-free shop at the airport when you enter the country.

**TELEPHONE:** The country code for Colombia is 57.

**FACTS IN BRIEF / Ecuador** 175

**GETTING THERE/GETTING AROUND:** The main entrance points are Bogotá, Barranquilla, Cartagena, Medellín, and Cali. The airlines providing direct or nonstop flights from the US to Colombia include *American, Avianca,* and *LADECO. Aerolíneas Argentinas, AeroPerú, Copa, Varig,* and *Viasa* offer connecting flights. The domestic line is *Avianca,* which services the capital, the Caribbean Coast, and the interior. Roads are in only fair condition and trains are not well maintained, so the best bet for getting around Colombia is by air.

**CLIMATE:** The Caribbean Coast averages a year-round temperature of about 80 F. Bogotá, 8,640 feet above sea level, ranges from the mid-50s F to the 70s F throughout the year. Colombia has two rainy seasons: one in March and April, the other in October and November.

**LANGUAGE:** Spanish. English is spoken widely in hotels, restaurants, and travel bureaus.

**ELECTRICITY:** 110 volts.

**MONEY:** Peso.

**CALCULATING COSTS:** Hotel rates are highest in Bogotá, Cartagena, and Medellín, ranging from $60 and up (plus a 15% value added tax) for a double room in the expensive range; $40–$60, moderate; under $30, inexpensive. Prices escalate (up to 25% higher) during *Carnaval* and the holiday season (December–January). Rates outside these cities can be very reasonable, from $50 to less than $20, although smaller hotels in remote areas often lack amenities like hot-water showers. Reservations outside major cities always are advisable. In Bogotá, an expensive dinner for two costs $40 and up (not including beverages and tip); moderately priced, $18–$35; inexpensive, $10–$15. Local beers cost less than imported wines.

**TIPPING:** In restaurants, tip 10% if no service charge is added to the bill; 5%, if a service charge is included. Porters get about 50¢ per bag; washroom attendants, about 30¢.

**BANKING/BUSINESS HOURS:** Banks are open Mondays through Thursdays from 9 AM to 3 PM,, and Fridays from 9 AM to 3:30 PM.. Bank hours do vary somewhat from city to city. Business hours are 9 AM to 6 PM, Mondays through Fridays.

**HOLIDAYS:** *New Year's Day* (January 1), *Epiphany* (January 4), *Wise Men Day* (January 11), *St. Joseph's Day* (March 22), *Holy Thursday* (April 8), *Good Friday* (April 9), *Easter* (April 11), *Labor Day* (May 1), *Ascension Day* (June 14), *Corpus Christi* (June 21), *Sacred Heart of Jesus* (July 5), *Independence Day* (July 20), *Battle of Boyacá* (August 7), *Assumption Day* (August 16), *Columbus Day* (October 18), *All Saints' Day* (November 1), *Independence of Cartagena* (November 15), *Immaculate Conception* (December 8), and *Christmas* (December 25). Many holidays which fall on a Sunday are observed by businesses on the following Monday.

**SPORTS:** Soccer, tennis, golf, auto racing, bullfighting, whitewater rafting, windsurfing, deep-sea fishing, and mountain climbing are most popular.

**SHOPPING:** Woolen ponchos *(ruanas),* leather goods, artisan products, and weavings can be purchased at the government-run *Artesanías de Colombia.* Emeralds mined and sold here are among the world's finest. Do not purchase gems from street vendors. Colombian coffee is almost as good as it gets.

**AIRPORT DEPARTURE TAX:** Domestic airport tax varies from city to city, ranging between $3 and $4; international: $15.

# Ecuador

**TOURIST INFORMATION:** *Ecuadorian Foundation for the Promotion of Tourism (FEPROTUR):* 7270 NW 12th St., Suite 400C, Miami, FL 33126 (phone: 800-553-6673; 305-477-0041 in Florida). *Ecuadorian Embassy:* 2535 15th St. NW, Washington,

DC 20009 (phone: 202-234-7200). *Ecuadorian Consulates:* 548 S. Spring St., Suite 602, Los Angeles, CA 90013 (phone: 213-628-3014); 870 Market St., Suite 860, San Francisco, CA 94102 (phone: 415-391-4148); 1101 Brickell Ave., Suite M102, Miami, FL 33131 (phone: 305-539-8214); 612 N. Michigan Ave., Room 716, Chicago, IL 60611 (phone: 312-642-8579); World Trade Center, 2 Canal St., Suite 1312, New Orleans, LA 70130 (phone: 504-523-3229); 18 E. 41st St., Room 1800, New York, NY 10017 (phone: 212-683-7555); 4200 Westheimer Ave., Suite 118, Houston, TX 77027 (phone: 713-622-1787).

*US Embassy in Ecuador:* Avdas. Patria and 12 de Octubre, Quito (phone: 2-560401). *US Consulate in Ecuador:* Avdas. 9 de Octubre and García Moreno, Guayaquil (phone: 4-323570).

**ENTRY REQUIREMENTS AND CUSTOMS:** US citizens are required to have a valid passport and an ongoing ticket for visits of up to 90 days. Travelers may bring in 300 cigarettes and 1 bottle of liquor.

**TELEPHONE:** The country code for Ecuador is 593.

**GETTING THERE/GETTING AROUND:** The main entrance points are Quito and Guayaquil. The airlines providing direct or nonstop flights from the US to Ecuador include *American, Ecuatoriana, United,* and *SAETA. Aerolíneas Argentinas, AeroPerú, Avianca, LADECO, Varig,* and *Viasa* offer connecting flights. Domestic lines are *SAN* (a division of *SAETA*) and *TAME.* The train ride from Quito to Riobamba, a half-day roller coaster ride through the Andes, is quite spectacular and well worth it if you have the time. Buses make the run from Quito to Guayaquil in 8 hours; airplanes, in 35 minutes. Air service is recommended for trips to the interior. The Galápagos Islands can be toured only by yacht or, in some rare instances, by cruise ship.

**CLIMATE:** The coastal lowlands have a year-round equatorial climate in the humid 80s F. During the rainy season, November through May, temperatures are hotter. Quito has a temperate, Andean climate, with an average yearly temperature in the 50s F. The dry season runs from May through October; June and July are the coolest months, but also the clearest in the highlands. In the Galápagos, temperatures are in the humid 80s F during the rainy season (January through March), and in the drier 70s F during the rest of the year. It can get very cool at night.

**LANGUAGE:** Spanish is the official language; Quechua is spoken by the Indian population.

**ELECTRICITY:** 110 volts.

**MONEY:** Sucre.

**CALCULATING COSTS:** A double room at a luxury hotel in Quito ranges from $90–$150; expensive, $70–$90; moderate, $35–$70; inexpensive, under $35. Guayaquil's prices generally are higher. Outside these cities, travelers can find very inexpensive accommodations (as low as $15 per night), but rooms tend toward the primitive, compared to US standards. Small country inns called *residenciales* are popular. Reservations for a stay in the Galápagos Islands should be made well in advance because of limited facilities. Happily, meals for two don't coincide with city hotel rates: expensive, $25 and up; moderate, $15–$25; inexpensive, under $15 (not including beverages, tax, and tip).

**TIPPING:** In restaurants, tip 10% if there is no service charge; otherwise, 5%, if the service is particularly good. Porters should get about 50¢ per bag, but never less than $1. Taxi drivers do not expect to be tipped.

**BANKING/BUSINESS HOURS:** Banks are open weekdays from 9 AM to 1:30 PM; some banks are open those days from 2:30 PM to 4:30 PM as well. Business hours are 8 AM to 12 noon, 2 to 6 PM, Mondays through Fridays. Some businesss are open on Saturdays from 8 AM to 12 noon; some stay open through midafternoon on weekdays and close at 5 PM.

**HOLIDAYS:** *New Year's Day* (January 1), *Carnaval* (February 20–23), *Good Friday*

(April 9), *Easter Sunday* (April 11), *Labor Day* (May 1), *Battle of Pichincha* (May 24), *Bolívar's Birthday* (July 24), *Independence Day* (August 10), *Independence of Guayaquil* (October 9), *Columbus Day* (October 18), *All Souls' Day* (November 2), *Independence of Cuenca* (November 3), *Founding of Quito* (December 6), and *Christmas* (December 25).

**SPORTS:** Soccer, bullfighting, horse racing, fishing, mountain climbing, and hunting.

**SHOPPING:** Quito's shopping district is ranked among the best in South America. The market at Otavalo is the best place to buy handmade weavings. The market, a colorful pageant, is active all week, although it reaches its peak on Saturdays. By all means bargain, but don't expect much of a break — prices are fairly standard, even in the markets. Ponchos, weavings, and straw items, including the famous Panama hat made here, are good buys all over the country, and available in markets and shops.

**AIRPORT DEPARTURE TAX:** There is no domestic airport departure tax; international: $25.

# French Guiana

**TOURIST INFORMATION:** *French Government Tourist Office:* 610 Fifth Ave., New York, NY 10020 (phone: 212-757-1125; 900-990-0040). *French Embassy:* 4101 Reservoir Rd. NW, Washington, DC 20007 (phone: 202-944-6000). *French Consulates:* 10990 Wilshire Blvd., Suite 300, Los Angeles, CA 90024 (phone: 213-479-4426); 934 Fifth Ave., New York, NY 10021 (phone: 212-606-3600).

There is no US consulate or embassy in French Guiana; this area is covered by the US Consulate in Martinique at 14 Rue Blenac, B.P. 651, 97206 Fort de France, Martinique (phone: 596-631303).

**ENTRY REQUIREMENTS AND CUSTOMS:** US citizens are required to have a valid passport and an ongoing ticket for visits of up to 90 days. A yellow fever vaccination certificate is required for stays longer than 2 weeks. Travelers may enter with 400 cigarettes and 1 liter of liquor.

**TELEPHONE:** The country code for French Guiana is 594.

**GETTING THERE/GETTING AROUND:** The main entrance point is Cayenne. The only airline serving French Guiana (from Miami) is *Air France*. *Cruzeiro do Sul* and *Surinam Airways* offer connecting flights. *Air Guyane,* the domestic carrier, is represented in the US by *Air France;* however, service is very limited. River trips from Cayenne to the Suriname border at St.-Laurent are among the most exciting expeditions in South America. The road system is limited to the coastal area; the only major road runs between Cayenne and St.-Laurent.

**CLIMATE:** Equatorial (tropical) climate throughout the year, with temperatures in the 80s F. The dry season lasts from August to December and the rainy season from January to June.

**LANGUAGE:** French and creole.

**ELECTRICITY:** 110 and 220 volts.

**MONEY:** French franc.

**CALCULATING COSTS:** Hotels here are small, quiet, comfortable — and few. A double room at an expensive hotel in Cayenne runs between $120 and $140. Moderate accommodations are available for $70–$90. Outside the cities, rates range from $70, expensive, to under $25, inexpensive.

**TIPPING:** In restaurants and hotels, a service charge will be included on the bill. Tipping taxi drivers is done at the passenger's discretion.

**BANKING/BUSINESS HOURS:** Banks are open from 7:15 AM to 11:45 AM, and

**178 FACTS IN BRIEF / Guyana**

from 2:30 to 5 PM, Mondays through Fridays, except Wednesdays, when they are open from 7 AM to noon. Business hours are 9 AM to 12:30 PM, 3 to 6 PM, Mondays through Fridays; 9 AM to 12:30 PM, Saturdays.

**HOLIDAYS:** *New Year's Day* (January 1), *Easter Sunday* (April 11), *Easter Monday* (April 12), *Labor Day* (May 1), *Fête de la Victoire,* which marks the end of World War II (May 8), *Whitsunday* (May 30), *Whitmonday* (May 31), *Ascension Day* (June 14), *Bastille Day* (July 14), *Assumption Day* (August 16), *All Saints' Day* (November 1), *Armistice Day* (November 11), and *Christmas* (December 25). In addition, some businesses may close for part of the *Cayenne Annual Festival,* held during the last 2 weeks of October.

**SPORTS:** Fishing, water skiing, windsurfing, and tennis.

**SHOPPING:** Since French Guiana is a department of France, most goods are imported from France and are very expensive. There are some good local crafts to be found — basketwork, hammocks, Indian pottery, Boni carved wooden objects, creole gold jewelry, and Asian embroideries.

**AIRPORT DEPARTURE TAX:** There is no domestic departure tax; international: about $15.

# Guyana

**TOURIST INFORMATION:** *Guyanese Embassy and Consulate:* 2490 Tracy Pl. NW, Washington, DC 20008 (phone: 202-265-6900). *Guyanese Consulate:* 866 UN Plaza, 3rd Floor, New York, NY 10017 (phone: 212-527-3215).

*US Embassy in Guyana:* 100 Young St., Kingston, Georgetown (phone: 54900).

**ENTRY REQUIREMENTS AND CUSTOMS:** US citizens are required to have a valid passport, an outward-bound ticket, and a tourist visa, which requires 3 forms and 3 photos and is issued by the consulate before arrival. Travelers may enter with 1 carton of cigarettes, 1 bottle of liquor, and 1 bottle of wine. If you plan to hunt, be sure to register your weapon at the Ministry of Home Affairs, Georgetown.

**TELEPHONE:** The country code for Guyana is 592.

**GETTING THERE/GETTING AROUND:** The main entrance point is Georgetown. The airlines providing direct or nonstop flights from the US to Guyana (from Miami and New York) are *Guyana Airways* and *British West Indian Airlines (BWIA)*. *Surinam Airways* offers connecting flights. Domestic service is provided by *Guyana Airways,* although service is very limited. Auto traffic follows the British system, with drivers keeping to the left. Bus service connects the main coastal cities. Boats travel the major rivers. Overland travel is the best way to get to the interior.

**CLIMATE:** Guyana has an equatorial (tropical) climate all year, with considerable humidity and a steady sea breeze. On the coast, temperatures range from the upper 60s F to the low 90s F, and, inland, temperatures reach the low 100s F.

**LANGUAGE:** English is the official language; a local patois of English-based creole also is widely spoken. The Amerindians still speak their own dialects.

**ELECTRICITY:** Major cities generally use 110 volts and rural areas use 220 volts.

**MONEY:** Guyana dollar.

Guyana now has a free foreign exchange system — a service unavailable a few years ago — whereby you can convert money. Foreign currency can be changed at *cambios* (exchange houses) located in Georgetown and other cities and at banks; the best rates are offered at *cambios*. However, because local currency is *not* convertible abroad (no bank in the US or elsewhere will convert Guyana dollars), hotels require foreigners to pay in hard currency (that is, from industrialized nations), as do local airlines. Be sure to come with US dollars in cash or traveler's checks and to change only the amount you actually need; otherwise you'll be left with useless Guyana dollars to show as souvenirs when you return home.

**CALCULATING COSTS:** Guyana is mainly a tropical jungle, so accommodations are fairly primitive. Considering the conditions, overnight rates in the interior are surprisingly expensive. In Georgetown a top double room runs about $120. Expect to pay $40–$60 per night for a standard room — without private bath. *Note:* Hotel bills must be paid in foreign currency.

**TIPPING:** Porters get 25¢ per item of luggage. Taxi drivers also are tipped a small amount.

**BANKING/BUSINESS HOURS:** Banks are open Mondays through Thursdays from 8 AM to 12:30 PM; Fridays from 8 AM to 12:30 PM and 3 to 5 PM. Business hours are 8 AM to 4:30 PM, Mondays through Fridays; 8 AM to noon, Saturdays.

**HOLIDAYS:** *New Year's Day* (January 1), *Republic Day* (February 23), *Mashramani* (February 23; this is the celebration of the attainment of the status of republic in Guyana, festivities last for 2 weeks), *Phagwah* (February or March), *Good Friday* (April 9), *Easter Sunday* (April 11), *Easter Monday* (April 12), *Labour Day* (May 1), *Eid-ul-Azah* (June), *Caribbean Community Day* (first Monday in July), *Freedom Day* (August 1), *Youm-un-Nabi* (September), *Deepavali* (late October or early November), *Christmas* (December 25), and *Boxing Day* (December 26).

**SPORTS:** Cricket is played primarily in Georgetown. Soccer and boxing are popular spectator sports as well. At *Easter,* there is an annual rodeo at the Rupunini savannah ranches. Fishing and hunting are the main participant sports.

**SHOPPING:** Native crafts — beads, woodcarvings, and straw weavings — can be purchased at reasonable prices at *Staebroek Market* in Georgetown. Be sure to bargain. Guyanese diamonds are another good buy.

**AIRPORT DEPARTURE TAX:** There is no domestic departure tax; international: about $10.

# Panama

**TOURIST INFORMATION:** *Panamanian Embassy:* 2862 McGill Terrace NW, Washington, DC 20008 (phone: 202-483-1407); *Panamanian Consulate:* 1212 Avenue of the Americas, 10th Floor, New York, NY 10036 (phone: 212-840-2450).

*US Embassy in Panama:* Av. Balboa and Calle 37, Panama City 5 (phone: 271777).

**ENTRY REQUIREMENTS AND CUSTOMS:** US citizens are required to have either a valid passport or other proof of US citizenship, and a tourist card. The tourist card can be purchased for $2 from any of the airlines serving Panama. Travelers may enter with 2 cartons of cigarettes and 2 bottles of liquor.

**TELEPHONE:** The country code for Panama is 507.

**GETTING THERE/GETTING AROUND:** The main entrance point is Panama City. The airlines providing direct or nonstop flights from the US to Panama include *American, Copa, Ecuatoriana, LAB, United,* and *Varig. Aerolíneas Argentinas, AeroPerú, Avianca, LanChile,* and *Viasa* offer connecting flights. The domestic line is *AeroPerlas.* Flamboyant buses connect the major cities; some are ramshackle, others air conditioned. Many cruise ships go through the Panama Canal on Caribbean sailings.

**CLIMATE:** Hot, muggy, tropical climate throughout the year, with temperatures in the 80s and 90s F; cool and pleasant in the highlands, with temperatures in the 50s and 60s F. The rainy season lasts from April to December.

**LANGUAGE:** Spanish is the official language, but many people speak English as well.

**180 FACTS IN BRIEF / Paraguay**

**ELECTRICITY:** 110 volts.

**MONEY:** US dollars (which are called balboas). The old balboa coins have no value and are for collectors only.

**CALCULATING COSTS:** Panama City has abundant hotel rooms, but many are costly — $90 and up per night for a double; moderate rooms go for $40–$70; inexpensive, under $30. Outside the city, rates dip to $20–$40 in the moderate range, while inexpensive translates to $20 or less. The capital's polyglot, international mix means dinner for two costs $30 and up in the expensive category; $20–$30, moderate; under $20, inexpensive (not including beverages and tip).

**TIPPING:** In restaurants, tip 10%. Porters get 25¢ per bag. Taxi drivers are not tipped.

**BANKING/BUSINESS HOURS:** Banks are open weekdays from 8 AM to 1:30 PM. Some banks are open on Saturday mornings. Business hours are 8 AM to 5 PM, Mondays through Fridays.

**HOLIDAYS:** *New Year's Day* (January 1), *Day of the Martyrs* (January 9), *Carnaval Tuesday* (February 23), *Good Friday* (April 9), *Easter Sunday* (April 11), *Labor Day* (May 1), *Revolution Day* (October 11), *Memorial Day* (November 2), *Independence from Colombia* (November 3), *Flag Day* (November 4), *Independence from Spain* (November 28), *Mother's Day* (December 8), and *Christmas* (December 25).

**SPORTS:** Baseball, horse racing, cockfights, soccer, and boxing are the most popular spectator sports. Water sports such as snorkeling and water skiing are popular at coastal resorts. Deep-sea fishing fans flock to the marlin-filled Pacific and Caribbean waters. Freshwater fishing in the rivers and lakes is good, too.

**SHOPPING:** Famous around the world for bargains in high-quality imported items, Panama's best buys are cameras, small electronic goods, watches, perfume, and luxury items — Irish crystal, Asian jade, and silk. Local handicrafts include appliqué cloth *(molas)* and bead necklaces *(chaquiras)*. For Panamanian crafts, visit *Artesanía Nacional* in the Old City or *Salsipuedes Market*. Gold jewelry (sold by the ounce) is a very good buy in the Free Zone of Colón.

**AIRPORT DEPARTURE TAX:** There is no domestic airport departure tax; international: $15.

# Paraguay

**TOURIST INFORMATION:** *Paraguayan Embassy:* 2400 Massachusetts Ave. NW, Washington DC 20008 (phone: 202-483-6960). *Paraguayan Consulate:* 1 World Trade Center, Suite 1947, New York, NY 10048 (phone: 212-432-0733).

*US Embassy in Paraguay:* 1776 Av. Mariscal López, Asunción (phone: 21-213715).

**ENTRY REQUIREMENTS AND CUSTOMS:** US citizens are required to have a valid US passport and a tourist card. The tourist card may be obtained when you enter Paraguay; it costs about $3. Travelers may bring in an unlimited amount of cigarettes and liquor for personal use (though according to the Embassy of Paraguay, these should be in "reasonable quantities").

**TELEPHONE:** The country code for Paraguay is 595.

**GETTING THERE/GETTING AROUND:** The main entrance point is Asunción. The airlines providing direct or nonstop flights from the US to Paraguay include *American* and *Líneas Aéreas Paraguayas (LAP)*, both of which fly to Asunción. *Aerolíneas Argentinas, LAB, LADECO*, and *Varig* offer connecting flights. There is no domestic air service. Roads in Paraguay connect the national highway systems of Argentina and Brazil, and overland travel is the best way of getting to remote sections of the country. Boat traffic plies the Paraguay and Paraná rivers. It is possible to travel to Buenos Aires, Argentina, on the Paraná River from Asunción.

**CLIMATE:** Humid and warm most of the year. Daytime temperatures are generally in the 70s and 80s F September through April, and in the 60s F May through August.

**LANGUAGE:** Spanish is the official language, but most Paraguayans also speak Guaraní, particularly along the Jesuit Mission Trail.

**ELECTRICITY:** 220 volts.

**MONEY:** Guaraní.

**CALCULATING COSTS:** In Asunción, an expensive hotel runs $90 and up for a double; moderate, $40–$90; inexpensive, under $40. Breakfast usually is included in moderate/inexpensive rates. Family-style *pensiones* are another affordable choice. In other parts of the country, hotels are scattered but small, comfortable, and reasonably priced — $45 and up, expensive; $25–$45, moderate; under $25, inexpensive. The exception is resort areas like the Golden Triangle, where rates are higher. Here, as elsewhere outside Asunción, advance reservations are a must. Locals relish eating out because of reasonable prices. Meals for two classed in the expensive range are $45 and up; moderate, $25–$45; inexpensive, under $25 (not including beverages and tip).

**TIPPING:** In restaurants tip 5% to 10%. Porters get 50¢ per piece of luggage. Round off the fare for taxi drivers.

**BANKING/BUSINESS HOURS:** Banks are open weekdays from 7:30 AM to noon; exchange houses *(casas de cambio)*, from 7:30 AM to noon and 3 to 6 PM. Business hours are 7:30 AM to noon, 3 to 7 PM, Mondays through Fridays; 7:30 AM to noon, Saturdays.

**HOLIDAYS:** *New Year's Day* (January 1), *San Blas Day* (February 3), *Heroes' Day* (March 1), *Holy Thursday* (April 8), *Good Friday* (April 9), *Easter Sunday* (April 11), *Labor Day* (May 1), *Independence Day* (May 14 and 15), *Chaco Peace Day* (June 12), *Foundation of Asunción Day* (August 15), *Columbus Day* (October 18), *Immaculate Conception* (December 8), and *Christmas* (December 25).

**SPORTS:** Soccer *(fútbol)*, tennis, golf, swimming, water skiing, and fishing.

**SHOPPING:** Two of Paraguay's specialties include *ñandutí* cloth in the form of tablecloths, bedspreads, handkerchiefs, and wall decorations, and *aó po'i,* an embroidered cloth.

**AIRPORT DEPARTURE TAX:** There is no domestic airport departure tax; international: about $12.

# Peru

**TOURIST INFORMATION:** *Peru Tourist Office Inc. (FOPTUR):* 1000 Brickell Ave., Suite 600, Miami, FL 33131 (phone: 800-854-0023 or 305-374-0023). *Peruvian Embassy:* 1700 Massachusetts Ave. NW, Washington, DC 20036 (phone: 202-833-9860). *Peruvian Consulates:* 444 Brickell Ave., Room M135, Miami, FL 33131 (phone: 305-374-1305); 215 Lexington Ave., 21st Floor, New York, NY 10016 (phone: 212-481-7410).

*US Embassy in Peru:* Corner of Avdas. Inca Garcilaso de la Vega and España, Lima (phone: 338000). The consular section is at 346 Grimaldo del Solar, Lima (phone: 443621).

**ENTRY REQUIREMENTS AND CUSTOMS:** US citizens require a valid US passport and round-trip airline ticket. No visa is required for visits of up to 90 days. A yellow fever vaccination is strongly suggested for travelers going to the central and southern jungles; for those who plan to stay for over a week, malaria pills also are essential. Travelers may enter Peru with 400 cigarettes, 2 liters of alcohol, and items intended for personal use not to exceed $300 in value.

**TELEPHONE:** The country code for Peru is 51.

**GETTING THERE/GETTING AROUND:** The main entrance points are Lima, the port of Callao, and Iquitos. The airlines providing direct or nonstop flights from the

## 182 FACTS IN BRIEF / Peru

US to Peru include *Aerolíneas Argentinas, American, AeroPerú, Faucett,* and *LanChile,* all of which fly to Lima. *Faucett* also flies to Iquitos. *Avianca, Ecuatoriana, LAB, LAP, Varig,* and *Viasa* offer connecting flights. *AeroPerú* and *Faucett* also offer domestic flights. The Pan-American Highway, paved but narrow, is clogged with trucks, buses, and frenetic drivers. Because of increased terrorist activity, the US State Department has recommended strongly against traveling by public bus. Since distances between Peruvian cities are long, domestic air service is the best way to get around. Train rides through the Andes are scenic but slow. River trips through the jungle in dugout canoes are great fun — and in some areas offer the only transportation — but be prepared to spend days in transit.

**CLIMATE:** Lima is foggy and humid during the fall and winter months (April through September). Spring and summer (October through March) tend to be somewhat clearer, with temperatures in the humid 80s F. Winter temperatures are in the 50s F. Several miles east of the capital, a dry, warm desert climate prevails year round. The Andes' dry season runs between April and November, with daytime temperatures in the 60s and 70s F. In June and July, the mercury may drop below freezing, and it occasionally snows. Summer is the rainy season in the Andes and in the jungle. The Amazon region is hot and rainy all year round, with temperatures in the 80s and 90s F; the flat jungle *(selva)* frequently gets as hot as the high 90s to low 100s F.

**LANGUAGE:** Spanish and Quechua.

**ELECTRICITY:** 220 volts. The major hotels have special 110-volt outlets, for the use of shavers only.

**MONEY:** The nuevo sol replaced the inti in 1991. Although you may still come across intis, they no longer have any value.

**CALCULATING COSTS:** As Lima's tourist trade has flourished, so has its hotel capacity. Although a double room in a luxury hotel now exceeds $100 per night, many accommodations average $35–$65. An overnight stay in the Cuzco area ranges from under $25 up to $80. Other parts of Peru are less expensive, commonly $15–$40 for a double room. Reservations outside the capital always are advisable. The real but hidden cost factor in Peru is the room tax and service charge — a whopping 30% in Lima in first class establishments, less in others. Good food is important to Peruvians, so eating virtually anywhere is a pleasure — and the bill won't spoil your appetite. On average, dinner for two runs between $15–$35 (not including beverages, tax, and tip) in Lima.

**TIPPING:** A 10% tip is added to the check by most restaurants; regardless, the total tip should be about 15%. Porters should get about 50¢ per bag, but never less than $1. Taxi drivers do not expect a tip.

**BANKING/BUSINESS HOURS:** Most banks are open weekdays from 9 AM to 12:30 or 1 PM and 3 to 6 PM, though some banks are open from 9 AM to 4 PM. Business hours are 9 AM to 5 PM, Mondays through Fridays; some businesses close at 1 PM and reopen at 3 until 6 PM; some shops are open daily except Sundays from 9 AM to 8 PM..

**HOLIDAYS:** *New Year's Day* (January 1), *Holy Thursday* (April 8), *Good Friday* (April 9), *Easter Sunday* (April 11), *Labor Day* (May 1), *Agriculture Day* (June 24), *St. Peter and St. Paul* (July 5), *Independence Day* (July 28 and 29), *St. Rose of Lima* (August 30), *Anniversary of the Death of Admiral Miguel Grau,* which observes the Battle of Angamos (October 8), *All Saints' Day* (November 1), *Immaculate Conception* (December 8), and *Christmas* (December 25).

**SPORTS:** Soccer *(fútbol),* volleyball, basketball, tennis, bullfighting, cockfighting, and horse racing are Peru's most popular spectator sports. The Andes attract climbers and trekkers from all over the world. Lima's beaches have a loyal crowd of surfers.

**SHOPPING:** Peruvian handicrafts — weavings, ponchos, woolen hats, hand-knit alpaca sweaters, leather goods, ceramics, and carvings — are somewhat better buys in Cuzco or an Andean market than in one of the more expensive Lima tourist shops, but the quality of market goods may be questionable. Lima's jewelry shops sell excellent hand-wrought gold and silver jewelry in Inca motifs, but check the silver items to make sure they have been carefully soldered, or they soon may fall apart. Another indigenous folk-art form, colorful *retablos* (miniature houses made of wood, with ceramic figures), are sold in Lima.

**AIRPORT DEPARTURE TAX:** Domestic: about $7; international: about $15. Both taxes are highly subject to change without notice.

# Suriname

**TOURIST INFORMATION:** *Suriname Embassy:* 4301 Connecticut Ave. NW, Van Ness Center, Suite 108, Washington, DC 20008 (phone: 202-244-7488). *Suriname Consulate:* 7235 NW 19th St., Suite A, Miami, FL 33126 (phone: 305-593-2163).
*US Embassy in Suriname:* 129 Dr. Sophie Redmondstraat, Paramaribo (phone: 472900).

**ENTRY REQUIREMENTS AND CUSTOMS:** US citizens require a valid passport, visa, and an outward-bound ticket. The visa can be obtained through the consulate or the embassy in Washington, DC. There is a fee of $17 and the visa is valid for 1 year. Travelers may bring in 400 cigarettes, 2 liters of liquor, 2 liters of wine, 50 grams of perfume, 1 liter of eau de cologne, 8 rolls of unexposed film, and 100 meters of recording tape.

**TELEPHONE:** The country code for Suriname is 597.

**GETTING THERE/GETTING AROUND:** The main entrance point is Paramaribo. *Surinam Airways* (note, there's no "e" at the end) flies from Miami to Paramaribo and also provides domestic service. *ALM Antillean, Cruzeiro do Sul,* and *KLM* offer connecting flights to Suriname. A coastal road connects Paramaribo with the borders of French Guiana and Guyana, and there are some roads to the interior; at the time of this writing, however, travel to the interior by roads was not advised due to civil unrest in the area. Domestic air service and boats along the rivers are the best alternatives.

**CLIMATE:** Hot, humid, and tropical with temperatures between the 70s and 90s F throughout the year. There are two rainy seasons: from April through June and from December through January.

**LANGUAGE:** Dutch is the official language, but there is a smattering of Chinese, Javanese, Sarnami Hindustani, Sranan Tongo, and Surinamese. English also is widely spoken.

**ELECTRICITY:** Most hotels use 110/127 volts. Some of the major hotels have outlets for shavers for both 220 and 110/127 volts.

**MONEY:** Suriname guilder or florin.

**CALCULATING COSTS:** US travelers will find that accommodations with creature comforts are very expensive in Suriname. Top rates in tourist-style resorts can rise to $180 per night for a double room (at the official exchange rate, not the black market rate); in the moderate range, $30–$80. Guesthouses, usually under $30, offer fairly primitive facilities.

**TIPPING:** In restaurants, tip 10% unless a service charge has been added to the check. Porters should get 50¢ per bag, but never less than $1. Taxi drivers are not tipped.

**BANKING/BUSINESS HOURS:** Banks are open weekdays from 7:30 AM to 2 PM. Business hours are 7 AM to 3 PM, Mondays through Fridays. Stores are open weekdays from 7:30 AM to 4:30 PM, and until 1 PM on Saturdays.

**HOLIDAYS:** *New Year's Eve* (December 31), *New Year's Day* (January 1), *Day of the Revolution* (February 25), *Carnaval* (February 20), *Holi Phagwah* (Hindu New

Year, in March or April), *Good Friday* (April 9), *Easter Sunday* (April 11), *Easter Monday* (April 12), *Labor Day* (May 1), *Idul Fitre* (Muslim New Year, in May or June), *Unity Day* (July 1), *Independence Day* (November 25), *Christmas* (December 25), and the day after *Christmas* (December 26).

**SPORTS:** Golf, fishing, tennis, cricket, and soccer.

**SHOPPING:** Imaginative woodcarvings, gold and silver jewelry, and woven fabrics are the best buys in Suriname. It is customary to bargain in the markets.

**AIRPORT DEPARTURE TAX:** There is no domestic departure tax; international: about $17.

# Uruguay

**TOURIST INFORMATION:** *Uruguayan Office of Tourism:* 541 Lexington Ave., Suite 356, New York, NY 10022 (phone: 212-755-1200, ext. 346). *Uruguayan Embassy:* 1918 F St. NW, Washington DC 20006 (phone: 202-331-1313). *Uruguayan Consulate:* 747 Third Ave., 21st Floor, New York, NY 10017 (phone: 212-753-8191).

*US Embassy in Uruguay:* 808 Abadie Santos, Montevideo 11200 (phone: 2-770950).

**ENTRY REQUIREMENTS AND CUSTOMS:** US citizens require a valid passport and a round-trip airline ticket. Travelers are entitled to bring in 2 cartons of cigarettes and 2 bottles of liquor.

**TELEPHONE:** The country code for Uruguay is 598.

**GETTING THERE/GETTING AROUND:** The main entrance point is Montevideo. Although there is no nonstop service from the US to Uruguay, *LanChile* and *United* provide direct flights to Montevideo. *Aerolíneas Argentinas, Iberia, LAB, LADECO, LAP, Pluna,* and *Varig* offer connecting flights. *Pluna* is the national airline, offering flights within South America and between Uruguay and Spain. Domestic routes are very limited. A good network of roads links the interior with the capital. There is ferry and hydrofoil service between Buenos Aires, Argentina, and Colonia. Bus service is reliable. Overland travel is the best way of reaching the interior. Boats travel to a number of ports along the Uruguay River, Carmelo, Mercedes, and Salto.

**CLIMATE:** Its warm, temperate climate and 200 miles of Atlantic Ocean beaches have earned Uruguay the nickname the "Riviera of South America." Daytime temperatures from December through February are in the 80s F, dropping into the 60s F at night. In winter, between June and September, the temperature drops into the 40s F and skies turn foggy.

**LANGUAGE:** Spanish is the official language. English also is widely spoken.

**ELECTRICITY:** 220 volts.

**MONEY:** Peso.

**CALCULATING COSTS:** Hotel rates are quite reasonable in Uruguay — averaging $40–$70 for a moderately priced double room. Coastal resorts are more expensive, especially in summer (December–March), ranging anywhere from $40–$165 for a double room. Advance reservations in season are essential. The welcome bargain in this country is its restaurants. The expensive classification covers a three-course meal for two (including wine and coffee) for $25–$35. Moderate meals cost between $15–$25; inexpensive ones, under $15. Restaurants in Montevideo are more costly; an expensive establishment can charge as much as $50 for two (not including drinks and tips).

**TIPPING:** In restaurants, tip 10% of the check. Tip porters 50¢ per bag. Taxi drivers get 5% to 10% of the fare.

**BANKING/BUSINESS HOURS:** Banks are open weekdays from 1 to 5 PM. (This varies slightly, depending on season: In summer, some banks open earlier, around 11 AM.) Business hours are 9 AM to 7 PM, Mondays through Fridays (some closing during midday between 1 and 3 PM); 9 AM to 1 PM, Saturdays.

**HOLIDAYS:** *New Year's Day* (January 1), *Epiphany* (January 6), *Carnaval* (February), *Holy Thursday* (April 8), *Good Friday* (April 9), *Landing of the Orientales Day* (April 19), *Labor Day* (May 1), *Battle of Las Piedras* (May 18), *Don José Gervacio Artigas's Birthday* (June 19), *Signing of the Constitution* (July 18), *Independence Day* (August 25), *Columbus Day* (October 18), *Immaculate Conception* (December 8), and *Christmas* (December 25).

**SPORTS:** Soccer, basketball, horse racing, rugby, polo, and hunting are the most popular participant sports. During the summer, swimming, surfing, and sailing attract enthusiasts from all over the continent. Deep-sea fishing is good throughout the year.

**SHOPPING:** Leather clothes and accessories, amethysts, and woolen sweaters, along with antiques and folk art, are good buys.

**AIRPORT DEPARTURE TAX:** For international departure: about $9.

# Venezuela

**TOURIST INFORMATION:** *Venezuelan Tourism Association:* PO Box 3010, Sausalito, CA 94966 (phone: 415-331-0100). *Venezuelan Embassy:* 1099 30th St. NW, Washington, DC 20007 (phone: 202-342-2214; hours are from 9 AM to 1 PM, and from 2 PM to 5 PM). *Venezuelan Consulates:* 1101 Brickell Ave., Suite 901, Miami, FL 33131 (phone: 305-577-0302); 7 E. 51st St., New York, NY 10022 (phone: 212-826-1660).

*US Embassy and Consulate in Venezuela:* Av. Francisco de Miranda, La Floresta, Caracas (phone: 2-284-6111 or 2-284-7111).

**ENTRY REQUIREMENTS AND CUSTOMS:** US citizens are required to have a valid passport, a tourist card (issued by airlines serving Venezuela), and a round-trip ticket. (Do not lose the tourist card, as it must be surrendered upon departure, and it's difficult to get through immigration without it.) Furthermore, whether your trip is for business or pleasure, it's far easier just to indicate on the card "pleasure." (Although when completing business transactions, a business visa may be required.) Travelers are entitled to bring in a reasonable amount of cigarettes and alcohol.

**TELEPHONE:** The country code for Venezuela is 58.

**GETTING THERE/GETTING AROUND:** The main entrance points are Caracas and Maracaibo. The airlines providing direct or nonstop service from the US to Venezuela include *American, Avensa, United,* and *Viasa,* which all fly to Caracas; *Avensa* and *Viasa* also fly to Maracaibo. *Aerolíneas Argentinas, AeroPerú, Avianca, LAB, LanChile,* and *Varig* offer connecting flights. Domestic lines are *Avensa* and *Viasa.* Intercity bus travel from Caracas is quite efficient.

**CLIMATE:** Tropical along the coast, cooler inland. Caracas, at 3,400 feet above sea level, has a consistent, warm climate most of the year, with the temperatures around 70F; nights are cooler in January and February, with temperatures in the evening around 60F. The rainy season is between May and November, but be prepared for sudden tropical downpours at any time. In the Andes, temperatures are in the 60s and 70s F during the day, dropping considerably at night. The rainy season begins in May and lasts until November.

**LANGUAGE:** Spanish, as well as some Indian dialects.

**ELECTRICITY:** 110 or 115 volts.

**MONEY:** Bolívar.

**CALCULATING COSTS:** Hotel rates depend on where you venture, but the average cost of a double room is between $25–$65 per night. East coast beachfront hotels, along with resorts on Margarita Island, are popular with vacationers and therefore more expensive — $50–$85 per night in high season. Advance reservations are suggested for these destinations. Caracas also is relatively costly, with rooms averaging $50–$125 for a double. A three-course meal for two in Caracas will cost $50 and up in expensive restaurants; inexpensive dinners are available for less than $35 (not including beverages and tip). Wine, as a rule, is vastly overpriced.

**TIPPING:** In restaurants, tip 10% if it's not already included in the bill. Porters should get 50¢ per bag, but never less than $1. Taxi drivers are not tipped.

**BANKING/BUSINESS HOURS:** Banks usually are open weekdays from 8:30 to 11:30 AM, and from 2 to 4:30 PM. Some banks are open on Saturdays from 8:30 AM to noon. Business hours are 8 AM to 5 PM, Mondays through Saturdays; some businesses close between noon and 2 PM.

**HOLIDAYS:** *New Year's Day* (January 1), *Carnaval* (February 22–23), *Good Friday* (April 9), *Easter Sunday* (April 11), *Declaration of Independence Day* (April 19), *Labor Day* (May 1), *Anniversary of the Battle of Carabobo* (June 24), *Independence Day* (July 5), *Bolívar's Birthday* (July 24), *Columbus Day* (October 18), *Anniversary of the Death of Bolívar* (December 17), and *Christmas* (December 25).

**SPORTS:** Horse racing, bullfights, and baseball are the most popular spectator sports. Swimming, snorkeling, scuba diving, water skiing, and deep-sea fishing lead the list of participant activities.

**SHOPPING:** Caracas is still a reasonable place to shop (though not as reasonable as Buenos Aires or Quito) due to the strength of the US dollar. Coffee, dark rum, and woolen *ruanas* (ponchos) offer fine quality. Handicrafts are best purchased in the markets of small towns. Margarita Island, off the Caribbean Coast, has a duty-free zone offering liquor, perfume, gold and silver jewelry, and Margarita pearls.

**AIRPORT DEPARTURE TAX:** Domestic departure tax varies from city to city and is between $1 and $2; international: about $10.

# PERSPECTIVES

# History

## PRE-COLUMBIAN ERA

Theories on the geographic formation of the Americas, as well as notions of how they became populated, are many. Some scientists say man first appeared in North America some 30,000 years ago (others say only 12,000) when the last glacial advance froze sufficient water to allow a land bridge to form between Asia and Alaska. The people who walked across the Bering Strait into what are now Alaska and Canada generally wandered south in nomadic bands, existing by hunting and occasionally warring among themselves for territory and game. Eventually they occupied even the southernmost regions of the continent. A more controversial notion put forth by a Portuguese scientist claims migration happened across the polar ice caps, that there was no need for a land bridge between Asia and the Americas. But these theories are constantly being reevaluated as new scientific discoveries shed light on how long humans have lived in different parts of the globe. Some anthropologists and archaeologists claim they have evidence of human populations in the Americas from as far back as 47,000 years. Norwegian explorer Thor Heyerdahl, among others, favors ocean migration theories that claim boats — not overland travel — were the key to spreading *homo sapiens* around the world. He postulates that South America — specifically Peru — may have been the key point in this population movement. Other seafaring migration explanations start with people living in coastal Siberia, claiming they sailed along the Pacific coast of first North, then South, America.

No matter which theory you accept, it is clear that ancient humans eventually occupied even the southernmost regions of the Americas; there is evidence of Stone Age hunters in Patagonia from as many as 20,000 years ago. According to archaeological findings of a formative sedentary agricultural community in the central Peruvian Andes, tribes began cultivating seeds for planting squash, corn (which is thought to have been brought from Mexico), beans, and peppers as far back as 5,000 years ago. The llama was domesticated as a draft animal and used as a source of meat and fleece around that time, too. And pottery, the solid clue of a settled culture, may have originated in Venezuela 4,000 years ago, an innovation that was adopted by other nascent civilizations in the Andean region that now forms Ecuador and Peru. In Peru, agricultural and fishing communities evolved into villages. Where food supplies were stable enough to permit expansion and specialization of production, some men became farmers, some became potters, and others, warriors. Peru and Ecuador perhaps have the oldest and most varied history of the continent. The spread of culture and the control of one group by another began early in northern Peru. By 1000 BC, the culture known as Chavín was influencing coastal development.

Chavín highlights two elements that became characteristic among pre-Columbian civilizations: an elaborate religion that usually assigned religious significance to natural phenomena — animals, weather, changes in the sun, moon, and planets — and finely developed artistic skills displayed in metalworking and ceramics and in the design and construction of massive buildings and temples. The influence of Chavín can be seen in many subsequent Peruvian civilizations; for example, the artistic style found in the Nazca culture of the 2nd century AD on Peru's southern coast clearly reflects Chavín.

Several groups that once existed have become known as the "forgotten peoples" of pre-Columbian history. Certain indigenous tribes, however, have perservered in the Caribbean area to this day. The Kuna tribe in Panama, for example, was until recent times cut off from contact with neighboring peoples because the isthmus of Panama formed a cultural barrier. To the north, the development of civilization was predominantly influenced by the Central American Olmec cultures (from 1000 to 500 BC) and later by the Maya. South of the isthmus of Panama, the Chibcha-speaking people of the Bogotá Valley in Colombia produced remarkable works of gold that led the 16th-century Spanish conquistadores to search for El Dorado ("The Golden Man"), the legendary ruler who was ritually bathed in gold. In the Atacama Desert of northern Chile and the area that is now northern Argentina lived a number of pre-Columbian tribes who now are virtually extinct. The indigenous inhabitants of the Colombian and Venezuelan coasts conducted trade with and later migrated to several Caribbean islands.

The extent of communication among these formative cultures and civilizations still is under investigation and the subject of keen debate. Nonetheless, there are sufficient clues — duplication of styles found in early Mexican, Ecuadoran, and Peruvian ceramics; apparent similarities in mythology and worship; the discovery of Chilean gemstones in the ancient graves of northern Peruvian Indians; and evidence of a seaborne trade from Ecuador — to surmise that social and commercial intercourse was as prevalent and crucial as conflict and conquest.

Yet the heart of the great South American civilization lies in Peru. The dry, overcast, sandy plains that form the coast of Peru experienced a continual refinement of culture. The evolution of Peruvian civilization can be accurately traced through the manifold techniques of ceramics: from the sculpted human likenesses of Mochica pottery (as early as 300 BC) found in the northern Lambayeque Valley to the depiction of animals, birds, and fish on the pottery of the later Nazca group. The Nazca civilization — whose mysterious line drawings scratched on the Peruvian coastal desert have stimulated fantastical speculation about the possibility of communication with outer space visitors — existed from the 3rd to the 8th century AD. There is an abundance of intact specimens of work dating from this period, work that allows scholars to pinpoint accurately separate periods of historical development. Weaving was a special Peruvian art; the finely crafted burial shrouds of the Paracas Peninsula south of Lima date back to 500 BC. They are woven of finely spun cotton on the once almost universally used backstrap loom. Many examples of this art exist, preserved in the arid soil of the Peruvian coast. The skill of the Peruvian weavers is considered unequaled to this day.

By the 9th century AD, two more complex groups appeared; the Tiahuanaco, on the plains of Bolivia near Lake Titicaca, and the Chimú in Peru. The city built by the Tiahuanaco poses an architectural mystery: The famed stone archway now referred to as "the Gate of the Sun" not only displays faint traces of the earlier Chavín but is clearly a precursor of the Inca. By the 11th century AD, the Tiahuanaco civilization somehow disappeared, either by conquest, disease, or simple attrition. The Inca, when questioned by the Spaniards, confessed that they knew nothing of the people who built the stone monoliths of Tiahuanaco except that they were a far older civilization.

The Chimú civilization evolved on the coast of Peru and was highly developed, more widespread, and more imperial than its forerunners. The Chimú kingdom, with its headquarters in the walled city of Chan Chan, was artistically the most advanced of the pre-Inca civilizations of Peru, and under Chimú overlords, metalworkers, potters, and jewelers made enormous progress. Again, the pattern of growth and organization was largely hierarchical. Chimú, like previous minor empires, was ordered: A priesthood and local autocracy headed a society divided into functional classes of soldiers, artisans, farmers, and workers.

Despite the presence of the great Chimú culture, in the mind of most tourists, Peruvian history actually began in about the 15th century AD, when a small tribe near the valleys north of Lake Titicaca began the conquest of the Andean Sierra. Rapidly achieving dominance in the mountains, this clan, called the Inca, swept down to the coastal regions and subjugated the powerful Chimú kingdom.

The Inca most likely originated from a tribe in the Cuzco area. Their mythology claims that they were commanded by Inti, the sun god, to found a capital where a golden shaft would be swallowed by the earth. This was Cuzco, and from here, divinely inspired and divinely led, they commenced their expansion.

To appreciate the Inca contribution to South American history, you must understand their attitude toward conquest and government. They believed strongly in the concept of nation, in bringing disparate peoples together under one allegiance and authority. The Inca often are spoken of longingly by contemporary South Americans; an atavistic current still runs through modern South American thought that glorifies the Inca as the "true" South Americans of the past.

The Inca were successful for various reasons, but an administrative genius and a creative eclecticism were of prime importance. Frankly not initiators, the Inca sought to preserve and consolidate the social and technological features of conquered territories that they found useful. Inca generals were magnanimous in victory, and through such policies as the *mitimae,* whereby entire vanquished tribes were transferred from their native lands to colonize and police new areas, the Inca created a vast empire.

The empire and state existed to serve the interests of the Inca, a term that refers to a hereditary ruling class rather than to a people or race. All productive resources, all energies in Inca society, were channeled to serve "the Children of the Sun," as the Inca dubbed themselves, and they in turn provided their subjects with a totally controlled, albeit safe, society. In this sense the state was a religious dictatorship, not a "socialist" society, as some have claimed. It has become fashionable to describe Inca history glowingly in modern terms, but for the individual citizen, life must have been hard, patterned, and predictable. Inca law was apparently unyielding: Flogging and execution were common punishments for rape, theft, sacrilege, and sheer laziness. Agricultural production was strictly controlled; the crops, which consisted mainly of potatoes, corn, and a cereal grain — *quinoa* (a form of amaranth), were divided into three portions: one-third for the people, one-third for the Inca, and one-third stored for the sun, the ultimate deity. The food management skills of the Inca were, in fact, one of their greatest achievements.

As builders, the Inca were unparalleled masters of stone. Roads were constructed between major population centers to speed the progress of armies and messages; they were invariably built high along mountain ridges for reasons of defense. Fortresses were erected at strategic points along the many valleys of their empire, named Tahuantinsuyo ("Empire of the Four Quarters" — the Inca divided their world into four sectors, with the center at Cuzco). Sacsayhuaman was one such fortress. All this construction took place *without* the use of the wheel.

The Inca were very conscious of the need for good defense; they had many enemies along the rim of their empire, which at its zenith of expansion encompassed Ecuador, Peru, Bolivia, and parts of Argentina, and extended as far south as the Maule River in Chile and as far north as what is now Colombia. Beyond the Maule lived the Arauca Indians, warriors who successfully resisted both the Inca and Spaniards until 1850, when a peace treaty was signed with the Chilean republic.

One of the most astonishing facts about the Inca dynasty was how long it lasted — barely more than a century. Inca legend claims that there were 14 Inca in the ruling dynasty, although the exact number may have been fewer. The population of Tahuantinsuyo is disputed by authorities, and estimates run from 1.5 million to more than 12 million. Recent finds indicate that agricultural techniques and irrigation under the Inca were more highly developed than previously thought (in fact, food output was definitely higher than modern levels). These data support theories that a population exceeding 8 million may not be inaccurate.

There is much that is not known about South America's pre-Columbian past. The unreliability of historical witnesses and the relative paucity of early records (since most pre-Columbian civilizations had no form of writing) leave many fields open to fruitful study and entertaining speculation. Improvements in dating methods and new archaeological excavations already have prompted researchers to alter some historical eras by hundreds of years. The Andean area, in particular, attracts anthropologists and archaeologists eager to sift through the Inca past. It is now clear that the Inca civilization that began in the 15th century was neither old nor auspiciously long-lasting. In a sense, a whole history stops at the end of the 16th century (with the arrival of the Europeans) and another begins.

## CONQUEST AND COLONIZATION

In the 15th century, European traders and sailors became very interested in finding a new route to the Orient through which they could obtain highly valued spices and other rare commodities. Trade with the Orient was lucrative, but travel there was expensive and time-consuming. Finally, in 1492, the Crown of Spain was convinced by an unknown Genoese named Columbus to underwrite his explorations for a shortcut *west* to the fabled Spice Islands. That the world was round was not in serious dispute in Columbus's time: However, the length of its circumference and the presence of an entire continent between the Orient and Europe were not known. Columbus's initial voyages to the Caribbean and the coast of Venezuela and subsequent missions by Amerigo Vespucci produced glittering, enticing reports of an earthly paradise, a realm of innocence and savagery, and a world of gold and immeasurable riches. The actual discovery of South America was a great accident, a monumental example of serendipity. Even the eventual naming of the continent was accidental: A German cartographer came upon one of Vespucci's many maps and began to call the lands America from Vespucci's Latinized first name, Americus. After a short period of probing and limited exploration, it was evident that the New World was indeed immense, and soon exploration became earnest conquest.

To understand the Spanish conquest, it's necessary first to picture 16th-century Spain at the moment of America's discovery. It was the most powerful kingdom in Europe, ruling half of Italy and Flanders. Spain's new monarch, Charles I, was concurrently Charles V of the Holy Roman Empire, defender of the faith. As such, he was responsible for preserving, militarily and politically, the realm of Catholic Christendom. Financial and religious reasons merged to compel Spain to take quick advantage in the New World. All discovered lands were considered part of the Spanish Crown. Thus, Vasco Nuñez de Balboa, the early conquistador who crossed the isthmus of Panama in 1513, claimed the entire Pacific Ocean and all contiguous lands for Spain. A board was established in Seville, the Casa de Contratación, to ensure that only selected Spaniards would be allowed on the new Spanish territory. Hispaniola (now Haiti and the Dominican Republic) was the site of the first Iberian colonies. Cuba and other Caribbean islands were invaded and quickly fell. So rapid was the pace of events that by 1516, a seaborne force of Spaniards was sailing up the Río de la Plata in what is now Argentina.

The pattern of conquest and colonization of South America was in many aspects similar to the process used to pacify Spain itself during the medieval struggle to win the country from the Moors. One feature transposed was the founding of strong urban enclaves, a tactic first used in Spain on conquered territory. (King Ferdinand advised Columbus from a siege city founded outside Granada.) This practice soon became widespread in America.

Through another Spanish tradition, individuals who participated in campaigns in the service of the Crown were rewarded with land and servant-retainers from conquered territories. In the New World, this custom engendered the *encomienda* system, whereby soldiers were awarded lands and Indian vassals as a labor force, with the added proviso that each lord *(encomendero)* care for the spiritual health of those assigned to him. Spanish

America, then, was originally organized along feudal lines according to an old, yet proven, policy. This assured that settlements were widely separated and extremely personalized — an extension of Spanish custom and character. The bureaucracy created to administer these new territories also reflected the strong desire to centralize administration so as to benefit the Crown. Refinements of this class structure are still evident today.

The conquistadores themselves, the military vanguard, were men capable of incredibly heroic yet barbaric deeds. Many possessed the crazed character that permitted feats such as the voyage of Francisco de Orellana, who, with a small band of men, sailed more than 2,000 miles down the Amazon River, plundering Indian villages all along the way in their feverish quest for El Dorado. The explorers were often veteran European infantrymen or simply penniless and nameless men lusting for personal recognition and the riches of gold. And to achieve those ends, they also were capable of intolerable cruelties.

The natives of the continent simply were unable to mount effective resistance to the conquistadores, who had the great advantages of armor, cannons, and horses. This last is perhaps the most salient factor in Spanish victories. (Hernando de Soto once actually won a battle by falling off his horse, terrifying the native onlookers, who believed man and mount were one being.) Mounted charges, cannonade, and quick, close combat usually were sufficient to defeat armed opposition, even though native armies often vastly outnumbered the invaders. The native populations often were immobilized by their own legends and superstitions, which frequently did as much damage to the local cause as European gunpowder.

On the heels of the conquistadores came the inevitable retinue of priests. The Catholic church, ubiquitous throughout the conquest and after, was responsible for some of the most detailed chronicles of the era. Its role in spreading Spanish culture, particularly through 3 centuries of a brutal Inquisition, almost equaled that of the king. Priests participated in mass baptisms and supervised the construction of churches and schools. In some cases, priests presented an earnest defense of Indian rights, a tradition that continues to this day with certain religious orders, such as the Maryknolls.

The most important chapter of the conquest of South America began in 1532, when Francisco Pizarro, an earlier comrade of Balboa's in Panama, landed with 180 men and 27 horses at Tumbes in northern Virú (now Peru) to search for the legendary kingdom of gold. Pizarro was fortunate. The last Inca, Huayna Capac, had died, leaving the empire split between his legitimate heir, Huascar, and his favored, but illegitimate son, Atahualpa, by a princess of Quito. Atahualpa warred against his half-brother (eventually having him killed), and the civil war that plagued Tahuantinsuyo at the time of Pizarro's arrival was exploited by the conquistador throughout the campaign — a situation and tactic successfully employed as well by Cortés in Mexico. The Spanish and Atahualpa met in the city of Cajamarca in November 1532. After a violent, quick battle, the Inca warrior was captured and eventually executed, and the reign of the divine Children of the Sun ended. Their empire rapidly disintegrated. Cuzco was occupied and plundered the following year; true to Spanish habit, however, Pizarro made his capital — Lima, City of Kings — on the coast.

Later expeditions, by Mendoza to Buenos Aires in 1535 and by Valdivia to Chile in 1540, resulted in the settlement and colonization of those areas. By the middle of the 16th century, Spain was secure in South America. Conquest and preliminary colonization were accomplished by no more than 30,000 European immigrants.

Although Spain was the major European influence in South America, Portugal's presence in the New World was secured by the early (1493) Treaty of Tordesillas. This was actually a papal decree granting the Portuguese rights to all lands east of a longitude some 370 leagues from the Cape Verde Islands. The Portuguese exploration and colonization of that area of the continent they called Brazil (from *braza,* or hot coal; the term described a certain tropical tree found on the coast) was sporadic and slow. There were Indian tribes to dominate but no wealthy empires to conquer. It was not until 1540 that the Portuguese Crown began to found settlements in earnest on the coastal areas of Brazil. The territory over which they had theoretical sovereignty was huge. Soon the English, the Dutch, and the French were establishing beachheads on the northeastern shores of the continent. These countries — now called Guyana, Suriname, and French Guiana — became the only non-Iberian enclaves on the continent.

## INDEPENDENCE

South America enjoyed (or suffered) colonial status for over 300 years. Spain instituted elaborate systems of management to exploit her territories effectively, dividing the continent into the viceroyalties of New Spain (Mexico); New Granada (Colombia, Venezuela, and Ecuador); Peru (Peru, Bolivia); La Plata (Argentina); and Chile. The Spanish king was sovereign, represented by his viceroys; however, local criollo (native-born of Spanish blood) authorities were always able to circumvent the maze of royal regulations that limited their activities. They became, in effect, individual barons in their own areas. The Crown's authority was respected but, more often than not, ignored. This was, again, a Spanish tradition that soon became a South American custom, exaggerated by the immense distance between Spain and her colonies.

Spain's long reign was considered peaceful, and few wars or incidents of violence marred the colonial period. Visitors to the colonies frequently would remark that the mail service was surprisingly swift and travel relatively safe. A rather indulgent viceroyal society grew up in those port cities founded by the conquistadores, often in complete isolation from the vast undeveloped hinterlands and in relative isolation from other royal capitals. Lima was considered the historical center of administration and trade, for Peru was the wealthiest and most valued viceroyalty, far richer in precious metals than the others. All trade filtered through Lima. Even products from Argentina were carried through Lima to Panama for eventual shipment to Seville. The Hispanicized cities flourished culturally and economically, especially the viceroyal cities, but the enormous countryside was largely ignored.

The Europeans' attitude toward the Indians in the rural savannahs and mountain villages was at least partially tempered by the religious conviction that, even though demonstrably inferior, the "childlike" natives did possess immortal souls. Church-inspired lip service, however, did not protect their underlings from enforced labor, disease, and suffering, especially in areas like Potosí in Bolivia, where silver miners spent virtually their entire lives underground. One social development was of critical importance: free intermarriage between the Spanish victors and the vanquished Indian. This was carried out with libertine fervor from the earliest days of the conquest. The mixed offspring — the mestizo (literally, "mongrel") — enlarged the population base and produced a cultural melding. As time went on, this offered a basis for the argument that South American society has a unique heritage and that a true Latin American consciousness has emerged through the centuries.

Despite this widespread intermarriage, power remained firmly in the hands of the Spanish and criollos, who became the dominating class. This group gradually began to resent Spain's economic control, especially its policy of buying raw materials inexpensively and selling finished goods at dear prices, so that "two cents of Peruvian cotton sent to Spain became a four-dollar handkerchief sold in Buenos Aires." In addition, trade with any country other than Spain was prohibited and taxes paid to the Crown were hefty. Spain was determined to isolate her possessions from the world and keep them subservient. Even those colonials who considered themselves loyal and patriotic Spaniards became estranged, their ambitions curbed by royal control.

Economic reasons for separation from Spain joined other motives, often conflicting in nature. Native merchants and landlords came to mistrust Spanish administration for the surprising reason that it was too liberal; strong laws protecting Indian rights jeopardized the ruling class's social and economic status. In an opposite vein, enlightened thought, born of the American and French revolutions, slowly became somewhat popular in the urban intellectual centers of South America. While the impact of such ideas should not be overstated, there were enough daring individuals who found democracy and federalism romantically appealing. An early example of the contradictory nature of the revolt was the uprising of Túpac Amaru, a Peruvian Indian *cacique* (a leader with political and commercial power), in 1780. Although his Indian army was dispersed after a year, his rebellion was carried out in the name of the king to protest the unfair advantages accumulated by the criollo minority of his country.

Another development in Europe hastened the movement toward emancipation: the deposition of the Spanish king by Napoleon in 1810 and the installation of Napoleon's brother as ruler. Here was a situation that all could deplore. War was declared on the French king holding a Spanish throne, and he was condemned as a threatening liberal and a usurper. Patriotism in the name of the mother country was converted to South American nationalism.

Serious attempts at rebellion began in Venezuela in the early 19th century. After several preliminary failures against Royalist forces led by Francisco de Miranda, the Venezuelan patriots, along with some British allies, rallied under the young Colonel Simón Bolívar.

Bolívar was an extraordinary individual — a period Romantic (he was greatly admired by the English poet Byron), a democrat, a well-traveled intellectual. He was all of these, but he was also a shrewd realist who recognized the shortcomings of his countrymen and the difficulties of waging war in America. He dreamed of a huge nation, Gran Colombia, with a central government modeled on the recently independent United States, and managed to lead his little army brilliantly to a series of hard-fought victories in Caracas and Bogotá, eventually advancing to Guayaquil in Ecuador.

At the same moment, General José de San Martín secured Argentina and began preparations for an epic campaign across the Andes to free Chile from Royalist control. San Martín was an accomplished soldier and a meticulous tactician (he had learned his craft in the Spanish army years earlier); he easily defeated the Spanish and Royalist garrison in Chile. He then turned north, taking his army by sea to Lima, and occupied the capital city, which had been abandoned by the Peruvian viceroy and his followers for the safety of the Andean Sierra.

Hitherto, the efforts of the two great patriots were separate and uncoordinated, but it was felt that a unification of forces would be necessary to successfully confront the strong Royalist army encamped in the mountains. A meeting was arranged in 1822 between the Great Liberator (Bolívar) and the Protector (San Martín). Perhaps it was inevitable, but the two could not agree on postwar policy; San Martín was somewhat of a monarchist, Bolívar, ever the republican. Sorely dejected, San Martín exiled himself to Europe, leaving Bolívar free to enter Peru and soundly defeat the Royalists at the Battle of Ayacucho in 1824.

The wars for independence ravished many areas of the continent. Venezuela was extremely hard-hit, with bands of armed men looting the countryside, burning villages, and settling regional rivalries and petty jealousies by force. The great conflict was actually a civil war, where a victorious minority "liberated" the majority against their will. The Spanish colonial apparatus holding the territories together was shattered, and with nothing immediate to replace it, so was Bolívar's dream of a great South American union. His postwar travels were telling: Upon his arrival in southern Peru, the entire area seceded from the old viceroyalty and, perhaps in misplaced gratitude, adopted the name Bolivia in honor of the Great Liberator. Bolívar's own Gran Colombia in the north split into the three sovereign Republics of Ecuador, Colombia, and Venezuela. The noblest efforts of great men were insufficient to overcome the centuries of local history, local enmities, and the sudden collapse of common authority. Writing near the end of his life (he died poor and alone), Bolívar expressed his misgivings and disappointment: "I was in command for twenty years, and during that time came to only a few definite conclusions. (1) I consider that, for us, America is ungovernable; (2) Whosoever works for a revolution is plowing the sea; (3) The most sensible action to take in America is to emigrate; (4) This country will ineluctably fall into the hands of a mob gone wild, later to fall under the domination of obscure small tyrants of every color and race."*

Brazil's experience was substantially different and somewhat more fortunate. Whereas Spanish America was under a relatively tight colonial system, Portuguese America prospered under a more pliant rule. The mother country had other important interests in Africa and in the Far East, so the Brazilians were largely left to themselves. One major factor that hastened Brazilian

*Carlos Rangel, *The Latin Americans* (New York: Harcourt Brace Jovanovich, 1977), p. 6.

development was that the port cities were open to shipping with all nations, which allowed a thriving trade with Great Britain. The other was that its independence, which again was in part the result of the Napoleonic invasion of Portugal, was relatively peaceful and orderly.

Dom João, the Regent of Portugal, fled his country upon Bonaparte's invasion, transferring his throne to Rio de Janeiro. Brazil became the legal seat of the sovereign, equal with Portugal itself. Brazilians welcomed Dom João's arrival and even lamented his eventual departure to recapture his throne, which meant that Brazil again would become a colonial appendage. Dom João, however, left his son, Dom Pedro, behind in Brazil as his regent; he quickly was elevated to be Emperor Dom Pedro I of an independent Brazil. The transition from colony to monarchy under the continuity of a single royal house was accompanied by the transfer of an intact colonial administration to national hands. Free from the disasters of combat, Brazil enjoyed qualitative advantages over its continental neighbors during its period of national infancy.

Any hopes for a union of the fledgling republics soon were dashed after the failure of the 1826 Conference of Panama, which Bolívar called to unite the republics by treaty and mutual agreements on trade and foreign policy. Only four nations sent representatives. Instead of concentrating their efforts on items of common interest and hemispheric solidarity, the new nations attempted to resolve their individual problems of reconstruction and eagerly defend their newly perceived self-interests and responsibilities or, conversely, defend historic claims.

The first 60 years of independence were marked by internal disorder, war, and a constant change of government. The familiar pyramid social structure of South America, the obvious legacy of the colonial era, was more firmly entrenched by the political behavior it inspired. Most of the republics fashioned constitutions similar to the US document (Argentina's was so like the US Constitution that Argentine jurists frequently quoted US legal precedent). In most cases, however, the criollo caste easily dominated national congresses and executive branches through deliberately limited suffrage. In practice, politics became caudillismo, strong man regimes, where the powerful and influential would seize the government and rule alone, couching their decrees in vague ideological terms. In many cases, the wars of independence created a military caste system, the armed forces being the symbol of nationhood and often the only instrument available to preserve order. Peru's political history has developed along such lines, divided between *militaristas* and *civilistas.* By 1879, Chile had a navy superior to the US fleet of the time, and was able to defeat Peru and Bolivia handily in the War of the Pacific. And in perhaps the saddest example of military adventurism, Paraguay, desiring primacy in the Río de la Plata region, challenged Uruguay, Argentina, and Brazil in the War of the Triple Alliance (1865–1870). In that bloody encounter, Paraguay lost most of its male population.

The Roman Catholic church was one institution that survived and prospered after emancipation, and in several cases it was constitutionally the only legally permitted faith. From the beginning, the church dominated all education and was actively involved in formulating social policies (the *encomienda,* for example). No political activity was possible without the assent of the ecclesiastics. The canonical attitude of Catholicism meshed with Spanish legalistic tradition to form an inherently strict, conservative factor in Spanish-American society.

Independence also thrust the republics into the arena of overseas foreign policy. Great Britain was the first nation to recognize the South American nations. With the opening of the ports to British vessels, a long, profitable period of British economic ascendency was under way. Argentina was the major beneficiary of British investment; by 1890, one-quarter of Argentina's population was foreign-born. Buenos Aires grew into a European-style capital, her upper classes very "English." By the same year, the British had built almost 6,000 miles of railroad to transport grain and refrigerated beef to the coast for shipment to Europe. Chile's early years were similar. While immigration to Chile was not as voluminous, a European-style society based on large farms and nitrate mining evolved to make it the second most developed Spanish-speaking country in Latin America.

Brazil, under Emperor Dom Pedro, was following a different course. The Spanish-speaking countries always have considered Brazil a separate entity with a distinct historical heritage. Brazilians, who happily proclaim that "God is Brazilian," gladly share the opinion. Successive booms in coffee and rubber propelled Brazil to wealth, and São Paulo became one of the largest, most industrial cities in the Southern Hemisphere. Slavery was a particularly Brazilian issue. The practice was not terminated until 1888. The following year, Dom Pedro was forced to abdicate, a republic was proclaimed, and Brazil began to resemble her Latin neighbors more closely.

The reaction of the US to Latin American independence was the 1823 promulgation of the Monroe Doctrine, which declared that the US would not tolerate European interference in hemisphere affairs or attempts at new colonization (which included a feared reconquest by Spain). It also announced, in vague principle, a commonality of interests between the US and the Latin American countries. The Monroe Doctrine certainly did not deter Britain from expanding its direct investments; it continued to dominate Latin American economic growth until the turn of the century. It was, however, an early statement of principle and attitude that the hemisphere was American, north and south, and that the US, from the beginning, rather unilaterally assumed the role of leader and protector, teacher and policeman, on its side of the globe.

## THE TWENTIETH CENTURY

The eventual ascendency of the US in hemispheric relations dates from the American victory over Spain in 1898. The US occupied Cuba and Puerto Rico (and, intermittently, Nicaragua and the Dominican Republic). Such open interventions were based on an addendum to the Monroe Doctrine known as the Roosevelt Corollary (named for Theodore Roosevelt), which stated that the US assumed the right to intervene in any hemisphere nation where disorder threatened North American interests. The great North American interest was the Panama Canal, and to protect that interest the US arranged for the creation of the Republic of Panama (Panama seceded from Colombia under the guns of a US warship). The canal was completed in 1914. In 1928, US State Department policy shifted, and the Roosevelt Corollary was declared to be inappropriate in terms of the Monroe Doctrine. Franklin Delano Roosevelt's 1933 inaugural address initiated the Good Neighbor Policy, which professed to respect the rights of other nations. This policy was seen as a reflection of government and public disenchantment with the Roosevelt Corollary.

The evolution of US involvement in South American affairs, and US interventionist behavior in particular, was noted with alarm in Latin America. Viewed within the context of the increasing "Americanization" of Latin American society, it demonstrates the often contradictory feelings held by the South toward the North. Latin Americans always have made analytical comparisons between their history and that of Anglo-Saxon Protestant North America, and while greatly admiring and emulating North American society, Latin Americans have not been able to compete, socially or economically, with the US. There have been real grievances in an inherently unequal relationship, yet the concept of a partnership still exists on an emotional and historical level, an affinity based upon all being "Americans."

By the early decades of this century, the US had eclipsed Great Britain as an influence in Latin America. It was largely US interests and capital that developed Venezuelan petroleum, Chilean copper, and Brazilian coffee. Political caudillos became business caudillos, and the wealthy class that produced so many leaders had its allegiance split between its nationalism and the world of international business. Latin America began an economic transformation, but investment was invariably in specialized sectors; it was growth but not development.

These same decades were marked by a hitherto muted demand for social and economic change. The European- and North American–dominated societies were conservative in nature and reluctant to change long-established custom or to threaten their decided economic advantages. But at the same time, they were open to (or vulnerable to) reforms, and in some cases revolutions, to better the plight of the growing numbers of urban workers and rural peasants who comprised the majority of the population. The demands came from different sectors: In Mexico, the *campesino* ("peasant") wanted land, while in Argentina the middle classes wanted a voice in the political process. In 1928, the Peruvian Victor Raúl Haya de la Torre founded the Popular Alliance for the American Revolution (APRA), based on Marxist principles, but tailored to the realities of semi-colonial societies. Venezuela's Acción Democratica party and Mexico's Partido Revolucionario Institucional (PRI) were founded along the same doctrine, but in modern times, this triad of political parties has split on philosophy. Still, APRA has continued to influence South American leftist political theory, for the core of APRA's ideology is an ever popular anti-imperialist stance (including international control of the Panama Canal) and a measured, gradual transition to socialism.

In other cases, change was effected through the old tradition of single-handed leadership. In Argentina, for example, the ultimate *personalista,* Juan Domingo Perón, based his political formula on the underclasses, the famous *descamisados* ("shirtless ones"), and his highly individual ideology encompassed terms ranging from communism to fascism. Caudillismo remained the most common, and perhaps the most effective, method of promoting or arresting change.

After World War II, which had brought undeniable prosperity to many Latin American countries, US global policy tended to ignore Latin America and concentrate instead on Europe and Asia, where communism was perceived as presenting a security threat. US policy in the Western Hemisphere was aimed toward promoting and strengthening regional organizations compatible with American interests.

Dreams of an effective program of inter-American cooperation remained alive after the ill-fated Panama Conference of 1826. In 1890 the first conference of Latin American diplomats was held in Washington. Successive meetings in Mexico, Buenos Aires, Lima, and Rio de Janeiro culminated in the founding of the Organization of American States (OAS) in 1948. Although begun under US auspices, the OAS provided a useful forum for discussion and cooperation in science and culture.

A new, troublesome chapter in hemispheric relations began on January 1, 1959, when the guerrilla army of Fidel Castro entered Havana, toppling the dictatorship of Fulgencio Batista. When it became evident that Castro was a dedicated Communist and clearly allied with the Soviet Union, the US reaction was severe enough to prompt an attempted invasion and even the threat of nuclear war. It was one of the very few times in the modern era that a major foreign power gained an ally in the hemisphere, and communism immediately became the dominant theme in inter-American politics.

In order to promote political and economic stability in Latin America, and thereby counter the growing Communist influence, the US under President John F. Kennedy upgraded the partnership concept by announcing the Alliance for Progress, a massive program of construction and development. Leaders in most hemisphere nations were at last becoming convinced that poverty and inequality bred dangerous social unrest and placed the political and economic status quo in jeopardy. The focus of political and economic responsibility began to shift toward ameliorating these long-standing conditions; reform programs and true developmental economic policies won acceptance and legitimacy. This sense of urgency was accompanied by Latin America's demand for continued US leadership and contributions in assisting its development, openly welcoming North American overtures.

The events of the 1960s and 1970s highlighted the growing love-hate relationship between Latin America and the United States, as well as the inseparability of their histories. As the wealthier, more powerful neighbor, the US still was held accountable for much of Latin America's difficulties; at the same time it was assumed that the US would, by good intentions, examples, and deeds, assist in providing solutions.

Expectations today are complicated by the diversity of Latin American interests, for the US has had a tendency to treat the continent as a semi-homogeneous bloc. New US policy suggestions, based on country-by-country appraisals, have served to improve relations. The 1978 Panama Canal Treaty, which grants Panama sovereignty over the canal by the year 2000, also has been favorably received, for it symbolizes the rectification of an old injustice. Though Panamanian political upheavals during the 1980s cast doubts on the future of the treaty, the US invasion of Panama in 1989 and the subsequent ouster of Panamanian strongman Manuel Antonio Noriega enabled the democratically elected president, Guillermo Endara, to take office. However, the prospect of Panamanian sovereignty over the canal remains unsettled. Because of the severe deterioration of its railroad and ports, there was talk of renegotiating parts of the treaty so that the US would retain some role in the running of the canal.

Contemporary Latin America features an ever-widening disparity of interests and levels of culture. The impelling force is nationalism, which shapes and directs the social and political paths Latin American nations follow today. Each nation is keenly aware of its own history and problems and its own heartfelt destiny. The experiences of four major nations illustrate this.

Brazil is clearly the largest and most populous of the Latin American republics. Brazil's experience has been qualitatively different, but Brazil has periodically taken part in what was once considered a Spanish-American tradition, that of military rule. The same forces of internal disorder — or fear of internal disorder — have caused Brazil to pursue repressive policies to protect its sometimes mighty, sometimes faltering, economy. The belief that Brazil is a first-rate power — even a nascent superpower — is strong and has been demonstrated. Brazil sent combat troops to Europe during World War II and today builds its own jet aircraft. Until the late 1980s, the US favored Brazil economically and strategically (hence ex-President Nixon's declaration: "As Brazil goes, so goes South America"), but the 1980s also saw nations of the Pacific Rim making investment inroads in this economically troubled nation. Brazil's current president, Fernando Collor de Mello, must contend with record-high inflation and a sky-high foreign debt. In an attempt to stop inflation, Collor froze wages and prices in early 1991. Whether he succeeds in staving off economic collapse with free market policies still remains to be seen.

These problems are exacerbated by the fact that its neighbors view Brazil with a mixture of envy and mistrust. The mere fact that all South American nations — except Panama, Ecuador, and Chile — share a border with Brazil is not overlooked.

Argentina is a nation with frustrated historical ambitions and presumptions of rather great proportion. Argentina's European society is more homogeneous and more educated than some of its sister republics, and Argentines have felt that their nation could have become the Colossus of the South, matching the US in wealth and prestige; its failure to do so led Argentina to the most sophisticated anti-Americanism. Argentine foreign policy has been unpredictably independent: Only under great prodding did Argentina declare war on Germany during the last war. The Argentine government, however, showed a willingness in 1991 to follow US wishes during the Persian Gulf war; it was the only South American country to send troops to the Middle East.

What the future politics will be in post–Falkland War circumstances remains to be seen; but meanwhile, the 1984 return of civilian government to Argentina by popular election was cause for cheering both here and abroad.

Democratic rule has endured, although when the Peronista Carlos Saúl Menem took on the Argentine presidency in 1989, he also inherited a legacy of runaway inflation and debt that had been accumulating since the 1970s. Austerity measures intended to prevent a crisis had been imposed at press time, but the success of those actions remained uncertain.

Chile's many decades of almost uninterrupted republicanism and prosperity ended in 1970, when it became one of the few South American nations to elect peacefully a self-proclaimed Marxist, Salvador Allende, as president. His government faced immense economic problems, many of which were induced by US intervention. Chile's troubles continued to mount and finally resulted in a *golpe de estado* (coup) in 1973 and the subsequent founding of a military government — the first dictatorship ever in the nation's independent history. To this day, many Chileans' response to the military government's repressive policies is: "We never thought it could happen here."

International censure directed at human rights violations by the regime, and continuing economic malaise, isolated Chile from several of its allies. Then in a historic plebiscite in 1988, the Chilean people voted against the wishes of General Augusto Pinochet, president since 1980, and called for democratic elections. Patricio Aylwin was elected chief of state in 1989 in the first presidential election in Chile in 16 years. The main issues this Christian Democrat faces in the 1990s aren't economic — unlike Argentina, Chile has experienced strong growth in recent years and is increasingly attracting foreign investment — but more likely will be political. It will be interesting to see how Aylwin appeases the Socialist and Communist elements of the alliance he formed before the election, and also how he deals with Pinochet's continued presence as commander of a Chilean military accused of widespread torture and murder during his dictatorship.

Peru is the heart of the empire of Tahuantinsuyo; it has, therefore, the largest Indian population among the various countries. This demographic group has not been integrated socially or economically with the cosmopolitan coast. Peru has always been a country of extremes. Even today, desert, jungle, and wealthy cities lie below a mountain "nation" that in many ways still lives in the 16th century. Lima and other urban centers have become clogged with people migrating from the bleak Sierra in search of jobs and a better future. Faced with a duality of cultures, the problem confronting Peruvians is: Which is the real Peru? Many feel that the Spanish-European influence has been alien and corrupting and would prefer to go back to the Inca past, re-creating Inca "socialism" in a contemporary form. The democratically run election of 1984 ended the long reign of Peru's military regime, and despite the ever-increasing burden of enormous economic problems and terrorist activities by members of the Maoist *Sendero Luminoso* (Shining Path) and the terrorist group *Tupac Amaru,* which believes in returning the country to native Indian culture, the present civilian government continues to survive — barely. In 1990, Alberto Fujimori, the son of Japanese immigrants, was elected President of Peru, defeating the novelist Mario Vargos Llosa in a run-off election. Fujimori, an agricultural engineer with no political background and strong left-wing support, has vowed to continue the battle against the Maoist terrorists that plagued his predecessor, and to finally set Peru's economy on a productive course. Shortly after his election, however, he surprised (and angered) his constituency by adopting a very conservative economic plan that required great sacrifices from the poorest classes in the country. And in April 1992, he declared martial law.

With some 300 million faithful followers, the Catholic church remains the most important enduring institution in Latin America, and in recent years it has become increasingly active in such temporal affairs as human rights and agrarian reform — largely through the efforts of such orders as the Jesuits and the Maryknolls. Although historically conservative, this new "Church of the people" may yet play a significant role in shaping the future for many South American countries, although it continues to block social programs, such as family planning and AIDS education.

The South American nations are undeniably mature members of the greater family of nations and participate in a variety of international organizations and endeavors. Many countries have become active in Third World affairs, often participating in the underdeveloped countries' voting bloc in the UN. Prominent South Americans, such as the Argentine economist Raúl Prebisch, have long been leaders in Third World research. Venezuela was a leader in the formation of the Organization of Petroleum Exporting Nations (OPEC), later joined by Ecuador. Intracontinental cooperation has grown: The republics of Venezuela, Colombia, Ecuador, Peru, and Bolivia have formed the Andean Common Market to coordinate trade and foreign investment policy (and in early 1992 these five countries set up a free trade zone), and the OAS has amplified its activities into creating training programs, export promotion, and the like.

Increasing international exposure and more sophisticated monitoring of internal affairs do place new pressures on South American governments. Through their political processes, several nations in the past and Chile in the present have not been able to deal constructively with dissent and have been accused of repeated human rights violations. On this count, major advances have been made in Argentina and Uruguay since civilians were elected to lead these countries.

## THE SOUTH AMERICAN FUTURE

A large Pan American middle class has been expanding for some time between the traditionally rich and the traditionally poor. Economic growth has led to increased mobility in most Latin American societies, and while the old families still tenaciously influence events, the consumer-oriented middle classes comprise new bases of political power and new sources of fashion and taste. But this phenomenon has also had its spiritual price. Latin Americans often harbor deep feelings based upon what they perceive as the tragedy of their history and the difficulties of modernizing their societies, where old and established habits co-exist uneasily with new social practices.

Latin Americans often feel insecure about their future, sensing that real progress in narrowing the gap between rich and poor classes, and rich and poor nations, is in fact slowing down. Economies still geared to the production of raw materials, coupled with global events beyond their control, have resulted in rates of inflation that would be intolerable for North Americans or western Europeans (often more than 1,000% per year!) — and that are becoming unbearable in many South American countries. Indeed, overextended bank loans, bearing interest rates that the debtor countries are unable to repay, have created both national and international crises of confidence. It is an uphill struggle for the newly elected governments that replaced former military regimes to meet even the basic needs of their people.

Cocaine, and to a lesser extent marijuana, is a billion-dollar industry in Bolivia, Colombia, and Peru, and current efforts to eradicate drug production surely will deprive the people of the Andean nations of a significant portion of their livelihoods unless industrialized countries open their markets to drug-crop substitutes. However, it's doubtful whether the transition from a drug economy to a non-drug economy in these countries will come about peacefully, as drug kingpins and guerrilla elements that profit from the drug trade continue to wage war on their antagonists in order to protect their interests.

At the same time, battles are being fought in the Amazon basin between those who want to exploit it and those who wish to preserve it. The earth's only remaining frontier, as the region has been called, is being opened up by migrant farmers from the south who burn forests to clear pastures, by gold miners whose mercury residues pollute the rivers and who seek to displace the indigenous population, and by industrialists who see the basin's hydroelectrical and petroleum-bearing potential. Environmentalists see the destruction of the Amazon as partly responsible for the stepped-up rate of global warming and depletion of the ozone layer worldwide; the government of Brazil views the region as having the potential for solving the nation's economic problems (although President Collor has pledged to protect the environment). Violence runs rampant in the region, as pioneers fight to protect their claims, and as settlers murder conservationists (such as the Brazilian Chico Mendes). Whether this conflict continues into the 21st century depends on the willingness of the combatants to compromise in a creative way. In this respect, the debt-for-nature swaps — such as the purchase of a portion of Bolivia's foreign debt by a US environmental group in 1987 in exchange for a commitment by the Bolivian government to protect millions of acres in the rain forest — seem a positive step.

Yet the generally unharried pace of life seems to indicate that Latin Americans will continue to live along predictable lines. The discomfort of altering expectations has been tempered by a long history of phlegmatic acceptance and justifiable pride in the many cultural achievements of Latin America. The pre-Columbian nations and their monuments are now appreciated more, and Indian culture, still sometimes a source of embarrassment to some, is undergoing a more respectful evaluation. Colonial art and architecture, the poems of Argentine Jorge Luis Borges, and the contemporary novels of the Colombian Gabriel García Márquez and the Peruvian Mario Vargas Llosa (the unsuccessful candidate for Peru's presidency, whose works are popular in North America and Europe) attest to the richness of the Latin American experience.

George Pendle, an author of many books on Latin America and longtime resident of South America, made perhaps the most concise and accurate appraisal: "The world will hardly look to the Latin American for leadership in democracy, in organization, in business, in science, in rigid moral values. On the other hand, Latin America has something to contribute to an industrialized and mechanistic world concerning the value of the individual, the place of friendship, the use of leisure, the art of conversation, the attractions of the intellectual life, the equality of races, the juridical basis of international life, the place of suffering and contemplation, the value of the impractical, the importance of people over things and rules."*

*George Pendle, *A History of Latin America,* 2nd rev. ed. (Pelican Original, 1971), p. 225. © George Pendle, 1963, 1969, 1971. Reprinted by permission of Penguin Books Ltd.

# Religion

Ever since South America was claimed for the Spanish and Portuguese Crowns, the continent has been officially Roman Catholic. Although historians tend to play down this fact, the new lands were claimed first for God, then for the king. The Spanish and Portuguese were every bit as zealous in their desire to save the souls of the pagan Indians as they were in any of their other endeavors. Ironically, it was a Spanish missionary, Bartolomé de las Casas, who wrote the first work in defense of the Indian, *Brevísima Relación de la Destrucción de las Indias* (Short History of the Destruction of the Indies). This work unleashed the *leyenda negra* ("black legend") that has plagued the Spanish in South America ever since, for it relates the familiar account of the Spaniards' greed and their mistreatment of the Indians. It has been used by many to justify a hatred of the Spaniards and all things Spanish.

The widespread conversion of the Indians may have been misguided, but it was in large part sincere. The Spaniards had to be sincere to last long in the Andes mountains and the Amazon jungle of 500 years ago. The missionaries were convinced that God saved only Catholic souls. They considered themselves members of a more enlightened race and felt it their responsibility to teach the Indians the true religion and to make them follow it. This enabled the Spanish and Portuguese to justify their conquest of the Indians through their feeling of religious superiority.

At any rate, the missionaries must never have heard the maxim about leading a horse to water. They may have gotten the Indians to convert by threatening, punishing, and beating them, but no one knows how many Indians today really believe in Catholicism or how many are just trying to avoid conflict or lessen the number of visits by the clergy. The same holds true for the African slaves converted by the Portuguese. How many of their descendants are sincere Catholics and how many still believe in the African cults is anybody's guess. To this day, there are Catholic missionaries out in the jungle attempting to contact and convert the remaining "pagan" Indians; at the same time, Protestant missionaries all over the continent are trying to reconvert Catholics to Protestantism. The 500-year struggle for lost souls thus continues. Despite all this, most South Americans say they're Catholic.

Unlike Spain and Portugal until just recently, the South American countries have allowed some form of religious freedom and separation of church and state ever since independence, so you will find people of almost every conceivable religion in all the South American nations. If you belong to any one of the major Western religions, you should have no trouble finding a place to worship in any of the larger cities. Many smaller religions are represented as well; but since the tragedy in Jonestown, Guyana, in 1978, most governments continue to keep a close watch on obscure cults, especially those from the outside.

Although the separation of church and state is more theoretical in some areas than in others, it does exist. South Americans tend to be anticlerical, for a number of historical reasons. Most North Americans have trouble understanding this concept and more difficulty in accepting it. South Americans themselves have no problem at all in balancing anticlericalism with a staunch faith in the Mother Church. But it's best to avoid a discussion of the subject. To avoid disturbing parishioners, try to visit churches and cathedrals when mass is not being said. Most likely no one will say anything to you if you interrupt the prayers, but it is one of the reasons for a dislike of tourists.

Whether or not you agree with the philosophy and methodology of the early missionaries, you will come across their influence almost everywhere you go in South America. No one denies their impact on art, architecture, literature, and history, either through their own works or through those of their Indian and African pupils. Jesuits, Dominicans, Franciscans, and others taught the natives and the slaves to read, write, sing, and compose church music. They also showed them how to play European musical instruments, paint on canvas, use new tools, and develop new forms of folk art, clothing, and architecture. A significant number of these students and apprentices went on to enjoy a certain amount of fame and respect.

The Indians, however, did not abandon their old ways immediately; in fact, they never completely gave them up. They rejected some Spanish and Portuguese customs and adopted others, just as the Africans did later.

When the Spanish and Portuguese first came into contact with the jungle Indians, they were horrified. The Jívaro Indians practiced their now infamous head shrinking; many other tribes carried trophy heads and ate their enemies. Human sacrifices and torture were apparently fairly common, although reports of these practices have probably been exaggerated to emphasize how savage and beyond salvation the Indians were. How many of these practices had religious significance is not known. At least some of the sacrifices must have been made to the supernatural spirits in an effort to ensure plentiful fish and game and to banish disease and natural disasters.

Although head shrinking is now illegal, the laws against it are probably not enforced in the jungle. Supposedly, most cannibalistic tribes have died out or have been subdued or converted to Christianity and are now living on missions. What has not been eliminated is the tendency to use hallucinogenic drugs to contact the spirits and supernatural forces. Neither has the dependency on shamans and magic been abandoned. The rites and rituals of most of the jungle tribes have not been organized into a formal cult. Almost everything centers around the magic of the shaman, who avails himself of a variety of herbs and drugs to produce different results. There are many small tribes, each with slightly varying rites and beliefs. If you find the works of Carlos Castañeda (a Brazilian anthropologist who wrote readable accounts based on true experiences with drugs) on the Yaqui Indians of Mexico interesting, you will be absolutely entranced (pun intended) by the South American Indians and their beliefs. The early Spaniards and Portuguese finally gave up most of their attempts to convert the jungle tribes, and many of the Indian practices survive almost unchanged to this day.

There were many Andean and coastal tribes prior to the Inca. Today we can at least partially reconstruct their religions through the myths and legends that have come down to us and through artifacts found at various archaeological sites. The vast number of burial sites in the Andean countries supports the theory that most of the tribes believed in an afterlife, since the bodies were all buried with their possessions to take to the next world.

The coastal tribes apparently worshiped the moon as their ruling deity because it controls the tides of the all-important sea. The sea itself must have had a guiding spirit, celebrated by certain rituals.

Several of the Andean tribes believed in a creator-god, Viracocha, who was later adopted by the conquering Inca. In general, when the Inca defeated another people, they did not try to destroy their religion. The Inca realized that this would cause no end of hatred and hostility — a lesson learned the hard way by the European conquerors. Instead, they incorporated the local deities into the state system of religion and allowed the defeated peoples to maintain their own temples. The most important temples were at Pachacamac, near Lima, and at Chan-Chan, near Trujillo, Peru. The Inca did require that a shrine also be built to Inti, the sun god, near any shrine dedicated to a local god.

It was Inti that the Inca were worshiping when the conquistadores arrived, hence the name Kingdom of the Sun given to their empire. (Contrary to a popular belief, Inca civilization wasn't called this because of the sunny climate of the Andes; the region has a very wet rainy season.) The Inca were as systematic about their religion as they were about everything else. Their subjects were organized into groups called *ayllus,* a sort of tribal arrangement based on kinship. Although each *ayllu* had its own sacred object, or *huaca,* to worship, all *ayllus* also paid tribute to both Inti and a special *huaca* at Huanacauri, near Cuzco. This special *huaca* has since disappeared or been overgrown with vegetation like Machu Picchu. A *huaca* could be almost anything as long as the members of a particular *ayllu* all agreed that it was sacred. *Huaca* also means burial ground, an obviously sacred site. Some Indians preserved the bodies of ancestors (*mallquis*) in stone towers called *chullpas*. Some *chullpas* are still standing at Sillustani in the Puno–Lake Titicaca region.

An *ayllu* could choose the god or spirit of a nearby lake, river, cave, or other natural formation as its *huaca*. All natural formations were believed to be inhabited by spirits, who also caused natural disasters. An earthquake meant that Pachamama ("Earth Mother") was angry. Avalanches, rainstorms, and floods brought about by melting snows were the work of the angry Apus and Aukis who lived on the mountain peaks. (These spirits are called Achachilas by Bolivian Aymaras.) Ccoa, a feline spirit, was believed to inhabit the Ausangate peak in Peru. In fact, all mountains and volcanoes had great religious significance for the Indians, and each had residing spirits. Ccoa caused lightning and hail to ruin Peruvian crops. Knuno, the god of snow, did the same in Bolivia. This animistic system allowed — and still allows — the Indians to believe that they had some control over their destiny. All they had to do to avoid natural disasters was to make offerings to keep the gods and spirits happy. Some of the offerings developed into formal communal rituals such as those that were held during the month of *Inti*

*Raymi* (June 22–July 22), the first month of the Inca calendar. (In modern-day Peru, it is a 1-day celebration that takes place outside Cuzco at the fortress ruins of Sacsayhuaman on June 24.)

While still disputed whether the Inca practiced human sacrifice, especially of young virgins and children, it is certain that animals, especially llamas, were sacrificial items. Llamas are still offered up during *Inti Raymi.* Now, however, the festival is celebrated on *St. John's Day,* and the masks used in the *Diablada* dance have the horns of the Christian devil.

The Indians have held to almost all their other beliefs, whether openly or in secret. Llama fetuses are used as sacred offerings. No Quechua-speaking or Aymara Indian would think of building a new house without burying a llama fetus under the cornerstone to ensure a happy and prosperous life. In fact, you can buy a llama fetus in almost any Indian market.

Another way to appease the gods is to offer them some drink. Before any Indian partakes of his *chicha* (home brew), he faithfully sprinkles a few drops on the ground for Pachamama. If no *chicha* is available, he can make an offering of the ubiquitous coca, a shrub whose leaves, when chewed, release a stimulant. (Although coca is the base for cocaine, coca leaves and their effect bear no resemblance to that of the chemically processed narcotic.) Coca can be used by diviners to foretell the sex of a baby and a number of other facts. Most Indians also believe in diviners, oracles, and omens. Superstition seems to be stronger in Bolivia than in Peru and Ecuador, but the farther you get from the urban centers and the white Catholic influence in any of these countries, the more ancient rituals you will observe. In the most remote areas, the priest comes through only once a year to marry couples, give communion, and bless the deceased.

By worshiping both the Christian God and the pagan gods, the Indians have it both ways. Before you dismiss them as religious hypocrites, however, think of the last time you threw salt over your shoulder, cried over a broken mirror, or crossed a street to avoid a black cat. The Indians reconcile their different religious beliefs just as we do. The missionaries made it easy by placing their cross on the mountain peaks also inhabited by the Apus or Achachilas, and by making religious holy days correspond to existing sacred days in the Indian religions. This mixture of witchcraft, native religion, and Catholicism is a complex, fascinating subject.

The blacks of Brazil have learned that their native African cults have commercial value among the tourists, and the Andean Indians are starting to find this out about their festivals. The *candomblés* of Bahia (West African in origin) and the *macumba* rites of Rio (from Angola and the Congo) often are arranged and practiced in advance, and tourist agencies sell tours that include a visit to one or the other. The blacks distinguish clearly between *candomblé* and *macumba,* but most whites think of them both as voodoo. A third type of ritual, *caboclo,* has been strongly influenced by native Indian cults and is looked down upon by practitioners of the other two. By all means go to these services if you have the chance. Each is slightly different, but they are all equally interesting.

You should bear in mind that the more sincere of these rituals are never performed when outsiders, especially whites, are present. As a result, what you will see is often more theater than religion. This is not to say that there is no sincerity in a staged rite; even there, a participant can feel a spiritual force, causing him or her to fall to the ground and writhe in ecstasy.

There are many more spiritualistic cults all over Brazil, whose members generally come from the lower classes of society. Most of these people also go to mass and worship as Catholics. All cult gods have two names, an African one and a Catholic equivalent. Like the Andean Indians, the black spiritualists have no trouble reconciling the two different beliefs. One helps them function in a Catholic-dominated world; the other allows them to maintain ties with their African heritage and be true to their roots.

If you are a very religious person, try to approach the black and Indian religions with an open mind. If you are black, you may already have the advantage of understanding the historical background on which these cults are based. But attending a ceremony for the purpose of reaffirming a preexisting prejudice does no one any good. These native religions have survived almost 500 years of persecution and are obviously necessary and vital to their followers. As such, they deserve tolerance and understanding.

# Legends and Literature

Modern South America has produced an exciting body of prose and poetry, especially over the last few decades. Chilean poets Pablo Neruda and Gabriela Mistral, the Colombian novelist Gabriel García Márquez, Nobel Prize winners all, and their contemporaries — the Brazilian Jorge Amado, the Peruvian Mario Vargas Llosa (an unsuccessful candidate for his country's presidency), and Argentine Jorge Luis Borges, among them — continue to delight lovers of literature around the world. Besides the works of modern authors, the most interesting aspects of South American literature are the traditional legends. The few masterpieces in the intervening 300 years stand out like pine trees in the Atacama Desert. Even so, there's enough good reading to keep you busy for quite some time.

Although the pre-Columbian tribes had no written language, a rich oral tradition of myths, legends, and folklore was carefully handed down from one generation to the next. Only certain members of each tribe were entrusted with the knowledge of this tradition, which they then committed to memory. The Inca were so systematic about this that, when a noble died, the *amautas* (wise men) met to decide which facts about his life would make it into the "official" Inca history. An ingenious device called a *quipu* was used as an aid to memory. It consisted of a series of knots on strings. The color, size, and way in which each knot was tied indicated something to the *quiposcamayo* (*quipu* reader). The Spaniards never bothered to write down the code of the knots, and the Indians stopped using the system. Why transmit a history of defeat, humiliation, and slavery? So, while *quipus* are displayed in several museums in both North and South America, no one knows how to read them. Much oral literature embodied in the *quipus* has thus been lost forever.

A few of the early legends were preserved by the Spanish chroniclers in their letters and books. Most were either ignored or scorned as the work of the devil. The Spanish scribes claim to have preserved the few surviving legends just as the Indians told them. The problem is that the Spaniards already had started teaching Catholicism to the Indians. So by the time the stories were copied, the originals had probably been influenced by church teachings. In addition, many of the Spanish chronicles have been lost, their pages reduced to dust over the years or destroyed in fires, earthquakes, and wars. (During the War of the Pacific, Chilean troops burned the library in Lima, turning many of the original records to ashes.)

The Indians also may have altered a legend or two to fit what they thought the Spaniards wanted to hear. The story of Atahualpa indicates that this would have been a wise course of action. According to the story, when Pizarro told Atahualpa that the Bible was the Word of God, the Inca chief put the book up to his ear. When he didn't hear anything, he disgustedly threw it to the ground. If it was the Word of God, why couldn't he hear it? This so angered a Spanish priest that he insisted on the chief's death.

Besides the legends rescued from oblivion by the chroniclers, countless others are still told whose origins are unknown. Experts surmise that all the South American tribes had myths about nature gods, especially the gods of the sun and the moon. There were also stories about supreme creator gods, but none of the tribes had a pantheon as organized as that of the Greek gods of Mt. Olympus. The functions of the gods in South American legends are confused by an overlapping of their names and deeds, so it's often hard to determine which god did what.

If you want to go to the source, the best chroniclers are Pedro de Cieza de León, *History of Peru;* Cristóbal de Molina, *Conquest and Settlement of Peru;* and, above all, Garcilaso de la Vega, *The Florida of the Inca* and *The Royal Commentaries of the Inca.* Garcilaso was the son of an Inca princess and a Spaniard, and he should not be confused with a famous Spanish poet of the same name who was a relative of the chronicler.

All the tribes had legends that explained their origins. When the Inca conquered other peoples, they borrowed or changed local legends to prove Inca supremacy. According to the Inca, the sun god Inti felt sorry for man when he saw people living in a barbaric, primitive state. Inti sent his own two children, Manco Cápac and Mama Occlo, to earth to teach man all the arts of civilization. They rose from Lake Titicaca, and from there they were to travel until they found the place where the long golden rod they were carrying would sink easily into the soil. (This is significant because the Inca depended almost entirely on agriculture.) The rod sank into the ground at Cuzco, so Manco Cápac and Mama Occlo founded their capital there. They taught civilization to the natives and converted them to the religion of the sun. As the direct descendants of the children of a god, the Inca believed they had the right to conquer and rule others.

The Tiahuanaco people lived near Lake Titicaca in Bolivia before the Inca came, but less is known about them. They did leave behind apparent irrigation canals and huge, carved stone monoliths over 6 feet high. According to the Inca, these huge statues were originally people who had disobeyed the laws of the creator god Viracocha. Angry at having been disobeyed, Viracocha turned them to stone. (Shades of Lot's wife and pillars of salt?) This same legend is supposed to explain stone statues at other South American sites. A different story states that these monoliths were Viracocha's mock-ups for the peoples he was planning to create.

Viracocha is a rather confusing god (or gods, since he appears in many places with slightly different names and guises). Among other legends describing a great flood are a number of Viracocha stories that are usually called the Deluge myths. At some long-forgotten time, man was evil and lived in sin. This upset Viracocha, so he sent a great deluge to destroy man. Only a select few survived. Viracocha, a white god with a beard, told these men he would return someday. This is supposed to account for the lack of resistance the Indians put up against the white-skinned, bearded Spaniards. In fact, many Indians called their Spanish overseers on the haciendas by the name Viracocha, an equivalent of the "my lord" used by medieval British serfs.

## PERSPECTIVES / Legends and Literature

Some tribes claim their origin from these survivors of the Great Deluge. Others claim to be descendants of lakes or mountains or other nature gods. When you are in the La Paz, Bolivia, region, be sure to take a good look at Illimani or the other great Andean peaks. Natural sites worshiped by the Aymara Indians are called *achachilas,* and these peaks fit into that category. Illimani was supposedly Viracocha's favorite. This is understandable, since it is the most beautiful mountain overlooking La Paz. When the nearby peak Mururata complained to Viracocha that he was jealous of Illimani, Viracocha punished him by breaking off his top, so now he is flat. (Mountains are either male or female, according to Indian beliefs. Two peaks that are close together are usually one of each and small peaks between them are said to be their offspring.) Most residents can point out the peaks to you, but it is the Indians who know the legends.

Since before the Inca conquest, Andean Indians chewed coca leaves, enabling them to better endure cold, hunger, and long hours of work. Supposedly, the Inca reserved the privilege of chewing coca leaves for their nobility. Coca leaves also have medicinal and, the Indians believe, magical powers, and they are used extensively in rituals. The origin of the use of coca, like other important aspects of Indian life, is explained in a legend. A long, long time ago, the subtropical Indians of the Lake Titicaca region moved to new areas in the Yungas, the valleys and foothills of the Andes. When they burned the vegetation to clear the land for planting, the smoke rose and contaminated the mountain peaks. The god of snow, Khuno, woke up and saw what had happened. In anger he flooded the Yungas and destroyed the Indians' homes. When the waters subsided the Indians could find nothing to eat. After much searching they came across a plant with bright green leaves. They discovered that chewing the leaves produced a sudden feeling of well-being. They returned to Tiahuanaco with the news of this wonderful plant, and Indians have chewed coca leaves ever since.

Legends of the Chibcha Indians of Colombia also have survived in one form or another. The creation of the beautiful Tequendama Falls near Bogotá is explained by the myth of Bochica, the chief of the gods. This time it was the god Chibchacum (the name varies) who was angry with the peoples of the Bogotá plateau and flooded their land. (No wonder South America has so many rivers and lakes.) The desperate people appealed to Bochica for help. He appeared in a rainbow, sent the sun to dry up the water, and opened a deep cleft in the rocks to allow the waters to recede. The Tequendama Falls still pour over this split in the cliffs.

The most famous legends of all concern El Dorado. One version appears to have been a Chibcha legend based on an annual ritual. Once a year, the body of a young Indian male would be entirely covered with gold dust. Placed on a raft laden with offerings of silver, gold, and precious stones, he would float into the middle of Lake Guatavita in Colombia. There he would throw the offerings overboard, then jump into the lake to wash off the gold dust. A piece of gold sculpture in the *Museo de Oro* in Bogotá seems to represent this ritual. It depicts a raft with an Indian in the center surrounded by offerings for the god of the lake. Don't miss it if you are visiting the Colombian capital.

Gold was plentiful all over central and northern South America, and it seems that every tribe had a legend of a golden city or a golden people. Also, the fame of the Inca empire, based on its enormous wealth, had spread all over the continent, giving rise to several El Dorado–type stories. Even so, the beauty of the metal itself and its representation as the sun god's rays were enough to inspire myths. It also has been suggested that the Indians repeated and embellished the legends just to watch the greedy Spaniards go trekking off into the dangerous mountains and jungles on wild goose chases. There are to this day dreamers who go off to South America in search of El Dorado, and there have been several fairly recent attempts to drain Lake Guatavita to recover the loot that is supposed to be there.

The Spanish and Portuguese brought several hundred European legends with them, mostly stories of the Virgin Mary and the saints. Once the missionaries discovered that the Indians already had a fondness for this kind of storytelling, they used the legends to help in conversion. The Indians' sensibilities seemed to be especially attuned to Mary because of the many stories of her miraculous appearances. Most European legends have undergone South Americanization, though a few are told in the original version. Others have simply served as inspiration for a South American counterpart.

When the black slaves were brought over from Africa, they carried their legends with them. In the area around Bahia in Brazil, where the African influence is strongest, many of the legends have remained intact since the days of slavery. The others were added to or combined with the large body of oral literature already in existence in South America.

South America's history itself often reads like a legend. The battles of the conquest, the Indian and slave rebellions, and the wars of independence all furnished heroes and other material for stories. Among the more colorful figures are the *bandeirantes* of the Brazilian *sertão* and the gauchos of the pampas of Argentina, Uruguay, and the Rio Grande do Sul of Brazil, as well as the *llaneros* of Venezuela. These men and occasional women loom so much larger than life, it is hard to believe they could ever have really existed. Yet it is with them that life, legend, and literature come together. Many of their names can be found in the history books, poems, novels, and legends time and time again.

The pampas of Argentina are a vast desert of thorny bushes, containing a number of trees and animals found nowhere else. The *sertão* is similar in its vastness, but life there is even harsher because the region is one of the most drought-plagued in the world. The origins of the gauchos and the *bandeirantes* — mestizos of Spanish and Indian blood — are not clear, but they certainly have been out on the pampas and *sertão* since the late 1700s. These cowboys and hunters were social outcasts with little or no formal education, no organized religion, and their own limited concept of law: an eye for an eye and survival of the fittest. It is easy to see how such men and women became the stuff of which legends are made. You had to be strong to survive.

In the case of the gauchos, the reverse was also true: Literature became life. The Argentine poem *Martín Fierro* (1872) was a literary creation of José Hernández, an educated man who had lived among the gauchos and admired them very much. This work is a classic of South American literature, and Argentine students still have to memorize portions of it for school. It is *the* gaucho epic: the story of Martín Fierro and his life out on the pampas, his time in the army during the wars of independence, and his desire for freedom. The poem also deals with the problems this desire causes him with the police and society in general. *Martín Fierro* became very popular and was recited frequently to the illiterate gauchos around their campfires and at their festivals and dances. This hero was so real to them that they began to believe in his existence, and many more legends grew up around his name.

Domingo Faustino Sarmiento's *Civilization and Barbarism: The Life of Juan Facundo Quiroga* is an excellent study of the gauchos and another South American classic. The book is a biography of sorts, but if you are interested in the gaucho, it is the place to start. The work is filled with the author's passion for his subject.

In Brazil, Euclydes da Cunha wrote *The Sertões* (1902), an equivalent study of the *bandeirantes* and their descendants. Unlike Sarmiento's book, da Cunha's is a novel, yet it lacks the personal passion that makes *Facundo* so readable. Da Cunha subscribed to the French naturalist school of thought and, like Emile Zola, thought that a novel should be a scientific study of man's behavior.

Gaucho and *bandeirante* legends have been around almost as long as the people themselves. But the people of these regions are not the only subject. The flora and fauna also have their own stories explaining their origins or unusual characteristics. The *ombú*, for example, is a tree that exists only in the pampas. It is a wonderful shade tree, a necessary shelter in a hot, dry climate, but its wood is of very little use. A myth tells that in the beginning all trees were alike. One day God was in a particularly good mood, and He decided to visit earth to give each tree its wish. He talked to the pine, the oak, and all the other trees; they all wanted to be tall, straight, beautiful, and have hard wood so they could not be cut down easily. Then God came to the *ombú* and asked what it wanted. The *ombú* answered that it wanted to be big so it could give shade to man, but it wanted soft, weak wood. God granted the request, but he was puzzled by it, so He asked the *ombú* why it didn't want to be strong. The *ombú* answered that it never wanted its wood to be used as a cross for the sacrifice of a saint. Ever since then, the *ombú* has had soft, weak wood, and no one bothers to cut it down.

*Bandeirante* and gaucho authors almost inevitably include legends in their works. It is well-nigh impossible to portray a believable gaucho or *bandeirante* without his guitar, his songs, and his stories. So you get two for the price of one: a good novel or poem and myths and legends as well. Because of the disappearance of gauchos, fewer works are being written about them and their lifestyle, and the gaucho is no longer the major theme in Argentine literature. The *bandeirante* held on a bit longer in Brazil, but he too is being replaced by other subjects.

The two outstanding authors of gaucho novels are Benito Lynch and Ricardo Güiraldes. In *Raquela, El inglés de los güesos* (The Englishman of the Bones), *The Romance of a Gaucho,* and *Los Caranchos de la Florida* (The Carrion Hawks), Benito Lynch has captured the language and customs of a dying breed. The epitome of the gaucho novel is *Don Segundo Sombra.* Güiraldes's hero, Don Segundo, is the ideal gaucho. He is a symbol, as his name *sombra* ("shadow") implies. The story really has no plot, but is a series of vignettes of gaucho life. The moment Don Segundo must take leave of his young apprentice is especially touching.

The inhabitants of the *sertão* — from the *bandeirantes* of the past to the present *sertanejo* — have been the subject of many novels. José de Alencar introduced the *sertanejo* to the world in 1870 with *The Gaucho*. (This figure isn't limited to Argentina's literature; he also shows up frequently in Uruguayan literature.) Since then, most of Brazil's leading authors have written about the *sertão*. Da Cunha's novel *The Sertões* (also known as *Revolt in the Backlands*) has already been mentioned. Writing about the same time, José Pereira de Graça Aranha produced *Cana,* a novel with much local color and particularly beautiful descriptions.

José Américo de Almeida started a true literary rebirth in Brazil (the birth had taken place in the early 1800s, just after independence) with his novel *A Bagaceira* (Cane Trash, 1928). The author was born in the *sertão,* so the problems he describes are based on firsthand knowledge.

Graciliano Ramos spent his youth in the *sertão*. He became a staunch defender of the poor and spent time in jail for his leftist views. *Vidas Sêcas* (Parched Lives, 1938) is the study of a poor, uneducated man (the typical *sertanejo*) and his family during two periods of drought. Character development is traced with a very skillful hand.

Rachel de Queirós is not only a regional writer of the *sertão,* but also one of South America's feminist authors, and her novels deal with the position of women in Brazilian society and the need for expanded women's rights. De Queirós herself is a strong character. In a land dominated by *machismo* (while the term is Spanish, the Brazilians understand it well), she published her first novel at the age of 18. *O Quinze* (The Year Fifteen, 1930) tells of the *sertanejos'* struggle for survival during the terrible drought of 1915. It is a strong, sober novel. She has since written the better-known *The Three Marys*.

The Brazilian João Guimarães Rosa wrote only one novel, but it is a masterpiece. Not unexpectedly, the subject is the *sertão*. Unjustly overlooked in its English translation, *The Devil to Pay in the Backlands, Grande Sertão: Veredas* (1956) is fully appreciated in South America. It is a long monologue in which the bandit Riobaldo looks back on his life in the *sertão*. He is convinced that he is a good man who sold his soul to the devil and, as a result, evil forces have plagued him all his life. But in the end he comes to realize that the devil is no more than his own instincts. As a psychological study, this novel is not easily surpassed, and it is still one of Brazil's leading novels.

Then there is Erico Veríssimo, another Brazilian, the novelist of the city, whose books are set in places like boarding schools and hospitals, where people are drawn together by circumstances and then separated. Veríssimo shows the influence of John Dos Passos or perhaps Aldous Huxley in his cross-sectional views of life. Some of his more famous works are *A Place in the Sun* (1936), *Behold the Lilies of the Field* (1938), and *Saga* (1940).

One of Brazil's greatest authors, Machado de Assiz, was also an urban writer. (His full name is Joaquim Maria Machado de Assiz, but he is so well known by his last name that no one remembers the first two.) All of his works have been translated into English and many other languages. The best known are *Memórias Póstumas de Braz Cubas* (Epitaph of a Small Winner), *The Heritage of Quincas Borba* (1890), and *Dom Casmurro* (1900). Machado was a cynic with an ironic sense of humor, and character development is his strongest feature. Some critics considered him Brazil's foremost psychological novelist.

Until recently, most great South American novels were regional in character, and two such other giants of Brazilian literature are José Lins do Rêgo and Jorge Amado. José Lins do Rêgo wrote of the northeastern sugar plantations near the *sertão*. He published what is still considered to be one of the greatest 20th-century South American works, *The Sugar Cane Cycle,* begun in 1932 with *Menino de Engenho* (Plantation Lad) and followed by *Doidinho* (Little Fool, 1933), *Bangüe* (1934), *O Moleque Ricardo* (1935), and *Usina* (Factory, 1936). Lins do Rêgo was raised on a sugarcane plantation and, like the other writers, knew his material well. With *O Moleque Ricardo,* Lins do Rêgo also produced what is perhaps the most interesting study of a black man to be found anywhere in Brazilian literature. The novel avoids all the clichés and stereotypes: Ricardo is not an exotic creature to be studied for his picturesque speech or African customs. He is an average Brazilian who happens to have black skin.

Lins do Rêgo's writing has a light touch, and his love of life shows through in his pages. It is his own childhood and youth that he is describing, and he obviously enjoys sharing it with us. Even such scenes as the young boys' discovery of sex in the barn with the cows are handled in such a way that we feel amused rather than scandalized.

This same sensual approach to life shows up in the works of Jorge Amado, the best-known contemporary Brazilian writer. Although his books are deeply rooted in the Salvador (Bahia) region, they have been translated into many languages. One of his novels, *Dona Flor e Seus Dois Maridos* (Dona Flor and Her Two Husbands), was made into a delightfully erotic film that earned itself an "X" rating in some US cities. Shot in Salvador (Bahia), the photography alone makes this film starring Sonia Braga worth seeing. But the novel is even better.

Amado also created Gabriela, the most popular female character in Brazilian literature. The heroine of *Gabriela, Cravo e Canela* (Gabriela, Clove and Cinnamon) is a charming, barefooted, free-loving spirit. Before Amado discovered the commercial value of sex in fiction, he wrote some of the best social protest work to come out of South America. He described the lives of the street urchins who eke out a living through petty theft and other crimes in *Capitães de Areia* (Beach Waifs). He then turned his attention to the plight of the workers on the cocoa plantations in *Cacau* and *Terras de Sem Fim* (Lands Without End) and to that of the wretched slum dwellers in *Suor* (Sweat). No one has captured the people and life of his native Salvador (Bahia) better than Amado. A recent work is *Tocaia Grande* (Showdown), a novel that traces the bawdy transformation of a frontier crossroads of prostitutes, gunfights, and runaway slaves into a full-size (and respectable) town. And now available in English is *The War of the Saints,* a funny romance novel.

In the Andean countries, the regional and social protest novels were known alternately as Indianist or indigenist. The Indian novel was first written from a point of view outside Indian culture by whites and mestizos. Under the guise of social protest, many of the earlier examples of this genre stressed the Indian's exotic and picturesque elements, which made him a curiosity to outsiders. The first writer to denounce openly the mistreatment of the natives was a woman, Clorinda Matto de Turner, the wife of an English hacienda owner. Although *Aves Sin Nido* (Birds Without a Nest, 1889) was no masterpiece, it did pave the way for what became the main Andean theme for quite some time. In Bolivia, Alcides Arguedas's *Raza de Bronce* is the leading novel of this type; in Ecuador it is Jorge Icaza's *Huasipungo*. While all three novels are noble attempts to awaken their societies to the plight of the Indian, none of them shows any real understanding of the Indians themselves. These writers were merely interested and accurate observers of behavior.

The principal Indianist writers, Ciro Alegría and José María Arguedas, are both Peruvians. Alegría's *El Mundo Es Ancho y Ajeno* (Broad and Alien Is the World) and Arguedas's *Los Ríos Profundos* (Deep Rivers) are masterpieces of Peruvian literature. Arguedas pointed out that since Alegría was writing about the northern Quechua-speaking Indians of the Andes and he about the southern, there was no basis of comparison between them. Although Alegría brings us closer to the Indian than any of his predecessors, it is Arguedas who finally takes us inside the Indian culture. He spent his childhood living among the Quechua, and Quechua was his first language. As far as Arguedas was concerned, the Indians were his people. His works are highly autobiographical, and several of his narrators are thinly disguised versions of himself. Arguedas became something of a martyr after he committed suicide in 1969, claiming that he could no longer help himself or the Indian because he could no longer write. He included pages from his suicide diary in his last, incomplete novel, *El Zorro de Arriba y el Zorro de Abajo* (The Fox from Above and the Fox from Below), referred to by most critics as *The Foxes*.

After Alegría and Arguedas, the Indian seems to have disappeared as an Andean literary subject, much as the Argentine gaucho did earlier. This is to be lamented for at least one reason: The literature included Indian legends and myths. (As an anthropologist and ethnologist, Arguedas had been especially active in collecting and preserving Indian legends.)

Lacking a common theme, the novels of the other South American countries were until recently grouped under the broad category of rural or regional novel. The most famous and still the most popular romantic novel of Colombia (and all of South America) is *María* (1867), by Jorge Isaacs. The plot would make a good opera. Ephraim, the hero, falls in love with his young, orphaned cousin María, an epileptic. When Ephraim is sent to medical school in Europe, María's condition worsens, and she is dying. Ephraim is sent for. Will he arrive in time? There lies the suspense of the novel.

Despite the idyllic setting of *María,* all was not well in the countryside. In *Doña Bárbara,* Romulo Gallego's novel of the Venezuelan llanos (plains), nature is okay, but man is ugly. Doña Bárbara, having been betrayed and savagely raped as a girl, declares vengeance on all men and becomes the most powerful figure of the region by committing all manner of crimes. When

Santos (saint) Luzardo moves to the area, Bárbara (barbarian) falls in love and repents her evil ways. Alas, Santos is not interested in her at all, but in her illegitimate daughter. This is the crux of the final conflict. Gallego's psychological study of Bárbara is one of the high points of the novel. *Doña Bárbara* was made first into a film and later into an opera; it is Venezuela's best-known novel.

*La Vorágine* (The Vortex, 1935), by José Eustasio Rivera of Colombia, is the jungle novel par excellence. Rivera describes the effects of the jungle on man's mind and body in great detail. Quicksand awaits the unwary, snakes hang from trees, and parasites are everywhere. Those who go in rarely come out. Rivera himself was lost for a time in the Colombian jungle, and he was unhealthy for quite a while after he did manage to get out. And, as if the jungle weren't enough to contend with, he describes the cruel and inhuman exploitation of the workers on the old rubber plantations deep in the jungles. These plantations no longer exist, but Rivera's novel is still compelling as a strong indictment of man's inhumanity to man.

Things are no better in today's cities if we are to judge by current works. Uruguay's two most prominent novelists, Juan Carlos Onetti and Mario Benedetti, write about life in Montevideo although they both are in voluntary exile in Madrid. Onetti's themes stress modern man's inability to communicate. In *Tan Triste Como Ella* (As Sad as She Was), *Los Adioses* (The Goodbyes), *El Astillero* (The Shipyard), and *La Vida Breve* (The Brief Life), his characters lead despairing lives. Man goes through the motions of living but never really succeeds at life. Benedetti's work stresses the impersonality of the modern city. The opening of *Gracias por el Fuego* (Thanks for the Light) is set in New York, but the emphasis is on the problems of Uruguayan society and on the inability of his own generation to remedy the situation.

Augusto Roa Bastos is Paraguay's foremost novelist, although he, too, is in exile. His *Hijo de Hombre* (Son of Man) is based on Paraguayan history, including the peasant uprisings of 1912 and the Chaco War of the 1930s. It tells the familiar South American story of the oppressed struggling against the ruling elite and is replete with Christian symbolism, myth, legend, and poetic effects. Paraguay is a place that few outsiders know anything about and even fewer visit, yet Roa Bastos's work has created a new interest in the country.

Current Peruvian fiction is dominated by Mario Vargas Llosa, a novelist and would-be-politician of international stature whose works have been translated into several languages. *La Ciudad y los Perros* (The City and the Dogs) is set in a Lima military academy — the "dogs" are the cadets. The academy is a microcosm of society's dishonesty, betrayal, violence, torture, and bestiality. *La Casa Verde* (The Green House) is set in both the jungle and a brothel in Piura. Vargas Llosa constantly shifts back and forth in time, breaking off a train of thought and picking it up later, thus destroying chronology. The lives of the main characters come together, crisscross, separate, and run parallel, as in life. *Conversation in the Cathedral* is an interesting, complicated series of intertwining conversations. There is a lighter side to Vargas Llosa. His *Pantaleón and the Visiting Service* is a very funny satire on a "service" that the Peruvian government provided for the workers in the jungle oil fields. Vargas Llosa carries his idea to its ludicrous extreme. The hero is originally in charge of a small house with a few prostitutes. As the service grows until he is the biggest pimp in South America, his military superiors must disguise and deny the whole operation. Another humorous novel, *Aunt Julia and the Scriptwriter,* details the misadventures of a young writer who marries his aunt. As in most of Vargas Llosa's works, there are autobiographical traces.

José Donoso leads the field in Chile, and his works are now being translated almost as soon as they are published. *Coronation* deals with the impotence of a ruling class that has outlived its usefulness. Chilean life now belongs to the young and to the working classes, not to the degenerate aristocracy. *The Obscene Bird of Night* deals with physical deformity, insanity, and similar subjects. The sexual scenes are ludicrous, repelling, and anything but erotic. Some of the technical effects are original, and Donoso has an active imagination and a macabre view of life.

Argentina has produced a great number of topnotch modern writers, among them the urban and urbane Jorge Luis Borges and Ernesto Sábato. Borges was one of the first writers to put South America on the map of world literature. His works are intellectual games played with his readers. Most of his writings are short story–essays that he called "fictions." Two of his favorite themes are labyrinths and mathematics. He enjoys destroying our concepts of time, space, infinity, and truth, using personal friends and other people as fictional characters, and quoting actual reference works to back up his invented theories. His mystery stories are especially enjoyable, as they take you through the whole process of solving a crime. For the skeptical Borges, life is tragic because it is limited by time and is irreversible, but we can relieve the tragedy by constructing games to distract ourselves. Borges's friend, Adolfo Bioy Casares, 1990 winner of Spain's Cervantes Prize for Literature, the highest literary award in the Spanish-speaking world, who shows up as a character in some of the fictions, also uses the detective story as a game. You occasionally get the impression that the two of them are trying to outdo each other and that the reader is just incidental to the process.

Ernesto Sábato's works are not fun and games, rather they are existentialist novels of people's self-punishment. While his masterpiece, *About Heroes and Tombs,* deals with a large segment of Argentine history, it stresses the 1920s and 1930s and pre-Perón Argentina. The heroine Alejandra is one of the most powerfully drawn women in South American literature. As the novel begins, Alejandra (who symbolizes Argentina itself) has set fire to the house and killed her father and herself. Then we learn the history of her unusual family. Buenos Aires, with its corruption, lies, and violence, is the real villain. Usually required reading at Hispanic literature classes at US universities is his first novel, the classic *The Tunnel.* This book launched a literary career that has spanned 45 years.

Julio Cortázar and Manuel Puig are the best of the younger Argentines, but keep your eye on Eduardo Gudiño Kiefer, whose popularity is rising. Cortázar, another game player, sets the tone in his titles: *End of the Game, Hopscotch, The Prizes, A Novel to Put Together. Hopscotch* is a series of episodes, dialogues, and monologues. Each section has two numbers. You can read the novel consecutively and get one story, or you can read the sections according to the second set of numbers, which skip around in a different order. Sometimes you jump forward and sometimes backward (as in hopscotch), thereby getting a different story. This technique is part of Cortázar's rebellion against literary convention. Characters invent their own games; Buenos Aires and Paris are interchangeable; anarchy abounds. *A Novel to Put Together* is, just as it says, a do-it-yourself kit for a novel.

Manuel Puig has written three novels that have received critical acclaim and commercial success: *The Buenos Aires Affair, Boquitas Pintadas* (Heartbreak Tango), and *The Betrayal of Rita Hayworth*. A fourth, *Kiss of the Spiderwoman,* was made into a movie directed by the Argentine-born Hector Babenco. The film followed the 1986 publication of an English translation of Puig's critically acclaimed novel, *Pubis Angelical* (Angel Hair), one of his last works before his death. Movies and novels are more real for Puig's characters than their own humdrum existence.

The most famous and popular contemporary South American writer is the Colombian Nobel Prize winner Gabriel García Márquez, author of the international best seller *A Hundred Years of Solitude.* For South Americans the story of Macondo and the Buendía family is an allegory of their continent. For others it is just an extreme pleasure to read, with all manner of strange happenings repeating themselves in defiance of all laws. García Márquez takes us through seven generations of this family. The author has a very offbeat sense of humor, allowing him to describe deaths and tragedies without upsetting the reader. The reader is compelled to move on to each unexpected event to see how the Buendía family copes with it. Equally funny and macabre is the more recent *Autumn of the Patriarch,* the story of a dictator who dies several times. But does he really die? He's been in the presidential palace so long that no one remembers when he wasn't. The dictator's character is based more than a little on the late Venezuelan strongman, Juan Vicente Gómez. *No One Writes to the Colonel* is an earlier work that is definitely worth reading. If you know Spanish, be sure to read García Márquez in the original. His style and use of language are incomparable.

The commercial and critical emergence of Latin American literature continued into the 1980s with names both familiar and new. Works that represent the best of this genre include *Love in the Time of Cholera,* García Márquez's more recent novel, and *We All Loved Glenda So Much,* a collection of short stories by the Argentine writer Julio Cortázar. Three female Latin American writers also emerged in North American publishing: Luisa Valenzuela, the Argentine short story writer whose book, *The Lizard's Tail,* has appeared on best-seller lists in the US; Chilean poet María Luisa Bombal, who finally has achieved recognition here not for poetry, but for short stories, in a collection entitled *New Islands;* and another Chilean, Isabel Allende. Now living in California, the niece of former President Salvador Allende has three novels available in English translations: *The House of the Spirits, Of Love and Shadows,* and *Eva Luna,* and a collection of tales, *Stories of Eva Luna.* They are all fascinating works that offer many insights into the overthrow of the Allende government in the mid-1970s.

In the early 1990s, Latin American literature continues to thrive in several genres, especially in the novel. Among those well-established authors who recently have published works are the Peruvian Mario Vargas Llosa, with his gigantic novel, *The War at the End of the World, El Hablador* (The Storyteller), which concerns a Lima anthropologist whose fieldwork takes him to the Amazon jungle, and *In Praise of the Stepmother,* a novel of passion. In addition, the Chilean exile José Donoso has published *A House in the Country.* Gabriel García Márquez's controversial novel, *The General in his Labyrinth,* chronicles the final days of Simón Bolívar, the Great Liberator.

If your real love is poetry, South America has plenty to offer. Even when no good novels were being produced, South America had an abundance of excellent poetry and several anthologies are available in English. Pablo Neruda (1904–73) and Gabriela Mistral (1889–1957), both Chileans, were Nobel Prize recipients. One of Neruda's best-known works, *Canto General,* was published in Mexico in 1950 (21 years before he won the Nobel Prize), and appeared in its English translation in 1991. The *Canto* relates the history of Latin America from 1400 into the 20th century through a Marxist perspective and focuses on the abuse of its indigenous peoples. It contains one of Neruda's most famous poems, "The Heights of Machu Picchu," in which he uses the Peruvian citadel as a spot from which to contemplate the Latin American experience. And a bilingual edition of *Spain in the Heart: Hymn to the Glories of the People at War* was published in the US in 1991. Written in 1937, this work condemns fascism in the context of the Spanish Civil War. Neruda was consul at the Chilean embassy in Madrid just before the outbreak of the war; when the fighting broke out, he moved to Paris and did relief work with Spanish refugees.

Gabriela Mistral was a schoolteacher whose work often concentrated on themes involving passion, universal love, children, and nature. Born Lucila Godoy y Alcayaga, she chose a pen name because she feared that she might lose her teaching job if it was discovered that she was the writer of such collections of emotional poetry as "Desolación" (Desolation), "Ternura" (Tenderness), and "Tala" (Despair), all now available in the US in translation. The last two were originally published by Mistral to raise funds for the Basque orphans of the Spanish Civil War. The first of her poems published in the US was in the volume, *Selected Poems of Gabriela Mistral,* translated by Langston Hughes. She won the Nobel Prize in Literature in 1945, the first Latin American recipient of the award, and when she died, Chile declared 3 days of national mourning.

Peruvian César Vallejo's poems appear simple and easy to read on the surface, but carry a profound examination of where people fit into the world. Argentine Alfonsina Storni, a friend of Mistral, filled her poems with images that were both cruel and beautiful — perhaps much like her own life, which ended in a suicide that moved her country.

South American literature now ranks with the world's best. Once you get to a big city in South America, check out the best-seller lists or talk to a book dealer to find out who the promising young authors are. Then, even after you are back in the US, keep an eye out for translations or watch for imports if you read Spanish or Portuguese.

# Music and Dance

South Americans come by their love of music naturally. With a triple heritage of Indian, European, and African influences, they have a terrifically varied background upon which to draw. Thus, each ethnic group has contributed its own rhythms, scales, and instruments to new musical forms that exist nowhere else.

And for almost every song there is a dance. So closely related are the two that the Quechua-speaking Indians of the Peruvian Andes have only one word, *taqui,* for both. South Americans are among the world's most graceful dancers — men as well as women. Indeed, unlike some North American men, South American men need no coaxing to get them on the dance floor. They rank dancing with eating, drinking, and lovemaking (not necessarily in that order). After watching the sensual movements of some of the dances, you will realize that for them dancing *is* a form of lovemaking. (Back in the days of watchful chaperones, a dance was the only excuse for having physical contact with one's fiancée.)

Music has always been an important part of South American life. Spanish chroniclers state that the Indians used drums, flutes, and rattles, especially in their religious ceremonies. (It has been said that some Indians carved their flutes from the leg bone of a particularly hated enemy.) The Inca, who had the highest musical development among the Indians, played complex panpipes, some with as many as 36 tones. Such instruments are still used in the Andes, as is the basic five-tone (pentatonic) scale used by many primitive tribes. Instruments played by the native South American Indians were those that could be blown, such as flutes (*quenas*) and horns (*cañas*), and percussive instruments, such as bells (*zacapas*) and a variety of drums (*tambors, bombas,* and *cajas*). Interestingly, there were no indigenous stringed instruments, either plucked or bowed.

The Spanish and Portuguese colonists brought the stringed instruments — the guitar, harp, mandolin, and violin — as well as the seven-tone scale and their own rich musical heritage. The Indians were quick to adopt the European instruments and to adapt them to their own tastes. The use of an armadillo shell as a sounding box resulted in the *charango,* a small, ukelele-like instrument that helps give Andean music its distinctive sound. The Andean harp, with only 36 strings, produces a rather strident pitch, but the Indians wanted the harp to be portable for their parades and street festivals, of which there are literally thousands. In the mountains all events, both pagan and Christian, are observed, usually with a curious compromise between the two traditions. The Indians appease both God and the gods with their music, just in case. And music helps them cope with the harsh realities of Andean life.

Since many Indian dances are symbolic, at major festivals each dance is performed in a different costume, the splendor of which will amaze you. Elaborately worked papier-mâché masks top outfits of neon colors with intricate sequin, bead, embroidery, and lace designs. The huge, carved-wood heads used in the *Diablada* (devil) dance would scare anyone. Two festivals to be considered are *Inti Raymi* (the festival of the sun god Inti, in Cuzco, Peru, June 24, which has become rather touristy) and the *Virgen de la Candelaria* (Lake Titicaca area, February 2–10). The *Diablada* is performed at the Oruro *Carnaval* in Bolivia, the Saturday before *Ash Wednesday.* (Be warned that any Indian festival is accompanied by much drinking. The Indians will sing, drink, and dance until they pass out. Since there is no taboo against it, the women get as drunk as the men. After a few glasses of home brew, the normally reserved Indians may want you to dance with them. Since a drunken person is always unpredictable, handle these situations with as much tact and grace as you can muster.) Regardless, the festivals are well worth attending for the music, the spectacle, and for the interest in a people that has for over 500 years struggled to maintain its traditions in the face of tremendous adversity. As the Indians come into contact with late-20th-century civilization, the typical Andean band of flutes, panpipes, violin, harp, drum, and *charango* slowly is being modified with the addition of brass and wind instruments common to the popular music of the US and Europe.

In the highlands of Peru and Bolivia, the *yaraví* and *huayno* are the most common songs. The *yaraví* or *haraví* (Quechua for "lament") is a ballad-like piece about death, lost love, or other unhappy themes. It can be sung or just played on a flute. Many aficionados feel that it is the truest expression of the melancholy Indian spirit. More popular is the *huayno,* which is both a song and a dance. The *huayno* begins with a slow *triste* (sad song) and ends with a quick-paced *fuga* (flight). The dance consists of small, quick steps executed close to one's partner but with little contact. Like unfamiliar food, the *huayno* is an acquired taste, for it is often sung with a whining quality. In Ecuador, a variation of the *huayno,* the *sanjuanito* (named for St. John, the patron saint of Ecuador) is the national song and dance. Andean music is also found in southwestern Colombia and northern Chile and Argentina with slight regional adaptations.

Admittedly, Andean music is not for everyone. Don't let internationally acclaimed vocalist Ima Sumac's highly touted five-octave range scare you off. Her voice is definitely unique, but she is a trained professional and in no way typifies folk singers. If you start with the hauntingly melodic flute music, then progress to the male vocalists, you should soon be ready for the higher-pitched wailing sounds of the female singers. Simon and Garfunkel's "El Condor Pasa" notwithstanding, excellent artists are now interpreting Indian music. North Americans who develop an appreciation of Andean music become lifelong devotees.

In Paraguay, Jesuit missionaries taught the Guaraní Indians to sing religious music and to play the harp. The Guaraní, like the Quechua-speaking Indians of the Andes, quickly adopted the instrument. Today, masters of the Paraguayan harp perform in concerts throughout the world. Paraguayan music is almost always gay and lilting. Many of the songs imitate bird calls, falling rain, and other sounds from nature. Add to this the melodious cadences of the Guaraní language and you have a combination that makes for pleasant listening. Jazz harpist Roberto Perera has adopted his country's traditional music into the contemporary recordings that he cuts in the US.

The *canción* (*purajhei* in Guaraní) is sung in Guaraní. The *galope* (gallop) and the *polka paraguaya* (Paraguayan polka), while sometimes sung in Guaraní, are really European in origin with a tropical touch added. They cannot be considered Indian in the same way a *huayno* or *yaraví* is. Even the popular *guaranía,* a ballad with a waltz-like beat, was created by professional composers who wanted to return to native melodies. The authentic Guaraní music, apparently slower and more melancholy in nature, was destroyed long ago. Its survival, though transformed, can be found in the classical music of Paraguay. One of the greatest Paraguayan composers and concert performers to make a name beyond his borders was the guitarist Augustín Barrios Mangoré (1885–1945), who scorned the traditional black tie attire in favor of full Guaraní regalia. (He also added another surname — Mangoré, which means "the chief" in Guaraní.) His charming compositions reflect the use of Paraguayan folklore fused with a Chopinesque neo-romanticism.

Traditional Indian melodies have nevertheless inspired much of the protest music coming out of South America. This movement, which calls itself the *nueva canción latinoamericana* (new Latin American song), had its origins in the folk song movement in Cuba during the 1960s, and made its way to southern South America and Chile, where it flourished under the Allende regime in the early 1970s. It rapidly became international, especially after the military junta executed or exiled most of the protest musicians in 1974. One of the most famous singers of Chilean protest songs, Victor Jara, was shot to death in the *National Stadium,* after he led thousands of political protestors in song when they were rounded up during the coup that overthrew Salvador Allende. Many political composers and singers are aware of the value of South America's Indian heritage and do not wish to see it destroyed in the name of progress. Their songs represent a fusion of the new and the old similar to our folk revival of the 1960s. These young, highly skilled musicians have produced some of the most creative and dynamic South American music around. (*Quilapayun* and *Inti-illimani* are the best-known groups in the US today.)

Creole — Spanish American (criollo) — music did not look to the Indian for its inspiration, although the rhythms brought to the continent by African slaves insinuated themselves into these tunes. Though born in South America, all criollos originally shared a southern European (mostly Iberian) heritage, and their music tended to cross national boundaries easily. First popular in colonial Lima, Peru, the *zambacueca,* with its name shortened to *cueca,* became the national dance of Chile. Once the *cueca* was firmly established as Chilean, the Peruvians changed the name of their *cueca* to *marinera* to avoid any reference to its rival to the south. In Argentina, the *zambacueca* gave rise to two dances, the *zamba* and the *cueca,* each slightly different. These dances are fun to watch because of the graceful, flirtatious waving of handkerchiefs and the playful, coquettish movements of the couples. Despite the increasing popularity of rock and disco in South America, the *cueca* and the *marinera* are still very much alive. Creole music has also resulted in some rather amusing combinations such as the *foxtrot incaico* (Inca foxtrot) — which appeared following the success of the foxtrot in the US during the 1930s, and has nothing of the Inca in it — and the *vals peruano* (Peruvian waltz), a romantic serenade.

No one, including leading ethnomusicologists, seems to have sorted out all the origins and influences found in criollo music. The musical crisscrossing of borders has only confused the issue. In Argentina, people simply ascribed all creole music, with the exception of the urban *milonga* and tango, to a romantic gaucho figure, the colorful *payador* (wandering ballad singer) of the pampa. He has now been replaced by radio and television. With him went the *contrapunto* (counterpoint), the last vestige of the troubador's art in South America. (If you scour the pampa of Argentina or the *sertão* of Brazil, you might be lucky enough to find a lone troubador still entertaining the people of the remoter regions.)

Many other creole songs and dances, whether gaucho or not, have been saved from oblivion in nightclubs, called *peñas*, which offer folklore shows (see *Nightclubs and Nightlife*, THE CITIES). The *vidala* or *vidalita* (my life), the *triste* (sad song), and the *estilo* (style) are slow, sentimental songs that describe life on the pampa or relate some event of national or regional importance. A *triste* is often a love song for one who is far away. The *gato* (cat) and the *pericón* (large fan) are very lively country dances that were extremely popular with the gauchos. They were frequently accompanied by songs of varied content, some of which were quite humorous. The *tamer cielito* (little heaven) and *cuando* (when) resemble a waltz and a minuet, respectively.

The music of rural Uruguay is similar to that of Argentina because this, too, is gaucho country. Like the American cowboy of the Far West, the gaucho sings to keep himself company while riding herd. Since this folklore is not written down, we have no idea how many gaucho songs there really are.

The urban music of Buenos Aires and Montevideo has little in common with the songs of the rural plains. When it was first introduced, the famous Argentine tango — which began as an adaptation of the *habanera* from Cuba and Spain's Andalusian tango during the mid-19th century — was considered scandalous. It even caused a furor because, for the first time, men and women danced with their entire bodies touching! Before the tango, most dances were done in lines or circles, and physical contact was limited. Even in a waltz the partner had been kept at arm's length. And when the lambada was the rage throughout the continent in the 1980s, the Catholic church condemned this dance that requires excessive body contact as immoral. With the advent of disco dancing, Buenos Aires became one of the disco capitals of South America. Consequently, even the tango found itself almost relegated to the realm of folklore. But a tango well done is still a thing of beauty and grace (see *Buenos Aires*, THE CITIES). Best-known of the tango orchestras that popularized the dance and transformed it into a sophisticated style during the 1930s was that of singer Carlos Gardel. More recently, until illness forced his departure from the concert stage, Astor Piazzolla (dubbed the "The Father of New Tango") delighted sold-out concert crowds for many decades with his innovative interpretations on the *bandoneón* — he instilled contemporary harmonies and rhythms into the traditional tango form. Piazzolla was also a prolific composer of classical music in addition to his work with his jazz/rock fusion band (*Quinteto Tango Nuevo*) and has been an influential voice for Latin American music abroad for several decades. In the US, his collaborations with jazz vibes player Gary Burton and the *Kronos Quartet* testify to the diversity of his musical endeavors.

As in Argentina, the folkloric music of Colombia and Venezuela is predominantly Spanish in style, but unlike Argentina, there are regions where the African influence is strong. Along the northern coastline the blacks have contributed more complex, syncopated rhythms to the popular music. Their influence is especially evident in the lively Colombian *bambuco* and *cumbia* and in the Venezuelan *joropo*. The *cuatro* (four-stringed guitar) and the *tiple* (five-stringed guitar) are played in both countries. Their peculiar sound, similar to that of the *charango*, may take a bit of getting used to. Despite this, Colombian and Venezuelan music is usually lively and lots of fun to dance to. Both countries also are havens for Caribbean merengue and salsa.

In any of the aforementioned countries, you can find clubs that offer flamenco and other elements of Spanish folklore should you want a taste of the mother country. The mother country of Brazil is Portugal, which offers not flamenco but *fados*, very sad, haunting melodies about homesickness or lost love. It is difficult to believe after seeing the bubbly craziness of the Brazilians that these melancholy, beautiful songs are part of their heritage.

Brazilians are the most musically oriented people in South America, and at no time does this stand out more than during *Carnaval*. There is no spectacle like it anywhere else on the continent. The samba is the predominant dance of *Carnaval*, and the costumes of the samba schools have to be seen to be believed, they are so incredibly ornate. Incredible also is the energy of the people, who sing and dance for 4 days and nights, literally nonstop. It is impossible to walk down the street without getting caught up in the rhythm and vitality of it all. Although the samba is always a characteristically syncopated dance, there are in fact a variety of tempos and moods. The *samba cancao* is a slow samba used to accompany ballads, the *batucada* is the lively form danced during *Carnaval*, and the *embolada* (rolling ball) begins slowly and gradually gathers speed until it reaches a frenzy. The flamboyant Carmen Miranda, with her trademark fruit basket headwear and high-high heels, popularized the samba in the US during the 1930s and 1940s with such great songs as '"Brazil."

Samba rhythms are the basis for the bossa nova melody "A garota de Ipanema" ("The Girl from Ipanema") by Antônio Carlos Jobim. Together with North Americans Charlie Byrd (guitar) and Stan Getz (tenor saxophone), and Brazilian João Gilberto (vocals and guitar), Jobim effectively changed the face of the jazz music scene in the US with the landmark recording *Jazz Samba* in 1962. Another ubiquitous bossa nova, "Black Orpheus," was popularized in the 1959 film of the same title, with music by Luiz Bonfá, and performed by Bola Sete.

When you think *Carnaval*, don't just think Rio. Salvador (Bahia) and other cities in the north have *carnavales* that are not as jammed with tourists and so overtly commercialized. In fact, the samba was started in the *favelas* (slums) of Rio by blacks who had originally emigrated from the north. Although by no means the only one, the samba is the South American dance most frequently associated with blacks, and *Carnaval* is really their festival. A lesser-known musical style found in northeast Brazil is *forró,* a form of rock 'n' roll played by small groups; it features the Brazilian button accordion, the *sanfonas.* The *forró* is a blues-style music similar to zydeco from Louisiana.

The samba is only one of the dances performed at *Carnaval.* The *marcha* and the *frêvo* also can be seen, although they are becoming increasingly overshadowed by the samba and the lusty, erotic lambada, which made its way to both US coasts in a peak of popularity several years ago. There are numerous other Brazilian songs and dances. After you recover from your *Carnaval* hangover, you can begin to discover them for yourself, one at a time. There is also special music that accompanies the various types of *macumba* (secret religious rites). See *Festivals,* DIVERSIONS; *Rio de Janeiro* and *Salvador (Bahia),* THE CITIES.

No other South American country has as many popular musicians and performers as Brazil. Astrud Gilberto, the voice of "The Girl from Ipanema," is still going strong — taking an updated bossa nova beat to sold-out concert and club engagements around the world. Although lesser known in the US, the pop singer Gilberto Gil and the extraordinary guitarist Baden Powell are certainly idols in their own right in Brazil. North Americans may be more familiar with those Brazilians who currently live in the US, such as vocalists Tania Maria and Flora Purim, percussionist Airto Moreira, and guitarist Laurindo Almeida. Many lesser-known performers, however, are prime examples of the incredible diversity and quality of Brazilian music. They include the jazz/classical guitarist Egberto Gismonti, the singer Milton Nascimento, pop vocalists Margareth Menezes and Nara Leão, and popular guitarists Caetano Veloso and Paulinho da Viola.

If you prefer some culture with your revelry, South America has many excellent symphony orchestras, chamber music ensembles, and concert soloists that often perform the works of the continent's composers. Although many of them never received much fame beyond their own borders, they all contributed to a high standard of musical life. During much of the 20th century, these composers participated in a nationalistic movement in the arts in which their own particular folklore was incorporated into classical musical forms. Those who achieved worldwide success were not only noteworthy for bringing fame back to their own country, but also for making their native folklore better known to North American and European audiences. Two such composers were Argentina's Alberto Ginastera (1916–1983), whose operas, ballet scores, chamber, and orchestral works used themes and rhythms from Argentine folklore, and Brazil's Heitor Villa-Lobos (1887–1959), one of the most prolific composers of all. Villa-Lobos is best known for his haunting "Bachianas Brasileiras No. 5" for Soprano and Eight Cellos and his exquisite guitar music. World class performers from South America include pianists Martha Argerich of Argentina and the late Claudio Arrau from Chile. There also is a rich tradition of guitar music; unsurpassed is Alirio Diaz, with his interpretations of his native Venezuelan dance music and the unparalleled compositions of his countryman Antonio Lauro.

In Lima, *zarzuelas* (operettas à la Gilbert and Sullivan) imported from Spain are performed. The *Teatro Colón* in Buenos Aires, one of the world's great old opera houses, features regular concert, opera, and dance performances by Argentine performers as well as by such groups as the orchestras and ballet companies of São Paulo and Caracas, which generally are considered to be the most sophisticated on the continent.

There is enough music in South America to keep your toes tapping and your hands clapping for the better part of your trip. When you find something you love, spread the word back home. South American music has been overlooked for far too long.

# Crafts

As South America slowly becomes more familiar and accessible, travelers are beginning to discover and delight in its remarkably varied handicrafts — historic, colorful, fine, crude, amusing, traditional, first- and second-rate. In many countries these handmade items embody artistic links to pre-Columbian and Hispanic heritages. And even if you were never before interested in handicrafts per se, seeing them on location may add a special dimension. A poncho will no longer be an ethnic item seen in fall fashion shows, but rather an essential garment to protect the wearer against the Andean cold. Cloth made of llama and alpaca wool somehow feels warmer once you've seen the animals grazing and the weavers weaving. Vicuña has become an endangered species, so don't expect to buy anything made from its wool during your visit.

In Latin America vital folk art traditions flourished centuries before the arrival of the Europeans and, despite the laments of scholars and purists, not all local skills are dying or dead. Certain crafts perhaps can be called "endangered species," compromised by synthetic fibers, machine looms, and plastic materials. But there is hope for others as governments and private citizens become aware of the cultural and economic value of handicrafts production. That hope will not be fulfilled, however, until the continent's tradition of exploiting the workers is revised so that they can make a living wage and function as independent craftspeople. (You may want to keep that in mind when bargaining — especially when buying directly from the artisan.)

Some ancient skills now are being revived; many craftspeople remain faithful to tradition while others are updating their products. The mixing of past and present can yield amusing results, as it did during the hot pants craze in the late 1960s. Indian women, dressed in their traditional layers of full-skirted *polleras*, busily knitted alpaca hot pants decorated with Inca motifs to sell to tourists.

Such novelties aside, the truly South American items will attract your attention with their bright colors, fine workmanship, and mysterious and/or primitive designs. Before you look around urban artisan centers or country markets, it is always interesting to visit local folk art museums. There are many very fine ones — in Quito, Recife, and Bogotá, for example — where costumes, utensils, and musical instruments are displayed by region and clearly and imaginatively demonstrate what is most important about handicrafts: their utilitarian or spiritual function.

Folk art reflects the variety of influences on the local artisan; the most dramatic change in South America came with the arrival of the Spanish and the introduction of Christianity. Indian artistic skills and imagination quickly took to the baroque trappings and awe-inspiring pageantry of the Catholic church. Even today, Indian handicrafts continue to interpret Christian themes with local dramatis personae: a cross, a bird-god, and a political figure may all appear on a Cuna Indian *mola* appliqué from Panama; Inca suns emblazon frames of colonial-style mirrors made in Peru; and llamas may guard the manger of Jesus in a nativity scene etched around an Ecuadoran gourd.

The most basic change between ancient and contemporary crafts is the separation of function and decoration. Isolated Amazon tribes, who were not part of either the Inca or Spanish conquest, continue to make objects — baskets, pottery, hunting weapons, and musical instruments — for practical purposes and decorate them in a traditional way. Objects that we call artistic, the tribesman would call useful. However, items crafted by artisans who *have* been exposed to colonial and modern influences may now be either utilitarian or ornamental.

Without doubt, all South American countries are not equally endowed with treasuries of superb folk arts. Historically, the finest come from the Andean centers of pre-Columbian cultures whose craftspeople excelled in weaving, pottery making, and gold- and silversmithing. Creativity was never simply applied to art for art's sake, but was devoted to enhancing things that were used in daily life and religious ritual. For these peoples, design and embellishment celebrated the close association between themselves and nature, between man and god. Folk art — ancient and modern — remains intrinsically linked with life, as you will see in the objects that continue to bloom in Colombia, Ecuador, Peru, and Bolivia. In addition, in some cultures like that of the Moches of Peru, pottery designs and crafts were a form of record keeping and storytelling for a people with no written language.

In Argentina, Chile, and Uruguay, it is the gaucho who has influenced the regional *artesanía*. Silver is used to decorate the harness and saddle trappings of his horse as well as his own costume. Watch for other gaucho paraphernalia: heavy belts fashioned from silver coins and chains (worn only by old-timers) and the silver gourd and *bombilla* (drinking straw) that are basic to making and taking maté on the range. Gaucho countries also are noted for their leatherwork. The hide of an unborn calf is most highly valued, but horsehide, kid, and snakeskin also are used in making clothing and furniture. These leatherwork skills have transferred easily into good workmanship on fur clothing.

Centuries ago, the Spanish and Portuguese nuns taught the Indian women embroidery and lace making and, in most countries, rich needlework patterns adorn women's and men's clothing. The delicate *ñandutí* lace and the *aó po'i* embroidery of Paraguay are among the finest on the continent, and the patterns of sequins, beadwork, and stitching on costumes for religious and folk ceremonies in Brazil, Bolivia, Ecuador, and Peru absolutely defy description.

Generally, the best places to find high-quality handicrafts are often the government stores, which serve as cooperative centers for marketing and distribution. These are headquartered mostly in capitals and major towns. Here also, from time to time, you will find the gallery of a contemporary craftsperson whose specialty is using ancient materials (such as beads and textile pieces found in pre-Columbian graves or colonial embroideries and metal religious objects) to fashion modern jewelry, clothing, or collages.

## PERSPECTIVES / Crafts

Yet nothing can beat the country market as a source for particular crafts. There you will find not only a wider selection of certain objects, but also lower prices. Bargaining is accepted, but haggling over pennies is certainly poor form when you consider the seller's time, effort, and annual income. Above all, in a village market, you can watch a craft emerging from the skilled hands of its creator.

Each South American country offers a handicraft specialty, although the best folk arts and crafts are concentrated in some half-dozen areas. We have focused on the leading craft countries, listing city centers and village markets where handwork is found and/or produced. The latter are particularly fascinating and colorful in the Andean regions — here you should make an effort to adjust your travel itinerary to accommodate the weekly market schedule. (The same is true for the annual festivals, where the finest items are worn or displayed in their appropriate functional/decorative framework.) For the location of and transportation to a town or village, you may want to refer to each country's DIRECTIONS section.

**BOLIVIA:** After you've caught your breath in La Paz, your next problem is to decide what to see first in this city of dramatic Andean peaks and fascinating, somber people. Make your first stop the *Museum of National Ethnography and Folklore,* a repository of folk arts — musical instruments, which are still played beautifully and frequently in local restaurants; contemporary costumes; and the masks of the *Diablada* (Devil) dance. Then head for the city markets — the *Artisans Market* off Plaza San Francisco, the *Mercado Negro* (Black Market), and the food market (on Av. Camacho) — which always are open for business. The best known is the *Mercado de las Brujas* (Witches' Market), where you may or may not want to buy sheep or llama fetuses, believed to bring fertility or good luck to new enterprises. At all these markets you'll recognize the sellers (female) by their black *boina* hats. Favorite purchases in the city are ponchos; sweaters; *chuspas* (coca pouches) decorated in interesting figurative and geometric patterns; wonderfully dressed dolls; and musical instruments, ranging from unusual strings to all kinds of pipes.

Many fine weavings — tapestries, rugs, and blankets — can be found in Cochabamba, Bolivia's third largest city. This is the home of Fotrama Cooperative, founded by a Maryknoll priest from the US, where the Indian women are taught advanced weaving and knitting skills. The nearby valley town of Villa Rivero produces the only tapestry weaving in Bolivia. In the area around Cochabamba many village markets are held, mostly on Sundays.

Sixty miles (96 km) by rail or road from La Paz is Oruro, where the region's big social event — the Wednesday markets — takes place. Oruro's annual *Diablada* performances held during *Carnaval* are probably the best in the country and the masks and costumes are among the most fascinating examples of folkloric arts.

**BRAZIL:** The best crafts found in the major visitor centers — Rio de Janeiro and São Paulo — come from another part of Brazil. This doesn't mean that you won't find good-quality crafts in Rio's specialty stores or at its *Hippie Market,* or at the Sunday market in the Praça de República in São Paulo. In fact the latter has good crafts from every region of the country, particularly leather bags and jackets from the immediate area. But the major arts and handicrafts center is Salvador (Bahia), whose wildly decorative arts allude to both Portuguese and African influences.

Go to Bahia's *Museu da Cidade* (City Museum) to see life-size models dressed in the opulent old Bahian costumes and headdresses — the ultimate in layered, embroidered fashion. The silver jewelry on display is probably close in quality to what you will find in the *Mercado Modelo* (Model Market). Other regional crafts that can be found in Bahia range from bejeweled dolls dressed as lavishly as the museum models to Bahian rug tapestries with primitive scenes woven in the warmest Gauguinesque colors. Oil painting is done in this same folkloric style, and both have rightly attracted the attention of international art collectors — prices have risen accordingly. Tilework, rendered in the more formal patterns and colors of Portuguese ceramics, is also good here.

The influence of the Africans who were brought to Brazil as slaves is most apparent in Bahia, and a common purchase is the *figa*, a charm bringing fertility or good luck and once worn by the slaves. Shaped like a clenched fist, the *figa* can be made of jacaranda wood and silver, solid silver, or colored quartz. Other charms are collected into a *penca* (bunch) and worn as a cluster on a neck chain or bracelet.

Brazil also is known for fine baskets and hammocks (the bed used most frequently in the tropics). At Fortaleza in the northeast, you'll find some of the most intricate, beautifully woven hammocks at the *Centro de Turismo*, the *Tourist Handicraft Center*, housed in an old prison whose cells are now little shops. Delicate Brazilian lace is sold in the vast *São José Market* in Recife, as are skillful woodcarvings — masks, statues, and utilitarian objects such as bowls, eating utensils, and platters — made from Amazon mahogany and jacaranda. In the Minas Gerais area, between Rio and Salvador, is a major craft center that specializes in pewter reproductions of antique vessels, such as tea and coffee pots, mugs, and pitchers.

**CHILE:** Chile is a country rich in high-quality raw materials from which many folk crafts are fashioned — wool, leather, wood, copper, and even lapis lazuli gemstones. Small crafts centers have sprung up from top to bottom of this long thin country; in *Chile*, DIRECTIONS, we have noted those towns and villages that have their own specialties.

In large cities such as Santiago, you will find a variety of crafts at the *CEMA* stores, a government-initiated project founded to help women earn household money. *CEMA* (Centro de Madres, or Mother's Center) basically distributes and markets artisan goods from all over the countryside. From Arica come ceramics modeled after the artifacts of the pre-Inca Diaguitas Indian culture; from the Central Valley come *boradores de Isla Negra*, fabric panels embroidered with scenes of rural Chilean life, as well as vicuña and alpaca garments — ponchos, sweaters, and jackets. From towns near Santiago come baskets, pottery, blankets, capes, and shawls and a variety of leatherwork and cowboy accessories such as ornamental stirrups. From the southern Lake District and the island of Chiloe off Puerto Montt come thick woolen knits, mostly sweaters, in muted shades of brown, white, and tan. *CEMA* also carries copperware, but the more interesting lapis jewelry is found in Santiago's specialty stores.

**COLOMBIA:** Bogotá, Colombia's capital — in spite of its reputation for drugs — is a gem of a city (and a city for gems — specifically emeralds) for the folk arts lover; almost everything you find here is as good — although perhaps not as inexpensive — as it is in the place of manufacture. Crafts traditions are rather well looked after and supported by the *Artesanías de Colombia Cooperative*, with shops in the international sector (Almacén San Diego, 26-50 Carrera 10) and downtown (at Almacén Las Aguas, 18-60 Carrera 3) in Bogotá. There also is a branch on the island of San Andrés. The stores offer a wide variety: traditional ponchos; *ruanas* — Colombian ponchos, which wrap like capes and come in wonderful single and mixed colors; straw baskets of every imaginable shape and woven design; rugs; and leather. The *Artesanías* were instrumental in encouraging the pursuit of fine appliqué work done in the coastal regions; whether window or wall size, these colorful depictions of local scenes are a joy.

The gift shop of the *Museum of Popular Arts and Traditions* near the Presidential Palace also sells fine textiles, basketry, ceramics, and woodcarvings. The museum, which occupies a former monastery, has one of the finest permanent folk art exhibitions on the continent, with emphasis on how people live in various regions and the household objects they use. As a visit to the *Gold Museum* will show, goldsmithing is an ancient Indian skill and, although it has gone far beyond folk art, the goldwork now produced in *galerías* that specialize in copies of pre-Columbian pieces is superb. *Galería Cano* in Bogotá (27-98 Carrera 13) is a pioneer in this craft, and there is a branch in Cartagena.

In Cartagena itself, the best place to shop is the crafts center located in the stalls of the *Bovedas* (restored dungeons in the fortifications). An hour from the coast is the city of San Jacinto, an important center for bags, hats, baskets, cotton weaving, and hammocks. Some years ago Peace Corps workers in this area originated cotton string wall hangings called *divisorios;* they were an overnight success and are now found everywhere, executed in two or more colors and geometric designs. Some are more interesting than others, so don't buy the first one you see.

The province of Boyacá is the leading crafts-producing area of Colombia and, if you don't want to stay in one of its charming colonial inns, at least take a day's excursion from Bogotá. Tunja, the provincial capital, has a lively Indian market on Tuesdays and Saturdays and is a good place to buy fine *ruanas;* rugs; *bolsas* (knitted bags); esparto grass baskets and hats; and *fique* (fiber from the century plant) items such as placemats, toy animals, large bags, and purses. From Tunja it is not far to Duitama, a furniture making center, from which reproductions of colonial pieces can be shipped. Other more portable and traditional Duitama woodcrafts are hand-carved plates, bowls, trays, and spoons. The pottery produced in the small town of Ráquira is famous, fragile, and fun: Clay birds can be blown as whistles, clay frogs make another kind of peep, and ceramic vessels are covered with all sorts of fanciful figures. The market in Duitama is held on Tuesdays; in nearby Villa de Leyva on Saturdays; and in Ráquira on Sundays.

En route to Boyacá is the Cocontá Monday market, known for its fine leatherwork, primarily found on horsemen's gear. Beautiful woolen shawls (*panolones*) with 3-foot macramé fringes also come from this area. In Chiquinquirá, local craftspeople make handsome guitars and tambourines inlaid with shell designs.

**ECUADOR:** Quito is probably one of the best craft-shopping capitals on the continent. Here you'll find everything from straw mats and hats to elegant little dolls, Indian beadwork, ceremonial drums and flutes, weavings, embroideries, fanciful ceramic nativities, jewelry, baskets, wooden statues, and bread sculpture. Be sure to pay a visit to the *Folklore Gallery* (260 Av. Colón, Quito; phone: 231767), which has a variety of goods to see and buy. Olga Fisch, the late grande dame of Ecuadoran folk art, designed rugs which were sold here. Since her death, her niece Gogo has continued to operate the store with her own original designs, incorporating regional material and motifs into their lovely patterns. They also carry crafts from all over the country, as does the government center *OCEPA* (Exportation of Ecuadorian Artisan Products; at 752 Washington) and at the excellent *La Bodega* (614 Av. Juan León Mera). Quito is the home of many other contemporary South American artists; their galleries — open to the public on request — are worth seeing and their work (particularly paintings) is internationally recognized.

With its large Indian population, Ecuador has an almost unending spectacle of markets, some three dozen from one end of the country to the other. You should leave enough time to visit either Otavalo or Ambato, both crafts markets, as well as a produce market such as Saquisili or Pujili.

Otavalo's big day is Saturday. Reserve well ahead through your travel agent or a local tour operator so that you can go on Friday and secure one of a limited supply of rooms in the area. Only in this way can you be up and in the marketplace at sunrise when the distinctively dressed *otavaleños* begin to sell their ponchos, wall hangings, thick wool sweaters, baskets, decorative woven pouches called *shigras,* rugs, blankets, lightweight, delicately woven scarves, and thick ropes of gilt and red glass beads that they themselves wear. En route to or from Otavalo, stop in Calderón where the flamboyant bread-dough figures (ideal as *Christmas* tree ornaments) are shaped, baked, and painted and in the woodcarving center of San Antonio de Ibarra. You might alos want to visit Cotacachi, the country's leather-producing town.

The *otavaleños* also carry their weavings to Ambato, but keep your eyes open here for locally made rugs and for tapestries made by the Salasaca Indians. This area produces fine leatherwork, and multicolored, woven belts — some with different patterns on each side. And, since the Ambato market is close to the Amazon jungle region, you will also find baskets and pottery.

At the Saquisili market (held on Thursdays), the emphasis is on supplying what the local people need, not what visitors want, so on sale here are fine baskets and mats made from Totora reeds. Pujili (Wednesdays and Sundays) is also a local supply market and one where you will see llamas. Other markets within easy reach of Quito are Latacunga (Tuesdays), Machachi, and Salcedo (Sundays).

The Canari people, famous artisans for centuries, live in the Cuenca region. They are weavers and leatherworkers; for the tourist trade they produce fine and interesting woven belts and macramé. There are other things to buy in Cuenca, including pottery and the misnamed Panama hat — you can watch both in production right in the city. Finally, there is an *OCEPA* craft store off the central plaza, and a good display of regional artifacts in the *Municipal Museum*.

**PANAMA:** The best selection of Panamanian crafts is the *Artesanías Nacionales* in Old Panama (City) and at the airport. The displays here include straw hats and bags, leatherwork, and ceramic and wood items. But nothing is more quintessentially Panamanian than the national costume; for women, this is the *pollera,* and for men, the *montuno*. The *pollera* is a wonderful multilayered dress with intricate embroidery that gives it a delicate lacy look. The *montuno* is a loose-fitting overshirt, also of finely embroidered cotton.

Another Panamanian specialty is the beautifully beaded collars worn and made by the Guaymi Indians who live in the central part of the country, about 4 hours from the capital. (The best buys are found on location.) The most famous handicraft from Panama, the *mola,* is an appliquéd square made by the Kuna Indians of the San Blas Islands. Set into the front and back of a woman's blouse, a good *mola* is made of four or five layers of colored cloth through which the pattern is cut. (This is different from conventional appliqués, in which layers are stitched one atop another.) The *mola* designs are pure fancy — taken from nature, from good and bad "spirits," even from patterns seen on food labels! Look carefully when you buy. Panama is now deluged with *mola*-style objects, from wall hangings to aprons, handbags, sun hats, and men's shirts and sport jackets. They are generally second-rate in workmanship; special attention and creativity is usually reserved for a woman's own apparel, which later may be bought by a visitor to the San Blas or an art collector. And certainly, in the islands, *molas* are *never* worn by men!

Another fanciful Indian craft is the birdcage made of the *piruli* reed by the people of the Chiriquí Highlands. Cages may be shaped like a bird, a plane, or their own *bohío* (thatch hut). Sunday is market day in that region.

**PERU:** Peru's artisans may produce the most interesting and varied crafts on the continent — indeed, some of the finest in the world. The official center is the nonprofit *Artesanías del Peru,* which has stores in Lima, Puno, Cuzco, Arequipa, and Iquitos. Some popular items are ponchos of various designs; woven belts from different regions; decorative woolen pillow cases and wall hangings; woven shoulder bags; copies of colonial knickknacks such as mirrors and altar candleholders; *tupos* (shawl pins, and try to find the old ones); and alpaca fur everything, from slippers to rugs. (The slippers are patterned in brown and white, and you will be lucky if they last a year in a centrally heated home.) Jewelry is also distinctive here, especially turquoise and silver designs. Lima's *Museo Nacional de la Cultura Peruana* has a fair collection of handicrafts, but to really understand why the country is the leading handicraft center, go to study pre-Columbian history at the *Museum of Anthropology and Archaeology;* ceramics at the *Larco Herrera Museum;* and textiles at the *Amano Museum* (by appointment).

Lima stores offer a wide selection of merchandise from throughout the country, but it is always fun to buy items where they are produced at prices that can be considerably lower. So, if you can, try to include the following places on your itinerary; each trip alone is worth consideration.

Most travelers to Cuzco go dashing off to Machu Picchu on a 2- or 3-day excursion and don't leave enough time to see the surrounding region or the former Inca capital. Cuzco is full of big and little treasures, including colonial antiques, which simply require browsing time to find. Crafts come to Cuzco from all over the highlands, but the most local items are *chuspas* (little pouches used by the Indians to carry coca leaves); wonderfully carved wooden locks; and all kinds of pottery. At the Sunday market in nearby Pisac, the plaza is filled with ponchos, blankets, highland woolen hats and slippers, and *varas,* processional staffs decorated with silver. Less of a crafts market but more of an all-Indian gathering is the Sunday market at Chincheros, where people come to mass and then picnic.

The very fine Ayacucho ceramic bulls, the carved gourds, and the famous *retablos* — miniature to grand in size, gaily decorated portable altars with doors that open into a divided scene of secular and religious carved figures — have become hard to find here, but keep looking; the price will be right. Rather than shopping in Ayacucho (better to avoid it because of the region's political problems), shop for the best bulls and *retablos* in Lima's better craft stores. (Try *Artesanías Huamanqaqa* on Av. Jirón Unión, as well as the *Los Alamos* gallery in the Urbanización Zarate district.) Near Ayacucho is the mountain village of Quinua, famous for its folkloric pottery.

If you take the train from Cuzco to Puno, try to buy one of Pucara's famous (and charming) pottery bulls. Just hang out the window of the train and a vendor is sure to appear. The Puno area itself is a knitting center, and the price is absolutely right for sweaters, vests, stocking caps, ponchos, and wonderful little, knitted, stuffed animals called *animalitos.* The women of Juli also embroider panels with primitive scenes of everyday life. Saturday is the big market day in Puno, Thursday in nearby Juli, and Sunday and Monday in Juliaca. The Lake Titicaca region in general is an excellent center for craft and festival folklore.

Huancayo, a wild and fascinating train ride from Lima, is another remarkable craft town, with market days on Sundays (although, for safety reasons, visitors recently have been discouraged from shopping here). Intricately etched gourds are also made here and the region is famous for rugs, blankets, tapestries, and knitted goods. For life and people, this is the most interesting market in Peru, but leave time to get used to the altitude.

**SURINAME:** At the central market in Paramaribo, sellers greet buyers in Dutch, Hindi, Sranan Tongo, Chinese, and Javanese. It is the linguistic chorus of a nation whose citizens hail from around the world. In the same market, you will find a variety of imported merchandise from those foreign shores, from Javanese bamboo and Indonesian batik prints to Indian saris and Dutch cheeses.

But this is also the central market source for local crafts made by the skilled hands of the Bushnegroes, descendants of the 17th- and 18th-century slaves, whose own African roots are reflected in their arts. Their finest work is woodcarving, and geometric designs cover tabletops, wall panels, stools, water containers, shields, and paddles. These items are less expensive when purchased in the local village markets along the banks of the jungle rivers, but if you're not going into the interior, you'll find the quality in the capital just as good.

Also locally made — and to be watched for — are native necklaces of seeds and kernels; bauxite jewelry; carefully woven straw baskets and mats; and the Suriname square nickel coins, which are mounted for charm bracelets.

**VENEZUELA:** When compared to many other countries on the continent, Venezuela is not a place where a wide variety of handicrafts is available. However, a representative selection of what is made — ceramics, baskets, pottery, and woolens — is housed in Caracas at the *Artesanía Venezolana*. The blankets, rugs, *ruanas,* and ceramics generally come from the highland regions; from the western area, you will find sisal products, seed necklaces, woodcarvings, and finely woven hammocks. From the Amazonas and the Delta Amacuro come graceful, yet sturdy baskets.

Venezuela shares the traditional *Diablada* ceremonies with Peru and Bolivia, and the home for this annual event on *Corpus Christi Day* is San Francisco de Yare. In June, the villagers dress as little Lucifers and dance in the streets, wearing grotesque masks that are intricately carved and exuberantly decorated. Masks can be purchased at the little shops in town or sometimes in the craftspeople's homes.

# Food and Drink

Few North Americans have sampled authentic South American cuisine in the US. Each country has its specialties, which vary from region to region. Depending upon the ethnic background(s) of the people and upon the crops, tastes range from bland to hellishly hot. At press time, however, the World Health Organization had issued a precaution advising against eating raw seafood because of the number of cholera cases sweeping the continent.

Most North Americans already know that Argentina has as many cows as Texas. A natural — and correct — assumption, then, is that Argentines eat a lot of beef. Don't pass up any opportunity to attend an Argentine *asado* (outdoor barbecue), at which the entire cow is roasted in the hide and literally everything but the hide gets eaten. Should you have any nonreligious prejudices about which animals or which parts of the animal are edible, put them aside and try everything once. You will be pleasantly surprised more often than not.

A favorite restaurant meal is the *parrillada mixta* (mixed grill), consisting of steaks, *chorizo* (spicy pork sausage), *morcilla* (blood sausage), and *mollejas* (sweetbreads). This last is especially worth trying. So is *bife a caballo* (beef on horseback) — a fried egg "riding" atop a steak. The plate may be garnished with *papas fritas* (French fries) or with slices of lettuce, tomato, onion, ham, and fried bananas. The meat usually is presented by itself and side dishes have to be ordered separately.

Argentines are also fond of lamb and chicken, whether baked, roasted, broiled, or in stews *(pucheros)*. *Pucheros* can have a corn, bean, or potato base, to which sausages and cuts of meat or chicken are added. A *puchero* is often a meal in itself. Beware: Argentines are heavy-handed with the salt shaker — even when it comes to salad. If you want dishes without salt, be sure to ask the waiter *sin sal,* or with very little salt, *poquito sal.*

Argentina produces good-quality wines. By all means sample any variety not readily available back home. Exercise some caution when you try *grappa,* a potent grape brandy brought over by the Italians.

South American coffee is excellent but strong. You can get *café americano* (North American–style coffee) or Nescafé in the larger cities, should you desire a weaker variety, one that does not keep you going all day. The national drink of Argentina, however, is *yerba maté,* a somewhat bitter herbal tea. Go easy on it at first. *Maté* has been known to give even the gauchos a mild case of *turista.* In spite of this minor inconvenience, *maté* is an acquired taste for many. It is not, as some advertisements suggest, an aphrodisiac.

Uruguay and southern Brazil are also beef-producing regions. Menus here are similar to Argentina's, although there are a few regional dishes not found elsewhere. In Uruguay, order a *carbonada,* a dish made with rice and fruit —

usually raisins, pears, and peaches. The inhabitants of these areas also drink *maté* and *grappa*.

In Chile, the beef is of a slightly inferior quality but still worth ordering. When you tire of *churrascos* (braised beef), try a famous Chilean empanada (pastry turnover), filled with ground beef, eggs, olives, and spices, or a *pastel de choclo* (corn pie), a meal similar to shepherd's pie with a flavorful corn mush replacing the mashed potatoes.

If you prefer seafood, Chilean menus offer great variety. *Chupe de mariscos* (seafood stew) is a favorite. The thin broth is full of *camarones* (shrimp), *langostinos* (crayfish), *jaibas* (crabs), *almejas* (mussels), whatever fresh fish is available, and chunks of potato and *choclo* (corn on the cob). If *caldillo de congrio* (conger eel soup) sounds too adventurous, choose a dish made from the more conventional *corvina* (sea bass).

Chileans and Argentines observe teatime (*té completo* in Argentina, *once* in Chile) should your sweet tooth crave *galletas* (cookies) and *pasteles* (pastries). Little round cakes called *alfajores* are considered the national dessert of Chile.

While Chilean beer is good, be sure to try the excellent wines, the best in South America. Red and white varieties are of equally high quality. Concha y Toro, Undurraga, and Cousiño-Macul are among the best labels.

In the countries to the north, different ethnic groups — Indian, African, Chinese, Dutch, Indonesian, and French — have made significant contributions to their respective national cuisines. Dishes in the north tend to be spicier (hotter) than those in the south. If past experience has told you that you cannot handle lots of chili pepper, now is the time to learn the important phrase *"No muy picante, por favor"* ("Not too hot, please").

Indian and African dishes tend to be both hot and starchy, with lots of beans, potatoes, rice, and corn. They are also interesting and not to be overlooked. The Andean Indians know more ways to serve potatoes than anyone else in the world (maybe because they lead the world in the number of varieties grown). *Chuño*, a boiled dinner of black balls of dehydrated potato, eggs, meat or fish, and cheese, is perhaps one of the more intriguing.

Since Bolivia is landlocked, fish is not abundant, but chicken and beef usually are. In Copacabana and other towns along Lake Titicaca and in La Paz, you can get freshly caught *trucha* (pink salmon trout). Giant frogs' legs from the lake are exported to France. Try a *picante de pollo* (chicken in *ají*, a very strong chili). Bolivians snack on *empanadas salteñas*, spicy pastry turnovers of beef, eggs, olives, peas, potatos, onions, and peppers. In La Paz try a *plato paceño* (the La Paz plate), a meal of corn, potatoes, beans, and cheese guaranteed to fill you for the rest of the day. For curiosity, sample a glass of *chicha blanca* (white *chicha*), the home brew made from corn. This potent drink accompanies every Indian festival from birth through death. It is not served in better restaurants.

In Peru there is also a nonalcoholic *chicha morada* (purple *chicha*) made from maize. Be sure to specify which *chicha* you want or you could be unpleasantly surprised. Peru also produces a soft drink called, of all things, Inca Kola. It is touted as having *el sabor nacional* (the national flavor). It has a yellowish color and a distinctive taste you will not confuse with anything else.

Peru has perhaps the most varied cuisine in South America. *Ceviche* (raw shellfish or white fish soaked in a spicy lemon marinade) and *anticuchos* (marinated kabobs and grilled beef hearts) are both a treat, although at press time it was unadvisable to eat raw fish because of the numerous cases of cholera reported in the country. Peruvians know how to prepare fish literally hundreds of ways, all delicious. *Corvina* (sea bass) is the most common fish, either stuffed with seafood (*almejas, choros, machos*), smothered in a sauce, or both. *Ocopa* (boiled potatoes or eggs in a spicy, cheese and peanut sauce), *ají de gallina* (shredded chicken in a hot pepper and cheese sauce), and *rocoto relleno* (stuffed hot pepper) are three hot items (*muy picante*) to try. Try anything prepared *a la chiclayana;* the cuisine of the Chiclayo region is generally acknowledged to be the best in Peru. *Chifas* are Chinese restaurants, and Lima has some of the best outside Asia. Don't be disappointed if the dish you order is not exactly what you are used to. Chinese food in Peru has not been Westernized to the extent that it has in the US, and it is actually more authentic. For the cocktail hour, *pisco* sours are an absolute must. *Pisco* (grape brandy) is also used in the popular *chilcanos* (with ginger ale) and *algarrobinas* (with carob syrup).

Andean Indian dishes are rarely found in tourist restaurants. If you come across them, try *tacu-tacu* (mashed rice and garbanzo patties), *cau-cau* (spiced tripe, potatoes, peppers, and rice), or *cuy* (guinea pig).

In Ecuador the national drink is nonalcoholic. Start your day with a glass of frothy *naranjilla* (a fruit of the tomato family, but tartly sweet, like an orange) juice — it's indescribably delicious. Indeed, the availability of fresh tropical fruits is one of the greatest pleasures of South American eating. Papayas, mangoes, *guanábanas* (custard apple), *lúcuma* (egg fruit), and many, many more are served all over South America in one form or another. *Dulce de membrillo* (sweet quince) and *pasta de guayaba* (guava paste) are frequent dessert items, best eaten with a piece of white cheese to balance the almost excessive sweetness of the fruit jelly.

While in Ecuador, sample *humitas* (similar to Mexican tamales), *locro* (a corn or potato and cheese soup, sometimes served with avocado), or the popular *llapingachos* (a patty of cheese and fried potatoes with peanut sauce and an egg on top). *Ceviche* is as common here as in Peru, but the spices in the Ecuadoran version are slightly different and the shrimp and lobster, fresh from local waters, are not to be missed. (With cholera becoming endemic, however, Ecuadorans have taken to cooking the fish that was used in preparing *ceviche.*)

Fish is abundant in Colombia as well, but residents tend to prefer meat and chicken. *Arroz con pollo* (chicken with rice) is found on most menus. Be sure to try a *piquete* (meat, potatoes, and vegetables in *ají*). Two hearty soups are the *cuchuco* (a thick barley and meat soup seasoned with peppercorns) and *mazamorra* (a similar soup thickened with a pap of ground maize). (To add to the confusion, in Peru *mazamorra* is a dessert made with the same maize pap and fruit.) No Colombian goes through a day without *arepas* (a cornmeal pancake often eaten in place of bread) or that great Colombian coffee. The local alcoholic brew is called *aguardiente* (literally, "fire water") and should be approached with caution.

*Arepas* — served with butter, cheese, or an array of fillings ranging from tuna salad to shredded beef — are also the mainstay in neighboring Venezuela. Wash them down with an icy cold Polar beer or some of that country's fine aged fum — the best on the continent. Or try the sweeter and milder *ponche crema* (egg nog). You do not have to wait until *Christmas* to drink it. Sweeter still is the dessert with the catchy name *bien me sabe* (it tastes good to me), made from coconut custard on cake and topped with meringue. Although Caracas is one of the most North Americanized cities in South America and you can find restaurants serving every cuisine under the sun, criollo menus rarely resemble ours. Try *mondongo* (tripe with lots of vegetables). Order a *sancocho* (fish or meat stew with squash, sweet potatoes, and plantain). or other favorites such as the national dish, *pabellón criollo* (shredded beef in spiced tomato sauce served with fried bananas, white rice, and black beans), and *cazuela de mariscos* (similar to Chilean *chupe de mariscos).*

In Brazil, Portuguese and African dishes will replace the Spanish and Indian meals of the other countries. The black influence is strongest in the region around Salvador (Bahia). One of the local specialties is *vatapá*, a peppery fish or chicken and shrimp stew seasoned with coconut milk, peanut and palm oils and served with manioc or rice powder. The Brazilian national dish, *feijoada,* carried to its ultimate complexity, can have some 20 or more different kinds of sausage and cuts of meat — tongue, pig's feet, or *chorizo* (sausage) — added to a black bean soup that is also served with the ever-present manioc powder. Be warned that a spoonful of moist manioc powder sticks to the roof of your mouth like peanut butter. (Best mix it in with the *feijoada.)* The variety of spicy sauces is what makes a *picadinha* (hash) worth ordering. The *comidas criollas* (creole cooking) are Portuguese in origin and tend to be bland. A *cozido* (stew) is a transplanted Portuguese dish of boiled meat and vegetables. It is identical to the *cocido* found in the Spanish-speaking countries.

Wash down your meal with *cachaça* (homemade sugarcane whiskey) if you dare, but no Brazilian considers a meal complete without a *cafezinho,* a demitasse of pure coffee extract (served loaded with sugar) almost strong enough to stand your spoon in. These are served in coffee bars, where you drink standing up. Brazilian beer is perhaps the best in South America, but Brazilians drink a lot of *batidas,* a potent drink of *cachaça* and fruit juice. One of the best is a *caipirinha* — *cachaça,* sugar, and lime. It's very potent. In Spanish, *batida* (sometimes *batido)* means an ice cream or fruit shake. (Don't confuse the two.)

In Paraguay, the local moonshine is *caña,* a rum made from sugarcane or honey. The national meal is *so'o-yosopy* (a Guaraní word), a meat soup. Try also *sopa paraguaya* (Paraguayan soup), which is more of a soufflé made from mashed corn, cheese, milk, eggs, and onions. The *surubí* fish is a delicacy prepared in a number of ways.

Paraguay and all the other northern countries have jungle regions. Should you venture off the usual tourist routes, you will be faced with armadillo, snake, monkey, and various other unidentifiable meats. People will tell you that you are eating meat or fowl. If it tastes good, don't ask any more. Try any and all of these dishes as long as they are well cooked. Do not watch them roast a monkey on a spit or you may lose your appetite. A jungle diet otherwise consists of fruits and starches (plantain, potatoes, rice, and lots of yucca). Tortoise egg omelettes are very good, although the consistency is rather spongy compared to those made with chicken eggs.

The Guianas are usually the least known, most overlooked countries of South America, but dining there can be an amazing experience because of the additional ethnic backgrounds. In French Guiana, old-style French cooking still predominates, while in Guyana you can order roast beef and Yorkshire pudding. Suriname offers a choice of Dutch, Indonesian, and Chinese meals. *Nasi goring* or *bami goring* (rice or noodles tossed with various cuts of meat) are both Indonesian in origin. All three countries offer some native Indian or black dishes as well.

The capitals and a few of the larger cities (such as Buenos Aires and Caracas) have restaurants that serve international fare. This usually means French or Italian dishes, but occasionally you can find German, Japanese, Greek, and other foreign establishments as well. Imported vodkas, gins, and whiskeys are served in all the better bars, but they are very expensive. Why not enjoy what is uniquely South American instead?

You will not have any unpleasant experiences with food or drink if you follow a few simple rules. The water supplies in the larger cities are fairly safe, but when in doubt, remember the two B's: boiled or bottled. Peel fruits before eating them, and avoid any with severely damaged skin. Anything that has been thoroughly cooked is safe so you need not worry if you find out that you just ate armadillo stew by mistake — and be sure to eat the food when it is still hot. The biggest danger is overeating and drinking too much at the higher altitudes. *Soroche* (mountain fever) is not fatal unless you suffer from heart problems, but no one will be able to convince you otherwise when you are feeling its effects. To help avoid *soroche,* eat *very* lightly your first day or two in the mountains. Tea and toast or chicken broth are highly recommended. Do not drink anything alcoholic unless you want to be higher than the Andes themselves. One *pisco* sour in Cuzco will have the same effect as three or four in Lima. After a day or two of taking it easy, you should be able to eat normally with no side effects. But always take care with alcohol.

We have included information on specific restaurants in the *Best in Town* section of each city report in THE CITIES. As Spanish-speaking South Americans say before a meal, *Buen provecho!* (May it benefit you!)

# THE CITIES

# ASUNCIÓN

The capital of Paraguay is still one of the best-kept secrets in South America. With a population of about 800,000 — one-fifth the national total — Asunción is small, clean, and provincial enough to have retained the atmosphere of a South American colonial town, yet it has all the amenities of a major capital.

Life still centers around the Plaza de los Héroes, with its many flowers, trees, fountains, box camera photographers, shoeshine men with elaborate chairs, lace vendors, and a mixed crowd of businessmen, schoolchildren in white uniforms, and a few Macá Indians. Spending just a few minutes on its four city blocks provides a feeling of how life used to be in the bigger cities of South America and how it still is in most small cities and towns. Surrounding the plaza are government buildings, shops, and restaurants. The most important business here is government, but the city is also a valuable port, and many light industries are located on the outer fringe of town. Key sources of revenue are the sale of liquor and imported electronics, much of which violates contraband laws (although they are not enforced by the government). The business section covers about 20 square blocks, but since there are no zoning regulations, the high-rise buildings blend with the low, stucco residential districts. The downtown area is becoming increasingly overrun with cars and pollution is on the rise; trolley cars and buses are the main form of municipal transportation. Multistory shopping centers filled with stores selling imported perfume, liquor, jewelry, watches, and electronics are springing up all over the city. Many flowering trees and palms line the streets. Gardens bloom with giant orchids and poinsettias. Although not a glamorous, exciting metropolis, Asunción's quaintness gives it a subtle appeal.

The people's work habits have evolved in response to the hot, humid climate. With hardly an exception, everyone wakes up early and goes to work before it gets hot. Everything shuts down tight at noon, and siesta is not over until 3 or 4 PM. Shops and some public buildings open again until 6:30 or 7 PM. The siesta is responsible for Asunción's four rush hours rather than the usual two. At 7 AM and noon, and again at 3:30 and 7 PM, the streets are jammed with cars and buses. Since everyone has a siesta, people dine late and generally don't go to bed until well past midnight.

Situated on a series of seven small, rolling hills on the east bank of the Río Paraguay, part of the Río de la Plata system that flows into the Atlantic at Buenos Aires, Asunción is practically in the center of South America, nearly equidistant from the Atlantic and the Andes. The city stands at an altitude of about 250 feet and covers about 45 square miles. Paraguay itself is about the same size as Montana, covering 150,000 square miles of rugged scrubland and jungle. Because most of its western portion, the Chaco, is remote and quite undeveloped, it is often called the last frontier of the Americas (see *Paraguay*, DIRECTIONS).

# ASUNCIÓN

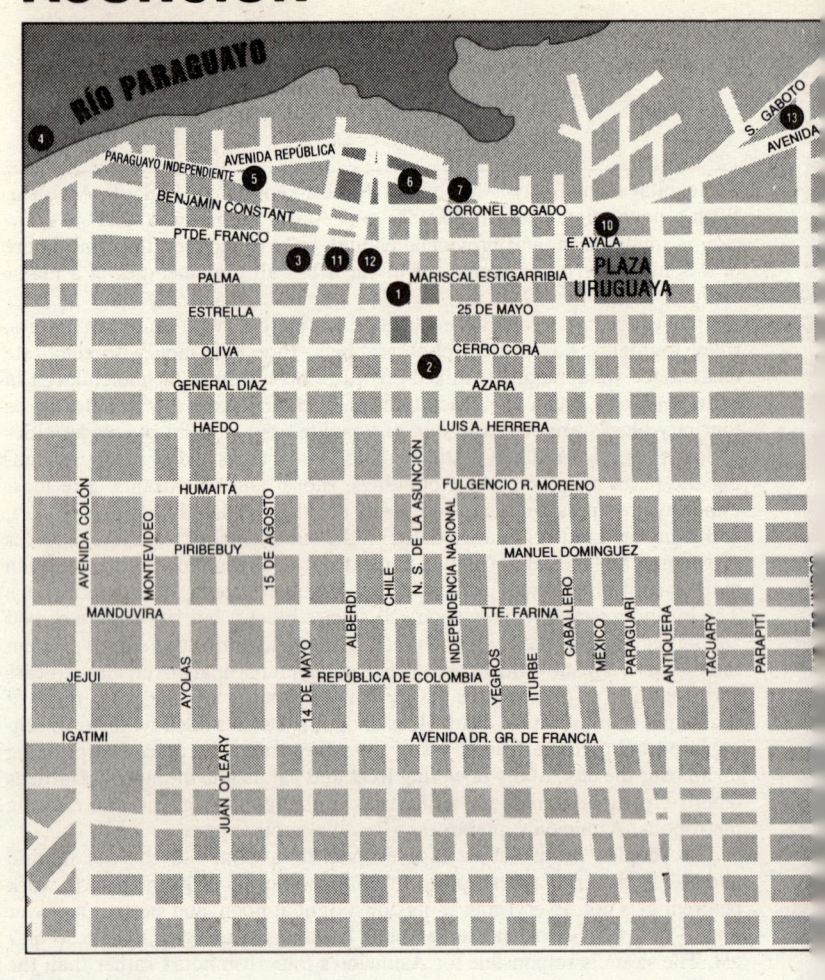

**Points of Interest**

1. Plaza de los Héroes; El Panteón/The Pantheon
2. Guaraní Hotel
3. Casa de la Independencia/Independence House
4. The Port
5. Palacio del Gobierno/Government Palace
6. Plaza Independencia/Independence Plaza
7. Catedral/Cathedral; Museo Bogarín/Bogarin Museum

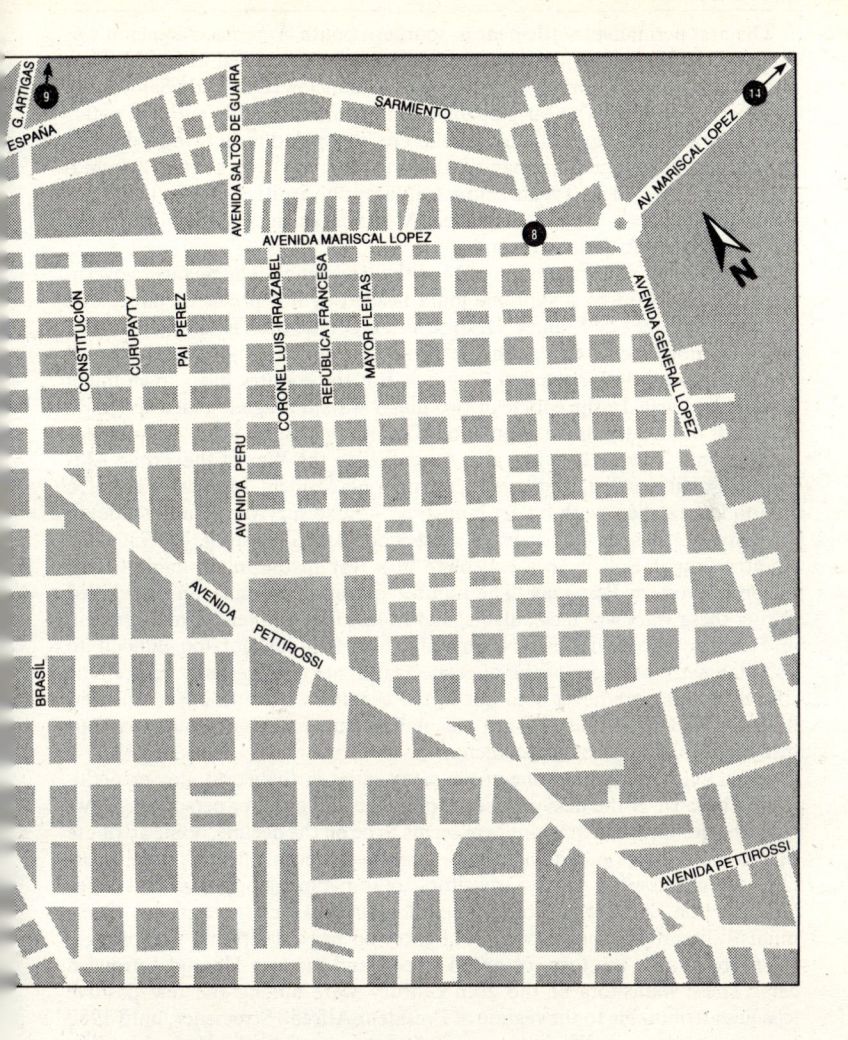

8. Villa Morra; Museo Histórico Militar/Military History Museum
9. Iglesia Recoleta y Cementario; Jardín Botánico/Botanical Gardens, Asunción Golf Club
10. Train Station
11. National Tourist Office
12. Asunción Teatro Municipal/Municipal Theater
13. Museo Etnográfico Andrés Barbero/Andres Barbero Ethnography Museum
14. Airport; Museo Paraguayo de Arte Contemporáneo/Paraguayan Museum of Contemporary Art; Museo del Barro/Barro Museum

The first permanent settlement in southern South America, Asunción was founded in 1537 by Spanish explorers seeking lost cities paved with gold. They named it Nuestra Señora Santa María de la Asunción (Our Lady Saint Mary of the Assumption). The early Spanish settlers mixed readily with the native Guaraní, and even today, most of the city's population is of mixed background and is bilingual in Spanish and Guaraní. Two years after its founding — still more than 60 years before Captain John Smith sailed up the James River in Virginia — Spain designated Asunción as the capital of its entire southern South American empire.

Independence was granted in 1811 without violence. The Spanish government was replaced by a supreme junta headed by a supreme dictator, José Gaspar Rodríguez de Francia. Despite his autocratic title, Rodríguez — who has gone down in history with the name "El Supremo" — held Paraguay together peacefully for the first 20 years. But the country has known much turmoil and war. In the course of two major wars, Paraguay twice lost more than half of its adult male population. During the 1860s, it put up a gallant fight against Brazil, Uruguay, and Argentina in the War of the Triple Alliance. In that conflict, Paraguay's greatest hero, Field Marshal Francisco Solano López, died (with his Irish mistress — who survived — at his side) in a decisive battle near the border of what is now Brazil. During the 1930s, the country fought Bolivia to a stalemate in a war in the inhospitable Chaco region of western Paraguay. The number of young Paraguayan men killed during these wars was incalculable, and to this day, women outnumber men in Paraguay. So male visitors generally find that it's not too difficult to socialize with members of the opposite sex. True, until recently respectable single women were never seen out in the evening without a chaperone, but times have changed, and single women now go out alone or in groups, without fear of social stigma or harassment.

Asunción is considered one of the safest cities in the world, day or night, in part because of the heavy presence of police and military personnel. However, the number of men in uniform seems to be on the decline. Some attribute this to the institution of an almost-democratic government. Still, it is important to keep passports handy, as visitors are sometimes stopped and asked for identification. Security agents have been known to search travelers for "Communist" literature, and inspection of carry-on bags at airports is thorough.

Progress takes the form of paved streets and modern US and European cars. These indicators of the 20th century were among the few positive legacies attributable to the regime of President Alfredo Stroessner, until 1989 Paraguay's supreme dictator — in fact if not in actual title. He had been in power since 1954 (and had been elected to a new 5-year term as recently as 1988), but was ousted in a bloody coup in February 1989. The new military rulers of Paraguay held elections (plagued with irregularities) on May 1, 1989, and General Andrés Rodríguez, head of the military group, was overwhelmingly elected. But there is some skepticism about true democracy returning to Paraguay — *The Economist* magazine reported that "the tinpot dictatorship is now a tinpot democracy." Paraguay was a notoriously unstable country before Stroessner took control, and there is great fear that it will lapse back to its unproductive political past. One ray of hope comes from the new president's promise to step down after this year (although at press time there was talk of extending the deadline to 1994), and to allow heads of state to serve for only one term thereafter. In addition, newspapers closed by Stroessner are publishing again, workers are allowed to strike, and the number of human rights abuses has decreased.

Asunción residents tend to be kindly disposed toward North Americans, and there is no sense that this relationship will change. This community numbers about 1,000, most of whom are embassy personnel, Peace Corps workers, and Protestant missionaries of various denominations. Even more noticeable are the large Asian and German communities in the city, both of which tend to keep to themselves. Many shops, restaurants, and hotels advertise in both Spanish and German. Missionaries from Germany — especially Mennonites — are active in the capital and surrounding countryside.

With such an international mix of residents and travelers, money flows freely in Asunción's *casas de cambio* (exchange houses), where visitors can obtain greenbacks for their traveler's checks. Change your money at the *casas de cambio* along Calle Palma rather than at the bank or your hotel, for they offer several more guaranís for your dollar, and it is all legal. (Be forewarned: US bills must be in good condition — without stains, drawings or written notes on them — or they will be flatly rejected in *casas de cambio* as well as hotels and shops that would normally accept dollars.) If you are heading on to Brazil, you also can pick up some cruzeiros here. Asunción is full of Brazilian tourists who fill up the *casas* with cruzeiros, so they are only too glad to have you take some off their hands, especially if you have dollar traveler's checks.

And one more thing: Bring your bathing suit for a swim in a hotel pool. Asunción is hot, hot, hot, except during the winter months of June, July, and August, when it is only slightly cooler.

# ASUNCIÓN AT-A-GLANCE

**SEEING THE CITY:** The best place to start your tour of Asunción is at the top of the *Guaraní* hotel on the main plaza, Plaza de los Héroes. From the 13th-floor lookout, you can see most of the city and Río Paraguay beyond. It is not difficult to imagine why the first settlers chose this high spot as the location for Asunción, with its natural vantage point over the low-lying flatland bordering the river to the north and south of the city. Take the lobby elevator to reach the 13th floor, which has an outdoor walkway circling the building. At times, this floor is used for private receptions and may be closed to the public; if so, ask at the front desk for permission to enter. Or drink a cocktail in the restaurant on the same floor, which provides a dramatic view of Asunción at night. The *Internacional* hotel (520 Ayolas; phone: 494113), with its 15th-floor garden-piano bar, is another great spot for seeing the city lights.

**SPECIAL PLACES:** You can see almost all the special places in Asunción on a walking tour beginning at Plaza de los Héroes. The downtown streets are laid out in a neat and orderly grid. As you stand in front of the *Guaraní* hotel with the plaza in front of you, you are on Calle Oliva. The next street down, crossing the heart of the plaza, is Calle Estrella, and the street at the bottom of the plaza is Calle Palma. Oliva, Estrella, and Palma — the olive, the star, and the palm — are the three symbols on the Paraguayan flag.

**El Panteón (The Pantheon)** – In a lower corner of Plaza de los Héroes sits the Pantheon where Paraguay's military heroes lie enshrined. It is a replica of Les Invalides, Napoleon's tomb in Paris. As you pass the smartly uniformed guards beneath the pillars, you enter a large rotunda. Below, in the center, is the tomb of the unknown soldier, commemorating the many Paraguayans who gave their lives for their country. On all sides are vaults containing the remains of national heroes, including Francisco Solano López, hero of the Triple Alliance War, and José Félix Estigarribia, hero of the Chaco War. On the upper walls are numerous plaques, gifts of friendly foreign governments. At the far side of the rotunda is a statue of the Virgin Mary, patron saint of Asunción. It is said that she holds the rank of marshal in the Paraguayan army. The statue was transported to Paraguay from Naples in 1742. Open daily from 6 AM until 6 PM. No admission charge. At Plaza de los Héroes, corner of Calle Palma and Calle Chile.

**Casa de la Independencia (Independence House)** – Here the Paraguayan revolutionaries plotted to overthrow the Spanish in 1811. Independence House is one of the few authentic colonial buildings still standing, and it has been fully restored. The entrance to the house is set off by a mural of Asunción in the 1700s, painted by Paraguayan artist José Laterza Parodi; the sitting room has a 150-year-old chandelier. Be sure to visit the room at the back, where the revolutionaries declared independence on the night of May 14, 1811. Open from 7:30 to 11:30 AM and from 3 to 6:30 PM except on Saturday afternoons and Sundays. No admission charge. Calle 14 de Mayo at Presidente Franco (phone: 93918).

**The Port** – For centuries before a road connected the capital with Brazil, Asunción was literally Paraguay's lifeline to the rest of the world. Here oceangoing freighters dock to unload manufactured goods and to load Paraguay's agricultural surplus: cotton, soybeans, tobacco, wood, and meat products. There are short, 3-hour yacht tours of the Bay of Asunción and the adjoining river which can be arranged through local travel agencies and the larger hotels. In addition, groups can charter a skippered cabin cruiser for this purpose from the *Casino Yacht y Golf Club Paraguayo* (phone: 36121). You also arrange a cruise at the tour desk in the lobby of the *Itá Enramada* hotel (phone: 33041 or 37265) and be picked up at the hotel's dock or you can book through *Travel Club* (phone: 494164; fax: 446146) and leave from the city dock. To reach the port, walk through the Customs Building, across the street at the end of Calle Colón, onto the dock. You are facing the Bay of Asunción. Río Paraguay lies out of sight behind a peninsula that forms the far shore of the bay.

**Palacio del Gobierno (Government Palace)** – Also known as the Palacio de López, it was constructed more than 100 years ago for Francisco Solano López by his father, and was intended to be his private residence, but the Triple Alliance War intervened, costing the younger López his life. The building became the offices of the president and the Ministry of Foreign Affairs. It was spruced up and returned to its former glory in late 1990 in honor of a visit from the King of Spain. Open Mondays through Fridays from 3 to 6 PM, although whether visitors are allowed in is arbitary. Visitors' passports must be left at the door. No admission charge. Calle El Paraguayo Independiente between Calle 15 de Agosto and Calle O'Leary.

**Plaza Independencia (Independence Plaza)** – The city's original plaza is almost on the waterfront, just down Calle Chile from the Pantheon. It sometimes is called Plaza Constitución, because of the tall monument commemorating the signing of the constitution in 1870. Take a seat on one of the dark green benches and just let the world go by. The plaza is surrounded by important buildings and contains several statues in honor of Paraguay's heroes. As you face the river, the Legislative Palace stands in front of you, the former military school is to your left, the cathedral to your right. Behind you are the main post office and police headquarters. This area, called Chacarita, is the closest thing you'll see to a slum in the capital. Asunción's relatively small population of 800,000, aided by migration to Brazil and Argentina and the government's successful voluntary rural colonization schemes, have helped to prevent the growth of slums that plague so many South American capitals. Plaza Independencia covers the 2-block area between Calle Chile and Calle Independencia Nacional on the river.

**Museo Paraguayo de Arte Contemporáneo (Paraguayan Contemporary Art Museum) and Museo del Barro (Clay Museum)** – Actually two collections under one roof, the pieces here range from old clay figures to modern art. The *Contemporary Art Museum* houses changing exhibits of contemporary Paraguayan artists. This collection is partly the effort of Carlos Colombino, the country's best-known painter/sculptor/printmaker. In the *Clay Museum,* there are many fascinating pieces of locally produced naïf religious art — saints with human hair, jointed limbs (the better to dress them in hand-stitched gowns as is still done today in South American churches), and glass bead eyes. There also are a few figures from the Jesuit missions, which are characterized by classical lines and unmistakable Indian features. One room is devoted to masks from the village of Tobatí known for its woodcarving. Used in religious and irreverent festivities in the countryside, the masks wear expressions ranging from humorous to grotesque. There also are erotic, decorative, and functional ceramics, wool and cotton weavings, fine *ñandutí* (spider's web lace), and jewelry. Be sure to stop by the gift shop (see *Shopping*) with its wonderful selection of locally produced ceramics. Open daily except Sundays from 4 to 8:30 PM. No admission charge. Calle Uno e Emeterio Miranda y Molas López (phone: 604244). To get here, take Bus No. 30A (marked "Airport"), get off at the 2800-2900 block of Avenida Aviadores del Chaco and follow the signs for 2 blocks.

**Catedral (Cathedral)** – The Catholic metropolitan cathedral is neither exceptionally large nor ornate by Latin American standards. Built in the 19th century, it is rather plain inside. Of note is the intricate carving of the altar, which contrasts with the edifice itself. Most people who are devout go to neighborhood churches scattered around the city. While there is complete freedom of religion and many Protestant churches in Asunción, the overwhelming majority of Paraguayans are at least nominally Roman Catholic. Open daily from 8 to 11 AM and 3:30 to 5:30 PM. No admission charge. Calle Independencia Nacional and Calle Colonel Bogado. More interesting than the cathedral itself is the *Museo Bogarín* (Bogarín Museum) next door, which houses a fascinating collection of religious sculptures and paintings from the colonial period, as well as some arms used during the Triple Alliance and Chaco Wars. Open Mondays through Saturdays from 8 to 11 AM (phone: 447716). No admission charge.

**Museo Etnográfico Andrés Barbero (Andrés Barbero Ethnographic Museum)** – If you want to know more about the Indians who roamed Paraguay before the Europeans colonized it, this museum has excellent collections of artifacts and historical exhibits. The Guaraní dominated an area far greater than today's Paraguay. Iguazú and Itaipú are two of many Guaraní Indian words still in use. (The Guaraní words are easy to recognize, as the accent is usually on the last syllable.) The museum also has an excellent library and photo archive. Open Mondays through Saturdays from 8 to 11 AM, Wednesdays from 3 to 6 PM. No admission charge. 217 Calle España at Mómpox. It's about a 15-minute walk from the main plaza or a quick trip on the *Las Mercedes* trolley line (phone: 441696).

**Villa Morra** – Asunción is not quite large enough to have suburbs as we think of them, but it does have interesting neighborhoods. To see Villa Morra, one of the best of these, go along Avenida Mariscal López. The street is lined with homes of some of Asunción's finest families, interspersed with embassies. At the crest of the hill of this avenue lined by jacaranda trees, about a dozen blocks from its start, is the Ministerio de Defensa (Department of Defense), which houses the *Museo Histórico Militar* (Military History Museum). On the right, a few blocks farther on, is the US Embassy (at the corner of Avdas. Kubitschek and Mariscal López). In the middle of the next block, on the right behind the big fence and all the shrubbery, is the sprawling compound where ex-President Stroessner lived before he was forced into exile. The current president refused to move into the former dictator's compound, preferring to remain in his sumptuous, château-like mansion in the Carmelitas district, near the Central Bank of Paraguay. A bit farther on is the imposing edifice of the Embassy of Japan, also on the right, followed shortly by the Recoleta Church and Cemetery. You will soon reach Avenida República Argentina, where you may wish to turn around and head back to the city center. But before you start back, visit the *Amandau* ice cream parlor, a few blocks to your right on Argentina. The ice cream is excellent, and there are several flavors you may never have tasted, such as prune or chocolate *bariloche,* a delicious chocolate with raisins and chopped almonds. Alternatively, continue down the street to *Sugar* (at the corner of De Las Palmeras), a clean and very "in" ice cream shop.

**Iglesia Recoleta y Cementerio (Recoleta Church and Cemetery)** – Here the well-to-do bury their dead, though, in fact, the dead remain above ground in caskets on the shelves of each family's mausoleum. Wander freely among the eerie and elaborate mausoleums, many as large as small houses. On *All Saints' Day,* November 1, and other religious holidays, thousands of people descend on the cemetery. Wealthy residents arrive early with folding lawn chairs, throw open the doors and windows of the mausoleums, and sit and fan themselves as the mourners stream past. Immediately to the left of the church is the memorial to Eliza Lynch, Francisco Solano López's Irish mistress. Erected during the early 1970s, the monument — topped by a modern statue of the heroine Paraguayans call "Madame Lynch" — is curiously out of sync with the adjacent cemetery, which was built in the 1850s. There are also many modest grave sites with simple tombstones. In front of the Recoleta Church is a flower market, where the mourners purchase small bouquets to place in vases before the mausoleums. Open daily. Av. Santísimo Sacramento and Av. Mariscal López. Take a taxi; it's only a 10-minute ride from downtown. Or, if you're not in a rush, catch any of the many city buses that ply Av. Mariscal López.

**Jardín Botánico (Botanical Garden)** – If the old saying "getting there is half the fun" has any truth, here is the proof. Asunción's Botanical Gardens are a somewhat run-down park sprawling over many acres, with two museums, a zoo, stables, and a golf course. The garden was once the López family estate, a typical country home with wide verandahs, which now houses a library and natural history museum. Taken all together, it makes a visit worthwhile, but the chief attraction is getting there — if you can catch the train. The old wood burner leaves from the station on the Plaza Uruguaya near the city center for the Botanical Gardens and points south every day at 12:15 PM. You can take a taxi or bus back. Check the train schedule before you set out (phone: 447316). Open daily from 8 AM to 7 PM. Admission charge. While at the garden, don't miss the *Museo de Historia Natural* (Natural History Museum), an eclectic collection of stuffed (and somewhat frayed) animals, plus jar upon jar of dissected creatures. Open daily from 8 AM to 7 PM. No admission charge. Once at the Jardín Botánico, hop aboard the new "tram," a bus designed to look like an old-fashioned trolley. For less than a dollar, you can take a ride through the city and back to the gardens (or take it back into town and ask the driver to drop you off downtown). At the corner of Av. General Artigas and Av. Santísimo Sacramento in the Trinidad neighborhood.

**Iglesia de la Santísima Trinidad (Holy Trinity Church)** – Built in 1853 so that then-president Carlos Antonio López would have a spot to attend Sunday mass close to his house, this is the most Paraguayan of Asunción's churches. Built in the style of a colonial house with a red tile roof, there are shuttered windows here instead of stained glass and side altars carved in the town of Yaguarón. Note the delicately hand-painted ceiling and the more psychedelic designs around the doorways. Lopez's remains were buried here until 1939, when they were moved to the Pantheon. Open daily from 8 to 11 AM and 3 to 6 PM. At the corner of Santísima Trinidad and Sacramento.

■ **EXTRA SPECIAL:** The estate where Marshal López kept his Irish mistress, Eliza Lynch, is well worth an afternoon fling. Now the *Gran Hotel del Paraguay,* the old estate's lush gardens and tropical vegetation are still flourishing. Although the elegance of the villa's interior has faded, it remains charming. From 11:30 AM to 2 PM, a buffet and an à la carte lunch, with warm, attentive service, is offered in the hotel dining room. At Madame Lynch's request, it was painted to resemble an arbor; this cavernous salon originally was used as the estate's theater. If the adjacent tennis courts aren't busy, you may be able to squeeze in a set. Ask the resident pro. Another possibility is to sip a cocktail or a fresh fruit drink beside the large outdoor pool. It might even be worthwhile to step back in time and spend a night in one of the big rooms of this once opulent mansion. A double room only costs about $30. Calle La Residenta and Padre Pouche (phone: 200051).

## SOURCES AND RESOURCES

**TOURIST INFORMATION:** For general information and tours, your best bet is *Inter-Express* (690 Yegros; phone: 490111 through 490115; fax: 449156), a travel agency whose personnel speak English and which offers a fleet of buses and private cars with drivers. *Inter-Express* can arrange tours of the city and its environs, as well as of neighboring Brazil and Argentina. Open weekdays from 7:30 AM to noon and 2:30 to 6:30 PM, Saturdays from 7 AM to noon. At the government's helpful national tourism office (468 Palma; phone: 441530; fax: 491230), you can find useful information on current and upcoming events, as well as brochures (some in English) and maps. The tourist office puts out a map of the city center, which is duplicated in most car rental brochures and is available from most travel agents. The office is open weekdays from 7 AM to 7 PM, Saturdays from 7:30 to 11:30 AM.

Another excellent English-speaking agency, more convenient to downtown, is *Americana Tours* (in its new location at 517 Alberdi; phone: 490672). English (and German) are spoken at the efficient Mennonite-run *Menno Travel Agency* (551 Azara; phone: 441210), open from 8 AM to 6 PM. In addition to travel arrangements and currency exchange, this office also provides a safer mail service than the city post office. *(Menno* mails letters only — no packages).

*TAP Guía,* a new guidebook with street maps, hotel and restaurant rundowns, and other information of interest to visitors, is available at newsstands and bookstores. The guide, which covers all of Paraguay, is printed in English, Spanish, German, and Portuguese; it costs about $6. *Land of Lace and Legend* (published by the American Women's Club of Asunción) is an English guide to the city and the country — it has two maps of Asunción, one with a key to major points of interest. It's on sale for about $6 at *Books* (in the shopping center *Villa Morra* on Av. Mariscal López; phone: 605794). If you read Spanish, the store also has a good collection of volumes on Paraguayan history and politics (and novels in English).

The US Embassy is located at 1776 Mariscal López (phone: 201041).

**Local Coverage** – The *Buenos Aires Herald* and the *Brazil Herald* are the only English-language newspapers available in Asunción. You can pick them up, along with the fortnightly English magazine *Guaraní News,* 1 day after publication at major newspaper stands (for example, those at the corner of Chile and Estrella, the *Guaraní* hotel, and the airport).

**TELEPHONE:** The city code for Asunción is 21. When calling from within Paraguay, dial 021 before the local number. The country code for Paraguay is 595.

**CLIMATE AND CLOTHES:** Asunción is hot except during the winter, June through August, when the weather is warm, though winter temperatures may dip into the low 50s F (around 10C) during a cold snap. It is also rather humid, so light clothes and air conditioned hotel rooms are recommended. Evenings are delightful, and much dining and entertainment takes place under the stars. An important note: When it rains in Asunción, it rains *hard,* and since the city has few storm drains, and a number of unpaved streets, make sure you bring along waterproof footwear. Mosquito repellent also will come in handy, especially during the rainy season.

**GETTING AROUND: Bus** – Virtually everything downtown can be reached on foot. Buses have hard, uncomfortable seats, and lack adequate shock absorbers for the cobblestone lanes, although for trips outside the center of town, they are an inexpensive alternative to taxis. Local trips within the urban area cost about 25¢. Be sure to keep your ticket until you get off the bus as inspectors periodically board for spot checks. The central bus station is located at the corner of Avdas. Fernando de La Mora and República Argentina (phone: 551732).

**Taxi** – For trips outside the city center, taxis are available at taxi stands and also may be hailed on streets. Generally, the price of a cab ride as listed on the meter, plus a small tip, is not expensive. The fare between the airport and downtown is about $15 to $20. Beware of drivers who leave the meter off, however, or claim they are unable to make change. Carry a supply of small bills.

**Car Rental** – If you want to drive, try *Hertz* (at the airport; phone: 206195, or at Km 4.5 of Av. Eusebio Ayala; phone: 605708); *Only Rent-a-Car* (503 Calle Palma; phone: 492731/2/3); *Touring Cars* (682 Calle Iturbe; phone: 447945 and 491394); or *National Car Rental* (501 Yegros; phone: 491379 and 491848). An international driver's license is not needed, but your US license and a major credit card are necessary, and you must be at least 22 years old. The *Touring y Automóvil Club Paraguayo* (at the corner of Avdas. 25 de Mayo and Brasil; phone: 200014) has maps for sale.

**Trolley** – Though old and rickety, the trolley is fun to ride and costs only a dime or so. There is one line, which runs along Calle España to Las Mercedes suburb. Avoid the trolley during rush hours. Unfortunately, it does not run Saturday afternoons, Sundays, or when it rains. The trolley operates regularly from 6 AM to 7 PM Monday through Friday.

**SPECIAL EVENTS:** Religious processions are held on *Good Friday* and on August 15, the anniversary of the founding of the city; check locally for details if you are here on either date. June 24 is *El Día de San Juan* (St. John's Day), commemorating the patron saint of fire. On the evening of June 23, bonfires are built and barefoot men and some women run across the hot bed of coals after the fire burns down. This ritual takes place at many locations; check locally. July and August are folk festival months, when many concerts, exhibits, and parades are held in towns in the interior. On September 21, the *Día de la Primavera* (Spring Festival Day) is celebrated with a youth parade and with flowers everywhere. The most special event is December 8 *(Feast of the Immaculate Conception);* on this day it seems as though the whole city walks or rides (the president flies by helicopter) 30 miles (48 km) to the shrine at Caacupé. Thousands go on foot, leaving after work the day before, arriving in Caacupé about sunrise, in time for the first mass at the large church with the blue Virgin over the altar. There usually are fireworks and the town takes on a carnival atmosphere with amusement rides, souvenir stands, and vendors selling *chipa* (bread) and sausages.

**MUSEUMS:** In addition to those described in *Special Places,* other museums of interest include the following:

**Museo Histórico Militar (Military History Museum)** – Artifacts from the War of the Triple Alliance and the Chaco War are on display here. Open Mondays through Fridays from 7:30 to 11:30 AM and 2:45 to 5:30 PM, Saturdays from 7 to 9 AM. No admission charge. Ministerio de Defensa, Avdas. Mariscal López and 22 de Septiembre.

**Museo Nacional de Bellas Artes (National Fine Arts Museum)** – This colonial building is slowly being restored. At press time, the permanent art collection was not on view to the public, and a date for reopening was unavailable. Call ahead to check the status. Housed in the same building is the *National Archive* with some of the first documents of the Spanish conquest, including an order from the Spanish crown, instructing the governor of Paraguay to educate the Indians. Open weekdays from 2 to 6:30 PM. No admission charge. Corner of Iturbe and Estigarribia (phone: 447716).

**Museo de Ciencia Natural (Museum of Natural Science)** – Open Mondays through Saturdays from 7:30 to 11:30 AM and 1:30 to 5 PM, Sundays from 8 AM to noon and 2 to 5:30 PM. No admission charge. Río de Janeiro and Mujer en la Conquista (phone: 290172).

**SHOPPING:** Asunción is tops for special souvenirs. Paraguayan lace is beautiful, lightweight, and fits easily into even overloaded suitcases. Craftspeople make rainbow-hued spiderweb lace called *ñandutí* into doilies, placemats, tablecloths, coasters, and other household items. Just as popular is *aó po'i,* embroidery work done on cotton cloth that is made into shirts, blouses, dresses, tablecloths, napkins, neckties, and breadwarmers. These items wash well and will not fade, though they may require ironing. There are also locally made leather products and straw and rattan goods as well as pottery and ceramics. But nothing compares with the lace. If you take home a dozen *ñandutí* doilies and half a dozen *aó po'i* breadwarmers, you will not regret it. You will never see the likes of it elsewhere, and the prices are low, especially for handmade goods. If you have the opportunity, visit the town of Itauguá, 30 minutes from Asunción, where much of the lace is made.

In Asunción, several shops along Calle Colón near the port carry a wide assortment of *ñandutí* and *aó po'i,* as well as hand-tooled leather goods and hand-painted ceramic hens. You also can make your purchases at the airport, where prices are only slightly higher, or from itinerant merchants at the Plaza de los Héroes along Calle Palma.

Modern, multistory shopping centers featuring imported electronic equipment, designer sportswear, jewelry, watches, and just about everything else, are cropping up all over Asunción, although you'll have to search hard for bargains that beat US prices. A concentration of shopping centers can be found on Calle Palma.

***Anahi*** – This small boutique features hand-embroidered women's fashions, *ñandutí* lace, and some of the prettiest tablecloths in the capital. Everything is made from natural fibers. 343 Caballero at 25 de Mayo (phone: 200791).

***Confecciones Catedral*** – Here you can have a shirt or blouse made to order in 24 hours, if you don't see anything on the shelves that strikes your fancy. Lace placemats and delicate embroidered napkins also are irresistible. Three blocks from the main plaza at 189 Calle Presidente Eligio Ayala (phone: 444747).

***Galería Arte Popular*** – Perhaps the finest quality *artesanía* shop in the city, this handicrafts store offers woodcarvings, clay ceramics, delicate baskets, and leather handbags, but the highlight is the room filled with superbly crafted *ñandutí* and *aó po'i.*

Magnificent tablecloths, stunning shawls, embroidered blouses, and baby clothes are just a few of the items on display. Also for sale are lovely photography books of Paraguay. 360 Ayolas at Palma (phone: 492548).

**Gift Shop of the Museo Paraguayo de Arte Contemporáneo and Museo del Barro** – Shelves crammed with locally produced ceramics — from the distinctive rotund women balancing jugs on their heads made by Virginia Yegros of Tobatí to the anonymous miniature erotic figurines — are the forte of this museum gift shop. The prices are incredibly low and your purchases support the local artist community. For hours and directions to the museum, see *Special Places*. Calle Uno e Emeterio Miranda y Molas López (phone: 604244).

**Victoria** – If you're in the market for Paraguayan *artesanía*, this shop has it all — handmade pottery, finely tooled leather, dolls in regional costume, and an entire brood of the distinctive, hand-painted ceramic hens said to bring good luck. Iturbe at the corner of Eligio Ayala (phone: 494360).

**SPORTS: Fishing** – The fishing in the Río Paraguay and its tributaries is excellent. The problem is getting there. There is fishing — particularly dorado and surubí — at Villa Florida, on the road to Encarnación, a 2-hour drive from Asunción. See the tourist agencies for more information. Overnight fishing trips to a lodge on the Paraná River are available through *Scotty's Sport Fishing* (153 Maldonado; phone: 602653; fax: 662947; Av. Costanera in Ayolas; phone: 72-2272; fax: 72-2274). Travelers are picked up at their hotels in Asunción. Three-day (or more) fishing trips on a yacht on the Río Paraguay can be arranged by calling *Yate El Marqués* (phone: 444200; fax: 446908). For information on fishing licenses contact the Ministerio de Agricultura (640 Av. 25 de Mayo; phone: 445214).

**Golf** – Asunción has two 18-hole golf courses: the public *Asunción Golf Club* (at the Botanical Garden; phone: 290251), and the *Casino Yacht y Golf Club Paraguayo* resort hotel (11 Av. del Yacht in the suburb of Lambaré; phone: 36117, 36121 through 36129, and 37161).

**Hunting** – Duck hunting is permitted fairly freely in the Chaco region, but a permit is required to hunt other animals. Permits can be obtained from travel agents or directly from the Ministerio de Agricultura (640 Av. 25 de Mayo; phone: 445214) in downtown Asunción.

**Soccer** – *Fútbol* is the national sport year-round — people passionately play, watch, and follow the game on the radio or TV. Professional soccer matches take place every Sunday afternoon. If you are going on to Brazil, Uruguay, or Argentina, you may want to wait until you get there to see soccer at its very best. Games are played at *Estadio de Defensores de Chaco* (Av. Juan Díaz de Solís and Martínez), *Estadio de Club Olimpia* (Av. Mariscal López near Sánchez), and *Estadio Cerro Porteño* (828 Av. de las Americas). Check the local newspapers for game schedules.

**Tennis** – If you want to play tennis, there are lighted courts at the *Itá Enramada* hotel (Calle Cacique Lambaré and Ribera del Río Paraguay; phone: 33041 through 33049) and at the *Casino Yacht y Golf Club Paraguayo* (11 Av. del Yacht; phone: 36117, 36121 through 36129, and 37161). Also contact the *Asunción Tennis Club* (1369 España; phone: 200585).

**THEATER:** Several theater companies perform at the *Asunción Teatro Municipal* (Municipal Theater; Presidente Franco near Alberdi; phone: 445169), *Teatro Arlequin* (DeGaulle and Quesada; phone: 605107), and *Teatro de las Américas*, which also hosts music performances (at José Berges; phone: 24772). Check the newspapers to see what's playing. Most presentations are in Spanish; the rest, in Guaraní. *Sala Augustín* (Barrios at 352 España; phone: 24772) sometimes shows free films in English, as does the *Centro Anglo Paraguayo* (457 España at Brasil; phone: 25525).

**MUSIC:** Don't miss the Paraguayan folk music. You can hear it live over a late dinner at many fine restaurants. Typically, groups of three — two guitarists and a harpist — sing in Spanish and Guaraní. Records of Paraguayan folk music, particularly the harp, make nice souvenirs; they're available at all record stores and at the airport. Handmade harps and guitars also can be purchased. Local groups play live jazz on Thursday nights in the summer at the corner of Cruz del Chaco and Pacheco. For information, call 605945.

**NIGHTCLUBS AND NIGHTLIFE:** Asunción's nightlife consists mostly of restaurant shows that start at 9 PM and go on past midnight (see *Best in Town*, below). There's a nightclub with dancing and entertainment, as well as a complete gambling casino, both open 7 nights a week at the *Boite Yasy* of the *Itá Enramada* hotel (Calle Cacique Lambaré and Ribera del Río Paraguay; phone: 33041 through 9). If you're looking for contemporary music from the US, the "in" place for the younger crowd is the *Caracol Club* discotheque (Av. General Perón y Felicidad; phone: 31905), about 20 minutes from downtown on the road to Itá Enramada. There is also a casino and a good small disco at the *Casino Yacht y Golf Club Paraguayo* (in the suburb of Lambaré; phone: 36121), and another at the *Excelsior* (980 Calle Chile and Calle Manduvirá; phone: 495632). Women pay no cover charge at the disco-pub *A Go-Go* (5318 Boggiani at R. Argentina; phone: 660936), currently popular with the younger set. The best-known folklore show, complete with the country's famous bottle dance, is at *El Jardín de la Cerveza* (Av. Argentina at Castillo; phone: 600752). Entertainment begins around 10 PM. Another club offering a show of traditional dance plus dinner is *Yguazú* (1334 Choferes del Chaco; phone: 601008).

# BEST IN TOWN

**CHECKING IN:** The choice of hotels in Asunción has broadened in recent years. You'll find the luxurious *Excelsior* in the heart of the capital, the out-of-town *Itá Enramada* resort, the *Presidente* — catering to businesspeople, and family-style *pensiones*. All entries have air conditioned rooms with private baths. Hotel prices are relatively modest in Asunción. Expect to pay $90 and up for two for a double in those places listed as expensive; between $40 and $90 in those hotels in the moderate category; and under $40 in inexpensive hostelries. Note that breakfast is included in the price of most hotels other than those in the expensive category. All telephone numbers are in the 21 city code unless otherwise indicated.

*Casino Yacht y Golf Club Paraguayo* – Asunción's modern resort hotel is just outside of town on the shores of the Paraguay River. Rooms range from comfortable doubles to deluxe suites. There are 4 restaurants, 5 bars, and a disco that swings until 4 AM on weekends. Other amenities include a casino, an 18-hole golf course, a squash court, lighted tennis courts, swimming pool, sauna, and water skiing and fishing on the Paraguay River, all 15 minutes from town in the suburb of Lambaré, at 11 Av. del Yacht (phone: 36117, 36121 through 36129, and 37161; fax: 36120). Expensive.

*Excelsior* – This downtown, 123-room hotel, with a pool and a fine restaurant is considered the best in Asunción. In a separate building are 15 additional rooms, a penthouse, 3 additional restaurants, a theater, convention facilities, discotheque, shopping area, sauna, massage room, and hairdresser. 980 Calle Chile (phone: 495632 to 495636; in the US: 800-44-UTELL; fax: 496748). Expensive.

*Guaraní* – This imposing, 13-story structure, with its angular lines, dominates the plaza and can be counted on for comfort. Visiting chiefs of state always stay at this government-run hotel. With rooms somewhat larger than those of the *Chaco* (below), it has both penthouse and lobby restaurants, and a large, outdoor swimming pool, as well as a sauna, massage room, and hairdresser. Reservations are advised. Try breakfast in the *Lapacho* restaurant in the lobby; its prices are inexpensive, although service is sometimes surly. A pianist plays at teatime. Calle Oliva, between Calle Independencia Nacional and Calle Nuestra Señora de la Asunción (phone: 491131 to 491139; in the US, 800-878-7449; fax: 443647). Expensive.

**Cecilia** – Now offering several suites in addition to its 50 other rooms, this hotel caters to families (it provides baby-sitting services). Amenities include *La Preferida* restaurant, spa, sauna, gym, swimming pool, and bar. 341 Estados Unidos (phone: 497111). Moderate.

**Chaco** – Run by the same people who run the *Itá Enramada*. It has a fine reputation, mostly based on its excellent restaurant (see *Eating Out*) and outstanding service. It must be doing something right since it is always full and reservations are a must. The rooms and indoor swimming pool are small. Everything looks quite modern. Av. Mariscal Estigarribia at Calle Caballero (phone: 492066 through 492069; fax: 444223). Moderate.

**Gran Hotel del Paraguay** – If you want to relive Asunción's past — and get away from modern accommodations — this is for you. This was Madame Lynch's home 100 years ago. The dining room (see *Eating Out*) formerly was the estate's theater; it was painted to look like an arbor. This 70-room hostelry is surrounded by beautiful grounds and has an outdoor pool. It is about 1 mile (1.6 km) from the downtown area — guests can walk or take a trolley or taxi. Calle de la Residenta and Padre Pouche. (phone: 200051 through 200053). Moderate.

**Internacional** – This modern, 100-room high-rise features a roof garden piano bar with great views, the *Cristal* restaurant offering international fare, sauna, gym, and outdoor pool. 520 Ayolas (phone: 494113 and 496597; fax: 494383). Moderate.

**Itá Enramada** – This resort property is set on 15 sprawling acres on the banks of the Río Paraguay, about 15 minutes south of the city. Facilities include a casino, nightclub, bar, restaurant, coffee shop, sauna, tennis courts, playground, and a gorgeous swimming pool. There are 150 rooms, each with a direct-dial phone, color TV set, and wet bar. The drawback is the distance from Asunción itself, but free shuttle buses go back and forth to the *Chaco* hotel downtown at regular intervals. The resort has a special arrangement allowing guests to take advantage of facilities and sports at the *Casino Yacht y Golf Club Paraguayo*. A boat tour on the river is available from the hotel's dock. Contact the tour desk in the lobby for information. Calle Cacique Lambaré and Ribera del Río Paraguay (phone: 33041 through 33049; in the US, 800-44-UTELL). Moderate.

**Paramanta** – Built in the colonial style, this spotless, German-run hostelry is in a lush setting midway between the international airport and the city. All rooms have color TV sets. A pretty pool, dry cleaning and laundry services, and a breakfast room round out the amenities. 3198 Av. Aviadores del Chaco (phone: 607053 and 607054; fax: 607052). Moderate.

**Presidente** – This 5-story, 55-room property aims to please the business traveler with direct-dial phones, fax service, a multilingual staff, and good corporate rates. *Oliver's* restaurant offers a buffet brunch every morning and the bar serves great coffee. Azara at Independencia Nacional (phone: 494931, 494932, and 494916; fax: 444057). Moderate.

**Gran Hotel Paraná** – Just up the street from the *Chaco*, it is similar, but somewhat drab. If the *Chaco* is full, try this place. No pool, but it does have its own restaurant and bar. Reservations unnecessary. Calles Caballero and Veinticinco de Mayo (phone: 444545 and 444236; in the US, 800-44-UTELL). Inexpensive.

**Residencial "El Lapacho"** – *Residencial* usually indicates an extremely modest hotel, which would be an injustice here. It is a house in a residential neighborhood with a dining room, patio, pool, garden, lots of grass, and 15 air conditioned rooms; rates include continental breakfast. Many Americans stay here, as it is close to the US Embassy. Especially recommended for visitors with children, it is about 15 minutes from downtown at 153 República Dominicana España (phone: 200721). Inexpensive.

**EATING OUT:** Paraguayans eat late, often under the stars, and enjoy live entertainment. The restaurants with shows do not start serving dinner before 9 PM; shows start at 10 PM. Other restaurants serve dinner from about 7 PM. Lunch counters are an option for those who prefer to eat earlier. A very popular section of town where you can rub elbows with lots of hungry Paraguayans is Avenida Brasilia off España. After 9 PM, the *parrilladas* lining the street will be packed. These open-air barbecues featuring grilled meat from Paraguay's ranches all are reputable, but many say *La Paraguayita* is the best. Wherever you go, be sure to get there a little before 9 PM to ensure getting a table.

There are a number of delicious local dishes including *sopa paraguaya* — which isn't a soup as the name implies, but a type of cornbread. Also good is *surubí* — a river fish similar to catfish — and the local cheeses (which come from Mennonite dairy farms). Try starting a meal with *palmito* (hearts of palm) and ending it with the local cane sugar liquor, *caña*.

Restaurant prices are reasonable. Expect to pay $45 and up at restaurants in the expensive category; between $25 and $45 in the moderate range; under $25 at places classified as inexpensive. Prices are for dinner for two, not including drinks, wine, or tips. All telephone numbers are in the 21 city code unless otherwise indicated.

**Chaco** – The restaurant on the second floor of this hotel serves very good international food and has live music on weekends. Open daily. Reservations advised in the evening, unless you arrive early or are staying at the hotel. Major credit cards accepted. Av. Mariscal Estigarribia and Calle Caballero (phone: 492066). Expensive.

**La Pergola Jardín** – Excellent dining from an international menu, and good service. Open daily, except Mondays, for lunch, tea, and dinner. Reservations advised. Major credit cards accepted. 240 Av. Perú (phone: 200777). Expensive.

**Talleyrand** – Considered by many to be Asunción's finest, and probably its most expensive. The food, mostly French, is good and the atmosphere is cozy, if a bit formal. Open daily. Reservations necessary. Major credit cards accepted. 932 Av. Mariscal Estigarribia (phone: 441163). Expensive.

**Tayi Poty** – A fine dining spot in the casino of the *Itá Enramada;* live music for dancing and typical Paraguayan music daily except Sundays. Reservations advised. Major credit cards accepted. Calle Cacique Lambaré and Ribera del Río Paraguay (phone: 33041 through 9). Expensive.

**Bistro** – A more leisurely alternative to the *Bolsi* (below), this charming little eatery with crisp white tablecloths and a polished, dark-wood bar offers good international food and excellent service. Open daily, except Sundays, from 11:30 AM to 2:30 PM and 7:30 to 11:30 PM. Reservations advised. Major credit cards accepted. Av. Estrella at 15 de Agosto (phone: 447910). Moderate.

**Il Capo** – This fine Italian eatery boasts a tempting array of antipasti (try the asparagus with parmesan), superbly prepared pasta and risotto dishes, and a reasonably priced list of French, Portuguese, and South American wines. Save room for the chocolate mousse or nut soufflé with zabaglione. Excellent service. Open daily for lunch and dinner. Reservations unnecessary. Major credit cards accepted. 291 Av. Perú at José Berges (phone: 213022). Moderate.

***Churrasquería Brasilera*** – Grilled meat is a favorite dish in Paraguay and this Brazilian restaurant is one of the most popular spots for that fare. Diners can choose between the huge main dining room outdoors with slabs of meat sizzling over hot fires or smaller, air conditioned dining areas. Chilean and Argentine wines are available in abundance to accompany a meal. Popular with families on weekends. Open daily from 11:30 AM to 3:30 PM and 6:30 PM to midnight. Reservations unnecessary. Major credit cards accepted. Av. Mariscal López at Tte. Zotti (phone: 601750). Moderate.

***Gran Hotel del Paraguay*** – Even if you don't stay in this hotel, at least take the time for a meal in the colonial dining room of the estate that belonged to Madame Lynch, the Irish mistress of former President Francisco Solano López — a woman who once tried to get herself declared Empress of Paraguay. Its cold buffet is terrific and its dessert cart is laden with tempting goodies. Although the usual fare is basic international, the curry — the Wednesday night special — is recommended. Entertainment and dancing Wednesday nights as well. Open daily. Reservations advised for Wednesday nights only. Major credit cards accepted. Calle de la Residenta and Padre Pouche (phone: 200051). Moderate.

***El Jardín de la Cerveza*** – Literally "The Beer Garden." This big hall offers passable food (and some excellent desserts) and its rousing 3-hour production of Paraguayan folk entertainment is recommended. Open daily. Reservations advised for large groups. It does not take credit cards, but does accept payment in dollars at the going exchange rate. Av. Argentina at Castillo (phone: 600752). Moderate, but note that there is a cover charge of about $5 per person.

***La Preferida*** – International food, featuring beef and freshwater fish. The decor is plain and there is no entertainment. Open daily. Reservations advised in the evening. Major credit cards accepted. 1005 Calle 25 de Mayo (phone: 210641). Moderate.

***Taverna El Antojo*** – This dark and bohemian Spanish *tasca* has the wackiest interior in the city — a conglomeration of stuffed animals, farm tools, and clay plates (with wonderful inscriptions). As if the decor weren't entertainment enough, there is live music every evening after 7:30 PM. Come for a drink and *tapas,* Spanish snacks such as fried squid or shrimp broiled in garlic, or for a full meal. The house specialty is seafood paella. Open daily for lunch and dinner. Reservations unnecessary. Major credit cards accepted. 631 Av. Ayolas (phone: 441743). Moderate to inexpensive.

***Di Trevi Café*** – A refuge from the hectic shopping and money-changing chaos of Palma Street, this multilevel establishment with marble-topped tables is just right for coffee, a cold beer, or a snack. If you don't want to be pestered by vendors, sit near the back. Open 7 AM to 1 AM (2 AM on Saturdays; closed Sunday mornings); there's piano music Thursday through Sunday evenings. No reservations. Major credit cards accepted. 573 Palma (phone: 491845). Moderate to inexpensive.

***Celestial*** – If you're looking for excellent Chinese food and don't care much about decor, this is the place. Opens for lunch, closes mid-afternoon, and then reopens again in the evening, every day but Sunday. No reservations. No credit cards accepted. Upstairs at 919 Luis A. Herrera (phone: 444633). Inexpensive.

***Heladerías Tropical*** and ***Anahi*** – Asunción has unusually good ice cream. Here are two popular places to sample it, right across the street from each other, away from the city's center. The *Tropical* offers superior ice cream plus sidewalk seating — perfect for watching late-night strollers — while the slightly more upscale *Anahi* has an upstairs, air conditioned dining room. Open daily. No reservations. No credit cards accepted. Av. Acuña de Figueroa and Parapité (phone: 71333, *Tropical;* phone: 72291, *Anahi*). If you're downtown, stop by *Anahi 2* (Presidente

Franco and Ayolas; phone: 495846). This location offers an adjacent bakery with tempting breads and rolls. Inexpensive.

**La Pergola del Bolsi** – Commonly called the *Bolsi*, it has a popular lunch counter — which serves excellent soup, empanadas, beef, and chicken — and an adjoining dining room in which tea with French pastries is served in the afternoon. There's also a fancy take-out bakery. It is a favorite of businesspeople who lunch at noon; it's less crowded in the evening. The typical Paraguayan bill of fare features especially good fish and a long wine list. Open daily. Reservations advised for lunch, but a table is usually available after a short wait. Major credit cards accepted in the dining room. 399 Estrella at the corner of Alberdi (phone: 491841 amd 494720). Dining room, moderate; lunch counter, inexpensive.

# BOGOTÁ

*Although the much-publicized violence from drug traffickers that plagued Colombia for most of the last decade subsided somewhat in the past year, terrorism from narcotics trafficking and a 35-year-old leftist insurgency continue to torment Colombia. As a result, the US State Department has issued an advisory warning US tourists against travel to certain parts of Colombia (primarily the interior), and to take precautions in other areas of the country. Bogotá is considered relatively safe, but travelers should be on the alert as there have even been random attacks in the capital. Travelers are advised to check with the US State Department's Citizens' Emergency Center (phone: 202-647-5225) prior to departure and with the American Citizens' Services Unit of the US Embassy in Bogotá (phone: 1-285-1300, ext. 206 and 215) upon arrival.*

Before the conquistadores arrived in quest of gold, a city already existed in the valley high in the Andes. Known as Bacatá, it was home to the Cacique Indian chief of the same name. In 1538, Gonzalo Jiménez de Quesada arrived at the Muisca city after following the Magdalena River upstream from its mouth in the Caribbean. The Spaniard was searching for the fabled land of El Dorado (The Golden One), a legend that is believed to have originated in the ritual consecration of a new Zipa. In the ceremony, the Zipa's body was coated in gold dust, and gold and emerald objects were offered to the gods by tossing them into the depths of Guatavita lagoon. Even though only 166 of the conquistador's 800-man expedition survived the journey, Bacatá was firmly under the control of the Spaniards a year later and had become Santa Fe de Bogotá, the seat of the Royal Audiencia. It eventually became the capital of the Viceroyalty of New Granada, and later, named simply Bogotá, the capital of the Republic of Colombia. In July 1991, the national assembly restored the city's name to its original — and more formal — 16th-century form; however, most Colombians continue to call it Bogotá.

Today, Bogotá is a city of over 5 million people, and a place where various races have merged. Contrasts of old and new, wealth and poverty, are dramatically obvious. Amid the soaring skyscrapers and fashionably dressed men and women on the street, visitors occasionally will still see burro-drawn carts reined by drivers who seem to have arrived right out of the colonial era. This is a place where the art treasures from centuries past are still found in colonial churches and museums, buildings that maintain their places alongside the modern office buildings, posh nightclubs, and luxury hotels. But Bogotá also has earned the reputation as a dangerous city, based on its popularity among drug traffickers and the existence of significant street crime.

Bogotá was officially founded on April 27, 1539, upon the arrival of expeditions led by Sebastián de Belalcázar from Quito, and by the German, Nicholás de Federmann, from Venezuela. Upon finding Jiménez de Quesada already here, the three leaders signed a royal warrant on the grounds that would first become the central market, and later the Plaza Bolívar.

Over the centuries, the square has been the scene of numerous events of moment. This was where a dispute over a flowerpot ignited the Creole uprising of 1810. (Creole, or criollo, refers to people of Spanish ancestry who were born in Colombia.) Here Simón Bolívar and Francisco de Paula Santander were greeted after their victory over the Spanish royalist armies in 1819; the political leader Jorge Eliécer Gaitán was assassinated in 1948, sparking the riots of Bogotazo; and the guerrillas and army fought in the takeover of the Palace of Justice in 1985.

Perhaps the most important statistic for a visitor to bear in mind is the city's altitude of 8,640 feet above sea level. (It usually takes at least a day to adjust to the effects of the change in oxygen. An afternoon nap, along with moderation in the consumption of alcohol or tobacco, are recommended.) The drive into the city from El Dorado Airport follows a wide avenue that reveals how far the population has spread from the city center. This rapid growth — in 1910, Bogotá had only 100,000 inhabitants — resulted from the vast numbers of people immigrating from the countryside to Colombia's industrial center. This, in turn, brought about a different migration, that of the city's wealthy, who left their colonial homes to move to the northern part of Bogotá in order to escape the increasing congestion and crime of the city's center. Today, this northern area is known for its well-to-do neighborhoods, but thanks to recent efforts to renovate the colonial houses, the downtown neighborhood of La Candelaria, with its patios and narrow streets, is once again becoming very desirable. La Candeleria also houses an abundance of small theaters, as well as restaurants and cafeterias which feature folk music, art exhibitions, or poetry readings.

Covering 111 square miles, Bogotá follows a north–south axis at the foot of the mountains along the Sabana de Bogotá, a 150-mile-long and 30-mile-wide plateau in the eastern range of the Andes. Such an inland location for a capital is unusual in South America; most are situated closer to the sea. To the west, away from the mountains, are the industrial plants, factories, and warehouses, and as far as the eye can see in a southerly direction are the shabby, makeshift homes of the poor. In contrast, Bogotá is also home to the personnel from diplomatic missions and numerous international organizations. Many of the latter have established regional offices in the city because of its importance on the continent and its strategic location. These foreign "communities," of which the US is the largest, contribute to the general cosmopolitan atmosphere of the city.

When the Spaniards reached the Sabana de Bogotá, they found the Muisca living in palisaded villages of wood-and-thatch houses. These Indians, who spoke Chibcha and are sometimes referred to by that name, cultivated the land, built temples, and mastered a variety of crafts and industry. They mined emeralds and salt, developed a textile industry, and traded with neighboring tribes. Their political and social organization included a class of serfs who became slave laborers under the Spaniards; those who resisted were exterminated or driven into the jungle and mountains.

The Muisca ruling class lived in large, well-constructed "palaces" and were

# BOGOTÁ

## Points of Interest

1. Plaza Bolívar
2. Museo del Oro/Gold Museum
3. Las Iglesias de San Francisco; La Veracruz/Churches of San Francisco; La Veracruz
4. Iglesia de La Tercera Orden/Church of La Tercera Orden
5. Carrera Séptima
6. Iglesia de Las Aguas/Church of Las Aguas
7. Museo Arqueológico/Archaeological Museum
8. Iglesia de San Agustín/Church of San Agustín
9. Palacio de Nariño/Presidential Palace
10. Museo de Artes y Tradiciones Populares/Museum of Popular Art and Tradition
11. El Monasterio de Santa Clara/Monastery of Santa Clara
12. Quinta de Bolívar
13. Capilla del Sagrario/Cathedral and the Sanctuary Chapel
14. Museo 20 de Julio/Twentieth of July Museum
15. Iglesia de San Ignacio/Church of San Ignacio; Museo de Arte Colonial/Museum of Colonial Art
16. Palacio San Carlos/San Carlos Palace
17. Teatro Colón/Colón Theater
18. Fundación Alzate Avendaño/Alzate Avendaño Foundation
19. Museo de Desarrollo Urbano de Bogotá/Bogotá Urban Development Museum
20. Casa de la Moneda/Royal Mint
21. Museo Nacional/National Museum
22. Iglesia de San Diego/Church of San Diego
23. Museo de Historia Natural and Galería Santa Fe de Bogotá/Natural History Museum and the Santa Fe de Bogotá Gallery
24. Museo de Arte Moderno/Museum of Modern Art
25. Museo de Arte Religioso/Museum of Religious Art
26. Plaza Santamaría Bullring
27. Galería Cano/Cano Gallery
28. Corporación Nacional de Turismo/National Tourist Corporation
29. Avenida 19
30. Bus Terminal
31. Train Station
32. Estadio El Campín
33. Chapinero
34. Teatro Nacional
35. Carrera 15
36. Museo del Chico
37. Unicentro
38. Boulevard Niza
39. El Dorado Airport

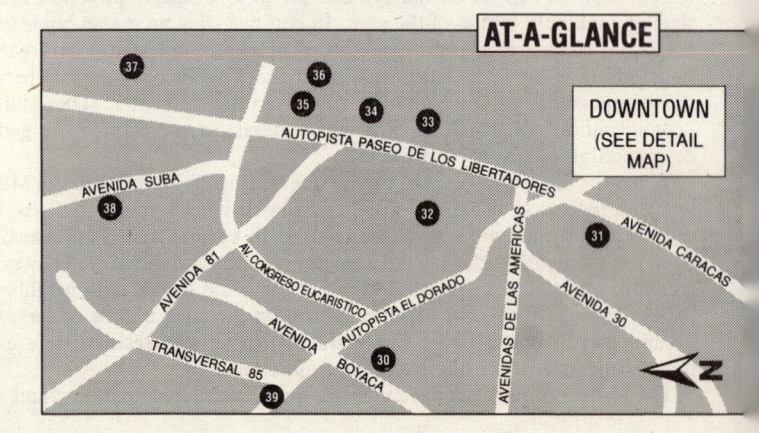

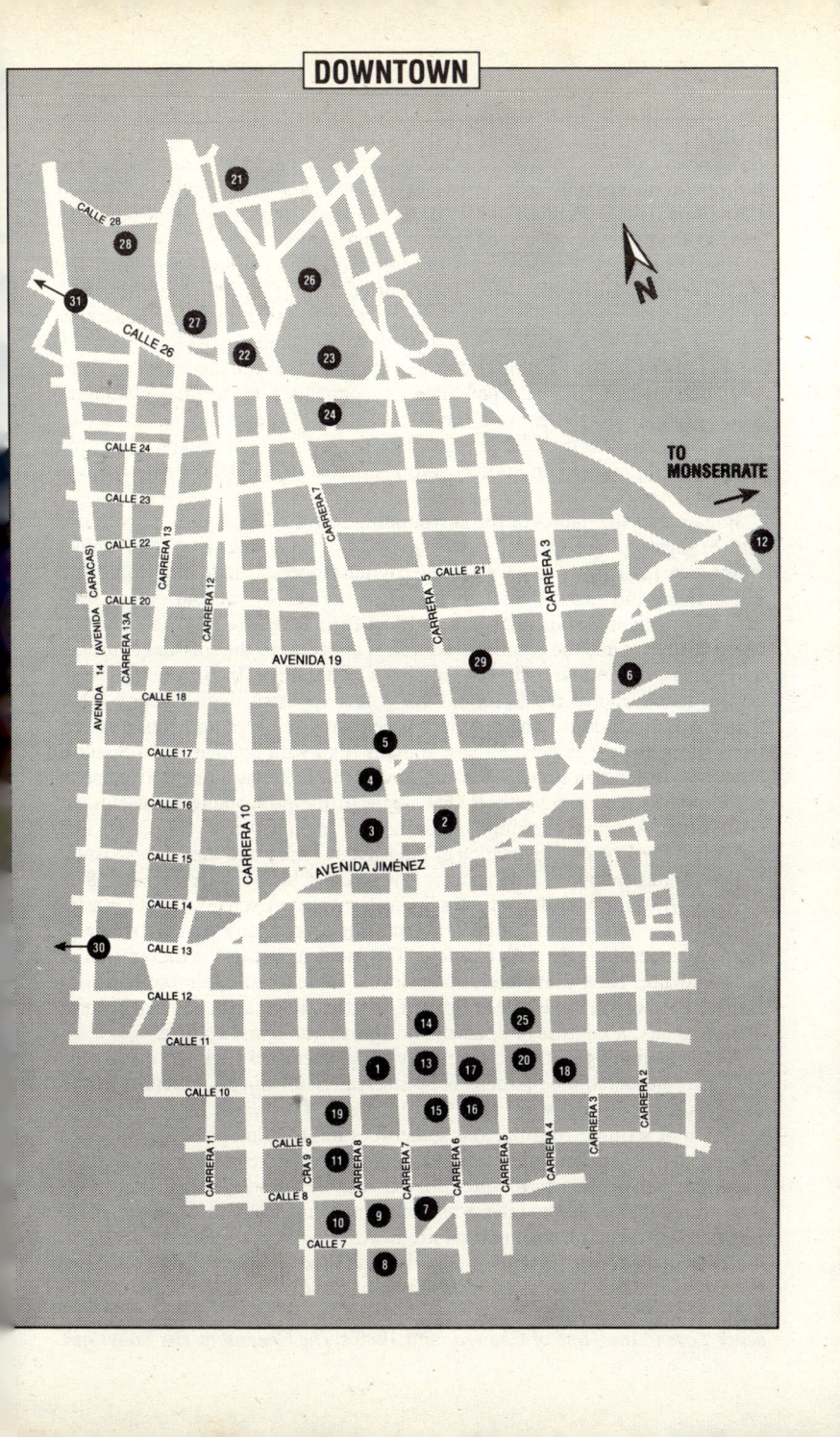

# DOWNTOWN

carried about in gold-covered litters. Their religion centered on a sun cult and included the sacrifice of valiant prisoners since it was thought that in this way the bravery of the conquered would be passed on to the victors. Caves, hilltops, and lakes were considered sacred places, and no site was more sacred than Guatavita, a circular lake 47 miles (75 km) from Bogotá that had been gouged from the top of a mountain by a huge meteorite.

Juan Rodríguez Fresle, in his chronicle of the conquest, explained the significance of Guatavita. After the future chief of the Muisca had lived in a cave and remained celibate for 6 years, he was taken to Lake Guatavita, where his body was covered from head to foot in gold dust. Thus prepared, he was rowed by four plumed nobles to the middle of the lake in a raft filled with offerings of gold and emeralds. Accompanied by a great clamor of drums, flutes, and rattles from the lake's shore, the new chief dove into the lake, giving his offering of gold and emeralds to the sacred waters. The ritual is depicted in one of the famous gold scuptures in the *Museo del Oro* (see *Special Places)*.

Bogotá and the names of the surrounding towns of Zipaquirá, Facatativá, and Fusagasugá are Indian, but Bogotá is not an Indian city. The Indian rulers gave their gold and jewels to the conquistadores, who then tortured and killed them and razed their temples when the supply ran out. Their serfs mixed with their Spanish masters and lost their language and their culture. Nevertheless, while the Spanish tradition is apparent in the colonial churches and homes, the Indian influence remains a subtle force. In Bogotá, the flamboyant machismo of the Latin culture is less apparent than in many other South American cities. The populace is generally reserved and conservative, traits more closely associated with Indians than with Spaniards. In Spanish churches, the Indian influence is still obvious in the lavish, decorative use of gold, mirrors, and sun symbols that relate to the pre-conquest sun cult.

In 1793, Antonio Nariño, a champion of independence, translated and published the French *Declaration of the Rights of Man and the Citizen.* But it took an argument over a flowerpot for revolution to blossom. On July 20, 1810, a Creole, Antonio Morales, struck a Spanish royalist merchant, José González Llorente, for refusing to lend a flowerpot for a ceremony paying tribute to Commissioner Antonio Villavicencio. The incident led to the declaration of independence. Nine years later, Spanish rule came to a tumultuous end with Bolivár's victory in the Battle of Boyacá. By then, Bogotá already had become a mestizo city, a mixture of Spanish and Indian blood and culture.

At the beginning of the 20th century, Bogotá earned itself the distinction of being considered the "Athens of South America," due to its refinement in customs and culture. More than anything else, this was a by-product of a tradition of writing, reciting, and sometimes improvising poetry maintained by the old, established families — those who refer to themselves as *santafereños* rather than *bogotanos.* Bogotá became an oasis of amateur poets who stimulated such fine talents as Guillermo Valencia and León de Greiff. Even today, recitations sometimes are heard after lunches and dinners. Colombia's best-known writer is the Nobel Prize winner Gabriel García Márquez. Author of *One Hundred Years of Solitude,* the epic acclaimed as Latin America's greatest modern classic; his other novels include the best seller *Love in the Time of Cholera,* and 1989's *The General in His Labyrinth,* an historical novel about the final days of Bolívar. After years of living in Mexico, García Márquez has returned to live part of the year in Cartagena.

The city's aristocracy also created a culinary tradition that enlivens Bogotá's kitchens. Recipes served with special pride include *chocolate santafereño* (rich cocoa with cheese floating on top, accompanied by yucca bread); *mazato santafereño* (a fermented drink made from maize or rice, and eaten with a special brown bun); tamales (spiced chicken and chopped vegetables in a steaming corn mixture, wrapped in a plantain leaf); and a corn and potato soup served with shredded chicken, avocados, and capers, called *ajiaco*.

Today, Bogotá's place in world headlines is mainly a result of a single product: drugs. Following the murder of presidential candidate Luis Carlos Galán in August 1989, the government declared an all-out war on drug traffickers. The leaders of the cartels fought back with a series of bomb attacks and a wave of kidnappings. By November 1990, the bombings appeared to have stopped, but more than 1,000 people had been kidnapped. One of these, a prominent journalist who was the daughter of a former president, was killed in January 1991. After the military attacked the headquarters of the Colombian Revolutionary Armed Forces (the country's largest guerrilla group) in December 1990, violence against the police escalated.

Since the surrender to the authorities of many members of the Medellín drug cartel in 1991, four leftist guerrilla groups, and a right-wing paramilitary death squad, Bogotá has become somewhat more peaceful. However, guerrilla warfare — especially in the countryside — and street crime continue to be big problems. Although attacks rarely are directed against visitors, travelers should exercise caution at the airport and in the areas around the major hotels — muggers and pickpockets frequent both regions. Drug- and guerrilla-related violence, as well as a high level of street crime, foster a feeling of lawlessness in Bogotá, which contrasts sharply with the city's pleasant surroundings and the elaborate courtesy of its inhabitants.

One result of the crime and violence is that all visitors entering public buildings, banks, museums, and the like, should expect to be searched thoroughly and have their handbags, briefcases, or camera cases checked as a matter of course.

Being constantly on guard against crime has not stopped Bogotá from maintaining its role as one of the cultural centers of Latin America. On weekend nights — which begin on Thursday here — the city is alive with dozens of plays and concerts, and art galleries feature the works of first-rate Colombian painters. In this sense, Bogotá remains one of South America's prime paradoxes.

# BOGOTÁ AT-A-GLANCE

**SEEING THE CITY:** The city is laid out according to a familiar grid system, so there's little difficulty getting around. *Carreras* (roads) run north-south, parallel to the mountains. *Calles* (streets) run east-west, toward the mountains, with numbers increasing as you move north from the city center.

*Calles* and *carreras* intersect at right angles. Carrera Séptima (Seventh Avenue) runs the entire length of the city, joining the downtown and colonial districts with the northern sector. Avenida Diecinueve (Nineteenth Avenue) passes through an elegant commercial center with many craft shops.

The best bet for transportation is a taxi, preferably one of the green and white tourist taxis that stand in front of the main hotels and have English-speaking drivers who also conduct tours of the city on request. Set the amount of time available for your tour, and find out what it will cost, in advance. These taxis charge considerably more for their services than metered cabs, which also offer guided tours (see *Getting Around*). Some hotels, such as the *Cosmos* and the *Travelodge Orquidea Real*, offer guided tours for guests. Taxis are reasonable, but the buses and microbuses are comfortable when they are not too crowded. A warning: Bogotá is known as a pickpockets' city. So infamous are the local practitioners that groups of New York and Los Angeles police are trained by the more experienced Bogotá police. By day, you should have no trouble in the areas discussed below, but it is wise to leave valuable jewelry at home (or at the very least in your hotel's safe); at night be wary of people "accidentally" bumping into or touching you.

A note about drugs: Colombia in general and Bogotá in particular have a well-earned reputation for drug trafficking. As a tourist, you will most likely not be affected, except for the possibility of time-consuming baggage checks while clearing customs. A common misconception is that tourists will be approached on the street by drug dealers. This is far more apt to happen in large cities in the US than in Bogotá. The only way you are likely to get in trouble regarding drugs is by looking for them. Don't.

**SPECIAL PLACES:** High above a sheer cliff of Monserrate, the mountain that stands behind the city like a drop curtain, is the shrine of Monserrate. It can be reached easily from the city center by funicular, a Swiss-made cable car, and the ride up is as exhilarating as the view from the top is superb. All of Bogotá lies at your feet: the skyscrapers thrusting up ambitiously, the colonial quarter looking lovely with its neat white walls and tiled roofs, and the rest of the city expanding exuberantly in every direction. Beyond, the magnificent, multihued plateau is fringed by distant mountains. On clear evenings, there is a breathtaking view of two snow-clad volcanoes of the Cordillera Central, some 74 miles (118 km) away. One of these, the Nevado del Tolima, is a perfect cone, like Japan's Fujiyama.

On Sundays, thousands of *bogotanos* swarm up Monserrate Mountain to "keep a promise" *("pagar una promesa")* to the *Fallen Christ*, a colonial figure sculpted by Pedro de Lugo y Albarracín, to whom the church is dedicated. Some carry crosses or climb on their knees. Besides a chapel and two restaurants, the top of the mountain is also home to a cobblestone street and buildings from the Candelaria neighborhood of the city that were taken apart and reconstructed on the mountaintop. There is also a jungle trail with stations of the cross and stories of Colombia's Indians.

The Plaza Bolívar is the centerpiece of the city. Surrounding the stone plaza are numerous historic buildings, including the neo-classical cathedral built in the early 1700s on the site of a Muisca temple. It contains many relics, such as the *Christ of the Conquest* statue, and an altar encrusted with gold, silver, and precious stones; the bones of Bogotá's founder, Gonzalo Jiménez de Quesada, also reside in the Cathedral. On the south side of the square is the colonnaded capitol building, home of the National Congress. Behind it is the Greco-Roman Nariño Palace, now the presidential residence. On the west side of the square is Alcaldia Mayor (City Hall), and on the north side will be the site of the new Palacio de Justicia (Palace of Justice) — much of the old one was destroyed by the army in 1985 while routing guerrillas who had taken control of the building.

## DOWNTOWN

**Museo del Oro (Gold Museum)** – If there is only time for one museum, make it this one. The 30,000 gold artifacts — the largest such collection in the world — give credibility to the legend of El Dorado. Glass-encased exhibitions reveal the rich traditions of the Muisca, Tairona, Quimbaya, Sinú, and Capuli. Having seen this museum, there will be little wonder at the fact that, at the time of the Spanish conquest, the Indian artisans were already familiar with every gold-working technique being practiced in Europe. The stunning highlight is the last room. Darkened upon entry, the lights slowly come up and the visitor is surrounded by dozens of glittering gold artifacts. Open daily, except Mondays, from 9 AM to 4 PM; Sundays, 9 AM to noon. Films in English at 11:30 AM and 2:55 PM. Admission charge. 5-41 Calle 16 (phone: 281-3600).

**Las Iglesias de San Francisco, La Veracruz, La Tercera Churches (Churches of San Francisco, La Veracruz, La Tercera)** – Three magnificent colonial churches stand opposite the *Museo del Oro,* reminding us that Spain's conquest was largely due to the devastating moral and physical power of her Church.

Built in 1567, San Francisco is the oldest and most beautiful of all. Its somber interior is lit by the countless candles of the faithful. By their light, you can see some of the fine sculpted figures that are venerated. The gilded wooden altarpiece *(retablo)* of the main altar is a rococo masterpiece by Ignacio de Ascucha built over an earlier work in the baroque style of the rest of the ornamentation. The San José altar is particularly splendid; the carved ceiling is also of great beauty; and there are paintings by Gregorio Vázquez, Gaspar de Figueroa, and others. Av. Jiménez and Carrera 7. La Veracruz and La Tercera both have rococo ornamentation. The latter is built on the site where the mass celebrating the foundation of the city was sung by Bartolomé de Las Casas, the famous bishop who denounced the atrocities committed against the Indian peoples. Carrera 7 and Calle 16.

**Avenida Jiménez (Jiménez Avenue)** – Located between Carrera 10 and the mountains, this is the business and financial center of the city. Colonial architecture like that of San Francisco and of the Plazoleta del Rosario contrasts with tall modern buildings such as the Bank of the Republic and the Banco Ganadero.

**Carrera Séptima (Seventh Avenue)** – Running the entire length of the city parallel to the mountains, this road joins the colonial district to the downtown areas, the international sector, and the north. It is the *bogotanos'* favorite street, along which the traditional *paseo,* or stroll, may extend from the Plaza Bolívar as far as the international sector. This entire stretch is alive with commerce, cafés, and restaurants, as well as the bustle and noise of countless street vendors.

**Avenida Diécinueve (Nineteenth Avenue)** – Between Carrera Séptima and the mountains is an elegant commercial center that has many shops of special interest, selling ethnic and craft wares, leather goods, and jewelry (especially Colombia's famed emeralds). A pleasant walk to the top of the avenue will take you past the Colombian American Center to the delightful little church of Las Aguas (18-66 Carrera 3). Flanking this church is a lovely cloister that houses the arts and crafts shop of *Artesanías de Colombia,* containing an extensive assortment of ethnic and craft wares from all over the country; another branch of the store is located in front of the *Tequendama* hotel (26-50 Carrera 10; phone: 284-3484). In the same building is one of the best restaurants for creole cooking, the *Casa Vieja del Claustro* (18-60 Carrera 8; phone: 284-3484).

## THE COLONIAL CENTER — LA CANDELARIA

Take your time and your camera to wander around the well-preserved colonial neighborhood of La Candelaria, with its delightful old houses nestling quietly around flowered patios in the old Moorish style. Much of the planning and plotting that shaped

Colombia's history occurred behind these broad adobe walls and under these graceful tiled roofs. You may come across some interesting antiques shops, too, and can have the best creole food in this same setting (see *Eating Out*). Calles 7 to 13 and Carreras 1 to 8.

**Museo Arqueológico (Archaeological Museum), in the Casa del Marqués de San Jorge (House of the Marquis of St. George)** – The finest and most interesting of the stately colonial houses of old Bogotá — built in the 17th and 18th centuries and admirably restored in recent years — is the setting of one of Latin America's most important collections of pre-Columbian pottery from Mexico, Colombia, Ecuador, and Peru. The exhibits are beautifully presented, and you will be totally enchanted as you wander through the whitewashed rooms — each with green woodwork and wooden floors, yet each different from the next — along corridors, onto balconies, and out into the typically Moorish patios with cool fountains and fresh plants. It's a perfect introduction to the old center of Bogotá. Also on the premises is a good and inexpensive restaurant, serving lunch only. Museum open daily, except Mondays, from 9 AM to noon and 1:15 to 5 PM; Sundays, 10 AM to 1 PM. Admission charge. 7-43 Carrera 6 (phone: 282-0740).

**Iglesia de San Agustín (Church of San Agustín)** – Just below the House of the Marquis of St. George you will come across the austere façade of the Church of San Agustín, first constructed in 1575 and remodeled in 1748 after an earthquake. The interior has fine baroque decoration, and among the more important pictures and wooden sculptures you will find a *Flight from Egypt* by Vázquez and the statue *Jesus of Nazareth* by Pedro de Lugo. Calle 7 and Carrera 7.

**Palacio de Nariño (Presidential Palace)** – Standing opposite San Agustín, this imposing edifice, reconstructed in 1979, is again the seat of government. Built in 1906, it was gutted by a mob in 1948, after the assassination of populist Liberal leader Jorge Eliécer Gaitán. This incident sparked off a bitter civil war that lasted nearly a decade. A bitter chapter in Colombia's predominantly peaceful history, it is known appropriately as *La Violencia* (The Violence). At press time, visits to the palace were suspended indefinitely. However, the changing of the presidential guard every afternoon at 5 PM, with more fanfare on Sundays, is well worth a visit and can be seen from outside the building. Calle 7 between Carreras 7 and 8 (phone: 284-3300).

**Museo de Artes y Tradiciones Populares (Museum of Popular Art and Tradition)** – Displayed here is a marvelous variety of craftwork produced in different regions of the country. Some have been made by inhabitants of remote sections of the interior. In an old monastery, the museum has a restaurant and a shop under the colonial archway that sells ethnic items and crafts. Open Tuesdays through Fridays from 8:30 AM to 5:30 PM; Saturdays, 9 AM to 5 PM. Admission charge. 7-21 Carrera 8 (phone: 284-5279).

**El Monasterio de Santa Clara (Monastery of Santa Clara)** – If you walk 2 blocks north along Carrera 8, passing the neo-classical Observatorio Astronómico, with its shroud of colonial and republican history, you come to the Monastery of Santa Clara. Part of this colonial church and monastery has been converted to a museum that houses interesting religious art. The museum, a chapel dating from 1629, is open daily except Mondays from 10 AM to 1 PM and from 2 to 5:30 PM. No admission charge. 8-90 Calle 8 (no phone).

**Quinta de Bolívar** – Built in 1800, here Bolívar resided from time to time. A museum today, it houses many of his documents, weapons, medals, and personal effects. The garden and scenery alone are worth the visit. Open daily, except Mondays, 10 AM to 5 PM. Admission charge. 3-23 East Calle 20 (phone: 284-6819).

**Capilla del Sagrario (Cathedral and the Sanctuary Chapel)** – Located on the Plaza Bolívar, the cathedral already existed in Bolívar's time. It stands on the site of an early Muisca temple, where the first Christian church of Bogotá was built in 1565.

The present neo-classical church was designed at the beginning of the 18th century by Fray Domingo de Petrés and contains some of the woodwork from the earlier church. In one of the side chapels is the tomb of Bogotá's founder, Gonzalo Jiménez de Quesada. The Sanctuary Chapel can be reached from inside the cathedral, though it actually predates the cathedral and has an impressive baroque screen and many of the paintings of Gregorio Vázquez Arce y Ceballos, the finest Colombian painter of the 17th century. Carrera 7 and Calle 10.

**Museo 20 de Julio (Twentieth of July Museum)** – Occupying a colonial house on the corner of Plaza Bolívar next to the cathedral, it was here, on the 20th of July, 1810, that an insignificant incident sparked rebellion among the Creoles. The Spanish merchant José González Llorente reportedly insulted the Creole family of one Francisco Morales, whose supporters rioted. The ensuing Act of the Twentieth of July called for an independent Colombian constitution and denounced the Spanish viceroy. The site of this historic argument, which eventually cost Spain half her colonial provinces in the Americas, contains many paintings and relics of those who participated in the events. Open Tuesdays through Saturdays from 10 AM to 6 PM; Sundays and holidays from 10 AM to 4 PM. Admission charge. 6-94 Calle 11 (phone: 334-4150).

**Iglesia de San Ignacio (Church of San Ignacio)** – Just off the other end of the Plaza Bolívar, opposite the beautiful Plazuela de San Carlos, stands the Jesuit Church of San Ignacio, which contrasts architecturally with the more rustic structures of the other churches of the same period (early 17th century). Inside are magnificent baroque altarpieces, some of which are attributed to Juan de Cabrera; many remarkable wood sculptures by the great Pedro Laboria, others by Pedro de Lugo and lesser artists; and some fine paintings by Gregorio Vázquez. Calle 10 and Carrera 6 (phone: 342-1639).

**Museo de Arte Colonial (Museum of Colonial Art)** – This building, just up the street from San Ignacio, was originally built to serve as a Jesuit university. After the expulsion of the Jesuits in 1768, it successively served as a national congress, a prison, a national library, a school, a natural sciences museum, a court of justice, and finally as the Ministry of Education before being converted to its present use. In the sober splendor of its halls and 2-story colonnade are the finest paintings, drawings, sculptures, carvings, furniture, and silverwork of the colonial period, including 160 paintings and drawings by Gregorio Vázquez. Open Tuesdays through Fridays from 10 AM to 1 PM and 2 to 5 PM; Saturdays from 11 AM to 3 PM; Sundays from 11 AM to 5 PM. Admission charge (free on Saturdays). 9-77 Carrera 6 (phone: 341-6017 and 284-1373).

**Palacio San Carlos (San Carlos Palace)** – Also known as the Casa del Libertador (House of the Liberator), because none other than Simón Bolívar himself resided here. Bolívar escaped an assassination attempt here by leaping from a balcony while his mistress, Manuela Sáenz, stalled the conspirators in the antechamber. In the garden is a tree that he allegedly planted. This was the presidential palace until 1979. Exhibits pertaining to Bolívar's life are on display. Carrera 6 and Calle 10 (phone: 281-7811).

**Galería Cano (Cano Gallery)** – A combination private museum and jewelry shop, it houses a collection of pre-Columbian artifacts gathered by the Cano family over the past 50 years. The shop sells gold reproductions of pre-Columbian jewelry. The museum includes a small theater where a film on pre-Columbian artifacts is shown. Open daily except Sundays from 10 AM to 7 PM. No admission charge. 27-98 Carrera 13 in the Bavaria building (phone: 342-9114).

**Teatro Colón (Colón Theater)** – A landmark in its own right, this elaborate 19th-century building is still *the* place for theater, opera, and ballet in Bogotá. It is the home of Colombia's *National Symphony,* and hosts visiting touring companies. Open to visitors weekdays from 10 AM to 5 PM. Across the street from Palacio San Carlos. 5-32 Calle 10 (phone: 284-7420).

**Fundación Alzate Avendaño (Alzate Avendaño Foundation)** – As you leave the Colón, stroll along Carrera 5 toward Calle 9, a picturesque colonial street. Head up cobblestone Calle 9 toward Calle 10. If you feel like some refreshment in a delightful setting, stop at the *Alzate Avendaño Foundation* cafeteria. The foundation houses an art gallery featuring works by painters living in La Candelaria. Open daily from 9 AM to 5 PM. No admission charge. 3-16 Calle 10 (phone: 342-5375).

**Museo de Desarrollo Urbano de Bogotá (Bogotá Urban Development Museum)** – Inside this colonial house are stunning old photographs, paintings, and exhibits concerning the city's early life. If your walk through contemporary and colonial Bogotá has aroused your curiosity about the old days, be sure to spend some time browsing here. Open weekdays from 8 AM to 5 PM. Admission charge. 9-83 Carrera 8 (phone: 286-5535).

**Casa de la Moneda (Royal Mint)** – Here gold was coined for the first time in Latin America. Its beautiful buildings (built in 1627) now contain the *Museo de Numismático* (Numismatics Museum), with a complete collection of all the money coined to date, and the *Museo de Artes Plásticas* (Museum of Plastic Arts). The museums were closed for renovations at press time; call the tourist office (phone: 283-9466) for current information. 4-93 Calle 11.

## INTERNATIONAL SECTOR

The tallest skyscrapers, the most elegant hotels, the best restaurants and cinemas, some of the most exclusive shops and nightspots, and every kind of tourist and business facility are concentrated in the international sector, which is close to Bogotá's center. Among its many other attractions is one of the city's best coffee shops, *Café Oma* (27-91 Carrera 10; phone: 343-8241), an excellent place to sample the best Colombian coffee and to buy coffee beans. It is open weekdays from 11:30 AM to 9:30 PM. The northern branch of this establishment (82-60 Carrera 15; phone: 256-6542) also has a magnificent bookshop.

**Museo Nacional (National Museum)** – Established in the Old City prison, this complex includes an excellent anthropological museum as well as interesting national history and fine arts museums. Open Tuesdays through Saturdays from 9:30 AM to 5:30 PM. Admission charge (free on Thursdays). 28-66 Carrera 7 (phone: 342-5925).

**Iglesia de San Diego (Church of San Diego)** – This is a pleasant example of early-17th-century colonial architecture with a fine altarpiece. Especially interesting is the Lady Chapel, dedicated to Our Lady of the Fields. Calle 26 and Carrera 7.

**Museo de Historia Natural and Galería Santa Fe de Bogotá (Natural History Museum and the Santa Fe de Bogotá Gallery)** – Both occupy part of the building of the *Planetario Distrital* (District Planetarium), which stands next to the *Plaza de Toros* (bullring). Few countries have as many varieties of flora and fauna as Colombia, so there are some fascinating exhibits. The *Santa Fe de Bogotá*'s temporary exhibitions invariably are interesting, and the stars never lose their magic. Open Tuesdays through Sundays from 9 AM to 5 PM. Parque de la Independencia on Calle 26 and Carrera 7 (phone: 284-7396).

**Museo de Arte Moderno (Museum of Modern Art)** – Just across the bridge from the planetarium, this museum was founded in 1981 by Colcultura, and is the country's principal modern art museum. There is a fine restaurant on the premises. Open Tuesdays through Saturdays from 10 AM to 7 PM; Sundays from noon to 6 PM. 6-55 Calle 24 (phone: 283-3109).

## THE NORTH

**Carrera 15** – From Calle 72 to Calle 100, this road is Bogotá's elegant busy commercial axis, with businesses and shops. It offers a wide variety of stores in a safe area, without the claustrophobia or sensory overload of a shopping mall. Veer east from Carrera 15 to Carrera 11, where between Calles 81 and 85 is the Zona Rosa (Pink

Zone), a large concentration of shops, restaurants, and discos. It is *the* place to be in Bogotá on weekend nights.

**Museo del Chicó (Chicó Museum)** – Formerly the home of the distinguished Doña Mercedes Sierra de Pérez, it now houses a chockablock collection of objets d'art amassed by the late matron during her world travels. Open Mondays through Fridays from 9 AM to noon and 2:30 to 5 PM. No admission charge. 93-01 Carrera 7 (phone: 236-7285).

**Museo del General Santander (Museum of General Santander)** – Francisco de Paula Santander, a somewhat obscure (compared to Bolívar, at least) liberator of the five Andean nations, was known as the "Man of Laws." Although born in Caracas, he is considered a national hero of Colombia. The colonial house, and the artifacts from Santander's life that it houses, provide an interesting look at Colombia's colonial past. Open daily, except Mondays from 10 AM to 5 PM. No admission charge. 150-01 Carrera 7 (phone: 258-2250).

**Unicentro** – This futuristic, highly exclusive shopping center has about 300 boutiques and other shops under one roof. If you get homesick for shopping malls, this is Colombia's biggest and the most similar to those in the US. It also houses a small indoor amusement park for children. Carrera 15 and Calle 127 (phone: 213-8800).

**Chapinero** – Bogotá's traditional center of commerce is still fairly active if not quite as glamorous as Carrera 15. Although, if you're hunting for bargains on leather goods, you will not find much of a difference in the prices between this area and downtown or Carrera 15 shops. Carrera 13 between Calles 57 and 68.

**Bulevar Niza** – Bogotá's most elegant shopping arcade. Designed in Art Deco style, it has trendy boutiques, restaurants, salons, and theaters. Av. Suba, Calle 127.

**Teatro Nacional (National Theater)** – Mostly Spanish-language plays are presented here, along with occasional concerts or mime performances. 10-25 Calle 71 (phone: 212-5930).

## ENVIRONS

**Catedral de Sal (Salt Cathedral of Zipaquirá)** – The Muisca Indians mined salt as well as gold. The mines of Zipaquirá ("the town of the chief") were producing salt long before the Spaniards arrived and they are still being mined today. In the heart of this vast mountain of salt is a unique cathedral with four aisles and a capacity of 8,000. Open Tuesdays through Sundays from 10 AM to 4 PM. Admission charge. On Carraterra Libertador, a four-lane highway, 31 miles (50 km) north of Bogotá.

**Salto del Tequendama (Tequendama Falls)** – The magnificence of this 448-foot waterfall and its extraordinary rock canyon surrounded by mists clinging to the Andean jungle make this an exciting, romantic place to visit. There's also a restaurant at the site that offers a wonderful view of the waterfall. Open Thursdays through Sundays from 11 AM to 6 PM. (For information on excursions from Bogotá, see "Getting Around" in *Sources and Resources.*) On the road to Mesitas del Colegio, 17 miles (27 km) from Bogotá.

**Villa de Leyva** – It's a longish drive, but you will never forget the scenery. Nor will you forget this lovely colonial town that has managed to preserve its beauty so perfectly. We suggest booking a hotel room from Bogotá and spending the night in one of the first class hotels: *Hostería el Molino de Mesopotamia* (phone: 213-3491), *Duruelo Hospederia* (phone: 288-1488), or *Mesón de la Plaza Mayor* (phone: 236-2177). About 86 miles (138 km) north of Bogotá near Tunja.

**Las Piedras de Tunja (Tunja Monoliths)** – Now a national archaeological park, the site was a sacred center of the Chibcha. Hieroglyphics are etched on the huge rocks. Located on the outskirts of the town of Facatativa, about 26 miles (42 km) from Bogotá on the Western Highway.

**Sasaima** – If you drive east, over the brink of the savannah, then wind down the eastern slopes of the Andes, the vegetation changes as you descend to this tropical mountain resort. Soon you will be stripping off layers of clothing. There is nothing more restful than dozing at the edge of a swimming pool in the warmth of the tropics. About 50 miles (80 km) from Bogotá.

**Llanos Orientales (Eastern Prairies)** – This is another longish drive, winding for 2½ hours down an impressive gorge, but the view from the final escarpment before you reach Villavicencio is like looking out to sea from a high cliff. And Villavicencio is just like a port, except that the "sailors" ride in on horseback after the long cattle drive, and spend all their money riotously on wine, women, and song in true cowboy tradition. The climate is warm and breezy, with all the fragrance and body of the tropics and none of its oppressiveness. There is good hunting in most areas and excellent fishing on some rivers. Villavicencio has some good hotels: the *Del Llano* (phone: 866-24409/10/11), *Centauros* (phone: 866-25106), the *Inambú* (phone: 866-24402/3), and the *Villavicencio* (phone: 218-8849).

■**EXTRA SPECIAL:** If you are beguiled by the myth of El Dorado, discover for yourself the lake where it all reportedly occurred. Torn from the top of a mountain by a giant meteorite, its great depths filled with emerald waters, Lake Guatavita perches at the top of an Andes peak. About 75 miles (120 km) from the capital, it has lost none of its mystery. Legend claims its fathomless bottom still retains its treasure. To get to the lake, go by jeep or hire horses near the new town of Guatavita la Nueva, and ride up to the lake's shores as did the Spanish, whose half-man, half-animal appearance so terrified the Muisca. It will take an hour each way, and the trip will be more pleasurable if you carry a picnic to enjoy at the top. Or plan to eat at Guatavita la Nueva upon your return. The old town of Guatavita was flooded in 1967 by an artificial lake, Lago Tominé, on whose banks stands a delightful modern town built entirely in colonial style, complete with church, cobblestone streets, and bullring. The taverns are excellent; the countryside, enchanting.

# SOURCES AND RESOURCES

**TOURIST INFORMATION:** Excellent general information, brochures, maps (in English, Spanish, German, and French), and exhaustive information on hotels and restaurants throughout Colombia (available in Spanish for a fee) can be obtained from the Corporación Nacional de Turismo (on the first floor of the Edificio del Centro de Comercio Internacional; 13A-15 Calle 28; phone: 283-9466). Personnel speak English and are helpful, although you will have to leave identification at the door and have your handbag searched when you enter the building. Less helpful is the Instituto Distrital de Cultura y Turismo (in the Candelaria area, 3-61 Calle 10; phone: 286-6555). Their most recent publication dates from October 1988. The national hoteliers' association, *COTELCO* (Asociación Hotelera de Colombia; phone: 212-8138), publishes the *Guía Hotelera Colombiana,* a complete guide in Spanish of hotels across the country, with prices and ratings. You probably will find a free copy of the bilingual *Guía de Bogotá* in your hotel room. Check at news kiosks for the *Cartur Map of Bogotá.*

The US Embassy is at 8-61 Calle 38 (phone: 285-1300).

**Local Coverage** – *El Tiempo* and *El Espectador* are the Spanish-language daily newspapers. The better hotels have the *Miami Herald* and the *International Herald*

## BOGOTÁ / Sources and Resources

*Tribune* (though a few days late). International editions of *Time* and *Newsweek* also can be found at many hotels.

**TELEPHONE:** The city code for Bogotá is 1. When calling from within Colombia, dial 91 before the local number. The country code for Colombia is 57.

**CLIMATE AND CLOTHES:** Bogotá is almost on the equator — but then, it is 8,640 feet above sea level, too, so you will feel the height more than the heat. Don't drink alcohol for the first 24 hours and you will adjust more comfortably. Days are spring-like, with an average year-round temperature in the 50s and 60s F (10C and 16C); the sun is prickly hot when it's shining, but the shade is always cold and nights are nippy. The only variation of climate is when it rains (and an *aguacero,* or cloudburst, can be as violent as it is short-lived!). It can rain anytime, but there is a rainy season between May and November. It rains somewhat less frequently during the summer, from December through March.

Casual city clothes are appropriate for daytime. *Bogotanos* enjoy dressing up for a night out, so bring evening wear (jackets and ties for men). Be sure to have a light coat or warm sweater for evenings.

**GETTING AROUND: Bus** – Bogotá buses stop at the green "Paradero" boards throughout the city. An especially scenic route is the "Capilla–Via La Calera" (Route 149), heading east of the city into the mountains. Fare is minimal, but you may find yourself standing. Unsubsidized buses, or *busetas,* charge a bit more.

**Taxi** – Because of the street crime in Bogotá, the US State Department advises visitors to take only official taxis — including green and white tourist cabs and metered ones. The best service is offered by the green and white tourist taxis that stand outside all major hotels (phone: 282-0151). Taxis are a real bargain here; the fare from the airport to your hotel in a metered cab should be around $4. The drivers generally speak a little English, and will take you on tours of the city or surrounding sights for about $4 an hour. Metered taxis are easy to hail in the street, or you can call *Radio Real* (phone: 243-0580) or *Radio-Taxi* (phone: 211-1111 and 411-1111).

**Car Rental** – *Hertz* has five locations: at the *Tequendama* hotel (26-21 Carrera 10; phone: 284-1080); *Travelodge Orquidea Real* (32-16 Carrera 7; phone: 288-5651); *La Fontana* hotel (21-10 Av. 127; phone: 274-9490); El Dorado Airport (phone: 266-9200); and the El Dorado Airport Shuttle Terminal (phone: 263-1779). *Dollar Rent-a-Car* (82-28 Carrera 13; phone: 218-4011); El Dorado Airport (phone: 268-7670); and the El Dorado Airport Shuttle Terminal (phone: 413-8524) also rents automobiles. Armed robberies of privately owned and rented cars are becoming increasingly common in Bogotá as well as other Colombian cities. Visitors should consider hiring a taxi for the day (see *Taxi,* above) as a safer and less expensive alternative.

**Excursions** – Two companies offer tours: *Granturismo* (27-51 Carrera 10; phone: 286-1099) and *Lowrie Travel Service* (19-29 Carrera 7; phone: 243-2546/7).

**SPECIAL EVENTS:** *Día de la Raza* (October 12) commemorates Columbus's discovery of America and the subsequent fusion of races; parades include Indians from tribes all over the country, folk dancers, and theater groups. During July and December, an excellent crafts fair is held in the Parque Nacional (Carrera 7 and Calle 36). July 20 is *Independence Day.* On even-numbered years, you can visit the *Feria Exposición Internacional* (International Commercial Fair; in Centro Nariño) from July 10 to 25. On Sundays and holidays (from

8 AM to 5 PM) you can browse at *El Mercado de San Alejo* (on Carrera 3 from Calle 19 to 24), a flea market where you just might find that very special bibelot you've been looking for everywhere.

**MUSEUMS:** Many of Bogotá's museums are described in *Special Places*. Others of particular interest include: the *Fondo Cultural Cafetero* (Coffee Growers' Cultural Foundation; 7-93 Carrera 8; phone: 281-6480); the *Museo Militar* (Military Museum; 4-92 Calle 10; phone: 281-3086); and the excellent *Museo de Arte Religioso* (Museum of Religious Art; 4-31 Calle 12; phone: 281-0556). All museums are closed on Mondays.

**SHOPPING:** *Unicentro* (Carrera 15 and Calle 127; phone: 213-8000) is a futuristic, exclusive shopping center with a choice of more than 300 boutiques; Colombia's most elegant. Another fine shopping arcade is along the Bulevar Niza (at Av. Suba, Calle 127). It's filled with trendy boutiques, theaters, and restaurants. The city's newest shopping mall is *Hacienda Santa Bárbara,* converted from an 18th-century country ranch house, with 431 shops and restaurants (Carrera 7 at Calle 116). Silverware is inexpensive but good in the small shops along Carrera 6 between Calles 12 and 13 and along Calle 12 between Carreras 6 and 7. There is a value added tax of 15% on all luxury goods. Other stores of interest include the following:

***Artesanías de Colombia*** – At these shops you will find very attractive woolen goods — knit purses, sweaters, embroidered folk tapestries, the traditional woolen *ruana,* or Colombian poncho — basketwork, hats, rustic and original pottery, leather, and the beautiful flowing gowns of the Guajira Indians called *mantas*. There are shops in the international sector (Almacén San Diego, 26-50 Carrera 10; phone: 286-1766) and downtown (Almacén Las Aguas, 18-60 Carrera 3; no phone).

***El Balay*** – Located in the Carrera 15 shopping district, this boutique consists of two shops next door to each other — one sells a wide variety of handicrafts and leather goods, the other, leather only. No credit cards accepted at the crafts shop; at the leather shop, VISA only. 75-63 Carrera 15 (phone: 248-3115).

***Boots 'n' Bags*** – A good place for wonderful leather. In the *Tequendama Hotel,* 10-42 Calle 26 (phone: 213-0276) and at 5-35 Calle 19 (phone: 241-6490).

***Clavia*** – Excellent prices on original artifacts and jewelry made from pre-Columbian beads and stones as well as a wealth of information on pre-Columbian art are what's offered at this shop that also has a branch in Cartagena. Sales in Bogotá are by appointment only. 9-10 Calle 45 (phone: 232-0356).

***Colombian Bags*** – High-quality leather goods. In the *Tequendama Hotel,* 10-42 Calle 26 (phone: 286-0894) and 93-07 Carrera 15 (phone: 257-9789).

***Cuerolandia*** – Another excellent source of leather goods at reasonable prices. Ten locations, including the *Tequendama Hotel* (*Local 108;* phone: 281-1068); *Unicentro* (*Local 1-177;* phone: 213-0165); *Travelodge Orquidea Real Hotel* (*Local 5;* phone: 232-7836); *Local 146* (Bulevar Niza); at El Dorado Airport (phone: 266-9200, ext. 2461).

***Galería Cano*** – Pre-Columbian gold ornaments and pottery including perfect gold-dipped replicas of the figures you saw in the *Museo del Oro,* produced by the same techniques. In the international sector at 27-98 Carrera 13, Tower B (phone: 284-4801).

***Galería Errazuriz*** – Authentic pre-Columbian artifacts, mostly necklaces and ceramics (complete with certificates of authenticity). In the *Tequendama Hotel,* 10-42 Calle 26 (phone: 334-1961).

***Gianni Valanti*** – Leather goods, many at bargain prices. Locations at *Centro Internacional Tequendama* (phone: 284-0092) and Bulevar Niza (*Local 2-05;* phone: 226-1970).

**BOGOTÁ / Sources and Resources** 279

***Greenfire*** – The place for excellent and exquisite emeralds. Two locations: In the *Tequendama Hotel,* 10-42 Calle 26, and the Bavaria Building, international sector.

***H. Stern*** – A renowned source for all kinds of precious stones and gold. Three locations: *Tequendama Hotel,* 10-42 Calle 26 (phone: 283-2819); the *Travelodge Orquidea Real,* 32-16 Carrera 7 (phone: 329894); and at El Dorado Airport (phone: 413-8812).

***Land Leather*** – All kinds of leather goods. 22-52 Calle 23 (phone: 268-1747) and 82-26 Carrera 14A (phone: 256-6570).

***Muzo*** – Another emerald source. In the *Tequendama Hotel,* 10-42 Calle 26 (phone: 341-0289).

***Sterling Joyeros*** – Emeralds and other precious stones and gold. Three locations: In the *Tequendama Hotel* (10-42 Calle 26; phone: 286-6895); *Bogotá Hotel* (phone: 364216); and at *Unicentro* (phone: 213-0696). Even better, visit the *Sterling* factory (68B-37 Calle 11; phone: 262-6700) for lower prices and a tour of the factory, where you will see the entire operation, from design through gold smelting and gem faceting to the finished product.

***TAB*** – For knitted, handwoven, and traditional Colombian goods of all kinds. 79-60 Carrera 14 (phone: 256-6700).

***Tibabuyes*** – More knitted Columbian products. 6-15 Calle 33 (phone: 245-8465).

**SPORTS: Auto Racing** – Mostly local competition and karting on Bogotá's circuit take place Sundays and holidays at the *Autódromo,* Autopista del Norte, about 9 miles (15 km) out of town.

**Basketball** – Club championships are held at the *Coliseo El Salitre.*

**Boxing** – Most tournaments also share the *Coliseo El Salitre.*

**Bullfighting** – Bogotá has a fine bullring in the international sector, and excellent programs are held Saturdays and Sundays in season. The festivals are in December and February. Plaza Santamaría.

**Fishing** – There's good trout fishing north of Bogotá at Lake Neusa, Lake Sisga, and Lake Tominé and at Lake Tota in the State of Boyacá. In addition, Lake Tota is the site for an international trout fishing contest held each November.

**Golf** – The best courses are those at the *Country Club de Bogotá* (phone: 258-3300) and the *Los Lagartos Club* (phone: 613-0266).

**Sailing** – Neusa, Muña, and Tominé lakes are the main sailing centers.

**Soccer** – *Fútbol* is one of Colombia's most popular sports and can be watched Sundays at *El Campín Stadium,* Calle 57 and Carrera 30 (phone: 235-6044).

**Squash** – Two good clubs, *El Club de Squash* (24-34 Carrera 5; phone: 284-5558) and *Squash Gym 85* (Carrera 7 and Calle 85; phone: 288-8285), are open to the public. They also have racquetball courts.

**Tennis** – Any number of good courts can be found in Bogotá's elegant clubs. If you want a game before or after business, the *America Tennis Club* is close to the city center at 4-06 Calle 51 (phone: 245-0608).

**Water Skiing** – *Los Lagartos Club* has top facilities on its spacious lakes (phone: 253-0077).

**THEATER:** There's no national theater company, but plenty of experimental theater. Check the papers to see what's on (almost always in Spanish). Visiting companies stop mainly at the *Teatro Colón* (5-32 Calle 10; phone: 284-7420). An amateur English-speaking theatrical group, *Community Players of Bogotá,* offers something like six plays a year. Check the local press. Variety theater on the lines of café-concerts is listed under *Nightclubs and Nightlife.* Movies are shown in their original language, usually with Spanish subtitles.

**MUSIC:** The *National Symphony Orchestra* plays weekly at the opera-style *Teatro Colón* (5-32 Calle 10, phone: 284-7420), alternating with visiting orchestras. Top-rank soloists and chamber groups appear at the beautiful *Concert Hall of the Luis Angel Arango Library* (Calle 11 and Carrera 4; phone: 342-0605). Another remarkable hall is that of the National University, which sometimes presents fine programs. Check the local paper for what's going on at the *Colsubsido Theater* (25-40 Calle 26; phone: 285-0100).

**NIGHTCLUBS AND NIGHTLIFE:** Some of the restaurants we recommend offer the opportunity to sample indigenous food and music at the same time. *Así es Colombia, Tierra Colombiana,* and *Noches de Colombia* specialize in creole cooking and dancing. The very chic *La Mirage* (93B-30 Carrera 11A; phone: 236-2063) offers a floor show and an international menu. There are many bars and discos in the Zona Rosa (Pink Zone) on and around Calle 82 between Carreras 12 and 15. The "in" discos in other parts of the city include the *Keops Club* (10-54 Calle 96; phone: 218-2258) and *Unicorn Topsi Club* (25-36 Av. 116; phone: 213-8575). A 15-minute drive into the mountains northeast of Bogotá brings you to the "Via La Calera," an area where bars and discos abound and the views are spectacular. The *Casa Colombia* (26A-40 Carrera 5, phone: 243-3562) is a super place for dancing to live Colombian folk rhythms. The *Galería Club* has blackjack tables and a good bar (27-27 Carrera 10; phone: 234-3526). If your Spanish is up to it, you may enjoy cabaret shows at *La Gata Caliente* (Calle 100 and Carrera 15; phone: 256-8496); and at *La Casa del Gordo* (90-34 Carrera 16; phone: 218-4384). The fashionable *Salón Monserrate* at the *Tequenadama* hotel (10-42 Calle 26; phone: 286-1111) has a good orchestra and guest performers in the evenings.

## BEST IN TOWN

**CHECKING IN:** Two hotels with very different styles have shared the scene since the 1950s: the *Continental,* in the heart of the business world, overlooking the colonial center, and the *Tequendama,* which pioneered the international sector. More recently, the lead has been taken by the *Travelodge,* the *Bogotá Plaza,* the *Cosmos 100,* and the *Bogotá Royal.* Expect to pay $100 for a double room at the *Travelodge Orquidea Real;* $75 to $95 at other hotels in the expensive category; between $40 and $60 at hotels in the moderate category; and under $30 (and as low as $10) at inexpensive hotels. A 15% value added tax is now in effect for accommodations and meals in the expensive category. All telephone numbers are in the 1 city code unless otherwise indicated.

**Bogotá Royal** – Opened in 1986, this impressive 80-room hotel, in Bogotá's World Trade Center, is an ideal choice for business travelers. There is an informal restaurant, the *Café Royal,* and *El Estudio,* a very inviting bar that includes a string quartet and looks more like a library than a drinking establishment. 8-01 Av. 100 (phone: 218-9911; fax: 218-3362). Expensive.

**La Bohemie** – This brand-new, 66-room establishment is in the heart of the Zona Rosa — the city's busiest shopping and nightlife district. The marble floors, flowered wallpaper, elegant chandeliers, and tinted windows are reminiscent of a fine French hotel. The guestrooms are small, but luxurious, and each has a mini-bar and double-glazed windows to block out the noise. The restaurant serves French fare. 12-35 Calle 82 (phone: 617-1177; fax: 618-0003). Expensive.

**Casa Medina** – Located in a magnificent, restored French country-style mansion.

It has 24 elegant rooms, personalized service, and an excellent restaurant (see *Eating Out*). 69A-22 Carrera 7 (phone: 217-0288; fax: 216-6668). Expensive.

**La Fontana** – In the North Bogotá area, opposite the *Unicentro Shopping Mall,* it has 130 rooms, of which 48 are suites. There also are well-equipped meeting and conference rooms, a plus as the hotel caters mostly to business travelers. 21-10 Av. 127 (phone: 274-0200; fax: 216-0449). Expensive.

**Tequendama** – More centrally located than the *Travelodge Orquidea Real* and inhabited by better shops, the address is at the core of the international sector. Its restaurants and cafeterias are very reasonably priced. The *Salón Monserrate* on the 17th floor has the most fashionable nightclub in town and a good orchestra and guest performers in the evenings. The 726 rooms all have attractive views over this part of the city and up toward the mountains. 10-42 Calle 26 (phone: 286-1111; fax: 282-2860). Expensive.

**Travelodge Orquidea Real** – Formerly the *Hilton International,* this is the only hotel with a heated swimming pool and a gym. Its 195 rooms all have wonderful views, and *Le Toit* restaurant (on the 42nd floor) has an unbeatable vista and offers very good French cooking (see *Eating Out*). Downstairs are quaint cafeterias, another restaurant, attractive lounges, and 3 spacious conference halls, as well as a number of very useful shops and agencies. International sector, 32-16 Carrera 7 (phone: 285-6020; fax: 287-7480). Expensive.

**Bogotá Plaza** – This very modern 148-room hotel is in a smart residential area well away from the city center, but it's easily accessible from the airport. This, and its excellent service, elegance, and comfort, make it an ideal stopover site. 18A-30 Calle 100 (phone: 257-2200; fax: 218-4050). Expensive to moderate.

**Charleston** – In a quiet, tree-lined residential area, this unassuming 5-story brick townhouse has a cozy atmosphere and the elegance of a private club. The 32 guestrooms each have a bar, a TV set, and arched windows through which guests can look out on gardens. There's also a small restaurant in a library-like setting, which features excellent international fare (see *Eating Out*). 85-46 Carrera 13 (phone: 257-1100; fax: 218-4050). Expensive to moderate.

**Cosmos 100** – In the northern residential area, with 128 very large rooms, 3 restaurants, 2 bars, and a sauna. All rooms have color TV sets and mini-bars. The top-floor *Saturno* restaurant offers an unusual view of the city and excellent service. 21A-41 Calle 100 (phone: 257-9200; fax: 257-2035). Expensive to moderate.

**Bacatá** – Also in a busy part of town, this very comfortable modern hostelry has 220 rooms, very good service, and a restaurant. 5-20 Calle 19 (phone: 283-8300; fax: 281-7249). Moderate.

**Dann** – Literally surrounded by some of the best shops downtown, it has much of the ambience and service of a luxury establishment at a much more modest price. The lobby and lounge are modern and distinguished. Its 145 rooms are very comfortable and all have TV sets. 5-72 Calle 19 (phone: 284-0100; fax: 282-3108). Moderate.

**Dann Colonial** – The 76 rooms at this place provide an air of local charm, and there is a good and inexpensive dining room. It's located in the colonial section. 4-21 Calle 14 (phone: 341-1680; fax: 334-9992). Moderate.

**Presidente** – Situated between the international sector and downtown, this place has 150 spacious rooms, a pleasant restaurant, a cafeteria, and a good bar. A TV set is optional in single rooms. 9-45 Calle 23 (phone: 284-1100; fax: 284-5766). Moderate.

**Continental** – The elegance of this 155-room hotel is subdued and a little old-fashioned, but both its restaurant and cafeteria are downtown meeting places for businesspeople. In part that's because the property is so convenient, standing at the top of Avenida Jiménez, Bogotá's main street, overlooking the Parque de los Periodistas and the colonial neighborhood. Shops and services are good and include a sauna. 4-16 Av. Jiménez (phone: 282-1100). Inexpensive.

**Del Duc** – Small and modern, with quite spacious and 54 agreeable rooms, a welcoming restaurant, and a bar and cozy lounges, it is central and gives excellent value for a reduced cost. TV sets must be requested. Reservations advised. 9-38 Calle 23 (phone: 334-0080; fax: 284-5169). Inexpensive.

**Hostería La Candelaria** – A delightful, restful 10-room hostelry in three restored colonial mansions, convenient to theaters, museums, and concert halls. 3-11 Calle 9 (phone: 282-7724). Inexpensive.

**San Diego** – In the international sector, this small hotel offers many advantages, most prominent being its low rates. The restaurant is undistinguished, but the 34 pleasant rooms all have a view. TV set in the lounge only. 24-82 Carrera 13 (phone: 284-2100). Inexpensive.

**Tundama** – Still quite comfortable and well attended though somewhat past its prime, the address is central, and the staff offers the same tourist and business services as the other modestly priced hotels. TV sets are optional in its 70 rooms. 8-81 Calle 21 (phone: 284-5900). Inexpensive.

**EATING OUT:** There is some excellent French and international food in town, but we recommend trying the creole (or criollo) food as well. The term criollo stems from the colonial era and refers to people of Spanish ancestry born in Colombia. Creole restaurants usually include a particularly attractive colonial atmosphere, and several offer dance shows that are entertaining. Keep in mind that all imported beverages, including wine, are expensive. Beer and other drinks produced locally are reasonably priced. Colombian creole cooking is far from exotic. On the whole, it consists of very simple meals delicately flavored with herbs — good, wholesome combinations that always have something delicious to remember them by. There is a saying in Colombia: *La comida entra por los ojos* ("The meal enters through the eyes"). It all looks so appetizing — food, earthenware dishes and pots, the large wooden ladles for serving — and the four branches of *La Casa Vieja* prepare it better than any other restaurant in the city. As an appetizer, Colombians typically have a fruit juice. If you want to do things right, have a *sorbete de curuba* before eating. A local fruit, *curuba* is really good news and grows nowhere in the world outside the savannah. Also appetizing is *maracuyá*, passion fruit juice with a tangy, acid flavor. Aperitifs are based on rum; excellent Chilean wines can accompany your meal; and the traditional *canelazo* (warm and anise-flavored) goes very well with dessert. We recommend the *ajiaco bogotano,* to begin. It will serve to acquaint you with the full flavor and dimension of this cuisine. Ingredients could not be more simple: three varieties of potato, chicken; and a corn cob. But there's some Muisca magic here, which may be the herb *guasca* or the thick cream, capers, and avocado. The *viudo* fish soup, the *sobrebarriga*, and *puchero* stew are also excellent. Here, too, is the perfect place to have a cup of Colombia's renowned coffee. Unless otherwise noted, reservations usually are not necessary, though during *Christmas* and *Easter* they're a must. Expect to pay $40 and up for a meal for two in those restaurants in our expensive category; $18 to $35 in those listed as moderate; and between $10 and $15 in those noted as inexpensive. Prices do not include drinks, wine, or tips. All telephone numbers are in the 1 city code unless otherwise indicated.

**Casa Medina** – Located in a converted residence in the hotel of the same name, this eatery boasts a varied international menu and excellent service. Open daily. Major credit cards accepted. 69A-22 Carrera 7 (phone: 217-0288). Expensive.

**Casa San Isidro** – The sun sets over the savannah, the city lights shimmer in the twilight, and the distant mountains appear silhouetted against the blood red of the dying day — that is supper here, on a cliff on the peak of Monserrate. If one forgets the very respectable French menu in contemplation of the view, the waiter will call attention to it. Open for lunch every day except Sunday, and for dinner on Thursdays through Saturdays, when there's a fire to warm this large old colonial house. Reservations necessary. Major credit cards accepted. Teleférico (phone: 281-9309, 281-9270). Expensive.

**Charleston** – Well worth a visit, this restaurant features elegant continental dining in a library-style setting. Although it's located in a hotel (of the same name), you feel as if you're dining in someone's home. Open daily. Reservations advised. Major credit cards accepted. 85-46 Carrera 13 (phone: 257-1100). Expensive.

**Chez Stefan** – With a limited, but carefully selected, menu featuring French food only, this is the "in" place to eat in Bogotá. Chef and owner Stefan personally takes individual orders and helps in the selection of the proper wine to accompany dinner choices. Open daily for lunch and dinner except Sundays and holidays. Major credit cards accepted. 82-10 Carrera 18 (phone: 236-1082). Expensive.

**Classic de Andrei** – Good international fare is served at this intimate dining spot where fish is the specialty — the trout and shellfish are especially noteworthy. With more than 90 dishes, the menu is probably Bogotá's most extensive. Closed Sundays and holidays. Reservations necessary. Major credit cards accepted. 4-31 Calle 75 (phone: 212-8152 and 248-6987). Expensive.

**La Fragata** – If seafood is your favorite, there is no better place in town. A fleet of fishing boats keeps this group of restaurants — and their sister operation in Cartagena — in fresh seafood, rushed from the coast every day. Main courses are complemented by excellent wines and good service. The decor is so nautical that diners don't know whether they're on land or at sea, but surely frigates were never this attractive or luxurious. Open daily. Major credit cards accepted. Three locations: Bavaria Bldg., 27-98 Carrera 13 (phone: 243-2959); 9-30 Calle 15 (phone: 241-0176); and 20-36 Diagonal 127-A (phone: 274-6527). Expensive.

**Hatsuhana** – Authentic Japanese food is served at this eatery that is divided into three rooms, each with its own specialty — in one, guests sit on tatami mats; in another, food is cooked in front of you (teppanyake); and in the third, sushi is served. An added attraction are the chefs who toss their utensils into the air while preparing the food. Closed Sundays. Reservations advised. Major credit cards accepted. 100-43 Transversal 21 (phone: 257-9469 and 610-3056). Expensive.

**Le Toit** – On the roof of the *Travelodge Orquidea Real* — the tallest and most elegant hotel in town — this is French in the grand style. It has a magical ambience, impeccable service, a fine wine list, and the most varied French menu in Bogotá. Open for lunch and dinner Mondays through Fridays; dinner only on Saturdays. Reservations advised. Major credit cards accepted. 32-16 Carrera 7 (phone: 285-6020). Expensive.

**Tramonti** – Thanks to its location high above the city, diners can enjoy a spectacular view while savoring Italian fare, although recent reports say that the food isn't as good as it once was. Open daily. Major credit cards accepted. 93-80 Carrera 1 on Via La Calera (phone: 218-2400). Expensive.

**Así es Colombia** – Good indigenous and international fare are served at this dining spot while typical Colombian dances are performed and live music played. Open daily except holidyas. Reservations advised. Major credit cards accepted. 116-59 Carrera 15 (phone: 214-9995). Expensive to moderate.

**Cactus** – For those homesick for a US-style diner, this place serves roast beef sandwiches and barbecued ribs and has a salad bar. It also offers international fare. Open daily. Reservations advised. Major credit cards accepted. 94-50 Carrera 15 (phone: 257-3032). Moderate.

**Café de Rosita** – Located in a restored house in colonial La Candelaria, this dining spot has a prix fixe menu that changes daily. You can sit either in a glass-covered interior courtyard or inside adjoining rooms. Open daily from 8 AM to 6 PM. No credit cards accepted. 3-11 Calle 9 (phone: 342-1727 and 286-1479). Moderate.

**La Casa Vieja** – The oldest of the four *Casa Vieja* restaurants on the Avenida Jiménez, it is on the fringe of La Candelaria and is in a quaint little house in which everything is curiously asymmetrical, down to the antique furniture and colorful decorations. Open daily. Major credit cards accepted. 3-73 Av. Jiménez (phone: 334-6171). Moderate.

**Casa Vieja de la Pepe Sierra** – The newest *Casa Vieja*. Open daily. Major credit cards accepted. 20-50 Carrera 116 (phone: 213-7855). Moderate.

**Casa Vieja de San Diego** – Just opposite the *Tequendama* hotel in the international sector, occupying another cloister, that of the Church of San Diego. Open daily. Major credit cards accepted. 26-60 Carrera 10 (phone: 284-7359). Moderate.

**Casa Vieja del Norte** – In the northern residential area. Open daily. Major credit cards accepted. 89-08 Carrera 11 (phone: 236-3421). Moderate.

**Giuseppe Verdi** – The decor isn't much to speak of, but the menu — some of the best Italian food in town — more than makes up for it. Closed Sundays. Major credit cards accepted. 5-35 Calle 58 (phone: 249-5368). Moderate.

**Gran China** – The only place for really good Chinese food in Bogotá, offering Szechuan and Cantonese fare. Open daily. Major credit cards accepted. 11-70 Calle 77A (phone: 249-5938 and 211-4807). Moderate.

**Le Grand Vatel** – For decades this has been one of the city's best French restaurants, and glamour still clings to the classical old house like the ivy on its façade. The food is excellent and the price very reasonable. Closed Sundays. Major credit cards accepted. 70-40 Carrera 7 (phone: 255-8142). Moderate.

**El Integral** – For vegetarians, this is the place. Open daily. Diners Club accepted. 95-10 Carrera 11 (phone: 256-0899). Moderate.

**Lomos** – An excellent steakhouse in northern Bogotá, with live music and gracious service. Closed Sundays. Major credit cards accepted. 100-23 Transversal 21 (phone: 256-3315 and 218-2450). Moderate.

**Noches de Colombia** – Dine on steaks and paella while watching a live show featuring typical Colombian music and dance. Open daily. Reservations advised. Major credit cards accepted. 97-65 Carrera 15 (phone: 610-6865). Moderate.

**Pierrot** – Just beyond the bullring and a favorite of Bogotá's show biz community. Take time from gathering autographs to try the chicken in mustard sauce — the house specialty. Closed Sundays. No credit cards accepted. 5-72 Calle 27 (phone: 334-4492). Moderate.

**El Pórtico** – On the outskirts of town, this beautiful old farmhouse in the savannah is surrounded by attractive parks and playgrounds and has a horse-drawn carriage and an ox-drawn cart to take you around. This is another restaurant that combines delicious creole food with a thoroughly bucolic setting. There's even a bullring for those who want to fight with calves and a real *trapiche* — a sugarcane press — that you can see at work. We recommend the *carne a la Fragua*, a delicious grilled filet served with potatoes called *papas chorreadas*. Open daily. Major credit cards accepted. At Km 16 on the Carretera Central del Norte (phone: 676-0752). Moderate.

**Pueblito de Yerbabuena** – If your Sunday is free and you want to change the city scene, here is a charming little village that turns out once a week to become virtually a village-wide restaurant, serving excellent creole food. Open Sundays and holidays only. No credit cards accepted. At Km 24 on the road to Tunja (phone: 863-0517). Moderate.

**Refugio Alpino** – Small, cozy, and with very friendly service, this place specializes in European food. Afternoons you'll find locals enjoying business lunches that tend to be very long and very liquid. Closed Sundays. Major credit cards accepted. Reservations advised. 7-49 Calle 23 (phone: 284-6515). Moderate.

**Samurai-Ya** – A small Japanese restaurant where the *yosanabe*, a stew prepared with fish, shrimp, chicken, beef, and vegetables, alone is worth the trip. Sushi and other dishes also are available. Open daily except Sundays and holidays for lunch and dinner. Major credit cards accepted. *Centro Internacional Tequendama* (phone: 243-8992). Moderate.

**Tandoor** – Good quality Indian food served in an elegant but relaxed setting. Excellent service. Closed Sundays. Major credit cards accepted. 84-53 Carrera 11 (phone: 218-9698). Moderate.

**La Teja Corrida** – The name roughly translates as "The Loose Screw," and it is a rather crazy place, serving creole food and drinks made from the local firewater. Music, especially on weekends, is mostly Colombian; however, if you feel a song coming on — in any language — just tell the waiter and suddenly the spotlight is on *you!* Downtown, just across the way from the bullring. Closed Sundays and Mondays. Major credit cards accepted. 26A-54 Carrera 5 (phone: 342-4783). Moderate.

**Tierra Colombiana** – In the elegant international sector, it offers a lively folk show and light music as well as both creole and international dishes. Closed Sundays. Major credit cards accepted. 27-27 Carrera 10 (phone: 334-9525). Moderate.

**Las Acacias** – Pop in at one of the 15 branches of this ubiquitous restaurant chain for typical Colombian food. Closed Sundays. Major credit cards accepted. For a list of their locations and a coupon for a complimentary dinner, call the main office (212-9187). Inexpensive.

**Brasa Brazil** – Enjoy an almost unlimited array of meat dishes, all for a set price. Daily except Sundays from noon to midnight, and if there's a good-size crowd, closing time usually stretches a bit. Major credit cards accepted. Av. 19 and Calle 118 (phone: 214-8064). Inexpensive.

**Café Color** – Sightseers in the Candelaria area should seek out this combination coffeehouse-crafts gallery located on the Plazaoleta del Chorro de Quevedo. Espresso, cappuccino, and a variety of mixed drinks, including *Cappucino Colores*, made with three different liqueurs. There is music in the evenings. Closed Sundays and Mondays. No credit cards accepted. 13-06 Carrera 2 (phone: 284-7312). Inexpensive.

**Crema y Lujuria** – Any restaurant called "Cream and Lust" can't be all bad. This is a place to indulge in mouth-watering pastries and ice cream concoctions. Open daily. No credit cards accepted. Two locations: *Unicentro Shopping Mall* (phone: 213-5074) and 6-47 Calle 124 (phone: 213-5286). Inexpensive.

**Donde Canta la Rana** – Translated, the name becomes "Where the Frog Sings," and it's a must for the truly adventurous diner questing for the most authentic native delicacies. Among the most notable items on the menu is a barbecue of "liver and lights," including cow's udder and bull's testicles. Anything but elegant, but it's a real culinary experience. Open daily. No credit cards accepted. 20-10 Sur, Carrera 24-C (phone: 239-1870). Inexpensive.

**O' Sole e Napoli** – The owner personally supervises the preparation of the excellent Italian fare he offers at good prices. It's also one of the few places in town that serves good pizza. Closed Mondays. MasterCard accepted. 11-58 Calle 69 (phone: 249-2186). Inexpensive.

**La Parrilla de Oro** – Although not even moderately comfortable, its excellent *churrasco* has made it highly popular. Many delicious preparations of the less refined creole cuisine are also offered at unbeatable prices. Open daily. No credit cards accepted. 17-94 Carrera 4 (phone: 243-9587). Inexpensive.

**Le Poivre** – A French restaurant with a reasonably priced menu. Open daily except

Sundays for lunch and dinner. Major credit cards accepted. 69-38 Carrera 10-A (phone: 249-8198).Inexpensive.

*El Zaguán de Las Aguas* – A fair variety of good creole dishes is the main attraction at this very central place. Try the *jaiba al Zaguán,* a giant crab done au gratin with a tasty cognac sauce. It also is a good place to be introduced to *ajiaco bogotáno* (stew) or to the *postre de nata* (custard with raisins). Open daily. Major credit cards accepted. Two locations: 5-62 Calle 19 (phone: 282-3020) and 20-52 Calle 100 (phone: 236-6138). Inexpensive.

■ **Deli-cum-Colombia:** There are several New York-style delicatessens in town that serve bagels and lox — a rarity in the middle of the Andes — as well as sandwiches. The *New York Deli* has three locations: at the World Trade Center (8A-49 Calle 100; phone: 226-9230 and 226-9280), at the *Parque Central Bavaria* (28-01 Carrera 13; phone: 288-6847 and 287-7724), and next to *Friday's* (82-15 Carrera 12; phone: 218-2512 and 218-2610). Also try *Teisty Bagel and Deli* (17-62 Calle 90; phone: 257-8494). They are all open daily. No credit cards and no reservations are accepted. Their prices range from moderate to inexpensive.

# BUENOS AIRES

Acclaimed by both residents and travelers as the Paris of South America, Buenos Aires is one of the most haunting and attractive destinations on the continent. The city shares a considerable number of architectural elements with its French nicknamesake: wide boulevards, flowers and foliage, large parks, and ornate, gray buildings dating from the 1930s with rococo and baroque decorations. Some Spanish colonial elements are detectable — most notably, the many government and religious buildings around the Plaza de Mayo — but the Parisian influence predominates. Just as Paris has its Eiffel Tower, B.A. (as Buenos Aires is called by English-speaking residents) has its own picture-postcard landmark: the towering obelisk in the center of the plaza where Avenida Corrientes intersects Avenida Nueve de Julio, the boulevard that city officials claim is the world's widest. The 40-mile Avenida Rivadavia, stretching from the Plaza de Mayo to the suburbs, is frequently referred to as the world's longest street, although a metropolis of such grand dimensions hardly needs hyperbole.

Bordered on the northeast by the Río de la Plata (River Plate), the city sprawls inland across 76 square miles. The Río de la Plata is not really a river, but a deep, wide estuary that receives the waters of both the Río Paraná, which begins in Brazil and flows south through Paraguay to northern Argentina, and the Río Uruguay, which flows south from the southern Brazil–northern Argentina border. Along the waterfront stretches one of the city's most famous neighborhoods, La Boca (The Mouth), the bawdy port that is home to many Argentine artists. As in Paris, each neighborhood is distinctive, with its own shops, restaurants, *confiterías* (cafés), and *ferias* (public food markets). The neighborhood of San Telmo is the site of numerous tango parlors. The luxurious Barrio Norte (North District), full of fashionable cafés, is where the rich fled in 1870 when they mistakenly concluded that the fog in wealthy neighborhoods near the river was causing a malaria and yellow fever epidemic.

The capital's lifestyle takes its rhythm from Paris, too. Restaurants, theaters, cabarets, shops, and art galleries line the ground floors of many buildings, few of which exceed 6 or 7 stories. The *Teatro Colón* (Colón Theater), one of the world's premier opera houses and concert halls, draws many international artists. More than 100 movie theaters present films ranging from Bergman's heavy dramas to grade B Italian sex comedies. There are several first-rate, if controversial, Argentine filmmakers, such as Leopoldo Torre Nilsson, who produced *Boquitas Pintadas* (Little Painted Mouths) in 1974, and Raúl de la Torre, with *Crónica de una Señora* (Chronicle of a Lady) in 1971. Director Luis Puenzo's *The Official Story,* which looked at the trafficking of political prisoners' children during the military dictatorship, won an Oscar for the best foreign-language film in 1985. And a year later, Julie

# BUENOS AIRES

## Points of Interest

1. Plaza de Mayo/May Plaza
2. Casa Rosada/Pink House
3. El Cabildo/Council House
4. La Catedral/Cathedral
5. Edificio del Congreso Nacional/National Congress Building
6. El Obelisco (The Obelisk)
7. Avenida Nueve de Julio/July Ninth Avenue
8. Teatro Colón/Colón Theater
9. Teatro Cervantes/Cervantes Theater
10. Plaza San Martín/San Martín Plaza
11. Avenida Lavalle
12. Plaza Dorrego; San Telmo district
13. La Boca district; El Caminito
14. Plaza Francia/France Plaza
15. Museo de Bellas Artes/National Museum of Fine Art
16. La Recoleta neighborhood; Plaza Vicente Lopez
17. Cementerio Recoleta/Recoleta Cemetary
18. Palermo Parks
19. Sociedad Rural/Rural Society Fairgrounds
20. Jardín Botánico Carlos Thays/Carlos Thays Botanical Gardens
21. Hipódromo Argentino/Argentine Racetrack
22. Jardín Japonés/Japanese Gardens
23. Parque Zoológico/Zoological Gardens

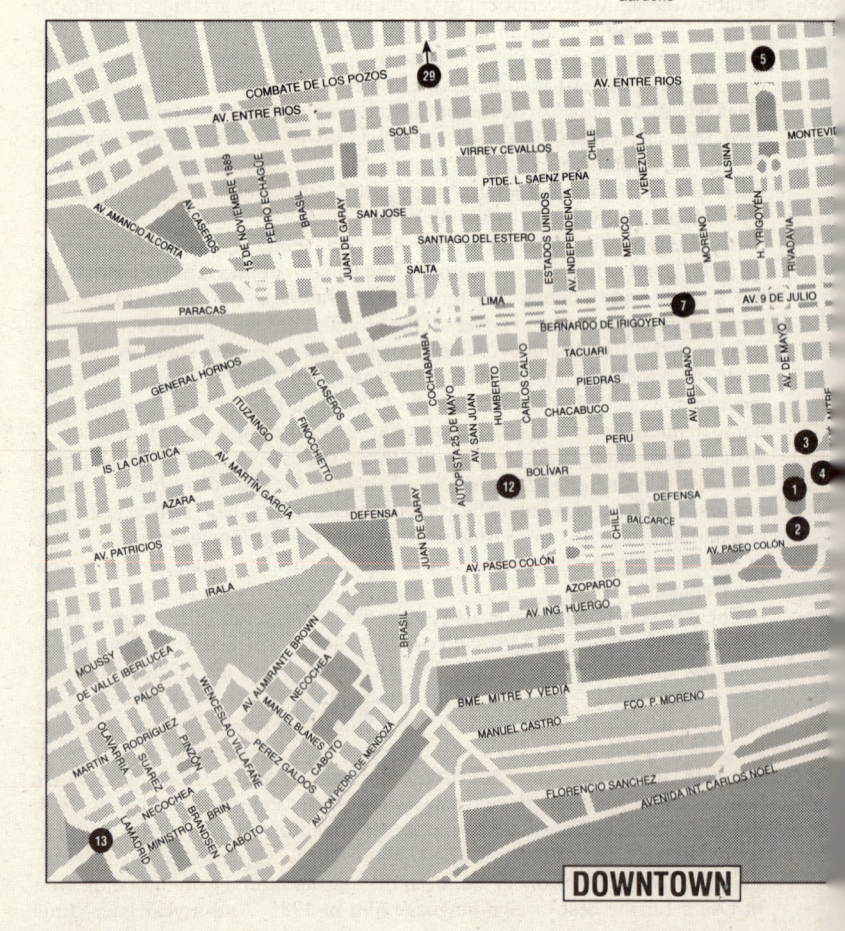

**DOWNTOWN**

24. Planetario Galileo/Galileo Planetarium
25. Teatro San Martín
26. Estación Terminal de Omnibus/Bus Station
27. Estación Retiro/Retiro Train Station
28. Aeroparque Jorge Newberry
29. Azeiza International Airport
30. Argentine National Tourist Office

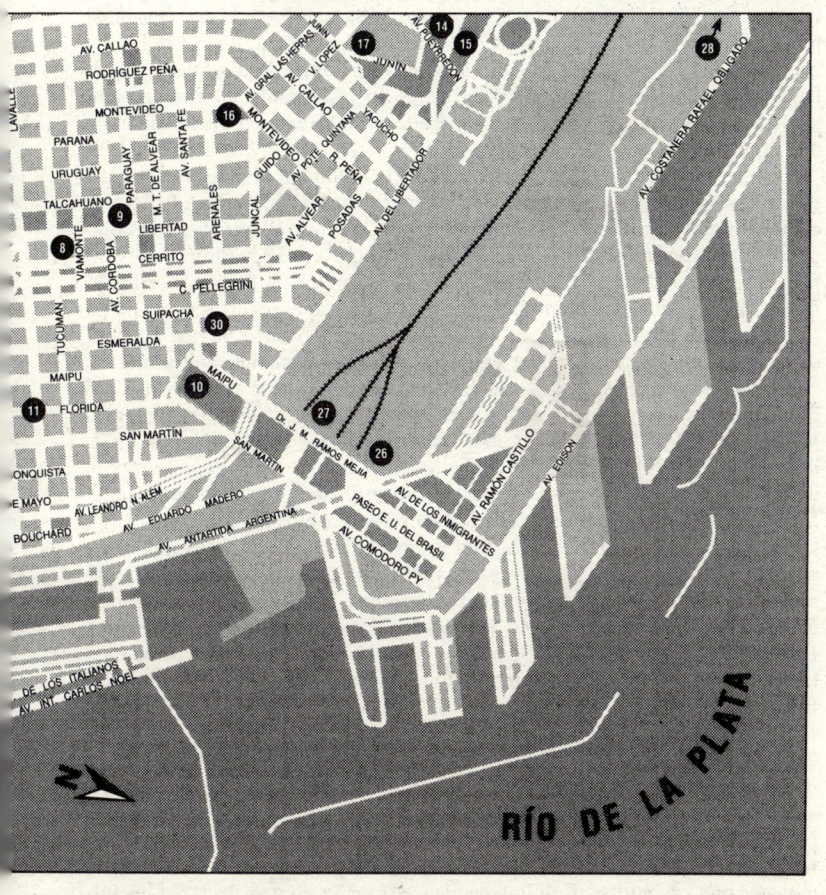

Christie played the lead role in yet another Argentine film, *Miss Mary,* directed by María Luisa Bemberg. With a national literacy rate of 94% and over 4,500 bookstores in the city, Buenos Aires ensures a lively cultural atmosphere.

The strong presence of the legitimate arts is enhanced by a proliferation of nightclubs, cabarets, and music halls that are responsible for B.A.'s reputation as "the city that never sleeps." A paradise for insomniacs, the downtown streets are busy practically 24 hours a day. Restaurants are accustomed to serving diners emerging from shows after midnight. Nighttime is devoted to window shopping (some stores stay open until midnight) or taking leisurely breaks over espresso at favorite *confiterías.* On weekends, groups of friends carouse until dawn, then stop for coffee and croissant-like pastries called *media lunas* (half moons) before retiring. There is nightlife for all tastes. And the streets are safe after dark, well lit all night, and usually busy with pedestrian traffic. Violent street crime is minimal, although there is an occasional purse snatching. Unlike Bogotá, Colombia, or Lima, Peru, it isn't normally necessary to remove jewelry before leaving your hotel. And while it is perfectly acceptable and safe for women to go to restaurants, *confiterías,* and movies without a male escort or chaperon, at night women customarily go out in groups.

Fueling this restive energy is Argentina's abundant beef, touted as the tastiest in the world; Argentines devour more than 176 pounds of beef per capita annually. Because it is so plentiful, beef is relatively inexpensive compared with other meat and fish, as a stroll through a *feria* readily reveals. In fact, Argentina claims to have about 1½ head of cattle for each of its 33 million inhabitants, and some Buenos Aires restaurants report serving half a ton of beef nightly! In addition to beef, Argentina produces a vast array of other foodstuffs, and is a major exporter of fruit, vegetables, and grain.

Most of Argentina's exports are shipped through Buenos Aires, which has become the country's main port and commercial center. The city struggled to reach this dominance. When first settled by Pedro de Mendoza in 1536, it was barely a dot on the map of the Spanish Empire. The first 5 years of its existence were less than auspicious, as the settlement was constantly under Indian attack. When the Indians finally succeeded in burning it down in 1541, the Spaniards simply left, and the first permanent settlement was founded by another Spaniard, Juan de Garay, in 1580. The town grew slowly. By the mid-17th century, the population barely reached 1,000. In that era, Spanish colonial life was controlled from the headquarters of the Spanish viceroy in Lima, Peru. Eventually, the Spanish colonies became too large to be controlled from one site, and in response to pressures from independent-minded Buenos Aires, a separate viceroyalty of the Río de la Plata was formed in 1776, headquartered in B.A.

The viceroyalty did not last long. By the beginning of the 19th century, the winds of revolution were whipping through Latin America. On May 25, 1810, a cautious Buenos Aires declared independence from the viceroy but wisely pledged continued loyalty to the Spanish crown. This forced the viceroy's resignation, resulting in the formation of a local government without the violence of a revolution. Full independence from Spain was declared on July 9, 1816, in the city of Tucumán in Argentina's interior. This event provoked a long battle between B.A.'s political leaders and those from the provinces who feared centralized control from B.A. as much as from Spain. A bitterly divided Argentina suffered a series of civil wars in which rival political leaders fought for national control. Buenos Aires did not become the permanent capital of the country until 1880.

For the next 50 years, the city developed as an important shipping center, but nothing of major significance occurred. The first waves of immigrants from Italy, Spain, and Eastern Europe began arriving around the turn of the century, lured by the Argentine government's offer of economic opportunity in a rich, new world. (Today, Italian immigrants and their descendants form the biggest ethnic block, about 50% of the population. And England — which forged strong economic and political ties with the country after Argentine independence — is regarded as a cultural model.) In the 1930s, the city's population swelled when thousands upon thousands of rural migrant workers poured into the capital in search of more profitable work.

These *descamisados* (shirtless ones) were the foundation of Juan Domingo Perón's formidable political base. Just one of a group of colonels who seized power from the elected Republican government in 1943, Perón was appointed labor minister. By endorsing the demands of the labor unions, he accumulated a broad and loyal political following, which later enthusiastically supported him for president. His totalitarian regime remained strong until the early 1950s, when it was seriously weakened by local economic conditions and the death of Eva ("Evita"), his wildly popular second wife. Perón himself soon disintegrated psychologically and conceded to a military takeover, preferring exile in Spain to a battle for power. While outside the country, Perón encouraged his supporters to aggressively confront the government, which had banned the Peronist labor unions and political parties.

Perón became leader of Argentina for a second time when President Héctor Cámpora stepped down in 1973. But his chaotic regime was short-lived. Perón died in 1974 and was succeeded by his third wife, María Estela de Perón, known as Isabelita. Whereas Eva Perón's dedication to the *descamisados* had won her folk-heroine adulation, Isabelita lacked any comparable following. In fact, her dependence on the minister of social welfare, José López-Rega, was said to be so great that the presidency was actually in his control, and her administration was widely viewed as one of the worst ever in Argentina. The military finally forced her to resign in early 1976, and seized power directly. In the 7 years of military rule that followed, Argentina's economic and political conditions deteriorated precipitously. Terrorist assassinations were followed by government-sanctioned "disappearances" of social and political opponents, in the course of which an estimated 20,000 people were detained for questioning and simply never reappeared.

The junta's defeat in the ill-advised Falkland Islands (Las Malvinas to the Argentines) war against Great Britain in 1982 ultimately forced the downfall of the military government. General elections were held in October 1983, and Raúl Alfonsín, a lawyer and human rights advocate, was elected president. Although Argentines appear better fed and more affluent than residents in other South American countries, the burgeoning debt and economic woes forced Alfonsín from office 5 months before his term ended in 1989.

The election ending Alfonsín's tenure marked the first time in 60 years that power in Argentina was transferred peacefully from one civilian-elected democratic government to another. The fact that the election of Carlos Menem brought the Peronistas back in control demonstrated the power of populism in Argentina, but also underlined the presence of the unhappy military lurking ominously in the background. The new president quickly managed to restore some economic stability (after prices had jumped 600% overnight), yet much to the displeasure of many Argentines, he calmed a jumpy military by pardoning officers awaiting trial in connection with the tortures and deaths that had taken place under the country's last military government. A year later, Menem freed the last of the former ruling junta members, once again provoking national criticism.

In this, the Third World's number three debtor nation, one of the major issues that continues to preoccupy the Argentines is the inflation rate and devaluation of the currency. In 1992, the currency changed from the austral to the Argentine peso. Its value is linked to the US dollar — 1 peso equals $1 US. While Argentina does not have to endure the street violence and terrorism that have scared tourists away from some other Latin American countries, it has always been subject to unpredictable price changes. Currently, Argentina's inflation has begun to diminish and, although the country is no longer an inexpensive travel destination, economists say a strong show on the Buenos Aires stock market and new foreign investment are signs that the economy is stablizing. Still, wealthy Argentines have not repatriated the estimated $50 billion they have socked away in bank accounts and investments outside the country.

At the end of 1990, in an attempt to reduce the country's foreign debt, the government began a program to privatize several publicly owned companies. ENTel (the phone utility) was sold to a consortium of foreign banks and telecommunications companies and control of *Aerolíneas Argentinas* given to a group led by *Iberia Airlines*. As we went to press, plans were under way to break up the giant state-owned oil company and parcel out the national rail lines, and President Menem had announced a huge deregulation program.

The tension between the indulgent lifestyle and political and economic realities of the *porteños* (as B.A. locals are called) seems to result in an air of sadness, a vein of melancholia in their vision of life. Buenos Aires's nearly 11 million residents have an uncanny (some might say incongruous) knack for expressing the dark side of life between mouthfuls of steak and potatoes, washing down the bitterness with mellow red wine. Some people attribute the *porteños'* stormy nature to the rains that dowse the city through much of the year; others theorize that the widespread melancholia is part of a middle class syndrome of people whose physical needs are abundantly filled and who brood incessantly over every emotional and personal setback. Yet another hypothesis is that *porteños*, caught in the crossfire of various national and ethnic heritages, are still in search of an identity. *Porteños* are often described as Italians who speak Spanish and think they are English. Whatever the reason, a *porteño* (or *porteña*) can dramatize a personal problem, such as a broken love affair, into a social tragedy. Nothing expresses this more eloquently than the tango.

As inextricably bound to B.A. as Dixieland jazz is to New Orleans, the tango was born at the turn of the century, the musical expression of the poor black population. But the music was adopted by successive waves of working class Europeans who had immigrated to Argentina to make their fortunes. The lyrics were a social barometer of their desires and aspirations. In the 1920s, optimistic tangos reflected a hopeful political situation. During the 1930s, after a populist party failed, tango lyrics mourned the desperate hardship of the Depression. Argentina became exceptionally prosperous immediately after World War II by providing food for Europe, thus generating the expression "rich as an Argentine." This minimized economic problems, increased the ranks of the middle class, and saw the evolution of a new style of tango that expressed the frustrations of modern life. One of the most famous tangos, *Cambalache* (Barter), evokes a powerful, nihilistic image of the 20th century as a big bazaar where values are swapped:

> Everything is the same.
> Nothing is better.
> A mule is equal with a great professor.

The song complains that today's heroes are those crooks, robbers, and swindlers who get away with it. The lyrics of another song lament:

> I know a city called Buenos Aires
> A city where my love was born.
> For the two of us along the city's solitary streets
> Love was born during a winter that had flowers in bloom.

After the love affair ends, the song grows bitter:

> This city doesn't exist anymore.
> It doesn't have streets for walking.
> It doesn't have homes to share happiness.

A natural for throaty female torch singers capable of squeezing tragedy and despair into their facial expressions, the tango also lends itself well to deep male voices expressing the pathos of unfaithful love. Lyrics are often written in *lunfardo,* the *porteño* slang that intertwines Spanish and Italian to form a third language full of twists and tricks. The key instrument of the tango is the *bandoneón,* similar to a concertina but slightly larger, with piano and violin accompaniment. The tango is no longer the dominant music it once was in Buenos Aires — young people seem to prefer the latest hits from the US and Europe — but it always will be a part of Argentine life. Carlos Gardel, who died in 1935, remains the most popular tango singer. His records are still played regularly on radio stations, and street vendors hawk his picture along with national flags, pennants, and banners at public events.

The *porteños'* heavy reliance on nostalgia for the past may be a sign of their discontent with the present, but it could also be only the sincere expression of their love for the city and its traditions. Despite decades of turmoil, Buenos Aires has retained its grace and dignity. When Pedro de Mendoza founded his settlement, he called it Nuestra Señora de la Santísima Trinidad de los Buenos Aires (Our Lady of the Blessed Trinity of Good Airs). Since the Spanish explorer planted his conqueror's cross, the settlement has grown tremendously and the name has shortened considerably. But throughout its growth (and despite its growing pains), this city has always retained something of its good air.

# BUENOS AIRES AT-A-GLANCE

**SEEING THE CITY:** The sheer vastness of Buenos Aires makes a sweeping, panoramic view from any one spot difficult to find. Since the city lacks true skyscrapers, getting a glimpse of even a significant section is not easy, either. For the best view of the downtown area, try the cocktail lounge on the top floor of the *Sheraton* hotel. To the east, you can see the docks and the shimmering waters of the Río de la Plata, which shines iridescent-silver under the full moon. To the west, you can get a good look at the tree- and flower-lined Plaza San Martín linked to a network of narrow, grid-webbed streets. It is courteous to order a drink while enjoying the view. However, no one will stop you from walking in, taking a look, and leaving. Open daily until 2 AM. 1225 San Martín (phone: 311-6311).

**SPECIAL PLACES:** Walking through the downtown area is easy: Streets are laid out in an orderly grid, and buses run up and down the alternating one-way cross streets and all the main avenues except Lavalle and Florida — the two pedestrian boulevards downtown. Private traffic is restricted on key streets during rush hours. However, taxis are plentiful; there are approximately 75,000 in Buenos Aires. They are not expensive, and can be hailed on the street. If you do not speak Spanish, write the address of your destination on a slip of paper and present it to the taxi driver.

**Plaza de Mayo (May Plaza)** – One block wide and 2 blocks long, the city's principal square and oldest park is surrounded by government and religious buildings. It was named to commemorate the date of independence from the Spanish viceroy — May 25, 1810. The most important gathering place in the country, South America's first "underground tramway" opened here on Dec. 1, 1913. A center of political activity during its various post-colonial incarnations, the plaza was the scene of huge demonstrations during the populist governments of Juan Perón (1946–55, 1973–76), when as many as 100,000 people jammed the square to hear their leader. Even after the overthrow of the Peronists in March 1976, the plaza retained its political importance. It was here that women — known as the *"madres de mayo"* — untiringly demonstrated during the last military government, demanding an end to the *"desaparecidos."* Protests by labor unions, militant retirees angered by the effect of the Menem government's economic policies on their pensions, and other groups seeking the attention of the president still draw thousands. Av. de Mayo and Calle San Martín.

**Casa Rosada (Pink House)** – Named for its color, this huge building facing the eastern side of the Plaza de Mayo houses the office of Argentina's president. A fortress in colonial days, it was constructed to protect the city from sea invasion via the Río de la Plata, which once lapped at its back door. The roof is equipped with a helicopter pad, numerous radar scanners, and large communications antennas, but the interior retains its original Spanish atmosphere, with courtyards full of flowers, fountains, and statuary. The courtyards, once open to the sky, are now enclosed. It is from the balcony of this building that Eva Perón once delivered her stirring rhetoric to the Argentine masses. The *Museo de los Presidentes* (phone: 469841, ext. 379) with memorabilia from former presidents is housed in the building. Open Wednesdays and Thursdays from 9 AM to 2 PM, Fridays and Saturdays from 2 to 6 PM; No admission charge. Visitors are required to show a passport to enter. Plaza de Mayo.

**El Cabildo (Council House)** – The house of the Spanish viceroys' counselors, this was where the counselors declared independence in 1810, running from the building to shout their jubilation in Plaza de Mayo. In 1940, the Council House was declared a national monument, redecorated, and converted into a museum containing mementos of the 1810 uprising. Its basement was once used as a jail, then as the city morgue. At press time, a group of North American archaeologists had begun excavating under the Cabildo in what are believed to be Jesuit tunnels that were blocked up more than half a century ago. On Fridays, handicrafts are sold in the garden behind the building. Open Tuesdays through Fridays from 12:30 to 6:30 PM, Sundays from 3 to 6:30 PM. Admission charge. 65 Bolívar (phone: 343-0593 and 343-1782). For guided tours in English, call 343-1782 or 343-0593.

**La Catedral (Cathedral)** – On the site of the second church built in Buenos Aires (ca. 1593), this Greek-façaded structure has gone through many renovations, the last of which took place after the cathedral and other Catholic churches were severely burned on June 16, 1955, by rampaging Peronists, who felt the church was a center of opposition to their government. The cathedral contains the tomb of General José de San Martín, the Argentine who, with Simón Bolívar, led the South American wars of independence from Spain in the 19th century; the paintings on its wall are said to be by Rubens. The cathedral also houses the Chair of Rivadavia, a symbol of the Argentine presidency. The chair belonged to Bernardino Rivadavia, the nation's first president, and is used when the current president attends official ceremonies at the cathedral. This occurs fairly frequently, as Catholicism is the state religion and the Constitution stipulates that the Argentine president must be a practicing Catholic. Often, on important national and religious holidays, the president and his ministers parade the 2 blocks to the cathedral, which fronts the Plaza de Mayo on the north, to attend services. Tourists are not permitted to enter the cathedral if they are wearing shorts, miniskirts, or other attire deemed inappropriate by church officials. 450 Rivadavia.

**Edificio del Congreso Nacional (National Congress Building)** – Finished in 1906, it is a square, block-long, white Greco-Roman structure at the end of Avenida de Mayo, the street that starts at Plaza de Mayo. Noteworthy are the Senate Chamber and the Salón Azul (Blue Salon). Free guided tours are conducted every half hour Monday through Friday mornings from 9 to 11 AM, and Monday, Tuesday, and Friday afternoons from 2 to 4:30 PM. 53 Entre Ríos (phone: 313-8300).

**El Obelisco (Obelisk)** – Jokingly nicknamed "the Argentine monument to the suppository" by bus drivers, this 70-foot structure stands in the heart of town. The most frequently photographed symbol of the city, it reminds some visitors of the Washington Monument and was built on the spot where the first flag of independent Argentina was flown in 1813. It marks the intersection of Avenida Nueve de Julio and Calle Corrientes, an active nightlife street.

**Avenida Nueve de Julio (July Ninth Avenue)** – One city block wide, this thoroughfare measures 425 feet across, which *porteños* claim make it the world's widest street. The boulevard has grassy squares in its center, each sectioned off and named after different provinces. It was built by tearing down square block after square block of downtown apartment and office buildings. Presently 26 blocks long, the avenue is still growing, and city planners seem determined that it fulfill some urban manifest destiny by cutting a swath through the city until it reaches the Río de la Plata. In addition to the obelisk, the avenue has two huge fountains with special lighting effects that can be seen for several blocks at night. An ideal place for strolling and people watching, the *confitería*-lined avenue has some terrific places to have tea, coffee, cocktails, and sandwiches while you watch the parade or catch up on the newspapers from the abundantly stocked kiosks. The *International Herald Tribune,* the *Miami Herald,* and *The New York Times* are among the many foreign publications on sale.

**Teatro Colón (Colón Theater)** – Filling almost 1 square block, this majestic building about 3 blocks from the obelisk is the center of the city's classical music life. One of the world's major opera houses for more than 80 years, it hosts touring concerts and ballets as well as works by its own ballet troupe, opera company, and symphony orchestra, whose repertoires are enhanced by frequent guest appearances of international artists; dance superstar Mikhail Baryshnikov has called it "the most beautiful of all the theaters I know." Underneath the theater, a maze of rehearsal halls, carpentry shops, tailor shops, and work areas are devoted to the vast number of tasks involved in launching any performance. The theater's main entrance is on Plaza Lavalle, a large tree-filled park whose fountain, decorated with statues of ballet dancers, commemorates an Argentine ballet troupe that died in a plane crash en route to Montevideo, Uruguay, in the 1960s. The rear of the building and its stage entrance overlook spacious Avenida Nueve de Julio. Along one side of the theater Calle Toscanini, a tiny street named after the world-famous symphony conductor, passes the entrance to the upper balconies. The highest balcony is called El Paraíso (Paradise) because it sits so close to the heavens. It is also paradise for students and other music lovers of humble means because the seats here are least expensive. Although dress codes are no longer strictly enforced, men customarily attend performances in black tie. The concert season runs from March through November. Tours of the *Colón* and its underground complex are available 10 AM to 6 PM weekdays. Inquire at the ticket office, open daily from 10 AM to 8 PM (phone: 355414). Admission charge for tours. 1111 Tucumán (box office phone: 352389).

**Teatro Cervantes (Cervantes Theater)** – Its venerable wood-paneled interior reeking of ages of glossy polish, this is the house of tried and true classical drama. The theater was opened in 1921 by a pair of Spanish actors, and its curtains, tiles, railings, and paintings were imported from Spain. Foreign companies on tour play the *Cervantes* stage. English-language programs with principals such as the late Sir Michael Redgrave have performed here. Spanish translations of the works of Shakespeare, Brecht, and other dramatists are also staged. Although the main season runs from March through November, it often has limited summer engagements. Open daily. 815 Libertad (phone: 454224).

**Plaza San Martín (San Martín Plaza)** – Named after Argentine liberator General José de San Martín, this park has a huge statue of its namesake at its western end. The statue is a favorite spot for visitors from other parts of Argentina to be photographed. Over a square block in size, the plaza is a popular gathering place for downtown residents. It is the center of the city's most fashionable area, but homeless people and young lovers seem to be taking over. Calle Florida and Av. Santa Fe will lead you from the plaza to some of B.A.'s most elegant shops. At the end of Maipú, between Maipú and Av. San Martín.

**Avenida Lavalle** – This downtown pedestrian-only street is the single most active stretch in the city. If you think it's crowded at breakfast time or for lunch, drop by after midnight. Lined with restaurants and shops, it also offers block after block of movie theaters and is a favorite gathering place for street musicians. No matter how late at night — or early in the morning — you go, there is always something to do on Lavalle between Avenida Florida and Nueve de Julio. Running a close second in popularity is the other pedestrian mall, Avenida Florida. Shops on both streets usually are open from 9 AM to 9 PM; many of the restaurants are open nearly until dawn.

**San Telmo** – The tango is alive and well in trendy San Telmo, with music 7 days a week. Fashionable *porteños* are rediscovering this area, which is the oldest in the city. San Telmo has retained its cobblestone streets, colonial manors that formerly housed cattle barons, and underground passageways where smugglers stashed loot from pirate ships. Antiques shops are concentrated around Plaza Dorrego, once the watering station for draft animals. The corner of Calle Humberto and Calle Defensa is the scene of a giant flea market on Sundays and holidays, where everything from a copper milking pail to a rare edition of an out-of-print *porteño* magazine is for sale. Bargaining is requisite. At night, San Telmo metamorphoses into a string of brightly lit tango bars and cabarets, with musical renditions so sensual they would make Rudolph Valentino blush. Be sure to stop in at *El Viejo Almacén* (The Old Grocery Store; 799 Calle Balcarce), in what was, 150 years ago, an English hospital and is now a delicatessen. It offers what amounts to a crash course in the tango, with songs, dances, and instrumentals. *Taconeando* (725 Balcarce; phone: 362-9596), owned by Bebe Bidart, the grande dame of tango, has a good tango show mixed with some gaucho dances and folk music. Tours of San Telmo that include nightclub stops can be arranged through most hotels. The district is several blocks south of the Plaza de Mayo.

**La Boca** – The old port area of the city faces the point at which the Río Riachuelo empties into the Río de la Plata. La Boca is the Italian district, many of whose inhabitants trace their ancestry to the northern Italian port of Genoa. Like any waterfront area, it has plenty of sleazy bars and nightclubs, but it also has gaily decorated homes and art galleries. The rainbow of colors used on the buildings comes from the poor fishermen's custom of touching up their houses with leftover boat paint. This was encouraged by artist Benito Quinquela Martín (he died in 1977), and brought international acclaim to the area. La Boca has long been favored by Argentine painters. It was the inspiration of these artists that created El Caminito — a street of artists' studios with neither sidewalks nor doors, but colorful windows, balconies, and plenty of street art, the site of weekend art fairs in warm weather. (Murals and an open-air rooftop exhibit of modern sculpture can be seen at the *La Boca Museum of Fine Arts* and *School La Boca,* founded with donations from Martín (1835 Calle Pedro de Mendoza; phone: 211080). It is perfectly safe to stroll through this neighborhood alone during the day; at night, you would be advised to travel with a group and stick to the well-lit main streets. It is difficult to get to know the residents of La Boca. They form a closely knit, independent, and somewhat insular community within the larger city. In fact, they only half jokingly refer to their neighborhood as the Independent Republic of La Boca. Traditionally, tourists visiting La Boca have stopped by the rowdy *cantinas* for home-cooked meals and generous quantities of wine. However, the quality of the food and service is hit and miss. (You may want to head out to another section of Buenos Aires when it's time to eat.) The most famous *cantina* is *Spadavecchia* (1180 Necochea; phone: 214977). Stay away from *La Cueva de Zingarella,* which has the reputation among *porteños* as a grossly overpriced tourist trap. Tours of La Boca, including a dinner at a *cantina,* can best be arranged through one of the travel agencies with desks at the major hotels.

**Plaza Francia (France Plaza)** – Particularly lively during spring and summer, this favorite park lures the locals to sunbathe, picnic, and nap. Students use it as a place to study, and young lovers as a site for trysts. About twice as big as Plaza San Martín, Plaza Francia has enough grass for children to play soccer. Situated on a long, sloping hill, its asphalt walkways make handy speedways for skateboards and go-carts, so be wary. Vendors sell popcorn, candy, coffee, and ice cream. Also on the plaza is the *Centro Cultural* (Cultural Center), housed at a site once occupied by a convent, which was turned into a hospital, and then a prison, a barracks, and a home for the aged (1930 Junín; phone: 803-1041). Nearby, clusters of *confiterías* and restaurants provide comfortable roosts for surveying the scene. The plaza is on the 1300 block of Av. Libertador.

**Museo de Bellas Artes (National Museum of Fine Arts)** – Across the street from Plaza Francia is Argentina's finest art gallery, with a very strong collection of modern Argentine painters and sculpted wooden artifacts from the provinces. Its collections of classical paintings and sculpture are poor in comparison to those found in major US and European museums, but the catalogue of the rest of its collection reads like a who's who of Impressionist and post-Impressionist painting, with major works by Monet,

Degas, Renoir, Toulouse-Lautrec, Gauguin, and Chagall. One of the greatest honors for a living Argentine artist is to have his or her work exhibited in the gallery, even for a brief time. Open Tuesdays through Sundays, 9 AM to 12:45 PM and 3 to 6:45 PM; closed in January. Admission charge. 1473 Av. Libertador (phone: 803-8814 and 803-8817).

**La Recoleta** – This lovely residential neighborhood, inhabited at the turn of the century by upper class families fleeing outbreaks of yellow fever and malaria in the riverfront areas, also boasts wonderful shopping. Knickknacks and antiques can be found on Vicente López, near the Recoleta Cemetery. On Saturdays, Sundays, and holidays, there are artisan fairs at the Plaza Vicente López. Fancy boutiques selling exclusive clothing are found on streets like Esmeralda, Presidente Quintana, Guido, Montevideo, and Alvear. While in the neighborhood, join well-heeled *porteños* for a cup of coffee or a glass of champagne at *La Biela* (at the corner of Junín and Alvear; phone: 804-4153), considered *the confitería* in this part of the city.

**Cementerio Recoleta (Recoleta Cemetery)** – If you liked Forest Lawn in Los Angeles, you'll love this place. About half a block from Plaza Francia on Calle Junín, this mausoleum is a venerated necropolis — a city of the dead — and *the* place to be buried in Argentina. The final resting place of patriarchs, presidents, and poets, no common graves are allowed — only crypts housing generations of famous families. Arranged neatly along walkways, the crypts range from the simple to the ostentatious, with architecture in every style from Arabian and Moorish to Greco-Roman, decorated with little pyramids, benches, and war memorials. The central lane of the cemetery, extending from the main Doric entrance, is lined with cypress trees. At the far end stands a bronze statue of the Resurrection. Every day fresh flowers are sold outside the cemetery walls for visitors to place on the graves. For a bit of history, stroll over to the crypt of former President Pedro Aramburu; a left-wing group stole his remains in the early 1970s as a political protest. Also pay a visit to the nondescript, black marble crypt of Eva Perón ("Evita"). Juan Perón's remains are at Chacarita, at the end of the *B* subway line, but visitors have been banned from the site since 1987, when someone broke into the crypt, stole the hands of the corpse, and demanded a ransom. No money was paid and the body parts — and the grave robbers — were never found. Open daily from 8 AM to 5:30 PM. Entrance is at 1822 Calle Junín.

**Palermo Parks** – When in Buenos Aires, do as the *porteños* do and head for the park — 1,100 acres of lakes, lawns, forests, and formal gardens — which, like the Bois de Boulogne in Paris, is within the city itself. The area had been nothing but an uninhabited swamp until 1836, when Argentina's iron-handed ruler Juan Manuel de Rosas began draining it to build a house there. Years later it was developed into a series of parks. Sports-loving Argentines flock to its golf courses and tennis courts, as well as to the racetrack, polo fields, and riding and walking trails. On Sundays, families come to picnic, grilling steaks on portable stoves and taking long siestas. The park can be reached via subway: Take the *D* line to Plaza Italia.

**Sociedad Rural (Rural Society Fairgrounds)** – The fairgrounds are the pride and joy of Argentine cattlemen, who take the annual national fair and rodeo, held for 3 weeks at the end of July and in early August, very seriously indeed. *La Sociedad Rural* (Rural Society), the major cattlemen's association, holds competitions during the fair to determine Argentina's best bull, cow, horse, sheep, and pig. The grounds runneth over with meat on the hoof and on the plate as fairground restaurants spring up to feed hungry cattlemen and cattle watchers. The most popular event is the gaucho bronco-busting competition, in which these famous Argentine cowboys, dressed in their leather trappings, baggy pants, and boots, ride bucking broncs — it's just like rodeos back home. The fairgrounds' exhibition halls serve as promotional centers for various companies' products — wineries, meat-packing houses, textiles, handicrafts, leather, and hand-carved bone. At other times, the fairgrounds host exhibitions ranging from dog shows to toy fairs. For information on the fair, check the newspapers or look for posters — it is advertised all around town. 3001 Av. Santa Fe, Palermo (phone: 771-6080).

**Jardín Botánico Carlos Thays (Carlos Thays Botanical Gardens)** – Flowers from around the world bloom in this municipally run garden. Plants are arranged in orderly rows with labels; one section specializes in Argentine flora. Plenty of benches line the walkway, so you can sit and breathe the floral-scented air. The gardens are a good place to relax or read outdoors, and many *porteños* come here to do just that. The place is home to several hundred cats fed by park workers and animal lovers. (You might want to apply mosquito repellent before your visit.) Open daily, 8 AM to 6 PM. No admission charge. Across from the fairgrounds at 3951 Av. Santa Fe, Palermo; take the *D* subway line to Plaza Italia (phone: 712951).

**Hipódromo Argentino (Argentine Racetrack)** – With a wooden clubhouse and grandstands that seat around 70,000 spectators, this racetrack is practically a functioning museum piece. Since Argentina is a major producer of thoroughbred horses, the *Hipódromo* is the site of most big races, including the *El Premio Nacional* (National Prize), Argentina's equivalent of the *Kentucky Derby*, held every year around October. It also is the site of premier international races for horses from other parts of Latin America. Meets take place throughout most of the year. In Palermo, the racetrack can be reached by a 10-minute suburban train ride from Retiro station downtown. Get off at the stop called Tres de Febrero. Av. Libertador just off Parque Tres de Febrero, Palermo (phone: 772-6022).

**Jardín Japonés (Japanese Gardens)** – A gift to Buenos Aires from the city's Japanese community, this lovely little park is best known for the antics of its voracious goldfish. Schools of them, in manmade lakes beneath wooden and stone bridges, follow visitors as they cross to the park's five artificial islands. The fish will even eat out of your hand — food pellets are for sale in the park. Refreshments are available in the pavilion. Open daily except Mondays from 10 AM to 7 PM. Admission charge. Av. Casares at Adolfo Berro.

**Parque Zoológico (Zoological Gardens)** – A favorite spot with locals on Saturdays and Sundays, this more-than-a-century-old zoo was built with careful attention to architectural detail. The park's gardens and buildings allegedly were inspired by the architectural styles of the countries from which their animal residents originated. Outside the zoo gates, horse-drawn carriages can be rented for tours of the area. Open Tuesdays through Sundays, 9:30 AM to 5 PM. No admission charge for children under 13. Av. Sarmiento between Avdas. del Libertador and Las Heras, Palermo (phone: 802-2174).

**Planetario Galileo (Galileo Planetarium)** – Just down Sarmiento from the zoo, this planetarium offers astronomy shows on Saturdays at 4:30 and 6 PM, and Sundays at 4:30, 6, and 7:30 PM. Tickets can be purchased in advance Tuesdays through Fridays, 9 AM to 6 PM, or weekends beginning at 2:30 PM. Children under 7 are not admitted. Av. Sarmiento at Roldán (phone: 771-6629).

## ENVIRONS

**Luján** – This well-loved Argentine town, one of the oldest in the Buenos Aires countryside, stands on the spot where a miracle occurred almost 350 years ago, when the wagon carrying the statue of the Virgin from one regional church to another suddenly stopped on the road and would not budge for man or beast. Taking this as a sign, the people built a modest shrine to the Virgin on this site, and the town grew up around it. On the site of the shrine is now an enormous Gothic basilica with towering spires, where the figurine that caused the stir is kept. More than 4 million of the faithful make the pilgrimage to Luján every December. In addition to its religious interest, Luján has some great antique automobiles, campsites, and recreational areas with swimming pools. Ancient trees line the banks of the Río Luján, inviting strollers to lie down in the shade, and boats are available for rental. Luján's other big tourist attraction is the *Museo Provincial, Colonial, e Histórico* (Provincial Colonial and Historical Museum), in what served as the Town Hall during the Spanish era and as the viceroy's residency when the English invaded Buenos Aires in 1806. The museum has 63 rooms displaying items linked to 16th-century life in Buenos Aires. Open daily except Monday from noon to 6 PM; admission charge (phone: 20245). It's downtown on Av. Lavalle, 1 block from the riverfront. Also worth a look is the Cárcel del Cabildo (Town Council Prison), no longer in use. Its list of former occupants include such notables as Bartolomé Mitre, later President of Argentina. To get to Luján, take Avenida Rivadavia west to Route 7 for about 43 miles (69 km). After you cross the white bridge in Luján, you will be on Calle Constitución. You can also take a city bus or one of the Ferrocarril Sarmiento trains that leave Buenos Aires from Plaza Once — Plaza Miserere stop on the A subway line. Be aware, however, that the train ride is slow — it takes 2 hours — with a change in Moreno. In Luján, stop by the more-than-a-century-old *La Paz* hotel for a coffee and snack or take a cab to *L'Eau Vive*, just outside of town (2106 Av. Constitución; phone: 21774). This excellent restaurant is run by Roman Catholic laywomen and nuns from Third World countries. The menu includes dishes from Asia, Africa, and the South Seas. At 11 every night (and 3 PM on Saturdays), the nuns sing "Ave Maria" to diners. Open noon to 3 PM and 8 PM to midnight daily except Sundays.

**San Isidro** – Take the suburban train from the Once station to the loveliest of coastal towns, about 10 miles (16 km) from Buenos Aires. Once the spot where wealthy *porteños* built their summer villas, San Isidro later became a year-round lure for visitors when a railroad connected it to the city. Behind the nearly 100-year-old Catedral de San Isidro is the Casco Histórico (Historic District), where stately old homes, draped in bougainvillea and surrounded by palm trees and gardens, are found on narrow streets. These whitewashed or pastel-colored villas have sweeping views of the Río de la Plata. One of the town's prettiest sites is the Quinta de Pueyrredón, a villa preserved in the style of the 18th century. Located on the corner of Riviera and Roque Sáenz Peña, it once was the home of independence hero Juan Martín de Pueyrredón. Open Tuesdays and Thursdays 3 to 7 PM and weekends 2 to 8 PM. There is a handicrafts fair in the town square on weekends. In the summer, try cooling off at one of the popular local ice cream parlors — *Olympia, Fragola,* or *Vía Flaminia* (in the town's center).

**La Plata** – This lovely town about 34 miles (55 km) from Buenos Aires, laid out on a 3-mile grid, became the provincial capital in 1882. It was renamed Eva — for Eva Perón — when her husband ran the country, but the original name was restored after he was overthrown. There's a natural science museum in the center of Paseo del Bosque that was founded in 1884, and it has an astonishing collection of prehistoric skeletons from the Argentine pampas. The museum is closed on national holidays. Another outstanding feature of the city is its buildings, most of which were designed in classical Greek style; take a walk down Avenida Séptimo (Seventh Avenue) to get the full effect. La Plata's most famous building is the Catedral, which combines Romanesque, Gothic, and Byzantine architectural styles and has a capacity of 14,000.

**Ciudad de los Niños (Children's City)** – Located 5 miles (8 km) from La Plata on Highway 1, this city was originally built on a small scale for orphans and abandoned children during the Perón government. Complete with a child-size airport, the city is now an amusement park.

■ **EXTRA SPECIAL:** On weekends throughout the year, *porteños* flock to the Paraná River Delta to enjoy boating, water skiing, fishing, and relaxing at vacation homes and many exclusive private clubs. The 5,000-square-mile delta, about 19 miles (30 km) from Buenos Aires, is made up of thousands of islands at the mouth of the Paraná River where it joins the Río de la Plata. The area is a lush, semitropical rain forest crisscrossed by dozens of smaller rivers and streams, making it a sanctuary for birds and world-weary humans. Many mysterious inlets tempt anglers and canoeists. Wealthy *porteños* discovered the delta at the turn of the century, and soon built elaborate vacation cottages on stilts and established rowing and boating clubs — some with sail-up bars.

Visitors can experience the delta in a variety of ways — from renting a kayak for individual exploring to cruising on a large riverboat. The Buenos Aires suburb of Tigre is the gateway to the delta. Going by train takes 1 hour and costs a pittance. Trains leave from the Retiro station, opposite the *Sheraton* hotel. Many bus companies also serve Tigre, and tour operators in Buenos Aires offer day and weekend packages. Bus and train stations are near the docks. The tourism office on the wharf can provide maps and information on the various boat companies, tour operators, and individual catamarans. One such firm is *Paraná's Delta Excursions* (phone: 749-0397). Top of the line is the cruiser *Humberto M,* which features a fine restaurant. It departs from a dock near the *Tigre* hotel on Saturdays and Sundays (phone: 749-5554). If you or a group of up to 30 want to rent your own luxury yacht — bilingual captain and crew included — a full-day private excursion can be arranged through *Rent-A-Yacht* (16012 Av. Libertador, San Isidro; phone: 743-3220 and 743-2055). En route, you'll pass pleasure boats, vacation homes, and beaches of private clubs. Buy some wine and cheese from shops on the dock before sailing. When you get on board, stake out a spot on the sundeck for tanning and eating. Many catamarans also make circuits from 1 to 4 hours.

Back at Tigre, be sure to take a leisurely stroll along the tree-lined waterfront. Dozens of outdoor cafés offer tempting pitchers of iced sangria, while vendors provide caramelized apples, peanuts, and popcorn. The *Museo Naval* (Naval Museum) along the waterfront boasts an extensive collection of warplanes, elaborate model ships, and maritime memorabilia. Open 8 AM to 12:30 PM Monday through Friday and 2 to 6 PM on weekends. Admission charge.

# SOURCES AND RESOURCES

**TOURIST INFORMATION:** For general information, brochures, and maps, contact the Argentine National Tourism Office (883 Santa Fe; phone: 312-2232, 312-5550, 313-6220; fax: 313-6834), open weekdays from 9 AM to 5 PM. There also are information counters at Ezeiza and Jorge Newberry airports, but they are open only sporadically. The offices have price lists of all major hotels in Buenos Aires and some other major Argentine cities. Most of the provinces in Argentina maintain tourism offices in Buenos Aires, where visitors can obtain maps and limited information before heading off on trips to other parts of the country. Check with the national tourism office for addresses and phone numbers. *Optar* (1067 Suipacha, 8th Floor; phone: 312-0837; fax: 311-7110), the tour operator connected with *Aerolíneas Argentinas,* arranges tours of the city and to other parts of the country, and also provides information.

On Calle Florida there are two kiosks run by the city, offering free tourist information weekdays from 8:30 AM to 8 PM and Saturdays from 9 AM to 2 PM. Ask for the Spanish-English booklet, *Buenos Aires Today,* or you can buy it at kiosks around town for about $5. The main Buenos Aires tourism office is at the *San Martín Cultural Center* (1551 Sarmiento, 5th Floor; phone: 453612). It is open Mondays through Fridays from 9 AM to 8 PM, Saturdays from 9 AM to 2 PM. Most hotels and tourist agencies provide free maps of the downtown area. Maps of Greater Buenos Aires, including subway and suburban train lines, are available at newsstands for around $4.

You can change money at banks from 10 AM to 1 PM and at exchange houses, which

## 302  BUENOS AIRES / Sources and Resources

are located primarily along Calle San Martín between Corrientes and Cangallo (Mondays through Fridays from 10 AM to 4 PM; some are open on Saturdays, usually until noon). Be sure to carry your passport when changing traveler's checks.

The US Embassy and Consulate are located at 4300 Av. Colombia (phone: 774-8811).

**Local Coverage** – The *Buenos Aires Herald,* an English-language morning daily, provides local and international news. It also contains a restaurant and shopping guide, movie listings, and schedules of major cultural events, including performances at the *Teatro Colón.* If you read any Spanish, the daily newspaper *Página 12* is also a good source for listings of cultural events.

**TELEPHONE:** Don't expect much from an overloaded telephone system that has not been able to expand fast enough to meet the needs of the rapidly growing city. What's more, seepage from heavy rains frequently causes short circuits in underground cables. Telephone numbers change often, and by the time the telephone book comes out, a staggering proportion of the numbers are already out of date. Telephone numbers are included with addresses in this chapter, but it is only fair to caution you: It is generally faster to visit someone than to try to contact him or her by phone. If the person is not in, you can leave a note. (Dropping in is socially acceptable.) On the other hand, international direct dialing is available in some homes, offices, and hotels. The telephone monopoly was sold to private companies in 1990 and some new high-tech lines appeared the following year, but officials say it will be years before there will be improved service.

The city code for Buenos Aires is 1. When calling from within Argentina, dial 01 before the local number. The country code for Argentina is 54.

**CLIMATE AND CLOTHES:** Keep in mind that Buenos Aires lies south of the equator, and its seasons are the reverse of those in the Northern Hemisphere.

When it is winter in the US, it is summer in Argentina. B.A.'s winter runs from June to September, with temperatures generally dropping into the 40s F (6C to 10 C). Rarely does it get colder. The average temperature during July, the coldest month, is 49F (9C). During the summer, from December to March, temperatures climb into the 80s F (27C to 32C), accompanied by high humidity. The mean annual temperature is 61F (16C). The average yearly rainfall is 38 inches, with the principal rainy season during the winter. Due to the city's proximity to the spot where the 275-mile-wide Río de la Plata meets the Atlantic Ocean, marking the largest coming together of fresh and salt water in the world, Buenos Aires experiences heavy rains. A raincoat or umbrella always comes in handy. In the fall and winter, carry sweaters as further protection against penetrating cold and dampness. Pack dressy clothes (jackets and ties for men) for evening wear if you intend to dine at the city's better restaurants or visit nightclubs. During the daytime, informal city dress (but not shorts) is appropriate.

**GETTING AROUND: Bus** – If you arrive at Ezeiza International Airport, you can take a bus to any of the major downtown hotels. Purchase a ticket at the tourist booth just beyond the customs area. The fare is under $15. Buses back to Ezeiza depart from the shuttle office at 509 Carlos Pellegrini downtown (phone: 396-2078) at least every half hour from 5 AM to 10 PM. Getting around Buenos Aires by bus is easy because of the city's well-organized grid system. Buses pass frequently, about every 5 to 10 minutes, but during rush hours they are overcrowded and slow-moving. Fares are based on distance and begin at 30¢. Exact change is not required, although drivers are reluctant to change big bills. A large, modern bus terminal next to Retiro Station serves city and national routes. City buses generally do not run between midnight or 1 and 5 AM.

**BUENOS AIRES / Sources and Resources** 303

**Car Rental** – Major international firms are represented: *Alamo* (367 Uruguay, 5th floor; phone: 402523); *Avis* (944 Maipú; phone: 311-1008); *Budget* (977 Pellegrini; phone: 313-8169); *Dollar Rent-a-Car* (520 Florida; phone: 394-4525; fax: 322-0847); and *Hertz* (451 Dr. Ricardo Rojas; phone: 312-1317; fax: 311-9323). A local car rental agency is *Ovalle Rent-a-Car* (925 Marcelo T. de Alvear, 5th Floor; phone: 312-6665).

**Subway** – Buenos Aires has an antiquated, but serviceable, subway system, outlined on most street maps. The subway, complete with wooden escalators, operates weekdays from 5 AM to midnight, Saturdays from 8 AM to 1:30 AM, and Sundays from 8 AM to 10 PM. On the street, its entrances are marked by "Subte" (for *subterráneo*). It consists of five lines, with one line crossing the others as a transfer line. Four of the lines meet at Plaza de Mayo. A suburban train system, outlined on most street maps, connects downtown with outlying residential areas. The trains leave from four major stations, each heading in a different direction. There are no formal street addresses for these four stations. Any taxi or bus driver will be able to find them by name. You can try to telephone for information, but the phone lines are as busy as *Amtrak* information in the US. It might be less frustrating to go to the Railway Information Center (CIFA; *Galería Pacífico,* 783 Calle Florida; phone: 311-6411).

**Taxi** – In Buenos Aires, taxis are plentiful, metered, and easy to hail in the street anytime. The meter will display a number corresponding to a fare on an official list that the driver has. Tipping is not customary, but *porteños* routinely round off the fare. A trip from the international airport to downtown can cost $40 to $45; the fare between Ezeiza and the domestic airport, Aeroparque Jorge Newberry, will run just under $40; and from the Aeroparque to downtown, about $10. Taxi rides around the 32-square-block downtown area cost from $5 to $10. If you do not speak Spanish, it is advisable to have the address of your destination written down for the driver. Also be sure to count your change before leaving the cab. Most taxi drivers are honest, but those who aren't are on the lookout for tourists. Taxis are black with a yellow roof. When available, they have a red flag visible in the windshield, or you can call a cab (*Radio Taxi;* phone: 903-1142 or *Teletaxi Pronto;* phone: 981-5440). You also can hire a chauffeured car at the airport for the trip downtown.

**SPECIAL EVENTS:** Argentina's *Revolution Day,* May 25 and *Independence Day,* July 9, are national holidays celebrated with religious services at the cathedral, and special performances at the *Teatro Colón.* The *Feria de la Sociedad Rural* (Rural Society Fair), around the end of July and into early August, is the occasion for mass family outings at the fairgrounds. *Día de la Tradición* (Tradition Day), November 10, honors the gaucho. It is celebrated with folkloric and cultural activities, especially in the town of San Antonio de Areco, an hour's drive west of the capital. The anniversary of the founding of Buenos Aires is celebrated on November 11, and there are folkloric dances, music, and historical exhibitions throughout the city the preceding week. The *Fiesta de Nuestra Señora de Luján* (Feast of Our Lady of Luján), a major religious celebration on December 8, is marked by a pilgrimage to Luján from Buenos Aires, with the pilgrims accompanied by colonial-style oxcarts and gauchos in rustic costumes on horseback (see *Environs*).

**MUSEUMS:** In addition to the *Museo de Bellas Artes* (National Museum of Fine Arts) and *El Cabildo* (the Council House), mentioned in *Special Places,* Buenos Aires has a number of other interesting museums. Winter hours are listed below; note that museum hours change during the summer season — December through March.

**Buque Fragata Pdte. Sarmiento (Frigate *Presidente Sarmiento*)** – This boat serves as a floating museum. Open weekdays from 2 to 7 PM; weekends from 2:30 to 6:30 PM. Admission charge. At Av. Costanero and Av. Viamonte (phone: 311-8792).

**Museo de Arte Decorativo (Museum of Decorative Arts) and Museo de Arte Oriental (Museum of Oriental Art)** – As the names imply, these two museums are stockpiled with European and Asian ornamental pieces, housed in a French-style building that is a replica of the one in which General San Martín lived while he was exiled in France. Open daily except Tuesdays from 3 to 7 PM; closed in January. Admission charge. 1902 Av. Libertador (phone: 802-0914 or 801-5988).

**Museo de Ciencias Naturales B. Rivadavia (B. Rivadavia Natural Sciences Museum)** – Contains zoological, marine, botanical, and mineralogical exhibits. Open Tuesdays, Thursdays, and Sundays from 2 to 6 PM. Admission charge. 470 Av. Angel Gallardo (phone: 982-5243).

**Museo Histórico Nacional (National Historical Museum)** – Contains General José de San Martín's uniforms and furniture. Guided tours in English available. Open Tuesdays through Sundays from 3 to 7 PM; closed January and February. Admission charge. 1600 Defensa (phone: 274767).

**Museo José Hernández (José Hernández Museum)** – Specializes in the culture of the gauchos, Argentina's fabled cowboys. José Hernández was the 19th-century writer who immortalized gaucho life in his classic, *Martín Fierro*. Call ahead to arrange for a guided tour in English. Open weekdays from 10 AM to 8 PM; weekends from 4 to 8 PM. Admission charge. 2373 Av. Libertador (phone: 802-9967).

**Museo Municipal de Arte Hispano Americano (Hispanic-American Art Museum)** – In a lovely reproduction of a colonial mansion, this museum specializes in colonial artifacts and silver. Call ahead to arrange a guided tour in English. Open Tuesdays through Sundays from 3 to 8 PM. Admission charge except on Thursdays. 1422 Suipacha (phone: 393-6318).

**Museo Municipal de Arte Moderno (Municipal Museum of Modern Art)** – This San Telmo loft houses a collection of major contemporary Argentine artists. Open Tuesdays through Sundays from 10 AM to 7 PM. Admission charge. 350 San Juan (phone: 494796 and 469426).

**SHOPPING:** Buenos Aires traditionally has been a good place to buy leather goods. All those cows that provide good eating also provide good tanning. Fine-quality leather is still inexpensive compared to prices for leather of comparable quality available in the US and Europe. Be sure to check the stitching on leather goods and clothes. As a cost-cutting measure, low-quality thread, which breaks easily, is sometimes used. The most expensive shops can be found on Calle Florida and along Avenida Santa Fe off Plaza San Martín. For the best quality in over-the-calf suede boots (*botas salteñas*) for men and women, hunt along Florida, Santa Fe, and M.T. de Alvear. Fur is another good buy. For bargains in clothing, check out the piles of merchandise in the bargain-basement stores of the Once (Eleven) district, starting around 2400 Corrientes. In clutter, friendly noise, and rock-bottom prices, the atmosphere is similar to that of a US flea market. But be patient: It takes determined hunting to locate the better-quality merchandise among the piles of junk. The 6-block stretch along Avenida Libertad to Córdoba is the place to find good antique jewelry shops; not bargain prices, but definite finds. On weekends from 10 AM to sunset (weather permitting), some 150 artisans display their handiwork at the *Feria Artesanal* in Parque Lezama (at the corner of Brasil and Defensa).

*Los Angelitos* – Shoppers nostalgic for tango and the days of native singer Carlos Gardel will find novel gifts and souvenirs at this store that specializes in arty T-shirts, ceramic tiles of San Telmo (where tango was born), Gardel commemorative tiles, the lyrics to famous tangos, and other tango memorabilia. 689 Maipú (phone: 393-7018).

*Artesanías Argentinas* – Folk crafts in leather or wool from the Argentine provinces are available at this nonprofit shop. 1386 Montevideo (phone: 812-2650), 770 Córdoba (phone: 325-8566), and in San Isidro.

**Art Petrus** – Precious stones are featured in these exceptional jewelry and artisans' shops. 971 Florida, in *Galería Larreta* (phone: 311-1918), and 1883 Av. M.T. de Alvear (phone: 804-5728).

**El Ateneo** – Not only does this large bookstore boast an extensive map and English-language guidebook section downstairs, but it has a very helpful staff. 340 Florida (phone: 325-6801).

**Casa López** – One of the best places to purchase quality leather. There is a branch in the *Sheraton Hotel*, 1225 San Martín (phone: 311-6310), at 945 Florida (phone: 312-2642), at 640 M.T. de Alvear (phone: 311-3044/45), and outlets at the *Alto Palermo Shopping Center* and *Unicenter Shopping Mall*.

**Charles Calfun** – A good place to buy Patagonia fox and spotted rabbit. 918 Florida (phone: 311-3388).

**Ciudad del Cuero** – More than 3 dozen manufacturers display and sell jackets, gloves, handbags, and belts at this "Leather City." 940 Florida (no phone).

**Enrico Morano** – Handmade shoes, snakeskin bags, and belts. 892 Suipacha (phone: 313-9957).

**Le Fauve** – High-quality leather and suede coats, jackets, skirts, and belts. Ready-made (alterations free) or made to order. 1315 Arenales (phone: 448-848) and 1226 Sarandi (phone: 277326).

**El Gato Negro** – On the way to the Once district, this shop has spices from all over the world, teas (mostly from Argentina) mixed by the store, canisters, and mugs. Frequented mainly by restaurant owners and gourmets. 1669 Corrientes (phone: 461730).

**Harrods** – Though not related to its London namesake, Buenos Aires's largest department store stocks leather goods, toys, cutlery, and a range of high-quality products. 877 Florida (phone: 312-4411).

**H. Stern** – High-quality jewelry at decent prices. Outlets at the *Plaza Hotel* (phone: 312-4595), the *Sheraton Hotel* (phone: 312-6762), and the *Alvear Palace Hotel* (phone: 804-4031).

**La Martina** – *The* spot for polo and riding equipment, as well as leather jackets, boots, moccasins, bags, and even Pendleton blankets. Serious equestrians — both North and South American — come here for saddles and polo wear. 661 Paraguay (phone: 311-5963).

**Patio Bullrich** – Formerly a cattle auction house, this upscale shopping center boasts 126 boutiques (including several specializing in leather goods), art galleries, restaurants, and two movie theaters. The more unusual stores include *Papel Plus* (store No. 203), with a variety of stationery items, *Carteras Italianas* (store No. 34), which carries chic designer handbags, briefcases, and wallets, and *Lion D'Or* (store No. 209) for knick-nacks and exotic bonbons. The complex also has a number of designer shops, including *Nina Ricci* and *Christian Dior*. The stores are open daily from 10 AM to midnight. Entrances at 750 Av. del Libertador and 1245 Posadas.

**Pullman** – This chain is a good choice for leather goods. At 321 Esmeralda (phone: 325-9818), 350 Florida (phone: 325-4111), and 985 Florida (phone: 313-3443).

**Ricciardi's** – Good jewelry at good prices. In the *Plaza Hotel* (phone: 312-3082) and 512 Marcelo T. de Alvear (phone: 311-1836).

**Rossi y Caruso** – Traditional leather goods are carried here. 1601 Av. Santa Fe (phone: 411538).

**URU Sweaters** – Despite its name, it sells all kinds of leather clothing. Free alterations. 978 Suipacha (phone: 311-8550 or 311-6998).

**Welcome** – The usual line of leather goods is sold in this shop behind the *Plaza Hotel*. At the corner of San Martín and Marcelo T. de Alvear (phone: 312-8911).

**SPORTS:** By far the most popular spectator and participant sport, soccer (*fútbol*) generates fevered passion among Argentines. Auto racing, *pato* — a unique Argentine combination of polo and soccer on horseback — and polo have large followings, and tennis is becoming more popular. For information on sports events, consult the listings in the *Buenos Aires Herald*.

**Golf** – Golf remains the domain of the privileged classes. The *Sheraton, Claridge,* and the *Plaza* hotels can arrange for guest passes to private clubs. The municipal golf course is at Tornquist and Olleros in Palmero Woods (phone: 772-7576). The Argentine Golf Association is at 538 Av. Corrientes (phone: 394-3743).

**Kayaking** – Clubs in the Paraná River delta in the Tigre suburb are the main places where people practice this sport. Daniel Urriza of *Hidrodiseño* (1712 Castelar, in B.A.; phone: 629-2532) organizes whitewater activities in the capital and outside the city (including Mendoza). In Tigre, contact *Lalos Parking Náutico* (1174 Túpuc Amaru; phone: 749-0411).

**Pato** – A combination of polo and soccer, *pato* is played on horseback. The object is to throw a soccer-size ball through the opponent's goal. Handles are attached to the ball so it can be passed from horseman to horseman. Allegedly the game got its name, which means "duck," because a live duck was used rather than a ball in the Argentine interior, where the game originated. The best time to see *pato* is during the national championships, held in November and December at the *Campo de Mayo, San Isidro,* and *Palermo* sports fields just outside B.A. Contact the Argentine Pato Federation, 530 Av. Belgrano, 5th Floor (phone: 331-0222).

**Polo** – This is one of the more pronounced Anglicisms in Argentine life, and has been played in the country since 1875. Some of the world's best polo players can be found on Argentine teams. The season runs from August through November and consists of a series of tournaments in which teams compete according to their handicap. The season climaxes in November with the *Open Championship* at the *Palermo Polo Fields*. For information, see the *Buenos Aires Herald* or contact the Argentine Polo Association, 636 H. Yrigoyen (phone: 343-00792 or 342-8321; fax: 331-4646).

**Racing (Auto)** – Around the second week in January, Buenos Aires hosts the opening race of the annual world *Grand Prix* championship at the *Autódromo Oscar Gálvez* (Autodrome; General La Paz and Puerto Ocho, Parque Almirante Brown; phone: 601-1273). National races are held throughout the year. Be sure to call before going — at press time, police officials, concerned about the track's safety, had begun efforts to close it.

**Racing (Horse)** – The major horse racing event, *El Premio Nacional* (National Prize), is run in September or October at the *Hipódromo* (Hippodrome; Av. Libertador and 3 de Febrero, Palermo), which holds 70,000 spectators. International races for horses from other parts of Latin America take place throughout the year.

**Rugby** – This rugged sport is quite popular in B.A. For information on matches, contact the Argentine Rugby Union, 2120 Pachecho de Melo (phone: 840463).

**Soccer** – Greater Buenos Aires has about ten major league teams, which create innumerable crosstown competitions. The strongest rivalry is between the *Boca Juniors* and *River Plate*. To celebrate victories, their fanatical fans drive around the city all night, blowing car horns and waving their team's pennants. In addition to the major leagues, some form of soccer tournament is going on all year long. The soccer fever is heightened by government-sponsored gambling. Weekly soccer pools offer *porteños* the chance to become rich overnight by guessing the winning teams. If you plan to attend a soccer match for the first time while in the city, bear in mind that the fans often become rowdy. The most frenzied game of all took place in 1978, when Argentina first won the *World Cup*, the symbol of international soccer supremacy, in a round-robin competition against the top teams from 15 other nations. Victory was especially sweet since the championships were held in Argentina, with B.A. the site of the final match. A second *World Cup* win in Mexico in 1986, made the Argentines more fanatical. Even President Menem got in on the act shortly after taking office, when he played alongside bad-boy international soccer star Diego Maradona in a charity game. A word of advice to first-timers: When in doubt, root for the home team.

**Squash** – This sport is growing rapidly in popularity. The following courts are open to visitors: *Olimpia Cancillería* (1042 Esmeralda; phone: 311-8687); *Posadas Squash Club* (1265 Posadas, 7th Floor; phone: 220548); *Tribunales Squash Courts* (556 Montevideo; phone: 498358); and *Hernán Dubourg Squash Center* (142 Perú in Acassuso; phone: 747-6484). The latter is owned by Argentina's top pro.

**Tennis** – On the upswing, thanks to the international tournament successes of Argentines Guillermo Vilas and, most especially, Gabriela Sabatini. The *Sheraton* hotel has tennis courts, and there are public courts at Parque Norte (on Cantilo and Güiraldes Sts. in the Costanera Norte; phone: 784-9653). The tourist office will provide directions to other city parks with tennis courts. Or contact the Argentine Tennis Association (1315 San Juan; phone: 261569).

**THEATER:** The few English-language productions, staged mostly by amateur groups, are listed in the *Buenos Aires Herald*. Occasionally professional English-language touring groups pass through town, performing at *Teatro Cervantes* (815 Av. Libertad; phone: 454224; see *Special Places*). *Teatro San Martín* (1530 Av. Corrientes; phone: 468611) occasionally stages plays in English. If you are comfortable with your Spanish, by all means, go to see an Argentine play. Argentina has produced its own theatrical form, "the theater of the grotesque," so called because many of its characters are physically ugly or deformed as a symbol of their tortured lives and souls. Similar to the early tangos, the basic themes of these *obras grotescas* (grotesque works) are the social aspirations and subsequent frustrations of the poor and working classes. From time to time, theaters stage excellent Spanish adaptations of famous foreign-language plays. For modern, lighter productions, visit the *Teatro Regina* (1235 Av. Santa Fe; phone: 812-5470). The *Centro Cultural San Martín* (1551 Sarmiento; phone: 461251), sponsors a number of works for the theater and is a good place to get overall information on other productions around the city. From January to mid-March, the city sponsors a variety of free outdoor concerts, dance performances, and plays performed by professional troupes. Information and schedules for the *Festival Musical de Verano* (Summer Music Festival) are available (at 1530 Av. Corrientes, 7th Floor; phone: 469268 or 453981). Complete theater listings are published daily in *La Nación, Clarín, La Prensa,* and *La Razón*.

**MUSIC:** Classical music and tangos dominate the music scene, though jazz is making inroads. Argentina's excellent chamber music group, *Camarata Bariloche,* performs regularly during the winter and fall season at *Teatro Coliseo* (1125 Marcelo T. de Alvear; phone: 393-7115). Opera is strictly the domain of the *Teatro Colón*, where performances are generally the best in Latin America (see *Special Places*). There are at least 38 tango clubs in B.A. Most of them, however, do not have a dance floor for patrons — guests are there to watch the tango performances, not to participate. B.A.'s foremost tango musician, singer Susana Rinaldi performs at various clubs during the fall and winter. Although another great, the controversial Astor Piazzolla no longer plays his *bandoneón* in concert or composes new music, he is still known as "the Father of New Tango," because he modernized tango music by adapting it to electronic instruments. His work has been panned by traditionalists, but praised by many music critics, one of whom called it "the closest to perfection that music can get." A classic spot on the tourist circuit for tango is *El Viejo Almacén* (799 Balcarce in the San Telmo district; phone: 362-3602). Visitors may not understand the jokes in the songs, but the art form speaks a universal language.

There are at least half a dozen other tango places on the same cobblestone street; tourists' favorites are the 2-hour cabaret at *Casa Blanca* (668 Balcarce; phone: 361-4621 and 361-3633) and *Taconeando* (725 Balcarce; phone: 362-9596), where shows start at 9 and 11 PM. Other clubs, frequented by *porteños,* are *La Davi* (474 Humberto Primo); *Café Pichuco* (237 Talcahuano; phone: 356307); and *La Catedral de Tango* in the suburb of Belgrano (6157 Villa Urquiza; phone: 687-9222). The clown princes of Argentine music, the group *Les Luthiers,* zanily spoof everything from opera to Muzak. They specialize in playing unusual, funny instruments — slide trombones made from vacuum cleaners and violins made from giant ham tins. To fully enjoy it, you need a working knowledge of Spanish. Although their musical high jinks and sight gags need no translation, many sketches depend on dialogue. Complete listings of *Les Luthiers'* scheduled engagements and other musical performances are found in the Spanish-language dailies and selected entries in the *Buenos Aires Herald.* Try the *Café Tortoni* (829 Av. 25 de Mayo; phone: 342-4328) for jazz and tango on weekends (see *Eating Out*).

**NIGHTCLUBS AND NIGHTLIFE:** Buenos Aires has been dubbed the city that never sleeps, and its downtown area is practically one big nightclub. *Michelangelo,* a reconverted old warehouse (433 Balcarce; phone: 331-5392), serves dinner and has a show. For disco, try *Le Club* (111 Quintana; phone: 222565), *Hippopotamus* (1787 Junín; phone: 804-8310), *Mau-Mau* (866 Arroyo; phone: 393-6883), and *Trumps* (2772 Bulnes, at Av. Libertador; phone: 802-2083), the place to go to be seen. For tango dancing (go escorted) and a tango show, try *Taconeando* (725 Balcarce; phone: 362-9596), which opens at 11 PM.

Vaudeville is alive and well in Buenos Aires. Known as *revistas,* these music hall revues of scantily clad women, double-entendre skits, and stand-up comics are exceptionally popular with *porteños.* Tickets should be reserved in advance. One of the most popular *revista* music halls is *Teatro Maipo,* 443 Esmeralda (phone: 322-4882).

Nightclubs exclusively featuring folk music from the provinces are *El Palo Borracho* (637 Calle Tacaurí; phone: 334-5901), and on weekends only, *Ollantaytambo* (541 Estados Unidos; phone: 362-2358) and *La Casa de Fanny* (391 San Lorenzo; phone: 362-0095). The latter two feature folk music from all over Latin America and Argentine food.

# BEST IN TOWN

**CHECKING IN:** Buenos Aires has downtown hotels aplenty for every pocketbook. However, the city's top-quality establishments are not exactly inexpensive; those bargain prices that proliferated a few years ago have climbed considerably. Argentina's roller-coaster inflation also produces unexpected hikes in hotel prices; figures quoted here are subject to change. Expect to pay up to $250 a day for a double room at a hotel in the very expensive category, $75 to $150 at a hotel listed as expensive, $50 to $75 at a hotel in the moderate category, and under $50 at a hotel listed as inexpensive. All telephone numbers are in the 1 city code unless otherwise indicated.

**Alvear Palace** – This 250-room, European-style hostelry in the heart of the Recoleta district remains an exclusive, though charming place to stay. Its rooms are spacious and its tearoom is a special afternoon stop. It also has 3 restaurants and a cocktail lounge. 1891 Marcelo T. de Alvear (phone: 804-4031; in the US, 800-44-UTELL; fax: 804-0034). Very expensive.

**Buenos Aires Bauen** – Modern and not far from the *San Martín* theater/cultural

## BUENOS AIRES / Best in Town

center. This 227-room property boasts good, reasonably priced meals at its 2 restaurants, it has an outdoor pool, and its nightclub attracts some of the most popular local and international entertainment. 340 Callao (phone: 804-1600; in the US, 800-44-UTELL; fax: 111134). Very expensive.

**Claridge** – The most venerable of Buenos Aires hotels, it always will be tops with some visitors. English elegance prevails, from the wood paneling and high ceilings to the prim uniformed maids (in starched caps) parading around the floors. The hotel has its own limousine service, with English-speaking drivers available (at prices substantially higher than taxi fares; rates are quoted in advance for trips to specific parts of town). Guestrooms are equipped with refrigerators stocked with soft drinks, beer, snacks, ice cubes, and liquor. You are charged for what you consume. The restaurant is one of the best in town (see *Eating Out*), and afternoon tea here is a delicious tradition. There is also an outdoor swimming pool and a health club with a gym and sauna (non-guests may use it for a fee). 535 Tucumán (phone: 322-7700; in the US, 800-223-5652; fax: 322-8022). Very expensive.

**Inter-Continental Buenos Aires** – Located in the historic section of the city's south side, this brand-new 315-room establishment features 3 restaurants, a bar, lounge, indoor swimming pool, and a fitness center with saunas, whirlpool baths, massage rooms, a gym, and squash court. Each guestroom has a mini-bar, satellite television, and a marble bathroom. 870 Alsina (phone: 800-327-0200 in the US). Very expensive.

**Libertador** – Now under German management, this hotel has 203 remodeled rooms. *La Pérgola* restaurant serves fine international food and there are 2 bars. Facilities include a rooftop swimming pool and solarium, sauna, and gym. 664 Av. Córdoba (phone: 322-2095; in the US, 800-44-UTELL). Very expensive.

**Park Hyatt Buenos Aires** – Recently built, this 157-room hostelry combines a modern high-rise with a cozier 19th-century French classical mansion whose 6 suites are furnished with antiques. Amenities include two executive floors for business travelers, a French restaurant, an Italian eatery, outdoor rooftop pool, fitness center, sauna, spa, juice bar, a billiard room, and in the mansion, a lounge with a fireplace. 1433 Cerrito (phone: 222541 and 222105; in the US, 800-233-1234; fax: 223738). Very expensive.

**Plaza** – All the rooms in this long-time favorite of locals and foreigners alike have been upgraded and redecorated. Centrally located, across the street from tree-filled Plaza San Martín, nothing is new about its longstanding reputation as the place to have afternoon tea in the *Café les Jardins*. Both the *Grill* restaurant (which claims to have one of the continent's largest wine cellars; see *Eating Out*) and the hotel's bar are popular. Sports facilities include a gym and sauna, and a pool. 1005 Florida (phone: 311-5011; in the US, 800-327-3573). Very expensive.

**Sheraton** – Contemporary comfort in a self-contained hotel environment makes this popular for conventions and package tour groups from the US. En route to its northern Italian *Cardinale* restaurant, new Japanese eatery, cocktail lounges, *Express* coffee shop, boutiques, wine and cheese bar, heated swimming pool, tennis courts, or sauna, you can expect to encounter groups of conventioneers shuttling from guestrooms to meeting halls. The lobby is usually crowded, too. Not the place to stay if you seek a quiet and intimate getaway or historic, picturesque ambience. The hotel offers limousine service, tour agencies, a business center with secretarial services, and a shopping arcade. 1225 San Martín (phone: 311-6311; in the US, 800-325-3535; fax: 311-6353). Very expensive.

**De Las Américas** – First class and centrally located, off Avenida Nueve de Julio and not far from the *Colón Theater*, with 150 fully air conditioned rooms, sauna, beauty salon, snack bar, restaurant, and auditorium. 1020 Libertad (phone: 393-3432; fax: 393-0418). Expensive.

***Carsson*** – Although not well known, this luxurious, wood-paneled downtown (centrally located) hostelry often has rooms available for travelers who arrive with baggage in hand. It also has a nice tearoom that serves cocktails. 650 Viamonte (phone: 322-3551). Expensive.

***Crillón*** – A favorite with business executives, location is the plus for this recently remodeled 110-room hotel facing Plaza San Martín. There is a friendly, no-nonsense staff, and amenities include a lobby bar, disco, and laundry, dry cleaning, and 24-hour room service. 796 Av. Santa Fe (phone: 312-8181). Expensive.

***Elevage*** – Considered by many to be the most deluxe establishment in town, though service isn't always first rate. The hotel is small (86 rooms and 12 suites) — each room has silk drapes and bedspreads and crystal ashtrays — with an outdoor patio and pool, bars, nightclub, and *L'Escoffier* restaurant. Just off Calle Florida and the Plaza San Martín at 960 Maipú (phone: 313-2082; in the US, 800-44-UTELL). Expensive.

***E'Toile*** – This "apart-hotel" (apartment/hotel) in the Recoleta district has 96 luxurious suites with kitchenettes and all the modern conveniences, such as air conditioning and cable television, plus a pool, sauna, and parking. Special rates for stays of at least 3 nights. 1849 R.M. Ortíz (phone: 805-2626; fax: 804-8603). Expensive.

***Gran Hotel Buenos Aires*** – Just off Plaza San Martín, it offers comfort and efficiency without much luxury. It is big, conveniently located, and usually has rooms available. Though it has no restaurant, there's a small breakfast room. 767 Marcelo T. de Alvear (phone: 312-3001 and 311-6220; in the US, 800-44-UTELL). Expensive.

***Lancaster*** – Certainly one of the best in its price category. Although the rooms are not very big, they are comfortable and well furnished. A spacious reading room set behind the small lobby is stocked with daily newspapers. A cozy breakfast room and bar behind the reading room serves breakfast, snacks, and drinks most of the day. There is a small, excellent restaurant. 405 Av. Córdoba (phone: 311-3021). Expensive.

***Panamericano*** – Almost opposite the obelisk, it has 208 rooms and 25 suites, each with a color TV set and a refrigerator. There are also 3 bars, a restaurant, a sushi bar, and a heated indoor pool, sauna, and gym. 525 Carlos Pellegrini (phone: 393-6017; in the US, 800-44-UTELL). Expensive.

***Plaza Francia*** – If you want to stay out of the commercial district, this hotel is within walking distance of Plaza Francia and the elegant shops at Marcelo T. de Alvear. It offers a good view of the avenue facing the *Museo de Bellas Artes.* 2189 Eduardo Schiaffino (phone: 804-9631; in the US, 800-338-2288). Expensive.

***Trianon*** – For tourists who want an at-home atmosphere for stays of at least a week, this complex has apartments with a living room, 2 bedrooms, kitchen, and maid service. 1869 Callao (phone: 415403). Expensive.

***Alpino*** – Clean and simple, this 40-room place has a very tranquil ambience. It is located in the Palermo Park area, which is also home to many restaurants. 3318 Cabello (phone: 802-2430). Moderate.

***City*** – If you are traveling on a budget but still want to experience the heritage of old-style elegance for which the grander hotels are famous, this is the place. Near San Telmo (the tango district), this old building has 400 big rooms, spacious, old-fashioned bathtubs, and noisy radiators. At one time among the foremost hotels in town, it retains the character of the old days, although the polish, snap, and performance of its former era of luxury are largely gone. 160 Bolívar (phone: 342-6480; fax: 331-5342). Moderate.

***Gran Hotel Dora*** – First rate service from an extremely accommodating staff distinguishes this hotel with more than 90 rooms. The nicely decorated guestrooms and baths are comfortable, as is the lobby area; reasons that make guests return year after year. 963 Maipú (phone: 312-7391; fax: 313-8134). Moderate.

**King's** – Across the street from the *Liberty*, this place has more of an English flavor than its neighbor. The small, cozy cocktail lounge and tearoom are worth visiting even if you are not a guest. 619 Corrientes (phone: 322-8161; fax: 393-4452). Moderate.

**Liberty** – Ideally situated on Av. Corrientes around the corner from Calle Florida, this modest hostelry features a small but popular bar that seems to be frequented by friends of the hotel's guests. Be sure to secure a room away from Corrientes or else the noise of the city that never sleeps will prevent you from catching even a few winks. 628 Corrientes (phone: 325-0261). Moderate.

**Regidor** – Conveniently and centrally located, it offers the additional advantage of not being on a street that is heavily traveled at night. If you are sensitive to noise, this is a better choice than the other downtown hotels in this category. 451 Tucumán (phone: 393-9615). Inexpensive.

**EATING OUT:** As dedicated night people, *porteños* love to eat out. Argentine food is abundant and tasty, and visitors have no trouble finding places to eat well. The main dish is beefsteak, usually accompanied by salad, wine, potatoes, dessert, and espresso. In fact, the all-pervasive aroma of beef led one Egyptian journalist to comment that B.A. smelled like a steakhouse. Although Argentina has excellent fish, most *porteños* prefer beef, and fish is only prepared well in specialty houses. The dinner hour is late by US standards; restaurants start serving the evening meal at 8 PM, though they really don't begin to fill up until well past 9 PM. For those unwilling to wait, try a *confitería* or pizzeria. Remember, too, that restaurants do not serve light soup and sandwich lunches as they do commonly in the US. In most places, the lunch menu is the same as the dinner menu. *Confiterías* are the best bet for light lunches and for cocktails. Restaurants serve cocktails, but do not specialize in mixed drinks. Argentines traditionally drink wine with dinner. Warning: Argentines are heavy-handed with the salt shaker, no matter what the dish. Tell your waiter you want dishes "*sin sal*" (without salt), and then season to taste at the table.

Because of inflation, restaurant prices have been fluctuating considerably in the past few years. Expect to pay more than $80 for dinner for two at the restaurants noted as very expensive, $60 to $80 at those places listed as expensive, $40 to $60 at moderate eateries, and up to $30 at those places noted as inexpensive. Prices do not include drinks, wine, or tips. All telephone numbers are in the 1 city code unless otherwise indicated.

**Au Bec Fin** – One of the finest in the city, this small but elegant French restaurant is located in a former residence whose rooms have been converted into intimate dining areas and are romantically lit by dozens of candelabra. The bar is on the ground floor; meals are served upstairs. Open nightly from 8 PM to 2 AM. Reservations advised. Major credit cards accepted. 1827 Av. Vicente López (phone: 801-6894). Very expensive.

**Catalinas** – Excellent French cuisine has made this place very popular among *porteños*. Among the specialties: trout, grilled seafood, lamb, and honey crêpes. Closed Saturday afternoons and Sundays. Reservations advised. Major credit cards accepted. 875 Reconquista (phone: 313-0182). Expensive.

**Claridge** – One of the best restaurants in town (in the hotel of the same name), with excellent food, service, and elegant atmosphere. As you enter, you pass the portable cold buffet table of appetizers — salads, marinated fish, and cold meats. Waiters deftly maneuver the plush armchairs so that you fit snugly around the tables. In addition to the ubiquitous plain grilled steak, a variety of other beef dishes — pepper steak, sliced steak, and cuts smothered in a variety of mushroom and wine sauces — are served. One of the best dishes, pressed duck, appears regularly on its international menu. The wine list includes an impressive, expensive selection of imported vintages. This is the dining place chosen by wealthy *porteños* for grand celebrations. Open daily from noon until 3 PM and from 8 PM until midnight. Reservations unnecessary. Major credit cards accepted. 535 Tucumán (phone: 322-8025). Expensive.

**Clark's** – *The* hangout for the jet set. A window filled with colorful exotic birds sets the style for lively dining. The food is quite good, though pricey. Open daily for lunch and dinner. 1777 Junín in Recoleta (phone: 801-9502). An offshoot of this restaurant, *Clark's II,* is in the heart of the downtown business district in an old-fashioned tailor shop. It's patronized by the city's leading business executives. Closed Sundays. Reservations advised. Major credit cards accpted. 645 Sarmiento (phone: 451960). Both are expensive.

**Hostal del Lago** – At this beautiful lakeside restaurant in Parque 3 de Febrero, there's music and dancing and international fare. During the summer, cocktails are served on the terrace under the trees. Open daily for lunch and dinner. Reservations advised. Major credit cards accepted. 6100 Av. Figueroa Alcorta, Palermo Woods (phone: 783-8760). Expensive.

**Pedemonte** – Opened more than a century ago, this classic, elegant eatery is where the leaders of the business community meet for lunch and where visiting celebrities frequently dine in the evenings. Typical Argentine dishes, as well as international favorites, are featured on the menu. The bar is topnotch. Open daily for lunch and dinner. Reservations advised. No credit cards accepted. 676 Av. de Mayo (phone: 331-7179). Expensive.

**Plaza Grill** – Alternating with the *Claridge* as the "in" restaurant of B.A., it still advertises such exotic dishes as wild boar and venison. You probably will be better off sticking to steaks, casseroles, and fish in wine sauces — all well prepared. The place is 100 years old, and carved wood and stained glass contribute to a castle-like atmosphere. Open from noon to 4 PM and from 8 PM to midnight. Reservations unnecessary. Major credit cards accepted. In the *Plaza Hotel,* 1005 Florida (phone: 311-5011). Expensive.

**El Refugio del Viejo Conde** – An unusual menu features caviar, salmon blintzes, smoked antelope, venison, and pheasant. Open for dinner only. Closed Sundays. Reservations necessary. Major credit cards accepted. 4453 Cerviño, Palermo, near the US Embassy (phone: 773-1362). Expensive.

**Tomo I** – An excellent, family-run, French restaurant in an elegant turn-of-the-century house. Specialties include wild boar with chestnuts. Open from noon to 3 PM and from 8:30 PM to 2 AM. Closed Sundays and Mondays. Reservations necessary. Major credit cards accepted. 3766 Las Heras (phone: 801-6253). Expensive.

**La Cabaña** – Founded in 1935, this is one of the city's most famous steakhouses. It specializes in huge *bola de lomo,* a tender filet. It also serves Argentine *parrillada,* a mixed barbecue of sausage, blood sausage, and parts of the cow not normally eaten in the US — intestines and brains, for instance. The off-cuts taste a lot better than they sound, so don't be squeamish about trying them. Another specialty is *matambre* — a generous slice of rolled veal stuffed with hard-boiled eggs, olives, pepper, salt, onion, garlic, and chili. As you enter, you will see rows of refrigerated cuts of meat from which you can select. Open daily for lunch and dinner. Reservations unnecessary. Major credit cards accepted. 436 Entre Ríos (phone: 372639). Expensive to moderate.

**El Caldero** – This medieval banquet hall allows you to serve yourself all you can eat from huge cauldrons of soup, casseroles, goulash, vegetables, and garnished meat. Musicians perform medieval songs. Open Tuesdays through Saturdays from 9:30 PM to 2 AM. Reservations necessary. Major credit cards accepted. 3972 Gorriti in Palermo (phone: 892335). Moderate.

**Cantina Norte** – A small restaurant serving excellent steaks and a limited international menu, among its foremost patrons has been B.A.'s most distinguished author, Jorge Luis Borges, who lived on the street behind the restaurant. The simple, folksy decor consists of hams hanging from the ceiling and shelves of wine lining the walls. To retrieve wine from the top shelves, the waiters tip the bottle with a pole and then catch it as it falls. They rarely miss. Stuffed homemade pasta, empanadas, and seafood round out the culinary repertoire. Open daily from noon to 3 PM and from 8 PM to midnight. Reservations unnecessary. Major credit cards accepted. 786 Marcelo T. de Alvear (phone: 312-8778). Moderate.

**E'Certo** – Formerly *Subito,* little has changed about this sleek northern Italian restaurant on the second floor of an elegant shopping gallery. It features a pasta chef who churns out spectacular homemade *tagliatelle* and fettuccine, plus a respectable Argentine wine list and a tempting dessert cart. Open daily, except Sundays, from noon to 4 PM and 8:30 PM to midnight. Reservations unnecessary. Major credit cards accepted. 640 Paraguay (phone: 313-6125). Moderate.

**La Estancia** – In the heart of downtown, near the movie and hotel district, this establishment features eye-catching cooks dressed as gauchos who roast steaks, chicken, goat, and pig. Try the roasted goat (*chivito*) and suckling pig (*lechón*). The *parrillada* and steaks are good, too. Open daily for lunch and dinner. Reservations unnecessary. Major credit cards accepted. 941 Lavalle (phone: 718015). Moderate.

**London Grill** – For a break from beef, try this English place, whose menu includes turkey, curry dishes, Yorkshire pudding, and leg of lamb. Open daily from noon to midnight. Reservations unnecessary. American Express and Diners Club accepted. In the heart of the banking district at 455 Reconquista (phone: 311-7481). Moderate.

**La Mosca Blanca** – Don't let the name ("The White Fly") turn you off. This is an excellent, comfortably priced steakhouse boasting the largest portions in the city (you can order half-portions). In addition to steaks, the menu offers pork chops, seafood, pasta, breaded beef cutlet stuffed with ham and cheese — enough to feed four people. Another hearty filler is the boiled meat and vegetable stew (*puchero*). The drawback here is the restaurant's location between two major railroad stations, which makes for a noisy background. Open daily from noon to 3 AM. Reservations unnecessary. Major credit cards accepted. 1430 Dr. J. M. Ramos Mejía (phone: 313-4890). Moderate.

**El Palo Borracho** – Folkloric nightclub entertainment is offered with meals featuring a hot, spicy meat and corn casserole (*locro*) from rural Argentina, and an assortment of goat cheeses (*quesos de cabra*). Open daily, except Mondays, from 9 PM to 3 AM. The show starts at 11 PM. Reservations advised. Diners Club accepted. 637 Tacuarí in San Telmo (phone: 334-5901). Moderate.

**El Recodo** – As you settle into one of the high, delicate, straight-back chairs, you can expect luscious international food and personal service. Meals are often preceded by complimentary sherry, but don't let it go to your head — you'll want to appreciate the appetizers of salads and cold meats that are wheeled to your table. We suggest you follow the starters with seafood. Smoked trout and salmon are the house specialties. An extensive wine list is available. Open daily except Sundays from noon to 4 PM and from 8 PM to 1 AM. Reservations advised. Major credit cards accepted. 130 Lavalle (phone: 312-2453). Moderate.

**Rey Don Luis** – At the side of the *Colón Theater,* this is a favorite of after-theater diners. Try *capelettis caruso* — macaroni covered with a thick tomato, meat, and mushroom sauce. Paella, the Spanish rice dish, is another good choice. The place is jammed at lunch. By 1 PM, all tables are full. In the evening, seating is no problem. Open daily from noon to 2:30 PM and from 8 to 11:30 PM. Reservations unnecessary. Major credit cards accepted. 1169 Viamonte (phone: 481806). Moderate.

**La Rural** – Meat roasting on an open blaze in the front of this *parrillada* restaurant downtown gives diners a good idea of what's in store. Service is good, the grilled meat is tasty, and the servings hearty. If you're really hungry, try the *parrilla especial* (grilled beef, goat, and chicken). Open daily. Reservations unnecessary. Major credit cards accepted. 453 Suipacha (phone: 322-2654). Moderate.

**Zum Edelweiss** – As its name suggests, this is a good place to sample decent German cooking (or a good steak, if you prefer). Its wide assortment of cold appetizers include pickled vegetables and marinated fish. The service is good and the waiters friendly; it's popular with artists and writers. Open daily from noon to 5 AM. Reservations necessary. Major credit cards accepted. 431 Libertad (phone: 353351). Moderate.

**La Bodega** – Aptly named "The Wine Cellar," the long, narrow interior is lined with wine bottles. Homemade pasta and steaks cooked in a variety of sauces and spices are the house specialties. In this male-dominated society, this restaurant observes the unusual practice of employing waitresses only. As it seats only about 100 people, the dining room fills quickly for both lunch and dinner. Open daily, except Sundays, from noon to 3 PM and from 8:30 PM to 12:30 AM. Reservations unnecessary. No credit cards accepted. 1286 Bartolomé Mitre, next to the *Lisboa* hotel (phone: 389995). Moderate to inexpensive.

**El Giardano** – One of the best of several vegetarian restaurants in the downtown area. The sumptuous and tasty veggie buffet includes salads and daily specials. 429 Suipacha (phone: 322-1819). Inexpensive.

**El Palacio de la Papa Frita** – As the name implies, there's no shortage of potato dishes here. There's beef, pasta, omelettes, generous-size salads, and wine as well. Open daily. Reservations unnecessary. Major credit cards accepted. An institution, at three locations: 1612 Corrientes (phone: 468063), 954 Lavalle (phone: 322-1599), and 735 Calle Lavalle (phone: 393-5849). Inexpensive.

**La Payanca** – A rustic, bi-level restaurant with a large bar–service counter downstairs and a family dining room upstairs. Bartenders clang a huge bell every time they are tipped. Upstairs is somewhat more subdued, but it's still not the place for a quiet meal. However, it is the best place in the city to taste northern Argentine cuisine, generally spicier than the food in Buenos Aires. The corn or wheat casserole with chopped meat and hot pepper (*locro*) is very good. Closed Sundays. Reservations unnecessary. Major credit cards accepted. 1015 Suipacha (phone: 312-5209). Inexpensive.

**Los Teatros de Buenos Aires** – Owned by tango lovers, this charming little restaurant always has tango music playing and the walls are adorned with huge photos of Argentine actors. With three theaters less than a block away, it's a favorite haunt of theatergoers and performers. The menu ranges from pasta to seafood to steaks. Portions are generous; split one with a friend. Open daily for lunch from noon to 4 PM and dinner from 9:30 PM until the last customer leaves (sometimes as late as 4 AM). Reservations unnecessary. Major credit cards accepted. 350 Talcahuano (phone: 464946). Inexpensive.

**Ying Yang** – This clean, bright, macrobiotic eatery is a pleasant change from the steakhouses throughout the city. The menu describes the philosophy of macrobiotics as well as certain dishes. There's a cafeteria in front that serves the same food as the restaurant (with a garden) in the rear. The fare includes stir-fry vegetables with tofu or chicken and brown rice, salad, vegetable loaves, pizza, empanadas, and desserts. Open daily except Sundays for lunch and dinner. Reservations unnecessary. Diners Club accepted. 858 Paraguay (phone: 311-7798). Inexpensive.

■ **Perfect Pastries: Confiterías:** No section on eating out in Buenos Aires would be complete without mentioning these cathedrals for the worship of teatime pastries. These tearooms, many in old, high-ceilinged buildings, specialize in afternoon tea, but also serve early morning coffee with *media lunas* (croissants), good sandwiches and sodas for quick lunches, and late-night brandy. As in Paris cafés, *confiterías* rather than bars are frequented by businesspeople stopping in for a cocktail after work. The person with a sweet tooth can get coffee with thick cream and an elegant plate of cookies, éclairs, or cream puffs. *Confiterías* are open from breakfast through midnight snack. The oldest and best-known *confitería* in the city is *Café Tortoni,* which was started in 1858 by a group of artists; it moved to its present location (829 Av. de Mayo; phone: 342-4328) a century ago and has been a meeting place of intellectuals for decades. Try its slightly alcoholic cider, or *sidra*. Another classic place is the opulent *Ideal* (384 Suipacha; phone: 396-1081). Other well-known *confiterías* are *Petit Paris Café* (774 Av. Santa Fe, off Plaza San Martín; phone: 312-5885); *Café Vitti* (1000 Av. Córdoba at the corner of Carlos Pellegrini; phone: 392-7139); and *Matisse Café* (902 Lavalle; phone: 392-9437).

■ **Beef Beat: Los Carritos de la Costanera:** Costanera is a broad avenue that winds alongside the Río de la Plata — a long cab or bus ride from downtown — and the word *carritos* refers to the modern, almost identical beef barbecue restaurants lining the sides of the road. The restaurants are so named because years ago men with pushcarts (*carritos*) containing grills used to barbecue meat for hungry railway and dock workers' lunches. The pushcarts have long since disappeared, but *los carritos* now serve the same fare. If you stroll along the Costanera, you will see about 20 such restaurants of varying quality. One of the liveliest and best-known is *Los Años Locos,* where late-night diners start lining up around 11 PM, and the rush hour continues until 3 in the morning. The house specialty is baby beef — a 2-pound plate of meat. Reservations advised (Costanera; phone: 784-8681 and 783-5126). *Look* is another spot that serves pasta and fish in addition to steaks. Reservations advised (Costanera; phone: 783-1375). The *carritos* have names, but are often referred to by number. They are open daily, with summer dining alfresco under a pavilion. Some accept credit cards. Moderate to inexpensive.

# CARACAS

The capital of Venezuela — the richest nation in Latin America and one of the world's largest producers of oil — is a contemporary, cosmopolitan city with chronic growing pains. New buildings are going up all the time. Businesspeople from all over the world pass through town, and many take up residence for periods of years. Yet despite the sleek sophistication for which Caracas is renowned, *caraqueños* (as residents are called) are frequently unable to praise their city at the same time they express affection for it. Raucous Caracas is one of those places that grows on you, they say. It's not a city you're likely to fall in love with at first sight.

But inhabitants of any city are generally too immersed in its day-to-day rhythms to be able to perceive it with the openness of a first-timer. They become accustomed to wrestling with the problems of traveling to and from offices, working, and raising families. Yet to outsiders, Caracas is extremely well suited to tourism, and since the collapse of the oil market in the early 1980s, Venezuela is coming to realize the importance of attracting travelers. The devaluation of the bolívar in 1983 sparked an increase in the number of visitors, and the nation is trying its best to accommodate them. The latest efforts include a spate of new hotel projects and a public education campaign — via television commercials, newspaper comic strips, and seminars for those involved in tourism — designed to teach Venezuelans to welcome tourists. One setback, however, is the rise in petty street crime, including purse and chain snatchings.

A city of about 5 million people (considerably more if you count illegal aliens), Caracas occupies a narrow, 9-mile valley that follows the east-west course of the Río Guaire. The Guaire rises about 20 miles (32 km) west of Caracas in El Junquito, flowing southeast through the city into the Río Tuy, which in turn flows into the sea. Covering about 45 square miles, the city stands about 12 miles (19 km) south of the Caribbean coast as the toucan flies, with a forested mountain, Mt. Avila (7,380 feet above sea level at its peak), separating it from the sea. The uniform greenness of Mt. Avila contrasts with the unrelenting "forest" of cement and steel girders of downtown Caracas. The city's elevation of about 3,400 feet gives the place a spring-like climate, with an average yearly temperature of 77F (25C). Unquestionably, the mountain, linked to the city by a *teleférico* (cable car), and the mellow weather are what *caraqueños* like best about the place.

A glittering valley at night, Caracas tends to be hectic, traffic-clogged, and polluted during the day, and even the fairly new subway system is overtaxed as this city grows faster than its services. Afternoons are more chaotic, especially during the rainy season (from May through December). Then, the so-called Ciudad de las Autopistas (City of Highways) becomes a frenzied, soggy mess.

Although oil was first discovered in Venezuela's Lake Maracaibo in 1917, Caracas began to be profoundly affected by the expanding petroleum industry only after World War II. From the postwar years until the present, Caracas has absorbed more than 1 million immigrants, mostly from Italy, Spain, Portugal, and the rest of Latin America. Many entered the country illegally from Colombia and Ecuador, lured by the prospect of employment in the oil fields; a smaller number of people arrived from the US, Northern and Western Europe, and the Orient. Although immigration laws have staunched the unchecked entry of foreigners, Latin Americans from poorer countries still view Venezuela as the promised land. Caracas also must accommodate emigrants from the Venezuelan interior, many of whom have settled in the shanties dubbed *ranchitos,* which cover the western part of the city and the slopes of the eastern hills. While many *ranchitos'* floors are dusty ground, and bathrooms are little more than washbasins or holes in the floor, plasterless walls are lined with posters of the latest rock and cinema stars, and intricate antennas adorn many roofs — a testament to the presence of TV sets.

Lining the valley, between these ramshackle shelters of the poor who comprise more than 50% of Caracas's population, are the business section (El Centro) and the affluent eastern residential area (El Este). Most of the snazzy shopping malls and private schools are concentrated in El Este, as are office buildings that strive to outdazzle each other with marble decorations and spacious penthouse executive suites.

El Centro, the oldest section of the city, contains most of the colonial buildings, historical monuments, museums, and churches. But unfortunately, these picturesque remnants of old Caracas are being methodically swallowed up by new office buildings, replaced by government projects and retail centers, and eaten away by automobile exhaust. Sadly, only a few of the older buildings in La Candelaria and La Pastora sections of town have been preserved and restored. El Centro is dominated by the two skyscrapers of Centro Simón Bolívar and the government-subsidized residential city of Parque Central: five high-rise buildings equipped with standard modern comforts, yet from time to time lacking such essential services as water, electricity, and elevators that function. Looking into the city from either of these two busy complexes at midday offers a more realistic idea of what life is like for most *caraqueños* than the wide-angle, long-distance view from Mt. Avila. Long lines of bumper-to-bumper cars, interlaced with motorcycles, give the streets the appearance of multicolored placards. Columns of people march up and down the sidewalks, and buses whose drivers sometimes seem depraved zigzag like ambulances through streets plastered with sexual graffiti–adorned commercial and political posters. Travelers be warned: Amid this chaos, especially since the country has hit harder times, pickpockets are on the rise. Motorcyclists also are known to hop over the curb and grab purses or packages from unsuspecting pedestrians. Avoid wearing jewelry; chain snatching is all too common and police will be of no help if you are robbed in the street. As far as the police go, don't be surprised if you are stopped from time to time and asked to present identification. It could happen anywhere. *Always* carry your passport and tourist card.

Although Caracas is in the federal district (Venezuela has 21 states, a

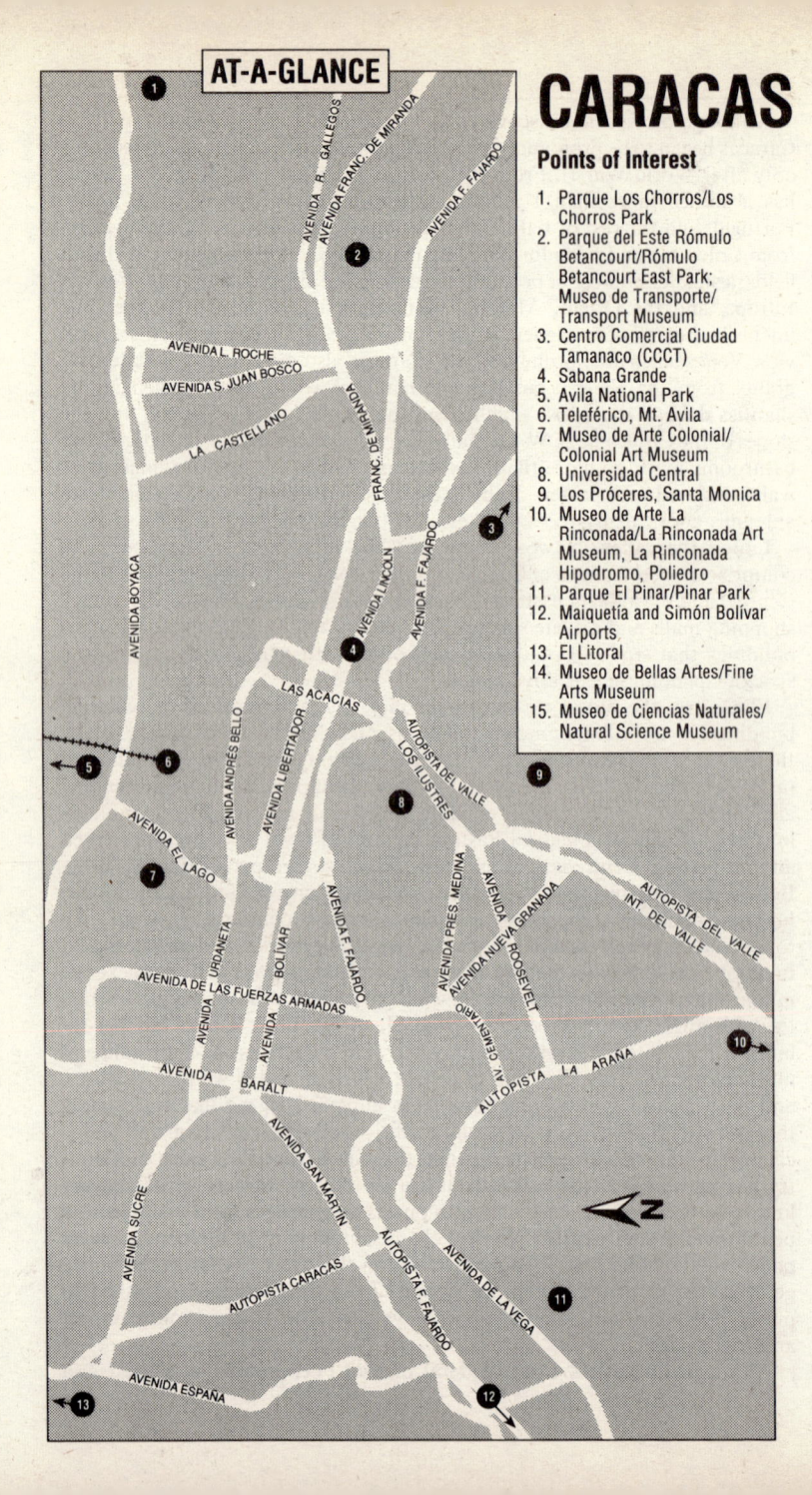

# CARACAS

## AT-A-GLANCE

### Points of Interest

1. Parque Los Chorros/Los Chorros Park
2. Parque del Este Rómulo Betancourt/Rómulo Betancourt East Park; Museo de Transporte/Transport Museum
3. Centro Comercial Ciudad Tamanaco (CCCT)
4. Sabana Grande
5. Avila National Park
6. Teleférico, Mt. Avila
7. Museo de Arte Colonial/Colonial Art Museum
8. Universidad Central
9. Los Próceres, Santa Monica
10. Museo de Arte La Rinconada/La Rinconada Art Museum, La Rinconada Hipodromo, Poliedro
11. Parque El Pinar/Pinar Park
12. Maiquetía and Simón Bolívar Airports
13. El Litoral
14. Museo de Bellas Artes/Fine Arts Museum
15. Museo de Ciencias Naturales/Natural Science Museum

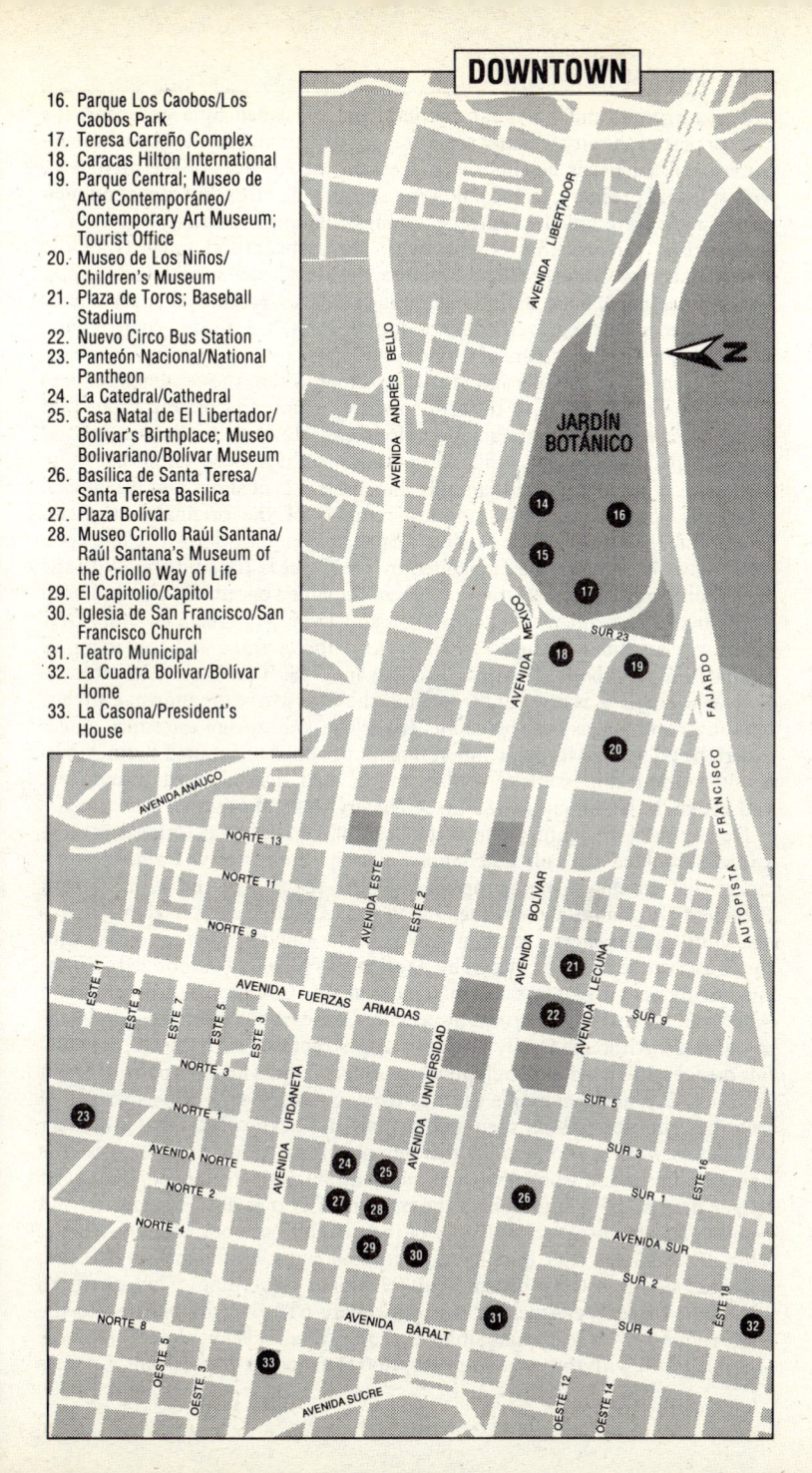

# DOWNTOWN

16. Parque Los Caobos/Los Caobos Park
17. Teresa Carreño Complex
18. Caracas Hilton International
19. Parque Central; Museo de Arte Contemporáneo/Contemporary Art Museum; Tourist Office
20. Museo de Los Niños/Children's Museum
21. Plaza de Toros; Baseball Stadium
22. Nuevo Circo Bus Station
23. Panteón Nacional/National Pantheon
24. La Catedral/Cathedral
25. Casa Natal de El Libertador/Bolívar's Birthplace; Museo Bolivariano/Bolívar Museum
26. Basílica de Santa Teresa/Santa Teresa Basilica
27. Plaza Bolívar
28. Museo Criollo Raúl Santana/Raúl Santana's Museum of the Criollo Way of Life
29. El Capitolio/Capitol
30. Iglesia de San Francisco/San Francisco Church
31. Teatro Municipal
32. La Cuadra Bolívar/Bolívar Home
33. La Casona/President's House

federal territory, and a federal district), and is headed by a governor, the eastern part of the city is under separate jurisdiction and is ruled by a municipal council. El Este's neighborhoods remain the enclaves of the privileged, with splendid greenery, tropical flowers, and singing birds, but recent municipal councils have failed to enforce zoning violations, resulting in a rash of construction projects that conflict with the architectural integrity of the suburbs, such as Country Club, Altamira, and La Castellana. Novelty shops, restaurants, clubs, bars, discotheques, and *areperas* (cornmeal snack stands that are Venezuela's equivalent of hot dog counters) are steadily encroaching. And, though some members of former municipal councils have actually been jailed for accepting payoffs and violating zoning codes, the residents of these districts are only beginning to form cohesive community organizations that could effectively halt commercial development. However, in the central and southern parts of the city, neighborhood groups have been somewhat more successful in stemming the seemingly inevitable tide of shops and businesses.

In this rush to high-rise, nothing remains of the original settlement, founded in 1567 by Diego de Losada, a Spanish conquistador who came upon the remarkable green valley inhabited by the Caracas Indian tribe. With the arrival of Spanish colonists, the settlement remained essentially tranquil until the War of Independence between 1803 and 1824. Venezuela's victory over Spain was attributable, in no small part, to the courage and leadership of Simón Bolívar, who was born in Caracas in 1783. The Great Liberator, as Bolívar was called, is revered throughout the city, where monuments, streets, buildings, and plazas bear his name. (Even the Venezuelan monetary unit is called the bolívar.) Although Simón Bolívar dreamed of a united Latin America, he found it impossible to realize, and he died, disenchanted, abandoned, and broke, in Colombia in 1830 (see *History,* PERSPECTIVES).

During the 19th century, life in the "city of red roofs," as Caracas became known, unfolded drowsily and happily among a conservative Catholic population that emulated the European elite. At the end of the 19th century, President Guzmán Blanco banned the Roman Catholic church from Venezuela, shutting monasteries and convents when he found himself in conflict with the conservative religious hierarchy. During this period of authorized secularism, many social patterns began to loosen up. Compared to other South American countries, Venezuela (especially Caracas) has been progressive for many years. Although family life is not as unstructured as in the US, *caraqueños* do not adhere to family relationships as formally as in other parts of South America. It is not uncommon for men to have mistresses as well as wives and to father children (whom they may or may not acknowledge) by a number of different women. (Some claim this stemmed from the disparity between the number of men and women in Venezuela, although the female population no longer dramatically outnumbers the male ranks.) It is also common to find people with one surname, indicative of their having been born out of wedlock. This in itself is a sign that having children outside of marriage is being accepted in the society rather than remaining something of which to be ashamed. Under Venezuelan law, illegitimate offspring are entitled to the same rights as their legitimate siblings, though the law is not always enforced.

Since 1959, with the election of Rómulo Betancourt as president, Caracas has been the seat of a popularly elected, democratic national government. In 1975, under the presidency of Carlos Andrés Pérez, Venezuela's oil reserves were nationalized. Oil accounts for more than 95% of the country's foreign exchange earnings (in 1991, Venezuela's national oil company, Petróleos de Venezuela, was ranked the third-largest oil enterprise in the world, surpassing Exxon), and while the Pérez administration channeled a large part of the money (reported to be about $10 billion) into the construction of steel plants, electrical power plants, shipyards, and the development of agro-industry designed to increase the country's self-sufficiency (so that it could cut down its food imports), the public became dissatisfied with reports of kickbacks being taken by high government officials, especially those in the Ministry of Defense. Pérez himself was implicated in some of the charges involving arms purchase deals. In December 1978, Luis Herrera Campíns was elected president for a 5-year term and took office in 1979. He was replaced in February 1984 by Jaime Lusinchi, a member of the opposing Acción Democrática party. Pérez was re-elected president in December 1988, and Venezuela continues to boast that its democracy has been functioning longer than any other on the continent. The fact is that Pérez's administration has been far from trouble-free; strikes by students protesting public transportation price hikes in late 1991 turned bloody. In addition, growing unrest over government corruption and the increasing cost of food and other necessities (at press time, more than half the country could afford only one meal a day) led to an attempted coup by military officers to oust the president (with the sympathy of many Venezuelans) in early 1992. The discontent continues.

But the vicissitudes of politics will more than likely be the last thing on your mind if you ascend Mt. Avila at dusk. At that time the capital, to the south, is just commencing its softer evening rhythm, a gentle glow of light shining from the valley. To the north, the turquoise Caribbean acquires a special, rich sheen. As the sea wind blends with the scent of tropical flowers, the reality of Caracas takes a different form. It becomes more of a vision, an enchanting place you once imagined but never thought you would find in real life.

## CARACAS AT-A-GLANCE

**SEEING THE CITY:** The most dramatic view of Caracas is from the *teleférico*, or cable car, that normally climbs to the 7,380-foot summit of Mt. Avila every day but Monday. Be forewarned that it usually is crowded on weekends and holidays; get an advance ticket for the ride from the station in the Maripérez neighborhood (phone: 781-8424). The *teleférico* operates from 8 AM to 9 PM. (Note: At press time, the *teleférico* was closed for repairs, so call to find out if service has resumed.) Travel by car is allowed if you have a permit; however, the road to the summit is hard to drive — it's best to go by jeep.

For another spectacular view, go to the *Caracas Hilton International*'s top-floor restaurant/nightclub, *Cota 880* (phone: 571-2322). The city is an impressive sight from there, especially at night when the shanty houses appear as thousands of glittering lights on the hillsides.

## CARACAS / At-a-Glance

**SPECIAL PLACES:** El Este (East Caracas) is far and away the swankiest section of the city. The historic district, El Silencio, stands to the west of the busiest commercial sector, El Centro. It's important to keep in mind that *caraqueños* do not use street addresses in the sense that we are accustomed to in the US, making a good city map indispensible for visitors. Each site is referred to by district, then (if necessary) by the main street and, occasionally, the nearest cross street. Every district has a main street called Avenida Principal. Street names are not always marked, and they change without notice. This makes driving very difficult for someone unfamiliar with its unusual address designations.

**Plaza Bolívar** – Built in 1567 by Captain Diego de Hanares on the instructions of Diego de Losada, Caracas's founder, this was a free market until 1865. Today the plaza is the meeting place for old-fashioned *caraqueños*. Smack in the middle is a statue of the Great Liberator on horseback. Perched on his squat shoulders are a handful of pigeons, and beneath his stirrups are shoeshine boys, beggars, and blind lottery salesmen. Surrounding this informal pageant of Venezuelan street life are the bastions of Venezuelan government — the National Congress, the governor's office, the Ministry of Foreign Affairs — and the local parish headquarters. Attractively lit at night, the plaza is busy any time of day and its palm trees provide shade from the warm sun. El Silencio.

**La Catedral (Cathedral)** – Built in 1575, this masterfully constructed church was rebuilt in 1637 and soon thereafter consecrated as a cathedral. Demolished by earthquakes early in the 19th century, the cathedral wasn't rebuilt until 1876, and since that time no major structural changes have been made. It is a colonial-style church with a sober but artistically decorated interior, with 8 chapels and 17 altars. The fine woodcarvings and the curved altar are adorned with paintings by Rubens and Arturo Michelena. Be forewarned — visitors in shorts will not be allowed into this or other churches. Open daily from 7 to 11 AM and 3 to 6:30 PM. Just east of Plaza Bolívar on Veroes at La Torre (phone: 824963).

**Basilica de Santa Teresa (Santa Teresa Basilica)** – Probably the most popular and venerated church in Caracas, it harbors the *Nazareno de San Pablo,* the oldest image of Christ in Venezuela. He is dressed in a purple velvet robe trimmed with gold embroidery, and he carries a cross. The basilica (actually a double church with a central altar serving the congregations of Santa Ana and Santa Teresa) is known as the Iglesia de los Milagros (Church of the Miracles). According to legend, during an epidemic, the statue was being carried in a procession and the cross got caught in a lemon tree. When people began eating the lemons, they were cured. It is believed that every year the statue bends farther under the cross's weight. The most devout followers attend 4 AM mass on *Holy Thursday* to give thanks for favors granted. Centro Simón Bolívar next to the *Teatro Nacional* (phone: 545-4380).

**El Capitolio (Capitol)** – This landmark is the home of the National Congress, inaugurated in 1873. Its gilded dome makes it one of the most attractive sights in the city. Inside, the elliptical room displays 52 oil paintings of Venezuelan patriots. The dome's ceiling is covered with scenes from the Battle of Carabobo, perhaps the most crucial event in the War of Independence from Spain. Virtually all of the paintings are the works of Martín Tovar y Tovar (1827–1902), one of Caracas's most extraordinary artists. Open daily except Mondays from 9 AM to noon and 2 to 5:30 PM. It is closed Wednesday and Thursday afternoons when Congress is in session. No admission charge. Plaza Bolívar (phone: 483-1275).

**Museo Criollo Raúl Santana (Raúl Santana Museum of the Criollo Way of Life)** – An institution whose title reads more like a short story than a museum, it depicts the traditions and ways of life of Caracas's past. There are houses and street scenes, reduced to miniature, in wood and other materials. Both city and rural life are masterfully re-created in three-dimensional, full-scale replicas. Open Tuesdays through Fridays from 9:30 AM to noon and 2:30 to 4:30 PM; mornings only on weekends. No admission charge. In the Concejo Municipal (City Hall) at the Los Naranjos corner of Plaza Bolívar (phone: 545-6706).

**Casa Natal de El Libertador (Bolívar's Birthplace)** – Not only is the Great Liberator's home one of the most outstanding examples of colonial architecture in Caracas, it is also one of the most charming, well-laid-out sites in the country. Much of the original home was destroyed by an earthquake in 1812, but a facsimile was built in the late 1800s. In its rooms, patios, and gardens, you can visualize the day-by-day life of the colonial aristocracy. The house (also known as the Casa de San Jacinto) contains memorabilia of the Great Liberator's childhood, and many of his early possessions can be related to his turbulent career as a politician, political and social theorist, and warrior. The halls are adorned with a variety of portraits and paintings, all of which depict the key personalities of the colonial and independence period, among them: *America's Discovery, El Padre de las Casas, Don Diego de Losada, 19 de Abril de 1810,* and *Generals of the Independence.* Bolívar was born here in 1783. The central patio is where he was baptized, and the other rooms are associated with innumerable incidents of his youth. Open daily, except Mondays, from 9 AM to noon and 2:30 to 5:30 PM. No admission charge. One block east of the *Museo Criollo Raúl Santana* on Calle Traposos at Calle San Jacinto (phone: 545-7693).

**Museo Bolivariano (Bolívar Museum)** – The documents, arms, and personal belongings of Bolívar are kept in this nationally renowned museum next to the Great Liberator's childhood home. The historical collection includes the gold medallion awarded to Bolívar and a lock of his hair (and one of George Washington's, as well). Open daily except Mondays from 9 AM to noon and 2:30 to 5:30 PM, and on national holidays — most of which, in one way or another, commemorate Bolívar. No admission charge. Next door to Bolívar's birthplace, on Calle Traposos and the corner of Calle San Jacinto (phone: 545-9828).

**Iglesia de San Francisco (San Francisco Church)** – Here Simón Bolívar was given the title of Great Liberator in 1813. Of interest are its delightful grounds, relics, sculptures, and luxurious tapestries. This is a fine example of a colonial-era church. Open Mondays through Fridays from 6 AM to 12:30 PM and 3 to 6:30 PM. Av. Universidad at the corner of Calle San Francisco.

**Panteón Nacional (National Pantheon)** – The site of Jimmy Carter's proclamations in Spanish to the Venezuelan people, this monument, built in 1874, is the tomb of Simón Bolívar. The front is sober and somewhat grim; the interior, of luxuriously adorned marble. It was a church from 1783 to 1874. You will quickly be aware of the reverence that Bolívar is accorded in his home country. Voices are kept to a whisper in the Panteón and military guards watch the tomb all day. Be forewarned — visitors in shorts and halter tops may be refused entry. Open Tuesdays through Sundays from 9 AM to noon and 2:30 to 5:30 PM. No admission charge. Av. Norte at El Ministerio in Altagracia, Plaza del Panteón (phone: 821518).

**Parque Los Caobos (Los Caobos Park)** – Here is Caracas's artistic hangout, home of the few real bohemians in this glittering, money-conscious town. It also happens to be one of the few places downtown where the smell of bus exhaust is not pervasive, thanks to its breathtaking foliage and cool lawns. In the open areas, people ride bicycles, roller-skate, skateboard to their heart's content, and even jog. The park adjoins the *National Gallery,* the *Fine Arts Museum,* the *Natural Sciences Museum,* and the National Cinematographic Library. Peace and art fill the air. Teresa Carreño and Paseo Colón (no phone).

**Museo de Ciencias Naturales (Natural Sciences Museum)** – This museum contains a varied collection of stuffed animals from Venezuela and many other parts of the world. Reptiles, insects, and birds adorn the corridors, interspersed with pre-Columbian archaeological exhibitions and neolithic and Miocene fossils. Open Tuesdays through Fridays, 9 AM to 5 PM; weekends, 10 AM to 5 PM. No admission charge. At the end of Av. México at the entrance of Parque Los Caobos (phone: 541-2563).

**Los Próceres** – Built to honor the fathers of Venezuelan independence, this is actually a promenade and knoll adorned with fountains, statues, and plaques honoring many Venezuelan patriots. Highlighting the promenade are two parallel, monumental marble walls surrounded by gardens and floral wreaths. A walk through this park is nothing less than a stroll through Venezuela's history. The home of the annual *North American Association* picnic and the site of various Venezuelan university graduations and spectacles, it is also the parade grounds of the nation. Av. Los Próceres, Santa Mónica.

**Parque El Pinar (Pinar Park)** – Though small (and its view marred by high-rise buildings), this hilltop zoo was the city's first. Tucked up against the foot of the mountain in El Paraíso, a couple of blocks from the national stadium behind Avenida José Páez. Closed Mondays. Open 9 AM to 5 PM. Admission charge. Av. Guzmán Blanco, El Paraíso (phone: 461-7794).

**Museo de Bellas Artes (Fine Arts Museum)** – Here is the city's best sampling of the work of Venezuela's creative artists as well as an attractive collection of Oriental ceramics and carvings of wood and marble. There also is European art, including a work by El Greco. The museum is a meeting place for Caracas's art lovers. The building also houses the *Cinemateca* (see *Theater*). Open Tuesdays through Fridays from 9 AM to noon and 3 to 5:30 PM, Saturdays and Sundays from 10 AM to 3 PM. No admission charge. Opposite the *Natural Sciences Museum*, adjoining Parque Los Caobos (phone: 571-0169).

**Museo de Arte Contemporáneo (Contemporary Art Museum)** – Entirely dedicated to channeling the currents of international modern art toward Caracas, its exhibits represent most of the recent trends and schools of art. Works by Léger, Matisse, Chagall, Miró, and Picasso are found along with those of Venezuelans such as Jesús Soto. From time to time, there are special exhibits of the works of renowned international artists. Guided tours for foreign groups and students can be arranged in advance. Open Tuesdays through Sundays from 10 AM to 6 PM. No admission charge. Parque Central, near the *Hilton* hotel (phone: 573-8289, ext. 257).

**Museo de Los Niños (Children's Museum)** – Internationally acclaimed as a must for adults and children alike (although the exhibits are geared for children 7 and older). Activities include being a DJ in a recording studio, learning how babies are created, and pumping a bike-powered generator to light up a string of bulbs. During school holidays, the lines can be staggering. Open 9 AM to noon and 2 to 5 PM; closed Mondays and Tuesdays. Admission charge. Parque Central (phone: 573-3434).

**Museo de Arte Colonial (Colonial Art Museum)** – Perhaps the most pleasant and refreshing place one can visit in Caracas. A beautifully kept colonial house (known as Quinta Anauco), it offers not only a handsome collection of period furniture, a coach house, and a blacksmith's forge, but also a delightful garden whose tranquillity provides a welcome escape from the bustle of the city. A long line of marquesses lived in this house until the last, the Marqués del Toro de Caracas, died in 1837. Simón Bolívar's last visit to this house also marked his final visit to Caracas. Open Tuesdays through Saturdays from 9 AM to noon and 3 to 5 PM, Sundays from 10 AM to 5 PM. Admission charge. Av. Panteón, San Bernardino (phone: 518517).

**Parque del Este Rómulo Betancourt (Rómulo Betancourt East Park)** – Magnet for joggers, a recreation center for children, and a comfortable place to read the Sunday newspaper, this park has a little something for everybody. As its name suggests, it's in the eastern part of the city and covers more than 494 acres. A choo-choo train chugs around the grounds carrying jovial passengers past families picnicking near an artificial lagoon in which floats a scaled-down replica of Columbus's ship, the *Santa María*. You can rent a rowboat to enact your own mini-voyage of discovery. Another special feature of the park, not yet well known to most *caraqueños,* is the terrarium — a congregation of snakes, turtles, and lizards displayed in thick glass cabinets. The park also includes a domed planetarium, a parrot cage, and a band shell. Puppet shows are performed regularly, and political speakers hold forth on Sundays. Open daily except Mondays from 6 AM to 6 PM. Admission charge. Between Av. Francisco de Miranda, Autopista Francisco Fajardo, and La Carlota Military Airport and *Aeroclub,* entrance on Francisco de Miranda (phone: 284-3022).

**Parque Los Chorros (Los Chorros Park)** – A gift from former President Caldera, this beautiful park is in the lush, eastern neighborhood of Los Chorros. Its freshwater cascades, streams, tropical vegetation, and cool breezes more than compensate for weariness of the soles acquired on any long ramble through the park. There's a snack bar where you can revive yourself, or from which you can buy a picnic to enjoy at the shaded tables. Bring insect repellent — it's a favorite spot for mosquitoes, too. Open daily, except Mondays, from 8 AM to 5 PM. Admission charge. Although the grandparents of today's youngsters used to come here by then-existent railways, now they reach the park by following Av. Boyacá or by winding up the mountain from Av. Francisco Miranda (phone: 361779).

**La Casona (President's House)** – Formerly a colonial cacao plantation, this modern mansion was restored in 1966 as the residence of the Venezuelan chief of state and the first lady. Various paintings and other works of art have been gathered here amid the gardens and fountains of this villa-estate. With an information center for tourists, an adjacent parking lot, and guides, La Casona is between the La Carlota and Santa Cecilia districts. Open Tuesday afternoons by prior arrangement; call in advance. No admission charge. You can get there by following Avenida Principal of La Carlota or by taking the Santa Cecilia exit of the Autopista Francisco Fajardo (phone: 284-6322).

**Sabana Grande** – This bustling, pedestrians-only street that stretches the mile between Plaza Venezuela and Chacaíto is *the* place to rub shoulders with *caraqueños.* There is constant activity from early morning to late at night. There are shops, theaters, fast-food eateries, and cafés, including the traditional outdoor meeting place, the crowded Gran Café (Gran Avenida near Av. Los Jabillos) — order a cappuccino topped with mounds of real whipped cream. Chess enthusiasts can learn the game or challenge the experts at the many tables on the promenade. Jewelry hawkers, street musicians, and the blare of salsa strains from record stores ensure the nonstop noise that's characteristic of the capital. Side streets off the boulevard have an exotic mix of ethnic cafés. If the motion of Sabana Grande becomes too overwhelming, duck into one of the several subway stops and head for a calmer area. But if you can stand the activity, buy an ice cream cone and wander up and down the wide mall, and window shop or people watch.

## ENVIRONS

**Avila National Park** – Between Caracas and the coast, this lush 210,000-acre mountainous park is a great escape from the smog and chaos of the city. It has several peaks, including Avila itself (7,380 feet), that are favorites of hikers and climbers. You can visit the park on foot, by car, or via the *teleférico,* when it's running (see *Seeing the City*). If you walk or drive, you'll need to buy a permit for a couple of dollars from the National Parks Office (Inparques) at the entrance to Parque del Este (see above). Maps of hiking routes also are on sale. Drive into the park from Llano Grande, above Cotiza, on the west side of Caracas on a wide, well-paved road with frequent lookout points that offer sweeping views of the city. There's a recreational center at Los Venados; a short walk will bring you to a hacienda, once a working coffee farm and now a museum with exhibits on coffee production, the flora, fauna, and indigenous people (now extinct) of the Avila. Above Los Venados is the tiny farming community of Galipán, founded 2 centuries ago by Canary Islands émigrés. The tidy farms grow flowers and fruits for Caracas's markets, and children sell cups of strawberries and mulberries by the roadside. There's also a small general store. Farther along on a very bumpy road is the *teleférico* (cable car) station. As we went to press, the *teleférico* was closed for repairs. Be sure to call to find out if service has resumed (phone: 781-8424). Hikers may wish to enter the park from the east side of Caracas, at El Marqués, Altamira, or Los Chorros above Avenida Boyacá. You'll walk up steep paths under a canopy of eucalyptus, juniper, mango, and mulberry trees, and be serenaded by the noisy chatter of *guacharaca* birds. Although it's possible to hike in Avila without special equipment or experience, be aware that attempting to scale the tree-covered peaks is best left to skilled mountaineers. There's a severe shortage of rangers in the park, so be sure not to stray from the paths.

**Zoológico de Caricuao (Caricuao Zoo)** – This is a favorite weekend spot for families with children. Although many species are still in caged areas, increasingly the animals are being moved to larger open areas; wildlife ranges from lions, elephants, and giraffes to deer, alligators, and jungle serpents. There are picnic areas and a restaurant. Open daily except Mondays from 8 AM to 5 PM. Nominal admission charge. Entrance next to the Zoológico subway station in the Caricuao neighborhood.

**El Litoral** – Thanks to the Caracas–La Guaira Freeway, it takes less than an hour (without traffic) to get from Caracas to the sunny central coast beaches on the Caribbean shore on the other side of Mt. Avila. The roads and beaches are packed on weekends and the water is polluted (although *caraqueños* swim anyway); a weekday trip for water sports (see *Sports*), sunbathing, or a seafood meal at one of the open-air restaurants that dot the area might be a better idea.

You might also want to roam around La Guaira, Venezuela's most important port city and one that retains vestiges of its past. Two forts here — El Vigía and La Pólvora — were once the only defense against maurauding pirates, until a ship from the flotilla of Sir Walter Raleigh infiltrated port security; then a wall was built around the city to prevent further incursions. The pirates came for the booty amassed by a group of traders and housed in the Casa Guipuzcoana, now one of the loveliest restored colonial buildings in the country. It was the headquarters for the colony's import house, a monopoly that controlled the port for nearly 6 decades. After touring Casa Guipuzcoana, stroll across the street to the *Museo Fundación John Boulton* (John Boulton Foundation Museum; phone: 31-25921), an 18th-century colonial home built by an Englishman who exported coffee and cacao and imported flour and brandy. It is open Tuesdays through Fridays from 9:30 AM to 1 PM and 3 to 6 PM; Saturdays and Sundays from 9 AM to 1 PM.

If you prefer to stay closer to the water than Caracas, consider getting a room at the *Meliá Caribe* or *Macuto Sheraton* at Caraballeda (see *Checking In*). Minibuses leave the Nuevo Circo bus terminal for El Litoral every few minutes.

■**EXTRA SPECIAL:** Although Caracas's sophisticated shops, restaurants, and nearby beaches are what usually attract visitors to Venezuela, a popular stop is the German mountain village of Colonia Tovar, 35 miles (56 km) from Caracas. This unlikely village resulted from the government's attempt to stimulate the agricultural sector by opening its doors to immigrants with farming expertise. The first German colonists settled in the highlands in 1843 — a group of Black Forest farmers, masons, and carpenters, who crossed the mountains by foot. The government's project went awry, but Don Felipe Tovar, the owner of the colonists' homestead, awarded them title to the property anyway and they named the town for him after his death. Karl Moritz, the botanist who contributed most to the scientific world's knowledge of Venezuelan flora, lived here. A fictionalized version of the village appears in Isabel Allende's novel, *Eva Luna*. The fresh mountain air will stimulate your appetite, so don't leave before eating a filling German meal. Wash it down with a beer; this was the site of the first Venezuela brewery. Or sip a cold *batido de fresa* (a whipped strawberry milkshake). Try to go to the town's hillside cemetery, where the grave markers are checkerboard tiles and people place bouquets of colorful flowers on top of them. The villagers have fair hair and blue eyes, and only German was spoken in the town until just 40 years ago, when a road finally opened it to outsiders. Colonia Tovar has become quite crowded on weekends, but it is still an enjoyable trip and a good place to buy fine crafts and ceramics. Try the *Alta Baviera* (phone: 33-51333 and 33-51483) or the *Selva Negra* (phone: 33-51415) if you want to spend the night.

# SOURCES AND RESOURCES

**TOURIST INFORMATION:** There's a branch of Corpoturismo (Venezuelan Tourism Corp.) at Maiquetía Airport. It usually has tourist brochures and personnel can assist visitors with hotel reservations. It is open daily 24 hours a day. Corporturismo's main office is downtown at Torre Oeste, 37th Floor, in Parque Central (phone: 507-8876). They also have set up a 24-hour multilingual tourist telephone line to answer questions (phone: 507-8829 and 573-8983).

The US Embassy is located at Av. Francisco de Miranda, La Floresta (phone: 285-2222).

**Local Coverage** – *The Daily Journal* is the city's English-language newspaper. If you read Spanish, try *El Diario de Caracas, El Nacional, or El Universal,* the largest of the daily newspapers. US news magazines are available at kiosks near the major hotels and on Sabana Grande. Major hotels have Cable News Network (CNN), which broadcasts international news in English 24 hours a day.

**TELEPHONE:** The city code for Caracas is 2. When calling from within Venezuela, dial 02 before the local number. The country code for Venezuela is 58.

**CLIMATE AND CLOTHES:** With an annual average daily temperature in the 70s F (20s C), Caracas's elevation of 3,000 feet accounts for its delightful climate. You will hardly ever need a sweater in the daytime, although in the evenings the temperature can drop to as low as the 50s F (between 10 and 16C). Like most tropical locations, Caracas's two seasons are dry and wet. The rainy season generally runs from May through November, although in lucky years the rain arrives and stops before the day has truly begun and often doesn't recommence until well into the afternoon.

As a general rule, the lighter the clothing the better. Blue jeans and American T-shirts are common attire for the young and the young at heart for sightseeing around town. Yet the cosmopolitan atmosphere that pervades Caracas makes it more formal than sporty. Venezuelans take pride in their appearance, and in the city you are expected to be well dressed, day or evening (men should wear jackets at the city's better restaurants). If you are staying at the beach, you can get away with casual resort attire.

**GETTING AROUND: Bus** – Unfortunately, the Caracas buses have been stereotyped as the working class mode of transport, but new minibuses and the metro have gradually been driving them to extinction. The city-run buses are big, unwieldy vehicles that look (and ride) like converted school buses.

They are the least expensive and slowest means of local travel, following designated routes and stopping at marked spots, or *paradas*.

**Car Rental** – If you're not sufficiently frightened by the traffic and want to get behind the wheel yourself, you'll find ample rental facilities. The major car rental agencies are *ACO* (Edificio ACO, Las Mercedes; phone: 919133); *Avis* (Edificio Xerox, Av. Libertador, 6th Floor, Bello Campo; phone: 283-9699); *Budget* (50 Av. Venezuela, El Rosal; phone: 951-6911); *Fiesta* (Av. Venezuela, El Rosal; phone: 951-6911); *Hertz* (Av. Principal El Bosque, Centro Commercial Chacaíto; phone: 952-5511 and 952-8611); and *National* (Edificio National, Av. Principal Los Ruices; phone: 223-0911 and 344611 to 344616).

**Por Puestos** – As a step above the buses and as an alternative to walking, there are collective cars and minibuses, called *por puestos*. At the same or sometimes twice the price of a bus, but still a fraction of what a taxi would cost, these cars have been getting more numerous as buses become fewer. Riders need to be knowledgeable about the city, as they have to shout out requests to the driver — in Spanish. *Por puesto* routes are fixed, but the stops are not; you must tell the driver where you want to get off.

**Subway** – The Caracas metro, which opened in the early 1980s, is the finest subway system in Latin America and one of the most efficient in the world. Still under construction, this French-engineered project extends the length of the city from Propatria in the west to Palo Verde in the east with a short north-south spur connecting El Silencio and ending at the Caricuao zoo. Complementing the subway are connecting metro buses. If you take a subway *and* a bus, make sure to ask for a *boleto integrado* (a special ticket good for a ride on both the subways and buses). Automatic machines also sell tickets, but be sure to have coins handy as the lines to get change can be very long. The metro operates daily from 5:30 AM to 11 PM; it is clean, quiet, inexpensive, and the fastest way to get around the city. It is crowded, however, at rush hour.

**Taxi** – Taxi meters have arrived, but not every driver uses them, or at least they seldom seem to be running. Ask if the meter works; if not, negotiate the fare before entering the cab. Because of the abundance of petroleum in Venezuela, transportation is relatively inexpensive. (Note: Many *taxistas*, or drivers, are not from Caracas and don't know their way around, so be prepared with good instructions. A 10% surcharge is levied on Sundays, holidays, and late at night.) To call a cab, dial *Tele-Taxi* (752-9122), or *Taxi Tour* (749411).

**SPECIAL EVENTS:** The 2 days and nights before *Ash Wednesday*, when *Carnaval* is celebrated, Caracas and the rest of the country close down. The same is true during *Semana Santa* (Holy Week), the week before *Easter*. In addition to Roman Catholic holidays, Venezuela observes *Declaration of Independence Day* (April 19), *Labor Day* (May 1), the *Anniversary of the Battle of Carabobo* (June 24), *Independence Day* (July 5), *Bolívar's Birthday* (July 24), and *Columbus Day* (October 12). Practically everything shuts down on *Christmas* and on *New Year's Eve*, a holiday traditionally celebrated with family at home parties.

**MUSEUMS:** In addition to those described in *Special Places*, other museums of note include the following:

**La Cuadra Bolívar (Bolívar Home)** – The rebuilt country home of the Great Liberator's family is an enchanting escape from the rigors of modern city life into the tranquillity of the past. Open Tuesdays through Saturdays from 9 AM to noon and 2:30 to 5:30 PM; Sundays from 10 AM to noon and 2:30 to 5:30 PM. No admission charge. Av. Sur 2 between Esquina Bárcenas and Las Piedras (phone: 483-3971).

**Galería de Arte Nacional (National Art Gallery)** – A permanent exhibition of the works of Venezuelan artists in this neo-classical building. Closed Mondays. Guided tours available by appointment on weekdays only. No admission charge. Near the *Fine Arts* and *Natural Sciences* museums in Plaza Morelos, Los Caobos (phone: 572-1070).

**Museo de Arte La Rinconada (La Rinconada Art Museum)** – This striking building at the racetrack houses a permanent exhibition of paintings, sculptures, pre-Columbian pieces, and ceramics by Venezuelan artists in addition to temporary international shows. Closed Mondays. No admission charge. Av. Intercomunal del Valle, La Rinconada (phone: 606-6111).

**Museo Arturo Michelena (Arturo Michelena Museum)** – A traditional 19th-century home open to the public. Michelena, one of Venezuela's most renowned 19th-century painters, lived here until his death in 1898 at age 35; his widow stayed on another 60 years. Open daily, except Mondays, from 9 AM to 5 PM. No admission charge. La Pastora (phone: 825853).

**Museo de Transporte (Transport Museum)** – On view are old cars and locomotives and scale models of Caracas as it was 100 years ago. Open Tuesdays through Sundays from 9 AM to 5 PM. Admission charge. Parque del Este, near Urbanización Santa Cecilia (phone: 342234).

**SHOPPING:** Caracas has some spectacular shopping centers, and with the devaluation of the bolívar visitors will find prices of some items attractive. The best shopping centers for spending some time (and perhaps a few dollars on a light snack) are *Centro Comercial Chacaíto; Sabana Grande; Concresa; Paseo Las Mercedes; Plaza Las Américas; Centro Plaza;* and Latin America's biggest to date, *Centro Comercial Ciudad Tamanaco,* known as *CCCT* (pronounced *Say-Say-Say-Tay*) and located near La Carlota Airport. The Avenida Urdaneta shopping district downtown has a more Latin flavor but is unappealing for its head-splitting pollution.

Venezuela produces fine rum and coffee; both make excellent gifts. Caracas is also one of the biggest recording centers on the continent and is a great place to pick up salsa and merengue tapes, as well as South American pop music. If you aren't familiar with the artists, ask the record store attendants to play sample tracks — they'll be happy to do it. Throughout the city, costume jewelry and shoes are two major Caracas bargains.

***Artesanía Venezolana*** – Full of folk art and crafts, including weavings by Guajira Indians and wicker basketry from Orinoco regions. Fine quality hammocks and the famous painted devil masks worn at the *Feast of Corpus Christi* in June are sold, along with just about everything else produced by craftspeople across the country. Plaza Venezuela (phone: 782-3810/1020/5732/9126).

***Audubon Society Store*** – The continent's oldest Audubon Society runs a shop at its Venezuela headquarters, selling books, magazines, postcards, and other products that focus on Venezuela's flora and fauna. The best coffee-table books, bird watching guides, and academic tomes (in English and Spanish) on subjects such as music and indigenous groups are found here. Paseo Las Mercedes, Sección La Cuadra (phone: 913813).

***Beltrami*** – Local outlet of this Italian designer of shoes and leather products. Major credit cards accepted. *CCCT* (phone: 959-0451).

***Charles Jourdan/Gucci*** – Casual and dressy shoes, bags, belts, and wallets from these two famous European sources, at bargain prices. Major credit cards accepted. *CCCT* (phone: 925405).

***La Francia*** – A 9-story building filled with small jewelry shops — 18-carat gold is a specialty. Most jewelry is sold by weight. There are some real buys here. Off Plaza Bolívar at Esquina Las Monjas.

***H. Stern*** – Fine gold and precious gems in stylized designs that carry international quality guarantees. Look for the intriguing pre-Columbian designs. In the lobbies of the *Caracas Hilton International* (phone: 571-2322) and the *Tamanaco Inter-Continental* (phone: 914444) hotels and at the Maiquetía international airport terminal.

**Nardi** – Quality shoes for low prices. Major credit cards accepted. *CCCT* (phone: 959-2137).

**Trevi** – Shop here for well-made and well-designed leather bags. Branches in *CCCT* and at *Centro Comercial Chacaíto*.

**SPORTS:** Unlike the rest of South America, baseball rather than soccer is the major spectator sport. The nearby Caribbean beaches are perfect for water sports, but be aware that all too often the ones nearest Caracas are polluted. It's better to travel out to more pristine areas, such as those at Morrocoy National Park.

**Baseball** – Venezuelan players David Concepción, Manny Trillo, Luis Aparicio, Vic Davalillo, and Antonio Armas have been stars in the US major leagues. Upcoming Venezuelan stars and athletes imported from the US get together in the winter leagues in Caracas to keep in shape. The local teams are quite colorful, and although the "raw" quality of play has declined somewhat in recent years, the color and spirit of the games never wane. Especially fascinating are the *Little League World Series* and the *Series of the Caribbean*, where teams from the region, mostly Spanish-speaking, vie for the number one slot. Even if you aren't a diehard *beisbol* fan, you'll enjoy the intensity of the crowd and the endless stream of snack vendors selling everything from roasted peanuts to fried bananas topped with ketchup and grated cheese. All games in Caracas are played at the Universidad Central campus (phone: 619811). The Venezuelan season runs from October through February; most games are played at night, except for Saturdays and Sundays, when afternoon games are held. For information, check the sports pages of *The Daily Journal*.

**Boxing** – Aspiring hopefuls, trying to fight their way to greater success, are to be seen at the *Poliedro*, next door to *La Rinconada* racetrack (phone: 681-8950).

**Bullfighting** – Depending on whether your sympathies lie with the man or the bull, you'll find these contests challenging or sickening. Superior performances and more elaborate displays can be found in other Venezuelan cities, but Caracas has its own bullring. (A word of caution: Watch your wallet.) Bullfights take place on Sunday afternoons at *Plaza de Toros* (Nuevo Circo, San Martín at the corner of San Roque). Maracay and Valencia have their own rings and the same fighters as Caracas.

**Deep-Sea Fishing** – You can charter a boat with tackle, gear, and crew (lunch and drinks included) from the *Marina Mar* (phone: 31-527097), next to the *Macuto Sheraton*.

**Golf** – There are no public golf courses, so be prepared to pay hefty fees at the private clubs. Ask your hotel to arrange privileges at the *Junko, Lagunita* or *Caracas* country clubs. The *Meliá Caribe* and *Macuto Sheraton* offer guests playing privileges at the 9-hole *Caraballeda* golf course, and the *Tamanaco* hotel can arrange for guests to play at the 18-hole *Valle Arriba* golf course, but only at certain hours. César Quijada at *Arelys Tours* (phone: 782-4680) can arrange privileges at *Junko, Caraballeda, and Izcaragua*. He also rents clubs.

**Horse Racing** – Millions of the billions of bolívars are spent weekly on the horses, both off the track (at the betting game known as the *Cinco y Seis*) and at *La Rinconada Hipódromo* itself. Surrounded by a green, rising plain, the racetrack is considered one of the best in Latin America and seats up to 30,000. Jackets and ties are required dress for gentlemen, and ladies must wear skirts or dresses in the clubhouse. Races are run every Saturday and Sunday afternoon. La Rinconada, El Valle (phone: 681-3333).

**Sailing** – Rent a sailboat or cruiser from the *Marina Mar* next to the *Macuto Sheraton*. Charter companies advertise in *The Daily Journal*, and some small adventure travel companies have their own flotillas of skippered boats. Contact *Alpi Tours* (phone: 283-1433) or *Caribbean Nimbus Tours* (phone: 310001) to rent sailboats or yachts.

**Snorkeling and Scuba** – Rent scuba equipment with a boat and guide from the *Macuto Sheraton* (phone: 31-944300, ext. 188). Other hotels along the Caribbean rent flippers and masks for a small fee.

**Swimming** – The Litoral coast has some terrific (and not so terrific) beaches (see *Special Places*). Most of the major hotels, including the *Caracas Hilton International, Meliá Caribe,* and the *Avila* allow non-guests to pay to use their pools. Towels are provided.

**Tennis** – Guests have first choice at the *Caracas Hilton International, Macuto Sheraton, Meliá Caribe,* and *Tamanaco,* but non-guests can play for a small fee. *Davis Cup* matches usually are held in Caracas in February.

**THEATER:** The *Ateneo* in the *Teresa Carreño* theatrical complex (opposite the *Caracas Hilton International;* phone: 573-4400/4600) has several stages and a varied repertoire — from classical drama to outrageous new comedies by young *caraqueño* playwrights. There are also dozens of smaller theaters scattered throughout the city, all of which have works in Spanish. Cultural associations such as *Humboldt* (phone: 527634) and *Alianza Francesa* (phone: 711773) often have productions as well. Look for details in *The Daily Journal* or the Spanish-language press (*El Diario de Caracas, El Nacional,* or *El Universal*). The *Caracas Playhouse,* an amateur group, periodically presents works in English at its stage on Calle Chivacoa, San Román (phone: 911311).

If movies, rather than nightclubs, are your thing, there's a good selection of domestic and foreign films. Try the small, arty *Cine Prensa* (Av. Andrés Bello, Las Palmas; phone: 782-2786) or the *Cinemateca,* housed in the *Museo de Bellas Artes* (Fine Arts Museum; adjoining Parque Los Caobos; phone: 571-0176) for offbeat shows and weeklong foreign film festivals at very low prices. Consult *The Daily Journal* "Movie Guide" for listings.

**MUSIC:** From the blast of salsa tunes that rock every *por puesto* to the superb symphony concerts of the *Teresa Carreño* complex, Caracas is a city that pulsates with music. Discos vibrate with salsas and merengues, in addition to US and European pop and rock music. Around *Christmas,* the seasonal *gaita* music is played in every criollo restaurant and club. Piano bars are gaining a following (see *Nightclubs and Nightlife*). International pop stars usually play the *Poliedro* (next door to *La Rinconada* racetrack on the south side of the city, off Autopista del Valle; phone: 681-8950/9782). A smaller pop/rock place is *Mata de Coco* (Av. Blandín, La Castellana, 1st Floor, phone: 321366 or 261-9398). Also popular with young rockers is the video bar *L'Attico* (Quinta Palic, Av. Luis Roche, Altamira; phone: 261-2819). The 2,400-seat *Ríos Reyna Hall* (in the *Teresa Carreño* complex) is the venue for big-name opera stars, classical concerts, touring dance companies, and the occasional pop celebrity. More intimate concerts and recitals are staged in *Teresa Carreño*'s 800-seat *Salon José Félix Ribas.* The *Teresa Carreño* is opposite the *Caracas Hilton International.* Call ahead to reserve tickets; the big shows are almost always sold out (phone: 574-9122/9133/9666 from 8:30 AM to 7 PM daily). In the neighboring *Ateneo,* check out *Café Rajatabla* (phone: 571-4219 or 572-8946) to hear the latest jazz and experimental sounds. In addition to the *Teresa Carreño,* classical concerts are held at the *Aula Magna* of the Universidad Central (south of Plaza Venezuela, go in the Ciudad Universitaria entrance from Av. Los Mangos; phone: 619811). The *Teatro Municipal* (at *Esquina Teatro Municipal* on Av.

Bolívar, near the south side of Centro Simón Bolívar, 1 block east of Av. Baralt; phone: 415384) is home to the *Caracas Symphony Orchestra*. Check newspapers for musical events.

**NIGHTCLUBS AND NIGHTLIFE:** Whatever else you might think or say about Caracas, it is certainly ideal at night. The city is full of bright lights and gaiety, with everything from sophisticated midnight shows to raunchy "welcome bars," where ladies of the evening ply their trade. The numerous discotheques play top American rock and Latin soul music. Some of the more exclusive discos have their own bands and occasionally offer a top international group. In El Este, there are two kinds of discos: those conducive to romantic interests exclusively (they are very dark and the music is quite loud) and those that provide quieter areas, where you can hold a conversation without having to scream. Music clubs, where there's dancing, eating, drinking, and watching videos on big screens are more popular with the older crowd, with discos being frequented by students. Piano bars are also extremely popular. Even on weeknights, you'll find Caracas vibrant at midnight. This is often perplexing to foreigners, who wonder how these same night owls can party so late, then go to work the next day. *Naiguatá* (at the *Tamanaco;* phone: 914555) puts on the best show in town, and on Mondays the *Caracas Hilton International* stages *Noches Caraqueñas* for guests. The most popular discos are *New York, New York* (*Centro Comercial Concresa,* Plaza Bolívar 1; phone: 979-7745 or 979-7778); *Red Parrot* (Av. Tamanaco, El Rosal; phone: 951-1953 or 951-2861); *Le Club* (*Centro Comercial Chacaíto,* Sotano; phone: 952-0807); *1900 My Way* (*Centro Comercial Ciudad Tamanaco,* Nivel C-2; phone: 959-0441); *Mazzo* (*Centro Comercial Chacaíto,* Sótano; phone: 723215); *Reflections* (Plaza Venezuela, Phelps Tower Mezzanine; phone: 782-7523); *The Flower* (Plaza La Castellana, Av. Francisco de Miranda; phone: 333013); and *Rainbow* (*Centro Comercial Bello Campo;* phone: 316088). The finest piano bars are *Juan Sebastián Bar* — which also has outstanding jazz bands and great bar snacks (Av. Venezuela, El Rosal; phone: 951-5575); *Crystal Club* (Av. Principal, La Castellana; phone: 314973); *Gypsy* (Paseo Las Mercedes, Nivel Trasmocho; phone: 929245); and *Magic* (Calle Madrid, Las Mercedes; phone: 928704). A posh piano bar (with an adjacent seafood restaurant) is *El Palacio del Mar* (San Juan Bosco between 3rd and 5th Transversales in Altamira; phone: 261-6460). For live bands (and *gaita* music around *Christmas*), try the *Nueva Esparta* (Av. Los Marquitos, Sabana Grande; no phone).

For a British pub atmosphere and a chance to quaff a pint with some English speakers, try the *Dog and Fox* (Av. Río de Janeiro, Las Mercedes; phone: 917319) or *La Bolera* (on Fuerzas Armadas, north of Av. Urdaneta), where reporters and editors from *The Daily Journal* hang out after work. Hardcore bullfight fans may get a change to toast one of the local *toreros* at *Los Cuchilleros* (Av. Urdaneta west of Plaza La Candelaria; no phone), a haunt of bullfighters and their groupies.

■**Female Facts:** Women traveling alone in Caracas can expect to encounter rude remarks, sneers, and lip-smacking noises during the day; the problem is exacerbated at night. *Caraqueñas* and women from other parts of the country suffer the same fate in the city. It is annoying but rarely dangerous, and usually it is possible to avoid confrontations by simply ignoring the provocation. Men generally assume that women out alone at night are looking for pickups; at the worst, they assume such lone travelers to be prostitutes. A woman who goes alone to a restaurant, bar, or nightclub can expect to be approached; unaccompanied women are often refused entry to bars, clubs, and discos. There are many cafés, however, especially along Sabana Grande and the commercial centers, where such sexist treatment is not the case. Exceptions to this unpleasant "rule" are *Café Morgana* (Centro Plaza; phone: 284-6590) and *Weekends* (Av. Luis Roche, Altamira; 261-6869).

# BEST IN TOWN

**CHECKING IN:** Even though Caracas has more hotels than ever, visitors are advised to book well in advance and to have some confirmation in writing. The *Sistema Nacional de Reservaciones* (National Reservation System) guarantees reservations at more than 300 hotels nationwide, and can send confirmed reservation vouchers to your home or business from 8 AM to 7 PM Monday through Friday (phone: 782-8433; fax: 782-4407). *Corpoturismo* (phone: 507-8876) also can assist with hotel reservations. Expect to pay about $75 to $150 for a double room in the hotels listed below as expensive, $35 to $75 at those places listed as moderate, and less than $30 at the places listed as inexpensive. All telephone numbers are in the 2 city code unless otherwise indicated.

**Caracas Hilton International** – Favored by businesspeople, this 912-room property has ballrooms, conference rooms, and a lounge on each of the top 6 executive floors of the newer tower (where rooms are more expensive than in the original building), plus good business services. Unfortunately, standard services can be spotty (phone messages are often not delivered to guests). Tennis courts are free for guests, and there's a large pool, sauna, and gym. The food is excellent, and the 15th-floor restaurant-nightclub, *La Cota 880,* offers continuous dancing and a spectacular view of the city (see *Eating Out*). Other restaurants in the hotel include *Los Caobos, La Rotisserie,* and *La Terraza.* The downtown location is convenient to the neighboring cultural complex, the Parque Central complex for shopping, and the *Contemporary Art Museum.* Av. Sur 25, El Conde (phone: 571-2322 or 574-2122; fax: 575-0024; in the US, 800-HILTONS). Expensive.

**CCCT** – Situated in the city's largest shopping center, this hotel offers a rooftop swimming pool, tennis, sauna, gym, a restaurant, and bars. The building is surrounded by boutiques of every kind, banks, and restaurants galore. *Centro Comercial Ciudad Tamanaco,* entrance at 1 Sótano (phone: 959-0651). Expensive.

**Eurobuilding** – This impressive luxury high-rise has counted Fidel Castro among its guests. It has 737 rooms and suites, plus 37 poolside cabañas, 3 restaurants, 2 coffee shops, 3 bars, a gallery of shops, sundeck, gym, sauna, and nightclub. Its services for business travelers include meeting rooms, telex, secretaries, translators, and banks. Calle La Guairita in Urbanización Chuao (phone: 959-1133; fax: 922069). Expensive.

**Lincoln Suites** – Service is still a bit uneven at this new all-suite hotel, but its location can't be beat. The only luxury property right in front of Sabana Grande Boulevard, it offers quiet rooms, a restaurant, bar, room service, and good security. It is within walking distance of two subway stops and close to many fine restaurants and shops. Av. Francisco Solano near Jerónimo (phone: 728576 through 728579; fax: 725502). Expensive.

**Macuto Sheraton** – A natural choice for beach lovers who prefer to visit Caracas proper at night, its complete range of aquatic sports facilities includes 2 swimming pools, sailboat rental, fishing, scuba diving, water skiing, and the beach. There are tennis courts, lighted for night play, and a bowling alley of sorts on the premises; golf privileges entitle you to play at a nearby course. The expected Sheraton accoutrements are all present in force: 3 restaurants, disco, nightclub, gift shop, bookstore, beauty salon, and travel agencies, but the service is seldom up to par with other hotels in the chain. It is 20 miles (32 km) from Caracas, in Caraballeda (phone: 31-944300; reservations, 31-781-1508; in Caracas, 782-9408; in the US, 800-325-3535; fax: 31-944318). Expensive.

**Meliá Caracas** – The latest Caracas property in this Spanish hotel chain, this one is geared toward both business travelers and vacationers, offering a restaurant, parking, and a wide range of services. It is ideally situated just off the Sabana Grande. Av. Casanova, Bella Monte (phone: 729314; in the US, 800-336-3542). Expensive.

**Meliá Caribe** – Another link in the Meliá chain, this is a competitor of the *Macuto Sheraton*. It has extensive facilities including a disco, and a wide variety of restaurants and bars. Facilities include a gym, tennis court, marina with sports facilities, pool and poolside bar, band, and buffet. It is 20 miles (32 km) from Caracas in Caraballeda (phone: 31-945555; in Caracas, 729314; in the US, 800-336-3542). Expensive.

**President** – This 165-room hotel has the business traveler in mind — it even has an airport meet-and-greet service that gets you through customs quickly as well as secretarial services, translators, photocopy and fax facilities. Other amenities include 2 restaurants, a bar with live music, a snack bar by the pool, whirlpool bath, tour desk, valet parking, barber shop and beauty salon, and mini-bars and cable television in all the rooms. Av. Valparaíso and Sabana Grande (phone: 782-6622; in the US, through *LARC,* 800-327-3573; fax: 782-6458). Expensive.

**Tamanaco Inter-Continental** – A favorite with foreign visitors, it offers above-average dining in 5 different restaurants, a great swimming pool and gym, tennis courts, a spectacular view of Caracas, shows, shops, and genuine Latin soul. Av. Principal, Las Mercedes (phone: 914555 and 208-7000; in the US, 800-327-0200; fax: 208-7951). Expensive.

**Residencias Anauco Hilton** – In Parque Central, the hotel has 317 suites, junior suites, and split-level apartments (with a living room, dining room, and 2 to 4 bedrooms), available for both long and short stays. The hotel has remodeled (and noise-proofed) all its rooms in a tropical decor — with remarkable results. Amenities include use of the *Caracas Hilton International*'s pool, sauna, tennis courts, gym (all right across the street), plus a good choice of restaurants. The complex also has shops, a cinema, and a supermarket. Parque Central (phone: 573-4111; fax: 573-7724). Expensive to moderate.

**Avila** – Pleasantly situated on a hill overlooking the city, this gracious, older hotel has plenty of original Venezuelan charm. Meals can be enjoyed alongside the swimming pool, while listening to the chatter of birds (instead of the perennial hum of traffic). There is a pleasant piano bar and an English- and Spanish-language newsstand in the lobby. It's the perfect alternative to supermodern, impersonal hotels. Av. Jorge Washington, San Bernardino (phone: 515128 and 515137; fax: 523021). Moderate.

**Continental Altamira** – Well situated in Altamira (and not to be confused with the unrelated *Altamira*), it features a swimming pool, restaurant, bar, and room service. Av. San Juan Bosco, Altamira (phone: 261-6019). Moderate.

**Crillón** – Neither as classy as the *Tamanaco* nor as flashy as the *Hilton*, this is a substantial, comfortable, modern (but not too modern) establishment near the Sabana Grande shopping district. Most of the accommodations are 2-room suites, complete with refrigerators and television sets. Almost all have terraces. Try the excellent Swiss restaurant, *El Chalet*. Av. Libertador and Av. Las Acacias (phone: 714411). Moderate.

**El Marqués** – Someone finally invested money in a "middle of the road" hotel and is making money. In an unlikely residential area of the city, it is charming and well run, catering mostly to business travelers. There's a bar, restaurant, and coffee shop. Av. El Samán and Calle Yuruarí, El Marqués (phone: 239-3211). Moderate.

**Paseo** – Pocketed in one of Caracas's finest shopping centers, this former *Holiday Inn* has no facilities for recreation, but it is within walking distance of the *Tamanaco* and provides guests with golf privileges nearby. Service is competent. Av. Principal, Las Mercedes (phone: 910177). Moderate.

**Tampa** – Near Plaza Venezuela and the Sabana Grande shopping district, this hotel's location and reasonable prices make it a good bet. Its Italian restaurant, *Rugantino,* is worth a visit. 9 Av. Francisco Solano López, Sabana Grande (phone: 723771). Moderate.

**El Cóndor** – With a convenient location in Chacaíto, near the subway, this hotel offers an Italian restaurant and a bar. Tercera ($3^{ra}$) Av. Las Delicias de Sabana Grande (phone: 729911). Moderate to inexpensive.

**Macuto** – Small, spotless, and simple, this is a good alternative for travelers who want to be close to the ocean in El Litoral (it's a couple of blocks away), but don't want to pay luxury hotel prices. The atmosphere is friendly and the restaurant features good criollo seafood dishes. Av. La Playa, Macuto (phone: 31-44561 and 31-44563). Inexpensive.

**Plaza Palace** – In a city where it is hard to find safe, clean budget hotels, this place is a secret bargain. It was recently renovated and has an English-speaking staff, 68 basic, but comfortable rooms with private baths (some have balconies), telephones, TV sets, and air conditioning. The restaurant is good, the bar friendly, and the location is within walking distance of the Sabana Grande and the subway. Be sure to book well ahead. Av. Los Mangos in Las Delicias (phone: 724821 through 724829; fax: 726375). Inexpensive.

**EATING OUT:** As far as food is concerned, *caraqueños* need not suffer any inferiority complex. The main problem with eating out in Caracas is the existential anguish of deciding which among so many restaurants to visit first. Most of the best are found in the east, and a proliferation of new eateries, especially in Las Mercedes and El Rosal, makes choosing even more problematic. On weekdays, the majority of diners are prosperous businesspeople, but on weekends all *caraqueños* come out in force. Caracas restaurants are moderately priced by US urban standards, and for even less expensive eating there is an abundance of soda fountains (don't leave without sampling their fresh fruit juices or fruit shakes called *batidos*), snack bars, and fast-food chains. Visitors cannot fail to notice the numerous *areperas,* informal restaurants selling deep-fat-fried cornmeal *arepas* stuffed with everything from cheese to chopped ham salad. The national dish, *pabellón criollo,* is a plate of shredded beef, rice, black beans, fried plantains, and *arepas.* If you want to sample finger foods such as *tequeños* (deep-fat-fried cheese sticks) along with a cocktail, ask the waiter for a list of *pasapalos.* It's also possible to eat informally and well in any of the many Spanish *tascas* (taverns) in La Candelaria or the Sabana Grande areas. But be forewarned — La Candelaria is not the safest neighborhood at night. If you wish to "dine out" with a three-course meal, expect to pay at least $50 for two at the restaurants listed below as expensive and $35 to $50 in the moderate range; anything less is considered inexpensive. Prices do not include drinks, wine, or tips. (Wine is on the pricey side in Caracas, and not normally of the best quality.) All telephone numbers are in the 2 city code unless otherwise indicated.

**La Atarraya** – One of the few really classy restaurants in the center of town, it serves traditional criollo dishes — *natilla,* cheeses from Coro with *arepas, cazón* (ground shark meat), and *pabellón* (a typical meat-and-bean plate). Government big shots abound, and the sangria is very good. Open daily. Reservations advised. Major credit cards accepted. Plaza El Venezolano, Esquina de San Jacinto (phone: 545-8235). Expensive.

**Aventino** – Located in a gracious villa, this Caracas classic features a French kitchen and the most extensive wine cellar in the capital. The house specialty, pressed duck, is so special that whoever orders it receives a certificate of gastronomy and is registered in a gold book. Open daily. Reservations advised. Major credit cards accepted. Av. San Felipe at the corner of José Angel Llamas, La Castellana (phone: 322640). Expensive.

***La Belle Epoque*** – This remains one of Caracas's finest French restaurants. Delicious asparagus and artichoke appetizers serve as a prelude to the main course. The trout here is particularly succulent. Enjoy the romantic atmosphere and lively music at night. Jackets preferred. Closed Sundays. Reservations advised. Major credit cards accepted. In Edificio Century on Av. Leonardo da Vinci, Colinas de Bello Monte (phone: 752-1342). Expensive.

***Cota 880*** – The refined dishes (mostly French and northern Italian), cosmopolitan atmosphere, panoramic view, excellent entertainment, and dancing to live music make this one of the best choices in Caracas. Buffets are served on Sunday evenings, and a jacket is required in the evenings. Closed Mondays. Reservations advised. Major credit cards accepted. On the top floor of the *Caracas Hilton International,* El Conde (phone: 571-0846). Expensive.

***Da Emore*** – A choice of Italian dishes is offered at this charming family-run eatery. There are only prix fixe menus. Closed Mondays. Reservations advised. Major credit cards accepted. In *Centro Comercial Concresa* (phone: 979-3242). Expensive.

***Gazebo*** – Prepare to dress for this very formal continental restaurant. Gourmands in Caracas's French community say the food — and prices — are as impressive as Paris's best. If you are going to Caracas on business, this is a good place to impress a client. Paul Bocuse has been among the stellar guest chefs at the restaurant's periodic gastronomic festivals. Closed Saturdays at lunchtime and Sundays. Reservations advised. Major credit cards accepted. Av. Río de Janeiro, Las Mercedes (phone: 925568 and 926812). Expensive.

***Lasserre*** – The finest classical French cuisine is served in an elegant yet intimate dining room, tastefully furnished with antiques. A fine cellar of French wines. Open daily. Reservations advised. Major credit cards accepted. Av. Tercera ($3^{ra}$) between Segunda ($2^{da}$) and Tercera ($3^{ra}$) Transversales, Los Palos Grandes (phone: 283-4558, 283-3079). Expensive.

***El Barquero*** – Spanish-style cooking, specializing in seafood, is what makes this spot so popular. The house is famous for its *pasapalos,* generous-size snacks of sausage, clams, shrimps, and mushrooms in garlic sauce. Open daily. Reservations advised. Major credit cards accepted. Av. Luis Roche, Esq. 5th Transversal, Altamira (phone: 261-4645). Expensive to moderate.

***Bogavante*** – Decorated as a fishing boat, this restaurant specializes in lobster, crab, shrimp, and fish filets. The Italian and Spanish wine list is quite good. Open daily. Reservations advised. Major credit cards accepted. Av. Venezuela, El Rosal (phone: 952-0146). Expensive to moderate.

***Casa Juancho*** – Large, popular, and in a garden setting, with a high-quality Spanish menu. The house specialty is suckling pig. There's live guitar music in the evenings. Open daily. Reservations advised. Major credit cards accepted. Av. San Juan Bosco, Altamira (phone: 334614). Expensive to moderate.

***La Cigogne*** – This place continues to command esteem — even though the decor could use an update. Its pâtés are superior, and other French dishes are worth a taste. Open daily, except Sundays, until midnight. Reservations advised. Major credit cards accepted. Av. Garcilazo off Av. Principal, Colinas de Bello Monte (phone: 751-3313 and 751-3242). Expensive to moderate.

***La Estancia*** – A converted colonial-style house and covered terrace make this a refreshing spot to enjoy excellent steaks — grilled at your table — and traditional criollo cuisine. The dessert cart is tempting. The proximity of the garden completes the escape from the bustle of the city. Closed Sundays. Reservations advised. Major credit cards accepted. Av. Principal, La Castellana, at the corner of Urdaneta (phone: 331937). Expensive to moderate.

***Hereford Grill*** – This fine steakhouse does prime meat to perfection. *Medallón de* *lomito al oporto* (steak in port) and *pollo deshuesado Hereford* (boned chicken) are special. Open daily. Reservations advised. Major credit cards accepted. Calle Madrid in Las Mercedes (phone: 929664). Expensive to moderate.

**El Hostal de la Castellana** – Don Quixote and Sancho Panza stand guard at the portals of this Spanish stronghold lined with conquistador souvenirs and audible flamenco overtones (the music starts at 8:30 PM). The gazpacho, paella, and *pierna cordero castellana* (leg of lamb) are commendable. Open daily. Reservations advised. Major credit cards accepted. Av. Principal at Plaza Castellana (phone: 334260). Expensive to moderate.

**Il Padrino** – Billed as the most beautiful restaurant in the world, it is certainly the most beautiful in Caracas. Originally designed as a Russian restaurant, its basic decor features vaulted ceilings. Some years back, it was converted to a Sicilian restaurant, and Italian hardwood furniture and lamps from Toledo, Spain, were added. Distinguished by its incomparable salad bar and antipasto (virtually a meal in itself), it has music for dancing, accordion-playing waiters, and wandering photographers. Don't go expecting a quiet, romantic evening. Open daily. Reservations advised. Major credit cards accepted. Plaza Altamira Sur (phone: 327684). Expensive to moderate.

**Altamar** – Superb seafood, paella, and a very enjoyable flamenco show are the draws at this time-honored favorite. Open daily. Reservations advised. Major credit cards accepted. Tercera ($3^{ra}$) Transversal between Bosco and Roche, Altamira (phone: 261-9765). Moderate.

**Comilona** – Conveniently located for the *Tamanaco* or the *Paseo* hotel at the end of Av. Principal Las Mercedes, it offers an Italian menu in a friendly atmosphere. Open daily. Reservations advised. Major credit cards accepted. Opposite Paseo Las Mercedes (phone: 921231). Moderate.

**Dama Antañona** – A genuine criollo menu is offered in this beautifully converted colonial house — its original rooms intact. Best at midday and popular for business lunches. Try the delicious sweet corn soup (available Fridays only). Very courteous service. Open daily. Reservations unnecessary. Major credit cards accepted. Downtown, at 14 Jesuitas at Maturín (phone: 563-5639 or 837287). Moderate.

**La Era de Acuario** – This vegetarian and macrobiotic eatery offers pleasant, informal surroundings and an extensive menu, from whole wheat pizza to salads to fish. Open daily from noon to 11 PM. Reservations unnecessary. Major credit cards accepted. Calle Madrid near Veracruz, Las Mercedes (phone: 912535). Moderate.

**La Jaiba** – Unlike many of Caracas's mid-priced restaurants, this one offers a peaceful setting conducive to conversation — perhaps that's why political heavyweights congregate here. Plenty of plants, airy spaces, and excellent seafood also make it a good choice for dining out. Try the *arroz negro* (black rice), a delicate paella dish with squid ink. Its appearance may not be appealing, but the taste is exquisite. Open daily. Reservations advised. Major credit cards accepted. Av. Principal del Bosque (phone: 719186). Moderate.

**Jardín des Crêpes** – Handsomely filled crêpes, both sweet and savory, plus meat and fish dishes tempt palates here. Sit at the open, plant-filled balcony, then drop by the bar for live music. Open daily. Reservations advised. Major credit cards accepted. Calle Madrid between New York and Trinidad, Las Mercedes (phone: 915509). Moderate.

**Kibbe Steak** – The Middle East can be found in Caracas at this quaint spot that features delicious Arabic food, as well as more conventional fare. Good jazz can be heard in the piano bar upstairs before heading for the cozy dining room. Belly dancing begins at 10 PM. Open daily from noon. Reservations advised. Calle Madrid, Las Mercedes (phone: 910519). Moderate.

***Lee Hamilton Steak House*** – If you're homesick for hamburgers or steaks, this Caracas institution is your place. It's known for well-aged steaks — T-bone, New York, sirloin — and a good salad bar. Luncheon specials. Open daily. Reservations unnecessary. Major credit cards accepted. Av. San Felipe, La Castellana (phone: 325227). Moderate.

***Nueva China*** – A favorite with locals for its tropical drinks and excellent Chinese food. Try the house specialty, *sopa de mongoles,* a multi-course meal prepared with flair on a grill at your table. Servings are generous, so be sure to come hungry. Open daily. Reservations advised on weekend nights. Major credit cards accepted. Av. Principal, Las Mercedes (phone: 751-6884). Moderate.

***El Portón*** – The owners claim that no important person who comes to Venezuela ever leaves without first tasting a criollo meal here. With criollo scenes painted all over the wall and the excellent food, you walk away feeling as though you've just had an especially delicious lesson in Venezuelan culture. This is one of the best Spanish-American restaurants in the city. A band plays in the evenings. Open daily. Reservations advised. Major credit cards accepted. 18 Av. Pichincha, at the corner of Calle Guaicaipuro, El Rosal (phone: 952-0027). Moderate.

***Seoul*** – Conveniently located, this is the only Korean restaurant in town. Those who prefer mild flavorings beware — the food is very spicy. Open daily. Reservations unnecessary. Major credit cards accepted. 10 Calle El Cristo, Sabana Grande (phone: 723222). Moderate.

***El Dragón Verde*** – Superlative Chinese food at one of the oldest Chinese restaurants in Caracas. Open daily. Reservations unnecessary. Major credit cards accepted. Edificio Ciné París, Av. Maturín, Los Cedros (phone: 718404). Moderate to inexpensive.

■ **Best Bakes:** Two bakeries that are worth a special stop are *Pastelería Danubio* (Calle Guaicaipuro, Chacao; phone: 322749) and *La Casa Brioche* (Calle Madrid in Las Mercedes; phone: 929481). The latter also serves continental breakfast and lunch. Both are open daily; reservations are unnecessary; and major credit cards are accepted.

# LA PAZ

Among the highest cities in the world, at an altitude of 12,500 feet, La Paz, Bolivia, is also one of the most exceptional. How well you respond to the place will depend most on your ability to adjust physically to the altitude and psychologically to the extraordinary human pageant that passes by every day. Its combination of Indian and Spanish cultures, the extreme effect of its altitude, and its rather astonishing location in a shallow bowl between spectacular mountains make it a city even visitors familiar with other South American cities view with wonder.

From the moment your plane lands at El Alto Airport — a "world's highest" titleholder at 13,200 feet — you will be aware of something different about the air — at this altitude, the oxygen content is significantly lower than that to which most North Americans are accustomed. This atmospheric thinness partially accounts for the moderately bumpy landings on El Alto's 2-mile airstrip. When you emerge from the airplane, you may feel lightheaded, somewhat breathless, and sometimes cold. If you take the time to catch your breath (literally), this first flash of *soroche* (altitude sickness) will soon go away. It is best to eat lightly for the first couple of days and to avoid smoking and drinking alcoholic beverages. If the symptoms persist, rest, aspirin, Tylenol, or *maté de coca* (coca tea) may help restore feelings of good health.

The original site of the La Paz settlement was, like the present airport, on the flatlands of the altiplano, a barren, windswept plateau fenced in by the Andes. But by 1548 the Spanish colonists found it too windy and moved it down into the valley below the tableland. A modern highway now connects the old site and the present city, winding down some 1,600 feet from the airport into La Paz.

Just before the road from Lake Titicaca — at 12,500 feet, another global altitude champion — reaches the rim of the bowl in which La Paz sits, it joins a freeway interchange that links La Paz with the mysterious ruins at Tiahuanaco (see *Bolivia*, DIRECTIONS). Unlike other cities, where the highest stretches of land become the mansion-lined residential districts of the wealthy, the higher neighborhoods of La Paz belong to the poor. In recent years, the barrio (neighborhood) of El Alto, on the high plateau near the airport of the same name, has grown to a population of more than 400,000 politically active residents. Their demands for improved roads, housing, sewage, and other municipal services led to El Alto being established as a separate city in 1988. The barrio now has just about everything that La Paz has, including shops, restaurants, and even movie theaters. Most of the inhabitants of these neighborhoods are Aymara Indians who have fled the countryside in search of a better life. As if in response to some of their demands, a reddish-brown prefab housing project spreads beside a hill on the side of the road

# LA PAZ

## Points of Interest

1. El Prado
2. Mercado Camacho/Camacho Market
3. Iglesia San Francisco/San Francisco Church
4. Mercado de Hechicería/Indian Witchcraft Market
5. Mercado Negro/Black Market
6. Museo Nacional de Arte/National Art Museum
7. Plaza Murillo
8. Catedral/Cathedral; Museum of Colonial Religious Art
9. Palacio Legislativo/Legislature Palace
10. Palacio de Gobierno/Presidential Palace
11. Templete Arqueológico Semisubterráneo/Semisubterranean Archaeological Temple; Estadio Hernando Siles/Hernando Siles Stadium
12. Pasaje de las Flores/Flower Passageway
13. Museo Costumbrista/Museum of Customs; Museo del Litoral Boliviano/Bolivian Coastal Museum; Museo de Metales Preciosos Precolombinos/Museum of Pre-Colombian Precious Metals; Casa de Murillo/Murillo's House
14. Museo de Etnografía y Folklore/Ethnography and Folklore Museum
15. Instituto Boliviano de Turismo/Bolivian Institute of Tourism
16. Estación Central/Central Train Station
17. Museo Arqueológico de Tiwanaku/Tiahuanaco Archaeological Museum
18. Museo de Instrumentos Nativos/Museum of Native Instruments
19. Teatro Municipal/Municipal Theater
20. Casa de la Cultura/House of Culture
21. Cinemateca Boliviana
22. Tesla—Los Escudos
23. Peña Naira
24. Peña Marka Tambo
25. Casa del Corregidor
26. Terminal Terrestre/Terrestre Bus Terminal
27. El Alto Airport

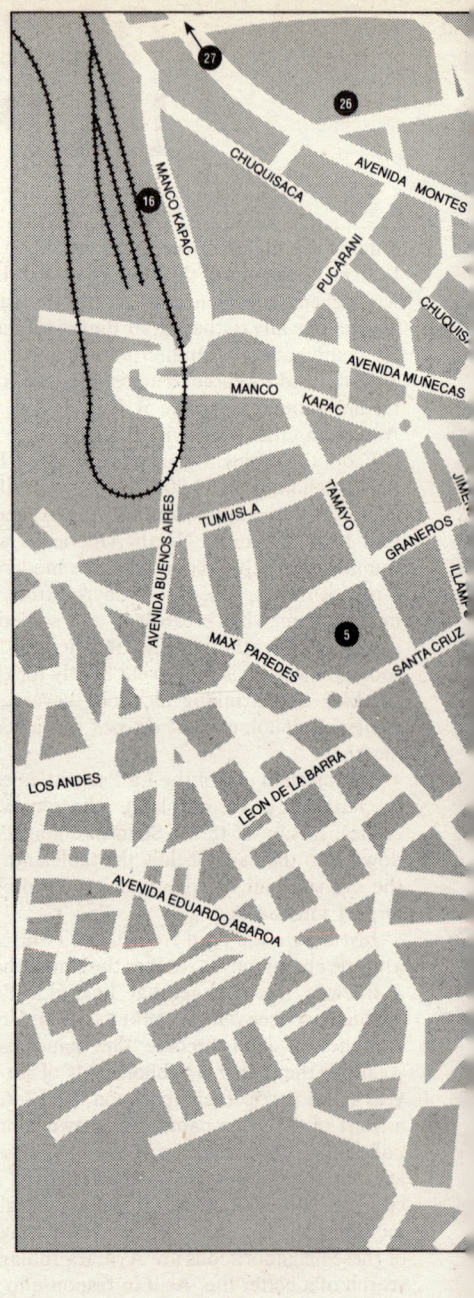

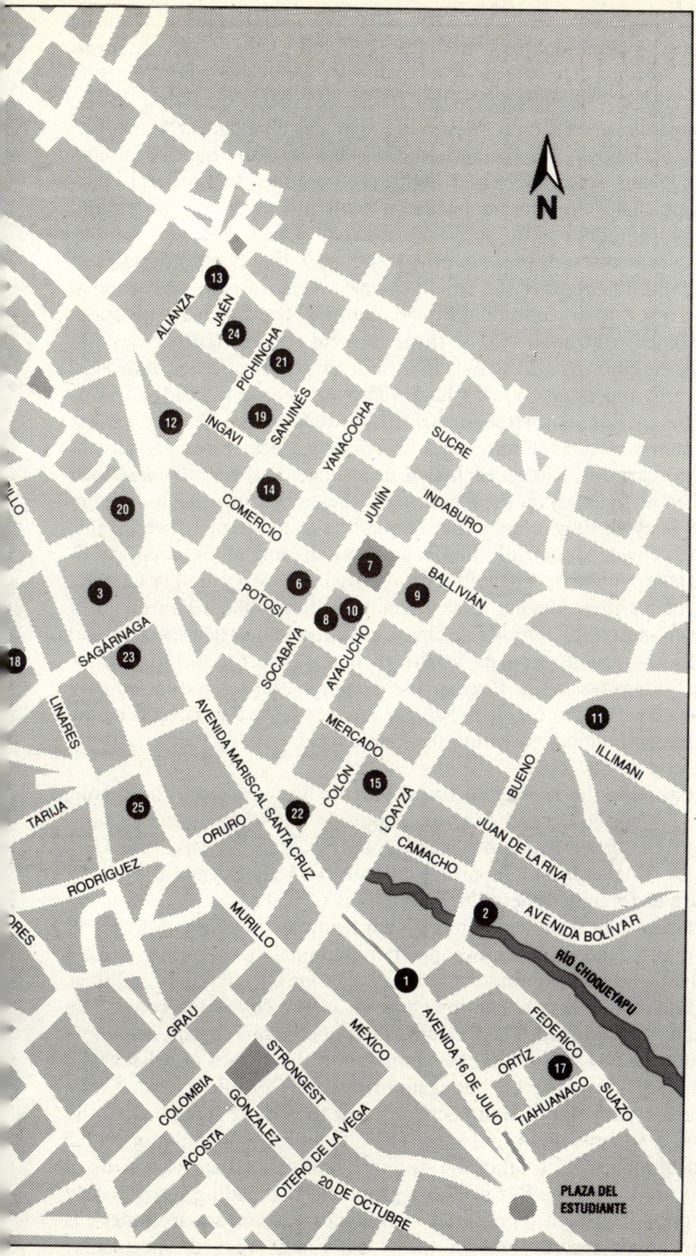
N
ALIANZA
JAÉN
PICHINCHA
SANJINÉS
INGAVI
YANACOCHA
SUCRE
INDABURO
JUNÍN
COMERCIO
BALLIVIÁN
POTOSÍ
SOCABAYA
AYACUCHO
SAGÁRNAGA
LINARES
MERCADO
ILLIMANI
BUENO
COLÓN
LOAYZA
AVENIDA MARISCAL SANTA CRUZ
TARIJA
ORURO
CAMACHO
JUAN DE LA RIVA
RODRÍGUEZ
AVENIDA BOLÍVAR
RÍO CHOQUEYAPU
MURILLO
GRAU
MÉXICO
AVENIDA 16 DE JULIO
FEDERICO
SUAZO
ORTÍZ
TIAHUANACO
STRONGEST
COLOMBIA
GONZALEZ
ACOSTA
OTERO DE LA VEGA
20 DE OCTUBRE
PLAZA DEL ESTUDIANTE
1
2
3
6
7
8
9
10
11
12
13
14
15
17
18
19
20
21
22
23
24
25

edging the city. As you look to your right, the flat altiplano suddenly drops away. Below, inside a huge crater, stands the city of La Paz, the sky above it a clean, icy blue. The rectangular tin roofs of Aymara huts cling to the crater's inner walls, glittering in the sun like spangles on a dancer's costume. About 1,000 feet below, near the bottom of the crater, stand high-rise apartment buildings and skyscrapers. (At night, the approach to La Paz is even more dramatic. The city shimmers like a bowl full of smoky topaz and glowing sapphire lights.)

The road winds through a eucalyptus grove, spiraling down at angles of between 50° and 80°, passing the small, chunky Aymara men and women, many of whom still wear traditional Indian clothing. The men leave peacockery to the women, who wear two or three cheerful *polleras* (petticoats) and skirts, striped or embroidered shawls in a rainbow of pinks, blues, reds, and yellows, and, to top it off, bowler hats. (This incongruous headwear was introduced by an English merchant before the turn of the century.) Most Aymara women wear their shining black hair in long, thick braids, and almost all seem to be carrying babies, each tied in an ingenious bundle of striped blanket (called an *aguayo*) on their backs. As you circle down the mountain, you will see busy throngs conducting commerce at numerous street stalls, hopping onto crowded, colorful microbuses, and bustling along steep, winding, cobbled thoroughfares. You will see tiny *cargardores* (porters) practically buried (except for their jogging legs) under what looks like a household of furniture or enough brick to build a school, children selling newspapers, and Indian vendors — usually women — with their wares spread out in front of them on the sidewalks of La Paz. In the evenings, the streets are equally packed as *paceños* (La Paz residents) gather to discuss the day's events or the results of a soccer match, generating the mad excitement of a block party on just about every street.

As you descend to the modern sector, the crowd becomes more cosmopolitan: engineers from the US and Australia, upper-middle class mestizo Bolivians, visitors from other South American countries, and tourists from Germany, France, England, and Japan intermingle with the Aymara. Nobody stops to stare at foreigners here. Nobody is out of place.

This is an ideal spot from which to get your bearings. Looking up, you will see the city surrounded by snowcapped mountains, the Cordillera Real (Royal Range), and you will understand why *paceños* affectionately call their city *La Hollada* (The Hole). The lowest point of the city is the confluence of rivers known as Calacoto. The Calacoto district contains elegant neighborhoods, residences of US Embassy personnel, and the homes of aristocratic Bolivian families. Then the city rises again toward the Cordillera Real. As the altitude increases, the population decreases, but the city is spreading to the mountains at a surprisingly rapid rate. The city's present population is 1.5 million (out of a national total of 6.5 million), and more than two-thirds of the residents are Indian. La Paz itself, geographically spreading across barely 10 square miles at present (compared to Bolivia's 424,200 square miles), is already starting to absorb some of the world's most rugged, spectacular scenery. Like Denver, Colorado, one of La Paz's finest features is its proximity to gorgeous mountain wilderness with extraordinary wildlife, especially birds. Southeast of La Paz stands the incomparable Mt. Illimani, the 21,200-

foot sentinel that can be seen from almost any point in La Paz. In 1961, according to local legend, the Mayor of La Paz led an expedition up Mt. Illimani by jeep, donkey, and foot to an Indian hut at an elevation of 19,800 feet in search of bear. Instead of bear, they found "a human footprint, eleven or twelve inches long," as described by one expedition member. The natives described "a fearful, two-legged creature between 10 and 11 feet high with tons of hair who sometimes came for food, chickens, sheep, and crops." This little-known Andean equivalent of the Himalayan Abominable Snowman has yet to be better documented.

Archaeologists, anthropologists, historians, and sociologists have long pondered the origins of the lost Tiahuanaco civilization that disappeared from the shores of Lake Titicaca (see *Bolivia*, DIRECTIONS) around AD 900. But succeeding Aymara and Quechua-speaking communities settled in the natural shelter carved by the Río Choqueyapu in what is now the city, using the valley to cultivate those sturdier varieties of potato and corn that the cold, dry, windy, rocky altiplano allows to survive. They were living there on October 20, 1548, when Captain Alonso de Mendoza founded La Paz after a long quest for gold. It soon grew to a mining camp of 20,000 Europeans. By the turn of the 17th century, around the time Jamestown, Virginia, was settled, La Paz had grown tremendously due to its unique geographical position between the gold and silver mines in the Oruro-Potosí area and the seaports in Peru. Upon entering the 19th century, La Paz became the national capital of the emerging nation of Bolivia, rivaling the "official" capital of Sucre. Bolivia began its lengthy war of independence in 1809. The Spanish did not easily surrender the colony that, they claimed, had given them enough silver to build a bridge of the precious metal between themselves and their colony.

Sixteen years later, La Paz became part of a newly independent Bolivia and began another phase of what developed into a confusing, violent history. In 1879, Chile went to war with Bolivia (which was allied with Peru), only to cease hostilities in 1885 after Bolivia lost its entire coastline, the factor that, more than any other, has determined the country's underdevelopment and retarded its modernization in the 20th century. When the 1983 expiration of the Hundred Year Treaty of the War of the Pacific was in sight, many Bolivians thought there would be an attempt to recapture their corridor to the sea and, indeed, in 1987 Bolivia offered Chile money, land, and water rights in exchange for the corridor and the port of Antofagasta, but the offer was refused. "It is part of the Bolivian mentality," a chauffeur in La Paz explained. "We cannot rest until we have our port back again." Nevertheless, in early 1992, Bolivia signed an agreement with Peru that gave the once landlocked country access to the Pacific through the port of Ilo.

However, Bolivian politics are rife with rumor. At one time during the 1970s, newspaper headlines in La Paz declared: BRAZIL PREPARES TROOPS TO INVADE BOLIVIA as La Paz residents strolled past newsstands as unperturbed as some New Yorkers glancing at a headline reading MASS MURDER IN QUEENS. *Paceños* intuitively know they can't believe anything until it happens. Although the city's name means "The Peace," La Paz has seen more than 160 revolutions, coups (violent and bloodless), and various overthrows of government, thus more than 60 different presidents have served since Bolivia's independence in 1825. Recently, however, in spite of isolated incidents, Bolivia entered one of the more stable eras in its political history, and now enjoys a relatively strong economy, no foreign debt problem, and increasing stability of the value of the boliviano against the dollar. The biggest problems facing the government today are the powerful drug traffickers who smuggle out Bolivian coca, and the dramatic poverty suffered by some of the country's residents (especially elderly Indians and children). In addition, there has been a limited outbreak of cholera in the La Paz area. Travelers are advised to drink only bottled beverages and be sure that vegetables and shellfish are well cooked and eaten while hot. For additional information, contact the *Centers for Disease Control's International Travelers Hotline* (phone: 404-332-4559).

The national election of 1989 that put Jaime Paz Zamora in power was perhaps the most peaceful and least divisive to be held in South America in a decade. Paz Zamora actually finished third but, under Bolivian law, the Congress gets to choose the president from among the top three contenders if none get more than 50% of the vote. In this case, the congressional decision went to the Social Democrat, a 52-year-old sociologist who previously was vice president of the country.

A certain innocence on the part of its residents to the ugly ways of the rest of the world helps make La Paz among the safest cities in all of South America. Although there have been reports of theft by pickpockets or purse snatchers in some areas after dark (among them, Plaza San Francisco, near the train station, and neighborhoods around the outdoor markets), it is generally safe for residents and tourists to walk in virtually any part of the city during the day. (Be wary, however, of pickpockets and backpack and purse slashers on crowded city buses.) While La Paz is generally safe, there is a widespread problem with police corruption in the provinces. There are increasing reports of tourists — especially young travelers — being "fined" by police for any number of fictitious infractions. It is, therefore, important to always carry your passport with you. Another problem travelers may face is the chronic strikes, including those of the transportation system, that set back their itineraries. This is a country that requires patience.

Although the city is almost entirely confined to its huge hole in the altiplano and its disadvantageous geophysical location would seem to preclude further development, the master plan for the future of La Paz (and El Alto) projects an expansion in all directions: toward the Cordillera Real, into the valleys, to the shores of Lake Titicaca, across the altiplano, and downriver to the agricultural areas. In spite of the chaotic, fragmented quality of its political history, La Paz continues to reign as the undisputed queen of the Andes.

# LA PAZ AT-A-GLANCE

**SEEING THE CITY:** The road from El Alto Airport — the highest commercial airport in the world — leads along the edge of the altiplano, where the city below fills every level and most inclined pieces of land. At night, these layers of light increase the unreality of this already unbelievable scene; you can visually trace one main artery of lights. From the highway, the road becomes Avenida Montes, then changes its name to Plaza Pérez Velasco, Avenida Mariscal Santa Cruz, El Prado or Avenida 16 de Julio, Avenida Villazón, and Avenida Arce, continuing down hundreds of feet to become the main street of the Obrajes and Calacoto districts. The Cordillera Real is visible just a few miles from the center of the city. The northern approach to the city, coming from El Alto, is called Ceja del Alto ("the eyebrow," or edge of the altiplano). Behind this sprawling suburb, the altiplano stretches to the north, south, and west until it meets the western Cordillera Occidental (Western Range) about 80 miles (129 km) away, that extends from north to south, dividing Bolivia from Chile and Peru. On clear days, you can see this and much more. During the rainy season, you can observe the awesome altiplano storms approaching from as far as 150 miles away.

Another spot affording a terrific view of La Paz is the *Alaya* restaurant atop the *La Paz* hotel (see *Eating Out*). Take the elevator to the 15th floor and enjoy the spectacle of city lights over dinner — or simply take in the panoramic views provided by the large windows in an open area outside the dining room entry.

**SPECIAL PLACES:** The downtown *(centro)* area is generally defined as being split by the avenue that starts out as Mariscal Santa Cruz, then changes its name to 16 de Julio (also known as El Prado), then Avendia Villazón, and eventually, Avenida Arce. Along the avenue are the city's best hotels, shops, and restaurants. The area 3 blocks north of Avenida Mariscal Santa Cruz is where Plaza Murillo and its colonial buildings, as well as many of the city's museums, are located.

## DOWNTOWN

**El Prado** – This 3-block-long stretch of Avenida 16 de Julio (La Paz's main avenue) has a median divider of flowers, benches, fountains, and statues. Considered the center of La Paz, it is lined with trees and increasingly tall buildings. As the international sector of the city it contains many of its higher-priced shops. This is a great place for a stroll, day or night, and an appropriate spot to begin exploring. Although, relative to other large cities, nothing is expensive in La Paz (except rent, cars, and real estate), there is a big gap between tourist-trap prices and those in other sections of town. Browse here, by all means, but spend your money elsewhere, where you'll be sure to get better value. There are several popular cafés along this stretch, including *Eli's* and *Heladería KreMrik* (see *Eating Out*).

**Mercado Camacho (Camacho Market)** – An unobtrusive gate marks the entrance to the city's central market. As you make your way past the Indian women, wearing braids and bowlers, who sit on the ground selling cheese empanadas (also called *llauchas),* you'll file down a narrow set of steps lined with stalls displaying steel wool, canned goods, powdered soup, pickled onions, green and black olives, lard, yogurt, Brazil nuts, wooden doors, garlic, sponges, toilet paper, Horniman's tea, bananas, grapefruit, lemons, macaroni, powdered milk, cans of Nescafé, cheese, and sausages. And that's just the beginning! Indoors, a covered market sprawls under a tin roof where vegetables and straw baskets are piled high and rotund Aymara women hack off sections of meat to order. Outside the market, kiosks sell wine or malt ale *(cervecina)* in a concoction know as a *batido,* a froth made by whipping the beverage with an egg — it is recommended for the "weak or anemic." Hungry tourists tempted by the array of fresh vegetables, fruit, or meat should remember that the residents are immune to the local bacteria, but you aren't. Open from 9 AM daily, with Saturday the most active day. Av. Camacho and Calle Bueno.

**Iglesia San Francisco (San Francisco Church)** – This huge stone structure undoubtedly has one of the most curious interiors of any South American church. The intricately carved, gilded wooden altars are eye-catching, but more interesting still is the very eclectic assortment of statues and side naves. Inside the door, to the right, is a small, plain image of San Francisco illuminated by dozens of devotion candles. The prone figure encased in glass beside the main altar is also the church's patron saint. Much of the decor in the church is rather garish — the conquistador in blue silk mounted on a hobby horse, San Antonio de Padua and the Christ Child with neon halos, and gilt-framed mirrors strategically placed to reflect light during mass. Note the bloody statues of the crucified Christ; the graphic detail is characteristic of Bolivian colonial art. The church is also a good place to people watch. Indian women remove their bowlers when entering; you may see them later selling goods in the busy plaza outside. But do be alert to the pickpockets and bag snatchers here. Church open daily from 6:30 AM. Plaza San Francisco, Av. Mariscal Santa Cruz at Sagárnaga.

**Mercado de Hechicería (Indian Witchcraft Market)** – One of the most fascinating streets in the world, Calle Linares (between Santa Cruz and Sagárnaga) is lined with Indian women selling the coca leaves, herbs, amulets, and magic charms so important to their culture. Need a charm to protect you from traffic accidents? Just ask and the vendors will prepare one and explain how to use it. (Be courteous and respectful when you ask. This is serious business for the Indians, and giggling tourists who make fun of what they see may find the vendors unwilling to either sell or explain their wares.) You will see plenty of grotesque, dried fetuses of llamas along with slabs of llama lard; both are burned in offerings. Interspersed among the street vendors are some of the best artisan shops in the city, where silky-soft alpaca sweaters and wall hangings, musical instruments, tin and silver jewelry and dishes, small handicrafts, and leather goods are available for sale. Open daily. Calle Linares between Sagárnaga and Santa Cruz.

**Mercado Negro (The Black Market)** – The name is legitimate. This section of town is dedicated to the sale of contraband — the irony is that the tourism office boldly notes it on its map for visitors. Although clothing and imported shoes seem to dominate in this market, this is the place to buy Kellogg's corn flakes, US and Canadian whiskies, and Japanese electronic goods. Hot items right now are bootlegged music tapes, snack foods, Brazilian chocolates, and Argentine and Chilean wines. Although visitors probably won't need to make purchases from this area, a walk through the market gives a good idea of the types of goods that either are not imported legally into Bolivia or are normally very expensive here. Open daily at 10 AM. Calle Max Paredes and Graneros.

**Museo Nacional de Arte (National Art Museum)** – Built in 1775 for a Spanish nobleman, it is considered La Paz's finest baroque building and now houses 3 floors of paintings and sculptures. The first floor is dedicated to contemporary art, the second to colonial art by Andean painter Melchor Pérez de Holguín and his students, and the third floor has a permanent collection of Bolivian artists' work. Be sure to see the stone sculptures of Marina Nuñez del Prado whose respresentations of *campesinos* (peasants) have won her international acclaim. The museum courtyard has an alabaster fountain surrounded by plants and flowers. Open Tuesdays through Fridays from 9:30 AM to 12:30 PM and from 4 to 7 PM; mornings only on Saturdays. Admission charge. Calles Socabaya and Comercio off Plaza Murillo (phone: 371177).

**Plaza Murillo** – This plaza is built on the spot where La Paz revolutionary and national hero Pedro Domingo Murillo was hanged by the Spanish after leading a fight to free the city from colonial rule. The colonial plaza is bordered by the presidential palace, the legislature, and the cathedral. The monument at the center is fronted by a cement sculpture of an open book containing the manifesto signed by Murillo and other revolutionaries; it remains one of the most scathing criticisms of Spanish colonial rule found in any South American plaza. (An English translation can be found in *Casa de Murillo.*) As much the property of pigeons as of humans, Plaza Murillo stubbornly maintains its uniquely *paceño* architectural heritage, but not far away the tall buildings creep ever closer. Bordered by Calles Comercio, Ballivián, Ayacucho, and Socabaya.

**Palacio de Gobierno (Presidential Palace)** – Also known as the Palacio

Quemado (Burnt Palace), this is the place from which Bolivia's many presidents and dictators have run the country. Built more than 130 years ago and subsequently gutted twice by fire, it is not open to the public but it is worth eyeing from the outside. On Plaza Murillo.

**Catedral (Cathedral)** – Although massive in size, this cathedral is much simpler in decor than those found in other major Latin American cities. The modern altar is framed by marble pillars, and even more impressive than the mammoth pipe organ are the delicate crystal chandeliers and the brilliantly colored stained glass windows. To the right as you face the main entrance and halfway down the street is the entry to the Museum of Colonial Religious Art, which has a spectacular collection of sacred silver ornaments. The cathedral is open daily from 8 AM to noon and 2:30 to 7 PM; the museum is open Tuesdays through Fridays from 9:30 AM to 12:30 PM and 3 to 7 PM; Saturdays 9:30 AM to 12:30 PM. Admission charge. Cathedral entrance on Plaza Murillo; museum entrance at 432 Calle Socabaya (museum phone: 341920).

**Palacio Legislativo (Legislature Palace)** – This colonial-style building and the neighboring cathedral and presidential palace contain stone blocks from Tiahuanaco in their foundations. Although in a bit of disrepair, the chandeliers, marble stairway, and classical statues of the Legislature pay tribute to its opulent design. Tourists must show their passports to get a visitors' pass (stop by the building and officials will assign you a visiting time, although it may not be for the same day). If the Senate and Chamber of Deputies are in session, guests may sit in the visitor's section and listen in on the debate. No admission charge. Calle Ayacucho.

**Templete Arqueológico Semisubterráneo (Semi-subterranean Archaeological Temple)** – Functioning as an open-air museum, this below-ground, roofless temple/plaza features monoliths and other stone carvings rescued from the ruins at Tiahuanaco. If you can't make it to the ruins themselves, this will give you an idea of what you are missing. Open daily. No admission charge. To reach the temple, which is near the *Estadio Hernando Siles* (Hernando Siles Stadium), follow Calle Comercio downhill to its end. (Note: Calle Comercio changes its name to Calle Illimani as you near the site.)

**Pasaje de las Flores (Flower Passageway)** – Diagonally across the street from the *Casa de la Cultura,* and a block from the San Francisco artisans' market, is a tiny walkway containing one flower vendor after another. The kiosks lining the passageway all bear the names of different flowers. This is a great place for an aromatic escape from the bustle of busy Avenida Mariscal de Santa Cruz, and you can always buy a bouquet to brighten up your hotel room. Open daily.

**Parque Mirador Laykacota (Laykacota Lookout Park)** – The steps up to this hilltop park look steep, but it's worth the climb. At the top of the stairway is an impeccably maintained park with a children's playground, flower gardens, refreshment stands, and wacky sculptures of headless *Carnaval* revelers (use your own head to complete the picture and have your photo taken). The park is also one of the finest lookout spots from which to see the city. Open daily, 9 AM to 6 PM. Admission charge. Near the end of Av. del Ejército, Miraflores.

**Museo Costumbrista (Museum of Customs)** – This neo-colonial building is the first of four adjacent museums, and the place to buy tickets to all of them. Using miniature clay sculptures, this museum offers glimpses of the clothing, customs, and lifestyles in La Paz during the colonial and republican eras. Although there are dramatic depictions of the hanging of revolutionary leader Pedro Domingo Murillo and a scene of the Spaniards ordering Inca Tupaj Katari to be drawn and quartered, most of the exhibits are scenes from daily life in La Paz: the people who carried water to the homes of the wealthy, bread sellers, and Indian "curers" reading coca leaves. Also included are antique photographs of Calle Comercio, the Alameda (now El Prado), Plaza Venezuela, and other sections of the city. Open Tuesdays through Fridays from

9 AM to noon and 2:30 to 6 PM, Saturdays and Sundays from 10 AM to 1 PM. Admission charge. Calle Sucre at Calle Jaén (phone: 378478).

**Museo del Litoral Boliviano (Bolivian Coastal Museum)** – This small museum pays painful tribute to the coastal area (now Antofagasta, Chile) that once belonged to the formerly landlocked Bolivia. In addition to exhibiting memorabilia from the Pacific War, the military encounter in which Chile won coastal land from both Bolivia and Peru, the museum contains documents, letters, and maps from around the world showing the oceanfront that Bolivians still claim as their own more than 100 years later. Open Tuesdays through Fridays from 9 AM to noon and 2:30 to 6 PM, Saturdays and Sundays from 10 AM to 1 PM. Admission charge. Calle Jaén at Calle Sucre (no phone).

**Museo de Metales Preciosos Precolombinos (Museum of Pre-Columbian Precious Metals)** – A small but fine gold museum, it exhibits masks, ornaments, and figurines. Along with the gold collection and an exhibit area devoted to silver, there are expositions explaining how the Tiahuanaco and Wankarani Indians developed mining and smelting operations long before the arrival of the Spanish conquerors. Other exhibits pay tribute to the delicate craftsmanship of the pre-Hispanic civilizations. Another area of the building displays Inca and Tiahuanaco ceramics. Open Tuesdays through Fridays from 9 AM to noon and 2:30 to 6:30 PM, Saturdays and Sundays from 10 AM to 1 PM. Admission charge. 777 Calle Jaén (phone: 371470).

**Casa de Murillo (Murillo's House)** – The onetime home of Bolivia's hero offers an excellent exhibit of restored colonial furniture, religious art, and housewares as well as a quick lesson in Bolivian history. The house contains the "Conspiracy Room" where Pedro Domingo Murillo and other city leaders planned the July 16, 1809 insurrection against the Spanish in La Paz — before their liberation force of 800 men was cut down by a Spanish army of 5,000 sent from Peru. The museum also has a fascinating exhibit dedicated to herbs and folk superstitions, and a room full of costumes and masks used in *Carnaval* celebrations. Open Tuesdays through Fridays from 9 AM to noon and 2:30 to 6 PM, Saturdays and Sundays from 10 AM to 1 PM. Admission charge. Calle Jaén (phone: 375273).

**Museo de Etnografía y Folklore (Ethnography and Folklore Museum)** – Housed in the former home of the Count of Villaverde, this colonial structure had been sold and resold so many times that it had become a commercial outlet full of tiny stores by the time the state rescued it and reclaimed it for use as a museum in 1962. The building now contains an excellent exhibit concerning the Indian cultures in Bolivia, with information on clothing, music, and customs. The museum delivers a scathing message of reproach (including strong criticism of Christian missionaries) for the damage that has been inflicted on indigenous groups by exposure to the "civilized" world. Before leaving the museum, walk upstairs and take a look at the ornately carved wooden doors to the library. Open Mondays through Fridays, 9 AM to noon and 2:30 to 5 PM. Admission charge. 916 Calle Ingavi at Calle J. Sanjinés (phone: 358559).

**El Montículo** – At the southern edge of the area we consider "downtown," there is a hill that juts into La Paz. The park, a small church, and an observatory *(mirador)* provide a beautiful view and a quiet respite from the nearby hustle of the city. Calles Lisimaco Gutiérres and Presbitero Medina. It's best to take a taxi; there are no buses that go directly to the park.

## ENVIRONS

**Valle de la Luna and Malasilla (Valley of the Moon and Cactus Garden)** – "Why go to the moon when you can go to La Paz?" And well you might ask. Intriguing beige and red spires of earth and rock sculpted by wind and water surround you, reaching for the sky. Between them lie gorges, dangerous drops, and narrow, steep paths connecting different parts of the valley. If you visit before sunset, you'll see a dazzling burst of light and color. Just around a bend in the road from the Valley of the Moon, at a

## LA PAZ / At-a-Glance

slightly lower elevation, the municipal cactus garden contains a fascinating concentration of regional flora. Erosion is a real threat here — the average rainfall from December to March is 17 inches — and the garden was planted as a land reclamation project. Open daily. No admission charge. Take a cab to the suburb of Calacoto and follow Avenida José Ballivián to Malasilla (about 30 minutes) or take the Nos. 11 or 130 microbuses to Mallasa. A private cab that waits for you should charge around $25 for a 2-hour outing. Make sure you have sturdy walking shoes; you also may want to take along drinking water. Several La Paz tour agencies offer daily bus trips to the valley for about $20. Some include a drive through the area as part of the full-day excursion to Tiahuanaco.

**Achocalla** – This is actually a huge hole in the altiplano, rather like the one that cradles La Paz. It provides even better views of the mountains than you'll find within the city itself. It is a pleasant spot for walking; boats can be rented on the small lake. Bring a picnic lunch, since there are no high-quality restaurants. There are several ways to get here: Take a bus (either one that says Achocalla or others that stop there — ask the driver) that leaves from the corner of León de la Barra and Vicente Ochoa Streets; rent a taxi for the day (about $50, round trip); or take the main avenue uphill to El Alto and follow the signs to the Oruro road. Then, after about 10 minutes, take the turnoff to Koritambo. The one-way trip takes from an hour to an hour and a half.

**Chacaltaya** – The world's highest ski slope, at 17,716 feet, it is a 90-minute drive from downtown La Paz on a rugged road that is definitely not for the fainthearted. Four-wheel-drive vehicles are the best way to get here, as the rocky, pitted, twisting, hairpin-turning, mind-blowing road will destroy a normal car (and a city-trained driver's nerves). The scenery en route is simply dazzling: splendid panoramic views of the city nestled in its crater, getting smaller and smaller as you ascend; tiny stone shacks clinging to the mountains near running streams. Just before you arrive at the rudimentary ski tow lift and the rustic lodge hanging on the edge of a precipice, you will pass the Bolivian Institute of Cosmic Physics. It's operated by the Bolivian Institute for Atomic Energy, a complex of white buildings high on a ledge, overlooking some weird instruments set among the black rocks to measure ultraviolet radiation. If you enjoy the challenge of driving on empty, tough roads, the trip is definitely worth it, if only to experience the vertiginous thrill of standing — not flying — at an altitude of more than 17,000 feet. If you're a hard-core downhill skier and can handle the very fast, steep run here, contact the *Club Andino Boliviano* (1638 Calle México; phone: 324682) for information. The club takes groups skiing on weekends. The trips normally begin at 8 AM at the club office and you're back in La Paz by 6:30 PM. The ski season runs from December through April — the rainy season (at lower elevations) — after that, it's too cold. By the way, even if you're accustomed to the altitude in La Paz, be prepared for some dizziness and *soroche* at Chacaltaya. You need to be in top physical condition to ski here. Take the road to Tiahuanaco at El Alto, then turn right on Avenida Chacaltaya (avenida is a euphemism) and continue until you come to a stone indicator at a fork in the road, where you bear right. Chacaltaya is about 19 miles (30 km) from La Paz. They're guaranteed to be among the most unforgettable 19 miles you'll ever ride.

■ **EXTRA SPECIAL:** Visitors to La Paz can't help but be drawn to the majestic mountains that form the backdrop to the city. The Cordillera Real, or "royal range," provides innumerable opportunities to see the Andes at their mightiest, to take stunning photos, or just simply to experience the thrill of reaching an altitude where you can see jungles behind snow-capped mountains. You can rent a car and explore the Cordillera yourself, or consider booking a package with a local travel agency. (Most excursions leave about 9 AM, return by 3 PM, and include a box lunch and bilingual guide for a $22 charge.)

The tours take travelers by minibus up to the city of El Alto, overlooking La Paz, then on to Alto Lima where there is an open-air market on Thursdays and Sundays. Past the town is a miner's cemetery; graves are marked by stark white niches roofed with red clay tiles. This is a wonderful spot for photos — the 20,000-foot Huayna Potosí (where daredevils ski down glaciers) is behind the scene and a mountain lake is visible to the side. Also on this excursion is the Zongo Pass that separates Chacaltaya and Huayna Potosí (with a view of the Bolivian jungle in the distance), a reddish-violet lagoon colored by waste minerals from abandoned tin mines, an emerald-green lake, a hydroelectric plant, and droves of llamas. A recommended agency is *Plaza Tours* in the *Plaza Hotel,* 1789 Av. 16 de Julio (phone: 378322; fax: 343391).

# SOURCES AND RESOURCES

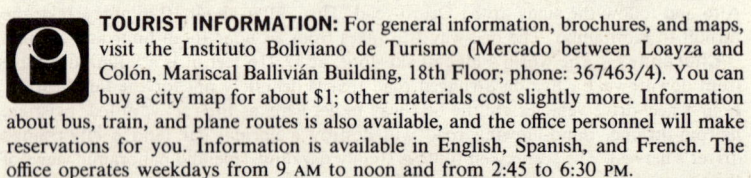

**TOURIST INFORMATION:** For general information, brochures, and maps, visit the Instituto Boliviano de Turismo (Mercado between Loayza and Colón, Mariscal Ballivián Building, 18th Floor; phone: 367463/4). You can buy a city map for about $1; other materials cost slightly more. Information about bus, train, and plane routes is also available, and the office personnel will make reservations for you. Information is available in English, Spanish, and French. The office operates weekdays from 9 AM to noon and from 2:45 to 6:30 PM.

Maps of Bolivia are rather hard to come by. The best bet is a road map costing about $3 that's available at *Los Amigos del Libro* (1315 Calle Mercado, across from the tourist bureau; phone: 320742; and 1603 Av. 16 de Julio; phone: 358164). You also can obtain maps from the Instituto Geográfico Militar (government cartography office; in the 1400 block of Av. 16 de Julio, beside the Banco de La Paz; phone: 364416). English-language tour books are few and far between, but an outstanding exception is the Spanish-English *Guía Turística* (Tourist Guide). Published by the Bolivian Institute of Tourism, it offers information on interesting sites, history, hotels, and more. It can be obtained for about $4 at the tourist office and at *Los Amigos del Libro.* Another recommended resource is *An Insider's Guide to Bolivia,* edited by Peter McFarren, the local *New York Times* correspondent and La Paz resident. It costs about $18.

**Local Coverage** – *Presencia, El Diario,* and *Ultima Hora* (all morning dailies) are the three top newspapers. *Selecciones Librería, Los Amigos del Libro,* and *Best Seller* (a news kiosk on Av. 16 de Julio near Citibank) sell *Time* and *Newsweek.* US newspapers, particularly the *Miami Herald,* are widely available on the date of publication or a day late. The *Plaza* hotel has cable TV service, which provides guestrooms with US network news programs and Cable News Network broadcasts.

The US Embassy is located in Edificio Banco Popular del Perú at Calle Colón at the corner of Mercado (phone: 350251).

Because of isolated terrorist incidents against US citizens, travelers to Bolivia are advised to contact the consular section of the US Embassy (phone: 320494) upon arrival to get the latest information.

**TELEPHONE:** The city code for La Paz is 2. When calling from within Bolivia, dial 02 before the local number. The country code for Bolivia is 591.

**CLIMATE AND CLOTHES:** Although we have discussed altitude sickness in passing in the essay, above, and in *Staying Healthy*, GETTING READY TO GO, be aware that this is an inevitable factor to consider when planning a trip. Altitude and overall human health is a relatively ignored subject. One important component of those symptoms attributable to high altitude is psychosomatic, but there is definitely an important physical element. People who have come from sea level or lower altitudes to live in La Paz attest to an acclimation period that ranges from 6 months to a year. It takes about that long for the red blood cell count to increase sufficiently. Since there is less air pressure at 12,000 feet, the altitude of Plaza Murillo, less oxygen enters the bloodstream, water boils at a lower temperature, and the atmosphere is drier and more electric. If you intend to explore the city and neighboring countryside, you should practice lung-enlarging exercises before your trip. Some heart accelerators are sold in La Paz, but these should only be used in emergencies. Before beginning your trip, you may want to consult your doctor. Most hotels supply coca tea (ask for *maté de coca*) to perk you up. If you have severe respiratory or heart disorders, you should avoid La Paz entirely. As a rule, the better your physical health, the more thorough and enjoyable your visit will be. Note, however, that travelers coming from Cuzco, Peru (via the train to Puno and across Lake Titicaca — a popular routing), will be acclimated to the altitude and should have little discomfort in La Paz and environs.

The temperature throughout the year ranges from 30F ($-1$C) to 70F (22C), with about a 20F (7C) difference between sun and shade. Evenings are cold enough to require a sweater almost every night of the year. It is perceptibly chillier at El Alto than in the city itself. You will need much warmer clothing from May through August. The winter months, June through September, are very cold and clear, with June and July the coldest. The climate in the mountains is comparable to that of the Arctic. High-altitude sun exposure, windburn, and snow blindness occur frequently, so bring sunscreen and sunglasses. The meteorological conditions do not follow the patterns to which you are accustomed at sea level. The rainy season starts in November and lasts until the middle of March, with cold torrential downpours and chilling fog throughout the season. Although storms are generally brief, weather changes are sudden so be sure to take a sweater and rain gear if you go out on a touring expedition. Spring temperatures are more moderate than those of the autumn and winter months, but La Paz can be uncomfortably cool if you are not prepared. The most beautiful days are generally in April and May and, if you don't mind the cold, June and July.

**GETTING AROUND: Bus** – The least expensive form of transport, buses fall into two categories: *micros* and the larger *colectivos*. Try to avoid *colectivos*, especially during the lunchtime rush hour, around noon. *Micros* and *colectivos* run until midnight, officially, but it is unlikely you will find one after 10 PM.

**Taxi** – There are two kinds of taxis: *trufis*, which run along an established route, stopping to discharge and pick up passengers so that the car remains full, and taxis. Sometimes a taxi driver will stop to pick up another fare while someone is in the car, but the cabbie will drop the first passenger at his or her destination first. *Trufis* cost about 50¢ and are easily distinguishable by the colored flags they display on their front bumpers. Taxis have red license plates and a white and black stripe runs around the car. If you want an "express" taxi — one reserved for you alone — bargain with the driver before hiring him or her. La Paz's cab drivers can be pretty fierce when it comes to overcharging gringos. Check with the Tourist Information Desk at El Alto Airport or with your hotel reception desk to find out the going rate for airport service. At press time it was about $10, but varies slightly depending on the time of day and quantity of luggage. If possible, have someone who works at the airport negotiate the fare for

## 352  LA PAZ / Sources and Resources

you before stepping into the cab. *Contrastur* minibus service (phone: 782570) also operates every half hour until 8 PM between the airport and the plazas along El Prado; the fare is less than $1. (If it's raining, a cab might be a better option. Luggage is stored on the roof of the minibuses.)

You also can call a radio taxi for private car service to anywhere in the city and its environs. Among the best are *Su Taxi* (phone: 355555 and 366666) and *El Chasqui* (phone: 355559). A private taxi to Tiahuanaco will cost about $50. A full-day tour with a private driver, guide, lunch, and admission fees will cost between $50 and $70 per person, and can be booked with most La Paz travel agencies. Only *Transturin, Ltda.* (1295 Mariscal Santa Cruz; phone: 320445; fax: 391162) and *Crillón Tours* (1223 Camacho; phone: 374566/7; in the US, 305-358-5353; fax in the US: 305-372-0053) offer combined bus/boat transportation via Lake Titicaca to Puno, Peru (to connect with the train to Cuzco). *Transturin* also can arrange a seat on a tourist bus between La Paz and Puno.

**Car Rental** – A jeep or equivalent four-wheel-drive vehicle is essential when tackling Bolivian roads, though driving yourself is not recommended. If you insist, *Oscar Crespo Rent-a-Car* (1865 Av. Simón Bolívar; phone: 350974) can provide Toyota Land Cruisers, Toyota sedans, Volkswagens, and other types of autos. *International Rent-A-Car* (1942 Calle Federico Zuazo; phone: 342406) rents cars and jeeps, as does *National Car Rental* (1935 Calle Federico Zuazo; phone and fax: 376581). *Kolla Motors* (502 Calle R. Gutiérrez; phone: 351701), rents jeeps. For more information on car rentals, contact *Automóvil Club Boliviano* (2993 Av. 6 de Agosto; phone: 326132 or 355502). Current jeep prices average between $55 and $75 a day, (or about $200 a week) — with some rates even higher; cars, $40 daily plus mileage. You need an international driver's license to drive in Bolivia; it can be obtained from any automobile association or affiliate in the US or South America (although it is more convenient to get the license before you go).

**Train** – Riding a train through the Andes is an unbelievable experience. Although it is not by any means the fastest way to travel long distances, a train is probably the best way to get a leisurely look at the countryside and people. Don't expect to get where you're going on time, either (see *Traveling by Train*, GETTING READY TO GO). Railroads link most parts of Bolivia, Peru, and Chile. The primary difficulty is the irregularity of service and frequent schedule changes. Don't count on any printed schedule, but instead, for information check with Estación Central (Av. Manco Capac; phone: 373068). A train goes to the northern frontier of Chile: *Ferrocarril Arica–La Paz*. The fare in Pullman class (definitely recommended) is no more than $20, and information and tickets are available at the main station. There is also a "ferrobus" — a gas-powered vehicle that runs on rail tracks — connecting La Paz, Oruro, Potosí, and Cochabamba three times a week. The tickets can be purchased in advance at the railroad office (1920 Plaza del Estudiante; phone: 367537), *Exprinter* (Edificio Herrmann, Av. 16 de Julio; phone: 355926), and *Zingara Travel* (1280 Av. Mariscal Santa Cruz; phone: 326287) in La Paz.

**SPECIAL EVENTS:** La Paz hosts many small festivals and fairs throughout the year. Two particularly noteworthy events are the *Feria Alacitas* (Alacitas Fair) from January 24 to February 7, which is dedicated to the Ekeko good-luck god. Miniatures of the god — a jolly fat man covered in tiny sacks of sugar and flour, money, and cooking utensils and often smoking a cigarette — can be found in shops all over the city. People believe that you can buy a miniature image of anything from a cow to a car at the *Alacitas Fair* and, if Ekeko favors you, you'll have the real thing by the end of the year. However, the very best luck is reserved for those who receive an Ekeko statue as a gift. In addition, there is the *Festival del Gran Poder* (Master of Great Power) that is held in June, and marked by processions of masked dancers throughout the town.

## LA PAZ / Sources and Resources

**MUSEUMS:** La Paz has a number of fine museums, most of which are listed in *Special Places*. You might also want to visit the following:

**Museo Arqueológico de Tiwanaku (Tiahuanaco Archaeological Museum)** – In a building reminiscent of the ancient pyramids, this museum displays a good collection of pre-Columbian artifacts. Open Tuesdays through Fridays, 9 AM to noon and 2:30 to 6:30 PM; Saturday mornings. Admission charge. On Calle Tiwanaku, at the corner of Federico Zuazo (phone: 329624).

**Museo de Instrumentos Nativos (Museum of Native Instruments)** – A collection of original Indian string, wind, and percussion instruments. Open Mondays through Fridays from 10 AM to noon and 2 to 6 PM, but it's best to call ahead. Admission charge. At the beginning of the *Indian Witchcraft Market* at Calle Sagárnaga and Linares (phone: 355776).

**Museo Mineralógico (Minerology Museum)** – In a country so dependent on mineral exports, it is not surprising that this collection is here. This museum was closed at press time for renovations. Call for reopening date and schedule of hours. No admission charge. At 6 de Agosto and Belisario Salina (phone: 365880).

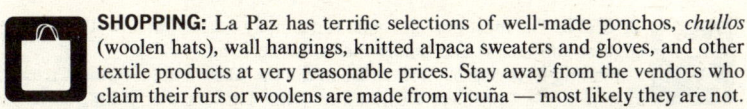

**SHOPPING:** La Paz has terrific selections of well-made ponchos, *chullos* (woolen hats), wall hangings, knitted alpaca sweaters and gloves, and other textile products at very reasonable prices. Stay away from the vendors who claim their furs or woolens are made from vicuña — most likely they are not. If they are, the product violates international laws aimed at protecting this endangered cousin of the llama, and may be confiscated at either US or South American customs. Also beware of street vendors who approach you with "antiques," which they often display from inside an open coat or wrapped in newspaper. It doesn't take an antiquarian to know that most likely the ceramics are fakes; in the rare event that they turn out to be authentic, their sale is against the law. As mentioned in *Special Places*, Calle Linares, where the *Indian Witchcraft Market* is located, has some of the best shops. Near the San Francisco church, across the street from the *Casa de la Cultura*, are two large artisans' markets. *Mercado Artesanal de San Francisco* has everything from silver spoons and devil dancers' masks to leather goods and fur jackets; next door, *Galería Artesanal de Paula* offers slightly higher-quality goods at higher prices. Fine gold and silver jewelry is displayed at the better hotels. It's wise to price them first, then shop around for similar merchandise at lower cost. But beware of silver plate that is sometimes passed off as sterling at the less pricey establishments. Commercial outlets usually don't open until 9:30 AM, but stay open at least until 7 PM, with a 2-hour siesta at midday.

***Los Amigos del Libro*** – A wide choice of travel books on Bolivia in English and Spanish is offered at this friendly shop. There also are US magazines ranging from the *Smithsonian* to *Premiere*, maps, English-language paperbacks, and high-quality postcards. Main store at 1315 Calle Mercado (phone: 320742) and branches at 1603 Av. 16 de Julio (phone: 358164) and at the airport (no phone).

***Fotrama*** – This weaving cooperative outside Cochabamba has two stores in La Paz that sell its finely knit and woven sweaters, hats, blankets, shawls, and gloves. The clothing is made from alpaca, llama, and sheep's wool using traditional weaving techniques. In the lobby of the *La Paz Hotel*, Av. Arce (phone: 356950) and at 1405 Av. 16 de Julio (phone: 325222).

***Icono*** – Fine alpaca sweaters and scarves in original designs, plus contemporary silver jewelry with pre-Columbian motifs. Sweaters have dollar price tags; all are hand-knit. Edificio Hoy, 2170 Av. 6 de Agosto (phone: 374900).

***Intiwara*** – A good spot for alpaca knits. In the *La Paz Hotel*, Av. Arce (phone: 327972).

***King's*** – For fine jewelry designs in silver and gold inspired by Tiahuanaco, Inca, Moche, and Nazca motifs, this is the place to stop. Adjacent to the *Sucre Hotel* at 1636 Av. 16 de Julio (phone: 328178).

**Maderma** – Alpaca sweaters, *Christmas* tree ornaments, a fine selection of books on Bolivia in English and Spanish, postcards, contemporary woven vests, and T-shirts are available at this friendly store. 1616 Av. 16 de Julio (phone: 352385).

**Mi Joyita** – A wide range of silver jewelry and gifts at exceptional prices are sold here. Silver dinnerware, filigree jewelry, ornaments, desk accessories, and good luck charms are just a few examples. There also are objects in bronze, copper, and pewter, and engraving is available. Edificio Litoral, Av. Mariscal Santa Cruz near Calle Colón (phone: 320442).

**Millma** – Upscale, exclusive New York–designed, high-quality, high-fashion alpaca knits for men and women at about a third of the US price. Two locations: *Plaza Hotel*, Av. 16 de Julio (phone: 321831) and Calle 225 Sagárnaga (phone: 342247). You can also visit the *Millma* factory (which was being relocated at press time) to see the knits being woven. Inquire at the shops for more information.

**Tiendas Bolivianas** – Quartered in a restored colonial house, with good sweaters, leather products, and regional crafts, including musical instruments. 2142 Av. Arce, across from the *La Paz Hotel* (phone: 326111).

**SPORTS:** The most popular sport is definitely soccer *(fútbol)*. The world's highest golf course and tennis courts are here, too.

**Fishing** – Great trout and catfish live in the lakes of the Negruni-Chacapa region of the Cordillera Real and in Lake Titicaca. For fishing on Lake Titicaca, stop by the *Yacht Club Boliviano* in Huatajata on the lake (phone: 811669). You will need a fishing license, valid for 1 year, from the Ministry of Agriculture (Av. Camacho), or from the US Embassy. Bring two passport-size photographs for the license.

**Golf** – *Golf Club Malasilla* has the world's highest 18-hole course. Be careful choosing clubs — there's less air resistance here, the ball carries farther, and it's easy to overshoot. Follow the road to Valle de la Luna, and bear right just before the tunnel. Malasilla (phone: 326111).

**Hunting** – Again, you need a license from the US Embassy or the Ministry of Agriculture. If you want to meet other hunters and anglers, go to the building in front of the *Golf Club* in Malasilla, which houses the *Club de Caza y Pesca* (Hunting and Fishing Club; no phone). There is also duck shooting on Lake Titicaca.

**Mountain Climbing** – During the dry season (from April to October), many expeditions leave for Huayna Condoriri and Mt. Illimani. The other mountains require more time and are not as popular. For information, contact the *Club Andino Boliviano* (1638 Calle México; phone: 324682), which also can provide hints on hiking and camping. The mailing address is 1368 Casilla in La Paz. *Tour Adventure World Agency* (*TAWA;* 701 Calle Rosendo Gutiérrez; phone: 391175) offers climbing trips and an extensive variety of treks . Another operator specializing in mountain climbing is *Expediciones Guarachi* (Edificio Santa Ana, Office 314, Plaza Alonso de Mendoza, phone: 320901).

**Sailing** – When the weather's good, the world's highest lake has brisk winds and cobalt blue waters. Boats can be hired from the *Yacht Club Boliviano* in Huatajata on Lake Titicaca (phone: 811669). You also can rent boats at Chúa on the lake (no phone).

**Skiing** – The world's highest slope, at Mt. Chacaltaya, is unusual by Bolivian standards because it has a lift. It is primitive, but preferable to walking up. (See *Special Places*, above.) A new ski station is at Mt. Mururata, which is an hour from La Paz and has a 9-month season. *Club Andino Boliviano* (1638 Calle México; phone: 324682) arranges ski outings to both spots, as well as to Condoriri. It also has a ski lodge set on a precipice of Chacaltaya. The weekend bus ride, ski rentals, and lift ticket cost about $25. The *Crillón* hotel also arranges day trips for its guests who are skiers.

**Soccer** – Soccer matches are held year-round, usually on Sundays, at *Estadio Hernando Siles* (Hernando Siles Stadium; across from the *Templete Arqueológico Semisubterráneo* at the end of Calle Comercio away from the downtown area). The newspapers and tourism office publicize the starting times.

**Swimming** – Mountain lakes, such as Titicaca, are not recommended because the water is always icy cold. *Golf Club Malasilla* also has the world's highest pool. The *Automóvil Club Boliviano* (Av. Ballivián at the corner of Calle 12, Calacoto; phone: 792126) has a pool. *Club Alemán* (German Club) has a pool, tennis courts, riding stables, and a soccer field. It's in Calacoto, near Calle 23, but you'd best call for directions (phone: 793999). The *La Paz* hotel (2100 block of Av. Arce; phone: 356950 and 356956) and the *Plaza* hotel (1789 Av. 16 de Julio; phone: 378310 to 378313) have small indoor pools for guests' use.

**Tennis** – Excellent for people with hearty lungs who prefer running after balls to hanging off cliffs, this sport is gaining in popularity, with a number of clubs now in operation. The world's highest is *Club de Tenis La Paz* (8450 Av. Arequipa, La Florida; phone: 793930). Also, *Sucre Tennis Club* (1001 Av. Busch; phone: 324483).

**THEATER:** Daily newspapers carry listings of performances. The *Teatro Municipal* (Municipal Theater; Calle G. Sanjinés; phone: 375245) presents operas and, occasionally, very good performances in Spanish (although the city has no theater company of its own). This is also where you can see Bolivia's national ballet and symphony. *Casa de la Cultura* (House of Culture; Av. Santa Cruz at the corner of Potosí; phone: 374668) has a theater that seats nearly 300. It also presents movies on Monday nights, film festivals, and changing displays of art and handicrafts. Good movies also are shown at the *Cinemateca Boliviana* (at the corner of Pichincha and Indaburo; phone: 325346). For new plays in Spanish, the *Tesla* is a good place to go (*Los Escudos* restaurant; phone: 322028).

**MUSIC:** The *peñas* — nightclubs specializing in Andean music and dance — offer the best regional music typically on Thursday, Friday, and Saturday nights. These shows are characterized by music played on reed flutes (*quenas* and *zampoãs*), accompanied by the ukelele-like instrument called the *charango*. *Peña de Cinco Estrellas,* an excellent 2-hour show featuring ethnic music from all over Bolivia, is staged each Friday at the *Plaza* hotel's *Penthouse* bar. Reservations are necessary (phone: 378310). Reservations also are necessary for what is usually a very rewarding night at perhaps the most authentic club, *Peña Naira* (161 Sagárnaga; phone: 325736), where the shows start at 10 PM, and at *Marka Tambo* (710 Calle Jaén; phone: 340416). Other good places for folk music are *Casa del Corregidor* (1040 Calle Murillo; phone: 363633), and *Peña Los Escudos* (Av. Mariscal Santa Cruz at the corner Ayacucho; phone: 322028). The *Casa de la Cultura* (House of Culture; Av. Santa Cruz at the corner of Potosí; phone: 374668) sponsors folk and classical music recitals.

**NIGHTCLUBS AND NIGHTLIFE:** The nightclub scene in La Paz can be a bit disappointing for travelers seeking trendy or chic spots. Disco clubs move in and out of favor and existence at a fast clip. A good spot to try is *Baccara* (1824 Av. 20 de Octubre; phone: 344039). Visitors staying at hotels have the benefit of gathering places such as the nightclubs at the *La Paz* (Av. Arce; phone: 356950); the *Arcón de Oro* at the *Plaza* (Paseo de Prado; phone: 378311); and the *Gloria* hotel's *Sky Room* (909 Calle Potosí; phone: 370010).

# BEST IN TOWN

**CHECKING IN:** Until several years ago, La Paz suffered from a frightful shortage of hotel rooms. But now there is a wide range of accommodations, making it relatively easy to book a room. Expect to pay between $95 and $125 for a double room in a hotel categorized as very expensive; between $60 and $95 for a double room in a hotel listed as expensive; between $35 and $60 at a place in the moderate category; and under $35 in an inexpensive place. All prices include tax and service. All telephone numbers are in the 2 city code unless otherwise indicated.

*La Paz* – Formerly the *Sheraton*, this high-rise has a flashy elegance. The lobby houses shops, newsstands, a travel agency, a foreign exchange desk, postal desk, telephone office, and bar. Fitness center facilities include a pool and sauna. Highlights of the ground floor decor are the polished rust-red granite floor, walls, and columns that were cut in Italy, and a $78,000 chandelier made in Vienna that is a twin to the one hanging in New York's *Metropolitan Opera*. The 345 rooms have great views of Mt. Illimani and the surrounding city. Although the hotel is well kept, service can be erratic, and it is a long walk uphill to the touristic highlights of La Paz. Do try its supper club/restaurant *Alaya* (see *Eating Out*). In the 2100 block of Av. Arce (phone: 356950 or 356956). Very expensive.

*Plaza* – Billing itself as the highest luxury hotel in the world, this is the most expensive hotel in town, and a lovely one indeed. It has 200 well-appointed rooms and suites with central heating, private bath, phone, and the only cable TV in any La Paz hotel (broadcasting US network news and CNN programs) — which is perhaps why TV anchor Peter Jennings stayed here on a recent visit. Facilities include Turkish baths and sauna, plus a heated indoor swimming pool. There's a good choice of bars and restaurants (see *Utama* in *Eating Out*), including those with top-floor views, and a shopping mall downstairs. The location is ideal. 1789 Av. 16 de Julio (phone: 378310 to 378313; *Utell International* in the US, 800-44-UTELL; fax: 343391). Very expensive.

*Libertador* – The best of the somewhat moderate hostelries, this 53-room place is well located in the commercial center. If you are looking for a downtown location, it leaves little to be desired and the *Sky Room* restaurant offers a good view of the city. 1421 Calle Obispo Cárdenas (phone: 343362). Expensive to moderate.

*Presidente* – With subdued contemporary decor, this 104-room luxury establishment has 2 roof-top restaurants, a disco, a complete health club, indoor pool and sauna, a 24-hour coffee shop, meeting and convention facilities, and a gallery of boutiques. 920 Calle Potosí (phone: 340675; fax: 355015). Moderate.

*Sucre Palace* – Centrally located, this 100-room property is a good value — although there are occasionally hot water problems. A small restaurant is on the premises. 1636 Av. 16 de Julio (phone: 363453 or 363409). Moderate.

*Crillón* – A good bet outside the priciest category, this 70-room hotel maintains a high standard. The lobby's polished floor and mirrored walls give it an inviting feel. The English-speaking staff at the front desk is extremely helpful and pleasant. The restaurant is good, too. 2478 Plaza Isabel La Católica (phone: 352121 through 352130). Moderate to inexpensive.

*La Estancia* – Well located, this hostelry has its own *parrillada* restaurant and is carefully attended by its owner. The 14 rooms are somewhat basic, but relatively modern, clean, and carpeted; all have private baths with warm water. 1559 Calle México (phone: 324308). Moderate to inexpensive.

*Eldorado* – Newly renovated from top to bottom, with a marble lobby and 80 clean, refurbished rooms, this conveniently located hotel features pleasant service and offers good value for the price. There's a restaurant, bar, and laundry service. Bilingual business assistance is available on request. Breakfast is included. It's named for the legendary Inca Man of Gold. Av. Villazón (phone: 363403; in the US through *SRS,* 800-223-5652; fax: 391438). Inexpensive.

**España** – Built in what was once an elegant turn-of-the-century mansion, the 23 rooms are adequate and clean, and all have private bath with warm — not hot — water (some of the beds are lumpy, though). Ask to see those rooms opening onto the back courtyard, which have polished wood floors and are by far the nicest. Breakfast is included in the room rate. 2074 Av. 6 de Agosto, a block from San Andrés University (phone: 354643). Inexpensive.

**Gloria** – Just across the street from the *Casa de la Cultura* (House of Culture; see *Theater,* above), this has a flashy, uninviting lobby, but 85 attractive, well-kept rooms (all with bath) and a top-floor restaurant with a lovely view of the Plaza San Francisco. A very good value and a fine location. 909 Calle Potosí at the corner of Calle G. Sanjinés (phone: 370010 through 370018). Inexpensive.

**Milton** – A good bet for the traveler on a budget, especially for its location. The 53 rooms can best be described as "okay," but the staff is friendly and helpful. A few blocks above Plaza San Francisco at 1124 Calle Illampu (phone: 368003). Inexpensive.

**Residencial Rosario** – Popular with the international backpacking crowd, this newly expanded property near the *Indian Witchcraft Market* is a real bargain. A labyrinth of cobblestone courtyards and balconies with flowering plants make it a pleasant place to stay. Other features include clean, comfortable rooms with hot water, a friendly staff, a casual restaurant (serving breakfast and dinner), and a good travel agency on the premises. Some rooms with shared baths are available to the budget traveler. 704 Calle Illampu (phone: 325348). Inexpensive.

**Sagárnaga** – Another good budget bet, this one is in the Aymara quarter, not far from Plaza San Francisco. It has an attractive lobby decorated with bright Inca motifs and a small restaurant. Some of the 35 rooms have baths but none have heat. 326 Calle Sagárnaga (phone: 350252 and 358757). Inexpensive.

**EATING OUT:** Even though La Paz has not been a small town for some time, it has, until fairly recently, been the kind of place where most people ate at home. But with more travelers and businesspeople heading here, the range of eating establishments has widened considerably, and *paceños* are eating out more and more. Not only are new restaurants opening, old ones are improving. Many restaurants tend to imitate Argentine cuisine, and delicious *parrillada* (barbecue) can be found almost everywhere. Restaurants usually open just before noon for lunch, then close promptly at 2 PM; they reopen for evening meals at 6 PM. Informal eateries often remain open throughout the day. Note that many places in the lower price range do no accept credit cards.

Expect to pay at least $40 for dinner for two, not including drinks or tip, at a restaurant categorized as expensive; between $20 and $40 at a place in the moderate category; under $20 at an inexpensive place. Taxes are included. All telephone numbers are in the 2 city code unless otherwise indicated.

**Alaya** – A handsome supper club atop the *La Paz* hotel, it offers an international menu, good service, and dancing far into the night. Also on the top floor is a lovely sunken bar and, from every side, the vistas are dazzling. Open daily. Reservations advised. Major credit cards accepted. 2100 block of Av. Arce (phone: 356950). Expensive.

**Arcón de Oro** – The *Plaza's* top-quality dining room, and one of the two best bets in town for a meal in the continental tradition. The rich, deep-red walls and carpet create an atmosphere of luxury. The menu is about 70% fish and seafood, and if you order the salmon trout from Lake Titicaca, it's possible to experience the best of the European and South American cuisines in one dish. Week-long gastronomic festivals highlight other cuisines every 2 months. Closed Sundays. Reservations advised. Major credit cards accepted. *Plaza Hotel,* Av. 16 de Julio, Paseo del Prado (phone: 378310). Expensive.

**Diego's** – The menu is international at this sophisticated bistro. Open daily. Reservations advised. Major credit cards accepted. 2123 Calle Capitán Ravelo (phone: 377173). Expensive.

**El Refugio** – This very small restaurant serves international specialties and is known for its *parrillada* of Argentine beef. Open daily. Reservations advised. Major credit cards accepted. 2458 Av. 20 de Octubre (phone: 355651). Expensive.

**Club Alemán** – Not to be confused with the private club of the same name, this place is located right behind the *Plaza* hotel. The extensive menu offers everything from Lake Titicaca trout to sauerkraut and rye bread, but don't be surprised if the preparation is a bit heavy-handed. The club-like dining room is a popular lunch spot. Open daily. Reservations advised. Major credit cards accepted. Calle Carlos Bravo (phone: 324397). Expensive to moderate.

**Maison La Suisse and La Suisse Gourmet** – Just across from the *La Paz* hotel are two restaurants at one address. Downstairs at *Maison La Suisse,* you'll find excellent fondue and other classic Swiss specialties. The *Suisse Gourmet,* upstairs, features meats cooked on individual tabletop grills. Closed weekends. Reservations advised. Major credit cards accepted. 2164 Av. Arce (phone: 353150). Expensive to moderate.

**La Paz** – This restaurant has quickly taken its place among the most popular in town. Although some international dishes can be ordered here, its forte is found in the many local specialties offered. Open daily. Reservations advised. Major credit cards accepted. 19 Goitia (phone: 343291). Expensive to moderate.

**Utama** – On the top floor of the *Plaza* hotel, this dining room offers spectacular views of the city. The menu features some Bolivian specialties and excellent fish and meats from the grill. Try the grilled Lake Titicaca trout topped with a sauce of white grapes and blackened butter. Open daily for lunch and dinner. Reservations advised. Major credit cards accepted. Av. 16 de Julio, Paseo del Prado (phone: 378310). Expensive to moderate.

**La Carreta** – One of several popular Argentine-style grill restaurants, it specializes in *parrillada* that keeps coming and coming to your table on wooden planks. Salad is wheeled to your table on a cart so you can choose what you like. Bring your appetite. This spot is a lunchtime favorite for business executives. Service is friendly. Open daily. Reservations unnecessary. Major credit cards accepted. 32 Calle Batallón Colorados (phone: 355891). Moderate.

**Casa del Corregidor** – In one of the oldest colonial houses of La Paz, this is a favorite place to come for European cooking and not too heavily spiced local dishes. It's also nice for listening to folk music in the evenings, except Sundays. Open weekdays for lunch and dinner; weekends for dinner only. Reservations unnecessary. Major credit cards accepted. 1040 Murillo (phone: 363633). Moderate.

**Giorgíssimo** – Popular for light lunches, snacks, and drinks, it caters to an international clientele — resident and traveling. Open daily for lunch and dinner. Reservations unnecessary, but it's a good idea to go early to be sure to get a table. No credit cards accepted. Calle Loayza at the corner of Av. Camacho (phone: 324456). Moderate.

**Naira** – Considered by many to be the most typically Bolivian restaurant in La Paz. The atmosphere is almost medieval — family-style dining at long wooden tables

## LA PAZ / Best in Town 359

set with locally made pottery. Bolivian cuisine features Andean potatoes and corn in a variety of soups and casseroles. The food itself is bland; the sauces, *picante* (very hot). *Escabeche,* a boiled chicken dish, will not harm your palate. After dinner, take a walk next door to the *peña,* featuring a dazzling variety of folk music and dance groups. Open daily, except Sundays, for lunch and dinner. Reservations advised. No credit cards accepted. 161 Calle Sagárnaga (phone: restaurant 350530; peña 325736). Moderate.

**Los Escudos** – A Munich-type beer hall with an inexpensive fixed-price lunch and evening folklore shows on Fridays and Saturdays, it is open for lunch and dinner every day but Sunday. Reservations unnecessary. Major credit cards accepted. In *Edificio Club de La Paz,* 1201 Av. Mariscal Santa Cruz (phone: 322028 and 350586). Moderate to inexpensive.

**Café La Paz** – For the best espresso in town, this quaint, old downtown café is the place to go. A favorite haunt of politicians, business executives, and labor leaders, this was the spot where Nazi war criminal Klaus Barbie often lingered — before he was expelled from Bolivia. Drop by for iced coffee, cake, or a light meal — try the *salteñas* (spicy, juicy meat turnovers). Open daily. No reservations. No credit cards accepted. At the corner of Ayacucho and Camacho (phone: 350202). Inexpensive.

**La Casa de los Paceños** – Upstairs in a building in the historic colonial district, this is the spot for Bolivian food and a favorite among *paceños.* Wood floors and hand-hewn beams add to the atmosphere. The food is excellent and the owners extend an exceptional welcome to all. Open daily for lunch and dinner. Reservations unnecessary. No credit cards accepted. Calle Sucre at the corner of Pichincha (phone: 328018). Inexpensive.

**Chez Lacoste** – Housed in an old colonial mansion, this French bistro is the talk of La Paz. Decor is elegant and subdued in soft apricot and green, and the kitchen staff's expertise complements the ambience. The emphasis is on fresh local fruits, vegetables, and fish. Open daily. Reservations unnecessary. No credit cards accepted. 2604 Av. 6 de Agosto (phone: 324667). Inexpensive.

**Eli's** – An institution for more than half a century, this is a simple, hearty café in which Bolivian food is served to a lively clientele of *paceños* and tourists under the watchful eye of US expatriate and longtime La Paz resident, Señor Harry. Steaks with an egg on top, hamburgers, and even chicken soup are available. If you want to meet the locals, make this the stop for your Sunday midday meal. The breakfasts and pastries here also are worth trying; the Dutch apple cake is a real treat. Open daily for lunch and dinner. No reservations. No credit cards accepted. 1497 Av. 16 de Julio (phone: 355468 and 352216). Inexpensive.

**Heladería Il Fiore** – Just across from the university, so you know it has to be good and inexpensive. A wide selection of Italian ice cream flavors, but the best deal here is the *almuerzo familiar* (home-cooked lunch). For about $2 there's salad, soup, a hot main dish, light dessert, and coffee or tea. Open daily from 8 AM to midnight. No reservations. No credit cards accepted. 1958 Calle Villazón (phone: 356880). A branch recently opened on the Plaza del Estudiante at 221 Landaeta (no phone). Inexpensive.

**Heladería KreMrik** – One block past Plaza del Estudiantes on Prado, this ice cream shop is a cut above the rest. In addition to a whole menu of ice cream creations, it offers scrumptious sandwiches and burgers, a long list of fruit juices, and tea and coffee served in china cups. Open daily for lunch and light dinners. No reservations. No credit cards accepted. 1987 Av. Villazón (phone: 374651). Inexpensive.

**Max Bieber** – Tasty snacks and filling meals come at an incredibly low price at this restaurant/ice cream parlor. The prix fixe menu of four courses plus tea or coffee costs under $3 and features such Bolivian treats as *chairo,* a hearty highland soup loaded with vegetables. Don't miss the superb homemade ice cream including the irresistible coconut, cinnamon, and fresh fruit flavors. With good food, a relaxing atmosphere, and exceptional service, it's easy to understand how this place has been a favorite with *paceños* since 1940. Open daily. Reservations unnecessary. No credit cards accepted. 2080 Av. 20 de Octubre (phone: 341661). Inexpensive.

**Pizza a la Piedra (Los Inmortales de Buenos Aires)** – An Argentine family of Italian extraction has brought their considerable skill to La Paz. Crusty, cheesy pizza comes in every description; cold beer comes in chilled mugs. Located in an interesting neighborhood of old villas, the eatery is small and cozy with white tablecloths and candles on the tables. Open Mondays through Saturdays from 3:30 to 10 PM. No reservations. No credit cards accepted. 349 Calle Fernando Guachalla, between 6 de Agosto and 20 de Octubre. Inexpensive.

# LIMA

*Because of continued terrorist attacks, and, at press time, the declaration of martial law, the US State Department has issued an advisory warning tourists planning to visit Peru. Travelers concerned about the political situation and the threat of violence should call the US State Department's Citizens' Emergency Center (phone: 202-647-5225), the South American Explorers Club (phone: 607-277-0488 in the US; 14-314480 in Lima), or the consular section of the US Embassy in Peru (phone: 14-443621) for updates on areas recommended off limits for tourists. In addition, due to the large number of cases of cholera, travelers are advised to drink only bottled carbonated water, and eat only cooked, hot food and peeled fruit. For further information, contact the Centers for Disease Control's International Travelers' Hotline (phone: 404-332-4559).*

For those who circle Lima's Jorge Chávez International Airport on a rare clear day, the first view of Peru's Pacific coast has the same purity and power that attracted the original Spanish settlers more than 400 years ago: white Pacific breakers buffeting desert sand beaches; an arm of the Andes reaching so far into the sea that its final peaks form the chain of islands of El Frontón, San Lorenzo, and the Palominos; and some 7 miles inland, in the lush oases of the Rímac Valley, Lima itself, dominating this panorama of sea, desert, and mountain just as it did when it was the capital of Spain's South American empire.

In 1621, when the Pilgrims were sitting down to their first *Thanksgiving* dinner, Lima had been the most important city in the Western Hemisphere for 80 years. Known originally as the City of Kings — because conquistador Francisco Pizarro established the site of the new city on January 6, 1535, *Epiphany,* or Day of the Kings — it was the center of Spain's viceroyalty from its founding until independence swept across the continent at the beginning of the 19th century. It picked up the name Lima soon after its founding by virtue of a mistake. The city was laid out along a river and a valley known to the Indians as Rímac ("Talking River"); the Spanish misunderstood the word as Limac, and before they corrected the error it was shortened to Lima.

The name was just about the only mistake Pizarro and his conquistadores made in planning the city. The sketch he drew with his pikestaff in the fertile fields around Río Rímac indicated a city built slightly inland from the coast served by an efficient port (Lima's seaport, Callao, is still one of the biggest in South America), surrounded by wide plains with plenty of space for growth (modern Lima covers 27 square miles and is still growing, unimpeded by natural obstacles), at a point midway along Peru's 1,400-mile coast. The city that emerged from these ambitious plans was protected, beautifully situated, and regally proud — one of the finest products of colonial culture in South America. Pizarro designed a city to stand for the ages.

# LIMA

## Points of Interest

1. Plaza de Armas / Armaments Plaza
2. Catedral / Cathedral
3. Palacio Municipal / City Hall
4. Iglesia y Monasterio de Santo Domingo / Church and Monastery of St. Dominic
5. Casa de Osambela / Osambela's House
6. Iglesia de San Agustin / Church of St. Augustine
7. Iglesia de La Merced / Mercy Church
8. Iglesia de San Pedro / Church of St. Peter
9. Iglesia y Monasterio de San Francisco / Church and Monastery of St. Francis
10. La Alameda de los Descalzos / Promenade of the Shoeless Friars
11. Plaza de Toros de Acho / Acho Bullring
12. Museo de la Inquisición / Inquisition Museum
13. Museo de Arte / Museum of Art
14. Government Tourist Information Office
15. Peruvian Health Sciences Museum
16. Desampardos Train Station
17. Segura Theater
18. Municipal Theater
19. Lima Sheraton
20. Crillón Hotel
21. Parque Salazar
22. Museo del Oro
23. Lima Golf Club
24. Museo de la Nación

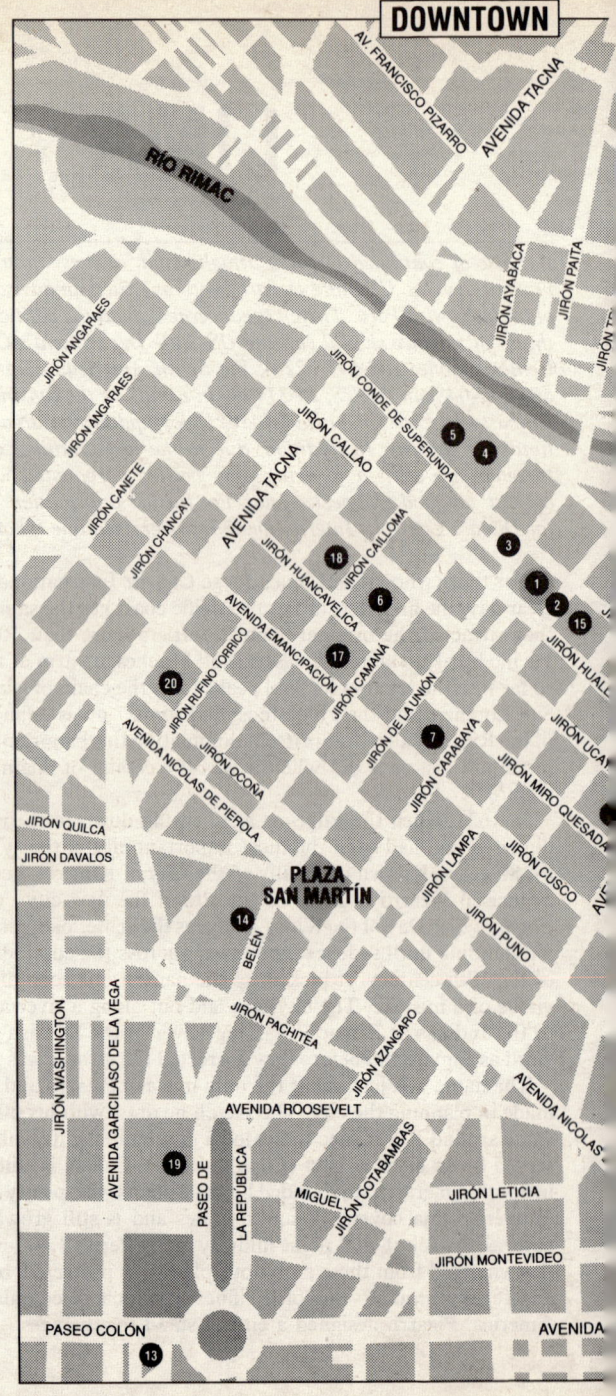

**SAN ISIDRO**

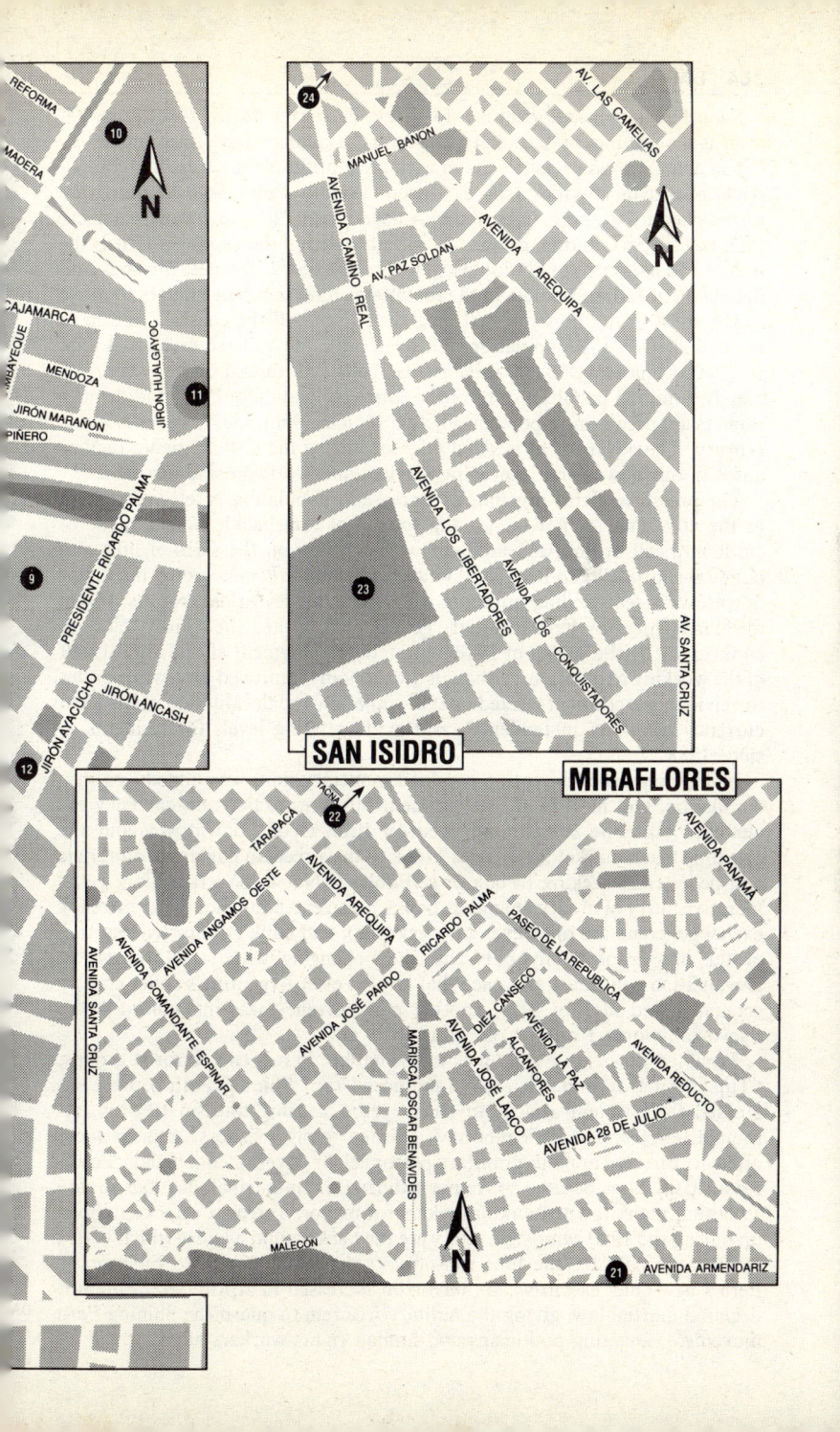

**MIRAFLORES**

Such foresight was fortuitous, for Lima has never ceased to be a capital even as the fortunes of the colony, and later the country, have risen and fallen. When contemporary *limeños* claim with great pride *"Lima es Perú,"* compatriots in provincial cities such as Cuzco, Trujillo, Puno, and Arequipa are forced ruefully to agree. Everything — government, finance, industry, education, newspapers, and magazines — is centralized in the capital, and it is the hub of the nation's population as well. For the last 2 decades, the sons and daughters of Indian farmers in the mountains have left their villages to move to the coast in the hopes of bettering their lives. All the coastal cities have been affected by this population upheaval, but none quite so much as Lima. In 1940, Lima had 500,000 inhabitants. Today, Greater Lima has approximately 7 million people, a third of the entire population of Peru, and demographers are predicting a population of more than 10 million by the end of this century. The government is slowly decentralizing the nation, giving regions autonomous power and improving services and roads outside the capital.

The pressure of this precipitous increase in population is felt everywhere in the city. *Pueblos jóvenes* (young towns) of ramshackle homes made of cardboard, oil drums, and adobe have sprung up on the sides of hills and beside the airport. Peddlers of all kinds, called *ambulantes,* crowd the major downtown streets selling anything from razor blades to handicrafts. Fiscal mismanagement by Peru's military government pushed the country close to bankruptcy by the spring of 1978, and underemployment affects almost half of the working population. Although the economy improved for a while under the civilian government elected in 1985, inflation and devaluation of the local currency have run in tandem — and at devastating levels for residents — since 1988.

In January 1986, the inti, a revalued monetary unit, was introduced into circulation, and in 1988 the government lifted restrictions on currency exchanges. *Casas de cambio* reopened on Jirón Ocoña downtown, and the one-time black market *"cambistas"* took to the streets to flag down motorists and pedestrians seeking to buy or sell dollars. Not to be left behind in the lucrative flurry of money changing, banks began extending hours for currency exchange (some are open even on weekends), and bank ads started warning of the danger of phony bills and short-changing with street *cambistas.* Devaluation continued at a pace that rivaled even Argentina's roller coaster economy, and in July 1991, another new currency was introduced — the nuevo sol, worth 1 million old intis.

Troubled times are hardly new to the nation. Peru's two terrorist groups, "Tupac Amaru" and "Sendero Luminoso" (or "Shining Path"), have increased their violent attacks in recent years, causing tourism to drop, although few terrorist incidents have affected foreign visitors. Attacks most often are directed at police, military personnel, or government officials. Political assassinations became so frequent during the municipal elections in late 1989 that many towns found no takers for mayor. Terrorist attacks stepped up during the 1990 campaign, and were the background against which voters went to the polls for the June run-off vote that elected Alberto Fujimori as Peru's new chief executive. As terrorism increased in April 1992, Fujimori declared martial law, giving the military free rein to quash the Shining Path movement, angering politicians and human rights workers alike.

Economic problems have continued to plague Peru, and Fujimori — who was elected on a wave of left-wing support — has instituted a free market austerity program. Using a team of economists known as the "Oxford Boys," the Fujimori government quickly cut tariffs, lifted foreign investment restrictions, and began to sell off state-owned companies. President Fujimori also resumed payments on the nation's foreign debt and began to court banks in the US and in Japan — the land of his ancestors — with some success. (Aid packages were halted after Fujimori's state of emergency decree until democracy is restored in Peru.) The social cost of the program has been high, however, and the economic squeeze has heightened crime in some areas.

> ■**Note:** Peruvian tourism officials advise visitors to be wary of pickpockets and thieves — including children. It is best not to carry too much money in the streets — and to conceal what you do have in a money belt or another hidden spot. Avoid wearing jewelry and keep watches covered up by the sleeves of a shirt or sweater. Carry your passport with you at all times; occasionally you will be asked to show it to officials. Finally, do not deal with any individual who calls your hotel room or approaches you in your hotel lobby claiming to represent a travel agency, guide service, or specialty shop.

Although close to the equator, Lima's climate is temperate, owing to the cold Humboldt Current that flows north from Chile toward Ecuador. Because of the current and the barrier of the Andes range that almost hugs the ocean, it rarely rains in Lima. However, between July and October (Lima's winter months), sunny days are rare. The skies are depressingly gray, and at times a misty rain makes the days even more overcast. Peruvians call the fog bank that hangs over the capital *garúa*. When the sun shines through the *garúa* unexpectedly on a winter day, the very pace of life on the streets quickens; people appear in bright clothes, and at least for a moment the city casts off its dreary gray garb.

What makes the *garúa* worth it is the city itself: the city center, a very South American combination of modern and colonial architecture; the mountains in the distance; and the string of suburbs along the Pacific coast. The suburbs' palm-lined streets, stately mansions, and modern, clean, high-rise apartment buildings contrast with the Spanish colonial and office-block gray of downtown. In the wealthier suburbs, the contemporary architecture contains certain colonial features — balconies, red tiles, latticework, and sculptured wood. Miraflores, the beachfront community that sits on a long cliff overlooking the Pacific, has an atmosphere similar to that of a resort town, with sidewalk cafés, boutiques, first class restaurants, cinemas, and surfers. Because the principal streets of Miraflores are well lit, more and more *limeños* go there to shop, to eat out, and to kick up their heels at night.

Bordering Miraflores is the group of beaches known as the Costa Verde. In the summertime they are packed with people, particularly on weekends. The best time to use the beach is Mondays through Fridays, but for swimming, stick to beaches from La Herradura on south. Closer to Lima the water is polluted — and very cold — though strolling is still fine here and the seaside restaurants and cafés offer some culinary treats at inexpensive prices.

The Costa Verde, linked to downtown Lima by a modern expressway, is less than a half-hour drive away.

Nearly 5 centuries old, Lima has lived through earthquakes and invasions, seen many changes of government, and experienced immense wealth and widespread poverty. It is a city burdened by economic woes, homelessness, and petty crime, yet the visitor who focuses on the positive will be dazzled by its fabulous history and impressed by the admirable industriousness of the *limeños*.

# LIMA AT-A-GLANCE

**SEEING THE CITY:** The spacious windows of the elegantly decorated dining rooms of the fine Chinese restaurant *El Dorado*, on the 20th floor of the building of the same name (2450 Av. Arequipa; phone: 221080), offer a wide-angle view of the entire city. Also known for their panoramas are *La Terraza* and the *Sky Room* (at the *Crillón Hotel*, 589 Av. Nicolás de Piérola; phone: 283290), and *La Azotea Bar* (at *César's Hotel*, corner of La Paz and Diez Canseco in Miraflores; phone: 441212). At all of these places you will have to order something in order to savor the view.

**SPECIAL PLACES:** You will need only a couple of days to visit Lima's special places. The first day could be spent in getting to know the heart of colonial Lima, starting with its main square, the Plaza de Armas, where you will find the Presidential Palace, the cathedral, the Archbishop's Palace, and City Hall. Near the Plaza de Armas, you can easily walk to a number of colonial churches and convents, such as Santo Domingo, San Agustín, La Merced, San Pedro, and San Francisco (the largest church and convent complex remaining from earliest colonial times), as well as the original seat of the Inquisition. Crossing the Río Rímac by one of its four bridges, you can easily get to the district of Rímac, known popularly as Bajo el Puente (Beneath the Bridge). Among the noteworthy sights are the promenade known as Alameda, the Convento de los Descalzos, and the famed *Acho* bullring.

The second day could be spent visiting some of the museums that are scattered throughout the city and suburbs.

You could reserve the third day for visiting archaeological sites or one of Lima's fine beach resorts (see *Peru*, DIRECTIONS). Or for a respite, you might want to escape to Chosica, a small sunny city a bit upland where well-to-do *limeños* have winter homes (see *Extra Special*, below).

Summer and winter visiting hours often vary; so before setting out on a walking tour, check schedules in the *Perú Guide*, available at no charge in all major hotels, travel agencies, and the national tourism office at 1066 Belén (phone: 323559).

## CENTER

**Plaza de Armas (Armaments Plaza)** – Planned by Francisco Pizarro in 1535, the plaza is flanked by three seats of power: the cathedral, the Palacio del Gobierno (or presidential palace, which is no longer open to the public), and City Hall. Among the attractions that make the plaza a must for visitors is the impressive architecture, including wooden balconies. An event worth timing a trip for is the daily changing of the Presidential Guard of Honor at 1 PM. Due to tightened security, visitors are not permitted to view the goose-stepping Hussars of Junín from the gates in front of the palace or from the plaza square, but the cathedral steps still offer a good vantage point.

**Catedral (Cathedral)** – On the spot designated for the building of the first cathedral by Pizarro, the present building was begun in 1746 after the first edifice was destroyed in one of Lima's many earthquakes. The carved choir stalls were a gift of Charles V to the first cathedral of Peru. On the right-hand side of the cathedral, as you enter, is the chapel where Pizarro's remains are kept in a glass casket. Both the cathedral and the *Museum of Religious Art* (inside) are open to visitors Mondays through Fridays from 10 AM to 1 PM and 2 to 5 PM, weekends from 10 AM to 3:45 PM. The admission charge includes guided tours in English, French, or Spanish. Plaza de Armas (phone: 275918, ext. 67).

**Palacio Municipal (City Hall)** – After surviving earthquakes and floods for nearly 4 centuries, the original City Hall was destroyed by fire in 1923. The present neo-colonial building was designed in 1944 by two Peruvian architects. Of special interest is the library which contains the record of Lima's founding, signed by Pizarro, and is graced with a beautiful rococo spiral staircase intricately carved from a single block of Nicaraguan cedar. No admission charge. Guided tours can be arranged at the city tourism office at 134 Pasaje Santa Rosa, just off the Plaza de Armas (phone: 276080, ext. 3).

**Jirón de la Unión (Union Street)** – Connects the Plaza de Armas with the other important square of central Lima, the Plaza de San Martín. This was Lima's elite shopping street before the flowering of the suburban Miraflores shopping area. Now the entire 5-block area is a pedestrian mall, with several large shopping galleries that include good *artesanía* shops and interesting restaurants. However, it is so chronically clogged with vendors selling everything from sweaters to dog collars that it could be overwhelming for some visitors. If you do go, be wary of pickpockets and jewelry snatchers. But do be sure to glance at the upper levels of the buildings to get an idea of their past charm.

**Iglesia y Monasterio de Santo Domingo (Church and Monastery of St. Dominic)** – One block west of the Plaza de Armas are the church and monastery of the Dominican friars, built in 1549. In many ways, the buildings are a rare oasis in a troubled city. For 45 years, the monastery was home to St. Martin de Porres who served as barber and pharmacist to the friars but was never permitted to become a priest himself because he was black. His remains, and those of Peru's other famous saint — Rose of Lima — are buried in the monastery. Here South America's oldest university, San Marcos, was founded in 1561. It is a fine example of colonial architecture and in it can be found tiles shipped from Spain in 1586, the music room ceiling made from 3,000 separate pieces of Nicaraguan cedar, and the city's oldest library. The church is open daily from 7 AM to 1 PM and 4 to 8 PM. The monastery and tombs are open Mondays through Saturdays from 9 AM to noon and 3 to 5 PM. Sundays and holidays, they are open in the morning only. Admission charge includes a guided tour in English or Spanish. 170 Jirón Camaná, Plazuela Santo Domingo.

**Casa de Osambela (Osambela's House)** – Formerly known as Casa de Oquendo, this excellent example of colonial rococo architecture was built between 1798 and 1808 and has been restored. It now serves as a cultural center and the main office for seven Peruvian cultural and historical institutes. Books from the home's library were added to those donated by General José de San Martín to form the National Library, and it was in this mansion that San Martín stayed after proclaiming Peru's independence from Spain in 1821. Open weekdays from 9 AM to 3 PM when cultural events (including lectures, art expositions, and films) are ongoing. Free tours of the house can be arranged. 298 Calle Conde de Superunda (phone: 277987).

**Iglesia de San Agustín (Church of St. Augustine)** – From the corner of Camaná and Superunda, turn left on Camaná and go down to Ica, where you will find this lovely church, which unfortunately was quite badly damaged in the earthquake of 1974.

Despite its having been renovated and painted a brilliant blue and pink, the interior remains surprisingly simple. Open daily from 8:30 AM to noon and 3:30 to 5:30 PM. 225 Jirón Ica.

**Iglesia de La Merced (Mercy Church)** – From the corner of Ica and Unión, walk 1 block to this famed church, with its great façade carved from granite brought from Panama. La Merced was opened in 1534, a year before the official founding of Lima. Open from 7 AM to 12:30 PM and 4 to 8 PM; the convent hours are from 8 AM to noon and 3 to 5:30 PM. 621 Jirón de la Unión.

**Iglesia de San Pedro (Church of St. Peter)** – Half a block from the Torre Tagle Palace, this baroque church was built by the Jesuits in the early 1600s. Its dome is a small replica of the great dome of St. Peter's Basilica in Rome. But most striking are its many wooden altars covered with gold. Open daily, 7 AM to 12:30 PM and 6 to 8 PM. 300 Jirón Ucayali.

**Iglesia y Monasterio de San Francisco (Church and Monastery of St. Francis)** – The brethren of St. Francis of Assisi were one of the first Catholic missionary groups to arrive in Lima. The present church of St. Francis, built on the site of the first one, constructed in 1546, was completed in 1674. Baroque and Andalusian architectural styles influenced its design. Both the church and monastery complex deserve a prolonged visit, for they have a great deal to offer: 15 chapels, elaborately carved choir stalls from Panamanian imported cedar, beautiful ceilings, and the eerie catacombs, a surprising bit of architecture, with galleries of 3 floors below the earth where once were buried the bodies of thousands. Before an earthquake blocked the secret passageway, the catacombs connected the monastery to the Palacio del Gobierno, the cathedral, and the Inquisition Tribunal. There are ongoing restorations at the monastery and a number of original frescoes are emerging from beneath layers of paint. Some of them are without faces, which were found on the walls in the cells of some overzealous monks who apparently had taken them from other parts of the monastery in order to have the faces close to them! Open daily, 10 AM to 1 PM and 3 to 6 PM. Admission charge includes a guided tour. After the tour, stop for coffee or a light snack in the outdoor café, *El Mesón del Fraile* (see *Eating Out*), on the monastery's Patio de Pimienta, which formerly was a spice market. 300 Jirón Ancash.

**La Alameda de los Descalzos (Promenade of the Shoeless Friars)** – Inaugurated in 1606 by the viceroy, the Marquis de Montesclaro, the Alameda was the "in" place for fashionable limeños of the 17th century. Here elegantly dressed, well-chaperoned young upper class society women promenaded to look at one another and to be seen by young gentlemen. While promenading yourself, you might want to visit Los Descalzos (the name stems from the friars' custom of wearing sandals rather than shoes), the church and monastery run by Franciscan friars. The monastery is open to the public and provides a wonderful look at colonial monastery life, including a pharmacy, library, and lovely inner courtyards. It also has a fine collection of 17th- and 18th-century paintings. A huge painting of a crucified Christ here allegedly prompted a legal battle over the value of life versus the value of art when the artist, seeking a better expression of pain on the face of his model, fatally stabbed the man posing for the work. He argued in court that the homicide was justifiable because the painting was so well executed. He was later sentenced to a lengthy jail term. Open daily except Tuesdays from 8 AM to 1 PM and 3 to 6 PM. Admission charge. The Alameda can be found behind the Palacio de Gobierno on the other side of the river, in the district of Rímac. Cross the bridge at the end of Jirón de la Unión (phone: 810441).

**Plaza de Toros de Acho (Acho Bullring)** – Not far from the Alameda, you will find the bullring in the Plaza de Acho, north of Balta Bridge. It is the oldest ring in South America, built by Viceroy Amat in 1764 and restored in 1945, with its original façade preserved and protected. The first bullfights in newly established Lima took place in 1540 (Pizarro himself took part as a toreador). From that time until the present, the bullfighting season has always brought together all that is traditional, colorful, and lively in Lima. It is the one time of the year when social distinctions disappear and all of Lima gives itself over to its two great passions — the October processions of the venerated image of the Lord of the Miracles and the bullfights. The season is October, November, and early December, when world-renowned toreadors come to *Acho* to compete for the prized Silver Scapular of the Lord of the Miracles. The cost of tickets is relatively high these days, and the best seats are reserved for those with season passes. The bullfights take place on Sundays and holidays during October, November, and early December at 3 PM. Ask for seats in the shade — *sombra*. Tickets are sold from 10 AM to 1 PM and 4 to 8 PM weekdays (284 Jirón Huancavelica; phone: 277580 or 276570). A number of hotels, including the *Lima Sheraton,* the *Crillón,* and *César's,* offer criollo buffet lunches before the fights and transportation to and from the *Plaza de Acho* ring.

**Museo de la Inquisición (Inquisition Museum)** – Leaving Acho by crossing the Puente de Balta (Balta Bridge), you will come to Avenida Abancay and Plaza Bolívar, formerly known as the Plaza de la Inquisición (Inquisition Plaza). Here stands the Palacio del Congreso (Congress Building). To the right as you face the Congress is the building that houses the *Museum of the Inquisition.* The Inquisition Tribunal of Lima was established in 1569 to "protect" the Catholic religion in the jurisdiction of the new viceroyalty. It endured until 1813 when it was abolished by royal decree, at which time *limeños* happily vandalized the building, destroying records and instruments of torture. In contrast to its grisly purpose is the building itself, with some of the most beautiful woodcarving in Lima. The ceiling of the Audience Hall is an exceptional piece of work dating from the 18th century. Visits to the prisoners' galleries and cells on the subterranean levels are also possible. Photographs are not permitted, and children under 12 must be accompanied by an adult. Note: This neighborhood has become a little down at the heels. Open Mondays through Fridays from 9 AM to 7 PM and Saturdays from 9 AM to 4:30 PM. No admission charge. 548 Jirón Junín at Plaza Bolívar (phone: 287980).

**Museo de la Nación (National Museum)** – For those who think Peru's Indian history began and ended with the Inca, Lima's newest museum is an eye-opener. Reportedly the largest in South America, this museum traces the country's development from prehistoric times through the Huari, Chavín, Chimú, Paracas, and other advanced civilizations up to the storied Inca Empire, using scale models of cities, pottery, textiles, and legends. One of the most dramatic displays is a life-size reproduction of the Lord of Sipán burial chamber that was uncovered in northern Peru in 1987. Another exhibit is dedicated to Spanish colonial days. The massive building, once home to the nation's important Ministry of Fishing, has a restoration center, library, audiovisual department, coffee shop, and handicrafts boutique. Open daily except Mondays from 10 AM to 6 PM. Admission charge includes a guided tour in Spanish, English, or French. Arrangements can be made for bilingual guides who sign for the hearing impaired. 2465 Av. Javier Prado Este, San Borja (phone: 377999 or 377969).

**Museo de Antropología y Arqueología (Museum of Anthropology and Archaeology)** – This fabulous museum has exhibits of rare pottery, weavings, and mummies. The unique tapestries from Paracas and Nazca are works of art in their own right, as are the gold and silver images and vessels. There is also an outstanding collection of Mochica pottery — ceramics that show the pastimes, diseases, marital practices, and food of that advanced Indian civilization. Open daily, 10 AM to 6 PM. Admission charge. Plaza Bolívar in Pueblo Libre (phone: 635070).

**Museo Arqueológico Rafael Larco Herrera (Rafael Larco Herrera Archaeological Museum)** – When this part of Lima was still farm country, this building used to be a hacienda. Now it has been transformed into a museum housing the famed collection of erotic pottery and other artifacts that belonged to Larco Herrera, one of Peru's most respected archaeologists. These ceramics date back to the so-called fluorescent era of Peruvian culture, which lasted from AD 200 to 600. Tucked away in a basement-level room next to the gift shop is an extensive collection of erotic art from the Moche culture. Open Mondays through Saturdays from 9 AM to 1 PM and 3 to 6 PM and Sundays from 9 AM to 1 PM. Admission charge. 1515 Av. Bolívar in Pueblo Libre (phone: 611312 or 611835).

**Museo de Arte (Museum of Art)** – Opened in 1872 as an exposition center for the *World Fair* being held in Lima that year, this building now houses collections of pottery, tapestries, gold and silver objects, weavings, mummies, and paintings illuminating Peru's 2,500 years of culture according to its historical epochs: pre-Inca, Inca, colonial, and republican. A cinema also offers some interesting evening features that include North American and European movies. Open Tuesdays through Sundays from 9 AM to 5 PM. Admission charge. Down the street from the *Lima Sheraton* hotel at 125 Paseo Colón (phone: 234732).

**Parque Japonés (Japanese Garden)** – A few blocks from the *Museum of Art,* this peaceful and charming garden was donated to the city by Peru's Japanese community in 1973 in honor of the 100th anniversary of diplomatic relations between the two nations. The garden offers a delightful collection of plants and flowers indigenous to the Far East and, although much of the exotic vegetation originally planted did not adjust to Lima's climate, the cherry trees, Japanese pine, and the flowering Sutsuki plants at the park's entrance are thriving. A dragon-shaped lagoon, filled with goldfish and a small waterfall, sits next to a ceremonial tea house. Open daily from 9 AM to 6 PM. Admission charge. Av. 28 de Julio.

**Museo del Oro (Gold Museum)** – Approximately 6,500 pieces of worked gold — figurines, bowls, cups, plates, and ceremonial objects — are found in this private museum. One awe-inspiring glimpse of such wealth and you will undoubtedly regret that European greed melted down, indiscriminately, other great works of art, such as the gold and silver garden in the Temple of the Sun in Cuzco. What remained — like the pieces collected here — was what was insignificant enough to be overlooked. Besides gold, there are ceremonial costumes of exquisite featherwork, ceramics (look closely for the erotic miniatures), and mummies. The upper floor of the museum also contains an extensive weapons collection, including Japanese armor and a sword believed to have belonged to Francisco Pizarro. Open daily from noon to 7 PM. Admission charge. A 20-minute cab ride from downtown at 1100 Av. Alonso de Molina, Monterrico (phone: 352917).

**Presbítero Maestro (Master Cemetery)** – An unusual escape from the bustle of Lima is a Sunday walk through one of the city's oldest cemeteries. Here you'll find the Heroes' Crypt — containing the remains of those who fought in the war against Chile — and the tombs of famous writers, presidents, and patriots. Elaborate headstones, some of them works of art in themselves, mark the graves of the wealthiest early *limeños*. Across the street is the newer Cementerio El Angel (Angel Cemetery) where the dead are interred in *pabellones* — or huge walls. Don't miss the dramatic monument that pays tribute to police officers who have fallen victim to terrorist acts. Stands filled to overflowing with brilliantly colored flowers line the outside of the cemetery gates. Open daily from 7:30 AM to 5 PM. Av. Cementerio.

## ENVIRONS

Leaving the center of Lima, take the Via Expresa, a modern, six-lane expressway uniting the center of Lima with Chorrillos and the beaches of the Costa Verde. Chorrillos, about 7 miles (11 km) from the Plaza de Armas, is one of downtown Lima's original summer resorts, beautifully placed on bluffs high above the Pacific Ocean. In between are some residential areas of Greater Lima: the working class neighborhoods of La Victoria and Lince, and the middle class and wealthier areas of Jesús María, Surquillo,

Miraflores, San Isidro, and Barranco. Surrounding these enclaves are the massive *pueblos jovenes* (young towns), a euphemism that describes those many square kilometers of shantytowns.

**Miraflores** – This suburb along the Pacific embraces contemporary and earlier architectural styles. Actually, it is a small, elegant city in itself. By comparison, the center of Lima is run-down, indeed. Miraflores's central shopping street, Avenida Larco, ends in a pleasant little park (Parque Salazar) overlooking the ocean where balloon sellers, ice cream vendors, and street artists offer their wares. The park is actually a landscaped section of a steep cliff, below which stretches a narrow strand of public beach. The beachfront road, called the *malecón,* is lined with very expensive apartment buildings and occasional grand colonial mansions. (Most of the truly splendid homes have been torn down to make way for more profitable apartment houses, but as you head farther north along the shore, you will come upon more houses.) Miraflores is spotted with many surprising little flowery parks. Archaeology buffs should stop at the pre-Inca temple, *Huaca Juliana* (Av. Arequipa between Calles Ayacucho and Tarapacá), particularly to see the excavated sections. There is a small museum at the site. Open Tuesdays through Sundays, from 10 AM to 5 PM. Admission charge. The best time to see Miraflores is after 4 PM, when the shops have reopened after the long lunch break and residents come in their best casual attire to shop and meet friends in the cafés. A favorite evening stroll is along Calle San Ramón (off Av. Diagonal), where outdoor pizza parlors are packed with people watchers. Often in the summer, Miraflores can be disappointingly misty, but hard-core surfers will find waves worth tackling along its shore. You can get to Miraflores along 60-block-long Avenida Arequipa, a lovely tree-lined street that becomes Avenida Larco.

**San Isidro** – Tucked between greater Lima and Miraflores, this suburb is neither as expensive nor as commercial as Miraflores — and it is the better of the two for enjoying neo-colonial architecture because it is far more residential. Wooden balconies, red tile roofs, decorative blue-and-white tiles known as *azulejos,* and huge flowering poinsettia bushes grace these homes. Especially intriguing is El Olivar, an area that has a quiet park and Tudor-style homes. The library overlooking El Olivar Park — formerly an olive grove — is a peaceful place to write postcards. An old olive press is on display in the park. San Isidro offers elegant dining in a colonial mansion at *Los Condes de San Isidro* restaurant, with its excellent selection of international and seafood specialties (see *Eating Out),* and good shopping in the city's best artisan shop — *Artesanías del Perú* cooperative (see *Shopping).* If you're interested in archaeology or ancient Indian cultures, visit *Huaca Huallamarca* on the corner of El Rosario and Nicolás de Riviera. It is a restored pre-Inca pyramid, with a small museum displaying Indian artifacts found during its excavation. Open daily except Mondays, 10 AM to 5 PM.

**Barranco** – Two miles (3 km) south of Miraflores, Barranco is a pocket of splendid old mansions built by the "beautiful people" of the Republican era. Note the many fanciful balconies, gables, and other English architectural touches that give the area unusual charm. Many of the mansions have been divided into smaller apartments. Although it was *the* summer resort a century ago, it is now part of metropolitan Lima, and is increasingly gaining fame as a bohemian enclave. In the summertime, Barranco is an enchanting, cool place to stroll. Highly recommended is the Puente de los Suspiros (Bridge of Sighs). This secluded lovers' lane filled with flowering trees is delightful. Under the wooden bridge is a walkway that leads down a cliff overlooking the Pacific Ocean from which you can often see gliders drifting gracefully down to the beach. While visiting the park, a stop at the jazz club *Nosferatu* or dinner at *El Otro Sitio* (see *Eating Out),* or a folklore show at *Karamanduka* (see *Nightclubs and Nightlife)* can be easily accomplished. To get to Barranco, turn left at the end of Avenida Larco and continue along the oceanfront road or take Paseo de la República to Avenida José María Egurén. The ocean is to the right.

**Costa Verde** – This handsome circuit of beaches is better for looking than for swimming. The water is polluted, often very cold, the undertow is strong, and a prolific community of jellyfish takes up residence at different times of the year. Still, it is very popular with residents, especially on weekends. If you visit, do so during the week, and bring a picnic lunch, or pick up a cold beer and a snack at one of the numerous restaurants and food stands along the beaches. The *Costa Verde* and the *Rosa Náutica* (see *Eating Out*), elegant restaurants with international standards, are worth trying. Costa Verde extends from the northern border of Miraflores at Avenida Brasil and the *malecón* to Barranco.

**La Herradura Beach** – Just south of the Costa Verde, this beach tends to be less crowded, although it's not deserted. Its name, "horseshoe," refers to the shape of the bay, in which some people practice surf casting. Here, too, you'll find food stands and restaurants along the shore; *El Salto del Fraile* (see *Eating Out*), a restaurant that allegedly takes its name from the spot where a love-struck priest mysteriously jumped to his death, is worth a visit. (The name is literally "The Friar's Leap.") No matter which beach you visit, be sure you leave all valuables in your hotel's safe. Esplanada, Chorrillos.

**Parque de Las Leyendas (Park of the Legends)** – This small zoo has, as its central motif, a vivid presentation of the three principal geographical regions of Peru: the desert coast, the Andes, and the Amazon jungle. Each area has a collection of animals that are not often seen in US zoos — herds of rare vicuñas, condors, jungle serpents, and brilliantly plumed Amazon birds. It is especially worth visiting if you're traveling with small children, for whom it provides a great geography lesson. Also of interest are the painted murals depicting Indian myths and legends. The roadway leading into the park is lined with stalls at which alpaca sweaters and Indian art and souvenirs are sold. Open daily, 9:30 AM to 5 PM. Admission charge. Av. La Marina, San Miguel (phone: 526913).

■ **EXTRA SPECIAL:** One of the most popular day trips from Lima, especially during the gray winter months, is the excursion to the mountain resort town of Chosica, 25 miles (40 km) from the center of town on the Central Highway (Carretera Central). About 19 miles (31 km) from Lima you will pass through Chaclacayo, a town of approximately 30,000 inhabitants, where the sun shines at least 350 days a year. It has a number of fine, modern houses, but it's not much to look at from the road. Chosica is a city of 150,000 that was Lima's select winter resort at the turn of the century, attested to by its Victorian houses. However, as more indigenous people settled in and around the town, its desirability as an exclusive winter resort lessened drastically, and the old families built new houses in Chaclacayo, down the road. Although Chosica is a bit faded, it remains a charming city, and train service from Lima's downtown station, an hour away, is available several times a day. (The route is lined with miles of cardboard shacks.) Its very large plaza is surrounded by many shady, impressive palm trees. Because it is 600 feet higher than Chaclacayo, its climate is even better. It has clearer air and brighter winter sunshine. However, it is more susceptible to the summer rainstorms that come swirling down from Cerro de Pasco and Huancayo in the Andes. It is worthwhile visiting the public market to get an idea of how mountain markets function in the daily lives of the people. Mention Chosica or Chaclacayo to most *limeños*, and they'll immediately say *"La Granja Azul,"* a lovely country restaurant that specializes in exotic drinks and delicious grilled chicken (see *Eating Out*). Next door is *El Pueblo Inn*, a delightful restaurant-resort complex in Santa Clara, which has two golf courses, two pools, squash and tennis courts, a bowling alley, horseback riding, a sauna, and pleasant rooms (see *Checking In*). It's ideal for an overnight rest. *El Pueblo Inn* also opens its grounds to non-guests daily, for a $1.50 entrance fee. Three mini-buses to the inn leave downtown Lima (in front of *Lima Tours* at 1040 Belén); the fare is $1.

# SOURCES AND RESOURCES

**TOURIST INFORMATION:** General tourist information in the form of pamphlets, brochures, and maps is available from the Government Tourist Information Office (1066 Belén; phone: 323559), weekdays from 8 AM to 7 PM. This office, with guides who speak six languages, should be the first stop for any visitor. In addition to the main office in suburban San Isidro (320 San Andrés Reyes; phone: 420143 and 424195) and the downtown location, information offices can be found at the international check-in booth at the airport. (The Belén office is poorly marked; look for the arcade that housed the now-defunct *Tambo de Oro* restaurant, and still is home to numerous artisans' shops.) In addition, Peru has a special force of tourist police who are trained to assist visitors with problems or those who wish to report a crime. In Lima, the office is at 1156 Av. Salaverry (phone: 714313).

The government hotel chain, EnturPerú (1358 Javier Prado; phone: 721928) will book the state-run *Turistas* hotels in over 2 dozen towns throughout Peru. These hotels also can be reserved through any local travel agency. Recommended are *Condor Travel* (677 Nicolás de Piérola; phone: 289845) and *Lima Tours* (1040 Belén; phone: 276624), with branches in Miraflores, San Isidro, and at the *Lima Sheraton* hotel. Reservations also can be made in the US (phone: 800-275-3123).

The *South American Explorers Club* has a local office (146 Av. República de Portugal, Breña; phone: 314480). Members can use the club's vast collection of firsthand travel reports and other information services, store equipment and valuables, and even purchase hard-to-find items left for resale by other members. The club also holds mail, helps arrange hotel accommodations, and confirms reservations. For more information, see *Planning a Trip*, GETTING READY TO GO.

*Perú Guide,* the country's monthly English-language tourist guide, is distributed free at the airport, tourist information office, travel agencies, and all the better hotels. Detailed maps of various areas of the city are found in the last section of the Lima white pages. Maps for walking tours and information about downtown hotels, restaurants, and museums are available at the city tourism office (134 Pasaje Santa Rosa, off the Plaza de Armas; phone: 276080, ext. 3). Adventure travelers in need of top quality maps can contact the National Geographic Institute (phone: 287993) or the Instituto Geográfico Militar (phone: 464785).

The US Embassy is located at the corner of Avenida Inca Garcilaso de la Vega and España (phone: 338000). The consular section is at 346 Grimaldo del Solar, Miraflores (phone: 443621).

**Local Coverage** – The *Lima Times,* published every Friday in English, contains local news, restaurant and film reviews, and a listing of the week's cultural events in Lima. Major US news magazines can be found on streetside newsstands and copies of the *Miami Herald* normally are available from the concierge at the *Crillón* hotel. For the Spanish-speaking visitor, the daily *El Comercio* has the most complete listings of movies, theater, music, and other types of entertainment. *Perú Guide* has a thorough listing of Lima's restaurants, categorized by specialty.

**TELEPHONE:** The city code for Lima is 14. When calling from within Peru, dial 014 before the local number. The country code for Peru is 51.

**CLIMATE AND CLOTHES:** Lima's climate is moderate, with seasons the opposite of those in the US and Europe. Clothes that you would wear during the spring and fall in the Northern Hemisphere are suitable for Lima's winter (July to October). Light clothing is the rule for the summer months, but shorts of any description for men or women are not acceptable streetwear in Peruvian cities. Bring a sweater for summer evenings (some days, too), just in case, and don't forget to pack a bathing suit.

**GETTING AROUND: Bus** – There are plenty of buses, both publicly and privately owned, but taking one is not recommended for the visitor who doesn't speak Spanish. Lima is a large city, and it's easy to get lost by taking the wrong bus. The buses definitely are *not* recommended for the claustrophobic, since they are often so full of passengers — especially at rush hour — that riders actually hang out the open doors.

**Taxi** – The best and easiest way to get around. Cabs lack meters, so the rider should determine (and negotiate) the price of any trip in advance. Ask the people at the reception desk in your hotel about the going rate for your destination. Gasoline prices have skyrocketed in Peru in recent years, so don't expect bargain fares. The best hotels offer a permanent taxi service called *taxis remisse*, which charge more than taxis hailed in the street (but are usually in better condition). To order a cab yourself, *Remisse* (phone: 366547), *Yellow S.A.* (phone: 229375), or *Camino Real* (phone: 402430) are good bets. Fares increase substantially after midnight and holidays. Lima cab drivers often overcharge foreigners by refusing to honor agreed-upon rates or by refusing to state fares in advance. If you can, ask a *limeño* to negotiate the price for you. Cabs at the airport charge a fixed fare, ranging from about $15 to downtown Lima and up to $20 for a trip to Miraflores. Although there also are unregistered taxis there, officials urge tourists to avoid taking them as there have been reports of occasional thefts. There is also a Miraflores-based hotel shuttle service (phone: 469872 in Miraflores and 518011 at the airport). Try to avoid rush hour travel.

**Car Rental** – Although we don't recommend too much self-driving in Lima, all the major chains have car rental offices near downtown and at the airport: *Avis* (at the *Lima Sheraton* hotel; phone: 327245); *Budget* (522 La Paz; phone: 444546); *Hertz* (550 Rivera Navarrete; phone: 424509); *National* (449 Av. España; phone: 232526); and *Dollar* (575 Las Flores, San Isidro; phone: 425729).

**SPECIAL EVENTS:** From January through March, the *Summer Festival of Ancón*, Lima's Nice on the Pacific, is celebrated with choreographed sea spectaculars, a song festival, art expositions, and world surfing championships (see *Peru*, DIRECTIONS). In April and November, the *Official National Competition of Peruvian Pacer Horses* takes place at Mamacona, south of Lima. The modern Peruvian *caballo de paso* is a descendant of the horses that the first Spaniards brought to Peru. They are noted for their fine lines, arrogant nature, and the graceful, dancing rhythm with which they walk. They are generally ridden by skilled jockeys called *chalanes*, who ride dressed all in white with straw hats and flowing ponchos.

In October, *Señor de los Milagros* festivals honor Our Lord of the Miracles. A painting of the crucified Christ, which was supposedly done on an adobe wall of the slaves' meeting place in the 1600s, has survived all of the great earthquakes in Lima (those of 1655 and 1746 being the worst) and thus is considered the *limeños'* special patron. Formerly, the Christ in the painting was called the Lord of the Abandoned, probably because it was primarily an object of devotion for blacks. But today, tens of thousands of *limeños* take part in the three great ritual processions that wind through the streets of Lima on October 18, 19, and 28. The 3-ton icon is borne by teams of men accompanied by incense bearers and a choir; the result is an amazing spectacle. Throughout October you will see many people either dressed in purple or with some touch of purple on their clothes to show that they are devotees of the Lord of the Miracles. *Turrón,* a delicious honey-drenched shortbread, is sold throughout the city during the festival. At the same time, the secular side of the feast is celebrated with the impressive Silver Scapular bullfights in honor of the Lord of the Miracles. During November of odd-numbered years, *Feria Internacional del Pacífico* (the International Pacific Fair) takes place at its own special fairgrounds, devoted primarily to the exposition of the industrial products and technical developments of the participating countries. Many bars and restaurants offer the typical food and drink of the participating nations, and the hottest Latin American bands and singers perform outdoors. There is an admission charge to the fair itself. Av. de la Marina (phone: 528140).

**MUSEUMS:** In addition to those described in *Special Places,* other outstanding Lima museums include the following:

**Museo de Osma (Osma Museum)** – This former French estate houses Lima's finest collection of art from the viceroy period. There is an abundance of gold, crystal, marble, and mother-of-pearl in the house, as well as 16th-century Spanish paintings and 17th-century wood sculptures. Guided tours by appointment only. Admission charge. 501 Av. Pedro de Osma, Barranco (phone: 670915).

**Fortaleza Real Felipe y Museo Militar (Real Felipe Fortress and Military Museum)** – Stands in Callao, the city's port. Built over a 30-year period in the 18th century, the immense pentagonal structure was used to defend the city against attacks by Dutch and English pirates. Several rooms of the fortress have been converted into the *Museo Militar* in which documents are exhibited that record the proud historic deeds accomplished at the site. Open Tuesdays through Thursdays from 9 AM to noon, weekends from 2 to 5:30 PM. No admission charge, but visitors must present photo identification. Callao (phone: 291505).

**Museo Yoshiro Amano (Yoshiro Amano Museum)** – Houses a private collection of weavings from Chancay and ceramics from various cultures, and is one of the best museums to visit if you have only a short time in Lima. Tours by appointment only, weekdays from 2 to 5 PM. No admission charge (but donations are accepted). 160 Calle Retiro, Miraflores (phone: 412909).

**Museo Nacional de la Cultura (National Museum of Peruvian Culture)** – Exhibits include a fine collection of folk art, costumes, and ceramics from all periods. Open weekdays from 10 AM to 5 PM, Saturdays from 9 AM to 5 PM. Admission charge. 650 Av. Alfonso Ugarte (phone: 235892).

**Peruvian Health Sciences Museum** – Tucked away on the second floor of a dusty building in the colonial section of downtown, this fascinating museum offers artifacts and English explanations of pre-Columbian medical practices and herbal healing. Open Wednesdays through Sundays, 10 AM to 4 PM. Admission charge. 270 Junín (phone: 270190).

**Museo del Banco Central de Reserva (Central Reserve Bank Museum)** – The big draw here — tucked into what once was the bank's vault on the lower floor — is an amazing collection of ceramics and textiles, including looted items returned to the country from the US, Australia, Japan, and other countries. Open Mondays through Saturdays from 10 AM to 5 AM, Sundays from 10 AM to 1 PM. No admission charge. 291 Ucayali (phone: 276250).

**SHOPPING:** Of greatest appeal are items of silver, gold, leather, and wood, as well as pottery, textiles, tapestries, and alpaca rugs and sweaters. The center of Lima is filled with *artesanía* (artisan) shops of all kinds. One of the main shopping streets is Avenida Nicolás de Piérola, better known as La Colmena, and Avenida Belén is even better. For excellent-quality goods (but also higher prices), stroll through the upscale *El Suche Galleries* (near the *El Condado* and *María Angola* hotels), a passageway filled with little shops. There you'll find gorgeous hand-knit alpaca sweaters, jewelry, and a wide range of gift items. Major credit cards accepted.

On the way to the airport, on the tenth block of Avenida La Marina, is *Mercado Artesanal*, a group of Indian markets offering hand-crafted products from various regions of Peru. There are many good buys, and the vendors are often willing to bargain. These shops are open daily until around 7 PM.

Artisan goods of all kinds can also be found in *Artesanías del Perú*, a cooperative dedicated to the development and sales of native handicrafts. Its principal store is at 610 Jorge Basadre, San Isidro (phone: 228874), but there also is a branch at the *Museo de la Nación* (2465 Av. Javier Prado del Este, San Borja; no phone) and at the international airport (no phone). Among the best (and least expensive) items to acquire are wooden bowls and spoons that have been carved by hand. Also, make sure to try on and/or carefully inspect all woolen sweaters.

Other fine shops include the following:

***A. Johari*** – Fine quality gold and silver jewelry in the city center. 851 Jirón de la Unión (phone: 288891).

***Alpaca 111*** – This shop, with two locations in Lima and branches in Arequipa and Cuzco, specializes in leather and fur, but its best selection is of alpaca sweaters, scarves, fabric, and knitting yarn. English-speaking staff. 859 Av. Larco in Miraflores (phone: 477163) and *Centro Comercial Camino Real*, Level A, San Isidro.

***Antisuyo*** – Specializing in high-quality jungle handicrafts, beautiful Chulucanas ceramics, and weavings by Taquile and Pomata Indians at Lake Titicaca and Cajamarca. 460 Tacna, Miraflores (phone: 472557).

***Artesanías Huamanqaqa*** – Perhaps the best crafts in Lima, with especially good tapestries and *retablos* (portable altars decorated with religious or secular scenes). 1041-A Jirón de la Unión, where the street name changes to Belén, across from the national tourism office (phone: 270026).

***Cabuchon*** – Elegant gold and silver goods, excellent jewelry, and some expensive handicrafts. In the *Libertadores Shopping Center*, 532 Libertadores, San Isidro (phone: 270086).

***Camusso*** – If you speak Spanish fluently, you can buy gold and silver plates, cutlery, vases, candelabras, goblets, and other gift items from the factory. At two locations: 679 Av. Colonial (phone: 276170) and 788 Av. R. Rivera Navarrete, San Isidro (phone: 420340).

***Casa Más*** – One of the better dealers of gold and silver jewelry, gifts, and souvenirs. 781 Av. Nicolás de Piérola (phone: 277561).

***Casa Welsch*** – Essentially offering the same wares as *Casa Más*. Prices run about the same at both places, but it's a good idea to do some comparison shopping. 498 Jirón de la Unión (phone: 276153).

***La Gringa*** – Run by a North American woman, this place features a fine selection of handicrafts from around the country. In the *Alamo Shopping Center*, across from *César's* hotel in Miraflores. 522 La Paz (phone: 442900).

***Helen Hamann*** – The fashionable, high-quality alpaca and cotton knit sweaters are expensive, but less so than in the US. The factory store is at 370 Tacna, Miraflores (phone: 468609). There is also a shop at the *Museo del Oro*, 1100 Av. Alonso de Molina, Monterrico.

***H. Stern*** – Fine gold and silver jewelry with exclusive Peruvian designs. Expensive but backed by an international guarantee of credit or exchange. Main lobby of the *Lima Sheraton* (phone: 324842); at the *Gran Hotel Bolívar* (phone: 282257); and *César's* hotel (phone: 441212). Other branches at *Museo de Oro* and Jorge Chávez International Airport.

**Mon Repos** – Finely made alpaca and cotton sweaters and handicrafts in both traditional and contemporary styles and colors. At two locations: *Museo del Oro,* 1100 Av. Alonso de Molina, Monterrico (no phone) and at the *El Suche Galleries,* 646 La Paz in Miraflores (phone: 442150).

**Murguía** – Gold and silver items. 553 Jirón de la Unión (phone: 275955).

**Las Pallas** – Selected crafts from around Peru. The quality of artisan works here is probably, overall, the highest in the Lima area. 212 Cajamarca, Barranco (phone: 774629).

**Silvania Prints** – Sophisticated contemporary textiles, incorporating ancient Peruvian designs, are sold by the meter or made into scarves, dresses, and handbags. Goods are expensive, but everything is well made and quite stunning. Three locations: 714 Av. Nicolás de Piérola (phone: 243926); 905 Conquistadores, San Isidro (phone: 226440); and in *César's* hotel, Miraflores (phone: 441212).

**Vasco** – Exclusive designs of contemporary gold and silver jewelry, plus silverware and gifts. Three locations, besides the *Gold Museum: Crillón* hotel (phone: 283290, ext. 569); *Diplomat* hotel, Miraflores (phone: 475552); and at the *Central Comercial Todos* in San Isidro (phone: 408652).

**SPORTS:** The most popular sports in Lima are soccer *(fútbol),* bullfighting, and surfing.

**Bullfighting** – One of the major rings in Latin America, the *Plaza de Toros de Acho,* is described in *Special Places.* The major bullfighting season is October, November, and early December on Sundays and holidays. Ticket sales: 284 Jirón Huancavelica (phone: 277580 or 276570).

**Cockfighting** – This "sport" has been outlawed in the US, but is practiced in Lima on Wednesdays, Fridays, Saturdays, and Sundays at 8:30 PM at *Coliseo Sandia,* 150 Calle Sandia (phone: 281204).

**Cricket** – Aristocratic Anglo-Peruvians play cricket at the *Lima Cricket and Football Club* (151 Av. León de la Fuente, Orrantia; phone: 610080). There are no regularly scheduled matches; check the *Lima Times.*

**Fishing** – Surf-cast at La Herradura Beach or travel to Pucusana 39 miles (62 km) south of Lima on the Pan-American Highway. You can rent boats with local fishermen as guides. Fishing boats also can be rented at Ancón (see *Peru,* DIRECTIONS).

**Golf** – As this is the sport of Peru's elite, there are no public golf courses. The two main private clubs are the *Lima Golf Club* (Camino Real, 7th Block; phone: 227800) and *Los Incas Golf Club* (Av. Golf; phone: 352046). These clubs make their courses available to non-members on weekdays; arrangements should be made through your hotel or travel agent. If you are really hankering for 18 holes and can't get into either club, try *Los Eucaliptos* (in San Isidro; phone: 404060) or take a trip to *El Pueblo Inn* (at Km 11 on the Carretera Central; phone: 350777), or *Huampaní Golf Club* (at Km 26 on the Carretera Central; phone: 910342).

**Horse Racing** – Races are held on Tuesday and Thursday evenings and Saturday and Sunday afternoons at the *Hipódromo Monterrico* (Av. Javier Prado; phone: 351035). Check at the reception desk in your hotel or consult the morning newspaper for race schedules. On Fridays and Saturdays, you can place bets on the winners in Sunday's La Polla sweepstakes. The betting office is near Plaza San Martín (175 Jirón Tambo de Belén; phone: 238041).

**Polo** – Ponies can be rented at the *Lima Polo and Hunt Club* (phone: 373066), Monterrico, near *Los Incas Country Club.*

**Sailing** – The main regatta season runs from January through March, although aficionados sail year-round. There is an international competition in even-numbered years for the *Admiral Miguel Grau Cup*. It's not possible to charter boats in Lima, but four major yacht clubs offer privileges to members of other clubs: *Lima Regatta Club* (Chorrillos; phone: 672545); *Union Regatta Club* (Plaza Gálvez, La Punta; phone: 290286); *Yacht Club Peruano* (Muelle Dársena, Callao; phone: 290775); and *Yacht Club de Ancón* (Malecón de Ancón; phone: 883071).

**Skin Diving** – The preferred beach is Santa María. For information on equipment and group dives, call the Peruvian Federation of Skin Diving (phone: 246688).

**Soccer** – Lima's three best teams are *Universitario, Alianza Lima,* and *Sporting Cristal*. Major games are played at the *Estadio Nacional* (National Stadium), Calle José Díaz (phone: 329177).

**Surfing** – You can see surfers on the waves along the Costa Verde beaches throughout the year, sun or fog. International competitions are held in Lima from time to time; Peru has been home to its share of champions in the sport. Note: The waters inevitably are cold, so don't forget a wet suit! For information, contact *Waikiki Club* (Bajada Baños de Miraflores; phone: 451149). The best surfing beaches are La Herradura, Macaja, Punta Rica, and Ancón.

**Swimming** – Good surfing beaches are not always best for swimming because the waves are pretty rough. There are swimming pools at the *Lima Sheraton* (Paseo de la República; phone: 328676); *Lima Country Club* (Los Eucaliptos, San Isidro; phone: 404060); *El Pardo* (420 Pardo, Miraflores; phone: 470283); *María Angola* (610 Av. La Paz, Miraflores; phone: 441280); *César's* hotel (463 La Paz, Miraflores; phone: 441212); *El Bosque Country Club* (at Km 33 on the Carretera Central, Chaclacayo; phone: 910682); *Los Cóndores Country Club* (Chaclacayo; phone: 910058); *Villa Country Club* (Chorrillos, just off the Pan-American Hwy. heading south at Km 22; phone: 670851); and *El Pueblo Inn* (Km 11, Carretera Central; phone: 350777). Also contact the Peruvian Federation of Swimming (phone: 249885) for information on public pools.

**Tennis** – In addition to the country clubs and golf clubs listed above, there are courts at the *Lawn Tennis Club* (744 Av. 28 de Julio; phone: 240906), which also has a swimming pool, and at the *Club Tenis Las Terrazas* (Malecón 28 de Julio, Miraflores; phone: 452997). *El Pueblo Inn* (Km 11, Carretera Central; phone: 350777) also has courts, as does *Country Club Los Eucaliptos* (in San Isidro; phone: 404060).

**Water Skiing** – Ancón is the best place in Peru for water skiing. Contact the *Yacht Club de Ancón* for details, Malecón de Ancón (phone: 883071).

**THEATER:** The *Lima Times* has listings of the occasional English-language productions performed in Lima but, for those who know Spanish, there are numerous theatrical productions to enjoy. These can be found by referring to the cultural section of the daily newspaper, *El Comercio*. The principal theaters in the center of Lima are *Segura* (255 Jirón Huancavelica; phone: 277437) and the *Municipal* (355 Jirón Ica; phone: 282303). The latter presents concerts, ballet, and folklore spectaculars, both Peruvian and from other nations. There are several theaters and café-theaters in Miraflores but most present only Spanish-language performances.

**MUSIC:** Peruvian music is as varied as the country's geography and ranges from the *marinera* from the coast to the popular *chicha* dance music common in the *pueblos jovenes* (shantytowns). But by far the most haunting tunes are those performed with *quenas* — reed flutes from the Andean highlands. Andean groups perform nightly at *Bar Restaurant 1900,* 1030 Calle Belén (phone: 233590).

The *Philharmonic Society* sponsors a series of concerts that features well-known North American and European orchestras and soloists. The office is open Mondays, Wednesdays, and Fridays from 10 AM to noon at 170 Porta, Office 301 in Miraflores (phone: 457395).

**NIGHTCLUBS AND NIGHTLIFE:** There are plenty of nightclubs and lots of nightlife, especially on the weekends, but not in the center of Lima unless you want to stay in your hotel: If it's the *Lima Sheraton,* you can go to the *Koricancha;* César's has *El Lúcumo;* and the *Crillón*'s nightclub is the *Sky Room,* which offers Lima's best folkloric show evenings, except Sundays, at 8 PM. Lasting more than an hour, elaborately costumed performers bring you the dances and music of the sierra and coastal regions of this diverse country. The show is complimentary to diners; otherwise there is a $6 cover charge. 589 Nicolás de Piérola (phone: 283290).

The better discotheques are *Ebony 56* (841 Las Magnolias, San Isidro; phone: 424695); *Las Rocas* (821 Las Magnolias, San Isidro; phone: 420906); and *Percy's* (125 Los Tulipanes; phone: 724568). They are jammed full of folks and are noisy, colorful, and expensive — very North American in style. Bring your passport for admission to these clubs. *Satchmo Jazz Bar* (530 La Paz, Miraflores; phone: 441753) offers national and international jazz names (with a stiff cover charge) in an elegant, New Orleans–style setting. Drinks and hors d'oeuvres are served in the bar, while its restaurant, *Sal & Pimienta,* has a menu emphasizing seafood. Reservations necessary.

There are two elegant spots for dinner and dancing in Miraflores: *Piel Canela* (120 Pardo; phone: 454331) and *Privilege* (beneath the *El Condado* hotel at 465 Alcanfores; phone: 443614).

Lima is a great city for *peñas* and no visit is complete without a stop at one of these restaurants offering nonstop entertainment ranging from Peruvian folk singers and Afro-Peruvian dances to energetic salsa in which the audience participates. The main attraction is definitely the music; the food and drinks are often overpriced and not as tasty as some found in the better restaurants. Consider eating first and going to a *peña* for after-dinner drinks. There are *peñas* all over the city, although some on the Av. del Ejército have become tourist traps. We recommend *Karamanduka* (135 Faustino Sánchez Carrión, Barranco; phone: 473227); *La Casa de Edith* (250 Ignacio Merino, Miraflores; phone: 410612); *La Palizada* (800 Av. del Ejército; phone: 410552); and *Sachún International* (657 Av. del Ejército; phone: 410123). *Hatuchay* (228 Trujillo, Rimac; phone: 247779), less flashy and more popular with *limeños,* also is good for a rollicking time Wednesdays through Saturdays. Most *peñas* have one show during the week, starting at 11 PM and two on weekends — the first beginning at 8 or 9 PM.

If you're in the mood for a drink or for some light food and people watching, try one of the popular outdoor cafés, all right in the heart of Miraflores: *Haiti* (160 Benavides; phone: 475052); *La Sueca* (759 Larco; phone: 459733); *La Tiendecita Blanca* (111 Larco; phone: 459797); and *Vivaldi* (258 R. Palma; phone: 471636).

**Note:** There are no singles bars in Lima, and if a woman is traveling alone and knows no one locally, she is somewhat restricted in her choice of nightlife. Women may be subjected to unsolicited attention if they go to a club or café-theater alone. Men or women are ill advised to go alone into the bars called *cantinas,* of which there are a number in the center of the city. It is much safer to go out with others at night since the crime rate has been increasing rapidly.

## BEST IN TOWN

**CHECKING IN:** Since the early 1970s, Peru has become an international tourism destination. People come from Japan, Germany, France, Italy, New Zealand, the US, and England at great cost to appreciate both pre-Columbian and colonial Peru. As a result, the major cities on the prime tourist route — Lima, Cuzco, and more recently Arequipa — have built several new hotels and hostels in all price categories. In Lima, expect to pay as much as $100 for a double room at those hotels classified as expensive; between $35 and $65 at hotels in the moderate category, and less than $35 at places in the inexpensive category. The expensive hotels charge a 30% tax on rooms and food. All telephone numbers are in the 14 city code unless otherwise indicated.

**César's** – One of Lima's most luxurious hotels (and undoubtedly the best) is in the elegant suburb of Miraflores. The 150 rooms are spacious, air conditioned, and handsomely furnished with replicas of the furniture that graced the fine mansions of colonial Lima. One of the bars, *La Estación,* is decorated like a first class coach car on one of the early English trains brought to Peru almost a century ago; there's lovely wood paneling and silver adornments — very British-Peruvian. The tearoom, *La Reja,* and the cafeteria-bar, *La Vereda,* have excellent Peruvian pastries and sandwiches. The hotel's elegant restaurant, *El Lúcumo,* offers both Peruvian and international menus. Or, if you want to see Miraflores from above, go up to the restaurant with a view, *La Azotea.* The hotel has its own drugstore, flower shop, barber and beauty shops, an open-air swimming pool, small stores, and parking. Reservations necessary. Major credit cards accepted. Av. La Paz and Av. Diez Canseco (phone: 441212; fax: 444440). Expensive.

**El Condado** – One of Miraflores's most elegant properties, with 50 rooms, 27 suites (some with saunas and Jacuzzis). It has a charming restaurant with wood beams and wrought-iron chandeliers, and an adjacent piano bar with deep leather sofas (see *Eating Out*). In the chic *El Suche Shopping Center,* it is within walking distance of virtually all of the better Miraflores eating and drinking spots. 465 Alcanfores (phone: 443614). Expensive.

**Crillón** – This was the first truly modern hotel in Lima and is on the Colmena, one of the city's principal streets, and because of the exceptional service and Swiss management it is a favorite, despite its 1950s decor. Twenty-two stories high, its 551 comfortable rooms and suites are attended night and day by devoted staff. Suffice it to say that your every request is answered practically as you make it. The hotel's roof garden restaurant has an excellent buffet weekdays from noon to 3 PM, from November through March, with a sumptuous spread of both Peruvian/creole and international food. In the evenings, the *Sky Room* on the 20th floor offers a superb view of downtown Lima and a good folkloric show. Try colonial Peru's unique contribution to the world's cocktails, the *pisco* sour, in the *Bar Don Pepe.* It will come accompanied by lots of tasty complimentary nibbles. Downstairs, the *Grill La Balsa* serves some of the best food in Lima (see *Eating Out*). 589 Av. Nicolás de Piérola (phone: 283290; in the US, 800-44-UTELL; or through *Latin America Reservations Center, LARC;* 800-327-3573; fax: 280682). Expensive.

**Diplomat** – Located in Miraflores, this is an attractive first class place associated with the Plaza hotel group. Its 130 large, clean rooms all have private baths and air conditioning. There are 2 restaurants, as well as a coffee shop. The decor is clean-lined and contemporary. 290 Alcánfores (phone: 478776; fax: 466767). Expensive.

**Gran Hotel Bolívar** – The name is Spanish but the influence is all British, for whom the Peruvians have a cultural affinity that dates from independence in 1821, when the British participated in the revolution and later built railroads throughout the country. An enduring and endearing custom is tea served with dainty petit fours by white-gloved waiters in the glass-domed rotunda every afternoon. The hotel bar is a popular meeting place and serves possibly the best *pisco* sours in the capital; the dining room serves fine Peruvian fare. Pass up a room overlooking the picturesque plaza in favor of a quieter one facing inside. Unfortunately, the elegant ambience has been diminished by a *Kentucky Fried*

*Chicken* outlet on the main floor. Conveniently located at Plaza San Martín (phone: 276400). Expensive.

**José Antonio** – This 56-room luxury hotel prides itself on service. There's a bar and restaurant and the location — in the heart of Miraflores — can't be beat. 398 Av. 28 de Julio (phone: 456870 and 468295; fax: 468295). Expensive.

**Libertador Lima** – A very pleasant and peaceful 52-room hostelry right next to the *Country Club,* overlooking the golf course, where guests can arrange to play. In addition to a rooftop restaurant, there is a piano bar and coffee shop. 550 Los Eucaliptos, San Isidro (phone: 416492; in the US, through *LARC,* 800-327-3573; fax: 423011). Expensive.

**Lima Sheraton** – This link in the Sheraton chain has few surprises as far as architectural design and its 490 rooms are concerned. However, its 20-story lobby is enlivened by striking sculptures by Delfin, one of Peru's best-known artists. Also very striking are the magnified copies of Nazca and Paracas tapestries, which decorate all of the public rooms as well as the far end of the lobby. On weekends, the *Korikancha* restaurant-nightclub presents a super show with internationally known Latin American stars. Reservations are necessary. The main dining room is furnished with colonial-style tables and chairs and decorated with some fine pieces of 17th- and 18th-century viceregal art. Dinner is always served by candlelight. The coffee shop, open 24 hours a day, serves American food. 170 Paseo de la República (phone: 333320 and 329050; in the US, 800-334-8484; fax: 336344). Expensive.

**María Angola** – Another Miraflores favorite, right down the street from both *El Condado* and *César's.* A medium-size hotel with good service, it has suites with saunas and hot tubs. There is a rooftop pool and *Los Faisanes* restaurant, one of Lima's finest (see *Eating Out*). 610 La Paz (phone: 441280; in the US, 800-44-UTELL). Expensive.

**El Pardo** – Still another of Miraflores's convenient properties, this 10-story, 120-room hostelry boasts a fine restaurant, rooftop swimming pool, gym, sauna, Jacuzzi, and satellite TV. It mainly caters to businesspeople, and offers services such as fax, telex, and meeting rooms. 420 Av. Pardo (phone: 470283; in the US, 800-44-UTELL; fax: 442171). Expensive.

**El Pueblo Inn** – The name, which means "the village," really reflects the physical nature of this hotel: It's constructed like a typical Andean colonial village (were the typical Andean village to have such beautiful antiques and carved doors and ornate, wrought-iron grillwork). Truly impressive, comfortable, and more Peruvian in flavor than any of Lima's luxury hotels, it is outside the city in the Rímac Valley, only 25 minutes from the airport. Surrounded by the low peaks of this part of the Andes chain, this place enjoys sun almost every day of the year, making its 18-hole golf course, horseback riding facilities, 2 pools, and other activities especially attractive. Besides rooms, there are 34 bungalows, 3 restaurants, a bread and pastry store, tearoom, cinema, billiards parlor, bowling alleys, Turkish baths, and a sauna. A few steps away is the well-known *Granja Azul* restaurant (see *Eating Out*). At Km 11 on the Carretera Central (phone: 350777; in Lima, 466427; fax: 355354; in Lima, 466396), or write 2585 Casilla, Lima 100. Reservations also can be made in the US through *Utell International* (phone: 800-44-UTELL). Expensive.

**Ariosto** – In the heart of Miraflores, this is a pleasant, medium-size hostelry, offering room and laundry service, car rental, and telex. A small criollo restaurant is open daily, and *La Pérgola Bar* serves drinks and hors d'oeuvres. 769 Av. La Paz (phone: 441416; fax: 441416). Moderate.

**Country Club** – Until several years ago, this was one of the most popular properties in Lima, sought after by visitors who wanted to enjoy tranquillity and the lovely green parks of San Isidro, one of Lima's most exclusive residential districts. Although no longer considered luxurious, it offers 2 restaurants, 2 bars, its own golf links in front of the hotel, tennis courts, a swimming pool, and sauna. Los Eucaliptos (phone: 404060). Moderate.

***Emperador*** – This new 20-suite hostelry in Miraflores is working hard to earn a reputation for service, but its comfortable price in this upscale area is the biggest draw. The hotel's *El Encuentro* restaurant features French fare; there also is a cafeteria and a bar. 240 General Suárez (phone: 478177; fax: 453880). Moderate.

***La Plaza*** – Only steps away from Plaza San Martín, it's a small, first class hostelry with a cozy cocktail lounge called *Don Eduardo* and a small restaurant, *La Placita*. All rooms are air conditioned. 850 Av. Nicolás de Piérola (phone: 286270). Moderate.

***Riviera*** – This modern hotel is close to the geographical center of Lima, with comfortable, clean rooms, 3 restaurants, including one with Peruvian music, and cafeteria service. One floor of rooms is set aside for nonsmokers. 981 Av. Garcilaso de la Vega (phone: 289460; fax: 314687). Moderate.

***Sans Souci*** – An immaculate 35-room hostel with small modern rooms and excellent service, just off Av. Javier Prado at 2670 Arequipa, San Isidro (phone: 226035). Moderate.

***Colonial Inn*** – A family place that offers 20 rooms and 2 suites, all featuring phones, TV sets, and private baths. There is a restaurant and a rooftop sundeck, and bicycle rental and laundry services can be arranged. It also has telex and fax services. A continental breakfast is included in the room rates. Not far from the beach, and just a few blocks from the main shopping district of Miraflores at 310 Av. Comandante Espinar (phone: 466666; fax: 451641). Inexpensive.

***Hostal Beech*** – This small, pink house has a lovely little garden and serves breakfast and light snacks. In the heart of San Isidro, it is owned by a North American. 165 Los Libertadores (phone: 405595). Inexpensive.

***Hostal San Francisco*** – Right across from the San Francisco monastery, this 46-room establishment is a favorite of students and budget-conscious travelers. Clean, well run, and with a fine lobby restaurant, this place is a good choice for those who want to stay downtown at a very good price. 340 Jirón Ancash (phone: 283643). Inexpensive.

***Hostal Torreblanca*** – Small and with an ocean view, this place also has a lovely interior garden. Owners are friendly and will keep baggage for those guests traveling to the provinces. The snack bar provides room service. 1453 Pardo (at the second *óvalo*) in Miraflores (phone: 479998). Inexpensive.

**EATING OUT:** Judged on its restaurants alone, Lima would have to pass as a very cosmopolitan city. Peruvians consider food an important part of life, and this attitude has influenced the development of restaurants in the capital, where a broad spectrum of cuisines spill out of kitchens around the city. The most pervasive is criollo, native Peruvian cooking, a combination of Spanish and Indian kitchens and unique for its delectable spicing. There are hundreds of criollo restaurants in Lima, and though atmosphere and quality vary widely among them, the basic ingredients are the same in all. Lima also has good French, Spanish, Italian, Argentine, Mexican, Swiss, Japanese, Chinese, and vegetarian restaurants. Don't leave Peru without trying ceviche — fish marinated in lemon, hot pepper, and onion — and the national cocktail, *pisco* sour, which is a blend of *pisco* (a grape brandy), lemon juice, egg white, and cinnamon.

Expect to pay $60 and up for a dinner for two at the restaurant in the expensive category; between $35 and $60 at those places we've classified as moderate; under $35, inexpensive. Prices do not include drinks, wine, tip, or tax. A fixed charge — *cu-*

*bierto* — is often added for place settings. Be forewarned — at press time, a whopping 30% tax and service charge was added to restaurant bills! All telephone numbers are in the 14 city code unless otherwise indicated.

**El Condado** – Wooden beams and wrought-iron chandeliers decorate this cozy restaurant in *El Condado* hotel. Their specialty is El Puñal de la Condesa (The Dagger of the Countess), a grilled brochette of shrimp, artichokes, and onion served on a bed of saffron rice. Before dinner, enjoy a cocktail on the deep leather sofas in the adjacent piano bar, where there's live music from 9 to 11 PM. Open daily for breakfast, lunch, and dinner. Reservations unnecessary. Major credit cards accepted. 465 Alcanfores (phone: 443614). Expensive.

**Los Condes de San Isidro** – If you'd like to relive the grace and charm of the colonial days and sample traditional Peruvian dishes at the same time, this is the place to go. The lovely mansion-restaurant has elegant dining in the main room or outside on the terrace by the garden. Its seafood is highly recommended. Open daily. Reservations unnecessary. Major credit cards accepted. 290 Paz Soldán, San Isidro (phone: 222557). Expensive.

**La Costa Verde** – Many say that this is the best of all Lima's fine seafood restaurants. Right on the beach, it is perfect for a relaxing lunch at a seaside table with one of the excellent piña coladas, or the ideal setting for a romantic dinner outdoors. Open daily. Reservations necessary. Major credit cards accepted. Barranquito Beach, Barranco (phone: 678218). Expensive.

**Pabellón de Caza** – One of Lima's luxury dining places, a few yards from the *Gold Museum* in Monterrico. The chef is French, and venison and other game (in season) are specialties of the house. The *Bwana Grill,* the latest addition to *Pabellón*, offers excellent grilled meats, a salad bar, and fine wines by either the bottle or the glass. Open Mondays through Saturdays for lunch and dinner, and Sundays for brunch only (10:30 AM to 4 PM. Reservations unnecessary. Major credit cards accepted. 1100 Alonso de Molino (phone: 379533 and 379477). Expensive.

**Rosa Náutica** – This popular and elegant Miraflores spot is built over an ocean breakwater and provides a view of the ongoing parade of surfers. Seafood, international, and Peruvian dishes are featured at lunch and dinner; there's also brunch on Sundays. Corvina (sea bass) is the house specialty. Open daily. Reservations advised. Major credit cards accepted. Espigón (Pier) No. 4, Costa Verde (phone: 470057 or 450149). Expensive.

**El Suche** – Elegant dining, a French and international menu, and piano music await patrons here. Open daily. Reservations advised. Major credit cards accepted. In the *El Suche Galleries,* 646 La Paz, Miraflores (phone: 455592). Expensive.

**La Granja Azul** – A must for anyone spending a few days in Lima who is looking for something different in the way of a restaurant. For one price, you can eat your fill of charcoal-broiled chicken, with plenty of hot sauce at hand if you like your bird spicy. Homemade bread is served straight from adobe ovens that you can see in the restaurant. In addition to good bar service, on weekends an orchestra plays, and there is dancing nightly. Open daily. Reservations necessary. Major credit cards accepted. At Km 11 on the Carretera Central (phone: 350777). Expensive to moderate.

**Blue Moon** – An unlikely name and an unlikely setting — the largely residential district of Lince. Once inside, though, you're in for a treat. The highlight of the decor is the ceiling — covered with more than 5,000 bottles of wines and liquors. The owners are Italian, so the pasta is tasty and you can get real Italian ices as well. Open daily; Sunday brunch from 1 to 4 PM. Reservations unnecessary. Major credit cards accepted. 2526 Pumacahua (phone: 701190). Moderate.

**Carlin** – This Miraflores eatery has an interesting international menu, but it is most famous in the neighborhood for mixing up a very good *pisco* sour, the Peruvian national drink. The atmosphere is a rustic blend of wooden beams, antique curiosities, and porcelain collectibles. It is in *El Suche Galleries,* where you can browse through the exhibits of handicrafts. Open daily for lunch and dinner. Reservations advised on Fridays and Saturdays. Major credit cards accepted. 646 Av. La Paz (phone: 444134). Moderate.

**Casa Vasca** – Particularly to be recommended in this Basque bistro is ceviche, a Peruvian specialty made with raw fish marinated in lemon juice, hot pepper, and onion and served with corn on the cob. Reservations advised. Major credit cards accepted. 734 Av. Nicolás de Piérola (phone: 236690). Moderate.

**Châlet Suisse** – The decor is "Swiss kitsch," and the clientele is mainly tourists, but the food is in the best of taste, with specialties from Swiss and Viennese cuisines. Commendable service. Open daily. Reservations advised. Major credit cards accepted. 560 Av. Nicolás de Piérola (phone: 312985). Moderate.

**El Cortijo** – Specializes in Argentine food, primarily charcoal-broiled baby beef served with large salads and a carafe of wine. Broiled chicken is on the menu, too. A pleasant, somewhat rustic spot quite a distance from the center of Lima. Open daily. Reservations unnecessary. No credit cards accepted. 675 Av. República de Panamá, Barranco (phone: 454481). Moderate.

**Los Faisanes** – Very elegant atmosphere with good, and sometimes excellent, French cuisine. Reservations unnecessary. No credit cards accepted. Downstairs in the *María Angola Hotel,* 610 La Paz, Miraflores (phone: 441280). Moderate.

**Giannino** – Solid, plain Italian dishes. The downstairs decor is plain; upstairs, schmaltzy elegant, but the food is of high quality and ample quantity on both floors. Closed Sundays and holidays. 899 Jirón Rufino Torrico (phone: 314978). Moderate.

**Grill La Balsa** – Although this elegant eatery is mostly frequented by tourists, it offers some of the best dining in Lima. It serves both international food and *"comida tipica"* (typical Peruvian fare) and specializes in fish. There is live folkloric music every night. Closed Sundays. No reservations. *Crillón Hotel,* 589 Av. Nicolás de Piérola (phone: 283290). Moderate.

**José Antonio** – For some of the best in criollo food and music, try this little jewel, tucked away in San Isidro. The atmosphere is colonial and the weekend crowds are lively. Closed Sundays. Reservations unnecessary. Major credit cards accepted. 200 Monteagudo (phone: 619923). Moderate.

**Matsuei** – The place to go for excellent Japanese cuisine. Reservations advised. Credit cards accepted. 236 Canadá, La Victoria (phone: 722282). Moderate.

**El Otro Sitio** – If you're out for a moonlight stroll through the picturesque Barranco and over the Bridge of Sighs, stop here for a good criollo dinner. Daily buffet of Peruvian food, live music. Closed Sundays. Reservations unnecessary. Major credit cards accepted. 317 Sucre, Barranco (phone: 772413). Moderate.

**La Pizzería** – Currently one of Miraflores's most popular nightspots, offering international, Italian, and Peruvian choices at very reasonable prices. Great people watching, too. Open daily. Major credit cards accepted. 322 Benavides (phone: 467793 and 467795). Moderate.

**El Puente** – Tucked under the romantic Bridge of Sighs in the bohemian suburb of Barranco, there's good food and music in one of the most tranquil corners of Lima. Major credit cards accepted. 343 Av. Bajada de los Baños (phone: 671886). Moderate.

**Rincón Gaucho** – Perched on a cliff overlooking the Pacific at the end of Avenida Larco, this spectacular Argentine restaurant serves terrific *parrillada* and steaks. Be prepared for long lines, especially around 8:30 and 9 PM. It's jammed on weekends, too. Open daily. No reservations. Major credit cards accepted. 1207 Larco at Parque Salazar, Miraflores (phone: 474778). Moderate.

**El Salto del Fraile** – Set on a cliff where legend has it that a love-struck friar leaped to his death, this fine eatery along Herradura Beach specializes in grilled seafood. A good spot to be at sunset (phone: 671355). Moderate.

**Las Trece Monedas** – In the center of Lima, this illustrious colonial mansion built in 1787 now houses one of the best truly Peruvian restaurants. The coat of arms over the main entrance contains 13 coins, from which comes the restaurant's name. The atmosphere is unexcelled, and the criollo food, superb. The international selections on the menu also are well prepared. Closed Sundays. Reservations necessary in the evenings. Major credit cards accepted. 536 Jirón Ancash (phone: 276547). Moderate.

**Valentino** – A charming eating place in San Isidro popular with both Peruvians and resident foreigners, it offers simple and delicious Italian fare with a Peruvian touch. Closed Sundays. Reservations advised. Major credit cards accepted. 215 Manuel Bañón (phone: 416174). Moderate.

**El Dorado** – Very good Peruvian-Chinese fare with a panoramic view of Lima. Try the crab claws (*uñas de cangrejo*). Reservations unnecessary. Major credit cards accepted. 2450 Arequipa, San Isidro (phone: 221080). Moderate to inexpensive.

**Lung Fung** – With private dining rooms and indoor gardens, it is the most dramatic of Lima's *chifas,* or Chinese restaurants. The wontons are good as is the shrimp *cristal,* light, deep-fried shrimp served with a piquant lemon sauce. Reservations unnecessary. Major credit cards accepted. 3165 Av. República de Panamá, San Isidro (phone: 226382). Moderate to inexpensive.

**Rosita Ríos** – In one of the oldest parts of Lima, the district of Rímac (across the river and behind the Presidential Palace), is this truly representative Peruvian coastal restaurant, with a large variety of pretty spicy dishes. Along with your meal, you are served a heaping portion of all kinds of Peruvian music. A favorite with the locals. Closed Mondays. Reservations advised. No credit cards accepted. 100 Cajatambo, La Florida (phone: 814105). Moderate to inexpensive.

**Bar Restaurant 1900** – This former US Embassy residence is a delightful spot tucked away in an arcade that also contains three courtyards and two dozen souvenir shops. The turn-of-the-century decor contrasts charmingly with the menu (which features seafood and Peruvian specialties) and the Andean music performed nightly. Lunch is served in the café; for dinner, patrons move indoors to the elegant dining room. Open daily, except Sundays, from 10 AM. Reservations unnecessary. No credit cards accepted. 1030 Calle Belén (phone: 233590). Inexpensive.

**Bircher Benner** – Installed in a charming old house, this vegetarian restaurant offers good meatless dishes, fresh juices, herb teas, and very good natural ice cream sundaes, all at very reasonable prices. There is also a natural foods store on the premises. Closed Sundays. Reservations unnecessary. No credit cards accepted. 598 Schell, Miraflores (phone: 477118 or 444250). Inexpensive.

**Centenaria Botica Francesa** – An offbeat escape from the hustle and bustle of Jirón de la Unión. It's a soda fountain and pharmacy under the same roof. Sandwiches are unimaginative, but the ice cream is scooped with a heavy hand. This is also a quiet spot for a coffee. No credit cards accepted. 451 Jirón de la Unión (phone: 289917). Inexpensive.

**L'Eau Vive** – Linked to the Argentine restaurant (in Luján) with the same name, this one offers French country cooking served by French nuns in a colonial building in the heart of downtown Lima. The decor is spartan, but the food — especially the desserts — is delicious. At 10 PM, just before the restaurant closes, the nuns gather in the dining room to sing "Ave María." Closed Sundays. Major credit cards accepted. 370 Ucayali (phone: 275612). Inexpensive.

**El Mesón del Fraile** – Nestled in the Franciscan monastery's Patio de Pimienta, where spices once were traded, this small eatery offers dining in a lovely courtyard or in a series of rooms decorated with altars. Criollo food is served daily from 10 AM to 6 PM, but guests also are welcome to enjoy coffee or a drink from the bar. No reservations. No credit cards accepted. Note: No admission charge to the monastery for those who come only to dine. Monasterio de San Francisco, 300 Jirón Ancash (phone: 272720 or 275254). Inexpensive.

*El Pacayal* – For a taste of the city of Arequipa without leaving the capital, try this friendly spot tucked inside a colonial house near the Bridge of Sighs in Barranco. The spicy Arequipan touch is applied to shrimp — the house specialty — and other dishes, so if you don't like it hot, be sure to tell the waiter. Open daily for lunch and dinner. Reservations unnecessary. Major credit cards accepted. 106 Pedro de Osma, Barranco (phone: 677114). Inexpensive.

*Raimondi* – If the gold brocade wall covering doesn't hit you, then the intricately carved ceiling will. The food here isn't the greatest in the city but the decor is worth the visit. Right downtown, just off Jirón de la Unión, this is where the secret lovers in Mario Vargas Llosa's novel, *Aunt Julia and the Scriptwriter,* met for coffee. Open daily. No reservations. No credit cards accepted. 158 Miró Quesada (phone: 277933). Inexpensive.

# MONTEVIDEO

Residents of Montevideo are fond of referring to their home as a place hardly anyone knows. The capital of the Oriental Republic of Uruguay, it is frankly overshadowed by Buenos Aires to the west and São Paulo to the north.

Uruguay is a land of low hills and rolling grassy plains with abundant pastureland and a temperate climate on the eastern bank of the Río Uruguay, its frontier with Argentina. This river, in turn, flows into the great estuary of the Río de la Plata, whose wide shores are shared by Buenos Aires and Montevideo. With an area of 68,037 square miles, Uruguay is one of the smallest countries in South America. Its population of about 3.5 million inhabitants is unevenly distributed: nearly 1.5 million people make their home in the capital; the remainder live in the cities in the interior and in the countryside.

If residents of the city and citizens of the country are sanguine about the relative obscurity of city and state, wedged between the trailing tail of Brazil and Argentina's overweening bulk, it may be because in the lifestyle sweepstakes they are doing quite well. In recent years, Uruguay has become a key offshore banking center for Latin American investors and "narcodollars" that are "helping" the country's economy. The country is predominantly middle class, and its people are extremely well nourished by international standards. Uruguayans are well educated, with a literacy rate of 94%, along with Chile and Argentina, the highest in South America. Life expectancy is 69 years, and there is a low infant mortality rate.

The first European to step on Uruguayan soil was Juan Díaz de Solís, who arrived in 1516. The Spanish explorer was sailing southward along the eastern coast of South America, seeking a strait leading to the other side of the New World; as soon as they landed, he and his party were attacked and killed by the Charrúa (Uruguayan Indians). Four years later, the Portuguese discovered the area. Captain Ferdinand Magellan, whose crew first circumnavigated the globe, sailed cautiously into the Río de la Plata. A sailor posted as lookout saw the hill that today's *montevideños* call the *cerro* and called out *"Monte vide eu"* ("I see a mountain").

From those days of Solís and Magellan to the coming of the British (who occupied the city for a brief 7 months in 1807), and the independence from Spain soon thereafter, the Banda Oriental del Uruguay (as it was then called) served as a natural arena of conflict between the Spanish and Portuguese empires.

Finally in 1828, with Great Britain's intervention, both Brazil and Argentina recognized Uruguay as an independent nation, a buffer state between two large and jealous neighbors. Despite the fact that independence had been

## AT-A-GLANCE

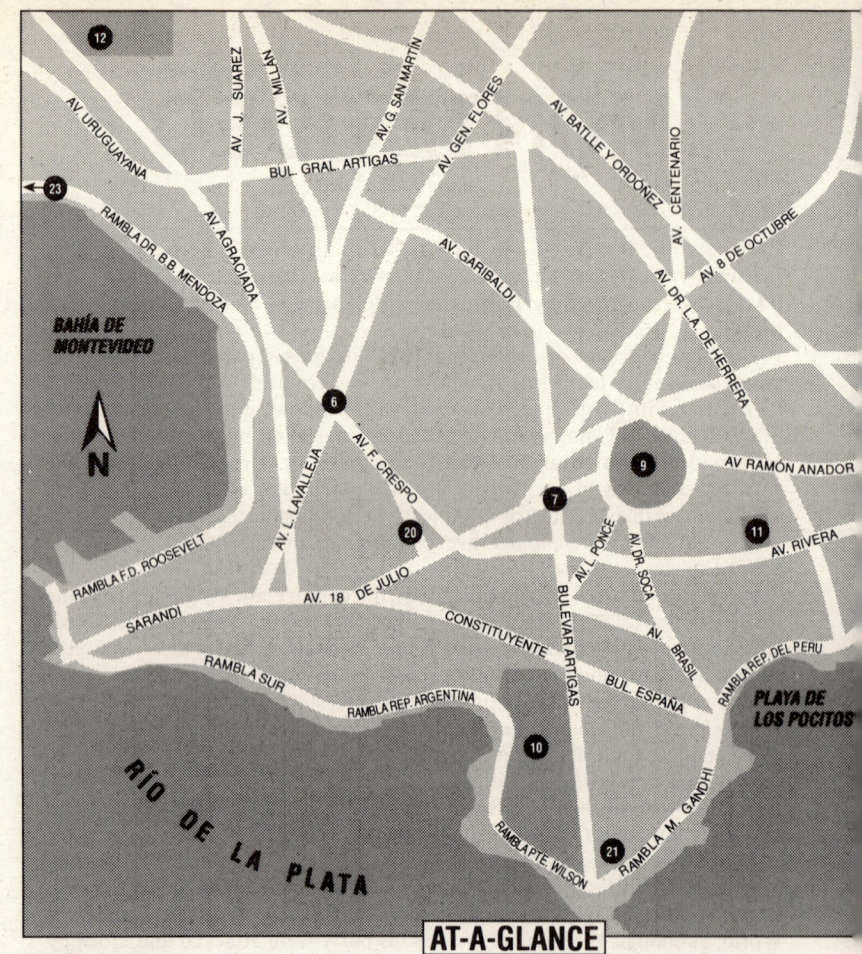

### Points of Interest

1. Mirador/Lookout Tower; Intendencia/Municipal Palace
2. Plaza Independencia/Independence Plaza; Mausoleo de José Gervasio Artigas/Mausoleum of José Gervasio Artigas
3. Cabildo/Town Hall
4. Catedral de Montevideo/Montevideo Cathedral
5. Museo Histórico Nacional y Museo Romántico/National Historical Museum and Romantic Museum
6. Palacio Legislativo/Legislative Palace
7. El Obelisco/Obelisk
8. Museo del Gaucho y La Moneda/Cowboy and Gold Museum
9. Parque José Batlle y Ordóñez; La Carreta Statue; Estadio Centenario
10. Parque Rodó/Rodó Park; Galeria Nacional de Arte/National Art Gallery
11. Parque Zoológico/Zoological Park
12. Parque Prado/Prado Park; Museo Municipal de Juan Manuel Blanes/Juan Manuel Blanes Museum
13. Teatro Solís/Solís Theater; Museo de Historia Natural/Natural History Museum
14. Museo Municipal de Arte Precolombino y Colonial/Municipal Museum of Precolumbian and Colonial Art
15. Plaza Cagancha; Tourist Information; Museo de Arte Contemporáneo/Museum of Contemporary Art
16. Plaza Zabala; Plaza Matriz Antiques Fair
17. Mercado del Puerto/Port Market
18. Carrasco Beach
19. Museo de Arte Decorativo/Decorative Arts Museum
20. Feria de Tristán Narvaja/Tristán Narvaja Market
21. Feria de Villa Biarritz/Villa Biarritz Market
22. Aerpuerto Nacional de Carrasco
23. Fortaleza General Artigas

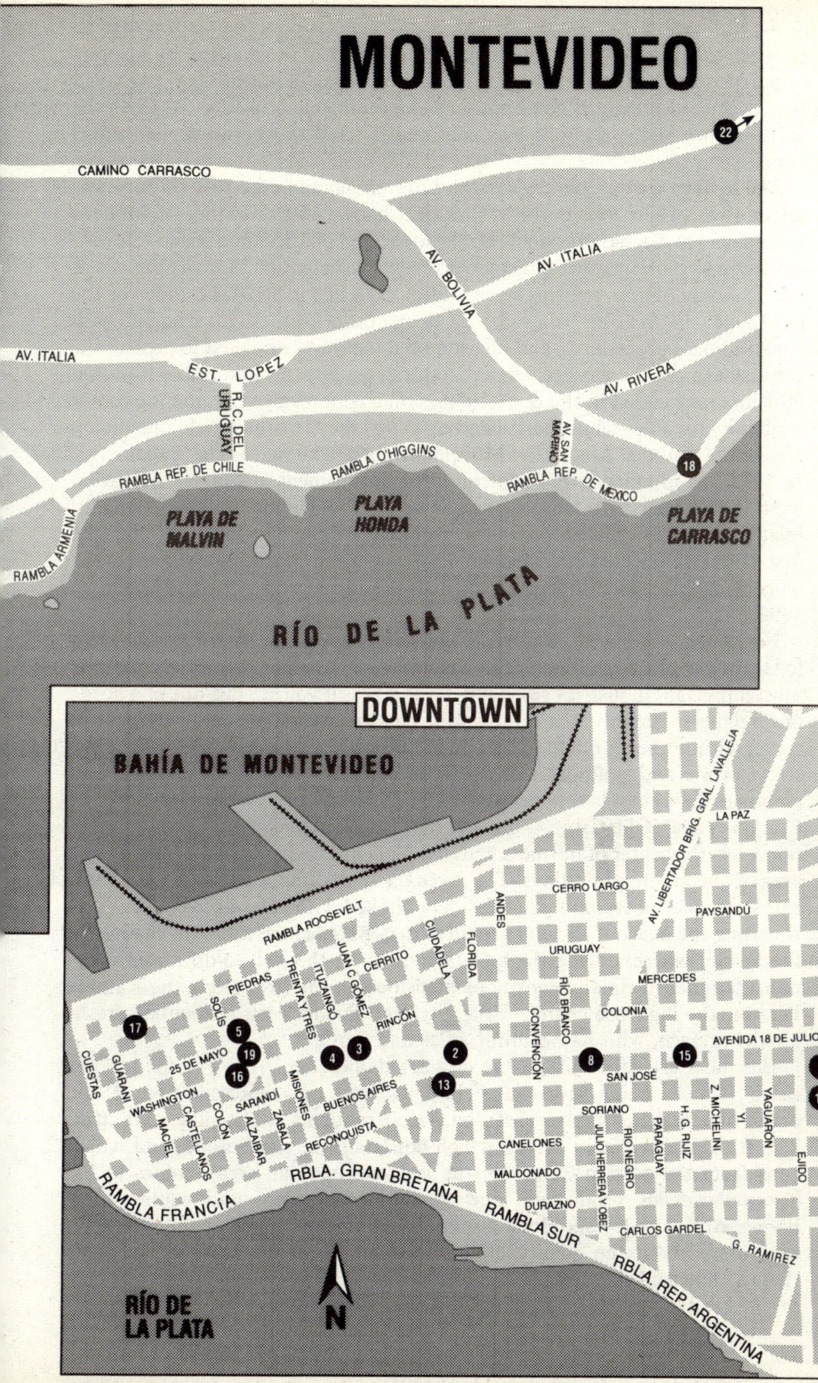
MONTEVIDEO
22
CAMINO CARRASCO
AV. BOLIVIA
AV. ITALIA
AV. ITALIA
EST. LOPEZ
R. C. DEL URUGUAY
AV. RIVERA
AV. SAN MARINO
RAMBLA REP. DE CHILE
RAMBLA O'HIGGINS
RAMBLA REP. DE MEXICO
18
PLAYA DE MALVIN
PLAYA HONDA
PLAYA DE CARRASCO
RAMBLA ARMENIA
RÍO DE LA PLATA
DOWNTOWN
BAHÍA DE MONTEVIDEO
LA PAZ
AV. LIBERTADOR BRIG. GRAL. LAVALLEJA
CERRO LARGO
PAYSANDÚ
RAMBLA ROOSEVELT
ANDES
CIUDADELA
FLORIDA
URUGUAY
PIEDRAS
TREINTA Y TRES
JUAN C GÓMEZ
CERRITO
ITUZAINGÓ
MERCEDES
RÍO BRANCO
CONVENCIÓN
COLONIA
SOLÍS
RINCÓN
AVENIDA 18 DE JULIO
17
5
19
4
3
2
8
15
1
25 DE MAYO
16
13
SAN JOSÉ
14
CUESTAS
GUARANI
WASHINGTON
SARANDÍ
MISIONES
BUENOS AIRES
MACIEL
CASTELLANOS
COLÓN
ALZAIBAR
ZABALA
RECONQUISTA
SORIANO
JULIO HERRERA Y OBEZ
RÍO NEGRO
PARAGUAY
H. G. RUIZ
Z. MICHELINI
YI
YAGUARÓN
EJIDO
CANELONES
MALDONADO
DURAZNO
CARLOS GARDEL
G. RAMIREZ
RAMBLA FRANCÍA
RBLA. GRAN BRETAÑA
RAMBLA SUR
RBLA. REP. ARGENTINA
N
RÍO DE LA PLATA

secured, the gaucho spirit, which played godfather to the political philosophy of independence in the 1820s, continued as a strong factor in the Uruguayan way of life. Although its constitution was promulgated on July 18, 1830, the early history of the republic was confused by civil war between rival presidents.

The pattern for the country's political development in the 20th century was set in 1903, when José Batlle y Ordóñez, known as the Father of Modern Uruguay, was elected president. Batlle advocated political and social reforms, extensive welfare measures, and government participation in many sectors of the economy. These reforms were still in evidence in 1970. Founder of the newspaper *El Día,* he believed in a democratic form of government with constitutional procedures, and he promoted measures designed to protect the country against the emergence of dictatorships. But this admirable tradition of democracy ended in the early 1970s, when Montevideo became the center of activity for a left-wing guerrilla group called the Movimiento de Liberación Nacional (National Liberation Movement), better known as the Tupamaros. In 1973, the military seized control of the government, dissolved the parliament, and began an intensive crackdown on the Tupamaros, their friends, relatives, and associates. However, military rule ended in 1985 after the first popularly elected president in 12 years, Julio Mario Sanguinetti, took office. Control passed to another civilian president, Luis Alberto Lacalle, in 1990.

Foreigners are always well received by *montevideños,* who are renowned for their warmth, friendliness, and hospitality. Tourism is one of the country's most important industries yet you'll never feel as if you are just one of a horde of foreigners. Happily, the capital still is a safe city and a single woman can travel without being made to feel uncomfortable. Currently free of both the street crime and political violence found in some other South American countries, Uruguay is an uncomplicated place to visit. During the day, the Ciudad Vieja (Old City) — the district between the main plaza and the port — is the center of business activity. You will find it a compact, walkable area of old and new buildings. The Avenida 18 de Julio is a bustling commercial street that is becoming increasingly choked with sidewalk vendors. Surrounding the heart of the city are three major residential areas: to the north, the Prado, where, during the late 19th century, the well-to-do raised enormous families in equally enormous mansions; to the east, along the Rambla Pocitos, the high-rise center of the city; and farther east, residential, fresh-aired Carrasco, with its beautiful villas and gardens.

But most crucial to life in the city are its beaches, from Pocitos to Carrasco (which, being river-water beaches, are not representative of the ocean-blue beaches farther east), on which residents study, play, and strut. The Rambla (riverfront drive), which borders these city beaches and which runs from the port to Carrasco (the last metropolitan area), comes to life as *montevideños* promenade during summer evenings and winter afternoons. And a long walk along a quiet beach in the middle of the afternoon says more about the quality of life here and the attitude of its residents than a thousand pictures.

# MONTEVIDEO AT-A-GLANCE

**SEEING THE CITY:** The best place to get a view of Montevideo is from the Mirador (Lookout Tower) on top of the Intendencia (Municipal Palace). Ride the glass elevators up to the observation deck on the 22nd floor, or to the tearoom on the 23rd floor, or the fine restaurant (see *Eating Out*) on its 24th floor. Enter the back of the building on Soriano between Santiago de Chile and Ejido. The main downtown avenue and shopping center, 18 de Julio, runs directly below you. Ten blocks to the left along 18 de Julio is the Plaza Independencia with its bronze statue of national hero José Gervasio Artigas. On the other side of the plaza is the Ciudad Vieja (Old City), which constituted the heart of the colonial city. Today it is the business and banking center of the country, where you will find the Banco República (the government commercial import-export bank), the Stock Exchange (Bolsa de Valores), the Central Post Office, the Customs House, the Central Bank, most of the foreign banks' central offices, and the shipping center. The telephone company, ANTEL, also has offices in this area that are open around the clock for placing long-distance calls. They are located at Rincón and Treinta y Tres.

**SPECIAL PLACES:** There is one main thoroughfare in downtown Montevideo (18 de Julio). Since the streets are laid out in an orderly way, it is easy for visitors to find their way around. Most Uruguayans are very helpful, so do not hesitate to ask anyone for directions. The streets you will use most (described as if you were standing at Plaza Independencia facing Avenida 18 de Julio) are Colonia, running parallel to and left of 18 de Julio, and San José, to its right. Behind you, Sarandí, which would be the continuation of 18 de Julio on the other side of the plaza, runs through the Ciudad Vieja and down to the port. Take note that many of the plazas have two names. Cagancha, for example, is also known as Plaza Libertad.

## DOWNTOWN

**Mausoleo de José Gervasio Artigas (Mausoleum of José Gervasio Artigas)** – Under the equestrian statue in the center of the main plaza, this solemn mausoleum, dedicated to Uruguay's national hero, is made entirely of marble and granite. Artigas became the leader of the gaucho movement between 1811 and 1821 that fought both the Spanish and the Portuguese to maintain Uruguayan independence. He is considered the father of Uruguayan nationhood and is credited with keeping alive the spirit of freedom during the darkest days of foreign dominance. The mausoleum's date inscriptions represent various stages of the hero's life and participation in the country's liberation. Guards stand vigil over the urn that holds the national hero's ashes. Open daily, except the first Monday of every month. No admission charge. Plaza Independencia.

**Plaza Independencia (Independence Square)** – With a gigantic mounted statue of José Gervasio Artigas in its center, the plaza — dotted by palm trees and fountains — is a favorite gathering spot for sunbathers and weary shoppers. The stately building with columns bordering one side of the square is the former Casa del Gobierno (Government House). Diagonally across from it is the Palacio Salvo, erected 60 years ago by an eccentric *montevideño*. This eclectic structure, originally viewed as an outrage and labeled the ugliest on the continent, is now benignly accepted by city residents. For many years it was Montevideo's tallest building. Opposite the Casa del Gobierno is the *Victoria Plaza* hotel, where members of local society meet for tea. The tree-shaded streets of Colonia and San José, parallel to 18 de Julio on either side, are home to tearooms, cafés, and shops. At the far end of the plaza are the remains of the original city wall — now the portal into the Ciudad Vieja (Old City). Formal military and diplomatic ceremonies take place at the plaza.

**Cabildo (Town Hall)** – An interesting exhibition of old Montevideo, from early Indian days until present times, with a brief resume of the country's history, and a display of paintings, antique pieces of furniture, costumes, and even a replica of the old Montevideo bastion. Open daily except Saturdays from 2 to 6 PM, although the museum is often closed for restoration work or to prepare for new exhibits. No admission charge. Plaza Matriz, Sarandí and J. C. Gómez (phone: 959685).

**Catedral de Montevideo (Montevideo Cathedral)** – Roman Catholicism is the main religion in Uruguay, although churches of various other denominations exist (recently Mormons, evangelical Christians, and Jehovah's Witnesses have gained converts). Since the days of Batlle in the early 1900s, there has been total separation between church and state. This large, boxy cathedral was built between 1790 and 1804. Though plain by South American standards, its otherwise somber olive green altar has gold-colored pillars and its pulpit is detailed brass. Uruguay's archbishops are buried here. Open daily from 3 to 7 PM. On the oldest plaza in the city, Plaza Matriz, at Sarandí and Ituzaingó.

**Palacio Legislativo (Legislative Palace)** – This superb piece of architecture is built on a rise on Avenida Libertador Lavalleja, 15 blocks north of 18 de Julio. Designed by the distinguished Italian architect Gaetano Moretti and inaugurated in 1925, this building combines 45 varieties of marble and granite in its mosaic floors and walls. Its stained glass windows depict historic events and are extraordinarily beautiful. The building cost approximately $17 million, an exorbitant figure in the 1920s! Open daily from 10 AM to 3 PM. Call first, as some activities are closed to visitors. No admission charge. Av. Libertador Lavalleja and D. Fernández Crespo (phone: 201334 or 409111).

**Museo Histórico Nacional y Museo Romántico (National Historical Museum and Romantic Museum)** – Once the home of an Uruguayan merchant, this 1831 mansion is now a museum (although it has two names, it is actually one museum) dedicated to both the romantic period of the 1830s through 1860s and historical pieces. It is filled with portraits (note the painting of a widower and his children — his deceased wife's portrait is part of the picture), costumes, furniture, ornate crystal dishes, and even a fan signed by Enrico Caruso, Sarah Bernhardt, Arturo Toscanini, and Isadora Duncan, among others. Open Tuesdays through Fridays from noon to 5:45 PM, Sundays from 2 to 5:45 PM. No admission charge. 314 Av. 25 de Mayo, near Zabala (phone: 954257).

**El Obelisco (Obelisk)** – Sculpted by Uruguayan José Luis Zorrilla de San Martín in 1923, it commemorates the signers of the country's first constitution. From here you can enter the Parque Batlle y Ordóñez. 18 de Julio and Bulevar Artigas.

**Museo de Artes Decorativos (Decorative Arts Museum)** – Actually two treats in one building, this museum has an intriguing collection of Old World glass, art, and artifacts, including a mummy from ancient Egypt and some anthropological exhibits related to Uruguay. But even better than the exhibits is the building they're in — the Taranco Mansion. Built in 1910 by a trio of wealthy brothers from Spain and modeled after an 18th-century French palace, this lovely home still has its original furniture, paintings from Spain, stunning marble pillars, gilt mirrors, and breathtaking chandeliers. Group tours in English can be arranged by appointment. Open Mondays through Fridays from 3 to 6:30 PM, but call ahead to be sure. No admission charge. Entrance at 1445 Primero de Mayo (phone: 951101).

**Museo del Gaucho y La Moneda (Cowboy and Gold Museum)** – Housed in the opulent Banco de la República building, this impressive collection pays tribute to two national assets — gold and the gaucho (or cowboy) — so essential in Uruguayan life.

It is considered by locals to be one of their most important museums and has the added plus of being housed in a fabulous late 19th-century mansion with marble stairways, a stained glass atrium, detailed woodcarvings, and antique light fixtures. From mid-April to mid-December it is open weekdays from 9:30 AM to 12:30 PM and 3:30 to 7 PM, weekends from 4 to 8 PM; the rest of the year, the museum is closed Mondays, open Saturdays from 4:30 to 8 PM, and Sundays from 4 to 8 PM. No admission charge. 998 18 de Julio (phone: 908764).

**La Carreta Statue** – Blending into the landscape above a reflecting pool in Parque José Batlle y Ordóñez, this bronze monument to the pioneers of Uruguay takes the form of three yokes of oxen drawing a covered wagon and a bearded gaucho. Parque José Batlle y Ordóñez, Avdas. Italia and Las Heras.

**Estadio Centenario (Soccer Stadium)** – If you hear that an important soccer (*fútbol,* literally football, in South America) match is to be played while you're visiting, don't miss it. It will be one of the best opportunities to see Uruguayans at their most passionate public moments. The largest stadium in the country, with a seating capacity of 75,000, it was built in 1930 to commemorate the nation's 100th anniversary and to host the *World Football Championship,* which took place that same year. It also houses the *Museo de Fútbol* (Museum of Football), a bicycle race track, and an athletics field. Open Thursdays, Saturdays, and Sundays from 2 to 7 PM. Parque José Batlle y Ordóñez, Avdas. Italia and Las Heras (phone: 801262).

**Parque Rodó (Rodó Park)** – Children will enjoy this amusement park on the *rambla,* with rides, an open-air summer theater, an artificial lake, and ponies for rent. This is one of the places where you can taste the typical *chorizos al pan* (very good sausages) and *churros* filled with *dulce de leche* (fried pastry tubes with a sweet filling). Opens daily around 4:30 or 5 PM. Admission charge for each ride. Rambla Presidente Wilson and Bulevar Artigas (phone: 416317).

**Parque Zoológico (Zoological Park)** – Leo, the first South American–born elephant, was born here in 1974 (he died a few years ago). On these same grounds is one of the best planetariums in South America, with evening shows on selected days. Open daily, except Mondays and Tuesdays, to 10 PM. Admission charge, except for children under 12. 3245 and 3275 Av. Rivera (phone for zoo: 629108; for planetarium: 629110).

**Asociación Rural del Uruguay (Rural Association of Uruguay)** – Here is where horse-breaking competitions are held during *Semana Criolla* (*Easter Week*); other activities include exhibitions of typical dances and folkloric music contests led by real gauchos. The other important event here is the *Exposición Rural* (Cattle Show), in August. As Uruguay is a cattle-breeding country, this event is of great importance to all breeders, and only the very best animals are shown. Evenings, there are the ever-present *parrilladas* (barbecues). 96 Lucas Obes in Parque Prado (phone: 393616).

**18 de Julio (18th of July)** – The city's main artery, this street runs through nearly every important plaza in Montevideo, and from here you can catch buses to Carrasco or the Palacio Legislativo. You also can sit at a *confitería's* window and watch the people go by or change money. Lined with newsstands, shops, movie theaters, restaurants, airline offices, and hotels, it's bustling from early morning until late at night.

**Feria de Tristán Narvaja (Tristán Narvaja Market)** – This flea market, about 10 blocks long, convenes every Sunday morning from 8 AM until noon. Here you can find anything and everything from live house pets to meat, vegetables, automobile spare parts, and priceless antiques. It is the city's most important open-air market, offering both new and used goods. Sundays only. Tristán Narvaja between 18 de Julio and La Paz.

**Feria de Villa Biarritz (Villa Biarritz Market)** – Similar to the *Tristán Narvaja Market,* with knitted clothing, handicrafts, carpentry, glasswork, and even homemade desserts. Saturdays only, from 8 AM to 2 or 3 PM. Located in the Parque Zorilla de San Martín, in the Pocitos neighborhood, on the south side of town.

**Teatro Solís (Solís Theater)** – Built in 1856, this beautiful work of architecture is the center of the city's regularly scheduled concerts and cultural activities. Unfortunately, no tours are offered but the complex is open around performance time (about 7:30 PM). Ask the guards to let you in for a quick peek at the plush burgundy boxes and the impressive crystal chandeliers. 678 Buenos Aires, just off Plaza Independencia (phone for the ticket office: 959770).

**Museo de Historia Natural (Natural History Museum)** – Designed especially for children and young students, it has a good display of archaeological objects, fossils, and Uruguayan flora and fauna. Call to check the schedule, though it's usually open Tuesdays through Saturdays from 2 to 6 PM. No admission charge. On the ground floor of the *Solís Theater*. 652 Buenos Aires (phone: 960908).

**Museo Municipal de Arte Precolombino y Colonial (Municipal Museum of Pre-Columbian and Colonial Art)** – An excellent exhibition of original art collections from the pre-Columbian and colonial periods, including religious paintings of the 17th and 18th centuries, set in buildings next door to each other. Closed Mondays. No admission charge. Beside the Post Office in the Palacio Municipal at 1322 and 1326 Ejido (phone: 989252 and 917518).

**Fortaleza General Artigas** – This is a great place to get a good look at Montevideo, except that it is slightly out of the way. Once a fort, this building stands on the *cerro* (hill) for which Montevideo was named. It is now a military museum with a good display of Spanish uniforms, guns, and artifacts dating from the era of the battle for independence. Open Wednesdays through Sundays from 2 to 7 PM. Admission charge. About a 30-minute ride from downtown. Camino de la Fortaleza (phone: 311154).

**Museo de Arte Contemporáneo (Museum of Contemporary Art)** – Also the home of a small theater, this art gallery has changing national and international exhibits. Open daily from 3 to 8 PM. No admission charge. 1164 Plaza Cagancha (phone: 985457).

**Plaza Matriz Antiques Fair** – With a flavor much like that of the San Telmo district in Buenos Aires, this open-air market, initiated in 1987, offers a variety of antiques. Open Sunday mornings. Plaza Zabala, between Zabala and Colón, in the Ciudad Vieja.

**Mercado del Puerto (Port Market)** – This sprawling 19th-century glass and cast-iron gallery is filled with the scent of wood smoke and meats sizzling on the grill, and the sound of guitarists playing. You may see workers carting in loads of firewood to fuel the dozens of stand-up *parrilladas* (grills) that are packed with sailors on leave and businesspeople from the nearby financial district. For more leisurely eating, choose from the pair of sit-down places flanking the entrance to the market: *El Palenque* (1579-85 Pérez Castellano), or *La Posada del Puerto* (1509 Pérez Castellano; phone: 954278). Most restaurants are across the street in the restored Republican-style building that has been turned into a complex of boutiques and art galleries. Around the corner, facing the port and the Customs House, is a string of dark and seedy sailor bars, one with the amusing name *El Perro Que Fuma* (The Smoking Dog). The indoor part of the *Mercado del Puerto*, which was originally shipped from England to be the city's train station, is open Mondays through Fridays from 8 AM to 8 PM, and Saturdays from 8 AM to 4 PM. The outdoor restaurants are open daily. At the intersection of Piedras and Pérez Castellano.

■ **EXTRA SPECIAL:** Carrasco, the popular Rambla beach area along the Río de la Plata, bordering Montevideo, has white sand and huge homes with manicured lawns. Take a cab, a bus (No. 104 Puente Carrasco), or drive 12 miles (19 km) down the Rambla to Carrasco, taking in the cool breezes, sun worshipers, and palm trees. Once polluted, new water treatment facilities have been installed and it is now safe to swim here — although *montevideños* tend to visit the area for the sun and sand, not the water. Mansions with red tile roofs, covered with flowering vines, grace the streets. Just a block up from the water in the heart of Carrasco, you'll find the palatial *Carrasco* hotel and casino (on Rambla República de México; phone: 616501 for the hotel; 601971 for the casino). Though its care has been neglected of late, its former glory cannot be denied. Unfortunately, the marble and hardwood floors have been covered by carpeting and the vaulted ceilings lowered, but the wood details and chandeliers still gleam. Don't miss the stained glass skylights overhead. Treat yourself to an overnight stay; it costs only about $40 a night for a double and $55 for an antiques-filled suite in this now city-run hotel. A bet of under $10 will get you into the hotel's small, but luxurious, casino. You may want to skip the gloomy hotel dining room and wander through the neighborhood in search of a restaurant (see *Eating Out*), an outdoor café, or ice cream at *Las Delicias* (at the corner of Arocena and Dr. Schroeder). Stop by the Carrasco branch of *Manos del Uruguay* (see *Shopping*), across the street from the hotel, for beautiful woolens and handcrafted souvenirs.

# SOURCES AND RESOURCES

**TOURIST INFORMATION:** For general information, brochures, and maps, contact the tourist information centers at Plaza Cagancha, also known as Plaza Libertad (phone: 905216) and at Carrasco Airport (phone: 603812). They are open weekdays from 8 AM to 8 PM and 9 AM to 1 PM on weekends. The Plaza Cagancha office can make hotel reservations around the country; it also distributes copies of the Spanish-language weekly entertainment guide, *Guía del Ocio.* Contact the *Asociación de Hoteles y Restaurantes* (Gutiérrez Ruiz 1217; phone: 982317) for information about hotels all over the country, including Montevideo. The staff at this office will make reservations for you; there is no charge for the service. Inquire also at your hotel about special events and recommended sites. Maps are on sale at gas stations, corner bookstands, and bookstores. The *Automóvil Club de Uruguay* has an office at Colonia and Yí (phone: 919020 or 989020). Also found in bookstores is *Uruguay,* a book published in France which describes the country in English and Spanish, with special sections in French and German; it costs about $50. By dialing 214, you can contact the Central Bureau of Information for an update on events and schedules. They will also answer your queries (in English) about bus and plane schedules, the weather, and tell you which gas stations and drugstores are open weekends and evenings. There are two English-speaking travel agencies, *Viajes Bueme's* (979 Colonia; phone: 921050) and *Turisport Ltd.* (942 Mercedes; phone: 920852 or 920829); the latter represents American Express in Uruguay.

The US Embassy is located at 808 H. Abadie Santos (phone: 236061).

**Local Coverage** – The only English-language newspaper is the *Buenos Aires Herald.* Available at most newsstands, it will not give you much information on Montevideo. *La Mañana, El País,* and *El Día* (all Spanish-language morning dailies) contain entertainment schedules. Available at the tourist information center at Plaza Cagancha, *Guía del Ocio,* the Spanish-language weekly entertainment guide, lists films, art exhibits, concerts, and theatrical productions.

**TELEPHONE:** The city code for Montevideo is 2. When calling from within Uruguay, dial 02 before the local number. The country code for Uruguay is 598.

**396 MONTEVIDEO / Sources and Resources**

**CLIMATE AND CLOTHES:** The weather is very pleasant, with temperatures ranging from a high of 90F (32C) in the summer (December through March) to a low of 41F (5C) in the winter (June through September). It is generally slightly humid, so bring light clothes for the warm weather and warm clothing during the cold and windy months. (The wind can make the air feel much colder than thermometers indicate, and old buildings often have poor heating systems.) Informal clothes, except for shorts, are suitable during the daytime. Men should wear a jacket and tie at the more exclusive restaurants in the evenings. A light raincoat and umbrella are handy in winter.

**GETTING AROUND: Bus** – There is regular, frequent bus service to practically every point in the city. Most buses pass through downtown at some point. Rates vary according to destination; though exact change is not required, have small bills and coins on hand.

**Car Rental** – Besides *Avis* (6337 Rambla Rep. de México; phone: 605060 or 608129) and *Hertz* (813 Colonia; phone: 916363), there is *Autorent* (1683 Yaguarón; phone: 920573); *Car Rental* (1363 Andes; phone: 907728 or 916588); *Dollar Rent-A-Car* (1432 Convención; phone: 984912 or 984376); *National Car Rental* (1397 Ciudadela at Rincón; phone: 900035); and *Punta Car* (1523 Yaguarón; phone: 902772 or 920726). A $1000 cash deposit or a major credit card is required. Most major credit cards are accepted. Some companies require drivers to be at least 23 years old.

**Taxi** – Service is very good. Taxis can be hailed in the street 7 days a week, though you may have more difficulty during rush hours or after midnight. There is an efficient, inexpensive *Radio Taxi* service (phone: 209421). Taxi drivers expect a 10% tip. Under a new government program, some taxi drivers have been trained as tour guides — they point out interesting sights, relate historical tidbits, and give out brochures and maps — at no extra charge.

**SPECIAL EVENTS:** During *Carnaval* week, before *Ash Wednesday,* do not miss the *Las Llamadas* parade. An interesting display of color, music, and rhythm, based on South America's African traditions, it takes place in the Barrio Palermo, where, along the narrow streets of Carlos Gardel and La Cumparsita, the dancing and the drums continue until the early morning hours. Be warned: Shops close down during the week of partying and hotel rooms are hard to come by, so reserve well ahead. *Fiesta Gaucha,* held *Easter Week,* highlights rodeo competitions in the Parque El Prado or Parque Roosevelt; the festivities include handicraft exhibits, outdoor barbecues, and music. The *Cattle Show* takes place in August at the Asociación Rural del Uruguay (96 Lucas Obes, in Parque El Prado). *Christmas* and *New Year's* eves are celebrated with firecrackers and drummers in the streets.

**MUSEUMS:** In addition those described in *Special Places,* the following are worth a visit:

**Casa de Don José Batlle y Ordóñez (Don José Batlle y Ordóñez's House)** – The home of the man known as the Father of modern Uruguay. Open Thursdays through Sundays from 2:30 to 6 PM. No admission charge. 3870 Teniente Rinaldi (phone: 224933).

**Galería Nacional de Arte (National Art Gallery)** – A collection of plastic and visual arts. Open daily except Mondays from 3:30 to 7:30 PM. No admission charge. Parque Rodó (phone: 716054).

**Museo Histórico Nacional (National Historical Museum)** – Housed in the 19th-century home of General Fructuoso Rivera, the building was restored in the 1940s and opened as the *Rivera Museum.* Open Tuesdays through Fridays from 1 to 7 PM. Sunday 2 to 6 PM. No admission charge. 1469 Zabala (phone: 951028).

## MONTEVIDEO / Sources and Resources

**Museo de Juan Zorrilla de San Martín (Museum of Juan Zorrilla de San Martín)** – The home of the author of major Uruguayan literary works. Open Tuesdays through Fridays and Sundays from 2 to 6 PM. No admission charge. 96 Ellauri (phone: 701818).

**Museo Municipal de Juan Manuel Blanes (Juan Manuel Blanes Museum)** – Home of the official painter of the republic. Open daily except Mondays from 2 to 8 PM. No admission charge. 4014 Av. Millán and Arroyo Miguelete, in Parque Prado (phone: 362248).

**Museo Oceanográfico (Oceanographic Museum)** – Open daily except Mondays from 3 to 7 PM. No admission charge. 4215 Rambla República de Chile, Puerto Buceo (phone: 720258).

**Museo de Transporte Fernando García (Fernando García Transportation Museum)** – Features vintage automobiles. Open daily except Mondays from 2 to 6 PM. No admission charge. 7005 Camino Carrasco (phone: 913711).

**SHOPPING:** Uruguay has an extensive textile industry, and the fabrics it produces are inexpensive, of excellent quality, and can be found in most downtown stores. Uruguayan nutria (a fur-bearing mammal) is one of the best of the breed in the world, with longer, thicker, softer hair, and better color than can be found elsewhere. And the fur is not expensive. The best shop for nutria is *Peletería Holandesa* (894 Colonia; phone: 902093).

A large US-style mall with more than 100 shops is the *Montevideo Shopping Center* (1290 Luis A. de Herrera). It is open daily except Sundays until 10 PM. Besides clothing, leather, and souvenirs, there are restaurants, a supermarket, a cinema, and an ice-skating rink.

In the Plaza Cagancha, to the north of the bus station, is the *Mercado de los Artesanos* (Artisans' Market) where craftspeople sell an assortment of handmade wares at stands inside a former warehouse. Every afternoon on the plaza itself, there are a variety of stalls, including those selling hand-knit wool sweaters, small leather goods, and jewelry. Beware of street vendors offering you watches, electric appliances, and perfume. It is preferable to pay more and buy these goods from an established source. Shops are normally open daily except Sundays from 9 AM until 7 PM.

***Arbiter*** – For women's shoes, stop at any branch of this store. 943 Av. 18 de Julio 943 (phone: 904200), 1310 Río Negro (phone: 982735), and in the *Montevideo Shopping Center* (no phone).

***Casa Mario*** – Well-made leather bags, as well as nutria and fox coats. In the Old City at Piedras and Bartolomé Mitre (phone: 962356).

***Casa Schiavo*** – For souvenirs and a wide range of leather goods. 1050 Uruguay (phone: 911494).

***Cuarzos del Uruguay*** – This shop carries an extensive selection of souvenir key rings, pendants, and such, and rare cuts of agates and amethysts. 604 Sarandí (phone: 959210). Note that several other shops selling these stones have sprung up along Sarandí (between Plaza Independencia and Ituzaingó). Jewelry made with these stones is relatively inexpensive since they both are mined in Uruguay.

***Libreria Linardi y Risso*** – This is a book lover's paradise, with rare, used, hard-to-find, and some English-language volumes tucked into ceiling-to-floor shelves. If you read Spanish and have been searching for an offbeat title, odds are that you'll find it here. There are also some English editions of Hemingway (among others), as well as photo books of Uruguary. In the Old City at 1435 J.C. Gómez (phone: 957129 or 957328).

***Louvre Antiguedades*** – Montevideo is a city in love with antiques, from fine silver jewelry and china vases to spurs studded with semi-precious stones and other gaucho finery. The best place for "finds" is at this wonderful place in the Cuidad Vieja (Old

City) — even if you're only window shopping. Certificates of authenticity are given with jewelry sales. 652 Sarandí at Bartolomé Mitre (phone: 962686).

*Manos del Uruguay* – A cooperative formed to give in-home employment to women in the Uruguayan countryside, it has high-quality, handwoven woolen products from all parts of the country — sweaters, rugs, ponchos, curtains, and modern tapestries. The sweaters are stunning hand-knits in contemporary designs, priced at about one-third of their stateside cost. The main shop is at the corner of J. C. Gómez and Reconquista (phone: 959522 or 960602). Three branch locations: 1111 San José (phone: 904910); in the shopping mall at Larrañaga and Rivera (phone: 620650); and in Carrasco at 1552 Arocena (phone: 613887). All accept credit cards.

*Sagaro* – This small sweets shop is chock-full of tantalizing *bombones* (bonbons), *caramelos* (caramels), and the national treat, *yema* (crystallized egg yolk). Choose your own mix for a beautifully wrapped gift box. Two locations: 2020 Av. 18 de Julio (phone: 416814) and 1329 Cuareim (no phone).

*Taborelli* – The place for finely crafted wallets and belts. 1184 18 de Julio (phone: 986156).

*Venet* – Elegantly made leather shoes. 1069 Av. de 18 Julio (phone: 986880) and in the *Montevideo Shopping Center* (phone: 728007).

**SPORTS:** Soccer (*fútbol*) is the national sport and games take place year-round. Try to see a *clásico* between the two most popular teams and traditional rivals, *Nacional* and *Peñarol*. Any hotel clerk or person on the street can tell you if a match is coming up.

**Basketball** – This sport has become almost as popular as soccer. Final and championship games are played either at the *Cilindro Municipal* (phone: 585169) or at the *Palacio Peñarol* (Calle Galicio, between Minas and Magallanes; phone: 493425).

**Golf** – The *Club de Golf del Uruguay* (379 Bulevar Artigas; phone: 701721 through 701725) offers a fantastic view of the city. Non-members are welcome.

**Horse Racing** – The *Hipódromo de Maroñas* has races on Thursdays, Saturdays, and Sundays. The biggest race of the year, held on January 6, attracts international spectators. It's about 20 minutes from downtown by taxi. 3750 J.M. Guerra (phone: 585890).

**Soccer** – Professional matches are held every weekend in the afternoons. You will undoubtedly see people playing it, especially in the residential areas, on any and every day of the week. Check the newspaper *El País* for game times, or contact the Asociación Uruguaya de Fútbol (1531 Guayabo; phone: 407101). The main stadium is *Estadio Centenario* (Parque José Batlle y Ordóñez, Avdas. Italia and Las Heras; phone: 784270).

**Swimming** – Carrasco's beach is the best; Playa Honda and Playa Malvin are next best. The finest in the country are found at Punta del Este, 80 miles (129 km) from Montevideo (see *Uruguay*, DIRECTIONS). There are no public or hotel pools in the city.

**Tennis** – The only hotel in the city with tennis courts is the *Hostería del Lago* (9637 Arizona; phone: 612210). If you want to watch some good matches (often featuring international players), try the *Carrasco Lawn Tennis Club* (6401 Dr. Eduardo J. Couture; phone: 600148); the *Círculo de Tenis de Montevideo* (Buschental in Carrasco; phone: 393500), or the *Club Biguá* (2968 José Vázquez Ledesma in Pocitos; phone: 702485). Tennis matches are publicized in the newspapers. Squash courts are available at the *Club Carrasco* (1539 Av. A. Arocena; phone: 600229).

**THEATER:** Naturally almost all performances here are in Spanish. If there is any visiting international production, it will take place at the *Teatro Solís* (678 Buenos Aires; phone: 959770). The *Comedia Nacional* (National Theater Group), the resident company of the *Teatro Solís*, is very good. *Teatro* *del Notariado* (1730 Av. 18 de Julio; phone: 483669) and *Teatro Circular* (1388 Rondeau, off Plaza Cagancha; phone: 915952) are some of the theaters that present Spanish works; check newspapers for their schedules.

Modern films are shown at downtown theaters — a cluster of them can be found near the Plaza Cagancha — and you will often find replays of good old films. The movies are always shown in their original language. The newspapers list what's playing.

**MUSIC:** Don't miss the tango, *camdombe* (a lively dance of South America blacks), and Uruguayan folk music. The best spot is *La Cumparsita* (on Calle Carlos Gardel; phone: 916245). You also can hear folkloric music at some of the local restaurants, but if there is any special show in some theater or concert hall at the time of your visit, don't miss it. For classical music, the *National Symphony Orchestra* plays at the *Solís*. The *Alianza Uruguay-EEUU* (Uruguay-US Alliance; 1217 Paraguay; phone: 902721) sometimes hosts musical (including some classical) performances.

**NIGHTCLUBS AND NIGHTLIFE:** Montevideo has a few good discotheques, known as boîtes, that admit couples only. Among the most popular are *Zum Zum* (1647 Rambla Armenia in Pocitas; phone: 621007); *Caras y Caretas,* an old French castle in Carrasco (5817 Friburgo; phone: 604121), open daily; and *Ton-Ton Metek* (9635 Arizona, near Carrasco; phone: 612328), on weekends only. Dinner and dancing are at *Makao del Hotel Oceanía,* from which you get a beautiful view (1227 Mar Artico; phone: 600444). If you plan to go on a Friday or Saturday night, make a reservation first. For a more typically US discotheque, try *New York, New York* (5521 Rambla República de México). It is open only on Friday nights and has no "couples only" rule. The restaurant *La Taverna de Chiche* (in *Galería Libertad;* phone: 916278) offers tango, bolero, cumbia, and other music from 10 PM until the early morning hours every Friday and Saturday. The pub, *Ley Seca* (Soriano and Río Branco; phone: 982481), also features live music Friday and Saturday nights starting at 10:30 PM. You can try your luck at roulette and blackjack or even bingo in either of the two informal casinos in town: the *Parque* hotel (Rambla W. Wilson; phone: 415953) and the *Carrasco* (Rambla República de México; phone: 610551).

# BEST IN TOWN

**CHECKING IN:** There is quite a variety of accommodations in Montevideo, from air conditioned luxury hotels to family-style *pensiones*. All hotels listed here have rooms with private baths. Reservations are essential during the summer months (December through March), when prices usually go up 10%. Expect to pay $85 and up for a double in those places classed as expensive; between $50 and $85 at places in the moderate category; under $50 in the inexpensive range. Bear in mind that many hotels offer two or three classes of service at rates ranging from inexpensive to moderate to expensive, depending on the size of the room, whether it is interior or exterior, and how picturesque the view is. Rates include breakfast and the 12% value added tax. All telephone numbers are in the 2 city code unless otherwise indicated.

**Hostería del Lago** – Only a 5-minute drive from Carrasco or 15 minutes from downtown, this modern and luxurious, all-suites establishment on the lake offers its guests a restaurant, tennis courts, a pool, water sports, and rooms with a view of the lake; 24-hour room service. 9637 Arizona (phone: 612210 and 612949; in the US, 800-44-UTELL; fax: 612880). Expensive.

**Victoria Plaza** – This 18-floor high-rise in front of the main plaza has a square, unimpressive, orange brick exterior, but its 357 rooms are air conditioned and the hotel boasts good service and an excellent view from its rooftop restaurant. Guests have included King Juan Carlos and Queen Sofía of Spain. Scheduled to open this year is a new 300-room tower, linked by a skywalk to the main hotel. On Friday and Saturday nights, there is entertainment in the *Restaurante del Victoria*. From November to March, there is a midday barbecue and a salad bar as well as a great view of the skyline, in its moderately priced *El Techo* restaurant (reservations necessary). 759 Plaza Independencia (phone: 920237; in the US, 800-44-UTELL; fax: 921628). Expensive.

**Lancaster** – Another downtown property, with smallish rooms, and a cafeteria downstairs. All rooms have mini-bars. 1334 Plaza Cagancha (phone: 920029; in the US, 800-44-UTELL; fax: 981117). Expensive to moderate.

**Balmoral** – Ideally located in the city center, this new 74-room modern high-rise has a parking garage for guests. There's no restaurant, but breakfast is included in the room rate. The only drawback is that it's right beside the busy *COT* bus terminal. 1125 Plaza Libertad (phone: 922393; in the US, 800-44-UTELL; fax: 922288). Moderate.

**Columbia Palace** – Newer than the *Victoria Plaza* (the other top hotel in town), some rooms face the Rambla and on a windy day offer an exciting view of the rough river water hitting its walls. Its 150 rooms are comfortable. It also has a good international restaurant. 468 Reconquista (phone: 960001 or 960192; in the US, 800-44-UTELL). Moderate.

**Cottage** – This comfortable, medium-size hotel has been restored to first class condition. All the guestrooms have direct-dial telephones, and there is a cafeteria, bar, and laundry service. In front of Carrasco Beach, on the Rambla. 1360 Miraflores (phone: 600804 or 610862; fax: 607218). Moderate.

**Embajador** – A basic, but comfortable, downtown establishment with 80 rooms. 1212 San José (phone: 920215; fax: 920009). Moderate.

**Internacional** – This first-rate, 90-room, air conditioned hostelry offers a good downtown location (not far from Plaza Independencia). 823 Colonia (phone: 905794 and 920001; fax: 921242). Moderate.

**Klee** – Owned by the same company as the *Internacional,* this 60-room and 10-suite hotel offers similar amenities and has the same reputation for service. Breakfast included in the rates. 1306 Yaguarón (phone: 910671; fax: 937377). Moderate.

**Lafayette** – This new property has 89 air conditioned rooms and 10 suites, all with satellite television, wet bars, and Jacuzzis. Facilities include a restaurant, lobby bar, indoor pool, gym, sauna, parking garage, and a friendly staff. 1170 Soriano (phone: 922351; in the US, 800-44-UTELL; fax: 921301). Moderate.

**London Palace** – Not luxurious, but very relaxing and conveniently located in the middle of downtown, with 84 rooms, a cocktail lounge, and a garage. 1278 Río Negro (phone: 920024). Moderate.

**Presidente** – The perfect place for shopping forays, with an entrance in *Galería Madrileña*. It has 80 rooms, air conditioning, laundry service, a coffee shop, and a bar. 1038 18 de Julio (phone: 920003; fax: 984850). Moderate.

**Oxford** – The same kind of relaxing atmosphere as the *Lancaster* or *Klee,* this hotel has 70 newly remodeled rooms, is well located, and has air conditioning, laundry service, a bar, and coffee shop. Breakfast included. Part of the Aragón chain that has several properties in Argentina. 1286 Paraguay (phone: 920046). Moderate to inexpensive.

**Balfer** – Very modest, but clean and has 75 air conditioned rooms. A bar and coffee shop are on the premises. Breakfast included in the rates. Near the Plaza Cagancha (Libertad) at 1328 Zelmar Michelini (phone: 912647; fax: 920009). Inexpensive.

**Casino Carrasco** – More than a gambling establishment, this palatial building on the Rambla in Carrasco is 20 minutes from downtown and the beach is just across the road. Inaugurated in 1921, it has 110 very spacious rooms. A casino, restaurant, and cocktail lounge are on the ground floor. Arrangements can be made to use the fairways at the nearby *Club de Golf del Uruguay,* as well as court facilities at the *Carrasco Lawn Tennis Club.* Rambla República de México (phone: 501261). Inexpensive.

**Ermitage** – For a beach stay that is closer to town than the beaches at Carrasco, this is your best bet. It is 1 block up from the Pocitos Beach, 10 minutes from downtown. Request a room facing the sea; the view of Pocitos Bay in the evening is enchanting. 779 J. B. Blanco (phone: 704021). Inexpensive.

**Parque Casino** – Not for gamblers only, this older luxury hostelry, renovated and remodeled several years ago, is very comfortable. Besides the *Carrasco,* it boasts Montevideo's only other casino. Unless you have a car, it is not too conveniently located. Rambla W. Wilson (phone: 497111; in the US, 800-44-UTELL). Inexpensive.

**EATING OUT:** Restaurants are a bargain. Special cuts of meat are reserved for restaurants, so the very best *pulpas* (boneless cuts of beef) can be sampled. Besides the restaurants listed here, a healthy, good, economical lunch or dinner is available at any café along the main street or downtown. Dinner is never served before 8 PM. Expect to pay $35 to $50 at restaurants in the expensive category, between $25 and $35 in the moderate range, and under $15 at places noted as inexpensive. These prices are for two, for a three-course meal (with meat) and coffee. They do not include drinks or tip. All telephone numbers are in the 2 city code unless otherwise indicated.

**Bungalow Suizo** – There are actually three "bungalows": one downtown, one in Carrasco, and one in Punta del Este. Try the Carrasco branch, which, though slightly out of the way, is built in Swiss-chalet style, with a very warm, cozy atmosphere and excellent food. The specialties are cheese fondue, smoked pork chops (an excellent choice), and Swiss potatoes. Closed Sundays and December through March. Reservations unnecessary. Major credit cards accepted. 150 Colonel Carrasco, Carrasco (phone: 611073). Expensive.

**La Camargue** – Very small establishment serving well-prepared French food. Closed Sundays. Reservations advised. Major credit cards accepted. 1133 Mercedes, corner of Rondeau (phone: 906120). Expensive.

**Club de Golf** – A 10-minute ride from downtown will get you to this luxurious not-for-members-only club with a wide variety of dishes, a buffet, and dessert table. French cuisine is a specialty. If you decide to go at midday, watch the golfers play right outside the French windows. Open daily for lunch only; members only on Saturdays and Sundays. Reservations advised. Major credit cards accepted. 379 Bulevar Artigas (phone: 701721). Expensive.

**Doña Flor** – One of the most expensive restaurants in town, with a very limited (but excellent) French menu. Try the special, *gratin de langostinos* (lobster au gratin). Closed Saturdays for lunch, Sundays, and during January and February. Reservations advised. Major credit cards accepted. In front of the Faculty of Architecture, 1034 Bulevar Artigas (phone: 785751). Expensive.

**Gran Cantón Chino** – The ever-present Chinese restaurant is alive and well in Montevideo. This one serves Cantonese fare. Although not up to international standards, the spring rolls and sweet and sour pork dishes are very good. Open daily. Reservations unnecessary. Major credit cards accepted. 2863 21 de Septiembre (phone: 707630). Expensive.

**Hawaii** – The excellent *parrillada* (grilled meat) is worth the trip to the Carrasco suburbs. The house specialty is stuffed chicken. Reservations advised. 6608 Murillo (phone: 606311). Expensive.

**Panorámico Municipal** – At the top of the Lookout Tower in Town Hall, this establishment offers an international menu. Open Thursdays through Sundays for lunch and dinner. Reservations advised. Major credit cards accepted. 1375 Soriano, at the corner of Ejido (phone: 920825). Expensive.

**Morini** – A very large dining spot on top of the *Mercado Central*. The seafood is extra special here. Open daily. Reservations unnecessary. Major credit cards accepted. 1229 Ciudadela (phone: 959733). Expensive to moderate.

**Del Aguila** – An old and traditional restaurant, frequently mostly by businesspeople at noon and theater patrons at night (it's next to the *Teatro Solís*). If you have a sweet tooth, order the omelette surprise. Open daily except Sundays for lunch and dinner. Reservations unnecessary. Major credit cards accepted. 694 Buenos Aires (phone: 959905). Moderate.

**Bellini** – One of the best Italian eateries in Montevideo, with live music most nights and a convival atmosphere all the time. A 5-minute taxi ride from the center of town — and worth it. Closed Sunday lunch and Mondays. Reservations unnecessary. Major credit cards accepted. 1644 San Salvador at Minas (phone: 412987). Moderate.

**Club Alemán** – The surroundings aren't too welcoming, but the German food is first class. Dancing on Thursday through Saturday nights. Closed Sundays. Reservations advised. Major credit cards accepted. 935 Paysandú (phone: 917496). Moderate.

**El Hórreo** – Great downtown spot for an informal seafood dinner and a flamenco show. Open Tuesdays through Saturdays for lunch and dinner. Flamenco show on Friday nights and music on Saturday nights. Reservations advised. Major credit cards accepted. 1137 Santiago de Chile (phone: 917688). Moderate.

**Ley Seca** – A cozy pub that is especially popular on Friday and Saturday nights, when there is live music starting at 10:30 PM. The menu is limited, but the bar offers a wide range of mixed drinks and coffee liqueurs. Closed Sundays. Reservations advised. No credit cards accepted. Soriano and Río Branco (phone: 982481). Moderate.

**La Mascota** – Tasty hot dogs, pizza, *chivitos,* and *parrillada.* Informal; frequented mostly by young people. Closed Sundays. Reservations unnecessary. No credit cards accepted. 1605 Arocena at Gabriel Otero (phone: 600335). Moderate.

**Otto** – Whether it's cocktails, lunch, tea, dinner, or a quick snack, the food is tasty and the service friendly at this cozy spot that specializes in beef stroganoff, grilled brochettes, and chicken. Good German-style pastries too. Open daily. Reservations unnecessary. Major credit cards accepted. 1301 Río Negro, at the corner of San José (phone: 901994). Moderate.

**La Suiza** – Ten varieties of fondue, including roquefort, chicken, and tomato, are among the delectable choices at this cozy little eatery with checkered tablecloths and candlelight. Save room for dessert — try the chocolate fondue, served with fresh fruit. A good place to sample Uruguayan wines. Excellent service. Closed Sundays and Monday dinner. Reservations unnecessary. Major credit cards accepted. 939 Soriano (phone: 911370). Moderate.

**El Viejo Turismo** – The best *asado* (roast beef with sauce) and *parrillada* (grilled meat). Also, don't miss the *pamplona.* Small and informal. Open daily. Reservations unnecessary. Major credit cards accepted. In Carrasco, at Costa Rica and Rivera (phone: 601514). Moderate.

**La Azotea** – The *parrillada* (grilled meat) is very good, as are the stuffed chicken and the seafood dishes. Another plus is that the staff speaks English. It's on the Rambla in Pocitos Bay. Closed Sundays. Reservations unnecessary. Major credit cards accepted. Rambla República del Perú 1063, Pocitos (phone: 796714). Moderate to inexpensive.

**El Entrevero** – An absolute must if you want to try a typical Uruguayan place. The *parrillada* (grilled meat) is particularly delicious. Open daily. Reservations unnecessary. No credit cards accepted. 2774 21 de Septiembre, Pocitos (phone: 700481). Moderate to inexpensive.

**La Taverna de Chiche** – A favorite with journalists and actors, who like its bohemian atmosphere, the informal dining here features full-course daily specials including wine, as well as pasta and sandwiches. Extremely friendly service. A music show featuring tango, bolero, and *cumbia* is offered every Friday and Saturday starting at 10 PM. Closed Sundays. Reservations unnecessary. Major credit cards accepted. 1329 Z. Michelini (formerly Cuareim) in *Gallery Plaza Libertad* (phone: 916278). Moderate to inexpensive.

**El Chivito de Oro** – Noisy and informal, but *the* spot to savor a mouth-watering *chivito* — a hot steak sandwich with whatever you choose to have on it. The grilled ham and cheese sandwiches (*sandwich caliente*) and the mixed cold sandwiches (*olímpicos*) are filling and succulent here, too. Open daily until 3 AM. No reservations. Major credit cards accepted. 1251 18 de Julio (phone: 905160). Inexpensive.

**Conaprole** – If you stay at one of the Carrasco-suburb hotels, this will be a convenient place to eat. It has a lovely location in a park and serves full meals — steaks, *chivitos,* and omelettes — as well as breakfast and afternoon tea. Open daily. Reservations unnecessary. Major credit cards accepted. Eduardo Couture, corner Av. Arocena Carrasco (phone: 600447). Inexpensive.

**El Emporio de la Pizza** – Casual, lively, and quite simply the best pizza place in Montevideo. In addition, they serve excellent empanadas and *faina,* a Uruguayan flatbread made with chickpea flour. Open daily. No reservations. No credit cards accepted. 1311 Río Negro (phone: 914681). Inexpensive.

**Oro del Rhin** – Do not leave Montevideo without having had breakfast or tea at this Old World *confitería.* The sandwiches and cakes and pastries are the pride of all Uruguay. Ask for a *té* or *café completo* (which consists of toast, marmalade, grilled sandwiches, cakes, pastries, and tea or coffee) or choose your own sandwiches and cakes from the front counter. If you like your coffee strong, order a *cortado.* Open daily. No reservations. Major credit cards accepted. 897 Colonia, at Convención (phone: 912054). Inexpensive.

**Soko's** – If you are looking for a place to have a cocktail before a meal, this popular spot serves tables full of excellent appetizers. Handy hint: Imported whiskey is very expensive; the local one, not anywhere near as good, is half the price. The piled-high ice cream sundaes must be seen to be believed, and one serving of the apple strudel is ample for two people. Closed Sundays. No reservations. No credit cards accepted. 1250 18 de Julio (phone: 905800). Inexpensive.

# PANAMA CITY

During the 1880s, when the French were in the midst of a doomed attempt to cut a sea-level canal across the steaming Isthmus of Panama, an outraged missionary described Panama City as a "hideous dung heap of moral and physical abomination." It was a place where the definition of a good time was as broad as the ocean the city overlooked, and tomorrow was a day whose arrival could not be expected with certainty.

While Panama City has grown from the striking collection of shacks and moldering colonial structures of a century ago to become one of the more exciting and cosmopolitan metropolises of Latin America, one thing has not changed — it is still a city dedicated to the pursuit of pleasure. So whether a visitor's tastes are high-brow or low-rent, classy cabaret or strip joint, hotel or flophouse, racetrack or bullring, seafood or honky-tonk junk food, casino or bingo hall, it's possible to indulge them in Panama City, where "gambling is not only a cornerstone of the country's economy, but a way of life."

At the more hospitable end of the world's most important nautical short cut, Panama City is home to more than 580,000 people — one-quarter of the entire population of Panama. The majority of the city's residents are mestizo, a mixture of Spanish and Indian. There is also a sizable black population, living primarily in the areas called Río Abajo and Parque Lefevre, an important minority of highly enterprising Chinese, and many Western Europeans. Although the Canal Zone ceased to exist as an American-governed enclave on October 1, 1979, thousands of *norteamericanos* continue to live there in the tropical equivalent of suburbia.

Large numbers of Panamanians still live in ramshackle tenements, teeming with humanity and humanity's laundry, scattered throughout the city, but these are gradually being replaced by new, concrete, government-built tenements (although at press time government money was scarce and the work was proceeding at a slow pace). In either case, they contrast starkly with the sleek glass and concrete high-rise office buildings, condominiums, banks, and hotels that dominate the city's skyline.

The present city is the second Panama City. The first was founded in 1519, 4 miles (6 km) east of the present site, 18 years after the Atlantic coast of Panama was discovered by Columbus. The city's founder was Pedro Arias Dávila, known as Pedrarias the Cruel, who murdered Vasco Nuñez de Balboa, discoverer of the Pacific Ocean at Darién in 1513. Pedrarias also began the grisly work that eradicated all but three of Panama's 60 indigenous Indian tribes during Spain's 300-year tenure. In 1524, the conquistador Francisco Pizarro began the plunder of the Inca empire from Panama City. The city became a storage terminal for the incredible golden treasures of the Inca and 200,000 tons of Bolivian silver, which were then taken across the isthmus by heavily guarded mule trains to be shipped to Spain. Although strongly garrisoned, the city was not built in a particularly defensible location. So after resisting several earlier attempts, the city was sacked and burned in 1671 by a horde of buccaneers led by Henry Morgan.

The city was rebuilt within a year, behind stout walls, at the tip of the peninsula that forms Panama Bay. It was never taken by force again. Panama was granted independence from Spain without violence in 1821 and joined the Republic of Greater Colombia, a federation of the countries that today forms Colombia and Venezuela. Panama separated from Colombia in 1903, with the help of the US, when Panama signed the Hay–Bunau–Varilla Treaty granting the use of the 10-mile-wide and 51-mile-long Canal Zone to the US permanently and exclusively.

The more-than-300-year-old Spanish colonial town of stucco, wrought-iron grillwork, and balconies overlooking narrow cobblestone streets is the core of modern Panama City. The peninsula on which the city stands extends south into the Pacific Ocean, with the bay to the east and the Panama Canal to the west. The city extends northeast across the peninsula and overflows into progressively newer and less frenetically crowded urban districts. The newest section lines a sleek boulevard and looks west across the placid bay toward the walls and spires of the colonial city.

Although the Canal Zone is no longer officially American sovereign soil, the enclave still contrasts sharply with the rest of Panama City. On one side of a six-lane boulevard are expansive lawns framing split-level homes, before which air conditioned Detroit monsters sit in paved driveways. On the other side of the street are tenements and crowded streets jammed with battered taxis, litter, and the most flamboyantly decorated buses in Latin America. In the former Canal Zone, now known as the Canal Area, Americanisms and Americans still prevail: Protestant churches, supermarkets, and the most southerly lodge of the Benevolent and Protective Order of Elks.

The gringos and their condescending ways were long a source of irritation to Panamanians, and the 15 years preceding adoption of the new canal treaties were marked by periodic episodes of violence. Except for anti-American demonstrations late in 1979, when Panama gave refuge to the deposed Shah of Iran, and in mid-1988 (when then-President Reagan halted all payments to Panama after President Eric Arturo Delvalle was ousted by the National Assembly of Panama, under the control of the now deposed military leader General Manuel Antonio Noriega), the mood of the Panamanian public toward the US generally has softened. The Americans, or Zonians, however, greeted the canal pact with belligerent dismay and displays of jingoistic patriotism, brought about by the realization that their own unique tropical paradise was finally coming to an end.

The 1978 pact (which left most Panamanians pleased and which elevated former US President Carter to a level of esteem uncommon even in his own country), grants Panama sovereignty over the canal by the year 2000. To Panamanians it symbolizes the rectification of an old injustice: the establishment of the canal as a neutral zone through which all vessels have equal right of passage (under the new treaty, traffic between the Atlantic and Pacific oceans will continue as always). Though the country's political upheavals during the last decade may have cast doubts on the future of the treaty,

# PANAMA CITY

## Points of Interest

1. Plaza Paitilla Inn
2. Plaza de Francia/French Plaza
3. Paseo de las Bóvedas/Promenade of the Dungeons
4. Iglesia de Santo Domingo/Church of Santo Domingo
5. La Presidencia/Presidential Palace
6. Plaza Independencia/Independence Plaza
7. Iglesia de San José/Church of San José
8. Balboa Monument
9. Museo Antropológico de Reina Torres de Araúz/Queen Torres of Araúz Anthropological Museum
10. Puente de las Américas/Bridge of the Americas
11. Panama Canal
12. Balboa Yacht Club
13. Panamá Viejo/Old Panama
14. Panama Tourist Bureau, Marriot Caesar Park
15. Estadio Juan Demóstenes Arosemena
16. National Theater
17. Plaza Santa Ana

**AT-A-GLANCE**

# SAN FELIPE

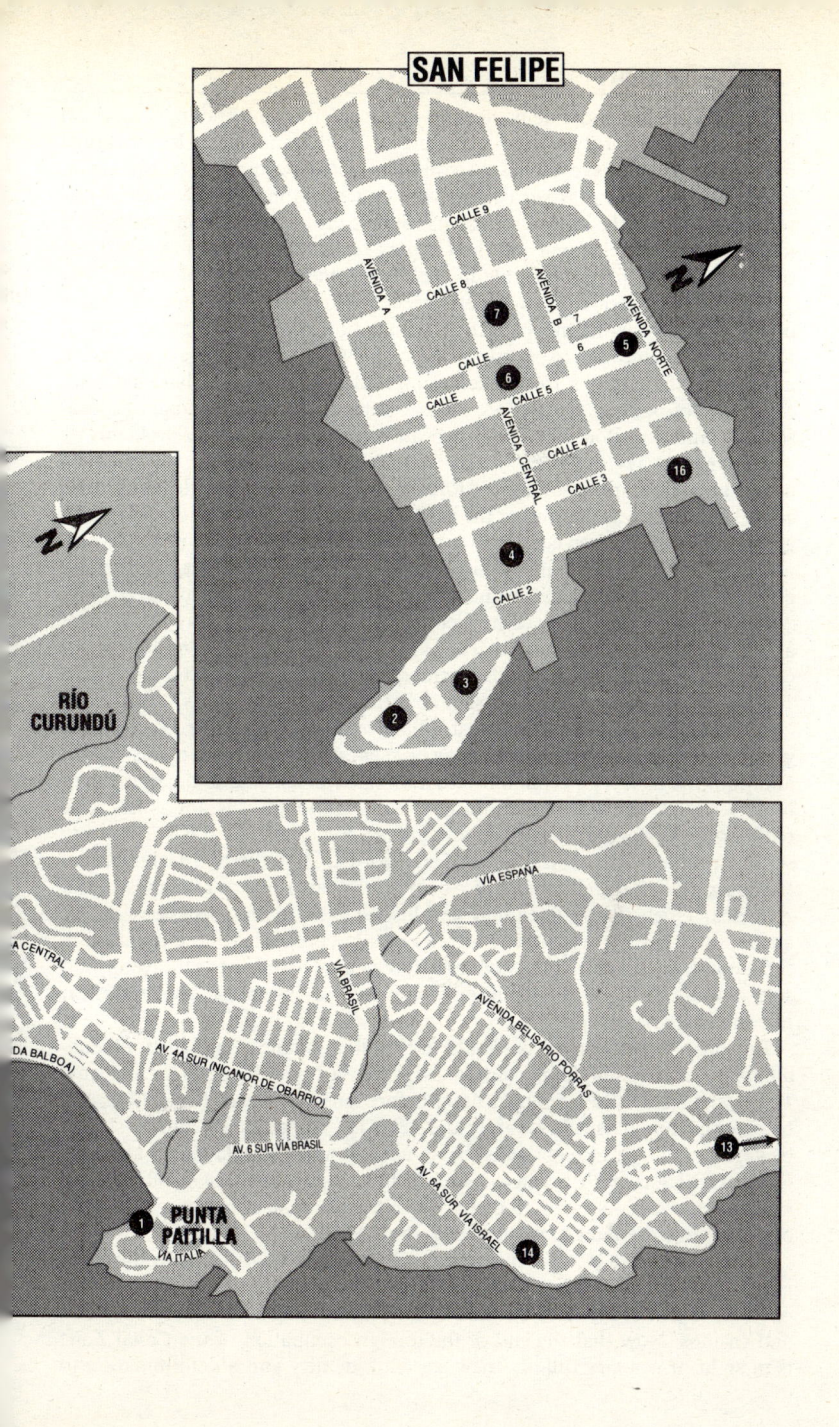

today's leadership under democratically elected President Endara is expected to be more conciliatory toward US interests in the Canal Area. International maritime officials have expressed concern over deterioration of the canal, including the canal railroad (which was shut down in 1990 because of disrepair and again, the lack of money has left its future in question), ports, and locks. As a result, Panama and the US may renegotiate parts of the treaty so that the US will play some role in the management of the waterway.

Despite some residual anti-American sentiment and increasing displeasure on the part of other members of the Organization of American States (OAS), Panama City continues to encourage tourism. Many travelers again are taking advantage of the city's free-wheeling nightlife and duty-free bargains and, regardless of politics, tourists are always welcome. English is taught in local schools, and a visitor who doesn't speak Spanish will have no problems.

Panama always has been a way station on a trade route traversed by adventurers, seafarers, soldiers of fortune, merchants, and gold seekers who came because it was one end of the shortest distance between the world's two great oceans. It has seen conquistadores and pirates, '49ers rushing to California gold fields, French canal builders, and American engineers, who finally conquered the jungle, malaria, and yellow fever to complete the canal in 1914.

Panama has never really controlled its own affairs. Even today, its internal affairs are strongly influenced by the US Government, by giant multinational corporations like United Brands (formerly United Fruit), and by more than 100 banks from more than 2 dozen countries.

As in any large city where great affluence and poverty live side by side, unwary travelers in Panama City may be separated from their possessions. In addition, the country's economic situation has worsened and unemployment has risen since the US invasion in late 1989. Although it is not as rife with petty crime as Bogotá, Colombia, or Caracas, Venezuela, theft is still a pretty serious problem, particularly in the areas of El Chorrillo and Calidonia on the south side of the city and Río Abajo on the eastern end. Like most Latin American cities, lone women may be whistled at more than occasionally. (Be aware, too, that at press time, isolated cases of cholera had been reported in the capital. Water in the city's major hotels is safe to drink; but avoid food sold in outdoor markets and eat only well-cooked vegetables, fish, and meat in restaurants.)

But these negative aspects should not inhibit anyone's enjoyment of Panama City. A few simple precautions will keep a traveler out of harm's way. Prices always should be agreed upon before a service is rendered. Bags and belongings should be held securely and never left unattended. Cameras should be kept out of sight, except when being used. Jewelry should be left at home. (Even eyeglasses with expensive frames have been stolen right off people's faces in crowds.) As in any big city, the odds are against becoming a victim of crime, but the danger is there and should be recognized.

Panama City is a city on the make, a city that hustles. As long as the canal is an important trade route, it will have a captive audience for the bazaar-like open-air markets, the sleek boutiques, the phantasmagorical discos, the bars, and casinos. Now that the end of the foreign occupation of the Canal Zone is in sight, it is a city full of a new sense of identity and a determination to

PANAMA CITY / At-a-Glance  409

grow into the grandiloquent sobriquet bestowed on it by the Panama Tourist Bureau: "Heart of the Universe."

# PANAMA CITY AT-A-GLANCE

**SEEING THE CITY:** There is a superb view of Panama City looking west across the bay toward the heart of the city, from the refurbished *Belvedere* rooftop lounge of the *Plaza Paitilla Inn* (Vía Italia and Winston Churchill at Punta Paitilla; phone: 691122); it is especially impressive at night and is usually open past midnight, but closing hours may vary depending on business.

**SPECIAL PLACES:** It would take the instincts of a lovelorn bloodhound to overcome the haphazard asymmetry of Panama City's streets. The canal can be found to the west of the city proper. Most of the streets of the major shopping district run east-west near Panama Bay. Many of the streets (*calles*) run along a north-south axis and are numbered; other streets have been renamed, and are referred to by both their old and new names. The addresses given here are the names commonly used on maps and by bus and taxi drivers.

**Plaza de Francia (French Plaza)** – At the southernmost tip of the peninsula on which the city is built, this is the heart of the old colonial section and a logical place to begin a walking tour. Shaded by red-flowering trees, the square contains monuments to Finlay, the conqueror of yellow fever, and former Panamanian President Pablo Arosemena and an obelisk dedicated to the French canal builders, who started work before the Americans. The Palace of Justice, where the Supreme Court meets, and a number of colonial buildings line the square. The city recently revitalized the area of San Felipe, which includes the Plaza de Francia, Paseo de las Bóvedas (Promenade of the Dungeons), and the Iglesia de Santo Domingo (Church of Santo Domingo).

**Paseo de las Bóvedas (Promenade of the Dungeons)** – This lovers' walk atop the Old City wall is reportedly not only for lovers these days, but pickpockets too — so beware! It can be reached by stone stairs from the Plaza de Francia and affords a good view of the bay and offshore islands. Beneath the wall are the old dungeons that give the promenade its name. Behind the Plaza de Francia.

**Iglesia de Santo Domingo (Church of Santo Domingo)** – Not far from the Paseo de las Bóvedas, this church, now in ruins, contains a flat archway, more than 350 years old, made of brick and mortar that stands without any internal support. The archway's durability was taken as proof that Panama was not endangered by earthquakes, and this was a conclusive argument for building the canal here instead of across Nicaragua. Av. A.

**La Presidencia (Presidential Palace)** – The president's palace is the most striking building in Panama City. Its main attractions are the gardens and fountains in its internal courtyard, where a flock of heron holds court for visitors. Tours of the palace can be arranged by calling the public information office (phone: 274487). Av. Norte.

**Plaza Independencia (Independence Plaza)** – The main square of colonial Panama City is the site of the cathedral that, with its mother-of-pearl twin towers, took 108 years to complete. The Archbishop's Palace, now a university, and the Central Post Office, headquarters for the French attempt to cut a canal through the isthmus, also front the square. Av. Central.

**Iglesia de San José (Church of San José)** – This church houses one of the greatest treasures of Panama and of all Central America — its magnificently convoluted gold baroque altar, the only gold in the first Panama City (Panamá Viejo, or Old Panama) that escaped the pirate horde of Henry Morgan in 1671. It was saved by a monk, who painted it black, and by the citizenry, who protected the ruse. Calle 8-A, just beyond the cathedral.

**Salsipuedes District** – This section, whose name means "get out if you can," is an area of narrow streets crammed with vendors who will sell you anything, including a deed to the canal. It is just outside colonial Panama in the older commercial section, where the Panamanians do their shopping. This is a particularly good place to visit at lunchtime, for it has many good Chinese restaurants of unassuming decor, moderate price, and excellent quality. Just off Av. Central. The largest camera and electronics stores are along Avenidas Central and President Kennedy.

**Balboa Monument** – In suitably heroic style, this marble monument depicts the discovery of the Pacific Ocean by Balboa in 1513. Then he stood "silent upon a peak in Darién." Now he stands just as silently upon a globe supported by representatives of the four races of man. The monument also offers a good view of the bay. Av. Balboa.

**Museo Antropológico de Reina Torres de Araúz (Queen Torres of Araúz Anthropological Museum, also known as the Museum of the Panamanian Man)** – Pre-Columbian gold, relics of the Spanish occupation, displays covering archaeology and ethnography of the many tribes that inhabited the isthmus make this the best museum in town. Open Tuesdays through Saturdays from 10 AM to 3:30 PM, Sundays from 2 to 5:30 PM. Admission charge. Plaza 5 de Mayo and Av. 7 Central (phone: 620415).

**Puente de las Américas (Bridge of the Americas)** – Honors the five-time US Representative from Kentucky, Maurice H. Thatcher, who was the youngest member of the Isthmian Canal Commission and author of the bill that authorized the canal's construction. This mile-long span joins the Pacific end of the Panama Canal. From it, there is a great view of the canal, the Canal Area, Panama City, and the offshore staging area where ships await their turn to make the 8-hour voyage to the Atlantic Ocean. If asked, taxi drivers will stop at scenic overlooks at either end of the span. Av. Amador.

## CANAL AREA

**Panama Canal** – It is unthinkable to visit Panama City without seeing the "Big Ditch," one of the certifiable wonders of the modern world. First suggested by the Spanish in 1524, the canal remained a dream for almost 4 centuries. It originally was attempted by the French hero of the Suez Canal, Ferdinand Marie de Lesseps. Two decades and tens of thousands of lives later, de Lesseps gave up in the wake of a political scandal that rocked France. It was the Americans in the era of Theodore Roosevelt's "Big Stick" diplomacy who finally joined the oceans with a 50-mile canal that rises and descends 85 feet through three two-lane sets of locks to cross the rocky backbone of the Americas. In the course of building the canal, the scourges of the tropics, malaria and yellow fever, also were conquered. The canal and the 5-mile strip on each side of it were ceded to the US "in perpetuity" by the 1903 treaty under which it was built. In the year 2000, the canal will revert to Panama.

There are a number of ways to see the canal, including a package tour, rental car, and boat. In the 1920s, one man swam it. It cost him 36¢ in tolls, which are (still) based on weight. The railroad was completed in 1855 to carry '49ers to California, and was the first "transcontinental" rail link. Running between Panama City and Colón, the railroad gave passengers a panoramic view of the canal for just $2 until it was shut down in 1990 for some much-needed repairs. Check with the tourist office (phone: 267000) for a reopening date. Buses to the canal cost 40¢ and leave frequently from the bus terminal at Shaler Plaza. It's a 15-minute walk from the bus stop to the Miraflores locks, where bleachers have been set up for spectators. Otherwise, rent a car or check with your hotel desk. Every tourist hotel offers transportation to the canal. A tour boat trip takes 8 hours one way.

**Balboa** – The chief city of the former Canal Zone, Balboa is not so much a city as an American suburb, homogenized, manicured, air conditioned, and all but hermetically sealed from the Latin disorder and passion that seethes along its borders. Although no longer strictly American property, it retains its character and most of its gringo population. If you have been too long on the road and need a fix of supermarkets and stainless steel cafeterias, Balboa is a good stop. Or ask for the army base and *Balboa Yacht Club,* underneath which is a wonderfully lazy gringo bar filled with characters straight out of Jimmy Buffet lyrics. Ft. Amador.

**Taboga** – This would be an unspoiled island paradise except for the heavy tourist traffic on weekends and national holidays, for there are no cars and no pollution. It does have fragrant blossoms (Taboga is also called the "Island of Flowers"); beautiful beaches; good snorkeling, scuba diving, and water skiing; delicious, juicy, ripe mangoes (best eaten in a bathtub or while wearing a raincoat) and pineapples; and ceviche (corvina, or sea bass, marinated in lime juice), a perfect accompaniment to a cold brew. The island has two air conditioned hotels — the recently refurbished *Taboga* (phone: 502122), a 70-room resort-like retreat with moderate prices, a pool, and open-air restaurant; and the venerable *Chu* (phone: 502035), a 2-story wooden hostelry with inexpensive rates. Visitors can use the changing facilities at the *Taboga* for $1 and rent a picnic hut for $5. Water taxis called *pangas* provide transportation around the island. Ferries to Taboga leave daily from Pier 18 in the Canal Area, and the fare is $2.50 each way. Contact *Argo Tours* (Calle 53; phone: 643549) for a schedule. *Reisa Tours* (PO Box 5007, Balboa; phone: 254728; fax: 272696) offers day tours of the island for $20.

**Barro Colorado Island** – An island that was created when the canal was built (the Chagres River was backed up to form Gatún Lake), today Barro Colorado is a research center of the *Smithsonian Institute.* Scientists come from all over the world to participate in various flora and fauna projects. Tours to the island, which include boat transportation, a guided nature walk, and lunch, can be arranged through the *Smithsonian Tropical Research Institute* (Box 2072, Balboa, Panama; phone: 623049). Write or call ahead in plenty of time — tours often are booked months in advance. *Eco-Tours* (PO Box 465, Panama 9A; phone: 363076) offers day trips for $85.

## OUT OF TOWN

**Panamá Viejo (Old Panama)** – This is the original city founded in 1519 by Pedrarias the Cruel. It was destroyed in 1671 by as ruthless a band of pirates as ever swashed a buckle. The city was rebuilt on a more defensible location farther west. What is left are the moss-covered remains of churches and residences, including the old Church of San José, which contained the golden altar now in colonial Panama's church of the same name. There is a stone bell tower and the ruins of the city's cathedral along with what is left of treasury houses and government buildings. The King's Bridge, which was the beginning of the mission trail known as El Camino Real, a muddy track that crossed the isthmus and was the most important road in the Spanish empire, still stands. Over this bridge marched the gold- and silver-laden mule trains and their escorts of halberd-clad Spanish soldiers. The area has been restored to a state of studied, moss-enshrouded ruin by the Panama Tourist Bureau. Free bilingual brochures about the ruins can be picked up at the *Bohío Turístico* restaurant next to the Morelos statue near the ruins. Vía Cincuentenario.

**Pacific Beaches** – So many people get intoxicated by the gambling and nightlife of Panama City that the beaches are still relatively uncrowded and unspoiled. Your best bet is to rent a car from one of the agencies and get a map from the tourist bureau. *Focus on Panama* and *Panama 2000* guides also carry maps. Several hotels and clubs on the ocean open their facilities to day tourists — these have the best beaches. The loveliest of all is the *Coronado Beach* (phone: 233175), with a golf course, restaurant, and villas. Call ahead and you will be welcomed. Other beachfront hotels are the *Motel*

*Punta Chame* in Punta Chame (phone: 231747); the *El Palmar* (phone: 237685) and *Río Mar* (phone: 642272) in San Carlos; and the *Playa Corona* (phone: 508037) in Corona. *Club Gaviota* (phone: 274969) on Coronado Beach has a pool and picnic huts, both available to visitors for a small charge, and an outdoor restaurant that features live music on Saturday nights. Plans are in the works to build a 120-room hotel next to the club's recreational facilities.

■ **EXTRA SPECIAL:** The Pearl Island archipelago 35 miles (56 km) south of Panama City was Balboa's base for his explorations of the Pacific coast. Once the source of a wealth of pearls, the islands now offer excellent snorkeling, water skiing, sailing, scuba diving, and fishing. There are more than 300 islands in the chain, and you can get to the principal ones by a 20-minute flight from Paitilla Airport or by tour boat. The gem of the Pearls is Contadora (which means "accountant" or "counter"), where pearls were counted before being shipped to the King of Spain. This island paradise was the retreat of the late Shah of Iran, and most recently the site of the Contadora Peace Conference in 1988. The island has 13 beaches, which have recently become popular with Panamanians, especially on weekends. The main resort is *Caesar Park Contadora* (phone: 504033; fax: 504000), a 133-room complex with a restaurant, open-air cafeteria, piano bar, 3 tennis courts, 9-hole golf course, pool, gym, marina, deep-sea fishing, dive shop, boat rentals, and windsurfing. Round-trip air fare from Paitilla Airport is about $44; contact *Aeroperlas* (phone: 696224 or 635363). For day tours, call *Reisa Tours* (phone: 254728).

# SOURCES AND RESOURCES

**TOURIST INFORMATION:** The Panama Tourist Bureau (in the *Convention Center — ATLAPA*, across from the *Marriott* hotel on Vía Cincuentenario; phone: 267000; fax: 263483), has city maps, information on scuba diving, fishing, and group tours, and two English-language guides — *Focus on Panama* and *Panama 2000*. It is open weekdays from 8:30 AM to 4:30 PM. Basic information is provided at the information stand at Tocumen Airport. Open daily from 8 AM to midnight.

**Local Coverage** – There are five Spanish-language dailies: *La Prensa, Estrella de Panamá, El Siglio, El Panamá América,* and *Crítica Libre.* An English version of the *Miami Herald* is available at most major hotels.

The US Embassy is located on Av. Balboa and Calle 37 (phone: 271777).

**TELEPHONE:** The area code for Panama is 507. (There are no city codes.)

**CLIMATE AND CLOTHES:** Tourist literature advertises the climate as "pleasantly tropical... from 73 to 81F (22 to 35C) in coastal areas. Nights are generally cool." Don't bet on it. Panama City's weather runs hot and muggy, with temperatures into the 90s F (30s C), which matches the humidity during the rainy season (from April to December), when it rains almost daily, but usually for brief periods (annual precipitation of 65 inches). The dry season is hot but uniformly sunny and generally comfortable. Dress for the tropics, casually, and in light cottons. In the rainy season, bring along a raincoat and umbrella. Synthetics are fashionable but will be uncomfortable in the outdoor heat. At night, casual is the rule, although a tie and jacket are appropriate in the best restaurants. Neither ties nor jackets are required in casinos. Women may find a sweater or shawl a good way to fight the air conditioning in theaters, restaurants, and nightclubs in the evening.

**GETTING AROUND: Bus** – Latin America's most picturesque — gaudily painted, hung with fringe, wrapped with Day-Glo vinyl, armed with air horns, and festooned with windshields that look like a cross between a religious gift store and a naughty postcard stand. More crowded than the winner's locker room after the *Super Bowl,* they would give claustrophobia to all but veterans of the Tokyo subways. Good fun for the adventurous and well worth the unbelievably low price of admission for those addicted to the best in local color, but definitely not for the fainthearted. The bus system goes everywhere.

**Taxi** – The best bets for getting from place to place are the flocks of battered taxis with no meters that roam the streets and hover around hotel entrances. Fares start at $1 and are governed by a zone system. There are two brands of taxi: big taxis and little taxis. They are priced according to the taxi's size and zone and are very reasonable. You can get to most places in the city for less than $5. Cabbies almost universally speak English and will gladly hire out by the day. They are also a good source of information on nightclubs and nightlife. Getting to outlying tourist attractions is easiest by taxi. An hourly rate is negotiable. Because of street crime, it is unwise to walk the streets at night, particularly downtown.

Most people enter Panama at Tocumen Airport, a modern facility 18 miles (29 km) from downtown. It is a 50¢ bus ride, $20 by cab. If you are willing to share a ride, the fare can go down to $8.

**Car Rental** – Driving in Panama City can be fun for the daring or torture for the timid. *Avis* (phone: 384037), *Budget* (phone: 384069), *Hertz* (phone: 384081), and *National* (phone: 384144) are represented at the airport (these numbers are all at the Tocumen Airport), as well as in many of the lobbies of the major hotels.

**SPECIAL EVENTS:** *Carnaval* begins the Friday before *Lent* and ends on *Ash Wednesday.* There is dancing in the streets, colorful costumes, all-night parties, and general revelry. Panama's *Independence Day Festival* is November 3. The *Underwater Fishing Tournament* takes place every year in April or May. The *International Fishing Tournament* draws anglers from all over the world and generally produces a world record or two during its August through October run. Check with your hotel or the tourist bureau.

**MUSEUMS:** The *Museo Antropológico de Reina Torres de Araúz* and the ruins of Old Panama are described in *Special Places.* Two other interesting museums are the following:

**Museo Historia de Panamá (Panama History Museum)** – With displays of the city's past. Open weekdays from 8 AM to 3:30 PM. Admission charge. Plaza de la Independencia Antiguo Palacio Municipal (phone: 628089).

**Museo de Arte Contemporáneo (Museum of Contemporary Art)** – Features exhibits by 20th-century artists. Open weekdays from 9 AM to 4 PM, Saturdays from 9 AM to noon. Admission charge for special exhibits. Av. de los Mártirez in the Canal Area (phone: 628012).

**SHOPPING:** Panama City has been called "the Hong Kong of North America." Prices are no lower than in other free ports such as the US Virgin Islands, but they're no higher either. Camera prices, however, are an exception — they actually are higher than at discount outlets in New York City. Still, if only for the number of stores and the quantity and variety of merchandise,

Panama City is a good shopping stop. Duty-free goods must be paid for at the store and picked up at the airport on your way out of the country. Regulations do not allow you to open your purchases until you and they are on the airplane; however, the head of customs in the airport will allow you to open and reseal any packages in his presence to make sure you got what you bought. Free port shops are extremely honest and reliable in making deliveries.

The main articles of trade are perfume, cameras, projectors, electronic goods, radios, lace, watches, china, chess and backgammon sets, and Oriental art. In late 1989, the duty on these and other items, such as bed and table linens and jewelry, was reduced to 2.5%. The main shopping area is along the Vía España. Other stores, especially camera and electronics stores, can be found along Avenida Central and Avenida de los Mártires. All the major hotels have shopping areas, too. You can bargain in most places.

For distinctive shirts, weavings, baskets, wicker, soapstone figures, necklaces, beaded collars, leather goods, straw, wooden figurines, ceramics, the distinctive appliquéd *mola* fabrics, and leather sandals, visit the *Salsipuedes* open-air bazaar (off Av. Central, see *Special Places)*. Offer half the stated price and try to meet somewhere in the middle. Those who want to purchase an authentic Panama hat will be disappointed. What we've come to know as a Panama hat is actually made in Ecuador, though the Panamanians make a very durable straw hat of their own, called a *pintado*.

Major US credit cards are cheerfully accepted everywhere except in the open-air markets.

**Artesanías** – Wide selection of wall hangings, bedspreads, pillowcases, and purses, all made from *molas*. In front of the *El Panamá* hotel on Vía Veneto (phone: 236963).

**Artesanías Nacionales** – Handicrafts of a more uniform quality than the *Salsipuedes* market, with predictably higher prices, can be purchased from this government-run cooperative for native artisans. In Old Panama and at the airport.

**El Especial** – Good collection of fabrics with designs inspired by the Kuna Indians. Closed Sundays. In the *Salsipuedes* bazaar off Av. Central.

**Salomon's** – A hodgepodge of imported goods, from Asian rugs to Indian tablecloths and garments. Closed Sundays. Next to *El Continental* hotel on Vía España (phone: 649663). Also outlets on Av. Central and Plaza 5 de Mayo.

**SPORTS:** Panama has just about every major outdoor athletic activity — from baseball and soccer to deep-sea fishing.

**Baseball** – Panama's best-known representatives to major league baseball include Rod Carew, Omar Moreno, Manny Sanguillén, and Juan Berenguer. Inflation has wiped out the Winter Leagues that included many US major and minor leaguers, but big league scouts still can spot some good prospects from among the teenage players who participate in the annual provincial baseball championships which begin in February. Games are played at the *Estadio Juan Demóstenes Arosemena* in Panama City and at stadiums in other provincial capitals.

**Boxing** – Panama has given the world at least four international champions. They mix it up regularly at the *Gimnasio Nuevo Panamá*, a huge indoor arena near the airport (no phone).

**Cockfights** – Take place every Saturday and Sunday from May through November at the *Club Gallístico* (Vía España; phone: 215652). Monday fights are added for the main tourist season, from December through April.

**Fishing** – Panama is an Indian name meaning "place where many fish are taken" and is the black marlin capital of the world. More than 40 world records have been taken in Panama's waters. Boat charters can be arranged through your hotel. Also, try *Club Pacífico* (on Coiba Island; phone: 610654) or *Tropic Star Lodge* (at Piñas Bay in southeastern Panama; phone: 645549). Gatún Lake has excellent bass fishing. Lists of boats for hire are available at the tourist bureau (see *Sources and Resources).*

**Golf** – At the *Panama* golf course (Cerro Viento; phone: 667777), the *Coronado Beach Golf Club* (phone: 646352), and *Brazos Brooks* (phone: 453858).

**Horse Racing** – Many of the world's top jockeys were either born or trained in Panama, so the citizens take the sport seriously. Races take place on Thursdays, Saturdays, Sundays, and holidays at the *Hipódromo Presidente Remón* (Vía José A. Arango; phone: 331600). Pari-mutuel betting is available.

**Snorkeling and Scuba** – Snorkeling, skin diving, and water skiing are available off Taboga Island and Contadora Island. Better to bring your own regulator and buoyancy compensator to ensure having good equipment. A couple of reputable places to rent are *Buzo* (phone: 618003) and *Scuba Panama* (phone: 613841).

**Soccer** – *Fútbol* is played at *Estadio Revolución,* near the airport. The game in the stands is sometimes more exciting than the one on the field. Check at your hotel for a schedule.

**Swimming** – Most hotels have swimming pools, and there are plenty of beaches. The Pacific beaches are still relatively uncrowded and unspoiled.

**Tennis** – There are courts at most major hotels.

**THEATER:** The wonderfully neo-classical *National Theater* (Calle 2-A; phone: 633582), in colonial Panama, periodically hosts performances — although odds are that unless it's the *Folkloric Ballet,* it is not really worth the time. The *Folkloric Ballet* features native folk dances and costumes and performs during February and March in Panamá Viejo. Check with the tourist bureau for events. The newspapers contain addresses of the movie theaters. All English-language movies are shown with Spanish subtitles.

**MUSIC:** The *National Symphony* is best left to itself. Outdoor concerts are held in the dry season in Plaza Santa Ana on Thursdays and on Sundays, in Parque Cathedral. There are outdoor dances and folkloric music shows at Panamá Viejo's ruins during February and March. Check at your hotel for schedules.

**NIGHTCLUBS AND NIGHTLIFE:** This is Panama City's specialty; the beat goes on all night. There are dancing and floor shows at the following: *El Continental* hotel, where a mighty Wurlitzer organ accompanies a light show nightly in the *El Sótano* nightclub (Vía España; phone: 639999); *Las Tinajas* (Calle 51, Bella Vista; phone: 637890), where women turned out in festival dress, dripping with gold combs and jewelry, and men topped with a straw hat (a *pintado*) perform *el tamborito,* the traditional Panamanian dance; *Plaza Paitilla Inn* (Vía Italia and Winston Churchill at Punta Paitilla; phone: 691122); and *El Criollo* (Villa María, Juan Díaz; phone: 211282). Discotheques are an ephemeral breed that go boom and bust, so check local listings, but some to look for are *Bacchus* (Vía España; phone: 639004 or 639005); *Magic* (Calle 50; phone: 636885); *Las Molas* (Los Angeles section C-41, near the Chase Manhattan Bank; phone: 602291); the *Disco Stelaris* at the *Marriott Caesar Park* (phone: 264077); and *Mai-Tai* at the *Gran Hotel Soloy* (phone: 271133).

Casinos are government-operated and honest. There is a $1 minimum bet and no tax on winnings. Slot machines, roulette, poker, blackjack, baccarat, craps, and a spin-the-wheel game called jackpot are available. There are casinos in the following hotels: *Plaza*

**416 PANAMA CITY / Best in Town**

*Paitilla Inn, Continental, Granada, Doral, Caribe, El Panamá, Soloy,* and *Marriott Caesar Park.*

## BEST IN TOWN

**CHECKING IN:** Panama City always has been a place to spend the night and have a drink or two, and there is no shortage of places in which to do that, although hotel rooms have become very costly. The city has more than 3,000 hotel rooms — more than other Latin American cities twice its size.

Panama City is one of the most expensive cities in Latin America, though several inexpensive and moderately priced hotels have sprung up in the area of the *Gran Hotel Soloy.* Expect to pay $90 and up for a double room at a hotel rated expensive; from $40 to $70 at a place in the moderate category; and under $30 at an inexpensive hotel. Major credit cards are accepted in all but the most inexpensive places. All telephone numbers are in the 507 area code unless otherwise indicated.

**El Continental** – It has 200 rooms, a shopping arcade, a bar, 6 dining rooms, lounges, international shows, a casino, and a terrazzo lobby. Vía España (phone: 639999; fax: 694559). Expensive.

**El Ejecutivo** – A 96-room hotel catering to businesspeople, it is fairly well priced and suitable for travelers without expense accounts. It has a pool, sun deck, and bar but no casino. Rooms have direct-dial phones, divan beds, and desks with swivel chairs. Calle 52 and Calle Aquilino de la Guardia (phone: 643333; fax: 691944). Expensive.

**Granada** – This medium-size, 180-room property has a small pool, casino, intimate bar, coffee shop, and a location from which you can safely walk to the diversions of the even more expensive hostelries nearby without paying their room rates. Calle Eusebio A. Morales, 1 block off the Vía España (phone: 644900; fax: 640930). Expensive.

**Marriott Caesar Park** – Adjoining the *ATLAPA Convention Center,* this 18-story place has 400 rooms near the ocean, a good view from the top-floor restaurant-lounge, and fine interior decor. It also has a casino, pool, tennis courts, and several choices of restaurants — *Le Trianon* is the best (see *Eating Out).* Vía Israel (phone: 264077; fax: 260116). Expensive.

**El Panamá** – Although the pink paint is faded on the outside, this hotel with 335 rooms, cabañas, and suites recently underwent a complete interior renovation. All the guestrooms have air conditioning, television sets, direct-dial telephones, and refrigerators. There also are 3 restaurants, a pool, tennis courts, a disco, and a casino. Vía España (phone: 231660 and 695000; fax: 236080). Expensive.

**Plaza Paitilla Inn** – Formerly the *Holiday Inn,* the only oceanfront hotel in the city proper, this 20-story, 274-room, round tower has a lofty vista of the bay and Panama City. Ask for a bayside room, however, or you may end up with a stunning view of the *Dairy Queen* and the technical high school. All rooms are air conditioned and have phones. Features include a pool, tennis courts, a lobby coffee shop, and the roof-top restaurant, Belvedere. Vía Italia and Winston Churchill at Punta Paitilla (phone: 691122; fax: 231470). Expensive.

**El Continental** – A 200-room hotel conveniently located near the airport, with good access to the city. It has a bar, restaurant, pool, and free bus service to the city (phone: 203333; fax: 205017). Moderate.

**Europa** – Centrally located, with 103 rooms, a bar, and a restaurant serving good food at reasonable prices. Singles, doubles, and suites come with telephones and

TV sets. Major credit cards accepted. Vía España and Calle 42 (phone: 636911; fax: 636749; telex: 3573 EUROPHTL PG). Moderate.

***Gran Hotel Soloy*** – Well situated, this 200-room tower has direct-dial telephones and a color TV set in every room. It also has a bar, restaurants, casino, and a fine view of the city and the canal from the top floor. Av. Perú and Calle 30 (phone: 271133). Moderate.

***Veracruz*** – Across from the *Gran Hotel Soloy,* this modern hostelry has 64 air conditioned rooms and a restaurant. Av. Perú (phone: 273022; fax: 272789). Moderate.

***Acapulco*** – A basic hotel with air conditioning and television sets in all 55 guestrooms and private parking, but no restaurant. Av. Perú and Calle 30 (phone: 253832 and 253834). Inexpensive.

***Bella Vista*** – Centrally located, next to the *Europa* hotel, with 48 rooms and a restaurant. Av. Central (phone: 644029). Inexpensive.

***Caribe*** – Probably the best of the budget hotels, it has 163 air conditioned rooms, a good dining room, and a lounge. It also has good service and is excellently located for shoppers. Av. Perú and Calle 28 (phone: 250404; fax: 273115). Inexpensive.

***Central*** – The city's funkiest and architecturally most interesting hostelry. What this 143-room relic lacks in convenience it makes up for in charm. In the heart of the colonial city, it has a restaurant, bar, and coffee shop. A good choice for the traveler on a budget. Plaza Independencia (phone: 226080). Inexpensive.

***Colonial*** – Another old establishment in the colonial city with the bare essentials, great prices, and a good personality, it does have a pool, a bar, and a restaurant, although not of the luxurious variety. Plaza Bolívar (phone: 229311). Inexpensive.

**EATING OUT:** Panama is a polyglot city with a hedonistic atmosphere, and eating out is almost a national pastime. Meals range from the simplicity, tang, and culinary adventure of pushcart vendors (scenic but rarely sanitary) to elaborate candlelit dining rooms. The quality is generally good, particularly in the moderate-price range, where competition is keenest. Seafood, the national specialty, reflects the Spanish influence and is usually excellent. The melting-pot nature of the city is reflected in good Italian, French, Chinese, and other cuisines. Although it is hard to find the really inexpensive meals that characterize other Latin American cities, the average meal still costs less than its US equivalent. A bill of fare is ordinarily posted at the door. A particularly wide selection of good restaurants may be found in the bayside area — for a gastronomic adventure, try walking into a restaurant that looks as if it would never be listed in a travel guide and ask for the specialty of the house. You probably will be pleasantly surprised. Panamanian beers — Panama or Soberana (both light), or the hearty Cristal Balboa — are very good. Local rums of the highest quality include Carta Vieja, Bacardi, and Tonel Vieja.

It costs $30 or more for dinner for two in those restaurants we've classified as expensive, including those in the top hotels. Expect to pay between $20 and $30 at those places in the moderate category; under $20, inexpensive. Prices do not include drinks, wine, or tips. Major US credit cards are accepted at almost all but the inexpensive restaurants. All telephone numbers are in the 507 area code unless otherwise indicated.

***Casco Viejo*** – This popular boîte run by two French citizens is centrally located. Excellent French cuisine and wines. Closed Sundays. Reservations advised. Calle 50 in the Mansión Danté Building (phone: 233306). Expensive.

***Korea House*** – A small cozy place close to the major hotels and banking center. Korean and Japanese food is served, including such dishes as roast beef, shrimp, chicken, or pork *bul-koki,* and sushi. Open daily. Reservations advised. La Vía Argentine, between La Vía Brazil and La Vía España (phone: 230176). Expensive.

***1985*** – Seafood is the specialty at this European-style restaurant, and it has a separate bar for sipping fine wines and brandies. Open for lunch and dinner on weekdays; dinner only on weekends. Reservations advised. Calle E. Morales (phone: 638541). Expensive.

***Rincón Suizo*** – A Swiss spot that specializes in fondues and Weiner schnitzel. Open for lunch and dinner Mondays through Fridays; dinner only on Saturdays and Sundays. Reservations advised. Calle Eusebio A. Morales (phone: 647529). Expensive.

***Sarti*** – A taste of Italy in the tropics, it has a pleasing atmosphere, good food, and fine service. Try the *fettuccine al pesto* or any of the excellent veal dishes. Closed Sundays. Reservations necessary. Calle Ricardo Arias (phone: 237664). Expensive.

***Le Trianon*** – The best in town, with a fine international menu. In the *Marriott Caesar Park* next door to the *ATLAPA Convention Center*. Open daily except Sundays for dinner. Vía Israel (phone: 691122). Expensive.

***Bajwa's Shamiana*** – An Indian curry house that specializes in exquisite tandoori dishes and curried meat. Open daily. Reservations unnecessary. Urb. Marbella and Calle 53 (phone: 638586). Moderate to expensive.

***Palacio Gran Bahía*** – Gone are the paper lanterns and the embossed felt wallpaper of what was once the *Gran China*. The restaurant has been remodeled with a modern, yet subdued touch. Chinese and Korean dishes are served. Open daily. Reservations unnecessary. Av. Balboa (phone: 272220). Moderate to expensive.

***El Pavo Real*** – Exclusive and with a European atmosphere, the specialties are homemade pâtés and quiche. Guests are urged to retire to the small pub on the premises for a game of darts and local or English beer. Closed Sundays. Reservations advised. Calle 51 Este, Campo Alegre (phone: 690504). Moderate to expensive.

***Bohío Turístico*** – Serves both continental and local specialties, with an emphasis on seafood. There is live music every evening. Open Mondays and Tuesdays at 4 PM, Wednesdays through Sundays from 11 AM. No reservations. Next to the Morelos statue in Old Panama. Vía Cincuentenario (phone: 265166). Moderate.

***La Casa del Marisco*** – Seafood cooked Panamanian-style; try the eel and squid. Open daily. No reservations. Av. Balboa (phone: 237755). Moderate.

***Granada*** – The Spanish decor looks as if it came out of a bottle, but the food is reasonably priced and the restaurant is very popular with locals. Open daily. Reservations advised. Calle Eusebia A. Morales (phone: 644900). Moderate.

***Matsuei*** – Several good Japanese restaurants have opened in Panama City. This one is patronized by local Japanese businessmen and specializes in fish dishes. Open daily. Reservations advised. Calle Eusebio A. Morales and Calle A-12 (phone: 649547). Moderate.

***El Pez de Oro*** – "The Golden Fish" serves seafood Peruvian-style in a pleasant atmosphere. Try the red snapper. Open daily. No reservations. No credit cards accepted. Vía Italia, Punta Paitilla, Centro Commercial, Bal Harbor (phone: 641372). Moderate.

***Siete Mares*** – Try the fish soups or the *corvina especial* (sea bass in a wine and shrimp sauce) at this seafood restaurant popular with movers and shakers. Closed Sundays. Reservations advised. Calle Guatemala (phone: 643032 or 640205). Moderate.

***Las Tinajas*** – The place to experience both typical Panamanian fare and the country's lively folkloric dancing. Appetizers like *carimañolas* (yucca croquets), *patacones* (green mashed plantains), *bollo* (corn timbals), and ceviche are followed by plates piled high with chicken and pork, seafood and shellfish. Several nights a week at 9:30 PM, elegant ladies and dashing gentlemen perform the traditional *punto* on a tiny stage to the delight of all. There is a $5 cover charge. Closed Sundays. Reservations advised. Calle 51, Bella Vista (phone: 637890 or 693840). Moderate.

**Palacio Rey Kung** – An addition to the city's long list of Chinese eateries. Go for the dim sum. Open daily. Reservations unnecessary. Vía España (phone: 690956). Moderate to inexpensive.

**El Dragón de Oro** – As you would expect from the name, it's Chinese. Meals are filling, plentiful, and cheap, making it one of the city's best food values. Open daily. No reservations. No credit cards accepted. Vía España (phone: 235719). Inexpensive.

**Napoli** – Not strictly Italian, but definitely one of the better bargains in Panama City. Food is plentiful, good, and the owner is said to have a pathological dislike for raising his prices. Closed Tuesdays. Reservations unnecessary. Major credit cards accepted. Calle Estudiante and Calle 58 (phone: 622446 or 622448). Inexpensive.

**Panamar** – Very good Panamanian seafood specialties are served in a pleasant, open-air dockside setting. Ask for whatever was caught fresh that day, prepared in the local style. Open daily. No reservations. Major credit cards accepted. Calle 50 (phone: 260892). Inexpensive.

# QUITO

When the Spanish conquistadores arrived in the heart of Ecuador's Central Valley at the beginning of the 16th century, they discovered Quito, today the capital, then the seat of government of the northern half of the Inca empire, governed by Atahualpa. When Atahualpa was killed by Francisco Pizarro in what is now Cajamarca, Peru, Atahualpa's general, Rumiñahui (whose name meant "face of stone"), continued the resistance against the invaders. Quito was razed in 1534 after Rumiñahui also was killed. After destroying the last vestiges of Inca resistance, the Spanish rebuilt the city, constructing homes over Inca foundations and building resplendent colonial cathedrals on one of the largest and most beautiful high plains of the Andes.

Although Quito retains many Spanish colonial buildings and considers itself the center of aristocratic Hispanic culture in Ecuador to this day, its roots go even deeper into the past than the relatively recent Inca civilization. And the pattern of destruction and reconstruction by both manmade and natural forces recurs throughout its recorded history.

More than 5,000 years ago, primitive hunters settled in a sheltered nook of the Andes at the foot of Pichincha volcano, on the site of what is today a modern housing development not far from Quito's Mariscal Sucre International Airport. It was the beginning of one of South America's earliest and most successful civilizations, the Cotocollao kingdom, which survived in the same area for the next 2,000 years, only to be replaced by successive Indian communities that culminated in the fabulous Inca empire. The Inca were destroyed by the Spanish, who in 1563 made the rebuilt city of Quito the seat of the royal *audiencia,* a judicial subdivision of colonial rule. But colonial rule proved no more secure than any of the earlier civilizations, and in August 1809 the first sparks of the anti-Spanish rebellion were struck in Quito. Some 13 years later, the final battle of the Independence War, the Battle of Pichincha, was fought on the mountain's slopes. Field Marshal Antonio José de Sucre led the fight, defeating General Melchor Aymerich on May 24, 1822, a date that has since become a national holiday.

Culturally and physically, Quito is a product of the 18th century, when the city reigned as a colonial capital. Now, 200 years later, the heart of colonial Quito is still largely made up of dignified colonial buildings, superb religious art, and beautiful Spanish architecture. It has been called "the Florence of the Americas," and its colonial art and architectural treasures earned Quito a place on the UNESCO list of World Cultural Heritage Sites. Modern development is contained by strict laws aimed at preserving the rich legacy of the past. Unfortunately, a 1987 earthquake and general economic decline have left Ecuador unable to keep up its old buildings, although you will see some restoration efforts under way. Visitors are often pleasantly surprised when they enter an apparently unkempt colonial building to find its interior in perfect condition.

Standing 15 miles (24 km) south of the equator and at an altitude of 9,350 feet, Quito's incomparable position between the only two Andean mountain ranges in Ecuador, the Cordillera Occidental (Western Range) and Cordillera Oriental (Eastern Range), has been the major factor in its independence and self-determination. In the distance glow the snow-covered peaks of the Andes — Cotopaxi, the world's highest active volcano (at 19,347 feet), and Cayambe, both of which are usually visible from the city on a clear, bright day, especially during the mornings. It is easy to understand the religious awe in which the conquistadores held this part of the world, where mountains are sculpted into vast panoramas and the very air seems to give objects far and near an animation slightly supernatural.

Quito has a population of 1.5 million, about a seventh of Ecuador's national total, and though it is the capital, it is not the largest or the richest city in the country. That honor belongs to Guayaquil, on the Pacific coast, a 35-minute flight from Quito. While the capital may lack industrial clout, it has so far held most of the political reins and certainly, in its mountain isolation, is one of the continent's loveliest cities.

With adequate room to grow, the heritage of different ages and cultures exists in Quito without noticeable strain. You will find supermarket chains and dawn street markets. Color television sets carry US network news, but Quechua, the language of the Inca, is heard in the streets. Auto repair shops may be housed in what once were the courtyards of colonial homes. The Ecuadoran economy boomed during the 1970s with the discovery of oil in the jungle regions; that boom brought a concomitant expansion of the middle class. Although the subsequent plummet of world oil prices in the early 1980s wreaked havoc with the country's economic development, Ecuador managed to stabilize its economy at the beginning of the 1990s. The wealthier sectors of Quito are steadily expanding northward, and a contemporary Andean architecture has developed, using plenty of airy arches, big windows, open patios, and split-levels in homes designed for affluent *quiteño* families.

Between the newer residential districts and the Old City spreads a mixed area, surrounding El Ejido and Alameda parks and the Avenida Amazonas shopping district. Called the Mariscal district, its pretty 19th- and early-20th-century houses stand beside modern office and apartment blocks, hotels, stores, and restaurants. Most of our recommended hotels, shops, and restaurants are in this area, which is quite safe for walking, even well into the evening hours.

Along with other Latin American countries, Ecuador now has a foreign debt, a huge budget deficit, and lots of social problems. Although there is poverty in Quito, there are few of the rambling shantytowns common to so many South American cities. An alarming number of children work, however, doing everything from shining shoes to selling chocolate bars, and in recent years Quito has drawn more and more indigents who may ask tourists for money. For now, the city lacks many of the social and political tensions that tend to breed violence, and the local scene remains among the safest in South America — although recent reports lead us to discourage walking alone (day or night) in the Panecillo Hill area, and to suggest that it's wise to avoid the historic colonial district at night as well where pickpocketing and

# QUITO

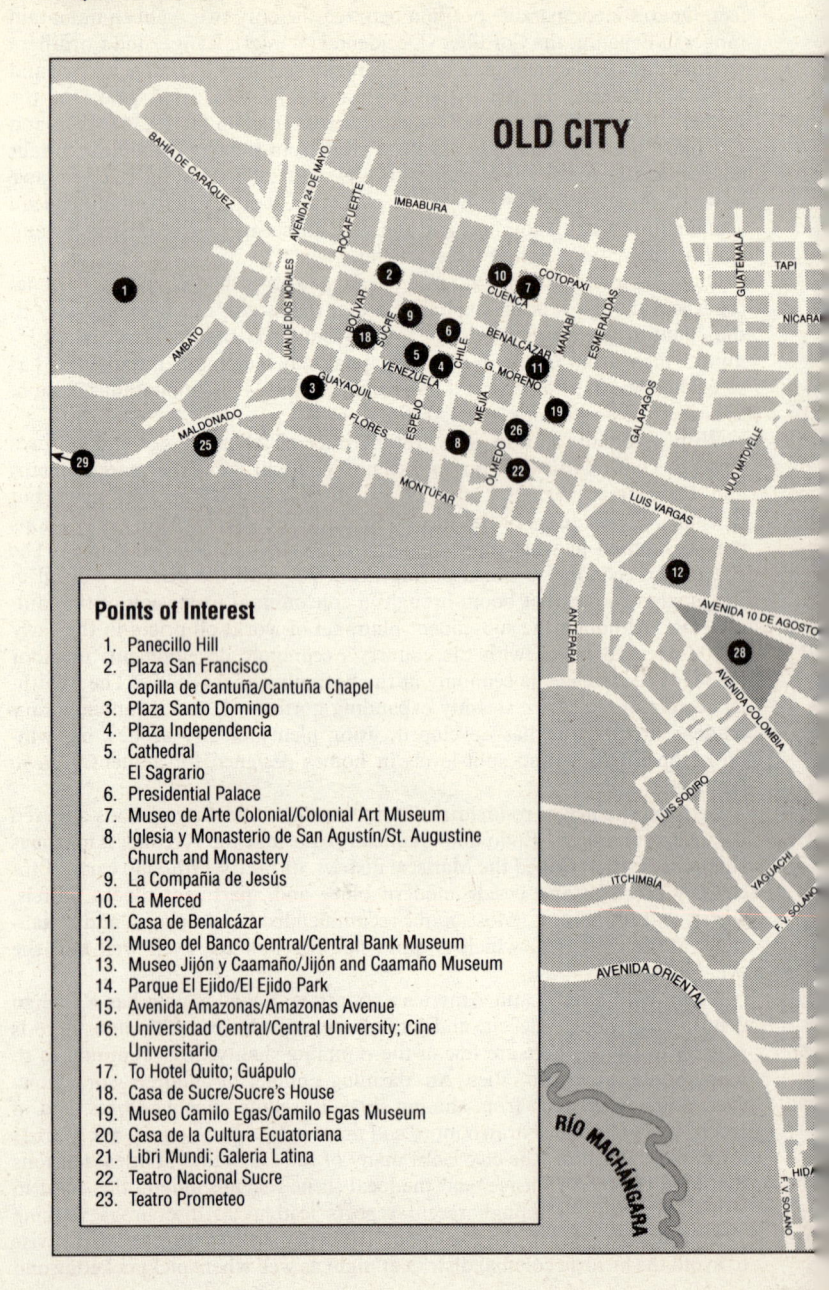

**OLD CITY**

## Points of Interest

1. Panecillo Hill
2. Plaza San Francisco
   Capilla de Cantuña/Cantuña Chapel
3. Plaza Santo Domingo
4. Plaza Independencia
5. Cathedral
   El Sagrario
6. Presidential Palace
7. Museo de Arte Colonial/Colonial Art Museum
8. Iglesia y Monasterio de San Agustín/St. Augustine Church and Monastery
9. La Compañía de Jesús
10. La Merced
11. Casa de Benalcázar
12. Museo del Banco Central/Central Bank Museum
13. Museo Jijón y Caamaño/Jijón and Caamaño Museum
14. Parque El Ejido/El Ejido Park
15. Avenida Amazonas/Amazonas Avenue
16. Universidad Central/Central University; Cine Universitario
17. To Hotel Quito; Guápulo
18. Casa de Sucre/Sucre's House
19. Museo Camilo Egas/Camilo Egas Museum
20. Casa de la Cultura Ecuatoriana
21. Libri Mundi; Galeria Latina
22. Teatro Nacional Sucre
23. Teatro Prometeo

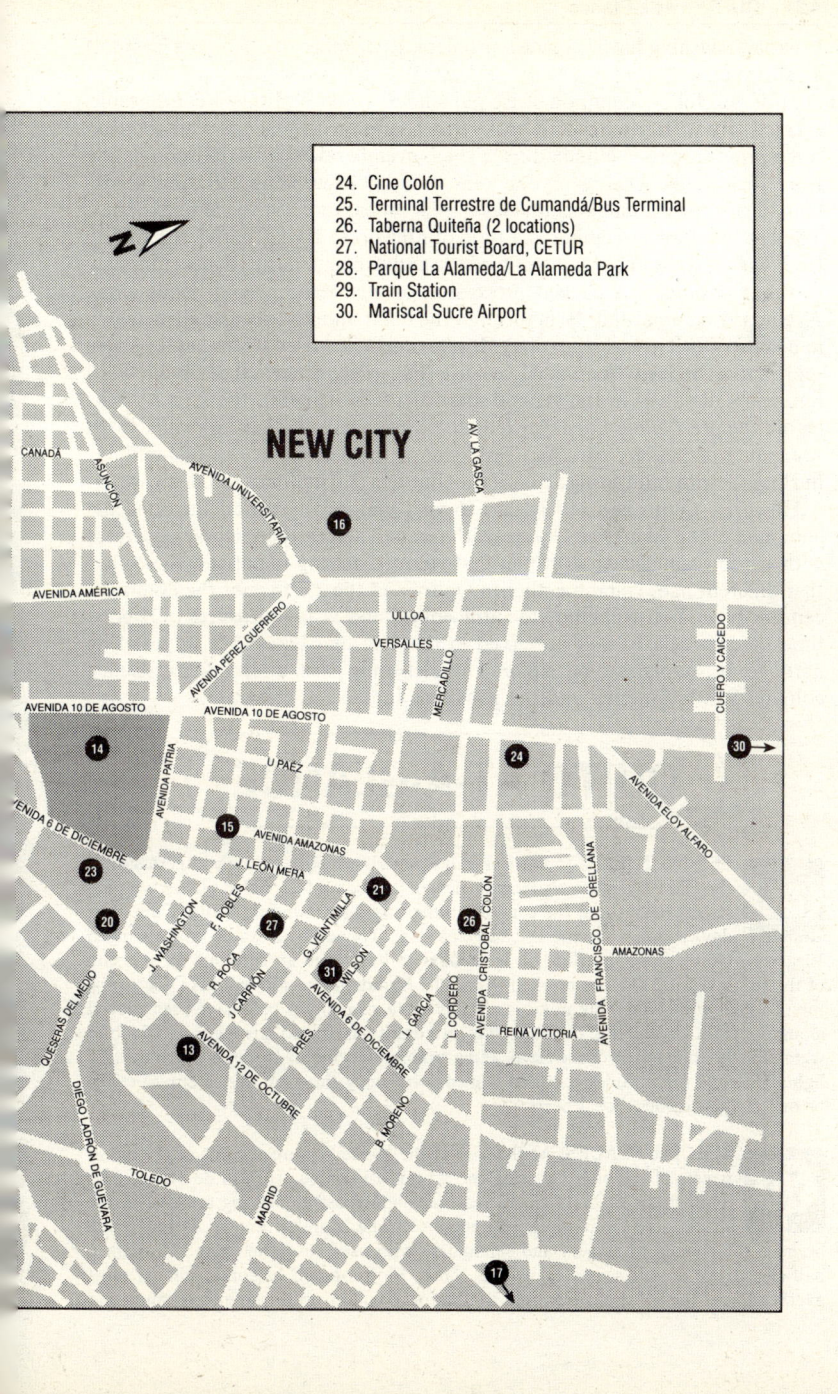

24. Cine Colón
25. Terminal Terrestre de Cumandá/Bus Terminal
26. Taberna Quiteña (2 locations)
27. National Tourist Board, CETUR
28. Parque La Alameda/La Alameda Park
29. Train Station
30. Mariscal Sucre Airport

# NEW CITY

backpack slashing have become a problem. Remember to carry your passport at all times.

So if you follow common sense guidelines, you'll find this a comfortable, relaxed city with squares and parks that sparkle with flowers. The *quiteños'* town pride reaches a climax during the November *Minga,* a tradition dating from Inca times, when everyone joins in a day of weeding, painting, scrubbing, dirt-clearing, and general cleaning in preparation for the annual fiestas. The first week of December is a time of fireworks, masks, parades, partying from bar to bar, and bullfights. Drinking and dancing in the streets culminate in the *Amazonazo,* a packed procession of mad dancers and bands along Avenida Amazonas that lasts through the night and leaves most participants in a state of collapse the next day. It is a time when friendships can be made more spontaneously than usual because the *quiteños'* normal reserve toward foreigners dissolves in the general merriment. In contrast, the 2 or 3 weeks before the pre-*Lenten Carnaval* tend to be more chaotic than enjoyable, with occupants of passing cars and residents of the second stories of buildings hurling — with infuriating accuracy — buckets and balloons full of icy water.

However, Quito is a lovely city to visit almost any time. The residents complain of the telephone service (with reason), and the bureaucracy operates with expected inefficiency. If you find yourself getting impatient, remember that different ages come together in Quito, and the 20th is not the dominant century here. You will enjoy the atmosphere and visual pleasures of bygone times — particularly well preserved in this city that takes care to guard its heritage. It is a place to be explored at a leisurely pace, a place to experience colonial South America and the ghosts of Indian civilizations.

## QUITO AT-A-GLANCE

**SEEING THE CITY:** The Panecillo (Breadloaf) Hill, on the southern side of the Old City, offers a sweeping view of the red roofs, cobbled plazas, winding streets below, and the rugged Andes ranges surrounding Quito. On a clear day, you can see the volcano Cotopaxi. Topped by a statue of the winged Virgen de Quito, the Panecillo Hill is thought to have been an Inca site for worship of the sun god Inti. The bus marked Mitad del Mundo–Panecillo will take you to the top. Though you could walk up, it is not advisable, as many people have been robbed along the path. On the hill, the *Panecillo* restaurant has a good terrace from which to watch the daytime bustle of the town, and a panoramic window through which the city lights glitter at night. Since the food is mediocre, enjoy the view over a cup of coffee or one of the excellent local beers.

**SPECIAL PLACES:** At the foot of the Panecillo spread some of the oldest streets of the city. Crossing the Avenida Veinticuatro (24) de Mayo, with its open-air markets where red crabs and roast guinea pig are among the snacks sold from stalls, you come to Calle Morales, known as La Ronda because the rounds of singers and serenaders who used to gather here. Through a half-closed eye it still seems to be the 1500s: Flower-laden balconies almost meet overhead, and the soft light from old iron lamps conjures up the sounds of spurs and hoofs on the cobblestones of the narrow street, which serves as the main artery off a maze of passageways in one of the most picturesque parts of Quito.

■**Note:** Don't wander around this area alone during the day, and especially after dark — pickpockets and muggings are common, and thieves often carry weapons.

## THE OLD CITY

**Plaza San Francisco** – Three blocks from La Ronda is the wide Plaza San Francisco, named for the magnificent Church and Convent of San Francisco, honoring St. Francis, the patron saint of Quito. In one corner of the plaza, which is crowded with street vendors, stands a statue of Flemish Friar Jodoco Ricke, the founder of the church and the man who first planted wheat in South America. Started in 1536 on the site of an Inca holy place, the church, which took 59 years to build (the monastery was the city's first), is the oldest in South America and is considered one of the world's masterpieces of baroque art. Every inch of wall and ceiling is painted or covered with gold leaf. (Note the images of the sun, which was the Inca divinity.) Its ornate altars are especially sumptuous, and the choir area is an impressive example of woodcarving, as is the pulpit. The unusual, winged image of the Virgin, by Bernardo de Legarda, is considered one of the finest works from the School of Quito. (Look closely; she has the facial features of an Indian woman.) The museum in the convent is packed with art from the 16th to the 18th century, including a gallery with 54 canvases depicting the life of St. Francis of Assisi. Paintings, sculpture, and more outstanding carvings can be seen in the Capilla de Cantuña (Cantuña Chapel). The church, convent, and some of the museum's artwork underwent restoration for the ceremonies marking the 500th anniversary of Columbus's journey to the New World. Open Mondays through Thursdays from 7 AM to noon and 3 to 6 PM; Fridays through Sundays from 7 AM to noon and 5 to 8 PM. Admission charge. Calles Cuenca, Bolívar, Benalcázar, and Sucre (phone: 212545).

**Capilla de Cantuña (Cantuña Chapel)** – Actually the atrium of the San Francisco church, this chapel is named after the Indian mason who built it. Legend has it that Cantuña agreed to finish the chapel by a certain date or risk a jail term. However as the deadline neared, the work was only half done. One night — the story goes — Satan appeared to Cantuña and in exchange for Cantuña's soul, agreed to send thousands of devils to finish the work before dawn the following day. When dawn arrived the next morning, the chapel was finished except for a single brick which rendered the satanic pact void and left Capilla Cantuña as the only (alleged) devil-built chapel on the continent. The chapel has a number of paintings and sculptures from the School of Quito, as well as the famed stone carving of Cantuña. To get to the chapel, enter through the finely carved wooden doors that are to the left of the main entrance of the church. Open Mondays through Saturdays from 6 AM to 1 PM; Sundays from 6 AM to 9 PM.

**Plaza Santo Domingo** – Head east along Calle Bolívar and you will come to this busy square, named for another of Quito's 86 exquisite churches filled with fine religious sculpture. The image of the Virgin in the church was a gift from Charles V of Spain. Connected to the church is the *Museo de San Francisco,* a museum with a fine art collection from the School of Quito. At press time, the visiting schedule was uncertain; call ahead for the hours. The road to the southeast has a carved stone arch that joins the houses over your head. Calles Rocafuerte, Flores, Bolívar, and Guayaquil (phone: 210723).

**Plaza Independencia** – More commonly known as Plaza Grande, this is the real center of the Old City. The square is flanked by the cathedral on the south, the Presidential Palace on the west, and the modern — and unimpressive — city administration building built in 1978 to replace the colonial building that was beyond repair.

On the north side of this well-kept plaza is the archbishop's palace — a good spot for people watching or a point of departure for a walking tour of Quito's older section. A monument dedicated to the 1809 declaration of independence depicts Victory raising her torch of freedom over the Spanish lion, and condors — symbolizing the native people — clutching the broken chains of bondage. Beware of pickpockets and backpack slashers. Calles Chile, Venezuela, Espejo, and García Moreno.

**Catedral** – This church is believed to have first existed as a wood and adobe structure before the official cathedral was built on the site in 1565. It has been restored twice since then because of earthquake damage, and sections of the building still are being repaired as a result of the tremors in 1987. The cathedral is filled with paintings and other artwork by some of Ecuador's finest early artists. One of the side altars contains the remains of Antonio José de Sucre, the Venezuelan statesman who led the liberation army that annihiliated the Spanish royalists in the Battle of Pichincha, the culmination of Ecuador's fight for independence. Open Mondays through Saturdays from 6 to 10 AM; Sundays from 6 AM to noon and 6 to 7 PM, although tourists are requested not to enter during mass. Plaza Independencia.

**El Sagrario** – Next door to the cathedral, this is the main chapel for the followers of the Blessed Sacrament. Statues and ornate columns grace its stone façade and the baroque interior has rich carvings of angels and foliage. The building was damaged very seriously in the 1987 earthquake and slow restoration — funded in part by the United Nations — has been underway since then. Check with the national tourist board to find out if the chapel is open to visitors and its hours. On Calle Moreno to the side of the cathedral.

**Presidential Palace** – Erected in 1621, this building is an odd mix of classical porticos, interior patios, a main entrance with martial guards, and a basement-level row of small stores selling Panama hats, postcards, handicrafts, and other souvenirs. It houses Ecuadoran artist Oswaldo Guayasamín's famous mosaic mural glorifying the Spanish discovery of the Amazon River. The palace guard's 18th-century blue, red, and gold shakoes and uniforms contrast sharply with their modern automatic rifles, which proved useless in repelling an attempted coup in September 1976. Tourists are usually able to look in the main door of the building, but entry to the area with Guayasamín's mural is prohibited. Plaza Independencia.

**Museo de Arte Colonial (Colonial Art Museum)** – Formerly the mansion of one of early Quito's wealthy families, this 2-story building has an excellent collection of 16th- through 18th-century School of Quito paintings and sculptures, including Miguel de Santiago's painting of the Virgin (surrounded by a border of flowers added by the artist's daughter), Caspicara's *Christ* (considered a perfect study in anatomy), and Legarda's *St. Rose of Lima*, which was banned by the Inquisition because its flowing skirt was considered "too vivacious." The artwork pioneered a number of techniques, including vegetable dyes and the use of lamb bladders to polish wood sculptures to a porcelain finish. A guided tour in English, Spanish, or French is included in the admission charge (although tips are appreciated). Open Tuesdays through Fridays from 9 AM to 12:30 PM and 3 to 6:30 PM; Saturdays from 10 AM to 4 PM. 915 Cuenca (phone: 212297).

**Iglesia y Monasterio de San Agustín (St. Augustine Church and Monastery)** – The only way to enjoy the center of Quito is by walking (parking is impossible in the narrow streets). A 1-block stroll along Calle Chile from Plaza Independencia leads to the San Agustín church and its monastery, site of the signing of Ecuador's Independence Act in 1809. Inside is a silent, flower-filled patio and colonnaded cloisters, with robed monks pacing between oils by master painter Miguel de Santiago, who spent most of his life in the monastery illustrating the life of St. Augustine. The third floor of one wing is now occupied by the restoration workshops of the Cultural Heritage Institute. Open Mondays through Thursdays from 8:30 to 11 AM; Fridays and Saturdays fro

2:30 to 5:30 PM; and Sundays from 4:30 to 8 PM. No admission charge. Calles Chile and Guayaquil (phone: 511001).

**La Compañía de Jesús** – Richly ornate both outside and in, this 18th-century Jesuit church is a masterpiece of baroque and *quiteño*-colonial art. In fact, it is one of the most splendid churches in Latin America, with nearly all its altars covered in gold leaf and its ceilings decorated with artwork so fine that it has been dubbed Quito's Sistine Chapel. The wood pulpit and confessionals are intricately carved, and the walls are covered with fine murals from the School of Quito — the art form that evolved from the colonial mix of Spanish and Indian styles — one of which depicts the Final Judgment. Open Mondays through Saturdays from 6 to 11 AM and 4 to 7 PM; Sundays from 6 AM to 12:45 PM and 4 to 9 PM Calle García Moreno, 1 block from Plaza Independencia.

**La Merced** – This church was one of the last constructed during Quito's colonial period — an era in which religious orders built so many huge monasteries and churches in the city that Quito became known as "the cloister of America." This Spanish-baroque structure, with Moorish touches, boasts the tallest church tower in the city and the largest bell. The walls are embellished with pink and white reliefs lending a fanciful, wedding cake appearance, and it contains more than three dozen gilt-framed paintings from the School of Quito. The adjoining monastery, considered one of the city's most beautiful, has the city's oldest clock and a large garden patio with a fountain of Neptune in its center — an unusual image for a Christian monastery. Open Mondays through Saturdays from 6 AM to noon and 3:30 to 8 PM; Sundays from 6:30 AM to 1 PM and 5:30 to 8:30 PM. Visits to the monastery must be arranged in advance. Calle Cuenca at Chile.

**Casa de Benalcázar** – With its traditional red tile roof, this adobe home was once the residence of city founder Sebastián de Benalcázar, whose statue remains in the small plaza adjacent to the house. Restored by Spanish architects, the colonial building now serves as headquarters for Ecuador's Institute of Hispanic Culture. Damage sustained by the 1987 earthquake is still being repaired, and the institute has dedicated its energies to trying to preserve and restore other colonial period buildings nearby. A small art museum connected to the institute is open occasionally. Corner of Benalcázar and Olmedo.

## THE NEW CITY

**Museo del Banco Central (Central Bank Museum)** – Actually, the Central Bank has two museums. Their most valuable treasure is a painting with a frame of precious stones and gold valued at more than $10 million. It rarely leaves the deepest vault. But you will find a well-laid-out display of the finest items of pre-Columbian art on the fifth floor. Remember, as you gaze, that these items have been selected from the tens of thousands of pieces stored in the basement. Clay figures from coastal cultures more than 2,000 years old show strong character and witty observation of personality. Some of the delicately ornamented double-bellied jugs have spouts with air holes worked to whistle as water is poured out. Display cards give clear histories and explanations in Spanish, but artistically, the items speak admirably for themselves. A sixth-floor collection contains religious and colonial painting, with examples from all the great painters of the School of Quito. Whenever archaeologists discover and excavate an important site, the museum puts on a new display and presents public lectures. Open Tuesdays through Fridays from 9 AM to 4:45 PM; Saturdays, Sundays, and holidays from 10:30 AM to 3 PM. Admission charge. There is a guided tour in English at 11:30 AM on Tuesdays. Av. 10 de Agosto, near the corner of Alameda Park (phone: 510302 or 510382).

**Museo Jijón y Caamaño (Jijón and Caamaño Museum)** – The Catholic University houses this collection, donated in 1963 by the family of Jacinto Jijón y Caamaño, a scholarly aristocrat whose life's work digging, analyzing, and classifying pre-Columbian remains provided the basic knowledge of Ecuador's different tribes and civilizations. His own books are now valuable rarities, though new editions of some are planned. Other departments of the university provide language courses for foreigners; Quechua is taught using audiovisual labs. Open Mondays through Fridays from 9 AM to noon and 2 to 6 PM; Saturdays from 9 AM to 4 PM. Admission charge. Guided tours in English are available for a small charge. Catholic University, Av. 12 de Octubre and Calle Rocca (phone: 521834).

**Avenida Amazonas (Amazonas Avenue)** – Green and cool under the tropical midday sun, Parque El Ejido (El Ejido Park) has dozens of families basking under the trees. Otavalo Indian women sell *fritada, papas, y mote* — small portions of meat, potatoes, and maize. For a snack or meal that won't upset your gastrointestinal system, head for the sidewalk cafés of Avenida Amazonas off the north side of the park, past the city's largest hotel, the *Colón Internacional*. *La Fuente* and *Manolo's Churrería* are popular spots for meeting friends, sipping cold beer, or people watching. The tiny snack shop *El Cocodrilo* (at the corner of Veintimilla) is one of the city's best stops for fresh-from-the-oven empanadas filled with herbs, cheese, or meat. Great cappuccino can be found up the street at *Stop* (2415 Amazonas). The half-mile of Amazonas, now a pedestrian mall, and the surrounding streets are filled with eating places, bookstores, international banks, travel agencies, airlines, offices, fashion boutiques, antique shops and craft stores, as well as art galleries. During the *Quito Festival* in December, Avenida Amazonas becomes one big open-air ballroom.

**Guayasamín Museum and Workshop** – Here you'll find an exhibit of posters, signed prints, and other works — some of which are for sale — by the exceptional Ecuadoran painter Oswaldo Guayasamín, as well as his private collection of archaeological artifacts and colonial religious art. Look for his four paintings, hung side by side, that include portraits of Ronald Reagan and Mikhail Gorbachev. Donated by the painter to the government, the building is one of the loveliest in the city. Its views of Quito's red tile rooftops alone makes it worth a visit. Connected to the museum is a small retail outlet for jewelry, handicrafts, and furniture produced by the artist's daughter and students at the Guayasamín workshop. Open Mondays through Fridays from 9 AM to 12:30 PM and 3 to 6 PM; Saturdays from 9 AM to 12:30 PM. 543 Calle José Bosmediano at José Carbo in Bellavista (phone: 242779 or 244373).

**Universidad Central (Central University)** – The left-wing politics of the student body here do not engender anti-US sentiment as violently as in many South American colleges. Everyone is welcome at *Cine Universitario* (University Cinema; phone: 236988), where films are changed frequently (sometimes, even daily). Close by, the *Mercado Santa Clara* (Santa Clara Market) sells the best fruit, vegetables, and herbs for *quiteños* in the northern sector of the city. Six blocks from Av. Amazonas on the lower slopes of Mt. Pichincha.

## ENVIRONS

**Hotel Quito** – On the other side of the city from Pichincha is the mountain pass used by Francisco de Orellana in 1542 for his jungle expedition that led to the discovery of the headwaters of the Amazon on his way to the Atlantic and then to Spain. (In 1977, an expedition led by another Spaniard reenacted the trek.) Orellana's road passes right by some of the choicest home sites, looking eastward to the next range and westward across the city from the ridge. The luxurious *Quito* hotel is in the best spot. Opposite it are an English pub, bar, and a Chinese restaurant. Several other small clubs and restaurants are within easy walking distance. Just over the ridge and down the hill is Guápulo, a village cluster of houses and a late-17th-century Guápulo church, built by Indian slaves. Its pulpit, by the sculptor Menacho, is famed as the finest piece of carving in Quito. Guápulo is where the Quito School of Art was founded 3 centuries ago. 2500 Av. González Suárez (phone: 230300).

**Centro Comercial Iñaquito (Iñaquito Shopping Center)** – Twenty blocks from downtown, Quito's answer to the US urban shopping complex is, by local standards, large and luxurious, but lilliputian to anyone who knows the real thing. Still, the range of goods on its two floors is good: European and American tobaccos, pipes, and rolling papers at the *Admiral Nelson Smokers' Shop,* a branch of the *Favorita Supermarket; McDonald's* and other fast-food outlets; and shops selling books, clothes, toys, car accessories, records, health food, plants, and pets. The nearby *Cine Iñaquito* often has good US movies. Three other shopping centers, the *Caracol, El Bosque,* and the *Naciones Unidas,* have joined *Iñaquito* at the same crossroads. *Dimpy* cafeterias in all the centers provide excellent coffee and good sandwiches. Av. Naciones Unidas and Av. Amazonas.

**Mitad del Mundo (Middle of the World Marker)** – The equator passes 15 miles (24 km) north of Quito, and a few commuters cross from one hemisphere to the other twice a day. There is a small monument (the closest one to the actual equator) commemorating this line on the road to Otavalo, and another on the road going out to the large ethnographic museum complex in the village of San Antonio de Pichincha. (You can have your picture taken here with one foot in each hemisphere.) From the top of the monument is a terrace with a lovely view of the countryside. Inside the building are 9 floors of handicrafts (and items for sale) and exhibits of Ecuador's different Indian populations. A planetarium near the monument has shows daily except Mondays. The area is exciting to explore, with volcanic craters and the ruins of Rumicucho, the site of a pre-Inca fortification. The museum is open daily except Mondays from 9 AM to 3 PM. Admission charge. Rent a cab from the *Hotel Quito Taxi Cooperative* (phone: 236492 or 237555) for about $8 an hour or take a tour car with a bilingual guide from any of the hotels or the bus marked Panecillo–Mitad del Mundo.

**Mt. Cotopaxi** – In the early Indian legends, the mountains are gods and goddesses, quarrelsome but revered. Mt. Cotopaxi's power to inspire reverence is unabated, as it majestically rears through the clouds. This active volcano about 40 miles (64 km) from Quito and surrounding stark *paramo* (moor) are now respected enough to have gained the status of a protected national park. Hire a taxi and head south on the Pan-American Highway (or hire a local tour operator); less than 1 mile (1.6 km) beyond the former NASA-station turnoff is a signposted road to the 19,347-foot peak of Cotopaxi that leads right up to the mountain refuge. At the gates to the national park administration office are the stables for a breeding herd of llamas. Some 150 usually can be spotted at the 11,000- to 12,000-foot level. If they have very new young, the mothers scurry them away and the old males spit defensively. Otherwise, they are friendly and elegant animals. Wild horses can sometimes be seen galloping across the horizon in the distance. Car engines often give up well below the snow level, and human lungs have to work hard to take you any higher, but the cold, desolate splendor is worth it. A mountaineers' refuge just above the snow line serves as a base camp for serious climbers. Combine the drive with a trip to Saquisilí village, a half hour away, where one of the prettiest Ecuadoran Indian markets takes place on Thursdays.

■**EXTRA SPECIAL:** What some call the continent's best Indian market is in Otavalo, 2 to 2½ hours north of the center of town by a speedy microbus that you can pick up at the corner of Avenida Patria and Avenida 10 de Agosto or on the regular interprovincial bus (at least a 2-hour ride) that leaves from the Terminal Terrestre (at Maldonado and Cumandá, near Plaza Santo Domingo in the Villa Flora district). Otavalo is a town at the center of a group of Indian villages with strong textile traditions whose work is now sold all over the continent and as far away as Europe. In addition to the well-known Saturday morning market, where you can purchase weavings and shining multiple strands of gold beads like those worn by Indian women, there are squares selling food and animals. On one corner you can see dealers haggling over sacks of squeaking *cuyes,* the ubiquitous Andean guinea pigs. Sometimes you can find bargains in fine, antique coral (see *Ecuador*, DIRECTIONS). You may find the prices on handicrafts hiked up a bit for tourists, but any purchase still will be a bargain. And remember, the *otavaleños* are shrewd businesspeople, but they love to bargain. A general rule is to start by offering 20% below their asking price, then haggle for something in between. Look for sweaters and wall hangings in brilliant blues and purples, delicate scarves, *quenas* (Andean flutes), and *Christmas* ornaments. Since the market starts before dawn on Saturdays, it is easiest to spend Friday night in the Otavalo area at a local hotel or hacienda (see *Ecuador*, DIRECTIONS). Advance reservations are essential.

# SOURCES AND RESOURCES

**TOURIST INFORMATION:** For general travel assistance, the National Tourist Board, CETUR (on the corner of Avdas. Reina Victoria and Roca; phone: 239044, 527002, and 527053; fax: 568198), is a place to start, although the office provides very little in the way of printed material. Open Mondays through Fridays from 8 AM to 4:30 PM. Detailed, large-scale maps can be purchased at the *Instituto Geográfico-Militar* (Calle Paz y Miño; phone: 522066). Open Mondays through Fridays, 8 AM to 3 PM.

In addition to its office in Lima, the *South American Explorers Club* has one in Quito (1254 Toledo, La Floresta; phone: 566076). This very helpful organization has maps, books, and other reference materials, and the clubhouse is a great place to meet fellow explorers. Membership is $30 a year; you can join the club in the US (phone: 607-277-0488), Lima, or Quito. Open Mondays through Fridays from 9:30 AM to 5 PM.

*Libri Mundi*, at 851 Calle Juan León Mera (phone: 234791) and at the *Colón Internacional* hotel (phone: 550455), carries virtually every publication in print on Ecuador, as well as a selection of books and magazines in English. Outdoor people are strongly recommended to obtain *The Fool's Climbing Guide to Ecuador and Peru*, by Michael Koerner (17212 Buckingham, Birmingham, MI 48009; $2); *Backpacking in Venezuela, Colombia and Ecuador*, by Hilary and George Bradt (54 Dudley St., Cambridge, MA 02140); and *Climbing and Hiking in Ecuador*, by Rob Rachowiecki (*South American Explorers Club*, PO Box 18327, Denver, CO 80218; $11.95).

The US Embassy is located at 120 Av. Patria (phone: 562890).

**Local Coverage** – Spanish dailies include *El Comercio* (morning daily), *Hoy* (morning daily), and *Ultimas Noticias*. *El Comercio*, with a business/commercial orientation, lists all cultural and social events. *Hoy* is generally seen as more liberal in orientation. The monthly Spanish-English magazine, *Qué Hacer*, on sale at *Libri Mundi* bookstores and some kiosks, has information on tourist sites in the capital and the provinces and lists current exhibitions at galleries, various nightlife activities, concerts, and theatrical productions. The *Miami Herald* (a day late) and *The New York Times* (a few days late) are available at the *Colón Internacional* and *Quito* hotels.

**TELEPHONE:** The city code for Quito is 2. When calling from within Ecuador, dial 02 before the local number. The country code for Ecuador is 593.

**CLIMATE AND CLOTHES:** Ecuador's proximity to the equator wipes out expected seasonal changes. In the dry season, roughly May through October, and sometimes in November and December, people with sensitive skin need a sunscreen to protect them from the ultraviolet rays that are so much stronger at this elevation. Even during the rainy seasons during the rest of the year, the sun is often very strong in the morning. Nights can be cold enough to require a thick sweater or poncho in the highlands, but daytime temperatures rarely stray from the upper 60s F (20C). Guayaquil and the rest of the coastal area are generally hot. A lightweight waterproof jacket or collapsible umbrella is essential. Give yourself enough time to adapt to the altitude. Get plenty of rest, especially when you feel a headache beginning. (See *Medical and Legal Aid and Consular Services,* GETTING READY TO GO.) Note: In recent years the pollution from cars and buses has worsened dramatically. Visitors with respiratory problems are strongly advised to avoid walking on the main streets of the city; opt instead for the less-congested side streets.

**GETTING AROUND: Bus** – Buses are inexpensive and cover all of the city, but they are crowded, uncomfortable, and few run after 9:30 PM. A useful route, though, is the Colón-Camal, which runs along Avenida Colón and Avenida 10 de Agosto to the center of the Old City and to the bus terminal. The *Amazonas* line — with modern, double-decker blue and white buses — runs from the center of Quito at El Ejido Park all along Avenida Amazonas to the airport and back. It is a good, safe, and comfortable way to travel.

**Taxi** – There are meters in all authorized cabs, and the fares around town and to the airport are inexpensive. If the driver claims his meter isn't working, be sure to agree on a fare before entering the taxi. Cab ranks are scattered at the obvious places: supermarkets, hotels, Plaza Independencia, Universidad Central. They also cruise for passengers. To phone for a cab, just select the nearest of the 50 or so cab cooperatives listed in the Quito telephone directory. For long-distance trips, the *Hotel Quito Taxi Cooperative* (phone: 236492 and 237555) will provide cabs for about $8 an hour.

**Car Rental** – *Budget, Dollar, Hertz, National,* and *Ecuacar* have representatives at the airport. Locations and other companies include: *Budget* (1140 Av. Colón; phone: 237026); *Hertz* (517 Santa María at Amazonas; phone: 545117); *National* (1613 Av. Colón at the corner of 9 de Octubre; phone: 549848); and *Avis* (1700 Av. Amazonas and Orellana; phone: 550238 or 550243). *Ecuacar* (1280 Av. Colón and Av. Amazonas; phone: 523673) offers cars, jeeps, and trucks. Most agencies have a 3-day minimum for rentals.

**SPECIAL EVENTS:** The *Quito Festival,* the first week in December, is the biggest fiesta of the year, with parades, street dances, and bullfights (it marks the beginning of the bullfight season). Culminating in the *Amazonazo,* a crowded procession of dancers and bands down Avenida Amazonas, this citywide party cultivates friendships, even with foreigners. December 28 through January 2 is the week for costumes and masks, with an effigy representing the previous year (usually bearing a remarkable resemblance to some unpopular politician) burned at hundreds of sidewalk parties on *New Year's Eve* — called, in Ecuador, *Año Viejo,* literally "old year." In San Rafael, near Quito, January 6 is a day of costumed processions celebrating the *Day of Three Kings* (Epiphany). Ambato's *Fruits and Flowers* festival is a floating holiday in February. Quito and the surrounding Andean countryside hold giant parades during *Semana Santa* (Holy Week), the week ending with *Easter.* This is a better time to visit than during the pre-*Lenten Carnaval.* There are a number of civic holidays in May, including *Labor Day* (May 1) and the *Day of the Battle of Pichincha* (May 24), a day that marks the turning point in the Independence Wars. Simón Bolívar's birthday is honored on July 24 and *National Independence Day* is August 10. The first week of September, Otavalo holds *El Yamor,* an annual harvest festival dating from pre-Columbian times. The festival culminates in the arrival of a *coraza* — a triumphant horseman whose face is covered with golden tinsel and who wears plumed, sequined, and fringed regalia. In November, in a tradition dating back to Inca times, *quiteños* join together to clean the streets in a festival known as *Minga*, in preparation for the week of festivities in December described above.

**MUSEUMS:** Many of the city's art and archaeology displays are described in *Special Places*. Quito has many other interesting museums.

**Casa de Sucre (Sucre's House)** – This renovated colonial building is where the soldier-statesman who helped free Ecuador from Spanish rule once lived. The bedrooms on the lower floor have been converted into a museum; the upstairs is used as an office and storage space. Open Tuesdays through Fridays from 9 AM to 4 PM, Saturdays and Sundays from 10 AM to 1 PM. No admission charge (but passports must be left at the door). At Calle Sucre and Venezuela (phone: 512860).

**Museo Camilo Egas (Camilo Egas Museum)** – Located in the colonial area, this museum houses a permanent exhibition exposition of the work of one of Ecuador's most famous contemporary painters. Open Mondays through Fridays from 10 AM to 1 PM and 3 to 5:30 PM, Saturdays from 10 AM to 4 PM. Admission charge. 1302 Calle Venezuela at Esmeraldas (phone: 514511).

**Casa de la Cultura Ecuatoriana** – This large, circular building houses some very interesting museums, including the *Museo de Ciencia Natural* (Natural Science Museum), *Museo de Instrumentos Musicales* (Museum of Musical Instruments), *Museo de Arte Contemporáneo* (Museum of Contemporary Art), and *La Biblioteca Nacional* (National Library). Occasionally it hosts film festivals; check the local newspapers. Open Tuesdays through Fridays from 9 AM to 6 PM, Saturdays from 9 AM to 1 PM. 9 de Octubre at Patria (phone: 565808 and 527440).

**El Convento y Museo de San Diego (San Diego Convent and Museum)** – A restored Franciscan convent that remains a cloister. Open daily except Mondays from 9 AM to noon and 2 to 5 PM. 117 Calicuchima at Farfán (phone: 212616).

**SHOPPING:** In addition to the market in Otavalo (see *Extra Special*), Quito has very fine crafts that can be purchased at a number of handicraft shops along Avenida Amazonas as well as at the following places:

*Angelo* – Finely crafted boots, wallets, bags, jackets, and luggage from Cotacatchi, Ecuador's leather center, can be found here at exceptional prices. Credit cards accepted. 662 Av. Amazonas (phone: 523614).

*La Bodega* – An intriguing selection of antiques, textiles, and Indian craft products. The owners also commission their own production of high-quality handknits in both cotton and wool, which are available in Quito for a fraction of what they would cost in fashionable US boutiques. A few blocks from the *Colón Internacional* hotel, at 614 Calle Juan León Mera (phone: 232844).

*Centro Artesanal* – Diverse, good selection of primitive paintings on sheep's hide canvases, hand-knit sweaters, imaginative ceramic ware, *Christmas* ornaments, and some excellent Ecuadoran coffee to buy. 804 Calle Juan León Mera (phone: 548235).

*Coosas* – This boutique with Dutch designer sportswear is the place for colorful and popular Galápagos T-shirts. 838 Calle Juan León Mera (no phone).

*El Español* – Stop by this well-stocked deli for delicious picnic items — aged meats and rounds of exotic cheeses, patés, several varieties of olives, home-baked breads and cakes, wines, and delectable sandwiches made to order. Try the garlicky marinated mushrooms. 863 Juan León Mora at Wilson (no phone).

*Folklore* – Also known as *Olga Fisch's Folklore Gallery*, it sells a variety of high-quality artisan products as well as contemporary-style clothing incorporating traditional designs and colors. The much-loved Hungarian Olga who opened the shop died in 1990, but her niece Gogó — a designer — continues to run the store. At press time, the upstairs was being turned into a museum honoring Olga herself. English- and

French-speaking staff. 260 Colón (phone: 541315) and in the lobby of the *Oro Verde Hotel*.

***Galería Latina*** – An art gallery that specializes in Bolivian and Peruvian textiles plus fine silver and gold jewelry by contemporary designers. There are also rooms and rooms of quality handicrafts. 823 Calle Juan León Mera (phone: 504206).

***La Guaragua*** – Antique musical instruments, jewelry, ceramics, colonial artifacts, and furniture. 614 Jorge Washington (phone: 520347).

***La Llama*** – Another shop with a large selection of handicrafts items at good prices. 149 Av. Amazonas (phone: 546273).

***Libri Mundi*** – Wide selection of maps and books in Spanish, English, French, and German — everything from fiction through science and history, plus its own photo book on the Galápagos. The staff is friendly and multilingual. Across the street from *Centro Artesanal*, at 851 Calle Juan León Mera (phone: 234791), with a branch in the *Colón Internacional Hotel*, Av. Amazonas and Av. Patria (phone: 550455).

***OCEPA*** – The nonprofit government center for Ecuadoran hand-crafted goods from around the country. 1236 Carrión (phone: 565961), with a branch at Av. Amazonas and Av. Jorge Washington (phone: 236334), and another near the *Quito Hotel* (phone: 235602).

***Productos Andinos*** – An Indian cooperative that offers handcrafted wares. Woolen articles are its specialty. 800 Robles (phone: 546337).

**SPORTS:** Soccer is Quito's favorite sport, with seasonal bullfighting running second. Ecuador's marlin fishing is legendary among anglers.

**Bullfighting** – The December fiestas attract big-name *toreros* from Spain and other Latin countries. Tickets should be bought well before the big *corridas* (bullfights). There are a few bullfights earlier in the year, and in some other towns. At village fiestas, where bulls are "fought" but not killed, amateur aficionados are sometimes allowed to try their skills. *Plaza de Toros,* Av. Amazonas and Av. Cofanes (no phone).

**Fishing** – Good-size trout can be caught in nearby mountain lakes and some rivers, especially south of Cuenca. Boats can be hired in Salinas for deep-sea excursions in pursuit of big marlin and swordfish in the Pacific. *Pesca Tours* offers week-long packages that include hotel, bait, and tackle on its seven boats. Contact Knud Holst, Dept. FS, at PO Box 487, Guayaquil, Ecuador (phone: 4-443365).

**Golf** – The *Quito Tennis and Golf Club* has an 18-hole course at El Condado, (Av. Ocidental, north of Quito; phone: 538120). Ask your hotel concierge for information.

**Horseback Riding** – Horses can be hired from the *Cusín* hotel, near the San Pablo Lake, 1½ hours north of Quito, and from the excellent *Hostería Chorlavi*, on the Pan-American Highway, near Ibarra (phone: 950777; in Quito, phone: 522703).

**Mountain Climbing and Trekking** – Climbing in Ecuador is excellent, with several local clubs and equipment available for hire: the *Cumbres Andinas Club* (841 Olmedo; phone: 517748); the *Agrupación de Montaña Pablo Leiva* (1240 Av. 6 de Diciembre; phone: 230758); and the *Universidad Católica Climbing Club* (corner of 12 de Octubre and Roca; phone: 529270). One of the continent's best-known mountaineers, Marco Cruz, leads climbs and treks; a complete description of those programs is available from *Metropolitan Touring*, 239 Amazonas, in Quito (phone: 560550; fax: 2-564655).

Trekkers also can tackle the highest active volcano in the world, crossing the ice fields of Cotopaxi at altitudes between 15,000 and 16,000 feet, just one of several programs offered by *Nuevo Mundo Expeditions*. Full details can be obtained from the tour operator at their Quito office (2468 Av. Amazonas; phone: 552617), or by contacting their US representative, *International Expeditions* (phone: 205-870-5550 in Alabama; 800-633-4734 in other states). The *International Hiking and Climbing Group* (209

Baron Von Humboldt; phone: 238397) has weekend mountaineering outings. The *South American Explorers Club* (1254 Toledo, La Floresta; phone: 566076) can help with equipment or refer you to an expedition.

**Soccer** – Matches take place Sundays at the *Estadio Olímpico Atahualpa* (Atahualpa Olympic Stadium), which is also used for athletic meets. Av. 6 de Diciembre and Av. Naciones Unidas (no phone).

**Swimming** – In addition to the *Quito Tennis and Golf Club,* the *Quito* hotel (2500 Av. González Suárez; phone: 230300), and *Colón Internacional* hotel (Av. Patria and Av. Amazonas; phone: 560666), have swimming pools. The *Quito Municipal Tennis Club* (see below) recently added a swimming pool that is open to non-members.

**Tennis** – The *Quito Tennis and Golf Club* (on Av. Occidental, north of Quito; phone: 538120) has 9 clay courts. Temporary membership is expensive, but worth it for use of the swimming pool and the social life, although the facility is far from the center of town. The *Quito Municipal Tennis Club* (1058 Av. Atahualpa; phone: 242918) has 6 courts and an expensive membership fee. The *Club de Tenis Buena Vista* (Charles Darwin and de las Alcabalas; phone: 430682/5) sometimes welcomes outside players. For a change of pace, the *Quito Racquetball Club* (Pasaje Oriente and Av. 10 de Agosto; phone: 433706) offers 6 courts.

**THEATER:** Quito's most important theaters are *Teatro Nacional Sucre* (Calle Flores and Calle Manabí; phone: 216668), where the *Ecuadoran Folklore Ballet* performs on Wednesdays, and *Teatro Prometeo (Casa de la Cultura,* 794 Av. 6 de Diciembre; phone: 565808). Stages at Quito's two universities — Universidad Central (Av. America; phone: 521590) and Universidad Católica (Av. 12 de Octubre and Calle Robles; phone: 529240) — often provide biting, witty political theater. The *Pichincha Playhouse* (758 Av. Colón; phone: theater 543689; office 211321), a good amateur English-language group, puts on several productions a year. Occasionally the British Council and Fulbright Commission sponsor English-language plays. Check at the Fulbright Commission (532 Av. 12 de Octubre at Andrade Coello; phone: 230119). Movie buffs will find a couple of dozen cinemas, some showing English- and other foreign-language films. Try the *Cine Colón* (Av. Colón and 10 de Agosto) or the Universidad Central's *Cine Universitario* (Av. América at the Plaza Indoamérica) for the best selection.

**MUSIC:** Visiting symphonies, ballet troupes, and opera companies play at *Teatro Nacional Sucre, Teatro Bolívar* (847 Espejo; phone: 210960 or 215778), the *Casa de la Cultura* (794 Av. 6 de Diciembre; phone: 543748) and the *Conservatorio Nacional de la Música* (1159 Madrid; phone: 564790). *Adventure Associates* (in the US, 800-527-2500) makes arrangements for the *Ballet Folklórico* (at the *Teatro Nacional Sucre),* as does *Metropolitan Touring* in Quito (phone: 560550). An $11 package covers the tickets and transportation costs. Traditional Andean music can be found in the *peñas,* an important part of a rather limited city nightlife. You will hear songs played on instruments like the *charango* — a five-string member of the guitar family that has an armadillo shell for its body — and the *rondador,* the South American pan pipes. *Peñas* tend to sprout up, then wither quickly. The most popular and best is probably *Pachacama* (530 Jorge Washington; phone: 234855), but there are others such as *Nuestra América* (149 Iñaquito, Amazonas) and *El Chúcaro* (1335 Calle Reina Victoria). Also popular is the *Taberna Quiteña,* which has two locations (in the colonial part of the city, at Calle Manabí and Luis Vargas and at 1259 Av. Amazonas). The folklore singing usually begins about 9 PM. Most *peñas* serve as normal bars do, but some restaurants have good Spanish-American and Indian music to accompany the fine Pacific seafood. Andean music fills the streets during the December fiestas. Radio Musical, a medium-wave pop station, occasionally gives news of rock concerts.

**NIGHTCLUBS AND NIGHTLIFE:** Discos spring up in Quito only to vanish swiftly. The best are still the oldest. *La Licorne* (at the *Colón Internacional* hotel; phone: 520666) has sufficient light and flash to come sporadically into fashion with high-society youth. Salsa and Latin dancing is found at *Son y Candela* (Carrión at Reina Victoria). *El Pub Inglés* (135 González Suárez, just across the street from the *Quito* hotel; phone: 523589) has for years been a magnet for English-speaking residents along with tourists from around the world. In the Mariscal district, popular spots with locals and foreigners are the *Taberna Bavaria* (1238 Calle Juan León Mera and García; phone: 233206), and the North American–run *Bar Reina Victoria* (530 Reina Victoria; phone: 233369). For a more intimate setting, try *Amadeus Pub* (1398 Coruña; phone: 230831), a piano bar. And for those with an urge for games of chance, gambling is popular and legal for those over 21, with casinos at the *Colón, Quito, Chalet Suisse, Alameda Real,* and *Tambo Real* hotels.

A sober note: Alcohol has swift and powerful effects at this altitude. That's something to remember when you're offered strong local brandies — *pisco* and anise-flavored *paico*. Oxygen tanks are sometimes needed for first-timers' hangovers. The *Colón* hotel serves the traditional restorative, *caldo de patas* (pig trotter broth), at dawn for suffering revelers.

## BEST IN TOWN

**CHECKING IN:** Not only has an aggressive tourism policy made Ecuador a major travel destination, but since the early 1970s, Quito has become a center for international meetings and conferences, putting pressure on available hotel room inventory. In addition, in the Mariscal or Amazonas area, travelers on a budget probably can find very inexpensive, but clean and safe, accommodations by checking small lodgings that are called *residenciales*.

Quito offers good value for the money and some pleasant surprises in the moderate price range. Expect to pay $90 to $150 (plus 20% tax and service) for a double room at those places we call very expensive; $70 to $90 at expensive hotels; $35 to $70 at those noted as moderate; under $35 and as low as $15 for a clean, simple room in the inexpensive category. All telephone numbers are in the 2 city code unless otherwise indicated.

*Colón Internacional* – This international class 450-room hotel has every amenity the most demanding traveler could want, including a modern conference center and an arcade of stores, lounges, restaurants, and galleries, as well as a pool and well-equipped gym. With the food of the *El Dorado* restaurant (see *Eating Out)*, the Sunday buffet lunch (around $7), the casino, a good 24-hour coffee shop, and the disco beneath it, this remains one of Quito's major social centers. Exceptional service now that the entire hotel system has been computerized. Major credit cards accepted. In the heart of the shopping and cultural districts, at Avdas. Amazonas and Patria (phone: 560666; in the US, 800-44-UTELL; fax: 563903). Very expensive.

*Oro Verde* – A sister to the deluxe hotel of the same name in Guayaquil, this elegant property in a lovely residential area has 241 rooms, an indoor and outdoor pool, sauna, complete fitness center, racketball and squash courts, 3 restaurants, a casino, and a bar with a live band. Also noteworthy is a center for business travelers that is equipped with computers, fax machines, and secretarial services. 1820 Av. 12 de Octubre at Cordero (phone: 566497; in the US, 800-327-9854; fax: 569189). Very expensive.

**Alameda Real** – Originally built as a condominium project, thus 83 of this hotel's 150 rooms are ample suites. Especially popular with business travelers, it boasts 7 channels of US network and cable television. Other amenities include a casino, coffee shop, restaurant, and the *Big Ben* bar. Along with the *Colón,* this place is within a few blocks of the restaurants and shops of the Mariscal district. 653 Roca and Amazonas (phone: 562345; in the US, through *Latin America Reservations Center (LARC);* phone: 800-327-3573; fax: 565759). Expensive.

**Quito** – High on the ridge over the village of Guápulo, this building is sometimes bathed in low clouds, sometimes in scorching sun. A casino, *La Llama* nightclub, a steakhouse, a large conference center, ballrooms, and the elegant rooftop *El Techo del Mundo* (The Roof of the World) restaurant (see *Eating Out)* put this member of the Best Western chain in the luxury class. Although all 226 rooms were recently enlarged by eliminating their balconies, each still has a spectacular view. Regular guests swear that what brings them back is the palm-shaded pool with vistas across the valley. Unfortunately, however, the neighborhood is not as desirable as it once was. 2500 Av. González Suárez (phone: 230300; in the US, 800-327-0200; fax: 567284). Expensive.

**Chalet Suisse** – An elegant, Swiss-managed, 50-room hotel offering good atmosphere and excellent service, especially in its first class restaurant (see *Eating Out*). Features casino and entertainment in the revolving jazz bar. The hotel now has a hot tub and sauna. 312 Calle Calama at Reina Victoria (phone: 562700). Expensive to moderate.

**Amaranta** – A 22-room apartment hotel with a piano bar, an international restaurant, and disco. 194 Leonidas Plaza and Jorge Washington (phone: 560585 or 527191). Moderate.

**Hostal Los Alpes** – This cozy, 22-room hotel is a real sleeper. Italian-owned and serving an international clientele, it also has an excellent restaurant. Very popular, so reserve in advance. 233 Tamayo and Jorge Washington (phone: 541126). Moderate.

**República** – A modern, 40-room property in the residential section near Avenidas Amazonas and República, a new and fast developing business and shopping area. Comfortable, pleasant, and efficient, it is one of the best choices in this range. Avdas. República and Azuay (phone: 457337). Moderate.

**Savoy Inn** – Not far from the airport, this 60-room property has its own travel bureau. Three conference rooms make it a popular choice for business meetings, and the sunny 100-seat restaurant is good enough to attract people from the other side of town. It has a small billiard and card room and a disco nearby. 304 Calle Yasuní at El Inca (phone: 246263). Moderate.

**Tambo Real** – The 90 rooms at this hotel, across from the US Embassy, are well-furnished and comfortable, making this the best mid-price choice. There is a restaurant (with a fine selection of national and international dishes), cafeteria, casino, and shopping. Av. 12 de Octubre at 670 Queseras del Medio (phone: 563-8222). Moderate.

**Casino Real Audiencia** – One of the few recommended hotels (37 rooms) in the heart of the Old City. Located on the Plaza Santo Domingo, it features a bar, restaurant, and coffee shop. 220 Bolívar and Guayaquil (phone: 512711 or 510590). Inexpensive.

**Embassy** – Especially pleasant for families. Some of the 60 suites are self-contained units with kitchenettes, fireplaces, and motel-style parking. It has an adequate restaurant and a good location. 441 Calle Wilson and 6 de Diciembre (phone: 525133 or 525555). Inexpensive.

**Inca Imperial** – The lobby of this 45-room hotel is exotic, with Inca architectural lines, pre-Columbian artifacts, and tooled leather furniture. Its restaurant features the same decor and an international menu. A good bet for budget travelers and those with a fondness for kitsch. 219 Bogotá (phone: 525019). Inexpensive.

**Santa María** – Located in a residential district about 10 minutes from the airport, this is an excellent inexpensive choice. All rooms have private baths, telephones, and TV sets, and there's a bar, restaurant, coffee shop, and even a sauna. 933 Inglaterra at Mariana de Jesús (phone: 529929). Inexpensive.

**EATING OUT:** National policies on fishing rights and frequent seasonal bans on lobster exports mean that seafood finds its way onto local tables at reasonable prices, and Quito eating places make extensive use of shellfish and crustaceans, although many restaurateurs still complain that they never get enough lobster to meet the demand. Traditional highland dishes provide some delicious lower-priced surprises, especially *llapingachos con hornado* — fried potato and cheese cakes with crackling roast pork. The *Colón Café* serves an excellent *sancocho quiteño*, a delicious chicken soup chock full of noodles, corn, and other vegetables. The sidewalk cafés along Avenida Amazonas and casual spots like *La Rana Verde*, just across from *La Bodega*, serve a variety of inexpensive snacks and light meals. Try them accompanied by *chicha*, a lightly alcoholic corn-based beverage.

Expect to pay $25 and up for a dinner for two in those restaurants noted as expensive; between $15 and $25 in the moderate category; under $15, inexpensive. Prices do not include drinks, wine, tips, or taxes. All telephone numbers are in the 2 city code unless otherwise indicated.

**La Belle Epoque** – Fine French food and a range of Chilean, Argentine, and French wines, with attentive but somewhat aloof service. The lobster is delicious, as are the profiteroles. Closed Sundays. Reservations necessary. Major credit cards accepted. 925 Calle Whimper and Av. 6 de Diciembre (phone: 233163). Expensive.

**Chalet Suisse** – Some of the best continental food in Quito is elegantly served in a pleasant atmosphere for serious gourmands. This is a good spot for sizzling steaks. A subdued piano and small casino in the adjoining hotel add to its popularity with diplomats and lovers. Closed Sundays. Reservations advised. Major credit cards accepted. 312 Calle Calama at Reina Victoria (phone: 516700 and 232053). Expensive.

**Costa Vasca** – Splendid Spanish food, with especially good prawns and *calamares* flavored liberally with garlic. Open daily. Reservations advised. Diners Club accepted. 553 Av. 18 de Septiembre between Páez and 9 de Octubre (phone: 564940). Expensive.

**El Dorado** – Formerly *El Conquistador*, this fine restaurant boasts a menu that highlights international cuisine as well as some tasty local dishes; every meal benefits from the country's fresh fruits, vegetables, and splendid fish and meat. A popular spot with the local people. Open daily. Reservations advised. Major credit cards accepted. *Colón Internacional Hotel*, Avdas. Amazonas and Patria (phone: 560666). Expensive.

**La Gritta** – Elegant European decor, a fireplace, and good atmosphere in what is probably the best Italian restaurant in Quito. The homemade pasta is superb, and the wine list commendable. Closed Sundays and for lunch on Saturdays. Reservations advised. Major credit cards accepted. 246 Av. Santa María (phone: 567628). Expensive.

**La Marmite** – Another elegant, well-appointed dining place, very popular with businesspeople, local VIPs, and tourists. The menu is international, but basically

French, with especially tasty seafood and meat dishes and excellent desserts. Closed Sundays and for lunch on Saturdays. Reservations advised. Major credit cards accepted. 287 Mariano Aguilera (phone: 237751). Expensive.

**Le Peche Mignon** – One of the best dining spots in Quito, specializing in French cuisine, it is small, cozy, and tastefully decorated. Very pleasant atmosphere. Closed Sundays. Reservations advised. Major credit cards accepted. 338 Bello Horizonte, next door to *La Ronda* (phone: 230709). Expensive.

**El Techo del Mundo** – The *Quito* hotel's so-called "Roof of the World" is so high on the ridge over the city that diners are sometimes surprised to see aircraft almost level with the windows as they make the turn to land. Seating 110, it is quietly elegant with unobtrusive live music. Good food, the splendid nighttime view, and wonderful service make a visit here worthwhile. Open daily. Reservations advised on weekends or for groups of more than four. Major credit cards accepted. 2500 Av. González Suárez (phone: 230300). Expensive.

**La Terraza del Tártaro** – This penthouse offers fine views of the city and, if you're lucky, the distant snow-capped peaks as well. The varied menu is strong on seafood and steak dishes. Closed Sundays. Reservations advised at dinner. No credit cards accepted. 1106 Calle Veintimilla and Av. Amazonas (phone: 527987). Expensive.

**La Vieja Castilla** – One of Quito's best Spanish restaurants, with a very nice atmosphere in which to enjoy the excellent dishes that emerge from its kitchen. Outstanding wine list and warm, attentive service. Open Mondays through Saturdays for lunch and dinner. Reservations advised. Major credit cards accepted. 435 La Pueta and Amazonas (phone: 566979). Expensive.

**Excalibur** – Another fine international dining experience in a cozy atmosphere. Excellent service is the hallmark. Open daily. Reservations advised. Major credit cards accepted. 380 Calama (phone: 541272). Expensive to moderate.

**Der Rhein** – Oswald Homolka, longtime chef at several major Quito hotels, embarked on his own venture and created a wonderful combination of German and Ecuadoran fare. Open daily. Reservations advised. Major credit cards accepted. 3467 Av. 6 de Diciembre and Bélgica (phone: 242597). Expensive to moderate.

**La Casa de Mi Abuela** – The best meat in Quito is served in this Argentine restaurant, with such generous helpings that diners tend to stagger out. Delicious salads. Open daily. Reservations advised on Fridays and Saturdays. Major credit cards accepted. 1649 Calle Juan León Mera (phone: 521922). Moderate.

**La Choza** – A good place to sample local dishes in a pretty Quito setting. Start with *empanadas de morocho,* drink some *chicha,* and try the *llapingachos* — potato and cheese cakes with a spicy peanut sauce; Saturdays and Sundays, lunch only. Definitely call to be sure they're open as the restaurant occasionally closes without notice. Reservations necessary on weekends. Major credit cards accepted. 1831 Av. 12 de Octubre at Cordero (phone: 230839). Moderate.

**Churrasquería El Tropeiro** – This informal Brazilian steakhouse serves only grilled meat and salads — in great variation and abundance. A waiter keeps your plate stacked with hot, juicy cuts of beef, pork, and chicken, while you serve yourself from a tasty and imaginative salad bar. Open daily. Reservations unnecessary. Major credit cards accepted. 546 Veintimilla (phone: 548012 or 545793). Moderate.

**Pekin** – Another small, unpretentious spot, this one serves delicious Chinese food. It ain't Beijing, but it's good. Closed Mondays. Reservations advised. No credit cards accepted. 197 Calle Bello Horizonte (phone: 545021 or 520841). Moderate.

**Rincón de Francia** – Considered by *quiteños* "the" place to see and be seen. The French kitchen serves up a different specialty each day, all of them worth trying. Closed Sundays. Reservations advised. Major credit cards accepted. 779 Av. General Roca at Av. 9 de Octubre (phone: 232053 or 554668). Moderate.

***Rincón La Ronda*** – One of the best spots in town for local fare, as well as live Latin music in the evenings. Open daily for lunch and dinner. Reservations unnecessary. Major credit cards accepted. 400 Bello Horizonte at Diego de Almagro (phone: 540459 or 545176). Moderate.

***Chantilly*** – An ideal place for coffee and a mouth-watering pastry. Lunches are served as well. Pastries and sweets are also on sale at the shop downstairs. Closed Sundays. No credit cards accepted. No reservations. 736 Calle General Roca and Av. Amazonas (phone: 528226). Inexpensive.

# RIO DE JANEIRO

*Cariocas* (as residents of Rio de Janeiro are called) say that one of the six days God needed to create the world was devoted to making Rio. No one yet has complained that the time was ill spent. Just under the brow of Brazil's long Atlantic coast, Rio washes inland on a tide of tawny beaches across the graceful valleys and hillsides of the tropical mountains that dot its 15-mile section of coast. Above the city, on Corcovado Mountain, the world-famous sculpture of Christ the Redeemer spreads its arms in an open embrace of the city and the sea beyond. The sentiment of the gesture — the radiant acceptance of something almost miraculous in its beauty — touches even the most casual first-time visitor. Mention Rio to a recently returned traveler and you are practically guaranteed a smile and a deep sigh of pleasure: "Ah, Rio!" It's a universal response.

Brasília is the capital of Brazil (at least since 1960; for the preceding 197 years that honor belonged to Rio); São Paulo is the country's conscience and keeper of its work ethic; but Rio is its soul, undisputed master of its heart. If *cariocas* sometimes seem giddy with pleasure and pleasure-seeking, be more sympathetic than censorious. Rio is not an easy city in which to be serious — or at least serious about anything except beauty. In a town so utterly devoted to and so generously endowed with glamour — and despite the increasing problems of crime, grime, and the deteriorating Brazilian economic situation — the business of being beautiful is taken very seriously.

The site of Rio de Janeiro — River of January — was discovered on Guanabara Bay by Portuguese sailors in January 1502, just 2 years after the first Portuguese incursions into northern Brazil at Salvador de Bahia. Though the Portuguese established settlements at Bahia, Rio actually was settled by the French, and only after numerous bloody battles during which the city changed hands several times did it become Portuguese in 1567. Salvador and many other settlements in early Brazil flourished by raising sugarcane, then tapping rubber, and by mining gold and gemstones. Coffee plantations were established in the area as well. In 1763 Rio replaced Salvador as capital of the colony.

The Portuguese ruled from Europe for 300 years, until Napoleon invaded Portugal in 1807 and the royal family fled to Rio for refuge. When Napoleon was defeated, King João VI returned to Portugal and left his son Pedro as regent. In 1822 Pedro, following the behests of the wealthy plantation owners, declared Brazil independent and named himself Emperor Dom Pedro I. An unpopular monarch, he had to return to Portugal to take the crown as Pedro IV, leaving his 5-year-old son, Dom Pedro II, whose 58-year reign was known as Brazil's golden era. Dom Pedro II fostered land reforms, encouraged mass education, and opened Brazil to immigration. In 1888 he abolished slavery, an act so unpopular with his wealthy supporters that he was forced to flee

Brazil for Paris, where he died shortly after. Many years later his body was returned for reburial in the cathedral in Petrópolis (a suburb in the hills outside Rio). In 1889, Brazil was declared a republic; Rio remained its capital. It was a boom time for Brazil, with coffee in high demand and the discovery of rubber in the Amazon bringing untold wealth into the country. Immigrants from Japan and Europe poured into Rio and São Paulo, bringing with them the creativity and industry of all immigrant peoples, and successive discoveries of a vast array of natural resources continued to fuel economic progress. Brazil's economic miracle did not divide the spoils equally among its citizens, however, and the recent 21-year military regime (1964–1985) did not resolve problems of unemployment, illiteracy, poverty, the largest foreign debt of any developing nation, and rampant inflation. Rising prices have now affected everyone — rich, poor, and tourist alike. Nevertheless, the happy-go-lucky atmosphere is not gone. In 1985, an electoral college selected a civilian, Tancredo Neves, as president. However, he died before his term began, and José Sarney, his vice presidential candidate, became president. Sarney was unable to curb Brazil's inflation (it reached a level of 1,800% in 1989) or lower its foreign debt (Brazil's is the largest in the Third World). In late 1989, Fernando Collor de Mello was elected president in the first democratic election in Brazil in 29 years. At his inauguration a few months later, he announced a sweeping economic plan to reduce inflation, install a free market economy similar to Great Britain's, and lower Brazil's foreign debt. In early 1991, in an effort to pull Brazil out of its worst recession in a decade, he froze wages and prices. Later that year, Collor started to implement one of the programs promised at his inauguration — he privatized the country's state steel company. The inflation rate decreased and in an attempt to bolster his government, in early 1992 he appointed a new cabinet, made up mostly of conservatives. Visitors from North America, however, probably won't be affected by the inflation rate — the dollar remains strong in comparison to the cruzeiro — and tourists usually can take advantage of the "parallel" or "tourist dollar" rate offered in exchange houses, hotels, and shops.

Certainly, Rio never seems to stop growing. Today the city has more than 5 million residents (a total of over 10 million in the greater metropolitan area) in beach communities and inland suburbs that stretch for miles around the downtown commercial center of Guanabara Bay, the site of the original Rio settlement. The city's incessant growth has been primarily to the south and west, where the beaches lie, and has been fed in part by Rio's position as the number one tourist destination in South America and in part by the *cariocas'* native craving for fine strands, as one after another of these small beach communities have become part of Rio's overall urban plan. During the 1940s, Copacabana Beach was the center of Rio's chic sun-worshiping life; today various beach communities, of different styles and degrees of development, are all part of Rio. They, along with other parts of the city — the airport, highways, and the telephone, sewage, and traffic systems — were given a facelift that coincided with *Earth Summit,* the United Nations' international ecology conference held here in June 1992. The most visible part of the program is Rio-Orla, a 20-mile pedestrian and bicycle path that runs the entire length of Rio's beachfront.

# RIO DE JANEIRO

## Points of Interest

1. Pão de Açúcar/Sugar Loaf Mountain
2. Corcovado/Hunchback Mountain Christ the Redeemer Statue
3. Morro da Urca/Urca Hill
4. Praia Vermelha Station—cable cars
5. Launch and Hydrofoil to Ilha Paquetá
6. Floresta da Tijuca/Tijuca Forest
7. Feirarte/Art Fair
8. Gemstone Tour
9. Avenida Rio Branco
10. Praça Mauá/Mauá Square
11. Mosteiro do São Bento/Monastery of São Bento
12. Igreja Nossa Senhora da Candelária/Candelária Church
13. Praça XV de Novembro/November 15 Plaza Paço Imperial/Imperial Palace
14. Downtown Shopping District
15. Largo da Carioca/Carioca Square; Igreja de São Franciso da Peniténcia/Church of St. Francis of the Penitence
16. Catedral Metropolitana/Metropolitan Cathedral
17. Teatro Municipal/Municipal Theater
18. Museu Nacional de Belas Artes/National Museum of Fine Arts

19. Cinelândia
20. Parque do Flamengo/Flamengo Park; Museum of Modern Art; National War Memorial; Military Museum
21. Museu da República/Museum of the Republic
22. Praia de Copacabana/Copacabana Beach
23. Praia de Ipanema/Ipanema Beach
24. Praia do Leblon
25. Santa Teresa; Chácara do Céu
26. São Cristóvão; Museu Nacional/National Museum; Jardim Zoológico/Zoological Garden
27. Jardim Botânico/Botanical Garden
28. Planetario/Planetarium
29. Tivoli Amusement Park
30. Museu Carmen Miranda/Carmen Miranda Museum
31. Museu do Indio/Indian Museum
32. Estádio Maracanã
33. The Jockey Club
34. Rio de Janeiro Tourism Office (RIOTUR)
35. Estacão Rodoviaria Novo Rio/Novo Rio Bus Station
36. Estacão Dom Pedro II/Dom Pedro II Train Station
37. Santos Dumont Airport
38. Galeão International Airport

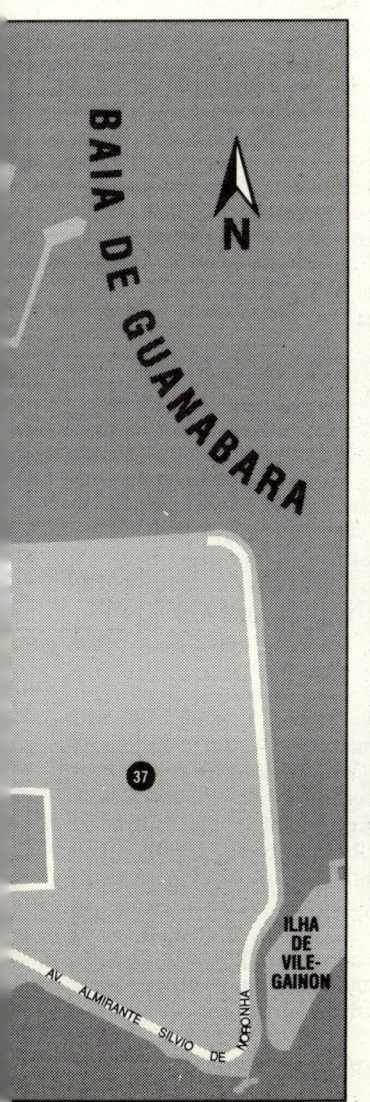

## AT-A-GLANCE

These communities stretch south of the bustling, noisy downtown area like beads on a string. That image is more than apt, in fact, because much of the city is connected by 13 tunnels, the quickest way to negotiate the mountains around which the city is splashed like paint from a profligate artist. Clinging precariously to the sides of these mountains are small homes made of wood and hammered tin. Although they appear gaily painted and picturesque, these *favelas* (shantytowns) are actually the slum dwellings in which poor *cariocas* live. Celebrated in song and in the haunting film *Black Orpheus,* the people who live here are a lot tougher and a lot less glamorous in real life than on screen. Many *favelados* have emigrated from other parts of Brazil to try to support destitute relatives, and life is hard. Thefts, stabbings, drug traffic, and contraband trade are all too common in the *favelas;* and, all too often, street crime overflows *favela* borders. Pickpockets are a constant threat on the beaches and the streets of Rio; tourists are advised to leave valuables at home — or to lock them in their hotel safes. Perhaps as a result of the increased poverty level among *cariocas,* other crimes against tourists — such as purse snatchings — are on the rise, so it is wise to take precautions.

Rio's downtown area (*centro* or *cidade* as the *cariocas* call it) is bustling, hectic, and noisy, and though it has a number of hotels, restaurants, shops, and night spots, the really chic establishments are concentrated in the more fashionable beach communities. The *centro* is devoted to business, where modern high-rises abut traditional Brazilian public buildings. Since most residents live outside the downtown area, traffic on weekdays always is heavy.

Adjacent to the downtown area are the beach communities of Flamengo and Botafogo, whose beaches face Guanabara Bay. Both areas are primarily residential, although they have some good older hotels and restaurants. During the 1930s and 1940s, they were the center of Rio's resort area.

Passing through the Botafogo Tunnel, you come to the Leme-Copacabana Beach strip, the "grande dame" and heart of Rio's resort area. World-renowned Copacabana is popular with *cariocas* from all walks of life and all age groups. The wide, black-and-white mosaic sidewalk lines Avenida Atlântica, site of the majority of Rio's fine hotels, excellent restaurants, sidewalk cafés, and nightclubs. Visitors inevitably spend a good part of their time in this area.

Around the corner is Ipanema, prime rival for popularity with Copacabana, and now considered more fashionable. Acclaimed in the hit song "The Girl from Ipanema," it is quieter than Copacabana, with fewer hotels, but is very popular with Rio's chic young crowd. It has the city's finest restaurants, boutiques, and a Sunday flea market. A modest beachfront apartment in either Copacabana or Ipanema rents for as much as $2,000 a month; prices escalate to $5,000 to $10,000 per month for grander establishments. During *Carnaval,* even a modest apartment can cost several thousand dollars for a month or less.

Next along the Atlantic strip, primarily residential Leblon is the home of many wealthy Rio residents. Posh apartment buildings facing the ocean along Avenida Delfim Moreira have duplex and triplex apartments, penthouses, and rooftop swimming pools.

Twenty-five years ago, the long beach at São Conrado was inhabited mostly by waterfowl and driftwood. As tourists poured into Rio during the early 1970s, the need for luxury accommodations became acute, and within a few months of each other, three resort hotels opened their doors on Avenida Niemeyer in 1971. These three — the *Sheraton Rio, Inter-Continental,* and *Nacional Rio* — led the building boom that made São Conrado Rio's newest fully developed beach community. Its skyline is littered with high-rises and the streets, lined with shopping centers and recreational areas. Rio's development isn't over, however. The story of São Conrado is now being repeated in Barra da Tijuca, even farther from the *centro.* Until recently, Barra was no more than a 10-mile strip of beach, honky-tonk bars, a few seafood restaurants, and various campgrounds. Now it is being developed as a major residential site, as Rio grows relentlessly toward the south and west.

As you stroll through these communities trying restaurants and browsing in the boutiques, art galleries, and antiques shops, you will savor the special rhythm, sound, and smell of each. Perhaps you will be drawn to one section above the others: Copacabana, with lithe sunbathers and soccer players; the sweet pineapples hacked apart by a machete; graceful papagallo kites soaring over the sand and water; or Ipanema, where the beach and streets are less crowded and even traffic jams are tamer, but the bathers younger, more beautiful, less inhibited.

And despite the recent development of the area, some say Rio's best beach can still be found in São Conrado at Praia do Pepino, which is isolated from the rest of the city by a long oceanside cliff (although some contend that Barra's remoteness makes its beaches the safest and least polluted). Here you can watch hang gliders soar from the rocky heights as you sip the milk of chilled coconuts sold on the beach.

Rio is truly a multiracial society in which the color of a citizen's skin is relatively unimportant and people of all shades live together in apparent harmony. Discrimination exists, but it is different from the racism of the US. Though the majority of *favela* dwellers are black and poor, among the growing middle class in Brazil are blacks, whites, mulattos, and Asians. Most Brazilians are mulatto, descendants of the black slaves, Indian tribes, and Portuguese, Dutch, and Spanish settlers. The opening of Brazil to immigration in the early 20th century and after both world wars brought large numbers of Eastern Europeans, Italians, and Japanese. There are large numbers of Europeans in Rio's business centers, shops, and restaurants, and a huge Japanese sector in São Paulo.

Portuguese is Rio's native language. But the *cariocas'* dialect, more closely akin to that of Portugal, is distinct from that of São Paulo's *paulistas,* which was influenced by the past immigration of Italians. Surrounded by Spanish-speaking neighbors, you would expect Spanish to be the second language here, but, surprisingly, English is more widely spoken. (A distant second to be sure, but English is taught in secondary schools, and many *cariocas* study it privately.) Hotels, better restaurants, and shops invariably have English-speaking personnel. If you speak some Spanish, try using it in a pinch, since *cariocas* in the tourist business deal with many Spanish-speaking visitors and the languages are similar. And, if you are fluent in Spanish, don't be surprised to find yourself gesticulating and trying to lip-read in an attempt to understand the lilting inflection of the unfamiliar-sounding Portuguese words. It is easier for Brazilians to understand Spanish than for Spanish speakers to understand Brazilian Portuguese. Both are Romance languages, with similar grammatical structures and many words that are written much the same, but pronunciation is usually quite different. Don't believe people who tell you that Portuguese and Spanish are identical. They are similar, yes; but it takes time and patience to learn the essential phonetic distinctions that will allow you to communicate effectively.

Much of the *cariocas'* leisure time is spent in pursuit of *la dolce vita,* Brazilian-style, their enthusiasm for the pleasures rather than the responsibilities of life no less earnest for the country's current economic problems. From dawn until dusk the easily accessible beaches are a kaleidoscope of color and activity, with men and women in brightly hued tangas and bikinis sunning, swimming, surfing, dancing, singing, and playing soccer, bongos, and guitars — it's a beehive of hedonistic activity.

The residents' incessant pursuit of pleasure makes Rio an easy place to meet people of the opposite or same sex. On the beaches, in sidewalk cafés, and in discotheques, people are busily engaged in the business of meeting people. The image of a young woman out on a date with a grim-faced chaperon two paces behind is not a picture of Rio. Young people here are free to enjoy themselves as they choose. In addition to the discotheques that cater to the young, pizza parlors and sidewalk cafés serve as meeting places. Flirtatious and frivolous, *cariocas* seem to have an innate sense of how to flatter and charm, quickly accepting newcomers into their circle of friends or family.

Although there is not a strong women's movement in Rio ("honor" killing — when a husband may murder his adulterous wife, pleading that he was defending his honor, and be acquitted — was rejected by Brazil's Supreme Court as a defense only in 1991), both men and women are sexually liberated. The women of Rio are known for their beauty, and they are quite open about their sexuality. Sex is readily available for anyone looking for it, male or female. A single woman will find more authentic acceptance in Rio than anywhere else in Latin America, and attention from men, on the beach or in a café, is usually friendly; it can be accepted or rejected. The only stumbling blocks for single women are in nightclubs. Many clubs do not permit single women to enter, and it is unusual for a woman to go to a club or bar unescorted. However, clubs usually allow female tourists to enter to see the show, especially in the big hotels.

Another of Rio's special features is the homegrown religious cult, *macumba*. While ostensibly Roman Catholic, many *cariocas* follow the rituals and practices of this sect, which is rather like voodoo. Its houses of worship, called *terreiros,* can be found throughout the city, and services are held nightly. *Macumbistas* believe that spirits affect all aspects of life and that there are good and evil spirits. They employ a medium to call down the good spirits to assist them. You should try and visit a *terreiro* during your stay in Rio; the ceremony is fascinating. *Macumba* festivals are held at various times during the year. The most important one, the *Feast of Iemanjá,* takes place on the beach on December 31, *New Year's Eve,* when, at midnight, gifts and flowers are sent out to sea in little boats as offerings to the goddess of the sea.

Soccer provides a different outlet for many people, who enjoy the sport as both participants and spectators. Every beach, most parks, and all school yards have soccer goal posts. They are constantly in use in impromptu as well as organized league games. Many are lighted for night play. These games are hard-fought, which you will sense immediately by the ferocity of the play. The hysteria of the fans at *Maracanã Stadium* during professional matches far surpasses that of *Super Bowl* and *World Series* crowds. The noise is deafening and the enjoyment contagious.

The most important event in Rio is *Carnaval*. While it is true that this pre-*Lenten* celebration lasts only for the 4 days preceding *Ash Wednesday,* some pre-*Carnaval* activities start as early as November, when costumes are designed and made, parties are planned, and nightclubs begin samba contests. All business comes to a halt as *Carnaval* begins. The entire city is festooned with colorful streamers and lights, and bandstands are set up for street dancing that lasts from dusk till dawn. Traditional *Carnaval* events take place downtown in the *Sambódromo,* a wide boulevard edged by permanent bleacher seats, constructed by the local government to promote and establish *Carnaval* as part of the Brazilian culture. During the year, classes are held in the bleachers and musical concerts in the square at the end of the boulevard. The *Carnaval* parade is now held on both Sunday and Monday evenings and is a spectacle worthy of Cecil B. De Mille. Samba schools, each consisting of several thousand members, strut, glide, dance, and samba down the avenue in elaborate costumes to original musical accompaniments, singing lyrics written by club members around an assigned theme. The multitude of spectators take an active part by singing and clapping. *Carnaval* is also the time for costume balls held at local social clubs, nightclubs, and fashionable hotels. The costumes range from whatever you have to gorgeous, opulent displays of feathers, bangles, and glitter. Sometimes costume competitions feature outfits costing tens of thousands of dollars, feasts for the eyes; otherwise, and especially at small clubs, celebrants dress as they wish.

Words can describe a museum filled with marvelous paintings or an ancient ruin, but Rio de Janeiro is an experience that enchants mind, soul, and body. The bubbly sensuality of the *cariocas;* the splendid colors of sea and mountains playing against the colorful crowds moving gracefully along the streets; the mingled scent of ocean and tropical flowers: These are all part of the elixir called Rio. It is a dynamic collage playing on all senses. It is alive; to be there, life-giving.

# RIO DE JANEIRO AT-A-GLANCE

**SEEING THE CITY:** *Cariocas* adore their city. They take pleasure in looking at it themselves and pride in showing it to visitors. There are several natural viewing points, as well as a number of man-made ones. Pão de Açúcar (Sugar Loaf), jutting into Guanabara Bay, and the peak of Corcovado (Hunchback) Mountain, farther inland, offer the most spectacular views and are Rio's major tourist attractions (see *Special Places,* below). The road leading up Corcovado has two viewpoints: the Vista Chinesa (Chinese View) at 1,300 feet, overlooking the lovely lagoon (*lagoa*) section, Ipanema, and Leblon; and, at 1,500 feet, the Mesa do Imperador (Emperor's Table). Both provide excellent panoramas for photographs. Many of the city's newest hotels have cleverly positioned nightclubs, first class restaurants, or quiet piano bars on their top floors. What better decor than a view of Guanabara Bay at sunset, the purple-hued mountain range, or the city's skyline? Visit the *St. Honoré* restaurant on the 37th floor of the *Méridien* hotel (1020 Av. Atlântica, Copacabana; phone: 275-9922), and the *Skylab* bar on the 30th floor of the *Rio Othon Palace* hotel (3264 Av. Atlântica, Copacabana; phone: 521-5522). *La Tour* (downtown, 651 Rua Santa Luzia; phone: 240-5493) is a revolving restaurant that makes its rounds once an hour. The view pans from Pão de Açúcar to Corcovado and the beach areas. Another restaurant (open only for lunch) with a stunning view of the downtown skyline and harbor is *Pão de Açúcar* (on Urca Hill, adjoining Sugar Loaf; phone: 541-3737). It's accessible by cable car from Avenida Pasteur.

**SPECIAL PLACES:** Rio has warm weather nearly all year, with hot, hot weather in the summer (December to March) months and a number of the finest beaches in the world, so you are bound to spend a good deal of your visit in a horizontal mode, playing footsies with the Atlantic's fine sands. But there is much else to see and do in Rio.

**Pão de Açúcar (Sugar Loaf Mountain)** – Rio's number one tourist stop is a brown gumdrop-shaped mountain at the entrance to Guanabara Bay. Standing at 1,325 feet, its summit is reached via two cable cars. Glass-enclosed and large enough to hold 70 people, the first car carries you from Praia Vermelha station to Urca, a sister peak 650 feet high. The ride takes only 5 minutes and the views of the bay area are lovely. At its peak, Urca is larger than Pão de Açúcar and is a popular picnic spot. It also has a small restaurant, a playground, and an open-air theater with bleacher seats and a dance floor. It's used for *Carnaval* balls, *New Year's Eve* parties, and samba or popular music shows throughout the year. On the second leg of the journey, the cable car from Urca to Pão de Açúcar seems to rise vertically. Although the peak is small, the views are nothing less than stunning — on one side, the harbor and downtown skyline; on another, the mountain range, with Rio's fabulous white beaches spread along the shore; still another, Corcovado Mountain and its famous Christ the Redeemer statue. On a clear day, you will swear you can almost see forever. The cable car runs daily, every half hour from 8 AM to 10 PM; it's crowded on weekends. Admission charge. Praia Vermelha station, Av. Pasteur, Botafogo (phone: 541-3737).

**Corcovado (Hunchback Mountain)** – Rivaling Pão de Açúcar in popularity, this is the mountain on which stands the 120-foot statue of Christ the Redeemer — restored 2 years ago because of cracks and stains caused by pollution. If you are familiar with Antônio Carlos Jobim's evocative jazz composition "Corcovado," you will undoubtedly place this higher than Pão de Açúcar on your itinerary. Built in the late 1920s with money raised in churches throughout Brazil, the statue is visible from most parts of the city, especially when illuminated at night. The views of the city from its 2,400-foot peak are perfect for photographers on clear days. The beach areas, Guanabara Bay with Pão de Açúcar beside it, Rio's lagoon, modern buildings, and huge ships are all within lens's view. By the way, wear comfortable shoes; there is a steep, arduous climb from the parking lot to the statue peak, but the reward is worth every huff and puff. To reach the statue the easy way, hop a 30-minute ride on a railroad that leaves from Cosme Velho station every half hour from 8:30 AM to 6 PM, making several stops at residential stations along the way. Admission charge.

It is worthwhile to explore the mountain as well as the statue, which you can do if you rent a car, cab, or come via tour bus. There is a good road up the mountain, with several lookout and picnic points along the way. As mentioned above, the two most popular lookout points are the Vista Chinesa (Chinese View) and the Mesa do Imperador (Emperor's Table). The Vista Chinesa is marked by a green pagoda with ferocious dragon heads. The Mesa do Imperador was a favorite picnic area of Emperor Dom Pedro II. Both overlook the city and you get better views than from the peak. Also on the way up is Largo do Boticário, a cluster of five lovely historic colonial houses. Open daily. No admission charge. Cosme Velho station, Corcovado (phone: 285-2533).

**Ilha Paquetá (Paquetá Island)** – For a different view of Rio, set aside a day and hop a motor launch for a relaxing ride through Guanabara Bay. The launch leaves from a downtown marina and heads into the sheltered waters of the bay under the Niterói Bridge, giving you a completely different perspective of the city. As you near Paquetá, you will see fishing boats, waterskiers, and snorkelers. One of the most picturesque islands of the 84 in Rio's bay, it has a population of 3,000, most of whom are fishermen. Some of the more fashionable homes belong to *cariocas,* who come on weekends. Since no cars are allowed on the island, the best way to get around is to rent a bicycle from one of the several rental offices near the dock. It costs about $2 per hour. A more relaxing, albeit slightly more expensive, way to see the island is to rent a horse-drawn carriage. The going rate is $5 for a 45-minute ride. You can bring a picnic or have a filling seafood lunch at the *Flamboyant* hotel (phone: 397-0087). The *Flamboyant* and the *Lido* hotels (phone: 397-0377) are modest but clean and comfortable enough for an overnight stay. Try to schedule your visit on a weekday since they are quite crowded on weekends. The launch leaves from Praça 15 de Novembro (downtown) near the *Alba Mar* restaurant (see *Eating Out*) Mondays through Saturdays from 5:30 AM to 10:30 PM, Sundays from 7:10 AM to 10:30 PM. Returning boats leave Paquetá from 5:30 AM to 8:30 PM. The trip takes 1¼ hours (phone: 231-0396). You can also visit Paquetá and other islands by hydrofoil in just 25 minutes. The hydrofoil leaves Praça XV for Paquetá at 10 AM, noon, 2 PM, and 4 PM.

**Floresta da Tijuca (Tijuca Forest)** – Only 20 minutes from downtown, Tijuca Forest gives city folk a perfect opportunity to stroll through a tropical forest along a road shaded by towering trees and lined with flowers. Tijuca Forest was cleared as a coffee plantation, but Mother Nature has reasserted herself here, and the forest has returned to its natural state. There are many types of trees, small waterfalls, narrow paths winding through the woods, picnic grounds, a hiking path, and even a 3,000-foot peak (Pico da Tijuca) to conquer. You can enter the forest at Alto da Boa Vista; the road winds past Taunay Waterfall (Cascatinha Taunay), whose waters are used to produce Brahma beer; the Mayrink Chapel; and *A Floresta* (phone: 258-0183) and *Os Esquilos* (phone: 258-0237) restaurants, the latter of which has the decor of a colonial house, complete with fireplace, lace curtains, and a garden where drinks are served. The area of the forest called Bom Retiro (Good Retreat) is a good picnic spot and also the starting point of the 2-hour hike to the peak. A cab from Copacabana costs about $15. All city tours include a visit to Tijuca. Alto da Boa Vista, Tijuca Forest.

**Feirarte (Art Fair)** – Formerly the "Hippie Market," *Feirarte* has outgrown its jeans-and-sandals image. This is the *carioca* version of a flea market, but you will be able to find a multitude of items ranging from the frivolous to the first-rate. Held every Sunday in Ipanema, the market draws enthusiastic shoppers, bargain hunters, and the curious. The vendors imaginatively display their wares in makeshift stalls, on rugs on the ground, and even on tree branches. Very popular are copper wall plates and mirrors, tapestries, hand-tooled leathers — bags, belts, sandals, and wallets — trays, and wood carvings. Silver jewelry, gaily painted ceramics, and kitchen utensils make excellent gifts. The market provides a gallery for the work of a number of very talented young artists not yet well enough known to command real gallery space but whose oil paintings — ranging from primitive to modern — are available at extremely reasonable prices and just could be valuable investments. Prices range from a few dollars to more than $100; what you pay will in large part depend on your ability to bargain. Nobody pays the first price here or the second. Bargain like crazy, and, as in most outdoor markets throughout the world, beware of pickpockets. The fair takes place on Sundays from 9 AM to 6 PM, Praça General Osório, Ipanema.

**Gemstone Tour** – Brazil is to gemstones what Saudi Arabia is to oil. This mammoth nation produces 90% of some of the world's colorful minerals — aquamarine, topaz, amethyst, opal, turquoise, agate, to name a few — as well as coral. Take a guided tour through several workshops to learn how and why Brazil sparkles. A real show is that of *H. Stern,* Rio's largest gemstone dealer and, with more than 100 shops in Latin America, the US, Europe, Asia, and the Caribbean, one of the world's largest jewelers as well. The very modern tour uses headphones that come in half a dozen languages, slides, and views of workers behind glass; it lasts about 15 minutes. It begins with an exhibit of a gemstone in its raw state, embedded in rock. Then you are shown the cutting, shaping, polishing, faceting, and the gem in its final form, ready to be set in a piece of jewelry. You'll learn how stones are graded and how new designs are planned in design workshops. Unless you are a jeweler, you'll probably be surprised to discover that not all amethysts are purple nor all tourmalines green. The tour is interesting even if you don't plan to buy any jewelry (there is no pressure to do so); if you do, it will give you some insights toward making an intelligent purchase. And you can't beat the price. The tour is offered during regular shop hours; closed Sundays. No admission charge. 113 Rua Garcia D'Avila, 3rd Floor, Ipanema (phone: 259-7442).

## DOWNTOWN AND FLAMENGO BEACH

**Avenida Rio Branco** – This is the major street of commercial Rio. During the day, the black-and-white-tiled sidewalks are filled with people rushing to work in the offices, banks, and public buildings. Traffic is heavy and so is pollution. At night, this street is very quiet. From its northernmost point in the Praça Mauá dock area, it runs south several miles to Avenida Beira Mar, near Flamengo Beach.

**Praça Mauá (Mauá Square)** – The older dock area is interesting to stroll through because the older, ornate gray architecture of the nearby streets is so different from that of modern Rio. Cruise ships dock nearby. Although the area is full of local color, it borders on the seamy, sleazy, and dangerous.

**Mosteiro do São Bento (Monastery of São Bento)** – Not far from Praça Mauá, this delightful religious complex contains one of the most beautiful baroque golden chapels in Brazil. Open daily from 8 to 11:30 AM and 1 to 6 PM. 68 Rua Dom Gerardo, Ladeira de São Bento (phone: 291-7122).

**Igreja Nossa Senhora de Candelária (Our Lady of Candelária Church)** – Built in the early 18th century, the church stands in the plaza that for many years was the starting point for the samba school paraders during *Carnaval.* The back entrance of the church faces the main street; the front doors open onto Guanabara Bay. The original church was built by mariners in the early 17th century after they had witnessed a shipwreck, and many of the paintings inside depict this terrible scene. Open weekdays from 7:30 AM to noon and 1 to 4:30 PM; weekends, mornings only. Praça Pio X at Av. Presidente Vargas (phone: 233-2324).

**Praça XV de Novembro** – This is the oldest square in Rio, ringed by little 16th-century churches and pastel-colored buildings.

**Downtown Shopping District** – Rio's major shopping area embraces several streets: Rua Ouvidor, Rua Gonçalves Dias, Rua Buenos Aires, and Rua Uruguaiana. The main flower market, Praça Olavo Bilac, is here, too. Shops specialize in handicrafts, *macumba* items, leather goods, records, and home furnishings of wood and stone. In the last few years, several fashionable boutiques have opened in this area (see *Shopping*). Rua Gonçalves Dias is a mall and good for browsing. The few streets that cross the shopping area are rather narrow. Drop in for a snack at *Confeiteria Colombo,* 32 Rua Gonçalves Dias (phone: 232-2300).

**Largo da Carioca (Carioca Square)** – This small concrete plaza near the shopping center area has benches to rest on, shoeshiners and faith healers plying their trades, and street vendors selling everything from candy to folk art. The nearby Convento e Igreja de Santo Antônio (St. Anthony's Convent and Church) is one of Rio's oldest, dating from the early 17th century. It has interesting blue tile work, indicating Portugal's influence, and some early paintings. Adjoining Santo Antônio.

**Igreja de São Francisco da Penitência (Church of St. Francis of the Penitence)** – Don't be discouraged by the uninspiring exterior of this church. Inside are restored carved altars and ceiling paintings by José de Oliveira, one of Brazil's outstanding artists. 5 Largo da Carioca (phone: 262-0197).

**Catedral Metropolitana (Metropolitan Cathedral)** – Rio's avant-garde cathedral was under construction for 15 years. The structure is conical, angular, and its only gesture to traditional design is the presence of four enormous stained glass windows. Services are held on Sundays at 10 AM, daily at noon. Open mornings for visits. Near Largo da Carioca at 245 Av. República do Chile (phone: 240-2869).

**Teatro Municipal (Municipal Theater)** – Modeled after the *Paris Opera House,* the *Municipal Theater* was built over an underground lake. Since it opened in 1909, it has been home to Brazil's best artists as well as visiting companies from North America and Europe. Opera, ballet, and concerts are performed here regularly. The theater underwent a major renovation in the early 1980s, and its interior has been completely modernized. You'll recognize the building on the skyline by the eagle on its bronze roof. Open by permission only; call to set up a visit. Av. Rio Branco at Praça Marechal Floriano (phone: 210-2463).

**Museu Nacional de Belas Artes (National Museum of Fine Arts)** – This impressive building houses over 800 paintings and other works of art. Many are reproductions of works by well-known artists. Open Tuesdays through Fridays from 10 AM to 5:30 PM; Saturdays, Sundays, and holidays from 3 to 6 PM. No admission charge. 199 Av. Rio Branco (phone: 240-0068).

**Cinelândia** – This is Rio's crowded downtown entertainment center, very busy around-the-clock. Clustered in this area are several large movie theaters, restaurants, hotels, pick-up bars, both straight and gay, and nightclubs. If you're in the area during the day, stop in at *Café Amarelinho* (558 Praça Floriano; phone: 240-8434), where the *centro's* office workers go. The scene can be somewhat seamy at night, although there are police at the ready. The main street, Rua Senador Dantas, begins at Praça Mahatma Gandhi and runs for several blocks.

**Parque do Flamengo (Flamengo Park)** – Built in 1965, on the 400th anniversary of Rio's founding, this bustling park has children's areas with playgrounds, a puppet theater, soccer fields, volleyball and basketball courts. A small tractor-pulled train takes you from place to place. Also in Flamengo Park are the *Museum of Modern Art,* the *National War Memorial,* and the *Military Museum.* The park stretches along Flamengo's shore.

**Paço Imperial (Imperial Palace)** – Housed in a 250-year-old former customs house, later converted into the emperor's administrative offices, this building was completely restored in 1985 and today is Rio's finest museum. Its exhibits change continuously. There are chamber music concerts in the afternoons. Open daily, except Mondays from 11 AM to 6:30 PM. Admission charge. Praça XV de Novembro (phone: 232-8333).

**Monumento dos Mortos da II Guerra (National War Memorial)** – Two 150-foot pillars supporting a curved bowl with an eternal flame mark the war memorial. Three statues of servicemen, one from each branch of the military, guard this flame and the crypt beneath it. Inside is the Tomb of the Unknown Soldier and the remains of Brazilian soldiers killed during World War II, in which Brazil fought with the Allies. These soldiers were killed and buried in Italy until reinterred here. Crypt open daily, except Mondays, from 10 AM to 5 PM. No admission charge. Flamengo Park, Flamengo (phone: 240-1283).

**Museu Militar do Monumento (Military Museum and Memorial)** – Near the memorial stands a small military museum with memorabilia from World War II, including touching photographs, captured weapons, and murals. Open daily, except Mondays, from 10 AM to 5 PM. Admission charge. Near the *Museum of Modern Art* in Flamengo Park, Flamengo (phone: 240-1283).

**Museu da República (Museum of the Republic)** – This historical museum is in the Catete Palace, which was designed by a German architect and built between 1858 and 1866. In its checkered career it has served as a bank and hotel before it became the home of Brazil's presidents for 63 years. In 1960, when Brasília became the capital, Catete Palace became a museum. The inlaid wood mosaic floors are so highly polished you can see your reflection in them. One room is the bedroom of former President Getúlio Vargas, who committed suicide here on August 24, 1954, while still in office; another, a huge banquet hall; a third, the former game room. The palace grounds are stunning. The garden has a series of royal palm trees, some as tall as 150 feet. Open daily, except Mondays, from noon to 5 PM. 153 Rua do Catete, Palácio (phone: 225-4302).

## BEACH COMMUNITIES

With countless beaches at your disposal, you can visit a different one each day. Each has a distinct atmosphere and rhythm. Closest to downtown are Flamengo and Botafogo. The calm waters of Guanabara Bay have been cleaned up and swimming is once again a pleasant experience. Farther south are Leme, Copacabana, Ipanema, Leblon, São Conrado, and Barra da Tijuca, where you will be swimming in the Atlantic Ocean. It is best to swim in the morning and use your afternoons and early evenings to visit Rio's other "must-see" attractions. Leave all valuables in your hotel when you come to the beach. Brazil's crime rate increases dramatically during the tourist-filled summer months (December to March), and though the city police have set up beach patrols to protect tourists, it's just asking for trouble to take cameras, watches, passports, and more than pocket money to the beach.

**Copacabana** – The heart of Rio's resort area, this community actually combines Leme and Copacabana beaches. The beach area is the longest and widest in the city. This is where the action is on sunny weekends all year. Avenida Atlântica, the wide, mosaic-tiled beachfront street, is lined with many fine hotels, excellent restaurants, sidewalk cafés, and elegant shops as well as fashionable apartment buildings. The area's major street however, Avenida Nossa Senhora da Copacabana, is a block back from the beach. Here you will find somewhat less expensive (but nonetheless chic) hotels, shops, cinemas, and art galleries. It is always crowded with people. Barata Ribeiro, 2 blocks from the beach, is a tree-lined street with take-out food stalls, antiques shops, and private homes. At some points, Copacabana is only 4 blocks wide due to an encroaching mountain range.

**Ipanema** – The crown princess of beach areas is chic Ipanema. Slightly narrower and less crowded than Copacabana, it draws young bongo players, singles, college students, and upper class *cariocas* with homes nearby. Avenida Vieira Souto, the beachfront street, has some good hotels and restaurants but is primarily residential. Rua Visconde de Pirajá, 2 blocks from the beach, is the chicest shopping area of the city. The 5-block stretch from Praça General Osório to Praça Nossa Senhora de Paz is lined with zany boutiques, shopping arcades, and small restaurants. Check out this area before buying anything, especially clothing. The *Feirarte* (see *Special Places*, above) is held in Praça General Osório every Sunday at 9 AM. Rua Maria Quitéria is an important cross street of boutiques, nightspots, and restaurants.

**Leblon** – Avenida Delfim Moreira, the oceanfront street, is lined with duplex and triplex apartment buildings in which many of Rio's wealthiest families live. Leblon is no longer the quietest of Rio's beaches, since several restaurants have opened on Avenida Ataulfo de Paiva, 2 blocks from the beach.

**São Conrado** – Until 20 years ago, São Conrado had a lovely beach, a golf club, and wide open spaces. Then the *Sheraton Rio, Inter-Continental,* and *Nacional Rio* hotels went up. Soon apartment complexes, a shopping mall, restaurants, nightspots, schools, and supermarkets were built, and a new area of the city was developed. Avenida Niemeyer, which runs along the beach, is easily accessible by buses that run frequently from Copacabana. You can use the tennis facilities, nightclubs, and excellent restaurants at these three hotels (see *Checking In*).

**Barra da Tijuca** – Rio continues to expand in a southerly direction, and Barra is the newest area undergoing rapid growth. The city fathers are making a concerted effort to develop this area in a controlled manner to avoid overcrowding. New residential complexes under construction already are changing the Barra skyline, and hotels also are on the increase here. Barra's beach is very long and very narrow, and camping is permitted at official camp sites. Several unimposing restaurants serving seafood are right off the beach. Although Barra is accessible by bus, sporadic bus crimes in the area — holdups and even murder — makes this a dangerous choice of transportation. Take a taxi.

## BEYOND THE BUSINESS CENTER

**Santa Teresa** – A visit to this picturesque area of the city, high up on a hill, offers some idea of what Rio de Janeiro was like in colonial times. The narrow, winding streets are lined with lovely old buildings and homes, very different from the modern glass structures found downtown and on the beaches. The delightful tree-lined streets contain excellent examples of 19th-century architecture. You get a bonus when visiting this area: a chance to ride one of Rio's last trolleys, which departs for Santa Teresa from Avenida República do Chile downtown. Take off watches and hold on tightly to bags because thieves spot tourists easily and strike quickly, jumping off the moving trolley with their loot.

**Chácara do Céu** – This museum, whose name means "small farm of heaven," occupies a lovely old mansion. Its major emphasis is on modern and Impressionistic works by Brazilian artists, although it exhibits Picassos, Monets, and Modiglianis from time to time, and some metal sculptures as well. The rooms of the mansion are elegantly appointed; the grounds, impeccably groomed; and the views of Botafogo from the rear garden, striking. After you take bus 433 or 464 from Copacabana to Avenida Chile and hop on the trolley, ask to be dropped at the museum (Largo do Corvelo stop). Open Tuesdays through Saturdays from 2 to 5 PM, Sundays from 1 to 5 PM. Admission charge. 93 Rua Murtinho Nobre, Santa Teresa (phone: 232-1386).

**Museu Nacional (National Museum)** – Set in a huge park, this museum, formerly the residence of Brazil's emperors, focuses on archaeology, anthropology, and the natural sciences, with exhibits like that of the Bendego meteorite, one of the largest ever found on earth. Particularly interesting are the displays of Amazon Indian tribes' weapons, clothing, and tools. Brazil's Amazon region has an astonishing variety of butterflies and birds, which also are on display. Open daily, except Mondays, from 10 AM to 4:30 PM. Admission charge. Quinta da Boa Vista, São Cristóvão (phone: 264-8262).

**Jardim Zoológico (Zoological Garden)** – The zoo occupies part of the Quinta da Boa Vista and has the usual assortment of tigers, lions, and gorillas as well as several rarer species, especially in its bird and reptile collections. It's worth a look, particularly if you visit the nearby *National Museum*. Open daily, except Mondays, from 9 AM to 4:30 PM. Admission charge. Quinta da Boa Vista, São Cristóvão (phone: 254-2024).

**Jardim Botânico (Botanical Gardens)** – A serene oasis in the middle of this big city where huge water lilies float in still ponds and you can find over 5,000 varieties of tropical plants, cacti, orchids, and banana plants. The paths are delineated by towering royal palm trees, and the aroma of the flowers is almost overpowering. On the grounds, the *Kuhlmann Botanical Museum* (phone: 274-8246) has exhibits describing the types of vegetation found in different areas of Brazil. It also houses a part of the *palma mater,* an original palm planted in 1808, when the gardens opened, by Portuguese King Dom João VI. The palm was struck by lightning in 1973 and had to be cut down. Open daily, except Mondays, 8 AM to 5 PM. No admission charge. 920 Rua Jardim Botânico, immediately inland from Lagao Rodrigo de Freitas; car entrance at 1008 Rua Jardim Botânico (phone: 274-8246).

**Planetario (Planetarium)** – This stop is worthwhile primarily to see the different constellations in the southern sky, of which the Cruzeiro do Sul (Southern Cross) is the best known. Open weekends only, with children's shows at 5 PM Saturdays and Sundays, and 6:30 PM Sundays; for adults, the show starts at 6:30 PM Saturdays. Admission charge. Take bus 591 or 592 from from Copacabana or Botafogo. 240 Rua Padre Leonel Franca, Gávea (phone: 274-0096).

**Tivoli Amusement Park** – More like an American amusement park than its namesake in Copenhagen, *Tivoli* has a hair-raising assortment of rides for adults and children. On the lagoon, there are some snack shops and fast-food counters. Fun to visit. Open daily, except Mondays, from 3 until 10 PM. Hours vary on holidays and during summer school vacation (January and February). Admission charge; rides extra. Lagoa, near the *Jockey Club.*

■ **EXTRA SPECIAL:** If you want to get away from Rio's crowded beaches without leaving the shore, head east on Route 101 and continue past the town of Niterói, with its 8-mile bridge. Niterói's beaches — Saco de São Francisco, Adão e Eva, and Icaraí — are popular weekend spots for *cariocas.* Historic sites include the 16th-century forts of Santa Cruz and Barão do Rio Branco. Continue east along the coast to Saquarema, a town with a boating and fishing lake as well as spectacular beaches. For a super view of the town, climb to the 17th-century Church of Senhora de Nazaré. Cabo Frio, 100 miles (160 km) from Rio de Janeiro, at the easternmost tip of this stretch of shore appropriately named the Sun Coast (Costa do Sol), is one of the most popular resort areas in the state of Rio. About 14 miles (22 km) to the east, Armacão dos Búzios, known locally as Búzios, is the hideway of wealthy *cariocas,* jet-set millionaires, and visiting celebrities. Its beaches — Brava, João Fernandes, Ossos, Tamoios, and Rasa — are justifiably famed. The most luxurious of the local hotels, called *pousadas,* is *Nas Rocas Club,* a 70-room property built into a rocky promontory overlooking the ocean. It offers everything from jogging and windsurfing to a sophisticated disco and heliport (phone: 253-0001 in Rio de Janeiro). Just outside of town, on Praia Bahia Formosa, is *Auberge de l'Hermitage,* another excellent *pousada* (phone: 246-231103). If you're looking for clean, modest accommodations, try *Estalagem Repouso do Lobisomem* (on the main drag in town, Rua José Bento Ribeiro Dantas; phone: 246-231181). Although at the last count Búzios boasted more than 40 *pousadas,* reservations are necessary on holiday weekends during the summer months. Every travel agency in Rio de Janeiro has its "pet" *pousada* and if you don't want to drive, it also will arrange for transportation — be it by car, bus, or even by plane (Búzios has its own airstrip). For eating, the best options are *Le Streghe* (no phone) and *Au Cheval Blanc* (phone: 246-231445; both on Rua José Bento Ribeiro Dantas). There also are many jazz clubs, music bars, and discos hopping from early at night to the wee hours.

Or go southwest from Rio on the Rio–Santos Highway (BR-101) to discover hotels well-loved by Brazilians along what is known as the Costa Verde — Green

Coast. Their favorites include the *Portogalo* (high on a hill overlooking Ilha Grande Bay; phone: 243-651022; 267-7375 in Rio de Janeiro); the *Hotel do Frade* (on its own beach on Angra Bay; phone: 243-651212; 511-5394 in Rio); the *Porto Bello* (located in Mangaratiba; phone: 243-789-1485; 267-7375 in Rio); and the *Porto Pousada Parati*, a restored colonial inn in the historic landmark town of Paratí (phone: 243-711205; 267-7375 in Rio). The first three are expensive and offer all the best of the sea; the fourth is moderately priced and one of several *pousadas* in this dream town. The *carioca* elite have their summer homes on the Archipelago of Angra dos Reis, which is dotted with hundreds of islands.

Day-long boat excursions to tropical islands near Rio are a relaxing and convenient way of enriching a visit to the city. Air conditioned buses pick up passengers at major hotels and take them to a yacht. The itinerary varies, but stops usually include the islands of Itacuruça and Jaguanum. Swimming on unspoiled beaches, nature walks in tropical forests, an all-you-can-eat buffet lunch at an island restaurant, and snacks and occasionally live music on board — all are included in the $50 fare. Book through travel agents, most hotels, or directly through *Rio Sightseeing*, 48 Av. Prado Junior, Loga 19, Copacabana (phone: 542-1393 or 541-5696).

Farthest down the Costa Verde, 3 hours by car from Rio, is Parati, a colonial, cobbled port that has preserved all its 17th-century charm. Artists, writers, and actors retire here, and many have opened restaurants, bars, and inns. A great place to spend *Carnaval*, Parati is where much of *Gabriela*, the Brazilian film based on the novel by Jorge Amado and starring Sonia Braga and Marcello Mastroianni, was shot (see also "The Costa Verde," in Brazil, DIRECTIONS).

# SOURCES AND RESOURCES

**TOURIST INFORMATION:** The Rio de Janeiro Tourism Office, (RIOTUR; 10 Rua da Assembléia, Room 814) has a phone service (242-8000) that will provide information such as the hours for museums, churches, and stores, as well as assistance in finding hotels and restaurants. A visit to their office will help with more detailed questions. Some of the staff speak English.

*The Insider's Guide to Rio de Janeiro*, by the British journalist Christopher Pickard, who has lived in Rio for many years, offers a detailed rundown of the city and its goings-on as well as good maps; the book is sold in hotel bookstores in Rio, as well as in a few bookstores in the US, for about $10. *H. Stern* jewelers (see *Special Places*) produces a simple map of Rio's main tourist areas that is available free at most hotels. *Guia Quatro Rodas*, which offers a map of Rio in Portuguese, is available at newsstands and hotel bookstores.

The US Consulate is at 147 Av. Presidente Wilson (phone: 292-7117).

**Local Coverage** – Many hotels carry the free bilingual monthly, *Este Mês em Rio/Rio This Month*, which lists events and other information. The Portuguese-language weekly news magazine, *Veja*, appears Mondays on Rio's newsstands with a Rio supplement. *This Week in Rio* and *Tourist Calendar Rio* are provided (free) by many hotels. The Brazilian Tourism Foundation (Funtur; 10/1212 Rua Da Assembléia; phone: 252-9296) has English-speaking staff members and provides information not only about Rio, but all of Brazil. *Time* and *Newsweek* magazines arrive on Wednesdays. *USA Today*, the *Miami Herald*, and the *International Herald Tribune* arrive daily and are available shortly after midday at major newsstands and hotel bookstores. Most major hotels offer CNN (Cable News Network).

**TELEPHONE:** Once a disaster, the telephone system in Rio de Janeiro is gradually improving; but telephone numbers change frequently, and chances are you will reach as many wrong numbers as correct ones. Phone booths are found on most street corners; use a *ficha*, or token, which you can buy at newsstands.

The city code for Rio de Janeiro is 21. When calling from within Brazil, dial 021 before the local number. The country code for Brazil is 55.

**CLIMATE AND CLOTHES:** Roughly on the same latitude as Puerto Rico but south of the equator, Rio de Janeiro has a tropical climate. Spring and summer, between October and March, have average temperatures of between 85 and 95F (between 29 and 35C). It does get much hotter, and it is sometimes very humid. Evenings are usually cool, with breezes sweeping in from the bay and ocean. Heavy rains start and stop quickly and frequently during the summer. Fall and winter, between April and October, are cooler, with temperatures falling into the low 70s F (around 22C) and occasionally as low as the 60s F (around 16C). In winter, it is less humid and rains less often. You can swim and sunbathe all year, although *cariocas* really do not consider October warm enough for the beach.

*Cariocas* have a flair for fashion and are well dressed. As in most tropical climates, informality is the key (even in the more expensive restaurants), but you will not feel out of place if you dress up. People feel free to dress to suit their mood, much as they do in New York. Bring comfortable, lightweight, colorful clothing. Most hotels have laundry service, but wash-and-wear clothing will prove much less expensive. Bring comfortable walking shoes for sightseeing.

**GETTING AROUND: Bus** – Plentiful and the least expensive mode of transportation, buses are always crowded and sometimes air conditioned. Buses go from all parts of the city to outlying beaches and parks. Be aware of pickpockets, and avoid riding buses to outlying areas. Bus stops are marked "Onibus"; passengers board through the rear door. The *Alvorada* bus line links the Galeão International Airport with hotels in the downtown beach areas.

**Taxi** – Ubiquitous and, except for peak hours, easy to hail. Most are VW beetles with the front passenger seat removed and meters installed. As a result of rampant inflation, taxi meters now display a number corresponding to a fare on an official list, rather than the amount in *cruzieros;* the list is updated monthly. There is a 20% surcharge (the driver raises the "#2" flag on the meter) from 10 PM to 6 AM daily, and all day Sundays and holidays, and for trips outside city limits. Rio cab drivers make breaking wild horses seem like a tame ride. Sit back and hang on. Yellow cabs are the least expensive (although their drivers usually don't speak English), but radio taxis are more reputable. Two reliable companies at the airport are *Cootramo* (phone: 270-1442) and *Transcoopass* (phone: 270-4888); passengers prepay at the airport. *Radio Taxi* (phone: 260-2022) goes by the meter and is considerably cheaper than the others.

**Car Rental** – You can rent a car from *Hertz* (334-B Av. Princesa Isabel, Copacabana; phone: 275-4996, and at Galeão Airport; phone: 398-3162); and *Avis* (150-A Av. Princesa Isabel, Copacabana; phone: 542-4249, and at the airport; phone: 398-3083). Rates start at $20 a day plus mileage for a Volkswagen. Larger cars are more expensive. Gasoline prices are in a constant state of flux — at press time, a gallon cost about $2.50.

**Trolley** – Rio has a few trolley lines that are fun to ride. The most interesting is from Avenida Chile to the Santa Teresa section (see *Special Places,* above), but be sure to take the necessary precautions to avoid theft — keep watches and jewelry out of sight and hold onto your bags with a tight grip.

**SPECIAL EVENTS:** *Carnaval,* Rio-style, is the granddaddy of all special events and the standard by which all others are measured. If you've ever been to *Mardi Gras* in New Orleans or other pre-*Lenten* celebrations in the Caribbean, multiply the excitement by 1,000 and you'll just be coming close to what happens here! It's as if the outside world fades away and nothing exists except the samba beat and the will to be part of unrestrained joy. People who've never danced before find themselves caught up in the tremendous outpouring of rhythm and gaiety. *Carnaval* officially takes place on the 5 days that precede *Ash Wednesday,* but the *Carnaval* spirit starts early in November, when preparations go into high gear at social clubs all over Rio. These clubs each sponsor a samba school — a huge group of singers, dancers, and musicians that will strut through the *Sambódromo* downtown on Sunday and Monday of *Carnaval* in frenzied competition with other outstanding clubs. Club members painstakingly create original lyrics, samba music, dance steps, and fantastic costumes around a theme chosen by each individual school. Each club has fans and admirers in the more than 200,000 onlookers sitting in bleacher seats along the street or standing on the sidewalks. They sing, clap, cheer, stamp their feet, whistle, and dance along with their favorites. You, too, will become involved very quickly. The refrains are repeated frequently, and since a school can have between 2,000 and 4,000 marchers, it can take an hour for a group to pass. The parades begin at 6 PM Sunday and Monday and may continue (with waits of up to an hour between groups) until noon the following day. The entire city is decorated with colored lights and streamers. Bandstands are erected on street corners to allow dancing in the streets. On those corners without bandstands, impromptu combos play. People in very skimpy costumes dance gaily through the streets on all 5 nights of *Carnaval.* Everywhere — from on the buses to on the beaches — samba is king. Business comes to a halt for the duration of the frenetic holiday in which *cariocas* welcome the world to participate with them.

Another exotic aspect of *Carnaval* are the fabulous balls held at the *Scala* nightclub and major club ballrooms. A few of the best are the *Vermelho e Preto* ball at the *Scala;* the *Yacht Club Ball,* a week before *Carnaval;* and *Baile de Pão de Açúcar* at Sugar Loaf. Wealthy and socially prominent *cariocas* attend in formal attire or fantastic costumes. Elaborate silk gowns, gem-encrusted tiaras, and even powdered wigs make this an incredible sight. If you plan to attend a ball, formal attire or a costume is suggested, although Brazilian ball-goers often dress informally: Men wear anything from T-shirts and gym shorts to caftans; women tend to be more festive, with feathers and plenty of glitter. In any event, dress coolly — the balls are crowded and hot. Since ball tickets can run $50 and up, you may prefer to spend the night club hopping. Many clubs have all-night samba shows in which the audience participates. On Tuesday night, the street dancing winds down, and when dawn breaks on *Ash Wednesday,* the city is strangely quiet. Another *Carnaval* is nearly history except that the group winners will be back at the *Sambódromo* the following Saturday night for the winners' parade.

*Cariocas* in exile can get accustomed to living without beaches, warm weather, and *feijoada,* but they cannot survive without celebrating *Carnaval.* The Brazilian communities in the US and Canada often flock to the Grand Ballroom of the *Waldorf-Astoria* in New York for a wild evening of samba schools, costume contests, and a leading *Carnaval* band imported from Rio de Janeiro. In fact, the pageantry of the northern *Carnaval* has become an attraction in its own right, with some *cariocas* traveling from Brazil to participate. ("After all," they claim, "we've seen *Carnaval* in Rio for so many years.")

If you are going to be in Rio any time between November and *Carnaval,* you should visit a samba school rehearsal for an inkling of what the main event is like. Samba schools are really social clubs; they can be found throughout Rio and are especially common in low-income areas and *favelas.* There are a great many of them and they are ranked. The top 14 clubs take part in the major *Carnaval* parade, while those with lower ranks dance in other parts of the city. Every August, each school chooses its own theme. The goal is to be judged best on *Carnaval* night. Winning means money for the club and, occasionally, fame for the top performers. Starting in November, rehearsals are well organized enough to permit visitors. While the costumes are not completed, the music, lyrics, and enthusiasm of the several hundred participants are contagious, and you'll soon be moving to the samba beat yourself. Many of these clubs have been taking part in *Carnavals* for over 100 years and are rich in tradition. The practice halls are far from Copacabana, unfortunately, but some can be reached in 30 minutes by car. *Mangueira,* one of the oldest clubs and winner of four recent *Carnavals,* practices Friday, Saturday, and Sunday nights from around 10 PM at the *Palácio do Samba* (1082 Rua Visconde de Niterói, Mangueira; phone: 234-4129). *Beija-Flor,* also a frequent prizewinner, has rehearsals on Friday, Saturday, and Sunday nights at 11 PM at *Quadra de Nilópolis* (1652 Rua Pracinha Wallace Paes Leme, Nilópolis; phone: 791-1353). *Salgueiro* rehearses Saturdays at 10 PM (104 Rua Silva Teles, Andaraí; phone: 238-5564). In addition, *Beija-Flor* and *Portela* samba schools hold rehearsals in Botafogo, which is more convenient for tourists to attend. Check your hotel for schedules.

*Macumba* is the ritual practiced by some 10 million Brazilians. Loosely related to voodoo and based on African and Indian rituals, *macumba* draws most of its followers from descendants of African slaves but has adherents in all levels of society. *Macumbeiros* believe that spirits affect all aspects of our lives, both good and evil. Alternately known as *candomblé, macumba* rituals allay the evil spirits and encourage good ones. A medium (called *cavalo,* meaning "horse") is used to call on the spirits to assist individuals in need. When the slaves tried to practice their own faith, slave owners and the Catholic church suppressed it, forcing the slaves to conduct secret ceremonies in the forests and on the beaches. To appear more orthodox, many *macumba* gods and goddesses were renamed with Christian biblical names. Over the years, African ritual intermingled with the Indian traditions, so *macumba* as practiced today is not akin to any African religion but to other regional religions such as voodoo. You can attend a *macumba* rite in houses of worship called *terreiros.* Outside each *terreiro* is a small house where the mischievous spirit (Exu) is held captive. Lighted candles placed outside the house are designed to keep Exu imprisoned during the ceremony. The *terreiro* itself is usually a large room dimly lit by candles. An altar in the center holds a crucifix as well as statuettes of Oxalá (the major god, comparable to Jesus), Iemanjá (the goddess of the sea, comparable to the Virgin Mary), and other figures. The ceremony opens with singing, interrupted by the white-robed *cavalos.* They grunt, grimace, and roll on the ground, speaking in strange tongues. By observing this business, adherents can tell which spirit has possessed the *cavalo.* As the *cavalos* position themselves around the *terreiro,* worshipers queue up to speak to the spirit guide from whom they need assistance. A cleansing ritual, chanting, and some herbal medicines are involved. The ceremony goes on for hours. *Pai Jerônimo* (423 Rua Barão de Uba, Praça da Bandeira, Zona Norte), a 20-minute cab ride from Copacabana, is a *terreiro* that permits visitors at its 10 PM ceremony. Wear white (no shorts), sit quietly, and don't cross your arms or legs, as this is believed to interfere with the arriving spirits. Leave your camera in the hotel — no photographs are allowed.

Other *terreiros* that permit visitors are *Tenda Espírita Mirim* (597 Av. Marechal Rondon, São Francisco Xavier) on Wednesday and Friday evenings at 8 PM, and *Yansa Egum Nitã* (152 Estrada de Santa Ifigenia, Jacarepaguá; phone: 342-2176) on Saturday evenings at 10 PM.

The *Festa de Iemanjá,* a major and highly visible *macumba* festival, occurs on December 31, when millions of *macumbeiros* come to Rio's beaches, starting at sunset and continuing until dawn. Lace cloths are spread along the tide line, and offerings of fruits, perfumes, colorful ribbons, and flowers are laid on them by the worshipers. Drums keep up a hypnotic beat as frenzied dancing begins. Candles placed on small mounds of sand flicker eerily. At midnight Iemanjá, goddess of the sea, sends a huge wave that either accepts (carries out to sea) or rejects the offering. The dancing and rituals go on until dawn. If you face Copacabana Beach, you have the best "seat." Also at midnight, spectacular fireworks explode over Copacabana Beach and from atop the *Meridien* hotel.

**MUSEUMS:** *The Imperial Palace,* the *Military Museum,* the *Museum of the Republic,* the *National Museum of Fine Arts, Chácara do Céu,* the *National Museum,* and the *Kuhlmann Botanical Museum* (Botanical Gardens) are described in *Special Places.* Other museums of special interest include the following:

**Museu Carmen Miranda (Carmen Miranda Museum)** – Filled with photographs from the motion pictures of the popular star of the 1940s. Her famous fruit-filled turbans and extraordinarily high platform sandals are on exhibit along with costumes and jewelry. Open Tuesdays through Fridays from 11 AM to 5 PM, Saturdays and Sundays from 1 to 5 PM. No admission charge. 560 Av. Rui Barbosa, Flamengo Park, Flamengo (phone: 551-2597).

**Museu do Indio (Indian Museum)** – Articles and scenes of contemporary Indian life in Brazil's Amazon region. Ceramics, utensils carved of jatoba wood, clay dolls, baskets, and religious articles still used by these primitive tribes are on display. Open Mondays through Fridays from 11:30 AM to 5 PM. 55 Rua das Palmeiras, Botafogo (phone: 286-8799).

**Museu de Farmácia (Pharmacy Museum)** – Contains old pharmaceutical equipment, apothecary jars, containers, scales, and an antique music box that plays eight different tunes. Open Mondays through Fridays from 8 AM to noon and 1 to 5 PM. 206 Rua Santa Lúzia, Centro (phone: 297-6611).

**SHOPPING:** Brazil is the world's leading exporter of gems, and they are easily the best buy here. Often referred to as semi-precious stones, they have become increasingly popular in recent years with both men and women. High-quality gems are set in 18-karat gold; less expensive ones, in silver. Designs are innovative and trendy. Bracelets, pendants, earrings, and rings in a multitude of colors sparkle in the windows of elegant shops. The most popular stones used in fine jewelry are aquamarine, in various shades of blue; tourmaline, of which the green are most popular; purple amethyst; and gold-yellow or brown topaz. Stones are classified by color as well as by size and degree of perfection. Turquoise, cat's-eye opal, and lapis lazuli are the gemstones most often set in popular silver costume jewelry.

Brazil's rich folk traditions are expressed in primitive paintings, woven wall tapestries, batiks, woodcarvings, and masks. These colorful items are not yet well-known in the US and make interesting home decorations. Other good buys are salad bowl sets, ashtrays, bookends, and serving platters made of Brazilian rosewood (jacaranda). Paperweights of chunks of rock with low-grade stones embedded in them are good gift items. Bikinis and *tangas* (micro-bikinis), T-shirts, leather shoes, and handbags are also highly prized Rio catches. The prices of these items are comparable to US prices, but the quality is good and the styles are Brazilian. No one should leave Rio without a *figa,* the Brazilian good luck charm — a clenched fist with a raised thumb. They come in any number of colored stones, carved in wood and even gold and silver, and make inexpensive, yet thoughtful, uniquely Brazilian gifts.

Boutiques and shops are scattered throughout downtown and the beach areas. However, three clusters of shops give you an easy way to browse and compare. The finest boutiques for clothing and accessories are on Rua Visconde de Pirajá, the main street of Ipanema, and its side streets. Small shopping arcades jut off the main street as well. Avenida Copacabana, 1 block from the beach, is the major shopping area of Copacabana, with native crafts stores, art galleries, and costume jewelry shops. The area near the old *Copacabana Palace* is thronged with shoppers in search of folklore items, jacaranda wood, and Indian artifacts (see *Special Places*). Prices here are slightly lower than in the other streets mentioned.

Stores open at 9 AM and usually stay open until 6 or 7 PM. Most are open on Saturdays until 1 PM. Rio's popular shopping malls are open Monday through Saturday from 10 AM until 10 PM. What follows is a list of leading shops and shopping malls. Undoubtedly, you will discover more as you browse.

**Amsterdam Sauer** – Specializes in pink topaz and emerald stones. 484 Rua Visconde de Pirajá, Ipanema (phone: 239-8999). Other branches throughout the city.

**Aquarela do Brasil** – Great for hand-embroidered items, including tablecloths, dish towels, and nightgowns. Top-quality work using traditional Portuguese and Italian methods. 206 Rua Henrique Oswaldo, Copacabana (phone: 235-5626).

**Barra Shopping** – Latin America's largest, and some consider most complete, shopping mall. There are hundreds of stores and boutiques here as well as representatives of the large Brazilian department stores, such as *Sears & Mesbla*. The mall also is one of Rio's main entertainment centers with movie houses, theaters, restaurants, and even an ice rink. In high season, the mall provides free bus service from the major hotels. Barra da Tijuca (phone: 325-5611).

**Copacabana Couros e Artesanatos** – A variety of leather items: Lamp shades, folding chairs, beanbag chairs, desk sets, briefcases, and footrests are the best sellers. Belts, wallets, and handbags are close behind. Everything is made on the premises. 45A Rua Fernando Mendes, Copacabana (phone: 257-3697).

**Feirarte** – Formerly the "Hippie Market," this is held every Sunday from 9 AM to 6 PM; it's as much an institution as Corcovado Mountain. Original oil paintings in modern and primitive styles, hand-tooled leather belts, handbags, sandals, wallets, carved wood statues, bowls, gaily painted ceramic planters, wooden boxes of all sizes, kitchen utensils, handmade aprons, and pot holders are all yours for the bargaining (see *Special Places*, above). Praça General Osório, Ipanema, near the subway station.

**Feira de São Sebastião** – A smaller version of *Feirarte*, it's held in one of Rio's most historical sections, downtown. Although you can get handicrafts of metal, leather, and straw, it is best known for its large selection of antiques, coins, and stamps. Open Thursdays and Fridays from 8 AM to 6 PM. Praça XV de Novembro.

**Folklore** – Costume jewelry and folklore items are sold together in this shop, owned by *H. Stern* jewelers. A lot of merchandise is crammed into a small space: *figas*, charms, and Indian artifacts, along with silver jewelry set with opal, cat's eye, and agate. If you are looking for a great gift for a young child, consider a set of small, polished gemstones sold with the raw material from which they came. It is also a good place to find eye-catching palm bark wall masks and papagallo kites. *Folklore* has branches throughout Rio in the major hotels — *Inter-Continental, Nacional, Sheraton Rio, Méridien, Rio-Palace,* and *Atlântica-Suite,* as well as at the airport and *H. Stern* in Ipanema (see below).

**Fórum de Ipanema** – A modern arcade of small boutiques that specializes in sportswear, bikinis, even briefer *tangas*, and T-shirts. Creative store windows depict the latest trends. 351 Rua Visconde de Pirajá, in front of the Praça Nossa Senhora da Paz, Ipanema.

**Northeastern Fair** – Those who can't get to the northeast of Brazil should stop in for a taste of its regional food (typical cheeses and *carne-de-sol*, sun-dried beef with beans), its music (an interesting combination of accordion, triangle, and drum — live), and its flea market mania (hammocks and leather goods proliferate). Homesick Northeasterners come here religiously. Open Sundays from 6 AM to 1 PM. Campo de São Cristóvão.

**Rio Design Center** – This ultramodern shopping center fills 3 floors with Rio's chic home (and office) furnishings stores. It also has a variety of art galleries and restaurants and is a good place to browse when it rains. 270 Av. Ataulfo de Paiva, Leblon (phone: 274-7893).

***Rio-Sul*** – After *Barra Shopping*, this is the city's largest mall and the most popular with visitors because of its easy access from both Copacabana and Ipanema. There are hundreds of air conditioned stores including *Mesbla, C & A, Lojas Americanas*, and a number of snack bars and restaurants under one roof. The *Rio-Sul* tower is now a Rio landmark and every taxi driver knows exactly where it is. 116 Av. Lauro Muller, Botafogo (phone: 295-3444).

***São Conrado Fashion Mall*** – Close to the *Inter-Continental Rio* and *Nacional Rio* hotels, this shopping mall offers an eclectic cross section of stores that includes fashion as well as gifts and books. Also present are a number of excellent restaurants, snack bars, and four movie theaters. Auto Estrada Lagoa-Barra, São Conrado (phone: 322-0300).

***Sidi*** – Carries items such as salad bowls and trays made of jacaranda, as well as souvenir items, including gemstones. Two locations: 1536-A Av. Atlântica (phone: 541-1998) and at *Shopping Cassino Atlântica*, 4240 Av. Atlântica, Copacabana (phone: 287-2444).

***H. Stern*** – Brazil's largest gemstone retailer, and the first stop if you are interested in buying jewelry. The classy main showroom, staffed by multilingual personnel, contains private viewing areas where tray upon tray of bracelets, rings, pins, or whatever your heart and wallet desire is presented for your appraisal. Their jewelry has extremely contemporary as well as traditional settings. There is no hard sell, but the gems are hard to resist. Prices start at $50 and go way up. Gems are set in 18-karat yellow gold, white gold, or platinum. You are issued a written guarantee, and your jewelry can be returned to any *H. Stern* outlet within 1 year of purchase. Since there are more than 100 shops worldwide, including one in New York, it is easy to have repairs done or stones matched. *H. Stern* maintains shops and service desks in virtually every hotel in Rio, but the main showroom is at 113 Rua Garcia D'Avila, Ipanema (phone: 259-7442). If you are not interested in buying gems, at least take the free workshop tour (see *Special Places*, above).

***Zuhause*** – For more unusual local crafts, as well as interesting dehydrated plants. Two shops in Copacabana: 303-A and 458 Rua Barata Ribeiro (both locations, phone: 256-9624).

**SPORTS:** Soccer, or *futebol*, is the major athletic passion in Rio. On every beach, soccer goalposts are in continuous use. In parks, plazas, and on quiet neighborhood streets, young boys are playing soccer, often still using a ball worn out by their brothers before them.

**Bicycling** – Bicycles can be rented on Paquetá Island (see *Special Places*, above). Avoid biking in Rio, where traffic is heavy.

**Fishing** – Marlin, bass, shark, and codfish are among Atlantic catches. Make arrangements with *Captain's Yacht Charters* (at the *Glória Marina;* phone: 252-2227)), where crewed boats and tackle can be rented starting from about $100 a day. Others to try are *Ponto Mar* (phone: 266-6066), *Glória Marina* (phone: 265-0797), or *Brasiltrek Expeditions* (phone: 779-1726) which offers fishing packages as well as diving and trekking vacations.

**Golf** – Most golf courses in Rio are part of private clubs and closed to non-members, except during the week. Rio's two golf courses within the city are the *Gávea Golf Club* (next to the *Inter-Continental* hotel; 800 Estrada da Gávea, São Conrado; phone: 322-4141) and the *Itanhanga Golf & Country Club* (Barra da Tijuca; phone: 399-0507). Visitors can play 18 holes on these lovely courses for about $50 in greens fees plus $5 for a caddy. Clubs may be rented and the better hotels will reserve tee times, although by world standards, Rio's golf courses are remarkably empty.

**Sailing** – The two big annual sailing regattas are from Rio de Janeiro to Buenos Aires in February, and from Rio to Santos in November. For information, contact the yacht club: *Iate Club do Rio de Janeiro*, 333 Av. Pasteur (phone: 295-7395).

**Soccer** – Brazil has an illustrious name in soccer lore, having won the *World Cup* three times. This enabled it to keep the trophy in the country. The culmination of hard-fought matches played all over the world during a 2-year span, the cup is awarded every 4 years. The site of the championship competition changes each time. Brazil has many outstanding players. Some play on professional teams in Brazil; others, in foreign countries. Pelé, the man acclaimed as the greatest soccer player ever, hails from Santos, Brazil. The world's best-known and then-highest-paid athlete (now retired), Pelé led Brazil to victory in three *World Cup* finals. He also played for the *New York Cosmos,* leading them to their league championship and helping to popularize soccer in the US. The pro soccer clubs of Rio and visiting national and international teams play matches at *Estádio Maracanã* (Stadium; São Cristovão; phone: 264-9962). Its 6 tiers hold 200,000 spectators, making it the largest stadium in the world. The team's aficionados wave banners, stamp their feet, hoot at the referees, and cheer their team. This is an exciting introduction to high-level soccer. Matches are held Wednesday and Saturday evenings at 9 PM and Sundays at 5 PM. Amateur but highly skilled players compete in league games at Parque do Flamengo on weekends.

**Swimming and Surfing** – Take your pick of ocean beaches, but remember that the Atlantic Ocean waves pound the shore in the afternoon. That's good for surfing, and you'll see any number of surfers along Ipanema Beach and at Praia do Pepino at São Conrado. If you are a serious swimmer who prefers to swim laps in calm water, you will do better at one of the large hotels' swimming pools. Most of the better hotels have pools, but the *Sheraton Rio* (Av. Niemeyer, Vidigal; phone: 274-1122), the *Inter-Continental* (São Conrado; phone: 322-2200), and *Copacabana Palace* (phone: 255-7070) have gorgeous ones in which you easily can spend hours if invited by a guest of the hotel.

**Tennis** – The *Inter-Continental* (São Conrado; phone: 322-2200) and *Sheraton Rio* (Av. Niemeyer, Vidigal; phone: 274-1122) hotels have tennis courts that can be rented for an hour by non-guests. Call the hotel to make arrangements. There are six illuminated courts at *Lob* (290 Rua Stefan Zweig, Laranjeiras; for reservations, phone: 225-0329) and many more courts scattered throughout town, especially out in Barra da Tijuca.

**Track** – The *Jockey Club,* Rio's racetrack (Praça Santos Dumont; phone: 274-0055), has quite a setting, more like a park than a track. It has towering palms, colorful plants, flowers, and even a small lagoon in the center. Races are held Saturdays and Sundays from 2:30 to 7 PM and Mondays and Thursdays from 7:30 to 9 PM. You can bet as little as $1 or as much as you want. "Win" windows are called *vencedor* and "place" windows are called *place.* There is no "show" bet. Admission is about $1 in the stands.

**THEATER:** Rio has excellent theater, all of it performed in Portuguese. Some good ones are *Cândido Mendes* (63 Rue Joana Angelica, Ipanema; phone: 267-7295); *Teatro Ipanema* (824 Rue Prudente de Morais; phone: 247-9794); and *Clara Nunes* (*Gávea Shopping Center;* phone: 274-9696). Look in the arts pages of *Jornal do Brasil* and *O Globo* newspapers for others.

**MUSIC:** Rio's *Carnegie Hall* is the 2,000-seat *Teatro Municipal* (Municipal Theater; Av. Rio Branco at Praça Floriano; phone: 210-2463), presenting operas, ballets, and concerts. Performances often feature touring companies from the US or Europe. Ticket prices start at $5 and run as high as $250 to hear a major star. Check the "Caderno B" entertainment section of the Portuguese-language daily *Jornal do Brasil* for current attractions. Chamber music is played at the *Sala Cecília Meirelles* (47 Largo da Lapa; phone: 232-9714).

**NIGHTCLUBS AND NIGHTLIFE:** Rio's nightlife is world-renowned. There are plenty of nightspots of all kinds, and since dinner is rarely started before 9 PM, most clubs don't get going until 11 PM and stay open until the last guest staggers out. Feel like dancing? Try a frenetic discotheque. Enjoy watching? Visit a club featuring a sex-charged samba show. Like your drinks with a stiff upper lip and darts? Drop into an English pub. The list and variety of clubs goes on and on — ranging from posh supper clubs to far-out discotheques to piano bars, gay and hetero pick-up bars, and even a German beer hall or two. Rio has a surprisingly large number of clubs that have remained jammed on weekends for over 10 years. It also has clubs that are very "in" for a short time and very "out" soon after.

Dress is informal, except at some supper clubs. In clubs with shows, there is a cover charge — usually about $8, sometimes more. Often, there is a two-drink minimum as well. By the way, Scotch is extremely expensive in Brazil (as are all imported liquors), so stick to locally made rum, gin, or vodka.

As in much of Latin America, nightclubs prefer to admit couples. Single women rarely are admitted by the doormen, who zealously guard the entrances. Sometimes single men are admitted. Still, the times they are a changin', and some clubs, particularly those with shows, will admit women if they are tourists.

Popular nightclubs with shows include *Canecão* (215 Av. Wenceslau Brás, Botafogo; phone: 295-3044), which comfortably seats 2,400 people at tables. After many years, *Canecão* remains Rio's hot nightclub by constantly and consistently delivering the top Brazilian and international entertainers. Reservations are important and show times vary depending upon who is performing and how many shows *Canecão* has scheduled. There may be up to three different shows in a night. Rio's second nightspot is the *Scala* (296 Av. Afrânio de Melo Franco, Leblon; phone: 239-4448). One of *Scala*'s rooms provides a first-rate Las Vegas–style show with Brazilian flair — lots of nudity and samba. Dining and dancing are also on the agenda; reservations advised.

*Oba Oba*'s (110 Rua Humaitá, Humaitá) famous show features long-legged mulatto showgirls in skimpy outfits, as well as samba dancers. Doors open at 8:30 PM. Shows start at 10:30 PM, with an additional show at midnight on Friday and Saturday nights; closed Mondays. Phone 286-9848 for reservations on weekends (a must). Better yet is *Plataforma I* (32 Rua Adalberto Ferreira, Leblon; phone: 274-4022), which features a nightly samba show at 11 PM; the doors open at 9 PM.

Two popular private clubs that might let you in are *Hippopotamus* (354 Rua Barão da Torre; phone: 247-0351) and the *Palace Club* (at the *Rio Palace Hotel*, 4240 Av. Atlântica; phone: 521-3232). If you are staying at one of the deluxe hotels have the concierge make a reservation for you. Another popular and trendy nightspot is *Caligola* (129 Rua Prudente de Morais, Ipanema; phone: 287-1369). Simpler and more relaxed is *Mikonos,* a club in a private house (177 Rua Cupertino Durão, Leblon; phone: 294-2298), which features jazz for listening upstairs, music to dance to downstairs. Open from 10 PM to 4 AM nightly. *Sobre as Ondas,* a club with live music on the second floor, which overlooks the Copacabana street scene (3432 Av. Atlântica; phone: 521-1296), is quiet and pleasant for listening or for dancing. *Circus Disco* is a swinging spot popular with the young Ipanema beach crowd. It's right above the *Bella Blu Pizza Parlor* (102 Av. General Urquiza, Leblon; phone: 274-7895). Rio's biggest disco, *Help,* on the busy Copacabana stretch (3432 Av. Atlântica; phone: 521-1296), draws a young crowd; its flashing lights can't be missed. Gay discos are *Boate Incontrus* (15 Praça Serzedelo Correia, Copacabana; phone: 257-6498) and *Sundays at Kitchnet* (543 Rua Barata Ribeiro, Copacabana; phone: 235-2045). For those who want to experience the special beat of the Northeast, there's *Forró Forrado* (235 Rua do Catete; phone: 245-0524), open Thursdays through Sundays at 10 PM. The regional music — played with accordion, triangle, tambourine, and drum — has its own skippy dance step and is considered Brazil's version of country-and-western music.

Couples of all ages flock to *gafieiras* on weekends. These large dance halls offer live music for good old twosome dancing. Two traditional *gafieiras* are *Elite* (upstairs at 4 Rua Frei Caneca, Centro; phone: 232-3217), and nearby *Estudantina* (79 Praça Tiradentes, Centro; phone: 232-1149), which draws a younger crowd. The newest and most sophisticated *gafieira* is *Asa Branca* (17 Av. Mem de Sá, Lapa; phone: 252-0966).

Besides its large dance floor, this club also features shows with some of the country's best singers.

Lambada, the music craze that hit Brazil (and the US, too) in the 1980s, is still danced at many clubs in Rio. Some clubs and discos have nights just for lambada, while others have lambada bands that alternate with samba and rock bands.

Jazz bars also are popular in Rio, probably because the quality of the music is so good. The most important jazz spots are the *Rio Jazz Club* (1020 Av. Atlântica, Copacabana; phone: 541-9046), below the *Meridien* hotel; *Jazzmania* (769 Rua Rainha Isabel Elizabeth, Ipanema; phone: 227-2447); and *Mistura Up* (15 Rua Garcia D'Avila, 15, Ipanema; phone: 267-6596).

Not a club devotee? You have plenty of other choices: English-language cinemas, sidewalk cafés with live music for only a small donation, *macumba* services, samba school rehearsals, sporting and cultural events of all kinds, and moonlight to do with what you wish. If you're alone, it's easy to find someone with whom to share the moonlight. What more can you ask for? *Lord Jim Pub* (63 Rua Paul Redfern, Ipanema; phone: 259-3047) is a popular meeting spot for English-speaking people living in Rio. A typical pub serves afternoon tea, has bars on both floors, darts, and steak and kidney pie on the upstairs restaurant menu — the feeling is strictly British.

In Copacabana, erotic shows are the draw at *Frank's* (185 Av. Princesa Isabel) and *Swing* (840-A Rua Gustavo Sampaio). Many couples come here for the shows, which include simulated sex and nude dancing. Both shows are attractive and offer late-night performances and women eager to join unattached men for a drink. Transvestite shows take place at *Teatro Alaska* (*Galeria Alaska*, 1241 Av. Nossa Senhora de Copacabana; phone: 247-9842) and *Boêmio* (760 Rua Sanata Luzia; phone: 240-7259). Warning: Many women (and men) in the area are "professionals," so be sure there are no "misunderstandings." Bear in mind that after the US, Brazil has the highest number of reported AIDS cases in the Americas.

# BEST IN TOWN

**CHECKING IN:** Rio has hotels to suit any taste or budget. A visitor can select a downtown hotel but would probably enjoy a nearby beach community more, a far cry from the hotel-upon-hotel scene of such places as Miami Beach or Honolulu. No hotel in Rio is directly on the beach. The majority of hotels on Copacabana Beach are discernible from the adjoining apartment buildings only by their lobbies. They offer beachfront accommodations and comfortable surroundings. Resort-style hotels began to open in Rio in the 1970s. Designed by Brazil's foremost architects, they were built on newly developed São Conrado and have swimming pools, tennis courts, beautifully landscaped grounds, boutiques, several restaurants, and nightspots. Although the areas around them have become more residential, these hotels still offer some measure of isolation, yet they're only minutes from the heart of Copacabana.

Choosing a hotel just a block or two off the beach can save a considerable amount of money and still assure clean, pleasant surroundings. All rooms are air conditioned and have private baths, unlike the small European hotels with communal bathrooms. An added bonus: Hotel rates usually include a delicious breakfast that is often served in your room, or as a buffet in the coffee shop. Breakfasts usually come in the continental style, with fresh fruit, cheese, warm rolls, and coffee.

Double rooms at hotels classified as expensive range from $100 to about $200; in the moderate category, from $65 to $90; and in the inexpensive category, under $60 (and

## RIO DE JANEIRO / Best in Town

as low as $40) nightly. All telephone numbers are in the 21 city code unless otherwise indicated. *Note:* Hotels listed in the expensive category receive satellite television broadcasts from the US and offer CNN (Cable News Network).

Note: Two US credit cards are known in Brazil by Brazilian names: MasterCard is called *Passaporte* and Visa doubles as *Cartão Elo.*

**Caesar Park** – This is Rio's top luxury hotel for businesspeople. A tall, ultracontemporary structure with a small rooftop swimming pool, its 221 rooms are all luxuriously decorated, with conveniences such as stocked refrigerators. It prides itself on excellent, personalized service, and the *feijoadacompleta* on Saturdays in the *Tiberius* restaurant (see *Eating Out*) is an event. The *Mariko* sushi bar serves some of the best Japanese food in the city, and *Petronius* (see *Eating Out*) offers very fine international fare. 460 Av. Vieira Souto, Ipanema (phone: 287-3122). Expensive.

**Copacabana Palace** – Now part of the Venice Simplon Orient Express group, this property has been totally renovated and restored to its former days of glory. To get an idea of luxury 1920s style, walk through the lobbies and public rooms of Rio's dowager queen of a hotel. This grand establishment occupies the entire block from Avenida Atlântica, Copacabana's beachfront drive, to Avenida Copacabana, and its rooms have 14-foot ceilings and most have a view of the beach or pool. It has its faithful following who return year after year (even during the years of renovation), despite some reports that the service can be spotty. The hotel has one of the best pools in Rio, and plans include the addition of a number of elegant restaurants and bars and a fitness center. 1702 Av. Atlântica, Copacabana (phone: 255-7070). Expensive.

**Everest Rio** – This 23-story building stands on a quiet street in Ipanema, but it is only a few minutes' walk to the action and the price is lower than for beachfront accommodations. There is a pool on the 23rd floor as well as a bar and coffee shop. Rooms are comfortable if undistinguished in decor, with TV sets and refrigerators. A good choice. 1117 Rua Prudente de Morais, Ipanema (phone: 287-8282). Expensive.

**Inter-Continental Rio** – Part of the superior worldwide hotel chain, the Rio branch holds up very well. Its well-kept grounds include first-rate recreational facilities: 3 tennis courts (lighted for night play), 3 pools (1 with a swim-up-and/or-sit-down bar), and a health club. The 483 rooms and suites are furnished in contemporary Brazilian style, all with balconies that face either the ocean or the mountains. The views are particularly lovely at dusk. For the gourmet, the hotel offers both the highly regarded *Monseigneur* (see *Eating Out*) and a branch of Rome's *Alfredo di Lello,* as well as 3 other restaurants and snack bars. The hotel has several bars, including the *Jakui* nightclub and the popular *Papillon* discotheque. There are conference and convention facilities, shops, and it is only a short walk from the *Fashion Mall.* 222 Av. Prefeito Mendes de Morais, São Conrado (phone: 322-2200). Expensive.

**Internacional Rio** – All 117 rooms and 13 suites have private terraces overlooking the ocean and Copacabana Beach. There's a rooftop swimming pool and sauna, as well as a restaurant with a view of the mountains and sea. The hotel prides itself on its personalized and efficient service. 1500 Av. Atlântica, Copacabana (phone: 295-2323; in the US, 800-87-HOTAC). Expensive.

**Marina Palace** – Not to be confused with its sister resort, *Marina Rio* (below), it is also subdued and elegant, with a good restaurant on the second floor, overlooking the beach. It's one of the few beachfront hotels in Leblon. 630 Av. Delfim Moreira, Leblon (phone: 259-5212). Expensive.

**Marina Rio** – With only 70 rooms and set on Rio's most subdued beach, Leblon, this is the place to go for a quiet retreat in understated surroundings. Even the music at the piano bar is muted, and waiters in the continental restaurant speak in hushed tones. Not everyone's idea of Rio, but it may be yours. 696 Av. Delfim Moreira, Leblon (phone: 239-8844). Expensive.

**Le Meridien Copacabana** – The outstanding French chain has a link on a major Copacabana thoroughfare. The *Café de la Paix* on the ground floor could settle in amid the brasseries of the Champs-Élysées, and Paul Bocuse's *Le St. Honoré* on the 37th floor serves classic haute cuisine (see *Eating Out*). Rooms are elegantly appointed, and the decor of the entire hotel is particularly stylish. The swimming pool on the fourth floor is edged by a comfortable sun deck and well-stocked bar. Rooms have radios, TV sets, and refrigerators. 1020 Av. Atlântica, Leme (phone: 275-9922; toll-free in Brazil, 11-800-1554). Expensive.

**Nacional Rio** – Oscar Niemeyer, the renowned Brazilian architect who created Brasília and designed the UN building in New York, is responsible for this hotel. Popular with package tour travelers, it is a round, glass, 26-story structure that blends perfectly into the surrounding area of mountains and pulsating Atlantic waves washing onto the beach (there also is a pool). With huge convention halls and banquet rooms, the lobby is always buzzing with many languages. 769 Av. Niemeyer, São Conrado (phone: 322-1000). Expensive.

**Rio Othon Palace** – Not to be confused with the sleek *Rio Palace* (see below), this has been a popular Rio stopping place since it opened its doors in 1976. From the rooftop pool and solarium to the *Pátio Tropical*, this place was designed for easy living. The rooms are large and many have ocean views. All are air conditioned, with TV sets and small refrigerators. The *Estância* restaurant is known for its gaucho-style barbecued beef. The colorful coffee shop is open late. 3264 Av. Atlântica, Copacabana (phone: 521-5522). Expensive.

**Rio Palace** – One of the best hotels in town and destined to be the center of attention for a long time to come. Its location at the junction of Copacabana and Ipanema beaches is excellent, and the 415 rooms have individual balconies offering a fantastic view of the beach. Duplex apartments are available for long-term rentals. An external glass elevator whisks you from the lobby to the sixth floor's 2 swimming pools, bar, health club, and tearoom. There also are several restaurants, including Gaston LeNôtre's *Le Pré Catalan* (see *Eating Out*), a shopping center, a large convention center, and a parking garage. The decor is very modern, using Brazilian woods and fabrics especially designed for it. It's quite a place. 4240 Av. Atlântica, Copacabana (phone: 521-3232). Expensive.

**Sheraton Rio** – It's possible to enjoy a terrific vacation and never leave the grounds here. Dramatically perched on a lovely (but narrow) private swimming beach, it also has 3 swimming pools, tennis courts, a sauna and health club, elegant shops, chic boutiques, a nightclub, excellent restaurants including the wonderful *Valentino's* (see *Eating Out*), *Edo*, a branch of the Japanese chain, the *O Casarão* barbecue house, and a late-night coffee shop. With 579 rooms and 61 suites, it is Rio's second-largest hotel after the *Glória*. All the rooms have a private balcony with a view of the sea. 121 Av. Niemeyer, Vidigal (phone: 274-1122; toll-free in Brazil, 11-800-1694). Expensive.

**Sol Ipanema** – This hotel uses Brazil's natural resources in a stunning blend of color and good taste. Lustrous jacaranda furniture is set off by colorful upholstery; Bahian tapestries provide the finishing touches. A small pool and a roof solarium are available for those who like their swimming *sans* sand. The hotel has 90 rooms spread over 15 floors. All have TV sets, and radios. 320 Av. Vieira Souto, Ipanema (phone: 267-0095). Expensive.

**Luxor Copacabana** – A 123-room, 11-floor hotel that uses rosewood on the walls, in the furniture, and even for the headboards of the beds. The rich warm tone sets off the vibrant colors of the ultramodern lamps and furnishings. With a terrace restaurant and beachfront location, this is a good value. 2554 Av. Atlântica, Copacabana (phone: 235-2245). Expensive to moderate.

**Bandeirantes Othon** – On a quiet street 2 blocks from Avenida Atlântica, this hotel is surrounded by apartment buildings, small restaurants, and antiques stores. Its 90 spotless rooms all have TV sets. 548 Rua Barata Ribeiro, Copacabana (phone: 255-6252). Moderate.

**Copa d'Or** – Since it opened several years ago, this 195-room hostelry has become popular with savvy business and vacation travelers because it is a good value for the money. There is a rooftop pool and sun deck, and conference and convention facilities. 875 Rua Figueiredo Magalhães, Copacabana (phone: 235-6610). Moderate.

**Debret** – Once a modern apartment house, it became a hotel in 1972 and has provided pleasant accommodations ever since. The lobby, tastefully decorated with works of sculpture and good paintings, is a cozy spot to sit in. The area of Avenida Atlântica on either side has sidewalk cafés that are popular hangouts for young people at night. 3564 Av. Atlântica, Copacabana (phone: 521-3332). Moderate.

**Glória** – This 630-room and 20-suite property is Rio's largest, but far from the center of the main tourist areas in Copacabana and Ipanema. It was once, along with the *Copacabana Palace,* one of South America's great hotels. The grande dame has lost much of her glitter and glory over the years but still is popular with business travelers and package groups on a limited budget with a penchant for large, traditional hotels. Four restaurants, 4 bars, and 2 swimming pools give an idea of the size of this historic property. Interestingly, the hotel used to be directly on the seafront until Flamengo Park was built. It offers terrific facilities and value for the visitor who does not mind being away from the heart of the action or prefers to be closer to the business center. 632 Praia do Russel, Glória (phone: 205-7272). Moderate.

**Lancaster** – A small, 74-room property, converted from an apartment house, this is a comfortable stop for people not concerned with luxurious atmosphere. Many of the large rooms have separate sitting areas, and those rooms facing Avenida Atlântica have terraces. All have TV sets. Its friendly service and good location bring people back again and again. 1470 Av. Atlântica, Copacabana (phone: 541-1887; toll-free, 11-800-8990). Moderate.

**Leme Palace** – In a quiet neighborhood adjacent to Copacabana, this 17-story hotel looks like a modern apartment building. It has only a small lobby, but it crams a lot into the small area. The 194 rooms are large, and the furnishings modern and attractive. The small refrigerator in each room is stocked with liquor, mixers, and snacks. Pay only for what you consume. The top-floor nightclub has a great view and the restaurant is highly regarded. 656 Av. Atlântica, Leme (phone: 275-8080). Moderate.

**Ouro Verde** – Considered the class hotel in its price range, this place is so spotless it could thrive in Zurich. Everything is meticulous, including the white gloves of the elevator operators. Service is impeccable, and the continental restaurant is highly respected (see *Eating Out).* A small sitting area in one part of the lobby is always stocked with international newspapers. You can relax in a leather armchair and catch up with the news. All 66 rooms have radios and telephones. 1456 Av. Atlântica, Copacabana (phone: 542-1887). Moderate.

**Trocadero** – The key word is convenient. Walk across the street and you are in the center of the Copacabana Beach strip, only 1 block from the major shopping section of Avenida Copacabana. Yet this 120-room hotel stands as a quiet oasis in Copacabana's pulsating heart. Rooms are large, comfortably furnished, and have refrigerators. The *Moenda,* one of Rio's finest Bahian restaurants, is in the hotel (see *Eating Out*). Its sidewalk café-bar is very popular at sunset. 2064 Av. Atlântica, Copacabana (phone: 257-1834). Moderate.

**Ambassador** – In the heart of the Cinelândia theater district, this is splendid for people who enjoy being in the center of things. A short walk leads you to the *Municipal Theater,* the downtown shopping center, and Flamengo Park. The 130-room hotel opened in 1949 and was a favorite of businessmen for many years. There's lots of traffic noise, so ask for a back room. 25 Rua Senador Dantas, Centro (phone: 297-7181). Inexpensive.

**Castro Alves** – A charter member of the Othon hotel chain, this place is a block from the beach, so it's less expensive than equivalent hotels on the shoreline. The 75 rooms are a good size and are furnished in motel-style modern. All have TV sets and stocked refrigerators. 552 Av. Copacabana, Copacabana (phone: 255-8815). Inexpensive.

**Florida** – In the Flamengo section, the 200 rooms are large, with parquet floors and big, tiled bathrooms. The furniture is undistinguished, but the rooms are bright and the hotel, clean and well cared for. 69-81 Rua Ferreira Viana, Flamengo (phone: 245-8160). Inexpensive.

**Novo Mundo** – Also in the Flamengo section, this hotel has 200 rooms, all with TV sets. It was outstanding when it opened in 1950, and its views of Guanabara Bay and Pão de Açúcar are still stunning. The main disadvantage is that guests must walk to Flamengo Beach or take a bus to an Atlantic Ocean beach. The furnishings are well worn, but spit-and-polish is evident in the care they receive. 20 Praia do Flamengo, Flamengo (phone: 205-3355). Inexpensive.

**Vermont** – A small 38-room hostelry, right on the main street of Ipanema, the building is marked by a canopy over the door. All rooms are carpeted, and while not exactly large, they are comfortable. Breakfast is served in your room. 254 Rua Visconde de Pirajá, Ipanema (phone: 521-0057). Inexpensive.

■**Note:** An alternative to the traditional hotel in Rio is the rental of "aparthotels" — unique 1-bedroom, furnished apartments with kitchen, as well as customary hotel services such as maid, laundry, front desk, and room service. Some have swimming pools and saunas, and all are in modern buildings. Mostly in the expensive-to-moderate price range, they have become a great option during peak seasons, when the hotels are full. Try *American Flat Service* (244 Rua Humaitá, Humaitá; phone: 274-9546 or 274-7222); *Atlântico Flat Service* (15 Rua Santa Clara, Copacabana; phone: 274-9546 or 274-7222); *Barrabela* (4700 Av. Sernambetiba, Barra da Tijuca; phone: 385-2000); *Barraleme* (600 Av. Sernambetiba, Barra da Tijuca; phone: 389-3100); *Copacabana Flat* (73 Rua Xavier da Silveira, Copacabana; phone: 257-8170); *Copacabana Hotel Residencia* (222 Rua Barata Ribeiro, Copacabana; phone: 256-2610); *Ipanema Sweet* (137 Rua Gomes Carneiro, Ipanema; phone: 287-9292); *Leblon Flat Service* (33 Rua Prof. Antônio Maria Teixeira, Leblon; phone: 259-4332); *Monsieur Le Blond Apart-Hotel* (325 Av. Bartolomeu Mitre, Leblon; phone: 529-3030); *Rio Flat Service* (332 Rua Almirante Guilhem, Leblon; phone: 274-7222 or 274-9546); *Rio Ipanema* (66 Rua Visconde de Pirajá, Ipanema; phone: 267-40150; *Santa Clara Flat* (212 Rua Santa Clara, Copacabana; phone: 256-2690); or *Tiffany* (Av. Prudente de Morais, Ipanema; phone: 521-4418). Or contact the agencies *Fantastic Rio* (phone: 541-0615); *Marlin Tours* (phone: 255-4433); or *Rent A Flat* (phone: 256-9986).

**EATING OUT:** Brazilians revel in the good life, and eating out plays a major part. Visitors cannot fail to be impressed by the sheer quantity of restaurants in Rio, all crowded with people enjoying themselves. The sophistication of the population is reflected in the variety of restaurants: Chinese, German,

Japanese, French, Italian, and Swiss are just a small sample. Many have English menus. Typical Brazilian restaurants serve tasty, unusual dishes.

Called Bahian, the local cuisine was created by slaves in the Bahia province of Brazil, north of Rio. Because beef was scarce, the dishes use seafood, poultry, nuts, fruits, coconuts, and milk. *Feijoada,* the national dish, consists of black beans and rice. *Feijoada completa,* traditionally served on Saturdays, adds sausage and pork to the beans and rice. *Xinxim de galinha* is another popular dish, featuring pieces of chicken in a white sauce. *Vatapá* is a creamy dish of shrimp or fish in coconut milk. *Siri* is a spicy and delicious stuffed crab appetizer. *Frango com arroz* is Brazil's version of chicken and rice. While you wait for your main course to arrive, have a *batida,* a mixed drink based on *cachaça* (a strong cane liquor) and fruit; or a *caipirinha,* made with *cachaça,* sugar, and lime. Brazilian fruits are superb on their own: *abacaxi* (pineapple), *mamão* (papaya), *carambola* (star fruit), and *goiaba* (guava). And be sure to sample Brazil's national soft drink, *Guaraná:* Very sweet, it's made from the seeds of a fruit that grows in the Amazon jungle. It's reported to be effective in combatting diarrhea because of the tannin it contains. (Another excellent remedy for diarrhea and dehydration is the refreshing *água de coco,* green coconut water, which you drink straight from the fruit with a straw.) *Churrascarías* are barbecue restaurants where excellent beef, lamb, and sausages are charcoal grilled.

Most restaurants have a cover charge *(couvert)* that ranges from $1 to $3. It is optional and covers bread, butter, a cold vegetable platter, and tiny quail eggs that are ubiquitous as side dishes as well as coffee.

While fast-food and counter restaurants are open continuously, most sit-down restaurants serve lunch from noon until 3 PM. Dinner is rarely eaten before 9 PM, and most kitchens remain open till 2 or 3 AM on weekends. Expect to pay $40 and up for restaurants in the expensive category; $25 to $35 in the moderate range; under $20 for inexpensive places. Prices are for dinner for two, without drinks, wine, or tips. All telephone numbers are in the 21 city code unless otherwise indicated.

Note: Be warned that Rio's restaurants don't all believe in plastic payment. Because of the high inflation rate, currently even many of the expensive restaurants simply refuse to accept credit cards. If you wish to pay with a credit card, be sure to double-check with the restaurant in advance.

**Antiquarius** – It's a very pleasant dining spot decorated with antiques. The bar area is small but comfortable, a nice place to sip a drink while waiting for your table. The Portuguese *bacalhau* (codfish) dishes are quite good. It gets crowded here. Open daily for lunch and dinner until 2 AM. Reservations advised. No credit cards accepted. 19 Rua Aristides Espinola, Leblon (phone: 294-1049). Expensive.

**Le Bec Fin** – Many *cariocas* would choose this as the best French restaurant in Rio. The lobster is unmatchable and the *canard* (duck) dishes run a close second. The horseshoe-shaped dining room doesn't allow for much privacy and the decor is unimpressive, but you definitely need reservations here. Open daily for dinner only. Major credit cards accepted. 178-A Av. Copacabana, Copacabana (phone: 542-4097). Expensive.

**Claude Troisgros** – Set in an attractive colonial house of *Jardim Botânico,* this Relais & Châteaux member offers French nouvelle cuisine with Brazilian overtones. It is considered one of the best restaurants not only in Rio de Janeiro, but in all of South America. The menu prepared by owner-chef Claude Troisgros (of culinary fame) changes constantly, and is a delight to behold for those interested in fine dining. Open daily, except Sundays, for dinner. Reservations necessary. No credit cards accepted. 62 Rua Custódio Serrão, Jardim Botânico (phone: 226-4542). Expensive.

**Clube Gourmet** – This eatery once was a cooking school, but its fame spread to such an extent that it led to the opening of this full-fledged restaurant. One of Rio's most popular dining spots, it offers a relaxed atmosphere and some of the best food in town. Portions are small and the ever-changing menu of international fare is limited, so at night choose the set menu of four courses. Closed Saturday lunch and Sunday dinner. Reservations essential. No credit cards accepted. 186 Rua General Polidoro, Botafogo (phone: 295-3494). Expensive.

**English Bar** – The one area of Rio not well represented by restaurants is the downtown business area. However, this eatery offers an air conditioned, cosy British atmosphere with a well-prepared selection of international dishes. The excellent service makes it a favorite haunt for business executives. Open weekdays for lunch only. Reservations advised. Major credit cards accepted. 11 Travessa do Comércio, Centro (phone: 224-2539). Expensive.

**Laurent** – French owner/chef, Laurent Suaudeau, was a pupil of the renowned French chef Paul Bocuse, and for a number of years was responsible for the kitchen of Bocuse's *Le Saint Honoré* in the *Meridien Copacabana*. His stint built him a faithful clientele who followed him to his own restaurant located in a large house in Botafogo. Traditional and nouvelle French cuisine are mixed on a menu that always offers exciting new dishes. Open daily, except Sundays, for lunch and dinner. Reservations advised. Major credit cards accepted. 209 Rua Dona Mariana, Botafogo (phone: 266-3131). Expensive.

**Madame Butterfly** – The center of Brazil's Japanese community is São Paulo, but Rio has some of the best restaurants of that ethnic stripe, including this very attractive spot. Ask to sit upstairs so you can eat in authentic Japanese style. Open daily for lunch and dinner. Reservations advised. No credit cards accepted. 472 Rua Barão da Torre, Ipanema (phone: 267-4347). Expensive.

**Maxim's** – Keep this place in mind for those very special occasions when the meal's presentation and service is as important as the food itself. Located on the roof of the *Rio-Sul* tower, it offers spectacular views from its balcony. Open daily, except Sundays, for dinner. Reservations advised. Major credit cards accepted. Torre Rio-Sul, Botafogo (phone: 541-9342). Expensive.

**Monseigneur** – In the *Inter-Continental* hotel, this is one of the city's outstanding restaurants. Offering an international menu with a distinctly French accent, this elegant eatery is popular not only with hotel guests, but with Rio residents as well. Open daily for dinner. Reservations unnecessary. Major credit cards accepted. 222 Av. Prefeito Mendes de Morais, São Conrado (phone: 322-2200). Expensive.

**Ouro Verde** – There are few restaurants in Rio with a better reputation than this long-time favorite on the second floor of the hotel of the same name. It doesn't need neon signs — the French food is prepared perfectly, the unobtrusive service, and quiet ambience are justly famous. Try the chateaubriand or a veal dish in wine sauce. And try to get a table overlooking the beach. You can't miss. Open daily from noon to midnight. Reservations advised. American Express accepted. *Ouro Verde Hotel*, 1456 Av. Atlântica, Copacabana (phone: 542-1887). Expensive.

**Petronius** – This restaurant in the excellent *Caesar Park* hotel offers a menu that holds some interesting surprises — the current mix of fare is international, seafood, and Swiss. Open daily for dinner. Reservations advised. Major credit cards accepted. 460 Av. Vieira Souto, Ipanema (phone: 287-3122). Expensive.

**Le Pré Catalan** – This charming restaurant, at the *Rio Palace* hotel, is known for its light French cuisine. French chef Gaston LeNôtre reviews the menu every 2 months. Open for dinner. Reservations advised. Major credit cards accepted. *Rio Palace Hotel*, 4240 Av. Atlântica, Copacabana (phone: 521-3232). Expensive.

**Le Saint Honoré** – On the 37th floor of the *Meridien* hotel, it is considered one of the finest restaurants in town and the best of hotel dining. The fare is French, with many dishes created by Paul Bocuse. *Pâté de caneton* and shellfish in delicious light sauces are recommended. Lovely views of the city and music at dinner add the right atmosphere to complement the delectable fare. The 3-course prix fixe lunch is a bargain. Closed Sundays; dinner only on Saturdays. Reservations necessary. Major credit cards accepted. 1020 Av. Atlântica, Leme (phone: 275-9922). Expensive.

**Le Streghe** – Rightly considered to be Rio's top Italian eatery, it offers Italy's *nuova cucina* in relaxed but elegant surroundings. One of Rio's most popular and loved restaurants for a number of years. Open daily for dinner. Reservations necessary. No credit cards. 129 Rua Prudente de Morais, Ipanema (phone: 287-7146). Expensive.

**La Tour** – The only dining spot in Rio where you can have your appetizer while gazing at Pão de Açúcar, your entrée under the outstretched arms of Christ the Redeemer high atop Corcovado, and dessert facing the downtown skyline. It is on the 37th floor of an office building, and revolves once every hour. The extensive menu lists Italian, French, and German dishes side by side, although the view is better than the food. At night, roving musicians play Latin melodies as you dine. Open daily for lunch and dinner. Reservations advised. Major credit cards accepted. 651 Rua Santa Lúzia, Centro (phone: 240-5795). Expensive.

**Valentino's** – Since opening in the late 1980s, this beautiful and elegant restaurant in the *Sheraton Rio* hotel has had an international menu, leaning toward Italian. Open daily for dinner. Reservations advised. Major credit cards accepted. 121 Av. Niemeyer, Vidigal (phone: 274-1122). Expensive.

**Antônio's** – Perhaps because it caters to Rio's artists, writers, and actors, this place is reminiscent of Greenwich Village restaurants. Wood-paneled walls lined with wine racks and framed posters, a dining terrace, and a very popular bar contribute to the feeling. The menu is in Portuguese, but some items don't need translations: fettuccine Alfredo, *scaloppine marsala,* and filet mignon *alla pizzaiola* come highly recommended. The maître d' speaks some English and can help you decide. Jackets are common, but ties are not required. Open daily, noon to midnight. Reservations necessary. Major credit cards accepted. 297 Av. Bartolomeu Mitre, Leblon (phone: 294-2699). Expensive to moderate.

**Café de la Paix** – On the ground floor of the *Meridien* hotel, this French brasserie with comfortable booths and tables loaded with Gallic charm offers a varied menu, good wines, pâtés, omelettes of all kinds, and absolutely scrumptious pastries. Open daily from noon to 3 PM and 7 to 11 PM. Reservations advised. Major credit cards accepted. 1020 Av. Atlântica, Leme (phone: 275-9922). Expensive to moderate.

**Castelo da Lagoa** – The name, "Castle on the Lagoon," says it all. Set in a large private home overlooking the lagoon, the attractive indoor dining room at this continental restaurant has brown leather chairs and gold tablecloths. After dinner, move next door to *Chico's Bar,* where the Brazilian music is live and good. Open daily from noon to 4 AM. Reservations unnecessary. Major credit cards accepted. 1560 Av. Epitácio Pessoa, Lagoa (phone: 287-3514). Expensive to moderate.

**Enotria** – Considered one of the best in Rio for Italian food, it has only nine tables, albeit elegantly decorated ones. The same owner runs a fine food shop next door for those who wish to take a snack back to the hotel. Open daily, except Sundays, for dinner. Reservations advised. No credit cards accepted. 115 Rua Constante Ramos, Copacabana (phone: 237-6705). Expensive to moderate.

**Grottamare** – One of Rio's most popular and crowded Italian seafood restaurants, this place draws a chic crowd. Recommended are fish served right off the grill, as well as the fresh green salads and pasta dishes. Open for dinner Tuesdays through Sundays, lunch on Sundays and holidays. Reservations advised. Diners Club accepted. 132 Rua Gomes Carneiro, Ipanema (phone: 287-1596). Expensive to moderate.

# RIO DE JANEIRO / Best in Town

**Maria Thereza Weiss** – Try the delicious fish and seafood cooked in the style of the Bahian region. Specialties include *bobo de camarão* (a shrimp stew in red sauce, served over rice), and *empanada de camarão* (shrimp empanadas). *Feijoada* also is offered. Live piano music on Sundays. Closed Mondays. No reservations. Major credit cards accepted. 152 Rua Visconde de Silva, Botafogo (phone: 286-3098). Expensive to moderate.

**Rive Gauche** – Offering a traditional international menu in comfortable surroundings, but the appeal of this place is the stunning view across the lake to Corcovado and the live music somewhere between jazz and bossa nova. Open daily for dinner. Reservations advised. Major credit cards accepted. 1484 Av. Epitácio Pessoa, Lagoa (phone: 521-2645). Expensive to moderate.

**Tiberius** – *Feijoada completa* is this eatery's most popular dish, served only on Saturday afternoons, although other dishes are equally delicious. Try the *bandeja imperial*, a platter of grilled seafood and shrimp, cooked in coconut milk and served over rice. Live jazz band on Saturday afternoons and Sundays. Open daily. Reservations necessary. *Caesar Park Hotel*, 460 Av. Vieira Souto, Ipanema (phone: 287-3122). Expensive to moderate.

**Alba Mar** – What better location for a seafood restaurant than overlooking the water? This circular building with a turret roof, located in the downtown dock area, was once the municipal market, but has since been converted into a 2-level restaurant. Many of the dishes are prepared Bahian-style, but if these don't suit your palate, you can stick to shrimp, crab, oyster, and fish dishes prepared in more familiar fashion. The main dining room is on the second floor. Closed Sundays. Reservations advised. American Express accepted. 184-186 Marechal Ancora, Centro (phone: 240-8378 or 240-8428). Moderate.

**Arataca** – If you can't make the trip to the northern Amazon, at least try some of the regional cooking here. The restaurant serves fish typically found in the Amazon, a duck dish called *pata de tucupi*, and *carne-de-sol*, a meat dish with beans. Ask about regional fruits, such as *cupuaçu, açai*, and *graviola;* they make great *batidas*, juices, and ice cream. Open daily. Reservations unnecessary. Major credit cards accepted. Two locations, at 135-A Rua Dias Ferreira, Leblon (phone: 274-1444), and 28-AB Rua Figueiredo Magalhães, Copacabana (phone: 255-7448). Moderate.

**Café do Teatro** – A lunch-only choice, it is in the *Municipal Theater*. The international fare and the Assyrian mosaic walls and lovely decor make it an excellent place to while away a few leisurely hours. Open weekdays from 11:30 AM to 3 PM. Reservations advised. Major credit cards accepted. Av. Rio Branco at Praça Floriano, Centro (phone: 262-4164). Moderate.

**Churrascaria Copacabana** – Easy to find, this is one of the most pleasant, informal beef places in town. Filet mignon and other juicy cuts are sizzled and brought to you by gaucho-costumed waiters. On Wednesdays and Saturdays, traditional *feijoada* is served. You get a good view of the comings and goings on one of Copacabana's most active streets. Open daily from 11 AM to 2 AM. Reservations unnecessary. American Express accepted. 1144 Av. Copacabana, Copacabana (phone: 267-1497). Moderate.

**Lagoa Charlie's** – Why eat Mexican food in Rio? Because the outdoor dining room is particularly gorgeous under a full moon and starry sky and you can gaze across the lovely lagoon. Deciphering the trilingual menu is fun, and so are the strolling mariachi players. But above all, good Mexican food is served here. Chili con carne (hot), spicy guacamole, and enchiladas (chicken and cheese) are just a few of the familiar items. If you have room, by all means order a *crêpe cajeta* (a hot pancake with ice cream and caramel) for dessert. Very informal. Open daily, for dinner only until 2 AM. Reservations unnecessary. Major credit cards accepted. 136 Rua Maria Quitéria, Lagoa (phone: 267-8777). Moderate.

**Lucas** – Rio would never be mistaken for Munich, but this place makes the effort. The indoor dining room is rather austere, but the outdoor terrace (covered by a roof) is very relaxed. Sausages and wine bottles dangle everywhere, and the aroma of wurst (*salsichas*), beer, and the salty ocean air will give you an appetite. A favorite dish is Wiener schnitzel (a fried, breaded veal cutlet) served with an egg on top, home-fried potatoes, and salad. Steak Leipzig is also fine. Home-baked brown bread and butter are the *couvert*. Open daily. Reservations advised. Major credit cards accepted. 3744 Av. Atlântica, Copacabana (phone: 247-1606). Moderate.

**Mariu's** – One of the few *churrascarías*, or barbecue spots, on the beachfront. The modern decor features lots of mirrors, and the view of Leme Beach is a delight. It's the place to stuff yourself on beef, pork, or chicken that has been grilled on a spit. The entrée comes with salad, rice, and other trimmings. Open daily from noon to 1 AM. Reservations advised. Major credit cards accepted. 290-B Av. Atlântica, Leme (phone: 542-2393). Moderate.

**Moenda** – Among the finest Bahian eateries in Rio on the second floor of the *Trocadero* hotel, overlooking Copacabana Beach. Fresh flowers on every table, hanging plants, comfortable high-back chairs, and low-beam ceilings create an inviting feeling. The friendly, traditionally clad waitresses will offer you a fruit punch of *cachaça* to start your meal. The maître d' speaks English and will gladly explain the special features of each dish. Open daily from noon to midnight. Reservations advised on weekends. Major credit cards accepted. *Trocadero*, 2064 Av. Atlântica, Copacabana (phone: 257-1834). Moderate.

**Panelão** – Great *feijoada* is served at this comfortable restaurant on Saturdays. Every day other typical Brazilian fare such as *vatapá* and *bobo de camarão* (shrimp with red sauce) is offered. Open daily from noon to 2 AM. Reservations necessary. Major credit cards accepted. 300A–B Rua General Venancio Flores, Leblon (phone: 294-0848). Moderate.

**Pizza Palace** – One of the most popular meeting places in Rio, this is a particular favorite of late-night revelers. Great pizza and pasta. Open daily from 11 AM until 5 AM. No reservations. Major credit cards accepted. Next door to the fashionable disco *Hippopotamus*, at 340 Rua Barão da Torre, Ipanema (phone: 267-8346). Moderate.

**Porcão** – These barbecue houses are not only among Rio's most popular but also among its best. Service is "rodizio" style, which means you pay one set price and they keep bringing you every imaginable cut of barbecued meat until you tell them to stop. Great value for the money and wonderful food. The most popular branches are in Ipanema and in Barra da Tijuca. Open daily. Reservations unnecessary. Major credit cards accepted. 218 Rua Barão da Torre, Ipanema (phone: 521-0999); 591 Av. Armando Lombardi, Barra da Tijuca (phone: 399-3355). Moderate.

**Real Astoria** – A peaceful eatery with wood paneling and a terrace overlooking a busy thoroughfare, it offers Spanish fare such as *paella valenciana* and *pouvo española*. Open daily. No reservations. No credit cards accepted. 1235 Rua Ataulfo de Paiva, Leblon (phone: 294-0047). Moderate.

**Rian** – Although this is a bustling place, the service is friendly. Specialties include *contrafile Oswaldo Aranha* (broiled steak with garlic sauce), *caldeirada* (Portuguese fish stew), and *bacalhau* (dried, salted cod served in many ways). Open daily from 11:30 to 12:30 AM. Reservations unnecessary. Major credit cards accepted. 18 Rua Santa Clara, Copacabana (phone: 237-4074). Moderate.

**Shirley** – Gigantic grilled shrimp are the draw here as well as other reasonably priced seafood. Open daily from noon to 2 AM. Reservations not accepted so be prepared to wait. No credit cards accepted. 610 Rua Gustavo Sampaio, Leme (phone: 275-1398). Moderate.

**Via Farme** – This Italian restaurant offers excellent carpaccio (sliced raw beef), as well as all kinds of pasta dishes, gnocchi, and *fruits de mer.* Open daily for lunch and dinner. Reservations necessary. Major credit cards accepted. 47 Rua Farme de Amoedo, Ipanema (phone: 227-0743). Moderate.

***Aurora*** – Frequented by the film set, this crowded and quaint café serves a variety of meat dishes. The menu is entirely in Portuguese. Open Tuesdays through Sundays, noon to 1 AM. Reservations unnecessary. No credit cards accepted. 43 Rua Cāpitao Salomão, Botafogo (phone: 226-4756). Inexpensive.

***Bar do Arnaudo*** – A great place to sample Bahian (and other Northeastern) specialties is this simple, crowded little eatery on the trolley line in Santa Teresa. The place is packed with paintings and *artesanato,* most of which is for sale. Menu specialties include *carne-de-sol* (sun-dried beef jerky) served with *manteiga de garrafa* (bottled liquid butter), rice, and beans; there's also *sarapatel* (pork stew) and other meat and fish dishes. Open Tuesdays through Sundays for lunch and dinner. Reservations unnecessary. No credit cards accepted. Take a taxi, or if you're feeling adventurous, the trolley to the Largo dos Guimarães stop and walk a block back down the hill. 316 Av. Almirante Alexandrino, Santa Teresa (no phone). Inexpensive.

***Bella Blu*** – In the same genre of good Italian spots serving pizza and pasta, fish, chicken, and veal in attractive surroundings, these places are only beginning to make it big on the tourist trail. Open daily from 11 AM to 2 AM. No reservations. No credit cards accepted. Three locations: 107 Rua Siqueira Campos, Copacabana (phone: 255-0729); 44 Rua da Passagem, Botafogo (phone: 295-9493); and 102 Rua General Urquiza, Leblon (phone: 274-7895). Inexpensive.

***Centro China*** – Among Rio's best Chinese restaurants, this 2-story establishment is on Lagoa Rodrigo de Freitas and has a few tables with views of the lagoon. Try the duck with hot sauce. Open weekdays for dinner, weekends for lunch and dinner. Reservations unnecessary. Major credit cards accepted. 1164 Av. Epitácio Pessoa, Lagoa (phone: 287-3947). Inexpensive.

***Churrascaria Jardim*** – The charcoal pits are on the left as you enter this barbecue grill. The decor amounts to plain tables on bare floors with some tables outdoors; others are under a tin roof. Choose beef steaks, lamb, or pork — all are superb. They are brought to your table on small ovens where they cook and stay hot till the final bite. French fries and tomato-onion salad are the typical side dishes. Open daily until 1 AM. Reservations advised. Major credit cards accepted. 225 Rua República do Perú, Copacabana (phone: 235-3263). Inexpensive.

***Colombo*** – An institution in downtown Rio, this is a "must" stop for at least one lunch during your stay. Head for the fast-food counter, where you can select tiny breaded chicken drumsticks or large breaded shrimp-stuffed crab goodies, meat or cheese pies, and many other delicacies. Take your lunch and a soft drink (*Guaraná,* perhaps?) and head for the nearest greenery to munch. Afternoon tea is served, a time to sit and relax in the beautiful, authentic Art Nouveau atmosphere. Open daily. No reservations. No credit cards accepted. 32 Rua Gonçalves Dias, Centro (phone: 232-2300). Inexpensive.

***El Faro*** and ***Rio Jerez*** – Like Tweedledum and Tweedledee, these adjoining eateries serve reasonably priced Spanish food. They both have indoor dining rooms, but the alfresco tables are always the most crowded. Start with gazpacho, then try some paella or *zarzuela de pescado* (fish stew). The sangria is a good buy. Open daily from noon to 3 AM. Reservations unnecessary. Diners Club accepted. 3806 Av. Atlântica, Copacabana; El Faro (phone: 267-1128); Rio Jerez (phone: 267-5644). Inexpensive.

***Garota de Ipanema*** – Among the many sidewalk cafés around the beach areas, this one stands out because here the hit tune "The Girl from Ipanema" was composed. Sidewalk cafés are almost always open, thanks to Rio's superb weather. They are most frequently jammed in the early evening and again late at night. Open daily. No reservations. No credit cards accepted. Corner of Prudente de Morais and Vinicius de Morais (which used to be Rua Montenegro but was renamed for the co-composer of "The Girl from Ipanema"), Ipanema (phone: 267-8787). Inexpensive. (If it's too crowded, wander over to Avenida Vieira Souto, where *Barril 1800* offers a good alternative.)

**Helsingor** – Sandwiches are the specialty, making this a perfect choice for a late-night snack or light lunch or dinner. You would be amazed at what the chef can fit onto a roll or bun — for example, filet mignon with sour cream and potato! Roast beef and turkey are also excellent. Cold platters and a complete smorgasbord are available, too. Red-and-white-checkered tablecloths and pretty posters of Denmark add a cheerful touch to the two indoor dining rooms and outdoor terrace. Open daily from 6 PM to 1 AM, Sundays for lunch also. No reservations. No credit cards accepted. 983 Rua General San Martín, Leblon (phone: 294-0347). Inexpensive.

**Mistura Fina** – During the day, this eatery has an inexpensive prix fixe lunch and a salad bar. Open Tuesdays through Sundays from noon to 6 PM. Reservations unnecessary. Major credit cards accepted. 15 Rua Garcia D'Avila, Ipanema (phone: 267-6596). Inexpensive.

**Oriento** – If you have a very large appetite or a very low budget, make a beeline straight here. Not only are the portions huge, but the food is well prepared. The egg drop soup is full of peppers, eggs, and mushrooms. The beef with green pepper and diced chicken with bean sprouts are delicious. Anything you order will be large enough to share. Chinese lanterns provide the decor. Open until midnight nightly. No reservations. Major credit cards accepted. 64 Rua Bolívar and Av. Copacabana, Copacabana (phone: 275-7798). Inexpensive.

**Oxalá** – This counter-only eatery downtown, on one of Cinelândia's narrow streets, has the best Bahian food in Rio. It packs in the natives at lunchtime. Specialties include delicious *vatapá, frigideiras* 6 inches high and generously stuffed with shrimp, *moqueca* (fish, oyster, or crab), and *carurú*. For dessert, don't pass up the *pudin*, a milk pudding you'll never forget. Reservations unnecessary. Major credit cards accepted. 36 Alvaro Alvim (phone: 220-3035). Inexpensive.

## OUTSIDE THE BUSINESS CENTER

If you're willing to travel for good food, consider a day trip to Pedra de Guaratiba, a fishing town on the outskirts of greater Rio. This is the home of delicious fresh seafood, and the two restaurants listed below are among the best. To get here, make taxi arrangements or catch the bus marked "Santa Cruz" on Avenida Atlântica in town.

**Cândido's** – Despite burning down during its 21st anniversary dinner in 1990, this eatery has rebuilt and reopened. Ask to be seated on the terrace; then settle back and watch the sunset as you dine on the daily catch. The owner of this popular place is a woman named Dona Carmen. Whether you make reservations through Carmen or an assistant, make them you must or you'll never get seated. Open daily from noon to 7 PM, Saturdays to 11 PM. American Express accepted. 352 Rua Barros Alarcão, Pedra de Guaratiba (phone: 395-1630). Expensive.

**Quatro Sete Meia** – A neighbor to *Cândido's,* this place is much smaller and just as popular. Its setting is a house and garden overlooking the sea; you can watch the local fishermen bring in their catch. The menu is limited to a few well-prepared dishes, mostly seafood. Try a *batida,* a drink made with *cachaça* (Brazilian rum), fruit juice or coconut milk, and honey. Open Mondays through Thursdays from noon to 5 PM; Fridays, Saturdays, and Sundays from noon to 11 PM. Reservations necessary. No credit cards accepted. 476 Rua Barros Alarcão, Pedra de Guaratiba (phone: 395-2716). Expensive.

# SALVADOR (BAHIA)

"Have you been to Bahia?," goes a well-known song by the beloved Brazilian composer, Dorival Caymmi. "No? Then go!"

Picture a fat thumb of land tapering southward from Brazil's northern Atlantic coast some 30 miles into the inky blue Atlantic. Along the eastern shoreline stretch mile after mile of golden sand beaches lined with tall coconut palms, while on the other side lies a vast bright blue bay studded with islands. And perched on the narrow tip of the peninsula in the state of Bahia, where 365 days a year the sea breezes blow from the ocean to the bay, is one of the loveliest cities in the world: Salvador da Bahia de Todos os Santos, known simply as Salvador — although some call it Bahia.

If Rio is the heart of Brazil and São Paulo its brain, Salvador is its spirit, for it was here that Brazil cut its first painful teeth and grew to potent young nationhood. And it was here in 1549 that the Portuguese founded the capital city and chief port of their new colony — and just in time, too, for in the next half century the young colony was attacked by the stubbornly persistent Dutch, who didn't make peace until 1647. Meanwhile, the city prospered, as Bahian sugar and cacao filled European kitchens. Vast fortunes were made with slave labor, both native South American and African, and much of the shameful slave trade was transacted here. The natives often preferred death to enslavement, but the resilient Africans endured and outlived it. Today, Salvador's colonial heritage remains alive not only in its glorious old buildings, but also in its beautiful brown-skinned citizens, with their unique mix of native American fortitude and European civility, both charged with the exuberance and sensual grace of Africa.

Bahians are infinitely hospitable, accepting with smiling patience all sorts of foreign intrusions and influences; but whatever comes to Bahia — human being or social institution — undergoes an almost imperceptible transformation, a very gradual and profound process of Bahianization. Witness the Roman Catholic church: Since the very beginning, the church has strewn its cathedrals, convents, monasteries, churches, and chapels all over the Bahian landscape; today there are some 500 throughout the state (over 150 in Salvador alone), many of them breathtaking examples of gold-encrusted baroque extravagance. Yet for every church there are several *terreiros* dedicated to the ancient African gods, houses of worship for the religion known here as *candomblé*. During *candomblé* ceremonies, devotees dance hypnotically to the specific drumbeat of each African god in turn, until the god being invoked suddenly "descends" into the body of his devotee, triggering, in some cases, a spectacular spasmodic reaction. Naturally the church frowned on all this for a long time, but Afro-Bahians, who were delighted to accept the Christian God and His Son (and especially the Son's mother and grandmother), have clung to both faiths; today they co-exist so amicably that the African gods and goddesses have been completely syncretized with the Christian saints and are worshiped under both names. With this potent blend of historical and cultural riches to draw on, it's no wonder that Salvador inspires so much of Brazil's first-rate art. Internationally acclaimed writers Jorge Amado and João Ubaldo Ribeiro live here, as do such highly gifted musicians and graphic artists as Carybé, Mario Cravo, Jr., and Jenner Augusto.

Although not nearly as large as Rio de Janeiro, some 1,022 miles (1,635 km) south, Salvador is a hardworking, modern metropolis. With the discovery of oil nearby and the founding of the $3 billion Camaçarí petrochemical complex, the city is growing northward at a galloping rate, and the new network of highways can barely keep up with the traffic. Between 1965 and the first years of this decade, Salvador grew from a cozy 400,000 to a very crowded 2 million, and there's no end in sight. Still, Salvador is in one of the poorest areas in Brazil and has very high birth and infant mortality rates. The city also has a crime problem ranging from armed robbery to pickpocketing and purse snatching by children, so be careful with your valuables (better yet, leave them home or in the hotel safe).

To get a sense of the city's layout, imagine that you are driving in from the airport along the beach road. You pass the pleasant beaches of Itapoã, Piatã, and Boca de Rio, each with its cluster of fishermen's houses and its scattering of luxurious summer villas; then come the middle class residential neighborhoods of Rio Vermelho, Pituba, and Amaralina, where little pink and blue and yellow houses snuggle up against newer white apartment buildings; then comes Ondina, where the new luxury hotels stare proudly over the ocean. Finally, at the squared-off point of the peninsula, is the elegant residential neighborhood of Barra, with expensive boutiques, trendy discos, and pretty little urban beaches. At this point the playful beach road curves around to the right, becoming the dignified Avenida Sete (7) de Setembro, which begins its gradual climb to the Upper City. Here it takes on the splendid trappings of colonial decor: great Portuguese palaces set in formal gardens, baroque churches, and carefully laid out parks and plazas. This stretch of broad avenue hugs the edge of the cliff overlooking the Bay of All the Saints, rewarding you with sudden, dazzling views between old mansions and new apartment houses. At the Campo Grande, officially called Praça Dois (2) de Julho (a sort of miniature tropical Central Park bordered by the very imposing Cardinal's Palace and the ultramodern theater *Castro Alves)*, it turns right, then left, and abruptly plunges into narrow streets crammed with modern banks, shops, and offices. All traffic inches along at a painful pace for several blocks, finally breaking free at the main plaza, Praça da Sé. Like Lisbon, the city on which it was modeled, Salvador is built into a cliff.

From Praça Municipal, the giant, public Lacerda Elevator carries you down to the Lower City in a few thrilling seconds, and you emerge onto a scene of frenetic activity: a thriving jumble of contemporary buildings and colorful open-air markets poised on the edge of a spectacularly beautiful harbor. In the streets of this area, you may catch an impromptu demonstra-

# SALVADOR
## (Bahia)

**Points of Interest**

1. Airport
2. Ocean Beaches
3. Igreja de São Francisco/Church of St. Francis
4. Igreja de Ordem Terceira de São Francisco/Church of the Third Order of St. Francis
5. Terreiro de Jesus
6. Catedral Basilica/Cathedral
7. Ladeira do Pelourinho/Pillory Hill
8. Museu do Convento do Carmo/Carmelite Convent Museum
9. Fundação Pierre Verger; Fundação Jorge Amado
10. Fundação Museu Carlos Pinto/Carlos Pinto Foundation Museum
11. Igreja e Convento de Santa Tereza/Church and Convent of Saint Teresa; Museu de Arte Sacra/Museum of Sacred Art

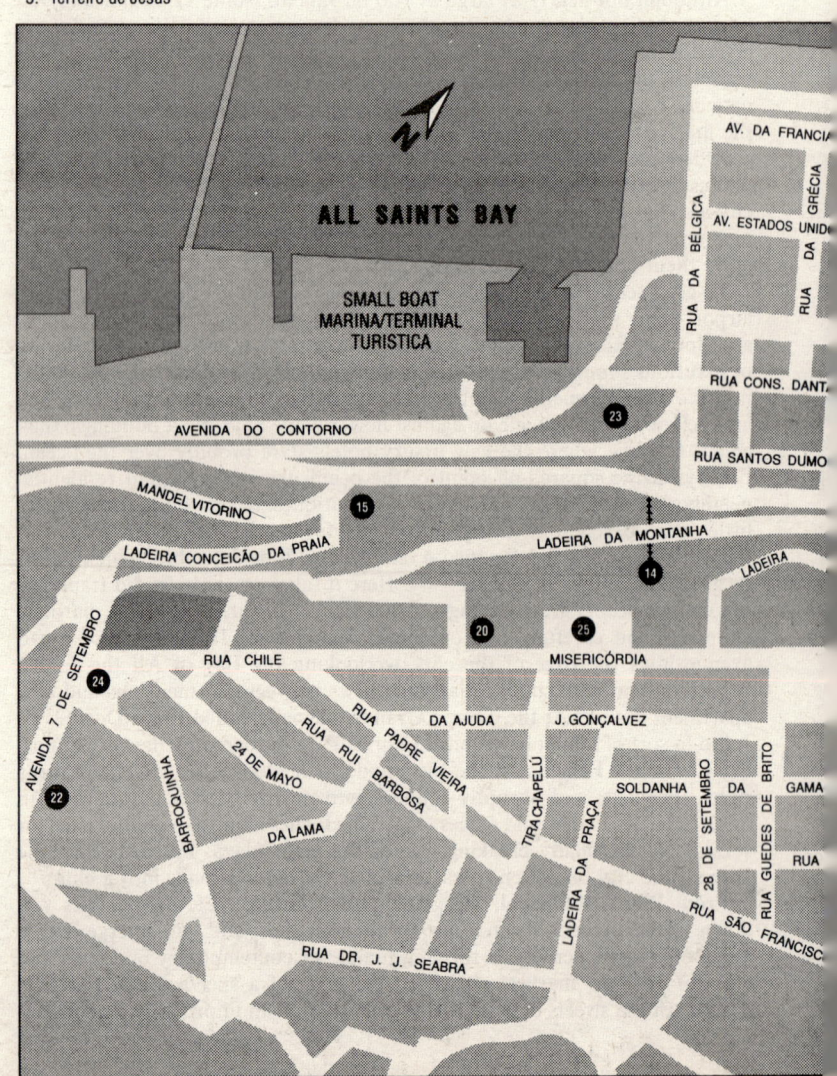

12. Igreja e Mosterio de Nossa Senhora da Graça/Church and Monastery of Our Lady of Grace
13. Forte de Santo Antônio da Barra/Fort of St. Anthony of Barra
14. Lacerda Elevator
15. Igreja de Nossa Senhora de Conçeição da Praia/Church of Our Lady of Immaculate Conception at the Beach
16. Bonfim
17. Feira de São Joaquim/São Joaquim Market
18. Igreja do Mont'Serrat/Mont'Serrat Church
19. Itaparica Island
20. Bahiatursa
21. Museu Afro-Brasileiro/Afro-Brazilian Museum
22. Museu de Arte da Bahia/Museum of Bahian Art
23. Mercado Modelo
24. Praça Castro Alvez
25. Praça Municipal

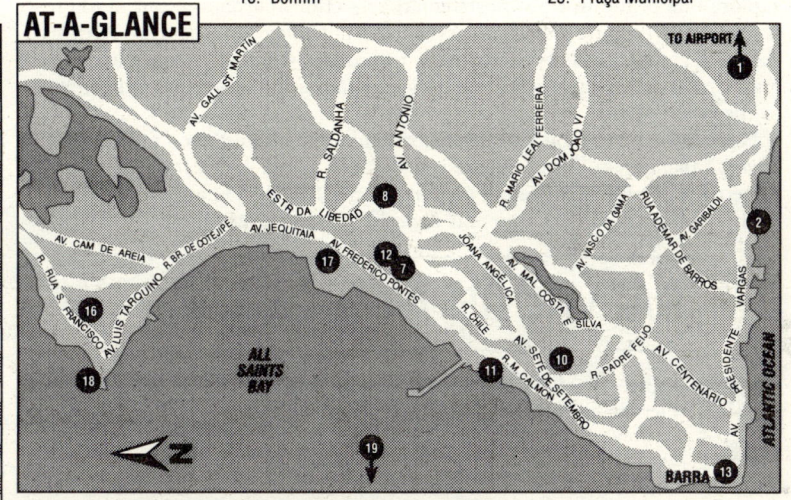

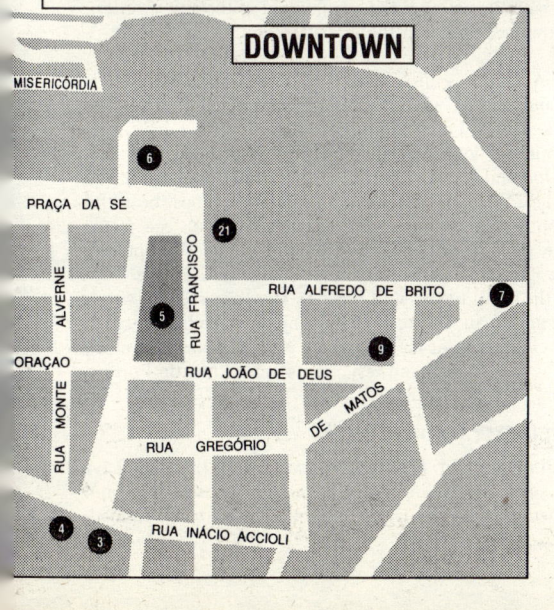

## AT-A-GLANCE

## DOWNTOWN

tion of *capoeira,* the ancient art of foot fighting that the African slaves (who were forbidden to fight by their Portuguese owners) cleverly disguised as a ritual dance. You're sure to see Bahian women dressed in traditional layers of brightly printed skirts and snowy, lace-trimmed blouses selling *acarajé:* plump crispy fritters of ground beans, fried in the bright gold oil of the *dendê* palm, and stuffed with *vatapá* — a soupy mixture made with dried shrimp, coconut milk, and spices, studded with fresh shrimp, and spiked, if you ask for it, with hot pepper sauce, which can be either a thrill or a disaster to the uninitiated stomach. And this is just the beginning, for in Salvador you can explore one of the world's most remarkable ethnic cuisines — but if you're trying it for the first time, go easy on the hot sauce. Invented by African slaves, it combines European cooking techniques with the rich oils and fragrant spices of Africa as well as with the vegetables and seasonings indigenous to the New World.

Not only are the food and layout of Bahia remarkable; even more so are *baianos* themselves. Their effervescence is not an act — it's for real. When someone from Bahia is feeling sad, his or her friends admonish cheerfully, "Why be depressed? Let's go and dance!" It works every time.

# SALVADOR AT-A-GLANCE

**SEEING THE CITY:** Because Salvador sprawls over so many different levels of terrain, there's no single vantage point that provides a bird's-eye view of the whole city. But you can get a panorama of the Upper City from the *Jangada* restaurant atop the *Meridien* hotel (216 Rua Fonte do Boi, Rio Vermelho Beach; phone: 248-8011); and from the Lacerda Elevator you'll get a fine view of the Lower City and the bay. Best of all is the terrific sight of the city's western face from Mont'Serrat (see below), especially in the late afternoon.

**SPECIAL PLACES:** A unique split-level city on a peninsula, Salvador is divided into Upper and Lower, with beaches on three sides. Catch a bus along the beach marked Itapoã or Aeroporto, or hire a car and driver and head for Bahia's 44 miles of golden beaches. You can stop and swim at any of the beaches, but watch out for undertows; it's best to swim only where you find Bahians. The two farthest beaches, Piatã and Itapoã, are probably the most beautiful and the longest, respectively; both offer plenty of restaurants where you can picnic royally on cooked crabs, lobster, shrimp, and the like. After Itapoã, the Metropolitan Region of Salvador begins. The Estrada do Côco, an asphalt road, runs parallel with the coast and connects most of the small towns with beaches. Here are a few to watch for — Ipitanga, at Km 2; Buraquinho, at Km 6; Jauá, at Km 15; Arembepe, at Km 26; Barra do Jacuípe, at Km 37; Guarajuba, at Km 42 (there's good camping here also); Itacimirim, at Km 49 (which has some hotels and restaurants); and Praia do Forte, a lovely resort near a 16th-century fort, at Km 83.

## UPPER CITY (CIDADE ALTA)

**Igreja da São Francisco (Church of St. Francis)** – *Baianos* joke that they have a church for every day of the year, and if you take all the religions and cults into consideration, it's probably true. Some of the larger Catholic churches are tremendously impressive. Two blocks from the Praça da Sé (walk past the whole line of buses and turn right) is one of the most famous 18th-century baroque churches in the world. Built by Franciscans with Portuguese stone, it's best known for the dazzling expanse of gold leaf that covers the interior. There are also some fine examples of hand-carved Brazilian rosewood and some charming scenes from the life of St. Francis in blue and white Portuguese tiles. The adjacent monastery has a very pretty tiled courtyard, which women may see only by peering through the door; men are welcome to tour the inner sanctum, accompanied by one of the Franciscans, from 7 to 11 AM and from 2 to 5 PM, except Sunday afternoons. The same hours apply for the church, although you may also attend mass before or after visiting hours. Closed during *Carnaval*. 1 Praça Padre Anchieta (phone: 243-2367).

**Igreja de Ordem Terceira de São Francisco (Church of the Third Order of St. Francis)** – Next door to the Church of St. Francis, this smaller church was completed in 1703; its façade, built of squared gray stone, is of the plateresque baroque style — the only such building in Brazil. Open from 8 to 11:30 AM and 2 to 5 PM, Saturdays from 8:30 to 11:30 AM. Largo de São Francisco at Rua Ignácio Accioli (phone: 242-7046).

**Catedral Basilica (Cathedral)** – Walk back from the Church of St. Francis through the Terreiro de Jesus, where on Sundays there's an open-air handicrafts market known as the "Hippie Fair." There you can pick up primitive paintings by Bahian artists that some critics predict will soar in value (as did Haitian art about 25 years ago). The massive church at the far end of the square is the cathedral, built from 1657 to 1672 by the Jesuits, who then lost it to the local archdiocese in 1759, when they were kicked out of Brazil. Here, too, is some splendid gold leaf, especially the high altar. Open daily from 7 to 11 AM and from 2 to 6 PM. Closed during *Carnaval*. Terreiro de Jesus (phone: 243-4573).

**Ladeira do Pelourinho (Pillory Hill)** – From the cathedral, it's just a short walk down Rua Alfredo de Brito, Pelourinho, a wonderful old neighborhood of gaily colored colonial houses jammed together on steeply twisting cobbled streets. A couple of centuries ago, the respectable ladies of the district would while away long afternoons on these pretty little balconies, observing the agonies of the disobedient slaves and other miscreants who were pilloried in the square below. Today these colorful streets harbor more than one juvenile pickpocket, and the ladies of Pelourinho are reputed to be not so respectable (some women might not feel entirely comfortable walking here alone, though they would certainly be in no actual danger). The government authorities, in an attempt to uplift the moral character of the neighborhood, are encouraging writers and artists to live and work here. The result has been a general face-lift of the neighborhood. Stop briefly at the *Fundaçõ Pierre Verger* to see its interesting collection of *candomblé* artifacts, among other things. Open daily, except Sundays, from 9 AM to noon and 2 to 5 PM. Admission charge. 45 Rua Gregório de Mattos (no phone). Just a couple of doors away is the *Fundaçáo Pierre Verger,* which houses memorabilia devoted to the Bahian writer, Jorge Amado. Open daily, except Sundays, from 9 AM to noon and 2 to 5 PM. No admission charge. 49-51 Rua Gregório de Mattos (phone: 321-0122).

**Museu do Convento do Carmo (Carmelite Convent Museum)** – From the bottom of Pelourinho, it's a short but steep walk up the Ladeira do Carmo to the Igreja do Passo (Church of Passo). Climb this impressive flight of steps and continue to the top of the hill. Here you'll find a beautiful Carmelite church, founded in 1585, with a delightful little museum containing many dolls in religious costumes; ceremonial objects in silver, gold, and precious stones; and a colorful exhibit explaining the syncretism of *candomblé* gods with Christian saints. Open daily from 8 AM to noon and 2 to 6 PM. Admission charge. Largo do Carmo (phone: 242-0182).

**Fundação Museu Carlos Costa Pinto (Carlos Costa Pinto Foundation Mu-**

seum) – This little jewel of a museum gives you a great way to see how the other half lives (or used to live). The descendants of Costa Pinto have built a showcase for the family's collection of 17th- and 18th-century furniture, Chinese porcelain, Baccarat crystal, dazzling jewelry, and a wonderful collection of silver *balangandãs* (fruit clusters). Open Wednesdays through Fridays from 2:30 to 6:30 PM; Saturdays and Sundays from 3 to 6 PM. Admission charge. 2490 Av. 7 de Setembro (phone: 247-6081).

**Igreja e Convento de Santa Tereza (Church and Convent of Saint Teresa)** – This compound was built in the 17th century for the Shoeless Carmelite's Order of Saint Teresa. The Federal University of Bahia has restored the church and convent and installed the *Museu de Arte Sacra* (Museum of Sacred Art). This is the most impressive of Bahia's museums, with an immensely valuable collection of religious art in various media: tiles, sculptures, paintings, and silver artifacts. Open Tuesdays through Saturdays from 10 to 11:30 AM and 2 to 5:30 PM. Admission charge. 276 Rua do Sodré (phone: 243-6511).

**Igreja e Mosteiro de Nossa Senhora da Graça (Church and Monastery of Our Lady of Grace)** – Considered the oldest church in Salvador, this 18th-century structure includes part of a 16th-century monastery. The sacristy houses a fine collection of famous paintings. Open daily, except Sundays, from 7 AM to 5 PM. Largo da Graça (phone: 247-4670).

**Forte de Santo Antônio da Barra (Fort of St. Anthony of Barra)** – Known locally as the "Farol da Barra" ("Lighthouse of Barra"), it's the oldest and most picturesque fort of Salvador. The *Museu Hidrográfico de Salvador* (Hydrographical Museum) was installed in it in 1975. Open daily except Mondays from 10 AM to 1 PM and 2 to 5:30 PM. No admission charge. Av. Oceanica, Farol da Barra.

**Centro Administrativo da Bahia (Administrative Center of Bahia)** – Originally constructed to encourage the growth of a new urban area of Salvador, this stark modern building is accented with sculptures and murals by Bahia's artists. The CAB was designed by Lúcio Costa and landscaped by Roberto Burle Marx, both of whom were involved in the development of Brasília. Av. Paralela.

## LOWER CITY (CIDADE BAIXA)

**Igreja de Nossa Senhora da Conçeicão da Praia (Church of Our Lady of Immaculate Conception at the Beach)** – As you exit from the Lacerda Elevator in the Lower City, turn left past a row of small shops and snack bars (the Brazilian soccer shirts in the sporting goods stores make nice gifts for US soccer fans) and you'll come to Conçeição da Praia, a magnificent Portuguese baroque church built by a Portuguese nobleman in honor of his daughter's wedding in 1739. Bahians also worship the sea goddess Iemanjá here. Open daily from 6:30 to 11:30 AM and 3 to 5:30 PM, except weekends and holiday afternoons. Largo de Conçeição da Praia (phone: 242-0545).

**Bonfim** – About 5 miles (8 km) from downtown Salvador, on a little hill overlooking the bay, is the most popular of all Bahia's churches, the Igreja de Nosso Senhor do Bonfim (Church of Our Lord of the Good Ending). For Bahians, Our Lord of Heaven, or Jesus of Nazareth, is identical with Oxalá, the father of the *candomblé* gods and goddesses. Worshipers often come here wearing the traditional costumes of that faith, especially in white and silver, Oxalá's colors. Bonfim has none of the gilded splendor of the powerful city churches, but there are beautiful scenes done in blue and white tiles. In the far right-hand rear corner is a tiny room full of grisly, but nonetheless moving, ex-votos, or mementos of "miraculous" cures, brought about by the guiding spirit of the place: wax castings of innumerable feet, hands, limbs, and organs, once mutilated or otherwise distressed, now completely recovered. The front steps look out over the city and bay. Aggressive women and children sell colorful Bonfim ribbons thought to bring luck to those who wear one tied around the wrist or ankle. As you put on the ribbon, make three silent wishs as you tie three knots. Who knows? Open daily from 6:30 AM to noon and 2:30 to 6 PM. Adro do Bonfim (phone: 226-0196).

**Feira de São Joaquim (São Joaquim Market)** – The largest market in Salvador, it's a vast sprawl of tiny stands crammed with strange, vivid fruits, vegetables, herbs, roots, and everything necessary to Bahian life. There are terrific bargains here on clay pots (some of them glazed on the inside for easy cleaning) and very funny little figurines from Maragogipe. Stop here on your way to or from Bonfim or come by taxi, but be prepared for the dirt, the smell, and being approached by beggars. The market is open daily from 6 AM to 6 PM, Sundays to 1 PM. Av. Jequitaia.

**Igreja do Mont'Serrat (Mont'Serrat Church)** – This church is just a few blocks away from Bonfim. The road winds past some lovely old hospitals and the Fort of Mont'Serrat (closed to the public), ending on a little point of land that juts out into the bay, where there is a tiny lighthouse and a sweeping view of the entire shoreline all the way to Barra, at the tip of Salvador's peninsula. Here, too, is the simple, 16th-century Chapel of Mont'Serrat, with its rough wooden benches and handsome Portuguese tiles. A few blocks away is the beach of Boa Viagem, where on Sundays (after mass at the Church of Bonfim) happy crowds gather to eat crabs and drink beer. Ponta de Humaitá (phone: 226-3051).

■ **EXTRA SPECIAL:** If you'd like to spend a cool and restful day away from the city, consider an excursion to the island of Itaparica. You can arrange (through your hotel or travel agent) a day's ferry cruise to several small islands, stopping in Itaparica for sightseeing, swimming, and lunch before returning to Salvador. The town of Itaparica is a sleepy little place, untouched by the galloping economic boom of the mainland. Be sure to visit the Fonte da Bica, a public garden in the heart of town where you can drink from a natural spring of mineral water. Pleasant beaches are within walking distance, and several modest hostelries offer excellent fresh seafood. There is also a fine *Club Med* resort on the island (see *Checking In*). Or you can cruise the bay on giant schooners (spelled *escuna* in Portuguese). They make the all-day trip to Itaparica, just as the ferries do; and they also make shorter cruises along the Salvador shoreline. Consult Bahiatursa (phone: 241-4333) or any travel agency.

# SOURCES AND RESOURCES

**TOURIST INFORMATION:** Bahiatursa, the official state tourist agency, has its most central office on Belvedere da Sé, off Praça da Sé (also known as Praça Tomé de Souza), in the elegant old Rio Branco Palace, just a few feet away from the Lacerda Elevator (phone: 241-4333). This agency has geared up for foreign tourists, and provides several pamphlets that occasionally include maps and a schedule of events (though only one is in English). The enthusiastic young staff members speak English and are eager to help travelers arrange guided or unguided tours and plan excursions. A map of the city is available for about $1. Bahiatursa has several other locations around town including stands at the airport (phone: 204-1244), the city bus station (phone: 231-2831), the Praça Azevedo Fernandes (phone: 358-0871), and the *Mercado Modelo* (phone: 241-0242).

It's possible, though not probable, that your hotel clerk will be able to give you up-to-date schedules for such events as concerts, folklore shows, and *candomblé* ceremonies. He or she can certainly put you in touch with travel agencies accustomed to guiding *norte-americanos* around town.

Many hotels carry the monthly *Itinerío Bahia,* which has a listing of special events and other information. The newsweekly *Veja* appears Mondays on Salvador's newsstands with a Bahia supplement. Both are in Portuguese, but places names and hours are decipherable.

**Local Coverage** – Salvador has no English-language newspaper, but *Time* and *Newsweek* arrive on Wednesdays or Thursdays. *USA Today,* the *Miami Herald,* and the *International Herald Tribune* arrive daily and are available from the city's major newsstands and hotels. Most of the major hotels also offer CNN (Cable News Network).

**TELEPHONE:** The city code for Salvador is 71. When calling from within Brazil, dial 071 before the local number. The country code for Brazil is 55.

**CLIMATE AND CLOTHES:** Thanks to the blissful coincidence of tropical sun and constant sea breezes, Salvador has balmy weather throughout the year, with highs usually in the 80s F (around 29C), lows in the 70s F (20s C). During the summer (December through March), temperatures can climb into the 90s F (30s C), but this is fine, clear summer heat, hardly ever the sticky sultry air that can be so oppressive in Rio. During these months, too, there are occasional fierce (but brief) rains — to be on the safe side, bring an umbrella. From June through September, the rains are more frequent, gentler, and longer-lasting.

Women travelers will be most comfortable in cotton or cotton-blend sundresses, shorts, or summer pants, with a light sweater or jacket for cool evenings and sturdy, flat-heeled sandals for steep, cobbled streets. Men can go virtually anywhere in lightweight pants and sport shirts, although Brazilian men of the upper classes often wear close-fitting dark suits and ties (never sport coats) to restaurants and the theater. For the beach, men and women alike wear the briefest of bikinis; and women often wrap themselves in a long swatch of cotton in bright tropical prints, known as a *kanga;* these do triple duty as long skirts, sarongs, and beach blankets.

**GETTING AROUND: Bus** – If you don't mind circuitous travel at breathtaking speeds, you won't mind the buses. They go virtually everywhere and cost very little. On most buses, you get on at the rear, pay at the turnstile, and exit at the front. (They will not change large notes on buses, so bring plenty of small change.) On the deluxe buses, called *seletivos,* or *executivos,* you board at the front and take a seat; a ticketseller collects the fare, generally about $1, en route. Many routes terminate at the Praça da Sé, where you'll see long lines of Bahians patiently waiting their turn to climb aboard with a restraint unknown in New York and other large cities. (A word of caution: When the buses get packed, they turn into a haven for pickpockets.)

**Taxi** – The best way to get around town, cabs are inexpensive and plentiful and drivers sometimes can be persuaded to drive at less than murderous speeds, which is not true of Salvadoran bus drivers. Because of rampant inflation, taxi meters now display a number corresponding to a fare on an official list, rather than the amount in *cruzieros;* the list is updated monthly. After 10 PM, on holidays, and when there are four or more passengers, the rate goes up by a fixed percentage, which the driver charges by raising the "#2" flag on the meter. For longer trips — along the beach road or to the Church of Bonfim — arrange a fixed price in advance; otherwise, pay only what's on the table. Reputable taxi companies include *Comtas* (phone: 245-6982), *Ligue Taxi* (phone: 359-7766), and *Radio Taxi* (phone: 243-4333).

**Car Rental** – Don't. Streets rarely are marked and traffic is impossible. However, if you insist, there is *Avis-Lokarbras* (1796 Av. 7 de Setembro; phone: 237-0154; and at the airport; phone: 249-2550), *Budget* (409 Av. Presidente Vargas; phone: 237-3396; and at the airport; phone: 891-1330), and *Hertz* (1 Rua Baependi; phone: 245-0448; and at the airport; phone: 204-1296).

## SALVADOR (BAHIA) / Sources and Resources

**SPECIAL EVENTS:** You're welcome to witness the colorful *candomblé* ceremonies at some of the major *terreiros*. Please remember that, despite the vivid costumes and spirited dancing, these are religious ceremonies. Dress conservatively, and don't take your camera. Men will be asked to sit on one side of the room, women on the other. Don't be nervous. This is a very friendly, humanistic religion, and most of the participants are Roman Catholics as well. Remember to leave a donation in the collection dish at the drummer's feet after the ceremony. If you prefer to go with a guide, check with any of the tourist agencies, which regularly sponsor evenings of *candomblé*. Try to arrive by 7:30 PM to get a seat. Most ceremonies begin around 8:30 PM and end between 11 PM and midnight. Arrange return transportation to your hotel in advance. To go on your own, call Bahiatursa for a list of current ceremonies (phone: 241-4333).

You'll see demonstrations of *capoeira*, an ancient and agile foot-fight-turned-ballet in any of the folklore shows (at the SENAC building, A Moenda, A Tenda dos Milagres); but if you get hooked on it, you can see more complete exhibitions (or even sign up for a course) at one of the official *capoeira* schools. Call Bahiatursa (phone: 241-4333) for up-to-date schedules.

Bahians celebrate every conceivable Roman Catholic and/or patriotic occasion with unbelievable enthusiasm. On these dates (which seem to occur every 10 days or so until December, and then go nonstop through *Carnaval*), taxis are harder to find, and buses are very infrequent. Try to allow a lot of time for getting around town; or just relax and let the full flood of Latin *alegría* flow over you. Besides *Carnaval* (the 4 days preceding *Ash Wednesday*), the most outstanding festivals include the following:

January 1, *Boa Viagem*, when a procession of boats carries the image of Our Lady of the Sailors across the bay to the beach at Boa Viagem, where the sailors carry her tenderly to her little church. Thousands of people eat, drink, and make merry.

On the Thursday before the third Sunday in January, *Bonfim*, costumed Bahian women wash the steps of the most popular church in the city, Nosso Senhor do Bonfim. This ritual is followed by feasting, which often goes on for days.

On February 2, the feast of *Iemanjá* is celebrated. To win the goodwill of the goddess of the sea and to bribe her not to swallow up their fishermen husbands, brothers, and fathers, Bahian women in traditional lace costumes assemble at the water's edge in Rio Vermelho and Itapoã and send little gifts of pretty cakes, combs, and scented soaps floating out to sea. General feasting goes on all day.

June 24 and June 29 are *St. John's* and *St. Peter's* days, respectively. The saints in these cases provide slender excuses for what are really harvest festivals, with bonfires, fireworks, and traditional dishes of *canjica* (a firm pudding made of sweet corn and coconut milk) and homemade fruit liqueurs.

On September 27, *Saints Cosme* and *Damian* are revered. Everybody feasts enthusiastically, and a lot of *carurú* (stewed okra) is consumed.

On December 8, *Conceição da Praia*, a religious procession to the church of that name, is preceded and followed by immoderate eating, drinking, and merriment in the area surrounding the *Mercado Modelo*.

**MUSEUMS:** In addition to those described in *Special Places*, Salvador's major museums include the following:

**Museu de Arte da Bahia (Museum of Bahian Art)** – A restored colonial mansion houses 18th-century tiles, furniture, ceramics, silver, and paintings from Europe as well as Bahia. Open daily, except Mondays, from 2 to 6 PM. 2340 Av. 7 de Setembro, Vitoria (phone: 235-9492).

**Museu de Arte Moderna (Museum of Modern Art)** – Works of contemporary artists are housed in what was once an old estate house. Open daily, except Mondays, from 1 to 5 PM. Av. do Contorno, Solar do Unhão (phone: 243-6174).

**Estácio de Lima** – Cultural anthropology, African culture, and criminology. Open weekdays 8 AM to 4 PM. Av. Centenário, near the police station, or Polícia Técnica (phone: 245-4144).

**Museu Afro-Brasileiro (Afro-Brazilian Museum)** – A historical portrayal of African influence on Brazilian society, including clothing, musical instruments, and photography. Open Tuesdays through Saturdays from 9 to 11:30 AM and 2 to 5 PM. In the old School of Medicine, Terreiro de Jesus (phone: 243-0384).

**SHOPPING:** Good buys are silver jewelry, gemstones, hand-carved rosewood, and (especially useful if your suitcases are stuffed to capacity) leather bags of all sizes and shapes. Bahia is also the home of many interesting artists. Among the galleries you might want to check are *Acervo* (37 Rua Alfonso Celso; phone: 245-2783), and *Epoca* (246 Rua João Gomes; phone: 245-5541).

***Barra Shopping Center*** – The newest and most modern of the city's malls, this one has movie theaters and discos, as well as boutiques representing the country's finest designers. Open weekdays from 10 AM to 10 PM, Saturdays from 9 AM to 9 PM. On Sundays, only the movie theaters and fast food places are open — from 3 to 9 PM. Av. Antiprário, in the Chame-Chame district.

***Gerson Shops*** – For silver of reliable quality at fixed prices, outside the chaos and bargaining of the market, these establishments may suit you better. There are branches in all the luxury hotels, in the *Museu do Convento do Carmo* (Carmelite Convent Museum), and on the third floor of the *Iguatemi Shopping Center*, on the road to the airport.

***Iguatemi Shopping Center*** – Bahians are very excited about this very big, very US-style shopping center. It even has a *Big Burger* restaurant on the ground floor, and every major store in town has an outlet in it somewhere. Most shops are open Mondays through Fridays from 9 AM to 9 PM, Saturdays to 6 PM.

***Instituto Mauá*** – This nonprofit organization is dedicated to preserving traditional arts and crafts of the Brazilian interior: embroidery, weaving, lace making, potting. It has branches at Porto da Barra (phone: 235-5440). Closed Sundays.

***Itaigara Shopping Center*** – Another modern, US-style shopping mall, it has 3 levels filled with shops. Not far from the *Iguatemi Shopping Center*, on Av. Antônio Carlos Magalhães, Pituba.

***Mercado Modelo*** – Destroyed by fire in 1984 and now reopened, it is the best place to stock up on silver or rosewood *figas* (traditional Brazilian amulets) for all your friends and relatives, to protect them from the evil eye. The smallest ones can be found for less than $1. Or you may want to harvest a collection of the lovely silver fruits known as *balagandãs,* which you see everywhere hanging in clusters from silver brackets *(pencas).* In colonial days, Portuguese swains gave these as tokens of appreciation to the slave women whose favors they enjoyed, and the women wore them at their waists as readily convertible assets, much the way some women today sport diamond rings. Be careful not to mistake acrylic for rosewood (jacaranda); or silverplate *(banhada de prata)* for real silver *(prata legítima, prata noventa).* There are also a couple of silver alloys widely sold in the market, known as *prata sessenta* and *alpaca;* these have the advantage of not corroding, and also cost less than real silver, but they don't much look like real silver, either. Other buys include regional musical instruments, embroidered cotton blouses and nightgowns, semiprecious stones, and religious icons. There are many Gypsies in this area who will want to tell you your fortune. It's best to ignore them as some may try to rob you. Open Mondays through Saturdays from 8 AM to 6 PM, Sundays from 8 AM to noon. On Praça Cairu, in the Lower City (phone: 242-3683).

## SALVADOR (BAHIA) / Sources and Resources 487

**SPORTS:** Salvador is just one soccer-mad city in a *futebol*-mad country.

**Soccer** – Don't miss a chance to attend a soccer match in the *Estádio Otávio Mangabeira*, which is as memorable for the passionate delight of the spectators as for the brilliant performances of the players. Games start at 4 PM on Sundays and at 9 PM on Wednesdays. Arrive an hour ahead of time, earlier for championships or other really big events, and pay the extra few cents for seats in the section marked "Numeradas." You won't be allowed to bring glass bottles into the stadium with you. Beer and snacks are sold by vendors throughout the game. Fonte Nova (phone: 243-7507).

**Swimming** – In addition to the beaches mentioned in *Special Places*, there are swimming pools at most of the better hotels listed in *Checking In*, below. Remember that the tropical sun is very strong, especially when reflected off sand and water. Unless you're already tanned when you arrive, you won't be able to spend more than a few minutes a day on the beach anyhow.

**Tennis** – There are courts at the *Meridien* hotel (216 Rua Fonte do Boi; phone: 248-8011); *Vela Branca* hotel (Av. Antônio Carlos Magalhães, Pituba; phone: 359-7022); and *Sofitel Quatro Rodas* hotel (Rua Pasárgada, Farol de Itapoa, Km 28; phone: 249-9611).

**THEATER:** The largest and most important theater is *Teatro Castro Alves* (Praça Dois de Julho, Campo Grande; phone: 235-7616), in the Upper City, which seats 1,700 people in air conditioned comfort. You almost always can get tickets for plays and concerts at the last minute. If you want to buy them in advance, the box office is open from 9 AM until noon and from 2 PM until the performance.

**MUSIC:** Among Brazil's best-known musicians, such internationally acclaimed Bahian music makers as Caetano Veloso, Maria Bethânia, and Gilberto Gil perform annually in Salvador; they pack the *Teatro Castro Alves* to overflowing. Check at your hotel to find out if any major Brazilian artists are appearing during your visit.

**NIGHTCLUBS AND NIGHTLIFE:** As throughout most of South America, disco has taken over the nightclub scene in Salvador. You're as likely to hear North American rock as you are bossa nova in the most swinging discos. Lambada is still danced at clubs all over Salvador. Some clubs and discos have nights just for lambada, while others have lambada bands that each evening alternate with samba and rock bands. At present, hot spots are *Le Zodiaque* and *Canoa* at the *Meridien* hotel (216 Rua Fonte do Boi; phone: 248-8011); *Hippopotamus (Bahia Othon Palace Hotel*, 2456 Av. Presidente Vargas; phone: 247-1044, ext. 1518); *Champagne (Salvador Praia Hotel;* 2338 Av. Presidente Vargas, Ondina; phone: 245-5033); *Churrascaría Roda Viva* (Av. Otávio Mangabeira, Jardim dos Namorados; phone: 248-3499); *Close Up* (84 Av. Presidente Getúlio Vargas, Barra; no phone); *Buall' Amour* (Av. Otávio Mangabeira, Corsário; phone: 231-9775).

At the following places, you can have a good meal (international or Bahian), as well as enjoy some fine music: *Berro d'Agua* (27-A Rua Barão de Sergy, Porta da Barra; phone: 235-2961), the "in" gathering spot for young *baianos* to talk and mingle; *Bistrô do Luís* (369 Rua Conselheiro Pedro Luís, Rio Vermelho; phone: 247-5900); *Dose Dupla* (2 Rua Bráulio Xavier, Vitória; phone: 245-5530), a discotheque for the young; and *Uauá* (46 Av. Dorival Caymi, Itapoã; phone: 249-9579), which has *forró* and *caipira* (traditional Brazilian dance music) on Fridays and Saturdays.

# BEST IN TOWN

**CHECKING IN:** By US standards, Salvador's hotels tend to be pretty expensive for the level of luxury they provide. Here, as in other places, you pay considerably more for a beachfront address than for similar comfort elsewhere in the city. And you may not use the beach enough to make the difference worthwhile. Furthermore, real beach enthusiasts won't want to limit themselves to the small urban beaches of the big hotels, with much more spectacular beaches only a few minutes down the road.

All the hotels listed here are air conditioned, unless otherwise noted. All provide complimentary breakfasts of fruit, coffee, and bread. All but the inexpensive ones accept American Express, Diners Club, MasterCard, and Visa. Expect to pay $100 and up for a double room in hotels we list as expensive; between $50 and $90 at those in the moderate category; and under $40 in the inexpensive range. All telephone numbers are in the 71 city code unless otherwise indicated.

Note: Two US credit cards are known in Brazil by Brazilian names: MasterCard is called *Passaporte* and Visa doubles as *Cartão Elo*.

**Bahia Othon Palace** – "Palace" is a good word for this sumptuous member of the Othon chain. Completely modern and elegantly appointed, it has nonetheless managed to incorporate into its architecture and decor many traditional elements of Bahia's urban landscape: the soaring stone arches of its cathedrals, beautiful ceramic tiles, pale rattans, polished woods, and vivid textiles. Perched on a hill at the edge of the sea, it offers a smallish beach, an immense pool, a legitimate massage parlor, several boutiques, a coffee shop, the excellent *Lampião* restaurant (see *Eating Out*), a couple of bars, and a nightclub. Each room has an ocean view. 2456 Av. Presidente Vargas, Ondina (phone: 247-1044). Expensive.

**Club Med Itaparica** – This tropical resort grows in popularity every year. There is air conditioning, a refrigerator, and an individual safe in each of the property's 346 rooms. Pastimes include a 9-hole golf course, swimming, horseback riding, windsurfing, yachting, and just about any other sport you'd expect from a beachside *Club Med*. There's supervised recreation for children. Two-night minimum stay. Km 13 on Estrada Nazaré (phone: 833-1141; in the US, 800-CLUB MED). Expensive.

**Enseada das Lajes** – Each of the 8 rooms in this charming member of the Relais & Châteaux group faces the sea. Furnished with Brazilian antiques, the rooms have wood floors, picture windows, air conditioning, mini-bars, and TV sets. There's a swimming pool, a private beach, and a classic Bahian dining room. Staff outnumber guests almost 2 to 1. 511 Av. Oceanica, Rio Vermelho (phone: 336-1027, 336-0654, and 336-0665). Expensive.

**Hotel da Bahia** – A member of *Varig*'s Tropical hotel chain, and currently the best property in the downtown area. It is tailored more to the businessperson than to the resort seeker. There are 282 rooms and very attractive public areas. 2 Praça Dois de Julho, near the *Castro Alves Theater*, Campo Grande (phone: 321-3699; in Rio de Janeiro, 21-240-7776). Expensive.

**Meridien Bahia** – Just up the beach from the *Bahia Othon Palace* this 426-room hotel is the city's largest. A member of the French hotel chain, it offers the same degree of luxury as the *Bahia Othon Palace* but on a much larger and jazzier scale with a beach, pool, boutiques, sauna, solarium, tennis courts, a marina, several excellent restaurants (see *Eating Out*), bars and clubs (see *Nightclubs and Nightlife*, above). The ocean view from the top floor is memorable. 216 Rua Fonte do Boi, Rio Vermelho (phone: 248-8011). Expensive.

**SALVADOR (BAHIA) / Best in Town 489**

**Salvador Praia** – Right next to the *Bahia Othon Palace* on the Ondina beach, this place is smaller but only slightly less expensive. Its comfortable rooms overlook the ocean and swimming pool. You'll find the predictable services: boutiques, beauty salon, coffee shop, restaurant, bar, and nightclub. 2338 Av. Presidente Vargas, Ondina (phone: 245-5033). Expensive.

**Sofitel Quatro Rodas** – The newest of Salvador's deluxe establishments is on Itapoã Beach, about a 40-minute drive from town. In addition to 195 rooms, this resort hotel has a pool, covered gym and other sports facilities, including tennis, volleyball, as well as its own 9-hole golf course. Other amenities are a baby-sitting service, an excellent restaurant, a satellite dish for international TV reception, and sand and sea out front. Rua Pasárgada, Farol de Hapoã (phone: 245-5033). Expensive.

**Manhattan** – Located 4 blocks from the upscale beach of Pituba, this recently opened 63-room apartment hotel has complete kitchen facilities, Jacuzzis, and satellite television in each unit, making it a good value for long-term stays, and appealing to those who want a firsthand glimpse of daily life in a pleasant residential neighborhood. There is a pool, tennis court, and health club. The Friday *feijoida completa* lunch at its *Madison* restaurant is one of the few places in town to sample the Brazilian national dish. 445 Rua Maranhão, Pituba (phone: 248-9911). Expensive to moderate.

**Praiamar** – Next door to the *Grande Hotel da Barra,* just a few steps removed from the beach, it is aggressively modern in decor. It, too, has a pool, bar, restaurant, and shops. 3577 Av. 7 de Setembro, Barra (phone: 247-7011). Expensive to moderate.

**Grande Hotel da Barra** – Also on Avenida 7 de Setembro, but all the way down the hill where it meets the sea in a posh residential section, this place has a split personality. There is the older, street side of the hotel, where rooms are less expensive but also shabbier and noisier; and there is the ocean side. Here, the attractive newer rooms have balconies overlooking either the adjacent beach, which is fine though crowded, or the inner courtyard and pool. Each side has its own reception desk, but guests in any of the rooms may use the various hotel services — pool, bars, or restaurant. By all means pay the extra $5 or so for a newer room. Little English is spoken. Av. 7 de Setembro at 2 Rua Forte de São Diogo, Barra (phone: 247-6011). Moderate.

**Hotel do Farol** – A walk across the street from this hotel will take you to the Farol do Barra beach, where a lighthouse (*farol*) at the far point makes for a lovely view at sunset. Fashionable boutiques and lots of pizza parlors make this a pleasant and popular neighborhood, and the hotel itself has a restaurant, bar, and pool. 68 Av. Presidente Vargas, Barra (phone: 247-7611). Moderate.

**Ondina Praia** – This is the budget version of the three big beach hotels. It sits across from the *Bahia Othon Palace* and the *Salvador Praia* on the other side of the perilous Avenida Presidente Vargas (people drive very quickly on this boulevard), which guests must cross to get to the beach. Small, pleasant, and ultramodern, it, too, has a pool, coffee shop, and gift shop. 2275 Av. Presidente Vargas, Ondina (phone: 247-1033). Moderate.

**Vela Branca** – This one feels more like a US motel than a Bahian hotel. A few minutes farther out of town than the more expensive beach hotels, it does have quite a good beach as well as a pool, restaurant, and bar. 585 Av. Antônio Carlos Magalhães, Pituba (phone: 359-7022). Moderate.

**Vila Velha** – A few doors down from the *Plaza* and a bit less expensive, this attractive little hotel is popular with North American families. No pool or beach, but a friendly ambience and all the necessary services. 1971 Av. 7 de Setembro, Vitória (phone: 247-8722). Moderate.

**Bahia do Sol** – Close to the *Vila Velha,* this smallish place has a pleasant ambience, reasonable prices, and services, with a bar, coffee shop, and restaurant. 2009 Av. 7 de Setembro, Vitória (phone: 247-7211). Inexpensive.

**Camping Club do Brasil** – If you are prepared to camp on the beach and prefer the convenience of campsites, the area has room for 350 tents, several caravan sites, showers and washing facilities, toilets, and a store. On Praia do Flamengo, about 31 miles (50 km) from town (phone: 249-2001). Inexpensive.

**EATING OUT:** To savor the full glory of Bahian cooking, the best bets are the modest restaurants popular with Bahians themselves; these include *Yemanjá* out on the beach road and the *SENAC* restaurant in Pelourinho. Among the more elegant establishments, *Lampião* also serves excellent local specialties. Alas, certain international restaurants tend to adulterate Bahia's brilliant sauces with canned condensed milk and, in a misguided effort to imitate European cuisine, garnish honest cuts of meat with limp, tasteless, canned vegetables.

Be sure to try a *moqueca,* freshly caught fish (or shellfish) simmered in golden dendê oil with what Bahians call "all the seasonings:" sweet peppers, onions, scallions, tomatoes, garlic, parsley, cumin, and fresh coriander. Like most Bahian dishes, your *moqueca* will arrive with a side dish of rice. If you like spicy food, ask for the hot pepper sauce (*molho de pimenta*) — but watch out. This stuff is *hot.* If you'd prefer to try the same seafood poached in fresh coconut milk (with the same seasonings), ask for an *ensopado.* Two other tasty Bahian dishes are *galinha ao molho pardo,* fresh-killed chicken in a savory brown sauce enriched with the chicken's own blood, and *xinxim* (pronounced sheen-sheen) *de galinha*, chicken in a thick, tasty sauce of ground peanuts or cashews, plus "all the seasonings." And for dessert, don't fail to order *quindim* (pronounced *keen-jeen),* a jewel-like custard of egg yolks, sugar, and coconut; or *papo-de-anjo,* which is the same thing without the coconut; or the rich coconut candies known as *cocadas.*

Lunch usually is served from noon until 3 PM, dinner from 7 until 10 PM, although all such hours in Bahia are approximate and variable. Except for major tourist stops, most places are closed on Mondays. You don't need a reservation or a necktie, although upper class Bahian men usually wear the latter to the fancier restaurants.

There's only one menu for both lunch and dinner. Bahians traditionally eat their big meal at noon. Portions are hefty; you probably won't need a first course. Besides, first courses can cost almost as much as entrées, since only tourists order them. Beware, too, of ordering drinks containing imported booze: They often cost $8 or more. Brazilian beer is excellent with Bahian food, as is the local firewater, *cachaça,* blended with fruit juice into a *batida*.

Expect to pay $30 and up for a meal for two at those restaurants we've categorized as expensive; between $10 and $20 for a meal at restaurants in the moderate category; under $10, inexpensive. This does not include appetizers, drinks, wine, or tips. All telephone numbers are in the 71 city code unless otherwise indicated.

Note: Be warned that Salvador's restaurants don't all believe in plastic payment. Because of the high inflation rate, currently even many of the expensive restaurants simply refuse to accept credit cards. If you wish to pay with a credit card, be sure to double-check with the restaurant in advance.

**Casa da Gamboa** – In an old colonial house with lace curtains and antique furniture, its atmosphere evokes a past era. Bahian specialties, such as grilled fish with carmelized pineapple and shrimp (*fruta e mel),* are served up by waitresses dressed in typical regional costume. There's an English-language menu. Open daily, except Sundays, from noon to 3 PM and for dinner until 11:30 PM. American Express accepted. 51 Rua Newton Prado (Gamboa de Cima), Aflitos (phone: 321-9776). Expensive.

**Chez Bernard** – This intimate little room feels more European than Brazilian.

## SALVADOR (BAHIA) / Best in Town

Prized by local cognoscenti for its consistently good French food, it also offers a spectacular view of the bay. Closed Sundays. Major credit cards accepted. 11 Gamboa de Cima, Aflitos (phone: 245-9402). Expensive.

**Jangada** – You get an impressive view of the city from up here on top of the *Meridien* hotel, and the French food is pretty good by local standards, but you'll certainly pay top dollar for it. Open daily, from 7 PM to midnight. Major credit cards accepted. 216 Rua Fonte do Boi, Rio Vermelho (phone: 248-8011). Expensive.

**Lampião** – Named for the Robin Hood of the Brazilian northeast, this handsome, bright red restaurant in the *Bahia Othon Palace* features delicious Bahian food beautifully presented. Try any of the *moquecas* here. It's too bad this place isn't open for lunch, because it looks out on a nice stretch of ocean. Dinner daily, from 7 PM to midnight. Major credit cards accepted. 2456 Av. Presidente Vargas, Ondina (phone: 247-1044). Expensive.

**Solar do Unhão** – Here you dine in a wonderful old sugarcane processing factory, where the waves of the Bay of All the Saints literally lap at the thick, hand-built stone walls. Elegant and comfortable, this place is a popular rendezvous for Bahian politicians and jetsetters. Stick to the simpler dishes on the international menu, although the buffet table with Bahian dishes and a seafood menu are promising. The highlight here is the floor show that has samba, *capoeira* (a traditional slow dance), and *maculele* (knife dance). If you come at lunchtime, be sure to visit the adjoining museum and art gallery. Dinner only on Sundays. Major credit cards accepted. Av. do Contorno, Gamboa (phone: 245-5551). Expensive.

**Baby Beef** – Owned by the Paes Mendonça chain, this sophisticated *churrascaría* (barbecue place) offers tempting meat dishes for those who've had enough of Salvador's seafood. Open daily for lunch and dinner. Major credit cards accepted. Av. Antônio Carlos Magalhães, Pituba (phone: 244-0811). Moderate.

**Iemanjá** – Also on the shore road, an excellent choice for both seafood and typical Bahian dishes. Here too you will find a lot of local color, though it's off the main tourist route. Open for lunch daily, except Mondays, from noon to 4 PM, and for dinner daily, except Sundays, from 7 PM to midnight. No credit cards accepted. Av. Otávio Mangabeira at Jardim Armação, Boco do Rio (phone: 231-5770). Moderate.

**Moenda** – Definitely on the tourist route, but worth a visit nonetheless, this place serves a wider variety of Bahian dishes than most of the fancier spots in town. Dinner includes a lively floor show of traditional dances, including sambas, usually starting about 9:30 PM. Closed Mondays. American Express accepted. Rua P, 21st Block, Boca do Rio (phone: 231-7915). Moderate.

**Tenda dos Milagres** – Similar to *Moenda,* with a 9:15 PM floor show, but you pay about $5 more for it, though the extra fee entitles you to one *batida* and one *acarajé*. The dance based on the pulling in of fishing nets is worth the price of admission all by itself. Open daily. American Express accepted. 553 Av. Amaralina (phone: 248-6058). Moderate.

**Paes Mendonça** – When your schedule, budget, or appetite dictates a light lunch or a quick snack, do as the Bahians do: Head for the nearest *Paes Mendonça*. These are a chain of formica-tiled fast-food places with all the charm of *McDonald's*, but they're efficient, clean, and very inexpensive. You can get a decent grilled cheese sandwich *(queijo quente,* pronounced *cage-ooh-ken-chee)* for about 50¢, as well as hot dogs, hamburgers, miniature (and not very Italian) pizza, hot fudge sundaes, and assorted junk food. One of the better sandwiches is the *Americano:* ham, cheese, sliced tomato, and fried egg. There are also special daily dinners for about $6, including meat, rice or potato salad, a little vegetable garnish, and a slice of bread. You have to know the procedure: Decide what you want, pay for it at the cashier, then take a seat and order it, presenting your receipt. The places in this chain are highly visible in virtually all the major plazas (most of them are linked to enormous supermarkets of the same name) and are open Tuesdays through Saturdays from 7:30 AM to 7 PM, Mondays from noon to 7 PM. No credit cards accepted. Perhaps most convenient for travelers is the branch directly across the street from the *Mercado Modelo* and the one facing the beach in Barra (no phones). Inexpensive.

**SENAC** – One of the best deals in town, and it should be one of your first stops. Sponsored by the Center for Professional Training in Tourism and Hospitality, it's a self-service cafeteria in an attractive colonial dining room. You pay about $5 for all the Bahian food you can shovel onto your plate from a buffet that contains about 40 items, all of them labeled, so make a note of the things you especially like so you can seek them out at other restaurants. As an added attraction, there are free folkloric shows downstairs every night at 8 PM, including exhibitions of *candomblé, capoeira,* and samba as well as frequent productions of plays by local playwrights. (Be forewarned — the area is extremely dangerous after dark.) Open daily, except Sundays, for lunch from noon to 3 PM and for dinner from 7 to 11 PM; from 5 to 8 PM there is also a *seia* — coffee or hot chocolate served with a variety of typical Bahian sweets, costing less than $2. Major credit cards accepted. 13-19 Largo do Pelourinho (phone: 321-5502). Inexpensive.

# SANTIAGO

*Because of the bombing of Mormon churches and other US-related properties in the not-so-distant past, at press time the US State Department had extended a caution for travelers to Chile. For the latest information, contact the US Embassy in Santiago (phone: 671-0133).*

Among Latin Americans, Chilean hospitality is legendary, and the reputation is well deserved. From one end of the country — narrow as a leaf and 2,600 miles long (like a blade, Henry Kissinger once noted, "pointed at the heart of Antarctica") — to the other, visitors are uniformly treated with a courtesy and patience found in few other parts of the world. Whether trekking through the surreal orange Atacama Desert in the north, or marveling at the magnificence of the icy green fjords and powder-blue glaciers of Tierra del Fuego in the south, travelers always find someone willing to give directions, offer a taste of Chilean wine, or steer them to an intriguing restaurant.

The best way to see Chile and to meet its inhabitants is to travel via the Pan-American Highway, the country's spinal column and the route that provides easiest access to at least 75% of this diverse land. Along this roadway, which begins in California and runs to the southern tip of the South American continent, are found Chile's fertile Central Valley and Santiago, the dynamic heart of Chilean activity.

Santiago, a splendid architectural collage of Northern European elegance, North American suburbia, and South American imagination and culture, is the home of more than 4 million *santiaguinos,* as residents are called. The city covers an area 40 miles from north to south and 20 miles east to west, surrounded by some of the most productive farmland in the nation and flanked on two sides by an overwhelming range of the Andes called the Cordillera.

Santiago owes its existence to a half-starved Spanish soldier-of-fortune who, under the sponsorship of King Charles III, staggered into a rich, fertile valley and grandly proclaimed the founding of Santiago del Nuevo Extremo on February 12, 1541. Its beginning was not without setbacks. Indians living along the Mapocho River did not take kindly to founding father Pedro de Valdivia and his motley group of armor-clad soldiers. They burned down the budding future capital of Chile twice. No sooner was it reconstructed and well on its way to becoming a permanent settlement than it was leveled in a savage earthquake in 1674. But the descendants of the early Spanish adventurers and the other Europeans who joined them in this New World did not give up easily, and by 1800 the city had become a major South American capital.

In its more recent political past, Chile was ruled (from 1970 to 1973) by the Socialist-Communist coalition government of President Salvador Allende Gossens, which was overthrown, with the help of the CIA, by the armed

# SANTIAGO

## Points of Interest

1. Cerro San Cristóbal/Saint Christopher Hill; Parque Metropolitana
2. Plaza de Armas
3. Post Office
4. Catedral
5. Museo Histórico Nacional/National Historical Museum
6. Museo de Arte Precolombino/Pre-Columbian Art Museum
7. Palacio de la Moneda/Presidential Palace
8. Casa Colorada/Red House; Museo de Santiago/Santiago Museum
9. Iglesia y convento San Francisco y Museo de Arte Colonial/San Francisco Church and Museum of Colonial Art
10. Paseo Ahumada y Paseo Huérfanos/Ahumada Passage and Orphans Passage
11. Cerro Santa Lucía/Santa Lucía Hill
12. Palacio Cousiño
13. Planetario/Planetarium
14. Parque Forestal;
    Museo Nacional de Bellas Artes/National Fine Arts Museum;
    Museo de Arte Popular Americano/Museum of Popular American Art;
    Museo de Arte Contemporáneo/Museum of Contemporary Art
15. Quinta Normal; Museo de Historia Natural/Natural History Museum;
    Museo de Ciencia y Tecnologia/Science and Technology Museum;
    Museo Ferroviario/Railway Museum; Museo Nacional Aeronáutico de Chile/National Aeronautic Museum
16. Universidad Católica/Catholic University
17. Teatro Municipal/Municipal Theater
18. Terminal Norte/Norte Bus Station
19. Terminal Santiago/Santiago Bus Station
20. Estación Central/Central Train Station
21. Museo Iglesia de la Merced/La Merced Church Museum
22. Chilean National Tourist Office
23. Arturo Merino Benítez Airport
24. Estadio Nacional

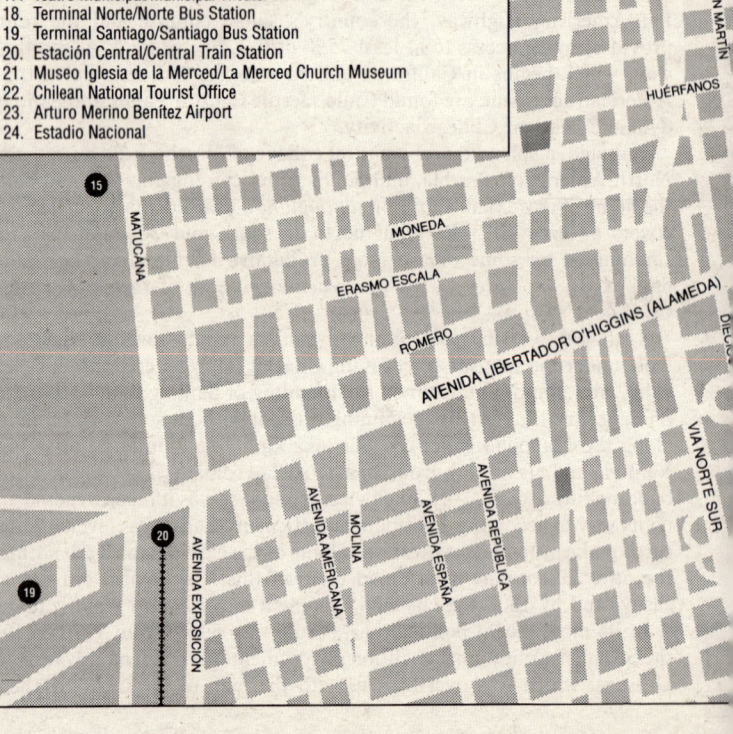

AV. PERÚ
N
1
FUNICULAR
DOMENICA
AVENIDA RECOLETA
AVENIDA LA PAZ
AVENIDA INDEPENDENCIA
SANTA FILOMENA
ANDRÉS BELLO
LORETO
CONSTITUCIÓN
BELLAVISTA
DARDIGNAC
BELLAVISTA
PIO NONO
22
AVENIDA SANTA MARÍA
CARDINAL J. M. CARO
AVENIDA ANDRÉS BELLO
AVENIDA PROVIDENCIA
14
AVENIDA VALDES VENGARA
21 DE MAYO
PUENTE
MONJITAS
MORANDE
BANDERA
3
CATEDRAL
2
4
5
6
MERCED
MACIVER
MIRAFLORES
BARRA
J. B. LASTARRIA
SUPERCASEAUX
SANTA LUCIA
21
COMPAÑIA
8
ESTADO
SAN ANTONIO
10
AHUMADA
11
MARCOLETA
AGUSTINAS
17
16
MONEDA
DIAGONAL PARAGUAY
AVENIDA FRANCISCO BILBAO
7
9
PARIS
13
ALONSO OVALLE
GENERAL JOFRE
MARÍN
TARAPACÁ
SAN ISIDRO
CARMEN
LIRA
AVENIDA GENERAL BUSTAMENTE
AVENIDA VICUÑA MACKENNA
SAN CAMILO
AVENIDA PORTUGAL
AVENIDA SANTA ROSA
SAN DIEGO
NATHANIEL COX
SERRANO
ARTURO PRAT
SAN FRANCISCO
AVENIDA DIEZ DE JULIO
AVENIDA M. ANTONIO MATTA
24

forces under General Augusto Pinochet, who then assumed the role of head of state. Amid citations of human rights abuses, charges of fraud by the opposition, and an outcry against a faltering economy, the military eventually yielded to the pressure of the populace. In 1988, a presidential plebiscite was called; Chileans voted "no" on whether Pinochet should remain in power and open elections were held at the end of 1989, making Patricio Aylwin Chile's first democratically elected president since Allende, although Pinochet remains in charge of the military. In 1991, a report was published that described more than 2,000 political murders, as well as countless human rights violations, that took place while Pinochet was in power — and talk of his resignation briefly surfaced.

During Pinochet's time in office, the strong presence of armed military personnel on the streets made Santiago a low-crime city day and night, but left foreigners — and doubtless many *santiaguinos* — uneasy. The Chilean capital remains relatively free of violent crime (although there have been increased concerns about street offenses), and border and customs officials intimidate visitors less now that democracy has returned to the country.

As in so many South American cities, contemporary Santiago is a confused jumble of colonial buildings in the grandest style competing for space and attention with modern corporate architecture. It is not just the surrounding snow-capped mountains that make Santiago's high-rises seem not so high. Like all areas that circle the Pacific Ocean, Chile is an earthquake zone, and the height of buildings is carefully controlled for safety reasons. The urban sprawl of Greater Santiago might remind you of one of the newer US cities west of the Mississippi, except for the shantytowns (*poblaciones*) in the northern and southern parts of town. Although compared with similar settlements in neighboring Latin American cities, Santiago's are relatively sturdy (and many even have television antennas), and there has been an attempt to block them from sight by constructing 5- and 10-story housing projects.

Like most North American cities, Santiago is primarily middle class, with a high proportion of university-educated adults. You will not see quaint Indian markets in this cosmopolitan capital. (At the government-sponsored *CEMA-Chile* shop, you can buy the best traditional and modern handicrafts from all over the country.) The native population — or *araucanos,* as the Spanish called them — were still fighting long after their counterparts in other areas of the continent were either dominated or driven to such remote regions that the conquering population ceased to worry about them. In Chile the battle lasted 300 years, which explains the reduced number of the original inhabitants. Nevertheless, the majority of Chileans are dark-haired, and many bear the wide cheekbones that speak of Indian blood. You also will encounter many Chileans who are tall, with light hair and eyes. (Don't be surprised by the number of redheads you see!) Early migrations of British, Germans, Yugoslavs, French, and — to a lesser extent — Italians have combined with the criollo (Spaniard born in Chile) and mestizo (mixture of Spanish and Indian) to produce a diversified and unusually attractive people. Chileans take great pride in extolling the beauty of their women. Pictures of women in skimpy bikinis adorn most Chilean travel brochures and posters, and Chilean men aren't bad looking either. And although machismo is a Spanish word that still applies to Chileans, the men generally are more polite and considerate toward foreign women than in other South American cities. By the way, no offense should be taken if you hear someone call you gringo or gringa. Chileans love to invent nicknames, and gringo usually refers to anyone with light hair, foreign or native. If you are African-American, you may feel somewhat uneasy, as black people are rare in this part of the world and often become objects of curiosity.

Chileans are fond of calling their country "the end of the world," and this vision has given them all, and especially *santiaguinos,* an outgoing frontier spirit. Like pioneers of the American West, they go out of their way to extend themselves to foreigners who have traveled thousands of miles to get here. What always impresses travelers is the genuine graciousness with which they are welcomed. This is what endures, and it is the reason why many visitors fall in love with Santiago.

# SANTIAGO AT-A-GLANCE

**SEEING THE CITY:** At 1,145 feet above Santiago, at the crest of Cerro San Cristóbal (Saint Christopher Hill), stands a beautiful statue of the Virgin Mary, her arms open to the city below. South of her feet lie the modern buildings of the downtown area, and on a clear day you can easily distinguish the nearest peaks of the Andes to the east and the more undulating slopes of the coastal mountain range to the west. The inauguration of this religious statue more than 80 years ago marked the opening of what has become one of the most impressive parks in Latin America. The principal entrance to this terraced park is at the end of Calle Pío Nono, from which you can either drive up or take the funicular. (There are also walking paths, but it is a strenuous hike.) A sky lift transports visitors to and from three stations, and each stop is worth a visit, including the zoo with a collection of more than 1,200 animals (most native to Chile), picnic grounds, hiking paths, and two hilltop swimming pools. The *Tupahue* public pool can accommodate 1,200 people and offers a breathtaking vista of the city below. Nearby, in the Chacarillas area of the park, which is accessible only by car, is the *Antilén* pool, which can accommodate 1,500 swimmers. The swimming season runs from December to March. There is an admission charge for both pools (phone: 777-6666).

Don't leave the park without stopping by *Enoteca,* a neo-colonial building tucked away behind a grove of palm trees, housing a wine museum, a salon for wine tasting, one of the city's finest restaurants and, in the evenings, a folklore show. The manager can suggest some good local wines to purchase. The restaurant is open daily; reservations are unnecessary, and major credit cards are accepted (phone: 232-1758). The park is open daily, generally from 9 AM to 9 PM, although some buildings have reduced hours on Mondays and the *teleférico* (skylift) stops operating at 7:30 PM on weekdays, 8:30 PM on weekends. The restaurant is open until 11 PM and a taxi service is available for late diners. You also can get a panoramic view of Santiago from *Giratorio* (2250 Av. 11 de Septiembre; phone: 232-1827), a revolving restaurant atop a 16-floor high-rise that is open for lunch and dinner (see *Eating Out*).

**SPECIAL PLACES:** The axis of the city lies along the Avenida Libertador O'Higgins which runs more than 40 blocks west from the Plaza Baquedano. From Baquedano to the Plaza Bulnes, more than 20 blocks away, a tree-lined boulevard splits this huge avenue to form what is known as the Alameda by Santiago residents. This boulevard is the main divider of the city and is a perfect place for an evening stroll; statues to Chilean heroes are stationed every few blocks, and one small plaza even contains a *moai* from Easter Island. One of the most beautiful buildings on the south side of the Alameda, just east of the Moneda subway station, is the Brazilian embassy, which long ago was the mansion of a mining magnate. The intriguing Art Deco building beside it is a members-only casino.

**Plaza de Armas** – The oldest plaza in Santiago contains the Liberty of America Monument, celebrating liberation from Spanish rule. On the northeast corner stands a bronze statue of Pedro de Valdivia, the city's founder. The plaza is bordered by the one-time presidential palace (now the post office), the cathedral, and the *Museo Histórico Nacional* (National Historical Museum). A great place to sit and write postcards (sold at the string of stands outside the post office) and people watch. On Thursdays and Sundays, musicians play in the gazebo in the plaza; you also can hear the cathedral bells ringing out tunes on the hour. In the center of downtown, where Ahumado crosses Merced.

**Catedral** – Finished in 1789, this is the fourth cathedral to stand on this site; the first three were destroyed by earthquakes and fires. The enormous interior contains altars of rose-colored marble, impressive stained glass, and detailed dark woodwork. The entrance on Calle Bandera also provides access to the neo-classical cathedral's museum of religious art and library (with historic documents signed by the country's founders). Cathedral open daily. Museum open Mondays only during the Chilean winter; Mondays and Wednesdays in the summer from 10 AM to 1 PM and 3:30 to 7 PM; No admission charge. On the Plaza de Armas at Calle Catedral.

**Museo Histórico Nacional (National Historical Museum)** – Here is an interesting stop for visitors who want to know more about the colonial period, Chile's independence from Spain, and the Pacific War with Peru and Bolivia. The 2-story museum contains furniture, works of art, and written material from both periods along with a collection of pre-Hispanic Indian ceramics and textiles. Open Tuesdays through Sundays from 10 AM to 5 PM. Admission charge. 951 Plaza de Armas (phone: 381411).

**Museo de Arte Precolombino (Pre-Columbian Art Museum)** – Housed here is a valuable collection of ceramics, textiles, jewelry, and artwork from the Indian cultures of both Chile and Peru. At the museum entrance, you can purchase guidebooks in English and Spanish explaining the exhibits or rent cassettes narrating the story of the pre-Columbian cultures. Open Tuesdays through Saturdays from 10 AM to 6 PM, Sundays from 10 AM to 2 PM. Admission charge. One block from Plaza de Armas at 361 Bandera (phone: 695-3627).

**Palacio de la Moneda (Presidential Palace)** – Initially designed by Italian architect Joaquín Toesca as the national treasury, this fortress-like building was severely criticized for its size and opulence when the Spanish crown completed the 15-year construction in 1799. In 1846, nearly 30 years after Chile was liberated from Spain, the building began to be used as the official residence of ruling Chilean presidents. La Moneda was bombed on September 11, 1973, during the coup that deposed President Allende; he died in his office. After this dramatic event, most of the interior had to be rebuilt. General Pinochet later had his headquarters in this historic palace. As you stroll through the courtyard, try to imagine the labyrinth of underground parking for the president and government officials, plus the notorious bunkers built during the Pinochet regime, beneath your feet. Visits by the general public have to be requested in advance, but the changing of the guard (which is quite a spectacle — a marching band performs a host of popular tunes) can be seen in the plaza facing La Moneda every other day, from 10 to 10:30 AM. Calle Moneda and Calle Teatinos (phone: 671-4103).

**Casa Colorada (Red House)** – This colonial building was the residence of Mateo de Toro y Zambrano, the most successful Santiago businessman of the late 1700s and the first president of the Spanish Junta Nacional de Gobierno. The house, restored in 1977, is considered the best preserved colonial home in the city. It is also the site of the *Museo de Santiago* (Santiago Museum), in which slides, historical documents, clothing, and maps are used to illustrate the history of the city. Open Tuesdays through Saturdays from 10 AM to 6 PM, and Sundays from 10 AM to 1 PM. No admission charge. 860 Calle Merced (phone: 330723).

**Iglesia y Convento San Francisco y Museo de Arte Colonial (San Francisco Church and Museum of Colonial Art)** – Built between 1586 and 1628 on the site of an earlier church that had been destroyed by an earthquake, this complex with Moorish touches has withstood the ravages of earthquakes and fires for over 4 centuries, making it the oldest building in Santiago. When Franciscan monks moved into the monastery, it was situated on the city's fringe, but today, due to urban growth, it is smack in the center of town. The principal altar contains the small statue of the Virgin del Socorro that conquistador Pedro de Valdivia carried from Spain in his saddlebag, making it the first European religious artifact to arrive in Chile. A door to the left of the main entrance on your way out marks the passage into the monastery and art museum which contains, among other works of art, a series of 53 paintings tracing the life of Saint Francis. The collection is considered to be the continent's finest example of painting from the School of Cuzco. Open Tuesdays through Saturdays from 10 AM to 1 PM and 3 to 6 PM, Sundays from 10 AM to 2 PM. Admission charge for the museum. 4 Londres (phone: 398737).

**Paseo Ahumada/Paseo Huérfanos (Ahumada Passage/Orphans Passage)** – These two intersecting streets, converted into pedestrian malls in 1977, are cobblestone walkways lined with shopping galleries, fountains, ice cream shops, outdoor cafés, movie theaters, banks, and currency-exchange establishments. Ahumada is home to Santiago's biggest department store, *Falabella,* and is a great place for people-watching. In the block of Ahumada between Agustinas and Moneda, the odor of coffee wafts out of *Café Haiti* and *Café Caribe* — two stand-up coffee bars frequented by businesspeople. (Coffee is not grown in Chile and is considered a special treat.) On Huérfanos, some of the finest shoe stores can be found — along with street vendors and roving musicians. The old, traditional *Café Santos* (downstairs, on the north side of the intersection of Ahumada and Huérfanos) serves a fixed-price buffet lunch. It usually is packed with businesspeople; for a more relaxing visit, go for coffee and a pastry during off hours. Note: Street crime after dark has become a problem on these pedestrian malls, and tourists and businesspeople are generally the targets. Travelers should avoid these streets at night.

**Cerro Santa Lucía (Santa Lucía Hill)** – This lovely park is sometimes referred to as "the lungs of Santiago," because of its oxygen-producing greenery. The park marks the spot where Spaniard Pedro de Valdivia founded Santiago. Entering off Calle Merced, one passes an ornate fountain and, following winding pathways to the top of the hill, a chapel built by the Chilean statesman Vicuña Mackenna, a small fortress built to protect the conquistadores from Indian attacks, and several fountains and plazas. At noon, a cannon on the hill is fired. By leaving the park via the exit on Avenida Libertador Bernardo O'Higgins, the visitor will see the Biblioteca Nacional (National Library) on the right (Guided tours in Spanish are available by prior arrangement; phone: 338957), the Universidad Católica (Catholic University) straight ahead, and the huge Diego Portales building to the left. Diego Portales, a modern steel, copper, aluminum, and glass structure, was built in record time for the United Nations Commission on Trade and Development. Not far from the Universidad Católica metro station at Av. Libertador O'Higgins and Calle Santa Lucia.

**Fantasilandia** – As its name implies, this is Santiago's version of *Disneyland.* The most modern amusement park in Latin America, it has mechanical rides (including the Russian Mountain, the Aquatic Splash, and the Toboggan), an artificial lake, and green surroundings. It is a great place for children of all ages. Open daily except Mondays from 10 AM to 9 PM. Admission charge. To get here, take Metro line 2 from the Los

## 500  SANTIAGO / At-a-Glance

Héroes station on Avenida Libertador O'Higgins to the station called El Parque. It is in Parque O'Higgins on the corner of Calles Tupper and Beaucheff (phone: 93035).

**Palacio Cousiño** – Don't leave Santiago without visiting this neo-classical mansion, a vestige of an era of great wealth in the Chilean capital. The mining magnate and vineyard owner who planned the palatial home died before it was completed in 1878, but his widow carried through with his plans and had it decorated with stunning furniture, paintings, porcelain, and draperies from Europe. The designs on the parquet floors differ from room to room, the porcelain tiles were handmade in Italy, and the gilt mirrors give an illusion of spaciousness. Since its sale to the city in 1940, the second floor of the mansion has been used to house visiting foreign dignitaries including Charles de Gaulle, Golda Meir, and Indira Gandhi; a fire caused by a short circuit in 1968 prevented Queen Elizabeth II from lodging here. The gardens outside the mansion are equally impressive. Open Tuesdays through Sundays from 9 AM to 1:30 PM for guided tours only (available in English). Admission charge. 438 Dieciocho (phone: 698-5063).

**Providencia** – Once a rural area, this posh shopping and residential district gets its name from the Sisters of Providence — nuns who opened a huge wood and adobe convent in the area in 1853. Today it's the place to find the homes of the well-to-do and their elegantly dressed inhabitants as well as the chic boutiques at which they shop. The avenue starts at Plaza Baquedano, a continuation of O'Higgins, and proceeds east for 15 blocks. The most exclusive shops are found on the blocks between Bucarest, General Holley, Suecia, and Los Leones.

**Planetario (Planetarium)** – Connected to the University of Santiago, this planetarium is among the best in world. The 300-seat auditorium provides visitors access to projected vistas that can be populated with nearly 5,000 stars and planets at once. Accessible to the handicapped. Shows on Wednesdays and Fridays at 7 PM, Saturdays at 5 and 7 PM, and Sundays and holidays at noon, 3:30, 5, and 7 PM. Admission charge. 3349 Av. Libertador O'Higgins, north of Estación Central metro stop (phone: 776-2624 and 681-2171).

## ENVIRONS

**Barrio Alto** – Farther east from Providencia are the swanky residential areas of Vitacura, Las Condes, and Los Dominicos, the home of many US expatriates, diplomats, and well-to-do Chileans. The *barrio alto* — or "high neighborhood," as it is called — reaches about 15 miles (24 km) east of the city to the foothills of the Andes. It derives its name from two factors: First, being closer to the Andes foothills, it is more elevated than the rest of town, which means cleaner air and a more refreshing breeze after the sun goes down. Second, this is where the upper class lives, shops, and dines. The *barrio alto* begins to the east of Calle Tobalaba and extends along Avenida Apoquindo, the extension of Avenida Providencia.

**Los Dominicos** – Beyond the twin spires of an old Dominican mission in the eastern part of the city, lies one of the most beautiful residential areas of Greater Santiago. Through its winding streets you can see the immaculate, manicured gardens with their fruit trees and sweet-smelling flowers that hide the homes of Santiago's elite. Sundays at noon, artisans gather here to sell ornamental clay figures. Beside the Dominican monastery is *Los Graneros del Alba,* a collection of workshops where visitors can watch 120 artisans plying their trades with such materials as leather, copper, lace, and even perfume. Musicians and singers serenade shoppers on Saturdays. The wares are for sale daily, except Tuesdays, from 10 AM to 6 PM (9085 Av. Apoquindo; phone: 246-4360). East of the city on Camino del Alba.

**Hacienda Los Lingues** – Don't miss a visit to this 17th-century hacienda, which has been owned by the same family for 400 years. This country estate is filled with antique furniture from the days of the conquistadores. It has its own little chapel and is surrounded by well-kept gardens and arbors. Take a day or even a weekend to wander around the estate, now also an Aculeo horse-breeding farm, see a horse show, dine on Chilean food, drink wine made from grapes harvested in the fertile valley outside Santiago, and listen to local folk music. This 18-room (it sleeps 30 people) working farm is the fourth South American property to become a member of the French Relais & Châteaux association. The hacienda is a 2½-hour drive from Santiago in San Fernando. Make reservations in Santiago (at 1100 Av. Providencia, Edif. Tajamar Torre C., Oficina 205; phone: 2-223-3518), or in the US through the *Latin America Reservations Center* (phone: 800-327-3573) or *UTELL* (phone: 800-44-UTELL).

■ **EXTRA SPECIAL:** Chile boasts some of the world's best wines, and its largest producer is headquartered in a former hacienda just outside Santiago. The Concha y Toro vineyard, in the sleepy town of Pirque, is open daily from 10 AM to 1 PM and 2 to 6 PM with free guided tours (in Spanish). Groups can made advance arrangements (phone: 223-3112 in Santiago). Although the tours center around the hacienda and not the fields, Concha y Toro has 10 extensive fields of grapes, including one that covers more than 1,100 acres. If you plan to buy wine — and this is the most economical place in the country to purchase the vineyard's fine Casillera del Diablo sauvignon blanc or the Marqués de Casa Concha cabernet sauvignon — make sure your visit does not take place on Monday, the only day the wine store is closed. (The shop accepts credit cards, but will not ship to the US.)

After passing the stainless steel vats where the white wine is fermented and the oak barrels where the red wine is aged, the tour goes on to the cellar where the founding family of this prestigious firm had its private wine stock 150 years ago. Pay special attention to the "Devil's Chamber" (Casillera del Diablo), which once held the family's most exquisite wine; to discourage theft, family members spread the rumor that the devil haunted the room. The adobe bricks in this, the oldest part of the complex, are mortared with egg white, and the temperature remains a constant 59F (15C) year-round.

English-language tours that incorporate wine tastings at Concha y Toro or other vineyards can be arranged through Santiago travel agents. The tour costs about $25 to $30. The visiting schedule for most vineyards is from 10 AM to 1 PM and 2:30 to 5 PM daily (phone: 223-3112, 235-5299). If you take such a tour, make sure it also includes a drive through the fertile Cajón del Maipo (Maipo Valley).

To get to Concha y Toro on your own, take a cab or a Puente Alto bus from the small terminal on the 700 block of Tarapaca near the corner of San Francisco. After a 55-minute ride, switch buses in Puente Alto to finish the last 10 minutes of the trip on a Pirque bus. The buses run every 5 minutes. (The tourist office can tell you how to take the longer, scenic route through the Maipo Valley in a bus.) A good place to lunch in Pirque is *La Vaquita Echá*, Calle Ramón Subercaseaux (phone: 850-3507).

# SOURCES AND RESOURCES

**TOURIST INFORMATION:** The Chilean National Tourist Office (1550 Av. Providencia; phone: 698-2151, and at the airport; phone: 601-9320), while not abundantly supplied with materials in English, can provide a variety of maps and brochures (many in Spanish), as well as information on hotels and public transportation for Santiago and the rest of Chile. Staff here is multilingual. The office in the city is open Mondays through Fridays from 9 AM to 5:30 PM; the airport office is open weekdays Sundays from 9 AM to 9 PM. The biweekly, Spanish-language brochure *Guiamérica* lists a variety of tourist and theater information. It is available free at hotels and the tourism office, and sold at newspaper kiosks throughout the city. If you're in need of special maps for hiking or mountain climbing or just about any other pursuit, you can buy them at *Instituto Geográfico Militar* (65 San Antonio; phone: 632-1956). The *Turistel* books on different parts of Chile are useful for those who read Spanish. Published jointly by the tourism office and the phone company, they are sold at bookstores and newsstands in downtown Santiago.

The US Embassy is located at 1343 Augustinas, Suite 529 (phone: 671-0133).

**Local Coverage** – *El Mercurio, La Tercera,* and *La Nación* (morning dailies), and *La Segunda* (afternoon daily) provide coverage in Spanish. Every Friday *El Mercurio* publishes a weekend section with suggestions of what to see and where to eat. Santiago publishes no English-language newspapers, but international papers and magazines are available at newsstands around the city. Cable News Network (CNN), the 24-hour television news station that broadcasts in English, is available at some hotels.

**TELEPHONE:** The city code for Santiago is 2. When calling from within Chile, dial 02 before the local number. The country code for Chile is 56.

**CLIMATE AND CLOTHES:** Santiago's climate tends to be sunny throughout most of the year, although the smog creates a hazy atmosphere even on the brightest of days. In winter (June through September), daytime temperatures may drop into the 30s F (around 0 C). In summer (December through March), the mercury may soar into the 90s F (around 34C). Winter rarely brings snow (though skiing is less than 2 hours away), but be prepared to get wet and pack sweaters and heavy clothing. You will need to wear sweaters indoors, since most Chilean heating leaves much to be desired, namely heat. In summer, the smog and lack of air conditioning can make the city seem hotter than it is, but you should bring a light jacket or sweater for the evening. Intermittent showers are common in fall and spring, so rain gear is needed if that's when you're traveling. Overall, Chileans dress rather informally, though men wear jackets and ties at the better restaurants.

**GETTING AROUND: Bus** – There is service within walking distance of almost any street in town. Buses are generally crowded and slow during rush hours. They also are marginally more expensive than the pleasant and efficient metro. Multiple signs in bus windows make it difficult to discern the route; people often board in the middle of the street. For long-distance trips, there are three bus stations: Terminal Norte (920 Amunátegui; phone: 671-2141) is primarily for service north; Terminal Santiago (3800 Av. Libertador O'Higgins; phone: 779-1385) and Terminal Alameda (1 block down at 3250 O'Higgins; phone: 776-1025) serve buses headed to Viña del Mar, areas south of Santiago, and out of the country. An airport bus, *Tour Express* (downtown terminal, 1529 Moneda; phone: 671-7380) runs at intervals of about 30 minutes, from 6:30 AM until 9:45 PM, when it operates according to flight arrivals and departures.

**Car Rental** – Major companies have offices throughout Santiago: *Hertz* (1469 Av. Costanera, Providencia; phone: 225-9328); *Avis* (at the *Holiday Inn Crowne Plaza,* 136 Av. Libertador O'Higgins; phone: 392268; the *Sheraton San Cristóbal,* 1742 Av. Santa María; phone: 274-7621); the *Plaza San Francisco* hotel, 816 Av. Libertador O'Higgins; phone: 393832; and at the airport; phone: 601-9050); *Budget* (4900 Av. Apoquindo; phone: 246-0888; at the *Carrera* hotel; phone: 698-2011, ext. 374; and at the airport;

phone: 601-9421); *National Car Rental* (212 La Concepción; phone: 251-7552). For trips outside the city, maps are available from the *Automóvil Club de Chile* (122 Marchant Pereira; phone: 274-4167). If traveling outside Santiago, call 133 for a report about major highways in the surrounding area.

**Metro** – Santiago's clean, modern subway system provides rapid crosstown transportation. Since only two lines have been completed, it's impossible to get lost. The *Pudahuel–Las Condes* line runs below Avenida Libertador O'Higgins–Providencia–Avenida Apoquindo artery and is the fastest way to whiz under traffic jams at rush hour. There's also a north-south spur from the central station, Los Héroes. In each station is a map of the city to help you find your way. There is no extra charge for transferring from one line to another; if you intend to transfer, however, make sure you get two tickets at the ticket booth. The trains run Mondays through Saturdays from 6:30 AM to 10:30 PM, and Sundays from 8 AM to 10:30 PM.

**Taxi** – Black and yellow taxis can be found just about anywhere and may be the easiest — though far from the least expensive — way of getting around. The cabs are metered; there is no bargaining over fares. Taxi service can be requested by telephone from three lines: *Taxis Andes Pacífico* (phone: 225-3064); *Taxis 33* (phone: 330585); or *Taxis Las Condes* (phone: 211-4404).

**Train** – Passenger service from Santiago only goes south. The train station (3322 Av. Libertador O'Higgins, at the corner of Calle Matucana; phone: 95199 and 95401) connects directly with the Estación Central metro (where you can buy your train tickets). They also are sold at a railway branch office (853 Av. Libertador O'Higgins; phone: 398427) and the Escuela Militar metro station (phone: 228-2983).

**SPECIAL EVENTS:** The fourth week of January is when the *Festival Nacional Folklórico* (National Folklore Festival) takes place. It is celebrated with 5 days of music and dance at the *Anfiteatro San Bernardo* (San Bernardo Amphitheater; 377 Av. Libertador O'Higgins). September 18 is the Chilean Fourth of July, celebrated with rodeos in San Bernardo and Melipilla as well as *fondas* — stalls where *huasos* (Chilean cowboys or farmworkers) dance the national dance (called the *cueca*) and drink both wine and the fresh grape cider (*chicha de uva*) or apple cider (*chicha de manzana*). *Fondas* appear all over Santiago, but the best — since Chile's national tradition has its roots in the rural population — are in the little farming towns along the Central Valley. This event is followed by a military parade in Santiago's Parque O'Higgins on September 19. The *Feria Internacional de Artesanía* (National Artisans' Fair), featuring art and craftwork from all over the continent, is held the second week of December, in Parque Bustamante at the corner of Francisco Bilbao, from 10 AM to 11 PM. All major Catholic holidays are celebrated, too.

**MUSEUMS:** Santiago could be nicknamed "the City of Museums" owing to the number and variety of museums found in its environs. Among its treasures are the *Museo Histórico Nacional* (National Historical Museum), the *Museo de Arte Precolombino* (Pre-Columbian Art Museum), the *Museo de Santiago* (Santiago Museum at Casa Colorada), and the *Museo de Arte Colonial* (Colonial Art Museum at the San Francisco Church). See *Special Places.* Other museums of interest can be found at the following places:

**Casa de la Chascona** – This lovely house was the home of Pablo Neruda, Chile's Nobel Prize–winning poet. Built on 3 levels of a hillside in peaceful Barrio Bellavista, it offers an intimate look at the life of the poet. His furnishings and books are just as they were when he lived and wrote here. Visits by appointment only. Admission charge. 192 Marqués de la Plata (phone: 777-8741).

**Museo de Artes Decorativos (Museum of Decorative Arts)** – Exhibits of everything from furniture to silverwork to religious artifacts, from the middle ages to the present. Open Tuesdays through Fridays from 10 AM to 1:30 PM and 2:30 to 5:30 PM, Saturdays and Sundays from 10 AM to 5:30 PM. Admission charge. 950 Av. Kennedy (phone: 224-3985).

**Museo Iglesia de la Merced (La Merced Church Museum)** – Although this small museum specializes in religious art, it has an intriguing collection of woodcarvings and artifacts from Easter Island. Lodged on the second floor of La Merced church, it is also a pleasant escape from the bustle of the city. Take note of the bell jars with religious statues inside. These crystal vessels, which survived the ocean voyage from Europe and all of Santiago's earthquakes, originally contained erotic figures that the pious Chileans quickly replaced with Roman Catholic icons. Open Tuesdays through Saturdays from 10 AM to 1 PM and 3 to 6:30 PM, Sundays from 10 AM to 2 PM. Admission charge. 341 MacIver (phone: 336633).

**Parque de las Esculturas (Park of the Sculptures)** – This open-air museum along the banks of the Mapocho River is filled with the monumental works of Chile's most notable sculptors. There also is a building at the park's entrance that houses changing exhibits by Chilean artists. Starts at 2201 Av. Santa María.

**Parque Forestal** – This huge park-promenade along the Mapocho River is the home of the *Museo Nacional de Bellas Artes* (National Fine Arts Museum; phone: 391946), which houses an excellent collection of Chilean art as well as art from other countries. The building itself — *Palacio de Bellas Artes* (Palace of Fine Arts — is worth seeing for its architecture; natural lighting is used expertly in some galleries. (An electronic security system buzzes when museum visitors move too close to a piece of art; it seems to be triggered continuously when schoolchildren take class tours.) It is open Tuesdays through Saturdays from 11 AM to 8 PM and Sundays from 10 AM to 6 PM. The park also serves as home to the *Museo de Arte Popular Americano* (Museum of Popular American Art; phone: 330138) on the second floor (at press time, the museum was closed for renovations; call to check its new hours) and the *Museo de Arte Contemporáneo* (Museum of Contemporary Art; phone: 331675); call for hours. Admission charge for all museums. Calle José Miguel de la Barra.

**Pueblito O'Higgins** – This village of small museums is found outside one of the city's largest public parks. In addition to a number of artisans' shops and restaurants offering Chilean food and entertainment, the "village" contains a museum dedicated to the Chilean cowboy culture, an aquarium, and a collection of exotic insects and mollusks. The *Museo del Huaso* has a collection of textiles, clothing, and artifacts typically found in Chile's cowboy world. It is open Tuesdays through Fridays from 10 AM to 5 PM, Saturdays and Sundays from 10:30 AM to 7 PM (phone: 555-0054).

The *Museo Acuario Municipal* (phone: 556-5680), with its intriguing exhibitions of sea life, is open daily from 10 AM to 8 PM, as is the *Museo Municipal de Insectos y Caracoles*. Here you'll find a chilling exhibit of scarabs, tarantulas, and scorpions, along with a fascinating display of butterflies from around the world (phone: 556-5685). No admission charge to the museums. The Pueblito O'Higgins is located at the Parque O'Higgins metro stop. Nearby is *Fantasilandia* amusement park (see *Special Places*).

**Quinta Normal** – Founded in 1830 as a site to cultivate plants not native to Chile, this park supports four museums. The *Museo de Historia Natural* (Natural History Museum) is in a building originally constructed for an *International Exposition* held in Santiago in the early 1800s, and it holds an impressive collection. It is open daily, except Mondays, from 10 AM to 5:30 PM. Admission charge, except on Sundays (phone: 681-4095).

In front of the park's lagoon is the *Museo de Ciencia y Tecnología* (Science and Technology Museum), which sponsors a series of participatory displays, making it fun for children as well as adults. Open Tuesdays through Fridays, 10 AM to noon and 2 to 5 PM, Saturdays and Sundays from 11 AM to 2 PM and 3 to 6 PM (phone: 681-6022). Sharing the same hours and phone number is the *Museo Ferroviario* (Railway Museum), with exhibits of antique locomotives and steam engines. Both museums have a small admission charge. Finally, everything that a visitor could want to know about Chilean aeronautics can be found at the *Museo Nacional Aeronáutico de Chile* (National Aeronautic Museum). Open Tuesdays through Sundays, 10 AM to 6 PM (phone: 681-5006). The Quinta Normal is located at 502 Av. Matucana, near the Los Héroes subway stop.

**SHOPPING:** Paseos Ahumada and Huérfanos, two intersecting streets, are pedestrian zones abundant with stores (although they have become increasingly clogged with street vendors). Huérfanos is home to some of the top shoe stores in the city (see *Gacel* below).

Although Providencia has the best shops in Santiago, especially on the blocks between Bucarest, General Holley, Suecia, and Los Leones (and some large shopping centers including the *Cosmocentro Apumanque* at 31 Av. Manquehue Sur at the end of Providencia), its boutiques offer little in the way of crafts or the work of local artisans. *Parque Arauco* (Av. Presidente Kennedy) is a popular new mall with more than 200 shops and restaurants.

Shops specializing in copper and jewelry — especially pieces made with lapis lazuli — are found along Calle Bellavista, between Pío Nono and Arzobispo. (The deep blue lapis stones are native only to Chile and Afghanistan.) More touristy trinkets are sold at kiosks at the Estación Central, the main train depot in Santiago, and in galleries at Portal Fernández Concha (the archway near Plaza de Armas). The best bargains in Chile are wine and copper and leather goods.

***Arkitec*** – This new 4-story design center houses eight different shops displaying the latest in style and both traditional and modern household gifts. 2895 Isadora Goyenechea (phone: 232-4325).

***Cariola's*** – The specialty here is fine lace table linen, including tablecloths and placemats. 148 Alberto Orrego Luco (phone: 251-5562).

***CEMA-Chile*** – This government-run store brings together women's handicrafts from all over the country. Its main emporium is in a well-kept, former colonial convent at 351 Avenida Portugal (phone: 222-2645). Open Mondays through Fridays, 9:30 AM to 1 PM and 3 to 6:30 PM, Saturdays from 10 AM to 1 PM. Other *CEMA* outlets are located at the airport and the Universidad de Chile subway station. (All *CEMAs* in Chile are closed the first week of January for inventory.)

***Falabella*** – Santiago's largest department store. Corner of Paseo Ahumada and Av. Libertador Bernardo O'Higgins (phone: 695-3636) and in the Las Condes neighborhood at 5413 Av. Kennedy (phone: 242-0889).

***Feria Chilena del Libro*** – Good selection of Spanish-language works by Latin American authors, as well as children's books, dictionaries, and lovely photo books on Chile tucked among the 2 stories of bookshelves. 623 Huérfanos (phone: 396758) and 2124 Av. Providencia (phone: 231-7197).

***Gacel*** – Excellent footwear at good prices. 2120 Providencia (phone: 231-9810) and 331 Huérfanos (phone: 383714).

***Los Graneros del Alba*** – Handmade leather, lace, and other items are for sale in this series of workshops located in one of the most beautiful areas in Greater Santiago. 9085 Av. Apoquindo (phone: 246-4360).

***Gucci*** – Good values from the Italian purveyor of leather goods. 31 Av. Manquehue Sur, Las Condes (phone: 246-2371).

***H. Stern*** – South America's prestigious jewelry chain has two hotel shops in Santiago that feature — among other precious and semi-precious gems — fine-quality lapis lazuli. In the lobby of the *Carrera* (phone: 698-0735) and at the *Sheraton San Cristóbal* (phone: 223-7579).

***Librería Inglesa Kuatro Ltda.*** – This English-language bookshop will satisfy your

## 506 SANTIAGO / Sources and Resources

craving for light or serious reading while on the road. Books of every genre are for sale. 669 Huérfanos (phone: 231-6270) and 47 Pedro de Valdivia (phone: 632-5153).

**Morita Gil** – *The* spot for original-design lapis lazuli jewelry and decorations. Prices are higher than at other shops, but the quality is superb. 1991 Los Misioneros, Pedro de Valdivia Norte (phone: 232-6853) and at the international airport (no phone).

**Sucamp** – Excellent bargains in capes, wool blankets, rugs, and fabric can be found at stores of this nonprofit distribution center for goods woven by *campesinas*. Several outlets (especially the one at 112 Av. República; phone: 671-6943) also offer some handmade leather items. No credit cards accepted. The surrounding district — once the wealthiest part of town — is dotted with huge mansions.

**SPORTS:** As in most South American countries, the national sport of Chile is soccer (*fútbol*).

**Car Racing** – The *Autodromo Las Vizcachas* has an international track 1 mile long for all kinds of car racing, held from April to December. It is 14 miles (22 km) from Santiago on the road to San José de Maipo (phone:774-1025). For racing information, contact the *Federación Chilena de Automovilismo Deportivo* (phone: 222028).

**Fishing** – The Laguna de Aculeo, about 40 miles (64 km) from Santiago, is a good place to fish for mackerel. It's near the coastal mountain range and offers a chance to breathe clean mountain air. Buses leave from the first block of Avenida San Alfonso. Take any one marked Santiago-Aculeo. The Embalse del Yeso, an artificial lake 60 miles (96 km) from the city in the Cajón del Maipo, is ideal for trout fishing. Private transportation is the only way to get there. On the road to El Volcán. There is marvelous fishing in the south (see *Fishing*, DIVERSIONS). To obtain a fishing license and information on the fishing seasons and restrictions, go to *Servicio Nacional de Pesca* (1349 Letelier, 2nd Floor; phone: 698-1103). It is open weekdays from 9 AM to 2 PM.

**Golf** – The *Prince of Wales Country Club* (Av. Ossa and Av. Francisco Bilbao), and the *Club de Golf* (Av. Americo Vespucio and Av. Presidente Kennedy), have private golf courses. Ask your hotel concierge to arrange greens privileges. The *Sheraton San Cristóbal* (1742 Av. Santa María; phone: 233-5000) offers a 7-hole putting green, and guests at the *Carrera* hotel may use the *La Dehesa Golf Club* course (2501 Camino Club de Golf) from Tuesdays through Fridays for about a $10 fee.

**Horse Racing** – Santiago has two racetracks: the *Hipódromo* and the *Club Hípico*. The *Hipódromo* races are run Wednesdays and Saturdays from 3 to 7 PM (1715 Av. Hipódromo de Chile; phone: 377078). The *Club Hípico* has Wednesday afternoon races on alternate weeks with the *Hipódromo,* and on Sundays between 2 and 9 PM (2540 Av. Blanco Encalada; phone: 91757; on racing days, 683-5586). Tea is served on the lawn to *Club Hípico* members and guests on racing days.

**Rodeo** – Accompanied by crafts fairs and indigenous Chilean foods, rodeos are held in Santiago from 9 AM to 7 PM on weekends from September through March. The rodeo rotates among 20 sites in the city, culminating in the national championship in Rancagua every March. Call the *Federación de Rodeo* (phone: 384639) to find out where.

**Rugby** – This sport is gaining more and more popularity in Chile. From March to November, weekend matches are held on a revolving basis at several fields, including *Stade Français* (phone: 233-7608), *Country Club* (phone: 227-2025), and *San Carlos de Apoquindo,* at the Universidad Católica. For information, call the *Rugby Federation* (phone: 699115).

**Skiing** – The season begins in June and lasts until September, which makes Chile a favorite with professional skiers from the Northern Hemisphere. Thirty very winding miles (48 km) from Santiago, at 6,700 feet, Farellones can be reached in about 1½ hours. Take Avenida Providencia east, then Avenida Apoquindo and Avenida Las Condes. After the turnoff to Barnechea, you will see a road sign to Farellones. La Parva,

## SANTIAGO / Sources and Resources

another ski resort, is just 3 miles (5 km) farther. There are also ski runs at Lagunillas, about 10 miles (16 km) from San José de Maipo in the Cajón del Maipo. You can spend the day skiing at any of these places and return to the city at night. Contact the *Federación de Andinismo* (77 Almirante Simpson; phone: 222-0888) or call the "Ski Report" (phone: 220-9501) to find out about ski conditions.

**Soccer** – Santiago is the home of numerous professional soccer clubs. Games are held Saturdays, Sundays, and sometimes on Wednesdays, starting at 4 PM, from March to December. Pro games in Santiago are held at the *Estadio Nacional* and the *Estadio de Santa Laura*. Schedule information can be obtained by calling the *Asociación Central de Fútbol* (phone: 221-7125).

**Swimming** – The rooftop pool at the *Carrera* hotel (108 Calle Teatinos; phone: 698-2011), is okay for a quick dip, as is the pool at the *Holiday Inn Crowne Plaza* (136 Av. Libertador O'Higgins; phone: 381042). The pool at the *Sheraton San Cristóbal* (1742 Av. Santa María; phone: 233-5000) is the nicest in town, but 3 newer additions include the indoor pool at the *Plaza San Francisco* hotel (816 Av. Libertador O'Higgins; phone: 393832) and the outdoor pools at the *Aloha* hotel (146 Francisco Noguera; phone: 233-2230) and the *Hyatt Regency* (4601 Av. Kennedy; phone: 218-1234). There are two public pools at Parque Metropolitana, mentioned in *Seeing the City*, above. Two other pools — one of which is for children only — are at Parque O'Higgins.

**Tennis** – The *Sheraton San Cristóbal* (1742 Av. Santa María; phone: 233-5000) and the *Holiday Inn Crowne Plaza* (136 Av. Libertador O'Higgins; phone: 381042) have tennis courts where visitors can play for a fee. Other courts are found at *Tenis y Squash Lo Cañas* (5000 Monseñor Escrivá de Balaguer; phone: 485323); *Tenis Cordillera* (13297 Av. Las Condes; phone: 472331); *Hans Gildemeister Tennis Club* (5970 Monseñor Escrivá de Balaguer; phone: 220-0757); and *Tennis El Aurora* (282 Las Perdices Parcela; phone: 273-1887). Contact the *Federación de Tenis* (36 Almirante Simpson; phone: 222-7279) for more information.

**THEATER:** Check the newspapers for a complete listing of cultural events and schedules. The *Teatro Municipal* (Municipal Theater; 149 Calle San Antonio at the corner of Augustinas; phone: 332804 or 381515) attracts international stars for performances at its 135-year-old location, restored after a fire in 1870 and an earthquake in 1906. The city ballet and orchestra, chamber music groups, and opera companies also perform here. The best live theater will be found at *Teatro Baquedano* (43 Providencia; phone: 344745); *El Conventillo I* and *El Conventillo II* (173 Bellavista; phone: 777-4164); the *Abril* (786 Huérfanos; phone: 335932); and the open-air theater run by the Catholic University (phone: 204-7601) in the summer. Its plays are held at 8 PM on weekends in Parque Manuel Rodríguez. Most plays and movies are in Spanish. Classic films are shown at the *Teatro del Angel* (786 Huérfanos, at the corner of San Antonio; phone: 333605).

**MUSIC:** Santiago has everything from classical to burlesque and from folklore to disco. The *Teatro Municipal* (Municipal Theater; 149 Calle San Antonio at the corner of Augustinas; phone: 332804) is the queen of serious music, concerts, opera, and ballet. From May to October, the *Beethoven Foundation* presents a series of concerts at the *Teatro Oriente* (Av. Pedro de Valdivia between Providencia and Costanera). For ticket information, stop at 2888 Marcel Duhault.

Also visit the old, quaint suburb of Barrio Bellavista, which has been turned into a bohemian quarter, with good restaurants, lots of interesting shops, art galleries, old book stores, and little cafés with folkloric, jazz, and modern music all featured. Turn-of-the-century houses have been restored, and there is a special ambience here during the first 3 weeks of January, when the barrio holds a festival of dance, theater, and music.

Some presentations take place on open-air stages. A recommended stop is *Café del Cerro* (192 Ernesto Pinto Lagarrigue; phone: 372240), where you can hear jazz, salsa, and rock performed by up-and-coming young musicians. The cover charge includes your first drink; sandwiches also are sold.

**NIGHTCLUBS AND NIGHTLIFE:** Music — whether classical, tango, or disco — is such an integral part of Latin American life that you simply have to choose which kind you most enjoy. *Balta's* (10690 Av. Las Condes; phone: 215-1091) plays disco as well as serving dinner; open Tuesdays through Saturdays from 10 PM. Other good discotheques are *Cassamila* (298 Alvara Casanova; phone: 273-2782), *Kasbba* (81 Suecia; phone: 231-7419), *Las Brujas* (9040 Príncipe de Gales; phone: 273-1072), and *Caledonia* (339 Av. Nueva Larraín; phone: 273-1888).

Santiago has several restaurants that also offer dancing and a show. One of the better known is *Los Adobes de Argomedo* (at the corner of Lira and Argomedo; phone: 222-2104), which has the best folk show in town, dancing, and Chilean specialties; reservations advised. Other Chilean restaurants with good weekend shows are *La Querencia* (14980 Av. Las Condes; phone: 471226) and *La Estancia* (13810 Av. Las Condes; phone: 471301). Steer clear of the *Bali Hai,* however, which offers the city's only Easter Island floor show. It has become an overpriced tourist trap with surly waiters, mediocre food, and a second-rate show.

# BEST IN TOWN

**CHECKING IN:** One of the most pleasant aspects of Santiago's hotel scene is the range of alternatives: from modern, snazzy buildings to old-fashioned, pretty hotels that remind you of romantic Paris. Expect to pay $175 and up for a double room at a place classified as very expensive; between $125 and $175 at hotels in the expensive category; from $80 to $125 at places in the moderate range; and under $80 at a hotel described as inexpensive. Breakfast is often included in room prices. All telephone numbers are in the 2 city code unless otherwise indicated.

**Carrera** – For many years, this was *the* hotel. In fact, journalists covering the 1973 coup used it as headquarters and filed stories to news organizations around the world from the telex desk in its lobby. It remains a top establishment, a landmark bordered by the Presidential Palace and still a favorite with many international businesspeople who like being at the center of the action. All 325 rooms (including 41 suites) were fully refurbished recently and a health club and beauty salon were added. In addition, it offers restaurants, a coffee shop, a popular bar, and a terrace swimming pool. The service is excellent, particularly in the 10th-floor business suites, where a host of English-speaking butlers assist with every need, from sending faxes to pressing clothes. 180 Calle Teatinos (phone: 698-2011; in the US through *SRS,* 800-223-5652; fax: 672-1083). Very expensive.

**Holiday Inn Crowne Plaza** – This hostelry offers 293 ultramodern rooms and special facilities that include floors for nonsmokers and executives, an Executive Club (with a bar, lounge, and pool table), a sauna, a pool under a glass dome, and tennis courts. Room service is very good, and there is a choice of bars, nightclubs, and restaurants. 136 Av. Libertador O'Higgins (phone: 381042; in the US, 800-465-4329; fax: 336015). Very expensive.

**Hyatt Regency Santiago** – Built around a circular 19-story atrium with a cascading waterfall, this new luxury 314-room hotel offers 2 restaurants — Italian and an informal café, a business center, health club, tennis courts, outdoor pool, and spa. 4601 Av. Kennedy (phone: 218-1234; in the US, 800-233-1234). Very expensive.

**Park Plaza** – Another new property — this one features 104 rooms and the atmosphere of a private British club, with a wood-paneled restaurant and lobby bar, and a sidewalk terrace that opens in warm weather. In every season, there's a host of business services that can't be beat — secretarial and translation services, an English-speaking concierge, fax machines, and conference rooms for up to 350 people. 207 Av. Ricardo Lyon, just off Av. Providencia (phone: 233-6363; in the US, 800-44-UTELL; fax: 233-6668). Very expensive.

**Plaza San Francisco** – Named after the 400-year-old church at its side and managed by the German Kempinski group, this is the latest and smartest addition to Santiago's downtown hotel scene, with 110 rooms (of which 16 are suites). This property was designed with executives in mind. Secretarial services, fax, telex, and modem hookups on all room phones are available. Amenities include an indoor pool, fitness center, sauna, the *Bristol* restaurant with good seafood and meat (as well as an extensive wine cellar), and parking. The hotel eventually plans to add another 70 rooms. 816 Av. Libertador O'Higgins (phone: 393832; in the US, 800-426-3135 or 800-44-UTELL; fax: 397826). Very expensive.

**Sheraton San Cristóbal** – Considered the best in town. At the foot of San Cristóbal Hill, its 339 rooms and 44 suites overlook the hotel's private swimming pool and lighted tennis courts on one side, the Mapocho River on the other. There also is a jogging path and a 7-hole putting green. While somewhat removed from the bustle of downtown, it's a stone's throw from the *"barrio alto,"* the city's poshest shopping and residential area, and only 2 blocks from a metro station. Its *El Cid* restaurant (see *Eating Out*) is outstanding. 1742 Av. Santa María (phone: 233-5000; in the US, 800-325-3535; fax: 234-1729). Very expensive.

**El Conquistador** – Yet another modern hotel with all essential comforts. Pleasant, with a tasteful, sober interior, it offers 120 rooms and suites, a multilingual staff, and is in the center of town — in one of Santiago's many pedestrian passageways. Don't miss the health-food restaurant, *Diet El Conquistador*, next door. 920 M. Cruchaga (phone: 696-5599; in the US, 800-44-UTELL). Expensive.

**Galerías** – Within walking distance of the business and banking center. The hotel has 162 rooms, bars and restaurants, plus a health center with a gym and sauna, a pool, and patio. 65 San Antonio (phone: 384011; fax: 330077). Expensive.

**Aloha** – Although this new inn has a rather spartan exterior, its 52 rooms and 13 suites are welcoming. There's a restaurant, bar, outdoor pool, gym, and sauna. It's located on a quiet, shady residential street in tony Providencia. 146 Francisco Noguera, off Av. Providencia (phone: 233-2230; fax: 233-2494). Moderate.

**Don Tito** – A very good choice for those desiring a small (25 rooms), intimate, first class hotel. The service, overseen by the English-speaking owner, is excellent. Centrally located, 1 block from Santa Lucía Hill. 578 Huérfanos (phone: 391987). Moderate.

**Foresta** – On the quiet end of the Santa Lucía Hill. Although small, each room has its own separate sitting room. The little reception area and its restaurant on the top floor are both tastefully decorated with antiques. This genteel quality gives the place a character all its own. Most rooms look out on the greenery below, as does the restaurant. 353 Av. Victoria Subercaseaux (phone: 396261). Moderate.

**Santa Lucía** – Meets international travelers' needs, and is surprisingly quiet for its downtown location. It does have a telex service in the building itself, which is helpful if you need to keep in touch with an office during your stay. Located in the heart of the city, above a shopping gallery. 779 Calle Huérfanos (phone: 398201; in the US, 800-275-3123). Moderate.

**Tupahue** – This deluxe 209-room hotel combines a central location with a striking modern interior of bright, bold color. Although the reception area is on the first floor, the hotel's restaurant, snack bar, and lobby are all located on the third floor along with the terrace swimming pool and a piano bar called *Chiloé*. 477 Calle San Antonio (phone: 383810 and 393861; in the US, 800-44-UTELL; fax: 395240). Moderate.

**Conde Ansurez** – Conveniently located just a block from the República metro stop, this no-frills hostelry has 39 rooms and 3 suites — all with direct-dial phones and color television sets — and a friendly staff. There also is a small dining room, bar, and laundry and room services. 25 Av. República (phone: 699-6368; fax: 698-3779). Moderate to inexpensive.

**Montecarlo** – Located on the quiet side of Santa Lucía Hill, it provides most creature comforts. Although there is no restaurant, it has 24-hour room service and drinks are served in its arched-ceiling lobby–sitting room. 209 Av. Victoria Subercaseaux (phone: 381176 and 339905; fax: 335577). Moderate to inexpensive.

**Libertador** – An old hostelry with 126 rooms and more local atmosphere than most. Its dining room serves international fare. Located near the Universidad de Chile metro station. 853 Av. Libertador O'Higgins (phone: 394211). Inexpensive.

**Metropoli** – Small, quiet, and centrally located, this establishment has very good personal service. 465 Calle Dr. Sótero del Río (phone: 723-9871). Inexpensive.

**Orly** – As its name implies, this intimate hostelry, a block from the exclusive Providencia shopping area, has a certain Parisian charm. 27 Av. Pedro de Valdivia (phone: 231-8947). Inexpensive.

**Riviera** – Although this tiny but endearing hotel has no real restaurant, its rooms are comfortable. 106 Calle Miraflores (phone: 331176). Inexpensive.

**EATING OUT:** In the downtown area, most shops and offices stay open for lunch. In other parts of town, businesses close from 2 to 4 PM. Most Chileans believe in a good, hearty lunch of several courses. If you feel like having something light, try *lomito*, the local version of the hamburger, the basis of which is roast pork. It is served in all the soda fountains that pepper the city center. Many of these little diners also serve a more substantial menu at lunchtime for about $5 per person. Dinner starts around 8:30 or 9 PM. Chileans are rather informal, so you do not have to wear evening clothes at restaurants or nightclubs, although jackets and ties for men are recommended at the expensive restaurants and at nightclubs.

Diners who enjoy a bohemian atmosphere should head for the Bellavista area at the foot of San Cristóbal hill. Seafood and Italian dishes are featured at the family-run bistros that draw local artists and intellectuals. In general, dinner starts a bit later in this area than elsewhere, and restaurants usually are open well past midnight.

While in Santiago, be sure to try any *mariscos* (seafood) and empanadas (meat pies). Other treats include *pastel de choclo* (a rich casserole with meat and corn) and a meat and seafood stew called *curanto* that is common on Easter Island. The best wines are those of the Concha y Toro, Cousiño-Macul, Santa Emiliana, and Undurraga vineyards. No matter what you order, you'll find Chilean food terrific — especially at the restaurants listed below. Expect to pay $50 and up at those places we've listed as expensive; between $30 and $50 at restaurants in the moderate range; under $30 at restaurants in the inexpensive range. Prices are for dinner for two and do not include drinks, wine, and tips. All telephone numbers are in the 2 city code unless otherwise indicated.

**Aquí Está Coco** – Just a stone's throw from Providencia, this is a fine choice for seafood. Plenty of it, and all sorts, are prepared in any number of delectable ways. Though not on the menu, ask for *percebes* (whelks); they're delicious. The wine selection is also quite good. Open daily, except Sundays, for lunch and dinner. Reservations unnecessary. Major credit cards accepted. 236 Calle La Concepción (phone: 465985). Expensive.

**El Cid** – An outstanding lunchtime buffet that features Chilean fare is served here, with service that can't be beat. In the *Sheraton,* the restaurant overlooks the hotel's grounds. Open daily for lunch and dinner. Reservations unnecessary. Major credit cards accepted. In the *Sheraton San Cristóbal,* 1742 Av. Santa María (phone: 233-5000). Expensive.

**Coco Loco** – This eatery specializes in seafood and the results are imaginative and tasty. Service is friendly and attentive. Open daily for lunch and dinner. Reservations advised. Major credit cards accepted. 554 Rancagua (phone: 491214). Expensive.

**Giratorio** – A revolving restaurant atop a 16-floor building, this is a special dinner spot if you want an impressive night view of Santiago. (At lunch, the view may be marred by the city's smog — especially in the summer.) The menu offers international dishes. Open daily for lunch, *once* (afternoon tea), and dinner. Reservations advised. Major credit cards accepted. 2250 Av. 11 de Septiembre (phone: 232-1827). Expensive.

**Maistral** – Small and intimate, this French bistro serves fine haute cuisine. Open daily, except Sundays, for lunch and dinner. Reservations advised. Major credit cards accepted. 485 Mosqueto (phone: 330870). Expensive.

**Martín Carrera** – Considered one of the very finest restaurants in Chile, its cooking is international *nouvelle.* Señor Carrera, the chef, has won quite a few gastronomic prizes, thereby invigorating the city's haute cuisine world. His wife, María Gloria, is his partner in the business, which is located in one of Santiago's prettiest suburbs. Open daily, except Sundays, for lunch and dinner. Reservations advised. Major credit cards accepted. 3471 Isidora Goyenechea (phone: 231-2798). Expensive.

**Da Renato di Vittoria** – Tucked away in a cul de sac in chic Providencia, this Italian eatery has it all — a charming country-style ambience, excellent service, exquisite food, and an imaginative wine list (Chilean wines only). Try the abundant antipasto selection, served from a heavily laden cart, and agonize over the many tempting pasta dishes. Be sure to leave some room for one of the luscious fruit and nut layer cakes. Open daily for lunch and dinner. Reservations unnecessary. Major credit cards accepted. 183 M. Fernández, between Suecia and Los Leones (phone: 232-2739). Moderate to expensive.

**Los Adobes de Argomedo** – Another place to find fine Chilean food and performances of traditional music in the evenings. Open daily, except Mondays, for lunch and dinner. Reservations advised. Major credit cards accepted. 411 Argomedo, at the corner of Lira (phone: 222-2104). Moderate.

**Da Carla** – Very good Italian food served in a setting replete with checkered tablecloths and an occasional exclamation in Italian from the direction of the kitchen. The homemade pasta and a wide selection of seafood are its mainstays. Open daily, except Sundays, for lunch and dinner. Reservations advised. Major credit cards accepted. 577 MacIver (phone: 333739). Moderate.

**Chez Henry** – This is really three distinct places: a delicatessen-wine shop, a restaurant, and a nightclub with nonstop dancing to a Latin beat. The restaurant is generally crowded at any time of day and any day of the week. Some travelers from the US may find the dining area noisy, but others will appreciate the liveliness that makes it a favorite of local residents. Open daily. Reservations advised. Diners Club accepted. Entrance is through the store (which is known as a good spot to purchase wine) under the archways that surround the Plaza de Armas. 962 Portal Fernández Concha (phone: 672-1992). Moderate.

**Confitería Torres** – Operating since 1879, this is Santiago's most traditional bar/coffeehouse where, at the turn of the century, the country's best known artists, writers, painters, and politicians met. Its dark wood walls and cast-iron lights give the impression that you have stepped back in time, and the antique phone and typewriter around the dining room are reminders of an era when intellectuals gathered here. A full menu is served and the restaurant is proud of its flaming crêpe desserts. It claims credit for inventing Chile's *barros luco* (beef with melted cheese) sandwich, naming it after Sir Ramón Barros Luco who always requested the combination. Saloon doors separate the dining room from the bar. Service is excellent. On Friday and Saturday nights there is live tango and bolero music. Open daily. Reservations unnecessary. No credit cards accepted. 1570 Av. Libertador O'Higgins (phone: 698-6220). Moderate.

**El Otro Sitio** – Bellavista's trendy dining spot offers Peruvian and international fare. Try a Chilean *pisco* sour cocktail, but beware — the grape-based liquor packs a potent punch. People come late here — it doesn't fill up until close to 11 PM. Open daily for lunch and dinner. Reservations advised. Major credit cards accepted. 53 Antonia López de Bello (phone: 777-3059). Moderate.

**Pinpilinpausha** – *The* Basque restaurant of Santiago. Its bistro atmosphere and tasty Spanish dishes make it a favorite of many international visitors as well as foreign residents. Service is a bit rushed — you may want to tell your waitress that you want to linger over your salad and wine before the main course is served. Open daily, except Sundays, for lunch and dinner. Reservations advised. No credit cards accepted. Centrally located in downtown Santiago at 62 Matias Cousiño (phone: 696-1835). Moderate.

**Yie Kung** – One of the best of the 2 dozen Chinese eateries in Santiago. Be sure to try the fried Chinese ravioli (*wonton frito*) as an appetizer. Dinner is served in a roofed-in garden. Open daily for lunch and dinner. Reservations unnecessary. Major credit cards accepted. Near Providencia at 62 La Concepción (phone: 223-3535). Moderate.

**La Pizza Nostra** – Serving much more than pizza, including tasty homemade pasta and tempting fresh salads, this Italian eatery recently opened a third branch just steps away from the Tobalaba metro station. Open daily for lunch and dinner. Reservations unnecessary. No credit cards accepted. At Av. Providencia and Pedro de Valdivia (phone: 231-9853); 6757 Av. Las Condes (phone: 229-7321); and 019 Luis Thayer Ojeda, at the corner of Av. Providencia (phone: 232-3556). Moderate to inexpensive.

**Los Buenos Muchachos** – Chilean food — empanadas, *mariscos* — in a Chilean environment, with the music of guitars and the Chilean harp. Closed Sundays, except in summer when it is open for dinner on Sundays. Reservations unnecessary. Major credit cards accepted. 1031 Calle Ricardo Cumming (phone: 698-0112). Inexpensive.

**Café Colonia** – If you find yourself craving real German apple strudel or cheesecake while in Santiago, head for this *confitería*. Take-out pastries and marzipan confections also are available. Open daily. No reservations. No credit cards accepted. 133 and 161 MacIver (phone: 397256). Inexpensive.

**Café Paula** – Satisfy your sweet tooth with an ice cream creation, pastry, or any of dozens of other desserts. There are several branches of these downtown tea houses and they are also good spots to have coffee. Open daily until 9 PM. No reservations. Major credit cards accepted. 235 Estado (phone: 398243), 915 Moneda (phone: 380537), and 302 Pasaje Matte (phone: 332215). Inexpensive.

**Diet El Conquistador** – Adjacent to the *El Conquistador* hotel, this eatery is perhaps the first and only in Santiago to feature cholesterol-free and diabetic menus. Try the luncheon specials — three-course meals and coffee — for a low fixed price. There's a selection of healthful juices, soup, fish, and lean meat on the à la carte menu. Very attentive service. Open daily for lunch and dinner. Reservations unnecessary. Major credit cards accepted. 920 Miguel Cruchaga (phone: 696-5599). Inexpensive.

***Naturista*** – The place for vegetarians, featuring a wide selection of omelettes. You can ask for your own concoctions if they aren't too complicated. No matter what your taste preference, you will enjoy a drink at the juice bar. Closed Sundays. Reservations unnecessary. Visa accepted. 846 Calle Moneda (phone: 698-4122). There's a second branch at 42 Orrego Luco Sur (phone: 231-8964). Inexpensive.

***Pérgola de la Plaza del Mulato del Gil*** – This is the spot for open-air dining in the summer months, and an eatery serving international fare where you'll rub elbows with Santiago's actors, authors, and lawyers. Open Mondays through Saturdays for lunch and dinner. Reservations unnecessary. No credit cards accepted. 305 Calle Lastarria (phone: 393604). Inexpensive.

***Venezia*** – Set in a lovely older neighborhood of quiet, tree-lined streets below San Cristóbal Hill. Abundant platters of beef, lamb, and pork and reasonable prices make this dining spot a favorite of artists who live in the area. Open daily for lunch and dinner. No reservations. Visa accepted. 200 Pío Nono (phone: 370900). Inexpensive.

# SÃO PAULO

A surprisingly humble site for an event as important as the proclamation of Brazilian independence in 1822, the city of São Paulo has since come to embody and celebrate the bold spirit of that action. In its 150-year transition from backwoods outpost to South America's largest city, São Paulo has cultivated its stubborn independence, held on to its brash pioneer tradition, and shed any semblance of humility. As recently as 1932, the city led a serious secessionist revolt. It continues to surprise and challenge just about everyone, from the national leaders in Brasília, who would like to tame this unruly dynamo, to the visitors, who must somehow reconcile the fact of a skyscraper jungle with their previous visions of Brazil as a country of silent Amazonian waterways and sensuous Rio de Janeiro sambas.

São Paulo defies both the silent and sensuous stereotypes. It is, instead, a roaring tumult of a city, an often-polluted perpetual motion machine of some 16 million *paulistas* (officially, *paulistanos*) who never seem to stop hurrying, honking, or building. With their impatience and unabashed materialism, the *paulistas* drive the economic locomotive that has pulled Brazil to its current place as the world's eighth-largest economy. In their state capital, they have joined the agricultural importance of a Chicago with the once industrial might of a Detroit to create a commercial center that they proudly call "South America's second country." Within the city's 580 square miles (approximately ten times the area of Washington, DC), they make up almost 10% of the country's population.

The reward for all this urban concentration and bustle: One of South America's highest standards of living, some of the best restaurants on the continent, and an active cultural and nightlife that some foreigners rate far superior to that of more famous Rio.

From the very beginning, when Jesuit Padre Anchieta climbed to the 2,400-foot Piratininga plateau to found his São Paulo Indian mission in 1554, the city has been different from the rest of Brazil. Instead of hugging the coast like the sugar planters of Rio, Recife, and Salvador, the São Paulo pioneers, the *bandeirantes,* penetrated the inhospitable frontier. And slowly they pushed the evangelizing Jesuits south into Paraguay, for they had their own uses for the Indian population — they married the women, sold the men into slavery, and adopted such tongue-twisting Tupí-Guaraní place names as Anhangabaú (An-yan-gab-ah-*oo*) and Itapetininga (*Ee*-tap-ay-tee-*neen*-gaa) for their streets and towns. For almost 3 centuries the *bandeirantes* had the region to themselves. The Portuguese crown profited first from the sugar plantations (as did São Paulo at the beginning of the 19th century) and then the gold mines of Minas Gerais, but not until 1850 did São Paulo play its economic trump card — coffee.

Coffee built São Paulo. To grow it, southern Europeans immigrated by the hundreds of thousands. To transport it, Englishmen built two railroads to the coast, the Santos-Jundiaí and the Sorocabana, then managed the warehouses and docks of the port of Santos. To enjoy its financial rewards, the now-wealthy *bandeirantes* divided their time between the state's immense plantations and Paris's elegant salons.

The 20th century brought a new wave of immigrants — Japanese, Syrian, and Lebanese Arabs — for whom trade and commerce were a far more palatable means of support than plantation life. King coffee had a competitor. While the Japanese continued the rural immigration pattern (cultivating many vegetables which were introduced into the Brazilian diet for the first time), the Arabs settled in the city, where industrial São Paulo was just emerging. Instead of allowing their rivers to flow south unimpeded over the 2,500 miles to Buenos Aires, São Paulo engineers dammed two of them during the 1920s, installed generating plants, and set São Paulo on its industrial path. Volkswagen, Ford, and General Motors have since set up shop in São Paulo, where they too are perpetuating the city's brash *bandeirante* spirit by pioneering the production of alcohol-driven cars. Multinational chemical corporations have chosen suburban Mauá, and innumerable manufacturers are in the city itself. In fact, 75% of Brazil's electrical goods, rubber, and machinery are produced within the city limits — all in all, a staggering 50% of the total industrial output of the nation. *Paulistas* like to boast that 70% of the money in Brazil circulates on Avenida Paulista alone. Greater São Paulo, easily acknowledged as the largest industrial region in Latin America, absorbs 75% of foreign investment. São Paulo state produces most of the coffee from which Brazil supplies nearly half of the world's need. Coffee futures and other commodities are traded in São Paulo. Tons of agricultural produce are shipped through the city and Santos, its port.

Billed as the world's fastest growing city (Mexico City might argue about the dubious title), São Paulo increases by at least 300,000 inhabitants per year, 70% of whom migrate from other parts of Brazil, particularly the Northeast. Although accurate statistics are hard to come by, the city has more than tripled in size from 1960, when it had 3.8 million residents compared to Rio de Janeiro's 3,307,000. (Rio is 272 miles — 435 km — north of São Paulo.) In 1970, there were 6 million *paulistas* and 4 million *cariocas* (residents of Rio de Janeiro). Estimates in 1990 put the population of São Paulo at 9 million, with the total for Greater São Paulo (which includes 37 surrounding towns) at 17 million. That's quite a change from 1872, when São Paulo numbered only 32,000 inhabitants.

With more than 7.6 million workers, São Paulo has a strong labor movement and outspoken and often courageous political leaders. Since May, 1978, when some 400,000 São Paulo workers held the country's first strike in 10 years, work stoppages have once again become legal and have spread to other cities such as Rio, Belo Horizonte, and Porto Alegre. Strikes, which had been declared illegal when the former military government was in power, are an important way in which São Paulo pushed more political freedom throughout the country.

A fearless spirit is part of the city's 20th-century history. The coffee aristocracy that built splendid mansions along then-residential Avenida Paulista had

# SÃO PAULO

**Points of Interest**

1. Edifício Itália/Italian Building
2. Praça Ramos de Azevedo
3. Praça do Patriarca
4. Praça da Sé/Cathedral Plaza
5. Asian District
6. Museu de Arte Sacra/Sacred Art Museum
7. Praça da República/Republic Plaza
8. Museu de Arte de São Paulo/São Paulo Art Museum
9. Feira de Pacaembú/Pacaembú Market Pacaembú Stadium
10. Memorial de América Latina/Latin America Memorial
11. Rua Augusta and the Jardins
12. Parque Ibirapuera/Ibirapuera Park

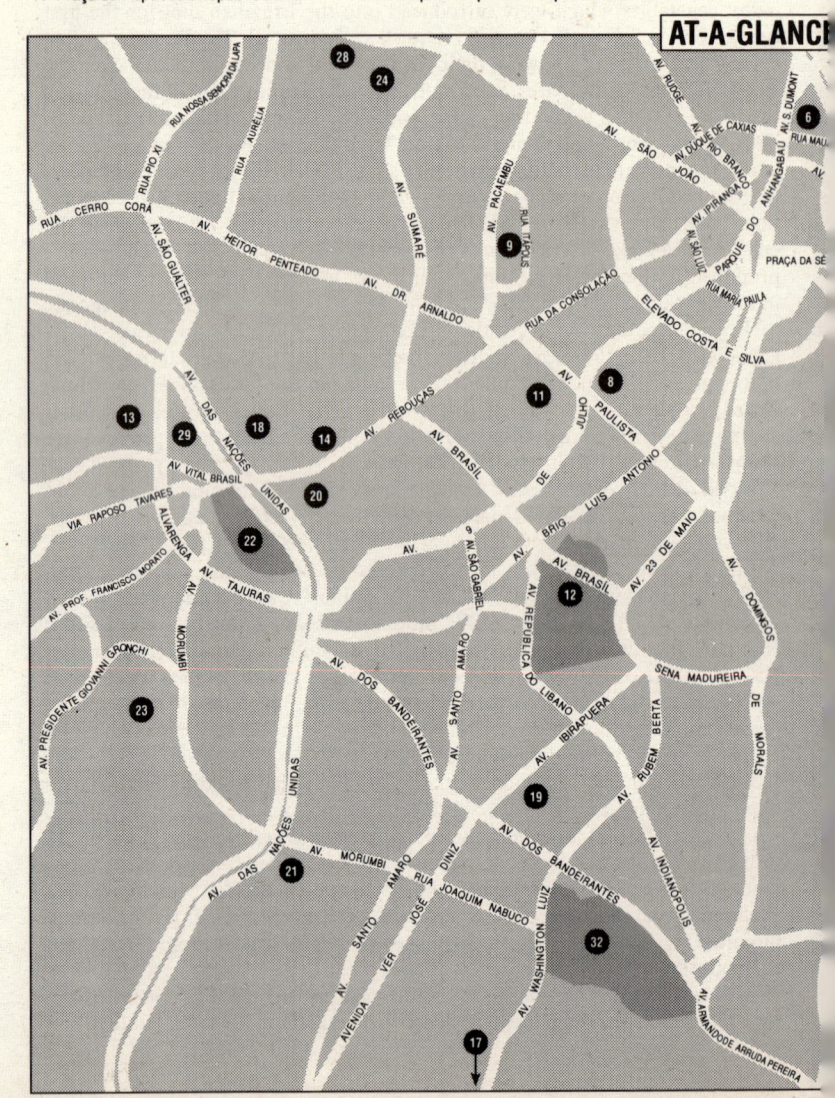

**AT-A-GLANCE**

## DOWNTOWN

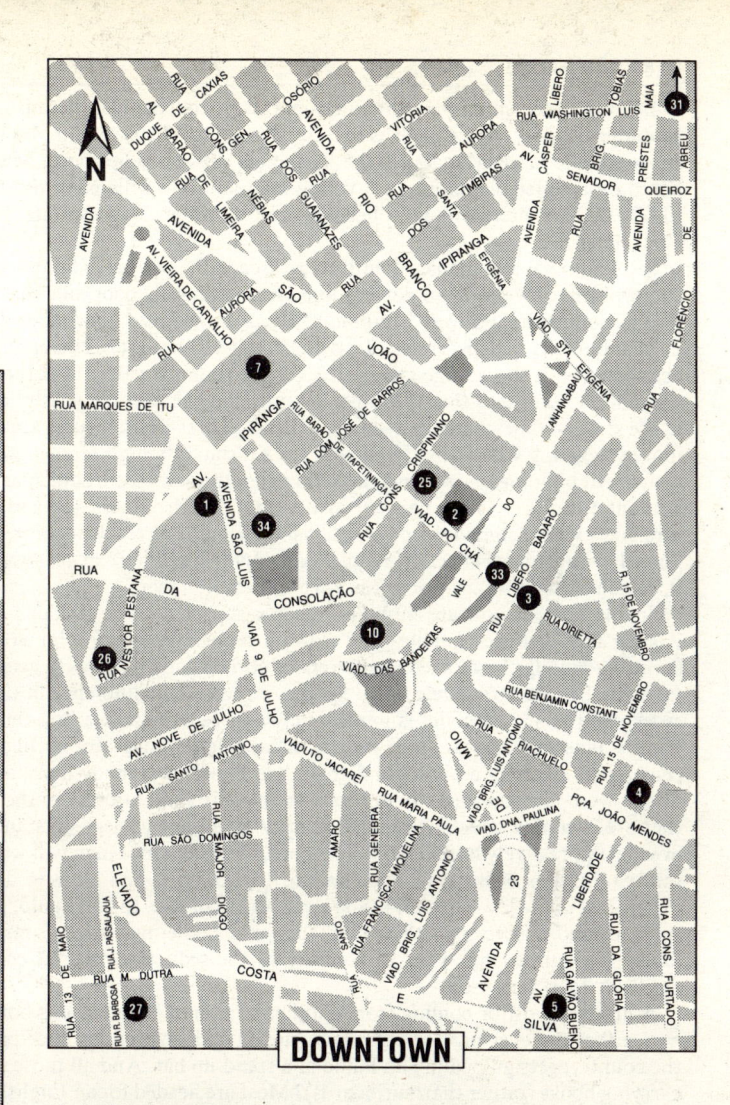

13. Instituto Butantã/Butantã Institute
    Casa do Bandeirante/Pioneer House
14. Museu da Casa Brasileira/Brazilian Home Museum
15. Jardim Zoologico/Zoo
16. Parque da Independência e Museu Paulista/Independence Park and Paulista Museum
17. Interlagos and Guarapiranga Reservoir
18. Shopping Center Iguatemi
19. Shopping Center Ibirapuera
20. Eldorado Shopping Center
21. Shopping Center Morumbí
22. Jockey Club de São Paulo
23. Morumbi Stadium
24. Antarctica Stadium
25. Teatro Municipal/Municipal Theater
26. Teatro de Cultura Artistica
27. Teatro Sérgio Cardoso
28. SESC Fábrica de Pompéia
29. Casa do Bandeirante/Pioneer House
30. Estação Rodoviária Tietê/Tietê Bus Station
31. Estação Luz/Luz Train Station
32. Congonhas Airport
33. Viaduto do Chá/Tea Viaduct
34. State Secretary of Sports and Tourism

to make way for empire-building immigrants — Italians like the millionaire Matarazzo family, Arabs such as São Paulo politician Paulo Salim Maluf, and Japanese like artist Manabu Mabe. A typical rags-to-riches hero, Mabe labored on a coffee plantation as a young man and now sells paintings for up to $30,000 to international collectors, one of whom was the late Nelson Rockefeller.

São Paulo has not managed entirely to escape the pervasive South American problem of widespread poverty and crime. It has its poor, like every city on this continent, and over 1 million *paulistas* crowd into homemade shacks in shantytowns called *favelas*. Less than half of the city's inhabitants are connected with the sewage system; 72% have running water. Half the city's population earns less than $200 per month, and the average yearly income in the state is somewhere between $2,000 and $3,000. These figures are all the more staggering when contrasted with the exorbitantly high rents in modern apartment buildings — as much as $800 a month for a 2-bedroom apartment without furniture. (Who can afford it? Only North Americans and other foreigners whose companies pay for housing, which, one resident commented, "has the unfortunate effect of giving landlords the idea they can get away with it, which in turn forces prices to skyrocket even higher.")

Surrounded by upward-mobility success stories on every side, it is no wonder that *paulistas* are obsessed with movement. A visitor who would be sprinting among the relaxed saunterers of Rio de Janeiro quickly gets overtaken by São Paulo's determined, jostling crowds. The difference in the two cities' tempos and lifestyles is immediately apparent, even to a first-timer. In Rio de Janeiro, *cariocas* (men *and* women) often lounge around like juicy centerfolds awaiting a photographer. In São Paulo, everybody looks as if he or she were late for work. In contrast to the shirts unbuttoned to the navel that are everyday street attire in Rio, *paulistas* wear business suits and ties, even on oppressively humid, hot afternoons. Occasionally a man will wear the top two buttons of his shirt open. Women wear skirts and blouses, demure in contrast to the low-cut shifts and *tanga* bikinis of Rio. In São Paulo, people walk around absorbed in their own thoughts, sometimes tired, sometimes lonely, sometimes annoyed. In contrast to the seductive, playful *cariocas*, *paulistas* look very real.

A first-time visitor coming from another section of Brazil also is bound to notice that the ever-present *cafezinho*, sipped and savored in other parts of the country, gets gulped in São Paulo at a stand-up bar. And all those people carrying books (rather than surfboards)? Most are headed for an English class or a professional course for an evening of study after a full day's work. One *paulista* eloquently summed up both cities: "In Rio, it's women, samba, and *cachaça* (sugarcane liquor). In São Paulo, it's work, work, work, 48 hours a day. No wonder the people are crazy!"

Returning to the city itself, a semblance of order does reign among the residential areas that ring the south and west of downtown (*centro*), although business activity continually encroaches. On hills reminiscent of those of San Francisco, apartment buildings and chic boutiques start at Avenida Paulista and give way to the quiet lanes of the residential neighborhoods, called *jardins* (gardens), before commerce returns at Avenida Faria Lima. Farther south, in the Zona Sul, *paulistas* have built suburbs on the US model — Morumbí, Santo Amaro, and Chácara Flora. However, they, too, are getting surrounded by commerce, as has already happened to the *jardins* and to the western suburbs such as Pinheiros, Pacaembú, and Sumaré.

This growing city will never be voted one of the planet's most attractive. Although it does have mosaic sidewalks with curved patterns laid into wide pedestrian walkways, palm trees, and grand boulevards, it is overpoweringly noisy, hectic, and anonymously modern. And the predominant color is gray from top to bottom: hazy sky melting into buildings melting into concrete. Even the most photographed site — the spectacular "S"-shaped Copan apartment building designed by Oscar Niemeyer curving sinuously across the street from the cylindrical tower of the *São Paulo Hilton* — can lose its dramatic appeal in the washed-out, unattractive daylight. Though architect Gian Carlo Gasperini's project for a new high-rise building — the Matarazzo Tower — may give the city a distinctive, postmodern skyscraper (if the Matarazzo family relinquishes its precious parcel of land on Avenida Paulista), the skyline for now remains nightmarishly monotonous. Like the majority of industrial cities around the world, São Paulo's appeal has nothing to do with its physical appearance; rather, its most impressive quality is the human energy that built it and keeps it moving. It's a city with heart. People love it despite its ugliness, which seems to go endlessly in office building after office building, apartment house after apartment house, and factory after factory. You can drive through São Paulo for an hour and be convinced that you are in the same part of town in which you started out, so identical are the sections of unrelieved urban landscape. Which makes it even more surprising when you get to the edge of the city and find a tropical forest with mist clinging to flower-filled gorges. Then you understand the triumphant, mammoth undertaking that has become São Paulo: It is a city hacked from jungle!

In the evening, *paulistas* head home to pockets of relative tranquillity to recuperate among traditionally tight-knit families. Except for an occasional late dinner, play, or concert at the magnificent *Municipal Theater, paulistas* abandon downtown to the city's poorer (and tougher) population at night. Similarly, on weekends the affluent flee to beach houses or country homes while the majority spend time among family or fellow soccer fans. Those who remain crowd the city's restaurants on Sunday — maid's day off. But beware the long weekend. At the slightest excuse, *paulistas* will descend to the coast en masse, creating 2- to 3-hour traffic jams when they return on Sunday night.

This very private and family-centered social life frustrates both the city's estimated 70,000 resident Americans and foreign visitors. The 550 US firms (such as Alcoa and IBM) that have personnel scattered throughout the city and the state try to solve the problem as wealthy *paulistas* do: They buy memberships in the city's many expensive sports clubs. Public recreational facilities are scarce.

A more viable alternative for tourists seeking casual but respectable encounters are evenings at what one American calls São Paulo's "California-type bars." (Less respectable encounters are well advertised for traveling businessmen in the hotel tourist pamphlets.) The action at these bars starts late, after 10 PM, and reflects traditional São Paulo society. The bars are away from downtown, mostly near Avenida Paulista and the *jardins* neighborhood, and socializing most often takes place in groups.

This paradoxical mix of modern business and traditional social customs is just one example of São Paulo's growing pains. Spectacular growth also has caused plenty of physical problems. Winter rains annually force thousands from their homes. Residents who enjoy an extensive public telephone system (tokens, called *fichas,* are sold at newsstands and lunch counters) may find it difficult to obtain a private line. And everyday concrete replaces more of the city's precious trees. As in other South American cities, street crime does exist, and tourists would be well advised to leave their valuables in the hotel safe — or better still, at home.

Yet São Paulo remains undaunted. Even with predictions of a population of 24 million by the year 2000, *paulistas* face the future with optimism and confidence — *bandeirantes* to the end.

# SÃO PAULO AT-A-GLANCE

**SEEING THE CITY:** Although only a plane can provide a complete view of the sprawl that is São Paulo, the top floors of the downtown Edifício Itália offer a good substitute. The city's hills swallow the suburbs, but at your feet lies the labyrinth of downtown streets, and to the southwest you should be able to spy the huge Itaú time and temperature sign that marks Avenida Paulista. A combination of two elevators will whisk you up to the 41st floor. From here you can choose the free and often windy view from the balcony, a soft drink or costly but scenic meal at one of the two restaurants, or a drink at the bar. The best time to go is at night, when everything sparkles. Open daily until 2 AM. 344 Av. Ipiranga (phone: 257-6566).

**SPECIAL PLACES:** With its tortuous traffic patterns and pedestrian malls, downtown São Paulo is best explored on foot. Wear sensible shoes and be prepared for the construction that can turn any sidewalk into an obstacle course. You'll do well to remember that the city is divided into named neighborhoods (downtown being *centro*) and that streets frequently change names — for example, Rua Augusta becomes Rua Colômbia, then Avenida Europa, and finally Rua Cidade Jardim before expiring at the river. Trust your map rather than generous but often uninformed residents, and don't forget that most museums open only in the afternoon and are closed Mondays. One final note: Don't wear valuable jewelry or carry large amounts of cash while walking around the city. Street assaults are rampant, especially downtown.

## DOWNTOWN

**Viaduto do Chá (Tea Viaduct)** – Here is the nonstop heart of nonstop São Paulo. It is people, people everywhere. Bustling Brazilians overflow from the sidewalks onto the already bus- and taxi-jammed streets. Vendors and beggars, bankers and delivery boys, are all fellow companions on the Viaduto do Chá. Linking the two major squares, Praça do Patriarca and Praça Ramos de Azevedo, it provides the primary downtown reference point. The Praça do Patriarca and the malls of São Paulo's lucrative financial district, the Old City, lie to the east. To the west, the Praça Ramos de Azevedo, the ornate *Municipal Theater,* and *Mappin* department store mark the beginning of the

New City and the downtown shopping area. The viaduct spans the 12-lane Anhangabaú traffic artery.

**Praça da Sé (Cathedral Plaza)** – Rebuilt in 1977 and inaugurated in 1978, the Praça da Sé is dominated above by South America's largest cathedral and below by the city's major subway station. Although the cathedral was completed in 1953, the design is European traditional. Grand in scale, its Gothic dome is 213 feet high and its two towers are 328 feet high. The cathedral's interior is also quite impressive, with its stained glass windows and colored mosaics. Contiguous to the financial district, both the fountains of the square itself and the vaulting coolness of the Gothic cathedral that holds 8,000 people offer a quiet interlude. The city's second subway line, partially functioning now and due for completion within the next few years, intersects the north–south subway line here. The subway entrance is to the left of the cathedral, and the ride (about 20¢) will provide ample demonstration of the vastness of the city. Wall maps at the entrance indicate the subway route; just watch the *paulistas* to learn how the computerized gates work. Two points of interest, the Liberdade district (Bairro Oriental) and the *Sacred Art Museum,* can be reached by subway. Two blocks east and south of Praça do Patriarca on Rua 15 de Novembro.

**Liberdade/Bairro Oriental (Asian District)** – Treats galore lie beyond the welcoming red lacquer gates of São Paulo's Asian district: tranquil rock gardens perched above the traffic din; herb stores stocked with mysterious remedies; and numerous Japanese, Chinese, and Korean restaurants that come alive under the glow of the district's Japanese lantern street lights. São Paulo state boasts the largest Japanese population outside of Japan, and Liberdade is its urban hub. Besides curio shops that sell both Brazilian and Asian souvenirs, numerous little shops feature delicate, handpainted kimonos. The nearby *Museu da Imigração Japonesa no Brasil* (Brazilian Museum of Japanese Immigration; 381 Rua São Joaquím; phone: 279-5233 or 279-5465) recounts the interesting 75-year story that has given the country some 800,000 Japanese-Brazilian citizens. Open Tuesdays through Sundays, 1:30 to 5:30 PM. A handicrafts fair fills the local square on Sunday afternoons. South of Praça da Sé along Praça da Liberdade and Rua Galvão Bueno.

**Museu de Arte Sacra (Sacred Art Museum)** – Locals claim that this museum, housed in the colonial Mosteiro da Luz (Convent of the Light), has the largest collection of religious art outside the Vatican. Carved wooden altars, statues, and several rooms of gold altarpieces are exhibited around an interior courtyard. If you call ahead, you may be able to arrange for an English-speaking guide. Open Tuesdays through Sundays, 1 to 5 PM. Admission charge. Across from Tiradentes subway station at 676 Av. Tiradentes (phone: 227-7694; 228-4063 for curator).

**Praça da República (Republic Plaza)** – This lovely square is full of exotic tropical plants and shaded by palm trees. There are many pleasant tourist shops around the edge and along the two nearby pedestrian shopping streets, Barão de Itapetininga and 24 de Maio. *H. Stern* sells exotic gems right across the street. In the nearby *Galería California* (at 222 Av. Barão de Itapetininga), more than a dozen souvenir shops offer typical items. If you're in town on a Sunday, don't miss the morning flea market Brazilians are fond of calling the "Hippie Fair." Leather craftsmen and local artists exhibit beside wizened coin and stamp collectors. Be cautious with your personal belongings as well as with the regional snacks sold by transplanted *baianas* — the sauces can be pretty fiery for an uninitiated stomach. Never wander here at night. Av. Ipiranga and Av. Barão de Itapetininga.

**Museu de Arte de São Paulo — MASP (São Paulo Art Museum)** – Balanced dramatically on four concrete pylons, this museum displays South America's most complete permanent collection of Western art — a Rembrandt, a Raphael, and a sampling of French Impressionist works. There are also examples of contemporary Brazilian art and frequent excellent traveling exhibitions. All paintings are mounted on plastic stands instead of hung on walls so that they appear to be floating. The *Degas* restaurant, in the basement, is a good place to have lunch. The museum is open Tuesdays through Fridays from 1 to 5 PM, weekends from 2 to 6 PM; special exhibits also open evenings. No admission charge. 1578 Av. Paulista (phone: 251-5644).

After taking in the galleries, enjoy the greenery of the Trianon Park across the street, and then stroll along Avenida Paulista — once the avenue of stately mansions, but quickly becoming a second financial district of adventurous, impressive contemporary architecture.

**Feira de Pacaembú (Pacaembú Market)** – This market offers everything from orchids to octopus, with luscious tropical fruits and vegetables in between. It's the biggest and best-known of São Paulo's numerous street markets, which are held on different days in different neighborhoods. Held Tuesdays, Thursdays, Fridays, and Saturdays in front of *Pacaembu Stadium* at Praça Charles Miller.

**Memorial da América Latina (Latin America Memorial)** – Designed by Oscar Niemeyer — of Brasília fame — this recently built, seven-building complex is a center for the dissemination of Latin American culture. On a Sunday afternoon, you might see a folk ballet from Argentina performed in the *Praça Cívica* amphitheater; on a weekday evening, there might be a Venezuelan chamber music concert in the 1,700-seat auditorium. The complex also has art exhibits, a library, and a restaurant. Adjacent to the Barra Funda subway station (west line) at 664 Av. Mário de Andrade (phone: 826-1822).

**SESC Fábrica da Pompéia (Pompéia Center)** – This sprawling old factory complex and fascinating piece of industrial architecture has been converted into a cultural center that is very popular with *paulista* artists and intellectuals. It's a great place to take in the latest contemporary theater, music, dance, or art, or just to have a *choppe* (draft beer) or *cafezinho,* people watch, or meet the local intelligentsia. Open Tuesdays through Fridays from 10 AM to 10 PM, weekends and holidays from 9 AM to 10 PM. No admission charge. 93 Rua Clélia (phone: 864-8544).

## SUBURBS

**Rua Augusta and the Jardins** – You'll see *paulistas* at one of their favorite occupations — shopping — as you descend the rather steep Rua Augusta from Avenida Paulista in the *jardins* district. Side streets such as Alamedas Tietê, Lorena, and Oscar Freire are filled with boutiques, native art stores, art galleries, informal lunch counters, and several good restaurants. Try the excellent Italian restaurant, *Massimo* (1828 Alameda Santos); or the ever-popular *Churrascaría Rodeio* steakhouse (1826 Rua Haddock Lobo). Cross Avenida Estados Unidos at Rua Bela Cintra to wander among the lush vegetation and modest mansions that mark the beginning of the residential *jardins* area.

**Parque Ibirapuera (Ibirapuera Park)** – After a morning of dodging the traffic and elbowing the downtown crowds, the willow-bordered lakes and eucalyptus groves of Ibirapuera Park provide a welcome respite. The park was designed by Oscar Niemeyer, architect of Brasília, and because it is such a large place (400 acres) you might take a taxi to a specific place — the *Contemporary Art Museum* (open Tuesdays through Sundays from noon to 6 PM; no admission charge; phone: 571-9610 or 544-2511) or the Pavilhão Japonesa (Japanese Pavilion), a reconstruction of Japan's Katura Palace. Then, with an ice cream purchased from a vendor, meander across the lawns to one of the museums or to the planetarium (nightly shows during the week by reservation only; open to the public on weekend afternoons and holidays). Try the roads that have been closed to traffic or, if you stay along the main thoroughfares, watch out for the motorcyclists. They are as enamored of this oasis as pedestrians — but they go a lot faster. Parque Ibirapuera.

**Instituto Butantã (Butantã Institute)** – Snakes are the specialty here: live ones that are "milked" for medicinal purposes, and stuffed specimens of poisonous snakes, spiders, and scorpions that are displayed for educational ends. The important snakes, though, are the live ones that sun themselves and slither around the open pits. Well protected by high leather boots, researchers extract venom from these creatures six times a day (schedule varies), and they delight in showing their fangs and darting tongues to the crowd. Walk behind the museum parking lot to get a view of the city horizon. Open Tuesdays through Sundays from 9 AM to 5 PM, Mondays from 1 to 6 PM. No admission charge. 1500 Av. Vital Brasil (phone: 813-7222).

**Casa do Bandeirante (Pioneer House)** – Within walking distance from Butantã, you can see how the *bandeirantes* lived. As this oversize reconstruction of an 18th-century pioneer home shows, they led a spartan, nomadic existence. These pioneers used uncomfortable but portable rope hammocks for beds and substituted well-traveled trunks for the chests and buffets of more settled city life. Scattered around the grounds, you'll discover the unwieldy oxcarts still used in Brazil's less-developed regions and three mills: one for sugarcane, another for corn, and one primitive, all-purpose mill. If you ask, the caretaker will turn on the water to show how this mill worked. Open Tuesdays through Sundays from 9 AM to 5 PM. No admission charge. Praça Monteiro Lobato (phone: 211-0920).

**Museu da Casa Brasileira (Brazilian Home Museum)** – In an imposing residence that was built in 1945 in 19th-century neo-classical style, this museum offers a good overview of how Brazil's elite has lived during the past 400 years. Excellent photographs of elegant Victorian drawing rooms and enlargements of 16th- and 17th-century sketches augment the museum's large furniture collection. Fashioned from beautiful native woods, they are notable for their immense size and the preponderance of religious pieces. English-speaking guides available. Open Tuesdays through Sundays from 1 to 5 PM. No admission charge. 774 Av. Brig. Faria Lima (phone: 210-2564).

**Jardim Zoológico (Zoo)** – A great source of pride for residents and a required stop for anyone remotely interested in tropical animals, the *São Paulo Zoo* is perhaps the best substitute for a trip up the Amazon. There are over 500 mammals (136 species) and 650 reptiles (40 species), including anteaters, sloths, tapirs, and cage after cage of spectacular birds, which currently number over 900 (240 species); among them toucans, parrots, and macaws (always paired, the macaws scream incessantly and vary in hue from brilliant blue to bright red). The scattered signs *Não Pise na Grama,* by the way, mean "Don't Walk on the Grass." Facilities include snack bars, picnic tables, playgrounds, and a museum. Be sure to pick up the useful map the ticket seller gives you. Open daily from 9 AM to 6 PM. Admission charge. 4241 Av. Miguel Estefano, Agua Funda (phone: 276-0811).

**Parque da Independência e Museu Paulista (Independence Park and Paulista Museum)** – There's a little of everything for history buffs here. The *Paulista Museum,* a converted palace, displays old maps, coins, firearms, colonial furniture, and art. Fountains and statuary dot the grounds, and you can walk through the preserved mud house where Dom Pedro I spent the night before giving the Cry of Ipiranga, the Brazilian Proclamation of Independence. Open daily, except Mondays, from 9 AM to 5 PM. Admission charge. Parque da Independência, Ipiranga (phone: 215-4588 or 215-4307).

**Wholesale Markets (CEAGESP and CEASA)** – Beware the trucks that rumble into São Paulo's wholesale produce market, *CEAGESP,* about midnight. The drivers are bringing food to Latin America's largest food distribution center. You'll see fruits and vegetables you've never heard of. On either a Tuesday or Friday midmorning visit to the adjoining wholesale flower market, *CEASA,* you'll see hundreds of delicate ferns and exotic birds of paradise. The *CEAGESP* restaurant (1946 Av. Dr. Gastão Vidigal, Marginal do Rio Pinheiros; phone: 261-9388) serves hearty, typical Brazilian meals. Closed Sunday afternoons; no credit cards accepted.

## 524  SÃO PAULO / At-a-Glance

**Interlagos and Guarapiranga Reservoir** – About 8 miles (13 km) south of the city along Avenida Atlântica, the reservoir affords a quick escape from the urban environment. The beaches and restaurants fill up on weekends, but most facilities are open all week long. Besides pleasure boats and sailboats for rent, there are hydroplane rides and pony trots for the kids (rentals can be found along Estrada de Guarapiranga). The *Interlagos* restaurant (on Estrada de Guarapiranga) is a good place for a meal or just a beer. The *Brazilian Formula I Grand Prix* is held at the nearby *Interlagos Raceway* (*Autódromo;* 259 Av. Senador Teotônio Vilela; phone: 521-9911 or 247-3766), which also hosts local car and motorcycle races.

**Embú** – This colonial town, about a half-hour drive from downtown, dates from 1554 and has a well-attended artisans' fair on Sundays and holidays as well as permanent shops that are open all week. At midafternoon on Sundays, the local oompah band serenades shoppers and townsfolk from the central bandstand. Art (especially primitive), antiques, and handicrafts fashioned from clay, leather, wood, metal, and rattan can be had at reasonable prices. Restaurants along the main square serve snacks or lunch on rustic tables. About 16 miles (26 km) west on Rte. BR-116.

**Itú** – After someone made a joke about the size of things in Itú several years ago, the city adopted the idea and now uses it as a successful tourism promotion gimmick. An immense telephone booth towers over the heads of visitors in the main square, restaurants sell 3-foot-long hot dogs, and all souvenirs come in gargantuan sizes. The narrow cobblestone streets and antiques stores provide plenty of interest. Eat at the *Bar do Alemão,* also called *Steiner* (575 Rua Paula Souza; phone: 482-4284). Some of the region's most beautiful campsites are located near Itú. About 70 miles (112 km), or 2 hours, west on the Castelo Branco Hwy.

■**EXTRA SPECIAL:** When *paulistas* want to escape to the shore, they don't have to go as far as Rio de Janeiro: The resorts of Guarujá, Santos, and São Vicente lie 43 miles (69 km) to the southeast. The road winds through hills of purple flowers and jungle vegetation, with fog and clouds rising steamily from the gorges. Santos, Brazil's largest port, is a frayed, seamy, tough Latin waterfront town with huge container ports, mechanics' shops, and storefront merchants selling tired little bananas. However, don't get too depressed as you travel through this part of town, for soon you will reach Gonzaga — a beachfront of white apartment buildings, with cafés like those in Rio de Janeiro and a long grassy plaza along the water, good for walking along or eating beside, but not for swimming. Guarujá, across the channel, is considerably more elegant. Nicknamed "the Miami Beach of Brazil," its nucleus of ubiquitous white high-rises contains well-tended cafés, restaurants, promenades, and surf shops. At the far end of a long road is a section of hillside villas clinging to cliffs that offer views as good as any at Big Sur. Halfway in between lies one of the ultimate, consummate resorts in the Americas: *Casa Grande.* A converted ivy-covered hacienda replete with white Victorian wooden verandahs, palm trees, alcoves with bird cages, and a palm-lined swimming pool, it faces a wide, clean, white beach with palms to shade you from an overly hot sun. *Casa Grande*'s eateries include a luncheonette featuring ingenious sandwiches on pita bread and a superb French restaurant that serves giant lobster in a hollowed-out pineapple. Pelé, Brazil's most famous athlete, is a habitué of its disco. American companies based in São Paulo hold conventions here, too (999 Av. Miguel Estefano, Praia da Enseada; phone: 132-86-2223). In São Paulo, you can make reservations at the *Casa Grande* office (571 Av. Europa; phone: 282-4277). If you are not up for driving (traffic jams are awful during the summer — December–February), there is frequent bus service from the city to Santos and Guarujá. Better yet, take an *Expresso Luxo* chauffeured car: They carry five passengers; the trip takes about 2 hours. Cars leave as soon as they're full throughout the day until midnight (932 Av. Ipiranga and Rua 7 de Abril, across the street from the Praça da República; phone: 222-7325 or 223-5161). Another option is to call *Radio Taxi* (phone: 251-1733). The Guarujá Peninsula can be reached either by land or by ferry. The ride across the channel, past multicolored fishing boats, sculling crews practicing rowing, and giant freighters, takes about 10 picturesque minutes. If you are driving, take the Anchieta or Imigrantes highway to Santos and follow signs to Guarujá.

# SOURCES AND RESOURCES

**TOURIST INFORMATION:** The State Secretary of Sports and Tourism maintains an information office (115 Av. São Luiz; phone: 257-7248 or 231-0044) with a helpful, multilingual staff; open weekdays from 9 AM to 6 PM. On weekends, contact one of their other offices (at Congonhas Airport; phone: 531-1242, ext. 195; open from 9 AM to 10 PM; or at Guarulhos International Airport; phone: 945-2111). The São Paulo city information office (154 Praça da República and the *Morumbi Shopping Center)* has maps and information on the city's attractions, and recommends guided tours. Ask for the English-language pamphlet *São Paulo Is All*. A number of brochures on São Paulo state's spas and resort facilities are available, too.

*Quatro Rodas Guia de São Paulo* is the best local guide and and has the most complete map of the city. Available for about $8 at most newsstands, the guide is written in both English and Portuguese. The main English-language city guide is *The Insider's Guide to São Paulo for the Business Executive* by the resident British author, Christopher Pickard. It is sold in hotel bookstores in both São Paulo and Rio for about $10. *Veja*, a newsweekly in Portuguese, appears on the newsstands Mondays with a São Paulo supplement. Probably the handiest map, though incomplete, comes with the tourist office's monthly *São Paulo* pamphlet.

The US Consulate is located in Edifício Conjunto Nacional, 933 Rua Padre João Manuel 01000 (phone: 881-6511).

**Local Coverage** – Two São Paulo morning papers, *O Estado de São Paulo* and *Folha de São Paulo,* cover the news and contain complete events listings. A freebie at most hotel reception desks, the *Este Mês em São Paulo/São Paulo This Month* pamphlet in Portuguese and English includes the most comprehensive monthly calendar of the city's cultural offerings.

Major foreign newspapers are available in the big hotels as well as at newsstands at the corner of Avenida Ipiranga and Avenida São Luís and on Avenida Paulista near Rua Augusta. Newsstands throughout the city sell both *Time* and *Newsweek*, as well as *USA Today,* the *Miami Herald,* and the *International Herald Tribune,* which arrive daily shortly after noon. The Sunday *New York Times* costs about $20. All major hotels broadcast CNN (Cable News Network) via satellite from the US.

**TELEPHONE:** The city code for São Paulo is 11. When calling from within Brazil, dial 011 before the local number. The country code for Brazil is 55.

**CLIMATE AND CLOTHES:** Located on the Tropic of Capricorn, São Paulo has a pleasantly moderate climate. The average summer temperature (December through March) is 75F (24C) and the average winter temperature (June through September) is only 10 degrees lower at 65F (around 18C),

## 526  SÃO PAULO / Sources and Resources

but the thermometer can swing drastically and quickly. In general, it's best to wear fairly light clothing and always carry a warm sweater or jacket. The lack of central heating can make the humid winter seem colder than the thermometer indicates. An umbrella is a must for the torrential rains that fall from October through March, and plastic boots also come in handy. For day, casual city attire is appropriate. Women wear skirts and blouses; men generally wear business suits with ties, although sport shirts and slacks are all right for sightseeing.

**GETTING AROUND: Bus** – It's not recommended, except as an adventure in itself, or as a test for those who expect to be reincarnated as sardines, though the newer, bright-red double-decker buses are a better, less expensive way to sightsee. Estaçao Rodoviária Tietê is the main bus station (1777 Av. Cruzeiro do Sul, subway station Tietê; phone: 235-0322). Because this number is often very busy, less time will be wasted by contacting the bus companies directly for information on inter-city service. The main companies are *Itapemirim* (phone: 298-7500 and 267-8466) and *Cometa* (phone: 299-0177). Bus service between Praça de República in downtown São Paulo and Guarulhos International Airport, between the square and Congonhas Airport, and between the two airports is provided by *Metropolitana de Trasportes Urbanos* (known as *MTU;* phone: 221-9103). Each of the three buses runs approximately every half hour from 6 AM to 10 PM; the fare is about $7 each way.

**Subway** – Again, an adventure rather than a useful mode of transportation. The supermodern, 15-mile-long subway merits a ride — get on at the Praça da Sé and go in any of the four directions — but it won't really get you to many of the places you want to go although it was recently expanded to, and along, Avenida Paulista.

**Taxi** – The best bet for travel within the city. All taxis have meters. Because of the recent rampant inflation, however, the meter no longer registers monetary value, but shows UTs *(unidades taximetros),* which are converted to cruzeiros on a *tabela* (table). The omnipresent Volkswagens are the least expensive; the orange and white *Radio Taxis* (phone: 251-1733) cost 25% more. The large Ford Specials (headquartered next to the *São Paulo Hilton* hotel; phone: 258-2885) charge only by the hour and their drivers are multilingual. Volkswagens will balk at carrying more than two passengers, and if a cabbie passes you by, he's probably off to eat or returning the cab to the company. Little "#2" flags that indicate a 20% fare rise go up on the taxi meter from 10 PM to 6 AM and on Sundays and holidays. It costs the equivalent of about $20 to get from Congonhas Airport or Guarulhos International Airport to the center of town in the medium-price cabs. Tips are not expected but are greatly appreciated. Cab drivers have to spend long hours in the grueling traffic.

**Car Rental** – Try *Hertz* (439 Rua da Consolação; phone: 255-8055, Congonhas Airport; phone: 531-6275, and Guarulhas International Airport; phone: 945-2700); *Budget* (328 Rua da Consolação; phone: 256-4355, and Congonhas; phone: 542-2525); or *Avis* (335 Rua da Consolação; phone: 256-4166, and Congonhas; phone: 241-1817, Guarulhos International Airport; phone: 945-2180). If you plan to travel on a weekend, be sure you have enough gas for Sunday, when many gas stations are closed.

**SPECIAL EVENTS:** In keeping with its industrial character, the city's most spectacular events are often the trade shows held periodically at the huge *Parque Anhembi Exposition Center,* north of downtown. Newspapers and the *Este Mês em São Paulo* pamphlet will give particulars on current trade fairs. Although nowhere nearly as spectacular a show as in Rio de Janeiro, *Carnaval* is celebrated with aplomb in Santos and Guarujá just before *Lent,* and the São Paulo *Carnaval* gets bigger and better every year. The *Bienal Internacional de São Paulo Festival,* held in odd-numbered years from October through December, is an important international contemporary art show, the only event of its kind in South America. Admission charge. *Bienal Pavilion,* Ibirapuera Park.

**MUSEUMS:** Most museums in São Paulo are open only in the afternoons and are closed Mondays. The *Museu da Imigração Japonesa no Brasil* (Brazilian Museum of Japanese Immigration), *Museu de Art Sacre* (Sacred Art Museum), the *Museu de Art de São Paulo — MASP* (São Paulo Art Museum), the *Museu da Casa Brasileira* (Brazilian Home Museum), *Casa do Bandeirante* (Pioneer House), and *Museu Paulista* (Paulista Museum) are all described in *Special Places*. In addition to the *Contemporary Art Museum,* Parque Ibirapuera (Ibirapuera Park) has on its grounds a *Museu de Folclore* (Folklore Museum; phone: 544-4212); *Museu de Arte Moderna* (Modern Art Museum; phone: 549-9688); *Museu de Aeronáutica* (Aviation Museum; phone: 570-3915); and the *Planetário* (Planetarium; phone: 544-4606).

Ibirapuera Park is also host to the *Bienal Internacional de São Paulo,* or *São Paulo Biennial*. Originally sponsored by the *Modern Art Museum (MAM)* but now run by its own private foundation, this international art exhibition has been held in the Oscar Niemeyer–designed *Bienal Pavilion* since 1951. Reflecting the country's political climate, the *Bienal* fell into relative obscurity until 7 years ago, when, with the reestablishment of a democratic government in Brazil, curator Sheila Lerner mounted an exhibition of art dealing with humanitarian subjects. Since then, like its counterpart in Venice, it has become predictably unpredictable and always good for a bit of highbrow hijinks.

**SHOPPING:** Visit the *Shopping Center Iguatemi* (1191 Av. Brigadeiro Faria Lima) or the fancier *Shopping Center Ibirapuera* (3103 Av. Ibirapuera), the *Eldorado Shopping Center* (Marginal Rio Pinheiros), or the *Shopping Center Morumbí* (Marginal Rio Pinheiros, near Morumbi Bridge), which have a variety of goods; check out the Sunday artisans' fairs at Praça da República, Embú, and Liberdade described in *Special Places*. São Paulo housewives still buy their produce at colorful outdoor markets that set up on different streets each day; one of the largest is held four mornings a week in the *Pacaembú Stadium* parking lot, not far from downtown at Praça Charles Miller (see *Special Places).*

Leather continues to be one of Brazil's best exports and one of the best buys in the country. Remember that most São Paulo shops are open from 9 AM to 6 PM weekdays and closed Saturday afternoons; shopping malls, however, are open all day on Saturdays. No stores are open on Sundays.

São Paulo's sophisticated boutiques line the streets that intersect Rua Augusta — particularly Alameda Lorena and Rua Oscar Freire. Two shopping centers — *Conjunto Nacional* and *Center 3* — on the 2000 block of Avenida Paulista, contain movie theaters, cafés, and a plethora of intriguing shops.

The most stylish fashions for the young can be found along Rua Clodomiro Amazonas, Rua Joaquim Floriano, and Rua João Cachoeira. For bargains in shoes, purses, and other leather items, go to Rua do Arouche, close to Largo do Arouche. In eastern São Paulo, Rua 25 de Março in the Jewish-Arab district offers bargain hunters a chance to get cut-rate merchandise of all kinds: toys, clothing, and cloth by the meter. Budget-conscious shoppers should also check out Rua José Paulino, near Luz Railroad Station and Rua Oriente, where wares are similar to those found on 25 de Março.

Other specialty shops include the following:

**Arte Nativa Aplicada** – Indian basket weaving and painting designs are incorporated into contemporary yard goods — scarves, shawls, beach wraps, tablecloths, placemats, and much more. Sports clothes with indigenous motifs, too. 351 Rua Mário Ferraz, Itaim Bibi (phone: 815-9727).

**Beneducci** – Good selection of women's leather shoes and handbags. This shop also

# SÃO PAULO / Sources and Resources

boasts a line of clothing made from leather and natural fibers. 1504 Rua Haddock Lobo (phone: 853-3241).

**Casa do Amazonas** – Quite a complete collection of Amazonian objects; the rare pieces are only for display, but the more common items are for sale. Near the *Shopping Center Ibirapuera* at 460 Av. Jurupis (phone: 572-3098) and 187 Av. São Luiz, in the *Galeria Metrópole* (phone: 258-9727).

**Dan Galeria** – An enormous selection of paintings by Brazilian masters and contemporary artists. Multilingual staff. 1638 Rua Estados Unidos (phone: 883-4600).

**Galería Jacques Ardies** – Run by an English-speaking Frenchman, this gallery specializes in Brazilian primitive art. Near Ibirapuera Park at 221 Rua do Livramento (phone: 884-2916).

**Mimosa Presentes** – Large selection of souvenirs at good prices. 275 Rua Joaquim Nabuco, Brooklin (phone: 616705).

**O Bode** – A Brazilian folk art bazaar specializing in handicrafts from the north. 2009 Rua Bela Cintra (phone: 853-3184).

**Pewter Shop — John Somers** – Hand-wrought pewter (shiny or antique finish), a far cry from the mass-produced pieces generally available. Everything made of pewter — from 2-foot-high candlestick holders to *Christmas* tree ornaments. 2973 Rua da Consolação (phone: 282-6108) and *Shopping Center Morumbi* (phone: 612945).

**Rendas e Fricotes** – Some of the finest handmade lace from Brazil's north — curtains, bedspreads, tablecloths, blouses, and nightgowns. 3459 Rua da Consolação (phone: 282-0330).

**H. Stern** – The gem king of Brazil, these shops offer the classiest objects of silver and precious stones. One large store can be found on Av. Ipiranga and Rua 24 de Maio, a pedestrian shopping mall open till 10 PM weekdays, across the street from Praça de República (phone: 258-1222). Other locations: 2340 Rua Augusta (phone: 853-5804), *Shopping Center Iguatemi* (phone: 210-0826), and *Shopping Center Ibirapuera* (phone: 543-7194), as well as at the luxury hotels.

**Sutoris** – Reasonably priced shoes and bags in a variety of colors and styles. 2710 Rua Augusta (phone: 883-7122) and 247 Rua Dr. Mário Ferraz (phone: 814-6161).

**Veruska** – A good leather boutique, for fashionable handbags, belts, and luggage in many styles and colors. 84 Rua do Arouche (phone: 220-1204).

**Zoomp** – Terrific designer jeans and trendy togs for the young look. 995 Rua Oscar Freire (phone: 641556) and at all shopping malls.

**SPORTS:** As in most of Brazil, soccer — or *futebol* as Brazilians label it — is the city's sport. The teams seem always to be battling through a state or national championship, and on weekend afternoons, fans drive the city streets waving huge, homemade team flags that flap beautifully in the breeze. Pelé's home team, *Santos,* plays in São Paulo from time to time. Informal beach leagues compete on the beaches of Santos every Sunday, with a big soccer festival every *Christmas.* For information on soccer and other sports, call the Sports and Tourism Secretary's Office (phone: 229-3011).

**Car Racing** – Most weekend afternoons throughout the year, there are races to be enjoyed. *Este Mês em São Paulo* lists schedules. 259 Av. Senador Teotônio Vilela, Interlagos (phone: 521-9911).

**Chess** – Team championships are played on Saturday afternoons and Friday evenings at the *São Paulo Chess Club* (154 Rua Araújo, 3rd Floor; phone: 259-6442). Open 2 PM to midnight.

**Golf** – São Paulo has seven golf clubs, all private, although visitors are permitted to play during the week (paying a greens fee of course). The most popular courses with the resident foreign community are the *São Fernando Golf Club* (Estrada Fernando Nobre, Cotia; phone: 492-5544), *São Paulo Golf Club* (540 Praça Dom Francisco de

Souza, Santo Amaro; phone: 521-9255), and *Clube de Campo* (3400 Av. Frederico Rene de Jaegher, Rio Bonito; phone: 520-3111).

**Horse Racing** – Thoroughbreds run on Monday and Thursday nights and Saturday and Sunday afternoons at the *Jockey Club de São Paulo* (1263 Av. Lineu de P. Machado, Cidade Jardim; phone: 211-4011). A well-attended track with a modern, computerized electronic scoreboard, the *Jockey Club* also sports an elegant restaurant where you can dine and bet at the same time.

**Soccer** – São Paulo has three stadiums and 3 days of *futebol* almost every week — Wednesday nights and Saturday and Sunday afternoons. *Morumbi Stadium* in the southern part of the city (Praça Roberto Gomes Pedroas, Av. Giovanni Gronchi; phone: 842-3377), is the third-largest private stadium in the world and can hold 150,000 spectators. *Pacaembú Stadium* (at Praça Charles Miller; phone: 256-9111), is the most centrally located. *Antarctica Stadium* is in the Agua Branca neighborhood (1840 Rua Turiaçu; phone: 263-6344). Check the newspapers for times.

**Surfing** – If the beaches of Guarujá and Santos are any indication, surfing is quite popular with local lads. There is a surf shop across the street from the beach in the center of Guarujá, near the Expresso Luxo station.

**Swimming** – You will find pools at the *Hilton* (165 Av. Ipiranga; phone: 256-0033), and *Brasilton* hotels (330 Rua Martins Fontes; phone: 258-5811), both under Hilton management. There are also pools at the *Caesar Park* (1508 Rua Augusta; phone: 285-6622); at the *Maksoud Plaza* (150 Alameda Campinas; phone: 251-2233); at the *Mofarrej Sheraton* (1437 Alameda Santos; phone: 284-5544); at the *Ca d'Oro* (129 Rua Augusta; phone: 256-8011); at the *Crowne Plaza* (1360 Rua Frei Caneca; phone: 284-1144); and at the *Transamerica* (18591 Av. Nações Unidos; phone: 532-4511). Obviously, the best place to swim is in the Atlantic Ocean at Guarujá (see *Extra Special*). One advantage to swimming in the city is the pools' proximity to saunas. *Paulistas* recently have developed an affection for saunas, but men and women have to sweat separately. The *Maksoud Plaza, Caesar Park, Brasilton, Hilton, Mofarrej Sheraton, Ca d'Oro, Crowne Plaza, Della Volpe,* and *Transamerica* hotels all have saunas. Other saunas are *YMCA (ACM;* 147 Rua Nestor Pestana; phone: 256-1011), and *Maria José* (562 Rua Barra do Tibagi; phone: 221-5421).

**Tennis** – The racquet rage has hit São Paulo in a big way. Court time usually costs from $15 (dollars) up and you get the luxury of ballboys, who should be tipped at about 50¢ per hour. *Hobby Sports* has courts at four locations (16111 Marginal de Pinheiros; phone: 246-6990; 463 Rua João Lourenço, Parque Ibirapuera; phone: 241-1094; 5104 Av. Santo Amaro, Brooklin; phone: 542-5435; and 148 Rua Luís Correia de Mello, Granja Julieta; phone: 246-6990). *Tennis SESC* has courts (89 Rua Lopes Neto; phone: 212-6454). Hotels with tennis courts include the *Transamerica* (phone: 523-4511), *Ca d'Oro* (phone: 256-8011), and the *Ibirapuera Park* (phone: 572-0111).

**THEATER:** Check with the *American Society* (phone: 246-2074) for the occasional English presentations and the local papers for plays in Portuguese. Generally, tickets must be purchased at the theater in advance, but the larger hotels can sometimes make arrangements for guests. The *Teatro Municipal* (Municipal Theater; in the Praça Ramos de Azevedo; phone: 223-7344) often has first class traveling opera, ballet, and other such entertainment.

**MUSIC:** São Paulo offers the music lover a little bit of everything — from classical to samba to Sunday afternoon concerts in the park. The *São Paulo Symphony Orchestra* and the *Municipal Symphony Orchestra* provide most of the classical music; the season generally runs from September to mid-December. From May through August, internationally renowned orchestras and soloists, sponsored by the *Mozarteum Brasileiro* and local businesses, perform at various

**530 SÃO PAULO / Sources and Resources**

venues in the city. Besides the *Municipal Theater,* halls such as the *Teatro de Cultura Artística* (196 Rua Nestor Pestana; phone: 256-0223), the *Teatro Sérgio Cardoso* (153 Rua Rui Barbosa; phone: 251-5122), and the *Anhembi Convention Center* (1209 Av. Olavo Fontoura; phone: 267-2122) also feature concerts and ballet. (Note: The acoustics of the last hall are not all they should be.) Ibirapuera and other parks often have free open-air concerts on Sundays, especially during the summer. For samba information, see *Nightclubs and Nightlife* below.

**NIGHTCLUBS AND NIGHTLIFE:** São Paulo nightlife, without question the liveliest in South America, could as appropriately be called morninglife, since few places hit their stride before midnight. A cover charge that may or may not include drinks is common. Warning: Brazilian whisky (always Scotch and never bourbon) is fairly poor quality, and you pay astronomical prices for the imported stuff. Too often nightclubs will pour local brew into an imported bottle; then both you and your pocketbook suffer. The safest bet is to stick with domestic beer, wine, gin, or vodka drinks.

Sambas can be melodic, snazzy, or frenetic. But whatever the tempo, the rhythm of the samba is unquestionably the heartbeat of Brazil. Samba *shows* are actually nightclub entertainment. Samba houses *(casas de samba)* are dance halls — and they're democratically jammed with working people and the middle class alike on weekends. One of the best shows in São Paulo is at the *Palladium (Eldorado Shopping Center,* 3rd Floor; phone: 814-9461), where a Brazilian orchestra and female mulatto dancers (wearing the bare minimum) perform nightly, except Sundays. Another spot for live samba and good music and dancing is *Plataforma I* (424 Av. Paulista; phone: 289-5238). Johnny Alf, one of the creators of bossa nova, plays nightly at the *Caesar Park* hotel bar. The *Maksoud Plaza* hotel bar is another good place for listening to more mellow samba and bossa nova.

Less chic than the places listed above, the samba houses are less expensive, less sophisticated, and more spontaneous. These are the places to samba: *Moema Samba,* closed Mondays (2124 Av. Ibirapuera; phone: 549-3744) and *República do Samba,* closed Sundays (1025 Rua Santo Antônio; no phone).

Lambada, the music craze to hit Brazil (and the US, too) just a few years back, is still danced at clubs all over São Paulo. Some clubs and discos have nights just for lambada, while others have lambada bands that each evening alternate with samba and rock bands.

The bar-lined streets of Henrique Schaumann and Treze de Maio are called the "beaches" of São Paulo (the only major city in Brazil, except for the capital, that is not directly on the coast). These are two of the best areas to go bar-hopping, because once there revelers will find a car unnecessary. Some of the best bars, many of which offer live music, along Rua Henrique Schaumann include *Halleluyah* (No. 431; phone: 282-5371); *Quincas Borba* (No. 170; phone: 282-6667); and *Barravento* (No. 311; phone: 64-3329). On Treze de Maio and its parallel, Rua Santo Antônio, in the traditionally Italian district called Bexiga, try *Café do Bexiga* (76 Rua Treze de Maio; phone: 259-6059), *Piu-Piu* (134 Rua Treze de Maio; phone: 258-8066), or *III Whiskey* (573 Rua Santo Antônio; phone: 347031). All three are open nightly.

*Clube do Choro* (763 Rua João Moura; phone: 883-3511), in the Pinheiros neighborhood, near Rua Henrique Schaumann, is a good choice for listening to another brand of Brazilian music, called *choro,* which is traditionally performed with a ukulele, tambourine, flute, guitar, and a Brazilian instrument called a *reco-reco* that sounds like a washboard. There are nightly performances during the week; Saturdays and Sundays, the club is open till the wee hours.

The city's top hot spot for jazz is *Opus 2004* (1187 Rua Pamplona; phone: 884-9086). There's also the *Cotton Club* (59 Rua Franz Schubert; phone: 814-0515). Popular houses include the *Palace* (213 Av. do Jamaris; phone: 531-4900) and the *Olympia* (1517 Rua Clélia; phone: 864-7333).

American-style "fern" bars can be found mostly in the Jardins neighborhood. One of the most chic (and expensive) is *Plano's* (811 Rua Oscar Freire; phone: 883-5322). Other good bars in the area include *San Francisco Bay* (30 Rua Barão de Capanema; phone: 853-4596); *Victôria Pub*, open nightly (1604 Alameda Lorena; phone: 881-3460); *Finnegan's Pub* (1529 Alameda Itú; phone: 853-7852); and *The Queen's Legs*, open nightly (490 Rua Dr. Melo Alves; phone: 280-0206).

São Paulo's most elegant discotheques are the *150 Nightclub* (at the *Maksoud Plaza Hotel*, 150 Alameda Campinas; phone: 251-2233); the *Gallery* (1626 Rua Haddock Lobo, Jardim Paulista; phone: 881-8833); and *L'Onorabile Societá* (5872 Av. Nove de Julho; phone: 282-9855). All three are private clubs open to card-carrying members only; well-dressed foreigners, however, especially those bearing a "passport" (a booklet given to guests at major hotels that describes the hotel's regulations, gives the room number, and basically proves that the bearer is a guest of the hotel) from the city's top hotels, usually have no problems whatsoever at the door.

Less formal, but equally popular spots (and you don't need to be a member) and where live music often is heard are *AeroAnta* (404 Rua Miguel Isasa; phone: 211-7084); *Berrante Brasil* (1016 Rua Margarino Torres; phone: 954-5453); *Nation* (2203 Rua Augusta; phone: 852-6345); *Dama Xox* (100 Rua Butantã; phone: 211-2725); *Madame Satã* (783 Rua Constante Ramalho; phone: 285-6754); *Ta Matete* (5725 Av. 9 De Julho; phone: 881-3622); *Up-and-Down* (1418 Rua Pamplona; phone: 881-3460); and *Woodstock Music Hall* (3247 Rua da Consolação; phone: 883-5419).

# BEST IN TOWN

**CHECKING IN:** Because business is São Paulo's business, the city's hotels cater to men in gray flannel suits — and to their expense accounts. As a result, travelers can pick and choose from comfortable, though rather pricey, hostelries, where a few extra dollars often provide the luxury of adequate soundproofing from the 24-hour traffic din. All prices include a continental breakfast (sometimes served in your room), and most also cover the traditional 10% service charge. Doubles at the expensive hotels start at $150, while the moderate rates fall in the $75 to $100 range; inexpensive hotels run less than $50. Hotels listed as "expensive" have satellite dishes for international TV reception. Most hotels fill up during the week, so reserve ahead. Weekends are a different story, however, and the leading hotels offer a number of good packages. All telephone numbers are in the 11 city code unless otherwise indicated.

Note: Two US credit cards are known in Brazil by Brazilian names: MasterCard is called *Passaporte* and Visa doubles as *Cartão Elo*.

**Brasilton** – Known as "the other Hilton," this is a fellow member of the international chain. About 3 blocks from the older *São Paulo Hilton*, it offers tastefully subdued decor with a fairly complete wet bar and refrigerator in its 251 guestrooms. The bathtubs have handles on the wall for the handicapped. All rooms have color TV sets. There's a swimming pool on the roof, and a sauna, masseuse, and an impressive program of activities for guests. *O Braseiro* restaurant features Brazilian grilled *churrasco* dishes. Everyone here, from doormen to telephone operators, is friendly. 330 Rua Martins Fontes (phone: 258-5811). Expensive.

**Ca' D'Oro** – Besides 2 swimming pools, 2 tennis courts (just for guests), Ping-Pong, a pool table, and an exercise room, the hotel also has a dog kennel. Rooms in the newer addition cost more, but you can request accommodations in the old wing, which has more Old World charm than any place else in São Paulo. Try the excellent *Ca' D'Oro* restaurant, one of the best in the city (see *Eating Out*). 129 Rua Augusta (phone: 256-8011). Expensive.

**Caesar Park** – Lush vegetation at the entrance and an elegantly subdued lobby greet a guest to this lovely and serene hotel owned by the Aoki Corporation of Japan. There are 177 rooms, and the efficient, multilingual staff provides excellent service. Amenities include a sauna, swimming pool, and health club. You can pick up free copies of the local papers or buy the most recent copy of *The New York Times* or *Wall Street Journal* to peruse over breakfast fruits beside a small garden. The coffee shop offers a lunch buffet, the sushi bar is among the best in town, and at night there's live music at the rooftop bar. 1508 Rua Augusta (phone: 285-6622). Expensive.

**Della Volpe Garden** – This modern 137-room hotel has a restaurant, 2 bars, a swimming pool, and even a 110-meter jogging track on the roof. 1199 Rua Frei Caneca (phone: 285-5388). Expensive.

**Holiday Inn Crowne Plaza** – Modern, with 223 rooms, this hostelry instantly makes international business executives feel at home. A restaurant, coffee shop, 2 bars, swimming pool, and sauna, are just a few of its facilities. The rooms are comfortable and large on the assumption that businesspeople will spend more time in their rooms using the 24-hour room service than the hotel's less impressive public areas. Located just off bustling Avenida Paulista. 1360 Rua Frei Caneca (phone: 284-1144). Expensive.

**Maksoud Plaza** – Without a doubt, this is São Paulo's "most" hotel — most luxurious, most architecturally daring, most security-conscious, and most expensive. Some 416 rooms and indoor gardens surround its 22-story atrium and a 1-ton, 40-meter suspended stainless steel sculpture by Brazilian artist Toyota. You can choose from 8 restaurants, including a 24-hour coffee shop, a Scandinavian smorgasbord, and the excellent *La Cuisine du Soleil*. For recreation, the hotel offers a swimming pool, sauna, shuffleboard, and even 2 rooftop squash courts (for emergencies, a doctor is on duty at all times). There are also mezzanine-level offices available for short term rental. Rooms on the top 2 floors have butler, maid, and valet service. 150 Alameda Campinas (phone: 251-2233). Expensive.

**Mofarrej Sheraton** – This 247-room deluxe property is one of the few located south of Avenida Paulista. Built by a Lebanese industrialist, there is more character (and more wood) than others in this international chain. It has 2 swimming pools (one outdoor and one heated indoor), a health club, sauna, and the highly rated *Vivaldi* restaurant, with one of the best views of São Paulo (see *Eating Out*), 2 bars, *Christine's* coffee shop, banquet and convention facilities. 1437 Alameda Santos (phone: 284-5544). Expensive.

**São Paulo Hilton** – The remodeled lobby beneath the hotel's 32-story tower bustles with tour groups and with local gatherings that use the hotel's convention facilities. Geared to tourist traffic, the hotel has several nice shops on the ground floor and a sauna and swimming pool on the tenth floor. There is also a rooftop restaurant with a good view of downtown. The hotel's location at the beginning of the city's red-light and gay district discourages evening strolls; although it is a block from Praça da República, the downtown park where the Sunday handicrafts fair takes place (see *Special Places*). 165 Av. Ipiranga (phone: 256-0033). Expensive.

**Transamerica** – Although outside the center of town, (but close to the city's southern industrial zone and the Centro Empresarial, an important business district), this 200-room hotel is the only one in São Paulo that is a mini resort — it offers tennis, squash, a health club, swimming pool, football, volleyball, and even

3 holes of golf. There are 2 restaurants, a coffee shop, and 2 bars. 18591 Av. Nações Unidas (phone: 523-4511). Expensive.

**Eldorado Higienópolis** – Near downtown in the tree-lined residential neighborhood of Higienópolis, this is certainly the quietest of the moderately priced hostelries. It boasts a lovely pool and an informal poolside restaurant. 836 Rua Marquês de Itú (phone: 222-3422). Moderate.

**Nikkey Palace** – One of the nicest in the Japanese section (called Liberdade), it's known for its restaurant, serving, needless to say, Japanese food. 425 Rua Galváo Bueno, Liberdade (phone: 270-8511). Moderate.

**Novotel** – In the upper class suburb of Morumbi, minutes away from the big industries, this is a convenient choice for the business traveler. 450 Rua Ministro Nelson Hungria (phone: 844-6211). Moderate.

**San Raphael** – Clean and comfortable, this hotel has 252 rooms. Its location in the downtown area makes for convenient shopping. 1173 Av. São João, corner of Largo do Arouche (phone: 220-6633). Moderate.

**São Paulo Center** – In the bustling heart of the city, this family-run place has 110 rooms decorated in a very modern Brazilian style. A complimentary breakfast includes every available tropical fruit and a selection of fresh pastries and sweet breads. 40 Largo Santa Ifigênia (phone: 228-6033). Moderate.

**Cambridge** – Long a gathering place for cost-conscious travelers, it has an international clientele and a central location. 216 Av. 9 de Julho (phone: 239-0399). Inexpensive.

**Samambaia** – More frequented by Brazilian travelers than foreign tourists, this 70-room hostelry is right off the Praça da República. 422 Rua 7 de Abril (phone: 231-1333). Inexpensive.

**EATING OUT:** Drawing on its diverse ethnic cuisines, São Paulo has become the unchallenged culinary capital of Brazil — perhaps of all South America, as some people claim. From barbariously generous barbecues *(churrascos)* to the delicate fare of the fashionable sushi bars, you hardly can go wrong. Restaurants routinely charge a $1 to $2 *couvert* (a bread, butter, and nibbles fee) that you can refuse if you like, and most include a 10% service charge on your bill, which is considered an adequate tip, unless you wish to reward especially good service. Imported liquor *(whiskey escocés* or *importado* instead of *whiskey nacional,* the Brazilian product) will swell your bill immediately. *Paulistas* generally dine after 9 PM. For dinner, dessert, and a Brazilian drink apiece, a meal for two at an expensive restaurant will come to at least $40. Expect to pay between $15 and $35 for two at those places we've listed as moderate; less than $15, inexpensive. Prices don't include wine or tips. Most restaurants close 1 day a week (usually Mondays), so it's advisable to call ahead. All telephone numbers are in the 11 city code unless otherwise indicated.

Note: Be warned that São Paulo's restaurants don't all believe in plastic payment. Because of the high inflation rate, currently even many of the expensive restaurants simply refuse to accept credit cards. If you wish to pay with a credit card, be sure to double-check with the restaurant in advance.

**Antiquarius** – One of Rio's most traditional and respected restaurants opened a branch here at the end of 1990. As in Rio, diners sit among beautiful antiques, many of which are for sale. Although the management bills this eatery as serving Portuguese fare, the menu really is international. Open daily for lunch and dinner. Reservations advised. Major credit cards accepted. 1884 Alameda Lorena (phone: 282-3015). Expensive.

**Bassi** – While *feijoada* comes from the coast, the roots of *churrasco* are in the southern Brazilian and Argentine pampas. It may be far from home, but it is definitely at its best at this steakhouse, where patrons choose their preferred cut of meat, which is served rare (unless requested otherwise), and seasoned only with rock salt. The array of salads and fresh raw vegetables served as appetizers are a meal in themselves, but gringos' stomachs should beware. Open daily. Reservations, accepted only until 8 PM, are advised. No credit cards accepted. 334 Rua 13 de Maio, Bela Vista (phone: 34-2375). Expensive.

*Ca' D'Oro* – Although hotel restaurants are not normally notable, this one in the hotel of the same name is an exception. Its elegant atmosphere, featuring individual lamps on the tables, creates a perfect background for succulent Italian dishes served by gracious waiters. Favorites include veal-stuffed ravioli, *bollito* (boiled meat stew), and pheasant with polenta. A tradition in São Paulo for 35 years. Exclusive wine list and a well-stocked bar. Men are requested to wear jackets and ties, although it's not obligatory. Reservations necessary. Major credit cards accepted. 129 Rua Augusta, Centro (phone: 256-8011). Expensive.

*Don Curro* – Former bullfighter Curro Dominguez owns this Spanish-style cantina, and his wife oversees the kitchen. It is a supremely successful partnership, for the seafood served here is among the best in the country. Among the many outstanding dishes on the menu, we particularly recommend the paella, the shrimp in garlic and mushroom sauce (it serves two to three people), and the grilled lobster (chosen from the tank in the entryway). Closed Mondays. Reservations advised. No credit cards accepted. 230 Rua Alves Guimarães (phone: 852-4712). Expensive.

*Fasano* – One of the most spectacular and luxurious restaurants in Brazil, if not in all of South America. Although the Fasano family only opened these doors in July 1990, it can trace its São Paulo restaurant roots back to 1903 with the modest *Brasserie Paulista*. The large, old bank building which houses this dining place represents an investment of over $2.5 million. Diners sit in an elegant surrounding of high ceilings, wood paneling, and marble floors. A number of superb food choices are offered — ranging from traditional to modern Italian fare. The wine cellar has over 160 different labels. Open daily for lunch and dinner. Reservations necessary. No credit cards accepted. 1644 Rua Haddock Lobo, Cerqueira César (phone: 852-4000). Expensive.

*Govinda* – Fireplaces and antique furniture set the stage for the best in Indian cuisine. Well-practiced waiters serve specialties such as Tandoori chicken, Bhuna king prawns, and *nan* bread to diners who are encouraged to specify the heat level of spice they prefer. Open daily, except Sundays, for dinner. Reservations advised. No credit cards accepted. 379 Rua Princesa Isabel, Santo Amaro (phone: 531-0269). Expensive.

*Komazushi* – Generally considered the best sushi and sashimi restaurant in São Paulo, a town where Japanese restaurants are outnumbered only by Italian ones. All seafood served in this tiny place has been caught the same day. Closed weekends and holidays. Reservations necessary. No credit cards accepted. 2050 Av. Brigadeiro Luís Antônio, in *Centro Comercial Paulista,* Centro (phone: 287-1820). Expensive.

*Marcel* – Chef Jean Durand displays his friend Paul Bocuse's portrait in this tiny restaurant with pride and justification. For 10 years Chef Jean has been serving the very finest French cuisine in the city. Shrimp dishes and delicate desserts are among the specialties. It's superb food in a simple setting. Open for lunch and dinner Mondays through Fridays, for dinner on Saturdays and holidays. Lunch reservations necessary. No credit cards accepted. Across from the *São Paulo Hilton* at 98 Rua Epitácio Pessôa, Centro (phone: 257-6968). Expensive.

*Massimo* – Continually rated by local restaurant critics as the best restaurant in Brazil and its owner, Massimo Ferrari, as the king of Northern Italian nouvelle cuisine. A glass-enclosed dining room filled with fresh-cut flowers and plants provides the showcase for carefully prepared meat, seafood, and pasta dishes. Those waiting to be seated relax in the adjoining bar, which features soothing piano music. Open daily. Reservations advised. No credit cards accepted. 1826 Alameda Santos, Cerqueira César (phone: 284-0311). Expensive.

**Paddock Jardim** – Good service and a limited but well-prepared menu of international dishes make this a favorite of São Paulo's elite. Comfortable, with music after 9 PM. Closed Sundays. Reservations necessary. Major credit cards accepted. Two locations: *Cal Center Shopping Center* on 1541 Av. Brigadeiro Faria Lima, Jardim Paulistano (phone: 212-0619) and in the Zarvos building at 258 Av. São Luiz, Centro (phone: 257-4768). Expensive.

**Roanne** – After his successful *Troisgros* venture in Rio de Janeiro, Frenchman Claude Troisgros decided to expand and open this branch in São Paulo. A French chef presides over the kitchen. The result is one of São Paulo's finest restaurants. Open daily, except Sundays, for dinner. Reservations advised. No credit cards accepted. 631 Rua Henrique Martins, Jardim Paulista (phone: 887-4516). Expensive.

**Rodeio** – The "in" *churrascaría* of discriminating *paulistas*, this is a meat lover's delight. Try *picanha na brasa* — São Paulo's best beef grilled right at the table. The hot *pão de queijo* that arrives automatically is a specialty of the state of Minas Gerais. Open daily. To avoid a long wait, get there before 1 PM for lunch and before 8:30 PM for dinner. No reservations. Major credit cards accepted. 1498 Rua Haddock Lobo, Cerqueira César (phone: 883-2322). Expensive.

**Rubaiyat Churrascarías** – "Baby beef" is this chain's boast. Open daily for lunch and dinner. No reservations. Major credit cards accepted. Centro: 116 Dr. Vieira de Carvalho (phone: 222-8333). Near Av. Paulista: 86 Rua Alameda Santos (phone: 289-6366); and Jardim Paulistano: 533 Av. Brigadeiro Faria Lima (phone: 813-2744). Expensive.

**Suntory** – A lovely rock garden beside the bar rivals the fine food as the main attraction at this popular Japanese place. You either can call ahead for reservations in one of the restaurant's three rooms — teppan-yaki, sukiyaki, and sushi — or you can come unannounced to enjoy a drink and then take whatever table becomes available. Open daily, except Mondays, for lunch and dinner. Reservations advised. Major credit cards accepted. 600 Alameda Campinas, Jardim Paulista (phone: 283-2455). Expensive.

**La Tambouille** – For over a decade this restaurant has been considered one of Brazil's best, offering an imaginative mix of Italian and French fare. Choose between the enclosed garden terrace or the more formal inner dining room. Open daily for lunch and dinner. Reservations advised. Major credit cards accepted. 5925 Av. 9 de Julho, Jardim Europa (phone: 883-6276). Expensive.

**La Trainera** – One of the top seafood restaurants in town. Super-fresh fish, shrimp, and lobster are transformed into creative, succulent dishes such as *paella valenciana* and fish chowder. The desserts also are excellent. Open daily. Reservations advised. Major credit cards accepted. Near the *Shopping Center Iguatemi,* 511 Av. Faria Lima, Jardim Europa (phone: 282-5988). Expensive.

**Vivaldi** – The rooftop restaurant of the *Mofarrej Sheraton* has had its ups-and-downs before getting firmly established as one of the city's major international dining spots. It also has one of the best nighttime views of São Paulo. Closed Sundays. Reservations advised. Major credit cards accepted. 1437 Alameda Santos, Cerqueira César (phone: 284-5544). Expensive.

**Bolinha** – *Feijoada* is the country's national dish (a tasty concoction of black beans and all cuts of pork), and an excellent one is served here every day of the week (most restaurants serve *feijoada* only on Wednesdays and Saturdays). You'll find a long line between 2 and 4 PM on Saturday. Just give your name to the maître d', order a *caipirinha* at the bar, and watch the bustle. Open daily for lunch and dinner. No reservations. Major credit cards accepted. 53 Av. Cidade Jardim, Jardim Europa (phone: 852-9526). Moderate.

***Clyde's*** – If you've been traveling long enough to yearn for a charcoal-grilled hamburger, onion rings, and a fudge brownie, this is the place for you. Modeled after the Georgetown (Washington, DC) eatery of the same name, it's a favorite of both the local Yankee community and young *paulistas*. Sunday brunch is a specialty. Open daily for lunch and dinner. Reservations advised in the evening. Major credit cards accepted. 70 Rua de Mata, Itaim Bibi; tell your taxi driver that it's a cross street at 5345 Av. 9 de Julho (phone: 883-0300). Moderate.

***Sushi-Yassu*** – One of the city's top sushi bars, this traditional Japanese restuarant, in the Liberdade (Asian district), also offers sashimi and other seafood specialties. Reservations unnecessary. No credit cards accepted. 110-A Rua Tomás Gonzaga, Liberdade (phone: 279-6622). Moderate.

***Almanara*** – If Japanese food doesn't tempt you but you still want something different, try this busy Arabic eatery off the Praça da República. It serves generous portions of hummus, stuffed grape leaves, and various sorts of *kibbe* (ground beef) at good prices. Near the bar, you order each dish separately while past the partition you pay a set price and watch the delicacies appear and reappear. Open daily for lunch and dinner; closed *Christmas*. No reservations. Major credit cards accepted. 70 Rua Basilio da Gama, Centro (phone: 257-7580). Inexpensive.

***America*** – Housed in a chic Art Deco version of a 1950s diner, it serves what many consider to be the best burgers and fried chicken in town. Teenagers and foreigners make up the bulk of the clientele here, where long lines form at regular meal hours. It's best to go for a mid-afternoon lunch. Open daily. No reservations. No credit cards accepted. Three locations: 5363 Av. Nove de Julho (phone: 280-3200); 957 Alameda Santos, behind the Citicorp Building on Av. Paulista, Cerqueira César (phone: 289-7900); and the *Iguatemi Shopping Center*, Itaim Bibi (phone: 210-4179). Inexpensive.

***Andrade*** – Located on the corner of Rua Henrique Schaumann, the street famous for its bars, this place offers a carefully prepared selection of meals from the Northeast region. Try the *carne-de-sol* (sun-dried beef), served with bottled butter, rice, beans, and squash; or the *moqueca de badejo* (spicy fish stew). On weekdays during dinner and at Sunday lunch, trios play lively *forró* music. Service can be slow, but the atmosphere and food are worth it. Closed Mondays. Reservations advised. No credit cards accepted. 874 Rua Arthur de Azevado, Pinheiros (phone: 648644). Inexpensive.

***Colonna*** – For São Paulo's lightest homemade pasta — *fettuccine verdi al pesto, ravioli alla parmigiana, cappelletti al triplo burro*. The *cassata* (an ice cream pie topped with walnuts) should not be missed either. Open daily for lunch and dinner. Reservations advised in the evening. Major credit cards accepted. 540 Rua Maranhão, Higienópolis (phone: 67-0547). Inexpensive.

***Genghis Khan*** – Although the city's Chinese restaurants generally can't compare with the Japanese establishments, this is one exception. On the second floor you can try a Chinese barbecue. Open daily for lunch and dinner. Reservations advised. Visa accepted. 3241 Av. Rebouças, Pinheiros (phone: 212-8951). Inexpensive.

***Konstanz*** – In the Moema neighborhood, near Ibirapuera Park, this charming *bierstube* has developed a reputation for huge portions and good draft beer at very reasonable prices. Specialties of the house include paprika schnitzel (pork tenderloin in paprika sauce) and orange duck with applesauce and cabbage. Closed Mondays. Reservations unnecessary. No credit cards accepted. 713 Av. Aratans, Moema (phone: 543-4813). Inexpensive.

***Vegetariano Sattva*** – This simple eatery boasts a daily special, although most regulars seem to always order the special salad — with a superb fruit dressing. Open daily, except Sundays, for lunch only. No reservations. No credit cards accepted. 3140 Rua da Consolação, Cerqueira César (phone: 883-6237).

# DIVERSIONS

# Introduction

For many travelers today, the point of a trip is not merely to visit someplace new but to participate in something special once they get there. Whether it's athletic, sybaritic, or educational — playing a challenging new golf course, lolling on a perfect crescent of beach, or examining ancient ruins with an experienced guide — activity-oriented vacations are becoming increasingly popular.

South America is an old yet still relatively young continent. Most of its cities were settled by the Spanish almost a century before the English landed on Plymouth Rock, and its colonial architecture and traditions predate those of the US. But the South American colonists (with the exception of those in mineral-rich Bolivia) preferred to remain along the continent's coastlines, and to this day most of the interior remains lightly explored and free of settlement or development. Populations are clustered in cosmopolitan centers hemmed in by dramatic topography — towering mountains, vast deserts, and lush rain forests. The visitor is confronted immediately by the juxtapositions of environment — modern urban and ancient rural cultures, deluxe and basic facilities. In South America, expect to find astounding diversity.

Which is not to say that all countries on this continent are equally endowed with natural wonders or tourist facilities. South America is largely a Third World continent, and many of its nations are only beginning to recognize the inherent value of their abundant natural resources as tourist attractions; other countries are in the process of developing tourist services, and still others, long familiar with the international traveler, have facilities as finely tuned as any in the world. Resort cities in Colombia, Venezuela, and Brazil offer golf, tennis, swimming, diving, and fishing with luxurious accommodations and a full complement of sophisticated *après* activities. And unparalleled wilderness experiences — at the top of the world or in the heart of a rain forest — are open to anyone willing to rough it through the far corners of Ecuador, Chile, Argentina, Peru, and other South American countries. It is just this choice — the variety of experience available in any single visit to the continent — that makes South America so appealing to the adventurous traveler.

Combining the right activity with the right place is something of an art, and most difficult in so diverse a continent as South America. The pertinent question is, "Where is the quality of experience highest?" In the following pages, we attempt to answer this question by suggesting the best places in South America to pursue 18 separate and distinct activities. Certainly the emphasis is on uniquely Latin American experiences — *Carnaval* or jungle excursions, wilderness trekking or exploring the continent's incredible Indian ruins — but not on these alone. Included in each section is all the information necessary to organize a trip, including the names of organizations that offer special interest package tours to South America. Whether you want to climb mountains, fish in the Pacific, hike through Andean villages, or observe wildlife in the jungle, the number of group tours to South America oriented around these activities is growing rapidly. Formerly out-of-reach, exotic parts of the continent are now accessible to travelers.

Joining a group ensures that reservations and facilities are arranged in advance. A package tour will also guarantee that at least one member, the tour escort, will speak Spanish (or, in the case of Brazil, Portuguese) — an important consideration when traveling out of the major city centers and off the beaten path. In addition, a tour devoted to a particular activity means traveling with a group of people who share your interests. Finally, it provides more security — a comfort to would-be adventurers who are discouraged by reports of crime, political unrest, and terrorist activity in some South American countries.

If you plan to travel on your own, it's still a good idea to consult a special interest travel organization when planning your trip. Each one is usually staffed with experts who know the field in which you are interested, and they can offer advice on the range of services and accommodations available. (See *How to Use a Travel Agent* and *Package Tours,* GETTING READY TO GO.)

Whether you travel independently or with a group, on a strict budget or with unlimited funds, it is important to remember that the diversions of South America are as varied as its topography, its individual countries, its ancient cultures, and its different paces of modernization. Above all, no matter what sport or activity you pursue, South American diversions will seldom fail to provide new adventures and experiences. Herewith, those places throughout the continent where the quality of experience is likely to be unusually high.

# For the Experience

## Quintessential South America

Mystery still abounds on this vast continent with its rich history and many cultures — there are Indian tribes that have yet to see outsiders, rivers aswarm with anacondas, untouched rain forests, and 3-million-year-old islands. All the once little-known wonders, sights, sounds, traditions, and arts of the South American countries are waiting to be discovered by those with a sense of abandon, adventure, and curiosity. The continent offers travelers an extraordinarily rich mosaic of experiences, but there are some activities here that uniquely capture the spirit of the people and the place, crystallizing them, and helping visitors understand why they are like no other. Experience them now, while they still retain the exotic flavor of the almost unexplored.

**THE LAST TANGO, Buenos Aires, Argentina:** Sinuous and sleek, tightly black-clad bodies dance together in one long controlled movement, partners exchange intense looks of concentrated passion meant only for each other — that's the tango. You needn't understand the words to the songs' soulful laments — the dancers' movements and expressions tell all — promises of love and lust, threats of abandonment, and lifelong despair. The melodic tones of the piano and violin, accompaniments to the wailing sounds of the *bandoneón,* an accordion-like instrument, complete your submersion into another era.

At the turn of the century, the tango was considered so scandalous (the Vatican had even banned it) that it was danced only by men; women watched and swooned. But that changed in the 1920s when the tango became popular with Argentina's upper classes and the dance became all the rage in New York and Paris. Watching it (or dancing it) today evokes memories of the Roaring Twenties — women with spit curls pasted on their foreheads (banded in beads or black velvet ribbon) and Rudolph Valentino insinuating himself around languishing, yet lustful females. Buenos Aires is still loaded with tango clubs, although most of them are strictly for spectators, not for dancing. But who knows? If you meet the right person, you too might be able to dance the last tango in Buenos Aires.

**ON THE AMAZON:** Dark and murky waters, their silence broken only by the splashing of angry alligators and perilous piranhas or the slithering of boa constrictors and the deadly fer-de-lance, the amazing Amazon River stretches across eight countries from the Andes Mountains to the Atlantic Ocean. You can sense their presence. The teeming, dense jungle, filled with giant liana vines and trees dripping down to the ground, comes alive with the screech of monkeys and green parrots, the snorting of wild boars, and the cries of jaguars. The Amazon basin occupies an area as large as the US west of the Mississippi and carries more water than any river in the world. Though the Amazon is becoming increasingly familiar from such recent cinema epics as *At Play in the Fields of the Lord* and *Medicine Man* (not to mention news reports about the destruction of its rain forests and resources), nothing short of being there can convey the vast expanse from the river to the horizon or the musty scent of the jungle. Navigated from its mouth at Belém, Brazil, as far upstream as Iquitos, Peru, the Amazon is no longer just the province of adventurers and scientists. Craft ranging from lazy river boats to luxury cruise ships offer unforgettable voyages to a teeming world of wilderness, exotic flora and fauna (the forest holds 10% of the world's species, 85% of which have yet to be identified), Indian villages, and the rough-and-ready human animals who have settled there.

**SUMMER SKIING, Portillo, Chile:** When the temperature hits the 90s in sweltering Chicago in July, it's peak ski weather at this ritzy resort in the Andes. Whether this upside-down season of granular-powder snow, dazzling sunshine, and dry mountain air with temperatures ranging in the 20s gives ski aficionados the chance to perfect their turns so they look like *Olympic* champs on the slopes back home in the North American winter, or to sit in an après-ski Jacuzzi and chuckle over the novelty of it all, is up for grabs. A ride on a chair lift brings into focus the skier's-eye view of the towering, snow-covered mountains; twirling ice skaters below on Laguna del Inca; the almost-45-degree angle of the craggy Roca Jack (one of the most difficult slopes in the world), whose precipitous incline drops into sheer nothingness; and the spectacle of Portillo: an urbane populace dressed in fashionable skiwear complete with color-coordinated goggles. You'll rub elbows with some of Santiago's most elegant citizens and members of the national ski teams from the US, Canada, and Europe. After a chilling day on the slopes, join the chic Chileans and Argentines and indulge in the magic of lolling on the sun-warmed deck of the restaurant at the bright yellow *Gran Hotel Portillo* on the lake while sipping a glass of fine Chilean *vino tinto*. Thoughts of steamy city streets will quickly slip away.

**CARNAVAL, Rio de Janeiro, Brazil:** A tremendous explosion of rhythmic energy takes over Rio as early as 5 days before *Ash Wednesday,* when the entire city starts moving to the sexy, scintillating beat of the samba. All of Rio gets caught up in this dazzling madness — nothing else matters but the nonstop gaiety that infects everyone during *Carnaval,* the event to end all events. Brilliant colors are everywhere — neon lights, flowing streamers, and especially in the glittering costumes of the samba school members who strut in front of the *Sambódromo* (designed by Oscar Niemeyer, best known as the architect of Brasilia) on Sunday and Monday. Thousands of musicians, dancers, and singers take part in the parade, moving to the incessant rhythm of the samba, perfectly choreographed, and all decked out in spectacular costumes that took months to make and cost a large chunk of the salaries of these people from Rio's *favelas*. The town almost closes down as the most lavish float parade and wildest street party in the world vie for attention with a stunning series of glamorous indoor balls. Festivities last all night and fans of the samba schools sing, clap, cheer, stamp their feet, whistle, and dance along with their favorites. The stands of the *Sambódromo* and the streets of the city resonate with the driving beat and the excitement.

To get in the mood, rent Marcel Camus's 1959 film, *Black Orpheus,* which lyrically transposes the Greek myth into the *favelas* that provide the backbone of these festivities. Although *Carnaval* itself has become increasingly institutionalized, the enthusiasm for it remains uncontained as a hypnotic and seductive samba beat emanates relentlessly from TV sets, radios, boom boxes, and live musicians all over the city straight into your soul. Be forewarned that service at hotels and restaurants wilts as Rio's summer heat intensifies and personnel become more concerned with the festivities than with their daily duties. But nobody seems to mind. They've all been swept away by the magic of *Carnaval.*

**IGUASSU/IGUAÇU FALLS, Argentine-Brazilian Border:** Torrents of water fall and crash with a thunderous noise onto the rocks below, sending sprays shooting back up to make exquisite rainbows. At Iguassu, the widest waterfalls in the world, walking through this tremendous roar drowns out all other sounds — the piercing calls made by swiftly flying birds and jungle animals amidst 4 miles of tropical rain forest that form the background, and the buzzing of the engines from the planes that carry visitors who want an aerial view of this spectacular phenomenon. People have been debating for years over whether the Argentine or the Brazilian side is more spectacular, but either way you look at the cataracts — and viewing them from *both* sides is a must — chances are that you'll never forget their mighty magnificence. From the cascades tumbling at your feet to the enveloping mist (slickers might be in order, except on a hot summer's day) to the multitude of magnificent arches of color that seem to come out of nowhere, Iguassu will take your breath away.

**SHOPPING FOR HANDICRAFTS AT AN INDIAN MARKET, Otavalo, Ecuador:** The exquisite hues of sunrise permeating the sky in Otavalo match the tones of the gaily colored woolens and *artesanía* from all over Ecuador that are on sale every Saturday morning at the best-known market on the continent. The artistry of the displayed goods is rivaled only by the distinctive, traditional dress of the *otavaleños* themselves who sell their wares. Women wear two layers of dark woolen skirts, a brightly embroidered blouse, a vivid woven belt, silver and copper rings, and — most captivating of all — necklaces made from gold-colored glass and coral beads. Men sport a white cotton shirt and calf-length woolen trousers, a blue woolen poncho, and a long braid down their backs. Walk through the Plaza de Ponchos, devoted exclusively to textiles — weavings (some still made in the traditional way with vegetable dyes and ancient looms), sweaters, and wall hangings in iridescent blues and purples, striped ponchos, decorative pouches, and blankets and rugs in muted tones. At Plaza Centerario are straw mats and hats (the *real* Panama hats that actually come from Cuenca in southern Ecuador) and the shining necklaces worn by *otavaleñas* themselves. The melodic sound of the *quenas* (Andean flutes) drifts through the squares; they also are for sale and perhaps a quick lesson on how to play one will be part of the deal. These might be the only sounds you hear at this omnium-gatherum — *otavaleños* conduct their business in low voices, a sharp contrast to the vivacious colors of the wares. Although the town is only 2 hours from Quito, it's best to spend the night in Otavalo and be at the market as day breaks to ensure getting the best, the brightest, and the bargains.

**FUTEBOL/FÚTBOL FEVER:** The exuberant passion unleashed by South Americans during a game of *futebol* (in Portuguese) or *fútbol* (in Spanish) is unparalleled — the suppressed energy that lays dormant until game time bursts forth in a single display of hysteria that surpasses that of *Super Bowl* and *World Series* crowds. And all this just for a weekly Sunday match. Tension accelerates to a feverish pitch — fans wildly root for their soccer stars, sing team anthems, unfurl banners, yell at referees, and shout with raw joy when a goal is scored. Aficionados' passions run deep, but surprisingly, their enthusiasm rarely reaches the level of violence it often achieves in Europe. When victory reigns, delighted devotees ride around in their cars, hanging out the windows, honking horns, and waving the winning team's pennant. Soccer rules are simple and South Americans will patiently and eagerly explain them to the uninitiated. Knowledge of the game, however, is almost irrelevant to the outside observer, as a trip to a soccer stadium such as Rio's *Maracanā* (seating 200,000, it is the world's largest) provides as much excitement in the stands as it does on the playing field. Call it religion, call it fervor, whatever it is, soccer is king all across the continent.

Brazil's Pelé, possibly the greatest soccer player of all times, is still revered as a god, although he has retired on the millions he earned from twice leading the country to victory in the *World Cup*. And of course, South Americans not only revel in watching the game, they love to play. It is their birthright and one that crosses all class lines — every child dreams of becoming the next Pelé or Maradona and attaining their glory and wealth. From young kids kicking the ball around on the dirt road in the *favelas* to the teenagers making head shots in the plush playgrounds of private schools, *futebol* fever flourishes throughout the continent. Every beach, park, and school yard has soccer goal posts, and amateur games are played with the same ferocity as professional matches. South America has produced numerous internationally known stars and its national teams have captured the *World Cup* more than any other continent (Brazil is a three-time winner and Argentina has claimed victory twice). Catch the fever.

**A WALK WITH THE WILDEST, WOOLIEST, AND WETTEST:** Picture tree-covered mountains and crystal-clear streams where llamas, vicuñas, alpacas, sheep, chinchillas, and red foxes pause along the sparkling waters to drink. These are the true denizens of the Andes, a chain of mountains that stretches across the vast continent — all the way from Panama to Tierra del Fuego at the southern tip of Argentina. Throughout the length of South America, trekkers and mountain climbers can find any or all of these beasties roaming with dignity and using the Andean streams as their trough. And for a glimpse of South American creatures that live in and along the continent's waters, the Valdés Peninsula in Patagonia on the Atlantic coast in central Argentina is host to several thousand blubbery sea elephants who live and breed here. Slink up to them as close as several yards as they sun themselves on the beach — the battle-scarred males are surrounded by a bevy of smaller females — they are unthreatened by upright, two-legged beings. On the open sea itself, and south of the peninsula to Golfo Nuevo, are the breeding grounds of whales (several operators offer whale watching trips from Puerto Pirámide). Farther south in Camarones are more than a million Magellanic penguins, the largest rookery in the world — that come here from Antarctica at the end of September. These docile black-tie birds breed and raise their young here until April. Wander among them in their natural habitat, it's a far cry from seeing them in a zoo back home.

Other sea wildlife wonders are found in the rocky, barren Galápagos Islands, 600 miles off the coast of Ecuador. Think Darwin: Take a step back in time to when the world was populated only with animals and there were no human disturbances — just the primal order of things. Swim in the icy waters with frisky sea lions, seals, penguins, and brightly colored fish; walk casually (visitors are required to go with guides) among the giant tortoises that gave these islands their name and with scaly, dinosaur-like iguanas whose colors change from gold to red; and watch a variety of birds, including the magnificent frigate, red- and blue-footed boobies, and 13 varieties of finches. In this natural wonderland of volcanic islands — mostly uninhabited and now a national park — are native species so rare and so exotic that at least half of them cannot be found anywhere else in the world. Or along Peru's Pacific coast, visit Paracas, the "poor man's Galápagos." Wildly exotic birds (including the white and brilliant red flamingos that allegedly inspired the colors of Peru's flag) flit about, condors soar overhead with the strong coastal winds, and friendly seals and sea lions frolic in the waters at this national park.

**THE LOST CITY OF THE INCA, Machu Picchu, Peru:** The first question inevitably asked by first-time viewers is how did this city of more than 200 structures, built 2,000 feet above the valley of the Río Urubamba — the sacred river of the Inca — get here? And without the use of the wheel! Even after you spend hours walking around its vast urban spaces set amid the spectacular terraces carved into the surrounding slopes, the answers only become more elusive. This is the inexplicable magic of this "lost" city of the Inca that sits perched atop a mountain spur — covered with lush vegetation — overlooking the Río Urubamba Valley. Imagine, too, in this quiet, tranquil setting what this thriving city was like several hundreds of years ago; you might even fall into a spiritual trance, overcome with its beauty and enchantment. See it at glorious dawn or dramatic dusk when you can almost feel the presence of the ancient Inca sun god Inti and his obedient subjects among the magnificent ruins of temples, baths, houses, plazas, warehouses, stairways, and a guardhouse, all harmoniously integrated into the countryside. Or sit at the *Turistas* hotel on top of Machu Picchu peak and sip a *pisco* sour under the stars. Unknown to the conquistadores, and "discovered" by Hiram Bingham in

### DIVERSIONS / Quintessential South America

1911, there is a mystical, magical timelessness in this isolated spot, particularly at sunset after the tour groups have gone.

**SUNNING AND SURFING IN THE SOUTHERN HEMISPHERE, Punta del Este, Uruguay:** Welcome to the continent's Riviera: Roaring surf on the Atlantic Ocean side of the peninsula, tranquil waters on the river side, and miles of beautiful golden-sand beaches, Punta del Este is *the* place for the South American set seeking summer sports. Forget about the December sub-zero temperatures north of the Mason-Dixon line and escape to the beaches between the wave-capped Atlantic and the silent-flowing Río de la Plata. The pine, mimosa, and eucalyptus trees that line the beaches offer respite from the midmorning sun (though sea breezes keep the temperatures comfortable), and taking in their fragrance allows fantasies to emerge. One day you might choose to leisurely soak up the sun on a *playa mansa* (gentle beach) and take an occasional swim or go waterskiing in calm waters. On another, you might be up for the challenge of surfing the gigantic waves in the ocean at a *playa brava* (wild beach).

**OPERA IN THE WILD, Manaus, Brazil:** Imagine an eclectic Beaux Arts–style opera house fashioned from Italian marble and crystal, French furnishings and decorations, Portuguese-style staircases and paving blocks, German tiles, Japanese and Chinese porcelain, Scottish iron, and US electrical wiring. Those lavish materials would create a dazzling effect anywhere, but they are all the more extravagant 1,000 miles up the Amazon River in the city of Manaus, when they went into the building of the *Teatro do Amazonas,* an opulent opera house, during the height of the rubber boom at the turn of the century. That event became the basis of Werner Herzog's 1982 movie, *Fitzcarraldo,* but the truth about the *Teatro do Amazonas* is even stranger than the screenplay. With all its embellishments, the *Amazonas* was considered one of the world's great opera houses; it was constructed after European prima donnas, who didn't know what to do with their new-found millions, complained (with good reason) about the primitive performing conditions in the jungle. Restored to its former glory after many years of renovations (including a 2,000-square-foot stage curtain painted by a set designer from the *Comédie Française* and a ballroom decorated with Venetian mirrors, Murano glass, and Carrara marble), the *Teatro do Amazonas* once again provides a sumptuous backdrop for performances. A sad note, however: like many arts centers, it suffers from a lack of funding, which has made its program rather erratic, but the amazing fact of the opera house's existence in its steamy surroundings is more dramatic than any libretto.

**THE CONTINENT'S COWBOYS:** Wearing wide-brimmed hats, brightly colored shirts, *bombachas* (balloon pleated pants with buttoned ankles), coin-studded belts, leather boots, jangling spurs, and a knife at their waists, South American gauchos confidently ride their horses at breakneck speed, twirling their *boleadoras* (lassos with steel balls), across the gentle plains of Argentina, Brazil, Colombia, Uruguay, and Venezuela. In Uruguay, they are worshipped as heros, and honored with parades and festivals. The proud Venezuelan *llanero* rides barefoot, braving the ever-present danger of rattlesnakes, with his big toe hooked through a small stirrup ring. Gauchos, especially *llaneros,* spend their free time sitting around a campfire, drinking maté (a bitter herbal tea), playing the guitar, telling stories of their glorious feats (real or imagined), and singing passionate songs. Although these proud cowboys are not the romantic figures they once were, gauchos are still very much a part of the cultural life of the continent. Many books have been written about them, detailing their life of herding cattle and sheep across the vast grasslands that are still home to these proud and solitary figures who, like their North American counterparts, work mostly as ranch hands. The flat pampas that are the gaucho's habitat stretch endlessly across the continent, the vegetatin growing in their fertile soil providing sustenance for the cattle. Looking at the land, it is easy to imagine a South American version of the macho world of Clint Eastwood or John Wayne.

# Luxury Resorts and Special Havens

As we have noted elsewhere, South America offers the traveler an extraordinary spectrum of experiences and pleasures. The range of accommodations is as varied as the landscape — indeed, in some cases, irrevocably linked to the landscape.

The choice of a vacation retreat is very personal. The places listed below include many of our particular favorites, as well as a few that have earned their stars through popular acclaim. Some are large hotels in famous resort areas that have a long-standing reputation for fine facilities and service. Others are small, one-of-a-kind places in unusually appealing surroundings. Most offer their rooms on the European Plan (no meals), but some include one or more meals. While many are expensive — in the $150-plus per night category for a double room — others offer some very attractive bargains. Without exception, both large and small vacation resorts should be booked far in advance, and be sure to leave additional time for reservations requested by mail.

In South America, whether your choice is a big hotel or a small inn, genuine hospitality and personal attention are the rule. Hotel managers are generally accessible and members of their staffs regularly extend their help in arranging sightseeing itineraries; recommending restaurants; and organizing fishing trips, boat rentals, or guest privileges at nearby golf courses and tennis courts. Guests will not, however, always find (either with hotel staffs or with fellow guests) that English is the lingua franca, as travelers from the US have come to assume. Still, there is a pervasive sense that people sincerely want you to feel welcome and will go to great lengths to make sure you do. Just the fact that you have come such a long way makes you a very special guest.

In keeping with our view of a multifaceted South America, our special havens are grouped not by country, but by physical environment and special interest.

## SEASIDE SWELLS

**COPACABANA PALACE, Rio de Janeiro, Brazil:** For anyone with a penchant for the past, this historic hostelry, renovated in 1991, is a triumph of preservation and restoration, though some say the service has not quite caught up yet. In the oldest part of the building, which was erected in 1923, remains a restored Beaux Arts façade, white marble lobby and staircases, ballroom-size hallways, soaring ceilings, and bedrooms facing the sea; to these, add ample Art Deco, including painted glass walls in the public areas. The hotel has one of the best pools in Rio as well as a number of elegant restaurants and bars. Conveniently located on Copacabana Beach at 1702 Av. Atlântica, Copacabana (phone: 21-255-7070). Reservations may be made in the US through *Venice Simplon–Orient Express* (phone: 800-237-1236).

**INTER-CONTINENTAL RIO, Rio de Janeiro, Brazil:** This 15-story structure on São Conrado Beach, in the resort area of a resort city, has a spectacular setting beside a white sand beach that stretches for several miles and a backdrop of towering peaks. It also overlooks the 18-hole *Gávea* golf course. The hotel's layout provides all 483 rooms with a view of the ocean and the hills, and the interior decor — with local wood and stone materials and native crafts — maintains the Brazilian atmosphere. Guest facilities include a swimming pool with a swim-up bar, and tennis courts lighted for night play. For dining, there is both the highly regarded *Monseigneur* and a branch of Rome's *Alfredo di Lello,* as well as 3 other restaurants and snack bars. The hotel has a number of after-hours boîtes including the *Jakui* nightclub and the popular *Papillon* discotheque. It has its own conference and convention facilities and shops, and is a short walk from the *Fashion Mall.* Hotel service here is among the best in Brazil. Twenty minutes by car and shuttle bus from Copacabana Beach. Reservations: *Inter-Continental* in the US (phone: 800-327-0200), or 222 Av. Prefeito Mendes de Morais, São Conrado, Rio (phone: 21-322-2200).

## DIVERSIONS / Luxury Resorts and Special Havens 547

**SHERATON RIO, Rio de Janeiro, Brazil:** An almost complete refurbishment program makes this a serious contender with the *Inter-Continental Rio* as the city's premier resort hotel. It is possible to enjoy a complete vacation here and never leave its grounds. Dramatically perched above its own beach and the first along the road from Ipanema and Leblon, this hostelry has an excellent swimming pool, with steps down to the sand. There are tennis courts, sauna, health club, elegant shops, and the *120-Nightclub*. Restaurants include *Valentino's*, *Edo* (a branch of the Japanese chain), the *O Casarõ* barbecue house, and a late-night coffee shop. With 579 rooms and 61 suites, this is Rio's second-largest hotel and all its rooms are furnished elegantly. All have private balconies and seaviews and some of the suites are decorated with a tropical theme. Reservations: 121 Av. Niemeyer, Vidigal (phone: 21-274-1122 or any *Sheraton* reservation office).

**CASA GRANDE, Guarujá, São Paulo, Brazil:** *Paulistas* say that they never need to go as far as rival Rio de Janeiro because they have their own beach resort at Guarujá, only 55 miles (88 km) away. On an island of white high-rises, this former hacienda, facing the Atlantic, provides an intimate and sumptuous retreat. Landscaped with tropical flowers and palms, the grounds have a swimming pool with terrace bar, sauna, tennis courts, golf links, and a heliport. The main restaurant serves spectacular lobster thermidor in a hollowed-out pineapple, and super-athlete Pelé comes from his home in nearby Santos to dance at the hotel disco. There's a piano bar with more mellow music, too. Manager Hans Schadler goes out of his way to make certain that each guest is very well cared for. Although he speaks perfect English, do not count on the same from everyone at the hotel. Reservations — a must for weekends and during the peak season of December through March — are made through *Casa Grande*'s São Paulo office, 571 Av. Europa (phone: 11-282-4277). In Guarujá, the hotel address is 999 Av. Miguel Estefano (phone: 132-86-2223).

**PORTO BELLO, Mangaratiba, Brazil:** An addition to the lineup of Frade hotels along the shores of the immense Bay of Kings, there are 86 rooms in 2-story buildings, a pool, 2 restaurants, and, best of all, nearly 2 miles of private beach. A soaring roof constructed of bamboo and thatch (in the style of Mexican *palapas*) encompasses the open-air public spaces. Warm touches in the decor include intriguing antique pieces used as accents, and a superb collection of hand-painted Brazilian pottery. Guests can make use of the windsurfers, kayaks, and dinghies, as well as tennis and horseback riding facilities available to them. Located about 1½ hours from Rio, at Km 48 of the Rio-Santos Highway. Reservations: *Porto Hotels,* 161 Rua Joaquim Nabuco, Rio de Janeiro, Brazil (phone: 21-267-7375) or in the US, through *F & H Travel Consulting,* 2441 Janinway, Solvang, CA 93463 (phone: 805-688-2441 or 800-544-5503).

**SOFITEL QUATRO RODAS, Olinda, Brazil:** Of all of the hotels in Brazil's Northeast, this property comes closest to being a self-contained resort — and one where English is widely understood. Its rooms are large, with balcony views of the ocean and beautiful gardens. Daytime activity centers around a nice big pool, served by a thatch-roofed snack bar with exotic fruit cocktails on tap. The hotel beach is the take-off point for sailors and windsurfers, and for the hardy, the hotel has lighted tennis courts for night play. There are several restaurant and bar settings, including the *Rilla d'Olinda* for international dishes and regional specialties, and the *Piano* bar and *Panoramic* restaurant for weekend dining and dancing. Two additional bonuses: boutiques well stocked with crafts, and proximity to Olinda — an architectural gem of a colonial town — just minutes away. Reservations: 2200 Av. José Augusto Moreira, Olinda 53130, Brazil (phone: 81-431-2955), or through *Utell International* (phone: 800-44-UTELL).

**ENSEADA DAS LAJES, Salvador (Bahia), Brazil:** Perched high on a cliff above the ocean in the Rio Vermelho district of Salvador, this intimate hotel was formerly an elegant private home and is still owned by the Castro Lima family. Their extensive collection of art and antique furniture remains, and each of the 8 rooms is individually decorated. A staff of 22 caters to the 16 guests. There is a swimming pool surrounded by lush gardens, and meandering paths lead to the beaches below. The hotel is a member of the worldwide Relais & Châteaux group of prestigious properties. For reservations, write to 511 Av. Oceanica, Rio Vermelho, Morro da Paciencia, Salvador (Bahia) 40210, Brazil (phone: 71-336-1027, 71-336-0654, or 71-336-0665).

**MERIDIEN BAHIA, Salvador, Brazil:** This is Salvador's largest and most luxurious hotel and part of the prestigious French chain owned by *Air France.* It has a beach, pool, boutiques, sauna, solarium, tennis courts, marina, several excellent restaurants, bars, and clubs. The ocean view from the top floor restaurant, *Jangada,* is memorable. Reservations: 216 Rua Fonte do Boi, Rio Vermelho, Salvador (Bahia) 41910, Brazil (phone: 71-248-8011).

**SOFITEL QUATRO RODAS, Salvador (Bahia), Brazil:** The newest of Salvador's luxury establishments is on the white sand Itapoã Beach, about a 40-minute drive from the center of town. In addition to 195 rooms, this deluxe resort property in an isolated setting has a pool, covered gym, and other sports facilities including tennis, volleyball, as well as its own 9-hole golf course. Other facilities include buggies-for-hire, babysitters, an excellent restaurant, satellite television, and sand and sea right outside. Reservations: Rua Passárgade, Farol de Hapoã, Salvador (Bahia) 40000, Brazil (phone: 71-249-9611; toll-free in Brazil, 71-800-8983).

**OCEANIC, Viña del Mar, Chile:** Clinging to rocks jutting out over the Pacific Ocean, this former villa is small and personal and is a marvelous hideaway for beach lovers who want to escape the trendy crowds at Viña. Most of the 20 rooms have enchanting floor-to-ceiling windows that offer superb sea views, oversize beds, and baths with tubs. Guests have at their disposal a gym, Jacuzzi, sauna, terrace, bar, and a French restaurant that excels with dishes using local fish. The staff speaks English. Reservations: 12925 Av. Borgoño, Viña del Mar (phone: 32-830006; fax: 32-830390).

**CARTAGENA HILTON INTERNATIONAL, Cartagena, Colombia:** Cartagena finally has a hotel with a beach. Even though it's a small one, the sand is soft and white — a luxury in a hard-sand resort area. In the El Laguito section of Boca Grande, this 289-room hotel is surrounded by water on three sides, and every room has a balcony with a view of the Caribbean. In typical Hilton style, there is a choice of dining rooms and lounges, a grand swimming pool with swim-up bar, 3 lighted tennis courts, and the wonderful beach. This section of Cartagena also has good restaurants, and the walled city and its massive fortifications are not far away. Reservations: *Hilton International* in the US (phone: 800-445-8667); or PO Box 1774, Cartagena (phone: 536-50660 and 536-54657; in Bogotá: 1-232-7902 and 1-285-6020).

**IROTAMA, Santa Marta, Colombia:** Take the setting here (sea out front, sierra behind), a simple, sybaritic lifestyle, and imagine the Caribbean of 20 years ago. Add modern, air conditioned, individual bungalows surrounded by tropical vegetation, clear blue water, and wide, clean beaches, and you've described this fine seaside retreat. There are several restaurant choices — open-air terrace dining; air conditioned, closed-in comfort; and beachside service — as well as a full range of facilities for sailing, diving, snorkeling, and deep-sea fishing. Day excursions to the neighboring Tairona National Park (with even more beautiful sandy coves) or into the hills to visit a coffee plantation are also possibilities. Reservations: PO Box 598, Santa Marta (phone: 54-237140; telex: 38871).

**SOLANA DEL MAR, Punta Ballena, Uruguay:** In a lovely resort area — quieter and prettier than its better-known neighbor at Punta del Este — this is a good vacation choice, especially for North Americans. The hotel is modern, comfortable, and wonderfully decorated, and occupies a superb setting, with a pine forest behind and the ocean and beach below. The food is excellent — important, because meals are on the Modified American Plan (MAP). However, it would be hard to imagine being here for long without a car to take an occasional run to Punta del Este for a night at the casino or to the yacht races in season. Other delightful excursions could include a day's boat ride to Lobos Island, with its colonies of sea lions, or to the fine beach (and ex–pirate hangout) on Gorriti Island. There also are plenty of resort activities, including windsurfing and kayaking. The whole coast here is jumping from *Christmas* to *Easter,* nearly deserted the rest of the year. But even in the off-season the weather can be good and the golf and tennis facilities not booked. Reservations: Ruta Interbalneario, Km 126.5 in Punta Ballena (phone: 432-788881, or 2-721187 in Montevideo).

**CUMANAGOTO, Cumaná, Venezuela:** Neighboring Puerto La Cruz and offshore Margarita Island (connected here by ferry service) are better known than historic Cumaná, but the last is our choice for a vacation in Venezuela. This 150-room, first class hotel is bordered by wonderful beaches, and the resort also has a super swimming pool surrounded by lovely grounds. Oceanside facilities include waterskiing and fishing boats. It is a short ride to town, the oldest city on the continent, and its sightseeing attractions include a Spanish fort and colonial churches. Cumaná also enjoys a lively *Carnaval* season, although an even finer example is 80 miles (128 km) farther east on the coast, at Carúpano. Reservations: Av. Universidad, Cumaná (phone: 93-653355 and 93-653115).

**GOLDEN RAINBOW MAREMARES, Puerto La Cruz, Venezuela:** A recent addition to the giant El Morro — the government's costly tourist complex — this resort is the most exciting in Puerto La Cruz. Its 500 rooms are spread out among a group of low-rise, Mediterranean-style, white stucco buildings with arches and tiled floors. The deluxe accommodations overlook an 18-hole golf course and marina and the lagoon-style pool boasts a wave machine; additional sports facilities include tennis and racquetball courts. There also is a fully equipped health spa. Everyone's dining choices can be met in the resort's 4 restaurants — there is a formal eatery that specializes in Italian dishes and fresh seafood, a dinner theater offering a prix fixe menu and show, a casual dining room offering buffet and à la carte service, and a poolside snack bar. Children are welcome here — baby-sitters are available. Reservations: *Complejo Turístico El Morro,* Puerto La Cruz, Venezuela (phone: 81-813022; in Caracas, 2-563-6042; in the US, 800-3-GOLDEN; fax in Caracas, 2-563-0738).

**MELIÁ, Puerto La Cruz, Venezuela:** About 9 miles (14 km) from the international airport at Barcelona, this is a smaller, though deluxe, version of the resort hotels near Caracas. All 222 rooms have private balconies. It has a full complement of facilities: sauna, gym, Turkish bath, nightclub, bridge and gamerooms, bars, tennis courts, swimming pool, golf, mini-golf, nautical sports, and a shopping center, as well as a fine beach. The hotel will organize a cruise to several Caribbean islands or a safari to the Venezuelan jungle. Reservations: *Meliá* hotels (phone: 800-336-3542; or in Puerto La Cruz, 81-691311; fax: 81-674401).

**PÁRAMO LA CULATA, Valle Grande, Venezuela:** Luxury has come to the Venezuelan Andes in the form of this lavish resort set in a 150-acre wooded area. Flowers are everywhere, especially orchids, for which Mérida is famous and brick pathways connect the buildings. The furnishings in each of the 93 villas are replicas of 19th-century, Andean pieces, yet the facilities are modern. A peaceful and restful spot, this is an ideal place to get away from the hustle and bustle of Mérida and indulge in a feeling of total privacy in the wilderness. There are 2 restaurants — one features local fare and the other is a formal eatery serving US fare — and 2 snack bars, a disco, 2 swimming pools (for adults and children), and 6 tennis courts. It's located just outside Mérida. Reservations: Valle Grande, Venezuela (phone: 74-446121; in the US, 800-275-3123; fax in Caracas, 2-261-5537).

## ISLAND IDYLLS

**POUSADA NAS ROCAS CLUB, Búzios, Brazil:** Part of a relaxed resort that attracts high-living guests, this small-scale hotel is located just offshore on its own island, and is reached by a 7-minute boat ride. Landscaping here is lush; facilities include a main lounge with restaurant and verandah overlooking the pool, a snack bar by the bay beach, and lovely double rooms and suites in *casita* or bungalow units. There is water skiing, windsurfing, sailing, and fishing, and, on the mainland, there are many choice small beaches to explore. Nightlife on the mainland in town is equally laid-back, and there are several good restaurants from which to choose when you venture off-island. Búzios is a 3-hour drive from Rio or a short flight via small aircraft. Reservations: Ilha nas Rocas, Búzios, Brazil (phone: 246-23-1303; in Rio, 21-253-0001) or in the US, through *F & H Travel Consulting,* 2441 Janinway, Solvang, CA 93463 (phone: 805-688-2441 or 800-544-5503).

**CASARÃO DA ILHA, Itaparica Island, Salvador (Bahia), Brazil:** A wonderfully relaxing spot on Itaparica, the largest island in All Saints Bay, as 25 miles of pristine white sand beaches stretch in both directions. Serenely Mediterranean in styling, the rooms of the hotel have whitewashed walls, tile floors, and simple furnishings. Ample windows open to the sea breezes. Palm trees dot the beaches, and tropical foliage surrounds the hotel. For reservations, write: *Nelmar Empreendimentos Turisticos Ltda.,* 1247 Av. Garibaldi, Edificio Anita Garibaldi, 4th Floor, Salvador (Bahia), Brazil (phone: 71-235-3200).

## HISTORIC HOSTELRIES

**POUSO CHICO REI, Ouro Preto (Minas Gerais), Brazil:** For those able to get a reservation at this lovely inn, it may well be the highlight of their visit to Brazil. (If you can't, try the *Luxor Pousada Ouro Preto* for a similar living-history experience.) The *Pouso Chico Rei* is an elegant old home furnished with colonial antiques and charm. There are no tennis courts and swimming pools here, but the inn is a perfect home base for a visit to this very historic town and art center of Ouro Preto — declared a national monument by the government. Spend several days exploring the town's churches, walking its cobbled streets and stairways, and plan at least one excursion through the beautiful countryside to other art centers of nearby Marina and Sabara. Reservations: Rua Brigadeiro, 90 Mosqueira, Ouro Preto (phone: 31-551-1274).

**PORTO POUSADA PARATI, Parati, Brazil:** A night in Parati, a perfectly preserved 18th-century colonial port town, is something special. Situated on the Rio-Santos highway about 3 hours from Rio, Parati flourished with the Brazilian gold rush, and when it died, the town simply shut down. Fortunately, its cobbled streets and shuttered homes are now protected by UNESCO as a world heritage site. The *pousada*'s 46 rooms, all with private baths and air conditioning, are tucked around a swimming pool and the patios of several old homes within the historic district. For reservations, contact *Porto Hotels,* 161 Rua Joaquim Nabuco, Rio de Janeiro, Brazil (phone: 21-267-7375), or in the US, through *F & H Travel Consulting,* 2441 Janinway, Solvang, CA 93463 (phone: 805-688-2441 or 800-544-5503; fax: 805-688-1021).

**POUSADA PARDIEIRO, Parati, Brazil:** A luxurious *pousada* with 24 air conditioned rooms furnished in colonial Brazilian style. The gardens are a delight, and the pool is a comfortable spot to relax after a full day of sightseeing and exploring. No children under the age of 15 are allowed. For reservations, write 74 Rua Comercio, Parati, Rio de Janeiro, Brazil (phone: 243-711370 or 243-711139).

**HACIENDA LOS LINGUES, San Fernando, Chile:** This beautiful estate, an elegantly restored manor house on a working farm, is the first member of the Relais & Châteaux group in Chile — and with good reason. From the furnishings in the vast living room and lounges to the silver used for candlelit dining, the hacienda is full of splendid antiques. Eighteen colonial-style rooms face a central patio, where there is a chapel with its own artworks. Stables provide mounts for riding into the hills as well as breeding stock for horse shows and rodeos. Other amenities include a pool, gameroom, hunting, nature walks, and the very personal attention of the owners. The hacienda is 78 miles (125 km) south of Santiago. For reservations, contact the owner, German Claro Lyon, *Hacienda Los Lingues,* 1100 Providencia, Torre C. de Tajamar,

Santiago, Chile (phone: 2-223-3518), or in the US, through *LARC* (*Latin American Reservation Center* (phone: in Florida, 813-439-2118; toll-free in the US and Canada, 800-327-3573) or *Utell International* (phone: 800-44-UTELL).

**HOSTERÍA EL MOLINO LA MESOPOTAMIA, Villa de Leyva, Colombia:** In the province of Boyacá and a 3-hour drive from Bogotá is Villa de Leyva, a deceptively sleepy-looking town that resembles a setting from *Don Quixote*. It has been designated a national monument, and this hotel, built in 1568 as a flour mill, is one of its loveliest treasures. The inn, set in lovely gardens with paths leading to private room entrances, is full of antiques such as decorative wooden canopied beds. Modern facilities include a pool; stables with horses for guests to take out on long country rides; a bar set in a cave; and a large dining room where the centerpiece is the original millstone. The dining room staff is dressed in period costume and the meals are delicious. Rates are very reasonable, as are prices at the regional market held on Saturdays in the vast cobbled town square. Reservations: Calle del Silencio, Villa de Leyva, Colombia (phone: 1-213-3491 in Bogotá).

**HACIENDA LA CIÉNAGA, Lasso, Ecuador:** Some 45 miles (72 km) south of Quito, Ecuador's oldest colonial estate has opened its historic doors as a country inn. The original manor house, built in the mid-17th century for the Marquis de Maenza, remains an elegant stone structure with cobbled patios, Moorish fountains, and grand windows with views of the snow-capped volcanoes of Cotopaxi province. Many original accessories decorate the mansion, and the estate even boasts its own church. Guest accommodations are in 27 rooms, all with private baths. Sports activities include riding and tennis. Also available are excursions to the wildlife area of Cotopaxi National Park and mountain expeditions up the Cotopaxi peak. Lively weekly markets are plentiful in the area. Reservations can be made at the hotel in Lasso by calling 2-801622, or, in Quito, 2-541337. *Nuevo Mundo Expeditions* in Quito organizes excursions to this area, including car and driver/guide. Contact the company at 2648 Av. Amazonas (phone: 2-552839 or 2-552617; in the US, 800-633-4734).

**HOSTERÍA CUSIN, San Pablo del Lago, Ecuador:** Just a 15-minute drive from Ecuador's bustling Otavalo Indian market, guests can relax at this manor house of a working hacienda. The original farmhouse, built about 100 years ago, has been incorporated into a 2-story addition surrounding the cobbled central courtyard. The hotel specializes in country elegance and family hospitality. Spacious guestrooms lead off a second-floor balcony overlooking flowers and fountain; bedroom windows frame peaceful views of the surrounding countryside — gardens, fields, and mountains. Furnishings are a mix of antiques and Ecuadoran handicrafts. Cocktails are served in the high-ceilinged central salon, which is dominated by a huge fireplace; dinners (prepared with homegrown produce) are taken in the adjoining dining room. Guests can also relax in a separate bar which resembles an intimate English pub. Bougainvillea and hibiscus bloom everywhere, and in the rear gardens there are several llamas in residence. A stable of horses is available for guest use. Reservations: in San Pablo del Lago (phone: 2-440672, and in Quito, 2-543107). Programs (minimum of 2 days), with meals and private car from Quito, can be arranged through *Unique Adventures,* 690 Market St., Suite 1100, San Francisco, CA 94104 (phone: 800-969-4900).

**LIBERTADOR, Cuzco, Peru:** Everyone knows that Cuzco is the gateway city to Machu Picchu, but few visitors linger long enough to see other ruins and the weekly markets in the area — or to really get to know this former capital of the Inca empire. It's worth the time, especially when it's possible to stay in a building that was the 16th-century home of a Spanish conquistador, built on the foundation walls of an Inca residence. The second floor of the colonial mansion has 18 grand, high-ceilinged suites. The newer rooms are comfortable, modern, and decorated with lively Peruvian textiles and crafts. The lobby, restaurant, and bar all have Inca walls and feature the hotel's collection of pre-Columbian artifacts as well as nice colonial touches. This is by far the best hotel in Cuzco. Reservations: 400 San Agustín (phone: 84-231961; in Lima, 14-420166 or 14-421995; fax: 84-233152). For reservations in the US, call *LARC* (phone: 800-327-3573, throughout the US and Canada; 813-439-2118 in Florida).

**LA POSTA DEL CANGREJO, Punta del Este, Uruguay:** Between the wave-capped Atlantic and the silent-flowing Río de la Plata is Punta del Este, just a 45-minute flight from Buenos Aires and a playground for rich, young Argentines. Out of the fray, in the suburb of Barra de Maldonado, is this very low-key Mediterranean-style inn, with comfortable and airy rooms overlooking its gardens and the beautiful, powdery sand beaches beyond. Guests relax and socialize in the sun-drenched, tile-floored public rooms and feast on excellent fare, under the supervision of co-proprietor Ana María Moya, once a student of Paul Bocuse. There is tennis and, for high rollers, gambling at the nearby *San Rafael* casino after midnight. Reservations: In Punta del Este (phone: 42-70021).

## LAKESIDE LODGES

**EL CASCO, San Carlos de Bariloche, Argentina:** The town of Bariloche is an alpine gem hidden in Argentina's Lake District; *El Casco* is its deluxe-plus hotel. A simple, white, stucco building gives way to 20 elegant guestrooms with lavish antique furnishings and individual sun terraces. Excellent food is served in the restaurant overlooking Lake Nahuel Huapi and landscaped woodlands stretch down to the beach. Guests may work out at the health spa on the premises, play golf and tennis nearby, or fish practically off the front lawn. There are 3 shops on the hotel's property that sell hand-knit clothes made from the famous wool of Bariloche. In winter, there is skiing at the country's leading center, Cerro Catedral, 15 minutes away. This is an expensive hotel, one that is booked far ahead, but it is well worth the price. Reservations: PO Box 634, San Carlos de Bariloche (phone: 944-61032/88/89/90; in Buenos Aires, 1-312-5768).

**RALÚN, Reloncaví Estuary, Chile:** In the heart of the Lake District, surrounded by grand forests and snow-capped mountains, this is one of the loveliest retreats anywhere on the continent. The main lodge sits on a hillside overlooking the point where ocean waters meet lakes. The hotel has stunning public rooms, all paneled in wood, with picture-window views. Luxury suites and double rooms in the lodge face gardens and water; separate cabins have a living room, kitchen, fireplace, and terrace. Come to enjoy swimming, sea and freshwater fishing, skiing, horseback riding, and nature itself. The hotel is an hour from Puerto Montt. For reservations in Chile, call 65-254001 in Puerto Montt, or 2-639-2345 in Santiago; fax in Santiago: 2-382428. In the US, call *LARC* (phone: 800-327-3573, throughout the US and Canada; 813-439-2118 in Florida).

## SPAS AND SPORTS SPOTS

**PORTILLO, Portillo, Chile:** South America's most prestigious ski resort stands in a valley at 9,233 feet above sea level, surrounded by peaks laden with the finest deep-powder snow on the southern continent. International skiing champions practice here from June through September. They train on the most challenging of all South American slopes, the incredible Roca Jack (see *Skiing*). Other less demanding slopes serve intermediates and beginners. Lessons are available, and the hotel stocks Rossignol skis and Head and Nordics boots for rent. Guests also can rent ice skates for a glide across the frozen lake that's just a few steps from the hotel's back door. Facilities include a sun deck, sauna, heated outdoor swimming pool, billiards, Ping-Pong, movies, a discotheque, and a cozy bar. Hotel accommodations range from chalets and suites to rooms with bath and dormitory-style sleeping. There are 650 beds, and reservations are at a premium in any price category. No matter when you plan to visit — although particularly in winter — bookings must be made almost a year in advance. Portillo is closed from November through January (phone: 562-243-3007, or in Santiago, 2-231-3411). For reservations in the US, including comprehensive ski packages, contact the *LanChile* tour desk (phone: 800-627-7780) or *Ladatco Tours* (phone: 800-327-6162).

**GRAN HOTEL PUCÓN, Pucón, Chile:** Remodeled and enlarged, this is the most complete lakeside resort in southern Chile. All of the 204 rooms and 24 suites face either the snow-capped Villaricca volcano or the placid blue Lake Villaricca. There also are 27 deluxe apartments with fully equipped kitchens, fireplaces, and terraces next to the main building. Guests have access to indoor and outdoor pools, a wide black sand beach, tennis, squash, and racquetball courts, a gym, sauna, Jacuzzi, boats for fishing and rowing on the lake, horses for riding, use of the neighboring 9-hole golf course (there are plans to expand it to 18 holes), and transportation to the ski slopes on the side of a live volcano and to the Huife hot springs. A restaurant, bar, casino, and disco round out the wide range of pleasurable pursuits here. Reservations: 190 Clemente Holzapfel, Pucón (phone: 45-441001; in Santiago: 2-232-6008; fax in Santiago: 2-246-6935).

**SOCHAGOTA, Paipa, Colombia:** Treat yourself to a long weekend (or a few mid-week days) outside of Bogotá to "take the waters" here. Hot mineral springs erupt in Paipa and are piped into the baths of this Boyacá spa. Each of the hotel's connecting villas has its own private atrium with plunge pool; other diversions include horseback riding, tennis, or the natural Lake Sochagota. Guests also can use the hot springs treatment and stay half a mile away at the *Casona del Salitre,* a 17th-century hacienda used by Simón Bolívar during one of his campaigns. The hacienda has been carefully restored and modernized. Both are managed by *Morales* hotels, a reliable and reasonable hospitality group, 6-62 Calle 75, Bogotá (phone: 1-248-1956 or 1-217-6200). For reservations, lakeside (phone: 87-850012 or 87-850172).

**PUNTA CARNERO INN, Punta Carnero, Ecuador:** The cool Humboldt and the warm equatorial currents meet around Salinas, north of Guayaquil, and the waters are full of striped marlin year-round. Black marlin, often weighing in at over 1,000 pounds, are in season in November, and the giant tuna are present from January through March. This hotel occupies an oceanside bluff near Salinas, and boasts 41 rooms with balconies, 2 tennis courts, and handsome public rooms. The fish dishes prepared by its kitchen are fresh and delicious. The hotel will arrange cruiser rentals and provide equipment, bait, and box lunch for fishing trips. In Salinas call, 4-785450; in Guayaquil, 4-327149; in Florida, 305-594-9240; elsewhere in the US, 800-327-7080. *CWT Vacation,* 1300 Coral Way, Miami, FL 33145 (phone: 305-858-9800; toll-free, 800-882-4665), offers a fishing package that includes a stay at *Punta Carnero.*

**LAS DUNAS, Ica, Peru:** Hang your poncho and sombrero in any one of the 120 rooms at this desert oasis, built like a small Moorish town around a twisting lagoon. There is no shortage of fresh water here — as dramatically demonstrated by the complex's 3 large swimming pools and abundant palm-studded acreage. The air conditioned rooms have separate dressing and bathing areas, and look out on Spanish patios and the landscaped gardens and dunelands beyond. Guests dine buffet-style, with open-grill cooking, or in a more intimate dining room decorated as a wine cellar. (The latter is appropriate since Ica is Peru's wine center; tours can be arranged to regional vineyards.) In addition to its 3 pools, there are 2 tennis courts, a 9-hole pitch-and-putt golf course, horseback riding, sauna, and health club. Some 150 miles from Lima down the Pan-American Highway, the hotel is in the middle of a major archaeological zone, and guests can fly directly from the hotel's landing strip to the famous Nazca line drawings or drive to Paracas on the Pacific Ocean for fishing, swimming, snorkeling, and wildlife viewing. Reservations: In Ica (phone: 34-231031; in Lima: 14-423090; fax in Lima: 14-424180); *LARC* (phone: in Florida, 813-439-2118; in other states, 800-327-3573); *American Express Travel* also can make your reservations (phone: 800-327-7737).

**EL PUEBLO INN, Santa Clara, Peru:** Just 9 miles (14 km) from the outskirts of

**554 DIVERSIONS / Luxury Resorts and Special Havens**

Lima, the sun shines year-round on this resort complex that resembles an Andean village, complete with gardens, fruit groves, 2 pools, and a golf course. Guests live in air conditioned bungalows with balconies or in white-stucco villas on the hilltop — reached by a funicular. The "town" is laced with hibiscus-lined paths and cobbled, lantern-lit streets; no cars are allowed. Everything is right here: a built-to-look-old bank, post office, shops, bars, cafés, restaurants, a church, a bakery, a discotheque — all tailored to a small village atmosphere. For recreation, there are saunas, a gym, massage, bowling alleys, cinema, tennis and squash courts, and riding. And just down the road is one of Peru's best-known restaurants, the *Granja Azul,* known for its chicken-on-the-spit, salad, and homemade bread. Buses shuttle guests to and from Lima, and the pre-Inca city sites in the valley can be explored by private car or on an organized tour. There is Cajamarquilla, a maze of crumbling adobe walls, and Puruchuco, a reconstructed palace of a former nobleman. There is also a historical museum at the latter site, and during the summer months, a folklore festival. Reservations: Km 11 on the Carretera Central (phone: 14-350777; fax: 14-355354), or write *El Pueblo* at PO Box 1306, Lima 18, Peru. Reservations also can be made from the US through *Utell International* (phone: 800-44-UTELL).

## JUNGLE JUNKETS

**ARIAÚ JUNGLE TOWER, Manaus, Brazil:** A 3-hour cruise up the Rio Negro brings travelers to the best of a number of properties on the river. The hotel is actually three towers built on stilts and that are connected by wooden catwalks. All 96 rooms and suites have balconies that overlook the jungle filled with monkeys and birds. The restaurant, which serves regional fare, and bar are located in one of the towers, and afford sweeping views of the surroundings, as does the special Tarzan's House, a double room in the treetops that is over 100 feet above the jungle floor. Two- and 3-night packages include transfers from the airport in Manaus (there is direct air service from the US), all meals, and escorted excursions in the Amazon. Reservations: *Rio Amazonas,* 42 Rua Silva Ramos, Centro, Manaus 69000 (phone: 92-234-7308), or in the US through *F & H Travel Consulting,* 2441 Janinway, Solvang, CA 93463 (phone: 805-688-2441 or 800-544-5503).

**TROPICAL HOTEL MANAUS, Manaus, Brazil:** This granddaddy of South American resorts is also on the Rio Negro, amidst thousands of acres of rain forest in the heart of the Amazon River basin, only 11 miles (18 km) from the heart of Manaus, a 30-minute ride on the hotel's own bus. The hotel offers every luxury imaginable. Architecture is colonial, which here in the jungle means wide, spacious hallways, patios of exotic birds, and graceful arches. In addition to air conditioned rooms, facilities include swimming pools and sauna, tennis courts, a floating river-bar (and other, stationary, cocktail lounges), restaurants, and a discotheque. Guests may choose from a wide array of sightseeing excursions or fishing expeditions along Amazon tributaries. Reservations from the US: *Varig Brazilian Airlines* (phone: 800-468-2744). In Brazil: *Tropical Reservations,* 368 Rua da Consolação, 4th Floor, São Paulo 01302 (phone: 11-231-5844); and at the hotel (phone: 92-238-5757).

**EXPLORAMA LODGE, Iquitos, Peru:** For those who prefer hotels built on solid ground, but still want to visit the Amazon, this one — located 50 miles downriver from Iquitos and a short ride up the Yanamono tributary — is worth a try. It is a charming and imaginative jungle inn and a miracle of supply and efficiency. Peter Jensen is the majordomo here, presiding over a lodge set among towering hardwood trees intertwined with vines, wild orchids, macaws, parrots, and a resident pet tapir. The facilities include 8 palm-thatched buildings connected by elevated and covered passageways; there are 3 guest pavilions for sleeping, and separate toilets and showers. Public rooms, like *La Tahuampa* (The Swamp) bar, are screened, as is the dining room, where the food is varied and good. Guests can swing in a hammock; join guided walks along interesting jungle trails; or ride boats to Indian villages, river islands, and inland lakes. They can even leave the lodge comforts for the more rugged *Explornapa* camp. Reservations: *Explorama Tours,* 340 Av. de la Marinas, Box 446, Iquitos, Peru (phone: 94-235471) or through its US representative, *Selective Hotel Reservations* (in Massachusetts, 617-581-0844; throughout the US and Canada, 800-223-6764).

**EXPLORER'S INN, Puerto Maldonado, Peru:** Thirty-five miles (56 km) from the tiny jungle town of Puerto Maldonado (fly there from Cuzco), this simple inn has comfortably designed twin-bedded rooms situated in 7 large bungalows built entirely of native materials. Though each room has a private bath, there is no electricity and only river-temperature water for showers, but the staff does an admirable job of supply and service, considering the logistical nightmare it faces daily. The emphasis here is on natural history, particularly bird watching, the Tambopata being rated by Audubon groups as one of the top spots in the world. Resident naturalists, mainly British, working on advanced research projects, act as guides for the guests, and therein lies its uniqueness. Reservations: *Peruvian Safaris S.A.,* 1334 Av. Garcilaso de la Vega, PO Box 10088, Lima 1, Peru (phone: 14-316330; fax: 14-328866; in Cuzco, 84-235342).

**CANAIMA, Angel Falls, Venezuela:** Guests can get to this rustic, but comfortable, cabaña resort only by flying over the 3,212-foot Angel Falls, and on a clear day the vista below is spectacular. Set next to a lagoon in a national park, the lodge facilities include a dining room serving good, hearty food at its single seating. With water, water everywhere, there is swimming, sunning, water skiing, boating, and fishing. Guests also may request a variety of excursions through the jungle on foot or to the splendid Orchid Islands by motorized dugout canoes. Taking a 1-week trip by jeep, foot, and canoe, it's possible (from May through November) to get right to the base of the falls. Reservations from the US: through *Avensa Airlines* (phone: 800-283-6727), *Lost World Adventures* (phone: 404-971-8586 or 800-999-0558; fax: 404-977-3095), or *Unique Adventures* (phone: 800-969-4900).

## WILDERNESS WHIMSY

**HOSTERÍA, KAU YATÚN, Calafate, Argentina:** Only a 15-minute walk from the center of town, this 46-room ranch-like inn sits in a meadow, surrounded by a carefully tended flower garden. You can laze indoors in the overstuffed chairs in the lounge or sip your mid-morning coffee on the terrace while soaking up some sun, chatting with the *hostería*'s international clientele. Each room is comfortably furnished, with country-style chintz draperies, coordinated bedspreads, and a private bath. There's a folkloric show and traditional lamb barbecue twice weekly, and horseback riding can be arranged. But most guests come to Calafate, on the the shores of Lago Argentino (Lake Argentina), to visit Glacier National Park, crammed with more than 300 glaciers. Open from September through April. Reservations: *Hostería Kau Yatún,* Provincia de Santa Cruz, El Calafate 9405, Argentina (phone: 902-91059; or in Buenos Aires, 1-394-6701).

**POUSADA CAIMÃ, Pantanal, Campo Grande, Brazil:** Once the farmhouse of the massive Miranda Ranch, this Mediterranean-style country house is now a 10-room hotel with a full program of excursions over the ranch's 53,000 hectares of protected forest, savannah, and lowland. The Pantanal, a vast grassland subject to annual flooding, is located in the midwestern part of Brazil, in the states of Mato Grosso and Mato Grosso do Sul. This cycle of renewal sustains an overwhelmingly lush habitat for thousands of species of flora and fauna. The air conditioned lodge, 125 miles (200 km) by road from Campo Grande, is truly elegant, yet comfortably furnished and appointed as befits a country manor. There's even a swimming pool. Reservations: *Roberto Klabin Hotéis e Turismo,* 1208 Rua Pedroso Alvarenga, São Paulo 04531, Brazil (phone: 11-883-6566).

**HOSTERÍA PEHOE, Punta Arenas, Chile:** Awesome natural wonders and wide open spaces are the big draw in this corner of the world, and lodgings often become a secondary concern. This 35-room inn, though simply furnished, is something very special. Located on a small island on Lake Pehoe and accessible only by footbridge, it is one of only two lodges (the other caters to the backpacking crowd) located within the boundaries of Paine Towers National Park. The park is best known for its sparkling glacial lakes, dramatic waterfalls, and snow-capped mountains. This spectacular series of peaks probably is best viewed from the large windows of *Pehoe*'s dining room. The huge main lodge is reminiscent of a Colorado ski lodge, with several fireplaces, a bar, and unusual hand-carved wooden furniture. Dotted among the island's trees and gardens are several single-story buildings housing the guestrooms, each with central heating and private bath (rates are higher for rooms with the best views). The hotel can arrange trekking, horseback riding, fishing, and a daylong boat trip (skirting floating icebergs) to reach Grey Glacier. From September until the first of April, this tip of South America cannot be beat for its combination of scenic grandeur, Old West romance, and simple comfort. Accommodations in the park are limited, so make plans well in advance. Reservations: In Punta Arenas, 1464 21 de Mayo (phone: 61-411390); in Santiago (phone: 2-671-8709).

**ISLA ESTEVES, Lake Titicaca, Puno, Peru:** The Lake Titicaca area finally has a hotel that brings comfort to the great experience of staying in this scenic and historic region. The hotel is on the island of Esteves, just offshore from the port town of Puno, and has central heating, air conditioning, first class rooms, and lounge areas; this is a marvelous spot at sunrise, or after dark when the shores of the lake are dotted with lights. For those especially interested in the Indian culture and with a taste for visiting archaeological sites or attending some of the most colorful weekly markets and Indian festivals on the continent, this inn perched close to the most sacred lake in Incan mythology is likely to prove perfect. Reservations: On the island (phone: 724); in Lima, *EnturPerú* (phone: 14-721928); in the US (phone: 800-275-3123).

**CLUB COTOPERIX, Choroní, Venezuela:** Actually three renovated colonial houses, this club provides comfortable — if spartan — rooms. Wonderful meals made from local ingredients, including fresh coconut, passion fruit, hearts of palm, avocado, and fresh fish. At night, the lush courtyards are a gathering place for guests to enjoy rum cocktails and piano music. The hotel takes groups into the thick tropical forest to the remains of what were once-booming cacao haciendas. Boats and drivers are provided for water sports, and journeys to lovely, palm-shaded beaches on blue lagoons are available. Make reservations in Caracas (phone: 2-573-5241).

**HACIENDA DOÑA ROSA, Mérida, Venezuela:** All the rooms at this old-fashioned hacienda open onto a large cobbled courtyard and their shutter-framed windows look out on the surrounding lush, flowered landscape. Meals of traditional local specialties, such as wheat *arepas,* are enjoyed family-style on an open-air terrace, with the sound of birds chattering in the trees. Make reservations through *Lost World Adventures* (phone: 404-971-8586 or 800-999-0558; fax: 404-977-3095).

**HACIENDA ESCAGUEY, Mucurubá (Mérida), Venezuela:** Located in an emerald-green mountain valley, this working, family-run hacienda is open to guests seeking an authentic Andean experience. The house is perched on a hillside with a commanding view of the valley. Although it is ancient, the house has been beautifully restored and meals are cooked from fresh and savory homegrown ingredients. Few guests leave without dining at least once on succulent trout taken from cold Andean streams nearby. Guests may observe the dairy operations, including cheese making, as well as other farming tasks. Make arrangements in Caracas through *Morgan Tours* (phone: 2-271-9265/7217).

**LOS FRAILES, Santo Domingo, Venezuela:** Typically, the mention of Venezuela conjures up images of sparkling beaches and azure waters. While the country does, indeed, have these assets in abundance, it also has an alpine region, with an alpine-style gem of a colonial South American inn (owned by *Avensa Airlines).* A half-hour above the town of Santo Domingo and 2 hours from Mérida, it is set on a 17th-century monastery site, with the central lodge housing a cozy bar and a fine restaurant. Rooms are connected by covered corridors and are carpeted, heated, and furnished with antiques and reproductions. There are flowers everywhere, and a little brook bounces along its mountain course right through the hotel. The views are grand, and many guests choose horseback riding as the natural way to get out and enjoy the Andean landscape. Especially during the *Christmas* holidays and *Semana Santa* (Holy Week), book well ahead, through *Avensa Airlines* (phone: 800-283-6727).

# Great Buys: Shopping in South America

South America has great buys in a wide variety of items — handicrafts (*artesanías*), fine quality leather goods, and precious and semi-precious stones. Each country has its own unique style; throughout the continent, there are wonderful things to buy, and in most countries, US shoppers will be amazed by the reasonable prices.

But visitors should be careful when making a purchase. More than one traveler has bought a handmade wool sweater at an Andean market only to discover later that the sleeves are vastly different lengths. Buying in exclusive, expensive boutiques is not necessarily a guarantee of quality. Even the best shops occasionally sell merchandise with flaws that purchasers might not notice until they get the item home. While shopping in South America, check at tourist offices for the locations of handicrafts cooperatives (some have outlets at major hotels, shopping centers, and museums). Cooperatives offer some of the most original designs around, and your purchases will help keep traditional crafts alive and will contribute to the local economies.

The art of bargaining is still practiced in most of South America. In some markets the prices are fairly equal, and there are few meaningful bargains obtained by haggling, but it's worth a try, and the seller may accept a price of about two-thirds to three-quarters of what he or she originally asked. When dealing with someone who actually made what's for sale, however, consider the time and labor involved, and don't try to shortchange the seller. In the big cities and at better stores, prices are set. In some places, when you ask if there is a discount, the merchant willingly marks off between 5% and 10%, particularly if you pay in cash rather than by credit card.

Remember, too, that skins or any article made of animals on the endangered species list cannot be brought back into the US. Get an up-to-date list before leaving from the US Fish and Wildlife Service, Department of the Interior, Washington, DC 20240. See also *Customs and Returning to the US* in GETTING READY TO GO. It is illegal to take pre-Columbian artifacts out of most South American countries. (If you buy copies, you might want to make sure your bill specifies that fact.) And bear in mind that international laws prohibit the sale of vicuña wool; any item sold as such is likely to be alpaca. In addition, check US customs for items on the Generalized System of Preference (GSP) list which can be brought into the US from Argentina, Bolivia, Brazil, Colombia, Ecuador, Guyana, Panama, Peru, Suriname, Uruguay, and Venezuela duty-free in addition to your $400 allowance. Some gems and handicrafts are on the list.

Below is a list of the best places to shop in South America.

**ARGENTINA:** There well may be more cattle than people in Argentina, and it may occasionally seem that most of the beasts have "donated" their hides to supply the endless array of shoes, jackets, coats, bags, handbags, and luggage for sale in downtown

Buenos Aires shops. Leather goods have long been the mainstay of tourist purchases in Buenos Aires, although angora sweaters and fur coats of fox and nutria are traditionally good buys in Argentina.

Whether just browsing or actually planning to purchase, a good place to start a shopping tour is on Calle Florida, in downtown Buenos Aires, heading north from Avenida de Mayo (1 block from the *Casa Rosada*). Florida really is a shopping mall that extends 10 blocks to Plaza San Martín. Along Florida, there is a great variety of merchandise — from some of Argentina's finest leather boutiques to blue jeans and sneakers shops. The closer to Plaza San Martín, the fancier the shops, but also the better the merchandise and the value. Some of the best handbags are found at *Rossi y Caruso* (1601 Av. Santa Fe) and *Welcome* (behind the *Plaza* hotel). *Harrods* (between Paraguay and Córdoba) is Buenos Aires's largest, most exclusive department store. It stocks leather goods, toys, cutlery, and a range of products similar to its high class, though unrelated, London namesake.

Heading west from Plaza San Martín, Santa Fe is one of the city's major shopping streets, with small, exclusive shops close to the plaza. Prices are higher than those in the shops in the arcades of the major hotels around the plaza. *Casa López* in the *Sheraton* hotel (at 945 Florida and at 640 Marcelo T. de Alvear) has fine, expensive bags. For cowhide rugs, try shops along Bartolomé Mitre in the 1300 blocks. Leather goods can be bought for less money at the factory outlets in the Once (Eleven) district, starting in the 2000 block of Corrientes. It takes a good eye and persistence to shop here, however. One successful shopper recommends *Majourno Hermanos* (3664 Lavalle).

Fascinating antiques can be found in the small shops around Plaza Dorrego in the San Telmo section. Many stores stock limited collections of very specific items — miniature bronzes, for example. Every Sunday and on holidays, at the *San Telmo Fair* in the Plaza Dorrego, dealers put their wares under canvas awnings and sit to hawk and chat. Knickknacks, antique and otherwise, also can be bought in the shops at 2102 Vicente López, and at 2188 Vicente López, near Recoleta Cemetery.

On Saturdays, Sundays, and holidays, artisans fairs are held in Plaza Vicente López, Plaza Britania, and Parque Lezama. Attractive displays of craft items include leather handbags and enamel jewelery. Stop in at the *Caminito Fair,* on the street of the same name in La Boca, for the Friday and Saturday art fair.

Fancy boutiques with exclusive clothing are along the streets between Plaza San Martín and Recoleta Cemetery. Particularly good streets are Esmeralda, Presidente Quintana, Guido, Montevideo, and Avenida Alvear.

Typical items — the maté cup, the silver *bombilla* straw for sipping maté, gaucho apparel, ponchos, the three-balled *bola lasso,* onyx ashtrays, and odds and ends — can be found along Paseo Leandro Alem. Even better buys on fine cashmeres and angora sweaters can be found in Bariloche, not to mention this ski resort's delectable chocolates — stop by *Benroth* (569 Beschtedt; phone: 944-22310) or *Abuela Goye* (157 Albarracín; phone: 944-22531). If you've developed a taste for tango, this is the country where you'll find the best tapes — ranging from the legendary singer Carlos Gardel to the contemporary composer and musician Astor Piazzolla.

**BOLIVIA:** La Paz has terrific buys on weavings, wall hangings, and ponchos; alpaca sweaters; and jewelry of silver and gold. The most interesting shopping streets are found behind the San Francisco Cathedral, going up on Calle Sagárnaga. About halfway up the steep street to Calle Linares is the so-called "Indian Witchcraft Market" (a misnomer), where Aymara Indian women sell wizened llama fetuses (for good luck), herbs, potions, and sundry magic charms. They don't always like to sell to foreigners, but it's great fun to browse here. The best shops for handicrafts line the bottom of Calle Sagárnaga, Calle Linares, and Calle Illampu. There are any number of tourist shops in the center of town offering the same goods at much higher prices, as is apparent after even a little comparative pricing.

In addition to the stalls and booths along the streets mentioned above, Indian craftsmen sell their wares from sacks tied to their backs. They are good sources from whom to pick up some rare, excellent weavings at prices lower than those in the shops. (Note: the US is restricting the import of antique Aymara weavings. Check with the US Embassy in La Paz to find out what you need to do to bring them back into the country). There are also some fine things to buy in the provinces in which most specific crafts originate, and the prices for them are right all over the country.

Alpaca sweaters and mufflers of exceptional quality (designed for the New York market and selling there for three times the price) for both men and women can be found at *Millma* (in the *Plaza* hotel and at 225 Calle Sagárnaga). Other interesting, fashionable alpaca knits are featured at *Intiwara* in the lobby arcade of the *La Paz* hotel. *Fotrama,* the weaving cooperative outside Cochabamba, has two shops in La Paz that sell its high-quality sweaters, hats, shawls, and blankets (in the lobby of the *La Paz* hotel and at 1405 Av. 16 de Julio).

*Tiendas Bolivianas* (2142 Av. Arce, across from the *Plaza* hotel), quartered in a restored colonial house, has good sweaters, leather products, and regional crafts, including musical instruments. Fine gold and silver jewelry is available at *King's* (1636 Av. 16 de Julio) and at *Mi Joyita* (Edificio Litoral on Av. Mariscal Santa Cruz near Calle Colón). *Icono,* at 2170 Av. 6 de Agosto, Edificio Hoy, has fine alpaca sweaters and scarves in original designs and contemporary silver jewelry incorporating pre-Columbian motifs.

**BRAZIL:** The country is known for its semi-precious stones — tourmalines, amethysts, aquamarines, topazes — and for diamonds and emeralds. Most of the jewels come from the state of Minas Gerais. Semi-precious stones — particularly topaz, aquamarine, and tourmaline — are available at bargain prices. When the stones are purchased already set, the setting is generally 18-karat gold. The best-known dealer, *H. Stern,* offers a free trip from any hotel to its cutting factories. *H. Stern* stores in Rio are on Avenida Visconde de Pirajá in Ipanema — its largest and where the group's headquarters are located — as well as stores in the international airport and most of the major hotels. *H. Stern* also has branches in São Paulo, Brasília, and other cities. The company offers a 1-year guarantee with worldwide service. *Amsterdam Sauer* (156 Av. Rio Branco in downtown Rio and on Av. Atlântica in Copacabana) is another top jewelry store chain.

In Rio, the high-fashion shopping district is between the Praça General Osório and the Praça Nossa Senhora da Paz in Ipanema. *Cariocas* for the most part, however, prefer to shop in the city's two giant malls, *Rio-Sul* and *Barra-Shopping,* which offer hundreds of stores of every imaginable type under one air conditioned roof. The malls also have the advantage of being open from 10 AM to 10 PM. On the side streets off Avenida Rio Branco, downtown, there are souvenir shops selling leather goods, wood carvings, and dolls. At the Sunday fair ("Hippie Fair") in the Praça Osório, Ipanema, there are all sorts of arts and crafts of varying quality. You might also want to buy a *figa,* the most traditional Brazilian amulet.

In São Paulo, the best shopping streets are Itapetininga, Augusta (especially its side streets, including Alameda Lorena and Rua Oscar Freire), and Paulista. There's a fair on Sundays from 9 AM to 1 PM on the Praça da República, where handmade leather, ceramic, silver, and other artisans' products are sold.

Salvador (Bahia) is the best place in Brazil to buy silver, woodcarvings, handmade lace, and native art. Practically everything is for sale in the *Mercado Modelo* — rosewood items, silver jewelry, embroidered linens, lace, dresses, and leather goods are the best buys. *Gerson's* in the *Convento do Carmo* museum also has an extensive line of silver jewelry, as well as Bahian handicrafts. Many Brazilian artists have shops here, but their work is expensive; however, handwoven rugs are usually a good buy.

In Belo Horizonte, there are not only semi-precious stones but pewterware. The town of São João del Rei, 110 miles (176 km) from Belo Horizonte, is known for its silver, pewter, leather, and straw goods, as well as handloomed bedspreads and tablecloths. Pewterware, wooden goods, and earthenware also are made in Tiradentes, 115 miles (184 km) from Belo Horizonte.

In the state of Ceará, in northeast Brazil, handmade lace is fashioned into various clothing and household articles, and embroidered goods are lovely and inexpensive.

**CHILE:** Chile's best buys are handsome, diamond-patterned, Mapuche wool rugs that come in all sizes, copper items, and jewelry of semi-precious, dark blue lapis lazuli. Unless you are going to Temuco, where the Mapuche rugs are woven, the best buys are found in the government-run *Centro de Madre (CEMA)* stores. At several locations in Santiago (351 Av. Portugal, the airport, and the Universidad de Chile subway station). There are also *CEMA* stores in towns throughout the country; these stock handicrafts and artisan works from all over.

Chile is noted for its lapis lazuli jewelry, dark blue stones with minute flecks of mineralization (not spots or streaks) that often are set in silver or made into attractive necklaces. *H. Stern* (at the *Carrera* and *Sheraton* hotels in Santiago) has a few good pieces on display. Pieces can be made to order in a few days in *Atelier Kot* (at 510 Huérfanos). Other shops specializing in lapis lazuli jewelry, as well as cooper, are found in Santiago along Calle Bellavista between Pío Nono and Arzobispo. Most highly recommended of all is the studio of designer Morita Gil for jewelry and superb stones (at 1991 Los Misioneros), near the *Sheraton San Cristóbal* hotel and at the airport.

*Sucamp,* a nonprofit cooperative, has an alluring selection of fine wool capes, ponchos, and blankets as well as wool cloth at 112 Av. República in Santiago.

Excellent bargains in bolts of fine wool can be found at the end of the winter season (August through September) in downtown Santiago shops. To the north of Santiago, in the town of La Ligua, there are some exceptional buys in alpaca sweaters and cloth at the *La Baltra* factory. Other shops have nice alpaca sweaters and ponchos, but unfortunately many are now mixing wool with synthetic fibers.

Chimbarongo, south of Santiago, manufactures wicker furniture and knickknacks. Roadside stands sell items for a song. In Puerto Montt, leave time for shopping for woolen clothing of every description and elaborately carved wooden stirrups in the stalls lining the port at Angelmó.

**COLOMBIA:** The country is considered the emerald capital of the world. These gems can be purchased at the *Central Bank* and at *H. Stern* shops in Bogotá, but beware the street hawker. *H. Stern* shops can be found in the *Tequendama* and *Travelodge Orquidea Real* hotels, and at El Dorado Airport. However, the most original jewelry designs (pre-Columbian reproductions) are at *Galería Cano*'s main store (at 27-98 Carrera 13), or its branch in the *Travelodge.* There is also superbly designed jewelry at *El Lago* (Avianca Bldg. at Carrera 7).

Colombia's most attractive artisan product is the multicolored *ruana,* or wool poncho, but the country also produces basketry, ceramics, straw goods, leather goods, and terrific coffee (pick up at least one can). In San Isidro, near Bogotá, there are a number of craft shops where bargains in gold and silver jewelry can be found, as well as reproductions of pre-Columbian artifacts, alligator and snakeskin shoes, belts, and bags. One of the finest Bogotá craft centers is in the *Museo de Artes y Tradiciones Populares* (Museum of Popular Art and Traditions; at 7-21 Carrera 8). The prices are right here and at *Artesanías de Colombia* across the street from the *Tequendama* hotel. Leather goods, particularly luggage, are also an excellent buy in Colombia. In Bogotá, try *Boots 'n' Bags* (at the *Tequendama* hotel and at 5-35 Calle 19), *Colombian Bags* (at the *Tequendama* hotel and at 93-03 Carrera 15), and *Land Leather* (22-52 Calle 23 and 82-86 Carrera 14-A). Both handicrafts and leather goods at reasonable prices are available at *El Balay* (at 75-77 Carrera 15).

Native handicrafts are a good buy in Cartagena, where there are a number of stalls near Plaza Bolívar, in the Old City. The government-operated *Artesanías de Colombia* has a wide selection of handicrafts at reasonable prices. In the Old City, leather goods and emeralds also are available. *Greenfire Emeralds* has stores in the *Pierino Gallo Shopping Center* in the Boca Grande area of Cartagena. Dennis Lynch, a former Peace Corps volunteer from California, runs a handicrafts store, *Artexpo,* at the entrance to the Inquisition Palace in Cartagena (but that doesn't mean he'll twist your arm to buy his goods). Other handicrafts stores are the *Tropicana* and *Galería Salomé* in Boca Grande and the *Oriental* in the Old City.

On San Andrés Island, off the Colombian coast, duty-free shops stock Swiss watches, perfume, china, crystal, cameras, and liquor.

**ECUADOR:** The *Otavalo Indian Market* on Saturday morning sells fine woolen and woven goods and is Ecuador's best-known shopping site. The town is 80 miles (128 km) north of Quito. Get there early in the morning, about daybreak, since the market disperses early. The Otavalo Indian goods are well known, so well known that other Indians will try to pass theirs off as *otavaleño* in order to get a higher price. There's a Saturday market in Riobamba.

Quito is one of the best shopping centers on the continent, and Avenida Amazonas is its main shopping street. Shops along the main avenue and in the colonial area just behind the *Alameda Real* hotel have a huge selection of fine handicrafts ("*artesanías*") from all over the country. Along with textiles, look for primitive paintings on cowhide, unique ceramic nativities, wonderful woodcarvings, and the diminutive bread dough *Christmas* ornaments and figures from nearby Calderon. One of the best shops is *La Bodega* (at 614 Calle Juan León Mera), which also commissions its own production of well-designed, hand-knit sweaters in wool and cotton at a fraction of their stateside prices. Just down the street, next door to *Libri Mundi,* is *Galería Latina,* specializing in fine Peruvian and Bolivian woven goods, both new and antique.

Up the hill, *Folklore* (260 Av. Colón) is the gallery of Olga Fisch. (There is a second store in the lobby of the *Oro Verde* hotel). Ms. Fisch was the grande dame of Ecuadoran crafts for many years and not only was instrumental in preserving Indian arts, but used their motifs imaginatively in clothing, jewelry, carpets, and decorative accessories. Since her death at age 90, her family has continued operating her shop where prices are not low, but the quality is high, and shipping is reliable. Finely crafted boots, wallets, bags, jackets, and luggage made in Ecuador's leather center, Cotacachi, are available in Quito at *Angelo's* (662 Av. Amazonas; phone: 2-523614).

Another "don't miss" is the hilltop museum-gallery of Ecuador's best-known painter, Oswaldo Guayasamín. His art prices match his reputation, but it's hard to resist his superbly designed jewelry. Every taxi driver knows where he lives.

Cuenca is the center for production of not only its famed "Panama" hats, but of weavings, embroidery, and all kinds of other unique objects made of toquilla straw. The most delightful small items are intricately detailed *Christmas* ornaments in the shape of angels, Santa Claus, and the Three Wise Men. These are available at *El Tucán* (7-88 Gran Colombia at Luis Cordero). Strolling down Gran Colombia, stop by *La Piel* (8-28 Bolívar for quality leather goods. *Exportadora Cuenca* (at the corner of Gran Colombia and Benigno Malo) is one of the best stores for Panama hats. The distinctive filagree jewelry of Cuenca is available at *Joyería Guillermo Vásquez* on the ground floor of the *El Dorado* hotel.

**PANAMA:** Panama City is the traditional free port shopping stopover for travelers heading to and from Latin America. Prices are comparable with other Caribbean free ports, though camera prices tend to be higher than those in discount stores in most US cities. But the endless array of perfume, cameras, projectors, electronic goods, radios, lace, watches, china, chess and backgammon sets, and Oriental art will entrance anyone who enjoys shopping. Camera and electronic stores cluster along the Avenida Central. Other good shopping areas are along the Vía España (in the El Panamá neighborhood) and Avenida de los Mártires. All major hotels have shopping arcades. Bargaining is a possibility at some stores.

Native handicrafts are found at the *Salsipuedes* open-air bazaar off Avenida Central. Crafts at higher prices, but of more uniform quality, can be bought at *Artesanías Nacionales,* the government cooperative with one shop at the airport and the other at the ruins in Panamá Viejo.

Crafts items include shirts, weavings, baskets, wicker goods, necklaces, beaded collars, leather goods, straw and wooden figurines, ceramics, and hand-appliquéd *mola* fabric appliqués. The *molas* are made by the Cuna Indians on the San Blas Islands (where they also can be purchased, as they're exhibited outside every Cuna cottage). The *molas,* with their stylized animals and birds cut through several layers of brightly colored cloth, are one of Latin America's most popular art forms. The *molas* have risen rapidly in price over the past few years, but it's possible to bargain for a decent price — and they are still considerably more expensive in New York.

When leaving Panama, duty-free goods will be delivered at the airport. Pick them up on the way out of the country, after paying for them at the time of purchase in the store. Regulations do not allow travelers to open packages until actually aboard the outbound airplane, but the airport customs official allows opening and resealing them *in his presence* to make sure you've received what you bought. Free port shops are extremely honest and reliable in making deliveries. (The airport itself offers no real bargains.)

**PARAGUAY:** *Nandutí* (spiderweb) lace weavings for table linen and wall hangings and the *aó po'i* embroidered cotton cloth are handsome souvenirs that can be purchased in downtown Asunción. The *ñandutí* is made in Itaguá, a small town near the capital where the *ñandutí* looms stand outside the doorways of the houses along the main street, making it seem as if each home is marked by a distinctive brightly colored giant spider web. The *aó po'i* cloth, white or colored, is used to make men's fancy summer shirts and women's dresses, skirts, and slacks. (You can machine wash it, but ironing is difficult; you may want to opt for dry cleaning.) Bright woven belts and sashes, *piri* straw hats, wooden articles, Spanish guitars, and gold or silver jewelry can be purchased at markets in Asunción and in many small towns. Hand-painted ceramic hens — said to bring good luck — are found in several colors and sizes. The best shops are found along Calle Colón. One of the most complete selections of *artesanía,* including woodcarvings, ceramics, leather, and superb *ñandutí,* is found at *Arte Popular* (360 Ayolas at Palma). Also recommended for every type of handicraft imaginable is *Victoria* (Iturbe at Eligio Ayala). *Confecciones Catedral* (189 Calle Presidente Eligio Ayala) will make a shirt or blouse to order in 24 hours. Fashionable hand-embroidered women's clothing and exceptionally pretty tablecloths are sold at *Anahi* boutique (343 Caballero at 25 de Mayo).

**PERU:** Silver, gold, alpaca sweaters and ponchos, and knit and woven goods of llama and alpaca wool are available in Lima. There are moderately priced handicrafts stalls at the *Mercado Artesanal* (sometimes called "La Marina") in Pueblo Libre on (Av. de la Marina). Items include knit socks, hats, scarves, blankets, sweaters, rugs, carved wood llamas, llama fur slippers, jackets, and llama rugs. The llama and alpaca sweaters and ponchos have small llama designs woven in. Be careful to check the quality of what you buy. An even better source of handicrafts is *Artesanías del Perú,* a cooperative located in the Lima suburb of San Isidro (610 Jorge Basadre) and at the *Museo de la Nación* in Lima.

In Lima, silver and gold trinkets can be found in the shops along the Avenida Nicolás de Piérola, approaching the Plaza San Martín from the *Crillón* hotel and the Jirón Camaná. These shops along the Avenida Nicolás de Piérola (also known as *La Colmena*) are packed with woolen sweaters. Some of the best crafts shops, including the excellent *Huamanqaqa,* are on Avenida Belén, right across from the tourist office. This is not an area for bargains, but on the other hand, nothing in Peru is expensive by US standards. There are lovely weavings, carved gourds, paintings, embroideries, and other crafts from around Peru. Also stop by *Mon Repos* and *La Gringa,* a fine crafts boutique owned and operated by a North American (both in the *El Suche* shopping complex of Miraflores) across from *César's* hotel.

Very nice jewelry can be found at *H. Stern* in the *Gran Hotel Bolívar* (on Plaza San Martín), as well as in the lobbies of the *Lima Sheraton* and *Cesar's* hotels. Other good shops line the side street to the left of the hotel facing the plaza.

Handicrafts, particularly rugs and sweaters, also can be bought in stores or from sidewalk vendors in Cuzco and at the Cuzco Indian markets. Puno has well-made, thick ponchos at prices even lower than those found in Cuzco, and the famous Pucara ceramic bulls come from this area. Well-known Sunday markets with excellent selections of handicrafts are found in Huancayo and Pisac.

Lima is where the colorful *retablos* are sold. The *retablo* is a gaily painted wooden frame (originally a portable altar) that looks almost like a miniature house with decorated double doors on the front. Inside are religious and secular scenes populated by handmade ceramic figures. Lima record shops are a good place to stock up on lovely Andean flute music cassettes.

**URUGUAY:** Uruguay is known as the country where leather and suede jackets, bags, belts, and shoes can be bought for even less than in Buenos Aires. Most of the better shops are in Montevideo between Plaza Independencia and Plaza Libertad. Very soft leather goods are made from *nonato* (unborn calf). Uruguay also produces nutria furs and good-quality amethysts. The best places to purchase nutria are *Peletería Pendola,* (1087 San José) and *Peletería Holandes* (894 Colonia). For agates and amethysts, visit *Amatistas del Uruguay* (Sarandi and J. C. Gómez).

Montevideo is also a haven for antiques aficionados, who are treated to a selection of shops with everything from period silver and turquoise jewelry to fine china vases.

*Manos del Uruguay,* a nonprofit cooperative, stocks high-quality items from around the country made of pure, hand-dyed and spun wool. Particularly enticing are its hand-knit sweaters, exported to high-fashion boutiques around the world; you'll pay about about one-third the price in Montevideo. There are four shops in Montevideo (including one in the beach suburb of Carrasco) and one in Punta del Este. *Manos del Uruguay* also sells a good selection of folk art and other handicrafts.

**VENEZUELA:** Once considered the most expensive of South American capitals, Caracas now ranks as more than reasonable. At the moment, items from clothes to cosmetics, imported or well made locally, offer grand savings over prices in the US. Margarita Island is designated as "duty-free," and the prices are indeed attractive for liquor, perfume, cigarettes, and shoes; however, for the last, and on most clothing and jewelry, buyers can do just as well in Caracas.

Caracas's shops and shopping centers are as sophisticated and deluxe as those anywhere in the world. There are any number of snazzy, well-stocked shopping centers offering the same sort of goods found in the US: *Centro Comercial Chacaito, Concresa, Plaza Las Américas, Paseo Las Mercedes,* and *Centro Comercial Ciudad Tamanaco* (especially good). There is a building full of jewelry shops (gold, sold by weight, glitters everywhere): the *Edificio Francia* on Plaza Bolívar.

A variety of handicraft shops cater to tourists, although Venezuela is not well known for highly developed artisan work. *Artesanía Venezolana* (at Plaza Venezuela on the Sabana Grande pedestrian walkway) has one of the most complete selections. Crafts shoppers will find woolen *ruanas* (like ponchos), baskets and hammocks, sisal products, rugs and blankets, masks, and some jungle seed jewelry.

Shoppers also would do well to leave the country with a can of Venezuelan coffee and a bottle of the country's fine, and very expensive, dark rum. Buy these at any supermarket.

# Fabulous Festivals

Splashy, miraculous, colorful, bizarre, intriguing, and musical — a festival anywhere in South America is likely to be an utterly extraordinary human pageant of celebration. Without a doubt, the most famous of all is *Carnaval*, in celebrated Brazilian style. Rio de Janeiro's tops the favorite list, but many aficionados of the mad pre-*Lenten* festivities insist that *Carnaval* in Salvador (Bahia) is, if anything, more exciting and less commercial.

What most foreigners don't realize is that *Carnaval* is celebrated, in one form or another, for between 3 and 8 days before the beginning of *Lent* throughout virtually all of South America. In Oruro, Bolivia, masked devil dancers perform the *Diablada*, in which good and evil wrestle for control. In Ecuador and Argentina, however, the main ritual (joyous only for perpetrators) consists of dropping water-filled balloons on unsuspecting passersby. But whether you prefer to samba in the streets or marvel at the demonic dancers, be sure to make reservations at least 6 months ahead of any *Carnaval* you intend to visit.

Plan ahead for other festivals, too, such as the continent-wide celebration in June of *Corpus Christi*, which, like *Carnaval*, is a moveable feast. When the Spanish priests first came to "civilize" the Indians, they found it expedient to move many of the saints' days nearer to existing local celebrations that had always accompanied planting and harvesting. Today, especially in the Andean countries, fiestas continue to mix Christianity and Indian rites, Western and Indian music and pageantry. Celebrations usually include the pomp and circumstance of a procession to Mass at the cathedral, as well as traditional dancing, feasting, and lots and lots of drinking.

For those lucky enough to find a room at festival time, or anywhere in the vicinity of a festival that is about to happen, chances are that it will be impossible to make a telephone call (since none of the operators will be working), buy gasoline (since all stores and shops will be shut), or find local transportation. It's inevitable, however, that every stranger will be invited to dance, drink, feast, and possibly even to marry. Take it all with good cheer and a fine sense of humor. After all, that's what festivals are for.

**ARGENTINA:** Argentines celebrate everything from soybean harvests to beer drinking to the founding of cities to a whole string of religious holidays and saints' days. Certain festivals are more important in different provinces. In Puerto Madryn, the new year starts with a *Deep-Sea Fishing Festival;* in Rosario del Tala, in the province of Entre Ríos, with a provincial *Tango Festival*, which takes place from January 1 to January 15 on a stage overlooking the Río Gualeguay. In Salta, where *Christmas* festivities begin on December 25 and end on January 15, tableaux and carol singing are staged throughout this period. On January 15, the 2-week *National Folklore Festival* begins in Cosquín, in the province of Córdoba. One of Argentina's most important national events, it attracts artists and musical groups from all over the country. An artisans' fair is held at the same time. Unfortunately, elements of this annual event have become commercialized.

The *Vendimia*, one of the country's largest festivals, celebrated in Mendoza during the first week in March, is held in honor of the harvest of the wine grapes. The vines are blessed, there is a parade of floats and antique cars, and a light-and-sound spectacle is held in an amphitheater at the foot of the Cordillera. The city is packed, so be sure to make hotel reservations well in advance.

*Carnaval* is not an official holiday in Argentina, but it is celebrated in some fashion or other in many towns, and most gaily in Corrientes, beginning on the Saturday before *Ash Wednesday*. In Buenos Aires and other towns, there are a series of balls and parties in hotels and clubs. Throughout most of Argentina, visitors must take care not to be

## DIVERSIONS / Festivals

the target of water-filled balloons. In the northern towns near the Bolivian border, *Carnaval* festivities begin in Tilcara at the end of January or beginning of February with the *Carnaval de Ablande:* a warm-up for the myriad of festivities that start in February in Humahuaca with a pilgrimage to the Virgin of Candelaria, supplemented by fireworks, traditional foods, and religious music. In Humahuaca, *Carnaval* starts the Friday before *Ash Wednesday* with a *chicha* festival and altiplano music. If you don't join in the drinking, you'll have to down a large cup in one gulp. In Tilcara, *hermitas* of flowers representing the stations of the cross are hung along the streets, and processions come down from the mountains on *Ash Wednesday.*

During *Semana Santa* (Holy Week) in Yavi and Abra Pampa, the northern Argentines and southern Bolivians meet to barter and exchange handicrafts and products. *Holy Week* also is celebrated with religious events throughout Mendoza province, San Javier in Misiones province, Salta province, and Aimogasta in La Rioja province.

On April 16, Salta celebrates its founding with a *Cultural and Sports Festival*. Corrientes marks its *Founding Day* on May 3 with a religious and popular arts festival.

In mid-June, *Semana Salta* (Salta Week), a gaucho festival, commemorates the death of General Martín Miguel de Güemes. Various contests are capped by a parade of *Gauchos de Güemes,* who light a bonfire at the feet of their hero's statue.

*St. John's Day* is celebrated on June 24 in a number of towns, but the most striking is in Formosa, where the faithful walk barefooted over a bed of hot coals without feeling the burns. Outside of Córdoba in Villa General Belgrano, the first 2 weeks of October mark the *Festival Nacional de Cerveza* (National Beer Festival). During the last two Sundays in October, at the *Manca Fiesta* (Festival of the Pot), the country's oldest festival in La Quiaca, Argentines from the altiplano and Bolivians from the south of their country come on burros and llamas loaded with merchandise for bartering.

On December 8, in the town of Luján, the festival of *Our Lady of Luján,* the patron saint of the Argentine Republic, is observed. It starts with a pilgrimage in which the devout are followed by old colonial carts and gauchos mounted on decorated horses. The week before, there's a parade of the old coaches from the *Museo Provincial, Colonial y Histórico* (Provincial Colonial and Historical Museum) in Luján, and townsfolk dress in colonial clothing.

The first week in December, the *National Sea Festival* in Mar del Plata is celebrated with sporting events, the blessing of the sea and sea gods, gatherings around bonfires at Laguna de los Padres, and the crowning of a queen. A *Snow Festival* is held in June in Bariloche at the height of the ski season.

An important Argentine event, although not a festival, is the annual *Livestock Exhibition* in July on the grounds of the Argentine Rural Society in the Palmero section of Buenos Aires, where prize cattle, horses, sheep, and pigs are shown and auctioned.

**BOLIVIA:** In Oruro on *Carnaval Sunday,* the *Diablada* (devil's dance) is performed. Dancers representing good and evil (often dressed as the Indians and the Spaniards) fight it out in a marathon of merrymaking that includes a parade and offerings of *chicha,* a corn liquor, to Mother Earth. This traditional festival kicks off an 8-day *Carnaval* celebration.

The *Diabladas* also are performed in La Paz during *Carnaval,* when special days are reserved for water fights. The *Diablada* dancers rarely rest in festival-filled Bolivia, performing also at Lake Titicaca during spring (November) fertility celebrations; and on major saints' days in Oruro.

*All Souls' Day* (October 31) and *All Saints' Day* (November 1–2) are occasions for honoring the dead who in pre-Columbian times were buried with many worldly goods and food provisions to sustain themselves in the next world. Bread is still placed on graves, along with special decorations and candles to light the way. At Cochabamba and around the Titicaca area, miniatures of reed boats are offered to ease the passage of souls across the lake. The cemeteries are the place to be.

During August, the *Dark Virgin of the Lake* at Copacabana is elaborately honored in her lakeside hometown and throughout the province. Other honors are bestowed on *San Roque,* protector of dogs, in Tarija, in September, a month before the *Festival de las Flores* — Tarija's flower festival. There always seems to be cause for celebration anywhere at any time in Bolivia. Other festivities during the year include the *Feria Alacitas* from January 24 to February 7 in La Paz, *Virgin of Candelaria* celebration in early February in Copacabana; a *Carnaval* celebration in the town of Tarabuco, near Sucre, in March; the *Fiesta del Gran Poder* (Festival of the Master of Great Power) in La Paz in June; and the *Fiesta of Urkupiña* in Quillacollo, near Cochabamba, in August.

**BRAZIL:** Some 10 million Brazilians practice the rituals of *macumba,* a Brazilian religious cult akin to voodoo. *Macumbeiros* celebrate *New Year's Eve* in Rio de Janeiro on Copacabana Beach by dashing into the ocean carrying offerings — flowers, mirrors, lipsticks, and other items designed to please a woman — letting the waves carry the gifts away to Iemanjá, the goddess of the sea. The celebrations begin a few hours before midnight, when thousands pack the beaches to sing and dance by candlelight.

In Salvador (Bahia), on the Thursday before the third Sunday of January, Bahian women gather on the front steps of the Bonfim Church to wash the steps. This *Lavagem do Bomfim Festival* includes 10 days of dancing and celebrating. On February 2, Bahians celebrate their *Festival to Iemanjá.* Beautifully dressed women put gifts to the sea goddess in boats and launch them from Salvador's Rio Vermelho and Itapoá beaches.

Other important Bahian festivals are the June 24 *Feast of St. John,* with fireworks, bonfires, and dancing; 3 days of festivities beginning December 4 in honor of *St. Barbara;* and the December 8 procession and feast in honor of *Nossa Senhora da Conceição* at the church of that name in the lower city.

*Carnaval* in Brazil, which begins the Friday before *Ash Wednesday,* needs no introduction. The days and nights of the parades of the samba "schools" (as groups from Rio's *favelas* are called) in glittering costumes that Brazilians begin planning a full year in advance make the picture pages of newspapers throughout the world. If you want to join these festivities, make reservations at least 6 months ahead; be prepared to pay steep, hiked-up prices for everything; and carry onto the streets only the money and documents you absolutely need — as, among other things, *Carnaval* is a pickpockets' field day. If the exuberant madness of Rio's *Carnaval* is a bit overwhelming, consider *Carnaval* in Salvador (Bahia) or other northern towns, where the street processions, dancing, and gaiety are equal to Rio's, even if the touristic glitter is not. A 7-day stay usually is required when booking hotel rooms during *Carnaval.*

**CHILE:** The main festival celebrated throughout Chile is the national holiday, the *Fiestas Patrias,* on September 18 and 19. All over the country, small open huts topped with tree boughs, called *ramadas,* are set up and people gather in the evening to drink the first fermentation of the grapes, *chicha,* and dance the traditional dance, the *cueca.* Celebrations reach the highest intensity in and around Rancagua, where there are rodeo competitions between *huasos,* the Chilean cowboys. Chileans also observe a series of religious festivals in the country's small towns. The best known honors the *Virgin of Carmen,* on July 16 in La Tirana, in northern Chile. Thousands flock to this Atacama Desert town, some walking barefoot or on their knees to repay the *manda* (promise) made to the Virgin for favors granted. There's dancing in traditional Indian costumes and elaborate devil masks.

In the town of Andacollo, southeast of La Serena, a spectacular procession of brightly costumed townsfolk combines Indian and Christian rituals on the day after *Christmas.* This festival, called the *Feast of the Virgin of Andacollo,* is most important in northern mining towns, as Our Lady of Andacollo is the patron saint of miners. (The statue used in the festivities is said to have been found by miners who were trapped underground for 5 days and survived.) A smaller version of the same festival is held the first Sunday of October.

On December 8 (the *Feast of the Immaculate Conception),* an impressive number of people walk barefoot or on their knees from Santiago and Valparaíso to the Lo Vásquez chapel on the road uniting the two cities, asking favors of the Virgin.

The *Cuasimodo,* a religious procession, takes place in the central zone the Sunday after *Easter.* The priest leaves the church in a horse-drawn carriage, carrying the host to his bedridden parishioners. He is followed by a procession of mounted *huasos* in full dress with decorated horses — and in recent years by bicyclists and motorcyclists. There are numerous processions in localities around Santiago.

The fourth week of January is when the national *Festival Folklórico* (Folklore Festival) takes place. It is celebrated with 5 days of music and dance at the *Anfiteatro San Bernardo* (San Bernardo Amphitheater) in Santiago, 377 Av. Libertador O'Higgins.

A popular international music festival, the *Festival Internacional de Viña del Mar,* is held in the beach resort of Viña del Mar during February. Up-and-coming singers (and some who will never arrive) come from all over the world to participate in week-long singing competitions. There's ample entertainment by well-known people to supplement the contestants' singing in the outdoor amphitheater in Quinta Vergara Park. To watch the festival, make hotel reservations as far ahead as possible. Even camping space is hard to come by.

The *Feria Internacional de Artesanía* (International Artisans' Fair), featuring art and craftwork from all over the continent, is held the second week in December in Parque Bustamante at the corner of Francisco Bilbao in Santiago.

**COLOMBIA:** Among a host of festivals, one of the most colorful is the August *Parade of the Chair Carriers* in Medellín, celebrating Antioquia state's independence from Spain. (Medellín is the state capital.) Hundreds of farmers come down from the hills carrying flower arrangements, including exotic species of orchids. There is a parade of marching bands, horsemen on thoroughbreds, and horse- and oxen-drawn floats. Also in August is the annual *Orchid Show.* Medellín, though infamous for drugs, is known as the orchid capital of the world. In February, the town celebrates the *Feast of the Candelaria,* the city's patron saint day.

*Holy Week* at the end of *Lent* is a time of religious observance all over Colombia. The most famous is in Popayán where the Indians from the countryside join the city elders in elaborate processions, and life-size saintly statues are taken from the churches and borne through the town. A festival of sacred music is held concurrently. Pre-*Lenten Carnaval* is also important to Colombians who celebrate to the Caribbean rhythms in Barranquilla and Cartagena. The latter now has an annual March festival highlighting Afro-Caribbean music, with visiting combos invited from all around the area. It's exciting music and the scene is lively.

During the last 2 weeks of June, Neiva holds its special festival featuring the *bambuco,* the country's national dance. In Ibague, at the end of June, troupes from the highlands, plains, and coast gather for the largest national spectacle of folkloric dances.

**ECUADOR:** The Indian festivals of Ecuador are important not only for religious reasons but also as social events. Many festivals are highly decorative affairs. An Indian man acquires social prestige by the amount he spends on the festivals and by taking on leadership posts in organizing and supervising them.

On January 6 *(Epiphany)* in San Rafael, near Quito, the *Three Kings Day* procession takes place. The "Kings" ride through the streets of the town. In Ambato, there's the *Festival of Flowers and Fruits* sometime during the first part of February, and *Holy Week* in Riobamba and *Corpus Christi* days in June are not to be missed.

On September 8, the Otavalo Indians of Imbabura province celebrate their harvest festival, *El Yamor.* This festival is Indian in origin and gives thanks for the harvest (it revolves around the special fermented corn liquor, *yamor.* The Spanish combined this celebration with the *Feast Day of San Luís,* the harvest's patron saint. In Latacunga, south of Machachi, the *Mama Negra* festival is held for 3 days in September. (The pious call this the *Festival of the Holy Virgin of Merced).* Bonfires, brass bands, and the designated Mama Negra (allegedly the Virgin Mary's cook) are central to the celebration of fertility.

In September, near Cuenca, at the Hermitage of Biblian, a festival honors the Virgin, who saved the people from drought. There are pilgrimages, and giant paper hot-air balloons are released.

In both Quito and Guayaquil, Ecuadorans ring in the *New Year* by forgetting about the old one. This juxtaposition of *el año viejo* and *el año nuevo* is great fun. Life-size papier-mâché figures of characters representing bad luck (often politicians) or particularly difficult events in the past year are ceremoniously paraded around on *New Year's Eve,* and then burned with great enthusiasm at midnight.

**PARAGUAY:** The celebration of the *Virgen Azul de los Milagros* (Blue Virgin of the Miracles) in the town of Caacupé is the biggest in the country. The faithful begin their overnight pilgrimage on foot from Asunción the night before and reach the basilica where the Virgin's statue is kept in time for morning mass. During the pilgrimage, there is music, dance, fireworks, and much merry making. Religious processions also are held on *Good Friday* and on August 15, the anniversary of the founding of Asunción. The night before the June 24th celebration of *St. John's Day,* the devout set bonfires and walk across hot coals. And *Día de Primavera* (Spring Day — remember, the seasons are reversed) festivities on September 21 are celebrated with a parade of youths and flowers everywhere.

**PERU:** In Lima, tens of thousands of worshipers clad in purple robes take part in a procession to honor *Nuestro Señor de los Milagros* (Our Lord of the Miracles) on October 18, 19, and 28. The festival honors a painting of Christ that, according to legend, has survived all of Peru's worst earthquakes. At the same time, the *Silver Scapular Bullfight Festival* takes place in the *Plaza de Acho,* Lima's biggest bullring.

In Cuzco, the *Inti Raymi* (Inca Sun Festival) is celebrated on June 24 at Sacsayhuaman, the fortress overlooking the city. Rituals honoring the solstice — singing, dancing, and much drinking of *chicha* (corn liquor) — are the order of the day. Make reservations well in advance of your intended time of arrival. (See *Peru,* DIRECTIONS.) (By the way, Cuzco is one of those places where *Carnaval* consists of dumping water and other objects on pedestrians, so it's a good time to be somewhere else.)

Before visiting Peru, it is worthwhile to investigate the possibilities of coordinating your stay with the dates of the summer and winter solstices, *All Souls' Day, Corpus Christi,* or any one of the many festival periods celebrated in all Andean countries. Cuzco, Puno, Arequipa, and the Huaráz area are major centers for colorful spectacles.

Puno is considered Peru's folkloric capital, and the principal festival is that of the *Virgin of Candelaria,* which begins on February 2 and lasts an entire week. The *Diablada* (devil's dance) is performed with giant masks and elaborate costumes and is the catalyst for a whole series of other dances. Celebrants come from all over the province. *Carnaval* is the next big season of folkloric explosion, but nearly every month in some part of the province of Puno there is at least one fiesta featuring one or more of these costumed dances. The most raucous *Carnaval* festival in the country is celebrated in Cajamarca, where residents throw water and talcum powder, paint one another with shoe polish, and spend days dancing, drinking, and making merry.

**SURINAME:** The country's festival calendar reflects its large Asian population of East Indians of the Hindu faith, Indonesians following Islam, and many Chinese. Each group rings in a different *New Year.* The Hindustanis seem to have more religious holidays than anyone: *Basant Panchami* during *Carnaval* and the harvest time; *Holi Phagwa* marking the beginning of spring; *Deepavali,* the festival of light, in the fall. Fireworks and dragon dances are part of Chinese celebrations for their *New Year's Day* and *Nationalist China Holiday* observance. Christians who trace their roots to Holland turn out for the arrival of *St. Nicholas,* who parades in with gifts on December 5.

**URUGUAY:** Not surprisingly, many of this country's festivals and special events focus on the gaucho — or cowboy — traditions. *Fiesta Gaucha,* held *Easter Week,* revolves around rodeo competitions although handicrafts exhibits, barbecues, and music are important facets. Every August, Parque El Prado in Móntevideo is the scene of the *Cattle Show* sponsored by the Asociación Rural del Uruguay.

Less representative of Uruguay but perhaps most popular is *Las Llamadas* parade during *Carnaval* week each year. Music and drum rhythms, based on African influences in Latin America, provide the scenario for dancing and merrymaking along two narrow streets — Carlos Gardel and La Cumparsita.

**VENEZUELA:** Venezuelans close down their offices during *Semana Santa* (Holy Week) and head to the beaches. They celebrate *Carnaval* the week before *Ash Wednesday.* The best *Carnaval* takes place in the beach city of Carúpano, which becomes jammed with residents and tourists dressed in wild costumes and with dancing in the streets. In addition to Roman Catholic feast days, important holidays include *Independence Day* on July 5, the anniversary of the Battle of Carabobo on June 24, *Simón Bolívar's Birthday* on July 24, and *Día de la Raza* (Columbus Day) on October 12.

In January, the *Paradura* (standing up) of the Christ Child is celebrated in Mérida. Peasants take the Infant Jesus statue through the streets to their farms to ask a blessing on the land. They return the statue to its crib, standing up. The procession is accompanied by music and firecrackers.

On February 2, the *Dance of the Vassals of Candelaria* in La Punta celebrates Venezuelan folklore.

The day before *Corpus Christi,* which falls in late May or early June, in the town of San Francisco de Yare, the 2-day *Festival of the Devils* takes place. The townspeople dress in cumbersome red papier-mâché masks depicting grotesque horned creatures. Some of the masks have asses' teeth. The dancers perform in front of the church until fatigued; then drunken revelry ensues.

# Casinos Royale

Most of South America's casinos are fewer and smaller than those found in Las Vegas. However, there's a certain cachet in gambling in exotic surroundings — Iguassú Falls, for example. Most of the casinos are in luxury hotels; in many, little English is spoken.

Gambling is not legal throughout South America — you won't be able to roll the dice in Brazil, Guyana, Peru, and Venezuela because it's against the law. It would be legal to do so in Bolivia and French Guiana, but there are no casinos.

**ARGENTINA:** All 15 casinos in Argentina are state-owned. The biggest, most modern, luxurious, and best known is the *Central Casino* at Mar del Plata (2252 Blvd. Marítimo Patricio Peralta Ramos; phone: 23-27011). Described by one Argentine as a "railroad station for gambling," *Central* has 108 roulette tables, 55 tables for a card game called *punto y banca,* 7 for dice, and 2 for "34." It's open from 5 PM to 5 AM all year except for a brief closing for maintenance. The admission charge is about $1; chips are issued in denominations from $20 to $100. Minimum and maximum bets, depending on the game, run from $1 to $500. The minimum age is 18 and casual dress is allowed. Two other Mar del Plata casinos are annexes of the *Central Casino:* (at 3545 Av. Martínez de Hoz; phone: 23-84031 or 23-84032); the other, in the luxurious *Provincial* hotel (2500 Blvd. Marítimo Patricio Peralta Ramos; phone: 23-24081). In the lake district resort of San Carlos de Bariloche, the *Bariloche Center* hotel (on the corner of Calle Gobernador Pagano and Calle San Martín) has roulette and *punto y banca.*

In the *Internacional Cataratas de Iguazú* hotel, on the Argentine side of Iguassú Falls, is a small casino with four roulette tables and two for *punto y banca.*

Other casinos can be found in Miramar (at 1343 Calle 9 de Julio); in Necochea (at the corner of Calle 4 and Calle 91); in Pinamar in the *Playas* hotel (at the corner of Av. Arquitecto Jorge Bunge and Calle Las Sirenas); in Alta Gracia (at the corner of Vélez Sarsfield and Carlos Pellegrini); in La Cumbre (at the corner of Vélez Sarsfield and Estanislao Olmos de Aguilera); in Paraná (at the corner of Costanera Alta and Córdoba); in Resistencia (at the international airport); in Puerto Madryn (at the corner of Julio A. Roca and Sarmiento); in Comodoro Rivadavia (at the corner of 9 de Julio and Rivadavia); and in La Rioja (at the corner of Quiroga and Sarmiento).

**CHILE:** There are five casinos in Chile. The *Viña del Mar* casino, one of the most outstanding in Latin America, is an elegant building with ample gardens; dress is *very* formal. The casino, right on the bay along Avenida San Martín, is open every night during the summer season from September 15 through March 14 and on weekends during the rest of the year. There are roulette, blackjack, baccarat, and slot machines. To enter the casino, players pay a $1 admission charge, but to enter the gameroom, a membership card for the season, which costs about $2, is necessary. The minimum age is 21. The minimum roulette bet is $1; for blackjack and baccarat it's $10. In Arica, there's a modern, smallish casino (955 General Velásquez). Coquimbo, near La Serena, is home to the elegant *Casino Municipal de Peñuelas,* open every night from September through March and weekends the rest of the year. There is another small casino in Puerto Varas as well as one at the ski lodge at the *Gran Hotel Pucón;* open year-round.

**COLOMBIA:** Among the casinos in Colombia, there's the informal *Casino del Caribe* (in the *Pierino Gallo Shopping Center* in Boca Grande). It's usually crowded until the 3 AM closing time. There are 10¢ slot machines with chips, roulette tables European-style (20 to 30 players long), and blackjack (minimum bet is about 80¢). The *Americano* hotel casino requires a jacket and tie.

The *Giradot* resort hotel in Lagomar El Peñon has a small casino, as does the *Nutibara* hotel in Medellín. Surprisingly, there are two casinos on relatively undeveloped San Andrés Island, where the atmosphere is casual, chips start at $1, and the casinos are set up for roulette, craps, blackjack, and poker from 9 PM to 3 AM. One is the *Casino Internacional* and the other the *Casino El Dorado-Monte Carlo* (both at the corner of Avdas. La Playa and Providencia). The minimum age in Colombia is 18.

**ECUADOR:** The major hotels in Quito, Guayaquil, and Salinas have casinos. Serious crapshooters and blackjack players prefer the atmosphere of Quito's *Colón* hotel casino, where the roulette wheels have two zeros. The hotel is one of Quito's major social centers (at the corner of Avdas. Amazonas and Patria; phone: 2-560666). There's a casino in the *Quito* hotel (2500 Av. González Suárez; phone: 2-230300). The new *Oro Verde* hotel in Quito also has a casino (1820 Av. 12 de Octubre at Cordero; phone: 2-566497). In Guayaquil, a lovely casino (brightly decorated and where single women will feel welcome), billing itself as Ecuador's largest, is open at the *Oro Verde* hotel (9 de Octubre y García Moreno; phone: 4-327999). The minimum age is 21.

**PANAMA:** This country's tourist bureau claims that "gambling is not only a cornerstone of the country's economy, but a way of life." In Panama City, try the casinos at the following hotels: *Soloy* (corner of Av. Perú and Calle 30; phone: 271133); *Marriott Caesar Park* (Vía Israel; phone: 264077); *Granada* (Calle Eusebio A. Morales; phone: 644900); *Continental* (Vía España; phone: 639999); *Doral* (Calle Monteserín; phone: 625133); *Plaza Paitilla Inn* (Vía Italia; phone: 691122); *Caribe* (Av. Perú; phone: 250404); and *El Panamá* (Vía España; phone: 231660). In the Chiriquí Highlands at Volcán, there are slot machines at the *Bambito* hotel (6 Calle Gerardo Ortega; phone: 235084 and 714265). The minimum age is 18.

**PARAGUAY:** Since gambling is illegal in Brazil, Brazilians who want to outfox fate at the tables cross the border to Paraguay where the minimum age is 21. Right across the line there's a rather basic casino in the *Gran Hotel Casino Acaray* (Ciudad del Este; phone: 61-2302). In Asunción, the luxury *Itá Enramada* casino (Cacique Lambaré and Ribera del Río Paraguay; phone: 21-33041 through 33049) has roulette, baccarat, 21, and slot machines. There also are casinos in the *Hotel Guaraní* (Plaza de Independencia; phone: 21-491131), the *Yacht y Golf Club Paraguaya* (11 Av. del Yacht in Asunción; phone: 21-36121), and, in San Bernardino, in the *Hotel Casino San Bernardino* (phone: 21-391 through 397).

**SURINAME:** There is a casino at the *Suriname Torarica* in Paramaribo (phone: 471500 or 477432) where stakes are moderate to expensive. The minimum age is 21.

**URUGUAY:** The casinos here range from very basic to deluxe and there are plenty of them. Two are in Montevideo: the *Parque Casino* hotel (Rambla W. Wilson; phone: 2-497111/2/3), and the *Casino Carrasco* hotel near the airport of the same name (phone: 2-610551). Uruguay's two other fancy casinos are in the seaside resort of Punta del Este: *Nogaró* (at Calles Gorlero and 31; phone: 42-41012), and the *Casino San Rafael* hotel (on the Rambla L. Batlle; phone: 42-821-6166). The beach towns of Atlántida, Carmelo, La Paloma, Coronilla, and Piriápolis also have small casinos. There is one in the *Casino El Mirador* hotel in Colonia (phone: 522-2004) and casinos in several of the smaller cities. The minimum age is 18.

# Amazonia: Jungle Adventure and Exploration

The huge Amazon basin stretches across the continent to encompass parts of Colombia, Ecuador, Peru, Bolivia, and vast tracts of land in Brazil. In fact, if "Amazonia" were a country, it would be the ninth-largest in the world. Each minute the Amazon River discharges 3.4 million gallons of water into the Atlantic, about one-quarter of the world's freshwater supply. Originating in the Andes of Peru and Bolivia, the river is just over 4,000 miles long and is drained by 200 major tributaries, 17 of which are themselves more than 1,000 miles in length.

The ever-increasing exploitation of the riches of the Amazon rivers and forests — gold, petroleum, fine hardwoods, and more recently grazing land — not only threatens our environment, but makes it more difficult to get into untouched areas. In most cases, you will enjoy the atmosphere of the jungle and its flora, and you'll often have exceptional opportunities for bird watching, but due to population pressures, it is increasingly difficult to see the most exotic of jungle wildlife.

There is a sense of mystery and magic about the jungle for most of us. And as interest in the Amazon grows, so too do the number of travel programs within the Amazon basin. When selecting a jungle excursion, expect the worst — heat, humidity, and bugs — though you may be pleasantly surprised. Decide just how much "roughing it" you can realistically take; various levels are offered, so it's possible to pick a program that provides the level of comfort you prefer. Ask your travel agent questions and look carefully at brochures, which often have pictures of the accommodations offered. You'll probably want an English-speaking guide, so determine if that is guaranteed in the program you choose.

Once you've booked your jungle adventure, plan carefully. In many cases you will be asked to bring a duffel or weekender, and to leave other luggage behind in the company's office or your port city hotel. All clothing should be lightweight, preferably cotton or cotton blends. Bring long-sleeve shirts (for sun and bug protection) and long pants that meet your socks. Unless you don't mind getting bitten, shorts are not a good idea in lodges, but may be suitable for boat trips, where river breezes clear out the insects. Also bring along a light pullover sweater and a waterproof windbreaker or rain poncho. The weather sometimes can be surprisingly chilly in the higher jungle areas of Peru. Sneakers that you don't mind throwing away are excellent for most jungle excursions, since you'll likely be traipsing through mud. Other useful items include a bathing suit, a hat or cap, sunglasses, sunscreen, binoculars, insect repellent, and certainly a camera with plenty of high-speed film. A good sense of humor and an ability to roll with the punches is a prerequisite for travel in Amazonia, whether you're cruising by boat or staying in a lodge.

Since a number or travel programs encompass more than one country (and the Amazon area is rapidly becoming a single destination — one region that knows no national borders), our coverage of Amazon travel opportunities in this chapter are divided between boat-based and lodge-based excursions. As a cross-reference, check the DIRECTIONS sections for each country.

Aside from luxury cruise ship itineraries on the Brazilian Amazon (see *Traveling by Ship*, GETTING READY TO GO), there are a number of other passenger *boats* (as opposed to cruise ships) operating on the Amazon and its major tributaries. The majority of the Brazilian boats operate out of Manaus, about 1,300 miles upriver from the Atlantic. The *Tuna* is a typical 2-deck wooden riverboat refurbished to provide comfortable travel while exploring the nearby Rio Negro, Cuieriras River, and Cachoeira Creek, all pretty much off the beaten tourist track. It has 10 cabins, each with 2 berths, air conditioning, and a private bath (with river-water shower) and a crew of seven. The *Tuna*'s trips (3 and 6 nights) are intended to provide an in-depth look at ecology, botany, ethnology, and even tropical medicine. For reservations and further information, contact *Sáfari Ecologico* at 204 Rua Lima Bacuri in Manaus (phone: 92-233-6910).

The two-hulled catamaran-style *Pará* and *Amazonas* of the Brazilian *ENASA* line were built in the early 1980s specifically for Amazon cruising. Each carries 138 passengers in inside and outside cabins equipped with air conditioning, private baths, taped music, and even a telephone. There is also a bar, a swimming pool, an exercise area, a boutique, and particularly good food aboard. The ships cruise between Manaus and Belém on 4- and 6-night programs, both of which include a day on Marajó Island, near Belém. For reservations and further information contact *ENASA*, at 41 Av. Presidente Vargas in Belém (phone: 91-223-3011).

The S/M *Iguana* also sails out of Manaus. A double-deck boat, it was built in 1986 to accommodate 10 passengers in 5 air conditioned cabins, sharing 2 full and 2 half baths, on 2-night "Escape Safaris." Social life centers around the below-deck lounge and dining room and the sundeck. Canoes carry passengers into ecological preserves. There is time for fishing and swimming, and excellent meals are prepared aboard.

On the Peruvian Amazon, boat trips typically operate out of Iquitos. There are 3- and 6-night cruises on the M/V *Río Amazonas* between Iquitos and Leticia, Colombia, and Tabatinga, Brazil (virtually next to one another on the river). The boat, reconstructed in 1981, offers casual, solid comfort for 55 passengers in 20 air conditioned cabins with private baths and 6 non–air conditioned cabins with shared bath. Though registry and the crew of 18 are Peruvian, the ship is operated as part of the *Amazon Camp Tourist Service* owned by Paul Wright, a North American who lives in Iquitos. There are twice-daily excursions on foot and by launch, and delicious meals of freshly caught fish. The refurbished, air conditioned M/V *Arca* and her sister ship, M/V *Delfin* have similar itineraries, but with more on-board activities and fewer excursions. You can contact *Amazon Camp Tourist Service*'s US representatives: *South America Reps* (PO Box 39583, Los Angeles, CA 90039; phone: in California and Canada, 818-246-4816 or 800-477-4470; elsewhere in the US, 800-423-2791), and *LARC* (PO Box 1435,

## DIVERSIONS / Amazonia: Jungle Adventure and Exploration

Dundee, FL 33838; phone: 813-439-2118 or 800-327-3573). *Tara Tours* (6595 NW 36 St., Suite 306A, Miami Springs, FL 33166; phone: 305-871-1246 and 800-327-0080) also books packages on the river boats.

Also on the Iquitos scene is the 16-passenger, air conditioned *Amazon Explorer,* a ship that began operating in early 1989. Four-day cruises from Iquitos travel up the Amazon to the mouth of the Ucayali and Marañon rivers, then up the Río Tigre to explore the Pacaya-Samiria National Park. The boat stops frequently for jungle excursions, fishing, and swimming. The *Amazon Explorer* is operated by *Amazon Lodge & Safaris,* PO Box 5232, Lima, Peru (phone: 14-419194); or in the US, PO Box 238, Mamaroneck, NY 10543 (phone: 800-548-3931).

If you have a month to spare, *Amazon Explorers* is the only company to take travelers on an organized journey all the way from Pucallpa, Peru, to Belém, Brazil. Utilizing four different boats of varying levels of luxury, the itinerary covers extensive areas of virgin jungle, while also allowing for several "hotel breaks" during the trip. This company is a veteran operator, with some 35 years in Amazonia, and the source of a wide variety of other programs. Contact *Amazon Explorers* (PO Box 815, 499 Ernstron Rd., Parlin, NJ 08859; phone: in New Jersey, 908-721-2929; elsewhere, 800-631-5650).

The *Flotel Orellana* is a comfortable "floating hotel" that now cruises the Aguarico River in Ecuador. Accompanied by trained naturalist guides, stops are made for jungle walks or visits to native villages. Owned and operated by *Metropolitan Touring,* the *Flotel* has first class food and facilities, and is probably one of the best of its kind. (See *Ecuador,* DIRECTIONS.) Contact *Metropolitan Touring* (239 Av. Amazonas, Quito, Ecuador; phone: 2-560550; fax: 2-564655), or its US office, *Adventure Associates* (13150 Coit Rd., Suite 110, Dallas, TX 75240; phone: in Texas, 214-907-0414; elsewhere, 800-527-2500; fax: 214-783-1286). Another outfitter, *Turtle Tours,* Box 1147, 9446 Quail Trail, Carefree, AZ 85377 (phone: 602-488-3688; toll-free, 800-283-2334), offers trips from Quito to Cuenca to Cajas National Park in the Andes (3 days on horseback), then down into the Amazon basin, with an optional Galápagos extension. Expedition members hike in the jungle (and eat native dishes) to Indian villages where customs remain unaltered by outsiders.

There are number of jungle lodges in Amazonia. Typically they are constructed of local materials like bamboo and hardwoods, with soaring, thatched roofs that allow for natural ventilation. Many lodges offer rooms or bungalows with private baths and showers that use river water; some have shared baths. Although some lodges operate a generator a few hours a day to provide electricity for the rooms, most depend upon kerosene lamps and candles. Most are surprisingly comfortable considering the ongoing difficulty of assuring dependable supplies of bottled water and drinks, fresh vegetables, and meat. The few inconveniences are more than offset by the experience, particularly the night sounds, the lush foliage, and the absolute foreignness of it all.

Most lodges offer programs of 2 or 3 nights, though these can be extended. Organized activities focus on the flora, bird, and Indian life. Some excursions are made by foot and others in small open-air *pamicaris,* which range from glorified versions of the dugout canoe (motor added) to a much larger flat-bottom wooden boat with an outboard motor and shaded seating. Sometimes there are nighttime ventures for cayman viewing; sometimes fishing and swimming.

The per-day cost of the lodge normally includes all meals, transfers from the gateway or port city to and from the lodge, accommodations, and a program of excursions by foot and by boat, led by a lodge guide/naturalist. It is important to ascertain just what type of accommodations you can expect and whether the guide speaks only Spanish or is a multilingual naturalist.

Peru leads the way in offering a selection of excellent jungle lodges, clustered around Iquitos, Pucallpa, and Puerto Maldonado. Two companies (both US-owned and -operated) run the majority of lodges around Iquitos, *Explorama Tours,* which has been operating in and around Iquitos for more than 25 years, and *Amazon Camp Tourist Services*. The *Explorama Inn* is 25 miles (40 km) from Iquitos. Opened in 1985, it has the distinction of being the only jungle lodge in Peru directly on the Amazon River. A bit farther away (and a bit more rustic) is the *Explorama Lodge,* 50 miles (80 km) from Iquitos, on a small tributary called the Yanamono. Kerosene lamps light the lodge buildings, built with 10 to 15 sleeping rooms each. Covered thatch-roof sleeping facilities (with excellent shower and bathroom facilities) and open-hearth cooking are available at the *Explornapo Camp,* another 45 river miles (72 km) beyond the lodge. Many guests spend a week, combining a stay at several of these lodges. Contact *Explorama Tours* (340 Av. de la Marina, PO Box 446, Iquitos, Peru; phone: 94-235471), or its US representative, *Selective Hotel Reservations* (phone: in Massachusetts, 617-581-0844; throughout the US and Canada, 800-223-6764).

Near the camp is the recently opened *Amazon Center for Environmental Education and Research (ACEER)* set in the Amazon Biosphere Reserve, a 250,000-acre tract of rain forest. Founded by individuals and companies devoted to preserving rain forests, the center is a research facility as well as an environmental preserve established to educate and increase visitors' awareness about the Amazon's flora and fauna. To make this happen, the center has built a 1,200-foot-long canopied walkway above the rain forest. Workshops in English are offered by the center. For information, contact *ACEER,* 10 Environs Park, Helena, AL 35080 (phone: 800-255-8206).

The *Amazon Camp* is a 42-room lodge on a quiet tributary near Iquitos. Each kerosene-lighted room has private facilities; showers are taken in a separate building. *Club Amazonia* is the company's holiday concept — a jungle lodge dedicated to a more vacation-oriented program of activities (if fun at the beach, why not in the jungle?). Each of the 20 thatch-roofed bungalows has a bathroom and a private balcony overlooking the river. Both can be booked with *Amazon Camp Tourist Service* (159 Prospero, PO Box 549, Iquitos, Peru; phone: 94-233931), or with its US office, *Amazon Tours and Cruises* (8700 W. Flagler St., Suite 190, Miami, FL 33174; phone: 305-227-2266 or 800-423-2791; fax: 305-227-1880).

*Wilderness Expeditions* offers adventure programs to *Tambo Safari Inn, Anaconda Lodge,* and *Yarapa Reserve* (a lodge as well as an area), all outside Iquitos. Contact them at 310 Washington Ave. SW, Roanoke, VA 24016 (phone: 703-342-5630 or 800-323-3241).

There are daily flights into Pucallpa, about 550 miles (880 km) northeast of Lima. Thirty minutes away is *La Brisa Lodge* (phone: 6457-6551, or in Lima, 14-276720); in the US, call *LADATCO Tours* in Miami (phone: 305-854-8422; toll-free, 800-327-6162). It is situated on the shores of Lake Yarinacocha. Its buildings are on stilts and are interconnected by a series of raised walkways. This is one of the best spots to visit Indian villages as well as to share in the excitement of market day in Puerto Callao.

Thirty-five miles (56 km) from the tiny jungle town of Puerto Maldonado (reached by air service), the *Explorer's Inn* is located on the edge of the Tambopata Nature Reserve. Simple, comfortably-designed twin-bedded rooms are situated in seven large bungalows built entirely of native materials. Though each room has a private bath, there is no electricity and only river-temperature water for showers. The staff, however, does an admirable job of supply and service, considering the logistical nightmare it faces daily. The emphasis here is on natural history, particularly bird watching, the Tambopata being rated by ornithologists as one of the top spots in the world. Those working in the Tambopata have recorded more than 570 species of birds since 1976. You also have a good chance of seeing several species of monkeys, capybara, coati, brocket deer, and anteaters. Resident naturalists, mainly British, working on advanced research projects, act as guides for the inn's guests, and therein lies its uniqueness. Reservations: *Peruvian Safaris S.A.,* 1334 Av. Garcilaso de la Vega, Lima, or by writing to PO Box 10088, Lima 1, Peru (phone: 14-316330).

### DIVERSIONS / Amazonia: Jungle Adventure and Exploration

In the southeastern part of Peru, Manú National Park and the adjacent reserve is now a UNESCO Biosphere Reserve, because it protects an entirely unhunted, unlogged region of rain forest watershed. Rain falls mainly from November through April. Excursions into Manú are most commonly aimed at the most adventurous of travelers (see *Trekking, Backpacking, River Rafting, and Camping,* FOR THE BODY), but there is one lodge there. It is reached from Cuzco on a 10-hour drive, and then by 2 days of river travel, with night camping along the way (you must start the drive from Cuzco at midnight in order to meet the river trip). Guests can be flown out to Cuzco by small twin-engined private planes from Boca Manú, about 4 hours by boat from the lodge. The lodge itself overlooks a tranquil oxbow lake and is built entirely of mahogany. It is comfortable, but there are only outdoor latrines. For information, call the owner, Boris Gómez, at 84-231549 or 84-234793.

# For the Body

## Sinfully Sensuous Beaches

Whether you are used to the sharp cliffs dropping into the Pacific on the Oregon coast, the muscle beaches of Southern California, the boardwalk madness of New Jersey's Atlantic shore, or the serenity of the Outer Banks off the Carolina coast, South America is bound to radically change your perceptions of a beach. Somewhere, whether on the Atlantic, Pacific, or Caribbean coasts, visitors are likely to find a beach that's just right for sunning, swimming, body surfing, riding a surfboard, floating lazily, gathering shells, or playing Robinson Crusoe.

By and large, the climates and waters of Peru and Ecuador (on the Pacific), Colombia (Pacific and Caribbean), Venezuela (Caribbean), and Brazil (Atlantic) from Rio de Janeiro north are warm enough for most North Americans to bask and bathe in all year, although many South Americans insist that the winter months are just too cold for jumping into the water. (Even hedonistic *cariocas* — residents of Rio de Janeiro — shudder at the thought of plunging their much-cared-for tans into the shimmering Atlantic in October, although the thermometer still hugs the mid-80s F.) Except for the northern desert beaches around Arica and Iquique, Chile's coastal waters are chilled by the icy Humboldt Current that sweeps north from Antarctica. Here, as in Argentina, Uruguay, and southern Brazil, visitors need to plan their visits around the warmer spring and summer months (late October through March). Remember that not all of South America is sunny and tropical. (For a full description of climate and terrain, see *What's Where* and *When to Go*, GETTING READY TO GO.)

There are innumerable varieties of beach topography — white, gray, black, yellow, fine grain and coarse grain sand, and foliage (especially coconut palms). Remember that the sun is particularly strong near the equator. Bring plenty of sunscreen to protect you from the ultraviolet rays.

Listed below are some of the choice spots on the continent. Some are very popular; others, little-known gems. They are by no means the only beaches. If you have a taste for adventure, ask some questions and use many of the following spots as jumping-off points for sniffing out new beach sites, often just beyond that next cove.

### ARGENTINA

**Mar del Plata** – December through March are the warmest and driest months at this world-famous resort of tree- and flower-filled plazas that is truly the center of Argentina's beach life. About 240 miles (385 km) south of Buenos Aires, its population of 500,000 easily swells to more than 3 million during peak season, so make reservations well in advance, whether you plan to bed down in luxurious hotels or less expensive *pensiónes* (boardinghouses). The 5 miles of clean, sandy beaches — including fashionable Playa Grande, Playa Perla, and Punta Iglesia — can get crowded at times, but it's always easy to find a more secluded spot by walking a bit.

**Costa Atlántida (Atlantic Coast)** – North of Mar del Plata, and considerably less crowded, the beaches still offer plenty of conveniences, good fishing, and swimming.

Best along this stretch are Villa Gesell, with beautiful dunes, pine forests, and friendly, small hotels; Pinamar, rapidly becoming a fashionable resort town with casinos; Miramar, another fast-paced vacation center with high-rise hotels, golf courses, and casinos; and Necochea, with about 15 miles of the best and cleanest beachfront.

**Pehuén-Có** – Some 43 miles (69 km) southeast of Bahía Blanca, this is just one of many spots on a huge stretch of an isolated, undeveloped shore, with shady pine trees and space to camp.

## BRAZIL

With almost 4,450 miles of coastline, the climate affecting Brazil's beach life exhibits a bit of variability. In the south, the hottest months (January to March) are also the wettest, and while the rain is never extreme, the heat can rise to well over 100F (37C) around Rio. This is the period when the beaches are most crowded. July and August are a bit cooler — not too cold for gringos, but cool enough to keep Brazilians home and the beaches relatively uncrowded. Along more northerly coasts, the temperatures are invariably even hotter throughout the year, so visits do not need to be planned around a calendar. Rain is intense when it comes, but its duration generally is short.

**Rio de Janeiro** – Copacabana and Ipanema are probably the best-known stretches of sand in the world. They are crowded in midsummer (December through February), and quite a few residents head for the more secluded beaches at Cabo Frio, Búzios, and Angra dos Reis. Not far from the city center — but far enough to make them quieter and cleaner than the better-known beaches — are Barra and Gávea. For a complete description of Rio's beaches and Cabo Frio, see *Rio de Janeiro*, THE CITIES.

**Itaipauaçú** – About 25 miles (40 km) north of Rio's Niterói Bridge, it has lots of empty, open, sandy beaches, good for camping. Swimming can be dangerous, as the surf is quite rough, but there are some great rocks from which to dive. There are a couple of little restaurants, but no hotels.

**Saquarema** – Seventy miles (113 km) east of Rio de Janeiro, this is *the* surfing beach, where international competitions are often held. The gigantic waves break on huge, wide, white beaches, where visitors can camp. There also are a number of small hotels and restaurants.

**Florianópolis** – This island state capital, about 433 miles (693 km) south of São Paulo, is full of serene bays and shores. Get to Praia Inglês on the far side of the island for greater privacy and good camping.

**Búzios** – The look and feel of a small fishing village remains, but whitewashed, tile-roofed Búzios is gaining recognition around the world for offering a choice of 17 fine beaches, a laid-back lifestyle, fine dining, and intriguing small inns. Just 110 miles (176 km) east of Rio (a 2½-hour drive), this is a favorite weekend haunt of wealthy *cariocas*. Among the recommended cozy inns here are *Auberge de l'Hermitage, Casas Brancas,* and *Pousada Moana, Le Relais la Boie,* and *Byblos.* The *Búzios Bauen Club* and the *Nas Rocas Club* are *Club Med*–style "villages," offering an international atmosphere and a variety of sports.

**São Sebastião** – Heading north from Santos, São Paulo's seaport, on the superb Rio-Santos highway, are plenty of unpopulated beaches where the tropical mountains meet the sea. São Sebastião, a small fishing village about 125 miles (200 km) north of Santos, is one of the prettiest along the route. Hotels along the route are modest. *Recanto dos Passaros* has a swimming pool, sauna, and a restaurant. 822 Av. Guarda-Mor Lobo Viana (phone: 124-522046).

**Angra dos Reis** – Fortunately, the completion of a nuclear power plant a few miles farther south hasn't destroyed this enticing spot about 120 miles (192 km) south of Rio. (The plant isn't operating because it was discovered not to have been built according to environmentally safe specifications!) The coast road twists around numerous small bays with quiet beaches, all within the arms of the immense Bay of Kings, which is dotted with hundreds of tropical islands, many easily reached by boat. Three hotels belonging to the family-owned Frade group are the best spots to stay along this route. Closest to Rio is the splendid *Porto Bello* (phone: 21-789-1485; in Rio de Janeiro, 21-267-7375; in the US, 800-544-5503), whose airy rooms open right onto the beach. Guests gather to dine and socialize under a huge open-air pavilion similiar in style to a Mexican *palapa* (see *Luxury Resorts and Special Havens,* DIVERSIONS). Farther south lie the clifftop *Portogalo* (phone: 243-651022; in Rio de Janeiro, 21-267-7375; in the US, 800-544-5503) and the beachside *Hotel do Frade* (phone: 234-65212; in Rio de Janeiro, 21-267-7375; in the US, 800-544-5503). At each hotel, schooners take guests for cruises among the islands, and there's also tennis, golf (at *Hotel do Frade*), horseback riding, windsurfing, and scuba diving.

**Salvador (Bahia)** – Terrific tawny sands surround the city, but beware of crime resulting from the extreme poverty in the area. See *Salvador (Bahia),* THE CITIES.

**Porto Seguro** – This beach, 440 miles (704 km) south of Salvador (Bahia), has become *the* spot for trendy young Brazilians. It is an old colonial town, with miles and miles of empty beaches and lodgings in all price ranges, and dance halls where visitors learn the sensual lambada. Two coral reefs keep the light blue water very calm and warm. Camping is possible almost everywhere, but there's maximum privacy out of town toward Santa Cruz Cabralía. The Franciscan monastery school puts up people for free when classes are not in session.

Leave town in the opposite direction and cross the bay to find more beautiful, uninhabited, white, sandy beaches below the bluffs of Nossa Senhora de Ajuda, an old, quaint place with great views of the ocean below and full of fishermen.

**Trancoso** – Hike another 11 miles (18 km) down deserted beaches, past red cliffs and up the bluff, to reach this splendid little fishing village with a population of just a few hundred. No lodgings, electricity, or restaurants, just a tiny store, some marvelous residents, gentle waves, and a jungle environment that's fine for camping. It is a good place for relaxing and learning how simply some people can live. Carry supplies with you so you can continue on to more isolated sands.

**Boa Viagem** – Eleven miles of clean, white sand beaches washed by warm Atlantic waters, just south of Recife. An up-and-coming resort area presently being promoted in the US, the beach is delightful for strolling, swimming, and people watching. The numerous hotels provide every amenity. It's usually possible to bargain for a ride on a *jangada,* the local fishermen's wooden sailing raft.

**Maceió** – Only Brazilians seem to know about the miles of clean, uncrowded beaches that surround this growing city between Salvador (Bahia) and Recife. Reasonably priced, pleasant spots that are recommended are the *Do Sol* (phone: 82-231-5577) and the *Jatiúca* hotels (phone: 82-231-2555).

**Itamaracá** – Near Recife, this is a somewhat touristy little fishing island town, with a few hotels and restaurants serving very good seafood. Weekend houses of the wealthy stand beside fishermen's shacks. A great reef beyond the horizon keeps the water placid along the narrow, but not particularly clean, beach. Camping is permitted anywhere, but for wider, cleaner beaches (and much more privacy), walk to the end of the island opposite the fort and look for a dirt road that heads up a bluff through the trees beyond the last house. This leads to a bay where, during the day, a ferryman carries workers from the coconut grove back and forth across the water in his canoe. Carry supplies you will need and ride his canoe to the other side, where you can camp under the coconut palms or in an empty hut. There are miles of gloriously empty beaches to walk down and plenty of coconuts to eat and drink.

**Natal** – Some of the most unusual sand formations in the country are near this city. Huge dunes, just right for rolling down, have been formed by the wind (many hotels and agencies rent dune buggies). There are no deluxe hotels in Natal, but the *Vilo do Mar,* right on the beach, 5½ miles (9 km) from town, comes close (phone: 84-222-3755).

**Morro Branco** – Multicolored craggy cliffs frame huge sand dunes on this lovely beach about 50 miles (80 km) southeast of Fortaleza. Dine on just-caught fish at tiny beachside bar/restaurants.

**Canoa Quebrada** – This tiny fishing town, between Natal and Fortaleza, is known for its outstanding blue waters and friendly natives, who are happy to take in guests and show them a bit of their way of life.

**Alcântara** – Another small fishing village, it is best reached by ferry from São Luís. Outside town is some of the best beachcombing in Brazil. Little shacks belonging to the fishermen can be rented for next to nothing. Old Portuguese ruins nearby provide something to focus on when the sun begins to fall.

**Ilha do Mosqueiro** – This fantastic, jungle-covered island near Belém has tiny hotels, some villas, and plenty of clean, sandy beaches.

## CHILE

**Arica, Antofagasta** – Unlike most of Chile's waters, these Pacific beaches in the northern Atacama Desert are lapped by warm waters and are perfect for swimming year-round. In the resort city of Arica, the best beaches are El Laucho and La Lisera, with their clean dark sand. Waterfront development farther south on the coast has left Antofagasta with the nation's longest — 12 miles — string of beaches and promenades. Bahía Inglesa, a bay at the port city of Caldera south of Antofagasta, offers good beaches for sunning and swimming year-round.

**Viña del Mar** – Not only is this the foremost beach resort in Chile, but it is one of the very best in all of South America, a refuge for thousands of tourists, both Chilean and international, during the spring and summer (October through March). A graceful town of flowers, trees, parks, and palaces, mixed with modern buildings, Viña also hosts many cultural events, including an annual international music festival that lures European jet-setters. There is a casino, one of the best racetracks in Chile, and hotels in every price range. Steep bluffs rise behind the city, and its 10-mile stretch of sandy shoreline includes the gray, sandy beaches of El Recreo and Caleta Abraca, crowded in spots, but with enough open space to move around. The most popular beach, however, is Reñaca.

**Santiago Province** – All the beaches here have wonderful climates in the summer and, like the rest of Chile, waters cooled by the Humboldt Current. Most are popular with Chilean vacationers and can get pretty crowded at the height of the season. At San Sebastián, Cartagena, Las Cruces, Isla Negra, El Tabo, and El Quisco, the sand ranges from gray to yellow to white. Another beach, Algarrobo, is exceptionally peaceful, and its waters are quite good for snorkeling and water skiing.

## COLOMBIA

**Parque Tairona, near Santa Marta** – The equatorial climate does not vary too much during the course of the year. December through April and July through September are the driest months on the Pacific as well as on the Caribbean coast. Parque Tairona is a national park on the jungle-bordered Caribbean coast in the shadow of the Sierra Nevada. Its many beaches are filled with little warm coves. Cañaverales Beach has freshwater showers, palm trees, and dangerous currents. Next door, Punta de la Concha offers some of the best snorkeling in the Caribbean. From Cañaverales visitors can hike for 2 hours through the humid jungle and arrive at Finca Martínez, a private beach with crystal Caribbean waters. Huts with hammocks and meals are available, and it's also possible to pitch a tent under the coconut palms. It's a good starting point for a hike along the coast to some really fine isolated beaches.

**Tolú** – This small fishing town south of Cartagena is on the magnificent Caribbean Gulf of Morrosquillo. Its miles of white sand and warm, blue waters are perfect for fishing and swimming. It is an out-of-the-way spot with some decent accommodations.

**San Andrés and Providencia** – Both of these Caribbean islands are far from

## ECUADOR

**Salinas** – The beaches and fishing offshore have made this one of Ecuador's best-known resorts. It is the haunt of affluent Ecuadorans, perhaps because of the *Copa Galápagos Regatta* to the islands of the same name that Salinas hosts in even-numbered years. It is busy both day and night — there's yachting, deep sea fishing, and two crescent-shaped beaches for those who like sun activities. In the evening, you can try your luck at the casino at the *Casino Miramar* hotel (on the *malecón)* or go to the *Barba Negra* disco (a block from the yacht club).

**Bahía de Caraquez** – Near Manta, in the province of Manabí, some 150 miles (240 km) north of Guayaquil, there are lovely stretches of beach here. Appealing mostly to Ecuadoran tourists, there are a few rustic accommodations and good spots for camping. A small first class hotel, *La Piedra,* is located on the beach (phone: 2-690418 or 2-560550 in Quito). There also are nice beaches in neighboring San Vicente.

**Atacames** – In the north, some 15 miles (24 km) south of Esmeraldas, this beach is primarily popular with Ecuadorans. Camping is easy under the palms, though somewhat crowded on weekends. Now there are a number of tourist-oriented facilities, including moderately priced, fully equipped beach cabanas. Recommended are the *Hostería Puerto Esmeraldas* (phone: 2-242694) and the *Castelnuovo* hotel (phone: 2-513588 or 2-512744). The surf is often good at Castelnuovo Beach, and local seafood dishes are delicious.

## PERU

Beaches in Peru range from a few chic resorts to wild stretches of beautiful sand, perfect for camping. Punta Sal, the country's most popular resort, is located near Tumbes in the north. There are individual beachhouses to rent, and the hotel restaurant serves fresh fish daily. Reservations should be made well in advance through *LARC* in the US (phone: 800-327-3573) or with *Peruvian Safaris* (1334 Av. Garcilaso de la Vega, PO Box 10088, Lima 1; phone: 14-313047 or 14-316330); fares should include round-trip air travel to and from Tumbes, plus a resort transfer car on arrival. Just a few miles away in Mancora, *Las Pocitas Beach Club* (phone: 14-426978 in Lima) offers ocean-front rooms, fishing, diving, and sailing. And farther south down the coast is Huanchaco, near Trujillo. Actually a fishing village, this is a good spot for sunning and surfing. Extremely popular with *limeños* is Ancón, 1 hour north of Lima. On weekends, day-trippers jam the public-access beaches here, so those who prize private relaxation should stick to weekdays. An hour south of Lima is the *Santa María Beach Club,* a fine day trip. More convenient are El Silencio or Punta Hermosa, with modest (but good) oceanside restaurants. Farther south, near the Paracas Wildlife Reserve, the *Paracas* (phone: 34-221736 in Pisco, 14-464865 or 14-465079 in Lima) is a charming small garden hotel. Lovely white sand beaches are a short drive away, and transportation is available on request.

## URUGUAY

**Montevideo** – This city has many tranquil beaches, of which Carrasco is the trendiest. Montevideo's best beach weather occurs between December and April although beach lovers here come for the sun, not swimming, despite new water treatment facilities aimed at cleaning up past pollution problems. (See *Montevideo,* THE CITIES.)

**Atlántida** – To the east of the capital, surrounded by magnificent pine and eucalyptus forests, this serene water resort has a small casino, tennis, a golf course, and fine fishing. Las Toscas and Parque de la Plata are its two best beaches.

**Piriápolis** – To the east of Atlántida, set around a horseshoe bay near some pleasant hills and rock gardens, this town has a casino, good restaurants, fishing off Punta Fría, an excellent swimming beach (second in popularity only to those of Punta del Este), and comfortable facilities.

**Punta del Este** – The internationally famous resort stands on a peninsula, with picturesque pine and eucalyptus trees shading white sand. The calm waters of Playa Mansa (on the bay) are excellent for swimming. Playa Brava (on the ocean) is good for surfing. La Barra de Maldonado, a beach to the east of the city, offers both a protected area for swimming and waves for surfers. From here, explore the coast north to Brazil. (See *Luxury Resorts and Special Havens,* DIVERSIONS, and *Uruguay,* DIRECTIONS.)

## VENEZUELA

**Choroní** – This colonial village on the coast a few miles from Cata is in the heart of a string of gorgeous palm-lined crescents of white sand beaches. The best — like Chuao — are reached by outboard launches that leave from the waterfront at Choroní.

**Los Roques** – The most pristine — and remote — beaches in all of Venezuela are found in this cluster of tiny cays 100 miles (160 km) offshore from La Guaira. White sand, turquoise waters, and coral reefs await the adventurous sun worshiper who is willing to get there by chartered yacht, plane, or helicopter (see *Venezuela,* DIRECTIONS).

**Morrocoy National Park** – Reached by launch from Tucacas or Chichiriviche, this park of coral reef islands is a paradise for snorklers and divers. Of the 7 major cays, Sombrero is the most popular. One side is crowded with fast boats and beautiful people; the other is more peaceful. Camping is permitted on all the cays.

**Playa Colorado/Playa Arapita** – Near the resort city of Puerto La Cruz, about 40 minutes by plane (or 5 hours by car) from Caracas, these beaches are magical. Most of the area is part of Mochima National Park, and thereby protected from development. There are several little islands offshore, and visitors can hire a local fisherman to provide the transportation to a day on a deserted isle.

**Margarita Island** – Smooth Caribbean shores at their most seductive bring Venezuelans here by the thousands. The big draw is the unique combination of white-on-white beach, mangrove lagoons, and duty-free shopping. The most isolated sections can be found in the north and in the mangrove lagoons along the Macanao Peninsula to the west (watch for the scarlet ibis and exotic seashells). The most popular spot is the Porlamar resort center to the southwest. El Agua is the recommended beach. Although the climate does not vary much, expect some rain from May through December. And Beware, mosquitoes can be bothersome. (See *Venezuela,* DIRECTIONS.)

# Best Depths: Snorkeling and Scuba

The clearest, warmest waters are found off South America's northern coast, abutting the Caribbean Sea. Here are abundant coral reefs and tropical fish, as well as some intriguing shipwrecks, especially off the Colombian and Venezuelan shores.

Diving equipment is available for rent at resorts in Colombia, Venezuela, and Panama, but such facilities are nonexistent in some of the key diving spots, so be prepared to bring your own gear. Snorkelers should remember to wear rubber-soled shoes if they plan to roam around shallow-water coral reefs.

Since scuba diving requires skill and knowledge to use high-pressure cylinders of compressed air and regulators that control the flow of oxygen during descent and ascent, reputable diving shops and expedition leaders require proof of the successful completion of a diver's certification course (upon the conclusion of which a "C" card is issued). It's easy to find a course in the US. Length of the course depends on the instructor; in order to get a "C" card, a person has to have had 11 hours of class time and 17 hours in the water. For information, contact: the *National Association of Underwater Instructors* (*NAUI;* 4650 Arrow Hwy., Suite F-1, PO Box 14650, Montclair, CA 91763; phone: 714-621-5801); the *Professional Association of Diving Instructors* (*PADI;* 1251 E. Dyer Rd., Suite 100, Santa Ana, CA 92705; phone: 714-540-7234); or your *YMCA/YWCA.*

For information and advice concerning fitness or preparation for diving, contact the *Divers Alert Network* (*DAN;* Box 3823, Duke University Medical Center, Durham, NC 27710; phone: 919-684-2948; fax: 919-490-6630). *DAN* also has a 24-hour hotline for diving emergencies (phone: 919-684-8111).

Panama has three decompression chambers. They are located in Gatún (phone: 507-435368), at the Panama Canal (phone: 507-525114), and at the US Army base in Panama City (phone: 507-856114).

**ARGENTINA:** A good place for organized scuba diving is Puerto Madryn, in the heart of the Welsh country in southern Argentina. During the first week of February, a diving and underwater fishing championship is held here. Remember to bring your own gear. A well-regarded local operator for diving is *Aguatours* on Muelle (Pier) Piedrabuena in Puerto Madryn (phone: 965-71001; in Buenos Aires, 1-322-6798; fax in Buenos Aires, 1-804-1514).

**BRAZIL:** Scuba is popular along the resort-studded coastline east and south of Rio de Janeiro, from Cabo Frio, 100 miles (160 km) east, to Angra dos Reis, 120 miles (192 km) south. The main spots are Búzios and Cabo Frio, about 2 hours by bus or car from Rio, and Angra, 3 hours to the south, centered around the *Portogalo* (phone: 21-267-7375) hotel. The big lure of the Cabo Frio area is the large number of wrecks; at least 80 have been charted. The water here is cold — in the 70s F — and clear. Bring your own equipment and a wet suit. *Brasiltrek Expeditions* (Box 94514, Rio de Janeiro; phone: 21-770-1726; fax: 21-262-6715) specializes in adventure programs in the state of Rio that include snorkeling and scuba.

The US-based expert on the entire Brazilian scuba scene is *Brazilian Scuba and Land Tours* (5254 Merrick Rd., Massapequa, NY 11758; phone: 516-797-2133 or 800-722-0205). The company maintains its own dive shop operation in Cabo Frio, and a shop and a 50-foot dive boat in Fortaleza, to the north. Bill Smith, the owner, calls the waters around Fortaleza "the new Bahamas — one of the best dive spots in the world." The area benefits from the swirl of equatorial currents from Africa, which produce heavy concentrations of fish. Visibility and light are excellent, even at 100 feet deep. The prime northern diving season is from January through July. With water temperatures in the low 80s F year-round, there is no need for a wet suit.

There's also good diving and surfing in the Bay of Dolphins off the island of Fernando de Noronha. Fly there from Recife, João Pessoa, or Natal for a day's outing, or stay in the *Posada de Esmeralda do Atlântico* (Alameida do Bodró; phone: 81-549-1138), a 34-room hotel on the island. Unfortunately, because of the hotel's size, it is frequently difficult to obtain reservations and there is a 7-day minimum stay requirement.

**COLOMBIA:** Cartagena, the walled city from which the Spanish colonials shipped precious metals home to the royal court, was a prime target for pirates. Eight miles offshore, there's a sunken Spanish supply ship with cannon still aboard. Jim Buttgen runs boat trips in the area. Contact *CaribeTours* (phone: 53-642966 or 53-641221). Also try *Caribe Divers* in the *Caribe* hotel (phone: 536-50155, ext. 783). This group offers full-day snorkeling tours to the nearby Rosario Islands.

San Andrés and Providencia, two tiny Colombian islands in the Caribbean that are closer to the Caribbean coast of Nicaragua than to their mother country, have palm-studded beaches and turquoise waters. San Andrés has great snorkeling. Nearby Johnny Key is known for lots of splendidly hued fish, and Haines Key for sea urchins. (Be sure to wear rubber-soled shoes for protection against reefs and wrecks.)

Conditions on the island can be primitive, but the *Bahía Marina* resort can supply craft and equipment. Write to *Bahía Marina Resort* (PO Box 597, San Andrés, Colombia; phone: 57-811-23539). The island is only 8 miles long and 2 miles wide, so what few hotels exist get booked ahead. Reservations are essential for visits in December, January, *Easter Week,* July, and August. The *Royal Abacoa* (phone: 57-811-24044) and the *El Dorado* (phone: 57-811-24155) hotels both have small casinos and some air conditioned rooms. Providencia is much farther out and requires an additional flight from San Andrés, but it's worth the ride for beautiful scuba diving.

**ECUADOR:** The Pacific waters contain the breeding and feeding grounds of hundreds of species of fish, undersea archaeological sites, and several wrecks from the days when the Galápagos Islands were a pirate stronghold. Guayaquil and Salinas are headquarters for all water sports. *See and Sea Travel Service* organizes 2-week diving trips to the Galápagos Islands. Escorted by a naturalist, divers explore pinnacles and caves where starfish, conch, anemone, whale, sunfish, and sea lion live. The expedition includes visits to the Charles Darwin Biologicial Research Station. The price does not include equipment. For information, contact *See and Sea Travel Service* (50 Francisco St., Suite 205, San Francisco, CA 94133; phone: in California, 415-434-3400; in other states, 800-348-9778). *Tropical Adventures* has scuba expeditions to the Galápagos that include a stop in Quito, a week on a motor sailer around the islands. Price includes use of equipment. Contact the group (111 2nd N., Seattle, WA 98109; phone: 206-441-3483; toll-free, 800-247-3483) for more information. *Lost World Adventures* (1189 Autumn Ridge Dr., Marietta, GA 30086; phone: in Atlanta, 404-971-8586; toll-free, 800-999-0558; fax: 404-977-3095) can organize 1-week dive trips to the Galápagos for a minimum of four people. *Galápagos Network* (phone: 305-592-2294 or 800-633-7972; fax: 305-592-6394), which is affiliated with *SAETA* airlines, operates the M/V *Vertigo,* an 8-passenger dive boat. Yachts also are for hire on Santa Cruz Island in the Galápagos for week-long diving trips. (However, take note that officials discourage novices from diving in the Galápagos because of strong currents, cold water temperatures, rocks, and pinnacles.) Be sure though to allow several days to make the arrangements. You may want to purchase the *South American Explorers Club* report ($6.50 for non-members, $4.50 for members) on the Galápagos Islands; it has all the specifics on boats, owners, tours, and even sample charter contracts. The club has a branch in Quito (1254 Toledo, La Floresta; its mailing address is Apartado 21-431 Eloy Alfaro; phone: 2-566076; in the US, 607-277-0488). Annual membership in the organization is $30; it includes a 1-year subscription to the quarterly magazine *South American Explorer.*

**PANAMA:** Good fresh water and salt water diving are available in Panama and it's possible to dive in the Atlantic and Pacific oceans in the same day! Gatún Lake, the second-largest artificial lake in the world, has an underwater town and train. Bocas Del Toro, Isla Mamey, Isla Grande, and the San Blas Islands on the Atlantic Coast all have beautiful coral reefs, and Portobelo has excellent coral and wreck diving with dive shops that fill tanks and rent equipment. On the Pacific Coast there is good diving and snorkeling off Corba, Taboga, and Contadora islands. *Buzo* (phone: 507-618003) and *ScubaPanama* (phone: 507-613841) have dive shops in Panama City and Portobelo. The main resort hotel on Contadora Island is the *Caesar Park Contadora* (phone: 507-695269; fax: 507-694721), 20 minutes by air from Panama City's Paitilla Airport in the Pearl Island archipelago.

**584 DIVERSIONS / Sailing**

A good source of information and possible dive buddies is the *YMCA* (phone: 507-281247). Remember, Panama has three decompression chambers.

**VENEZUELA:** The best diving and snorkeling in the country center around Tucacas and Chichiriviche, gateways to the Morrocoy National Marine Park. This spectacular area is only a 3½-hour drive west of Caracas. It has hundreds of reefs and tiny offshore cays with palm trees. *Lost World Adventures* (1189 Autumn Ridge Dr., Marietta, GA 30066 (phone: in Atlanta, 404-971-8586; toll-free, 800-999-0558; fax: 404-977-3095) operates dive programs in the cays in conjunction with veteran diver Mike Osborn. Visitors can stay in decent hotels in Tucacas, or arrange with a local fisherman to be deposited on one of the tiny islets that's perfect for camping. A few miles beyond is the beach resort of Chichiriviche, which boasts the better hotels and also serves as a departure point for the cays.

Los Roques, a tiny atoll in the Caribbean, can be reached by boat from La Guaira, or by air from several spots on the mainland, via *Aerotuy*. There is a small hotel, but many divers arrange for day trips (about $120) with local travel agencies. *Lost World Adventures* (see above) can arrange an all-inclusive package featuring a live-aboard charter for Los Roques diving.

# Sailing

Opportunities for chartering yachts are somewhat limited in South America compared to Mexico and the Caribbean islands. The most extensive facilities are on the Caribbean coast, where water sports facilities are more fully developed. But the prime lure of sailing in these waters is that it allows travel at a very leisurely pace into open blue sea, anchorages alongside tiny, palm-filled islands, and exploration of the coasts from an entirely personal perspective.

Keep in mind that during peak season (November through March), chartering a boat at any of the major resorts is going to be more expensive than in the off-season. However, in Argentina, southern Brazil, and Uruguay, the fall and winter months offer far from optimum sailing conditions.

**ARGENTINA:** It is possible to rent small sailboats in Bariloche for trips on the larger lakes, such as Nahuel Huapi. For information, contact the national tourism office (883 Av. Santa Fe, Buenos Aires; phone: 1-312-2253). The *Club Naútico* (phone: 23-800323), in the super-plush seaside resort of Mar del Plata, rents yachts and sailboats.

**BOLIVIA:** There are two ways to sail the world's highest navigable lake, Lake Titicaca. One is to bring your own boat, as did Welsh sailor Tristan Jones in 1974. (He sailed up the Amazon, then hauled the boat by road to the Peruvian side of the lake, where he launched it — to the great wonder of the Quechua-speaking Indians.) Unless you have many free months, this is not a very feasible plan. But boats may be chartered (with a skipper-guide who knows the inlets and islands of the lake) at Copacabana. Stroll down to the dock and ask around. There is a yacht club — *Yacht Club Boliviano* (phone: 2-811669) — in the town of Huatajata. You also can rent boats in the town of Chúa on the lake.

**BRAZIL:** The renowned *Iate Club do Rio de Janeiro* (Rio Yacht Club, 333 Av. Pasteur; phone: 21-295-4482), is in the heart of the city, directly beneath Pão de Açúcar (Sugar Loaf Mountain) in the Botafogo Inlet. Sailboats can be chartered for cruises from the city's marina through *Glória* (phone: 21-265-0797), *Captain's Yacht Charters* (phone: 21-252-1155), *Ponto Mar* (phone: 21-266-6066), or *Brasiltrek Expeditions* (phone: 21-779-1726) south to Angra dos Reis and the Green Coast, which is speckled with dozens of small islands, of which Ilha Grande is the best known. Numerous charter boats are found at Cabo Frio and Búzios, weekend resorts for wealthy *cariocas*. Contact the *Strelitzia Travel Agency* (Praça Dom Pedro II) for information or wander down to the docks at Rua Jonas Garcia in Búzios. About 6 miles (10 km) out of town, there is a marina at Arraial do Cabo on Anjos Beach and Armação de Búzios. At Interlagos, outside São Paulo, boats may be rented at the marina at *Parque de Guarapiranga* (no phone).

In Salvador (Bahia), no individual rentals are available, but a tour of the bay, on large schooners that carry between 20 and 30 passengers, can be arranged. Contact the Bahiatursa office at the airport or at the *Mercado Modelo*.

Sailing and windsurfing are two of the many sports enjoyed at *Club Med*'s resorts on Itaparica Island opposite Salvador and at Angra dos Reis. One- and 2-week all-inclusive vacations can be booked by calling 800-CLUB MED.

**COLOMBIA:** Sailing is popular in Colombia's Caribbean waters, and there are a number of spots where boats can be rented. On San Andrés, the small island far off the northwest coast, all sorts of charters and equipment can be rented from *Bahía Marina Resort* (PO Box 597, San Andrés, Colombia; phone: 811-3539 or 811-3657). Then cruise to Bolívar Key, about 45 miles northwest of San Andrés, and Albuquerque Key, 15 miles east. In Cartagena, sailboats of all sizes are available for rent. From Cali, sailing and motorboat tours on the Cauca River, where egrets and other birds come to nest at sunset, are popular. The *Club Náutico* in Cali sponsors this; arrange a tour through your hotel or travel agent. There also are facilities for sailing at the Calima Reservoir, near Cali. Lake Tominé, at Guatavita, about an hour's drive from Bogotá, has sailboats for rent at its marina. In Cartagena, a Canadian sailor named Norman makes daily trips to the nearby Rosario Islands on his 60-ft. schooner, the *Silva*. Ask for him at the *Club Náutico* in Manga.

**ECUADOR:** For races, regattas, fishing, cruising, and simply enjoying the company of the yachting crowd, the only place in Guayaquil is the *Yacht Club* on the *malecón* (phone: 4-515225). The *Casino Miramar* hotel in Salinas (phone: 4-772115) caters to sailors. The *Punta Carnero Inn* in Punta Carnero (phone: 4-785450) has a fleet of Sunfish, cruisers, and fishing boats.

Private yachts that carry from 4 to 40 passengers can be chartered to tour the Galápagos Islands, 600 miles west of the Ecuadoran coast. National Park regulations require a crew and certified naturalist to accompany each charter vessel. Visitors will have time for swimming, sailing (although a crew does the actual navigating), and hiking, along with fascinating hours spent close to the unique wildlife, which differs from island to island. A small flotilla of luxury yachts is available from *Galápagos Inc.* (7800 Red Rd., Suite 112, South Miami, FL 33143; phone: in Florida, 305-665-0841; in other states, 800-327-9854; fax: 305-661-1457). Five yachts sailing from San Cristóbal are represented by *Tumbaco Inc.* (PO Box 1036, Punta Gorda, FL 33950; phone: in Florida, 813-637-4660; in other states, 800-247-2925). *Adventure Associates* (13150 Coit Rd., Dallas, TX 75240; phone: in Texas, 214-907-0414; in other states, 800-527-2500; fax: 214-783-1286) offers a wide range of yachts, including the newly refitted 36-passenger *Delfin II* and the 34-passenger, 166-foot *Isabella II*. *Inca Floats* (1311 63rd St., Emeryville, CA 94608; phone: 510-420-1550) is another good source for charter excursions.

**PERU:** Guest privileges are extended to members of other sailing clubs at *Lima Regatta* (Chorrillos, Lima; phone: 14-672545); *Unión Regatta* (Plaza Gálvez, La Punta; phone: 14-290286); *Yacht Club Peruano* (Muelle Darsena, Callao; phone: 14-290775); and *Yacht Club de Ancón* (Malecón de Ancón; phone: 14-883071).

**VENEZUELA:** Sailboats are for rent at the *Margarita Concorde*, the luxury hotel at Porlamar on Margarita Island. Write to them (Apartado 570, Porlamar; phone: 95-613333). In Puerto La Cruz, try the *Golden Rainbow Maremares* resort (Complejo Turístico El Morro; phone: 81-813022; in Caracas, 2-562-6042) for boats. Marina Mar

**586 DIVERSIONS / Tennis**

next to the *Macuto Sheraton,* in Caraballeda, on the beach outside Caracas, rents Sunfish or catamarans (phone: 31-527097). The *Caracas Hilton International* (phone: 2-571-2322) will arrange boat rentals upon request.

There are smaller marinas at Morrocoy, Chichiriviche, and Maracaibo. Morrocoy has delightful cays and tropical scenery.

# Tennis

Tennis courts, ranging from adequate to excellent, can be found in all of South America's major cities and luxury resorts. With the exception of Argentina, this sport is not as popular in South America as it is in the US, and there are very few package tours designed specifically for serious tennis players. But if you regard travel as an opportunity to sample different courts in different settings, there is enough of a selection around South America to justify taking along a tennis racquet.

**ARGENTINA:** Public tennis courts are found at Parque Norte on Cantilo and Güiraldes streets in the Costanera Norte section of Buenos Aires (phone: 1-784-9653). The tourist office here can provide directions to other city parks with courts. Buenos Aires's *Sheraton* hotel (1225 San Martín; phone: 1-311-6311) also has courts.

**BOLIVIA:** For players in truly excellent physical shape, the challenge of the world's highest court awaits in La Paz: *Club de Tenis La Paz* (8450 Av. Arequipa, La Florida; phone: 2-793930). Another tennis facility in La Paz is *Sucre Tennis Club* (1001 Av. Busch; phone: 2-324483).

**BRAZIL:** Two hotels in Rio de Janeiro have tennis courts: the *Inter-Continental Rio* (222 Av. Prefeito Mendes de Morais, São Conrado; phone: 21-322-2200), and the *Sheraton Rio* (121 Av. Niemeyer, Vidigal; phone: 21-274-1122). Both hotels' courts overlook the Atlantic Ocean and are lighted for night play. For those not staying at these hotels, ask at the following clubs for permission to play: the *Rio Country Club* (1697 Prudente de Morais; phone: 21-239332), the *Caiçaras* (in Ipanema), or the *Paissandu Club* (in Leblon).

In São Paulo, several hotels have tennis facilities: the *Caesar Park* (1508 Rua Augusta; phone: 11-285-6622), the *Cá d'Oro* (129 Rua Augusta; phone: 11-256-8011), the *Transamerica* (18591 Av. Nações Unidas; phone: 11-532-4511), which also has squash, and the *Ibirapuera Inn* (1355 Rua Sena Madureira; phone: 11-572-0111). The *Maksoud Plaza* has squash (150 Alameda Campinas; phone: 11-251-2233).

In São Paulo, commercial courts are a booming business. Court time usually costs $15 and up per hour. Ballboys should be tipped the equivalent of about $1 per hour. *Hobby Sports* has courts in four locations (148 Rua Luís Correia de Mello, Granja Julietta; phone: 11-246-6990; 463 Rua João Lourenço, Parque Ibirapuera; phone: 11-241-1094; 5104 Av. Santo Amaro, Brooklyn; phone: 11-542-5674; and 1611 Marginal de Pinheiros; phone: 11-246-6990). There's also the *Academia Paulista de Tênis* (89 Rua Lopes Neto; phone: 11-212-6454), *Tennis Center* (114 and 166 Rua Tenete Negrão; phone: 11-853-4471 and 11-853-6488), and *Tennis Place* (1325 Rua Borges de Figueiredo; phone: 11-274-6799). Professional instruction is available at all the São Paulo courts but not always in English.

At *Club Med Itaparica* (phone: 11-833-1141; toll-free in the US, 800-CLUB MED), on an island off Salvador (Bahia), there are 12 tennis courts for guests, as well as 2 paddle tennis courts. Tennis lessons are free. The deluxe *Meridien Bahia* hotel (phone: 11-248-8011) also has tennis facilities, as does the equally deluxe *Tropical Hotel Manaus* (phone: 92-238-5757), on the Rio Negro tributary of the Amazon. There is also riverside tennis at the *Das Cataratas* hotel (phone: 455-742666) at Iguaçu Falls.

The *Casa Grande* resort hotel in Guarujá, outside São Paulo, 999 Av. Miguel Estefano (phone: 132-862-2239; in São Paulo, 11-282-4277), also has tennis courts.

In Recife, there are fine courts at the beachfront resort property of the *Quatro-Rodas Hotel,* 2200 Av. José Augusta Moreira (phone: 81-431-2955).

In Brasília, the *Centro Deportivo Presidente Medici* (Setor Diversoes Norte, Parque Rogiero Pithon Farias; phone: 61-224-9860) has spectacular courts designed for tournament play.

**CHILE:** The *Sheraton San Cristóbal* hotel, set on a grassy hilltop overlooking Santiago (1742 Av. Santa María; phone: 2-274-5000), has 2 courts lighted for night play, and the *Holiday Inn Crowne Plaza* (136 Av. Libertador O'Higgins; phone: 2-381042) in town also offers tennis. Other courts are *Tenis Cordillera* (13297 Av. Las Condes; phone: 2-472331), *Hans Gildemeister Tennis Club* (5970 Monseñor Escrivá de Balaguer; phone: 2-220-0757), and the *Tenis y Squash Lo Cañas* (5000 Monseñor Escrivá de Balaguer; phone: 2-485323), and *Tenis El Aurora* (282 Las Perdices Parcela; phone: 2-273-1887).

**COLOMBIA:** Arrangements to play tennis at most private clubs usually can be made by securing guest cards from a hotel, airline, or tour operator. Bogotá's main clubs are *Los Logartos* (phone: 1-613-0266), *Country Club* (phone: 1-258-3300), and the *American Tennis Club* (phone: 1-232-2829 and 1-285-6309).

In Cartagena, there are 3 tennis courts at the *Cartegena Hilton.* Your hotel can arrange guest privileges at the *Country Club,* the *Club Cartagena,* and the *Club Naval.*

Clay courts are available for play at the *Gaira Golf Club* and the *Irotama* hotel (phone: 54-237190) in Santa Marta.

On the island of San Andrés, there are 4 public courts at the *Tennis Club,* near the *Isleño* hotel (on the Av. de la Playa). They are open to all for a nominal fee.

In Cali, there are courts at the *Country Club, San Fernando Club,* and the *Tennis Club;* in Cúcuta at the *Tennis Club;* in Medellín at *El Rodeo,* the *Country Club,* the *Llanogrande, La Raza,* and *La Macarena* hotels. In Medellín, there are also public courts available at the *Inter-Continental* hotel (phone: 4-266-0680), at the *Club de Tenis de la Sociedad de Mejoras Públicas,* and at the *CONFAMA* recreation center in Copacabana. The *Lagomar El Peñón* resort complex in Giradot and the *El Prado* hotel (phone: 58-456533) in Barranquilla have courts.

**ECUADOR:** It's possible to purchase an expensive temporary membership at the *Quito Tennis and Golf Club* (Av. Ocidental; phone: 2-538120), that will provide access to the 9 clay courts and the swimming pool. You also may want to check out the *Club de Tenis Buenavista* (Charles Darwin and de las Alcabalas; phone: 2-430682) or the *Quito Racquetball Club* (Pasaje Oriente and Av. 10 de Agosto; phone: 2-433706). For a fee, play is permitted at the *Quito Municipal Tennis Club*'s 6 courts (1058 Av. Atahualpa at the corner of Av. 10 de Agosto; phone: 2-24918). For guest cards for tennis clubs, ask at your hotel in Quito.

**PANAMA:** Most major hotels in and around Panama City have tennis courts. There are also courts at the *Caesar Park Contadora* hotel on Contadora Island (phone: 507-695269; fax: 507-694721).

**PARAGUAY:** There are composition courts at the *Itá Enramada,* a luxury hotel just outside Asunción (phone: 21-33041 or 21-33049). The hotel will arrange a tennis partner if you need one. Near the *Itá Enramada,* there is also tennis and squash at the new *Yacht y Golf Club Paraguayo* hotel (phone: 21-36121 and 21-37161).

**PERU:** There are tennis courts in Lima at *Lawn Tennis Club* (744 Av. 28 de Julio; phone: 14-240906). In the suburbs: *Club Tenis las Terrazas* (Malecón 28 de Julio, Miraflores; phone: 14-452997); *Country Club* (Los Eucaliptos, San Isidro; phone: 14-404060); and *El Pueblo Inn* (at Km 11 on the Carretera Central, Chosica; phone: 14-350777). The *Las Dunas* hotel (phone: 34-231031) in Ica, near the famous Nazca lines, has 3 courts.

**SURINAME:** The *River Club* hotel/motel (phone: 597-451959), 7 minutes by car from Paramaribo near the mouth of the river, has tennis courts.

**URUGUAY:** In Montevideo there are courts at *Carrasco Lawn Tennis Club* (6401 Dr. Eduardo J. Couture; phone: 2-600148); *Círculo de Tenis de Montevideo* (Buschental in Carrasco; phone: 2-393500); and *Club Bigúa* (2968 José Vázquez Ledesma, Pocitos; phone: 2-702485). The only Montevideo hotel with courts is *Hostería del Lago* (9637 Arizona; phone: 2-612210). Punta del Este's best courts are at *Cantegril Country Club* (for members only).

**VENEZUELA:** For a nominal fee, non-guests may play on the 3 courts of the *Tamanaco Inter-Continental* hotel (Av. Principal, Las Mercedes; phone: 2-914555), which have night lighting; the *Caracas Hilton International*'s 1 court (Av. Sur 25, El Conde; phone: 2-571-2322 or 2-574-1122); or the *Macuto Sheraton*'s 2 courts (Caraballeda; phone: 31-944300 or 31-781-1508). Hotel guests are given preference. *CCCT* (*Centro Commercial Ciudad Tamanaco;* phone: 959-0651) has 1 court. The *Meliá Caribe* also has courts (phone: 31-945555).

The mammoth *Margarita Concorde* hotel on Margarita Island has 5 tennis courts (phone: 95-613333). In Puerto La Cruz, there are courts at the *Golden Rainbow Maremares* (Complejo Turístico El Morro; phone: 81-813022), *Doral Beach Villas* (Pozuelos Bay; phone: 81-666333), *Meliá* (Paseo Colón; phone: 81-691311), and *Rasil* (Calle Monagas at Paseo Colón; phone: 81-672422). In the Andes, Mérida's new *Páramo La Culata* (Valle Grande; phone: 74-446121) offers 6 courts. And if you can take the heat of Maracaibo, there are courts at the *Inter-Continental del Lago* (Av. El Milagro; phone: 61-912022) and the *Maruma* (2 Av. Circunvalación; phone: 61-349011).

# Great Golf

For any one of the thousands of Americans who cheerfully lug heavy bags full of clubs to airports in anticipation of trying new golf courses, it will be a delight to discover that it's easy to play your way around South America, teeing off in nearly every major city. But keep in mind that courses range in quality from luscious, hilly, 18-hole tournament class courses — such as the *Club de Golf de Panamá* — to simple 9-holers that most serious golfers would not consider enough of a challenge to be worth teeing up for.

To most South Americans, golf remains a sport exclusively for the wealthy, and the supremely manicured greens, fairways, and surroundings form an important part of the privileged realm in which most South American golfers circulate. Membership in private clubs is extremely expensive — for example, the *Caracas Country Club* charges a $30,000 initiation fee — but your hotel, travel agent, or airline usually can arrange guest privileges for a charge.

**ARGENTINA:** Mar del Plata has four 18-hole golf courses; check at the tourist office at Bristol Beach across from the *Central Casino* (2252 Blvd. Maritimo Patricio Peralta Ramos) for directions. In Buenos Aires, the *Sheraton, Claridge,* and *Plaza* hotels can arrange for guest passes to private clubs. The municipal golf course is at Tornquist (at Olleros in Palermo Woods; phone: 1-772-7576). The *Argentine Golf Association* is located here (at 538 Av. Corrientes; phone: 1-394-3743).

**BOLIVIA:** Not far from the heart of the world's highest capital, La Paz, stands *Golf Club Malasilla*, which is the world's highest course. But don't even attempt to play its 18 holes unless you are in truly excellent physical condition. And even if you are, be sure to allow a couple of days rest after arriving in La Paz to acclimate to the altitude.

When teeing off, remember that the air is thinner, the ball sails farther, and overshooting a target is a fairly common problem. The golf course is in Malasilla (phone: 2-792124). Take the road to Valle de la Luna, just before the tunnels. Bear right at the fork. Several thousand feet lower, at Santa Cruz, there is a good 18-hole golf course at the *Los Tajibos* hotel (phone: 3-351000).

**BRAZIL:** Brazil has many golf clubs, most of which are private. However, these clubs often will allow a foreign visitor to play if the golfer is willing to pay the "guest" greens fee. A full list of Brazilian golf clubs is available from the *Brazilian Golf Federation* (282 Rua 7 de Abril in São Paulo; phone: 11-255-0744). There are 2 golf courses in Rio: the *Gávea Golf Club* next to the *Inter-Continental* hotel (800 Estrada da Gávea in São Conrado; phone: 21-322-4141), and the *Itanhanga Golf & Country Club* (Barra da Tijuca; phone: 21-399-0507). Visitors can play 18 holes on these lovely courses for a greens fee of about $50, plus $5 for the caddy. Golf club rental is available and the better hotels are able to reserve tee times.

São Paulo has 7 major golf clubs. Among the most popular courses with the resident foreign community are *São Fernando Golf Club* (Estrada Fernando Nobre, Cotia; phone: 11-492-5544), *São Paulo Golf Club* (540 Praça Dom Francisco de Souza, Santo Amaro; phone: 11-521-9255); and *Clube de Campo* (3400 Av. Frederico Rene de Jaegher, Rio Bonito; phone: 11-520-3111).

**CHILE:** If you're staying in Santiago, the *Prince of Wales Country Club* (Avdas. Ossa and Francisco Bilbao) and the *Club de Golf* (Av. Americo Vespucio at Av. Presidente Kennedy) have private golf courses. Ask your hotel concierge to arrange greens privileges. Guests at the *Carrera* hotel in Santiago may use the *Dehesa Golf Club* courses (2501 Camino Club de Golf) 4 days a week.

**COLOMBIA:** Golf courses are part of private clubs here, but guest cards are generally available from your hotel, tour operator, or airline. In Bogotá, there's the *Lagartos Club;* about an hour out of town is the country's highest course, the *San Andrés* golf course. Barranquilla has two 18-hole courses, one at the *Country Club* in the city and the other at the *Club Lagos de Cavrajal,* a short distance from town. The country club at Cartagena has a 9-hole course.

Medellín has four private clubs with courses; the *Club La Macarena,* the *El Rodeo Club* (both 18-hole courses), and the 9-hole country club and *Club Llanogrande* courses. The Colombian Tourist Bureau recommends making arrangements through your home club by asking for exchange privileges on Medellín courses.

At Santa Marta, there's the 9-hole *Gaira Golf Club* course, a short drive from the *Irotama* resort hotel. Foreign visitors can play here without arranging for exchange membership privileges. There are also 18-hole courses in Cali at the country club, in Manizales near Medellín, and in Bucaramanga at the *Club Campestre.*

**ECUADOR:** The *Quito Tennis and Golf Club* (Av. Ocidental; phone: 2-538120) has an 18-hole course on the leeward side of Mt. Pichincha. The thin Andean air makes 9 holes sufficient for most visitors; those brisk few hours are usually enough to pick up a tan.

**PANAMA:** The *Club de Golf de Panamá* (Cerro Viento; phone: 667777), where international tournaments are played, is in Panama City; the *Coronado Beach* golf course (phone: 507-646352) is at Coronado, off the Pan-American Highway. *Brazos Brooks* (phone: 507-453858) is near Colón.

**PARAGUAY:** There is a 9-hole course at the *Yacht y Golf Club Paraguayo* hotel (Av. del Yacht 11 in Lambaré; phone: 21-36121 and 21-37161). The *Asunción Golf Club* (Jardín Botánico; phone: 21-290251) is a public course, open from March through November. It's not that great, but it's the only one in town and it's worth playing, if only for the social coup of being able to tell your friends that you birdied the 5th in Asunción.

**PERU:** In Lima, the most popular course is the somewhat flat, 18-holer at the

*Country Club* (Los Eucaliptos, San Isidro; phone: 14-404060). Many travelers take a trip to *El Pueblo Inn* (Km 11 on the Carretera Central, Chosica; phone: 14-350777) for another 18-hole course. There are private courses at *Lima Golf Club* (Camino Real, 7th Block; phone: 14-227800); at *Los Incas Golf Club* (Av. Golf; phone: 14-352046); and at *Huampaní* (Km 26 on the Carretera Central, Chosica; phone: 14-910342). Farther south, in Ica, the elegant *Las Dunas* hotel (phone: 34-231031) offers guests a 9-hole pitch and putt course. In northern Peru, in Trujillo, arrangements sometimes can be made for small groups of non-members to use the course at the *Golf y Country Club de Trujillo* (phone: 44-241322).

**URUGUAY:** Guest cards are available at the *Club de Golf del Uruguay* (379 Bulevar Artigas; phone: 2-701721 through 2-701725).

Golf is also excellent in Punta del Este at the *Cantegril Country Club* (for members only).

**VENEZUELA:** The better hotels in Caracas sometimes can arrange for guests to play at the private courses at *Junko, Lagunita,* or the *Caracas* country clubs. The greens fees are stiff; caddies and club rental are extra. Guests at the *Tamanaco Inter-Continental* hotel (phone: 2-292-4522) can play at the 18-hole *Valle Arriba Golf Club*. Note: Private club playing has become more difficult to arrange in Caracas.

Guests at the *Macuto Sheraton* (phone: 31-944300) can use the facilities of the *Caraballeda Golf and Yacht Club*'s 9-hole course, about 5 minutes from the hotel. Arrangements to play and for equipment rental for the *Junko, Izcaragua,* and *Caraballeda* courses can be made through César Quijada at *Arelys Tours* in Caracas (phone: 2-782-4680). The *Hilton International* hotel in Caracas (phone: 2-571-2322 or 2-571-1655) can arrange play on any of the 18-hole courses in the city or on the 9-hole *Caraballeda* course, Mondays through Fridays.

There is a small golf course, as well as an 18-hole course, overlooking the Caribbean near the *Meliá* hotel in Puerto La Cruz (phone: 81-691311; for reservations in the US, 800-336-3542).

# Fishing

South America offers unbelievably varied fishing grounds: from the deep-sea Caribbean waters off the shores of Venezuela, Colombia, Suriname, French Guiana, Guyana, and Panama, to the sparkling mountain lakes and streams of Chile and Argentina and the exotic rivers of the interior. And the entire South American continent is bordered by thousands of miles of Pacific and Atlantic Ocean, just teeming with countless numbers of fish.

Whether planning a fishing tour on your own or purchasing a package, check to find out where a particular species is running during the regular fishing season. When chartering a boat, make sure to fully discuss all of the following points: price; what the captain of the boat will provide (tackle, bait, food, drink); what fish are running; how the catch will be divided; and cancellation terms. Also, be sure to check on any permits that may be required in certain waters.

For advance planning, consult *The PanAngler,* a monthly newsletter updating the fishing scene in South America (and other parts of the world), issued by specialists in arranging fishing expeditions. The subscription rate is $20 per year or $36 for 2 years. Contact *PanAngling Travel Service* (180 N. Michigan Ave., Room 303, Chicago, IL 60601; phone: in Illinois, 312-263-0328; in other states, 800-533-4353). The *Angling Report,* a monthly publication promising no commercial ties to anyone in the fishing business, contains reports on top fishing spots and outfitters throughout the world. Annual subscriptions cost $39. Contact the *Angling Report* (666 Fifth Ave., 35th Floor,

## DIVERSIONS / Fishing

New York, NY 10103). The *International Fishing Journal,* published annually, is actually *Fishing International*'s catalogue. However, it contains in-depth destination coverage of top fishing spots around the world, including South America, and is well worth saving. Contact *Fishing International* (4010 Montecito Ave., Santa Rosa, CA 95404; phone: 707-542-4242 or 800-950-4242).

**ARGENTINA:** There are three main fishing areas. In the northern rivers, the prime catch is dorado, the strongest freshwater game fish in South America. The season runs from July through October. In the southern Lake District, there are trout, salmon, and perch waiting to be caught. The trout season runs from November 15 through April 15; January and February are the most outstanding months in Patagonia and Tierra del Fuego. In the Atlantic Ocean off the coast of Mar del Plata, Argentina's biggest seaside resort, anglers can catch hake *(merluza),* sea bass *(corvina),* and shark *(tiburón).* The best month for deep-sea fishing is October.

In Chascomus, outside Buenos Aires, there is a 12-acre lake full of pejerrey, although there are also catfish and the aggressive *tararira,* which is similar to pike. Amateur fishing contests are held here during the winter; Chascomus was host to the *South American Fishing Championship* in 1988.

The southern lakes and rivers have salmon and rainbow, brown, and brook trout. The largest rainbow trout caught in Argentine waters weighed almost 28 pounds, and the largest salmon about 35 pounds. The best trout fishing from mid-November to mid-April centers around Bariloche and includes San Martín de los Andes and Esquel. An Argentine firm, *Corcovada Fishing* (phone: 945-94014 and 945-94016), picks up anglers in Esquel for Pacific salmon fishing in Patagonia from mid-November through March. Guests stay in bungalows on Lake Corcovado, and fishing licenses, equipment, and boats are handled by the company. Meals also are included. Farther south, in Tierra del Fuego, there is superb sea-run brown trout fishing. Probably the largest company in the US specializing in deluxe fishing trips around the world is *Frontiers* (PO Box 959, 100 Logan Rd., Wexford, PA 15090; phone: in Pennsylvania, 412-935-1577; in other states, 800-245-1950; fax: 412-935-5388). In San Martín, *Frontiers* has a trip that hosts anglers at two well-appointed privately owned ranches for 6 days of trout fishing, with a 2-day add-on for landlocked salmon at a third ranch. South of Bariloche, in Esquel, the *Frontiers* program includes several days at a remote lodge within Los Alerces National Park. *Fishing International* (4010 Montecito Ave., Santa Rosa, CA 95404; phone: 707-542-4242 or 800-950-4242) specializes in 2-week fishing safaris in this part of Argentina, led by expert Ken Schoenauer, a North American who has spent the last 15 years there.

One of the best current programs is a tour for wade fishing with fly or spinning tackle to Bariloche, operated by *Laddie Buchanan* (2948 Las Heras, Apartado 4H, Buenos Aires 1425; phone: 1-456721 and 1-457249). Arrangements for fishing trips with Mr. Buchanan also can be made through *PanAngling Travel Service* (180 N. Michigan Ave., Room 303, Chicago, IL 60601; phone: 312-263-0328 in Illinois; 800-533-4353 in other states). *PanAngling*'s specialty is custom-designed fishing excursions anywhere in Patagonia, led by local expert Carlos Sanchez.

There is continuous open season on trout and pejerrey at Sierra de la Ventana, except for a 90-day spawning period from September 1 to November 30. The Río Sauce Grande outside Córdoba also has good trout fishing. January and February are the best months to fish the fighting sea-run brown trout in Tierra del Fuego. Record catches are being recorded by fisherfolk headquartered at the comfortable *Kau Yatún* outside Calafate (phone: 902-91059) on 6-day programs exclusively marketed by *Frontiers* (see above).

Up the Paraná River lives the dorado, a real fighter that can reach 60 pounds or more. Known in Argentina as the "Tiger of the Paraná," it can be fished from the

## 592 DIVERSIONS / Fishing

provinces north of Buenos Aires — Corrientes, Missiones, and Entre Ríos — between the beginning of August and the end of October. One favorite fishing spot near Corrientes is Paso de la Patria, where fishing boats and gear can be rented at *Le Apart* hotel (1201 25 de Mayo; phone: 783-94171). (For a description of this region and a list of hotels along the river, see *Argentina*, DIRECTIONS.) *Laddie Buchanan* (see above) runs a dorado fishing tour on the Paraná, as does *Holditur* (834 Tucuman in Buenos Aires; phone: 1-322-2254; fax: 54-6-322-5572).

In the Mar de Ajó, near Buenos Aires, red and black sea bass *(corvina)* can be caught. The best time to go is the beginning of October, when an annual fishing championship is held. Prize catches of up to 101 pounds have been hauled from these waters. In Mar del Plata, *Club Náutico* arranges private charters for shark fishing. The lakes around Puerto Madryn and the Valdés Peninsula coast in Chubut have good freshwater and saltwater fishing.

A permit is necessary for fishing anywhere in Argentina; contact the national park office at 24 San Martín in Bariloche (phone: 944-23111) or in Buenos Aires at 680 Santa Fe (phone: 1-322-4668).

Recently, fishing enthusiasts have turned their attention to the river and ocean opportunities in the Falkland Islands, where 12-pound sea trout are common and 20-pounders are not unheard of. Other popular catches are smelt, rock cod, hake, skate, and whiting. The fishing season runs from October to April. Packages are not available from the US but can be arranged by two British tour operators: *Abercrombie & Kent Travel* (Sloan Square House, Holbein Place, London, England SW1W 8NS; phone: 71-730-9600; fax: 71-730-9376) or *Sport Elite* (Woodwalls House, Corscombe, Dorchester, Dorset, England DT2 ONT; phone: 935-89477; fax: 935-89797).

Fishing in the Río de la Plata around Buenos Aires is prohibited because of pollution.

**BOLIVIA:** Trout fishing in Lake Titicaca has been getting mixed reports lately. Some people claim the fish are just not biting these days; others claim the catch is still good. You'll need a license, available from the US Embassy (Calle Colón and Mercado, La Paz; phone: 2-350251) or the Ministry of Agriculture (Av. Camacho, La Paz). For fishing on Lake Titicaca, stop by the *Yacht Club Boliviano* (at Huatajata on the lake; phone: 2-811669). There are plenty of mountain lakes outside La Paz, on the road to Chacaltaya, where fishing for catfish, trout, and perch is reportedly excellent. Near Cochabamba, around the Corani Dam, trout fishing is also good. Local adventure travel operators are just beginning to open up Bolivia to the international fisherperson. There is excellent fishing in the Beni River for the fighting dorado and *pacu*, as well as *surubí, piraba,* tarpon, and the two giant catfish that range up to 200 pounds, the *azulejo* and the all-white *blanquillo*. A complete package, including airfare, transfers, and accommodations, can be booked with *Plaza Tours* of La Paz, which also owns the deluxe *Hostal Tacuara* in the jungle town of Rurrenabaque and the twin-engine turboprop plane that flies between there and La Paz. Contact *Plaza Tours* at the *La Paz* hotel (1789 Av. 16 de Julio; phone: 2-378322; fax: 2-343391). The tour operator also can arrange for trout fishing at Lake Titicaca.

**BRAZIL:** Whether you prefer deep-sea fishing or the challenge of exotic rivers, Brazil has it all, although fishing has not been offered extensively as a tourist attraction. Along the coastline of the states of Rio de Janeiro and Espíritu Santo, north of Rio, underwater and deep-sea fishing for marlin, swordfish, and other big-game fish is excellent. Underwater fishing championships are frequently held at Cabo Frio. Other good spots are the Ilha Grande, Angra dos Reis, Itacuraca, Itacoatiara, Saquarema, Armação dos Búzios, and Macaé.

During the first half of January, a national deep-sea fishing tournament is held off the coast of the state of Espiritú Santo. The best places for deep-sea fishing in this state are Jacaraipe, Nova Almeida, and Santa Cruz.

Surf casting is excellent off the shores of Salvador (Bahia). Fortaleza and João Pessoa, in the northeast, are the country's major commercial fishing areas. The catch includes lobster and shrimp as well as ocean fish. Boats can be chartered for day excursions at the docks.

In the southeast, Ilhabela is popular with surf casters. Squid is quite plentiful. Cassino, an Atlantic resort town near Rio Grande do Sul, has good deep-sea fishing. Charters are available.

Giant catfish and dorado can be caught in the Amazon. For rare tropical species, however, it's hard to beat the Araguaia River, near Aruana in state of the Mato Grosso. Standing along the banks of the river at dawn or sunset should yield any number of unusual fish: *tucanaré* (a rare catfish), dogfish, the one-eyed *soia, poraquê* (an electric fish), *tambarana* (a fighting fish), *pacu,* and *pirarucú.* (They have no English names because these fish are found only in the South American interior.)

Development of Brazilian lodges, camps, and inclusive river fishing programs by US companies is still in the nascent stages. Most of the activity is centered in the Pantanal and Mato Grosso. A good tour operator will be able to provide detailed and up-to-date information on this growing industry.

**CHILE:** With its 2,600-mile coastline and its extensive southern lake region, Chile provides anglers with many different options: deep-sea fishing, beach fishing, surf casting, underwater fishing, dry-fly and wet-fly casting, and trolling. The lake district has some of the most outstanding trout fishing in the hemisphere. The first stop for anglers in Chile should be the local office of the *Servicio Nacional de Pesca,* better known as *SERNAP* (1349 Valentín, Santiago; phone: 2-698-1103), for the required permit to fish. Police make regular spot-checks of anglers for permits, as well as for minimum-size and catch-limit violations. There are special licenses for tourists, or there is a season license. *SERNAP* can advise on local variations on the inland fishing season, which generally runs from November 16 through April 15. The season varies in certain districts, and for certain species of fish. There's also a 10-fish or 44-pound catch limit. The minimum size depends on the species. The national tourism office has brochures on favorite fishing areas and catches.

The ocean is open all year; there is no season for deep-sea and coastal fishing. Deep-sea fishing is most common in the north of Chile, where anglers bag swordfish, long-finned and big-eyed tuna, bonito, and shark. World records have been broken at both Iquique and Tocopilla, the Chileans claim. Despite the fishing potential of the area, there is not yet an adequate infrastructure to promote fishing tourism in the north. Northern deep-sea fishing is best from April to September.

Surf casting and beach fishing are common from La Serena, at the fringe of the northern Atacama Desert, along the coast as far south as Concepción. Ocean and river mouths in the central area have sea bass *(corvina),* sole, perch, tunny, and scad. Los Choros Beach, near La Serena, is famous for scad fishing. Other popular beach fishing spots are Tongoy, Los Vilos, Papudo, Quintero, Algarrobo, El Tabo, Cartagena, Las Cruces, Rocas de Santo Domingo, Navidad, Pichilemu, Cahuil, Bucalemu, Llico, Iloca, Constitución, Curanipe, Colquecura, Dichato, and Concepción. In the central region's inland streams, pools, and rivers, there are carp, trout, and various other species.

The focus of the Chilean fishing tourist trade is the lake region of Chile, beginning at Lake Villarrica, just south of Temuco in the town of Pucón. As early as the mid-1930s, this was a hot spot for serious anglers, many of whom stayed at the (recently renovated) *Gran Pucón* hotel. Although good trout is still found in the lake and surrounding rivers, fishing packages generally offer programs farther south. A relatively uninhabited region of impressive scenery, southern Chile always seems to offer yet another lake, river, or stream to the adventurous angler in search of brown, rainbow, or brook trout, as well as perch. *Frontiers* specializes in deluxe tour programs for ardent trout fisherfolk (phone: in Pennsylvania, 412-935-1577; in other states, 800-245-1950). The best fishing is in November and December and March through

## 594  DIVERSIONS / Fishing

May. Showers are frequent even during the December to February summer months, and are almost constant during the cold winter months of June through August — when few but the hardiest even think of fishing. Popular spots are in the Toltén River flowing into Lake Villarrica, Lake Panguipulli, Lake Ranco, Llifén, and Lake Calafquén. There are ample modest and first class hotels in the lake district, although reservations are almost always needed during the summer season, from December through February. All hotels have a list of locals who act as guides and boatmen. For information on fishing in all waters off Chile, contact *Turismo Cocha* (PO Box 1003, Santiago; phone: 2-698-3341; fax: 2-699-3290), or *Frontiers* (above).

Chilean operator *DMC* (3144 Napoleón, Santiago; phone: 2-242-9043; fax: 2-246-6935) offers Pacific salmon and trout fishing packages; anglers are lodged at the new *Salzburg* hotel in Frutillar, on the banks of Lake Llanquihue. Fishing equipment, boats, and licenses are provided.

Adrian Duffloq also runs a superb lodge that offers stream and river fishing for trophy brown and rainbow trout on the Cumilahue River. The lodge is small (10 guests at a time) and well-run, according to American tastes. Inquiries in the US can be made through *PanAngling Travel Service* in Chicago (phone: in Illinois, 312-263-0328; in other states, 800-533-4353). In addition to the Cumilahue, other rivers within a short car ride can be fished and experienced; English-speaking guides are available to guests.

*Río Puelo Lodge,* a new 12-room lodge owned by entrepreneur Adrian Duffloq, recently opened near Puerto Montt. Its packages are pricey, but everything is deluxe, from the fleet of light planes to the food. For information in the US, contact *Angling Travel and Tours* (phone: 800-288-0886).

For those seeking a combination raft and fishing trip, check into *Mountain Travel/Sobek*'s rafting trip along the Bío-Bío River in southern Chile. In between shooting whitewater rapids, it's possible to cast for brown and rainbow trout. Write to them at 6420 Fairmount Ave., El Cerrito, CA 94530 (phone: 510-527-8100 and 800-227-2384).

**COLOMBIA:** Both ocean and river game fishing are possible. At the upper reaches of the Amazon and its tributaries around Leticia you can go after giant, spotted and yellow catfish, *pirarucú, tucanaré,* and native species similar to bass, trout, tarpon, and amberjack. Fishing in the Caribbean off the eastern coastline usually will net marlin, wahoo, kingfish, grouper, amberjack, and red snapper.

There's no off-season for fishing in the Caribbean, but conditions are better during the spring and summer seasons. In the deep-sea waters off Cartagena, there are sailfish, tuna, wahoo, mackerel, and the dolphin-like dorado, which is completely different from the freshwater dorado found in Paraguay, Bolivia, and Argentina. In the shallower waters, barracuda, pompano, tarpon, and bonefish swim.

Caribbean fishing can be arranged in Cartagena, Santa Marta, and on San Andrés Island. San Andrés has very deep waters just 3 miles off its shores, but there is limited hotel space — the main hotels are the *De Camerón, Casa Blanca, Gran Hotel Internacional, Royal Abacoa* (phone: 57-811-24044), and the *El Dorado* (phone: 57-811-24155) — so reserve well ahead for December, January, *Easter Week,* July, and August. In the deep waters are marlin, sailfish, wahoo, bonito, amberjack, and dolphin; in the reefs around the island, grouper, jewfish, and red snapper. In the flats there are large bonefish. Fishing charters can be arranged through the *Bahía Marina Resort* (PO Box 597, San Andrés; phone: 811-23539).

For Caribbean fishing in Cartagena, book charters through the *Club de Pesca* in the San Sebastian fortress or through Pepino Mogollón (phone: 536-42966). Mogollón captains a Bertram 31 with two diesel engines and radio-telephone, and has fished Colombian waters for years. Rent a boat for cruising and fishing from *Acuatur,* next door to the *Caribe* hotel.

In Santa Marta, go to El Rodadero Beach and ask for the office of Captain "Pancho" Ospina, who charters a variety of crafts at a variety of prices. He'll arrange for ocean game fishing or river fishing for tarpon, snook, and *mojara*. (When arranging charters in Colombia, as anywhere, be sure to know in advance exactly what you're paying for and that you and the captain agree.)

For surf casting in Santa Marta, try Rodadero Beach or Irotama Beach. There's also surf casting off the Tairona National Park's Arrecifes beach. The park begins about 20 miles (32 km) northeast of Santa Marta and stretches along the Caribbean coastline almost to Taganga, spreading inland to cover 37,500 acres. It's open from 8 AM to 5 PM, although it's possible to camp at the park with the permission of INDERENA, the government agency in charge of national resources, which has an office at the entrance gate, or in Bogotá, 20-30 Carrera 10 (phone: 1-286-8643 or 1-286-283-0969). INDERENA rents huts on jungle hills overlooking the beach, with spectacular views and a delightful breeze. There are public restrooms with showers for campers. Access to the beach is by horseback or foot, however, as cars are not allowed in the park. Bring your own gear.

The inland fishing scene really centers around the Orinoco drainage, and many rivers make up this system. In the last few years, the Orinoco has proven to be among the best providers of exotic fishing in the world, with many world-record *pavon* and *payara* taken here — some far larger than even experienced world anglers thought existed. The local operator is Erland von Sneidern; the US representative is *PanAngling Travel Service* (180 N. Michigan Ave., Chicago, IL 60601; phone: in Illinois, 312-263-0328; in other states, 800-533-4353). At present, von Sneidern's headquarters is called *El Morichal*, a modern camp with main lodge and individual cabins, near Puerto Carreño, on the eastern coast of Colombia. Excellent *tucanaré* (or peacock, butterfly, and speckled *pavon*) fishing is available within a short run of the camp. In addition, anglers can catch near-world-record class *payara*, which can tip the scales at up to 30 pounds, plus *arawana, pacu, sardinita,* and giant catfish among other species. The best fishing months are June through December; bring your own heavy- and medium-weight tackle and equipment.

**ECUADOR:** Renowned for exceptional ocean fishing for marlin, swordfish, big-eyed tuna, and dorado, its inland lakes and rivers also have ample trout. The waters off Salinas are among of the best spots on the continent for deep-sea fishing, which reaches its peak from May through January. July through November are best for striped marlin, and January, March, and May through December for black marlin. Along with the big ones, 20- to 45-pound dolphin reportedly are biting to the point of being annoying. *Pesca Tours* is the best-equipped local operator to handle the needs of US fisherfolk. Contact Knud Holst, *Pesca Tours, S.A.* (Dept. FS, Box 487, Guayaquil, Ecuador; phone: 4-443365), or make arrangements through *CWT Vacations* (1300 Coral Way, Miami, FL 33145; phone: 305-858-9800 in Florida; toll-free, 800-882-4665). *CWT* offers an attractively priced long weekend of fishing with *Pesca Tours*.

There are jungle safaris to the tropical Oriente region. Fish here include peacock bass, piranha, dorado, and giant catfish that weigh up to 300 pounds. Bring your own gear. The local operator is *Sam Hogan Safaris* (PO Box 122-A, Quito; phone: 2-450242), who runs superb jungle safaris for the adventuresome who can live off the land with a skilled guide (Hogan). There is fast fishing and exotic wildlife in the area. These trips can be booked in the US through *PanAngling Travel Service* (phone: in Illinois, 312-263-0328; in other states, 800-533-4353) in Chicago. The best trout fishing in Ecuador is in Las Cajas National Park near Cuenca. At altitudes over 10,000 feet, the dramatic landscape was carved by volcanic and glacial activity over centuries. There are nearly 300 lakes there, about 50 of which yield trout typically weighing 8 to 10 pounds, and some ranging to 16 pounds. Fishing is good year-round, but generally the best from March through July, when there are more cloudy days. Overnight trips include transportation by horse or on foot, and camping is the only overnight alternative. All arrangements can be made by the congenial owners of Cuenca's *Crespo*

*Internacional* hotel (793 Calle Larga, Cuenca, Ecuador; phone: 7-835984). They also arrange fly-ins from Cuenca to the Oriente for fishing.

To fish in Ecuador, it's necessary to get a license from the Ministry of Industry. Consult your tour operator about obtaining one.

**PANAMA:** In a local Indian tongue, Panama literally means "place where many fish are taken." In contemporary English, it is known as the black marlin capital of the world. And any number of other species of big-game fish can be found off its shores, too. World records are frequently set during the July through September *International Fishing Tournament*. In April and May, the *Underwater Fishing Tournament* is held. Boat charters can generally be arranged through your hotel.

The best fishing tour of the moment is to the *Tropic Star Lodge* in southeastern Panama (phone: 507-645549); or contact *Tropic Star Lodge* (693 N. Orange Ave., Orlando, FL 32801; phone: 305-843-0124). Or, book through *Frontiers* (phone: 412-935-1577; toll-free, 800-245-1950). One of the finest lodges in Latin America, it has air conditioned bungalows; a fleet of diesel-powered, 31-foot Bertrams for charter; and heavy and light tackle for rent are on Piñas Bay, 150 miles (240 km) south of Panama City, where black marlin, striped marlin, sailfish, roosterfish, amberjack, wahoo, dolphin, and rainbow runners can be caught. The season for marlin runs from early December through March; for sailfish from April through June; for all others, throughout the year. Weekly packages, including charters, run from Panama City to camp.

The luxurious *Caesar Park Contadora* resort, 20 minutes by air from Panama City, is on 220-acre Contadora Island in the Pearl Island archipelago. The 150-room hotel has a 24-foot open diesel-powered boat for fishing marlin, sailfish, amberjack, wahoo, barracuda, and cubera snapper. Spearfishing equipment can be rented on Taboga Island or Contadora Island, but on the other islands it's necessary to bring your own gear. Gatún Lake has some of the best freshwater bass fishing in the world.

**PARAGUAY:** Although it's a landlocked country, Paraguay offers good fishing in the Paraguay, Paraná, and Tebicuary rivers. Anglers here go after dorado (which average 20 pounds but can weigh as much as 50, and measure 4 feet long), *surubí* (similar to catfish), of comparable size or much larger, piranha, and salmon. The dorado usually is found in fast waters and below waterfalls. Many anglers head for Villa Florida, on the Tebicuary River 100 miles (160 km) from Asunción, and stay at *Las Mercedes,* a rugged lodge about 2 miles (3 km) off the highway into Villa Florida (phone: 83-220).

There are year-round possibilities for fishing, but the best are available from August through March. *PanAngling Travel* advises that it is using a local operator who offers excellent freshwater dorado trips, with catches in the 20-pound (and larger) range possible. The operator uses four-wheel-drive vehicles and boats to get anglers to the best fishing grounds. Tours operate out of Ascunción and include 5 days of fishing. Utilizing the superior *Ayolas Lodge* (with swimming pool), *Scotty's Sport Fishing* (153 Maldonado, Asunción; phone: 21-602653; in Ayolas, 72-2272; fax in Asunción, 21-662947; in Ayolas, 72-2274), undoubtedly the premier operator in Paraguay, reports astounding angling on the Paraná River. Packaged fishing trips include licenses, when necessary. To get a license on your own, contact the Ministry of Agriculture (640 Av. 25 de Mayo, Asunción; phone: 21-445214).

**PERU:** There's sport fishing in Peru in the Tambopata Natural Wildlife Preserve at Puerto Maldonado, a 45-minute flight from Cuzco. The waters here have *surubí,* dorado, piranha, and peacock bass. There is a tour to the *Explorer's Inn,* which provides very comfortable accommodations in simple cottages, and boats for fishing and exploration. The local operator is *Peruvian Safaris S.A.* (1334 Av. Garcilaso de la Vega, PO Box 10088, Lima; phone: 14-313047). From September through November, José Rada takes groups fishing on the headwaters of the Amazon near Puerto Maldonado. An 8-day package excluding air fare runs about $920. Contact Rada at *Pan American Safaris* (240 Av. 2 de Mayo, San Isidro, Lima; phone: 14-221542 and 14-

417309; fax: 14-422438) or the Peru Tourist Board in Miami (phone: 305-374-0023; fax: 305-374-4905).

There is marlin fishing at Mancora, on Peru's northern coast. Contact *Las Pocitas Beach Club* (phone: 14-426978 in Lima). José Rada arranges day outings on his 28-foot boat for deep-sea fishing enthusiasts off Tumbes, where marlin feed. Trout fishing is popular on Paca Lagoon in the Andes mountains near Jauja; boats are available from the *Turistas* hotel at the lagoon (phone: Jauja 232741; in Lima, 14-721928).

**SURINAME:** Fishing is good in the inland waters, where the most popular catch is a swamp fish called *kwie-kwie*. The best season runs from July 16 to March. There is little offshore sport fishing. Suriname has a minimum catch size of 12 centimeters for all species and other special minimums depending on the species, ranging from 10 centimeters for crobia to 32 centimeters for tarpon. The legal minimums shouldn't bother anyone, since travelers are inevitably after the big ones, such as the record 7-foot-3-inch, 240-pound tarpon caught in Suriname waters. Native *Djuka* (Bushnegro) guides, who are skillful in white water with their dugout canoes, are necessary if you want to go after the most adventurous fishing that Suriname has to offer. At press time, because of political turmoil, the US State Department issued an advisory to travelers heading to Suriname not to go outside the big cities. However, even prior to that warning, there were no organized programs to Suriname, and making local arrangements was very difficult, according to expert sources. If you are nonetheless determined to try, contact Mr. Ramdhami at the *Suriname Hotel and Tourism Association* (30 Neumanpad, Paramaribo, Suriname; phone: 476011 or 476223) or *N.V. Mets* (8 Waterkant, Paramaribo, Suriname; phone: 471163, 474751, or 478421).

**URUGUAY:** The inland rivers and lakes provide excellent freshwater fishing for dorado, *pacu*, pejerrey, *surubí*, and others. Particularly good spots are the Río Negro, Rincón del Bonete, Salto Grande, Nueva Palmira, Río Cuareim, Río Uruguay, and Fray Bentos. Seasons vary according to the species, but the Dirección Nacional de Turismo (National Tourist Office; Plaza Cagancha, Montevideo; phone: 2-905216) can provide a chart. Other information on catches and tackle can be obtained from the main office of the Federación Uruguaya de Pesca Amateur — a sports fishing association with offices across the country (its headquarters is in the Casa de los Deportes Artigas (980 Canelones in Montevideo (phone: 2-920877).

Surf casting off Uruguay's Atlantic coastline, and in the Río de la Plata from Montevideo north to the Brazilian border, yields sea bass, conger eel, pompano, bonito, and many other species. The best beach fishing spots are Atlantida, Punta Negra and Punta Rosa near Piriápolis, Punta Ballena at Punta del Este, the mouth of the Río Arroyo, La Paloma, and La Coronilla. The *Yacht Club*, at Buceo Port, Montevideo (phone: 2-780415), arranges charters for deep-sea excursions.

**VENEZUELA:** This is the hot spot of South American fishing. White marlin, especially during August and September, and other big-game fish can be tackled in the Caribbean. There are any number of places along Venezuela's 1,800-mile coast where boats can be chartered. The best-known ones are the Marina Mar beside the *Macuto Sheraton* (Caraballeda; phone: 31-527097); the *Margarita Concorde* hotel (Porlamar, Margarita Island; phone: 95-613333); and the *Meliá* hotel (Puerto La Cruz; phone: 81-691311). In many places, a less expensive price can be negotiated at the local docks than at the luxury hotels.

Both *PanAngling Travel Service* and *Frontiers* (see above) arrange bill-fishing trips to Venezuela. *PanAngling* arranges for daily charters on 35- to 45-foot sport fishing boats, and reports outstanding fishing for white and blue marlin. *Frontiers* utilizes a small, very comfortable guesthouse in La Guaira for its clients, and charters boats with *Keene International.*

The bone fishing in the area of Los Roques is cited by *Frontiers*' fishing experts as being as good as exists anywhere in the world (with the exception of Christmas Island, which, they point out, is much harder to reach). Clients fly in from Caracas aboard private chartered aircraft, and stay at a renovated private home now called the *Lodge at Frances Cay* for 6 days of fishing. Contact *Frontiers,* PO Box 959, 100 Logan Rd., Wexford, PA 15090 (phone: in Pennsylvania, 412-935-1577; in other states, 800-245-1950; fax: 412-935-5388).

Bone fishing at the *Los Roques Light Tackle Club* is available from *Fishing International,* as is tarpon fishing, cited as among the best in the world. The company takes clients to the *Orinoco Tarpon Camp,* a luxurious fishing camp. The beachside *Río Chico Tarpon Camp* is their other destination. Contact *Fishing International,* 4010 Montecito Ave., Santa Rosa, CA 95404 (phone: 707-542-4242 or 800-950-4242).

The high streams of the Andes and the western llanos have superb *pavón* (peacock bass) and some trout fishing, especially around Santo Domingo and Mérida. So do the Caroní and Paraguay rivers in the state of Guayana, in the Gran Sabana. Smaller freshwater fish (catfish, perch, and several local species) can be found in the streams of Barinas and Portugesa states. In the jungle area, there is outstanding peacock bass fishing from early December to April. Watch out for piranha, although they are more likely to go after your catch than any part of you. Poisonous stingrays inhabit some rivers.

Another of the special lures of Venezuela is the outstanding "exotic" fishing in the jungle areas, particularly for *pavón. PanAngling Travel Service* takes fisherfolk to three different, good-quality camps, the most deluxe of which is *Puedpa Fishing Club,* situated on the Guri Reservoir in the midst of an 90,000-acre private *estancia* (ranch). A much more modest camp that offers excellent fishing is *Peacock People,* located on the Cinaruco River. *Manaka Lodge,* on the Orinoco–Ventuari River system, can be booked with either *PanAngling* or *Frontiers* (see above). Another operator featuring programs at Guri, Los Roques and in the Andes is *Lost World Adventures* (1189 Autumn Ridge Dr., Marietta, GA 30066; phone: 404-971-8586 or 800-999-0558; fax: 404-977-3095).

The fishing season runs from March 16 through September 30. Licenses are issued by the Ministry of Agriculture (Torre Norte, Centro Simón Bolívar, Caracas; phone: 2-483-2458). The ministry, however, can be sticky about letting anglers into unexplored regions for fishing, and the red tape can be long, but operators can obtain licenses for you prior to your arrival in Caracas.

# Because It's There: Mountain Climbing

For those hearty souls who cannot bear to see a mountain just standing there, minding its own business, without contemplating an assault on its summit, the Andes of South America are an irresistible magnet. A 4,500-mile ridge of some of the world's most glorious mountains, the Andean chain is commonly referred to as the backbone or spinal column of the Southern Hemisphere.

While the Andes are indeed challenging, there are all grades of climbing in South America. Naturally, the level of personal expertise will determine whether you sign on for a simple afternoon climb or a difficult high-altitude expedition that lasts for weeks. Keep in mind that some climbing in the Andes is done on ice, rather than rock, and requires knowing how to use ropes, ice axes, crampons, pitons, nuts, and chocks. In fact, there is very little actual rock climbing, and even a so-called easy climb is likely to be well beyond the skills of a novice.

Whether you choose an organized expedition or prefer to arrange one with friends, be sure to bring along a comfortable pair of broken-in mountaineering boots. As far as other equipment is concerned, check with each outfitter when inquiring about climbing trips to find out what kind of gear is included in the cost of a trip.

Probably the best source for organized South American climbing programs is the *American Alpine Institute* (1212 24th St., Bellingham, WA 98225; phone: 206-671-1505), which is North America's largest operator of guided technical climbing trips. At least one of the company's staff of 35 US-trained climbing experts accompanies every one of its trips.

*Mountain Travel/Sobek*'s founders are accomplished climbers, and the company continues to offer climbing trips. Contact *Mountain Travel/Sobek*, 6420 Fairmount Ave., El Cerrito, CA 94530 (phone: 510-527-8100 or 800-227-2384).

The center of mountaineering in South America is the Cordillera Blanca in Peru. The town of Huaráz is where climbers meet, exchange information on conditions, and form expeditionary teams. More climbers are also tackling the numerous peaks of Bolivia's magnificent Cordillera Real (Royal Range) and imposing Mt. Aconcagua, the continent's tallest peak — straddling the Chilean-Argentine border — increasingly has lured daring climbers. June and July are considered the best (driest) months in the Andes, but they are also the coldest. In comparison to the Himalayas, the Andes have more reliable weather during the dry season (June through October). When fair weather arrives, it normally lasts for weeks at a time. There is also less danger of storms and avalanches than in the Himalayas.

Experienced climbers are most likely to find others of similar skill in Huaráz. (It is possible to travel to the Andes alone and be fairly certain of encountering climbing mates.) It is less expensive to form your own team than to sign on with one of the many operators in the mountaineering business, but again, you should be truly expert to attempt it, and a guide is always recommended.

Below is a list of climbing associations, outfitters, and peaks. It should be noted that while local associations are good sources on the spot, they rarely answer written requests for information.

**ARGENTINA:** The highest peak in the Western Hemisphere, Mt. Aconcagua, at 22,834 feet, has challenged mountaineers from all over the world. There are also frequent locally organized expeditions (usually during January), although climbing permits are not easily obtained. Contact the *Club Andinista Mendoza* (Calles Pardo and Ruben Lemos, Mendoza, Argentina; phone: 61-241840) for information, and leave plenty of time for them to reply. The Mendoza city tourism office (1143 Av. San Martín; phone: 61-242800) is promoting mountain climbing and may also be able to help with permits and guides. The *American Alpine Institute* offers one Anconcagua ascent each year, as well as climbing in Patagonia. *Mountain Travel/Sobek* (6420 Fairmount Ave., El Cerrito, CA 94530; phone: 510-527-8100 or 800-227-2384), also offers an Anconcagua ascent. *Southwind Adventures* (1861 Camino Lumbre, Santa Fe, NM 87505; phone: 505-438-7120) specializes in Aconcagua climbs too, as does *Genet Expeditions* (PO Box 230861, Anchorage, Alaska 99523; phone: 800-33-GENET; fax: 907-561-1948).

**BOLIVIA:** The most popular climbing trips from La Paz are to 19,975-foot Huaya Potosí and to 21,100-foot Mt. Illimani. *Club Andino Boliviano* (1638 Calle México, La Paz; phone: 2-324682), puts climbers in contact with one another and arranges expeditions. *TAWA (Tour Adventure World Agency),* the major Bolivian adventure operator (PO Box 8662, 701 Calle Rosendo Gutiérrez, La Paz, Bolivia; phone: 2-391175), is actually a French-Bolivian company, which does offer some climbing trips as well as an extensive lineup of treks . Another La Paz operator, *Expediciones Guarachi* (Plaza Alonso de Mendoza, office 314, Edificio Santa Ana, La Paz; phone: 2-320901) also arranges climbing tours. Bolivia's *Plaza Tours* (1789 Av. 16 de Julio, La Paz; phone: 2-378322; fax: 2-343391) organizes a number of climbing expeditions. The major US outfitter that organizes trips to Bolivia is the *American Alpine Institute* (1212 24th St., Bellingham, WA 98225; phone: 206-671-1505).

**BRAZIL:** Although not in a class with the Andes, Brazil's mountains attract some climbers. Mountaineering is not an industry here, so it's usually necessary to bring your own gear. The mountains, such as they are, can be found in the Serra dos Orgãos National Park region around Teresópolis, halfway between Rio de Janeiro and São Paulo in Parque Itatiaia, and at Nova Friburgo, where the 7,575-foot Pico da Caledônia stands. *Brasiltrek Expeditions* (Box 94514, Rio de Janeiro; phone: 21-779-1726; fax: 21-262-6715) specializes in adventure programs in the state of Rio that include walking, trekking, and mountain climbing.

**CHILE:** Although the southern Andean peaks are as dramatic as any in the entire chain, climbing is neither as well organized nor as popular as in neighboring Peru, Argentina, or Bolivia. Parque Nacional Torres del Paine (Paine National Park) has challenging peaks. For information on mountain climbing, the best bet is to contact the *Federación de Andinismo* (727 Almirante Simpson, Santiago; phone: 2-222-0888). *Mountain Travel/Sobek* (6420 Fairmount Ave., El Cerrito, CA 94530; phone: 510-527-8100 or 800-227-2384; fax: 510-525-7710) has several climbing expeditions to Chile. The *American Alpine Institute* (1212 24th St., Bellingham, WA 98225; phone: 206-671-1505) also offers mountain-climbing trips to Chile's Patagonian region.

**ECUADOR:** The snow-capped Ecuadoran ranges offer everything from scrambles to climbing volcanoes. Mt. Cotopaxi, at 19,347 feet, is the world's highest active volcano. The highest peak in Ecuador is 20,577-foot Mt. Chimborazo. The tropical eastern slopes of the mountains endure abrupt changes in weather conditions. It's wise to get a licensed guide or travel with a local climbing group or organized expedition. Locally, Oswaldo Muñoz of *Nuevo Mundo Expeditions* (2468 Av. Amazonas, Quito; phone: 2-552839 or 2-552617) is extremely knowledgeable about all aspects of outdoor adventure in Ecuador. If his company doesn't have a climbing trip on the agenda, he should be able to put you in contact with a reliable guide. One of the best climbers and guides on the continent is Marco Cruz, whose expeditions are represented in the US by *Adventure Associates* (13150 Coit Rd., Dallas, TX 75240; phone: in Texas, 214-907-0414; in other states, 800-527-2500). Also contact *American Alpine Institute* (1212 24th St., Bellingham, WA 98225; phone: 206-671-1505) and *Mountain Travel/Sobek* (6420 Fairmount Ave., El Cerrito, CA 94530; phone: 510-527-8100 or 800-227-2384; fax: 510-525-7710). In Quito, you may also want to contact *International Hiking and Climbing Group* (209 Baron Von Humboldt; phone: 2-238397), the *Cumbres Andinas Club* (841 Olmedo; phone: 2-517748), the *Agrupación de Montaña Pablo Leiva* (1240 Av. 6 de Diciembre; phone: 2-230758), or the *Universidad Católica Climbing Club* (12 de Octubre and Roca; phone: 2-529270). For information on climbing sites, contact the *South American Explorers Club* (1254 Toledo, La Floresta; mailing address: Apartado 21-431, Eloy Alfaro, Quito; phone: 2-566076; in the US, 607-277-0488).

**PERU:** The most active mountaineering center in South America is the Cordillera Blanca near Huaráz, where more than 30 peaks reach heights of more than 20,000 feet. Mt. Huascarán, at 22,206 feet, is the nation's tallest. Contact travel agencies in Huaráz or the *South American Explorers Club* (146 Av. República de Portugal, Breña, Lima; phone: 14-314480; in the US, 607-277-0488). You might also want to contact the *Peru Mountain Guides Association* (225 Av. Paz Soldán, San Isidro, Lima; phone: 14-418831) or the *Casa de Guías de Huaráz* (Huaráz House of Guides; Zona Comercial 28G, Apt. 123, Huaráz; phone: 44-418831). Two US operators offering packages are *Iowa Mountaineers* (30 Prospect Pl., PO Box 163, Iowa City, IA 52244; phone: 319-337-7163) and *Mountain Travel/Sobek* (6420 Fairmount Ave., El Cerrito, CA 94530-3606; phone: 415-527-8100 or 800-227-2384; fax: 510-525-7710).

**VENEZUELA:** Although not an organized sport, mountain climbing is acquiring numbers of participants in Venezuela. Mt. Avila, the 7,380-foot mountain right in

Caracas, is eminently climbable. Visitors driving along the Cota Mil Highway in Caracas often see climbers practicing on a certain limestone face beside the road. They are usually friendly and helpful. There is some snow climbing in the Sierra Nevada de Mérida. Many of the *tepuís* (vertical cliffs), towering thousands of feet, in the Gran Sabana are unclimbed, but there growing interest in the region. *Lost World Adventures,* which specializes in Venezuela, offers several climbing programs. Contact the operator at 1189 Autumn Ridge Dr., Marietta, GA 30066 (phone: in Georgia, 404-971-8586; toll-free, 800-999-0558).

# The Wild Continent: Trekking, Backpacking, River Rafting, and Camping

South America is indeed a wild continent: from the coastal deserts to the perpetually ice-glazed faces of the Andean chain's southern tip in Chile and Argentina, to the snow-capped cones of Bolivia's and Ecuador's volcanoes, to the thousands of square miles of jungle, to the walls of the Patagonian glaciers.

The fact that all this wilderness exists on a developing continent has advantages and disadvantages that should be realistically appraised while planning a trip. One thing that is immediately apparent is how easy it is to lose the urban crowds if you really want to. Quite simply, there are far fewer people climbing around in the South American hills or floating down its rivers than in the US. Campsites littered with beer cans are few and far between, (although popular routes, like the Inca Trail, are beginning to show the effects of increased traffic). Sadly, it is more often the locals who do the littering, rather than the travelers on the well-managed North American expeditions.

It is primarily this remoteness that can make traveling difficult, unless a four-wheel-drive vehicle is available. Transportation is not always available or frequent, and it's rarely punctual. But the *campesinos* (peasants) scattered throughout the small villages that dot the countryside do have to get to the markets in the larger towns, so it's usually possible to find a bus, train, or boat to drop you somewhere near a good spot to begin a jungle hike or volcano climb. The train may not leave on the precise day you prefer (or even that week), but in South America travelers quickly learn that flexibility and adaptability are their most useful pieces of luggage. And whether traveling in your own Land Rover or using public transportation, the road will inevitably be rocky, dusty, bumpy, and fascinating.

The wilderness travel business is now a multimillion-dollar industry. Organized backpacking, trekking, and camping trips enable travelers to meet in the US and travel through one of the South American wilderness areas with experienced, English-speaking guides. Whether you want to hike around the base of Mt. Aconcagua, camp along the shores of an Amazon tributary, or walk in the footsteps of the Inca, there's probably a North American outfitter who has just the trip. Some of the best practical information is found in the South America backpacking guides by *Bradt Enterprises.* The guides cover Venezuela, Colombia, and Ecuador, Peru and Bolivia, and Chile and Argentina. This company also publishes two guides for South America river trips. Most are available from bookstores or from the *South American Explorers Club,* 126 Indian Creek Rd., Ithaca, NY 14850 (phone: 607-277-0488).

The major US wilderness travel organizations that conduct trips to South America include: *Wilderness Travel* (801 Allston Way, Berkeley, CA 94710; phone: in California, 510-548-0420 or 800-247-6700; fax: 510-525-7710); *American Alpine Institute* (1212 24th St., Bellingham, WA 98225; phone: 206-671-1505); *Mountain Travel/Sobek* (6420 Fairmount Ave., El Cerrito, CA 94530; phone: 510-527-8100 or 800-227-2384); and *Above the Clouds Trekking* (PO Box 398, Worcester, MA 01602-03998; phone: 508-799-4499 or 800-233-4499).

Whether you plan to travel with an organized group, with friends, or on your own, what follows is a list of South America's prime wildernesses along with the top organized programs operating there. (For more information on camping, see *Camping and RVs, Hiking and Biking* in GETTING READY TO GO.)

## ARGENTINA

Both the southern Andean cordillera and the Lake District border on Argentina and Chile.

**Parque Nacional de los Glaciares (Glaciers National Park)** – The park contains Lago Argentino, and at the far end of the lake, the huge Perito Moreno Glacier, one of the few on the planet that's still advancing. With a thunderous sound, walls of ice "calve," or break off from the glacier, every half hour or so, crashing into the lake and creating enormous waves. The glacier is also famous for the ice bridge it builds every 3 or 4 years, sealing off one end of the lake from the other, until the pressure becomes so great that a cataclysmic explosion of ice and water occurs, uniting the two halves of the lake once again. The park can be reached from the town of Calafate by bus. See park headquarters there for more information.

Moving east from the mountains into the heart of Argentina's Patagonia, geographic similarities with Chile fade. The weather here is often blustery and cold even during the somewhat drier summer months; the fjords, channels, and islands seem to transform into a barren, flat, gray, and desolate plain. Transportation can be difficult without your own vehicle. Bus service is limited but relatively inexpensive. Travel along the coast is the most intriguing route. This is one of the most magnificent wilderness areas in the world, a pristine region of glaciers, forest, huge ice-blue lakes, and coastal fjords reminiscent of Alaska.

*Overseas Adventure Travel* (349 Broadway, Cambridge, MA 02139; phone: in the Boston area, 617-876-0533 or 800-221-0814) plans a Patagonia expedition beginning in Argentina and ending in Chile that includes hiking and camping, whitewater rafting, trout fishing, wildlife photography, and an excursion by motorized sailboat along the fjords of the Chilean coast.

**Valdés Peninsula and Camarones** – Thousands of Magellanic penguins harbor here on the Patagonian coast from September until the end of March, when they head south for the winter. Colonies of sea lions continuously perform their antics on the rocks of the *loberia* (sea lion refuge). It's possible to sight whales at their breeding grounds at Golfo Nuevo, south of the peninsula. Blubbery sea elephants waddle their way in and out of the bone-chilling sea. Sea birds favor San José, the gulf on the northern side. See park officials at Valdés for more information about camping. The *Automóvil Club de Argentina,* with offices in larger cities, supplies information and maps. *Elite Custom Travel* (2817 Dumbarton St. NW, Washington, D.C. 20007; phone: 202-625-6500; fax: 202-625-2650), a US operator, also offers packages that include the peninsula. Those who miss walruses at Valdés Peninsula can see them at Punta Tombo, a large Magellanic penguin rookery.

**Lake District** – Farther north and deeper into the mountains, this area full of lakes and forests is popular with tourists, but it's easy to slip away from the crowds into some amazing countryside. Much of the region is devoted to a national park. Snow-capped peaks surround the trout-filled lakes: Nahuel Huapi, Correntoso, Gutiérrez, Mascardi, and Guillelmo. Lake Futulafquen in Las Alceres National Park is an especially good fishing spot. Lanín Park, outside of San Martín de los Andes, contains the Lanín

## DIVERSIONS / Trekking, Backpacking, River Rafting, and Camping 603

Volcano (12,000 ft.). Visit the *Club Andino de Bariloche* in Bariloche (phone: 944-24579) for more information, including maps of hiking trails. It is also possible to go by boat and bus to the Chilean lake district. From October through May, *Southern Cross Expeditions* (phone: 800-359-0193) offers horseback riding treks with stopovers at ranches and mountain hotels.

Virtually every tour operator with Argentine programs offers tours to the highlights of the southern wilderness areas. Those that include much hiking and camping are primarily available from *Wilderness Travel* (phone: 800-247-6700) and *Mountain Travel/Sobek* (phone: 800-227-2384).

**The Chaco** – North and east of Salta are swamps, very deep forests, grassland, some of the hottest temperatures on the continent, lots of birds, and unusual vegetation. Visitors usually arrive from the east via the Río Paraná or from the west via Tucumán.

**The Pampas** – Would-be gauchos can saddle up for 11-day horseback riding trips across the Argentine plains to the lush Ibera marshlands, noted for their bird life. The rides are offered from October through May by *Southern Cross Expeditions* (phone: 800-359-0193).

## BOLIVIA

Here, where the Andes are their widest and road transportation is possibly the worst on the continent — only 300 miles (480 km) of Bolivian roads are paved — the topography can be exceptionally strange and fascinating.

**Altiplano** – Lake Titicaca — at 12,500 feet, the world's highest navigable lake — must be visited (see *Bolivia*, DIRECTIONS). But the lake is only one feature of the stark, seemingly endless altiplano. A long, bleak, windswept plain cutting through the Peruvian and Bolivian Andes, the altiplano is inhabited by sheep, red fox, llama, alpaca, vicuña, chinchilla, and some hardy Quechua-speaking and Aymara Indians. Travel from Cuzco, Peru, by plane, bus, train, or *collectivo* to the shores of the lake and from there to the Bolivian capital (see *La Paz*, THE CITIES). Then take a train from La Paz to Antofagasta, Chile. The track traverses the altiplano, passing the snow-capped mountains that form its border. With a four-wheel-drive vehicle, it's possible to visit many traditional Indian villages. The mountains are driest and coldest between April and November. June through August are the clearest (but chilliest) months. The lowlands receive their heaviest rains from November through March. The *Club Andino Boliviano* (1638 Calle México in La Paz; phone: 2-324682) can provide information.

**La Cumbre to Coroico** – This is a different type of hike, leading from the cold, upper reaches of La Cumbre pass, at 13,510 feet, downhill into the semitropical Yungas Valley. Trekkers walk along an Inca or pre-Inca stone road, pass several ruins, and see plenty of Indian towns. The first day of this 3- or 4-day trek is spent crossing the snowy pass to a super view of the eastern slopes, with lots of bright birds and butterflies.

Although technical climbing trips to Bolivia can be arranged in the US (see *Because It's There: Mountain Climbing*), few overland camping and trekking expeditions are offered by stateside tour operators. That is not to say there aren't plenty of well-organized trips, but you'll most likely have to arrange a program with a Bolivian company in La Paz. A recommended operator is *Plaza Tours, Plaza Hotel,* 1789 Av. 16 de Julio, La Paz (phone: 2-378322 or 2-378311; fax: 2-343391).

Bolivia's biggest adventure tour operator, *TAWA* (*Tour Adventure World Agency* and short for *Tawantinsuyu*, the name the Inca gave their empire), has an extensive lineup of trekking and camping programs throughout the entire Cordillera Real. Contact *TAWA* at 701 Calle Rosenda Gutiérrez, PO Box 8662, La Paz, Bolivia (phone: 2-325796).

**Train from Santa Cruz to Corumbá, Brazil** – The "Death Train," as it is fondly nicknamed by those who regularly ride on it, rolls through some of the wildest parts of Bolivia. Jungle birdlife abounds along this 400-mile (640-km) ride through a frontier region that has only recently been vacated by Indians. Train service has improved of late, and derailments now occur with far less frequency than was once common.

There are only a few lodges in the Bolivian jungle that are worth describing, one of which is owned and run by *TAWA* (see above). Located on the Tuichi River, a tributary of the Beni, the camp offers an authentic backwoods existence, the only contact with the outside world being by shortwave radio. The company offers programs of jungle camping, trekking, and exploration combined with a few nights in the "luxury" of the camp. The most intriguing is a trek down the original Inca gold route — stairways, paved paths, and all — ultimately connecting to the camp at Santa Rosa de Tuichi by river.

**River Trip to Trinidad –** Perhaps one of the most exotic regions in South America, the jungle lowlands of Bolivia are called "the forgotten corners" by the residents themselves. Clouds of brightly colored butterflies shimmer in the clear light; villagers gather to welcome travelers; and utterly exotic species of wildlife — wild boar, armadillo, giant tortoise — sun themselves on the banks of the rivers. Travel from Cochabamba to Puerto Chipiriri by road, a distance of about 120 miles (192 km). From there, it is about 4 days' journey up the Río Grande to Trinidad. Bring a sleeping bag and plenty of mosquito repellent. It's also possible to travel by *peque-peque* (motorized dugout canoe) along the Río Madre de Dios from Peru into Bolivia (see *Peru* and *Bolivia* in DIRECTIONS).

## BRAZIL

Although this is one of the few South American countries in which the Andes do not crowd the horizon, one-third of Brazil (whose landmass occupies almost half of the southern continent) is part of the Amazon basin. In fact, 1979 was declared the International Year of the Amazon by a group of Brazilian environmentalists and journalists. About 15% to 20% of the total Amazon jungle — an area larger than Holland — has been deforested for development projects. In 1989 the president of Brazil's rubber workers union was murdered, allegedly by ranchers, because of his campaign to end the destruction of the rain forest. In early 1991, the two men accused of killing him were found guilty and sentenced to 19 years in prison.

In recent years, ecologists and conservationists from all over the world have been drawing attention to the increasing destruction of wildlife, foliage, and human habitation patterns. President Fernando Collor de Mello has introduced various measures in an attempt to stop this trend and to preserve the forest. A Vermont-based company, Community Products, Inc. (created by Ben and Jerry of ice cream fame), is doing its part to protect the rain forest — it produces "Rainforest Cashew & Brazil Nut Crunch." The nuts used in this mix are bought directly from the Indians, thus giving them a much higher income for their labors. In addition, 40% of the company's profits go to environmental organizations that work for the preservation of the rain forest. From the Rainforest, an environmentally conscious food company that manufactures fruit and nut products, also has devoted itself to using the market system to benefit indigenous people of the rain forest.

The vast Amazon River system has been the main transportation route for people living in the world's largest rain forest since humans first settled the region, and it is still the most practical route of passage. Today, deluxe boat trips on the Amazon are almost as easy to book as Caribbean cruises. These trips can be arranged through a travel agent (see *How to Use a Travel Agent*, GETTING READY TO GO). For a complete description of Amazon travel, see *Amazonia*, DIVERSIONS, and *Brazil*, DIRECTIONS.

Any real exploration of the region requires a trip up the tributaries of the river. It's possible to set up individual day trips by hiring a guide in Manaus who has his own *peque-peque* (motorized dugout canoe). Another inexpensive way to scout the area is

## DIVERSIONS / Trekking, Backpacking, River Rafting, and Camping

to go on a milkboat that leaves daily around 5 AM, stops at several villages accessible only by water, and returns to Manaus in the afternoon. It's also possible to stay overnight at one of the villages.

Travelers with a bit of gumption can take a ferry through the Meeting of the Waters, where the brown Amazon meets the black Rio Negro, and continue by bus to Manacapurú, a small fishing village on the Rio Negro. Go to the dock area and ask among the fishermen for one who lives deeper into the interior. More than likely, he will be pleased to provide a lift farther upstream into the wilds, for a nominal fee. Carry everything you need with you — from there you are on your own.

São Francisco River, from Pirapora in Minas Gerais to Juazeiro in Bahia, is another beautiful river trip. Bring a hammock and prepare to relax for 4 or 5 days as you float through some inspirational countryside. November to April is the best time. (Other routes into the Brazilian interior are described in *Brazil*, DIRECTIONS.)

### CHILE

In the course of winding your way down this elongated country, you will come across some dramatic contrasts. In the north, there is rainless desert devoid of vegetation. Moving south and into the mountains, the Andes build to a height that peaks at over 20,000 feet and then begin tapering down as the trail leads into the more active volcanoes of the stunning, forested lake district south of Santiago. Still farther south is a maze of dense forests, glaciers, islands, fjords, channels, and the Straits of Magellan, finally arriving at the blustery, raw, often stormy tip of the continent, Tierra del Fuego, where the heavily glaciated Andes come to an end.

**Tierra del Fuego Region** – A popular way to see Chilean Patagonia, the area between Puerto Montt and Tierra del Fuego, is to take the ferry. Check with *Navimag* (phone: 65-253318) or *Empremar* (phone: 65-252548) for ships and schedules. Bring along a copy of Darwin's *The Voyage of the Beagle* to get real insight into the region, plenty of warm clothes, and enough food so that you won't have to buy all your meals on the ship. The mildest months for the journey are between November and March. Another way to follow the same routing, but in greater comfort (though at greater cost), is aboard the *Skorpios I* with 38 cabins for 74 passengers or the *Skorpios II*, a newer, more luxurious, 160-passenger, 5-deck Chilean ship. Each sails Saturdays year-round from Puerto Montt. For reservations and information, call *Naviera y Turismo Skorpios S. A.* (phone: in Santiago, 2-338715; fax: 2-336752), or have your travel agent contact *Ladatco Tours* (phone: in Miami, 305-854-8422; elsewhere, 800-327-6162), *Tara Tours* (phone: in Miami, 305-871-1246; in Florida, 800-228-5168; elsewhere, 800-327-0080), or *4th Dimension Tours* (1150 NW 72nd Ave., Suite 250, Miami, FL 33126; phone: 305-477-1525 or 800-343-0020). A new 58-passenger catamaran, *Patagonia Express*, features 7-day land and cruise packages. Contact *Patagonia Connection* in Santiago (phone: 2-223-5567; fax: 2-274-8111).

**Parque Nacional Torres del Paine (Paine National Park)** – Accessible from Puerto Natales (reachable by bus from Punta Arenas), the park has mini-icebergs; abrupt rock escarpments; guanacos (similar to llamas); *avestruz* (ostrich-like birds); red and gray fox; some pink flamingos; and the huge Gray Glacier, an awesome, gnarled mass of rock and ice dropping 150 feet into the water. Rock and ice climbing can be attempted on the Torres del Paine Mountains. Visitors who arrive after the tourist season (December through February) may have to finagle a bit to find transportation out to the park. But check with park headquarters in town. They are very helpful and can supply some maps, and usually a lift on a supply truck that heads to the park once or twice a week. Note that some lodgings are not open year-round. *Mountain Travel/Sobek* (phone: 510-527-8100 or 800-227-2394) offers a strenuous trip in the park.

**Island of Tierra del Fuego** – Half owned by Chile, half by Argentina, the fjords,

**606 DIVERSIONS / Trekking, Backpacking, River Rafting, and Camping**

glaciers, waterfalls, mountains, and sea lions here are most easily explored from the Argentine city of Ushuaia, one of the southernmost outposts in the world (after nearby Puerto Williams). Ushuaia is served by plane or bus. Go to the *Club Andino de Ushuaia* for more information.

The same tour operators working in Argentina offer hiking and camping trips to Chilean Patagonia and the Lake District, often in combination with Argentina. For complete information, check the listings under "Argentina" in this section.

**Río Bío-Bío** – Located in south-central Chile, just north of the famed Lake District, the Bío-Bío is known by whitewater enthusiasts all over the world. The river cuts through a scenically spectacular area with hot springs, waterfalls, lakes, and virgin forest, all crowned by towering snow-capped volcanoes. Most US-based trips include a few days in Santiago and 7 days on the river. Contact *Mountain Travel/Sobek* (phone: 800-227-2384) for more information. Eighteen-day trips are available from *Sport International* (314 N. 20th St., Suite 300, Colorado Springs, CO 80904; phone: 719-520-1784). Other outfitters include *Steve Currey Expeditions* (PO Box 1574, Provo, UT 84603; phone: 801-224-6797) and *Nantahala Outdoor Center Adventure Travel* (PO Box 41, Bryson City, NC 28713; phone: 704-488-2175).

## COLOMBIA

Generally more developed than the other countries in the Andean group, Colombia has better roads, buses, and more extensive tourist information; it also has more than its fair share of narcotics-related crime and rebel activity. Check with the US State Department's Citizens' Emergency Center before planning any overland travel to make sure that the areas you wish to visit are considered safe. Here, at the northeast end of the continental landmass, the Andes split into three mountain ranges. A climber can move from the *tierra fría* (cold country) of the mountains to the *tierra caliente* (hot country) of the valleys in a matter of hours. (For those heading south on an overland trip through South America, Colombia offers the first opportunity to enter the Amazon basin.) The mountains are driest and clearest from December through March, which is the jungle's rainiest season. The jungle usually gets some rain every day, no matter what time of year. *Rana Tour Operators* (27-27 Carrera 10; phone: 1-282-3377) arranges trips to La Guajira, the Amazon, the Sierra Nevada, and San Agustín, which, as we went to press, were *not* the safest parts of the country.

**San Agustín** – From this little town, famous for its archaeological sites and leatherwork, backpackers can hike or ride horseback in almost any direction and find something special. In the market, you can arrange horses and a guide for a 5-day journey up the steep and lovely Magdalena River valley — past mountain vegetation, an emerald lake, waterfalls, and archaeological sites. *Hospedaje* (food and lodging) usually can be found in little villages along the way.

**Los Llanos** – The great grassland is the intermediary zone between Colombia's mountains and the eastern jungle. Poisonous snakes, alligators, pumas, and jaguars are all part of the landscape. Trips start from Villavicencio.

**Leticia** – Where the borders of Colombia, Peru, and Brazil meet is one of the best jumping-off points for trips into the Amazon jungle. *Avianca* and *Intercontinental de Aviación* both fly there.

To see how the Indians live and get to know some of the world's most exotic wildlife, it's necessary to travel into one of the tributaries of the Amazon River with someone who knows the Indians well. There are regular trips to Monkey Island and to Tacuna and Yagua Indian villages, but even more isolated areas can be reached with the right guide. Guide service tends to be less expensive here than in the Manaus region of Brazil — about $30 per day, with a group, compared to $60. Ask at the *Parador Ticuna* or *Anaconda* hotel for someone to lead your trip, or check with Earl Hanks, manager of *Lowrie Travel Service,* 19-29 Carrera 7, Bogotá (phone: 1-243-2546/7).

## DIVERSIONS / Trekking, Backpacking, River Rafting, and Camping

### ECUADOR

A mountain climber's and alpine hiker's haven, this country has more than 30 huge, volcanic peaks, not all of which are dormant. The equatorial latitude affects the climate at higher altitudes, so it's possible to travel through the Andes without encountering weather changes as severe as those in the south, where the sun's rays are less direct. May through September are filled with crisp, dry days. Late November and December are often pleasant, too. Good maps are available at the Instituto Geográfico Militar, Calle Paz at Calle Miño in Quito (phone: 2-522066).

**Mt. Cotopaxi** – This snow-covered cone last erupted during the 1940s. A visitor can see where the mass of lava and melted ice washed away the tiny village that lay below. If you have your own vehicle, you can drive to 13,000 feet; otherwise take a bus from Quito that stops at the entrance of Parque Nacional Cotopaxi. Hiking and climbing are not technically difficult, but the lack of oxygen is. Acclimatize to the altitude in Quito for a week or so before attempting any strenuous activity.

Hiking in this area offers much to the adventurous. Besides breathtaking scenery, there are tiny Indian settlements, and travelers may even get to see the great Andean condor. *Nuevo Mundo* offers a 3-night Chimborazo trek and a 4-night Cotopaxi trek utilizing local porters, deluxe tents, and excellent meals. The emphasis is on the unique natural history of these high mountains so near the equator. Contact *Nuevo Mundo* (2468 Av. Amazonas, Quito; phone: 2-552617); or their US representative, *International Expeditions* (phone: 205-870-5550 or 800-633-4734). *Metropolitan Touring* offers a 6-day trek by foot and on horseback around Chimborazo. For information, contact the operator directly (239 Av. Amazonas, Quito; phone: 2-560550) or its US representative, *Adventure Associates* (phone: 800-527-2500). You may also want to get in touch with local climbing groups based in Quito. They include the *Cumbres Andinas Club* (841 Olmedo; phone: 2-517748) and the *Universidad Católica Climbing Club* (12 de Octubre and Roca; phone: 2-529270).

**Oriente** – Ecuador is not all mountain. The Oriente (or jungle) is very accessible, and there are possible river trips that do not require guides. The gateway to this region is the ramshackle town of Misahualli, on the Río Napo, reached by bus from Tena. There is motorized canoe service downriver to the muddy town of Coca every few days. From there, it's necessary to ask around in the port for someone continuing downstream. By traveling in this manner, there is a good chance of spending a few nights with a family living in a bamboo hut along the riverbank. Carry your own supplies. *Metropolitan Touring* in Quito has expanded its repertoire of jungle tours. Contact the operator directly (239 Av. Amazonas; phone: 2-560550) or its US representative, *Adventure Associates* (phone: 800-527-2500).

The jungle also can be reached on flights to Coca or Lago Agrio.

Three hours down the Río Napo from Coca is Limoncocha, home to the Amazon Research Station, where regional plants and animals are studied. Nearby is Limoncocha's alligator- and piranha-inhabited lake. Cofan and Secoya Indian tribes are not far away, either.

Other excursions begin in Misahualli. To see this primitive area in relative comfort, talk to Señor Jorge R. Hurtado of *Natura Turismo* in Tena. He will describe how to contact Douglas Clark, a gringo (in name only) guide on Anaconda Island, about an hour downstream from Misahualli. Clark's tours include meals, and nights are spent in huts with flush toilets. He will also take you to meet a *bruja* (witch), drink *chicha de yucca* (the local firewater), or to eat guavas with the Alama Indians. He knows the jungle well and can point out the spectacular vegetation and wildlife.

Douglas Clark or one of the other guides in Misahualli also can act as a guide on a rigorous 4-day hike to an Auca Indian village. These people have only recently begun to accept white people in their territory. It is a demanding trip up and down what is

**608 DIVERSIONS / Trekking, Backpacking, River Rafting, and Camping**

often mucky countryside. But, as always, it's necessary to get off the well-trodden paths to see what is most unusual.

One of the newest organized camping programs in the Oriente goes to the Cuyabeno Nature Reserve, a network of lakes and rivers, jungle and rain forest. The gateway is Lago Agrio, reached by a short flight on *TAME* from Quito. *Nuevo Mundo,* a top Ecuadoran tour operator, maintains a transient jungle camp inside the reserve by special arrangement with the government. The camp utilizes deluxe six-person tents, built atop wooden platforms for protection from the mud, for every two persons, along with a large dining tent. All food is carried in from Quito. At Cuyabeno there's the chance to see some animal life, along with freshwater dolphins, profuse plant life, and hundreds of species of birds. This trip is recommended from April through November, and requires a minimum of four persons. Contact *Nuevo Mundo* in Quito or *International Expeditions* in the US (see above).

**Las Cajas National Park and Mazan Forest Reserve** – Though only 18 miles (29 km) from the southern city of Cuenca, it feels like 200. The park's sweeping high terrain (10,000 to 14,000 feet) has been created by volcanic and glacial action over thousands of years, and is dotted with some 300 lakes. There are wonderful opportunities here for fishing, hiking, camping, and horseback riding. *Nuevo Mundo* also emphasizes the natural history and unique flora of this high-altitude environment on its 3-night horseback riding program here. Participants can either camp or spend nights in a rustic lodge, complete with hot running water. It is even possible to arrange similar excursions once you reach Cuenca. Contact the owners of the *Crespo Internacional Hotel* (793 Calle Larga, PO Box 221, Cuenca; phone: 7-8359843) or get in touch with *Rootours* (at the corner of Calle Larga and Benigno Malo, Cuenca; phone: 7-835888 and 7-835533).

## PERU

In contrast to the rather solitary volcanoes scattered across the face of Ecuador, the Peruvian Andes are arranged in formations more favorable to backpacking trips of several days' duration rather than single mountain climbs. The highly organized Inca Empire carved a road network into the mountains, which makes Peru one of the best backpacking areas in South America. Trails formerly used by the Inca are now the well-tramped routes of international hikers. For extensive information, see *Backpacking in Perú and Bolivia,* by Hilary and George Bradt.

> ■**Note:** As we went to press, warnings issued by the US State Department in response to recent urban terrorist activity, as well as incidents throughout the central Andean region (including parts of the Inca Trail), were still in effect. Caution is advised. Since unaccompanied hikers have reported robberies, it is recommended that you join an organized group to hike the trail. *Travelers should also be aware of the large number of cases of cholera in Peru and are advised to drink only bottled carbonated water, and eat only cooked food served hot and peeled fruit.*

**Inca Trail** – This well-worn path is still one of the world's greatest. It skirts several Inca ruins along the way, culminating with the hiker entering the grandeur of Machu Picchu through the same stone archway the Incas used 500 years ago. Take the "Indian train" from Cuzco and ask to be let off at Km 88. From there it is a 3- to 6-day hike, depending on your pace, and how much time is spent dawdling along the Inca highland trails.

Bring a tent and cook stove. May and June are the best months to do it, but don't forget — it is a popular route, so there's little chance of being alone. Hiking in the less crowded rainy season has its advantages, but dry socks is not one of them. The tourist

## DIVERSIONS / Trekking, Backpacking, River Rafting, and Camping

bureau in Cuzco issues a map, but it is not very good. It is available at all hotels, too. Take along all the reference material available because so many people have gone the wrong way that the incorrect path is often better detailed than the right one. Stock up on dried bananas, oranges, and D'Onofrio chocolates from the *supermercado* on the plaza in Cuzco. Or, if you prefer, arrange to make the hike in conjunction with a Cuzco tour operator who will provide food and supplies.

To tread a section of the Inca Trail that allows hikers to sleep at an abandoned temple beside a waterfall, climb to the guardhouse at the top of Machu Picchu and follow the track along the ridge overlooking the sacred Urubamba River to the Inca gate. Looking back, notice how the lost city has diminished in size. Once through the Inca gate (the original entrance to the city) the descent leads down a set of slimy, irregular steps carved into the cliff. These end right in the middle of a green rain forest with climbing vines and leaves bigger than a human head. The trail is very hard to follow since it is overgrown with tangled vegetation, but turn right at the bottom of the steps and keep going to eventually emerge onto a dry trail similar to the one connecting Machu Picchu to the Inca gate. Take this path over the ridge to Huiña y Huayna, a most remarkable set of ruins. Here is the place to recover from the 8-hour trek, pitch a tent, and spend the night. Bring plenty of mosquito repellent, and don't litter at any campsite or anywhere along the trail. Recently, tours have been organized just to clean up this historic highway.

*Mountain Travel/Sobek* (phone: 510-527-8100 or 800-227-2384), *Overseas Adventure Travel* (phone: 617-876-0533 or 800-221-0814), and *Wilderness Travel* (phone: 510-548-0420 or 800-247-6700), among others, have organized, escorted treks along the Inca Trail to Machu Picchu.

**Colca Canyon** – Four hours north of Arequipa is Colca Canyon, one of the continent's most dramatic areas. Cut by the Colca River, it is twice as deep as the mighty Grand Canyon. Like the early Indians, today's travelers walk through this moonscape region in the shadows of the Misti and Chachani volcanoes. There are ancient Inca farming terraces here, and *CanoAndes Expeditions* runs a series of rafting and hiking trips in the area. A member of this organization was the first non-Peruvian to travel the whole Amazon River — from its source north of Colca to the Atlantic — by kayak. Contact *CanoAndes Expeditions*, 310 Madison Ave., Suite 1916, New York, NY 10017 (phone: in New York, 212-268-9415; toll-free, 800-242-5554).

**Parque Nacional Huascarán** – In the north of Peru are many spectacular hikes through the Cordillera Blanca, of which Mt. Huascarán, at 22,206 feet, is the highest. The hikes, which cover between 8 and 40 miles, can last from 1 to 6 days and venture as high as 15,000 feet. All trails start at the Callejón de Huaylas Valley.

One favorite hike, from Yungay to Caraz via Calcabamba, leads past Mt. Huascarán and Lake Llanganuco, which has great camping and trout fishing. It is the base camp for expeditions to the surrounding peaks. The trek will take about 6 days (not recommended for beginners). The remnants of the brutal 1970 earthquake are visible, as are tiny mountain villages, and there are few gringos. Additional information and maps are available at Huascarán Park headquarters in Huaráz.

A strenuous trek in the Cordillera Blanca is offered by *Mountain Travel/Sobek* (see above for information) as is most of the other trekking in Peru's other ranges — the Carabaya, the Cordillera Vilcabamba, and the Cordillera Huayhuash. As we went to press, no tour operator is offering trips to Cordillera Huayhuash because of increased guerrilla activity in the region. Each tour operator clearly states the level of endurance and experience required by each expedition. Believe them and don't overestimate your strength or stamina, especially at altitudes over 15,000 feet. *Wilderness Travel* and *Mountain Travel/Sobek* (see above for information) offer these more advanced trekking programs in other parts of Peru.

**Iquitos** – Follow the route of the Amazon explorer Francisco de Orellana to the

*Explorama Lodge,* 50 miles downriver from Iquitos, and then along the tributary of the Napo to *Explornapo Camp.* Accommodations at this base camp are hammock- or floor-mat-style in mosquito-net covered, elevated, thatch-roofed huts without walls. *Explorama Tours* operates a basic 5-day circuit jungle itinerary, but arrangements can be tailored to group needs. This is a favorite tour for biologists, researchers, and ornithologists (some of whom are given almost free lodging). Guides accompany all expeditions into these Amazon backwaters and jungle trails. For information, contact *Explorama Tours* (Box 446, Iquitos, Peru; phone: 94-235471) or its US representative, *Selective Hotel Reservations* (phone: in Massachusetts, 617-581-0844 or 800-223-6764).

**Madre de Dios/Manú National Park** – A rough, mountainous jungle region with sparkling rivers and unusual trees, butterflies, and wildlife, Madre de Dios Province is accessible by truck from Puno or Cuzco, or by air from Cuzco (see *Peru,* DIRECTIONS). The best way to see the area is via the river. *Wilderness Expeditions* (310 Washington Ave. SW, Roanoke, VA 24016; phone: in Virginia, 703-342-5630 or 800-323-3241) is one of the few outfitters with offices in the US offering river rafting on the Tambopata River. Descending by raft from its headwaters for 8 days of camping, whitewater thrills, and exploration, participants then spend several nights at the *Explorer's Inn,* a lodge in the Tambopata National Wildlife Refuge.

The Manú National Park, declared an international biosphere area by UNESCO, is one of the most remote and undisturbed areas of South America, providing a sanctuary for many species that have vanished elsewhere in the Amazon. *Wilderness Travel*'s excellent Manú program combines overnight camping with a few nights in a simple jungle lodge. There are opportunities to see large numbers of monkeys and many tropical birds. Contact *Wilderness Travel* (801 Allston Way, Berkeley, CA 94710; phone: 510-548-0420 or 800-247-6700).

## VENEZUELA

Some of the last, really wild frontier on the continent can be found in the Venezuelan interior, and with the increasing interest in natural history and adventure travel, Venezuela is one of the "up-and-coming" destinations.

**Amazon** – Actually part of Amazonas Territory, the trackless jungle is a sparsely inhabited area, full of rivers, falls, plateaus, and Indians. The upper Orinoco River can be navigated by small craft. Check with *Lost World Adventures* (1189 Autumn Ridge Dr., Marietta, GA 30066; phone: 404-971-8586 or 800-999-0558; fax: 404-977-3095) for organized excursions into the vast Orinoco drainage.

**Gran Sabana** – Also known as the highlands of Guayana, this is another relatively unexplored area of more than a half-million square miles, one of the world's largest national parks. The topography consists of pink massifs, jungle, and flat-top sandstone mountains called *tepuis.* It's about a 10- or 12-hour drive from Caracas to Upata, on the edge of the Gran Sabana (see *Venezuela,* DIRECTIONS).

Cascading from one of these *tepuis* (Auyan Tepui) is Angel Falls, the world's highest waterfall (15 times higher than Niagara), named for a daring North American pilot, Jimmy Angel, who discovered it in 1935. *Mountain Travel/Sobek* offers a 6-day trekking expedition to the top of this impressive mountain, using Indian porters from a local mission, followed by a 3-day boat trip to the base of Angel Falls via the Akanan River. Contact *Mountain Travel/Sobek* (6420 Fairmount Ave., El Cerrito, CA 94530; phone: 510-527-8100 or 800-227-2384). *Lost World Adventures* (phone: 800-999-0558), the Venezuelan expert, has a canoe/camping trip out of *Canaima Camp* to the base of the falls, as well as a tougher 12-day overland trek to Auyan Tepui mesa and a trek to Mount Roraima, described by Arthur Conan Doyle in his classic *The Lost World.*

**Andean Region, near Mérida** – Venezuela also has a mountainous region with rugged snow-capped peaks. *Lost World Adventures* has trekking, horseback riding, and even mountain biking programs there, most of which involve some camping.

**Llanos** – The central plains of Venezuela are the legendary domain of the rugged *llanero*, the barefoot cowboy. They also are home to incredible bird species such as the hoatzin and to the the alligator-like caiman, the capybara (the world's largest rodent), howler monkeys, and the elusive jaguar. *Lost World Adventures* (phone: 404-971-8586 or 800-999-0558; fax: 404-977-3095) offers a stay at a working *hato* (very large ranch), *Doña Bárbara,* where you can saddle up with the *llaneros* or go bird watching. This is a very rewarding program for the nature lover who is willing to rough it.

# Parrots, Penguins, Piranhas: Wildlife Expeditions

More and more people are traveling around the world specifically to observe wildlife in its natural environment, and South America offers some of the finest and most unique opportunities for wildlife expeditions. Wildlife tours, which take bird and animal watchers to sanctuaries, preserves, and wilderness areas, are becoming increasingly popular. The eminent ornithologist Dr. Roger Tory Peterson attributes the evolution of this special interest branch of the travel industry to "hard-core birdism." Those birders who spend half the year traveling in search of new species constitute a new kind of traveler. "If you're obsessed with natural history, you want to keep seeing different species," he observes.

Although preparations for a bird watching or nature expedition vary with the destination, certain factors are common to all such trips. Whether you plan to observe iguana in the Galápagos, penguins in the Falkland Islands, or monkeys in the Amazon, consider the following:

1. Choose binoculars with care. For most trips, binoculars of $7 \times 30$ or $8 \times 40$ are good. Steadier hands can manage a 10- or 12-power. Zeiss, Leitz, and Nikon are best.
2. Carry a field guide. Although some of the more remote sections of South America have not yet been covered, many favorite bird watching areas have been catalogued. Contact the *National Audubon Society,* 700 Broadway, New York, NY 10003 (phone: 212-832-3200), for a list of books.
3. Travel with someone who knows the area. Tours are escorted through the area by guides who know the local species. Throughout South America, there are knowledgeable natives and long-term foreign residents who can help.
4. Study records and cassettes of birdsong. Familiarize yourself with the sounds before leaving home or carry a small tape recorder. Bird records and cassettes are available from the *National Audubon Society.*
5. Carry a camera. Although not necessary for sighting birds, a camera enhances the enjoyment of any expedition. Unless you plan to construct a blind and wait for a close-up, you should have a 300-mm or 400-mm lens and a tripod. Penguins are the one exception. It's possible to get very close to them because they don't seem to be afraid of people.

Although wildlife tourism is not as developed in South America as in Africa, a number of organizations offer well-planned tours to different parts of the continent. Some of the major tour companies specializing in wildlife tours include: *Nature Expeditions International* (PO Box 11496, Eugene, OR 97440; phone: 503-484-6529 or 800-869-0639); *Holbrook Travel* (3540 NW 13th St., Gainesville, FL 32609; phone: 904-377-7111 or 800-345-7111 in Florida; in the rest of the US, 800-451-7111); *Questers Tours and Travel* (257 Park Ave. S., New York, NY 10010; phone: 212-673-3120 or

800-468-8668); *Victor Emanuel Nature Tours* (Box 33008, Austin, TX 78764; phone: 512-328-5221 or 800-328-VENT); *Society Expeditions* (c/o *Abercrombie & Kent*, 1520 Kensington Rd., Oak Brook, IL 60521; phone: 800-426-7794); and *Wilderness Travel* (801 Allston Way, Berkeley, CA 94710; phone: 510-548-0420 or 800-247-6700). Trips offered by these companies emphasize natural history and wildlife viewing and are frequently escorted by experts in the field, who give lectures along the way.

Below is a list of the best areas for wildlife expeditions in South America.

**ARGENTINA:** It's possible to observe the sea lions, sea elephants, Magellanic penguins, and whales on and around the Valdés Peninsula. The *Society Explorer* cruises from here to Antarctica with *Society Expeditions* (c/o *Abercrombie & Kent*, 1520 Kensington Rd., Oak Brook, IL 60521; phone: 800-426-7794). A deluxe, escorted land program in Argentine and Chilean Patagonia — plus a stay at the Chilean Antarctica Station at Lt. March Base — is offered by *Travcoa* (2350 SW Bristol, Santa Ana Heights, CA 92707; phone: locally, 714-476-2800; in California, 800-992-2005; in other states, 800-992-2003). Its 30-day tour concludes with a 6-day cruise among the dramatic Chilean fjords. *Questers Tours and Travel* (257 Park Ave. S., New York, NY 10010; phone: 212-673-3120 or 800-468-8668) has a 22-day tour to Tierra del Fuego and Patagonia in Argentina, with an emphasis on wildlife viewing and photography. *Holbrook Travel*'s program there is escorted by an ornithologist experienced in research expeditions around the globe. Contact *Holbrook Travel* (3540 NW 13th St., Gainesville, FL 32609; phone: in Florida, 904-377-7111 or 800-345-7111; in the rest of the US, 800-451-7111).

**BRAZIL:** There are some exceptional wildlife specimens visible in the extensive Amazon jungle. Tourist agencies in Belém and Manaus can arrange expeditions. Daily flights from Belém or Manaus, on *Cruzeiro do Sul*, *TransBrasil,* and *Varig* airlines, go to numerous towns in the Amazon.

From Manaus, there are boat excursions to Parrots Island, where thousands of parrots flock at sunset. Longer trips can be taken to bird-rich Oriole Island and up the Rio Negro from Manaus. The Rio Negro is a black tributary of the brown Amazon, and both colors are visible where the two rivers flow separately into the same riverbed, along whose banks live alligators, kingfishers, butterflies, and parrots.

From Belém, there are excursions by air (30 minutes) and *ENASA Line* riverboats (5 hours) to Marajó Island, where there are jaguars, monkeys, anteaters, sloths, ocelots, parrots, giant armadillos, and tropical birds by the thousands. There are a few water buffalo ranches *(fazendas)* that accept guests for 1 night or more. Inquire at a travel agency in Belém or have your travel agent contact *LADATCO Tours* in Miami (phone: in Miami, 305-854-8422; toll-free, 800-327-6162), which can arrange programs to *Fazenda Bom Jardim*. *Brazilian Adventures* ("Brazil Nuts") offers a variety of Amazon excursions where the emphasis is on the tropical flora. Contact the tour operator (1150 Post Rd., Fairfield, CT 06430; phone: in Connecticut, 203-259-7900; elsewhere, 800-553-9959). Travel to Jaguar Island is also possible by boat from Belém, along the Pará River.

Even more exotic than the Amazon are the less well-known Brazilian states of Mato Grosso and Mato Grosso do Sul. Here is the Pantanal, a vast lowland plain in the center of the South American continent. It is flooded annually (January–March) by the Paraguay River and its tributaries, creating one of the world's lushest breeding grounds for wildlife. Virtually undiscovered and undeveloped until very recently, now there is increasing interest in travel to the Pantanal; consequently, the infrastructure is being developed to handle incoming tourists. For birders the best time to visit is from July through October, during the dry season. Birdlife is impressive here, with many large species such as the jabiru stork, which stands some 5 feet tall. Animal viewing is often better during the flood season, when animals congregate on the few remaining high spots. The most outstanding floral displays are during February and March, once the rains have started, although orchids flower in October and November. It is hot and humid year-round in the Pantanal, with temperatures up to 95F (35C) in the rainy season and about 80F (26C) in drier months; nighttime temperatures drop to 60F (31C).

*Brazilian Adventures* offers Pantanal expeditions by boat with cabin or hammock accommodations during the rainy season, and by overland vehicle the rest of the year, as well as lodge-based safaris. Probably the most elegant spot to stay in the entire region is the *Pousada Caiman* (see *Special Places),* a 10-room hotel housed in a sprawling, privately owned country manor. Game runs are made twice daily, along with slide and video presentations by guides. Contact *Robert Klavin Hotéis e Turismo* (1208 Rua Pedroso Alvarenga, São Paulo, CEP 04531, Brazil; phone: 11-883-6566). *Focus Tours,* run by US-born ecologist Douglas B. Trent, also offers nature tours of the Pantanal and other regions of Brazil. Contact Douglas or Andrew Whittaker (502 Rua Grão Mogol, Sala 223, Belo Horizonte, Minas Gerais; phone: 31-223-0358).

**COLOMBIA:** The jungle areas and eastern prairies are home to jaguars, tigers, wildcats, ocelots, tapirs, pumas, black panthers, leopards, deer, beavers, possum, several types of monkey, parrots, alligators, armadillos, iguanas, turtles, anacondas, boar, ducks, and pigeons.

The Amazon town of Leticia is one of the best bird watching areas, with 1,500 species (120 of which are hummingbirds). The *Turamazonas* tourist agency runs bird watching tours and trips to *Monkey Island Lodge,* a monkey preserve of 1,000 acres where there are also thousands of green parrots. Contact the agency through the *Parador Ticuna* or ask Earl Hanks at *Lowrie Travel Service,* 19-29 Carrera 7, Bogotá (phone: 1-243-2546/7).

There are a number of observatories for watching wildlife in Tairona National Park, which runs east from Santa Marta for about 20 miles (32 km) along the Caribbean coastline almost to Taganga, ending at the mouth of the Piedras River. Sea turtles can be glimpsed off Playabrava and Mayuey points. The park is closed to vehicles, so it's necessary to walk or ride horseback to the observatories. For information, contact INDERENA, the government agency in charge of national resources, which has an office at the entrance gate.

■ **Note:** At press time, the rural area around Santa Marta was the site of continuing guerrilla violence. Check with the US State Department's Citizens' Emergency Center (phone: 202-647-5225) or the US Embassy in Bogotá before traveling.

**ECUADOR:** Ecuador's Galápagos Islands, where Darwin formulated his "survival of the fittest" theory, is a dream trip for nature lovers. Giant tortoises, weighing over 500 pounds and perhaps more than 100 years old, land iguanas, marine iguanas, penguins, cormorants, blue-footed boobies, sea lions, and fur seals are part of the pageant of fauna inhabiting the archipelago's 14 largest islands. Galápagos means "giant turtles," although few have survived on the volcanic islands, which have both 40-foot cacti in dry, coastal desert areas and creepers and ferns in dense rain forests a few miles inland. The islands are a national park area. Should you wish to design your own tour, purchase the *South American Explorers Club* report on the Galápagos. (The club is located at 1254 Toledo, La Floresta, in Quito; phone: 2-566076; in the US, 607-277-0488; its mailing address is Apartado 21-431 Eloy Alfaro). The report costs $6.50 ($4.50 for members).

Several boats ply the waters around the islands, stopping for nature observation in accordance with national park laws. For a complete rundown of the yachts and ships operating regularly in the Galápagos, see *Ecuador,* DIRECTIONS.

Ecuador's Amazon region is also good for wildlife trips. The *Flotel Orellana,* a

**614 DIVERSIONS / Wildlife Expeditions**

comfortable boat-hotel, cruises the Aguarico River, stopping often for jungle walks and visits to native villages, accompanied by trained naturalist guides. Owned and operated by *Metropolitan Touring* of Quito (phone: 2-560550), the *Flotel Orellana* has first class food and facilities. Its US representative is *Adventure Associates* (phone: 214-907-0414 or 800-527-2500; fax: 214-783-1286). *Metropolitan Touring* has two jungle camps offering bird watching and wildlife tours. If you get farther off the beaten track in the Ecuadoran Oriente, you'll have a much better chance to observe wildlife. There is excellent bird watching and a chance to see the famous freshwater dolphins in the Cuyabeno Nature Reserve during a 5-day camping program organized by *Nuevo Mundo* of Quito. Guides accompanying these expeditions are sensitive to the protection of the environment and knowledgeable about the flora and fauna of the reserve. Contact *Nuevo Mundo* (2468 Av. Amazonas; phone: 2-552617), or their US representative, *International Expeditions* (phone: 205-870-5550 or 800-633-4734).

**PERU:** In Peru's eastern areas, part of the Amazon River basin, there are tropical birds, monkeys, deer, peccaries, capybaras, tapirs, and other animals. Among the tours to the Amazon region is one by *Peruvian Safaris* (1334 Garcilaso de la Vega, PO Box 10088, Lima; phone: 14-31-6330), which takes you to the excellently staffed *Explorer's Inn* in the Tambopata Wildlife Preserve from Puerto Maldonado. From the *Explorama Lodge*, which is 50 miles downriver from Iquitos, guides take groups for more rugged exploring to the *Explornapo Camp*. (See *Peru*, DIRECTIONS.) Closer to town is the *Explorama Inn*, where guests usually stay for 1 or 2 nights. This is the departure point for Amazon River cruises aboard the M/V *Margarita* and the MV *Río Amazonas*, which sail between Iquitos and Leticia, Colombia. These Amazon programs can be booked through US tour operators. Another great spot for bird watchers is at the Lagoons of Mejía, on the Pacific Coast just 90 miles (144 km) from Arequipa. There are hundreds of exotic species at this bird sanctuary. This trip can be taken independently or arranged through local operators in Arequipa. Some of the most fabulous wildlife can be seen at the Manu National Park.

**SURINAME:** Suriname has five nature preserves administered by the Foundation for Nature Preservation in Suriname (STINASU). Four of the preserves have basic accommodations, from hammocks to bungalows, where visitors may stay while observing the wildlife. STINASU makes a real effort to see that each trip is educational. It has published nature guides to the reserves and provides field trips, films, and lectures. A trip can be self-service or organized, as desired, simply by arranging to cook food in bungalow kitchenettes or going on a completely catered tour. For information, write STINASU (10 C. Jongbawstraat, PO Box 436, Paramaribo; phone: 475854). You can also consult *Surinam Airways* (5775 Blue Lagoon Drive, Suite 320, Miami, FL 33126; phone: 305-262-9792; toll-free in Florida, 800-432-1230; toll-free in other states, 800-327-6864).

■**Note:** As we went to press, the US State Department had issued an advisory warning against travel to Suriname. Because of political turmoil, it is dangerous to travel oustide the major cities. North Americans who visit Suriname are urged to register with the consular section of the US Embassy (129 Dr. Sophie Redmondstraat, Paramaribo). Currently, the only wildlife expedition available is to the Wia-Wia Reserve, northeast of Paramaribo (see below).

The 14,820-acre Brownsberg Reserve is 90 miles (145 km) south of Paramaribo and can be reached by car in 2½ hours. It stands at an elevation of 1,500 feet on the Mazaroni plateau. There are brocket deer, agouties, peccaries, large gray-winged trumpeters, black curassows, and many other birds, giant toads, communal spiders, and seven species of monkey and jaguar.

At an elevation of 375 feet above the jungle, the Voltzberg Reserve can be reached only after a 3-hour trek on foot up to the top of a granite mountain. There are monkeys, trumpeter birds, and crickets living amid the surrounding rock slopes and granite plateaus.

Set among rivers, rapids, and waterfalls are the 149,000 acres of the Raleigh Falls Reserve, on the upper Coppename River. The reserve's headquarters and guest lodge are on Foengoe Island, a site replete with many birds. Travelers get to the Raleigh Falls Reserve by a 1-hour flight from Paramaribo or a 120-mile drive through savannah and jungle, followed by a 4-hour boat trip in a motorized dugout canoe.

There are two lodges on the 90,000-acre Wia-Wia Reserve, one at the mouth of the Matapica Canal and the other, Krofajapasi, on the west side of the reserve. These can be reached by a 2½-hour STINASU boat trip from Paramaribo or by road with a short boat trip. This reserve is home to scarlet ibis, egrets, herons, woodstorks, black skimmers, and thousands of migratory birds: roseate spoonbills, herons, storks, kites, terns, and crab-eating hawks, among others. Giant turtles also nest on the beaches.

Giant turtles are the attraction at the 10,000-acre Galibi Reserve. There are lodges at Galibi and nearby Babuensanti. This reserve is accessible by a 2-hour boat trip from Albina that passes by several Amerindian villages. As many as 500 Olive Ridley sea turtles were seen one night nesting on the Eilante Beach in the reserve. At both the Wia-Wia and Galibi reserves, the turtles come ashore to lay their eggs between February and July, but they can best be seen from March through June.

Prices at the reserves' lodges are moderate, but in some places it's necessary to bring along bedding. (Bedding costs extra.) At some places, you must also bring your own food. Transport in Suriname is fairly inexpensive. At this writing, travel through the interior is not very safe (see above).

**VENEZUELA:** Venezuela is a natural history lover's paradise just waiting to be discovered. There is an excellent system of national parks throughout the country, protecting jungle, mountain, grassland, and marine environments. Morrocoy National Park near Chichiriviche and Tucacas encompasses islets, lagoons, mangroves, caves, bays, and beaches that offer fine snorkeling with excellent visibility. Henry Pittier National Park has high mountains close to the Caribbean Sea between Maracay and Choroní. There is an extraordinary variety of plant and animal species, many of which are endemic to the park. Other important parks are Paria, Mochima, and Los Roques Marine Park.

Canaima National Park has enormous waterfalls including Angel Falls (the world's highest at 3,212 feet), thick jungle, tropical forests, powerful rivers, and ancient rock formations. *Avensa,* a Venezuelan airline, operates a jungle resort in the park that can only be reached by air from Caracas. The lodge is rustic but comfortable, with space for 150 guests. The food is good and there's an opportunity to see jungle wildlife on a variety of excursions run by local tour operators, ranging from a few hours to more than a week. These can be short river trips, one full-day trip in a motorized dugout canoe to Orchid Island, or a week-long trip on foot, by jeep, and in dugout canoes. You can also make arrangements to fly over Angel Falls through *Avensa* (phone: 800-283-6727, in the US) or *Unique Adventures* (phone: 800-969-4900, in the US). *Aerotuy Airlines* uses the Pemon Indian camp, Kavac, as a base for its Angel Falls programs that range from 1 to 4 days. Book through *Lost World Adventures* (phone: 404-971-8586 and 800-999-0558; fax: 404-977-3095).

Perhaps the most exciting area of Venezuela for the naturalist is the llanos grassland. Located in the center of the country, the llanos are an enormous extension of plains bordered by the Andes and the Orinoco River, similar to Brazil's Pantanal. A number of rivers cross the plains to finally drain into the Orinoco. The wet season (when most of the land is flooded) runs from May to October (May being the most colorful time), the dry season from November to April. The incredible variety and sheer quantity of wildlife here make this a paradise for birders and nature enthusiasts. Large congregations of ibis, heron, and egret festoon the trees, and the rivers are packed with the large swimming rodent, the capybara, and caiman. Hato Piñero is a working cattle ranch that also cooperates with the World Wildlife Fund in a program of wildlife preservation. *Bio Tours Llanos* offers an array of trips to this and another large ranch in the llanos, with excursions for wildlife viewing and photography by jeep, horseback, and launch. For more information, write to *Bio Tours* (at its office, Torre Diamen, 1st Floor, 1-9 Av. La Estancia, Chuao; phone: 2-916965 or 2-916854; or write to PO Box 52-1308, Miami, FL 33152-1308, attn: Ani Villanueva; or Apartado 64597, Caracas 1060 A, Venezuela). A young company, *Bio Tours* was founded in response to a need for well-organized bird watching tours in Venezuela. The company has expanded to include special interest tours to most of the major national parks. *Lost World Adventures* (1189 Autumn Ridge Dr., Marietta, GA 30066; phone: 404-971-8586 or 800-999-0558; fax: 404-977-3095) also offers tour programs to the llanos. They are based at the large working cattle ranch, *Hato Doña Bárbara,* where guests saddle up with the *llaneros* and go bird watching on foot, in four-wheel-drive vehicles, or by boat.

# Downhill Skiing

When it's sweltering at home and the favorite North American slopes have long turned green, it is peak ski season in South America. Whether dedicated skiers want to iron out the kinks so that they look like pros when winter comes back home, or whether the main appeal is merely the novelty of it all, it's great fun to ski in South America during July through September. What's more, it's a snap to combine a sightseeing trip to Buenos Aires, Argentina, or Santiago, Chile, with a side trip to an Andean ski resort.

Mention South American skiing to anyone even vaguely knowledgeable about it, and two places come immediately to mind: Portillo, Chile, and Bariloche, Argentina (see *Chile* and *Argentina* in DIRECTIONS). Although these are far and away the best-known ski resorts, there are a number of others, mostly in the southern Andean region known as the Switzerland of South America or the Lake District. Up-and-coming are Las Leñas in Argentina and Farellones, Valle Nevado, and Pucón in Chile.

There are slopes for skiers of all levels of expertise. Novice, intermediate, and once-a-year skiers will do well at San Martín de los Andes and Esquel in Argentina and at some of the smaller Chilean resorts. Ski bums, intermediate, and expert skiers rave about Portillo, especially the extremely difficult Roca Jack slope. There are other challenging runs at Bariloche. Families prefer the more organized facilities at Portillo, Bariloche, and San Martín de los Andes. Experts and hard-core downhill enthusiasts in search of a challenge even tackle the glaciers at Chacaltaya, Bolivia, the world's highest ski slope at 17,500 feet, one near Mérida, Venezuela, at 14,400 feet (see *Venezuela,* DIRECTIONS), or the Patagonian Ice Cap (skiing elevation averages about 5,000 feet), a challenge that involves a climb up to the ice cap in sometimes variable, impassable snow conditions before cross-country skiing through unspoiled mountain terrain.

Officially, the season at most South American resorts opens in early July. But some places have better snow conditions later in the season. Portillo's light, deep powder is reputedly among the finest anywhere, especially in early July. San Martín de los Andes and Esquel, Argentina, have better spring skiing in September and sometimes October. Argentina has granular powder snow. The best time to ski Chacaltaya is September to March; Mérida, in July and August.

Facilities range from ultra-luxurious to downright rustic. The most elegant hotels are in Portillo, Bariloche, and Las Leñas. Comfortable, clean accommodations can also be found near the slopes in other parts of Chile and Argentina. The village of Pucón offers a ritzy range of accommodations, and Valle Nevado has well-equipped new lodges. Most resorts are accessible by car, on pretty good roads. Others are close enough to major cities to be suitable for a day trip. Most ski areas have ski patrols, first-aid stations, and instructors who speak English, Spanish, and German.

To ski at the larger, better-organized places in Chile or Argentina, it's unnecessary to weigh yourself down with excess equipment. Just pack a parka, heavy sweater, and ski pants or warm-ups. All equipment, from skis to boots, can be rented right at the mountain. Professional skiers from the US report that some Andean resorts (particularly Portillo) have a nasty habit of overcharging on rentals, and you should keep a close eye on anything you do own, as equipment and clothing often get ripped off. There are no rental facilities in Bolivia, Venezuela, or at the smaller Chilean and Argentine resorts.

Inflation and currency fluctuation make it difficult to provide accurate prices for lift tickets or rental fees. Argentina's prices are generally the highest; expect to pay between $20 and $30 for an all-day lift ticket.

Ski tours to Argentina can be booked through *Path Tours* (phone: in California, 818-980-4442 or 800-521-6215; west of Texas, excluding California, 800-843-0400); ski trips to Bariloche can be booked in the US through *Latin America Reservations Center* (phone: in Florida, 305-825-4767; in other states, 800-327-3573). An Argentine-owned New York travel agency books comprehensive ski programs to all four resorts detailed below, and provides lift tickets and equipment rentals, if desired. Contact *Columbus Tours* (330 W. 58th St., Suite 6H, New York, NY 10019; phone: 212-765-8835). Or you can obtain brochures and information from the tour desk of *Aerolíneas Argentinas* (phone: in Florida, 305-577-9595; in other states, 800-333-0276). Chilean tours, particularly to Portillo, are available from *Traveluxe, Inc.* (phone: 212-269-1409), *Nova World Tours* (phone: 305-374-8300 or 800-727-7736), *Continental Ski Network* (phone: 800-275-3121), and *Ladatco* (phone: 800-327-6162). To make arrangements for the Patagonian Ice Cap, contact *Inner Asia* (2627 Lombard St., San Francisco, CA 94123; phone: 800-777-8183) or *Patagonia Wilderness* (610 Av. Julio Roca, 8th Floor, Buenos Aires; phone: 1-334-5134). Travel agents in Buenos Aires and Santiago also can arrange ski trips.

## ARGENTINA

**Bariloche** – A Swiss-like village perched on the southern shore of Lake Nahuel Huapi in the Argentine Andes, this resort is exceptionally crowded during the peak season. The Cerro Catedral slopes are about 12 miles (19 km) from town and are easily reached on good, paved roads. Several major hotels offer transportation to the slopes. The *cerro* (hill) derives its name from the natural formation of rock, which resembles a cathedral. The peak itself stands nearly 8,000 feet above sea level, with a range of 3-mile ski runs from novice to expert. Facilities include a cable car with a 25-person capacity and 9 double chairs along with T-bars and pomas for a total capacity of 20,000 people per hour.

The official ski season opens on July 9 every year and continues through September, snow conditions permitting. Cerro Catedral is frequently the site of national and international competitions. The colorful *Fiesta de la Nieve* (snow festival) takes place in August and should not be missed. Bear in mind that because Bariloche has become so popular with Argentines and other South Americans, interminable hours can be wasted waiting in lift lines during July and early August. However, restaurants and refuges midway down the slopes are refreshing places to stop, refuel, and avoid the crowded lines at the base of the mountain. Argentine and Austrian ski instructors give classes in Spanish, English, and German.

The *Catedral Ski* hotel (phone: 944-22322), at the base of the lifts, is adequate and offers après-ski nightclub entertainment. There is also a hostel at Punta Condores, on the side of the mountain. During July and August accommodations are scarce, so book ahead. For other hotels in Bariloche, see *Argentina,* DIRECTIONS.

**Cerro Chapelco, near San Martín de los Andes** – Smaller than Cerro Catedral, less expensive, and much less crowded, Chapelco has good spring skiing through September and offers a variety of slopes for novice, intermediate, and once-a-year skiers, with virtually no wait in any lift line. From the top of Chapelco (which means "land of melting ice and floating waters" in the Mapuche Indian dialect), it's possible to see the Lanín Volcano and Lake Lácar, which cross the Chilean border a few miles away.

Skiers can reach the 6,396-foot slopes by a triple chair lift, double chair lift, a T-bar, and poma lifts. The longest run, some 3.8 miles, is wide and gentle in most parts. There are smaller, more difficult offshoots to test even expert skiers.

Projects are under way to expand the mountain resort and add chalets and hotels around the base lodge, but there are still no hotels at the slopes. The town of San Martín de los Andes is only about 7 miles (11 km) down the mountain, snuggled at its base along the shores of Lake Lácar. There are comfortable lodgings here, some with meals, at very reasonable rates. Bungalow communities rent cabins with complete kitchens (including utensils), which can sleep as many as eight people for less than $70 per day. *Cabañas Lácar,* 2 blocks from the lake, is one of the best. *Los Pinos,* across the street, is also popular with skiers. It has clean, inexpensive rooms and good food.

The *Manolo* refuge, halfway down the main ski run, serves hearty lunches and snacks, so it's unnecessary to go all the way back to the base lodge. The cafeteria at the base serves decent, inexpensive meals. The *Jockey Club* restaurant, behind the central bank in San Martín de los Andes, offers a buffet: all you can eat for around $6.

In contrast to Bariloche's active nightlife, San Martín closes early, but the *Sol Jet* hotel (used primarily by *Sol Jet* ski tours) has a casino and nightclub. It's on a hill on the road to Cerro Chapelco.

Chapelco regulars recommend avoiding late July and early August — during school vacation break — unless you're coming for the annual *Fiesta de la Montaña* snow festival on August 5.

Ski equipment can be rented at the mountain's base lodge or at any of the ski shops along the main street of San Martín. If you don't speak Spanish, ask a resident to help you negotiate a price so that you are not overcharged. Ski students can take lessons from English-, Spanish-, or German-speaking Argentine or Austrian instructors.

**Las Hoyas, Esquel** – Much less well known, and certainly less jammed than either Chapelco or Catedral, these slopes are popular with learners, intermediate skiers, and infrequent skiers. The slopes are about 9 miles (14 km) from Esquel, which is about 160 miles (256 km) south of Bariloche. They have limited skiing, with a chair lift and T-bar to carry skiers up the slopes.

Its southern locations makes Las Hoyas ideal for spring skiing; in fact, the season lasts through October. Many spring skiers, finding no snow at Catedral or Chapelco, make their way to Las Hoyas to finish the season. Equipment can be rented at the mountain and at Esquel. The Argentine instructors are quite good.

**Las Leñas** – South of Mendoza and near the Chilean border, this 15,000-acre ski complex is now South America's largest and most extensive ski resort. The Austrian, French, Swiss, and American Olympic ski teams train here. Accommodations for more than 3,000 skiers are available in deluxe and first class hotels along with four apartment complexes featuring fully equipped kitchenettes. A shopping arcade, numerous restaurants and bars, and a disco also are located at the base of the lifts. There also is a deluxe hotel with indoor/outdoor heated pool, Jacuzzis, sauna, restaurants, and an international casino. Beginning at a base of 7,382 feet and climbing to 11,253 feet, the lift system at Las Leñas carries 9,200 skiers per hour. Prime time is June through October. For reservations, contact *Valle de Las Leñas* (238 Suipacha, 4th Floor, Buenos Aires 1003; phone: 1-311-8232 or 312-2259); for information and reservations in the US (phone: 800-862-7545, except in Florida where the number is 305-864-7545); or contact *4th Dimension Tours* (1150 NW 72nd Ave., Suite 250, Miami, FL 33126; phone: 800-343-0020; 305-477-1525, in Florida).

For more information about skiing in Argentina, write directly to the ski resorts or to the *Federación Argentina de Ski* (1560 Viamonte, Buenos Aires; phone: 1-407127). In Buenos Aires, Bariloche, or Neuquen, check with any travel agent. Or contact Argentina's Tourist Board office in New York (phone: 212-603-0400).

## BOLIVIA

**Chacaltaya, near La Paz** – After skiing Chacaltaya, everything else is tame. Billed as the "world's highest ski slope," the glacial run at 17,716 feet is only for very accomplished skiers in peak condition, and it really cannot be described as great skiing. It's a short run, and to be negotiated more for the feeling of accomplishment afterward than for the pure sport. Relatively undiscovered, the slope is about a 90-minute drive from one of the world's highest cities (La Paz), on difficult, empty roads that challenge the brave and instill terror in anyone with even a mild fear of heights. The road is actually dangerous, with mind-bending hairpin turns twisting around sheer green shale cliffs that drop thousands of feet. Those who survive the ride, and do not succumb to altitude sickness, will probably find the spartan restaurant and ski hut next to the Bolivian Institute of Cosmic Physics complex a fascinating change from more sophisticated resorts. There are now two hook tows which take skiers from the edge of a cliff to the top of the Chacaltaya Glacier to begin the descent. The best times to ski are October or November through April. Later in the season, it gets too windy and icy. Bring your own equipment, since the ski rental shop is open only on weekends. For more information on skiing, contact the *Club Andino Boliviano*, 1638 Calle México, La Paz (phone: 2-324682).

## CHILE

**Portillo** – Probably the best-known South American ski resort, this is also the toughest. Many national and international competitions have been held here, including *World Cup Ski Championships*. A world speed record, 124 mph, was set here by American Steve McKinney in 1978, although it has been broken many times since. The most recent time was 142.49 mph, clocked by Michael Prufer at the *1992 Olympics* in Les Arcs, France.

Some 91 miles (146 km) northeast of Santiago in the Cordillera de los Andes, 9,348 feet above sea level, Portillo's granular powder slopes have challenged skiers for more than 40 years. The seven main runs are reached by seven lifts, including a double chair, T-bars, and tows. Lift lines are shorter than at Bariloche in Argentina. Although the season runs from June to October, depending on snow conditions, expert skiers agree that the period from July to early August is best.

But it's not necessary to be a dynamite skier to try the slopes. Beginners can start on an 861-foot run along a 305-foot slope served by a tow lift, graduating to the Plateau, a 2,736-foot run with a 981-foot slope served by a ski chair. Juncalillo, the longest and best intermediate slope, is a run of 4,595 feet with a slope of 1,105 feet. Other slopes are Enlace, 1,040 feet with a 266-foot slope, and Nido de Condores, 1,170 feet with a 513-foot slope. The most challenging slope of all is Roca Jack, 2,405 feet, of which 1,000 feet are vertical. For those who have never skied, there's a bunny hill of 845 feet and a 211-foot slope. Siggi Grottendorfer, an Austrian, operates a ski school where there are private or group lessons in beginning, intermediate, and advanced skiing. The Roca Jack and Plateau runs come together at the bottom, forming a "V."

Despite its glamorous reputation as a jet-set resort, Portillo is more popular with Argentines and Chileans than with Europeans and Americans. Professional US skiers have been openly expressing disappointment about the way skiers are overcharged for renting skis and for using the facilities at the one hotel. They also caution that theft of clothing and equipment is now a big problem. So keep your eye on everything that's yours, and don't leave anything lying around.

Robert Purcell, an investment banker whose New York holding company took financial control of Portillo in the early 1960s, now runs the entire mountain-hotel resort complex. The 650-bed *Portillo* hotel (at Km 61 on International Rd., Portillo; phone: 562-243-3007), on the shores of the blue glacier lake, Laguna del Inca, has several restaurants, a cinema, nightclub, swimming pool, sauna, and medical station. Reservations can be made at its office in Santiago (phone: 2-231-3411; fax: 2-231-7164). Or in the US, contact the *LanChile Airlines* tour desk (phone: 800-255-5526) for ski package information or *Ladatco Tours,* which works in conjunction with Chile's *Ladeco Airlines* (phone: 800-327-6162). For a full description of Portillo, see *Chile,* DIRECTIONS.

**Farellones, near Santiago** – About a 90-minute drive from downtown, this is an ideal day trip, and thousands of Chileans descend on the place on winter weekends. There are three easy runs (good for beginners and intermediates), the longest of which is 5,576 feet. All can be reached by a T-bar and tow lift. Reservations can be made at the *Farellones Hotel,* 1998 Av. Las Bandurrias in Farellones (phone: Farellones 211-2726; in Santiago, 2-246-3344).

**La Parva, near Santiago** – Another very popular weekend ski area, its five runs (beginner and intermediate) have about 1,640 feet of vertical drop. Contact *Condominio Nueva La Parva,* 77 Nueva La Parva (phone: La Parva 220-8510; in Santiago through *Centro de Ski La Parva,* 2-233-2476; fax: 2-231-3233).

**El Colorado, near Santiago** – Actually, it's between Farellones and La Parva. There are four slopes reached by a chair lift and a T-bar; the longest is 6,560 feet. Contact *Centro de Ski El Colorado-Farellones,* located at 4900 Av. Apoquindo, Local 47-48 in Santiago (phone: 2-246-3344).

Farellones, La Parva, and El Colorado are interconnected by lifts and by shuttle bus service, offering a choice of runs for all levels of experience. With no other surrounding high peaks, skiers enjoy exposure to the sun throughout the day.

**Lagunillas, near Santiago** – This small ski station, only 6,560 feet above sea level, 37 miles east of the city, is relatively new. Only two slopes have currently been prepared for skiing. The road to Lagunillas winds around the Cajón del Maipo, one of the most enchanting valleys in Chile (see *Santiago,* THE CITIES). The *Club Andino de Chile* runs a clean, inexpensive refuge. For reservations, contact the club at 24 Enrique Foster Sur (phone: 2-228-5449).

**Termas de Chillán** – Located 300 miles (480 km) south of Santiago and 50 miles (80 km) from the city of Chillán, this is also a spa resort known for its thermal hot springs and is just now joining the ranks as one of Chile's prominent ski resorts. The new 48-room hotel, *Pirgallo* (phone: 42-223887), has color TV sets, a restaurant, bar, sauna, tennis, and a swimming pool. There is good off-track helicopter skiing here, too. Reservations can be made in Santiago (at 2237 Av. Providencia; phone: 2-251-5776) or in the US through *Ladatco Tours* (phone: 800-327-6162) and *Continental Ski Network* (phone: 800-275-3123).

**Valle Nevado, near Santiago** – New in 1989, this resort is about a 2-hour drive from Santiago, and is the brain child of the French developers of Les Arcs. The *Valle Nevado* hotel, next to the slopes, offers everything from ski equipment and classes to a bar, restaurant, and disco. The recently opened 130-room *Puerta del Sol* hotel and the *Mirandor del Inca* condominiums also provide upscale lodging for skiers. Make reservations in Santiago (at 441 Gertrudis Echeñique; phone: 2-206-0027; fax: 2-228-8888). Billing itself as the "ski capital of the Southern Hemisphere," the resort encompasses 21,000 acres of skiable terrain, and more than 16 miles of ski runs. *Brendan Tours* in Los Angeles offers comprehensive ski packages in cooperation with *LanChile.* Check with *LanChile*'s tour desk (phone: 800-735-5526) or *Brendan Tours* (phone:

800-421-8446). *Ladatco Tours,* in conjunction with *Ladeco Airlines,* also has packages (phone: 800-327-6162), as does *4th Dimension Tours* (1150 NW 72nd Ave., Suite 250, Miami, FL 33126; phone: 305-477-1525 or 800-343-0020). *Cavalcade Tours* (phone: 800-822-6754) also has week-long packages to Valle Nevado.

**Antuco, near Concepción** – Three slopes run down the side of an inactive volcano, the Volcán Antuco, 9,790 feet above sea level. All can be reached by a T-bar. There are two small refuges, one sponsored by *Club de Ski de Los Angeles* (phone: 43-322651). The other is sponsored by *Inversiones Camapanil,* at the Universidad de Concepción (196 Ongulmo, Concepción; phone: 41-234881).

**Pucón** – A chair lift and T-bars take skiers up to the slopes on this live volcano surrounded by brilliant blue lakes. The runs provide a challenge for beginning and intermediate skiers, who can later soak their weary muscles at hot springs on the outskirts of Pucón, explore the friendly town in full view of the Villarrica volcano, or try their luck at the casino at the *Gran Hotel Pucón.* Ski packages are available through *DMC* (3144 Napoleón in Santiago; phone: 2-242-9042; fax: 2-246-6935). February is the trendiest time for skiing in Pucón; it's almost impossible to book lodgings during that month — so plan ahead.

**Antillanca, near Bariloche, Argentina** – Nowhere as large as the resorts across the border, this is one of the loveliest ski resorts in Chile. There is a trio of lodges at the ski center, the largest being *Hotel Antillanca* (at Km 98, southeast of Osorno; phone: 64-235114; in Santiago, 2-672-7812 or 698-8072). Make reservations through the *Club Andino* offices in Osorno (phone: 64-232297).

# Hunting

Hunting laws and regulations in Latin American countries are subject to change. So just before planning a trip, re-check current laws, prohibitions, regulations, and seasons. Some governments have limits on the number or types of guns, or on the amount of ammunition a hunter can bring into the country, but most tour organizers who specialize in hunting trips will assist with all of these details. Contact the consulate of the country in which you plan to hunt to arrange to bring your weapons along with you. It probably will be necessary to supply information on the make, model, caliber, and serial number of your arms, as well as your passport number, home address, addresses in the country you are visiting, arrival and departure dates, and the places you plan to hunt. Check with the consulate to see whether you must register with local police or other organizations once you get into the country. If the consulate doesn't know, try other sources — hunting organizations or travel agents — and by all means, check again once you get into the country.

Note that United States federal law prohibits the import of any animal or bird considered an endangered species. For a list, write the US Department of the Interior, Fish and Wildlife Service, PO Box 28006, Washington, DC 20005.

**ARGENTINA:** Hunting is permitted for deer, puma, wild boar, peccary, partridge, duck, and wild turkey. Although jaguar and tapir exist, hunting them is now prohibited. Deer hunting season runs from March through April in Neuquén, the southern lake district, La Pampa, and along the Atlantic coast. The black buck can be hunted all year south of Santa Fe and in Buenos Aires province. Wild boar can be hunted all year in La Pampa and along the coast of the province of Buenos Aires and Bahía Blanca; puma, throughout the year, everywhere it is found. Puma hunting is best in La Pampa, Río Negro, and Neuquén. Peccaries are hunted all year in the northern provinces of Salta, Santiago del Estero, and Formosa.

Partridge season runs from May 1 to August 1. The bird is found all over the country.

## DIVERSIONS / Hunting

Duck and geese can be hunted April, May, and June throughout much of the country, and through August in some parts. Wild turkey is hunted during May through July in Chubut province, especially in Trevelin. There are limits on hunting partridge and wild turkey.

Red deer does with their young cannot be taken, nor red deer with less than 12 points, and a hunter is not allowed to bag more than two red deer per season.

Firearms must be registered with the Registro Nacional de Armas (3301 Figueroa Alcorta, Buenos Aires 1425) before a hunter enters the country. Be sure to secure a permit from this office. Send your name, nationality, passport number, and home address; temporary address in Argentina; length of stay; where and how (plane, train, bus) you will enter the country; the type, model, caliber, and serial number of your arms; and type, caliber, and quantity of ammunition. A hunter is allowed to bring two big-game, two small-game, and one hand gun into Argentina.

To secure hunting permits, go to the National Park Service if you wish to hunt in a national park or to the provincial tourist office in the province in which you wish to hunt. In Buenos Aires, call the *Federación de Cazadores* (Hunting Federation) for information (phone: 1-653-7198 and 1-785-6014). The provincial tourist office can also help you locate a hunting guide. If you want a guide in the San Martín de los Andes area, go to the National Park Service (at 690 Santa Fe, Buenos Aires; phone: 1-311-0303 or 311-8853), the *intendencia* of the Lanín National Park, or the tourist information office (883 Av. Santa Fe, Buenos Aires; phone: 1-312-2253).

Special tours for waterfowl and wild bird hunting are offered by *Frontiers* (phone: 412-935-1577, in Pennsylvania; elsewhere, 800-245-1950) to Esquina, Goya, Bahía Blanca, San Martín, and Choele Choel. The season for Esquina and Goya is from February to August; the other sites, April to August. *Frontiers* also offers year-round dove shooting near Córdoba. Hunting tours also are available from *Holditur* (834 Tucuman, Buenos Aires; phone: 1-322-2254; fax: 54-1-322-5572) and from Monica Knüll (2963-6B, Av. Las Heras, Buenos Aires; phone: 1-804-3882; fax: 1-802-8872).

**BOLIVIA:** Hunting or fishing in Bolivia is permitted with a license, good for one calendar year, available from the US Embassy or the Ministry of Agriculture (on Av. Camacho in La Paz). You need two small photographs and must pay a nominal fee. If you want to meet other hunters, visit the *Club de Caza y Pesca* (Hunting and Fishing Club) in front of the golf club in Malasilla. There is duck hunting on Lake Titicaca.

**BRAZIL:** Hunting has been prohibited in Brazil since 1989.

**COLOMBIA:** The list of game animals and birds in Colombia is extensive and ranges from water to prairie to jungle fauna: jaguar, tiger, wildcat, ocelot, tapir, puma, black panther, leopard, deer, beaver, possum, several types of monkey, parrot, alligator, armadillo, iguana, turtle, anaconda, boa, duck, goose, dove, partridge, and wild pig. Hunting jaguar, tiger, and monkey is prohibited.

In the swamps and prairies around Cartagena are duck, geese, deer, and wild boar. To hunt this area, contact Jaime Borda (phone: 59-47937 or 59-41979). Borda speaks English, has gear, and knows the best hunting spots. For safaris into the Sierra Nevada, contact Captain "Pancho" Ospina at his beachstand on El Rodadero Beach in Santa Marta.

Around Cali, there is small-game hunting for duck, dove, and partridge. Contact *La Rivera Club* through your hotel for assistance. *Frontiers* (phone: in Pennsylvania, 412-935-1577; in other states, 800-245-1950) and *Caribbean-Pacific Safaris* (phone: 205-540-2240) operate dove-hunting tours to the Cauca Valley, near Cali. They report incredible numbers of birds day in, day out. However, at press time, the Cauca River Valley was among the areas considered dangerous by the US State Department.

Another dove-hunting tour in the Cauca Valley, around Cali, is sponsored by *Safari de Colombia* (Box 777, Cali; phone: 23-641749 or 23-861806). A hunter can rent guns and purchase shells locally. The 5-day tour runs throughout the year, as there is open season on doves.

**ECUADOR:** There's pigeon shooting near Quito, partridge and deer hunting in the highlands. During the dry season (September through March), for a jungle safari in the Oriente to hunt capybara, paca, peccary, and tapir, contact *Sam Hogan Safaris,* PO Box A-122, Quito (phone: 2-450242).

To hunt in Ecuador, get a permit from the *Dirección de Parques Forestales,* Ministerio de Agricultura, 5th Floor, Guayaquil 1740 (phone: 4-517200).

**PARAGUAY:** The Chaco region is the place for hunting in this country. Wild duck from 8 to 12 pounds are a draw, as are peccaries. The duck are best found along the Río Paraguay. The national tourism office (468 Palma, Asunción; phone: 21-441530 or 441620) can provide information on how to arrange hunting trips and where to get necessary licenses, or contact the Ministry of Agriculture (640 Av. 25 de Mayo, Asunción; phone: 21-445214).

**SURINAME:** Tapir, deer, wild boar *(pingo),* capybara, jaguar, and a genus of crocodile called caiman live in Suriname. The season for most big game is March 1 through September 30, although jaguar and caiman can be hunted all year (except for black caymana, which is a protected group). There's also hunting for waterfowl, jungle cats, and howler monkeys. The hunting season for wild duck runs from September 1 through March 31; for the Amazon parrot, from July 1 through December 31. The hunting season for most birds is September 1 through April 30, except for the wild dove, which can be hunted all year. The hunting of flamingos and ibises is prohibited, as is the killing of most types of turtle. No hunting is permitted in nature reserves.

Big-game hunting parties can be arranged with the help of local tour operators. The Suriname Consulate in Miami has a list of referrals and is also the source of all paperwork necessary to obtain hunting licenses and gun permits. Contact the Suriname Tourism Department (8 Waterkant, Paramaribo; phone: 471163 or 478421). They will require the make and caliber of your guns, and the number of cartridges you plan to carry into the country. Shotguns can be provided by tour operators, or you can bring your own into the country free of charge for up to 3 months. No rifles or sidearms are permitted. *Note:* At press time, because of the current guerrilla activity and recent political upheaval, there are likely to be severe restrictions on bringing firearms into the country.

**URUGUAY:** Hunting trips for North American tourists are not widely developed as yet in Uruguay, but what's available is topnotch. There is excellent walk-up hunting with dogs for partridge near Colonia, and from May through August, waterfowl hunting in the eastern part of the country is also very good. Information about restrictions and hunting regulations are available from the Ministerio de Agricultura, 1476 Constituyente in Montevideo (phone: 2-404155 and 2-404159).

# For the Mind

## Lost Worlds: The Archaeological Heritage of South America

Even more fabulous than the legends of Golden Empires that lured the Spanish and Portuguese to South America in the 15th and 16th centuries were the indigenous civilizations that flourished at that time and earlier.

The mysteries of pre-Columbian history can best be appreciated by visiting any one of the archaeological sites scattered throughout the Southern Hemisphere. Massive stonework, intricately carved into dazzling shapes by unknown masons, stand piled in patterned formation. Some are in areas so remote and sparsely settled that it's an authentic mystery how anyone ever decided to build there.

The fascination with the people who actually built and lived in the complex structures of these vanished civilizations draws thousands upon thousands of visitors to South America every year. The archaeological site with biggest box office appeal is Machu Picchu, a terraced complex of stairways, temples, and aqueducts on a mountainside not far from the Andean city of Cuzco, Peru. Machu Picchu is one of many archaeological sites with competently guided tours of its ruins, and in Peru in particular — and the Andean countries in general — the guides employed by tour operators are, for the most part, well trained and knowledgeable. Read about the places you plan to visit before your arrival, since there is very little (if any) historical information distributed at the sites. Generally, they are very far off the beaten path. Whenever possible, spend a day in the capital visiting the archaeological museums for background, and consider taking along an English-Spanish dictionary since exhibits are generally described in Spanish. Check the bookstores for locally published guides; some are very good.

Other major sites are at Tiahuanaco, near La Paz, Bolivia; San Agustín in Colombia; the Nazca Desert line drawings in southern Peru; and Easter Island, off the coast of Chile. But there are dozens of smaller ruins, many of which are still being excavated — and more that have not yet been discovered. This is the place where the really adventurous actually have come upon previously undiscovered lost worlds. In 1988, the *National Geographic Society* announced the discovery of a Moche warrior-lord's tomb in Sipán, Peru — the richest burial excavation in the Americas. And in late 1991, archaeologists announced there were at least half a dozen probable tombs at the same site. *Archaeological Tours* offers a continually changing list of trips to various countries, including Latin American destinations. The tours are led by anthropologists, archaeologists, and art historians. For the latest schedule of tours contact the company at 30 E. 42nd St., Suite 1202, New York, NY 10017 (phone: 212-986-3054).

### ARGENTINA

Although not the first stop on an archaeological itinerary, Argentina does have some notable pre-Columbian and colonial ruins. Visits to many of the best-known ruins can be arranged through *Lihué Expeditions* (262 Belgrano, Suite 104, San Isidro, Argentina; phone: 1-747-7689). Another Argentine operator offering specialized packages, including archaeological trips is *Appel* (848 Av. Corrientes, Oficina 1201, Buenos Aires, Argentina (phone: 1-394-5172 or 1-612-6782; fax: 1-325-5219).

**Incahuasi** – Some 4 miles (about 6 km) northeast of the Ingeniero Mauri Railroad Station in Salta, it has extensive remains of a stone Inca fortress.

**Tafí Valley** – An hour from Tucumán in the Parque de los Menhires are 60 stone monoliths, believed to be about 2,000 years old, inscribed with symbols that archaeologists still have not translated.

**Morohuasi** – These ruins of pre-Columbian dwellings, Inca roads, walls, and art are about 3 miles (5 km) south of the Quebrada del Toro and 7 miles (11 km) northeast of the Diego de Almagro Station in Salta. Tours can be arranged in Buenos Aires through *Holditur* (834 Tucumán; phone: 1-322-2254).

**Tolombon** – About 131 miles (210 km) from Salta, in the Santa María Valley, some pre-Hispanic ruins are scattered to the east of town. The best way to get there is to walk from the town of Santa María.

**Tilcara** – About 50 miles (80 km) north of Jujuy, is the Pucara, a restored Indian fortress with pre-Columbian ruins — chambers, stairways, tombs, and terraces.

**Uquia** – Inca ruins are still visible at Peñas Blancas, 3 miles (5 km) from Uquia, a small town in the Quebrada de Humahuaca in the state of Jujuy.

**Cayasta** – About 52 miles (83 km) northeast from Santa Fe stands the city founded by Juan de Garay in 1573 to serve as a stopover between Asunción and the kingdoms of Peru. The city became quite developed for its time, but because of the attacks from Indians and the floods from the Paraná River, it was transplanted a century later and became what today is Santa Fe.

**Aconquija** – About 20 miles (32 km) from Concepción, in the state of Tucumán, at an elevation of 13,448 feet, are some small dwellings and ancient roads.

## BOLIVIA

**Tiahuanaco** – The capital of a civilization believed to be more than 3,000 years old, this 50-acre site — Bolivia's most impressive archaeological zone — has yet to be fully excavated. The center of the pre-Inca Aymara empire, it reached its peak between AD 600 and 900. The major sections are the Gateway of the Sun, a massive doorway carved from a single piece of stone, with square figures surrounding a central figure said to represent the god Viracocha; some stone monoliths between 9 and 12 feet high; and the ruins of Kalasasaya Palace, a 442-by-426-foot rectangular plaza marked by 20-foot-high perpendicular stones. Nearby stands the Akapana pyramid. About 45 miles (72 km) from La Paz, Tiahuanaco is accessible by a rugged road. A number of La Paz operators offer guided tours (see *Bolivia,* DIRECTIONS).

**Islands of the Moon and the Sun, Lake Titucaca** – According to Inca legend, Inti, the sun god, created Manco Cápac and his sister-consort, Mama Occlo, whom he placed on the Island of the Sun. Then he gave a golden staff to the sun's children, commanding them to found an empire on the spot where the staff would vanish into the earth. In the course of their journey, Manco Capác and Mama Occlo came upon a valley where the staff disappeared. There they founded their capital, the city of Cuzco, "Navel of the World." The Island of the Moon, or Coati, in the lake, was consecrated by the Inca to their deities, with priestesses (*ñustas*) in charge of ceremonies of worship. The ruins of the Palace of the Vestal Virgins and a temple to the Moon Mother also can be found on the Island of the Moon. About 100 feet below the surface of the water, divers have found submerged stone walls, believed to be the original Inca city. Lake Titicaca trips that stop at the Island of the Sun can be arranged through *Transturin* (295 Mariscal Cruz, La Paz; phone: 2-320445; fax: 2-391162) or *Crillón Tours* (1223 Camacho, La Paz; phone: 2-374566/7).

## CHILE

**Pucara de Lasana** – This pre-Inca fort, to the east of Chuquicamata, has been declared a national monument.

**San Pedro de Atacama** – The highlight of Chilean archaeological sites, this town, 60 miles (96 km) southeast of Calama, houses an archaeological museum of mummies, skeletons, and artifacts excavated from the Atacama Desert. Originally inhabited by the Cunza or Atacama Indians, then the Inca, the town was conquered by Don Diego de Almagro in 1536. About 20 miles (32 km) south of San Pedro de Atacama, at Toconao, is a section of the original Inca Highway. *Ladatco Tours* offers packages to the site (phone: 800-327-6162).

**Guaiquivilo** – Not far from Parral, at an elevation of 9,840 feet, stand the so-called talking stones. These are actually huge chunks of rock from the Andean Cordillera, carved with symbols; their markings have not yet been deciphered.

**Rapa Nui (Easter Island)** – About 1,000 giant stone gods called *moai*, each between 30 and 40 feet high, are scattered all over the island. They are covered with unintelligible inscriptions, although anthropologists, archaeologists, and laypeople have begun to unravel the mystery of how the *moai* moved. Legend decrees that the *moai* walked to their destination, but archaeological findings reveal that they were transported on wooden boards pulled like a sled by ropes made of tree fibers. At dry spots, cooked potato was rubbed along the bottom of the boards to make them more slippery. Other *moai* may have been moved on top of rolling logs. The biggest ones, measuring around 150 feet in height, can be found in Vinapu and Tongariki. Other stone constructions, ancient tombs, and funeral monuments can be found in other parts of the island (see *Chile,* DIRECTIONS).

## COLOMBIA

**San Agustín National Park** – The most elaborate stone carvings in South America are found here, in the Valley of the Statues, about 145 miles (233 km) from Neiva. A few hundred stone figures of men, animals, and gods are scattered over 14 widely separated sites. Many appear to bear strong similarities to the Tiahuanaco carvings. According to carbon 14 dating methods, the earliest section of San Agustín is Alto de Lavapatas, which dates back to 600 BC. The *lavapatas,* or foot-washing fountain, is a series of small water ducts carved in the face of a huge, relatively flat rock about 550 square feet in area. The ducts carried water from a stream into terraced pools. It takes about 3 or 4 days to see the most important sites and statues. The archaeological zone is accessible only by four-wheel-drive vehicle or horse. Nineteen miles (30 km) away is the recently discovered Alto de los Idolos, a site covered with statues, coffins, and tombs (see *Colombia,* DIRECTIONS). Note that the US State Department considers the rural Huila department, where the park is located, an unsafe area. For additional information at the time of your trip, call the State Department's Citizens' Emergency Center (phone: 202-647-5225).

**Tierradentro** – From either starting point, Neiva or Popayán, the road is rough to San Andrés de Pisimbala and the burial caves of Tierradentro. But the scenic trip is worth every bump, and the cave paintings are fantastic; bring a flashlight for viewing. Area artifacts are housed in the small *San Andrés Museum,* where it's possible to camp out or stay in the nearby tourist hotel (see *Colombia,* DIRECTIONS).

**Sierra Nevada de Santa Marta** – To prevent looting, the Colombia government has sealed off one of the largest ancient lost cities ever found. Reliable sources working at the excavation report that the pre-Columbian center was once populated by hundreds of thousands of people. The most impressive site, called Ciudad Perdida (Lost City), is situated on a lush mountain ridge at about 3,000 feet. Again, the north coast area of Colombia, with the exception of major tourist areas such as Cartagena, Santa Marta, and Barranquilla, is considered dangerous for travelers.

**Tairona National Park** – Twenty-five miles (40 km) northeast of Santa Marta is a national park whose jungle vegetation and crystal-white beaches make it one of Colombia's most beautiful spots. There are paths through the jungle — ideal for strolling — refreshment stands along the beach, and huts to rent for those who wish to spend the night.

## ECUADOR

**Ingapirca** – About 43 miles (69 km) from Cuenca, in the province of Canar, stands a stone fortress inn built by Huayna Cápac, the last legitimate Inca, during the 15th century. Reachable by car or bus, the ruins are positioned along the Inca road network in the midst of rough, impressive Andean scenery. Its design, uniquely fashioned chambers, and engraved stones are all being excavated by scientists and studied. This is Ecuador's most important Inca site. Not far from Cuenca, archaeologists have uncovered golden crowns, breastplates, and weapons (see *Ecuador*, DIRECTIONS). *Metropolitan Touring* offers 1-day trips to the sites from Cuenca (phone: in Quito, 2-560550).

**Rumicucho** – Outside Quito, near the Equator Monument at San Antonio de Pichincha, are the ruins of the Temple of Rumicucho, which is one of the largest pre-Columbian sites in the country. There is a museum at the site. For tours, contact *Rootours* in Cuenca, at the corner of Avdas. Larga and Benigno Malo (phone: 7-835533 and 7-835888).

## PANAMA

**Punta Escosés** – In the hot, steamy jungles of Darién Gap, a group of explorers led by Lieutenant-Colonel John Blashford-Snell and Vincent Martinelli of New York's *Explorers Club* uncovered a remarkable set of ruins. In 1978, they discovered the remains of Fort St. Andrews, the site of a Scottish colony founded in 1698 on the northern coast of eastern Panama. Keen to know more about the ill-fated colony that ended with the death of some 2,000 men, the expedition members explored deeper into the isthmus and discovered what are believed to be the first remains of the lost city of Acla, founded by Balboa around 1509, prior to his discovery of the Pacific. Defying schools of barracudas and inquisitive sharks, the expedition's divers also found traces of sunken vessels in the area. Other finds included a fort's moat, a lookout and defensive position built out of coral blocks cut from nearby reefs, a cannonball of the type used in Scotland in the late 17th century, pieces of glazed pottery, and fragments of glass. A complete excavation of the site has been impossible because it is so overgrown by the jungle. One hypothesis of the Fort St. Andrews saga suggests that some of the colonists survived, intermarried with the Cuna Indians, and sired a unique, now lost tribe of red-haired, blue-eyed, dusky Scottish Indians.

## PERU

Unquestionably the South American nation with the richest archaeological heritage, Peru is the home of the incomparable lost city of the Inca, Machu Picchu, one of the most visited destinations on the continent. But the discovery of lost cities has not ended in Peru, and new sites are uncovered yearly, such as the new sites of the Chanca culture which were found in the Chicah Valley north of Cuzco; or, in the northern province of San Martín, the newest of the old lost cities, Gran Pajaten, which was occupied by an unknown people from AD 500 to 1500. There also are the ongoing excavations on the northern coast at Túcume and Sipán, the most dynamic digs on the continent.

When Pizarro and his conquistadores arrived in Peru in 1527, the Inca empire, Tahuantinsuyo, stretched along the Pacific coast, through the Andes, as far north as the present northern border of Ecuador and as far south as the Maule River in central Chile.

## 628 DIVERSIONS / Archaeological Heritage

Though the most famous, the Inca civilization was only the latest of the early South American cultures, reaching its height between AD 1100 and 1500. Around 1470, the Inca conquered the Chimú Indians, whose central city, Chan-Chan, still stands. Predating both groups, the Paraca and Nazca Indians flourished in the deserts of southern Peru 3,000 and 4,000 years ago. Their pottery, exquisite woven textiles, mysterious line drawings, and mummies can still be seen (see *Peru*, DIRECTIONS).

**Machu Picchu** – Accessible in a few hours by train from Cuzco or after a 4- or 5-day hike, this incredible complex of temples, houses, baths, hundreds of stairways, and a guardhouse rises 2,000 feet above the valley of the Río Urubamba, the sacred river of the Inca. Discovered in 1911 by North American Hiram Bingham, it has more than 100 acres of hard granite block buildings, walls, and plazas. Dr. Bingham separated the city into three distinct sections: the Ingenuity Group, so called because of ingeniously constructed houses set on giant rocks at 45-degree angles and linked by numerous stairways; the Princess Group, which includes the circular tower built into a rock, a sundial in a cave under the tower, and several stairways; and the Religious Group, containing the Temple of the Three Windows and the priest's house. Finds, dating from the 15th and 16th centuries, include vast agricultural terraces and a ritual center with 30 tombs. A number of travel companies offer tours to Machu Picchu, including *Maya Route Tours,* 18 E. 41st St., Suite 1606, New York, NY 10017 (phone: 800-537-2297).

**Huayna Picchu** – For the best view of the whole city of Machu Picchu, hike up this steep mountain (unless you suffer from vertigo, in which case the hike is definitely not recommended). The strenuous exercise is well worth the effort. At its summit, there are stairways that date from Inca times, stonework, and three small caves. (Note that the approach to this site is dangerous; climb with caution.)

**Huiñay-Huayna** – A 3-hour hike from Machu Picchu, this smaller, abandoned Inca city, whose name means "growing boy," is set on a hillside next to a waterfall, in superb isolation. Overgrown with jungle vegetation, Huiñay-Huayna consists of stone buildings, arches, doorways, and stairs (see "Peru," *The Wild Continent: Trekking, Backpacking, River Rafting, and Camping,* DIVERSIONS).

**Ollantaytambo** – About halfway between Machu Picchu and Cuzco, this giant fortress stands on a hill overlooking the valley. The remains of circular defense towers guard the lower slopes. But the most unusual section is a wall formed by six huge polished slabs set upright, with stone wedges in between. The boulders are said to come from quarries on the opposite side of the mountain. Contact *Lima Tours* (phone: 14-276624 in Lima; 84-228431 in Cuzco).

**Sacsayhuamán** – This impressive fortress, with three gateways and the remains of three towers, stands on a hill overlooking Cuzco. To the east, the Inca temple of Kenko consists of a large boulder set upright on a platform in front of a group of other boulders, with many steps cut from the stone. About 1 mile (1.6 km) beyond Kenko, the small fort of Puka Pukará dominates two valleys, where there are entrances to tunnels that are said to be connected to Sacsayhuamán and Cuzco. According to legend, at least one of the Inca tunnels went all the way to Ecuador. Contact *Lima Tours* (see above).

**Pisac** – The largest of the fortified cities that guarded Inca Cuzco, the stone complex sits high above the town of Pisac. A road leads about 7 miles (11 km) to the foot of the multi-terraced ruins that include a sun temple, baths, guard towers, royal dwellings, and a cliff-burial cemetery.

**Pucará** – At Km 285 of the Cuzco-Puno Highway, this was the ceremonial center or fortress of another lost city that is believed to date to the second century AD. Artifacts resembling those of Tiahuanaco were discovered in May 1976. Carved rocks, pyramids, and streets cover an area of 2½ square miles at an altitude of 12,792 feet. Several monoliths, one 4½ feet high, stand around the area. Archaeologists believe they were sacred symbols. A temple of carved red rocks, 115 feet in diameter, has also been unearthed.

**Sillustani** – Heading north from Puno on the shores of Lake Titicaca, follow the turnoff to Lake Umayo. About 15 miles (24 km) from Puno stand the *chulpas* (pre-Inca funeral towers) of Sillustani, a puzzling sight. Don't miss it.

**Paracas** – South of Lima, Paracas is the center and burial place of an Indian culture that flourished more than 3,000 years ago. In the cemetery, Paracas Necropolis, mummies buried in elaborate textiles have been discovered. There's a good museum here, as is the small one in nearby Ica. Tours here are frequently planned through the *Californian Institute for Peruvian Studies,* 9017 Feather River Way, Sacramento, CA 95826 (phone: 916-362-2752).

**Tambo Colorado** – Between Pisco and Paracas lies one of the best-preserved palace complexes of pre-Columbian Peru; some of the original wall paintings remain. This is a worthwhile detour off the coastal road south from Lima.

**Nazca** – The famous Peruvian line drawings are in the desert plains between Nazca and Palpa. The Pan-American Highway goes through the heart of the area, but visitors will not be able to see anything from the road. Contact *Aero Condor,* with flights to and over Nazca (at the *Sheraton Hotel,* Paseo de la República, Lima; phone: 14-329050). The designs are believed to have been made as long as 2,500 or 3,000 years ago. The purpose of the lines is subject of constant speculation: Some say they could have served as a calendar or are linked to the constellations. Straight lines, huge triangles, animals, and spiral forms can be seen over the entire area. For guests staying at the *Las Dunas* hotel in Ica, *Aero Condor* runs a flight over the Nazca drawings; the plane departs from the hotel's landing strip. A complete 2-night package that includes round-trip transportation from Lima can be booked with *LARC* hotels (phone: in Florida, 813-439-2118; in other states, 800-327-3573). (See *Peru,* DIRECTIONS.) *Aeroica* (phone: 14-243777) also has flights over the lines.

**Chan-Chan** – Near Trujillo, the adobe ruins of Chan-Chan cover 11 square miles, making it the largest adobe city in the world when the Spanish stumbled onto it. Formerly the center of the Chimú empire that stretched from Guayaquil, Ecuador, to the south of Peru, this walled city contained reservoirs, temples, and gardens. It reached its height around AD 1300. The city was discovered by the Inca around 1470, but ultimately was destroyed by the Spanish, who also stole the silver and gold ornaments. Today, the massive adobe walls (originally almost 50 feet wide) enclose ruins of the city, including temples, ceremonial plazas, and bas-relief of fishing nets, birds, and fish. To the north of Chan-Chan, at the mouth of the Chicama River, Huaca Prieta contains subterranean houses lined with stone and roofed with earth. Several US firms offer tours to the site, including *ATS* (phone: 800-223-9657) and *Maupintour* (phone: 800-255-4266).

**Chavín de Huantar** – The stone carvings found at the site of this Indian temple are believed to be 3,000 years old. The Chavín civilization appeared at almost the same time as the Olmec civilization in Mexico, and their architecture, sculpture, and carved ceramics were similar. The temple is about 38 (61 km) miles from Huaráz, on the road to Recuay.

**Pachacámac** – About 19 miles (31 km) from Lima, this was Peru's largest coastal city prior to the arrival of the Spanish and was the most important coastal worship center in both pre-Inca and Inca cultures. The complex contains a pyramid built around the 1300s, the Temple of Pachacámac, the Inca Temple of the Sun, and the House of the Virgins of the Sun. Contact *Vista Tours* in Lima (phone: 14-276624).

**Sipán** – In the northern Peruvian desert outside Chiclayo, this excavation became one of the world's most talked-about digs when the *National Geographic Society* announced that archaeologists uncovered the tomb of a Moche warrior-lord in 1988. The richest tomb ever found in the Americas, however, may be outdone. By late 1991, four tombs had been uncovered and archaeologists are fairly certain that there are several more. Tours can be arranged in the US through *Maupintour* (phone: 800-255-4266), *Brendan Tours* (phone: 800-421-8446) and *International Expeditions*

(800-633-4734). In Chiclayo, contact *Indiana Tours* (phone: 74-242287; fax: 74-240833).

**Túcume** – Norwegian archaeologist Thor Heyerdahl and his team of Peruvians and Europeans currently are excavating at a site of 27 ancient adobe pyramids in the valley at Túcume, just outside Chiclayo in northern Peru. This burial area has not been invaded by looters for centuries, and Heyerdahl predicts invaluable artifacts will be recovered. Tourists are welcome at the site. Packages can be arranged in the US with *Path Tours* (phone: 800-843-0400), *Fourth Dimension* (phone: 305-477-1525), and *Magellan Tours* (phone: 800-521-5963) or, in Chiclayo, with *Indiana Tours* (phone: 74-242287; fax: 74-240833) or *Aero Andino* (phone: 74-233161).

# Memorable Museums

Compared to Europe, South America has a limited selection of excellent museums. There are, however, some notable collections. The gold museums in Bogotá and Lima are among the most famous in the world, and Brazil has several unusually fine art museums. Where available, buy English-language guides, particularly for the archaeological museums.

## BRAZIL

**Museo Emílio Goeldi (Emílio Goeldi Museum)** – For those who venture no farther up the Amazon than its mouth, this collection of Amazonian Indian relics and exhibits on Amazon life and history (adjoining a zoo with animals from the region) provides an idea of what the interior is like. Closed Mondays. Admission charge. 376 Av. Magalhães Barata, Belém (phone: 91-224-9233).

**Arquidiocesano Museu (Archdiocese Museum)** – The works of Brazil's foremost colonial sculptor, Antônio Francisco Lisboa — known as Aleijadinho, or "the Little Cripple" — and of his contemporary, painter João Ataíde, can be found here along with Portuguese silverware and religious art. Closed Tuesday mornings. Admission charge. The museum is in Mariana, a few miles from Ouro Preto, on Rua Frei Durão (phone: 31-557-1237).

**Ouro Preto** – The center of the Brazilian revolution against the Portuguese in 1822, Ouro Preto is so densely packed with colonial history and art that the entire town has been declared a national monument. Many of Aleijadinho's works are found in the São Francisco de Assis church, most notably the altar and carvings. Others can be found in the Carmel, São José, and All Souls churches. The *Teatro Municipal,* actually an opera house, is the oldest theater in Brazil. Rua Brig, Mosqueira. The Casa dos Contos, built in 1782, is one of the best examples of Brazilian colonial architecture. The *Museu de Minerologia* (Minerology Museum at the Mining School) contains 2,500 different types of stones from all over the country. Praça Tiradentes. Open daily from 1 to 5 PM (phone: 31-551-1666). (For a complete description of Ouro Preto, see *Brazil,* DIRECTIONS.)

**Museu do Ouro (Gold Museum)** – One of Brazil's richest museums stands in Sabará, about 15 miles (24 km) from Belo Horizonte, a town founded by the *bandeirantes* (pioneers) who were one of the largest suppliers of gold to Portugal. In a house built in 1730, it contains a complete collection of relics and documents from the gold rush era, as well as gold bars imprinted with the Portuguese royal seal. Open Tuesdays through Fridays. Rua da Intendencia, Sabará.

**Museu Imperial (Imperial Museum)** – The summer home of the former royal family houses the Imperial Crown and other items from the royal era. There are also a library and extensive park grounds. Closed Mondays. Admission charge, except Tuesdays. 220 Rua da Imperatriz, Petrópolis.

**Museo do Homem do Nordeste (Museum of Anthropology of Northeastern Man)** – A complex of superb exhibitions, with excellent displays of the costumes, folklore, music, and general lifestyles of the different peoples settled in this Brazilian region. In addition, there is the *Sugar Museum,* which traces the industry from the days of the colonial mills and slave labor to more modern modes of production. Closed Mondays. 2187 Av. 17 de Agosto, Recife (phone: 81-268-2000).

**Jardim Botânico (Botanical Gardens)** – An outdoor nature museum that has thousands of varieties of plants and trees. The Victoria Regia water lilies that grow up to 6 feet in diameter are white the first day they bloom; pink on the second day; red, the third. Open daily. No admission charge. Rua Jardim Botânico, Rio de Janeiro (phone: 21-294-4898).

**Museo Carmen Miranda (Carmen Miranda Museum)** – Quirky and charming, this place is filled with exotic mementos of the woman who made high-wedged shoes and fancy, fruit-filled headpieces her trademark. Closed Mondays. Admission charge. 560 Av. Rui Barbosa, Parque do Flamengo, Rio de Janeiro (phone: 21-551-2597).

**Museu de Arte Sacra (Sacred Art Museum)** – This important collection of religious paintings, sculpture, furniture, and objects wrought of gold is housed in the monastery and church of Santa Teresa. Some items were brought from the Old World; others were made nearby. Closed Sundays and Mondays. Admission charge. 276 Rua do Sodré, Salvador (Bahia) (phone: 71-243-6310).

**Museu do Convento do Carmo (Carmelite Convent Museum)** – A beautiful Carmelite church on top of a hill has dolls in religious costumes, ceremonial objects of gold, silver, and precious stones, and an exhibit on the relationships between *candomblé* gods and Christian saints. Open daily. Admission charge. Largo do Carmo, Salvador (Bahia) (phone: 71-242-0182).

Contemporary Bahian art, among the most distinctive in Brazil, can be found in many art galleries in the Upper City. See *Salvador (Bahia),* THE CITIES.

**Museo de Arte de São Paulo (São Paulo Art Museum; MASP)** – Arguably the best art museum on the continent, its extensive collection contains works from the Middle Ages to the present. Works by Rembrandt, Toulouse-Lautrec, Renoir, El Greco, Cézanne, Van Gogh, Modigliani, and several modern Brazilian painters are mounted on plastic stands rather than hung on the walls — to give a free-floating feeling. Closed Mondays. No admission charge. 1578 Av. Paulista, São Paulo (phone: 11-251-5644).

**Museo Paulista (Paulista Museum)** – A converted palace, this museum contains old maps, coins, firearms, colonial furniture, and art. It's set in Independence Park, where graceful fountains and statues stand amid the foliage. A sound and light show is presented in the evenings. Closed Mondays. Admission charge. Parque da Independência, Ipiranga, São Paulo (phone: 11-215-4588 or 11-215-4307).

**Casa do Bandeirante (Pioneer House)** – A large, reconstructed 18th-century *bandeirante* home, it has rope hammocks, trunks, and authentic furniture. Oxcarts are scattered throughout the museum grounds, along with three old-fashioned mills. The *bandeirantes* were the first settlers in the São Paulo region. Closed Mondays. No admission charge. Praça Monteiro Lobato, Butantã, São Paulo (phone: 11-211-0920).

**Museu de Arte Sacra (Sacred Art Museum)** – *Paulistas* claim that this convent-turned-museum houses the largest collection of altars, statues, and altarpieces outside the Vatican. English-speaking guides can be reserved in advance. Closed Mondays. Admission charge. 676 Av. Tiradentes, São Paulo (phone: 11-227-7694 or 11-228-4063 for the curator).

## CHILE

**Palacio Cousiño** – This neo-classical mansion built by a mining magnate more than a century ago is what remains of the tremendous wealth once found in Santiago. Filled with stunning European furniture, paintings, porcelain, and linen, the house was converted into a museum in 1940. The mansion's huge gilt mirrors create optical illusions and the parquet floor patterns are different in every room. Closed Mondays. Admission charge. 438 Dieciocho, Santiago (phone: 2-698-5063).

## COLOMBIA

**Museo del Oro (Gold Museum)** – One of the "must" sights that any trip to South America should include. More than 25,000 pieces of pre-Columbian goldwork from the Muisca, Tairona, Quimbaya, Sinú, and Capuli cultures, worth tens of millions of dollars, are housed in the 3-story museum. Objects in the form of frogs, insects, animals, serpents, birds, masks, armor, shields, human figures, and instruments are carefully displayed for maximum impact. The choicest items are kept in an intricately illuminated special vault. All the items are carefully labeled, with additional synopses on Indian culture providing background. For a thorough lesson in pre-Columbian culture and art, plan to spend at least a few hours in this museum. Closed Mondays. Admission charge. 5-41 Calle 16 Bogotá (phone: 1-281-3065).

**Museo Arqueológico (Archaeological Museum)** – A restored 17th–18th-century home is the setting for one of Latin America's most stunning collections of pre-Columbian ceramics from Colombia, Ecuador, Peru, and Mexico. Open Tuesdays through Saturdays, 9 AM to 12:30 PM and 1:30 PM to 5 PM, Sundays from 10 AM to 1 PM. Admission charge. 7-43 Carrera 6, Bogotá (phone: 1-282-0740).

**Museo de Artes y Tradiciones Populares (Museum of Popular Art and Tradition)** – The best place to sample the many different styles of craftwork produced in many regions of the country, the museum has a shop selling ethnic items and crafts. Closed Sundays and Mondays. Admission charge. 7-21 Carrera 8, Bogotá (phone: 1-284-5279).

**Museo de Arte Colonial (Colonial Art Museum)** – Originally a 17th-century Jesuit university, this is where Colombia's first president was named and the country's first constitution was written. The collection of Spanish and native arts and crafts includes 300 pieces of furniture and carvings. Open Tuesdays through Saturdays from 9:30 AM to 6 PM. Admission charge, except Saturdays. 9-77 Carrera 6, Bogotá (phone: 1-341-6017 and 1-284-1373).

## ECUADOR

**Museo del Banco Central (Central Bank Museum)** – Actually two museums under the same roof, the most impressive piece here is a painting framed by precious gems and valued at more than $10 million (it rarely leaves the vault). The museum also includes a fifth-floor exhibit of archaeological pieces from prehistoric times to the Spanish conquest. Some of the best remaining religious art pieces from the School of Quito are housed on the sixth floor. Guided tours in English are available on Tuesdays at 11:30 AM. Closed Mondays. Admission charge. Av. 10 de Agosto near the corner of Parque Alameda, Quito (phone: 2-510302 or 2-510382).

**Museo de Arte Colonial (Colonial Art Museum** – This former mansion houses an excellent collection of 16th- through 18th-century School of Quito paintings and sculptures. Open Tuesdays through Fridays from 9 AM to 12:30 PM and 3 to 6:30 PM; Saturdays from 10 AM to 4 PM. Admission charge. 915 Cuenca, Quito (phone: 2-212297).

**Museo de Jijón y Caamaño (Jijón and Caamaño Museum** – The Catholic University houses the work of Jacinto Jijón y Caamaño, a 20th-century explorer and anthropologist who spent his life studying Ecuadoran Indians. Closed Sundays. Admission charge. Catholic University, at the corner of Av. 12 de Octubre and Calle Ventimilla, Quito (phone: 2-521834).

**Museo de Arte Religioso (Museum of Religious Art)** – Housed in the Convent of the Sisters of the Conception in the city of Riobamba, this collection of paintings, sculpture, and goldwork is outstanding. The convent and gardens have been completely restored. Closed Mondays. Admission charge. On Orozco at España in Riobamba.

## PARAGUAY

**Museo Paraguayo de Arte Contemporáneo y Museo del Barro (Paraguayan Contemporary Art Museum and Clay Museum)** – Housed under the same roof, these two collections are heads above any other museum in Paraguay. In part the effort of leading Paraguayan artist Carlos Colombino, the *Contemporary Art Museum* offers changing expositions of work by local painters, printers, photographers, and sculptors. The *Clay Museum* is a fascinating collection of locally producted naïf religious art — including centuries-old artifacts rescued from Jesuit missions — and nonreligious popular pieces such as masks and ceramics. Open daily except Sundays from 4 to 8:30 PM. No admission charge. Calle Uno at Emeterio Miranda y Molas López, Asunción (phone: 21-604244).

## PERU

**Museo de la Nación (Museum of the Nation)** – This excellent museum uses scale models of temples, ruins, and archaeological sites, as well as pottery, weavings, and legends to trace the history of Peru's most important and advanced pre-Hispanic civilizations. This is the most complete display of pre-Inca cultures in the country. Admission charge. 2465 Av. Javier Prado, San Borja, Lima (phone: 14-377999 or 377969).

**Museo del Oro (Gold Museum)** – Amazingly, a private collection. Displayed here are golden treasures from the earliest Peruvian civilizations, as well as splendid feathered costumes, ceramics, textiles, and a weapons collection, all housed in a subterranean museum. Open daily. Admission charge. In the Lima suburb of Monterrica, 1100 Av. Alonso de Molina, Monterrico, Lima (phone: 14-352917).

**Museo Arqueológico Rafael Larco Herrera (Rafael Larco Herrera Archaeological Museum)** – Popularly known as the "Museum of Primitive Erotic Art," it actually houses one of the first collections of ceramics and other items from the pre-Hispanic coastal cultures of Peru. About 44,000 items are on exhibit. Open daily except Mondays from 10 AM to 6 PM. Admission charge. 1515 Av. Bolívar, Lima (phone: 14-611312 or 14-611835).

**Museo de Antropología y Arqueología (Museum of Anthropology and Archaeology)** – This is one of the foremost archaeological museums in South America. More than 80,000 objects — rock sculptures, ceramics, basketry, wool and cotton woven goods, jewels, tools, weapons and gold, silver and copper items with precious stones — are on display. Open daily. Admission charge. Plaza Bolívar, Pueblo Libre, Lima (phone: 14-635070).

**Museo Yoshiro Amano (Yoshiro Amano Museum)** – A private collection of woven fabric from the Chancay Valley north of Lima and ceramic objects from pre-Hispanic Peruvian cultures, it can be visited Mondays through Fridays by appointment only. Call a day ahead to arrange a visit. No admission charge, but donations accepted. 160 Calle Retiro, Miraflores, Lima (phone: 14-412909).

**Museo de Brüning (Brüning Museum)** – Besides astonishing textiles and ceramics, this museum has many of the precious artifacts found in the region that was the continent's most important gold-working center in pre-Inca times. This is the permanent home of the fabulous gold, silver, copper, and turquoise riches rescued by archaeologists at the nearby Sipán excavation. Open weekdays from 9 AM to 6 PM, weekends from 9 AM to 1 PM. Admission charge. Av. Huamachuco in Lambayeque (phone: 74-282110).

## URUGUAY

**Museo Histórico Nacional y Museo Romántico (National Historical Museum and Romantic Museum)** – Once the mansion of a wealthy Uruguayan merchant, this home has been turned into a museum (although it has two names, it is actually one museum) that has two collections — one dedicated to the Romantic era of 1830 to 1860 and the other to historical pieces. It displays costumes, furniture, porcelain, and even a fan signed by Enrico Caruso and Sarah Bernhardt (among others). Open Tuesdays through Fridays from noon to 5:45 PM, Sundays from 2 to 5:45 PM. No admission charge. 314 Av. 25 de Mayo, Montevideo (phone: 2-954257).

**Museo del Gaucho y La Moneda (Cowboy and Gold Museum)** – Housed in an opulent mansion that is now owned by the Banco de la República, this impressive collection pays tribute to two national assets — gold and cowboys. Uruguayans consider it their most important museum. Open weekdays from 9:30 AM to 12:30 PM, Saturdays from 3:30 to 7 PM, and Sundays from 3 to 7 PM from mid-April to mid-December; the rest of the year, the museum is closed Mondays; open Saturdays from 4:30 to 8 PM and Sundays from 4 to 8 PM. No admission charge. 999 18 de Julio, Montevideo (phone: 2-908764).

## VENEZUELA

**Casa Natal de el Libertador (Simón Bolívar's Birthplace)** – Mementos from Bolívar's youth and military career are preserved here. Murals depict scenes from the Great Liberator's life, and the inner courtyard is a fine example of colonial architecture. Closed Mondays. No admission charge. Calle Traposos at Calle San Jacinto, Caracas (phone: 2-545-7693).

**Catedral (Cathedral)** – The cathedral, built in 1575 and rebuilt in 1637, contains three notable paintings: *The Resurrection* by Rubens, *The Presentation of the Virgin at the Temple* by the Spanish painter Murillo, and *The Last Supper* by Venezuelan painter Arturo Michelena. Open daily. One block east of Plaza Bolívar, Caracas (phone: 2-824963).

**Galería de Arte Nacional (National Art Gallery)** – One of the few museums in Latin America deliberately established to foster national cultural identity, it was opened in May 1976 by the National Board of Culture. Works by more than 40 Venezuelan painters are displayed in the contemporary and popular arts sections. The older *Museo de Bellas Artes* (Museum of Fine Arts), containing an international collection, adjoins the gallery. Closed Mondays. No admission charge. Parque Los Caobos, Caracas (phone: 2-572-1070).

**Museo de Arte Moderno Jesús Soto (Jesús Soto Museum of Modern Art)** – Found in Ciudad Bolívar, in the middle of the jungle in the state of Guayana, this extremely attractive museum consists of six rooms surrounding a central patio designed for its function and light. Plastic interpretations of notable kinetic artists are on display. Open daily except Mondays from 9 AM to 5 PM. No admission charge. Avdas. Mario Briceno Iragorry and Germania, Ciudad Bolívar (phone: 85-24474).

**Museo de Arte Contemporáneo (Contemporary Art Museum)** – Dedicated to current trends in international modern art, the museum's exhibits represent most schools of art. There are occasional shows of top international names. Parque Central, near the *Anauco Hilton*, Caracas (phone: 2-573-8289, ext. 257).

# DIRECTIONS

# Introduction

The Pan-American Highway is a vast road system running approximately 16,000 miles down the western side of both the North and South American continents. Its road links are of varying quality, with some fine sections and some poor ones. Most of the secondary roads through the mountains and to the jungle are very difficult, and during some seasons they are impassable. However, if you especially enjoy driving and prefer to explore the Americas by car, it is possible to drive from Alaska all the way to southern Chile (with a break between Panama and Colombia where vehicles must be shipped from Colón or Balboa to ports in Colombia). While the Pan-American is South America's most important highway, and the focal point of the west coast road network, visiting drivers find that there are other good national highway systems on the continent, such as those in Brazil and Argentina, where a through road connects the two via Paraguay.

Although nowhere in South America are there long stretches of six-lane freeways comparable to those in the US or Europe, it's hard not to be impressed by the roads that have been built in some of the most out-of-the-way places imaginable. Perhaps even more amazing are many of the railway routes that traverse the Andes like a roller coaster. Whether you travel by car (in your own vehicle — not recommended — or one rented locally), by bus (and there are some fine deluxe services, particularly in Chile, Argentina, and Brazil), or by train, you will discover that some of the world's most breathtaking scenery is in South America.

Certainly the easiest way to travel between countries is by air, and along the west coast even the bird's-eye view is spectacular. South American airlines also have recognized the attraction of seeing the continent by air and a few offer air passes that let tourists travel between countries or, alternatively, to several cities within one country. These passes must be purchased in the US (see *Traveling by Plane,* GETTING READY TO GO). Flying point to point, you can rent a car in each country to drive where you want, or where the road system will permit.

On the following pages we have outlined driving tours of rural sections of each South American country, including Panama, which forms the land bridge from Central America to the southern continent. Each tour generally requires several days' travel time, and is designed to direct the traveler to the continent's most interesting areas. From Colombia's sparkling Caribbean Coast to the snow-capped volcanoes of the Ecuadoran Andes, from the vast Amazon jungle to the glaciers of Tierra del Fuego, we have tried to outline tours that start from South America's major cities, with suggested side trips and short journeys. Entries are not exhaustive but they do discuss the highlights of the route, including useful suggestions for shopping and dining; in *Best en Route,* they suggest accommodations at the best available hotels, inns, and lodges along the way.

## 638  DIRECTIONS / Introduction

Entries are organized by country, with an introduction explaining the routes that follow. Since each country is divided into several routes, it is possible to string them together into longer itineraries. But if you are pressed for time, following any single itinerary will introduce the most notable spots (and attractive accommodations) in the area.

> ■ **Note:** Car rental companies throughout South America, with very few exceptions, do not allow their cars to leave the country in which they are rented. If you plan to travel by car and to cross borders, rent a car in each country that you visit.

# Argentina

The second-largest country in South America, Argentina's 1,068,302 square miles are wedged into a triangular shape that is wide at the north, then narrows to a long skinny tail at the south. The country is bordered by the Atlantic Ocean and Uruguay to the east, Paraguay to the northeast, Brazil to the north, Bolivia to the northwest, Chile to the west, and the Antarctic Ocean to the south. At the southernmost extreme of the continent, Argentina shares the Tierra del Fuego archipelago with Chile.

Argentina is separated into four distinct sections. To the east are the white, sunny coastal beaches; to the west, the snow-capped peaks of the Andes, including South America's highest, 22,834-foot Mt. Aconcagua. The Lake District in the west, also known as the Switzerland of South America, is one of the most popular skiing and fishing resort areas on the southern continent. The 400-mile Río Colorado runs from west to east, cutting the country in two, with the humid jungle (the *chaco*) and fertile plain (pampas) to the north, and the dry, craggy, infertile cattle fields, small mountains, and moor-like scenery of Patagonia to the south. The farther south you go, the starker the land becomes. By the time you reach Tierra del Fuego, across the Strait of Magellan, the country becomes cold and gray. Daylight rarely arrives before 9 AM in winter (June to September), and the temperature during the summer (December to March) hardly ever rises above 52F (11C), just about one-half that found in the north, where it tops 100F (38C). If you continue south to the slice of territory Argentina claims on the Antarctic continent, you'll find snow, icebergs, and subzero weather. The only farmable thing here is the kelp, produced in the cold Antarctic waters.

Cold or hot, Argentina is a cosmopolitan country. Its 33 million people — of Spanish, German, Italian, and English descent — are among the most educated in South America; the literacy rate is over 90%.

Buenos Aires, on the Río de la Plata (actually the mouth of the Río Paraná and Río Uruguay, which flow into the Atlantic Ocean on this part of the coast), is Argentina's capital. More than 11 million people live in greater Buenos Aires. One of the world's largest seaports, it exports tons of fruit, tanning and leather goods, wool, lumber, paper, rubber goods, iron, steel, oil, and other manufactured goods. Musically, Buenos Aires is the birthplace of the graceful, sensuous tango. (For a complete report on Buenos Aires, see THE CITIES.) Argentina's other major cities are: Córdoba (pop. 1,200,000), Rosario (pop. 975,000), Mendoza (pop. 700,000), and Mar del Plata (pop. 500,000).

Discovered in 1516 by Spanish explorer Juan Díaz de Solís (who anchored in the Río de la Plata), Argentina's first settlement was not founded until 1536, when Pedro de Mendoza came to what is today Buenos Aires. Argentina, like other South American countries, remained under Spanish rule until

1810, when the Spanish viceroy, who had jurisdiction over the Argentine area, was forced by the populace to resign. Independence was declared in 1816 by the Congress of Tucumán, after a fiery, 6-year revolution led by José de San Martín, who went on to liberate Chile and Peru.

Argentina's 20th-century political course has been fraught with violence, rebellion, and repression — which eroded the country's great economic potential until the mid-1980s. Juan Domingo Perón, a strong political figure, headed a dictatorial regime from 1946 until his ouster in 1955. During his administration, many companies were nationalized, and labor unions were established. His second wife, Eva (Evita), was a heroine among the large working class that constituted Perón's strongest following. Following a 17-year exile in Spain, Perón returned to Argentina and ruled for a year. When he died in 1974, his third wife, María Estela (known as Isabelita) became president of an industrially developed nation whose fortunes continued to slide under her inept leadership. She was deposed in 1976 during a military coup headed by General Jorge Rafael Videla, whose authoritarian rule neither won applause in world human rights circles nor resolved the country's economic woes. Following the military's attempted takeover of the British-ruled Falkland Islands (Las Malvinas), Argentina's government fell. Elections held in 1983 put an end to military rule. Democratically elected President Raúl Alfonsín held office until 1989, when the country's economic problems forced him to leave before the end of his term. Carlos Menem, elected president in mid-1989, introduced the new peso in 1992 (its value is linked to the US dollar — 1 peso equals $1 US), battled sky-high inflation with some success, and privatized several national companies — an ironic twist for a Peronist politician.

The eight routes in this chapter suggest itineraries that will enable you to explore the different areas of Argentina as fully as possible. Although you can drive yourself, it is important to know that distances between towns can be great; if you break down, you may have to wait a very long time for someone to come along to drive you to the nearest source for assistance. Touring is often better done via an excellent network of buses, railroads, and domestic airlines that connect even the remote towns and villages.

The first route in this chapter starts in Buenos Aires and heads south on the coastal highway through Mar del Plata, Argentina's largest seaside resort, to Bahía Blanca. The second route takes you from Bahía Blanca west across the Río Colorado valley, where you can see the geological separation between pampas and Patagonian desert, to Bariloche and the Lake District. The Patagonia route runs from Carmen de Patagones south through Santa Cruz to Tierra del Fuego (Land of Fire) and the town of Ushuaia, the self-proclaimed City at the End of the World. From Patagonia you can board a ship heading straight through the Beagle Channel to Antarctica.

If you don't care to rough it, the northern routes offer more comfortable alternatives. The first heads northeast from Buenos Aires to Mesopotamia, that section of Argentina sandwiched between the Uruguay and Paraná rivers, to Iguassu Falls, stopping at the ruins of magnificent Jesuit missions along the way. Other routes go west, passing through the fertile Mendoza and Córdoba areas, continuing north to historic Tucumán.

If you are driving, be sure you have the proper insurance and that your *carnet* (customs pass) and insurance policy are in order and easily accessible should you have an accident (see *Traveling by Car*, GETTING READY TO GO).

■ **A note on prices:** Travelers should be aware that because of a roller-coaster economy, hotel, restaurant, and other prices quoted here are subject to change.

# Buenos Aires to Bahía Blanca

The 390-mile (624-km) route from Buenos Aires to Bahía Blanca is rich in history, land, and industry. The heartland of Argentina's earliest settlements, the area's natural resources are fully developed: The Río de la Plata, the northeastern river boundary separating Argentina from Uruguay, is the country's chief inland shipping route; the lush, fertile soil of the pampas provides the basis for a thriving farm industry; the Atlantic beaches of Mar del Plata, Miramar, and Necochea are filled seasonally with international and local travelers.

Discovered by Juan Díaz de Solís in 1516, the 550-mile Río de la Plata is the second-largest river system in South America (the Amazon ranks first). On the river, Buenos Aires was settled in 1536 by the Spanish conquistador Pedro de Mendoza; it remained the provincial territory capital until declared the nation's capital in 1882. La Plata, a coastal city 35 miles (56 km) southeast of Buenos Aires, succeeded as the provincial capital, and today it is a major cultural and import-export center.

The economic growth of Buenos Aires was spurred by two events: its status as federal capital and the rapid development of the surrounding pampas into farms and ranches. Cattle, horses, and mules were raised on huge *estancias* (ranches) built in the flatland; alfalfa, barley, oats, maize, linseed, and sorghum seed were imported for planting.

More than 68% of the Argentine population inhabits the pampas in the Buenos Aires area, and the contributing nationalities are diverse: Spanish, Italian, German, Dutch, Portuguese, and Yugoslavian. Sadly, there are few native Argentines, for the colonials literally exterminated the Indians. The Campagna del Desierto (1878–1883) was responsible for the founding of most of the cities and towns from Buenos Aires to Bahía Blanca, and many of the large *estancias* originated as spoils of war for victorious military officers.

Pampas towns are usually treeless, although in the Sierra de Tandil there are pine forests and eucalyptus trees, both imported from Australia.

When you travel to the Atlantic Ocean from the pampas, the landscape changes from browns to greens, from dry to moist, and the beach resorts begin to appear. Coastal Route 11 goes to the popular resorts of Pinamar and Villa Gesell, which offer fishing, swimming, and sailing. Mar del Plata, known as "the happy city," has 5 miles of beaches, parks, and campsites. Farther south is Necochea, growing in popularity as a rival to Mar del Plata as a favorite summer retreat.

The city of Bahía Blanca (White Bay), at the head of a large bay where the

Naposta River flows into the Atlantic Ocean, is not much to look at, but nevertheless is the most important town in southern Argentina. Here, a variety of merchandise, from fruits and vegetables to petroleum products, is exported to every part of the world.

Leaving Bahía Blanca, a trip 139 miles (222 km) inland on Route 33 west leads toward the pampas and a small lake resort area. There, Carhué's 162-acre Lago Epecuén is so heavily mineralized that its salt content is 20 times that of an ocean.

The 240-mile (384-km) path south from Buenos Aires to Mar del Plata on Route 2 is dotted with vacation resorts. However, we recommend the longer circuit that encompasses the pampas town of Chascomus then follows the coast on Route 11 through the resorts of Mar de Ajo, Pinamar, and Villa Gesell before you reach Mar del Plata.

Argentina has more than 100,000 miles of developed highway, mostly paved and modern and good. Road travelers are advised to drop into the *Argentine Automobile Club* in Buenos Aires (1850 Av. del Libertador; phone: 1-801-0701) for route maps and road information. As an alternative, the country is equipped with an excellent domestic airline network, more than 27,000 miles of railroad, and comfortable cross-country bus service.

**CHASCOMUS:** Chascomus, the birthplace of ex-President Raúl Alfonsín, is fewer than 70 miles (112 km) south of Buenos Aires on Route 2. It sits on a 12-acre lake of the same name and its best catch is the pejerrey fish, although there also are catfish and the aggressive *tararira,* similar to pike. (Amateur fishing contests are held here during the winter season; it was the site of the *South American Fishing Championship* in late 1988.) Camping grounds and bathing beaches are at Monte Brown, on the lake's far side. Speedboats, rowboats, water skis, and sailboards are available for rent. Across the lagoon from Monte Brown is the *Regatta Club* (Av. Costanera). Stop by the *Museo Pampeano* (Pampas Museum; in the Parque de Libres del Sur), dedicated to just about everything linked to life on the Argentine pampas. The museum building is a replica of a 19th-century stagecoach inn. The houses around Chascomus's city square are a blend of architectural styles.

**En Route from Chascomus** – At this point, swing southeast to coastal Route 11, which goes through Mar de Ajo, a favorite place for clamming. Impressive catches of red and black sea bass also have been reported. Continuing south, you arrive at the coastal resort of Pinamar, a summer playground for families who stay in chalet-type houses, although more hotels and resorts are being built as the area gains in popularity. There are plenty of small spots to go for tea or a meal, including *Status Playa* (Av. del Mar at the waterfront) and the *Casona del Tío* (Libertador and Av. Bunge).

Continue south to Villa Gesell. This town was founded and developed by Carlos Gesell during the early 1950s. Today it is one of the more popular youth resorts in the area. It offers a respite from the bustle of other resorts, and its 10-mile beach and woods of cypress, pine, eucalyptus, and acacia provide quiet moments. In the summer, *Aerolíneas Argentinas* has several daily flights from Buenos Aires or the 252-mile (403 km) trip can be made by bus. Approximately 78 miles (125 km) farther south is Mar del Plata.

**MAR DEL PLATA:** Argentines call this "the happy city," and well they might. With its 5 miles of beautiful beaches, parks, shopping galleries, and restaurants, Mar del Plata is equipped to make people smile. From December through *Easter* it's a lively resort, where the Argentine elite have met for the last 300 years and where big money can be won — or, unhappily, lost — at the gaming tables of its fabulous casinos. (The city's off-season population of about 500,000 swells to more than 3 million in the summer; make hotel reservations early.)

Originally founded by wealthy Argentines as a retreat from Buenos Aires, Mar del Plata today caters to the rich and less rich alike. There are 1,500 hotels in the city, and their prices depend on their proximity to the beach. Hard-core Mar del Plata addicts are exhilarated by the throngs of people who flock here to sit by row after row of colorful beach umbrellas and cabanas, and swing to the frenzied nightlife, particularly in the casinos, theaters, and movies.

The largest gambling establishment in the world is the casino at Bristol Beach, and it rakes in hundreds of thousands of dollars a night. (Believe it or not, all profits are forwarded to the Welfare Ministry.) For a small entrance fee ($1 at press time), you can enter just to look, not play. The minimum bet is $2, maximum $20. The *Provincial* hotel (see *Best en Route*) next door has rooms reserved exclusively for high rollers, and together both places can handle up to 9,000 gamblers at a clip. The casinos are open from 5 PM to 5 AM.

There are also convention and exhibit halls in Mar del Plata as well as a roller-skating rink and gymnasium. For shoppers, the primary consumer items are sweaters, made in Mar del Plata and sold throughout Argentina. If you notice an abundance of these in sky blue and white, it's no coincidence; Argentines, especially Buenos Aires youth, are partial to sweaters that sport the colors of their flag. The latest trendy offering in this status-conscious city is Argentina's first *Fonobar* (1825 San Luis), where you can make a phone call or send a fax — domestic or international — while savoring cocktails, coffee, cakes, and sandwiches.

Mar del Plata is also the home of *alfajores*, cookies filled with *dulce de leche* (caramel à la Argentina) and topped with chocolate. Argentines confide that there is a hierarchy of *alfajores;* the best are Havanna brand (nothing to do with Cuba — they're made by a wealthy Greek family); Trassens are very good, too. *Alfajores* are also made in Santa Fe and Córdoba. The *Havanna* candy factory (3298 Brandsen) is open by appointment only, but there are *Havanna* outlets throughout the city — one (Buenos Aires and Rivadaria) is open 24 hours a day, and another (at the airport) sells gift boxes.

Too many *alfajores?* Walk them off or rent a bicycle at Plaza Mitre for $9 an hour. Mar del Plata is filled with plazas of trees and flowers. General San Martín and General Arias parks are at elegant Playa Grande, and polo grounds and golf clubs are in the vicinity. Mar del Plata has four 18-hole golf courses. In the extreme north of the city, the sports center of Parque Camet has polo, rugby, and *pato* (the national sport) fields, with ample space for horseback riding. The stadium, built for the *1978 World Cup* soccer games, holds 41,500 spectators.

Mar del Plata is also a working port — a bustling, colorful place filled with bright yellow fishing boats with red trim gleaming in the sunlight. The boats return to the harbor daily at 3 PM, followed by herds of seals barking happily and vying for the crews' rejected fish. Bring your camera; on a clear day, this scene makes a beautiful shot.

The tourist office (2267 Boulevard Marítimo P.P. Ramos; phone: 23-21777) operates from 7 AM to midnight during the summer.

South of the port, the combination of sand, sea, and rocks continues to the point of Punta Mogotes, whose lighthouse guides ships along the irregular coast.

Some 240 miles (384 km) south of Buenos Aires, Mar del Plata is about 4½ hours by car — a direct route, but driving can become slow, unsafe, and uncomfortable in summer. A 4½-hour train ride on the *El Marplatense* express from Constitución station in Buenos Aires ($10) or the 5-hour trip with stops might be preferable. A bus ride (La Costera Criolla is recommended) takes about 5 hours and costs $11. The shortest and most expensive trip is the 45-minute plane ride. Outside the Mar del Plata airport a fleet of taxis awaits, but if you're in no hurry and want to save money, hop aboard bus No. 542. It goes right downtown, past the casino to near the hotels. Restaurants to try here are *Noa Noa* and *Don Diego* (both on Av. 3).

**BALCARCE:** You can reach Balcarce by following Route 226 northwest from Mar del Plata. Forty miles (64 km) inland from the seaside resort, this small (pop. 20,450) pampas town serves as a good base for hikers who wish to explore the area. An interesting spot to visit is Cinco Cerros, five strangely shaped hills. The tourism office (634 Calle 13) can give you more information about hiking, fishing, and boating.

**TANDIL:** Continuing west from Balcarce on Route 226 (or traveling from Mar del Plata directly by train), you reach Tandil. Nestled in hill country, this town (pop. 65,700) is a leading cheese-producing center in Argentina.

Tandil is the Arauca Indian term for "high hill." It was settled in 1823 during the Indian Wars when General Martín Rodríguez extended the western frontier as far as Sierra de la Ventana and built Fuerte Independencia (Fort Independence) in Tandil. In the *Museo Fuerte Independencia* (845 4 de Abril) are documents, arms, and antique carriages related to Tandil's often bloody history. (Open daily except Mondays, 4 to 8 PM.)

From the central Plaza Moreno, follow the avenue that leads down the hill and pass through a stone archway donated by the town's Italian community to commemorate Tandil's 100th anniversary. Beyond the arch, Parque Independencia offers some interesting sights. The stairway leads to a terrace dominated by the statue of General Rodríguez, and there is a good view of the countryside and a restaurant atop Castillo Morisco's hill. The hillside harbors the *John Kennedy Amphitheater,* which can accommodate 5,000 spectators.

Tandil's best-known holiday is its spectacular *Semana Santa* (Holy Week Festival), held prior to *Easter.* The predominant religion throughout South America is Roman Catholicism, and during this week, from *Palm Sunday* to *Easter Sunday,* thousands of pilgrims flock here for processions to El Cerro Calvario (Calvary Hill), where a 49-foot cross at the summit supports a Christ figure sculpted in French marble. To the left of the cross stands a replica of the Holy Sepulcher and a sculpture representing the Stations of the Cross stands nearby. The hillside itself is covered with groves of eucalyptus and olive trees.

Inaugurated in 1943, Calvary Hill and the sculptures were conceived by Pedro Redolatti, a local businessman, and his cousin, Monsignor Fortunato Devoro, a local priest. You can reach the hill by following Avenida España to Avenida de Calvario.

**En Route from Tandil** – Leaving Tandil, continue west on Route 226 to Azul, then on Route 3 south; you will arrive at Tres Arroyos, an important wheat and cattle center on the pampas with a thriving Dutch community.

Tres Arroyos is not a major tourist site, but there is good reason to come here if you enjoy fishing. An annual fishing contest, *24 Horas de la Corvina Negra* (black bass), is held every February. Information on the event is available from the *Club de Cazadores* (285 Calle Vélez Sarsfield), or the tourism office (1 Av. Rivadavia).

Tres Arroyos is named after three streams that flow into the Río Claromeco, about 46 miles (74 km) north of the town of Claromeco. The three streams — Seco, Orellano, and Del Medio — are popular fishing areas. Regular fishing expeditions are organized, and equipment can be rented in town.

**CLAROMECO:** This resort, south from Tres Arroyos on Provincial Route 73, is a favorite with beachgoers because north winds bring balmy weather, and a current from the Brazilian coast keeps the water warmer here than at most other beaches in the area. The dark sands backed by high dunes stretch smooth and soft along the coast. The town is easy to navigate; all streets are numbered and follow each other in logical sequence. To rent bikes and mopeds, inquire at the tourism office on Calle 28 between Avenidas 9 and 11.

Dining and dancing are Claromeco pastimes. Fresh fish, the local specialty, is served at the *Juanillo* restaurant (Calle 9 between Avdas. 28 and 30), *Claromeco* hotel (Calle

7 and Av. 26), and at the *Cabaña de Fermín* (Calle 11 between Avdas. 7 and 8). The tango haunts include *Don Mateo* (Calle 28 between Avdas. 21 and 2) and *Claromeco* (Calle 26 between Avdas. 23 and 2).

A visit to the lighthouse offers a good view of Claromeco's coast, if you're willing to climb 278 steps for it. If you're not exhausted afterward, cross the bridge that fords Río Claromeco to Dunamar, a forest wildlife reserve.

If you wish to return to the coast and Mar del Plata, retrace your route to Tres Arroyos and pick up Route 228 east to Necochea.

Home to a large Danish community, Necochea is a popular beach resort (pop. 50,000). It has a waterfront casino that rivals that of Mar del Plata. The casino is part of a public complex that includes a swimming pool, Turkish baths, restaurants, and a nightclub. The beach is 15 miles long and is reportedly one of the best in the country — not only for swimming but for fishing. Ask the tourist office, 2969 Calle 56 (phone: 262-22220).

From Necochea you can take Route 88 back to Mar del Plata or pick up Route 2 and travel south to Bahía Blanca.

**BAHÍA BLANCA:** The most important city south of Buenos Aires, Bahía Blanca (White Bay) is a modern seaport that sits at the head of a large bay where the Naposta River flows into the Atlantic Ocean. From its five docks — Arroya, Pareja, Ingeniero White, Galvin, and Rosales — fresh produce sails to all ports in the world.

The city was founded in 1828 by Colonel Tomás Estomba and a small band of soldiers, who were searching for a strategic site for a frontier fortress. Today, Bahía Blanca has a population of 300,000. Most residents earn their living in port-related employment and at the naval base, suerto Belgrano. Another major and growing industry in and around the city is petroleum. Argentina, now almost self-sufficient in petroleum production, has two important refineries and a research center in Puerto Galván.

Although Bahía Blanca is a cultural center for the southern pampas and Patagonia is home to the Universidad del Sur and several technological institutes specializing in oceanographic studies — it is not a popular tourist destination. However, anglers may enjoy its freshwater streams.

If you stay overnight, take time to visit the *Museo Histórico* and the *Museo de Ciencia Natural* (History and Natural Science Museums; both in the basement of the *Teatro Municipal,* 116 Calle Dorrego; phone: 91-23963). Here you can wander through permanent exhibits featuring fossils, maps, and travel diaries relating to Patagonia's past.

The *Museo de Bellas Artes* (Fine Arts Museum; 65 Calle Alsina; phone: 91-20110) displays paintings, sculpture, and drawings of respected Argentine artists, including Sforza, Castagnino, and Quiros. You can visit the museums most days of the week, but check their hours before going.

Bahía Blanca has some very good restaurants. *Taberna Baska* (284 Lavalle; phone: 91-21788) has seafood and tasty international fare. *Gambrinus* (174 Arribeños; phone: 91-22380) is a popular beer hall. You can't miss at any of the fish cantinas along Puerto Ingeniero White. Especially good is *Cantina Micho* (3875 Av. G. Torres; phone: 91-70346), which also offers Greek specialties.

**En Route from Bahía Blanca** – If you're not rushing toward any destination, plan to stay an extra day or two to explore the countryside around Bahía Blanca, especially Route 3 east and Route 33 north. Sign names signal the Indian origins of most towns and villages in the pampas.

Pehuén-Có, or "pine and water" in the Arauca dialect, is a stretch of beach dotted by small chalets some 43 miles (69 km) southeast on Route 3. The beach is well shaded by a grove of pine trees growing near the shore. When you're finished sunning, take a stroll along the Avenida de los Pinos and sample any number of refreshing drinks in the small cafés.

Monte Hermoso is one of several resorts in the small lake district found on provincial Route 78, a detour off Route 33 north. You can rent fishing or beach equipment along the boardwalk extending down Avenida Costanera. Be careful if you go swimming. Jellyfish are known to annoy swimmers during the summer season, even though underwater barriers have been built.

If possible, visit Monte Hermoso around October 15 to be on hand for the *Fiesta de la Llanura,* complete with fireworks, dancing, and special foods.

Some 139 miles (222 km) north of Bahía Blanca, Carhué's Lago Epecuén covers 162 acres and is 20 times saltier than the sea (and too salty to support fish). Its Arauca name means "almost burning" (*carhué* is Arauca for "strategic place") and testifies to the water's stinging qualities if accidentally swallowed or rubbed into your eyes. Numerous health spas along the lakefront treat guests for skin problems and rheumatism. Unfortunately, severe flooding in recent years has diminished the appeal of the area.

From Carhué, continue southeast to Sierra de la Ventana.

**SIERRA DE LA VENTANA:** This is a small town with a surrounding reserve that offers spectacular views and freshwater fishing. The Ventana peak gets its name from a natural opening in its apex that is shaped like a window, or *ventana.*

You can drive through this cultivated region on good asphalt roads, and there is a variety of inexpensive and free sports facilities in the area: swimming pools, a 9-hole golf course, horseback riding trails, mountain climbing trails, and trout fishing in the Río Sauce Grande. In Sierra de la Ventana, it's continuous open season on trout and pejerrey fishing, with the exception of the 90-day spawning period from September 1 to November 30.

## BEST EN ROUTE

Hotels in the Bahía Blanca region range from expensive ($65 to $110 per night for a double), to moderate ($45–$65), to inexpensive (under $45), and provide modern facilities. Travelers, however, are reminded that popular resort areas often raise prices as high as 40% in the summer, so check prices in Claromeco and Necochea if you plan to visit at that time. And Mar del Plata has two sets of high-season prices — one for December and March, and another, slightly higher one for January and February.

### PINAMAR

*Arenas* – A modern, sophisticated hotel with room service, a pool, tennis courts, disco, and even baby-sitters. 700 Av. Bunge (phone: 254-82444 and 254-82621; 1-312-3001 in Buenos Aires; fax: 254-86770). Expensive.

*Del Bosque* – This modern luxury resort features a restaurant, pool, and everything you'll need for a relaxing stay. 1550 Av. Bunge (phone: 254-82179; fax in Buenos Aires: 1-312-4384). Expensive.

### VILLA GESELL

*Austral* – Open December through April, this 38-room hostelry is at the waterfront. Calle 306 at Camino de la Ribera (phone: 255-68050). Moderate.

*Luz y Fuerza* – This 3-story hotel has balconies with sea views. Open year-round. Playa and 111 (phone: 255-62685). Moderate.

### MAR DEL PLATA

*Bisonte* – Centrally located, this elegant high-rise property has 80 rooms. 2601 Belgrano, at the corner of Córdoba (phone: 23-24065). Expensive.

*Château Frontenac* – An 84-room hotel, with private baths. Open year-round. 2010 Alvear, at the corner of Moreno (phone: 23-519828). Expensive.

*Hermitage* – This elegant Old World–style hotel has a pretty marble lobby and 210 comfortable rooms. A casino, bar, and restaurant round out the amenities. Breakfast is included in the rate. 2657 Blvd. Marítimo P.P. Ramos (phone: 23-519081). Expensive.

**Flamingo** – Near the casino, with 150 rooms. 2155 Moreno (phone: 23-41080). Moderate.

**Gran Hotel Provincial** – Next to the casino sits this newly renovated, 500-room hotel conveniently open year-round. Amenities include a bar and outdoor swimming pool. 2500 Blvd. Marítimo P.P. Ramos (phone: 23-24081; 1-417121 in Buenos Aires; fax in Buenos Aires: 1-393-0827). Moderate.

## BALCARCE

**Balcarce Gran** – This 48-room property is the best in town. At Gen. Balcarce and Mitre, in the vicinity of Cinco Cerros (phone: 266-22055). Moderate.

## TANDIL

**Hostal de la Sierra de Tandil** – It has 14 air conditioned rooms, with a spa and solarium on the premises. Open year-round. 931 Av. Avellaneda (phone: 293-22330). Moderate.

**Libertador** – A choice of 56 rooms, as well as suites and apartments can be found at one of the best lodgings in Tandil. At 545 Mitre (phone: 293-22127). Moderate.

**Plaza** – The rooms face Plaza Independencia; all have private baths and air conditioning. Snack bar. Located at 438 Pinto (phone: 293-27160). Inexpensive.

## TRES ARROYOS

**Alfil** – This 43-room property is in the downtown area. 142 Rivadavia (phone: 983-7001). Expensive.

**Catalina** – A 42-room hotel. 187 Maipú (phone: 983-7025). Moderate.

## CLAROMECO

**Claromeco** – Open only during the summer, December through March, it features a good restaurant. Calles 7 and 26 (phone: Claromeco 7). Moderate.

**Residencial La Perla** – A 17-room lodging, open December through March. Right off the beach at Calle 9, at the corner of 28 (phone: Claromeco 14). Moderate.

## NECOCHEA

**Corona** – Private baths and air conditioning are at this 30-room lodging open December through March. 371 Av. 75 (phone: 262-22646). Moderate.

**San Martín** – A 56-room hotel considered one of the best in town. Calle 6 at the corner of 86 (phone: 262-22042). Moderate.

**Doble-J Campsite** – Less than 1 mile (1 km) from the wharves; facilities include hot running water. Inexpensive.

## BAHÍA BLANCA

**Austral** – Modern downtown hotel with 100 rooms, restaurant, and bar. 159 Av. Colón (phone: 91-20241; fax: 91-24749). Expensive.

**Argos** – A full-service 40-room hostelry, with its own restaurant, snack bar, and parking. 151 España (phone: 91-28384; fax: 91-45369). Moderate.

**Belgrano** – This 100-room hotel has a family-style restaurant, bar, and parking. 44 Av. Belgrano (phone: 91-20240). Inexpensive.

## MONTE HERMOSO

**La Goleta** – This 32-room hotel on the seashore is open year-round. Costanera, at the corner of Calle 10 (phone: 11-8284). Moderate.

**Nauta** – A 15-room hostel at 653 Av. Dufaur (phone: 11-81083). Moderate.

### SIERRA DE LA VENTANA

***Don Diego Caravan Camp*** – This campground has all modern conveniences and is a member of the *Argentine Automobile Club* (phone: 91-821-6061). Boasts a natural swimming pool formed by two streams right on Route 72.

# Bahía Blanca to Bariloche

The 1,186-mile (1,898-km) cross-country excursion along Route 22 from Bahía Blanca west to Neuquén will be particularly interesting to geographers. It runs parallel to Río Colorado, the boundary between northern and southern Argentina. You'll notice a difference in the terrain of the two areas immediately. To the north stretch the flat lands of the pampas and to the south, the mountainous slopes of northern Patagonia, where the *estancias* are so far from each other that the country resembles a frontier land.

Patagonia is an area whose main distinction is a lack of local color; travelers generally find it boring. The monotony of the countryside ends only at Neuquén, the capital of Patagonia's northernmost province of the same name, which marks the entry into Argentina's Swiss-style Lake District.

Here, at the foot of the Andes near the Chilean border, tens of thousands of *norteamericanos* and Europeans flock every winter (remember that Southern Hemisphere seasons are the opposite of those of the Northern Hemisphere). The district encompasses the western end of Patagonia; south to Lago Argentino and Glaciers National Park in Santa Cruz; to Lanín National Park in Neuquén province; and Los Alerces National Park in Chubut province (for more detailed information, see *Patagonia to Antarctica,* below). The focal point of the district is San Carlos de Bariloche, which sits at the southernmost end of Lake Nahuel Huapi in the national park of the same name.

Bus and train service are available to Neuquén on a regular basis from Buenos Aires. You also can fly to Neuquén daily on *Austral* or *Aerolíneas Argentinas* and make a connection to Chapelco on the provincial carrier *TANSE. CATA* also has air service to Bariloche.

**NEUQUÉN:** Straddling the Neuquén and Lima rivers, the capital of Patagonia's northernmost province (pop. 90,000) is noted for its apples — especially red delicious and Granny Smith. Pears and, to a lesser extent, peaches and cherries also are grown here. The Fuder apple factory, 9 miles (14 km) west of the city on Route 22, lets travelers look at its shipping and packing operations. In town, visitors should stop at the *Museo Histórico Provincial del Neuquén* (Provincial Historical Museum; 163 Santa Fe). The museum has six salons featuring exhibits on art, ethnography, folklore, and local history.

For those who want to buy local souvenirs, the artisans' market at 291 San Martín features a moderately priced variety of woven ponchos, spreads, clothing, woodcarvings, and sweaters. Even if you're not planning any purchases, it's interesting to watch the craftspeople at work.

Restaurants in Neuquén — moderately priced — include *Rincón Colonial* (110 Alberdi) and the *Del Comuse* (387 Av. Argentina). The *Del Castillo* (50 Diagonal 9 de Julio) is also worth a try. Wherever, try some of the local wine, either Rey del Neuquén or Relmu Lagrim del Limay, and the apple cider.

For diversion, we recommend an interesting side trip to Lago Pellegrini, an artificial lake with campgrounds 9 miles (14 km) north of Neuquén. Cross at Dique Ingeniero Ballester and continue on Route 151 south. When you arrive at the town of Cinco Saltos, follow the road as it bears left. The lake sits beyond the village. You're permitted to swim, water ski, and fish on Lago Pellegrini.

While you're here, take some time and wander into neighboring Cipolletti, a small village just above the lake on Route 151 south. Founded in 1904, Cipolletti boasts a mansion imitating France's Petit Trianon. The mansion is at the end of Calle Yrigoyen in the midst of a park and it houses a provincial museum containing exhibits and documents about Patagonian history.

Leaving Cipolletti, a ride down Route 151 north to Route 234 south returns you to Neuquén.

**En Route from Neuquén** – A 115-mile (184-km) jaunt on Route 22 west will take you to Zapala, a major railroad crossing that links the southeastern part of Patagonia with railroads from Bahía Blanca and Buenos Aires. Founded on July 12, 1913, the town has two museums, archaeological and historical. Fortin Regimenteo 21, the town's landmark, was constructed during the Indian Wars.

Leaving Zapala and heading toward Argentina's Lake District you have a choice: Continue northwest to the Andes and Chilean border, or head south on Route 40 to the lakes.

Should you decide to head northwest, don't overlook two sites: Copahue National Reservation, with thermal baths and an extinct volcano; and Laguna Blanca National Park, a haven for animals and birds, particularly flamingos and black-necked swans. For guided tours of Laguna Blanca, contact the Neuquén Tourism Office (182 Calle San Félix at Av. Río Negro; phone: 943-24089). Camping also is available in the park.

**LANÍN NATIONAL PARK:** Immense (980,000 acres), with 12 lakes and numerous rivers, this park can be reached by continuing south from Zapala on Route 40, then heading north on Route D. Lago Huechulafquen, the park's largest lake, is a primary fishing area, and divides into two smaller lakes, Paimun and Epulafquen, where camping is available near the Andes Cordillera. Lanín is one of the country's best-developed national parks for sports activities — swimming, boat rentals, and mountaineering (there are refuges for climbers) are available to visitors. There's also a hostel in the southeast sector for overnight stays (see *Best en Route*).

**JUNÍN DE LOS ANDES:** Twenty miles (32 km) east of Lanín Park and north of San Martín de los Andes on Route D is the tiny fishing village of Junín de los Andes. The nearby Río Chimehuin possibly is the country's best known fishing hole. Brown and rainbow trout and salmon are the big catch. Black-neck swans, ducks, geese, falcons, and the occasional condor can be spotted in the area.

A side trip from Junín on Route H will take you 84 miles (134 km) through the Tromen Pass to Lake Villarrica and the city of Pucón in Chile. The high point of the trip is passing the 12,388-foot Lanín Volcano, now extinct.

**SAN MARTÍN DE LOS ANDES:** Continue 17 miles (27 km) southwest from Junín de los Andes on Route D, and you will arrive at San Martín de los Andes, right on Lago Lácar. Try the slopes at Cerro Chapelco ("land of melting ice and floating waters"); it has both alpine and cross-country skiing and is a good spot for novices. (There's a ski school with 150 instructors and equipment rental.) Though growing in popularity and equipped to handle 11,600 skiers an hour, Cerro Chapelco has fewer people and lower prices than Bariloche. Information is available from the resort (phone: 541-350021 and 541-350025; fax: 541-356620).

*La Raclette* (see *Best en Route*) has an excellent restaurant that provides a menu as diverse as the tourists' nationalities: dishes borrowed from France, Germany, Switzerland, Italy, China, England, Hungary, and Argentina.

*El Barrelito de Oro* also serves an international menu. As an added touch, Jaime Muñoz, the owner, personally attends his clientele. The *Kopper Kettle* offers brownies, lemon pie, cakes, and sandwiches in the afternoon; at night there are cheese empanadas, pancakes with cream, fondue, and chocolate and lemon mousse. Travelers aching for pizza, empanadas, or a sandwich in the middle of the night can visit *Doscientos 65* (on the main avenue). Homemade candies are sold throughout town, the most delicious being Mamusia chocolate. Contact the tourist office (San Martín at J.M. de Rosas; phone: 972-27166) for information on hotels and other areas of concern to travelers.

**NAHUEL HUAPI NATIONAL PARK:** Continuing south on Route D, you come to Nahuel Huapi National Park, a sprawling 4,867-square-mile reserve adjacent to Lanín National Park on the Argentina-Chile border. Opened in 1903, the park contains spectacular natural attractions: lakes ranging in color from deep blue to emerald green, glaciers, waterfalls, torrents, rapids, and age-old forests. It offers a visitors' center, museum, picnicking and camping grounds, swimming, fishing, mountaineering, and skiing (with equipment rental available).

Lake Nahuel Huapi, the park's largest lake, stretches 45 miles northwest to southeast and is up to 1,436 feet deep — easily navigable by catamarans and steamers. The lake divides into eight *brazos,* or arms, that poke into surrounding mountains.

The largest island on the lake is Isla Victoria, which has dense forests, a subsoil of volcanic rock, and cliffs stretching 164 feet into the air on its western side. Red deer — some with enormous antlers — run free on the 9,259-acre island.

Cruises to Isla Victoria run every day. The boats leave from Puerto Pañuelo, 18 miles (29 km) north of Bariloche, and dock at Puerto Anchorena on the island in time for lunch. Dress warmly. It can be chilly here even when the sun is shining.

The boat makes a quick stop at the Quetrihue Peninsula, which is thickly covered with *arrayanes* trees. A carefully constructed catwalk, which protects the delicate root systems, winds through the forest, providing a close look at the cinnamon-colored trees. Found only in this area, the *arrayanes'* unusual coloration is said to have so inspired Walt Disney that he featured them in the forests of his movie *Bambi.*

Should you wish to make your cruise to Victoria an overnight affair, stop at the *Huaiquil* lodge on the lakeshore. It has a restaurant specializing in trout, a snack bar (where you can also buy provisions for a picnic on the island), and a kiosk that sells film and souvenirs.

Another side trip is a boat excursion to Puerto Blest, on the eastern arm of Nahuel Huapi, and the waterfall of Los Cantaros. *Turisur Co.* (227 Quaglia; phone: 944-26110 or 944-24879) offers catamaran cruises on Nahuel Huapi. A short drive from the western end of Puerto Blest south on Route H leads you to Laguna Frías, a small lake near the Chilean border. The waters are a striking green, the result of a vein of copper at the lake's bottom. From here, you can see Mt. Tronador, "the thunder maker," a snow-capped mountain, 11,600 feet high.

The base of Mt. Tronador can be reached by taking Route 258 west from Bariloche, which passes Lake Gutiérrez (where there is a grotto to the Virgin of the Snows) and Lake Mascardi. Both lakes are good for fishing.

From Mascardi, take Route 254 west along the lake on to Pampa Linda and the Valley of the Vuriloches to the Black Glaciers, huge blocks of ice in every shade of gray, and the Devil's Gorge, a dare for the mountain climber.

**BARILOCHE:** On the southern end of Lake Nahuel Huapi, this community of 50,000 people is the heart of the Lake District's resort life. Founded in 1895 by Carlos Wiederhold, it resembles a European ski village, with its wood and stone chalet-like houses, and it's plain why Bariloche is known as "the Switzerland of South America." The only difference is that here the steaks are thicker, the wine is heartier, and the number of cuckoo clocks is fewer.

The Town Hall is in the middle of the plaza which routinely is filled with keg-carrying Saint Bernards. Crowds gather for one of Bariloche's daily and most popular events — the noon ringing of the town clock. Four wooden figures emerge from the clock tower and rotate as the hour hand reaches 12. The figures represent the region's people: an Indian, a colonist, a conquistador, and a missionary.

The nearby *Museo de Patagonia* (Patagonian Museum) in the Centro Civico contains 11 rooms of Indian artifacts and exhibits, including a photo history of the colonization of Bariloche. Housed in the same building is the Domingo Faustino Sarmiento Library. The Church of Our Lady of Nahuel Huapi is at 450 V. Almirante O'Connor.

Mountain climbers and hikers can obtain information from *Club Andino Bariloche* (30 Av. 20 de Febrero; phone: 944-24579 or 944-24531; fax: 944-22266). It is open Mondays through Fridays from 9 AM to noon and 3 to 8 PM. For a $10 fee, the club offers guides and transportation for novice hikers who wish to make day climbs; experienced hikers and climbers may choose longer treks. *Club Andino* maintains several mountain hut refuges and also offers a number of winter and summer outings — from a day of cross-country skiing to a mountain drive and barbecue in warm weather.

Shoppers should know that Bariloche's most important street is Bartolomé Mitre. Boutiques sell wool, leather, and ski jackets called *camperas*. The sweaters and ski coats are unrivaled and cost less here than in Buenos Aires. If price is a concern, stop first at *Arbol* (in the mall at 263 Bartolomé Mitre) for woolen goods. Down the street, at *Manos del Uruguay* (339 Bartolomé Mitre; no phone), a handicrafts cooperative, handmade sweaters from Uruguay are sold. Beautiful knitwear also can be found at the two shops at the *El Casco* hotel (7 miles/11 km out of town on the road to the village of Llao-Llao on Av. Ezequiel Bustillo), *Les Belles Choses* and *B.R. Fashion & Gifts* (phone at *El Casco* hotel for both: 944-61032). Both stores also have cotton clothing and ceramics. Also stop in at another *El Casco* store, *Cerámica Tero-Tero* (phone at the hotel: 944-61032), for a wonderful variety of multicolor knit sweaters, dresses, and coats. A shop for leather goods is *Cuero's* (77 Bartolomé Mitre; phone: 944-23096).

Chocolate lovers will cry with delight as they discover stores whose floor-to-ceiling glass showcases are stocked with all kinds of chocolate. The aroma alone is mouthwatering. Prices are, surprisingly, quite moderate. A local treat is *papas de chocolate*, nuggets of milk chocolate with nut cream centers. For goodies with the most cocoa and the least butterfat, go to *Benroth* (569 Beschtedt; phone: 944-23326). If you fancy chocolate studded with whole nuts, raspberries, raisins, or other goodies, go to *Abuela Goye* (157 Albarracín; phone: 944-22431). For an almost overwhelming selection of chocolates in every shape and flavor, plus a stand-up coffee bar and a deli that sells locally produced jams, stop by *Del Turista* (239 Bartolomé Mitre; phone: 944-22124).

The town also is known for ceramics. *Cerámica Bariloche* (290 San Martín; phone: 944-22310; and 1605 Anasagasti; phone: 944-24085) carries various pottery items. *Cerámica Burton* (Km 4 on Av. Ezequiel Bustillo; phone: 944-23002) sells works by local artists who use clay from the area. Other novelty goods available in the city include toiletry items made from local lavender on sale at *Gourmandaise* (shop No. 7 in the gallery at 242 Quaglia; no phone) or one of the area's largest collections of Bariloche handicrafts at *Fitz Roy* (18 Bartolomé Mitre; phone: 944-22335). For more local artisan work as well as crafts from other South American countries, stop by *Huitral-Hue* (250 Villegas; no phone).

Bariloche restaurants dish up good, hearty food to the summer and winter resort crowds. Most feature barbecues. *El Jabalí,* (130 Av. San Martín; phone: 944-22256), and *El Viejo Munich* (102 Bartolomé Mitre; phone: 944-22336) serve both venison and trout in season, and *La Casita Suiza* (342 Quaglia; phone: 944-26111) concentrates on Swiss specialties such as fondue. For a change, go to a fine vegetarian restaurant, *La Huerta* (362 Morales; phone: 944-23128), right in Bariloche's center. Outside of town, try the *Tres Monedas* or *La Casona*. For pub drinks and rock 'n' roll in a beautiful setting on Lake Nahuel Huapi, go to *Playa Bonita* (Av. Ezequiel Bustillo, Km 8 on the road to Llao-Llao; phone: 944-61027).

Another point of interest is Bariloche's music camps, where people gather to play outdoors. Here, too, is the home of the *Camerata Bariloche,* a world-famous chamber music group that performs free during the *Snow Festival* in August. Bariloche also claims a one-of-a-kind establishment in South America — the Bernabé Méndez Park Keepers' Training Center.

The fishing season in Bariloche lasts from mid-November to mid-April. Lakes and rivers are kept well stocked with brown trout, brook trout, rainbow trout, and salmon. The record catch, a 35-pound salmon, is exhibited at the *Nahuel Huapi Fishing and Hunting Association* in Bariloche. A permit must be purchased. Detailed fishing information is available from the national park office, 24 San Martín (phone: 944-23111).

Sport fishers can choose from a range of trips offered by *Safaris Acuaticos* (phone: 944-25521). Eight-day fishing packages in the Bariloche region start at about $300 a day (airfare from the US not included). Guides speak English and all equipment, lodging, meals, and licenses are provided. In the US, book through *Angling Travel and Tours* (phone: 503-666-9936 or 800-288-0886); *Mel Krieger's Club Pacific* (phone: 415-752-0192; fax: 415-752-0804); or *Angler Adventures* (phone: 203-434-9624 or 800-628-1447; fax: 203-434-8605).

The Bariloche area is the most popular place to ski in Argentina, particularly at Cerro Catedral: With its 3-mile runs and 3,280-foot incline, the slope is internationally famous, and ski competitions are held here throughout the season. Equipped with all modern facilities, chair lifts ferry skiers to the mountain's top, 8,000 feet above sea level. There are runs for every level of expertise, and up to 20,000 skiers an hour can be accommodated. There's a ski school that has 250 instructors, equipment can be rented, and part of the slope is lit for night skiing. The Cerro Catedral information center (at the base of the hill; phone: 944-60005) can answer all your questions.

Take the chair lift to the top of the 3,600-foot Cerro Campanario and enjoy a magnificent view of the lake district. Be sure to stop at the café at the top of the mountain for delicious hot chocolate and homemade cakes. The *Snow Festival,* featuring a torchlight parade, has become an internationally known sporting, cultural, and social event.

There are a total of 1,000 beds in the ski village at the mountain's base, including *Catedral Club* (see *Best en Route*). *Club Andino Bariloche* has a lift and station that can be reached by an unpaved road at the base. Cerro Otto, on the outskirts of Bariloche, and Cerro Colorado, south of Cerro Otto, also are recommended slopes. Numerous ski tours are offered by various clubs and airlines throughout the season. Check with a travel agent for information. Some tours combine Bariloche and the Chilean ski resort of Portillo.

In summer, the entire district is overcome with campers, swimmers, anglers, and other outdoors fans, lured to the blue-green lakes, snow-peaked mountains, and clear air. But despite its beauty, or maybe because of it, the Lake District suffers from that one flaw — too many tourists. The year-round popularity of Bariloche, Lake Nahuel Huapi, and Cerro Catedral has produced surplus visitors, and people who know the area well recommend more remote places, like San Martín de los Andes and Junín de los Andes. Because of Bariloche's popularity and wide sports offerings, visitors are advised to book hotel accommodations well ahead.

The city tourist office (in the Centro Civico; phone: 944-23022) sells *Datos,* a helpful book (in Spanish) that lists hotels, restaurants, shops, and general information. It is open seven days a week. The provincial tourism office (605 Av. 12 de Octubre; phone: 944-25973) has maps and material on spots outside of town. The *Argentine Automobile Club* (785 Av. 12 de Octubre; phone: 944-23000 and 944-23001) also provides a map with routes in the district.

Air service is available to the Lake District via *Aerolíneas Argentinas, CATA,* and *Austral;* all connect Bariloche with Buenos Aires by jet in 2 hours. Flights to San Martín de los Andes and Esquel, north and south of Bariloche respectively, also are offered. Train service has always been good, with an express run making the 1,472-mile trip in 29 hours. There is a daily bus between these two cities — a 28-hour ride — and other buses serve the route with many stops in between.

The Lake District trip (also described in *Chile*, DIRECTIONS) can be taken starting from Argentina, with boats departing from below the Llao-Llao peninsula. The trip can take 1 or 2 days or longer; tour companies usually offer this lake excursion for a 1- or 2-day period, and you travel by boat and bus. *Catedral Turismo* (399 Bartolomé Mitre; phone: 944-25443, 944-25444, and 944-25445) is the preferred operator. Guides speak fluent English, the buses and boats are clean and safe, and the bus/boat transfers are handled smoothly. Their Bariloche–Puerto Montt, Chile trip takes about 13 hours, including a stop at a hotel for lunch (the meal is not included in cost of the trip). The route takes travelers by bus along the shore of Lake Nahuel Huapi, passing beautiful vacation houses with lush flower gardens, and-if skies are clear — the snow-capped Cerro Catedral. At Puerto Pañuelo, a catamaran takes visitors to the western finger of Lake Nahuel Huapi — which resembles a Norwegian fjord. You'll also cross tiny Lago Frías where condors may be seen swooping down from the snow-crusted cliffs lining the shore. After the border crossing to Chile and lunch at Peulla, the boat will pass one ice-capped volcano after another, culminating in the nearly perfect cone of Osorno (8,793 feet high). Transferring back to a bus, travelers will go by Puerto Varas and then stop at Saltos del Petrohue National Park for a look at Petrohue Falls and the emerald green rapids. The trip costs $36, with an additional fee for optional hotel stays at Puerto Varas or Puerto Montt.

**CIRCUITO CHICO and CIRCUITO GRANDE:** For travelers who use Bariloche as the base for their visit to the Lake District, there are two highly recommended land excursions. Circuito Chico, or small circuit, provides an afternoon's outing to the charming, picture postcard village of Llao-Llao. Circuito Grande, or large circuit, is an all-day affair encompassing a northern route through the the park. Both circuits begin and end in Bariloche. If you prefer to sit back and enjoy the scenery while someone else takes care of driving along the winding roads, any travel agency in Bariloche will be able to book a motorcoach tour for you. The price is set at $14 for the small circuit and $27.50 for the large.

For Circuito Chico, follow coastal Route H west to Llao-Llao, at the foot of Cerro López on the peninsula of Lakes Nahuel Huapi and Moreno. It is famous for its trout fishing in the Limay River. Llao-Llao has its own port, Puerto Pañuelo, and a 9-hole golf course. Travelers making the Lake District trip between Argentina and Chile depart from the Pañuelo dock.

Returning to Bariloche, you'll pass Cerro López, a good mountain for beginning skiers on the north shore of Lago Gutiérrez, and Cerro Catedral and Punto Panorámico.

Circuito Grande leads north from Bariloche along Route 237, following the winding Limay River. The drive is much more rustic and uncluttered than the route to Llao-Llao. You'll pass the Anfiteatro (Amphitheater), with a wide view of the river, then go through Valle Encantado (the Enchanted Valley), with its curious limestone rock formations, including the Finger of God and Indian Chief. The Indians believed that the rock shapes were people, frozen long ago by the angry gods. *Safaris Acuaticos* (phone: 944-25521), leads full-day rafting trips on the river. This is an easy trip with no big rapids, suitable for beginners. A barbecue is included in the $35 charge. They also offer novices a raft trip on the Manso River, in a very remote and beautiful area about an hour's drive from Bariloche. The cost for a full-day trip with lunch is $60. Skilled rafters can takle the Manso's Class IV rapids for the same price. Book through your hotel or any Bariloche travel agency.

After passing Valle Encantado, turn left onto Route 1 at the small village of Confluencia. The route will take you north to 20-mile-long Lake Traful, famous for its salmon. Facing the lake at an altitude of 495 feet, you can observe a curious phenomenon: Any light object thrown out over the lake is caught in a strong ascending current of air and returned to its point of origin.

Continuing south on Route H leads you near Lakes Correntoso and Espejo and Villa la Angostura, on the northeast shore of Lake Nahuel Huapi. From there, the road follows the lake to the tip of Brazo Huemul, then reconnects with Route 237 south, returning you to Bariloche.

**LOS ALERCES NATIONAL PARK:** Continuing south on Route 40 from Bariloche, you reach Los Alerces National Park, a 700,000-acre reservation in the northwest corner of Patagonia's Chubut province. This remote park rewards determined travelers with unspoiled natural wonders — numerous lakes, streams, rapids, and cascades. It's accessible only from early December to mid-March or April. In the spring, fields of tulips bloom, adding brilliant swatches of oranges and reds to the green backdrop of the forest. The northern gateway to the park is the town of El Bolson, 78 miles (125 km) south of Bariloche, which offers a few small hotels and rooming houses (see *Best en Route*). There are two gorgeous lodges with superb views of Lake Futalaufquen inside the park and a visitors' center at the lake. If possible, take a launch tour from Pto. Limonado that crosses the lake and cruises up the River Arrayanes to tiny Lake Verde and then across to Lake Menéndez. The scenery is splendid. For information, ask at *Hotel Futalaufquen* (no phone) or *Tehuelche Viajes y Turismo* (574 Av. Fontana in Esquel) or *Esquel Tours* (just down the street at 764 Av. Fontana; phone: 945-2704). Fishing in the area is good; rainbow trout and salmon are the best catches. A 15-day license costs $30.

Lake Menéndez, deep in the park, has two outstanding sights: the high peak of Cerro Torrecillas, with its large glacier ripe for climbing, and forests that contain the 1,000-year-old larches for which the park is named. If these larches are as old as is estimated, they are the second oldest living trees in the world after California's sequoias. (A National Geographic study is underway to determine if there are alerces even older than the sequoias.)

**ESQUEL:** This small (15,000-person) village 160 miles (256 km) south of Bariloche on Route 40 was once an offshoot of the Welsh settlements in Chubut, 400 miles (640 km) east on the Patagonian coast. Thirty-six miles (58 km) east of Los Alerces National Park, the town provides no public transportation except boats (and bus and air links to the outside world), but hotel accommodations and restaurants are reasonable. La Hoya ski slopes, about 9 miles (14 km) away, are ideal for spring skiing. Snow remains after it's disappeared from Catedral and Chapelco, so many skiers finish their seasons here. In Esquel, travelers with a sweet tooth may want to stop by the *Confitería Suiza* (569 Antártida Argentina; phone: 945-2727). The city's tourism office is at the corner of Alvear and Fontana (phone: 945-2369).

## BEST EN ROUTE

Hotels and guesthouses range in price from very expensive ($80 to $120 per person), to expensive ($60–$80), to moderate ($35–$60), to inexpensive (under $35). Prices often vary according to season. During the peak ski period (July and August), prices may be double the summer rate. The ranges mentioned reflect this possibility. Breakfast often is included; be sure to ask when booking. Accommodations are adequate in the larger resort areas, like Bariloche, but be prepared to pay for rooms without private baths elsewhere.

Once again, you must make reservations well in advance to stay at a major resort. There's a reservations center for Bariloche hotels in Buenos Aires (upstairs at 520 Florida; phone: 392-1786 or 392-8115).

Camping is available in all major parks, but check with authorities if you wish to camp at an unofficial camping site: A permit is needed.

## NEUQUÉN

***Del Comahue*** – Rooms for up to 200 guests in this modern high rise; a remodeled restaurant, gallery of shops, and a small pool are on the premises. 387 Av. Argentina (phone: 943-22439). Moderate.

***Iberia*** – This lodging has 50 rooms with air conditioning and a snack bar. 294 Av. Olascoaga (phone: 943-22372). Moderate.

***Royal*** – A 40-room hotel with a bar, laundry service, and bilingual staff. 143 Av. Argentina (phone: 943-22408). Moderate.

***Hostal del Caminante*** – Outside of town, this comfortable hotel has 35 rooms and a bungalow that sleeps six. There's a laundry service, a small swimming pool, and English-speaking personnel. On Route 22 (phone: 945-33118). Inexpensive.

***Posta Arroyito*** – Also outside of town, this 32-room motel has a small swimming pool. On Rte. 22 (phone: 19, via public phone). Inexpensive.

## LANÍN NATIONAL PARK

***Hostería El Ciervo*** – A hostel in the park's southeastern section, near Lago Melinque, it is operated by English personnel (phone: 944-93267). Moderate.

## JUNÍN DE LOS ANDES

***Hostería Chimehuin*** – With only 16 rooms, this intimate inn near Río Chimehuin is an almost legendary gathering spot for fishermen. Its dining room is better known for its wine list than for the food, but the biggest draw is the chance to hear — and share — fishing tales. Suárez and 25 de Mayo (phone: 362-91132). Inexpensive.

## SAN MARTÍN DE LOS ANDES

***El Sol de los Andes*** – Hilltop hotel that offers 117 rooms and good food. Open year-round. Rte. D (phone: 972-27460). Expensive.

***Caupolicán*** – This 31-room lodge-like hotel has two fireplaces, a sauna, laundry service, and a snack bar. 969 Av. San Martín (phone: 972-27658 or 972-27900; in Buenos Aires, 1-962-4728). Moderate.

***Hostería la Masía*** – A small lodging place (17 rooms) with a teahouse and bakery. 811 G. Obeid (phone: 623-7688 or 623-7979). Moderate.

***La Raclette*** – The restaurant at this hostelry offers a multitude of international dishes. 1178 Coronel Pérez (phone: 972-27664). Moderate.

## NAHUEL HUAPI NATIONAL PARK

***El Casco*** – Furnished with Spanish colonial antiques, this exclusive, 20-room hotel is in the Nahuel Huapi National Park. Each room is named for the color in which it's decorated (for example, "La Violet") and every suite or room has its own private sun terrace overlooking the lake. Reserve well ahead. At Km 11 on the route to Llao-Llao (phone: 944-61032/88/89/90; phone and fax in Buenos Aires: 1-312-5768). Very expensive to expensive.

***La Cascada*** – One of the newer properties in the area, this 25-suite hotel features a balcony and Jacuzzi in every room. There is a restaurant, coffee shop, piano bar, and a private pier on Lake Nahuel Huapi for fishing and boating excursions. The hotel can arrange ski lessons and offers free transportation to the Cerro Catedral slopes; it also organizes guided fishing trips, hunting at private reserves, horseback riding and lessons, and golf at nearby courses. Km 6 on Av. Bustillo (phone: 944-41088 and 944-41220; in Buenos Aires, 1-826-5537; in the US, 800-44-UTELL; fax: 944-41076; in Buenos Aires, 1-826-5510). Expensive.

***Tunquelén*** – A cozy, 50-room stone lodge on the shores of Lake Nahuel Huapi. The restaurant, tennis court, shops, and free transportation to the ski runs are welcome features. At Km 24.5 on the route to Llao-Llao (phone: 944-48233; in Buenos Aires, 1-312-4997; in the US, 800-44-UTELL; fax: 944-48106). Expensive.

**Lago Villarino** – A chalet-style 8-room hotel near the forest research station that offers lunch for boat tour visitors and a fabulous view of the mountain ridge on the opposite shore (phone: 944-27299 or 944-27333). Inexpensive.

## BARILOCHE

**Bariloche Ski** – This 50-room property, with a bar and roof garden, also has ski rentals. During fishing season, guides can be arranged through the hotel. 352 San Martín (phone: 944-22913). Expensive.

**Bella Vista** – Near downtown Bariloche, a good 58-room hotel, with all the amenities, including *El Quicho* restaurant, which serves traditional Argentine *asado* (grilled meat) and has folk dancing and tango shows, a bar, and sauna. 351 Rolando (phone: 944-22435). Expensive.

**Edelweiss** – On the lake, this 93-room chalet-style place offers a swimming pool, gym, and sauna. *La Tavola* restaurant serves international fare; there also is a bar and coffee shop. There are rooms with a view of the lake, but they are on the street and you might have to put up with some noise. 232 San Martín (phone: 944-26165; in the US, 800-327-3573; fax in Buenos Aires: 1-393-4158). Expensive.

**Interlaken Palace** – An 84-room resort hotel with a restaurant, 1 block from the lake. 383 O'Connor (phone: 944-26156). Expensive.

**Panamericano** – A hotel with rakish lines and luxurious amenities. All 180 rooms have views of Lake Nahuel Huapi. Ten are suites equipped with Jacuzzis and fireplaces. There's a rooftop swimming pool and solarium, a sauna (and masseur), a wine cave, 2 restaurants, a shopping arcade, and 24-hour room service. Continental breakfast is included. 536-70 Av. San Martín (phone: 944-25846 or 944-25850; in Buenos Aires, 1-393-6017 or 1-393-6062; in the US, 800-44-UTELL; fax in Buenos Aires: 1-393-6570). Expensive.

**Sol-Bariloche** – Private baths and first class service are offered at this 135-room hotel. 212 Bartolomé Mitre (phone: 944-22507). Expensive.

**Apartur** – In the center of town, this 110-suite hostelry offers a restaurant with regional and international dishes, a pub, spa, sauna, 24-hour room service, and color television sets. Transportation to the ski slopes is provided and fishing, golf, and tennis can be arranged. Continental breakfast included. 685 Bartolomé Mitre (phone: 944-26190). Expensive to moderate.

**Tres Reyes** – On the lakeshore, its 57 rooms have private baths. 135 Av. 12 de Octubre (phone: 944-26124). Expensive to moderate.

**Residencia Flamingo** – A 42-room hostelry that serves breakfast. 24 Bartolomé Mitre (phone: 944-22334). Moderate.

**El Retorno** – Nestled among the trees beside Lake Gutiérrez, this small chalet-style place offers an idyllic setting for travelers seeking to avoid the crowds and be close to a golf course a mile away, and to the Cerro Catedral slopes 3 miles (5 km) down the road. There is a restaurant, bar, a variety of water sports, hiking, and horseback riding. Seven miles (11 km) from Bariloche at Villa Los Cohiues (phone: 944-41262 in Bariloche). Moderate.

**Slalom** – Every room in this contemporary property has a lake view. The lounge has huge picture windows and a fireplace. There's also a snack bar. 194 Salta (phone: 944-24574). Moderate.

## CERRO CATEDRAL

**Catedral Club** – A 68-room and 76-apartment hotel at the foot of the ski slope. Three restaurants, 2 bars, 2 nightclubs, shops, 2 tennis courts, a pool, and a sauna round out the amenities. Villa Catedral (phone: 944-60004 or 944-60006; in Buenos Aires, 1-393-9048; fax in Buenos Aires: 1-322-9469). Moderate.

## EL BOLSON

***Hostería Steiner*** – Small rooming house, but provides adequate services. 300 Av. San Martín (phone: 944-92224). Moderate.

***Hostería Amancay*** – All 15 rooms have private baths. 3217 San Martín at Cervantes (phone: 944-92222). Inexpensive.

## LOS ALERCES

***Futalaufquen*** – Ideally situated in the Los Alerces National Park on the lake, this comfortable hostelry has 37 rooms and 2 bungalows. Try to get a room with a balcony overlooking the water. Half board available. Open November through April. Near the Puerto Limonado boat launch (no phone). Moderate.

***Hostería Quimé Quipán*** – Each of the 29 rooms in this rustic lodge on Lake Futalaufquen has a spectacular view. Favorite of fishing enthusiasts. One meal is included in the rate. On the lake (no phone). Moderate.

# Patagonia to Antarctica

Southern Patagonia is not a resort center like Bariloche, but a territory for the stalwart adventurer. The northern region of lush forests and numerous lakes gives way to rugged, stark mountains and the drier stony countryside of the southern mountain region. This area is dominated by huge, isolated *estancias*, often covering thousands of acres, most run by the descendants of English and Welsh immigrants. Travel accommodations are scarce, and not as comfortable and elaborate as those in the Lake District. Backpack camping becomes a requisite for anyone who wishes to enjoy the region at close range.

Patagonia is spread over 301,158 square miles, from south of the Río Colorado and Bahía Blanca in the northeast to the island territory of Tierra del Fuego in the south. The region also encompasses the provinces of Neuquén in the northwest (for more information, see *Bahía Blanca to Bariloche*, above), Chubut in the central area, and Río Negro in the northeast. So uninhabited is the area that it has only 400,000 people, most of whom live in the small cities and towns. Santa Cruz province, for example, is about the size of Yugoslavia, yet the total population is 145,000. The largest city is Comodoro Rivadavia, with 100,000 residents.

Patagonia was "discovered" by Ferdinand Magellan in 1519, during his voyage around the world. The Strait of Magellan was named after him, for he used the Strait (which separates Tierra del Fuego from Chile and Argentina) as a corridor between the Atlantic and Pacific Oceans. Magellan named Tierra del Fuego — Land of Fire — after he sighted smoke from the Indian campfires along the coast. Because the natives covered their feet with thick hides and furs, the European sailors nicknamed them Patagones, or "people with big feet," and the moniker stuck. The Indians continued to live on the coast, successfully driving away other settlers and explorers until the Indian Wars 400 years later, when they were all but exterminated. Today, their few remaining descendants inhabit Argentina's far north portion of Tierra del Fuego.

The first Spanish settlement in Patagonia was at Carmen de Patagones in Río Negro on the northeastern coast in the early 1820s. A Welsh settlement followed in 1865 in Puerto Madryn, south of Carmen de Patagones. Additional settlements were established by immigrants from Scotland, Wales, and England from Bahía Blanca southward.

Patagonia retains a Wild West atmosphere, and legends about outlaw bandits abound. In 1915, a ferocious female outlaw called "La Inglesa" ("The Englishwoman") was shot to death, thus ridding the territory of a personality — the story goes — that frightened the toughest men.

As in the 19th century, most Patagonian land is used for sheep raising; in recent years, though, the discovery of petroleum, the commercialization of fishing, the promise of industrial growth, and tax incentives encouraged more people to migrate from northern Argentina, helping transform Patagonia into a modern, industrial frontier land. More recently, efforts have been made to boost tourism as an industry in the area. The only agriculture to speak of here is in the north, in the Colorado and Río Negro valleys. Irrigation has been very successful in the Río Negro Valley, which produces great amounts of fruit, especially apples and pears. The area's alcoholic apple cider (*sidra*) is popular throughout the country.

Tourism and business ventures in this part of the continent have Argentines and Chileans working together — a far cry from when the two countries were heatedly disputing the ownership of three Atlantic islands near the Beagle Channel off Tierra del Fuego (the channel was named after Charles Darwin's *Beagle* expedition in the early 19th century). The trio of islands had been up for grabs since the late 19th century when Argentina got control of most of the large island of Tierra del Fuego and Chile was awarded authority over the Strait of Magellan. Chile, a Pacific nation, was given Lennox, Nueva, and Picton islands through international negotiation in 1972, and its control over them was reaffirmed after Pope John Paul II mediated the dispute.

The weather in Patagonia can be chilly or mild, depending on how near you are to the equator or the Antarctic Circle. Summer daytime temperatures reach as high as 81F (27C) in the Río Negro valley; 59F (15C) in Santa Cruz; and as low as 52F (11C) in Tierra del Fuego. Travelers in the southernmost regions will be treated to an interesting phenomenon around Río Gallegos: This section of Patagonia is so far south (at the 52° latitude mark) that sunrise occurs at 9 AM.

Not always in top condition, roads in Patagonia have good connections to the north; bad weather, however, can close even the most direct roads, and screen windshield protectors are requisite on gravel surfaces (protectors are available in Bariloche and Comodoro Rivadavia). The recommended road is Route 3, which extends south from Buenos Aires to Ushuaia. Along it you'll see a wide variety of wildlife roaming freely on the range: guanacos, rheas (a type of ostrich), large rabbits, foxes, and, on the beaches of the Valdés Peninsula, seals, sea elephants, walruses, and penguins. For an unusually perceptive tale of one man's travels through this remote part of the world, read *In Patagonia,* by the late Bruce Chatwin (Summit Books). Written with consummate grace, it describes his personal odyssey in the 1970s.

There are numerous ways to travel through Patagonia besides going by car. The *Transportes Patagones* bus line leaves daily from Buenos Aires for the 50-hour trek through port towns along the coast as far south as Río Gallegos.

Buses depart from Estación Terminal de Omnibus in Retiro Square. Flights leave Buenos Aires (Jorge Newberry city airport) regularly for all parts of the region, but reserve seats well in advance. Rail service, however, is more limited; it's available in the northwest only, to Neuquén and Bariloche.

Further travel information can be obtained from the national tourism office in Buenos Aires, 883 Av. Santa Fe (phone: 1-312-2232).

Travelers heading for Patagonia should also consider an expedition to Antarctica. A number of excursions are available to the world's Fifth Continent; generally, they are wildlife and scientific expeditions. Tours here are discussed further under Antarctica.

**CARMEN DE PATAGONES:** On the southern tip of Buenos Aires province, 96 miles (154 km) south of Río Colorado, this was the first settlement in Patagonia. It faces the town of Viedma, the capital of Río Negro province, just across the Río Negro. Ex-president Raúl Alfonsín commissioned a study to move Argentina's capital to Viedma in order to relieve crowding in Buenos Aires and to encourage development in the southern part of the country. The proposal was estimated to have cost $5 billion and the plan was tabled by the current administration because of overwhelming economic problems. Both towns are irrigated agricultural centers, not of interest to tourists, although you might want to visit Las Mercedes cathedral in Viedma, or one of its five museums. In summer, there is swimming at the public beach along Río Negro and at beaches along the coast.

A monument on Cerro de la Caballada in Carmen de Patagones commemorates a Brazilian military attack on both towns in 1827.

**SAN ANTONIO OESTE:** Going west on Route 3 to Route 23 leads you to San Antonio Oeste, a small town on the San Matías Gulf. With only 4,000 people, it is linked with the Río Negro by a canal. There is excellent fishing all along the coast — from Carmen de Patagones to San Antonio Oeste — as well as in the Río Negro. Simple, inexpensive lodging can be found in San Antonio Oeste.

**PUERTO MADRYN:** Retracing your steps to Route 3 south, drive to Puerto Madryn, 108 miles (173 km) away on the Golfo Nuevo in Chubut province. The locals earn their livings mainly from fishing or working in the aluminum plant, although tourism is becoming increasingly important. Founded in 1865 by Welsh immigrants, this seaport town of 30,000 inhabitants still has many families who speak Welsh. A statue of a Welsh woman on the waterfront pays homage to its settlers; it was they who first implemented the irrigation techniques that made the Chubut Valley fertile.

While in town, be sure to sample the fresh seafood. *Las Aquilas* (Av. San Martín between 28 de Julio and R.S. Peña), favored by locals, serves tasty shellfish, homemade pasta, and Argentine wines. Stop in at the helpful tourist office (444 Av. Julio A. Roca; phone: 965-73029) for more information about the city.

A side trip from Puerto Madryn on Route 256 east leads you to the Valdés Peninsula via Punte Norte, 106 miles (170 km) away. Joined to the mainland by a 5-mile-wide isthmus, the peninsula has the continent's only colony of sea elephants (thousands of them) that live and breed here. You can observe them from a distance of several yards while they loll on the beach. Each battle-scarred, 2- or 3-ton male has a harem of 1 dozen smaller females. It's also possible to sight whales at their breeding grounds in the Golfo Nuevo, south of the peninsula. Seabirds favor San José, the gulf on the northern side. Because of its crystal clear waters, the peninsula is a good place to go diving. Large clusters of giant algae and a great variety of fauna are found in the waters, which are clear down to 100 feet.

On the way to the Valdés Peninsula, you pass through Puerto Pirámide. Several companies there offer whale watching trips from June through December. Information is available through a seafood restaurant, *Cantina El Salmón* (phone: Puerto Pirámide 7, in town). All the local operators are said to be reputable, but one highly recommended company is *Aguatours* (phone: 965-71001, 1-322-6798 in Buenos Aires; fax in Buenos Aires: 1-804-1514). At press time, all operators were charging $20 for each passenger for an hour-long trip. Tours depart as boatloads of about 20 are filled.

**En Route from Puerto Madryn** – Returning to the port, continue south on Route 3 to Rawson, a small (pop. 2,500) port that serves as the capital of Chubut province, then west on Route 25 to Trelew (pop. 80,000), which is Welsh for "Town of Lewis," and is allegedly named for Lewis Jones, the city's credited founder. Like Puerto Madryn, Trelew was settled by the Welsh. Located on the Chubut River, the city is the air-service hub for the area. The highway continues to Gaiman, the most authentic Welsh town in Patagonia today. It has a Welsh museum and holds fast to the tradition of afternoon tea.

Returning to Route 3 south, those who missed the walruses at the Valdés Peninsula will find them at Camarones. The largest rookery of Magellanic penguins in the world is at Punta Tombo. More than 1 million penguins migrate here from Antarctica at the end of September and stay until April to breed and raise their young. Visitors are welcome to wander around the colony of these docile birds.

**COMODORO RIVADAVIA:** One of the newest communities in the Patagonia area, this small (pop. 100,000) city 249 miles (399 km) south of Rawson on Route 3 is a bustling town. Petroleum was discovered in 1907, and today 28% of Argentina's entire oil supply comes from here. A 1,095-mile pipeline carries natural gas to Buenos Aires. This city, on the Gulf of San Jorge, is noted for its ceramics, soap, and lime factories; in addition to oil, frozen meat, wool, and hides are exported.

Bus and air transportation are available to Buenos Aires and Bariloche from Comodoro Rivadavia.

Puerto Aysen in Chile can be reached by heading west via Paso Río Mayo. The tiny (5,500 people) town is in mountain and fjord country.

**En Route from Comodoro Rivadavia** – Continuing south on Route 3 leads to Fitz Roy, 68 miles (109 km) away. Due west of Fitz Roy is the Pinturas River, along which are many important prehistoric sites. The most famous is called Cueva de los Manos (Cave of the Hands). The cave walls are covered with murals of hunters — little more than stick figures — stalking guanacos with lances and stones. There are zigzag lines, geometric shapes, and human hands, the latter formed when the Toldense people — the earliest inhabitants of southern Patagonia — spread solutions of ocher and other minerals around their hands, using straw made from reeds. The oldest paintings date back more than 7,000 years and the most recent to AD 1000, but the black, yellow, and red dyes are still distinct. Back at Fitz Roy, you have a choice of two routes to Tierra del Fuego. If you continue on Route 3's corridor, Route 281, you will reach Puerto Deseado and Río Gallegos; then make a left turn into Punta Delgada. A 40-minute crossing by *ENAP* oil boats will take you to Punta Espora (check daily schedules for tide changes). From there, the route leads to Río Grande and, finally, Ushuaia.

The alternate journey (through Chile) is to take Route 3's corridor Route 282 from the spectacular jagged peak of Mount Fitz Roy (10,125 feet) — a short cut that bypasses Puerto Deseado into Río Gallegos, followed by Punta Arenas. Take the regular ferry crossing into Porvenir in Chile, across the Strait of Magellan. From Porvenir, the 135-mile (216-km) Route 3 alternate continues into Río Grande in Argentine Tierra del Fuego.

**PUERTO DESEADO:** Have you ever wondered how the penguin got its name? Well, *pengwyn* is Welsh for "white head"; the name was coined in the 16th century when a member of an English expedition spotted the bird here at Puerto Deseado, southeast of Comodoro Rivadavia. Unfortunately, an oil spill in late 1991 killed at least 16,000 penguins (and possibly even twice that number), alerting environmentalists to the depletion of these birds, as well as other forms of wildlife, in Patagonia. The small town (pop. 10,000) is of interest for the international ornithological community. The Deseado River is the only place in the world where five species of the cormorant are found. West of Puerto Deseado is the Monumento Nacional Bosques Petrificados (National Monument of the Petrified Forests). This eerie fossilized forest contains the 70-*million*-year-old remains of araucaria trees that preceded the formation of the Andes! The area is accessible only in the spring and summer. While in town, stop by the *Museo de la Fragata Swift* (Frigate Swift Museum). Its exhibits include an hourglass that was retrieved from the English vessel of the same name, which was shipwrecked off the coast in the 1700s.

**PUERTO SANTA CRUZ:** Another 282 miles (451 km) south on Route 3, this town has supposedly one of the best harbors in the country at the mouth of the Río Santa Cruz, which flows into Lago Argentino. Bahía Grande, south of the city, was chartered by Magellan during his voyage.

Continuing south, Magellan wintered at San Julián, some 200 miles (320 km) north of the Magellan Strait. The town marks the 563-mile (901-km) point between Comodoro Rivadavia and Río Gallegos.

**RÍO GALLEGOS:** The capital of Santa Cruz province, this is the largest city (75,000) south of Puerto Madryn and is known as a primary sheep-raising center, exporting wool, sheepskin, tallow, and processed frozen meat. In 1991, the Hudson volcano in the Chilean Andes erupted, spreading its ash across a large portion of Santa Cruz province, and killing about a million sheep (40% of the area's woolly population) and adversely affecting farming in the region. Río Gallegos has a centrally located tourist office (1551 Av. Roca; phone: 966-22702) and a variety of coffee shops and restaurants. A museum sits at the corner of Calle Tucumán and Calle Belgrano, and that is about as interesting as the town gets.

There are daily flights from Buenos Aires on *Aerolíneas Argentinas* and *Austral Airlines* to Río Gallegos.

Because Río Gallegos is so far south, the sun usually rises between 8 and 9 AM. Stars this far south are incredible, too, especially the Southern Cross, which rotates on an axial star one complete turn throughout the night; sailors used to depend on it as a guide.

One note: If you're interested in learning about the stars in the Southern Hemisphere, buy a celestial guide *before* coming to South America. There simply are none to be found once you're here.

**En Route from Río Gallegos** – Before descending to Tierra del Fuego — an excursion to be considered only in the summer months (November through March) — you may want to take a side trip to Río Turbio, some 156 miles (250 km) west from Río Gallegos on Route 293. This small mining town is located at the site of the country's largest coalfield and is just starting to be developed as a ski area. Río Turbio is on one of the routes to Lago Argentino; and also by taking Route 3 from here, you can cross the border into Chile to Puerto Natales, the gateway to Parque Nacional Torres del Paine (Paine Towers National Park). This route is impassable in winter.

**GLACIER NATIONAL PARK/LAGO ARGENTINO:** Immense glaciers — over 300 in all — highlight the park, one of Argentina's most important scenic attractions. You easily can visit four of them in 2 days, using the town of Calafate as your operational base. Be sure to dress properly — it is cold in this area, even in summer. Gloves, hat, trekking boots, and a warm coat are a must. If you didn't come prepared, consider buying one of the lovely — and warm — sheepskin coats sold locally. A 12-hour bus-and-boat excursion operated by *Nova Terra* (39 Nueve de Julio; phone: 902-91155 in

Calafate) visits Upsala (the biggest, with a surface of nearly 1,000 square miles), Onelli (where the lake is filled with hundreds of icebergs), and Spegazzini glaciers. Any travel agency in Calafate can make reservations. As an alternative, you might consider contacting the local youth hostel in Calafate, *Albergue del Glacier* (Calle Los Pioneros; phone and fax: 902-91243). Staff there can also arrange horseback riding excursions as well as trips to the best known of the glaciers, Perito Moreno — one of the few in the world still advancing. It is 20 miles long, and has 3-mile frontage on the water and a height of between 160 and 200 feet. About every 4 years, the glacier calves — huge chunks of its face crack off and drop into the channel below with an astounding rumble. The next calving season is expected in 1996, but because of warming due to the damage to the ozone layer, the date is uncertain.

Instead of booking an excursion to Perito Moreno, you can take a 2-hour, twice-daily bus from Calafate over a dirt and gravel road. Once at the glacier, you can make arrangements with various operators for trekking excursions across the ice, boat rides to the face ($20 each), and a 15-minute helicopter ride over the glacier ($40). Nature lovers, however, discourage the latter because of its impact on the area's fauna. If you choose to enter the park on your own (after paying a small fee), there are several wooden walkways that lead to different views of the glacier. All are excellent vantage points for picture taking.

Lago Argentino itself is 75 miles long and an average of 12 miles wide. Two long arms reach toward the Andes and the glaciers. Camping is permitted in two areas. A recommended private campground that offers a cafeteria, horseback riding, fishing, and boating is *Camping Lago Roca*, about 30 miles (48 km) outside of Calafate on the road to Perito Moreno. Reservations can be made in Buenos Aires (1054 Cerritos; phone: 1-415352) or locally; there is a daily bus from Calafate to Lago Roca. For information on campsites and permits, contact the park's office in Calafate. If you have enough time, head into the northern part of the park to Lago Viedma, which is larger than Lago Argentino, and to Mount Fitz Roy, named for the young English captain of Charles Darwin's ship, the *Beagle*. Scenic hiking trails lead to both Fitz Roy and Torre mountains. There is daily bus service (4 hours) between Calafate and Chaltén where you can find accommodations in two comfortable hostels with shared baths. Though there are two small restaurants, it's a good idea to bring food from Calafate. The park is closed from May 1 to September 1.

Skilled skiers might relish the challenge of taking on Patagonia's ice cap. It is a cold and wet experience, best negotiated during the so-called dry season (November through March). *Inner Asia* (2627 Lombard St., San Francisco, CA 94123; phone: 800-777-8183) or *Patagonia Wilderness* (610 Av. Julio Roca, 8th Floor, Buenos Aires; phone: 1-334-5134) can arrange tours that include a stay at the restored ranch house *Estancia Cristina* (see *Best en Route*).

**CALAFATE:** This small (pop. 3,000) town on the southern shore of Lago Argentino is the region's touristic center, boasting a dozen hotels, and an assortment of restaurants and tearooms. Calafate is 192 miles (307 km) northwest of Río Gallegos and is reached over an all-weather road (6 hours) or via *LADE* (the air force transport) from Río Gallegos (45 minutes; advance arrangements — best made in Buenos Aires — are essential). *Inter-Lagos Turismo* (1175 Av. Libertador; phone: 902-91018) also operates twice-daily, 40-seat first class buses between Río Gallegos and Calafate.

Aside from the excursions throughout the national park, there is little of interest in Calafate itself, although there is a bird reserve on the edge of town with flamingos (seeing their brilliant color against the gray background is truly a memorable experience), ducks, and other birds native to Patagonia. Follow Bustillo away from downtown until you arrive at a marshy area (or ask anyone in town; it is not clearly marked). Also, there are some ancient Tehuelche Indian paintings in the caves of Gualicho at the *25 de Mayo Ranch*, about 3 miles (5 km) outside Calafate. Horses can be rented at *Hostería*

*Kau Yatún* (see *Best en Route*). *La Tablita,* at the town's entrance, is a great spot for barbecue. The restaurant at the *Michelangelo* hotel (Gob. Moyano at the corner of Cmte. Espora; phone: 902-91045; see *Best en Route*) is excellent. Another recommended spot for a good meal or drink after a day's outing is *El Refugio* (963 Av. Libertador), located on the city's main avenue (and only paved street). Delicious chocolate bars and confections are made locally. The best can be bought at *Sur Pagatonicos* (827 Campa del Desierto; phone: 902-91216). A good travel agency for making arrangements in the Calafate area is *Eves* (702 Tucumán, Buenos Aires; phone: 1-393-6151, 1-393-6251, or 1-393-6202).

**USHUAIA:** The southernmost city in the world according to Argentines (Chileans make a similar claim about about Puerto Williams), the capital of Argentine Tierra del Fuego sits at 55° latitude south: a rustic, coastal town set in the midst of waterfalls, glaciers, snowclad mountains, and beech forests with rich, red foliage in autumn. Its principal industries are sheep raising, timber cutting, fishing, and trapping. In the late 1980s, Ushuaia became a boomtown as the government sought to increase Argentina's presence near Antarctica by giving tax breaks to citizens who settled here. That plan was reversed, then reinstated, although at press time the tax incentives for the city's 30,000 residents were again in doubt. Ushuaia was formerly a Protestant mission town; it was founded in 1884, some 40 years after Charles Darwin's famous expedition on the *Beagle.* Planes make the 1,450-mile trip here from Buenos Aires in 5 hours (a new airport is scheduled to be built, but the economic crisis may set that plan back as late as the year 2000); ships take 5 days. Sailings around the tip of the continent are offered by major cruise lines; ships travel through the strait and dock in Ushuaia. *Cruceros Australis* (178 Miraflores, 12th Floor, Santiago, Chile; phone: 54-2-696-3211 or 54-2-337004; fax: 54-2-331871) is promoting luxury cruises through areas of the Strait of Magellan and the Beagle Channel that are off-limits to large US and European ships. It offers popular 7-day voyages (from Ushuaia or Punta Arenas, Chile) aboard the *Terra Australis.* This 126-passenger vessel has all outside cabins in a variety of categories — fares start at $1,600. Be sure to book well in advance; most cruises are sold out early. The *Ushuaia Aero Club* offers short flights over the Beagle Channel and air tours of the area. Check with the information desk at the airport.

Ushuaia is a rather desolate town, although the atmosphere is far more festive in summer, when cruise ship passengers and tourists fill its long shopping street, Avenida San Martín. A couple of the lines taking tourists to Antarctica also call at Ushuaia. Although the town is a duty-free port, North Americans won't find any bargains. You probably can have more fun stocking up on penguin souvenirs (T-shirts, mugs, and baseball caps) at shops like *El Viejo Lobo de Mar* (302 San Martín; phone: 901-22376). The store also sells *Tierra del Fuego,* a book by Rae Natalie Prosser Goodall that details the island's natural and political history. Though the houses are painted warm, pastel colors, the weather is chilly year-round. Winter sports such as downhill and cross-country skiing and skating are possible. Rental cars are available from *Rent Austral* (1022 Gobernador Paz; phone: 901-22422). Taxi drivers will take you anywhere you want after much pleading on your part, for they dislike traveling the bad roads at any price. Behind town there is a glacier — a 2½-hour hike away.

Excellent seafood is served at a couple of restaurants, including *Angela e Pietro Masciocchi* (857 San Martín; no phone) and *Moustacchio* (San Martín and Gob. Godoy; phone: 901-23308). The local specialties are *centolla* (king crab) and *cholgas* (giant mussels) prepared in a variety of ingenious ways — including as empanada fillings. A few miles outside of town, within the confines of the Estancia Río Pipo, the *Refugio Tolkeyen* (phone: 901-22408) has a scrumptious all-you-can-eat lamb barbecue lunch. Lamb halves roasting on spits over an open fire make a fine photo opportunity as well as a filling meal. Reservations are essential.

In the city, stop by the *Museo Territorial Fin del Mundo* (End of the World Museum;

donation requested; Av. Maipú and Rivadavia; phone: 901-21863) for a briefing on local fauna and the region's indigenous peoples. Or, for an unusual outing, head north of Lago Fagnano to the world's southernmost hot springs. Details are available from the provincial tourism office (at Maipú and Laserre; phone: 901-21423) or the city tourism office (638 San Martín; phone: 901-23303).

To explore a bit of the famed Beagle Channel, take the excursion boat *Ana B.* It sails daily in the summer months from Ushuaia. Take the full-day trip in order to see the penguins, sea lions, and large flocks of sea birds. The journey ends with tea at *Estancia Harberton,* once the home of British pioneers. Contact *Rumbo Sur* (342 San Martín; phone: 901-22275). There are also excursions to Tierra del Fuego National Forest (entrance fee). It is Argentina's only national park on the sea coast and includes Lapataia Bay. The park has a number of trails that you can explore on your own. A bus (under $10 round-trip) leaves several times daily from in front of the *Canal Beagle* hotel (590 Maipú) and drops you at the *confitería* ("the world's southernmost") in the park. Rangers provide maps with suggested routes for half- or full-day circuits. The park is closed during the snow season — normally May through early September. A good local agency for tours on the island and to Antarctica is *Antartur* (638 San Martín; phone: 901-92668), or contact their Buenos Aires office (351 Esmeralda; phone: 1-394-4273 or 1-394-4275).

An island itself, Tierra del Fuego also encompasses the islands off the Strait of Magellan. It divides more or less down the middle, the western part belonging to Chile; the eastern, to Argentina. It is large: 250 miles long and 280 miles wide. At the extreme south is Cape Horn, a rather unimpressive hunk of gray rock in a stormy sea.

If you plan to go on to Chile from southern Patagonia (a region called Magallanes in Chile), there is a good road from Río Gallegos to Punta Arenas, as well as bus service. From there you can fly north to Puerto Montt, which is the gateway for crossing the Lake District to Bariloche. You also can travel north to Río Grande and then west across the island to Porvenir, where the ferry leaves daily at 1 PM for Punta Arenas. The trip takes 8 hours over an unpaved road. You will have to leave Ushuaia in the middle of the night in order to clear the border crossing and arrive in Porvenir in time for the ferry. There are local buses that do make the trip, but you may have to overnight in Río Grande. That's good news if you happen to like to fish. The area is renowned for trout, and there's even a *Festival de Trucha* (Trout Festival) the third Sunday in February. As long as you're traveling south, you should consider a trip to Antarctica.

**ANTARCTICA:** Its summertime temperature never exceeds 40F (4C); its winter temperature plummets to −127F (−88C). Still, the desolate iceland of the Antarctic continent has been an international hotbed of controversy ever since English explorer James Cook discovered it in the late 18th century. The issue: territorial domination of a country of 5,500,000 square miles, with no native human population, but rich in natural resources that include petroleum, minerals, and krill, tiny shrimp that are predicted to become one of the world's largest protein staples.

The 1959 Treaty of Antarctica was signed by 12 nations, including the US, the Soviet Union, Argentina, and Chile. It established the Antarctic as a region to be used "for peaceful purposes, for international cooperation in scientific research, and not the scene or object of international discord." So far, the treaty has worked pretty well and the number of signatories has climbed to 39. But with the discovery of offshore oil (potentially greater than the supply in Alaska) and mineral resources, national interests are pushing claims to the cold, southern turf. Environmentalists, however, point to the need for intensive studies before any exploration or exploitation projects are implemented, since the area has a critical influence on global climate, and its ecosystems are highly vulnerable. The UN Conference for the Law of the Sea instituted discussions on internationalizing Antarctica so that its resources become available for the common good rather than for the benefit of the few. Third World nations are in accord with this approach and tend to regard the Antarctic Treaty powers as "colonial." With the exception of New Zealand, the signatory nations believe that they have the right to any resources; New Zealand proposes that Antarctica become an international park. The current Antarctica Treaty was extended in 1991 after signatories agreed to a provision that banned mining and mineral exploration for 50 years; meanwhile, the South Pole continues to be barraged by scientific expeditions. Ecuador, Peru, and other Latin American nations plan to use their research as the basis for permanent territorial claims in the region.

Antarctica's closest neighbors, Argentina and Chile, fervently favor territorializing the continent and both have taken steps to establish settlements or camps. Their interests are founded on a papal bull that transpired in 1493, giving all nations west of the 46th meridian to Spain. Argentina claims that Antarctic Argentina has been a part of that country since the founding of the Argentine Republic in the 19th century. Formal claims were filed in 1908; these added to original Spanish rights and geographical proximity and affinity support the Argentine argument. Chile bases its claims on 16th-century exploration. Both claims — each totaling one-eighth of the continent — overlap each other between the 80° and 20° latitudes.

Entrance into the Antarctic Circle can be made by boat or plane from Ushuaia through the Beagle Channel into the Drake Passage, and to the Antarctic Peninsula. A trip to the continent is geared only to the serious traveler-explorer interested in environment and wildlife. The weather and winds can be challenging. There are no hotels, no highways, no airports, and no restaurants. Tours must be arranged beforehand; they usually are sponsored by a scientific organization or wildlife-oriened group.

Several US organizations offer cruises to Antarctica. Groups aboard the ships visit glaciers, penguin rookeries, and various research stations, including the American Palmer Station in Admiralty Bay. Contact *Society Expeditions* (c/o *Abercrombie & Kent*, 1520 Kensington Rd., Oak Brook, IL; phone: 800-426-7794); *Salén Lindblad Cruising* (333 Ludlow St., Stamford, CT 06912; phone: 203-967-2900 or 800-223-5688); *Ocean Cruise Lines* (1510 Southeast 17th St., Ft. Lauderdale, FL 33316; phone: 800-556-8850 or 800-338-1700); and *Travel Dynamics* (132 E. 70th St., New York, NY 10021; phone: 212-517-7555 or 800-367-6766). An outfitter for the adventurous traveler with time and money is *KSAR Expeditions*, owned by the French ex-captain of Jacques Cousteau's *Calypso*. His 42-foot sailing vessel has a steel hull designed for Antarctic waters. It can be chartered for a minimum of 7 days for a trip between Ushuaia and Cape Horn. Contact Jean-Paul Bassaget (460 Gov. Paz, Dpto. 12, 9410 Ushuaia; phone: 901-21876).

## BEST EN ROUTE

Accommodations in Patagonia are limited to the widely scattered settlements, and are typically simple in style and spotlessly clean. It is imperative that you make reservations in advance; empty rooms are a rarity in the high season (November through March). In some areas, many hotels are closed from *Easter* to October 1. Expect to pay $100 and up per night for a double room in hotels listed as very expensive, $65 to $85 at an expensive place, $45 to $65 in a moderate hotel, and under $45 in an inexpensive place. Camping is allowed in areas such as Glaciers National Park, but permits are needed elsewhere.

### CARMEN DE PATAGONES

*Percaz* – Basic and considered the best lodgings in town. 348 Rivadavia (phone: 462-195). Moderate.

## VIEDMA

***Austral*** – The best in town, this 100-room waterfront hotel offers private baths and a tearoom for its guests. 25 de Mayo at Villarino (phone: 920-22019; in Buenos Aires, 1-466746). Expensive.

***Comahue*** – Just a few blocks from the public beach at the Río Negro. 355 Av. Colón at Garrone (phone: 920-22184). Moderate.

***Peumayen*** – Small hostelry with a bar and a bilingual staff. 334 Buenos Aires (phone: 920-22839). Inexpensive.

## PUERTO MADRYN

***Península Valdés*** – A centrally located, full-service hotel, this 70-room establishment represents the plushest accommodations available in the area and is quite expensive by local standards. 163 Av. J. A. Roca (phone: 965-71292). Expensive.

***Costanera*** – Set near the sea, this 40-room hotel has a restaurant and snack bar. 759 Brown (phone: 965-72234). Moderate.

***Playa*** – Not far down the street from the *Península*, this hostelry is clean and comfortable, offering heat and private baths. 181 Av. J. A. Roca (phone: 965-71446). Moderate.

***Yanco*** – A straightforward downtown hotel with a snack bar and disco. 626 Av. J. A. Roca (phone: 965-71581). Moderate.

## TRELEW

***Rayentray*** – The best choice in town, its 120 rooms have color televisions and mini-bars. Other amenities include a heated pool, sauna, and 3 restaurants. Located at San Martín where it meets Belgrano, a block from the Plaza de Armas (phone: 965-34702). Expensive.

## COMODORO RIVADAVIA

***Austral*** – This property, with 115 rooms and suites, has conference facilities and a snack bar. 190 Rivadavia (phone: 967-22021). Moderate.

***Comodoro*** – Featuring 104 rooms with an ocean view, a lobby bar, TV sets, and conference facilities. 777 Av. 9 de Julio (phone: 967-22061). Moderate.

***Hostería del Sur*** – Only 10 rooms at this small hostelry. 1083 Maipú (phone: 967-24119). Inexpensive.

## RÍO GALLEGOS

***Comercio*** – One of the largest hotels in town, there are 55 rooms with heat and private baths as well as telephones, a restaurant, and bar. 1302 Roca (phone: 966-8209). Moderate.

***Santa Cruz*** – Downtown 53-room hotel with a tearoom, restaurant, bar, and sauna. 701 Calle Roca (phone: 966-20601/3). Moderate.

***Oviedo*** – Small, downtown establishment located at 746 Libertad (phone: 966-20118). Inexpensive.

## CALAFATE

***Posada Los Alamos*** – An attractive 88-room hotel with a beautifully decorated lobby "living room," bar, breakfast room, and restaurant. Half board (lunch or dinner at $10–$15 per person) is mandatory for guests; meals are served in the *Restaurante La Fosta* across the street. Be aware that there's hallway noise from early-rising guests setting off on excursions. Located just a short walk from the bird sanctuary. Gob. Moyano and Bustillo (phone: 902-91144; in Río Gallegos, 966-20159). Expensive.

***Michelangelo*** – A small hostelry with the best dining room in town — the chef has a restaurant in Buenos Aires, too. Rooms, simply furnished, have private baths. Gob. Moyano at the corner of Cmte. Espora (phone: 902-91045). Moderate.

## LAGO ARGENTINO

***Estancia Cristina*** – Midway between Mount Fitz Roy and Perito Moreno glacier, northwest of Calafate, this ranch has been converted into a lodge for up to 15 guests. Most rooms are triples (only one has a private bath). Meals are prepared on wood stoves and water is heated with a wood-fired boiler. Rates include full board. Closed May through September. Reserve through *Inner Asia Expeditions* (2627 Lombard St., San Francisco, CA 94123; phone: 415-922-0449 or 800-777-8183) or *Patagonia Wilderness* (phone: 1-334-5134 in Buenos Aires). Very expensive.

***Hostería Alta Vista*** – There are 6 doubles and 1 suite — all with private baths — in this antiques-filled house with custom-made china and linen. Rates includes full board, liquor, and laundry. Horses are available for hire at $20 an outing. Closed May through September. Located 45 minutes from the Perito Moreno glacier. Reserve through *S.A. Importadora y Exportadora de la Patagonia* (547 Av. Roque Sáenz Peña; phone: 1-344-2688 and 1-344-8617 in Buenos Aires; in the US, 305-667-0912). Very expensive.

***Los Nostros*** – This cozy lodge has three 4-room cabañas and serves great meals with a view of Perito Moreno glacier. The split-level restaurant/bar features friendly service and a tasty menu — from homemade soup to steaks to cappuccino. After trekking the glacier, stop for a warming drink and *alfajores,* a local sweet made with *dulce de leche* (crème caramel). Breakfast included; half board available. Closed May to mid-September. In front of the Perito Moreno glacier, on the road through the park (phone: 902-91437, 1-812-2166 in Buenos Aires; fax: 1-814-0317). Very expensive.

***Hostería Kau Yatún*** – Just outside town on the shore of Lago Argentino, it has 46 rooms decorated in Victorian style, each with private bath, a comfortable indoor bar-lounge, and wide terraces overlooking the flower garden. Horses also can be rented and excursions in small planes can be arranged. Closed May through August. Estancia 25 de Mayo (phone: 902-91059, 1-394-6701 in Buenos Aires). Expensive to moderate, depending on the season.

## USHUAIA

***Albatros*** – Good full-service hotel, with a lobby that has native hardwood floors and soaring windows with harbor views, 75 newly refurbished rooms with private baths, attractive decor, and mini-bars, 24-hour room service, a bar, and a coffee shop. Breakfast included. 505 Av. Maipú (phone: 901-22504). Very expensive.

***Gran Hotel Ushuaia*** – Luxury has come to the southernmost city in the world. This property is the finest around, but costs twice as much as other accommodations and is a long walk from downtown. All rooms have a TV set, and there's a restaurant, snack bar, and beauty salon. Breakfast included. 933 Lasserre (phone: 901-22024). Very expensive.

***Canal Beagle*** – Overlooking the harbor area, this modern property is also a good choice. There is a restaurant, coffee shop, and even two television channels. Breakfast included. 590 Av. Maipú (phone: 901-21117, 1-802-6061 in Buenos Aires; fax: 901-21120, 1-802-0553 in Buenos Aires). Expensive to moderate.

***Río Pipo Villa*** – About 2 miles (3 km) outside town, this 16-cabaña property is perfect for the sports-minded guest, with opportunities for cross-country skiing, fishing, yachting, and nature excursions. A snack bar and nightclub offer additional comforts. Located on Ruta Nacional No. 3, Km 5 (phone: 901-234111).

Reservations through *Río Pipo Tours* (388 Maipú, Buenos Aires; phone: 1-325-1899). Moderate.

**Hostería Monte Cervantes** – Accommodations with a Tudor-style façade on the main street. There are 20 small, attractive rooms, all with carpeting, private baths, and central heating. Breakfast included. San Martín at Sarmiento (phone: 901-22153). Moderate to inexpensive.

**Hostal Malvinas** – Central heating, plenty of warm water, and a central location are the pluses of this small, economical inn with a restaurant. 615 Deloqui (phone: 901-22626; fax: 901-22485). Inexpensive.

# The Falkland Islands/Islas Malvinas

Although by no means back to normal diplomatic ties, an effort to reestablish air and naval traffic from Argentina to the Falkland Islands (or Islas Malvinas, as they are known in South America) in 1991 signaled a new era in relations between England and Argentina following the war over the sovereignty of the islands in the spring of 1982. Britain and Argentina had earlier restored some trade ties — particularly those related to fishing — and abolished visa requirements, and began to seek ways to jointly participate in oil exploration in the waters around the islands. But, at press time, the sovereignty issue had not been decided, and Argentina informed Britain that it wanted to have the dispute resolved by an international arbitration organization. Since the war, Chile has served as the closest air link and supply point for the islands and it is still possible to reach the islands via a twice-monthly air service from Punta Arenas in southern Chile. Contact *Aerovias DAP* in Punta Arenas (1022 Ignacio Carrera Pinto; phone: 61-223958). In the US, *Society Expeditions* (c/o *Abercrombie & Kent*, 1520 Kensington Rd., Oak Park, IL 60521; phone: 800-426-7794) offers cruises that include the Falklands in its itineraries. Other cruises that stop at the islands are offered by *Ocean Cruise Lines* (1510 SE 17th St., Ft. Lauderdale, FL 33316; phone: 800-556-8850 or 800-338-1700). Since conditions remain unstable, we suggest you double-check the availability of all tours, cruises, and flights mentioned herein. For the latest update, contact a British consulate in the US or write to the Falkland Islands Tourism Information Service (14 Broadway, London, England SW1H OBH; phone: 71-222-2542; fax: 71-222-2375).

A group of more than 700 islands 350 miles east of Tierra del Fuego, with a total landmass of 6,500 square miles, the Falkland Islands have an oceanic climate. Extremes here are unknown. Temperatures range from 36F (2C) in midwinter to 49F (9C) in midsummer. Snow rarely falls, and heat waves and heavy frosts are unheard of. The only catch is the rain. The sky frequently is overcast, and rain falls, usually as a light drizzle, 250 days of the year. November, at the onset of the Falkland summer, is the driest month.

The vista is strongly reminiscent of the western highlands of Scotland or the outer Hebrides Islands. The rolling, windswept hills with their springy turf lure the hiker and explorer; beaches of fine, white sand and the deeply eroded, dramatically shaped cliffs provide superb scenery. The atmosphere is clear and clean; one can often see for vast distances. There is a pervasive spirit of solitude here, broken only by the calls of sea birds and the muttering of the surf. A walk in the Falklands, with a keen wind blowing, is exhilarating and refreshing. The islands are noted for their high winds, which come mostly from the west and south, but fortunately there are many sheltered harbors in the deeply indented coastlines that protect small vessels.

The soil is peat and often spongy, due to an underlying layer of clay. The peat is a vital source of fuel for the islanders. Many ponds and salt lagoons, often of considerable size, support large populations of waterfowl. While there are no native trees, most of the land is covered by grasses, shrubs that rarely reach a height of 5 feet, and a variety of ground plants. Trees planted around the settlements are wind-stunted, but they do provide the shelter essential to keeping land birds on the islands.

A plant of considerable interest is tussock grass, which grows in dense turf as high as 12 feet from its root crowns and is used as shelter by a variety of birds. From a distance, these clumps look like treetops, which led some early explorers sailing by to report that the islands were densely wooded. Unfortunately, sheep and cattle are very fond of this grass, but although it has been extirpated from some areas, it still grows where the farmers have fenced it in.

Sheep farming is the main industry of the islands, and to the dismany of environmentalists, who say they are destroying the habitat of rare species of birds, there are 750,000 sheep; wool is the principal export. Mutton is constantly on the menu, and people say that it is served 364 days of the year — with lamb on *Christmas*. The rest of the yuletide meal includes a variety of homegrown vegetables, fresh-baked bread, and the local specialty — diddle-dee jelly made from the berries of a plant with the same name. Lunch and dinner are broken up by "smoko" — tea or coffee served with delicious homemade cakes. The commercial harvest of squid in the waters off the Falklands also is an important local industry.

The total population of the Falklands is about 2,100. Mainly of Scottish descent, these people are staunchly British and the Falklands have been a British dependency since the early 19th century. More than half live in Port Stanley, the only town of any size. The rest of the population is scattered throughout the islands, living in small farm settlements. Since there are no telephones, contact is maintained through radiotelephone, Beaver float seaplane, and small inter-island boat traffic. A traveling teacher system provides for the education of small children in the settlements; medical attention can be called for when necessary.

Apart from a road from the airport at Mount Pleasant to Stanley, islanders move around in four-wheel-drive vehicles or horseback on rough, boggy tracks. Travel among the islands is by dinghies or 9-passenger planes that fly from Port Stanley to grass or beach landing strips in "the camp" — as islanders call everything outside the major settlements. The Falklands also are a good spot for hiking, although there are military mine fields at Port Howard, Fox Bay, Fitzroy, and outside Stanley. The fields are fenced off and marked and mine field maps may be obtained at the tourism office in Stanley (56 John St.; phone: 22215).

To see wildlife at its best, visit the Falklands between November and February, when most of the birds are nesting. Species include the rockhopper, gentoo, and Magellanic penguins, quaint birds that nest in closely packed colonies. Penguins, however, nest in burrows. The large and handsome king penguin, once exterminated from the islands by seal hunters, is making a comeback, and a colony of birds now are reestablished on East Falkland Island. A fifth penguin type, the macaroni, often can be found breeding among the rockhoppers. The dignified, black-browed albatross also nests in huge concentrations, and the tame bird can be approached gently within a few feet of its nest without being disturbed.

Despite former persecution by farmers the upland geese are again a common sight here. Three other kinds of geese — the ruddy-headed, ashy-headed, and Kelp — also breed. Of particular interest is the striated caracara, a hawk-like scavenger with long legs and a good stride. It has a strong addiction to shiny articles such as cameras, knives, and binoculars, which should not be left unattended. In addition, up to 17 species of land birds can be found, ranging from the black-throated finch to the long-tailed meadowlark — a striking, red-breasted bird.

Marine mammals are another source of interest. The southern fur seal and southern sea lion can be found here, but Ian Strange, a Falklands Islands environmentalist, has documented a dramatic decline in their numbers. He found 63,000 sea lions on the islands in a 1960 survey and only 8,000 during a count in 1990. He has no clear explanation for the decline, but he is pushing to have some of the islands declared national reserves as a way to protect the area's flora and fauna. Elephant seals can still be seen on the beaches. Although whales are no longer abundant, occasionally they can be seen cruising close to shore, especially the killer whale. The little Peale's and Commerson's dolphins are still plentiful, and they delight in playing around the bows of small vessels. More recently, fishing enthusiasts have turned their attention to the Falklands, where 12-lb. sea trout are common, smelt abound, and rock cod, hake, skate, and whiting are taken out at sea. The game fishing season is from October to April and the best rivers are the Murrell near Stanley, the San Carlos on East Falkland, and the Warrah and Chartres on West Falkland.

■**Note:** It is not possible to dial direct to the Falkland Islands from the US; have an international operator place the call for you. Also, credit cards are *not* accepted anywhere on the islands.

**PORT STANLEY:** On the east coast of East Falkland Island, this tiny town (1,100 people) is mostly British. It is the sole town in the island system, the official government seat, and the official port of entry. There are two usable docks on the island; behind them are warehouses operated by the Falkland Islands Company and a small museum. There is a large department store and several smaller stores (woolens, crafts, prints, and posters are popular tourist items) on the main street, which borders the waterfront; the post office and government building lie farther to the right. Money can be exchanged at the Standard Chartered Bank. You can get a feel for local life at one of the many British-style pubs in the area.

Port Stanley is of considerable historical interest. The museum documents much of the nautical history of the past 150 years while the hulls of several clipper ships end their days along the shoreline. In both World Wars I and II, Port Stanley was involved in major naval battles between British and German forces. Due to the frequent winter gales, accompanied by 80-foot waves called "greybeards," and the treacherous reefs, hundreds of wrecks are scattered around the coasts, and much rescuing has been performed by local seamen.

**CARCASS ISLAND:** Access to this tiny, 4,300-acre island from Port Stanley is either via boat or seaplane. At the northwest end of the system, the island is a bird watcher's dream spot, the home of several gentoo and Magellanic penguin rookeries close to the shore. Geese, brown pintails, teal, and crested and steamer ducks live in the ponds and along the coast. Brown skuas are so fearless that they will swoop by the heads of intruders when nests are approached; the friendly tussock bird is also very much in evidence.

**WEST POINT ISLAND:** This 3,100-acre island, only a few miles from Carcass and one of the peninsulas of West Falkland, houses great, noisy rookeries of rockhopper penguins, and albatross. These birds are both interesting and very photogenic; they can be approached closely without disturbing them. It is expecially impressive to watch the busy rockhopper traffic in and out of the sea, which breaks heavily on the rocky coast. A favorite vantage point for bird watching is a rocky promontory known as the Devil's Nose, where you must watch every step to avoid nesting albatross.

**NEW ISLAND:** At the southwest end of the Falkland Islands, this settlement offers the remains of a whaling station and several shipwrecks. A short walk to the windward side brings you to rockhopper rookeries, which are spread up the cliff slopes and far into the surrounding hills. Careful searching will reveal a few pairs of Macaroni penguins, their bright orange head plumes sticking out among the rockhoppers. From the cliffs, sea lions can be watched as they prey upon penguins, seizing them in their jaws and literally shaking them out of their skins. On the northeast side of the island is a rookery of fur seals. Several large gentoo and rockhopper penguin colonies are on the north coast.

**KIDNEY ISLAND:** A few miles north of Port Stanley Harbour at the entrance of Berkeley Sound, this small island is a nature reserve. Kidney is only three-quarters of a mile long and one-quarter of a mile wide), but it supports an amazing variety of breeding birds; 28 species have been found nesting, including five types of petrel, three shearwaters, three gulls, and six land birds. This high productivity is due to the growth of tussock grass, which covers 90% of the island, as well as to the absence of predatory animals. Taking in Kidney is an all-day trip and quite strenuous. Visitors must use inflatable boats to reach the island, then trek across rough terrain. Trips can be arranged through the tourist office in Stanley.

**PEBBLE ISLAND:** Run as a sheep farm by about 20 settlers, this 17½-mile-long island is an attractive spot with a mountainous western half that contrasts with the grassy eastern plains. Black-necked swans and red-backed hawks can be photographed here.

**MOUNT PLEASANT:** This town on East Falkland is home to the archipelago's airport and a base housing about 2,000 British military personnel. The armed forces' vehicles and occasional helicopters belong to this base.

**PORT HOWARD:** Much of this island is taken up by the Port Howard Farm, where travelers can visit a sheep ranch. There is a small museum that offers the British side of the Falklands/Malvinas conflict. Walking, horseback riding, windsurfing, and fishing outings can be arranged through Robin Lee, a local guide and owner of the *Port Howard Lodge* (see *Best en Route*).

## BEST EN ROUTE

Lodging in the Falklands is pricey and limited, so it is best to book in advance. In the hotels listed as expensive, expect to pay more than $80 per person a night; moderate places are in the $55 to $80 range; and inexpensive ones run under $50.

***Pebble Island*** – Run by naturalists John and Ann Reid. Meals are included at this hotel. Pebble Island (phone: 41097). Expensive.

***Port Howard Lodge*** – Though spartan, this is a comfortable hostelry. Meals are included. Port Howard Settlement, West Falkland (phone: 42150). Expensive.

***Upland Goose*** – A hearty breakfast comes with the rooms here. Try diddle-dee jelly on your toast. On Ross Road, Stanley (phone: 21455). Moderate.

***Emma's Guest House*** – This simple, white wooden house with lace curtains has a restaurant where homemade Falkland dishes are served. On Ross Rd, Stanley (phone: 21056). Inexpensive.

# Mesopotamia

Like its ancient Asian namesake in the Tigris-Euphrates Valley, Argentina's Mesopotamia is sandwiched between two rivers: the 1,827-mile Paraná and the 1,000-mile Uruguay. The rivers run parallel to each other from Alto Paraná in the north, forming a base southward before flowing into the Río de la Plata, a distance of 690 miles. The distance between the rivers along this route is narrow — only 241 miles in the north to 130 miles near Santa Fe, on the west bank of the Paraná.

High in the northeastern pocket of Argentina, Mesopotamia borders Paraguay, Brazil, and Uruguay. The region encompasses the provinces of Entre Ríos to the south, Corrientes to the northwest, and Misiones to the northeast, where one can gaze at the majestic Iguassu Falls, sitting on the border between Argentina and Brazil.

Topographically, Mesopotamia is divided into three parts. Tropical jungles fill Misiones; sloping, grassy hills and marshes dominate Corrientes; dry grass and pastures dot the Entre Ríos countryside. Agriculturally, Mesopotamia plays an important role in Argentine citrus production; non-citrus fruit, linseed, and fowl also are raised here, and rice is grown along the banks of the Río Paraná, between Corrientes and Posadas, the capital of Misiones. Corrientes also produces about 9 million head of cattle and sheep annually. Mesopotamian weather is often humid, with little rainfall, and it is hot in the summer, reaching 100F (38C) by day, dropping to a cool 70F (21C) at night. The Misiones forests are filled with exotic birds and animals: monkeys, toucans, parrots, pumas, and tapirs. Argentines visit the area for good fishing, canoeing, and windsurfing.

Historically, Mesopotamia plays as important a role in Argentina's settlement as does Tucumán and the northwest region. The importance, however, is more religious than political in nature. Where Tucumán is the site of the declaration of Argentine independence, Mesopotamia is the site of a heavy concentration of Roman Catholic missions, mostly Franciscan and Jesuit, founded by Spanish missionaries in the 17th, 18th, and 19th centuries. The missions had two purposes: to convert the Guaraní Indians (most of whom were exterminated during the 19th-century colonial campaign) and to become a source of spiritual security for explorers and settlers (although several missions were set aflame by marauding Indians). The ruins of San Ignácio Miní in Misiones are a national monument; this was a Jesuit mission for the

## DIRECTIONS / Argentina 673

Guaraní during the 18th century. The mission padres, by the way, were the first producers of the beverage maté (made from holly trees) in Argentina; the trees are still grown in Mesopotamia today.

Traveling north from Buenos Aires, it is possible to take in Mesopotamia by a number of routes. Route 9 runs north up the west bank of the Río Paraná to Rosario (see *Córdoba,* below) where Route 11 goes to Santa Fe, then crosses the river by tunnel to the city of Paraná and continues north up the river's eastern bank as Route 12, passing through the river towns of La Paz and Corrientes. At this point the route turns east to Posadas, then continues north to Puerto Iguazú and the falls. Or you can take Route 9 north until it merges with Route 11 north at Rosario, then continue up the Río Paraná's east bank to Resistencia, crossing the river there to Route 12 and Corrientes. Either way, Route 12 will take you into Paraguay and Encarnación, an important border city.

If you prefer to explore Mesopotamia by boat, an excursion on the Río Paraná is recommended. The largest river in Argentina, it is a major traffic artery connecting Buenos Aires and Brazil, Paraguay, and Uruguay. The Río Uruguay, however, is geared more to small boats and vessels.

Tours to Mesopotamia can be booked through *Flight Tours* (986 Rivadavia, 10th Floor; phone: 1-380866 or 1-380912) or *Lanusse Turismo* (240 San Martín; phone: 1-331-2669 or 1-331-2886), both in Buenos Aires. It also is possible to reach the area on daily *Aerolíneas Argentinas* and *Austral* flights to Posadas and Iguassu Falls.

**SANTA FE:** On the west bank of the Río Paraná on Route 11, the capital of Santa Fe province is not a Mesopotamian city but is linked to Paraná by a 5-mile canal. Founded by Juan de Garay in 1573, Santa Fe was once the center of Jesuit missions and an outpost against the Indians, providing the seat of the constitutional assembly in 1853. The port, actually on Río Salado, is somewhat larger than Paraná.

La Merced and San Francisco, mission-era churches (built in 1680 with materials brought down the river from Paraguay), are worth a visit. While in Santa Fe, also visit the *Museo de Bellas Artes* (Museum of Fine Arts), where local artists exhibit, and the *Museo Histórico Provincial* (Museum of Provincial History). Also worth seeing are the painted glass windows in the Church of Nuestra Señora de Guadalupe.

**En Route from Santa Fe** – Before crossing the Río Paraná into Paraná and continuing upriver on Route 12, consider the alternate route: following the river's west bank north, then east into Corrientes.

Resistencia, 365 miles (584 km) north of Santa Fe on Route 11, is the capital of El Chaco province and parallels Corrientes on the Paraná's east bank. A hot and dusty railroad junction for the north, this city of 94,000 manufactures tannin and trades in lumber, cotton, and hides. Cattle, quebracho wood (used in tanning), and lead are exported from its port on the Paraná.

Resistencia's international airport has several weekly flights to Salto, Uruguay; check the schedule. Rail and bus service are available to Santa Fe, with train connections available to La Paz and Santa Cruz, Bolivia; full bus service is slated for Posadas, Tucumán, Formosa, and Salta, Argentina, and Asunción, Paraguay.

**PARANÁ:** Across the river from Santa Fe (they're connected by a tunnel) and 235 miles (376 km) northwest of Buenos Aires, the capital of Entre Ríos province is a shipping center of beef and cattle grain. Founded in 1730, Paraná (pop. 200,000) was the capital of the Argentine confederation from 1853 to 1862.

Find time to stroll around the center of town: Plaza San Martín is full of fountains, and there is a statue of the Great Liberator. The cathedral east of the plaza is worth a stop, as is the city tourism office (across the street; phone: 43-221632), but an even more impressive plaza is the one named after a Argentine hero General Urquiza. A statue of him is at the site.

Paraná can be reached from Santa Fe by taking the connecting tunnel.

**CORRIENTES:** Continuing north along Route 12 from Paraná leads to Corrientes, where, it is said, Indians who tried to burn down the cross housed in the pilgrim Church of La Cruz in 1808 were struck by lightning — which appeared, literally, out of a clear, blue sky. Founded in 1588, the capital (pop. 200,000) of Corrientes province is 648 miles (1,037 km) north of Buenos Aires, and 25 miles (40 km) below the merging of the Alto Paraná and Río Uruguay: Passengers en route upriver must change to smaller boats because of the shallow water. Corrientes is also reputed to be the setting for Graham Greene's novel, *The Honorary Consul.*

A good time to visit Corrientes is during the pre-*Lent Carnaval,* generally the end of February or beginning of March. Sponsored by wealthy families, the *Carnaval* is patterned after those held in Río and Bahía. The streets are filled with parades, music, and dancing. Vividly colored costumes and floats add a gala touch to the raucous celebration.

Directly north of Corrientes, Paso de la Patria provides good waters for dorado fishing. Fishing boats and gear can be rented at *Le Apart* hotel (1201 25 de Mayo; phone: 783-94174). Fishing information is available at the local tourism office (462 25 de Mayo; phone: 783-94007).

**POSADAS:** Continuing north along Route 12, the bend along the Alto Paraná leads to Posadas, the capital of Misiones province, 226 miles (362 km) east of Corrientes. This steamy (in summer) port and border city is in the heart of a maté- and tobacco-growing area and is now linked to the Paraguayan city of Encarnación.

It's possible to take a train from Buenos Aires to Posadas. You also can get here by bus: Be prepared for a 27-hour ride. The bus lines will change your money to cruzeiros if you plan to enter Brazil. By far, air is the most convenient way to get to this city; *Aerolíneas Argentinas* and *Austral* have daily flights from Buenos Aires.

Posadas (pop. 200,000) is a friendly city with a number of good restaurants, including a fine traditional steakhouse, *La Querencia* (on the main plaza at 322 Bolívar; phone: 752-34955) and the post-modern *La Ventana* (in the 400 block of Bolívar), a delightful eatery with an extensive menu with delicacies such as homemade pasta and patés.

Natural history and science buffs may want to stop by the newly renovated *Museo de Ciencias Naturales* (Museum of Natural Sciences; in the 1900 block of San Luis; phone: 752-23893). At press time, the streets were being renumbered, and the old address — still on the building — is 384 San Luis. The museum is open Tuesdays through Fridays from 7 AM to noon and 2 to 7 PM, weekends from 9 AM to noon. (It's best to visit in the mornings to avoid school crowds.)

The city also has a casino (1872 Félix de Azara; phone: 752-26919), botanical gardens, a public beach, and an artisans' market. Amethysts are mined nearby at La Libertad. There is an impressive and reasonably priced selection at *Edel Stein* (at the Posadas Airport; no phone).

But the reason most people flock to Posadas is to see what remains of the 17th- and 18th-century Jesuit missions in the surrounding countryside. To get an idea of what these highly developed settlements were like, make a quick visit to the *Museo Arqueológico e Historico Andrés Guacurari* (Andrés Guacurari Archaeological and Historical Museum; 1865 General Paz; phone: 752-3548). The museum houses models of the Jesuit complexes, religious statues, and some of the finely carved stones that once adorned the mission buildings. If you read Spanish, you can learn about Guaraní Indian legends and how the invading Europeans not only destroyed the self-sufficient Guaraní lifestyle, but left behind a legacy of disease and social problems.

The best-known and best-preserved Jesuit mission is San Ignácio Miní (see below), but there are three others to visit en route if you have your own transportation. Details on these routes are available from the city tourist office at 393 Colón (phone: 752-30504).

About 2½ miles (4 km) north of Posadas on Route 12 is the Paraguayan city, Encarnación. Founded in 1862, Encarnación has become the country's third-largest city, thanks mainly to the nearby Yacyreta hydroelectric complex. There is a bridge connecting it to Posadas.

**En Route from Posadas** – Route 12 connects Posadas with San Ignácio Miní. About 13 miles (21 km) outside Posadas, there is a sign indicating *ruinas* (ruins) down a dirt road to your right. This is what remains of the Nuestra Señora de la Candelaria mission. Trees have taken over much of the site, but you can still see the fine stone carvings on the portals and get an idea of how the mission was laid out. Originally there were more than a dozen missions in the area, each supporting up to 2,000 Indians in highly organized settlements. Archaeologists are still studying the ruins.

Return to Route 12 and continue another 13 miles (21 km) to the turnoff for the Santa Ana ruins. The bridge just off the main road sits on a base of stones taken from the mission site. There also is a small museum. Back on Route 12, head 5 miles (8 km) until the exit for San Loreto. Take this road 2 miles (3 km), but be forewarned — the road is impassable after a rain. Don't risk it if it looks muddy. Follow Route 12 another 4 miles (7 km) to San Ignácio Miní.

**SAN IGNÁCIO MINÍ:** First founded in Brazil, this mission was reestablished in 1632 by the Jesuits here to escape Brazilian marauders. By 1731, it had reached the height of its prosperity, swiftly declining by 1777, when the priests were forced to leave the territory under orders from Charles III. No Indians were left by 1810, and the settlement was burned 7 years later by the troops of Paraguayan dictator Francia. The ruins lay hidden in the jungle until they were discovered in 1897. The Argentine government has maintained the mission as a national monument since 1943; it is open to the public and tours are free of charge, although guides should be tipped. There is a daily sound-and-light show in Spanish at 7:30 PM.

In their own way, the ruins are as spectacular as Iguassu Falls. The large, open plaza (1,076 square feet) is flanked by remnants of buildings. Constructed from local red and yellow sandstone, the walls take on a burnished sheen as the sun sets — a highly recommended time for a visit. A preference for bas-relief is much in evidence. In its heyday, the mission contained 4,356 people; today it stands empty. But the town that took its name still is home to 20,000 people.

Though the roofs disappeared long ago, the walls, some 37 inches thick, are still as high as 30 feet in places. The empty rooms were once classrooms where 2,700 Indians were taught in their own language, priests' quarters, workshops, printing shops, barracks, arsenals, 1-room dwellings, and storerooms for crops, which included corn, rice, tobacco, maté, and citrus fruit. A huge, baroque church on the site dates to 1724; note the remnants of intricately carved doorways and windows — the faces of the angels have Indian features. A cemetery (without headstones) is next to the church and there also is a small museum with a few relics, including carvings and ceramics.

Other Jesuit ruins are São Miguel in Brazil and the Jesús and Trinidad missions of Paraguay. Misiones Regional Tourism Office in Buenos Aires (989 Av. Santa Fe; phone: 1-393-1615) distributes maps and brochures on these other ruins.

San Ignácio Miní is also home to the *Casa de Horacio Quiroga* (Horacio Quiroga House), where the famous Uruguayan writer and storyteller lived. Now a wax museum, the *casa* is dedicated to the story of the Jesuit settlement of the area and to the indigenous culture. It also bears witness to the array of hobbies in which Quiroga indulged, including carpentry, taxidermy, photography, and pottery. The museum is open daily from 7 AM to 7 PM.

**En Route from San Ignácio Miní** – Continuing on Route 12 to Puerto Iguazú and Iguassu Falls, stop at the tiny burg of Wanda, a short dirt road turn off Route 12. Wanda is home to a number of mines and amethyst and quartz excavations, where visitors can see these stones made into jewelry, which is for sale in town.

Farther north on Route 12, Puerto Iguazú provides the Argentine doorway to Iguassu Falls.

**LAS CATARATAS DEL IGUAZÚ (IGUASSU FALLS):** A visit to Iguassu is a thrilling and humbling experience, and a trip most easily made from Buenos Aires via one of the daily flights offered by *Aerolíneas Argentinas* or *Austral* (although there is also bus service to the falls). Depending on flight routes and weather, you may catch a glimpse of the falls before touchdown. Discovered by conquistador Alvar Nuñez Cabeza de Vaca in 1541, Iguassu comes from the Guaraní Indian expression for "big water"; justly so since it is considered the widest waterfall in the world, extending well over 4 miles and claiming 275 cataracts. As you approach, you can hear the roar of the falls and can see a huge cloud of mist rising up over the surrounding jungle. A long system of concrete catwalks, built in 1965, winds along the edge of the Río Paraná and skirts the falls, providing a safe perch from which to view (and photograph) the giant cataracts tumbling at your feet. A 2-hour hike will take you past all the falls visible on the Argentine side as well as through the tropical jungle. Brilliant butterflies and birds flutter about — as do some rather determined mosquitoes. (Swab on repellent before venturing out.) The cataract called Gargantua del Diablo (Devil's Throat) is the most magnificent and a good spot to catch some of the rainbows that grace these cascades. A lesser known, but perhaps even more magnificent, vista is from behind the *Internacional Cataratas de Iguazú* hotel. More information about the falls is available from the Argentine Tourism Office in Puerto Iguazú, 396 Av. Victoria Aguirre (phone: 757-2800).

Several companies, including *Turismo Caracol* (563 Av. Victoria Aguirre; phone: 757-20064) and *Emitur* (396 Av. Victoria Aguirre; phone: 757-28000) offer tours of Iguassu, although travelers who enjoy walking can see the Argentine side on their own. The falls lie within a national park and trips in four-wheel-drive vehicles with park ranger guides can be taken to look at the exotic flora and fauna in the tropical forest surrounding the cascades. Alternatively, you can rent a mountain bike and explore on your own. When there is a full moon, park rangers guide visitors on (free) night walks to the falls. For information, check at the Visitor's Center at the park's entrance.

For a spectacular view of the falls, take the 15-minute ($30 per person) or 50-minute ($120 per person) helicopter ride from the Puerto Iguazú airport offered by *Misiones Helicópteros* (phone: 757-20618) or *Helicópteros Turísticos* (phone: 1-450045 in Buenos Aires). Helicopters are a controversial issue here and park authorities are trying to eliminate them from the area because the noise not only ruins the mood for tourists, but disrupts animal habitats as well.

There is also a ferry ride from Puerto Iguazú to Foz do Iguaçu on the Brazilian side or a 20-minute *colectivo* taxi trip to the same destination. From Brazil, you can cross the Puente de la Amistad (Friendship Bridge) into Paraguay to spend a couple of hours shopping, taking advantage of that country's low import duties. Transportation — especially cabs — is very expensive in Iguassu; alternatively, you may wish to take a tour bus.

■**Note:** Plan to visit the falls between August and November; May to July is the area's flood season.

## BEST EN ROUTE

Hotel accommodations in Mesopotamia are small (often lacking single rooms and air conditioning) but adequate; when one finds luxuries, however, one pays dearly for them. Hotels will cost from $100 to $150 for a double in places listed as very expensive, $75 to $100 for those rated as expensive, $40 to $75 for moderate, and under $40 in the inexpensive category. It's wise to make arrangements through agencies in advance. Many hotels offer breakfast; check when booking.

## PARANÁ

**Mayorazgo** – This 110-room luxury hotel has a casino, a swimming pool, ample sports facilities, a restaurant with a view, and a hairdressing salon. Av. Etchevehere at Miranda (phone: 43-21611 or 43-21614; in Buenos Aires, 1-311-7546). Expensive.

**Gran Paraná** – All 200 rooms in this hostelry are doubles, with central heating and air conditioning, and phones. 976 Urquiza (phone: 43-223900). Moderate.

## POSADAS

**Julio César** – The best in town, despite its gloomy lobby, this 12-story property boasts the only hotel pool in Posadas. All 150 rooms are air conditioned, and there is a floor of mini-suites and a penthouse presidential suite. An international restaurant and a bar round out the amenities. Breakfast included. 1951 Entre Ríos (phone: 752-33609; fax: 752-36740). Expensive to moderate.

**Continental** – It has 186 rooms and 20 suites, all air conditioned and with phones. There is a restaurant and bar, and next door is a lively sidewalk café. 314 Bolívar (phone: 752-38966). Moderate.

**Libertador** – This small downtown hotel with 31 rooms has air conditioning and a snack bar, and is another good bet. 1208 San Lorenzo (phone: 752-37601). Moderate.

**Posadas** – A medium-sized hostelry, this is a good runner-up to the *Julio César*. Right in the heart of downtown, all the rooms have air conditioning, refrigerators, and color television sets. There also is a snack bar. 1949 Bolívar (phone: 752-30801). Moderate.

## SAN IGNÁCIO MINI

**San Ignácio** – Simple but comfortable lodgings (some with private baths) and a dining room; close to the Jesuit ruins. 823 Sarmiento (phone: San Ignácio Miní 47). Inexpensive.

## IGUASSU FALLS

**Internacional Cataratas de Iguazú** – The falls can be seen from half of the 180 balconied rooms in this hotel; book well ahead to ensure that you get one of them (they cost more, but the view is worth it). Other comforts include air conditioning, private baths, pool, bar, and a fine restaurant. Located in Parque Nacional Iguazú (phone: 757-2748). Reservations can be made in Buenos Aires (1020 Av. Madero; phone: 1-311-4259; in the US, 800-448-8355; fax in Buenos Aires: 1-312-0488). Very expensive.

**Cataratas** – This large, deluxe inn has comfortable rooms with air conditioning and mini-bars, plus an elegant international restaurant, a snack bar, and a coffee shop. There also is a pool, gym, and paddle tennis. Located between the town of Puerto Iguazú and the national park. Ruta 12 at Km 4 (phone: 757-21220; fax: 757-21100). Expensive.

**Esturion-Iguazú** – Another hotel in the jungle, but not right at the falls, it has 114 attractive and air conditioned rooms, a swimming pool, nightclub, Viennese tea shop, baby-sitting service, shopping gallery, tennis courts, and restaurant. (For dinner, order the local specialty, dorado, a fish caught in the waters of the Río Iguazú.) 650 Av. Tres Fronteras (phone: 757-20020 or 757-20161). Reservations can be made in Buenos Aires (265 Av. Belgrano, 10th Floor; phone: 1-343-4919 or 1-342-0815). Expensive.

*El Libertador* – Located in the town of Puerto Iguazú, this 108-room property has a swimming pool, bar, night club, and restaurant. Perito Moreno at Bonpland (phone: 757-20823 or 757-20416). Moderate.

# Mendoza

The adobe gateway to Mendoza province for travelers arriving from the east bears the slogan: *"Bienvenidos a Mendoza, Tierra del Sol y del Buen Vino"* ("Welcome to Mendoza, Land of Sun and Good Wine"). There's no more fitting description for the wine-producing center of Argentina, a title shared with San Juan and La Rioja provinces, to the north. And under the warm *mendocino* sun are wonders of nature that beckon mountain climbers, viticulturists (or just plain viticonnoisseurs), hikers, and even convalescents (there are plenty of curative thermal springs). Stark, jagged mountains (among them Aconcagua, the highest peak in the Western Hemisphere) and bountiful, irrigated valleys make this one of the country's loveliest places.

Mendoza (pop. 700,000), 636 miles (1,018 km) northwest of Buenos Aires, is rated among the most beautiful cities in Argentina, and has been the lovely backdrop for a number of international meetings. In late 1991, the foreign ministers of Argentina, Brazil, and Chile met here to sign a pact banning the development or use of chemical weapons. Founded in 1561 by a Spanish officer, Mendoza was named for García Hurtado de Mendoza, the Governor of Chile (not for Pedro de Mendoza, who founded Asunción and the first successful colony of Buenos Aires). Mendoza was destroyed by an earthquake in 1861 and, as protection against possible quakes in the future, the city was rebuilt with 1- or 2-story office structures. In 1816, General José de San Martín equipped his army of 40,000 men at nearby Potrerillos before crossing the Andes to liberate Chile and Peru. To help him, the women of Mendoza collected their jewelry and presented it to him. The street Patricias Mendocinas was named in commemoration of this event: It means "patriotic women of Mendoza" (*patrician*, or "rich," would also be appropriate).

Today, Mendoza is the largest city in western Argentina. Its beauty stems from a combination of low buildings on seemingly endless tree-lined streets, with green, artistically designed plazas interspersed throughout. The trees are special: In a given city block, there are ten on each side of the street, often touching overhead, and their presence has given Mendoza the nickname "City of Trees." City officials take the title seriously and have embarked on a campaign to plant enough trees so that there are three for each resident. Environmentalists say the trees help contain air pollution in this urban area and Mendoza has become a model for other cities, among them Los Angeles and Mexico City, where tree planting is one of the efforts aimed at reducing smog. Extensive, open drainage canals run along the streets, removing excess rainwater and giving the tree roots a good dousing. Because the canals and trees extend to the outskirts of the city, Mendoza hasn't just one pretty part; it's all lovely. But be careful when crossing the street in the middle of the block — you can fall into a canal!

Mendoza's surrounding province complements the city. The hot springs of Cacheuta and Villavicencio to the west are set amid picturesque mountain settings. At Puente del Inca (Bridge of the Inca) one imagines trolls hiding under its curved, shadowed arch of rock. To the north, the wine country of San Juan has a dry, Mediterranean climate — excellent for vineyard maintenance.

Mendoza can be reached by air. Jets fly out of Buenos Aires three times a day, and *Aerolíneas Argentinas* has flights connecting the city to Bariloche twice weekly. The *San Martín* railway follows a trans-Andean route from Buenos Aires to Mendoza, but no longer crosses into Chile. There is quick and comfortable bus service in and out of Mendoza. Traveling by car, Route 7 west from Buenos Aires goes to Mendoza and straight on to the Chilean border. Route 40 north of Mendoza leads you through the wine country of San Juan and La Rioja provinces.

For further information, contact the main tourism office (1143 Av. San Martín; phone: 61-242800) or the tourism office at the airport (phone: 61-306484). A tourism booth at the bus station (phone: 61-313598) has information on hotels and other lodging.

**MENDOZA:** Up to 40% of Mendoza's irrigated land is devoted to grape cultivation, which helps make Argentina the fifth largest producer of wine in the world. Accompanied by much hoopla, including processions, sports events, theater, and concerts, the *Fiesta de la Vendimia* (Grape Harvest Festival) has been held every March since 1936. It is preceded by a wine festival in mid-February. Open-air concerts, performed nightly in a Greek-style theater that seats 22,000, are a highlight of this annual event. Some wineries are open to the public and offer informative tours followed by free samples of their products. One of the best bodegas (wine cellars) to visit is Arizu — it's also one of the largest in the world. At 1515 San Martín in barrio Godoy Cruz (phone: 61-293460), it's a 10-minute ride on bus Nos. 1, 4, or 7 from Plaza Independencia. At the bodega, visitors congregate in a room resembling the dining room of a Spanish colonial hacienda, where they meet their guide. Later, they return to toast one another around the wooden table. The tour itself weaves through areas where the grapes are processed, past huge, wooden French vats that line the dimly lit passageways of the earthquake-proof winery. Light streams in from skylights above, and the smell of the fermentation is heady. The only letdown: The wine is served in plastic cups. (Arizu is open to tourists Mondays through Fridays 9 AM to 4 PM and Saturdays from 9 AM to 1 PM.)

Giol Bodega (1040 Ozamis; phone: 61-972493), one of the largest wineries in South America, offers tours weekdays from 9 AM to noon and 3 to 6 PM and Saturday from 9:30 AM to noon. Take bus Nos. 15 or 16.

Besides wine, Mendoza is famous for olives and fruit. The best place to shop for them is at the central market: It's a wonderland of fresh vegetables, fruit, eggs, cheese, *matambre* (cold cuts), and prepackaged and precooked foods, such as empanadas and pizza. You can sit and eat your food here.

Look for good buys on Mendoza sweaters and shoes at stores on Las Heras and Avenida General San Martín. The *Artesanías Mendocinas* (on the basement level of 1133 San Martín — the same building that houses the tourism office) is a nonprofit organization dedicated to preserving artisan traditions and serves as both a shop (phone: 61-243645) and a museum. If you make a purchase, ask for a certificate of authenticity. The same street is dotted with a good selection of *confiterías* (tearooms) where you can stroll in and rest after spending your money.

For sightseers, the *Museo Sanmartiniano* (San Martín Museum; 1843 Av. San Martín; phone: 61-257947) provides insight into the life and times of the Great Libertador and into the Mendoza of that period. Open weekdays from 9 AM to noon and 5 to 8 PM.

One of the most impressive sights in all of Mendoza is the statue atop Cerro de la Gloria (Hill of Glory), which celebrates Argentina's independence from Spain and pays homage to San Martín. Massive yet not overpowering on the forested hilltop, the stone and bronze work by sculptor Juan Manuel Ferrari portrays the victory as the the goddess of liberty, with broken chains dangling from outstretched arms. Behind her flies a condor; on each side frenzied horses bolt. Bas-reliefs surround the statue's huge base; one depicts the women of the city offering their jewels to San Martín. In front of the statue, San Martín sits on his horse, arms crossed over his chest.

Buses travel frequently to Cerro de la Gloria, but you must wait at the base of the hill for another bus to take you up the winding road to the top. Your best bet is to walk down at your own leisure and enjoy the scenery, which includes the soccer stadium built for the *1978 World Cup* games.

Mendoza's zoo is at the foot of the mountain. Animals — many surprisingly tame — roam in miniature versions of their own habitats. A trail goes uphill and down and is well marked. You might be standing at the top of an abrupt drop of land only to find yourself eye to eye with a giraffe. Monkeys and bears woo you for a snack, and there are guanacos (part of the llama family), elephants, and North American buffalo. As you arrive at the trail's end, be sure to see the Argentine rabbits, odd-looking little animals with rabbit heads and deerlike bodies. The zoo also has a pet chimpanzee that welcomes visitors and drinks *yerba maté* (stimulating herb tea) like a pro (phone: 61-250130).

You really should take a stroll through Mendoza's parks. Parque General San Martín, 10 blocks west of Plaza Independencia, has giant portals, tall palms, winding lanes, and well-kept grounds bespeckled with fountains and statues. Around the man-made lake grow *ceibo* trees, which bear the pretty red blossoms that are Argentina's national flower.

The *Museo de Historia Natural* (Natural History Museum) is at the corner of the Playas Serranas Park, near the lake. Although small, it boasts a fine archaeological collection. Open Tuesdays through Fridays from 9 AM to 1 PM and weekends from 3 to 7 PM (phone: 61-255241).

Mendoza has no shortage of good eating establishments. For a first class meal with faultless service, try the pasta at *Vecchia Roma* (1619 Av. España; phone: 61-251491); another good Italian restaurant is *Trevi* (68 Las Heras; phone: 61-233195). In both these places, you'd do well to have the waiters make wine selections. The best spot for an elegant night out is *La Bodega del 900* (it's just outside the city in Guaymaller; phone: 61-262775), where entertainment accompanies the meal.

One word about local tours: Agencies offer them for a reasonable price; the guides are young and well informed; and buses will pick you up at your hotel early in the morning. The outings take a full day, however, and the same scenery can be viewed on the 7-hour bus trip from Santiago, Chile — which is cheaper, too.

Two interesting side trips from Mendoza lead in opposite directions but reach very similar destinations. Cacheuta is 45 miles (72 km) southwest on alternate Route 7. It is known for its hot springs, but you cannot enter them until the doctor at the site has given you a quick examination and instructions. (Individuals with high blood pressure, for example, are not permitted to bathe in the springs.)

The mineral springs of Villavicencio are 27 miles (43 km) northwest of Mendoza on alternate Route 7. Nearby is an old amphitheater once the site of Indian rituals.

**En Route from Mendoza** – By far the best excursion from Mendoza is 96 miles (154 km) west on Route 7 toward the Chilean border and Puente del Inca (Bridge of the Inca). The route follows the Río Mendoza through its valley up into the mountains, climbing from 2,518 feet above sea level to 8,195 feet (bring an extra sweater for the chill and sturdy shoes for walking). If you get a headache, it might be from the change in altitude.

As you get near the Chilean border, the mountain range becomes increasingly formidable — a gray, barren beauty. Impressive peaks along the way include 22,310-foot Tupungato, 18,500-foot Tupungatito, and 18,000-foot Los Penitentes. More and more, Los Penitentes is becoming a popular ski spot; its 21 slopes are located near a complex of hotels, restaurants, and shops. The ski season normally runs from June through October, although in the summer months, trekking, biking, horseback riding, and kayaking are becoming increasingly popular. Information on skiing and lodging at Los Penitentes is available in Mendoza (1194 Av. España; phone: 61-231580) or in Buenos Aires (643 Lavalle, Office 2C; phone: 1-393-5204).

Aconcagua (Watchman of Rock), near the Chilean border at the Uspallata Pass, is the tallest mountain in the Western Hemisphere. At 22,834 feet with a dazzlingly white blanket of snow, it was first conquered by Matthias Zurbriggen in 1897. Not all its alpinists were successful, though, and a small cemetery at the base of Aconcagua pays tribute to those who died trying to scale its peak. The best time for climbers to tackle it is from mid-January to mid-February. For more information, check with the *Club Andinista* in Mendoza (the corner of Lemos and Pardo; phone: 61-241840), or write in advance to the club c/o *Refugio Mausy* (917 Casilla de Correo, Mendoza 5500; no phone).

**PUENTE DEL INCA:** This is a mountain, carved by the Río Mendoza into a natural bridge 65 feet high, 70 feet long, and 90 feet wide. Mineral springs gurgle out of the earth, making the rocks appear copper and gold tinged with green.

The bridge is set back from Route 7, and must be reached on foot. Over the bridge and up a small hill are the ruins of a community destroyed by an avalanche. However, an army base hinders examination at close range. Legend has it that the bridge was formed when the mineral-laden waters washed over Indians who had formed a human chain to allow an Inca ruler to cross the river with his ailing son. Sold here as souvenirs are ceramic figurines, soaked in these waters to give them the legendary hard finish.

From the bridge there are a number of manmade and natural points of interest. Los Penitentes, the statue *Cristo Redentor* (Christ the Redeemer, also known as Christ of the Andes), and Laguna de los Horcones, a green lake at the base of Aconcagua, are each within a 20-minute walk of Puente del Inca.

The work of Mateo Alonso, *Cristo Redentor* stands on the border of Argentina and Chile, a symbol of peace between the two countries. Erected by Argentine workers, the statue bears the inscription: "These mountains will crumble before the Argentine and Chilean people break the peace sworn by them at the feet of *Christ the Redeemer.*" The statue portrays a beautiful, rugged Christ.

Bad weather often bars access to *Cristo Redentor* except during the summer, and it is virtually impossible to see the statue from the train, although it is visible from a car or bus entering Argentina from Chile.

Unless you want to go to Chile or visit *Cristo Redentor,* ignore the border town of Las Cuevas, a bleak, barren cluster of about 15 buildings on either side of a narrow road, which is actually Route 7. The orange roofs are a sharp contrast to the surrounding barren land and gaunt mountains. This village, however, is the proposed site of a ski resort. One hotel with a restaurant, *Hostería del Inca,* already exists, as well as a ski lift. Look up and you might see condors.

From Las Cuevas, Route 7 continues into Chile. Route 7 branches into two roads;

the main road runs along the railway route; the alternate, which is not as modern, goes over La Cumbre Pass. The trans-Andean railway ends at Los Andes, where other transportation connections can be made for Santiago and Valparaíso.

**SAN JUAN:** Those wishing to see more of Argentina's wine country and to feel more of a dry, Mediterranean climate should take Route 40 north of Mendoza and head toward San Juan province, 106 miles (170 km) away.

An Argentine expression says that when a man is drunk, he is "between San Juan and Mendoza." Besides good wine, San Juan has a paleontological treasure called Moon Valley in the Andean foothills of the Ischigaulasto region. Thirty-six miles long and 9 miles wide, the valley was a lake 100 million years ago. Severe droughts brought death, and today the remains of former inhabitants — petrified carcasses of enormous reptiles and fossils of gigantic ferns — are strewn about. You will need a car to enter the park, and a guide must accompany you through the valley (included in the entrance fee; no charge for children under 12).

Founded in 1562, the city of San Juan (pop. 142,000) was destroyed in an earthquake in 1944, but was rebuilt. Domingo Faustino Sarmiento, president of Argentina from 1868 to 1874 and a renowned historian, was born here; his birthplace now houses the *Museo Sarmiento* (Sarmiento Museum).

Regularly scheduled buses and trains travel to San Juan from Buenos Aires 1,297 miles (2,075 km) away.

**LA RIOJA:** The capital of still another wine province is a 6½-hour drive from San Juan — from Route 40 north to Route 607 east (at the village of Jachal), turning onto Route 74 south at Nonogasta, and finally going north on Route 38 at Patquia. Founded in 1591, the city (pop. 45,000) contains a folk museum and the ruins of a Jesuit church. Its *palo borracho* (drunken stick) trees are intriguing because of the cotton-like substance that hangs from them (it's used to stuff mattresses); the same tree can be found at Plaza San Martín in Buenos Aires. There are a number of museums in Rioja, a casino, and an artisans' market.

An unusual dry wine is produced in the province.

**MALARGUE:** Because of its proximity to one of Argentina's fastest growing ski areas, this town draws many visitors. The focus is Las Leñas, a ski resort opened by a French consortium in 1972. It hosted the *1989 Pan American Winter Games*. In winter, charter planes bring ski buffs into Malargue Airport, from where they are bused to lodges and the slopes. The resort has five hotels and six "apart-hotels" for long-stay guests, as well as equipment rental, ski classes, shops, several restaurants, coffee shops, laundry service, pool, sauna, gym, casino, disco, and post office. Seven lifts take skiers up to altitudes of 10,000 feet, and there are runs for skiers of every skill level. Information on booking is available in Mendoza (1233 Av. San Martín, second level of the *Galería Caracol;* phone: 61-231628) or in Buenos Aires (707 Arenales; phone: 1-313-2121; fax: 1-311-2626). In the US, reservations can be made through *SkiL Internacional* (phone: 305-864-7545 or 800-862-7545; fax: 305-861-2895).

It isn't necessary to stay at Las Leñas to ski at the resort, and many top South American skiers don't. An alternative is the less expensive Los Molles complex not far away, where the perfect end to a day on the slopes is soaking in the hot mineral springs that have long brought attention to this spot. Open year-round, Los Molles has added a third hotel to its lodging inventory, and half board is included in its price tag — as is daily transportation to and from Las Leñas. Arrangements for transfers to Los Molles's hotels from the Malargue Airport can be made when booking. In Mendoza, stop by the Los Molles reservations office (12 San Lorenzo, 1st Floor, office 8; phone: 61-257348 or 61-292580); in Buenos Aires (330 25 de Mayo, 6th Floor; phone: 1-325-0344 or 1-325-6285).

## BEST EN ROUTE

Hotel prices in the Mendoza area are $75 to $100 for a double room in places listed as expensive, $40 to $75 for those noted as moderate, and under $40 for those in the inexpensive category. Most accommodations are clean and comfortable, and since the area draws business meetings and conventions there is a broad selection. Camping also is available; check at the tourist office in Mendoza.

### MENDOZA

**Aconcagua** – Modern, air conditioned, and with a pool. It offers 152 rooms and 8 suites, a restaurant, tearoom, and snack bar. 545 Av. San Lorenzo (phone: 61-243833; in Buenos Aires, 1-322-0046; fax: 61-311085). Expensive.

**Plaza** – Considered the best in town, this classic 86-room hotel on the shady main plaza has air conditioned accommodations, a restaurant with marble floors, bar, and a casino. 1124 Chile (phone: 61-233000). Expensive.

**Alcasa** – Offering rooms with private baths, this property also has a 24-hour snack shop and a laundry service. 1469 Perú (phone: 61-234808). Moderate.

**Cervantes** – Here's European charm in downtown Mendoza and it is clean and has good service. Cable television, bar, and central air conditioning are pluses. 65 Amigorena (phone: 61-244700; fax: 61-240131). Moderate.

**Palace** – Downtown 56-room hotel, with clean accommodations. 70 Las Heras (phone: 61-234200). Moderate.

**Rosario** – A modest place with a plentiful supply of hot water; the 33 rooms have private baths but are on the gloomy side. The main attraction is the low rate. 1579 Chile (phone: 61-254765). Inexpensive.

# Córdoba

In the heart of Argentina, Córdoba province has maintained its 17th-century reputation as an important agricultural center. Founded in 1573 by Don Jerónimo Luis de Cabrera, the province produces port wine, cattle, peanuts, millet, grain sorghum, alfalfa, wheat, birdseed, barley, oats, sunflower, flax, soybean, cotton, tobacco, rye, potatoes, and so on. The list is endless, and much of the produce is shipped to the US, Germany, France, and Belgium.

Industrially, Córdoba is important for one main reason: The first locomotives in South America were built here. There now exists a steadily increasing production of automobiles by IME (Industrias Mecanicas del Estado): Fiat Concord Argentina, and Renault, a good part of which are imported by Uruguay, Brazil, and Chile. The hydroelectric power of the province is also reaching its potential: Up to 19 dams have been built on the province's rivers; the principal thermoelectric plants include Pilar, Dean Funes, Las Playas, Río Cuarto, San Francisco, and Isla Verde.

Geographically, the province is split into two regions. The mountains in the west incorporate three chains: the Sierras Chicas to the east, the Sierras de Pocho (which become the Sierras de Guasampampa) to the west, and the Sierras Grandes, the central chain (they all run parallel to each other, north and south). To the east is the extension of the Argentine pampas.

The Punilla Valley, which stretches between the Sierras Pocho and

Grandes, houses a number of rustic mountain towns. There is a large dam at each end of the valley: the San Roque in the south, Cruz del Eje in the north. The tops of the mountain ranges are flat, which earns them the nickname "pampas."

Córdoba's tourist industry is second only to that of the coastal (Mar del Plata) area, with about 3 million visitors a year. Outdoor enthusiasts come for the invigorating fresh air and for the swimming, hiking, fishing, camping, and horseback riding, available in the health resorts of La Cumbre and Capilla del Monte. Places like Córdoba and Carlos Paz have a thriving nightlife as well.

The Traslasierras region, the heart of Córdoba's farming area, centers around Villa Dolores, south of the capital, a small farming town that produces, among other things, peanuts, corn, and tobacco. Neighboring San Javier is a major producer of herbs.

Transportation to Córdoba is no problem: Trains, buses, and planes depart from Buenos Aires and surrounding provinces daily. In Córdoba, there are offices for *Aerolíneas Argentinas* (520 Av. Colón; phone: 51-45003 or 51-813676) and *Austral* (59 Buenos Aires; phone: 51-228008 or 51-228529). The bus and train terminals are close to each other on Bulevard Reconquista.

To take in all of Córdoba's tourist attractions by car — from the northeast to Carlos Paz, Capilla del Monte, and Cruz del Eje down toward Villa Dolores, Río Cuerto, and Alta Gracia — would take about 5 to 7 days. To do this effectively, we recommend a circular route. This takes you, first, west of Córdoba on Route 20 to Carlos Paz, continuing north on Route 38, winding your way north, then southwest, from Cruz del Eje to Salsacate and Taninga, continuing south on Route 146 from Yacanto to Route 7 east, then taking Route 8 northeast, coming up north on Route 36 to Río Cuarto and Alta Gracia, and returning, finally to Córdoba.

Although the route starts in Córdoba, one major city cannot be overlooked: Between Córdoba and Buenos Aires lies Rosario, the capital of Santa Fe province.

**ROSARIO:** With a population of 975,000, Rosario is the third-largest city in Argentina. On the west bank of the Río Paraná, it is the major port for exporting produce from the central provinces (including Córdoban products) and plays a key role as a clearinghouse for shipments to Argentina's island territories.

Attractions in Rosario include the *El Monumento de la Bandera* (Monument of the Flag; at Córdoba and 1 de Mayo; phone: 41-214972), a riverbank monument honoring the spot where, on February 27, 1812, General Belgrano first raised the Argentine flag he designed; the Rose Garden in Parque Independencia; and the municipal and provincial museums. On weekends and holidays, boat excursions around the river islands near Rosario leave from near the Monument of the Flag.

**CÓRDOBA:** The second-largest city in Argentina, Córdoba (pop. 1,200,000) is a 192-mile (307-km) drive from Buenos Aires northwest on Route 9. The capital of Córdoba province, it was founded in 1573 and is in the center of the country. It became somewhat of a metropolis by the 17th century, an important crossroads and center of religious and intellectual life. Universidad Nacional de Córdoba, one of the oldest universities in South America, was established in 1622 from the roots of a Jesuit seminary. Today, 40,000 students are enrolled here, and the institution retains its reputation as one of the most prominent schools on the continent. Stroll through the university area near the main plaza, San Martín, for a taste of student life, Córdoba style. You'll find interesting bookstores, cozy coffee shops with walls covered with political and humorous graffiti, inexpensive salad and sandwich bars, plus dozens of ice cream parlors.

Like other early Argentine settlements, Córdoba was planned on a grid, an easy route for city sightseers. Plaza San Martín, similar to other Argentine plazas, contains a statue of El Libertador and is graced with shady trees and flowering shrubs. On the western side of the plaza is the cathedral, its 18th-century architecture depicting the Moorish influence on Spanish art at that time. The building, unfortunately, is neither well kept nor always open to the public, so check with the tourist office for details. La Compañía church (ca. 1650), with its impressive ceiling, is also near the plaza, on Obispo Trejo, a pedestrian street. East of the church is Casa del Virrey (House of the Viceroy), now the *Museo Marqués Sobramonte* (Colonial Museum; phone: 51-44837). The Natural History section of the *Museo Provincial* (Provincial Museum; phone: 51-221428), on the top floor of the *cabildo* (Town Hall), is beside the cathedral.

Two churches north of Plaza San Martín, La Merced (Calle Rivadavia), with its intricately carved wood pulpit painted in bright colors, and the Church and Convent of Santa Teresa (ca. 1770), are colonial institutions worth examining. Santa Teresa was built by Captain Juan de Tejeda y Mirabel — on the site that was originally his home — after his daughter was miraculously cured of an illness.

At Plaza Vélez Sarsfield, a tiny square with a statue honoring the jurist who wrote Argentina's civil code, are the *Academy of Fine Arts,* Córdoba's theater, *Teatro de Libertador General San Martín* (built in 1890 and the city's main center for musical and theatrical activities; phone: 41-44770), and the Olmos School. The *Museo de Bellas Artes* (Museum of Fine Arts) is at Plaza Centenario. East of it is the landscaped Parque Sarmiento, where you can get a good view of the entire city. The *Jardín Zoológico* (Zoo) is here, and you can pass the afternoon enjoyably among the lions and hippos.

Shoppers will be interested to know that Córdoba was the first Argentine city to turn one of its main streets into a pedestrian mall full of shops and galleries. Several streets downtown are closed to cars. The prettiest — and one of the most exclusive — is 9 de Julio (which later becomes 25 de Mayo) which is sheltered under a long arbor of bougainvillea. Fine leather goods, designer fashions, and perfumeries rival the selection in Buenos Aires.

The city's tourism office on Plaza San Martín (39 Rosario de Santa Fe; phone: 51-35031) is helpful. The provincial tourism office also is good, and is located in the large, modern bus terminal (250 Bulevar Reconquista; phone: 51-34169 and 30532). Both offer maps and are open daily from 7 AM to 9 PM.

Córdoba is only 1 hour from Buenos Aires by air, and flights operate daily: Córdoba's airport is an international one, second in importance only to Buenos Aires's. The *Mitre Railroad,* which passes through Rosario on the Río Paraná, makes the 434-mile (694-km) trip in about 12 hours.

A possible side trip is to Jesús Maria, 31 miles (50 km) from the city (north on Route 9 to Route 38 west). Of interest are the national *Museo Jesuitico* (Jesuit Museum), containing more than 15,000 articles of archaeological, historical, and artistic value, and the annual *Doma y Folklore Festival* the first 2 weeks in January, a time of native music and horse shows. Along the way, you'll pass Saldan, famous for its mineral waters and the walnut tree that San Martín rested under during his journey to Chile; Río Ceballos, the site of La Quebrada Dam; Candonga, with its restored chapel (ca. 1720) at the former Jesuit ranch of Santa Gertrudis, declared a national monument; Ascochinga, a charming township that dates back to colonial times; and Santa Catalina, a magnificent 17th-century Jesuit mission.

On the way to Mar Chiquita, you'll pass Cerro Colorado, which contains reddish sandstone cave drawings of animals, people, and curious designs left by Indians who once lived in the area.

**En Route From Córdoba** – After an outing in Córdoba, head away from the city on Route 8.

**CARLOS PAZ:** On the south shore of Lake San Roque (formed by the San Roque Dam), this resort town is noted for its boîtes (nightclubs) and casinos. It is also called the noise capital of Córdoba. Its main street claims to have the largest cuckoo clock in the world — a boast as yet unchallenged — and crowds gather here on the hour to watch it strike (that is, if their hangovers will let them). A lift up one of the mountains offers grand views of the valley; at the top, a nightclub and tearoom await you.

The *Festival Folklórico* (Folklore Festival) from January 7 to 14 always attracts large crowds. Depending on the season, the area may be filled with sports enthusiasts, pursuing tennis, golf, windsurfing, boating, or fishing. The resort is also a good place to buy such handmade items as bags and pottery.

Just 3 miles (5 km) outside of town on Route 20 is *Peko's,* a tourist complex built in a "castle" that has everything from a garden maze to a tearoom offering regional sweets. It's very commercial, but travelers with small children might find a visit worthwhile.

**En Route from Carlos Paz** – Continuing north on Route 38 leads you past the health resorts of Bialet Masses, Santa María, and Villa Bustos.

Cosquín, 38 miles (61 km) north of Córdoba at the foot of Pan de Azúcar (Sugar Loaf Mountain), is another resort village known for its therapeutic air. Swimming and camping are allowed here, and the village holds a huge *Festival Folklórico Argentino–Latinoamericano* (Argentine–Latin American Folklore Festival) annually during the second 2 weeks in January.

La Falda, 51 miles (82 km) north of Córdoba, is the site of the Universidad Nacional de Córdoba's holiday center, frequented year-round by students from around the world. The resort is known for its golf and swimming. The *Museo Arqueológico de Ambato* (Ambata Archaeological Museum; 1469 Calle Cuesta del Lago) has a collection of Indian tools, ceramics, and artifacts, as well as illuminated displays of cave paintings and petroglyphs.

Huerta Grande, 2 miles (3 km) north of La Falda (continuing on Route 38), is famous for its medicinal waters; fishing and camping are allowed.

From here, a right turn onto alternate Route 38 will lead you to the resorts of La Cumbre (with neighboring Cruz Chica) and Los Cocos.

**LA CUMBRE:** Sixty miles (96 km) north of Córdoba, the village of La Cumbre adjoins the health resort of Cruz Chica, which also has one of the best English boys' schools in the country. Here, trout streams attract fishing enthusiasts from November to April, and swimming, tennis, and golf are major attractions.

Traditionally, La Cumbre has been known as a refuge for writers and the elite. The famous Argentine writer Mujica Laines resides here; he is best known for his novel *La Casa* (The House).

The city tourist office is located on General Paz (phone: 548-51154).

**LOS COCOS:** The next stop on this alternate route, the *Gran Mansión el Descano* hotel (see *Best en Route*), has a small park containing imitation Roman statues, a honey shop that sells honey goodies (displaying a beehive within glass walls), and a labyrinth made of intertwining hedges. You can wander through the park for a small fee. If you get lost among the hedges, you end up providing free entertainment for other travelers: When a guide leads you to the safety of the cupola, you discover that other people have been watching and laughing at your self-inflicted misery. Altogether, there are something like 28,000 hotel rooms in the Punilla Valley area. Check with the tourist office in Córdoba for more information.

**CAPILLA DEL MONTE:** Continuing on alternate Route 38 north leads you to the main route and Capilla del Monte, with thermal springs, waterfalls, and grand vistas. Only 64 miles (102 km) from Córdoba, it is in the heart of the Sierras of Córdoba, a line of slopes and hills that rise out of the pampas and contain a wealth of resort activities, including fishing (especially at Los Alazanes Dam), swimming, camping, and hiking. El Zapato rock offers a wide view of the surrounding area; horseback riding tours are available from locals.

**En Route from Capilla del Monte** – A left turn northwest leads onto a small, unmarked, provincial route that connects Capilla del Monte with the San Roque Dam. Here is San Marcos Sierras. The center of Argentina's honey-producing region, San Marcos is the site of the *Festival de Miel* (Honey Festival) held every February.

Cruz del Eje, just west of San Marcos Sierras, is the heart of Córdoba's southern olive-growing region and the site of the annual *National Olive Festival* the last 2 weeks in July. The nearby Cruz del Eje Dam provides a lake for swimming and fishing; it also marks the end of the Punilla Valley.

Salsacate and Taninga, about 72 miles (115 km) from Cruz del Eje, are in a region of palm trees and dry, tropical air, unlike the sierra resorts.

Continuing south on Route 38 takes you farther into Traslasierras Valley, the farming region of Córdoba. Dique la Viña, the first stop, is the highest dam in South America at 335 feet above sea level. Las Rosas, farther south, is the heart of the most important tobacco-growing region in Córdoba.

**VILLA DOLORES:** Some 116 miles (186 km) southwest of Córdoba, Villa Dolores is the most important town in this region. Despite its small size (pop. 10,000), it is an agricultural center on the Río de Sauces that produces corn, peanuts, wheat, tobacco, and fruit. Wine is another industry here.

**YACANTO:** South of Villa Dolores, Yacanto is at the foot of Mt. Champaquí (9,459 feet), the highest peak of the Sierras of Córdoba. You can swim, ride, climb, play tennis, golf, and fish or enjoy the thermal springs.

**En Route from Yacanto** – A trip down Route 146 south to Route 7 east will lead to Mercedes and the junction of Routes 7 and 8. Take Route 8 north until you reach Río Cuarto; then pass through a series of small villages to Río de los Sauces. From here, head north on Route 36.

**RÍO TERCERO LAKE:** This lake resort on Route 36 has the country's second electroatomic center on its southern shore. Fishing and boating are permitted on the lake formed by the Río Tercero Dam.

Villages along the lakeshore include Rumipal, Villa del Dique, and Embalse.

**VILLA GENERAL BELGRANO:** North of Río Tercero Lake on Route 36, Villa General Belgrano hosts the annual festival popular with Argentina's hops consumers — the *Festival Nacional de Cerveza* (National Beer Festival) — the first 2 weeks in October. Settled by Germans, this village is distinguished by its European ambience and customs.

**ALTA GRACIA:** Only 29 miles (46 km) southwest of Córdoba, Alta Gracia was once the site of a Jesuit ranch; the colonial church and some dwellings remain and are open to visitors. Beside the colonial edifices are a casino and numerous nightclubs and coffeehouses. The *Sierras* hotel has a 9-hole golf course (see *Best en Route*).

Continuing north on Route 36 leads directly into Córdoba.

## BEST EN ROUTE

Double rooms in hotels listed as expensive cost from $70 to $100, from $40 to $70 for moderate-priced accommodations, and under $40 for inexpensive places.

## CÓRDOBA

**Crillón** – A 120-room hotel that provides excellent service and a pleasant sidewalk café with a fountain and umbrella-topped tables. The restaurant has an international menu; the staff is bilingual. 85 Rivadavia (phone: 51-240907). Expensive.

**Nogaró Córdoba** – This 128-room operation is right downtown, with a bar, tearoom, and room service. Breakfast included. 137 San Jerónimo (phone: 51-221746). Expensive.

**Sussex** – Conveniently located right downtown and offering comfortable amenities including air conditioning, a pool, *Maxim's* restaurant with a panoramic view of the plaza, tearoom, and tennis courts. 125 San Jerónimo at the corner of Buenos Aires (phone: 51-229071, 229071, and 229072). Expensive.

**Claridge** – A 51-room hotel with neither heat nor air conditioning. 218 Av. 25 de Mayo (phone: 51-45471). Moderate.

**Gran Astoria** – Convention facilities, an international restaurant, a bar, and a coffee shop are featured at this 100-room property in the heart of downtown, near the plaza. 168 Av. Colón (phone: 51-45091; fax: 51-240697). Moderate.

**Plaza** – A tennis court, sauna, and pool are pluses at this first class establishment. 79 Buenos Aires (phone: 51-45035/6). Moderate.

**Miramar** – More than 3,000 hotel rooms and campgrounds are at this popular lakeside resort. Contact the Córdoba Tourist Office (phone: 51-35031) for details.

## CARLOS PAZ

**Portal del Lago** – All the amenities of a first class hotel, including a pool and international restaurant, are offered at this 84-room property. Gob. Alvarez and J.C. Cabrera (phone: 541-24931 or 541-24932). Expensive.

**Platino** – Just a block from the casinos, this hotel offers rooms with private baths and phones, heat and air conditioning, a dining room, and a swimming pool. 60 Las Heras (phone: 541-24077). Moderate.

## LOS COCOS

**Gran Mansion el Descano** – This small resort hotel is entertaining: It has Roman statues, a honey shop, and a small park filled with landscaped hedges to get lost in. Moderate.

**Los Piños** – A 34-room hostelry with a swimming pool. Av. Grierson (phone: Los Cocos 2). Moderate.

**La Esperanza** – Eight rooms and a swimming pool just about sum it up. Av. Grierson (phone: Los Cocos 16). Inexpensive.

## ALTA GRACIA

**Sierras** – This modern 135-room property has a 9-hole golf course and restaurant. 57 Carlos Pellegrini (phone: 547-21001). Moderate.

**Liguria** – Comfortable and centrally located 28-room hotel near the public swimming pool. 797 Carlos Pellegrini (phone: 547-21766). Inexpensive.

# Northwestern Argentina

High near the border of Bolivia, the northwestern section of Argentina is a hodgepodge of topography. The interplay of mountain and plain in El Norte is dramatic: The mountains of Tucumán province are laced with a multitude of fresh streams; mountains wind and plummet through Salta and Jujuy provinces, which are also partly covered with cacti-filled, arid pampas and moist, Scottish-type moors. Toward the Bolivian border, the jagged Quebrada de Humahuaca produces a deep river valley; the mountains range from blue to red to green, the result of their high mineral content. In fact, one town, Maimara, is named after the Coya term for "painter's palette." The region's climate is invigorating; summer days are hot, often reaching up to 100F (38C). Nights are a refreshing 70F (21C).

Tucumán was among the earliest provinces to be settled by Spanish explorers traveling south from Bolivia and Peru in the 1500s. The towns of Salta, and Jujuy are steeped in colonial history. Many churches, government buildings, and houses date from the 300-year period of settlement.

Some of the few remaining Indian towns are north of Jujuy, near Bolivia: The Coya (slang for "Indians") resemble their southern Bolivian neighbors and resent being treated as tourist attractions. They were converted to Chrisitianity by missionaries, and their *Holy Week* and *Carnaval* celebrations are vivid, filled with colorful parades and candlelight processions.

The Coya and some Indian villages in Patagonia and Tierra del Fuego are all that remain of Argentina's indigenous people, after the colonial exterminations of the 1800s. Coya villages include Humahuaca, Purmamarca, and La Quiaca.

Since the north region was settled earlier than Buenos Aires, the northwestern region conducted a large trade with Bolivia and Peru during the settlement period. Salta was the heart of commerce, thanks to its two rivers, Salado and Dulce. Most business centered around mules, which grazed in the pampas region near Rosario, Santa Fe, and Córdoba (for detailed information, see *Córdoba,* above) and were later shipped to the northern mining towns. Maize, alfalfa, and tobacco were also important products.

Tucumán was the seat of the country's sugarcane industry. More than 140 acres of cane were harvested yearly, the land irrigated by the streams of Sierra de Aconquija. Today, some sugar is produced, but the region is better known for harvesting alfalfa and maize for fodder, and it is cattle, not mules, that cross the pampas. And, in contrast to its brisk commerce in earlier centuries, it is now one of Argentina's poorest provinces.

Northwestern Argentina is easily accessible from Buenos Aires. Buses travel as far as Córdoba, with connections made there to Tucumán — a 15-hour trip. The Rayo de Sol and the Estrella de Norte trains offer nightly rides that take about 13 hours. You also can fly to Tucumán from Córdoba.

If you drive, you can take Route 9 northeast from Buenos Aires. The route will take you into Salta and Jujuy and eventually straight up into Bolivia. The more scenic way to travel north, however, is to take Route 38 south at Tafi del Valle and continue north on Route 307 to Route 40, which leads through mountains and valleys, archaeological ruins, and small villages.

**TUCUMÁN:** The largest city in the north, San Miguel de Tucumán sits on the banks of the Río Dulce at the foot of Sierra de Aconquija, whose streams once irrigated more than 141 acres of sugarcane fields. Founded in 1565 by Spanish conquistadores from southwest Peru, the city was moved after the area was hit by a flood in 1580. The existing buildings of the densely populated (500,000 people) province date back as far as the 18th century.

True to its Spanish heritage, the city is laid out on a grid: The main Plaza Independencia is bordered by a cathedral (Calle 24 de Septiembre), Government House (Calle 9 de Julio), and a tourist office (484 Calle 24 de Septiembre; phone: 81-218591 or 81-225300). The office distributes maps and brochures on the area. Across the street and 1 block west is the *Museo Provincial Folklórico* (Provincial Folklore Museum).

*Casa Histórica* (181 Calle Congreso, between Calle Alvarez and Calle San Lorenzo) is a museum incorporating the rooms and furniture where the country's declaration of independence from Spain was signed in 1816. The historic event is reenacted each evening with special lighting and recorded music and words. The audience stands in patios of the museum for each part of the presentation. One of the patios contains a bas-relief portraying the congressional delegates proclaiming national independence to the people.

There are more sights in downtown Tucumán: Santo Domingo Church, 1 block west of *Casa Histórica* (Calle 25 de Mayo); the *Museo Provincial de Bellas Artes* (Provincial Museum of Fine Arts; Alvarez and 25 de Mayo); the *Museo Prehistórico de Antropológia y Arqueología* (Museum of Prehistoric Anthropology and Archaeology; 25 de Mayo, between San Juan and Santiago); La Merced Church (24 de Septiembre and Rivadavia); and La Casa de Cultura (Calle San Martín).

Parque Centenario 9 de Julio (Av. Soldati, between Av. Gobernador del Campo and Benjamin Araoz) contains the house of Bishop Colombres, who introduced sugarcane to Tucumán in the early 1880s. In front of the house is the giant steam press he imported from France in 1883. His first, crude attempt at building his own is in the house.

Any sightseeing trips outside the city can be done on your own. However, local tourist agencies (there are several on 24 de Septiembre, near Plaza Independencia) offer tours, and a guide is always a good idea. Buses also run to tourist attractions, but not always daily. The bus station is at Avenidas Benjamin Araoz and Sáenz Peña. If you need a map, stop in at the *Automobile Club of Argentina* office at the corner of Alvarez and Salta (phone: 81-311522).

If you're planning to take a side trip, try the resort town of Villa Nougués, outside of Tucumán where rich Tucumán residents used to spend their summers. In nearby Raco, a town famous for its cheeses, horseback riding is available. Another good excursion leads north of Tucumán on Route 9 to Cadillal Dam, about 15 miles (24 km) outside the city. Here you can boat, fish, swim, camp, and browse through a museum. A large amphitheater, canteen, and a modern sculpture of a woman look out over the serene water, ringed by the mountains of the sierra. Just beyond Cadillal (the next stop on the local bus) is a favorite picnic-bathing spot for Tucumán residents along a Río Dulce tributary. Tables, barbecue grills, running water, and a bath house (a small fee is charged if you change clothes) are available. No food is sold, so bring your own. The river is refreshing for swimming; the water is cool even on the hottest days, but the current is swift and can be dangerous.

One note about Tucumán province: Be prepared for a lot of holidays. The residents are a festive people, and there's a feast for every occasion. The biggest is July 9, Argentina's *Día de Independencia* (Independence Day), but there are a host of local feasts. Crafts fairs are held every Saturday morning in Simoca, just south of Tucumán on Route 157. Tafí del Valle holds a cheese festival in midsummer. Amaicha del Valle, on Route 307 in the Valles Calchaquies, hosts the *Festival de Pachamama* throughout the *Carnaval* season. And, usually in February, Trancas's annual festival (near San Pedro de Colalao on Route 9) is held at the beginning of autumn. Tucumán observes *Semana Santa* (Holy Week) with processions and holds a music festival every September.

In addition, folk festivals are held in Lules, Monteros, Aquilares, Alberdi, and Tafí Viejo. Inquire in the Tucumán Tourist Office for their dates and other information.

**En Route from Tucumán** – Continuing north on Route 9, you come to Salta, some 200 miles (320 km) away. En route you pass San Pedro de Colalao (left on Route 311 west); horseback riding and camping are available on the banks of the Río Tacanas. Farther north is Rosario de la Frontera, a small resort town with sulfur springs.

Although Route 9 is the most direct way to Salta, the route via Tafí del Valle and Cafayate is more scenic. It is highly recommended, even though the road is unpaved much of the way. The route swoops south (Route 38), then north (Routes 307 and 40) through mountain scenery, then past rolling cattle country and archaeological ruins. If the archaeological aspect interests you, stop in the Tafí Valley's Parque de los Menhires, where there are immense, carved stones. The menhirs, or stone monoliths, with as yet undeciphered inscriptions, were gathered from all over the valley. They are believed to be about 2,000 years old. The route enters barren, mountainous land, where giant cacti grow beside the road. It isn't unusual to see Indian women weaving or baking bread outdoors in an adobe oven.

**CAFAYATE:** Surrounded by vineyards, this little town is just across the Salta provincial border on Route 40. Restaurants in the area serve delicious empanadas. The craft center right on the square, *Mercada Artesanal Municipal* (81 Av. General Güemes; no phone), sells the work of local artisans; several other handicrafts stores can be found around the plaza. There is an interesting wine museum (at the corner of Avdas. General Güemes and Chaca Buco; open daily from 9 AM to noon and 6 to 9 PM.) The tourist office is located in a kiosk on the square. All attractions are within walking distance.

Professor Rodolfo Bravo, a citizen of Cafayate, maintains a private museum of Calchaqui Indian archaeology in his home on Calle Colón; it is open to the public — there are no fixed hours, stop by if you want to visit this museum. One room holds artifacts from the surrounding area; Professor Bravo shows a film on the Cayo Indians followed by audience discussion, in another room.

Two bodegas (wine cellars) worth a visit are *El Recreo* and *La Rosa* (the vineyard where Michel Torino wines are produced), just north of the town's camping area; tours and samples are available on request.

**En Route from Cafayate** – There are two ways to get to Salta and both have spectacular scenery. One is an easy route that heads east of the city, then north along paved Highway 68 to Salta; the other leaves Cafayate to the west then goes north on curvy, unpaved Highway 40 (best avoided from December to April, when rains make it impassable at points). Both are described below. You also can combine the two for a 2- or 3-day circular excursion that loops up to Salta and returns to Cafayate.

The shorter route along Highway 68 takes 4 hours and runs through canyons and past hills of futuristic-looking sandstone formations, eerie and monumental — not unlike the Badlands in the US. As the road gets closer to Salta, however, the terrain softens dramatically and becomes green and fertile.

Just 36 miles (58 km) before you reach Salta is the town of Colonel Moldes, known for its reservoir that draws anglers from all over the northern part of the country. The town boasts the *Hostería Cabra Corral,* a comfortable motel with a pool and a good all-you-can-eat buffet at lunchtime. An English-speaking staff person at the tourist office in Salta (phone: 87-215847) can reserve a room for you here. It's also a good place to stop if you are running low on fuel, or *napta,* as gasoline is known here — stations are few and far between along this road.

All along this roadway you'll see indications of how the rural people live — their rounded clay ovens sitting next to the sides of rustic houses, herds of goats and sheep wandering along the roadside, and adults and children passing on horseback. Visits to any of the villages along the route are bound to be pleasant.

Although the other route takes at least 12 hours on windy gravel roads, the scenery is more varied and spectacular — you'll reach altitudes of almost 12,000 feet, often amid cloud cover, and traverse valleys where irrigated fields add green to otherwise forbidding terrain. Be sure to take along plenty of film and be prepared for a bumpy ride with long stretches of not seeing a gas station or another car. Although human companionship is in short supply, quails, hawks, rabbits, guanacos, foxes, and goats run or glide over the roadway. And, if you're lucky, you might even see a condor or eagle soaring above.

Nearly halfway along the route is Molinos (which means mill), a delightful small town with a historic church and a colonial home that was converted into a small hotel, the *Hostería Provincial* (across the street from the church; no phone). If the 12-hour drive seems too long, call the tourist office in Salta (phone: 87-215847) and ask one of their English-speaking staff to make reservations for you to spend the night at what was once the residence of the last Royalist governor in the region. The hotel also has a restaurant, handicrafts shop, and a room (known as the *museo*) that houses artifacts from the colonial and pre-colonial period.

Some 23 miles (37 km) north of Molinos is the turnoff for the tiny town of Seclantas. As you drive, you'll pass small markers where motorists have been killed — probably from going too fast around the loose-gravel curves or from accidents during inclement weather. (It's a good idea to honk before going around the road bends.) Seclantas is noted both for its handwoven *ponchos de Güemes* (red and black blankets) and because it was from this town that 30 residents, including children, set out on a religious pilgrimage some years ago and were killed in a tragic traffic accident farther along the road to Salta. You can't miss the eerie spot where the deaths occurred — a huge wooden cross and monument on the side of the road bear the inscriptions of the names of each of the victims.

Continue on to Cachi, on the banks of one of Argentina's longest rivers — the Cachaquí. It's worth a stop just to see the church with its unusual cactus wood ceiling and confessional. Hardwood is scarce in this area, so residents improvise with what's available — the giant *cardón* (candelabra cactus). On the main plaza, the *Cardón* restaurant is a pleasant spot for a drink or meal. Also on the square is a good archaeological museum, which houses ancient Indian pottery, including Inca *aríbalos* and the huge jars used to bury the dead.

Seven miles (11 km) past Cachi is the junction with Highway 33. Head 90 miles (144 km) toward Salta, winding along mountainsides, driving in and out of cloud cover at high altitudes. A river-fed valley below provides a pastoral setting with horses drinking at the water's edge and white herons flying overhead. At eye level there are striated mountains where intense blue, green, and red lines of mineral deposits lie exposed. Above, shrubs and cacti grow.

**SALTA:** Founded by Hernando de Lerma in 1582, this city of 345,000 retains its colonial character. People build in the style used almost 300 years ago — they get a tax break if they do! Houses with wrought-iron grating in the windows and stately churches are everywhere. Salta, along with Jujuy to the north, is a paradise for people who love to explore historic churches.

Salta is 140 miles (224 km) north of Tucumán and can be reached from Buenos Aires via *Aerolíneas Argentinas* and *Austral*. The province is a center for farming, lumbering, livestock raising, and mining. In fact, Salta province has large deposits of minerals — petroleum, iron (Rosario de Lerma), and copper (San Antonio de los Cobres). The area is equally rich with historical significance. It was here that General Manuel Belgrano defeated the Spanish royalists in 1812 and General Martín Miguel de Güemes led the gauchos in seven successful battles against the Spanish in 1814 and 1821.

Salta's first *cabildo* (Town Hall) was constructed in 1582, followed by a number of others. The present building (575 Caseros on Plaza 9 de Julio) dates to 1783 and has been declared a national monument, housing both the provincial and national museums. If you look closely, you'll notice that the wooden columns on the first and second stories aren't aligned; for some reason, there are 15 on top and only 14 on the bottom. The museums offer details about the lives of national heroes such as Güemes, colonial furniture, and religious artifacts.

Convento San Bernardo (on the corner of Caseros and Santa Fe), also a national monument, was at one time a hermitage, then a hospital, before housing Carmelite nuns. The massive, wooden double doorway (which originally belonged to a private home, not the convent), hand-carved by the Indians, dates from 1762. San Bernardo hill at one edge of Salta is where the faithful claim the city's patron saint miraculously appeared to scare away fierce Indian warriors who had attacked the city.

San Francisco church has the highest belfry in South America — 174 feet. First built in 1625 (with an addition in 1674), the original church was destroyed by fire in the mid-1750s, after which the present church was erected. The most fascinating aspects of this structure stem from the optical illusions added during that last construction. Note the phony draperies carved out from stone hung over the entranceways and the trompe l'oeil interior windows. Inside lie the remains of Don Francisco de Gurruchaga, founder of the Argentine Navy. Declared a national monument in 1941, the church is an easy landmark to spot — not simply because of its belfry, but because the building is painted a plum color and trimmed with yellow.

Salta's cathedral (596 Calle España) built in 1858, contains the images of Cristo del Milagro (imported from Spain in 1592) and the Virgin Mary, which are paraded through the streets each September in commemoration of a miracle that occurred in 1692, when a similar procession with the images purportedly quelled a large earthquake.

Worth a visit is the *Museo de Bellas Artes* (Fine Arts Museum; No. 20 on the Calle Florida pedestrian mall; phone: 882-214714), where a collection of works by painters from northern Argentina is housed in an 18th-century colonial home. Look up at the wood ceiling beams in the main gallery — some are decorated with carved Indian faces. The museum is open daily from 7:30 AM to 12:30 PM and 2 to 8 PM.

Salta's monument to the Battle of Salta, or 20 de Febrero, sits in the center of Parque 20 de Febrero in remembrance of Belgrano's victory in 1812. The base is made of rock from surrounding mountains and is topped by a bronze statue of a female Victory carrying a laurel branch high above her head.

A monument to Güemes stands at the foot of Cerro San Bernardo. Güemes is portrayed in bronze, dressed in typical gaucho garb. Behind the monument, a steep path leads to the top of Cerro San Bernardo or you can take the *teléferico* (skylift) to the top of the hill and enjoy a view of the city with the mountains in the background (it operates only in the afternoons). Behind the Güemes statue is the fine *Museo de Antropología* (Anthropology Museum; at the corner of Polo Sur; phone: 87-222960). The exhibits include pottery made by pre-Columbian cultures, including the Inca. Open Mondays through Fridays from 8 AM to 6 PM, Saturdays from 9 AM to 1 PM, and Sundays from 10 AM to 1 PM.

Salta boasts several good restaurants, including *La Posta* (476 España), the *Restaurante Italiano* (95 Buenos Aires), and *Casa Moderna* (674 España), a deli with hams hanging from the ceiling and a dining area offering tidbits of meat and cheese to accompany a glass of wine or beer. *La Casa de las Empanadas* (12 de Octubre, near the train station) is noted locally for its empanadas and *humitas* (corn tortillas).

If you enjoy shopping, try the *Mercado Artesanal* (2555 Av. San Martín) — a nonprofit wonderland of handmade goods — wall hangings, ponchos, *salteños* (boots), gloves, socks, leather and woven belts, Indian headbands, pottery, and much more — all reasonably priced — and certified as authentic by the regional tourism authority. The market is open Mondays through Saturdays from 7 AM to 7 PM.

*Vino casero* (homemade wine) is sold in the markets for just a little more than the manufactured stock; you might try it before you frequent *La Peña La Herencia* (500

**694 DIRECTIONS / Argentina**

Buenos Aires), a renowned nightclub where local residents go for tango and gaucho dances, accompanied by grilled meat, *empanadas,* and plenty of local wines. The music begins at 10 PM.

Before beginning your sightseeing, stop at the tourist office on Calles Alvarado and Buenos Aires, 1 block from Plaza 9 de Julio.

There are some interesting side trips you can take from Salta. One of the most popular is the "Tren a los Nubes" (Train to the Clouds). The 14-hour adventure starts at 7 AM every Saturday, April through November. The round trip takes passengers through stony gorges, past decaying Jesuit churches, and through cacti-covered countryside before reaching Concordia Mine at 13,000 feet above sea level. Tickets can be purchased a Salta travel agencies or at the provincial tourism office (93 Av. Buenos Aires; phone: 87-215847). Food is sold aboard the train. Check with the tourist office; at press time, the train was not running while tracks were being relaid.

**En Route from Salta** – Route 9 leads directly north to Jujuy and to La Quiaca at the Bolivian border, passing the Quebrada de Humahuaca (Humahuaca Ravine). The small towns you pass don't have much in the way of accommodations for travelers, so you may prefer to use Salta as your home base.

**JUJUY:** Founded in 1593, San Salvador de Jujuy (pronounced Hoo-hoo-ey) is the capital of Jujuy province, the northernmost province in Argentina and one of the most rural; its population is 200,000, many of them Coya. Nicknamed the Silver Cup, Jujuy is rich in minerals — many as yet untapped.

Facing Plaza Belgrano, the Government House has the first Argentine flag, which General Belgrano, a patriotic leader during the independence movement, created. Note the impressive statues sculpted by Lola Mora. The cathedral, a colonial structure on the west side of the plaza, has a fabulous wooden pulpit carved and painted by the Indians. The doorway to the *Museo Provincial Histórico* (Provincial History Museum; 200 Calle Lavalle) marks the place where General Juan Lavalle, former governor of Buenos Aires province, was killed by an assassin's bullet in 1848 in the campaign against Juan Manuel de Rosas. The museum is open Mondays through Saturdays.

There is a small daily artisans' market in a tent near the cathedral on Plaza Belgrano.

Another attraction in Jujuy is the casino (1056 Av. Fascio; phone: 882-23212). It is open Tuesdays through Sundays from 10 PM. You must be 18 to enter; there is an admission charge.

The tourist office (690 Belgrano; phone: 882-28153), open daily from 8 AM to 8 PM, is very helpful.

*Aerolíneas Argentinas* provides daily air service to Jujuy from Buenos Aires. *Austral* also serves the area. Bus and train service are available to Jujuy from the capital, although not on a daily basis. There is also bus service from Jujuy to Iguassu Falls (see *Mesopotamia,* above).

**En Route from Jujuy** – The real attraction of the province of Jujuy is not its capital but the northern countryside and small towns that stretch along Route 9 to the Bolivian border.

Termas de Reyes, 12 miles (19 km) north of Jujuy, contains hot springs supposedly used during Inca days. Today, the springs pour into a concrete swimming pool.

The spectacular Quebrada de Humahuaca (Humahuaca Ravine) begins north of Termas de Reyes and continues for about 102 miles (163 km), also along Route 9. A major tourist attraction, the ravine follows a narrow, deep river valley between high mountains that become more and more variegated in color because of a high, diverse mineral content. Along the route, tropical vegetation gets sparse until only shrubs, pygmy herbs, thorny plants, and the local *cardon* (thistle) remain.

Towns along the route are primarily Indian — tiny, with narrow, cobbled streets and adobe houses that gleam white in the sun. Tumbaya, one of these towns, contains some old churches that date from the late 1700s.

As you continue north on Route 9, a montage of mountains of strikingly different hues — red, green, blue, purple, and pink — announces the approach to Purmamarca.

**PURMAMARCA:** Just beyond Tumbaya, this town is noted for its colorful mountain range. Purmamarca is a well-kept town with a simple church built in 1648 and white houses with orange roofs. Residents sell their reasonably priced wares along the streets.

**TILCARA:** North of Purmamarca on Route 9 and a short distance north of Maimara, Tilcara's major attraction is the Pucara, a restored Indian fortress within walking distance of the town. Like the Inca, the Coya lived in stone houses. Around Tilcara's main plaza are a number of museums, including a folklore museum and the *Museo Arqueológico de Eduardo Casanova* (Eduardo Casanova Archaeological Museum), which exhibits artifacts found in Pucara, as well as those from Bolivia, Peru, and Chile.

Try to plan your trip to the northwestern regions of Argentina around *Holy Week*. Most festivities, especially those in Tilcara, are beautiful and touching, with many processions and masses throughout the week.

**HUMAHUACA:** Nestled in the mountains at 9,062 feet, 76 miles (122 km) north of Jujuy on Route 9, Humahuaca's main tourist attraction is a mechanical, wooden statue of St. Francis Solano that appears daily at noon on the church tower to lift his hand as though blessing the people. The center of town contains a memorial to the Indians, topped by a powerful statue of an Indian brave; a long flight of stone steps leads to the monument.

**LA QUIACA:** About 175 miles (280 km) north of Jujuy on an unpaved stretch of road, La Quiaca is the border town next to Bolivia; a concrete bridge connects it with Villazon, where you can visit for the day and glimpse the Bolivian Indians with their stiff bowler hats.

If you're entering Bolivia, remember that clocks there are set an hour earlier and bring an overcoat, since the high altitude makes the area cool year-round. Rail connections are available from La Quiaca to La Paz, and both Argentine pesos and US dollars are accepted across the border.

## BEST EN ROUTE

As far as accommodations go, hotels in northwestern Argentina are small but comfortable; although not all have private baths. Rates for a double room are classed as very expensive (over $100), expensive ($70–$100), moderate ($40–$70), and inexpensive (under $40).

### TUCUMÁN

*Metropol* – A highly regarded 100-room hotel. 524 Av. 24 Septiembre (phone: 81-311180). Expensive.

*Gran Hotel del Tucumán* – This 140-room establishment has private baths and air conditioning, although it is a bit far from downtown. 380 Av. de los Próceres (phone: 81-245000). Moderate.

*Hotel del Sol* – One of the better lodgings in the city, offering private baths and basic comforts. 32 Laprida (phone: 81-311755). Moderate.

### CAFAYATE

*A.S.E.M.B.A.L.* – Small, tidy, and friendly, this inn is just a couple of blocks from the main plaza. It has a notable restaurant in its enclosed central courtyard, and a bar. Corner of Avdas. Güemes and D. de Almagro (phone: 868-21065). Inexpensive.

**Asturias** – A 70-room hotel at 154 Av. Güemes (phone: 868-21040). Inexpensive.

**Gran Real** – This is a 50-room property with a pool. 128 Av. Güemes (phone: 868-21231). Inexpensive.

## SALTA

**Salta** – Facing the main square, it's a first class hotel with colonial charm, a pool, 90 rooms, and a 50-year reputation for service. All rooms have air conditioning, phones, mini-bars. Suites have cable TV sets. The restaurant has an international menu; food also is served in the bar and adjacent sidewalk café. 1 Calle Buenos Aires (phone: 87-211011; in Buenos Aires, 1-312-0220; fax: 87-225241). Very expensive to expensive.

**Portezuelo** – A modern hotel with an old-fashioned flavor, featuring a restaurant with an international kitchen, a cafeteria, and conference facilities. 1 Av. del Turista (phone: 87-310105). Expensive.

**Provincial** – An outstanding downtown lodging with a restaurant, *confitería,* parking, and bilingual staff. 786 Caseros (phone: 87-218400; in the US, 800-44-UTELL). Expensive.

**Victoria Plaza** – Pleasant and also first class, it has 80 rooms, a nursery, and a tea house open 24 hours. 16 Zuviria (phone: 87-211222). Moderate.

**Residencia Elena** – Just a block off the main plaza, this quaint and quiet hostel is a good value. Blue and white Spanish-style tiles line the foyer and plants grace the patio. All rooms have private baths. Although there is no restaurant, it is within walking distance to the city's best dining spots. Book ahead for weekend stays. 254 Buenos Aires (phone: 87-211529). Inexpensive.

## JUJUY

**Fenicia** – This 100-room high-rise has an international restaurant, a piano bar, a tearoom, and laundry service. 427 Av. 19 de Abril (phone: 882-28102). Expensive.

**Gran Hotel Panorama** – The best in Jujuy, with 64 modern rooms and 3 suites, all with private baths and air conditioning, a pool, convention facilities, a restaurant offering both regional and international dishes, a bar, and a tearoom. 1295 Belgrano (phone: 882-25517). Expensive.

**Alto la Viña** – A 70-room hostelry with private baths and a swimming pool, located 2 miles (3 km) from Jujuy at a slight elevation that offers a panoramic view of the town. Unfortunately, the service is not always up to par. At Km 5 on Route 56 (phone: 882-26588). Moderate.

**Internacional Jujuy** – Air conditioning and private baths are offered at this 110-room modern high-rise hotel located on the main plaza. 501 Belgrano (phone: 882-22004). Inexpensive.

# Bolivia

There is an ever-shrinking club of countries that still qualify as lands for the adventurous traveler. Bolivia remains a charter member and treats visitors to an authentic South American experience of Indian cultures and dramatic, superlative landscapes.

There is no danger of falling into a tourist trap when traveling anywhere in Bolivia. It is not the place to find gaming tables, beaches bathed in eternal sunshine, or historic sites packed with tour groups. What Bolivia is, banal as it sounds, is a country of astounding contrasts. You can get lost in the crowds of the downtown markets of La Paz, or you can stand remote from all earthly things in the stillness of the pre-Columbian monoliths of Tiahuanaco, just 45 miles (72 km) away. The climate ranges from the extreme aridity of the plains of the Chaco in the southeast to the dense humidity of the rain forests of the eastern foothills.

Bolivia is the breathtaking beauty of Lake Titicaca in the north and the brackish lakes and salt beds of Salar de Uyuni in the south. And, while the country has a navigable river system, it was one of the two South American landlocked nations (Paraguay is the other) until early 1992, when Bolivia and Peru signed an agreement that gave it free access to the sea at Ilo, Peru. It borders Brazil on the north and east, Paraguay and Argentina on the south, and Chile and Peru on the west.

Bolivia is a 424,164-square-mile land about the size of Texas and California combined, or twice the size of France, with a population of 6.5 million. About 70% of the inhabitants are of indigenous Indian descent (proportionally the largest in South America) and 25% are mestizo; about 5% are of European descent. While it's the fifth-largest South American country, it is one of the continent's most sparsely populated and the region's poorest nation.

The dominant feature is mountains, stretching for nearly 400 miles from east to west down the Bolivia/Chile border. Divided into two ranges, the Cordillera Oriental (Eastern Range) and the Cordillera Occidental (Western Range), the Bolivian Andes take in some lofty heights. Among them are Sajama (21,391 feet), Illimani (21,201 feet), and Illampu (20,958 feet). The Cordillera Real (Royal Range) includes more than 600 ice-covered peaks higher than 15,000 feet.

Between the two ranges lies the heartland of the nation, the 500-mile rust-colored altiplano, a remote, almost surrealistic plain battered by brutal winds that have swept the land almost bare. But all is not bleak. When the sun hits the altiplano as you travel between Cuzco in Peru and Lake Titicaca, the land, bordering mountains, is streaked by such a brilliant orange that you wonder why you'd ever thought the altiplano was ugly.

Moving across the altiplano to the Cordillera Oriental, the picture is slightly different. To the northeast, the massive peaks of this range fall away sharply, down toward the Amazon basin's heavily forested slopes, which are indented with fertile valleys known as the Nor Yungas and Sud Yungas (North and South Valleys). In these lush, semitropical valleys drained by the Beni River system, cacao, sugar, coffee, tropical fruits, and coca — from which cocaine is derived — are grown. In fact, Bolivia and Peru are the only countries in the world where the cultivation of coca is legal; however, the authorized harvest is far outstripped by the illegal crops sown to feed the drug traffic.

In the river valleys farther south lie Santa Cruz and Cochabamba, the second and third most important cities in the nation, as well as the large town of Tarija, one of the oldest settlements in Bolivia and the heart of the wine-producing region.

When the Quechua-speaking Inca conquered the Aymara Indians around Lake Titicaca in the 13th century, they found them living among ancient ruins. As archaeologists and historians piece the story together, it appears that there was a rich civilization in this area some 600 years or more before the arrival of the Inca, who appeared during a second phase of Aymara civilization. During this earlier period, they produced extraordinary pottery, textiles, and metalwork as well as massive stone buildings and monolithic monuments.

The Aymara in Bolivia resisted the Inca so fiercely that it took nearly 100 years to subdue them — until the reign of Túpac Yupanqui (1471–93). As in other instances of civilizations overpowered by the Inca, the Aymara were allowed to keep their own language and most of their social structures and were permitted to fight for the Inca under their own officers. Only the Inca religious practices were imposed upon them — perhaps more easily than imagined since worship of the sun and natural forces was common to all pre-Columbian cultures.

Before visiting Bolivia, keep a couple of things in mind. This is a rugged land — difficult to know well, yet fascinating to see. The altiplano and La Paz altitudes of 12,000 feet (and up) may produce *soroche* (altitude sickness), characterized by dizziness, shortness of breath, nausea, or even a first-day headache. Veteran travelers suggest the following: Upon arrival, take time to catch your breath; don't start running around the city. Walk slowly, eat lightly the first day, rest, and avoid alcoholic beverages. Carry headache and nausea pills with you and make certain, in advance, that your hotel is equipped with oxygen (most are). Drug stores also sell a lozenge, Coramina, that helps alleviate *soroche* symptoms. A heart stimulant called Micoren is sold without a prescription; consult your doctor before using it. For many visitors, a cup or two of *maté de coca* (coca leaf tea) is all that is needed. Physical orientation normally takes about 24 hours, but for some it takes up to 3 days.

Transportation in Bolivia is limited. Some areas only can be reached by railroad, and the trains are generally old, dirty, and uncomfortable — but "picturesque" and the best way to travel overland. All of the major cities and towns are linked by rail, and many by the reliable and fairly inexpensive air services of *Lloyd Aereo Boliviano (LAB)*. Most areas of greatest interest to visitors are accessible by road; the condition of the road, however, is another matter. Only one-sixth of all Bolivia's roads are paved or surfaced with gravel — very rough gravel — and even the popular route from La Paz to Tiahuanaco by public bus or taxi is a bumpy ride. Overland trips as short as 100 miles (160 km) can take more than 4 hours; travelers going by bus or car should allow plenty of time.

Note that because of isolated terrorist incidents involving US citizens, the US State Department has issued a caution for travelers to Bolivia. Visitors should contact consular section of the US Embassy in La Paz (phone: 2-320494) to get the latest information.

# The Highlands

The altiplano is an area of paradoxes. It is limited agriculturally but rich in mineral deposits; plagued with a harsh, cold climate by night and a fierce, burning sun by day, yet blessed with bracingly fresh air. The following route winds through the altiplano, west from La Paz to Lake Titicaca — the world-famous site of Tiahuanaco — then south to Oruro, Potosí (once the world's silver capital); on to Sucre, Bolivia's official capital; and finally to Tarija, an isolated farming community in a fertile river valley noted for its vineyards, but cut off from the rest of the country by forbidding mountain ranges.

**LA PAZ:** La Paz is Bolivia's movable capital. It was originally established in 1543 at Laja, 22 miles (35 km) away and at an even higher altitude. However, the conquistadores soon found the fierce winds of the altiplano too much and in 1548 moved the settlement down to its present location in a deep, natural basin. Actually, La Paz is the country's unofficial capital (Sucre is the legal capital), its center of government and commerce. And in its "capital" role it is the world's highest, at 12,500 feet above sea level.

The city spreads across 10 square miles and has a population of 1.5 million. Most routes in this section use La Paz as a starting point. From La Paz there is daily air service to Cochabamba and Santa Cruz and flights every day but Sunday to Sucre and Tarija on *Lloyd Aereo Boliviano (LAB)*. For a detailed report on the city, its hotels and restaurants, see *La Paz,* THE CITIES.

**TIAHUANACO:** Also known by Tiwanaku, Tiawanacu, and a variety of other spellings, this awesome pre-Inca site is reached by a bone-shattering, 45-mile (72-km) stretch of road — some of it paved, some gullied. When the Inca arrived to conquer the Aymara Indians, they found a city that had been constructed using architectural techniques superior to their own. The vanquished people also had devised their own calendars, hieroglyphics, and a system for processing minerals. Modern archaeological studies indicate that the Indians who inhabited this city, which is believed to have been the capital of a series of small towns in the area, were here from about 1580 BC to AD 1170. Although the area now is impoverished, Alan Kolata, a US archaeologist from the University of Illinois at Chicago, believes that the highland plain once supported a population of 125,000 people who had advanced irrigation and farming techniques.

There is an incredible loneliness to this site, near the southern end of Lake Titicaca. With its rolling plateau and yellow grass whispering in the wind, you feel isolated, alone with the gods of the high Andes. There's a stillness over the air, as if something is there, hanging, waiting to be resolved.

Though the Bolivian government has not had the resources needed to thoroughly restore the site, in the early 1960s, the reconstruction of the semi-subterranean temple that first greets visitors to the ruins was completed. Its walls are adorned with carved-stone heads, its drainage system rivals those of contemporary times, and the original stone construction contains no mortar. (The sections where cement has been added are those where the rock had deteriorated significantly.) The Kalasasaya compound also has been partially reconstructed.

The best-known symbol of the Tiahuanaco civilization is the Gate of the Sun, a 10-ton slab of andesite depicting a god figure in the center, 48 attendants approaching him from each side, with a low doorway carved in the center. This is one of the largest single carved pre-Columbian blocks (7 feet high, 11 feet wide) in existence. The relief figure is said to represent the creator-god Viracocha. The Colla (descendants of the Tiahuanaco culture) say that the stone works were built by a race of giants who incurred Viracocha's wrath and were destroyed by him. The god is depicted with cheeks streaked by bands containing tiny circles that look like tears. Heads hang from his belt. In each hand he carries a staff, topped by a condor's head. Archaeologists say there are indications that a metal door once hung at the gate.

It baffles many that the gate leads to nothing — it just stands there in the middle of the altiplano. One thought is that the gate once led to a palatial structure designed for meetings; another is that it was the entrance to a temple. Some believe it is a religious monument, with figures representing a pre-Inca calendar.

The main ruin is the Kalasasaya ("standing stones") compound, a rectangular earth mound. Its plaza alone runs 442 by 426 feet, squared off at the edges by perpendicular stones about 20 feet high. Archaeologists like Kolata, who began investigating the site in 1985, believe Kalasasaya was a temple and the burial spot for Tiahuanaco nobility. Other ruins are the 2-tiered Akapana pyramid, the top of which has been hollowed out, allegedly by the Spanish conqueror-bandit Pedro de Vargas, who thought it was filled with gold, and the Ponce monolith, named for the government archaeologist who found this finely carved statue erected on a mound facing the Gate of the Sun. During excavations, the headless remains of 16 bodies — probably human sacrifices — were found near Akapana. The evidence of the temples and symbolic artifacts unearthed by scientists lead to the conclusion that Tiahuanaco was a great religious center.

Beyond Kalasasaya is Putani, which scientists are fairly certain was once a small palace. A limited amount of excavation has been done at this site and at the nearby Kantatayita — now little more than a pile of stone slabs, although it is believed to have been, at one time, a four-sided building whose corners coincided with points directly north, south, east, and west.

The museum on the site contains some of the ceramics rescued from the ruins along with a large number of other carved-stone pieces. Archaeologists lament, however, that much of what was once Tiahuanaco was pillaged centuries ago. Smaller stone slabs were hauled off to become the foundations of homes, sidewalks in nearby towns, or parts of local roads. Today, children — and even workers at the excavation sites — will offer tourists small statues and amulets they claim have been discovered in the ruins; archaeologists say, however, that almost all are imitations and have no value except as souvenirs. In the rare instance that you might purchase an authentic artifact from Tiahuanaco, keep in mind that doing so would be breaking Bolivian law and that the object can be confiscated by officials.

A few miles southwest are the ruins of Puma Punku — literally, the Door of the Puma — the two pyramids of which are said to be part of a lost city. The massive 100-ton blocks of stone were probably part of a temple, and there are ancient Indian legends that claim Puma Punku was once connected underground to Cuzco, Peru. Scientists still have not figured out how the stones were transported to the area since the nearest source of stone of that type is more than 6 miles (10 km) away. However, in late 1989, scientists announced they had discovered the purpose of mysterious furrows across miles of broad pampas (plain) spreading from outside Tiahuanaco to Lake Titicaca. With the help of agronomists, they concluded that they were drainage and irrigation canals — part of an elaborate network that served one of the most sophisticated and productive agricultural systems of ancient times. As a result, archaeologists also have determined that Tiahuanaco had an elaborate underground sewer system.

Several tour agencies in La Paz offer guided day trips to Tiahuanaco on a seat-in-car or bus-basis for as little as $15 per person. Contact *Condor Tours* (232 Juan José Pérez; phone: 2-354034); *Diana Tours* (328 Sagárnaga; phone: 2-375374); *Turismo Balsa* (1036 Av. 18 de Julio; phone: 2-345049; fax: 2-391310); or *Turisbus* (in *Residencial Rosario,* 704 Calle Illampu; phone: 2-325348). A full-day tour with a private car, driver, and guide will cost between $50 and $70 per person, including lunch and entrance fees. Contact *Transturin, Ltda.* (1295 Mariscal Santa Cruz, 3rd Floor; phone: 2-320445; fax: 2-391162). A taxi from La Paz will cost about $50. You also can take the daily bus to Copacabana, which will stop at Tiahuanaco, from Calle José María Asín, near the Puerta del Cementerio (main cemetery entrance), for a few dollars. Tickets for this bus must be purchased at the *Autolíneas Ingavi* office (Calle Policarpio Eyzaguirre; phone: 2-328981), from which the buses depart up to four times a day, starting before 7:30 AM. The trip there takes about 2 hours. The difficulty with the bus is that although there are regular departures to Copacabana early each morning, afternoon returns may be canceled if there is an insufficient number of passengers, leaving you stranded at Tiahuanaco. If you want to risk the bus route, wait for the return vehicle down the road from the ruins in the town of Tiahuanaco. The ruins close at 5 PM. An entrance fee of about $2 lets you wander about the seven excavation areas at Tiahuanaco, enter the archaeological museum at the site, and visit Puma Punku. There is a small cafeteria at the ruins. The trip, including transportation time, merits a full day, and is not nearly as meaningful without a local guide. Be sure to apply sunscreen liberally before heading off to explore.

**LAKE TITICACA:** The Inca called Cuzco "the navel of the world" and Lake Titicaca "the womb of mankind," and lakeside dwellers today regard themselves as the "oldest people in the world." Like many places in Bolivia, Lake Titicaca takes another "highest" championship — it is the world's highest navigable lake (12,500 feet). From every part of the shoreline — indented with bays and inlets and covered with farms from waterside to terraced hills — you will see snow-capped Andes in the distance. The lake is 110 miles long and 40 miles wide; slightly over half of it is in Peru.

Two companies offer Bolivia–Peru transportation with a lake crossing: *Transturin, Ltda.* and *Crillón Tours.* Both operate their own boats with guides from the port of Huatajata, 47 miles (75 km) from La Paz. (They'll pick you up at their offices in La Paz and drive you to the port.) Each makes a short stop at the Island of the Sun, where passengers can go ashore to see the ruins there and drink from the Inca spring, a supposed source of eternal youth, and each includes lunch in Copacabana. *Transturin* (1295 Mariscal Santa Cruz, 3rd Floor, La Paz; phone: 2-320445; fax: 2-391162) utilizes catamarans equipped with with comfortable seating, restrooms and a snack bar inside, and open decks (an advantage) for its crossing from Huatajata to Copacabana, followed by bus transportation to Puno. The price is $75 per person for the boat and bus ride to Puno. *Crillón Tours* (1223 Camacho, La Paz; phone: 2-374566/7; in the US, 305-358-5353; fax: 2-391039; fax in the US, 305-372-0054), with over 30 years in the business, operates hydrofoils that cross from its own port in Huatajata to Copacabana, then to Juli, Peru; passengers continue to Puno by bus. The craft is well maintained and equipped; the service is high quality but expensive by local standards; prices, including land and sea transportation, are about $160 per person.

You also can drive or take the bus from La Paz to Huatajata (about 1½ hours), eat lunch at a lakeside café, and continue to Copacabana via the Strait of Tiquina, which is a ferryboat point for people and produce — a colorfully chaotic scene. Visitors who arrive at noon will be treated to the daily performance of the local brass band at the waterfront. You can stay overnight in Copacabana, return the same day to La Paz, or, best of all, continue along the western shore to Puno. There are some lovely colonial towns en route as well as Peruvian customs. *Note:* Do not make the trip via the Bolivia–Peru border at Desaguadero. Not only is the trip less scenic, but this border crossing is one of the ugliest on the continent, and if a traveler is delayed, it offers only one hostelry and one restaurant (which isn't open every day).

The best known of Titicaca's islands are those of the Sun and the Moon, places where, according to Indian legend, the sun and the moon sought refuge during times of flood. The former, dotted with ruins, is the shrine of the early Indians, who say their first emperor, Manco Cápac, rose from the lake and was planted on the island with his sister-consort before they set off to find what would be the capital of the Inca empire — Cuzco. The ruins of the Palace of the Vestal Virgins and of a temple dedicated to the Moon Mother are on Moon Island. The Indians claim there is a city 100 feet below the surface.

The lake's northern shore at Sillustani, Peru, holds mysterious, tall (30 feet), round burial towers called *chullpas,* built by the Colla culture. The Uro Indians live by this part of the lake on reed islands that drift about in the water or are anchored by long taproots. They fish from reed boats or rafts made of rushes and hunt birds with bolas (similar to slingshots). Once they have captured the bird, they kill it, drying the meat to trade with farmers for potatoes, corn, and millet. The Uros Islands can be visited, but travelers should note that the residents are very poor and revenue from tourists is crucial to their survival. The island children, who are clever and have learned phrases in a variety of languages, will sing for visitors or allow their photos to be taken — then demand tips. Fresh fruit, pens, and notebooks are good choices (the children go wild over the last two). Don't worry about who gets what; the Uro believe all belongings are common property.

Over the centuries, the lake has receded; there is a theory that at one time it flowed up to the ancient city of Tiahuanaco. (By the way, cramming in a visit from La Paz to both Tiahuanaco and Lake Titicaca in a day does justice to neither.) While at the lake, you can go to Suriqui, whose islanders (led by the Limachi brothers) built Thor Heyerdahl's raft *Ra II* for his Atlantic crossing, as well as a similar boat, the *Tigris,* for his trip from Iraq to the Red Sea. Natives sell replicas of these craft, which Heyerdahl used to document his theories of ancient world migrations. Boat service to Suriqui Island is available from the restaurant, *Hostal Balsa,* in Puerto Pérez, about 40 miles (64 km) from La Paz. The 1- and 2-day Lake Titicaca tours offered by La Paz agencies generally include a visit to Suriqui and sometimes one to the ruins on the neighboring island of Kalahuta. To arrange your own boat outing on the lake, contact the *Yacht Club Boliviano* in Huatajata (phone: 2-811669).

**COPACABANA:** You can get to Copacabana, a central Titicaca lakeside resort by car. As it is a 4-hour drive from La Paz over a curving, dirt road, you may prefer to spend the night; there are a number of little hotels, most of them somewhat spartan. The people are very friendly and are sure to escort you to a hotel "with running water" the moment you alight from the bus (a few dollars by regular bus, or under $10 on a tourists' bus from La Paz). The running water may turn out to be in a courtyard of the pension and run only at certain times of the day, but in this crazy little town, it won't matter; you'll be having too much fun to get upset.

There is a tone of gaiety here, and you feel as though you're at a carnival when you encounter these incredibly cheerful people, who pack their calendar with many fiestas. The largest one celebrates the Dark Virgin of the Lake, also known as the Virgin of Candelaria. This dark wood statue is enclosed in glass in the cathedral. (Indians believe that removing the statue from the church will cause Lake Titicaca to flood; a copy of the statue is used in many of their year-round processions.) On August 5, a 3-day festival is held in her honor. Indians travel by foot from all around the Titicaca basin and from as far away as Cuzco to pay homage to her image. The dark-wood statue, said to have been carved by the descendant of an Inca, wears a gold crown and is draped in embroidered robes and inlaid with precious stones. Besides the religious attributes of this fiesta, it provides an excellent opportunity to witness regional dances. Beware of street crime during festival days.

Everything in this joyous little town is within walking distance from the town plaza — indeed, local residents do not use street names to describe locations. Five blocks from the plaza, heading straight for the lake, is the beach where boats dock for the half-day trip to the Island of the Sun or the day-long trip to the islands of the Sun and the Moon. The small boats carry up to 8 persons each; the shorter trip costs about $5, and the price of the longer one depends on the number of people traveling and the itinerary worked out by the boat owner. Expect to pay about $35 per person on a full boat. A walk along the beach at dusk is recommended, for its dramatic sunset on the lake.

Also within walking distance of the plaza is an archaeological site known as the Asiento del Inca (Inca's Chair), another ruin on the road out of town toward La Paz, and a religious walk — El Calvario, which marks the Roman Catholic stations of the cross — to a hilltop with a dramatic view of the town and Lake Titicaca. A tourism kiosk can be found in the town plaza.

**YUNGAS:** Turning northeast from the capital, the road winds down to the warm Yungas — or Valley — provinces 60 miles (96 km) from La Paz, about a 4-hour drive. Natives use this road to bring their crops to the capital, and it's a spectacular trip (though not for the fainthearted), traveling over snow-capped Andean peaks before a steep descent of more than 10,000 feet over 50 miles (80 km) to Coroico, a peaceful village that serves as the capital of the tropical Nor Yungas region. This is an agricultural area, producing coffee and fruit at 4,500 feet. Stop by the Convento de las Madres de Clarissa (Convent of the Mothers of Clarissa), where the nuns sell homemade bread, peanut butter, and wine. Located right near the Prefectoral (prefect), 2 blocks up the hill from the main plaza. Or walk down to the river for a swim. An hour's drive farther, 80 miles (128 km) from La Paz, is the jungle village of Chulumani, the capital of Sud Yungas and the center of an area rich in citrus fruit and coffee. Between the two capitals is Coripata, the coca-growing center of northern Bolivia. La Paz tour agencies offer 1- and 2-day trips to the Yungas, or you can go by bus for about $5. In La Paz contact *Flota Yunguena* (phone: 2-312344). A large number of the residents in the Yungas are Bolivians of African ancestry. They are the descendants of slaves who were brought to work in the silver mines, but when they couldn't adjust to the climate, they were taken to the Yungas to work in the coca and coffee fields. Although some speak dialects with African roots, most converse in Aymara and dress in traditional Bolivian Indian fashion with *polleras* and bowler hats.

Returning south to La Paz, you pick up another road at El Alto, on the rim of the crater in which the capital lies. This road leads to Oruro.

**ORURO:** Some 100 miles (160 km) south of La Paz, Oruro is set on the slopes of a hill 12,000 feet above sea level. It is the site of Bolivia's first tin smelter, and its population of 108,000 Indians still work the area's tin, silver, copper, lead, and tungsten mines (although, in recent years, there has been epidemic unemployment in the city). The name Oruro is derived from *Uro*, which refers to the Indians used as laborers in the mines. In 1871, the Indians joined forces with the mestizos and staged an uprising against the Spanish authorities, sending Sebastián Pagador to demand that the workers receive more administrative posts. Pagador has become Oruro's folk-legend hero and the symbol of freedom. Simón Bolívar's tutor, Simón Rodríguez, founded a boys' school here, and the town also has a university known for its engineering and mining schools.

Oruro is also a rail center with connections to the Bolivian cities of La Paz, Cochabamba, and Potosí as well as to other important South American destinations including Tucumán, Rosario, and Buenos Aires, Argentina. (The rail station phone number is 52-60605.) In addition, it is a city that mixes modern customs with folk and Indian traditions. On the fringes of the city are animal-shaped rocks — particularly those in the form of frogs or rabbits — where offerings are made in attempts to obtain health, work, and happiness. Although the region's main industry is mining, farming (barley, potatoes, and other tubers) and sheep ranching also play a role.

Oruro's *Carnaval* is the most famous in Bolivia. Participants spend months rehearsing dances and making their costumes for the festival. On the Saturday before *Ash Wednesday*, all work stops for *La Diablada*, the parade of the devil dancers who, dressed in wild costumes and grotesque masks, depict the story of the battle between good and evil. *La Diablada* begins with a a procession of the statue of the Virgin of Socavón (the patron saint of miners), continues with a musical rendition of the Spanish conquest, then the rebellion of the devils, and ends with the victory of Archangel Michael over the devils. This spectacle, which dates from colonial times, is full of the naturalistic elements of a pagan past. During another part of the festival, participants make offerings of liquor, cigarettes, and coca to the spirit that haunts the mines. There also is a sunrise Andean ritual at which the revelers ask ancient gods for happiness and protection.

Seats can be booked for these spectacles at the Oruro Town Hall, but hotel reservations should be made months in advance. (*Note:* There are water shortages in Oruro and some hotels have water only in the mornings; ask when making reservations.) Tour agencies in La Paz also book 1-day trips to see the devil dancers. If you aren't in the city for *Carnaval*, you might want to stop by the *Museo Arqueológico Vivero Municipal* (Calle Lizarraga near the zoo) to see its collection of *Diablada* masks. The museum also has a distinguished collection of pre-Columbian archaeological artifacts. More treasures can be found at the *Casa de Cultura* (House of Culture; Calle Soria Galvarro at Ayacucho), a neo-classical building that once belonged to tin magnate Simón Patiño. Colonial art, ancient art, and Patiño's belongings round out the museum exhibits.

The city tourism office is located in Edificio Prefectural (Plaza 10 de Febrero; phone: 52-51764), and can provide a good city map.

**En Route from Oruro** – Two roads lead into southern Bolivia and its three main communities — Potosí, Sucre, and Tarija. The most commonly used road spins off the main paved highway (part of the Pan-American route) east of Oruro, turns south, and divides: One fork leads south to Potosí; the other southeast to Sucre. The second road picks up farther down the main highway, toward Cochabamba, at Epizana, about 85 miles (136 km) from La Paz. The 140-mile (224-km) route to Sucre, like the Oruro road, is stony, dusty, and a tight squeeze in many places. Both are scenic, however, and each will take you about 7 or 8 hours. On this roller-coaster journey, the views are spectacular.

**POTOSÍ:** This is Bolivia's silver city. Legend says that the Indian Diego Huallpa discovered silver in 1544 while searching for a stray llama. Huallpa lit a fire to keep warm and a nearby "stone" (silver vein) melted into a pool of the precious metal. The word got out and the Spanish arrived to mine at Cerro Rico (Rich Hill). But it is likely that even before the Spanish found the silver, the Inca mined here. Myth has it that work was called off when the mountain shuddered and a deep voice called, "The Lord guards the treasures for one who will come later." From then on, the mountain was called Potosí, meaning "exploding sounds" in Quechua.

When New York City had a population of 150,000, Potosí's numbered 200,000. At an altitude of more than 14,000 feet (higher than La Paz and, with Lhasa, Tibet, one of the highest cities in the world), the climate is often frigid, with nightly temperatures sometimes falling below zero degrees Fahrenheit during July and August.

Potosí was regarded as Spain's most valuable city in South America in the 17th century, when immense amounts of silver were torn from Cerro Rico, a mountain of 70% silver. The wealth was so great here that women wore Flanders lace and Chinese silk; homes were decorated with Persian rugs and Dutch linen. There is a tragic side to the story, however. During this epoch, it is estimated that some 8 million Indians lost their lives because of deplorable conditions in the mines. (And when it was feared that there wouldn't be enough labor for the mines, 17,000 African slaves were taken to Potosí. They never adapted to the cold or altitude — some died, and the rest were sent to the Yungas.) For several hundred years, silver was shipped to the port of Antofagasta (now in Chile) and on to Spain. Pirates preyed on the ships, waiting for the silver cargo to come around the Horn. There is a sweeping panoramic view of Potosí from the top of the Cerro Rico, which can be reached on foot or by jeep.

By the 19th century, the lodes began to give out and Potosí's importance decreased, and for a century it ranked as no more than a second-rate provincial town. Then, in 1905, Simón Patiño, a mestizo working for a German trading firm, discovered a metal ignored by the Spanish — tin. The rich tin deposits, as well as sizable amounts of copper, lead, and still minable quantities of silver, revived Potosí and made Patiño one of the world's richest men. It was his uncontrolled takeover of South American, North American, and European tin interests that prompted Bolivia to nationalize its mines in 1952. Today, Potosí is a relatively prosperous community of 118,000 residents, and despite 5,000 mine tunnels and more than 440 years of exploitation, the Cerro Rico is still producing ore, although the decline of tin prices in 1985 dealt a harsh blow to the industry and left tens of thousands of miners — many in Potosí — on the streets without work. Tours to a tin mine, usually lasting 3 hours, can be arranged locally; the government-run Pailaviri Mine outside of town has tours Mondays through Fridays from 9:30 AM to noon.

In its heyday, churches, convents, and palaces were erected that made Potosí one of the most beautiful cities on the continent. Most of these buildings have been preserved, including the *Casa Real de la Moneda* (the Royal Mint), built from 1750 to 1773 and renovated in 1959; it is now a museum. The first-floor salon, which is the main art gallery, is so rich and impressive that it overwhelms the paintings it contains. On exhibit are the huge wooden presses that produced the strips of silver from which colonial coins were made; the coin dies themselves; and smelting houses with carved altarpieces from a number of Potosí's churches that fell into ruin. Open to the public weekdays from 9 AM to noon and 2 to 5 PM, and Saturdays from 9:30 AM to noon and 2:30 to 5 PM, but it can only be toured with a guide (wear warm clothes as the building is not heated). The tour costs about $1. Located on Calle Ayacucho (between Bustillo and Quijarro; phone: 62-22777). Also worth visiting is the *Museo y Convento de Santa Teresa* (Museum and Convent of Santa Teresa; on Calle Chichas, at the corner of Ayacucho; phone: 62-23847). It is open to the public Mondays through Saturdays, 4 to 5 PM. Elsewhere in the city there are nearly 2 dozen other fine baroque churches typical of the Andean or mestizo architecture of the 18th century.

The religious fervor that the Spanish conquistadores brought with them is also evident in the cathedral at the Plaza 10 de Noviembre — the same plaza where the Palacio de Justicia (Palace of Justice) is located and where the Royal Mint was originally found. The City Hall, another fine colonial building on the plaza, was once the royal vault. A block away, on Calle Sucre, is a colonial mansion called the Palacio de Cristal (Crystal Palace). The office of the Banco Nacional de Bolivia on Calle Junín was once the home of the Marquis de Otavi and its elaborate entryway is unrivaled for fine detail.

Also worth a visit is the *Museo Universitario* (University Museum) on Calle Bolívar, with its displays of paintings, pottery, musical instruments, and artifacts from the area. It is open Mondays through Saturdays, 10 AM to noon and 3 to 5 PM (phone: 62-22284).

Shopping at the town market and at the merchants' stalls along Calle Bustillos is rewarding, particularly for those interested in silverwork — including coins and jewelry — and woven native textiles. There is also an artisans' market off Calle Omiste.

It is possible to go for a swim at the Tarapaya hot springs 15 miles (24 km) outside of Potosí. Daily bus transportation from Plaza Chuquimia is available to the lake and the outdoor swimming pool, not far away.

The Potosí Tourism Office is located in Edificio Cámara de Minería, 2nd Floor (phone: 62-25288 or 62-26392).

**En Route from Potosí** – It is a little less than 100 miles (160 km) to Sucre, although the trip takes 4 hours by car or bus over a bumpy, dusty, but scenically spectacular road. Private taxis generally charge $100 or more for the trip. The best and most comfortable alternative is the daily tourist bus service operated by *Soltrans,* a division of *Solarsa Tour.* This is a nonstop, first class, air conditioned bus, radio-equipped in case of a breakdown. Contact the tourist office in Potosí or *Soltrans* in Sucre (6 Nicolás Ortiz; phone: 64-30500). There is also train service (the trip takes 5 hours) between the two cities several times a week, but the schedule is unpredictable. Check with the rail station in Potosí (phone: 62-23101) or in Sucre (phone: 64-31115).

**SUCRE:** Still Bolivia's legal capital (although the president and congress work out of La Paz, 45 minutes away by plane), Sucre stands at an altitude of about 9,000 feet. Its climate is mild, averaging 55F (13C). During the rainy season, late October through March, the days are typically warm, with evenings mild. From April through September, days are sunny but nights are quite cold. It was because of the inviting climate that the wealthy, who made their fortunes from the mines in Potosí, installed their families here. For those who stayed in colder Potosí, not a single European child born there in the first 50 years of the Spanish colonization lived beyond 2 weeks.

In 1809, residents of Sucre issued the continent's first formal cry for independence from Spain and in 1825, Bolivia's Declaration of Independence was signed here. San Xavier University — a breeding ground for intellectual and revolutionary thought — dates from the 17th century, yet even during the 16th century the town was the cultural center of South America and Spanish families sent their children here to school.

Founded in 1538, Sucre has long been known as La Ciudad Blanca (White City) because by law most of its buildings, including private homes, must be whitewashed. The earliest Spanish settlers were titled families (the titles in those days were purchased from the Vatican), and each represented an order of the Church. Generally, each titled family would build a church dedicated to the saint or order it represented. During the pre-*Lent* holidays, church ornaments and tons of silver from the wealthy families of the town are carried by burro in the *Parade of Silver* to the cathedral to be blessed for the coming year. In an appendage of the cathedral, besides its museum, is the 17th-century Chapel of the Virgin of Guadalupe (31 Nicolás Ortiz). The image of the Virgin is staggering — swathed in diamonds, pearls, and rubies. Donated by Sucre's wealthiest residents over a period of 3 centuries, this painting is said to be worth millions of dollars and is believed to be the most valuable religious icon in the Americas. The cathedral itself is guarded by the 16 statues in its towers; local legend has it they are the 12 apostles and saints of Sucre. Adjacent to the cathedral, the *Museo de la Catedral* (Cathedral Museum), holds a collection of colonial paintings, parchment, and furniture decorated with mother of pearl. There is a nominal admisssion charge, but you must pay extra to take photos. To tour the church, make an appointment with Padre (Father) Tesorero. Visiting hours for the cathedral are 7:30 to 9:15 AM daily; those for the museum are weekdays from 10 AM to noon and 3 to 5 PM; Saturdays from 10 AM to noon.

Even though Sucre has a population of 120,000, it retains an atmosphere of antiquity — a certain quiet, dignified, colonial charm. Its public buildings are impressive.

What's more, the infusion of money into the community, as a result of the completion of a gas pipeline from the fields at Monteagudo to the southeast, has enabled these buildings to be maintained.

Foremost among the architectural sites is the Casa de La Líbertad (House of Liberty), or Legislative Palace, located on the main square (Plaza 25 de Mayo), where the country's Independence Act was signed, and where a copy of that document is now preserved. Even earlier, in the 16th century, the building housed the first university established in Bolivia; the scholars' gilded chairs still remain in the principal salon. Between the artifacts from its university days and the memorabilia from the independence struggle, you can easily spend several hours here. The museum is open Mondays through Fridays from 9 AM to noon and 2:30 to 6 PM and Saturdays from 10 AM to noon. There is a small admission charge but here, too, you must pay extra to take photos. Ask for the services of an English-speaking guide; the cost is included in the price.

Just off the Plaza 25 de Mayo (at 10 Calle Arenales) is the Iglesia de San Miguel (Church of St. Michael), reportedly the oldest church in use today in South America. Closed for more than a century, San Miguel has been restored to its original state, with carved and painted wooden ceilings, intricate Moorish designs, glistening white walls, and a fine gold and silver altar. The church is open daily to tourists from 6:30 to 7:30 PM.

Another early church worth seeing is San Francisco (like San Miguel, it has carved wooden Moorish ceilings). San Francisco's bell cracked when it was rung to rally Sucre's citizens to join the independence revolution and is now silent. To tour these sights, you should arrive early, since most churches in Sucre are closed by 10 AM except on Sundays or holy days. (San Francisco reopens from 4 to 7 PM but tourists are asked not to enter during mass.) At the center of Plaza 25 de Mayo is a statue of the revolutionary leader Antonio José de Sucre, who helped write the 1825 Declaration of Independence, and for whom the city is named. Tarabuco Indians from the nearby countryside are sometimes found here selling their weavings and stringed instruments, known as *charangos*.

Other buildings of interest are the *Teatro Gran Mariscal Sucre*, Junín College, and the more modern Palacio del Gobierno (Government Palace) and Palacio de Santo Domingo (Santo Domingo Palace), also known as the Palace of Justice, where Bolivia's federal judiciary, including the Supreme Court, has its seat.

In fact, the Palace of Justice is the starting point of one of the loveliest parks in the city — the Parque Bolívar. Follow the park downhill from the huge, white Supreme Court building and you'll find throngs of students studying on park benches, well-tended flower gardens, a goldfish pond, and a miniature Eiffel Tower that can be climbed for a breathtaking view of colonial Sucre. This is a good place to buy a *salteña* — a juicy, spicy meat turnover sold throughout Bolivia — before continuing the walk past pine and palm trees. The park ends at the train station.

For another amazing view of Sucre, walk up to the Convento Recoleta (Recoleta Monastery), high above the city, and stroll along its archway, which serves as a lookout and a lovers' lane. The Franciscan monastery was built in 1601 on the site where the city was founded 63 years earlier — a hill the Indians called "beautiful hilltop." Inside are lovely cloisters, interior patios and flower gardens, and exquisitely carved choir stalls. Behind the monastery is Cerro Churuquella, a hill covered with eucalyptus trees and topped by a statue of Christ. The monastery is open to visitors Mondays through Fridays, 9 to 11:30 AM and 4 to 7 PM. There is an admission charge and guided tours are available. You also can see the city's roofs from the top of the 17th-century San Felipe Neri Church (located at 165 Nicolás Ortiz), open daily from 4:30 to 5:30 PM. Get permission from the city tourism office located at 102 Potosí (phone: 64-25983). There is an admission charge.

A number of shops opposite the Church of San Francisco have interesting handicrafts. On Calle Arenales, at the *Residencia San José,* you can buy alpaca clothing woven at nearby Yotala. Be on the lookout for antique woven items. This is also a good city to buy jewelry made from Potosí silver. Stop by the *Caserón de la Capellanía,* a complex with shops and restaurants across from the Santa Teresa church on Calle San Alberto at Potosí.

**En Route from Sucre** – It takes nearly 2 hours by taxi to drive the 36 miles (58 km) to Tarabuco, which has one of the most colorful Sunday Indian markets in South America. Buses also leave Sucre daily in the morning and return in the afternoon. Here, in addition to being able to buy ponchos and other typical native garments, you'll see Indian men strolling about playing the *charango,* a stringed instrument that has an armadillo shell for a soundbox. The woven skirts and belts of the women, duplicates of which can be purchased, are among the most unusual in Bolivia. The action at the market begins around 9 AM and continues in full force until at least noon. There are several "passable" restaurants on the main plaza where you can have lunch. Special festival days are in late February or early March, during *Carnaval.*

**TARIJA:** As Bolivia's wine-producing center, this is the last relatively accessible major community of touristic interest in the Sucre-Potosí area (the departure point is Potosí). And for fans of the movie, *Butch Cassidy and the Sundance Kid,* rumor has it that the remains of Butch and the Kid have been found in the area. The 230-mile (368-km) trip south over a bad, unpaved road takes about 10 hours, depending on weather conditions. You also can fly here from La Paz, Cochabamba, Santa Cruz, or Sucre. At the foothills near the landing strip, be sure and look out for a giant cut-out billboard of Pope John Paul II. It was erected in honor of the pontiff's visit to this devout region, in 1988.

Founded in 1574 to guard the colonists against the Chiriguano Indians, Tarija (pop. 80,000) is one of the oldest communities in Bolivia, yet its residents (called *chapacos*) were not officially absorbed into the country until Bolivian Independence in 1825. They declared independence from Spain in 1807 and founded their own little republic. This led to a fierce struggle with colonial powers and ultimately, after the Spanish were defeated, to Tarija's absorption into the new nation. The original residents of Tarija were tall, fair-skinned people known for their hospitality and horsemanship, and today its inhabitants look more like southern Europeans or Levantines than the usual Indian or mestizo Bolivians. They compare their city and its agricultural environs to those in Spain's Andalusia and are known in Bolivia for their relaxed attitude and the melodic quality of their speech.

Tarija has a mild climate (average temperatures are in the 60s and 70s F [15–26C] most of the year). At an altitude of about 6,000 feet in the heart of a fertile valley of flowers, orchards, and vineyards watered by the Río Guadalquivir, the town is the center of a productive agricultural area. It is also the source of Bolivia's best wines, although unfortunately there are no organized tours of the vineyards. A variety of distilled liqueurs — especially *singani* (made from grapes) — are popular. Every February, the city holds a wine festival.

Spring holidays are Tarija's big moment. The most colorful one is the celebration of *San Roque,* which begins on the first Sunday of September and lasts most of the month. Bolivia has a patron saint for everything, and San Roque is the protector of dogs. On the first three Sundays of the month, a series of processions carry the saint's statue, clad in ornate vestments, through the streets of the town, led by residents dressed in costumes with cloth turbans and veils; the mutts wear colored ribbons. The processions begin at San Roque church; its viewing balcony was used as a sentry post during the Republican era. In another, the *Festival de las Flores,* a carpet of flowers is thrown on the ground as a statue of the Virgin of Rosario is carried through the streets. It is held the second Sunday in October.

There is a local tourism office (883 Calle General Trigo; phone: 66-25948). Tarija is a jumping-off point for road trips to Argentina, some 150 miles (240 km) away.

## BEST EN ROUTE

Except for those in La Paz, there are few first-rate hotels along this route. In some areas you're in a deluxe accommodation (by Bolivian standards) if running water is available. On rare occasions you'll come across a property with a pool, tennis courts, and a restaurant. Expect to pay up to $85 for a double room in a place listed as very expensive; between $40 and $55 for an expensive hotel; $25 and $40 for a moderate listing; and under $25 in an inexpensive place. Note that hostels serve only breakfast, which is included in the rates.

### LAKE TITICACA

*Inca Utama* – At *Crillón Tours*' port in Huatajata, this 45-room hotel is used primarily for those taking tours or hydrofoil trips through the agency. Rooms are heated, but electric blankets are also given to guests. There also is a restaurant, bar, and shop. The program for overnight guests includes an early wake-up to view the sunrise over the lake, a visit to the company's own altiplano museum, and meals. Reservations through *Crillón Tours,* 1223 Camacho (phone: 2-374566/7; in the US through *LARC,* 800-327-3573). Moderate.

*Titikaka* – This attractive spot in Masani has 24 rooms, each featuring private bath, hot water, and color TV set. Its *Suma Uru* restaurant is known for its trout, served fresh from the lake. Conference rooms can handle up to 100. Reservations: PO Box 1724, La Paz (phone: 2-343172). Moderate.

### COPACABANA

*Playa Azul* – A clean but rustic property; at least there is hot water, and some rooms have private baths. Located just a block from the beach, close enough to hear the sounds made by Lake Titicaca's giant frogs. Full board is possible (phone: 2-320068). Moderate.

*Prefectural* – One of the government-owned group of tourist properties, this old hotel has a lovely lake view. There are private baths and hot water, a good restaurant, pool tables, a sun deck, and live music on weekends. Reservations at the hotel (phone: 2-362041); in La Paz (phone: 2-374586). Inexpensive.

### COROICO

*Prefectural* – This pleasant little hostelry has a pool, and the food is quite good. Meals normally required but the cost remains moderate. Ten minutes north of the town. For reservations, call 2-374586 in La Paz. For transportation from La Paz, call 2-312391. Moderate.

### CHULUMANI

*San Bartolomé* – The nicest accommodations in Chulumani are in this attractive, small resort with cottages for families, a swimming pool, mini-golf, tennis, and volleyball. Reservations through *Plaza Tours,* at the *Plaza Hotel,* 1789 Av. 16 de Julio, La Paz (phone: 2-377499 or 2-378311). Very expensive.

*Prefectural* – This hotel has cabañas with private baths and a swimming pool. Reservations, in Chulumani (phone: 2-324539) or through *Diana Tours,* 328 Sagárnaga, La Paz (phone: 2-375374). Moderate to inexpensive.

### ORURO

*Terminal* – By the bus station, this place offers private baths with hot water and is definitely the best in town. There is a different price for Bolivian nationals so don't be confused by the dual tariff. Calle Reyka Vakovic (phone: 52-53209 or 52-53127). Moderate.

**Repostero** – Its German owners offer good food and service. Singles are available, with or without bath. There is no hot water here but the staff will boil you some for bathing. 370 Calle Sucre (phone: 52-50505). Inexpensive.

## POTOSÍ

**El Solar** – Offers guestrooms with telephones, private baths, and plenty of hot water. 41 Calle Wenceslao Alba (phone: 62-27456). Expensive to moderate.

**Colonial** – Built in an old colonial house, this was the best place to stay in town before the *Tambo* came on the scene. Rooms have heat, carpeting, and private baths. 8 Calle Hoyos (phone: 62-24265). Moderate.

**Tambo** – This is the town's first property edging on the luxurious. Km 5 of the Oruro Hwy. (phone: 62-25186). Moderate.

**Turista** – This property has private baths, heat, and hot water. The manager is a walking well of tourism information and service here in general is very friendly. 19 Calle Lanza (phone: 62-22492). Moderate.

## SUCRE

**Crúz de Popayán** – A charming small hostel in a colonial mansion, with rooms built around a flower-filled patio; it is also very quiet. Private baths. 881 Calle Loa (phone: 64-25156). Moderate.

**Libertad** – Comfortable hotel with phones, private baths, TV sets, and mini-bars in every room, a block from the main plaza. You'll hear Sucre's chiming church bells here. 99 Calle Ancieto Arce (phone: 64-23101). Moderate.

**Sucre** – This hostel's 2 stories also are constructed around a colonial patio, and it boasts that many years ago European royalty stayed here. The location is a bit noisy. At 113 Calle Bustillos (phone: 64-21411). Moderate.

**Municipal** – In a wonderfully quiet location near Bolívar Park, this hotel is no more than a 10-minute walk to the center of town. Its 39 rooms, all facing the patio and gardens, are pleasant and clean, and have private baths, TV sets, and telephones. The restaurant is good, and there is room service, too. 1052 Av. Venezuela (phone: 64-25508 or 64-21216). Inexpensive.

## TARIJA

**Prefectural** – Just outside the city center, it is the largest hotel in Tarija. All rooms have a private bath, and there is a pool and restaurant, although there have been complaints about the service. 1252 Calle La Madrid at the corner of Av. Las Américas (phone: 66-22461 or 66-22789). Moderate.

**Victoria Plaza** – On the main square, an old but comfortable hotel, the atmosphere is ritzy by Tarija standards. Calle Madrid at the corner of Sucre (phone: 66-22600 or 66-22700). Moderate.

**Residencial Bolívar** – A homey, comfortable place; you can get a hot bath here. 256 Calle Bolívar (phone: 66-2741). Inexpensive.

# Cochabamba and Santa Cruz

The highland landscapes, with their colonial centers and folkloric traditions, may be the Bolivia of picture books, but the lowlands also have great charm and interest. The centers of Cochabamba and Santa Cruz shouldn't be missed, whether you visit by air or road from the easiest departure point, La Paz.

**COCHABAMBA:** This was the early home of the tin king, Simón Patiño, one of the few Bolivian Indians with the cunning to cash in on the area's native resources. But he did it by exploiting his own people and virtually enslaving them in the mines, a tale outlined in Augusto Céspedes's novel *El Metal del Diablo*. The Patiño Foundation is housed in Los Portales, the sumptuous mansion that Patiño built for himself but never lived in. The French-designed palace (1450 Av. Potosí; phone: 42-43137) is now the sight of cultural events and activities. Los Portales, finished in 1927 after a decade of work, is open to the public for tours Mondays through Fridays from 5 to 6 PM; Saturdays from 10 to 11 AM; and Sundays from 11 AM to noon.

Cochabamba, with a population of about 350,000, is one of Bolivia's garden spots. Vegetation is lush, the climate mild. The best view of the entire area is from the top of San Sebastián Hill on the south edge of the city, where a monument commemorates the Bolivian women who fought and died during the War of Independence in the 19th century. These heroines are honored every May 27.

There's great shopping at the *Mercado Municipal* (Municipal Market) and at the retail market at La Cancha, open Wednesdays and Saturdays. The best buys are woolen blankets, ponchos, and carved and painted wood figures of llamas and other animals. (Be forewarned that pickpockets and petty thieves often turn up at these markets in search of unsuspecting tourists.) The Maryknoll fathers and several other organizations have introduced the local women to the art of knitting. Hand-knit sweaters from high-grade alpaca wool are the specialty; prices are substantially lower than in the US and many styles are available only in Bolivia and Peru. But bear in mind that Cochabamba, in general, is one of Bolivia's most expensive cities. There is a 25-year-old cooperative in the suburb of Cala Cala, complete with an alpaca ranch; goods from the Fotrama Cooperative are available at its shop (at the corner of Heroinas and 25 de Mayo; phone: 42-25791). Fotrama goods are sold in stores in Santa Cruz and La Paz and provide income for 1,500 artisans.

This area is Bolivia's biggest producer of grain and fruit. It's also the site of Inkallajta, Inca ruins 75 miles (120 km) from Cochabamba that are seldom visited by outsiders, probably because there's a 2-hour walk up to the mountain site. For those interested in ruins and the like, but not anxious to take this hike, a fine archaeological museum with an intriguing collection of prehistoric pieces and pre-Inca textiles is found in Cochabamba at the Universidad Mayor de San Simón.

A popular excursion an hour or so outside the city is to the thermal baths at Liriuni. You can continue to La Cumbre pass (13,510 feet) for a superb view of Mt. Illimani, hundreds of miles away. Check with the tourist office, in the Edificio Prefectural (Plaza 14 de Septiembre; phone: 42-23364). If you're an angler, fishing can be arranged at the Cabaña del Club Angostura, 17 miles (27 km) from the city on the highway to Santa Cruz.

**En Route from Cochabamba** – The 300-mile (480-km) road to Santa Cruz is fairly well paved, but badly maintained, and skirts the Inca temple ruins of Inkallajta, just off the main road, about 85 miles (136 km) from Cochabamba. Back on the road, you climb to the top of Siberia Pass; you'll think you're in the clouds as you watch their formations skim over the surrounding peaks. From here the road gradually descends over 200 miles (320 km) down to the largely undeveloped plains around Santa Cruz. A second (and newer) route to Santa Cruz is entirely paved, but again badly maintained. It goes over a high pass and down into the Chapare and through Villa Tunari and Yapacani to Santa Cruz. Chapare has the highest rainfall in the Amazon basin, some 195 to 235 inches yearly, so it's very green and very humid. *Lloyd Aereo Boliviano (LAB)* also has daily flights between Cochabamba (at press time, a modern airport terminal was scheduled to be completed) and Santa Cruz (be forewarned that there is no currency exchange at the airport here). In addition, there is "ferrobus" (rail car) service betweeen La Paz and Cochamba. For information on routes, check at the Cochabamba train station (phone: 42-22402).

**SANTA CRUZ:** Though it was founded in 1560, 25 years ago Santa Cruz looked like a town on the Texas Panhandle — horses roamed the dusty streets, few people could be seen, and about the only noise was that of the howling wind. Then came the discoveries of oil, natural gas, and illegal cocaine trafficking, which have since turned this remote, sleepy outpost into Bolivia's boomtown. Its population has grown to almost 400,000, making it Bolivia's second-largest city, and it has one of the best hotels in the country, *Los Tajibos* (see *Best en Route),* where US oil engineers stroll about in baseball caps. Located at an altitude of only 1,250 feet, Santa Cruz is hot and tropical except when cold *surazo* winds blow in from the Argentine pampa from May to August. Among Bolivians, the city enjoys its reputation as fun, energetic, and "with it," thanks, perhaps, to the more salubrious climate. At any rate, Santa Cruz is said to have the best nightlife and highest prices in Bolivia.

Today there are several oil fields — including those at Colpa and Caranda, within 30 miles (48 km) to the north and northwest of the city — and a large gas field at Río Grande, some 25 miles (40 km) southeast, that are being exploited in the department of Santa Cruz. This has led to the construction of a government-run oil refinery in Santa Cruz, accompanied by the extensive development of transportation and communications systems and the improvement of all of the city's facilities.

In addition to access by a mostly paved road via Cochabamba, there is domestic and international air service including direct flights to Miami on *Lloyd Aereo Boliviano (LAB),* a railway, and a dirt road (not recommended) running almost 400 miles (640 km) east to Corumbá, Brazil, on the Río Paraguay. Another rail line extends more than 300 miles (480 km) south to Yacuiba on the Argentine border. Information is available at the train station (phone: 3-348047).

All of these factors have increased integration and altered the population mix of Santa Cruz. At one time, the rural people living here were descendants of the area's first Spanish settlers and are still known as *cambas,* people who live in the tropical lowlands. When the government initiated settlement programs in the 1960s, things began to change as land was made available on a first-come, first-served basis. Other projects offered houses, schools, potable water, medical care, farming aid, and even long-term loans. The Indians of the altiplano were urged to overcome their fear of the heat and mosquitoes of the lowlands in exchange for a prosperous way of life.

By the 1970s, the character of Santa Cruz had undergone a radical transformation. Where once highlanders settled in only for the 3- or 4-month sugarcane harvest, they now came with their entire family. Mennonites from Canada and different parts of South America also came to stay. Northwest of Santa Cruz, near Montero, there's a colony of Japanese from Okinawa. Near Abapó Izozon, 150 German families have formed a community that's roughly the size of Holland. This influx of residents has made Santa Cruz the fastest-growing area of Bolivia.

Many settlers have entered agricultural enterprises, raising cotton, sugar, rice, and coffee. Cattle ranching and timber processing have also become important. Deposits of iron ore and magnesium were found near the Bolivia–Brazil border, bringing even more industry into the region. Along with new discoveries came more settlers, including more highland Indians, who now seem to find Santa Cruz less threatening.

Visitors will find that amusements in Santa Cruz swing to a 20th-century beat. There is tennis, swimming, and golf at hotels or at the *Club Los Palmas* (outside the city on the road to Cochabamba), tennis at the *Club de Tenis,* and horseback riding at the *Club Hípico* outside town. When the sun goes down, the lights go up nightly at the *Paladium* (83 Calle Boquerón; phone: 3-340034), *Fiz* (Av. Román Vaca; phone: 3-332510, and *Swing* (Km 4.5 on the Cochabamba Hwy.; phone: 3-329150) discotheques. The Santa Cruz *Carnaval* is celebrated in a wild frenzy of masquerade balls, parades, and street dances during the 2 weeks before *Lent.*

Shopping is also worthwhile. The modern *Los Pozos Market* deserves a visit, particularly in the summer, when tropical fruits are on sale, including papaya and pineapple and some local oddities such as *ambaiba,* which looks like a glove (the meat is sucked out of the "fingers"), and *guayperú,* which is like a cherry. More durable buys are leather goods, baskets, hammocks, contraband Brazilian goods, and carvings and furniture made from guayacan and jacaranda. Be on guard against purse snatchers in the market.

Stop in the local tourism office (Edificio Chasal, 215 Calle René Moreno; phone: 3-348644). *Note:* Always carry your passport with you. There have been reports of police officers imposing a $50 fine on students and young tourists who cannot produce their documents upon request. If you have any problems, contact the US consulate here (Edificio Oriente, 3rd Floor; phone: 3-330725).

In the suburb of San Carlos is one of South America's most acclaimed zoos. It features native species in an open, park-like setting, and an outdoor restaurant and play area for children. Take bus No. 8 or 16 from the *Terminal de Buses* on the corner of Cañuto and Irala (phone: 3-340772).

About 68 miles (109 km) southwest of Santa Cruz (on a mostly paved road) is Samaipata, an immense carved rock formation dating from the brief period of Inca occupation of the country. The carvings include feline shapes, geometrical figures, and niches that may have held religious objects. Archaeologists continue a lively debate about the interpretation of the site; some insist it was a fortress, while others maintain that Samaipata was a setting for religious or fertility rites. In the nearby village of the same name is a small archaeological museum highlighting several pre-Columbian cultures. A bus from Santa Cruz takes nearly 2 hours. Call the *Terminal de Buses* (phone: 3-340772) for departure times.

## BEST EN ROUTE

You should have no trouble finding accommodations in Cochabamba or Santa Cruz. However, if you're traveling on a tight budget, be aware that hotels in the oil boomtown of Santa Cruz tend to be pricier than elsewhere in Bolivia. Expect to pay up to $110 for a double room in the hotels listed as expensive; between $45 and $70 at a place listed as moderate; and under $45 for an inexpensive place.

### COCHABAMBA

**César's Plaza** – This modern downtown property only 2 blocks from the central plaza is one of the better hostelries in town. It has a restaurant with an international menu, bar, coffee shop, and shopping arcade. 210-213 Av. 25 de Mayo (phone: 42-24558 or 42-26547; fax: 42-22646). Expensive.

**Portales** – A luxury option, located in a pleasant residential area just behind the Patiños's former palace, Los Portales; it has a pool, 2 restaurants, convention center, disco, gym, sauna, racquetball courts, and attractive gardens. 1271 Av. Pando (phone: 42-48700 or 42-48507; fax: 42-42071. Expensive.

**Gran Hotel Cochabamba** – On the outskirts of town amid lush gardens, each of its 50 rooms has a private bath. Suites are available. Facilities include tennis courts, swimming pool, bar, grill, and banquet room. Plaza Ubaldo Anze (phone: 42-43300 and 42-43303). Expensive to moderate.

**Aranjuez** – This small hotel is housed in a Spanish colonial-style building in a residential neighborhood. It has balconies off some of the guestrooms, lovely gardens with fountains, and terraces. There also is an international restaurant and bar featuring live jazz. E-0563 Av. Buenos Aires (phone: 42-41935); in La Paz through *Plaza Tours* (phone: 2-377499 or 2-378311; fax: 42-40158). Moderate.

**Emperador** – A small hotel, with 30 comfortable rooms, each with bath; restaurant and bar. 864 Av. Colombia (phone: 42-29343). Moderate.

**Gran Hotel Ambassador** – Offers all the comforts of home in a garden setting, plus a central location. Its 70 rooms have private baths, hot water, and telephones; there are tennis courts, a swimming pool, and a good restaurant on the property. 349 Calle España (phone: 42-48777; fax: 42-28778). Moderate.

**Residencial Ollantay** – Simple, clean, with good service, this is a good choice for the traveler on a budget. 211 Calle Baptista (phone: 42-23188). Inexpensive.

## SANTA CRUZ

**Los Tajibos** – On the outskirts of town, this luxurious 170-room resort hotel on 7 acres of land has air conditioning, restaurant, bar, casino, a gorgeous figure-eight pool, an 18-hole golf course, sauna, whirlpool bath, racquetball courts, and meeting rooms. The carpeted rooms have private baths and telephones. 455 Av. San Martín (phone: 3-351000 to 351004; in La Paz, 2-325974; in the US, 800-44-UTELL; fax: 3-336994). Expensive.

**Las Palmas** – A few blocks from the center of town, this hotel has a pool, a sauna, and a good restaurant. Av. Trompillo at the corner of Chaco (phone: 3-330366; fax: 3-330533; in La Paz, 2-373693). Expensive to moderate.

**Asturias** – Solid, clean, bungalow-style motel with 2 pools and air conditioning. It is a favorite of families. The *Parrillada* (grill) restaurant draws hungry diners from all over Santa Cruz. 154 Calle Moldes (phone: 3-339611). Moderate.

**Caparuch** – Located outside the center, this hostelry has comfortable, air conditioned rooms. There's a small outdoor pool, sauna, and hot tubs, as well as the *Caparuch* restaurant. Breakfast buffet included. 1717 Av. San Martín in the Sirari neighborhood (phone: 3-333303; fax: 3-351735). Moderate.

**Cortez** – On the edge of town, with 81 rooms and 11 suites, this old inn is quiet and unpretentious. There is a restaurant, cafeteria, swimming pool, and air conditioning. Breakfast included. 280 Av. Cristóbal de Mendoza (phone: 3-331234; fax: 3-351186). Moderate to inexpensive.

# Brazil

Covering more than half the continent, Brazil is not only the largest country in South America, but in terms of its people, customs, and physical terrain, it is one of the most diverse countries in the world. Within its boundaries are Indians who have never seen 20th-century Western men and women; cosmopolitan cities larger than the biggest urban centers in the US; jungles in which the vegetation is so thick that sunlight never reaches the ground; settlements where poverty and starvation exist beside startling examples of ostentatious wealth; and religions that incorporate elements of Catholicism as well as African animism. The country is bordered by the Atlantic on the north and east; Uruguay to the south; Paraguay, Argentina, and Bolivia to the southwest; Peru and Colombia to the west; and Venezuela, Guyana, Suriname, and French Guiana to the north.

Nearly equal in size to the continental US, the bulk of Brazil lies in the tropics, with the equator crossing the country in the north and the Tropic of Capricorn in the southeast. The Amazon basin contains the world's largest rain forest. It has an equatorial climate, with constant rain and wilting heat. Temperatures climb into the 90s and 100s F (30s C). The splendid 4,603-mile Atlantic coast notched with azure bays has some of the most delectable beaches on the continent. Although the seaboard accounts for less than 10% of Brazil's terrain, more than one-third of the population lives here. The cities of Rio de Janeiro, Salvador (Bahia), Santos (the port for São Paulo), Recife, Fortaleza, and Porto Alegre have grown up around natural harbors.

One cannot generalize about a country so large; each region has its own character. Although Brazilians are a complex variety of ethnic types, there is relatively little racial tension, partly because of a tradition of intermarriage started by the Portuguese. Brazil enjoys a homogeneous society, with distinctions based not on race but rather on pride in home states. They like to describe themselves as *paulistas* (from São Paulo); *cariocas* (from Rio); *mineiros* (from Minas Gerais); and *nordestinos* (from the northeast). They are predominately young, with half the population of about 148 million under 20.

Brazil's population, once expected to reach 200 million by the end of the 20th century, is now projected to fall somewhat short of the mark. A few factors have led officials to believe in this projected change: Television has penetrated into the remote regions of the country, with its subliminal message (in soap operas and sitcoms) that two or three children is the trend, rather than ten or twelve. A worsening economy and wider access to contraceptives also have contributed to reducing the birth rate from 6 children per woman in 1970 to about 3.2 today.

The country is divided into five geographical regions: the north, northeast, west central, southeast, and south, which are further divided into 27 *estados* (states).

In the north, travel through the dense Amazon rain forest is restricted to boats. While a few travel agencies have comfortable excursion boats for tourists, most Amazon travel is by twice-monthly government or private vessel. In this remote region you will find 2,000 species of fish, colorful parrots, and exotic animals such as capybaras, crocodiles, tapirs, and anacondas. The majority of the country's remaining Indian population (220,000, according to the Indian protection agency FUNAI) lives in reservations in this area, but generally you cannot visit them for health reasons, as they are terribly susceptible to communicable diseases. Other Indians have long since intermingled with settlers, and their descendants have given a distinctly Indian appearance to the general population of the north.

The government sends groups to visit the Indians and attempt to bring them out of their isolation, exchange gifts with them, and inoculate them against these destructive diseases. The government also hopes to preserve their lands while balancing the economic interests of gold miners and ranchers who seem bent on destroying the area's ecology. In a show of support to the Indians and environmentalists in 1991, President Collor de Mello set aside two vast tracts of lands as reservations for two tribes — an area the size of Portugal for the approximately 9,000 Yanomami and a tract the size of Switzerland for the 500 Kaiapó, displeasing a number of politicians.

The Northeast (the country's one geographic area that always is referred to formally), with 30% of the national population, is the poorest section of the country. Note: at press time, the cholera epidemic that has swept the continent had hit northeastern Brazil. Although travelers to the area are unlikely to be affected, they are advised to drink only bottled water and eat only hot, cooked food. Many of the poor from here migrate to the southern part of Brazil. The oldest cities, such as Salvador (Bahia) (pop. 1.8 million), Recife, Natal, and São Luís, contain stunning examples of colonial architecture. Here you will find the origins of Brazil's folklore and customs, such as the spiritualistic religion *macumba,* which is practiced throughout the country by all classes of people. The majority black population in the Northeast not only has retained many African traditions but also has had a profound influence on the rest of the country in terms of art, music, philosophy, and religion. The area also has a distinctive cuisine, many deserted beaches, and few foreign tourists.

The west-central (Mato Grosso) region is still a frontier, with savannah grasslands crossed by meandering rivers and a fauna-rich area known as the Pantanal, the world's largest wetlands, which is increasingly trying to develop tourism. There is some cattle farming here, but it is quite rugged. The city of Brasília (pop. 1.6 million), constructed on the edge of the Mato Grosso, became the nation's capital in 1960. (Previously, Rio de Janeiro was the capital.) Also in this region are the mining city of Belo Horizonte and the historic town of Ouro Preto, a national monument.

The heart of industrial, commercial, contemporary Brazil is the southeast, with Brazil's two largest cities, Rio de Janeiro (pop. 10.2 million in the greater city area) and São Paulo (pop. 15.3 million in the greater city area). The most visited destination in South America, Rio is famous for its beaches (among them Ipanema and Copacabana), glittering *Carnaval* celebrations, and the restored statue of Christ the Redeemer on Corcovado Mountain. São Paulo, the largest city in South America, is also one of the world's fastest-growing cities.

There are many European settlers in the south. It is an agricultural region of cattle pastures, coffee plantations, and vineyards, with picturesque communities such as Curitiba, built for the pedestrian, and Porto Alegre, a modern industrial city that has a far slower pace than São Paulo.

When Portuguese explorer Pedro Alvares Cabral first landed in the state of Bahia in 1500, he thought he had found a large tropical island. Portuguese colonists followed over the next 100 years, bringing slaves imported from Africa. They created large sugar and lumber plantations in the northeast as far south as São Paulo, building the cities of Salvador (Bahia) and Recife as monuments to their wealth. Salvador remained the capital for the next 200 years, until population shifts made Rio de Janeiro the country's economic center. With further economic growth, inland cities grew. One was Manaus, strategically placed in the rubber-producing Amazon River basin; Ouro Preto, once a center of gold and diamond mining, and Goiás, another gold-mining area, were two others. The spread of coffee growing and, later, cattle grazing was responsible for the expansion of the region south of São Paulo, now one of the most densely populated areas in the country.

Brazil remained a colony until 1822, when Pedro I, the son of the Portuguese monarch, declared himself the emperor of an independent nation. Due to the abolition of slavery in 1888 and a subsequent financial crisis, the monarchy failed, and the following year the Brazilian Federative Republic was created. The country remained a liberal democracy until 1964, when, after a period of social and economic upheaval, the military took over.

Under the military regime, the country experienced rapid economic growth, known as the Brazilian Miracle. Evidence of that prosperity has been especially prominent in major cities in the south, such as São Paulo and Rio. Brazil has the largest iron ore deposits on earth, ranks third in automobile production, and is a primary supplier of coffee, soybeans, cotton, cocoa, and sugar.

However, while the economic boom brought prosperity to some, 65% of the population continues to struggle for bare economic survival. Unemployment is high, and staggeringly high inflation rates have pushed the cost of staples such as rice and beans almost out of reach. As the poor from the Northeast flock to the more prosperous south in search of work, huge *favelas* (poor housing areas, some of which are shantytowns) have grown up on the outskirts, and sometimes within the confines, of metropolitan areas. The dwindling Indian population, officially protected by a government agency that requires them to live on reservations, consistently resists "citizenship" in a country that does not acknowledge their rights. Ultimately, they face the loss of their land and culture, particularly in the Amazon region, where agriculture and cattle raising are taking hold as major industries. In 1975, Chico Mendes, a rubber tapper and one of the forest dwellers, organized a mass effort to stop the deforestation. Although successful in saving thousands of acres, Mendes was murdered by landowners, one of whom was brought to trial, found guilty, and sentenced to prison. Other activists, however, continue to meet Mendes's fate as landowners resort to violence in order to preserve their holdings.

Military rule in Brazil ended in 1985, some 2 decades after it had begun. In that period, five army generals led the country, and the last, João Baptista Figueiredo, initiated a gradual return to a democratic government. In 1985, a 686-member electoral college made up of the Chamber of Deputies, the Senate, and delegates from each of Brazil's 23 states elected a civilian, Tancredo Neves, as president. However, he never began his term: The night before his swearing-in ceremony in March of that year, Neves was hospitalized with an intestinal disorder and died soon after. José Sarney, his vice presidential running mate, became president, only to be faced with the continuing overriding problem of inflation, which hit 230% in 1985 and threatened to jump to 500%. Early in 1986, Sarney went on the attack, introducing wage and price freezes and a new currency, the cruzado, in place of the cruzeiro. The Sarney administration attempted a total of three wage and price freezes, yet by the end of 1989, annual inflation was rapidly approaching 1,800%, and the novo cruzado was introduced. At that time, Fernando Collor de Mello was elected president for a 5-year term in Brazil's first democratic election in 29 years. He promised to bring economic growth back to Brazil, largely through a program of free market economy that would curb inflation and reduce the country's enormous foreign debt — the largest in the Third World. In March 1990, Collor introduced yet another new currency, once again called the cruzeiro.

Inflation, however, continues to plague Brazil. Criticizing government spending, Collor reduced the number of government ministries; on a nationwide level, he enacted strict wage and price controls which met with varying degress of success. (Brazilians at times seem to be more interested in the juicy private lives of their leaders than their political abilities.) Collor also pledged to preserve the land rights of the Amazon Indians and to protect the area's rain forests from destruction. As a show of good faith, President Collor stopped the construction by Japanese industrialists of a highway through untouched hardwood forests. Collor has pledged to protect Brazil's rain forest, as well as the rubber tappers and Indians who rely on the area for their livelihood. "Chico Mendes did not die in vain," Collor said. "We must and will put a stop to ecological crimes." In June 1991, in an attempt to bolster his standing with the environmentalists (as well as reduce some of Brazil's overwhelming debt), he introduced a "debt for nature swap," which would enable the country's debt to be exchanged for financing ecology programs.

Still, of all the South American countries, Brazil has the most sophisticated infrastructure for tourists. Quality hotels can be found in most cities and resort areas. An efficient internal air network connects all parts of the country. Whenever large distances are involved, flying is definitely recommended. You can take buses, trains, and freighters into the interior. The southeast has decent paved roads, but in other areas overland travel is considerably more rugged, particularly during the rainy months. Gasoline and service stations are few and far between in remote parts of the country. If you plan to drive the Trans-Amazon Highway, remember that it is in no way comparable to a US road. Be sure to carry the necessary spare parts, and be prepared to make repairs yourself. Check that your insurance papers and *carteira* (driver's license) are in order. And don't go during the rainy season, when large sections of road are completely washed out. Travelers should be aware that prices may vary as a result of Brazil's high inflation and the value of the US dollar against the cruzeiro.

The eight routes in this chapter are the Amazon, which leads from Belém to Manaus; the Northeast, from Recife to São Luís; from Rio de Janeiro to São Paulo along a spectacular coastal route — the Costa Verde; from Rio de Janeiro to Belo Horizonte, which goes through the mining district and Ouro Preto; from Belo Horizonte to Brasília; from Brasília through the Mato Grosso; from São Paulo to Uruguay, passing through Curitiba, Porto Alegre, and Rio Grande do Sul; and Iguaçu Falls.

# The Amazon: Belém to Manaus

One of the most exotic and still unexplored regions on earth is the Amazon basin, where the world's largest river and its thousands of tributaries dominate an area of more than 2.3 million square miles, roughly two-thirds the size of the continental US. The area's main feature is its equatorial forest, which creates a landscape of vegetation and wildlife without equal; in some places the foliage is so dense that sunlight never reaches the ground.

The intriguing and exotic notion of anacondas, man-eating piranhas, and species of birds found nowhere else lures many visitors to this area. Such wildlife probably only will be seen in the region's zoos, but the 1,200-mile river excursion from Belém to Manaus still gives one a sample of a part of the earth that remains unconquered by man.

The Amazon River was discovered by the Spaniard Francisco de Orellana, one of Pizarro's lieutenants, in 1592. He had heard reports of a great inland sea that existed on the other side of the Andes. Captains sailing off the coast of Brazil noted fresh brown water mixing with the green ocean as far as 200 miles offshore. Orellana was sent into the jungle from Quito in Ecuador to help Pizarro find the lost city of El Dorado, the mythical Indian community so fabulously wealthy that each night its residents bathed their chief in gold dust. Orellana separated from Pizarro to explore the mighty river and search for the famed warrior women, the Amazons, who were reputed to live there. The explorer's river and jungle adventures, including the battles with the Indians and the hardships that forced the men to eat their shoes and saddles to fight off starvation, were reported by Fray Gaspar de Carvajal, a Dominican priest on the expedition. Later groups of adventurers and gold seekers entered the Amazon basin to explore its riches and mystery and were never seen again.

The Amazon begins as melted snow high in the Peruvian Andes. Before spilling the brownish-yellow silt into the Atlantic, 4,000 miles away, it is fed by over a thousand tributaries, which make it the world's largest river in terms of water volume. At its mouth, near the city of Belém, the river is 200 miles wide. It provides 25% of the world's fresh water and 30% of its oxygen.

The existence of saltwater fish that have adapted themselves to fresh water, supports the theory that before the Andes rose in the west, a salty Mediterranean-like Amazon separated the top third of the South American continent from the rest of its landmass. The jungle, stretching for more than 180 miles along the Atlantic and reaching nearly 1,200 miles inland, has the oldest formation of plant life on earth and is virtually unchanged since the Tertiary Era.

The Amazon region is one of nature's last preserves of wildlife, hosting 1,500 species of fish, 250 species of mammals, 15,000 species of insects, and 1,800 birds (including 319 types of hummingbirds). The jungle's more renowned inhabitants — the jaguar, margay, capybara, tapir, wild boar, river dolphin, and anteater; exotic birds such as the mountain cock, morphus eagle, and macaw parrot; reptiles including the anaconda, boa constrictor, alligator (called *jacaré*), and turtles; and fish such as tambaqui, piranha, and electric eel — are usually unseen by the river traveler, but extensive zoos in Manaus and Belém display much of the wildlife in natural environments.

Although the river and jungle represent 18% of Brazil's total area, the region holds only 4% of the country's population. On a river excursion, visitors see occasional homes on stilts or families traveling to nearby towns via dugout canoe. It is not uncommon to find farms as large as 1,235,000 acres where cattle and water buffalo are raised. Introduced to Brazil in the late 19th century, the water buffalo has proved particularly adaptable to the Amazon region due to its resistance to disease and fondness for aquatic vegetation. Here and there, signs of modern technology are creeping into this lazy river scene, and visitors may see mining expeditions in search of iron ore, bauxite, manganese, tin, and oil. The reclusive American billionaire Daniel K. Ludwig made news when he floated a completely self-sufficient factory from Asia up the Amazon to a large tract of the jungle he purchased from the government (and subsequently sold back).

Visitors may sample areas that still are unchanged since Orellana's time, but now facilities and transportation are more modern and convenient, and resorts in major cities along the Amazon offer sophisticated comforts.

A voyage up the Amazon sounds exciting and adventurous and is really the only way to see this mighty river at first hand. But the 6-day excursion from Belém to Manaus includes parts of the river that are so wide that you may not even see the shore, not to mention the area's famed wildlife. You can shorten the trip to 4 days by embarking in Manaus and sailing downstream to Belém, but the boats stay far in the middle of the river in this direction to take advantage of the swift currents.

A recommended way of going is on the government's weekly *ENASA* line (41 Av. Presidente Vargas, Belém; phone: 91-223-3011), diesel passenger boats that also carry some cargo. The *ENASA* boats have first class accommodations, which include a stateroom, bed, three meals a day, and access to the upper decks of the ship. Classe Popular passengers must bring a hammock for sleeping (available in Belém for $6) and be prepared to sandwich between bodies swinging on all sides. *ENASA* also has two catamaran vessels, the *Pará* and the *Amazonas,* offering 138 passengers first class travel between Belém and Manaus. The 4- and 5-day cruises operate year-round. The cruise from

Belém to Manaus (upriver), however, does not include a day's stop at Marajó Island. Boat facilities include air conditioned cabins with bath, lounge, snack bar, nightclub, bar, solarium, pool, and sun deck. The boats are comfortable, not luxurious, and the cost is roughly $500 per person for a double cabin.

If you don't want to wait for an *ENASA* boat, there are sometimes small private boats, such as *Fé em Deus IV* (Faith in God), that take passengers upriver. They are found by asking around the *cais do Porto* (Belém docks) near the *Ver-o-Peso Market* on Travessa de Breves. These smaller boats will take you as far as Santarém, where there are boats just about daily to Manaus. You also can check with the *capitania do porto* (captain of the port), whose office is just off Av. Presidente Vargas near the *ENASA* office downtown. This office can tell you about larger freighters that sometimes take passengers upstream. You will need written permission from the *capitania* to gain access to the pier if you care to do your own soliciting of freighter captains, but beware — you will sample Brazilian bureaucracy at its worst. If you are berthing in less than first class, traveling on one of the smaller private boats is usually more pleasant, with more diverse food and eased restrictions. First class on these smaller boats entitles you to hang your hammock in a cabin, but many prefer the open deck, with its cool evening breezes. Bugs never seem to be a problem, and if a shower comes along, canvas flaps are dropped to close up the sides of the ship. The private boats usually are less crowded, and the mess chefs may even include a few green vegetables in the day's fare. Also, the smaller private boat usually gives you a better opportunity to mix with the local people, who are very friendly if you extend yourself to them.

No matter what class you're in, the day begins at sunrise with *café da manhã* (breakfast). It will be the meals, no matter how uninspired, that define your day, so after breakfast it is best to occupy your time until lunch with books, magazines, chess, a sketch pad, camera, or whatever you fancy. After lunch, most people pass the hottest part of the day in the famous South American institution of a siesta, an afternoon nap, which is an easy habit to acquire when the only sounds are the steady engine, a few birds, and the Amazon swooshing around the boat. After midafternoon coffee, the most pleasant hours of the day are spent watching the water and sky change color. As the sun lowers toward the horizon and the temperature drops, the jungle colors deepen to a dark greenish gray and the sky becomes a pinkish red. With darkness, the air on open decks can be brisk — even in the tropics — so it is best to bring a blanket or sleeping bag for sleeping in hammocks. During the evening, many people form groups for games of dominoes, playing music, drinking, or quiet conversation. By 10 PM most passengers have turned in, and if you are not crowded by nearby hammocks, the gentle swaying of the ship and the Amazon's fresh air provide the perfect sleeping tonic.

During the voyage, the boat will occasionally stop to pick up and discharge passengers. While the ship is never in port long enough for you to go ashore, you will get an opportunity to see a family welcome home a son or daughter from the big city or see a schoolteacher reunited with her students.

*A word about health:* Although malaria is considered a hazard only for those going into the jungle itself, you still should be taking anti-malaria pills as a precaution on a river trip. Aralen is one of the brand names (chloroquine-phosphate, 500 mg) for which you need a prescription. Start taking one pill each week for 5 weeks before entering the area, one every day while you are there, and one each week for 6 weeks after you leave. Though yellow fever shots are not required for Brazil, vaccination 10 days before going to the jungle region is highly recommended. In this region, as in most of Brazil, do not drink unbottled water, and avoid fruits and vegetables that aren't or can't be peeled, such as lettuce, tomatoes, and apples, and don't eat uncooked food. The humid tropical climate is a good breeding ground for hepatitis and dysentery; consult your physician before leaving home.

If you think the complete 5-day ride too much, the trip can be shortened by picking up a boat at Santarém, exactly midway between Belém and Manaus. Santarém, Manaus, and Belém are connected by *Taba, Varig-Cruzeiro,* and *VASP* airlines. If your starting point in Brazil is Manaus, you can fly there directly from North America on *Varig* or *Transbrasil* or from other Latin American cities by *Air France, Avianca, Transbrasil, Varig-Cruzeiro,* and a number of other carriers.

**BELÉM:** At the mouth of the mighty Amazon River, this city of 1.12 million is the recipient of all the gifts of the jungle and perhaps the best representative of this area. Eighty miles (128 km) from the open sea, Belém is on the southern side of the river as it surrounds Ilha de Marajó before pouring into the Atlantic. The Portuguese founded the city a few days after *Christmas* in 1616 on the feast of *Our Lady of Bethlehem.* The name Belém is Portuguese for Bethlehem.

In the midst of tropical foliage, the city boasts white colonial buildings with red tile roofs, tree-filled public squares, scraggly buzzards in place of pigeons, and the leisurely pace characteristic of most towns in the north of Brazil. Only 1½° south of the equator, the heat and the humidity slow most people down, and showers are almost a certainty every day, occurring with such regularity that people in the city often arrange their appointments around the afternoon shower.

Belém is the capital of the state of Pará and the outlet for all the produce from the Amazon. In port you will find freighters loaded with lumber, nuts, dozens of different fruits, jute, fish, cattle, minerals for industry, and orchids. Away from the slow pace of the public plazas, the port is thriving with constant activity as oceangoing vessels pass small fishing boats with multicolored sails. One of the most intriguing sights is the largest outdoor market in Brazil, *Ver-o-Peso* (on Av. Castilho França), where stalls four and five deep offer fish and produce, flowers, meat, fruit, and cooked food. There are also hammocks, crocodile teeth, dried boa constrictor heads, sea horses, shell rosaries, handmade clothing, pottery, and charms made by practitioners of *macumba,* Brazil's version of voodoo, guaranteed to solve any love or financial problem. Come early in the morning and plan to spend a good part of the day poking around the blocks of amazing wares, mostly agricultural.

The central plaza, Praça da República, bordered on one side by Avenida Presidente Vargas, is shaded by mango trees and dotted with gazebos, lush plants, and flowers. The square is the gathering place for old men sharing stories, young mothers playing with children, lovers strolling, and workers eating during lunch hour. To plan a walking tour from here, contact PARATUR, the regional government tourism bureau (Praça Kennedy; phone: 91-224-9633), for a map of the city and suggested tours; there is also an adjoining craft shop.

One of the relics to survive the rubber boom that boosted this area around the turn of the century is the white marble *Teatro Paz* on the plaza. This wonderfully restored, interesting theater is one of the largest in Brazil and still hosts classical and folkloric concerts and ballet and visiting theater troupes.

Continuing up Avenida Presidente Vargas toward the port, you will find street vendors with interesting and inexpensive specialties of Bahia. There is a delicious shrimp dish called *vatapá* made with coconut milk; *moqueca,* a fish stew cooked in palm oil; and *empadinhas de camarão,* a fried shrimp pastry. At just about every corner, vendors of *sorvete* and *sucos,* ice cream and juices made from the dozens of fruits native to this area, offer a variety of unusual and delicious concoctions, such as *bacuri, açai, manga, maracujá, goiaba, graviola, guanabana,* and *cupuaçu.*

The *Museu Emílio Goeldi* (Emílio Goeldi Anthropology Museum) and its adjoining zoo (376 Av. Magalhães Barata; phone: 91-224-9233) are a must to understand the profusion of wildlife and flora that exists in the Amazon jungle. The museum has an exhibit of Indian clothing, pottery, and weapons and graphic accounts of the various tribes that inhabited the Amazon basin. Next to the zoo, which houses a good selection of jungle animals, is the Paraiso das Tartarugas, where 3,000 turtles, from hatchlings to old-timers, live in natural environments. The zoo itself houses most of the animals that are hard to catch a glimpse of even when traveling on the river, such as anacondas, tapirs, exotic birds, alligators, and several varieties of monkeys. Closed Mondays.

Some of the most exotic food in South America is available in the towns along the Amazon, so if you want to sample one of the regional delicacies, such as turtle in its many varieties, the restaurants of Belém are an excellent place to start. There are turtle legs, turtle sauce, minced turtle meat, and even pancakes and a dessert made of turtle eggs. *Lá em Casa* (247 Av. Gov. José Malcher; phone: 91-223-1212) serves several of these regional dishes at reasonable prices. Seafood is particularly good and quite inexpensive in Belém (more so than in the rest of Brazil), and there is a wide selection at *O Outro,* right next door to *Lá em Casa* (same address and phone number), considered the best in town.

There are a number of excursions from Belém that shouldn't be missed if you have time. A 5-hour ride on an *ENASA* boat (41 Av. Presidente Vargas; phone: 91-223-3011) brings you to the largest island in the Amazon estuary, Switzerland-size Ilha de Marajó. It is home to great herds of water buffalo and zebu, thousands of colorful birds, fishing villages with lovely waterfront homes, and large-scale cattle ranches *(fazendas).* Visit the island during the dry season, July to December, and stay at one of the ranches that accepts guests. One of the nicest is that of Eduardo de Castro Ribeiro, whose family owns *Fazenda Bom Jardim.* (Contact him at 882 Av. Presidente Vargas, Belém, Pará, CEP 66000; phone: 91-224-2111 or 91-228-0011.) The ranch house accommodations are comfortable, and his wife is a superb cook. Both the air taxi from Belém and the boat also land at the town of Soure, which has a very good hotel with a pool, *Pousada Marajuara* (9 Rua 4 Marajó; phone: 91-741-1287). The town of Macapá lies directly on the equator, and here you can ride water buffalo with the locals and climb 16th-century Portuguese fortifications that still seem to protect the town. About 3 hours from Belém by bus is Ilha do Mosqueira. Attached to the mainland by a causeway, it is another jungle island with good beaches, but Marajó is more unspoiled.

The town of Salinópolis, 4 hours by bus from Belém on the Atlantic, has the closest beach of any note, with small beachfront restaurants that feature inexpensive regional specialties.

**En Route from Belém** – The first 2 days of boat travel from Belém will be the most interesting for those who want an idea of how the river supports and nourishes its people. In this section of the Amazon basin, appropriately called the Narrows, the boat weaves through a labyrinth of tiny islets, passing close to the jungle shore and frequently encountering the small fishing boats that bring their catch to the port of Belém. When the Narrows gives way to the Amazon's full girth, flat-topped mountains appear in the distance, as well as small villages that sit in jungle clearings, such as Monte Alegre. At the point where the clear waters of the Rio Tapajos meet the muddy Amazon (an interesting natural phenomenon, though not as dramatic as the meeting of the Rio Solimões and the Rio Negro near

Manaus), you have reached the exact midpoint of your journey, the town of Santarém. Passengers on the *ENASA* boat will not have time to disembark, but if you are doing the trip in two or three stages, Santarém is worth a visit.

**SANTARÉM:** This city of 240,000 was settled in 1865 by an odd mixture of Portuguese and residents of South Carolina and Tennessee who fled the Confederacy when slavery was abolished. Brazil permitted slavery for only 23 years after the Southerners' arrival, but they still prospered and helped build a town that has become an important trading center. It now serves as a supply center for miners, gold prospectors, rubber tappers, Brazil nut gatherers, and the jute and lumber industries. Several bars display the Confederate flag, and you still occasionally meet the settlers' descendants, who mixed with the multiracial Brazilians and have names like José Carlos Calhoun. Their graves can be visited in the town cemetery.

The city itself lacks much of the sophistication of Belém and Manaus, but therein lies its charm. Remaining distinctively small-townish with its winding unpaved back streets, friendly slow-paced people, and remnants of colonial architecture, Santarém's center is its bustling port, with small fishing boats and dugout canoes delivering a day's catch or produce from one of the interior settlements, both jostling with the large oceangoing cargo ships loading fruit and huge balls of crude gray rubber. Wooden signs and a roving loudspeaker proclaim the next departure for Manaus as vendors shout the lowest prices of bananas and fish. From the port you can look at the river and see the blue, clear waters of the Tapajos, which is 15 miles wide at Santarém, joining the Amazon in a parallel journey before they merge a mile downstream.

You can sail on the tributaries of the clear Tapajos for a breathtaking look at the jungle, which hugs the shore in this area. Your hotel should be able to inform you about boat trips up this river. Prices vary.

*Mercado Modelo* is the open-air market in the center of town. While not as extensive as the one in Belém, it is still worth a visit to see the local produce and the people socializing. Along the eastern sea wall, a walkway with benches and flowering shade trees is a good place to relax after lunch during the hottest part of the day.

Restaurants in Santarém are much simpler than those in Belém and Manaus, but you can eat fresh fish at *Mascote* (10 Praça do Pescador; phone: 91-522-1997), or try the Japanese menu at *Lumi* (1683 Av. Cuiabá; phone: 91-522-2174). Good food also can be found at the *Tropical* hotel (4120 Av. Mendonça; phone: 91-522-1533; see *Best en Route*).

Santarém was put on the map at the end of 1991 when an international team of archaeologists discovered fragments in a nearby village of the earliest pottery found in the Western Hemisphere. The shards are believed to be some 7,000 or 8,000 years old and disprove the current theory that the tropical rain forest's resources were too scant to have sustained human settlement.

**En Route from Santarém** – On this last 3-day stretch of river travel to Manaus, the ship passes several tiny villages, stopping for 15 to 30 minutes to pick up and discharge passengers. The only city of any note along this route is Obidos, a town of less than 30,000, sitting on the red banks of the Amazon. On the boat's regular schedule, you will pass the town at night (there is not much to see even if you are awake). Finally the boat swings onto the Rio Negro, the largest of the Amazon's tributaries, and docks 10 miles (16 km) beyond in Manaus.

**MANAUS:** In the very heart of the Amazon region, this city of 1.1 million is in the midst of its second boom. Turn-of-the-century buildings, remnants of the once-lucrative rubber trade, sit beside the modern high-rises indicative of present commercial operations in this Free Trade Zone.

Manaus's history is a classic story of a boom-and-bust one-crop economy. Rubber, made from a milky juice that flows from the *Hevea Brasilensis* tree, was known to the explorers accompanying Columbus, who saw Indians playing with hollow rubber balls in Haiti. In the early 1800s, with Charles Macintosh's invention of the raincoat and the development of shoes that could withstand the snows of European winters, rubber became an important Brazilian export. But the rubber boom really began in earnest when Goodyear discovered the process of vulcanization and car and bicycle wheels could be made consistently pliable.

Because the Amazon forest was the only place to get the rubber, foreigners flocked to the area and made enormous fortunes overnight. The residents grew fabulously rich and built a lavish jungle city that competed architecturally and culturally with major European capitals. They brought marble from Italy, tiles from Portugal, and the best china from England and constructed huge mansions in the jungle, a few of which still stand between the skyscrapers in the hilly section of the city. But the greatest remaining monument to this era is the grand, ostentatious opera house, *Teatro do Amazonas*. Dozens of foreign artists and architects were brought to the jungle in 1892 to create a splendid building. Italian marble, English porcelain, French furniture, and wrought iron were imported to adorn the elaborate structure. The ceiling and walls of the lobby were decorated with mirrors and murals of harp-playing angels and Amazon Indians, and the huge dome was painted in gold leaf with green and yellow tiles. Besides the $10 million spent on construction, the city paid exorbitant sums to lure world-famous performers such as Sarah Bernhardt and Pavlova. Opening night in 1896 saw Manaus society at its most resplendent, the ladies dressed in Paris gowns and the men sweltering in woolen tailcoats. And then, with the end of the rubber boom, the opera went bust and the building stood empty. Remodeling of the opera house began in 1962 and continued off and on until it finally reopened in March 1990, 2 days after President Collor's inauguration. But just 7 days later, the theater fell victim to Collor's austerity measures, and it closed once again. Today there are sporadic performances. (For current information, call 92-234-3525.) It is open to the public for tours Tuesdays through Sundays from 9 AM to 6 PM. The *Teatro do Amazonas* is at Praça São Sebastião.

Manaus lost its monopoly on rubber in the early 1900s, when rubber tree seeds were smuggled out of Brazil to Ceylon. The effective cultivation of these trees, lower taxes, a lack of health hazards, and better access to shipping lanes made the Ceylonese rubber a quick success and vastly diminished the Amazon market. Brazil was producing 88% of the world's rubber in 1910, but 3 years later it exported less than half. Fortunes faded, the Europeans left, and the city survived on what could be taken from the river and jungle.

As capital of the state of Amazonas, Manaus has become a major northern center of commerce, exporting Brazil nuts, black pepper, jute, rubber, and lumber. The city's second boom occurred in 1965, when the government decided that if Manaus were to become a thriving city once more, something was needed to encourage industry and money to flow back in. It was decided to turn the city into a free port, with generous tax incentives and duty-free trading. Subsequent years have seen Manaus transformed. There are now hundreds of large and small shops packed with foreign merchandise — clothes, watches, cameras, television sets, air conditioners, boats, motorcycles, cars — as well as a host of locally assembled electronic goods made with imported components, and almost anything else you can imagine.

Manaus's harbor is laden with oceangoing vessels that sail up the river some 1,000 miles from the Atlantic, bringing food and other staples for the residents (everything here is very, very expensive due to the high cost of transportation). The city's most fascinating sight is the floating market, where each day people deliver fish, fruit, vegetables, and crafts to the vendors' stalls via dugout canoe. The city also boasts the world's largest floating port, a massive concrete pier constructed in 1906 by British engineers. A few blocks from these floating structures is the *Mercado Municipal* (City Market; on Rua dos Bares), a remnant of the rubber era. Its entire structural framework was imported from Europe, and architecturally it is one of Brazil's most unusual indoor markets. In an Art Deco setting is an exotic array of medicinal herbs, caged exotic birds and animals, regional farm produce, arts and crafts, and many varieties of fish. You should come early in the day to see it at its best and plan to spend some time walking around the docks.

The jungle creeps up on the city. To get an idea of the plant and animal life around you, plan to explore the museums, botanical gardens, and zoos. The *Museu do Indio* (Indian Museum; Av. 7 de Setembro and Rua Duque de Caxias; phone: 92-234-1422) has authentic Indian costumes, weapons, crafts, and art objects dating from the discovery of Manaus. Closed Sundays. The *Parque Zoolólogico do CIGS* (CIGS Zoological Garden), on the outskirts of town (Estrada da Ponta Negra; phone: 92-238-4149), houses 300 animals, including jaguars, tapirs, monkeys, snakes, and varieties of parrots. Turislândia, a 20-minute drive from downtown in the Aleixo District, features groves of Brazil nut trees and cocoa, rubber, and guaraná trees. One of the most natural settings in the Amazon region in which to observe the ecological system is at Salvadore Lake, where a reserve is open to the public. The reserve, about 5 miles (8 km) from the *Tropical Hotel Manaus* (see *Best en Route*) and operated by it, is near the Rio Negro and has an exotic variety of Amazon animals, such as tapirs, jaguars, boars, monkeys, alligators, turtles, snakes, and parrots, which can be seen from floating pavilions. The reserve has a picnic area and hiking along a forest trail about 2 miles (3 km) to the Guedes River narrows. Tours can be arranged through the *Tropical Travel Agency* at the *Tropical* hotel (phone: 92-238-5757).

Some unusual handmade artifacts can be found in Manaus's gift shops. One shop worth visiting is *Casa de Beija-Flor* (House of the Hummingbird, 224 Rua Quinto Bocaiuva). The English-speaking owner has stocked his store with Indian weapons, masks, crafts, piranhas, rings, and tropical fish. *FUNAI*, an Indian organization of the Brazilian government, runs a small store (957 Rua Major Gabriel; phone: 92-232-4890). The store sells handicrafts made by Indians from the interior.

A sight not to be missed is the "Meeting of the Waters" boat trip, one of the most memorable experiences on the Amazon. About 12 miles from the port of Manaus, the Rio Solimões and the blackish Rio Negro, both about 2 miles wide at this point, converge with terrific force, causing whirlpools of black and brown swirling water. These two waters flow side by side for more than 5 miles before mixing, because of their differing velocity and density. Eventually they become a muddy brown, or the *café com leite* (coffee with milk) color of the Amazon. Boating excursions can be arranged through most of the main hotels in Manaus. A popular trip is on the 26-berth *Tuna* that has 3- and 6-day cruises on the upper Rio Negro out of Manaus (phone: 21-240-6785 in Rio de Janeiro). Overnight trips to the ever-growing number of jungle lodges can be booked through any US travel agency. Among the best and the most popular lodges are the *Amazon Lodge* (phone: 92-232-1454; in Rio de Janeiro, 21-235-2840), *Amazon Village* (phone: 92-232-1454; in Rio de Janeiro, 21-235-2840); *Araiú Jungle Tower* (phone: 92-234-7308 or 92-233-3825); *Pousadas dos Guanavenas* (phone: 92-236-2352); and *Tepiri Pousada* (phone: 92-234-8639).

Manaus has the most interesting and best organized hunting and fishing facilities in the Amazon region. *Tucanaré* are caught by trolling from outboard-powered canoes. Piraiba, pirarara, surubim, and dorado weighing up to 180 pounds require heavy tackle and may be caught in these areas. Most tour companies in Manaus offer fishing excursions; ask at the tour desk of any of the major hotels.

There are a few notable dishes in Manaus, such as *mixira* (manatee meat dish); *pirarucú* and *tucanaré* (river fish); *tacacá*, a snack food prepared with shrimp, tapioca, jambu herb, and *tucupi* sauce; and *maniçoba*, similar in taste to the Brazilian favorite *feijoada*, made from pork, calves' feet, animal innards, bacon, sausage fat, vegetables, and beans. Restaurants here are quite expensive, but more plentiful than in Belém or Santarém. *Piauí* (202 Rua Dr. Moreira; phone: 92-234-2133) specializes in fish from the region, as does *Panorama* (199 Blvd. Rio Negro; phone: 92-624-4646), where you should try the *tucanaré* and *tambagui*, as well as the *creme de cupuaçu*, a tropical fruit dessert. Ask the cab driver for *Panorama* by the river; it has a view, while its sister restaurant of the same name is on a loud, busy street corner. If you're set on barbecued meats, try *Roda Viva* (1005A Av. Ajuricaba, Cachoeirinha; phone: 92-232-2687) or *Bufalo* (628 Av. Joaquim Nabuco; phone: 92-234-8154). The best food in Manaus, however, is still found in the restaurants of the *Tropical* hotel.

For further information about Manaus and the state of Amazonas, contact the tourist board, EMAMTUR, 379 Av. Taruma (phone: 92-234-5503).

## BEST EN ROUTE

Thanks to the government's program to promote tourism in Brazil, and in particular, what it calls "ecological tourism," tourist facilities are improving. In major cities, such as Belém, Santarém, and Manaus, visitors will find a few high-caliber and moderate hotels and many pensions. Prices are generally higher here due to the high cost of transporting food, materials, and personnel to this remote part of the country. In hotels categorized as expensive, expect to pay $100 or more a night for a double room with a private bath, air conditioning, a television set, radio, restaurant, pool, hairdresser, and nightclubs; moderate, from $50 to $90 per night for a private shower, air conditioning, and TV set; and inexpensive, below $40 per night for hotels ranging in quality from the bare minimum to adequate, and generally having no restaurants, bars, or TV sets.

New hotel projects are constantly underway in Brazil, especially in the Amazon area. Expected to open in spring 1994 is the lavish *Maksoud Plaza* in Manaus.

### BELÉM

**Equatorial Palace** – Modern, first class and renovated back in 1980: 211 rooms with refrigerators and air conditioning, pool, tennis courts, nightclub, restaurant, and snack bar. 612 Av. Braz de Aguiar (phone: 91-241-2000). Expensive.

**Hilton Internacional Belém** – The most luxurious establishment (360 rooms) in Belém, pampers guests with satellite TV, a swimming pool with hydromassage, sauna, exercise room, hair salon, barbershop, and coffee shop. 882 Av. Presidente Vargas (phone: 91-223-6500). Expensive.

**Novotel Belém** – Modern and near the river, its 121 rooms are fully air conditioned, with wheelchair access, pool and sauna, boating facilities, restaurant, and meeting space for 300. 4804 Av. Bernardo Sayao (phone: 91-229-8011). Expensive.

**Excelsior Grão Pará** – Offers 140 air conditioned, well-decorated rooms overlooking Praça da República, excellent dining, a bar, hairdresser, private telephone, and a TV set in every room. 718 Av. Presidente Vargas (phone: 91-222-3255). Moderate.

**Vanja** – A downtown hostelry — 105 air conditioned rooms with TV sets. It has dining facilities, a bar, beauty salon, and barber. 1164 Rua Benjamin Constant (phone: 91-222-6688). Inexpensive.

### MACAPÁ

**Novotel** – All 76 rooms in this property have air conditioning, television, and mini-bar. There's a restaurant, bar, swimming pool, tennis, volleyball, and soccer. 17 Av. Eng. Azarias Neto (phone: 96-223-1144). Moderate.

### ILHA DO MOSQUEIRO

**Chapeu Virado** – Small and directly on the beach of Mosqueiro, with nicely decorated rooms, each with private bath. Praia do Virado (phone: 91-771-1202). Inexpensive.

**Farol** – Another small hotel on the beach, it has 6 double rooms with private baths and 12 without. Praia do Farol (phone: 91-771-1219). Inexpensive.

**Murubira** – Across the street from the beach, this place also has a pool and a fairly good restaurant. Av. Beira-Mar (phone: 91-771-1256). Inexpensive.

## SANTARÉM

**Santarém Palace** – If the *Tropical* is full, this 48-room hostelry is an acceptable alternative. 726 Av. Rui Barbosa (phone: 91-522-5285). Moderate.

**Tropical Santarém** – The best in the city and hard to beat for luxury in the Amazon region. The 120 air conditioned rooms all have balconies. Facilities include a circular tiled pool, a nightclub, gamerooms, a movie theater, an indoor-outdoor restaurant, and a houseboat cruiser for day or overnight trips. 4120 Av. Mendonça Furtado (phone: 91-522-1533); contact *Varig* for reservations. Moderate.

**Uirapuru** – A clean, modest place with 23 rooms, 15 of which are air conditioned. 140 Av. Adriano Pimentel (phone: 91-522-5881). Inexpensive.

## MANAUS

**Novotel Manaus** – Adequate, 168-room establishment, 10 minutes from the city center; air conditioning and refrigerator in rooms, pool, and restaurant with dining terrace. Popular with business travelers who want to be near Manaus's commercial area. 4 Av. Mandii, Grande Rótula (phone: 92-237-1211). Expensive.

**Taj Mahal Continental** – Located across from the *Teatro do Amazonas,* this recently opened property has 170 rooms, including 28 suites (the 2 presidential suites overlook the opera house). The top floor houses a revolving restaurant, the *Noor-e-Jahan,* and a swimming pool. Other facilities include a sauna, steamroom, nightclub, discotheque, piano bar, beauty salon, travel agency, duty-free boutique, 6 meeting rooms, and an auditorium. 741 Av. Getúlio Vargas (phone: 92-233-8900; fax: 92-233-5125). Expensive.

**Tropical Hotel Manaus** – The largest and one of the most exclusive resorts in South America, with 616 air conditioned rooms and suites with colonial furnishings of natural wood. The grounds, on the Rio Negro, are beautifully landscaped, with 40,000 orchid plants, tropical patios, 2 swimming pools, a natural zoo, shops, a floating river bar, and cruisers for jungle river trips. On the beach of Ponta Negra, 12 miles (19 km) from downtown (phone: 92-238-5757); or contact *Varig* (phone: toll-free, 800-468-2744; in Brazil, 92-234-1116). Expensive.

**Amazonas** – The property, while nothing special, has 182 air conditioned rooms, a bar, and a restaurant. It has a pool; it is near shops and docks downtown. Praça Adalberto Valle (phone: 92-234-7679). Moderate.

# The Northeast

The Northeast of Brazil — or *O Nordeste,* as it's called in Portuguese — is composed of nine states: Ceará, Rio Grande do Norte, Piauí, Paraíba, Pernambuco, Bahia, Alagoas, Sergipe, and Maranhão. Together they form the bulge of Brazil's coastline that includes its most easterly point, which is the continental spot closest to Africa in the Western Hemisphere. This geographical fact has profoundly influenced the culture of certain sections of the Northeast.

An area of over 1 million square miles harboring one-third of Brazil's population, the Northeast has been and still is the scene of great joy and heartbreak for Brazil. Over 200 out of every 1,000 babies in the Northeast die in their first year; life expectancy is 50 years; the illiteracy rate ranges from 33.8% in urban areas to 66.2% in rural areas. These are overall statistics, though. The Northeast is actually made up of two distinct regions, the Northeast coast and the *sertão,* which have developed separately and unequally due to one factor: rainfall. The 150-mile-wide Northeast coast is bordered by the Atlantic on the east and by Brazil's Great Escarpment on the west, extending from Ilhéus in the southern part of Bahia to Fortaleza in Ceará. The early Portuguese sailors quickly realized that its rich soil and humid tropical climate tempered by ocean breezes would be ideal for the cultivation of sugarcane, as indeed it was. The crop flourished, and by the mid-1600s, Portugal's colony was a power on the world's sugar market. The areas of Olinda in Pernambuco and Salvador in Bahia became especially prosperous as a result, and great individual fortunes were made by the end of the century.

This wealth attracted the Dutch, who took advantage of Portugal's temporary domination by Spain in the 1630s to invade and hold the area. By 1654, the Portuguese, who had once again gained control of their portion of the Iberian Peninsula, succeeded in driving the Dutch from the region. Unfortunately for the Northeast, the invaders who had been expelled carried the knowledge they had acquired during their occupation to the Antilles. There, along with Jewish technicians who had been driven from Brazil during the Inquisition, they started their own sugarcane plantations. By the 1750s, the sugar grown on these farms, together with the English and French West Indian production, cut into Brazil's sugar markets. While the crop is still important today, it has been in a slow decline for the last 200 years.

The societies that grew up along the Northeast coast can be compared to those that formed around the southern cotton plantations in the US. Large tracts of land were often presented to favorites of the Portuguese crown as rewards for helping rid the area of bandits. Within the family-owned sugarcane plantations *(fazendas)* a semi-feudal world developed, complete with aristocracy, slaves from Africa, and free laborers and artisans who were dependent on the *fazendeiro* for protection. These semi-independent economic units scattered along the coast usually consisted of the *fazendeiro*'s mansion, shacks for the slaves, small houses and shops for the artisans and laborers, and the ever-present church. Additionally, each *fazenda* usually had its own sugar refinery, cattle, and crops. In these closed communities, incest and miscegenation were a matter of course. Paralleling the Virginia plantations in the US, the *fazendas* produced many of the statesmen of the day.

By the end of the 19th century, the family-owned *fazenda* began to lose its place as the foremost economic institution of the Northeast. With the development of large steam-powered refinery equipment, the smaller farmers, whose profits had been slipping anyway, found themselves being usurped by the large concerns that eventually became the huge corporations that today control sugar production.

Remnants of the wealth that sugar brought to the region still can be found in the *fazendas* with their abandoned sugar mills that dot the countryside and in the magnificent baroque-tiled buildings that adorn Salvador and Recife. Probably the most enduring and colorful vestiges of the sugar era are the surviving elements of African culture that arrived with the slaves, brought by the thousands to work in the sugarcane fields. Slavery in Brazil, while perhaps not as brutal as that in North America, was certainly more widespread. Africa's presence can be felt not only in the areas surrounding Salvador and Recife, where huge slave markets existed, but in the African-rooted samba that is popular throughout Brazil. In Rio de Janeiro, *macumba,* a fusion of West African voodoo elements with Christianity, is widely practiced. Two cousins of *macumba* that have many adherents are *candomblé* in Bahia and *xangô* in Pernambuco.

Also from Africa is *capoeira,* which in Angola was originally a type of one-on-one combat and today is a dance performed in the midst of a clapping circle of onlookers in streets all over the Northeast. Planters forbade the original kicking duel, which could permanently injure one of the contestants. The participants, however, learned how to mask their battles. When the *fazendeiro* came too close during a *capoeira* duel, the combatants would pull their kicks up short of landing and brush their legs just over the opponent's head, feigning harmless exercise. This disguised form of combat has evolved into the high leg-sweeping, hip-spinning, tumbling ballet that is performed to the twangy beat of the *berimbau,* a one-stringed African instrument.

African cuisine has become a tasty, permanent fixture in the Northeast. The following dishes are most characteristic of the state of Bahia, which has the most slave descendants in Brazil: *vatapá,* a creamy shrimp dish made with *dendê,* an oil from a certain type of palm tree; *acarajé,* a deep-fried shrimp and bean batter mixture served with extremely hot sauce; *carurú,* okra with fish or shrimp and minced herbs and spices; *abará,* banana leaves surrounding a stuffing of bean paste, peppers, and palm oil; *xinxim,* a chicken ragout; and *cocada,* a sweet made from coconuts and sugar. Cholesterol crises, all!

Oral traditions are also rich with African folklore — stories of goblins, spells and fantastic journeys. The hand-carved, sacred wood sculptures make you wish you had some extra room in your suitcase.

The area in southern Bahia surrounding Ilhéus is considered a subregion of the Northeast coast. It had its own single-crop boom — cacao. For many years the dense forests and hostile Indians kept settlers away, but by the late 1800s, migrants from drought-stricken regions of the Northeast had cleared land for small farms. Cacao transplanted from the Amazon did not do particularly well, but by 1907, with the introduction of sturdy Ceylonese cacao and the wide markets provided by the burgeoning chocolate industry in the US and Europe, a major boom was under way.

A violent era followed, with clan wars, assassinations, and false documents used to usurp precious cacao lands. Brazil's gifted Jorge Amado, born in Ilhéus in 1912, has written several novels of the cacao days, including *Cacao* and *São Jorge dos Ilhéus.* In the latter, he describes the city in its heyday:

> Ilhéus and the cacao zone swam in gold, bathed in champagne, slept with French ladies from Rio de Janeiro. At the Trianon, the city's chicest cabaret, Colonel Maneca Dantas lit cigarettes with 500,000-reis bills, repeating the gesture of all the country's rich *fazendeiros* during the previous rises in coffee, rubber, cotton, and sugar prices.

The most precious and certainly the most famous of Amado's treatments of the epoch is in *Gabriela, Clove and Cinnamon,* which portrays the end of the violent days and the beginning of "civilization" in Ilhéus through a rich cast of characters headed by the splendid Gabriela, a mulatto migrant from the drought region, played by Brazilian star Sonia Braga in the movie version.

Large *fazendas* developed here, as they did in the north, but with a difference. The resident slaves were replaced by mobile migrant workers from other sections of the Northeast, who left when the harvest was in. A mercantile elite developed among the *fazendeiros,* known as "colonels," who passed on their great estates to their heirs.

But soil erosion and foreign competition put an end to Ilhéus's glory. Prices fell and land changed hands as exporters bought farms from ruined *fazendeiros.* Today, Ilhéus has only its old palatial mansions to attest to the era.

Along the shores from Ilhéus to Natal and then on to Fortaleza and São Luís are some of the most varied, beautiful, and isolated beaches in South America (and perhaps the world). You can pick from white sand, red sand, yellow sand, flat shores that let you walk out a mile, steep coconut-studded dunes, built-up beaches with modern facilities, desolate expanses where the only footprints you see are your own, pounding surf or little laughing waves. If you care to get away from the more "civilized" beaches that surround the larger cities, you can head for an outlying fishing village and enjoy a more down-home surfside scene. Adventurous travelers can put on a broad-brimmed hat, pack some supplies, and start hiking in one direction or another from a fishing village down miles of uninhabited beach. Eventually, one day or the next, you will hit another village. Along the way is ample opportunity for uninhibited abandonment. Watch out for the sun, though. In many areas of the Northeast, the ultraviolet rays are so intense from 11 AM to 3 PM that all but the minimum exposure can be dangerous.

## THE SERTÃO

Things have not been nearly as cheery in this drought-plagued region of Brazil's Northeast, sometimes referred to as the "other" Northeast. It is an arid land of low mesas and sloping terrain spotted with scrub forest called *caatinga,* thorny bushes, and cactus beginning 150 miles from the coast. The *sertão,* which means "hinterland," is often referred to as *o polígono das secas* ("the polygon of drought") in government studies due to the rough geometric shape of the region.

Rainfall here is completely unpredictable, but when it does arrive, violent torrents run quickly through the eroded soil, providing minimal relief. Droughts run in cycles and can last from 1 to 5 years. During these periods, when the last drops of water have disappeared and the scrawny cattle that form the fragile economic backbone of the region have died off, there are mass migrations to the Amazon Valley, the mountains, or the coast to find relief and work. Over the years, these unfortunate migrants have been brutally exploited upon their arrival in more prosperous areas.

A typical migration will mean the movement of from 15,000 to 20,000 people, but the numbers can swell. During the devastating drought from 1877 to 1879, over 100,000 *sertanejos* were forced to leave their homes and as many as 500,000 died. In *Barren Lives,* Graciliano Ramos writes with stunning vividness of one destitute farmer and his family during the drought of 1938 — a story of their journey to nowhere. This book was made into a classic Brazilian film.

Today, the Northeast migrant often is recruited as a laborer for the great building boom in the south, especially in Rio and São Paulo. For 2 to 3 years he will leave his family and head for the big city, where he lives and eats in a shed right on the job site and is paid from 35¢ to 50¢ per hour, depending on how skilled he is. He hopes that at the end of his job he will have something to bring back to his family in the north.

Strangely enough, with all the adversity of this region, the *sertanejo* still seems to love his home. When the drought ends, he can once again be found returning to the *sertão,* which has the highest rural population density in Brazil.

The *vaqueiro,* a hearty, horse-riding, dust-covered cowboy shrouded in worn leather, is the economic mainstay of the *sertão.* He usually tends the cattle herds for an absentee landlord. His life is often seminomadic, and, as is true of many of the people of the region, he is usually a squatter on the land that he does occupy. The *vaqueiro* probably does some farming to feed his family, and when he is not doing that or tending the herds, he will be collecting *carnaúba* and *licuri,* which are a source of wax, and *oiticica,* used in the production of paint and varnish, from local trees.

The history of the *sertão* is similar in some respects to the holdups (or "bangie-bangie," as Brazilians like to call it) of the American Wild West. Bandits roamed the region as hired guns for the *fazendeiros* or robbed the gold and diamonds transported through the *sertão* from the mines in Minas Gerais.

These bandits, who sensed the inequality between the landowners and the landless, were an early breed of South American revolutionary. Like Robin Hood, they were transformed into legendary figures. The most famous of these was Virgulino Ferreira da Silva, better known as *Lampião* (Lightning), who, from 1920 until he was killed in 1938, tore through the countryside stealing from merchants and giving amply to charities while urging the people to wake up to what was happening around them.

In this land of suffering and uncertainty, the people often have embraced a messianic leader to help them through troubled times. The village of Canudos, under the direction of its "savior" Antônio Conselheiro, battled the federal government for years in a struggle for secession that ended finally in its crushing defeat in 1896. This struggle has been described effectively by Euclides de Cunha in *Rebellion in the Backlands.*

Another popular figure at the turn of the century was Padre Cicero in Juazeiro do Norte. Even though he had been excommunicated by the church, he had 50,000 followers when he tried unsuccessfully to take over the state of Pernambuco.

More recently, in the early 1960s, peasant leagues were formed under the leadership of Francisco Julião. These groups took possession of some Northeast lands by legal expropriation and helped the peasants pay their debts. Sensing a threat in the growing political awareness that the poor gained from their exposure to the leagues, the government has moved to placate the people by creating an economic development program called SUDENE. Various projects of SUDENE, such as the construction of dams and hydroelectric plants, have been started to provide relief and alleviate some of the devastating effects of drought.

Other books that give some historical perspective on the region are *The Devil in the Backlands,* by João Guimarães Rosa; *Death in the Northeast,* by Josue de Castro; and *Sharecroppers of the Sertão,* by Allen W. Johnson.

Because the *sertão* is so severe an area and probably of more interest to the sociologist or anthropologist than the casual traveler, our tour will primarily follow the more pleasant route, along the sands of the Northeast coast. The roads in this region (BR-101, 116, 222, 343), generally two-lane blacktops, are by far the best found in the more remote areas of South America. Travel is almost exclusively via buses, which are at least as comfortable in Brazil as any you will find in the US. And though not all are air conditioned, you usually can travel at night, when the air is cool. There is the occasional inconvenience caused by a washed-out bridge, especially in the midst of the rainy season. This may require putting your bus on a barge to ford the river or taking a potholed detour on a dirt road. The journey begins in Ilhéus.

**ILHÉUS:** With a population of 146,000, this city lies 287 miles (459 km) south of Salvador. As noted above, its history is rich, but its present state is not particularly glorious. The beautiful beaches and tours to the abandoned cacao *fazendas* in the countryside make it a nice place for a short visit.

**En Route from Ilhéus** – Heading northwest, you soon pass Itabuna (pop. 150,000), the trading center for the cacao region. From there, take the newer BR-101 rather than the Rio-Bahia Highway, passing through some magnificent elevated countryside of Brazil's Great Escarpment, with villages that still retain a colonial flair, such as São Felix, Cruz das Almas, and Cachoeira. Feira de Santana is 20 miles (32 km) beyond Cachoeira and 72 miles (115 km) northwest of Salvador. Try to arrive here for the Monday market, which is quite colorful and offers some excellent leather handicrafts and other native products. There is also a handicrafts fair at the *Centro de Abastecimento,* every day except Sundays from 7 AM to 7 PM. Continue north across Bahia's border into the tiny state of Sergipe and stop off in Aracaju, 221 miles (354 km) north of Salvador.

**ARACAJU:** The capital of Sergipe, Aracaju has a population of 400,000. While this symmetrical city has no great tourist attractions, it is a good base from which to explore some wonderful nearby beaches. Offshore oil rigs can be seen from the town's waterfront and are just a part of the industry that has been attracted to the region through financial incentives. Restaurants here are simple, but you can't go wrong with seafood. One of the best in town is *O Miguel* (340 Rua Antônio Alves, Atalaia Velha; phone: 79-223-1530) as well as the *Adega do Antônio* (235 Rua José Sotero; phone: 79-222-6844).

**En Route from Aracaju** – Continuing on BR-101 on the way to Maceió, you cross the Rio São Francisco between Propria and Porto Real do Colegio. From Maceió, via Palmeira dos Indios — or in a bit more complicated fashion from Penedo, a nice little town 37 miles (59 km) east of Propria off BR-101 — the Falls of Paulo Alfonso on the river can be reached by bus and boat.

**FOZ OF PAULO AFONSO:** Upstream on the Rio São Francisco, this set of four falls cascades 260 feet and is separated by spires of boulders, a very spectacular sight. Centuries of gushing water have polished the granite walls of the cavern through which the falls flow, creating caves and a deep gorge that has inspired many local Indian legends. The surrounding area, a mat of tropical vegetation, is now a national park. The falls are grandest in the wet months of January and February. The Alagoas bank to the north offers the best view.

Returning to the land route and crossing into the tiny state of Alagoas, you arrive at its capital, Maceió, 190 miles (304 km) north of Aracaju.

**MACEIÓ:** This sugar port has a population of 528,000. Here (and throughout the Northeast) you will see baroque colonial buildings with familiar red tile roofs. Though high-rises do dot the skyline, Maceió has managed to preserve some of its earlier flavor. There is a lighthouse in the center of town, near the Government Palace and the Church of Bom Jesus do Mártires, all worth a visit. The refurbished waterfront, where large cargo ships are berthed, is very pleasant, as are the seafood restaurants, the town lake, and Pajuçara Beach. All the beaches in this area are delightful, with coral reefs a half-mile offshore to keep the water calm. From December 20 to January 6, regional folk plays and dances are performed in the public squares.

In Maceió there are fishermen, called *jangadeiros,* who can be seen on their strange *jangada* boats all along the coast to Belém. They just manage to squeeze out a living on these raft-type sailboats made of six logs some 24 feet long, fitted together with wooden pegs and tapered at one end to form a bow.

Sometimes out for days at a time, the *jangadeiros* and their rafts bob like floats on the water, usually anchored to a good fishing spot with a stone. When they finally return home, they use two dry logs on the beach as rollers on which to haul their *jangadas* past the high tide's reach. Several of the town's more enterprising *jangadeiros* take small groups out to the sandbar a mile offshore, where other equally enterprising *jangadeiros* await, their boats transformed into floating bars. It's a wonderful way to spend a Maceió morning; departures from Pajuçara Beach.

Brazilian tourists have started to discover Maceió. The city has responded by building hotels (see *Best en Route*) and restaurants to meet the demand. For great seafood, try a local favorite, *Alípio* (321 Av. Alípio Barbosa; phone: 81-221-5186), a casual eatery outside town on Mundaú Lake.

Continue north through several tiny fishing towns, enter the state of Pernambuco, and 177 miles (283 km) from Maceió you'll reach the state capital of Recife.

**RECIFE:** With a population of 1.35 million, this city is the main port and commercial capital of the Northeast and the largest city on the route. Though the Brazilian tour brochures proclaim Recife to be the Venice of Brazil, a bit of an overstatement, waterways do run through the city. Split by the Capibaribe and Tijipió rivers, Recife, meaning "reef" and named for the great natural coral mass that lies off its shore, is made up of three sections: Freguesia do Recife, which is a peninsula; Santo Antônio, an island between Freguesia do Recife and the mainland; and Boa Vista, on the mainland. Bridges of stone and iron connect the three sections. In 1975, the Capibaribe and Tijipió catastrophically flooded Recife, but a series of dams have since been constructed that should prevent such a recurrence.

The city was founded by fishermen and sailors in the first half of the 16th century and grew quite rapidly as sugarcane cultivation became profitable. As the closest point in Brazil after João Pessoa to West Africa, Recife became a huge center for the slave trade, and much of its present population are descendants of those slaves. Sugar and cotton are still the main crops of the region.

Recife is still expanding rapidly, and it is getting more and more crowded as skyscrapers nudge out the beautiful colonial mansions, monuments to the sugar era. Wide boulevards, such as Ruas Nova and Imperatriz, have been built to try to cope with the intense traffic jams, but more construction will be necessary to alleviate the problem. As the poor people of the countryside continue to stream in looking for employment, a more *tranquilo* Recife does not seem to be in the cards.

Several very special folkloric traditions of the Northeast are centered in this city: *Frevo* is wildly accelerated music with syncopated rhythms, and its name comes from the Portuguese *ferver*, "to boil," which is just what it does. *Maracatu* is a traditional dance drama, similar to the Portuguese *fandango*, practiced usually during *Carnaval* by the people of the surrounding area who come to the city to celebrate. *Caboclinha* groups perform their folkloric dance in bright feathers, red tunics adorned with medals, and animal-tooth necklaces. Theirs is a leaping, spinning performance played to the beat of banging bows and arrows.

Recife boasts more than 60 splendid churches that deserve a look. A few of the best are Nossa Senhora da Conceição dos Militares, built around 1710 in a baroque-rococo style (on Rua Nova in Santo Antônio); Nossa Senhora do Livramento (on Rua do Livramento), built in 1692 and refurbished in 1735, has a classic style with interiors worked in granite and wood; and Capela Dourada on Rua Imperador, completed in 1734, is another church of baroque design with some splendid gold leaf paintings and carved cedar.

Some other attractions in Recife include Fort Brum, erected by the Portuguese and finished by the Dutch when they took over the city; Fort São Tiago das Cinco Pontas, built by the Dutch and completed by the Portuguese in 1677 in the shape of a pentagon; Pátio de São Pedro, in the center of the city across from the Church of São Pedro dos Clerigos, a gathering place of the intellectual and artistic crowd of Recife, with good restaurants nearby, weekend folk music concerts, and poetry readings; Sitio da Trinidade, in the districts of Casa Amarela and Parnamirim, the nicest park in town and the former site of the Dutch invasion. *Casa da Cultura,* a 3-story restoration of a 19th-century prison (Rua Floriano Peixoto), is a good place to buy souvenirs and handicrafts. Each of the prison cells has been turned into a tiny specialty shop. The *Museu do Açúcar* (Sugar Museum; 2187 Av. 17 de Agosto) has examples of colonial sugar mills, slave torture devices, and many other historical, social, and scientific exhibits related to sugar production. Next door is the *Museu do Homem do Nordeste* (Anthropology Museum of Northeastern Man; 2187 Av. 17 de Agosto; phone: 268-2000), which has exhibits on the culture and daily life of the peoples who settled the region. Closed Mondays. Don't miss the *Teatro Santa Isabel* (on the Praça da República), built by French architect Louis Leger Vauthier and first opened in 1850. Guided tours available in English (phone: 81-224-1020). Boa Viagem is the fashionable southern suburb that sports a 5-mile ocean promenade, scenic views, coconut palms, and villas of the wealthy. Some good eating establishments are here, too.

Beaches are one of the area's greatest attractions and the major reason for a visit to Recife. Those within the city limits include Pina, to the south and Boa Viagem, mentioned above. Farther south, in an area filled with coconut palms and clean sand, are Piedade, Venda Grande, Candeias, and Barra de Jangada. Still farther, near the town of Cabo, 20 miles (32 km) from Recife, are Itapuama, with interesting rock formations, lots of coconuts, and full facilities for the traveler; and Gaibu, the most famous in the area and perhaps the most beautiful. There are natural spring pools here, and it is possible to rent *jangadas*. Nazaré is even more remote, with ruins of an old lighthouse and a church built in 1612. Suape is also an isolated blue cove surrounded by green hills and miles of empty beach.

Another excursion from Recife is to Olinda, the original capital of Pernambuco. Founded in 1537, it lies just 4 miles (6 km) north of Recife. It is a delightful town built on hills and has been preserved in its early elegance. Many local artists have chosen to live on its winding cobblestone streets lined with tile-faced buildings. The spirit of the old days returns each November during Olinda's colonial festival.

This place abounds in old churches, convents, and monasteries. Some of the recommended spots for exploration include the monasteries of São Bento and São Francisco, full of woodcarvings and paintings; the *Pernambuco Contemporary Art Museum,* with a good collection of painted ceramic figurines; the Church of Nossa Senhora do Rosário dos Pretos, built in 1715; and Bica de São Pedro, the colonial public fountain.

Recife has a number of good restaurants, ranging from seafood cooked in various ways to grilled meat to continental fare. Besides the top hotel eateries, a good place for fish and regional cuisine is *Canto da Barra,* on Candeias Beach, just south of the city at 9150 Av. Bernardo Vieira de Melo (phone: 81-361-2168).

Clean local beaches are Barro Novo, Carmo, Casa Caida, Farol, Rio Doce, São Francisco, and Milagres.

**ITAMARACÁ:** Small and pretty, this island is 38 miles (61 km) from Recife just off the mainland and reached easily via causeway. Fort Orange, built by the Dutch in 1631, is one of the attractions, but its fame lies in its beaches. Vila de Pilar is the main town on the island, shared on weekends by poor fishermen and wealthy vacationers from Recife. It has a tourist hotel and plenty of good seafood. The cleanest and most remote beaches are reached by walking beyond Jauaripe, a tiny village just a mile or so from Vila de Pilar. The travel agency at the hotel can arrange a day cruise to Itamaracá that includes lunch.

**FAZENDA NOVA:** This is a tiny town 2 hours west of Recife. The sole reason to visit this place in the middle of the arid region is to see its open-air theater-town of Nova Jerusalem, which has been constructed as a replica of Ancient Jerusalem. During *Easter Week* each year, thousands flock to the village to witness the spectacular *Passion of Christ* play. A hotel, the *Grande,* complete with air conditioning and swimming pools, has been built to handle some of the tourists (Av. Poeta Carlos Pena Filho; phone: 81-231-1388). Most visitors either camp at the *Empetur* campgrounds or stay in hotels at Caruaru or Recife (see *Best en Route*).

**CARUARU:** If you are visiting Fazenda Nova, you will want to stop here, too; it is just a few miles away. The Wednesday and Saturday markets, open 5 AM to 7 PM, offer some good buys in the leather and pottery of the region. Visit the *Mestre Vitalino Museum,* an homage to the sculptor responsible for creating the traditional distinctive clay figures of peasants sold at the market. From December 23 to January 1, the city hosts a festival featuring Pernambuco folklore, and in March, an *International Handicraft Week* is held.

**En Route from Recife** – The road north toward João Pessoa passes through some lovely coconut palm–filled country. Just 24 miles (38 km) from Recife, Igarassu is reached. Filled with colonial buildings, including the first church built in Brazil, much of the town has been declared a national monument. It is a pleasant place to stop for a few hours.

Continuing north, you will arrive at Paulista, yet another old city with some nice inviting beaches. The last stop before João Pessoa is at Goiana, 44 miles (70 km) from Recife. It has churches dating back to 1595, and the clean, easygoing beaches of Catuama, Carne de Vaca, and Pontas de Pedras are not far away. Thirty-one miles (50 km) on the road north from Goiana is João Pessoa on the Paraíba River.

**JOÃO PESSOA:** With a population of 440,000, this is the capital of Paraíba state. Again, there is the juxtaposition of high-rises and the baroque, wealthy homes of a city on the move. Plenty of palms still line the streets, but the state government is providing many incentives to attract business to this region, which has as its major industries fishing, cattle breeding, and the cultivation of cotton, sisal, pineapples, corn, beans, and sugar. Huge stacks of modern sugar mills can be seen on the outskirts of town.

Continuing up the coast, you will be constantly tempted to try a new succulent variety of tropical fruit. Sometimes the same fruit will bear a different name in a town just 100 miles away. Besides the old standbys like bananas, watermelons, and pineapples, in João Pessoa you might experiment with new tastes, like *graviola, bacuri, açai, manga, cupuaçu, goiaba* (guava), or *maracujá* (passion fruit). The fruit is put into a blender with some milk and made into a smooth drink called a *suco*. (*Note:* It's usually safe for visiting stomachs, as the fruits are peeled before going into the blender.)

October is the beginning of the summer season, which is greeted by the election of the Queen of the Beaches, jalopy races, a *jangada* regatta, and plenty of *batidas,* a favorite Brazilian drink combining the local firewater, *cachaça,* with any of the above-mentioned fruits.

Tambaú is a beach resort just half an hour from town. The beach is extensive, the fishing and bathing excellent, the palm trees sway constantly, and all complemented by excellent facilities. Cabo Branco is another beautiful nearby spot.

Campina Grande is 2 hours west of João Pessoa and another fast-growing sugar manufacturing center. Its weekend market is quite lively and a good place to pick up artifacts from the Northeast.

Juazeiro do Norte lies another 314 miles (502 km) west of Campina, deep in the heart of the *sertão,* but its elevation makes it an oasis of green. Here, Padre Cicero's stand against the government is commemorated by an open-air mass and pilgrimage to his statue each November 2. It is from Juazeiro — if you care to skip the rest of the Northeast — that you can take a relaxing 9- to 10-day paddlewheel boat ride 500 miles down the legendary Rio São Francisco to Pirapora in Minas Gerais. This river valley is actually a subregion of the *sertão,* and forms a navigable waterway that has served to unite the north and south of the region. Along its banks and within its narrow flood plain, river agriculture avoids the droughts that afflict the rest of the *sertão.* Bring malaria pills and a hammock for a glide through some inspirational countryside that is still much as it was in the days of Lampião.

As the road moves away from the coast a bit, you pass Guarabira and 115 miles (184 km) after leaving João Pessoa, you arrive in Natal, the capital of the state of Rio Grande do Norte.

**NATAL:** Sitting on the Rio Potengi just inland from the coast is this city of 580,000 people. The surrounding area is the largest sea salt–producing region in Brazil, and huge, flat tracts of the white salt dominate the countryside in Macau to the north. Important regional products are manioc, sugarcane, black beans, and fruit.

Natal is a pleasant city that still has a lot of green foliage. Its beaches are its real claim to fame, with Praia do Genipabu the finest. Huge sand dunes, which you can cruise aboard rented buggies, are shaded by coconut palms that offer an ideal place to camp.

Restaurants here offer mainly local cuisine — seafood and *carne-de-sol* (sun-dried beef jerky). One good spot, which features live *sertanejo* music Thursdays through Saturdays at dinnertime, is *Raizes,* 609 Av. Campos Salles, Petrópoli (phone: 84-222-7338).

**En Route from Natal** – As the elevation drops and the temperature rises, you move closer to the equator along this route to Fortaleza. Although nighttime driving is not normally recommended in Brazil, here, try to travel during the cooler evening hours. About 90 miles (144 km) outside Fortaleza, after you have passed Mossoró, a salt-processing center for the area, and have crossed the border into Ceará, you arrive at the turnoff for the tiny fishing village of Canoa Quebrada.

**CANOA QUEBRADA:** While there are no formal facilities for the traveler here, this is the perfect spot for someone who cares to rough it a bit and get to know the local people. The beaches are magnificent and unspoiled and the fishermen hospitable, offering you space in their simple homes and food for a ridiculously low price. Although European tourists have discovered the beach, it has managed to remain largely unspoiled.

Continuing beyond Canoa Quebrada for a few hours brings you to Fortaleza, the capital of Ceará.

**FORTALEZA:** This port of 1.8 million people grew as a center for the export of sugar, caraúba wax, cotton, castor oil, and salt. Today, lobsters and cashew nuts, both marketed worldwide, are the most important sources of income, along with manufacturing and tourism. Fishing is also excellent here, and the state government has built new port facilities to protect the fishing fleets and lessen layover times for large cargo ships. While the city does have some old colonial buildings and plenty of red tiles on its roofs, it does not possess the historic and artistic flavor of the other colonial cities in the Northeast.

Many *jangadeiros* of Fortaleza became famous in Brazil for refusing to carry slaves from shore to ship after 1850, when the importation of slaves was banned and the local *fazendeiros* sought to make a profit by bringing their slaves to Rio de Janeiro for sale. Today, the *jangadeiros* can be seen from Iracema beach bringing in their catch at sunset.

The *Northeastern Handicrafts Fair* is held in Fortaleza at a different time each year. Local art is displayed, and folk groups perform. At *Christmas,* a nativity play with singing and dancing is enacted.

There are several sights in Fortaleza worth seeing, such as the *Mercado Central* (14 Rua Gen. Bezerril), where you can bargain for stunning handmade lace, embroidery, and hammocks (the best in Brazil), and the *Tourist Center* (350 Rua Sen. Pompeu), in Fortaleza's old prison, with an interesting popular art museum, shops that sell folkloric items, and good restaurants. Both are open daily, except Sunday afternoons. One of the best restaurants in the city, *Alt Heidelberg* (498 Rua Vicente Linhares, Aldeota; phone: 85-224-6953), offers German fare. For seafood and live music every night, try *Trapiche* (3956 Av. Pres. John Kennedy, Mucuripe; phone: 85-244-4400) or the more upscale *Sandra's* (555 Av. Eng. Luís Vereira; phone: 85-234-6555).

The beaches in and around Fortaleza are excellent. Within about 7 miles (12 km) of town are Iracema, Meirelles, Mucuripe, do Futuro, and Caça e Pesca. More outlying beachcombing awaits in Aquiraz, 20 miles (32 km) away, on the beaches of Prainha and Iguape; Beberibe, 49 miles (78 km) away, with the beaches of Morro Branco combining sand dunes and freshwater waterfalls; and in Cascavel, 37 miles (59 km) away, with Capanga Beach. Not to be missed are two very different spots: *Beach Park* (Porto das Dunas, 13 miles/21 km from Fortaleza; phone: 85-360-1150) has an aquatic park, dune buggies; sailboards, surfboards, and motorized hang gliders for rent, and good food. In the other direction are the pristine beaches of Cumbucco (23 miles/37 km miles north of Fortaleza) which can be reached and explored only by dune buggy.

Another quite worthwhile trip is the 19-mile (30-km) drive to the mountain of Serra de Maranguape, which has tropical vegetation and an excellent view of the city.

**En Route from Fortaleza** – You travel deep into the *sertão* on your way to São Luís, the final stop on this route. After passing the city of Sobral, the climate becomes pleasantly cool as you ascend Serra da Ibiapaba. As if by magic, the arid scrub landscape becomes a lush green tropical scene, complete with banana and mango trees. The pleasure is short-lived, through, as the descent from the hills plunges you into the even hotter and dustier environment of the state of Piauí. On BR-222, between Piracuruca and Piripiri, are the Sete Cidades.

**SETE CIDADES (THE SEVEN CITIES):** This national park is a strange moonlike area of dried eroded earth formations that are symmetrically arranged over 11.4 square miles and look like the ruins of seven cities intersected by streets and avenues. Even stranger are the carvings on some of the formations — hands, animals, and other figures. Scientists have been unable to identify their origin, but one imaginative theory is that they may have been left by ancient Phoenicians.

A waterfall with some refreshing bathing pools is right on the site, and you can camp for a nominal fee.

**En Route from Sete Cidades** – There is no good road that leads directly to São Luís, so you will have to continue south to Terezina, a brutally hot, dry city of 378,000 that offers nothing particularly appealing to the traveler, then north toward the cool breezes of the coast once again. Roughly 665 miles (1070 km) from Fortaleza, you arrive at São Luís, the capital of Maranhão.

**SÃO LUÍS:** Technically, this city of 625,000, sitting on an island between the bays of São Marcos and São José, is considered part of northern Brazil, but because it is such a nice spot, it makes a good finish for the Northeast tour route.

A pleasant, low-key place with a minimum number of high-rise buildings, São Luís has managed to preserve a bit of its past. The older part of town, built on steep flagstone streets, still has many beautiful baroque mansions, complete with blue tile façades, interior gardens, wrought iron, and hand-carved woodwork. The narrow, winding avenues have plenty of palm shade cover.

Claimed in 1612 by Frenchman Daniel de la Touche for the French regent Marie de Médicis, who desired a tropical paradise of her own, the city was named in honor of King Louis XIII. The port is now too shallow to accommodate modern ships, unlike in the beginning of the 19th century, when hundreds of boats entered and left the harbor annually. These ships hauled the tons of cotton that were the source of the tremendous one-crop boom that shook the area just as sugar and cacao stimulated other sections of the Northeast. Supported by slave labor, the São Luís region flourished, producing enough writers and poets — including former President José Sarney, a published poet in his own right — to be called the "Athens of Brazil". As with all the single-crop booms that Brazil has experienced, this one crashed ultimately as a result of the large-scale cotton production on US plantations. Today, the most important products of the area besides cotton are babacu nuts, rice, and manioc.

There are some 380 miles of tranquil water beaches to the east and west of São Luís. Some extend out for miles when the tide is low, and, closer to town, others are the scene of perpetual parties. Dune buggies cruise up and down the shoreline past the many *barzinhos* (little bars), most of which serve delicious seafood.

The region never seems to get too hot; even after the winter rains have ceased in April and the sun begins to shine for 8 months, a gentle breeze keeps the air circulating almost constantly. The city is now the scene of a reverse migration, moving from south to north, as many *paulistas* (people from São Paulo), disheartened with the fast-paced life, look for a more relaxed existence in the north.

June 15 to July 10 is a special time. The festival of *Bumba-Meu-Boi* is celebrated with a pastoral play. Its principal theme, the death and resurrection of the bull, has a mixture of Portuguese, African, and native elements. The players are divided into three classes: human, animal, and fantasy. They dance, sing, and talk to the accompaniment of percussion instruments. A good place to sample the local cuisine, especially seafood, is *Base do Germano,* Av. Wenceslau Brás, Canto da Fabril (phone: 98-222-3276).

A 1½-hour boat ride across the Bay of São Marcos brings you to Alcântara, a tiny, quiet fishing community. With its rich treasury of colonial buildings and ruins of Portuguese forts, it has been designated a historical monument. There are many nice beaches here, too. For those who want to visit and return, the boat leaves at 7 or 8 AM and returns 1 and 3 PM, depending on the tide.

## BEST EN ROUTE

The Northeast is still developing facilities for tourism, and present hotels range from a few top-quality places in the major cities to the most primitive accommodations in general. Restaurants, when they exist in hotels, have continental cuisine with regional specialties, primarily seafood. Hotels categorized as very expensive will cost $100 or more per day for a double room; expensive from $80 per day for a double room; moderate, from $50 to $75 per day; and inexpensive, under $40 per day.

### ILHÉUS

***Transamerica Ilhéus*** – This 140-room modern resort sprawls across one end of the practically deserted Comandatuba Island. Water sports, sailing, and fishing are among the amenities offered, as well as all the trappings of a modern, international class hotel. There's also a mini-zoo on the property. Estrada para Canavieiras, Ilha de Comandatuba (phone: 73-212-1122; toll-free in Brazil, 11-800-3437). Very expensive.

*Jardim Atlântico* – With a great view of the beach, this 30-room hotel offers a variety of water sports, satellite TV, a bar, and shops. Estrada para Olivença (phone: 73-231-4541). Expensive.

*Ilhéus Praia* – A comfortable hostelry with air conditioning, TV sets, and refrigerators in its 64 rooms. Praça D. Eduardo (phone: 73-231-2533). Moderate.

*Britânia* – All 40 rooms are clean and have air conditioning; most have a private shower. 16 Rua 28 de Junho (phone: 73-231-1722). Inexpensive.

## ARACAJU

*Beira-Mar* – Right on the beach, this place is pleasant, and it has a nightclub. Av. Rotary, Atalaia Velha (phone: 79-243-1921). Expensive.

*Da Ilha* – Its island location makes this a relaxing retreat, with 90 rooms and 30 chalets, restaurant, bar, sports facilities, and special activities for kids, including a mini-zoo and train. Atalaia Nova, on Santa Luzia Island (phone: 79-262-1221). Expensive.

*Parque dos Coqueiros* – This comfortable and modern 94-room resort hotel is located right on the beach. It also has a pool, tennis, sauna, and volleyball court. 1075 Rua Francisco Rabelo Leite Neto, 1075 (phone: 79-243-1511). Expensive.

*Palace* – Comfortable and centrally located, it has 74 air conditioned rooms, a good restaurant, and bar. Praça General Valadão (phone: 79-224-5000). Moderate.

*Oasis* – In the central part of town. This place has private baths and air conditioning. 466 Rua São Cristóvão (phone: 79-224-2125). Inexpensive.

## PENEDO

*São Francisco* – A 52-room hostelry; each room has a private bath and air conditioning. Bar and restaurant. Av. Floriano Peixoto (phone: 82-551-2273). Inexpensive.

## MACEIÓ

*Jatiúca* – For luxury, try this beachfront property. Its 95 rooms are in 2-story structures half hidden from one another by the lush vegetation and coconut palms. A poolside drink here while watching the local children's ballet perform folk dances is a must. It also offers volleyball and tennis courts. 220 Lagoa da Anta (phone: 82-231-2555). Expensive.

*Matsubara* – Though not directly on the beach, this place more than compensates with luxury as well as topnotch service. Av. Brigadeiro Eduardo Gomes (phone: 82-231-6178). Expensive.

*Melia Maceió* – This newest member of the Brazilian Sol Melia hotel chain opened last year. In addition to 240 rooms, it has a restaurant, swimming pool, tennis court, sauna, shops, travel agency, car rental, and convention center. 2991 Alvaro de Otacilio (for reservations call 11-813-3088 in São Paulo or fax 11-813-3323). Expensive.

*Beira Mar* – Located on the central beach and run by the congenial Britto family, it has 88 rooms, a restaurant, bar, and hairdresser. Ask for a room with a view. 1994 Av. Dugue de Caxias (phone: 82-221-0101). Moderate.

## FOZ DE PAULO AFONSO

*Grande Hotel de Paulo Afonso* – First-rate and set in a national park at the falls, it has a good restaurant, bar, pool, and air conditioning. All 46 rooms have a private bath. Parque da Chesf (phone: 75-281-1914). Inexpensive.

## RECIFE

***Petribu Sheraton*** – The newest of Sheraton's three Brazilian properties, this 16-story structure is the only deluxe hotel in the greater Recife area located directly on the beach. There are 197 rooms, 2 restaurants, 2 loungers, an outdoor pool, health club, business center, ramps for the disabled, a tour desk, and free parking. There are courtesy transfers to the Recife airport 6 miles (10 km) away. 1624 Av. Bernardo Vieira de Melo (phone: 81-361-4511; in the US, 800-325-3535). Very expensive.

***Quatro Rodas–Recife (Olinda)*** – One of the nicest resorts on the Atlantic coast, this property of the Quatro Rodas chain is just outside Recife, in Olinda. The hotel is most attractive, as are the beachfront grounds, which include a large pool with snack bar and refreshments. Rooms face the sea, and the service is attentive, with a mostly English-speaking staff. Boutiques offer unusually good selections. 2200 Av. José Augusto Moreira (phone: 81-431-2955). Very expensive.

***Recife Palace*** – Sister hotel to Rio de Janeiro's luxurious *Rio Palace,* it has quickly become popular with both business and tourist travelers for its high level of service and style. There are 294 rooms, a swimming pool, 2 restaurants, a bar and nightclub. Located on Boa Viagem Beach. 4070 Av. Boa Viagem (phone: 81-325-4044). Very expensive.

***Internacional Othon Palace*** – A member of the countrywide Othon chain, and a good one, on Boa Viagem Beach with 264 rooms. 3722 Av. Boa Viagem (phone: 81-326-7225). Expensive.

***Miramar*** – Well situated on a beach, all 120 rooms have private bath, music, air conditioning. The hotel has a pool, international restaurant, nightclub, bar, hairdressers. 363 Rua dos Navegantes (phone: 81-326-7422). Expensive.

***Grande*** – Fully air conditioned with a bar and restaurant. All 107 rooms have private bath. 593 Av. Martins de Barros (phone: 81-224-9366). Inexpensive.

## JOÃO PESSOA

***Tambaú*** – The best in town, right on the beach and part of *Varig's* Tropical Hotel group. All 110 rooms have private bath, with air conditioning, TV set, radio. Plus a great restaurant, pool, and bar. 229 Av. Alm. Tamandaré (phone: 83-226-3660). Expensive.

***Sol-Mar*** – Simple yet comfortable with 60 rooms that have private baths, stocked refrigerators, TV sets, and air conditioning. 500 Av. Rui Carneiro, Tambaú (phone: 83-226-1350). Moderate to inexpensive.

## CAMPINA GRANDE

***Ouro Branco*** – The 60 rooms have private baths, TV sets, radio. Bar and restaurant. 20 Cel. João Lourenço Porto (phone: 83-321-4304). Moderate.

***Rique Palace*** – This hostelry has 41 rooms with private showers and TV sets. There is also a bar and restaurant. 287 Venâncio Neiva (phone: 83-341-1433). Inexpensive.

## NATAL

***Vila do Mar*** – On a pleasant beach right outside of town. It has 150 rooms, each with a color TV set and mini-bar. At Km 4.5, on the Via Costeira, Bareira d'Aqua Beach (phone: 84-222-3755). Expensive.

***Luxor*** – A tall, round, modern hotel in the center of downtown. A quick cab ride gets you to the beach. 634 Av. Rio Branco (phone: 84-221-2721). Moderate.

***Reis Magos*** – Great location overlooking the ocean, it has a good restaurant, pool, bar, and nightclub. All 91 rooms have a private bath, TV set, and air conditioning. 882 Av. Pres. Cafe Filho (phone: 84-222-2055). Inexpensive.

## FORTALEZA

***Cesar Park*** – Opened last year at a prime beachfront location, this modern luxury hotel has 230 rooms (many with ocean views), 40 deluxe suites, and a sumptuous presidential suite, all with air conditioning, radios, and TV sets. There are 3 restaurants — one with an international menu, another offering the cuisine of Japan (the hotel's owners are Japanese), and a third featuring a piano bar. Other facilities include a fitness center, massage, Jacuzzi, swimming pool, shops, a business center with computer, fax, and telex services, and a meeting room that can accommodate up to 600 people. 4000 Av. Pres. Kennedy (for reservations phone: 21-800-0789 in Rio de Janeiro; in São Paulo, 11-800-1164). Expensive.

***Esplanada Praia*** – A modern 244-room property with balconies overlooking the sea. The hotel has a restaurant, bar, nightclub, and 2 pools. 2000 Av. Pres. John Kennedy (phone: 85-224-8555). Expensive.

***Imperial Othon Palace*** – This modern hotel has 117 rooms, all with private baths, music, TV sets, and air conditioning. There is a bar, pool, restaurant, and nightclub. 2500 Av. Pres. John Kennedy (phone: 85-224-9177). Expensive.

***Praia Verde*** – A tastefully designed resort property located away from the hotel cluster of Praia de Meireles in the more unspoiled Praia do Futuro area. It has 150 modern rooms, a swimming pool, tennis court, volleyball court, and gameroom. 3860 Av. Dioguinho (phone: 85-234-5233). Expensive.

***Beira-Mar*** – Pleasant and on the main drag. The pool and outdoor restaurant are good for people watching. 3130 Av. Pres. John Kennedy (phone: 85-244-9444). Moderate.

***Colonial Praia*** – It has 40 comfortable rooms with private baths. Plus bar, restaurant, sauna, and pool. 145 Rua Bar. de Aracati (phone: 85-211-9644). Moderate.

***Magna Praia*** – A 124-room property on Iracema Beach with a TV set and mini-bar in every room. 1002 Av. Aquidaba (phone: 85-244-9311). Moderate.

***São Pedro*** – One of the best in town in its price range. There are 102 rooms with private showers, as well as a great restaurant, bar, pool, and hairdresser. 81 Rua Castro e Silva (phone: 85-211-9911). Inexpensive.

## TERESINA

***Luxor Hotel do Piauí*** – A first class property, all 87 rooms have private baths, air conditioning, TV sets, and music. Facilities include a good restaurant, bar, and pool. 310 Praça Marechal Deodoro (phone: 86-222-4911). Moderate.

***Rio Poty*** – Situated on the bank of a river, and the best in town. All 105 rooms have satellite TV and mini-bars. 555 Av. Marechal Castelo Branco (phone: 86-223-1500). Moderate.

***Teresina Palace*** – This hotel's 95 comfortable rooms have private showers, air conditioning, and TV sets. Has a bar-restaurant. 1219 Rua Paissandu (phone: 086-222-2770). Inexpensive.

## SÃO LUÍS

***São Luís Quatro Rodas*** – This exclusive member of the Quatro Rodas chain is located on an excellent beach far from the madding crowd. It offers satellite TV sets and a mini-bar in every room, a top restaurant, bar, nightclub, hair salon, pool, other sports facilities, and a mini-zoo. Calhau Beach (phone 98-227-0244). Expensive.

***Vila Rica*** – Near the old colonial section of the city, this comfortable hotel offers easy access to cobblestone streets along which you'll find museums and "hidden-away" restaurants. There is a coffee shop, sauna, and hairdresser. 229 Praça Dom Pedro II (phone: 98-232-3535). Expensive to moderate.

***São Francisco*** – This 90-room riverfront property is among the best in town.

Among its amenities are a bar, restaurant, and 3 swimming pools, plus color TV sets and mini-bars in the rooms. 77 Rua Dr. Luís Serson (phone: 98-232-3855). Moderate.

**Central** – The 108 simple rooms are available with a variety of bathroom facilities. Also has a restaurant and bar. 258 Av. Dom Pedro II (phone: 98-222-5644). Inexpensive.

# The Costa Verde: Rio de Janeiro to São Paulo

Some of the most spectacular and dramatic scenery in Brazil is found along BR-101, more commonly known as the Rodovia Rio-Santos or Rio-Santos Highway. Most of it is a well-paved road that curves westward along the Atlantic from Rio de Janeiro to Santos, the port serving the city of São Paulo. Justly called the Costa Verde, or Green Coast, the area features lush tropical greenery sweeping magnificently down from hills and mountains to the water's edge, where coves hide unpolluted beaches and pockets of civilization. Out at sea, hundreds of islands are scattered thickly as far as the eye can see, while the land offers a number of historic colonial towns, including Parati, one of the most captivating on the continent.

Until recently, the Costa Verde had been a well-kept secret to outsiders. For the privileged residents of Brazil's two largest cities — Rio de Janeiro and São Paulo — it has been a popular weekend and holiday playground since the early 1970s, when the Rio-Santos Highway opened to make the area more accessible to tourism. Now it is slowly being discovered by foreign visitors who prefer the splendor of the 375-mile (600-km) coast road between the two cities to the shuttle plane or the 270-mile (402-km) inland highway — shorter but less interesting — called BR-116 or Via Dutra.

This route begins in Rio de Janeiro (for more details about Rio and its beach communities, see *Rio de Janeiro,* THE CITIES), heading west along the coast and then inland to São Paulo. (It may, of course, also be driven in the opposite direction, from São Paulo to Rio de Janeiro.) The first stop is Itacuruçá, a quaint fishing village that is also a departure point for schooner excursions to tropical islands in the bay. Trips to the islands are a highlight all along the Costa Verde, either going with a group or chartering your own yacht. The route meanders past luxury resorts, the historic port of Angra dos Reis, Serra da Bocâina National Park, the unspoiled town of Parati, and the playground towns of Ubatuba and Caraguatatuba. Moving inland, it then passes through the countryside to São José dos Campos, and on to São Paulo. It also covers an optional stretch of less well-maintained highway (with an increasingly developed beachfront) between Caraguatatuba and Santos.

Without stopping, the route can be traveled in about 8 hours. To be fully enjoyed, however, it is best spaced out over a period of a few days or even a week. At a pleasurable and practical pace, the trip could take 5 days and 4 nights, leaving Rio de Janeiro mid-morning on a Monday to avoid the city's rush-hour traffic (be sure not to enter or leave Rio de Janeiro or São Paulo during the grid-locked peaks of Friday and Sunday nights) and arriving in São Paulo mid-morning on Friday. Accommodations suit all tastes and budgets — everything from charming and simple inns called *pousadas* to flashy luxury resorts. Beaches are virtually deserted during the week most of the year except in the villages and at the main hotels. Many of the towns and hotels covered are destinations in themselves and can also be used — as *cariocas* and *paulistas* do — as weekend getaways from the two larger cities.

**En Route from Rio** – Heading west, for the first hour or so out of the city, BR-101 (also known as RJ-071 in the state of Rio de Janeiro) runs through a morass of Brazilian-style urban sprawl. It is of passing interest in its own right — close enough to the highway to satisfy the curiosity of amateur anthropologists, yet far enough away to keep the somewhat seamy sights at a safe distance. The landscape includes roadside *favelas* (shantytowns), honky-tonk trysting spots known as *motels*, and ramshackle restaurants with little to recommend them to outsiders.

**ITACURUÇÁ:** Forty-three miles (69 km) west of Rio de Janeiro is the turnoff for this sleepy fishing village, the point of departure for *saveiros*, Brazilian schooners that tour the tropical islands near the mainland. As an alternative to a group tour, hire your own boat through one of the local agencies — *Itacuruçá Turismo* (439 Rua Raphael Levy Miranda; phone: 21-780-1710) or *Passamar* (37 Rua Evelina, loga A; phone: 21-780-1776). Most of the islands off the coast are either unpopulated or inhabited only on weekends when wealthy *cariocas* and *paulistas* sail out to their beachhouses.

**En Route from Itacuruçá** – The spectacular scenery that continues all the way to Caraguatatuba 175 miles (280 kms) farther west begins just outside Itacuruçá. The beauty seems endless, with waves crashing onto clean, white-sand beaches dotted with coconut trees on one side of the road, and lush green mountains on the other. Twenty miles (32 kms) past the town, near the village of Mangaratiba, are two of the area's newest and most sophisticated resort complexes, the *Club Méditerranée Village Rio da Pedras* and the *Porto Bello* (see *Best en Route*).

**ANGRA DOS REIS:** Continue west on BR-101 for 35 miles (57 km) to Angra dos Reis, a town of 80,000 that was an important port (its name means Bay of Kings) during colonial times. Unappealing industrial architecture has taken over most of the few colonial remains, but there are a few historical monuments, including a 17th-century chapel, Capela de Santa Luzia (194 Rua do Comércio); a 16th-century convent, Convento de Nossa Senhora do Carmo, the 17th-century Nossa Senhora do Carmo church, and an 18th-century monastery, Convento de São Bernardinho de Sena (all at Morro de Santo Antônio); and the 17th-century Igreja Matriz de Nossa Senhora da Conceição (Praça General Silvestre Travassos). Angra dos Reis also serves as a jumping-off spot for excursions to Ilha Grande (also accessible by ferry from the docks) and other bay islands where you can enjoy the pleasures of swimming in emerald waters, strolling on shockingly white beaches, or fishing in groups or with private charters. Agencies such as *Green Coast* (392 Rua do Comércio; phone: 243-652613) and *Mar de Angra* (38 Rua da Conceição; phone: 243-651350) can arrange these trips.

**En Route from Angra dos Reis** – Just west of Angra dos Reis, stretching north of BR-101, all the way to Parati, is the Serra da Bocâina National Park. Established in 1971, the park has some 250,000 acres of jungle and mountains, with waterfalls cascading into the Mambucaba River as a backdrop to its abundant wildlife. Near sea level, monkeys, parrots, and tapirs thrive in tropical hardwoods; farther up, otters, wild boars, and hedgehogs roam pine forests; at the summit of the mountains, deer and wild hares feed in meadows of lichens and wildflowers. Many hotels in Angra dos Reis can arrange expeditions to Serra da Bocâina —

either on foot, horseback, or with a four-wheel-drive vehicle. In stark contrast to this environmentalist's paradise is a sight from BR-101, after the village of Cunhambebe — the abandoned Angra dos Reis nuclear reactor, shut down after it was discovered to be environmentally unsafe.

Fifteen miles (24 km) west of Angra dos Reis is Marina Bracuhy, the main marina complex in the area, used as a base for many yacht charter companies, including *Captain's Yacht Charter* (phone: 21-252-1155), *Angra Yacht Charters* (11-258-8887), and *Yacht People* (21-512-1363). The marina has its own hotel with a pool, the 20-room *Porto Bracuhy* (BR-101 Sul, Km 115; phone: 243-65-1675). Four miles (6 km) west of Bracuhy is the *Hotel do Frade,* the first resort hotel to be built in the area (see *Best en Route).*

**PARATI:** Continue on BR-101 46 miles (74 km) to the major historical attraction along the route. Considered by UNESCO to be one of the most important intact remains of colonial architecture in the world, Parati (pop. 27,000) is a living monument to the 16th, 17th, and 18th centuries, when the town was an important port from which gold from the mines of the inland state of Minas Gerais was shipped. No new structures are allowed to be built in this beautiful town, thereby preserving Parati's architectural integrity. The tourist office on Praça Macedo Soares at the corner of Avenida Roberto da Silveira (phone: 243-711266) sells simple maps of the major sites for about $1.

Among the charms of Parati are its cobbled streets, built so that the sea would wash them at high tide. (Be sure to park out of harm's way during such times.) The streets are especially appealing in the 6-square-block historical center, a pedestrian-only zone. Parati is often used as a location for period movies, among them *Gabriela,* based on Jorge Amado's novel *Gabriela, Clove and Cinnamon,* with Marcello Mastroianni and Sonia Braga.

Parati's restaurants offer simply prepared fare, largely based on seafood, at somewhat less than simple prices. Among the best are *Hiltinho* (233 Rua Mal. Deodoro; phone: 243-711432); *Chez Régine* (38 Rua Dr. Pereira; phone: 243-711608); and *Brik a Brak* (267 Rua Dr. Samuel Costa; phone: 243-711445).

The town can be easily seen in a day; or if you choose to savor it more slowly, a stay at one of Parati's many *pousadas* is an ideal way to soak up the colonial character. There are some 24 inns, so reservations are not always necessary, except on weekends and during high season. Most of the *pousadas* are fairly similar in service and style — tastefully and comfortably decorated in colonial style.

Parati is another departure point for schooner rides to the nearby islands — *Antigona* (Praça da Bandeira; phone: 243-711165) can arrange an excursion. Another highlight is a visit to the *Fazenda Murycana* (4 miles/7 km outside of town on Estrada Cunha; ask for directions; phone: 243-711153), a 17th-century farm that produces its own *pinga* or *aguardente,* the sugarcane aquavit for which Parati is also famous. The farmhouse also has an ethnological museum, a small zoo, horseback riding, and a good restaurant.

**En Route from Parati** – West of Parati, the Rio-Santos Highway enters the state of São Paulo and becomes officially known as SP-55. Along this section of the route, the mountain scenery is spectacular — made more so because the beaches are obscured by luxury condominiums built by wealthy *paulistas.* Be careful when driving on the section of highway between Parati and Caraguatatuba during the winter (June through September) — the road is often obscured by fog and landslides.

**UBATUBA:** Forty-seven miles (75 km) west of Parati is the next resort town along the route. Ubatuba (pop. 38,000) is popular with *paulistas,* who sail their yachts and play other sports on its sheltered cove, Saco da Ribeira, 20 minutes from downtown.

Excellent seafood is served at the restaurants of the *Solar das Aguas Cantantes* and *Sol e Vida* hotels (see *Best en Route).* Like the rest of the coast, the surrounding waters are rich in tropical islands, which can be visited by making arrangements through local tour agencies such as *Corsário* (34 Av. Beira-Mar, Saco da Ribeira; phone: 124-420311), *Escunatur* (18 Rua Sete Fontes, Saco da Ribeira; phone 124-420238), and *Mykonos* (17 Rua Flamenguinho, Saco da Ribeira; phone: 124-411388).

**CARAGUATATUBA:** Thirty-three miles (53 km) farther ahead is Caraguatatuba, another *paulista* resort town of about 50,000. Rich in accommodations, the town also serves as a base for basking on a number of nearby sandy beaches and excursions to the tropical island of Tamandua, 1½ hours away by boat. Caraguatatuba is also the site of Brazil's *National Fishing Tournament,* which takes place in early October, and the *Orchid Fair and Exposition,* which follows 2 months later in early December.

From here, either take the inland road to São Paulo or continue along the coast on SP-55 to Santos, and then head to the interior.

**En Route from Caraguatatuba** – The most pleasant and best-maintained route to São Paulo from Caraguatatuba heads inland 115 miles (184 km) from the coast. The first 56-mile (90-km) stretch winds through a series of small lakes on SP-99 to São José dos Campos, the center of Brazil's aviation industry — Empresa Brasileira de Aeronautica (EMBRAER; 2170 Av. Brigadeiro Faria Lima, phone: 123-25-1610). It is open to visitors by appointment Tuesdays through Thursdays from 4 to 5 PM. The route then intersects with BR-116, where it continues for another 59 miles (95 km) of heavy traffic to São Paulo.

If you're not going directly to São Paulo from Caraguatatuba, continue on SP-55 for more beaches and resort towns. The newest such resort is Riviera de São Lourenço, which was being built at press time. When completed, it will accommodate up to 50,000 people (most of which are entrepreneurs from São Paulo), with hotels, high-rises, and single-family units. Developers have made efforts to preserve the area's flora and fauna and to keep its waters unpolluted. *Note:* the roads from Caraguatatuba west are often unpaved and best negotiated in a four-wheel-drive vehicle.

**SÃO SEBASTIÃO:** Another 17 miles (27 km) from Caraguatatuba is this city of about 27,000. Much of its colonial past is on display at the *Museu de Arte Sacra* (Museum of Sacred Art; 90 Rua Sebastião Silvestre Neves; no phone); open daily except Mondays from 8 AM to noon and 2 to 6 PM. Another historical monument is the 17th-century church, Igreja de São Sebastião (15 Praça Major Luis Fernando).

Although there some 30 beaches in town, a better choice for sunbathing and water sports is Ilhabela, a 30-minute ferryboat ride from São Sebastião. Justly named Beautiful Island, Ilhabela is a tropical paradise with some scattered historical buildings, but it is better known for its marine wildlife. The island's inns — *Itapemar* (341 Av. Pedro Paula de Morais; phone: 124-721329) and *Mercedes* (Prainha Mercedes; phone 124-721071) — can arrange diving equipment rental.

**GUARUJÁ:** Continue on SP-55 for 79 miles (126 km) to Guarujá, a glitzy resort city of 207,000. Unlike the other, simple towns along the route, Guarujá has chic beaches, similar to Rio de Janeiro. The best is Pitangueiras — in the city itself — (where people promenade and sample ice cream in its many *sorveterias* or ice cream parlors) and Pernambuco, 5 miles (8 km) from the center of town and therefore even more exclusive. Nightlife is almost as important here as surfing and sunning for the affluent *paulistas* who escape here on weekends — try *Aquarius* (913 Rua Mareschal Floriano Peixoto; phone: 132-864148) and *Boate Caixa Lote* at the *Casa Grande Hotel* (999 Av. Miguel Stefano, Praia da Enseada; phone: 132-862223).

**SANTOS:** Eight miles (13 km) west of Guarujá is Santos (pop. 483,000), São Paulo's port, and Brazil's largest and most active harbor. Connected to the mainland by bridges, Santos's magnificent beaches are next to high-rise apartment buildings and wide, tree-lined streets. Among the more historic sights here are *Museu de Arte Sacra* (Sacred Art Museum) in the Mosteiro de São Bento (795 Rua Santa Joana d'Arc; phone: 132-338578), the late-16th-century Convento do Carmo and its adjacent 18th-century Capela da Ordem Terceira (16 Praça Brigedeiro do Rio Branco), and the early-17th-century Capela de Nossa Senhora do Monte Serrat (33 Praça Correia de Melo).

From Santos, SP55 continues 45 miles (72 km) up gently sloping terrain to São Paulo.

## BEST EN ROUTE

Accommodations along this route range from simple inns to luxury resorts. The best reflect the most attractive aspects of the Costa Verde — they are located on secluded beaches or, as in Parati, in colonial-style buildings in the town's historic center. Expect to pay $80 to $130 for a double room in an expensive hotel; $65 to $80 in a moderate place; and $40 to $65 for inexpensive lodgings. Breakfast is usually included in the price of the room.

### ITACURUÇÁ

**Elias C** – Located on the island of Itacuruçá (*not* the town of the same name on the mainland), this simple, but well-equipped hotel has 30 rooms and 8 chalets and offers facilities for water sports and nature walks. Praia Cabeça do Boi, Ilha de Itacuruçá (phone: 21-780-1003). Moderate.

**Hotel do Pierre** – Also located on the island, with its own beach and private garden, this unassuming 51-room hotel offers a restaurant, a full range of land and water activities, and a playground for children. Coroa Grande, Ilha de Itacuruçá (phone: 21-788-1560). Moderate.

### MANGARATIBA

**Club Méditerranée Village das Pedras** – Attractively landscaped, this 324-room member of the worldwide group was built in colonial style a few years ago. It has its own beach, an extensive pool area, and offers the usual array of *Club Med* sports, including sailing, windsurfing, water skiing, snorkeling, scuba diving, tennis (9 lighted courts, 3 of which are indoors), squash, soccer, volleyball, basketball, archery, cycling, and a fitness center. There are separate facilities for children ages 4 to 10 and 10 to 12. Minimum stay Thursday through Sunday; weekly stays run from Sunday to Sunday. Km 55, BR-101 (phone: 21-789-1635; in Rio de Janeiro, 21-297-5337; in São Paulo, 11-813-7311; in Salvador, 71-247-3531; in the US, 800-258-2633). Expensive.

**Porto Bello** – This 86-room hotel sits on its own 2-mile beach and the guestrooms are luxuriously situated in two buildings that also house 2 restaurants, a bar, and a swimming pool. A soaring bamboo-and-thatch roof dramatically defines the public spaces, which are accented with antiques and hand-painted pottery. Recreational facilities include windsurfing, boating in kayaks and dinghies, tennis, and horseback riding. Km 47, BR-101 (phone: 21-789-1485; in Rio de Janeiro, 21-267-7375; in the US, 800-544-5503). Expensive.

### ANGRA DOS REIS

**Hotel do Frade** – A pioneer in luxury resort accommodations on the Costa Verde, it has 117 attractively decorated rooms and 17 suites, its own beach, an 18-hole golf course, facilities for water sports, horseback riding, and cycling. BR-101, Km 123 (phone: 234-651212; in Rio de Janeiro, 21-551-5394; in the US, 800-544-5503). Expensive.

**Portogalo** – Splendidly located on a cliff overlooking the Ilha Grande Bay, this 100-room hotel has a chair lift that links the property's beach, where it also operates a marina and seafood restaurant. Km 123, BR-101 (phone: 243-651022; in Rio de Janeiro, 21-267-7375; in the US, 800-544-5503). Expensive.

***Pousada Mestre Augusto*** – This simple and pristine little hotel is located just outside the town of Angra dos Reis on Praia Grande beach, and offers boating and windsurfing. It's a good idea to book ahead — the inn has only 6 rooms. 4509 Estrada do Contorno (phone 243-650619). Moderate.

## PARATI

***Pousada Pardieiro*** – What distinguishes this peaceful 24-room *pousada* from others in town with similar facilities (small size, colonial-style decor, restaurant, air conditioning, and swimming pool) is its own private garden. Children under 15 are not allowed. 74 Rua do Comércio (phone: 243-711370; in Rio de Janeiro, 21-240-7749; in São Paulo, 11-258-7966). Expensive.

***Porto Pousada Parati*** – The 46 rooms at this historic inn surround an outdoor swimming pool and relaxing patios. There also is a restaurant serving Brazilian fare — the emphasis is on fish — a bar, and parking. Rua do Comércio (phone: 243-711205; in Rio de Janeiro, 21-267-7375; in the US, 800-544-5503). Moderate.

***Refúgio das Caravelas*** – Just outside town, this 14-room hostelry offers simple beachside accommodations, a special blessing during hot weather or high season when the well-worn streets of Parati clatter with well-heeled *cariocas* and *paulistas*. Estrada para Ubatuba (phone: 243-711270). Moderate.

## UBATUBA

***Sol e Vida*** – Ubatuba's most luxurious hotel has 41 rooms as well as a beach, swimming pool, tennis, volleyball, soccer, and child care, all of which attract many *paulista* families. Its seafood restaurant, *Cassino Sol e Vida,* is considered the best in the area. Km 9, Praia da Enseada (phone: 124-420188). Expensive.

***Solar das Aguas Cantantes*** – Slightly smaller than *Sol e Vida,* with just 21 rooms, this hotel has similar facilities, including a popular seafood restaurant. Km 14, Praia do Lázaro (phone: 124-420178). Expensive.

***Wembley Inn*** – Located on a hill that slopes down to a beach, this 45-room property offers a restaurant, and a full line of sports and health facilities, including a pool, tennis, and sauna. Km 8, Praia das Toninhas (phone: 124-420198). Expensive to moderate.

***Bonhotel*** – The best low-price option for those to want to be near the pricey and flashy resort scene. This 17-room hotel is shares the same beach as *Sol e Vida* and has a TV set in each room, a bar (but no restaurant), and parking. Km 9, Praia da Enseada (phone: 124-420011). Inexpensive.

## CARAGUATATUBA

***Pousadas da Tabatinga*** – This 24-room beachside hotel offers water sports as well as tennis, basketball, and soccer. Km 17, Estrada para Ubatuba, Praia Tabatinga (phone: 124-241411; in São Paulo, 11-289-7786). Expensive.

***Jundu*** – Located right on the beach, this 14-room hotel also has a simple restaurant and gameroom. Km 10, Estrada para Ubatuba, Praia de Massaguacu (phone: 124-361134). Moderate.

## SÃO SEBASTIÃO

***Porto Grande Hotel*** – The best accommodations in town. This modern hotel on the beach offers 31 rooms, a restaurant, bar, and swimming pool. 1440 Av. Guarda-Mor Lobo Viana, Praia de Porto Grande (phone: 124-521101). Moderate.

## GUARUJÁ

***Casa Grande*** – Lushly landscaped with tropical flowers and palms, this 162-room luxury resort offers golf and tennis as well as fine dining and a discotheque. The crowd of wealthy *paulistas* that frequent this spot makes reservations a must, especially on weekends and from December through March. 999 Av. Miguel Estefano (phone: 123-862223; in Sao Paulo, 11-282-4277). Expensive.

# Rio de Janeiro to Belo Horizonte

The 290-mile (464-km) route from Rio de Janeiro north to Belo Horizonte is one of the most scenic and historic in South America. Starting at Avenida Brasil in Rio, BR-040 winds its way through tropical and subtropical flora and spectacular mountains to the 19th-century "imperial" city of Petrópolis (pop. 240,000), 40 miles (64 km) from Rio and 2,748 feet above sea level.

In Petrópolis you already can see the odd mixture of tropical, subtropical, and even temperate-zone flora that excited the scientific interest of Brazil's great post-independence ruler Dom Pedro II. From Petrópolis to Belo Horizonte is another 250 miles (400 km) of increasingly temperate but continuously mountainous terrain. Crossing the border between the states of Rio de Janeiro and Minas Gerais just after Três Rios, 50 miles (80 km) from Petrópolis, you enter the industrial region around Juiz de Fora. Approaching the state capital of Belo Horizonte, the land begins to take on the iron-red color that is typical of Minas Gerais (which means literally General Mines), one of the great mineral centers of the world.

The state's iron ore reserves are estimated to be an astounding 38½ billion tons, but Minas Gerais also produces nickel, tin, chrome, silver, gold, and diamonds. The state's fabulous mineral production and processing industry is also of interest to tourists, since metalwork handicrafts as well as precious and semi-precious stones are traditionally good buys.

In the hilly, red-tinted Serra da Mantiqueira region between Juiz de Fora and Belo Horizonte, a distance of 150 miles (240 km), lies one of Brazil's most important historical treasures, the Old Minas region, which includes the colonial cities of Ouro Preto, São João Del Rei, Tiradentes, Congonhas, and Mariana, preserved for the benefit of historians and tourists.

It was in 1695 that gold was first discovered in Minas Gerais, which led, in the 18th century, to the first significant development of the state. Many of the cities and towns of Old Minas trace their beginnings to the time of the gold rush and to the long period of prosperity that followed. It was also here in 1789 that a group of merchants, clergymen, and planters plotted the famous Inconfidência Mineira (Independence Movement), one of the first colonial revolts against the Portuguese crown. The political leader, Joaquim José da Silva Xavier, better known as Tiradentes (literally "Tooth-puller," for he was a dentist), was arrested and executed in Rio de Janeiro. Tiradentes is one of the great heroes of Brazilian history, and his name is used liberally for towns, plazas, and roads throughout the state.

In more contemporary times the state of Minas Gerais (Brazilians usually say simply "Minas") has served as one of the political and economic capitals of Brazil, supplying the nation with presidents, artists, and some of the nation's most distinguished bankers. The people of Minas, with their distinctive accent, are regarded by other Brazilians as being somewhat stubborn and tenacious, although extremely courteous and intelligent.

The state is also one of the most important artistic centers of the nation. In Ouro Preto, Congonhas, and the other towns of Old Minas, some of the best-preserved and most important works of Brazil's baroque and rococo periods in art, sculpture, and architecture can be seen. Particularly noteworthy are the world-famous sculptures of Antônio Francisco Lisboa, known as Aleijadinho ("the Little Cripple"), whose 18th-century religious works are among the highlights of any visit to Brazil. Belo Horizonte, on the other hand, is more modern. During a characteristically energetic urban renewal campaign in the early 1940s, Belo Horizonte's mayor, Juscelino Kubitschek (who served as Brazil's president from 1956 to 1961), commissioned world-famous architect Oscar Niemeyer to design a number of structures in the city's Pampulha District that still seem futuristic today.

The highway from Rio to Petrópolis is extremely steep, but the road conditions are generally good. The entire route from Rio to Juiz de Fora has been widened to four lanes and provides good driving conditions. After Juiz de Fora, the highway has two lanes and passes through mountains for its entire length, although it is not as steep as the initial Rio-Petrópolis segment.

The best local guidebook to the region is the trilingual — English, Portuguese, Spanish — *Guia Quatro Rodas,* which includes detailed information on routes, attractions, and accommodations for the entire country. It can be purchased at newsstands for about $10.

**PETRÓPOLIS:** This historic 19th-century city (named after Brazil's two emperors, both named Pedro) lies 40 miles (64 km) west of Rio de Janeiro on the well-paved but sinuous highway BR-040. At an altitude of 2,748 feet, the city is noted for its moderate climate and rich flora.

Petrópolis (pop. 290,000) was founded in 1843 by Dom Pedro II, the second emperor of Brazil, and its earliest settlers were Germans. A number of street and district names — Westfalia, Bingen, and Darmstadt — still reflect this heritage. During the latter part of his 49-year reign, Emperor Pedro II used the city as his summer residence. It was here in 1889 that the liberal monarch was first informed that Brazil's First Republic had been proclaimed in Rio de Janeiro. He left the city for the last time in November of that year and died in exile in France 2 years later. Since 1940, his summer palace has been an official historical site, and in 1947 it was the meeting place for the signing of the Hemispheric Mutual Assistance Treaty — the historic "Rio Pact," which has aligned US and Latin American military and political interests ever since.

The junction of the Petrópolis-Teresópolis bypass road and BR-040, 7 miles (11 km) outside the city, affords a spectacular view of the tropical valleys below and the heights of the Serra Fluminense ahead. After reaching the plateau a few miles beyond, the road approaches the first important suburb of Petrópolis, Quitandinha, the site of the memorable, Normandy-style *Quitandinha Club* (Rua Coronel Veiga). Once one of the most elegant hotels in the world, the picture-postcard structure is now a private club but the public is welcome to visit this extraordinary property.

Busy Avenida Quinze de Novembro is the heart of Petrópolis. On the west side is the emperor's lushly overgrown Botanic Gardens, and just beyond, on 220 Rua da Imperatriz, is the Imperial Palace. Open from noon to 5:30 PM every day except Monday, the interior of the palace has been faithfully preserved as its last occupant left it. The major attraction is the room that houses Pedro's crown — a remarkable work of craftsmanship that sparkles with 77 pearls and 629 diamonds. Across the street is the private residence of the Bragança family, the legitimate heirs to the Brazilian throne.

Up the street from the palace is the Catedral de São Pedro de Alcântara on (Av. Tiradentes), a Gothic cathedral that is Pedro I's burial site. Farther up the road, beyond the turnoff to Itaipava, is the Crystal Palace, erected by the royal family for musical and horticultural exhibitions. The entire glass and metal structure was imported from France in pieces and assembled in Brazil.

Also worth seeing are the *Santos Dumont House,* a museum (at 124 Rua do Encanto; closed Mondays), and the castle-like *Weapons Museum* (on BR-040 12 miles/19 km from the city on the Rio side). Largely forgotten outside Brazil, Santos Dumont was the father of Brazilian aviation, one of the most important inventors and daredevils of the early days of flying. His home, built in 1918, features a collection of aviation relics and memorabilia. The *Weapons Museum* (phone: 42-6564; visits by appointment only) is noted for its collection of early military hardware as well as for its commanding valley view.

**En Route from Petrópolis** – Six miles (10 km) beyond Petrópolis on BR-040 is *Tarrafa's Churrascaria,* which features reasonably priced barbecue dishes according to the traditional Brazilian *rodizio* plan ("running skewer" — all you can eat of a variety of meats) and, at night, entertainment by nationally known musicians. On the highway 2 miles (3 km) before *Tarrafa's,* look for the turnoff to *Florilândia* (on Rua Barão do Rio Branco), a marvelous, almost hidden rose garden with an alpine-style restaurant and a well-stocked but high-priced gift shop.

Another 13 miles (21 km) down BR-040 is Itaipava, a small town noted for its good buys in ceramics and home decorations. Itaipava marks the junction of BR-040 and BR-486, the northern cutoff that extends 25 miles (40 km) through magnificent scenery to the city of Teresópolis, in the heart of Serra dos Orgãos National Park.

**TERESÓPOLIS:** With a population of about 130,000, Teresópolis stands at an elevation of little more than 3,000 feet, but it is surrounded by an impressive set of sheer peaks that are collectively known as the Dedos de Deus ("Fingers of God"), the highest of which is the 7,422-foot Pedra do Sino. Also notable here is the *Von Martius Natural History Museum* (inside the park 8 miles/13 km from the city). Good restaurants include the *São Moritz* (also a hotel, Km 41 of the Teresópolis–Nova Friburgo Hwy.) and the *Margo,* an excellent German restaurant downtown (259 Rua Heitor de Moura Estevão; phone: 21-742-7414). Other restaurants are on Avenida Lúcio Meira downtown. Rugged RJ-130 begins east of the city and runs 66 miles (106 km) to Nova Friburgo.

**NOVA FRIBURGO:** At 2,778 feet above sea level, Nova Friburgo (pop. 160,000) is the third city of the Serra Fluminense. In both its architectural and its natural setting, Nova Friburgo retains the alpine aspect that first drew Swiss settlers to its picturesque valley in the early 19th century. The city is noted for its mountain scenery and its resorts, which offer sports, mountain climbing, and hiking programs. The highest mountain is the 7,575-foot Pico da Caledônia. A 2,132-foot cable car (which operates 9 AM to 5:30 PM) takes passengers from Praça dos Suspiros downtown to Morro da Cruz, which commands views of the city and countryside. Restaurants are around Praça Getúlio Vargas.

**En Route from Nova Friburgo** – The Petrópolis–Belo Horizonte road continues for another 62 miles (99 km) to the Rio-Minas border, passing a small railroad museum near Paraíba do Sul on the Rio side of the border. After another 27 miles (43 km) of well-paved, four-lane highway you arrive in the industrial city of Juiz de Fora (pop. 300,000) in Minas.

**JUIZ DE FORA:** Set in a deep valley at an elevation of 2,227 feet, Juiz de Fora (pop.

**752 DIRECTIONS / Brazil**

380,000) can be a good stop for lunch. Try the *Brasão* (2262 Av. Rio Branco) in the heart of downtown or the *Adega do Minho* (in the *Ritz Hotel,* 549 Rua Floriano Peixoto; phone: 32-212-8223). *Mariano Procópio Museum* (Rua Dom Pedro), a former mansion containing a number of Brazilian and European paintings, is set on a swan-graced lake. Its original owner was the engineer who built the first Rio-Petrópolis highway in the 19th century. Open every afternoon except Mondays (phone: 32-211-1145). Three miles (4 km) outside town is a statue of Christ atop the Morro do Imperador similar to the statue on Corcovado in Rio de Janeiro.

**En Route from Juiz de Fora** – BR-040 is two lanes all the way to Belo Horizonte, a distance of 150 increasingly rugged miles (240 km). Driving at night can be particularly hazardous since reckless truck drivers dominate the road. Beyond Santos Dumont, 25 miles (40 km) from Juiz, the road begins to climb again until you reach the horticultural center of Barbacena, 72 miles (115 km) from Juiz.

**BARBACENA:** Nine miles (14 km) before this city of 115,000 lies an area of small rose and chrysanthemum farms that form the basis of a unique export industry. The farms, some of which can be visited on request, produce 150,000 dozen roses a month from October to March. Most of the crop is shipped to Rio in refrigerated trucks; some are sold there, and some are placed in refrigerated containers and flown on to Europe. Every October this city of 86,000 celebrates its major industry with a 3-day *Rose Festival* in Senador Bias Fortes Exposition Park. Worth visiting for a good lunch is the *Grogotó SENAC* restaurant (phone: 32-331-7755) 2 miles (3 km) from town on the main road. The busy spot is completely staffed by service trainees and hence is reasonably priced. In the middle of town, is the Basílica de São José Operario (on Praça Dom Bosco), and in the city's shops are good buys in leather, ceramics, and wood handicrafts.

**En Route from Barbacena** – An obligatory side trip for anyone on this route is a journey into the historic region of Old Minas, accessible via BR-265 to the west of Barbacena. You first come to São João Del Rei, the beginning of the historical and artistic heart of Minas. The rich history of Old Minas is open today to the tourist. The hilly, red-tinted setting is bracing and spectacular. Unlike most of Brazil, the Old Minas region is often quite cool during the winter, with temperatures averaging in the 60s F (15–21C) and sometimes dipping into the 50s or 40s F (5–15C). During the summer, average temperatures are in the 70s F (21–27C).

Like most Brazilians, the *mineiros* love to eat, and unique local dishes are served everywhere. The dairy products here are the best in Brazil, originating in the rich pasturelands in the western part of the state. *Feijão tropeiro* (black beans in bean sauce), *frango ao molho pardo* (brown sauce and chicken), and *lombo de porco e torresmo* (luscious pork loin and sauce) are among the most popular.

**SÃO JOÃO DEL REI:** Famous for its baroque churches, this city of 82,000 is 36 miles (58 km) west of Barbacena, at an altitude of 2,942 feet. Its most notable church is the Igreja de São Francisco de Assis (on Praça Frei Orlando; phone: 32-371-3966), built in 1774. It contains several works by Aleijadinho, and visitors should know that the priests have been known to bar tourists who wear short-sleeve blouses or shorts. Nossa Senhora do Pilar on (Rua Getúlio Vargas), noted for its gold-encrusted altars, was opened in 1721. Nossa Senhora do Carmo (on Praça Carlos Gomes), completed in 1732, includes a small museum. The city is one of the oldest in Minas and has 11 churches in all, but, unlike nearby Tiradentes or Ouro Preto, it also has been penetrated by modern buildings. Good buys here include wood, silver, and pewter handicrafts and flatware. Eight miles (13 km) away is the Fazenda Pombal, where the patriot Tiradentes was born. An interesting sidelight is the *María Fumaça,* a coal-burning train that runs Fridays, weekends, and holidays to Tiradentes at 10 AM and 2:15 PM from the RFFSA station (366 Hermilio Alves; phone: 32-371-2888).

**TIRADENTES:** Nine miles (14 km) from São João Del Rei and 33 miles (53 km) from

Barbacena, this city of 10,000 boasts an almost completely preserved 18th-century façade. Places worth seeing include the baroque Igreja de Nossa Senhora das Mercês (on Praça das Mercês), the Matriz de Santo Antônio (on Rue Santissima Trindade) with its golden altars and 18th-century organ, and the Tiradentes House (on Praça Berço da Liberadade). Some of the churches contain furnishings that were uniquely crafted, without either nails or glue. The city also is noted for its many fountains and is surrounded by picturesque hills.

**CONGONHAS:** Seventy-two miles (115 km) from São João Del Rei on BR-383 or 60 miles (96 km) from Barbacena on BR-040 is Congonhas, one of the most important cities of Old Minas. With a population of 41,000 and elevation of 3,243 feet, it is the home of the Santuário do Bom Jesus (Church of the Good Child Jesus; on Praça da Basílica). Outside the church are famous statues of the Twelve Prophets, and inside, 66 sculptures of the Passion of Christ. All the soapstone statues are the work of Aleijadinho, who completed them in his early sixties. The incredible figures seem to come alive as the viewer approaches them, and the graceful esplanade that is the showcase for the Twelve Prophets is a work of art in itself. (Church closed Mondays.) The city is also noted for its festivals, including the annual *Aleijandinho Jubilee* in the first half of September, but the Prophets are the town's main attraction. Other notable churches include Nossa Senhora da Conceição, built in 1745 (on Praça 7 de Setembro) and the 17th-century Rosário (on Rua do Rosário).

**OURO PRETO:** The capital of Old Minas until 1897, Ouro Preto ("Black Gold") is a perfectly preserved 18th-century colonial city with a current population of 68,000, 60 miles (96 km) from Belo Horizonte or 85 miles (136 km) from Congonhas on the circuitous BR-040 cutoff route. Ouro Preto is the home of some of the most important artistic and historical treasures of Brazil. Begin the journey through Ouro Preto at the Igreja de São Francisco de Assis, the most important church in the city, in the heart of town (on Largo de São Francisco). The church contains works by Aleijadinho and his noted associate, the painter Ataíde, including the latter's *Glorification of the Blessed Virgin*. Also interesting is the *Museu de Minerologia* (Minerology Museum; 20 Praça Tiradentes; phone: 31-551-1666), formerly the governor's palace, which was finished in 1742 and is now part of the state Minerology School. The museum is open every afternoon except holidays. The baroque Church of Nossa Senhora do Carmo (on Rua Costa Sena) includes some of Aleijadinho's last works. The tile paintings there were done by Ataíde. Nossa Senhora de Conceição (on Rua Bernardo Vasconcelos) is the site of Aleijadinho's tomb and includes a museum annex devoted exclusively to the great artist. Nossa Senhora do Pilar (on Praça Monsenhor Castilho Barbosa not far from the central Praça Tiradentes) houses the city's silver museum whose interiors are rich in gold and silver work. The most imposing museum in town (at the site of a former penitentiary) is the *Museu da Inconfidência* (Museum of the Rebellion; 139 Praça Tiradentes; phone: 31-551-1121), which houses a collection of sacred art. Open daily except Mondays from noon to 5:30 PM. Half the sights are open mornings, half afternoons; check at the tourist office.

Ouro Preto is a town to be walked through and savored. In addition to the main attractions, there are countless 18th-century houses and public buildings along the cobbled streets and hills. In 1933 Ouro Preto was declared a historical city, and justly so. It has 13 churches, 11 chapels, 18 fountains, and numerous byways such as Rua São João and Rua Conde de Bobadela, where you'll find the famous *Calabouço* restaurant, which got its name from the fact that it used to be the city jail (132 Bobadela; phone: 31-551-1222). The *Casa do Ouvidor* (42 Rua Conde de Bobadela; phone: 31-551-2141), is also a good spot for a meal. Festivals here include several events during July as well as *Tiradentes Day* (April 21, the date of his execution in 1792) and *Holy Week*. On April 21, Ouro Preto becomes the state capital again — for 1 day. Good buys include soapstone statues at prices much lower than in the big cities. If the city of Ouro

Preto looks at all familiar, especially the main square, this is where US film director Paul Mazursky shot *Moon Over Parador.*

**MARIANA:** Only 11 miles (18 km) from Ouro Preto along a steep road, Mariana (pop. 34,000; elevation 2,286 feet) is said to be the oldest town in Minas (founded in 1696). The Igreja de São Francisco de Assis (on Praça João Pinheiro) includes paintings by Ataíde. The cathedral (on Praça Dr. Cláudio Manoel) has works by both Aleijadinho and Ataíde and maintains an ancient organ that is operated by a hand bellows. Praça João Pinheiro is also the site of Nossa Senhora do Carmo and of the old Governor's Palace. The *Museu Arquidiocesano* (Archdiocese Museum; 49 Rua Frei Durão) also displays works by Aleijadinho and Ataíde. Open daily. For shoppers, the bargains here are rugs. One of the oldest of Brazil's few remaining active gold mines is just outside of town.

**SABARÁ:** Another city on the Old Minas circuit is Sabará, 15 miles (24 km) outside Belo Horizonte off BR-262. From the hilltop just before you reach the town of 81,000, you'll set a magnificent view of Belo Horizonte and the surrounding countryside. The Igreja Nossa Senhora do Carmo (on Rua do Carmo) includes works by Aleijadinho, most notably his famous *Four Evangelists.* On a hill overlooking the town is the noted *Museu de Ouro* (Gold Museum; on Rua da Intendência; no phone); it is open Tuesdays through Sundays from noon to 5 PM. Rua Pedro II has some of the best colonial homes. Rua Caquende is the site of the legendary Caquende Fountain, but don't sample it: The legend says that those who drink from its waters will never leave Sabará. Below the *Gold Museum* (on Largo de Nossa Senhora do O) is the church of the same name, displaying an uncanny Oriental influence. *Holy Week* in Sabará is especially festive.

**BELO HORIZONTE:** The state capital of Minas since 1897, Belo (pop. 2.34 million) is one of the great cities of Brazil and the first to be completely planned and built from scratch in the country's interior. The city also went through a significant face-lift in the 1940s during the administration of Mayor Juscelino Kubitschek (later President of Brazil and the man responsible for the construction of Brasília). The two most important changes were the creation of an industrial park in the Contagem District and the opening of a modernistic park area around Pampulha. Downtown Belo Horizonte is a busy financial and administrative center, with the Municipal Park (bordered by Avenida Afonso Pena, the city's main street, and Alameda Ezequiel Dias) as its heart. Overlooking the park is the *Othon Palace* hotel (see *Best en Route*). The park is noted for its 2,000 varieties of trees, its beautiful gardens and ponds, and a Sunday morning arts and crafts fair that offers bargains in all types of handicrafts. Tree-lined avenues radiate from the park.

A few blocks away is the Praça de Liberdade, the Governor's Palace, and the city's library. The approach to the plaza is impressively lined with royal palms. Important churches in downtown Belo include Nossa Senhora de Lourdes (on Rua Espírito Santo), featuring attractive stained glass windows; and the nearby Nossa Senhora de Boa Viagem, which has a plant fair and sale every Saturday. Also located in the downtown area is the fascinating *Museu de Mineralogia,* a gem and mining museum housed in the old City Hall. Open daily from 8 AM to 5 PM (1149 Rua da Bahia; phone: 31-212-1400). In sharp contrast to this part of downtown Belo is its modernistic Pampulha District, 7 miles (12 km) outside town around a beautiful lake. The setting there is dominated by the *Governor Magalhães Pinto Stadium* — known locally as *Minerão.* The stadium is supposed to be the second-largest in the world (surpassed by the *Maracanã* in Rio de Janeiro), seating 110,000 noisy soccer fans (phone: 31-441-4866). On another part of the lake is the famed Igreja de São Francisco de Assis. Its rounded surfaces portend the stylistic breakthroughs made later by its architect, Oscar Niemeyer, when he designed Brasília. Inside are works by Brazil's great 20th-century artist Cândido Portinari. Other notable structures include the Casa do Baile and the *Museu de Arte Moderne* (Modern Art Museum; phone: 31-443-4533), both designed

## DIRECTIONS / Brazil

by Niemeyer as well. Slightly removed from this area are the city zoo and, on the opposite side of the lake, the Pampulha Airport. The entire district was laid out and landscaped by another noted Brazilian artist, Roberto Burle Marx, who also participated in the design of Brasília some 15 years later. The *Modern Art Museum,* incidentally, was a gambling casino until gambling was outlawed in Brazil in 1947.

## BEST EN ROUTE

This region of scenic towns and panoramic views is fast becoming a heavily traveled route for both Brazilian and foreign tourists, so there are modern, sophisticated hotels. You should try to make advance reservations during the summer, December through March, especially in the smaller towns, where there are not many places to stay. Hotels listed as expensive will cost $80 per night and up for a double room; moderate will cost from $40 to $75; and inexpensive, usually under $35.

### PETRÓPOLIS

*Casa do Sol* – Just outside the city, this hotel has a nice view, a swimming pool, and sauna. Estrada Rio-Petrópolis, 115 Quitandinha (phone: 242-435062). Expensive to moderate.

*Margaridas* – Accommodations with a pool and good food. 235 Rua Bispo D. José Pereira Alves (phone: 242-424686). Moderate.

### TERESÓPOLIS

*Rosa dos Ventos* – Considered to be one of Brazil's best country house hotels, this Relais & Châteaux member was made popular by the foreign community of Rio who were looking for weekend retreats. All 41 rooms private bathrooms. There is a pool, restaurant, tennis, and horseback riding. No children under 16. Located at Km 22.6 of the Teresópolis–Nova Friburgo Hwy./RJ-130 (phone: 21-742-8833). Expensive.

*São Moritz* – A pool, sports facilities, a boutique, and good food, included in the price of your room. At Km 41 of the Teresópolis–Nova Friburgo Hwy. (RJ-130), 16 miles (26 km) from the city (phone: 21-741-1115; in Rio de Janeiro, 21-239-4445). Expensive.

*Caxangá* – Pleasant place with a restaurant, pool, and sports facilities. 68 Rua Caxangá (phone: 21-742-1062; in Rio de Janeiro, 21-257-4732). Inexpensive.

### NOVA FRIBURGO

*Bucsky* – There is a pool, horseback riding, and good food included in the price. Nova Friburgo–Niterôi Hwy. (RJ-116), 3 miles (5 km) from the city (phone: 245-22-5052; in Rio de Janeiro, 21-252-5053). Expensive.

*Sans Souci* – Sports, pool, horseback riding, movies, and a good restaurant included in the price. Jardim Sans Souci, 1 mile (1.6 km) from the city (phone: 245-227752; in Rio de Janeiro, 21-239-2089). Expensive.

*Camping CCB* – Comfortable camping facilities surrounded by exceptional natural beauty. Nova Friburgo, at Km 69 on Niteroí Hwy. (RJ-08) near the *Mury Garden* hotel. Inexpensive.

*Mury Garden* – A pool, boutique, horseback riding, and a good restaurant included in the price. Nova Friburgo–Niteroí Hwy., 5 miles (8 km) from the city (phone: 245-421120; in Rio de Janeiro, 21-220-2234). Inexpensive.

### JUIZ DE FORA

*Ritz* – Despite its name, a relatively unassuming hostelry, but it's the best in town. The 180 rooms have air conditioning and color TV sets. 2000 Av. Barão do Rio Branco (phone: 32-212-7300). Moderate to inexpensive.

***Imperial*** – A simple hotel with a restaurant. Rua Batista de Oliveria 605 (phone: 32-215-7400). Inexpensive.

## BARBACENA

***Grogotó SENAC*** – Highly recommended, it has a restaurant, and is staffed by hotel and restaurant students from government training programs. Service is excellent throughout, and it's hard to get a table. BR-040, at Km 699, 2 miles (3 km) from the city (phone: 32-331-7755). Inexpensive.

## SÃO JOÃO DEL REI

***Novotel Porto Real*** – This pleasant place has a restaurant featuring an international menu. 254 Av. Eduardo Magalhães (phone: 32-371-1201). Moderate to inexpensive.

## TIRADENTES

***Solar da Ponte*** – Recommended hostelry, but it has no restaurant (though the rate does include breakfast and afternoon tea). The address is simply Praça das Mercês (phone: 32-355-1255). Moderate.

## OURO PRETO

***Estrada Real*** – The best property in the area is located in a park right outside of town. It offers both rooms and chalets, and 3 of the rooms are accessible to the handicapped. Sports facilities, including 2 swimming pools, are the main attraction, along with 3 bars and a restaurant. Inconfidentes–Belo Horizonte Hwy., 5 miles (8 km) from town (phone: 31-551-2122; in Belo Horizonte, 31-273-1144). Moderate.

***Luxor Pousada*** – An historic hotel converted from a colonial mansion, with simple, rustically furnished, air conditioned rooms with refrigerator and phone; popular restaurant and bar. 16 Rua Doutor Alfredo Baeta (phone: 31-551-2244; toll-free in Brazil, 21-800-3073). Moderate.

***Grande Hotel Ouro Preto*** – Built in the modern style of famed Brazilian architect Oscar Niemeyer. 164 Rua Senador Rocha Lagoa (phone: 31-551-1488). Inexpensive.

***Pouso Chico Rei*** – A colonial home converted into a 6-room hotel (3 with private bath), but without a restaurant. Highly recommended. 90 Rua Brigadeiro Mosqueira (phone: 31-551-1274). Inexpensive.

## BELO HORIZONTE

***Brasilton Contagem*** – TAn affiliate of Hilton International), this 145-room hotel is in a resort setting 9 miles (14 km) out of town. There is a pool, health club, and entertainment. Rod. Fernão Dias, CP 2220 (phone: 31-396-1100; toll-free in Brazil, 31-800-5850). Expensive.

***Othon Palace*** – A link in the Othon chain, it opened back in 1978 and features complete hotel services and a view of the city's park. With 309 rooms, this place is Belo Horizonte's largest hotel. 1050 Av. Afonso Pena (phone: 31-273-3844; toll-free in Brazil, 31-800-2318). Expensive.

***Real Palace*** – A luxurious 256-room property in the center of town, with a pool, health club, and restaurant. 901 Rua Espírito Santo (phone: 31-273-3111). Expensive.

***Del Rey*** – Considered one of the best in town, it includes shops, convention room, and a restaurant. 20 Praça Afonso Arinos, downtown (phone: 31-273-2211; toll-free in Brazil, 11-800-1441). Moderate.

***Normandy*** – Noted for its fine restaurant. 212 Rua Tamoios, downtown (phone: 31-201-6166). Moderate to inexpensive.

# Belo Horizonte to Brasília

From Belo Horizonte to Brasília there is a long stretch of relatively new road built to link the new inland capital with the rest of the country. While the 472-mile (755-km) trip can be made in 12 to 14 hours with few stops, you have to make some lengthy detours to see the main sights.

Highway BR-040 takes you diagonally across the state of Minas Gerais (shortened to "Minas" by residents), one of the most historically important areas in Brazil and the center of vast mineral deposits. From Belo Horizonte the terrain is mountainous, with peaks of 9,000 feet that contain the state's valuable deposits of iron ore, gold, limestone, manganese, and bauxite. This is Brazil's hottest and driest region, where temperatures of 100F (38C) are common during the dry season (May to November) and unpredictable torrential downpours cause extensive flash-flooding.

In 1698, gold was discovered in Minas by explorers from São Paulo, starting a great influx of Brazilian and Portuguese settlers in search of quick wealth. In the early 1700s, large quantities of diamonds were found in what is now the city of Diamantina, north of Belo Horizonte. In the next hundred years, the mines in this state yielded over 3 million karats of diamonds and 100 tons of gold. The mineral reserves were so important to the Brazilian economy that in 1763 the capital was moved from Salvador to Rio de Janeiro, the main port and access route to Minas. Today, iron ore is the source of wealth for the state, accounting for 10% of Brazil's total exports. Although the amount has greatly diminished, gold and diamonds are still mined there as well as semiprecious stones, such as topaz, aquamarine, and tourmaline.

**En Route from Belo Horizonte** – Instead of taking the main highway, BR-040, north from Belo Horizonte, you might consider making a visit to Gruta da Lapinha and Gruta de Maquiné, two of the 400 caves in the whole of Minas. Take the road from Belo Horizonte to Vespianino and Lagoa Santa. The first group of caves is at Gruta de Lapinha, only 25 miles (40 km) from the city. The caves themselves, with colorful stalactites and stalagmites, are open from 9 AM to 5 PM. At the nearby town of Lagoa Santa there is a lake with a sandy beach and good camping facilities. *Castelinho* (phone: 31-681-2075), near Gruta da Lapinha, is a good place to eat. From Lagoa Santa you can continue directly to Diamantina, almost a must for the traveler going to Brasília.

**DIAMANTINA:** This town, as its name suggests, was the very center of Brazil's diamond mining industry and is well worth a visit. You may find that while Diamantina is probably the best-preserved colonial town in Brazil, it does not have the splendor of Ouro Preto (see *Rio de Janeiro to Belo Horizonte,* above). This town of 39,000 is the birthplace of Juscelino Kubitschek, builder of Brasília. The town's economy still centers around the mining and processing of semi-precious stones, and these are good buys if you know quality. Worth seeing is the *Museu de Arte Popular* (Museum of Popular Art); 10 Praça Juscelino Kubitschek), part of the city public library, and the *Museu de Diamante* (Diamond Museum; on Rua Direita), open Tuesday through Sunday afternoons.

**En Route from Diamantina** – You must return to the main Belo Horizonte–Brasília highway to reach the federal capital. The road passes just below the hydroelectric dam that contains the waters of the Rio São Francisco to form Três Marias Lake. The small town of Pirapora, 200 miles (320 km) from Belo, is the next stopping place, a point where the river becomes navigable. Here the wood-burning, paddlewheel riverboats end their inland journey of 6 or 7 days from Juazeiro in Bahia.

**BRASÍLIA:** Since the beginning of the 19th century, successive Brazilian governments had planned to move the federal capital to the central plateau. But it was only with the government of Juscelino Kubitschek in the late 1950s that the dream became a reality. The former capital, Rio de Janeiro, had become so overcrowded that enlarging the various ministries was physically impossible. An equally important reason for moving the capital inland was to develop the interior of this immense country, where to this day 80% of its 148 million people live within 50 miles of the seacoast. It was felt that the new location would start people looking inland for their inspiration instead of toward Europe or North America. Unfortunately, the expected migration to the new city still hasn't materialized. In fact, some say the best thing about Brasília (pop. 1.57 million) is that it's only a 1½-hour flight to Rio.

In Brazil, where presidents cannot run for reelection, a president has had to move quickly to ensure that a project be near enough completion so that it cannot be abandoned by his successor. Kubitschek, born in the state of Minas (which would most benefit from the building of Brasília), started the project with the construction of the BR-040 Highway to the site of Brasília. To ensure the inauguration of the city during his presidency, Kubitschek got the buildings up as rapidly as possible; today some of the city's original buildings already are showing serious signs of age and the forced timetable of building. Many have had to be partially rebuilt due to flaws such as cracking cement. Sidewalks have been replaced and roads done.

Brasília is designed for tours by car; it is almost impossible to see it on foot. It has been built on the principle that there is plenty of space that should all be used, resulting in long distances between buildings. The contest to design the city was won by Lúcio Costa, who laid it out in the shape of an airplane, spacing residential districts out along the "wings" and the major government buildings on the "fuselage." The well-known Brazilian architect Oscar Niemeyer designed the major public buildings, including the *National Theater* and the houses of government. The major commercial districts — including banks, hotels, office buildings, cinemas, and shops — are at the intersection of the "wings" and the "fuselage," near the busy Brasília bus station.

Flying into Brasília, you have a very good panoramic view of the city, spreading out in a sort of giant bowl with the artificial Lake Paranoá as a backdrop. If you are arriving by car, you come upon a city that looks like an enormous oasis — a mirage that you cannot believe is true, especially after the very long and rather tedious drive from Belo Horizonte. As you approach, the first signs of habitation are the new lots marked for development on the fringes of the city; building within the confines of Brasília itself is strictly limited. The original area of the city — the Pilot Plan, as it is called — is completely developed now, and there are almost as many residents on the outskirts of Brasília as there are in the city proper.

Coming from Minas, you enter the city itself at the southern tip. To get to the center where the hotels are, there are several routes to choose from. The fastest way is to travel along the Eixo Monumental, but you can follow the Avenida das Nações (Avenue of the Nations) if you wish to pass closer to the lake and see the elegant embassies that line its shore. The street numbering and names are quite confusing to the newcomer, but once the code has been deciphered, getting around the city is very easy indeed. Brasília is divided into a series of blocks running from the center to each "wing" tip: They go from 1 to 16. This number forms the last two digits of a three-digit locating number. The first digit indicates where buildings lie on several parallel roads. There are also letter symbols for each of the various central districts. SHS, for example, is Setor Hoteleiro Sul, the hotel area in the southern "wing." SCS is Setor Comercial Sul, the southern commercial sector. All the hotels are in the same area and all business is done within one very small area, which does simplify locating the buildings. After selecting a hotel, make a quick tour of the city to get your bearings.

The easiest course is to drive around the Eixo Monumental (Monumental Axis), a one-way route where virtually all the buildings of importance and interest in central Brasília lie. Leaving your hotel, drive north along the axis, following the signs to Palacio Burity. The whole city is linked by fast expressways, and there are very few intersections with traffic signals to slow you down.

The first major building is the 600-foot-tall Torre de Televisão (Television Tower), in the very center of the axis near the bus station. This is one of the tallest communications towers in the world; you can take an express elevator to a viewing platform 225 feet above the ground. Another elevator takes visitors to a restaurant and bar with a panoramic view of the city, although the restaurant changes hands so often that it frequently is closed. At the highest level you can see as far as the horizon. This is one of the best places for you to get an idea of Brasília's layout. The best time to visit the tower is near sunset, when the whole city and the surrounding areas are illuminated with a beautiful golden light. It is the perfect time to take color photographs of the downtown area, stretched away from the tower to the Praça dos Três Poderes (Square of the Three Powers), where the congressional buildings, the president's palace, and other major administrative buildings are located. Because Brasília is not yet overcrowded with tourists, the TV tower is seldom busy. On the distant horizon you may see columns of smoke rising where areas of scrubland are being cleared for new building projects. At the foot of the TV tower on Saturdays, Sundays, and public holidays, a handicrafts fair is held, with articles for sale from all over Brazil. Particularly good buys are handmade leather shoes and sandals, glasswear, metal and semi-precious stones, jewelry, leather, furniture, and baskets. You also will find the famous dried flowers of Brasília, although a better selection is available daily on the square in front of the cathedral.

The next building of interest on the axis is the convention and leisure center, completed in 1979, with an auditorium for 2,000 delegates and other conference facilities. But part of this building is now also open to the general public, thereby providing the large public gathering place that has been absent so long in Brasília. There is a large recreation area with a tree-lined "lovers meeting area," complete with an open-air bar and dance floor. The city's planetarium and the *FUNARTE Theater* for Brazilian culture are part of this complex, which has a number of pools and waterfalls — particularly welcome in a city that is bone dry most of the year.

Opposite the convention center is Brasília's sports area, with a soccer stadium with seating for 100,000 spectators and a gymnasium. Nearby is a motor racetrack. On the axis at Praça do Cruzeiro is the Juscelino Kubitschek monument and museum in honor of the capital's founder.

Continuing on the axis to its end, the last building is the railway station, now also the interstate bus station, one of the select buildings designed by architect Oscar Niemeyer, appropriately enough, in the shape of a railroad car. At this point, turn around and head back on the southern side of the axis road. Leaving the TV tower on the left, the road passes beside the Estação Rodoviária (city bus station), the point of arrival and departure for the majority of Brasília's residents, who have come far to live here. Here you see the city as it really is. Long-distance buses arrive and depart for the distant Northeast, Amazonas, and the more civilized Southeast. Some of the vehicles, many of which are old and battered, will be traveling on rough direct roads for the next 48 hours or more, running through deep mud in the rainy season. If you do not want to drive around the city by car anymore, you can take the city bus to points of interest. With few exceptions, all the bus lines in Brasília start and finish here, and there are some circular trips that take you around the city. Buses marked "Três Poderes Universidade de Brasília" (University of Brasília), "Avenida das Nações" (Avenue of the Nations), and "Aeroporto" (Airport) are among the most interesting. Also in the bus station is one of the stores run by FUNAI, the Indian foundation. Here you can purchase pottery, baskets, bows and arrows, musical instruments (notably flutes), and ornaments. These latter generally are made from fish scales and bones as well as from a wide range of berries and nuts from the forest, feathers, and butterfly wings, all at very reasonable prices. The tourist office is also in the bus station, adjacent to the Indian shop. The staff will make hotel reservations for the visitor in need of a room, as well as provide maps and guides to the city.

Continuing past the bus station toward the Três Poderes, the first major building is the Cathedral of Brasília. This building is in the form of a crown of thorns, and the nave is below ground. The roof is surrounded by water, making this one of the many places in Brasília where visitors can find relief from the dry, hot city. Before reaching the main circular nave you still follow a darkened passage called the Passage of Reflection. The St. Peter statue, suspended from the roof, is one of the main features in this light and airy structure. The marble altar and marble blocks spaced around the nave for temporary seating are prominent features in the rather stark but restful interior. The glass panels of the roof reflect the water in the surrounding pool, and the buildings of the city beyond shimmer in the pool's reflection.

Proceeding farther down the axis, the foreign ministry, Itamarati Palace, the last of these buildings on the way to Three Powers Square, should not be missed. This is one of Brasília's most notable buildings, rising out of beautiful water gardens that hold Brasília's best-known and most-photographed piece of sculpture, the *Meteor*. In the Itamarati Palace is one of the best collections of Brazilian art, including magnificent paintings by Portinari, one of Brazil's most important painters. Register at the reception desk a day before visiting. In the center of the Monumental Axis just below the Itamarati Palace are the Congress buildings, composed of the House of Deputies, the Senate, and the various offices housed in a huge, marble-coated tower, also rising out of the lake. These buildings can be visited by appointment, between 2:30 and 5 PM (phone: 61-211-6640 or 61-221-4432). Black and white swans, offspring of a gift from the British government, glide peacefully in the water gardens.

Behind the Congress is Three Powers Square. On one side is the Planalto Palace, the office of the president; the other holds the Supreme Court. There are several important pieces of sculpture on the square, including the *Two Warriors* and a statue of justice. There is also a curious-shaped dovecote, the home of hundreds of pigeons. The birds can sometimes be persuaded to fly in the right direction for taking interesting photographs of the buildings in the foreground. The Planalto Palace (Uplands Palace) is one of the most graceful buildings in Brasília, its roof supported by one of the several varieties of marble pillars that are the hallmark of Brasília's architecture. Changing-of-the-guard ceremonies take place in front of the palace on Tuesdays and Fridays at 8:30 AM and 5:30 PM.

Just below Three Powers Square is the capital's giant flagstaff, a controversial structure of steel that rises 300 feet from the ground and holds a massive 3,000-square-foot flag. On the first Sunday of each month, the flag is lowered and replaced by a new one, donated by the governors of each of Brazil's 24 states in turn. From this end of the Monumental Axis, the visitor can either turn around and travel back up the axis, visiting the buildings on the other side, or make a short drive to the president's official residence, the Alvorada (Dawn) Palace, one of the most beautiful buildings in Brasília. However, President Collor maintains his own Brasília abode. Designed by Niemeyer and set on the banks of Paranoá Lake, it cannot be visited, but you can get a good view from the main gates. En route to the palace, you pass one of the best restaurants in the city, *Churrascaria do Lago* (Lake Barbecue). Here, the usual procedure is to have a *rodizio* meal, where you pay a set price and are served assorted barbecued cuts of beef, chicken, and sausage as well as plates of assorted salads, rice, vegetables, and garnishings. The price for this typical meal ranges between $5 and $10 per person, a very good value. *Rodizio*, however, should be avoided if you just want a light meal. There are other restaurants on the lakeside as well as clubs that are usually restricted to members; several are housed in spectacular buildings, notably those of the various armed forces. On the way back to the Monumental Axis, your next stop should be at the Palácio da Justiça (Ministry of Justice), another of Niemeyer's structures. This building is remarkable because of the huge water shoots emerging from its walls at different levels and cascading to a delightful water garden below. The building, its water gardens, and vegetation are open to the public weekday afternoons and 9 to 11 AM and 2 to 5 PM on weekends. It's a good idea to call in advance (phone: 226-8015).

At the intersection of the avenue with the main east-west throughway is the *Teatro Nacional* (National Theater). This building was left unfinished for many years, but its three auditoriums, restaurant, and exhibition area finally opened to the public in March 1979. It has one of the finest stages in the country in its main auditorium, and the building itself, shaped like an elongated Aztec pyramid, is one of the most interesting in the city. The rooftop restaurant is one of Brasília's most attractive and inviting eating places, comparable to the TV tower restaurant.

The Galeria dos Estados (Gallery of States) is a section of town that can only be seen on foot. It links the central commercial district of business buildings with the banking district and has shops for each of Brazil's 22 states. This 200-yard-long mall has displays of handicrafts at reasonable prices. The most beautiful wares are from Pernambuco, Ceará, Maranhão, Pará, and Bahia. The Ceará shop has good buys on hammocks and handmade lace. The Amazon state of Pará has some of Brazil's most interesting pottery, which has its roots in Indian designs. Other states whose stores are especially good are those of Rio Grande do Norte, Maranhão (for baskets), Mato Grosso, and Goiás, Brasília's home state.

Several impressive buildings are nearby, including the huge bulk of the Banco Central (Central Bank), similar to the Federal Reserve Bank in the US, and completed in 1979. This building has a money museum on the first floor, is shaped in the design of a doubloon, and is the largest structure in Brasília. The eighth floor is home to an art gallery, featuring nearly 5,000 works by artists such as Cândido Portinari and Salvador Dalí. The gallery is a result of the Banco Central amassing works of art for years, largely as partial debt payment from failed financial institutions. Open Mondays through Fridays from 10 AM to 5 PM.

There are three drives around the city that are worth taking. One is along Avenida das Nações where the majority of the foreign embassies have been built on land donated to each country by the Brazilian government. Competition to build an outstanding structure has produced some delightful variations in architecture. It all depends on one's taste, but the Italian, Spanish, and some of the Middle Eastern and Asian embassies all have been called the best.

If time permits, a fun trip in Brasília is the drive around Lake Paranoá, a 50-mile (80-km) excursion. On the far side of the lake are some of the most impressive individual homes, where the very wealthy and foreign ambassadors live. There is also a dam that holds back the waters of the artificial lake. The Dom Bosco Chapel, near the dam, at the geographical center of the country, is a nice place from which to view the city outline rising up from the lake.

The University of Brasília has many notable buildings of futuristic, even extravagant, architecture. These include the main library and lecture hall, which are nicknamed *o minhocão* ("the big worm") because they are almost a quarter-mile long and curve unevenly. If you are interested in architecture, the refectory and the exact science facility are worth a visit.

A visit to Brasília would not be complete without a short tour of the "superquadra" residential area. Brasília was designed so that a group of blocks of flats, none of which can be more than 6 floors high, would have all facilities available to residents, thereby avoiding travel to other areas for necessities. Each block has a school, shops and restaurants, and other utility buildings within easy reach of all the complexes. Each block, sometimes with dozen or so in a group, forms a "superquadra." There are also gardens and play areas between each block. The access of vehicles is controlled so that the whole area is safe for children's play, something that is especially welcome to Brazilians from crowded cities. If you do not want to stay in a hotel in Brasília, there is a large campsite behind the sports area and the motor racetrack. Rogerio Pithon Farias Park is a favorite spot for picnickers, and there are other sporting facilities, including a swimming pool with a wave-making machine for those nostalgic for the beaches of Copacabana, Ipanema, and Flamengo. Open daily 6 AM to midnight.

From Brasília, you can drive to Salvador (Bahia) in the Northeast or to the less-developed state of Mato Grosso in the west.

## BEST EN ROUTE

There are few hotels of any note before Brasília, but the federal city itself has modern facilities in all price ranges, built within the last 20 years in either the Southern or Northern Hotel Sector. While not as luxurious as the tourist hotels of resort areas (few contain pools and other recreational facilities), they are on the whole modern and efficient. Hotels listed as expensive will cost $70 per night and up for a double room; moderate, $35 to $60 per night; and inexpensive, below $30 per night.

### DIAMANTINA

**Tijuco** – The best in town, with a bar, restaurant, private showers. 211 Rua Macau do Meio (phone: 37-931-1022). Moderate.

**Dália** – A small hotel with television sets, and private showers. 25 Praça Juscelino Kubitschek (phone: 37-931-1477). Inexpensive.

**Grande** – Another small hotel with a restaurant. 70 Rua da Quitanda (phone: 37-931-1520). Inexpensive.

### PIRAPORA

**Canoeiros** – Moderately comfortable hostelry near the river, it has 84 rooms with private bathrooms. 3 Av. Salmeron (phone: 37-741-1946). Inexpensive.

### BRASÍLIA

**Carlton** – Brasília's best, it offers a fine, top class health club, swimming pool, bar, restaurant, nightclub, and hairdresser. Southern Hotel Sector (phone: 61-224-8819). Expensive.

**Eron Brasília** – One of Brasília's most spectacular hotels, with an outside elevator made of glass for a good view of the city. All 203 rooms have air conditioning and refrigerators. Other features are a hairdressing salon and nightclub. Northern Hotel Sector (phone: 61-321-1777; toll-free in Brazil, 11-800-1036). Expensive.

**Kubitschek Plaza** – Brasília's newest hotel is named after Juscelino Kubitschek, who was President of Brazil when this city was being built as the country's capital. This 300-room property also has a restaurant, bar, pool, and health club, and baby-sitters are available. QD2, Setor Hoteleiro Norte (phone: 61-321-7676; in the US, 800-544-5503). Expensive.

**Nacional** – Facilities include a nightclub, good restaurants, swimming pool, air conditioning, sauna, hairdresser. Beneath it is one of the city's best shopping arcades. Southern Hotel Sector (phone: 61-321-7575; toll-free in Brazil, 11-800-1441). Expensive.

**Américas** – Modern accommodations, all 154 rooms are air conditioned and have a refrigerator. Southern Hotel Sector (phone: 61-321-3355). Moderate.

**Aracoara** – A comfortable hotel with 165 rooms, all air conditioned and with refrigerators. Northern Hotel Sector (phone: 61-321-9222). Moderate.

**Torre Palace** – One of Brasília's better places, with a swimming pool and a refrigerator in each of the 160 rooms. Northern Hotel Sector (phone: 61-321-5554). Moderate.

**Aristus** – A small hostelry with 50 rooms. Near the *Conjunto Nacional Shopping Center*, Northern Hotel Sector (phone: 61-223-8675). Inexpensive.

**El Pilar** – Very basic but comfortable, with 70 rooms. Northern Hotel Sector (phone: 61-224-5915). Inexpensive.

**Planalto** – Simple and with few frills. Southern Hotel Sector (phone: 61-225-6860). Inexpensive.

# Brasília to Cuiabá: The Mato Grosso

Traveling from Brasília to Cuiabá through the west-central region of the Federal District — the states of Goiás, Tocantins, Mato Grosso, and Mato Grosso do Sul — is like weaving through a time warp. The area holds much of human history, combining the futuristic capital and Stone Age Indians, satellite stations and wild frontier towns like those of pre-1900 Texas, *artesanatos*, or handicrafts fairs and remnants of the colonial Portuguese past, luxurious hot spring spas, primeval swamps, and forests untouched by man.

The 700-mile (1,120-km) route west across this region of striking contrasts begins 3,500 feet above sea level on the red earth of the central plateau that covers much of the territory. In Goiás, the terrain slopes gently in alternating levels of hilly plateau, scrub-grass flatlands, and tropical riverbeds carved by the many tributaries that flow north through the newly created state of Tocantins to the Amazon or south to the Paraná–La Plata system. At the eastern border of Mato Grosso the route crosses the Rio Araguaia before climbing to the plateau, where the elevation offsets the heat of the latitude. Near Rondonópolis the road begins a final descent to Cuiabá and the low-lying plain and swamps of the Pantanal that cover most of southwestern Mato Grosso and northwestern Mato Grosso do Sul.

The 936,000 square miles of the west-central region was first visited in the 16th and 17th centuries by *bandeirantes* (pioneers) from São Paulo, who traveled in tightly organized, armed expeditions in search of Indian slaves and precious stones. These adventurers rarely formed permanent settlements, but their discovery of gold in the early 18th century brought an influx of people who established colonial towns like Cuiabá and Goiás near the mines. By the 19th century, a primitive grazing economy had been developed on the savannah plains of Goiás and Mato Grosso do Sul, but the dense tropical forests in the northern part of both states remained inhabited exclusively by primitive Indians.

It was only at the beginning of this century that the west-central region began to be integrated with the rest of the country. Under the leadership of Cândido Rondon, telegraph wires were laid across the territory, and 150,000 Indians were subdued, opening up the area to settlers with their families. Rondon, who was part Indian and twice nominated for the Nobel Peace Prize, established the Indian Protection Service at the government's request and organized 100 service posts in the interior. The peaceable Rondon told his agents, "Die if you must, but never kill." Despite his motto and principles, the destruction of Indians and their way of life has continued throughout this century, reducing tribes like the Paco d'Arco from 3,000 to one old woman with bitter memories.

While this area has been one of Brazil's fastest-growing regions during the past 2 decades, with new roads, railroads, airports, and modern cities like Brasília rising rapidly on the plains, the gains have often been made at the cost of human life and dignity.

It is best to begin the journey in the cool, dry months of July through September if you intend to take side trips on the dirt roads that lead off the paved highways. This is particularly true when exploring the Pantanal, where rivers overflow and cause flooding from October to early April. Brazilians also suggest, half kiddingly, that the safest way to begin your journey is with a brief detour to a suburb north of Brasília called Vale do Amanhecer (Valley of Dawn). Here you may seek the blessings of a religious cult started by a woman truck driver, a *macumbista,* or practitioner of the popular religion that combines voodoo with Catholicism. That visit, plus a *figa,* the common clenched-fist amulet designed to ward off the evil eye, should guarantee a good trip into the wild west.

**En Route from Brasília** – Begin your drive in the southern part of the city on Routes 40-50-60 that starts near the zoological garden. A short distance ahead on the right is Saída Norte (north exit), a single-lane exit road that joins the Brasília-Belém highway and is paved all the way to the mouth of the Amazon 1,450 miles (2,320 km) away. A little farther on the left is the single-lane paved road that becomes Routes 40 and 50 going south to Belo Horizonte, but you should continue on the double-lane Route 60 toward Anápolis.

Route 60 is heavily trafficked but in good condition, passing through an urban area that is 9 miles (14 km) from the capital. On the left is a city officially called Nucleo Bandeirante, but generally known as Cidade Livre (Free City).

**CIDADE LIVRE:** Prior to the building of Brasília, the unskilled, uneducated northeasterners flocked here to escape the drought and poverty of their own region. Desperate for food and money, they lived in wooden shacks and worked 15 hours a day to build Brasília in 3 years.

Cidade Livre, which quickly grew to 100,000 people, was a dusty, rough city, reminiscent of Hollywood's version of a Wild West town. Its clapboard storefronts had false second stories; hundreds of bars served hordes of men who arrived in jeeps instead of on horseback. On payday, lines formed at the bordellos at the far end of town, where men often fought over the few prostitutes in residence.

Government officials planned to dismantle Cidade Livre after the completion of Brasília, but it stands today as an unofficial monument to the men who built the new city. In fact, it remains because the capital's planners did not realistically allocate housing for anyone earning less than $10,000 a year.

**En Route from Cidade Livre** – Continuing on Route 60, you pass additional satellite communities such as Taguatinga, Ceilândia, and Braslândia, which hold the overflow of poor migrants from the Northeast. Take the turnoff to Gama (which ends in Belo Horizonte), bypassing the dirt road exits for Cidade Eclética and Santo Antônio do Descoberto. The shift to these dirt roads reflects with sociological precision the emergence of slums around the metropolis. The most primitive and recent are farthest out, with housing of cardboard and tin that will someday become adobe when the occupants have some economic success. The next wave of migrants will begin the process again as squatters in a new ring of slums even more remote from the employment that initially drew them to the city.

After the turnoff to Gama and Belo Horizonte, Route 60 becomes a single-lane road all the way to Cuiabá. The road is kept in good condition, with well-marked signs and asphalt exits. After leaving the Federal District at Luziânia and entering the state of Goiás, the road starts to wind as you lose altitude. The landscape is the same arid red earth found in Brasília, with low scrub brush and twisted trees that barely cover the soil. A number of small streams intersect the route, and the vegetation along their banks is more tropical. Here you may see monkeys, parrots, and snakes if you decide to wander along one of the streams.

Along this route before Anápolis, there is little to see except the small towns of Alexânia and Abadiânia, where the only attractions are filling stations and stores with the most basic supplies. Here there are also meat stores that attract people from Brasília, who buy at lower prices to try to offset their very high cost of living. Just outside Anápolis, take the main highway to the right — the main road to Belém.

**ANÁPOLIS:** Some 100 miles (160 km) from Brasília, Anápolis is a growing city of 250,000. It is a prime example of the economic boom that came to the region with the building of Brasília. The city has become a manufacturing center, supplying Brasília with processed food, furniture, fabrics, ceramics, and beer, as well as a center of agricultural produce. The area around Anápolis is a region of large farms that produce Brazilian staples such as rice, beans, eggs, and dairy products.

Besides the military, manufacturing, and agricultural installations here, there is little to see, but interesting excursions can be taken to Jaraguá and Pirenópolis, two colonial towns near the old gold mines north of Anápolis. Stop for lunch at the *Estância Park* hotel (see *Best en Route*).

**JARAGUÁ:** About 55 miles (88 km) from Anápolis, this city of 68,000 has provincial architecture and two churches of note, Igreja da Conceição and Igreja do Rosário. Prior to *Carnaval,* the *Festa de São Sebastião* (Feast of St. Sebastian) is celebrated in January and features street dancing and sales of arts and crafts. Hotels and dining spots are pretty bad (for emergency use only).

**PIRENÓPOLIS:** About 40 miles (64 km) from Anápolis, this town of 28,000 has more extensive examples of colonial architecture, including the Igreja do Carmo in the downtown area and the *Museum of Religious Art* and the Igreja da Matriz, built in 1728, in the central district. The city is also the site of the *Cavalhada,* a medieval pageant that originated in Portugal and is still celebrated with jousting tournaments, clowns, and jesters. The festival, which takes place 40 days after *Easter,* lasts for 1 week, and is one of Brazil's outstanding folklore events.

**En Route from Anápolis** – Take Route 60 for the 35-mile (56-km) journey to Goiânia through low, rolling hills. The main approach to the city is startling — you top a hill of scrub brush and find a city of skyscrapers rising before you.

**GOIÂNIA:** This growing city of 920,000, capital of the state of Goiás, was one of the first planned cities in Brazil and was created in 1937 as a result of President Getúlio Vargas's "to the West" campaign. The charismatic president, affectionately called "Father of the Poor," broadcast radio messages urging western expansion to change the economic lot of the millions of peasants flooding to southeastern cities.

City planners designed Goiânia with symmetrical streets marked with white divisions for bus lanes. Although the city was planned for easy movement of automobiles, the population grew way beyond the original dimensions. Goiânia has a large number of parks, botanical gardens, and areas for outdoor relaxation. Educativo de Goiânia (Al. das Rosas) has a good zoo, playground, and park. Mutirama, also a park, has a large amusement area for children (Av. Araguaia; phone: 81-223-2214). You can water ski on Jão Reservoir. Locally made arts and crafts are displayed each Sunday morning in the Praça Civica at the *Feira do Hippi* ("Hippie Fair").

Several restaurants have good reputations for indigenous food. For regional dishes, there's *Forno de Barro* (570 Rua Henrique Silva; phone: 81-224-7155). Try *Chopim* (3612 Rua 87; phone: 62-241-6460) for *churrasco*. Goiânia is a cosmopolitan city and has a good Chinese restaurant, *Muralha Chinesa* (1585 Av. República do Líbano; phone: 81-223-6841). The top restaurant in town, featuring an international menu, is the *Bougainvillea* at the *Castro's Park* hotel (phone: 81-223-7766) — see *Best en Route.*

Centrally located Goiânia is a good starting point for trips into less-populated areas — the more remote regions of the Araguaia and Tocantins rivers for wildlife; Goiás, the old state capital and former gold-mining center; and Caldas Novas, an area known for luxurious hot springs resorts. If you wish to travel in a group, several tourist agencies in Goiânia can arrange tours, including *Incatur* (151 Av. Goiás; phone: 81-225-2622) or *Cardealtur* (182 Av. Goiás; phone: 81-225-8633). Both sponsor fishing and hunting packages.

If you wish to visit Caldas Novas, an area of therapeutic hot springs, take BR-153 south from Goiânia through broad farmland. The two-lane highway is paved and kept in good condition. Turn left at Morrinhos to complete the 110-mile (176-km) journey to Caldas Novas. Near the city are two other well-known mineral bath resorts, Fontes de Pirapetinga, a few miles away, and Rio Quente, which has the most luxurious accommodations. The temperature of these springs ranges from 98 to 115F (36 to 46C) as the bubbling water emerges from caverns in the base of the adjacent mountains and meanders through natural pools and lakes.

Goiás, the former state capital, is well worth visiting for its colonial architecture. Take the road from Goiânia; the paved road ends midway on the 90-mile (144-km) trip. Goiás (pop. 43,000) has narrow, winding streets with low, 2-story houses. The most spectacular of its churches is Igreja de Nossa Senhora da Boa Morte, now a museum of sacred art featuring the works of José da Veiga, as well as many works in gold. Igreja de São Francisco de Paula (Praça Zaqueu Alves de Castro) is the oldest in town, erected in 1761. The *Museum of the Bandeiras,* is dedicated to the early pioneers (on Praça Brasil Caiado, to the right of the central water fountain). Around the city you can still see remains of the mortarless stone walls built by the slaves of landowners.

There are several adequate restaurants here, including *Vila Boa* (Morro Chapéu do Padre; phone: 62-371-1000), with a spectacular view, and *To-Ka* (231 Rua Dr. Americano do Brasil; phone: 62-371-1408) for *churrascos.*

If you're set on exploring the Aruanã and wildlife preserves by car, be prepared for few luxuries, although the roads north of the Aruanã are paved and marked. The village of Aruanã (pop. 7,000) has few tourist facilities. Get a good supply of gas in Goiás for the 90-mile (144-km) trip and plenty of insect repellent, since Aruanã is on the Rio Araguaia. It is the central point for river fishing and hunting expeditions and has a few basic tourist lodges, eating spots, and camping facilities. Located 15° south of the equator, the town's favorite activity is swimming off the white sandy beaches that line the river, but beware: Some of the warmer, stagnant pools near shore have piranha. The area also has sting rays that measure up to 2 feet in diameter, with long, poisonous tails.

You are almost guaranteed a good catch of fish on the Araguaia, especially at dawn or sunset, when the calm river is tinged reddish yellow. You will find a variety of unusual fish, including striped *tucanaré,* with their large painted mustaches; dogfish with enormous teeth used by the Indians for decorative purposes; *soia,* a fish with only one eye; *poraquê,* an electric fish; and *tabarana,* considered by many to be the area's most powerful fighting fish. Fishermen boast of catches of all sizes, from the tiny *pacu* to the *pirarucú* that are sometimes 6 feet long and weigh 200 pounds.

You can rent small motorboats with a guide for about $10 a day. Larger excursion boats that make 1- and 2-week trips on the river can be reserved through tourist agencies in Goiânia or Brasília. *Botels* — hotels constructed on large, flat-bottom boats — are more comfortable. You can also combine a weekly river excursion with an escorted trip to the Rio Tocantins valley, which has good hunting.

On a river excursion through a rain forest, you will see wildlife such as turtles, parrots, gulls, and alligators along the banks as the widening river approaches the Amazon. You also will pass the world's largest river island, Bananal, which measures 8,000 square miles. Inhabited by Carajá and Javae Indians, the island is a good stopping point and has small villages with tourist lodgings. The Carajá make interesting orange and black clay dolls and feather headdresses. You'll find them very hospitable to visitors. Remember, however, to get permission to visit them from FUNAI (the national Indian foundation) in Brasília, which maintains strict control over outsiders mingling with Indians to protect them against disease. The common cold, a routine illness of non-Indians, killed 177 Meinaco Indians 1 year, and when measles carried by a traveler broke out among Gavião Indians on the Rio Tocantins, 60 died overnight. Be very sure you are in good health before visiting any tribe even if you do have permission.

**En Route from Goiânia** – Rejoin Route 60 and travel west through the farming areas characteristic of this region. The two-lane highway is still heavily traveled and well maintained, with gas stations approximately every 25 miles. You may want to visit Pirenópolis, a small community a few miles off the main road, that celebrates a tournament between Moors and Christians 40 days after *Easter.* There is little to do in these small towns, so the inhabitants make annual celebrations big events. The *St. John's Day* celebration on June 23 is dedicated to the saint believed to have enjoyed good music and drink. Bonfires and firecrackers at night are thought to awaken him so he will join in the fun of mock marriages performed by drunken priests and irate fathers holding shotguns.

Continuing on Route 60, you pass through the small farming communities of Guapó and Posselândia and the town of Indiara, which is intersected on the right by a dirt road that leads to Parauna, 38 miles (61 km) away. Parauna is one of the best places to view the eroded rock sculptures typical of the red rock highlands north of this route.

You cross the Capivari and Turvo rivers on Route 60, but unlike in less-developed regions, there are bridges instead of ferries. You might want to stop for a swim or to fish in one of the rivers, although there are few tourist facilities here or at the Rio Verdão beyond Acreun. After crossing the Verdão, you will pass the town of Santo Antônio da Barra and two paved highways before Rio Verde.

**RIO VERDE:** After leaving Goiânia, you'll find this city of 100,000 is one of the best and most interesting places to stop for food. It has a large community of Mennonites, who fled Prussia, the Ukraine, and other European countries and who have maintained their strict religion. The Japanese, a major immigrant group to Brazil since World War II, own many of the outlying farms, where they grow vegetables and fruit. This area, known as *campo cerrado,* has become an important area for agriculture despite the fact that the red soil and arid climate have to be enhanced by fertilizers and irrigation.

Here, as in most of Brazil, agriculture is characterized by huge landholdings. Some 37% of the farmland is owned by 1% of the population. These enormous properties are typical of the west-central region. The only powerful group that protests land distribution is the liberal wing of the Catholic church which, along with some left-wing political parties, has been lobbying for land reform.

**En Route from Rio Verde** – Continuing on Route 60, the next stretch is a long haul as you pass through the flat plains typical of the cattle country in the western and southern parts of the region. The 300-mile (480-km) route has few diversions before Rondonópolis, but road conditions are good and there is little traffic. At Jataí, the road changes to Route 364, and there is a good alternative overnight and restaurant stop. The most adequate hotel/restaurant is *Rio Claro* (678 Av. Goiás; phone: 62-631-1208). On the longest stretch of the road, between Portelandia and Alto Araguaia, you cross the border into the state of Mato Grosso.

**RONDONÓPOLIS:** This town of 118,000 was named after the first Indian protector, Cândido Rondon, who attempted to save vanishing Indians from the advances of white settlers. The town makes a good stop on this long stretch of road. There are a number of Indian crafts for sale, and you can try to get permission to visit nearby tribes at the local FUNAI office.

About 500 miles (804 km) north of Rondonópolis is one of the largest Indian reservations in the world, the Xingu National Park. In an area the size of France, the remains of a once-enormous tribe continue their civilization. There are an estimated 30,000 Indians here and perhaps 8,000 more who have not yet made contact with the white man. It is very doubtful that FUNAI will permit you to visit this reservation.

**En Route from Rondonópolis** – The last stretch of Route 364 crosses a flat plateau with cotton, rice, bean, corn, and soybean farms and an increasing number of cattle ranches. You will pass through the small farming communities of Santa Elvira, Juscimeira, Dom Auino, S. Pedro da Cipa, and Jaciara. A possible stopping point on this 132-mile (211-km) trip is Aguas Quentes, which has health resorts and hot mineral baths. Then the road twists as you enter the flood plain. Cuiabá lies in a basin, abutted on the south by low mountains.

**CUIABÁ:** The capital of the state of Mato Grosso, a sparsely populated area of 353,000 square miles, Cuiabá grew as a center of gold mining in the 18th century but today gets its wealth from the Amazon rain forest as the center of rubber and palm nut harvest. Mato Grosso has been integrated into the Amazon region to benefit from the area's federally funded projects. Before 1978, Mato Grosso also included Mato Grosso do Sul, which is now a separate state with a population of 1.8 million.

Cuiabá is a modern city of 330,000 on the Rio Cuiabá. Except for the cost of meat, prices are much higher than those in São Paulo. Cuiabá is the geographic center of South America, but to add a little cultural confusion, the city also has a large community of Middle Eastern people and a large mosque near Praça Moreira Cabral. There are three museums worth visiting, including the FUNAI *Museu do Indio* (Indian Museum;, Av. Fernando Correia da Costa; phone: 65-815-8321) on the university campus; *Museu de Pedras Ramis Bucair* (Pedras Ramis Bucair Museum; 195 Rua Galdino Pimentel; phone: 65-624-1711); and the *Museu de Arte e Cultura Popular* (Museum of Popular Culture and Art; on the university campus; phone: 65-361-2211, ext. 137). They're open Mondays through Saturdays, from 8 to 11:30 AM and from 1:30 to to 5:30 PM. Indian handicrafts can be purchased in shops and at an outdoor market on Saturdays. The environment in the surrounding region is the real point of interest here. Travel agencies, like *Cuiabá-Tur* (63 Rua General Mello; phone: 65-322-8723), can arrange excursions to outlying areas.

There are several very good restaurants in town, such as *Peixaria de Queiroz,* an all-you-can-eat fish place (Praça Jaime Figueredo, Lixeria; phone: 65-322-6420), and the *Aurea Palace* hotel (63 Rua General Mello; phone: 65-322-3377).

Two hours south of the city are the tablelands of Guimarães — mountains suitable for climbing — with a spectacular waterfall, the Véu da Noiva (Bride's Veil), 180 feet high.

The Pantanal, a marshland with a wide variety of birds and animals, is half the size of Minnesota and can be crossed on the Trans-Pantaneira Highway. The trees along this wet savannah make natural aviaries for many bird species, including the spoonbill, the red wood ibis, and the gray heron. The region also has alligators, deer, capybara, and jaguars. It is one of the best places in the country to see (and photograph) native animals in their natural habitat. Accommodations in the region range from air conditioned villas to rustic hunting lodges to combination house boats–fishing boats called *botels*. *Focus Tours* leads tours of the Pantanal that includes a naturalist guide, binoculars, and spotlights (502 Rua Grão Mogol in Belo Horizonte; phone: 31-223-0358). The agency is run by US-born ecologist Douglas Trent, who also offers tours of the Amazon and Atlantic coastal forest regions.

Rio Teles Pires is one of the best rivers in Brazil for fishing, although the area does not have the extensive facilities for groups and individuals that other rivers have.

The Porto Velho Road is treacherous driving but has several interesting towns — Vihelna, Pimenta, Bueno, Cacoal — that will give you a good taste of contemporary frontier life. Southwest of Vihelna on the Rio Galarea are archaeological ruins currently under excavation. The caves, which are not open to tourists, have walls carved with symbols that indicate the people were sun- and women-worshipers.

The Interior, north of Vilhena, is the area Theodore Roosevelt explored by canoe in search of the lost Inca treasure, described in his book *In the Brazilian Wilderness*. Nearby is the site where British Colonel Percy Fawcett mysteriously disappeared, leaving behind accounts of a white god of the Xingu tribe. The area is only a little tamer now. It is spotted with FUNAI posts, such as Serra Morena; research centers like Humboldt Scientific City; and homesteading towns like Aripuana. This area and the region farther north are crossed by the Trans-Amazonia Highway and are slowly being developed. It can be explored by air taxis out of Cuiabá via government planes that usually fly in supplies. Get a yellow fever vaccination, anti-malaria medicine, and plenty of insect repellent. If you are adventurous and do not mind some discomfort, this is where the trip to the Wild West really begins.

## BEST EN ROUTE

Since this is not one of the more heavily traveled parts of Brazil, there are few hotels, and most are in the larger cities. Exceptions are the resorts around health spas. Hotels listed as expensive will run about $80 per night and up for a double room; moderate, about $30 to $70 per night; and inexpensive, under $25 per night.

### ANÁPOLIS

*Estância Park* – Located outside the city in a natural setting, this 31-room hotel is a good place to relax. It has 2 swimming pools, a jogging track, and a mini-zoo. Its restaurant is decent, considering the remoteness of the area. Km 2 of the BR-414 Hwy. (phone: 62-324-7624). Moderate to inexpensive.

*Itamaraty* – A pleasant place with 59 rooms; private baths, telephone, TV sets; breakfast included in the price. 209 Rua Manoel da Abadia (phone: 62-324-4812). Inexpensive.

*Príncipe* – Another simple hotel, with 45 rooms, all with private baths and hot water. 145 Rua Engo Portela (phone: 62-324-0611). Inexpensive.

### GOIÂNIA

*Castro's Park* – The best in town, with a health and fitness center including European-style vapors, 4 bars, 3 restaurants, and 2 swimming pools. 1520 Av. República do Líbano (phone: 62-223-7766; toll-free in Brazil, 11-800-8618). Expensive.

*Bandeirantes* – Comfortable and in the center of town, with air conditioning, a bar, boat rental, and a decent restaurant with an international menu. 3278 Av. Anhanguera (phone: 62-224-0066). Moderate.

***Umuarama*** – Another comfortable spot with convention facilities, parking, air conditioning, and a bar. The restaurant serves so-so food. 492 Rua 4 (phone: 62-224-1555). Moderate.

## CALDAS NOVAS

***Pousada do Rio Quente*** – One of the best in the hot springs area, in a scenic park with a swimming pool, boat, football field, playground, bar, and simple restaurant. Estr. P/Morrinhos, at Km 28 (phone: 62-421-2255) Expensive.

***Turismo*** – In a scenic park setting, with pool, air conditioning, bar, sports facilities, and a simple restaurant. Estr. P/Morrinhos (phone: 62-421-2244; in the US, 800-544-5503). Expensive.

## GOIÁS

***Vila Boa*** – Small hotel with panoramic views, air conditioning, a restaurant, bar, pool, and playground. Morro do Chapéu do Padre (phone: 62-371-1000). Inexpensive.

## PIRENÓPOLIS

***Municipal Campsite*** – Has room for 50 tents. Rio das Almas. Praça Emanuel Lopes. Inexpensive.

***Quinta Santa Bárbara*** – A group of 10 chalets in a scenic location with its own orchards, this establishment has a swimming pool, sauna, bar, and luncheonette. 1 Rua do Bonfim (phone: 62-331-1304). Inexpensive.

## ARUANÃ

***Recanto Sonhado*** – A simple hostelry, nicely located on the river, with restaurant, sauna, and 3 swimming pools. Av. Altamiro Caio Pacheco (phone: 62-376-1230). Inexpensive.

## RIO VERDE

***Rio Verde Palace*** – With 73 rooms, this is the best lodging in town. 599 Rua Nizo Jaime Gusmão (phone: 62-621-2722). Inexpensive.

## JATAÍ

***Rio Claro*** – Each of its 58 rooms has a color TV set and air conditioning. Good bar and restaurant. 671 Av. Goiás (phone: 62-631-4147). Moderate to inexpensive.

***Itamaraty*** – You can choose from among 10 rooms with private showers. 96 Rua José Carvalho Bastos (phone: 62-631-2502). Inexpensive.

## RONDONÓPOLIS

***Estância Canta Galo*** – This converted farm features a swimming pool fed by water from a hot springs. Each of its 16 bungalows has air conditioning, a color TV set, and a stocked refrigerator. Km 240 on the BR-364 Highway, Aguas Quentes district (phone: 65-361-5262). Moderate.

***Rondonópolis Palace*** – Plain but adequate, with air conditioning and a bar. 625 Rua Fernando Correia da Costa (phone: 65-421-2878). Inexpensive.

***Thaani*** – Reasonably comfortable accommodations with bar, air conditioning, and sauna. 472 Av. Amazonas (phone: 65-421-9288). Inexpensive.

## CUIABÁ

***Aurea Palace*** – The best in town, this comfortable 70-room hotel has a coffee shop, color TV sets, and refrigerators in the rooms. 63 Av. General Mello (phone: 65-322-3377). Expensive.

**Fazenda Mato Gross** – On a real farm, this inn offers fresh milk and cheese every day as well as horseback riding, a mini-zoo, team sports, rowing, playground, bar, and restaurant. Half of its 50 rooms have TV sets and refrigerators. 1200 Rua Antônio Dorileo, Coxipó (phone: 65-361-2980; toll-free in Brazil, 11-800-8880). Moderate.

**Excelsior** – A simple yet comfortable hotel with a good restaurant. 264 Av. Getúlio Vargas (phone: 65-322-6322). Inexpensive.

# São Paulo to the Uruguay Border

There are many places of interest in the three southern states of Brazil, and the road from São Paulo to Porto Alegre passes within a stone's throw of almost all of them. There is little of special interest in the first half of the trip from São Paulo to Curitiba, but the rewards farther south make the journey a memorable one, for the route passes through mountains that skirt the sea and a series of beaches. The city of Curitiba is pleasant, and from there to Porto Alegre you drive through lovely towns populated by German- and Italian-speaking people to the scenic beaches of Santa Catarina and its capital city of Florianópolis. The road goes through summer resorts along the coast before becoming a modern highway for the final 60 miles (96 km) to Porto Alegre, a city with many tourist attractions.

With all the interesting side trips possible on this route, you may want to devote a week to seeing the area. It will take the better part of one day to cover the 250 miles (400 km) from São Paulo to Curitiba. You will probably want to spend 2 nights in Curitiba, with a day's side trip to Paranaguá. A third night could be spent in one of the towns that has retained its German influence, such as Joinville or Blumenau. Plan to stop in Florianópolis for at least a big lunch of seafood at one of the restaurants by the lake. If you want to avoid metropolitan areas such as Porto Alegre, you can try one of the resort hotels in Gramado, stop in the wine region at Caxias do Sul, or stay in a seaside resort in Camboriu or Torres. From Porto Alegre you will find modern, paved roads to Montevideo, Uruguay, a distance of 530 miles (848 km), and to Buenos Aires, 641 miles (1,026 km) away.

The best tourist guides and maps in Brazil are the trilingual *Quatro Rodas Guides,* published annually by Editora Abril. The editions for the coming year appear on the newsstands by December. Most of the guides are published in Portuguese, with a condensed portion in English at the back of each book. Bring a dictionary. The most useful guidebook for southern Brazil is the Quatro Rodas *Guia do Sul* (Guide to the South), which covers the states of Paraná, Santa Catarina, and Rio Grande do Sul as well as parts of Paraguay, Uruguay, and Argentina. The *Guia do Sul* contains more descriptive information about the south than the *Guia Quatro Rodas do Brasil,* which covers the whole country.

The best time to visit southern Brazil is in summer, from November to April, when the climate is warm and dry, much like southern Europe. Many tourist facilities close in the winter, when you may even find occasional snow in the far south.

**En Route from São Paulo** – From the center of São Paulo, take Ipiranga Avenue south to Consolação Avenue, which turns into Rebouças Avenue, crossing the Rio Pinheiros. Beyond the *Jockey Club,* turn left onto Professor Francisco Morato Avenue and begin route BR-116 to Curitiba. For the first 19 miles (30 km) the highway is divided. The town of Embu, 16 miles (26 km) from São Paulo, is a historical town with a noteworthy church, Nossa Senhora do Rosário, dating to 1680. A haven for artists and artisans, the town has a weekly crafts fair on Sundays when you can buy everything from primitive art and ceramic sculpture to wicker furniture and antiques. The restaurants around the main square are all good. Once the divided highway ends, driving is tedious because of heavy traffic and slow-moving trucks. Fortunately, on most hills there is a third lane, and trucks obligingly move over, but there are many steep inclines and much traffic. São Paulo lies at an elevation of more than 2,500 feet, and by the time the road reaches the Rio Juquiá and the town of Registro, 15 miles (24 km) away, you are at sea level.

**REGISTRO:** This town of 58,000 is the largest between São Paulo and Curitiba. It lies on the south bank of the Rio Juquiá, about 40 miles (64 km) from the Atlantic, and is a river town with a port for shipping much of the produce from the region. The largest industry is tea processing, and the area is a major agricultural region; its principal crops are rice, bananas, and tea. Several truck stops along BR-116, such as *Petropen* and *Gaúcha Altaneira,* serve big steak dinners at low prices.

**CURITIBA:** They say that the *paulistas,* the residents of São Paulo, work all the time so that the *cariocas,* the residents of Rio, can play all the time. Of the *curitibanos,* one could say that they live all the time, for Curitiba, with 1.4 million people, is one of the most livable cities in Brazil. In fact, with adequate space for its people and no pollution, Curitiba is often cited by Brazilians as a model of how to do things right. The city center with its pedestrian mall has often been copied by other cities, but with less success. Here, cars are prohibited, and special bus lanes move commuters back and forth efficiently. Even the climate is more moderate, cooler in the summer than Porto Alegre. It is only about an hour's drive to the beaches along the coast, and Iguaçu Falls is less than 6 hours west over a well-paved road (which does not explain why many *curitibanos* have never made the visit). The city has no spectacular tourist sights, but by visiting it you are able to see a modern, well-organized Brazilian city that is moving with its people in a progressive direction. One of the several museums worth visiting is the *Paranaense,* in the old City Hall built in 1916. Here you will find paintings, sculptures, weapons, and coins. It is on Generoso Marquês Plaza downtown. Open weekdays from 10 AM to 6 PM; weekends from 1 to 6 PM.

There are several day trips from Curitiba; the best is the rail ride down to the major coffee-exporting port of Paranaguá. Trains leave Curitiba from the station (on Av. Afonso Camargo) at 7 AM and 8:15 AM, but be sure to check the time of departure when you make the reservations, which you should do at least 5 days in advance (phone: 41-234-8441). There are many short tunnels and fine views of the seacoast during the 3-hour trip through the mountains. Have lunch at *Danúbio Azul* (95 Rua 15 de Novembro; phone: 41-422-0992) in Paranaguá, which features inexpensive seafood and has a panoramic view. After lunch, take a taxi to the port or walk to the *Museu de Arqueologia e Artes Populares* (Archaeology and Popular Arts Museum), which dates from 1740 and is housed in a Jesuit monastery (575 Rua 15 de Novembro; open daily). The train station in Paranaguá (Av. Artur de Abreu; phone: 41-422-0892) has departures every day at 4:30 PM.

Take another worthwhile excursion to the state park of Vila Velha, 50 miles (80 km) from Curitiba. Wind has eroded the red sandstone rocks into grotesque and fantastic shapes, and a trail threads around their bases for several miles of wonderful hiking. There are also daily tour buses and public buses to the park.

**En Route from Curitiba** – You can rejoin Route BR-116 to get to Porto Alegre, but the more scenic route, the coastal BR-376, is much more interesting for sightseeing. This route leaves BR-116 just south of Curitiba. Signs are few and far between as you leave Curitiba; if you think you're lost, stop and ask for the road to Joinville or Florianópolis. Because the paved two-lane road is heavily trafficked, plan for a slow but scenic drive.

Watch for the striking Paraná tree, called *araucária* locally. This unique member of the pine family has a long, straight, limbless trunk with beautiful uplifting branches at the top. In April the trees bear fruit; their large cones are composed of many long, narrow nuts that taste like roasted chestnuts when cooked. Roadside vendors sell them by the quart for a pittance. About 50 miles (80 km) from Curitiba the road crosses the border into Santa Catarina state, an agricultural region with many German communities. At this point the road number changes to BR-101.

**JOINVILLE:** This city, settled in the 19th century by German immigrants, is 77 miles (123 km) from Curitiba. Joinville is one of the best known of southern Brazil's German communities and worth an overnight stop. Though it has become a bustling industrial center, many original buildings with their European architecture have been maintained. Joinville has more bicycles per inhabitant — of which there are 345,000 — than any other city in Brazil.

There are several museums of note, including *Museu de Arte de Joinville* (1400 Rua 15 de Novembro; phone: 474-225626), with a permanent exhibit of art, sculpture, and prints, and *Museu do Sambaqui* (600 Rua Dona Francisca; phone: 474-220114), with local archaeological finds. Both closed Mondays. If you like flowers, be sure to visit the private orchid collection at the *Orquidário Joinvilense* (590 Rua Placido Gomes; open daily).

The best German restaurant in town is *Bierkeller* (497 Rua 15 de Novembro; phone: 474-221360). For good seafood, all you can eat, try *Da Lagoa,* nicely situated on a lake 5½ miles (9 km) outside town (Rua Prefeito Balthazar Buchle; phone: 474-271422).

**En Route from Joinville** – The road is almost flat after Joinville and soon reaches the sea and Santa Catarina's beautiful beaches. Rice and bananas are the principal crops of this area. At the summer resort towns of Picarras and Penha there are many sandy beaches. If you prefer quiet and miles of secluded beach, stay along here; if you prefer wall-to-wall people on the beach, lots of young folks, nightlife, and classier hotels, push on to Camboriu.

**THE ITAJAÍ VALLEY:** Before reaching Camboriu, the road passes the city of Itajaí at the mouth of the Rio Itajai, 123 miles (197 km) from Curitiba. Itajaí, an important fishing and boatbuilding center, was settled by German immigrants whose architecture, customs, and language have survived. The most important town in the valley and the best known of all the German towns in Brazil is Blumenau, 26 miles (42 km) from Itajaí. Locally made linen and crystal are good buys, and there are several decent hotels and restaurants, most of which were built to accommodate the increasing numbers of tourists to the town, many of whom come for the annual *Oktoberfest* celebration. For restaurants, investigate the good German cuisine of *Cavalhinho Branco* (165 Alameda Rio Branco; phone: 473-224300); the touristy *Moinho do Vale* (66 Rua Paraguai; phone: 473-223337), with its imitation Dutch windmill; or the fantastic views of the river valley from the hilltop *Frohsinn* (on Morro do Aipiu; phone: 473-222137), half a mile from town.

**BALNEÁRIO DE CAMBORIÚ:** Ten miles (16 km) beyond Itajaí, Camboriú offers Brazil's most "in" beach south of Ipanema. The 4-mile stretch of sand is lined with restaurants, hotels, bars, houses, and condominiums, most of which went up in the past

10 years. Reservations are a must in summer, but in winter the place is deserted. If Camboriú Beach itself is too crowded, there are others in both directions (though the surf gets a bit rough to the north). The best seafood restaurant in Camboriú is *Sinhá Maria,* 522 Rua Dom Afonso, Vila Real (no phone).

**En Route from Camboriú** – Beyond this point, the road follows the sea and is very scenic, with beautiful beaches and resorts at every turn including Itapema. The road continues past several other small towns before reaching Florianópolis, the state capital.

**FLORIANÓPOLIS:** Part of this city of 237,000 is situated on an island and part on the mainland. To reach the city center, turn left off the main road and take one of the two bridges to the island, where the downtown section is quieter than that on the mainland. On the island are many fine beaches, a Jesuit monastery, several forts, and a beautiful blue lake, the Lagoa da Conceição. Excellent shrimp is available at the seafood restaurants along the lake on Rua Henrique Veras, such as *Oliveira.* If steak is your meat, try *Ataliba,* on the beach (Rua Jaú Guedes da Fonseca; phone: 482-442364), instead. The city's top seafood restaurant, *Martin Pescador,* lies 9 miles (14 km) out of town (Beco de Sirfosta, Estrada de Joaquina). Don't let the simple accommodations fool you — the food is excellent.

**En Route from Florianópolis** – The road continues along the coast, but the sea itself is not visible until you reach Imbituba, 224 miles (358 km) from Curitiba. Imbituba is in a coal-mining region and has several nice beaches. The next important town is Tubarão (Portuguese for "shark"), another coal-mining town with many hot springs nearby. To reach the popular hot springs at the town of Gravatal, turn right on the paved road at Tubarão for a 12-mile (19-km) side trip. The road beyond Tubarão passes many small villages before reaching Araranguá at 301 miles (482 km) away, a town with long, sandy beaches and good fishing. After another 33 miles (53 km), the road crosses the border into the state of Rio Grande do Sul, a cattle ranching area with cowboys similar to the gauchos of the Argentine pampas. Rice, corn, wheat, and grapes are also grown here. Just beyond the border there is a mobile information booth on the right side of the road during the summer. Stop there for maps and free brochures.

**TORRES:** This resort town of 39,000, also just beyond the state border, is named after the basalt towers that jut out into the sea and afford fine views of the area. Both the long beach and the towers can be reached on foot from the town's hotels. From May to October, it is just too cool to lie on the beach, and Torres and other resort towns to the south shut down for the winter.

**En Route from Torres** – Beyond Torres, the road runs between the sea on the left and several lakes on the right, passing the turnoffs to other beach resort towns. However, these are overcrowded because of their proximity to Porto Alegre. If you are going to stay at the beach, stay in Torres or in Santa Catarina. At the town of Osório, BR-101 becomes a modern, divided, toll highway for the rest of the drive to Porto Alegre, turning westward away from the coast and changing its number to BR-290. Osório is 411 miles (658 km) from Curitiba and just 64 miles (102 km) from Porto Alegre. The highway turns into Avenida Bento Gonçalves as it approaches downtown Porto Alegre.

**PORTO ALEGRE:** This is the largest city in south Brazil (pop. 1.37 million) and the state capital of Rio Grande do Sul. It is a booming, modern industrial center on the banks of the Rio Guaiba with access to the sea via the Lagoa dos Patos.

For a good view of this hilly city, take a boat trip to the islands in the Rio Guaiba. Porto Alegre has several museums, including the *Varig Airlines Museum* (800 Rua 18 de Novembro; open Wednesdays and Sundays), which has a collection of airplane parts and miniature airplanes. For the shopper, Porto Alegre is a good place to pick up leather goods, agates, and mounted butterflies.

The city has many fine restaurants that feature giant portions of steak and local wines. Some of the best local beef is served at *Quero Quero* (171 Rua 24 de Outubro; phone: 512-221934) and *Capitão Rodrigo (Plaza São Rafael* hotel); the German influence is still strong at *Floresta Negra,* in the Moinhos de Vento (Windmills) district (905 Av. 24 de Outubro; phone: 512-227584), while the Italian influence is best represented at *Etruria* (421 Rua Santo Antônio; phone: 512-219132).

While you are in Rio Grande do Sul, don't fail to take an excursion to the mountain region just north of Porto Alegre. The trip can be made in a day, but an overnight stay is recommended. Take BR-116 north from Porto Alegre through the heavily industrialized northern suburbs. The last of these, Novo Hamburgo, 28 miles (45 km) north of Porto Alegre, offers good buys in shoes at its factory outlets. Farther north, the road rises rapidly into the hills, reaching an altitude of 2,000 feet in the town of Nova Petrópolis 64 miles (102 km) from Porto Alegre. Turn off here to the twin mountain resort towns of Gramado and Canela, literally "the grassy place" and "cinnamon town." In summer, the roadside is covered with beautiful hydrangeas.

**GRAMADO and CANELA:** Gramado is 22 miles (35 km) from Nova Petrópolis on a paved road that continues 5 miles (8 km) to Canela. These towns have attractive gardens and Bavarian architecture, and the road is dotted with shops offering original handicrafts. There is a striking waterfall in the Caracol State Park on the outskirts of Canela that should not be missed. The water cascades over the lip of a giant cave and crashes on the rocks more than 300 feet below. Spend the night in Gramado.

**CAXIAS DO SUL:** To reach the wine country, retrace your route to Nova Petrópolis and continue north on BR-116 for 20 miles (32 km) to Caxias do Sul. The city (pop. 300,000) has several wineries open to the public, such as *Château La Cave* (Rte. BR-116 North at Km 143; phone: 54-222-4822), open every weekday morning and afternoon. All the wineries, called *adegas,* have a tour and offer free samples (most are closed Sundays). You also can visit the *Experimental Grape and Wine Center,* where new varieties of grapes are grown and tested. In February, there is an annual wine festival in Caxias do Sul. For some good food, try *Don Jon* at the *Alfred Palace* hotel (2302 Rua Sinimbu; phone: 54-221-8655), or the lively *Alvorada* (200 Os Dezoito do Forte; phone: 54-222-4637), which specializes in roast chicken.

To get to the vineyards, take the paved road west past the village of Farroupilha and turn north, when the road forks, to the town of Bento Gonçalves. Surrounded by vineyards, this town has several wineries of its own and an annual wine festival to rival the one in Caxias do Sul. The next stop is the ski slope at Garibaldi, 6 miles (10 km) south of Bento Gonçalves. To return to Porto Alegre, either retrace your steps to Caxias do Sul or continue south on the paved road from Garibaldi for 46 miles (74 km) until the road rejoins BR-116 just below Novo Hamburgo. If you want to stay overnight in the grape-growing region, do so in Caxias do Sul.

The complete trip from São Paulo to Porto Alegre, including the round-trip excursion to the mountains from Porto Alegre, is 928 miles (1,485 km).

## BEST EN ROUTE

Since this is one of the more heavily traveled areas of Brazil and more developed due to European immigrants, hotels tend to be more modern and numerous, including facilities such as swimming pools, television sets, and good restaurants. Hotels categorized as expensive will cost about $75 per night and up for a double room; moderate, about $40 to $70 per night; and inexpensive, under $30 per night.

### EMBÚ

***Rancho Silvestre*** – To avoid downtown São Paulo or get a head start on your way south, this is the place to stop. On the outskirts of Embú, about 45 minutes from downtown São Paulo in a parklike setting with a small lake, there are only 42 rooms, so reservations are a must. Facilities include a tennis court, swimming pool, playground, and sauna. 700 Estrada Votorantim (phone: 11-494-2911; in São Paulo, 11-210-1440). Moderate.

## CURITIBA

*Bourbon* – Best suited to the business traveler because of its downtown location and support services, the city's top hotel offers amenities such as 3 restaurants, a swimming pool, and color TV sets and mini-bars in the rooms. 102 Rua Cândido Lopes (phone: 41-223-0966; in São Paulo, 11-223-2244; in the US, 800-544-5503). Expensive.

*Iguaçu Campestre* – The best in town for rest and relaxation. Sauna, massage, miniature golf, lake fishing, horseback riding, and myriad other sports. Rte. BR-116, at Km 92 (Alto), 5 miles (8 km) from the city (phone: 41-262-5313; toll-free in Brazil, 11-800-8618). Expensive.

*Caravelle Palace* – Centrally located hostelry with 99 rooms. Reservations recommended. 282 Rua Cruz Machado (phone: 41-223-4323; in São Paulo, 11-289-0366). Moderate.

## JOINVILLE

*Tannenhof* – With 103 air conditioned rooms, a pool, and an excellent restaurant, it's the best in town. 340 Rua Visconde de Taunay (phone: 474-228011). Moderate.

*Colón Palace* – Comfortable and clean with 84 rooms, a small pool, and a good restaurant. 80 Rua São Joaquim (phone: 474-226188). Inexpensive.

## PIÇARRAS

*Imperador* – A pleasant resort hotel on the beach. Its 98 rooms are full most of the summer, and reservations are recommended. 380 Av. José Temistocles de Macedo (phone: 473-450037). Moderate.

## BLUMENAU

*Plaza Hering* – Owned and operated by the Hering family, who also owns the large Hering Glass Company and the Knitworks, which exports around the world. It is a large, modern facility with 134 rooms, satellite TV, a swimming pool, and a swanky restaurant. Reservations advised in summer. 818 Rua 7 de Setembro (phone: 473-221277). Expensive.

*Grande Hotel Blumenau* – On the left just as the road enters town, with 76 rooms and a swimming pool. Reservations advised in summer. On the crossroads of Rio Branco and Av. 15 de Novembro (phone: 473-220145). Moderate.

## BALNEÁRIO DE CAMBORIU

*Marambaia Cassino* – Right on Camboriu Beach, where the action is; though in spite of its name, there is no casino (gambling is illegal in Brazil). Its 117 rooms are full all summer. It has a swimming pool if you tire of the beach, and a good restaurant. During the tourist season (*Christmas* through *Carnaval*), a minimum stay of 7 days is required. 300 Av. Atlântico (phone: 473-66-4099; in São Paulo, 11-258-6587). Moderate.

*Fischer* – A pleasant hotel, right on the beach, with a restaurant. Reservations necessary in summer. 4770 Av. Atlântico (phone: 473-660177). Inexpensive.

## ITAPEMA

*Plaza Itapema* – A deluxe beach resort hotel, fancier than anything along the more popular Camboriu Beach. It has 162 air conditioned and heated rooms, with 4 swimming pools (one heated), sauna, tennis, golf course, volleyball court, restaurant, 3 bars, and a nightclub. Km 144 BR-101, Praia da Ilhota (phone: 473-442222). Expensive during high season; moderate the rest of the year.

## FLORIANÓPOLIS

*Cabanas da Praia Mole* – Located directly on the beach at Conceição Lake, it offers chalets that sleep up to six people each and have kitchens and TV sets. There's a variety of water sports and a special recreational program for children. 2001 Estrada da Barra da Lagoa (phone: 482-320231). Expensive.

*Florianópolis Palace* – A simple, downtown hotel, it has a good restaurant. Reservations advised. 2 Rua Artista Bittencourt (phone: 482-229633). Moderate.

## GRAVATAL

*Internacional de Gravatal* – At the hot springs near the village of Gravatel. Many Brazilians come here from as far away as Porto Alegre and Curitiba to bathe in the hot springs, which many believe have therapeutic value. It has 118 rooms, 2 heated swimming pools, sauna, gameroom, volleyball, football, tennis, bike track, a restaurant, bar, and barbecue. Km 4 of Termas de Gravatal Hwy. (phone: 486-422155; in Porto Alegre, 512-275257). Expensive.

*Gravatal Termas* – A country resort hotel with a satisfactory restaurant and room rates that normally include all meals. There are 96 rooms, tennis, swimming pool, and sauna. About 2 miles (3 km) from town on Av. Pedro Zappelini (phone: 486-422112; in Porto Alegre, 512-275257). Moderate.

## ARARANGUÁ

*Morro dos Conventos* – On the beach, with its own restaurant. Reservations recommended in summer. About 8 miles (13 km) from Araranguá (phone: 485-220989). Moderate.

## TORRES

*Dunas* – The best hotel in Torres, but back from the beach. Good restaurant. Reservations necessary in summer. 247 Rua 15 de Novembro (phone: 51-664-1011). Moderate.

*Do Farol* – Beautiful views of the beach and the sea from this *"Lighthouse"* hotel. Good restaurant. Reservations necessary in summer. 240 Rua José A. Picoral (phone: 51-664-1240). Moderate.

## PORTO ALEGRE

*Plaza São Rafael* – The most luxurious in Porto Alegre, a large downtown property with 284 rooms and 2 fine restaurants. Reservations necessary. 514 Av. Alberto Bins (phone: 512-216100). Expensive.

*Plaza* – Another good, large downtown hotel with a good restaurant, it has 176 rooms. Reservations advised. 154 Rua Senhor dos Passos (phone: 512-261700). Moderate.

*Porto Alegre City* – Still another good downtown place, with 146 rooms and a good restaurant. 20 Rua Dr. José Montauri (phone: 512-242988). Moderate.

## GRAMADO

*Serra Azul* – Definitely second place behind the *Serrano* (below), but a good choice nonetheless; it's also closer to town. Good restaurant, swimming pool. Reservations necessary in summer. 152 Rua Garibaldi (phone: 54-286-1082). Moderate.

*Serrano* – An 84-room resort in a garden setting in the mountain town of Gramado.

Full all summer. Swimming pool. Reservations necessary. 1112 Av. Coronel Diniz (phone: 54-286-1332). Moderate.

### CAXIAS DO SUL

**Alfred Palace** – Pleasant hotel with sauna, bar, hairdresser, and wine cellar — in the heart of the city. 2302 Rua Sinimbu (phone: 54-221-8655). Moderate.

**Samuara Alfred** – This beautiful 80-room property is in the forest on the road to Farroupilha. Swimming pool. Reservations a must during summer and fall. Good restaurant; most guests eat at the hotel. Six miles (10 km) from downtown (phone: 54-225-2222). Moderate.

# Iguaçu Falls

Three waterfalls in the world surpass the rest: Niagara, Victoria, and Iguaçu. While the argument as to which of the three is the most spectacular may never end, one thing is for certain: Iguaçu is awesome. The tropical rain forest provides the ideal setting for the torrents of water that fall and crash with a thunderous noise onto the rocks below, sending spray shooting back up to make beautiful rainbows. The Rio Iguaçu, a tributary of the Paraná, widens to a distance of 2 miles just above the precipice over which the river drops almost 200 feet, to create Iguaçu Falls. Since the lip of the precipice is uneven, the water doesn't fall in one great curtain, but rather in dozens of cataracts, interspersed with jungle greenery. The most spectacular cataract is Garganta do Diabo (Devil's Throat).

The panoramic view of these falls from the Brazilian side is breathtaking, but perhaps even more thrilling is the walk along the Argentine side. In 1965 the Argentine government built a system of catwalks alongside and over the falls. Each step on the catwalk affords an excellent view of the cataracts; every time you round a bend, you're surprised by a vista even more beautiful than the last. Possibly the most spectacular way to see the falls is by helicopter. *Helisul* at Km 16.5 Rodovia das Cataratas, Iguaçu (phone: 455-742414 and 455-741786; fax: 455-744114) offers a 7-minute ride for about $40 per person.

While any time is a good time to go to Iguaçu, the optimum months are August to November when you can climb around the falls more easily than during the highwater months of May and June. However, during this period the air is filled with butterflies, including many in lovely iridescent blues. The Rio Iguaçu forms the border between Brazil and Argentina and the areas on both sides of the river are national parks.

Iguaçu is served by two airports. The larger of the two is the international airport on the Brazilian side, midway between the falls and the city (in the border town of Foz do Iguaçu). *Varig, Vasp,* and *Transbrasil* have daily flights from Rio de Janiero and São Paulo to Iguaçu. The airport on the Argentine side, serving both the falls and border town of Puerto Iguazú, has daily flights to and from Buenos Aires on *Aerolíneas Argentinas. Cruzeiro do Sul* flies from Buenos Aires to Iguaçu Falls, Brazil. You can also take the bus from Asunción to the falls, crossing the international bridge at Ciudad del Este into Brazil at Foz do Iguaçu. A full 48 hours is recommended if you wish to see the falls from both sides. If you only see them from one side you have only seen half the show, since the two views are completely different.

**IGUAÇU — THE BRAZILIAN SIDE:** The best panoramic view of the falls is immediately in front of the *Hotel Das Cataratas* in the national park (see *Best en Route*). The well-manicured path and steps down to the falls start directly in front of the hotel. The steps lead to the very edge of the river, and at one point a catwalk goes right out over the river. Wear a raincoat or rent one from a vendor on the path. The path leads to the head of the falls, where an elevator takes you to the top for a small charge. From here it is a short walk upstream to the small boats that will take you out in the river for an even closer look. To return to the hotel, either retrace your steps or walk along the paved road; it's about 1 mile (1.6 km) each way. Take your movie camera.

**En Route from the Brazilian Side –** The trip to the Argentine side takes about half a day. Allow at least 2 hours on the catwalks, which pass many waterfalls before stopping just short of the Devil's Throat, the most violent waterfall of them all. Add an hour for lunch, an hour for shopping, plus time to rest. To get to the Argentine side, visitors can cross the 1,600-foot Ponte Presidente Tancredo Neves (Puente de Fraternidad in Argentina) spanning the Rio Iguaçu. (The ferry, which previously transported drivers and their cars across the river, is no longer running.) There's also a bus that runs four times an hour between the Terminal Urbana in Foz do Iguaçu in Brazil and the terminal of Av. Cordoba in Puerto Iguazú in Argentina; fare is about 75¢. You will have to go through customs as you are leaving Brazil. If they stamp your passport when you leave, which is unlikely, make sure it is stamped again when you return.

Once on the Argentine side you need to go through customs. After that, take a taxi to the falls some 12 miles (19 km) away. Only a short distance from the river is the town of Puerto Iguazú. Soon after leaving the town, the road enters the national park. The parking lot is next to an aging hotel, and the falls are a short walk across a field.

Once you have crossed the field, it is more than a mile on the catwalks leading past various falls out to the Devil's Throat. Take along suntan lotion, a hat, a camera, and perhaps a canteen or flask of water to keep you refreshed. The catwalks are all on the level above the falls leading to the Devil's Throat. There are other catwalks that descend immediately from the field to the bottom of the falls.

By the time you get back to the hotel you will be ready for lunch and a good rest (a light lunch of a sandwich or two is suggested). Sit on the verandah, have a snack, write postcards (no stamps available), and watch the other tourists. In due course, head back, stopping at the village of Puerto Iguazú to shop, especially if you do not make it to Montevideo or Buenos Aires. Puerto Iguazú's shops carry beautiful wool sweaters, sheepskin coats, and leather goods. There is no need to have Argentine pesos; you can pay with Brazilian currency, dollars, traveler's checks, and perhaps even with an American Express credit card. From here it is only a 5- or 10-minute walk down the hill to the ferry. Once again, it's time to go through Argentine customs, ride the ferry, and go through Brazilian customs. If transportation back to the hotel was not prearranged, taxis are available.

**IGUAÇU — OTHER ATTRACTIONS:** If you enjoy gambling, there is a full-fledged casino nearby in Paraguay, in the border town of Ciudad del Este. Transportation is available at all hotels on the Brazilian side for an evening across the Rio Paraná at the gambling tables. Many Brazilian and Argentine tourists visit Ciudad del Este by day to buy Scotch whisky, French perfume, and Japanese calculators at low prices. (Prices are not low by US standards, and therefore this border town holds no particular attraction for the American tourist.)

The Brazilian border town of Foz do Iguaçu (referred to simply as Foz by the local folks) is not much better. It is growing by leaps and bounds and now boasts several high-rise apartment buildings. The construction boom is due only in part to the tourist industry. Not far upstream from the confluence of the Iguaçu and Paraná rivers at Foz do Iguaçu, the Itaipú Dam is now completed, with a generating capacity of 12.6 million kilowatts, making it the largest hydroelectric power generating facility in the world. Organized tours are available, and tour buses even drive across the top of the dam. Check at your hotel for more information or in downtown Foz at the offices of Itaipú Binacional, a commission composed of an equal number of Paraguayans and Brazilians responsible for the Itaipú project. The better vantage points for viewing are on the Brazilian side, where a giant canal was carved out of the rock and the entire Rio Paraná was diverted into it on October 20, 1978. The new dam flooded, doing away with the Sete Quedas, or Seven Falls, once rated by *The Guinness Book of World Records* as the greatest waterfall in the world. A tour boat leaves from Porto Meira below the Iguaçu Falls and runs down the Rio Iguaçu, to the confluence of the Paraná, and then runs up the Paraná to the Itaipú construction site. Inquire at your hotel or at Porto Meira when crossing over to see Iguaçu Falls from the opposite side.

## BEST EN ROUTE

You're going to pay for the comfort you seek at Iguaçu Falls, and it doesn't matter what side you're on: Argentine, Brazilian, Paraguayan. The most expensive rate is around $80 per night for a double room; moderate is about $50 to $60; and inexpensive is under $40. All the hotels are in excellent condition and have spacious rooms with private baths, swimming pools, and that extra-plus amenity of a wonderful view of the falls. Make reservations before you visit, since the falls are one of South America's most breathtaking attractions.

### BRAZILIAN SIDE

*Bourbon* – This luxury motel has 180 rooms, a swimming pool, and a tennis court. The property is about 4 miles (6 km) from Foz de Iguaçu on the road Rodovia das Cataratas to the falls (phone: 455-741313; toll-free in Brazil, 11-800-8181; in the US, 800-544-5503). Expensive.

*Hotel Das Cataratas* – Because of its location alone, this is the outstanding choice on this side. Reservations are hard to obtain. This 200-room hotel has front rooms with a view, private baths, and a restaurant that has a smorgasbord every evening. Right on the *cataratas* (phone: 455-742666; in São Paulo: 11-231-5844; or write *Hotel Das Cataratas,* Foz de Iguaçu, Paraná, Brazil). Expensive.

*Salvatti* – For those who prefer to stay in the city of Foz, rather than on the road between the city and falls, this place is centrally located, with adequate facilities. 651 Rua Rio Branco (phone: 455-742727). Inexpensive.

*San Martín* – A 141-room motel, with a swimming pool. About 10 miles (16 km) from the falls and from Foz de Iguaçu, near where the road to the airport branches off (phone: 455-743030). Moderate.

### ARGENTINE SIDE

*Esturion–Iguazú* – This first class resort hotel near the riverbank has 114 air conditioned rooms with private bath; facilities include a restaurant, nightclub, swimming pool, and tennis courts. 650 Av. Tres Fronteras (phone: 757-20020 or 757-20161; in Buenos Aires, 54-1-304919 or 54-1-340815). Expensive.

*Internacional Cataratas de Iguazú* – With grand views of the falls and jungle (ask for a falls view); its 180 rooms have air conditioning and private baths, and facilities include a bar, casino, restaurant, and pool. 585 Reconquista (phone:

757-2790 or 757-2748; in Buenos Aires, 54-1-311-4259; in the US, 800-448-8355; fax in Buenos Aires: 54-1-312-0488). Expensive.

## PARAGUAYAN SIDE

*Casino Acaraí* – Well known for its gambling casino, this hotel also has a swimming pool and features live entertainment in its dining room. Turn left as you go up the main street of the town from the Rio Paraná, then follow the signs for about 1 mile (1.6 km) on an unpaved road to the hotel, which has a fine view of the river. Ciudad del Este (phone: 61-2302). Moderate to inexpensive.

# Chile

Chile, a 2,600-mile-long country on the southwestern edge of South America, extends from Peru and Bolivia in the north to Tierra del Fuego in the south. Its eastern boundary with Argentina is formed by the Andes; its western by the Pacific Ocean. Within its borders, Chile contains some extremely varied terrain: from the mineral-laden Atacama Desert in the north to the rich vineyards and farmlands of the Central Valley, where Santiago, the capital, is located. More than 4 million of the country's 13 million inhabitants reside in the capital; nearly three-quarters of the population lives in the central valley. (For a complete report on the capital, see *Santiago,* THE CITIES.) To the south of Santiago are the lake district and the fjords and glaciers of Patagonia and the Tierra del Fuego archipelago. Easter Island, the site of mysterious giant stone figures called *moai,* is a Chilean possession, as are the Juan Fernández Islands, the supposed setting of *Robinson Crusoe.*

The climate, too, varies considerably from region to region. The central area is temperate, with seasons reversed from those in the Northern Hemisphere. Summer temperatures average in the 90s F (32 to 37C) between November and March; winter temperatures between May and October can get as cold as the 20s F (−7C). Spring and fall are in the 60s and 70s F (16 to 26C). Visitors are attracted to Chile's beaches, especially those at the resort city of Viña del Mar and ultrachic Reñaca along the coast, and to Portillo, the most famous ski resort in South America. Gaining in popularity is the ski center at Pucón, where slopes are located on the live Villarrica volcano, and Valle Nevado, a French-owned ski complex with a European flair. The Atacama Desert is hot and dry throughout the year. Southern Chile is rainy even during the summer (December through March). During the winter (June through September), heavy snows are frequent.

Tawantinsuyo, the Inca Empire, extended as far south as Chile's Río Maule, but the Inca were unable to conquer the Araucano Indians, who inhabited most of the present-day country. In 1531, a colleague of the Spanish conquistador Francisco Pizarro headed south from Peru into what is now Chilean territory, but it wasn't until Pedro de Valdivia arrived in 1541 that the first Spanish settlement was built in Santiago. His path of conquest came to an abrupt and brutal end in 1544 with his capture by the Araucano (also known as the Mapuche). The conflict between settlers and Indians continued until the 17th century. Chile became part of the vice-royalty of Peru and remained under Peruvian jurisdiction until the late 18th century when immigrants from Spain, Great Britain, and Germany arrived to settle the country. Bernardo O'Higgins, a Chilean patriot, initiated a revolt against Spain in 1810, and the Argentine General José de San Martín helped Chile gain independence. In 1879, Chile seized control of nitrate fields in the Atacama Desert that belonged to Bolivia. Waging a successful military campaign, the

Chilean armed forces gained control of Bolivia's Pacific seaport Antofagasta and the coastal town of Arica, which had been part of Peru. The enduring enmity among these three countries continues to this day, a legacy of the War of the Pacific that ended in 1883.

Until 1973, Chile prided itself on a 150-year tradition of democracy in which presidents and legislators were freely elected. Unlike other Latin American countries, Chile was not prone to military takeovers of the government. But after a period of strikes, riots, and economic troubles, the elected government of Marxist President Salvador Allende was overthrown in a bloody military coup, assisted by the US, that cost Allende his life on September 11, 1973. For the next 15 years a junta headed by General Augusto Pinochet imposed tight state control and rule by military decree until a plebescite opened the way for elections at the end of 1989. Chile, the most economically developed of the South American countries, returned to democracy when Patricio Aylwin was elected president that year and took office in early 1990.

The Pan-American Highway, which cuts the country from north to south, ending at Puerto Montt, is the main road, and is used primarily by commercial vehicles such as trucks and buses. It is generally well maintained and has restaurants, gas stations, and other facilities for travelers. However, in some cases the distance between stops is long, and since there is a significant stretch through the Atacama Desert, it is important that drivers keep the gas tank full and have plenty of drinking water on hand. Wherever you drive, be sure to carry spare parts and to have your insurance papers and *carnet* in order (see *Traveling by Car,* GETTING READY TO GO).

Rather than driving north-south, travelers may opt to fly from one major city to another, then take a bus, train, or *colectivo* to nearby towns or resorts. The Chilean carriers, *LanChile* and *LADECO,* are known for their first-rate in-flight service, making air travel here an especially pleasant option. Note: Rail service is only available south of Santiago on *Ferrocarriles Chilenos,* with the exception of service to Bolivia and Argentina from Antofagasta. Those who travel as far as Puerto Montt can get a boat or plane farther south to Tierra del Fuego or, from November to March, to Antarctica via Punta Arenas. Easter Island and the Juan Fernández Islands are accessible only by air or sea.

For those who prefer to keep their feet on the ground and to see as much as possible, Chile may be the best spot in the hemisphere to travel by bus. Several buses depart daily to and from most cities, and most lines in the country provide service in spotless vehicles. In fact, the competition for business is so fierce that it is rare when the fare does not include meals and snacks. The buses are well-appointed and spacious, and most have attendants who distribute pillows and soft drinks, and make sure that passengers are comfortable. At night, curtains are drawn so weary travelers can recline their seats and sleep. Some bus lines even offer their patrons video screens and music, and they expedite paperwork at the numerous police control points in the north where travelers must check in. (*Note:* It is now common practice on some routes for the bus driver to collect passports from passengers upon departure and return them only upon arrival at the passenger's destination.)

The nine routes in this chapter crisscross the country. The North takes you south from the Peruvian frontier at Arica through the Atacama Desert, to the port city of Antofagasta (pop. 200,000), and through the resort town of La Serena. The Central Valley runs from Valparaíso (pop. 350,000), Santiago's port, to the seaside resort of Viña del Mar and nearby Reñaca Beach. Portillo leads from Santiago to South America's best ski resort, with a description of facilities and slopes. Ovalle to Talca explores the country's fertile farming and ranching region; Concepción to Laja Falls runs through the country's third-largest city. The Lake District route passes through mountain lake resort towns, including Temuco, the ski center at Pucón, Valdivia, Osorno, and Puerto Montt. Chilean Patagonia and the Tierra del Fuego archipelago describes a journey through the glaciers and fjords leading to the Chilean Antarctic. Easter Island, its statues and settlements, and the Juan Fernández archipelago are described in detail.

# The North

The northern third of Chile, that 1,640-mile stretch from Arica to La Serena, encompasses the Atacama, the driest desert in the world. It looks like no-man's-land but don't let it fool you. The desert's story is a dramatic and often bloody one, filled with tales of fortunes made and lost, of vicious battles fought for the enormous mineral wealth stored beneath the rock and sand. The Inca were the first to know of the desert's secrets; they mined copper from the open pit of Chuquicamata long before conquistador Diego de Almagro claimed it for the Spanish throne in 1536. (According to legend, de Almagro had his horses shod with copper shoes here when he led his troops back to Cuzco.) Eventually, the Spanish exploited the area's mineral wealth. Although they found nothing like the rich gold and silver deposits of Bolivia, there was still ample silver treasure in the Inca Huantahaya mines.

The Spanish were exultant over this mineral discovery, but nothing could beat the mining boom that followed the 1809 discovery that the sodium nitrate found on the altiplano (desert plateau) near Iquique could be converted into gunpowder. At the time, Iquique belonged to Peru, as did all of Chile north of Antofagasta (the territory south of the city belonged to Bolivia). Demand for the gunpowder dropped after the colonial independence wars in the 1820s, however, and a mining lull continued until the next decade, when nitrate became important for its value as a fertilizer.

A century of profit taking began following this discovery, but territorial rivalry over the desert's mineral wealth brought about the War of the Pacific in 1879. During the 6-year conflict, Chilean troops pushed as far north as Lima in an attempt to solidify their claim on the Atacama. The soldiers successfully occupied the Peruvian capital and claimed for themselves the rich nitrate fields in the desert, which Chile holds to this day.

You can travel the arid Atacama by picking up the Pan-American Highway (Rte. 5) at the Peruvian border and continuing south. You'll enter Chile about 12 miles (19 km) north of the seaport of Arica. Controls at the border have been reinforced to discourage contraband traffic and the illegal exchange of currency between Chile and Peru, and because of problems with the Mediterranean fruit fly in Chile, travelers are prohibited from carrying any fruit from the northern part of the country south as far as La Serena. Also, because of the unresolved military antagonism between Chile and Peru (left over from the War of the Pacific in 1879), the border area is mined, so don't stray off the road.

If you're entering from Peru, you'll receive a 90-day tourist card (renewable for another 90 days) at the border or on the plane. The route south leads through the coastal city of Arica, with its tantalizing beaches, to the seaport of Iquique, to the world's largest open-pit copper mine of Chuquicamata and its mining town, Calama, then on to Copiapó, where the river of the same name forms an oasis in the desert. These towns are in the Norte Grande (Great North Desert) part of the Atacama, where there is no rainfall. The next 200 miles (320 km) south through the colonial city of La Serena to Ovalle is Norte Chico (Little North Desert), where a visitor can swim and fish off La Serena's beaches or visit Vicuña, the home of the late Nobel Prize–winning poet Gabriela Mistral. In the Atacama's Norte Chico, rainfall makes the desert sprout with vineyards, olive groves, and mango and papaya trees.

In spots, Chile's road network is unmarked and unpaved. The Pan-American Highway, however, is, for the most part, well maintained. First class hotels do exist in the Atacama, although few and far between, mainly in Arica, La Serena, Calama, Antofagasta, Iquique, and Copiapó (see *Best en Route*).

What you lack in physical comfort will be made up for in sights. In this flat and tan-gray desert land, you'll find wildlife ranging from the near-extinct giant condor of the Andes to mountain lions, vultures, llamas, alpacas, vicuñas, skunks, falcons, pheasants, and hummingbirds. When you reach the Pacific coastline, look for dolphins, whales, sea lions, penguins, and otters, among other sea mammals and birds. A trip through the Atacama may appear boring; it steadily becomes a diversified and fascinating excursion. And there are few places in the world that rival the dramatic show when the sun sets on this desert.

**ARICA:** A constantly sunny climate where the temperature hardly ever dips below 66F (19C) has earned this town the nickname City of Eternal Spring. Arica (population 140,000) means "desired land" in Quechua. The northernmost city of Atacama, it is really an oasis filled with flowering gardens on the edge of the Pacific. The clean, dark-sand beaches (El Laucho and La Lisera being among the best) are good for swimming, for, unlike most Chilean shores, Arica's waters are warm. Neighboring and landlocked Bolivians are particularly fond of Arica because it serves as their main port (although at press time Peru and Bolivia had signed an agreement giving Bolivia access to the sea at Ilo, Peru) and seaside resort, offering a casino (at 955 General Velásquez), outdoor markets, and cafés featuring Chile's famous empanadas (meat-filled turnovers).

If you don't intend to snooze on the beach all day, go see some of the historical monuments in the area. The most famous spot is El Morro, a high bluff overlooking the sea, where the Chileans won one of the most decisive battles of the War of the Pacific (1879–83), resulting in Arica being taken from Peru and becoming one of Chile's important seaside cities. Legend has it that the Chilean soldiers downed a concoction of *aguardiente* (moonshine) and gunpowder. Thus fortified for war with the devil, they successfully scaled the steep precipice of El Morro to attack and defeat the Peruvians who were holding the fort. This legend, however, is more macho myth than reality. History books show that the Chileans actually took a less precarious route up a gradual incline at the side of the hill, away from the sea. You can climb El Morro, too, but forget the gunpowder and take the back route. The plaza atop the hill offers a panoramic view of the town and coast and is especially dramatic after sunset. There's also a small museum on the hilltop, the *Museo de Armas* (Armaments Museum), that has weapons, uniforms, flags, and other war memorabilia on display.

The Gothic-style church in the square at the base of El Morros, San Marcos, was built in 1868 to replace the original 1640 church, which was swept into the sea by a tidal wave. The second church actually was shipped prefab from England, and the iron steeple was designed by Alexandre Gustave Eiffel years before he built his famous Paris tower. Only the church's door is wooden — the rest is made of metal.

For shoppers, Arica has some local craft centers where goods are reasonably priced; the best is *CEMA,* the Centro de Madres, or Mothers' Center, designed to aid women from impoverished areas in earning money for their households. In the Arica *CEMA* (Av. Azola; phone: 58-41784), you can purchase ceramics whose shapes and designs are modeled after artifacts of the pre-Inca cultures.

On the edge of town, near where 21 de Mayo and Avenida Capitán Avalos join at the Pan-American Highway south, is the *Pueblo Artesanal* (Artisan Village) — a collection of 12 white houses where you can buy weavings, ceramics, carvings, and other craft work. The shops are open from 9:30 AM to 1 PM and 3:30 to 7:30 PM. There is also a folklore nightclub that is only open on weekends (at 9:30 PM).

One good restaurant in Arica is *D'Aurelio* (369 Baquedano; phone: 58-31471), a cozy eatery specializing in Italian food. While you're in town, enjoy some of the locally grown fruit, such as mangoes, guayabas, and midget bananas. Local seafood dishes are tasty: Try *perol de mariscos* (seafood pot) with *locos* (abalone), mussels, clams, sea urchins, and rock lobsters (*langostinos*). You also can have swordfish in black butter (*albacora a la mantequilla negra*).

To wash it down, try *pusitunga,* the local aperitif made from an inland *aguardiente; pisco* sours are made with lemon, beaten egg white, and *pisco,* a grape brandy. Wine fermented in the Codpa Valley 30 miles (48 km) from Arica is known as *pintatani.*

The lone train station in Arica (at 51, 21 de Mayo) is the terminus for trains to La Paz, Bolivia — a 10-hour trip. While the coaches, with their gas lights and wood paneling, may look like the original cars from 1913, travel on the route is comfortable and the views are spectacular. This La Paz train originates in Calama. There also is an 11-hour ferrobus (a motor vehicle that runs on rail tracks) service between Arica and La Paz.

The tourist office in Arica is at 375 Calle Prat (phone: 58-232101).

You can take two side trips from Arica. The first is a 7-mile (11-km) trek east of the city along a paved road to the Azapa Valley, an important olive-growing area. Connected to the Universidad del Norte is the *Museo Arqueológico San Miguel de Azapa* (San Miguel de Azapa Archaeological Museum), which contains a collection of items from pre-Inca cultures dating back to 5000 BC. Its exhibits include textiles that have been preserved for centuries by the desert dryness, as well as Andean ceramics and mummies.

The second side trip is about 50 miles (80 km) east of Arica on Route 11, a gravel road that is best traveled from March to April and September to December (poor weather in other months makes driving almost impossible). The altiplano scenery includes snow-capped volcanoes and a variety of wildlife, including Darwin's fox, *pudu* (miniature deer), and pumas, on the way to Lauca National Park, just past Putre. A

340,000-acre reserve, the park was opened in 1970 to provide a protected area for Chile's dwindling vicuña population. The first vicuña census at the park counted only 400 of them; the herd is now estimated at 10,000. Also east of Arica, in the Valle de Lluta, are Indian rock drawings, or petroglyphs.

**En Route from Arica** – The 180-mile (288-km) ride south on the Pan-American to Iquique takes you through the arid Atacama, so be sure your tank is full and your car is in good shape. The highway is paved, but it's a boring ride, more so with no gas stations around. Be sure to pack a sweater: Nights can plummet to a chilly 57F (14C).

To reach Iquique, take Route 16 at the Pan-American junction (Km 177) and continue west 47 miles (75 km).

**IQUIQUE:** Arriving here is like landing a small plane. The steep, winding descent from the coastal plain to the city is abrupt, and the bright reaches of the ocean come as a big surprise. Iquique, with 140,000 people, is the capital of the first region (Arica to the Loa River) and the site of numerous annual deep-sea fishing competitions. It is also Chile's main fishing port, with an annual catch of 580,000 tons, accounting for 35% of the nation's fish production, and it claims to be the world's leading port for fish meal shipments. The city has a duty-free import zone, but there's a catch: Leaving the area, you run right into a customs check. If you're carrying more than US $240 in purchased goods (check with the *carabineros* — customs officers — as the limit changes periodically), you have to pay some stiff taxes, and bribery in Chile will get you nowhere. A good spot for duty-free purchases is Zofri, an area bordering Avenida Salitrera Victoria. While there, stop at *Los Módulos* — a 3-story shopping center with everything from household appliances and auto parts to perfume.

One cautionary note about Iquique: The breezes off the ocean lower the heat to an average temperature of about 67F (19C), but the sun is still fierce. Bring a hat for protection.

Of all of Iquique's beaches, the best is Cavancha. On the waterfront on the opposite side of town is the sailor's monument, a memorial to the naval battle of May 21, 1879, during the War of the Pacific. The Chilean naval hero Arturo Prat captained the *Esmeralda,* which was rammed by a Peruvian ship until it sank offshore here. Prat died when he jumped aboard the Peruvian ship as it hit the *Esmeralda.* Plaza Prat, named for the hero, houses *Casino Español;* the building's architecture is as Moorish as the Alhambra. Launches leave from the Edificio de Aduana (Maritime Authorities Building) at the waterfront to take visitors to the spot where the *Esmeralda* went down. The 45-minute cruise around the bay costs less than $10. After the ride, try the homemade empanadas at *María Graciela's* pierside kiosk.

There are two museums in Iquique worth visiting. The *Museo Regional* (Regional Museum; on Baquedano between Wilson and Zegers; phone: 57-21018) has a collection of archaeological artifacts as well as displays on the Indian cultures in Chile and the history of nitrate mining. The *Palacio Astoreca* (Astoreca Palace; on Calle Baquedano at Avenida O'Higgins) is a mansion built and conserved in the style of that period; it also serves as a cultural center, with listings of concerts, new books, and poetry readings.

The city tourism office is at 436 Pinto (phone: 57-21499).

Iquique's wide streets and brick houses may seem odd to visitors. Homes were all wood frame during the nitrate boom years, and it wasn't until the 1920s that bricks were used. Set on narrow streets, the wooden houses were fire traps, and serious fires in 1875 and 1880 wiped out large portions of the city. In rebuilding the city, architects borrowed English Georgian, rococo, and Greek revival styles. A French visitor in 1866 wrote home to say that the balconies and small colonnades made the houses look like opera stages.

Interesting spots also can be found outside the city. Pica, 68 miles (109 km) away, at an oasis with the same name, has thermal springs, and there is another oasis with four hot springs, including one that legends say cured an Indian princess who had gone blind. You can bathe in the mineral waters at the *Salitre* hotel in Mamiña, 76 miles (122 km) to the east, or in the public pools. Mamiña is home to the Nuestra Señora del Rosario (Our Lady of the Rosary) — one of the few Andean churches on the continent with two bell towers. It was built in 1632.

**En Route to Chuquicamata** – Continuing east on Route 16 to the Pan-American, you come to the small town of Pozo Almonte (pop. 1,500), sitting by itself on the vast expanse of the nitrate fields, or Pampa de Tamarugal. As its name implies (*pozo* means well), this was an important watering hole in the desert. It is now an equally important junction for motor vehicles needing water and gasoline before continuing across the desert. In nearby Santa Laura you can visit an old nitrate office that is exactly the way the English left it, complete with cricket field.

La Tirana, near the Route 16–Pan-American junction, is the scene of the annual July 16 feast honoring the Virgin of Carmen. More than 30,000 pilgrims come here for the colorful festivities; townsfolk dance wearing costumes and masks, and people walk barefoot or on their knees into town to repay their *mandas* (promises) to the Virgin for granted favors. A legend says that "La Tirana" (the tyrant) was a nickname for an Inca princess who led a resistance effort against the Spanish conquistadores and was renowned for her cruelty. The sobriquet stuck until she fell in love with one of her European prisoners and was executed by her Indian followers.

South of La Tirana, the Pan-American passes through Salar de Pintados, a dry salt lake. About 150 miles (240 km) outside Iquique, take Route 23 east to Chuquicamata.

**CHUQUICAMATA:** The green slopes of cast-off ores that make up the embankment around the world's largest pit copper mine — a 9,840-foot hole — are startling against the tan and gray Atacama Desert. An Inca mine before the Spaniards claimed it, the pit was further developed by the Guggenheim Consortium. The mine (phone: 52-322291) now produces more than 500,000 tons of copper annually (47% of Chile's total output) to make the government-owned copper company — Codelco–Chile — one of the 100 largest companies in the world. Two-hour tours of the mine leave in small buses from Puerta No. 1 daily at 10 AM. The tours are free but a small donation for social programs in town is appreciated.

It is a 9-mile (14-km) drive south to Calama, the mine's support town. As you approach, posters promoting Chile's copper business dot the roadside.

**CALAMA:** About half of the more than 120,000 residents work in or around the mine, and the Calama resembles the hybrid of a Pennsylvania mining town and a frontier town out of the Old (US) West. Much of the remaining population works in industries related to sulphur, borax, and salt mining. Tiny stone houses are close together; there are wooden sidewalks, saloons with swinging doors, and general stores stockpiled to the ceilings with food and supplies.

Calama is set on an oasis along the bank of the Río Loa, the only river running through the Norte Grande. In town, a small archaeological museum on Ramírez Street, above the library, contains a chronologically arranged collection of pre-Inca artifacts (pottery, utensils, and so on). Also of interest is the Indian village of Chiu-Chiu, 20 miles (32 km) northeast of Calama. The Inca highway passed through this town. It later was an important stop on the silver route from Bolivia to the coast (and as such had 10,000 pack animals). But its heyday ended in 1890 when the railway service began. Follow the dirt road east through Lasana, another Indian village with low, adobe houses that was once a 12th-century *pucara* (Indian fortress settlement), then swing south to San Pedro de Atacama.

**En Route from Calama** – On an unpaved road between Calama and San Pedro de Atacama lie the Tatio geysers, marked by countless plumes of water and steam rising from an otherwise uninviting terrain. Travel agencies in Calama and San Pedro de Atacama can arrange tours in four-wheel-drive vehicles. Take a bathing suit along; most tours include a stop at the Puritama hot springs. About midway between the two desert cities lies the desolate landscape known as Moon Valley on the sides of the Domeyko mountain range. The crater-like terrain and salt formations can be visited through local tour operators.

**SAN PEDRO DE ATACAMA:** A Spanish-Indian town, built on an oasis of the Río San Pedro, it is famous for its *Museo Arqueológico* (Archaeological Museum) founded in 1963 by a Belgian priest, Gustavo Le Paige. He worked until his death in 1980 at age 77, collecting an estimated 380,000 artifacts from the area, which was inhabited some 10,000 years ago. On display are several mummies that have been well preserved by the desert dryness, Indian ponchos over 1,000 years old, and a collection of gold figurines. The most famous mummy is of a young woman whose beauty is so well preserved that she is known fondly as "Miss Chile." The museum is open weekdays 8 AM to noon and 2 to 6 PM, and Saturdays and Sundays 10 AM to 1 PM and 3 to 7 PM.

**En Route from San Pedro de Atacama** – To continue to Antofagasta, retrace your route to Calama. From there, take the paved Route 55 southwest 66 miles (106 km) to the Pan-American. Then it's another 66 miles (106 km) to Antofagasta.

**ANTOFAGASTA:** This port city of more than 200,000, which may strike you as unexpectedly modern, exports nitrates and the copper from Chuquicamata. From the railway station, trains leave for Salta, Argentina, and every Wednesday for La Paz and Oruro in Bolivia, making this the most important city in the desert. There is steamer service to Valparaíso, Iquique, and Arica.

Vigorous urban renewal has left Antofagasta with the nation's longest — 12 miles (19 km) — waterfront development of parks, beaches, and promenades. In addition to swimming and deep-sea fishing, there are two museums. The *Museo Regional* (Regional Museum; at the corner of Balmaceda and Bolíva, on the waterfront beside the yacht club) is open Tuesdays through Saturdays 10 AM to 1 PM and 2 to 7 PM and Sundays 10 AM to 1 PM. The *Museo Arqueológico* (Archaeological Museum; on 482 Prat) is open Mondays through Fridays 10:30 AM to 1 PM and 3:30 to 7 PM. There is a local tourism office (360 Baquedano, 2nd Floor; phone: 55-226-4044).

Antofagasta is filled with strange attractions. Plaza Colón contains a replica of Big Ben, presented by the British in 1910. If you take a walk along Avenida O'Higgins, look closely at its gardens. The soil comes from different parts of the world, carried as ballast on nitrate cargo boats that returned home empty. At the port, the old customs house resembles a strange combination of Spanish colonial and Swiss chalet architecture. It was built during the last century with prefabricated materials so it could be taken apart and moved. Drydocked on the Avenida Costanera, *El Galeón* is an old ship converted into a disco bar.

For a different dining experience, try the *Shangay* (2426 Latorre; phone: 55-262547), a small Asian restaurant with a relaxed atmosphere, icy cold Chilean beer, and excellent service. Closed Wednesdays. Or, for more elegant surroundings, *Club de la Unión* (474 Calle Prat; phone: 55-221258) is a good choice.

Antofagasta's major holiday is the June 29 *Fiesta de San Pedro* (Feast Day of St. Peter), the fishermen's patron saint. His statue is carried across the water in a motorboat procession, and a blessing is given for the fishermen's catch and well-being. A festival is held afterward. Some 24 miles (38 km) east of Antofagasta is a landmark indicating the Tropic of Capricorn.

From Antofagasta you'll start your second long journey down the Atacama: the

340-mile (544-km) trip through the Norte Grande to Copiapó and La Serena in Norte Chico.

**En Route from Antofagasta** – You've reached the fringe of the Atacama when you've arrived in Copiapó, an oasis on the river of the same name. While no rain falls in the Norte Grande, the Norte Chico gets occasional sprinkles. Temperatures are mild, and there are valleys running east-west along the length of the desert that are good planting grounds for olive trees and grapevines. As you travel south on the Pan-American, you'll pass through Taltal, once an important nitrate port, now mainly known for the large swordfish and sea bass caught off its shores.

**COPIAPÓ:** The Pan-American Highway turns inland at Copiapó; you get a better feel for what an oasis is really like here. In Copiapó, you're surrounded by sand dunes as far as the eye can see. A city of some 69,000, it was founded by Pedro de Valdivia in 1540. It wasn't until the 1700s, however, that silver and gold were discovered, and in 1832, Juan Godoy found the rich Chañarcillo silver mines south of the city. Plaza Godoy bears a statue of the prospector, and Copiapó's other plaza, Plaza Prat, is considered one Chile's prettiest, complete with its own pool of Carrara marble imported from Italy, statues representing the four seasons, and centenary trees. Today, the city is the capital of a region dedicated to mining and agro-industry.

The imposing Casa Matta, a colonial-style house built at the end of the 1800s and restored in 1982, serves as the *Museo Regional de Atacama* (Regional Museum of Atacama; 630 Calle Atacama), which features displays of minerals and metal tools used by the Indians as well as old mining equipment. Open Saturdays 3:30 to 6 PM. The most complete mining museum in the country, the *Museo Mineralógico* (Mineralogy Museum), is also in Copiapó (on the corner of Colipi and Rodríguez). Open Tuesdays through Saturdays 10 AM to 1 PM, and 4 to 8 PM, and Sundays 10 AM to 1 PM. Among its exhibits is a meteorite. The train station on Avenida Atacama was restored in 1982 to put a new shine to the wood structure built in 1854. A museum at the station has been opened, where you'll find photos tracing the history of one of the first railways in South America. It is open Mondays through Saturdays 8 AM to noon and 2 to 6 PM from December to March; for visits during the rest of the year, appointments must be made through the city tourism office (691 Los Carreras; phone: 52-212838). The locomotive *Copiapó* — the first operative locomotive in South America when it set off on its maiden voyage on *Christmas Day* in 1851 — is parked at the end of Avenida Copayapu, a few blocks down from the train station, and is open to visitors.

About 42 miles (67 km) west of Copiapó on the Pan-American Highway is the port city of Caldera and the nearby beach area of Bahía Inglesa. This unspoiled bay, visited by English corsairs in the 1600s, is warm year-round and offers several good beaches for sunning and swimming, including La Piscina, El Chüncho, Playa Blanca, and Las Machas. Good seafood can be found at *El Coral*, overlooking the bay on Avenida Morro (phone: 52-315331). Down the street, the *Britannia English Pub* has a variety of international beers, as well as dominoes and darts — and English owners.

**En Route from Copiapó** – Continue on the Pan-American for 200 miles (320 km) to reach La Serena.

**LA SERENA:** On entering the city, you can't miss the Alameda Francisco de Aguirre Boulevard; there are nearly 3 dozen marble sculptures lining the street like an open-air art museum. The road is indicative of the rest of the city. Founded in 1544, La Serena has preserved or remodeled buildings in the Spanish colonial style, and there are many churches and museums. A 16th-century cathedral can be found keeping watch over the Plaza de Armas. Sitting serenely on Balmaceda Street, the 17th-century San Francisco church houses the *Museo Colonial de Arte Religioso* (Colonial Museum of Religious Art), open Mondays through Fridays 10 AM to 1 PM and 4 to 8 PM, Saturdays 10 AM to 1 PM. The museum has poet Gabriela Mistral's death mask on display. The excellent

*Museo Arqueológico* (Archaeological Museum; at Cordovez and Cienfuegos Sts.; phone: 51-212393), with an extensive collection of pottery and tools from the pre-Inca Atacama and Diaguita Indian cultures, and a history section containing manuscripts of Chile's Nobel Prize winner in Literature, Mistral, is open Tuesdays through Saturdays 9 AM to 1 PM and 4 to 7 PM, Sundays 10 AM to 1 PM. Tourists with a special interest in the poet may want to take the short trip to the nearby town of Vicuña. The *Museo Gabriela Mistral* (Gabriela Mistral Museum) was opened in 1984 to honor her (759 Calle Gabriela Mistral; phone: 51-3123); beside it is the house where she was born. At the University of La Serena, the small *Museo Geológico de Ignacio Domeyko* (Ignacio Domeyko Geological Museum; 870 Anfión Muñoz; phone: 51-211868) houses more than 2,000 mineral specimens. Open Mondays through Fridays 8 AM to 1 PM and 2:30 to 6:30 PM. For more information, the tourist office is located at a kiosk in the Edificio de Servicios Públicos (on Calle Matta; phone: 51-213134), facing the Plaza de Armas.

Atop the garden-covered Santa Lucía Hill sits a *moai,* a 10-foot stone figure brought back from Isla de Pascua (Easter Island). At the base of the hill is the farmer's market, where picnickers can pick up fresh fruit and cheese, along with Serena's home-brewed *campanarios,* a fruit liqueur, to wash it down. Legend has it that a friar used the brew to boost the courage of a group of soldiers fearful of pirates who centuries ago repeatedly pillaged the area.

If you follow the Pan-American Highway south for 5 miles (8 km) you'll come to Coquimbo, La Serena's twin city and home of La Herradura (Horseshoe) beach. Its tourist draw is the elegant *Casino Municipal de Peñuelas,* with roulette tables, slot machines, and dining facilities, and ample gardens. (Dress is formal.) The casino is open every night from September through March and weekends the rest of the year.

Because of the clarity of the atmosphere, three international observatories are near La Serena, and in 1986 it was a popular site for viewing Halley's Comet. *Observatorio El Tololo* (El Tololo Observatory; 53 miles — 85 km — east of La Serena; phone: 51-213032) has the largest telescope in South America and can be visited Saturdays from 9 AM to noon and 1 to 5 PM if arrangements are made at least 24 hours in advance. A third observatory, *La Silla,* allows visits the first Saturday of every month (phone: 51-213832). Permission also can be arranged in person at the Colina El Pino building (behind the University of La Serena). *Observatorio Las Campanas* (Las Campanas Observatory) is 86 miles (138 km) north of the city just off the Pan-American Highway.

**En Route from La Serena** – Winding up your tour of the Atacama, take Route 43 east of La Serena and travel the 50 paved miles (80 km) to Ovalle. Along the way, you'll pass the town of Andacollo, which is the site of three yearly festivities. December 26, the *Fiesta de la Virgen de Andacollo* (Festival of the Virgin of Andacollo), is the most noted feast day in the Norte Chico. A smaller version of the celebration is held the first Sunday in October, complete with unusual Oriental dances and colorful costumes. The more than 300-year-old statue of the Virgin carried through the streets is said to have been found by miners who were trapped underground for 5 days and survived. It reportedly belonged to a Spanish soldier who got lost in the foothills of the Andes. During October there's the *Fiesta Chica,* the equivalent of the German *Oktoberfest.*

## BEST EN ROUTE

Any hotels you find on your journey through the Atacama will be small, frequently with shared bathrooms, except in larger towns. If you land a hotel with all the facilities in your room, however, you can expect to pay $55 to $90 for a double room in the expensive category, and about $30 to $55 in the moderate category. Those without these facilities are categorized as inexpensive, between $10 and $30. In most cases, breakfast is included in the price. Reservations usually aren't needed, except from December through March, when Chileans take their vacations, or during special festival times in the cities.

## ARICA

*Azapa Inn* – There are 71 rooms, some deluxe, all with private bath, and a swimming pool in this hotel; in a lovely shaded area on the outskirts of the city. 660 Calle Guillermo Sánchez, Valle de Azapa (phone: 58-222612). Expensive.

*Hostería Arica* – Private baths in its 70 rooms and 20 cabañas, and a dining room, as well as tennis courts, pool, and free transporation to the beaches. 599 Av. Comandante San Martín (phone: 58-231201; in Santiago, 2-696-6826; fax: 58-231133; in Santiago, 2-696-5599). Moderate.

*El Paso* – Part of the Cristóbal Inn chain, it's the best choice in town, with 40 double rooms, a restaurant, bar, and room service. 1109 Av. General Velásquez (phone: 58-231965; in Santiago, 2-333001). Moderate.

## IQUIQUE

*Cavancha* – Just about the best on the North Zone beach; 43 rooms plus a restaurant and room service. 250 Los Rieles (phone: 57-21158; in Santiago, 2-229-8745). Expensive.

*Arturo Prat* – Offers 55 small, comfortable rooms, as well as a restaurant and bar. 695 Av. Anibal Pinto (phone: 57-421414; in Santiago, 2-225-9432). Moderate.

*Eben Ezer* – You can get a US-style breakfast at this hotel, a rarity among rarities in Chilean hospitality. Beachfront at 981 Fuenzalida (phone: 57-29111). Inexpensive.

## CALAMA

*Calama* – Just 3 blocks from the plaza, this hotel has a good restaurant, bar, Jacuzzi, and attentive service. 1521 Latorre (phone: 82-211511). Inexpensive.

## ANTOFAGASTA

*Antofagasta* – A swimming pool, breakfast in bed (108 rooms), and a view of the city and port. Another member of the Cristóbal Inn chain. Beachfront. 2575 Balmaceda (phone: 55-224710; in Santiago, 2-330906). Moderate.

*Plaza* – A full-service, medium-size hotel, with a restaurant, cafeteria, bar, pool, Jacuzzi, sauna, squash court, and beauty salon. There's room service, too. 461 Baquedano (phone: 55-222058; in Santiago, 2-274-2509; fax: 55-266803). Moderate.

## COPIAPÓ

*Diego de Almeida* – Yet another of the hotels in the first class Cristóbal chain. It has 41 rooms, a restaurant, bar, and other amenities. 656 Av. O'Higgins (phone: 52-212075; in Santiago 2-330906). Moderate.

## LA SERENA

*Francisco de Aguirre* – The best in town, this 90-room property is situated along the avenue that looks out over the water. Amenities include a restaurant, coffee shop, bar, pool, sauna, discotheque, and laundry service. A member of the Cristóbal Inn chain. 210 Av. Cordovez (phone: 51-212351; in Santiago, 2-222991). Moderate.

# Valparaíso and Viña del Mar

On your Chilean tour, you should leave Santiago and head 70 miles (112 km) northwest to the major seaport of Valparaíso and its sister city, Viña del Mar. Actually, these two cities are more opposite than they are alike. Valparaíso is a brawling seaport, filled with closely built, weatherbeaten houses crawling over numerous hills. Nicknamed "Pancho" by its residents, the city preserves its past in English street names and European architecture. Viña del Mar, 5 miles (8 km) north across the bay, is a posh resort town, with clean, well-tended gardens, a casino, and long stretches of beach along a 10-mile coastal highway.

Viña del Mar is the spawn of Valparaíso, which precedes the town by more than 350 years. Founded in 1536 by Diego de Almagro, Valparaíso and the surrounding area already were inhabited by the Chango, an Indian tribe that lived off the sea and traveled the shore in canoes made of sea lion skins. The port had a rather dull, uneventful life until English pirateers started to plunder the South American coastline in attacks against the Spanish throne. Sir Francis Drake robbed, among other things, the chalice out of Valparaíso's church in 1578, and Richard Hawkins pillaged his way down the coast 15 years later. Finally the Spanish had to build the town's first real fortress, San José, overlooking the sea. With this, Valparaíso officially became a commercial port, docking boats regularly from as far north as the Peruvian port of Callao. By 1800, it had become Chile's most important international port.

A lot of Chilean firsts happened in Valparaíso. The first Chilean newspaper, *Aurore de Chile,* was published here on the country's first printing press in 1811, at the start of the Independence War; Valparaíso was the stage for its first battle in 1813. After the war, Chile's first naval squadron sailed from here in 1818 under the command of Captain Manuel Blanco Encalada. The first steamship to sail the Pacific arrived in Valparaíso in 1822, and Charles Darwin passed through during his 6-year voyage on the HMS *Beagle* in 1834. What's more, as the commercial and financial center of the nation, Valparaíso was the first city to get electricity, telephone, and telegraph service, and to have a train. During the height of its importance, it also boasted Chile's most splendid mansions, some of which are still scattered around the area.

It wasn't until 1874 that little Viña del Mar was even a gleam in Valparaíso's eye. That year, the town government gave José Francisco Vergara the go-ahead to build from village plans he had submitted. (Before then, Viña del Mar was no more than the hacienda of a wealthy port resident.) The resort was founded in 1878; since then, it has become popular with affluent tourists from all over Latin America.

The climate in Valparaíso and Viña del Mar is milder than that of Santiago; the temperature rarely falls below 30F ($-1$C) in winter and averages about 59F (15C) throughout the year. The summer heat (if any) is tempered by constant ocean breezes, and the Humboldt Current-chilled waters make sunbathing more popular than swimming at the beaches.

To reach these two cities from Santiago, the best route is to take a 90-

minute scenic trip along Route 68 northwest, going through the Lo Prado tunnel instead of over the hill. Along the way, you'll pass the town of Curacavi, known for its meringue sweets, and the small farming town of Casablanca, with its Lo Vásquez church. Every December 8 you share the road with pilgrims approaching the church, many on their knees, for the annual observance of the *Fiesta de la Imaculada Concepción* (Feast of the Immaculate Conception). There is one expensive toll along this route (about $4), so make sure you have your money ready. Alternatively, the trip can be made by bus. From 6:30 AM to 11 PM, buses leave the terminal at the University of Santiago metro stop every 5 minutes. City buses travel between Valparaíso and Viña, a 10-minute ride. For a novel trip to Viña, it is possible to fly from Santiago and along the Pacific coast in the small charter planes of *Spasa*. Make arrangements in Santiago at 1009 Catedral (phone: 2-695-3400; fax: 2-699-2121).

**VALPARAÍSO:** The first view as you enter this city of 350,000 people is Avenida Argentina, the major road, lined with monuments dedicated to, among others, Queen Isabella of Spain, Christopher Columbus, Lord Cochrane, Admiral Blanco Encalada, and the French and British colonists who settled here in the 19th century.

The city center is Plaza Sotomayer, with the main entrance to the port on one side and the gracious, wedding-cake Intendencia (Government House) on the other. In the middle is a monument to the Heroes of Iquique, where Captain Arturo Prat and the others who died in 1879 at the Battle of Iquique are buried. Every May 21 the Chilean navy stages commemorative events at the monument. Facing the plaza is Muelle Prat, the wharf where you'll find a line of artisans' shops as well as the city's tourism kiosk.

If you cross the plaza to the front of the Intendencia and turn right, you're headed south on Serrano Street, the oldest in the city. Two blocks down is the Plaza Echaurren, where La Matriz church stands at the site where the first chapel in Valparaíso was built in 1559. The current church was built in 1842, but the statue of Christ is from the 1600s.

Four blocks farther is the Plaza Aduana, with the old customs building. From here you can take a funicular railroad up to the top of Cerro Artilleria, where there's a terrace (Paseo 21 de Mayo) overlooking the city and bay. While you're in the port area, you can climb some of the other hills — but beware of purse snatchers and pickpockets, as visitors have been the targets of street crime. To the right of the Intendencia as you face it is Cerro Cordillera. Perched on top of the hill in a colonial-era villa is the *Museo del Mar Lord Cochrane* (Lord Cochrane Sea Museum), with its scale models of historic ships from around the world.

Be sure to ride at least one of the many public elevators that transport Valparaíso residents up the steep hills of the city. El Peral elevator is at Plaza Justicia, where you'll also find the *Museo de Bellas Artes* (Fine Arts Museum), which houses a collection of Chilean art, as well as European paintings from the 19th and 20th centuries. The modern art gallery is at 1550 Condell. Perhaps the most picturesque — and difficult to find — elevator is the Ascensor Polanco, which has an entrance on Avenida Argentina. If you can't find it, ask any Valparaíso resident; Chileans are most hospitable, and the ride is worth the effort. From a lookout that affords one of the best views of the city, the elevator drops through a solid rock shaft cut into the hillside to an underground walkway to Simpson Street.

A longer walk around Valparaíso will take you along the coast road west. From the Plaza Aduana, take Avenida Antonio Varas, which becomes Avenida Altamirano when it reaches the shore. There are a number of restaurants in this area. *El Membrillo* (1569 Av. Altamirano) is a fishermen's cooperative and has fresh seafood at low prices — try the *sopa de mariscos,* a seafood soup. As you walk back to the main dining room, a bare porch over the water, you'll see the beach where the fishermen draw up their long, brightly painted boats, guarded by a statue of San Pedro (St. Peter), which is taken out to sea every June 29 (the saint's feast day) to bless the water, the catch, and the fishermen. Here, as elsewhere in Valparaíso and Viña del Mar, you can get *congrio* (conger eel), *corvina* (sea bass), *almejas* (clams), and *cholgas* (mussels).

On Sundays it's worth strolling over to Plaza O'Higgins, where there is an antiques fair, a host of coin and stamp collectors, and some serious chess matches. The plaza is on Avenida Pedro Montt.

One of the city's newest attractions is the large, glittering Congress building erected by the outgoing military government to keep the politicians away from Santiago. (The old Congress building in downtown Santiago now is used as the Ministry of the Interior.) The massive size and correspondingly hefty price tag has made this structure on Avenida Brasil a controversial one. Guards at the front door allow visitors to enter (after leaving their passports) on Tuesdays, Wednesdays, and Thursdays when Congress is in session.

By the way, an exciting time to be in Valparaíso is *New Year's Eve,* when the city greets the new year with the wailing of ships' horns accompanying fireworks set off over the port. A good place to be is the Mirador de O'Higgins, a lookout point behind the city, where the roads from Viña del Mar and Valparaíso meet before heading on to Santiago.

Transportation is such in Valparaíso that you can go anywhere you want in the world, with steamers available to Los Angeles and New York; London; Guayaquil, Ecuador; or to Punta Arenas and Arica here in Chile. Buses also run between here and Viña del Mar, Santiago, and Concepción.

Leaving Valparaíso, take the paved road north to Viña del Mar, the little resort of 280,000 that is one of the most popular adult playgrounds in South America.

**VIÑA DEL MAR:** This resort is interesting from the moment you enter it: You'll pass a sundial of flowers planted on a small, raised plot of land; it keeps perfect time and is the resort's hallmark. North of the clock on Cerro Castillo overlooking the water is the summer presidential home, also called Cerro Castillo, a Spanish colonial mansion on the former site of the Collao fort. After Cerro Castillo, you will come to the *Museo de la Cultura del Mar* (Naval Museum; Av. Marina; phone: 32-625427), which is installed in an English Tudor castle-like building, Castillo Wolff, on a small peninsula overlooking the sea. The museum contains paintings and drawings, uniforms, medals, books, maps, and documents pertaining to Chile's naval history. Avenida Marina ends at a bridge crossing the Marga-Marga inlet; to the left is Avenida San Martín, which runs north to the beaches.

On the left of Avenida San Martín as you cross the bridge is a casino (phone: 32-973565), open every night during the summer season (mid-September to mid-March), and weekend nights the rest of the year. The casino is a gambler's haven for blackjack, baccarat, and roulette tables; there are also a gaming room for *tragamonedas* (one-armed bandits), a bar, dining facilities, and a floor show. You do have to pay admission at the door (a small gamble for a good time), and you have to pay for a membership card that gives you access to the gameroom. The minimum roulette bet is $1; $10 for blackjack and baccarat.

If you turn right from Avenida Marina and nix the casino, you'll find yourself on Schroeders Street. At the end of the second block, turn right onto Valparaíso Street, which will take you into the town's main shopping center and Plaza Vergara, where you can trot around in a colorful, horse-drawn carriage (*victoria*) decked with roses.

At one side of the plaza is the municipal theater, built during the town's early years. If you're not planning to attend a performance, at least take a peek inside the theater. This neo-classical building is decorated in an eclectic but pleasing style, and was renovated following the severe 1985 earthquake. Just south of the Plaza Vergara, 1 block past the railroad tracks, is the Quinta Vergara garden park. Here the *Museo de Bellas Artes* (Fine Arts Museum) is in one of the mansions where the founding Vergara family lived. The building was badly damaged in a 1971 earthquake but has been repaired and looks much as it did when the family lived was in residence. There is a large collection of European and Chilean paintings and antique furniture. The Vergara's first mansion has been converted into the stage and amphitheater used for Viña's annual international music festival.

Take Avenida Libertad to 4 Calle Norte to see the city's *Centro Cultural* (Cultural Center), consisting of the library, an archaeological museum (open weekdays from 10 AM to 6 PM, weekends from 10 AM to 2 PM), and a natural sciences museum housed in a restored mansion. Open Mondays through Fridays from 10 AM to 1 PM and 2 to 8 PM, Saturdays from 10 AM to 1 PM and 4 to 8 PM, and Sundays from 10 AM to 2 PM. In front of the museums is a carved stone *moai* from Easter Island. It was moved here from Avenida Marina after sea spray started to damage the statue. If you take a left onto 3 Calle Norte, 3 blocks down on Quillota you will find Rioja Park and the Rioja mansion.

Three blocks from Rioja Park is the *Sporting Club* (404 Av. Los Castaños; phone: 32-976047), with its racetrack and playing fields for rugby, tennis, hockey, polo, and soccer. (There are horse races on Fridays and Sundays.) Nearby is Lake Sausalito, a popular spot for boating and picnics under the willows. It also is the site of the *Sausalito Stadium,* with a capacity of 30,000. Beyond the lake are the municipal park, the golf club, and the *Granadilla Country Club*. For tennis, stop by *Tenis Sausalito* (next to the lake and stadium of the same name; phone: 32-976249).

The city tourism office (507 Av. Valparaíso; phone: 32-684117) is open weekdays from 9 AM to 2 PM and 3 PM to 8 PM; Saturdays from 9 AM to 1:30 PM and 4 to 7 PM; and Sundays from 9 AM to 1:30 PM.

There are many restaurants and cafés in Viña del Mar, but a traditional gathering spot is the *Samoiedo* shop (637 Av. Valparaíso; phone: 32-684610). You'll know it when you see it — it's the one with the stuffed animals in the window and crowds of young people outside. *Viñamarinos* and tourists take tea and cocktails here about 5 PM every day; one Chilean cocktail to try is a sherry punch, *vaina,* made with egg, milk, and sherry. This city is a haven for vegetarians, who can enjoy its numerous "natural" food restaurants and shops, as well as a "natural" food bakery, *Sol del Pacífico,* in the nearby town of Quilpué. For those with a sweet tooth, Viña's bakeries can't be beat. Many provide old-fashioned wicker baskets for shoppers to fill with breads and sweets. And for French cuisine, try *La Maison de France,* in a Victorian house shared by the French Consulate (366 Quinta).

Hotel reservations are always recommended during the summer season at Viña — and especially in February, when the city hosts its annual popular music festival in the *Quinta Vergara Greek Theater*. Attracting singers from all over the world, the event sells out and it's even difficult to find a camping spot in the area. The town goes crazy, with mobs of young people jamming the streets and having a good time.

If you're heading out to the beach — and usually you'll have to wait until early afternoon if you want sun — take Avenida Libertad north to the end and turn left at the Regiment Coracero onto Calle 15 Norte. In 1 block you're on Avenida Jorge Montt, the road along the coast.

The coastal ride is exhilarating: You drive along a winding road over the crest of Viña del Mar's rocky shoreline, the surf pounding to your left and a cliff with woods or houses with colorful gardens on the right. The first beach is Las Salinas. While there, stop at the restaurant of the seaside *Oceanic* hotel (12925 Av. Borgoño; phone: 32-830006) with its splendid view of the sea and Viña del Mar in the distance (see *Best en Route*); try the house specialty, *congrio oceanico* (conger eel with artichokes) and a bottle of Chilean wine. Farther down the road is Reñaca, one of the most popular, with a fairly wide strip of sand and a series of little shops selling ice cream and beer. As you hit the Reñaca area, a honky-tonk conglomeration of pizza parlors, hamburger dens, and dancing spots remind you of the crowded US Atlantic coast. Along here is the *Anastassia* restaurant (15000 Av. Borgoño; phone: 32-832191), a great setting for a drink while you enjoy the ocean view.

On the hill above Reñaca Beach is the area's most famous spot for dancing, *Discotheque Topsy* (501 Santa Luisa; phone: 32-902255). Perched at the top of a very high cliff, one of its many rooms has a superb view of the bay, with the lights of Valparaíso in the distance. Each room is decorated differently; in one, you skip over little ponds to dance and retire for your drinks to little caves. There's a 2-story slide to take you from one floor to another.

**En Route from Viña del Mar** – The fastest way back to Santiago is east on Route 68. However, you might want to take the scenic Agua Santa road that winds around the hills of Viña del Mar back to that route rather than return to Valparaíso to pick up the same road. If you leave Viña del Mar in the evening at sunset, you'll see a phenomenon for which Valparaíso is noted: The setting sun reflected on the windows of Valparaíso's homes seems to set the city's hills afire.

If you want to explore a bit more of the coastline east of Santiago, take the road that turns south off Route 68 just a few miles beyond Casablanca. This will take you to Algarrobo, a less noted, less crowded, and now fashionable beach resort, and on to the quiet and progressively less fashionable beaches of El Quisco, El Tabo, Las Cruces, and Cartagena. Isla Negra, where poet Pablo Neruda had his home, is a little south of El Quisco. Despite its name, Isla Negra is not an island, and you can visit Neruda's home and the women there who make the small, embroidered-cloth and hand-sewn scenes of rural Chilean life, the *bordadores de Isla Negra*. Neruda's home, Casa de Isla Negra, is open daily except Mondays. Make an advance appointment in Santiago through the Neruda Foundation (phone: 2-777-8741); travel agencies in Santiago also book tours.

From here, it's about 25 miles (40 km) from the turnoff to Algarrobo and another 25 miles (40 km) to the port of San Antonio, Chile's fourth-largest seaport (pop. 50,000). Just south of San Antonio is the small summer town of Rocas de Santo Domingo, a garden spot perched on a cliff overlooking the sea. This is a summer village of private homes of well-off Chileans, and it's a fabulous place for a seafood lunch or dinner.

From San Antonio you can return to Santiago in about 2½ hours, taking Route 78 through the Central Valley farming district.

## BEST EN ROUTE

In the resort area you'll need advance reservations, more so in the summer months (mid-September to mid-March) and especially in February, when Viña del Mar hosts the *Festival Internacional de Viña del Mar*. Hotels in Valparaíso are a lot less expensive than those in Viña del Mar — you can find a comfortable, clean room for about $15 a night — but the better properties are in the resort town and it is expensive. Viña del Mar hotels are priced from over $80 for a double room in the expensive category, from $50 to $80 per person in the moderate category, and under $50 in the inexpensive category. You get private baths, telephones, and often coastal views and excellent service.

### VALPARAÍSO

*Prat* – Elegant for Valparaíso, but pricey by local standards, this property has 100 rooms facing bay and sea. 1443 Condell (phone: 32-253081). Moderate.

## VIÑA DEL MAR

**Miramar** – Right over the water, here are 100 single and double rooms, private baths, phones, dining rooms, bars, terraces, and walk-ups to rocky cliffs overlooking the ocean. Caleta Abarca (phone: 32-664077; in Santiago, 2-671-3165; fax: 32-665220). Expensive.

**Oceanic** – Formerly a private villa, this little gem of a hotel is perched on a cliff beside Las Salinas Beach. Nearly all the 20 rooms have breathtaking, floor-to-ceiling ocean views, oversize beds, and bathrooms with tubs. There's a fine international restaurant, bar, pool, gym, sauna, and Jacuzzi. The attentive staff speaks English and there's 24-hour room service. Book well ahead. 12925 Av. Borgoño (phone: 32-830006; fax: 32-830390). Expensive.

**O'Higgins** – A 300-room hotel with private baths, phones, a dining room, bar, valet service, pool, discotheque, and other amenities. Plaza Vergara (phone: 32-882016; in Santiago, 2-671-3165; in the US, 800-44-UTELL; fax: 32-883537). Expensive.

**San Martín** – Private baths and phones in its 180 rooms. A dining room and bar service are there when you need them, as well as a gym and sauna. 667 Av. San Martín and Calle 8 Norte (phone: 32-972548; fax: 32-972772). Expensive.

**Hotel Español** – The quaintest lodging (18 rooms with private bathrooms) on the main plaza. The hotel is beside the *Cabeza de Buey* restaurant, which specializes in grilled meat and seafood and features an outdoor café for people watching. 191 Plaza Vergara (phone: 32-685145). Moderate.

**Alcazar** – Near the railroad station, this 75-room hotel offers a friendly atmosphere. 646 Alvarez (phone: 32-685112). Inexpensive.

## ROCAS DE SANTO DOMINGO

**Las Rocas** – Basic, clean, friendly, on a cliff overlooking the sea, it is the traditional hotel in town. A good spot for lunch. Open September to March only. 130 La Ronda (phone: 35-31348). Moderate.

# Portillo

Ski enthusiasts throughout the world smile knowingly or wistfully at the mention of Portillo, Chile's renowned ski resort nestled in the highest peaks of the Chilean-Argentine Andes. Just 91 miles (146 km) northwest of Santiago, looming 9,230 feet above sea level, beginners and pros alike have challenged the jagged, hair-raising slopes. The extra thrill for North Americans is skiing at its best — in July and August. There's something in Portillo for everyone: You can live a life of leisure and hang out by the fire in the *Gran Hotel Portillo* and skate on Laguna del Inca; or you can brave one of the toughest slopes in the world — 2,405-foot Roca Jack. If the thought of descending on a near-45-degree angle doesn't scare you, then perhaps the local lore about the slope will: "Jack" was an old-time local skier who used to ascend the slope every morning, then stand there and admire the Andean view until he had enough guts to parallel down.

Since Portillo has the most challenging ski slopes around, the best skiers converge here annually to keep themselves in shape. It is the summer home for national ski teams from the US, Canada, and Europe; its ski school is headed by Austrian Hartmut Helmsteit, formerly of Vermont's Sugarbush resort, and it has 40 international instructors. There are trails for skiers of all classes, but the most famous runs include the one going 9 miles cross-country to the Christ of the Andes monument on the Argentine border and another 4-mile track down Mt. Ojos de Agua. The *Gran Hotel Portillo* (see *Best en Route*) has been owned by Robert Purcell since the early 1960s. Purcell is a Rockefeller-affiliated investment banker who fell in love with the area while here on business. Today, his nephews operate the resort. Purcell himself has been known to sneak a few snowplows down the slopes.

The skiing season here lasts from June through October, with the *Ski Carnaval* held in August. Several airlines, including *LanChile,* offer 14- to 28-day ski packages to Portillo alone or to Portillo and Bariloche, Portillo's resort rival east across the Andes in Argentina. All flights bring you into Santiago; from there, you're bused up into the mountains or you can rent your own car.

Before packing yourself off to the plane, however, there are two important things to keep in mind. First of all, part of the resort, except for a small restaurant, is shut down from November through January; after that, several rooms containing bunk beds are opened from January through May for any visitors trekking through. The beds are in an octagonal building near the main hotel, where the downstairs cafeteria is open for dining. The summer entertainment is swimming in the resort's pool or gazing at the clear, Andean scenery — and it is superb.

The second important reminder is this: If you do visit Portillo during the winter, be prepared to overstay. Snowstorms are known to hold up activities, and if you're snowed in beyond your reservation, you're going to have to pay for the extra time spent there. One particular blizzard in 1978 lasted 20 days, and traffic to and from the hotel was cut, period. Desperate skiers who were either broke or suffering from cabin fever finally were flown out by helicopter.

There are two routes to Portillo. You can take the Pan-American Highway northwest out of Santiago to La Calera, exploring some of the Central Valley towns before heading east on Highway 60 to San Felipe and Los Andes; or you can take paved Route 57 north from Santiago to Los Andes, making an 11-mile (18-km) detour west to visit San Felipe before continuing on to Los Andes and Portillo on Route 60 once again.

The first route takes you 51 miles (82 km) out of Santiago to your first stop, the small village (10,000 people) of Llay-Llay. The town received its name from the way the Indians said the wind sounded as it blew through the valley. The valley is a rich fruit-producing area, although the village itself owes its existence to three copper kilns and a railway depot.

A few miles south of La Calera on Route 62 are three swimming holes. Farther south are the garden hills of Quillota and Limache; during the September 18 and 19 *fiestas patrias* (patriotic festivals), the rodeo shows are fun. East of Limache on a gravel road is Olmue, where there's a *huaso* (cowboy) festival during the second half of January and rodeos in November and February. From here, return to Llay-Llay and continue east on Route 60 to San Felipe, which was founded in 1740 as a central location for the schooling of the children of the scattered hacienda owners. Continuing west on Route 60 you'll reach Panquehue and the vineyards that produce some of

Chile's best wine. Hacienda Panque, owned by the colonial Toro-Mazote family until 1870, was once the world's largest vineyard owned by a single family. Today, the hacienda has wine shops where samples are offered.

A paved route north from San Felipe runs to the small colonial town of Putaendo, where the 4,000-strong army of liberators San Martín and O'Higgins rested in February 1817 after crossing the Andes from Argentina. From here, the troops marched to the south side of Chacabuco Hill to stage a comeback by defeating the Spanish. Three hundred years earlier, the Inca Huayna Cápac arrived in the village and declared the area part of the Inca empire, which at that time stretched as far north as Ecuador. East of San Felipe on a paved road are two small copper-, gold-, and silver-mining towns, Santa María and Catemu; north of Santa María are the Jahuel Hot Springs, and a full-service resort (see *Best en Route*). If you take the Route 60 stretch east of San Felipe for about 15 miles (24 km) you'll reach Curimon, where a Franciscan colonial church (Calle Real) houses a colonial religious museum. From here, it's on to Los Andes.

**LOS ANDES:** Founded in 1791, this town is an important transportation center for rail and road traffic to Argentina. The road from here that crosses the border is the only link between La Serena and Talca, and much of the Chile-Argentina tourist trade passes this way.

There's little for a tourist to do here other than wander through the town's plazas, admire the hand-painted Cala ceramics, and rest before taking the steep ascent from Los Andes, 2,400 feet above sea level, to Portillo. Stop in at the *Cerámica Cala* store (on Calle Freire near Av. Independencia; phone: 34-421630). It is open Mondays through Saturdays.

**En Route from Los Andes** – It's about 40 miles (64 km) — all uphill — from here to Portillo. The sky gets increasingly bluer, reaching an astonishing intensity for eyes used to gazing up through city smog. The paved road parallels the Río Aconcagua to Río Colorado. You then follow the Aconcagua past the Salto del Soldado waterfall and on to Río Blanco, where the Blanco and Juncal rivers join to form the Aconcagua. The road then runs along the Juncal to Portillo; it is increasingly steep, with many hairpin turns. During the winter, the snowdrifts reach above the roof of a small car, and sometimes the road is blocked. But it's paved all the way and in good condition.

**PORTILLO:** Despite the altitude, the bright yellow *Gran Hotel Portillo*, a curved slice of sunshine at the end of the road, is set in a valley with mountain peaks that tower to great heights on three sides. To the right as you come up the hill are the beginner and intermediate slopes; to the left, the craggy face of Roca Jack.

By the time you get this far, you'll be able to get a glimpse of Mt. Aconcagua, which at 22,834 feet is the highest mountain in South America, just over the border in Argentina.

Portillo gets its name from the Portillo Cordillera in Argentina, higher than the separate Peuquenes Ridge on the Chilean side. A short distance beyond Portillo, along paved Route 60, the border is marked by a large statue of Christ the Redeemer, erected in 1904. The statue, cast from the bronze of cannon used in the independence wars against Spain, bears the legend: "These mountains will crumble before Argentines and Chileans break the peace sworn at the feet of Christ the Redeemer." Well, the mountains haven't crumbled yet, the northern Atacama Desert dispute between Chile and Peru is quiet for the moment, and the southern Beagle Channel argument between Chile and Argentina has been resolved by a treaty negotiated by the pope. However, ownership of Antarctica is a hot issue, and Chile has already warned Argentina and Peru of its determination to retain its rights at the South Pole.

Behind the hotel at Portillo is Laguna del Inca, 3 miles long and about a mile wide. If you're here in the spring and hear some strange groans coming from the lake, don't worry: It's only the ice. That is, white men say it's the ice, but Indian legend says it's Illi Yunqui you hear, crying for his lover Kora-llé, who lies at the bottom of the lake. She died when she fell from one of the precipices surrounding the water, and poor Illi decided the only fitting burial place for her was in the lake. As Kora-llé's body sank to the bottom, the water turned emerald green, taking the color of her eyes. The lake, with three snow-covered mountains rising from its shores, is one of the most dramatic scenes in Chile.

Skiing is of prime interest from June to October. The highest of the resort's 11 lifts takes you to a chilling elevation of 10,700 feet. The ski school offers group and private lessons for beginning, advanced, and expert skiers. Ski equipment can be rented. You also can spend your days lounging and tanning on the deck; swimming in the heated outdoor pool; or shooting pool indoors. Or you can dine, take in a movie or disco, or simply keep watch at the bar (open from 11 AM to 10 PM). There's just one rule at the hotel: Wear a jacket to dinner. You can't escape this even if you're on a national ski team. You also might want to dine at the mountaintop restaurant off Plateau lift. Its specialties come from its open-air barbecue, accompanied by Chilean wine.

When you can't stay in Portillo much longer, and if you don't have a car, there is scheduled bus service, a 2-hour trip one way, operated by *Gray Line;* ask at the *Gran Hotel Portillo.* The bus also operates from Santiago, picking up passengers at major hotels. Make reservations with your concierge.

## BEST EN ROUTE

The best service in any Chilean hotel is rendered at the only hotel in Portillo. Guests have to pay the price, whether it be the basic $28 and $100 reservation fee for a bunk with common bath or the very expensive $227 private-room rate, double occupancy. Reservations are mandatory. Keep in mind that the *Gran Hotel Portillo* shuts down from November through January, with only some accommodations open from January until May, the start of the ski season; however, inexpensive, basic bunks with shared baths are also available in the train station. In other areas, a double room in an expensive hotel is $100 and up; $60 to $100 at a moderate place; and under $55 in the inexpensive category.

### LOS ANDES

*Plaza* – Small and comfortable, with a restaurant and a view of the city's plaza. 367 Calle Esmeralda (phone: 34-421929). Inexpensive.

### PORTILLO

*Gran Hotel Portillo* – A 650-bed phenomenon: ski lessons, rentals, and slopes; swimming, ice skating, pool tables, Ping-Pong, disco, bar, movie theater, nursery, sauna, and more. At Km 61 on the International Rd., Portillo (phone: 562-243-3007). The address in Santiago is 2911 Roger de Flor, Las Condes (phone: 2-231-3411; fax: 2-231-7164). In the US contact *LanChile* (phone: 800-627-7780) for ski package information. Very expensive.

### JAHUEL

*Termas de Jahuel* – This 70-room resort features therapeutic hot springs, a restaurant, bar, large pool, tennis courts, horseback riding, mini-golf, and a sauna. North of Santa María on the San Felipe road (phone: 34-511240; in Santiago, 2-392829). Moderate.

# Ovalle to Talca

The 400-mile (640-km) stretch of land from Ovalle south to Talca leads to the heart of Chile's Central Valley, comfortably sandwiched between the Chilean Andean Cordillera (ridge) and the Pacific coast. More than 70% of Chile's population of 13 million lives here; more than 4 million alone in the Greater Santiago area (for detailed information, see *Santiago* in THE CITIES). Considered a fringe town of the Atacama, Ovalle is the meeting point of desert and fertile valley; a number of oases here have been transformed into national parks, including Parque Fray Jorge and Parque Talinay. When you head south on the Pan-American Highway and reach La Ligua, 150 miles (240 km) away, you run into the start of a mild, rainy zone that stretches past Talca to the southernmost end of the desert and Concepción (see *Concepción to Laja Falls,* below). Vegetation becomes greener south of Santiago, thanks to the many rivers that irrigate the area. You'll cross water a dozen times between here and Talca. This part of the valley is the country's fruit-growing, grain-raising, and cattle district — a multitude of *fundos* (farms). The scenery is breathtaking: rows of poplars bending in the southwesterly winds; groves and groves of eucalyptus trees; and an occasional weeping willow drooping by the water. Between La Ligua and Santiago lies a trio of trendy ski areas — Farellones, El Colorado, and La Parva. Nearby, but higher up in the mountains, there is the French-owned resort of Valle Nevado, one of the fastest-growing ski centers in South America. Because of their proximity to the Chilean capital, all four resorts are popular with day trippers and crowded on weekends.

Agriculturally, Chile is a fairly well-developed country, and during recent years exports of agricultural produce have increased substantially due to improvements in agricultural techniques. As recently as 1969, however, there existed large haciendas where the majority of wealthy, absentee owners exploited peasant labor; the Araucano Indians who were previously indentured into serfdom on the farms gave in to the *inquilino* (tenant farmer system) rather than work in the owner's employ.

An agricultural reform program instituted under the presidency of Eduardo Frei (1964–70) continued through the ill-fated leadership of Salvador Allende (1970–73) and, despite the military junta led by General Augusto Pinochet Ugarte that deposed Allende, continued to the end of 1978. An active Pinochet government policy to stimulate agricultural exports modernized farming in the Central Valley, resulting in the appearance of Chilean fruits and vegetables in US stores. Today, Chile's economy remains dependent on fruit exports.

Chile's colonial heritage is strongly felt in the Central Valley: Landowners (descended from the early Basques and Castilians) pushed strongly for independence from Spain and the viceroy of Lima, who ruled colonial Chile.

Many of the independence war's important battles were fought here, and on February 12, 1818, Bernardo O'Higgins signed Chile's Declaration of Independence at Talca.

Continuing your tour from the Atacama on the Pan-American, you'll pass through some of the oldest towns in Chile. Talca dates to 1692; San Fernando, 1742; Rancagua and Curicó, 1743. Most of these towns are craft centers, and you can pick up a variety of ponchos, baskets, and ceramics. At times, the highway will flirt with the Pacific coast, taking you to some small resorts, including Papudo and Zapallar, known for their fishing and sailing.

**OVALLE:** This town of 66,000 people signals the start of the Central Valley. The arid desert of the Atacama blends into green, fertile valleys and pastures; the area around Ovalle is ripe with orchards of various fruit, from apples to oranges and mangoes; there are even vineyards. It is also Chile's center for the production of *pisco,* a grape-based *aguardiente* (home-brewed liquor similar to grain alcohol).

Ovalle's biggest attraction is its privately owned *Museo Arqueológico* (Archaeological Museum; 329 Calle Independencia), which features displays of pre-Inca items from an Indian cemetery discovered at a stadium construction site in 1962. Pieces include artifacts and relics from various Indian cultures, including the Valle del Encanto, Huentelauquén, El Molle, and Diaguita. Open Tuesdays through Saturdays from 8 AM to 1 PM and 3 to 7 PM, Sundays from 10 AM to 1 PM.

Ovalle is also a good spot for shopping. *CEMA* (beside the tourist information office at the corner of Aguirre and Vicuña Mackenna) has fine woven and hand-knit goods as well as delicate reed baskets and mats. Across town, at the fairgrounds, onyx, turquoise, and lapis lazuli stones and jewelry are sold along with fruit, cheese, and livestock.

The town is a good base for visiting the nearby national parks, which are reached by paved roads. Parque Nacional Fray Jorge (Friar Jorge National Park) is 18 miles (29 km) west of Ovalle; it is a natural forest in the middle of the Atacama fringe. Parque Talinay, another oasis-type park, is 35 miles (56 km) southeast.

If you prefer, you can take a 20-mile (32-km) ride down the Pan-American south of Ovalle until you come to a small, paved road that will take you — in less than a mile — to Termas de Socos, noted for thermal, therapeutic springs.

**En Route from Ovalle** – A paved road leads to the coast, where you can pick up the Pan-American south to La Ligua. On the way are thin, rocky beaches and the fruit-growing town of Huentelauquén, site of an excavated Indian cemetery and famous for its papayas and cheese. About 100 miles (160 km) south of Ovalle is Los Vilos, a fishing village with 8,400 inhabitants, wide, sandy beaches (camping is permitted), and a pair of islands to which boat excursions can be arranged. Isla de los Lobos is home to 1,400 sea lions. (If you have binoculars, they'll come in handy here.) There's a picnic site, so stock up on goodies in Huentelauquén and treat yourself to an afternoon in the open air. Los Vilos has become a popular weekend destination for Santiago residents wishing to escape the city. A short road north from the village leads to Conchalí Bay, where the beach is protected from coastal winds by a cover. Some 15 miles (24 km) south of Los Vilos, Pichidangui Beach offers deep-sea fishing and diving. If you fall in love with the white, sandy shore, you'll find camping facilities, hotels, and several good restaurants. From here, it's another 30 miles (48 km) to La Ligua.

If you prefer, take an alternate paved road to La Ligua and skip the beach. This road parallels the Pan-American, traveling over some rough, hilly territory that eventually leads to Combarbalá. This town, established 200 years ago to bring together mining families that were spread out over the area, serves the same purpose today. Note the unusual octagonal plaza decorated with Diaguita Indian designs and the local artisan work in *combarbalita* rock — which resembles a colored marble. Forty-five miles (72 km) south of Combarbalá on the same road is Illapel, a farming town of 15,000 on the Río Choapa. A nearby petrified forest contains *petroglifos* (rock etchings). From Illapel, another road southwest leads into Los Vilos and the Pan-American, which you'll ride until you come to La Ligua.

**LA LIGUA:** This small, heartland town is famous for its brown and gray vicuña and alpaca garments: ponchos, sweaters, jackets, coats, and even bolt wool. And you can forget about your diet: The *alfajores,* cookies made with layers of *manjar blanca* (blancmange) from cooked milk, are irresistible. Both clothing and food are sinfully inexpensive.

After you've finished indulging yourself, a 12-mile (19-km) drive northeast along a dirt road will take you to Cabildo, where you'll digest while wandering among the old-style Araucanian houses of straw and adobe. Fifteen miles (24 km) southwest of La Ligua on the same road are the resorts of Papudo and Zapallar, with white-sand beaches and calm waters perfect for swimming. Six miles (10 km) apart, both are noted for water skiing and sailing. While Papudo caters to the middle class vacationer, Zapallar is visited by a more wealthy clientele, who own large homes that date back 100 years. At Zapallar, you can set up casual arrangements with townspeople for a boat ride to nearby Isla de los Lobos and watch the sea lions if you didn't make the trip from Los Vilas.

You'll have to return to La Ligua before continuing south on the Pan-American another 147 miles (235 km) through Santiago to Rancagua.

**En Route from La Ligua** – Via the Pan-American you'll reach the Río Colina and Huechun Reservoir, about 25 miles (40 km) north of Santiago. There's good trout fishing here, so if you've packed your rod, you'll find some action.

To continue, you can take a road northeast toward Santiago's own little ski resort, an area containing three slopes: Farellones, El Colorado, and La Parva. The slopes are connected by lifts, and there is skiing for the beginner, novice, and pro. Farellones is an easy day trip from Santiago and a popular weekend spot with beginning and intermediate skiers. If you choose to stay overnight, the *Farellones* hotel on the slopes is a good bet; it has both regular hotel rooms and suites with kitchen facilities (phone: 2-211-2726; in Santiago through the *Centro de Ski El Colorado-Farellones;* 2-246-3344).

Between Farellones and La Parva is El Colorado, where a chair lift and T-bar lead up to four trails — the longest of which is 6,560 feet. The *Centro de Ski El Colorado-Farellones* provides information on ski conditions as well as transportation to the slopes. La Parva has five runs that also draw weekend skiers with beginner- to intermediate-level skills. Contact the *Centro de Ski La Parva* in Santiago (phone: 2-233-2476; fax: 2-231-3233).

Higher up in the mountains just past the trio of ski centers is the fast-expanding Valle Nevado, with nine lifts and 16 miles of ski trails. Like Farellones, El Colorado, and La Parva, the turnoff from the main road is well marked and the 66-mile (106-km) trip to the slopes is on paved, well-maintained roads.

**VALLE NEVADO:** Just a 2-hour drive from Santiago, this French-owned resort draws skiers from around the world from mid-June to as late as mid-October. Snow-covered Andes peaks, elegant hotels, and upscale restaurants and nightclubs make this an all-inclusive ski resort. Valle Nevado has 25 slopes that are accessible by chair lifts and T-bars. Guides are available at the ski school for classes in paragliding, snowboarding, and heliskiing; there also are children's instructors and baby-sitters. After a day on the slopes, skiers can swim in a heated pool and use the saunas and Jacuzzis at either of the resort's two hotels, the 53-room *Valle Nevado* and the new 130-room *Puerta del*

## DIRECTIONS / Chile

*Sol* hotels — they both offer luxury accommodations in comfortable guestrooms with terraces overlooking the mountainside — or the *Mirador del Inca* condominiums, available for groups or those wanting to stay awhile. The resort has 6 restaurants, ranging from an elegant French dining room to a mid-slope grill where hardcore skiers can stop for lunch. Ski packages include a complete meal plan.

The only drawback is that some people may have trouble with the altitude — the resort is located more than 10,000 feet above sea level. (Even those who have no trouble with heights should take it easy for the first few hours after arriving.) Reservations for Valle Nevado can be made in Santiago at 441 Gertrudis Echeñique (phone: 2-206-0027 and 2-228-1228; fax: 2-228-8888). Several US operators also offer ski packages (also see *Downhill Skiing,* DIVERSIONS).

**En Route from Valle Nevado** – To continue on to Rancagua, return to Santiago and head southwest on Route 78 to Maipú, where the decisive battle of the independence war was fought against the Spaniards in 1817. Legend says that liberator Bernardo O'Higgins, who later became Chile's first head of state, prayed to the Virgin of Carmen before the battle and promised that, if the Chileans won, he would erect a shrine in her name on that site. Today, the ground floor of the shrine houses the *Museo del Carmen* (Carmen Museum), which is full of colonial weapons, furniture, clothing, and historical documents. Religious embroidery from the 19th century and earlier and a collection of horse-drawn carriages are also featured. Open 3 to 6 PM Saturdays and 11 AM to 6 PM Sundays (phone: 2-557-4612).

Continuing southwest along Route 78 are two small villages famous for their crafts. Talagante, 26 miles (42 km) southwest of Santiago, makes ceramic figurines representing the traditional Chilean *huaso* (cowboy) festival, which takes place throughout central Chile on *Cuasimodo,* the Sunday after *Easter.* The brightly painted figures portray the ceremony, which includes a priest carrying the Host throughout town to the bedridden faithful accompanied by *huasos* on horseback or, where villages are more modern, on bicycles and motorcycles.

Another road you can take southeast from Santiago goes through the Cajón del Maipo (Maipo Canyon). This road stretches about 60 miles (96 km), then ends at the Morales hot springs, Baños Morales, at the fringe of the Cordillera, the Andes mountain range. The springs are 6,800 feet above sea level, with temperatures ranging as high as 77F (25C). The springs are recommended for rheumatism, bronchial problems, and nerves, and the canyon is a frequent weekend destination for Santiago residents. The springs are open to the public. No admission charge.

**RANCAGUA:** Essentially, this is the support town for El Teniente copper mine, Chile's third-largest mine, 42 miles (67 km) to the northeast. Operating nonstop since 1906, El Teniente has the distinction of being the world's largest underground copper mine, with an annual output of 29 million tons and shaft elevators that hold up to 450 workers at a time. (Tourist visits are not allowed.) About one-half of the city's 140,000 people depend directly on the mine for their livelihood. Founded in 1743, Rancagua was the site of the famous 1814 battle between Bernardo O'Higgins's revolutionary troops and Spanish royalists, in which the Chilean forces were defeated. The plaza, known as the Plaza de Héroes, is significantly different from other plazas in Chile in that two main streets form a cross through the middle, where a statue of O'Higgins stands. The colonial *Museo Histórico* (on the corner of Estado and Ibieta) is installed in an 18th-century house known as the Casa del Pilar de Piedra (House of the Stone Pillar), which contains many O'Higgins items.

You can eat well-prepared Chilean food in the *Mi Ruca* restaurant (Av. Cachapoal). If you prefer to dine on the road outside of town, ask for the *Munich* restaurant at the tourist office (277 Germán Riesco; phone: 72-225777).

Rancagua and the area south are known as *huaso* land, strong in cowboy tradition, and many places have a *media luna* (corral), with weekend rodeos. Rancagua's *media luna* is the most important in Chile, and every March the national rodeo championship is held here.

There are a few noteworthy towns east of Rancagua, good choices for a day trip. Machali does a good tourist trade during the *fiestas patrias* (patriotic festivals), the September 18 and 19 commemoration of Chilean independence. The town becomes an incarnation of the *huaso* tradition, with dancing and *chicha* drinking in the *ramadas*, open-air huts covered with tree branches. *Chicha,* a potent wine brewed from the first grapes of the season, goes down as easily as punch — a wallop, that is.

About 13 miles (21 km) west of Rancagua is the town of Doñihue, which is known for its elaborately embroidered and woven *huaso chamantos* (ponchos), some of which take up to 4 months each to complete. Eight miles (13 km) farther east is the turnoff for the Cauquenes hot springs, where the hot waters vary from 104 to 122F (40 to 50C) and are said to be good for kidney, skin, and nerve disorders. The springs allegedly have drawn such notables as Bernardo O'Higgins, General José de San Martín, and, later, Charles Darwin.

**En Route from Rancagua** – The area around the 60-mile (96-km) stretch of the Pan-American Highway between Rancagua south to Curicó is strewn with little towns devoted to some type of craft, whether it be wicker, straw works, weaving, pottery, or making the massive, wooden Chilean stirrups. You'll pass the broom-making town of Rengo first, 18 miles (29 km) from Rancagua. Farther on, you'll be greeted by a short stretch of wicker furniture lining the road, obviously begging to be bought. This is Chimbarongo, where prices are about a third of those in Santiago. If you're in the market for artisan goods, however, an alternative is to wait until you hit the markets at Curicó.

**CURICÓ:** The market in this town of 60,500 takes up an entire block between Rodríguez and Pena Streets. You'll find basketry from Panimávida, pottery from Cauquenes, blankets and capes from Talca, ponchos and shawls from Quinamávida, and stirrups from La Lajuela. Smoked delicatessen meats also can be purchased, and you even can hail a *calesas* (taxi) — a horse-drawn carriage, that is.

From Curicó it's a 40-mile (64-km) drive to Talca.

**TALCA:** Many mementos from the War of Independence are preserved here. In the crypt near the main altar of the small town's brick and concrete cathedral is the birth certificate of Bernardo O'Higgins. The *Museo O'Higginiano* (O'Higgins Museum; 875 Calle Uno Norte), formerly the childhood home of Bernardo O'Higgins and now a historical museum, once served as the headquarters of Chile's first government junta and was the place where O'Higgins signed the act of independence. The museum houses other colonial items and a collection of Chilean paintings. It is open Tuesdays through Saturdays from 9:30 AM to 1 PM and 3 to 8 PM; Sundays from 10 AM to 1 PM.

You can buy some local goods at the marketplace, but the area menu outshines the baskets. The dish to sample is *chancho en piedra,* pork with a sauce of tomato, onion, garlic, and *aji*. The recipe's name is derived from how it's made, on a grinding stone. If you don't care to try it in the market, then ask for it in any of the restaurants that line the Río Claró, near Urzua Park. The tourist office (in the Edificio Intendencia on the Plaza de Armas; phone: 71-233669) is happy to assist you.

About 95 miles (152 km) southeast of Talca down a paved road is Maule Lake, a popular spot for trout fishing and camping. For fishing information or a license, stop by SERNAP — the government office in charge of sports fishing (865 1 Sur, Office 111; phone: 71-234029). On the coast east of Talca is the beach resort of Constitución, at the mouth of the Río Maule, surrounded by small hills covered with pine trees. On the north bank of the river are the Quivolgo and Junquillar beaches, with some striking rock formations: seagulls, a church, and a lover's arch. The restaurants here are known for their seafood, especially sea bass, *erizos* (sea urchins), and *locos* (abalone).

As you leave Talca and Constitución and continue south, you're going to hit Chile's rainy regions. Be forewarned and carry rain gear, even in the summer.

## BEST EN ROUTE

There are more so-so hotels than good ones in this part of the Central Valley. Prices are for the most part moderate — about $25 to $40 for a double room and meal. Hotels charging over $40 are categorized as expensive. The smaller, more primitive places cost anywhere from $10 to $25 a night; they aren't listed here because of their poor quality. If you're staying in this area, your best bet would be to make reservations in Santiago.

### OVALLE

**Turismo Ovalle** – Small and first class, it offers both single and double rooms. 295 Victoria (phone: 51-620159). Moderate.

### TERMAS DE SOCOS

**Termas de Socos** – A health resort that offers thermal pools, topnotch accommodations, a good restaurant featuring spa cuisine, and wide terraces for relaxing. In a tree-shaded setting at Km 368 on the Pan-American Highway (phone: 71-620040; in Santiago, 2-681-6692). Expensive.

### TALCA

**Plaza** – This 45-room property is the best in town, and offers a bar, a restaurant, valet, and laundry services. 1141 Poniente (phone: 71-231515). Moderate.

# Concepción to Laja Falls

The Pan-American Highway, heading south from Concepción to Laja Falls where the Central Valley meshes into the start of the forest and Lake District, crosses territory laced with horror stories of the Spanish attempt to dominate the Indians. One such tale belongs to conquistador Pedro de Valdivia, who in 1551 crossed the Río Bío-Bío and set up cities at Imperial, Angol, Villarrica, and Valdivia, and forts at Tucapel, Buren, and Arauco.

Now de Valdivia, who founded Concepción the previous year, was after the heads (if not the hearts) of the Araucano Indians, otherwise known as Mapuche. The Mapuche put up stiff resistance, and when they destroyed the forts at Tucapel and Arauco under the leadership of Cacique (Chief) Caupolicán, de Valdivia rushed to Tucapel with reinforcements. Cacique Lautaro, whom de Valdivia had imprisoned at Concepción, escaped and went on to lead his tribe in bloody battle in December 1555. Not one Spaniard escaped alive, and de Valdivia was captured as he fled from the battleground. As he pleaded for mercy from Caupolicán and Lautaro, another chief came up from behind and bashed his head in with a club. Lautaro's troops then overran Concepción and moved on to take Santiago; Lautaro, however, was betrayed by one of his men on the banks of the Río Mataquito, outside Curicó. His head was carried off by the Spanish on a pike to Santiago. Caupolicán himself was impaled on a stake after he was taken prisoner in 1558.

The area's violent history continued into recent years in the fights between a revolutionary peasant movement and the landowners (1971–73), followed by incidents between the military and the leftists after the 1973 coup deposing President Allende.

Despite the past violence, the countryside now is peaceful, with golden wheat fields and groves of eucalyptus, pine, and the native *alerce* and *araucaria* trees. Hardwoods unknown to the rest of the world — *coigüe, raulí, lingue, canelo* — grow here. The only thing missing is the wildlife, largely exterminated as farmers cleared the land for planting and pasturing domestic animals. A number of rivers irrigate the land, and fish, including several varieties of trout, pejerrey, and perch, are abundant.

This route will take you from Talca south to Concepción, a city populated by the descendants of the German immigrants who came here in the 1800s. From Concepción, you will go through the coal mines of Coronel and Lota to Cañete and a small lake district, then on to Laja Falls, a popular honeymoon area. The first city you'll come to on the Pan-American Highway is Linares.

**LINARES:** This town of 46,500 is worth a stop if you're interested in colonial history. One of the first battles of the Independence War was fought in the Plaza de Armas; the *Museo de Arte y Artesanía* (Art and Artisan Museum; 580 Av. Valentín Letelier) contains works of Chilean artists dating back to the 1820s. The town's cathedral is the replica of one in Milan, Italy, and the marble altar was partly donated by Pope Pius XII. One of the continent's largest mosaics graces the cathedral's interior.

**En Route from Linares** – The Pan-American from Linares to Chillán is another 60 miles (96 km); along the way, you'll come to Parral, the birthplace of Chile's second Nobel Prize–winning poet, Pablo Neruda (1905–73); the house where Neruda was born is near the railroad station. From here, you can take Route 128 west to Cauquenes, some 33 miles (53 km) away, where artisans from Pilén, a town 25 miles (40 km) west of here, sell their black clay pottery at the Saturday market. If you follow a dirt road 24 miles (38 km) northwest, you'll come to Pelluhue, a small beach with black sand. You can eat seafood — raw or cooked — brought in by the fishermen right at the wharves. A gravel road east along the Pacific coast leads to Constitución (see *Ovalle to Talca,* above). If you retrace your steps, the Pan-American will lead into Chillán.

**CHILLÁN:** A rather modern city of 150,000, Chillán is noted for its famous natives: Bernardo O'Higgins; Captain Arturo Prat; contemporary pianist Claudio Arrau; painter Pacheco Altamirano; and writer Marta Brunet. Its low, modern architecture reflects the tragic history of the city, which was leveled repeatedly by dueling colonists and earthquakes until 1939. Following the 1939 earthquake that claimed 15,000 lives and destroyed 90% of the buildings in Chillán, Mexico raised money to rebuild a public school, and Mexican muralists David Alfonso Siqueiros and Xavier Guerrero painted frescoes on its wall. *Escuela México* (Mexican School; at Vega de Saldias and Av. O'Higgins) is open weekdays when school is in session.

The marketplace (779 Av. 5 de Abril) is a good place to sample the local dishes. You can try pork with *pebre* (a spicy onion-tomato sauce), sea bass filled with sausage, and two ground corn dishes: *humitas* (corn tamales wrapped in leaves) and *pastel de choclo* (corn and meat casserole). Some of the local drinks include *malicia* (coffee laced with the local *aguardiente*) and *chicha* made from *michai,* a local bush. Crafts sold in the *Feria Libre* adjoining the market include black and white pottery from Quinchamali, horsehair and vegetable fiber figures from Rari, and baskets from Mehuin.

Down Avenida O'Higgins, away from the center of town, is the Parque Monumental

Bernardo O'Higgins (Bernardo O'Higgins Park), located where the birthplace of the Chilean soldier and ruler once stood. Here too is a historical cultural center and the tourism office (250 Av. Bernardo O'Higgins; phone: 42-223272).

Chillán has become increasingly popular with ski enthusiasts, most of whom go to Termas de Chillán, a resort with hot springs at the base of the Chillán volcano. Ski packages are available in the US through *Ladatco Tours* (phone: 800-327-6162; in Florida, 800-432-3881) and through *Continental Ski Network* (phone: 800-275-3123).

Leaving Chillán en route to Concepción, follow the Pan-American south for about 16 miles (26 km) before turning west onto Route 148. From the turnoff, it's about 50 miles (80 km) to Concepción.

**CONCEPCIÓN:** The third-largest urban center in Chile, this city of 265,000 (mostly German descendants) is 354 miles (566 km) southwest of Santiago and is known for its sometimes violent rainstorms. Not unduly cold, summer temperatures range from 57 to 75F (14 to 24C); during the extended rainy season (April to September), the temperatures drop to between 46 to 66F (8 to 19C). Take note of Monterey pines that feed the area's timber industry. They were mistakenly introduced to the city in 1886 when a French exporter improperly filled a small order for Douglas firs. Although they have made forestry a mainstay here, a century ago the pines were poorly received by Concepción residents who feared that the firs would overwhelm native trees.

One of Concepción's prime tourist attractions is the Universidad de Concepción. The landscaped school grounds are a park in themselves, with a pond sheltering black-necked swans from the Chilean south. The city's art gallery, *Casa del Arte* (on Lamas at Larenas, near the university campus) has an impressive collection of Chilean paintings and merits a visit. It is open Tuesdays through Fridays 9 AM to 1 PM and 3 to 7 PM, Saturdays and Sundays 10 AM to 1 PM.

The Plaza Independencia (Independence Plaza), the largest of seven plazas here, houses the city's cathedral, built in 1940 with a gold and ceramic mosaic in the central nave. Six blocks from the plaza on the other side of Parque Ecuador (Ecuador Park) you can climb the 300-foot Cerro Caracol for a good view of the city and a glimpse of the shimmering Bío-Bío River in the distance.

Founded in 1550, Concepción was the capital of Chile for nearly a decade. It was here that Bernardo O'Higgins declared Chile's independence in 1818. Unfortunately, violent earthquakes in 1939 and 1960 destroyed most of the city's colonial structures.

Train service is available from Concepción to Santiago, Temuco, and Valdivia daily; to Puerto Montt, it runs on a thrice-weekly basis, so check schedules. A mural depicting the city's history is painted on the wall at the railroad station. *LanChile* offers daily service to Santiago (connections in Valdivia and Puerto Montt) year-round; if you prefer, you can hop a bus for the 9-hour trip to Santiago. The national tourist office is at 460 Aníbal Pinto, near Plaza Independencia (phone: 41-227976).

Visitors should venture out of Concepción to the *Parque Hualpén* (Hualpén Park), a few miles from the city overlooking the mouth of the Río Bío-Bío. Now a museum, it was the estate of famed adventurer Pedro del Río Zañartu and contains items he collected during his three round-the-world voyages. He donated everything to the city on his death in 1918. The house is open Tuesdays through Sundays, 9 AM to 12:30 PM and 2 to 6 PM. No admission charge.

South from here along a progressively impoverished road is Lebu, founded as a village-fortress by the Spanish and twice destroyed by the Araucano. This coal-mining center has a dramatic beach, Millaneco, that is accessible by motorboat or by walking 2½ miles (4 km) along Avenida J. Carrera Pinto. Bordering the beach on either end are two impressive caves — Cueva de Benavides is large enough to drive through and offers access to Millaneco; the smaller Cueva del Toro earned its name from the sound the sea makes as it crashes against the rock. The strong waves and rugged surf make this area better suited to photography than swimming.

You'll have to head back by Route 148 to Chillán from Concepción before continuing the 170 miles (272 km) to Temuco, with a stop some 45 miles (72 km) south of Chillán at the Laja Falls.

**LAJA FALLS:** These falls are considered one of Chile's most beautiful natural attractions; you can spot them from the highway. Salto del Laja cascades about 120 feet before crashing into a rocky gorge, a rainbow forming above in the fine spume.

**En Route from Laja Falls** – Continue east another 19 miles (30 km) to Los Angeles, one of Chile's fastest-growing cities, thanks to tourism and agriculture. Its population now nears 71,000. From here, you can take a side road 111 miles (179 km) northeast to the inactive Antuco Volcano and its three ski runs.

Then you can get on the Pan-American, which leads east onto a gravel road to the hot springs of Tolhuaca. Returning to the Pan-American takes you into Temuco and Chile's favorite lake resort area, which also is an up-and-coming ski spot.

## BEST EN ROUTE

From Concepción into the Lake District, you're going to have to make hotel reservations beforehand, since the area is popular with Chileans and foreigners alike. Don't expect a small-town hotel to be the *Ritz,* but you can have very comfortable accommodations (a double room with a private bath) for $80 and up in places listed as very expensive, $60 to $80 in those hotels categorized as expensive, and $40 to $60 at those places categorized as moderate. As you get into the Lake District prices are going to rise, and you'll probably find yourself paying about $15 more for a room here than you would up north.

### LINARES

*Turismo* – A small hotel on the plaza offering rooms with private baths. 522 Manuel Rodríguez (phone: 73-210636). Moderate.

### CHILLÁN

*Pirigallo* – In a Shangri-la setting at the base of the Chillán volcano, 5,904 feet above sea level, this hotel is the heart of Termas de Chillán, long famed for its thermal springs. Termas de Chillán has achieved prominence as one of the leading ski centers in South America — claiming it has the continent's longest ski slope — and one of the most popular resorts in southern Chile. Guests enjoy an unusually wide range of facilities, including lounges with fireplaces, a comfortable dining room, a disco, and a video cinema. Best of all, after a demanding day skiers can ease their tired muscles in the heated outdoor pool or in the individual or family indoor thermal baths. Advance reservations are essential and best booked through Santiago tour operators. Thirty-one miles (50 km) east of Chillán at Km 83 on Route 148 (phone: 42-232234; in Santiago, 2-251-5776; in the US, 800-327-6162). Very expensive.

*Isabel Riquelme* – A 68-room hostelry that offers single and double rooms with private baths; additional amenities include smoking and dining rooms. 600 Arauco (phone: 42-213663). Moderate.

### CONCEPCIÓN

*Araucano* – Provides private baths and telephones in its 168 rooms; swimming pool, restaurant, and disco. 521 Caupolicán (phone: 41-230606). Expensive.

### LAJA FALLS–LAJA

*Hostería y Cabañas Lagunillas* – Eighteen alpine-style cabins housing up to 8 people each make up these accommodations located just 3 miles (5 km) from the

Antuco ski lifts and right inside Laja National Park. There are 2 small pools — one indoor and one outdoor. Camping is available. Antuco Rd., 48 miles (77 km) east of Los Angeles at Km 90 (phone: Laja Falls 2; in Antuco, 42-233606; in Santiago, 2-231-5973). Moderate.

**Salto del Laja** – Spread over several acres of wooded area where herds of deer and llama roam, this comfortable but rustic hotel is located right at the waterfall. Its 80 rooms and suites all have central heating and televisions. Ask for one of the rooms in the new annex — they're larger. Chilean and international food are featured in the restaurant. Pan-American Hwy. at Salto del Laja (phone: Laja Falls 1). Moderate.

## LOS ANGELES

Two ski lodges on the Antuco Volcano offer accommodations, and you can make reservations either here at the *Club de Ski de Los Angeles* (phone: 43-322651) or at the *Inversiones Campanil* at 196 Ongulmo, Concepción (phone: 41-234881) at the Universidad de Concepción.

**Mariscal Alcázar** – A 25-room hotel with private baths and a dining room. 385 Lautaro (phone: 43-321275). Moderate.

# The Lake District

The Pan-American route between Laja Falls and Temuco signals the start of Chile's Lake District, called the South American Switzerland, with snow-capped mountains, clear lakes, and wooded hillsides. The only difference between the European and Chilean settings, however, is that the inhabitants here are not the rich, St.-Moritz–types you find in the Alps. On the contrary, the 1.3 million people living here are poor, and the "Swiss" scenery is interrupted by teams of oxen pulling heavy loads along rain-gutted roads, often stalling your journey. Be grateful for the animals, however, since these teams are known to have rescued sinking cars from the treacherous mud.

Let's face it: It rains in Temuco — and rains and rains. Unlike dry Santiago, the rainfall averages about 100 inches a year here, so be prepared and bring a raincoat. Most of the roads you'll be taking will be gravel or dirt, and the constant rain makes for muddy driving. Although there are many campsites in the south, you're better off camping only during the drier, summer months of December and January. Even then, be prepared for a shower or two, and if the rain doesn't get to you, the horseflies will, so bring plenty of repellent.

You'll find that you can spend the day here just admiring the view. The lakes (and there are 10 major ones) are magnificent, ranging from crystal to green to blue, reflecting the mountains and both active and dormant volcanoes of the eastern Andean Cordillera. When glaciers receded from the earth, the large depressions became lakes and rivers set deep into forests of cypress, *alerce, coigüe, raulí,* and *canelo.* You'll see an occasional fox skitter up to a lakeshore and *peucos* (one-banded buzzards) and *choroyes* (slender-billed parakeets) winging overhead.

The people here are just as colorful. There are nearly 300,000 Araucano Indians (noted for their silver jewelry and handwoven rugs) living around Temuco and the descendants of German immigrants are centered around the

**812 DIRECTIONS / Chile**

Puerto Montt and Valdivia areas. (The Germans came to Chile in 1850 at the urging of the Chilean government, which set up an immigration office in Kassel, Germany, in 1848 to lure farmers.)

You can divide this journey through the Lake District into four routes of about 3 days each. The first goes from Temuco south to Villarrica and the lake of the same name, to the trendy resort of Pucón, where ski runs crisscross a live volcano and tired skiers recuperate at hot mineral springs, then on to Calafquén, Panguipulli, and Riñihue before continuing to Valdivia, where the second route begins. From Valdivia, head southeast to Paillaco, to Lake Ranco, and to Llifén. You return to the Pan-American for the third route, through Osorno east on Route 215 to Lake Puyehue; then turn southeast along a gravel road to Entre Lagos and Lake Rupanco and Llanquihue, where you continue south to Puerto Octay to Frutillar and Puerto Varas, picking up Route 225 to Ensenada. The fourth and final route goes south down the Pan-American from Puerto Montt to the island of Chiloé.

**TEMUCO:** You're going to meet many Arauca men here, wearing diamond-patterned Mapuche rugs draped over their shoulders. Sometimes they'll offer the rug off their backs for sale. If you're in the market for one, buy it; you'll get a better offer from the individual seller than you will at any of the blanket stores here.

Temuco is a city of 158,000, and houses the largest Indian population in Chile. *The Museo Regional Araucano* (Araucano Regional Museum; 84 Av. Alemania) contains a collection of Arauca pottery and tools and a photographic history of the area. Open in the summer Mondays through Saturdays 9:30 AM to 1 PM and 3 to 6:30 PM, Sundays 9:30 AM to 1 PM. Shopping is another Temuco attraction: Try the *CEMA* (Balmaceda and Caupolicán Sts.), the municipal market (Aldunate and Rodríguez Sts.), and the *Feria Libre* (in front of the train station). At all three, you'll find Indian rugs and ponchos, as well as silver goods. Sometimes there are antique silver items and religious artifacts in the markets. To see the artisans at work, stop by the Catholic University's Escuela de Artesanía (422 Av. Alemania), where items featuring traditional Indian designs are crafted. There also is a city tourism office (at 586 Bulnes; phone: 45-211969).

For a hearty meal, try *La Estancia* (02340/A Av. R. Ortega, on the northeast side of the city), which many claim has the best *parrilla* (grilled meat) in southern Chile. If you're fond of German food, try *Club Alemán* (772 Senador Estabanez).

Less than 1 mile (1 km) north of the Plaza de Armas, Cerro Nielol is a hill covered with red, bell-shaped *copihue,* Chile's national flower. From here, you can see all of Temuco and the Río Imperial, which flows through the city. On one side of the hill sits Agua Santa (Holy Water), a small lake: Legend decrees that if you drink the water three times from a cupped hand, all your worldly aspirations will come true. The park at the lake also has restaurants, playgrounds, and trails for strolling.

From Temuco, travel 50 miles (80 km) east along a gravel road (that branches off to the Pan-American, north of the city) to the 10,153-foot Llaima Volcano.

**En Route from Temuco** – Leaving the city, continue south along the Pan-American Highway for 18 miles (29 km) to Freire, where you turn southeast along a paved road for 35 miles (56 km) to Villarrica, at the southwestern tip of Villarrica Lake. You'll know you're there when you see the towering, 9,230-foot active volcano on the southeastern edge of the lake.

**VILLARRICA:** This town of 36,000 is one of Chile's favorite resorts; you can swim in the chilly Andean waters or rent a boat and skim over them. Fishing is excellent on the Toltén River and rafting is a favorite pursuit here and at several nearby streams. In January, this is the site of the *Mapuche Cultural Festival,* with handicrafts displays, music, and dance. At the *Museo Municipal* (Municipal Museum; 1050 Av. Pedro de

Valdivia), historical displays focus on the Mapuche culture, including ceramics, jewelry, leatherwork, and musical instruments.

Villarrica has the feel of an Old West town in the US — its streets are lined with wooden houses and shops and all but the main street are covered with dirt and gravel. It even has a bit of history similar to some Old West towns — the founders gave the site the name Villarrica ("Rich Village") in 1552 because they thought it was rich in gold and silver (some gold was panned from the area's rivers). However, the city was abandoned twice because of the warring Araucano before it was destroyed in 1602 by the Indians. They remained in control of the area until 1883 when a treaty was signed and the Chilean government peacefully took over.

In modern times, German immigrants have had a hand in the city's development, as evidenced by the many businesses and shops that have German names. *Club Social Treffpunkt* (640 Av. Pedro de Valdivia; phone: 45-411081) is a good spot to soak up local atmosphere while downing a cold *chopp* (draft beer).

Follow Avenida Pedro de Valdivia away from the lake to Avenida Cerrera; turn right, go three blocks, and to the left is the Rodrigo de Bastidas bridge — a great spot to take pictures of the city, lake, and volcano.

If you skirt the southern shore around Lake Villarrica for 16 miles (26 km), you'll reach Pucón, currently the trendiest ski resort in southern Chile. There are a number of campgrounds along the way; for information contact the Villarrica Tourist Office (Avdas. Pedro de Valdivia and Acevedo; phone: 45-411162).

**PUCÓN:** Perched on lovely Lake Villarrica and in full view of its active, snow-topped volcano, Pucón is one of the latest areas to catch the eye of resort developers and travelers alike. Although it was first "discovered" in the 1930s by fisherfolk (until they moved farther south), it wasn't until several years ago that its potential was recognized. Its slopes run along the side of the volcano; in summer, the area offers beautiful lakeside beaches, thermal springs, trout fishing, water sports, and horseback riding — all within a setting of spectacular scenery.

While the town has not yet bowed to the demands of tourism (there are no designer boutiques here as in other resorts), Pucón's 13,000 residents are charming and friendly, and lovers of the outdoors will be astounded by the abundance of greenery. In summer, the town explodes with roses, bougainvillea, and chrysanthemums. In winter, a cool drizzle wets the valley and snow blankets the Villarrica volcano. Year-round, wisps of white smoke rise from the volcano's peak and, at night, a red-orange glow can often be seen over the crater.

While in Pucón, try some of the local fare, including river trout and salmon. At the top spot for trout, *Brasil* (477 Calle Fresia near Av. Bernardo O'Higgins; no phone), the chef prepares it seven different ways. Artisans' shops line Avenida O'Higgins, a street that ends at the public beach, which has black volcanic sand and docks for pleasure craft. Visitors with a sweet tooth will find a private paradise at *Holzapfel Bäckerei* (524 Clemente Holzapfel; no phone), a German chocolate shop and bakery.

*Gran Hotel Pucón* (190 Clemente Holzapfel) is the scene for nighttime action — there's a casino (formal wear not required, but shorts and jogging suits not allowed) and a disco.

From Pucón, you can take a gravel road 10 miles (16 km) south to the ski site located in the Parque Nacional Villarrica — a national park. The ski center and school opened in 1986. There are now 16 runs for all skill levels, the longest nearly 6,200 feet, served by chair and tow lifts, and a series of cross-country trails. A modern lodge offering a bar, cafeteria, ski school, and equipment rental is located at the slopes. Even non-skiers will marvel at the view of the volcano with Lake Villarica in the distance. For information on activities in the area, contact the Pucón Tourist Office (115 Av. Brasil; phone: 45-441916) or the *Gran Hotel Pucón* (phone: 45-441001 in Pucón; 2-232-1787 or 2-232-6008 in Santiago).

Just 13 miles (21 km) from Pucón is Lago Caburgua, a crystalline body of water.

Residents swim here in the summer and sunbathe at the two beaches, which are appropriately named Playa Blanca — with its white sand — and Playa Negra — where the volcanic sand is dark. About 19 miles (30 km) east of Pucón, over mostly dirt roads, is the charming Termas de Huife — hot springs next to an icy, narrow river tucked into a forested area. The *termas* consist of two outdoor pools of hot mineral water and a series of private baths inside small enclosed rooms, with windows overlooking the river. Massages are available and overnight stays are possible in the 20 cabañas at the springs (see *Best en Route*).

Return to Villarrica.

**En Route from Villarrica** – A rough, gravel road will take you south, then east, from Villarrica into Licán-Ray on the shores of Lake Calafquén, a small, summer resort of about 800 people, mostly Chileans who own or rent cottages. You can hire a boat from private owners down at the water, or take a swim across the lake. Looking to your north, you'll see the Villarrica Volcano; to the east, Argentina's Lanín Volcano towers above you.

Camping is available along the eastern road, which takes you to the lake's eastern tip at Conaripe (the Villarrica Tourism Office can give you details). From there, you can turn onto a dirt road and head south to a pair of towns and lakes with the same names: Panguipulli and Riñihue. Here take the 18-mile (29-km) jaunt down a paved road to the Pan-American, continuing south another 27 miles (43 km) to Valdivia, the start of your second Lake District route.

**VALDIVIA:** The broad, rolling Río Valdivia calmly flows by this city of 111,000. Founded by Pedro de Valdivia in 1552, Valdivia became more European than South American in the late 1800s when the Germans built Chile's first factory, the Anwandter Brewery. After a 1960 earthquake, most of the houses in Valdivia were rebuilt of lumber, in contrast to the concrete and stucco in the northern areas. There are parks and the grounds of old estates on Teja Island, in the middle of the Río Valdivia; you can reach it by crossing a bridge. Off the bridge is the *Museo Austral* (Austral Museum), housed in the 150-year-old mansion that once belonged to German colonist Carl Anwandter. The exhibits trace the European immigration to the area; behind the museum on the German School grounds is the Anwandter's private cemetery where the first German settlers are buried. The museum is open daily in the summer from 10 AM to 1 PM and 3 to 7 PM; in the winter, it is open only Tuesdays and Fridays.

*Café Haussman* (394 O'Higgins) is a small, centrally located diner recommended for its *kuchen,* a German cake with fruit filling that Chile has adopted as its own.

The docks are a short walk from town, and the morning activities there are lively. Large rowboats pull up with catches of fresh fish and loads of fresh vegetables and fruit, all of which are sold in stalls on the concrete promenade along the riverbank. Slightly upriver from the fruit and fish stands, passenger boats steam by to the villages of Niebla, Corral, Mancera, Amargos, and Cancahual. Take either a fancy cruiser or one of the standard small ferries. There is also a 1-hour cocktail cruise every evening. The tourism office (555 Prat; phone: 63-213596), can make arrangements.

Daily express rail service is available from Valdivia to Santiago; *LanChile* and *LADECO* also offer regularly scheduled service to Santiago from Pichouy Airport.

**En Route from Valdivia** – The second Lake District route leads around the lake area from here to Osorno. Take the Pan-American Highway 27 miles (43 km) southeast to Paillaco, where you continue on a road 50 miles (80 km) across the northeastern sector of Lake Ranco to Llifén. While you're here, try the Río Calcurrupe for fishing.

Continue around the lake past Lake Ranco to Río Bueno (with its Spanish castle-fort) and 48 miles (77 km) to the Pan-American Highway for the trip to Osorno and your third Lake District excursion.

**OSORNO:** Founded in 1558 by de Valdivia, this city of 124,000 is another major

German outpost. German is Osorno's second language, and more often than not, you'll find it on a street sign beside the Spanish name. This area is dairy land, so rich that it provides three-quarters of Chile's milk and cheese products. At the Plaza de Armas, a *canelo* tree was planted by Nobel Prize–winning poet Gabriela Mistral in honor of the Mapuche Indians. The *Museo Municipal* (Municipal Museum; 809 Calle Manuel Antonio Matta) contains Indian and German exhibits, and on the banks of the Río Rahue is the Spanish Fuerte Reina María Luisa (Queen Maria Luisa Fort), built in 1793.

For those who want a bite to eat before continuing, there is excellent German food at *Peter's Kneipe,* 1039 Manuel Rodríguez (phone: 64-232297).

The tourist office here is in the provincial government building, near the main plaza (phone: 64-234104). Those interested in skiing should contact the *Club Andino de Osorno,* weekdays from 8:30 AM to 12:30 PM and 2:30 to 6:30 PM (phone: 64-2297).

**En Route from Osorno** – Take paved Route 215 east along the southern shore of Lake Puyehue, in a national park. A short distance from the town of Puyehue (southern shore) are the Puyehue hot springs (and the Antillanca area). From here, the gravel road runs another 26 miles (42 km) to the Argentine border. North of here stands the 7,280-foot Puyehue Volcano.

Backtrack to Puyehue and Entre Lagos; from here, take the gravel road south to Rupanco, where the Río Rahue flows into Lake Rupanco. From here, you can get a good eyeful of the Osorno Volcano, the district's tallest and most perfectly shaped volcano, wedged between Lake Llanquihue, and the green, green waters of Lake Todos los Santos. To reach Llanquihue, take the gravel road south that allows you to cut over to Puerto Octay. A 112-mile (179-km) road encircles the lake; as you travel around, you'll see both the Osorno Volcano and another 6,549-foot volcano, Calbuco.

**PUERTO VARAS:** Founded as a German settlement, 11 miles (18 km) north of Puerto Montt, this is the City of Roses, and in season (summer) you'll be struck by the profusion of flowering arbors. From here, you can take boat rides across Lake Llanquihue to the small towns of Frutillar and Puerto Octay, or simply stay in port and try your luck at the gambling casino in the *Gran Hotel Puerto Varas* (see *Best en Route*), open year-round (there's dining and dancing, in addition to betting and beating the odds). You can also stroll to the top of Monte Calvario for a splendid view of the volcanoes and lake.

You can pick up paved Route 225 to tiny Ensenada, at the southeastern tip of the lake; from here, a 10-mile (16-km) gravel road heads to Salto del Petrohue (Petrohue Waterfalls), where brilliant green waters (laden with suspended minerals) cascade over and through a series of rock formations and channels. Nearby is the town of Petrohue, a small Indian settlement full of crystalized volcanic rock at the western edge of Lake Todos los Santos.

There's camping in Petrohue and a few basic hotels (a tourism kiosk at the dock can help you out). You can take motor- and sailboat rides along the lake to the town of Vuriloche or to a beach at Cayutue, where you can rent horses and trot into the woods. There's also a catamaran across Lake Todos Los Santos to Peulla on the eastern edge of the lake, where there is a hotel with a restaurant. From there, Route 225, another gravel road, continues east to the Pérez Rosales pass and the Argentine border.

From Puerto Varas take either a gravel road or the Pan-American Highway south to Puerto Montt for your fourth and last route in the Lake District.

**PUERTO MONTT:** This city of 106,000 is reminiscent of a Bavarian village with weathered wood homes. Here, too, the ocean meets the island's shore with a roaring, almost Teutonic crash, unlike other, quieter surfs along the Chilean coast.

Small but vital, Puerto Montt is the beginning of the Chilean Patagonian region and the starting point for tour groups crossing the lakes to Argentina. To arrange a 1- or

**816 DIRECTIONS / Chile**

2-day trip from Puerto Montt to Bariloche, crossing Lago Todos Los Santos, Lake Nahuel Huapi, and passing the region's volcanoes, contact *Andina del Sud* (437 Varas; phone: 65-257797; in Santiago, 2-697-1010; fax: 2-696-5121). An isolated village of German immigrants until 1912, when a rail line connected Puerto Montt to the rest of the country, it now maintains communication through good transportation. Rail and bus service to Puerto Varas, Osorno, and Santiago is scheduled regularly; *LanChile* and *LADECO* offer flights to Santiago, Valdivia, Concepción, Punta Arenas, and elsewhere. From here, you also can book a cabin on one of the steamers heading south into Patagonia and Punta Arenas.

Tourist cruisers offer a variety of trips from Puerto Montt to the fjords to the south. A 7-day voyage round-trip from Puerto Montt, through the fjords and as far south as Laguna San Rafael, is available on the *Skorpios II*. All 160 passengers have outside berths, important because the scenery is spectacular. The smaller and considerably less luxurious *Skorpios I* makes the same run and fares are lower. Book through *Turismo Skorpios Ltda.* (484 MacIver, Office 5, 2nd Floor, Santiago; phone: 2-336187, 2-393105, or 2-338715; fax: 2-336752). Other agencies making reservations for fjord cruises include *Andina del Sud* (see above); *Varastur* (437 Varas; phone: 65-252918); and *Empremar* (1450 Diego Portales; phone: 65-252548). The newest cruise experience in the area is a 7-day trip on the 58-passenger catamaran, *Patagonia Express,* operated by *Patagonia Connection* (reservations in Santiago; phone: 2-223-5567; fax: 2-274-8111). More information on sailings from Puerto Montt is available at the tourism office (on the second floor of the Edificio Intendencia annex; phone: 65-254580) or from Chile's main tourism office in Santiago. In the US, *4th Dimension Tours* (1150 NW 72nd Ave., Suite 250, Miami, FL 33126; phone: 305-477-1525 and 800-343-0020) offers round-trip cruises from Puerto Montt through the glacier and fjord-studded area of southern Chile.

You can take a short trip from the docks at Puerto Montt to Tenglo Island, right off the coast, for a picnic, and view the area from the top of the island's hill. If you're in luck, they'll be serving *curanto,* a mixed bag of seafood and shellfish steamed over rocks and leaves nestled in a sand pit.

**En Route from Puerto Montt** – If you're up to an interesting 4-hour trip, you're ready for Chiloé Island. You can get there by boat through the Chacao Channel to the port of Ancud; or you can drive south to Bahía Pargua along the Pan-American Highway and cross the channel to the island's extension, some 35 miles (56 km) from Ancud.

**CHILOÉ ISLAND:** Foggy and chilly — a constant 50F (10C) — Chiloé, which translates as "island of seagulls," is rich with hardwood and evergreen forests and fjords. It is the second-largest island on the continent, except for Tierra del Fuego. Founded in 1567, Ancud and Castro were stopping places for ships continuing through the Strait of Magellan. Jesuits who conducted a count in 1609 found 12,000 residents on the island — mostly Mapuche Indians. But measles and other epidemics, the sorry remnants of European colonization, slowly eroded the original population; by 1935 there was no longer anyone on Chiloé who spoke the Mapuche language. Today the islanders fish, farm potatoes, grow apples for making *chicha de manzana* (apple cider), or raise domestic livestock and welcome the occasional traveler.

Ancud, with nearly 3,400 people, is the first village you'll hit. This is the site of Fort San Antonio, the Spanish stronghold guarded by bronze cannon and the last fort where the Spanish flag flew in South America; it is a town of skilled fishermen and sailors who know their way around the Patagonian fjords. The small *Museo Regional* (Regional Museum), displaying colonial items and local handicrafts at the Plaza de Armas (where you'll also find the cathedral), is open weekdays 9 AM to noon and 2:30 to 6:30 PM, weekends 10 AM to 12:30 PM and 3 to 6 PM. The nearby market, on Calle Diéciocho, is known for its expensive stone chimneys, which Santiago residents proudly install in their homes. Handicrafts are for sale at *Centro Artesanal Moai* (439 Baquedano; phone: Ancud 570). The tourism office is in the Transmarchilay Building (665 Libertad; phone: 656-2665).

From Ancud, there's a paved road that leads 46 miles (74 km) south to Castro (pop. 3,600), the capital of Chiloé. A recommended stop is the *Museo Municipal* (Municipal Museum; on Blanco St.), containing archaeological and natural history collections. The museum is open Mondays to Saturdays, 9 AM to 2 PM and 3 to 8 PM. Some homes in Castro are constructed on stilts. In January or February, Castro is the site of a spirited rodeo festival, which includes music, dance, and typical island dishes. Take a walk to the town's hilltop cemetery to see the unusual tombstones and to get a panoramic view of Castro. Head to the docks where you'll see not only the fishing boats, but also local crafts, including items made of cypress. During the colonial era, the town's cypress chests for storing clothes made it famous. The tourist office is at 549 O'Higgins (phone: 657-5699).

You'll have to return to Puerto Montt to proceed by car to the Chilean Patagonia and the Tierra del Fuego archipelago.

## BEST EN ROUTE

Room rates in the Lake District fluctuate with the seasons — the peak is during the summer (mid-December to mid-March) and in the ski period (July to mid-October). During these times, expect to pay over $120 for a double room a hotel in the very expensive category; $80 to $120 in the expensive range; $50 to $80 at a moderate place; and under $50 at an inexpensive hotel. In other months, rates can drop by as much as 50%. Breakfast is often included and some resorts offer full board. Check with the local tourist office or ski clubs for information on the various camping sites available throughout the area.

### TEMUCO

**De La Frontera** – Here are 60 recently renovated rooms with private baths, a cafeteria, restaurant, and bar. Beside it is the newer, larger, and more expensive, *Nueva de la Frontera,* under the same management. 733 M. Bulnes (phone: 45-210718; in Santiago, 2-232-6008; fax: 45-212638; in Santiago, 2-246-6935). Inexpensive; *Nueva de la Frontera,* moderate.

### VILLARRICA

**El Ciervo** – Perhaps the best in town, all its guestrooms have a lake view, heat, television sets, and phones. An English-speaking staff and room and laundry services also are highlights. Breakfast included. 241 G. Körner (phone: 45-411215). Moderate.

**Yachting Club** – Most of the rooms in this recently remodeled property on the edge of Lake Villarrica have a lake view. The hotel terrace offers a spectacular vista of the volcano. Its *La Castalia* restaurant specializes in French fare, there is a new bar, and the staff speaks English. 802 San Martín (phone and fax: 45-411191; phone in Santiago, 2-696-0205; fax: 2-699-2808). Moderate.

### PUCÓN

**Antumalal** – Secluded 18-room hotel on Lake Villarrica that has welcomed Queen Elizabeth II and numerous other international dignitaries. The furnishings are from the 1950s, but every room has a fireplace and lake view. There's a terrace restaurant, covered pool, tennis, windsurfing, and water skiing. Camino Pucón–Villarrica, Km 2 (phone: 45-441011; fax: 45-441013). Very expensive.

**Interlaken** – This rustic resort is situated in a beautiful park and its simple, but comfortable, lodge-like rooms and suites are spread over several buildings, lending an intimate atmosphere to the property. All guestrooms have mini-bars, safes, and color television sets; the suites feature 2 bathrooms (1 with a tub), and a balcony or solarium. The à la carte restaurant offers Italian specialties, and there's also a bar. Room and laundry services are available. Sports facilities include bicycles, miniature golf, archery, and a pool. Av. Caupolicán (phone: 45-441276; fax: 45-441242). Very expensive.

*Gran Hotel Pucón* – The most complete resort in the area, this newly enlarged and remodeled lakeside property has it all — indoor and outdoor pools, a wide, black sand beach, boating, horseback riding, tennis, racquetball, squash, gym, sauna, and Jacuzzi, and golfers have use of the nearby 9-hole course (at press time, there were plans to expand to 18). The 204 rooms and 29 suites face the snow-capped Villarricca volano or the placid blue lake. For families or guests who require plenty of space, there are 27 deluxe apartments with fully equipped kitchens, fireplaces, and terraces adjacent to the hotel. A restaurant, bar, casino, disco, gameroom, and boutiques complete the facilities. Transportation to the ski slopes and spa with hot springs at Huife can be arranged. 190 Clemente Holzapfel (phone: 45-441001; in Santiago, 2-232-6008; fax: 2-246-6935). Expensive.

*Termas Huife* – Two large pools of natural thermal springs and a lush mountain setting are the star attractions at this relaxing spa on the edge of the bubbling Río Liucura. Each of the 20 guest cabañas has its own thermal tub, terrace, wood stove, king-size bed, and mini-bar. A massage room with small private thermal tubs is available for day visitors. The terrace restaurant beside the large pools features a tempting menu of Chilean dishes and there's also a lounge and adjacent billiards and gameroom. Full board available. 19 miles (30 km) from Pucón near Huife (phone: 45-44122; in Santiago, 2-233-2288; fax: 2-251-7736). Expensive.

## LAKE CALAFQUÉN

*El Conquistador* – This family-oriented complex consists of lodge-style cabañas — each accommodating up to seven people — in a forested area on Lake Calafquén. The restaurant specializes in grilled meat and salmon. Guests can arrange lake excursions for fishing and water sports, and the resort itself has two swimming pools, tennis courts, a putt-putt golf course, volleyball, supermarket, drugstore, and bakery. Transportation to Licán-Ray every half hour is available. On the road into Licán-Ray (phone: Licán-Ray 1; in Santiago, 2-331542 and 2-338492). Moderate.

## VALDIVIA

*Pedro de Valdivia* – Offers private baths in its 85 rooms, a good dining room, and a bar. 190 Carampangue (phone: 63-212931). Moderate.

*Villa del Río* – The best in Valdivia, with 60 rooms and cabañas, rental boats, tennis courts, and a sauna. 1025 Av. España (phone: 63-216292). Moderate.

*Melillanca* – Simple hostelry featuring 43 rooms, all with private baths, phones, and color TV sets. There is a coffee shop and bar. 675 Av. Alemania (phone: 63-212509). Inexpensive.

*Schuster* – An old, Victorian hostelry that offers comfortable amenities and a bar, but no restaurant. 60 Maipú (phone: 63-213272). Inexpensive.

## OSORNO

*Rayantú* – This luxury hotel features a dining room, bar, pool, sauna, therapeutic massage, beauty salon, shops, and room service, as well as facilities for children. 1462 Patricio Lynch (phone: 64-238114; in Santiago, 2-672-8838; fax: 64-238116). Expensive.

*Gran* – Here are 100 rooms with private baths, plus a dining room. 615 O'Higgins at Ramírez (phone: 64-232171/2). Moderate to inexpensive.

## ANTILLANCA

*Antillanca* – Formerly a ski lodge, and now converted into a hotel right in the heart of the ski area. There is a sauna, heated pool, and cafeteria. Week-long packages available. Parque Nacional Puyehue at Km 98 Sur Este (phone: 64-235114). Reservations also can be made in Osorno (1673 Mackenna; phone: 64-232297) or in Santiago (phone: 2-672-7812). Moderate.

## PUERTO VARAS

*Cabañas del Lago* – Considered the best in Puerto Varas, offering 10 cabañas and 20 first class double rooms, all with private bath and fantastic views over Lake Llanquihue and the magnificent Osorno Volcano. 195 Klenner at Bellavista (phone: 6523-2291). Moderate.

*Gran* – Giant by local standards (106 rooms), it offers dining, a bar, casino, and a view of the Osorno Volcano. Open year-round. 351 Klenner (phone: 6523-2524; in Santiago, 2-696-1793). Moderate.

## PUERTO MONTT

*Río Puelo Lodge* – This new 12-room lodge is an angler's dream come true. Everything is deluxe — from the private fleet of four light planes and helicopters that takes guests to pristine lakes and trout streams, to each of the guestrooms that has a view of the lake and a balcony, to the exquisite food. Activities include horseback riding, whitewater rafting, and escorted tours of the area. Near Puelo (phone: 65-258500; in the US, 800-288-0886; fax: 65-258499). Very expensive.

*Burg* – The 20 rooms at this downtown hotel all have private baths and phones; some of which face the lake. There is a restaurant and bar. 56 Pedro Montt, corner of Diego Portales (phone: 65-253813). Moderate.

## RALÚN

*Ralún* – On the Reloncaví Estuary about 60 miles (97 km) from Puerto Montt, it's a wonderful modern timber lodge, beautifully decorated and grandly comfortable. There is a choice of rooms in the main building or separate cabins, all overlooking gardens, water, and mountains. (The cabins have fireplaces.) The food is excellent, and excursions along the estuary to nearby villages, as well as fishing trips, horseback riding, and mountain-bike tours are organized by the hotel (phone: in Puerto Montt, 65-254001; reservations in Santiago, 2-392345; in the US, 800-327-3573; fax: 2-382328). Expensive.

*Hostería Ancud* – This warm and cozy inn is a good refuge on chilly Chiloé Island. It has a restaurant, cafeteria, and bar, and room and laundry services are available. 30 San Antonio (phone: 656-2340 and 656-2350; in Santiago, 2-671-3165; fax: 2-696-5599). Moderate.

# Chilean Patagonia and the Tierra del Fuego Archipelago

Few but the hardiest travelers venture into the South American Patagonia and Tierra del Fuego archipelago, the southernmost section of the continent shared by Chile and Argentina. It is a gray land filled with forest and moor where the sun does not shine until 9 AM in the winter; most days are drizzly, hazy, and cold. Biting winds can chill summer days as they whip as high as 70 miles an hour.

Every explorer to brave this area has had rough going. The first European was the Portuguese Fernão de Magalhães — Ferdinand Magellan — who, in the employ of the Spanish crown, discovered the area in 1520 as he was traveling east to west along a narrow, 330-mile waterway that separated the mainland from a large, rocky island from which bonfires filtered through the haze. The waterway became known as the Strait of Magellan; the island, Tierra del Fuego (Land of Fire). The mainland was christened Patagonia after the big-footed Indians on the coast (*patagones* means "big feet"). The name was an error, however, for the Indians had normal-size feet but covered them in animal pelts for warmth. Eventually Spain took possession of the strait for both itself and Chile, and the Indians, who were hostile to settlers, were gradually eliminated, first in battles with the Spanish and later by assassins hired by companies eager to search for gold on Indian land. The Europeans also brought illnesses such as smallpox and diphtheria, against which the Indians had no natural defenses, so that by 1920, only 279 Ona (from an original population of 4,000) remained. The Indians now are extinct.

For political purposes, the Spanish kept the strait a well-guarded secret until Francis Drake led an expedition through in 16 days, giving English names to the islands. English ships continued to use the passage until 1594, when the Spanish took control of the seas by force and the British pirate raids along the South American coast ceased.

Despite the dangers and hardships of the strait, its passage was an impressive experience, especially for Charles Darwin, who wrote extensively on the area after the HMS *Beagle*'s voyage, during which the captain, Robert Fitz Roy, discovered the Beagle Channel. The passage, to the south of the strait, has been long disputed by Chile and Argentina. Stopping short of war over possession of three tiny islands in the channel in 1978, both parties finally accepted the mediation of Pope John Paul II and signed a treaty in 1984 declaring the islands Chilean.

The discovery of oil in 1945, and the subsequent contruction of a Chilean oil pipeline that twice crosses the Straits of Magellan, prompted an economic boon in the area, which now provides half the oil used by the entire country.

The expansive Southern Patagonia Ice Field, a remnant of the last great Ice Age, stretches for some 250 miles (400 km) south of Puerto Montt, and the route will pass into Argentine territory before again turning south and returning to Chile. Leaving Puerto Montt, you take a rough road southeast to Punta Arenas and a ferry from there across the Straits of Magellan to tiny Porvenir on Tierra del Fuego. Continue east across the island into Argentine territory or retrace your steps to mainland Patagonia, where Pan-American alternate Route 9 leads northwest toward Puerto Natales.

There is frequent first class bus service between Punta Arenas and Puerto Natales, as well as biweekly buses to Puerto Montt. In Punta Arenas, check with *Buses Victoria Sur* (798 Colón; phone: 61-226213), or *Buses Fernández* (930 Chiloé; phone: 61-222313). Both companies also have offices in Puerto

Natales. Or book passage aboard *Naviera Magallanes*'s cargo/passenger ferry the M/S *Tierra del Fuego,* which operates between Puerto Natales and Puerto Montt, with stops in Chacabuco and Puerto Eden. *Navimag* has offices in Santiago (phone: 696-3211), Puerto Montt (phone: 65-253318), and Punta Arenas (830 Independencia; phone: 61-226600).

**PUNTA ARENAS:** A stark little port that is the capital of the Magallanes region, this town of 100,000 people is the entry point into Lower Patagonia. Five Indian tribes inhabited southern Patagonia and Tierra del Fuego at one time: the tall Tehuelche — the first to be seen by Darwin — who wore virtually nothing except guanaco capes over their shoulders, their faces painted with red and white bands and charcoal streaks, the Ona, the last of the tribes, who disappeared only a few years ago, the Yaganes, and the Alacalufe. Now due to successive waves of immigration from Europe, the population is almost one-third Yugoslav.

There are several museums in Punta Arenas. Both the Instituto de la Patagonia (Patagonia Institute), with an open-air colonial museum and a fine library and bookstore (*Los Flamencos,* across from the university; open Mondays through Fridays from 9 AM to noon and 3 to 5 PM) and the *Museo de Mayorino Borgatello* (Museum of Mayorino Borgatello) contain remnants of the Indian cultures that once thrived here. The *Museo Regional de Mayorino Borgatello* (corner of Sarmiento and Bories, beside the church), kept by Salesian friars, also has a magnificent collection of flora and fauna of the region, as well as a history of the now disappeared indigenous people; it is open to visitors Tuesdays through Saturdays from 11 AM to 4 PM, Sundays from 11 AM to 1 PM. Also not to be missed is the city cemetery, with its monumental mausoleums. A lone marker indicates the site where the last of the Ona Indians are buried.

In town, walk up Cerro La Cruz and look at the hillside planted with an assortment of native flowers and plants. Punta Arenas's municipal park is named after María Behety, one of the founding families; it has a small zoo housing guanacos, penguins, and *ñandu,* or rhea, a variety of ostrich native to the area. On the Plaza de Armas is the nearly 100-year-old Palacio Sara Braun, constructed by a French architect using materials shipped from Europe. Once the home of livestock pioneer José Nogueira and his wife, Sara Braun, the mansion now houses the *Club de la Unión* (716 Plaza Muñoz Gamero; phone: 61-221682). A block north, at 949 Magallanes, is the *Museo Braun Menéndez* (the Braun Menéndez Museum), another mansion that has been preserved as a museum of regional history. Fans of poet Gabriela Mistral might want to stop by the Liceo de Niñas, where Mistral once served as schoolmistress. Traveling south from Punta Arenas for 45 miles (72 km), you reach Fort Bulnes, which has been restored and contains a museum with documents and artifacts from the colonization period.

Back in town, try some of the local seafood specialties. *Sotito's* (1138 O'Higgins; phone: 61-223565), formerly an old mansion, is undoubtedly the best in restaurant in town, and opens its door to the public by reservation. You can arrange to have dinner here and to tour the still-elegant ground-floor rooms. The big treat at *Sotito's,* king crab, is generally eaten as an appetizer with mayonnaise or *salsa verde,* but it's such a sweet, succulent, reasonably priced dish that we recommend ordering it as a *plato fuerte* (main course). You also can try *locos* (abalone), *congrio* (conger eel, which is delicious) in cognac or blackened butter, *erizos* (sea urchin), or a mouth-watering *chupe de mariscos* (a thick seafood chowder). There is excellent local calamari (squid), served steamed as an appetizer or cooked in its own ink. Fish lovers also will want to sample pejerrey, a small mild white fish similar to sole, or the local salmon. Meat lovers can feast on local lamb.

When your stomach's filled, shop at the *CEMA* kiosk (741 José Menéndez; phone: 61-222618) for a limited selection of handicrafts, such as wood and shell carvings. Other than the *zone franca* (duty-free zone) at the edge of town, which is open Mondays through Saturdays from 10 AM to noon and 3 to 8 PM, there isn't much other good shopping in Punta Arenas.

There's no shortage of winter or summer sports in Punta Arenas. About 5 miles (8 km) south of town you can enjoy the ski slope on Mirador Hill; it's the world's southernmost run, and the season lasts from June through September. Check with the *Club Andino,* Km 8 outside Punta Arenas (phone: 61-223700).

Though there's little time for winter skiing, the 19-hour summer days (4 AM until 11 PM) are great for water sports: Deep-sea fishing, sailing, and other aquatic delights are offered at the *Nautical Club* (about 20 miles/32 km south of Punta Arenas).

If you want, you can take tours to the Antarctic and around the Tierra del Fuego archipelago from here before proceeding onto the island to Porvenir. The schedule depends on the weather and in any case is only operative in summer (from November through March). There are frequent boat tours to Puerto Williams, Whiteside Channel, the d'Agostini Fjord, and the Beagle Channel. Check with *Turismo Cabo de Hornos* (1039 Plaza Muñoz Gamero; phone: 61-222599) or *Turismo Comapa* (840 Av. Independencia; phone: 61-224256). You also can inquire about renting small planes for flights over the archipelago. *EcoAmerica Expeditions* (986 Local 25; phone: 61-228159) specializes in natural history expeditions, including cruises to Cape Horn.

*Cruceros Australis* (178 Miraflores, 12th Floor, Santiago; phone: 2-696-3211 or 2-337004; fax: 2-331871) offers luxury cruises in the region aboard the *Terra Australis,* a 100-passenger vessel with all outside cabins in a range of categories. The 7-day voyages are round trip from Punta Arenas (or alternatively, from Ushuaia, Argentina) and explore areas of the Strait of Magellan and the Beagle Channel that are off limits to large US and European ships. Fares start at $1,300; the season is from September through March. US travel agents can book the trip for you.

For those more included to adventure travel, another new company, *Akra Patagonia* (886 Roca, Loc. 7, Punta Arenas; phone: 61-226370), features cruises in the small sailing vessels M/V *Trinidad* and *Compass Rose.* They also arrange helicopter tours of the archipelago.

Cargo boats go from Punta Arenas to Puerto Montt and may take some passengers; if you're interested in returning to the north in this manner, check with *Empremar* (1336 Lautaro Navarro; phone: 61-221608). The tourist office (689 Calle Waldo Seguel; phone: 61-224435) maintains an information center (at the corner of Colón and Magallanes; phone: 61-223798).

From Punta Arenas, you can take the daily ferry across the strait (it leaves between 9 and 10 AM) to Porvenir. Check with *Transbordadora Austral Broom Ltda.* (924 Roca; phone: 61-22720 or 61-228166) or the tourist office. The trip takes 2½ hours. A highlight is observing the loading process; private vehicles squeeze between huge trucks laden with 600-pound bales of unprocessed wool, and passengers board with all manner of luggage. Porvenir and Punta Arenas also are linked by air. *DAP* airlines (1022 Ignacio Carrera Pinto; phone: 61-223958) flies every Monday and Saturday. *DAP* has connections from Punta Arenas to Puerto Williams every Tuesday.

**PORVENIR:** This port town (pop. 6,400), the jumping-off point for exploring both the Chilean and Argentine sides of Tierra del Fuego, was born as a police headquarters during a gold rush in the late 1800s. From Porvenir, you drive across the flat, Chilean side of the island to Parque Nacional Pinguinos (Penguins National Park), about 22 miles (35 km) northwest of Punta Arenas. The 37-square-mile park is made up of *coigüe* and *canelo* forests; both trees are native hardwoods and take centuries to grow. Near the park are the smaller islands of Magdalena and Santa María, where penguins line the coasts standing guard while sea lions and dolphins frolic in the waters.

Another side trip from Porvenir is to the oil camps at Cerro Sombrero and Manantiales, where the Chileans first discovered oil in 1945. En route, you'll pass the Lago de los Cisnes (Lake of the Swans), where the black-necked birds are part of the drab landscape; the depressing picture is enlivened, however, by pink flamingos.

Backtrack to Porvenir, but before taking the return ferry to Punta Arenas, meander through the town. The *Museo de Tierra del Fuego* (Tierra del Fuego Museum) features displays that trace the chronology of the gold rush days and the history of Porvenir. The tourism office (402 Samuel Valdivieso) maintains an information center on the corner of the central plaza. To see the direct effects of the recent petroleum boom, visit the nearby company camp of Empresa Nacional de Petróleo (ENAP), which is 700 workers strong. This self-sufficient development encompasses 150 homes for the workers and their families, a solarium, swimming pool, and gymnasium, as well as stores, a movie theater, a hospital, a church, and an airport. Visitors who want to spend some time in the community often are allowed to stay in one of the simple lodgings built for truckers who travel to and from the encampment. To make arrangements for an overnight stay, inquire at ENAP's central office in Puerto Arenas (1101 José Nogueira; phone: 61-222640). Before leaving Porvenir, stop for a meal at the old *Club Yugoslavo* (542 Calle Señoret at the edge of the bay; phone: 61-580053), which specializes in hearty food, including Yugoslav cuisine. To continue on to Puerto Natales, 145 miles (232 km) away on the mainland, you must return to Punta Arenas and head north along the Pan-American alternate Route 9.

**PUERTO NATALES:** This small town of 15,000 sheepherders and coal miners (who work in the Río Turbio mines across the border in Argentina) is famous for its Cueva del Milodón (the Milodón Cave), 15 miles (24 km) east. Discovered in 1896, the cave contained the well-preserved remains of a prehistoric animal, the mylodon, otherwise known as the giant sloth. You can visit the cave, where's there's a full-size replica of the beast (the real thing is at the *British Museum* in London). The site has been declared a natural monument, because it contained a living thing.

Back in town, the national tourism office maintains an information center (near the waterfront, at the corner of Pedro Montt and Phillipi).

Though the region around Puerto Natales is intriguing, most visitors come here en route to Parque Nacional Torres del Paine (Paine Towers National Park), an 85-mile (136-km) drive from town. Along the road you'll see sheep, an integral part of the Patagonian landscape and the region's major industry. Inside the park, the granite towers rise sharply from the golden grassland to heights over 7,000 feet. Snow-capped year-round, they often are lost in the clouds, so some luck with the weather is needed to fully appreciate the beauty of the place. Wildlife abounds: Herds of guanacos (rarest members of the camelid family), flamingos, and the majestic Andean condor frequently are sighted. A string of glacier- and spring-fed lakes provides superb fishing. The park is open from early October to sometime in April, when snow closes the road for the winter. During the summer months, there is regular daily bus service (except Mondays) between Puerto Natales and the park (about $5). It's also possible to continue via bus from Paine to Calafate, Argentina, and Glacier National Park. The 20-seater is operated thrice weekly by *Lake Travel* of Calafate and costs about $45. In the park, check with *Turismo Pehoe* (at *Hostería Cisne de Cuello Negro;* phone: 61-411965). The operator offers a variety of programs in the area, ranging from 3 to 6 days. Also, several companies offer full-day boat trips from Puerto Natales to view the glacier at the end of Ultima Esperanza Fjord. The best bet is *Arka Patagonia* (49 Eberhard; phone: 61-411984).

East of Puerto Natales on Route 250, you can head for Río Turbio in Argentina. On Last Hope Sound, this mining town is where most of the Puerto Natales working population earns its keep. Or you can return to Puerto Natales and Punta Arenas and catch a *LanChile* or *LADECO* jet back to Santiago.

**PUERTO WILLIAMS:** Claimed by Chileans to be the southernmost settlement on this side of the globe (Argentines claim Ushuaia is), Puerto Williams is actually on Isla

Navarino in the Beagle Channel and serves as a naval base. You can fly there from Puerto Arenas. Although small, with only 2,000 residents, Puerto Williams boasts a fine anthropological museum, the *Museo Martín Gusinde* (Martín Gusinde Museum), housing much of the collection of priest-anthropologist Martín Gusinde, who spent an extended period of time with the now-extinct Ona and Yagane Indians. Four-wheel-drive excursions as well as boat trips can be made around Isla Navarino to see the glaciers west of the Beagle Channel. Yachts take travelers to Cape Horn via Picton, Lennox, and New Islands.

## BEST EN ROUTE

Hotels categorized as expensive throughout Patagonia and Tierra del Fuego will cost $60 to $80 a night. First class, moderate hotels will cost $40 to $60 for a double room with private bath and often breakfast. There are some second class, inexpensive (under $40) hotels here; if you don't have a private bath, at least you'll have a clean room and friendly service. Wherever you stay, however, it's a good idea to reserve well in advance. If you're roughing it, you can camp anywhere in the area; that's the norm in the Patagonian heartland.

### PUNTA ARENAS

***Cabo de Hornos*** – Luxury in the wilds: 110 carpeted rooms with private baths, phones, one of the best restaurants in town, a gym, sauna, and a bar. On the main plaza. 1025 Plaza Muñoz Gamero (phone: 61-22134; fax: in Santiago, 2-338480). Expensive.

***Los Navegantes*** – A slightly less expensive alternative to *Cabo de Hornos*, this modern hotel has a bar, restaurant, central heating, and 50 rooms with private baths. 647 José Menéndez (phone: 61-224677). Expensive.

***Hostal Estrecho de Magallanes*** – A budget option, with 9 clean rooms sharing several baths, located near the main square. 1048 José Menéndez (phone: 61-226011). Inexpensive.

### PUERTO NATALES

***Capitán Eberhard*** – Shares the same magnificent view as the *Juan Ladrilleros*, but the walls of its 22 clean rooms are paper-thin. 25 Pedro Montt (phone: 61-411209). Moderate.

***Hostería Cisne de Cuello Negro*** – This century-old, English-style inn 2 miles (3 km) north of Puerto Natales has 17 basic but comfortable rooms and a salon/dining room with a fireplace. On the road to Torres del Paine (phone: 61-411965; through *Turismo Pehoe* in Punta Arenas, 61-224223; in Santiago, 2-671-8709; fax in Punta Arenas, 61-248052). Moderate.

***Juan Ladrilleros*** – The best choice in town, this 14-room hotel has a cozy bar and restaurant, plus a splendid view of Ultima Esperanza Fjord. Polished wood and marine blue accents are reminiscent of a ship's interior. 161 Pedro Montt (phone: 61-411652). Moderate.

### PAINE TOWERS NATIONAL PARK

***Hostería Pehoe*** – This first class lodge is situated on a small island (accessible by footbridge) in Pehoe Lake, in the middle of Paine National Park. The rustic dining room–bar has a fireplace and huge windows offering superb views of the soaring granite towers. The 35 rooms are somewhat spartan, but each has a private bath and central heating. Note: Rooms with the best views cost more. Open from September to April (phone: 61-411390; in Santiago, 2-671-8709). Expensive.

***Hostería El Pionero*** – Once the *estancia* (ranch) home of a pioneering British family, shaded by huge poplars and surrounded by flowering gardens, it has 9 rooms, most with private baths. Three have the original woodburning fireplaces. Guests use the home's comfortable living and dining rooms. Near Billa Cerro Castillo, on the Argentine border (phone: Torres del Paine 1; in Puerto Natales, 61-411594). Expensive.

**Posada Río Serrano** – A 38-bed gathering spot for budget travelers and backpackers, located within the National Park. Most rooms share baths, though each of the 4 rooms in the back house has a private bath and heating. There's a bar and a little store for supplies. Km 399 on Ruta 9 (phone: Torres del Paine 1; in Puerto Natales, check at 210 Arturo Prat; phone: 61-411355). Moderate.

**Tres Pasos** – There are 9 immaculate rooms sharing several spotless baths — it's a rural charmer, complete with white lace curtains and polished wood floors. Hot coffee is served with fresh, steamed milk; good food. At Km 38 from Puerto Natales (phone: Tres Pasos 1). Moderate to inexpensive.

### PORVENIR

**Los Flamencos** – Single and double rooms with private baths, restaurant, and bar in a pleasant atmosphere. Teniente Merino (phone: 61-580049; in Santiago, 2-339119; fax: 2-338480). Expensive.

### PUERTO WILLIAMS

**Hostería Patagonia** – This small inn with a roaring fireplace in the salon is your only choice in town. It has hot water, a restaurant, bar, and laundry service (phone: Puerto Williams 1; in Punta Arenas, 61-224926). Moderate.

# Easter Island

Easter Island isn't quite as isolated as it was 20 years ago, when virtually its only contact with the outside world was a Chilean navy that visited once a year with provisions. Still, despite the advent of organized tourism, the island remains far from civilization: 2,300 miles west of the Chilean coastline and 1,200 miles from the nearest speck of land, Pitcairn Island. The only way to get there is by plane or cruise ship.

Adding to its isolation is its landscape: The island was born when three volcanoes emerged from the sea to form a triangular wedge, with the cone of Rano Kao Volcano at the southwestern point of the triangle, Pua Katiki at the eastern point on the Poike Peninsula, and Rano Aroi forming the third point toward the north. The island is hardly more than a barren sweep of land covered with volcanic black rock and ash and two small sand beaches — one at Anakena Bay on the island's northern coast and the second, under the cliff at Ovahe, where the surf is treacherous.

Easter Island received its name from the Dutch explorer Jacob Roggeween, who anchored his three ships at the island on *Easter Sunday*, 1722. His crew were the first Europeans to step onto the island. They were met by what appeared to be a tall, racially mixed group of natives, some with dark skins and others quite fair. They all were naked, with tattoos of birds and figures across their bodies. Some wore reed hats on their heads; others wore feathers. They lived in reed huts, kept fowl as domestic animals, raised bananas, sugarcane, and sweet potatoes, and traveled about in canoes. Some anthropologists believe they came from Polynesia or Malaysia; others contend they were a pre-Inca Indian culture from Peru that moved to the island to escape either natural disaster or internal war. The debate rages on. The island became Chilean territory in 1888.

If the natives are intriguing, their *moai* — the stone figures that line the island's coast — are more so. Apparently some 600 *moai* were erected along the coast, standing sentry on *ahus* (pedestals), with some reaching as high as 150 feet and weighing as much as 30 tons. The monoliths were carved from stone at the Rano Raraku Volcano; about 53 are still affixed to the rock there. The details of the face and body were finished before the statues were chipped away at the back and set loose from the stone. *Moai* still dot the roadway, waiting for some long-gone transport to the shore below the quarry, where there seemed to be a storage lot from which they were taken to their final destination, atop the *ahus*. Southeast of the volcano is the only kneeling *moai*, found during one of the early expeditions Norwegian Thor Heyerdahl made to the island.

Although legend decrees that the *moai* walked to their destination, archaeological diggings reveal that they were dragged on wooden boards pulled like a sled from ropes made of tree fibers. At dry spots, cooked potato was rubbed along the bottom of boards to make them more slippery. Other *moai* might have been rolled on two round logs, with one log placed ahead of the other until the destination was reached. There, the statues were hoisted into place by ropes.

*LanChile* flies to the island every Sunday and Friday, with increased service in the summer according to demand. The trip takes 5 hours, and outbound flights continue to Tahiti. Confirm reservations for leaving the island if your time is limited; flights occasionally are overbooked, and some travelers have remained on the island longer than they wished. All flights depart from Santiago, and you can make reservations at *LanChile* offices there or in the US.

Tour operators include Easter Island in their South America programs. Among them are *Society Expeditions* (c/o *Abercrombie & Kent*) Oak Brook, IL; *Travcoa*, Santa Ana Heights, CA; *Unique Adventures*, San Francisco, CA. For more information, see tour listings in *Package Tours*, GETTING READY TO GO, or call the *LanChile* tour desk in Miami (phone: 800-735-5526).

The island is about 70 miles square, and the most comfortable way to get around is on horseback. Tradition has it that the first king and queen sailed to Easter Island on a fiber boat. The modern-day islanders built such a boat in 1988 and ushered it home with song and dance. About 2,000 people now live there — far fewer than the 15,000 who basked in this subtropical climate generations ago. Some are from the mainland, but three-quarters appear to be of Polynesian origin. The main settlement is at Hanga-Roa, and here and there you'll see small children, three at a time, astride horses trotting across the rocky terrain. The weather brings everybody out: Winter temperatures never fall below 60 to 65F (15 to 18C), and summer temperatures are a comfortable 72 to 83F (22 to 28C). Rainfalls may be heavy at times, but they're always brief. Be sure to bring a bathing suit and, for treading on the volcanic rock, sneakers. Those planning to explore caves should bring flashlights.

In addition to visiting the Rano Raraku Volcano and the *moai,* you can go to Orongo, next to the Rano Kau Volcano at the southwestern tip of the island. This was the site of the ceremonial village, and stone carvings still remain that depict the island's "birdmen." From the Orongo cliff, the island's young men would dive into the sea to swim on reed floats out to three tiny islands offshore in search of the first egg of the year laid by the sooty tern. The lucky guy who found it became a god — the "birdman" — for almost a year. His head was shaved and painted red, and he was taken to a hut at the foot of Rano Raraku, where he was given anything he wanted. The only catch was that he wasn't allowed to mingle with the villagers during that time.

You'll also want to see some of the caves where the villagers lived during what is believed to have been long periods of civil war on the island. The Atan Cave (near Hanga Roa), the Lázaro Cave (near Hanga Oteo at the north point of the island), and the Santiago del Este Cave (at Vaihu) all housed villagers fleeing from ravages and death. A cave of more temperate times is the Cave of the White Virgins, in the northeast sector of the island. Young girls were hidden here from the sun for years to keep their skin white. These "bleached" girls then exhibited their white bodies during ceremonial occasions. Stop by the church to witness a hybrid of Catholic and Polynesian ritual — the midday Sunday mass is celebrated in the language of the islanders, and the songs have a Polynesian rhythm.

Hanga Roa's *El Museo* (The Museum) exhibits photos and prints illustrating island life, as well as a rare female *moai.* During his early excavations some 30 years ago, Thor Heyerdahl discovered the headless body, bought it, and carted it home to Oslo, Norway, where it rested until 1988 in his *Kon Tiki Museum.* That year he returned the *moai* to Easter Island to be reunited with its head, which he finally uncovered on a recent dig. The islanders greeted the *moai* with a celebration fit for a queen.

At the waterfront in Hanga Roa, snorkeling equipment and boats, which often come with guides, can be rented. At the *Hotu Matua* hotel, there are horses for hire. For faster transportation, motorcycle owners frequently are willing to rent their bikes for a few hours or a day.

Reservations are advised if you plan to remain on the island. Since tourism is an established trade, everything, from local items to imported food, beer, and wine, has a high price tag. There is a tourism information office on the island, at the corner of Tu'u Maheke and Apina (phone: Hanga Roa 255).

## BEST EN ROUTE

The only hotels on Easter Island are in Hanga Roa. One, the *Hanga Roa* (noted below), towers above the others in Western amenities and in price. The cost of everything here is at least three times mainland prices. Lodgings can run from $100 to $200 a night for a double room, with meals, in the expensive category. Under $100 is moderate. Reservations should be made in advance. If you prefer, you may be able to stay at an islander's house or rent a tent from a hotel and camp out. Ask at the information desk at the airport.

**Hanga Roa** – Considered to be the best hotel on the island, this property sleeps 120 guests, and meals are included. Located right on the ocean, there's also a pool for cooling off after a day's exploring. Av. Ponto (phone: Hanga Roa 299; in Santiago, 2-396834; *LARC* in the US, 800-327-3573; fax: in Santiago, 2-395334). Expensive.

**Iorana** – A modern, 21-room hotel offering carpeted rooms with private baths and sea views. Amenities include a restaurant, bar, saltwater and freshwater swimming pools, and laundry and room services. Calle Ana Magaro (phone and fax: Hanga Roa 312; in Santiago, 2-632-1048; fax: 2-332650). Expensive.

**Hotu Matua** – A smaller hostelry that offers clean accommodations. Av. Ponto (phone: Hanga Roa 242). Moderate to expensive.

**Residencial Rosita** – Another small place in the village that offers clean and comfortable lodgings. Te Pito Te Henua (phone: Hanga Roa 250). Moderate.

# The Juan Fernández Archipelago

Just 500 miles west of Valparaíso in the green Pacific, the three volcanic islands of the Juan Fernández Archipelago — Robinson Crusoe, Alejandro Selkirk, and Santa Clara — offer a quiet haven to anyone seeking isolation, lush green surroundings, and warm, 71F (21C) swimming waters. Discovered in 1574 by the Spanish navigator Juan Fernández, the islands' outward calm belies their historic notoriety: Spanish, English, and Dutch pirate ships harbored here in the 16th, 17th, and 18th centuries. Since 1935, the island group has been designated a national park.

The islands' most famous resident was an English seaman who asked to disembark here because he couldn't stand the mistreatment he was receiving from his ship's captain. Alexander (or Alejandro) Selkirk was marooned by the ship *Cinque Ports* in 1704; 4 years later, he was rescued by another English ship and returned to England, where tales of his island exploits inspired Daniel Defoe to write *Robinson Crusoe*, published in 1719. Defoe changed the location of the island, but it's generally accepted that Selkirk was the Crusoe prototype, and the cave where he allegedly lived on Robinson Crusoe Island is shown to visitors today.

More than one man suffered hardship here. The survivors of two English shipwrecks lived on Robinson Crusoe for 5 months in 1721; the island also served as a prison camp for Chilean patriots in the Independence War and for Spanish prisoners once the war was won. Both parties lived wretchedly in caves that can still be seen along the Bay of Cumberland. Colonial settlements were also started at this time.

There is one amusing chapter in the islands' history. In 1877, German Baron Alfred Von Rodt arrived and fell in love with the archipelago. He decided to stay, and died here at the age of 65. Not only does his ship remain, but numerous de Rodts — the blue-eyed descendants of the baron's two wives — make up some of the 600 residents of Robinson Crusoe Island.

Robinson Crusoe is the only island in the archipelago visited by travelers and the only inhabited one. The main industry on the island is lobster fishing, and the catch is considered the tastiest in the world. Until 1966, the only way you could reach the archipelago was by boat or seaplane, but the construction of an airstrip now allows surface landings. The islands are linked to the mainland by a few boat trips monthly from Valparaíso during the summer season. Book packages through *DMC Tours* (3144 Napoleón; phone: 2-242-9042; fax: 2-246-6935); included are air transportation, lodging, full board (with at least two lobster meals), and two excursions. Prices start at $795 per person for 3 nights; $915 for 4 nights. The islands are accessible to visitors from September through April.

**ROBINSON CRUSOE ISLAND:** Formerly known as Más a Tierra (Closer to Land), this island is small — about 36 square miles — and west of Alejandro Selkirk Island, or Más Afuera (Farther Out Island), by about 109 miles. It's a desolate place with fabulous rocky beaches visited only during the lobster season (October to May) by fishermen. This island doesn't expect tourism competition from Santa Clara Island (also called Goat Island), either — a tiny southwesterly speck with no vegetation and no water.

The starting point for adventure here is San Juan Bautista village in the Bay of Cumberland, a small area that takes in the entire island population. Robinson Crusoe is triangular, with one angle pointing north; the bay is on the northeastern slope of the triangle. Selkirk, who spent his island vacation in the bay, was merely "let off" at the stop, so to speak, armed with his Bible, gun, knife, ax, gunpowder, tobacco, and clothes; you'll have to take a 90-minute motorboat ride from the landing strip on the southwestern tip of the island. You'll be impressed during the trip by the striking, nearly vertical cliffs of up to 1,000 feet that ring the island. Only at the Bay of Cumberland and three other spots does the ground slope gently to the sea, providing access to the island. In the center of the cliffs' towers is the 3,000-foot Yunque (Anvil) Hill, the island's highest peak, which is always covered by clouds.

The island does provide tourist accommodations in the Cumberland Bay area, but if you're dealing with islanders, take into consideration that they are not cash-oriented. Until a few years ago, the main currency was lobster. There is still no bank, so money doesn't have much value. Even today, islanders may choose to rent you a horse or take you fishing or deep-sea diving on their motorboats in exchange for some item you have that strikes their fancy. And whether you can rent a horse to ride or take that boat trip will depend on whim: Sometimes you can and sometimes you can't. If you do rent something, say, for 8 AM, don't get upset if it doesn't show up on time. Islanders are known for showing up with their goods as late as the following day.

If you do go fishing, you're in for a treat. Archipelago waters are noted for their abundance of fish — pompano, tuna, moray eel, rock salmon, dogfish, flying fish, and octopi. The crystalline waters make snorkeling a delight. You're also going to see a lot of sea lions, *lobos marinos de dos pelos;* these little fellows at one time numbered about 3 million, but North American sealing expeditions in the 19th century rapidly diminished that number. Some years ago, the Chilean government banned the hunting of seals; their population is now close to 1,000.

Unfortunately, the island's fragrant sandalwood tree was never given the opportunity to propagate; all the trees were chopped down by traders. Today, the Chilean government protects the *palmera chonta* (chonta palm) to keep it from the same fate, but items made of its dark wood occasionally can be bought in Chile. One natural feature still thriving in the constant 67F (19C) weather, fortunately, is the giant fern. More than 60 varieties of fern grow on the island, and some even grow to tree size. In fact, because of the vegetation, Darwin, who made the archipelago one of his many stops during the *Beagle*'s voyage, later commented that he was more impressed with these islands than with the Galápagos archipelago.

You can get a good look at the vegetation by taking a 90-minute climb from the Bay of Cumberland to the top of Selkirk's old lookout, the Mirador de Selkirk. A slightly shorter walk to the west from the bay will bring you to Puerto Ingles and the Robinson Crusoe Cave. On the Bay of Cumberland, at one end of San Juan Bautista village, are buried some sailors from the *Dresden,* a German ship that retired to the island for repairs during World War I. When some British vessels approached in 1915, the Germans dynamited the *Dresden* to keep it from falling into enemy hands. The crew stayed here for the rest of their lives. Parts of the ship were resurrected in 1964, and on clear days the ship's towers can be spotted in the bay where it sank. A few pieces of Krupp artillery from World War II and some old cannon also are buried in the bay.

The ruins of two other forts are a good hike from Cumberland Bay. Centinelas Fort ruins are near Puerto Ingles; the ruins of San Carlos are at the extreme eastern tip of the island at Puerto Francés.

## BEST EN ROUTE

Most hotels on Robinson Crusoe Island charge about $50 per person per night. If you arrange to stay with an islander, expect to pay anything — from money to your camera to your false teeth or water wings. There are no phones on the island, so confirm your hotel reservations through the national tourism office in Santiago (1550 Av. Providencia; phone: 2-698-2151) or arrange a package through *DMC Tours* in Santiago (3144 Napoleón; phone: 2-242-9042; fax: 2-246-6935).

### ROBINSON CRUSOE ISLAND

***Aldea Daniel DeFoe*** – A smaller, modest hotel that provides basic lodgings.

***Hostería Green*** – Four guestrooms with private baths, a parlor, and dining room all under one roof make up this clean — but basic — lodging run by Reinaldo Green. Electricity is sporadic, but lobster is served at meals.

***Hostería Pangal*** – Considered the best on the island, this 10-room lodge with private bathrooms has a lounge, a balcony overlooking the sea, and a restaurant that serves lobster in more ways than imaginable. Reservations in Santiago through *Taxpa* (phone: 2-273-4309 and 2-273-4354).

***Robinson Crusoe*** – Just outside town, this 25-room hotel serves 47 guests, provides private baths, hot water, and electricity, and offers a choice of rooms: single, double, small, medium, even a suite.

# Colombia

*Although the much-publicized violence from drug trafficking and guerrilla wars that plagued Colombia for most of the past decade decreased in the past year, the US State Department has issued an advisory warning US visitors against travel to certain parts of Colombia (primarily the interior), and to take precautions in other areas of the country. Travelers are advised to check with the US State Department's Citizens' Emergency Center (phone: 202-647-5225) prior to departure and with the American Citizens' Services Unit of the US Embassy in Bogotá (phone: 1-285-1300, ext. 206 and 215) upon arrival. Note also that at press time, cases of cholera had been reported in scattered areas throughout the country. Tourist areas have remained largely unaffected, but travelers are advised to drink only bottled beverages and eat only cooked hot food and peeled fruit. For further information call the Centers for Disease Control's International Travelers' Hotline (phone: 404-332-4559).*

Colombia covers 440,000 square miles of both tropical and mountainous terrain. Bordered on the north and west by the Caribbean, Panama, and the Pacific, on the south by Ecuador and Peru, on the east by Brazil, and on the northeast by Venezuela, it is famous for its fabulous emeralds and delicious coffee, and infamous for its pure cocaine. Less well known, but responsible for a substantial contribution to the country's economic growth, is its production of coal and oil, resources that have been developed in the Guajira Desert over the past decade (and in 1991, a huge oil field was discovered in the Cusiana region in the east — the largest of its kind in the Americas in more than 2 decades). The country's great variety of attractions, from the towering peaks of the Sierra Nevada chain to the tiny ports bordering two seas, as well as the treasures of a rich pre-Columbian and colonial past, are less publicized and also deserve attention.

Out of a national population of 32.3 million, about 5.5 million people live in the capital, Bogotá. In the center of the country, in an Andean valley, Bogotá stands at an elevation of 8,640 feet above sea level, an altitude that is responsible for the city's perpetual springlike climate, despite its near-equatorial latitude. Here is the *Museo del Oro* (Gold Museum), which contains thousands of gold objects that escaped the melting pots of the conquistadores, making it one of the most impressive and complete collections of gold objects in the world. Despite this wealth, shantytowns called "barrios" surround the city. Overflowing with poor migrants from rural areas, they typify the abysmal contrast between wealth and poverty that is common in Latin American society. In recent years, the Colombian government has instituted a number of programs to improve living conditions in the barrios. Electricity, sewage systems, and home improvement projects have helped somewhat, as have community action programs that enable barrio residents to participate in municipal activities. (For a complete report on Bogotá, see THE CITIES.)

Colombia has three Andean ridges: the Cordillera Occidental (Western Range), the Cordillera Central (Central Range), and the Cordillera Oriental (Eastern Range). In addition, a range separate from the Andes — the Sierra Nevada de Santa Marta mountains — rises in the north from the Caribbean Coast. It is in this range that the Sierra Nevada de Cocuy, one of Colombia's highest mountains, rises to 18,201 feet. Bogotá is situated in the Eastern Range while the second largest city in the country, Medellín (pop. 2 million), the self-proclaimed orchid capital of the world, stands in a Central Cordillera mountain valley. The country's third-largest city, Cali (pop. 1.8 million), is in a valley in the Western Range. Nearly half of all Colombians reside in these particular Andean valleys.

Bordering both Pacific and Caribbean coasts, Colombia has a couple of resort areas, Santa Marta (pop. 350,000) and Cartagena (pop. 800,000), as well as a thriving Caribbean port, Barranquilla (pop. 1.5 million). See DIVERSIONS for more about them. In the Amazon region of Colombia, the landscape consists of miles and miles of unbroken jungle. In 1990, the Colombian government recognized the rights of the Indians who live there to one-half of the overall area (thus tripling their former living area), acknowledging that the Indians are the best protectors of the region's ecology. The largest settlement within this jungle is Leticia (pop. 20,000), Colombia's prime Amazon port.

Historically, Colombia is the land that gave the world the legend of El Dorado (literally, "The Golden One"). The myth that attracted the gold-hungry Spaniards in the 16th century is believed to have come from an actual ritual in which Muisca Indians covered their chief in gold dust and tossed precious gold objects into a deep, sacred lake as offerings. In 1500, Alonso de Ojeda was the first Spaniard to sail into Cartagena, but the Indians drove him away. In 1538, Gonzalo Jiménez de Quesada founded Santa Fe de Bogotá. Later, when Colombia became the kingdom of New Granada and Panama (under Spanish rule), the country went through a relatively peaceful colonial era during which prosperity was ensured by regular shipments of gold to Spain.

Except for the problems of piracy, Colombia remained undisturbed until early in the 19th century, when the first battles for independence began. Simón Bolívar, the Great Liberator, waged a lengthy campaign on Colombian soil in 1812, but it was not until December 17, 1819, that he was able officially to declare the country's independence from Spain. He established the Republic of Gran Colombia, which included Venezuela, Colombia, Panama, and Ecuador, but he was unable to maintain a cohesive whole. In 1886, the Colombian constitution went into effect. It was rewritten in 1991 by a nationally elected group of 73 Colombian men and women. The new constitution seeks to limit official abuse of power and open up the country's political system to previously excluded minorities. The two traditional parties, the Conservatives and the Liberals, still dominate the government despite significant electoral gains by indigenous and left-wing groups.

No commentary on Colombia is complete, however, without mention of the drug trade *(narcotráfico)*, which has had a major effect on the country's economy and has meaningfully eroded the rule of law. The drug traffickers *(narcotráficantes)* control personal armies and fortunes that rival the national debt, oversee social programs for the poor, and ruthlessly kill their enemies. During 1989 and 1990, when the government carried out an extensive campaign against the drug cartels, bomb attacks and kidnappings were frequent occurrences. The head of the notorious Medellín drug cartel, Pablo Escobar, and 17 of his associates surrendered to authorities in 1991 in exchange for government leniency (which in Señor Escobar's case extends to non-convict, custom-built accommodations, complete with all of the creature comforts of a drug lord's castle). Even so, drug terrorism has not ended: killings continue among rival *narcotráficantes* fighting for turf. At press time, large-scale battles were still being fought between guerrillas and government troops in the interior, making those areas unsafe for travelers. Cruise ships, however, which had stopped putting in at Cartagena because of fears of violence, are docking there once again, and this Caribbean resort is seeing a resurgence of foreign visitors.

Although it's possible to drive through Colombia yourself, the country has an extensive system of buses, *colectivos* (chauffeured cars that carry four or five passengers), railroads, and internal domestic airlines that connect even the most remote towns and villages. The use of public transportation is highly recommended, because road service for private cars is very scarce and breakdowns in remote areas can be dangerous. Those who do drive should be sure to have their *carnets* (customs passes) and insurance policies in order and easily accessible should there be an accident. Also, bring spare parts and be prepared to make repairs without outside help.

Colombia is one of the most exotic and geographically diverse countries on the continent, with more than 50 different Indian tribes still holding steadfast to their traditions. However, the country's illicit drug traffic has contributed to its reputation as a particularly dangerous place. In Colombia's major cities, visitors should be particularly cautious with their valuables in public places. Checking them into the hotel's safe is a good idea. Passports especially should be kept out of sight. For non-Spanish-speaking visitors, travel with a tour group is an option that should be considered.

This chapter contains five routes. The first runs along the Caribbean Coast from Cartagena to Santa Marta, via Barranquilla. The second explores a not-often-traveled desert route from Riohacha in the Guajira Desert to Villa de Leyva in the dry foothills of the eastern Andes. The Bogotá-to-Medellín route travels through Colombia's agricultural region, where there are huge orchards and fields of coffee beans. Neiva to Cali includes several Colombian archaeological zones. Finally, the Amazon section offers several suggestions for exploring that region.

# Cartagena and the Caribbean West Coast

A trip to the Caribbean Coast of Colombia presents a startling contrast for a traveler who has just seen Bogotá. Descending from the mountains to sea level, the climate becomes balmy and the atmosphere Caribbean-casual. Behind the walls of Cartagena is South America's best-preserved and largest colonial city. Along the coast leading from the city are long stretches of white sand beach that extend to the resort city of Santa Marta and beyond into a vast national park that rises from the coast up into the Sierra Nevadas.

The residents of Colombia's Caribbean Coast are known as *costeños* and consider themselves to be distinct from the mountain dwellers. Generally speaking, they are known for their bold native dances, their exquisite cuisine, and for a lifestyle characterized as *muy alegre* (very merry). Visitors can follow plenty of paths to excitement here, from exploring the jagged *páramos* (barren mountaintops) of the Sierra Nevada, to gambling in the casinos and disco hopping, to joining in the revels of any of the many annual festivals such as the pre-*Lenten Carnaval* in Barranquilla during February and March.

There are a number of ways to start this Caribbean journey. There is airline service from New York and Miami to Barranquilla or Cartagena. If you intend to drive through Colombia, remember that many regions (particularly the entire north coast) are considered dangerous, particularly for nighttime travel. However, the major tourist areas, such as Cartagena, Baranquilla, and Santa Marta are considered safe. Before beginning any car journey, check with the US Embassy in Bogotá or the US State Department. The best road trip starts from Cartagena. From there, continue north to Barranquilla and on to Santa Marta, the oldest European-founded settlement in South America. Along this route live many different types of people: white and mestizo, black (slave descendants), mulatto (black and white), and zambo (black and Indian). *Costeño* music — like many of the people — is a happy blend of black and Spanish, sounding more like salsa and African tribal than Andalusian or Castilian Spanish music.

To drive the entire Colombian route, be sure to have a Mobil road map or the Codazzi Institute's set of route maps covering main highways and highlighting places of interest. There are many highways in Colombia, but only about one-quarter of the 100,000-mile network is paved; the rest is narrow, often poor, and unmarked. Any travel assistance needed, as well as maps, can be obtained from the national tourist office in Bogotá, 13A-15 Calle 28, 15th Floor (phone: 1-284-0716).

Just one word about this route: Petty crime is an ugly fact marring the beauty of the Caribbean Coast. Pickpockets and muggers thrive in most of the cities, so be prepared, and try not to wander about alone. Have a good time, but guard your personal belongings. If you do get robbed, report it to the authorities; the police can be quite cooperative. Don't let fear ruin your trip but, on the other hand, an "it can't happen to me" attitude about valuables only invites trouble.

**CARTAGENA:** Founded by Pedro de Heredia in 1533, the "Heroic City" was built as a Spanish base for the conquest of the continent — an impregnable port with a heavily armed garrison to protect the gold routes and slave trade established by the Spaniards. Within 30 years, a branch of the Río Magdalena joining the Bay of Cartagena to the main channel 90 miles inland was dredged. The result, the Canal del Dique, connected Cartagena with the interior, and made the city the main port for merchandise shipped from Spain for the conquest of the South American north and for treasures shipped back to the mother country. The city also was granted a royal monopoly as a slave port and market.

To protect the riches, the citizens and their slaves built a series of forts and a massive limestone wall around the city. These were aimed at stopping direct attacks by outside forces. Nonetheless, Cartagena faced its share of buccaneers: It was sacked by pirate Robert Baal in 1544, then by Martin Côtes a few years later; other English, French, and European pirates also contributed their bits of aggravation. The most famous (or infamous) of these renegades was the English privateer Sir Francis Drake who, with his 1,300-man force, pillaged the port in 1586, then "mercifully" decided not to burn the city to the ground once he was presented with 10 million pesos, which he ferried home to Queen Elizabeth. He also took with him an enormous emerald, which he gave to the Virgin Queen as a *New Year's Day* gift.

By the mid-17th century, the Spaniards finally had completed the forts and wall around the city. An adjacent circle of wall was constructed around the neighborhood of Getsemaní in 1656, and the small, eight-cannon Castillo de San Lázaro became the formidable Castillo de San Felipe de Barájas, bristling with 70 pieces of artillery. It was the strongest fort in all the Spanish colonies. As testimony, Don Blas de Lezo, with 2,500 troops, successfully defended the city against 27,000 British soldiers, but the battles cost him nearly half his body. Today, a statue of the one-eyed, one-armed, one-legged leader stands at the base of the fortress of San Felipe, the scene of his triumph. The British attack was led by Edward Vernon, one of whose regiments was composed of Americans commanded by Lawrence Washington, George's half-brother. Vernon was so confident of victory that medals proclaiming "The forts of Cartagena destroyed by Adm. Vernon" and "They took Cartagena, 1741" were stamped in advance. The loss apparently didn't deter George Washington from naming the family home, Mount Vernon, in the admiral's honor.

Cartagena has expanded in every direction, and today is a dynamic city of 800,000. Broad avenues, elegant residential areas, and tall, tourist complexes border the Caribbean. However, the walled Old City has changed very little since the colonial days of gold shipments and pirate attacks, and has been declared a World Cultural Heritage Site by UNESCO. It's a great place for a walking tour (but keep careful track of your personal belongings), beginning with the inner walled city at the Torre del Reloj (Clock Tower) entrance. The portal is near Plaza de los Coches, once a slave market, which now houses the City Hall and some arcades. Inside the wall, near the portal, is the Plaza de la Aduana, the city's old parade ground, which contains a stone statue of Christopher Columbus. Behind it are the narrow streets of El Centro, an elegant little neighborhood with 2-story, balconied colonial buildings. Plaza San Pedro Claver, behind El Centro, houses a church and monastery built by the Jesuits in 1603 and later dedicated to San Pedro Claver, a Spanish-born priest who ministered to the blacks brought from Africa as slaves. Claver, whose body rests in a glass coffin on the church's high altar, was the first person to be canonized in the New World.

There are a number of colonial churches and buildings in the San Pedro area. At the Palace of the Inquisition, located at the Plaza Bolívar, the Holy Office held its "trials" for suspected witches, starting in 1610. The present building dates from 1706. It's a wonderful example of colonial baroque, with balconies, cloisters, patios, stone entrances, and wooden doors. Rather than housing monsignors carefully scrutinizing the sins of *cartageneros,* the office today offers travelers a library and a museum; the latter includes paintings that vividly depict the excesses of the Inquisition and the machines of torture used by the Holy Inquisitor and his assistants. The palace is open daily (closed from noon to 2 PM for siesta); admission charge.

The city's cathedral, also in Plaza Bolívar, was started in 1575, but was partly destroyed by Francis Drake in 1586. The church has a fort-like exterior, and its museum houses models of weapons used by the English admiral Edward Vernon and his men, who laid siege to the city in 1741. The Church of Santo Toribio de Mongrovejo (Calle del Sargento Mayor) sports a real Vernon memento — a cannonball that was fired while mass was being said and imbedded itself in a central column of the church, where it remains to this day. Santo Domingo (Calle de la Universidad) is reputedly the oldest church in the city; it was taken over by the University of Cartagena in 1827. Santa Clara (Parque de San Diego) was a monastery transformed into a hospital, but the building still retains its carved altar.

The best place for shopping for crafts is the Plaza de las Bovedas, which also provides a good idea of the strength of the city walls — they're 40 feet high and 50 to 60 feet thick. Twenty-four bomb-proof vaults are faced with an elegant neo-classical portico that now contains shops for tourists. The *ruanas,* or woolen ponchos, at *Artesanías Bochica* (3 Plaza de la Bovedas) are a good bet, as are the leather goods at *La Garita* (23 Plaza de las Bovedas).

The plaza marks the end of the tour within the walls and the start of a walk through Gethsemane (named after the olive grove where Jesus Christ prayed after the Last Supper), the outer walled city. Today, only the eastern side of the neighborhood is walled, where the working class live in single-story *casas bajas,* typical of colonial architecture. Here visit the Chapel of Espíritu Santo (Calle Espíritu Santo) and the colonial Church of Santísima Trinidad, located on its own colonial plaza.

Outside the walls, across Avenida Pedro de Heredia, visit the Castillo de San Felipe de Barájas, which has a son et lumière (sound and light show — the equivalent of an audiovisual presentation) Saturdays at 8 PM, featuring the history of Cartagena and San Felipe. Once considered the city's most important fortress, the fort was built between 1536 and 1657. Today, its remarkable network of tunnels and passageways, its water system, its storage and munitions rooms — the sheer mass and ingenuity of the battlements and fortifications — make for a fascinating guided tour. Note that the Castillo de San Felipe recently has begun charging foreigners an admission fee that is more than double what Colombians pay. Outside the fortress stand an enormous pair of stone shoes honoring poet Luis Carlos López, who once said in a poem that the city inspired as much affection and comfort as an old pair of shoes. Bus tours to the fort are available in Spanish and English for about $6, or if you insist, take a taxi to get there on your own.

For the best view of the city, take a taxi to the top of La Popa, the hill outside the Old City. Also visit Manga Island to view the turn-of-the-century and older architecture, where some of the mansions still are occupied by Cartagena's first families. The old fort there, San Sebastián de Pastelillo, is now the *Club de Pesca* (Fishing Club), which serves a good seafood dinner (try the paella — a hodgepodge of rice, clams, mussels, and lobster). Consider taking a 2-hour trip to Boca Chica Bay (the eastern waterway that provides the only outside access to Cartagena) for swimming and sunning. The beaches are cleaner and fresher here than on Boca Grande. There also are two colonial forts, San Fernando and the Batería San José. Also, half-day trips to the Rosario Islands, outside the bay, are available. It's safest to buy tickets from the companies sponsoring trips and not from vendors on the street. Another boat trip follows the Canal del Dique, a favorite excursion for bird watchers.

While out on Boca Grande, check out *Greenfire* (in the *Pierino Gallo Shopping Center),* the gem store that sells those famous Colombian emeralds for a pretty fair price. The manager of the shop, Lee Miles, is an American from San Francisco who publishes a twice-a-year, English-language newspaper about Cartagena, *The Voice of the Spanish Main.* The latest edition and other tourist information are available at the store along with a large selection of emeralds. (On Monday evenings at 7:45 PM from October to May, *Greenfire* offers a film and lecture on emeralds. Call the store for more details.) In the same plaza, located near the *Caribe* hotel, are *Land Leather* (phone: 53-654321) and *Boots and Baggage, Ltd.* (phone: 53-650297), two shops specializing in leather goods. *Clavia* (in the *Pierino Gallo Shopping Center;* phone: 53-650308) and *Galería Cano* (at the *Cartagena Hilton International;* phone: 53-650666) sell pre-Columbian artifacts — originals and replicas. If you like shellfish, *La Fonda Antioqueña* (6-164 Carrera 2; phone: 53-651392) is guaranteed to satisfy your palate with their lobster, mussel, and clam dishes. For the gambler, there are the roulette wheels and baccarat tables of the *Caribe*'s casino, located in the nightclub and restaurant district of Boca Grande.

*Cartageneros* love to party, and some big celebrations are held during the year. In addition to the standard Roman Catholic and political holidays, Cartagena has its own fiestas, with plenty of eating, drinking, dancing, and general hell-raising. Cartagena goes crazy during *Carnaval* season, before *Lent*. Then, in mid-March, the city plays host to one of its most interesting celebrations, the *Caribbean Music Festival*, which runs for several days and brings in musicians from all over the Caribbean. September 9 is the *Feast of San Pedro de Claver* and features religious processions. From November 11 to 14 is the city's *Independence Day* feast when a national beauty queen is selected.

The city boasts a wide variety of very good seafood restaurants. The catches to try are lobster, red snapper, crab, and barracuda, which often are accompanied by coconut rice. The *Bodegón de la Candeleria* (Calle de las Damas; phone: 53-647251), located in the flower-filled courtyard of a colonial mansion, has good food and live music. Other spots for seafood are *Club de Pesca* within an old fort outside the Old City in La Manga (Fortress del Pastelillo; phone: 53-642961), and *Nautilus* (Calle San Martín; phone: 53-642961) in the Old City. For excellent Italian food and personal attention, stop in at *Giovanni O Sole Mio* (4-66 Av. San Martín; phone: 53-655671).

Hotels in Cartagena are of mixed quality. Some are small, in need of renovation, lacking hot water and shower stalls, and more often than not, lacking in security; at the other extreme is the posh *Cartagena Hilton International*. There are a variety of comfortable, moderately priced hotels in between, most of which are located on Boca Grande. Rates rise 25% to 30% during the *Christmas* and *Easter* holidays; reservations for these times should be made well in advance (see *Best en Route*).

Before taking a 90-mile (144-km) drive along the coastal Route 2 to the larger port of Barranquilla, you might fly from Cartagena to the island of San Andrés, 298 miles north of the Colombian coast.

**SAN ANDRÉS:** White beaches, palm trees, and blue skies aren't all that lure travelers to this happy Caribe resort island: Welsh privateer Henry Morgan harbored here during his 17th-century raids on Spanish strongholds. Legend has it that he left over $1 billion worth of gold bullion buried in a cave, either here or on one of the island's many tiny adjacent cays. You're welcome to hunt for the booty, but most people prefer to skip the cave and relax instead in the 75F (24C) weather, tempered by trade winds.

Discovered in 1527 by Spanish explorers on the eve of the *Feast of St. Andrew*, the tiny island — 8 miles long and 2 miles wide — became part of Colombia in 1827. Its population of 60,000, a mix of black slave descendants, English, and Spanish, is boosted by a large number of foreign and Colombian tourists. The island was cut off from any consistent means of communication with the mainland until the 1950s, when regular domestic air service was established by *Avianca*.

Sightseeing and water sports are the island's biggest draws. It's possible to hire a taxi or your own mini-jeep, motorbike, or bicycle for as low as $15 a day for a jaunt around the island's paved coastal road. Along the way, stop and visit Morgan's Cave and the Hoyo Soplador (Blowhole), formed by compressed air spouting through an opening in the sea floor near a number of underground tunnels.

As for sports, you can rent scuba gear at the *Aquarium Dive Shop* (Av. de Colombia) on San Andrés; diving excursions take place on the *Karina*, a 40-foot boat owned by Pablo Montoya (PO Box 1692, Isla San Andrés, Colombia). Pablo requires proof of certification and is very safety conscious. There are numerous dive sites, including one to a crashed 747. You also can go deep-sea fishing for marlin, sailfish, bonito, or red snapper. The *Bahía Marina* resort (PO Box 597, Isla San Andrés, Colombia; phone: 811-23539 or 811-23657) provides charters for fishing, water skiing, scuba diving, and snorkeling that cost anywhere from $12 an hour to $110 a day.

If you prefer, simply wander around the downtown area of the island. The free port area has over 600 stores containing foreign imports and domestic crafts, from china and porcelain to watches, jewels (plenty of Colombian emeralds), liquor, and even canned goods. Some of the stores worth browsing through include the *Carolina Duty-Free Shop* (Av. Costa Rica Colón) for porcelain, watches, and jewelry; and the *Casa Amberes* (2-131 Av. Colón) and *Artesanías de Colombia* (2-144 Av. Colón) for handicrafts from all over Colombia.

A $4 fare will purchase a ride on the public launch to Johnny Key for a picnic. On Sundays there's a fish fry, but every day is a party day on Johnny Key. There's plenty of singing and dancing, and the day turns into a mini-fiesta for no reason except the fun of it all. For nightlife, the main island has a quiet assortment of entertainment that ranges from dining to catching a show at the cinema.

Don't miss trying some of the local dishes on San Andrés. *Miss Bess* offers home-cooked specialties, including crab soup and ceviche (marinated fish that makes palates smart). *Patacones* (fried plantains), *rondón,* a vegetable stew, and coconut bread also are on the menu. Other restaurants feature interior Colombian dishes such as *mondongo* (tripe), *sobrebarriga con papas* (creole potatoes and steak), and *arepa* (corn cakes). Incidentally, in the Spanish-English patois spoken in San Andrés, seafood is known as *sifú.*

San Andrés hotels are clean and comfortable. Although some provide private baths, hot water is scarce, and the drinking water is often putrid, although the completion of a desalinization plant has improved the situation somewhat. All of the hotels are geared toward the tourist and include a number of game rooms, water sports equipment, discos, casinos, and bars (see *Best en Route*). There are also two casinos with very low minimum bets ($1) — the *Caribe Internacional* and the *Casino Eldorado–Monte Carlo*.

**PROVIDENCIA:** From San Andrés, it's possible to fly to Providencia, a mountainous rural island. The 45-minute flight costs about $40 round-trip. Providencia is a scenic escape with few tourists, and you'll find the English-speaking residents to be friendly and helpful. Fishing, diving, horseback riding, swimming, and eating are the primary activities, but be sure to take a boat ride around the island and see Morgan's Head, a rock formation with humanoid features. You also can swim in Morgan's Cove nearby. Stroll through the village of Santa Isabel and walk across the Rainbow Bridge to the picturesque island and fishing village of Santa Catalina. Accommodations are limited and most visitors to Providencia stay at the pensions at Bahía de Agua Dulce (Sweet Water Bay) — see *Best en Route.*

Next, return to Cartagena, where you can pick up the highway route or continue by jet up to Barranquilla, Colombia's number one port, at the mouth of the Río Magdalena.

**BARRANQUILLA:** Unless you're a quiet introvert who can't stand crowds, you're going to love the madness, mayhem, and assorted carryings-on that accompany this city's best-known and best-loved fiesta, *Carnaval*. Colombia's major port, 8 miles (13 km) from the Caribbean on the west bank of the Magdalena, goes wild during the 4-day festival, calling itself *Ciudad Loca* (Crazy City) with puffed-up pride. After all, not only do the city's 1 million inhabitants disguise themselves and roam the noisy, music-filled streets, but a lot of other people from neighboring Caribbean towns stagger in for the fun, as do the hard-core celebrants from Bogotá. Everyone, it seems, stages balls; every neighborhood schedules at least one parade filled with flower-decked floats. Water bombs blast passersby, and wandering, inebriated groups go from door to door in search of more rum and *aguardiente*. If you're invited to join a *parranda* (revel), go along and don't ask questions; after all, *Carnaval* is the equivalent of an adult's mischief night, so ease your conscience and have some fun — everyone else does.

The rest of the year, skip Barranquilla. Founded in 1629, it is an industrial city that produces textiles, glassware, perfume, beer, and ships. There really is little to do here but visit the colonial cathedral (Plaza Bolívar), wander through Parque 11 de Noviembre, and look around the interesting port zone. If you are driving, beware of the roads. They suffer from years of neglect.

The tourist office, should you need it, is at 75-45 Carrera 54 (phone: 58-57378).

**En Route from Barranquilla** – Leaving the city, head up coastal highway Route 2 north to Santa Marta, crossing the long bridge over the Río Magdalena. On the far side, you will enter Ciénaga Grande (Great Marsh) National Park, a startling and sad example of ecological devastation. When the coastal road was built, engineers were unaware that they were altering the mix of salt and fresh waters in the marsh; the road destroyed the park, and now acres of dead trees stand in the ruins of what was once home for sea birds, turtles, alligators, and howler monkeys.

Beyond this park, the land revives, and the desolation is replaced by beautiful Caribbean beaches. Forty miles (64 km) north of Barranquilla is Ciénaga, a small agricultural town of 68,000 people that produces bananas, cotton, and cocoa. Eighteen miles (29 km) beyond Ciénaga is Santa Marta and the jagged spur of the Sierra Nevada that juts out of the Caribbean coastline.

**SANTA MARTA:** The sight of a snow-capped, 16,420-foot Cordillera rising out of the ocean will probably astound you the way it did conquistador Rodrigo de Bastidas, who founded this first settlement in Colombia in 1525. When the Spaniards landed on Colombia's Caribbean Coast, they found a widespread network of more than 300 Tairona Indian villages, built on a series of circular stone platforms and interconnected by a system of stone roads that led into the Sierra Nevada. Today, the Tairona are considered to have been master ecologists who developed a means of land preservation that allowed them to farm the mountain slopes and to successfully reuse the land year after year. It is estimated that a total of 700,000 Tairona inhabited the region at the time of its conquest.

Although the Spaniards' search for gold left little room for appreciation of the highly advanced culture of the Tairona, the Indians' culture did not go unnoted. Brother Pedro Simón, one of the chroniclers of the conquest, wrote: "And if there is an earthly paradise in these lands of the Indians, this must indeed be it . . . Everywhere around is crowned with high peaks . . . slopes and mountains covered by populous towns of Indians, all of which could be seen from all sides with their slopes and pleasing views." He also spoke of the cities' "cleanliness and neatness, as shown in their courts paved with very large, dressed stones . . . and also in their paths made of slabs." Nonetheless, by the early 17th century the Tairona had been decimated and all that remains of their world are the ruins of cities, only now being unearthed, and the words of the chroniclers — once considered fantasy, but now understood as fact.

Eleven years after the arrival of Rodrigo de Bastidas, fellow Spaniard Gonzalo Jiménez de Quesada set off from here into the interior in his search for the mythical El Dorado. Later, the blue-watered harbor became the final resting ground of Simón Bolívar, who died in 1830 at the age of 47 at nearby Quinta San Pedro Alejandrino.

Today, Santa Marta (pop. 350,000) has some fine colonial buildings, but they're not as well preserved as those in Cartagena. Quinta San Pedro Alejandrino, where Bolívar died penniless and disillusioned with the collapse of his dream of a Gran Federación, sits on a road 2½ miles (4 km) north of the city, and today houses a museum dedicated to the Great Liberator. His body was kept in the town's cathedral for 30 years before it was removed to Caracas, but his heart remained in Santa Marta, at the request of the townspeople, in a leaden casket that mysteriously disappeared when the artifacts kept in the cathedral were salvaged during a fire in 1872.

Visitors usually go to Santa Marta not so much for the city as for the recreational pleasures available in its environs; these range from beachcombing, fishing, and scuba diving, to trekking in the Tairona National Park or into the Sierra Nevada. The park is less than an hour from the city by car, its beach is undeveloped, and camping is available.

The nightlife in Santa Marta is subdued. There is one casino at the *Tamacá Inn* at El Rodadero. The *cumbia,* Colombia's alternative to the rumba, originated here. The best time to see the dance — and try it yourself — is during the pre-*Lenten Carnaval,* Columbia's *Independence Day* (July 20), or the *Festival of the Sea* in July.

Within 25 miles of the coast, the snow-capped peaks of the Sierra Nevada soar to more than 17,800 feet, with Pico Colón and Pico Bolívar, the highest mountains in Colombia, rising above all others. The most impressive Tairona site, called Ciudad Perdida (the Lost City), is located along a lush mountain ridge at about 3,000 feet but is not accessible by road.

A rugged jaunt into the Sierra Nevada can afford opportunities to glimpse the jaguars, pumas, howler monkeys, and brightly colored parrots that live in the dense forests. The Sierra sits at the foot of the bleak, black *páramos* that precede the snow-capped peaks. You also can take a 20-mile (32-km) ride northeast of Santa Marta on Route 2 into Tairona National Park, an area on the beach that has been left in its virgin state. A more adventurous and rugged excursion climbs high into the Sierra Nevada, once the home of the Tairona Indians. Another possibility for exploration are the guided 5-day hikes available through a hotel called *La Ballena Azul* (The Blue Whale), which is located in the fishing village of Taganga, near Santa Marta. *La Ballena Azul* is a treat in itself, operated by a Quijote-inspired Frenchwoman. For information on the hikes, or for reservations at the restaurant and hotel, contact *La Ballena Azul,* 799 Apartada Aereo, Santa Marta, Colombia (phone: 54-33987).

From El Rodadero you can charter a boat for $15 an hour, or $30 daily, and go out for sailfish, wahoo, kingfish, amberjack, or red snapper. The boats are rented from Captain Ospina at his beachstand. If you'd prefer to skip the fishing, the jolly skipper will be happy to take you on a half-day driving tour through the vast Tairona National Park or into the Sierra Nevada.

Shopping is not one of Santa Marta's strong points, but *El Cocodrilo* in the downtown area sells soapstone statuettes of Tairona gods, chiefs, and animals, along with other Colombian crafts.

There are two tourist offices in Santa Marta (3-10 Calle 10; phone: 54-27291, and 16-44 Carrera 2; phone: 54-35773).

**En Route from Santa Marta** – You can continue your Colombian excursion in one of two directions. The first way is to backtrack to Ciénaga and Barranquilla, where you either can hop a plane to Bogotá or can take Route 11 east to Route 61, continue southeast on Route 51 via Pamplona, then pick up Route 71, alias the Simón Bolívar Highway, alias the Pan-American Highway (all to be discussed in *Riohacha to Villa de Leyva).* But if you take this route, you're missing a trip around the northern Caribbean Coast and the semiarid Guajira Peninsula, a weird, definitely romantic spot with its own Indians, beaches, and history. If you're in the mood for a little adventure — and possibly a lot of problems — delay your flight to Bogotá for a few days, and head north along the coast, where the first stop will be Riohacha, capital of the Department of La Guajira.

# BEST EN ROUTE

Rates for a double room in this part of Colombia range from $60 to $80 at hotels listed in the expensive category, $50 to $60 at places listed in the moderate category, and $20 to $30 at places in the inexpensive category. In Cartagena, the expensive range is $60 to $80; and keep in mind that rates go up at least 25% during *Carnaval* and during the high season (December 20 through January 31) — for everybody, not just tourists. (The exception is the *Cartagena Hilton International*, whose prices can rise to over $100 for a double room during the high season.) On Providencia, the inexpensive rooms are $12 or under. Most of the hotels have telephone numbers; however, it's better to write or make arrangements through a travel agent or the local tourist office, since phone connections from the US to Colombia frequently are bad. Once you're at the hotel, don't forget to keep an eye on personal belongings, and to check valuables in the hotel safe. Keep in mind that many hotels on Colombia's Caribbean Coast do not have hot water showers, and some don't have air conditioning.

## CARTAGENA

**Capilla del Mar** – This 198-room property offers a French restaurant, a coffee shop, disco, meeting facilities, and TV sets in the guestrooms. 18-59 Carrera 1 (phone: 53-651140 or 53-653866). Expensive.

**Caribe** – This traditional Cartagena hotel, built in 1939, was renovated a few years ago and now boasts a total of 361 rooms. Convenient to town and across the street from the beach, its amenities include a lush garden, Olympic-size pool, poolside restaurant, gym, and a variety of shops. 2-87 Carrera 1 (phone: 53-650155). Expensive.

**Cartagena Hilton International** – The city's best, with 289 rooms with balconies, 2 pools, 3 tennis courts, and a good, if small, beach. El Laguito, Boca Grande (phone: reservations in the US, 800-445-8667; in Cartagena, 53-650666 or 53-654657). Expensive.

**Don Blas** – Nearest of the "strip" hotels to the Old City. The rooms have balconies with views. 10 Carrera 10 near Capilla del Mar (phone: 53-665-4400). Expensive to moderate.

**Las Velas** – Set right on the beach, with a pool and rooftop bar. It has 100 rooms, with air conditioning and private baths; suites come with kitchenettes. 1-160 Calle 1 (phone: 53-665000). Expensive to moderate.

**Barlovento** – Close to the beach, it has 48 rooms with air conditioning, a bar, pool, and restaurant. 6-23 Carrera 3 (phone: 53-653965). Moderate.

**El Dorado** – A high-rise beachfront property favored by Colombians, it recently underwent an expansion which added another 206 rooms, in a separate annex, to the existing 326. There also is a restaurant. 4-41 Av. San Martín (phone: 53-650914 and 53-650752; fax: 53-650479). Inexpensive.

## SAN ANDRÉS

**El Aquarium** – A delightful spot, with 112 rooms constructed on pilings over the water. Also good food (phone: 811-26923). Expensive.

**Royal Abacoa** – Two wings with a total of 74 rooms: The newer wing has air conditioning; the older one doesn't. All rooms, however, are doubles with baths, and there's a restaurant with nightly entertainment and a casino. Av. Colombia (phone: 811-24044). Expensive to moderate.

**Los Delfines** – Features 26 suites with kitchenettes, air conditioning, TV sets, and balconies. A swimming pool, good dining room, and probably the friendliest service on the island round out the amenities. Av. Colombia (phone: 811-24083). Moderate.

**El Dorado** – The 66 bungalows here have fans and no hot water; a casino and restaurant also are on the property. 1A-25 Av. Colombia (phone: 811-24155). Moderate.

**Isleño** – Air conditioning and hot water are available at this 47-room property. The front desk will arrange passage to Providencia upon request. 5-117 Av. La Playa (phone: 811-23991/2). Moderate.

***Malibú*** – This 22-unit hotel provides air conditioning, hot water, and a restaurant. 4-65 Av. Nicaragua (phone: 811-24342). Moderate to inexpensive.

## PROVIDENCIA

Reservations for the following establishments on Providencia may be made on San Andrés.

***Aqua Dulce*** – The front rooms look out onto Sweet Water Bay. Agua Dulce (phone: 811-48160). Inexpensive.

***Cabañas El Recreo*** – Clean, simple accommodations. Located on Sweet Water Bay. Cabañas de Recreo (phone: 811-48010). Inexpensive.

***Posada del Mar*** – A well-kept, 8-room establishment — the best on the island — surrounded by lush vegetation and just a short walk from the beach. A restaurant adjoins the courtyard. Posada del Mar (phone: 811-48168). Inexpensive.

## BARRANQUILLA

***El Prado*** – A large suburban hotel, it has 171 rooms (single and double), a nightclub, swimming pool, and tennis courts. 70-10 Carrera 54 (phone: 58-456533). Expensive.

***Cadebia*** – Barranquilla's most elegant, with 110 very large rooms, color TV sets, conference rooms, supper club, pool, shops, and a casino. 41D-79 Calle 75 (phone: 58-456144). Expensive to moderate.

***Royal Lebolo*** – In the El Prado area, it has 74 rooms, a bar, pool, restaurant, and disco. 68-124 Carrera 54 (phone: 58-457500). Expensive to moderate.

***Caribana*** – This 170-room centrally located property offers reasonable singles and doubles, including private baths and occasionally hot water. 40-02 Carrera 41 (phone: 58-414277). Moderate.

## TAIRONA NATIONAL PARK

Campgrounds are available with hot water, electricity, and a restaurant. Huts can be reserved by calling *INDERENA,* Colombia's government environmental agency (phone: in Bogotá, 1-284-1700 or 1-284-8029).

## SANTA MARTA

***Irotama*** – The 130 cottage-type units have single and double rooms, air conditioning, living and dining rooms. There's also a restaurant. At Km 14 on Rte. 2 (phone: 54-237140). Expensive to moderate.

***Santamar*** – A plush resort hotel with 105 air conditioned rooms, 3 pools, 2 restaurants, a grill, a coffee shop, and 24-hour room service. Located next to the *Convention Center.* Vía a Rodadero, Pozos Colorados, Apto. 5056 (phone: 54-237098). Expensive to moderate.

***La Sierra*** – With 75 air conditioned rooms and hot water, plus a seafood restaurant and bar. At El Rodadero (phone: 54-227960). Moderate.

***Sompallón*** – A simple place with 14 rooms, no air conditioning, but with a good restaurant. 10B-57 Carrera 1, El Rodadero (phone: 54-237195). Moderate.

***Tamacá Inn*** – Single and double rooms (a total of 86), a swimming pool, casino, dining rooms, and coffee shop are offered here. 11A-98 Carrera 2, El Rodadero (phone: 54-227015). Moderate.

# Riohacha to Villa de Leyva

*Some of the routes described in this section lie within areas described as dangerous for travelers by the US State Department. Check with its travel advisory service (202-647-5225) or with the US Embassy in Bogotá (1-285-1300, ext. 206 or 215) before making any overland journey.*

Rimmed by the Caribbean and blessed with groves of graceful coconut palms, the highway east of Santa Marta to the Venezuela border belies its gentle appearance: Only rugged, risk-loving (and, frankly, irresponsible) travelers should venture on this course into the Guajira Desert. The isolated area, favored for smuggling cocaine, marijuana, and other contraband that includes emeralds, cattle, and electrical appliances, has been transformed into a battlefield between warring smugglers and local authorities. Police constantly patrol the border and the entire desert; even the Caribbean Sea is watched by the Colombian and US navies on the lookout for any ships ferrying illegal cargo up to Panama and the eastern US coast. For this reason, the police are edgy, nervous, and highly suspicious. If that's not enough, two other potentially dangerous groups also are in the region: leftist guerrillas and bands of disenchanted Guajira Indians. At best, the Guajira is like the rugged Old (US) West; at worst, it's like the front lines of a war zone.

You can avoid this route and travel from Santa Marta back to Barranquilla, taking the Barranquilla-Bogotá highway southeast to Bogotá, then reverse the route described below and travel from Bogotá to Villa de Leyva. The diehard traveler, however, will continue along Route 2 through Riohacha, capital of the Department of La Guajira, east across the desert to Maicao and Cúcuta.

En route through the desert, the traveler will see the nomadic Guajira Indians on the roadside. The women wear billowy, colorful gowns that reach to their feet, and some also paint their faces black below the eyes. Upon first glimpse, you might think that you've somehow been magically transported to an Arab land. Small, open-sided thatch huts along the desert roadside mark places where the Guajira sell soft drinks or beer. When you stop at one of these stands, be sensitive to the fact that the Guajira are camera shy; don't take any photographs without first getting permission.

Also, don't stop near any gathering of more than two or three people. The Guajira have attacked and robbed outsiders, assuming that they were associated with the large-scale coal mining operation that has come to the area. Although this mining operation has brought some menial jobs for the Guajira, it also has altered their way of life and resulted in occasional hostilities. The coal mine, known as Cerrejon Norte, is owned by Colombia, but is managed by Exxon, and about 150 Americans reside in this desolate and dangerous region. In an effort to overcome the social problems, Exxon recently helped start an Indian-controlled textile and crafts cooperative in Riohacha. The colorful fabrics made by the women at the cooperative factory are now being exported. In addition, a fishing project aimed at improving equipment and productivity has been established.

A unique sight along the road are the colorful, painted billboards bearing messages in both Spanish and Guajira. These messages usually are warnings to the local residents not to graze their sheep on the railroad tracks.

Entering the area that is near the Venezuelan border, the route ascends steadily up into the mountainous range of the Cordillera Oriental, the Andean ridge that continues through Colombia south to the Ecuador border. Encompassed in the Cordillera's *páramos* are the coffee-, oil-, and emerald-rich departments of Norte de Santander and Santander, named after Colombia's revolutionary hero, General Francisco de Paula Santander. The route winds down these departments by a number of good highways that intertwine with the Pan-American (Route 71) — through the Santander capital of Bucaramanga, where you can sample the local delicacies of fried and jellied ants, on through Boyacá, a rich historical department. In the Battle of Boyacá Bridge in 1819, the forces of Simón Bolívar were victorious over the royalist troops, thus defeating Spain's last attempt to hold Colombia. Set high in the Cordillera at 9,000 feet, Tunja was once the home of one of the Muisca chieftains who was annually initiated in ceremonies that produced the legend of El Dorado. The route from Tunja goes south to the small market villages of Chiquinquirá and Ráquira, through the Candelaria Desert, and into Villa de Leyva, an exquisitely preserved, colonial town. The whole lovely province of Boyacá can be visited easily by car or local bus from Bogotá.

**RIOHACHA:** Once the pearling center of Colombia, this port of 104,000 did not escape the licks of Francis Drake when he ravaged Santa Marta, 104 miles (166 km) to the east, in 1586. Today, the pearlers have all but disappeared, and Riohacha's role is that of a seaport and fishing town on the fringe of the semiarid peninsula. The temperature rarely dips below 90 to 95F (32 to 35C), and the dry, listless land is laced with occasional palm and almond trees.

The Guajira Indians basically keep to themselves by farming or raising cattle and goat. They used to be housekeepers and servants for the colonists on the peninsula, and some intermarried with the Spaniards. Living in white, thatch-roofed houses, they are known for their textile crafts, including the women's loose flowing dress, the *manta guajira,* as well as bright belts, sashes, and bags that can be purchased in the Indian market at Riohacha.

Other than wander through the town or play on the white sand beach, there isn't much to do in Riohacha.

**En Route from Riohacha** – Route 2 leads east some 40 miles (64 km) to the small town of Maicao, near the Venezuelan border. At least three and a half times the size of Riohacha, Maicao's numbers are inflated by approximately 10,000 citizens whose sole occupation is smuggling. Contraband goods are ferried in and out of Colombia. This is a rugged, really sleazy town that should be glanced at, gulped at, and gotten out of — or better yet, avoided. Before leaving, however, check out the legal Guajira market and try some of the local dishes, like *friche* (goat) and fish stew. If you're interested in crossing the border into Venezuela, do so legally by obtaining a visa (either in Cartagena or Barranquilla) and an exit stamp from Colombia and an entry stamp into Venezuela.

From Maicao, follow Route 167 southwest for 90 miles (144 km) to Valledupar; the highway turns into Route 51 and proceeds another 155 miles (248 km) until you reach the junction of a paved road that heads east some 110 miles (176 km) to the frontier town of Cúcuta.

**CÚCUTA:** This city of 600,000 and capital of the Department of Norte de Santander is another smugglers' hangout. Founded in 1724, Simón Bolívar passed through during his 1813 campaign, and a statue marks the spot where he addressed his soldiers. Most of the colonial buildings were destroyed by an earthquake in 1875, so many of the buildings are modern.

From Cúcuta, either travel northeast into Venezuela (get the necessary exit stamp at the immigration office, Av. S and Calle 15) or drive south along the Pan-American Highway — known here as Route 71 — some 42 miles (67 km) to Pamplona.

**PAMPLONA:** Unlike Cúcuta, this town of 50,000 is chilly, with temperatures hovering constantly around 48F (9C). Most of Pamplona's colonial buildings also were wiped out in the 1875 earthquake, although the former monasteries of San Agustín, San Francisco, and Santo Domingo are still intact. The recently restored cathedral is a colonial jewel.

From Pamplona, there are two routes to follow down to Tunja. One continues on the Pan-American Highway, passing through the small towns of Concepción, Málaga, and Capitanejo; Route 61 west, however, is better, continuing south through Chitagá to Bucaramanga, the next stop.

**BUCARAMANGA:** The capital of Santander, this city of 600,000 was founded in 1622 by a member of the party of the German explorer Nicolás Federmann, although this fact doesn't actually explain the local perchant for eating fried and jellied ants. An archaeological museum, where Bolívar lived for 2 months during his 1813 campaign, now houses pre-Columbian pottery and other artifacts.

Bucaramanga has an airport, and there are flights back to Bogotá; buses for the 9-hour trip also are available. It also has a tourist office, at the corner of Carrera 19 and Calle 35 (phone: 76-424366 or 76-338461).

**En Route from Bucaramanga** – Continuing south on Route 61, you'll pass Aratoca, a colonial town that looks the way it did during the settlement period. San Gil is 14 miles (22 km) south. The weather gets warmer as you head into the Central Valley in the Department of Boyacá: San Gil and Socorro and Barbosa are in fruit- and coffee-producing areas.

From here, continue south on Route 61 until it merges with the Pan-American Highway (Route 71) and leads to Tunja.

**TUNJA:** Only 90 miles (144 km) north of Bogotá, this was once the home of one of the two legendary Muisca kings, the Zaque, renowned for the legend of El Dorado. Settled by the Spanish in 1539, this city of 150,000 is a chilly one when the harsh Cordillera winds blow through its avenues filled with white colonial haciendas, stone churches, and tree-filled plazas.

Although the outskirts of Tunja are not impressive, the center retains the colonial elegance it had when it was founded by Captain Suárez Rendón, and many of the original 16th-century mansions and cathedrals are intact or are undergoing restoration. Many of the houses' façades still contain the carved coats of arms of their conquistador owners and are open to the public for small admission fees (about 25¢). Rendón mansion, across from Plaza de Bolívar (open daily from 8:30 AM to 6 PM, with 2 hours off for siesta, beginning at noon), contains vivid gold- and red-frescoed ceilings in the second-floor salons that overlook an enclosed courtyard filled with red geraniums. The mansion of Don Juan de Vargas (Calle 20), the oldest son of the first governor general, Don Diego de Vargas, also has elegant frescoes of red, gold, and blue (open from 8:30 AM to 6 PM; closed between 12:30 and 2:30 PM). The mansion of Don Juan de Castillanos, a major poet of the 16th century, is also worth seeing (Calle 1).

Tunja's churches are as lavish as its mansions. The cathedral (Plaza de Bolívar), was built between 1576 and 1607 and contains a very splendid gold, rococo repository. Built in 1574, the Santa Clara convent (Calle 19) was a former mansion whose paneled roof is typical of Sevillan churches from that period. Next to the convent choir is the cell of Sister Francisca Josefa, a famous writer and mystic known as the Colombian St. Theresa.

Tunja's Indian market — held Tuesdays and Saturdays — is a colorful hodge-podge stretching for blocks around the main market building. Look for especially good buys on ponchos *(ruanas)*.

The capital of the Department of Boyacá, Tunja was one of the first Colombian cities to declare war against Spain during the battle for independence. Plaza de Bolívar contains a statue of Simón Bolívar, who stayed in the nearby Holguín Maldonado

House (now the private *Club Boyacá*) when he came here prior to the Battle of Boyacá. Visits are allowed only with permission of the club's manager. The office of the national tourist board, on the central square, can assist in obtaining this permission.

You'll want to drive north through the city to the Teacher's College and Donato's Well. According to Muisca legend, the well was formed after Chief Unzahue fell in love with his sister and they ran away together. When they returned some months later, the daughter got into a dispute with her mother, who gave her a good wallop, knocking over *chicha* she was mixing with a wooden spoon. The spilled corn beer formed the pond, which the Muisca believed was bottomless. Don't drink its water, though, since you're likely to walk away with a case of Muisca Mama's Revenge. A few miles west of the city is Los Cojines (The Pillows), a 60-foot semicircle hewn out of rocks, used by the Chibcha chieftains in their homage to the sun god. The stone throne was used by the priest officiating at the rite.

Both bus and car service are available from Tunja south to Bogotá for about $5 (bus) or $12 (car). Or delay continuing to the capital and take a short side trip 50 miles (80 km) along a paved road to Lake Sochagota, where you can swim, fish, sail, and water ski. Also, there is a good Indian market and *Archaeological Museum* at Sogamoso. If you make this side trip, be sure to include a visit to two quiet colonial villages, Tópaga and Monguí, and to Lake Tota, high in the mountains, for a lunch of freshly caught trout. The *Don Lucho* restaurant in Aquitania is highly recommended. There are good accommodations in both Tota and Duitama, down the road (see *Best en Route*). It's necessary to return to Tunja, however, before proceeding to Villa de Leyva.

**En Route from Tunja** – Continuing south along the Pan-American, you come next to Puente de Boyacá, where, on August 6, 1819, Bolívar defeated the royalists during the Battle of Boyacá. From here, continue on an unpaved road west to Villa de Leyva, or backtrack through Tunja for the 45-minute drive to Villa de Leyva on a paved road. A more attractive alternative, however, is to take the unpaved road west past Lake Fúquene to the craft market town of Chiquinquirá, where green-glazed earthenware as well as *tagua* (ivory-type) figurines are sold. The town also holds two important religious celebrations: October 7 is the *Feast Day of the Virgin of Chiquinquirá*, patroness of Colombia; December 8 is the *Feast of the Immaculate Conception*. On both occasions, pilgrims flock to the cathedral on their knees to pay their respects and hear mass.

From Chiquinquirá, continue west along this unpaved road to Ráquira, another market town, this one renowned for its ceramics. The area around Villa de Leyva, the Candelaria Desert, is named after the Candelaria convent founded in 1604 by Friar Mateo Delgado, which is a short distance past Ráquira. The church, now a historic monument, contains many paintings from the 17th century and is open to the public daily, from 8 AM to noon and from 2 to 6 PM. The Candelaria may be the most fertile desert in the world; it was once a vast sea of which Lake Maracaibo is all that remains. A rich, olive-growing basin where the temperature never exceeds 65F (18C), it is surrounded by barren, fossil-filled mountains. Located outside Villa de Leyva is a fossil of a 15-foot-long prehistoric marine reptile. To find it, follow signs for "El Fósil."

**VILLA DE LEYVA:** Founded in 1572, this town was the home of several Colombian patriots, including Antonio Nariño, who helped start the independence movement when he translated the French declaration, *The Rights of Man,* into Spanish in 1794. His home — open to the public daily, except Mondays, from 8 AM to noon and from 2 to 6 PM — contains colonial memorabilia. It's also possible to visit the Iglesia Mayor, the 16th-century manor house where Colombia's first Congress met in 1812.

If there is only one place you visit in Boyacá, make it Villa de Leyva. The whitewashed houses and cobblestone streets are a colonial treasure, the stone plaza at the center of Villa de Leyva the largest in the country. The area is known for its fossils, and many are imbedded in the walls of buildings. One "fossil" that gives the town an ironic air is the carved Spanish coat of arms that is over the main entrance to the Royal Distillery. The still is gone and so are the royalists; today the building houses a small museum (open daily, except Sundays, from 8 AM to noon and 2 to 6 PM). Another convent, Santo Ecce Homo, was founded in 1620 by the Dominicans. It is worth a visit for its adobe and stone Andean-type architecture.

**En Route from Villa de Leyva** – It's necessary to backtrack to the Pan-American Highway to reach the outskirts of Bogotá, where you'll pick up Route 1 northwest to Manizales, a drive that leads through Colombia's more fertile region, the Magdalena Valley.

## BEST EN ROUTE

Most of the hotels on this route are small and simple (some lack private baths and hot water), but clean, comfortable, and very moderately priced, with double room rates of no more than $25 at a hotel listed in the moderate category, and many under $15 for a hotel listed in the inexpensive category, except in the province of Boyacá, where rates can go as high as $60 for accommodations in the expensive range. While not necessary, it's still a good idea to call ahead for reservations, especially on weekends and holidays. There are lovely country inns in old colonial homes in the Boyacá region; in Paipa, considered to be the tourist center of Boyacá, there are 2,500 hotel rooms. Some of the hotels have offices in Bogotá, so you can call there rather than risk poor connections in the smaller towns. Try not to linger in Riohacha or Cúcuta because of the contraband and drug problem, and remember to avoid irritating the police.

### RIOHACHA

*Gimaura* – Breakfast and clean, beachfront accommodations are offered at this 36-room hotel. Av. La Playa (phone: 56-72266). Inexpensive.

### CÚCUTA

*Arizona* – Modern, with 69 air conditioned rooms. 7-62 Av. O (phone: 75-731884). Moderate.

*Bolívar* – A swimming pool and comfortable accommodations are featured at this 141-room motel. Av. Demetrio Mendoza (phone: 75-743991). Moderate.

*Tonchalá* – This 208-room property has air conditioning, a pool, Turkish baths, and sauna. Calle 10 and Av. 0 (phone: 75-722005). Moderate.

*Villa Antigua del Rosario* – A clean hotel with 51 small rooms. Autopista San Antonio (phone: 75-742128). Inexpensive.

### PAMPLONA

*Cariongo* – Good service is provided at this quiet 32-room hostelry. 9-10 Carrera 5 (phone: 78-62645). Moderate.

### BUCARAMANGA

*Bucarica* – There are 72 refurbished rooms, a pool, and a restaurant. Calle 35 and Carrera 19 (phone: 76-423111 and 76-423114). Moderate.

*Chicamocha* – Offers 200 air conditioned rooms, pool, and TV sets. Its *Bar Cepitá* is decorated like a local farmhouse and is the place to try the area's delicacy, fried or jellied ants. 3124 Calle 34 (phone: 76-343000). Moderate.

*San Juan de Girón* – Clean, this 80-room hotel has a swimming pool and restaurant. On the Autopista a Girón, at Km 6 (phone: 76-366430; in Bogotá, phone: 1-257-3311). Moderate.

*Andino* – Seventy-four rooms and good service. 18-44 Calle 34 (phone: 76-422142). Inexpensive.

## SAN GIL

***Bella Isla*** – A small hostelry with 71 pleasant double rooms, a restaurant, bar, cafeteria, and a swimming pool. On the road from Bogotá to Cúcuta. Contact the Bogotá office for reservations (phone: 1-257-3311). Inexpensive.

## BOYACA

Reservations for recommended hotels in the area can be made by contacting *Boyacá Servicios Hoteleros,* 77-90 Carrera 15, in Bogotá (phone: 1-218-0321).

## TUNJA

***Hunza*** – A comfortable hotel with 53 rooms, a swimming pool, and Turkish baths. 10-66 Calle 21-A (phone: 87-424120; in Bogotá, 1-283-2200). Moderate.

***Centenario*** – This 29-room property has a restaurant. 16-81 Calle 10 (phone: 792-2271). Inexpensive.

## PAIPA/LAKE SOCHAGOTA

***Estelar Paipa and Centro de Convenciones*** – The place has 105 rooms, a pool, thermal baths, a convention center with a 1,000-person capacity, and a striking view of the lake (phone: 987-850944; in Bogotá, 1-232-8250). Expensive.

***Sochagota*** – A 58-room hotel with a hot-mineral-water swimming pool, convention facilities, and a helpful, friendly staff. Lakeside (phone: 987-850012 or 987-850013; in Bogotá, 1-217-6200). Moderate.

***Casona del Salitre*** – Rustic, charming, but basic, this converted hacienda with 12 rooms is the place where Bolívar stayed after the Battle of Bogotá. Salida al Pantano (phone: 987-850012). Inexpensive.

***Panorama*** – A total of 32 rooms, with pool, thermal baths, sauna, and spa. The decor is definitely of the plastic persuasion, but it is a good buy (phone: in Bogotá, 1-235-8976). Inexpensive.

## TOTA

***Pozo Azul*** – A beautiful and romantic property with a perfect view of the lake. There are 20 guestrooms, and the lobby boasts a huge circular fireplace that adds to the coziness of this mountain retreat. Four cabins with fireplaces also are available. Boat rentals can be found at the lake. Lakeside on the Laguna de Tota (phone: in Bogotá, 1-218-0321). Moderate.

***Rocaslindas*** – Offers 14 rooms on the edge of the lake; fresh trout is a specialty of the dining room. The temperatures at 9,000 feet are nippy, and in the evenings you'll be grateful for the roaring fire in the lounge and the handwoven blankets on the beds (phone: in Sogamosa, 87-2245; in Bogotá, 1-258-8563). Moderate.

## DUITAMA

***San Luis de Ucuengá*** – An old converted farmhouse with 22 rooms, surrounded by breathtakingly beautiful rose gardens. Family owned and run, with good food and a peaceful atmosphere (phone: 87-603260; in Bogotá, 1-218-0376). Moderate.

## VILLA DE LEYVA

***Hostería el Molino la Mesopotamia*** – A restored old mill that has 28 rooms with bath and telephones, a restaurant, swimming pool, and great atmosphere. 6-33 Calle del Silencio 117 (phone: in Bogotá, 1-213-3491). Expensive.

***Duruelo Hospederia*** – A picturesque 66-room Swiss-style hotel that overlooks the city. Its Carmelite-priest owners take fine care of the facilities, and the adjacent restaurant serves large portions of meals typical of the region (phone: in Bogotá, 1-288-1488). Moderate.

***Mesón de la Plaza Mayor*** – Right on the main square, this 14-room hotel is in an ancient building. Huge rooms, boiling hot water, and delicious food make guests feel right at home (phone: in Bogotá, 1-236-2177). Inexpensive.

# Bogotá to Medellín

*Many of the areas described in this route have been designated as dangerous by the US State Department. They include the northwestern Cundinamarca department, eastern Caldas, and all of the Antioquia department, where the city of Medellín, headquarters of the infamous drug cartel, is located. The US Embassy in Bogotá advises that these areas should be avoided. For those travelers who persist, be forewarned.*

The next route through Colombia begins in the Tunja-Bogotá area of the Cordillera Oriental and travels through some of the country's most fertile valleys. One of these, the Magdalena, is wedged between the Eastern and Central Cordilleras and borders Río Magdalena, which flows 1,000 miles to the Caribbean Sea. Honda, once a principal port on the west bank of the river, is today the heart of the fruit-producing valley; its warm temperatures averaging 84F (29C) and mild rainfall are ideal for growing coconuts, papayas, and other tropical tidbits.

The trip from the valley over the jagged, snow-capped *páramos* of the Central Cordillera is breathtaking as well as chilly — about 30 degrees lower than in Honda. Above, the black and white Andean peaks fill the blue, cloud-laced sky; below stretches the valley and the river — a mere silver sliver wandering through the green orchards. Manizales straddles the Cordillera like a man with a leg caught in the mud: Its buildings stand on stilts, and their backs slope down, down, down into the mountainside. This is coffee-growing country. Small farms dot the area, their coffee beans ripening for harvest under the shade of trees planted for the sole purpose of protecting them from the strong equatorial sun.

Isolated deep in the heart of Colombia, this area had little involvement in the country's fight for independence, but its prominent department, Antioquia, was founded through curious circumstances. In the mid-17th century, a group of Jews from Bogotá came here to escape the onslaught of the Spanish Inquisition, which was intent on purifying members of the Roman Catholic church and persecuting anyone who was not. As time passed, the immigrants became excellent farmers, heavily propagating among themselves to strengthen their work force, refusing to own slaves, and building up a reputation as hard workers with successful businesses. A wave of migration into the southern section of central Colombia during the 19th century resulted in the formation of additional departments, including Caldas, Tolima, and Valle. Medellín, the Antioquian capital — though renowned as the orchid capital of the world — is also the home base of the infamous Medellín Cartel of drug traffickers. Be forewarned.

**En Route from Bogotá** – Start this phase of the journey by taking Route 1 west from Bogotá through Facatativá, a small town of 22,000 about 25 miles (40 km) from the capital. Here, visit the Piedras de Tunja, an amphitheater formed by stones; then continue west across the ridge until you overlook the wide chasm of the Magdalena Valley. From this point, the snows of the Nevado del Tolima and Nevado del Ruiz in the Central Cordillera are visible. The eruption in November 1985 of the latter resulted in an avalanche of melted snow and volcanic mud that destroyed the town of Armero and caused great loss of life and property damage. Descending into the valley, you come into the coffee belt, pass the small towns of Sasaima and Villeta, then cross the broad valley of Guaduas into the Magdalena Valley itself and Honda.

**HONDA:** Known as the city of bridges because 14 of them span the Río Magdalena, this was an important port until the start of the 20th century. Now it's primarily a fishing town, and a number of Bogotá residents and other Colombians flock here every February with their bait, rods, and tackle. They gather in numbers along the west bank of the river, playing and chatting in the warm weather like children playing hooky.

Honda also has some colonial buildings in its downtown area, including the El Rosario Church, Casa Consistorial, and Calle de las Trampas (Street of the Traps), built for defensive purposes.

**En Route from Honda** – The scenery in the Magdalena Valley is remarkable: Flat cotton fields broken by strangely eroded table mountains skirted with jungle growth. Heading west toward Manizales, you'll come to Mariquita, the valley's fruit-producing area, known for its mangoes, papayas, pineapples, and coconuts.

Leaving Mariquita, you enter the rest of the fruit-bearing region, stretched out along a number of gently rolling hills not unlike those of Kentucky. You reach the small town of Fresno, the first of a series of towns set into the mountains of the Cordillera Central.

The view from the Cordillera is great: Black, snow-capped *páramos* loom high above the green valley of sparkling river waters and ripe fruit orchards. The highest point of the highway is at 10,000-foot Páramo de Letras. A left turn north leads below the snowline of El Ruiz Mountain. From here, the route dips down the other side of the Cordillera into the Department of Caldas and its capital of Manizales.

**MANIZALES:** Sitting on the side of the Cordillera at 7,000 feet above sea level, this city's population of 400,000 dwells in 2-story buildings that stand on stilts, then slope backward into the mountains to become 3 and 4 stories tall. It is surprising to learn that all of these buildings are made out of concrete and stone, thanks to a local ordinance imposed after two separate fires virtually wiped out the entire city's wooden structures in the 19th century.

Founded in 1848 by peasants from Medellín, which is 164 miles (262 km) north, the largest industry here is coffee. Introduced in 1865, the beans thrive in the moist, 60F (16C) temperature and mild rainfall of the Cordillera and are grown mostly on the 8-acre farms owned by *campesiños* (peasants), who are exemplified in Colombian folklore by Juan Valdez. The National Federation of Coffee Growers runs an experimental farm in Chinchiná, 15 miles (24 km) outside Manizales; it is open to the public Mondays through Fridays. This small town also suffered considerable damage from the November 1985 eruption.

**En Route from Manizales** – From Manizales it's possible to go in one of two directions: Traveling south, you go through the Cauca Valley into the archaeological parks of San Agustín and Tierradentro (discussed in *Neiva to Cali,* below). Otherwise you can continue along Route 1 west toward Medellín, picking up the Pan-American Highway at Risaralda. There is heavy traffic on this route, which only recently was paved all of the way into the city. The road winds up the Alta de Minas Pass at 8,000 feet, then winds down over the Cordillera Central until it descends 5,000 feet into Medellín.

**MEDELLÍN:** This city of 2 million people, aptly nicknamed "the City of Flowers, Friendship, and Eternal Spring," is the orchid kingdom of the world; its mild temperatures of 70F (21C) and its rainfall are perfect for floral cultivation and for the growth of coffee beans on the slopes of the mountains. Medellín also ranks second to Bogotá in industrial importance, being a major manufacturer of textiles, pharmaceuticals, woodwork, metallurgical products, and rubber goods. Unfortunately, it is also renowned as the infamous hometown of the Colombian drug traffickers, known as the Medellín Cartel.

Founded in 1675, most of the settlers here were Jewish refugees seeking isolation and a chance to develop their own way of life without too much pressure from Spanish feudal overlords. Contrary to the pattern set by the conquerors who exploited slave and serf labor, the settlers did their own work. The few Indians in the area were primitive nomads who made poor agricultural laborers, and the settlers refused, on ethical grounds, to use black slave labor. The land was therefore divided into small, family-size farms; the *antioqueños,* as they are called, maintained an extremely high birthrate in order to increase the work force, and there was very little intermarriage with the Indians or blacks.

Medellín has a number of museums. *Museo de Antioquia* (Calle 52 at Carrera 53; phone: 40241-2710) contains paintings by local artists and Indian pottery; it is open, with an admission fee, Tuesdays through Fridays from 9 AM to 1 PM and 3 to 6 PM, Saturdays from 9 AM to 2 PM. Fernando Botero, Colombia's foremost painter/sculptor, donated 15 of his finest paintings and 24 sculptures to this museum, making it a *must* stop for anyone visiting Medellín. *Museo de Antropología,* on the campus of Antioquia University, contains pre-Columbian pottery; it is open Mondays through Fridays from 10 AM to noon and 2 to 6 PM; no admission charge. *Museo de Ciencias Naturales* (30-1 Calle 55), exhibits over 300 stuffed animals, birds, and insects from the area. The museum is closed to the public, but private tours can be arranged (phone 4-390417 for an appointment). *Museo El Castillo* (Loma los Balsos in El Poblado) contains a collection of European and American art, crystal, porcelain, and priceless rugs. It is in the former mansion of Don Diego Echevarría Missas, an entrepreneur, and is open weekdays from 9 AM to noon and 2 to 5 PM.

One place not to be passed up is the Jardín Botánica Joaquín Antonio Uribe (73-298 Carrera 52), where there is a collection of orchids under the Orquideorama, a pavilion designed for growing and maintaining this exotic flower. The gardens also house a replica of a colonial Antioquian village, an azalea patio, fern gardens, and aviaries. Open daily from 9 AM to 5:30 PM; admission is 15¢ for adults, 10¢ for children. On a visit to the Santa Fe Zoo (20-63 Carrera 52), you'll come face to face with South American apes, rare black jaguars, and the fierce, almost extinct Andean condor. Open daily from 9 AM to 5 PM; admission is 20¢. Cattle auctions are held here Tuesdays and Thursdays; admission charge.

There also are many colonial churches in Medellín. Basílica Metropolitana (56-44 Carrera 49) is a huge, 15,000-square-foot Romanesque structure, with a 3,478-flute organ and marble altars; Basílica de la Candelaria, built in 1766, is more moderate in style, displaying a gentler creole touch in the altar's silverwork. Iglesia de la Veracruz (Calle 51 at Carrera 52) is a 17th-century church with a stone façade surrounded by pillars and arches.

There is still one public place here that is off limits to women through a centuries-old custom: The European-Mediterranean sanctuary of the café is for men only, and while women travelers stomp their feet and pout outside, their male companions are welcome to wander inside, grab a cold beer or quaff a *tinto* (strong demitasse coffee served black) while having their shoes shined, and even can buy a ticket to the lottery. More obliging — and less sexist — are the numerous discos in the city, including *Carousel* (Centro Comercial San Diego), *El Infierno* (69-20 Calle 50), *Timaná* (71-190 Calle 50), and

*2002* (651-30 Calle 50), all of which are open until dawn. But for some real high life, don't miss *Kevin's* (phone: 4-249-3420), a vibrant mixture of restaurant, art gallery, disco, bar, and more. On a high hill near the *Inter-Continental Medellín,* its surrounding glass walls provide a panoramic view of the sparkling city lights (see *Best en Route*).

Downtown Medellín is a shopping complex in itself, and travelers can pick up a number of craft items, from the Antioquian *carriel,* a leather pouch used by both men and women, to the *ruana* (poncho) and other leather and woolen items. Flea markets also are reaching popular proportions here, especially the *Mercado Popular Los Toldos de San Alejo,* held in Bolívar Park on the first Saturday of every month; you can buy rare coins, antiques, Indian artifacts, and even exotic pets like ocelots and *pericos ligeros,* koala-like bears found in the high sierra. Even those not shopping will want to visit the *Villa Nueva Shopping Center,* which not long ago won an international architectural prize for its conversion from a staid old brick seminary to a modern shopping complex. One of the attractions is an excellent restaurant in what was once the chapel (Av. Oriental and Carerra 50). Called *The Chapel,* it has waiters dressed as monks and Gregorian chants for background music. Beverages other than holy water are, however, available.

Golf and tennis are available at Medellín's private clubs, so if you're a member of a club at home, bring along a letter from your home pro or club president requesting hospitality and reciprocity. One unusual game open to the public is the cockfight; it's legal throughout South America, although banned in the US. There are three cockfighting arenas in town: *Guadalajara* (89-49 Calle 52), *Cantaclara* (Carrera a Bello), and *Villa Julia* (11SA-45 Carrera 52). Fights are scheduled regularly; check the newspapers — but don't go unless you have a strong stomach.

The people of Antioquia are no somber lot. They love to party, and at least six major festivals are held in Medellín throughout the year. The *Feria de la Candelaria,* held in February, commemorates the feast of the city's patroness with bullfights and 8 days of parades and musical celebrations. It's an occasion to don Spanish Coroban hats and shawls. The *Festival del Tango* in June commemorates the death of Argentine singer Carlos Gardel, who was killed in an airplane crash at the Medellín airport in 1935. The city goes tango crazy, and everybody, from professionals to the bar drunks, tangos all day and all night. Antioquia's independence is celebrated in the *Desfile de los Silletros* (Parade of the Chair Carriers) in August; parades are filled with floats of orchids, carnations, and other flowers; there are bands, singers, horsemen, and the typical gathering of beauties for the trip. *Feria Colombiana de la Confección,* held in September, is a salute to the textile and garment industries. The *Festival del Recuerdo* is a "nostalgic" fete, commemorating the city's past, held at different times throughout the year. The *Christmas* holidays are celebrated from December 20 through January 7; everyone, it seems, comes to the mountains on vacation. Dinners are flavored with aniseed *aguardiente,* and parades take place around the city.

It's no secret that the infamous Medellín Cartel — Colombia's drug traffickers — has had a corrupting effect on the local youth. As in Barranquilla, Bogotá, and the other big cities, the professional pickpockets have a field day in Medellín, so watch your belongings. Don't wander into slum neighborhoods if you can avoid it; and try not to hail just any old cab in the city — use the green and off-white cars assigned to hotels or you may be taken for a real ride. If you're doing your own sightseeing, rent a car from *Hertz* (23-50 Carrera 43A; phone: 4-232-4864), where you can get a Renault or other make for about $40 a day, or $200 a week, plus mileage. Other rental car agencies are *Alqui-Car* (43-32 Calle 53; phone: 4-393281), and *Rent a Car* (49-50 Calle 58; phone: 4-254-5766).

If you need assistance, stop by the tourist office, 49-84 Calle 55 (phone: 4-254-0800).

Unlike some Colombian cities, there are a number of good restaurants in Medellín. On the menu at *La Posada de la Montaña* (16-22 Carrera 43B; phone: 4-231-8086) are local dishes including *arepas* (corn griddle cakes), *frijoles* (red beans cooked with pork), *mazamorra* (corn soup that's very thick), *patacones* (fried plantains), and *chorizos* (sausages). *La Res* (64-A51 Calle 50) specializes in barbecued kidneys and Argentine grilled steaks. Strangely enough, this city far from the coast boasts an excellent seafood restaurant, *Frutos del Mar* (11-61 Carrera 43B; phone: 4-266-5766).

Some side trips from Medellín include a ride to El Ranchito, 7 miles (11 km) south of Medellín on the Pan-American in the small town of Itaquí, which has over 50,000 orchids. About a mile (1.6 km) before El Ranchito is Envigado, a village where craftsmen still make the traditional *carriel* (belt pouch). Bello, 4 miles (7 km) north of Medellín up the Pan-American, houses the hut where Marco Fidel Suárez, President of Colombia from 1918 to 1922, was born. The hut is encased in glass to preserve it. If there's time, make a side trip (about 3 hours each way) down the mountainside to Santa Fe de Antioquia, on the banks of the Cauca river. Founded in 1541, this perfectly preserved colonial town takes you back to a time of cobbled streets and thick-walled houses surrounding flower-filled patios. This jaunt may be done as an all-day excursion, or there are pleasant accommodations at *Hostería Mariscal Robledo* and *Lago Tours* hotel (see *Best en Route*).

**En Route from Medellín** – For the next leg of the Cauca Valley adventure and the mysteries of San Agustín and Tierradentro, there are several choices. Either drive back to Manizales and Bogotá, or fly (*Avianca* has daily flights from the José María Córdova Airport, which is over an hour away from downtown Medellín). Another possibility is to drive directly from Medellín to semitropical Cali; the road is good and well paved.

## BEST EN ROUTE

As on the previous route, hotels in this part of Colombia are economical in small towns and reasonable in cities, with a double room ranging up to $85 at a place classified as expensive, $30 to $50 at a moderate place, and under $25 in an inexpensive place. Most of the hotels in larger cities have private baths and hot showers in double and single rooms; some have fairly good restaurants. Here, as everywhere else in Colombia, it's a good idea to make reservations beforehand and to check security at the hotel to make sure your belongings will be safe.

### HONDA

*Campestre Cabañas El Molino* – A 23-room hotel with cabins, 5 swimming pools, and a game room. Carretera a Manquita (phone: 8951-3165; in Bogotá, 1-235-2105). Inexpensive.

*Ondama* – This comfortable 58-room property has a swimming pool. Calle 16 and Carrera 13 (phone: 8951-3127). Inexpensive.

### MANIZALES

*Las Colinas* – Its 65 rooms are clean and comfortable. Carrera 22 between Calles 20 and 21 (phone: 68-842009). Moderate.

*Hostería Villa Kempis* – On the city's outskirts, this 35-room retreat is very quiet and provides a view of the city from its hillside site. Salida a Pereira, 19-22 Carrera 23 (phone: 68-32961). Inexpensive.

*Tama Internacional* – Next to the city's cathedral; 36 rooms. 22-43 Calle 23 (phone: 68-822273). Inexpensive.

### MEDELLÍN

*Inter-Continental* – The best in town, although outside the center, with 300 rooms, a bar, health club, tennis courts, dining room, and a Turkish bath. Variante Las Palmas (phone: 4-266-0680). Expensive.

***Amaru*** – Modern, with 91 air conditioned rooms, a good restaurant, a cozy bar, and a shopping arcade. 53-45 Carrera 50A (phone: 4-231-5311). Moderate.

***Gran*** – A 112-room hotel with a bar, a restaurant, and homey service. Set right downtown, it's popular with the executive crowd. 45-92 Calle 54 (phone: 4-251-9951). Moderate.

***Europa Normandie*** – Not too large, with 154 rooms (singles and doubles) with private baths, hot water, and large closets. Dining room. 49-100 Calle 53 (phone: 4-241-9920). Inexpensive.

***Nutibara*** – Overlooking the main park, this 90-room property offers deluxe single and double rooms, with tile baths and antique furniture. There's also a sidewalk café, nightclub, casino, and a restaurant serving T-bone steaks for under $3.50. 50-46 Calle 52A (phone: 4-231-9111). Inexpensive.

***Veracruz*** – Private baths and hot water are features of its 134 rooms; an open bar, restaurant, and swimming pool. 54-18 Carrera 50 (phone: 4-235-2250; fax: 4-231-8881). Inexpensive.

### SANTA FE DE ANTIOQUIA

***Lago Tours*** – Twenty minutes away from Santa Fe de Antioquia, this pleasant country place has 10 bungalows, each with a tree growing through its roof, and 15 regular rooms. There's a good dining room, a pool with a giant slide, a cock-fighting pit, a lake with all water sports, and a billiard room (phone: 41-62004; in Medellín, 1-232-3069). Moderate.

***Hostería Mariscal Robledo*** – Named for the founder of the town, with 37 big, high-ceiling rooms; an Olympic-size pool; and a surprisingly good dining room. A block away from the central square. Calle 10 and Carrera 12 (phone: 41-1609). Inexpensive.

# Neiva to Cali

*Some of the areas described in this route have been designated as dangerous by the US State Department and should be avoided. They include the departments of northwestern rural Huila and Valle del Cauca. The city of Cali, although home to one of the country's largest drug cartels, is in the "relatively safe" category, as are Neiva and Popayán. Again, travelers are forewarned.*

The next route south from Bogotá leads through the lower part of the Magdalena Valley into the humid Department of Huila and the archaeological zone of San Agustín National Park. The site of many mysterious stone monoliths of men, monsters, and beasts was left by an isolated culture that cropped up between 600 BC and AD 1200, then suddenly disappeared. Very little is known about who or what these people were, but the 30 or so sites unearthed by archaeologists have determined that the Indians were farmers who harvested corn, yucca, and peanuts. The men wore loincloths; the women, short skirts, and they adorned themselves with necklaces, bracelets, and pectorals. They were devoted to death rites, burying their dead in elaborate tombs and artificial mounds, according to their status within the society. They had a polytheistic religion, and strolling along the park's forest paths, you will come upon a host of gods, including monkeys (fertility), eagles (fire and light), and cats (the underworld). A similar mystery is Tierradentro, some

100 miles (160 km) northeast of San Agustín, where several underground chambers housing human bones have been discovered; these possibly relate to the one situated at San Agustín. Their similarities can be seen in the carvings embedded in the hypogeums (chambers).

It takes a few days to explore and enjoy these sites. The "fastest" way to reach them is to take a plane from Bogotá to Neiva, then drive for about 5 hours down a paved highway to San Agustín.

From there, continue a round-robin circuit that heads west over the Cordillera Central into the fertile Pubenza and Cauca valleys, a spring-like area where the 70F (21C) climate is good for farming. The northern section of the valley is green and wet enough to grow sugarcane; along the 84-mile (134-km) stretch of the Pan-American north from Popayán to Cali are bamboo and palm trees. Ducks, doves, and partridges fly in the blue skies, into which juts the 18,860-foot Nevado de Huila, a snow-capped, wintry contrast to the tropical scenery.

Some of the oldest Colombian cities are in this area, founded in the mid-16th century by conquistadores in their search for El Dorado: Popayán was the birthplace of a number of Colombian patriots; Cali, the most important city, is a large producer of sugar, rice, coffee, and cattle. This is the "hottest" nightlife spot and ranks in the number one position as Colombia's Sport City, with a huge, multistadia sports complex constructed for the *Pan-American Games* of 1971. Leaving Cali, either return to Bogotá by plane (25 minutes) or continue east by car to the capital, completing the surface route.

Along this route, like all others in Colombia, there are good and bad roads, hotels with and without baths and hot water, and poor to fine restaurants. Actually, be prepared for excellent to horrible in all three categories. If any assistance is needed along the way, contact the tourist offices in any of the major cities and at points of interest such as San Agustín National Park. Also remember that exchanging a car route for an air itinerary is probably in your favor, since Colombia's 24 private carriers provide better passage than its roads in most cases.

**NEIVA:** This city of 228,500 was founded in 1539 by Sebastián de Belalcázar, while en route to Bogotá from Popayán. The climate is a relatively warm 80F (26C), and the city is a major producer of coffee. Many holidays are celebrated here, including *Bambuco* (June 29–28), the national dance festival, which lures Colombians from every part of the country. Sandwiched into the event schedule are the June 20 *Feast of San Pedro y San Pablo* and the June 24 *Feast of San Juan.* On both days there are masses and religious processions, followed by the usual merrymaking, fireworks, and bullfights.

Neiva's airport, La Manguita, has flights to and from Bogotá. You also can catch a bus to the capital; the trip, however, takes about 6 hours.

**En Route from Neiva** – Proceeding to San Agustín National Park on Route 61 south, the highway leads toward the headwaters of the Río Magdalena. Along the way are a number of small, green valleys and towns that include Garzón and Pitalito, about 88 miles (141 km) south of Neiva. From here, drive into the town of San Agustín: The national park is 3 miles (5 km) away. It's a minimum 5-hour drive from Neiva.

**SAN AGUSTÍN NATIONAL PARK:** Hire a horse or jeep, or take the tour on foot, to spend at least a full 1 or 2 days wandering along the park's well-tended forest paths crossed by small silvery streams. At each turn is another delightful surprise. The monoliths and carvings stand randomly throughout the area, as though the original dwellers here left them for our amusement. Be sure to take a walk through the Bosque de las Estatuas (Forest of Statues). Here stands the carved statue of a lizard, eyes glaring, ready to flick its tongue; here is a carved man who looks more like a primitive baseball player than an Indian, clutching a long, batlike stick in his hands. Salamanders squiggle underfoot, and they, along with lizards and various wizened humans, scurry across the face of the *lavapatas,* the foot-washing fountain, a water-washed basin that was once a shrine dedicated to the water gods. Not far from the fountain on the path is a stone toad that seems to be pointing a finger at the fountain. Some 15 miles (24 km) away is the Salto de Bordones waterfall.

A short drive 19 miles (30 km) north of the park leads to the town of San José de Isnos, where the Alto de los Idolos site is covered with statues, coffins, and tombs decorated in red, black, and yellow. North of the area and near the same town is Alto de las Piedras, which contains monuments to the local fertility goddess. Northeast of here you can cross El Estrecho, a small wedge through which the Río Magdalena flows furiously.

San Agustín's inhabitants were believed to be preoccupied with death: Villagers were buried according to social rank; the greater their affluence, the more elaborate the tomb. Similar to the ancient Egyptian practice of entombing a dead pharaoh's wealth with him, the dead here also were buried with their jewels, chains, necklaces, and ceramics. There is a good map of the ruins and a guidebook available at the park entrance or at the tourist office in San Agustín at 11-41/45 Calle 3A.

**En Route from San Agustín** – From here, it is best to backtrack to Garzón before continuing to Tierradentro. Along the way are the small towns of Inzá and La Plata, where you'll find the Cascada Azufrada, a sulfurous waterfall. From La Plata, drive 40 minutes to San Andrés de Pisimbala, the central town of Tierradentro.

**TIERRADENTRO:** Literally "beneath the ground," this archaeological zone contains up to 200 burial chambers that house bones of still other, unidentified ancient inhabitants of the area. Like the monoliths of San Agustín, the hypogeums, or underground tombs, are carved with designs similar to those of the other statues, hinting that some type of Augustinian influence was felt here. Again, you can hire a horse or walk up steep inclines to the areas of interest.

The museum in San Andrés de Pisimbala, the center of the burial area, displays various ceramics discovered in the tombs. About 15 minutes from the museum is Segovia, the most prominent site in the area, with about 15 tombs. Various catacombs are found in El Duende and Alto de San Andrés, both of which are within a 30-minute walk from the museum. You also can take a 90-minute hike up El Aguacate, a mountain from which the entire area, and the most elaborate tombs, can be seen.

San Andrés de Pisimbala is interesting in itself as the home of the Paez Indians, the tribe that now inhabits the area but has no relation to the pre-Columbian culture that left the tombs. The Indians, once fierce opponents of the white man, are today farmers and weavers, and a number of their crafts are for sale during the Wednesday market here.

**En Route from Tierradentro** – The 140-mile (224-km) drive on Route 68 west to Popayán is over rough, unpaved road and takes at least 4 hours. Along the way, stop in Puracé National Park, where you can horseback ride beneath or walk around the Coconuco volcanoes, a string of snow-capped craters with Puracé at one end and Pan de Azúcar (Sugar Loaf Mountain) at the other. There are a number of waterfalls and thermal springs here as well as wildlife, including the Andean condor, eagles, hummingbirds, black bears, rabbits, deer, and tapirs. From here, it's just a few short miles to Popayán.

**POPAYÁN:** Founded in 1536 by de Belalcázar in the rich and temperate Pubenza Valley, this city of 200,000 people somehow managed to guard its colonial beauty throughout the years. In 1983, on *Good Friday,* the town's sleepy atmosphere was disrupted by a massive earthquake that severely damaged all of its 2-story, Spanish colonial buildings, churches, and museums. However, thanks to numerous international donations, the town has risen from the ruins, even more sparklingly white than before.

It won't be the first time the town has had to recover from a crisis. After surviving the attacks of the Pijao Indians in the early years, Popayán went on to become a major social and cultural center. By 1540, it was a provincial capital, subject to the Audiencia de Quito, and was an obligatory stopover between Cartagena and Quito. In addition, the city attracted the wealthier Spanish families from the tropical sugar estates to the north, who came to live in the better climate and establish an aristocratic and cultural center by founding schools and a university. The city was an important gold-producing area until the mid-1750s. It managed to change hands at least 22 times during Colombia's fight for independence and was the birthplace of seven presidents and some outstanding citizens, including Francisco José de Caldas, who discovered how to determine altitude using variations in the boiling point of water.

Be sure to visit the churches, cloisters, and museums in Popayán. The Church of San Francisco (Calle 4 and Carrera 9) has a bell that can be heard from one end of the valley to the other; its pulpit is carved with the delightfully graceful figure of the *canefora americana,* a Creole girl carrying a basket of tropical fruit on her head. Other masterpieces of baroque wood sculpture are the *retablo* (altarpiece) of the Señor de la Coronación and Bernardo de Lagarda's *Virgin of the Immaculate Conception,* who seems to dance as she triumphs over the devil. In contrast to the baroque splendor of these works are the simple and highly spiritualized stone carvings on the outside of the church, done by the contemporary soldier-sculptor Roque Navarrete. The sacristy also has some treasures, including the stone-studded, gold monstrance by José de la Iglesia.

The Church of San Agustín (Calle 7 and Carrera 6) also contains a stone monstrance; Santo Domingo (Calle 4 and Carrera 5) has a carved colonial doorway; the cloistered Monastery of San Francisco, now the *Monasterio* hotel (Calle 4 and Carrera 10), and that of the Dominicans, next to the entry of Santo Domingo, have fine colonial architecture. The Dominican monastery now houses the university, founded in 1640.

Popayán has several interesting museums, including the *Casa Mosquera Colonial Museum* (Carrera 5 and Calle 3), which contains an ethnological section. The *Museo Guillermo Valencia* (2-69 Carrera 6) and the *Natural History Museum,* (opposite Cauca University), also are worth a visit.

Popayán is famous for its *Holy Week* celebrations, which vie with those of Spain in splendor and solemnity. The first procession occurs on *Palm Sunday,* when two images are brought down from the Chapel of Belén to the cathedral; every evening there are processions, with bearers carrying 11 or more images at a time.

In recent years, a *Festival of Sacred Music* with top rank musicians has been organized during *Holy Week.* The celebrations attract country folk in their typical dress from a wide area; they also attract Colombians from all over the country and many foreign visitors.

There is a tourist office (5-72 Calle 3A; phone: 282-2251) if you need any assistance.

One incredibly good restaurant in the city is *Mey Chow* (10-81 Carrera 10A, phone: 282-22604), which serves Chinese dishes — a welcome contrast to the staid Colombian diet of rice, potatoes, and, too often, tough beef. An ice cream shop on the main square offers tasty flavors, too, including *arequipe* (milk pudding). Also try *La Herrería* restaurant (under the Humilladero Bridge), a converted blacksmith shop. For a starter, ask for *empanadas de Pipián,* small meat pies with a peanut sauce.

Take a side trip to Silvia, 40 miles (64 km) northeast of Popayán on the dirt turnoff from the Pan-American at the town of Piendamó. Silvia is the small settlement of the skilled Guambino Indians. You can buy their carpets, woolen products, *chaquiras* (beads), and pendant crosses of beaten silver at the Tuesday morning market.

**En Route from Popayán** – The road leads in one of two directions: south to Pasto and the Ecuador border, or north to Cali, both of which are off the Pan-American Highway. Heading south to Pasto, the trip is 155 miles (248 km) and takes about 5 hours. The capital of the Department of Nariño, Pasto lost many of its colonial structures to modernization. Today a city of 370,000, it was very active during the battle for independence. During the early days of the fighting, Antonio Nariño, a Colombian patriot, attempted to take the royalist stronghold here. He was deserted by half his army, led to Pasto, clapped in irons, and shipped off to Spain to rot in prison for 6 years. When independence had been won in the rest of Colombia, royalists in Pasto put up a long and bitter resistance; later, when Ecuador split from Gran Colombia, the people here wanted to go with it but never did.

Those continuing on to Ecuador must stop in Ipiales and the customs post (6-19 Carrera 6) to have their *carnets* (passes) stamped. The Colombian exit stamp is obtained from the DAS at the frontier post of Rumichaca, about 2½ miles (4 km) south.

Nearby is the Santuario de Nuestra Señora de Las Lajas, an incredible, castle-like church built directly over a deep chasm. It resembles a medieval structure poised over a moat rather than a church. It's awesome and eerie, more so if you stand on its bridge and look down. It has been described by a famous poet as "a triumph of faith over gravity."

Going north from Popayán, it's a 90-mile (144-km) trip to Santander de Quilichao, a town inhabited only by blacks, descendants of runaway slaves.

**CALI:** The third-largest city in Colombia, with a population of well over 1.8 million people, Cali is a thriving center of commerce and industry and is filled with lively and friendly people who make the good life mandatory. Founded by de Belalcázar in 1536, the city is modern, with a matching mentality, and since the arrival of the railway early in this century, it has ridden a remarkable economic boom. It's the sugar capital of the country, and has developed a dynamic commercial sector of paper production and publishing.

There are a number of special places in Cali, ranging from the historic to the scenic to the lively. Plaza Caicedo, with tall palm trees, contains a statue of Joaquín Caicedo y Cuero, one of the leaders of the Independence movement. The cathedral, next to the plaza, is the oldest church in the city, revamped through the ages from the baroque style to the neo-classical.

Cali sits on the banks of the Río Aguacatal, and you can visit El Orquideal, a garden filled with thousands of orchids. For shopping, try the market around the plaza, which overflows with woolen goods from *ruanas* to skirts, *carriels* and other leather goods, and even emeralds.

If it's nightlife you're after, there are a number of discos and clubs between Calle 9 and Carrera 3 — the neon area has quickly earned a reputation as the city's "sin pot" or "fire zone." Locals frequent the *Papeto Show Bar* (6N-38 Calle 43 Norte; phone: 23-652451/2), a club that has live music; open Thursday, Friday, and Saturday nights until late. During the day on Sundays, the town goes crazy at Juanchito, a small port on the Río Cauca just a few minutes from downtown. There's plenty of eating, dancing, and drinking. Try the *sancocho de gallina,* a rich soup made from fowl, plantains, and several mysterious things.

Cali is known as the sports center of Colombia, and everything, it seems, is available here. The *Pan-American Sports Complex,* built in 1971 for the internationally acclaimed games, contains the 60,000-seat *Pascual Guerrero Stadium,* a 7,000-seat gymnasium, a 4,000-seat baseball diamond, swimming pools, a field hockey stadium, and a track for bicycle racing. A number of tennis clubs and golf clubs are spread throughout the city as well.

Cali is blessed with a number of good restaurants. *Cali Viejo* (near the *Inter-Continental* hotel) offers tamales and empanadas; they're not as spicy as the Mexican versions, but just tasty enough. Also try some *pan de bono* (cassava bread) while being serenaded by a band of roving musicians. *Embajada Antioqueña* (40-15 Av. Roosevelt; phone: 23-394619) and *Las Torres* (in the Chipre section of the city), feature regional dishes that include red beans served with pork, a favorite dish from the Department of Antioquia. *El Campanario* (also near the *Inter-Continental*) has seafood and rice specialties along with a wine cellar. *Carnes do Brasil* (Av. 8 Norte and Calle 18 Norte) serves beef in seven different varieties in a type of all-you-can-eat buffet. With scantily clad waitresses and samba music, close your eyes and you could be dining in Rio de Janeiro. *El Orquideal* (Carretera Aguacatal; phone: 23-808662) serves creole and international fare in a lovely outdoor setting. The same management runs a seafood restaurant, *Los Girasoles,* and a steakhouse, *Las dos Parrillas* (both at Av. 6 Norte and Calle 35 Esquina). Another good place for steak is *El Fuerte* (15A-06 Av. 8 Norte).

If you haven't a car already (or want to drop off the one you've been using), then go to *Hertz* (2-72 Av. Colombia; phone: 23-823225) or *Rayda Rent-a-Car* (at the *Inter-Continental* hotel; phone: 23-808971). Renaults and other makes are available from $36 per day, and from $225 per week, plus mileage. Additionally, there are lots of flights between Cali and Bogotá and other Colombian cities. International carriers serving Cali include *Avianca* and *American.*

One interesting side trip to take before heading to Ibagué and back to Bogotá is to the Pacific port of Buenaventura, about 54 miles (86 km) west of Cali. The warm (84F/29C) port is the major Pacific center for exporting coffee and sugar. The port is reachable either by car or by taking a bus (for about $8) over the Cordillera Occidental (Western Range) mountains or through the jungle. Then continue by launch: The port is on an island 10 miles out in Buenaventura Bay. From here, backtrack to Cali or fly to Bogotá.

Also on the Pacific coast, about 62 miles (100 km) southwest of Buenaventura, is the spectacular jungle island of Isla Gorgona. Once the site of a notorious maximum security prison, this lush island is now a national park and a popular international center for marine research. From June through November, it's an ideal place to watch whales and dolphins mating, but tourism is restricted and the island can only be reached by boat or helicopter. Local travel agencies can help travelers attain the necessary permit from INDERENA, Colombia's environmental agency. In Cali, contact *La Torre del Turismo* (phone: 23-675625, 23-675626, and 23-680861) for information. Accommodations on the island are limited to cabañas rented through INDERENA.

**En Route from Cali** – Take the Pan-American and continue through the Cauca Valley over the Cordillera Central to the Magdalena Valley and Ibagué, the capital of the cattle-raising Department of Tolima, at the foot of the Nevado del Tolima. A city of 350,000, Ibagué hosts the *National Folklore Festival,* held annually during the last week of June.

From Ibagué, it's a short 141 miles (226 km) to Bogotá and the completion of the circuit.

## BEST EN ROUTE

With the exception of Cali, where some hotels are in the expensive category ($40 to $80 a night for a double room), most of the hotels along this route are in the moderate range ($20 to $40) or inexpensive class (about $20). Most hotels are clean and comfortable and offer hot water, baths, and air conditioning. It's wise to make reservations before arrival, more so during the festivals from January through June. Also, don't forget to safeguard your belongings, since pickpockets are rampant throughout Colombia.

## NEIVA

**Hostería Matamundo** – A converted hacienda with 27 rooms, it has air conditioning and a restaurant. Carretera al Sur (phone: 88-722037). Inexpensive.

**Plaza** – Offers 142 air conditioned rooms and a swimming pool. 4-62 Calle 7 (phone: 88-723980). Inexpensive.

**Residencias Pacande** – This 30-room hotel has a swimming pool. 4-39 Calle 10 (phone: 80-729140). Inexpensive.

## SAN AGUSTÍN

**Cabañas Alto de las Guaduas** – The cabins here hold up to 4 people each. Make reservations in Neiva at 5-07 Carrera 9 (phone: 88-723430). Inexpensive.

**Osoguaico** – This place has 25 rooms and a good dining room. Via Parque Arqueológico (phone: 88-373069). Inexpensive.

**Yalconia** – A state-owned hotel with 36 rooms and a swimming pool; camping is permitted on the grounds, between San Agustín and the park. Make reservations in Bogotá (phone: 1-610-0830). Inexpensive.

## SAN ANDRÉS DE PISIMBALA

**Refugio de Pisimbala** – A 7-room hotel that is comfortable and provides hot water. In the archaeological park (no phone). Inexpensive.

## POPAYÁN

**Camino Real** – Owned by a North American, this restored colonial mansion has 29 balconied rooms and a restaurant serving international fare, with the emphasis on trout and shellfish. Charming and comfortable. 5-59 Calle 5 (phone: 282-240816). Moderate.

**Monasterio** – A converted monastery with 50 rooms, doubles and singles, with high ceilings and tiled baths, and a pool. Calle 4 between Carreras 9 and 10 (phone: 28-242190 and 28-242191). Moderate.

**La Plazuela** – Another restored colonial house, this one with 27 rooms. It is so small, its restaurant so excellent, and the service so friendly that stopping here feels more like visiting friends than staying in a commercial establishment. 8-13 Calle 5 (phone: 28-240912). Moderate.

**Los Balcones** – A modern, small hotel with 14 rooms, all very comfortable. 6-80 Calle 3 (phone: 28-242030). Inexpensive.

**Residencias Americanas** – Private baths are provided with the 25 rooms here. 2N-12 Carrera 6 (phone: 28-221645). Inexpensive.

## SILVIA

**Turismo** – Small and centrally located, with 27 clean and comfortable rooms. 1-18 Calle 10 (phone: 39-51076; in Cali: 23-771677). Inexpensive.

## PASTO

**Agualongo** – Sixty-seven rooms, doubles and singles. Carrera 25 and Calle 18 (phone: 27-35216). Moderate.

**Morasurco** – Offers 60 rooms, doubles and singles. 17-30 Carrera 23 (phone: 27-235017). Moderate.

## IPIALES

***Hostería Mayasquer*** – A 31-room hotel that is on the road (Pan-American) to the frontier (phone: 2725-3984; in Bogotá, 1-610-0830). Inexpensive.

***Pasaviveros*** – This 20-room hostelry is clean and has hot water. 16-90 Carrera 6 (phone: 304-2622). Inexpensive.

## CALI

***Inter-Continental*** – Large and deluxe, with 394 double and single rooms, air conditioning, a swimming pool, tennis courts, Turkish baths, and a sauna. 2-72 Av. Colombia (phone: 23-823225). Expensive.

***Aparthotel Dann*** – There are 90 air conditioned rooms, with spectacular views of the city. The restaurant, bar, pool, and downtown location make it a favorite with businesspeople. 1-40 Av. Colombia (phone: 23-823230; fax: 23-830129). Expensive to moderate.

***Americana Cali*** – A small property: 53 double and single rooms with tiled baths, cafeteria, and bar. 8-73 Carrera 4 (phone: 23-823063). Moderate.

***Aristi*** – There are a total of 167 double and single rooms, with air conditioning, tile baths, shower stalls, a rooftop pool, and a restaurant. 10-04 Carrera 9 (phone: 23-822521). Moderate.

## BUENAVENTURA

***Estación*** – The traditional choice at this Pacific port, it has been restored to its turn-of-the-century splendor and features 75 air conditioned rooms overlooking a pool and palm trees. 1A-08 Calle 2 (phone: 222-23935; fax: 222-23975; in Bogotá: 1-232-8250). Moderate.

## IBAGUÉ

***Ambalá*** – Air conditioning, a nightclub, sauna, and Turkish baths can be found at this 135-room hotel. 2-60 Calle 11 (phone: 82-638822). Moderate.

***Lusitania*** – Sixty-three rooms with air conditioning. 15-55 Carrera 2 (phone: 82-639166). Inexpensive.

# The Amazon

The Amazon basin lies deep in the southeastern section of the country. The teeming, dense jungle, filled with giant liana vines, comes alive with the screech of monkeys and green parrots, the snorting of wild boars, the splashing of angry alligators, and the quiet slithering of boa constrictors and the deadly fer-de-lance. Adventurers love superlatives, and the Amazon is full of them. The 3,700-mile network literally flows from one ocean to the other. The second-longest river in the world, it discharges enough water from its mouth to flood Texas to the depth of an inch or to supply New York City with water for 9 years. In just 3 hours, it would fill Lake Ontario. There are more species of fish in the river than in the Atlantic Ocean.

Each country the Amazon flows through has dozens of wild tales of lost tribes, Amazonian women warriors, primitive headhunters, and pink dolphins (real and locally revered inhabitants) that metamorphose into men and impregnate young women. Some of the stories are taller than others. Take, for instance, the story of Francisco de Orellana, the first white man ever to trek down the river's course. It was his supposed encounter with a band of warrior women that led him to name the river after the Amazons of Greek myth. Maybe he did meet a tribe of macho lovelies, but he didn't name the Colombian port of Leticia after a woman he captured. In fact, the port was named after the lost sweetheart of an engineer in the party of the Peruvian Captain Benigo Bustamante, who founded the port in 1867. Once part of Peru, Leticia was ceded to Colombia by treaty in 1922; it was retained by Colombia even after a bloody border skirmish in the 1930s was settled by the League of Nations. Today, the town is a lively frontier outpost with 20,000 inhabitants. It's a good place to purchase a number of Colombian and imported items, not to mention a few handicrafts made by the local Ticuna, Yagua, and Chama Indians, including bark masks, necklaces, blow guns, arrows, and snake and jaguar hides.

It's not possible to get to the Amazon and Leticia by car from Bogotá, more than 620 miles (992 km) to the northwest. The best option is to take a plane from the capital to Leticia, then take a cab into town for about $3.50. Or interrupt your flight at Villavicencio, the capital of the Department of Meta. Here, a long stretch of Llanos Orientales — the grassy, cattle-raising plain roamed by *vaqueros,* the Colombian version of the US cowboys — is on the side of the Cordillera Oriental (Eastern Range) that separates the rest of the country from the Amazon. With the exception of short, local roads, major highways simply don't exist in the Amazon.

Leticia is like something out of the North American Old West. The town consists of several rough dirt roads surrounded by clapboard buildings. Instead of horses, however, scooters are the main mode of transportation and the streets are full of them. Since it is the only port for miles, it's a center of commerce. A colorful, often muddy, market is located on the banks of the Amazon below the town. Nearby are anchored a hodgepodge of Amazon boats along with a surprising number of sleek, high-power motorboats, the most visible manifestation of the town's role as a major base for cocaine transportation.

Spending a couple of days in Leticia is a strange experience for even the best-traveled adventurer who believes that he or she has seen it all. You are very likely to meet foreigners who will say that they are tourists, just like you, but who are actually drug agents checking to see what you are doing here. You may also encounter locals who will think that you are one of the drug agents posing as a tourist. What all this means is that you should keep your wits about you, especially at night. Two journalists from Chicago who wrote a popular book about the Amazon wrote that, when in Leticia, they stayed in their hotel room with the door locked and the curtains drawn. In short, Leticia is an adventure.

Among the ways to enjoy Leticia is hiring a boat and captain for a local river excursion, or taking part in one of the many safaris offered by *Turamazonas* (through the jungle, to Monkey Island, up nearby tributaries), or booking a fascinating 3-day stay with the Yagua tribe. Don't just roam aimlessly through Leticia, for there are a lot of worthwhile things to do. Go catch butterflies in the surrounding jungle; take a 3-hour cruise upriver to the

Taraporto lakes, where you can fish for your own dinner of yellow catfish, *pirarucú,* trout, and amberjack; or simply gape at the giant lily pads *(Victoria rejias)* that grow in the nearby Yaguacaca lakes. They grow to as much as 5 feet in diameter. *Turamazonas*'s itinerary can very well wind up in the Brazilian villages of Marco and Benjamin Constant for a tour of a rubber plantation. You'll also be taken in to Arara village, where the Ticuna Indians live; if you're lucky, you'll get a glimpse of one of the ceremonies that include the *pelazón,* an initiation rite where young women have their hair plucked out by family and friends. Or hike or drive the short distance to the village of Tabatinga in Brazil, or cruise 30 minutes downriver to the Brazilian Ticuna village at Mariacú. More primitive, however, are the Yagua of the Río Atacuari, which forms the natural border between Colombia and Peru; these people still hunt with blow guns.

If you do not want to return or proceed to Bogotá from Leticia, take a short ride to the Tabatinga Airport, on the Brazil side of the jungle, and fly to Manaus, but remember to secure your entry visa in advance. Otherwise, either fly from Tabatinga to Iquitos in Peru and take an Amazon cruise. For information on a 4-day cruise, contact *Tara Tours,* 6595 NW 36th St., Suite 306-A, Miami Springs, FL 33166 (phone: in Florida, 305-871-1246 or 800-327-0080).

You also can arrange, in advance, a 3-night cruise from Leticia to Iquitos, Peru, through *Amazon Tours and Cruises* (8700 W. Flagler, Suite 190, Miami, FL 33174; phone: 305-227-2266 or 800-423-2791). The ship, the M/V *Río Amazonas,* is a 95-year-old Scottish cargo vessel that was converted to a 3-deck cruise liner with 20 air conditioned cabins. It is owned by Paul Wright, a former Los Angeles travel agent who has made his home in Iquitos on and off for more than 20 years. The *Amazonas* also makes the 6-night round trip from Iquitos to Leticia weekly.

## BEST EN ROUTE

Make reservations before traveling to the Amazon; there are very few hotels, and they get filled with adventure-seekers very quickly. The hotels listed below range from $20 to $45 per person a night. They are small and lack hot water, but are air conditioned.

### LETICIA

*Anaconda* – A 49-room hotel that offers large rooms and all the cold water you can stand. Carrera 11 and Calle 7 (phone: 819-7119; in Bogotá, 1-218-4679 and 1-218-0125).

*Parador Ticuna* – Though this 31-room property has become run-down, it does have refrigerators in its rooms, a bar, swimming pool, and an informal dining room that creates Yankee comfort in the jungle. Check out the mini-zoo in back. 6-11 Av. Libertador (phone: 819-7284).

### MONKEY ISLAND

*Monkey Island Lodge* – With free service to and from Leticia, this 31-room lodge runs on full-board plan, and all the chattering monkeys, parrots, and wild orchids on the island are at your disposal. Make reservations at *Parador Ticuna* (above).

# Ecuador

Sitting directly on the equator, Ecuador (Spanish for "equator") is bordered by the Pacific Ocean in the west, Colombia on the north, and Peru to the south. It is a geographical meeting place of high sierra, Amazon basin jungle, and coastal plain. Traveling north to south, the traveler is treated to the sight of the snow-capped volcanoes of the Andes, which stretch 410 miles in two parallel ridges called the Cordillera Occidental (Western Range) and the Cordillera Oriental (Eastern Range). The tallest mountain, Chimborazo, towers at an altitude of 20,577 feet and is always covered in snow. Wedged between the Cordilleras is the sierra, or mountain highlands, the most fertile area of Ecuador. Here, grains are harvested for domestic and foreign use along with the production of livestock, poultry, maize, sugar, and other products. Small Indian villages dot the highway, and some, such as Otavalo, are inhabited by people who were there long before the Inca or the Spanish and whose men and women wear distinctive clothing and are well known for their excellent handicrafts. These include ponchos, shawls, sweaters, embroidered blouses, and wood carvings sold at traditional weekly markets in the villages on different days.

About 45% of Ecuador's more than 10 million people live in the sierra. Of the entire population, 40% are mestizo (part Indian, part Caucasian), another 40% are Indian, and the remaining 20% are split evenly between Caucasians and the descendants of black slaves ferried in from Africa during the colonial period. While the sierra is considered to be the agricultural center of Ecuador, only 5% of it has been cultivated, and food supply and distribution to the country's people remains a major problem. For the most part, the rural population lives in small, thatch-roofed huts, and produce moves on the backs of the inhabitants from family farms to central villages. In hopes of raising the low standard of living, government job programs have been instituted in low-income areas. Recently, Ecuador's Indians have become a vocal force and are demanding distribution of the estate lands, acknowledgment that Ecuador is a multinational country, control over archaeological sites, and money for bilingual education. The landowners are not pleased with this threat to their property and are fighting it. Negotiations are continuing.

East of the Cordilleras lies the Oriente, a lowland covered with jungle vegetation and laced with Amazon tributaries of the Napo, Pastaza, and Curanay rivers. This area produces a wealth of tropical fruits that include avocados and papaya and is inhabited by exotic animals, such as pumas, jaguars, and deer that roam through forests of cedar, mahogany, and rubber trees. To add to the primeval atmosphere, the Auca (or, more formally, the Huaorani), another pre-Inca tribe — who in the past were rather savage — live deep within this jungle. The Oriente is also the home of the Jivaro, or Shuar, Indians, who once were headhunters.

Unlike the Oriente, the tropical coastal lowlands (El Litoral) benefit from the Pacific's proximity and are cooler and milder. Guayaquil, Ecuador's largest city (pop. 2.5 million), is also the country's major exporting seaport; the nearby beach resorts of Salinas and Playas provide *guayaquileños* with year-round seaside recreation. And, perhaps most intriguing of all, are Ecuador's Pacific islands — the volcanic Galápagos archipelago. Residents of the islands include ancient tortugas — lizards found nowhere else on the globe — and penguins.

Ecuador's climate is relative to its altitude, and two seasons prevail — dry and rainy. The rainy season in the highlands lasts from December through March, and temperatures vary, from the sierra's 40 to 60F (4 to 15C) to the Litoral's 90 to 95F (32 to 35C). If this sounds like paradise, there is a catch: Ecuador, like all Andean countries, suffers from occasional earthquakes. The one in 1987 destroyed the country's crucial trans-Andean oil pipeline, and officials are still repairing some museums, colonial churches, and other important buildings that were damaged.

For the total feel of Ecuador, time should be spent in each of the three major regions — the sierra, the coast, and the jungle — for each is uniquely intriguing. Frequent, inexpensive air service between Quito, Guayaquil, and Cuenca, Ecuador's third-largest city, as well as small plane service into the Oriente, make exploration relatively easy (although it sometimes is difficult to confirm return flights from Cuenca and schedules to and from the Galápagos Islands are unreliable). For those with plenty of time, there is nothing like the overland trip south from Colombia, on the Pan-American Highway, crossing the border into Ecuador at Tulcán, continuing through the Indian villages of Ibarra and Otavalo to Quito (for detailed information see *Quito*, THE CITIES). Beyond, there is a beautiful drive down the Valley of the Volcanoes to Ambato. Then you can take the highway west at Cajabamba, beyond Riobamba, to the coastal region and Guayaquil. If you're arriving in Ecuador by plane or steamer at Guayaquil, you may want to explore the coast first, then take the highway east to the Pan-American. Excursions into the Amazon basin can also be made from Quito, east, then south through the jungles until the Oriente Highway links up with the Pan-American outside Cuenca.

Traveling the Pan-American Highway south of Quito, you head down Ecuador's fascinating El Camino Real, the Royal Road that connected Quito with the Inca capital of Cuzco in Peru. The narrow path was a footroad used by teams of *chasquis* — relay runners — carrying messages between both kingdoms; following Spanish colonization, the road was paved with cobblestones and was later converted to the Pan-American Highway.

Be prepared for some rough riding in Ecuador if you're traveling by car or bus. Generally, 87% of Ecuador's 12,400-mile road network is passable year-round; the remaining 13% can wash out during the rainy season. This doesn't mean the road system is mostly a modern one. The Pan-American is a narrow, two-lane road, often good and just as often poorly paved (and sometimes unpaved). Ecuadoran highways are poorly marked and gravelly; through many villages, the highway is the main street. More often than not, they appear where no roads are indicated on the map. Still, you need a map, available in bookstores (try *Libri Mundi* in Quito; see THE CITIES), at the tourist office headquarters (CETUR) in Quito, or from the Military Geographical Institute, Calle Paz and Miño in Quito (phone: 2-522066).

Note that unlike its neighbor Peru, Ecuador has had only a few reported cases of cholera. Visitors, however, should be careful and drink only bottled water and eat only hot, well-cooked food, and peeled fruit.

# The North: Tulcán to Machala

From the Colombian border at Tulcán to the Peruvian border at Huaquillas, through the tiny Indian villages and marketplaces, this exciting and beautiful route leads through the remnants of the ancient civilizations of the Andes. Along the way, the most famous of the Indian markets is Otavalo, where traditional Indian goods are sold by the weavers of the region.

**TULCÁN:** Leaving Colombia, you travel over the natural stone bridge of Rumichaca. Papers are checked at the immigration office at the bridge. The border is supposed to be open 24 hours a day, but the immigration office usually stamps passports only during the day. Busloads of tourists and trucks with cargo can lengthen the time it takes to cross the border.

The route passes through Tulcán, a village of 35,000 in the heart of a rich agricultural district. Don't miss the cemetery; its hedges are trimmed in the shapes of animals, birds, geometric designs, and archways. The effect is bizarre and intriguing. Next to the cemetery is a sports field where paddleball games are held on weekends. You'll get a kick out of the curious implements — the big spiked paddles and the tiny soft ball — used in this homegrown sport. There are also open-air markets to visit on Thursdays and Sundays. The tourist information office is at Amazonas and Abdón Calderón (phone: 2-886323).

**En Route from Tulcán** – Continuing south to Ibarra on the Pan-American Highway, you pass Lago Yahuarcocha, the Lake of Blood. Legend has it that the lake turned red with the blood of the native Cara Indians during their futile fight to block the Inca conquest. The recent drop in the lake's water level continues to be a source of scientific study.

**IBARRA:** Every Saturday this village near the Imbabura volcano comes alive around 5 AM, when Indian merchants flock here to sell their produce and handicrafts. The village streets become cluttered with displays of ponchos, shawls, embroidered blouses, rope sandals, and woodcarvings from neighboring San Antonio de Ibarra. (A century ago, a man from this town went to Quito to learn the craft of woodworking. Upon his return, he accepted apprentices and began a tradition of fine woodworking that now involves a large number of Ecuadorans.) Prices are reasonable, and this local market draws fewer tourists than the one in Otavalo. Here and there, are the native Indian men (and a few women) sipping *chicha,* a liquor fermented from dried corn. Needless to say, there are a few happy, singing voices — and headaches — by the end of the morning. Ibarra is called "the White City," presumably because it is so clean.

Ibarra is known for its *helados de paila,* ice cream that is made by stirring fruit juice in shallow bronze pans that are resting on a bed of ice and straw. Another local ice cream recipe calls for adding add dry ice directly to the fruit mixture; you'll sometimes see young women tirelessly stirring huge bronze pans from which thick clouds of smoke are rising. Two other local favorites for those with a sweet tooth include *nogadas* (walnut nougats) and *arrope de mora* (blackberry syrup).

When traveling through Ecuador, try some of the local potables — they're quite good. One excellent beer is Cerveza Pilsener; *hervidas* are cocktails made with rum and fruit; and *canelazo* is a sugarcane liquor drink made with cinnamon. As you near the larger cities, what looks like the soy sauce on your restaurant table is probably concentrated coffee. Just pour it into your cup of boiled water and stir.

You can catch a bus in Ibarra and head to Otavalo and Quito or take the Pan-American Highway 14 miles (22 km) south to Cotacachi, Ecuador's most famous leather town.

**COTACACHI:** When the conquistadores came to the area, they forced many Indians to leave their farms and settle in small villages where the Spanish thought they could be better controlled. The Indians moved to Cotacachi were charged with supplying the Spaniards with leather goods, including saddles and boots, and that industry has dominated the town every since. Cotacachi's main street, Avenida 10 de Agosto, is lined with shops that sell everything imaginable in leather. In most of the shops, you can bargain over the prices of briefcases, satchels, handbags, jackets, skirts, boots, belts, and key rings.

Before or after shopping, try Cotacachi's most popular dish — *carne dorada* (sun-dried ham served with toasted corn kernels). *Chicha de jora* (corn liquor) is the focus of the annual September 13 *Festival de Jora,* when costumed townspeople form a parade, and engage in dancing, musical entertainment, much *chicha* consumption, and general round-the-clock merrymaking. Cotacachi is home to the lovely *La Mirage* hotel (see *Best en Route),* and at press time, two more hotels were under construction as the town's reputation for producing quality leather goods draws more and more visitors.

**OTAVALO:** The Saturday morning markets have become very popular with visitors, and rightly so, for they offer perhaps Ecuador's finest selection of Indian crafts. Goods come from all over the country, just as the *otavaleños,* world-famous weavers, travel all over the world with their produce. You can sometimes spot them in South American airports, where they wear the traditional provincial dress. For the man, it's white calf-length pants, white shirt, and blue woolen poncho, and hair drawn into one single braid falling down his back. (Interestingly, these Indians are not exempt from military conscription but they are allowed to keep their braid; it is a startling contrast to see *otavaleños* in army garb.) The woman's costume is even more captivating. She wears two dark woolen skirts, a brightly embroidered blouse, strands of colored glass and coral beads entwined around her neck, and brightly colored woven belts wrapped around her waist. Children wear pint-size versions of the same garb.

One big square in the market has nothing but textiles, some now made on big Spanish looms with synthetic fibers and dyes. However, many vendors still have only weavings of pure sheep's wool — hand carded, vegetable dyed, and woven in the traditional patterns on ancient backstrap looms.

Other squares hold the food and animal markets, and instant alfresco "kitchens" are in business all day. On one corner the dealers haggle over sacks of squeaking *cuyes* (guinea pigs), and in another, over trays of the ubiquitous coral or glass beads worn by the women. The Otavalo market was famous even before the Inca conquest and, in recent years, it has sparked the opening of several Indian-owned artisan shops. Although market merchants may have packed up their wares by early afternoon, you still can visit their shops. (Markets in Ecuador begin at sunrise, and the action usually is over by 1 PM.) To mark the end of the corn harvest, the city celebrates the *Festival of Yamor* on September 8. A fermented drink made with seven varieties of corn and sweetened with cane syrup, *yamor* is the centerpiece of the festivities (it is believed to have originated in pre-Inca celebrations). During the festival, men dress up as the legendary *corazas* — Indian princes who wore lavish garments.

*Otavaleño* sport is rough; illegal in the US, cockfights are habitual here and throughout Ecuador; bullfights are normally held in June, along with regattas on nearby Laguna de San Pablo.

If you're hungry on the way out of town, stop at *Puerto Lago,* a small lakeside inn with an excellent restaurant that boasts a wonderful view of Lake San Pablo and Mt. Imbabura (see *Best en Route).* From here, make a 3-mile (5-km) detour north, on the country road that runs parallel to the Pan-American Highway, to the town of Peguche. The Otalvo Indians who live here are renowned musicians. But the reason most visitors stop in Peguche is to see — and buy — the weavings of José Cotacachi (ask anyone where his workshop is located). This master weaver designs his own patterns based on traditional Otavalo motifs. He uses only natural dyes and traditional weaving techniques which, sadly, have been abandoned in other parts of the country. His signed weavings, jackets, sweaters, and purses are lovely and inexpensive.

This area of the Imbabura province is filled with eucalyptus trees which scent the air, and dotted with *tolas.* These large mounds — or hills — that rise up from flat fields were built by the Inca for three reasons: to cover the graves of important people, to grow crops during floods, and to use as a vantage point over the fields. There are more than 3,000 *tolas* throughout Imbabura.

**En Route from Otavalo** – Continuing south, the Pan-American Highway takes you through the winding, up-and-down countryside of the sierra on the way to Quito and the equatorial line.

Guayllabamba grove is noted for its harvest of avocados. In Cayambe, a dairy products center, there are shops selling good cookies and cheese.

Nineteen miles (30 km) north of Quito, Calderón is known for its painted bread-dough sculptures, modeled after the decorated breads made in Ecuador commemorating November 2, *Día de los Muertos* (Day of the Dead). These *"guaguas de pan"* (literally, "bread babies") are sold as decorations, jewelry, and *Christmas* ornaments and often are found in shapes representing figures in a traditional nativity scene. Most of the shops along the main street sell the images and 60% of Calderón's population makes its living from the craft.

**EQUATORIAL LINE:** You can't feel it or see it (save for one, lone monument), but the equatorial line is about 15 miles (24 km) north of Quito at the village of San Antonio de Pichincha. The monument is set at the line determined by the French explorer Charles de la Condamine in 1735. Condamine, however, was not totally accurate, for the imaginary line dividing the Northern from the Southern Hemisphere actually runs several hundred feet away. Nevertheless, the monument has never been moved, probably out of respect for Condamine's well-educated guess.

Closer to Quito is a newer, larger monument — Mitad del Mundo — marking the equatorial line contains two entrances, one on each side of the line. One door is marked NORTHERN HEMISPHERE; the other, SOUTHERN HEMISPHERE. You might try entering one door and exiting through the other, just for fun, or have your photograph taken with one foot in each Hemisphere. The terrace on top of the monument is a great spot to take photos of the surrounding area. The interior houses an ethnographic museum of present-day Ecuadoran Indian life, which is worth a visit. The museum (open daily except Mondays from 9 AM to 3 PM;) also contains information concerning the Inca sun cult. Just a few miles from the monument outside the town of San Antonio de Pichincha, you can visit the original Inti-Yan, or Road of the Sun, the ancient equatorial line recognized by the early civilizations that populated the area. On it sits the now-excavated pre-Inca ruins of Rumicucho and South America's largest crater, Pululahua. There also is a planetarium near this monument; it has three shows daily, Tuesdays through Fridays; and five on Saturdays and Sundays.

A paved road leads from the monument south to Quito; if you prefer, you can continue on the Pan-American Highway into the city.

**QUITO:** (For a detailed report on the city, its hotels and restaurants, see *Quito,* THE CITIES.) After you've enjoyed the city, either continue south to Cuenca; or drive south to Cajabamba and pick up the paved road that runs to Guayaquil; or continue on the Pan-American Highway south to Peru. In 1802, German explorer Alexander von

Humboldt christened the valley between Quito and Riobamba "the Avenue of the Volcanoes." Today, driving along the highway, you can glimpse 11 major volcanic cones, provided the weather is not overcast; some travelers claim the most dramatic view is in early evening. (You can also see the Avenue of the Volcanoes from above — an astonishing sight — as you peer into craters right and left while on the inexpensive, 30-minute *SAETA* flight between Quito and Guayaquil.) Quito is also an ideal base of operations for 1- and 2-day excursions north to Otavalo and south as far as Riobamba. There is frequent bus service, and taxis are easy to negotiate. Local tour companies also offer a wide range of programs highlighting the colorful Indian villages and market life of the sierra.

**En Route from Quito** – Machachi, 25 miles (40 km) south of Quito, is noted for its Sunday markets and therapeutic mineral springs. The water here has gone somewhat the way of commercialism, for it is bottled and sold under the name Agua Güitig (pronounced Wee-Teeg) and is the best-known carbonated mineral water in the country. You can try the village's fresh cheeses or catch a cockfight on Sunday afternoon.

South of Machachi, a minor road turns east off the highway toward Parque Nacional Cotopaxi. Here, you can see the famous Cotopaxi, the world's highest active volcano, its snow-capped peak towering 19,347 feet above sea level. Returning to the Pan-American Highway, you'll pass San Agustín Hill, believed to be a pre-Columbian pyramid. In Latacunga, the soil is laden with gray lava rock; it's used to build houses and public buildings. From town, you may be able to spot as many as nine volcanic cones. It will take a bit of luck though; the summits often are concealed in clouds. For 3 days in September this colonial city lets its hair down with the *Mama Negra Festival,* called the *Festival of the Holy Virgin of La Merced* by the pious. The streets come alive with bonfires, brass bands, clowns, and the designated Mama Negra (according to legend, a figure based on the Virgin Mary's cook) roams about squirting revelers with donkey's milk — said to symbolize fertility and virility. Special masses are also held at the Church of La Merced.

Northwest of Latacunga sits Saquisilí, an excellent Thursday market place — a riot of fresh fruit and vegetable colors. Its 11 plazas become jammed with people examining various merchandise (ponchos, shawls, rope shoes, and so on); the regional Indians can be identified by their red ponchos and white felt hats.

You can visit a host of smaller towns before returning to the Pan-American Highway. Most of these places, however, lie deep in the mountains of the Cordillera Occidental on almost nonexistent roads. It's best to take a bus into this area or, better yet, a guided tour, and let the locals do the driving — to the Sunday market at Pujilí, or to Zumbagua, where there is a good Saturday market with a lot of llama selling. This is probably the most authentic and totally Indian market in all of Ecuador. Nearby you can hike the volcanic crater–filled lake at Quilota.

**AMBATO:** A major earthquake in 1949 destroyed this city of 122,000; the survivors picked themselves up, dusted off, and reconstructed the area. The fourth-largest city in Ecuador and a 2½-hour drive from Quito, Ambato was once known as the "City of Flowers and Fruit," probably because the colonists lined the streets with parks and flowers. Ambato still has a *Fiesta de Frutas y Floras* (Festival of Flowers and Fruits) every February. The rich suburb of Miraflores is on the Río Ambato; from here, you can see the peaks of both Chimborazo and Tungurahua volcanoes. Ambato is also proud of its famous scions, and bills itself as the home of Ecuador's "three Juans:" writer Don Juan Montalvo, journalist Juan Benigno Vela, and Juan León Mera, author of the national anthem.

Market day (the biggest in Ecuador and one of the largest on the continent) is Monday; most of the buying and selling is carried on in the center plaza. Try to arrive the night before to watch the produce markets being set up. Crafts are grouped separately, with weavings the most abundant item. Genial haggling over prices is expected. While in Ambato, stop by the rug factory.

Don't forget to try some local dishes while you're in the sierra. *Llapingachos* is a treat of mashed potatoes and cheese, and *secos* are tasty chicken, lamb, or goat stews served with rice and potatoes. Another specialty is *fritada y mote,* fried chunks of pork with hominy.

Before leaving the area, an interesting side trip is the bus ride to Baños, known for its thermal pools that reputedly have miraculous — speaking in the religious sense — cures. Be forewarned, though, that most of the pools can be crowded and are not well maintained — even dirty. Your cleanest bet is *Piscina Salud.*

Take a camera: The placid, picturesque village of Baños is located at the foot of the volcano Tungurahua (see *The Oriente,* in this chapter) and offers some fine opportunities for day hikes; for example, a good trek begins at Martínez Street. (Avoid the hike to the crosses at the roadside shrine outside town — there have been reports of wild dogs biting travelers.) For tourist information in town, the best person to contact is a Shuar Indian guide named Sebastián (he can be found next door to the *Pensión Patty).*

For those interested, mountain climbing expeditions can start from Ambato (or Riobamba) for Chimborazo or other mountains. Take adequate mountain-climbing equipment and make sure you know what you're doing — Chimborazo is not for the sometime-climber. Allowing 4 days for the trip and arranging for an expedition and guide in advance are recommended. Information is available from the national tourist office in Ambato (beside the *Ambato* hotel, Av. Guayaquil at Roca Fuerte; phone: 2-821800); in Quito, from the *Agrupación de Montaña Pablo Leiva* (1240 Av. 6 de Diciembre; phone: 2-230758), the *Cumbres Andinas Club* (841 Av. Olmedo; phone: 2-517748), the *Universidad Católica Mountain Climbing Club* (12 de Octubre and Calle Roca; phone: 2-529270), or the *South American Explorers Club* (1254 Toledo, La Floresta, Quito; phone: 2-566076). Contact *Metropolitan Touring* (239 Av. Amazonas, Quito; phone: 2-560550; fax: 2-564655) for information about their 6-day trek by foot and horseback; or book through their US representative, *Adventure Associates* (13150 Coit Rd., Suite 110, Dallas, TX 75240; phone: 214-907-0414 or 800-527-2500).

A side trip 8 miles (13 km) east of Ambato goes to Salasaca, the village of the Salasaca Indians, whom the Inca brought from Bolivia as laborers in the 15th century. The natives here dress in white shirts, black ponchos, and flat white, wide-brimmed hats. Their skill as weavers is legendary. In the 1960s, Peace Corps workers organized the Salasaca into weaving cooperatives and their products are available at *Artesano de Salasaca,* near the church.

**RIOBAMBA:** In order not to miss the Saturday market here, take the 4-hour trip from Quito on Friday and spend the night. If you do stay over, make hotel reservations in advance; you'll find many other visitors have the same idea (see *Best en Route*). By 9 AM there's selling and bartering in all of the town's 11 plazas, each one reserved for different merchandise: ponchos, shawls, leather goods, animals, food, baskets, raw wool, and sheepskins. Different Indian groups from nearby towns bring their goods to market; you'll be able to single them out by the distinctive hats worn by the women. If you're hungry, grab a snack at one of the open-air restaurants: the local favorites are roast pig and grilled guinea pig. If you stay in Riobamba on Saturday night, drive out on Sunday to the Indian market at Lake Colta for the most vivid local color.

A major religious center, Riobamba (pop. 148,000) is particularly interesting during *Holy Week.* However, anytime (except Mondays, when it is closed) is right for visiting the beautiful *Museum of Sacred Art,* housed in a cloister of the Convento de la Concepción at Orozco and España. A guide who may speak some English will show you about; there is a small admission charge and guides expect tips. A special train, the *Expreso Metropolitan,* with refitted parlor cars, meal and snack service, and bathrooms, runs from Quito to Riobamba Tuesdays and Saturdays (returning Wednesdays and Sundays); it is operated by *Metropolitan Touring*. The *autoferro,* best described as a bus adapted to run on train tracks, lacks these amenities, but runs daily except Sundays. There is also regular bus service to Quito and to the coast, as well as special tourist itineraries. Riobamba has become a popular base for trekking, especially 6-day walks on the Chimborazo glacier fields or a 6-day walk along the Inca Road toward Cuenca.

**CAJABAMBA:** Actually, this is the site of the original Riobamba and was the capital of the country before Quito. Founded in 1534, the town was leveled by an earthquake in 1797; the new Riobamba was moved 12 1/2 miles (20 km) northeast.

**En Route from Cajabamba** – The Pan-American Highway running south to Cuenca passes through scores of little scenic villages. Guamote is on little Lake Colta; Alausi is a popular mountain resort and the spot where the *Nariz del Diablo* (Devil's Nose) steam rail line begins on its route to Guayaquil (see *Guayaquil*).

Azogues, the start of the southern sierra, is notable for being one of the Ecuadoran centers of "Panama" hat manufacturing. You can buy them at the market that takes place every Saturday in the town plaza.

**CUENCA:** Eighty-eight miles (141 km) south of Azogues sits the country's third-largest city (300,000 people); it is a charming colonial town, surrounded by four rivers — the Tarqui, Yanuncay, Tomebamba, and Machangara.

Founded in 1557, the city is filled with squares, monuments named for poets, streets christened after literary figures, small museums, and historical churches. El Carmen, a Carmelite convent (533 Calle Sucre), dates to 1682 and contains much of its original furniture. Nuns will sometimes take you through the building, showing you the dining room and "doctor's room," where the sisters used to receive medical treatment. A small Nativity scene enclosed in a wooden box, with wooden figures adorned in silver and gold brocade, highlights the tour. Check with the archbishop's office on Plaza Abdón Calderón (beside the cathedral) for permission to visit the convent. Two cathedrals, one lofty and new and the other old, face each other on Plaza Calderón in the center of the city. The older cathedral was built in 1557 and is still used for some cultural events, but not for religious purposes. Its tower was used by French scientists in 1739, during a study of the arc of the meridian on the equator in an attempt to end an ongoing debate with the British over the shape of the globe. Today it is particularly interesting during the various saints' days celebrations. The newer cathedral, a hulking structure with a pink marble façade, was begun in 1880 and remains unfinished because of architectural snafus — its towers ended up being too heavy for the building to support, thus thwarting the plan to make this South America's largest church. Less than a block away, in the tiny Plaza del Carmen, is the daily flower market, a blaze of nature's colorful bounty just crying to be photographed.

One of Cuenca's most colorful citizens, the late Padre Crespi, founder of the former *Salesian Museum,* had some interesting theories about early Ecuadorans. He believed that the Phoenicians and other Mediterraneans entered Cuenca from the mouth of the Amazon around 1000 BC. He said that expeditions he led in the Oriente produced pharaonic Egyptian chairs and artifacts from the Babylonians, Greeks, Etruscans, and even Mesopotamians! His collection has been moved to the *Archaeological Museum of the Banco Central,* next to the Pumapungo ruins, which are thought to be the Inca remains of a Huayna Cápac palace. The museum (located at Calle Larga and Av. Huayna Cápac) is open Tuesdays through Fridays from 9 AM to 4 PM and Mondays from 1 to 4 PM.

The Immaculate Conception monastery, at Calles Presidente Córdova and Hermano Miguel, houses a superb collection of religious art from the 17th and 18th centuries, well-lighted and organized, although without English explanations. The convent has been carefully restored and is itself a museum that illustrates the daily lives of 400 years ago. It is open Mondays from 1 to 4 PM and Tuesdays through Fridays, 9 AM to 4

PM. A wide range of regional crafts and artisans' work from across the country can be seen at the *Museo de Artes Populares* (at Escalera Hermano Miguel). The museum, which periodically holds workshops related to native crafts, is open daily from 8:30 AM to 12:30 PM and 2:30 to 6:30 PM. The city's modern art museum — in a former religious retreat house that dates back to colonial days (at Sucre and Colonel Talbot) is open daily.

The Church and Convent of San José de la Merced (1306 Calle Rafael Arizaga) is a smaller replica of La Merced in Quito. The main altar contains small sculptures and silver heads, arms, and legs — small tokens of thanks to the saint for granting favors.

Cuenca is a major handicrafts center and the original home of the Panama hat. (The hats were misnamed "Panama" because they were shipped to that Central American country — and sold there — en route to the California gold rush customers.) The city itself is famed not only for the crafts of its residents, but for those brought in by Indians from neighboring towns. For shopping, take a walk down Gran Colombia. *La Piel* (8-28 Bolívar) is excellent for leather goods, and *Exportadora Cuenca* (at the corner of Gran Colombia and Benigno Malo) is one of the best shops for Panama hats. *El Tucán* (7-88 Gran Colombia and Luis Cordero) carries a wide variety of Ecuadoran handicrafts, including the tiny *Christmas* tree figures crafted from the *toquilla* (palmetto) fiber. *La Carroza* (7-39 Borrero) specializes in regional art and antiques. A good spot for hand-embroidered items is *Doña Eulalia's* (15-84 Padre Aguirre). A dependable jeweler with a wide selection of the distinctive filigree designs of Cuenca is *Joyería Guillermo Vásquez* (on the ground floor of the *El Dorado* hotel). Market day in Cuenca is Thursday. Head for the Plaza Rotary for a stunning selection of handicrafts from around the country.

Delicious white corn with huge kernels called *mote* forms the backbone of Cuencan cuisine. Try *motepillo*, steamed kernels cooked with onion and eggs, or *mote pata*, a thick soup of corn cooked with beef knuckles, at *Los Capulíes* (Córdova and Borrero; phone: 7-831120). For international food and lovely atmosphere, try *El Jardín* (7-23 Presidente Córdova; phone: 7-824883). For dessert, sample *higos con queso*, sweetened fresh figs stuffed with mild, local white cheese.

There's a branch of the national tourism office (CETUR) at 725 Benigno Malo (phone: 7-827414).

**INGAPIRCA:** A 2-hour trip northeast from Cuenca and 6 miles (10 km) off the Pan-American Highway leads to Ecuador's only major Inca monument. Ingapirca (literally "the Inca wall") is a stone, fortress-like temple, religious site, and administrative center with walled terraces, stone aqueducts, and courtyards. The engraved stones are fitted together in a circular shape without any binding material between them. One of the great mysteries raised by Ingapirca is how the Inca managed to move the stones to the site from a faraway quarry, since they had no knowledge of the wheel. This archaeological site, which is still being excavated, is well worth a visit for those interested in ruins, with artifacts from the excavations housed in a fine small museum nearby. The museum also has an informative audio presentation in English.

Among the artifacts remaining at Ingapirca are two Intinahui (Eyes of the Road) — stone faces that seem to guard the fortress. The Ingachungana (Inca Game) is a stone chair that contains canals carved into the armrests; circular objects were apparently rolled down them to entertain royal guests.

From the road to Ingapirca, do as many faithful pilgrims do and make a short detour to Biblián, whose pilgrimage church is cut high into the rocks above the town. The view is worth the climb up the steep stairs to the church. Here, September 8 is fiesta day, honoring Our Lady of the Morning Dew.

Less than an hour from Cuenca is the picturesque colonial town of Gualaceo and, just beyond, the crafts village of Chordeleg, both of which have Sunday markets.

**CHORDELEG:** The site of Chordeleg was revered as holy ground by the Cañari Indians who were forced to assimilate into the Inca culture but managed to preserve their skills in metallurgy and weaving. They buried their dead in tombs with exquisite gold pieces and finely woven fabrics. At the close of the last century, significant relics were unearthed during a building boom in the town. Decades later, the Organization of American States (OAS) designated Chordeleg a "community museum," with the goal of fostering preservation. In a corner of the dusty main plaza is a museum dedicated to the local crafts of ikat (weaving done with tie-dyed cotton thread or wool) and ceramics. You can ask here for directions to nearby workshops. The local women are known for their magnificent handwoven ikat shawls with long, intricately designed macramé fringe. The metalworking tradition also lives on; local shops offer a good selection of gold and silver filigree jewelry; and many of the best pieces in Quito jewelry stores are from here.

Only 18 miles (29 km) west of Cuenca is Las Cajas National Park, a stunning area of some 300 natural lakes and streams at altitudes of up to 14,000 feet. Las Cajas is especially appealing to trout fishermen and hikers. Horseback riding and camping excursions can be arranged through the *Crespo* hotel in Cuenca (see *Best en Route)* or through *Rootours* (corner of Calle Large and Benigno Malo, Cuenca; phone: 7-835888 or 7-835533).

## BEST EN ROUTE

In most smaller villages of Ecuador, hotels are tiny, and many lack private bathrooms. For the most part, they are inexpensive — about $25 or less for a double room. The better hotels are in the larger towns and are a moderate $40 to $75 for a double. Unless you're in Quito or Guayaquil, you won't pay much more than this. Hotels categorized as expensive run $75 and up for a double. Remember to book well ahead if you're planning to stay in Otavalo on Friday (the night before market). Charming accommodations in restored haciendas are also available throughout the region.

### OTAVALO AREA

**Hostería Cusin** – A lovely working hacienda surrounded by spectacular gardens. Main rooms and upstairs bedrooms are furnished with antiques. Elegant but friendly atmosphere, though the lodge itself can be cold at night. There are several llamas in residence and a stable of horses is available for guest use. Six miles (10 km) from Otavalo (phone: 2-440672; in Quito, 2-543107; in the US, 800-969-4900). Moderate.

**Puerto Lago** – Right on lovely Lake San Pablo, ringed by mountains, this small and well-run inn is a real treat. The suites in its red-tile-roof chalets are charming and decorated with local crafts. The food and the service at the restaurant, which faces right onto the water, are first-rate. Even for those not planning an overnight stay, it's worth a stop to photograph the llamas wandering around the grounds or to indulge in some fresh lake fish. Boat rentals, fishing, and horseback riding can be arranged. Just outside Otavalo on the Pan-American Hwy. N. (phone: 2-920920 or 2-920900). Moderate.

**Mesón de las Flores** – Private bathrooms are a plus at this attractive, 15-room country inn. García Moreno and Sucre, Cotacachi (phone: 2-915009). Moderate to inexpensive.

**Ajaví** – A somewhat plastic, 60-room hotel with modern amenities, including telephone and bar-restaurant. 1638 Av. Mariano Acosta, just outside the town of Ibarra (phone: 2-952485; in Quito, 2-548477). Inexpensive.

**Hostería Chorlaví** – An old hacienda charmingly converted into a country inn with 44 rooms and a swimming pool set on lovely grounds. Its restaurant is excellent. Reservations necessary on Fridays nights; the atmosphere generally is much more relaxing during the week. At Km 4 of the Pan-American Hwy. S., near Ibarra (phone: 2-950777). Inexpensive.

***Otavalo*** – Though the rooms are rather dark and some don't have private baths, it's a friendly, budget hotel with a series of inner courtyards. Beds are scarce on Fridays without reservations. The restaurant serves up some good meals and there is an informal coffee shop that opens on to the street. Calle Roca (phone: 2-920415 or 2-920416). Inexpensive.

## COTACACHI

***Hostería La Mirage*** – Hand-tatted lace, sheer cotton canopies on the four-poster beds, and antique furniture add an enchanting touch to the 12 suites at this hotel. It was intentionally designed to resemble an old hacienda, but it has plenty of modern touches, including cable TV, telephones in every room, and an outdoor swimming pool. The hotel's dining room is as elegant as the guestrooms and the food is superb. The best touch is the garden of blooming flowers that surrounds the property. The inn's shop specializes in sachets made from these blossoms, as well as handmade lace and linen. At the end of Av. 10 de Agosto, Cotacachi (phone: 2-915237; fax: 2-915065). Expensive to moderate.

## LASSO

***Hacienda La Ciénaga*** – Near Lasso, between Quito and Ambato and in the foothills of the massive Cotopaxi volcano, this former colonial estate has 27 rooms and suites. The massive structure is built with 6-foot-thick volcanic stone walls. Public rooms are colonial or Victorian in decor, and the massive, intricately carved wooden doors are said to be among the most valuable in all of Ecuador. A restaurant, bar, shop, and gardens round out the facilities at Km 72 on the Pan-American Hwy. S. Reservations advised (phone: in Lasso, 2-801622; in Quito, 2-541337 or 2-549126; in the US, 800-969-4900). Moderate.

## SALCEDO

***Hostería Rumipamba de las Rosas*** – Also on the road to Ambato, this 30-room charmer has a pool, sauna, tennis court, restaurant, and bar. Arrangements can be made for horseback riding, fishing, mountain treks, and hunting. Each of the 5 suites has a fireplace, but all rooms have heat, which can be important at this altitude. Km 100 of the Pan-American Hwy., about 60 miles (96 km) south of Quito (phone: in Salcedo, 2-726128; in Quito, 2-566497; in the US, 800-327-9854; fax: 2-727103). Moderate.

## AMBATO

***Ambato*** – This modern 60-room hotel offers a host of amenities, including telephones, color TV sets, a restaurant, coffee shop, and conference rooms. The best in town by far. Av. Guayaquil at Roca Fuerte (phone: 2-823351 or 2-827598). Moderate.

***Villa Hilda*** – Surrounded by spacious, luxuriant, riverfront gardens, this German-run 50-year-old bungalow-hotel has 60 rooms, telephones, TV sets, heat, a good restaurant, and a pool. In the Miraflores neighborhood on Av. Miraflores (phone: 2-824065). Moderate to inexpensive.

***Miraflores*** – A 33-room hotel with private baths, a restaurant, and bar. In the Miraflores neighborhood at 71 Av. Miraflores at Las Rosas (phone: 2-824395). Inexpensive.

## RIOBAMBA

***Hostería La Andaluza*** – There is a fine view of the Chimborazo volcano from this country inn that features Spanish-style architecture, including dark wood ceiling beams and fireplaces in every guestroom. Formerly a private hacienda, this 450-year-old estate houses 30 rooms, 6 suites, a rustic but charming restaurant, a sauna, and a small gift shop specializing in leather goods. Km 16 of the Pan-American Hwy. N. (phone: in Riobamba, 2-904223 and 2-904284; in Quito, 2-564214; fax: 2-904234). Moderate.

*El Troje* – This country inn features 29 rooms, all with private baths, as well as a swimming pool, tennis court, restaurant, and bar-lounge. It can be quite cold at night. At Km 4 on the road to Chambo (phone: 2-960826 and 2-964572). Moderate.

**Chimborazo Internacional** – The best downtown choice, it has 33 comfortable rooms with private baths, a restaurant, bar, disco, and coffee shop. Corner of Argentinos and Nogales (phone: 2-963473/4). Inexpensive.

*Zeus* – Small and clean, with a restaurant, coffee shop, telephones, and TV sets. 4129 Daniel León Borja (phone: 2-962292 or 2-963100). Inexpensive.

## CUENCA AND ENVIRONS

*El Dorado* – The city's best. Right in the center of town, it has 90 rooms with carpeting, telephones, TV sets, and private baths, plus a coffee shop, a rooftop restaurant, disco, and sauna. The bilingual staff is helpful and the hotel has a special ticketing desk (and quota of tickets) for daily flights on domestic carriers *TAME* and *SAN*. 780 Gran Colombia at Luis Cordero (phone: 7-831390; in Quito, 2-550969; in the US, 800-44-UTELL; fax: 7-831-663). Expensive.

*Hostería Uzhupud* – Forty-five minutes from Cuenca in Paute, this is a charming, hacienda-style country inn. Its public rooms, grand staircase to the pool area, and separate chapel were originally part of an old estate mansion. The owners offer tours of their extensive orchid collection, which is housed in what was once the estate's glass-enclosed swimming pool. There are 49 lovely rooms and suites as well as a bar-lounge, disco, shops, and a good restaurant, along with tennis courts, volleyball, sauna and steamroom, and horseback riding. A convention center has been added to the complex. Paute (phone: in Paute, 4-250339 and 4-250329; in Cuenca, 7-807784; in the US, 800-327-3573). Expensive.

*La Laguna* – A lovely hotel whose attractive guest and public rooms overlook a small lake. Just outside the city center (taxi necessary to town), with 79 rooms, 2 restaurants, fishing, row boats, Turkish bath, children's play area and a pool. The Swiss-managed property is very well run. Av. Ordóñez Lasso (phone: 7-830200; in the US, 800-327-9854; fax: 7-832849). Expensive.

*Crespo Internacional* – Perched on a hillside overlooking one of Cuenca's four rivers, this 60-room hotel is a dramatic remodeling of an old mansion. It provides a 19th-century atmosphere but with modern comforts in the rooms, including telephones, private baths, and TV sets, as well as an excellent dining room. Trout is the specialty. Arrangements for trekking, horseback riding, and fishing can be made. 793 Calle Larga (phone: 7-827857). Moderate.

*Presidente* – A pleasant, modern property with amenities such as telephones, TV sets, a restaurant, and a ninth-floor bar with a great view. 659 Gran Colombia at Borrero (phone: 7-821066). Moderate.

*Las Américas* – Your basic budget hotel. The rooms have private baths, and there's a coffee shop and a restaurant. 1359 Mariano Cueva (phone: 7-825160 or 7-826753). Inexpensive.

# The Oriente

Some North American oilmen and Indians in Ecuador have one thing in common: They occupy the Oriente, that wild, tropical stretch of jungle east of the sierra that makes up at least 50% of Ecuador. Primarily undeveloped, the region saw few white men — other than Spanish explorers and heathen-converting Roman Catholic missionaries — until the 20th century. Then the discovery of oil deposits near Lago Agrio sent US corporations scurrying to the *selva* (jungle) for their stake in "black gold," which Ecuadorans refer to as their "oildorado."

The white man first came to the Upper Amazon basin in search of golden treasure in the 16th century; Francisco Pizarro's brother Gonzalo dispatched Francisco de Orellana into the *selva* to hunt for the precious metal in 1541. With his complement of 500 Spaniards and 4,000 Indians, Orellana trekked off, drifting down the Río Napo toward the mainstream of the Amazon River — the first white explorer to dare the jungle and survive — all the more amazing because he did it despite numerous intrigues and mutinies in his band. This expedition was one of the bloodiest and most brutal in colonial history. When not assassinating and executing one another, the explorers attacked and looted Indian villages. In the end, Orellana and the survivors of his band found the Amazon River and, thus, a waterway to the Atlantic Ocean. It was for this feat that Ecuador adopted the title "Amazon Country" (although, paradoxically, since 1941 the land that offers access to the Amazon is really part of Peru). Still crazed with gold fever, Orellana went back a second time, around 1546, never to be seen again.

Had Orellana been a modern explorer, he really might have struck it rich, for large petroleum deposits were discovered in 1967. Five years later, an oil pipeline was laid between the Oriente and the Pacific port of Esmeraldas, 311 miles (498 km) away. Texaco and Gulf Oil set up a consortium with the Ecuadoran government to maintain the fields. Today, the US investment in Ecuador is more than $850 million. The Oriente provided an impetus for economic growth in the 1970s but the boom was short-lived thanks to the oil surplus of the 1980s. Ecuador has since made attempts to diversify: Large tea plantations have been encouraged near Puyo, and considerable investment has been made in cultivating the African palm. However, the nation still produces 500,000 barrels of crude oil daily and Ecuador is one of only two OPEC countries on the continent (Venezuela is the other).

Shell-Mera and other petroleum towns look rather like a cross between a North American frontier town and the Panama hat and ceiling fan images often depicted in "banana republic" films: There are boardwalks for sidewalks, saloons with swinging doors, and even an occasional brothel or two. Such stereotypes, however, are somewhat modified by the appearance of discos in town and military security checkpoints at the Shell-Mera airport.

The road network in the Oriente is, to say the least, not first class. Long stretches of road are paved but very narrow, and some eventually wander into dirt tracks that turn to mud during the rainy season. While the temperature in the *selva* isn't impossibly hot — 85 to 90F (29 to 32C) — the humidity is very high, and the dust of the roads clings to you and your sweat-dampened clothes. Anyone venturing into the Oriente without a confirmed tour/accommodations program would be wise to bring a backpack, sleeping bag, mosquito repellent, and netting. Also, the deeper you wander into the jungle, the worse the roads get, until they're nothing but footpaths smothered in jungle flora. It's best to plan your trek around canoe or motorboat transport once you get near the rivers and let one of the missionaries or natives guide you around.

The number of organized excursions into the Ecuadoran Oriente has increased in recent years with the soaring interest in "soft adventure." Most jungle lodges detailed below offer programs that include meals, transportation, and river and jungle excursions with a local guide. A well-run 5-day program has been launched by *Nuevo Mundo* in the Cuyabeno Nature Reserve from its gateway at Lago Agrio. Here is a chance to see freshwater dolphins, monkeys, fantastic flora, and lots of birds. The company has received permission to build its own campsite deep in the jungle, and provides deluxe large tents that sleep two, inflatable mattresses, and fresh linen, as well as excellent meals. The best months are April through November. Contact *Nuevo Mundo* (2468 Av. Amazonas, Quito; phone: 2-552617; fax: 2-552916), or their US representative, *International Expeditions* (phone: 205-870-5550 in Alabama; 800-633-4734 in other states). *La Selva,* a lodge owned and operated by a North American (2816 6 de Diciembre or write to PO Box 635, Suc. 12 de Octubre in Quito; phone: 2-550995 or 2-554686; fax: 2-563814), provides a chance to experience the Amazon basin while staying in comfortable accommodations. *Metropolitan Touring*'s *Flotel Orellana* (often described as a 3-story floating raft) carries 40 passengers on jungle river tours out of Lago Agrio to new lodges built deep in the Amazon. The vessel is now operating on the pristine Aguarico River. Book through the operator (239 Av. Amazonas, Quito; phone: 2-560550), or in the US with *Adventure Associates* (phone: 214-907-0414 or 800-527-2500). A travel agency concerned with jungle preservation, *Caento's Excursions* in Quito (phone: 2-569960; fax: 2-569956), offers an intriguing trip from Quito — overland to Puyo and then by propeller plane into the jungle. Travelers sleep in tents, catch the fish they cook for dinner, travel in dugout canoes, and meet and talk with the Huaorani Indians in the town of Palm Beach — a settlement where five North American missionaries were speared in 1956. The guide is a multilingual Huaorani Indian. For further details, see *Amazonia,* DIVERSIONS.

Small-plane service is available to the Oriente from Quito and Guayaquil on a charter basis. *TAME* flies regularly to Macas, Lago Agrio, and Coca. There is also bus service to some interesting gateway towns, such as Baños and Puyo.

**PUERTO FRANCISCO DE ORELLANA:** At the mouth of the Coca and Napo rivers, the port was named after the conquistador credited with baptizing the Amazon River. (Ecuadorans still use its former name, Coca.) Here you can rent a canoe and drift down the river to Limóncocha, home to hundreds of bird species and a type of caiman that is said to grow as long as 13 feet, to Pañacocha (Piranha) Lake, and to the Peruvian border post of Nueva Rocafuerte (passports stamped here). If you prefer, you can reach the port of Coca on a direct flight, or via a 10-hour bus ride, from Quito.

At Limóncocha National Park, there is a jungle boardwalk connecting the Napo River with Limóncocha Lake. (The bright red eyes of caimans sometimes are seen here at night.) Arrangements can be made for evening boat excursions, as well as canoe and fishing outings; there is also swimming here. To the east of Limóncocha is Pañacocha

Lake, a paradise for serious bird watchers. Canoe trips into this jungle region allow travelers to snap photos of monkeys, fish for the ferocious creatures that give the lake its name, or simply marvel at the exotic wildlife.

Heading north to Lago Agrio then west to the Quito–Lago Agrio Highway will bring you to a fork halfway along the route. Continuing west, you will reach Quito. Continuing south, you will arrive in Tena.

**TENA:** The capital of Napo province is quiet; the town is inhabited by the Quijo Indians (a Yumbo tribe). They speak Spanish, but generally the common language is Quichua, a dialect of the Inca Quechua language. More often than not they reside in houses of bamboo and grass, making their living harvesting *naranjillas* (a citrus fruit in the tomato family) and selling them to truckers. (In the cities, *naranjilla* juice is a thirst-quenching drink found on most menus.) Some pan for gold in small streams. Between 30,000 to 50,000 Yumbo are thought to live in the Oriente today. Head south to Puyo.

**PUYO:** Now a major Oriente center, this was once a frontier town, and the swinging saloon doors still remain. The shops sell a variety of souvenirs, ranging from stuffed animals to feathers, baskets, and interesting pottery. The drive to Puyo from Tena or Baños is on a rough but scenically splendid road. The best overland travel in this region is by bus or chauffeur-driven car.

**SHELL-MERA:** Thirty-one miles (50 km) west of Baños, this oil camp houses an airport and an Ecuadoran military checkpoint. (At one time, special passes were needed to enter the Oriente.) There's a bar and disco in town. Outside town is an archaeological site — a mound-shaped *tola* that is a ceremonial complex located on a tea plantation, and open to visitors. Similar to those in the rural area north of Quito, this *tola* was built by ancient Indians. They were often the burial grounds for important Inca and pre-Inca honchos; at other times, *tolas* were used as high ground for planting during flood times or as vantage points for Inca foremen to oversee those who farmed.

A ride south along the Río Pastaza leads out of the Oriente to Baños.

**BAÑOS:** More on the fringe of the Cordillera Oriental (Eastern Range) than in the Amazonian plains, this is a health resort originally noted for its thermal baths and hot springs (at the foot of the volcano Tungurahua), but more popular today as a base for hikers and climbers. The church here has interesting murals depicting Nuestra Señora de Santa Agua performing miracles; you can sightsee or, if you're in hearty shape, take a walk up the volcano and camp there for the night. Also available and for sale here is a rich selection of the work of local artisans. (Also see *Ambato* in this chapter.)

From Baños, you can continue either west to Ambato and pick up the Pan-American Highway or eastward to the Oriente, where your next stop is Macas.

**MACAS:** The Sangay Volcano and the Salesian Sevilla and Don Bosco missions upriver on the Río Upano are the major attractions in this village. One note about the Amazonian tributaries: Unlike some rivers around Ecuador, you can swim in them (many others are very polluted).

**SUCÚA:** This upriver village is the home of the "tamed" Jívaro, or Shuar, Indians. They're a very passive, Christianized lot these days, but still display the evidence of wilder days — shrunken heads. This much is known about the head-shrinking process: The skull is removed, and the skin is dried out by a hot stove. This way, the skin shrinks yet retains its features. The mouth is sewn shut. Any shrunken heads you find today are animals, generally monkeys, cooked up for the tourist trade.

There are about 45,000 Jívaro left in the Oriente; they speak both Shuar and Spanish. For the most part the Indians are farmers, growing crops of cotton, tobacco, and fruit, and raising guinea pigs. Though Christianized, they still honor pagan ways, and their sociological system is chauvinistic: Either women are sold to their husbands or the prospective grooms are employed by future fathers-in-law for a certain period of time before the ceremony.

These Jívaro share the jungle with their cousins, the Auca (or Huaorani), once a fierce tribe that murdered several missionaries in 1956.

When you're ready to leave Sucúa, a turn west will lead you back to the Pan-American Highway and Cuenca. You can now continue south to Peru.

## BEST EN ROUTE

There are very few places offering accommodations in the Oriente. Unless you've booked a lodge, your best bet is to plan to camp or to stay at one of the several missions that dot the jungle. If you camp, be sure to bring plenty of mosquito repellent and netting with you, and begin taking quinine pills before your arrival.

Any "hotels" (as opposed to jungle "lodges" with excursions, programs, canoes, and so on) will be very primitive and inexpensive — about $10 to $15 for two people sharing a double room. A hotel categorized as moderate would cost about $25 for a double; however, an expensive hotel will cost about $60 per person. Check hotel availability with a travel agency in Quito.

### LAKE IRIPARI

*Iripari Lodge* – Built by *Metropolitan Touring*, this new lodge is used mostly for *Flotel* passengers. It offers 20 cottages with twin beds, each with a private bath and terrace. Ecological concerns are addressed here — a wooden walkway to the restaurant was built over the jungle floor to prevent damage to the flora and the lodge is powered by solar energy. Book with the *Metropolitan Touring* office (239 Amazonas, Quito; phone: 2-560550; fax: 2-564655) or through their US representative, *Adventure Associates* (13150 Coit Rd., Suite 110, Dallas, TX 75240; phone: 214-907-0414 or 800-527-2500). Moderate.

### IMUYA LAKE

*Imuya Camp* – This remote camp is also mainly for *Flotel* passengers, with a stopover at *Iripari Lodge* en route. Basic but comfortable, the camp's main draw is its proximity to pristine nature and possibilities for bird watching, photo safaris, and visits to indigenous communities. Book with the *Metropolitan Touring* office (239 Amazonas, Quito; phone: 2-560550; fax: 2-564655) or through their US representative, *Adventure Associates* (13150 Coit Rd., Suite 110, Dallas, TX 75240; phone: 214-907-0414 or 800-527-2500). Moderate.

### TENA

*Amazonas* – A jungle hotel, where you'll get a bed and be able to sleep safe and sound from things that go bump in the *selva* night, near the main square at Juan Montalvo and Juan Vela (phone: 2-886439). Inexpensive.

### BAÑOS

*Sangay* – Set near a waterfall, this hotel is also a health resort. There are 40 rooms, a restaurant, tennis and squash courts, a pool, sauna, and massage. 101 Plazoleta Ayora (phone: 2-740490; in Quito, 2-432066; fax in Quito: 2-740056). Moderate.

*Villa Gertrudis* – Undoubtedly the best in Baños, it has 18 comfortable, spacious rooms, all with private baths, as well as a swimming pool. Normally booked with meals, which are renowned in Ecuador. No children. 2975 Montalvo (phone: 2-740441). Moderate.

*Palace* – With a pool and a restaurant, this is a fine budget alternative to the neighboring *Sangay*. The meals are quite good and very reasonably priced 2003 Montalvo (phone: 2-740470). Inexpensive.

## MISAHUALLI

*Anaconda Lodge* – From Misahualli, it's an hour's ride downriver via motorized dugout canoe to this lodge on Anaconda Island in the Napo River. Comfortable accommodations in thatch bungalows with bath and shower; central lodge for meals. A typical program here includes transportation from Quito to Misahualli, daily jungle and river excursions, and meals; it can be booked by major tour operators in Ecuador such as *Gordon Tours* (phone: 4-373550 or 4-373555; fax: 4-284835) in Guayaquil, *Nuevo Mundo* (phone: 2-552617), *Ecuadorian Tours* (phone: 2-560488), and *Metropolitan Touring* (phone: 2-560550; fax: 2-564655) in Quito. Expensive.

# El Litoral

The easiest way to proceed southwest from the sierra to the coastal region (El Litoral) of Ecuador is to follow the Quito-Guayaquil Highway from Cajabamba and the Pan-American Highway. The 290-mile (464-km) journey will take you from the cattle ranges of the Cordillera Occidental (Western Range) through the marshy rice plantations that cover the lowlands. The 350-mile coast that stretches from Esmeraldas to Guayaquil is the heartland of Ecuador's major exports.

Barely 100 miles wide, El Litoral encompasses the provinces of Esmeraldas, Manabí, Los Ríos, Guayas, and El Oro, a mix of jungle, rolling hills, lowlands, beach, and desert. Hot and humid, El Litoral is tempered by the cool Humboldt Current. The average yearly temperature is 79F (26C) and is, in fact, about 10 degrees warmer but more comfortable than the Oriente, where the high humidity often makes it feel as though you're immersed in an eternal steambath. El Litoral is warmer than the Andes, since the temperature increases about 1 degree for every 320-foot descent. The coastal plains are also the home of exquisite varieties of birds and a number of colorful animals, ranging from the coatimundi, kinkajou, fox, and otter to the weasel and skunk.

There are several seaports along the Pacific coast. The farthest north, Esmeraldas, exports wood and bananas and houses the terminal of the 311-mile trans-Andean petroleum pipeline from the Oriente. At one time, the Santa Elena Peninsula south of Guayaquil contained a large number of oil deposits, but that quantity has declined, leaving the deposits in the Oriente to be explored and exploited. Manta and Puerto Bolívar, south of Esmeraldas, export frozen fish and shrimp, coffee, and castor beans.

But it is Guayaquil, Ecuador's largest city (pop. approximately 2.5 million) and seaport, that handles up to 65% of all exports and 90% of the imports. Passing through Guayaquil's Puerto Nuevo are bananas, sugar, beans, cocoa, fish, wood, Panama hats — a list of everything from soup to nuts. Guayaquil is seated on the west bank of the Río Guayas; ships ply in and out from the Gulf of Guayaquil, which eventually leads to the Pacific Ocean.

El Litoral exports a host of minerals. Azuay province has large copper and limestone deposits. Gold has been mined in Portoviejo in El Oro province since the 16th century; silver and salt deposits can be found in Guayas province.

Shrimp, which have become one of Ecuador's major exports, and fish, especially tuna, are taken from "national" waters that the government says extend 200 miles into the Pacific. Several US fishing boats have been picked up by Ecuadoran patrols in past years in this never-ending dispute over high seas sovereignty.

More than 52% of Ecuador's 10 million people live in El Litoral; of these, nearly 2,000 are Indians from the Cayapa and Colorado tribes along with a few migrant Yumbo from the Oriente and Coayquero from Colombia. Most of them live in the jungle or along riverbanks; many are farmers and fishermen, although the Cayapa are known for their basket weaving. They rarely mingle with whites, are baptized Roman Catholics, and live in houses of thatch roofs and open walls. The rest of the coastal population is made up of *montuvios* — coastal mestizos — who are mostly farmers and fishermen. The white population is generally concentrated around Guayaquil, Manta, and the resorts of Salinas and Playas.

Like the rest of Ecuador, the roads in El Litoral are partly paved, partly incomplete, unmarked, often impassable in the rainy season, with one or two lanes. The most interesting drive is from Quito to Guayaquil, which will take you past the river towns of Babahoyo and Daule, down into the port. From Guayaquil, you can journey to the resort towns of Playas, Salinas, and Punta Carnero, continue up the coastal highway to Manta, then inland to Quevedo, Santo Domingo de los Colorados, and north to Esmeraldas.

There are a number of flights to Guayaquil daily from Quito and Cuenca. But the best way to make this scenic excursion is on the *Nariz del Diablo* (Devil's Nose) narrow-gauge railroad, a roller-coaster ride that makes a 45-degree incline leading down to the coastal plains of Bucay and Durán just across the Guayas River from Guayaquil. The train passengers take a ferry from here to the coast. The trip is a real treat; it's the engineering feat of two North Americans, Arthur and John Harmon. Unfortunately, both men died before the road was completed in 1908, but you remember them every time that train creeps down a steep *cerro* or makes a vertical climb. Take a bus from Quito to Alausi where the 8-hour train ride starts.

Originally the train began in Quito, but torrential rains in 1983–84 unleashed damaging mud slides that destroyed much of the track between Quito and Guayaquil. The government has abandoned plans to repair the track.

Be sure to bring extra food with you, although a wide variety of local produce is sold on platforms at train stations (and this steam train stops with great frequency to get water to make it run). Full food service is available in the *Expreso Metropolitan* deluxe car that runs on the scenic route between Riobamba to Quito twice weekly. The *autoferro,* a kind of one-car rail bus run on gasoline, travels both ways between Quito and Riobamba daily except Sundays. You are allowed to sit on the roof with the baggage in case you want to take pictures or get away from the crowd. The cars, which carry a maximum of 40 passengers, can be specially chartered from the bus company's offices in Quito, 443 Bolívar at García Moreno (phone: 2-216180).

**GUAYAQUIL:** Ecuador is the largest banana exporter and second-largest shrimp exporter in the world, and it is through Guayaquil that the nation's most important commodities are shipped; so Guayaquil is used to heavy cargo traffic as a way of life.

It is, in fact, the largest port on the South American Pacific Coast. Still, the city's new port, Puerto Nuevo, is reputed to be the cleanest harbor in the world, despite the tons and tons of animals, minerals, crops, equipment, and people that plow through it daily. The first steamboat ever to run in Latin America was built here; also, the first submarine, the *Hippopotamus,* was tested in the Gulf of Guayaquil.

Guayaquil played an important role in South American independence in the 19th century. A military junta was formed against Spanish rule in 1820 after the signing of a declaration of independence in Ecuador; liberators José de San Martín and Simón Bolívar were invited to join the revolt. An army dispatched by San Martín helped overthrow the Spanish government in Quito in 1822. Soon afterward, San Martín and Bolívar held a secret meeting in Guayaquil to see who would claim credit for liberating Peru. San Martín wanted it to join Chile and Argentina in setting up a constitutional monarchy, but Bolívar wanted it as part of his Federación de Gran Colombia (Great Colombian Federation). No one ever knew what the two statesmen said to one another, but Bolívar became Peru's Great Liberator and San Martín exiled himself to Europe and never returned.

A waterfront monument (Av. 9 de Octubre and Malecón) commemorates the secret meeting between the two heroes. The rotunda of the monument is erected in such a way that two people can stand at opposites sides, whisper, and hear one another.

If you like museums, there are several here. The *Municipal Museum* (Calle Diez de Agosto y Pichincha) houses pre-Columbian artifacts discovered along the coast, including clay seals, molds for gold masks, and shrunken heads of *tzantzas.* It is open daily except Mondays from 8:30 AM to 4:30 PM. The *Museum of the Ecuadoran House of Culture* (1200 Av. 9 de Octubre) contains a gold exhibit, with objects such as snake-shaped bracelets, nose rings, chest shields, and masks on the seventh floor. Most of the gold artifacts in these museums were taken from excavations in the Santa Elena Peninsula; dating suggests that the pre-Columbian culture may be more than 5,000 years old. The *Museo Banco Central of Guayaquil* (Central Bank Museum) houses some of these golden artifacts as well as archaeological exhibits from coastal cultures. It's in a modern building on 9 de Octubre near the *Oro Verde* hotel. The Escuela Superior Politécnica del Litoral (Polytechnic University; 205 Rocafuerte at Loja; phone: 40-309558 and 40-563733, ext. 190) has a small museum with changing archaeology and art exhibits; open weekdays from 9 AM to 4 PM; no admission charge. Another fine museum is the *Museo Nahim Isaías Barquet* (Nahim Isaías Barquet Museum; 2nd Floor of the Filanbanco on Av. Aguirre at Pichincha; phone: 4-329099, ext. 353). It was named for the founder of the bank where the museum is housed — a businessman from Guayaquil who was kidnapped and killed by terrorists some years ago. It is open Mondays through Saturdays from 10 AM to 5 PM; no admission charge.

Take a taxi over to the huge, domed Centro Civico on Avenida Quito between Calles Venezuela and El Oro to see the two large outdoor sculptures by Oswaldo Guayasamín, Ecuador's most famous contemporary artist. The undulating white scupture with stained glass mosaics is representative of the Andes mountains; beside it is the sculptor's tribute to the Ecuadorian family. The domed Civic Center, which took 21 years to build, regularly stages musicals and live theater. Be aware that this is not an area to walk around in alone at night; there have been crime problems reported in the high-rise buildings across from the Civic Center.

It is also not wise to wander alone in the market area or the contraband selling section of town — La Bahía — unless you leave all valuables at your hotel. *Guayaquileños* recommend wandering through the outdoor market, where vegetables, fruits, and healing herbs are displayed, to see the metal building next to it where the fish market is housed. It was designed in 1905 by Gustave Eiffel, of tower fame, and shipped to Guayaquil from France. At La Bahía, chaos and noise reign and pickpockets are in profusion. Local authorities suggest going first with empty pockets to check out the merchandise, then returning later with just the exact amount of cash to make the purchase. Items with phony designer trademarks are mixed in with the real thing here.

A treat is in store for visitors who take a break from their city tour to rest in the Parque Seminario (Seminary Park) at Calle Chile and Calle 10 de Agosto. A lovely park, donated to the city in 1894, it encircles a statue of the Great Liberator Simón Bolívar on horseback. However, the most curious aspect of the park is its fauna. Besides the small pond filled with turtles, iguanas roam free, scurrying across the sidewalks and around the trees. Children will get a kick out of this stop while adults rest their weary feet.

You also can wander through Guayaquil's churches. The cathedral (Calle 10 de Agosto between Boyacá and Chimborazo) is a modern, Gothic church with white towers and impressive stained glass windows. In the old district of Las Peñas is the church of Santo Domingo, the first church erected in Guayaquil, in 1543.

The bohemian district, called Las Peñas, is famous for its winding stone streets and cramped houses. Many of the wooden houses along this walkway have been converted into artists' studios and workshops with balconies overlooking the river. Jasmine bushes scent the air here, and you will see the homes of two former presidents on the *malecón*. Unfortunately this charming area is also host to petty criminals. It's wiser to visit Las Peñas with a guide or as part of a group. This neighborhood got its name, which means "the pains" or "the woes," because it was here that the cemetery, jail, and hospital all were located. Like Las Peñas, the Government Palace is found along the boulevard facing the Guayas River. A stroll along this boulevard is pleasant; when you pass the waterfront clock tower, climb its steps to the top for a fine view of the city. The cemetery on Avenida Julián Coronel is also worth a visit. Nearly all its opulent marble tombs and grave markers are of a startling white stone.

Good eating in Guayaquil centers around the wealth of fresh seafood and fish and the abundance of local tropical fruits. The pineapple literally drips with honey-sweet juice, and banana chips, now a popular "health food" snack in the US, originated in Guayaquil, where they are made from a special green banana. You can try local specialties (ask for a *comida tipica*) at *La Piñata* in the *Unihotel* or the *Continental* hotel coffee shop. They include *hayaca*, made from cornmeal dough filled with chicken or pork and then steamed in a banana leaf (like a Mexican tamale), and *pan de yuca*, a tasty bread made from manioc flour. Delicious seafood includes river and stone crab, lobster, and huge shrimp. By far the best seafood restaurant in Guayaquil is *El Caracol Azul* (1918 Av. 9 de Octubre at the corner of Los Ríos; phone: 4-280461). Try the lobster bisque.

Guayaquil offers good prices on watches, cosmetics, cologne, and other items commonly found in duty-free shops; check the boutiques along Avenida 9 de Octubre. The city is sprouting modern shopping malls that offer good buys on Ecuadoran-made cotton casual wear and shoes. And if you have some spare time, you can arrange a manicure and pedicure for about $3. Visitors in the market for souvenirs should steer clear of the phony Inca relics. High-quality handicrafts can be found in the boutique of the *Oro Verde* hotel. But the best handicrafts shop is *Manos* in the Urdesa neighborhood (at 305 Cedros at Calle Primera; phone: 4-381567). This store sells a variety of goods from all over the country, including jewelry carved from *tagua*, the cream-colored nut nicknamed "vegetable ivory." Ecuador has begun exporting items made from *tagua* with the blessing of naturalists who say it may help to stem the illegal traffic of elephant ivory around the world.

As in other parts of Ecuador, Guayaquil celebrates the national holy days and festivals. There's a lot of merrymaking, and people have a good time drinking beer and *aguardiente* (moonshine sugarcane whiskey). But it's on July 23 and 24 that Guayaquil really rocks, as it celebrates its *Foundation Day*. Hotel reservations are an absolute must, but worth the effort — particularly for the chance to view the myriad sidewalk art displays. This is the best time to explore the streets of Las Peñas (they're full of people) and to see the interiors of these colonial buildings turned artists' studios.

Since Guayaquil is Ecuador's largest port, a number of steamers arrive in the harbor daily from all over the world. Simón Bolívar Airport, near the city, handles international traffic. A new airport, out in the country and equipped to handle wide-body jets, is in the works. Ecuador has many carriers of its own: *Ecuatoriana* and *SAETA,* both of which provide service between North and South America; *TAME (Transportes Aéreos Militares de Ecuador),* the largest domestic carrier, which flies to some 20 cities; and, in addition, *SAN (Servicios Aéreos Nacionales),* which offers daily jet service to Quito and Cuenca from Guayaquil (as does *SAETA).*

CETUR, the once ineffective national tourist office, has moved to a new location (on the corner of the *malecón* and Av. Aguirre; phone: 4-328312) and considerably upgraded its services. Although it has only one English-speaking staff person, multilingual guides are available to groups that contact the office in advance. The office has brochures on Guayaquil as well as other areas of Ecuador. You'll get much more useful information from the offices of the major Ecuadoran tour operators in Quito, such as *Ecuadorian Tours* (339 Av. Amazonas; phone: 2-560488; they also have an office in Guayaquil at 1900 Av. 9 de Octubre; phone: 4-39711) or *Metropolitan Touring* in Quito (239 Av. Amazonas; phone: 2-560550; fax: 2-564655). And at *Gordon Tours* in Guayaquil (2009 Av. 9 de Octubre; phone: 4-373550, 4-373555, and 4-373596; fax: 4-284835), there is no problem with English. If you read Spanish, the monthly entertainment guide *Tiempo Libre* is available at bookstores and kiosks for under $1, but it generally sells out at Guayaquil bookstores during the first 2 weeks of the month. The *Unihotel* here provides it to all guests, free of charge.

■ **A few final words to the wise:** Because of its status as a port city, Guayaquil has a higher level of crime than Quito. It also has a red-light district. Beware of pickpockets hanging around hotels and take care when visiting the market area. Use common sense while strolling after dark. Also, the male population of this city far outnumbers the female population, so unescorted women travelers may find themselves the objects of unwanted attention.

There's a wealth of excursion possibilities in the Guayaquil area. Visits can be arranged to the acres of shrimp growing pools surrounding the city. This is particularly exciting at night, when growers harvest the shrimp with the aid of huge searchlights. This area was home to the Valdivia Indian culture, which was never conquered by the Inca. For sailing, stop by the *Yacht Club* on the *malecón* (phone: 4-515225).

You may have traveled past Babahoyo and Daule on your way into Guayaquil by bus or car, but you can rent a boat and journey up the Guayas for a look at these riverfront villages.

In the style of Mississippi River boats, a new boat — the *Pedregal* — plies Guayaquil's Guayas River every afternoon; tickets for 1-hour cruises are sold along the *malecón*. Afterward, stop by the *Muelle No. 4* restaurant (right beside the *Pedregal*'s dock) and have some seafood or a cocktail and watch the sunset. Handicrafts are sold at the pier. Along the waterfront, there are small cargo vessels being loaded with food and other supplies for the Galápagos Islands. When they have room, they'll take passengers; although the 2-day trip is an adventure — you'll have to sleep on your own hammock strung on deck and be sure to pack food for the voyage. To make arrangements, just walk down to the boats and ask to speak to the captain.

Babahoyo, 119 miles (190 km) north of Guayaquil, is uninteresting in itself, but its tropical setting sells it. It's all there — the river, flocks of parrots and toucans brightening the jungle trees, plantations of rice, cocoa, sugar, and bananas (all you need are a gin and tonic, a Panama hat, and a Humphrey Bogart film). A few miles down the river, Daule, filled with banana plantations, is a pictorial repeat of Babahoyo.

Just 20 miles (32 km) from downtown Guayaquil on the outskirts of the city is the Jardín Botánico (Botanic Garden), which features a conservation center for tropical trees and plants; there are 150 species of orchids alone. The gardens are open daily from 8 AM to sunset from May through December; no admission charge. And a half-day's drive south is the newly developed Puyango Petrified Forest. To get there from Guayaquil, take Highway 70 west to Santa Elena; then follow Highway 1 north along the coast. The road eventually narrows and becomes an unnumbered continuation of Highway 1. Along here — between Puerto López and Puerto Cayo — is this 6,600-acre wildlife area filled with giant petrified ferns, trees, and plants, as well as 120 species of birds, deer, armadillos, and wild boars. Special permission from the government is needed to enter the area. Getting a permit is a long and involved process — it's better to book a trip through a local travel ageney, such as *Gordon Tours* (2009 Av. 9 de Octubre at the corner of Los Rós, Guayaquil; phone: 4-373550, 4-373555, and 4-373596; fax: 4-284835). The forest is open daily from 8 AM to sunset. Another fascinating nature area, only 14 miles (22 km) from Guayaquil via Highway 70 toward Salinas, is the Cerro Blanco Wildlife Preserve. Like the Puyango Petrified Forest, visitors need permission to enter this new "dry" forest sanctuary; *Gordon Tours* can make the arrangements. A tropical dry forest has high temperatures, low precipitation, and is filled with plant and animal life that survive under these conditions, including cactuses, carob trees, bromeliads, and exotic birds. Higher level areas of the reserve have bamboo, moss, and sea birds, and there are marked hiking trails throughout. Open daily from 8 AM to sunset.

Returning to Guayaquil, you're ready to pack your bags and head on to the resorts.

**PLAYAS:** Less than 60 miles (96 km) south of Guayaquil down the Peninsula Highway, this resort was once a lively fishing village. Today, fishermen still return in the afternoon with their catch stacked high on their canoes, but for the most part, the inhabitants here are sun-seeking *guayaquileños*. The beaches and salt flats of Playas are habitats for wild parakeets, gulls, terns, and other shore birds.

**SALINAS:** About 40 miles (64 km) west of Playas, this modern resort sits on a crescent-shaped beach and offers some of the best sport fishing in the world. Black marlin, tuna, and dolphin (the fish) abound. In fact, the world's record catch for black marlin (a whopping 1,560 pounds) was hauled in off the coast in 1953; this stood until late 1991, when a 2,000-lb. catch was officially listed as the new record. In recent years, Salinas has hosted a number of deep-sea fishing competitions and the *Copa Galápagos Regatta* to the islands of the same name. A seven-boat charter fleet, *Pesca Tours,* offers week-long all-inclusive charters (transportation from Guayaquil to Salinas, lodging at *Samarina* or *Punta Carnero Inn,* bait, tackle). Contact Knud Holst, *Pesca Tours S.A.* (Dept. FS, Box 487, Guayaquil; phone: 4-443365). Billfishing season is from May to January; September through November are the peak months. Like Playas, buses leave every 15 minutes from Guayaquil's bus terminal to this resort. A scrumptious seafood lunch is available at the seaside hotels and restaurants at both beaches. Especially notable (and pricey) is the *Mar y Tierra* restaurant on the *malecón*. Salinas also has an active nightlife. A favorite discotheque is *Barba Negra,* a block from the yacht club.

**PUNTA CARNERO:** About 6 miles (10 km) south of Salinas on the Santa Elena Peninsula, this resort has a 9-mile beach and plenty of surf and black marlin, dolphin, and bonito deep-sea fishing.

**En Route from Punta Carnero** – The coastal route forks at Santa Elena village; from here, you can head back to Guayaquil or continue north as far as Manta. This coastal road, however, is not very good during the rainy season — in fact, it disappears entirely. If you take it, do so in the dry season, and at low tide only.

**MANTA:** This port in Manabí province has grown steadily to handle almost 10% of the country's fruit and fish exports. It is an excellent spot for fishing enthusiasts; between July and November, giant blue and striped marlin are in abundance. (In May 1985, a 1,014-pound blue marlin was pulled in on an 80-pound test line.) The tourist office in the Edificio EMAPA can provide details on fishing trips. There really isn't much to see here, but Manta does have a beach where you can go swimming and watch the shrimp fleets off on the horizon. Vast shrimp beds were discovered about 10 miles off the coast 10 years ago. Archaeology buffs will be interested in the *Museo del Banco Central*'s (Museum of the Central Bank, in the modern building on 9 de Octubre near the *Oro Verde* hotel) collection of artifacts from the Manteña culture, the indigenous group living here when the Spaniards arrived.

Bahía de Caráquez, a small port north of Manta, has a tennis club and is the home of world tennis star Pancho Segura. It also has some lovely stretches of beach. There are nice beaches and reasonable accommodations in neighboring San Vicente, a town known for its thermal springs.

**En Route from Manta** – From Manta, continue inland south through Portoviejo, then north to Santo Domingo de los Colorados, where the highway (if you can call it that) eventually leads you northeast to Esmeraldas.

Jipijapa, the first town on this route, is a small fruit-processing center famous for Panama hats. Hats have been made here since the 1500s, using the same procedure. Leaves from the *paja toquilla*, a palm tree, are dried, then woven.

Montecristi, 20 miles (32 km) north of Jipijapa, also produces the hats. Here they're sold in distinctively painted balsa-wood boxes.

**PORTOVIEJO:** The road leading north from Montecristi eventually reaches a farm-produce processing center of 120,000 people.

**QUEVEDO:** This town of 70,000 is a junction for routes leading to Quito, Guayaquil, and Esmeraldas. It is known for its prominent Chinese community.

Ecuador has a number of foreign minority groups: A large, established Lebanese community resides in Guayaquil (where they are known as *turcos*, or Turks); and several thousand Germans and Spanish immigrated here during World War II and the Spanish Civil War. Here and there you'll also find native Ecuadorans with English, Irish, and French surnames.

**SANTO DOMINGO DE LOS COLORADOS:** The most colorful attraction here is the Colorado Indians. They paint their bodies with red dye from the *achiote* plant, thought to ward off unfriendly spirits. The men, who traditionally wear brief skirts and cloths slung over their shoulder, keep their hair short, parted in the middle, and smeared with the same red paint, giving a clay effect. The hard, protruding shelf of hair acts like a visor in this sunny region. The women wear their hair and skirts long. In the old days, many of the women romped around bare-breasted; because of a few missionaries, however, more and more are covering up.

Most of the Colorado farm for their living; others supplement their incomes posing for *turista* photographs for a few sucres. They're a very docile group and even appear to enjoy mingling with foreigners. In fact, they have mingled so much that tribal customs are now mostly for show. Many of the Colorado have left this area, however, in order to retain their traditional lifestyle, and it's not advisable to make this trip on the promise of seeing many of them. What is worthwhile is the dramatically changing flora as the road climbs as high as 11,000 feet and later descends into this fertile valley. The area also supports numerous species of birds, making the trip of particular value for bird watching and botanical studies. The Sunday morning *mercado de frutas* (fruit market) is filled with an astounding variety of tropical fruits, many of them unfamiliar to North Americans.

If you're returning to Quito by road — a 79-mile (126-km) trip — watch out: The road washes out during the rainy season. The road is better on the route northwest to Esmeraldas.

**ESMERALDAS:** A long 279 miles (446 km) from Guayaquil, the "emerald" province is continuously green — lush, tropical vegetation grows down to the shore of the Pacific. It's not as hot and humid here as it is in Guayaquil; temperatures stay at a constant 80F (26C). Unfortunately, mosquitos and malaria are problems, so start quinine treatments before visiting and take plenty of insect repellent with you (the local ones aren't as effective as what is sold in the US).

The second-largest seaport in Ecuador (pop. 80,000), its prime exports are wood, bananas, cacao, and tobacco, and the trans-Andean pipeline ends at Balao Port. Historically, the area is noteworthy as the first place in the country where Spanish conquistadores landed.

Esmeraldas has become a popular tourist spot for Ecuadorans, and there are at least 10 hotels with swimming pools in the city (see *Best en Route*). Its main boulevard is closed to traffic between 7:30 and 9:30 PM, so you can stroll through the street without worrying about being hit by a car, bus, or a rickety truck laden with bananas. Most of the Esmeraldans are blacks, the descendants of shipwrecked and freed slaves brought in by Spain during the 16th century to work the plantations. They have been assimilated into the Ecuadoran mainstream, contributing wonderful music, which you might have the good fortune to enjoy at an impromptu gathering, as well as handicrafts, including delicate gold jewelry.

There are a number of small, white sand beaches nearby (the most notable being Las Palmas) where you can step into the Pacific for a swim or simply bask in the sun. Atacames and Sua are about 15 miles (24 km) south of the city and make an excellent day trip. More information is available at the national tourist office in the Palacio Municipal (City Hall; phone: 2-714528).

Esmeraldas is a favorite destination of ornithologists — there are about 400 species of birds in the province. The Esmeraldas antbird and the blue-tailed torgan are among the prized sights.

For pre-Columbian treasures, visit La Tolita (Little Indian Mound) in the far north pocket of the province. La Tolia is located on a small island on the right bank of the mouth of the Santiago River and is believed to date back as far as 500 BC. The civilization that once lived here had advanced metallurgy skills and even worked with platinum. A town and ceremonial center, the area was unfortunately looted heavily before modern times. The *Museo del Banco Central de Esmeraldas* displays some remains of the 2,500-year-old La Tolita culture.

Another side trip from Esmeraldas is north to the banana-exporting town of Limones (also known as Valdez, on some maps). There you can arrange a canoe trip upriver to see the Cayapa Indians, subjects of current ethnographic study. Like the Colorado, Cayapa women wear long skirts and nothing else.

There is bus transportation along the coast between Guayaquil and Esmeraldas. Air service between Esmeraldas and Guayaquil or Quito also is available.

## BEST EN ROUTE

El Litoral has the widest variety of hotels found in Ecuador; it's possible to book a first class, double room (with private bathroom) in Guayaquil for a very expensive $100 to $150 a night; an expensive room would run up to $100; a first class, modern room with bath in a gulf hotel for a more moderate $35 and up a night; or a small, second class, not-so-private affair in a small town for about $15. Not all these hotels have telephones. If possible, make reservations at the city hotels in advance. Ask about air conditioning; Guayaquil is hot and sticky. Hotels, by the way, add the standard nationwide 20% tax. Guayaquil's hotels are more expensive than those in Quito.

### GUAYAQUIL

*Continental* – This first class, 91-room downtown hotel offers private baths, air conditioning, a cocktail lounge, conference rooms, service shops, and car rentals. Its *El Fortín* restaurant is excellent and its 24-hour cafeteria serves fine Ecuadoran fare. 300 10 de Agosto and Chile (phone: 4-329270; in Quito, 2-560666; in the US, 800-333-1212; fax: 4-325454). Very expensive.

**Grand Hotel Guayaquil** – Fully air conditioned, it offers friendly service, an excellent 24-hour coffee shop, cocktail lounge, restaurant, a huge gymnasium, and 2 squash courts. Outdoor barbecues are accompanied by music, and the pool is dramatically walled by the city's cathedral. 1600 Boyacá at 10 de Agosto (phone: 4-329690; in the US, 800-44-UTELL; fax: 4-327251). Very expensive.

**Oro Verde** – A truly deluxe property, it's also Guayaquil's most expensive by far. There are 250 tastefully decorated, air conditioned rooms, an outdoor pool, sauna, gymnasium, several restaurants (don't miss the Sunday brunch), and a friendly casino that bills itself as Ecuador's largest. Its business center has personal computers, typewriters, fax and telex services, a copy machine, secretaries, and translators. 9 de Octubre and García Moreno (phone: 4-327999; in the US, 800-327-9854; fax: 4-329350). Very expensive.

**Unihotel** – Part of a downtown shopping complex, it is located 2 blocks from the *malecón* and Avenida 9 de Octubre near the main cathedral. Its *El Parque* restaurant (one of three in the hotel) offers wonderful views into Parque Seminario's trees, which house the resident iguana population. This deluxe property has 77 air conditioned rooms and 47 suites with kitchens. Other facilities include 24-hour room service, a solarium with whirlpool bath, sauna, a small gym, a children's play area with rides, and a casino. 406 Clemente Ballén and Chile (phone: 4-327100; in the US, 800-223-5852; fax: 4-328352). Expensive.

**Casino Boulevard** – Besides a popular casino, there are 90 suites — all well equipped and comfortably furnished — as well as a coffee shop. 432 Av. 9 de Octubre at Chimborazo (phone: 4-306700; in the US, 800-223-9868). Expensive to moderate.

**Doral** – This hostelry has 126 rooms with private baths, a restaurant, and a coffee shop. 402 Chile and Aguirre (phone: 4-327175). Moderate.

**Palace** – Private baths are a feature at this 80-room hotel, plus air conditioning, and a 24-hour cafeteria. 216 Chile at Luque (phone: 4-321080). Moderate.

**Plaza** – Relatively comfortable and conveniently located downtown, it has 48 rooms, all with private baths, and a coffee shop. Check-out time is a convenient 3 PM. 414 Chile at Clemente Ballén (phone: 4-327140). Moderate.

**Ramada** – A comfortable property overlooking the Río Guayas, with 186 rooms, air conditioning, a restaurant, cocktail lounge, indoor pool, and health club. *Malecón* and Orellana (phone: 4-312200; fax: 4-322036). Moderate.

**Sol de Oriente** – Nothing special on the outside but the rooms are large, clean, air conditioned, decorated in an Oriental style, and have private baths. There is a Chinese restaurant, a coffee shop, and a bar. 603 Aguirre and Escobedo (phone: 4-325500; fax: 4-329352). Moderate.

## SALINAS

**Samarina** – The best bet in town, it features 190 rooms and 10 family bungalows, a tennis court, pool, restaurant, and bar. Av. 9 de Octubre, La Libertad–Salinas (phone: 4-785167; in Guayaquil, 4-327140). Moderate.

**Casino Miramar** – Located on the beachfront boulevard, this 62-room resort hotel offers private baths, telephones, a casino, a restaurant, coffee shop, and pool. Equipment for water skiing, windsailing, snorkeling, surfing, and biking can be rented at its marina. On the *malecón* (phone: 4-772115). Moderate to inexpensive.

**Salinas Costas** – One block from the beachfront, it offers private baths and telephones. At General Enríquez G. and Calle 27 (phone: 4-774268). Moderate to inexpensive.

## PUNTA CARNERO

**Punta Carnero Inn** – This 78-room hotel features private baths, air conditioning, and balconies overlooking the sea. There is also a pool, a restaurant specializing in local seafood, and a bar. Deep-sea fishing charters can be arranged (phone: 4-785450; in Guayaquil, 4-327149; in the US, 800-327-7080). Moderate.

## SANTO DOMINGO DE LOS COLORADOS

**Tinalandia** – A 32-room hacienda outside town that's hard to find but worth the trouble. It features a golf course and a restaurant. It's particularly suitable for birders and naturalists. Price includes three meals daily. It can be booked only by telegram — ask at major travel agencies in Quito. Quito–Santo Domingo Hwy. at Km 112 (no phone). Moderate.

**Zaracay** – Very attractive, 44-room hostelry on the edge of town with a swimming pool surrounded by gardens. It also has a bar, restaurant, and casino. Reservations are advised. 1639 Av. Quito (phone: 2-750316 or 2-750023; in Quito, 2-401948). Moderate.

## ESMERALDAS PROVINCE

**Castelnuovo** – On the beach of Castelnuovo in Atacames, this is one of the few first class hotels in the north. It has 26 rooms, a bar-restaurant, 3 pools, and air conditioning. Km 3 of Via Atacames (phone: 2-513588 or 2-512744). Moderate.

**Hostería Puerto Esmeraldas** – On the same beach as the *Castelnuovo*, it has 9 small bungalows, with kitchens, suitable for up to four (phone: 2-242694). Moderate to inexpensive.

## MANABÍ PROVINCE

**Coco Solo** – In Cojimies, this property has 5 bungalows with private baths. Special fishing and horseback riding excursions can be arranged by the owners, as can transportation from Guayaquil or Manta. Restaurant and bar on premises. Km 20 of Via Pedernales (phone: in Quito, 2-565504 or 2-564444). Moderate.

**La Piedra** – On the principal seaside boulevard in Bahía de Caraquez, a first class, 32-room beachside property with private baths, air conditioning, a pool, and a bar-restaurant (phone: 2-690418; in Quito, 2-560550). Moderate.

# The Galápagos Islands

To some they are ugly clusters of volcanic rock smothered by dry, thorny brush and coarse, yellow grass. But there is a certain magnificence in this stark landscape. Here on the equator colors seem stronger and the light purer, enhancing the contrast of sky, sea, and land. Here live native wildlife species so special that almost half of them cannot be found anywhere else on earth and whose lonely, isolated development has provided the basis for the theory of evolution. The sounds of the surf are broken by the harsh low barks of sea lions and the squawks of ocean birds. These are the fascinating Galápagos Islands, 13 major islands and dozens of small islets 600 nautical miles west of Ecuador, comprising a 3,029-square-mile natural wonderland. They may be the only remaining habitat of substantial size where man has conserved huge quantities of wildlife without upsetting the delicate balance of nature.

Discovered by the explorer Tomás de Berlanga in 1535, the islands were named Galápagos, the Spanish word for the giant, lethargic tortoises that sunned themselves on the rocks. They were later nicknamed the Bewitched Isles, or Las Islas Encantadas. The meeting of the cold, antarctic Humboldt Current with the warm, northerly El Niño Current churned the waters to create the hypnotic illusion that the gray, jagged boulders were swaying. During the 16th, 17th, and 18th centuries, British and French pirates used the islands as hideaways, explaining the non-Spanish names of some of the islands. In the Republican period, one island was used to confine political prisoners. More savage visitors harbored there in the 19th century: Whalers, and later oilers, moored in the island coves for the sole purpose of slaughtering tortoises (and thanks to these human predators, the *galápagos* are nearly extinct today).

A more pacific visitor did explore the islands in 1835 — 26-year-old Charles Darwin — a naturalist aboard the HMS *Beagle* during its 6-year voyage around the world. Darwin was fascinated with the local wildlife, and the variety of subspecies of animals and birds helped him formulate his theory about natural selection and the process of evolution; that is, animals, plants, and birds adapt to an environment for survival. It was Darwin's work that threw these islands into the world limelight. About 50% of the animals — mostly iguanas, tortoises, and sea mammals — were original residents of the islands, and other bird and marine species eventually were carried here by wind, water currents, or visiting ships.

The islands are estimated to be more than 3 million years old. In early 1992, scientists discovered evidence that there are still older islands (9 million years old!) that are now below the ocean's waves. This would explain the mystery of how the wildlife evolved at what scientists once thought was too rapid a pace. These "new" islands are 370 miles closer to the mainland than the existing chain. Tortoises and iguanas here may be the direct descendants of prehistoric animals. The land and marine iguanas look like miniature dinosaurs, and their scaly hides give them a beastly appearance (the land iguana turns itself from gold to brownish red). Having never developed a fear of man, these lizards and other island inhabitants seem virtually tame, with a tendency to be drawn to, rather than away from, two-legged visitors.

The list of wildlife tenants is endless: In addition to tortoises and iguanas, there are flightless cormorants, penguins, albatrosses, red- and blue-footed boobies, finches (13 varieties), frigate birds, swallow-tailed gulls, and more. Some "imported" trees and fruits crop up along some of the inhabited islands: bamboo, bromeliads, breadfruit, papaya, avocado, and orange. (Freshly squeezed orange juice is a daily treat on the inhabited islands.) Here and there a tropical rain forest adds lushness to the bare lava landscape.

Claimed by Ecuador in 1832, the Galápagos (also known as Archipelago Colón) were designated one of Ecuador's 20 governmental provinces during the 1970s. In 1964, the Charles Darwin Foundation, with the aid of the Ecuadoran government and UNESCO, established a biological research station on Santa Cruz Island. The entire Galápagos territory was designated a national park shortly afterward.

Of all the islands, only five are inhabited, by about 8,000 Ecuadorans and

English and German immigrants. Less than half of that population resides on the capital island of San Cristóbal where the naval base is located; the rest live on Santa Cruz (the central island), Baltra (the air base), Isabela, and Floreana. Most of the islands have both Spanish and English names: San Cristóbal (Chatham), Santa Cruz (Indefatigable), Isabela (Albemarle), and Floreana (Charles). Isabela, 75 miles long, is the largest island and contains the highest peak, 5,600 feet above sea level. It and the uninhabited islands of Fernandina, Santiago, Marchena, and Pinta have their own active volcanoes. In fact, the islands continue to be considered among the most volcanically active spots on earth. Visitors can fly directly to the Galápagos from Miami on *SAETA* or *Ecuatoriana* airlines or from New York, Chicago, and Los Angeles via *Ecuatoriana*. Most travelers, however, go to the islands in conjunction with visiting other parts of Ecuador.

Visitors who come to the islands by plane from Quito or Guayaquil land at Baltra (via *TAME)* or on San Cristóbal (via *SAN)*. Because there is no plane or scheduled boat service between islands, some 98% of the visitors to the Galápagos travel by sea, in vessels ranging from 4-passenger sailboats to 90-passenger motor cruise ships, and when the Ecuadoran government permits, the occasional large passenger vessel. Regardless of the size of the ship, national park regulations require that all passengers be accompanied by a park-certified and licensed naturalist-guide. This not only assures that visitors respect the carefully selected and clearly designated trails on each island, it also substantially enhances the visitor's experience.

Visitors also can fly to the islands and stay in one of the few small hotels on either Santa Cruz or San Cristóbal. There are limited but good accommodations in both Academy Bay (Santa Cruz) and Puerto Baquerizo Moreno (San Cristóbal) — see *Best en Route*. From these two spots day trips to neighboring islands can be arranged. Camping also is available, but first check with the national park office for authorized sites. A traveler should check upon arrival with local captains at the harbor. There is a national park fee of $80 (payable in US cash or traveler's checks) for all visitors arriving at either airport gateway. Air fares to the islands remain high and virtually never are discounted.

In 1991, the government made an exception to its policy of not allowing large foreign ships into the Galápagos. *Ocean Cruise Line* (1510 SE 17th St., Ft. Lauderdale, FL 33316; phone: 800-556-8850) was the first to announce that it would be including the islands, together with ports on mainland Ecuador (a stipulation in the government's decision), in its itineraries. Although this was not the first time the country had granted cruise rights to big vessels, the decision unleashed protests from conservationists and ecotourism operators alike. On a regular basis, there are two relatively large ships (that carry a maximum of 90 passengers each) operating in the islands and numerous smaller yachts, ranging from very basic with shared facilities and seawater showers to first class with private facilities and hot-water bathing. Larger ships offer 3- and 4-night cruises, while the yachts typically average 7- to 10-night cruises (although there are some exceptions, described below). Some yachts can only be chartered; others take individual bookings. The choice between a large ship or a yacht is very individual. There is more room and less chance of seasickness on the larger ships; the smaller ships, however, can visit at least five locations closed to larger ships. Note that some local fisherfolk have converted their boats to carry visitors to the islands; however, for safety purposes, we strongly advise that you go with an established ship or yacht — such as one of those mentioned below. At least a week in the islands is highly recommended if you have more than a passing interest in the wildlife.

The *Galápagos Explorer* is a clean, comfortable, and well-run mini-liner that has 3-, 4-, and 7-night cruises out of San Cristóbal. Originally a Greek island cruise vessel for 90, the ship was totally refitted in late 1987 and has a swimming pool and comfortable staterooms. Five scientists act as guides and give lectures. In addition, there's a good library on board. Reservations through *Canodros* (1418 L. Urdaneta and Av. del Ejército, Guayaquil; phone: 4-280143), and in the US through *Galápagos, Inc.* (phone: 305-665-0841 or 800-327-9854; fax: 305-661-1457). *Galápagos, Inc.* also represents seven first class yachts, each of which carries 8 to 16 passengers. *Metropolitan Touring*, the oldest operator in the islands, offers several of the most popular charter yachts and cruises. Among its fleet are the 90-passenger *Santa Cruz*, smaller than the *Galápagos Explorer;* the newly refitted, 36-passenger *Delfin II;* the *Isabella II*, a 166-foot deluxe, 34-passenger boat with salon-bar, dining room, and 20 outside twin cabins, each with private bath; and the 10-passenger schooner, *Encantada*. The company also has half a dozen smaller yachts. Contact *Metropolitan Touring* (239 Amazonas, Quito; phone: 2-560550; fax: 2-564655) or its US representative, *Adventure Associates* (13150 Coit Rd., Suite 110, Dallas, TX 75240; phone: 214-907-0414 or 800-527-2500). For the *Isabella II*, call *Fourth Dimension Tours* (phone: 800-343-0020).

*Nuevo Mundo* in Quito (2468 Av. Amazonas; phone: 2-552617; fax: 2-552916) represents the 12-passenger *Gaby* and other 12- to 20-passenger yachts. Reservations in the US through *International Expeditions* (phone: 205-428-1700 or 800-633-4734). *Tumbaco, Inc.* in the US can arrange reservations on five air conditioned boats sailing from San Cristóbal: the 10-passenger *Nortada* and the 12-person *Mistral* yachts (both 66 feet long); the 52-foot *Solitude*, a motor sailer; and two other yachts, the 73-foot *Resting Cloud*, which carries 10 passengers, and the 93-foot, 18-passenger *Lammer Law*. Contact *Tumbaco* at 813-637-4660 or 800-247-2925.

*Galápagos Network*, affiliated with *SAETA* airlines, has three luxurious, air conditioned 20-passenger yachts based in San Cristóbal. The operator offers special airfares from Miami in conjunction with its 3-, 4-, and 7-night cruises. And for experienced divers only, it operates an 8-passenger dive boat. For information, call *Galápagos Network* (phone: 305-592-2294 or 800-633-7972; fax: 305-592-6394).

Once in Guayaquil, the best bet for last-minute Galápagos arrangements is *Gordon Tours*, 2009 Av. 9 de Octubre at the corner of Los Ríos (phone: 4-373550, 4-373555, and 4-373596; fax: 4-284835).

Since luggage storage space on the smaller boats especially is limited, larger bags should be left in your hotel in Quito or Guayaquil. A soft-sided duffel is ideal for a week-long cruise. Be sure to pack sturdy rubber sole shoes, rubber beach thongs, a wide-brimmed hat, mosquito repellent, sunglasses, and sunscreen (buy it in the US) with a protection factor of at least 15 (this is the equator and the sun is strong!). Also suggested are cotton clothing, bathing suit, sweatshirt, and windbreaker. The larger ships generally have snorkeling gear for rental; bring your own if you have it. And bring plenty of film; even if you are able to restock in port (film is often unavailable) it will be very expensive. A good pair of lightweight binoculars enhances the trip immensely. There is little else to buy other than T-shirts and books at the *Darwin Center.* Bring some US cash as well as sucres. Most shops in Puerto Ayora (Academy Bay) take credit cards.

Below are descriptions of some of the prominent islands.

**BALTRA:** Notable only because it is home to one of the archipelago's two airports, this small island is north of Santa Cruz.

**SANTA CRUZ (INDEFATIGABLE):** From Baltra it's a short ferry and a 1½-hour bus ride into Academy Bay to visit the Charles Darwin Biological Research Station, which coordinates all scientific work on the archipelago. Open to visitors Monday through Saturday mornings (hours vary), the station, among other things, houses a tortoise egg hatchery with incubators, and tortoise pens. Few of the *galápagos* are alive today, thanks to the marauding whalers, but the station hopes to regenerate the species through controlled reproduction and replacement in natural breeding grounds.

Soon after the islands were established as a national park, the foundation formulated a master plan for the area in an attempt to set up a comfortable balance between the ecosystem and invading travelers. As a result, the islands were separated into zones. For instance, Academy Bay and the Darwin Research Station, along with the residential village (pop. 3,000-plus) and hotels, are open to visitors, but the rest of Santa Cruz is restricted. Within the last several years, the number of tourists visiting the islands has increased to at least 60,000 annually (the government-imposed quota), and further efforts are being made by park naturalists to curb growth. Tourists are prohibited from touching or feeding the animals (a huge temptation when the animals waddle, stroll, or slink right up to you) or from taking chunks of lava, black coral, and seashells home with them.

At the station, you'll be able to get a good look at the tortoises. They set themselves on the rocks, their old-man necks protruding from their shells, squinting at the sun — and you — through half-shut eyes. They look as if they're bearing the weight of the world on their backs — but so would you if you had to tote that massive shell around for 100 years or so. On Santa Cruz you also can arrange a tour by horseback to the tortoise reserve in the Highlands.

You can camp on the island, but check with the rangers to make sure you're not in a restricted area.

It is possible to book day trips on local yachts once in Santa Cruz; however, the safety standards of some of these vessels have been questioned. It's advisable to make arrangements in advance of your arrival with an established operator who booked the same boats over a long period of time. Another drawback — it may take you up to a week if you are trying to arrange a longer charter cruise, while you wait for the right boat and captain to be available, negotiate an acceptable price, and gather an adequate number of passengers to join you. The islands are widely scattered, so be prepared for some rides that last 6 or 7 hours; if you are prone to seasickness, bring plenty of preventive medication. Should you decide to design your own tour, we suggest you purchase the English-language *South American Explorers Club* report on the Galápagos Islands. It has all the specifics on boats, owners, tours and even sample charter contracts. The club has a branch in Quito (1254 Toledo, La Floresta; phone: 2-566076). The report costs $6.50 ($4.50 for members).

**SAN CRISTÓBAL (CHATHAM):** Puerto Baquerizo Moreno is this island's main city as well as the capital of the Galápagos. It also is the site of a navy base and home to the islands' second airport. San Cristóbal is one of the oldest islands in the group and home of the Galápagos's only freshwater lake, Laguna Junco — about an hour's bus ride from Puerto Baquerizo Moreno. Contact any of the local travel agencies to find out about half-day tours to the lake (take a sweater, it's quite cool in the highlands). Another place to visit, and within walking distance from town (take the main road that goes past the beaches), is the island's sea lion colony. Any of the local tour guides — found all over the island — will be happy to escort you. For a break from the midday heat, there are two inviting beaches in this friendly, slow-paced town. One of them is in front of the island's best inn, *Grand Hotel San Cristóbal* (see *Best en Route*); the other is a 10-minute walk farther along the town's only road until you reach the path to the beach. Wear sturdy shoes for walking on the sharp volcanic stones.

For those interested in the formation of the Galápagos, stop by the *Museo de Raphael ChaixFaure* (adjacent to the church) to view its collection of native flora and fauna and displays dedicated to the animals brought in by humans over the centuries (such as goats, pigs, rodents, etc.) to the islands. The museum also houses documents (in Spanish) about the islands and has a pleasant reading room upstairs where visitors can peruse them. The museum is open Monday through Saturday and there is an admission charge.

The waterfront is lined with simple hotels and small restaurants that serve notable seafood dishes. Native fare also includes excellent avocados and oranges. One of the town's best is the small (3-table), family-run *Café Nathaly* (Av. Northia at Merville). In the morning, ask for *morocho,* a warm, sweet drink made from boiled corn, milk, raisins, and cinnamon (it tastes better than it sounds). The *batidos* (fruit milkshakes) also are terrific.

**BARTOLOMÉ:** There's a good swimming beach here with excellent snorkeling just offshore and around Pinnacle Rock, perhaps the most distinctive landmark in the islands. Chances are good that you'll see (and swim with) penguins and sea lions. Sharks also have been sighted in the shallows. It is a fairly easy climb to the summit for an awe-inspiring view of the beaches and Pinnacle Rock.

**FERNANDINA (NARBOROUGH):** Wildly convoluted, relatively recent (less than 100 years old), lava flows here support little plant life other than the distinctive lava cactus. Flightless cormorants nest here and share the landscape with sea lions and the Galápagos' largest colony of marine iguanas. This island is considered the "purest" as there are no non-native plants or animals.

**RABIDA (JERVIS):** Most of this island is covered by dense, thorny vegetation and aromatic Palo Santo trees. It's home to some nine species of Darwin's finches. A salty lagoon on the north side supports flamingos; and sea lions populate the red sand beaches. There also are pelican feeding grounds.

**NORTH SEYMOUR:** This flat island has the largest colony of magnificent frigatebirds in the Galápagos. With luck, you'll see the males courting their ladies by puffing out their brilliant red chests. This is also a nesting area for blue-footed boobies and swallow-tailed gulls. Despite the rough surf, sea lions and iguanas are found along the shore.

**SANTIAGO (JAMES):** Lava cones and craters combine to make this island one of desolate beauty. Ships anchoring within secluded Buccaneer Cove cannot be spotted by those passing outside, probably the reason it was a well-known pirate sanctuary for several centuries. Saltwater lagoons harbor pink flamingos near Espumilla Beach. Salt was mined at Puerto Egas in the 1960s. Four goats from a visiting ship escaped to this island in 1813, and the present goat population is about 100,000. Because this animal's grazing has upset the ecological balance on the islands, goat hunting is permitted, even encouraged.

**GENOVESA (TOWER):** Large colonies of nesting oceanic birds — red-footed boobies, shearwaters, storm petrels, and frigatebirds — are found on Genovesa, the most remote of the northern group and a birder's paradise. It is acutally a huge volcano crater, most of which is submerged in the sea.

**ISABELA (ALBEMARLE):** The archipelago's longest island; an active volcano erupted here in April 1963. Until 1958 there was a convict colony on Isabela, and today about 1,000 people (all free and respectable) reside on the southern tip of the island in Villamil, where flamingos can be seen. At the Alcedo volcano, there are 4,000 Galápagos tortoises — one of the largest colonies of this ancient reptile in the world. The cliffs near Tagus Cove are home to thousands of blue-footed boobies and brown pelicans, along with sea lions and Galápagos penguins. Hikers will have spectacular views over a saltwater crater nestled within yet another larger crater.

**FLOREANA (CHARLES):** In 1793, whalers opened a post office here in a barrel, and letters have been dropped off and carried onward in one ever since — no stamps are necessary. A far juicier point of interest is the story-turned-legend of a small group of lusty German settlers (some still living on the island), who are chronicled in John Treherne's potboiler, *The Galapagos Affair*. Point Cormorant is a bird watcher's dream and also is considered to be the best snorkeling spot in the islands. The island sometimes is called Santa María.

**ESPAÑOLA (HOOD):** Scientists now say that it is one of the oldest islands in the Galápagos — between 3 and 5 million years old and almost every species of bird, including blue-footed and masked boobies and albatross, are found here. Its wild cliffscapes are alive with iguana and sea lions. Inland is the only nesting site of the waved albatross, the largest and some say the most spectacular Galápagos bird. Española is the only major island in the group that has no volcanic craters, but there is a picturesque geyser of water created by waves rushing into a hole in the shoreline rocks — a favorite backdrop for photos.

**SOUTH PLAZA:** Tourists are allowed here, and there is plenty of wildlife, highlighted by nesting red-billed tropic birds and lots of sea lions. Land iguanas can often be spotted.

**SANTA FE (BARRINGTON):** Here are found some of the largest Galápagos tree cacti and a unique species of land iguana who are observed during their 6-month long reproductive season by a group of European scientists who set up tents (with the government's approval). And you're likely to spot many sea lions. There is good snorkeling on the northeastern shore.

## BEST EN ROUTE

The only places to stay comfortably are in the tourist area on Santa Cruz Island and in the town of Puerto Baquerizo Moreno on San Cristóbal. Be prepared for water shortages and possibly for bathing in cold water as hot water is an almost unheard-of luxury. Visitors arriving without advance arrangements will have to inquire at Balta Airport about how to cross to Santa Cruz Island; it's not always easy. It is easy, however, to walk into town from the airport on San Cristóbal if you can't catch a ride with a local bus. Expect prices to be anywhere from $55 to $75 for a double room at those places categorized as expensive, from $25 to $55 at places in the moderate category, and under $25 at inexpensive places. The *Delfin* and the *Galápagos* hotels have programs of varying lengths that combine a cruise aboard the *Santa Cruz* and a land package. This gives visitors a chance to visit the Darwin Research Station (a tour is included in the price) and to take an optional tour to the Tortoise National Reserve in the highlands.

These days, it's recommended that plans for a Galápagos tour be made 6 months in advance, since the islands are popular and boat tours fill up rapidly. Tour operators hold blocked space for their programs, but they are compelled to release cabins 45 days prior to departure. So check them for cancellations.

## SANTA CRUZ (INDEFATIGABLE)

**Delfín** – Located a bit away from town and accessible only by small boat. Choose from 20 attached bungalows and rooms with private baths (but no hot water). Amenities include central dining, bar and lounge area, and three meals daily (picnics packed for boat excursions); cove beach swimming (phone: 2-245805 in Quito; or contact *Chasquitur* in Guayaquil, 4-281084 or 4-281085; in the US, 800-527-2500; *Chasquitur* fax: 4-285872). Expensive.

**Galápagos** – Definitely the best island accommodations — 14 cottage rooms with private baths and hot showers, and good laundry service. The rooms are immaculate and attractively decorated. The complex sits on several garden-covered acres (complete with gazebo and hammocks) on the edge of Academy Bay and is personally supervised by the owners. The central building houses a bar-lounge, a library, and a restaurant that serves excellent meals. Reservations in Quito (phone: 2-545777; fax: 2-502449; telegram or telex: 2302 COLTUR ED). Expensive.

**Sol y Mar** – There are cabin accommodations for 20 people, divided into doubles, triples, and quadruples, with private baths but no hot showers. Nice simple oceanfront restaurant. Breakfast is included. Contact *Chasquitur* (phone: in Guayaquil, 4-281084 or 4-281085; fax: 4-285872). Moderate.

**Cabañas de Gusch Angermayer** – It's best to ask about reservations at the Darwin Station for one of the 20 beds here, offered by a friendly and helpful English-speaking German immigrant, Mrs. Angermayer. A popular spot with the backpack crowd (no phone). Inexpensive.

## SAN CRISTÓBAL (CHATHAM)

**Grand Hotel San Cristóbal** – On the beach overlooking the port and bay, this small hotel has 11 rooms with private baths. It is usually the only spot in town with hot water for showers. There's a small bar and restaurant that has erratic hours. Book it through *SAN* in Guayaquil (phone: 4-329855 and 4-325364). Moderate.

**Cabañas Don Jorge** – These bungalows house up to 24 guests and each one has a private bath. The property generally is a cut above the other very simple hotels on the island. Next door to the *Grand Hotel San Cristóbal* (phone: in Quito, 2-239308). Inexpensive.

# French Guiana

French Guiana, that tiny, 35,135-square-mile relative of Suriname (its western neighbor) and Guyana, is meant to satisfy the traveler seeking an exotic, offbeat spot in the Western Hemisphere. After all, it has all the components to thrill the most jaded explorer: a jungle that is penetrable only by motorized, native canoe; exotic birds that include parrots and macaws; stunning orchids that block your way along the river path; Amazonian varieties of jaguar, ocelot, tapir, anteater, cayman (the South American alligator), the frightening howler monkey; snakes (including the anaconda); and the passive, lovely, blue morpho butterfly. Humid and constantly rainy (the best months to visit are from late June to November), the country sits slightly north of the equator, bordered to the south and east by Brazil (400 years ago, it was part of Brazil) and by the Atlantic on the north. Cayenne, the country's capital, sits on the banks of the Cayenne River and the Atlantic Ocean. If the name Cayenne sounds familiar to you, you're probably a cook: Cayenne is the red, hot pepper exported from French Guiana from as far back as the 17th century.

No stranger to European eyes (the Guianas were first sighted by Amerigo Vespucci in 1496), French Guiana was settled by the French in 1604. After that, its history is a stormy one, the land of jungle, marsh, and sand constantly passing back and forth among the French, Dutch, and English. Captured by the Dutch in 1676, the country was finally returned to the French, then taken by the English; a final resolution (thanks to the Treaty of Vienna of 1815, following the Napoleonic Wars) returned the land to the French. In 1946, French Guiana became an overseas department of France, with its own prefect (or governor) sitting in Cayenne.

Despite the lure of its jungle, French Guiana — with a minuscule population of about 125,000 (75% scattered in and around Cayenne), a mixture of Creoles, Asians, Amerindians, Bushnegros, and whites — still lacks extensive tourist accommodations. Travelers now have the amenities of modern air conditioned hotels in Cayenne, Kourou, and St.-Laurent. Aiding in the development of the coast is the French space center at Kourou, which launches and monitors satellites. (To visit the space center, talk to any of the tour companies mentioned below or call the Public Relations Department of the *Centre Spacial Guyanais;* phone: 594-334200.) In addition, several new roads have been built to exploit the boundless tracts of lumber and other resources to be extracted from the bush.

Any adventure in French Guiana starts in Cayenne. Before heading off into the jungle, take a look around the capital as well as Kourou and St.-Laurent. Whatever you do, *don't* — repeat, *don't* — forget a trip to Devil's Island, the infamous French penal colony, also known as the Dry Guillotine, about 12 miles offshore from Kourou.

If you do intend to travel into the jungle, it's wise to plan far in advance for local guides and boatmen. On a typical trip upriver, expect to visit lumber camps that bustle during the harvest of jungle hardwood logs that are floated downriver in rafts. Also you will see picturesque Indian and Bushnegro villages, where very interesting handicrafts can be purchased. Farther upriver comes the reward of wildlife, roaring cataracts, and rapids during the rainy season from late December to early August.

Camping is the rule upriver. Don't expect easy living here: Sleeping is in hammocks strung from the uprights of *carbets* (a jungle version of a lean-to), and sleeping on the ground is not recommended. There are few pesky insects, however, and mosquitoes are not a big problem as long as the swampy areas are avoided. Actually, the scourges of malaria and yellow fever are now mostly a thing of the past, but it's best to get inoculations and pills anyway. Today, the biggest health problem for the traveler is overexposure to the sun. When sitting in a dugout engrossed in photographing, birding, and observing, it is easy to forget the strength of the equatorial sun. Essentials for any river trip include a good insect repellent, sunscreen lotion, long-sleeve shirts and long pants, sunglasses, sun hats, a poncho or rain suit, plenty of plastic bags to protect cameras, and so on. An inflatable cushion (most dugouts have no seats) and camping equipment, including hammocks, are available locally: Consult with tour operators on other items, since proper equipment is most important. Dugouts or *pirogues* only can carry so much, and at many points portages must be made to bypass rapids and cataracts. The best time to observe birds and animals is early in the morning or late in the afternoon, when the jungle life seems to gravitate to the riverbanks to drink and feed.

Additional tour information is available from the French Government Tourist Office (610 Fifth Ave., New York, NY; phone: 212-757-1125), or from the regional tourist office in Cayenne (12 Rue Lalloutte; phone: 594-300900). The office is open weekdays from 9 AM to noon and 4 to 6 PM.

If you prefer not to rough it on your own, be aware that tour operators occasionally book tours through the area and cruise ship itineraries sometimes include Devil's Island. If you prefer to wait until you're in Cayenne, contact *Takari Tour* (Colline du Montabo; phone: 594-311960). The company also has offices (open evenings only) at the *Novotel Cayenne* hotel (Rte. de Montabo; phone: 594-303888) and at the *Des Roches* hotel (Bord de Mer, Kourou; phone: 594-323157); they also have a mailing address (BP 513, Cayenne 97300). Local travel agents ready and willing to help you in Cayenne include *Somarig* (1 Pl. L Heder; phone: 594-302980) and others located in the *Air France* office (Pl. des Palmistes; phone: 594-302740).

One offbeat attraction for adventure tourists is the country's wide variety of unusual insects. Jean-Marie and Odette Beloup (Villa Clery, Rte. de Cabassou, 97300 Remire, Guyane Française; phone: 595-354321), who describe themselves as "passionate entomologists," have set up a tourist facility on Kaw mountain for insect watchers. They promise a "rendezvous with these fabulous diurnal insects."

Note: There currently is no ferry service to Suriname because of civil unrest in that country.

*Surinam Airways, Air France,* and Brazil's *Cruseiro do Sol* all fly from Paramaribo, Suriname, and Belém, Brazil. *Air France* offers service from

Lima, Peru and, together with *Minerve* airlines, has direct flights to Cayenne from Paris. For travelers coming from the US, *Air France* has four direct flights a week from Miami, and connecting flights from Martinique, Guadeloupe, Haiti, and Puerto Rico. Air travel within French Guiana is limited, but *Air Guyane* (2 Rue Lalouette; phone: 594-317200) has daily service to St.-Georges, Regina, and Maripasoula, three flights a week to Saul, and one to St.-Laurent-du-Maroni.

If you do fly, start by driving or taking a taxi or bus in from Rochambeau International Airport, about 11 miles (18 km) outside of the capital.

**CAYENNE:** The first sight to greet you in this city of 38,000 people is the imposing statue of Felix Adolphe Eboué (1884–1944), the African Free French sympathizer who served as governor-general of Martinique and Equatorial Africa. He stands in the Place des Palmistes, the city's main palm-filled square. Surrounding the square are sidewalk cafés, and beyond the square is the city's main street, with little shops and a museum (closed Mondays). Adjoining Place des Palmistes is Place de Grenoble, equally picturesque with its old whitewashed governor's mansion and post office. Down the main street are the city cemetery, the hospital, and a small botanical garden and zoo.

A few blocks west of the main street is the older part of town, called La Crique after a tidal creek that flows through the area and provides safe haven for multicolored Brazilian fishing boats, called *les tapouilles*. Here indeed is the color of Cayenne, with its animated market, selling pottery, spices (including pepper), parrots and other tropical birds, as well as pelts of ocelot and jaguar. Chinese and Lebanese shops supply the surrounding populace, as well as the lumber camp workers and miners of the hinterland. Weekends are particularly animated in Cayenne compared to working days, which are dull, except after dusk, when the sidewalk cafés come to life in the cool of the evening.

**En Route from Cayenne** – Leaving town, you cross a long bridge spanning the Cayenne River, then travel northwest along the paved coastal highway 40 miles (64 km) to Kourou. As you speed along the lush jungle plain, which alternates with a few patches of cultivated clearing, you suddenly approach a horizon filled with antennas and tracking mechanisms, used by the nearby space center for tracking the communications and weather satellites orbited here. At present, this is the world's most active space-satellite launching center.

**KOUROU:** Once a small fishing village, the present town was built near its "older brother" on reclaimed, swampy land, spreading out at the very mouth of the river on a peninsular point. This Kourou is a modern whitewashed concrete town, with several shops (where you can buy jewelry, butterflies, and cigarettes), boutiques, bank, and post office. There are the ever-present cafés, all catering to a community of more than 10,000, the majority being either employees at the space center or French Legionnaires who come to town to relax.

Sit back and enjoy the river view here: Marsh and sea birds zoom into its banks for landings among the thick mangroves along the shoreline. Rent a dugout canoe at the *Des Roches* hotel for cruising.

You should definitely arrange at the hotel for the 1-hour launch ride out to Devil's Island (one of Les Iles de Salut); reservations are recommended, since space on the boat is limited, and space center employees and Legionnaires like to laze away their weekends on the islands. The boat departs Kourou at 8:30 AM and leaves the islands at 5 PM, depending on the tide, except during launches from the space center.

**DEVIL'S ISLAND:** Les Iles de Salut (the Isles of Salvation) are really a trio of islands: Royale (the largest), St. Joseph, and Devil's. Its name originated in the 17th century, when settlers fled the mainland to take refuge from the disease-ridden jungle.

On Royale, visit the commandant's house and the houses of the prison staff, the hospital, chapel, children's cemetery, lighthouse, and space center tracking station, and perhaps swim in a sheltered, ocean-fed pool, constructed by the prisoners for the staff. Overnight accommodations are provided in the converted guards' quarters. The entire island is circled by a passable footpath that can be walked in an hour (at a slow pace).

From Royale, a short motor launch goes to St. Joseph, where there are the remains of the huge, solitary confinement compound, with cells and a common area with its roof almost rusted away. Huge tree roots and vines make it difficult to enter. Facing the ocean is the prison staff cemetery and rocky beach, a cool place to picnic.

Tide and currents permitting, you may be lucky enough to visit Devil's Island itself, which now contains the ruins of 13 cottages once used for political prisoners, including Alfred Dreyfus, the Jewish French army officer who was convicted of treason and imprisoned here in 1895 until further investigation proved his innocence. Almost completely cut off from Royale and St. Joseph, the prisoners here raised their own vegetables and poultry. Today, the incarcerated have been replaced by rather aggressive bees.

**En Route from Devil's Island** – Returning to Kourou, you can visit the space center, which stretches 6 miles (10 km) west along the coast. Owned by the French, the center launches weather and communication satellites. Employees here boast that their location is far better than that of the Kennedy Space Center in Florida, since it is closer to the equator, and the greater thrust of the earth's rotation here makes launches easier and more successful. Visitors are allowed on the site for tours on Mondays through Thursdays at 8 AM, except during launches (phone: 594-334200). Tours are in French, but there is a 30-minute film in English. From the center, the coastal highway proceeds northwest along the plain, passing small farms and fishing villages. At Sinnamary, on the river of the same name, there is a Javanese settlement. One favorite restaurant here is Indonesian with an Art Nouveau decor, owned and operated by a retired Javanese soldier named Papa Chef. After leaving you will pass two more small villages, Iracoubo and Organaba, and come to the city of St.-Laurent on the Maroni River, which divides French Guiana from Suriname.

**ST.-LAURENT-DU-MARONI:** This frontier town is the starting point for a trip down the Maroni River, the supply route of the many Indian and Bushnegro villages dotting the shore. The quay is bustling with boats. Parquet flooring is the main industry here. As we went to press, the ferry connecting St.-Laurent with Albina (across the river in Suriname) remained closed as a result of the continuing civil unrest in that country. There are, however, daily flights on *Gum Air* (phone: 341840) from St.-Laurent to Zorg-en-Hoop Airport in Paramaribo, the Surinamese capital.

St.-Laurent was a larger community during the prison era: It was the receiving station for sentenced convicts. The remnants of the prison still stand. Prisoners were received, classified, and served sentences here; incorrigibles were shipped to the Salvation Islands. For a view of what prison life here was like, visit the *Camp de la Transportation* (Rue du Lt.-Colonel Chandon, near the waterfront). The onetime cells now are inhabited by squatters. Next door is the hospital, built to take care of the prisoners. Now used by the general public, it was being renovated at press time.

Except for the busy waterfront, St.-Laurent still maintains a sleepy look, enlivened in the evening when the bistros come to life. Here travelers make a final check of supplies and equipment for the trip up the Maroni River. For information on trips upriver, as well as excellent detailed material on hotels and restaurants in St.-Laurent, visit the Office du Tourisme (Rue Auguste Bordinot; phone: 594-342398).

**En Route from St.-Laurent** – The river is about 3 miles wide at St.-Laurent, and as you proceed upriver, the width, with a few exceptions, stays fairly constant. Close to the banks you get a good view of life along the river, with chattering naked children playing and bathing; women washing clothes and carrying water, firewood, and other unbelievable loads on their heads. The tailored, clean villages always have ornately carved decorations on the individual doors and walls and a ceremonial hut and granary that is always more ornate than the common dwellings.

For the next 130 miles (208 km) upriver you pass Bushnegro villages; you may be lucky enough to buy a painted paddle called a *pagaie,* a two-bladed affair with one end handsomely carved in a beautiful symmetrical design and the blade on the opposite end painted in a multicolored design. These paddles are an intricate part of village life, and usually the carving and painting carry deep meaning. For example, a *pagaie* with a house painted on it means a proposal of marriage when presented by a young man to the maiden of his choice.

After 3 or 4 days of river travel you arrive at Maripasoula, where accommodations are provided at a simple riverside inn. Maripasoula is the gateway to the Wayana Indian country, which stretches south upriver for hundreds of miles into Brazil. The Wayana culture is based on hunting (rarely with the use of firearms), sacred tribal rituals in colorful head regalia, and a natural red, rouge-like paste called *roucou.* The Wayana are a hospitable people, so much so that even though a visitor may break their daily routine, he or she would never be aware of the imposition. Since Maripasoula has an airstrip, return to Cayenne in a small, single-engine plane, or retrace your route downriver.

*Note:* A river trip to Maripasoula will involve passing by areas — particularly Stoelman's Island, where the Lawa and Tapahoni rivers meet — that were held by Surinamese insurgents as we went to press. Be sure to check with the tourist office in St.-Laurent beforehand about the advisability of making such a trip.

## BEST EN ROUTE

Tourist facilities in French Guiana still are limited, but several new hotels have been built in recent years. In Cayenne, expect to pay between $120 and $140 for a double room at the *Novotel Cayenne,* classified as expensive, a moderate-priced hotel will cost between $70 and $90. Outside the capital and Kourou, hotels mostly are limited to small rooms without private baths. However, what you get is comfortable and, if you're not fussy, likable. The most expensive places will run at least about $70 a night for a double room; more moderate prices are between $30 and $60; and anything under $25 is considered inexpensive. It's a good idea to make reservations; if you're booking with a tour, it will be done for you.

### CAYENNE

**Novotel Cayenne** – Two miles (3 km) outside town, on the sea, Cayenne's newest hotel has 100 air conditioned rooms, with 4 equipped for handicapped guests. Amenities include a pool, 2 tennis courts, cable television, an excellent restaurant, bar, and conference facilities. Rte. de Montabo (phone: 594-303888; fax: 594-317898). Expensive.

**Motel du Lac** – Located 5 miles (8 km) outside town, with 32 air conditioned rooms with private bath, a restaurant, and a pool. Rte. du Montjoly (phone: 594-380800). Expensive to moderate.

**Le Polygone** – The main draw of this 34-room hostelry outside town is its zoo with exotic animals. All the guestrooms have air conditioning, a private bath, and a television set. There also is a restaurant, tennis and racquetball courts, and a gym. Two miles (3 km) from town. Carrefour du Larivot (phone: 594-351500; fax: 594-315850). Expensive to moderate.

**Amazonia** – A small, pleasant hotel near the centrally located Place des Palmistes, it has 78 air conditioned rooms. The staff speaks English. Weekly rates available. 26-28 Av. du Général de Gaulle (phone: 594-310000; fax: 594-319441). Moderate.

***Central*** – Relatively new and right in the heart of the city (as the name suggests), this 35-room property has a television set, telephone, air conditioning, and sound-proofing in all rooms. Telex and fax facilities are available. At the corner of Rues Mole and Becker (phone: 594-313000; fax: 594-311296 or 594-307776). Moderate.

## KOUROU

***Des Roches*** – A large property with 100 rooms and 10 seafront bungalows, an elegant and very good restaurant, swimming pool, and tennis courts. Pointe des Roches (phone: 594-320066; fax: 594-320328). Expensive.

## DEVIL'S ISLAND

***L'Auberge des Iles du Salut*** – Once the administration building for the French penal colony, it now offers guestrooms, all with balconies and private bath, in dormitory accommodations (phone: 594-334530 and 594-321100). Moderate.

## ST.-LAURENT-DU-MARONI

***Julienne*** – A 6-room guesthouse. Rte. des Malgaches (phone: 594-341153). Expensive to moderate.

***Star*** – This 38-room hotel offers clean and simple accommodations. Rue Thiers (phone: 594-341084). Expensive to moderate.

***La Tentiare*** – Formerly a prison, this completely renovated hotel with 24 rooms — all with air conditioning, private bath, and television set — is the best in town. 12 Av. Franklin-Roosevelt (phone: 594-342600; fax: 595-341509). Expensive to moderate.

***Le Toucan*** – There are 20 rooms in this guesthouse, most without air conditioning or private bath. The staff is helpful, but the place could be cleaner. There's a pleasant sidewalk café and bar downstairs. Av. du Généeral de Gaulle (phone: 594-341007). Moderate.

# Guyana

Guyana is a country for serious adventurers, although an infrastructure for intrepid travelers currently is in the fledgling stages. The wild beauty of its jungle interior is visited at a price of rigorous — and sometimes dangerous — effort. Though only 83,000 square miles in area (about the size of Idaho or Kansas), travel is difficult. The rain forests and savannahs make air or river travel the only viable means of transport and, at press time, the best way to do either was with an organized group. Few of Guyana's 700,000 residents venture into the jungle interior; the exceptions are those who work for a growing number of gold and diamond mining companies, oil prospectors, and loggers. Those who do contend with tropical heat and humidity — temperatures range from 63 to 105F (17 to 41C), and rainfall averages as much as 105 inches annually — tropical insects, and (hardly surprising in such jungle) the risk of malaria.

Bordered by Venezuela to the west, Suriname to the east, Brazil to the south, and the Atlantic Ocean on the north, Guyana (pronounce "Guy" as in "eye") was called British Guiana before it gained independence in 1966. Until late 1991, its socialist government appeared to want to discourage tourism. Even in Georgetown, the capital, data on tourism was hard to find until recently, when the Ministry of Trade and Tourism started to encourage the private sector to create a tourist industry. The major hotels and tour operators responded, with the government's blessing, by formally launching the Tourism Association of Guyana.

Large-scale tourism is hardly a question in Guyana, although the new association is trying to encourage ecotourism by offering short trips to the interior as part of packages that also include nearby Caribbean destinations. There is a lamentable shortage of accommodations outside the capital and the rush of bad press at the time of the Jonestown massacre (in November 1978) has never quite subsided. For whatever reason, strangers — and that includes any travelers — are met in most interior towns and river ports by the police, who take a careful look at entry papers. The police are friendly and helpful, but vigilant. In Georgetown, be aware of attacks by "choke and grab" thugs on the city's streets. There seems to be no pervasive pattern to such incidents. Just be particularly careful after dark, even in a taxi.

Guyana is an Indian word meaning "land of many waters," and these many waters are the major thoroughfares of the country. All tours to the interior begin in Georgetown, the nation's port of entry by air or sea. With only two roads of any consequence (one along the coast, the other joining Georgetown to the bauxite mines in Linden, 65 miles/104 km away), visits to the interior must be made by air. Once there, travel is by boat, horse, or jeep. By the end of 1991, however, a dirt road had been cut through the jungle to the Takatu River at the Brazilian border. Plans call for a bridge to be built across the river; the road will then link Georgetown with the state of Roraima in northern Brazil. At press time, there were additional plans to turn it into a paved highway when funds become available. When the highway is completed, the interior of the country will be accessible to travelers with cars.

Despite its small size, Guyana offers a variety of landscape and vegetation. It is fanned by trade winds that keep the temperatures almost bearable along the 270-mile coast. In many places, the land is below sea level. The ingenuity of the first Dutch settlers (the first Europeans to colonize the country in 1621) still is evident in the form of floodgates, or *kokers,* set around Georgetown.

Because so many rivers empty into the Atlantic along Guyana's coast, the coastal waters are for the most part murky and muddy, a long shot from the fine Caribbean beaches that bring so many swimmers, divers, and sun worshipers to the Venezuelan and Colombian shores west of Guyana. But if sun worshippers are disappointed, river lovers thrive here.

Guyana's interior is forest, mountain, and savannah. Most mountainous is the southwestern corner of Guyana's border with Venezuela, where the mountains are characteristically primordial, steep and sharp along the inclines, and flat on top. Mt. Roraima, the 9,094-foot mountain near the juncture of the Guyanese, Venezuelan, and Brazilian borders, so caught Sir Arthur Conan Doyle's imagination that after seeing it he wrote *The Lost World,* envisioning the mountaintop inhabited by prehistoric animals.

The savannahs, in the northeast and southwest parts of the country, sustain cattle herds tended by cowboys who are really Indians. In fact, agriculture is one of the country's first, and still major, industries. Following the Dutch colonization and the founding of the Dutch West India Company, slaves were imported to work the plantations, which still produce sugar, cotton, and coffee. Today, more than 150,000 people are involved in the sugar industry; rice, rum, and timber are also profitable trade.

Mining is another major industry. The production of bauxite started in Linden in 1916 is still going strong but not at great profit because of low prices on the world market. In recent years, gold and diamond mining have increased.

Romantic? Exciting? Wild? Yes. But one must remember that a trip to Guyana is no fool's holiday. Certain precautions should be taken while traveling here. Visitors are warned to dress in field gear in the interior. Rainwear and insect repellent are requisite, and tennis shoes, not boots, should be worn for river transportation (boots are hazardous if a canoe tips over). Malaria tablets are essential, and a yellow fever inoculation is required when entering from Venezuela or Suriname.

Money is another concern. Guyana has a free foreign exchange system whereby you can change money (which you couldn't do just a few years ago). Foreign currency can be changed at *cambios* (exchange houses) located all over Georgetown and other major cities and at banks, but you'll get a better rate at *cambios.* However, because the local currency is not convertible abroad (no bank in the US or elsewhere will convert Guyana dollars), hotels require foreigners to pay in hard currencies (i.e., from industrialized nations), as do many local airlines. Be sure to come with US dollars in cash or traveler's checks and change only the amount you actually need; otherwise you will be left with useless Guyana dollars as souvenirs when you return home.

To ease the trials of a visit, visitors are urged to arrange travel, sightseeing, and accommodations through Guyanese travel agents. Try *Frandec Travel Services* (29 Main St.; phone: 592-2-52526) or *Swim Tours* (in the *Forte Crest* hotel; phone: 592-2-52853 through 592-2-52859). The Tourism Association of Guyana (in the *Forte Crest* hotel; phone: 592-2-52853 through 592-2-52859) also will answer queries.

**GEORGETOWN:** At the mouth of the Demerara River in the center of the coastline, Georgetown is the capital and commercial heart of Guyana. The city covers an area of 1,612 acres and has a population of 190,000, more than one-quarter of the national total.

Once called the "Garden City of the Caribbean," Georgetown is a quaint combination of Victorian elegance — the legacy of its British heritage — and tin-roofed mining town. Both aspects are worth a visit, and you can plan to spend a couple of days roaming the town. A walking tour should begin at the seawall near the *Forte Crest* hotel (formerly the *Guyana Pegasus*) on High Street. A stop at the top floor of the hotel will give you an overall view of the city. The seawall originally was built in 1882 to protect the city, which is 5 feet below the high-tide mark.

Leaving the hotel, observe the large, circular thatch building to your right. Patterned after the dwellings of the Indians in the interior, it was built some years ago at the request of the government to be used as an auditorium; it is a good example of Guyanese architecture. In contrast, colonial homes on High Street are trimmed in Victorian gingerbread.

When you reach the old railroad tracks, note the station, built in 1848 — the first such erected on the South American continent. At the tracks, High Street changes to Main Street and passes more Victorian homes; you can peer through the guarded hedge at Guyana House, home of the presidents, but you can't enter the grounds. By the time you reach the *Park* hotel (on the right at the corner of Main and Middle Sts.), you'll probably be ready to take a break at the hotel, an ideal resting spot. The *Park* is a glorious old place with a huge, wooden porch (see *Best en Route*). Sit under the rotating ceiling fans in a wicker chair, order a drink made with the local rum (rated "E" for "Excellent"), or indulge in tea and cakes. It is the tropical life as played out in a dozen different novels. There are often some miners or other breed of fortune hunter nearby, and they'll eagerly share some of their adventures with you, usually for the price of a cool drink and willing ear.

If you can pull away, resume your trip along Main Street to the *Tower* hotel (No. 74 on the left; see *Best en Route*). Straight ahead is the Bank of Guyana, the place to cash checks and change currency. A bit farther, Main Street once again becomes High Street.

Off Church Street is the *Georgetown Museum*. Open daily except Sundays, the museum contains exhibits on the country's prehistory, history, and flora and fauna.

St. George's Anglican Cathedral (across Main Street) is considered by the Guyanese to be the tallest wooden building in the world. That is probably an exaggerated claim, but the church, which opened in 1892, towers a magnificent 142 feet above the street. Inside, a huge stained glass window casts a many-colored glow on the simple wooden pews. Over half the Guyanese population is Christian, with Anglicans predominating. One-third of the citizens are Hindus; slightly under 10% are Muslim. English, however, is the official language.

Beyond the cathedral, High Street becomes the Avenue of the Republic. On your right is the tiny, charming police station that resembles a Victorian dollhouse and several other gingerbread buildings, including the City Hall (1887) and Tudor-style law courts.

The Botanic Garden and Zoo (on Vlissegen Rd.) completes the walking tour. The

180-acre garden is covered with bougainvillea, flamboyant trees, orchids, and other tropical plants. Afloat in the ponds are huge, umbrella-size lily pads. The zoo, open daily from 6 AM to 6 PM, has another pond loaded with sea cows, which swim over to take grass from your hand. Band concerts are held on Sunday afternoons around the little gazebo. Adjacent is the excellent *Cultural Centre*.

Shopping is a "don't miss" in Georgetown. Upon reaching Brickdam Street, take a right and pass the Parliament Building. Straight ahead is *Stabroek Market*, a glorious display of agricultural products and some handicrafts, but not the safest place for foreigners.

Two other fascinating shops carry only local handicrafts at absurdly low prices. Next door to the market is the *Amerindian Handicrafts Centre* (1 Water St.), run by the Interior Development Department. On the second floor of an austere, gray building, it looks more like a museum than a shop. Spears, blowpipes, beadwork, carvings, and feather headdresses made by the Indians are available. The *Guyana Crafts Co-op* (at the corner of Brickdam and the Ave. of the Republic) has lovely baskets and hammocks, as does *Houseproud* (6 Ave. of the Republic). Another place is *Creations Craft* (7A Water St.) for baskets and woodcarvings.

**En Route from Georgetown to Linden** – Bauxite mining, a major Guyanese industry, was started in Linden in 1916. Visitors can visit the nationalized plants there via a 65-mile (104-km) highway or by buses that leave frequently from Georgetown's *Stabroek Market*. A tour at the mines is a 2-hour affair.

**En Route from Georgetown to the Interior** – At press time, there were only two ways to go into the interior — by chartering a plane at a prohibitive price (the Tourism Association of Guyana at the *Forte Crest* hotel in Georgetown can make the arrangements; phone: 592-2-52853 through 592-2-52859) or traveling with an organized group. Previously, *Guyana Airways*' planes served some 20 domestic airfields and held 19 passengers each, but the high cost of doing business has grounded the airline's domestic flights.

*Swim Tours* at the *Forte Crest* hotel in Georgetown (see phone above) currently offers a variety of tours to the interior. Packages include a trip up the Demerara River to *Timberhead*, an overnight lodge. If you choose to stay, activities include bird watching, hiking on nature trails, and fishing at night the traditional Indian way — with a spear and a torch. Part of the same excursion is a stop at the *Shanklands* guesthouse and camp on the Essequibo River, where there is water skiing, swimming, fishing, and river trips to several historical and picturesque sites.

Another option are packages offered by Venezuela-based *Alechiven* (Local A-18, Centro Comercial Siglo XXI, La Viña, Valencia, Venezuela; phone and fax: 58-41-217018) or through its US representative, *Lost World Adventures* (1189 Autumn Ridge Rd., Marietta, GA 30066; phone: 404-971-8586 or 800-999-0558; fax: 404-977-3095). Most of *Alechiven*'s trips require leaving from Caracas (or combining travel through both countries). The 4-day, 3-night Guyana portion includes Georgetown, Kaieteur Falls, and traveling by wooden boats with outboard motors down the Essequibo River to see old Dutch forts on Fort Island and Kyk-over-al, before visiting the gold mining town of Bartica. Also available are 1-week trips that include road travel on the coastal highway to the border with Suriname (visiting a sugar factory en route), and a stop in the Mabura Hills with its virgin forests.

If you choose to charter a plane, make sure to get clearance through a travel agent to visit the interior, because many areas are off limits. The government does not want Jonestown to become a tourist attraction for obvious reasons, and some Indian reservations also are restricted. When you arrive at the outposts, show your credentials to the police, who will probably meet you at the plane anyway. Most of them will steer you to nearby attractions; they are also there for your protection in areas that sometimes resemble the wild, wild American West.

## DIRECTIONS / Guyana

**KAIETEUR FALLS:** On the Potaro River, a tributary of the Essequibo, about 150 miles (240 km) from Georgetown, the Kaieteur Falls, 740 feet high and nearly five times as high as Niagara, are Guyana's most famous attraction. The trip to Kaieteur certainly should not be missed. To get there, either charter a plane in Georgetown or book a trip through one of the tour operators in the capital. *Swim Tours* offers a 1-day excursion to the falls for $120, which includes a guide, food, and drinks. The small plane will bump to a landing on a rocky strip. The traveler is then left to walk across a desolate area and through a dense jungle along a trail surrounded by towering trees draped in moss. After a 10-minute walk, which includes clambering over rocks, the jungle opens, and you see the falls roaring below.

Sometimes diamond and gold miners congregate in tents at the top of the falls on the smooth, rocky bluff, and they usually can be persuaded to part with their finds for cash. But the falls is the main attraction. It varies considerably in size from the rainy to the dry season (the rainy seasons run from April to August and November to January), but is spectacular when flowing deep and fast. The water is stained brown by decaying vegetation, and branches of trees are swept along the cliff to oblivion at the falls' bottom. Dense spray rises from the white foam as the waves crash onto the boulders at the base of the gorge, and rapids twist away from the falls. Tiny birds flit around the edge of the falls to reach the huge cave that has been carved out underneath by years of erosion.

The truly adventurous don't have to make the return trip immediately. They can wait and spend several days camping with the miners at the top of the falls. The climb from the river to the top of the falls takes about 2 hours. There are no provisions in the area (except a plenitude of water), but the stay will allow time to follow the path to the base of the falls and along the roaring river downstream. If you come prepared, it can be an exceptional, otherworldly stay. But be sure your return flight is assured on another plane or with another *Swim Tours* group.

At press time, the government had plans to preserve the area as a national park with assistance from international conservation organizations.

**IMBAIMADAI:** A trip to Imbaimadai is also time well spent. The (US) Old West must have been much like this diamond- and gold-mining town on the Mazaruni River in western Guyana. The town consists of shanties, three bars (where gin in condensed milk is a popular breakfast drink), the diamond buyers' office — and a pool table.

Along the Mazaruni are dredges for gold mining. Divers spend entire days at the bottom of the river, handling the hoses that suck mud to the surface. The mud is strained, then panned by hand to separate the grains of gold, which are melted down in coffee cans.

The diamond hunters operate mainly along the riverbanks, digging holes and sifting the sand for the tiny glittering gems. Most of the diamonds are small, but they are of excellent quality. Usually a man will spend several weeks in the bush collecting, sell his finds, spend the money in a few days, then go into the wilds again. It is a cruel life — as cruel, it would seem, as the wild Guyanese environment surrounding the miners. Not even the three men who discovered Guyana's largest diamond have enough money to buy shoes today. (The 8-karat gem was discovered 25 years ago, only to disappear mysteriously. One of those three discoverers frequently passes through Imbaimadai, still searching for new riches.)

The Indians or some of the miners in the town — which has a population of about 200 — are happy to guide travelers to Imbaimadai's tourist attractions: Maipuri Falls (*maipuri* is the Arawak Indian word for the tapir), 80 feet high and 90 feet wide; and the Temehri cliff drawings, on the way to the falls; and nearby Kawaio Indian villages. The falls and the cliff drawings must be reached by the river, and at least two Indian paddlers — both familiar with the river — are necessary. Don't try to go by yourself.

The Temehri cliff paintings date from the 14th century, and the Indians claim the glistening, quartzite cliff was painted not by men, but by the god Ama Livaca, who visited Guyana during a great flood. The paintings extend over a width of 50 feet to a height of 25 feet, and they depict animals, groups of dancing figures, and hundreds of handprints. The half-hour hike from the river to the cliff is as impressive as the paintings themselves. The trail leads through the heart of the rain forest and across a chasm, stopping on the way only for a cool drink from a cold spring in a cave.

To get to the Indian villages, it is a good idea to have a motor rather than paddle boat. Gasoline is expensive because it must be flown in from Georgetown, but the trip is fascinating. The chief of the village will take you on the tour himself, showing you the peanut farm and the women making cassava bread (cassava is the plant whose root provides the stock for making tapioca).

At press time, the only way to get to Imbaimadai was by chartering a plane. Contact the Tourism Association (phone: 592-2-52853 through 592-2-52859) for assistance. The flight over the jungles, past the flat-topped mountains encircled by mist, is awesome.

**RUPUNUNI SAVANNAH:** In the southwest corner of Guyana, bordering Brazil, the Rupununi is part of the vast Río Branco savannah. One hour's plane ride from Georgetown to the town of Lethem (by charter plane or through a 2-day *Swim Tours* package that includes transportation, accommodations, and meals for about $200) brings you to the savannah and *Dianne McTurck's* guesthouse, one of the few remaining Amerindian houses on the savannah. Visitors to the guesthouse can fish, swim, ride horses, bird watch, and go on excursions in the area. One popular trip from the ranch goes by jeep to a tropical forest of the Kanuku Mountains to visit one of the oldest Indian settlements in the country. The Wai-Wai Indians, a branch of the Amerindian tribe, are known for their colorful use of bird feathers in their dress. Nearby, the Macushi Indians will take you on a 20-minute walk from the village to Moco Moco Falls, which has clear swimming pools surrounded by boulders.

In Lake Pan, you can go swimming or fish for *lukunani*, tasty fish that are caught easily with fly-fishing gear from the shore. If you're too lazy for the sport, however, you still can watch the natives fish for giant *arapaima* the old-fashioned way, with bows and arrows.

One word about the Rupununi waters: Beware when you bathe; some very unfriendly creatures lurk here. The *perai* is a 6- to 9-inch creature lured by the smell of fresh blood. Stingrays and electric eels — the 500-volt variety — also inhabit the otherwise tranquil waters.

Another short excursion from the guesthouse takes you to Schomburgk's Peak. The 3,000-foot climb to the top takes about 4 hours, winding past huge trees, balata and wild cocoa, covered with orchids.

Near Lethem is the Takatu River, the border with Brazil. Many floating shops can be found anchored along the Brazilian side.

## BEST EN ROUTE

A visit to Guyana is fun, if rugged, when planned properly. Accommodations are adequate in Georgetown, where the best hotel, the *Forte Crest* (formerly the *Guyana Pegasus*), runs $135 a night for a double room, while lodging in the interior borders on the primitive and can be disproportionately expensive. Hotels in the moderate category can range from $50 to $90 a night for a double. Remember that tourists are required to pay their hotel bills with foreign currency (US dollars, French francs, or other hard currency).

### GEORGETOWN

*Forte Crest* – Owned and operated by Forte Hotels, this 150-room air conditioned property has a swimming pool, tennis courts, restaurant, pub, and cocktail lounge.

Seawall and High Sts. (phone: 592-2-52853 through 592-2-52859; for information and reservations in the US, 800-225-5843). Expensive.

**Park** – A wide wooden porch runs the expanse of this 82-room hotel in a lovely colonial building. There is a restaurant and bar (serving high-quality Guyana rum) and room service. Breakfast included. Main St. (phone: 592-2-54911 to 592-2-54916). Moderate.

**Tower** – This hotel has 90 rooms, a swimming pool, and restaurant. The spare furnishings and the presence of security guards on each floor create a prison-like atmosphere, which hopefully will be softened by current renovations. 74 Main St. (phone: 592-2-72011 through 592-2-72015). Moderate.

**Woodbine** – A neat, cozy hostelry with 40 rooms, 31 of which are air conditioned. There is a restaurant and bar. The only drawback is its location on the edge of a dangerous slum neighborhood. 41 New Market St. (phone: 592-2-59430; fax: 592-2-58406). Moderate.

# Panama

Traversing the 340-mile (544-km) section of the Pan-American Highway linking the Costa Rican frontier at Paso Canoa with the Panama Canal provides a very different perspective of this 28,753-square-mile republic (about the size of South Carolina) of 2 million people. This is the Panama of lush mountain ranges, dormant volcanoes, trout-filled streams, and wide beaches, where the Guaymi Indians still farm and practice native arts of embroidery and hand-crafted jewelry and live in houses of thatch roof and bamboo construction, as their ancestors have for 10 centuries.

It's not until the highway winds its way east to Arraiján, and then drops a few miles down forest-cool slopes to the Bridge of the Americas across the canal, that travelers get a taste of the more traditional Panama — Columbus, Spanish gold-seekers, Henry Morgan's pirates, Colombian profiteers, and French and US canal builders.

Spain's interest in Panama as anything more than an interoceanic shortcut was perfunctory. What little gold the isthmus yielded was mined mostly in what today is the Colombian border area. The interior — in Panamanian usage, that part of the republic between the canal and the Costa Rican border entry at Paso Canoa, on the Pacific side of the Continental Divide — meant nothing to Madrid's gold-mad bureaucrats. Anyone who settled there was on his own.

Independence in 1821 brought a marginal change of status from a Spanish colony to a distant province of politically unstable Colombia. Bogotá's bureaucrats cared no more than their Madrid predecessors for anything Panamanian, except rapid transit. *Interioranos* were still on their own until 1903, when US President Teddy Roosevelt proved an adept puppeteer in the separation of Panama from Colombia.

So the Panama the road traveler sees between Paso Canoa and the canal, with Panama City close beside it, is not . . .

- the Panama of Balboa's discovery of the Pacific Ocean in 1513 — that's 93 miles (150 km) beyond the canal;
- the Panama of treasure raids by those "redistribute the wealth" economists, Sir Francis Drake and Lieutenant Governor Sir Henry Morgan;
- the Panama of the canal — the crushing French failure of Suez-builder Ferdinand de Lesseps, followed by the triumph of Teddy Roosevelt's US engineers and, most of all, the US doctors who controlled malaria and yellow fever;
- the Panama of two world wars and the passenger liner era, when ingenuous itinerants' tall tales promoted the city as rife with honky-tonks on a par with those of Port Said, Marseilles, and Macao.

No. The Panama glimpsed from the Pan-American Highway formed its character as a farming frontier, with no proud fortresses, no costly social pretensions. Self-reliance was the only way to get from one rugged day to the next.

Which has much to do with why the proud Texan-type folks of Chiriquí, the rich farm province adjoining the Costa Rican border, have been heard to scoff at three generations of to-ing and fro-ing between the US and Panama over canal issues. "Turn control of the republic over to us *chiricaños,*" they say, "and it would be so abundantly ranched that the canal would not matter much one way or the other."

This sturdy spirit has had culinary consequences. For most of the way along the highway, it is hitching-rail cuisine. Diners don't show up on cow ponies (pickups, four-wheel-drive farm vehicles, and trailer rigs, yes), but Pan-American Highway roadside restaurants — many of which double as open-air dance halls on weekends — are for hard, hard men. Hotel-hopping is, therefore, prudent — at least until the highway crosses the former Río Hato airstrip and sets off along the beach resorts, about 70 miles (112 km) from Panama City.

The best tourist guide is the twice-yearly *Focus on Panama,* which is available at the Paso Canoa frontier post and in the better hotels. At Paso Canoa, the tourist information office also hands out a road map. It's not as informative as the Shell road map of Panama, but since the latter is only available from the company's Panama City office, you may have to make do with what you can get.

One phone book serves the whole country. The number of any hotel in any town is there on its pages, and can be dialed directly for reservations.

Street addresses are less helpful. Newly installed mayors in Panama come with a built-in compulsion to manifest their authority. Since the municipal coffers usually tend to be empty, the least expensive way to exercise this urge is to change the names of the streets. In Panama City, for example, it is not uncommon to see a street sign bearing three names or numbers.

Another thing to keep in mind: The Pan-American Highway is not just part of Panama's highway system. It *is* the system. No sector of the interior, whether of tourist, industrial, farming, or commercial significance, can be reached by land from either the Costa Rican frontier or the capital without traveling part of the way on the Pan-American. However, the highway has any number of convenient turnoffs that lead to most of the nation's major attractions.

By and large, the signs on the highway are clear and accurate. But there is no guarantee that a given signpost might not suffer a little adversity the night before you come rolling by, so signposts should be augmented by a good map.

Panama is, with a single exception (La Herradura), bereft of trailer parks — an aspect of tourism that has yet to take root here. While an annual convoy of campers and motor homes from the US is given special treatment — much as Portobelo used to arouse from its slumbers to greet the Spanish galleons bearing treasure centuries ago — today's camper would do better to navigate from hotel to hotel, where power and water are assured.

As a frontier town, Paso Canoa is as ramshackle a place as Dodge City ever was. The border runs down its one and only street, and Panamanians and Costa Ricans buy whatever is least expensive in the cinderblock stores lining each side of the border. It is, however, one of Latin America's less nitpicking frontiers for international travelers. A busload can be cleared through both Costa Rican and Panamanian customs and immigration posts in about an hour. For those moving by car, motorbike, or thumb, the frontier delay is a matter of luck — depending on how many trucks, buses, and other vehicles are in line. It can be as brief as 5 minutes on a light traffic day.

There's a Paso Canoa tale that, in a statesmanlike effort to speed up the customs process, the two countries agreed to synchronize the lunch hour of border officials. Noon to 1 PM was decided upon, rather than the previous noon to 1 PM for the Costa Ricans and 1 to 2 PM for the Panamanians. So everyone lunched from noon to 1 PM, an exercise in bureaucracy that extended the midday border closing time from 1 to 2 hours. Someone had forgotten that, year-round, Panama is on eastern standard time, Costa Rica on central standard. Well, it's a funny story, but these days the frontier is a 24-hour operation, traffic having increased twentyfold over the past 10 years.

Panama has undergone some heat over the treaty, which (in the year 2000) changes US authority over the canal to control by the republic (the US already has turned over some buildings and land in the Canal Area to Panama). While Panamanians were, for the most part, delighted with the new pact, some resident Americans left the Canal Zone (now called the Canal Area), disenchanted. Others took early retirement and moved into one of the condominiums proliferating in the republic. But most of the Americans employed and living in the Canal Area have stayed on, rather than uprooting families and jobs.

Since the installation of democratically elected President Guillermo Endara in 1989, economic improvement has come slowly to Panama. The US-imposed sanctions during strong man Manuel Noriega's regime nearly crippled the Panamanian economy. While the government expects a healthy growth in years to come, at least one in five Panamanians is unemployed and few feel President Endara has done enough to help the country's poor. Most Panamanians, however, see Endara's administration as a transition and are looking hopefully toward next year's presidential elections.

Note: The outbreak of cholera that has hit some South American countries has spread to Panama as well. The Darién jungle in the southern Darién province has the most reported incidences, but there also have been isolated cases on some of the less-visited coastal islands. Travelers should be careful to drink only bottled water, eat only well-cooked vegetables, fish, and meat, and avoid food sold by street vendors.

# The Pan-American Highway

**PUERTO ARMUELLES:** Turn right off the Pan-American Highway about 2 miles (3 km) after entering Panama and head for Puerto Armuelles, one of the republic's chief ports, on the coast of the Gulf of Chiriquí in the Pacific Ocean. Created (and at one time owned) by United Brands (formerly United Fruit), the town is one of the few in the area with a population of more than 10,000 and is now controlled by national authorities.

If you've never seen one of Central America's big-time banana farms, Puerto Armuelles rates a look. Most of the plantations are today owned by those who work them. But the Chiriquí Land Company, the local arm of United Brands, remains the only customer of consequence and keeps a close eye on quality control. Chiquita Banana's Big Brother almost always is watching.

A question not to ask in Puerto Armuelles: "Where is the best hotel and restaurant?" They don't exist. Instead, take the question back to David, 55 miles (89 km) northeast, the capital of Chiriquí province.

**VOLCÁN and CERRO PUNTA:** The turnoff into the hills of Concepción, 17 miles (27 km) from the Costa Rican frontier, leads 22 miles (35 km) up into the hills to El Hato del Volcán, the rarely mentioned full name of the little town everyone calls Volcán. Bring a sweater; the altitude here is 5,000 feet. Farther up the road, about 11 miles (18 km), is Cerro Punta, 1,000 feet higher than Volcán.

If you've spent recent days in the green, crisp uplands of Costa Rica, Volcán and Cerro Punta may be a repetition. But for someone who has just barreled across Central America's scorched coastal plains, these two towns are a lofty haven where not only is the air like wine, but the strawberries are like strawberries. It doesn't take long to understand why the Indians called the region Chiriquí, the Valley of the Moon.

The volcanic soil of the slopes of the extinct Barú Volcano, at 11,411 feet Panama's highest mountain, and the farming skills of Yugoslav and Swiss communities that settled the high valleys generations ago, have made the region Panama's fruit and vegetable garden. Nowhere else in the country is there land so meticulously tilled. Nor, except in air conditioned city offices, do Panamanian girls wear woolen ponchos. It is roughly equivalent, in improbability, to an Aleut maiden in a bikini.

What to do in the area today? The steadiest tourist trade from the US is bird watching groups. Though it is only the fourth-largest country in the mid-Americas area (after El Salvador, Belize, and Costa Rica), Panama has close to 800 species of native birds. Another 200 or so spend the northern winter here or stop over on their southward migration. Chiriquí is the southernmost habitat of the quetzal, a gorgeous Central American bird with brilliant bronze, green, and red plumage.

Hunters and fishermen also head for the Chiriquí hills. Favorite targets are the torcaza (a white-tailed pigeon) and migratory waterfowl. The torcaza is known locally as *rabiblanco*. To explain to immigration officials that you are visiting the country to shoot *rabiblancos* will not quite do. The term is also slang for members of Panama's wealthy, traditional ruling class.

The fishing runs from brown trout — not found in the warmer, slothful streams where the Continental Divide dips toward the canal — to black bass, found in the tarns around Volcán. In both Volcán and Cerro Punta, horses can be hired for trail riding.

Climbers can try scaling the slopes of Barú. Guides are available. Groups should make it a 2-day venture, camping out overnight on the mountain. The climb is more like an uphill march than an alpine feat, but it's man against mountain all the way. Keep in mind there are no cabins or comforts of any sort along the trails. Bring what you need.

Volcán also can be reached by a road that runs up the line of the Costa Rican frontier from Paso Canoa to Río Sereno, and from there along the hillsides to Volcán. Sections of this route are slide-prone. The road from Concepción is more reliable.

**DAVID:** Sixteen miles (26 km) along the Pan-American Highway from Concepción, David (pop. 88,000) is Panama's principal city before the Canal Area, as well as Chiriquí's capital. Many highway-riding tourists make it their first Panama stopover.

David refuses to let tourists get on its nerves. It proudly remains a nine-bank, unreconstructed farm town. To capture its flavor, don't look for theaters or art galleries. Check the number of pickup trucks in the parking lots of the *Nacional* hotel (see *Best en Route*).

The big civic event of the year is the mid-March *Feria de San José de David*. It goes on for a week or more, and Costa Ricans and other Central Americans participate. Dancing in the streets till dawn? Feckless jubilation? Hardly. Cattle, farm equipment, and produce. Regional handicrafts, such as saddles, is what the David fair is all about.

Chiriquí looks to the future. Its Cerro Colorado copper deposits are said to be among the largest in the world. Near Cerro Colorado is Panama's costliest hydroelectric dam, the $236 million, 255-megawatt La Fortuna plant.

David's San José church stands as a symbol of the town's self-reliance. Built centuries ago, the structure's belfry was set apart from the church as a defense against hostile Indians.

The best David has to offer in the currency of the past are a small archaeological museum (Calle Octava; phone: 757839) — most exhibits of Chiriquí's pre-Columbian art are in museums in Panama City — and a modest historical display in the house where Francisco Morazán lived for a while between his 1838 ouster as the last President of the United Provinces of Central America and his subsequent engagement with a firing squad in Costa Rica. Central Americans, the majority of David's foreign tourists, do not come to Panama to inspect mementos of presidents who got shot. They can do that at home. Tourist attractions are the stores with household appliances and electronic equipment, either unobtainable or heavily taxed at home.

For non-drivers, transport from David to Panama City is abundant. Three flights daily, on *Chiricanas* (phone: 646448) and *Aeroperlas* (phone: 694555), offer a total of about 200 seats. Trunkline buses, some air conditioned with reclining seats, make the run down the Pan-American Highway in about 5 hours. No-frills buses that pick up and deposit passengers along the way, and stop for meals, take a little longer. For information about both kinds of buses, contact *Transportes Panamá* in David (phone: 629436).

**BOQUETE:** At an altitude of 3,800 feet, Boquete is a half-hour drive up into the foothills from David. It's the tranquil preference of many visitors having business in David; of escapees from the canal hotlands; of Pan-American Highway travelers; of bird watchers, fern collectors, and orchid fanciers; and of hunters of the feathered species.

Locals call Boquete and the misty mountain walls of its half-hidden valley the Land of the Rainbows. At times, seven rainbows can be seen at once. And in a way, it does come with a pot of gold for some. Some of the Forty-niners who reached Panama bound for the California gold fields decided that life in these hills would be somewhat steadier than in the gun-toting West. As a result, the Boquete section of the phone book carries a larger proportion of non-Spanish names than is true in most small Panamanian communities.

On the road from David, closer to Boquete, stop at *Coffee Bean* (phone: 701624). It has good food and a caged lioness named Elsa.

This place is known as the flower capital of Panama. The *Flower Fair* in mid-April, the brightest event of its kind in the republic, draws exhibitors from Central American neighbors and even from Japan.

As in Volcán and Cerro Punta, guided ascents of El Barú can be arranged.

**BOCAS DEL TORO and CHANGUINOLA:** They say that Bocas del Toro and Changuinola are "somewhere over the rainbow," probably because the only way to get here is by plane. Bocas Town, as natives refer to it, is in northwest Panama, some 300 miles (480 km) from Panama City on the Atlantic side of the isthmus, directly across from Boquete. Access from David is by DC-3.

Columbus stopped by Bocas del Toro on his fourth and final voyage in 1502, and not much has happened since. The archipelago of Bocas del Toro and the Chiriquí Lagoon, its islands' guard, provide as fine an anchorage as can be found on the coast. Fittingly, it's named Bahía Almirante (Admiral's Bay). Unhappily, once a ship is moored here, there is nothing much for it to load except bananas from the Chiriquí Land Company's Changuinola farms (Chiquita's headquarters) and cocoa.

For the tourist there's reef fishing, snorkeling, turtle steaks, a largely English-speaking population, and no danger of getting caught in traffic.

*Chiricanas* and *Aeroperlas* fly from Bocas del Toro to Panama City. For those tired of the highway and happy to devote a day or so to watching an 18-inch tide rise and fall, take this detour en route to Panama City.

**En Route from David-Boquete** – During the drive from the David-Boquete intersection down the Pan-American Highway, use one of the several gas stations thereabouts to ready car and riders for the 188-mile (301-km) run down a fine stretch of highway to Santiago de Veraguas, the next town in which gas stations and restaurants will be found.

This leg of the journey follows a gentle roller coaster over what was empty land until a new section of the highway opened a few years ago. The first 44 miles (70 km) of road hugs the base of the mountains, passing La Chorcha waterfall, a lovely sight when it is rushing, full of rainy-season water. On the right, Panama's richest cattleland stretches to the sea. The San Félix turnoff leads to the beaches of Las Lajas, where seaside tourism facilities are planned for the future. This shoreline is so attractive that, during major Panamanian fiestas, as many as 10,000 holidaymakers camp here despite the lack of organized accommodations. The next highway turnoff of significance is at Guabalá, about 7 miles (12 km) farther on. This turnoff was the old central highway to Santiago, through Soná, and it's in rough condition compared to the highway that replaced it. It has its attractions for the pastoral-minded, despite what the road does to car and passengers. The area serves fine farmland that one day will be brought into production by farmers cashing in on the Pan-American Highway access.

Tolé, gathering place of the Guaymi Indians, is just a few hundred yards off the Pan-American Highway, 3 miles (5 km) past the Guabalá turnoff. The Guaymi definition of a *caserío*, or village, comprises a couple of huts on one ridge, a couple more on another (with a 2,000-foot gorge between them), and a farther hut up a slope and virtually hidden by clouds. Some of these villages are as much as 14 trail hours by pack pony from the nearest road.

Saturdays and Sundays are market days in Tolé. The Indians gather to sell produce, buy goods, and gossip. Guaymi women wear floor-length, shapeless, varicolored, Mother Hubbard dresses. Among the best buys from the Guaymi is the *chaquira*, a shoulder-wide collar in beaded geometrical patterns, and the *chácarra*, also known as *mochila*, basically a string bag. Drivers buying souvenirs don't even have to go into Tolé. Close to the turnoff, the Indians have set up souvenir booths near the highway.

From the Tolé turnoff to Santiago, 59 miles (94 km) of empty land lie ahead.

**SANTIAGO:** This city is the capital of Veraguas, Panama's only sea-to-shining-sea province, in the center of the republic. Across the range lies Belén (sometimes called Bethlehem), where, at the mouth of the river of the same name, Columbus established Panama's first European community. Since 1914, Santiago has been the educational center of the republic. The Normal School was moved here in that year, and since then it has been the sole supplier of the republic's public school teachers. The decentralized National University has a campus here. The late General Omar Torrijos Herrera, President of Panama for 10 years (a record for this category of public office) until his resignation in 1978, was born and raised near Santiago. Both his parents were teachers.

About 7 miles (12 km) down the highway toward the canal is the turnoff for Atalaya. The village church there is probably the nearest thing to a Panamanian shrine. Panamanians from all social strata come here to solicit or give thanks for divine favors.

**AZUERO PENINSULA:** Down the highway 23 miles (37 km), mostly running between sugar fields, is Divisa, the turnoff for the Azuero Peninsula. The region is sketchily developed. Los Santos, a little beyond Chitré and 27 miles (43 km) from Divisa, is old Spanish Panama, tile-roofed and charming. It is the site of Panama's 1821 proclamation of independence from Spain, and its little museum recalls those times.

Business-oriented Chitré, a farming center, makes no effort to lure tourists. It serves more as a hot water base from which to prowl the peninsula. The hometown airline, *Chitreana* (phone: 263069; at the airport, 264116), flies twice daily to Panama City's downtown Paitilla Airport, a 40-minute flight.

The most enduring of Panama's music and dance stem from Azuero's mestizo heritage. Increasingly, Panama's *Carnaval,* virtually a week-long fiesta that folds at sunup on *Ash Wednesday,* is shifting into the interior in general and to Azuero in particular. Hotel space at this time is scarce. *Semana Santa* (Holy Week) is the other time of year when the chance of finding an empty hotel room in the interior is slender. The where-to-stay problem is not insoluble. Guararé in mid-September and Ocú in mid-January celebrate their respective saint's day with small-town happiness. Hotel rooms will be available in Santiago or Chitré or Penonomé or Aguadulce or Los Santos or Las Tablas, none of which is more than a few hours' drive from these festivities.

After folkloric celebrations, Azuero's major attraction is broad miles of people-free beaches. Local folk, busy with cows and crops, take the beaches for granted.

**AGUADULCE:** Fourteen miles (22 km) down the Pan-American Highway from Divisa is Aguadulce. Both the decor and the menu of the *Interamericano* hotel are attractive to veteran travelers, who make this their prime dining spot on the run between the canal and David. Aguadulce's additional claims to fame include: a salt industry based on running the Pacific tide of up to 20 feet into salt pans and letting the sun evaporate it; a small river port; the heart of the republic's sugar industry; and a battlefield from the Colombian civil war, the War of 1,000 Days.

**En Route from Aguadulce** – Through the sugar fields 6 miles (10 km) down the highway is Natá, and what some say is the oldest church in continuous use on the American continent. While the claim is questionable, there's no question that the church reflects its age and warrants a visit. In contrast to the venerable edifice is the nearby Nestlé plant, the biggest processor of Panamanian agricultural and dairy products.

**PENONOMÉ:** This area, 11 miles (18 km) farther east along the highway, was the heart of Panama's Indian culture long before (and during) the time Columbus was setting up a handful of grass huts in Belén as a symbol and example of Western civilization. For archaeologists, it has been the most fruitful site on the isthmus, and a considerable proportion of the exhibits in the *Museum of the Panamanian Man,* arguably Panama City's best museum, are from Penonomé. *Huacas,* the gold ornaments that traders promoted into symbols of Panama in days gone by, were obtained for the most part by grave-robbing in the area of the Penonomé Indian civilization.

**LA PINTADA:** A short drive into the hills from Penonomé leads to La Pintada, home of the *pintado*. These straw hats, worn by Panamanians and other isthmus residents, have a black pattern woven into the white straw with multicolored cords and thongs. In La Pintada, a visitor can be measured and can order a hat bearing the buyer's name and/or any pattern. Delivery takes a while, though.

**FARALLÓN:** Where the highway runs plumb across the Río Hato airstrip, about 12 miles (19 km) down the highway from Penonomé, it is close to history of modern vintage. By the seaward end of the strip, right on the beach of the Gulf of Panama, is the home that ex-President Torrijos used as his Camp David during the canal treaty negotiations. Named Farallón, for the islet off the end of the airstrip, it was here that US senators, congressmen, negotiators, and assorted VIPs came for treaty talks. Farallón is not a national monument battlefield; it's a Defense Forces post. Close by, however, is a chain of beach resorts that stretches 50 miles along the Pacific coast to Punta Chame.

As beaches, those between Farallón and Punta Chame are neither so broad nor so beckoning as those of the Azuero Peninsula or Las Lajas.

**En Route from Farallón** – From west to east, after Farallón, the beaches with cabins and other holiday facilities are: Santa Clara, 71 miles (114 km) from Panama City, with the *Vista Bella* cabin complex; Río Mar, 58 miles (93 km) from Panama City, with swimming in both river and ocean, and the *Río Mar* cabins and restaurant; El Palmar, 57 miles (91 km) from Panama City, with cabins; San Carlos, which is practically contiguous with El Palmar and retains a rural charm with shaded tables and a restaurant among beach facilities set up by the national tourist office; and Coronado, Panama's most ambitious beach development, 50 miles (80 km) from Panama City. Many of the houses would be elegant in any exclusive suburb. The golf course at *Club de Golf Playa Coronado* (phones: 646352 or 233175) is one of the three best on the isthmus, and facilities include an airstrip and supermarket, and its restaurant is the best for maybe 50 miles in any direction. Rentals, including apartments in a multistory building, can be negotiated at the development manager's office. Gorgona, 43 miles (69 km) from Panama City, features the *Jayes* hotel (see *Best en Route)* and the *Ocean Blue Cabins.* Punta Chame is reached from a highway turnoff at Bejuco, 40 miles (64 km) from Panama City. To get to the development at its western tip requires about 12 miles (19 km) of backtracking down the Chame Peninsula. There's ocean swimming on the southern side of this 10-mile tongue of sandy land, and calm-water swimming on the north side on the bay. By air, this is the closest resort beach to the capital. By road, Gorgona is the closest beach.

**EL VALLE:** Once tired of the beaches, just swing off the highway 3 miles (5 km) before the Río Mar turnoff, cross the mountains, and drive up to El Valle, at an altitude of 2,000 feet. The Sunday morning market here is the interior market best known to "canalsiders," and a good proportion of the shoppers are US citizen–residents of the isthmus. Bright bead necklaces, straw items, soapstone animal carvings, and all manner of produce are sold. Golden frogs are said to leap about beneath the area's odd, squarish trees, though they are rarely seen outside of the bush. Overlooking El Valle is the towering Sleeping Maiden Mountain, where it is said that a young Indian woman died from grief after her father forbade her to marry a dashing Spaniard. Legend has it that after her death the mountain took on her shape.

**En Route from El Valle** – Getting back on the Pan-American Highway at the Bejuco turnoff (the entrance to the Punta Chame resort), it's about a 40-mile (64-km) drive to Chorrera, a sprawling dormitory for Panama City, where the road turns into the patched and potholed remains of a time-worn thoroughfare. About a 10-minute drive farther is *La Herradura,* Panama's only trailer park, with plug-in facilities, a pool, restaurant, and riding horses for hire. Mobile home and camper travelers stop off here in the countryside to rest up and organize before heading on to Panama City, where standard mobile home facilities are nonexistent.

**PANAMA CITY:** For a detailed report on the city, its hotels, and restaurants, see *Panama City,* THE CITIES. As the Pan-American Highway winds its way to Arraiján, and then on down the cool, green slopes of Ancón Hill, you'll come upon "the Crossroads of the World," Panama's number one city with a population of more than a half million, standing near the Pacific entrance to the canal. This place hasn't had an easy time of it since its 1519 founding by the Spanish on the Pacific side of the canal.

Sacked by Henry Morgan and his merciless cutthroats in 1671, the Spanish picked up the pieces and took the city 7 miles east, set it up on a peninsula, and surrounded it with huge walls to keep out the likes of Morgan and his rowdies. As a center of commerce, Panama prospered until the late 18th century, when Spain decided to reroute its vessels around the Horn. Things looked bleak until the gold rush of 1849. Prosperity returned as settlers went through Panama on their way to the West Coast.

But the rush was short-lived, and the town's economic fortunes declined until the canal began to be built in earnest in 1903.

The result of the trauma undergone by the city is that today it wears three faces: old Panama, comprising the few remnants left by Morgan (the King's Bridge, the ruins of the Convent and Church of San José, and the Cabildo); colonial Panama, with its 108-year-old cathedral, iron-laced balconies, cobblestone streets (remnants of the walls still stand); and modern Panama, with wide boulevards, elegant shops, restaurants, hotels, casinos, and contemporary office buildings. A marble statute of Balboa looks out at the ocean he discovered.

**En Route from Panama City** – Beyond Panama City, the highway is in good shape for about 62 miles (99 km), passing the Tocumen International Airport and going on to where it bridges the lake backed up behind the Bayano hydroelectric dam and comes to an end. Construction on the road has all but halted since the US invasion in 1989, but the government still has plans to extend the highway through Darién, the republic's easternmost province, to connect it with Colombia. As it is, the swamps and wilderness of Darién today are harder to traverse than when Balboa crossed to stand silent upon a peak. Balboa had more Indians — therefore more trails and guides.

**SAN BLAS ISLANDS:** Off Panama's coast in the Caribbean are the San Blas Islands and their Kuna Indians, among Panama's most exotic attractions. The island chain is a sort of 130-mile coral-based Venice, dotted with bamboo huts. Panamanians say there are as many islands as there are days in the year. About 30 are permanently inhabited, and on them it's 100% occupancy — no room to build another hut.

Visitors can fly over for a single-day excursion or make arrangements to stay at one of the two hotels on the islands (see *Best en Route*). Canoes also can be hired for day trips to small atolls. The islands are indeed lovely and interesting, with rustic, but comfortable, accommodations, and the Kuna welcoming. Check with *Margo Tours* (phone: 696704); *Gordon Dalton Travel Agency* (phone: 282555); *Agencias Giscome* (phone: 640111); *Turista Internacional* (phone: 274929 or 274969); or *Caribe Travel* (phone: 693011). All are in Panama City.

Uncommon among Indian races, the Kuna can take civilization or leave it alone. A Kuna who has lived and worked on a US army post, with a color TV set in his barracks (as many have), returns to his island lifestyle without any apparent sense of loss. One aspect of this lifestyle, as closely adhered to in the islands as in the canalside cities, is a firm commitment to cash. While the men work on plantations on the mainland or fish, the women make *molas* — hand-stitched in reverse appliqué, and multicolored — which they price in line with big-city inflation. Photos of *mola*-clad Kuna will cost about 25¢ per person photographed — so count your change before they line up six children to pose for your picture.

**COLÓN:** The second city of Panama (pop. 100,000) is at the northern terminus of the canal. This place could have itself declared a monument to Joseph Conrad and Somerset Maugham — it could easily serve as a movie set for any of their novels of men and mores coming ungummed in the tropics. There's nothing much for a tourist to do around Colón except to savor its raunchy disarray, visit the Free Zone, and watch his wallet (be forewarned — muggings occur in Colón even during the daytime). A tour of the city takes about 15 minutes.

The *Panamanian Railrod,* which linked Panama City to Colón, used to take passengers across the isthmus until it was closed in 1990. However, express buses run daily between the two cities, leaving the capital from Calle O in Calidonia and departing Colón at Avenida Amador Guerrero. The fare is $1.75 each way. The city has four good restaurants: in the *Sotelo* hotel (in the center of town); in the *Washington Hyatt* hotel (on the waterfront); the *VIP* (on Front St., right by the railroad crossing); and the *Canal Zone Yacht Club* (beside the failed French canal in adjacent Cristóbal).

**PORTOBELO:** Some 30 miles (48 km) northeast of Colón, Portobelo was one of the great treasure ports of the Spanish Main. Then for 2 centuries or more it became a sort of Brigadoon, awakening only once a year for its *Black Christ Festival* on October 21. The town (whose fair, when the treasure fleet was in, handled the silver and gold of Peru and the products of the wealthiest cities of Europe) in these two sleeping centuries did not even have a road to Colón. The road exists now, although it is not in very good condition — there are a fair number of potholes and areas where there's more dirt than cement. You can ride to see the forts that blasted away at the all-star buccaneers of their era. You can also see the harbor mouth islet near which Drake was buried at sea, after dying aboard his ship in the harbor. There are good beaches and fine wreck scuba diving here. Stop at *Los Cañones* ("The Cannons," on the road to Portobelo from Colón) for fresh seafood and a fantastic view. Farther up the same road and overlooking the bay, the restaurant's owners have opened a new hotel — *El Hostal Los Cañones* (phone: 695655) — with 8 rooms and 3 cabañas.

**ISLA GRANDE:** Off the coast, near Portobelo, this island has a beautiful beach and is excellent for scuba diving. Although there's a small town with a couple of bodegas and a lighthouse, its main draw is the outdoor water sports. Panamanians come to the islands on weekends to escape the heat of the city. To get there, take the unpaved road (frequented by cattle) past Portobelo 10 miles (16 km) to the village of Guaira, where you can hire a boat from one of the locals.

## BEST EN ROUTE

There are a number of especially fine or interesting accommodations at your disposal in Panama, for the most part in the moderate range: $20 to $40 for a double with bath. The going rate for a double with bath which we classify as expensive is $50 to $100; $7 to $17 is inexpensive. Some of these prices are based on the American Plan, which includes three meals a day. Most of the larger hotels accept major credit cards. Except where noted, rooms are modest and low key. All telephone numbers are in the 507 area code unless otherwise indicated.

### VOLCÁN

*Bambito* – A modern hotel, complete with resort facilities that include tennis courts, a pool, and slot machines, as well as such activities as horseback riding, fishing, and hunting. Reservations through *Moonlight, Inc.*, 6 Calle Gerardo Ortega, Panama 4 (phone: 235084 or 714265; fax: 414207). Expensive.

*Dos Ríos* – A mountain rill ripples clear and cool below the bedrooms, past the bar and dining room. Beside it the soil is rich and the grass is soft and the flowers are bright. The 16-room hotel is at the western end of the village, where the road heads for Río Sereno. Both American and European Plans are available (phone: 714271). Expensive.

*California* – No frills, no discomforts, at this 24-room motel. Patronized by independents who rise and rest at eccentric hours, such as hunters and bird watchers. The restaurant and bar are sympathetic to them (phone: 714272). Inexpensive.

### CERRO PUNTA

*Cerro Punta* – About 5 miles (8 km) farther up the mountainside and a few degrees colder than Volcán is this restful haven with 12 rooms. There's also a cabaña that houses a fine restaurant at which strong coffee laced with brandy is the favorite digestive. Jackets and wool sweaters are needed during the winter months. The inn can arrange tours to visit the many flower gardens or for bird watching (phone: 712020). Moderate.

## DAVID

***Fiesta*** – Located right on the Pan-American Highway at the turnoff to David, it has 58 air conditioned rooms, bar, restaurant, swimming pool, and casino (phone: 755454). Moderate.

***Nacional*** – Just off the Pan-American Highway, it has 76 rooms and the best restaurant in town; it's also air conditioned and equipped with a tennis court, pool, bowling alley, and casino. Apartado 37, Panama City (phone: 752221). Moderate.

## BOQUETE

***Panamonte*** – Almost two generations of canalside Americans have sublimated their longing for the soft, quiet hills of home at this gracious, 15-room haven. An old residence among flowers and close to the coffee plantations, its contrast with company housing and sun-scorched locks is therapy. In the bar-lounge is the rediscovery of a household fixture that youngsters from the hot country may never have seen — a fireplace. Both European and American Plans available, depending on time of year (phone: 701327). Moderate.

***Los Fundadores*** – Not a hotel beside a dancing stream so much as a hotel (31 rooms) bestraddling a dancing stream. The brook is as all-pervading here as a better-known waterway is farther down the isthmus (phone: 701298). Inexpensive.

## LOS SANTOS

***La Villa*** – The most picturesque town on the Azuero Peninsula deserves the most pleasant hotel on the peninsula. With 49 rooms, it is air conditioned and has a bar and restaurant (phone: 968201). Moderate.

## RIO MAR

***Río Mar Cabins*** – The 13 cabins are as unadorned as a surfboard. The restaurant, on a bluff with a clear view out to sea, is held by many to offer the best eating along the 50-mile suntan lotion coast. San Carlos (phone: 642272). Moderate.

## CORONADO

***Villas-Golf Club*** – Set on the republic's most ambitious beach development, the eight 2- and 3-bedroom villas are elegant. The club features a bar, restaurant, pool, tennis courts, and a golf course — one of the three best on the isthmus. Apartado 4381, Panama 5 (phone: 233175). Expensive.

## GORGONA

***Jayes*** – The closest approximation to a hotel rather than beach cottages between Farallón and Punta Chame, though a casual, seaside style prevails. Hammocks swing lazily around the pool, and a band entertains. Air conditioning (phone: 237775). Moderate.

## PUNTA CHAME

***Punta Chame*** – A 20-room cabin-style motel, with restaurant and bar on the beach where you can fish, boat, surf, hike, and skin dive. The chef will cook your deep-sea catch to your taste while you take in the terrific view of the mountains across the water. Apartado 10520, Panama 4 (phone: 231747). Moderate.

## EL VALLE

***Club Campestre*** – A tranquil retreat surrounded by trees, flowers, and birds. The 19-room inn has its own golden frogs that are kept in an elaborate cage filled with lush foliage and a fountain. There also is a restaurant and lounge (phone: 936146). Moderate.

***El Greco*** – This lodge-like 22-room property is set back against the valley wall in ample grounds, with a view over the valley and most that goes on therein. Not much does. Visitors here are content to exchange a civil nod with such golden frogs that may chance by their rockers and to contemplate the growth rate of any square trees to be seen from the porch or bar. Huge fireplaces and a color TV set are in an adjacent sitting room (phone: 936149). Moderate.

## WICHUB WALLA ISLAND

***Wichub Walla*** – Not bad for a place in the San Blas Islands. All the rooms in the 2-story building around the pool are comfortable and have electricity; only some have baths. Boat transfer from the Porvenir Airport (phone: 223096). Moderate.

## COLÓN

***Carlton*** – Another old hotel that has been remodeled and modernized. It has 64 rooms, a restaurant, and bar. Calle 10 and Av. Meléndez (phone: 450717). Moderate.

***Washington Hyatt*** – Built by the Isthmian Canal Commission during the early days of canal construction, it has been remodeled several times and now offers 81 rooms (some air conditioned), a tennis court, swimming pool, bar, and one of the best restaurants in town. Located right on the waterfront (phone: 471868). Moderate.

***Sotelo*** – While there's nothing fancy here, the 45-room hotel is comfortable, sits in the heart of town, and the price is right. Casino, restaurant, bar, coffee shop. Av. Amador Guerrero and Herrera (phone: 417702). Inexpensive.

## ISLA GRANDE

***Isla Grande*** – Right on the main beach (it also has a private beach on the south side of the hotel), this property has 9 cabins that sleep two people and 10 bungalows, each housing four. There is a restaurant and bar (phone: 475227). Expensive.

# Paraguay

Paraguay, like its northwestern neighbor, Bolivia, is a landlocked nation. Relatively unknown as a tourist destination, Paraguay shares other borders with Argentina to the south and Brazil to the east. Its 157,047 square miles contain primarily barren plains, subtropical farmland, and thick jungle. Daytime temperatures are in the 90s and 100s F (32 to 39C) from November through March, and in the 70s and 80s F (21 to 28C) the rest of the year, although it can be quite chilly at night. Demographically, it is a young country, with about 70% of its residents under the age of 30! About 800,000 inhabitants out of a national population of 4.2 million live in the capital, Asunción, a port on the Río Paraguay (for a complete report, see *Asunción*, THE CITIES).

When discovered by the Spanish conquistador Juan de Ayolas in 1524, Paraguay was inhabited by the Guaraní Indians, a mostly peaceful people who welcomed the Europeans. During the next 2 centuries, the Jesuits exerted a strong presence in the southern part of the country, where they built a number of missions with the cooperation of the Indian workers and craftsmen. The Indians proved to be magnificent artisans, contributing their own distinctive touches to the plans of the Jesuit brothers. Thus, statues with strong Indian facial features and columns adorned with intricate designs of native plants lend the monuments a fascinating hybrid flair. Paraguay gained independence from Spain in 1811, a liberation that was significantly less bloody than the devastating War of the Triple Alliance against Brazil, Uruguay, and Argentina 50 years later. During the 1930s, Paraguayan forces fought the Bolivians in the Chaco War; they won the conflict and thus avoided occupation of the western territory by the Bolivians. Since independence, Paraguay's history has featured a cast of flamboyant dictators. The last in the line of *caudillos* (leaders) was General Alfredo Stroessner, president from 1954 until 1989, when he was deposed in a bloody coup and exiled. General Andrés Rodríguez, head of the military, is the current president. Whether the country becomes a true democracy depends partly on whether the general keeps his promise to hold elections this year. At press time, congressional representatives had already taken office following democratic elections and work had begun to draft a new constitution, but there was talk of delaying the presidential race until 1994.

One of Paraguay's most distinctive characteristics is the endurance of its Indian language, Guaraní. Although you will have no trouble if you speak Spanish, this is the only Latin American country where nearly everyone outside the capital prefers to use the ancestral tongue. In Asuncíon, both Spanish and Guaraní are spoken. TV and radio programs, however, are principally in Spanish.

Paraguay has three main highways that connect Asunción with the two other large cities, Encarnación and Ciudad del Este (formerly Ciudad Stroessner). Together, these roads comprise what is referred to as "The Central Circuit," which covers about 520 miles (832 km). Another important thoroughfare is the well-paved Trans-Chaco Road, from Asunción to Mariscal Estigarribia, the principal town in the Paraguayan Chaco; it covers about 220 miles (352 km) and extends up to the Bolivian border. The rest of the roads in Paraguay are, at best, partially paved and mostly in bad condition. Therefore, unless you plan to stay close to the main road, it is recommended that you fly or take bus or river transport to the interior. Travel agencies in Asunción, such as *Menno Travel Agency* (551 Azara St.; phone: 21-441210 or 21-493504; fax: 21-446618), can provide trips in vehicles suited to rough terrain. Rental cars are adequate if you stick to well-traveled routes (see the *Golden Triangle,* below).

There are four routes in this chapter: The Golden Triangle, which takes you on a 125-mile (200-km) tour from Asunción through Yaguarón (along the way is one of the oldest and most attractive Franciscan churches built in the 16th century); Chololó, with the natural beauty of its water jumps and landscape; Caacupé, with its modern Catholic basilica and the center of the national religious pilgrimage; San Bernardino, the best-known summer resort in the area, with its famous Lake Ypacaraí; and Itaguá, where *ñandutí,* or spiderweb lace, is made. To tour our second route, the Chaco region (west of the Río Paraguay), either fly or drive from Asunción to Filadelfia, visit the Mennonite colonies, and enjoy a photo safari (organized excursions where groups use cameras — instead of guns — to shoot animals) in the thick jungle, or fish in the Monte Lindo River.

Our third route, the "Central Circuit," runs from Asunción through Villa Florida (a fisherman's paradise famed for its prized golden dorado), located by the sandy shores of the Tebicuary River, to Encarnación, an important city on the Paraguay-Argentina border. The route continues to Ciudad del Este, a duty-free zone for liquor, electronic goods, perfume, tennis shoes, and watches that draws hordes of Brazilian and Argentine shoppers. From there we recommend a visit to Itaipú, the world's largest hydroelectric dam, and the Iguassu Falls, the giant and spectacular cataracts on the Paraguay-Brazil-Argentina border. Itaipú, which became operational in 1991, is proving to be one of the most important revenue sources for the country. Paraguay and Brazil split equally the cost of constructing the dam, but Paraguay only uses about 2% of its share. Sales of the rest (to Brazil right now, although Argentina and Uruguay could be next) provide about a third of the government's revenues. For a more detailed description of this area, see *Argentina* and *Brazil,* DIRECTIONS. The final route goes through cattle country to the Paraguay River port of Concepción and the Brazilian border town of Pedro Juan Caballero, where visitors can stay at a working *estancia* (ranch).

# The Golden Triangle

To travel through eastern Paraguay is to turn the clock back a century or more. The landscape is dotted with neat little villages, many as old as 300 years, each with its own central plaza and large Catholic church. Crude oxcarts and horse-drawn carriages are a common sight, and women wash the family clothes in streams at the side of the road, with jagged rocks as their only clotheslines. One-horsepower sugarcane refineries stand beside simple, thatch-roofed homes.

But even in rural Paraguay times are changing. Tractors are an increasingly common sight, and the introduction of modern farming techniques is boosting the production of cotton, tobacco, soybeans, and sugarcane on the fertile soil of the Paraguay and Paraná river valleys. Just east of Asunción is beautiful Lake Ypacaraí: The area here abounds with pretty waterfalls and is a center of the fine Paraguayan handicrafts, including *ñandutí,* the delicate spiderweb lace.

Isolated for much of its history, Paraguay really didn't make the international tourist scene until about 25 years ago, with the completion of a network of roads that formed a triangular route joining various lakes and other attractions. Hence the area became known as Circuito de Oro, the Golden Circuit or Golden Triangle, as it is more commonly known in English. It's easy to cover this route in 1 day and, fortunately for the tourist, the entire route is a paved, two-lane highway: You can either rent a car in Asunción or take one of the many minibus tours operated by the larger tourist agencies, including the Mennonite-owned *Menno Travel Agency,* 551 Azara St. (phone: 21-441210 or 21-493504; fax: 21-446618).

If you do prefer to go it alone, then obtain a map from the Instituto Geográfico y Militar, available at many *librerías* (bookstores) in Asunción. You might also want to do a little reading; try *The Land of Lace and Legend,* available from *Books,* in the *Centro Comercial Villa Mora* (Villa Mora Shopping Center; 914 Casilla de Correo in Asunción). The book costs about $6.

**En Route from Asunción** – Follow the main highway that starts at Asunción and runs due east to Brazil. About 5 miles (8 km) from the city, Paraguay's second major highway branches off to the southeast, and it is here that the Golden Triangle begins. The first leg goes through rolling hill country; small farms dot the landscape, and you pass several houses with sugarcane refineries in their yards. A single horse provides the power to drive the machine that crushes the cane. About 20 miles (32 km) from Asunción the highway passes through the town of Itá, a center of pottery production. Because most shops sport their wares right on the curb, you won't miss them as you drive through town. There is a large variety of decorative pieces as well as functional items that you can buy here. The good luck hand-painted ceramic hens are popular, but you can also pick up other animal figures, flower pots, water jugs, bowls, and so on. The pottery is low-fired, so be careful, since that means it is fragile.

About 7 miles (11 km) beyond Itá is the ancient colonial town of Yaguarón.

**YAGUARÓN:** Founded in 1539 (2 years after Asunción), this town, set on a river in an orange-growing region, is known mainly for its Franciscan church. You'll see it on the right just beyond the downtown area. Completed in 1720, it took 50 years to build and remains a prime example of Spanish colonial architecture: The large edifice is flanked by covered verandahs, and a bell tower sits in front of it. The intricate carvings on the altar and elsewhere are interesting. The original Indian vegetable dyes used in the colorful decoration remain remarkably vivid. Open from 7 to 11 AM and 2 to 7 PM. Near the church is the *Museo de Doctor Francia* (Museum of Dr. Francia), in the restored home of Dr. José Gaspar Rodríguez de Francia, who ruled Paraguay from its independence in 1811 until his death in 1840. Since the museum's hours are irregular (it's officially open on Tuesday, Thursday, Saturday, and Sunday afternoons, as well as Sunday mornings), inquire at the church for opening times.

**En Route from Yaguarón** – Continue 9 more miles (14 km) through the rolling hills to the town of Paraguarí and turn left, onto the second leg of the triangle — the narrow, winding road that eventually ends at the Asunción-Brazil Highway. From Paraguarí, the road climbs steadily higher into the hills, offering fine views of the countryside. The local folk call these rather modest hills La Cordillera (The Ridge).

Continue on the highway for another 14 miles (22 km) to a sign for Chololó Falls and a restaurant, *Chololó,* on your left. The restaurant is a fine place to stop. Not only does it have a good view of Chololó Falls, but the dining room was constructed over a small stream that tumbles across the rocks and through lush, tropical shrubbery among which the tables are set. If you want to enjoy the fresh water of Chololó Falls, there are bathhouses, complete with showers, for changing your clothes. There is a small fee for use of the facilities.

About 1½ miles (2 km) farther is the turnoff to the right for the Pirareta Falls (Pirareta is Guaraní for "place of fish"). The entrance is marked by an archway and sign for Colonial Pirareta (the Pirareta Farm). From here, it's a long 6 miles (10 km) over a rough road to Pirareta, which is somewhat larger than Chololó. The pools here are large enough for real swimming, but you'll have more fun at Chololó (and there are no overnight facilities in Pirareta).

From Pirareta, the narrow, winding road continues north past the town of Piribebuy, which has a church and the small *Museo Pedro Pablo Caballero,* both located on the central plaza. Now a peaceful village with lovely waterfalls, this was the scene of bloody fighting during the War of the Triple Alliance. Some of the museum's exhibits are dedicated to that unfortunate era; photographs and religious themes make up most of the rest of the collection. From here, it's about 9 miles (14 km) to the junction with the Asunción-Brazil Highway. Turn left at the dead end, and you are now on the third leg of the Golden Triangle. After 6 miles (10 km) on this busy two-lane road you enter Caacupé.

**CAACUPÉ:** The holiest of Paraguay's shrines is the Catholic church at Caacupé, with its Virgen Azul de los Milagros (Blue Virgin of the Miracles). Every December 8 (at the *Feast of the Immaculate Conception*), thousands of the faithful descend on Caacupé from all directions (including Argentina and Brazil), starting out on foot after work on the evening of the 7th and arriving in Caacupé at sunrise, in time for the first mass on the morning of the 8th in this copper-domed church. The less devout, less healthy, or less adventuresome make the trip by bus or car, and the President of Paraguay visits the shrine by helicopter. The religious solemnities are broken by carnival rides, fast-food stalls, and nighttime fireworks.

The church with the Virgen Azul (Blue Virgin) is 1 block above the main plaza, on your left as you drive through town. The small statue of the Virgin stands above the altar. During the December 8 holiday, some devout come to the church in light blue capes in imitation of the Virgin's dress. Others carry blue or white candles up to the altar to pray for favors. Street vendors peddle religious souvenirs, including posters and photos of the statue, at the side of the church. The outdoor market next door sells some locally made pottery. If you want a hearty meal, go to the *Uruguayo* hotel (at Presidente Eligio Ayala and Asunción in the center of town).

If you have time, take the side trip from Caacupé to the village of Tobatí, 10 miles (16 km) over a paved road. Take the main road back to Asunción, and turn right at the sign for Tobatí. This branch of the road takes you even farther into the hinterland. The chief attraction in Tobatí is the *santeros* (saint makers), who carve small wooden statues of saints. Teams of oxen (as many as six) and oxcarts laden with logs are beautiful, but too large to fit in your suitcase. There are also animal and bird statues and a variety of pots and vases, but the saint makers are best known for their holy images, which are unique and small enough to take home with you. The grand master of the saint makers is Zenón Páez Esquivel, a third-generation *santero*. One of his few nonreligious works, a chess set, was given by the Paraguayan government as an official gift to Spain's king and queen in 1979. In other villagers' homes you can purchase carved wooden masks. You also can visit the old church on the plaza or the Shrine of the Virgin off the road at the base of a cliff that is on your left on the road from Caacupé to Tobatí. Look closely at the names of shops, ice cream parlors, and even storehouses in Tobatí. Influenced by the *santeros*, the owners have given them saints' names.

**En Route from Caacupé** – As you leave Caacupé, you slowly climb a long hill with large eucalyptus trees on either side. This is the Escuela Nacional de Agronomia (National School of Agronomy), a well-known Paraguayan center for agricultural research and training. As you cross the crest of the hill and start down, you will catch your first glimpse of Lake Ypacaraí. At the bottom of the hill turn off the highway onto the paved road for about 1 mile (1.6 km) to reach the picturesque former German colony of San Bernardino on the lake's shore.

**SAN BERNARDINO:** Perhaps the loveliest city in Paraguay, this resort town is the weekend haunt of Asunción residents looking for fun in the sun and an escape from the sometimes intolerable heat of the capital. Beautiful weekend villas of the wealthy dot the road into town, but most of the action is along Lake Yparacaí. Here crowds, especially during the summer months of December through February, sunbathe, swim, windsail, rent pedal boats, picnic, and water-ski. The lake is somewhat polluted now so you may opt to swim in the pools of *Condovac Aparthotel Casino San Bernardino* hotel or at the outdoor pool of the charming old *Hotel del Lago*.

The town is full of ice cream shops and restaurants, especially open-air lakeside eateries that specialize in fish and grilled meat (the fish served comes from the lake — so it might be safer to order other dishes). In the evenings, there is plenty of casino action at the *San Bernardino* hotel on the roadway heading into the city. The tourism office is located on the corner of Calles Yegros and Vaché (no phone).

From San Bernardino you can hire a launch from local boat owners for a trip to the pottery center of Areguá, on the north side of the lake. Established a year after Asunción, this resort town has several genuine colonial houses — with extended tile roofs supported by columns — like those once found in the capital. It also is known for its candies.

Alternatively, Areguá (and San Bernardino) can be reached on a slow, but easy, trip on an authentic steam engine train. The train leaves Asunción's station at 12:15 PM daily except Sunday and chugs along past squatters' homes and grazing cows, while tropical hard woods are tossed into the fire that stokes the historic engine. (The return trip can be made on any of the buses that frequently leave from Areguá's main intersection).

**En Route from San Bernardino** – If you're traveling by car and want to continue the circuit, retrace your steps to the main highway, turn right, and head toward Asunción, passing the lakeside town of Ypacaraí. Continue until the town of Itauguá, just 18 miles (29 km) east of Asunción.

**ITAUGUÁ:** This is the place to purchase the beautiful, finely woven *ñandutí*, as it is known in the Guaraní Indian vernacular. Legend has it that the original *ñandutí* lace was spun by a spider to rescue a servant girl who had accidentally ruined her mistress's mantilla.

The art of making *ñandutí* was introduced from Spain and Portugal by the nuns in the 1700s, who then taught it to the Indian women. Lace weaving is now an important livelihood for the Indians. The delicate lacework is embroidered in small circular and floral patterns on large looms and comes in colors such as violet, yellow, and red, although many foreigners consider the traditional white and beige lace as the most attractive. It should not be confused with *aó po'i* embroidery, designs embroidered on clothing and pieces of cloth, although you will also find *aó po'i* here. This tradition of embroidered clothing dates back to the early 1800s when President José Gaspar Rodríguez de Francia banned such imports. Local residents combined traditional sewing techniques and fashions to produce *aó po'i*. Prices start at $30 for small, simple fabrics and climb to several hundred dollars for larger and more intricate *ñandutí* works.

You'll see the large (10-foot-long) *ñandutí* lace tablecloths draped over wooden racks at the roadside. They're quite inviting, but before you purchase one, be advised that they are difficult to iron. They say in Asunción that the Paraguayan Embassy in London used to return the lace tablecloths to Paraguay by ship to be washed, pressed, and stretched on the racks in Itauguá after each dinner party. Fortunately, there is a great variety of smaller items from which to choose; prices do vary, so shop around. The less pretentious looking shops often have the same quality goods at lower prices. However, there is no uniformity of quality in the handicrafts, so check the workmanship of each placemat, napkin, hammock, or whatever before you buy. There is some room for bargaining. If you're interested, stop by the church and market for a look before heading on. The church has a small museum with a collection of religious images.

**En Route from Itauguá** – It is only about 25 minutes back to downtown Asunción. As you approach the capital the highway becomes increasingly crowded, and there is little of special interest along the way.

## BEST EN ROUTE

On all routes in Paraguay, hotels are few and far between. Most are small, comfortable, and very reasonable. Expect to pay about $110 for a double room in the very expensive *Aparthotel Condovac,* $65 to $90 for a double in the expensive category, $35 to $60 for a double listed as moderate, and under $35 for a double room that is rated as inexpensive. Most travelers prefer to spend their nights back in Asunción, but for those who plan to overnight on the road, it's wise to make advance reservations in any one of the hotels listed below. If there are no phone numbers, consult your travel agent or the tourist office in Asunción.

### CAACUPÉ

***Uruguayo*** – Small and clean, this hostelry is fairly basic, but it's the best in town. It has a restaurant famous for its hearty meals. In the center of town at Pdte. Eligio Ayala and Asunción (phone: 511-222). Inexpensive.

### LAKE YPACARAÍ

***Aparthotel Condovac*** – This new, luxury all-suites hotel is just 1 block from the beach. Each of the 101 suites has a kitchenette, balcony with a barbecue, satellite TV, and mini-bar. There is a restaurant, snack bar, disco, swimming pool, gym, tennis courts, and a sauna, as well as 24-hour room service, and laundry service. Pedal boats, kayaks, and sailboards for use on the lake can be rented. Av. Eugenio Garay at Decoud (phone: 512-2761 through 512-2765; in the US, 800-44-UTELL; fax: 512-2766). Very expensive.

***Casino San Bernardino*** – Surrounded by gardens, this deluxe lakeside 104-room property has beautiful views, a swimming pool, tennis courts, sauna, restaurant, casino, piano bar, and discotheque. By far the best hotel on this circuit. Lakeside (phone: 512-391 through 397; in Asunción, 21-95354). Expensive.

***Del Lago*** – A charming, colonial-style hotel with a rustic atmosphere that will remind you of a bygone era, in much the same way as does the *Gran Hotel del Paraguay* in Asunción. It has 26 rooms, a pool, restaurant, snack bar, and shops.

The staff can arrange fishing and hunting trips. Lakeside on Calle General E.A. Garary (phone: 512-2201). Moderate.

# The Chaco

The area west of the Río Paraguay is a harsh, desolate plain called the Chaco, encompassing all of the western section of the country and extending into Bolivia and Argentina. It's hot — about 100F (37C) — dry and windy. The first 150 miles (241 km) are grasslands, and beyond that are scrubby forests. The Chaco is best known for the bloody Chaco War between Paraguay (the victor) and Bolivia in the early 1930s. The closer to Bolivia, the more inhospitable the Chaco becomes. However, its isolation has served as a protective oasis for increasingly rare animal species such as the puma, jaguar, and tapir.

There has been some optimism that the oil industry could provide jobs and boost economic development in this region. In late 1990, Phillips Petroleum signed an oil exploitation agreement with the Paraguayan government. At press time, construction of an oil pipeline was planned if sufficient quantities of crude oil are found in the Chaco.

Sparsely populated, the principal settlement in the Chaco is the area around the towns of Filadelfia and Loma Plata, about 300 miles (480 km) northwest of Asunción via the area's lone major roadway, the Trans-Chaco Highway. Most of the people are Mennonites, who came from Canada, Russia, Germany, and other countries searching for freedom to practice their religion, which includes, among other things, exclusion from military service. Today, there are about 10,000 Mennonites in the Chaco; their principal languages are German and Platt Deutsch (a cross between Dutch and German), rather than Spanish. Despite the harsh living conditions, they manage to battle the constant dust storms and have developed a thriving economy based mostly upon cooperatives that farm or produce soybeans, peanuts, dairy products, and cattle.

The Chaco is an interesting place to visit — for about 2 days. There is only one way to get to Filadelfia and that is by road, and there is only one place to go to make proper arrangements — the *Menno Travel Agency* in Asunción (551 Azara St.; the mailing address is 713 Casilla, Asunción; phone: 21-441210 or 21-493504; fax: 21-446618). The agency will book your round-trip bus tickets, as well as your stay in Filadelfia at the *Florida* (see *Best en Route),* the best of the very few hotels in the area. Bear in mind that tourists are rare here, although the presence of the highway has opened the Chaco to more outsiders.

It is possible, however, to drive the Trans-Chaco Highway to Filadelfia yourself. The road is entirely paved to Filadelfia. In good weather the trip can be made in 6 to 7 hours. (For car rental information, see "Sources and Resources" in *Asunción,* THE CITIES.) In Filadelfia, the *Museo de Unger* (Unger Museum), open Tuesdays and Fridays, traces the history of the Mennonite colonization of this region. Treat yourself to delicious homemade ice cream, made from local milk, at one of Filadelfia's many ice cream parlors.

**FILADELFIA:** About 25 miles (40 km) north of the Trans-Chaco Highway, here you will want to visit the small, flourishing agribusinesses, including the cheese-making and peanut oil factories. If you can, hire someone to drive you out to see the farms in the surrounding area. These Mennonite farming communities are made up of neat, small homes with wooden shutters, flowers, and orchards. The most important crops, besides soybeans and peanuts, are castor beans, cotton, and jojoba. Beef and dairy cattle also are raised, and the meat and dairy products are shipped out to Asunción.

While driving around, you also can visit the other Mennonite settlement, Loma Plata, south toward the highway. Nearby is a Swiss-run inn with a restaurant. Inquire at Loma Plata for directions, or alternatively, head southeast 50 miles (80 km) to Boquerón where there is a small hotel — *Los Pioneros* — and more Mennonite farms outside town. Back in Filadelfia you can sit in on a Mennonite service if you wish. You'll enjoy the singing even if you don't understand what is being said.

## BEST EN ROUTE

There are very few places to stay in the Chaco. In the two moderate-priced hotels we list, expect to pay up to $25 for a double room.

### FILADELFIA

*Florida* – Ask for a room in the newer wing of the best hotel in town — they all have air conditioning and private baths (in the older part, baths are shared). The restaurant has decent fare, including good German cake. Filadelfia (phone: 91-258; in Asunción, through *Menno Travel,* 21-441210 or 21-493504; fax: 21-446618).

### BOQUERÓN

*Los Pioneros* – Small, comfortable, and immaculate, this hostelry offers air conditioned guestrooms with private baths, TV sets, and mini-bars. There also is a good restaurant and the staff can arrange excursions and photo safaris in the Chaco. Km 415 of the Trans-Chaco Hwy. (phone: 94-820; in Asunción, 21-605740).

# The Jesuit Mission Trail/The Central Circuit

In 1588 the Spanish (actually, the Jesuit order of priests) began to filter into Paraguay. They found the area already occupied by the Guaraní Indians, a nomadic and pacific people who did not resist the Spanish invaders. Instead, the Guaraní formed an alliance with the Spanish, intermarried, and even went so far as to defend the Spanish forts against marauding Indians from nearby Brazil. However, the Jesuits were eventually expelled and many Guaraní were slaughtered by the Portuguese or captured as slaves. Today, there are some 27,000 Guaraní left as well as 23,000 other Indians, who, combined, represent 2% of the entire Paraguayan population. Guaraní is still a prominent language here, as Quechua is in the Andes.

The Jesuits set up numerous *reducciones,* or missions; they taught the Guaraní how to farm and speak Spanish and converted them to Catholicism. In return, the Indians built great stone churches in the forests. For a time, the missions served as havens, protecting the Guaraní from the slave traders.

They are impressive complexes which were once artistic workshops — there are Catholic statues with Indian faces, elaborate 3-tiered altars and baroque art. The construction of these churches, however, was halted in the mid-18th century, when the Jesuits began to criticize the divine right of the Spanish throne. Angered at their "rebellion," King Charles III of Spain ordered them out of Paraguay in 1767. After the Jesuits left, the *reducciones* were taken over by the Dominicans and four other orders. But in fewer than 15 years, 23 of the 30 original missions disappeared. They were mismanaged by the new overseers, abandoned by the Indians, who feared living there without the sanctity of the priests, and burned and sacked by *banderaintes* — Brazilian gold scavengers and slave traders who pillaged the area.

Today, these fine churches and missions — in southern Paraguay, southwestern Brazil, and northeastern Argentina — lie in ruins, but bit by bit are being restored by national and international organizations (such as the United Nations). The most extensive restoration, and the mission most visited today, is San Ignácio Miní, in the town of San Ignácio, across the Río Paraná in the Mesopotamia section of Argentina. (See "Mesopotamia" in *Argentina*, DIRECTIONS.) Three of the missions in Paraguay, Trinidad, Jesús, and San Cosme y Damián, are accessible from Asunción via Encarnación; the trip takes 2 nights (or 3 days), and tours are available from the major tourist agencies in Asunción. If you need any help, contact the tourism office in Asunción (468 Palma; phone: 21-441530; fax: 21-491230).

The following route goes from Asunción to the Paraguayan ruins and back over the Asunción-Encarnación Highway. For the first 38 miles (61 km) of this trip between Asunción and Paraguarí, you take the first leg of the Golden Triangle. Instead of turning left at Paraguarí, however, continue straight ahead through the town of Carapegua until you reach Villa Florida, on the banks of the Río Tebicuary, almost 100 miles (160 km) southeast of Asunción.

**VILLA FLORIDA:** If fishing is your thing, then 1 or 2 days here should be a joy. Paraguay's rivers are teeming with fish, but the rivers are for the most part inaccessible and facilities are not well developed, with the exception of Villa Florida. The prize catch is the dorado, which often weighs 15 to 20 pounds, puts up quite a fight, and makes excellent eating. Other fish commonly caught in the Tebicuary are the *surubí* (similar to catfish), often larger than the prized dorado, and the infamous piranha fish, which is often used in soups. For those who prefer swimming to fishing in the Río Tebicuary, head to Punta Paraíso — there is a more than mile-long beach with white sand and a shallow riverbed (it's especially appealing for children who want to go wading). There are several places to stay (see *Best en Route*), and you can get a good meal at the restaurant adjoining the Shell station on the left-hand side of the street as you drive through Villa Florida.

**En Route from Villa Florida** – Just 11 miles (18 km) beyond is the small village of San Miguel, one place in Paraguay where handwoven woolen articles are still found. In the shops you'll find roughly finished blankets, ponchos, and sweaters that are very inexpensive.

From San Miguel, you enter the Jesuit mission area. The towns bear the names given to them by the Jesuits: San Juan Bautista, San Ignácio (not to be confused with the better-known San Ignácio, Argentina), and Santa Rosa. In the first week of September, San Juan Bautista celebrates the *Fiesta de la Tradición Misionera*, a commemoration of mission life that somewhat curiously focuses on rodeo events and contests of skills. The next 75 miles (120 km) are an important cattle-raising area. Toward the end of this stretch the highway passes through rolling hills, where you will catch your first glimpses of the Río Paraná and Encarnación.

Fishing enthusiasts may want to make a detour to Ayolas after passing through the Jesuit mission area (turn off at Km 262, just after San Patricio). Situated on the Paraná, it is noted for *surubí* and dorado. *Surubí* is a sports fish that can reach 10 ft. in length and weighs up to 300 lbs. The dorado here regularly exceed 35 lbs.; the current world all-line class catch is a 51-lb. dorado taken in this region. Another sports fish, the *pacu,* weighs up to 35 lbs.

Most travelers looking for good fishing head to *Scotty's Lodge* in Ayolas. The lodge also can arrange 40-minute charter flights to and from Asunción (see *Best en Route*).

**ENCARNACIÓN:** This is Paraguay's third-largest city, the heart of the mission country, and the birthplace of the former president, General Stroessner. Although its population is only about 70,000, it is growing steadily due to the construction of the Yacyreta hydroelectric complex, a short way downstream. While not as high as the Itaipú Dam, Yacyreta is about 60 miles wide, to confine the mighty Paraná. There is nothing of particular interest to the tourist here, but those wishing to spend the night will find modern and comfortable accommodations in the *Novotel.* Alternatively, those willing to push on another 12 miles (19 km) toward the Paraguayan Jesuit ruins can stay at the *Tirol,* a resort hotel built of stone (see *Best en Route* for both hotels).

Or you can cross the Paraná on a bridge at Encarnación to Posadas, Argentina.

**En Route from Encarnación:** To reach the Paraguayan Jesuit ruins and the *Tirol* hotel, take the Encarnación Highway. The 150-mile (240 km) route was inaugurated in 1985 and affords some very worthwhile sightseeing.

At the 12-mile (19-km) mark, take the right-hand turnoff for the *Tirol* and continue for 6 miles (10 km), where you will come to the village of Trinidad and the first major Jesuit mission in the area. The mission is the best preserved in Paraguay: Most of the original walls are still standing, and some of the wooden statuary has been restored. Completed in 1745, the church contains many examples of the excellent stone carvings found in Jesuit churches throughout Paraguay. When the mssion was at its peak, 4,000 people lived here. Restoration of Trinidad began in 1982 and visitors can watch the work still in progress. The church at this mission was flanked by the priest's house and workshop on one side and, on the other, the hospital, a house for widows and orphans, and a cemetery. Indian homes bordered the big plaza in front of the church that contains the original pulpit — the remnants of which were discovered in 1,500 pieces and put back together.

From Trinidad, go 7 miles (11 km) down a dirt road off the left-hand turnoff of the highway to the tiny village and ruins of Jesús.

**JESÚS:** The largest of all the Jesuit missions, this church was not yet completed when the Jesuit order was expelled from Paraguay in 1767. The tropical vegetation and tree roots still cover much of the unrestored ruins. It is believed some 3,000 Indians worked on building the mission. Sunday is the busiest day here for tourists.

From Jesús, it is possible to make the 250-mile (400 km) return trip to Asunción or continue north on Route 7 to Ciudad del Este (known as Ciudad Presidente Stroessner until its namesake was deposed in 1989) and the gateway to Brazil and Iguassu Falls.

Alternatively, return to Encarnación and head west 36 miles (58 km) on Route 1 to the San Cosme y Damián mission. The buildings have been restored and mass is celebrated on Sundays in the ruins of the church.

**CIUDAD DEL ESTE –** Colorful, chaotic, and commercial, this city is little more than a huge shopping center for Brazilians and Argentines who cross the border here in search of duty-free (and contraband) liquor, electronic equipment, and perfume. Even the city's small casino plays second fiddle to the shopping, although North American and European travelers generally find neither price nor selection too appealing.

What most attracts US tourists is the Puente de Amistad (Friendship Bridge), which leads directly to Iguassu Falls. Worth a stop en route is Itaipú Dam, the world's largest hydroelectric complex when it went on line in 1991 after 18 years of being under construction. It boasts a 60-story building, a 5-mile long pair of dams, and 18 turbine generators — surpassing the combined power of Egypt's Aswan Dam and the Grand Coulee Dam in the US in power production.

At Itaipú, 12 miles (19 km) north of the city, there are morning and afternoon audiovisual shows about the dam; local travel agents can arrange interesting visits to the site, including hydrofoil rides on the reservoir-lake.

## BEST EN ROUTE

While a few hotels along the Jesuit trail cost more than $30 for a double room, most are less. Hotels are small, but have comfortable rooms with private bath. Prices for double rooms in the expensive category are $50 and up; double rooms listed as moderate are between $30 and $50; inexpensive ones are under $30.

### VILLA FLORIDA

*Las Mercedes* – This property's air conditioned bungalows are perched right along the river and guests are free to take a dip in the water — or fish — when the urge hits. Rustic, but comfortable, these are the best accommodations in town; there's a restaurant, too. At Punta Paraíso Beach (phone: 83-220). Expensive.

*El Dorado* – Like *Las Mercedes,* this property offers riverside bungalows and a restaurant, but has fewer amenities. (At press time, guestrooms had only fans, but there were plans to add air conditioners.) Popular with families. Right along the river (phone: 83-217). Inexpensive.

*Villa Florida* – Near the river, this small hotel has comfortable rooms with private baths and an outdoor swimming pool. Km 161 on Mariscál Solano López Ruta No. 1 (phone: 83-207). Inexpensive.

### AYOLAS

*Scotty's Lodge* – Situated along an 8-mile-wide river, this is a haven for fishing enthusiasts. The 16 double rooms and 4 suites at the lodge (also known as the *Ayolas*) are air conditioned in summer and heated in winter. Other amenities include a pool, restaurant, snack bar, tennis courts, boats, fishing equipment rental, and fishing guides. Av. Costanera (phone: 72-2272; in Asunción at 153 Maldonado, 21-602653; in the US, 305-491-8622; fax: 72-2274; in Asunción, 21-662947; in the US, 305-491-1963). Expensive.

### ENCARNACIÓN

*Novotel* – A first class hotel with 110 rooms and suites, a pool, tennis courts, restaurant, and bar. On Rte. 1 at Km 361 (phone: 71-4131; fax: 71-4224). Expensive.

*Tirol* – This resort-type property has stone chalets and a motel-like structure with 3 spring-fed swimming pools. Six cabins hold up to eight people each, and a large dining room, sitting room, gameroom, bar, and verandah overlook the valley. Rooms have air conditioning, baths, and TV sets. Charming, but the place has seen better days. Before Encarnación, on the highway from Trinidad, Capitán Miranda, Rte. 6, Km 20. (phone: 71-2388). Expensive.

*Viena* – A good, budget alternative to the classier *Novotel.* 568 Caballero (phone: 71-3486). Inexpensive.

### CIUDAD DEL ESTE

*Casa Blanca* – This neo-colonial building overlooking the Río Paraná is a great spot for travelers looking for peaceful surroundings and personal attention. All 11 suites have air conditioning, TV sets, telephones, and mini-bars. There is no restaurant, but amenities include an outdoor swimming pool, guest access to a nearby golf course, and a hot tub. Excursions to Iguassu Falls can be arranged. Outside town next to the golf course (phone: 61-60317 and 61-63632). Expensive.

**Gran Hotel Acaray** – Although this hostelry outside town appeals to those visiting Iguassu Falls, there is plenty to do on the property itself. The well-appointed rooms have balconies overlooking the manicured grounds and the Río Paraná. There is an international restaurant, nightclub, casino, and a large outdoor swimming pool. 11 de Setiembre at Río Paraná (phone: 61-61471 to 61-61475; in Asunción through *Inter-Express,* 21-490111 through 21-490115; fax: 61-61471; in Asunción, 21-449156). Expensive.

**Residence de la Tour** – This comfortable hotel has television sets, telephones, and mini-bars in all 15 guestrooms. The Swiss management makes sure that the grounds are well tended and the restaurant's food and service are first-rate. An outdoor swimming pool, bar, and laundry service round out the amenities. Next to the *Paraná Country Club* (phone: 61-60316; fax: 61-62193). Expensive.

# Cattle Country

Like Argentina and Uruguay, Paraguay is a major beef producer, with thousands of head of cattle roaming the vast countryside east of the Paraguay River and north of the main highway to Iguassu Falls. A trip to this region takes visitors on the roller coaster of red clay roads that wind through cattle country from Asunción to Concepción — once one of Paraguay's most important river ports, or, alternatively, to Pedro Juan Caballero on the Brazilian border. The latter thrives on commerce in contraband and duty-free goods, thanks to the relaxed frontier that allows shoppers to enter either country merely by crossing the street. (The Brazilian half of these twin towns is Ponta Porá.)

To travel through cattle country by car, you'll need a four-wheel-drive vehicle and the nerve to maneuver over hilly and often rutted dirt roads for long, desolate stretches. The less adventurous might opt to fly from Asunción to Concepción or Pedro Juan Caballero via the small propeller planes of *TAM,* the military domestic carrier (which also carries civilian passengers), and travel by motorcoach between these two northeastern towns.

Along the paths of cattle country are flowering fruit trees, exotic birds, gauchos on horseback, and farmers and their families piled into horse-drawn wagons carrying their fresh produce to the nearest town — which is likely none too near. Schoolchildren walk along the dusty red roads, sometimes accompanied by their mothers, who may be balancing the day's shopping in baskets atop their heads. Fields of cotton and corn come into view, but most of all there are miles of pastureland with hundreds of cows. Be prepared for both heat and insects — take along a hat, long-sleeve cotton shirt, and bug repellent.

One of the best ways to see the cattle country up close is to spend a few days at a working *estancia.* There currently are about three or four cattle ranches that open their doors to guests who are invited to go on horseback (or horse-drawn wagon) to watch the gauchos at their chores — branding cattle, shearing sheep, roping strays, and all the other activities that keep the *estancia* economy flourishing. Although the frontier is quiet nowadays and cattle rustling is rare, don't be surprised to discover these rough-riding Paraguayan cowboys toting pistols — it's a tradition in these parts.

Evenings are spent under the stars at the job the gauchos describe as their favorite — the *asado,* where sides of beef and pork are roasted over red hot coals in an open-pit barbecue. The doe-faced, humped-back zebu cattle, introduced from India, are ideally suited to the region's often intense heat, and Paraguayans claim their steaks — produced without the growth hormones used in other countries — are the tastiest around. You'll have to be the judge.

On an *estancia,* visitors can see the fascinating ritual of the *tereré,* the cold herbal beverage that the gauchos sip through tin straws when they stop on the heated range. A single cow's horn used as a glass is passed from gaucho to gaucho, with each one adding cold water from a Thermos to the thick, tea-like concoction.

*Raya Uno,* one of these *estancias,* offers packages combining a ranch stay (minimum 4 nights) with a 2-day tour of Asunción and optional excursions to Iguassu Falls, Itaipú Dam, and Río de Janeiro. Roundtrip transportation from Asunción is included. For information and reservations, contact Jean Paul and Marie Laura Thole, *Consultour,* Box 1324, Asunción (phone: 21-604272; Telex: 5307 PY).

**En Route from Asunción** – Head east on Route 2 from Asunción on the main highway for Iguassu Falls. After 86 miles (138 km), turn north onto Route 8 at the junction with Colonel Oviedo. The paved highway continues to Tacuará before becoming a dirt road for the long and lonely stretch to the village of Yby Yaú. Be sure to gas up and have something to drink; on this portion of the route, there are no rest stops. At Yby Yaú, make the choice between turning west on Route 5 to Concepción or east to Pedro Juan Caballero and Brazil. We recommend heading first to Concepción, then backtracking to Yby Yaú and continuing to Pedro Juan Caballero.

**CONCEPCIÓN:** Before dirt roads cut through this region, people and goods moved along the rivers and Concepción was one of Paraguay's most important ports. Although it now is little more than a small market town, with pigs and chickens roaming the dusty streets, it retains traces of its colonial past. Faded pastel-colored mansions, with their floor-to-ceiling windows covered in fancy grillwork and delightful patios with stone fountains and blossoming foliage, bear witness to the Republican era.

A stop in Concepción is not complete without a glimpse of the market where the *carretas* (horse-drawn wagons) are parked, providing shade to the rows of vendors hawking squash, watermelon, bananas, and chickens. Beef is sold here — by butchers who slice cuts with hand saws. There is no refrigeration and the aroma of the market is not for the fainthearted.

No longer a busy stop on the Paraguayan waterways, Concepción nonetheless still serves as a port. It's possible to walk down to the once-elegant terminal building to watch the cargo boats unload everything from store merchandise to wooden chairs onto the ubiquitous horse-drawn carts. And if Concepción's incessant heat leaves you parched, retire to the peaceful restaurant at the *Francés* hotel (902 Pte. Franco at C.A. López) to quench your thirst.

**En Route from Concepción** – Leaving Concepción, travel east back on Route 5 to Yby Yaú. There it becomes paved for the last 64 miles (103 km) to Pedro Juan Caballero. You'll enjoy easy driving to this active little town that serves as a gateway to Brazil, as well as the northeast's air link to Asunción (and Ciudad del Este).

This section of the route from Yby Yaú to the border is perhaps one of the most scenic in Paraguay. The rolling plains are peppered with pine trees, palms, cacti, and flowering shrubs as you reach this country's lone mountain range, the Cordillera Amambay. These separate and flat-topped peaks are not impressive by mountain standards (especially if you've seen the Andes), but they're certainly curious looking as they spring from the otherwise level terrain. Many schools will come into view — one of the more positive legacies of the Stroessner era.

About midway between Yby Yaú and Pedro Juan Caballero is the turnoff for Cerro Corá, where one of Paraguay's most infamous dictators, Francisco Solano López, died in the prolonged War of the Triple Alliance against Brazil, Argentina, and Uruguay — a mid-19th century conflict that decimated the majority of Paraguay's male population (even today, women outnumber men). A white obelisk marks the spot where a bullet ended the dictator's life. His Irish mistress, the notorious Eliza Lynch, had been with him nearly until the end, but managed to escape unhurt. She fled the country and later died penniless in Europe.

**PEDRO JUAN CABALLERO** – This frontier town has a Brazilian twin, Ponta Porá, that can be reached merely by crossing the street. There are no border formalities, but officials on either side may stop you for identification, so be prepared with the proper papers (US and Canadian citizens are required to have a visa to enter Brazil). Both Pedro Juan Caballero and Ponta Porá thrive on the sale of duty-free and contraband goods, with shop after shop selling electronics, perfume, watches, liquor, and clothing. North American visitors won't find the selection too tempting, however, compared to the variety and prices in US stores. Gambling is another mainstay of the local economy. Try the casinos at the *Casino Amambay* hotel (Av. Dr. José Gaspar Rodríguez de Francia and José Berges) or at *La Siesta* hotel (Calle Alberdi at Av. Dr. José Gaspar Rodríguez de Francia).

The town has a small airport with a dirt landing strip, open-air waiting room, and white picket fence, while Ponta Porá's airport is a bit larger and flashier. *TAM* is the name of both the Paraguay and Brazilian airlines, but the companies are unrelated — just another curiosity of this remote frontier region. Paraguay's *TAM* flies to Asunción and Ciudad del Este; Brazil's *TAM* to São Paulo.

## BEST EN ROUTE

Expect to pay $45 or more for a double in hotels listed as expensive and $25 to $45 for those listed as moderate.

### CONCEPCIÓN

*Francés* – This hotel is quiet, comfortable, and the best in town. All the rooms are air conditioned and offer private baths and phones. Other amenities include a good restaurant and laundry service. 902 Pte. Franco at C.A. López (phone: 31-2383). Moderate.

### PEDRO JUAN CABALLERO

*Casino Amambay* – The best lodgings in town, this modern property boasts a casino, pool, and restaurant. Av. Dr. José Gaspar Rodríguez de Francia and José Berges (phone: 36-2573 and 36-2983; fax: 36-2963). Expensive.

*La Siesta* – Breakfast comes with the room at this breezy, modern hotel with a casino on a main street. Make sure to ask for an air conditioned room as it can get quite warm here. Calle Alberdi at the corner of Av. Dr. José Gasper Rodríguez de Francia (phone: 36-3021 and 36-3022). Expensive.

# Peru

*The US State Department has issued several advisories on travel throughout Peru in response to terrorist activities by the Sendero Luminoso (Shining Path) and the Tupac Amaru Revolutionary Movement groups. Travel by public bus in some areas, particularly, is not recommended. Travelers are advised to check the latest status with the US State Department (202-647-5225), the consular section of the US Embassy (phone: 14-443621), or the South American Explorers Club (phone: 14-314480) when they arrive in Peru. Note also that at press time, martial law had been declared. Also, due to the widespread incidences of cholera, travelers are advised to drink only carbonated bottled water, and eat only cooked, hot food and peeled fruit. For further information call the Centers for Disease Control's International Travelers' Hotline (phone: 404-332-4559).*

Few countries in the Americas can match Peru in diversity of historic and natural attractions. Covering 496,223 square miles, the country is bordered by the Pacific Ocean to the west, Chile to the south, Bolivia and Brazil to the east, and Colombia and Ecuador to the north. Geographically, Peru is divided into three distinct regions: a narrow coastal strip of desert that extends the entire length of the country; the Andean sierra, where nearly half the Peruvian population of more than 20 million people live; and the jungle, which accounts for nearly two-thirds of the land.

Three climatic zones correspond to the topographical regions. Along the coast, temperatures climb into the 80s F (around 28C) between October and May, then drop to around 50F (10C) between June and September. In the Andes, winter, which runs from June through September, is the dry season, with temperatures frequently falling into the 20s F (−9C) at night and daytime highs in the 60s F (17C). During the rainy season, from November through April, temperatures are somewhat warmer. The jungle, which starts along the eastern slopes of the Andes, has temperatures ranging from the 80s to the 100s F (27 to 40C) throughout the year. It rains constantly, but most heavily between November and April.

Although it's in the arid coastal region, Lima, the capital (pop. 7 million), is enshrouded in fog (called the *garúa*) roughly from June to October. (For a complete report, see *Lima,* THE CITIES.) Peru's other major cities are Trujillo, the most important northern city; Arequipa, in the southern highlands; Iquitos, the leading Amazon port; Cuzco, the former Inca stronghold; and Puno, on the banks of Lake Titicaca.

While the Inca civilization with its headquarters in Peru is far and away the best known in South America, it was the last of an illustrious line of pre-Columbian cultures. Among others, the Lambayeque, Moche, Chavín, Chimú, and Nazca Indians predated the Inca by many centuries. However, when Spanish conquistadores Francisco Pizarro and Diego de Almagro arrived in Peru in 1532, the Inca empire extended from Ecuador in the north to Chile in the south. The conquistadores killed the last Inca, Atahualpa, and went on to found Lima in 1535.

Peru was one of the most important centers of the Spanish colonial realm in the New World until the early 19th century, when the struggle for independence began. Helped to a large extent by Argentine General José de San Martín and the Venezuelan Simón Bolívar, Peru gained its liberation from Spain in 1826 after years of fighting. In 1879, Peru allied with Bolivia against Chile to fight the War of the Pacific, which ended in 1883 with Peru's loss of the coastal town of Arica (now in northern Chile) and a strip of the mineral-rich Pacific coast. In 1945, another border war resulted in the Rio de Janeiro Treaty which delineated the political boundaries between Peru and Ecuador (its terms are still being debated today). The hostility between Peru and her northern neighbor has never completely abated, and in late 1991, minor confrontations surfaced. As a result, both countries have asked the United Nations to review the Peru-Ecuador border situation. In the meantime, both countries have armaments along their mutual frontier. However, tempers have become calmer on the Chilean border.

In the 20th century, military intervention has frequently occurred in national political affairs. The most recent military junta seized power in 1968, toppling the regime of President Fernando Belaúnde. In 1975, a shift in military factions resulted in the overthrow of General Juan Velasco by General Francisco Morales Bermúdez. The Morales government failed to assert effective financial and economic control, and Peru was officially on the verge of default in 1978, when the International Monetary Fund instituted austerity programs designed to stabilize the country in the face of the emergency. Peru experienced a return to democracy with the reelection of Fernando Belaúnde to the presidency in 1980, and the ensuing 1985 election of the young and charismatic Alan García. Increasing public dismay over rising prices, devalued local currency, and mounting terrorism, however, made the 1990 presidential election campaign a heated one, and pitted political conservative and novelist Mario Vargas Llosa against university rector Alberto Fujimori, neither of whom had had any political experience. Riding on a wave of left-wing support, Fujimori emerged as Peru's new chief executive. The new president surprised his supporters when he immediately instituted a series of unexpected price hikes and austerity measures, and the term "Fuji shock" became part of the Peruvian vocabulary. Relying on a Peruvian team of Oxford-trained economists, the Fujimori government resumed payments on the nation's foreign debt, instituted a free market economy, and lifted tariffs and import restrictions. Although these efforts won the new president US support and the promise of aid, it dealt a drastic blow to Peru's poor who, at one point, saw gasoline prices rise to $2.50 a gallon while the minimum wage remained at only $63 a month. And in April 1992, Fujimori further angered Peruvians — and stunned the US — when he declared martial law.

Although Peru is one of the most fascinating countries on the continent, it is also one of the most frustrating for travelers in a hurry. Because of road conditions and isolated cases of highway robberies, the US Embassy in Lima has discouraged car rentals for travel outside the capital. Trains are still an alternative, especially between Arequipa, Cuzco, and Puno, but they are slow, uncomfortable, crowded, and tickets are in short supply. *Ormeño* and *Tepsa* bus lines have countrywide service, and local airlines *AeroPerú, Faucett, Americana,* and *Andrea* have service all over the country. Be forewarned that train tickets should be purchased at least a day ahead of departure, and all plane tickets must be reconfirmed 48 hours before leaving. Travelers might consider booking trips with tour agencies that run their own buses.

In this chapter you'll find seven routes. The Outskirts of Lima describes several trips into the surrounding countryside, to the ruins of Pachacámac and Incahuasi, to the beach resorts of Ancón and Santa Rosa, to the mountain resort towns of Chaclacayo and Chosica, and on to the mountain market town of Huancayo. Lima to Cajamarca takes you north from the capital along the Pan-American Highway, with a side tour to Huaráz and Mount Huascarán (Peru's highest Andean peak), to the colonial city of Trujillo and Chan-Chan, onto the exciting archaeological dig at Sipán, and ends up in the charming mountain town of Cajamarca. Lima to Nazca describes a trip south of the capital to the curious area where huge line drawings appear in the Nazca Desert, passing the famous Paracas Peninsula, where mummies and more mysterious drawings were found — and explains how to arrange for a flight over the Nazca pampa. Arequipa to Puno takes you from this "White City" in the southern part of the country to the shores of Lake Titicaca, the world's highest navigable waterway. Puno to Cuzco and the Inca Ruins describes a voyage to the former center of the Inca empire, its surounding ruins, and a visit to the lost city of Machu Picchu and the peaceful Urubamba Valley. And the Amazon and Madre de Dios are trips through the jungle regions where oil and gold are mined, monkeys chatter in the trees, and some of the continent's most impressive natural reserves are found.

# The Outskirts of Lima

When Francisco Pizarro, the Spanish conqueror of Indian Peru, established the City of the Kings — now called Lima — beside the Río Rímac in 1535, he bypassed the existing large native population center of nearby Pachacámac. Apparently Pizarro wanted a capital that would be completely Spanish in its physical design and social character from the beginning: hence imperious, arrogant, viceregal, Spanish Lima.

Lima has already been discussed in a chapter all its own (see *Lima,* THE CITIES). A circuit around the outskirts of the capital is your next destination, and the trip takes you in just about every interesting direction. To reach Pachacámac, travel south on the Pan-American Highway into the Rímac and Lurín valleys, which once housed the Cuisamancu kingdom, a pre-Columbian civilization known to us only through remaining artifacts. Continue down the Pacific coast to the cotton-growing Cañete Valley and Herbay Bajo Hacienda (the Palace of the Inca King) and other Inca ruins, all about 68 miles (109 km) from Lima. If you continue north along the highway, you reach the

Peruvian beaches of Santa Rosa and Ancón. An alternate northern route leads to Canta, a small mountain town. Cantamarca, a bit outside of the town, is a mysterious archaeological site that was at one time a deserted fortress, town, or temple. The 2,000-foot climb to the ruins is strictly for the hearty. Near Ancón, San Pedro is reputedly the oldest inhabited site in the country.

The three major highways in Peru that lead south, north, and into the interior form a great T-shaped figure. The central part or the Central Highway (otherwise known as Route 2) connects Lima with the lands in the eastern Andean slopes. Leaving Lima and heading east, you begin to climb steadily, flanked by the peaks of the Andes. This part of the route will take you to Chosica, a mountain resort very popular with the *limeños* 80 years ago, and (many hours later) to Huancayo, a central business village where farmers and manufacturers in the area come every Sunday to sell their wares. The highways in all directions are asphalted, but, alas, are only two lanes wide and are not always well maintained. Those travelers who wish to take a break from driving or riding on the bus might consider the train trip from Lima (or Chosica) to Huancayo. Although it is a long trip, it cuts through some amazing scenery on the highest rail line in the world. Note that at press time, tourist officials in Peru warned against visiting Huancayo because of terrorist activities in the area.

For short trips, you can stay in Lima (see *Lima,* THE CITIES). This doesn't mean accommodations outside the capital are uniformly terrible, however. Many hotels are owned by the state and provide good service and clean rooms; they are inexpensive and also more comfortable than the basic accommodations you'll find on other routes in Peru.

Your first route from Lima goes south, to the mysterious Pachacámac. The easiest way to reach the highway is via either Avenida Javier Prado or the Avenida Primavera to the Pan-American Highway. Alternatively, *VISTA* offers daily guided bus tours to the ruins. For reservations, phone 14-276624 or contact a local travel agent. It's a good idea to take a guided tour, as the structures at the ruins are not identified and guidebooks (both in English and Spanish) on sale at the site are cursory at best. Pachacámac is 19 miles (30 km) outside the capital. Since the highway parallels the Pacific Ocean, you can get some good views of the fishermen going out to net the elusive anchovies that end up in fishmeal plants in Callao. Just before you reach the archaeological ruins, you'll pass Villa El Salvador. Once a shantytown, the squatters here organized, set up a local government, and transformed the poor settlement into a model community with sidewalks, streetlights, wide avenues, trees, and parks. The United Nations uses Villa El Salvador as an example of how grass-roots efforts in developing countries can be successful. The weather along the way will be pleasant, about 73F (23C) from December to March and about 55F (13C) the rest of the year.

**PACHACÁMAC:** What remains of the temple was probably built by the faithful under the orders of the head of the Cuisamancu kingdom around the middle of the 1300s, although archaeological data show this was an important pilgrimage center several hundred years before the beginnings of Christianity — and it was unquestionably the most important religious sanctuary on the coast. Hernando Pizarro, Francisco's brother and the first Spaniard to view the massive shrine, called it a mosque (having known the Moorish mosques in southern Spain); and indeed it was, in the sense that it was "Mecca" for the peoples of the various kingdoms before and after their conquest by the Inca. They came from as far north as Ecuador and from as far south as Chile. Truces were arranged among the warring kingdoms so that the pilgrims could fulfill their religious duties to the great god and his oracle. Peruvian linguists suggest that the name of this site is derived from two words: *pacha,* meaning "world" or "earth," and *camac,* meaning "maker" or "creator." Indeed, historians describe Pachacámac as a supreme god, "the creator of the universe." Earthquakes were an expression of his anger. So great and fearsome was this god that no one was allowed to look at him — and only high priests could consult him and interpret his proclamations to the people. The sacred chambers of the complex were protected by "doors" that were actually intricate weavings decorated with gold, seashells imported from present-day Ecuador, and semi-precious stones. At the entrance to Pachacámac, there is a small museum displaying the statues and delicately woven cloths found at the ruins from when archaeological excavations began in 1963. Perhaps most interesting is the carved wooden oracle on display in the museum. This column — male on one side and female on the other — was consulted by priests acting as intermediaries for individuals seeking divine favors.

The ruins, which are open daily except Mondays from 9 AM to 5 PM, encompass the Temple of Pachacámac, the Inca Temple of the Sun, the House of the Virgins of the Sun (also an Inca addition), the remains of the surrounding city, and other secondary temples. Most of the restoration and reconstruction at the site has been done at the Casa de las Mamaconas (House of the Virgins) where anywhere from 80 to 200 chosen women — or *mamaconas* — dedicated their lives to the sun god. A single door allows entrance to the labyrinth of rooms and, in Inca times, eunuchs guarded the complex. Hidden under the drifting sands are the remains of a large, ceremonial-like square. The first temple is a pyramid constructed of small adobe bricks. Climbing it, you reach the holy chamber where sacrifices of llamas in honor of the god were made.

The quadrangular Temple of the Sun is particularly attractive because of its massive stone foundations, upon which were erected the five great adobe brick platforms at varying levels. At the top of this terraced pyramid, there is a striking view of the Pacific and of the lush surrounding Lurín River valley.

Hernando Pizarro, and later his brother, came seeking the temples' legendary treasures. Both went away disappointed, for if there were great golden stores, they had been well hidden by the temple priests. Atahualpa, the conquered Inca, had sent Hernando to Pachacámac to collect the gold necessary for the Inca's presumed ransom. Some historians say that the Inca knew there were no riches there, but Atahualpa was trying to buy time to engineer his release. Later, the Spanish priests ordered wholesale destruction of the site, and its contents, as part of their campaign to rid the New World of pagan religions.

When the Pizarros first approached Pachacámac, the city had a population of 30,000. The year the fifth viceroy arrived in Lima, 1569, the city's population had been reduced to 100. Thus the "barbarian" Inca empire was tamed by the "civilized" Europeans.

**En Route from Pachacámac** – Continuing south on the Pan-American, you come upon some of the more pleasant and less crowded beaches near Lima: Punta Hermosa, Punta Negra, and San Bartolo, all about 28½ miles (46 km) from Lima; another 20 miles (32 km) bring you to the beaches of Santa María del Mar and Pucusana. If the weather is good, bring along a picnic lunch and enjoy a swim and some restful hours. Pucusana is a good spot for snorkeling, fishing, and diving. Stay clear of the small, very modest restaurants that serve local seafood dishes.

If you really want to take a good day's outing, continue south another 68 miles (109 km) to the Cañete Valley, on a seacoast bluff on what was known as the

Herbay Bajo Hacienda, or the Palace of the Inca King, as it was called in the 1800s. From what little remains of the adobe walls and foundations, you cannot visualize what kind of structure once stood here, but there is an early testament from the chronicler Pedro Cieza de León (and in 1863, with the eyewitness report of E. G. Squier, a North American archaeologist) that this was the site of the "most beautiful and ornate citadel to be found in the whole kingdom of Peru, set upon great square blocks of stone, and with very fine gates, entranceways, and large patios." From the top of this royal edifice, a stone stairway descends to the sea. By the time Squier saw it, the adobe walls, the 15-foot-high doorways, and some of the roof beams remained; the stone upper structure had long since disappeared.

Fifteen miles (24 km) inland, following the road along the Río Cañete (a popular river for rafting), you reach Incahuasi, once called New Cuzco by its Inca founder. This is a great complex of buildings, including the Houses of the Chosen Women, ceremonial sites and residences, a large storage area, and a square where apparently animal sacrifices took place. Incahuasi (House of the Inca) is the largest area of Inca constructions on the entire coast; the site covers some 5 square miles.

The best restaurants in Cañete are in the Plaza de Armas. They're modest and clean, offering good food at low prices. Just stay away from uncooked food such as lettuce, tomatoes, and unpeelable fruit. The food normally is prepared in pots of cooking oil, which makes it a bit greasy for North American stomachs, but it is savory. Try *Oasis* or *Le Paris* on Plaza de Armas; no reservations are necessary at either.

From here, you have to return to Lima to continue north. For a day trip from Lima in this direction you have the choice of two routes: Either turn off onto the asphalt road that leads to Santa Rosa de Quives and Canta, or continue straight ahead to the Santa Rosa beach and Ancón. If you have to choose, take the trip to Canta, since the Río Chillón valley is wonderfully green after the monotony of the coastal desert. The road is good, though winding (one should drive with care and sound the horn before arriving at the curves). Forty-six miles (74 km) later, you'll arrive at Santa Rosa de Quives, a bucolic spot with a small, graciously built church in honor of Saint Rose of Lima, who spent part of her short life here more than 300 years ago.

Though you may not have noticed, you have been climbing steadily since the turnoff from the north Pan-American Highway; when you reach Canta, some 24 miles (38 km) ahead, you will be 12,600 feet above sea level. Because the climb has been gradual and slow, you should not experience even slight *soroche* (altitude sickness).

Canta offers the first taste of small-town Andean life. On weekdays it is rather deserted, for the majority of people are busy with their farming duties outside town. There is nothing exceptionally inviting about Canta, but a bit farther is Cantamarca, the reason for coming here.

**CANTAMARCA:** This is one of those mysterious archaeological sites that abound in Peru, a deserted town or fortress or temple, abandoned but intact except for the ravages of the passing centuries. When you arrive, you will have to climb about 1,000 feet to reach the fortress-town (this climb is recommended only for the physically fit). If you don't want to climb, be sure to bring binoculars so you can get some impression of the town at the top. Once you reach the peak, you discover a series of cylindrical stone structures, the doors of which are set so low that you have to crouch to get inside. The interior roof beams are stone and spoke-like and go from the outside wall to a central pillar that incorporates a small fireplace with its flue. The roofs are sod placed on top of the beams: The grass growing on top of the sod must have served as camouflage. Before leaving this area, which archaeologists believe to be at least 1,000 years old, take a good look into the surrounding valleys to understand why the unknown builders chose this site for their town. It could have been conquered only by a prolonged siege that would starve out its inhabitants. The scenery is indeed overwhelming — a good introduction to the majestic beauty of the Andes. The climb up takes about 2 hours; the walk-at-a-run down will take less than half an hour.

**En Route from Cantamarca** – If you want to find the place where Lima's beautiful people water-frolic with great style and much display, it's at Santa Rosa Beach; beyond Km 35 turn left for Ancón.

**ANCÓN:** As you approach the resort, you will be surprised to see skyscrapers of residential apartments and many seaside villas sprouting up out of the dry desert sands, with the crude houses of the fishermen off to one side, although a dramatic rise in the number of slums has prompted wealthy *limeños* to seek summer escapes farther down the coast. This harbor resort hosts special *Holy Week* festivities and processions. The bay that has tamed the battering Pacific waves is flanked by a grand esplanade, along which the aristocracy of Lima — formerly known as the oligarchy because of their possession of both political and economic power — promenade in the cool sea breezes of the summer evenings. Arrangements for water skiing can be made at the *Yacht Club de Ancón* on the waterfront (phone: 14-883071).

**En Route from Ancón** – When you return to the Pan-American, be sure to stop briefly to visit the ruins of a small town on the site of the mountain called San Pedro. This town is considered by some archaeologists to be the earliest inhabited area on the South American continent. Many remains of the various Peruvian cultures that predate the Christian era have been discovered.

From here, return again to Lima to start the next excursion: the Central Highway. Your first stop will be Puruchuco.

**PURUCHUCO:** Head straight out the Central Highway to Km 8 to visit the reconstructed country mansion and farm center of an Indian chief. According to the many relics that have been found, the original house dates from the 900s. Built of adobe, the customary construction material used on the coast, the house is a geometrical triumph of straight lines and right angles and trapezoidal niches in the walls. The numerous corridors and alleys, with horseshoe-shaped doors and windows, add to the enchantment of the restored farm center. The adjacent museum displays artifacts, costumes, and musical instruments excavated in the area; they represent all the generations who have lived here — pre-Inca, Inca, conqueror, and colonial. Open daily, except Mondays, from 9 AM to 5 PM; admission charge.

**En Route from Puruchuco** – Continuing east on the Central Highway for 2 miles (3 km), you come to a road on the left. This will take you to the ruins of an enigmatic site like the one at Cantamarca. When discovered by the Inca, the huge complex of walls, squares, underground storage areas, and houses was empty. Unfortunately, because of financial limitations the site has not been scientifically investigated.

Back on the Central Highway and continuing toward the Andes to the east, you go less than 1½ miles (2 km) to find another group of ruins on the right-hand turnoff. This group is called Pariachicuiyo, built in a style similar to that of Puruchuco. The complex consists of two large residences and a group of isolated houses. The large residence has been restored, so you can appreciate the large rectangular patio, with its two successive platforms united by a short ramp. From the platforms you enter a group of rooms by a series of passageways.

Chaclacayo, a small town of about 30,000 people, is a favorite winter weekend spot of *limeños,* but there is more of interest in the traditional resort in Chosica, Chaclacayo's neighbor.

**CHOSICA:** City of the Sun and the Gateway to the Andes, this city of Victorian houses was Lima's winter resort at the turn of the century. Access to Chosica was easy then because it was only an hour away by train. However, as more indigenous people settled in and around Chosica, its desirability as an exclusive winter resort lessened drastically, and the old families built new houses in Chaclacayo. If you are pressed for time and can visit only Chosica, you might consider making the trip on one of the daily trains that runs from downtown Lima.

Chosica, though somewhat faded, remains charming. Its very large plaza is especially handsome because of the many palm trees that give it both shade and impressiveness. Because it is 656 feet higher than Chaclacayo, its air is clearer and winter skies sunnier. It is worthwhile visiting the public market to get an idea of the role the mountain markets play in daily life.

If you're tired of the sun at Chosica, push on up the Central Highway for 24 miles (38 km) east to Matucana solely for the sheer joy and excitement of knowing a little bit more of the fantastic variety of cultivated plants, wild flowers and trees, and chameleon-colored rocks of the Andes. The small city of Matucana is an enchanting introduction to the simplicity of life and the physical vastness of the Andes mountains and valleys. The climate is dry and brisk. When the sun shines in the Andes, it is normally hot from 10 AM to 2 PM. But as soon as you pass from sun to shadow, after 2 or 3 in the afternoon you will feel the chill.

**En Route from Matucana** – From Matucana the Central Highway, or Route 2, winds southeast to become Route 7 to Huancayo (pop. 360,000) — the major marketing center for the central Peruvian highlands. Some 192 miles (307 km) southeast of Lima, this city, at 10,750 feet above sea level, has many chilly afternoons, cold nights, and tempestuous rains. If you'd rather skip the car ride (and it's a hairy one), then backtrack to Lima and take the train from the station (207 Ancash; phone: 14-276620). Trains leave Lima daily, except Sundays, at 7:40 AM, and, having made the 12-hour trip, return on the same day; the voyage back is a couple of hours shorter since the route to Huancayo is mostly uphill. This narrow-gauge rail line — an engineering marvel — zigzags through the Andes as it goes from Lima, nearly at sea level, to its apex at Ticlio, a silent, imposing spot at an altitude of nearly 16,000 feet. Ticlio is not a depot but, if you haven't been affected by altitude sickness, you'll know you've arrived when you see a Peruvian flag atop a desolate mountain peak. If you do have *soroche* — usually characterized by a headache and flu-like symptoms — you can ask the medical personnel on the train for oxygen. (You'll see them rushing up and down the aisles with bags of it.) We recommend that you eat lightly (food is served on the train) and travel only when well-rested; also some visitors find that reading during this trip aggravates the symptoms.

Even those who have no difficulty coping with the lack of oxygen will find their breath taken away by the scenery. The train passes through valleys, over mountains where llamas graze, and through tiny mountain villages where the train — designed by an eccentric North American named Henry Meiggs — is the main conduit for outside contact for their inhabitants. Past the halfway point, the rail passes Oroya, Peru's mining center. Rather than heading straight on to Huancayo, you might stop and wander around in Jauja.

**JAUJA:** The Spanish wanted to make this lovely little village the capital of Peru but, bowing to pressure from soldiers who feared Indian uprisings and insisted on an easy escape route by sea, officials relented and declared Lima the capital. Still, Jauja, which was founded prior to today's capital city, bears some of the faded trappings of the short-lived Spanish presence here.

Its cathedral, on the Plaza de Armas, is impressive, with 14 side altars. Strolling around the plaza, stop and sample some of the mouth-watering breads sold by the women on the square; or try an *emoliente,* a thick, herbal drink containing alfalfa (ask for the boiling hot *"emoliente caliente"*).

Jauja was once the site of Peru's principal tuberculosis sanitarium, which now serves as a hospital. Tuberculosis sufferers, aided by the fresh, dry air and the mountain sunshine, frequently found that the disease went into remission when visiting here; this town was the place in which Peruvian author Ciro Alegría wrote his novel *Los Perros Hambrientos* (The Hungry Dogs), while seeking treatment for his own respiratory problems.

From Jauja, take a *colectivo* (taxi) to the peaceful Franciscan monastery in Ocopa, to the Laguna de Paca (where legend has it that 11,000 gold-laden llamas drowned while carrying Atahualpa's ransom to the Spanish), to the little town of Ingenio, famous for its trout farms, or to San Jerónimo, where fine silver filigree is tooled. (*Note:* Most of these trips require a bus change in the nearby town of Concepción.) There is a small government-run *Turistas* hotel on the banks of the Laguna de Paca, and boats can be hired there for trout fishing (phone: Jauja 232741; in Lima, 14-721928).

**OCOPA:** The smell of eucalyptus trees and a calming silence greets visitors to this village where, in 1725, Franciscan missionaries founded a training center for priests destined to be sent to the jungle to convert the Indians to Catholicism. Several of these monks documented paths through unknown regions, and explored areas previously unseen by white men.

The monastery has some impressive architecture, religious icons, and paintings, but without a doubt its library is its prize. With leatherbound volumes dating back to 1490, this library is one of the finest in South America, and the cool, dry air in the mountain village acts as a natural preservative for its 25,000 books. (Needless to say, there is a very strict no-smoking policy in and around the monastery.) The complex also contains an intriguing rain forest museum filled with stuffed animals, clothing, butterflies, and Indian artifacts collected by the missionaries. Open 9 AM to noon and 3 to 6 PM daily, except Tuesdays.

**HUANCAYO:** In recent years, this market town has grown into an active city with all the problems of a large urban area — plus a high level of terrorist activity, although it is still home to one of the finest artisans' markets in the country. Every Sunday, on Calle Huancavelica, top-quality workmanship will be found on such things as carved gourds, alpaca blankets and sweaters, clay figurines, textiles, and silver jewelry. After the market closes in the late afternoon, there is frequently music and dancing at the *Municipal Coliseum*.

Although it is the market that draws thousands of visitors every weekend, Huancayo bears its share of historical significance as well. In 1854, a decree made it the first community in Peru to outlaw slavery. It was also here in 1882 that three national heroes were killed by invading Chilean soldiers during an important battle of the Pacific War.

Don't leave Huancayo without trying its most famous dish, *papa a la huancaína*, a filling fare of potatoes covered in a spicy cheese sauce. For the daring, the city is also known for a variety of plates featuring *cuy*, better known as guinea pig.

Note: Because of reports of terrorist activities in the city at press time, visitors were discouraged from going there. Check with the consular section of the US Embassy in Lima or the *South American Explorers Club*.

As Huancayo has brought commerce to this poor, mountain region, it has also brought crime. Tourists should take care, especially in the evenings on Calle Real and outside the *Turistas* and *Presidente* hotels. Calle Tambo — a popular spot for thieves — should be avoided entirely; robberies also are not uncommon inside the *Andino* and the *Cine Real* movie theaters downtown. However, the Plaza de Armas is safe both day and night. The Policía de Turismo (Tourist Police; 162 Av. Ferrocarril; phone: 64-234521) are a good source for answering questions on safety issues.

## BEST EN ROUTE

Most hotels you'll come across on this route are small, with basic accommodations (room, bed, maybe a private bath, and meals). A very expensive hotel on this route will run about $50 to $75 a night for a double room; an expensive one about $30 to $50 a night, a moderate one about $20 to $25, and one listed as inexpensive under $20 a night. It's a good idea to make reservations before you go.

## SANTA ROSA DE QUIVES

**Turistas** – Comfortable rooms and a dining room are provided at this government-owned hotel. Centrally located on the highway into town at Km 64 of the Carretera Central (phone: 14-721928 in Lima; 800-275-3123 in the US). Expensive.

## CHACLACAYO

**El Pueblo Inn** – This impressive property was built to resemble a typical colonial village — it has antique furniture, carved doors, and ornate wrought-iron grillwork. A bakery, bookstore, chapel, an 18-hole golf course, horseback riding, 2 pools, bowling, billiards, Turkish baths, a sauna, 3 restaurants, and a tearoom are all on the grounds. At Km 11 of the Carretera Central (phone: 14-350777; in Lima, 14-466427; fax: 14-355354; in Lima, 14-466396). Very expensive.

**Los Cóndores Tambo Inn** – Cabin-type accommodations, with dining, swimming, and horseback riding. 900 Garcilaso de la Vega, Los Cóndores (phone: 14-910786; in Lima, 14-463913). Expensive.

## CHOSICA

**Fidel** – This 12-room hostelry provides private baths, a dining room, and a swimming pool in its garden. 200 Jr. Las Flores (phone: 14-910106). Inexpensive.

## LAGUNA DE PACA

**Turistas** – On the banks of the Paca lagoon, a small getaway spot for those who want sunny skies, mountain air, and peace. Legend has it that this lagoon is where 11,000 llamas were drowned while carrying a gold ransom for the release of the Inca Atahualpa; the Indians sent the pack animals and their load to a watery grave when they discovered the Spanish had already executed the Inca chief. Boats are available at the hotel for trout fishing or outings on the lake. (phone: Jauja 232741; in Lima, 14-721928; in the US, 800-275-3123). Moderate.

## OCOPA

**Monasterio de Ocopa** – This monastery opened its doors to overnight guests and is a peaceful setting for a night's stay. There are no private baths, but there is hot water. Check in advance for room availability (phone: Ocopa 1002; ask the operator to connect you with the monastery). Inexpensive.

## HUANCAYO

**Presidente** – No restaurant, but clean, reliable, and the best in town. 1138 Calle Real (phone: 64-231736). Expensive to moderate.

**Turistas** – Colonial decor, clean rooms, and meals are provided in this lovely 72-room, state-owned hotel. 729 Ancash (phone: 64-231072; in Lima, 14-721928; in the US, 800-275-3123). Expensive to moderate.

**Kiya** – Rooms with baths, restaurant for lunch and dinner; clean and neat, but noisy. 107 Calle Giraldez (phone: 64-231431). Moderate.

# Lima to Cajamarca

A voyage to Peru brings the traveler into contact with the mysteries of human origins on the South American continent: There are almost as many theories about those beginnings as there are books about early Peruvian civilizations. Although we know a great deal about the Inca Empire, there is precious little exact knowledge of the pre-Inca Andean cultures and of the coastal kingdoms other than what their buildings (mostly ruins) and their tombs (now largely plundered) have revealed to archaeologists. The use of carbon 14 in arriving at dates has been significant, but because the Peruvian civilizations didn't leave written documents, scholars have had to construct their cultural dimensions from ceramics, textiles, jewelry, food remains, metallurgy, building styles, and materials. Many of these artifacts, including mummies, are on display in museums in Lima, Cuzco, Ica, and Lambayeque.

The Peruvian coast, from Nazca in the south (see *Lima to Nazca*) through the valleys clustered around modern Lima (see *The Outskirts of Lima*) to Piura close to the northern frontier of Peru, is of singular interest to travelers fascinated with the roots of mankind in the Americas. Heading north from Lima to Trujillo offers the opportunity to learn and appreciate the majesty and the mystery of the ancient Peruvian coastal kingdoms; in Trujillo itself, the visitor also is offered an opportunity to see the sharp contrast between the Indian civilizations of Peru and the Spanish colonization that replaced them. Meanwhile, the southern coast is the region of creole Peru, an area with a distinctly black flavor because of the great number of slaves brought here to work the sugar and cotton plantations centuries ago. Within the first few years following Pizarro's arrival in 1532, the majority of the coastal Indians perished — victims of European diseases, firearms, and swords.

The trip north from Lima to Trujillo covers a distance of 341 miles (546 km) along the asphalt Pan-American Highway. If traveling by car, you can stop and savor the pre-Columbian and post-Conquest towns and cities at your own pace. There is bus service, but you will only get glimpses of the fragments of early Peruvian culture. *Tepsa* (129 Paseo de la República; phone: 14-321233) and *Ormeño* (177 Carlos Zavala; phone: 14-275679) offer reasonably comfortable service. Reservations are necessary to guarantee your seat. If you prefer to travel with a guide, contact a local tour operator who also can provide transportation. Reputable operators are listed in the *Perú Guide*, which is available for free at all major hotels and tourist information centers. In Lima, *APOTUR*, the organization of local tour operators, also can provide information on reliable operators (114 Libertad, office 28, Miraflores; phone: 14-460422). If you have little time, take the 60-minute flight to Trujillo instead. Once you arrive, you at least can tour the nearby adobe ruins of Chan-Chan. *Faucett Airlines* (865 Av. Wilson, Lima; phone: 14-336364) and *AeroPerú* (Plaza San Martín, Lima; phone: 14-317626) offer daily flights. *Americana* (345 Av. Larco, 5th Floor, Miraflores; phone: 14-471919) and *Andrea Airlines* (1200 Av. Angamos Oeste, Miraflores; phone: 14-223210) also have several flights a week to Trujillo. Book ahead, reconfirm your flight 48 hours before departure, and get to the airport early — especially on Friday evenings and Monday mornings.

Accommodations en route are comfortable and modern but not all have private baths. If you need any assistance, contact the national tourist office at 1066 Calle Belén, Lima (phone: 14-323559).

Proceed north along the Pan-American; before reaching the turnoff for

Ancón (see *The Outskirts of Lima*) you arrive at a bypass called Variante Pasamayo, 10½-mile (17-km) long; at its end are the Baños de Boza, recommended for their curative sulfurous waters. Crossing the Río Chancay, you find yourself in one of the usually narrow but lush valleys where the coastal cultures began and flourished. Because the major portion of the Peruvian coast is desert, these small valley oases were essential to the survival of the settlers. Therefore, the inhabitants devoted great time and effort to developing irrigation canals to bring precious water from the mountains in order to increase the amount of arable land. Some say that before the Spanish arrived there was more coastal land under cultivation than there is today because the Spaniards let the irrigation systems deteriorate. The beginnings of the Chancay culture, which is closely related to that of the Lurín and Rímac valleys, date back to 300 BC. There are some handsome examples of Chancay textiles in the *Museo Amano* in Lima (160 Calle Retiro, Miraflores; phone: 14-412909).

Chancay, a city of 20,000 farmers and fishermen, is about 51 miles (82 km) north of Lima: A number of factories are devoted to processing fishmeal, one of Peru's biggest exports. Near the main square, you encounter the well-known *Castillo de Chancay,* a colonial building that is now a restaurant serving shellfish (mainly shrimp). This is a good place for an early lunch. Two other restaurants, *Astoria* and *Marco* (both at Km 82), also feature local seafood.

Continuing north, you go through the village of Las Salinas de Huacho, filled with salt deposits.

**HUACHO:** Ninety-one miles (146 km) north of Lima, this fishing center of 37,000 inhabitants is a picturesque old sea town, surrounded by peaceful countryside, which offers a good spot to stop and rest. The restaurant in the *Centenario* hotel (836 Av. 28 de Julio; phone: 34-3012 or 34-2728) and the *La Libertad* restaurant (600 Av. 28 de Julio; phone: 34-2946) serve particularly good river shrimp. Try the *chupe de camarones* (thick, freshwater shrimp chowder).

**En Route from Huacho** – Three miles (5 km) north you'll pass the small village of Huaura, known to Peruvians as the capital of *la guinda,* a delicious if oversweet liqueur made from the cherry-like guinda fruit, which grows abundantly in this area. The liberation forces of General José de San Martín landed in this village on July 28, 1821, and it was from the famous Balcón de Huaura (Huaura Balcony) that San Martín first proclaimed Peru's independence from Spain. The house where this balcony is found is open to visitors daily.

As you travel north, you will be struck by the aridity of the surrounding desert area between the valleys. Often the wind will have formed sand drifts across the highway or heaped the sand into dunes. The soil of this desert is very rich; it just lacks water. Soon you'll reach Pativilca; a few miles north is the great adobe fortress of Paramonga — once the southern frontier of the Chimú kingdom.

**PARAMONGA:** Built of adobe and forming a series of ascending terraces, pyramid-style, the Paramonga fortress-temple is one of the best-preserved ancient buildings on the coast. A silent witness to the majesty and power of the kingdom of Chimú, it has beautifully decorated exterior walls, ceremonial terraces, subterranean passages, immense foundations, and a number of small rooms at the top where the walls bear some faint hints of their once brightly painted birds and animals. From the fortress-temple, its priests and soldiers had a commanding view of both the land and sea approaches.

The Inca found it exceedingly difficult to break the resistance of the defenders of Paramonga in their first try at conquering the Chimú territories; but around 1470, the fortress was breached by the Inca armies coming from the north, and the kingdom of Chimú was reduced to a province of the Inca Empire. On the hills around Paramonga are other buildings, probably houses and storage areas and granaries.

**En Route from Paramonga** – Leaving the small valley, follow the Pan-American Highway across one of the most desolate sections of the northern desert coast, 49 miles (78 km) of dunes and arid wasteland.

**CASMA:** A small city of 22,000 inhabitants; this crossroads handles commerce to and from the north and the south with Huaráz, 91 miles (146 km) — a 4-hour trip — to the east in the Callejón de Huaylas. Because of its hot, dry climate and fertile farmland, Casma is a cotton- and vegetable-producing center. Much of the historical significance of this area has been lost due to nearly constant looting in recent centuries. Casma residents still tell of the "pirate" Edward Davis, commander of an English flagship that sacked the town in 1683. Four miles (6 km) east, on the highway to Huaráz, are the formidable ruins of Sechín. Little archaeological work has been done here but preliminary radiocarbon dating pegs the ruins at between 3,400 and 3,700 years old. The colossal stepped pyramid — more than 10 stories high — is the largest building pertaining to Andean Indians ever found. This may have been a temple that influenced the design and decoration of the famous temple at Chavín de Huantar, which was an important pilgrimage site around 1,200 years ago.

What you find at Sechín now is a temple consisting of two great terraces, the smaller one imposed upon the lower and larger terrace. The upper terrace is striking for the catlike figures painted there, but the lower terrace is truly impressive for the stone carvings representing priests and warriors. Sechín is being excavated now, and its recently opened museum is well worth a visit.

In the Casma Valley, visit other ceremonial centers equally important in that early period: Moqeke and Pallka as well as the Canquillo Fortress and Monte Grande, a sanctuary that occupies about 7½ acres. Excavations are being led by Thomas and Shelia Pozorski, a husband-and-wife archaeological team from Pan American University in Texas. (Before beginning your tour of the Casma Valley, inquire in Casma itself about Canquillo Fortress and Monte Grande, since they are not usually visited by people other than archaeologists and, therefore, are not noted on maps.) All the temples are built in the pyramid style, with slight variations.

**En Route from Casma** – Take the well-paved Carretera 106 (Highway 106) toward Callejón de Huaylas and the city of Huaráz.

**HUARÁZ:** Callejón de Huaylas, an area rich in history, is the cradle of the amazing Chavín Indian civilization. It is home to Mount Huascarán — Peru's highest Andean peak — and a series of deep blue mountain lakes. The region is a favorite for mountaineers, trekkers, whitewater experts, hang gliders, and the most daring skiers. From May to October, the weather is temperate (the perfect time to scale the peaks) — the skies brilliant blue and sunny, the air crisp and clear. The largest city in the Callejón de Huaylas is Huaráz. It is believed that it was founded by the Huaráz Indians on the spot where Simón Bolívar organized and resupplied his troops before the important battles of Ayacucho and Junín. Nearly 300 years earlier, the Spanish conquistadores had come to this mountain valley after hearing of rumors silver mines. (The Spanish priests subsequently destroyed much of the Indian areas of worship at Chavín de Huantar in their quest to rid the valley of pagan religions.)

Less than 1½ miles (2 km) outside Huaráz, the "Mirador de Rataqueña" — a lookout point — offers a panoramic view of the city. In town, stop by the Templo de la Soledad, a church with a statue of Christ that the locals believe looks alive. The *Museo Regional de Huaráz* (Huaráz Regional Museum) in the Casa de Cultura (Culture House) on the main plaza has a collection of ancient ceramics and monoliths. Once a picturesque mountain town with narrow streets and adobe houses, Huaráz was nearly leveled by a 1970 earthquake and was rebuilt as a modern city with broad avenues.

The best place to eat in Huaráz is the restaurant at the *Turistas de Monterrey* hotel (see *Best en Route*). *Packchakas' Pub* (290 Centenario) and *Ticino Pizzería* (651 Av. Luzuriaga) are less formal but good; the latter is known for its house wines, tasty salads, pizza, and lasagna. *Ticino* receives tough competition from *Mama Mía* (808 Av. Luzuriaga), where the Italian-born cook says the dry mountain air gives his pizza dough (baked in a brick oven) a special texture.

Some of the most intriguing spots — including the Chavín de Huantar ruins 60 miles (96 km) away — are found in the valleys outside the city. Ask at the tourism office (on Avenida Luzuriaga in the post office building; phone: 44-721031) for directions to the ruins (they are 3 hours from Huaráz). A local tour operator also can help; contact *Cordillera Blanca Adventures* (Parque Ginebra, Lote 30; phone: 44-721934). The ruins were a temple/fortress that is now partly submerged in the earth as a result of a 1945 earthquake. Most of the temple — one of the oldest in the Western Hemisphere — has been excavated. Grotesque head sculptures once dotted the walls (one is still intact), and carved stone designs feature felines, condors, and serpents. A granite slab in the Chavín plaza has several roundish indentations that reflect the constellations when filled with water. The *lanzón,* an intricately carved granite monolith, also was found at this site.

The next stop on the route is Huascarán, the continent's second-highest Andean peak — 22,206 feet — in Huascarán National Park. For information on trekking, visits to the park, or a list of tour agencies, contact the local guides association, *Casa de Guías de Huaráz* (office 123, Zona Comercial 28G; phone: 44-721333) or the *Peru Mountain Guides Association* (225 Av. Paz Soldán, Lima; phone: 14-418831).

Huascarán National Park is a hauntingly beautiful protected area and a favorite of mountain climbers and trekkers because, aside from the crowning peak, there are 30 other snow-topped mountains with clear, cold rivers and cascades at their bases. The first person to scale Huascarán's north peak was North American Annie Peck, who accomplished this feat in 1908 when she was in her fifties. First class skiers have tried the treacherous slopes here; a new ski station, Pastorilla, opened in late 1990.

You can rent hiking and camping equipment in Huaráz from *Andean Sports Tour* (571 Av. Luzuriaga; phone: 44-721612). Prices are about $15 a week for tent rental, $5 a day for a guide, and $3 a day for donkeys. The favorite treks range from the 9-mile (14-km) day hike from Catac to Carpa, to the 5-day, 40-mile (64-km) journey from Yungay to Caraz via Llanganuco, Portachuelo, Huaripampa, and Santa Cruz.

Yungay, the loveliest of the towns in the valley, was wiped off the map by the 1970 earthquake and an accompanying mudslide. Within minutes, thousands were dead and all that remained after the earth swallowed up the village were the tops of the three palm trees that had graced the Plaza de Armas. The palms are still visible, not far from where the Yungay survivors have rebuilt their town. Meanwhile, in Caraz, there are brilliant flowers grown for export to the US. It also is a good spot for bargains on handicrafts and wool items. Llanganuco are twin emerald lakes within the park area and reportedly they offer good fishing. Check with the tourist office. Arrange for your hike to take you past fields of the bizarre *paya raimondi,* an Andean cactus that grows to 26 feet and, when not in bloom, resembles an elongated pine cone with a grass skirt. Alternatively, head the 11 miles (18 km) from Huaráz to the hot springs at Monterrey and take a soak.

For more information on Huascarán, read the bilingual book, *Parque Nacional Huascarán,* written by California native Jim Bartle, who makes his home in Huaráz. This 40-page paperback has stunning photos reminiscent of those that gave Bartle the nickname "the postcard man" for his other notable project, a set of 16 postcards depicting scenes of the area.

**En Route from Huaráz** – Return north to the Pan-American Highway and you get to Chimbote, the capital of the fishing and steel industry in Peru.

**CHIMBOTE:** Four decades ago, Chimbote was a sleepy little fishing village, but the commercialization of Peru's fish-laden Pacific waters turned it into the nation's fishing capital — a significant honor in a country that has frequently been the world's top fish exporter. This distinction changed during the regime of the military government in the 1960s, when mismanagement and overfishing of anchovy left many of Chimbote's residents unemployed. During the 1980s, however, the industry flourished once again. But 1991 brought the worst disaster ever to the city: Early in that year, cholera was reported in Chimbote, beginning an outbreak that swept the country and spread to other South American nations. For Chimbote residents, it brought not only hundreds of deaths in and around their city, but also a screeching halt to the fishing industry. After epidemiologists suggested that the cholera had come to the city from garbage that had been dumped from an Asian boat offshore, it was discovered that Pacific coast fish carried the bacterium. Developed nations immediately banned Peruvian fish imports and once again, Chimbote residents found themselves unemployed.

Aside from a pleasant climate and good swimming at Vesique and Santa beaches, Chimbote has little to offer travelers. During the cholera epidemic that has since been contained, the strong fish odor that had been Chimbote's claim to fame disappeared; by late 1991, fishing resumed (although not a previous levels) and the sweet smell of possible success is slowly coming back.

**En Route from Chimbote** – Before reaching Trujillo, you pass through the Virú Valley, where some of the earliest remains of prehistoric Peru have been found. (Supposedly, the name Perú is derived from the name of this valley; somehow it was given to the whole territory of the Inca in a case of mistaken identity on the part of the Spaniards.) Ruins dating back to AD 200 have been discovered in the valley, and there are 14 pyramidal sanctuaries in the area.

From here, it's a short, 30-mile (48-km) trip up the Pan-American Highway to Trujillo, founded in 1535 by the Spaniards near the monumental adobe city of Chan-Chan.

**TRUJILLO:** Named after Francisco Pizarro's Spanish hometown, even today it is referred to as the "Lordly City of Trujillo" in tribute to its rich colonial past. With an excellent climate, Trujillo averages 70F (21 C) December through April, and 58F (14C) the rest of the year, disturbed only by the high humidity that can make your tour through its colonial buildings a damp but enjoyable romp.

Because the surrounding Moche Valley is agriculturally rich, immense plantations devoted to the cultivation of sugar, cotton, rice, and cereals semicircled the city to the north, west, and south. They brought great wealth to the area, and plantation owners maintained elegant Spanish-style homes with large patios, luxurious reception rooms, and magnificent façades of sculpted wooden balconies and lovely lacelike wrought-iron window grilles. In the old city, which was surrounded by high walls topped with 28 watchtowers (a small section of the wall remains), there are still traces of the aristocratic luxury that was once synonymous with this viceregal city, probably the most Spanish of all the Peruvian cities during the colonial period.

However, government expropriation of farmland following agrarian reform in 1969 affected the plantations in the Trujillo area (Casa Grande, the property of one German immigrant family, was as large as the state of Rhode Island). The proud hacienda families have either left the country or retired to their mansions in the wealthy sections of Lima, and Trujillo has undergone industrialization and modernization.

Trujillo, certainly one of the most spotless cities in the country, has some handsome colonial churches and monasteries, but most of what is worth seeing can be done in a day. And, once that sightseeing is complete, there are two fine beaches for swimming: Buenos Aires and Las Delicias.

Among the sights to see are the winding lines of the ancient wall that Viceroy Don Melchor de Navarra ordered built in 1687 to defend the city from pirates. The Plaza de Armas, one of the largest in Peru, is dominated by a cathedral, a fountain, and the country's most unusual monument — a winged messenger whose legs were purposely made disproportionate to the rest of his body so that the statue would not stand higher than the cathedral across the street. The cathedral is not as impressive as those found in other South American cities, but it does have some fine paintings from the School of Quito. The cloistered Convent and Church of Carmen, on the corner of Jirón Bolívar and Jirón Colón, offer the best examples of high-colonial religious art in the city; their wooden altars are covered with gold leaf and their pulpit and some sculptures are made from the marble-like Huamanga stone found in Peru. The church was restored recently and at press time, there were plans to open a portion of the cloister to public view after nearly 270 years of isolation. The church and its art gallery, which take up an entire city block, are open Tuesdays to Saturdays from 9 AM to 1 PM and 4 to 7 PM; Sundays and holidays from 9 AM to 1 PM.

Diego de Almagro, the Spaniard who founded Trujillo in 1532, took advantage of the area's location midway between Lima and Piura and capitalized on its fertile land for use as a farming district. Five years later, King Carlos V of Spain bestowed the title "Most Noble City of Trujillo" on the area, thereby reaffirming its position as a city destined to be home to much of the Spanish nobility in Peru.

While visiting the churches mentioned above as well as the Church of San Francisco (which has a 300-year-old baptismal font), you will pass many of the better-preserved colonial mansions, among them the Casa del Mayorazgo (at Bolognesi and Pizarro), which houses the nation's most valuable stamp collection. Other colonial mansions permitting visitors include that of Sir Luis Fernando Ganoza (in front of the Church of San Francisco); the home of the Count of Aranda (621 Bolívar); the archbishop's palace (Plaza de Armas); the Palacio Iturregui (Junín and Pizarro); the Casa Emancipación (corner of Pizarro and Gamarra); and the newly restored Casa de Orbegoso (corner of Orbegoso and Bolívar). One of the most intriguing details is the intricate grillwork on the buildings' windows. Also note the wooden balconies that permitted the upper-class women to look out, but prevented their jealous husbands' rivals from looking in.

The *University Archaeological Museum* (349 Jirón Pizarro) presents an excellent collection of pre-Columbian art; it is open weekdays from 9 AM to noon and from 4 to 5:30 PM. The *Museo José Cassinelli* (601 Jirón Nicolás de Piérola) offers a private collection of 1,200 ceramics from the various ancient Peruvian civilizations. This collection, housed in the basement of a gas station, can be seen Mondays through Saturdays from 8:30 AM to noon and from 3 to 5 PM.

Surely you will get hungry as you stroll around Trujillo. At the coffee shop in the lovely *Turistas* hotel (see *Best en Route),* you can eat breakfast while looking out onto Plaza de Armas. *Gamarra* (777 Jirón Gamarra), the bar-restaurant *Demarco* (725 Jirón Pizarro, phone: 44-234251), and the bar-restaurant *Romano* (Jirón Pizarro; phone: 44-2445) can be recommended for the quality of their food, their cleanliness, and their moderate prices. Also recommended are *El Mesón de Cervantes* (654 Pizarro; phone: 44-257156) and *Kalorías* (4172 Av. América del Sur; phone: 44-211038).

In addition to the tourist office (628 Independencia; phone: 44-241936), information about the city also is available from a specially trained tourist police station (402 Francisco Pizarro; phone: 44-257372).

About 7½ miles (12 km) north of the city is the picturesque port of Huanchaco, which also has a decent beach. Its waves attract surfers from around the world; it is the site of an international surfing competition. One of its attractive features is the *caballito de totora,* a reed-constructed boat made by the residents and used for fishing. The boat's history goes back over 1,000 years, as evidenced by the pottery of the pre-Columbian Moche tribe. Good restaurants here are *Lobo Marino, Sunkelia,* and *El Poseidón,* right along the waterfront.

If you're looking for fiestas, plan to be in Trujillo during the third week in January, when *trujillanos* celebrate the *Festival of La Marinera,* a sensuous courting dance of African and Hispanic origins, in which couples circle each other waving handkerchiefs. It reminds one of the Spanish flamenco, but it is performed in a more leisurely manner. All schoolchildren on the coast learn the *marinera* at an early age, and its graceful (if strenuous) steps are Peru's major contribution to the ballet-like dance form. To discover what colonial social life was really like, visit Trujillo's *Spring Festival,* held the last 2 weeks of September. It offers all kinds of music and dance presentations, bullfights, cockfights, competitions, and lots of food and drink, including the corn liquor called *chicha.* One of its main attractions is the exhibition of Peruvian Paso horses, an elegant breed whose special gait and smooth ride has made it famous. A special program in northern California uses these gentle horses in its treatment of emotionally ill adolescents.

Your next stop in this area should be at Chan-Chan, onetime capital of the ancient kingdom of Chimú, about 2½ miles (4 km) from Trujillo. Public minibuses to the site leave every few minutes from Avenida José Gálvez at Avenida Las Incas. You also can take a cab from the same spot.

**CHAN-CHAN:** In its heyday, around AD 1300, this site was larger in size and population than any European city. Try to turn back the clock 650 years and imagine yourself, for the first time, descending the Andean mountain slopes to the Pacific Ocean. There, spread out over many square miles, sits the sophisticated Chimú city — actually a series of walled citadels or districts enclosed by a thick adobe wall. Surrounded on all sides, as far as the eye can see, by emerald green fields crisscrossed by aqueducts and irrigation channels, the city is a great bouquet of red, yellow, orange, and green, embellished by the continual glinting of gold and silver that adorn the palaces and temples — in an area that is actually quite parched.

Encircled by walls almost 50 feet high, immensely thick and covered with bas-reliefs of fish, birds, moons, and fishnets, the splendor of the city will make you gasp, for nowhere else in the Andean province can such a marvel be seen. You can imagine entering by one of the massive gates and find yourself caught up in the swirl of the city's busy life. To the right and left are small artisan factories where skilled hands are creating beautiful costume jewelry; hand-painting delicate pottery; renewing the weapons of the royal army; or weaving, with intricate patterns, soft mantles and shirts. Patient women are chewing the corn that ferments with their saliva. This chewed corn is deposited in great earthen vessels and becomes the *chicha* (corn liquor) so cherished by ruler and commoner alike.

When the Spanish came upon this majestic city, they called it Candia, a name that went through several revisions before 1892, when German scientist Ernest Middendorf translated the name as Chan-Chan, or "Sun-Sun." Other scientists and linguists, however, say that the name probably really means "House of the Serpents." An ancient legend holds that the city was a huge sacred plain dedicated to the Goddess of the Moon, whose silvery light reflects off Chan-Chan's adobe buildings in the evenings. It is believed that Chan-Chan was designed to be an earthly complement to the celestial universe, and that astronomy played an important part in this seaside civilization of fishermen and farmers. The four-star Southern Cross, for example, represented the four social classes within the city, with the two brightest stars standing for the two classes of nobility and the smaller, weaker pair representing the two classes of commoners.

As you enter each of the ten districts of the clay and adobe city, the pattern of life is repeated. The plan of each district is basically the same: The great central plaza was the center of political and religious life; the temples of the Moon Goddess (who controlled the tides) and lesser gods and the palaces of the princes; the courts of justice, where an "eye for an eye and a tooth for a tooth" punishments were dealt out; the marketplace with immense water reservoirs; the cemeteries, principally reserved for the notables. When still populated, the city's nobility were carried around on adorned litters, lived in palaces, and wore lavish clothing and ornaments (gold and silver nose and ear rings, and colorful turbans topped by proud sprays of exquisitely colored plumes). This was truly an empire, for its political and economic power spread far beyond its territorial limits, Paramonga in the south and Tumbes in the north.

What were the origins of this splendid city and kingdom? According to archaeological studies, the Chimú's great predecessor was the Moche civilization (sometimes called the Mochica culture), which flourished in the first eight centuries of this era. Fortresses and temples in the Moche style (pyramidal) abound throughout the Trujillo area. The most important remnants of this civilization are its marvelous ceramics, including their so-called "erotic *huacos*" and wall bas-reliefs, which provide a complete panorama of the daily life of the Moche people: ceremonial rites (both religious and political), work and recreational habits, war and hunting procedures, sexual practices, and burial customs. If you did not get to the *Museo Arqueológico Rafael Larco Herrera* (Rafael Larco Herrera Archaeological Museum) in Lima (1515 Av. Bolívar in the Pueblo Libre neighborhood; phone: 14-611312), be sure to do so upon your return, for it has a fine collection of Moche pottery, as does the *Museo Brüning* in Lambayeque, to the north (see below).

Chan-Chan today has suffered destruction at the hands of the gold- and relic-seekers, squatters, and from the rains (called El Niño storms) on the Peruvian coast. With roofs long rotted away by the humid and salty air, the buildings no longer are protected, although archaeologists are experimenting with a cactus-based sealant that they have painted on sections of the ruins to prevent further deterioration. However, you still can perceive the magnificence that was Chan-Chan in the several restored portions, and in the once monstrously thick walls, now somewhat reduced in height. Chan-Chan also has the great Moche temples of the Sun and the Moon, the first constructed of about 500 million adobe bricks. Do not wander off alone into the ruins at Chan-Chan; stick with the guided groups (official licensed guides can be hired at the entrance to the ruins). Robberies of visitors have been reported. A new museum (also at the entrance to the ruins) offers a glimpse of the Chimú civilization and its building and farming techniques.

In the same area are the Temple of the Dragon (its walls adorned with bas-reliefs of the dragon symbol, so common to the ancient Chinese and Mesopotamian civilizations) and the Emerald Temple. Other Moche and Chimú urban centers and irrigation projects are near Trujillo; their remains offer further confirmation of the political, economic, and artistic heights reached by these two ancient Peruvian cultures.

**En Route from Trujillo** – Although a roadway connects Trujillo to Cajamarca, the conduit is unpaved in spots, curves sharply as it crosses the highlands, and often is plagued by falling rocks. It's especially tricky to maneuver during the rainy season, October through May. Local officials say the difficulty of transportation is what keeps Cajamarca so culturally "pure." Instead of driving, consider the short *AeroPerú* flight or the 6-hour bus trip. As an alternative, you may want to continue north to Chiclayo and on to the latest — and most exciting — of Peru's archaeological discoveries. From there you also can turn east to Cajamarca.

**CHICLAYO:** This growing city is one of the most important commercial centers in northern Peru. Not far from the sea and linked to Lima by daily flights on *Faucett, AeroPerú, Americana,* and *Andrea* airlines, there is activity day and night, ranging from merchants arriving to collect wares destined for Cajamarca (in the Andes to the east) to scientists and tourists lured by the now world-famous archaeological excavations north of the city.

Chiclayo also is known for its religious festivals. The most important one is the *Cruz de Chalpón,* celebrated the first week in August, and drawing hundreds of religious pilgrims. In addition, this is a spot where herbal healing and white magic are the norm. As evidence, stop by the *Mercado Herbolario* (Herbal Market) at the city's large outdoor produce market where you'll find herbal ointments, hallucinogenic cacti, love potions, natural contraceptives, and sulphur soaps. It is located at Arica and Juan Cuglievan and is open daily from 7 AM to 6 PM. Be on the alert for pickpockets.

Besides spiritual sustenance, Chiclayo offers visitors a variety of tangible and tasty local dishes, ranging from the irresistible ceviche (fish marinated in lemon, onion, and hot pepper) to plates traditionally associated with the north — *pato a la chiclayana* (duck stewed with scallions) and *seco de cabrito* (goat served with rice and richly seasoned beans). For dessert, "King Kong" is the local favorite — a cake made from cookies and layers of sugary fillings, including molasses and *manjarblanco,* a milk sweet. Try the excellent *Le Paris* (716 Jr. M.M. Izaga; phone: 74-235485), a cozy restaurant with international specialties (including a superb *fettuccine Alfredo).*

For the traveler, Chiclayo is the hotel and restaurant — see *Best en Route* — stop for the 7-mile (11-km) trip outside the city to Lambayeque and the most talked-about archaeological excavations of the decade. Buses and cabs can take you to this dusty little village; contact the national tourist office (FOPTUR) in Chiclayo (830 Elías Aguirre, office 202; phone: 74-2227776) for details. Also, you can arrange trips through two local operators — *Indiana Tours* (774 Izaga; phone: 74-240833), which has a mini-van that picks up passengers at major hotels, and *Aero Andino* (191 Los Cipreses; phone: 74-233161).

**LAMBAYEQUE:** This tiny town is nestled among five desert valleys — Jequetepeque, Zaña, Lambayeque, La Leche, and Motupe — peppered by hundreds of archaeological sites, most of which still have not been explored (except, perhaps, by grave robbers). The slow-paced town is itself home to Peru's noted gold collection, the *Museo Brüning* (Brüning Museum; Av. Huamachuco; phone: 282110). Besides astonishing textiles and ceramics, it contains many of the precious artifacts found here in what was — in pre-Inca times — the continent's most important goldworking center (much of the inventory of the *Museo del Oro* (Gold Museum) in Lima, in fact, comes from the looted Batán Grande tombs in La Leche valley). At the *Brüning* you can find out about visiting the two excavations in progress outside Lambayeque — Túcume and Sipán, the latter being home to the most valuable pre-Inca tombs ever found intact in the Americas. When Dr. Walter Alva Alva, curator of the *Museo Brüning,* and his team of archaeologists (funded in part by the *National Geographic Society)* began excavating in 1987, they never expected to find the wealth of gold, jewelry, and ceramics buried with the Moche warrior lord interred at Sipán. The dig was launched after police contacted Alva Alva about amazing gold pieces nabbed from antiquities thieves; before the saga ended, at least one grave robber was dead (killed in a confrontation with police), and archaeologists, fearing retaliation, posted armed guards at the treasure trove. In 1988, the researchers found a tomb of the "Priest," followed in 1990 by the discovery of a third burial chamber — the most fabulous to date — that of the "Old Lord of Sipán," nicknamed the "Spiderman" because they found a gold necklace adorned with ten spiders on the top layer of funerary offerings. A fourth tomb has been uncovered, but at press time, officials had not made its contents public. They have determined, however, that there was an elaborate guard system, indicating that it was an important burial chamber. Archaeologists have also said that it was clear that the tomb had been opened before — by the Moche, not grave robbers — apparently to take out the original body and replace it with a higher-ranking person. Archaeologists have now begun work on yet a fifth burial area. A small on-site museum opened in Sipán in late 1991 (admission charge). The Sipán project, like many scientific/cultural ones in Peru, has been plagued by insufficient funding — so much so that some archaeologists have worked for as little as $40 a month. The *Museo Brüning* is now the administrative office for the Sipán Foundation, an organization set up to raise funds to continue the excavation. Note that there is only one authorized set of Sipán postcards, the profits from which go to the dig, and they also are best purchased at the museum, where you also can buy reproductions of the gold and turquoise ear ornaments found in the first two graves.

Just a few miles away at Túcume, Norwegian explorer Thor Heyerdahl — who decades ago sailed on his reed boat *Kon Tiki* from Peru to Polynesia to prove it could have been an ancient migration path — is working with Alva Alva on another dig. At a site where tourists can visit (a picnic area, piped-in water, and a hewn rock lookout point have already been installed), the scientists are excavating several of the 27 adobe pyramids that legend says were a part of one of the most important kingdoms in the region, and whose mysterious leader appears on the *tumis* (sacrificial or ornamental knives) found in the designs on Peruvian artisan work, ceramics, and textiles. Currently, a small museum is being built at Túcume.

Returning to Chiclayo, head east to Cajamarca in the highlands. *AeroPerú* has service between the two cities.

**CAJAMARCA:** A gem of a city, not only because of its beautiful valleys and rich farmland, but because it was one of the most important cities in the Inca empire, and the spot where the Inca and Spanish powers had their showdown. Known as the northern "vacation" spot for the Inca rulers, a thousand years earlier the Cajamarca region had been the cradle of several advanced Indian cultures whose pottery techniques are being recovered and whose architectural ruins are still under investigation. It is also the site of Peru's most raucous *Carnaval* every March.

When the Spanish reached this northern city full of Inca palaces, they awaited Atahualpa — the last Inca ruler — who arrived on a gold litter borne by admiring subjects. He refused Spanish attempts to take over his kingdom and, according to legend, offended the conquistadores by taking a Bible and touching it, smelling it, holding it up to his ear, and then throwing it onto the ground as a useless item. Atahualpa was taken hostage and garroted in what is now the Plaza de Armas — despite the fact that the Spanish had accepted a massive ransom for his release.

The Spanish converted the city into a colonial community that derived its wealth from mining until the late 18th century. It has since become one of the most important beef and dairy farming regions of Peru.

The city is best seen from Cerro Santa Apolonia, a hill with gardens and walkways leading up to a lookout point with carved stone seats where the Indian rulers allegedly watched out over their domain. The center of this city of 120,000 is the Plaza de Armas, where the cathedral is located.

Opened in 1776, the cathedral has carved wood altars covered in gold leaf and an intricately hewn volcanic rock façade. Most surprising is the obvious absence of any bell towers; they were left unfinished in a protest against Spain's tax on churches.

Across the plaza, known for its entertaining topiary (look for the bush with the *campesino* beside a llama), is the San Francisco church. More ornate than the cathedral, this 17th-century church and monastery complex has a *Religious Art Museum*, open daily except Sundays until 5 PM. The entrance ticket includes a guided tour and a visit to the catacombs.

A block away, the Complejo Belén (Belén Complex) is a group of museums and workshops that also houses the Institute of Culture. The church in the complex is the loveliest in the city, with brightly painted statues and carved stone details. The connecting building (Hospital de Varones), formerly a colonial-era hospital for men, consists of an altar with a series of alcoves along its side walls. Patients were placed in alcoves on animal-skin beds under the images of saints (whose healing powers corresponded to their illnesses). In a gesture that surely did not inspire optimism, the sickest individuals were placed closest to the altar — near the door leading out to the cemetery.

Across the street is a women's hospital — used primarily for maternity cases in the past — that has now been converted into an intriguing anthropology museum. In this same complex of buildings, the monastery's kitchen is a gallery displaying work by Cajamarca artists.

The Belén Complex (phone: 4492-2601) also contains an artisan shop run by a local cooperative and offers the best buys on postcards (by Cajamarquino Víctor Campos); books on the province are available in the editorial office of the Cultural Institute. The institute's archaeology office is a good place to get information about nearby digs that tourists can visit, including the University of Tokyo archaeological excavations at Huacaloma and Kuntur Wasi. (Bear in mind that no work takes place during the rainy season from October to May.)

There are artisans' shops with baskets, pottery, and leather goods on and near the Plaza de Armas, but the most fascinating (and most reasonably priced) spot to buy pottery and ceramic work is outside the city at Aylambo. The brainchild of ecologist Pablo Sánchez of the University of Cajamarca, this area is a series of experimental workshops in environmentally balanced settings. Sewage at the workshops, for example, is recycled to make the gas used to generate heat and light. The fine pottery, made by "apprentices" who range in age from 9 to 90, includes pieces that incorporate ancient traditional designs.

Also outside the city is Llancanora, 8 miles (13 km) from Cajamarca, with enchanting scenery and the Ventanillas of Otuzco, 4 miles (7 km) northeast of the city. The latter, a pre-Inca necropolis, is a series of curious burial "windows" that the ancient Indians carved into cliffsides.

Another must stop is Cumbemayo, a valley through which runs a pre-Inca irrigation ditch of carved rock considered by hydraulic engineers to be a marvel unsurpassed in modern times. The same valley has a sanctuary where pre-Inca cultures performed rituals to their gods, as well as unusual rock formations which, due to centuries of erosion, have taken on the shapes of hooded monks, frogs, dinosaurs, and castles.

If you reach Colpa — once the area's most important dairy hacienda and now a cooperative — before 2 PM, you can watch the cows being called in from the fields. The daily ritual involves calling each animal by name; they respond by meandering up to the milking areas assigned to them.

No visit to Cajamarca would be complete without a stop at Los Baños del Inca (the Inca baths). These mineral springs — so hot at their source that locals use them to boil eggs — have been diverted to small enclosed private pools and a large outdoor city swimming pool where you can take a dip for a small admission charge. The springs can be reached in collective cabs from the Plaza de Armas in Cajamarca or in city buses that run a block from the plaza on Amazonas Street.

For dining, stop by the *Salas* restaurant on the Plaza de Armas for fast service, bargain prices, and the best home cooking in the city. Try the *panqueques* (sweet crêpes) with *manjarblanco* or the *quesillo* with *miel* — a saltless cheese with a sweet syrup topping. Other local dishes include guinea pig (*cuy*), beef ribs (*costillas*), and potato herb soup (*chupe verde*). In the evenings, the restaurant at the *Hostal Cajamarca* behind the Belén Complex and the *Cajamarqués* on Amazonas at the side of the San Francisco church are your best bets. The *Hostal Cajamarca* has a small bar — *El Sitio* — where impromptu music is provided by local musicians and tourists alike (see *Best en Route*). The *Emperador* nightclub features folkloric music and dance shows.

During *Carnaval* in Cajamarca, there is no need to look for evening entertainment. Music, dance, drinking, and merrymaking go on around the clock for days. Residents celebrate by throwing water and talcum powder at each other, dressing in bizarre costumes, and painting one another with shoe polish. If you plan to visit Cajamarca during this time, come prepared to join in the fun, and be sure to make reservations well in advance.

Cajamarca's tourism office is located off the plaza outside the Belén Complex church (at 158 Jr. Silva Santistéban; phone: 4492-2228). To arrange guided visits to sites in and outside the city, stop by *Cajamarca Tours* (323 Jr. Dos de Mayo; phone: 4492-2813); *Cumbemayo Tours* (635 Amalia Puga; phone: 4492-2938); and *Intertours* (Plaza de Armas; phone: 92-2777).

## BEST EN ROUTE

Expect to pay from $25 to $40 for accommodations for two listed as expensive, $15 to $25 at a place listed as moderate, and under $15 at an inexpensive place. Expect clean rooms, some private baths, and restaurants on the premises. Again, make reservations before traveling.

### HUACHO

*Centenario* – This small hotel has a restaurant where seafood is the specialty. 836 Av. 28 de Julio (phone: 34-323731). Moderate.

### HUARMEY

*Turistas* – A state-owned place with clean rooms and good service. Centrally located at Km 270 of the Pan-American Hwy. (phone: Huarmey 31; in Lima, 14-721928; in the US, 800-275-3123). Moderate.

### HUARÁZ

*Turistas de Monterrey* – Where ex-president Fernando Belaúnde Terry stays when he's in the valley. Run by the state Turista chain, it offers 60 rooms, a swimming pool, good meals, and access to spectacular hiking trails. Located at Km 5 on the road to Caraz outside Huaráz (phone: Monterrey 1; in Lima, 14-721928; in the US, 800-275-3123). Expensive.

*Andino* – The most expensive and elegant accommodations in the city, it boasts the *Chalet Suisse* restaurant (try the fondue, but be forewarned — it's pricey). This property offers a fantastic view of Huascarán; climbing and hiking gear are available for rent. Jointly owned by German and Swiss nationals. 357 Pedro Cochachín (phone: 44-721662; in Lima, 14-459230). Moderate.

*Turistas de Huaráz* – The rooms are large and clean in this government-run hotel, but it's best to avoid the food. Av. Centenario, Cuadra 10 (phone: 44-721640; in Lima, 14-721928). Moderate.

*Albergue Juvenil La Monteñesa* – Clean and basic, this is a popular spot for adventure travelers who don't mind bunk bed and sharing a bathroom. 210 Centerario at A.B. Leguía (phone: 44-721287; in Lima, 14-755343). Inexpensive.

### CHIMBOTE

*Turistas* – Modern and pleasant, with private baths, restaurant, and a bar. 109 Calle Gálvez (phone: 44-323721; through *EnturPerú* in Lima, 14-721928; in the US, 800-275-3123). Expensive.

### TRUJILLO

*El Golf* – An elegant hotel with 120 pleasant rooms, a restaurant, and a bar, it is some distance from the center of town, but free transportation downtown is provided hourly. Urbanización El Golf, Manzana J-1 (phone: 44-242592; in Lima, 14-317872). Expensive.

*Turistas* – This modern and comfortable hotel, housed in a rebuilt colonial structure, features 80 rooms with TV sets, plus a sauna, swimming pool, and a bar. 485 Jirón Independencia on the Plaza de Armas (phone: 44-232741; in Lima, 14-721928; in the US, 800-275-3123). Expensive.

*Hostería El Sol* – A warm, comfortable, small hotel where many visiting archaeologists stay. 224 Los Brillantes, Urbanización Santa Inés (phone: 44-231933). Moderate.

**Opt Gar** – Small and centrally located, this place offers clean rooms, a restaurant, bar, and good service. 595 Jirón Grau (phone: 44-242192; in Lima, 14-478760). Moderate.

**Chan-Chan** – Spacious rooms, a restaurant, and a bar are here. 304 Av. Sinchi Roca and Huayna Cápac (phone: 44-242964). Inexpensive.

## HUANCHACO

**Caballito de Totora** – An oceanfront hostelry with nice gardens, a swimming pool, and a cafeteria. A good spot for surfing. 217 Av. La Rivera (phone: in Lima, 14-459869). Inexpensive.

## CHICLAYO

**La Garza** – Modern and clean, this 71-room hostelry, decorated in a colonial manner, has a lovely outdoor pool, a bar, restaurant, and a color television in every room. Quieter than the *Turistas*. 756 Av. Bolognesi (phone: 74-228172; fax: 74-228171). Moderate.

**Turistas** – Though unappealing to look at, this modern place is clean, well maintained, and the choice of visiting archaeologists. It is comfortable, has a pool and a good restaurant, and is just 1 block from the *Centro Cívico* (Civic Center), although it's about a 10-block walk from the Plaza de Armas. Unfortunately, there's a lot of street noise. 115 Av. Federico Villareal (phone: 74-234911; in Lima, 14-404630; in the US, 800-275-3123). Moderate.

**Sipán** – The newest hotel in town, it has a swimming pool and restaurant. 150 Virgilie D'All Orso (phone: 74-242564; fax: 74-242408). Inexpensive.

## CAJAMARCA

**Laguna Seca** – Though slightly rustic in appearance, this is the city's best lodging place and one of the most fascinating hostals in Peru. Located near the Baños del Inca, it has hot water from the mineral springs piped into the bathtubs in every room as well as into its large outdoor pool. In March, when the hotel is busiest, there are cockfights and bullfights at the small ring at the onetime hacienda. There also are eucalyptus saunas, a dining room, bar, weight lifting room, and free transportation to downtown. Av. Manco Cápac, Baños del Inca (phone: 4492-3149; in Lima, 14-463270). Expensive.

**Continental** – This modern building with 52 rooms clashes with the city's colonial architecture, but it is a recommendable place for a night's stay. Located next door to the *Cajamarqués*, the best restaurant in town. 760 Jr. Amazonas (phone: 4492-2758). Moderate.

**Turistas** – Right on the Plaza de Armas, this state-run place has a charming lobby, furnished in antiques, and a satisfactory restaurant. 773 Jr. Lima (phone: 4492-2470; in Lima, 14-721928; in the US, 800-275-3123). Moderate.

**Cajamarca** – Run by a young couple, this large property has a fine restaurant and bar with music. Once the home of a wealthy *cajamarquino*, the rooms in this colonial mansion retain their original wooden floors. 311 Jr. Dos de Mayo (phone: 4492-2532; in Lima, 14-623572). Inexpensive.

# Lima to Nazca

This route goes from Lima south on the Pan-American Highway to the valleys of the Pacific coast. The area is an archaeological treasure trove, filled with the remains of pre-Columbian cultures that developed here at least 9,000 to 10,000 years ago. No one knows the origins of the Nazca and Paracas groups. Presumably they settled here after migrations across the Bering Strait — probably a land bridge at the time — and down the American continents, living in nomadic fashion on the coast here. As they progressed from a survival existence based upon fishing, hunting, and food gathering, they began to lay the agricultural foundations of what would become the great Peruvian coastal and highland civilizations.

Perhaps the more mysterious culture of the two was the Nazca, whose people settled in five valleys along the coast: Nazca, Santa Cruz, Palpa, Ingenio, and Poroma. Very little is known except that they emerged between 1,000 BC and AD 500, a group of master craftsmen who made pottery in the shape of animals, men, and vegetables. The designs etched into the Nazca Pampa Colorado plain — figures of men, circles, and birds that can only be seen in their entirety from the air — are faithful to the designs found on Nazca ceramics and textiles. Although the who, when, and how of the making of the Nazca lines is becoming clearer, scientists and anthropologists still have many questions to answer.

The Paracas Peninsula, a dry, windswept piece of land about 125 miles south of Lima, was the center of Paracas culture. Like the Nazca, the Paracas Indians became master artisans. Little is known about this group except that once in about 300 BC people began to use the peninsula as a burial ground. They interred their mummified dead in baskets in chambers receding into the Cerro Colorado, a huge, reddish mountain. The tombs within the *cerro* also were discovered to be like those of the Egyptians, with anterooms, patios, and main chambers.

Travel this route by bus or through a tour operator from Lima. *Tepsa* (129 Av. de la República; phone: 14-321233) and *Ormeño* (177 Carlos Zavala; phone: 14-275679) lines have daily morning and evening departures. *Colectivos* (buses) that carry five passengers can be taken from 561 Montevideo in Lima (phone: 14-281423). Two operators that offer packages to this area are *Lima Tours* (1040 Belén; phone: 14-276624) and *Receptour* (889 R. Torrico; phone: 14-312022). Another possibility is to fly directly to Nazca from Lima on *Aero Condor* (phone: 14-425663) or *Aeroica* (phone: 14-273292).

If you're traveling in the daytime, summer clothing is comfortable from December through March; however, from April through November you had better carry along a couple of sweaters, one light and one heavy.

If you're traveling by land, you may want to take the Pan-American south to Cañete, 89 miles (142 km) from Lima (buses and *colectivos* follow this route). Just before reaching Chincha Alta, another 33 miles (53 km) to the south is the tiny village of San Pedro de Grocio Prado, which is famous for woven-cane baskets and mats. You may want to stop to shop, or just to watch the artisans at work. Chincha Alta, a town of about 80,000 inhabitants, was once the center of the small Chincha Empire, a pre-Columbian culture composed of the neighboring Chincha, Pisco, Ica, and Nazca valleys. In its heyday, the empire was renowned for its fierce soldiers. Tambo de Mora, the onetime capital of the empire, 7 miles (11 km) to the west, is now a small port and has several ruins, including a temple. The port's original adobe structures have survived the centuries well because of the dry desert air. Nearby is the site of El Centinela, a well-preserved Inca Temple of the Sun; and, to the east is Carmen, a farm town whose inhabitants are descendants of black slaves. The town is known for its *frejol colado,* a dessert made from beans.

**CHINCHA ALTA:** The town is home to the former plantation of San José, the most notable of several such colonial estates in the area. The hacienda, with its grand salons and private chapel, is open to tourists. The estate, now owned by the Cillóniz family, has underground tunnels that connect the plantation to the port at Tambo de Mora. Chincha, whose predominantly black population reflects its slave roots, is famous for its boxers and soccer players; it has been the hometown of some of Peru's finest athletes.

Continuing south from Chincha Alta for 19 miles (30 km), you'll arrive at the turnoff for Pisco. Before entering the city, however, take the left-hand side road marked Castrovirreyna. About 29 miles (46 km) inland is Tambo Colorado, the best-preserved Inca ruin on this part of the coast. Save for the thatch roofs that once crowned the buildings, this site is still intact, its red and yellow walls testifying to the excellent preservative quality of the desert air. If you travel straight into Pisco on the Pan-American Highway (or if traveling by bus), a taxi from the city to Tambo Colorado can be hired for about $25.

**PISCO:** Although Pisco was an important city for the Inca and, later, for the Spanish, its major fame is linked to its production of a grape brandy that bears the city's name. The wine industry started in this area when the Spanish brought grapevines from the Canary Islands to see if they would adapt to the Peruvian climate. It is likely that the first harvest did not result in the dry vintage the Spanish sought but rather in a smooth, quick-fermenting liquor they found just as appealing. The traditional cocktail made from this libation, a *pisco* sour, contains sugar, lemon, egg whites, and bitters along with the *pisco* brandy. Modern variations include *pisco* daiquiris.

Continuing on to the port of Pisco, down the same road, you'll pass the air force base used for international flights when fog closes the airport in Lima, and you will also drive past a string of kiosks serving fish and shellfish plates. This marks the town of San Andrés, where more than 4,000 fishermen head out in boats each morning to earn their living from the sea, just as their parents and grandparents did — and as their children and grandchildren will in the future.

Eleven miles (18 km) to the south is the palm-lined beach city of Paracas, the starting point for those who want to explore the pristine beaches and mysterious markings at the national preserve of the Paracas Peninsula.

**PARACAS:** Were a traveler to walk about this peninsula, innocent of any knowledge of its history, he or she might be shocked to find an occasional human bone in the path. This desolate area was once a great burial ground, dating back some 2,500 years to an age when an advanced pre-Inca civilization wove exquisite textiles and mastered cranial surgery, using metal implants to plug holes in the skull.

This extensive city of the dead was unearthed in 1925 by Julio C. Tello and Toribio Mejía Xesspe, leading archaeologists in Lima. They found priceless ceramics and textiles made of vicuña and alpaca wool and fine-spun, coastal cotton — a long fiber and one of the world's best for weaving. (Archaeologists say that because of the special qualities of this cotton, the dyes in ancient tapestries have retained their brilliant colors.) Mummies, buried in a sitting position, were placed in reed baskets and covered with cotton blankets. At the *Julio C. Tello Museum,* just south of the city of Paracas, visitors can see burial displays of mummies, along with other items found at the dig, including brightly colored woven mantles, some embroidered with purple and red wool, with checkerboard or condor patterns.

After a stop at the *Tello Museum,* walk behind the building to see the remains of the necropolis and the burial chambers.

Heading down the asphalt road for another 6 miles (10 km) leads to Lagunillas, known for its sandy beaches and deep, blue Pacific waters. There are fish stands and some simple restaurants here and, like most of the peninsula, this is a fine spot from which to watch the dramatic sunsets. It may be possible to drive another 3 miles (5 km) southwest of this point before leaving your vehicle and crossing the final short distance on foot to what is known as the *Mirador de Lobos* (or "Sea Lion Lookout") where, looking down, you can see groups of sea lions on the rocks below. Occasionally, a condor will sweep by in search of a sea lion carcass.

It was in the bay of Paracas that General José de San Martín disembarked to begin his fight against the Spanish. Legend has it that the exotic red and white flamingos on the peninsula inspired him to choose red and white for the liberation flag's colors.

Boat excursions off the peninsula, especially to the islands of Ballestas and Punta Pejerrey, are recommended. Ballestas Island, 2 hours by boat, is inhabited by sea lions, pelicans, and Humboldt penguins. A boat off Punta Pejerrey provides the needed vantage point from which to see the mysterious Candelabro (i.e., candelabra) drawing etched into a mountainside overlooking the ocean. Excursion boats leave from the *Paracas* hotel and *Hostería Bahía*. Guides also can be hired for land tours of the peninsula. This is a good spot for skin diving and snorkeling. Check at the *Paracas* hotel for information about renting equipment. Paracas is a favorite spot for camping during the *New Year's* holiday.

**En Route from Paracas** – You have to backtrack to San Andrés to catch the road that will take you back to the Pan-American Highway and on to Ica. This trip entails a desert crossing, and some recommend that the drive be accomplished before midday (or in the evening) to avoid not only the heat, but also the daytime "*paracas,*" strong gusts of wind that lift clouds of sand and impair visibility. Eleven miles (18 km) south of where you reconnect with the main highway is Pozo Santo, literally the "holy well." An oasis with small restaurants and a deteriorating clay church, this marks the spot where, according to legend, a friar caused water to gush miraculously out of the desert, saving the lives of the group of pilgrims accompanying him.

From this point until you reach Ica, just a little more than 27 miles (43 km) to the south, you will be passing through the Pampas of Villacuri — an area of vast dunes interrupted only by tiny oases that is frequently compared to the desert of North Africa. Amazingly, as you near the city you will be in one of the main wine-producing regions of Peru.

**ICA:** This city has had more than its share of natural disasters. In 1664, it was destroyed by a tremendous earthquake; nearly 300 years later, horrendous floods from the nearby Ica River again devastated the town. To recover from the most recent destruction, traditional lines of zoning and styles of architecture were disregarded and Ica was transformed into a modern city with crazy street patterns. Few colonial homes are found here, not only due to natural destruction, but because the city has always been an enclave of anti-Spanish sentiment and therefore never became a home preferred by viceroys and other titled officials.

Although modern in appearance, this city has an occult tradition that dates back to the days of slavery. Even today, Ica is known to be a center of witchcraft and of healing cults; it is rumored that a European ambassador annually books a room at one of the area's finest hotels in order to spend several nights consulting with practitioners of black magic.

Ica occupies one of those wondrous fertile valleys that enliven the long Peruvian desert coast and is best known for its grapes and the wines it has produced for four centuries. Two wines, Tacama and Ocucaje, are both very good and are exported to other South American countries as well as to North America. Each year, Ica residents celebrate the grape harvest with an enthusiastic festival that lasts the entire second week of March. It features folk dancing and music, cockfights, equestrian events, and *pachamancas* barbecues in which wrapped meat, surrounded by sizzling coals, is baked in underground pits. Tasting tours of the Tacama, Ocucaje, and Vista Alegre vineyards can be arranged. Also, take time to visit the fine archaeological museum on Prolongación Ayabaca (around the corner from the *Turista* hotel). Ica is a region rich in prehistoric artifacts — one of the greatest troves in Peru. Giant fossils have been found scattered throughout the area, and scientists recently discovered a decorated flute believed to date back 9,000 years. The city tourism office is at 148 Av. Grau (phone: 34-235247).

**En Route from Ica** – The climate here is dry, but not excessively hot — about 85F (29C). At its height, the pre-Columbian culture (between AD 400 and 1000) that existed here was definitely related to the Nazca culture, and there are still remains of the ancient city of Pampa de Tate. Backtrack about 2½ miles (4 km) toward the ocean and you'll arrive at Huacachina, which has medicinal waters once frequented by the Inca and still popular with Ica residents. The odor is sulfurous, but the site is handsome: The spa is a small lake surrounded by sand dunes and palm trees.

South of Ica are desolate desert regions that lead to the valleys of Nazca, Santa Cruz, Palpa, Ingenio, and Poroma. This is a most important archaeological zone, influenced both by the Paracas and by the Wari. The various developments in the Nazca culture reveal a homebound people, democratically inclined (at least in death, for there are no marked distinctions among the graves), without any strong authoritarian influences in their public life (there are no pharaonic public works such as you find under the government of the Inca), with sufficient leisure time to produce remarkable ceramics and textiles. The potteries are delicately colored in varying pastel shades and reveal an unexpected elegance. The Nazca textiles are among the finest in workmanship and design.

Some 53 miles (85 km) after Ica, you approach the Quebrada de Santa Cruz (Canyon of the Holy Cross). Within it is a ruin that fills the entire canyon. To get a good idea of its immensity and various structures, climb above it and look down. When the highway intersects with the Río Ingenio, turn to the left to investigate the Tambo (way station) El Ingenio, a typical Inca construction, but of adobe.

After passing the small town of Palpa, about 3 miles (5 km) later, you will come upon the Nazca Plain.

**NAZCA:** On the edge of this dusty city is Pampa Colorada, the plain where the Nazca lines and drawings were sketched into the earth over a period of 300 years, as much as 5,000 years ago. There has been much speculation as to exactly who drew these lines on the dry desert floor. Perhaps the most fantastical theory is that of Erich von Daniken, who speculated in his book *Chariots of the Gods* (Putnam; 1970) that the lines were drawn with the aid of extraterrestrial beings: He claimed one of the drawings depicts a man resembling an astronaut with a life-support system strapped to his back. A more recent far-fetched theory (by members of the *Explorers Society* of Coral Gables, Florida) says that Indians first strung out the lines on small plots of land, then were guided in drawing the finished products by observers who flew above them in hot-air balloons filled with smoke. The society went so far as to reconstruct a Nazca balloon, with the help of drawings found in Nazca burial chambers and *totora* reeds (cattails) from the shores of Lake Titicaca, but it couldn't stay up in the air long enough to prove anything.

German-born mathematician Maria Reiche was the person most associated with this delicate desert sketch pad and she has been declared the "Keeper of the Pampa" by Peruvian officials. Reiche (now retired due to poor health) spent nearly 5 decades documenting and interpreting the array of animal and geometric drawings etched onto the desert floor, speculating that they have astronomical significance. Signed copies of

*Mystery of the Desert,* her book on the Nazca lines, is available from the author at the *Turista* hotel (at Jr. Bolognesi) in Nazca. These days you may see the new "guardian" of the lines, North American astronomer Phyllis Pitluga, wandering near the pampas.

Virtually nothing of the drawings can be seen from the ground. However, at Km 420 on the Pan-American Highway, there is a small observation tower at the side of the road for those who want to try to distinguish the markings. *Note:* Do not walk or drive on the pampas.

You can fly up and see the Nazca lines for yourself in *AeroCondor*'s tours above the plains in a single-engined plane. Make sure you take the flight before 2 PM. Visibility is best then and the buffeting afternoon winds (that have left many a tourist feeling queasy) have not yet started. Takeoff is from Lima, Ica, or Nazca; reservations can be made at the *AeroCondor* offices in Lima (741 Juan de Arona; phone: 14-425663) or at *Aeroica* (677 Nicolás de Piérola, Office 102, Lima; phone: 14-273292). For *AeroCondor* in Ica, check at *Las Dunas* hotel (phone: 34-231031), and in Nazca at the *Condor's Nest* (phone: Nazca 134) in front of the airport. *Aeroica* also has flights from Nazca (476 Tacna; phone: Nazca 64). Or you can wander over to the Nazca airstrip and hitch a ride with one of the local pilots; agree on the price before takeoff.

It's a breathtaking tour. From above, the lines become a series of rectangles, squares, circles, and drawings of fish, whales, insects, and birds. The interpretation of the lines probably depends upon your own imagination and knowledge. Because coastal peoples worshiped the "cool" moon (night brought daily relief from the desert heat), it is possible that the lines do have astronomical significance. Reiche has theorized that the drawings contain hidden messages for the gods looking down from the heavens.

The small city of Nazca itself is modern and has 40,000 inhabitants. Before you leave, take a visit southeast to Cahuachi, where there is an unusual forest of planted, cut trunks of trees placed in orderly lines; its purpose is puzzling. The trunks and stakes have been here for more than 500 years — or maybe twice that long. The area is believed to have been a ceremonial center for the Nazca. On the opposite side of Nazca, by the Aja River, lies Orcona — part of an elaborate water canal system also believed left by the ancient Indian civilization. Meanwhile, sand dunes southeast of Nazca have drawn the attention of sand surfing fans.

## BEST EN ROUTE

Accommodations along this route are the standard Peruvian fare — prices range from $75 to $110 for a double room in those establishments listed as very expensive; $45 to $75 in those noted as expensive; $20 to $45 at hotels in the moderate category; and under $20 at hotels in the inexpensive category. Most are clean, with good-size rooms, modern facilities including private baths, and restaurants. As elsewhere, it's a good idea to make reservations before you arrive, either by phoning direct or having your travel agent make the arrangements.

### CHINCHA

*El Sausal* – A basic, 37-room *hostal.* On the Pan-American Hwy. at Km 205 (phone: 34-262451). Moderate.

*Turismo San José* – This former estate is in a country setting. On the Pan-American Hwy. at Km 205 (phone: 34-713487; in Lima: 14-411327). Moderate.

### PISCO

*Pisco* – Basic and clean; offering a good breakfast, friendly service, and a disco. Plaza de Armas, 115 San Francisco (phone: Pisco 2018; reservations in Lima, 14-355135). Moderate.

## PARACAS

***Paracas*** – An acceptable place that, with a little loving care, could be absolutely wonderful. Everything is just a little run-down, but the rooms, situated in bungalows dotted around the spacious gardens, are comfortable and clean. There is a swimming pool, an airy restaurant, tennis court, fishing boat rentals, and a dock from which boats leave on excursions to the Islas Ballestas. Rivera del Mar, outside Paracas (phone: 34-221736 in Pisco; reservations in Lima, 14-464865 or 14-465079; fax: 14-476548). Expensive.

***Hostería Paracas*** – Overlooking the bay, this hotel has a swimming pool and is recommended for families. Av. Los Libertadores (phone: in Lima, 14-276624). Moderate.

## ICA

***Las Dunas*** – Popular with *limeños* on weekends, here is a fully equipped resort — the only first class property in this entire area. Rooms, in buildings clustered around lush gardens and rolling sand dunes, are large and airy. There are 3 pools, several restaurants, tennis, horseback riding, and golf, as well as a private airstrip where flights can be arranged over the Nazca lines. The hotel arranges wine cellar tours and trips to horse breeding farms and the Paracas Nature Reserve. At Km 300 of the Pan-American Hwy., 5 minutes from the center of Ica (phone: 34-231031; in Lima, 14-424180 or 14-423090; fax: 14-424180). Reservations in the US through *Latin America Reservations Center* (phone: 813-439-2118 in Florida; 800-327-3573 elsewhere). Very expensive.

***Turistas*** – This state-owned hotel has 58 clean rooms, a swimming pool, a restaurant, bar, and disco. Av. Los Maestros (phone: 34-233330; in Lima, 14-721928; in the US, 800-275-3123). Expensive.

## NAZCA

***Turistas*** – A cozy, 68-room hotel, with a restaurant that has an especially good, thick, shrimp soup. Its lovely gardens, cool modern lobby, and casual poolside café make it a favorite lodging. The guardian of the Nazca lines, Maria Reiche, lives here. She occasionally can be seen walking assisted around the patio or swimming. Jr. Bolognesi (phone: Nazca 60; in Lima, 14-721928; in the US, 800-275-3123). Expensive to moderate.

***De la Borda*** – Formerly the hacienda of the family that still owns it. Outside the city, on the way to the Nazca lines, at Km 447 on the Pan-American Hwy. (phone: in Lima, 14-408430). Moderate.

***La Maison Suisse*** – Small and favored by Europeans and located across the street from the airport. There's a little swimming pool. On the Pan-American Hwy., at Km 445 (phone: 34-232; in Lima, 14-243777). Moderate.

# Arequipa to Puno

Diego de Almagro, Francisco Pizarro's first partner and later, bitter enemy (because of a dispute over dividing the riches of the Inca Empire), was probably the first Spaniard to enter Arequipa. It was a small but very important junction in the Inca road system: The Chilean road came from the south, and toward the north, it went through the now-pacified coastal kingdoms; eastward it ascended the high Andean passes to arrive at Cuzco.

The Spaniards established a small community in what is known today as the barrio of San Lázaro, the name of the first church erected. In 1540, the principal square was laid out, and the Spanish town of Arequipa was formally established. In 1541 King Carlos gave the "Beautiful Town of Arequipa" the rank of a city. "This city," writes Cieza de León, "is situated in the best and coolest spot suitable . . . and the location and climate of this city are so good that it is reputed the healthiest and pleasantest in which to live." And more than 4 centuries later, his words still ring true for this city of 600,000 residents.

Arequipa, 7,590 feet above sea level, is one of those rare places where "eternal springtime" reigns. Temperatures vary between 54 and 70F (12 and 21C) throughout the year, and the city rarely has a day where at least a few hours of brilliant sunshine do not illuminate turquoise skies and warm the *sillar* colonial houses and churches in the heart of the old city. *Sillar* is the white volcanic stone resulting from the lava overflow of the three volcanoes — Chachani, El Misti, and Pichupichu — that surround the city and were immensely active centuries ago. Even today El Misti, Arequipa's Vesuvius (and the resemblance to Vesuvius is striking), smokes from time to time.

Because of the *sillar* material, the city is called La Ciudad Blanca (The White City). But there are some who point out that the real origin of that title lies with the town edict passed a few years after the city's founding, limiting residency within the city to the Spanish whites and their Indian servants. All other Indians who had business in the city (artisans, mechanics, builders, and manual laborers) had to retire at the close of each day to their encampments beyond the city walls. Be that as it may, Arequipa merits its title today for the concerted effort to restore to their pristine loveliness the *sillar* mansions and churches that abound in the center.

*AeroPerú, Faucett, Americana,* and *Andrea* have daily flights from Lima to Arequipa. Like the tourist arriving in Cuzco by airplane, the visitor flying to Arequipa may experience a bit of *soroche,* or altitude sickness; sometimes the coca tea called *maté de coca* can help alleviate the symptoms. Because almost all the magnificent architecture is centrally located, a tourist can do practically all sightseeing on foot. And except for the market of San Camilo and the immediately surrounding streets, Arequipa is a safe city for travelers. The tourist office, open Mondays through Fridays, is at 112 Portal Municipal (phone: 54-213101).

**AREQUIPA:** The Plaza de Armas, with its trees and pretty fountains, is among the most beautiful central-city squares in all Peru. From the plaza you get a good view of the volcanoes that form Arequipa's background: the famous El Misti and the Chachani and Pichupichu. The cathedral dominates the plaza; rebuilt in the last century, after a fire, its unusual façade is impressive. The interior is 19th-century pseudo-baroque, with an Italian marble altar, detailed wood pulpit, and Belgian organ.

The heart of the plaza, although not immediately on it, is the Jesuit church, La Compañía. The church, begun in 1650 and finished 48 years later, has a front and side entrance, both remarkable for the *sillar* carvings above the doors. The interior of the church shines with quiet dignity because of the unadorned *sillares;* it's further distinguished by the principal and side altars of carved wood covered with gold leaf.

At the upper end of the left-hand aisle are two sacristies. Passing through the first, adorned with paintings, you will enter the second, which must be one of the most beautiful rooms in the entire country. If you can speak some Spanish (or use sign language), ask the caretaker to turn off the lights so that the second sacristy is dim when you go in. Then ask him to turn on the lights and you literally will gasp at the brilliance, freshness, and vividness of the colors. The sacristy, also known as St. Ignatius's chapel, is a polychromatic "high." It should not be missed during your visit to Arequipa. The church is open from 9 to 11:30 AM and from 3 to 5:30 PM, Mondays through Fridays; there is an admission charge.

On the Moral Street side of La Compañía are the church's restored cloisters, which breathe the starkness of the spiritual exercises of Loyola, the founder of the Jesuits, and contrast sharply with the exotic beauty of the Chapel of St. Ignatius in the church. However, the columns and their crowns offer excellent examples of the high artistic level that stone carving had reached in 17th-century Spanish Peru.

Among other churches and cloisters worth the visitor's detailed study are Santo Domingo (at the corner of Calle Santo Domingo and Calle Piérola) and San Francisco (in the small plaza and at the end of the street). Both churches are *sillar,* but what is most attractive is the combined use of red brick and white *sillar* within. The main altars are of sculpted wood covered with thin sheets of beaten silver. San Francisco has spacious cloisters; those of Santo Domingo are more intimate and garden-like. The art museum in San Francisco offers some fine examples of both the 17th-century *limeño* and *cuzqueño* schools of painting; its library has 20,000 volumes. Also you will see two illuminated psalters with pages of lamb's skin. The Chapel of the Sorrowful Virgin in the Church of San Francisco is another of those small chapel jewels one discovers in the dimly lit corners of so many of Peru's churches, especially in the Andes. An interesting ecclesiastical "novelty" is the group of saints and angels surrounding the image of the Virgin. The whole scene is mounted in a gilt Cinderella-like coach, which is drawn through the streets of colonial Arequipa on the Franciscan-inspired *Feast of the Immaculate Conception* on December 8.

The most interesting colonial architectural complex is the Convent of Santa Catalina, just 3 blocks from the main plaza, on the street of the same name (no. 301). It was founded in 1579 as a cloister principally for the daughters of well-to-do families. Except for the daily tolling of its bells, Santa Catalina meant little to the vast majority of the population until 1971, when the government opened a large portion of the ancient cloisters to visitors. The 2 dozen nuns who were left retired to the new convent built for them in one corner of the extensive grounds, leaving the rest for visitors to discover that 400 years of history had bypassed this corner of Arequipa.

The Convent of Santa Catalina is really a small, late-16th-century Peruvian city of mestizo architecture, and is a paradise for photographers. It has houses, streets, cooking areas, cloisters, a church, and the traditional isolated cells. The wealthy young women who entered Santa Catalina in its first 250 years of existence brought their serving maids and cooks with them, as well as large dowries. You can judge the social and financial status of some of the sisters by the size and richness of their quarters, the spiritual values of others by the ascetic cast of their cells. The convent is open from 9 AM to 4 PM daily, and there's a small admission charge. Guided tours in English are available. The other churches are open from 7 AM to noon and from 4 to 7 PM, but check with your hotel first to verify the time.

In a more secular vein, the Casa del Moral, on the street of the same name, is a restored colonial mansion well worth visiting. Its name comes from the ancient "mora" — or blueberry — bush on its patio. The building now houses the Banco Industrial, but is open to visitors.

If you're in Arequipa in mid-August, you'll be able to join in the city's annual birthday celebration, marked by a parade, concerts at Santa Catalina, and topped by a folk dance festival.

The choice of restaurants in Arequipa is far more diverse than anywhere else along this route. *La Chopería* (103 San José, Cerro Colorado; phone: 54-217667) serves German and Peruvian dishes. A great place for lunch outdoors is *Restaurant Campestre El Labrador* (at Km 3.5 of Camino Chilina; phone: 54-228474), where you get a beautiful view of the surrounding mountains. For vegetarian fare, try *La Vie Claire* (at Pasaje la Catedral), and *Chalet la Nonna* (132 Villa Hermosa). *Cerrito de los Alvarez* serves Italian food.

Among many of the *picanterías,* country-type restaurants, which only serve long, leisurely afternoon lunches, are *El Roho* in the suburb of Tiabaya, *La Capitanita* in the suburb of Antiquilla, and *La Cantarilla* (106 Calle Tahuaycani, Sachaca). (Any taxi driver will know where they are.) The *picantería* serves typical *arequipeñan* food, with or without hot sauce, that include *chicharrones* (fried bits of pork or chicken), *ocopa* (boiled potatoes with a piquant peanut sauce), *rocoto relleno* (hot red peppers, boiled and stuffed with ground beef, onions, raisins, and boiled egg), *tostado* (deep-fried corn kernels), and *cuychactado* (fried pressed guinea pig; you might want to remove the head and paws before eating).

Perhaps because of the usually cold nights (except in the summer) or because of the tradition of parties and dances at home or at the *Club de Arequipa,* nightlife in Arequipa hardly swings. However, the best discotheque in town is the *Piscis Club,* in the second patio of the "Claustros de La Compañía" — a series of patios beside the La Compañía church (no phone). In the third patio of the same complex is the *peña, Los Montaneros,* where highland music and dance are performed on Friday and Saturday nights.

If you like sweets, buy some chocolates at *La Ibérica* (on the corner of Moral and Jerusalén). Among the better artisans' shops are *Arte Perú* (at Los Claustros de La Compañía — the Jesuit Cloisters); *Artesanías del Perú,* the government-managed organization that sells directly for the artisans (120 General Morán); *Casa Sechi* (111 Calle Mercaderes); and *Inti* (202 Calle Zela, across from the small square beside the Church of San Francisco). Two other artisan shops are in the passageway behind the cathedral, *Quero Arte Popular* at 199 and *Artesanías* at 119. The *Galerías Colonial* (in the second block of Calle San Juan de Dios) has a number of small shops specializing in particular handicraft products, like leather goods, for which Arequipa is famous. *Alpaca 111* (115 Jerusalén; phone: 54-212347) sells fine fabrics, yarn, sweaters, scarves, and furs.

The best way to see the old suburbs of Arequipa is to take a taxi. Arrange this through your hotel — for route, hours, and price. One route takes you through Yanahuara on to Cayma and then to Yura, where there is the pleasant *Hotel de Turistas* on Calle Principal (phone: 54-109) and thermal baths. Just over a mile (1.6 km) outside the city, Yanahuara and Cayma have impressive colonial churches, built with the ubiquitous *sillar* and with graciously sculpted portals. The plaza in Yanahuara is singularly beautiful and offers a good view of the city. Another route takes you out to Tingo and Tiabaya, famous for their *picanterías,* which specialize in delicacies such as *chicharrones, cuychactado,* boiled corn, and lima beans served with cheese, as well as beer and *chicha.* Also see Sabandía, which is close to the city and has a lovely restored flour mill, near pre-Inca farming terraces which still are being used.

Bird watchers will find a treasure trove at the lagoons at Mejía, on the coast. It's a 90-minute drive from Arequipa and well worth the time since hundreds of species of birds, many very unusual, can be sighted here.

**COLCA CANYON:** Four hours overland from Arequipa, this rediscovered treasure is reportedly twice as deep as the Grand Canyon. When the railroad came through this region more than a century ago, the cargo trail in and around the canyon was forgotten — leaving the Indian villages on that route isolated and frozen in time. Visitors can pass through these unspoiled communities, where traditions remain from the era of the Spanish colonizers. Be sure to note the pre-Inca farming terraces on the sides of the

Colca valley, and watch the powerful condors that soar above the canyon from Cruz del Cóndor (Condor Cross). The whole area now is a condor sanctuary.

It is preferable to arrange this trip through a travel agency, and allow at least 2 or 3 days for the visit. The best way to see part of the canyon is by mule or horseback, passing through areas where there are caves with prehistoric paintings and herds of vicuña. You can stay overnight in the valley at the government-run *Turistas* hotel. To arrange trips, contact *Lima Tours* (120 Santa Catalina in Arequipa; phone: 54-242293); *Receptour* (118 General Moran; phone: 54-215752); or *Transcontinental Arequipa* (213 Santa Catalina; phone: 54-213843).

Kayakers can tackle the Colca River that careens through the canyon, although it is an adventure only for the bravest. In 1981, a Polish expedition thoroughly documented the journey, naming sections of the canyon after Polish places and personalities (e.g., Pope John Paul II). A 1987 expedition by Italians on the river was nearly thwarted when an earthquake and its aftershocks churned up the Colca waters. These whitewater experts discovered the abandoned raft of earlier adventurers who had lost their lives on the river. The Italians, accompanied by cinematographers, returned in 1990 to film an adventure/romance movie set in Peru. The canyon also has slowly begun to attract cyclists. Be forewarned that in winter (June through August), dawn temperatures drop below freezing, but the summer months (January through March) are warmer.

For travelers who do not have enough time to make the extraordinary Colca trek, *AeroCondor* offers flights over the canyon. For information, contact the airline's Lima office (phone: 14-329050).

To continue on to Lake Titicaca, travelers must return to Arequipa.

**En Route from Arequipa** – This is a journey for the adventurous, since airline tickets sometimes are hard to get and none of the other three transportation options — car, bus, or train — is perfect. Driving this 233-mile (373-km) stretch is not advised; the roadways are in generally poor shape and, during the rainy season (December through April), sometimes impassable. Another alternative is suffering on one of the buses between Arequipa and Puno. The trip is shorter than that by train, but much less comfortable. Never book a trip on *Morales Moralitos;* even Peruvians curse the service on this bus line, which frequently leaves passengers stranded and oversells tickets, then refuses to pay refunds.

That leaves the train, the preferred mode of transportation on this route after flying. Make sure to buy tickets for first class coaches; do so a day ahead of schedule, and be at the station to claim your seat an hour before the train leaves. This is a long journey — about 10 hours. The heating system in this train never quite works properly, and its food service leaves much to be desired. Approach the trip with an adventurer's outlook, keeping in mind that this is not a tourist service; rather, it is the way Peruvians get themselves and their bundles across the mountains. Pack your own food and water, and take along jackets or ponchos to keep warm as you cross the Andes. The night train leaves at 10 PM, and arrives at Juliaca just before 6 AM; you might opt for a sleeping car. From Juliaca, you take another train direct to Cuzco, or stay on this one and continue to Puno and Lake Titicaca. There's also a more comfortable day train that leaves Arequipa three times a week at about 7:30 AM and arrives in Puno at about 5 PM. Keep an eye on your belongings; theft on these trains is not uncommon. *AeroPerú, Faucett,* and *Americana* have flights from Lima (via Arequipa) or from Cuzco to Juliaca; it's a 40-minute shuttle bus ride from the airport into Puno.

**JULIACA:** The commercial and transportation center of the southern Peruvian Andes, this city of 250,000 has long been an important crossroads. At one time, it even had its own imperial Inca residence. It has since shed its pre-Inca heritage, its Inca vestiges and, finally, its colonial character. The Juliaca of today is a bare, rather ugly, Andean market town that belies its importance as a wealthy commercial center. Market days are Sundays and Mondays here, but vendors are always outside the train station. Among the best offerings are woolen goods and llama ponchos.

Aside from the market, there is not much reason to stop here, unless you need medical attention — Juliaca has an excellent medical center, La Clinica Adventista de Juliaca, located at Calle Loreto. If you do end up spending time in the town, you might wander over to the *Emperador,* a restaurant on the plaza. Be wary of thieves and pickpockets during your stay in town. From here, it is 28½ miles (46 km) to Puno, the highest town on the route.

**PUNO:** Confronted by an altitude of 12,500 feet above sea level, it is wise to avoid physical exertion for a while — rest and eat lightly — in this city of 100,000. The local residents also believe that *maté de coca* — tea brewed from coca leaves — helps alleviate the effects of altitude sickness. Eventually, climb slowly up Cerro Huajsapata, the hill 3 blocks from the main square, for a fine view of the city and Lake Titicaca.

Puno itself is not noteworthy architecturally, and what there is to be viewed can be seen in 1 day. On the Plaza de Armas is the cathedral, which dates from 1757. It is late-colonial baroque in style, and has a lovely marble altar with a silver-plated frontal; it is open daily from 9 AM to noon and from 3 to 5 PM. The name in the doorway attests that Simón de Asto designed the building, making this cathedral one of the few for which the name of the architect has been preserved through the years. Although mistreated by time and weather, its carved-stone façade remains impressive.

Next to the cathedral is the Balcón del Conde de Lemos (Balcony of Count Lemos) on the old house where this Spanish aristocrat allegedly stayed after arriving in Puno in 1668 and proclaiming the Spanish founding of this city. While on the Plaza de Armas, take a look into the museums there. All are under the same roof and they are closed Sundays. The *Museo Municipal* has some pre-Inca pottery and has been combined with the private collection of pre-Columbian ceramics and other artifacts of the late Carlos Dreyer, a Puno resident. Open Tuesdays through Saturdays from 8 AM to 12:30 PM and 2 to 5:30 PM.

Finding independent restaurants in Puno is a problem. The cleanest choices for decent food are the restaurants in the hotels (see *Best en Route*). If, however, you want to eat outside your hotel in spite of the cold, the best food at low prices is found at the *Café Internacional* and *Ito's,* both on the square. Other choices are *El Lago* (third block of Jirón Puno) and *Samary* (on Jirón Deustua). You might also try *Kimmamo* (507 Arequipa) for excellent apple pie and other pastries, or *Chiomi* (near the Plaza de Armas) for good cake and coffee.

As for shopping, you might well be captivated by the marvelous representations of the masks used in some of this region's famous folk dances. Reproduced on a smaller scale, there is a good selection of these and other handicrafts at the *Sociedad de Artesanos* (Calle Arequipa in front of the *Municipal Theater*). Other places to pick up similar items are the *Artesanías Puno-Corpuno* (544 Calle Lima); *Artesanías La Sirena* (576 Jirón Deustua); *Artesanías Folklóricas de Perú Andino* (44 Jirón Lambayeque); and *Artesanías Puno* (on Teodoro Valcarcel). Open-air handicrafts markets are found daily along the railroad tracks on Cahuide and by the post office on Ugarte. Also worth a visit is the *Mercado Cutra* (Market of Bribes; Av. El Sol), where contraband items smuggled in from Chile, Bolivia, and Brazil can be found. Chilean wine, fine whisky, electronics goods, and inexpensive film and batteries are good buys. Unlike other black markets in Peru, this one is safe from pickpockets and purse snatchers — be sure to take along your camera. More information is available from the tourism office (314 Arequipa; phone: 5435-3804).

Puno's fame rests on its cultural traditions. It has been rightly named by one of Peru's best modern writers, José María Arguedas, the symbolic capital of Latin American dance. The many Puno folk dances (in this context Puno refers to the whole department) find their inspiration in the daily life of fishing, farming, hunting, and sheep herding. The dances also give the Aymara (the largest ethnic group in the Titicaca region) an opportunity to reaffirm this distinctive tradition.

The principal fiesta is that of the Virgin of Candelaria, which begins on February 2 and lasts an entire week. The *Diablada* (the devil's dance) is performed with giant masks and elaborate costumes and is the catalyst of a whole series of dances; the *pandilla,* the Puno version of the lively coastal *marinera;* the *kallahuaya,* the medicine men's dance; and many others. *Carnaval* season offers the next big folkloric explosion of dancing, performed with such exuberance in the streets and plazas that some think the color and high spirits equal those in Rio de Janeiro. With much gusto, this city also celebrates *November 4* — the date of its founding by the Spanish. The holiday usually is marked by yet another burst of colorful dancing, the reenactment of Indian legends, and dance competitions. Each month, except February and April, in some part of the department there is at least one fiesta featuring one or more of the special costumed dances, which number at least 300. The most popular reason for visiting Puno, however, is to see legendary Lake Titicaca — the world's highest navigable body of water and the lake at which the Inca empire reportedly began.

Four particularly interesting trips outside the city are available: the floating islands of the Uro on Lake Titicaca; the burial towers at Sillustani; the churches of Juli and Pomata; and Taquile Island, famous for its textiles. You can combine the first two in a day, with a morning trip to the islands, and an afternoon trip to the towers. Actually, Puno is the most important Peruvian town on Lake Titicaca, at 12,506 feet above sea level. This lake was especially precious to the Inca, whose first ancestors, Manco Capác and his sister-consort, Mama Ocllo, supposedly were created by Father Sun on the Isla del Sol where Inca ruins are still being found.

At the mouth of the Río Huili (which leads into Lake Titicaca) are the 15 reed islands of the Uro. The floating islands house a tribe of some 600 Uro Indians, a very old lake civilization famous for its use of the indigenous totora reeds in building huts, boats, and rafts. Each island contains a small, cone-shaped reed hut and a small plot for potatoes and other tubers, which, along with fish, make up the daily diet. The children here are quite bright (some have picked up several foreign languages). Some experts theorize that this unusual intelligence comes from their high phosphorus diet — important for brain development. The Uro rarely leave their islands, visiting the mainland only on religious occasions. Legend has it that their blood is black, thereby enabling them to tolerate the bitter-cold nights on the lakes and preventing them from drowning. They have little contact with others except for the Adventist missionaries, who provide medical care, and the tourists who venture out to see them to purchase some small replicas of their sailing boats or weavings. If you visit, be prepared for an onslaught of young children selling miniature *balsas* (boats) and handmade postcards and others who demand tips for having their pictures taken. On these impoverished islands, tourism is an important source of income. Take pens, pencils, and small notebooks to give the children — they are more useful and appreciated than money. Fruit also is welcome. The women here sell embroidered tapestries.

The most important and interesting island for visitors is Taquile — the "Island of Weavers." The tourism jump here began when the islanders took control of promoting their culture. Taquile residents run the boat service to the island, open their homes to overnight guests (there are no hotels), and prepare meals for tourists. On Taquile, visitors can purchase textiles from the island's weaving cooperative and visit their two small museums which display antique weavings and traditional costumes. The islanders on neighboring Amantani are expert basket weavers and many also open their homes to overnight guests. Amantani craftspeople sell impressive creations made with polished stones. If you decide to spend the night on either island, take a sleeping bag or plenty of blankets. The temperature plunges after sunset.

You also might want to stop at the island of Esteves, connected to the mainland by a bridge and home to the *Isla Esteves* luxury resort hotel (see *Best en Route*).

Seventeen miles (28 km) north of Puno on Lake Umago, the burial tombs of Sillustani, called *chulpas,* were built probably before the Inca conquests of the Colla tribes. Either round or square, they are of adobe or stone and sometimes a combination of both. One of these mausoleum towers is 40 feet high. When the underground sections of the towers were filled with the cadavers and all the paraphernalia they needed for the next world (including wives and servants as well as food, drink, and clothing), they were packed with rocks and closed. This is one of the biggest necropolises in the Americas and archaeologists still are unsure of the age of these funereal monuments.

**En Route from Puno** – Since there are no car rental services available in Puno, we recommend that you arrange a tour to Juli and Pomata through a local tourist agency (particularly as Juli has no tourist services, not even a restaurant). This is a "must" trip. The road, dusty and curvy, follows the shoreline of Lake Titicaca, and the background of the magnificent snow-capped Andes off in the direction of Bolivia offer some wonderful scenery. In Ancora are the fine colonial Church of San Pedro and more tombs. Farther on, in the town of Ilave, is the handsome façade of the local church. But the high point is Juli, 51 miles (82 km) south of Puno, where there are five magnificent churches: San Juan, originally built by the Dominicans at the end of the 16th century and later remodeled by the Jesuits, and four Jesuit churches. The interior of one of the latter, San Pedro, is a marvel of gold, silver, and bronze, where a 400-voice Indian choir once sang. These churches, as well as the one at Pomata, 25 miles (40 km) beyond Juli, are superb examples of the blending of Spanish and Indian genius for art and architecture. The sculptured arches and portals with their wealth of detail of animals, birds, and fruit are exotically exuberant. Héctor Velarde, one of the greatest defenders of colonial architecture in Peru, has categorized the Pomata church as one of the finest examples of Indian themes found in a Christian place of worship. The doorway is an interweaving of figures not unlike those found in Inca temples, with heads of Indian rulers hidden among the sculpted fruits and flowers. Hydrofoils to Bolivia leave from Juli.

Twenty-five miles (40 km) beyond Pomata one reaches Desaguadero (unquestionably one of the ugliest border towns on the continent) and the Bolivian border. From here, it is possible to cross into the lovely lakeside resort of Copacabana to take a launch ride out to the Isla del Sol with its temple, fortress, and Inca spring, and to drive to the Tiahuanaco ruins in Bolivia. To continue on to Cuzco, the best bet is to fly or take the train. The latter, an 11- to 12-hour trip, is a bit of an ordeal, but the opportunity it provides to see some dramatic Andean scenery makes it worth the effort. The train leaves at 7:25 AM daily except Sundays, when there is no service. The route affords vistas of the rich, rugged hillsides populated with alpacas and llamas, and the views of the area's people are no less fascinating — glimpses of women in their *polleras* (numerous skirts one on top of another) — as they cook or wash clothes outdoors.

Plan to buy your ticket through a travel agency or at the station a day in advance. Book the "buffet" or "tourist" car, both considered first class and both guaranteeing you a reserved seat. It is best to carry all your luggage with you rather than to check it (the tourist car has much larger luggage racks), and keep your eyes on your belongings during the trip; theft is not unknown. Be especially alert and protective of your belongings in the train stations. You can buy a hot lunch prepared aboard the train for about $5; soft drinks, beer, mineral water, and snacks also are sold. It's a long day, though, so carry some food with you. Fruit, cookies or crackers, chocolate bars, and bottled water are good in a pinch; bring some tissues and toilet paper, too.

**PUCARÁ:** The train stops in Pucará, famous for its small, ceramic figurines of bulls adorned with flowers. In colonial days, the town was an important center for both pottery and cattle, and the bulls were used in ceremonies linked to the fertility of the cattle herd. In those days, authentic bull figurines came in only two colors: the bodies a light pink, the horns brown. Over the years, however, artisans have altered the pigmentation because brilliant tones were more attractive to tourists. If you hop off the train to bargain for a Pucará bull, you might be surprised to be told that they are actually made 6 miles (10 km) down the road, in the town of Santiago de Pupuja.

Pucará is also known for its archaeological site: the stone-and-adobe remains of what was a great fortress and temple, probably dating from the 2nd century. What is most physically impressive about this village is the tall, red sandstone monolith that rises behind the town.

When the train finally pulls into the Urcos station in Cuzco, children will be just outside the cars selling fresh-from-the-oven *chuta* bread. Buy a loaf — it is mouthwateringly good.

If you do not head to Cuzco, you may opt for a trip from Puno to La Paz, Bolivia.

**En Route from Puno to Bolivia** – About 80% of the visitors to La Paz, Bolivia, travel from Cuzco to Puno, and then from Puno by boat and/or by bus to Bolivia. Two La Paz–based travel companies offer Peru–Bolivia transportation with a lake crossing: *Transturin, Ltda.,* and *Crillón Tours* both feature a lunch in lovely Copacabana (Bolivia) and a stop at the Isla del Sol (Island of the Sun). *Transturin* takes passengers from Puno to Copacabana by bus, and from Copacabana to Huatajata by catamaran motor cruisers. Passengers continue on to La Paz by bus. *Transturin* has a La Paz office (1321 Camacho; phone: 2-328560 or 2-363654); another in Puno (149 Jirón Tacna; phone: 5435-352771); and one in Cuzco (109 Portal de Panes; phone: 84-222332). *Crillón Tours,* with over 30 years in the business, starts out in Puno and transports passengers by bus to Juli. Passengers take the hydrofoils that cross via Copacabana to Huatajata, then continue on to La Paz by bus. In La Paz, *Crillón* has a convenient office (1223 Camacho; phone: 2-374566/7). In the US, contact its Miami representative either by calling 305-358-5353 or sending a fax to 305-372-0054. You also can take the bus from Puno (via Copacabana) to La Paz, which is scheduled to depart twice daily, mornings and afternoons, though the afternoon run may be canceled if there is an insufficient number of passengers. The steamship *Mariscal Santa Cruz* goes from Puno to Guaqui. Reservation and schedule information is available in Lima at the *Velha* office (2575 Av. Arequipa; phone: 14-228350).

## BEST EN ROUTE

Not being on a heavily traveled route, the hotels and restaurants between Arequipa and Juliaca, in general, aren't particularly special, and there really aren't any worth recommending between Juliaca and Cuzco (those that do exist aren't particularly clean). It is possible, however, to find accommodations in varying price ranges that will be more than just places to spend the night. Arequipa has its share of good places to stay and, while hotels in Juliaca are passable, it's better to wait until you're in Puno. Better yet, pack a lunch and leave Juliaca in the morning so that you can reach Cuzco by evening. Most of the hotels have hot water (although even the best can surprise you with none when you want it), but some will not have central heating. Rates for a room for 1 night for a double room in hotels listed as expensive will run $40 and higher; moderate means $20 to $40; and a classification of inexpensive indicates rates under $20. Advance reservations are not absolutely essential unless you're arriving during festival times.

## AREQUIPA

*El Portal* – A modern, 64-room hotel on the Plaza de Armas, it has a good bar and restaurant; some rooms have balconies with views. 116 Portal de Flores (phone: 54-215530; in Lima, 14-406447). Expensive.

*Turistas Arequipa* – This lovely, large property is just outside the city in the Selva Negra neighborhood, but within comfortable walking distance. It has an outdoor swimming pool, colonial façade, and bar. Plaza Bolívar (phone: 54-215110; *Entur-Perú* in Lima, 14-721928; in the US, 800-275-3123). Expensive.

*El Conquistador* – Not far from the Plaza de Armas, the 28 rooms at this colonial-style *hostal* have private baths and phones. There also is a cafeteria. 409 Mercaderes (phone: 54-218987). Moderate.

*Crismar* – Centrally located, with clean rooms and good service. 107 Calle Moral (phone: 54-215290). Moderate.

*Posada de Puente* – Cozy, downtown hostelry with 22 rooms. 101 Av. Bolognesi (phone: 54-217444). Moderate.

## COLCA CANYON

*Turistas de Colca* – Very pleasant hotel in the Colca Valley, good for those who want to enjoy the natural wonders of the valley and canyon. Reservations must be made in Lima through *EnturPerú* (phone: 14-721928) or in the US (phone: 800-275-3123). Expensive.

*Albergue de Achoma* – Open April to November only, this spot in the valley offers heat, hot water, and electricity. Meals can be arranged. Staff can be unfriendly. Make reservations in Arequipa at 207 Piérola; in Lima at 125 Samuel Velarde in San Isidro (no phone). Inexpensive.

*Turistas de Yura* – Basic and low-budget, with baths and meals. There are hot mineral springs in this town 18 miles (29 km) from Arequipa. Calle Principal in Yura (phone: Yura 109; in Lima through *EnturPerú*, 14-721928; in the US, 800-275-3123). Inexpensive.

## JULIACA

*Turistas* – A clean and comfortable small hotel, with a restaurant and good bar service. 335 Av. Manuel Prado (phone: Juliaca 435; *EnturPerú* in Lima, 14-721928; in the US, 800-275-3123). Expensive to moderate.

## PUNO

*Isla Esteves* – For anyone looking for more than the most basic of accommodations, this is the only place to stay in Puno. Situated on an island just off the shore (connected by a causeway), this 126-room hotel has a design as stark and dramatic as its locale, with soaring roof lines and whitewashed walls, decorated with the hotel's collection of *Diablada* masks from around the province. Unfortunately, most guests arrive late and depart early, leaving little time to enjoy the sweeping lobby, discotheque, shops, and more. Dinners here are tasty but expensive by Peruvian standards (phone: 5435-724; *EnturPerú* in Lima, 14-721928; in the US, 800-275-3123). Expensive.

*Don Miguel* – The place is passable for a night or two. The 20 average rooms have private baths, but whether you get hot water is questionable. The restaurant isn't bad, though. 545 Av. La Torre (phone: 5435-371). Moderate to inexpensive.

*Sillustani* – This spot has hot water, private baths, and fairly good food in the restaurant. 195 Jr. Lambayeque (phone: Puno 5435-792; in Lima, 14-276720). Moderate to inexpensive.

# Cuzco and the Inca Ruins

The year was 1479, and Indians from as far as the arid Pacific coast, from the magnificent waters of Lake Titicaca, from the distant kingdom of Quito, and from the steamy jungles of the lower eastern slopes were arriving at the brink of the Cuzco hills and throwing themselves on their knees as they contemplated the gold and silver spectacle below them. Gazing down at the narrow valley, they cried out their pounding faith and burning reverence: "Cuzco, Oh Great City, We Salute You!" For that was the year the empire of the Inca was reaching its apex under the masterly rule of Cápac Inca Túpac Yupanqui, which translates to "The One and Only Child of the Divine God of the Sun." In 1445 his father, Pachacútec, had begun massive agrarian reform and the great expansion of the small Inca principality of Cuzco, spreading eastward to encompass all of Bolivia and the northern provinces of Argentina. It was an almost incredible military feat, one considered to be on a par with the conquests of Alexander the Great, the Romans, and Napoleon.

However, Inca domination over indigenous Indian groups throughout that area was relatively brief and not strong enough to counter the 1532 "invasion" of Francisco Pizarro. With his small band, Pizarro destroyed the mightiest empire ever built in the Western Hemisphere.

The following year, the Spaniards entered Cuzco itself; within 30 years, the city no longer existed — apart from some walls of the various palaces and temples and the great fortress of Sacsayhuamán — once the jewel of the City of the Sun. From 1534, Inca Cuzco was replaced by Spanish mansions and squares and churches. However, the Spaniards never quite replaced the Inca spirit of the city; even to this day, the Quechua language, the lingua franca of the Inca empire, is as prevalent as Spanish in Cuzco's streets.

To set the record straight, the Spanish under Pizarro probably could not have captured this mighty empire as easily as they did had it not been for the fratricidal civil war between the two sons of Huayna Cápac: Huáscar, the legitimate heir, and Atahualpa, the pretender (at least to Quito and the northern territories of Tahuantinsuyo, or the Kingdom of the Four Quarters, as the Inca empire was called). The Spanish arrived at the moment when Atahualpa not only had destroyed the armies of Huáscar but also had undermined the governing principle of the Inca empire — namely, that the Inca emperor was the child of the sun and, therefore, divinely appointed to his authoritarian role as the one and only ruler of these great provinces. Once Huáscar, the "son of the sun," was captured and killed by Atahualpa, the underlying basis of all Inca rule was destroyed. The Sun God either no longer had the power to protect his divine child or he had withdrawn his supernatural support. The empire began to collapse from within, a process that began even before the Spanish arrived.

The conquerors' primary motive was the search for the great stores of gold throughout the empire. They had no interest in Inca culture and almost casually destroyed the great palaces and temples. The destructive process was accelerated when the conquerors fell to disputing among themselves over the distribution of lands and treasures, quarrels that eventually erupted into full-scale war between the followers of Pizarro and those of Diego de Almagro in 1538.

The chaos that prevailed in and around Cuzco and throughout the empire in these turbulent years included the demolition of the great aqueducts, irrigation canals, and roadways and of the planned economy whereby the agricultural system and the interchange of all kinds of merchandise adequately served the needs of all the citizens of the empire. Many of the marvelous terraces were torn down by the Spaniards, so that great areas of arable lands were lost. Irrigation was abandoned, and the storehouses of food and clothing were burned. The result: death through both war and starvation.

This capsule view of the events that occurred in this historic area 500 years ago may not prepare you for the Cuzco of the late 20th century. A city of 225,000 people, Cuzco is a blend of Indian, Spanish, and mestizo, a charming city 11,000 feet above sea level. What is encountered today are subtle reminders of its 1,000-year-old history at the turn of almost every corner. Sit on a bench in the Plaza de Armas, close your eyes, and you can be carried back to when this square was called Huacaypata and was bounded on all sides by the sumptuous palaces of the dead and mummified Inca and the imperial residences of the living Inca. If you listen carefully, you will hear the muffled drums and the mournful wails of the great days of penance, when all foreigners were forced outside the city while the Inca emperor and his people begged for forgiveness and blessings from the Creator God Viracocha and from Inti, the Sun God. Or your eyes will be caught by the rich and dazzling colors worn by members of the court and by the glitter of shields, spears, and images, as the *Feast of Inti Raymi* (June 24), the day of the return of the Sun to his people in Cuzco, is celebrated with joyful songs, animated dancing, and drinking. Off in a far corner you see the somber, finely cut walls of the House of the Chosen Women, where some 3,000 women and girls served their divine spouse, the Sun, or waited to be called by their earthly spouse, the divine Inca. On a more gruesome note, another part of this plaza's memory must include the Spaniards' drawing and quartering of rebellious Túpac Amaru, said to be one of the last Inca descendents, as he tried to flee the city with his pregnant wife.

The reveries of yesterday are dissolved by the shouts of the plaza's ice cream peddlers or shoeshine boys, and you open your eyes to the magnificent sight of the cathedral. The House of the Chosen Women has become the Monastery of Santa Catalina, while the palaces have been replaced by Spanish mansions whose first floors are occupied by small stores and restaurants. The hoofbeats of the conquerors' horses no longer ring against the square's cobblestones; the clashing swords and thundering blunderbusses have been silent for 4 centuries.

Despite its beauty and brilliant history, Cuzco today suggests a poverty that rages through Peru. Its population grows daily with the arrival of more and more disillusioned Indian peasants who can no longer survive on the land. The city also has a sizable floating population of foreigners and young Peruvians from the coast who come for a few months — or even years — to soak up the "spiritual" atmosphere of Cuzco, Machu Picchu, and Urubamba.

Drugs may play a part in attracting some of these semipermanent residents. Innocuous coca tea, legal in Peru, is offered to visitors as an effective aid in acclimating to the altitude, and most Indians in the Andes chew coca leaves. However, the use of cocaine — derived from coca — is illegal and the penalties extremely stiff, especially for foreigners who are sometimes accused (rightly or not) of smuggling (see *Drinking and Drugs*, GETTING READY TO GO).

If Cuzco alone is your destination, it can be reached by road from Lima via the Central Highway to Huancayo, although it goes through Ayacucho, where terrorist activity is centered and is not a recommended route. The best way to reach Cuzco is by plane — *AeroPerú, Faucett, Americana,* and *Andrea* have 50-minute flights from Lima.

Traditionally, tourists dedicate 2 days and 2 nights to Cuzco, first touring the interior city and later exploring the Inca ruins at the city's outskirts. One day is devoted fully to visiting Machu Picchu — by a 3-hour train ride, either alone or with a tour group. At the ruins there is a small government-run *Turistas* hotel, which offers its guests a chance to have Machu Picchu to themselves from 2 PM, when the train to Cuzco departs, until 9:30 AM, when the next train arrives, and is well worth the extra time. Reservations are a must and can be made in Lima through *EnturPerú* (phone: 14-721928) or any local travel agency. In Aguas Calientes, the small town just half a mile from the base of the ruins, *EnturPerú* runs a clean and inexpensive youth hostel (open to all ages).

Like other cities in Peru, hotels in Cuzco are a mixed bag — some excellent, most basic, and some bathless. The attraction of the area is in its pre-Columbian and colonial artifacts and architecture; a tourist's comfort is secondary. To get a feel for the area before you visit, you might look at any of a number of books, including *The Ancient Civilizations of Perú,* by J. Alden Mason (Plata Publishing Ltd., Switzerland); *Perú under the Incas,* by C. A. Blurland (Putnam's); *Lords of Cuzco,* by Burr Cartwright Brundage (University of Oklahoma Press); *The Conquest of the Incas,* by John Hemming (Macmillan); *The Royal Road of the Inca,* by Victor W. Von Hagen (Gordon and Cremonesi, London); and *The Incas of Pedro de Cieza de León,* translated by Harriet de Onis (University of Oklahoma Press). Also highly recommended is *Exploring Cuzco,* by Peter Frost (available in bookstores in Lima and Cuzco). An excellent book on walking tours through Cuzco was published by William G. Evans (Editorial Universitario Lima); copies are still available in some of the mustier Cuzco bookshops. In addition, you might want to get a copy of *The Lost City of the Incas,* by Hiram Bingham (Greenwood Press), which details his discovery of Machu Picchu. A wide selection of guides and other material in English and Spanish is on sale at the *Peruvian Times* office in Lima (156 Pasaje los Piños, Floor B, Miraflores; phone: 14-472552). *Documental del Perú* (Cuzco volume) is a good guide, with maps, photographs, and historical information. *Documental* is a 25-volume series found in most Peruvian bookstores; it is available only in Spanish.

Because the center of Cuzco, where all the main tourist attractions are located, is not very big, it is easy to get around on foot — that is, if climbing up and down hills does not bother you at such a high altitude. We strongly suggest that you spend a few hours walking around the town at a leisurely pace, soaking in Cuzco's very special atmosphere. Travel with a friend to the central market area, near the station for the trains to Machu Picchu. Be alert, as there are plenty of pickpockets about, awaiting the unwary solitary tourist. This is also true of the train station itself here, and of the other one for Puno departures. In Cuzco, plenty of self-taught guides will happily show you around and help you to spend more money on handicrafts than the goods merit. If you don't know enough Spanish to make your purchases, you are better off sticking to the well-known artisan shops in the center of the city.

On-the-spot tourist information can be had from the national tourism office on the Plaza de Armas (115 Portal Belén; phone: 84-237364). In addition, many travel agencies in Cuzco can provide information and make arrangements, although ideally these should be made from Lima before your arrival in Cuzco.

One of the best local tour operators is *Milla Turismo* (673 Av. Prado, PO Box 348, Cuzco; phone: 84-231710 or 84-222566). Owner Carlos Milla, a *cuzqueño* by birth, not only runs an efficient business but is very much in tune with the grandeur and mysticism of the Inca civilization. He also speaks fluent English. *Lima Tours* (567 Av. Sol; phone: 84-223791) also is recommended.

**CUZCO:** Start your tour of the city at the Plaza de Armas, with the cathedral and its accompanying churches of El Triunfo and the Holy Family. On the site of Viracocha's Palace, the cathedral is considered by many to be the Western Hemisphere's finest mix of the Spanish Renaissance style and Indian stonemasons' skills. The cathedral took almost 100 years to build, and many of its stones were quarried at Sacsayhuamán, the immense Inca fortress overlooking the Sacred City. Many sculptures and paintings are within the building; of particular interest is the flame-blackened image of Christ Crucified, revered by the *cuzqueños* under the title *Lord of the Earthquakes*. The famous María Angola bell in the north tower, cast in 1659 from a mixture of gold, silver, and bronze, weighs over a ton and is the largest bell in South America: Its deep, melodic tone can be heard up to 25 miles away. The cathedral is home to the Gran Custodia, a priceless altarpiece made of gold and encrusted with more than 1,000 precious gems. It also has one of the world's most unusual renderings of the Last Supper. Look carefully and you'll see Christ dining on guinea pig, hot peppers, and Andean cheese. Within the painting is a picture of the crucifixion, which made the man who had commissioned it so angry that he refused to pay the artist. In revenge, the painter put the man's face on the figure of Judas. The church is open to the public from 6 AM to noon and from 3 to 6:30 PM daily.

To the right of the cathedral is El Triunfo, the first church built by the Spanish in Cuzco; the present building dates from 1733. Originally the church (its name means "The Triumph") commemorated the 1536 victory of the Spanish soldiers over the troops of Manco II, whose men attacked the storage tower where the Spaniards were hiding out, throwing red hot rocks at the thatch-roofed building. The desperate conquistadores, however, called upon the help of the Virgin Mary, and especially their patron of Spain, St. James the Apostle, both of whom are said to have appeared to save them, preventing the roof from blazing up and frightening the Indian soldiers. El Triunfo was built on the site.

The Church of the Holy Family, on the other side of the cathedral, dates back only to 1733. Looking up the hill beside the church, you will see an imposing Spanish mansion, the Palacio del Almirante (Palace of the Admiral; at the corner of Ataúd and Tucumán). Built in the early 1600s, the house was badly damaged in the 1950 earthquake but has since been restored. Following Tucumán past the palace, which houses the *Museo Histórico Regional* (Regional Historical Museum) with its paintings and antiques, you reach the Plaza de las Nazarenas. On the left, across the square, is the House of the Serpents, so called because of the seven snakes carved on the wall; they supposedly protected the house and its occupants from evil. The house is open from 9 AM to noon and from 3 to 6 PM daily. On the same plaza is the restored House of Jerónimo Cabrera (open Tuesdays through Saturdays from 10 AM to noon and 3 to 6 PM). Visitors can view its collection of colonial art and temporary exhibits as well as Inca ceramics, textiles, and ceremonial artifacts.

Turn right on the Calle Palacio leading off the plaza and walk downhill 1 block to the *Museo de Arte Religioso* (Museum of Religious Art; at the corner of Hatunrumiyoc and Herejes), originally the site of the Palace of Inca Roca, the sixth Inca. The museum is a lovely example of the finest in Peruvian architecture and merits close observation: the carved doors and balconies, the Moorish patio and fountain, the tiles throughout the building. In addition, there is a fine collection of paintings belonging to the so-called Cuzco school that flourished from the 16th through the 18th centuries. The paintings offer a fine example of the *mestizaje* (crossbreeding) in art; that is, Catholic religious scenes peopled by saints with Indian faces. The museum is open Tuesdays through Saturdays from 9:30 AM to 12:30 PM and 3 to 5:30 PM; Sundays from 3 to 5:30 PM.

Outside the principal door of the museum, to the right and a few paces up, you will discover embedded in the foundation wall the magnificent Twelve-Angled Stone, a fabulous example of the best in Inca stonecutting. The imperial stonemasons had mastered the art of fitting irregular stones so perfectly that no mortar was needed.

The Church of San Blas (2 blocks down Hatunrumiyoc from the *Museo de Arte Religioso*) is home to an awesomely ornate pulpit, carved from a single block of wood in the 18th century. Although its sculptor is unknown, some historians attribute it to Juan Tomás Tuirutupa, an Indian leper. The church is open from 9 AM to noon and 3 to 5 PM daily except Sundays. In this section of the city you will discover the splendid little studios used today by Cuzco artists.

Returning to the Plaza de Armas you will find the Jesuit church, La Compañía, considered by many to be the most beautiful church in Cuzco. If not the most beautiful, it is certainly the most representative of Cuzco baroque architecture. Situated on the site where the palace of Huayna Cápac stood in Inca times, the church took almost 100 years to complete because of its intricate interior; gold leaf covers the finely carved wood of the altars and the balconies. On the other side of this narrow street (once called the Street of the Sun, because it led from Cuzco's main plaza to its most sacred structure, Koricancha, the Temple of the Sun) is the wall of what was the House of the Chosen Women. The church is open daily from 9 AM to noon and 3 to 5 PM daily except Sundays.

Follow Loreto 2 blocks to Koricancha, upon whose Inca foundation now stands the Santo Domingo church. Koricancha means "Enclosure of Gold" and included not only the Temple of the Sun, but also that of the Moon Mother, Rainbow, God of Thunder, Lightning, Rain, and the Morning Star. There were smaller houses or chapels for the lesser gods, including those of the captured peoples of the empire.

The Enclosure of Gold must have been the most impressive group of buildings in the holy city of Cuzco. Walls were sheeted with gold; a garden of flowers and animals was cast in silver and gold, as was the area where llamas were kept to be sacrificed. You can get some idea of the structural plan of Koricancha by the restorations taking place within the cloisters of Santo Domingo. It's open from 9 AM to noon and from 2 to 5 PM daily except Sundays.

Back on the Plaza de Armas, turn right onto the Calle Santa Catalina Angosta to visit the cloistered convent of Dominican nuns who came from Arequipa in 1605 and built their complex on what was the Inca House of the Chosen Women of the Sun. The convent has been restored and is open to the public Mondays through Saturdays from 9 AM to noon and from 3 to 5 PM.

The Church and Cloisters of Our Lady of Mercy — La Merced — merit a place on your tour, especially the cloisters, which are among the most beautiful of viceregal Peru. The most famed possession of the cloister is the religious vessel known as La Custodia, made of 48 pounds of pure gold and containing 1,518 diamonds and some 600 emeralds, pearls, topazes, and rubies. This is also the place where the remains of several conquistadores, including Gonzalo Pizarro, are buried. The church is open from 5 to 10 AM and 6 to 8 PM daily; the cloisters and its *Museo de Arte Religioso* (Museum of Religious Art), from 9 AM to noon and 3 to 5 PM daily except Sundays.

A $10 entrance ticket allows a tourist to see the *Regional Historical Museum,* Santa Catalina, the *Museum of Religious Art,* the cathedral, San Blas, Koricancha, and the ruins at Sacsayhuamán, Puka Pukará, Tambo Machay, Pisac, Kenko, and Ollantaytambo. Buy tickets at any of the sites.

The stores in Cuzco specialize in alpaca and sheep's wool products. The *Galerías Turísticas* (103 Av. El Sol) has a good display of the most typical handicraft products of the Cuzco area. Fine pottery is available in the *Fábrica de Artesanías de Ruíz Caro* (387 Calle El Triunfo; phone: 84-224361), and beautiful alpaca skin rugs, bedspreads, and the like can be obtained at the *Fábrica de Artesanías de Federico Alarco* (567 Calle Pavitos; phone: 84-225411), at *Artesanía Pérez* (218 San Andrés; phone: 84-232157), and at the local outlet for the *Artesanías del Perú* cooperative (359 Plateros; no phone). If you want something special, go to *Plazoleta* (634 San Blas), behind the church of the same name, to make a choice from the pottery figures made by the family of the late Hilario Mendívil. Other fine artisans also work in the area; just walk around and look.

For entertainment, two small theaters specialize in the folkloric dances of the area: *Centro Qosco* (604 Av. Sol; phone: 84-227901) and *Peña Folklórica* (114 Montero). Presentations at both theaters begin at 8 PM. If you'd rather do the dancing yourself, there is the disco *El Muki* (114 Santa Catalina Angosta), half a block from the Plaza de Armas and decorated to simulate a salt mine. Its two dance floors are filled with younger *cuzqueños* and tourists until 4 AM. The best nightclub in town is *El Truco* on the Plaza Regocijo; it has both a small restaurant and live Peruvian music and dance (phone: 84-232441).

One of the most interesting night spots is the *Qhatuchay* in the Plaza de Armas (233 Portal Confitería, 2nd Floor). The attractiveness of the place is not so much in the surroundings but in its clientele and its show, which sticks to Andean and coastal and Latin American music. There's no rock 'n' roll. Beer and *pisco* are the only beverages served, accompanied by tasty, often hot hors d'oeuvres and bread and cheese. Open from 8 PM until 4 AM; you have to go early to get a table.

While Cuzco has relatively decent hotels, restaurants are sometimes disappointing. *El Truco* (247 Plaza Regocijo) — the nightclub with a restaurant — is fine, as is *La Taberna del Truco* next door. Also recommended are *Pizzería La Mama* (177 Portal Escribanos) and *Mesón de Espaderos* (105 Espaderos), and for delicious local fare try *Quinta Eulalia* (lunchtime only) away from the center of town — any cab driver knows the spot. Try the *chupes* (thick soups), local Andean lake trout, and *anticuchos* (shish kebabs of grilled beef heart). A diverting stop for a beer is the *Cross Keys Pub* (at Portal Confitería), a hangout for expatriates, scientists, guides, and trekkers.

To get around, local bus service is good in Cuzco but only if you can ask directions and understand the Spanish answers. Car rentals are available through the major hotels and through *Avis Rent-a-Car* (395 Av. El Sol; phone: 84-231381) or *National Rent-a-Car* (108 Portal Espinar; phone: 84-224591). All the better hotels have their own bus service meeting each flight at the airport. Organized group or private tours are available through local tour operators. Check the *Perú Guide* for a list of the best operators in

Cuzco or ask at the national tourism office (115 Portal Belén; phone: 84-237364). To get around, taxis are available and usually inexpensive (about $5 an hour in town); but fix the price for the trip before starting out.

**En Route from Cuzco** – After a good look at Cuzco, get out into the hills and visit the Inca ruins. A pleasant, second-day circuit will take you through the Sacred Valley of the Inca, the Urubamba. It is best to arrange this tour with a travel agency. Your first stop will be at overpowering Sacsayhuamán, or the Fortress of the Speckled Hawk, on the northern outskirts of Cuzco, 5 miles (8 km) from the city.

**SACSAYHUAMÁN:** One of the most stupendous structures of pre-Columbian America, it is a fortress begun by the first great conqueror of the known worlds, Pachacútec, sometime after 1445. Seventy-five years later it was still under construction, during the reign of Huáscar, the last of the legitimate pre-Conquest Inca. When the Inca were not off warring somewhere in their vast empire, there were probably 20,000 construction workers (most likely prisoners of war) constantly adding to the vast edifice — quarrying the great blocks of stone, dragging them to the site, and fitting them in place. Sacsayhuamán is an incredible heap of engineered masonry, and before its destruction by the Spaniards — who used it as a quarry for the stone needed to build Cuzco, 5 miles (8 km) down the road — it was the most wondrous complex in the whole Tahuantinsuyo (an Inca word meaning the four corners of the earth; it's used to refer to the Inca Empire). A limited amount of archaeological work still goes on at the site; in late 1990, a number of large ceramic urns for storing *chicha* were unearthed. The modern reproduction of the ancient Inca *Feast of Inti Raymi* on June 24 is staged with this brooding fortress as a background.

Of all the holidays observed in the Cuzco area, *Inti Raymi* is perhaps the most important. Coinciding with the *Feast Day of San Juan Bautista* (St. John the Baptist), this was once the time for the Inca observance of the winter solstice. The week leading up to the *Feast of Inti Raymi* is a time for partying, parading, drinking, and dancing. On the 24th, there's a costumed replay of the ancient procession and a symbolic sacrifice to the sun. (Hotel space in Cuzco is at a premium at this time.)

The shrines around Cuzco are linked to the Inca calendar. There are 328 shrines in all, set in a circular pattern around the city. They are believed to be spread out along 41 lines, each shrine representing 1 day of the Inca year; the lines, representing 1 week, and three sets of lines representing 1 month (the Inca year was 12 months divided into 3 weeks each, or 36 weeks a year).

*Inti Raymi* is not the only Inca holiday celebrated in Peru; *Kapaq Situa,* the Inca month of purification, occurs in August, and various acts of penance are performed by the Indians. *Koya Raymi* (the Festival of the Queen) coincides with the September 8 *Feast of the Nativity of the Blessed Virgin;* festivities center around Cuzco's Twelve-Angled Stone.

**En Route from Sacsayhuamán** – About 4 miles (6 km) east is Kenko, another Inca shrine that dates back to the days of Huayna Cápac; it is an amphitheater believed to have been used for religious rites. Take a look at the great stone block almost 18 feet high; local residents claim that it resembles a puma.

Puka Pukará, about 3½ miles (6 km) north of Cuzco, is what's left of a small fortress that probably guarded the road down to Pisac and the Sacred Valley of the Inca. You get another view of the hillside terraces, stairways, tunnels, and towers so common to Inca architecture. It is believed that tunnels from Puka Pukará went to Sacsayhuamán and Cuzco; legend has it that at least one of the Inca tunnels went all the way to Ecuador! Because of the color of its stone, it also is known as the red fortress.

Tambo Machay, a bit farther north, was a bathing place for the Inca and royal women of the court who were involved in the water cult. A handsome place, it offers in miniature some of the rich engineering details of the architecture of the Inca. Its aqueduct system feeds crystal-clear water to a series of showers. Look carefully, and among the llamas and alpacas roaming the site (along with Indian children who allow you to take their pictures for a fee), you may see a rare *warizo* — a cross between the two animals. It is a lovely, gentle camelid.

Leaving behind these lovely Inca ruins, head down the road — and it really is down, for you will be descending almost 1,500 feet — to the village of Pisac in the Urubamba Valley. In the rainy season it is best to find a driver who has a happy relationship with hairpin curves. Pisac, 19 miles (30 km) from Cuzco, has glorious terraces climbing up the mountainside, which is topped by the largest Inca fortification in the valley.

Pisac offers not only ruins and a Sunday market (with an enthusiastic albeit offkey brass band), but often a chance to hear a church mass in Quechua. About 50 miles (80 km) from Cuzco at Chincheros is an interesting Indian market, which is also held on Sundays and features some very fine weaving. This market is held in a plaza bordered by an Inca wall with 10 rectangular niches; the snow-capped peaks of Chicon and La Veronica are seen in the distance. Chincheros's church dates from the 16th century. Because weekly markets break up around noon, the distance between the two makes it difficult to do both the Chincheros and Pisac markets on the same day. The area fishing is good, and you might like to match wits with the fighting trout of the Vilcanota River. While in Pisac, stop by *Frank's Café* (619 Av. Pardo). Profits from the café go to an emergency care fund for local children.

Continuing from Pisac you pass through the village of Urubamba. Particularly pleasant for lunch is the *Alhambra 111* hotel in Yucay.

But your destination is the great fortress of Ollantaytambo — about 45 miles (72 km) from Cuzco — one of the very few Inca towns still distinctively Inca and inhabited. The fortress, intricate and elegantly constructed from rose-colored granite, is one of the dozen places in Peru that lends itself to dreaming of the great empire that was Tahuantinsuyo. The ruins here include temples, baths, and military defenses.

Now go back to Cuzco to depart for the most famous of them all — Machu Picchu. The tourist train from Cuzco now goes all the way to Machu Picchu and takes 3 hours. It leaves Cuzco daily at 6 AM, returning to Cuzco at about 5 PM. Advance reservations for the Cuzco–Machu Picchu train can be made at the Lima station, 207 Ancash (phone: 14-276620.)

**MACHU PICCHU:** Nothing written in the Spanish chronicles, which depended upon the oral histories of the Indians, prepares you for this dramatically isolated city of the Inca, unseen by Occidental eyes for centuries. Apparently the Indians who lived in the vicinity knew of the citadel, so loftily placed above the Río Urubamba and shrouded by clouds that envelope the more than 200 buildings of the city during the rainy season, but it is inexplicably absent from Spanish accounts. As the crow (or the condor) flies, Machu Picchu is only about 15 minutes from the cold heights of Ollantaytambo, but it has the climate of the semitropical, richly foliaged, eastern slopes of the Andes.

The theories about the city are varied, but each one, though somewhat romantic in detail, is basically sound. It *could* have been one fortress in a chain of fortresses erected by the Inca to protect the jungle flanks of the empire from the savages who made sporadic raids into the national territory; it *could* have been a great religious sanctuary administered by a group of Chosen Women of the Sun, for a disproportionate number of female skeletons have been found in its burial places; it *could* have been a training school for the noble youth of the empire; it *probably* was the last way station for the final Inca ruler and his nobles as they escaped from the Spaniards into what appeared to be the security of Vilcabamba in the jungle.

All we *know* is that Machu Picchu is an imposing architectural complex set in an awesome natural setting; it deservedly has helped Cuzco earn fame as a major archaeological capital of the world. The granite forts, temples, altars, squares, fountains, and aqueducts were rediscovered in 1911 by Yale University's Hiram Bingham, guided by Peruvian Melchor Arteaga, who used to live in the area of the citadel (Bingham's journal of the trip has been published as *The Lost City*). So inspirational were the ruins, so fascinating their anonymous blueprints, that world architects and planners chose Machu Picchu as the site for the signing of a 1977 charter to improve universal living conditions.

The peak you see in photographs of Machu Picchu is called Huayna Picchu. It's a steep climb, but the view from the top is hard to beat. Another more level walk follows the original Inca trail behind the ruins — about 2 hours to what may have been the lone entrance gate to the site. While at the ruins, note the Intiwatana, or stone sundial, as well as the condor stone where sacrifices were made. The ruins are divided into the urban and agricultural sections, with squares, temples, warehouses, workshops, stairs, streets, and water canals. The farming area is notable for its terraces, which allowed cultivation on the steep slope and prevented erosion. The sacred Sun Temple is a semicircular building that is one of the highest points in the city. It was built on a massive slab of granite, with niches and other stone work details, similar to Koricancha in Cuzco. Chronicles handed down from the Indians suggest that the wall once may have been encrusted with gems. Under the temple is a hidden cave that contains royal tombs. The Temple of the Three Windows, considered one of the most important sections of the city, is on the eastern edge of the main plaza. It has three open windows and two false windows that probably were used to display icons. The temple's stonework is particularly impressive.

Machu Picchu lies 70 miles (112 km) northwest of Cuzco; the only way to get there is by the narrow-gauge railroad that leaves Cuzco's San Pedro Station each day at 6 AM, arriving at approximately 9 AM, after passing through the beautiful "Sacred Valley of the Inca" en route. There is also a daily local train, although we *don't* recommend it — the trip is longer, it is more crowded and uncomfortable, and robberies are a common occurrence. Because the return train leaves at 2 PM, bring lunch with you from Cuzco or grab a bite at the *Turistas* hotel. Or you might want to get a return ticket for the next day and spend the night at the hotel. The trip to Machu Picchu is striking and full of scenic contrasts; try to sit by a left-hand window for the choicest views. Be prepared for rain from December through March, but even in the rain, the citadel is awe-inspiring.

It is well worth the effort of making advance reservations and reconfirmations with *EnturPerú* (phone: in Lima, 14-721928) to get a room at the one and only hotel on the mountaintop. The small *Turistas* hotel has grown from 17 to 31 rooms — scarcely enough supply to meet the demand. The hotel is fair, the food is just as fair, and neither factor is important as long as you can have the ruins basically to yourself when the tourist train leaves before sunset. Sunrise is even more spectacular.

If the hotel is booked, try your luck at the rustic hostels and boardinghouses in the town of Aguas Calientes, at the base of the mountain. Your best bet may be the government-run hostel, *Albergue Aguas Calientes*. The town — translated literally as "hot waters" — has hot springs; a morning dip, with Andean peaks rising around you, is recommended, so take your bathing suit. Bear in mind that there is no transportation between Machu Picchu and Aguas Calientes, but the half-mile hike down the train tracks between the two is an easy one. If you spend 1 night or more, you can take the local train back to Cuzco at 1 PM instead of the tourist train at 3 PM. Although more picturesque, the trip is longer. You share the car with resident Peruvians and even their live produce. Book first class for a cushioned seat, and take along a lunch packed by the hotel.

There is one other way to reach Machu Picchu; the way Bingham did — on foot. Treks are organized from Cuzco; take the train to Km 88 and walk the next 20 miles (32 km) on the Inca trail. The best time to take this trip is from May to September, before the rainy season starts. Depending on your stamina, you can take the high or low road, and organized expeditions are complete with the mandatory guide and a dozen or more bearers. Cuzco agencies that arrange Inca trail treks include *Explorandes* (N-17 Urb. Magisterio; phone: 84-226599); *Peruvian Andean Treks* (705 Pardo; phone: 84-225701); and *Tambo Treks* (589 Atocsaycuchi, San Blas; phone: 84-237718). There are no supply points along the way, so do not attempt the Inca trail alone (see *The Wild Continent*, DIVERSIONS) and for safety reasons, do not stray from the route. This trek normally takes 3 to 5 days.

Many travelers returning to Cuzco from Machu Picchu opt to take a train or plane to Puno, continuing on to Lake Titicaca (see *Puno)*. Tickets for the 10-hour train trip should be purchased a day in advance. The train route is cold and uncomfortable — be sure to take warm clothes and food. And keep your eye on your belongings. Air tickets are available from either *Faucett* or *AeroPerú*.

## BEST EN ROUTE

Hotels in and around Cuzco are very tourist-oriented. Several are very good, but some are poorly maintained and space can be hard to find. They generally provide hot water and private baths, but the city has problems with water pressure, so don't be surprised by chronic plumbing snafus; there's an occasional restaurant. What hurts, however, is that you pay for what you don't get: Prices for a double room range from an expensive $55 to $80; for moderate, figure $25 to $55; and for a double room in the inexpensive category, anything under $25. Make reservations beforehand, more so if you plan to be in the area in June during the *Feast of Inti Raymi*.

### CUZCO

**Alhambra II** – Here are 45 rooms with bath furnished in colonial style, as well as a restaurant that presents a nightly folklore show during dinner. It can be a bit chilly, but the hotel is one of the best in the mid-price category. 594 Av. El Sol (phone: 84-224076). Expensive.

**El Dorado Inn** – In the heart of town, it offers heated guestrooms with private bath, colonial-style public rooms, and a dining room and bar. This is one of the better choices in town. 365 Av. El Sol (phone: 84-231232 or 84-233112; in Lima, 14-421393; in the US, 800-44-UTELL). Expensive.

**Libertador** – Without question the best hotel in Cuzco, so reservations are a must. Much of the hotel is housed in a restored 16th-century colonial mansion — built on Inca foundations — that belonged to Spanish conquerer, Francisco Pizarro. A modern addition contains most of the pleasantly decorated rooms. The lobby, bar, and restaurant are graced with Inca walls and attractive pieces from the hotel's collection of pre-Columbian artifacts. 400 San Agustín (phone: 84-233152 or 84-231961; in Lima, 14-420166 or 14-421995; in Florida, 813-439-2118; in other states, 800-327-3573; fax: 84-233152). Expensive.

**Picoaga** – Just a short walk from Cuzco's main plaza, you'll find pleasant accommodations and receive good service in what was once the colonial home of the Marquis of Picoaga. The bar and restaurant offer a great view of the surrounding mountains. 344 Santa Teresa (phone: 84-232312; in Lima, 14-286314; in the US, 800-344-1212 or through *Latin America Reservations Center (LARC)*, 800-327-3573). Expensive.

**San Antonio de Abad** – Cuzco's newest hotel and the only government-run accommodations in the city, this 120-room facility is in a converted colonial-era monasatery with a red tile roof and two picturesque patios. Plaza las Nazaranas; no phone at press time. For reservations, contact *EnturPerú* (phone: in Lima, 14-721928; in the US, 800-275-3123). Expensive.

**Savoy Plaza** – This property has 139 rooms, double and single, with private bath and shower. It's rather far from the center of town and requires a taxi ride to and from the main plaza, but it is comfortable, although service can be hit-and-miss. The hotel will arrange tours of the city and nearby ruins for guests. 954 Av. El Sol (phone: 84-224322; in Lima, 14-467965). Expensive.

**Espinar** – Only a block from the Plaza de Armas, it has 36 rooms with private bath, and its restaurant has a fine view of the plaza. 142 Portal Espinar (phone: 84-233091). Moderate.

**Inti** – This place has been redecorated, and its 26 rooms have private baths and a cozy, family-like atmosphere. Both its restaurant and location are good. 260 Calle Matara (phone: 84-228401). Moderate.

**Royal Inka I** – Built within the hull of a colonial building, and quite nice, though some of the rooms are a bit small. Be sure you book into this hotel, which faces a little plaza where Indian women sell their wares and not to a sister property, the *Royal Inka II*, which is just up the street. Although it has a lovely central courtyard restaurant, the rooms are dismal, dark, and noisy. 299 Plaza del Cabildo (phone: 84-231067; fax: 84-234221). Moderate.

**San Agustín** – Centrally located, it has 53 rooms, each with bath and telephone. 390 San Agustín at the corner of Calle Maruri (phone: 84-222322; in Lima, 14-442066). Moderate.

## PISAC

**Chongo Chico** – This small hotel, housed in a former farmhouse, is less than a mile (1 km) outside town on the road to the ruins. It has clean rooms, good food, and a breathtaking view. Breakfast is included (no phone). Moderate.

## URUBAMBA

**Centro Vacacional de Urubamba** – State-owned resort with a swimming pool, bar, and restaurant. Jirón Cabo Alfonso Concha at Chatupa (Km 70 on the highway; phone: Urubamba 227191; in Lima, 14-441199). Expensive.

**Alhambra 111** – A lovely little hostelry in Yucay, set in a converted colonial hacienda. Each room, with private bath, opens onto a flower-filled patio. 123 Plaza Manco II (phone: Urubamba 224076). Moderate.

**Naranjachayoc** – This attractive hacienda has 6 spotless rooms, good food, and a pool. At Km 69 on the road between Pisac and Urubamba (no phone). Moderate.

## MACHU PICCHU

**Turistas** – The one and only place to stay at Machu Picchu is comfortable but small. Its restaurant can accommodate up to 300 people for self-service lunch. The food is unimaginative and expensive. At the ruins. Reservations must be made through *EnturPerú* (phone: Machu Picchu 31; in Lima, 14-721928; in the US, 800-275-3123). Expensive.

## AGUAS CALIENTES

**Albergue de Turistas** – Basic accommodations consisting of bunk beds and shared bathrooms located a short distance from the thermal springs. Bedding is provided, but towels must be rented. Make reservations through *EnturPerú* (phone: in Lima, 14-721928; in the US, 800-275-3123). Inexpensive.

# The Amazon

Peru's Amazon territory is a vast watershed of rivers and canopied rain forest in which more than a thousand species of unique plant and animal life flourish. Exceeding the size of Spain, France, and West Germany combined and covering almost 60% of Peru's landscape, La Selva (as it is known locally) is the home of some half-million people, largely adventurers, explorers, romantics, missionaries, and members of 35 known indigenous Indian tribes who have only superficial contact with the modern world.

This eastern Peruvian jungle consists of the basins of four great rivers. Far to the north, the Río Putumayo rises in the Colombian Andes and forms the border between Peru and Colombia. In the south, the Madre de Dios, known to the Indians as the River of Serpents, begins in the Andes near Cuzco and has as its major port Puerto Maldonado, near the Bolivian border (see *Madre de Dios,* below). Between these two rivers is the Infierno Verde (Green Hell) watered by the Marañón and Ucayali.

Peruvians have long dreamed of colonizing the Amazon territory, but the jungle, with its allies of rivers and mountains, has proven to be a worthy adversary. Even Carlos Fitzcarraldo, a man who devoted much of the immense wealth he amassed from the rubber boom to realizing his obsession with creating a link between two Peruvian rivers, was thwarted by the terrain. In the northeast, the important port of Iquitos, Peru's navigation outlet to the Atlantic, has no connecting road system — the idea of building a road from the Pacific west coast has been abandoned as an impossible dream. During October to May, the Río Marañón can rise 30 to 60 feet, flooding everything in its path; so even if the Andes could be conquered, the river cannot.

For travelers, Peru's Amazon region spells adventure but not danger to all but the foolhardy. Jaguars and other large animals have retreated deep into the rain forest; boa constrictors, fer-de-lance, and bushmaster snakes avoid people; dangerous Indian tribes are few and are almost never encountered even by those who seek them out. In the river, electric eels, rays, piranha, *carnero,* and crocodiles are hazardous — but there are some safe swimming areas. Although the areas normally visited are not teeming with animals, Peru's rain forest remains — by law and economic obstacles — one of the best protected areas of the Amazon. (It is too costly to exploit the lumber and oil in the region to any great degree).

What travelers to the jungle will encounter is a pioneer spirit among residents and the knowledge that here nature, not man, is in charge. It is believed that the Inca, respecting nature's dominion, never penetrated this jungle. In their relentless quest for gold, however, the Spanish did do battle with this area. A curtain of green vegetation is everywhere, as are the hum, squeak, screech, and buzz of bird and insect life. Indians with brightly painted faces and bodies smile and offer to trade goods. And then there is the ever-present heat and humidity, 82F (28C) average.

There are several ways to reach the Amazon and Iquitos from Lima. You can fly directly to the town on one of the four daily flights offered by *AeroPerú* and *Faucett,* or you can take one of those carriers — or one of the new airlines, *Americana* or *Andrea* — to Pucallpa, 489 miles (732 km) from Lima, finishing your trip by riverboat down the Ucayali; it's possible to travel by air to either Huánuco or Tingo María (about halfway to Pucallpa), mixing air and surface travel, or you can go all the way from Lima to Pucallpa by ground along the Carretera Central (Central Highway, also known as Route 2), traveling east from Lima (although this route is *not* recommended).

There are several ways to travel by road to Pucallpa. You can travel by *camión* (truck); the price is about as rock bottom as the comfort, and it is a long, dragged-out affair since the truck driver starts and stops anywhere he likes — depending on how far he's going and how long he decides to take getting there. The trucks are usually 4-ton types with wooden slat sides: They hold a lot of cargo, human and otherwise, and because they're open, they can be absolutely miserable in wet and cold weather. You "rent" one of these by simply standing along the road and flagging one down.

Or — though strongly *not* recommended — you can go by bus. Since this is not a popular tourist route, the vehicle may resemble a rejected school bus and is just as noisy. It is likely to be outfitted with a luggage rack on the roof, overhead racks inside, and a shrine to the Blessed Virgin on the dashboard (considering the road and the way the driver controls the bus, you'll need it). There may or may not be springs in the seats, mufflers, or headlights, and the quarters are tight. This method of traveling is a real endurance test; the buses seldom stop for meals, so when one pulls into a town, vendors flock to the windows with food for hardy stomachs. Needless to say, do not count on onboard toilet facilities.

Actually, the best way to get to the Amazon is to fly to Pucallpa or, if you insist on a more scenic route, by *colectivo* — taxis that take at least five passengers bound for the same destination. The *colectivos* make stops at little cafés for lunch and dinner: They also have specific runs, which means you have to hunt for another car when one segment ends. Prices, however, are inexpensive and negotiable.

This is not a route for the comfort-seeking traveler, but the scenery is perhaps the most extraordinary in Latin America. You cross mountains, plateaus, and ravines. Vegetation is bright or nonexistent; the terrain is harsh and chipped or soft and flowing. There are mountain villages lying in pastoral surroundings and homes hanging dangerously from cliffs.

Larger cities have adequate (no luxury or first class) hotels, and modest restaurants.

A direct trip by *colectivo* can take as little as 20 to 24 hours nonstop, but double that time is the average. The trip should be made in three sections of 3 days. The first stage, Lima to Huánuco, should take 10 hours. Next, it's Huánuco to Tingo María in 4 or more hours. And finally, it's Tingo María to Pucallpa in 10 hours, more or less.

To avoid the heavy rains that cause havoc in the mountains and jungle, the best time to travel is from April to November. July to October is ideal. By then, the rock slides usually are removed and the washouts repaired.

For special information, road maps, and itineraries, contact *Touring y Automóvil Club del Perú* (699 César Vallejo, Lince, Lima; phone: 14-403270).

Maps are also available at the *Instituto Geográfico Nacional* (1190 Av. Aramburú — 1 block from Av. Panamá, Lima; phone: 14-287993).

Advice, good sense, and arrangements are also provided by *Lima Tours* (1040 Belén, Lima); *Receptour* (889 Rufino Torrico, Lima); and *Condor Travel* (in the Galerías Comerciales of the *Lima Sheraton* hotel).

Now that you've been prepared for the horrors and excitement of traveling to and through the Amazon, there are three books that are must reading to get the feel of it. One, *The Rivers Amazon,* by Alex Shoumatoff (Sierra Club Books; 1978), is a fascinating account of a young naturalist's voyage down the Amazon and its tributaries and his encounters with various Indian tribes. A bit more bizarre is *Keep the River on Your Right,* by Tobias Schneebaum (Grove Press; 1969), an account of self-discovery in the jungle. It has been an underground cult favorite for many years. Finally, there is *The Cloud Forest* (out of print, but check your local library for a copy), Peter Matthiesson's exploration of South America, from Brazil's rain forest to the Andes to Tierra del Fuego.

**HUÁNUCO:** The capital of the department of the same name, this city of some 45,000 people lies in a mountain valley 6,300 feet above sea level. It sports a temperate climate and is a popular tourist center for people of the *montaña*. As in all the cities of the *montaña,* what is oldest and best preserved are the churches, and two good examples of colonial architecture are San Cristóbal and San Francisco (they are, however, no match for the great cathedrals of the major cities).

The city is known for its folkloric festivals and especially its popular ballet — *Negritos de Huánuco* — seen on January 8 and 16 and on other festive days. The Dance of the Negroes reenacts slaves calling for their liberation. Each dancer wears a mask to represent certain characters — the overseer, traveler, and nobleman. The music is Afro-Peruvian.

The city is irrigated by the Huallaga and Higueras rivers and is surrounded by large hills and green, spreading fields of sugarcane and grain. For the angler, the rivers are filled with fish; arrangements can be made at the hotels for tackle and bait.

The Huánuco area abounds in ruins. Just before entering the city, a turnoff to the left leads to Kotosh, an important, pre-Inca temple that is still undergoing restoration. Following a small road (ask directions) from the city center to adjacent flatlands will bring you to a series of ruins known as Huánuco Pampa, that cover an area some three-quarters of a mile wide. Here you'll find an Inca fortress, a royal palace, and baths, all badly decayed.

In Huánuco, there is a tourism office on the Plaza de Armas, 714 General Prado (phone: 6452-2124).

**En Route from Huánuco** – Two roads, one following the left bank of the river (passing the airport) and the other following the right bank, join the Central Highway again. The road continues its ascent through a terrain of cacti and small shrubs into the foothills of the Carpish Mountains, some 32 miles (51 km) from Huánuco. There is dense forest and a long tunnel (badly lit), which opens up into wooded hills and lush vegetation at an altitude of some 9,000 feet.

A side road leads to the top of Puente Pardo, some 12 miles (19 km) from the Central Highway. The dirt road is narrow and vegetation clogged; the climb, steep. The prize at the end is Cueva de las Lechuzas, or the Owls' Cave, inhabited by large birds known as *guácharos,* which are distant relatives to owls and almost extinct.

Back on the Central Highway, is the small village of Bella. Here on the banks of the Río Huallaga is the Playa de Bella, a beautiful white sand beach surrounded by wild flowers. It's worth a swim (although a bit cold), but you must hire someone at the village to take you there because there is no road. From Bella, the Central Highway descends sharply to Tingo María.

**TINGO MARÍA:** Born in various stages of this century, this rainy city has a population of some 25,000 people, most of whom work on the coffee and tea plantations and the farms producing sugarcane and bananas. The Río Huallaga widens at this point, providing an area for recreation. The city is nominally under the control of the Bureau of Mountain Lands and Colonization, which has had some success in encouraging people to settle in the area. Japanese immigrants have demonstrated that tea plantations can be run successfully.

The city lies at the base of a mountain dubbed "The Sleeping Beauty" owing to its similarity to the silhouette of a prone woman, and it is just such surrounding scenery, not the city itself, that attracts, for this area is a paradise of lush, subtropical green vegetation. Called the *ceja,* or eyebrow, of the *montaña,* magnificent glaciers extend into the clouds. The Peruvian *montaña* covers some 30,000 square miles of virtually unsettled area, but its rich, well-watered soil and temperate climate — about 70F (21C) — offer incredible potential for both agriculture and tourism (if recreational facilities can be developed).

**En Route from Tingo María** – The Central Highway heads toward the northeast with varying degrees of construction under way along the route to Pucallpa (a likely state of affairs for several years). Little villages on the road such as Naranjillo, Pumahuasi, and Las Delicias on the banks of the Río Huallaga are passed before the road begins an ascent into the Cordillera Azul, passing by great areas of coffee and tea cultivation. At La Divisoria, 39 miles (62 km) away at 5,000 feet, there is a marvelous panoramic view: On a clear day to the east, the green-blue plain of the Pampa de Sacramento is visible, and it is here that the Amazon plain begins.

The road descends slowly as it comes to and passes through the incredible natural pass, Boquerón Abad, which has to be one of the natural wonders of the world. The green-covered rock cliffs jut straight up, almost blocking out sunlight. Once through the pass, you are out of the Andes.

The road passes through magnificent vegetation and over the Río Aguaytia by way of the longest bridge in South America (2,290 feet). There is another bridge over the Río San Alejandro before the road ends at Pucallpa on the Río Ucayali.

**PUCALLPA:** This cluster of mud and thatch buildings, on the west bank of the wide, muddy-green Río Ucayali, thrives — in heat, humidity, and frontier spirit — as Peru's second-most important jungle riverport after Iquitos as well as the last navigable port for oceangoing vessels on the Amazon. It is also an important lumbering area.

The oil camps, scattered throughout the basin into northeastern Peru, are groups of huts spread out in a village-type grid. Some are no more than tents; all, however, have their general stores (or huts) and even shacks for prostitutes. If you're a woman, and manage to come upon one of these barrios, ignore the macho stares, whistles, and occasional propositions that will be thrown at you.

Most of Peru's oil fields, located near the Ecuadoran border, were, by the way, captured in a bloody border skirmish in 1922. Every once in a while controversy flares up anew between these two old adversaries, and feelings of hostility will hang in the air until negotiations settle disputes between the two countries or tempers simply cool down.

But why worry about international affairs now — you're in Pucallpa, on the fringe of the Amazon, where everything has that lusty smell of slow decay of earth and vine. The city's population of 60,000 is a rather off-and-on group of pioneers, Indians, and mestizos. Along the river is a collection of canoes, *peque-peques* (motorized launches — their name describes the sounds they make), barges, houseboats, small steamers, and workers loading and unloading a collection of jungle goods, including lumber and round gray-black balls of wild rubber from Ibena up north.

On musty store shelves everything is for sale: Japanese radios, English chocolate, stuffed crocodiles, pinned butterflies and beetles, feathered arrows, blowguns, and insect repellent (the latter may be the most important buy of all, because the Ucayali is not nicknamed the Mosquito River without reason).

In the city, sightseeing is limited to the exotic riverfront cargo and the Hospital Amazónico Albert Schweitzer, a 28-plus-bed hospital and research center devoted to helping jungle people, mostly members of the Shipibo and Cashiba Indian tribes. A staff member will be happy to show visitors around. Pucallpa has a tourism office at 298 Saénz Peña (phone: 6457-5008).

About 2½ miles (4 km) back on the route to Huánuco, a dirt road leads you 6 miles (10 km) to the lake, the basic center of activity around Pucallpa. Once an arm of the Río Ucayali (it's still possible to get out to the river during high tide), the lake offers boating, fishing, and a look at the natives.

The main village of the Shipibo, San Francisco, is about 6 miles (10 km) from Pucallpa by boat. En route, the mestizos have shacks along the reedy margin of the lake, and the warm waters break with leaping dolphins. Soon, the wood and palm-leaf houses of the Shipibo are visible. They are open-sided, have bamboo floors, and are high off the ground to prevent rats and snakes from entering. The Shipibo wear clothing with geometric designs that are also patterned on their enormous glazed pots. Dugout canoes line the banks; on land one must travel over log bridges. In the village, yuca beer is made, and a cooking pot may contain a brightly colored toucan, with beak and head attached. Often the Shipibo will trade their 8-foot blowguns for something you have that they like, and it is usually possible to purchase pottery and textiles.

Ten minutes or so by canoe (these can be hired for day trips) takes one to the off-and-on settlement of a band of Cashiba, a tribe that generally is found farther west. It is best to ask if they are around before venturing out into the jungle.

Lake Yarinacocha is also the base of the Summer Institute of Linguistics, a Wycliffe mission of translators who adapt the Bible into aboriginal tongues. From here the missionary-linguists fan out to work with some 35 jungle tribes of the *selva*. In the main office of the screened bungalow settlement, an orientation greets the visitors with the institute's philosophy: "To help prepare Indians for the severe adjustment they face as roads and planes threaten their isolation." The institute can be reached by writing Instituto Lingüístico de Verano (2492 Casilla, Lima 100, Peru); its jungle address is simply Yarinacocha (phone: 6457-6550). Spy-novel enthusiasts might be interested to know that local rumor has it that the institute has CIA ties.

By Lake Yarinacocha, live comfortably in the jungle at *La Brisa Lodge* and take river expeditions and bird watching trips in dugout canoes. The lodge was lovingly built, and is run, by California attorney Connor Nixon; accommodations are in 2-story screened bungalows or in the main lodge (202 Casilla; phone: 6457-6551, or in Lima, 14-276720). For information in the US, call *LADATCO Tours* in Miami (phone: 305-854-8422; toll-free, 800-327-6162).

Do anything you want in Pucallpa, but don't stop your Amazon trip here: On the contrary, the best part, that trek into the roadless jungle, is just beginning.

**En Route from Pucallpa** – Flying to Iquitos from Lima may be the fastest and easiest way to get to your next destination. Your other option, the 533-mile (853-km) journey downriver via the Ucayali to the Amazon's principal port, is wearisome but exotic. At best, the trip takes 4 to 5 days in high-water April to November, when the river is filled with vessels of all types taking advantage of the freight-carrying waters from the summer rains.

In the other months, when the water is low, the trip often takes 8 days, because sandbars make travel at night impossible. From the voyage's beginning to its end, the riverbanks are covered with jungle growth. There are always the vibration of the ship's motor and the cries of the jungle animals. River plantations with grazing cattle, the inevitable dugout canoe with Indians, fishermen hauling nets, the small, stilted houses of jungle villages are passed. Occasionally crocodiles are visible, as are tapirs and flocks of birds. There are also the plague of mosquitoes and flies and intense heat that is pacified only by river breezes.

No matter how one gets downriver, there will be problems. The biggest is booking. There is virtually no way to book before reaching Pucallpa, and then it's necessary to negotiate with the captain of the vessel (generally the monies become his sole property).

Almost any type of vessel takes passengers if there is room. There are Peruvian army steamships, oceangoing vessels, and *lanchas* (2-story houseboat-barge combinations). Passage on these will mean a bunk (if there is one) or a place to hang a hammock (your own). Food will be from the jungle and water from the river, so antidysentery medicine and canned food are mandatory. One can always travel by *colectivo* (large motorized passenger canoes or barges that function as water taxis). Several *colectivos* will have to be taken to make the entire trip, and nights will be spent in a hammock on the porch of an Indian's hut (visitors are a welcome sight on the river). Food must be brought or bought, and a sleeping bag, hammock, and tarpaulin are recommended.

Besides Iquitos, connections may be made for the downriver ports of Contamana, Reguena, and Omaguas on the Ucayali and Yurimaguas on the Huallaga. Upstream are the ports of Puerto Bermúdez and Atalaya.

**IQUITOS:** Some 2,000 miles (3,200 km) from the mouth of the Amazon River and the Atlantic Ocean and almost 1,000 miles (1,600 km) from Lima, Iquitos would seem the most isolated of places. Yet even before "Slim" Faucett opened up the air lanes between Lima and Iquitos in 1922 (today both *Faucett* and *AeroPerú* send in two daily flights), the city had a memorable history.

Started as the Jesuit Mission of Santa María de Iquitos in the 1750s, the town suffered the raids of the headhunting Jívaro Indians. In 1876, Iquitos had only 1,500 permanent residents, hardly a reason for the city to be called the Pearl of the Amazon. But just 4 years and 24,000 residents later, this steaming capital of the District of Loreto was indeed the Pearl.

From 1880 to 1917, Iquitos lavished in the rubber boom, as steamers as large as 1,000 tons called regularly from New York and Liverpool. There were resident consuls from ten foreign countries. The city imported everything from common foodstuffs like ice cream and fried chicken to champagne and caviar, and the *Gran Hotel Malecón Palace,* a luxury hotel covered in Venetian tiles, was shipped from Paris in pieces and reassembled on the banks of the Amazon. Its ballroom boasted performances by Sarah Bernhardt and the *French Grand Opera.*

There's a dark side to the boom, however, one which even today is ignored in many history books. Tens of thousands of Indians were enslaved to harvest rubber. If they didn't maintain the daily production quota — 42 pounds — they were whipped or starved. The most infamous company, the Peruvian Amazon Rubber Company, was owned by Julio César Arana. It is estimated that as many as 30,000 Indians died at his hand. In 1907, a US journalist was dispatched to investigate the situation. After a near-fatal beating by local thugs, he never filed a word. Although allegations of brutality continued to surface, Arana never was prosecuted. In fact, he held a respected position in the community and even was elected senator.

Today, Iquitos's 300,000 inhabitants benefit somewhat from oil discovered by PetroPerú. But the single most important export is lumber, with secondary products being orchids, raw rubber, wicker furniture, medicinal plants, barbasco (the source of Rotenone for insecticides), and tropical fish.

The port on the left (north) bank of the river is merely a shadow of its past. The *malecón,* the river promenade, with its balustrade and wrought-iron lanterns, guards a certain antiquity, but vegetation and the river have already undermined its foundation. The grandiose houses along the *malecón,* with cupolas, façades of Portuguese *azulejo* tile, and ornate wrought-iron balconies from England are now military headquarters. (It is prohibited to photograph these houses without permission from the army.) Statues to forgotten men stand in neglected squares.

The center of Iquitos, 1 block from the riverfront, is the Plaza de Armas — the business and social center. It was from the plaza that the city grew to its present dimensions. Santa Ana church, the Municipal Hall, banks, retail stores, and restaurants face the plaza, along with the tourism office (163 Próspero; phone: 94-288523); the main business district is centered on three streets extending south. Here, too, is the abandoned Casa de Fierro (Iron House), a metal structure built by Gustave Eiffel for an 1889 exposition in France. It was bought by a rubber baron, taken apart, and shipped to Iquitos where it rusted in the steamy heat. Five blocks away (on Plaza 28 de Julio) is Iquitos's first locomotive (it was used to transport rubber) — another trace of the past. The exotic really comes to light at the local market. Offerings include: sapodillas, mangoes, papayas, melons, and hearts-of-palm are recognizable. But there are also spiny fruits, nuts, roots, and cacti competing for space on the stalls with armadillos, snails, grubs, slugs, monkeys, piranhas, and turtles, not to mention love charms, coagulant bark, coca leaves, curare poison, and even popular aphrodisiacs.

For a look at stuffed denizens of the jungle plus popular crafts and archaeological items, there is the overcrowded *Amazon Museum* (349 Jirón Lima). Examples of jungle handicrafts are sold at *Artesanías del Perú* (128 Putumayo). To see what's in the waters surrounding Iquitos, a visit to the *Aquarium* (16 Jirón Ramírez Huitado) is worthwhile. In the Plaza Armas, note the fountain dedicated to the preservation of the endangered Amazon River dolphins.

Perhaps the most picturesque — and at the same time the most desperate — site in Iquitos is the waterfront slum of Belén. Previously a must stop for visitors, increased robberies at the site have officials now advising travelers to steer clear. If you insist on going, you will see a floating village (of some 15,000 people) made up of balsa rafts held in place with long poles. The average rise and fall of the Amazon here is about 40 feet, with the low point in August and September, when Belén sits on a bed of mud. At all times the village is a mass of humanity, but at high tide its floating market, with canoes canopied with palm thatch, serving as a storehouse for bananas, coconut, fish, and vegetables grown upriver. The whole scene reminds one of an exotic bazaar.

Water skiing is possible on nearby Río Nanay, and Moronococha is known for its sunsets. While visiting Iquitos, try *chuchuhuasi,* a drink made from fermented roots and rumored to have aphrodisiacal powers. The favorite local dish is *juane,* a jungle tamale with rice, chicken, olives, and eggs. And don't leave the city without trying *picadillo de paiche* (chopped cooked *paiche* fish seasoned with vegetables and herbs). A good eating and drinking spot is *Gran Maloka,* an outdoor restaurant on the *malecón.*

It is outside the city that the attraction of Iquitos is strongest. The jungles of the coffee-colored Amazon River offer visits to Yagua and Jívaro camps. The Yagua, the larger tribe, are famous blowgun hunters and their native dress is highlighted by the men's colorful rush skirts. When the Spanish conquistadores first explored this area, they were met by fierce Yagua warriors. Expedition leader Francisco de Orellana mistook the skirt-clad Indians for the Amazon women of legend and named the river accordingly.

The Jívaro, in the Río Napo area, were the once-feared headhunters of the jungle.

Now peaceful and quite civilized, they live in small village units much as they always did, without headhunting.

Visitors to the Amazon will find the area downriver from Iquitos brimming with environmentalists, bird watchers, biologists, and wildlife specialists who are awed by the rich and exotic flora and fauna. One of the biggest lures is the rare hoatzin bird, with its punk-like crest of feathers. As nestlings, the hoatzins have claws on their wings and cannot fly. When danger is near, they dive from their nest into the river, swim underwater, then crawl back up the tree to their nest. If you find an ecstatic ornithologist at your jungle lodge, it is most likely that he or she has just spotted one of these bizarre creatures.

The chance of spotting rare flora and fauna was increased by the construction of a 1,200-foot-long canopied walkway — 100 feet above the ground — in the rain forest. The walkway and a newly opened research and education laboratory were built by the Foundation for the Conservation of the Peruvian Amazon Biosphere; both are located behind the *Explornapo Camp* (see *Best en Route*). To visit the lab and walkway, contact the *Explorama Lodge* through *Selective Hotels Reservations* in the US (phone: 800-223-6764) or in Iquitos (Box 446; phone: 94-235471; fax: 94-234968), or the *Amazon Center for Environmental Education and Research* (10 Environs Park, Helena, AL 35080; phone: 800-633-4734).

An unusual tourism firm, *Wilderness Expeditions*, offers tours to jungle reserves it has purchased with its profits. This organization is dedicated to preserving the Amazon and its wildlife, and funds an orphanage south of Iquitos. The organization has a US office (310 Washington Ave., Roanoke, VA 24016; phone: 703-342-5630), and an Iquitos office (133 Putumayo; phone: 94-236918).

On the river there are commercial fishermen with huge nets suspended between boats, native dugouts and water taxis, occasional barges, and military boats. Along the shore the green wall of trees is broken now and then by clearings where cattle graze, a stilted river house stands, or where there's a government school whose pupils arrive by canoe. Every now and then the water breaks from the leap of a freshwater porpoise, which, a native will tell you, is the most dangerous of animals, capable of transforming itself into a man and impregnating swimming women. The same pink dolphins are said to emerge from the water at night, dress up as women, and go about town seducing men with perfect ease. They take them on a picnic at the water's edge or to a restaurant overlooking the river. There they lull them with sweet talk and take them home to a watery grave. Such is the steamy, fantasy-laced way of the jungle.

Undoubtedly the best way to see the rain forest outside of Iquitos is to book a stay in one of the jungle lodges, or take a 4-day or week-long cruise down the Amazon and its tributaries. The best-known and most recommended camps are those run by *Explorama* and *Amazon Camp*. The former, which has three different types of accommodations — an inn, a rustic lodge, and an isolated camp, *Explornapo* — is run by US expatriate Peter Jenson who visited the jungle nearly 3 decades ago and decided to stay. Jenson is keenly interested in rain forest preservation and offers his lodges free to scientists studying the region's flora and fauna. They, in turn, give *Explorama* guides lectures about their findings; and consequently, *Explorama* guides are among the best in the Iquitos area.

*Amazon Camp* also has good, multilingual guides. The camp is owned by *Amazon Tours and Cruises* in Miami (phone: 305-227-2266; fax: 305-227-1880), which also operates a trio of riverboats that cruise the Amazon and its tributaries between Iquitos and Brazil. Air conditioned cabins with private bath for two people, on-board meals, and three daily outings are part of the package. Like the lodges, the boat excursions include fishing for piranha, swimming in quiet rivers, hiking through virgin rain forests, bird watching outings, visiting missionary villages and jungle hospitals, and taking boat excursions at night in search of caiman (a South American crocodile) or walks to listen to the sounds of the Amazon.

**DIRECTIONS / Peru 993**

Travelers to the lodges or passengers aboard the M/V *Arca,* M/V *Delfin,* and M/V *Río Amazonas* can also visit the Yagua, Witoto, and Bora Indians, who perform native dances and give blowgun demonstrations. They also sell their crafts. Even if you don't need anything, consider buying or bartering for a necklace — they don't cost much and the sale will encourage the Indians to continue making their traditional wares. Sometimes the Indians will accept only cash, but if possible, barter. T-shirts, caps, and makeup are popular items, but fishing line and outdoor equipment, including knives, mess kits, and plastic ponchos, are more useful. The children are almost certain to ask for *caramelos* (candies) or *globos* (balloons).

## BEST EN ROUTE

Hotels in the Amazon region of Peru are a mixed lot, ranging from rustic to adequate to very comfortable. In some places, accommodations come with private bath and hot water, but in the interior, lodging can be very basic. The price of a double room listed here as expensive is over $40; moderate, $20 to $40; and less than $20, inexpensive. Jungle lodges are generally booked for 2-night stays; prices include all meals and, when necessary, transport to the lodge (in Iquitos particularly, book ahead, preferably through a US travel agent or through a travel agent in Lima).

### HUÁNUCO

***Turistas*** – This 34-room hotel provides private baths and a dining room. 775 Damaso Beraún (phone: Huánuco 2410; call *EnturPerú* in Lima, 14-721928; in the US, 800-275-3123). Moderate.

### TINGO MARÍA

***Turistas*** – Offers hot water and private baths with its clean, comfortable rooms. At Km 1 on the Carretera Tingo María (phone: Tingo María 2047; call *EnturPerú* in Lima, 14-721928; in the US, 800-275-3123). Moderate.

### PUCALLPA

***Turistas de Pucallpa*** – A swimming pool is featured. 552 San Martín (phone: 6457-5154; in the US, 800-275-3123). Reservations can also be made through *EnturPerú* in Lima (phone: 14-721928). Moderate.

***Mercedes*** – Amenities include a bar and restaurant. It's clean, but a bit noisy. 610 Raimondi (phone: 6457-6191). Moderate to inexpensive.

***Inambu*** – Offers rooms and a good restaurant. 271 Federico Basadre (phone: 6457-6822; reservations in Lima, 14-246803). Inexpensive.

### LAKE YARINACOCHA

***La Brisa*** – This lodge on an island in the middle of the lake offers bungalows in thatch-roofed huts, a restaurant, swimming, and fishing and jungle tours. In Lima, call 14-276720, or write to Connor Nixon, 202 Casilla, Pucallpa, Peru (phone: 6457-6551; or in the US, 800-327-6162). Moderate.

***La Cabaña Hotel/Lodge*** – A lakeside bungalow-resort that offers water sports, food service, jungle trails. Travelers usually reserve in 3-day packages. Write to the hotel at Apartado 43 in Pucallpa (no phone). Moderate.

### IQUITOS

***Amazonas Plaza*** – Owned by a Spanish hotel chain, this 120-room property provides swimming pool, tennis courts, and rooms with private baths. Although these are the most comfortable lodgings in the city, this place is outrageously expensive and the service poor. Abelardo Quiñónes at Km 2, about 4 miles (6 km) outside Iquitos (phone: 94-231091; in Lima, 14-404559). Expensive.

***Acosta*** – A small hotel, it also has a restaurant. Calles Huallaga and Calvo (phone: 94-231761). Its sister hotel, *Acosta II*, is closer to the riverfront at 252 Ricardo Palma (94-232904). Best options in town for service and price. Moderate.

***Ambassador*** – Another small hostelry, it has 25 rooms, a convenient location, and fairly good service. 260 Calle Pevas (phone: 94-233110; in Lima, 14-283029). Moderate.

***Turistas*** – A government-owned property that retains the musty, frontier ambience that has made it a long-time favorite with visitors. All of its 80 rooms have private baths, and there is a bar and dining room. Ask for a room with an air conditioner (although they can be noisy). Malecón Tarapacá (phone: 94-230111; in Lima, 14-721928; in the US, 800-275-3123). Moderate.

## DOWNSTREAM

***Amazon Lodge*** – Provides accommodations for 90 people in thatch-roofed huts, and it has a bar and restaurant, as well as walking trails. River trips, visits to an Indian village, and outings to fish or spot crocodiles can be arranged. Ninety minutes downstream from Iquitos. Make arrangements at *Amazon Lodge and Safaris Travel Agency* at 165 Putumayo in Iquitos (phone: 94-233032; in Lima, 14-419194). Expensive.

***Amazon Village*** – A village with 34 bungalows, a thatch-roofed common house, and open-air bar — all on the Momon River. For information, contact the US sales office of *Hotels Promoting Peru* (phone: in Florida, 813-439-2118; elsewhere in the US, 800-327-3573; in Lima, 14-441199; in Iquitos, 94-235731). Expensive.

***Explorama Inn*** – The best in the Iquitos area, this is the only lodge on the main Amazon River. Located 25 miles downriver from the city, where the Amazon meets the Yanamono, each of its 25 separate bungalows has a private bath and shower. The flora and fauna here are unsurpassed in the greater Iquitos area. Make arrangements at 340 Av. La Marina in Iquitos (phone: 94-235471; in Lima, 14-244764); or in the US, call *Selective Hotel Reservations* at 617-581-0844; toll-free, 800-223-6764). Expensive.

***Jungle Amazon Inn*** – Some 30 miles from Iquitos — a 1½-hour trip downriver and some 3 hours back — it has 29 bungalows with private bath, as well as a restaurant and bar. Make reservations at 132 Putumayo in Iquitos (phone: 94-232249); in Lima, 14-408068; fax: 14-479870). Expensive.

***Amazon Camp*** – Thatch-roofed accommodations with semiprivate bath, central dining, and jungle walks, run by the *Amazon Camp Tourist Service*. On Río Momon tributary, 45 minutes from Iquitos's dock. Reservations through *Amazon Tours and Cruises*, Miami, Florida (phone: 305-227-2266; fax: 305-227-1880; or in Lima, 14-407202). You also can make reservations at their office in Iquitos at 151 Próspero (phone: 94-233931; fax: 94-231265). Moderate.

***Explorama Lodge*** – Part of Explorama's trio of lodges (the other two are the *Explorama Inn* near Iquitos and the *Explornapo Camp*), this property has 10 pavilions of rooms. There are separate, rustic (but clean) bathrooms, and beds draped with mosquito netting. Hammocks strung outside give guests a place to relax as the sun goes down, when kerosene lamps are lit. Visitors may then go to the bar for Peruvian music and drink. This is the longest operating of the jungle accommodations and its food is unsurpassed. Five hours farther downstream is the more rustic *Explornapo Camp*, with tents and open-hearth cooking; a favorite of bird watchers and naturalists. Make reservations for all 3 lodges at 340 Av. La Marina in Iquitos (phone: 94-235471; in Lima, 14-244764); or in the US, call *Selective Hotel Reservations* at 617-581-0844; toll-free, 800-223-6764). Moderate.

# Madre de Dios

Cuzco is the jumping-off place (by air or land) for Peru's southeastern jungle of the Río Madre de Dios, a 700-mile-long tributary of the Amazon that runs northeast through Peru. The department of Madre de Dios, established in 1912, is a wide, 29,640-square-mile area no different than the Amazon — hot and humid, with a drenching rainy season. It has attracted oil and gold prospectors who daily combat jungle conditions in their search for fortune and fame. In recent years, it also has lured adventure tourists interested in traveling through the incomparable Manú National Park. Overland, the southern edge of the park is 154 miles (256 km) from Cuzco, passing through Paucartambo. The rest of the area's 40,000 inhabitants are farmers, who grow *cascarilla, castañas,* Brazil nuts, vanilla, cacao, coffee, cotton, and sugarcane. In addition, there are *siringeros,* the rubber farmers of the Río Tahuamanú near the town of Iberia on the Bolivian border, who still tap and produce *goma,* or organic rubber, using old-fashioned methods. Oddly enough, many of these rubber farmers are Japanese, descendants of the immigrants during the organic rubber boom of the early 20th century. During the expansion of the Inca empire, Túpac Yupanqui (Inca warrior and ruler) pushed as far as the Madre de Dios, which he called Amarumayo (Snake River). The Spanish conquistadores made several attempts later to enter the region but it wasn't until the 19th century that the first outside mission established a settlement here.

One way to see the Madre de Dios area is to take a boat trip from Puerto Maldonado, the capital of the department, 350 miles downriver, across the Bolivian border to Riberalta, an isolated Bolivian rubber-tapping center some 40 miles from the frontier. It's a glorious adventure, especially if you've ever dreamed of floating down a mammoth, muddy jungle river where shy, soft-spoken Indians shoot crocodiles with bows and arrows. The old-fashioned way to travel is by dugout canoe, taking about 7 days to complete the journey. By motorized launch, you can reach Riberalta in about 4 days. Although no regular transport service exists along the river, it isn't difficult to charter a boat, complete with necessary jungle river travel amenities that include a guide, cook, hammock, and (most importantly) a mosquito net. If you're looking for a detailed published route, forget it!

Another trip is to use Puerto Maldonado as the jumping-off point for visits to the Manú National Park, considered by many (including UNESCO) to be one of the most intriguing pieces of virgin rain forest on the planet, as well as for fishing at the headwaters of the Amazon. Unfortunately, Puerto Maldonado is not a pleasant town in which to relax. The people are friendly, but a quick walk around the square, grid layout of the dusty streets and the unexciting clapboard architecture should help inspire you to explore further.

There are a number of ways to reach Puerto Maldonado. You can take a 25-minute flight (depending on weather) from Cuzco aboard *AeroPerú, Faucett, Americana,* or *Andrea,* or any of airlines' flights from Lima that make connections in Cuzco. There are also tour agencies, including *Manu Nature Tours* (C-7 Ovalo de Tio; phone: 84-231549), that organize plane trips to

Puerto Maldonado. *AeroPerú* flies out daily, *Faucett* operates on Tuesdays, Thursdays, and Saturdays, and *Americana* and *Andrea* fly 6 days a week. In addition, the Peruvian Air Force — Air Group No. 8 — offers a passenger service aboard its cargo planes on a first-come, first-served basis every Thursday. The same service is available from Puerto Maldonado to Cuzco on Saturdays. Check at the airport for times.

However you go, consume a fair number of vitamin B pills *(tiamina)* as a deterrent against mosquitoes (it works) and check with the Centers for Disease Control or your local health department to see if they recommend quinine pills to ward off malaria. A medicine kit with antiseptic, insect repellent, a snakebite kit, and some antifungus cream might also be a good idea. There is little formal health care. However, the International Red Cross conducts boat cruises of the Madre de Dios system.

**PUERTO MALDONADO:** The sleepy, ramshackle, riverside port with 7,000 inhabitants is the shipping point for jungle products from the deepest reaches of the rain forests — and it is also a point for airlinks to Bolivia and Brazil. Founded in 1902 and the easternmost of Peru's cities, it lies where the Madre de Dios and Tambopata rivers meet.

In the surrounding area, about 3 hours by river, is the Tambopata Natural Wildlife Preserve, established in 1977. This is the place for jungle safaris and visits to the villages of the Huaraya Indians. Their main village lies on the Palma Real, a red-soil plateau overlooking the Madre de Dios. It is a clearing of huts with nearby fields under cultivation in the slash-and-burn method. The Indians are peaceful, but have had only limited contact with civilization. Trips to the preserve can be arranged through *Peruvian Safaris* (1334 Av. Garcilaso de la Vega, PO Box 10088, Lima 1; phone: 14-313047) and start at about $40 a day. This company also arranges for launches for about $10 an hour for those who want to go birding or fishing for catfish, piranha, and peacock bass. From September through November, Peruvian jungle veteran José Rada leads groups of 15 on fishing, bird watching, and photo safaris to Madre de Dios and the headwaters of the Amazon. The 7-day adventures involve a certain amount of roughing it — travelers sleep in tents by the riverside. The fishing target is the toothy, tarpon-like tigu fish, which resembles the African tiger fish. The safaris depart from Puerto Maldonado and the package costs about $1500 per person, not including airfare or fishing tackle. Contact Sr. Rada at *Pan American Safaris* (240 Av. 2 de Mayo, San Isidro, Lima; phone: 14-221542 and 14-417309; fax: 14-422438) or the Peru Tourist Board in Miami (305-374-0023; fax: 305-374-4905).

Farther into the rain forest is the Manú National Park, a 30-minute plane ride from Cuzco or several days by boat from Puerto Maldonado. But note before you go that the Peruvian Foundation for the Conservation of Nature has issued guidelines for visitors to this special region. Travelers are asked to try to see — and photograph — animals and birds as discreetly as possible, to avoid making noise, and not to leave trash in the park. In addition, hunting or capturing wild animals is forbidden by law. The best way to make the trip into Manú is through a local tour operator in Cuzco, Lima, or Puerto Maldonado, or through packages available in the US.

**MANU:** The park comprises some 4,800 square miles and extends from altitudes of 1,000 to 12,000 feet. The base of the Dirección Forestal de Perú, which runs the park with financial aid from the World Wildlife Fund, is where the Panahua and Manú rivers join. The national park was set up in 1967; 6 years later UNESCO declared it an International Biosphere Reserve.

Much of the park is unexplored cloud forest where bear, puma, tapir, and spider monkeys roam. Also in the area are hostile Amahuaca Indians, said to occupy the area of the Río de las Piedras near the Isthmus of Fitzcarrald. In the lowland jungle are such rare animals as giant otter and black caimans. Around Lake Cochacascho, the forestry department has built an observation post that has become the best spot in the *selva* for viewing rare hoatzin, a reddish yellow marsh bird, and oropendola. Bird watchers should note that it is believed that 460 species of birds live here, in an area of only 1 square mile.

Your first contact with the park will come at a point known as the Mirador de Tres Cruces (Three Crosses) where, on a clear day, it is possible to see the Amazon plain stretch as far as 60 miles in the distance. Following a serpentine route to the river Alto Madre de Dios, you'll come upon a spot known as Shintuya, where small boats are available for lunch trips into the park area. Another of the forestry department's bases is at Takakume, en route to Sotilya Lake (a giant otter haven), a good day's canoe ride from Panahua. Near the base is the only known collective settlement of the Machiguenga Indians, who generally live in separate family units. These primitive hunters have only had contact with the outside world for the last 20 years.

At a spot known as Pokitza, there is a park office where information is available, but unescorted treks into the park are discouraged. Miraculously, Puerto Maldonado and the immediate vicinity are not excessively plagued by mosquitoes and bugs. Cool nighttime breezes periodically sweep down from the not-too-distant snow-capped Andes and keep the insect population down. However, equip yourself with mosquito nets and long-sleeved shirts when you go on any expedition.

The temperature hovers in the 85 to 90F (29 to 33C) range year-round, but the months of June, July, and August constitute South American winter. Occasionally the "southern winds" will blow for 3 or 4 days and the temperature will dip to about 50F (10C). Although the locals complain about these cold spells (called *friaje),* they are most definitely welcome. Most important, avoid visiting the area during the summer rainy season, which lasts from November through March.

**En Route from Puerto Maldonado** – Sightsee here and take the side trips, but the natural termination of this trip is downriver at Riberalta, Bolivia. You'll see lots of fascinating wildlife once you're on the river: Black bears roam the jungle recesses and you might encounter freshly killed, ferocious-looking jungle cats. On some occasions baby vicuña stride down to drink at the river at sunset. You'll also see furry, two-toed sloths hanging upside down by their oversize claws. Armadillos, tapirs, crocodiles, and turtles also live in the area, and if you stop at a village (be prepared to stay since you'll be warmly invited), you might be treated to a bit of one of these as a snack.

The river literally is swarming with fish. Piranha are not particularly numerous since they favor clearer waters, where the oxygen content is higher, but other equally unfriendly aquatic specimens — such as the freshwater stingray — are prevalent. Three species of crocodiles exist, although their numbers are dwindling. July is the time for the migration of large schools of fish that the locals call salmon. These tasty 20-pound monsters can be hooked as they swim up the clearwater tributary side streams to spawn. July and early August is also when the turtles lay their eggs on the sandbars at night.

Probably the noisiest and most colorful of the nonhuman inhabitants are the birds. This is an area where birdlife proliferates, yet little ornithological work has been done. Butterflies glide past in rainbow-colored clouds, enveloping the equally breathtaking orchids that dangle from the fallen tree trunks along the banks. The air sparkles, and the scent of flowers is magical.

Before leaving Puerto Maldonado, be sure you have received your official stamps and *laissez-passer* exit papers that will be required at the frontier post at the Peru-Bolivia border. The terrain for 50 miles (80 km) on either side of Puerto

Heath is the wildest area of the entire route. The merchant boats do not pass through this section of Madre de Dios, and consequently, occasional groups of pure-blood, non-Spanish-speaking Amerindians have remained almost untouched in this part of the jungle. One such civilization is at Pan Marial, a population of less than 1,000 who retain their traditional language, religion, and customs and are extremely hospitable. Essentially oblivious to the cash economy and the outside world, they eke out a subsistence livelihood from their untamable environment in much the same way that their ancestors did.

**RIBERALTA:** This fairly pleasant town, whose economy is based on rubber and nuts, is perched at the confluence of the Beni and Madre de Dios rivers. A passable dirt road crosses the border from Brazil at Guayaramerin. No road, however, links the town with the rest of Bolivia. Consequently, although the dirt streets are wide and symmetrical, there are very few automobiles. Motorcycles, on the other hand, are quite common. For under a dollar you can go almost anywhere on one of the many "moto-taxis" that cruises throughout the municipality.

Unless you enter Riberalta by bus or jeep from Brazil, the only access is via airplane. Several passenger and cargo flights arrive every week from La Paz, Cochabamba, and Trinidad, Bolivia. The restaurants on the plaza all serve palatable food. There is even an ice cream and coffee shop serving delicious cappuccino.

The town is better maintained than Puerto Maldonaldo. Pickup trucks spray water on the dirt streets to keep the dust to a minimum. The main center of activity is the tastefully laid-out central plaza. During the cool evening hours, the entire population strolls up and down the plaza. The hottest nightspot is *El Disco,* just off the plaza. It is a neon-decorated, thatch-hut nightclub with genuine American soul music.

Forty-five minutes away by moto-taxi is the spectacular lake of Tumi Chucua, a perfect place to swim during the heat of the day. A US missionary group (the Wycliffe Bible translators) has established a small open colony at this heavenly spot. In blatant contradiction to the jungle setting, there are washing machines, hot dogs, diving boards, and Styrofoam sailboats.

Riberalta and its immediate environs have a rather congenial frontier atmosphere. Very few tourists venture this far into the jungle, so the townspeople are extremely friendly and eager to meet visitors. Don't be surprised at dinner invitations or conversations with strangers at neighboring tables.

The best time of year to visit is during the first 10 days of August, when Bolivian *Independence Day* is celebrated. For 4 days, August 4–7, all business activities shut down. All the *riberalteños,* in a truly hedonistic South American frontier style, take to the streets, eating, drinking, dancing, and laughing all through the night.

## BEST EN ROUTE

Transient accommodations are virtually nil along this route. With the exception of one hotel in Puerto Maldonado and some jungle lodges, there are no decent properties; even these, although inexpensive (about $14 a night and under for a double room), provide no hot water. You must also write to them for the required reservations or try to make arrangements through your travel agent.

### PUERTO MALDONADO

***Turistas*** – A 16-room government-run lodge on the Río Tambopata, providing basic room and food service. On León Velarde (phone: Puerto Maldonado 29; in Lima, through *EnturPerú* at 14-721928; in the US, 800-275-3123).

### DOWNSTREAM

***Albergue Cuzco Amazónico*** – This jungle lodge, 50 miles (80 km) downstream of Puerto Maldonado on the left bank of the Madre de Dios River, provides thatch-roofed accommodations, and package rates include meals. Trails lead into the surrounding jungle; hiking and canoe rides are offered. Stays are available in 1- and 4-day packages (phone: in Lima, 14-462775 or 14-477193).

## TAMBOPATA NATURAL WILDLIFE PRESERVE

***Explorer's Inn*** – Bungalow huts at the edge of the jungle park offer mosquito protection (netting), and the food is good; meals are included in package rates. Planned activities include jungle walks, visits to Indian camps, animal and bird watching, alligator spotting at night, and trips to Cocococha to see toucans, parrots, monkeys, and boas. This wildlife area has recorded sightings of 547 species of birds, 1,110 butterflies, and 103 dragonflies. Contact *Explorer's Inn,* 1334 Av. Garcilaso de la Vega, PO Box 10088, Lima 1 (phone: in Lima, 14-313047 or 14-316330; in Cuzco, 84-235342; fax: 14-328866).

## RIBERALTA

***Riberalta*** – A small hotel that offers clean rooms. In the center of town.
***Santa Rita*** – Another small place in the center of town that provides clean rooms and air conditioning.

# Suriname

*As we went to press, the US State Department had issued an advisory warning for travel to Suriname. Although the situation in the countryside is currently stable, because of a lack of sufficient police authority, US citizens are advised to exercise caution when traveling outside the main cities of Paramaribo and Nieuw Nickerie and to avoid unaccompanied travel to the interior. North Americans who visit Suriname are urged to register with the consular section of the US Embassy at 129 Dr. Sophie Redmondstraat, Paramaribo (phone: 477881).*

A tiny, 63,037-square-mile piece of land on the northern coast of South America, Suriname — formerly Dutch Guiana — is one of those countries you don't just drive into. It cannot be reached by car from the surrounding countries: Neither Guyana (to the west) nor French Guiana (to the east) is connected with the Pan-American Highway. And there is little reason to go to the expense of shipping a car in and out. Although there are good coastal highways (for the most part paved), they are cut by large rivers flowing from the mountains in the south to the Atlantic Ocean; the roads often can be crossed only by ferry.

Suriname itself is not an old country, gaining total independence from the Netherlands as recently as 1975. But its roots stretch back as far as the late 16th century, when Dutch expeditions repossessed Spanish territory that included not only Suriname, but Guyana (formerly British Guiana). The Dutch did their best during the next 400 years to preserve their stronghold, but to no avail. Constant British attacks against the coast and an unsuccessful slave revolt in the mid-1700s contributed to the erosion. Suriname finally was lost to the British in the 17th century, and the Dutch only regained it — named Serrinam by the British — when they traded it for their island of Manhattan in 1667. In 1863, an already torn Suriname endured a successful slave revolt that resulted in the Dutch granting the colony its own parliament 2 years later. This ultimately led to the country's total independence in 1975, which ended — for the moment — a long period of civil stress and racial strife.

The country had a two-party system until February 1980, when a group of army sergeants toppled the government and installed a military dictatorship. This government lasted until 1987, when a new civilian administration was elected. However, the military remained the dominant power, and in December 1990 the army again seized formal power, promising to hold elections within 100 days. Democratic elections were held in May 1991, and a coalition of three parties won 30 of the 51 seats in the National Assembly. The coalition formed a new government and elected Ronald Venetiaan president. At press time, Venetiaan had made a proposal to the assembly that the constitution be changed to strip the military of its power. Popular opinion holds that it is almost certain to pass, thus paving the way for Suriname to return to a democratic system of government. Prior to the coup, the only challenge to the military came from a lingering guerrilla revolt by Bushnegroes in the eastern and southern parts of the country, and the recent emergence of Amerindian insurgents in the west. The war has ended and as we went to press, peace was being negotiated; the area is no longer off limits to curious, albeit cautious, travelers.

The Suriname of today is a cultural melting pot of Bushnegroes (the term is absolutely valid, since it stems from the 1863 fight for independence by ex-slaves-turned-guerrillas who hid out in the jungle bush), Chinese, Indonesians (descendants of laborers brought to work on the tobacco, rice, and coffee plantations), Amerindians (or Suriens, descendants of the indigenous tribes), and Europeans (Dutch, Portuguese, and Jews). The official language is still Dutch. The local language is Sranan Tongo, or Taki-Taki; and there are a few dialects spoken by small tribal groups. Most of the country's 370,000 inhabitants are centered around Paramaribo, the coastal capital.

The country itself is a tropical, pretty place: a blend of forest-covered land, savannahs, sparkling rivers and streams, sandy beaches, lagoons, mangrove forests, and murky swamps. The leading industries are bauxite mining and aluminum processing along with forestry and the production of rice, bananas, plantains, citrus fruits, coconuts, and maize. Even before the guerrilla struggle began in 1986, tourism was almost nil.

The easiest way (a relative term) to get there is on *Surinam Airways,* the national carrier, with service between Miami, Amsterdam, and Paramaribo. *KLM, Cruzeiro do Sul,* and *ALM Antillean* all have connecting flights from the US via Caribbean points. Bus service from Paramaribo is available into the country's interior, although it is safer to travel to these areas in a group, and there is daily service by launch across the Corantijn River separating Suriname from Guyana.

The main road from Paramaribo south crosses, after some 75 miles (120 km), the Afobaka Dam, which backs up the waters of the Suriname River to form an artificial lake to generate electrical power on behalf of the bauxite mining industry. Whoever wants to go farther south into the jungle, where there are still quite a number of Amerindian and Bushnegro villages (Bushnegroes and their tribes — including chiefs — are recognized by the central government), must travel either by outboard canoe or plane. Airstrips built for survey and development work are numerous in the interior, and many are open to tourists.

The best place to start a tour through Suriname is from Paramaribo. Any questions you have can be answered by *Surinam Airways* (5775 Blue Lagoon Drive, Suite 320, Miami, FL 33126; phone: 800-327-6864 or 175-61 Hillside Ave., Suite 320, Jamaica, NY; phone: 718-658-3530 or 800-339-8052) before you leave the US, or at the tourism department in Paramaribo (8 Waterkant, phone: 597-471163 or 597-478421). Unless you're the rugged type, stay in a hotel, not in a guesthouse, which often lacks private baths and very much comfort.

Paramaribo is about 30 miles (48 km) from Johan Adolf Penegel, the international airport. The drive will take 45 minutes. The airport lies in a savannah where the trees do not grow very tall and the land is interspersed by white sand and swamp water. Alongside the road to Paramaribo some Bushnegroes have set up small workshops where they produce woodcarvings. Made on a flat cedar board, each intricately carved piece is different, depending on what the artist wants to express. Love and eroticism play a large role in this, as in daily life. The men produce these carvings for their women, using them to express their feelings. Crude utensils such as forks, combs, ladles, and paddles are also made (the last do not necessarily express feelings).

Near the Creole settlement of Onverwacht, one passes the ruins of the main station of what was the railway to the abandoned gold mines farther south. Nearby lies Bernharddorp, an Amerindian village, where on festive occasions the women may still don traditional brightly colored dresses. Nearer the city, stretched across both sides of the road, Hindustanis (as the East Indian immigrants are called) have small vegetable farm plots. There are also several Hindu temples. A few miles before reaching Paramaribo lies the 9-hole golf course of the *Golf Club Paramaribo*. Tourists may be introduced by members and pay only a small greens fee for using the well-kept course.

As the city comes into view above the water tower, the main reservoir of the waterworks sticks out above the surrounding buildings. The industrial area, it includes the plant of the British-American Tobacco Company and, by the river, the mills of the Bruynzeel Lumber Company. After crossing the Saramacca Canal, you are in Paramaribo.

**PARAMARIBO:** This interesting city has many wooden buildings in the typical colonial style, particularly in the center of the old town. In Sranan Tongo, the native lingua franca, Paramaribo is called Foto, "fort," since the city was built around Fort Zeelandia, lying in a bend of the wide Suriname River some 12 miles from the ocean. Fort Zeelandia was initially a small garrison of French colonists; later it became the English Fort Willoughby and then was captured by Abraham Crynssen from Zeeland in 1667. Strengthened afterward, the stone walls of the pentagonal fort are many feet thick and have bastions at the corners. When there was no further use for the fort as such, Zeelandia was used as a prison, then restored as a museum and, sadly, now reoccupied by the military. The area around the fort is lovely, with tall mahogany, mango, and tamarind trees, and the old residences of the officers — still in use — have been well maintained. To the left of the fort, the former army barracks, built in 1970, now house the Military Police. Behind the fort are the modern buildings and grounds of the Cabinet of the Commander of the National Army, which look out not only on the river but, on the land side, on Independence Square, one of the most beautiful squares on this side of the ocean. In the old times it used to be called Esplanado or Place d'Armée, for the army used to parade here, but the name was changed several times — for instance, into Government Square and Oranjeplein (after the Dutch House of Orange) — until the country became independent. The large grass field — a gathering place on festive occasions — is dominated by the Presidential Palace, the home of the president of the republic, built in 1730 but repeatedly remodeled and expanded since then.

The west side of the square is taken up by three old, typical colonial buildings: the Court of Justice, the Ministry of Finance, and the Ministry of the Interior. The first was built with red brick stone, which was brought to the country as ballast in sailing ships. The imposing Ministry of Finance in the center, with tall columns and a 104-foot tower, was originally the Town Hall. The Ministry of the Interior, built of wood, is at least as old as the Court of Justice (1774).

Visitors do not have far to go to find quiet in the middle of the busy city. Right behind the Presidential Palace are the Palm Gardens, with dozens of tall royal palms. Coming back past the palace and turning into the Gravenstraat, other colonial buildings, each 2 to 3 centuries old, catch the eye: the Parliament Building, on the corner with the Grote Combeweg, and the Ministry of General and Foreign Affairs, where the vice president has his office. Farther down the street is the Roman Catholic Cathedral of St. Peter and St. Paul, with its tall spires. It is said to be the largest completely wooden cathedral in South America. Now restored, it forms quite a contrast to the modernistic building of De Surinaamsche Bank next door. Go inside and admire its unpainted cedar interior with high curved ceilings in neo-Romanesque style, its pillars and high, glass-paneled windows each in a different pattern and the carved gate to the baptismal font.

Around the corner on Kerkplein is the Reformed church, an octagonal building that dates from 1835. Inside, the pews rest on historical gravestones covering the floor. With an old mahogany pulpit, brass chandeliers, and a big organ, it is only natural that Suriname's independence was proclaimed here in the presence of Queen Juliana of the Netherlands and that the University of Suriname also uses it on special occasions. Other interesting religious buildings include Hindu temples at Koningstraat, a mosque at Keizerstraat, and a synagogue, built over a century ago, at Herenstraat.

The Kerkplein is surrounded by some modern buildings, including the ABN Bank, the Central Post Office, a department store, and the main office of the electric company.

*Orlando's Coffee Shop*, with its coffee terrace, is a gathering place for lunching hotel guests. To have a hearty lunch or dinner, cross the street to *Iwan's* restaurant, which specializes in Chinese dishes.

On the other hand, if you're hankering for native dishes, ask for *Roline's* restaurant. Take a taxi for the 5-minute drive to the northern border of the city. The dining room is small, but the food is great. Some of the dishes you'll want to try are *pom*, which contains fried chicken and a potato-like vegetable, and *nasi goreng*, with either meat or chicken with vegetables, all ingredients fried.

In the center of the city are several cafeterias, including *Spanhoek's* soda fountain, *Chindy's Fountain*, and, in the Domineestraat (the main shopping street), the *Macoland* and *Hola* cafeterias, where you can sit and look down on the city's busiest intersection, the girls driving by on their fast scooters, and the vendors selling shaved ice. The *Hola* is next to a supermarket of the same name. *Alegria* (on Keizerstraat) is yet another good cafeteria.

For those wishing to try the Indonesian rijsstafel, a multi-course dish including the *nasi goreng*, try the *Deli* (on Watermolenstraat) or *Sarinah's* (on Verlengde Gemenelandsweg). Order a taxi to go there, however, for *Sarinah's* is quite a distance beyond Via Bella with its modern villas.

Surrounding Paramaribo are the modern residential areas, including Zorg en Hoop, site of a small international airport, and Elisabethshof. Driving beside the Suriname River toward the ocean one also sees beautiful villas on the Anton Dragtenweg all the way to Leonsberg, where the *River Club* hotel with its cozy restaurant and a lively discotheque are located (see *Best en Route*). On the edge of the river rests another bar-restaurant-discotheque, the *Leonsberg*. But go upstairs unless you want to mix with the local boys having a good time or waiting for the ferry to cross to Fort Nieuw Amsterdam and its open-air museum. (But upstairs the prices are higher!)

What you should not miss in Paramaribo is the central market, where you will see all the different people of the country, all the produce with its exotic smells and the stalls with fish brought in every morning from the river or barbecued if you want. Also, at the central market you will hear all of the country's languages being spoken.

From the central market all your shopping is available within a few blocks. It is better

**1004 DIRECTIONS / Suriname**

to walk here, as it is difficult to find a parking place. There is great variety — from large department stores to small souvenir and jewelry shops. There are also imports from the Orient such as batik, jade, and ivory (the latter is prohibited import to the US) as well as dress fabrics from all over the world.

**En Route from Paramaribo** – Traffic in Suriname drives on the left. When driving to Albina, a border town on the broad Marowijne (Maroni) River, look out, since the neighbors in French Guiana drive on the right and may forget when they cross the border. This route, closed from late 1986, was reopened by the military in late 1990 after the guerrilla war had subsided.

Traveling from Paramaribo, you have to cross the Suriname River first by car ferry to Meerzorg. From there, the East-West Highway leads straight to Albina, some 90 miles (144 km) away. The road leads past Hindustani settlements, with their temples and mosques, as well as the large, Indonesian village of Tamanredjo.

The widest river to cross in between is the Commewijne, but since a bridge has been built, people are no longer held up by the ferry, which was used for over 15 years. Apart from small farms and a few Bushnegro huts, there is not much to see between the Commewijne and the bauxite-mining town of Moengo. The Surinam Aluminum Company, a subsidiary of Alcoa, runs this American-style community. Stopping on the hill beyond the bridge over the Cottica River, one can see a small golf course, a ranch with the best cattle anywhere in Suriname, and a milk plant as well; to the left, down the Cottica River, are the smokestacks of the bauxite-crushing plant. If time permits, drive around Moengo; be sure not to miss the White House, the company club, situated on a hill and surrounded by a valley.

Near Moengo lies the Indonesian village of Wonoredjo, where on occasion you can see Javanese dances performed to the tinkling of *gamelan* music. Going on to Albina, you pass the bauxite mines and several Bushnegro villages. At one of them called Negerkreek, Bushnegro fire dances are staged (if arrangements have been made in advance). It is usually too costly for individuals to do so, therefore tour operators do it for groups only.

Nearing Albina, you cross a hill: The town can be seen with the river behind it and St.-Laurent-du-Maroni on the other side.

**ALBINA:** Formerly a popular vacation spot for Surinamese, this sleepy riverfront town largely was abandoned in 1986, when it was first seized by guerrillas and later retaken by the army. If peace is assured in eastern Suriname, Albina could resume its role as a jumping-off point for trips across the Marowijne River to neighboring French Guiana, or upriver to Amerindian and Bushnegro villages. Although one popular Marowijne River resort, Stoelman's Island, has been the headquarters of Bushnegro guerrillas since 1986, *Surinam Airways* started flying there again after rebel activity ceased in 1991.

At night, the *Anjoemara Club,* on a river beach, offers disco music. Tastefully decorated with driftwood and other crude material, it is practically the sole place of entertainment apart from a movie house.

On Albina's waterfront — which gets a constant breeze — hire a canoe to travel either downriver to some Amerindian village or to the beaches where the turtles lay their eggs, or upriver to other Amerindian and Bushnegro villages. A real adventure is the canoe trip to Stoelmansisland and beyond, up the Tapanahony River to the Gran Holo Falls, which takes several days. It may be easier to fly from Paramaribo on *Surinam Airways* for a 3-day tour.

**En Route from Albina** – If you backtrack to Paramaribo and take the highway west, you come to Nieuw Nickerie, a town on the western border nestled between the Nickerie and Corantijn rivers, the latter forming a natural border with Guyana. The road is dotted with many small farms; although a bridge now crosses the Saramacca River, you have to cross by ferry at the mile-wide Coppename

Estuary. On the other side of the river lies the Coronie district, called the land of milk and honey because of its coconut groves. The district is inhabited mainly by Creoles and Indonesians; signs along the road bearing Scottish names such as Inverness and Totness remind you of the first settlers.

Soon you reach the Nickerie district. Wageningen is the biggest fully mechanized rice farm in the world, and the polders, where rice is grown, seem endless. When you cross the bridge over the Nickerie River, you'll reach more rice fields before getting to the town of Nieuw Nickerie itself, which looks much like a western boomtown. It is Suriname's second-largest city, with a population of 30,000.

An interesting place to visit is Brownsberg, a 14,820-acre nature park about 2½ hours south of Paramaribo. The park can be reached by driving yourself or, better yet, by taking a combination bus and van tour. The park is a tropical rain forest filled with giant toads, communal spiders, monkeys, jaguars, jacamars, macaws, and the colorful, wide-billed toucan. There is an admission charge.

The park is operated by STINASU, the foundation for nature preservation in Suriname. Maps are available at the park office, and a guidebook to the birds in Brownsberg may be purchased at the STINASU office in Paramaribo (14 Cornelis Jongbawstraat; phone: 597-471856 or 597-475845). STINASU operates tours to nature preserves throughout Suriname. A worthwhile day trip is to Matapica in the Wia-Wia Reserve northeast of Paramaribo.

The Wia-Wia Reserve offers a look at five species of turtles (the reserve is their nesting ground), and some wonderful bird life, including wild ibis, flamingos, spoonbills, kites, terns, and storks. To get to the reserve from Paramaribo, make arrangements for a day trip, including transportation and lunch, with STINASU.

## BEST EN ROUTE

Because of the huge disparity between the official and parallel (read: black market) exchange rates in Suriname, hotels and other tourist facilities have become very expensive. At hotels in Paramaribo, expect to pay (at the official exchange rate) up to $180 a night for a double room categorized as expensive. More moderate hotels vary widely in price, from as low as $30 to $50 a night, up to $70 to $80. Guesthouses generally are inexpensive, less than $30.

### PARAMARIBO

*Krasnapolsky Paramaribo* – The 85 air conditioned rooms, including 3 suites, contain private baths; European and American Plans are both offered. Centrally located (phone: 597-475050; fax: 597-478524). Expensive.

*Suriname Torarica* – A gambling casino, swimming pool, meeting facilities, and a restaurant are among the amenities in this 132-room hotel. About 5 minutes from downtown (phone: 597-471500 or 597-477432; fax: 597-411682). Expensive.

*Ambassador* – It has 42 rooms, a bar, the *Rachel* bistro, meeting facilities, air conditioning, and showers. 66-68 Dr. Sophie Redmondstraat (phone: 597-477555). Moderate.

*River Club* – This 119-room property has air conditioning, showers, and 25 bungalows with kitchenettes. Bar, restaurant, lounge, swimming pool, and golf, tennis, and other sports facilities are also on the premises. On the river estuary about 7 minutes outside the city. Reservations: Box 914 (phone: 597-451959). Moderate.

### NIEUW NICKERIE

There are a few comfortable guesthouses worth checking out, including *Ameer Ali's* (G.G. Maynerdstraat; phone: 597-231642; fax: 597-231066) and *Hotel de Vesting* (6

Balatastraat; phone: 597-231265); others in the area are not recommended. Both guesthouses are inexpensive.

## BROWNSBERG PARK

***Central Lodge*** – Cottages and bungalows sleep eight to ten people and provide kitchen facilities, showers, toilets, and beds. In the park. Moderate to inexpensive.

# Uruguay

One of the smallest countries in South America, Uruguay covers only 68,037 square miles of hilly meadows, broken by streams and rivers and a strand of beaches along the coast. A roughly triangular country, it is bordered by Argentina on the west and south, Brazil on the north, and the Atlantic Ocean on the east and south. The capital, Montevideo, has a population of nearly 1.5 million out of a national total of 3.5 million.

Most of the country is grazing land for sheep and cattle. Salto (pop. 60,000) is the center of the cattle-raising area. Uruguay's colorful cowboys, the gauchos, congregate here. There also are 400 miles of beach, and the major seaside resort, Punta del Este, draws hordes of vacationing Argentines, as well as Uruguayans. The country has a temperate climate, with summer temperatures climbing as high as 90F (32C) between November and March, dropping to the low 40s F (around 5C) between June and August.

The Spanish explorer Juan de Solís landed in Uruguay in 1516, but he and his band were promptly attacked and killed by Charrua Indians. The first real exploration took place in 1520, when Ferdinand Magellan sailed up the Río de la Plata to the site on which Montevideo now stands. Although accurate records of the exact date have been lost, the capital was founded sometime in the early 18th century. Until the early 19th century, Uruguay was little more than a buffer zone between rival Spanish and Portuguese interests.

José Gervasio Artigas led a grass-roots movement for independence from Spain between 1811 and 1821, but Uruguay was annexed to Brazil until 1828, when independence finally was declared formally.

Uruguayans have experimented with various democratic institutions of government and, for a time, were popularly known as the Swiss of South America — because the country was run by a Swiss-inspired national council from the 1920s until 1966. During the 1970s, Uruguay suffered from horrific outbreaks of urban violence, and the adoption of dictatorial methods by President Juan María Bordaberry proved inadequate to quell the disorder. He was ousted in 1976 by a military coup that restored a certain amount of stability; the military government itself became one of oppression. However, the first popular election in years was held in 1984, when Julio Mario Sanguinetti was elected to a 5-year term. In a quiet election in late 1989, Luis Alberto Lacalle won the presidency.

As you drive through the countryside, you'll discover a wide variety of wildlife. Green parakeets nest high in eucalyptus trees; partridges can be seen walking across the road; red oven birds' 2-room nests perch on telephone posts; *ñandúes* (a species of small ostrich) gallop in the fields; and wood pigeons are practically everywhere. You also can see, among others, the small *apereá* (a rat-like rodent) scurrying into the bushes as the cars approach, hares in the fields, skunks, and the tasty *mulita* (a breed of small armadillo).

For the most part, Uruguay maintains the pace of the small, agrarian society that it is. English rarely is spoken in any of the smaller villages. Although you can change dollars at some banks in the interior, it is usually best to do so in Montevideo; credit cards are of little value except in the capital and Punta del Este.

One way to get around Uruguay is to rent a car. In Montevideo, in addition to *Avis* (6337 Rambla de Rep. de México; phone: 2-605060 or 2-608129), *Hertz* (813 Colonia; phone: 2-916363), and *National Car Rental* (1397 Ciudadela at Rincón; phone: 2-900035), *Autorent* (1683 Yaguarón; phone: 2-920573) is reliable; however, unless you hold a major credit card, you must pay a $1000 deposit. Expect to pay more than you would in the US for the rental and for gas (at press time, about $3 a gallon). When traveling in the interior, don't count on frequent wayside cafés or service stations; most of these are in towns.

The long-distance bus service is an efficient alternative to driving. Buses are comfortable and reliable, though you may have to buy your ticket in advance. The biggest bus companies are *ONDA* and *COT*. In Montevideo, both have offices on Plaza Cagancha (also known as Libertad).

Brochures and maps are available at the tourist information center in Montevideo (Plaza Cagancha; phone: 2-905216), or at the office in Carrasco Airport (phone: 2-603812).

The two routes detailed below run from Montevideo to Salto and from Montevideo to La Coronilla. The Montevideo-Salto route heads west from the capital through the potato farms of Rincón del Pino, through Nueva Helvecia (also known as Colonia Suiza, a Swiss pioneer town founded in the 1860s where *Nirvana,* Uruguay's finest country inn, is located — see *Best en Route*), to Colonia (founded in 1680), to the 16th-century cattle-ranching town of Carmelo, to Mercedes and Paysandú (both agribusiness centers), and to the gaucho town of Salto, with its noted thermal springs.

The route from Montevideo to La Coronilla takes you east from Montevideo along the Riviera of the South American coast, past the summer residences of Piriápolis, to Punta del Este, with its casino and nightclubs, to La Paloma, a smaller resort, and to La Coronilla and nearby Santa Teresa National Park.

# Montevideo to Salto

Most tourists come to Uruguay from neighboring Argentina and Brazil in search of the good vacation life: sun, beaches, food, wine, and song. If this is what you want, you should take off to the eastern Atlantic coastline, for there you will find the beaches (see *Montevideo to La Coronilla,* below). If, however, you are more interested in learning about Uruguay's grasslands and gauchos (cowboys), you should explore the river coastline west from Montevideo.

This route leads through the vast, fertile grasslands that produce the country's main exports, beef and wool. The most dramatic figure you'll see on this gentle landscape is the gaucho himself; gauchos are everywhere, confidently astride their horses, trekking cattle by the roadside. Under wide-brimmed hats, with a poncho, wide *bombachas* (pantaloon-type pants gathered at the ankles), leather boots, *facón* (knife) carried in their belt, and jangling spurs, they make impressively romantic figures. Uruguay's plains are famous for their ranches (called *estancias*). Visitors who wish to stay at an *estancia* where they can go horseback riding, fishing, and on photo safaris should contact *CEPLATUR* (1483 Minas in Montevideo; phone: 2-43088 or 2-414946), *C.R.Z. Viajes* (1313 Bacacay; phone: 2-963011; fax: 2-963012), or one of the tourist information centers (see "Sources and Resources" in *Montevideo*, THE CITIES).

There are some 60 cattle auctions held every month throughout the country, and even if you don't plan to take a cow home, you should attend one to get a flavor of Uruguay's cattle world. Large cattle auctions are always well advertised in the newspapers (try *El País*), and as cattle markets dot the countryside, it is easy to plan a visit to one en route.

The trip from Montevideo to Salto described here can be done easily in 5 days. The places of most interest to the tourist are Colonia, Paysandú, and Salto, and none of these very different towns should be missed. Although you can make this trip at any time of the year, the countryside is possibly most attractive in the middle of spring (November). Hotel reservations are a good idea.

Route 1 due west begins just beyond the toll bridge over the Río Santa Lucía. It takes you through Libertad, Rincón del Pino (where most of Uruguay's potatoes are grown), and on to Colonia Valdense, where there is a good wayside restaurant, *Brisas del Plata*. Turn right along Route 53 to Nueva Helvecia (New Switzerland).

**NUEVA HELVECIA:** Known as Colonia Suiza and founded in the 1860s by Swiss pioneers, the town bears the profound imprint of its founders and is well known for the cheese, cold meats, and wine it produces. Make a quick visit to the home of Eva Leitch de Muller (Camino de la Totorra) to see her antiques. This is a private home, but Mrs. de Muller usually is delighted to show visitors her collection of music boxes, coins, and lace. You can buy locally made music boxes in the town. If you're there on August 1, be sure to join in the annual celebration of Switzerland's national day.

Follow Route 51 back to Route 1 for the 36-mile (58-km) trip to Colonia del Sacramento.

**COLONIA DEL SACRAMENTO:** Known simply as Colonia, the town was founded in 1680 (before Montevideo) by Portuguese seeking to gain control of the Río de la Plata estuary. It was conquered by the Spaniards and became the most important city of southwestern Uruguay and a connecting point to Buenos Aires, which it remains today, with many daily crossings to the Argentine capital by ferry or airplane. Colonia has a few small industries and is a strategic port, but its main interest for a visitor is the colonial architecture, carefully restored and protected, that is part of the original 17th-century city known as Ciudad Vieja (Old City), one of the loveliest historic city areas on the continent. Well worth a visit are the lighthouse, Calle de los Suspiros (Street of Sighs), the Iglesia Matriz, Uruguay's oldest church (it dates to 1680), the city walls, and the section's four museums located in colonial buildings. The *Museo Municipal* (Municipal Museum; 77 Del Comercio) specializes in documents of the colonial period, while the *Museo del Período Español* (Spanish Period Museum; San José, corner of España) and the *Museo del Período Portugués* (Portuguese Period Museum; 124 Av. 25 de Mayo) each has collections of relics from the Spanish and Portuguese periods of colonization. At the *Museo de Azulejo* (Museum of Azulejo Tiles; on Misiones de los Tapes at the waterfront) there are two rooms of blue-and-white porcelain tiles with original 18th- and 19th-century Spanish and Portuguese designs. The collection is housed in a historical Portuguese building. All of the museums are open Thursdays through Mondays from 11:30 AM to 6 PM.

Colonia also possesses Uruguay's only bullring (*Real de San Carlos*), now a piece of historic architecture since it has not been used in over 50 years (bullfighting was abolished shortly after the ring was built). Near the bullring is an enormous building that houses a *cesta-punta* court (it's a deadly Basque ball game; international matches are held here in the summer). Colonia is also a good place for river fishing because of the Río Uruguay. There are beaches, but remember that although the Río de la Plata is 25 miles wide at Colonia, it is still a river and has very muddy waters at times. Maps and tourist information are available from the city's tourist office (corner of General Flores and Rivera; phone: 522-2103). It is open daily from 8 AM to 8 PM. There are daily ferry and hydrofoil services from Colonia to Buenos Aires — *Aliscafos* and *Buquebus* offer passage from the wharf in Colonia, starting at $35. *LADA* and *Pluna*, commuter airlines, provide shuttle service between the two cities for about the same price; for an additional charge, you can make a bus connection to Montevideo.

If you want to eat beef (you should in Uruguay), try *Pulpería De Los Faroles* (102 Del Comercio; phone: 522-2103) in the old part of town. It has juicy steaks. For a coffee or a snack, stop by the nearby cozy *La Casona del Sur* (143 Calle de las Misiones de los Tapes), which overlooks the lighthouse. Nightlife is restricted to gambling at the *Mirador* hotel (Av. Roosevelt).

**En Route from Colonia del Sacramento** – Take Route 21 north, but if it rains heavily, you'll have to wait for the flooded Manga stream to recede or take the much longer route through the town of Tarariras. About 12 miles (19 km) out of Colonia there is a turnoff left for the national park of Anchorena, a great place for a picnic lunch. If you are quiet, you may see wild pig or deer roam nearby. On the grounds you will find a watchtower that offers a wonderful view of the park and the Río Uruguay. From here it is just over 31 miles (50 km) along Route 21 north to Carmelo.

**CARMELO:** Now a small, sleepy agricultural town, it has had some important moments. Just south, at Arroyo de las Vacas, cattle were introduced into Uruguay in the 16th century. The parents of José de San Martín, the Argentine national hero, lived here (you can visit the ruins of their farmhouse in Calera de las Huérfanas); and both Charles Darwin and Giuseppi Garibaldi (Italy's liberator) visited here in the 19th century. Today the town offers little for a visitor, but it does have a lively yachting harbor in the summer.

As for restaurants, try the *Casino Hotel*, Calle Rodó (phone: 542314).

From Carmelo, follow Route 21 for some 62 miles (99 km) to Mercedes.

**MERCEDES:** An important center of business for the surrounding agricultural community, Mercedes has a few agribusinesses, including a sugar mill and milk pasteurizing plant. A drive along the riverfront is worthwhile, and the colonial cathedral on the main square is also interesting. The Castillo Mauá, built in 1857, gives you an idea of how fortress-like the farmhouses were when Uruguay was settled.

For a meal, try *El Estribo de Castro y Carreaga* (corner of Artigas) or the *Club Remeros* on the riverfront (949 de la Rivera; phone: 532-2198) — both specialize in steaks.

**En Route from Mercedes** – From here, follow Route 2 north 20 miles (32 km) to Fray Bentos, a small town that grew as a result of its meat packing plant. While in town, you might want to check if there are any productions scheduled at the

*Teatro de Miguel Young* — an impressive building — or its outdoor amphitheater. Fray Bentos also has a small casino. From here, you can cross to Argentina by means of the General San Martín Bridge 3 miles (5 km) north; the distance by road from the bridge to Buenos Aires is just over 186 miles (298 km).

Continue on Route 2 to Highway 24 and north to Paysandú.

**PAYSANDÚ:** This town was founded by Europeans in 1769, although Indians, now extinct, lived in the area previously. During the 19th-century wars of independence, it was a center of much fighting; in the early decades of this century, it became the main industrial town of the interior. Today, it maintains this position, though threatened by the recent growth of Salto. The industries that form the backbone of Paysandú are mostly related to agriculture (leather, wool, sugar, beer, and milk). Summer temperatures can soar to well over 100F (38C)!

The attractive cathedral on the main square is reputed to have one of the best organs in the country and cannonballs are imbedded in its walls, souvenirs of the 1865 siege by Brazil when Paysandú was held by Paraguay. The old cemetery (Monumento a la Perpetuidad) has a great number of statues and massive mausoleums.

Fishing on the Río Uruguay, mostly for dorado, *boga, dientudo,* and *surubí,* is said to be very good. From here, you can cross by the bridge for a day in Argentina. More information is available from the tourist office (1226 Av. 18 de Julio; phone: 722-6221).

For restaurants, *Artemio's* (985 Av. 18 de Julio; phone: 722-3826) is regarded as the best (try the pepper steak). You should not leave Paysandú without trying its famous *postre chajá* (buy it across the road from the *Centro* bar), a delicious cream cake.

**En Route from Paysandú** – Follow Route 3 north; at Km 404 there is a turnoff to the small waterfall of the Río Queguay, a lovely place to have a picnic and fish. About 25 miles (40 km) farther along Route 3 are the camping grounds of Guaviyú. The main attractions here are the thermal springs, but there are even better facilities farther north in Arapey. On Km 463 of Route 3 is a turnoff to the "Meseta de Artigas." This is the place where Artigas (the national hero) made his headquarters in 1815; it is an attractive spot from which to watch the Río Uruguay. Some 28 miles (45 km) farther is Salto.

**SALTO:** Until recently, this was almost exclusively a cattleman's town, serving the surrounding department as an administrative and commercial center. Lately Salto has had noticeable growth, mostly due to the hydroelectric dam (one of the largest in the world) being built on the Río Uruguay. The power generated is being shared by Uruguay and Argentina and will help supply Montevideo and Buenos Aires. It is an impressive structure and well worth a visit, with excellent guided tours around the works twice a day (no need to book in advance). Once the dam is completed, a large tourist complex is to be built on the reservoir. The local tourist office (1052 Uruguay; phone: 732-4096) can direct visitors to the dam.

The people of Salto pride themselves on the cultural facilities in their town. There are a number of museums worth visiting: *Museo de Bellas Artes y Artes Decorativas* (Fine Arts and Decorative Arts Museum; 1067 Uruguay), which exhibits mostly paintings, sculptures, and wooden cabinets (by Pacot) in what was once the French-style mansion of a rich rancher; *Museo Histórico Municipal* (Av. Paraguay y Ruta General Artigas), which has items pertaining to the history of the city itself; and the *Museo del Hombre* (Brasil and Zorrilla), which deals with anthropological topics. The theater, *Teatro Larrañaga,* built in 1882, was famous for its early acoustical design and lack of columns. There are also the ruins of two plants (Costanera Sur) that date back to the 1870s, where meat was salted and sent to feed slaves in Cuba and northern Brazil. Watch for attractive pieces of raw amethyst or polished agate in the shops.

The thermal grounds near Salto are worth a visit. Some pilgrims to the springs seek pure relaxation, while others come for cures prescribed by physicians. A limited number of the baths are accessible only to those with written medical permission. The nearest bath is at Daymán, 12 miles (19 km) north of Salto; it has rather limited facilities. The best is called Termas del Arapey, 60 miles (96 km) northeast of Salto (it is signposted from Route 3). The facilities there are very good. Not only can you have therapeutic baths in these waters rich in bicarbonated salts, calcium, and magnesium, but you can play tennis, basketball, or football. You can either camp or rent bungalows. (For reservations, contact the tourist information center at Plaza Cagancha in Montevideo; phone: 2-905216.) Long-distance buses go straight to Daymán from Montevideo, but reservations at the spa are always a must.

A pleasant drink at night can be had by the river at *Parador Ayuí* (Costanera Norte). For restaurants, try the *Chef* at the *Gran Hotel Salto* (5 25 de Agosto; phone: 732-3251), *Los Pingüinos* (708 Uruguay), or *Club Remeros* (Av. Costanera at Belén; phone: 732-3418). For good barbecued meat, try *Parrillada El Cerro* (619 Zorrilla).

**En Route from Salto** – There are two recommended routes back to Montevideo, both different from the way you came. The faster is to take Route 3 south until it meets Route 1 and then head east to Montevideo. The distance is 310 miles (496 km) and normally takes 6 hours (there is a very bad stretch of road just before the town of Trinidad). A modification of this choice is to take Route 3 to a point 16 miles (26 km) south of Paysandú, then follow Route 24 through Mercedes to Route 2. Follow Route 2 to Route 1, then east to Montevideo. A good place to stop for lunch is in Cardona, at the *Elizondo* hotel; ask if they have partridge (*perdiz*). The second route is 16 miles (26 km) longer than the first.

## BEST EN ROUTE

Hotels on this route are somewhat less expensive than those in Montevideo. Those classified as expensive will cost $55 and up for a double room per night; moderate, from $35 to $55; and inexpensive, under $35. Breakfast is usually included, but check when booking to be sure. Prices in some towns go up about 10% in summer months — December through March. It's a good idea to make reservations before arriving.

### COLONIA SUIZA

*Nirvana* – One of the best hotels in the country is set on 60 acres of lovely grounds. Tennis, horseback riding, and swimming are offered during the summer (December through March), and the restaurant features Swiss food. Follow the signposts off Route 1 at Km 118 (phone: 522-4052; in Montevideo, 2-987578). Expensive.

### COLONIA

*Mirador* – This modern 80-room hotel features a swimming pool, tennis courts, and a casino at night. All rooms are air conditioned. The food is very good, especially the cold buffet. All meals included. Av. Roosevelt (phone: 522-2004). Expensive.

*Plaza Mayor* – The most charming spot in town, this new 16-room inn is in a historic building in the Old City. Exposed stone walls, brass beds, and porcelain door handles are some of its fine details. The rooms that open on the patio have no windows but compensate with air conditioning. There is no restaurant, but breakfast is included. 111 Calle del Comercio (phone: 522-3193; in Buenos Aires, 54-1-834015). Expensive.

*Posada del Gobernador* – Formerly an elegant private colonial home, this small inn on a shady, cobbled street has 30 very cozy and comfortable rooms (some even have brass beds), all with private baths and mini-bars. There's a friendly breakfast room and lounge. 205 Av. 18 de Julio (phone: 522-3018). Expensive.

*Leoncia* – All 45 clean rooms have air conditioning and private baths in this comfortable hostelry. 214 Rivera, at the corner of Flores (phone: 522-2049). Moderate.

## CARMELO

***Casino Carmelo*** – A large 90-room hotel set in a pleasant park by the Río Uruguay. Good cooking and a casino are pluses. Calle Rodó (phone: 542-314). Moderate.

## MERCEDES

***Brisas del Hum*** – On the main square, this very plain hotel features comfortable rooms. Good yacht harbor nearby. 205 Artigas (phone: 532-2740 or 532-2741). Moderate.

## FRAY BENTOS

***Gran Fray Bentos*** – A small casino is the plus at this pleasant property that looks onto the Río Uruguay. 3272 Calle Paraguay (phone: 535-2358). Expensive.

## PAYSANDÚ

***Gran Paysandú*** – Centrally located, it is a functional hotel with a casino, good dining facilities, and a popular coffee room. 958 19 de Abril (phone: 722-3400 or 722-2614). Moderate.

## SALTO

***Los Cedros*** – Open year-round, this is a modern hostelry with 76 rooms and meeting areas. 657 Uruguay (phone: 732-3984 and 732-3985). Moderate.

***Gran Hotel Salto*** – Right on the square, this place has air conditioning, a pool, bar, laundry service, and a good restaurant. 5 25 de Agosto, corner Uruguay (phone: 732-4333). Moderate.

# Montevideo to La Coronilla

From Montevideo to the Brazilian border is a coastline of nearly 218 miles filled with many wonderful beaches that attract *montevideanos* who want a relaxing weekend by the sea and foreign visitors who want the traditional summer seaside vacation. The farthest resort, La Coronilla, is only 4 hours from Montevideo by car, on well-surfaced and -marked highways. Book hotels well in advance. The beach season is December to mid-April.

The first 68 miles (109 km) of the road to Piriápolis is a continuous series of small villages with summer houses, owned by Uruguayan families who idle away the summer months by the sea. The largest resort along the way is Atlántida. Twenty-four miles (38 km) east of Piriápolis is Punta del Este, the internationally famous resort with casinos, nightclubs, and a pleasant beach. La Paloma, 142 miles (227 km) from Montevideo, is set around a beautiful cove and tends to attract those fleeing the larger resorts. La Coronilla, about 186 miles (298 km) from Montevideo, is quiet even at the height of the summer season and sufficiently near the Santa Teresa National Park to attract those interested in camping in such beautiful surroundings. You can rent a car in Montevideo (see "Sources and Resources," *Montevideo,* THE CITIES) or take a bus.

The route begins at Atlántida, 31 miles (50 km) from Montevideo.

**ATLÁNTIDA:** Surrounded by pine and eucalyptus forests, this small resort, so near Montevideo, attracts people year round. The genial atmosphere of the town is as calm as the waters along its beaches, with such pleasant diversions as golf and tennis and tea at the town's best restaurant, *Country Club* (on Rte. 11, just north of the Interbalnearia; phone: 342-2173). A small casino in the center of town (on Calle No. 1) opens in the evening. And if you're out walking at night, you can't help but notice the lovely gas lamps downtown.

**En Route from Atlántida** – Some 23½ miles (38 km) past Atlántida (just past the second toll on the Interbalnearia), take the turnoff left and drive through the seaside village of Solís at the mouth of the river of the same name. This is a long beach with good fishing. If you stop to eat, be sure to go to the well-decorated *Chajá* (the only hotel and restaurant in the town proper). Then, as the road turns left along the beach, you'll see the waves breaking just over a half mile (1 km) from the road.

As you drive through the hamlet of Las Flores, look for the houses built of pebbles. Six miles (10 km) farther lies Piriápolis.

**PIRIÁPOLIS:** Laid out in wooded hills, this well-planned town with red-clay roofs was founded at the end of the 19th century and retains its Victorian atmosphere. Its beaches are second only to those of Punta del Este; in summer, Piriápolis's population of 7,000 quadruples. It is a popular resort for people with very young children because the waters of the bay are protected, quiet, and safe. Fishing is good off Punta Fría. Contact the *Club Nautico y Pesca* on the waterfront (phone: 432-3177) for fishing information. The club also rents water sports equipment. San Antonio Hill, also known as Cerro del Inglés (Hill of the English), has a statue of the Virgin Stella Maris at its base. A chair lift goes up to the top, where there's the *Parador San Antonio* restaurant (phone: 432-3403) and a tearoom, discotheque, swimming pool, and the view of the whole bay, town, and surrounding countryside; you can drive up if you prefer. Pan de Azúcar (Sugar Loaf Hill) on the outskirts of town (take Route 37 north) has only a very steep footpath in the bush leading up to the cross that crowns the hill. The view is spectacular and worth the 2-hour climb, but beware of snakes. You also can take the internal stairway into the arms of the cross and see the area from the viewing windows. This hill has been designated a reserve to protect endangered animals. For information on the park's activities, and hiking and driving routes, call 42-21921 or fax 42-29132. The town's third hill is Cerro del Toro (Bull Hill); named because a cascade of mineral water runs down from the mouth of a 3-ton bull sculpture, brought to this wooded spot from France.

In the evenings, the street known as Rambla de los Argentinos is the spot for strolling; it is lined with restaurants, sidewalk cafés, and boutiques. There also is dining and casino action at the *Argentino* (see *Best en Route*). *La Langosta* (1214 Rambla; phone: 432-3382) and *Puerto Don Anselmo* (on the waterfront; phone: 432-2925) have great seafood, but if you want to get away from the crowds, try one of the small cafés on the coast road. Seafood is their specialty, but Uruguay's most popular sandwich, *chivito* (beef tenderloin garnished with ham, cheese, lettuce, tomato, and peppers) is available at every restaurant and snack bar. The municipal office down the street from the *Argentino* provides general tourist information (along the waterfront; phone: 432-2560). It is open from 9 AM to 10 PM during high season and from 10 AM to 1 PM and 3 to 8 PM the rest of the year.

**En Route from Piriápolis** – Take Route 93 to get onto the Interbalnearia. On the left, at about Km 120, you pass a large lake, Laguna del Sauce, near an air force base (which also serves as the commercial airport for Punta del Este). The lake is a good place for boating and fishing. Farther on you will come to the steep climb up Punta Ballena; at the top take a camera stop, for the view of Portezuelo Bay is beautiful. On Punta Ballena itself (take the first right after the climb off the Interbalnearia) you will find an excellent site for snorkeling. Also there is Casa Pueblo, a beautifully designed Moorish house that clings to the cliff — it is the spectacular home of Carlos Páez Vilaró, a well-known Uruguayan artist. The *casa* houses a gallery and museum of his contemporary sculptures (they also are for sale). It is open to the public from 10 AM to 6 PM in summer. From Punta Ballena, Punta del Este is only 10½ miles (17 km) across the bay.

**PUNTA DEL ESTE:** This is one of the world's best seaside resorts, yet it is one of the least known, possibly because Uruguay itself is so far off the jet set's flight pattern. However, it has always been a place where wealthy Argentines and Brazilians come in the summer and either rent or own homes and where heads of state congregate for regional summits and world trade meetings. On a peninsula that juts out into the sea (here the Río de la Plata officially ends and the Atlantic Ocean begins), Punta del Este is surrounded by lovely pine forests. When it began as a resort area almost 100 years ago, houses were built only on the peninsula itself. Now the town has spread out and high-rise condominiums abound. But there are also hundreds of beautiful mansions — some with swimming pools and tennis courts, particularly on the outskirts of town. (A favorite pastime of Uruguayans visiting Punta del Este is driving around looking at the luxurious homes of the rich.) The town has a permanent population of about 100,000, but in summer over 400,000 people visit the resort; most of the summer visitors rent houses or apartments, and many stay for the whole summer (December through March). It will be too chilly swim, but perfect for strolls along the beach. Note that during off-season, some restaurants and business establishments have reduced hours, but if you don't like crowds, consider visiting early or late in the season (late November or March and April). You'll know when you reach Punta del Este because a huge hand will appear, rising from the sand. The sculpture is the work of Chilean artist Mario Irarrazabal.

On the western side of the peninsula (Playa Mansa), the waters are safe and calm enough to allow water skiing (try renting at I'Marangatú Beach), but on the eastern side (Playa Brava), the Atlantic Ocean has 10-foot waves: great for surfing, but intimidating for many swimmers. The two beaches are about a 30-minute walk from each other.

Punta del Este offers abundant outdoor sports. Arrangements for non-members to use the golf course can be made at *Club de Golf* (Barrio Parque del Golf past the suburb of San Rafael; phone: 42-82121). Tennis can be played on a number of public courts; information is available at the city tourism desk at the bus station near the waterfront. Fishing along the coast is excellent. Roll-cast from the coast or inquire about deep-sea fishing at the *Club de Pesca de Punta del Este* (Rambla Costanera, 3 Parada; phone: 42-81731).

For the person who only has a day to spend in Punta del Este, there are three "must do" activities: Go to the beach — Playa Brava — for a midmorning swim-and-sun; after a good meal take a taxi or drive yourself through the neighborhoods around the *San Rafael* hotel and the golf club to see some of the gorgeous houses; and in the evening, take a walk down Gorlero to get a feeling for the place and look at the shops. When you reach the casino, cross the street and peek in *Manos del Uruguay* (phone: 42-41953), a cooperative store. Its sweater and handicrafts are beautiful and of excellent quality.

There are four side trips from Punta del Este for a visitor with more time. Gorriti Island is about 2 miles off Punta del Este in the bay. This quiet island has two protected beaches and the ruins of an 18th-century colonial fortress. A second trip is to another island, Isla de Lobos, 6½ miles off Punta del Este, a government-run natural reserve for some 500,000 sea lions. It literally is covered with animals. You can go to both islands by boats that leave from the city dock, referred to by locals as the "puerto." About two boats go to Gorriti each hour starting at 8 AM, the last leaving around 5:30 PM in summer. At least one boat (more if there are passengers) goes to Isla de Lobos daily — it departs in the morning. Also visit La Barra de Maldonado and its inverted

W-shaped bridge some 6 miles (10 km) east of Punta del Este on the mainland. Manantiales, a few miles farther east, also is becoming fashionable and has some beautiful contemporary homes in the Spanish-Moorish style. A fourth trip to Maldonado, 3 miles (5 km) due north of Punta del Este, will show you how the other half lives; most of the population is year-round. While in Maldonado, stop in at the *Museo de Arte Americano* (American Art Museum; Calle Dodena, Esquina 33; phone: 42-22276), which brings together pre-Columbian, colonial, and contemporary art in a collection housed in a colonial mansion with lovely gardens. The town is full of shops (less expensive than Punta del Este) and has a beautiful cathedral on the main plaza that is well worth visiting at night to see the dancing waters of the musical fountain. There are also colonial ruins, such as El Vigía (The Watch Tower) and the windmill, as well as the *Museum Mazzoni* (789 Ituzaingó; phone: 42-23405). The tourist office (Av. Francisco Acuña de Figueroa at Burnet; phone: 42-20847; fax: 42-29132) can provide more information.

No matter how long you stay, be prepared to dine late — from 10 PM on. Eating in Punta del Este should be considered seriously, for there is a great choice of excellent restaurants (everyone dresses informally). For seafood, the best restaurants are *Mariskonea* (Calles 26 and 21; phone: 42-40408) and *Los Caracoles* (Calle 20 at the corner of Calle 28; phone: 42-45275), which is actually two separate restaurants — a seafood house and a *paradilla,* or café. *La Fragata* (800 Av. Gorlero; phone: 42-40001) is good for both fish and meat and has sidewalk tables that are excellent for people watching. *Bungalow Suizo* (Av. Roosevelt and the rail tracks; phone: 42-82358) is well known for fondue and other Swiss food. *Doña Flor* (Plaza París, San Rafael; phone: 42-84720), *La Bourgogne* (Av. del Mar and Av. Pedragosa Sierra; phone: 42-82007), and *El Floreal* (Av. Pedragosa Sierra, San Rafael) are all famous for haute cuisine. A good inexpensive restaurant is *Club Ciclista* (27 Calle 20; phone: 42-40007); try the *mejillones à la provenzal* (fresh mussels in parsley sauce), washed down with a local white wine. Quite good, too, are the seaside *Blue Cheese* (Calle 23 at Rambla de Circunvalación; phone: 42-40354), with an excellent salad bar and international fare that is served on a terrace facing the bay, and *Dakel* (719 Calle 20; phone: 42-40356). New restaurants, cafés, pubs, and music spots open every summer for the season; be sure to ask at your hotel about the latest, or check the local newspaper, *Peninsual.*

If you get restless spending a day on the sand, do as the locals do and repair to the *paradores,* small cafés along the coast which are popular spots for music, eating, drinking, and people watching. Among the most popular are *Postozuelo* (on the malecón); *"31"* (at 31 Parada); and *Posto 5* (at 5 Parada).

At night Punta del Este has a refreshing breeze (you will need a sweater). There are many after-dark diversions, and Avenida Gorlero is still crowded with people at 3 AM. Discotheques are geared mostly for couples and young singles. The most popular places include *Le Club* (by the sea at San Rafael; phone: 42-84869) and *Swan* (Rambla Pacheco at 8 Parada). Another form of entertainment is found in clubs like *Caras y Caretas* at the port, *Brujas* (Av. Roosevelt and Chiossi), and *Piano Bar J.R.* (downtown on Rincón y Cebollati in Maldonado; phone: 42-25215), where you can have a few drinks and listen to live music. In the port area, music spills out into the street until the wee hours of the morning from at least half a dozen bars that offer live entertainment. There is gambling every night — roulette, blackjack, and baccarat — at the *Casino Hotel San Rafael* (a coat is required for men) or at the *Casino Nogaró* (Gorlero and Calle 31).

**En Route from Punta del Este** – Drive to Maldonado and then north toward San Carlos. Drive through San Carlos and take Route 9 to Rocha. If you are tempted to visit Lago José Ignacio, be warned that the turnoff from Route 9, about 15½ miles (25 km) from San Carlos, is a very bumpy road. If you have time, stop for a drink or lunch at *La Posada Del Mar.* You'll love it. On the outskirts of Rocha you will come across the groves of palm trees that are dotted about the eastern part of the country — an unexpected sight. From Rocha, turn south along Route 15 for another 15½ miles (25 km) until you come to La Paloma.

**LA PALOMA:** This small summer sports resort is set in a beautifully wooded area surrounding a small bay protected by La Tuna island, a convenient natural design that allows water skiing in the bay and surfing at the beaches outside the bay. There is an excellent port and even better fishing — deep sea or shore casting. Species in local waters include *anchoa* (anchovy), bonito, *pargo* (red snapper), *sargo, brótola* (hake), *pescadilla* (whiting), *manta, luna, corvina blanca* (sea bass), *cazón* (tuna), *palometa, pez martillo* (hammer fish), *tiburón* (shark), and *raya* (ray fish). There is a very popular camping site, Parque Andresito, that is within walking distance of both the center of town and the beach. You can rent bungalows here inexpensively.

Try the fish in the restaurant of the *Cabo Santa María* hotel (Av. Nicolás Solari). Nightlife is somewhat restricted to the casino at this hotel and at various modest discotheques.

**En Route from La Paloma** – There are two possibilities from here. The first is to go back to Rocha and then turn east along Route 9 to Castillos, a 53-mile (85-km) trip that can be done in a little over an hour. The second is to take Route 10 east from La Paloma. Although it is about the same distance, the road is unpaved and the journey takes longer. There are, however, two very worthwhile side trips: Some 3 miles (5 km) out of La Paloma you will drive through La Pedrera, a tiny resort very popular with Argentines. It resembles Biarritz (ca. 1905!). Some 28 miles (45 km) beyond you will come to a sign reading Cabo Polonio. Don't attempt driving there unless you have a four-wheel-drive vehicle. Sooner or later, a horse-drawn taxi service will appear out of the sand dunes. Take it. After 6 miles (10 km) of going through the dunes you come upon the Atlantic Ocean and approach the cape and a lighthouse, where you will see thousands of sea lions; their playful roars rise above the dry crying of the seagulls and the thunder of the ocean waves. Unfortunately, there is nowhere to stay in the adjacent fishermen's village.

Once back on Route 10, heading to Castillos, you come to Aguas Dulces, an unusual summer village; the houses are thatched, wooden, and cramped (a few feet from the ocean) on the beach itself. Have a snack of fried fish at one of the small cafés on the main street. Don't bother to stop in Castillos, but follow Route 9 for 28 miles (45 km) and turn left at the sign for Punta del Diablo. Follow the unpaved road to this small fishing village — its economy is based on sharks caught from little boats out at sea. The fish are gutted and sun-dried into what is wrongly called *bacalao* (cod). This is consumed in vast quantities during *Holy Week,* when Uruguayans reluctantly leave their meat dishes aside and eat fish. You can find interesting handicrafts made of shark's teeth and vertebrae here. There is a restaurant, *Restaurante del Mar,* looking onto the sea. Once back on Route 9, the turnoff for Santa Teresa National Park is only 6 miles (10 km) away.

**PARQUE SANTA TERESA:** This is a lovely national park with many kinds of vegetation and over 300 species of trees. It is the ideal place for those who enjoy camping, although you also can rent cottages in summer. Among the 2 million trees in the park are scattered hothouses, a bird sanctuary, and some delightful freshwater swimming pools. Nearby is Laguna Negra, an excellent lake for fishing. The main attraction, though, is the colonial fortress built by the Portuguese in 1762. It changed hands many times among Spaniards, Uruguayans, Argentines, and Brazilians. Restored in 1921, it is now a museum of the colonial period. The park itself has palm-lined roadways.

If you do not want to camp, you can stay at one of the hotels in La Coronilla, only 9 miles (14 km) away (see *Best en Route*).

**LA CORONILLA:** A collection of summer houses with some nice hotels right on the beach, this is a good base for visiting Parque Santa Teresa and Chuy as well as for

**1018 DIRECTIONS / Uruguay**

enjoying the beach itself. The beaches here are vast and wild, and the fishing probably the best in Uruguay, especially shark and black corvina. There is little nightlife (except for the casino at the *Costa del Mar* hotel) and few restaurants, but these are not the main reasons for a visit.

There is a side trip worth your time to the border town of Chuy, which is half Brazilian and half Uruguayan. Then take Route 19 north for 6 miles (10 km) and visit the Park and Fortress of San Miguel, built about 30 years before the Fortress of Santa Teresa but by the Spaniards. It is smaller and very well kept, and free (as are most museums in Uruguay). Ask to see the small carriage museum on the grounds.

**En Route from La Coronilla** – You have two alternatives. First, you can return to Montevideo along Route 9, which will take about 6 hours. The second, a longer — by 62 miles (99 km) — but more picturesque way to Montevideo (going first through marshland and then hilly terrain), is to take Camino de los Indios (Routes 14 and 13) through to Aiguá and then Route 8 to Montevideo, which will take close to 9 hours due to the gravel roads on the first third of the journey. (A good spot for lunch is an isolated restaurant just outside Aiguá called *Pororó*.)

## BEST EN ROUTE

Hotels in Uruguay's coastal resorts are more expensive than those found in Montevideo. Double accommodations, in summer particularly (December through March), can run from $100 to $165 at a hotel in the expensive category; between $60 and $100 at a hotel in the moderate category; and under $60 at an inexpensive hotel. Room rates often include breakfast. Most are clean, comfortable, have private baths, restaurants, and a variety of sports. It's a good idea to make reservations ahead, especially for the summer.

### BELLA VISTA

***Hostería Bella Vista*** – A good hotel on the beach, run by an English-speaking management, it offers bungalows and good food, but a restricted menu for the day. Tennis courts and horseback riding are offered. Located 3 miles (5 km) from Solís toward Piriápolis (phone: in Balneario, Solís 52; in Piriápolis, 432-3192). Moderate.

### PIRIÁPOLIS

***Argentino*** – This large 60-year-old seafront property has a saltwater swimming pool, an indoor hot springs pool, ice skating, tennis courts, a well-known buffet restaurant, and casino action at night. Ask for a corner room or one on the newly remodeled second, third, and fourth floors. Room rate, which includes half board, goes up about 20% in high season. Rambla de los Argentinos (phone: 432-2572; in Montevideo, 2-904422; fax: 432-3107; in Montevideo, 2-902237). Expensive to moderate.

### PUNTA BALLENA

***Solana del Mar*** – Quiet, attractive, and modern rooms or bungalows in a lovely setting with pine forest behind and ocean and beach below. Plenty of resort activities, including tennis, windsurfing, and kayaking are available, plus a restaurant and bar. Km 126½ of Ruta Interbalneario (phone: 432-7888; in Montevideo, 2-721187). Expensive.

### PUNTA DEL ESTE

***L'Auberge*** – The most luxurious and charming accommodations in Punta del Este, this 30-room exclusive hotel (which resembles a small Swiss castle) has excellent service and a good French restaurant. Teatime here is de rigueur; the specialty is

Belgian waffles. There is a cozy bar in the hotel's tower. Barrio Parque del Golf (phone: 42-82601; fax: 42-83408). Expensive.

**Casino San Rafael** – Large, beautiful, first class accommodations, on the seafront, with facilities for meetings (usually held in winter). The 140 rooms are comfortable and have air conditioning and satellite television; tennis and basketball courts, a swimming pool, nightclub, 3 restaurants, and a casino are pluses. Rambla Lorenzo Batlle (phone: 42-82161 to 42-82166; fax: 42-82166). Expensive.

**La Capilla** – Small, but very comfortable, and only 2 blocks from the beach. Besides very good service, there is a swimming pool, sauna, bar, and an excellent restaurant. Open year-round. Viña del Mar, corner Buenas Artigas (phone: 42-84059; fax: 42-87953). Expensive to moderate.

**Porto Bari** – Excellent service is found at this hostelry facing the beach at San Rafael suburb. Mar Adriático at Ipanema (phone: 42-84304). Moderate.

**La Posta del Cangrejo** – A small hostelry, very near the beach on the outskirts of Punta del Este, that provides clean, airy rooms. Barra de Maldonado (phone: 42-70021). Moderate.

**Salto Grande** – A first class, 64-room property, convenient to both downtown and the beaches. It offers a restaurant, snack bar, and swimming pool in a wooded setting. Av. Italia — formerly Av. Salto Grande — Parada (Stop) 3½ on the Costanera (phone: 42-82137; fax: 42-88431). Moderate.

**San Marcos** – This hotel has comfortable rooms, all with a private bath and telephone, a swimming pool, tennis courts, barbecue, restaurant, and meeting facilities. It is closed during the low season, from *Easter* to mid-December. 191 Av. Mar del Plata, corner Buenas Artigas (phone: 42-82251). Moderate.

**Tanger** – This new, centrally located hotel offers 42 rooms with air conditioning, wet bars, and satellite television. Other amenities include a small restaurant, a pool, gym, and sauna. Open year-round. Breakfast included. Parada 1 on the Costanera (phone: 42-40601; fax: 42-40918). Moderate.

**Palace** – In the heart of Punta del Este, this is a well-run, renovated old hotel with comfortable rooms. Closed from *Easter* until mid-December. Av. Gorlero, Esquina (Corner) 11 (phone: 42-41919). Moderate to inexpensive.

**Alhambra** – Comfortable and in an excellent location, just off Gorlero and 2 blocks from the beach. A good place to stay if you don't have your own vehicle. Open year-round, it has 50 air conditioned rooms, a restaurant, and a bar. 573 Calle 28 (phone: 42-40094). Inexpensive.

**Embajador** – One block from the beach, it provides standard accommodations, including private bath and phone. Risso, corner La Vía (phone: 42-81008). Inexpensive.

**Gran Hotel España** – A small but comfortable hostelry in downtown Punta del Este. All rooms are air conditioned and have private baths. Snack bar and laundry service. 660 Calle 9 (phone: 42-40228). Inexpensive.

**Grumete** – Just 2 blocks from the beach and open year round, standard accommodations are available at this 20-room hotel. 797 Calle 20 (phone: 42-41009). Inexpensive.

**Playa** – Spacious and in front of the beach, but within walking distance of the center of Punta del Este. It has a restaurant, *Iris del Este,* bar, pool, and tennis court. Closed during the low season. Continuación Gorlero (phone: 42-82231). Inexpensive.

## LA PALOMA

**Casino Cabo Santa María** – One of the better hotels in town, it has large rooms, private baths, and a good restaurant (try the fish). The casino is open at night. Av. Nicolás Solari (phone: 473-6151). Inexpensive.

**Porto Bello** – All the guests at this property enjoy a splendid view of the sea (a few blocks away) and the pool. Tennis courts count among its amenities. Room rate includes meals. Calle Las Tres Marías (phone: 473-6159). Inexpensive.

**Yeruti** – A good value, this beachfront property has simple, nice rooms with private bathrooms. Its small restaurant is recommended. Las Grullas (phone: 473-6235; reservations in Montevideo through the national tourist office; phone: 2-905216). Inexpensive.

## PUNTA DEL DIABLO

**Hostería del Pescador** – If you want peace and quiet, this small, family-type place is ideal. But you will need a car, as there is almost no public transport. Good food. Km 298 on Rte. 9 (phone: Santa Teresa 17). Inexpensive.

## LA CORONILLA

**Costa del Mar** – This small hotel faces the sea and is open all year. It has a good restaurant and a pool, and its casino is open at night. Beachfront at Km 314 on Rte. 9 (phone: Coronilla 11). Moderate.

# Venezuela

For a range of geographical spectacles in a relatively small, accessible area, no South American country can match Venezuela. Covering 352,150 square miles, this tropical nation, with a fairly steady average yearly temperature in the 80s F (27 to 32C), is bordered by the Caribbean Sea to the north, Colombia to the west and southwest, Brazil to the southeast, and Guyana to the east. In Caracas, the capital, which stands at an elevation of 3,400 feet about 12 miles from the Caribbean, reside nearly 5 million of the country's 20 million inhabitants. (For a complete report, see *Caracas,* THE CITIES.)

In the southeast are the vast and dramatic Guayana Highlands, or Gran Sabana, an ancient plateau of rolling savannah, forest, and valley that covers almost half the country. The landscape is punctuated by massive rock formations with sheer walls and flat tops called *tepuis,* formed from sandstone hardened by intense heat. Angel Falls, the highest waterfalls in the world, tumbles more than a half mile over the side of the Auyan Tepui. The source of many rivers, the Guayana Shield is one of the oldest landforms on earth. To the botanist, the highlands are a paradise; to diamond miners, they are El Dorado.

In the northern and western parts of the country is the northernmost section of the Andes, which stretch from the Caribbean to Tierra del Fuego. This mountain range bunches in southern Colombia into a complex volcanic knot that eventually unravels into several spurs in Venezuela. One, the Sierra de Perijá, tracks north to the Guajira Peninsula on Venezuela's northwestern frontier; the other, the Cordillera de Mérida, makes a broad northeasterly arc, falling into the Caribbean just northeast of Caracas. Within the "V" formed by the two spurs is Lake Maracaibo, lying in a vast depression that is the major source of Venezuela's oil. A lesser spur, the Cordillera de la Costa, runs just to the south of Caracas, entering the sea off eastern Venezuela on a line with the Windward Islands.

Between the Andean highlands to the west and north and Guayana to the south is an immense area of low alluvial plain called the llanos, the basin of the Orinoco and Apure rivers. A harsh land, it is flooded 6 months of the year, drought-stricken the other 6 months, and always hot.

The territory that now comprises Venezuela was spotted by Columbus, on his third voyage in 1498. He sailed along the coast of the Delta Amacuro (where the Orinoco empties into the Atlantic) and rounded the Paria Peninsula in the east, near the islands of Trinidad and Tobago. The following year, Alonso de Ojeda and Amerigo Vespucci mapped the coast of the Guianas and Venezuela to Lake Maracaibo. Here, at what is now Sinamaica, they found Indians living on the water in palm-thatched huts supported by stilts, a phenomenon found also in the Delta Amacuro. All commerce was conducted by water and dugout canoe, as it still is today. Ojeda and Vespucci named the land Venezuela, which means "little Venice." From 1500 on, adventurers from Spain began roaming the difficult terrain in a relentless search for gold.

The first permanent settlement on the Venezuelan mainland was at Cumaná. The Germans assumed control of the land for a time and produced a couple of notable explorers, but they also fought a great deal and founded no towns. A Spanish colonizer from Curaçao founded Coro, at the base of the Paraguaná Peninsula, in 1523, but he was forced to flee. There were two main thrusts of colonization, one inland from the region of Coro, and the other from Pamplona (founded 1849), in what is now Colombia. The latter saw the establishment of the elevated aeries of Mérida and Trujillo in 1558 and San Cristóbal 3 years later.

Colonizers from the coast founded Barquisimeto in 1552, pushed east to Valencia (1555), also in an Andean valley, and, under the command of Diego de Losada entered the valley of Caracas in 1561. The *cacique* (chieftain) of the Caracas Indians, Guaicaipuro, defended his emerald paradise fiercely but eventually was killed near what is now La Carlota Airport and his head paraded about on a spear. Nonetheless, such was the ferocity of his resistance that Guaicaipuro is considered one of Venezuela's greatest heroes. The city of Santiago de León de Caracas was founded in 1567, and within a few decades every sizable valley along the spine of the Andes had bred a settlement.

The Andes gave birth to the caudillos who, until well into modern times, ruled their lofty valleys as fiefdoms, paying tribute to no one, least of all to one another. As late as the 1890s, the caudillo of Petare, now a suburb of Caracas, could be at war with the president of the republic in Caracas.

Politically, Venezuelans are proud of the fact they have the longest running democracy on the continent. It should be noted, however, that in early 1992, an unsuccessful coup led by the military did not go unappreciated by many of the country's citizens. The last dictatorship in Venezuela fell in 1958 with the overthrow of General Marcos Pérez Jiménez. Since then, presidents have been elected every 5 years (Carlos Andrés Pérez is the current leader); voting is required of all persons over the age of 18. The form of democracy is a highly centralized one. Corruption among appointed government officials is a virtual institution; however, while payoffs are commonplace, tourists generally are unaffected. At the same time, the government is continuing its campaign to ensure that tourists are not gouged by taxi drivers, hotels, restaurants, or tour agencies.

Economically, Venezuela's fortunes have varied dramatically. Though the conquistadores found little gold in the region, oil was discovered 400 years later. The abundant supply dramatically raised the economic standards of the country. When the price of oil soared in 1974, Venezuela reached its peak in prosperity, and for a decade enjoyed the highest standard of living on the continent. However, the collapse of the world oil market in 1983 spelled economic disaster. The bolívar was devalued, and the currency has fared poorly ever since (although it has done better here than in other countries). In early 1989, a dramatic hike in prices resulted in an uneasy week of street violence — primarily the looting of Caracas stores. The incident, however, was seen as an isolated occurrence and tourists were unaffected. In general,

Venezuela remains relatively peaceful and, with the exception of last year's attempted coup, freer from both the political and the social turmoil found in its poorer Latin American neighbors.

Although Venezuela has an extensive road network, driving in the interior is a rugged experience. Gasoline, while inexpensive, is not sold in many rural towns, and road services in more remote areas are very basic. If you do drive, make sure your car is in proper running condition before venturing out of the major cities, carry the spare parts needed in the event of a breakdown, and be prepared to make repairs yourself. Be sure to have your US or international driver's license and the proper insurance, and check to see that your insurance papers and *carnets* (customs passes) are in order and easily accessible. When driving in the interior, you must stop at *alcabalas* (military checkpoints). Also keep in mind that while English is understood by some in Caracas, in rural areas a basic knowledge of Spanish is extremely helpful. Driving in Venezuela is generally safe, except along the Colombian border, and rush-hour traffic in the capital can be hair-raising. Air transportation is fast becoming a favored method of travel and, owing to the abundance of petroleum in the country, is inexpensive.

The ten routes in this chapter are designed to enable you to plan varied itineraries through the Venezuelan countryside. The first one, Caracas to San Francisco de Yare, goes from Caracas west and south to the sulfur springs at San Juan de los Morros (home of the *llanero,* the Venezuelan cowboy), to Lake Valencia and the mountains around Cata, to the beaches in the colonial town of Choroní, and to the city of Valencia; then east to the beach area of Barlovento and Higuerote, and east to the village of San Francisco de Yare, in the Tuy River valley, and finally offshore to Los Roques Islands. The second route, the Andes, goes from Valencia through the cowtowns of San Carlos, Acarigua, and Guanare to the garden village of Boconó and the hill resort of La Puerta, and through the Aguila Pass of the Andes to the Apartaderos Andean valley, the mountain village of Santo Domingo, the fishing area of Laguna Negra, the historic mountain city of Mérida with its *teleférico* (cable car) to the Pico Espejo (15,634 feet above sea level), the restored colonial village of Jají, the city of San Cristóbal, and finally the Segovia Highlands, center of the María Lionza cult, one which draws all types of people — from students to businessfolks. The third route, the Western Coast, goes from Valencia to Chichiriviche along the Morrocoy reef, the sand dunes of Coro, and the Paraguaná desert. The fourth route describes a trip around the Maracaibo region off the Guajira Peninsula, where oil was discovered in 1917, changing the entire Venezuelan economy. The fifth route, the Eastern Venezuelan Coast, goes from Caracas east to Barcelona and Puerto La Cruz, a vast beach resort (see *Luxury Resorts and Special Havens,* DIVERSIONS), Cumaná, the first Hispanic settlement in Venezuela, the *Carnaval* city of Carúpano, the Paria Peninsula, and the Guácharo Cave. The sixth route, the Lower Orinoco, goes through Ciudad Bolívar, a river port, along the Río Paragua, through Ciudad Guayana, the Warao Indian town of Tucupita and through the Amacuro delta to Barrancas. The seventh route, the Gran Sabana, one of the most isolated sections of Venezuela, passes by towering massifs and tropical highlands and goes through the savannah town of Upata

**1024 DIRECTIONS / Venezuela**

and the jungle town of El Callao, to the outposts of El Dorado (the former penal colony where Papillon lived) and Santa Elena, and to the Brazilian frontier. The eighth route describes a trip to Canaima, site of Angel Falls. The ninth route covers Margarita Island, Venezuela's most famous Caribbean resort, and the tenth route explores the Venezuelan Amazon.

# Caracas to San Francisco de Yare

This route is a series of day trips around the Caracas outskirts, starting in the west, then heading south to the grassy llanos (plains) and continuing east along the Caribbean coast. Wedged between the base of the snow-capped Andes and marshy lowlands of the 1,700-mile Orinoco River, the llanos harbor a special breed of Venezuelan — the *llanero* (cowboy). He is an independent, proud character who rides his horse barefoot, herding his zebu (hump-backed cattle) through dust storm and flood and braving the dangers of ever-present rattlesnakes. The *llaneros* are quite a contrast to the coastal residents of Barlovento, who generally take life at an easier pace.

En route to the ocean is Lake Valencia, the second-largest lake in Venezuela. Here, Juan Vicente Gómez, one of the last, great, infamous military dictators, made the lakeside city of Maracay his unofficial capital after deciding Caracas was just ungovernable.

As there is only one short passenger-train route in Venezuela, between Puerto Cabello and Barquisimeto, it's better to fly between major cities or rent a car in Caracas (see "Sources and Resources," *Caracas*, THE CITIES) and drive from there. There are hotels in most of the major towns on this route, and their rooms — spacious, catering to double occupancies, and equipped with private showers — are more than adequate (see *Best en Route*).

Sun worshipers, sailors, and snorkelers who like out-of-the-way beaches should consider spending a few days in Los Roques, the coral-reef archipelago 100 miles (160 km) offshore from Caracas's port city, La Guaira. These remote, unspoiled cays can be reached only by charter yacht, plane, or helicopter.

For tourist information in Caracas, go to the *Venezuelan Tourism Corporation* (Corpoturismo; on the 37th floor of Torre Oeste in Parque Central; phone: 507-8876). The office is open Mondays through Fridays from 9 AM to 5 PM. The best maps are sold in giftshops of the major hotels and at CVP gas stations.

**En Route from Caracas** – Take the Caracas-Valencia *autopista* (freeway) or the Pan-American Highway, which leaves the *autopista* at the suburb of Coche, between Los Próceres and the Rinconada racecourse.

Fifty-seven miles (91 km) west of Caracas — 7 miles (11 km) beyond La Victoria — is San Mateo, where the hacienda of Simón Bolívar is open daily except Mondays to visitors. This is where the Great Liberator was raised, where he returned with his bride from Europe in 1802, and from where he fled to Paris after her death from yellow fever 6 months later. From La Encrucijada, 1 mile (1.6 km) away, Route 5 leads south to San Juan de los Morros, 30 miles (48 km) away.

**SAN JUAN DE LOS MORROS:** This town, named for the shape of the nearby mountains (which resemble Moorish castles with their tall, spiral peaks), is noted chiefly for its 1,500-gallon-per-hour, 95F (35C) sulfur springs; it is also the gateway to the llanos. The *llanero* will tell you that he is the true Venezuelan and his hardy and happy people herd some 5 million head of cattle (zebus) under immensely trying conditions. For 6 months of the year, the 125,000-square-mile plains are largely under water, and the herds must be moved to higher ground. The *llanero* rides barefoot (because wet feet inside soggy boots are subject to fungus infections) with the big toe hooked through a small ring stirrup. The other 6 months the plains are dry, and the herds are driven into the Central Highlands and fattened for sale. The music of the llanos is among the best in Venezuela: passionate ballads relating the tales of hell-bent men and evil women, odes to the ubiquitous rattlesnake (which are deadly to barefoot *llaneros*) and to the *llaneros'* other enemy, the jaguar. These songs are belted out by a soloist (preferably female), accompanied by maracas, *cuatro* (four-string guitar), and a harp, Venezuela's national instrument. There is a dance called the *joropo*, involving the vigorous stomping of feet. Another tradition is the *toros coleados*, a kind of rodeo whose object is (believe it or not) to throw a bull by its tail. Venezuelan writer Rómulo Gallegos immortalized the *llanero* in his celebrated novel *Doña Bárbara*.

The llanos are famous for their abundant wildlife. Scientists from around the world come to study this complex ecosystem and bird watchers and photographers have field days here. Howler monkeys, the alligator-like caiman, and the capybara, a huge swimming rodent, are among the most interesting creatures of the llanos. Once abundant, the capybara was nearly hunted to extinction after the Catholic church decreed that because the animal swims, it could be consumed on meatless Fridays during Lent. Thanks to the protectionist efforts of environmentalists, the capybara population has rebounded.

Bird watchers will find the llanos to be one of the most rewarding spots on earth. The scarlet ibis, maguari stork, sun bittern, hoatzin, and several varieties of macaw are only a few of the hundreds of fascinating species found at the water holes and along the rivers of the region.

For those who want a unique experience, the *Hato Doña Bárbara*, an immense cattle ranch near San Fernando de Apure, has opened its gates to guests. At one time the property of Pancha Vázquez, the tough plainswoman on whom the literary character Doña Bárbara was based, it is now owned by the nationally prominent Estrada family. The ranch is a wealth of historical and natural wonders. Guests can go birding, boating, hiking, and horseback riding next to the *llaneros* as they perform their daily chores, and family members are available to take visitors on daily excursions, such as bird watching at sunrise and four-wheel-drive treks into the forest to spot howler monkeys. All the food — featuring, of course, the famous beef — is produced at the ranch. Book packages through *Lost World Adventures* (1189 Autumn Ridge Dr., Marietta, GA 30066; phone: 404-971-8586 or 800-999-0558; in Caracas, 2-718644; fax: 404-977-3095; in Caracas, 2-717859).

**En Route from San Juan de los Morros** – Continue north on Route 5 to the junction of Route 9, and north toward the town of Cata, 36 miles (58 km) beyond Maracay, a commercial center on the eastern shore of Lake Valencia. Dictator Juan Vicente Gómez (1909–35) favored Maracay, building a zoo, a bullring, an opera house, parks, and fountains. Gómez maintained a vacation home here and took the precaution of ordering a road built over the mountain to the sea in case he needed to make a quick escape. He also started Venezuela's first air service to Maracay, Maracaibo, and Ciudad Bolívar. The *Museo de la Fuerza Aérea Venezolana* (FAV Museum) in Maracay houses the plane Jimmy Angel used when he accidentally discovered what later was named Angel Falls.

Lake Valencia itself is the second-largest in Venezuela, covering some 140 square miles and with 22 islands. Although for some years the lake was drying up, the situation is starting to stabilize, thanks to a multimillion-dollar cleanup and conservation campaign.

From here, the route runs 36 miles (58 km) north by way of Gómez's spectacular mountain drive. You'll go past waterfalls, over streams that wash across the road, and under a splendid canopy of towering bamboo. These mountains (the highest of which is about 4,200 feet) are in the Henri Pittier National Park. The region is beautiful, thickly forested with giant figs, lianas, and tree ferns. There are at least 14 identifiable vegetation zones, surmounted by one of the world's rare cloud forests. Along the road is Rancho Grande, an unfinished mansion that Gómez ordered built for purposes that were never clear. Part of it is now a natural history museum (not generally open to the public), part a laboratory, and the rest the range of forest wildlife.

This road ends at the resort village of Cata.

**CATA:** Very popular and one of the most beautiful beaches in Venezuela, Cata stretches along a wide, blue bay with fine white sands and coconut palms. Unfortunately, two very ugly condominiums rising above the beach detract from the beauty of the shoreline. Cata makes a good day excursion, with an overnight at the *Inter-Continental Valencia* (see *Best en Route*). The beach has lifeguards, a restaurant, changing rooms, and a dock where boats can be hired for journeys to the small, pristine bayside beach of Catita.

**En Route from Cata** – A few miles east of Cata is Choroní. Since there is no coast road, the approach to Choroní is from Maracay, 36 miles (58 km) back along the Valencia Highway. Coming directly to Choroní from Caracas, take Route 6 via the Henri Pittier Park.

**CHORONÍ:** A lovely colonial town, Choroní has accommodations available in reconstructed old houses that serve fresh fish from the coast and locally grown vegetables and fruits. They also employ only local residents in a pilot program to stimulate the once-moribund local economy and discourage young people from heading to Caracas for work. Most visitors head to Playa Grande, the main beach in town, or the more isolated Playa Escondida (Hidden Beach), although the best beaches in the area — gorgeous palm-lined crescents — are reached by outboard launches available at the waterfront. One of these, Chuao, was at the heart of the cacao-growing district in colonial times. Coffee and sugar also were products of this fertile area. Deep in the jungle are the crumbling remains of once-proud haciendas, which were supported by backbreaking slave labor. Dutch and Spanish merchant ships plied the coast and were subject to frequent raids by English pirates — explaining why most of the coastal towns, including Choroní and Chuao, were set back from the shore in order to afford some protection from pillaging.

Today Choroní draws sun worshipers to its beaches by day, while its seductive *tambores* lure dancers to the town's sea wall at night. *Tambores* — hollow logs beaten to Caribbean and African rhythms — are a special treat and the exotic and erotic dancing that accompanies them should not be missed.

Return to Maracay; 39 miles (62 km) west on Route 9 is the city of Valencia.

**VALENCIA:** Today an industrial city of nearly 500,000 people, Valencia is on the banks of the Río Cabriales, near Valencia Lake. It is a historical treasure trove, with a 200-year-old cathedral, a 1772 state capitol originally built as a convent, an 1894 theater resembling a scaled-down *Paris Opera House,* the second-largest bullring in Latin America (after Mexico City's *Plaza de Toros*), and a tragic past. After its founding by the Spanish, fierce Caribe Indians attacked the city 2 years in a row; later measles decimated the population. In 1677, French pirates attacked and burned Valencia, destroying all records of its history. And in 1812, an earthquake leveled the area. About 15 miles (24 km) south of the city is the battleground of Carabobo, where two battles were fought during the Independence Wars: one in 1814, the other in 1821, and both led and won by Bolívar. Shortly after the first war, José Tomás Boves ("The Butcher") charged from the llanos, slaughtering thousands and driving Bolívar clear out of the country. The second victory, won with the aid of the lancers of llanos strongman José Antonio Páez, definitively established Venezuela's independence. There is a large and impressive monument on the field that depicts scenes from the battle in high relief. Shortly before you reach the field is a safari park, with many black bears, animals from Africa (giraffes and the like), and Bengal tigers. The city's municipal theater merits a visit. Built in 1892 in European style, it was closed in 1971 to be renovated in time for the 150th anniversary of the Battle of Carabobo. Five years later it was temporarily closed for what was to have been 6 months; however, the repair work took 8 years! The building's ceiling, painted by Herrera Toro, is so striking that it has been declared a national monument. The theater is located where Calle Colombia meets Avenida Carabobo.

A possible side trip from Valencia follows a narrow road 18 miles (29 km) north to Vigirima, where there are petroglyphs; it's one of the many pre-Columbian sites to be found in the Valencia Valley.

**En Route from Valencia** – Return to Caracas and head east to Barlovento, a secluded beach area set on the seacoast that stretches from *Los Caracas* (a holiday camp) on the Litoral (see *Caracas,* THE CITIES) to the town of Higuerote.

**BARLOVENTO:** Cacao has been harvested in Barlovento for 3 centuries. The inhabitants of this area are the descendants of the black slaves shipped from Africa to work on the cacao plantations. For those in search of isolated beaches, Barlovento is a good one. The holiday camp of *Los Caracas* has its own, guarded entrances (all you have to do, however, is tell the guard you're passing through, and he'll let you by). There is an old mule track, winding up, down, and around steep headlands, fording several streams; the road is very rough, so take care. Camping is the mainstay of weekend beachcombers here, although there is a handful of small, basic hotels along the coast.

**HIGUEROTE:** This is a pleasant, bustling resort on a magnificent bay of long, white beaches. Its appearance is tranquil despite the rush to development. The city's waters have been polluted (partly by the number of yachts that dock here), but take a launch to one of the nearby islands where the water is clear and warm. The tranquillity of the Caribbean Sea here is what makes this an attractive spot for families with small children. Everything seems to be more expensive on this part of the coast, so watch how you spend your money, especially around the *Tambores de San Juan* festival in June.

According to tradition, the festival's origin dates back to the days of slavery, when liberty was granted for 1 day each year on the *Feast of San Juan*. The festival is one of the most popular in Venezuela, with its focal point here in Higuerote and in nearby Curiepe. This feast is a wild one, beginning at noon on June 23 with the ringing of bells and the pounding of large drums. Rum is consumed with gusto; the dancing in the streets and the constant throbbing beat of the *tambores* never stops until dawn on June 26, when the village returns to its usual tranquil self.

**En Route from Higuerote** – From here, retrace your steps to Caracas and proceed east on Route 9 through the Tuy Valley, following the Río Guaire valley to Santa Teresa, 34 miles (54 km) away — a pleasant drive. Continue another 9 miles (14 km) up the Tuy to San Francisco de Yare.

**SAN FRANCISCO DE YARE:** The best time to come to the town is in June, around the *Feast of Corpus Christi,* for the 2-day festival of the devils. The devils, in this case, are men wearing large multicolored masks of papier-mâché shaped like nightmarish animals. Each has two or more horns, and the more elaborate ones are fitted with the asses' teeth. The devils dance in front of the church, repent, defy the church again, and again repent. In the end, they say the hell with it, and everyone gets drunk.

# DIRECTIONS / Venezuela

Sadly, the origin of this festival is obscure, although it is assumed to have been invented by a medieval-minded missionary who imagined — and rightly so — that such a thing might prove diverting to the heathen. The masks, which can be bought at local craft stores, are unique to Yare. The village's heritage is a mix of Spanish, Indian, and African, and all the traditions blend together in this unusual festival. The headquarters for the dancers — who form the oldest active devil dancing society in the Americas — is in a building near Plaza de Armas where there is a also a museum. Its bright red façade makes it easy to find.

If the beat of drums on the coast or the smog of the capital is making your head throb, skip across the waves to the placid Los Roques National Park.

**LOS ROQUES:** The most pristine — and remote — beaches in the country are found in this cluster of tiny cays 100 miles (166 km) offshore from La Guaira. White sand, turquoise waters, and coral reefs await the intrepid sun worshiper who is willing to get there by chartered yacht, plane, or helicopter. Don't expect any luxuries in this archipelago that is a national park; be sure that the charter or package you choose includes all meals and drinks. Should you charter a plane or helicopter — try *Helicópteros del Caribe* (Simón Bolívar International Airport in Maiquetía), or *Alpi Tours* (phone: 2-283-1433) — be sure to take plenty of provisions. Don't forget the sunscreen — the rays on Los Roques are relentless and there's little shade — and while here, as elsewhere in Venezuela, be on guard against possible thefts on the beach. The best way to visit these cays is by yacht; you can sail to deserted ones to swim and explore, then spend peaceful nights at anchor. If you prefer to sleep ashore, *Morgan Tours* (phone: 2-261-9265 or 2-261-7217) has a package including lodging at a charming bungalow. *Aerotuy Airlines* (phone: 2-716231 or 2-718043; fax: 2-725254) offers packages with the option of yacht or land lodging. To charter a yacht, inquire at the Caraballeda marina near the *Macuto Sheraton* hotel in El Litoral, ask the concierge at your hotel, or check the classified section of the English-language *The Daily Journal* in Caracas. A note of caution: the daylong voyage to Los Roques against the current can be rough.

## BEST EN ROUTE

Hotels along this route are reasonably priced. Occasionally, one runs a very expensive $50 or $60 for a double room, but most cost from $30 to $50 a night (expensive); $20 to $30 (moderate); or under $20 (inexpensive). They're small, clean, and comfortable, and many have private baths. It's a good idea to make reservations in advance, especially during the festival season.

### SAN JUAN DE LOS MORROS

*Ana* – A small, 14-room hotel with double rooms and private baths. Av. Los Puentes (phone: 46-35037). Inexpensive.

### CHORONÍ

*Club Cotoperix* – Actually 3 renovated colonial-era houses, this club provides comfortable rooms and wonderful meals made of locally grown ingredients and fresh fish. Water sports are available. In Puerto Colombia, the tiny port village for Choroní. Make reservations in Caracas (phone: 2-573-5241). Moderate.

*Note:* A number of local residents have turned their homes into rustic hotels — some have rooms with private baths and a few serve meals. Don't expect hot water or air conditioning, though. The establishments are clearly labeled " HOTEL" or " PENSION." There is no way to make advance reservations; for a weekend stay, it is best to arrive on Friday night to ensure a bed. Prices start around $15 for a double.

## VALENCIA

***Inter-Continental*** – For both businesspeople and tourists, located in front of the *Viña Shopping Center*. It offers 158 rooms, a restaurant, jogging track, a bar and a piano bar, a gym and a sauna, and a swimming pool. Av. Juan Uslar, Urb. La Viña (phone: 41-211033; in the US, 800-327-0200). Expensive.

***Aparthotel Ucaima*** – This is a business hotel with 75 air conditioned suites with kitchenettes and TV sets; amenities include a restaurant, piano bar, tennis courts, sauna, and pool. 141-80 Av. Boyacá, La Viña (phone: 41-227011). Moderate.

## HIGUEROTE

***Barlovento*** – No frills, just a 25-room hostelry with a swimming pool, restaurant, and bar. Beachfront (phone: 34-21161). Moderate.

***Sol Mar*** – Clean double rooms for the night can be found in this 20-room hotel. Beachfront (phone: 34-21030). Moderate.

# The Andes

The elevated lands of Mérida are the frosty crown of the Venezuelan Andes. The *páramo*, or land beyond the treeline, known to geographers as the alpine moor, is a starkly beautiful region of mountain after mountain, falling here and there into narrow valleys beneath the snow-capped peaks. The principal vegetation is a fur-covered plant with yellow flower called the *frailejón* (great friar). The cold, gray *páramo*, carpeted with these *frailejones* in bloom, is a breathtaking sight. With its mountain streams and mirror lakes filled with trout, the region attracts fisherman and hiker alike.

There are only two seasons in the Andes: rainy and dry. The rainy season (May to November) is wet, often snowy; while the dry season (December to April) is cold, crisp, and clear.

The best way to reach the Andes is to fly or go by car, shunning the bus that takes travelers up and down what seems like a shaky roller coaster ride over the dozens of sharp zigzags, or switchbacks, along the Andean highway. The crafty traveler gets up at dawn to start his or her route and catches morning light, when visibility is at its peak.

**En Route from Caracas** – Start this trip by heading south along Route 5 out of Caracas; continue southwest through Valencia in the Central Highlands through the llanos (plains), skirting the foothills.

Continuing southwest from Valencia, you pass through the small towns of San Carlos, Acarigua, and Guanare (cowtowns all), whose streams offer fishing (as well as piranha). Guanare is the center of worship of the country's patron saint (since 1942), the Virgin of Coromoto.

**GUANARE:** The Virgin first appeared in the area in 1561, when the Indian *cacique* (chief) Coromoto spied a splendid lady with a radiant infant walking toward him on the surface of a stream. He was less impressed, perhaps, than he should have been, but after soliciting advice he commanded the baptism of everyone in his tribe, except himself. Obviously displeased, the Virgin appeared to him again, whereupon he lunged for her and she disappeared — leaving in his hands her image on parchment. Today, that same parchment — faded almost to the point of appearing blank — is still venerated, and the faithful make pilgrimages here in January and September. The legendary parchment is displayed at the Basílica de la Virgen de Coromoto (Basilica of the Virgin of Coromoto; Plaza Bolívar).

**En Route from Guanare** – Four miles (6 km) out of Guanare, head north, leaving the heat and scrub of the llanos to climb to the cool, rich green of the Andes. This is a land of flowering trees and coffee plantations clinging to the side of precipitous ridges; tiny villages perch on little plateaus that jut out over terrible gorges. A bizarre artwork — the painted skeletons of cattle — occasionally decorates fronts of houses. More bizarre, perhaps, are the boys on the side of the road who sell baby *cachecamos* (armadillos), considered tasty morsels.

At the village of Biscucuy the road once agains swings south, continuing to Boconó.

**BOCONÓ:** This garden town is reputed to have the prettiest girls in the country. The valley, set at the waters of the Río Boconó, is very narrow, and the town seems to tumble down the side of a long steep ridge. Trees sprout Spanish moss in the plaza, and mosses and airplants cling about the church.

The market here, open daily, is worth a visit for its good, traditional earthenware: pots, cups, bowls, and for its trays of woven *páramo* (high plain) grass. The *Casa Artesanal* (Calle 1 and Av. 3) gives demonstrations of wool and cotton weaving. It is open weekdays from 8 AM to noon and 3 to 6 PM, and Saturdays from 8 AM to noon.

**En Route from Boconó** – About 45 miles (72 km) north by northwest (the road winds itself in these directions, so don't worry about turns) is the turnoff for Trujillo; although the capital of this state, it is small and economically unimportant but old — dating back to 1557. About 20 miles (32 km) from the turnoff, continuing west through Trujillo, is Valera, the wheat and coffee center of the Andes. It is an unattractive town, but set in a picturesque river valley that's ringed by heavily forested mountains above and the Río Momboy below.

Another 14 miles (22 km) southwest is La Puerta.

**LA PUERTA:** Aptly named "The Door," this village is filled with the high, steep ridge of the *páramo*, which suddenly recedes to reveal a broad, green glade. La Puerta is a hill resort for the people of Maracaibo; at one end of town is a startling tract of prefabricated, concrete Bavarian houses.

Stores are filled with stocks of Andean *ruanas* (woven blankets) and blankets.

**En Route from La Puerta** – An early morning drive that winds through 14 miles (22 km) of zigzags from here to Timotes is a spectacular trip. Etched starkly in the morning light, the alluvial terraces are visible — small, and improbable — suspended from the sides of mountains on the edge of deep and narrow gorges; they are cultivated right to the edge by farmers using wooden plows and oxen.

Timotes is a good place to have breakfast. Try the regional specialty of wheat *arepa,* a kind of round unleavened bread that's very tasty — in contrast to the maize *arepa* found in the rest of Venezuela, which is definitely an acquired taste. *Arepas* can be eaten plain, with butter, or filled with just about anything, including cheese, meat, chicken, and *caraotas* (black beans).

From Timotes, it is about 28 miles (45 km) south to the Aguila Pass, where in 1819 Simón Bolívar crossed — in the hazardous snows of winter — to do battle against Royalist forces in Colombia on the plains of Boyacá. The zigzags in the road are sometimes severe, but on the whole it is a slow ascent, passing from verdant ranges to the harsh moonscape of the Páramo de Mucuchíes, where only *frailejones* can grow. On occasion, a deep valley will appear.

There comes a point in the wasteland where you reach a rise overlooking a long rugged valley and catch the first sight of snow on the cap of Pico Mucuñuque — miles away behind Laguna Negra. The peak to the left is Gavilán, at 14,000 feet, and off to the right is the Pico El Aguila at 13,500 feet. The Aguila (Eagle) pass farther on is cold, very windy, and impassable in snow. Here is a monument to

Bolívar in the shape of a condor (the pass actually is misnamed). There also is a pleasant way station where hot chocolate for the cold and glucose for altitude sickness are dispensed. About 4 miles (7 km) farther is the valley of Apartaderos.

**APARTADEROS:** In the arid brown landscape of the *páramos,* the sides of this valley are extremely steep and eroded, and a crystal stream runs by several small villages. Their houses are old and whitewashed, with worn red-tiled roofs that with time have sagged to gentle undulations. Massive stone fences crisscross the valley. The people grow wheat on the sides of the ridges, and in January they thresh the grain on round, stone threshing floors as they have done for centuries. By night, the *páramo* resembles a forbidding moonscape and is very silent and eerie when the fog rolls in.

Overlooking the valley from a 12,000-foot pass on the left is the *Sierra Nevada* hotel; across the road is an Andean handicrafts display and cafeteria where *ruanas* and *gorros,* a kind of Andean balaclava much more elegant than the Turkish variety, are sold. Near the *Mucubají* hotel in the valley is an antiques shop. Apartaderos is known for its cold cured ham; pick some up in one of the local *charcuterías* (delicatessens).

From here, the road leads southwest to the pretty village of Santo Domingo, set in wooded surroundings at 7,000 feet. From Apartaderos, take the road past the *Sierra Nevada* hotel heading south 15 miles (22 km) and down. En route is *Los Frailes* (The Friars) hotel, on the site of a monastery founded in 1620. The valley is somewhat wooded with the *páramo* only a step away; furry llamas roam with dignity — and at will. Horses are for hire at the hotel, which has elegant old-style buildings and walls surrounding a compound built about a brook. The rooms are exquisite and heated, with thick plastered walls and heavy exposed beams (see *Best en Route*).

Return to Caracas from Santo Domingo via Barinas on the llanos about 40 miles (64 km) from Santo Domingo, 64 miles (102 km) west of Guanare.

**LAGUNA NEGRA:** Down the ridge from the *Sierra Nevada* is the trail to Laguna Negra (the Black Lagoon), a mirror lake at the foot of a tall and snow-capped peak (a lure to photographers and trout fishermen). Aim to be at the lake before 10:30 AM when the sun strikes it. The early morning sun is strong and hot while frost crackles underfoot.

A 20-minute walk (or shorter drive) leads first to the Laguna Mucubají, a large glacial lake. Take it easy because at this elevation you can tire quickly or succumb to *soroche* (altitude sickness). Within 10 minutes there is a fork in the trail: Bear right and upward. Ten minutes later you overlook a rugged valley and the beautiful Laguna Negra. Filled and emptied by stepped waterfalls, the lake is fed by the snows of 15,000-foot Pico Mucuñuque, standing behind. Above it is another lagoon, the Laguna de los Patos (Duck Lagoon), which is worth a visit if you feel up to the 90-minute climb.

**En Route from Laguna Negra –** About 38 miles (61 km) south the road comes down to the town of Mérida. On the way, the vegetation changes, but the villages remain much the same: old whitewashed cottages with weathered, red tile roofs. The largest village (several blocks in size and very old) is Mucuchíes, a name lent to a breed of Andean dog that resembles a Saint Bernard. Mucuchíes, at an elevation of 10,000 feet, has one hotel and a pretty blue cathedral on the plaza. There's a well-known statue dedicated to Bolívar that depicts the patriotic Indian Tinjacá and his Mucuchíes dog, Nevado. The Indian and his canine were given to the Great Liberator when he passed through the area on a campaign. Legend has it that Tinjacá and the dog loyally served Bolívar until both were killed on the battlefield.

At the approach to Mérida, the valley broadens to include stately trees and manicured pines lining the stony beds of streams. Be on the lookout for patches of ivory lilies and bright fields of chrysanthemums. Except for the peaks that soar steeply and ruggedly on either side, you could believe this was England. To the south is the Sierra Nevada de Mérida, the only range in the Venezuelan Andes that is snow-capped year-round. Crowning the sierra is Pico Bolívar, at 16,427 feet the highest mountain in Venezuela.

**MÉRIDA:** If you should fly into Mérida during the day, you're in for a real treat. Be sure to reserve a window seat so you can see the emerald-green valleys set into the rugged mountains. Founded in 1558, this is one of the oldest cities in Venezuela. Unfortunately, little of the colonial town remains. It has one of the oldest universities in the Americas, the University of the Andes, established in 1785. At the entrance to the university, on the Plaza Bolívar, is a stained glass window with the biblical words (written in Latin): "You cannot hide a city which is on top of a mountain." Mérida also boasts many gardens, museums, and parks. The Parque Los Chorros de Milla is quite beautiful. According to legend, its springs and cascades are the tears Princess Tibisay shed for her love, the *cacique* Murachí, who was struck down by conquistadores. The Parque de las Cinco Repúblicas on Calle 13 contains soil from the five countries liberated by Bolívar; it was the first place in the world where a monument was erected to him (in 1842). The cathedral on the Plaza Bolívar has statues of dour, bloody saints, crucified Christs (with blood pouring out of heads and wounds), and suffering martyrs of the church, all grotesquely real. Architecturally, the cathedral is uninteresting ("rebuilt colonial," twice destroyed by earthquakes) but many devout Venezuelans will tell you it's the loveliest in the country. *Fiesta Week* here falls around December 8. Visitors should be sensitive to the fact that Mérida is one of Venezuela's most formal and traditional cities. It is best to avoid wearing skimpy clothing; shorts will draw looks of disapproval. Respect for the Great Liberator remains strong. If you cross a plaza that has his statue — particularly the main square — do not carry suitcases or large bundles as this is considered ill-mannered (and the police will tell you so!).

The real beauty of Mérida and the reason to visit the city is the Sierra Nevada and the quaint villages within a few hours of the city. Residents of the villages, presumably related to the Chibcha Indians of Bogotá, are set in their Andean traditions. They are a tough people: short, serious, supremely self-sufficient. Still, life is not easy in these cold, misty climes, and the higher you go into the Andes, the more poverty you will see. In the fertile valleys, however, there are terraced fields of every kind of vegetable. The small white potatoes grown near Mérida are famous for their sweetness. Don't leave the area without trying them; they're usually served with trout, the local delicacy. Although not native to Venezuelan waters, rainbow trout has been farmed with great success here for a couple of decades. You can visit the trout farms of Paraíso and Mucunutan, where big Mucuchíes dogs stand guard over the tanks fed by icy spring water piped in from the mountains. The trout raised here supply restaurants in Mérida, Caracas, Miami, and New York.

If you're interested in touring a working hacienda, Andean Rolando Araujo Pisani, a Caracas attorney, has opened his family estate at Mucurubá to paying guests. Visitors stay in the old but beautifully restored *Hacienda Escagüey* and can observe dairy operations, including cheese making, as well as farming tasks. Make arrangements in Caracas through *Morgan Tours* (phone: 2-271-9265). Another country hacienda that accepts guests is the charming *Doña Rosa,* where rooms open onto a cobbled courtyard and the dining room overlooks the lush, flowering landscape. Book through *Lost World Adventures* (1189 Autumn Ridge Dr., Marietta, GA 30066; phone: 404-971-8586 or 800-999-0558; in Caracas, 2-718644; fax: 404-977-3095; fax in Caracas, 2-717859).

A delightful sidetrip from Mérida is the jam factory, El Valle, on the Carretera El Valle en route to the *Valle Grande* hotel. Here, agricultural engineers José and Rhoda Ramírez grow the fruit, and process and package it into over 200 varieties of jams and marmalades. You'll find oddities such as angel hair (similar to cotton candy) and tamarind, and old favorites like rhubarb and strawberry. There's a tasting room, and you won't be able to resist buying several jars to enjoy on your travels (phone: 74-446144).

Travelers going into the sierras should bring a map; one is available at the Mérida climber's supply store. The map outlines walking trails — often blazing with wildflowers — across the *páramos,* the ascent to the Pico Bolívar, and takes in the length of the valley and sierras from Santo Domingo to Mérida. For organized hikes, ice climbing, and skiing excursions, and mountain biking packages, contact *Montaña Tours* (Av. las Américas, Edificio Las Américas, 1st Floor; phone: 74-631740) or their US representative, *Lost World Adventures* (1189 Autumn Ridge Dr., Marietta, GA 30066; phone: 404-971-8586 or 800-999-0558; in Caracas, 2-718644; fax: 404-977-3095; in Caracas, 2-717859)

Those preferring not to walk can see the sierras via a fantastic cable car ride.

**SIERRA NEVADA DE MÉRIDA:** Mérida boasts the highest and longest *teleférico* (cable car) in the world, running from an elevation of 5,000 feet to Pico Espejo (Mirror Peak), 15,634 feet high. It operates daily, except Mondays and Tuesdays, but occasionally is out of commission. If it's not running one day, return the following morning; mechanical difficulties are often minor. Get in line early, by 7 AM at the latest. The four-stage ascent takes 1 hour, if you go straight to the top. The first car leaves at 8 AM, the last at 2 PM. Bring warm clothes. It can be balmy in Mérida and snowing at the peak. Stop at the snack bar at the end station for a hot chocolate. After you've warmed up, take a short walk to the statue of *La Virgen de las Nieves* (The Virgin of the Snows).

The view from Pico Espejo is magnificent. With the massive splintered rock pile of the Andes all around and the alluvial plain of Mérida far below, you feel you are standing on top of the world. Far to the south is a haze, which is the heat rising up from the llanos, yet it is cold and windy. Across the gap and 1,000 feet above is Pico Bolívar. Several trans-Andean trails originate from the *teleférico* stations. Don't be surprised to see fully outfitted mountaineers embarking on great expeditions.

There are four well-known ascent routes from Pico Espejo, none of them exceptionally difficult for experienced climbers, but beware — ice-climbing equipment is necessary. The north face is the hardest, ice all the way with an unbroken fall of several thousand feet. The south face, Ruta Weiss, is the easiest. On top of the peak is a bronze bust of Bolívar. The next two peaks along are Jahn and Abanico. The south face of Abanico (16,000 feet) is almost vertical and a favorite with rock climbers. The *Club Andino de Mérida* takes parties of a maximum of three people to the top (ask at the alpinists' store) or contact *Montaña Tours* (Av. las Américas, Edificio Las Américas, 1st Floor; phone: 74-631740). You should camp at the *teleférico* station on Pico Espejo and set out at dawn. Permits from the local forestry commission and the Defensa Civil are necessary.

**JAJÍ:** A half-day excursion from Mérida (you can hire a taxi for the 27-mile/43-km drive), Jají is built on a point overlooking a valley and appears snow white in a blazing sun, with old buildings, a grassless plaza (named Bolívar, not surprisingly), and a church. The entire town, restored by the government as a way to draw tourists, surrounds the plaza. Small boys in the plaza hire out mule rides; little girls peddle traditional Andean sweets made from fruit and milk; and stores stock diverse souvenirs. Two restaurants serve Andean trout.

**En Route from Jají** – Return to Mérida and continue west through the tranquil valley of the Río Chama. From here, head toward the state of Táchira, an isolated, backwoods region. As with all border areas in Venezuela (and this one's near Colombia), there is a quality of anarchy here.

Believe it or not, Táchira has been more influential on Caracas than Caracas on Táchira. Its provincial mountain culture, with remnants of feudalism, recalls the 19th-century, tyrannical caudillos, whose portraits hang in the bodegas (grocery stores); and it becomes very clear that the democratic hurly-burly of Caracas is, indeed, far away. No less than five military strongmen from Táchira — including the most notorious, Juan Vicente Gómez and Marcos Pérez Jiménez — have seized the highest office in the land. Venezuela's current (and democratically elected) president, Carlos Andrés Pérez, also was born in Táchira, in Rubio.

Actually, even Mérida is far away — the road more or less disappears at Bailadores, just short of the Táchira line, about 60 miles (96 km) west of Mérida.

**BAILADORES:** This small, neat village lies at the end of a fertile valley; its plaza, smothered with flowering trees and bougainvillea, is among the prettiest in the country.

Just out of the town in a forest is a small park, built up, but in a minimal way, with paths, bridges, and shelters, and there is a fan-shaped waterfall. The *Toquisai* hotel is one of the nicest in the country and the principal reason for stopping here (see *Best en Route*). The restaurant is very good, and at night the locals drink at the bar. In this convivial atmosphere you find yourself sharing a table with *contrabandistas* and the self-proclaimed relatives of infamous guerrillas, all stout fellows and apparently upstanding citizens. This is not yet Táchira, but in the bodega on the plaza is a portrait of former dictator Pérez Jiménez.

**En Route from Bailadores** – The roads into Táchira are not good. Fourteen miles (22 km) from Bailadores is the Mérida-Táchira border, and here the paved road ends. Go left, continuing to the end at La Grita, on a twisting road that is paved in some stretches, covered with gravel in others.

La Grita (the Cry) is over 400 years old, a major trading center for the area and not very attractive. Thirteen miles (21 km) farther is El Cobre, a town in an arid landscape on the side of a ridge, sweltering under a hot midday sun with no trees in sight. The two spacious plazas are grassy oases, and the large Church of San Bartolomé, dominating one of the plazas, boasts some intricately carved doors. The houses are very old, and through a quality of the local stone the entire village is pink.

Another 35 miles (56 km) south is San Cristóbal, an equal distance from the Colombian border.

**SAN CRISTÓBAL:** Founded in 1561, some colonial streets remain in this town, but on the whole it is a modern, thriving city. Built on a terraced plateau in the broad, rolling valley of the Río Torbes, it has many parks and plazas. The cathedral (in the center of town) appears colonial, but the façade is not the original one. The most interesting building is the Casa de Gobierno (Government House) on Plaza Sucre. Completed by a cousin of the dictator Gómez, the imposing structure is topped by statues of lions — earning it the local nickname, Palacio de los Leones.

In late January, there is a week-long festival, dedicated to patron saint San Sebastián, that is vastly overrated but features good bullfights. At that time of the year it is very difficult to find a room, so make reservations before coming.

The Pan-American from San Cristóbal offers two routes; one to Maracaibo in the north; the second, heading south, leads to Llanos, returning to Caracas.

**SEGOVIA HIGHLANDS:** If you are feeling really jaded, bored with Haitian voodoo rites and *macumba* on the Copacabana, and seek something more macabre, visit the Sorte Mountains in the northeastern Andean foothills in the state of Yaracuy (its capital is San Felipe). Two miles (3 km) west of the junctions of Routes 1 and 11 is the village of Chivacoa, the home of the semipagan cult of María Lionza, whose statue stands in the middle of an eight-lane *autopista* in Caracas. Atop a 20-foot column, she sits naked astride a rampant tapir — a warrior queen brandishing aloft the bones of a male pelvis. Called Queen, Mother, and Goddess, María Lionza was an Indian princess whom her people thought a witch and cast out. It came to pass that she was loved by a serpent. There was a great flood, and she was saved from drowning, nursed, and raised by a tapir. As a result she is renowned as mistress of the elements. Should you make a pact with her, she grants you favors, including riches — if they are shared with the poor. She demands fierce fidelity.

Her altars include a distinguished pantheon: Jesus, Mary, and the Roman Catholic saints (especially Peter); the great Indian *caciques;* Simón Bolívar; the Negro Primero, Pedro Camejo (a slave who rose to be a general under Bolívar); the Negro Miguel, who led a slave revolt in 1552 (and who is sometimes identified as María Lionza's husband); and José Gregorio Hernández, a doctor who lived at the turn of the century and, after his death in a traffic accident, was credited with miraculous healing powers. The Vatican elevated him to the status of Venerable, an early step on the way to canonization. Several divinities are imported directly from the Santería Cubana cult, which is said to have had its origins in Nigeria. Commanding all this is María Lionza, who occasionally is represented on the altar by a photograph, said to have been posed for by a medium of 1930s vintage who was a concubine of the dictator Gómez. These highlands are the focal point for this cult.

The supplicant seeks intercession from mediums through whom the appropriate spirit acts. The supplicant goes barefoot, perhaps on his or her knees. Men are bare to the waist. Rum is used liberally as a purifier, and cigars are a major tool. Faith healing is common. María's followers believe that the rivers descending from the Sorte Mountains near Chivacoa have curative powers. Traditionally, pilgrimages are made to this area in June and the pilgrimage site has been declared a national monument.

The cult is not considered dangerous — although witnessing the participation of children in the rites is disturbing — and it has a wider following than a stranger might suspect. The newspaper space reserved for paid ads proclaiming gratitude to the Holy Ghost for favors granted generally includes several addressed to María Lionza. Scattered around Caracas are little "pharmacies" dealing solely in magic potions — love, fortune, health, and what have you — in countless combinations. People come in with prescriptions written on paper torn out of an exercise book.

San Felipe is about 78 miles (125 km) from Valencia on the Pan-American Highway. Take Route 5 heading south, turning right on Route 11 some 10 miles (16 km) later. Alternatively, take Route 3 to the coast as far as Morón, then Route 1 west.

## BEST EN ROUTE

There are a lot of hotels in the Andes; most are small, but comfortable, providing modern facilities and clean accommodations. They're not costly (except for the very expensive *Páramo La Culata* in Mérida that will run about $95 for a double); figure about $40 at a hotel listed here as expensive; $25 to $40 in a hotel listed as moderate; and under $25 at an inexpensive hotel. Make reservations in advance.

### GUANARE

*Coromoto* – A 76-room hotel with a swimming pool. Av. Francisco de Miranda (phone: 57-55231). Moderate.

### TRUJILLO

*Trujillo* – Private baths, a disco, bar, restaurant, and a pool in a 32-room hotel in the city. Av. Carmona (phone: 72-33576). Expensive.

### LA PUERTA

*Guadalupe* – A comfortable, 30-room hostelry with private baths, food, and a clay tennis court. Av. Principal (71-83825). Moderate.

*Las Truchas* – Excellent service, food, and facilities at this 10-room property. On the La Puerta edge of town (phone: 74-89158). Moderate.

### APARTADEROS

*Mucubají* – Very basic, but quaint and clean 16-room hotel, overlooking the valley on the southern edge of town (no phone). Moderate.

***Sierra Nevada*** – A pleasant 15-room hostelry offering food. Popular with fisherfolk and bikers. Near the *Mucubají* hotel (no phone). Moderate.

## SANTO DOMINGO

***Los Frailes*** – Considered one of the best in Venezuela, this charming 47-room hotel has cobblestone courtyards, fountains, balconies, a restaurant, and a cozy, rustic bar (order the *ponche páramo* — warm, sweetened milk spiked with *miche* liquor and cinnamon). On the highway between Santo Domingo and Apartaderos (phone: 74-88144). Reservations through the *Hoturvensa* hotel organization in Caracas (phone: 2-562-3022; fax: 2-562-3196), in the US, through *Avensa* (phone: 800-283-6727) or *Viasa* (phone: 800-432-9070 in Florida, 800-327-5454 in the rest of the country). Expensive.

***Moruco*** – Popular 23-room hotel that is not as pretty as *Los Frailes*. It has a good restaurant, which features the local trout. Just outside of town. Book in Mérida (phone: 74-88070). Expensive.

## MÉRIDA

***Páramo La Culata*** – Luxury comes to the Andes at this new deluxe resort that features 93 lavish bungalows, 2 restaurants, 2 snack bars, a bar, a disco, 2 swimming pools, and 6 tennis courts, all set in a 150-acre wooded area about 10 minutes from the airport. At Valle Grande, just outside Mérida (phone: 74-446121; in the US, 800-275-3123; fax in Caracas: 2-261-5537). Very expensive.

***Prado Río*** – With 60 rooms and cabañas, a pool, lovely gardens, and a mountain setting, among the nicest accommodations in town. Av. Milla (phone: 74-520704). Expensive.

***Park Hotel*** – A pleasant 125-room hotel with a good restaurant, and a coffee shop, bar, and disco. Located on Calle 37 at the Parque Glorias Patrias (phone: 74-632400). Reservations in Caracas through *Venantur* (phone: 2-979-3246; fax: 2-978-1497). Moderate.

***La Pedregosa*** – With 75 rooms, 25 cabañas, and 2 suites, this is a comfortable Andean hostelry. Amenities include an outdoor coffee shop, piano bar, an international restaurant, and disco. There's a gym, fishing, and horseback riding. Av. Panamericana in Urb. La Pedregosa (phone: 74-630525; *The National Reservations System* in Caracas at 2-782-8433; fax: 74-639936). Moderate.

***Valle Grande*** – Eight miles (13 km) outside Mérida, in a deep pine forest, this combination of lodge-plus-bungalows provides cozy accommodations, and the dining room serves fine food. There is also a bar and disco, and for the sports-minded, putt-putt golf and horseback riding are available. Km 10, Carretera El Valle, Mérida (phone: 74-635930). Moderate.

***La Sierra*** – Old, 37-room hotel, providing excellent service. Calle 23 and Av. 2 (phone: 74-23625). Moderate to inexpensive.

## JAJÍ

***La Posada de Jají*** – The best food in Jají is served in the restaurant of this 6-room hotel on the plaza. Try the fried trout stuffed with ham and the smoked cheese (*queso ahumado*). Live music on Sundays. Very pleasant and personal. Book in Mérida (phone: 74-35182). Moderate.

## BAILADORES

***Toquisai*** – Excellent service, good rooms, and private baths are features of this 20-room property. In a quiet setting, on the edge of town (phone: 75-71818). Moderate.

## SAN CRISTÓBAL

**Las Lomas** – A 50-room motel with a swimming pool. Av. Libertador (phone: 76-435775). Moderate.

**El Tamá** – This 112-room hotel with an Olympic-size swimming pool is at the edge of the city in Urbanización Pirineos and offers fine views, plus a restaurant, bar, shops, and disco. Av. 19 de Abril (phone: 76-554477 and 74-554335). Moderate.

## UREÑA

**Aguas Calientes** – Accommodations that include 32 rooms, 2 suites, and private baths, this property is 10 minutes from the San Antonio airport and an hour from San Cristóbal. The baths are fed by three hot springs. There are 2 swimming pools — one for adults and one for children — a bar, and a restaurant. Four miles (6 km) north of Vreña (phone: 76-86401). Expensive.

# The Western Coast

This route travels along the western Venezuelan coastline, starting some 27 miles (43 km) north of Valencia at Puerto Cabello, continuing on to the fishing/resort village of Chichiriviche and Morrocoy National Park, then to the Paraguaná Peninsula, a sandy, windswept area, barely above sea level. Inland are the dank, cave-filled badlands, inhabited only by rattlesnakes, oil birds, and burros. It was once the home of leftist guerrillas. A dry, often desolate route, this would be a boring trip if not for the small, picturesque resort towns fringing the Caribbean Coast and the lovely, palm-fringed cays just offshore.

From Valencia, the Pan-American Highway leads some 27 miles (43 km) north to El Palito, then 7 miles (11 km) east to Puerto Cabello.

**PUERTO CABELLO:** Set amid miles of palm-shaded beaches, this port of 70,000 people figured importantly in Venezuela's Independence War. Today, it is one of the country's loveliest cities with pastel-colored colonial buildings, including many with wooden balconies and intricate window grilles. On quaint Calle Lanceros, there is an unusual architectural detail — two colonial buildings across the street from each other are joined at their second floors via a small bridge.

During the Spanish conquest, galleons were loaded here with gold, silver, and other riches bound for Europe. To fend off British pirates, the Castillo Libertador fort was constructed; after the revolution, it became a political prison that was filled to capacity by Venezuela's ruthless dictators. Today, the fort is open daily and is a short ferry ride across the canal from the beachwall. There are guides (some bilingual) who can take you around the fort; they should be tipped about $1 per person. Messages scratched into the stone walls of the prisoners' cells are still visible. Not far from the fort, small boats are available for hire to take beachcombers to a variety of offshore islands, including Isla Blanca. There is also Quizandal Beach on the mainland with a coral reef. No matter where you go, take plenty of sunscreen — the rays are merciless here.

After a day at the beach, relax at one of Puerto Cabello's excellent seafood restaurants. For a memorable experience, dine alfresco at sunset at *Mar y Sol,* beside the beach at the end of the wall. To work off some of the shrimp drenched in garlic butter or fresh fried fish, do what local residents do and stroll along the *malecón* (promenade) at the water's edge. There are benches that are ideal for sitting to watch people strolling by and artisans selling their work, or to gaze at bubbling fountains.

At the end of the *malecón*, near the naval base that oversees the fort, is the Aguila — or Eagle — Monument dedicated to ten North American mercenaries who were paid by Venezuelan hero Francisco de Miranda to help overthrow the Royalist forces. They were executed in Puerto Cabello in 1806, but their deaths only fueled the revolutionary fever in this town where streets bear names like Independencia and Democracia.

Puerto Cabello also has the distinction of being on the country's only rail line, which runs from the port of Barquisimeto, 4 hours away. Travelers are *not* encouraged to take this trip — it is not a particularly scenic route and some of your fellow passengers will probably be pickpockets and purse snatchers.

**En Route from Puerto Cabello** – Continuing 31 miles (50 km) north, you soon reach the resort town of Tucacas, a run-down place of about 50,000 inhabitants noted as a jumping-off point to the palm-shaded, lush cays of Morrocoy National Park. Veteran diver Mike Osborn runs a well-known shop in Tucacas (6 Calle Ayacucho; phone: 48-84082 and 48-84679), where he rents equipment and operates beach and boat dives in the cays. Prime diving periods in Morrocoy are during June and December, when visibility is best. Book in the US through *Lost World Adventures* (1189 Autumn Ridge Dr., Marietta, GA 30066; phone: 404-971-8586 or 800-999-0558; fax: 404-977-3095).

Tucacas is just beginning to follow the lead of the coastal village of Chichiriviche, a few miles farther north on the Pan-American Highway — it has started to develop in order to attract international travelers.

**CHICHIRIVICHE:** This little fishing village boasts several resort hotels and, like Tucacas, is a gateway to Morrocoy. Take a launch at the waterfront to go out to one or more of the park's seven major cays. The price of about $20 per boatload is based on 10 passengers, but the amiable skippers are willing to strike a bargain to take a smaller group. Be sure to let the boat captains know where and when to pick you up later in the day.

The cays are coral reef islands. They are flat and lie very low in the crystal-clear water. There is excellent snorkeling and scuba diving around the Perasa, Borracho, and Sombrero cays. The distant Sombrero is the most popular. The near side of the island is packed with fast motorboats and people; the far side is favored by families, and by beachcombers who prefer stringing a hammock between the palms and avoiding the crowds.

Be sure to bring plenty of sunscreen (the rays are very intense), drinks, and food for day or camping trips. There are occasional vendors, but there is only one small snack bar on the cays at Sombrero.

Camping facilities are minimal to nonexistent. Many visitors prefer to stay overnight at one of the hotels in Chichiriviche (see *Best en Route*) and make day trips to the cays.

Another 120 miles (192 km) west on the Pan-American is the port of Coro and the Paraguaná Peninsula.

**CORO:** Like Puerto Cabello, this town saw action during the independence battles. It was the first capital of the province of Venezuela (before the country became independent). Founded in 1523, a large section of its colonial buildings have been preserved, along with cobblestone streets and grand old houses of sunburned brick and red-tiled roofs. The 16th-century cathedral has a tower that once doubled as a fort during the privateer attacks of Francis Drake, Henry Morgan, and Walter Raleigh. It was the country's first cathedral and is still being used. The Coro Jewish Cemetery is the oldest Jewish burial ground on the continent. Calle Zamora is the best street for viewing colonial houses, including the Casa de las Ventanas de Hierro (House of the Iron Windows; on the corner of Calle Colón). This was one of the first homes in the country to use iron grilles, instead of wood, which caused quite a sensation in the old days.

Today these are found everywhere. If you're there on the weekend, be sure to stop in and see the colonial furnishings. The *Museo Diocesano* (69 Calle Zamora) has an interesting collection of religious artifacts, including a fascinating group of saints carved by locals. Closed Mondays.

North of the city, at the base of the low-lying desert of the Paraguaná Peninsula, are the famous *médanos* of Coro, a 30-square-mile region of giant sand dunes that is designated a national park. Constantly shifted by unceasing winds, the dunes have already consumed three roads and are working on a fourth. You can hire a camel for a 20-minute ride over the dunes from near the Plaza de la Madre entrance to the park. The Paraguaná Peninsula itself is a vast, low desert connected to the mainland by only a narrow strip of sand. Its greater part is barely above sea level. The peninsula's highest point, rising abruptly to 2,500 feet from an immense flat plain, is the Santa Ana Mountain. At the foot of the mountain, 37 miles (59 km) from Coro, is the village of Santa Ana, founded about 1546. If you're interested in a guided hike up the mountain, ask around in town. Locals will take groups for a small charge.

There is a wealth of colonial houses with interesting architectural details in the peninsula's small villages. The beaches are great for shelling, if not swimming — the surf can be rough and the winds brutal. The best bathing and sunning beaches are near Adicora on the east side of the peninsula and just north of the oil refining center, Punto Fijo, on the west (try Villa Marina or El Pico). *Chivo* (goat) prepared in many different ways is the specialty on Paraguaná. Goatherds are everywhere.

**En Route from Coro** – Ferries on irregular schedules leave from Punto Fijo and the Muaco pier near Coro for the islands of Curaçao and Aruba in the Netherlands Antilles. Check at *Ferrys del Caribe* (Av. Independencia; phone: 68-519676); it's best to book a week ahead. In order to enter either Aruba or Curaçao, you must have a ticket showing that you're continuing on to another destination.

The southern road continues to the commercial city of Barquisimeto, 180 miles (288 km) from Coro in the Andes. It is known as the music capital of Venezuela because of the many noted singers and instrumentalists who come from here. En route is the turnoff to Siquisique, notable only in lending its name to the local tequila — a brew more commonly known as *miche,* which means "skunk juice," more or less.

The highway west of Coro leads to Maracaibo, 158 miles (253 km) away.

## BEST EN ROUTE

Hotels in the western coastal area sometimes lack hot water, but have cold showers, double rooms, and, in some cases, restaurants. They are reasonably priced — ranging from $40 and up for a double room at a hotel categorized as expensive; $25 to $40 for a hotel listed as moderate; and under $25 at an inexpensive one. Make reservations before arriving.

### PUERTO CABELLO

***Suite Caribe*** – This hotel has air conditioning, though it's not on the beach. 21 Av. Salón, Urbanización La Sorpresa (phone: 42-613346; fax: 42-613131). Expensive.

***Miramar*** – This 20-room property is on its own beach. El Palito (phone: 42-3853). Inexpensive.

### CHICHIRIVICHE

***La Garza*** – Down the street from the *Mario,* this hostelry is slightly smaller and older but offers basically the same amenities, including optional full board. Av. Principal de Chichiriviche (phone: 42-86126; fax: 42-86347). Moderate.

**Mario** – Modeled after a *Howard Johnson's* (note the orange-and-blue details), this ever-expanding property has a dining room serving bountiful buffet breakfasts, a disco, gift shop, and pool. Divers are welcome; there are lockers for scuba gear. Tours to the cays can be arranged. The meals are good — you may want to choose a package with full board if you're not planning to be in Morrocoy National Park all day. Av. Principal de Chichiriviche between Calle 6 and 7 (phone: 42-86114/5; fax: 42-86096). Moderate.

**Náutico** – Favored by divers, this little inn is perched right at the water's edge. It's basic, but clean and friendly with a restaurant (full board available) and bar. Only 3 of the 20 rooms have air conditioning, but fans in the rest provide a good breeze. Sector Playa Sur (phone: 42-86024). Inexpensive.

### CORO

**Miranda** – Opposite the airport, this 86-room, government-run hotel has a restaurant, pool, and tennis courts. Av. Josefa Camejo (phone: 68-516645; in Caracas, 2-507-8815). Expensive.

**Caracas** – Old and elegant, this 14-room hotel has a beautiful courtyard, is air conditioned, and serves meals. 17 Calle Toledo, on the edge of the colonial section (phone: 68-59545). Moderate.

**Los Médanos** – Located on the eastern fringe of Coro at the edge of the sand dunes, this property has 40 guestrooms in three buildings, as well as several cabañas. There's air conditioning, a restaurant, and bar. Av. Esteban Smith (phone: 68-59949). Inexpensive.

# The Guajira Peninsula

Fed by Andean streams in the south and open to the Gulf of Venezuela in the north, 5,000-square-mile Lake Maracaibo is the largest in South America. Its shores are heavily forested in the south (with the highest rainfall in the entire country) and desert-covered to the north — a desert that is hot, windless, and humid, but laden with riches. Oil was discovered here in 1917, and for a long time Venezuela was the world's leading exporter of petroleum. Today, 70 percent of the country's petroleum comes from this region.

A few words best describe this area: sweltering, desert, oil-rich, and dangerous. The peninsula, shared by Venezuela and neighboring Colombia to the west, has for years been a smugglers' haven; drugs, like cocaine and marijuana, have just about replaced the emeralds, cattle, and electrical appliances that were in such high demand during the 1960s. So much illegal traffic has crossed the borders recently that war has erupted between the authorities and the *contrabandistas,* transforming what was an interesting desert circuit into a dangerous zone best avoided by travelers.

This route, which starts with lakeside Maracaibo, is approachable from the Andes or from Coro on the western Caribbean coast. Maracaibo also is easily — and inexpensively — accessible by plane from Caracas. Some 438 miles (701 km) northwest of the federal capital, it has its own Indians (the Guajiro), who are related to the Colombian Guajiro, and whose women wear long, colorful *mantas,* or flowing caftans. Both Colombian and Venezuelan groups are nomadic and extremely independent. They consider themselves neither Colombian nor Venezuelan, but Guajiro, and the two governments allow them to cross the border without passports. The Spanish heard in rural areas along this route is almost incomprehensible — a quaint, archaic form of Castilian. Predominant in the culture is the *gaita*, often heard throughout the country during *Christmastime*, a song filled with humorous verses that are generally topical and often political. More than one controversial *gaita* has been banned from the radio. *Gaitas* are rendered by a soloist and chorus, and are accompanied by *cuatros* (a four-string guitar), maracas, drums, and *furrocos* (a drum with a pole extending vertically from the hide, played by moving the hand up and down the pole).

The first stop is Maracaibo.

**MARACAIBO:** On the western shore of the lake, this city of 1.7 million (Venezuela's largest urban area after Caracas) is only 25 feet above sea level and extremely hot — tempered only by a breeze that moves in at about 5 PM. Founded in 1570, Maracaibo ranks highly in the bygone romantic histories of Caribbean ports, but only around the docks is any trace of the colonial past still to be found.

One enters the city across the mouth of the lake via the 5-mile (8 km) Rafael Urdaneta Bridge, with the longest prestressed concrete span in the world.

Maracaibo remains an important business center, although centuries ago it was a charming colonial city. Maracaibo's oldest neighborhood fell to the wrecker's ball in 1973, but a few multicolored adobe homes can be found along the edges of Plaza Bolívar. The cathedral on the plaza marks the beginning of the 7-block walkway known as the Paseo de Las Ciencias, ending at the Basílica de la Nuestra Señora de Chiquidquirá. The century-old cathedral, remodeled in recent years, is home to the famous 16th-century statue of the *Cristo Negro* (Black Christ). Legend has it that the church where the statue originally stood was burned down in a fiery Indian raid in 1600. The figure of Christ survived, albeit discolored by smoke and flames, and the devout believe the statue has miraculous powers. To one side of the white-domed church is the Casa de Gobierno, the state capitol, also dubbed the Palacio de las Aguilas because of the two eagle figures that adorn its roof. It houses the national tourist office (phone: 61-22541). Next door is the *Casa de Morales* (no phone), which served in the 18th century as the residence of the Royal Governor of Maracaibo province; it is now a historical museum, and occasionally mounts art exhibits in the courtyard. Tours of the house (in Spanish only) are available on weekdays. Open weekdays from 8 to 11:45 AM and 2:30 to 5:45 PM; no admission charge.

It was in Maracaibo that the Spanish Armada capitulated to the independence forces following a naval battle on Lake Maracaibo in 1823. Folk history claims that a servant, Ana María Campos, yelled across what is now Plaza Bolívar for Spanish General Francisco Tomás Morales and his men to give up the fight. Morales had not yet decided what action to take and was so infuriated by her action that he had the young woman snatched from the house, stripped, flogged, and dragged across the plaza and down 2 blocks to the Convento de San Francisco, a monastery located in what is now the colorful outdoor market, the *Mercado Central*.

Next to the *Casa de Morales* is the *Teatro Baralt*, a plush theater that has been under restoration for several years. Built in 1883 to celebrate the centennial of Simón Bolívar's birth, the theater was replaced in 1929 with an 800-seat Art Deco building. During Venezuela's oil booms of the 1930s and 1940s, the legendary Argentine tango singer Carlos Gardel and the famous pianist Teresa Carreño performed here.

For a cool respite from the city's merciless heat, stroll along the Paseo de las Ciencias — dotted with concrete benches, hibiscus bushes, palm trees, and flowers. At the end is the Basílica de la Nuestra Señora de Chiquinquirá, with its false, painted,

Romanesque façade. Every November 18, the basilica is the springboard for the week-long *Feria de la Chinita*. The festival allegedly started in 1749 when a young girl found a floating board in the lake and took it home. As the story goes, a few days later the image of the Virgin of Chiquinquirá (or La Chinita for short) appeared on the wood. Now kept in the basilica, the image is taken out for the festival and carried through Maracaibo's streets.

Predominant among the Indians in the city are the Guajiro, who live in the native quarter of Ziruma. The Guajiro maintain traditional ways (those living in urban areas, however, have adapted mainstream Venezuelan lifestyles), and their weavers make a tidy living selling brightly colored hammocks, dresses, wall hangings, and rugs — some of which have been exhibited in the US. The infamous Papillon, a prisoner on Devil's Island, hid among the nomadic Guajiro on his first (unsuccessful) escape from the penal compound in French Guiana.

You can catch a glimpse of the oil derricks on Lake Maracaibo by taking Route 3 to Cabimas and continuing on to Lagunillas. Several miles after leaving Cabimas, there is a stretch of the lake dotted with derricks as far as the eye can see. Although oil is still pumped from under the lake, these first derricks are defunct — vestiges of the oil boom and subjects for photos.

**En Route from Maracaibo** – A road heading north from Maracaibo leads toward the Guajiro desert beaches and on into Colombia.

Off to the right is the 17th-century fortress of San Carlos, which saw action and lengthy siege against pirates and republicans and which, under the dictatorships, became a notorious prison. Twenty-five miles (40 km) from Maracaibo is the mouth of the lagoon at Sinamaica, the "little Venice" described by Alonso de Ojeda when naming the country. The Indians here live in houses woven from reeds and supported on stilts. Recommended is a boat trip on the Río Limón to visit the "city on stilts," known as Laguna de Sinamaica. To reach it, drive or take a taxi to Puerto Mar outside Sinamaica, a 45-minute trip from Maracaibo, then bargain for a launch to the lagoon.

The larger part of the wild and arid Guajira Peninsula is in Colombia. The road crossing into Colombia is at Maicao, 7 miles (11 km) beyond the frontier. However, Maicao is considered one of the most dangerous border towns on the continent and visitors are strongly urged to steer clear of the area.

## BEST EN ROUTE

Hotels on this route are few — mostly in Maracaibo — and are more expensive compared to those on other routes, ranging from $60 and up for a double room at a hotel in the expensive category; $35 to $60 at a hotel in the moderate category; and under $35 at a hotel in the inexpensive category. Because of the influx of business travelers here, reservations are a must.

### CABIMAS

***Cabimas Hilton International*** – On Lake Maracaibo, this property has 128 rooms and a full range of amenities and facilities, including a heliport. Av. Andrés Bello (phone: 64-45692; in the US, 800-HILTONS). Expensive.

### MARACAIBO

***Inter-Continental del Lago*** – On Lake Maracaibo (366 rooms), with a swimming pool, tennis courts, a gym, sauna, and 8 meeting rooms. The *Window*, considered the best restaurant in the city, is one of several located here. Av. El Milagro (phone: 61-912022; in the US, 800-327-0200). Expensive.

***Maruma*** – Five minutes from the airport, this deluxe hotel has 90 rooms and suites and caters mainly to business travelers. There's a gym, sauna, tennis court, disco, coffee shop, and bar. 2 Av. Circunvalación (phone: 61-349011). Expensive.

**El Paseo** – This neighbor of the *Inter-Continental del Lago* has a pool, disco, and bar. Atop the 54-suite tower sits the *Girasol,* a revolving restaurant with a spectacular view of the city, including the 5-mile bridge that spans Lake Maracaibo. Av. El Milagro at Av. 2 (phone: 61-919744). Expensive.

**Kristof** – Room service is available at this 327-room hotel; plus a pool, restaurant, bar, disco, gym, and sauna. 8 Av. Santa Rita (phone: 61-72911). Moderate.

**Astor** – Cold showers; and some of its 25 rooms are doubles. There's a coffee shop and bar. Calle 78, opposite Plaza República (phone: 61-914530). Inexpensive.

# The Eastern Venezuelan Coast

The eastern coast of Venezuela far outranks its western counterpart in terms of scenery. There are the sparkling, deep lagoons and coconut palm trees of Costa Azul; the vast, salt flats of the Araya Peninsula; and the Guácharo Cave, home of the blind guácharo, or oil bird. The stretch along the Caribbean has some of the loveliest beaches in the country, although it is not developed enough to handle the weekend vacation crowd that streams in from Caracas to laze on the sand, swim, and deep-sea fish for the coast's renowned marlin. So popular is the area, in fact, that several tourist developments along the coastal region between Barcelona and Puerto la Cruz have been completed or are being built. Among these is the El Morro complex. The country's most ambitious tourism project, it was started more than 2 decades ago and still is underway.

Start this route by heading east out of Caracas along the *autopista* that runs through the Central Highlands (Caracas to Guarenas) and to Route 9, an alternate of the Pan-American Highway, continuing along the flat, steamy, lagoon-filled coast until reaching Barcelona, 198 miles (317 km) away.

**BARCELONA:** Formed in 1671 by joining together two villages — Nueva Barcelona del Cerro Santo and San Cristóbal de Cumanagota — this busy commercial center is rich in colonial architecture. The ruins of the Casa Fuerte (Av. 5 de Julio at Plaza Bolívar) are one of the best examples. It was a Franciscan monastery until 1811, when the independence forces kicked the friars out because of their vocal support for the Spanish Crown. They turned it into a revolutionary fortress until 1817, when Spanish troops destroyed the monastery, killing 1,600 men, women, and children who had taken refuge there.

Also on Plaza Bolívar is the Iglesia San Cristóbal, a cathedral that was completed in 1773 after 25 years. The small chapel connected to the church contains the remains of the Italian martyr San Celestino, brought from Rome to Barcelona in 1777. Nearby is the *Museo de la Tradición* (Calle Juncal), erected in 1671 and now the oldest colonial home left standing in the city. Although damaged by an earthquake more than 150 years ago, the house has been restored and is now a museum with colonial art and furniture. It is open daily from 8 AM to noon and 3 to 6 PM; no admission charge. The museum also has the silver spurs that allegedly belonged to José Tomás Boves, the renegade fighter who had been shunned by the upscale mestizos when he first came to Venezuela from the Canary Islands. He got his revenge by recruiting blacks and Indians to fight Bolívar's forces and slaughtered droves of mestizos. Bolívar eventually made a series of concessions (most of them based on improving the social conditions of blacks and Indians) to Boves's troops so that they would join the revolutionary army in the fight against the Spanish.

It's another 6 miles (10 km) to the resort town of Puerto la Cruz.

**PUERTO LA CRUZ:** Tucked along Pozuelos Bay, this once-sleepy fishing town has in recent decades become a bustling commercial port and resort city with nearly 200,000 residents. A seaside refinery constructed here to handle oil pumped from the southern fields led the city's first transformation; tourism is at the forefront of its second. Lovely beaches and good weather make this an ideal spot for travelers seeking sun and sand, and the city also offers a charming peek at a particular slice of Venezuelan life.

The focus of much of the city's social life is Paseo Colón — a seaside boulevard lined with *marisquerías* (seafood restaurants), soda fountains, hotels, and nightclubs. After sunset, Puerto La Cruz residents leave their homes to stroll along the *paseo* where children play, adolescents flirt, and vendors sell locally made hammocks, jewelry, and souvenirs. The beach along the *paseo* is lovely, especially at sunset, but don't go in the water — it's badly polluted.

There are a number of beaches on the edge of the city. Isla Plata, a small island accessible by a ferry service that operates every 10 minutes from the far east side of Puerto La Cruz, has clear, calm water, but the beach is small and the roped-off swimming area is tiny. And, unfortunately, the view is unattractive — another rocky island with an ugly oil refinery. Nevertheless, the locals seem to love and heartily recommend it to visitors.

Other nearby islands, such as Las Borrachas, El Faro (also known as La Chimana), and Monos have coral reefs for snorkeling. Renting boats to go to the islands is easy — ask at the waterfront. You can also book day trips (including food and beverages) with local travel agencies.

There is a terminal for the 4-hour ferry ride to Margarita Island — try *La Vikinga* service (at the Américo Vespucio Marina in El Morro; no phone) or *Conferry* (phone: 81-668767). Ferry arrangements can be made at the *Meliá* hotel (phone: 81-23747). *Avensa* and *Aeropostal* serve Puerto La Cruz from Caracas and other major cities.

The huge coastal development, visible as you approach Puerto la Cruz from Barcelona, is the government's costly El Morro tourist complex. Other smaller, private developments are under construction. When El Morro was started in 1971, it was expected to cost $500,000 and plans were to build lagoons, Mediterranean-style houses, golf courses, 35 hotels, 40 motels, 2,000 vacation homes, and facilities for 60,000 tourists. The ambitious plan has been bogged down by construction and funding delays and some of it remains unfinished.

By backtracking all the way to Barcelona, you can take a highway south to the lower Orinoco River.

**En Route from Puerto la Cruz** – This 51-mile (82-km) drive east to Cumaná winds around the steep headlands of the spectacular "La Ruta del Sol." Standing along the coast are great jagged rocks eroded from the coastline. There are several good beaches, notably the Playa Colorada, 22 miles (35 km) outside Puerto la Cruz — a long blue lagoon with red sands lying in the shade of coconut palms and the beach most often shown on Venezuelan postcards. Hire a small, motorized launch for an unforgettable trip to less accessible beaches in Mochima National Park, including those on Isla Arapito and Isla Arapo or just laze on the beach. There is a small admission charge for cars entering Playa Colorada, camping is permitted, and there is a restaurant. Shortly before Cumaná the route cuts through the mountains along "the highway of the *muñecas*" (dolls) where local craftswomen make rag dolls and sell them along the roads.

**CUMANÁ:** The first Hispanic settlement on Venezuelan soil was perhaps the first in

South America, dating as far back as 1520 or 1521, when Spanish troops landed. However, ecclesiastical history records a settlement here in 1513 by two Dominican friars who were massacred, but a group of Franciscans returned in 1515 and somehow managed to survive. Cumaná, at the mouth of the Cariaco Gulf, has had a devastating history of war, revolution, pirates, and earthquakes.

Low and hot, parched Cumaná is shaded by coconut groves and cooled by Caribbean breezes. The Río Manzanares runs through the center of town, with the Parque Ayacucho and markets on either side. The city's residents are descendants of slaves, and Cumaná's customs, music, and food reflect Afro-Caribbean traditions. This is also a city where people work with their hands and fine crafts can be purchased.

The newer section of town by the airport (which has an excellent tourist kiosk) is barren and unpleasant, except for San Luis Beach. But the colonial architecture in the older part of Cumaná is fascinating. It is clustered around the foot of the hill topped by the fortress, Castillo de San Antonio. Built in 1678 to protect the city from British, French, and German pirates, it was here that Bolívar's General José Antonio Páez was imprisoned for opposing the Spanish governor during the Independence Wars. The fort is open to visitors (although the opening hours are sporadic; no admission charge) and is beautifully floodlit at night. Be sure to tip the volunteer guides who give short tours. Across the gulf from the fort you can see the arid Araya Peninsula, the source of Venezuela's salt. The salt harvester's lot was an unhappy one (laboring in the glaring flats naked, because clothing was destroyed by salt). Tunnels, long ago obliterated by earthquakes, once linked Castillo de San Antonio to the older, smaller complex of Santa María de la Cabeza. You can walk by this fortified area, but visitors aren't allowed inside — it's in ruins and there are no funds to restore it.

Cumaná is also the home of the ruins of the Convento de San Francisco (Calle Sucre at Plaza Ribero), built from 1669 to 1673. The first University of Cumaná was established here in 1812; after Venezuela's independence, it became a public school. The cathedral on Plaza A. Eloy Blanco, the main square, houses the so-called Cross of Pardon. Legend has it that a sinful woman repented and hugged the cross, and couldn't be separated from it. Onlookers took this as a sign that she had been forgiven and it is now believed that anyone who embraces the cross will be automatically pardoned for his or her wrongdoings. The cathedral was also the site of much bloodshed in the early 1800s. Three months after José Tomás Boves and his army routed the population of Caracas, Boves celebrated his arrival in Cumaná with the massacre of more than 200 people who had taken refuge in the cathedral.

At the Plaza Bolívar, beside the *Cine Pichincha,* is the colonial home of one of Venezuela's best-known poets, Andrés Eloy Blanco. One of his works, "Píntame Angelitos Negros," in which he asks the town artist to paint black angels around a white Madonna, has been set to music and recorded by a number of performers, including Roberta Flack in the US. Eloy Blanco's birth place now is a museum and cultural center. It is open weekdays.

The city beach is good for sunning and swimming and Cumaná has a variety of handicrafts for sale, including the *cuatro* (Venezuela's four-string guitar), hand-rolled cigars, and palm fiber hammocks (*chinchorros*). The tourist office is in the Palacio del Gobierno (Calle Bolívar at Plaza Bolívar; phone: 93-23799 and 93-236616).

*Conferry* (on the wharf in Terminal Puerto Sucre; phone: 81-661262) offers ferries (2 hours) and hydrofoils (1 hour) from here to Margarita Island.

**En Route from Cumaná** – A road leads south from here to the Guácharo Cave. Before heading there, however, take the coastal highway some 42 miles (67 km) east, skirting the shore of the Cariaco Gulf, where dry, thorny ridges seem to plunge into the water; across the gulf is the ridge of the Araya Peninsula.

In the shallows is a variety of marine life, notably grazing mollusks as big as a hand, very attractive and soft to the touch. The largest town is San Antonio del

Golfo, with neither luxury hotels nor tourists. At the eastern end of the gulf is Cariaco, with an unpaved road that goes to Araya 60 miles (96 km) away. A winding road through the highlands returns to the coast at the lovely port town of Carúpano, 74 miles (118 km) from Cumaná.

**CARÚPANO:** This prosperous town of 85,000 residents flourishes with beautiful woods and dates to the 1500s with narrow streets, old and elegant buildings, and tree-shaded plazas. It was here in 1816 that Simón Bolívar freed the slaves on the condition they join him in fighting. Bulevar Bermúdez along the waterfront not only is a popular spot for strolling and people watching, but an excellent vantage point for seeing Carúpano's lovely sunsets.

Carúpano is far from Caracas, and its people seem more gentle, tolerant, and friendly; it's renowned for its traditional pre-*Lenten Carnaval*, with days of dancing in bizarre and elaborate costumes, lusty encounters, and partying. The enthusiasm is probably enhanced by the best rum in the country, distilled right here in Carúpano.

Carúpano's beach is wide and desolate. From Maturincito Mountain, just a few minutes outside the city, there is a fantastic view of the region's beaches. The best of these include coconut tree–lined Puerto Santo, about 6 miles (10 km) east of Carúpano — the surf here is strong. Balneario Los Uversos has food and changing facilities. Other good beaches include Playa Copey, Playa de Oro, Playa Caribe, Playa Grande, and Caracolita in Río Caribe — a small, old fishing port, with houses neatly painted in pastel colors, 13 miles (21 km) from Carúpano. To the east is the Paria Peninsula; to the south, in the highland, is the Guácharo Cave.

**PARIA PENINSULA:** The stretch between Carúpano and the marshes of the Paria Gulf — about 34 miles (54 km) — is a startlingly luxuriant lowland forest, quite unusual for the Venezuelan coast. Stands of tall bamboo with their feather-like fronds crowd against the paved road, and great trees fringed with Spanish moss arch over the isolated, drab houses. Six miles (10 km) from Carúpano, rounding a headland, you see El Morro de Puerto Santo, a tiny village on a narrow strip of sand between a rocky island offshore and the coast. (Avoid the temptation to swim here; there have been numerous drownings.) From here, descend into the forest and on to the gulf, where the terrain becomes drier.

Sixty-three miles (101 km) from Carúpano on the gulf is Irapa, in a field of coconut palms. It was here that Papillon landed after his escape from Devil's Island in 1945. Now it is an important fishing area. Another 31 miles (50 km) brings you to Güiria, a fishing town where there is a boat across the strait of Dragon's Mount to Trinidad, if there are a sufficient number of passengers. It generally leaves for the 5-hour journey on Tuesdays.

**En Route from Irapa** – Head back to Carúpano and then go south, then northwest to get to the Guácharo Cave, 166 miles (266 km) away, just outside the town of Caripe. The cave, first described by missionaries in 1657, is over 8,500 feet long from mouth to source and has been designated a national monument. Visiting hours are daily from 7 AM to 5 PM. In 1799, Alexander von Humboldt penetrated it to a depth of 1,550 feet and it was tracked to its source by cave explorers in 1957.

This cave is one of the several known haunts of the guácharo (*Steatornis caripensis*) or the oil bird, a blind, nocturnal, and noisy specimen that flies from the mouth of the cave at dusk to feed on fruit far afield, returning to the cave at dawn because it can't stand sunlight. The birds have improvised their own radar system by clacking their beaks.

The first part of the cave is a tubular gallery 2,500 feet long and 150 feet in diameter called the Hall of the Guácharos. Stalactites and stalagmites abound. There are guácharos and rats and spiders, plus a vegetation sown by the birds. Contrasting with the boisterous uproar here is the Hall of Silence, 800 feet long, with a diameter of 6 to 20 feet. Farther on is a complex arrangement of galleries called the Salón Precioso; most notable is the Hall of the Caribe Vidal, renowned for stalactites as transparent as ice. The celebrated Well of the Wind, 3,300 feet from the entrance, is a 22-foot passage, 10 feet high and 5 feet wide. Stalagmites make the passage difficult to negotiate. About 230 feet farther is the most spectacular part of the cave, the Great Hall of the Landslide, a gallery 650 feet long, 150 feet wide and 80 feet high. Here is a silent enclosed moonscape of mountains and crags with enormous stalactites in red and white marblized colors. In the center is the smaller Hall of Towers, celebrated for its 10 cream stalagmites. Another 4,000 feet or so beyond is the source of the cave, well worth the trip but dangerous after a heavy rainfall. Be sure to take a coat; it is cold in the cave and a full tour takes up to 2 hours.

## BEST EN ROUTE

Accommodations along the eastern coastal route are comfortable, ranging from $65 to $100 for a double room at a hotel categorized as expensive; to between $35 and $65 at a hotel categorized as moderate; and under $35 at a hotel in the inexpensive category. Make reservations before arriving. Note: At press time, a new luxury hotel, *Fiesta Inn Aguasal* in Puerto La Cruz was under construction; for information, ask at the airport tourist information office.

### PUERTO LA CRUZ

**Doral Beach Villas** – A huge development with 1,312 rooms and suites on the Caribbean coast at Pozuelos Bay. Facilities include an 18-hole golf course, tennis, water sports, gym, mini-club for children, restaurants, bars, and disco (phone: 81-666333; in Caracas, 2-781-1444; in the US, 305-759-8071). Expensive.

**Golden Rainbow Maremares** – This new, low-rise, 500-room resort offers deluxe accommodations overlooking an 18-hole golf course and marina. Other sports available include a lagoon-style swimming pool with a wave machine and tennis and racquetball courts. There also are 4 restaurants, a nightclub, and baby-sitting services. Complejo Turístico El Morro (phone: 81-813022; in Caracas, 2-563-6042; in the US, 800-3-GOLDEN; fax in Caracas: 2-563-0738). Expensive.

**Meliá** – Deluxe, 222-unit property on the beach, it has a bar and restaurant, sauna, 2 tennis courts, pool with poolside bar, nightclub, and disco. All rooms have private balconies. Golf facilities are available. Paseo Colón (phone: 81-691311; in the US, 800-336-3542; fax: 81-674401). Expensive.

**Vista Real** – A 112-room property in the El Morro district, this hotel offers spectacular views of the Caribbean, a restaurant, and most of the amenities expected at luxury establishments. Part of the Venezuelan Hotels de Luxe chain. Complejo Turístico El Morro (phone: 81-811721; in Caracas, 2-261-1962; fax: 81-675058). Expensive.

**Cristina Suites** – Don't be fooled by the ugly exterior of this sister property of the *Vista Real*. It has 250 rooms and suites, a restaurant, snack bar, discotheque, pool (and bar next to it), and fitness center. Golf privileges at a nearby course can be arranged as well as water sports and equipment rental. The staff is friendly and efficient. Av. Municipal at Maneiro (phone: 81-674712; in Caracas, 2-261-1962; fax: 81-675058). Expensive to moderate.

**Caribbean Inn** – Just 2 blocks from Paseo Colón, this modern 102-room hotel has air conditioning, satellite television, a restaurant, bar, and small outdoor pool. Calle Freites between Libertad and Honduras (phone: 81-691848 and 81-691464). Moderate.

**Rasil** – This hotel has 348 luxury air conditioned rooms, 3 restaurants, a gym, sauna, tennis courts, and a gallery of shops. Calle Monagas at Paseo Colón (phone: 81-672422; fax: 81-673121). Moderate.

**Riviera** – A 44-room air conditioned hotel across the street from the beach. Ask for one of the larger rooms facing the ocean. 33 Paseo Colón (phone: 81-22268 and 81-22039; fax: 81-691337). Moderate.

**Neptuno** – Right on the Paseo Colón, this is perhaps the best value around for travelers on a budget. The restaurant specializes in Italian food. There also is a bar. Paseo Colón (phone: 81-23773). Inexpensive.

## CUMANÁ

**Los Bordones** – On a secluded beach, this hotel has a restaurant, coffee shop, bar, and nightclub as well as a swimming pool and tennis courts. Final Av. Universidad (phone: 93-653622). Moderate.

**Cumanagoto** – A 150-room hotel with a swimming pool, restaurant, bar, and water sports at its private beach. Av. Universidad (phone: 93-653355 and 93-653115). Moderate.

**Villamar** – Small beachfront hostelry with 30 rooms and a swimming pool. Located a fair distance from downtown on Av. Universidad (phone: 81-22147). Inexpensive.

## CARÚPANO

**Victoria** – Although somewhat rundown, this beach hotel offers 65 rooms and suites, a restaurant, bar, and pool. Av. Rómulo Gallegos (phone: 94-39554, or the *National Reservation System* in Caracas, 2-782-8433). Moderate.

## CARIPE

**El Guácharo** – A 34-room hotel with a swimming pool. Centrally located at the entrance to the Caripe Hwy. (phone: 92-51218). Moderate.

# The Lower Orinoco

The Orinoco River is the second-longest river in South America. Rarely narrowing to less than a mile, it widens in places to as much as 10 miles. Its waters rise to an altitude of about 3,000 feet above sea level in the Sierra Parima on the far southeastern border of the Amazonas territory, and tumble over the western edge of the Guayana watershed. One branch of the river flows into the Amazon while the main artery joins the Apure River. There it becomes a big brown stream that meanders across the scrubby flats of the llanos, then spills into the Atlantic 1,300 miles from its source. In its several-thousand-square-mile delta, canoes are the usual means of transport, and Indian villages are built on stilts along its banks. The paddle steamers that plied the river for decades exist no more, and only in the lower and upper reaches do boats take passengers any great distance. Some luxury cruise ships offer itineraries featuring the Orinoco that also include charter flights to Angel Falls and Canaima. Contact *Society Expeditions* (c/o *Abercrombie & Kent*, 1520 Kensington Rd., Oak Brook, IL 60521; phone: 800-426-7794); *Clipper Cruise Line* (7711 Bonhomme Ave., St. Louis, MO 63105; phone: 800-325-0010); *Salen Lindblad* (333 Ludlow St., Stamford, CT 06912; phone: 203-967-2900 or 800-223-5688).

It is an immense tropical river, for the most part free of deadly animals, but dangerous and impressive when flooded. It is the home of the Orinoco crocodile and the freshwater dolphin.

This route traverses the central llanos, south from San Juan de los Morros in the Central Highlands to Ciudad Guayana, on the river. A number of tours into this area can be arranged by *Happy Tours* in Puerto Ordaz (Calle Urbaba, 8 Edificio Tony, 1st Floor; phone: 86-23257), or at the *Happy Tours* office in Caracas (phone: 2-782-3342).

**En Route from San Juan de los Morros** – Starting out, a 31-mile (50-km) drive south from San Juan de los Morros brings you to the crossroads of Los Caminos. Swing east toward El Tigre, 259 miles (414 km) across the llanos. The road is a speedway, flat and fairly straight, and you make good time (but beware of *alcabalas,* the Venezuelan military checkpoints that will slow you down). El Tigre, the center of an old and sizable oil field, is reminiscent of a US midwestern town — until the clerks come out to hang their hammocks at siesta time.

Here the road joins the Pan-American Highway to Ciudad Bolívar, a fast 81 miles (130 km) away. There is also another 104-mile (166-km) route to El Tigre on the Pan-American south from Barcelona on the eastern coast.

**CIUDAD BOLÍVAR:** On the banks of the Orinoco River, this is an old, very romantic town, steeped in history. The capital of Bolívar is a major port and trading center for rubber from the forests and gold and diamonds gouged from the rivers and flats of Guayana. It retains much of its colonial character and has the *Museo de Ciudad Bolívar* (on Paseo Orinoco at the corner of Calle Carabobo), with the printing press Simón Bolívar used to publish Venezuela's first newspaper, *Correo del Orinoco,* in 1818–20. There's a fine collection of kinetic art at the *Museo de Arte Moderno Jesús Soto* (Jesús Soto Museum of Modern Art; Av. Mario Briceno Iragorry at Av. Germania).

It was in Ciudad Bolívar, in 1817, that Bolívar established his capital after a series of defeats suffered under the Royalists. He was soon joined, however, by legionnaires from Britain and the greatly feared and bloodthirsty *llaneros* of José Antonio Páez (the Centaur), who formerly fought for the Spanish Crown. From here Gran Colombia was declared independent, and from here Bolívar marched a ragged, starving army of 2,500 men across the sweltering llanos and over the Andes to engage a 5,000-strong Spanish army on the heights of Boyacá, near Bogotá. The Battle of Boyacá was the turning point in the Independence Wars, which in the end took the lives of one-quarter of the Venezuelan population.

During Bolívar's time, Ciudad Bolívar was called Angostura (Narrows), because the Orinoco slims down to less than a mile wide here; today it is spanned by the white and elegant Angostura suspension bridge. The city's previous name became legend when, in 1824, a German physician invented the famous bitters. The city is very hot, but at 4 in the afternoon a delightful breeze blows in from the river and, in the evenings, families stroll through the streets or sit on their doorsteps. A popular gathering place — especially for young people — is the Mirador Angostura, a riverside lookout where there's an open-air soda fountain with tables. Line markings on a calibrated rock here shows the height of the Orinoco. The waterfront teems with activity — markets, gold and diamond buyers, Indians peddling bows and arrows, baskets, and *sebucanes* (basket-woven presses used to extract the poison juices from cassava root).

Looking out over the river it's common to see dolphins cavorting in pairs. A short and intense fishing season begins at the rainy season (about June), when the very tasty sapoara migrate to spawn. The river is so thick with them, they say, that the rattle of scales against scales can be heard as they fight their way upstream. Here the river rises as much as 45 feet during the flood season. For those who prefer to see flashing hoofs, head for the *Angostura* racetrack where Ciudad Bolívar's long tradition of horse racing is alive and well.

This city is the best place in Venezuela to buy gold. A common souvenir is a brooch hand-beaten from green, pink, and yellow gold into the shape of the national orchid. It's rare, however, to find a bargain in diamonds. The local specialty is *pastel de morrocoy*, a tasty tortoise pie — but conservationists advise against ordering this dish as local tortoises are decreasing in number.

Ciudad Bolívar can be a jumping-off point for some excursions. One is a trip to the Gran Sabana and Canaima and Angel Falls. A shorter trip, however, is the 130-mile (208-km) drive south on a very scenic road to the Río Paragua. En route is Cerro Bolívar, the great iron mountain that is the crux of Venezuela's second industry, iron. The Río Paragua is a major source of diamonds, and a very primitive, strictly dry-weather track on the far side leads to the diamond camps. Five miles (8 km) short of the Paragua there is a dirt road leading east to San Pedro de las Bocas, 34 miles (54 km) away, at the confluence of the Paragua and the Caroní rivers. The best gemstones come from San Pedro.

*Happy Tours* in Puerto Ordaz (phone: 86-23257) runs a 4-day car and canoe tour to a campsite on the Paragua fields (minimum eight people). You can explore the mines and Indian villages, and fish.

**En Route from Ciudad Bolívar** – The industrial complex of Ciudad Guayana lies downstream from Ciudad Bolívar, about 67 miles (107 km) by road. After 43 miles (69 km) there is a crossroads. The right-hand fork is an alternative route to the Paragua; continuing straight ahead leads to the Río Caroní (crossed by punt), and on to the town of Upata, 49 miles (78 km) away, en route to the Gran Sabana. The left fork goes to Ciudad Guayana.

**CIUDAD GUAYANA:** This industrial town of about 500,000 people is Venezuela's newest city. Founded in 1961 by the Corporación Venezolana de Guayana by incorporating the modern river port of Puerto Ordaz and the old town of San Félix (also known as Puerto Tablas), it is home to two of country's largest industries — steel and aluminum.

Nearby are the breathtaking waterfalls of the Río Caroní known as Salto La Llovizna in Parque Llovizna, best reached by boat from the *Inter-Continental* hotel (see *Best en Route*).

A couple of hours downstream from Ciudad Guayana are the Castillos de Guayana, two Spanish forts. One was built in the 17th century on a rock in the river; the other, in 1747 on a nearby hill. History has it that in 1618 Sir Walter Raleigh, ailing and his fortunes waning, sent a party through here in search of gold. There was a bloody clash with the Spaniards, and Raleigh's elder son was killed. (In order to appease Spain for the fiasco, in which the Spanish governor lost his life, Raleigh himself was beheaded later the same year in England by James I.) The forts, the presumed site of the clash, lie about 22 miles (35 km) from San Félix via dirt road.

**En Route from Ciudad Guayana** – A car ferry crosses the Orinoco — here about 2 miles wide — at San Félix. Proceed north to the Mata Negra crossroads 42 miles (67 km) away. (The road goes on through a vast oil field to the eastern coast.) This is all low-lying llanos, very wet and humid cattleland. Another 40 miles (64 km) southwest, then 34 miles (54 km) northeast brings you to Tucupita in the Delta Amacuro. This former territory became Venezuela's 21st state in 1991.

**TUCUPITA:** This hot little town's population swelled to 30,000 after 1968, when the 7-million kilowatt Guri Dam opened 200 miles (320 km) away on the Caroní River. However, the dam slowed the Orinoco's momentum so that salt from the Atlantic Ocean backed into the delta, ruining the fishing and farmland of the Guarano or Warao Indians. Some have been relocated to government land (expropriated, with difficulty, from the cattle ranchers) near Tucupita. Others have moved into the town proper but have found it difficult to adjust to the strange new way of life. The Warao are fine craftspeople, making baskets of durability, utility, and beauty that have been exhibited in such faraway places as New York. The baskets, as well as comfortable, flexible hammocks woven from the fibers of the *moriche* palm, are sold in Tucupita.

All transport here is by river: speedboat, barge, and dugout canoe.

The delta is a maze of narrow and mile-wide channels, great and little islands, tangled vegetation and marshes. Traffic is considerable. Indians can be seen transporting their small cattle herds tied down in dugout canoes. One moment the river is like glass, the next it is very choppy. One moment you are solidly drenched by a sudden rainstorm, then the steam rises off you under a blazing sun. Dolphins frolic through the water, as occasionally do *babas* (small alligators), and many birds are visible. At the Indian villages, where the Warao live in *palafitos* (pile houses perched over the water and connected by walkways), there are tame peccaries (wild pigs), toucans, parrots, and agoutis (little rodents); women weave baskets from the fiber of the *moriche* palm, and men carve animals from balsa wood. A missionary on a houseboat may invite you to tea. There is a 2-day journey to Pedernales, a National Guard outpost and sometime prison on the far northern coast of the delta, less than 30 miles (48 km) across the Serpent's Mouth from the coast of Trinidad.

About 40 miles (64 km) upriver lies Barrancas.

**BARRANCAS:** The Orinoco widens to a mouth before spilling into the delta at this village. Though the view is obscured by islands, the river here is at least 10 miles across at its widest point. Barrancas is a small town, fairly clean, and very quiet. A day-long journey to the island of Curiapo is rather sobering but worth the effort. Lying in the mouth called the Boca Grande, Curiapo is the largest Indian village in the delta, where most people live in *palafitos*.

## BEST EN ROUTE

Expensive hotels here run as high as $55 to $75 a night for a double room. Hotels categorized as moderate cost from $35 to $55; inexpensive accommodations, under $35. It's best to make reservations.

### CIUDAD BOLÍVAR

*Río Orinoco* – This elegant 122-room property is the best in town. It has deluxe amenities, air conditioning, a restaurant (*Los Cornieles*) that specializes in river fish, a snack bar, disco-bar, and swimming pool, plus a location close to the airport. Distribuidor San Rafael on the Vía Perimetral (phone: 85-42011; the *National Reservation System* in Caracas, 2-782-8433; in the US, 800-275-3123; fax: 85-42844). Expensive.

*Bolívar* – Recently refurbished accommodations consist of 65 air conditioned rooms plus a view of the Orinoco River. Restaurant, bar, and disco. Paseo Orinoco, on the waterfront (phone: 85-20100). Moderate.

*Laja Real* – This 73-room city hotel near the airport is a good bet. Besides a restaurant, bar, coffee shop, and popular disco, it has a large pool with a waterslide. Av. Jesús Soto (phone: 85-27911 or 85-27944; fax: 85-28778). Moderate.

### CIUDAD GUAYANA

*Inter-Continental* – There are 205 rooms with great views and 24-hour room service, a bar, restaurant, tennis courts, gym, jogging track, and a pool (from which you can see La Llovizna Falls) — all on a beautiful lagoon at Puenta Vista, between Puerto Ordaz and San Félix (phone: 86-222280 and 86-222244; in the US, 800-327-0200). Expensive.

*Rasil* – A 350-room hotel with a pool, a good restaurant, and disco. Unfortunately, the service is often spotty. In a residential area, between downtown and the airport, at Centro Cívico (phone: 86-222568; fax: 86-227703). Moderate.

***Dos Ríos*** – This 74-room business property offers a bar, restaurant, pool, and downtown location. Calle México at the corner of Ecuador (phone: 86-220679; fax: 86-229713). Inexpensive.

## TUCUPITA

***Amacuro*** – Fairly good, 42-room hostelry with air conditioning. 23 Calle Bolívar (phone: 87-21057). Inexpensive.

# The Gran Sabana

The highlands of Guayana, the original "Lost World" immortalized in Sir Arthur Conan Doyle's novel of the same name, became cherished by and enchanting to Victorian England. Although the highlands extend along the southern frontiers of the three Guianas — French, Suriname, and Guyana — along the northern border of Brazil and into Venezuela to the Orinoco River, their greater and more interesting part is in Venezuela. The ancient tabletop mountains, or *tepuis,* are an awesome sight, rising thousands of feet above the surrounding savannahs. They are the remains of an extensive plateau that once covered millions of square miles. Their sides are so vertical that many have yet to be climbed and several are considered virtually impossible. Their summits are tabletop but seldom flat, often laced with streams and treacherous crevices; some are scrubby at the top; others, swampy or forested. Around the base are steep escarpments called talus, the accumulation of rubble and great sandstone blocks that have split from the cliffs in ages past.

The *tepuis* are a bonanza to ornithologists and botanists. Because of the *tepuis'* flat tops being isolated from the surrounding rain forests for millions of years, distinctive flora and fauna have evolved. More than 7,000 varieties of orchids are known to grow here. There is a species of frog that walks instead of hops, lays its eggs on land, and bypasses the tadpole stage; orchids that grow on the ground; and an insect-eating pitcher plant that is thought to date from the time when South America and Africa were connected.

So broad and extensive are the highlands (500,000 square miles) that this route will focus on only one of the principal areas, an enormous low tract in the east, the 10,000-square-mile Gran Sabana. Its northern escarpment lies about 230 miles (368 km) south of San Félix on the lower Orinoco, stretching some 120 miles (192 km) south to the Brazilian border, 800 miles (1,280 km) south of Caracas.

Although buses are available from Ciudad Bolívar to Santa Elena, the town near the Brazilian border, schedules are irregular, and the length of the trip (12 to 14 hours) depends on the weather. It's better to fly to Santa Elena from Ciudad Bolívar via *Aeropostal* or — if you're hardy — to rent a four-wheel-drive vehicle or Volkswagen in Caracas (see "Sources and Resources," *Caracas,* THE CITIES) and drive yourself. In recent years small adventure tourism companies have sprung up that arrange transportation and Indian guides. Unless you're a daredevil, we recommend this secure — but still adventuresome — approach to the Gran Sabana. One reputable and experienced operator is *Lost World Adventures* (1189 Autumn Ridge Dr., Marietta, GA 30066;

**En Route from San Félix** – Leaving San Félix, a 35-mile (56-km) drive through lone, rolling savannah brings you to the township of Upata, a good place to halt when coming from Caracas at the end of a 10- or 12-hour trip. This is a prosperous cattle-breeding, mining, and commercial center, founded in 1792 by Capuchin friars. There is a good hotel, the *Kukenán,* and the best food stop is at the restaurant at the *Comercio* hotel (Calle Ayacucho). Nowhere in Guayana is there hot water, and water of any temperature is severely rationed in Upata.

A 65-mile (104-km) drive from Upata leads to Guasipati, a little town that went through a gold rush in 1853 that lasted 3 decades, and still is an administrative center for Venezuela's gold- and diamond-producing region. By now, you have left the savannah and are driving through a thick lowland forest. Ten or 12 miles (16 or 19 km) farther is El Callao.

**EL CALLAO:** Though only a couple of hundred yards off the road on the other side of the Río Yuruari, the forest here is so high and thick you can't see the town and could drive right by. But that would be a mistake: El Callao is a pretty, romantic little place, one of the loveliest in the country and certainly the loveliest in the Guayana Highlands. The town is not much bigger than the plaza. It is very clean, the houses are brightly painted, and the obligatory rusted iron roofs are picturesque. In the cool of the evening the townsfolk gather in the plaza for the traditional Latin stroll, when young men contrive to catch the eye of a strolling *señorita.* Here, too, a Trinidadian population, going back several generations, brings an exotic, calypso flavor to the pre-*Lenten* February *Carnaval.* Because of the reopening of the gold mines, you will find no shortage of handguns visibly stuffed in waistbands. There is one restaurant, which serves chicken-on-a-spit and beer.

**En Route from El Callao** – A fast drive on a straight road across the broad alluvial plain of the Yuruari leads to the town of El Dorado, 67 miles (107 km) south of El Callao. The town swelters on the forested banks of the Río Cuyuní. It continues to exist by sheer persistence and by virtue of its gas station. On an island surrounded by rivers and swamps is the prison where Papillon — Henri Charrière — served the last of his many prison terms, imprisoned by the Venezuelan authorities after his escape from Devil's Island. Life was easier before the gold ran out and before they let the prisoners go.

An Englishman, Sidney Coles, owns the *El Dorado* hotel and tourist camp (see *Best en Route*). He will arrange 1-day and half-day river expeditions. Nowadays, he is not enthusiastic about arranging long river journeys — unless you have a well-equipped party of 9 or 10.

Erich Irady, an operator in Puerto Ordaz, also arranges river tours for 10 to 15 people (phone: 86-692465). Passengers travel up the Cuyuní to the highlands, down to the Guayanese frontier, up the Yuruari to the Paraván Falls. Along the way *tepuis,* gold mines, orchids, howler monkeys, parrots, toucans, and rivers the color of cognac can be seen.

Fifty-five miles (88 km) from El Dorado is an isolated outpost called Km 88, at the foot of the Escalera (staircase), the pass leading up to the Gran Sabana.

**KM 88:** This directly abuts the talus (steep escarpments) of the Gran Sabana. The rim of the plateau proper is about 25 miles (40 km) away by road up the Escalera, but only a mile or so away laterally and a bit over a mile vertically.

The size of Km 88 belies its importance as a crossroads and provisioning center. Not long ago, there was nothing here except a rough dirt track at the end of which lived a *brujo* (witch doctor) named Albilio. A small stream of clients were the only travelers to these parts when Señor Francisco Vargas, a miner, opened his bodega (general store)

20 years ago. Now, thanks to gold miners and backpackers, there is a garage next door to the bodega, a hotel, a gas station, and several houses. There is a certain amount of military traffic, and trucks haul timber in from Brazil. A restaurant on the porch of the bodega serves excellent meals. Not exactly a boomtown, however, it has the less savory elements of Venezuelan outposts — prostitution, overpricing and, increasingly, malaria.

**En Route from Km 88** – This is the last chance to fill up with gas before heading on to Santa Elena, 140 miles (224 km) south. Plan on a 6-hour drive; the first 40 miles (64 km) of this stretch must be driven in first gear.

Now you start your journey up the Gran Sabana's Escalera. For many decades, Km 88 was considered the end of the road. Diamond prospectors would stock up on provisions here and then set out for the plateau, searching for the pass to the top. Many never returned, falling prey to jaguars, snakes, disease or the elements. From time to time, at the bidding of various dictators, convicts were ordered to build a road, but they always were defeated by the hard sandstone that couldn't be blasted. In the end, the task was undertaken by a corps of army engineers. The road, an essential link in the now-almost-completed Pan-American Highway, was opened in 1973.

If you don't have a Volkswagen or a jeep, and if it has just rained, it may well be difficult to reach the top. The plateau escarpment is thickly forested, teeming with orchids and the long, hanging nests of turpials, the national bird. On the left near the top is a stream and a set of falls called the Salto Danto (*danto* means "tapir"). A very pretty spot with moss and mists, it is a sampling of what a rain forest offers. From the top, the stream seems deceptively gentle, but it narrows and rifles through a gap like a breaking dam.

A pathway leads to the bottom. From above the falls you look north across 100 miles of forest and savannah splashed with the pink and yellow of *apamate* and *araguaney* flowers, and you see that you're hanging from the almost vertical side of a great sandstone mountain rising from the wilderness: Welcome to the Gran Sabana.

**GRAN SABANA:** When you emerge from a close, heavily timbered fissure onto the open, rolling savannah of the Gran Sabana, the effect is startling. This is one of the most silent places on earth. Nothing lives here, save the occasional grasshopper by day, lightning bugs at night, and small, bony fish in the streams. The vegetation, except for trees along watercourses and *moriche* palms on the far escarpments, is largely confined to bromeliads. A great bushfire that swept through here in the 1920s is partly responsible for its sparseness.

You should come prepared to spend the night under the stars. When the morning mist lifts, if it lifts far enough, you see great *tepuis* rising several thousand feet from the rim of the plateau. Off to the west lies a vast highland crowned by the massifs of Sororopentepuy and Ptaritepuy, the latter the highest at 8,500 feet, its summit considered inaccessible. Other *tepuis* lie to the southwest. To the east, on the border with Guyana only a couple of miles away, is the Cerro Venamo, quite low at 6,200 feet.

Your view across the savannah is impeded by low ridges; from the higher ones you can see a surface broken by the gorges of streams. These are tributaries of Venezuela's second river, the diamond-rich Caroní, which rises here on the Gran Sabana.

A couple of hundred yards from the top of the Escalera is a campsite with round thatch huts, now considerably deteriorated. But there is no fresh water, and you'd be better off pitching a tent by the side of any stream. A few miles farther is a large *alcabala*, and just beyond that a track leading to the west that takes you, after a half-day's drive, to the Kavanayén mission on the Río Camá, which has facilities for travelers at a price. En route you pass the impressive 300-foot falls on the Río Aponguao (or Apanguao). From Kavanayén you can see the great bulk of Auyan Tepui rising from the forest.

**En Route from the Gran Sabana** – Farther south (on the road to Santa Elena) is the Río Yurnaní, also with falls and fine for swimming. This is called Quebrada Pacheco, 23 miles (37 km) south of the Camá. As you cross a vast open plain between here and the slopes, you may see, off to the left, the massive formation that includes Roraima. The mountain to the left and closer is Irutepuy. The long, monstrous formation on the right is Roraima, which is 9,094 feet high and the greatest of the red sandstone *tepuis* in the Gran Sabana. Its name means "Mother of Raging Torrents"; contiguous to it on the left is Cuquenán. (For the energetic these are worth a side trip.) To the south is a deep, fast stream that is crossed by raft powered by passengers (pulling on a rope) and an outboard-rigged *curiara* (dugout canoe). The system looks a trifle unsafe, but a cable to windward so far has arrested the tendency of the vessel to escape downstream. The system closes down after a heavy rain and you can find yourself stranded on the wrong side of the river. Above the crossing arch the thundering horseshoe falls that can be reached by a path on the northern bank.

A little farther, lying out on a flat, is the Indian settlement of Yurnaní. The Indians will sell you baskets, bows, and arrows. A few hundred yards south is a track leading off to the left. This is the starting point for a trip to Roraima. About 6 miles (10 km) from the village is San Ignacio.

You descend the southern slopes through a region of *moriche* palm to re-enter the forest near the Brazilian frontier. In the midst of the forest is the fascinating mining and frontier town of Santa Elena de Uairén.

**SANTA ELENA DE UAIRÉN:** This is about 37 miles (59 km) south of San Ignácio. Lucas Fernández Peña set out on foot in 1923 from Ciudad Bolívar to look for diamonds. He crossed the savannah and unexplored forest of the lowlands, ascended the Escalera, and in the forest near Brazil he found his fortune. He built a house, a large thatch structure of wattle and daub, founded a town, and fathered 27 children.

It is a small but growing town where you'll find every race of people — refugees (from Eastern Europe, war, justice, the din of Caracas, ulcers), miners, prospectors, diamond buyers. Prospectors come and go here. For 20 years now they've been tramping through the forest, searching, with the aid of diverse occult devices, for the "pipe," a volcanic formation that is the presumed source of the diamonds that sprinkle the greater length of the Río Caroní.

It rains at least 9 months of the year, and all is mud. Small diesel plants generate electricity, and there are no phones. Rather quiet through the week, Santa Elena comes alive on a Saturday night, when miners emerge from the jungle to drink.

Next door to the *Mac-King* hostelry is a very pleasant little restaurant called *La Gran Sabana*. Of the several watering holes, *Fanny's* bar is the best.

The Santa Elena mission on Colina Akurima (Akurima Hill) is a good place to stop if you need help or information. The priests there also let travelers fill water containers from the mission's pipeline that runs from the river.

At the edge of town is a pool and a small waterfall.

**En Route from Santa Elena** – Take the exit toward Brazil, then a marked fork to the right that directs you on a westerly course along the southern frontier. It's a 60-mile (96-km) drive. For a time you pass through a tall, impenetrable jungle, which is very dark when the sky is overcast. The foot-long structures hanging from the trees are the nests of turpials, and the darting patches of iridescent blue you see are the fabulous morpho butterflies. About halfway along this road you reach a high point, a desolate region of *tepuis* and sparse savannah, the birthplace of the Río Surucán. This is a region famous for diamonds and the source of the largest ever found in Venezuela. The 154.15-karat stone (about 1 inch in diameter), called the Barrabás, or Libertador, was discovered by Jaime Hudson (also called Barrabás) in 1942. Four stones were cut, the largest a 40-karat emerald cut. Six miles (10 km) farther is Pauji, inhabited by a number of Europeans and Americans. You descend toward the source of the Icabarú, an area very rich in diamonds.

Icabarú is a smaller, muddier version of Santa Elena, with few amenities. The mining here is typical of the Río Caroní. Large rafts carrying suction pumps are anchored on the water, with divers directing operations. The divers work in darkness at depths of 50 to 100 feet — and it's dangerous work. Another town near Santa Elena is the Tauripan Indian settlement of Peraitepuy.

**PERAITEPUY:** A day's walk from the Santa Elena Road (the name Peraitepuy is derived from the *paray,* footwear used during the dry season by the villagers). The road to the Río Chirimá is negotiable by Volkswagen or short-wheelbase jeep. Life here is simple; the houses are thatch-roofed wattle and daub; water is fetched by hand from streams 1½ miles away and several thousand feet down; and the little desks in the schoolhouse and the occasional sheet of galvanized iron have been carried on foot from Santa Elena, some 70 to 80 miles (112 to 128 km) away.

Peraitepuy's *cacique* (chief), may greet you upon your arrival and offer you a shot of *cachire* — a semi-fermented drink concocted from yams — in a calabash, and he will certainly place a hut at your disposal. If you need anything else, however, you will have to pay or trade for it. Cast-off clothes and shoes make the best trades. Through the local school teacher you may negotiate the help of a guide, probably a member of the Ayusco tribe, who generally do not speak Spanish, but instead Tauripen, the local dialect.

From here you can proceed up the Roraima Formation, the region's largest summit area of about 18 square miles. The north face of Roraima Mountain (an extremely difficult climb) was first scaled in 1973; however, there is a manageable ascent route from Paraitepuy. As we went to press, Roraima was officially closed to climbers because of environmental damage and litter caused by too many expeditions. However, travelers are still unofficially making the ascent and some tour companies are turning a blind eye to the ban. Let your conscience be your guide, but be aware that if you choose to make the climb and, in the unlikely event that you get caught, you might face some problems with the law.

Some distance out of the village you reach a high point of 4,500 feet and begin your descent, fording several streams. Four hours later you come upon an old Mines Ministry camp that can be reached in a day from the Chirimá. Two hours farther you reach the Río Cuquenán in the shadow of the massifs. Just short of the crossing is a trail to the left that leads to Cuquenán. En route is a cave, ideal for camping.

If the river is high, you lose half a day by crossing at a ford downstream. A steep 2,500-foot climb from the river brings you to a meadow (suitable for camping) at the foot of the cliffs, just to the right of the falls. The ascent begins in a wood at the northern edge. A rather unpleasant scramble through the wet, dank forest, over and under boulders, across tree trunks and treacherous vegetation, takes you higher, to the beginning of an ascending ledge. Five hundred feet up, the ledge maneuvers around three spurs and descends to a point where a stream from the mountain falls onto the path. Traversing this obstacle, you ascend sharply toward the summit on a path that can prove very slippery. You pass between the cliff face and great flakes that form a false front. At 8,625 feet you reach the summit.

The sight is staggering. You are in a vast amphitheater of rippled stone, occupied by great black boulders and pinnacles eroded into fantastic shapes. From any vantage point they stretch as far as you can see. Exploring this trackless labyrinth is dangerous at any time, but especially when the mist settles in. Here and there are small streams, waterholes and marshes, no trees, and few animals. Close to the top of the ledge the Río Camaiwá leaps from the mountain.

The current *comandante* of the region asks travelers to report their departure and return to the *alcabala* (military checkpoint) at San Ignacio.

## BEST EN ROUTE

For the most part, hotel accommodations along this route are very rustic. Cold showers are provided; in some cases, there are a few private baths. The most expensive hotel costs about $25 a night for two people; all, therefore, can be considered inexpensive.

### EL CALLAO

*Italia* – This centrally located 10-room hostelry provides only cold showers (no phone). Inexpensive.

### EL DORADO

*El Dorado* – In a beautiful location at the confluence of two rivers, this 6-room property run by an Englishman has its own beach. Some rooms have been added and there are reportedly chronic problems with the water supply to them (no phone). Inexpensive.

### SANTA ELENA

*Fronteras* – A quiet, 40-room hotel with private baths and a good restaurant. Centrally located (phone: 86-694323). Inexpensive.

*Mac-King* – This rustic 8-room lodge provides only 1 bed per room, plus rings for slinging hammocks (bring your own), and a restaurant. Center of town (no phone). Inexpensive.

### KM 88

*La Clarita* – Very basic 8-room hotel with 3 beds to each room, and 2 bathrooms. Hurricane lanterns are provided. Centrally located (no phone). Inexpensive.

# Angel Falls

In 1935, an adventuresome American bush pilot named Jimmy Angel flew up the canyon of the Río Cherún Merú and saw below him the great waterfall that now bears his name — Angel Falls. At the time, however, Angel was more interested in the mountain from which it sprang, the massive Auyan Tepui, about 160 miles (256 km) due south of Ciudad Guayana. Like many others, Angel was looking for a mountain of gold. Two years later, with a small party that included his wife, he attempted a landing on the summit. He crashed, and the plane remained, half-submerged in a bog, until 1970 when the *Fuerza Aérea Venezolana* retrieved it. The restored plane is displayed in the *Museo de la Fuerza Aérea Venezolana* (FAV Museum) in Maracay.

Eleven days after the crash, when the party emerged from the forest, the major treasures they had discovered were the 15 or 20 highest waterfalls in the world. The tallest, Angel asserted, was a mile high. In 1949, a *National Geographic Society* expedition set out to verify the matter, concluding that Angel Falls was indeed the highest in the world, with an unbroken fall of 2,648 feet and a total height of 3,212 feet. Since that measurement was only three-fifths of a mile, Jimmy Angel was disappointed, despite the fact that the falls were 15 times taller than Niagara Falls.

Equally celebrated in this interior part of Venezuela are the names Rudy

Truffino and Charlie Baughan. Baughan (who founded the diamond-mining town of Icabarú on the Gran Sabana — see *The Gran Sabana,* above) was also a pilot and discovered the beautiful wine-red lagoon about 2 days downstream from Angel Falls on the Río Carrao. He named it Canaima, and he and Truffino founded a tourist camp on its shores. They befriended the Indians (the Camarata, a people renowned for their gentleness) and introduced fruit cultivation. Canaima is an Indian name for the goddess of the jungle, a fierce deity who swallows everything in her path. Today, Canaima is also the name of a 6-million-acre park. The traveler with a taste for the jungle and the wild natural beauty of southern Venezuela should stay there.

For the most part, the only practical access to Canaima is by air. *Avensa* flies a DC-9 in daily for a price that includes airfare, accommodations, and meals. Weather permitting, passengers on these flights have a chance to see the spectacular park and waterworks as pilots make several passes by the falls and over the mountain's summit. In Caracas, you can book the excursion package with *Avensa* (phone: 2-562-3022; in Ciudad Guayana, 86-25780 or 86-25957). In the US, book through *Avensa* (phone: in Miami, 305-381-800l; toll-free, 800-283-6727) or *Viasa* (phone: in Florida, 800-432-9070; in other states, 800-327-5454). *Aerotuy* (Bulevar de Sabana Grande, 174 Edificio Gran Sabana, 2nd Floor, Caracas; phone: 2-716231 and 2-716247; fax: 2-725254) operates day tours and 3- or 4-day programs with a flight by the falls and a visit to the Pemon Indian camp, Kavac. In the US, book through *Lost World Adventures* (1189 Autumn Ridge Dr., Marietta, GA 30066; phone: 404-971-8586 and 800-999-0558; fax: 404-977-3095). Private pilots at the Canaima airport offer 5-passenger Cessna plane flights over Angel Falls and Canaima. Similar flights also are available from Puerto Ordaz. For the *very* adventurous, Bruce Means (1313 N. Duval St., Tallahassee, FL 32303; phone: 904-681-6208) leads backpacking tours to the summit of Auyan Tepui.

This route starts by flying into the *Avensa*-run Canaima campsite from Caracas, a 1½-hour flight, stopping in Ciudad Bolívar.

**CANAIMA:** Baughan and Angel are now dead (both having died with their flying goggles on), and "Jungle Rudy" Truffino has his own camp (see *Best en Route*) at Ucaima above Hacha Falls, an hour's walk upstream from here. (Regular guests include fashion designer Carolina Herrera.) The *Avensa* camp is on a beach at the lagoon. About 120 tourists arrive on the daily flight, and there are several guide companies that lead trips, including staff members from "Jungle Rudy's," *Excursiones Chérún-Verún,* and other locals who greet travelers at the airport. In addition, the tour desk at the *Tamanaco Inter-Continental* hotel in Caracas (phone: 2-914555) can arrange trips.

Fed by seven rose waterfalls and set against a backdrop of two *tepuis,* the lagoon is breathtaking, with pink sand beaches. Be prepared for water the color of iced tea — due to its high tannin content. Never fear; it's clean and safe to swim in. You can cruise the lagoon in large, motorized dugout canoes. You'll ride close to the falls and will probably get sprayed a little, so dress appropriately. If you go in May, you can see orchids blooming in the lush jungle. Jungle Rudy's camp at Canaima is a smaller operation, more expensive and more intimate than other lodgings. Skiing and sunfish sailing are available.

**En Route from Canaima –** There are several half-day, full-day, and longer river excursions both upstream and down from both camps, led by knowledgeable and multilingual guides. You shoot rapids, swim in the river, walk behind waterfalls, see a variety of wildlife (notably the macaws), and sail along the battlements of *tepuis.*

Auyan Tepuí (the setting for some parts of the book *Green Mansions*) is one of the largest of the *tepuis,* almost 9,000 feet high. Angel Falls springs from the northern wall. A fairly easy route up the southern escarpments has been known since 1938, but the overhanging northern wall wasn't climbed until 1971 (by a party of four, including alpinist David Nott). Read Nott's chilling account of the experience, *Angels Four* (Prentice-Hall). Though it's out of print, check at the library. Standing at the foot of the falls you can't help but feel a bit overwhelmed. The twin plumes of water shoot out into space from a half-mile above you.

On any excursion to Angel Falls you might meet Alejandro Laime, who has been living in the area now for more than 30 years and who guided the 1949 expedition to the foot of the falls. He lives in a cabin looking out on the mountain's soaring wall, decorated with a dozen glittering cascades — undoubtedly the most spectacular front yard on earth. Although he had a hand in opening the region to the outside world, the aging Laime has become disillusioned by the negative impact of tourism on this once-pristine wilderness. He laments the disappearance of tapirs and deer, which were abundant not long ago. Perhaps Laime's presence can serve as a reminder to travelers of the importance of working to preserve such natural wonders.

For another unique adventure, go to Kavac, a Pemon Indian camp that is set on a clearing ringed by *tepuis* and forests of orchids, waterfalls, and crystalline pools. Pemon guides in loincloths lead visitors on nature walks, photo safaris, and trips in dugout canoes. *Aerotuy* (Sabana Grande, 174 Edificio Gran Sabana, Caracas; phone: 2-716231 and 2-716247; fax: 2-725254) offers 1-, 3-, and 4-day programs with flights in and out of this remote site, accommodations in basic — but comfortable — huts at the camp (with private bathrooms), meals, and excursions included. In the US, reserve through *Lost World Adventures* (phone: 404-971-8586; toll-free: 800-999-0558; fax: 404-977-3095).

From here, return by plane to Caracas.

## BEST EN ROUTE

*Avensa* has a 150-bed camp at Canaima, where 2- to 5-night package tours are available, including air fare, accommodations (cold showers), and good meals (if you provide your own transportation). You also can stay at the camp at a per diem rate, or at Rudy Truffino's 3-bungalow camp at Ucaima on the Carrao River for $93 per person per night, including meals. Reservations are necessary at both sites. Contact either the *Avensa* offices in Caracas (phone: 2-525-1559) or *Truffino,* also in Caracas (PO Box 61879, Caracas 106; phone: 2-562-3022). Information is also available from the *Avensa* office in Miami (800 Brickell Ave., Suite 1109, Miami, FL 33131; phone: 305-381-8001; toll-free, 800-283-6727).

# Margarita Island

A 325-square-mile island, 18 miles north of the Araya Peninsula off the eastern Venezuelan coast, Margarita Island is the country's favorite tourist spot (although the country's best beaches remain those that are mostly undeveloped on the mainland). Venezuelans flock here in droves on weekends, attracted by its beaches and mangrove lagoons, but mostly by its free-port status. In spite of reports of pesky mosquitoes, it is becoming increasingly popular with tour groups from North America and Europe. The weather is excellent, with almost no rain (water is piped in from the mainland), and the mean temperature never exceeds 82F (28C). Traditionally, residents were both fishermen and pearl divers, but the oyster beds, once famous throughout the country, have diminished as tourism has flourished. Only the fishermen remain.

It's very easy to reach Margarita. There are almost 20 daily flights to Porlamar from Caracas via *Avensa* or *Aeropostal,* or a straight-through ticket can be purchased at the Nuevo Circo bus station in the capital. From there you'll be driven to Puerto La Cruz, then ferried out to Margarita. There are departures several times a day from Puerto La Cruz and twice daily from Cumaná. Hydrofoils, which take about half the time — 2 hours — depart from both cities every day. *Conferry* (Av. Casanova at Las Acacias, Torre Banhorient, Sabana Grande, Caracas; phone: 2-782-8544) arranges ticket reservations for those taking their own cars; offices are also in Puerto La Cruz (phone: 81-668767), Cumaná (phone: 81-661462), and Porlamar on Margarita (on Calle Marcano near the *Bella Vista* hotel; phone: 95-619235). Tickets also can be purchased for *La Vikinga,* a passenger-only vessel with an office in the *Centro Comercial Marbella* (no phone). Round-trip reservations are essential on weekends, at *Carnaval* time, during *Semana Santa* (Holy Week), July 1–September 15, and December 15–January 6.

This route starts at the thriving Margarita resort of Porlamar and continues on to La Restinga Lagoon, the historic village of La Asunción with its old cathedral, and ends at Punta de Piedra where you can take a ferry back to the mainland.

**PORLAMAR:** Founded in 1536 by a Franciscan priest, this was once a quiet fishing port and is now a thriving commercial and tourist center. There are bustling and pleasant shopping streets lined with boutiques, restaurants, and ice cream parlors, but the city is very congested with vacationers and shoppers here for duty-free imported bargains. If you're looking to get away from it all, this is the last place to be. But if you like nightlife, good dining, or duty-free bargains, you can book a hotel here and escape to the beaches during the heat of the day.

Hotels line the stretch of beach bordering El Morro Bay, and you can buy anything you want here — from Parisian perfume and Colombian emeralds to Andean *ruanas* and blowguns. Liquor, fine perfume, and embroidered linen are particularly good bargains. Some of the finest shops are along Avenida Santiago Mariño, between Avenidas 4 de Mayo and Igualdad.

On Igualdad you also will find the *Museo de Arte Contemporáneo Francisco Narváez* (Francisco Narváez Contemporary Art Museum), named for the Porlamar-born painter/sculptor who received attention and acclaim outside Venezuela. The museum has more than 4 dozen of Narváez's pieces, as well as works by other Venezuelan artists. Even if you don't get to the museum, you can catch a glimpse of one sculpture — four pigtailed girls dancing in a ring — outside the *Bella Vista* hotel. The city's most impressive landmark is Faro de la Puntilla (a lighthouse at the end of Calle Fajardo).

For a taste of the island's renowned seafood, try *Da Gaspar* (Av. 4 de Mayo; phone: 95-613486). The restaurant also specializes in pasta.

**En Route from Porlamar** – The fast, straight *autopista* west of the city returns you toward Punta de Piedra; 4 miles (6 km) short of Punta de Piedra is a road leading off toward the Macanao Peninsula. You skirt the Tetas de María Guevara, two conical hills shaped rather like breasts (*tetas*) that once served to identify the island to mariners. About 8 miles (13 km) along is a bridge crossing the sea mouth of La Restinga Lagoon, and on the other side is the port of Boca del Río on the peninsula.

**LA RESTINGA LAGOON AND NATIONAL PARK:** A narrow, 12-mile (19-km) lagoon enclosed to the north by a long narrow isthmus composed, apparently, mostly of seashells, La Restinga is about 24 miles (38 km) from Porlamar and is reachable by car, cab, *por puesto,* or in an arranged tour. The *por puestos* leave from Calle Mariño near Porlamar's waterfront and leave passengers near the dock where launches set out through the lagoon. The five-passenger motorboats pass through the salty canals where oyster beds cling to the underwater roots of trees and, if requested, will drop passengers off at La Restinga Beach and pick them up an hour later. That's enough time to wade along the shore, take pictures, and get a snack at kiosks dotting this shell-strewn beach. The boats also go through the mangroves, a natural bird sanctuary where the colorful scarlet ibis, pelicans, cormorants, frigatebirds, great blue herons, egrets, flamingoes, and gulls wing their way overhead. The price of the outing depends on the length of the cruise. If you speak Spanish and want to take the trip on your own, contact the tourist information desk at the airport for details; if not, it might be better to book a tour with a bilingual guide through your hotel or one of the travel agencies in downtown Porlamar.

**En Route from La Restinga Lagoon** – The large Macanao Peninsula is wilder, drier, and more mountainous than the rest of Margarita, very photogenic, and little inhabited; there are many secluded beaches, particularly at the western end near Boca de Pozo.

From here, return to Porlamar for a trip around the northern end of Margarita, where your first stop is La Asunción, 5 miles (8 km) outside Porlamar.

**LA ASUNCIÓN:** Coastal residents, who were constantly menaced by pirates, founded this inland capital in 1565. It is a quaint and quite beautiful town in the Santa Lucia Valley with a number of fine old colonial buildings. In front of Plaza Bolívar is the cathedral honoring its namesake, Nuestra Señora de la Asunción (Our Lady of the Assumption). One of the oldest churches in the country, it was started in 1571 and took almost 50 years to complete. Visitors may enter when mass is not in progress. The city's San Fransisco monastery also dates to the 16th century. The Puente de Piedra (a stone bridge still in use), sundial, and what is now the *Nueva Cádiz Museum* (corner of Calle Independencia and Calle Fermín) all are from the 16th and 17th centuries. The museum, formerly the seat of government and later a jail, has a varied collection which runs the gamut from pre-Columbian artifacts found on the island to colonial religious icons to stuffed birds to local handicrafts to antique diving equipment used when pearls were the island's most important asset. It is open daily from 8 AM to noon and 2 to 5 PM; no admission charge.

Shortly after La Asunción was founded, the fortress Castillo Santa Rosa was built to protect the city and, in the years that followed, it was the scene of many battles. During the Independence Wars, the pregnant young wife of revolutionary hero Juan Bautista Arismendi was held hostage in the fort's dungeon. A plaque marks the cell where the woman's baby daughter was born — and died. The fort is an excellent spot for panoramic views of the valley.

Between Porlamar and La Asunción is El Valle del Espíritu Santo (Valley of the Holy Spirit) with an oft-visited shrine, the sanctuary of the Virgen del Valle (Virgin of the Valley) and an adjacent small museum (open afternoons) that displays the Virgin's jeweled costumes. Legend has it that she was bound for Peru, was mistakenly unloaded on Margarita Island, and inexplicably turned up in a cave in El Valle; she is considered the patroness of eastern Venezuela. Her festival is held from September 7 to 15. On the feast day, September 8, thousands of Venezuelans flock to the island to pray to the Virgin and ask favors, especially those related to curing ill health. Silver offerings in the shape of the ailing body parts adorn the sanctuary; note the pearls in the form of a leg — allegedly the offering of a fisherman whose leg was bitten by a shark.

Between Porlamar and La Asunción on the coastal road is the deepwater port of Pampatar, scheduled for tourist development. Here two forts overlook the sea, the smaller called Caranta and the larger, the fortress of San Carlos Borromeo (17th century). There are several stillwater beaches here; Pampatar is the home of Cristo del Buen Viaje (Christ of the Safe Voyage), venerated by fishermen. To the north of Pampatar, reached by road from La Asunción, is an ocean beach at Guacuco.

**En Route from La Asunción** – A road leads north from La Asunción to Manzanillo, 12 miles (19 km) away on the island's northern extremity. About 8 miles (13 km) along is the fishing port of Puerto Fermín, also called El Tirano (The Tyrant) after Lope de Aguirre, a bloodthirsty rebel-adventurer who landed here and took the island by storm in 1561. At both Manzanilla and El Agua, a couple of miles south, are long ocean beaches with a powerful surf. The sun is very strong, and here, as at all beaches on Margarita, there is little shade. At El Agua Beach, you can rent umbrellas and chairs or stay in the shaded areas of the seafood restaurants lining the sand beach. Many visitors consider El Agua to be the best beach on the island, although the undertow is a bit strong.

A 9-mile (14-km) drive northwest of La Asunción leads to the village of Pedro González, on a quiet little bay with a stillwater beach and an ocean beach not far away in the village of Las Arenas. A few miles southwest, beyond the town of Santa Ana (known as Villa del Norte in accounts of the Independence Wars) is the beautiful bay and town of Juangriego, celebrated for its vivid sunsets. The town is fairly large by island standards, and the beach is long, white, popular, and attractive. Overlooking the town is the Fortín La Galera (Galera Fort), a well-known site to watch the sunset. Galera Beach, just past Juangriego, is known for its tranquil setting and quiet waters. For a few bolívars, children will recite a poem detailing the history of the town. If you take a cab to Juangriego, make sure it is a licensed one. You should be able to see their registration card at the corner of their front window and taxi drivers should have a photo identification inside their cabs. There have been reports of tourists taking "*piratas*" — unregistered taxis — and getting robbed (you can tell the "legal" cabs by the registration stickers that are displayed in the corner of the cab's front window).

About 8 miles (13 km) down the coast is La Guardia Isthmus, on the eastern end of the seashell spit that doubles as the sole connection between the main island and the Macanao Peninsula and as the wall separating La Restinga from the sea. Seven miles (11 km) inland, east of La Guardia, is the village of San Juan Bautista, an area of large date plantations.

This road then returns to the east-west *autopista* and Punta de Piedra, where you can take a ferry back to the mainland. Two islands worth visiting are Coche and Cubagua, between Margarita and the mainland, both scheduled for heavy tourist development. Coche has major salt mines and pearl fisheries; its town, San Pedro, is on a beautiful bay with quite nice beaches.

Ferries to Coche leave Punta de Piedra in the morning, returning in the late afternoon. Somewhere off the shores of the island lies the Spanish warship *San Pedro Alcántara,* sunk in 1815 during the Independence Wars.

Cubagua, Coche's twin, was the site of South America's first town, Nueva Cádiz, which appeared in response to the frenzied search for pearls in the 1520s and 1530s. The Spanish conquistadores forced the Indians on the 13-square-mile island to dive for oyster-bearing pearls and those who returned empty-handed were brutally beaten or sometimes killed. By 1533 the pearl beds were exhausted, and the city was on its way to becoming a ghost town. Eight years later an earthquake and tidal wave flattened what was left of Nueva Cádiz, before its San Francisco church was even finished. The ruins of the town lay under sand for centuries until archaeological excavations began in 1949. In 1979, Nueva Cádiz was the subject of a study conducted by oceanographer Jacques Cousteau. Generally the island has been largely ignored — until now. Cubagua has been slated for a $4.9-billion tourism project encompassing several hotels, cottages, swimming pools, nautical clubs, spas, and recreation areas. The fate of the archaeological site at Nueva Cádiz is unsettled and the 28 fishing families who live on the island will have to be relocated to new homes. There is no regular ferry service yet to Cubagua, but there are boats for hire in Porlamar.

## BEST EN ROUTE

Expect accommodations to be as costly on Margarita Island as on the mainland, with expensive lodgings ranging from $65 to $100 a night, double occupancy, to $35 to $65 for moderate, and under $35, inexpensive. Since the island is one of Venezuela's more popular tourist and shopping haunts, it's wise to make reservations ahead. There are reasonably priced vacation packages available from *Avensa* and *Viasa* airlines, if booked in the US. Check at the tourist information desk at the Porlamar Airport or at *Corpoturismo* in Caracas (various locations, including at the airport and at Torre Oeste, 37th Floor, in Parque Central; phone: 2-507-8876)

### PORLAMAR

**Bella Vista** – This government-owned hotel near the downtown area has 321 rooms, restaurant, shops, bar, disco, its own swimming pool, and is right on the beach (that, sadly, is polluted). Av. Santiago Mariño (phone: 95-22292; in Caracas, 2-507-8815). Expensive.

**Caribe** – Near the *Concorde*, this new twin-tower high-rise boasts deluxe rooms, 3 restaurants, 2 bars, 2 Olympic-size pools, 3 tennis courts, sauna, boutiques, and a disco. Av. Bolívar (phone: 95-91516; in the US, 800-275-3123). Expensive.

**Concorde** – A 475-room luxury property with a swimming pool, tennis, a marina, and its own beach. It boasts the island's most complete water sports facilities and a range of rental equipment. Dine and dance at the club atop the hotel and savor the panoramic view. Av. Raúl Leoni, El Morro Bay (phone: 95-613333; in Caracas, 2-751-9211; fax: 2-913617). Expensive.

**LagunaMar Beach** – This new hotel has 401 suites, 6 restaurants, 7 pools (including slide and wave), as well as a beach and saltwater lagoon, a spa, and tennis courts. Windsurfers, Sunfish, and water skiing equipment also are available. There is free shuttle service to the airport and the duty-free shopping areas. A convention center has facilities for up to 2,000 people. Via Pompatar, Sector Apostadero (phone: 95-620711; in the US, 800-44-UTELL). Expensive.

**Margarita Hilton International** – On the waterfront at Playa Moreno, this 280-room hotel features 24-hour room service, 2 restaurants, 2 bars, a disco, shops, a beauty salon, and all the other amenities for which the chain is noted. All rooms have balconies with ocean views. There's a pool, 2 lighted tennis courts, a fitness center, various water sports, and even an art gallery with changing exhibits. Playa Moreno, Calle Los Uveros, Porlamar (phone: 95-615387 and 95-615822; in the US, 800-HILTONS). Expensive.

**For You** – A good value, its 90 rooms are just a stone's throw from the beach; it has air conditioning, a restaurant, and money exchange office that will give you competitive rates on the US dollar. Guests can use the pool at the *Tizzi* hotel a block away. Special excursions can be arranged by the reception desk. Av. Santiago Mariño (phone: 95-618120). Moderate.

**Colibrí** – With 58 rooms and a fairly good restaurant, it is located near the best shopping areas and just 1 block from the beach. Av. Santiago Mariño (phone: 95-616346). Inexpensive.

**Coral Inn** – A budget-priced alternative that offers many resort luxuries — kitchenettes in the 101 junior suites, a seafood restaurant, 2 pools, and a small disco. Av. Guayacan, Urb. Costa Azul (phone: 95-93242; in the US, 800-275-3123). Inexpensive.

## PAMPATAR

**Flamingo Beach** – One of the newest luxury hotels on the island, with 163 rooms, 2 restaurants, 2 bars, and a disco. The elevated pool gives the impression that it was dropped into the middle of the Caribbean; in fact, a bridge connects the pool area to the sea. There also are facilities for tennis, snorkeling, sailing, and windsurfing. Calle El Cristo, Sector La Caranta (phone: 95-624822; in the US, 800-44-UTELL). Expensive.

**Villas Pampatar** – These 101 fully equipped villas with kitchenettes come in 1-, 2-, and even 3-story models. An international restaurant, a tavern featuring local libations and snacks, 2 pools (1 for children), and a small casino complete the property. Calle Cateo and Av. San Martín in Urb. El Paraíso (phone: 95-93897; in the US, 800-275-3123). Moderate.

## JUANGRIEGO

**Aparthotel Villa El Griego** – Right on the beach, this lavish development offers 168 studio suites and 50 townhouses, each with its own kitchen. There are 4 adult and 4 children's pools, plus an elegant restaurant, 2 snack bars, a piano bar, and disco. A travel agency and car rental office are on the premises. Calle Pica Quinta at Calle El Sol (phone: 95-54349; in the US, 800-275-3123). Expensive.

# The Upper Orinoco (The Venezuelan Amazon)

The wild, not entirely explored Amazonas Territory is Venezuela's last frontier and your next route, also known as the other half of the unique Roraima Formation, a little-inhabited region of vast, trackless jungle and marvelous wildlife, rivers, falls, *tepuis* (tabletop mountains), and nomadic Indians. Leading the geographic highlights is the Orinoco River itself. As early as 1531 the Orinoco was navigated to half its 1,700-mile length to the mouth of the Meta River, widely considered at the time to be the site of El Dorado by Diego de Ordaz; by the middle of the 18th century its larger tributaries had been explored, including the sprawling Ventuari basin in the northern half of Amazonas and the Casiquiare, the channel joining the Orinoco to the Amazon River system.

But for centuries, as with the White Nile in Africa, the source of the Orinoco remained a great mystery. It wasn't until 1950 that a joint Venezuelan-French expedition tracked the last unexplored 120 miles of its course to the Sierra Parima on the eastern frontier with Brazil. There, at a height of 3,400 feet trickling down the side of a mountain they called Delgado Chalbaud, was a small rivulet, the source of the Orinoco River.

With the notable exceptions of the Atures and Maipures rapids near Puerto Ayacucho, the greater part of the upper Orinoco is navigable by small craft. The Casiquiare connection is also navigable, and in 1956 a couple of Americans successfully (give or take some problems with authorities who locked them in jail for a short time) canoed from the Orinoco to the Río de la Plata in Argentina. The Ventuari is largely navigable, with a couple of fairly spectacular falls in its upper reaches.

Among the more spectacular mountains is Sarisariñama, one of a cluster of *tepuis* near the southern frontier in Bolívar state at the source of the Río Caura. About 130 square miles in area and about 7,200 feet high, the mountain is thickly forested on the summit and figures greatly in widespread Indian legend, which claims a manlike beast — a giant — lived in the forest. At night he would come down from the mountain and eat people, making a *sari sari* sound as he munched.

It was first climbed by the explorer and naturalist Félix Cardona in 1942. In 1964, a bush pilot named Harry Gibson discovered the phenomenon for which Sarisariñama has since become famous: gigantic holes punched violently into the emerald green surface of the plateau. They are 1,000 feet deep and 800 feet wide with vertical walls. The first descent into the larger hole was made in 1975 by the explorers Charles Brewer Carias and David Nott.

Toward the northern border of the Amazonas Territory is the *tepui* (or *jidi,* as this type of mountain is called by the Indians of this region) called the Autana. This 4,000-foot column resembles the trunk of an immense petrified tree. About 300 feet from the summit is a complex system of caves passing clear through the mountain, and it is said that at a certain time of year the setting sun shines directly through the hole. The caves were first explored in 1971 by Brewer Carias, who descended from the top, aided by a helicopter (the Autana has not been climbed). The Autana caves and the holes on Sarisariñama point to the existence of a vast underground river system in epochs past.

On the southern frontier of Amazonas (shared with Brazil) are the Sierra de la Neblina (Mountains of the Mists), the highest non-Andean peaks in Venezuela and the highest mountains in Brazil: The loftiest point, a few hundred yards inside Brazil, is Pico Phelps, with a height of just under 10,000 feet. Though La Neblina belongs to the Roraima Formation, it is not in the classic *tepui* mold, but presents a fantastic vista of mountains rising up from mountains, of vertical walls and impenetrable forests, and of a great canyon, which one visitor described in 1956 as rivaling the Grand Canyon of North America. The summit of La Neblina is about 230 square miles.

Among the several Indian nations here are the Piaroa, who in 1985 called a historic meeting to request the governor to give them protection from encroaching criollo (Spanish-American) settlers. The governor advised the tribe that policy demands that they assimilate, but as in neighboring Brazil, the Indians have refused to surrender their lands. The fierce Yanomamo, living on the southern frontier with Brazil, are an isolated people with a primitive culture that includes the use of *yope,* a drug that is snorted through the nose, like cocaine. In an unusual, precedent-setting decree, Venezuelan President Carlos Andrés Pérez in 1991 proclaimed a large portion of Yanomamo land off-limits to miners and developers. Anthropologists and conservationists have hailed the ban, although some are dubious that it will be enforced.

Be forewarned that in order to enter into the Amazonas you must obtain a permit from the Oficina Regional de Asuntos Indígenas (Bureau of Indian Affairs; in the Education Ministry, Torre Este in Parque Central in Caracas). Technically, such permits are available only for scientific expeditions. The process takes at least a full day. Some of the larger tour operators in Puerto Ayacucho, the territorial capital, may be able to get the permit for you. All transport in the Amazonas Territory is by river, air, or on foot, and the only good overland way to get to Puerto Ayacucho, the territorial capital, is by air. You can fly from Caracas or from San Fernando de Apure, on the Río Apure, a major tributary of the Orinoco itself, which can be reached by road from San Juan de los Morros in the central highlands, a 164-mile (262-km) drive. As an alternative to flying, a barge can be taken from Cabruta, a 3-day trip (there are buses to Cabruta from Caracas). Near the mouth of the Apure is Caicara, on the Orinoco, also connected to the north by road. You can take a vessel from Caicara to Puerto Ayacucho.

**PUERTO AYACUCHO:** On the edge of the forest, this is your typical jungle border town: small, fairly rough, and very hot — about 100F (37C). It has a population of 20,000 (roughly a quarter of the entire Amazonas population).

The *Museo Etnolólogico* (Ethnological Museum) near the church downtown, houses interesting exhibits on several of Amazonas' many indigenous groups. The market (be sure to go very early in the morning) offers some Indian handicrafts.

One of the major and most competitive "industries" here is religion. Catholic and Baptist missionaries are busy converting and, unfortunately, confusing the Indians. The Baptists are known for their aggressive conversion tactics, while the Catholics have painted pagan symbols on the outside of the church to lure the skeptical. The longer you stay, the more you become caught up in the drama of the quest for souls. Getting provisions to Puerto Ayacucho is a complicated and costly undertaking, so don't be surprised by the high price tags in the stores. For great people watching, nurse a drink at the poolside bar of the *Gran Hotel Amazonas* — you'll see a good cross-section of border-town characters, including missionaries, scientists, military personnel, bush pilots, and petty hustlers.

The Atures rapids are just south of town, and there is quite a good road to the impressive rapids at Maipures, about 40 miles (64 km) away.

**En Route from Puerto Ayacucho –** Amazonas on the whole offers little to the casual tourist but much to the rugged adventurer. However, legend has it that whoever drinks from the Atabapo River, eats the fruit of the temare plant, and dines on toucan soup never will be able to erase the Amazonas from his or her memory. Getting malaria is another, decidedly less romantic, way to remember the Amazonas. It's advisable to start quinine treatments before your visit. (You also may want to check with your local health department to find out if yellow fever vaccinations are recommended.)

A popular day trip — for locals and visitors alike — is to the natural jungle water slide, *Tobogán de la Selva.* It's located just off the road to Samariapo, about 22 miles (35 km) south of Puerto Ayacucho. Other activities at the site include swimming and hiking on the nature trails, and refreshments are for sale.

Several small pueblos have a fairly regular air service — San Fernando de Atabapo, an old rubber trading town where the Atabapo meets the Orinoco (pop.: about 1,600); San Simón de Cocuy, in the deep south on the borders of Venezuela, Colombia, and Brazil; La Esmeralda on the upper Orinoco near the 8,000-foot Mt. Duida; and Cacuri on the upper Ventuari. At *Campamento Camani* on the Ventuari, anglers can fish for *pavón* (peacock bass) while staying in comfortable, traditional-style dwellings (see *Best en Route*). Downstream from Cacuri are the Oso Falls and Tencua Falls, the latter about 300 feet high and very impressive.

About 80 miles (128 km) upstream from La Esmeralda and deep in the virgin forest is the mission of Platanal, which has costly ($40 a night) accommodations for travelers. There are also accommodations in the camp at Yutajé.

**YUTAJÉ:** Due east of Platanal, in the rugged highlands of the northern Amazonas at the source of the Río Mapaniare, this is a very beautiful area, long considered bewitched with spirits by the Indians. The camp is set in the "V" between the Mapaniare and its short tributary, the Río Yutajé; both rivers tumble over falls at their source. The word *yutajé* in the Piaroa dialect means "twin falls," and the spectacular falls on the Yutajé, only 10 minutes by boat from the camp, are reckoned to be the second highest (Angel Falls ranks first) in Venezuela (exact height as yet unknown).

The camp has accommodations for about 35 people in thatch-roofed cabins, with a restaurant and bar. You can choose between sleeping quarters: a rectangular, enclosed version and a round, Indian-style hut open to breezes. The principal attraction at Yutajé is the fishing, including night fishing with spotlight and spear. Canoes, pedalboats, swampboats (for the flooded areas beside the rivers), wagons, and horses are available, and there is swimming in a broad deep pool below the falls of the Mapaniare (which produce a foam considered by the Indians to be good for the skin) and in shallow pools below the falls on the Yutajé.

Excursions include a 3-day (return) hike to the top of the giant falls and a 3-day stay at an Indian village as guests of the Maquiritare. Among the wildlife thriving in the area are the beautiful macaws and parrots, peccaries, tapir, monkeys, and giant anteaters.

## BEST EN ROUTE

Except for the rundown, but impressive (in a decayed, tropical way), colonial *Gran Hotel Amazonas* (phone: 48-21962) in Puerto Ayacucho — which has a bar, a mediocre restaurant, swimming pool, and air conditioned rooms — accommodations along the upper Orinoco River are scarce.

Not far from Tobogán de la Selva is *Camturma Lodge,* with guest cabins modeled after Indian huts, but with air conditioning and hot water. Excursions are available. Book through *Lost World Adventures* (1189 Autumn Ridge Dr., Marietta, GA 30066; phone: 404-971-8586 and 800-999-0558; in Caracas, 2-718644; fax: 404-077-3095; in Caracas, 2-717859). You'll also find rooms at the mission at Platanal ($40 a night); Rudy Truffino arranges reservations (in Caracas; phone: 2-562-3022). The camp in Yutajé, with room for 30 guests, offers a restaurant and bar for about $100 a night, including meals. For a minimum stay of 3 days, groups of ten can stay for $80 to $90 a night. For reservations, call Johann Mikuski in Caracas (phone: 2-723727 or 2-723735).

*Campamento Camani* is a fishing resort located on the Río Ventuari, famed for its *pavón* (peacock bass). Guests must fly in — the nearest road is hundreds of miles away. Still, there's comfortable lodging in *churuatas* (traditional, thatch-roofed Piearoa Indian dwellings) equipped with private baths; there's even a pool. Book in Caracas (phone: 2-284-2804; fax: 2-283-1905).

# Index

Accommodations, 116–22
  bed and breakfast establishments, 119–120
  calculating costs, 71–72, 119
  with children, 107–8
  discounts, 119
  home exchanges, 120–21
  home stays, 121–22
  jungle lodges in Amazonia, 573–75
  luxury resorts and special havens, 546–57
  Relais & Châteaux, 117–18
  rental options, 118–19
  tipping, 140–42
  *See also* hotels *entry under names of individual countries*
Aconcagua peak, Argentina, 599, 639
Aconquija, Argentina, 625
Advanced Purchase Excursion (APEX) fares, 19
Aguadulce, Panama, 916
Aguas Calientes, Peru, hotels, 982, 984
Airline clubs, 26
Airplane travel, 14–35
  bartered travel sources, 34
  charter flights, 27–29
    bookings, 28–29
  with children, 106–7
  consumer protection, 34–35
  courier travel, 30
  flight insurance, 83
  fly/drive package, 57–58
  generic air travel, 33–34
  hints for handicapped travelers, 91–92
  last-minute travel clubs, 32–33
  net fare sources, 30–31
  scheduled flights, 14–27
    airline clubs, 26
    APEX fares, 19
    baggage, 25–26
    consolidators and bucket shops, 31–32
    delays and cancellations, 27
    discounts on, 29–34
    fares, 16–21
    frequent flyers, 21
    getting bumped, 26–27
    international flights and gateways, 14–15
    low-fare airlines, 21
    meals, 25
    national and intra-continental flights, 15–16
    reservations, 22–23
    seating, 23–24
    smoking, 24–25
    taxes and other fees, 21–22
    tickets, 16

Airport departure tax. *See entry under names of individual countries*
Albina, Suriname, 1004
Alcântara, Brazil, 579
Alcoholic beverages, 138
Alta Gracia, Argentina, 687
  hotels, 688
Altiplano, Bolivia, 603, 697
  *See also* Highlands (Altiplano) route (Bolivia)
Altitude sickness, 130–31
Amazon jungle exploration, 554–55, 571–75
  boat-based excursions, 572–73
  lodge-based excursions, 573–75
Amazon route, Belém to Manaus, Brazil, 719–28
  hotels, 727–28
Amazon route, Colombia, 861–63
  hotels, 863
Amazon route, Peru, 985–94
  hotels, 993–94
Ambato, Ecuador, 869–70
  hotels, 874
Anápolis, Brazil, 765
  hotels, 769
Ancón, Peru, 942
Andes Mountains, 10
Andes route, Venezuela, 1029–37
  hotels, 1035–37
Angel Falls route, Venezuela, 1057–59
  accommodations, 555, 1059
  jungle resorts, 555
Angra dos Reis, Brazil, 577–78, 744–45
  hotels, 747–48
Antarctica, Patagonia (Argentina) to, route, 657–68
  hotels, 665–68
Antillanca, Chile, 621
  hotels, 819
Antofagasta, Chile, 579, 789–90
  hotels, 792
Antuco, Chile, 621
Apartaderos, Venezuela, 1031
  hotels, 1035–36
Aracaju, Brazil, 733
  hotels, 740
Araranguá, Brazil, hotels, 777
Archaeological sites, 624–30
  Argentina, 624–25
  Bolivia, 625
  Chile, 626
  Colombia, 626–27
  Ecuador, 627
  Panama, 627

# 1070 INDEX

Archaeological sites (*cont.*)
  Peru, 627–30
Arequipa to Puno route, Peru, 964–73
  hotels, 972–73
Argentina, 9, 169–70, 639–96
  airport departure tax, 170
  archaeological sites, 624–25
  automobile clubs in, 52
  bank/business hours, 170
  beaches, 576–77
  Buenos Aires, 287–315
  calculating costs, 71–72, 169
  casinos, 569–70
  climate, 13, 14, 169
  driving routes, 639–96
  electricity, 169
  emergency telephone number, 133
  entry requirements and customs, 169
  festivals, 564–65
  general data on, 169–70, 639–41
  holidays, 170
  language, 169
  local transportation, 169
  money, 169
  railway offices and special routes, 45
  shopping, 170, 557–58
  sports, 170
  telephone, 169
  tipping, 170
  tourist information, 169
  transportation to, 169
  wildlife, 612
Argentina, Northwestern route, 688–96
Arica, Chile, 579, 785–87
  hotels, 792
Arquidiocesano Museu (Archdiocese Museum), Mariana, Brazil, 630, 754
Aruanã, Brazil, hotels, 770
Asunción, Paraguay, 247–63
  climate and clothes, 256
  general data on, 247–51
  hotels, 259–61
  local transportation, 256
  map, 248–49
  museums, 257
  music, 259
  nightclubs and nightlife, 259
  places of special interest, 251–55
  restaurants, 261–63
  shopping, 257–58
  special events, 256–57
  sports, 258
  telephone, 256
  theater, 258
  tourist information, 255
Atacama desert route, Chile, 784–91
  hotels, 792
Atacames, Ecuador, 580
Atlántida, Uruguay, 581, 1013–14
Automatic teller machines (ATMs), 115–16
Automobile clubs, 52
Automobile insurance, 83–85

Ayolas, Paraguay, 931
  hotels, 932
Azuero Peninsula, Panama, 915–16

Backpacking. *See* Trekking, backpacking, river rafting, and camping
Baggage and personal effects insurance, 80–81
Bahia, Brazil. *See* Salvador (Bahia), Brazil
Bahía Blanca, Buenos Aires to, route, Argentina, 641–48
  hotels, 647–48
Bahía Blanca to Bariloche route, Argentina, 648–57
  hotels, 654–57
Bahía de Caráquez, Ecuador, 580
Bailadores, Venezuela, 1034
  hotels, 1036
Balcarce, Argentina, 644
  hotels, 647
Balneário de Camboriu, Brazil, 773–74
  hotels, 776
Baltra, Galápagos Islands, Ecuador, 893
Bankruptcy and/or default insurance, 82–83
Baños, Ecuador, 878
  hotels, 879
Barbacena, Brazil, 752
  hotels, 756
Barcelona, Venezuela, 1043–44
Bariloche, Argentina, 552, 617–18, 650–53
  hotels, 656
Bariloche, Bahía Blanca to, route, Argentina, 648–57
  hotels, 654–57
Barlovento, Venezuela, 1027
Barrancas, Venezuela, 1051
Barranquilla, Colombia, 838–39
  hotels, 842
Bartered travel sources, 34
Bartolomé, Galápagos Islands, Ecuador, 894
Beaches, 576–81
  Argentina, 576–77
  Brazil, 577–79
  Chile, 579
  Colombia, 579–80
  Ecuador, 580
  Lima, 365
  Montevideo, 394–95
  Panama City, 411–12
  Peru, 372, 378, 580
  Rio de Janeiro, 454
  Salvador, 477, 480
  Uruguay, 580–81
  Venezuela, 581
  water safety, 131–32
Bed and breakfast establishments, 119–20
Beer, 138
Belém to Manaus route, Brazil (the Amazon), 719–28
  hotels, 727–28
Bella Vista, Uruguay, hotels, 1018
Belo Horizonte, Rio de Janeiro to, route, Brazil, 749–57
  hotels, 755–57

**INDEX 1071**

Belo Horizonte to Brasília route, Brazil, 757–63
   hotels, 762–63
Biking, 67–70
   organized trips, 68–69
   renting, 68
   road safety, 67–68
   tours, 69–70
Blumenau, Brazil, hotels, 776
Boa Viagem, Brazil, 578, 735
Bocas del Toro, Panama, 914–15
Boconó, Venezuela, 1030
Bogotá, Colombia, 264–86
   climate and clothes, 277
   general data on, 264–70
   hotels, 280–82
   local transportation, 277
   map, 266–67
   museums, 271–75, 278
   music, 280
   nightclubs and nightlife, 280
   places of special interest, 270–76
   restaurants, 282–86
   shopping, 278–79
   special events, 277–78
   sports, 279
   telephone, 277
   theater, 279
   tourist information, 276–77
Bogotá to Medellín route, Colombia, 849–54
   hotels, 853–54
Bolivia, 9, 170–71, 697–714
   airport departure tax, 171
   archaeological sites, 625
   automobile clubs in, 52
   calculating costs, 170–71
   climate, 13, 14, 170
   craft specialties, 233
   driving routes, 697–714
   electricity, 170
   emergency telephone number, 133
   entry requirements and customs, 170
   festivals, 565–66
   general data on, 170–71, 697–99
   holidays, 171
   language, 170
   La Paz, 339–60, 699
   local transportation, 170
   money, 170
   railway offices and special routes, 46
   shopping, 171, 558–59
   sports, 171
   telephone, 170
   tipping, 171
   tourist information, 170
   transportation to, 170
Books, recommended, 149–52
Boqueron, Paraguay, hotel, 929
Boquete, Panama, 914
   hotels, 920
Boyacá, Colombia, hotels, 848
Brasília, Belo Horizonte to, route, Brazil, 757–63
   hotels, 762–63

Brasília to Cuiabá route, Brazil, 763–71
   hotels, 769–71
Brazil, 9, 171–73, 715–81
   airport departure tax, 173
   automobile clubs in, 52
   banking/business hours, 173
   beaches, 577–79
   calculating costs, 172
   climate, 12–14, 172
   craft specialties, 233–34
   driving routes, 715–81
   electricity, 172
   emergency telephone number, 133
   entry requirements and customs, 171
   festivals, 566
   general data on, 171–73, 715–19
   holidays, 173
   language, 172
   local transportation, 172
   money, 172
   museums, 630–31
   railway offices and special routes, 46
   Rio de Janeiro, 440–75
   Salvador (Bahia), 476–92
   São Paulo, 514–36
   shopping, 173, 559–60
   sports, 173
   telephone, 171
   tipping, 172–73
   tourist information, 171
   transportation to, 172
   wildlife, 612–13
Brazil, Northeast, route, 728–43
   hotels, 739–43
Brownsberg Park, Suriname, 1005
   accommodations, 1006
Bucaramanga, Colombia, 845
   hotels, 847
Bucket shops, 31–32
Budgets. *See* Costs, calculating
Buenaventura, Colombia, 859
   hotels, 861
Buenos Aires, Argentina, 287–315
   climate and clothes, 302
   general data on, 287–94
   hotels, 308–11
   local transportation, 302–3
   map, 268–69
   museums, 297–98, 303–4
   music, 307–8
   nightclubs and nightlife, 308
   places of special interest, 294–301
   restaurants, 311–15
   shopping, 304–5
   special events, 303
   sports, 306–7
   telephone, 302
   theater, 307
   tourist information, 301–2
Buenos Aires to Bahía Blanca route, Argentina, 641–48
   hotels, 647–48
Bus, traveling by, 48–49
   accommodations and fares, 49

## 1072 INDEX

Bus (cont.)
  booking, 49
  bus service, 48
  hints for comfortable travel, 48
  hints for handicapped travelers, 93
Business hours. See banking/business hours entry under names of individual countries
Búzios, Brazil, 454, 549–50, 577

Caacupé, Paraguay, 925–26
  hotels, 927
Cabimas, Venezuela, hotels, 1042
Cafayate, Argentina, 691
  hotels, 695–96
Cajabamba, Ecuador, 871
Cajamarca, Lima to, route, Peru, 945–58
  hotels, 957–58
Calafate, Argentina, 662–63
  hotels, 555, 666–67
Calama, Chile, 788–89
  hotels, 792
Caldas Novas, Brazil, 766
  hotels, 770
Cali, Colombia, 858–59
  hotels, 861
Cali, Neiva to, route, Colombia, 854–61
  hotels, 859–61
Cameras and equipment, 155–57
Campina Grande, Brazil, 737
  hotels, 741
Camping. See Trekking, backpacking, river rafting, and camping
Campo Grande, Brazil, hotels, 555
Canaima, Venezuela, 555, 1058–59
  campground, 1059
Canela, Brazil, 775
Canoa Quebrada, Brazil, 579, 737
Cantamarca, Peru, 941–42
Capilla del Monte, Argentina, 687
Car, traveling by, 49–58
  automobile clubs, 52
  automobile insurance, 83–84
  breakdowns, 52–53
  car permits and checkpoints, 51
  with children, 107
  gasoline, 54
  hints for handicapped travelers, 92–93
  license, 50–51
  maps, 51–52
  rental, 54–58
  road safety and highway conditions, 53–54
Caracas, Venezuela, 316–38
  climate and clothes, 327
  general data on, 316–21
  hotels, 333–35
  local transportation, 327–28
  map, 318–19
  museums, 322–24, 328–29
  music, 331–32
  nightclubs and nightlife, 332
  places of special interest, 322–27
  restaurants, 335–38
  shopping, 329–30
  special events, 328
  sports, 330–31
  telephone, 327
  theater, 331
  tourist information, 327
Caracas to San Francisco de Yare route, Venezuela, 1024–29
  hotels, 1028–29
Caraguatatuba, Brazil, 746
  hotels, 748
Carcass Island, Falkland Islands, Argentina, 671
Carhué, Argentina, 646
Caribbean coast, 9–10
Caribbean West Coast and Cartagena route, Colombia, 833–42
  hotels, 840–42
Caripe, Venezuela, hotels, 1048
Carlos Paz, Argentina, 686
  hotels, 688
Carmelo, Uruguay, 1010
  hotels, 1013
Carmen de Patagones, Argentina, 659
  hotels, 665
Carmen Miranda Museum, Rio de Janeiro, Brazil, 459, 631
*Carnaval*, Rio de Janeiro, Brazil, 11, 225, 447, 457–58, 541, 566
Carrasco, Uruguay, 394–95
Car rentals, 54–58, 638
  automobile insurance, 83–84
  calculating costs, 71–72
  costs, 56–57
  fly/drive packages, 57–58
  hints for handicapped travelers, 93
  requirements, 55–56
  See also local transportation entry under names of individual cities
Cartagena, Colombia, 834–37
  hotels, 548, 841
Cartagena and the Caribbean West Coast route, Colombia, 833–42
  hotels, 548, 840–42
Caruaru, Brazil, 736
Carúpano, Venezuela, 1046
  hotels, 1048
Casa do Bandeirante Museum (Pioneer House), Brazil, 523, 631
Casa Natal de El Libertador (Simón Bolívar's Birthplace), Caracas, Venezuela, 323, 634
Cash machines (ATMs), 115–16
Casinos, 569–71
  Argentina, 569–70
  Chile, 570
  Colombia, 570
  Ecuador, 570
  Panama, 570
  Paraguay, 571
  Suriname, 571
  Uruguay, 571
Casma, Peru, 948
Cata, Venezuela, 1026

Catedral (Cathedral), Caracas, Venezuela, 322, 634
Cattle Country route, Paraguay, 933–35
   hotels, 935
Caxias do Sul, Brazil, 775
   hotels, 778
Cayasta, Argentina, 625
Cayenne, French Guiana, 899
   hotels, 901–2
Central Circuit/the Jesuit Mission Trail route, Paraguay, 929–33
   hotels, 932–33
Cerro Catedral, Argentina, 652, 653
   hotels, 656
Cerro Chapelco, Argentina, 618, 649
Cerro Punta, Panama, 913
   hotels, 919
Chacaltaya, Bolivia, 349, 354, 619
Chaclacayo, Peru, hotels, 945
Chaco, the, Argentina, 603
Chaco route, the, Paraguay, 928–29
   hotels, 929
Chagas' disease, 129–30
Chan-Chan, Peru, 629, 952–53
Changuinola, Panama, 914–15
Charter flights, 27–29
Chascomus, Argentina, 642
Chavín de Huantar, Peru, 629, 949
Chichiriviche, Venezuela, 1038
   hotels, 1039–40
Chiclayo, Peru, 953–54
   hotels, 958
Children, traveling with, 104–8
   accommodation and meals, 107–8
   getting there and getting around, 105–7
   planning, 104–5
   publications for, 104–5
Chile, 9, 173–74, 782–830
   airport departure tax, 174
   archaeological sites, 626
   automobile clubs in, 52
   banking/business hours, 174
   beaches, 579
   calculating costs, 174
   casinos, 570
   climate, 13, 14, 173–74
   craft specialties, 234
   driving routes, 782–830
   electricity, 174
   emergency telephone number, 133
   entry requirements and customs, 173
   festivals, 566–67
   general data on, 173–74, 782–84
   holidays, 174
   hotels, 548, 550–51
   language, 174
   local transportation, 173
   money, 174
   museums, 632, 786, 787, 790–91
   railway offices and special routes, 46
   Santiago, 493–513
   shopping, 174, 560
   sports, 174
   telephone, 173
   tipping, 174
   tourist information, 173
   transportation to, 173
Chile, North route, 784–92
Chilean Patagonia and the Tierra del Fuego Archipelago route, 819–25
   hotels, 824–25
Chillán, Chile, 808–9
   hotels, 810
Chiloé Island, Chile, 816–17
Chimbote, Peru, 950
   hotels, 957
Chincha Alta, Peru, 960
   hotels, 963
Chordeleg, Ecuador, 872–73
Choroní, Venezuela, 581, 1026
   hotels, 556, 1028
Chosica, Peru, 372–73, 942–43
   hotels, 945
Chulumani, Bolivia, 703
   hotels, 709
Chuquicamata, Chile, 788
Cidade Livre, Brazil, 764
Circuito Chico, Argentina, 653
Circuito Grande, Argentina, 653
Ciudad Bolívar, Venezuela, 1049–50
   hotels, 1051
Ciudad del Este, Paraguay, 931–32
   hotels, 932–33
Ciudad Guayana, Venezuela, 1050
   hotels, 1051–52
Claromeco, Argentina, 644–45
   hotels, 647
Climate, 12–14
   average temperature in °F, 13
   clothes and, 85–87
   See also climate and clothes entry under names of individual cities and countries
Cochabamba and Santa Cruz route, Bolivia, 710–14
   hotels, 713–14
Colca Canyon, Peru, 609, 967–68
   hotels, 973
Colombia, 9, 174–75, 831–63
   airport departure tax, 175
   archaeological sites, 626–27
   automobile clubs in, 52
   banking/business hours, 175
   beaches, 579–80
   Bogotá, 264–86
   calculating costs, 175
   casinos, 570
   climate, 12, 13, 14, 175
   craft specialties, 234–35
   driving routes, 831–63
   electricity, 175
   emergency telephone number, 133
   entry requirements and customs, 174
   festivals, 567
   general data on, 174–75, 831–33
   holidays, 175
   language, 175
   local transportation, 175

**1074 INDEX**

Colombia (*cont.*)
  money, 175
  museums, 632
  railway offices and special routes, 46
  shopping, 175, 560–61
  sports, 175
  telephone, 174
  tipping, 175
  tourist information, 174
  transportation to, 175
  wildlife, 613
Colón, Panama, 918
  hotels, 921
Colonia del Sacramento, Uruguay, 1009–10
  hotels, 1012
Colonial Art Museum, Colombia, 273, 632
Colonia Suiza, Uruguay, 1009
  hotels, 1012
Colonia Tovar, Venezuela, 326–27
Combination insurance policies, 84–85
Comodoro Rivadavia, Argentina, 660
  hotels, 666
Computer services, 153
Concepción, Paraguay, 934
  hotels, 935
Concepción to Laja Falls route, Chile, 807–11
  hotels, 810–11
Congonhas, Brazil, 753
Consolidators, 31–32
Consulates. *See* Embassies and consulates
Copacabana, Bolivia, 702–3
  hotels, 709
Copiapó, Chile, 790
  hotels, 792
Córdoba route, Argentina, 683–88
  hotels, 688
Coro, Venezuela, 1038–39
  hotels, 1040
Coroico, Bolivia, 709
  hotels, 709
Coroico, La Cumbre to, Bolivia, 603
Coronado, Panama, hotels, 920
Corrientes, Argentina, 674
Corumbá, Brazil, train from Santa Cruz, Bolivia, to, 603–4
Costa Atlántida, Argentina, 576–77
Costa Verde, Rio de Janeiro to São Paulo, Brazil, 743–49
  hotels, 747–49
Costs, calculating, 71–72
  car rentals, 56–57
  ship travel, 35–36
  *See also* calculating costs *entry under names of individual countries*
Cotacachi, Ecuador, 867
  hotels, 874
Crafts, 231–38
  Bolivia, 233
  Brazil, 233–34
  Chile, 234
  Colombia, 234–35
  duty-free items, 145
  Ecuador, 235–36
  Panama, 236
  Peru, 236–37
  Suriname, 237
  Venezuela, 237–38
Credit and currency. *See* Money; money *entry under names of individual countries*
Crime, 140
Cruises, 35–44
  to and around South America, 38–40
  freighters, 43–44
  specialty and regional cruises, 40–42
  South America's inland waterways, 42–43
Cúcuta, Colombia, 844
  hotels, 847
Cuenca, Ecuador, 871–72
  hotels, 875
Cuiabá, Brasília to, route, (the Mato Grosso) Brazil, 763–71
  hotels, 769–71
Cultural activities
  archaeological sites, 624–30
  museums, 630–34
  *See also* museum *entry under names of individual cities*
Cultural background of South America
  crafts, 231–38
  food and drink, 239–43
  legends and literature, 212–23
  music and dance, 224–30
  religion, 143, 207–11
  *See also* History of South America
Cumaná, Venezuela, 1044–45
  hotels, 549, 1048
Curicó, Chile, 806
Curitiba, Brazil, 772–73
  hotels, 776
Currency, 109–10
Customs and returning to the US, 79–80, 143–47
  clearing customs, 145–46
  duty-free articles, 144–45
  duty-free craft items, 145
  forbidden imports, 146–47
Cuyabeno Nature Reserve, 608
Cuzco and the Inca Ruins route, Peru, 974–84
  hotels, 551–52, 983–84

Dance, music and, 224–30
David, Panama, 913–14
  hotels, 920
Default and/or bankruptcy insurance, 82–83
Devil's Island, French Guiana, 899–900
  hotels, 902
Diamantina, Brazil, 757–58
  hotels, 762
Diarrhea and stomach upsets, 128–29
Discounts
  for older travelers, 102–3
  on scheduled flights, 29–34
Drink, food and, 239–43
Drinking, 138
Drinking water, 129
Drugs
  illegal, 138–39
  prescription, 134, 139
Duitama, Colombia, hotels, 848

## INDEX 1075

Duty and customs. *See* Customs and returning to the US
Duty-free articles and craft items, 144–45
Duty-free shops, 142–43

Easter Island (Rapa Nui), Chile route, 825–28
  archaeological sites, 626
  hotels, 827–28
Ecuador, 9, 175–77, 864–96
  airport departure tax, 177
  archaeological sites, 627
  automobile clubs in, 52
  banking/business hours, 176
  beaches, 580
  calculating costs, 176
  casinos, 570
  climate, 12–14, 176
  craft specialties, 235–36
  driving routes, 864–966
  electricity, 176
  emergency telephone number, 133
  entry requirements and customs, 176
  festivals, 567–68
  general data on, 175–77, 864–66
  holidays, 176–77
  language, 176
  local transportation, 176
  money, 176
  museums, 632–33
  Quito, 420–39, 868–69
  railway offices and special routes, 46–47
  shopping, 177, 561
  sports, 177
  telephone, 176
  tipping, 176
  tourist information, 175–76
  transportation to, 176
  wildlife, 613–14
Educational programs (studying abroad)
  for older travelers, 103
  for single travelers, 98–100
El Bolson, Argentina, 654
  hotels, 657
El Callao, Venezuela, 1053
  accommodations, 1057
El Colorado, Chile, 620
El Dorado, Venezuela, 1053
  accommodations, 1057
Electricity, 126–27
  Argentina, 169
  Bolivia, 170
  Brazil, 172
  Chile, 174
  Colombia, 175
  Ecuador, 176
  French Guiana, 177
  Guyana, 178
  Panama, 180
  Paraguay, 181
  Peru, 182
  Suriname, 183
  Uruguay, 184
  Venezuela, 185
El Litoral route, Ecuador, 880–89
  hotels, 887–89

El Valle, Panama, 917
  hotels, 920–21
Embassies and consulates
  South American (in the US), 148
  US (in South America), 136–38
  *See also* tourist information *entry under names of individual countries*
Embú, Brazil, 772
  hotels, 775–76
Emílio Goeldi Anthropology Museum, Belém, Brazil, 630, 723
Encarnación, Paraguay, 931
  hotels, 932
Entry requirements and documents, 77–80
  *See also* entry requirements and customs *entry under names of individual countries*
Equatorial line, Ecuador, 868
Esmeraldas, Ecuador, 886–88
  hotels, 889
Española (Hood), Galápagos Islands, Ecuador, 895
Esquel, Argentina, 654
Excursion fares, 18

Falkland Islands/Islas Malvinas route, Argentina, 668–72
  hotels, 671–72
Falls of Paulo Afonso, Brazil. *See* Foz of Paulo Afonso, Brazil
Farallón, Panama, 916
Farellones, Chile, 506, 620
Fazenda Nova, Brazil, 736
Fernandina (Narborough), Galápagos Islands, Ecuador, 894
Festivals, 564–69
  Argentina, 564–65
  Bolivia, 565–66
  Brazil, 566
  Chile, 566–67
  Colombia, 567
  Ecuador, 567–68
  Paraguay, 568
  Peru, 568
  Suriname, 568–69
  Uruguay, 569
  Venezuela, 569
  *See also* special events *entry under names of individual cities*
Filadelfia, Paraguay, 929
  hotels, 929
Film and tapes, 156
First-aid kit, 128
Fishing, 590–98
  Argentina, 591–92
  Bolivia, 592
  Brazil, 592–93
  Chile, 593–94
  Colombia, 594–95
  Ecuador, 595–96
  Panama, 596
  Paraguay, 596
  Peru, 596–97
  Suriname, 597
  Uruguay, 597

# 1076 INDEX

Fishing (*cont.*)
  Venezuela, 597–98
  *See also* sports *entry under names of individual cities*
Flight insurance, 83
Floreana (Charles), Galápagos Islands, Ecuador, 895
Florianópolis, Brazil, 577, 774
  hotels, 777
Food, 239–43
  calculating costs, 71–72
  with children, 107–8
  drink and, 239–43
  precautions for, 129
  *See also* restaurants *entry under names of individual cities*
Foreign exchange, 110–11
Fortaleza, Brazil, 737–38
  hotels, 742
Foz of Paulo Afonso, Brazil, 733–34
  hotels, 740
Fray Bentos, Uruguay, 1010–11
  hotels, 1013
Freighters, 43–44
French Guiana, 9, 177–78, 897–902
  airport departure tax, 178
  banking/business hours, 177–78
  calculating costs, 177
  climate, 12, 13, 177
  driving routes, 897–902
  electricity, 177
  emergency telephone number, 133
  entry requirements and customs, 177
  general data on, 177–78, 897–99
  holidays, 178
  language, 177
  local transportation, 177
  money, 177
  shopping, 178
  sports, 178
  telephone, 177
  tipping, 177
  tourist information, 177
  transportation to, 177
Frequent flyers, 21

Galápagos Islands route, Ecuador, 889–96
  hotels, 895–96
Galería de Arte Nacional (National Art Gallery), Caracas, Venezuela, 328–29, 634
Gasoline costs, 54, 56–57
Generic air travel, 33–34
Genovesa (Tower), Galápagos Islands, Ecuador, 895
Georgetown, Guyana, 905–6
  hotels, 908–9
GIT. *See* Group Inclusive Travel fares
Glacier National Park, Argentina, 602, 661–62
Goiânia, Brazil, 765–67
  hotels, 769–70
Goiás, Brazil, hotels, 770
Golden Triangle route, Paraguay, 923–28
  hotels, 927–28

Golf, 588–90
  Argentina, 588
  Bolivia, 588–89
  Brazil, 589
  Chile, 589
  Colombia, 589
  Ecuador, 589
  Panama, 589
  Paraguay, 589
  Peru, 589–90
  Uruguay, 590
  Venezuela, 590
  *See also* sports *entry under names of individual cities*
Gorgona, Panama, hotels, 920
Government tourist offices in the US, 148
Gramado, Brazil, 775
  hotels, 777–78
Gran Sabana route, Venezuela, 610, 1052–57
  hotels, 1057
Gravatal, Brazil, 774
  hotels, 777
Ground transportation, handicapped, 92–93
Group Inclusive Travel (GIT) fares, 19
Guaiquivilo, Chile, 626
Guajira Peninsula route, Venezuela, 1040–43
  hotels, 1042–43
Guanare, Venezuela, 1029–30
  hotels, 1035
Guarujá, Brazil, 746
  hotels, 748–49
Guayaquil, Ecuador, 881–85
  hotels, 887–8
Guyana, 9, 178–79, 903–9
  airport departure tax, 179
  banking/business hours, 179
  calculating costs, 179
  climate, 12, 13, 178
  driving routes, 903–9
  electricity, 178
  emergency telephone number, 133
  entry requirements and customs, 178
  general data on, 178–79
  holidays, 179
  language, 178
  local transportation, 178
  money, 178–79
  shopping, 179
  sports, 179
  telephone, 178
  tipping, 179
  tourist information, 178
  transportation to, 178

Handicapped travelers, hints for, 88–94
  ground transportation, 92–93
  by plane, 91–92
  planning, 88–91
  by ship, 92
  tours, 93–94
Handicrafts. *See* Crafts
Health care, 127–36
  altitude sickness, 130–31
  Chagas' disease, 129–30

diarrhea and stomach upsets, 128–29
emergency treatment, 132–33
first aid, 128
helpful publications, 35, 135–36
hints for older travelers, 101–2
infectious hepatitis or jaundice, 129
insects and other pests, 131
malaria, 130
pharmacies and prescriptions, 134, 139
prevention and immunization, 127–28
sunburn, 130
water safety, 131–32
Highlands (Altiplano) route, Bolivia, 699–710
hotels, 709–10
Higuerote, Venezuela, 1027
hotels, 1029
Hiking, 67
Historic hostelries, 550–52
History of South America, 189–206
conquest and colonization, 193–95
the future, 204–6
independence, 195–99
pre-Columbian era, 189–92
the twentieth century, 199–204
Holidays. *See* holidays *entry under names of individual countries*
Home exchange organizations, 120–21
Honda, Colombia, 850
hotels, 853
Hostelries, historic, 550–52
Hotels
luxury resorts and special havens, 546–575
historic hostelries, 550–52
island idylls, 549–50
jungle junkets, 554–55
lakeside lodges, 552
seaside swells, 546–49
spas and sports spots, 552–54
wilderness whimsy, 555–57
surcharges for telephone calls, 125–26
tipping, 141
useful words and phrases, 159–60
*See also* hotels *entry under names of individual cities*
Huacho, Peru, 947
hotels, 957
Huancayo, Peru, 944
hotels, 945
Huanchaco, Peru, 951–52
hotels, 958
Huánuco, Peru, 987
hotels, 993
Huaráz, Peru, 948–49
hotels, 957
Huarmey, Peru, hotels, 957
Huascarán National Park, Peru, 609, 949
Huayna Picchu, Peru, 628, 982
Huiñay-Huayna, Peru, 628
Humahuaca, Argentina, 695
Hunting, 621–23
Argentina, 621–22
Bolivia, 622
Brazil, 622
Colombia, 622
Ecuador, 623
Paraguay, 623
Suriname, 623
Uruguay, 623
*See also* sports *entry under names of individual cities*

Ibagué, Colombia, hotels, 861
Ibarra, Ecuador, 866–67
Ica, Peru, 961–62
hotels, 553, 964
Iguaçu Falls, Brazil, 542–43, 778–81
hotels, 780–81
Iguassu Falls, Argentina, 542–43, 676
hotels, 677–68
Ilha do Mosqueiro, Brazil, 579, 723
hotels, 727–28
Ilhéus, Brazil, 733
hotels, 739–40
Imbaimadai, Guyana, 907–8
Immunization requirements, 127–28
Imuya Lake, Ecuador, 879
Imports, forbidden, 146–47
Incahuasi, Argentina, 625
Inca Ruins and Cuzco route, Peru, 608–9, 974–84
hotels, 983–84
Inca Trail, Peru, 608–9
Infectious hepatitis or jaundice, 129
Ingapirca, Ecuador, 627, 872
Insects and other pests, 131
Insurance, 80–85
automobile insurance, 83–84
baggage and personal effects, 80–81
combination policies, 84–85
default and/or bankruptcy insurance, 82–83
flight insurance, 83
personal accident and sickness, 81–82
trip cancellation and interruption insurance, 82
Ipiales, Colombia, hotels, 861
Iquique, Chile, 787–88
hotels, 792
Iquitos, Peru, 609–10, 990–93
hotels, 554–55, 993–94
Isabela (Albemarle), Galápagos Islands, Ecuador, 895
Isla Grande, Panama, 919
hotels, 921
Islands of the Moon and the Sun (Lake Titicaca), Bolivia, 625, 702
Islas Malvinas. *See* Falkland Islands/Islas Malvinas route, Argentina
Isthmus of Panama, 9
Itacuruçá, Brazil, hotels, 747
Itaipauaçú, Brazil, 577
Itajaí Valley, Brazil, 773
Itamaracá, Brazil, 578, 736
Itaparica Island, Brazil, 483, 550
Itapema, Brazil, hotels, 776–77
Itauguá, Paraguay, 926–27
ITX fares, 19–20

# 1078 INDEX

Jají, Venezuela, 1033
  hotels, 1036
Jahuel, Chile, 800
  hotels, 801–2
Jaraguá, Brazil, 765
Jardim Botanico (Botanical Gardens), Rio de Janeiro, Brazil, 453–54, 631
Jataí, Brazil, hotels, 770
Jauja, Peru, 943–44
Jaundice (infectious hepatitis), 129
Jesuit Mission Trail/the Central Circuit route, Paraguay, 929–33
  hotels, 932–33
Jesús, Paraguay, 931
Jesús Soto Museum of Modern Art, Ciudad Bolívar, Venezuela, 634, 1049
Jijón y Caamaño Museum, Quito, Ecuador, 427–28, 632–33
João Pessoa, Brazil, 736–37
  hotels, 741
Joinville, Brazil, 773
  hotels, 776
Juan Fernández Archipelago route, Chile, 828–30
  hotels, 830
Juangriego, Venezuela, 1062
  hotels, 1064
Juiz de Fora, Brazil, 751–52
  hotels, 755–56
Jujuy, Argentina, 694
  hotels, 696
Juliaca, Peru, 968–69
  hotels, 973
Jungle, 10–11
Jungle exploration of the Amazon, 571–75
  boat-based excursions, 572–73
  lodge-based excursions, 573–75
Jungle junkets, 554–55
Junín de los Andes, Argentina, 649
  hotels, 655

Kaieteur Falls, Guyana, 907
Kidney Island, Falkland Islands, Argentina, 671
Km 88 route, Venezuela, 1053–54
  hotels, 1057
Kourou, French Guiana, 899
  hotels, 902

La Asunción, Venezuela, 1061–62
La Catedral (Cathedral), Caracas, Venezuela, 322, 634
La Coronilla, Montevideo to, route, Uruguay, 1013–20
  hotels, 1018–20
La Cumbre, Argentina, 686
La Cumbre to Coroico hike, Bolivia, 603
Lago Argentino, Argentina, 662
  hotels, 667
Laguna de Paca, Peru, hotels, 945
Laguna Negra, Venezuela, 1031
Lagunillas, Chile, 507, 620
Laja Falls, Concepción to, route, Chile, 807–11
  hotels, 810–11
Lake Calafquén, Chile, hotels, 818
Lake District, Argentina, 602–3, 653
Lake District route, Chile, 811–19
  hotels, 817–19
Lake Guatavita, Bogotá, Colombia, 276
Lake Iripari, Ecuador, 879
Lake Sochagota, Colombia, hotels, 848
Lake Titicaca, Bolivia, 701–2
  hotels, 556, 709
  Islands of the Moon and the Sun, 625
Lake Yarinacocha, Peru, 989
  hotels, 993
Lake Ypacaraí, Paraguay, 926
  hotels, 927–28
La Ligua, Chile, 803–4
Lambayeque, Peru, 954–55
Language. See language entry under names of individual countries
Lanín National Park, Argentina, 649
  hotels, 655
La Paloma, Uruguay, 1017
  hotels, 1019–20
La Parva, Chile, 506–7, 620
La Paz, Bolivia, 339–60
  climate and clothes, 351
  general data on, 339–44
  hotels, 356–57
  local transportation, 351–52
  map, 340–41
  museums, 346, 347–48, 353
  music, 355
  nightclubs and nightlife, 355
  places of special interest, 345–50
  restaurants, 357–60
  shopping, 353–54
  special events, 352
  sports, 354–55
  telephone, 350
  theater, 355
  tourist information, 350
La Pintada, Panama, 916
La Puerta, Venezuela, 1030
  hotels, 1035
La Quiaca, Argentina, 695
La Restinga Lagoon and National Park, Venezuela, 1061
La Rioja, Argentina, 682
Las Cajas National Park, Ecuador, 608, 873
Las Cataratas del Iguazú (Iguassu Falls), Argentina, 676
  hotels, 676–78
La Serena, Chile, 790–91
  hotels, 792
Las Hoyas, Esquel, Argentina, 618, 654
Las Leñas, Argentina, 618–19, 682
Lasso, Ecuador, hotels, 551, 874
Legal aid and consular services, 136–38
Legends, 212–18
Lethem, Guyana, 908
Leticia, Colombia, 606, 613, 862–63
  hotels, 863
Lima, Peru, 361–86
  beaches, 365
  climate and clothes, 374

general data on, 361–66
hotels, 379–82, 939
local transportation, 374
map, 362–63
museums, 369–70, 375, 633
music, 378
nightclubs and nightlife, 379
outskirts of, 938–45
places of special interest, 366–73
restaurants, 382–86
shopping, 376–77
special events, 374–75
sports, 377–78
telephone, 374
theater, 378
tourist information, 373
Lima to Cajamarca route, Peru, 945–58
hotels, 957–58
Lima to Nazca route, Peru, 958–64
hotels, 963–64
Limóncocha, Ecuador, 607, 877
Linares, Chile, 808
hotels, 810
Literature, 218–23
Lodges, lakeside, 552
Los Alerces National Park, Argentina, 654
hotels, 657
Los Andes, Chile, 800
hotels, 801
Los Angeles, Chile, 810
hotels, 811
Los Cocos, Argentina, 686
hotels, 688
Los Llanos, Colombia, 606
Los Penitentes, Argentina, 681
Los Roques, Venezuela, 584, 1028
Los Santos, Panama, hotels, 920
Luggage, airplane travel, 25–26, 74–75

Macapá, Brazil, hotels, 727
Macas, Ecuador, 878
Maceió, Brazil, 578, 734
hotels, 740
Machala, Tulcán to, Ecuador north route, 866–75
hotels, 873–75
Machu Picchu, Peru, 544–45, 628, 981–83
hotels, 984
Madre de Dios/Manu National Park, Peru, 610, 996–98
Madre de Dios route, Peru, 995–99
hotels, 998–99
Magazines, 152
Mail, 123–24
Malargue, Argentina, 682
Malaria, 130, 721–22
Manabí Province, Ecuador, hotels, 889
Manaus, Belém to, (the Amazon) route, Brazil, 719–28
hotels, 554, 727–28
Mangaratiba, Brazil
hotels, 747
luxury resorts, 547

Manizales, Colombia, 850
hotels, 853
Manta, Ecuador, 885–88
Manu, Peru, 996–98
Maps, 4–5, 248–49, 266–67, 288–89, 318–19, 340–41, 362–63, 388–89, 406–7, 422–23, 442–43, 478–79, 494–95, 516–17
*See also* map *entry under names of individual cities*
Maracaibo, Venezuela, 1041–42
hotels, 1042–43
Mar de Ajo, Argentina, 642
Mar del Plata, Argentina, 576, 642–44
hotels, 646–47
Margarita Island route, Venezuela, 581, 1059–64
hotels, 1063–64
Mariana, Brazil, 754
Mato Grosso (Brasília to Cuiabá) route, Brazil, 763–71
hotels, 769–71
Mato Grosso, Brazil, 9
Mazan Forest Reserve, Ecuador, 608
Medellín, Bogotá to, route, Colombia, 849–54
hotels, 853–54
Medellín, Colombia, 851–53
Medical aid, 132–36
*See also* Health care
Mendoza route, Argentina, 678–83
hotels, 683
Mercedes, Uruguay, 1010
hotels, 1013
Mérida, Venezuela, 1032–33
hotels, 556, 1036
Mesopotamia route, Argentina, 672–78
hotels, 676–78
Metric to US measurements (conversion table), 154–55
Misahualli, Ecuador, hotels, 880
Money, 109–16
cash machines (ATMs), 115–16
credit cards, 113–15
currency, 109–10
foreign exchange, 110–11
sending money abroad, 115
tip packs, 111
traveler's checks, 111–13
*See also* money *entry under names of individual countries*
Monkey Island, Colombia, hotels, 863
Monte Hermoso, Argentina, 645–46
hotels, 647
Montevideo, Uruguay, 386–403
beaches, 394–95, 580–81
climate and clothes, 396
general data on, 387–90
hotels, 399–401
local transportation, 396
map, 388–89
museums, 392–93, 394, 396–97
music, 399
nightclubs and nightlife, 399
places of special interest, 391–95
restaurants, 401–3
shopping, 397–98

# 1080 INDEX

Montevideo (*cont.*)
  special events, 396
  sports, 398
  telephone, 395
  theater, 398–99
  tourist information, 395
Montevideo to La Coronilla route, Uruguay, 1013–20
  hotels, 1018–20
Montevideo to Salto route, Uruguay, 1008–13
  hotels, 1012–13
Morohuasi, Argentina, 625
Morro Branco, Brazil, 579
Morrocoy National Park, Venezuela, 581, 1037, 1038
Mountain climbing, 598–602
  Argentina, 599
  Bolivia, 599–600
  Brazil, 600
  Chile, 600
  Ecuador, 600
  Peru, 600
  Venezuela, 600–1
  *See also* sports *entry under names of individual cities*
Mt. Cotopaxi, Ecuador, 607, 869
Mount Pleasant, Falkland Islands, Argentina, 671
Mucurubá, Venezuela, 556, 1032
Museo Arqueológico (Archaeological Museum), Bogotá, Colombia, 272, 632
Museo Arqueológico Rafael Larco Herrera (Rafael Larco Herrera Museum), Lima, Peru, 369–70, 633
Museo Carmen Miranda (Carmen Miranda Museum), Rio de Janeiro, Brazil, 631
Museo de Antropología y Arqueología (Museum of Anthropology and Archaeology), Lima, Peru, 369, 633
Museo de Arte Colonial (Colonial Art Museum), Bogotá, Colombia, 273, 632
Museo de Arte Colonial (Colonial Art Museum), Quito, Ecuador, 426, 632
Museo de Arte Contemporáneo (Contemporary Art Museum), Caracas, Venezuela, 324, 634
Museo de Arte Moderno Jesús Soto (Jesús Soto Museum of Modern Art), Ciudad Bolivar, Venezuela, 634, 1049
Museo de Arte Religioso (Museum of Religious Art), Riobamba, Ecuador, 633, 870
Museo de Artes y Tradiciones Populares (Museum of Popular Art and Tradition), Bogotá, Colombia, 272, 632
Museo de Brüning (Brüning Museum), Lambayeque, Peru, 633–34, 954–55
Museo de la Nación (National Museum), Lima, Peru, 369, 633
Museo del Banco Central (Central Bank Museum), Quito, Ecuador, 427, 632
Museo del Gaucho La Mondea (Cowboy and Gold Museum), Montevideo, Uruguay, 392–93, 634
Museo del Oro (Gold Museum), Bogotá, Colombia, 271, 632
Museo del Oro (Gold Museum), Lima, Peru, 370, 633
Museo Historico Nacional y Museo Romántico (National History Museum and Romantic Museum), Montevideo, Uruguay, 392, 634
Museo Jijón y Caamaño (Jijón y Caamaño Museum), Quito, Ecuador, 427–28, 632–33
Museo Paraguayo de Arte Contemporáneo (Paraguayan Contemporary Art Museum), Asunción, Paraguay, 253, 633
Museo Paulista (Paulista Museum), São Paulo, Brazil, 523, 631
Museo Yoshiro Amano (Yoshiro Amano Museum), Lima, Peru, 375, 633
Museu de Arte Sacra (Sacred Art Museum), Salvador (Bahia), Brazil, 482, 631
Museu de Arte Sacra (Sacred Art Museum), São Paulo, Brazil, 521, 631
Museu do Convento do Carmo (Carmo Convent Museum), Salvador (Bahia), Brazil, 481, 631
Museu do Ouro (Gold Museum), Sabara, Brazil, 630, 754
Museu Emílio Goeldi (Emílio Goeldi Anthropology Museum), Belém, Brazil, 630, 723
Museu Imperial (Imperial Museum), Petrópolis, Brazil, 630–31
Museum of Anthropology of Northeastern Man, Recife, Brazil, 631, 735
Museu Nacional de Belas Artes (National Museum of Fine Arts), Rio de Janeiro, Brazil, 451
Museums, 630–34
  Brazil, 630–31
  Chile, 632
  Colombia, 632
  Ecuador, 632–33
  Paraguay, 633
  Peru, 633–34
  Uruguay, 634
  Venezuela, 634
  *See also* museums *entry under names of individual cities*
Music and dance, 224–30
  *See also* music *entry under names of individual cities*

Nahuel Huapi National Park, Argentina, 650
  hotels, 655–56
Natal, Brazil, 578, 737
  hotels, 741
Nazca, Lima to, route, Peru, 958–64
  hotels, 963–64
Nazca, Peru, 629, 962–63
  hotels, 964
Necochea, Argentina, 645
  hotels, 647
Neiva to Cali route, Colombia, 854–61
  hotels, 859–61
Neuquén, Argentina, 648–49
  hotels, 655
New Island, Falkland Islands, Argentina, 671

# INDEX 1081

Newspapers, newsletters, and magazines, 152–53
Nieuw Nickerie, Suriname, 1004–5
  accommodations, 1005–6
Nightclubs and nightlife. *See* nightclubs and nightlife *entry under names of individual cities*
North Seymour, Galápagos Islands, Ecuador, 894
Nova Friburgo, Brazil, 751
  hotels, 755
Nueva Helvecia, Uruguay, 1009
  hotels, 1012

Ocopa, Peru, 944
  hotels, 945
Older travelers, hints for, 100–3
  discounts, 102–3
  health, 101–2
  planning, 100–1
Ollantaytambo, Peru, 628
Oriente route, Ecuador, 607–8, 875–80
  hotels, 879–80
Orinoco River routes, Venezuela
  lower, 1048–52
    hotels, 1051–52
  upper, 1064–67
    accommodations, 1067
Oruro, Bolivia, 703–4
  hotels, 709–10
Osorno, Chile, 814–15
  hotels, 818–19
Otavalo, Ecuador, 429–30, 543, 867–68
  hotels, 873–74
Ouro Prêto (Minas Gerais), Brazil, 630, 753–54
  hotels, 550, 756
Ovalle to Talca route, Chile, 802–7
  hotels, 807

Pachacámac, Peru, 629, 939–40
Pacific coast, 10
Package tours, 58–64
  biking, 69–70
  handicapped, 93–94
  older traveler, 103
  single traveler, 95–96
Packing, 85–88
  climate and clothes, 85–86
  hints for packing, 87–88
  sundries, 86–87
Paine Towers National Park, Chile, 600, 605, 823
  hotels, 824–25
Paipa, Colombia, 553, 848
Palacio Cousiño, Chile, 500, 632
Pampa Colorada, Peru, 962–63
Pampas (grasslands), 9, 11, 603
Pampatar, Venezuela, hotels, 1064
Pamplona, Colombia, 845
  hotels, 847
Panama, 9, 179–80, 910–21
  airport departure tax, 180
  archaeological sites, 627
  banking/business hours, 180
  calculating costs, 180
  casinos, 570
  climate, 12, 13, 14, 179
  craft specialties, 236
  driving routes, 910–21
  electricity, 180
  emergency telephone number, 133
  entry requirements and customs, 179
  general data on, 179–80, 910–12
  holidays, 180
  language, 179
  local transportation, 179
  money, 180
  Panama City, 404–19, 917–18
  railway offices and special routes, 47
  shopping, 180, 561–62
  sports, 180
  telephone, 179
  tipping, 180
  tourist information, 179
  transportation to, 179
Panama, Isthmus of, 9
Panama Canal, 405, 410
Panama City, Panama, 404–19, 917–18
  beaches, 411–12
  climate and clothes, 412–13
  general data on, 404–9
  hotels, 416–17
  local transportation, 413
  map, 406–7
  museums, 410, 413
  music, 415
  nightclubs and nightlife, 415–16
  places of special interest, 409–12
  restaurants, 417–19
  shopping, 413–14
  special events, 413
  sports, 414–15
  telephone, 412
  theater, 415
  tourist information, 412
Pan-American Highway route, Panama, 637, 912–21
  hotels, 919–21
Paracas, Peru, 629, 960–61
  hotels, 964
Paraguay, 9, 180–81, 922–35
  airport departure tax, 181
  Asunción, 247–63
  automobile clubs in, 52
  banking/business hours, 181
  calculating costs, 181
  casinos, 571
  climate, 13, 14, 181
  driving routes, 922–35
  electricity, 181
  emergency telephone number, 133
  entry requirements and customs, 180
  festivals, 568
  general data on, 180–81, 922–23
  holidays, 181
  language, 181
  local transportation, 180
  money, 181
  railway offices and special routes, 47
  shopping, 181, 562
  sports, 181

## 1082 INDEX

Paraguay (*cont.*)
 telephone, 180
 tipping, 181
 tourist information, 180
 transportation to, 180
Paramaribo, Suriname, 1002–4
 hotels, 1005
Paramonga, Peru, 947–48
Paraná, Argentina, 673–74
 hotels, 677
Paraná River Delta, Argentina, 300–1
Parati, Brazil, 745
 historic hostelries, 550
 hotels, 748
Paria Peninsula, Venezuela, 1046–47
Parque Nacional de los Glaciares, Argentina, 602, 661–66
Parque Nacional Huascarán, Peru, 609, 949
Parque Nacional Torres del Paine, Chile, 600, 605, 823
Parque Santa Teresa, Uruguay, 1017
Parque Tairona, Colombia, 579, 627, 840
Passports, 78–79
Pasto, Colombia, hotels, 860
Patagonia, 9, 11
Patagonia to Antarctica, route, Argentina, 657–68
 hotels, 665–68
Patagonia (Chilean) and the Tierra del Fuego Archipelago route, Chile, 819–25
 hotels, 824–25
Paulista Museum, São Paulo, Brazil, 523, 631
Paulo Afonso, Falls of, Brazil, 733–34
 hotels, 740
Paysandú, Uruguay, 1011
 hotels, 1013
Pearl Island archipelago, Panama, 412
Pebble Island, Falkland Islands, Argentina, 671, 672
Pedro Juan Caballero, Paraguay, 935
 hotels, 935
Pehuén-Có, Argentina, 577, 645
Penedo, Brazil, hotels, 740
Penonomé, Panama, 916
Peraitepuy, Venezuela, 1056
Personal accident and sickness insurance, 81–82
Peru, 9, 181–83, 936–99
 airport departure tax, 183
 archaeological sites, 627–30
 automobile clubs in, 52
 banking/business hours, 182
 beaches, 580
 calculating costs, 182
 climate, 13, 14, 182
 craft specialties, 236–37
 driving routes, 936–99
 electricity, 182
 emergency telephone number, 133
 entry requirements and customs, 181
 festivals, 568
 general data on, 181–83, 936–38
 holidays, 182
 language, 182

Lima, 361–86
 local transportation, 182
 money, 182
 museums, 633–34
 railway offices and special routes, 47
 shopping, 182–83, 562–63
 sports, 182
 telephone, 181
 tipping, 182
 tourist information, 181
 transportation to, 181–82
 wildlife, 614
Petrópolis, Brazil, 750–51
 hotels, 755
Piçarras, Brazil, hotels, 776
Pinamar, Argentina, 642
 hotels, 646
Pirapora, Brazil, hotels, 762
Pirenópolis, Brazil, 765
 hotels, 770
Piriápolis, Uruguay, 581, 1014
 hotels, 1018
Pisac, Peru, 628, 981
 hotels, 984
Pisco, Peru, 960
 hotels, 963
Plains, 11
Planning a trip, 72–75
 with children, 104–5
 hints for handicapped travelers, 88–91
 hints for older travelers, 100–1
 recommended reading, 149–53
Playa Colorado/Playa Arapita, Venezuela, 581
Playas, Ecuador, 885
Popayán, Colombia, 857–58
 hotels, 860
Porlamar, Venezuela, 1060
 hotels, 1063–64
Port Howard, Falkland Islands, Argentina, 671, 672
Portillo, Chile, 619–20, 800–1
 spas, 552–53
Portillo route, Chile, 798–802
 hotels, 552–53, 619–20, 801–2
Porto Alegre, Brazil, 774–75
 hotels, 777
Portobelo, Panama, 919
Porto Seguro, Brazil, 578
Portoviejo, Ecuador, 886
Port Stanley, Falkland Islands, Argentina, 670–71
Porvenir, Chile, 822–23
 hotels, 825
Posadas, Argentina, 674–75
 hotels, 677
Potosí, Bolivia, 704–6
 hotels, 710
Providencia, Colombia, 579–80, 838
 hotels, 842
Publications
 books, recommended, 149–52
 children, 104–5
 freighter travel, 43–44
 handicapped traveler, 90–91

health care, 135–36
newspapers, newsletters, and magazines, 152–53
single traveler, 96
Pucallpa, Peru, 988–90
  hotels, 993
Pucará, Peru, 628, 972
Pucara de Lasana, Chile, 626
Pucón, Chile, 621, 813–14
  hotels, 553, 817–18
Puente del Inca, Argentina, 681–82
Puerto Armuelles, Panama, 912–13
Puerto Ayacucho, Venezuela, 1066
  hotels, 1067
Puerto Cabello, Venezuela, 1037–38
  hotels, 1039
Puerto Deseado, Argentina, 660–61
Puerto Francisco de Orellana, Ecuador, 877–78
Puerto la Cruz, Venezuela, 1044
  hotels, 549, 1047–48
Puerto Madryn, Argentina, 659
  hotels, 666
Puerto Maldonado, Peru, 555, 996
  hotels, 555, 998
Puerto Montt, Chile, 815–16
  hotels, 819
Puerto Natales, Chile, 823
  hotels, 824
Puerto Santa Cruz, Argentina, 661
Puerto Varas, Chile, 815
  hotels, 819
Puerto Williams, Chile, 823–24
  hotels, 825
Puno, Arequipa to, route, Peru, 964–73
  hotels, 972–73
Puno, Peru, 969–71
  hotels, 556, 973
Punta Arenas, Chile, 820–22
  hotels, 555–56, 824
Punta Ballena, Uruguay
  hotels, 548–49, 1018
Punta Carnero, Ecuador, 553, 885
  hotels, 889
Punta Chame, Panama, hotels, 920
Punta del Diablo, Uruguay, hotels, 1020
Punta del Este, Uruguay, 545, 581, 1015–16
  hotels, 552, 1018–19
Punta Escosés, Panama, 627
Purmamarca, Argentina, 695
Puruchuco, Peru, 942
Puyo, Ecuador, 878

Quevedo, Ecuador, 886
Quito, Ecuador, 420–39, 868–69
  climate and clothes, 430–31
  general data on, 420–24
  hotels, 435–37
  local transportation, 431
  map, 422–23
  museums, 426, 427–28, 432
  music, 434–35
  nightclubs and nightlife, 435
  places of special interest, 424–30
  restaurants, 437–39
  shopping, 429–30, 432–33
  special events, 431–32
  sports, 433–34
  telephone, 430
  theater, 434
  tourist information, 430

Rabida (Jervis), Galápagos Islands, Ecuador, 894
Ralún, Chile, hotels, 552, 819
Rancagua, Chile, 805–6
Reading, recommended for travelers. *See* Publications
Recife, Brazil, 734–36
  hotels, 741
Recreational vehicles (RVs), 66–67
Registro, Brazil, 772
Relais & Châteaux, 117–18
Religion, 143, 207–11
Reloncaví Estuary, Chile, lakeside lodges, 552, 819
Resorts, luxury, and special havens, 546–57
  historic hostelries, 550–52
  island idylls, 549–50
  jungle junkets, 554–55
  lakeside lodges, 552
  seaside swells, 546–49
  spas and sports spots, 552–54
  wilderness whimsy, 555–57
Restaurants
  with children, 107
  tipping, 141
  useful words and phrases, 160–61
  *See also* restaurants *entry under names of individual cities*
Riberalta, Peru, 998
  hotels, 999
Riobamba, Ecuador, 870–71
  hotels, 874–75
Río Bío-Bío, Chile, 606
Rio de Janeiro, Brazil, 440–75
  beaches, 452–53, 454, 577
  climate and clothes, 456
  general data on, 440–47
  hotels, 464–68, 546–47
  local transportation, 456
  map, 442–43
  museums, 451–52, 453, 459
  music, 462
  nightclubs and nightlife, 462–64
  places of special interest, 448–55
  restaurants, 468–75
  shopping, 459–61
  special events, 457–59
  sports, 461–62
  telephone, 456
  theater, 462
  tourist information, 455
Rio de Janeiro to Belo Horizonte route, Brazil, 749–57
  hotels, 755–57
Río Gallegos, Argentina, 661
  hotels, 666

# 1084 INDEX

Riohacha to Villa de Leyva route, Colombia, 842–49
  hotels, 847–49
Río Mar, Panama, hotels, 920
Río Tercero Lake, Argentina, 687
Rio Verde, Brazil, 767
  hotels, 770
River rafting. *See* Trekking, backpacking, river rafting, and camping
Robinson Crusoe Island, Chile, 829–30
  hotels, 830
Rocas de Santo Domingo, Chile, hotels, 798
Rondonópolis, Brazil, 768
  hotels, 770
Rosario, Argentina, 684
Rumicucho, Ecuador, 627
Rupununi Savannah, Guyana, 908

Sabará, Brazil, 754
Sacsayhuamán, Peru, 628, 980
Sailing, 584–86
  Argentina, 584
  Bolivia, 584
  Brazil, 584–85
  Colombia, 585
  Ecuador, 585
  Peru, 585
  Venezuela, 585–86
  *See also* sports *entry under names of individual cities*
St.-Laurent-du-Maroni, French Guiana, 900
  hotels, 902
Salcedo, Ecuador, hotels, 874
Salinas, Ecuador, 885
  hotels, 888
Salta, Argentina, 692–94
  hotels, 696
Salto, Montevideo to, route, Uruguay, 1008–13
  hotels, 1012–13
Salvador (Bahia), Brazil, 476–92
  beaches, 477, 480, 578
  climate and clothes, 484
  general data on, 476–80
  hotels, 488–90
  island idylls, 550
  local transportation, 484
  luxury resorts, 547–48
  map, 478–79
  museums, 481–82, 485–86
  music, 487
  nightclubs and nightlife, 487
  places of special interest, 480–83
  restaurants, 490–92
  shopping, 486
  special events, 485
  sports, 487
  telephone, 484
  theater, 487
  tourist information, 483–84
San Agustín, Colombia, 606
  hotels, 860
San Agustín National Park, Colombia, 626, 855–56
  hotels, 860
San Andrés, Colombia, 579–80, 837–38
  hotels, 841–42
San Andrés de Pisimbala, Colombia, hotels, 860
San Antonio Oeste, Argentina, 659
San Bernardino, Paraguay, 926
San Blas Islands, Panama, 918
  hotels, 921
San Carlos de Bariloche, Argentina, 648
San Cristóbal, Venezuela, 1034
  hotels, 1037
San Cristóbal (Chatham), Galápagos Islands, Ecuador, 894
  hotels, 896
San Fernando, Chile, historic hostelries, 550–51
San Francisco de Yare, Caracas to, route, 1024–29
  hotels, 1028–29
San Gil, Colombia, hotels, 848
San Ignácio Miní, Argentina, 675
  hotels, 677
San Juan, Argentina, 682
San Juan de los Morros, Venezuela, 1025
  hotels, 1028
San Martín de los Andes, Argentina, 649–50
  hotels, 655
San Pablo del Lago, Ecuador, 551
San Pedro de Atacama, Chile, 626, 789
Santa Clara, Peru, spas, 553–54
Santa Cruz Province, Argentina, 657
Santa Cruz, Bolivia, train to Corumbá, Brazil, 603–4
Santa Cruz and Cochabamba route, Bolivia, 710–14
  hotels, 713–14
Santa Cruz (Indefatigable), Galápagos Islands, Ecuador, 893
  hotels, 896
Santa Elena de Uairén, Venezuela, 1055
  hotels, 1057
Santa Fe, Argentina, 673
Santa Fe (Barrington), Galápagos Islands, Ecuador, 895
Santa Fe de Antioquia, Colombia, hotels, 854
Santa Marta, Colombia, 839–40
  hotels, 548, 842
Santarém, Brazil, 724
  hotels, 728
Santa Rosa de Quives, Peru, hotels, 945
Santiago, Chile, 493–513
  climate and clothes, 502
  general data on, 493–97
  hotels, 508–10
  local transportation, 502–3
  map, 494–495
  museums, 498, 499, 503–5
  music, 507–8
  nightclubs and nightlife, 508
  places of special interest, 497–501
  restaurants, 510–13
  shopping, 505–6
  special events, 503
  sports, 506–7
  telephone, 502

theater, 507
tourist information, 501–2
Santiago, Panama, 915
Santiago (James), Galápagos Islands, Ecuador, 894
Santiago Province, Chile, 579
Santo Domingo, Venezuela, hotels, 556–57, 1036
Santo Domingo de los Colorados, Ecuador, 886
hotels, 889
Santos, Brazil, 746–47
São João del Rei, Brazil, 752–53
hotels, 756
São Luís, Brazil, 739
hotels, 742–43
São Paulo, Brazil, 514–36
beaches, 524
climate and clothes, 525–26
general data on, 514–20
hotels, 531–33
local transportation, 526
map, 516–17
museums, 521–22, 523, 527
music, 529–30
nightclubs and nightlife, 530–31
places of special interest, 520–25
restaurants, 533–36
shopping, 527–28
special events, 526–27
sports, 528–29
telephone, 525
theater, 529
tourist information, 525
São Paulo Art Museum (MASP), Brazil, 521–22, 527, 631
São Paulo (Brazil), Rio de Janeiro to, route, 743–49
hotels, 747–49
São Paulo (Brazil) to the Uruguay Border route, 771–78
hotels, 775–78
São Sebastião, Brazil, 577, 746
hotels, 748
Saquarema, Brazil, 577
Sarisariñama, 1065
Scuba diving. *See* Snorkeling and scuba diving
Segovia Highlands, Venezuela, 1034–35
Sertão, the, Brazil, 731–33
Sete Cidades (the Seven Cities), Brazil, 738
Shell-Mera, Ecuador, 878
Ship, traveling by, 35–44
Amazon (jungle exploration), 571–75
cabins, 36–37
with children, 107
cruises, 38–44
to and around South America, 38–40
freighters, 43–44
specialty and regional, 40–43
dress, 38
facilities and activities, 37–38
hints for handicapped travelers, 92
meals, 37–38
sanitation aboard ship, 38
shore excursions, 37
tips, 38

Shopping, 557–63
Argentina, 170, 557–58
Bolivia, 171, 558–59
Brazil, 173, 559–60
Chile, 174, 560
Colombia, 175, 560–61
duty-free, 142–43, 144–45
duty-free articles, 144–45
Ecuador, 177, 561
French Guiana, 178
Guyana, 179
Panama, 180, 561–62
Paraguay, 181, 562
Peru, 182–83, 562–63
Suriname, 184
Uruguay, 185, 563
useful words and phrases, 161–62
Venezuela, 186, 563
*See also* shopping *entry under names of individual cities*
Sierra de la Ventana, Argentina, 646
hotels, 648
Sierra Nevada de Mérida, Venezuela, 1033
Sierra Nevada de Santa Marta, 626
Sillustani, Peru, 629
Silvia, Colombia, hotels, 860
Single travelers, hints for, 94–100
studying abroad, 98–100
women, 97–98
cautions for, 332
hints for, 97–98
working abroad, 100
Sipán, Peru, 629–30
Skiing, 616–21
Argentina, 617–19
Bolivia, 619
Chile, 619–21
*See also* sports *entry under names of individual cities*
Snorkeling and scuba diving, 581–84
Argentina, 582
Brazil, 582
Colombia, 582–83
Ecuador, 583
Panama, 583–84
Venezuela, 584
*See also* sports *entry under names of individual cities*
South America, map, 4–5
South American embassies and consulates in the US, 148
*See also* tourist information *entry under names of individual countries*
South Plaza, Galápagos Islands, Ecuador, 895
Spas, 552–54
Special events. *See* special events *entry under names of individual cities*
Sports
fishing, 590–98
golf, 588–90
hunting, 621–23
mountain climbing, 598–601
sailing, 584–86
skiing, 616–21

Sports (*cont.*)
 snorkeling and scuba diving, 581–84
 tennis, 586–88
 trekking, backpacking, river rafting, and camping, 601–11
 wildlife expeditions, 611–16
 *See also* sports *entry under names of individual cities and countries*
Sports resort hotels, 552–54
Stomach upsets, 128–29
Students, hints for, 97–98
 studying in South America, 98–100
Sucre, Bolivia, 706–8
 hotels, 710
Sucúa, Ecuador, 878–79
Sunburn, 130
Suriname, 9, 183–84, 1000–6
 airport departure tax, 184
 banking and business hours, 183
 calculating costs, 183
 casinos, 571
 climate, 12, 13, 183
 craft specialties, 237
 driving routes, 1000–6
 electricity, 183
 emergency telephone number, 133
 entry requirements and customs, 183
 festivals, 568–69
 general data on, 183, 1000–2
 holidays, 183–84
 language, 183
 local transportation, 183
 money, 183
 shopping, 184
 sports, 184
 telephone, 183
 tipping, 183
 tourist information, 183
 transportation to, 183
 wildlife, 614–15

Tafí Valley, Argentina, 625
Tairona National Park, Colombia, 579, 627, 840
 campgrounds, 842
Talca, Chile, 806–7
 hotels, 807
Talca, Ovalle to, route, 802–7
 hotels, 807
Tambo Colorado, Peru, 629
Tambopata Natural Wildlife Preserve, Madre de Dios, Peru, hotels, 555, 999
Tandil, Argentina, 644
 hotels, 647
Tarija, Bolivia, 708–9
 hotels, 710
Telephone, 124–26
 hotel surcharges, 125–26
Temperature. *See* Climate
Temuco, Chile, 812
 hotels, 817
Tena, Ecuador, 878
 hotels, 879

Tennis, 586–88
 Argentina, 586
 Bolivia, 586
 Brazil, 586–87
 Chile, 587
 Colombia, 587
 Ecuador, 587
 Panama, 587
 Paraguay, 587
 Peru, 587
 Suriname, 588
 Uruguay, 588
 Venezuela, 588
 *See also* sports *entry under names of individual cities*
Tequendama Falls, Colombia, 275
Teresina, Brazil, hotels, 742
Teresópolis, Brazil, 751
 hotels, 755
Termas de Chillán, Chile, 620
Termas de Socos, Chile, hotels, 807
Terrain, 9–11
Theater, tickets for, 148–49
 *See also* theater *entry under names of individual cities*
Tiahuanaco, Bolivia, 625, 699–701
Tickets, special event, 148–49
Tierra del Fuego Archipelago and Chilean Patagonia route, Chile, 9, 605–6, 663–64, 819–25
 hotels, 824–25
Tierradentro, Colombia, 626, 856
Tilcara, Argentina, 625, 695
Time zones, 122–23
Tingo María, Peru, 988
 hotels, 993
Tipping, 140–42
 on ships, 38
 tip packs, 111
 *See also* tipping *entry under names of individual countries*
Tiradentes, Brazil, 752–53
 hotels, 756
Tolombon, Argentina, 625
Tolú, Colombia, 579
Torres, Brazil, 774
 hotels, 777
Tota, Colombia, hotels, 848
Tourist information. *See* tourist information *entry under names of individual countries and cities*
Tourist offices, 148
 *See also* tourist information *entry under names of individual countries*
Tours
 bike tours, 68–70
 hints for handicapped travelers, 93–94
 package, 58–64
 single travelers, 95–96
Train, traveling by, 44–48
 accommodations and fares, 45
 hints for handicapped travelers, 93
 railway offices and special routes, 45–48
Trancoso, Brazil, 578

Transportation, calculating costs, 71–72
   *See also* Airplane travel; Bus, traveling by; Car, traveling by; Car rentals; Ship, traveling by; Train, traveling by; local transportation *entry under names of individual countries*
Travel agents, how to, 75–77
   cruise specialists, 36, 44
   family specialists, 105
Traveler's checks, 111–13
Trekking, backpacking, river rafting, and camping, 601–11
   Argentina, 602–3
   Bolivia, 603–4
   Brazil, 604–5
   camping, 65–66
      equipment, 65
      organized trips, 66
   Chile, 605–6
   Colombia, 606
   Ecuador, 607–8
   Peru, 608–10
   Venezuela, 610–11
   *See also* sports *entry under names of individual cities*
Trelew, Argentina, 660
   hotels, 666
Tres Arroyos, Argentina, 644
   hotels, 647
Trinidad, Bolivia, river trip to, 604
Trip cancellation and interruption insurance, 82
Trujillo, Peru, 950–52
   hotels, 957–58
Trujillo, Venezuela, hotels, 1035
Tucumán, Argentina, 689–90
   hotels, 695
Túcume, Peru, 630
Tucupita, Venezuela, 1050–51
   hotels, 1052
Tulcán to Machala route, Ecuador, 866–75
   hotels, 873–75
Tunja, Colombia, 845–46
   hotels, 848

Ubatuba, Brazil, 745–46
   hotels, 748
Uquia, Argentina, 625
Ureña, Venezuela, hotels, 1037
Urubamba, Peru, hotels, 984
Uruguay, 9, 184–85, 1007–20
   airport departure tax, 185
   automobile clubs in, 52
   banking/business hours, 184
   beaches, 580–81
   calculating costs, 184
   casinos, 571
   climate, 13, 14, 184
   driving routes, 1007–20
   electricity, 184
   emergency telephone number, 133
   entry requirements and customs, 184
   festivals, 569
   general data on, 184–85, 1007–8
   holidays, 185
   language, 184
   local transportation, 184
   money, 184
   Montevideo, 387–403
   shopping, 185, 563
   sports, 185
   telephone, 184
   tipping, 184
   tourist information, 184
   transportation to, 184
Uruguay Border, São Paulo (Brazil) to, route, 771–78
   hotels, 775–78
Ushuaia, Argentina, 663–64
   hotels, 667–68
US Embassies and consulates in South America, 136–38
US to metric measurements (conversion table), 154–55

Valdés Peninsula and Camarones, Argentina, 602, 660
Valdivia, Chile, 814
   hotels, 818
Valencia, Venezuela, 1026–27
   hotels, 1029
Valle Grande, Venezuela, 549
Valle Nevado, Chile, 620–21, 804–5
Valparaíso and Viña del Mar route, Chile, 793–98
   hotels, 797–98
Venezuela, 9, 185–86, 1021–67
   airport departure tax, 186
   automobile clubs in, 52
   banking/business hours, 186
   beaches, 581
   calculating costs, 185–86
   Caracas, 316–38
   climate, 12–14, 185
   craft specialties, 237–38
   driving routes, 1021–67
   electricity, 185
   emergency telephone number, 133
   entry requirements and customs, 185
   festivals, 569
   general data on, 185–86, 1021–24
   holidays, 186
   language, 185
   local transportation, 185
   money, 185
   museums, 634
   railway offices and special routes, 47
   shopping, 186, 563
   sports, 186
   telephone, 185
   tipping, 186
   tourist information, 185
   transportation to, 185
   wildlife, 615–16
Venezuelan Amazon route. *See* Orinoco River routes

Venezuelan Coast routes
 eastern, 1043–48
  hotels, 1047–48
 western, 1037–40
  hotels, 1039–40
Viedma, Argentina, 659
 hotels, 666
Villa de Leyva, Colombia, historic hostelries, 551, 848
Villa de Leyva, Riohacha to, route, 842–49
 hotels, 847–49
Villa Dolores, Argentina, 687
Villa Florida, Paraguay, 930
 hotels, 932
Villa General Belgrano, Argentina, 687
Villa Gesell, Argentina, 642
 hotels, 646
Villarrica, Chile, 593–94, 812–13
 hotels, 817
Viña del Mar and Valparaíso route, Chile, 793–98
 hotels, 797–98
Viña del Mar, Chile, 548, 579
Volcán, Panama, 913
 hotels, 919

Water safety, 131–32
Weights and measures, 153–55
 conversion tables (metric to US measurements), 154–55
West Point Island, Falkland Islands, Argentina, 671

Wilderness whimsy, 555–57
Wildlife expeditions, 611–16
 Argentina, 612
 Brazil, 612–13
 Colombia, 613
 Ecuador, 613–14
 Peru, 614
 Suriname, 614–15
 Venezuela, 615–16
Wines, 138
Women, single. *See* Single travelers, hints for
Words and phrases, useful (in Spanish and Portuguese), 157–65
 checking in, 159–60
 colors, 162–63
 days of the week, 164–65
 eating out, 160–61
 getting around, 163–64
 greetings and everyday expressions, 159
 months, 165
 numbers, 165
 personal items and services, 164
 shopping, 161–62
Working abroad, 100

Yacanto, Argentina, 687
Yaguarón, Paraguay, 924–25
Yellow fever, 130
Yungas, Bolivia, 703
Yutajé, Venezuela, 1067

Zapala, Argentina, 649